W9-ACT-650

INDEX OF

REVOLUTIONARY WAR

PENSION APPLICATIONS

TAYLOR (continued)
William, Va., res. Jefferson Co., Ky., in 1818, Louisville in 1820, m. Elizabeth (or Eliza) Courts, 3/29/1849. Children Robert H. C., Eleanor Madison, Caroline Jefferson, Louise Washington, Eliza Ormsby and Richard W. Ferguson. Pension due mother was allowed the following surviving children—Richard F. Taylor, Eleanor M. Berry and Eliza O. Horning. D. 3/29/1830 in Oldham Co., Ky. W6233; BLWt. 2501-400 Mjr. Issued 12/8/1797
William, Va., b. May 1754, res. Moreland Twsp, Lycoming Co. Pa., in 1818, d. there 3/31/1839. M. Sarah in Amwell Twsp., N. J. in Nov. 1783 or 84 W4603
6 William Tarlton, Va. (?), res. Wayne, Co., Ky. in 1836, Elizabeth, R10414 (This file contains a leaf from a family Bible with many records)
8 Zachariah, Va., also 1794, m. Susannah Jarrell (or Gerrill), 12/19/1792, W6237; BLWt. 11195-160-55
7 Zachariah, Va., res. Woodford Co., Ky., in 1818 at age 62, Elizabeth, son John, Dau. Philadelphia, and other children not named. S31408
9 Zalmon, Conn., widow Hannah pens. from N. Y. (m. Hannah 10/26/1780) d. 5/10/1816 in Putnam Co., N. Y. W25470
10 TAYNTOR, Jedediah, Mass., Mary, W15418
11 TAYS, Samuel, N. C., S1594
TEACHEY
12 Daniel, N. C., Mary, W4082; BLWt. 19907-160-55
13 ** TEAFEE (or TEAF), Henry, Pa., Mary, W2025
TEAGUE
14 Beni, Mass., S38428
15 Daniel, Mass., S33785
16 Jacob, Va., S41235
17 Jesse, Mass., S42468
1 John, S. C., BLWt. 12632-100. Issued 10/7/1795; BLWt. 13811-100-1795
2 William, S. C., Elizabeth, W208
TEAL
4 Emanuel, N. C., Martha, R10440
5 Jeremiah, Pa., BLWt. 10488. Issued 7/27/1789 to Richard Platt, assne. No papers
6 (or TEEL), John, Pa., Catharine W2703; BLWt. 26003-160-55
8 Joseph, Conn., Hannah, W18119
9 Leonard, Pa., BLWt. 10478. Issued 3/29/1792 to Barnard Slauch, assne.
10 (or TEALL or TEEL), Nathan, Conn., Polly, W19438; BLWt. 18221-160-55
11 see DEAL, Samuel
TEALL
12 Joseph, Conn., S46473
13 Oliver, Conn., S11529
14 TEALS (or TEAL), Joseph, Conn., BLWt. 6536. Issued 4/22/1793 to William Judd. No papers
15 TEAM, Adam, N. C., S. C., S21528
16 TEANEY, Daniel, Pa., Catharine, W6252
17 TEARCOT, Francis, Cont. (Canada), Mary, W22390; BLWt. 14511-160-55 (Name spelled TAUCOT, TARCOT, TAUCO, and TERCO)
18 TEARNEY, Gilbert, Ga., Elizabeth, W9850
19 TEAS (or TEAZ), William, Cont. (Pa.), Sarah, W1663; BLWt. 2262-100;
20 TEASLY, Silas, N. C., S32009
21 TEATOR, Henry, N. Y. S11530
23 TEAZOR, Aaron, Del., BLWt. 10889. Issued 9/2/1789
TEBBETS
25 (or TIBBETS), Nathaniel, Mass., S19125
26 (or TIBBETTS), Samuel, Cont. (Mass.), S11560
28 † (or TIBBETTS), Ephraim, Mass., Rachel, W6286
1 TEBBITS, (or TEBBETS, TIBBETTS), Ephraim, N. H., S43201
3 TEBBS, (or TIBBS), Willoughby, Va., Betsey, W6284
4 TEDDERTON, John, N. C., R10441
TEDFORD
5 John, Va., S3776
6 (or TELFORD), Joseph, Va., Mary, R10447
7 Robert, Va., S3775
8 TEDRICK, Michael, N. C., S32242
TEED
9 John, N. J., S6205
10 William, N. Y., R10442
11 TEEDER, Michael, Pa., Agcy., Dis-
TEEL
12 (or TEAL), Adam, Pa., S23453
13 Ezekiel H., Navy, Sea Service (N. J.), S23968
15 Joseph, Mass., S29501
16 Lodrick, N. C., R10443
18 TEEPENING, Mary, former widow of Isaac SEAMENS, N. Y., W15851, which see.

Handwritten annotations: Box 3707; Box 3708; Box 3709; Roll 793; Roll 2354; Roll 2355; Teal, Adam, See Teel. 3; John Jeremiah, Penn. See Thiels 7; Teaz, Wm., Cont. (Pa.), See Teas. 22; Tebbets, Ephraim NH S43201 See Tebbits. 27; Tebbs, John, Va., BLWt 2132. See Tibbs. 2; John, Penn., W2703 Catharine. See Teal 14; Nathan, Conn. See Teal 17; 27 Wm., N.H., W23424, Allice. See Tibbetts. 29 Tebbetts, Isaac, Mass., S40579, See Tibbetts

* First five items in box 3707 are listed on p. 1144 and 1145. Each item is preceded by a Roman numeral. See Box 3707.
† Surname is shown as Tebbetts
** Surname is shown as TEAFFE.

Sample page of original Index showing extensive revisions incorporated in this edition.

Special Publication No. 40

Index of Revolutionary War Pension Applications in the National Archives

Bicentennial Edition (Revised & Enlarged)

National Genealogical Society
Washington, D. C.
1976

International Standard Book Number: 0-915156-00-8

Library of Congress Catalog Card Number: 75-43393

Second Printing 1977

Third Printing 1979

Printed and Bound in the United States of America

This Bicentennial Edition

is dedicated to all who had a part

in the establishment of

American Independence

and

to those in later years who have

preserved, arranged, codified and indexed

the evidences of Revolutionary War services

for those named herein

INTRODUCTION

As set forth at length in the first edition of this work, this *Index* originally appeared as sixteen-page supplements to the *National Genealogical Society Quarterly* from March 1943 through December 1962. Mrs. Margaret M. H. Finck of the National Archives cooperated with the compilers and contributed a brief preface to the first installment. From 1943 to 1945 Max Ellsworth Hoyt and Frank Johnson Metcalf produced the *Index*. From 1945 to 1954 Mr. Hoyt worked alone, and from his death through 1959, Mrs. Hoyt, the former Agatha Brouson, continued it. In 1960 Mabel Van Dyke Baer contributed to two issues. From 1960 through 1962 Miss Sadye Giller completed it. Miss Giller also furnished three installments of Additions – mostly Bounty Land Warrant Applications – in 1964, and a volume of Corrections (Special Publication No. 31) in 1965. William H. and Louise Marks Dumont incorporated Miss Giller's Additions and her Corrections into the comprehensive *Index*, which appeared in 1966 as Special Publication No. 32.

When the National Archives microfilmed the Revolutionary War Pension and Bounty Land Warrant applications and the items related to them, so many cross-references, corrections, and additions, and changes of order occurred that it became necessary to make a completely new index. While the material was being assembled for microfilming, a copy of the original *Index* was revised at the National Archives. A photocopy of one of the revised pages appears as the frontispiece of this edition. From photocopies of the revised pages, Mrs. Janis H. Miller made the typescript here reproduced in reduction. Her expertise as a genealogist, her deep interest in the Society, and her accuracy as a typist made this volume possible. The chief proofreading was done by Past President Kenn Stryker-Rodda, and the final collation of pages performed by Miss Helen Michaels.

As the original 1340-page edition had proved unwieldy, triple columns were adopted for this revision. Several self-evident abbreviations were used to save space: e.g., Pa., Ct. instead of Conn., Cont. for Continental Line, BLWt. for Bounty-Land Warrant, and ass. for assignees. Also, because of the availability of the originals on film and print-outs, the abstracts of pensions that appeared in the *Quarterly* for some years, starting in March 1920, have not been referenced.

Advice and encouragement by James D. Walker of the National Archives and a member of the Society's Council, by President Virginia Davis Westhaeffer, Nettie Schreiner-Yantis, and other members of the Council, are gratefully acknowledged.

The introduction written for the microfilm edition of the applications (M 804) follows. It is reprinted in full. Since it was written by Howard H. Wehmann, Clifford Neal Smith has edited two volumes in the *Federal Land Series* (Chicago: American Library Association, 1972, 1973) that show how many of the bounty-land warrants were used by the veterans or their assignees.

REVOLUTIONARY WAR PENSION AND BOUNTY-LAND-WARRANT APPLICATION FILES

On the rolls of this microfilm publication are reproduced an estimated 80,000 pension and bounty-land-warrant application files based on the participation of American military, naval, and marine officers and enlisted men in the Revolutionary War. Most of the records in the files are dated between 1800 and 1900. The files are part of Record Group 15, Records of the Veterans Administration.

Pension and Bounty-Land-Warrant Legislation and Administration Relating to Participation in the Revolutionary War

Pension Legislation

For more than a century before the beginning of the Revolutionary War, British colonies in North America provided pensions for disabled soldiers and sailors. During and after the Revolutionary War, three principal types of pensions were provided by the U. S. Government for servicemen and their dependents. "Disability" or "invalid pensions" were awarded to servicemen for physical disabilities incurred in the line of duty; "service pensions," to veterans who served for specified periods of time; and "widows' pensions," to women whose husbands had been killed in the war or were veterans who had served for specified periods of time.

On August 26, 1776, the first pension legislation for the American colonies as a group was enacted. A resolution of the Continental Congress provided half pay for officers and enlisted men, including those on warships and armed vessels, who were disabled in the service of the United States and who were incapable of earning a living. The half pay was to continue for the duration of the disability.

On May 15, 1778, another resolution provided half pay for 7 years after the conclusion of the war to all military officers who remained in the Continental service to the end of the war. Enlisted men who continued to serve for the duration of the conflict were each to receive a gratuity of $80 after the war under the terms of the same enactment. The first national pension legislation for widows was a Continental Congress resolution of August 24, 1780, which offered the prospect of half pay for 7 years to widows and orphans of officers who met the requirements included in the terms of the resolution of May 15, 1778. On October 21, 1780, the Continental Congress resolution of May 15, 1778, was amended to provide half pay for life to officers after the war; but on March 22, 1783, the half-pay-for-life provision was changed to 5 years' full pay.

Pension legislation during the Revolutionary War was designed to encourage enlistment and acceptance of commissions and to prevent desertion and resignation. After the war, pensions became a form of reward for services rendered. Both during and after the Revolution, the States as well as the U. S. Government awarded pensions based on participation in the conflict. The records reproduced in this microfilm publication pertain only to pensions granted or paid pursuant to public and private acts of the U. S. Government. Public acts, under which the majority of such pensions were authorized, encompassed large classes of veterans or their dependents who met common eligibility requirements. Private acts concerned specific individuals whose special services or circumstances merited consideration, but who could not be awarded pensions under existing public acts.

On September 29, 1789 (1 Stat. 95), the First Congress of the United States passed an act which provided that invalid pensions previously paid by the States, pursuant to resolutions of the Continental Congress, should be continued and paid for 1 year by the newly established Federal Government. Subsequent legislation often extended the time limit. An act of Congress approved March 23, 1792 (1 Stat. 243), permitted veterans not already receiving invalid pensions under resolutions of the Continental Congress to apply for them directly to the Federal Government. On April 10, 1806 (2 Stat. 376), the scope of earlier invalid-pension laws pertaining to Revolutionary War servicemen was extended to make veterans of State troops and militia service eligible for Federal pensions. The act superseded all previous Revolutionary War invalid-pension legislation.

Before 1818 national pension laws concerning veterans of the Revolution (with the exception of the Continental Congress resolution of May 15, 1778, granting half pay to officers for service alone) specified disability or death of a serviceman as the basis for a pension award. Not until March 18, 1818 (3 Stat. 410), did the U. S. Congress grant pensions to Revolutionary War veterans for service from which no disabilities resulted. Officers and enlisted men in need of assistance were eligible under the terms of the 1818 act if they had served in a Continental military organization or in the U. S. naval service (including the Marines) for 9 months or until the end of the war. Pensions granted under this act were to continue for life.

The service-pension act of 1818 resulted in a great number of applications, many of which were approved. Congress had to appropriate greater sums than ever before for Revolutionary War pension payments. Financial difficulties and charges that applicants were feigning poverty to obtain benefits under the terms of the act caused Congress to enact remedial legislation on May 1, 1820 (3 Stat. 569). The new law required every pensioner receiving payments under the 1818 act, and every would-be pensioner, to submit a certified schedule of his estate and income to the Secretary of War. The Secretary was authorized to remove from the pension list the names of those persons who, in his opinion, were not in need of assistance. Within a few years the total of Revolutionary War service pensioners was reduced by several thousand. An act of Congress approved March 1, 1823 (3 Stat. 782), resulted in the restoration of pensions to many whose names had been removed under the terms of the 1820 legislation, but who subsequently proved their need for aid.

Congress passed another service-pension act on May 15, 1828 (4 Stat. 269), which granted full pay for life to surviving officers and enlisted men of the Revolutionary War who were eligible for benefits under the terms of the Continental Congress resolution of May 15, 1778, as amended.

The last and most liberal of the service-pension acts benefiting Revolutionary War veterans was passed on June 7, 1832 (4 Stat. 529), and extended to more persons the provisions of the law of May 15, 1828. The act provided that every officer or enlisted man who had served at least 2 years in the Continental Line or State troops, volunteers or militia, was eligible for a pension of full pay for life. Naval and marine officers and enlisted men were also included. Veterans who had served less than 2 years, but not less than 6 months, were eligible for pensions of less than full pay. Neither the act of 1832 nor the one of 1828 required applicants to demonstrate need. Under the act of 1832 money due from the last payment until the date of death of a pensioner could be collected by his widow or by his children.

The time limit for making claims under the Continental Congress resolution of August 24, 1780, which promised half-pay pensions to widows and orphans of some officers, expired in 1794. For many years thereafter, unless a private act of Congress was introduced on her behalf, a widow of a veteran was limited to receiving only that part of a pension that remained unpaid at the time of her husband's death. By an act of Congress approved July 4, 1836 (5 Stat. 128), some widows of Revolutionary War veterans were again permitted, as a class under public law, to apply for pensions. The act provided that the widow of any veteran who had performed service as specified in the pension act of June 7, 1832, was eligible to receive the pension that might have been allowed the veteran under the terms of that act, if the widow had married the veteran before the expiration of his last period of service. An act of July 7, 1838 (5 Stat. 303), granted 5-year pensions to widows whose marriages had taken place before January 1, 1794. These pensions were continued by acts of March 3, 1843 (5 Stat. 647); June 17, 1844 (5 Stat. 680); and February 2, 1848 (9 Stat. 210).

On July 29, 1848 (9 Stat. 265), Congress provided life pensions for widows of veterans who were married before January 2, 1800. All restrictions pertaining to the date of marriage were removed by acts of February 3, 1853 (10 Stat. 154), and February 28, 1855 (10 Stat. 616). On March 9, 1878 (20 Stat. 29), widows of Revolutionary War soldiers who had served for as few as 14 days, or were in any engagement, were declared eligible for life pensions.

Pension Administration

During the Revolution and in the period between the conclusion of the war and the establishment of the Federal Government, administration of the pension laws enacted by the Continental Congress was left largely to the individual States. The act of Congress approved September 29, 1789 (1 Stat. 95), which provided for the continuance of such pensions by the newly established Federal Government, stipulated only that they should be paid "under such regulations as the President. . . may direct." The act of Congress approved March 23, 1792

(1 Stat. 244), which permitted the addition of new names to the existing list of Revolutionary War pensioners, specified that the Secretary of War was to administer its provisions. For most of the period between 1793 and 1819, Congress reserved to itself the power of final decision with respect to the allowance of claims. Thus an act of February 28, 1793 (1 Stat. 325), required the Secretary of War to send lists of claims to the Congress for action. The service-pension act of March 18, 1818 (3 Stat. 410), gave the Secretary of War the authority to approve applications submitted under that law, and by an act of March 3, 1819 (3 Stat. 528), he was similarly empowered to place invalids on the pension list without prior Congressional approval.

Within the Office of the Secretary of War, pension matters were handled as early as 1810 by a unit called the Office of Military Bounty Lands and Pensions. Between 1810 and 1815 the unit was also referred to as the Section (or Branch) of Military Bounty Lands and Pensions. In 1815 the Branch was divided into two units: a Pension Bureau and a Land Warrant Bureau; after 1816 the Pension Bureau was generally referred to as the Pension Office. Not until March 2, 1833 (4 Stat. 622), did Congress formally provide for the appointment of a Commissioner of Pensions to execute pension laws under the general direction of the Secretary of War. When an act of Congress provided for the establishment of the Department of the Interior on March 3, 1849 (9 Stat. 395), the Pension Office was transferred to it. On July 21, 1930, by Executive Order 5398, the Bureau of Pensions (formerly called the Pension Office) was consolidated with other agencies also serving veterans, and the Veterans Administration, an independent executive agency, was established.

Two pension acts pertaining to Revolutionary War servicemen were not initially administered by the Pension Office. Responsibility for executing the provisions of the act of May 15, 1828 (4 Stat. 270), was vested in the Secretary of the Treasury until authority was transferred to the War Department on March 3, 1835 (4 Stat. 779). The Secretary of the Treasury was also named to administer the act of June 7, 1832 (4 Stat. 530), but a Congressional resolution on June 28, 1832 (4 Stat. 605), relieved him of that function and transferred it to the Secretary of War.

Application procedures followed by would-be pensioners varied according to the acts under which benefits were sought. Generally the process required an applicant to appear before a court of record in the State of his or her residence to describe under oath the service for which a pension was claimed. A widow of a veteran was required to provide information concerning the date and place of her marriage. The application statement or "declaration," as it was usually called, with such supporting papers as property schedules, marriage records, and affidavits of witnesses, was certified by the court and forwarded to the official, usually the Secretary of War or the Commissioner of Pensions, responsible for administering the specific act under which the claim was being made. An applicant was subsequently notified that his application had been approved, rejected, or put aside pending the submission of additional proof of eligibility. If an applicant was eligible, his name was placed on the pension list. Payments were usually made semiannually through pension agents of the Federal Government in the States. An applicant rejected under the terms of an earlier pension act often reapplied for benefits under later, more liberal laws.

Bounty-Land-Warrant Legislation

Bounty-land warrants—rights to free land in the public domain—were granted under acts of the Continental Congress and of the Federal Government to veterans and to heirs of veterans for Revolutionary War service of specified periods of time. The promise of bounty land during the Revolutionary War was another inducement to enter and remain in service; after the war, bounty-land grants became a form of reward. Most warrants were issued to servicemen or their heirs who met common eligibility standards established by public acts passed between 1776 and 1856. Some warrants were issued to individuals as a result of private acts passed by Congress. States also granted bounty land to Revolutionary War veterans, but the records reproduced in this microfilm publication pertain only to bounty-land warrants made available under acts of the U.S. Government.

On September 16, 1776, the Continental Congress passed a resolution that provided for granting land to officers and soldiers who engaged in military service and continued to serve until the end of the war. Representatives of officers and soldiers who might be slain by the enemy were also entitled to land. The resolution specified that each noncommissioned officer and soldier should be entitled to 100 acres, an ensign to 150 acres, each lieutenant to 200 acres, and other officers to proportionate amounts of land up to 500 acres for a colonel. By a resolution of August 12, 1780, the provision was extended to include generals, and the grant was to be 850 acres for a brigadier general and 1,100 acres for a major general. The resolution of September 16, 1776, was the basic law under which Revolutionary War veterans were granted bounty-land warrants by the Federal Government until 1855, although numerous acts were passed in the interval providing claimants with additional time in which to apply for or to locate warrants.

On March 3, 1855 (10 Stat. 701), the U.S. Congress went beyond merely satisfying the former pledge of the Continental Congress and authorized the issuance of bounty-land warrants for 160 acres to soldiers, irrespective of rank, who had served for as few as 14 days in the Revolution or had taken part in any battle. Widows and minor children of such veterans were also eligible. An individual who had received a warrant under previous bounty-land legislation was limited by the act to receiving a second warrant for only such additional acreage as would total 160 acres. An act of May 14, 1856 (11 Stat. 8), extended the benefits of the 1855 act to include Revolutionary War naval and marine officers, enlisted men, and their widows and minor children.

Bounty-Land-Warrant Administration

On July 9, 1788, a supplement to a Continental Congress land ordinance of May 20, 1785, authorized the Secretary of War to issue bounty-land warrants to eligible veterans of the Revolutionary War or to their assigns or legal representatives. When the First U.S. Congress authorized the establishment of a Department of War in the newly formed Federal Government on August 7, 1789 (1 Stat. 50), the Secretary of War was given the responsibility of issuing bounty-land warrants. By 1810 the Office of Military Bounty Lands and Pensions had been formed within the Office of the Secretary of War to examine claims and to issue warrants. In 1815 the pension and bounty-land duties of the War Department were assigned to separate bureaus, and bounty-land matters were handled thereafter by an administrative unit known successively as the Land Warrant Bureau, the Section of Bounty Lands, and the Bounty Land Office. On November 1, 1841, the Secretary of War placed the bounty-land functions under the direction of the Commissioner of Pensions. This arrangement was formally authorized by an act of Congress approved January 20, 1843 (5 Stat. 597). The laws relating to the granting of bounty-land warrants were administered by the Department of the Interior after the Pension Office was transferred to that Department in 1849.

Depending upon the period in which a claim was made, claimants for bounty-land warrants based on Revolutionary War service sent applications for adjudication to either the Secretary of War, the Commissioner of Pensions, or the Secretary of the Interior. Affidavits of witnesses testifying to service performed, marriage records, and other forms of evidence, were also forwarded by some applicants. Property schedules were unnecessary as indigency was not a requirement for the award of a Revolutionary War bounty-land warrant. A claimant whose application was approved was issued a warrant for a specified number of acres. He could then "locate" his warrant; that is, he could select the portion of the public domain that he wished to have in exchange for his warrant. The Treasury Department, and after 1849 the Interior Department, accepted warrants and issued patents to the land. Many recipients of Revolutionary War bounty-land warrants did not choose to locate the warrants and to settle on the public domain; instead, they remained in their old homes and sold the warrants.

Pension and Bounty-Land-Warrant Application Files

Types of Files

The term "files," as used in this microfilm publication, denotes 10" x 14" envelopes containing applications or other records pertaining to claims for pensions or bounty-land warrants; 10" x 14" cards summarizing information about claimants for whom no original application papers exist; and 10" x 14" cards that serve as cross-references to envelopes and summary cards. A file can therefore be a single card or it can be an envelope containing from 1 to 200 or more pages of records. The typical file is an envelope containing about 30 pages of records, consisting generally of the application or applications of one or more claimants, other documents submitted as evidence of identity and service, and papers showing actions taken by the Government concerning the claim or claims. Each file pertains to one or more claims by one or more persons for pensions or bounty-land warrants based on the service of a single person, usually in the Revolution, although some files relate to claims based on post-

Revolutionary War service.

Before 1910 Revolutionary War pension application papers were folded and placed in numbered jackets arranged in three series. One series was reserved for approved applications of "survivors," as Revolutionary War veterans were called. The second series held approved applications of widows, and the third contained rejected applications of both survivors and widows. The series were arranged by file numbers; therefore, in order to withdraw a specific pension claim from a series, index books arranged by the first two letters of the surname of a claimant had to be laboriously examined for the pertinent file number. To eliminate the necessity of using the books and to protect the records from damage caused by frequent unfolding and refolding, the Bureau of Pensions flattened and refiled Revolutionary War pension application papers in a single series of linen-lined envelopes arranged alphabetically by surname of veteran. The project was completed in 1912. As part of the work, pension application papers of a survivor and a widow were consolidated in a single envelope if the claims seemed to be based on the service of the same person. Approved Revolutionary War bounty-land-warrant application papers were also flattened and consolidated with, or interfiled among, pension application papers at this time; previously, they had been maintained apart from the pension claims. The records reproduced in this microfilm publication are from the one large series of Revolutionary War pension and bounty-land-warrant application files that resulted from the flat-filing project.

Survivors' pension application files in the series have headings normally consisting of the name of the State or organization for which a veteran served; his name; and the letter "S" for survivor, followed by a file number. A file of this type ordinarily contains one or more post-1800 approved applications of a veteran for an invalid or service pension. The file may also contain affidavits by other veterans or persons testifying to the service or disability claimed; documentary evidence of service submitted by the applicant, such as a commission or a discharge certificate; printed briefs summarizing the service claimed; property schedules; paper jackets formerly used to hold application papers before the flat-filing project of 1910-1912; certified copies of the veteran's service record provided by State officials; powers of attorney; letters from attorneys, Congressmen, and other interested persons relating to the progress of the claim; letters from genealogists and other researchers seeking information available in pension papers; and copies of replies from the Pension Office, the Bureau of Pensions, or the Veterans Administration concerning such inquiries. A fire in the War Department on November 8, 1800, apparently destroyed all Revolutionary War pension and bounty-land-warrant applications and related papers submitted before that date. Applications and related records submitted after 1800 are occasionally missing from survivors' and other types of files because papers were sometimes returned to applicants by the Pension Office.

Widows' pension application files have headings usually consisting of the name of the State or organization for which a veteran served; his name; his widow's name; and the letter "W" for widow, followed by a file number. Usually only a widow's given name appears on an envelope, but if she remarried, her second husband's surname is also included, with the notation "Former Widow." A widow's pension application file may contain records normally found in a survivor's file, especially if the widow's file is a consolidation of her papers and those of the pensioned veteran who had been her husband. Whether a widow's file represents such a consolidation or relates only to pension claims made by her, it will generally contain one or more approved post-1800 applications for a pension made by the widow. Incorporated in or attached to some widow's applications is a copy of a marriage record made by a town clerk, a clergyman, or a justice of the peace. Sometimes family-record pages from Bibles and other books were also submitted by a widow as proof of marriage.

Rejected pension application files have headings usually consisting of the name of the State or organization for which a veteran served; his name; the name of his widow if the file relates to an application or applications submitted by her; and the letter "R" for rejected, followed by a file number. Each of these files normally contains one or more post-1800 rejected pension applications that were submitted by a veteran, his widow, or an heir, and that were based on the Revolutionary War service of the former serviceman. The "R" symbol on the face of the envelope usually indicates that the latest application in the file was rejected. There may be one or more approved pension applications in the file, however, if they were approved before the last application was rejected.

Pre-1800 disability-pension application files are envelopes that have headings generally consisting of the name of the State or organization for which a veteran served, his name, and the file symbol "Dis. No Papers." The symbol indicates that a veteran's original disability-pension application and related papers are not extant, presumably as a result of the War Department fire of November 1800. In place of the missing papers, most of the files contain one or more small cards that give information about an invalid pensioner or veteran (former rank, unit, enlistment date, nature of disability, residence, and amount of pension). The data were transcribed by the Bureau of Pensions from the Congressional publication *American State Papers, Class 9, Claims* (Washington, 1834). The volume contains information from War Department pension reports based on original application papers and submitted to Congress between 1792 and 1795. Some invalid-pension application papers submitted after 1800 were apparently destroyed in another War Department fire in August 1814. For some of these applications, pertinent entries in the 1835 *Report From the Secretary of War . . . in Relation to the Pension Establishment of the United States* (23rd Cong., 1st sess., S. Doc. 514) were copied and placed in the files that were also labeled "Dis. No Papers." Copying was done by the Veterans Administration, but it seems this was done only in response to and in the form of replies to inquiries concerning specific veterans.

Bounty-land-warrant application files for approved applications submitted after November 8, 1800, are envelopes that have headings consisting of the name of the State or organization for which a veteran served, his name, his widow's name if she applied for the warrant, and the symbol "B. L. Wt." for bounty-land warrant. This symbol is followed by two or three numbers, separated by hyphens, which represent the warrant number, the number of acres granted, and the year 1855 (usually written "55") in the case of warrants issued pursuant to the bounty-land act of that year. Records in the files may include applications by veterans, their widows, or heirs; family-record pages from Bibles; copies of marriage records; copies of State records showing the service of the veteran; affidavits of other persons testifying to the length or kind of service claimed; annotated paper jackets used to hold bounty-land-warrant papers before they were flat-filed, which show action taken on claims; commissions, discharges, and other original service papers; and powers of attorney.

Bounty-land-warrant files for approved officers' applications submitted before the War Department fire of November 1800 are mainly 10" x 14" cards that show the name of the State or organization for which an officer served, his name, the symbol "B. L. Wt." followed by the warrant number and the number of acres granted, the officer's rank, the issue date of the warrant, the notation "No Papers," and sometimes the name of a person other than the officer to whom the warrant was delivered or assigned. The original application papers are presumed to have been destroyed in the fire of 1800. About 1917 the cards were complied by the Bureau of Pensions from entries in a surviving register listing bounty-land-warrants issued to officers before November 8, 1800. After the cards were compiled it seems that upon the receipt of an inquiry pertaining to one of the officers, the card relating to that officer, the letter of inquiry, and a copy of the reply were placed in an envelope bearing the same heading as the card. As a result, some bounty-land-warrant application files for approved officers' applications submitted before November 8, 1800, are envelopes. Sometimes the card was discarded after the information it contained was added to the envelope file.

Bounty-land-warrant files for approved applications of enlisted men submitted before the War Department fire of 1800 are 10" x 14" cards headed "BOUNTY LAND WARRANT RECORD CARD." Each card usually gives the name of the soldier, his rank, and the name of the State or organization for which he served; the warrant number; the number of acres granted; the issue date of the warrant; and sometimes the name of a person other than the soldier to whom the warrant was delivered or assigned. The original application papers were apparently destroyed in 1800. The cards were compiled by the National Archives from entries in three registers of bounty-land warrants issued to enlisted men before November 8, 1800. Sometimes a card was placed in an envelope containing pension application papers based on the service of the same soldier. In such a case the warrant number on the card was added to the heading on the envelope.

Bounty-land-warrant applications submitted pursuant to the act of March 3, 1855, and approved were interfiled among or consolidated with pension application papers as part of the Bureau of Pension's flat-filing project of 1910-12. The files in which these approved applications may usually be found have been described in the paragraph concerning approved bounty-land-warrant applications submitted after November 8, 1800. Most bounty-land-warrant applications submitted in accordance with the act of 1855 and rejected are in manila envelopes, the headings of which generally consist of the name of the State or organization for which a veteran served, his name, the symbol "B. L. Reg." (or "Rej.") for bounty-land register, the register entry number assigned to the application, and the year 1855 (sometimes written "55"). The face of each envelope also has a section containing military service information. The rejected applications are similar in content to those that were approved, but paper jackets accompanying rejected applications do not show warrant numbers. Some of the rejected bounty-land-warrant applications were placed in envelopes containing pension application papers based on service of the same veteran.

Consolidated files of pension and bounty-land-warrant applications and related papers are numerous and the contents vary. Almost any combination of two or more pension and bounty-land-warrant files already described may have been consolidated. Frequently, a widow's approved pension application papers, which normally comprise a "W" file, are consolidated with approved bounty-land-warrant application papers relating to a claim made by her under the act of 1855. The resultant consolidated file bears a heading that includes both "W" and "B. L. Wt." symbols and numbers. Approved pension applications of veterans were consolidated with approved bounty-land-warrant applications of veterans or their heirs to form files with headings consisting of "S" and "B. L. Wt." symbols and numbers. Rejected pension application files may also contain approved or rejected bounty-land-warrant application papers.

"Former Widow" cross-reference cards are another type of file unit reproduced in this microfilm publication. The cards normally show the name of the State or organization for which a veteran served, his name, the surname his former widow acquired upon remarriage, the symbol and number of the file (usually a "W" file) in which pension or bounty-land-warrant application papers or information can be found, and the notation "Former Widow." These cross-reference cards are arranged by the surname of the former widow's latest husband, not by the surname of the veteran for whose service a pension or bounty-land warrant was claimed.

Cross-reference cards also exist for variant spellings of a veteran's name. A card generally gives the name of the State or organization for which a veteran served, the spelling of his name by which that card is arranged, the spelling by which the file containing papers or information relating to his service is arranged, and the symbol and number of the latter file.

There are files with headings different from those already described whose contents reflect such differences. Some files, for instance, are labeled "Not Rev." or "Not Rev. War" and contain pension or bounty-land-warrant application papers based on post-Revolutionary War service. The service period is usually shown on the face of the file. A number of pension files are overprinted with the statement "This Envelope Includes FINAL PAYMENT VOUCHER Received from GAO." Such vouchers, which were removed from a separate series of General Accounting Office records, sometimes give the date and place of death of a pensioner and names of heirs.

Some pension application files reproduced in this microcopy have headings that include instructions to "See N.A. Acc. No. 874" followed by a number between 050000 and 050201, the name of the veteran, and the notation "Half Pay" or "Not Half Pay." These instructions refer to a separate series of pension application files that are also in Record Group 15. The records in these files relate mainly to claims made by heirs under an act of Congress approved July 5, 1832 (4 Stat. 563), which provided half-pay pensions for Virginia veterans of the Revolutionary War, and to claims made by heirs for arrears due veterans of Virginia and other States under other pension acts. The files in this separate series were transferred from the Adjutant General's Office of the War Department to the National Archives in 1941 and are not reproduced in this microfilm publication. Abstracts of their contents are in Gaius Marcus Brumbaugh, *Revolutionary War Records, Volume I: Virginia* (Washington, 1936).

A few other pension application files in this microcopy have headings that include instructions to "See N.A. Acc. No. 837–Virginia State Navy," followed by the name of the veteran and the notation "YS File Va. Half Pay." The instructions refer to another small series of Revolutionary War pension application files in the same record group. The contents of these additional files relate mainly to half-pay pension claims of heirs of Virginia State Navy officers under the act of July 5, 1832. The "YS" files, so designated by the Department of the Navy in accordance with a Navy classification scheme, were sent to the National Archives in 1941 by the Office of Naval Records and Library. The files have not been microfilmed or abstracted. All files for Revolutionary War claimants in both the "YS" and the Adjutant General's Office series are referred to in the headings of related files reproduced in this microfilm publication.

Records Withdrawn From the Files

Between 1894 and 1913 several types of records were withdrawn from Revolutionary War pension and bounty-land-warrant application files and sent by the Bureau of Pensions to other Departments or Agencies of the Federal Government. The records were generally documents of historical value dated 1775-83. Between September 6, 1894, and January 16, 1913, muster rolls, payrolls, returns, orders, and miscellaneous personnel lists and papers were sent to the War Department pursuant to acts of Congress approved July 27, 1892 (27 Stat. 275), and August 18, 1894 (28 Stat. 403). On March 22, 1907, some lists of names of seamen taken from the files were sent to the Navy Department in accordance with an act of June 29, 1906 (34 Stat. 579). Diaries, journals, orderly books, account books, and other bound records removed from files were transferred to the Library of Congress on February 9, 1909, under the terms of an act of February 25, 1903 (32 Stat. 865). There are cross-reference slips in the files to describe the records that were transferred and to indicate the Government Department or Agency to which they were sent.

Informational Value of Records in the Files

The records contain both historical and genealogical information. Historical information pertaining to the organization of military units, movement of troops, details of battles and campaigns, and activities of individuals may be obtained from application statements of veterans; from affidavits of witnesses; and from the muster roll, diary, order, or orderly book that was occasionally submitted as proof of service and was not sent by the Bureau of Pensions to another Government Department or Agency. Naval and privateer operations are documented by applications, affidavits, and orders in some files based on service at sea. A few files contain letters written to or by soldiers and sailors during the Revolutionary War, which give firsthand accounts of military, naval, and civil events and conditions. Furloughs, passes, pay receipts, enlistment papers, discharges, commissions, warrants, and other original records of the period 1775-83 are also in some of the files.

Genealogical information is usually available in a file containing original application papers. A veteran's pension application normally gives—in addition to his former rank, unit, and period of service—his age or date of birth, his residence, and sometimes his birthplace. Property schedules often give names and ages of a veteran's wife and children. The application of a widow seeking a pension or a bounty-land warrant may give her age, residence, maiden name, date and place of her marriage, and date and place of death of her husband. A copy of a marriage record made by a town clerk, a clergyman, or a justice of the peace often accompanied the widow's pension application. Application papers submitted by children and other heirs or dependents seeking pensions or bounty-land warrants generally contain information about their ages and residences. Family-record pages from Bibles and other books submitted by pension and bounty-land-warrant applicants give the dates of birth, marriage, and death of family members. In a few pension files are final payment vouchers that sometimes contain information about the date and place of a pensioner's death and names of heirs.

Arrangement and Selection of Files and Records

Each file that is a single 10" x 14" summary or cross-reference card and all envelope files in the series of Revolutionary War Pension and Bounty-Land-Warrant Application Files have been reproduced in this microfilm publication. The files, with the exception of "Former Widow" cross-reference cards, are arranged in alphabetical order by the surname of the veteran. When two or more veterans have the same surname and given name, the further arrangement of the files based on their service is generally alphabetical by the name of the State or organization for which a veteran served, or by the word "Continental," "Navy," or some other service designation placed in the heading of some files above or before the name of a State. "Former Widow" cross-reference cards are arranged by the surname that the former widow acquired upon remarriage.

Within files, the records are unarranged. However, in each envelope file containing more than 10 pages of records, the more significant genealogical documents were filmed first, preceded by a target headed "SELECTED RECORDS." The documents may include pension applications, jackets showing the acts under which pension payments were made, bounty-land-warrant applications, jackets showing the warrant numbers of warrants granted, property schedules, family-record pages from Bibles or other books, copies of marriage records, and final payment vouchers. All remaining documents in that file were filmed after a target headed

"NONSELECTED RECORDS." No distinction was made between selected and nonselected records in filming the envelope files that contained 10 or fewer pages of records; these files can be recognized by a star next to the veteran's surname in the heading.

The "SELECTED RECORDS" in files containing more than 10 pages of records, except those portions of them having no apparent genealogical value (such as attestations or endorsements), have also been reproduced in another microfim publication, Selected Records From Revolutionary War Pension and Bounty-Land-Warrant Application Files (Microcopy 805). Records in files containing 10 or fewer pages of records were reproduced in Microcopy 805 in their entirety, as were all files that consist of a single 10" x 14" summary or cross-reference card. Upon request and for a fee, the National Archives can provide reproductions of the genealogical records filmed in whole or in part in Microcopy 805 relating to a specific veteran or other claimant.

Related Records and Sources of Information

Also in Record Group 15 are letterbooks, registers, and other administrative records of the Pension Office and its successors relating to Revolutionary War pension and bounty-land-warrant applications. Bounty-land warrants are in Record Group 49, Records of the Bureau of Land Management. Pension payment books and final payment vouchers are in Record Group 217, Records of the United States General Accounting Office. Correspondence of the Secretary of War and of the Secretary of the Interior concerning their supervision of pension and bounty-land-warrant matters is in Record Group 107, Records of the Office of the Secretary of War, and in Record Group 48, Records of the Office of the Secretary of the Interior.

Military service records for Revolutionary War soldiers are in Record Group 93, War Department Collection of Revolutionary War Records. Naval and marine personnel records are in Record Group 45, Naval Records Collection of the Office of Naval Records and Library, and Record Group 127, Records of the United States Marine Corps. For additional records of Revolutionary War service and for records of applications made to individual States for pensions or bounty land, researchers should communicate with State archival agencies.

Information of a general historical nature concerning pension and bounty-land-warrant legislation and administration is available in Gustavus A. Weber, *The Bureau of Pensions* (Baltimore, 1923); Gustavus A. Weber and Laurence F. Schmeckebier, *The Veterans' Administration, Its History, Activities and Organization* (Washington, 1934); William H. Glasson, *History of Military Pension Legislation in the United States* (New York, 1900), and *Federal Military Pensions in the United States* (New York, 1918); and Payson J. Treat, *The National Land System, 1785-1820* (New York, 1910). Many of the laws relating to pensions and bounty-land warrants granted for Revolutionary War service, and regulations established by the Secretaries of War, the Treasury, and the Interior for administering them, are compiled in Robert Mayo and Ferdinand Moulton, *Army and Navy Pension Laws, and Bounty Land Laws of the United States . . . From 1776 to 1852* (Washington, 1852).

These introductory remarks were written by Howard H. Wehmann and used here by permission of the National Archives.

AARON, William, Va., Rebecca, W10287; BLWt.67675-160-55
AARONS, Abraham, Va., S30813
ABBE, Eleazur, Ct., BLWt.267-100
Jeduthan, Ct., W22125, Lucretia Roberts, former wid., BLWt. 5371. Iss. 2/5/1790
Mason, Ct., S32628
Nathaniel, Ct., W26215, Nancy Little, former widow
Reuben, Mass., Joanna, See ALBE
Richard, Ct., Lydia, W17197
Thomas, Cont., Ct., S38105
ABBEE, William, Cont. Ct., Lydia, W20556
ABBEY, Edward, Cont., Va., S34621
Eliphalet, Pvt., Sheldon's Cont. Dragoons, Ct., BLWt.5391 iss. 2/9/1797 to Jeduthan Abbey, Sally Bunce, Martha Vibbert, Rebecca Abbey, heirs
George, Ct., S11931
Hezekiah, Ct., S21034
James, See Joseph James
Joseph James, Ct., R 1
Samuel, Ct., W5150, Margaret Mitchell, former wid.; BLWt. 101726-160-55
ABBOT, Abner, Cont., Mass.; Dorcas J., W693; BLWt.26835-160-55
Abraham, Cont., Mass., S30240
Amos, Mass., S5223
Amos, N.H., S12901
Benjamin, Drum Major, Mass. BLWt.3638 iss. 3/25/1790
Beriah, Cont., N.H., Martha,W25365
Caleb, Cont., Mass., S29569
Daniel, Mass., Elizabeth, W1201; BLWt.6434-160-55
Elijah, Va., S35167
Ephraim, Cont., Mass., Esther, W20552
Ezra, N.H., S45489
George, Cont., Mass., S32627
Henry, Pvt., Mass., BLWt.3628 iss. 7/20/1789 to R. Lilley, ass.
Isaac, Mass., S5222
Isaac, Mass., S295681; BLWt.13211-160-55
James, Ct., S17229
James, Mass., Patty/Martha, W20555
John, Mass., S28613
John, Drummer, N.H.,BLWt.2911 iss. 10/30/1789 to Ephraim True, ass.
John, N.J., S11929
John, N.C., S39925
John, Vt., S11934
Joseph, Mass., Ruth, W26972
Joseph, Mass. & N.H., Lucy, W26973
Joseph, N.H., S17807
Josiah, Mass., Anna, BLWt.17-150, W20554
Levi, Pvt., Md.; BLWt.10930 iss. to Francis Sherrard, ass.
Mary, former wid. of Solomon Cole, which see
Moses, Cont., N.H., S16592
Moses, Mass., Allice Lane, former wid., R6117

ABBOT (continued)
Nathan, Mass., S29570
Nathaniel Chandler, N.H., Hannah, W15502
Nehemiah, Mass., S5224
Reuben, N.H., S17808
Reuben, Pvt., Va., BLWt.11862 iss. 8/20/1791
Richard, N.J., BLWt.8086, iss. 8/10/1792
Samuel, Mass., S45831
Samuel, N.Y., S11932
Timothy, N.H., Sally, W20560
William, Mass., S45491
William, N.H., R11334, Mabel Wesson, former widow
ABBOTT, Aaron, Ct., S38101
Asa, Ct., Elizabeth, W20558
Bancroft, N.H., Lydia, W23389
Benjamin, Ct. & N.Y., S11933
Benjamin, Cont., Mass., S17230
Cato, Mass., S52625
Daniel, Mass., S45490
David, Cont., Mass., S32626
Ebenezer, Mass., S2027
Elias, N.H., S45488
Ezra, N.H., S16305
George, N.H., BLWt.2384-100
Henry, Cont., Mass., BLWt.26812-160-55; Lydia, W1347
Jeremiah, N.H., Elizabeth, W15868
Jeremiah, N.H., Betsey, W23387
John, Ct., Temperance Tarbox, former wid., W22434
John, Cont., Rachel, W4110; BLWt. 26714-160-55 & 34974-160-55
John, Cont., N.C., S32089
John, Mass., Betsey, W15504
John, N.H., Phebe, W16801
John, N.J., Alice, W880
Joseph, Ct., Nancy, W20553
Joshua, Mass., N.H., Nancy, W21598
Moses, Cont., N.H., S16592
Nathaniel, Mass., S36881
Nehemiah, Mass., Sarah, W23391
Pardon, R.I., S38102
Peter, Cont., N.H., Phebe, W16091
Philip, N.H., Experience, W23392; BLWt.26748-160-55
Silas, Cont., Mass., S36880
Solomon, S.C., S17806; BLWt. 15188-160-55
Stephen, Ct., S17231
Stephen, Mass., BLWt.14-300-Sgt.
William, S.C., S30239
William, Vt., Sarah, W15501; BLWt.3829-160-55
William, Va., Mary, W5616
ABBY, Eleazur, Ct., BLWt.267-100
Jeduthan, Ct. See ABBE
ABEEL, David, Navy, S46662
Garrett, N.Y., S28210
ABEL, Azel, Vt., Mary, W1348; BLWt.26581-160-55
David, Cont., Ct., S10314
John, Ct., S4257
John, Pa., R 9
Matthias, N.J., S2028
Thomas, Vt., Eunice, R 8

ABEL (continued)
Thomas, Va., Elizabeth, W4109
William, Ct., Lois, W20559
ABELL, Abel, Ct., S11930
Elijah, Ct., S17805
Garrett, N.Y. See ABEEL
John, N.J., S35760
Preserved, Mass., Lucy, W20557
Simon, Ct., Betsey, R 7
Thomas, Vt., R 8
ABER, Israel, N.J., Phebe, W16800
Morris, N.J., S2525
ABERCROMBIE, James, Mass., S14047
ABERNATHY, David, N.C., S1609
Robert, Va., S8006
ABERNETHIE, John, N.C., R 10
ABERTY, Frederick, See ALBARTY
ABLE, John, N.J., See ABELL
John, Pvt., N.Y., BLWt.6732 iss. 7/30/1790 to Edward Compston, ass.
Thomas, Va. See ABEL
ABNER (See EBNER/ABNEY)
Casper, Cont., Pa., S42693
ABNEY, George, S.C., S16591
Paul, Va., Rhoda, W23390
William, Cont., Va., Judith, W1202
ABOIRE, Pratt, Pvt., Hazen's Regt. BLWt.12718; iss. 1/22/1790 to Benjamin Mooers, ass.
ABORN, Ebenezer, Cont., Mass., S23624
Samuel, Ct., S38103
ABOTT, Stephen, Mass., See ABBOTT
ABRAHAM, James, N.J., Elsie, W235
Judith, S.C., former wid. of Moses Cohen, which see
Woodward, Navy, S32623
ABRAMS, Gabriel, Pa., R12
John, N.Y., Hannah, W16167
ABRO, Benajah, Pvt., Ct., BLWt. 5365 iss. 2/20/1790 to Solomon Goss, S38104
ABSALOM/ABSOLAM, Edward, Va., BLWt.2257-100
ABSHIRE, Abraham, Va., S6459
ABSTON, John, Va., R 14; BLReg. 196760-55 & 277661-55
ACART/ACHEHEART, Frederick, See HEART
ACHER, See ACKER
ACHERSON, Abram, N.Y., R17
ACHMET, Hamet, Ct., S38107
ACHOR/ACOR, Jacob, Ct., S39144, BLWt.1146-100
ACKART, Solomon, See ACKER
ACKELBARNER, Joseph, See EICHELBERGER
ACKEMAN, William, See ACKERMAN
ACKER, Albert, N.Y., Sarah, R 15
Benjamin, Cont., N.Y., S11936
Christian, Pa., S22073
Conradt, Pvt., N.Y., BLWt.6743 iss. 6/30/1790
Henry, N.Y., R 16
Jacob, N.Y., Mary, W2046. See her former husb., John Vanderbilt
Jacob, N.Y., Johannah, W16804
Peter, N.Y., S31510
Solomon, N.Y., S15351

ACKERMAN (AUKERMAN/OKKERMAN)
Andrew, Pvt., Hazen's Regt. BLWt.12719 iss. 5/20/1795
Christopher, Pa., Susanna, W26779
Daniel, Pvt., N.Y., BLWt.6763 iss. 9/6/1791 to Wm. Gilliland, admr.
Effy, former widow of David Marinus, W385, which see
Francis, Pvt., Hazen's Regt., BLWt.12712 iss. 9/22/1791
John, N.J., S16028
Wm., Pvt., Lamb's Art. N.Y., BLWt.6761, iss. 8/20/1790 to William Cumming, assignee
William, N.Y., S44545
ACKERS, Amos, Corp., N.J., BLWt. 8083, iss. 5/17/1800 to John Duncan, assignee
ACKERSON, See also ACHERSON
Cornelius, N.Y., Mary, W23393
Derick, N.Y., Leah, W15750
John, N.Y., Mariah Elizabeth, R18
John, N.Y., Maria, W21053
ACKERT, See ACKER
ACKLER, See ECKLAR/ECKLER
John, N.Y., Gertrude, W19214
John, Pvt., N.Y., BLWt.6752 iss. 8/27/1790 to Nicholas Fish, ass.
Leonard, N.Y., Catharine, W25335
ACKLEY, Abraham, See ACLY
Ahira, Ct., Miriam, W4872
Bezaleel, Pvt., N.J., BLWt.8075, iss. 8/14/1789
Champin, Pvt., Ct., BLWt.5362 iss. 12/6/1791 to Stephen Thorn
Champion, Ct., Abigail, W5197
Edward, Ct., S11935
Elihu, Ct., S44544
Isaac C., Ct., S17232
Ithamer, Ct., S28614
Jacob, N.Y., BLWt.6731, iss. 11/27/1790
Jacob, N.Y., See AKLEY
Joel, N.Y., S33959
Joel, Pvt., N.Y., BLWt.6748 iss. 8/4/1790 to John N. Blecker, ass.
Lewis, Pvt., Ct., BLWt.5361, iss. 4/11/1792 to Martin Kingsley
Nathaniel, Ct., R 20
Samuel, Cont., Mass., See AKLEY
Simeon, Ct., S18680
Stephen, Ct., Mehitable, W17198
Thomas, Ct., S38106
Thomas, Corp., Ct., BLWt.5369 iss. 2/5/1790
Thomas, Pa., BLWt.13883-160-55; Sarah, W12181 (or ACKLLYE)
ACKLING, Francis, Pvt., N.Y., BLWt. 6751, iss. 7/26/1790 to Gerit H. Van Waggenen, assignee
ACKRIGHT, Isaac, Md., R 22
ACLY, Abraham, Cont., Mass., S44543
ACOCK, Robert, N.C., S35168
ACOR, Jacob, Ct., See ACHOR
ACORD, Cornelaus, Md., S39145
ACORN, George Michael, Cont., Mass. Margaret, W23394; also 2nd U.S. Inf. 1813-1815
Michael, See George Michael
ACRE/ACREE/ACREA
Cronamus, Md., S39145
James, Va., Esther, W694, BLWt.

ACRE/ACREE/ACREA (continued)
BLWt.26051-160-55
John, Va., Lucy, R 21
Philip, Va., Catharine, W9690; BLWt.26293-160-55
William, N.C., Edith or Edy, W25334; BLWt.26998-160-55
ACRES, George, Pvt., Mass., BLWt. 3634. Iss. 8/3/1797 to S. Wyman, assignee to heirs
ACRON, Gabriel. See EAKINS
ACTON, Henry, Md., S2337
Smallwood, Md., Nancy, W26658; BLWt. 34590-160-55
ADAIR, James, S.C., S9264 (See ADARE)
John, N.C., S1158
John, S.C., Catharine, W2895 BLWt.24750-160-50; Indian War, 1792; Kentucky, War of 1812
William, S.C., Catharine, W9691
ADAMS, See also ADDAMS
Aaron, Green Mt. Boys, Vt., Sarah, W9323
Aaron, Mass., Vt., Lydia, W20573
Aaron, Pvt., N.H., BLWt.2903, iss. 3/25/1790
Aaron, St. Clair's War, Old War Invalid File 24446
Abigail, Mass., former widow of Hanmer Lanson
Abigail, Mass., former widow of Samuel Wyman, R 23, which see
Abijah, Ct., R.I.?, R24
Abner, Mass., Sarah, W3489
Abraham, Ct., S14914
Adam, Md., S34623
Amos, Cont., Mass., S18681
Andrew, Mass., S14915
Ansell, Navy, Mass., S32631
Asa, Mass., S22076
Asa, Mass., Elizabeth, W23103
Asa, N.J., Ann, W133
Bartholomew, Pvt., Del., BLWt. 10693. Iss. 9/2/1789; S35761, res. of Sussex Co., Del.
Benjamin, Cont., Ct., Susan, W20570
Benjamin, Va., S35169
Bryant, N.C., S6468
Daniel, Cont., N.H., S45494
Daniel, Mass., S17233
Daniel, Mass., Hannah, W23406
David, Ct., BLWt.30-400, Surgeon, No papers
David, Pvt., Ct., BLWt.5396, iss. 4/12/1792 to Stephen Thorn
David, Ct., S45171
David, Cont. N.H., S45169
David, Sgt., N.H., BLWt.2909, iss. 11/7/1796 to Joseph Thomas, ass.
David, N.H., Alice, W10349
David, N.J., Elizabeth, W4873
David, N.C., S34622
David, Pa., S30815
Deliverance, Ct., N.J., S45170
Dudley G., N.H., Sally Osgood former widow, W26599
Ebenezer, Cont., Ct., S37647
Ebenezer, Ct., N.Y., S11939
Ebenezer, N.H., S45649
Edward, Mass. & N.H., Privateer

ADAMS (continued)
Patty, W20567
Elias, Mass., S30241
Elijah, Ct., Sarah, W21604
Elijah, Ct., Mass., S2494
Elijah, Ct., N.Y., Sarah, R46, BLWt.34592-160-55
Elijah, N.Y., S11942
Elisha, Ct., R 28
Elisha, Va., S12903
Ellison E., Va., S37649
Emanuel, Pvt., N.Y., BLWt.6742, iss. 8/23/1796 to Jos. Roberts, assignee
Emanuel, N.Y., S45172
Enoch, Mass., S16593
Ezekiel, Vt., S23091
Francis, (French), Nancy, W8313
Francis, S.C., Mary, W5198; BLWt. 29034-160-55
Gavin, Va., R 31
George, N.C., S16594
George, Pa., BLWt.8911, iss. 1789
George, Pa., Elizabeth, R 29
George, Va., Nancy Bramblet, former widow, W8393
Gideon, Cont., Ct., Rhoda, W23395
Hannah, former wid. of Wm. Spaulding, W23401, which see
Heman, Mass., Lucy, W2047
Henry, Mass., Surgeon, Sarah Besly former wid. W8129; BLWt. 18-400 & BLReg. 191261-1755
Henry, N.Y., See ADAMY
Henry, N.C., Susanna, R 48
Henry, Va. Rebecca, W5595
Hitty, former widow of Asa Hoskins, Ct., W25366, which see
Isaac, Mass. Sea Service, S17811
Isaac, Mass. Sea Service, R 32
Isaac, Pvt., N.H., BLWt.2910, iss. 4/5/1796 to Oliver Ashley, ass.
Isaac, N.H., Polly, W23405
Isaac, Vt., Hannah, W20562
Issacher, Mass., Melisent or Millisent, W20566; BLWt.6105-160-55
Jacob, N.H., R 33
Jacob, Pvt., N.J., BLWt.8073 iss. 8/27/1796 to David Craig, ass.
Jacob, Pvt., Va., BLWt.11863 iss. 1793 to Robert Means, ass.
James, Ct., S11937
James, Cont., Mass., Susan, W28414
James, Mass., S5231
James, Mass., S22075
James, N.J., S11943
James, Pvt., N.Y., BLWt.6738 iss. 7/24/1790 to John Lawrence, ass.
James, Pvt., N.Y., BLWt.6739 iss. 9/28/1790 to Bartholomew & Fisher assignees
James, N.Y., Invalid, no papers
James, N.C., S8007
James, Pvt., Va., BLWt.11860, iss. 1/7/1793 to Robt. Means,ass.
James, Va., R 31 1/2
James, Va., S16306
Jedediah, Cont., Ct., S49293
Jedediah, Mass., Rebecca, W23412
Jeremiah, ---, R 34

ADAMS (continued)
Jeremiah, N.C., BLWt.19776-160-55
Elizabeth, W8093
Jesse, Cont., Mass., Meriam, W20565
Jesse, N.C., Unicy, W 66
Joel, Ct., Rejected
Joel, Mass., S45495
Joel, Mass., Jemima, W23402
John, Ct.,S11947; BLReg.191722-55
John, Ct., S15728
John, Cont., N.H., S45493; BLWt. 4-200, no papers
John, Cont., N.Y., Mary. See ADDOMS
John, (French), Esther, R 30
John, Pvt., Md., BLWt.10935 iss. 2/9/1792
John, Pvt., Md., BLWt.10938 iss. 3/11/1791
John, Md., S30816
John, Md., Pa., BLWt.61125-160-55 Ann or Nancy, R 25
John, Md., Privateer, R 38
John, Md. Sea Service, S6466
John, Mass., S5230
John, Mass., Prudence, W1529
John, Mass., Molly, W16490
John, Mass., Hannah, W23415
John, Mass., S28962
John, Mass., S12906
John, Mass., S5229
John, N.H., Molly, W16093
John, N.J., R 39
John, N.Y., R32, See ADAMY
John, N.Y., Elizabeth, BLReg. 291114-1855
John, Pa., S39926
John, Pa., Margaret, W1691; BLWt. 30603-160-55
John, Va., S35763
John, Va., Calarine, W 881
John, Va., Suckey, R 41
John Carroll, S.C., Sarah, W8312
Jonas, Cont., N.J., See ADDOMS
Jonas, Mass., S22617, Mary, R 42
Jonas, N.H., Disability, no papers
Jonas, N.H., S41400
Jonathan, Cont., N.J.; BLWt. 8904-100, no papers; and BLWt. 301-60-55; Margaret, W5596
Jonathan, Mass., Elizabeth, W23396
Jonathan, Mass., Abigail, W15869
Jonathan, Mass., S29572
Jonathan, Pvt. Moylan's Dragoons, Pa., BLWts.301-60-55 & 8904, iss. 1/28/179-
Joseph, Ct., BLReg.268665
Joseph, Ct., Rebecca, R 45
Joseph, Cont., Mass., S29571
Joseph, Cont., Mass., S32630
Joseph, Mass., S36882
Joseph, Mass., S36883
Joseph, Mass., Dorothy, W21603
Joseph, Mass., Molly, W15513
Joseph, N.H., Elizabeth, W16092
Joseph, R.I., S41401
Joseph, R.I., Hannah, W17199
Joshua, Ct., BLWt.13201-160-55, Sarah, W25337
Joshua, Mass., See ADDAMS
Joshua, Mass., S38486

ADAMS (continued)
Josiah, Mass., S11940
Lemuel, Mass., S29573
Levi, Ct., Vt., S11941
Levi, Cont., Ruth, W3913; BLWts. 217-60-55; 5392-100
Levi, Cont., N.H., S38485
Littleton, Va., Harriet W., W5597
Luke, Ct., S37652
Mark, Md., Navy, N.J., Privateer, Hannah, W2896
Martin, Vt., Mercy, W23409
Mary, former wid. of John Hutchinson, Ct., W20571, which see
Mathew, N.Y., S28212
Matthew, N.J., Mary, W882
Micajah, N.C., S1783
Moses, Cont., Ct., S45174
Nathan, Del., BLWt.371-300, Sarah (pensioned)
Nathan, Mass., Polly, W25336, BLWt.30592-160-55
Nathaniel, Mass., S33249
Nathaniel, Mass., Zebiah, W20563
Obadiah, Mass., S32633
Oliver, Mass., N.H., Catharine, R27
Paul, Mass., Privateer, S28965
Peleg, Pvt., N.Y., BLWt.6725,iss. 11/1/1791 to Asa Ballard, ass.
Peter, Cont., Mass., S45176
Peter, Md., BLWt.372-450
Peter, Mass., Peggy or Margaret, W15512
Peter B., (or F), Va., S30814
Philemon, Mass., Betsey, R 26
Philip, Cont., N.H., S38484
Philip, N.C., S8008
Phinehas, Mass., Patience, W15511
Reuben, Ct., Abigail, W23399
Reuben, Ct., Lydia, W20568
Reuben, Mass., S28964
Reufus, Cont., Mass., N.H., Martha, W21601
Richard, Md., S11938
Robert, Corp., Pa., BLWt.8910 iss. 11/5/1789
Robert, Va., S45175
Roswell, Ct., Privateer, Eunice, W23411
Samuel, Ct., See Samuel C.
Samuel, Cont., BLWt.69-450 Surgeon in General Hospital
Samuel, Cont. Ct., S38483; BLWt. 955-100
Samuel, Cont., Mass., S23508
Samuel, Cont. Mass., Abigail, W3490; BLWt.5204-160-55
Samuel, Mass., S17810
Samuel, Mass., S23090
Samuel, Mass., Susanna, W23413
Samuel, Mass., Navy, S28961
Samuel, Cont., N.H., Sarah,W23408
Samuel, N.H., Elizabeth, W20564; BLWt. 3-200
Samuel C., Ct., S11948
Sarah, Mass., former wid. of John Green, W15510, which see
Seth, Mass., S23509
Shubael, Ct., S28615
Silas, Ct., S12905
Silas, Mass., Lucy Dodge, former

ADAMS (continued)
widow, W19189
Solomon, Mass., S11945
Solomon, Mass., W17200, Hannah; BLWt.11256-160-55
Stephen, Cont. Mass., Sally,W23404
Stephen, Mass., S28963
Stephen, N.H., S45177
Sylvester, Va., S30243; BLWt.26361 -160-55
Thomas, Mass., BLWt.36527-160-55
Thomas, Mass., BLWt.49473-160-55
Thomas, Mass., S11949
Thomas, Mass., S22074
Thomas, Mass., Esther, W15515
Thomas, Mass., Sarah, W23397
Thomas, R.I., See ADDAMS. Abigail Larkin, former wid. W13615
Thomas, Va., Salley, W4111
Timothy, Ct., Susannah, W21600
Timothy, Mass., Privateer, S18682
Timothy, Mass., Joanna, W20572
Titus, Ct. & Mass., R 50
Titus, Mass., Anna, W23398
Walter, N.C., S30242
William, Ct. or N.Y., S11946
William, Ct., S45173
William, Cont., Mass., S32634
William, Cont., Mass., Anna,W23410
Wm., Cont., Mass., Esther,W21602
William, Md., BLWt. 373-200
Wm., Mass., Mary or Molly, W15514
William, N.J., R 51
Wm., Pvt., N.Y., BLWt.6740 iss. 9/28/1790 to Bartholomew & Fisher, assignees
William, N.Y., S35764
William,N.C., Mary, R 43
William, Pa., BLWt.47-400, Surgeon No papers
William, Pa., S5232
William, Pa., S30817
William, Pa., R 52
William, S.C., S17812
William, Va., R 53
Wm., Pvt., Va., BLReg.254310-55
Wm., BLReg.246961-55, Margaret
Winborn, N.H., BLWt.6-450, Lt. Col No papers
Zebediah, Mass., S21037
ADAMY, Henry, Pvt., N.Y., BLWt. 6737, iss. 7/30/1791
Henry, N.Y., S44287
John, N.Y., Elizabeth, R 37
ADARE, James, S.C., S9264
ADCOCK, John, Va., S39146
John A., Va., S21036
Joshua, N.C., S6467
Thomas, N.C., S1612
William, Va., S37648
ADDAMS, See also ADAMS
Benjamin, See ADAMS
David, See ADAMS
John, See ADAMS
Joshua, Mass., BLWt.247-100
Thomas, R.I., Abigail Larkin former widow, W13615
ADDEE, See ADYE
ADDINGTON, Wm., S.C., Delilah, W5598
ADDIS, Richard, S.C., S21594

ADDIS (continued)
Simon, N.J., S586
ADDISON, Jacob, Del., S16029
Richard, Va., S37651
William, S.C., BLWt.61311-160-55; Nancy, W5599
ADDITON, Thos., Cont., Mass., S18683
ADDOMS, John, Cont., N.Y., Mary, W16805
Jonas, Cont., N.J., BLWt.33-200-Lt. No papers. Sur. Cert. No. 26
ADEE, Aner, Pvt., Ct., BLWt. 5387 iss. 9/8/1789
ADER, Morres/Morris, Pvt., N.J., S44289; BLWt.8074 iss. 7/7/1790 to John Crawford, ass.
ADERTON, John, Mass., Mercy, W23407
ADKIN, Samuel, Cont., Mass., S44288
ADKINS, Charles, N.C., See ATKINS
David, Ct., Cont., S12012
Henry, N.C., R69
Hezekiah, Va., R290
Isaiah, Ct., BLWt.649-100; 30th U.S. Inf., S49292
Jabez, Pvt., Ct., S33248; BLWt. 5368, iss. 5/10/1798
James, Va., S1157
James, Va., Elizabeth, R56
John, Vt., Mercia, R 57
Luther, Ct., Azubah, W23400
Stephen, Del., S31512
Thomas, S.C., Ruthey, R 58
William, N.C., S6469
ADKINSON, David, Cont. Va., S35762
James, N.C., S41399
James, Va., See ATKINSON
William, --- Disability. No papers
ADKISSON, Ellis, Va., S12904
ADLEY, Peter, N.Y., War of 1812, BLWt.6265-160-55; Sally or Sarah, W5199
ADLINGTON, John, Navy, Mass., S32629
ADLUM, John, Pa., S11944
ADNER, George, N.Y., R 59
ADRIANCE, Isaac, N.Y., R 60
ADYE, Caleb, Ct., S6465
John, Ct., S21595
AEISLA, See ISSLEY/ISELEY
Coonrod, N.C., R 61
AERY, Joshua, Ct., Rachel, See AREY
AFRICA, Cash, Pvt. Ct., BLWt.5375 iss. 10/7/1789 to Benjamin Tallmadge
AGAR, Hugh, Pvt., N.J., BLWt.8076 iss. 9/7/1790 to Wm. Barton, ass.
AGARD, Hezekiah, Ct., S23092
John, Ct., R 62
Joseph, Ct., N.Y., S45179
Noah, Ct., N.Y., S45180
AGEE, Jacob, Va., S6470
Joshua, Va., R 63
AGENS, James, Md., N.Y., S33960
AGER, Hugh, N.J., S33961
AGGLESTON, Ct., Cont.
Jemima, See EGLESTON
AGIN, James, N.J., S2029
AGLE, Philip, Cont., res. N.C., S41402
AGNEW, George, Cont., S.C., S10315
John, Va., S37653

AGNEW (continued)
Robert, Pa., R64
AGREY, Thomas, Corp., Mass., BLReg. 230-465-55
AHART, Jacob, Va., S6471
AHEARN, William, Pvt., Md., BLWt.10920 iss. 2/7/1790
AHL, John Peter/John P. Venall, Cont., S5234
AIKEN, Andrew, Cont., N.H., S45497
Israel, Mass., Susanna, W25339
James, Mass. & Vt., S12908
James, N.Y., Amy, See AKIN
John, Pa., S2190
John, ---, Disability, No papers
Jonathan, Vt., S10316
Phinehas, N.H., BLWt.2383-160-55 Elizabeth
Samuel, Cont. N.H., S45496
Samuel, Cont., N.H., Martha, W16806
Solomon, Mass., War of 1812, S38488
Thomas, Ct., S4258
William, S.C., Hannah, See AKIN
AIKENS, James, N.C., Va., Dyce, See AIKIN
Nathaniel, Mass., Vt., Mary, W21605
AIKIN, Eliakim, Mass., S38487
James, N.C., Va., Dyce, W26780; BLWt.67617-160-55
Solomon, Mass., See AIKEN
AIKINS, Ebenezer, Mass., Chloe, See AKEN
Nathaniel, Mass., Vt., Mary, See AIKENS
Samuel, N.Y., See AKINS
AILER, Michael, Bombardier in Artillery, Pa., BLWt.8907 iss. 11/26/179- to Francis Kirkpatrick, ass.
AILESWORTH, George, Va., See AILSWORTH
AILSTOCK, Absalom, Va., S6475
AILSWORTH, George, Va., Susannah, W37
AIMES, John, Pvt., N.J., BLWt. 8085 iss. 6/16/1789 to Aaron Ogden, ass.
AINGER, Jesse, Cont., Mass., BLWt. 1260-100; S38489
AINSWORTH, Amariah/Amaziah, N.H., S22077
Benjamin, Mass., Sally/Silvey Crawford, former wid., W22863; Her other husb. Wm. Crawford also pensioned
Edward, Ct., Polly, R67
Moses, Mass., S15729
AIR, George, Pvt., Mass., BLWt. 3646, iss. 5/31/1790 to Theo. Fowler, ass.
AIRS, George, Cont., Maine res. in 1794. Disability. No papers
William, Cont., Mass., See AYER
AITCHLEY, Abraham, See ATCHLEY
AKALEY, John, Cont., res. Pa., BLWt.179-100; S39927
AKE, Wm., Del., BLWt.2043-100; Esther, W2898
AKEHART, Frederick, Ct., See

AKEHART (continued)
Frederick A. Heart; or John See Fred A. Heart
AKELEY, Benjamin, N.Y., S22619
Francis, N.H., S41934
John, Cont., Mass., Miriam, W25340
Thomas, Mass., Vt., S21596
AKELY, John, Cont., See AKALEY
AKEN, Ebenezer, Mass., Chloe, R66
AKENS, James, N.C., Frances, W4625
AKER, John, N.Y., S11950
AKERD, Andrew, Va., S19178
AKERLEY, Daniel, N.J., R9560, See SICKLES
AKERMAN, Peter, N.H., S20583
AKERS, John, Va., S6474
William, N.J., Pa., S22078
AKIN, James, Ct., N.Y., BLWt.24991-160-55; Amy, W1349
James, Va., S31513
Thomas, Ct., S16595
William, S.C., Hannah, W8314
AKINS, Henry, N.C., See ADKINS
James, Pvt., Lamb's Artillery, N.Y., BLWt.6758 iss. 7/12/1792
John, N.H., S17813
Matthew, Mass., Meriam, W20574
Samuel, N.Y., S45181
Seth, Ct., Sally, W25341
William, N.C., S.C., BLWt.30624-160-55; Elizabeth, W5600
AKLEY, Jacob, N.Y., S45182
Samuel, Cont. Mass., BLWt.16102-160-55; S17809
ALBAN, George, Va., S8019
ALBARTY, Frederick, N.C., Elizabeth W3749; BLWt.26841-160-55
ALBE, Reuben, Mass., Joanna, W10346 BLWt.40906-160-55
ALBEE, Asa, Cont., Mass., Abigail, W1351
Caleb, Mass., BLWt.6104-160-55; Marcy, W15519
Eleazer, Cont. Mass., S45189
Eleazer John, Mass., Privateer; BLWt.1762-100; S41404
Ichabod, Mass., Lona, W12192
John, Mass., See Eleazer John ALBEE
Jonathan, Mass., S36891
Obadiah, Mass., Privateer, S29578
Salathiel, Mass., S11960
Thomas, Mass., S23094
William, Mass., S20278
ALBEN, John, N.Y., R 70
ALBERT, Jacob, Pvt., Pa., BLWt.8887 iss. 6/14/1791
Jacob, Pa., Mary, W9326
John, Cont. Pa., S44293
William, Pa., S37659
William, R.I., S21038
William, Va., R-?
ALBERTSON, Abraham, N.J., S2904
Early, N.C., Elizabeth, W32; BLWt. 36519-160-55
George, Pvt., Pa., BLWt.8890 iss. 8/22/1791 to John McCleland, ass.
Jacob, R.I., S21597
Richard, Cont., N.Y., S12914
ALBERTY, Frederick, See ALBARTY
ALBEY, Reuben, Mass., See ALBE
ALBRECHT, Martin, Sophia, R 71
ALBRIGHT, Adam, Pa., Margaret, W20599

ALBRIGHT (continued)
Henry, N.C., S6485
Jacob, Pvt. Hazen's Regt., BLWt. 12720 iss. 11/14/1792 to George Schaffer, ass.
Jacob, Pvt., N.Y., BLWt.6724 iss. 7/24/1790 to John Lawrence, ass.
John, Pvt. Hazen's Regt., BLWt. 12713 iss. 1/5/1791
John, Corp., N.Y., BLWt.6722 iss. 9/3/1790
John, N.Y., S46365
John, Pa., Mary, See LAMBRIGHT
Ludwick, N.C., Elizabeth, W5609
William, N.C., S6492
ALBRITTON, John, S.C., See ALLBRITTON
Mathew, N.C., R 72
ALBRO, Andrews, R.I., S45188
Clark, R.I. Disability, No papers
Job, Cont. R.I., S46019
John, R.I., S11961
Stephen, R.I., S45190
ALBY, John, Pvt., Md., BLWt. 10933 iss. 2/1/1790
ALCOCK, David, Pvt., Ct., BLWt. 5360 iss. 3/2/1795 to Eneas Munson, Jr.
David, Ct., S45186
Robert, Md., S8017
Thomas, Va., S15731
ALCORN, George, S.C., S31516
William, Pvt., Del., BLWts.8891 & 10692, iss. 9/2/1789
ALCOX, John Blakesley, Ct., Lois, W17209
Samuel, Ct., Lydia, W17211
ALDAY, Seth P., Va., Sarah, R73
ALDEN, Alpheus, Mass., Elizabeth, W20594
Barnabas, Mass., Mehitable, W23433
Benjamin, Cont. Mass., Polly, W20578
Benjamin, Mass., R 74
David, Mass., Susannah, W5607
Ebenezer, Mass., S32650
Eliab, Cont. Mass., BLWt.6431-160-55; Mary, W20581
Elijah, Mass., Rebecca, R75
Humphrey, Cont. Mass., S32648
Ichabod, Cont. Mass., BLWt.24-500-Col., Mary Partridge former wid. W21903
Isaiah, Mass., S29583
John Adams, Mass., Hannah, W20589
Judah, Cont. Ct., BLWt.1150-300
Judah, Cont. Mass., BLWt.1716-300, S46364
Mason F., Pvt. Ct., BLWt.5356 iss. 9/8/1790
Moses, Mass., S12919
Nathan, Mass., S29576
Oliver, Cont., Mass., S41410
Roger, Ct., Elizabeth, W4113
Silas, Mass., BLWt.30928-160-55, Charity Mayhew, former wid. W7396
Simeon, Mass., S30246
ALDENDARFER, ---, Pa., R 76
ALDER, George, Md., Lucy Ann, W20580
James L., Md., S8022
Jeremiah, Pvt. Hazen's Regt.,

ALDER (continued)
BLWt.12723 iss. 3/1/1792 to Nathaniel Grimes, ass.
ALDERMAN, Daniel, N.C., Sarah, W9696
Ephraim, Ct., S45185
Gad, Cont., Ct., S32639
Timothy, Ct., Ruth, R77
ALDERSON, Simon, Sgt., N.C., BLWt.11884 iss. 6/1/1790 to Abishai Thomas, ass.
Simon, N.C., BLWt. 192-100
Thomas, Va., S8020
ALDIS, Amey, R.I., former wid. of William Gadcomb, which see
ALDMAN, Thomas, Pvt., Lee's Legion, Va., BLWts.11865 & 13966 iss. to Robt. Means, ass.
ALDRED, Henry, Va., S44291
John, N.C., See ALLRED
ALDREDGE, William, N.C., S16308
ALDRICH, Aaron, R.I., R 81
Abel, R.I., S38492
Amasa, Cont., Mass., Urana (or Amana) Whitcomb, former wid. W16467
Asquire, R.I., S18685
Benjamin, Mass., R12086
Caleb, N.H., S20584
Caleb, R.I., BLWt.96096-160-55; Lovey, W2510
Clark, R.I., Polly, W2740
Elisha, Navy, R.I., W20811, Content Burlingame, former wid.
Gideon, R.I., Mercy, W20591
Gustavus, Mass., Susan, W1692; BLWts.16267-160-55; 1882-100
Henry, Mass., S36889
Henry, Pvt., Mass., BLWt.3627 iss. 3/25/1790
Israel, R.I., Anna, W15516
Jacob, N.Y., R 80
James, Mass., S32646
Jesse, Mass., S11971
Joel, R.I., S21043
John, Ct., Navy, S21601
Joseph, R.I., S17236
Joshua, R.I., Ruth, W23426
Nathaniel, Cont. Mass., Mary, W23431
Noah, Mass., Susanna, W20585
Noah, R.I., Huldah, W15521
Olive, R.I., See JACOB GOFF, former widow of
Phinehas, Cont., Mass., Hannah Cook, former wid., R2255; BLReg. 202613-1855
Richard, R.I., S21041
Richard, R.I., Orphan, W15527; BLWt.2347-160-55
Robert, N.Y., R 82
Rufus, Mass. & R.I., S19520
Silas, Mass., Hannah, W16811
Simon, R.I., S21598
Solomon, N.H., S23512
William, N.H., See ALDRICK
ALDRICH/ALDRICK, Wm., N.H.,S45499
ALDRICKS, George, N.H., BLWt. 2-300, Capt., iss. to Benj. Whitcomb, no papers
ALDRIDGE, Caleb, Sgt., N.H., BLWt. iss. 11/7/1796 to Joseph Thomas, ass.

ALDRIDGE (continued)
Elisha, See ELDRIDGE
Eseck, R.I. res. 1794, Disability No papers
Francis, N.C., S35170
John, Pa., BLWt.1831-100; Elizabeth, W25342; BLWt.66-60-55
John/John Simpson, Va., Mary, W9698
Joseph, Pvt., Hazen's Regt., BLWt.12716 iss. 1/11/1791
Peter, Pvt., N.C., BLRej. 308762-55
William, Va., S12921
ALEN, Eleanor, R.I., former wid. of Samuel Short
ALESHIDT, Henry, Va., See ALESHITE
ALESHITE, Henry, Va., S29579
John C., Va., S17816
ALEXANDER, Abraham, Mass., Betsey, W5611; BLWt.2039-100
Abram, N.C., S8013
Asa, Ga., S32092
Benjamin, Ct., Cont., R84, Elizabeth
Benjamin, S.C., S10320
Charles, N.C., S21599
Charles, N.C., S6488
Dan, N.C., S2905
Dan, S.C., Sarah, R 88
Eldad, Mass., Mary, W20598
Elijah, N.C., Sarah, W5201
Eliphaz, Mass., S28617
Elisha, Mass., Sally, W8325; BLWt.19505-160-55
George, S.C., Rebecca, W8324; BLWt.24619-160-55
Henry, Mass., R.I., S11953
Hugh, N.H., Betsey, BLWt.71162-160-55
Isaac, Md., N.C., S.C., R86
Isaac, N.C., S6487
Isaac, N.C., Chloe, W2899
Jabez, Mass., N.H., Betsey Mack former wid. W7384; BLWt.9046-160-55
James, Ct., S38490
James, Ct. & R.I., S16599
James, N.C., Rhoda, W12190
James, N.C., Pa., S8014
James, Pvt., Pa., BLWt.8893, iss. 6/29/1789 to Al McConnell, ass.
James, S.C., Mary, W9327
James, Va., S37660
James, Va., Jerusha, W8322
James R., Md., N.C., Dorcas, W2901
Jeremiah, Va., S31515
John, Del., Pa., S44294
John, Mass., S41409
John, N.C., Susanna, W20586; BLWt.19775-160-55
John, N.C., Susannah Katherine, R89
John, Pa., S30820
John, Va., Rej. B.L.---
Jonathan S., N.Y., Bathsheba, W---. This woman's children by first husband were pensioned See JOHN HAGER, Mass.
Joseph, N.C., Martha, R 87

ALEXANDER (continued)
Joseph, Pa., S32091
Joseph, Pa., Va., Sarah, W5613; BLWt.40922-160-55
Joseph, S.C., S15355
Martha, Mass., former widow of Nathaniel Evans, which see
Mathew, S.C., Eleanor, W324; BLWt.36632-160-55
Nathaniel, Cont., BLWt.70-300 Surgeon's Mate. No papers
Nathaniel, Cont. Mass., BLWt. 23-300. Capt. S45166
Peter, Va., Jannett, W8323
Philip, Mass., Deborah, W16095
Philip, N.H., Olive, W20587
Quartus, Mass., Mary, W1794; BLWt.26808-160-55
Robert, Pa., S11970
Rufus, Mass., N.H., N.Y., S45191
Samuel, N.C., Jean, W1530; BLWt. 21836-160-55
Sarah, Mass., former widow of John Cummings, W21610, which see
Simeon, Mass., S28966
Solomon, Cont. Va., S46420; BLWt.1914-100
Solomon, Pvt., Mass., BLRej. 234897-55
Stephen, N.C., Martha, W20583
Susannah, N.C., former widow of John Bush, N.C., which see
Thomas, Cont., Mass., S15353
Thomas, Mass., Disability. No papers
Thomas, N.C., S6495
Thomas, Pa., R90
William, Cont., BLWt.3610
William, Md., Elizabeth, R 85
William, Pvt., Mass., BLWt.3610 iss. 3/25/1791 to D. Quinton, ass.
William, Mass., Esther, W21612
William, ?, Rebecca Jacobs, former widow, R---, N.H. res.
William, N.C., BLWt.64-200, Lt. No papers
William, N.C., S1893
William, N.C., S.C., S6496
William, N.C., S.C., S361
William, Pa., BLWt.41-400, Major No papers
William,Pa., Margaret, W9697
William, Pa., Va., Elizabeth, W4623
William, Va., S2344
William, Va., S1785
William, Va., S36398

ALFIN, William, N.C., S8018

ALFORD, Alexander, Ct., Green Mt. Boys, Elizabeth/Eliza, W20600
Asahel, Mass., S45184
Benedict, Ct., Mass., Vt., S8016
Eber, Ct., Cont., S11966
Elijah, Cont., Mass., R 92
George, Vt., S28968
Jacob, Va., Nancy, W386
John, Ct., S39932
John, Pa., S44290
John, Va., S1744

ALFRED, George, Vt., See ALFORD
Thomas, Sea Service, Va., Susan, R93. Other husbband was Jesse Kennedy

ALGER, Asa, Ct., Mass., Sarah, R94
Daniel, Mass., Sarah, W15526
Elijah, Ct., S11962
James, Mass., S32638
James, Mass., Mary, W15520
Jonathan, Mass., R.I., S21040
Nathaniel, Ct., Dorcas, W5612; BLWt.20593-160-55
Nicholas, R.I., Rebecca, W20590

ALGIER, Nathaniel, Dorcas, See ALGER

ALGOOD, John, Va., See ALLGOOD
William, Cont., Ga., S41408

ALING, Stephens, Cont., Ct. See ALLING

ALISON, John, Pa., Mary, See ALLISON

ALKINS, Shadrick, N.C.,See ELKINS

ALKYSER, George, Pvt., N.Y., BLWt.6745 iss. 10/2/1790

ALLAN, John, Cont. Pa., Va.,S45196
Moses, Va., S2487

ALLARD, Andrew, Mass., Zerviah Frail, former wid., W14753

ALLAY, Samuel, Va., S2903

ALLBAUGH, Zachariah, Md., Pa., S2902; BLWt.26125-160-55

ALLBEE, Jonathan, Mass. See ALBEE

ALLBEY, Reuben, Mass., See ALBE

ALLBRIGHT, Adam, Pa., See ALBRIGHT
John, Pa., R 96

ALLBRITTON, John, S.C., S31517

ALLCOX, Asa, Cont., Ct., S23513

ALLD, Benjamin, Cont., Mass., N.H., S45498
William, Mass., N.H., Hannah Clark, former wid., W23824

ALLDER, George, Md., Lucy Ann, See ALDER

ALLEE, David, Va., S16596

ALLEMBAUGH, Peter, Va., S36401

ALLEN, Abel, Ct., Phebe, See ALLING
Abel, Cont., Mass., Mary, W23432 BLWt.7063-160-55
Abel, Cont., N.H., S45500
Abiel, Cont., Ct., Lydia, W16807
Abijah, Mass., S15356
Abner, Ct. Cont., Lucy, W20588
Abner, Mass., S21600
Adam, Pa., S44295
Alexander, Md., Winifred, W15524
Alice/Else, former widow of Melzar Byram, which see
Almissey/Amisey, Pvt., N.Y., BLWt.6744 iss. 9/25/1790
Amasa, Ct., N.Y., S44547
Ambrose, Mass., Sea Service, Privateer, Mary, W20577
Amos, Ct., Hannah, W20582
Amos, Ct., Mass., S28619
Amos, Cont., Mass., S17818
Amos, Mass., S45197
Amos, Mass., Abigail, W23422
Ananias, N.C., R 100
Andrew, Mass., Elizabeth, W15975

ALLEN (continued)
Andrew, Sea Service. Disability. No papers
Archibald, Va., R 102
Arnold, Mass, S12913
Arthur, N.C., R 103
Asahel, Ct., Eleanor, W25346
Asaph, Mass., Persis, W20584
Asher, Ct., Elizabeth, W9325
Azor, Ct., Anna, W20592
Barnabas, Navy, Pa., Mary, W8315
Barnett, R.I., Elizabeth, W23436
Barsham, Mass., Navy, S29581
Bartlett, N.C., S8012
Benjamin, Ct., S46171; S45201
Benjamin, Mass., Lucy, R 128
Benjamin, N.C., S41407
Benjamin, R.I., Olive Barden, former widow, R 491
Benjamin, Va., R 106
Cady, Ct., Parthenia, W16094
Caleb, Mass. (& Jacob), S29586
Champion, N.C., Lucy, See ALLIN
Charles, N.C., S2900
Charles, S.C., S17819; BLWt. 15187-160-55
Charles, Va., S16597
Charles, Va., S36399
Content, N.Y., former widow of Edward McDonald
Cyrus, Ct., Eleanor, W8094
Daniel, Ct., S11956
Daniel, Ct., S37656
Daniel, Cont. Va., BLWt.11867-100; S37657
Daniel, Ga., N.C., S32093
Daniel, Mass., S36884
Daniel, Mass., S17817
Daniel, N.C., Alattica/Alathea, W325; BLWt.34971-160-55
Daniel, Pvt., Va., BLWt.11867 iss. 5/29/1792 to Francis Graves, ass.
David, Ct., S5241
David, Ct., S39930
David, Ct., Desire, See ALLYN
David, Ct., Lydia, W17212
David, Mass., S45198
David, N.H., S2; BLWt.1609-300
David, N.C., S16601
David, Pa., S22082
David, Va., BLWt.153-200
David, Va., S35172
David S., N.Y., Pa., S22081
Diarca, Ct., S12917
Ebenezer, Ct., S11968
Ebenezer, Ct., S37662
Ebenezer, Ct., Huldah, W8095
Ebenezer, Mass., S18688
Ebenezer, Mass., Esther, W17203
Ebenezer, Mass., Mary, W15531
Ebenezer, N.H., Lorana, W23434
Edmund, Mass., Molly, W27320
Edward, Ct., Abigail, W20596, BLWt.682-100; BLWt.87-60-55
Eleanor, former wid. of Samuel Short, R.I., which see
Eleazer, Ct., Cont., S35171
Eleazer, Mass., S28616
Eleazer, Mass., Navy, S15730
Elias, Ct., Privateer, Amy, R99

ALLEN (continued)
Elihu, Cont. Mass., TryphenaW2511
Elihu, Vt., BLWt.85061-160-55; Orelana, W10351
Elijah, Cont. Mass., S32647
Elijah, Mass., S12912
Elijah, Mass., Vt., S11958
Eliphalet, Ct., R 109
Elisha, Mass., W18024, Miriam Holbrook, former widow
Emanuel, Pvt. Md., BLWt.10926, iss. 8/12/1795 to Francis Sherrard, assignee
Enos, Ct., Mabel, W17207
Ethen, Cont., BLWt.1601-500 Green Mountain Boys
Eve, N.Y., former widow of Lambert Swayer, W15751, which see
Ezra, Ct., Mass., W27628
Ezra, Mass., S41403
Gabriel, Ct. Sea Service, S12915
George, Ct., Cont., Sabra, see ALLYN
George, Pvt., Lamb's Artillery, N.Y., BLWt.6753 iss. 2/21/1792 to William Campbell, ass.
George, Mass., S41406
George, N.J., S2488
George, N.Y., S12909
George, N.C., S2345
Gideon, Cont. Mass., S45202
Gideon, Vt., S6500
Hannah, former wid. of Zebah Thayer, which see
Herman, Cont. Ct., Green Mt. Boys Abigail Wadham former wid. W18285
Henry, N.J., R115
Henry, Va., Catharine, W20579
Hezekiah, Ct., S23093
Hezekiah Peters, Cont. Mass., Susannah, W23435
Hooper, Mass., Sarah, W23425
Howard, Ct., S45204
Ichabod, Ct., BLReg. 127696-1855
Isaac, Cont., S37654, Ct. res.
Isaac, Cont., Mass., S28967
Isaac, Pvt. Hazen's Regt. BLWt. 12707 iss. 4/11/1792 to Martin Kingsley, assignee
Isaac, Mass. Sea Service, S29582
Isham, Va., Elizabeth, W2900
Israel, Mass., S21044
Jabez, R.I., S11954
Jacob, Cont. Mass., BLWt.752-300
Jacob, Cont. Mass., Susanna, W5200
Jacob, Cont. Mass., N.H., S28618
Jacob, Cont., N.J., S39929
Jacob, Md., S34624
Jacob, Md., Elizabeth, R111
Jacob, Mass., BLWt.3631-100, Pvt. No papers
Jacob, Mass., S16598
Jacob, Mass., S29584
Jacob, Mass., R117
Jacob, Mass., Armenia, R24697
Jacob, N.J., Margaret, W5604; BLWt.1865-100
James, Ct., R12085
James, Cont. Mass., Anna, W21609
James, Cont. Mass. Navy, S36887
James, Pvt., Md., BLWt.10928 iss. 2/7/1790

ALLEN (continued)
James, Mass., R 118
James, Mass., Polly, W23418
James, N.Y., Susannah, W23423
James, Pa., S2489
James, R.I., Mary, W20575
Jared, Ct., R.I., S11967
Jason, Mass., Martha Doane, former widow, W22960
Jedediah, N.J., R 123
Jeffrey, Navy, Sarah, R142; R.I. res. in 1818
Jeremiah, Mass., R 119
Jeremiah, Mass., Martha, W3491; BLWts.297-60-55; 3639-100
Jesse, N.Y., Elizabeth, R 112
Job, Ct., Abigail, See ALLYN
Job, Mass., S28620; BLWt.12711-160-55
John, Pvt., Artillery Artificers, BLWt.12724 iss. 8/10/1792 to John Allen
John, Ct., Cont., Elacta, W25347
John, Ct., Mass., S17235
John, Ct., N.Y., W23429, Persis Coolidge, former widow
John, Cont., S17815; Mo. Agency and res.
John, Cont., Mass., S32641
John, Cont., Mass., Rachel, W21607
John, Cont., N.J., Mary, W883
John, Cont., N.Y., or Pa., R120
John, Cont. Pa., See ALLAN
John, Cont. Va., Nancy, W8319
John, Md., Mary, W4114
John, Mass., S19521
John, Mass., S36886; BLWt.1708-100
John, Mass., Bethiah Berry, former widow, W20697
John, Mass., Cynthia, W25368
John, Mass., Polly, W23420
John, Mass., R.I., Sally, W23424
John, Navy, R.I., S45501
John, Pvt., N.H., BLWt.2904 iss. 3/25/1790 to John Allen
John, N.H., S38491
John, N.H., Mary, W23416
John or John Allen Tailor, N.J., N.C., Elizabeth, R 113
John, Pvt., N.Y., BLWt.6734 iss. 7/15/1790 to Jerk Van Rensselar, assignee
John, N.Y., Mary, W16491
John, N.C., S6481
John, N.C., S17820
John, N.C., Polly, See ALLIN
John, Pvt., Pa., BLWt.8913 iss. 10/19/1789
John, Pa., S22622
John, Pa., S23511
John, Pa., R 122
John, Va., S4259
John, Va., S30818
John, Va., S39147
John, Va., Va. Half Pay, admitted
John, Va., Half Pay, R12048
John, Va., R-- Va. Half Pay
John, Va., Ann, W5603
John, Va., Jane, W8316
Jonathan, Ct., S12910
Jonathan, Ct., S32094

ALLEN (continued)
Jonathan, Ct., Cont., S45203
Jonathan, Cont. Vt., Green Mt. Boys, Margaret, W16809
Jonathan, Pvt., Hazen's Regt. BLWt 12708 iss. 4/11/1792 to Martin Kingsley, ass.
Jonathan, Mass., R124
Joseph, Ct., S11963
Joseph, Ct., Lucy, R 130
Joseph, Cont., N.H., S36890
Joseph, Mass., S32649
Joseph, Mass., Dorcas, W2578; BLWt.11413
Joseph, Pvt., Mass. & Crane's Artillery, BLWt.3643 iss. 1/25/1790 to John May, ass.
Joseph, Mass., R.I., Phebe, W15522
Joseph, Mass., R.I., R125
Joshua, N.C., R 126
Josiah, Mass., S45502
Josiah, R.I., Elizabeth, W23421
Lathrop, Ct., BLReg. 210493-1855
Lathrop, Ct., N.Y., Abigail,W17208
Levi, Ct., S11969
Luke, Ct., S16030
Luke, Ct., S18296
Lydia, Vt. Widow of Ezra Allen. Former wid. of Benjamin Stevens
Matthew, Mass., Jane, W15529
Moses, Cont., S37658, applied Va.
Moses, N.J., Sarah, W3125
Moses, Va., See ALLAN
Nathan, Md., S8011
Nathan, Mass., S30245
Nathan, Mass., S45194
Nathan, Mass., Abigail, W15530
Nathan, N.H., Vt., Deborah, W21608
Nathan, N.Y., Vt., S18684
Nathan, N.C., Apsabeth, R101; BLWt.45591-160-55
Nathaniel, Cont. Mass., S32635
Nathaniel, Mass., S32645
Nathaniel C., Mass., BLWt.13-300 Capt. No papers
Nehemiah, Mass., S30821
Noah, Cont. Mass., BLWt.10-400, Major, S32642
Othniel, Ct., Phebe, W17202
Parley, Ct., Catharine, W17206
Parmerly, Vt., Deborah, W9693
Patrick, Md., Pa., R133
Paul, N.C., S8010
Peter, Cont. Mass., S36885
Peter, N.J., R 97
Peter, N.J., Margaret, W5202
Peter, Pa., R134
Phebe, N.J., former widow of Rice Price, which see
Philip, Mass., S17814
Philip, Mass., R.I., BLWt.6388-160-55, Mercy, W20597
Philip, Va., See ALLIN
Phineas, Ct., S45200
Phinehas, Ct., Mass., S45199
Phinehas, Mass., S17234
Reuben, Ct., See Ruben ALLEN
Reuben, Ct., N.Y., R137
Reuben, Pvt., Va., BLWt.11877 iss. 7/6/1793 to Robert Means, ass.
Richard, Cont., N.J., Navy,S33251
Richard, N.C., S6490

ALLEN (continued)
Richard, Va., R138
Richard, Va., S1784
Robert, R.I., BLWt. 1-100
Robert, Vt., Mary, W4624
Robert, Va., S37661
Ruben, Ct., Rebecca, R 136
Salmon, Mass., R 141
Samuel, Pvt., Ct., BLWt.5393 iss. 3/3/1797
Samuel, Ct., Susan, W17201
Samuel, Cont., Mass., S18686
Samuel, Cont., N.J., Hannah,W5606
Samuel, Cont., N.Y., Margaret, W16168
Samuel, Mass., Lois, W25345
Samuel, Pvt., N.H., BLWt.2902 iss. 1/26/1796 to James A. Neal, ass.
Samuel, N.J., Nancy, W 443
Samuel, N.Y., Pamela, W23428
Samuel, N.C., S6480
Samuel, Wayne's Indian War (1794) Ky. Militia, BLWts.57093-80-50; 37734-80-55
Samuel, Pvt., Pa., BLWt.8889 iss. 5/14/1793
Samuel, R.I., R 140
Samuel, Va., S6484
Samuel F., see R14194 of Jacob Fleming, N.J.
Samuel G., Pvt., N.H., BLWt.2907 iss. 3/1/1790 to Elihu Mather,ass.
Samuel G., N.H., S41405
Seth, Ct., S11952
Seth, Cont. Mass., S29577
Seth, Mass., Abigail, R 98
Sluman, Ct., BLWt.32226-160-55, Hannah, W20576
Stephen, Ct., S11964
Stephen, Ct., S12920
Stephen, Ct., R.I., S11965
Stephen, Cont. Mass., Catharine, W23430
Thomas, N.C., R 144
Thomas, N.C., Bedith, R 105
Timothy, Ct., S29580
Timothy, Ct. Cont., See ALLYN
Timothy, Mass., S32640
Timothy, Vt., BLWt.52613-160-55 Julana, W5601
Titus, Ct., BLWt.19760-160-55; Abigail B., W25367
Vincent, Va., Elizabeth, W9692
William, Ct., Rebecca, W10353
William, Md., BLWt.1356-100
William, Mass., S20279
William, Mass., S29575
William, Mass., R 148
Wm., Mass., Elizabeth Brown, R1296
William, Mass., Privateer, R146
William, N.C., S30822
William, N.C., Martha, W20593
William, Pa., R147
William, Pvt., R.I., BLWt.14086 iss. 11/4/1794
William, R.I., BLWt.8-300, Capt. No papers
William, S.C., Mary A., W10288
William, Va., S6486
William, Va., S37655
William, Va., Frances, W8318

ALLEN (continued)
William, Va., BLWt.36625-160-55 Dolly, W25344
William Cornelius, Ct., S45195
Wright, Cont. Mass., Ruth, W23417
Zachariah, Indian Wars, 1785-1794, Dinah, R149
Zoheth, R.I., S12922
ALLER, Conrad, Va., S22080
ALLERTON, John, N.J., Mary, R151
Jonathan, N.Y., Bathsheba, R150
ALLEY, Abram/Abraham, Va., S11955
Ephraim, Mass., S36888
Isaiah, Va., S1939
James, N.C., Massey, W256
John, Va., R152
Samuel, Va., BLWt.36631-160-55; Mary, W9694
Shadrick, N.C., Va., S6499
ALLGAIER, Sebastian, Pa., S23510
ALLGOOD, John, Va., S15357
John, Va., R153
John, Va., BLWt.36518-160-55; Seleta, W1350
ALLICE, Bastin, S.C., R154
ALLIN, Champion, N.C., Lucy, R129
David, Ct., Desire, See ALLYN
David, Ct., Lydia, See ALLEN
Enos, Ct., Mabel, See ALLEN
Isaac, Va., R116
John, N.C., Polly, R135
Phillip, Va., S31514
Samuel, N.C., Va., S2343
Thomas, N.C., S12923
ALLING, Abel, Ct., Cont., Phebe, W20595
Daniel, Ct., See ALLEN
Ichabod, Pvt., Lamb's Artillery, N.Y., BLWt.6757 iss. 9/13/1790 to John Smith, ass.
John, Pvt., N.Y., BLWt.6755 iss. 8/24/1790 to Glenn & Barent Bleeker, adms. of Isaac Paris, ass.
John, N.J., S33250
Stephen, Cont. Ct., S37664
ALLIS, Aron, Mass., S45187
Lemuel, Mass., S32636
Moses, Mass., S8021
Russell, Mass., S11957
Stephen, Mass., BLWt.30617-160-55 Rachel, W25343
ALLISON, Burch, Md., S6493
David, N.C., R155
Gauyn, Pa., Va., R156
Hugh, S.C., R157
Isaac, N.Y., Mary, W16493
James, N.C., S6491
James, BLReg. 98417-1855
James, Pvt., Pa., BLWt.8888, iss. 3/19/1792 to A. Wechter, ass.
James, Pa., Mary, R 161
Jeremiah, Cont. N.Y., R158
John, N.Y., BLWt.1657-100, S45193
John, N.C., S32090
John, N.C., S16309
John, N.C., Sarah, W 8
John, Pa., S36400
John, Pa., S39931
John, Pa., Mary, W2512
John, Va. service about 1807; BLWt.86789-160-55

ALLISON (continued)
John, Va., Rebecca, W4112; BLWt.2159-450, Lt. Col.
Joseph B., N.Y., S22620
Richard, Pa., BLWt.44-300, no papers
Robert, Cont. Pa., Catharine, W3207; BLWt.43-200
Robert, Md., Martha, R160
Robert, N.Y., S45192
Thomas, Pa., S22079
ALLMAN, Edward, See ALMOND
Thomas, N.C., Judy, R164
ALLMAND, Thomas, Cont., S46540
ALLPHIN, Ransom, Va., S36402
Zebulon, Va., BLWt.45597-160-55; R162
ALLRED, Elias, N.C., S16307
John, N.C., R79
ALLSHOUSE, Henry, Pa., S2032
ALLSOP, Joseph, Md., Mary Casey, former wid., W3129
ALLSTATT, John, Pa., Margaret, See ALSTOTT
ALSTOTT, John, Pa., Margaret, W9695
ALLTON, Benjamin, Mass., Susannah, See ALTON
ALLUMBAUGH, Peter, Va., See ALLENBAUGH
ALLVIS, John, Va., Nancy, See ALVIS
ALLWINE, Laurance, N.J., Phebe, W511; BLWt.11273-160-55
ALLWORTH, Thomas, N.Y., Mary, R172
ALLYN, Charles, Ct., S14916
David, Ct., Desire, W15533
George, Ct., Cont., Sabra, W21606
Job, Ct., Abigail, W17210
John, Pvt., Ct., BLWt.5384 iss. 12/24/1796
John, Mass., S45205; BLWt.567-100
Jonathan, Mass., Privateer, S11951
Robert, Ct., BLWt.29-200. Lt. No papers
Timothy, Ct., Cont., BLWt.82-300 Ctf. 301
William, Mass., See William ALLEN Elizabeth Brown, former wid.
Wolcott, Ct., S18687
ALMAN/ALMON, Willis, N.C., Nancy, R166
ALMOND, Edward, N.C., S6489
John, Va., Lizza, W12193
Nathan, N.C., Winnifred, W5610
Thomas, N.C., Judy, See ALLMAN
William, Va., S2031
ALMY, John, R.I., Va., Abigail, W1531
Peleg, R.I., Hannah, R165
Sanford, Mass., R.I., S21039
ALSDORPH, Lawrence, N.Y.,S10318
ALSHOUSE, David, Pa., S39928
ALSOBROOK, Jesse, N.C., S16600
ALSON, Powell, Pvt., N.J., BLWt. 8082 iss. 6/16/1789 to Aaron Ogden, ass.
ALSOP, Benjamin, Va., S9269
James, Va., S12916
ALSPACH, John, Pa., S2033
Michael, Pa., Eva M., W2513; BLWt.27575-160-55

ALSTON, Joseph John, N.C., S6498
ALSWORTH, Andrew, Pa., S22621
ALTER, Jacob, Pvt., Pa., BLWt. 8897 iss. 1/25/179- to Christian Hubbert, admr.
ALTHOUSE
Matthew, Pvt., Pa., BLWt.8905 iss. 6/10/179- to Daniel Stever, ass.
ALTIGH, Michael, Pa., S34626
ALTIZER, Emery, Va., Mary, W4720
ALTOM, James, N.C., Sarah, See ALTORN
ALTON, Benjamin, Mass., Susannah, R167
James, N.C., Sarah, See ALTORN
William, Ct., Sarah, W17205
ALTOP, Thomas, Pvt., Va., BLWt. 11889 iss. 7/6/1793 to Robert Means, ass.
ALTORN, James, N.C., Sarah, W21611; BLWt.24167-160-55
ALVERSON, Elijah, Va., BLWt.26122-160-55; Wina or Nina, W10365
George, Mass., S29574
James, Va., Sibitha, W8326
John, R.I., S21042; BLWt.26070-160-55
John, Va., S5236
John, & Frances, Va., S39148
John S., Va., S30819
ALVEY, John, Va., Frances, W8320
John Durham, Postmaster to the Amer. Army, Hetty Fassett former widow, R3460
Josias, Md., S34625
Robert, Va., Susan, W8321
Thomas Green, Md., S35766
Traverse, Pvt., Md., BLWt.10927 iss. 8/14/179- to Francis Sherrard, assignee
ALVIS, Elijah, Va., Elizabeth,W5608
Henry H., Va., R 168
Jesse, Va., S35765
John, Va., Nancy, W1203; BLWt. 3752-160-55
Zachariah, Va., S8015
ALVOOD, Thomas G., Pvt. Lamb's Art. N.Y. BLWt.6760 iss. 7/9/1790 to Theodosius Fowler, ass.
ALVORD, Daniel, Cont.,Mass.,S45183
Eleazer, Mass., S29585
Eliab, Mass., S32644
Elijah, Mass., S32643
Jehiel, Mass., Dorothy, R 169
Job, Mass., BLWt.21-300. Capt. No papers. Justin Alvord, Admin.
John, Ct., S15354
John, Pvt., Mass., BLWt.3611 iss. 8/15/1796
John, BLWt. (no number) probably related to BLWt.3611
John, Mass., Rhoda, W15532; BLWt.32225-160-55
Phineas, Ct., S18295
Phineas, Mass., S5242
Phineas, Mass., S12911
Seth, Ct., S11959
Thomas G., Cont. N.Y., Nancy, W16492
Thomas G., Sgt. Lamb's Art. N.Y. BLWt.6759 iss. 7/9/1790 to

ALVORD (continued)
Theodosius Fowler, ass. See Thomas ALVOOD
Timothy, Mass., S32637
ALWARD, Benjamin, N.J., Sarah,R171
Samuel, ---, Catharine, R 170
ALWORTH, James, Pa., S22083
AMACKER, John, S.C., S9270
AMADON, Jonathan, Keturah, See AMIDON
Titus, Mass., Sabra, See AMMIDON
AMAN, John, Cont., Canada, S33962 N.J. Agency and res.
AMBERGEY, John, N.C., Elizabeth See AMBURGEY
AMBERMAN, See AMMERMAN
AMBERSON, Johnson, Pvt., Pa., BLWt.8909 iss. 7/13/1789
William, Pa., S39933
AMBLEMAN, Derick, Margaret, See AMMERMAN
AMBLER, James, Ct., Cont. N.Y., S11977
John, N.Y., S11978
Moses, Vt., Abigail, W20603
Peter, Pvt., Artillery Artificer Regt. Ct., BLWts.5370 & 12726 iss. 6/27/1791
Peter, Cont., Hannah, W25369
Squire, Pvt., Art. Artificer Regt. Ct., BLWt.12727, 5373 & 194-60-55 iss. 6/27/1791 to Jerusha Beers, former wid., W2056. See Phineas Beers.
Stephen, Pvt. Art. Artificers Regt., Ct., BLWt.5366 & 12725 iss. 6/27/1791
Stephen, Cont. Ct., S37665
AMBROSE, David, Drummer, N.C., BLWt.11882 iss. 7/1/1799 to Isaac Cole, ass.
David, N.C., S37667
Sarah, Mass., mar. Robt. Ambrose, former wid. of Joseph Cleasby
AMBURGEY, John, Elizabeth, R174 See BURGEY
John, N.C., Elizabeth, BLReg. 213350-1855
AMBURN, Samuel, Pa., S32095 BLWt.50811-160-55
AMEDON, Asenath, Cont. Ct., former wid. of Simeon Skeels, which see
AMELIN, Baptiste/Charles, Cont. Canada, Agathe, W20604
AMENT, Anthony, Pa., S1159
George, Pa., Ester, W3643
Henry, Pa., S22085
Philip, Cont. Pa., S30823
AMERMAN, Derick, See AMMERMAN
Powel J., N.J., Charity, R175
AMES, Aaron, Mass., BLWt.26304-160-55; Elizabeth, W20602
Amos, Ct., Cont., BLWt.2396-100; S45505
Asa, Ct., S11973
Asahel, Ct., S45207
Benjamin, Mass., Dorcas, W15536
Burpee, Mass., S22084
Daniel, Ct., S17237
David, Ct., S11975
Deborah, Cont., Mass. Sea Service, former wid. Alexander Orr

AMES (continued)
Eleazer, Mass., Sarah, W16096
Elijah, Ct., Cynthia, W5615; BLWt.50810-160-55
Elisha, Mass., Elizabeth, R176; BLWt.1293-100
Ephraim, Mass., Margaret, W9704; BLWt.2069-100
Everit, Ct., S37666
Jacob, Mass., S20280
James, N.C., S12924
John, Mass., S31518
John, Navy, Ct., BLWt.28544-160-55, Sarah/Sally, W20601
Joseph, Ct., Hannah, W17231
Joseph, N.H., S45504
Joshua, Pvt., Mass., BLWt.3612 iss. 9/8/1789 to D. Sturges
Joshua, Mass., S45206
Jotham, Cont., Mass., BLWt.1410-200; Keziah, W15819
Levi, N.Y., Ruth, R 177
Nathan, Mass., See EMES
Nathaniel, Ct., BLWt.5215-160-55 S11979
Peter, N.H., N.Y., & R.I., S23514
Prince, Pvt., Mass., BLWt.3626 iss. 7/21/1789 to Jnon[a] Cass, ass.
Prince, Mass., Eunice, W23439; BLWt.13220-160-55
Samuel, Ct., Axsa/Acksa, W25348
Samuel, Ames or Buck, Cont., Mass. S16603
Solomon, Cont., Mass., S45503
Spafford, Mass., S11974
Stephen, N.H., S44297
Zebulon, Ct., S41413
AMESBURY, Brownell/Brownwell, Armsby, Mass., Navy, S18297
AMET, Anthony, Pa., See AMENT
AMEY, David, Pvt., N.J., BLWt. 8072 iss. 6/22/1789
AMICKS, Matthew, Va., See AMYX
AMIDON, Jacob, Ct., Hannah, W23438
Jacob, Mass., Privateer, See also AMMIDON
Jedediah, Ct., S14917
Jonathan, Ct., Keturah, W23441
Moses, Ct., S11976
Titus, Mass., Sabra, See AMMIDON
AMLEN, Baptist, Pvt. Hazen's Regt. BLWt.12709 iss. 1/22/1790 to Benjamin Mooers, ass.
AMLIN, Baptiste, Cont. See Charles AMLIN
Charles, Cont., Canada, S45209 N.Y. res. and agency
AMMERMAN, Cornelius, Pvt., N.Y., BLWt.6726 iss. 3/7/1792 to Dirick Ammerman, admr.
David, N.J., S939
Derick, N.Y., Margaret, W23440
AMMIDON, Jacob, Mass., Privateer, Esther, W21613
Philip, Mass., Rhoda, R 178
Titus, Mass., Sabra, W15534
AMMINET, John, Va., S16602
AMMON, Christopher, Va., S8025
AMMONDS, Peter, Pvt., Va., BLWt. 11871 iss. 12/27/1794
AMMONETT, Charles, Va., BLWt. 26946-160-55; Phoebe, W3492

AMMONS, Joshua, S.C., S21045
Lucy, Md., former wid. of Clement Edeline, which see
Thomas, S.C., Catharine, R 179
AMONETTE, Charles, Va., Phoebe, See AMMONETT
AMOS, Elizabeth, Md., former wid of Thomas B. Hugo, which see
Isaac, Mass., Navy, S32651
John, N.C., S41414
Mordecai, Md., S2034
AMOSS, Martin, Va., S8024
AMPLE, John, Cont., Pa., Barbara. See Barbara SAMPLE
AMSDELL, Abner, Mass., See AMSDILL
AMSDEN, Abraham, Cont. Mass., Submit, W4115
Adam, Mass., Esther, W25349
Benjamin, Mass., Lucy, W15977
Isaac, Cont., Mass. Sea Service (?), S41412
Isaac, Mass., S11972
John, Mass., Lovisa, W15535
Noah, Mass., S45208
Silas, Mass., Dis. No papers
Simeon, Mass., Abigail, W5617
AMSDILL, Abner, Mass., S45210
AMY, George, N.H., S45869
Heman, N.H., S41411
William, N.H., Vt., S19524
AMYX, Matthew, Va., S6501
ANDERS, James, N.C., S6516
ANDERSON, Abraham, S.C., Vilinda, R 202
Adam, Cont. Pa., S39939
Alexander, Md., Va., S2340
Alexander, N.Y., Pvt., BLWt. 6727 iss. 4/21/1791
Alexander, N.Y., S12927
Alexander, N.Y., S45215
Allen, N.H., S22087
Andrew, Pa., S8026
Andrew, Pa., R 181
Archibald, Md., BLWt.390-400
Armstead, Va., S30825
Asa, Ct., S15732
Augustine, Cont. N.J., S44300
Bailey, Ga., S.C., Va., S30826
Charles, Cont., N.Y., S28621
Charles, Va., R 183
Daniel, Ct., S14919
Daniel, Cont. Pa., S44302
Daniel, Va., S37677
Darius, Pvt., N.J., BLWt.8081 iss. 6/16/1789 to Thomas Coyle, ass.
David, Cont. Va., Lucy, W5625
David, Mass., Olive, W20624
David, N.Y., S45211
David, S.C., S6515
Denney, S.C., Elizabeth, W9700
Edward, Mass., Mary, W25353
Enoch, Del., Eleanor, W3204
Enoch, Pa., S39937
Ephraim, N.J., BLWt.2673-300, Capt., Rezina Harris, late wid. and devise, no papers
Ezekiel, Pvt., N.J., BLWt.8071 iss. 8/21/1790 to Abel Belknap, ass.

ANDERSON (continued)
Ezekiel, N.J., N.Y., Hannah See ANDRASON
Frances, S.C., former widow of John McBride, which see
Francis, N.C., See ANTRICAN
Francis, R.I., S21604
George, N.J., S2913
George, N.Y., Elizabeth, R185
George, N.C., S46684
George, N.C., S2914
George, Pvt., Pa., BLWt.8912 iss. 7/9/178-
George, Pa., S39938
George, Pvt., Va., Artillery, Va. BLWts.11872 & 13990 iss. 10/21/1792 to Francis Graves, ass.
George, Va., Mary, W5627
Henry, Va., S44301
Isaac, Pa., Euphemia, W4628
Isaac, Pa., Mary, R 196
Jacob, Cont. N.J., N.C., BLWt. 10218-160-55, Rebecca, W2048
Jacob, Va., S37675
Jacob, Va., Frances, W2428; BLWt.26741-160-55
Jacob, Va., Christiana, R 184
James, Ct., Abigail, W23451
James, Ct., Cont., S37671
James, Cont., BLWt.68-200, Lt. No papers
James, Mass., S28972
James, Mass., Marcy, W15539
James, N.J., S33963
James, N.C., S1786
James, N.C., S12930
James, N.C., S2915
James, N.C., BLWt.36553-160-55; Dicey Plummer, former wid. W9232
James, Pvt., Pa., BLWt.8901 iss. 5/13/1794 to Jacob Sellers, ass.
James, Pa., R 190
James, Pa., Rachel, W513; BLWt. 26999-160-55
James, Pa., Mary, W3064
James, Pa., Esther, R 186
James, Pa. & War of 1812, Letty, W2902; BLWt.34969-160-55
James, S.C., Jane, W9699
James, Va., S32096
James, Va., S30827
James, or Asher Crockett, Va., Sarah, W2533; BLWt.31439-160-55
John, Ct., Linda, W20621
John, Cont. N.Y., S46682
John, Cont. N.Y., Lydia, R 194
John, Cont., N.Y., Sarah, W16812
John, Pvt., Md., BLWt.10932 iss. 2/1/1790 to Ann Tootle, admx., James Williams & Jos. Dawson, admrs. of James Tootle, late ass.
John, Pvt., Mass., BLWt.3634 iss. 10/1/1791
John, Mass., S45212
John, Mass., N.H., S2036
John, N.J., S798
John, Pvt., N.Y., BLWt.6754 iss. 7/12/1792
John, N.C., S6511
John, N.C., Sarah, W9329
John, Pa., S2035
John, Pa. Sea Service, See John

ANDERSON (continued)
Anderson Smith
John, S.C., Va., Ann, W884
John, Va., S16310
John, Va., BLWt.54-300, Capt.
John, Va., S44299
John, R192, Vt. res. at appl.
Jordan, Cont., Va., S6504
Joseph, Mass., Hannah, W21615
Joseph, See Joseph Insla Anderson only P. for wid. name, W23449
Joseph, Va., R193
Joseph, Va., S37676
Joseph Insla, N.J., BLWt.36633-160-55; BLWt.36-300. Capt. iss. 5/14/1790. No papers. Widow P. W23449
Lemuel, Ct., Rachel, W20615; BLWt.14662-160-55
Leonard, Cont., Va., N.C., Rosanna W8329
Lewis, N.J., S2037
Martha, S.C., former wid. of James Wilson, which see
Michael, Pvt., Md., BLWts.10929 & 12711 iss. 4/12/1796
Nathan, Va., Mariana, W5626
Nathaniel, Va., Sally, W9701. She m. 2nd William Anderson
Peter, Va., R199
Peter, Va., S2912
Richard, Cont., Mass., S45213
Richard, Md., S10059; BLWt.51-300 Capt. No papers
Richard, Pvt., Mass., BLWt.3614 iss. 6/6/1789
Richard, Va., Martha, W23448
Richard Clough, Va., BLWt.53-450 Lt. Col., No papers. Sally,W1356
Robert, Ct., S10325
Robert, Mass., S30824
Robert, N.H., S17821
Robert, N.C., Va., BLWt.34821-160-55; Nancy, W2579. Her first husb. said to be a soldier of the Rev., John Brown, Va., died 1811, which see
Robert, Pa., Elizabeth, W5628
Robert, Va., Molly, W28
Robert, Va., Mary, W276
Samuel, Ct., R200
Samuel, N.J., S39936, BLWt.8078 iss. 1/13/1792
Samuel, Pvt., N.Y., BLWt.6741 iss. 2/14/1791
Samuel, N.Y., S45214
Samuel, Pa., R201
Spencer, Va., S37672
Thomas, Ct., S37668; BLWt.28-200. Lt. No papers
Thomas, Ct., Vt., BLWt.12849-160-55; Alice, W17216
Thomas, Cont., Pa., S39940
Thomas, Del., S39941; BLWt.39-200 Lt. No papers
Thomas, Mass., BLWt.3981-160-55; Eunice, W1352
Thomas, N.H., Elizabeth, W16169
Thomas, Pvt., Pa., BLWt.8898 iss. 3/5/1791 to Stephen London, ass.
Thomas, R.I., S38497

ANDERSON (continued)
Thomas, Va., S21603
Timothy, Ct., Privateer, S31522
William, Ct., Dis. No papers
William, Pvt., Cont. Mass., Crane's Artillery, BLWt.3644 iss. 2/29/1792 to M. Beard, ass.
William, Cont. N.J., S12926
William, Ga., BLWt.6448-160-55; Mary, W512
William, (colored), Md., R203
William, Mass., S23518
William, Pvt., N.J., BLWt.8080 iss. 6/16/1789 to Thos. Coyle,ass
William, N.J., S2339
William, N.J., BLWt.38-150. Ens. No papers, Elizabeth, W3065
William, N.Y., Isabella, R188
William, N.C., S6512
William, N.C., Sarah, R204
William, Pa., S2342
William, Pa., R205
William, Va., S30828
William, Va., S36403
William, Va., R206
William, Va., Nancy, R197
William, Va., Elizabeth, W5204
ANDRASON, Elijah, N.J., S33965
Ezekiel, N.J., N.Y., Hannah,W23456 See N.A. Acc. No.874, 050003
ANDREAS, Jeremiah, Ct., Cynthia, W25350; BLWt.36630-160-55
ANDREKIN, Francis, N.C. See ANTRICAN
ANDRESS, David, Ga., R219
Ebenezer, Ct., See ANDREWS
Evin/Evan, N.C., S45832
ANDREW, Abner, Pvt., Ct., BLWt. 5364 iss. 12/14/1789 to Richard Platt
Adam, Pa., R207
Jeremiah, R.I., S21602
John, Ga., S.C., Mary O.,W5623
John, N.J., Elizabeth, R209
John, Pvt., Pa., BLWt.8892 iss. 4/16/1792
John, Pa., BLWt.258-100
John, Pa., S44305
Louden, N.Y., Vt., S28970
Sylvester, R.I., S15735
ANDREWS, Aaron, Mass. Sea Service, S15358
Abigail, N.H., former widow of Hubbard Carter
Abner, Cont., Ct., See ANDRUSS
Abraham, Mass., Sally, W3173
Adam, Cont., Va., S37674
Ammi, N.H., S16605
Amos, Pvt., Ct., BLWt.5374 iss. 9/9/1790 to James F. Sebor
Amos, Ct., S37679
Amos, Mass., Joanna, W15537
Amos, Mass., N.Y., S45216
Andrew, Ct., Mary, W15538
Arthur, Pa., S23517
Asa, Mass., S16031
Asa, N.H., Olive, W15540
Ashbel, N.Y., S45217
Athelstan, Mass., S1620
Benjamin, Ct., S17239
Benjamin, Cont., Vt., See ANDRUS

ANDREWS (continued)
Benjamin, Privateer, R.I., S38500
Benjamin, Va., Elizabeth, W4627
David, Pvt., Ct., BLWt.5376 iss. 8/3/1795 to Wm. Walsworth
David, Ct., Cont., See ANDRUS
Ebenezer, Ct., R 221
Ebenezer, Green Mt. Boys, Vt., S22086
Ebenezer, Mass., S11984
Eli, Ct., S11989
Elijah, Ct., S12935
Elijah, Ct., R5836, Mabel Kellogg former wid. Her last husband, Phinehas Kellogg, Mass. was pensioned under Act of 3/18/1818
Elisha, Ct., S11985
Elisha, N.Y., S12925
Elkanah, Sea Service, Va., S6507
Ephraim, Ct., Asenath R., W1795 BLWt.26503-160-55
Ephraim, Cont., Va., BLWt.415-100
Ephraim, Mass. Privateer, S17238
George, R.I., Ruth, W20616
Giles, Ct., R1493, Patience Bunnell, former widow
Henry, Mass., Navy & R.I., S5246
Hester, Cont., N.Y., R 211, former widow of David Welch
Hezekiah, Ct., Rhoda, W17215
Hugh, N.C., S6514
Humphrey, Pa., R20026
Isaac, Cont., N.J., S33964
Isaac, Mass., N.H., BLWt.14536-160-55, Sarah, W5205
Isham, Va., Mary, W5620
Israel, Mass. Sea Service, Mary, R 216
James, Ct., Cont., Lois, W15542
James, Cont., Mass., S38499
James, N.J., S39934
James, Pa., R 212
James, Pa., R 213
Jeremiah, Mass., S36893
Joel, Cont., Mass., N.H., Anna, W2741
John, Ct., Sarah, W5621; BLWt. 16257-160-55
John, Cont., Ct., R214
John, Cont., Ct., S11990
John, Ct., Mass., See ANDRUS
John, Cont., Ct.,Lydia, See ANDRUS
John, Cont., Mass., Betsey, W23453
John, Ga., S.C., See John ANDREW W5623
John, Pvt., Md., BLWt.10934 iss. 11/29/1790 to Geo. Windham, Adr.
John, Mass., S32656
John, Mass., Esther, W1693
John, N.Y., R 215
John, N.C., Nancy, W9702
John, Corp., Sheldon's Cavalry, Ct. BLWt.5397 iss. 12/10/1789
John, Va., S2908
Jonathan, Cont.,Mass.?, S38498 R.I. residence
Jonathan, Pvt., Invalid Regt., BLWt.12729 iss. 11/2/1791 to John Heaton, assignee
Jonathan, R.I., S11993
Joseph, Ct., Mercy, See ANDRUS
Joseph, Cont., Mass.,BLWt.2073-200

ANDREWS (continued)
Joseph, N.Y., Betty, W16173
Joshua, Mass., S16606
Josiah, Ct., S16032
Josiah, Cont. Ct., BLWt.86-100; S37670
Lemuel, Mass., BLWt.36618-160-55; Elizabeth, W5619
Lilburn, Mass., BLWt.3801-160-55; Sarah, W20618
Louden, N.Y., Vt., See ANDREW
Ludin, Mass., Lois, W20623
Mark, Mass., Privateer, S12929
Moses, Ct., Mass., S30247
Moses, Vt., Lydia, W23445
Nancy Ann, Va., former widow of William Clark
Nathan, Mass., R.I., S29590
Nathaniel, Ct., Jerusha, See ANDRUS
Nathaniel, Mass., S28971
Nehemiah, Cont., Mass., Elizabeth W25354
Owen, S.C., S16311
Phinehas, Ct., S12928
Reuben, Cont., Olie, W20608 Mass. res. and agency
Robert, Mass., S20282
Robert, Va., Half Pay, R12123
Samuel, Ct., S45218; BLWt.15424-160-55
Samuel, Ct., Privateer, Mary Lee, W25351
Samuel, Cont., Mass., S17822
Samuel, Mass., S29587
Samuel, Mass., Asenath, W5618; BLWt.14762-160-55
Samuel, N.Y., S12932
Samuel E., Cont., N.H., Hannah, W23447; BLWt.30586-160-55
Solomon, N.H., Sarah, W23457; BLWt.12726-160-55
Squire, Cont., R.I., Sarah,W20619
Stephen, Cont., Mass., S36892
Stephen, Mass., S29588
Stephen, N.H., Sally, W8228; BLWt. 86123-160-55
Thomas, Ct., Cont., S45219
Thomas, Pvt., Corps of Invalids BLWt.12731 iss. 12/6/1799 to Noah A. Phelps, assignee
Thomas, Mass., S32654
Thomas, Va., S6506
Thomas, Va., Margaret, W2985
Timothy, Ct., Mary, W20620
Varney, Va., S11992
William, Ct., S11981
William, Ct., See ANDRUS
William, Ct., Rosetta, See ANDRUS
William, Ct., Cont., BLWt.19-200 Lt. Crane's Regt. Art. No papers
William, Cont. Md., S37673
William, Cont. Mass., S16604
William, Mass., S19182
William, N.J., Abigail, W5622
William, Va. sea service, R---
William, ---, Dis. no papers; Va. & Ga. residence
William Fuller, Mass., Joanna, W15541; BLWt.15158-160-55
ANDRIKEN, Francis, N.C., See ANTRICAN

ANDROS, Thomas, Ct., Cont.
Privateer, S5247
ANDRUS
Benjamin, Ct., S11988
Benjamin, Cont., Vt., S39149
Clement, Ct., Mass., S44304
Daniel, N.Y., R220
David, Ct., S46495
David, Ct., Cont., S5244
Eldad, Vt., Sophia, R223
Elijah, Ct., S11983
Elisha, Cont., Ct., Anna, W16172;
BLWt.587-100
Ephraim, Ct., Asenath R., See
ANDREWS
Ethan, Ct., S23515
Hezekiah, Ct., Rhoda. See ANDREWS
Joel, Cont., Mass., N.H., Anna,
See ANDREWS
John, Cont., Ct., Mass., S38501
John, Cont., Ct., Lydia, W23442
Jonathan, Ct. Cont.,Sophia, W17214
Joseph, Ct., Mercy, W20612
Joseph, Vt., S11987
Josiah, Cont., Ct., See ANDREWS
Nathan, Ct., R.I., S19525
Nathaniel, Ct., Jerusha, W4117;
BLWt.19753-160-55
Richard, Ct., S12931
Richard, Ct., Catharine, W21616
Samuel, Ct., Elizabeth, R222
Samuel, Ct., N.Y., S11980
Samuel J., Ct., S11982
Theodore, Cont. Ct., Dis. No
papers
Thomas, Ct., S12933
William, Ct., S37678
William, Ct., Cont.,Rosetta,W23450
ANDRUSS, Abner, Cont., Ct., S19899
1/2
Ebenezer, Ct., R221, See ANDREWS
Giles, Ct., Patience Bunnell
former widow
Theodore, Ct., S37669
William, N.J., Abigail, See
ANDREWS
ANGEL, Abiather, Cont. Mass.,
Lucy, W20614
Augustus, Mass., Triphena/
Tryphena, W23444
Daniel, Mass., See ANGLE
Daniel, R.I., S23516
Henry, Mass., S8027
Jacob, Cont., Mass., S32653
John, N.C., Mary, W20622;
BLWt.30602-160-55
Joseph, Corp., R.I., BLWt.2916
iss. 4/20/1790 to Joseph Angel
Lawrence, N.C., S31519
ANGELL, Elisha, R.I., Catharine,
W1204; BLWt.26074-160-55
Ezekiel, R.I., Abigail, W25370
Fenner, R.I., Amey, W5630;
BLWt.29038-160-55
George, R.I., Elizabeth, W15544
Israel, Cont., R.I., S38496;
BLWt.7-500. Col. No papers
James, Pvt., Va. Artillery, Va.
BLWts. 11874 & 13996 iss.
10/31/1792 to Francis Graves,
ass. or Robert Means
Pardon, R.I., Susanna, W1353;

ANGELL (continued)
BLWt.26279-160-55
Stephen, Mass., S29589
Stukley, R.I., S18691
ANGIER, Charles, Cont. Mass.,
Elizabeth, W20609
John, N.H., R224
ANGLE, Charles, N.C., BLReg.
103293-1855
Daniel, Mass., S6510
ANGLEA, William, N.C., S.C.,
S8028
ANGLEMAN, Jacob, N.J., S 940
ANGLEN, John, N.C., Elizabeth,
See ANGLING
ANGLES, Thomas, R.I., S38495
ANGLETON, Sarah, Va., former
widow of John Robertson
ANGLEY, Peter, Pvt., N.J., BLWt.
8077 iss. 7/17/1797 to Abraham
Bell, assignee
ANGLIN, Henry, Ga., S31521
Philip, Va., R 225
ANGLING, John, N.C., Elizabeth,
W696; BLWt.32211-160-55
ANGST, Nicholas, Pa., S39947
ANNABEL, John, Mass., S32652
ANNABIL
Ebenezer, Ct. Sea Service, Ann
W5629
ANNABLE, Edward, Mass., S44548
Ephraim, Mass., S28622
John, Mass., Minah, W23446
Robert, Cont., Mass., S32655
ANNIN, Daniel, N.Y., S11991
Joseph, N.J., S2909
Samuel, N.J., S5245
ANNIS, Elizabeth, Ct., former
widow of Jason Harris
Isaac, Mass. & N.H., S45506
Jacob, Mass., Deborah, W387
John, Mass., S10323
Levi, Va., Sea Service, BLWt.
411-100, Peggy, W5624
Micajah, Va., S34627
Michael, N.H., S22088
Phinehas, Mass., Hannah, W23452
Stephen, Mass., S28969
ANSART, (DeMaresquelle) Lewis,
Cont. French, Catharine, W20611
ANSLEY, John, N.J., R 226
ANSON, John, N.J., Pa., R 227
Silas, N.Y., R 228
ANSPACK, Peter, Cont., BLWt.34-
200. Lt., Col. Lamb's Regt.
Art. No papers
ANSTEAD, Henry, Cont. N.J.,
Elizabeth, W21620
ANSWERT, Apollos, Ct., S32657
ANSWITZ, Appolas, Pvt., Ct., BLWt.
5367 iss. 5/5/1794
ANSWORTH, Benjamin, Pvt., Mass.,
BLWt.3617 iss. 4/15/1795 to E.
Answorth, assignee
ANTE, Philip, Pa., S6519
ANTHONY, Abraham ?, Mary McKee
former widow, R 6747
Burrington, R.I., Susannah, W20613
David, Mass., R 230
Frederick, Pa., BLReg.240-516
George, Cont., N.J., S44303
George, N.Y., S2341

ANTHONY (continued)
Gideon, R.I., S6503
Israel, N.Y., Elizabeth, W20607
Jack, colored, Ct., BLWt.297-100
Jacob, Mass., S23097
James, Mass., S38494
James, N.C., Elizabeth, W3914
John, Cont., N.Y., S12934
John, Pvt., N.Y., BLWt.6735 iss.
7/14/1790 to Richard Platt, ass.
John, N.Y., S44549
John, S.C., Mary, W21614
Michael, Pvt., R.I., BLWt.2917
iss. 7/20/1790 to Michael Anthony
Michael, R.I., S10322
Peter, Pvt., N.Y., BLWt.6736 iss.
9/21/1790 to Benj. Elwood, ass.
Peter, N.Y., S44550
Philip, N.J., R 232
Philip, N.C., S21046
Richard, N.Y., BLWt.32217-160-55
Martha, W2352
Samuel, Ct., S14918
ANTILL, Edward, Cont., BLWt.67-450,
Lt. Col. Hazen's Regt., no papers
Jacob, Va., Dorcas, W8328
ANTONY, Jack (colored) See ANTHONY
Michael, R.I., Margaret, W20617
ANTRICAN/ANDRICAN/ANDREKIN/ANDER-
SON/ENDERKIN/MC CAJAKIN
Francis, N.C., S4261
ANTRIM, John, Cont., Pa., BLWt.
8900-100, Pvt.; BLWt.12704
No papers. Margaret, W2742
AORSON, Aaron, N.Y., BLWt.32-300.
Capt. No papers
APGAR, Conrad, N.J., S 941
Peter, N.J., R 233
APLEBY, Thomas, Pvt., Pa., BLWt.
8896 iss. 7/9/1789
APLEY, Josiah, Ct., S16607
APLIN, Stephen A., R.I., S17240
APP, Michael, Pa., Sophia, R 234
APPELGATE/APPLEGATE,
William, N.J., S 588
APPELL, Peter, French Navy, Sea
Service, Ct., U.S. Revenue
Service, R 235
APPERSON, John, Va., Alcey, W24128
Peter, Va., S37680
Richard, Va., BLWt.386-300
William, N.C., Elizabeth, W3915
APPLE, Daniel, N.C., S6520
Henry, N.Y., N.J., S44551
APPLEBEE, Simeon, Mass. Navy,
S16608
Thomas, Cont., Mass., Judith,
W2580; BLWt.10009-160-55
Thomas, N.H., Margery, W20625;
BLWt.3426-160-55
APPLEBY/APPLEBEY, John, Pvt., Md.
BLWt.10919 iss. 8/12/1795 to
Francis Sherrard, assignee
John, R.I., Elizabeth, W17217
Michael, Mass., R 236
Thomas, R.I., Wait, W25371
William, N.H., S14920
APPLEGATE, Andrew, N.J., Elizabeth,
W5631; BLWt.26678-160-55
Asher, N.J., S846
Bartholomew, N.J., S2347

APPLEGATE (continued)
Benjamin, N.J., S33967
Benjamin, Cont., N.J., Phebe, W9706; BLWt.8069-100, Pvt. iss. 2/23/1791 to John Polhemus, atty.
Daniel, Musician, N.J., BLWt. 8084 iss. 3/13/1799 to Abraham Bell, ass. S46197
Daniel, N.J., S34628
Daniel, N.J., Esther Minor, former widow, W497
David, N.J., S848
Ezekiel, Not Rev., War with France, 1799-1807, Phebe; BLReg.30796-50
Garrett, Pa., Va., S32098
Henry, N.J., R238
James, Not Rev., N.W. Ind. War, 1791, Ky. agency, Old War Inv. file 6522
John, N.J., S 847
Joseph, N.J., S8029
Joseph, N.J., S33966
Joseph, N.J., Pa., Ann, W1354; BLWt.10217-160-55
Moses, N.J., S44552
Robert, N.J., Rhoda, W3916
Robert, Pa., Va., S32097
William, N.J., See APPELGATE
William, N.J., Elizabeth, W885
William, Indian War, 1790, Mary, BLReg. 181229-55
Zebulon, N.J., Rebecca, W10367 BLWt.29044-160-55
APPLEMAN/APPLEMON
David, N.J., S2346
APPLETON, Abraham, N.J., BLWt. 37-200, Lt. No papers
Benjamin, Mass., Molly, R 239
APPLEWHAITE, John, Va. Sea Service, Va. half pay, R 12129
APPLIN, Timothy Brown, N.H., Anna, W20626
APPLING, John, Mass., S30829
APTHORP, James, Mass., Lydia,W20627
ARAY, James, N.J., S33969
ARBEGAST/ARBIGUST, Ludwig, ---, Pa. Agency, S2923
ARBOGAST, Adam, Va., S8037
ARBOUR, Michael, Cont., Canadian, S36895
ARBUCKLE, James, Va., S37683
Matthew, Va., no claim for pension See claim of Wm. Richmond, Va. S9088. Much info of Matthew there
Samuel, Cont., Mass., Abigail Roberts, former widow, W13864. Married Charles Roberts
Thomas, Va., S16609
William, Va., R241
William, Va., R242
ARCHABALD, John, N.H. See ARCHIBALD
ARCHBOLD, Thomas, Pa., S2348
ARCHELUS, James, Pvt., Mass., BLWt. 3618 iss. 8/10/1789 to Richard Platt, ass.
ARCHER, Amasa, Ct., S17242
Crippen, Ct., Jemima, W21617
Edmund, Va., S12936
Evans, Va., S41415
Isaac, Va., S39151
James, N.Y., R20193
John, Pa., Hannah, W4629

ARCHER (continued)
John, Va. sea service; Va. half pay, Elizabeth Martin former widow, W5348
Joseph, Va., BLWt.2120-200
Michael, Mass., S38505
Obadiah, Ct., S28623
Peter Field, Va., BLWt.300-200
Richard, Va., BLWt.58-150; Ensign, iss. to Henry Lee, exec. of Alex. Skinner, ass. No papers
Stephen, Navy, Pa., Va.,BLWt.11056 -160-55; Martha Rice former widow W11133
Zachariah, Pa., Jane, W23462
ARCHIBALD, Ebenezer, Pvt., Hazen's Regt., BLWt.12717 iss. 8/3/1789 Wm. I. or J. Vredenburgh, ass.
John, Cont., N.H., S45576
Thomas, Pa., See ARCHBOLD
ARCULES, James, Mass., S32658
ARENDALL, Nathan, N.C., Susannah, R243
ARES, Wm., Ct., Cont., S37685
AREY, Cornelius, Navy, N.Y., S38502
Joshua, Ct., Rachel, W9335; BLWt. 36616-160-55
ARGOE/ARGOR, Levin, N.C., S.C., S17825
ARGUBRIGHT, George, Va., Christina, W25357
Jacob, Va., S12907
ARINGTON, John, Va., Susanna, See ARRINGTON
ARMAN, Thomas, Cont., Va. Charity W8332
ARMAND, Charles, Marquis de la Rouerie, Cont. French; BLWt. 2291-850
ARMANTROUT, Charles, Va., Christena See ARMONTROUT
ARMBRUSTER, Matthias, Pa., S39942
ARMENTROUT, Charles, See ARMONTROUT
ARMINGTON, Joseph, Mass., Deborah W20628
ARMISTEAD, Richard, Va., Elizabeth W20633
Thaddeus, Va., R244
Thomas, Va., Va. half pay, BLWt. 1846-300, R12157. Dau. Martha B. Fowler also claimed for War of 1812 serv. of her husband, John Fowler and Rev. serv. of uncle, Gregory Smith. Papers herewith
Westwood, N.C., Lucy, W8100
William, Va., half pay, R12155
William, Va., S10326
ARMITAGE, Shewbart, Cont., Pa., Sarah, W5206; BLWt.95501-160-55
ARMON, Thomas, Va., Charity, See ARMAN
ARMONTROUT, Charles, Va., Christena, W5641; BLWt.26823-160-55
ARMOR/ARMOUR, James, Pa., BLWt. 1383-200
ARMSBEY, Ebenezer, Ct., R.I., Experience. See ORMSBEE
ARMSBURY/ORMSBY, John, Cont., Mass., R.I., Priscilla, R246
John, R.I., S38504
Thomas, Cont., R.I., Susannah R247

ARMSBY, Brownell, Mass., Navy, See AMESBURY
ARMSTEAD, Westwood, See ARMISTEAD
ARMSTED, William, Va., S12001
ARMSTRONG, Abel, Cont. Va., S2039
Adam, N.Y., S44554
Adam, Pvt., N.Y., BLWt.6747 iss. 7/26/1791
Adam, Pvt., Va., BLWt.11870 iss. 4/12/1792 to Robt. Means, ass.
Alexander, N.C., R 248
Alexander, Pa., S16033
Alexander, Va., S31525
Ambrose, Va., S14921
Archibald, N.Y., BLWts.162-60-55 & 6746-100. No papers. Sabra, W1355
Bela, N.Y., S22625
Daniel, Ct., S37681
Daniel, Pa., Nancy, R 257
Ebenezer, Ct., Cont., S44298
Edward, N.Y., S28231
Edward, Pa., BLWt.35-200. Lt. iss. 5/30/1789. No papers
Elias, Mass., S32659
Elisha, R.I., Mercy, W5639; BLWt.19713-160-55
George, N.J., R249
George, Pa., S12005
Henry, Va., S30248
Isaac, N.J., S2038
Isaac, N.Y., Amy, W16174
Isaac, Va., S16312
Jabez, Ct., R250
James, Ct., Cont., Miriam,W25360
James, Ct., Cont., Nabby, W25372
James, Cont., BLWt.45-300. Capt. No papers
James, Cont., Va., Nancy, R258
James, N.Y., Pa., R251
James, N.C., BLWt.594-500
James, Pa., S22089
James, Pa., S2916
James, S.C., S2926
James Francis, Md.,Susannah,W5638
Jeremiah, Ct., S21610
Jesse, R.I., S21047
Jesse, Pvt., Lee's Legion, Va., BLWts.11883 & 14017 iss. 11/2/ 1792 to Robert Means, ass.
Jesse, Va., BLWt.2000-100
John, Cont. Pa., S17823; BLWt. 40-400. Major. No papers
John, Pvt., Md., BLWt.10922 iss. 3/11/1791 to John Armstrong
John, Pvt., Md., BLWts.10925 & 11932 iss. 8/7/1794 to Henry Purdy, ass.
John, Pvt., N.Y., BLWts.6730 & 6633 iss. 8/3/1790 to Cornelius Van Dyck, ass.
John, N.Y., S23095
John, N.Y., S44553
John, N.Y., Hannah, R253
John, N.C., BLWt.60-450. Lt. Col. No papers
John, N.C., Jane, W8229; BLWt. 19543-160-55
John, Pvt., Artillery Art. of Pa. BLWt.12733 iss. 7/27/1789 to Richard Platt, ass.
John, Pa., U.S.A. St. Clair's War

ARMSTRONG (continued
BLWt.42-200. Lt. No papers
Tabitha Lockhart, former wid. W10202
John, Va., S6529
Jona, Pvt., N.Y., BLWt.6762 iss. 1/2/1792
Joseph, N.C., R255
Joseph, Pa., R 254
Joseph, Pa., 1791-95, S22090
Joshua, Pa., Sarah, W23461
Martin, N.C., Mary, R256
Mathew, N.C., S8035
Nathan, N.Y., S6524
Robert, Pvt., Hazen's Regt., BLWt. 12710 iss. 9/2/1789
Robert, N.C., S.C., Nancy, R259
Samuel, Mass., BLWt.16-200
Solomon, N.Y., S12002
Thomas, N.J., R260
Thomas, N.Y., S12004
Thomas, N.C., BLWt.62-300. Capt. iss. 2/22/1798 to Peter Armstrong, guard. in trust for Thos. Jones Armstrong, only child & heir of soldier. No papers
Thomas, N.C., Janet, R 252
Thomas, N.C., Pa., S2925
Timothy, Mass., Dolly, W15547; BLWt.9476-160-55
Tobias, Pvt., Va., BLWt.11879 iss. 10/26/1795 to John Stockdell, ass.
William, Ct., BLWt.5379 iss. 9/8/1789 to Joseph Buell
William, N.C., S---; BLWt.61-300 Capt. iss. 1/16/1797 to Daniel Wheaton, ass. No papers
William, N.C., S30831
William, Pa., R261
William, Pa., Sarah, W8334; BLWt. 11160-160-55
William, S.C., S6534
William, Va., S8032
ARNAUD, John Peter, Md., Privateer, S31523
ARNDT, Abraham, N.Y., Anna, W20639
ARNEL, William, Del., S35767
ARNET, Thomas, Pa., S8036
ARNETT, David, Va., S14924
John, N.C., S.C., S31527
Samuel, Cont. Md., Nancy, R 262
ARNEY, Christian, N.C., S8023
ARNO, John, Mass., BLWt.39471-160-55; Miriam, W5633
ARNOLD, Aaron, Navy, BLWt.12734-160-55; Amey, W2581; R.I. res.
Aaron, N.C., S21051
Abimelech, N.Y., R.I., R 264
Abraham or Abram, N.Y., Lorana, W23458; BLWt.5376-160-55
Abraham, Pa., S6533
Alexander, Mass., R.I., S23519
Alford or Alfred, Cont., Mass., S38503
Anthony, R.I., S21605
Benedict, R.I., Elizabeth, W20629
Benjamin, S.C., Va., S2920
Caleb, Cont., R.I., S12003
Caleb, R.I., S21607
Caleb, R.I., Avis, W2582; BLWt. 26169-160-55

ARNOLD (continued)
David, Navy, R.I., Anna, W23465
David, N.C., S41417
Edward, Mass., S17241
Edward, R.I., Mercy, W20631; BLWt.7087-160-55
Elisha, Cont., Mass., S28974
Elisha, R.I., S21048
Elisha, Va., S6523
Fenner, Mass., Ct., S5250
Francis, Va., Elizabeth, W106
George, Cont. Md., Eve, W25356, BLWt.29041-160-55
Henry, Pa., S2919
Hezekiah, Va., S8034
Isaac, Ct., S31526
Israel, R.I., S21050
Jabez, Ct., Cont., Mass., S14922
Jabez, Cont., R.I., Rachel, W20630
Jacob, Pa., R 265
James, N.J., S942
James, Va., S30830
Job, R.I., S15359
John, Ct., S19183
John, Cont., Va., S37682
John, Pvt., Pa., BLWt.8894 iss. 6/29/1789 to A. McConnell, ass.
John, R.I., S21608
Jonathan, Ct.,N.Y., BLWts.212-60-55 & 887-100; Polly, W8102
Jonathan, Cont., Ct., or Mass., Lucy, W17218
Joseph, Cont., Mass., Ruth,W15546
Joseph, R.I., S21049
Joseph, R.I., S23096
Joseph, R.I., R 266
Josiah, Va., S35768
Levi, Ct., Privateer, BLWt.67536-160-55; Fanny P. Harris, former widow, W9050
Lindsey (Lindsay), Cont. Va., Elizabeth, W3750; BLWt.11869 iss. 1/7/1793 to Robt. Means, ass.
Moses, R.I., Sarah, W21618; BLWt. 9486-160-55
Nathaniel, Mass., S28973
Nathaniel, R.I., S14923
Nicholas, R.I., Hannah, W12213
Noyce, Cont., BLWt.5-200. Lt. iss. 5/8/1792 to Isaac Bronson ass.; also entered as above under BLWt.2607. No papers. Erroneous entry for soldier under BLWt.1577
Oliver, R.I., S21612
Oliver, R.I., Susannah, W15548
Oliver, Vt., S21611
Owen, R.I., S22623
Remington, R.I., S21606
Reuben, R.I., S6532
Richard, N.J., Pa., Mary, W10289, BLWt.28532-160-55
Richard, R.I., Hannah, W4118; BLWt.15170-160-55
Robert, Cont., Mass.,N.H., S36894
Robert, Pvt., Mass., BLWt.3622 iss. 4/18/1798 to Chris. S. Thom, ass.
Samuel B.P., Ct., S31524
Seth, Ct., Privateer, S18690
Solomon, N.C., Mary, W12208
Stephen, N.J., S33968

ARNOLD (continued)
Sylvania, Mass., W25355, former wid. of David Lamb, BLWt.15405-160-55
Thomas, Mass., Martha, W15978
Thomas, R.I., S8031
Thomas, R.I., BLWt.9-300-Capt. iss. 12/31/1789. No papers
Thomas, S.C., Mary, W5640
Timothy, Ct., Mass., Anna,W15549
William, N.C., S37684
William, not Rev., N.W. Indian War 1790, Ky. Mil., Old War Inv. File No. 6509
William, R.I., S17243
William, R.I., S21609
William, Va., R272
Ziba, N.J., S30832
ARNOT, David, N.C., See ARNOLD
Henry, N.J., N.Y., S8030
ARNOTT, Christian, N.Y., R268
Samuel, Md., Nancy, BLReg.50406-1855
ARRABY/ARRIBAS,
Jack, Pvt., Ct., BLWt.5381 iss. 9/24/1789
ARRANCE, James, Pvt., Lee's Legion Va. BLWts.11861 & 12734 iss. 1/15/1793
ARRANT, Peter, S.C., S17824
ARRASMITH, Massey, Va., S46321 or Massa Arra Smith, BLWt.1820-100
Nancy, Md., Va., BLWt.49468-160-55, former wid. of Casper Potterf, which see
ARRAY, James, N.J., See ARAY
ARRINGTON, Adler, Va., S6505
John, Va., Susanna, W5653; BLWt.28552-160-55
Samuel, Va., S8033
Thomas, Va., R269
William, Pvt., Va., BLWt.11878 iss. 1/7/1793 to Robt. Means,ass.
ARROSMITH/ARROWSMITH
Edmond, N.J., S12006
Nicholas, Cont., N.J., BLWt. 58690-160-55; Eliza R., W10356
ARROWSMITH, Edmond, N.J. See ARROSMITH
James, Va., Levina. See James Arrow SMITH
Nicholas, Cont., N.J., Eliza R., See ARROSMITH
ARSKINE, Alexander, Cont., Mass., Mary, W23459
ARTHER, James, Va., S6527
Catherine, Va., R270, former wid. of Walter Mackay
ARTHUR, James, Cont., Va., S2922
James, Md., Elizabeth, W5634
James, Va., See ARTHER
Joel, Va., S16034
John, Pa., Va., S39944
John, Va., Elizabeth, W5635
Richard, N.C., Clarkey, W1122; BLWt.26339-160-55
Stephen, Va., R271
Thomas, Va., Sally, W5636
William, Va., S6528
ARTIS, Isaac, Cont., Va., S39943
John, N.C., S41416
ARTISS, John, S.C., S39150

ARTMAN, Justice/Justus, Cont. N.Y., S22624
ARTWICK, Lawrence, N.Y., Martha, See HARTWICK
ARTWYCK, Lawrence, Pvt., N.Y., BLWts.6749 & 268-60-55 iss. 8/28/1790. BLWt.6749 to Exr's of Chr. Yates, ass.
ARUNDALL, John, Cont., Pa., Jemima, W5642
ARWIN, David, N.H., Isabella, See ERWIN
ARWOOD, John, N.C., S6535
ASAY, Samuel, N.J., R273
ASBERRY, William, Va., BLWts. 77-60-55 & 11873-100 iss. 7/7/1792 to Robt. Means, ass. No papers. Susan Bateman, former widow, W2988
ASBURY, George, Va., Mary, W5644
ASH, Francis, Va., Elizabeth, R274
Henry, Pvt., N.Y., BLWt.6756 iss. 6/17/1791 to H. Fisher, admx. of George Fisher, ass.
John, Privateer, R.I., S6547
William, N.H., Susan, W23463
William, S.C., Jane, W5645
ASHBERRY, John, Pvt., Mass., BLWts. 3615 & 10918 iss. 3/31/1797 to James DeBanfre, ass.
ASHBROOK, George, Va., R277
Thomas, Va., S31528
ASHBURN, Luke, Va. Sea Service, Susan, W5649
ASHBY, Benjamin, Va., BLWt.55-200 Lt., iss. 7/28/1790. No papers
Daniel, Va., S14927
Fielding, Va., S30249
John, Cont. Mass., Esther, W15712
John, Va., Half Pay, R12159
Joseph, Va., S8039
Peter, Va., pensioned as ASHLEY. Winnifred, R 285
Stephen, Va., BLWt.2420-300
Zebulon, N.Y., S6536
ASHCRAFT, Amos, Pa., Va., S16610
Daniel, Va., Sally. See ASHCROFT
John, Pa., S6537
Uriah, Pa., Va., R 278
William, Ct., Cont., Navy, S37687
ASHCROFT, Daniel, Va., Sally, W23466
John, Pa., See ASHCRAFT
ASHE, John Baptiste, N.C., BLWt. 2247-450
Samuel, N.C., Elizabeth H., W514; BLWt. 1233-200
ASHER, Bartlet, Va., Margaret, W23465
Canada/Canady, Mass., S32662; BLWt.676-100
Charles, Va., S30833
David, N.C., R279; BLReg.31137-55
Gad, Ct., S17244
ASHERST, William, Va., BLWt.27613-160-55; Mary Ashurst, W25361
ASHLEY, Abner, Ct., R.I., S18298
Barnabas, Mass., S32661
Daniel, Ct., R.I., S14928
Daniel, Mass., S44555
Elisha, Green Mountain Boys, Vt. Beulah, W23464

ASHLEY (continued)
James, Pvt., Md., BLWt.10924 iss. 8/14/1795 to Francis Sherrard, ass.
John, Mass., S18299
John, Va., Pvt., BLWt.11864 iss. 5/29/1792 to Robt. Means, ass.
Joseph, Ct., R.I., S14926
Martin, N.H., Theodosia, W20632
Moses, Mass., BLWt.11-400. No papers
Noah, Cont. Mass., S29592
Percival, Mass., S32660
Peter, Va., Winnifred, See ASHBY
Robert, N.C., Sarah, W4874; BLWt. 13016-160-55
Robert, S.C., R282
Samuel, Ct., Lucy, W17219
Thomas, Va., S35173
William, Cont. Md., Agnes, W9708
William S., Vt., BLWt.40928-160-55; Aurelia, R284
Zenas, Vt., S22091
ASHLOCK, James, Va., Charlotte,W886
Jesse, N.C., BLWt.110865-160-55, S1160
William, Va., S1161
ASHLY, John, S.C., Eleanor, R281
William, Green Mt. Boys, Vt.,R283
ASHMAN, Samuel, N.Y., Parthenia, W25362
ASHMORE, Jabesh, N.J., Hester,W5647
John, Pvt., Md., BLWt.10931 iss. 8/12/179- to Francis Sherrard, ass.
ASHPILL, Thomas, Pvt., Armand's Corps, BLWt.12702 iss. 1/12/1792 to Peter LeBarbier Duplessis, ass.
ASHPORT, Cuff, Cont., Mass. Lydia/Elizabeth Cuff, W27332
ASHTON, Alexander, N.C., See ASTON
Benjamin, Pvt., Pa., BLWt.8895 iss. 2/14/1791
George, N.J., Hannah, W3327
Isaac, N.J., Mary, W444
James, N.C., See ASTON
James, Pvt., Pa., BLWt.8899 iss. 1/5/1791
John, Pa., BLWt.49-200. Lt. iss. 8/24/1792. No papers
John, Va., S37686
Joseph, Pa., BLWt.46-200, Capt., Lt., Pa. Regt. Arty. Iss. 10/17/1789. No papers
Robert, N.J., Sarah, W15871
Samuel, Mass., Sea Service, Elizabeth, W15711
Thomas G., N.Y., S19184
ASHUR, Gad. Pvt., Ct., BLWt.5377 iss. 1/6/1797
John, N.C., R 280
ASHURST, William, Va., Mary. See ASHERST
ASHWORTH, Harrison, Cont., Va., Elizabeth, W5648
Joel, Va., Milly, W10290
ASK, Samuel, Ct., S10327
ASKEW
Constance, maiden name Mercer, widow of Josiah Askew. Former widow of Barnaba Barron

ASKEW,
James, ---, Disability. No papers
Peregrine/Perrey, Pvt., Md., BLWt.10937 iss. 2/1/1790
William, N.C., S8038
ASKINS, Alexander, Cont., Mass., See Mary ARSKINE
George, S.C., Mary, W9334
Robert, Sea Service, Margaretta, R21982
ASLIN, Thomas, Va., S39152
ASLINE, Priesque, Cont., Canadian, Mary, W15820
ASPENWALL, John, Pvt., Va., BLWt. 11868 iss. 12/13/1791 to Francis Graves, ass.
Samuel, Ct., Jane, W20634
ASPINWALL
Aaron, Ct., S44556
John, Cont., Mass., Nancy,W17220
Samuel, Ct., Jane, See ASPENWALL
ASPLEY
John, N.C., Sarah, W2903
ASRE, Jonathan, N.C., Va., R276
ASSELIN, Priesque, Cont. Canadian Mary, See ASLINE
Thomas, Va., See ASLIN
ASSLIN, Priesque, Cont. Canadian, See ASLINE
ASTIN, Thomas, N.H., Ruth, See AUSTIN
ASTON, Alexander, N.C., R286
Alexander, Va., S2927
James, N.C., R287
ATAYATAGHRONGHTA, Lewis, Indian, BLWt.12-450, Lt. Col. iss. 3/8/1792. No papers
ATCHERSON, Thomas, Mass., Pa., Privateer, S39153
ATCHINSON, Joshua, Mass., BLWt. 2484-100
Timothy, Pvt., Pa., BLWt.8902 iss. 9/26/179- to John McClel-and, ass.
ATCHLEY
Abraham, Va., R68
Thomas, N.J., Va., Lydia, W257
ATHELL, Benjamin, Va. See ETHELL
ATHERTON
Caleb, Mass., S5255
Joel, Mass., Nancy, W23472
Joel, N.J., S46020
John, Cont. Mass., S38506
John, Mass., S19185
Jonathan, Cont. Mass., Phebe W23473
Jonathan, Mass., Rhoda Tarbell, former widow, W16078
Joseph, Mass., Miriam, W15716
Matthew, Mass., Jemima, W5207; BLWt.3803-160-55
Philip, Mass., S32663
Sarah, N.Y., former widow of Nathaniel Plumsted
Thomas, Mass., S30250
ATHEY, James, ---, Va. res. in 1834. R289
William, Va., S34629
ATHY, Thomas, Va., S37689
ATIS, London, Mass. Sea Service, Eunice, W23468

ATKERSON, John, Cont. Mass., Privateer. Mary Neale, former wid., W15115; she was also pensioned as widow of other husband, James Neale, Cont. Mass., which see
ATKINS, Alexander, Va., S35175
Ambrose, Va., S6543
Charles, N.C., S31511
Chauncy, Ct., S10328
Cornelius, Pvt., Mass., BLWt. 3609 iss. 7/6/1791 to S. Pepoon, ass.
David, Ct., Cont., See ADKINS
David, Cont., Ct., S12013
David, Cont., Ct., S45224
David, Pvt., Sheldon's Artillery Ct., BLWt.5388 iss. 6/25/1789
Edward, Va., S35174
Isaac, Ct., S22092
Jehu, Va., S21613
John, Va., S37690
John, Va., R291
John J., or John Priest, Cont. Mass., Abigail, W16813
Joshua, Mass., Sea Service, S32665
Josiah, Pvt., Ct., BLWt.5372 iss. 12/24/1796
Josiah, Ct., S45223
Josiah, Ct., W17673, Sarah Culver former widow
Lewis, N.C., S2929
Lewis, Pvt., Va., BLWt.11866 iss. 11/17/1794
Robert, Mass., Polly, W23471
ATKINSON, Amos, Cont., Mass., Anna, W15715
Amos, N.C., Edith, W5651
Charles, Pa., Elizabeth, W4875
Daniel, Va., S10065
Elisha, N.C., S30834
Isaac, Va., Anna, W3494; BLWt. 19784-160-55
James, Pvt., N.Y., BLWt.6750 iss. 1/25/1791
James, Va., S15352
John, Mass., S5254
John, N.C., Elizabeth, W10358
John, N.C., Pheraba, BLReg. 338228-55
John, Va., S37688
John, Va., Mary, W5650
Joseph, N.C., Martha, R292
Joshua, Va., S30835
Mathew A., Pa., R293
Nathaniel, Mass., N.H., S14929
Reuben, Cont. Va., S6544
Richard Thomas, Va., S37691
Samuel, N.H., Sarah, W17221
Samuel, N.J., S943
Stephen, N.H., Nancy, W20635
Stephen, Pvt., N.H., BLWt.2906 iss. 10/21/1790 to Stephen Atkinson
Theodore or Theoder, Hannah, W21619; BLWts. 12568-160-55 and 1706-100
Thomas, Va., S5253
William, Pvt., Md., BLWts.12714 & 14093 iss. 1/28/1795 to Francis Sherrard, ass. of Ann Colemore, admx.

ATKINSON (continued)
William, Mass., Anne, W23470; BLWt.29033-160-55
William, Pvt., Va., BLWt.11876 iss. 3/26/1792 to Francis Graves, assignee
William, Va., R296
ATKISON, Henry, Va., S31529
ATSET, Joseph, Mass., R 297
ATTIGH, Michael, Pa., See ALTIGH
ATTWATER, John, Ct., Lucy, See ATWATER
ATTWELL, Charles B., Va., S10064
ATTWOOD, Lydia, R.I., former wid. of Samuel Lee
ATWATER, Benjamin, N.Y., S14931
Hannah, Pa., former widow of Henry Harding, which see
Holbrook, Cont., Ct., Mehitable, W16494
Ichabod, Ct., Electa, W699; BLWt.26184-160-55
John, Ct., Lucy, W698; BLWt. 26949-160-55
Jonathan, Ct., R298
Russell, Ct., S23238
Stephen, Ct., S12014
ATWELL
Charles, Va., See ATTWELL
John, Mass., Dolly, W515
Joseph, N.Y., S12009
Oliver, Cont., Ct., S19526
Oliver, Pvt., Sheldon's Cont. Dragoons, Ct., BLWt.5398 iss. 2/22/1790 to Theodosius Fowler
Paul, N.Y., S12008
Samuel, Ct., Betsey, W1205, BLWt.19805-160-55
ATWILL
Peter, Cont., N.Y., S12007
ATWOOD, Amos, Mass., S45225
Ebenezer, Ct., Demarest, W23469, BLWt.36626-160-55
Elijah, Ct., S39945
Gideon, Mass., S11893
Hannah, N.H., former widow of Francis Adam Drew
Isaac, Ct., Mass., Elizabeth, W20636
Jabish, or Jabez, N.Y., S6542
James, Vt., S21614
Jedediah, N.Y., R300
Jesse, Ct., Cont., Mass., Rachel, W17222
Jesse, Mass., Lois. See WOOD
John, Ct., Candace, W15718
John, R.I., Roby, W23467
Jonathan, Ct., S15361
Joshua, N.H., S12010
Moses, N.H., S12011
Nathan, Ct., Mass., S36896
Oliver, Vt., Miriam, BLWt.52614-160-55
Philip, Ct., Mass., S18689
Philip, Cont., Mass., S15360
Ruth, Mass., former widow of William Wethrell
Samuel, Ct., Mass., Vt., S14930
Sophia, Mass., N.H., See Samuel GRIFFIN
Thomas, Mass., Ruth, W20638
Wait, Cont. Mass., S32664

ATWOOD (continued)
Zaccheus, Mass., S21052
AUBONY, Thomas, Pvt., Va., BLWt. 11881 iss. 12/13/1791 to Francis Greaves, assignee
AUBREY, John Frederick, N.H., Sarah, R311
AUCHMUTY, Samuel, Pa., S39946
AUGER, Felix, Ct., Esther, See AUGUR
Justus, Ct., Cont., S38507
AUGHE, Harmon, Pa., R312
AUGIN, Isaac, Mass., BLWt.667-100
AUGUR, Felix, Ct., Esther, W20610
Justus, Ct., Cont., See AUGER
AUGUSTINE or GUSTINE
Joel, Ct., Ann Taylor
William Matthew, Pa., Sarah, R12178
AUGUSTUS, Ceaser, Jr., Pvt., Ct., BLWt.5363 iss. 11/30/1795 to Timothy Pitkin, Jr., Admr.
AUKERMAN, Christopher, Pa., Susanna, see ACKERMAN
AULD, James, Pa., S22093
AUMOCK, Abraham, N.J., S12015
John, N.J., S590
Tunis, N.J., S589
William, N.J., S946
AURAND/AURANDT, John Detrick, Pa., Catharine, W3291
AURYANSEN/AURIGANSEN, Resolvent, N.J., S944
AUSBURN, Robert, N.C., Jane See OSBORNE
AUSLEY, Jesse, N.C., W27520, Mary, BLWt.78031-160-55
AUSTIN/AUSTEN
Aaron, Ct., S37692
Abiathar, Mass., S12017
Alexander, N.C., R 314
Amos, Ct., S22626
Andrew D., Ct., S5257
Apollos, Ct., Sarah, W20644; BLWt.56512-160-55
Asa, Mass., Mary, W15709
Benjamin, Ct., Susannah, W2514
Benjamin, Mass., S36897
Benjamin, N.Y., R316
Benjamin, N.C., S6548
Caleb, Cont. N.Y., Martha, W3495
Caleb, Mass., S20593
Caleb, R.I., Sarah, W20640
Catharine, Ct., War of 1812, former widow of Wm. Wooldridge
Climena, Ct., former widow of Serajah Comstock
Dan, Ct., S29594
David, Cont. Mass., Judith Cashman former widow, W10574
David, N.Y., S39948
David, R.I., Judy, R323
Ebenezer, Ct., Amy, W20642
Edward, Ct., Mary, W16171
Elias, Ct., S12019
Elijah, R.I., R317
Eliphalet, Ct., Sibell, W3918
Eusebius, Cont., Ct., S45221
Ezekiel, Mass., N.Y., S21615
George, Mass., R.I., S28975
George, R.I., Lydia, W4876; BLWt. 15194-160-55

AUSTIN (continued)
Hannah, Ct., former widow of Abel Tharp
Harris, Pvt., Md., BLWt.10921 iss. 8/14/1795 to Francis Sherrard, ass.
Holmes, Pvt., N.Y., BLWt.6723 iss. 2/24/1791
Holmes, N.Y., S45220
Isaac, Mass., S28976
Isaac, N.Y., S12018
Isaiah, N.C., S5259
James, Ct., Hannah, W20643
James, Ct., N.Y., R.I., S19186
Jedediah, Ct., R.I., S21616
Jeremiah, R.I., Ester, W8105; BLWt.67608-160-55
Job, N.Y., S23520
Joel, Va., Anne, W3375
John, Ct., Esther, W15674
John, Ct., N.Y., Vt., R322
John, Cont. Mass., BLWt.1943-200
John, Cont., Mass., S36898
John, Mass., N.H., S22094
John, N.Y., S45222
John, Privateer, R.I., Priscilla, W2904
John, R.I., S18300
John, Va., S39154
John, Va., Elizabeth, R318
John, Va., Polly, R325
Jonah, Mass., S16611
Jonathan, R.I., S28624
Joseph, R.I., S15734
Joshua, Cont. Mass., S39165; BLWt.878-100
Moses, Cont., Mass., N.H.,S45507
Nathan, Ct., S14932
Nathaniel, Ct., S19902
Nathaniel, Ct., Margaret, W1695
Nathaniel, Mass., Vt., S18692
Percis, R.I., S21053
Phenas, Pvt., Ct., BLWt.5359 iss. 4/15/1796 to Amos Mussey
Philip, Cont., Mass., N.Y., S16035
Phineas, Ct., S44557
Phinehas, Mass., S19527
Picus, R.I., Grizell, R319
Polepos, R.I., S21054
Richard, Ct., Mary Phelps former widow, W17445
Richard, Md., S6513
Samuel, Ct., Cont., S2931
Samuel, Mass., S10330
Samuel, Pa., R328
Seth, Ct., Hannah, R320
Solomon, Mass., S12016
Stephen, Cont., N.C., S2040
Stephen, Mass., S30836
Thomas, N.H., Ruth, R326
Walter, Va., S37693
William, Mass., S28977
Zephaniah, Mass., S10324
AUTEN, Fulcard, N.J., Pa., R330
John A., N.J., S945
Thomas, N.J., Amy, R329
AUXER/AUXTIER
Samuel, Va., BLWt. 28516-160-55, and 26765-160-55; Sarah Phillips former widow, W8516
AVARY, Gardener/Gardner, Cont. Mass., S44559

AVARY (continued)
Nathan, Ct., Cont., Aliff. See AVERY
AVEREL, Jonathan, Ct., Navy, Privateer, S2933
Joseph, Mass., Sarah, R302
AVERELL, Ebenezer, R.I., Sarah, See AVERILL
Ezekiel, Mass., S36901
William, Ct., Navy, Privateer, Abigail, W20645
AVERILL, Daniel, Ct., S12027
Daniel, N.H., Mary, W1796; BLWt. 36634-160-55
Ebenezer, Ct., Privateer, S28625
Ebenezer, R.I., Sarah, W16816
Elijah, N.H., Mehitable Upton former widow, W7365
Ephraim, Pvt., Sheldon's Dragoons Ct., BLWt.5395 iss. 1/1/--
Ezekiel, Mass., See AVERELL
Jesse, Cont., Vt., S44562
Jonathan, Ct., Navy, Privateer, See AVEREL
Joseph, Mass., Sarah, See AVEREL
Josiah, Vt., Catharine, R301
Moses, Cont., N.H., S36900
Nathaniel, Ct., S12938
Robert, Cont., Vt., Green Mt. Boys, S38510
Shadrack, Cont., Mass., Hannah, W23479
Thomas, N.Y., Vt., S28627
William, Ct., Navy, Privateer, Abigail, See AVERELL
Wyman, Cont., Vt., BLWt.24623-160-55. Eunice, W27548
AVERY
Abel, Ct., Elizabeth, W23476
Abner, Ct., S12025
Abraham, Ct., Cont., Mass. & Privateer, S28626
Amos, Ct., Betsey, R12189
Amos, Ct., Eunice, R305
Amos, Ct., Mary, W25374
Amos, Ct., Cont., S12023
Benjamin, Pvt., Ct., BLWt.5383 iss. 10/4/1796 to Jacob Griggs
Benjamin, Ct., S44558
Caleb, Ct., Mary, W25363
Charles, Pvt., Ct., BLWt.5357 iss. 2/17/1797 to Theophilus Woodward
Charles, Ct., Mary, W23478
Christopher, Ct., S22627
Christopher, Ct., Cont., S49280
Constant, Ct., Zipporah, W1696
Daniel, Ct., S19903
Daniel, Ct., S44560
David, Ct., S12022
Denison, Ct., Hannah, W23474
Ebenezer, Ct., BLWt.782-160-55; S12021
Ebenezer, Ct., S19906
Elihu, Ct., Thankful Rogers former widow, W15955
Elisha, Ct., Sybil, R310
Ezekiel, Ct., S5261
Gardiner, Cont., Mass. See AVARY
George, Ct., Mass., Vt. BLWt. 26129-160-55; Mary, W23477
George, N.C., Elizabeth, W8335; BLWt.19824-160-55

AVERY (continued)
Griswold, Ct., R308
John, Drummer, Ct., BLWt.5378 iss. 3/21/1799 to Elnathan Fitch
John, Cont., Mass., Beulah, W5208; BLWt.12579-160-55
John, Cont., N.H., Mary, W15979
John, N.C., Sarah, W4119; BLWt. 56511-160-55
Jonathan, Ct., Cont., Parmela, W20646
Jonathan, Ct., Navy, Privateer, See AVEREL
Joseph, N.H., BLWt.2317-100
Joshua, Ct., Rachel, See AREY
Miles, Pvt., Ct., BLWt.5358 iss. 2/25/1797
Miles, Ct., S32666
Moses, N.H., Betsey, R303; BLWt.29902-160-55
Nathan, Ct., S10331
Nathan, Ct., Rebecca, R308
Nathan, Ct., Cont., Aliff, W17223
Nathaniel, Ct., S18693
Nathaniel, Ct., Cont., BLWt.34521-160-55; Amy, W700
Nicholas, Pvt., N.Y., BLWt.6729 iss. 7/30/1790 to Ed. Cumpston, ass.
Oliver, Ct., S16613
Park, Ct., S19904
Peter, Ct., S12024
Ransford, Cont. Mass., Polly, W8106; BLWt.30616-160-55
Richard, Mass., Maritta, W20647
Robert, Cont. Vt., Green Mt. Boys See AVERILL
Robert, N.C., R309
Roger, Pvt., Ct., BLWt.5386 iss. 6/29/1792 to Stephen Thorn
Roger, Ct., S44561
Rufus, Ct., S12939
Samuel, Ct., Lydia, R307
Samuel, Cont., N.H., S36899
Samuel, N.H., Anna, W23475
Shadrack, Cont. Mass., Hannah, See AVERILL
Simeon, Ct., BLWt.1143-200
Simeon, Cont., Ct., BLWt.5210-160-55; Sarah Bigelow former widow, W23615
Stephen, Ct., S12026
Stephen, Ct., Mary, W6890; BLWt. 19764-160-55
Submit, N.H., W15980, former wid. of James Barnes
Thomas, Ct., Cont., S5260; BLWt. 313-200
Uriah, Ct., Navy, S16612
Williams, N.Y., S12020
AVIS, Robert, Va., S38509
AVIT, Richard, Cont., Pa., Navy, S36404
AWALT, Michael, N.C., Eve, W326
AWBRY/AWBEY
Samuel, Cont. Va., S30837
AWTRY, Absalom, N.C., R531
AXE, Frederick, Pa., S23521
AXON/AXSON, Samuel J., S.C., BLWts.1250-300; 1830-100
AXTELL, Elizabeth, Mass., former wid. of Ephraim Minor, which see

AXTELL (continued)
Henry, Pvt., Mass., BLWt.3632 iss. 8/7/1797 to T.H. & Louisa Axtell heirs and children
Henry, Mass., S44563
Samuel, Mass., S12028
AYCOCK, Abner, N.C., Sarah, W9710
AYER, Benjamin, Mass., S19189
Darius, Md., R332
Ebenezer, Cont. Ct., Achsa, W8589; BLWt.26027-160-55
Elijah, Mass., S30838
Jonathan, Mass., BLWt.22-200 Lt. iss. 10/18/1796 to John Coats, assignee. No papers
Moses, Navy, Mass., Lydia, W12225 BLWt.27609-160-55
Peter, Ct., Temperance, W15872
Thomas, Mass., Esther, W21621
William, Cont., Mass., Mary,W15722
AYERS, Ebenezer, Cont., Ct., Achsa See AYER
Elihu, N.C., Lydia, See AYRES
Ezekiel, N.J., Eleanor, R333
Francis, Va., Mary, R26086
Frederick, Pvt., Md., BLWt.10939 iss. 1/15/1793 to John Wright, ass. of Hugh Mc Coy, Admr.
Jedediah, Cont., Mass., S44565
John, Ct., BLRej. Abigail Pelton, former wid. She was pensioned as wid. of Joseph Pelton, Ct. W26303
John, N.J., S14933
Joseph, Mass., S5251
Lewis, N.J., S799
Reuben, N.J., S47933
Reuben, N.J., Mary, W388
Thomas, N.J., N.Y., S17245
AYLESWORTH, Arthur, N.Y., R.I., Polly, W16495
AYLOR, Jacob, Va., S8040
AYLWARD, ---, Mass. Sea Service, Elizabeth, former wid. of Jeremiah Dayley, which see
AYMOND, John, Pvt., Hazen's Regt. BLWt.12715 iss. 4/28/1795
AYRES, Ebenezer, Cont. Ct., Achsa See AYER
Elihu, N.C., Lydia, R335
Enos, N.Y., Julia, W20649
Ezekiel, N.J., Eleanor. See AYERS
Francis, Va., Mary,See AYERS
Frederick, Pvt., Mass., BLWt.3637 iss. 3/25/1790
Henry, Va., Susan, W445
Jacob, N.J., S849
James, S.C., Va., R334
Jedediah, Cont., Mass. See AYERS
John, Ct., Abigail Pelton, former widow
John, Ct., Martha, W1357; BLWt. 27614-160-55
John, Del., Md., S45226
John, N.J., S28628
John, Va., Jane, W4120
Joseph, Mass., S5251. See AYERS
Nancy, former wid. of James Russey, which see
Nathaniel, N.C., R336
Reuben, N.J., Mary. See AYERS
Reuben, N.Y., Elizabeth, W1797; BLWt.8016-160-55

AYRES (continued)
Robert, N.J., S2041
Robert, N.Y., Sarah, See AYRS
Samuel, Cont., Mass., S38511
Samuel, Corp. Mass., BLWt.3621 iss. 8/3/1789 to ___ Vredenburgh, assignee
Thomas, Cont., N.Y., S44564
Thomas, Pvt., Md., BLWts.10923 & 274-60-55 iss. 6/9/1789
Thomas, Md., Elizabeth, W8346; BLWt.274-60-55
Thomas, N.J., N.Y. See AYERS
William, Ct., Cont., See ARES
AYRS, Robert, N.Y., Sarah,W20648
AZELIP, Richard, Md., Cont., S34630

B

BAARS, John, Mass., S9272
BABB, Benjamin, Mass., Rachel, W5764
Christopher, N.C., S6685
Moses, N.H., Merribah, W24636
Peter, Mass., Thankful, W24639
Seth, Va., Mary, W327
William, N.H., Jemima, W17243
BABBET, See BABBITT, Edward, Ct., S31545
BABBETT, Abijah. See BABBITT
BABBIDGE/BAVIDGE, Courtney, Mass., Catharine, W9346; BLWt.13439-160-55
BABBIT, Asa, Mass., Ruth, R337
Edward, Ct., S31545. See BABBET
Ira, Cont., Mass., Sabra, W1129
Joel, Cont., Mass., S38518
John, Fifer, N.Y., BLWt.6851 iss. 7/9/1790 to Charles R. & G. Webster, ass.
John, N.Y., Sylvia, W4633
Joy, Cont., Mass., S44609
Sanford, Mass., Mary, R338; BLWt.35841-16-55
Seth, Ct., R.I., S12956
Snellem, Mass., S29595
Uri, Mass., Lydia, W18555
BABBITT, Abijah, Mass., Betsey, See claim of Betsey Babbett or Babbitt, pensioned as former wid. of Benjamin Norton, Mass., R.I., W14256
Elijah, R.I., Amey, W21630
Isaac, Mass., S30848
Samuel, Mass., Mary, W20690
BABBS, John, Md., S45241
BABCOCK, Amos, Mass., S29606
Azariah, Ct., N.Y., Sabra, W25198 BLWt.3753-160-55
Benjamin, Mass., S17835
Beriah, Sg., Ct., BLWt.5539 iss. 2/19/1799 to Samuel Dorrance,ass.
Beriah, Cont., Ct., S12034
Caesar, R.I., R339
Caleb, Ct., R.I., S23112
Christopher, R.I., S12032
Christopher, R.I., Polly, W21643
Daniel, Ct., S12102
Daniel, Ct., Tryphena, R345
Daniel, Ct. R.I., R340
Ebenezer, Mass., Rhoda, R342
Elias or Elisha, Mass., Huldah, W15676; BLWt.5207-160-55
Elisha, Ct., R.I., Anna, W681; BLWt.26693-160-55
Elisha, N.Y., S6029
Ephraim, Ct., S37709
George, Ct., R.I., Content, W5210; BLWt.2350-160-55
Hannah, Mass., former widow of Benjamin Blodgett, which see
Henry, R.I., S21629
Horace, Ct., Elcey, W23513
Ichabod, R.I., S17262
Isaac,Cont., R.I., Amy, W4631
Isaac, N.Y., Mary, W20666 BLWt.27596-160-55
James J., N.Y., Mary, R341
Jason, N.Y., S28635
Jeremiah, Cont., Mass., S36904

BABCOCK (continued)
Jesse, R.I., S21621
Job, Ct., Cont., S44576
John, Ct., Lydia Barnard, former widow, W25187
John, Ct., Lydia Edgerton or Egerton, former widow, W17749
John, N.Y., Sarah, W20684
Jonas, Cont., Mass., S10352
Jonathan, N.Y., S6589
Jonathan, R.I., S28985
Joseph, Cont., Mass., S32679
Joshua, R.I., Nancy, W16496
Lemuel, Mass., S18699
Nathaniel, Ct., Mass., S2367
Oliver, Ct., Cont., Marcy Brown, former widow, W16865
Paul, R.I., S21630
Prime or Primus (colored) R.I., S37698; BLWt.2974, iss. 1789
Reuben, Ct., S28978
Reuben, Mass., Hannah, W14254 BLWt.30618-160-55
Robert, R.I., R343
Roger, Ct., S12107 (or BADCOCK)
Samuel, Mass., Sylvina or Sylvinia W23546
Sarah, Vt., former widow of Sampson Marble, W15874
Sherman or Shermon, Ct., R.I., Vt., S17246
Simeon, R.I., Mary, W14221
Simon, R.I., S15735
William, R.I., Cont., S44575
William, Cont., R.I., Phebe, W25191; BLWt.26801-160-55
William (or BADCOCK), N.Y., R346
BABER, James, Va., Milley or Melley, W3754
James, Pvt., Md., BLWt.10940 iss. 2/1/1790 to Ann Tottle, admx.; James Williams & Jos. Dawson admrs. of James Tottle dec'd, late ass.
Obadiah (or BEAVER), Va., Hannah, R347
BABER/BARBER, William, Va., S10333
BABIT, Isaac, Mass., See BABBITT
BACCHUS/BECKER, Benjamin, Cont. Pa., R695
BACCHUS/BACKUS/BOACHUS, George, N.Y., S39951
William (or BACCUS), N.C., Celia, W67
BACHE/BEACH, Samuel, Cont., Green Mt. Boys, S38512; BLWt. 79
BACHELDER, David, N.H., Susanna, R353
Jethro, Cont., N.H.,Dorothy,W17250
John, N.H., S15310
John, N.H., Martha, W389; BLWt. 6019-160-55
Joseph, N.H., Susanna, W23507
Josiah, Cont., N.H., Deborah, W1127; BLWt.16258-160-55
Stephen, Cont., N.H., S19193
William, N.H., S45236
William, N.H., Martha, BLReg. 55, CL.273093. She rec'd BL & pension acct. of former hùsband John Wadleigh, W27661; BLWt. 42-60-55, N.H.

BACHELDOR, Gideon, Ct., Mass., S36903
BACHELDOR/BATCHELDER, James, N.H., S45510
Samuel, Mass., Anna, R 348
BACHELER/BACHELDER, John, N.H., Martha, W389; BLWt.6019-160-55
BACHELLER/BATCHELDER, Ruppe, R.I., S23526
Theophilus, Mass., S17258
BACHELOR, Abel, Pvt., Ct., BLWt. 5515 iss. 10/7/1789 to Benjamin Tallmadge
Cornelius, Mass., R349
Frances, ---, former widow of William Wooten, R350
Susannah, N.C., former widow of Abram Hay, W17262
BACHER, Jacob, Pa., S23534
BACHMAN/BAUGHMAN, George, Pa., Barbara, W4632
BACHUS/BECCHUS, Jacob, Pvt., N.Y., BLWt.6777 iss. 7/30/1790 to Ed. Cumpston, ass.
John, Mass., N.Y., S9810
John, N.Y., Magdalena, W16497
John, N.Y., R354
Josiah, Ct., S8058
Ozias, Ct., Elizabeth, W17227
Samuel, Ct., S16036
Stephen, Ct., Privateer, S18704
Timothy, Mass., S38513
BACK, Elisha, Ct., S44605
John, Va., S32103
Lyman, Ct., Eunice, W23540
BACKENBAUGH/BECKENBAUGH/PECKINPAUGH
Leonard, Md., Catharine, W4122; BLWt.27681-160-55
BACKER, Jacob, See BACHER
BACKMAN/BUCKMAN, Jacob, Mass.,R1409
BACKUS, Abner, Ct., Jemima, W2049; BLWt.3794-160-55
Clark, Mass., Elizabeth, W21622
Elijah, Ct., S38514
BACKUS/BOACHUS, George, N.Y., See BACCHUS
George, Pvt., N.Y., BLWt.6863 iss. 8/4/1790 to Henry Hart, ass.
BACON, Abel, Cont., Mass., S38525
Abel, Pvt., Mass., BLWt.3764 iss. 2/13/1799
Abner, Ct., S37728; BLWt.2639-300 Capt., iss. 3/27/1794 to Samuel Dorrance, ass. No papers
Andrew, N.J., S39966
Ebenezer, Ct., S30849
Ebenezer, Ct., Cont., S44569
Ebenezer, Cont., Mass., S32673
Edmund, Mass., Vt., Tamma, R360
Elias, Cont., Mass., S32682
Elijah, Cont., Mass., S44568
Ephraim, Mass., Annah, BLWt. 19829-160-55
Eunice, Mass., former wid. of James Davis, W15982
Francis, Ct., S12981
George, Navy, Mass., S1636
Henry, Ct., R.I., S29604; BLWt. 2138-100
Isaiah, Mass., Ruth, W2052
Jabez, Mass., S30254
Jacob, Ct., Privateer, S15306

BACON (continued)
Jarib (Josiah Bacon on the roll submitted) Mass., S44567
John, Cont., Mass., Zeruah, W14230
John, Mass., S32667
John, Mass., Elizabeth, W14234
Jonathan, Mass., S12070
Jonathan, Mass., S44570
Jonathan, Mass., Submit, BLWt. 61228-160-55
Joseph, Ct., Betsey, R355
Joseph, Cont., Ct., Eleanor,W25190
Joseph, Mass., S32675
Joseph, Mass., R356
Joseph, Mass., Nancy Evans, R3389; BLWt.36741-160-55
Josiah, Ct., Mass., S17263
Josiah, Cont., Mass., S32689
Josiah, Pvt., Mass., BLWt.3677 iss. 1/7/1796 to C. Sanger, ass.
Josiah, Mass., S30842
Lemuel, N.Y., S49267
Levi, Cont. Mass., Esther, W21626
Lot, Mass., Naomi, W14251
Matthias (or BAKEN), N.J., R357
Nathaniel, N.H., S45513
Nehemiah, Ct., S45239
Norman, Mass., Jane, R358; BLWt. 38824-160-55
Oliver, Cont., N.H., Rebecca, W16822; BLWt.74-200 Lt., iss. 1/16/1793 to Samuel Emery. No papers
Olivia, Mass., former wid. of Benjamin Witt, W14260
Philo, Mass., S32676
Richard, Pvt., Ct., BLWt.5506 iss. 2/22/1799
Richard, Va., S16625
Robert, Pvt., Va., BLWt.11900 iss. 11/5/1789
Rufus, Mass., Eleanor, W20673
Samuel, Cont., Mass., S29610
Samuel, Mass., N.Y., Anna, W20681
Silas, Mass., S28981
Simeon, Mass., Easter, R359
Solomon, Mass., Margaret, W20653
Thompson, Mass., Martha, W14236
Thompson, Sgt., N.Y., BLWt.6820 iss. 9/28/1790 to McAnly & Brown, assignees
Timothy, Cont., Mass., S32669
Timothy, Mass., S36906
Timothy, Mass., Sibbel, W23498
William, Ct., S23525
William, Ct., S37694; BLWt.101-100
William, Ct., Cont., S45566
William, Pvt., N.Y., BLWt.6682 iss. 2/21/1792 to Moses Wells, assignee
BACOT, Peter, Capt. N.C., BLWt. 291-300 iss. 12/31/1796; S39166
BADCOCK, Amos, Ct., S44577
John, Abiah, R360 1/2, N.Y. res. of widow in 1837
Jonas, Mass., S4937
Jonathan, Ct., S12108
Robert, Ct., S23105
Roger, See BABCOCK
Seth, Cont., Mass., S29615
William, N.Y. See BABCOCK, R346
BADEAU, Elias, Cont., N.J., S44611

BADEL/BEDEL, Moody, N.H., Mary, W9349; BLWt.13859-160-55
BADGELY/BADGLEY, Joseph, N.J., S33254
BADGEN, Lemuel, see BADGER
BADGER, Benjamin, Ct., Mass.,S12121
Charles, Cont. Md., S34632
Charles, Pvt., Hazen's Regt., BLWt 12790 iss. 6/18/1792 to Jacob Miller, Admr.
Charlotte, Mass., former widow of Joseph Johnston, W4126
Gideon, Cont., Mass., S34641
John, Ct., Mass., S15301
John, Mass., Mary, W15568
Jonathan, Ct., S22104
Joseph, Ct., Cont.,Mass., S44336
Lemuel, Mass., Sabra, W17242
Obadiah, Mass., S32687
Stephen, Mass., Charlotte, S12945; BLWt.28643-160-55
William, Cont., Mass.,R.I., S32674
BADGERO/BADGERRO, John, N.Y., Sally, W1801; BLWt.156-60-55
BADGET, Thomas, Va., S6593
BADGETT/BADGET, Peter, N.C., S6559
William, N.C., S6552; BLWt. 10308-160-55
BADGLEY, Jonathan, N.J., Hannah, Littel, former widow, W8047
Joseph, N.J., See BADGELEY
BADIDGE, Courtney, See BABBIDGE
BADLAM/BADLUM, Sylvanus, Pvt., Mass., BLWt.3673 iss. 2/11/1797 to C. Sanger, ass.
Sylvanus, Cont., Mass., Hannah, W25188
William, Cont., Mass., Elizabeth, W15821
BAER, Henry, Md., S8051
Jacob (BEAR/BARE), Cont., Pa., Catharine, R364
Jacob, Pa., S5263
BAGBY, John, N.C., S31532
John, Va., Matilda, W2997; BLWt. 10263-160-55
BAGDEN, Ceaser, Pvt., Ct., BLWt. 5465 iss. 2/24/1795 to Eneas Munson
BAGENT/BEGEANT, John, Cont., Va., S37747
BAGG, Oliver, Mass., S28991
BAGGARLY/BAGGERLY, David, Md., Rebecca, W8120; BLWt.29860-160-55
BAGGER, John, See BADGER
BAGGETT, James, S.C., S39159
BAGGS, James, Pa., S44346
BAGGS/BIGGS, John, Pa., Isabella, R 830
John, R.I., Dis. No papers
BAGLEY/BAGLY, Aaron, Mass.,S21624
Asher, Pvt., N.J., BLWt.8140 iss. 4/5/1793
Asher, N.J., S46367
Azor, Cont., N.Y., S44341
Barnard, Ct., N.H., S10341; BLWt.73588-160-55
Enoch, N.H., R365
John, Ct., Cont., Mass., N.H., S12096
John, Cont., Mass., S30263

BAGLEY/BAGLY (continued)
Jonathan, Mass., S39164
Josiah, N.Y., BLWt.164-200-Lt. iss. 11/11/1791 to Samuel Broom, ass. No papers
Peter, Mass., S21623
Philip, Mass., S28979
Richard V., N.Y., R366
Samuel, Mass., S15743
Thomas, Mass., N.H.,Olive, W20672
BAGLEY/BIGLEY, Winthrop, N.H., Maria, W20682; BLWt.30591-160-55
BAGNAL, John, S.C., Mary, R367
BAGNALL/BAGNELL, Richard, Mass., Bethiah, W21633
BAGUM, Henry, Md., S5269
BAGWELL, Frederick, N.C., Mary, W10386
Isaiah, Va. Sea Service, S6550
John, N.C., S6571
William, N.C., S21057
BAHR/BARR, John, Cont., Va., BLWt. 284-100
BAILES/BAILIS, Eldridge, S.C., Sarah, W6099; BLWt.33565-160-55
Robert, Cont., Mass., R.I.,S44585
BAILEY, Aaron, N.J., BLWt.3144
Abijah, N.H., S21061
Adams, Mass., BLWt.102-300-Capt. iss. 12/31/1795 to Jos. & Allen Crocker, ass. No papers
Alexander, N.C., S32101
Amaziah/Amasiah, Mass., S12031
Ansolem/Ansalem/Anselm, Va., S37702
Benjamin, Cont., Mass., S32684
Benjamin, Cont., N.H.,Vt.,S22111
Benjamin, N.C., BLWt.295-300-Capt. iss. 2/19/1800 to Othniel Lassell, exec. in trust for the devisees. No papers
Bethia, N.Y., former widow of Elind Tryon, W16183
Caleb, Ct., Elizabeth, BLWt. 77004-160-55
Cesar (or Dickinson), Mass., Hager, R371
Christopher, Ct., S12098
Christopher S., Vt., Abigail, W4129; BLWt.32227-160-55
Daniel, Mass., N.H., S12065
BAILEY/BAYLEY, Daniel, Mass., Susannah, W24638
BAILEY, Daniel, N.J., N.Y., S28632
BAILEY/BALEY, Daniel, N.C., R369
David, Ct., Eunice, W18552; BLWt.71016-160-55
BAILEY, David, Mass., N.H., R642
BAILEY/BALEY, David, Mass., N.H. Sally, W16176
BAILEY, Ebenezer, N.Y., S---
Ebenezer, Pvt., N.Y., BLWt.6790 iss. 8/23/1796 to Joseph Roberts, ass.
Ebenezer, N.Y., Tryphena, R395
Eliakim, Ct., S17264
Elijah, Ct., S44573
Elijah, Mass., Susannah Barton former widow, W16823
Eliphalet, Cont., Mass., S32672
Eliphalet, Cont., N.H., S29596

BAILEY (continued)
Eliphalet, Pvt., Mass., BLWt. 3767 iss. 8/1/1789 to Thomas Cushing, ass.
Elisha, Va., Hannah, W8344
Enoch, Ct., S12072
Ephraim, Cont., Mass. Dis. No pension papers. BLWt.485-100
George, Pa., S23523
George, R.I., S21058
Henry, Ct., BLWt.1594-100
Henry, Va., S8053
Ichabod, Pvt., Ct., BLWt.5459 iss. 1/7/1802 to Nath. Bailey & others
Ichabod, Ct., Patience, W20667
Isham, Va., S12965
Ishmael, Va., Julina/Juliana, W5779
Israel, Mass., S29614
Israel, Mass., Lucy, W24637; BLWt.12840-160-55
Jacob, Ct., Sarah, W15875
James, Ct., Cont., Thedee or Theede, W1799; BLWt.3795-160-55
James, Cont., Mass., Barthenia, W16180
James, Md., Christiana, W9342
James, Md., Elizabeth, W5214
James, Pvt., Mass., BLWt.3690 iss. 2/5/1790
James, Mass., War of 1812, S28246; S44572
James, Mass., Lucy, W14261
James, Pvt.,Pa., BLWt.8991 iss. 9/7/1796
James, Pvt., Va., BLWt.11948 iss. 7/6/1793 to Francis Graves, ass.
James, Va., S2945
James, Va., S6577
Jared, Ct., R.I., Elizabeth, W4884
Jesse, N.H., Sarah, W17251
Jesse, N.Y., R375
Job, Mass., N.H., S6582
Joel, Mass., N.H., Mary, W16499
John, Clark's Ill. Regt. Nat. Archives Acct. #874
John, Cont., N.H., S6581
John, Pvt., Md., BLWt.10979 iss. 6/11/1790 & BLWt.10991 iss.8/14/1795 to Francis Sherrard, ass.
John, Mass., S32678; BLWt.744-100
John, Mass., Dis. No papers
John, Mass., BLWt.88-500. No papers
John, Mass., Abigail, W24632
John, Mass., Sarah, W23514
John, Mass., Lucy Roberts former widow; W1893
John, N.Y., Hannah, W17249
John, N.C., Penelope, W18562; BLWt.2460-100
John, R.I., Dorcas, W1022; BLWt.61307-160-55
John, Va., R377
John G., Vt., Abigail, R368
John M., N.H., S12056
Jonas, Mass., S5265
Jonathan, Mass., S28994
Joseph, Cont., Mass., S32680
Joseph, Cont., Mass., S46707
Joseph, Cont., Mass., Elcy, W20663

BAILEY (continued)
Joseph/Josephus, Md., S34633
Joseph, Mass., N.H., Mary, R382
Joseph, N.H., R379
Joseph, Pvt., N.Y., BLWt.6789 iss. 9/15/1790 to John S. Hobart et al, Exr's of Alex. McDougall, ass.
Joseph, R.I., S21059
Josephus, Md., See Joseph
Joshua, Ct., S10347
Joshua, Vt., S22112
Josiah, Mass., Mary, W475; BLWt. 32214-160-55
London, Sgt., BLWt.5481 iss. 7/7/1789
Loudon, Ct., Navy, S37703
Luther, Capt., Cont., Mass., BLWt.101-300 iss. 11/24/1795 to Nathl. Olcott, ass.; S32688
Luther, Vt., S21617
Manoah, Va., R381
Martin, N.C., Va., Susannah, R394
Matthias, Pa., Indian Wars 1791 & 1795, R383
Moses, N.H., Lucinda, BLWt.105586-160-55
Moses, Va., S16626
Nathaniel, Pa., R385
Noah, Cont., Mass., Lucy, W2584, BLWt.203-60-55
Noah, Va., S6556
Orsamos/Orsamas, N.H., Vt., Margaret, W20688
Peter, N.C., Va., S21618
Philip, Va., S5266
Prince (or Dunswick/Dunsick), Mass., Hannah, W17230
Rebekah, R.I., former widow of Samuel Black, W23535
Reuben, S.C., S37716
Richard, Va., S30841
Richard, Va., R387
Robert, Ct., S39953
Robert, Ga., N.C., S32108
Robert, R.I., S39156
Samuel, Ct., Mass., S39177
Samuel, N.H., Green Mt. Boys, Mary, W23525
Samuel, Mass., Lucy Burden, former widow, W25308; BLWt.9485-160-55
Samuel, Pvt., N.J., BLWt.8111 iss. 10/17/1789 to John Pope, ass.
Silas, Mass., S12042
Silas, R.I., R390. Wife's name not given, was widow of Joseph Marks, a Rev. sold., Ct. No papers except those in env.
Southy, Va., BLWt.1253-100
Thaddeus, Mass., S18696
Thomas, Pvt., Md., BLWt.10957 iss. 8/14/1795 to Francis Sherrard, ass.
Thomas, Md., S34634
Thomas, Va., S6578
Thomas, Va., S10334
Thomas, Va., Nancy, W2991
Timothy, Ct., S44574
Timothy, Mass. See claim of Martha, wid. of John Barnard, W15550

BAILEY (continued)
Timothy, Mass., N.Y., Jane, W15752
Ward, Vt., Mary, W15555
William, Pvt., Ct., BLWt.5480 iss. 5/3/ or 23/1797 to John Duncan
William, Ct., Cont., Rachel Goodsell, former wid., W25640
William, N.C., Elizabeth, R372
William, S.C., R396
William, Pvt., Va., BLWt.11942 iss. 4/16/1794
William, Va., S2053
William, Va., S.Ctf. 14296
William, Va., Nancy, W5778
William, Va., Sarah, W5777
William, Va., Emily, R373
William, Va., Margaret Porter, former wid., R8348
BAILIS, Eldridge, S.C., See BAILES
BAILY/BAILEY, Callam, Va., S12947
David, Va., S16616
Hezekiah, Ct., Cont., Adah, W9340 BLWt.30596-160-55
John, Va., R19354, Va. Half Pay
Samuel, Cont., Mass., Eleanor, W21629
Stephen, N.C., S41420
Thomas, Va., S21627
William C., Va. & U.S. Army from 1792 to 1808; S44342
BAIN/BAINE, Casparus, N.Y., Mary, W1125; BLWt.26579-160-55
John, N.C., Pa., S22110
BAINBROOK/BENBROOK, Ezekiel, N.C. R397
BAIRD, Absalom, Cont. Pa., BLWt. 2246-400. Iss. 2/25/1839
Alexander, Pa., R398
Asa, Mass., Abigail, W14241
David, N.J., S2352
David, N.J., S32100
Francis, Pa., Margaret, W3210 (not same as Francis Beard)
Henry, Cont., Pa., Elizabeth,R668
John, N.J., Catharine, W7227
John, N.J., Mary, W27877
John, Pa., S2058
Joseph, N.J., Jane, W5759
Robert, Pa., S2052
Stephen, Cont., Pa., S39959; BLWt.178-100
Thomas, Pa., Va., Jane, W9712
BAITH/BARTHE/BATHE, George, Pa., Va., Susanna, R572
BAKE, George, N.J., S853
John, N.J., S31538
BAKEHORN, Jacob, Pvt., N.Y., BLWt. 6861 iss. 8/8/1791 to Gabriel Furman, ass.
BAKEMAN, Daniel Frederick, N.Y., S17265. Last pensioned soldier of the Revolution.
Henry, N.Y., Jane, R400
BAKEN, Matthias, N.J., See BACON
BAKER, Abel, Ct., S10338
Abial/Abiel, R.I., Lois, W14262
Abner, Cont. Mass., Hannah, W20668
Abner, Mass., S8045
Abraham, N.Y., R403

BAKER (continued)
Abraham, R.I., R404
Absalom, Mass., Rebecca, W16829
Absalom, N.C., S35184
Albert, N.Y., S28989
Alpheus, Ct., R---
Amos, Mass., S4922
Andrew, Ct., Mary Walden, former widow, W22524
Anthony, Va., S12957
Asa, Pvt., Ct., BLWt.5462 iss. 11/2/1791 to Titus Street
Asa, Ct., S12127
Asa, Ct., Cont., Zilla Pangburn former widow, W21893
Beal, N.C., Sarah, W5212
Benjamin, Cont., N.H., S45516
Benjamin, Mass., N.H., Abigail, R401
Benoni, Mass., Navy, Abigail, W14237
Bolin/Bowling, N.C., S12950
Bradford, Cont., Mass., S29607
Charles, N.Y., S12109
Charles, N.C., S31536
Charles, N.C., Catherine, W9337
Christian, Pvt., Pa., BLWt.8917 iss. 5/14/1793
Christopher, Pvt., N.Y., BLWt. 6843 iss. 8/20/1790 to James Lowry, ass.
Daniel, Ct., Jerusha, W3922
Daniel, N.J., Hannah, W4121; BLWt.26737-160-55
Daniel, N.Y., S23099
Daniel, Vt., S19197
David, Cont., N.J., S2353
David, Va., Dorothy, W1802; BLWt.8170-160-55
Dempsey, N.C., R408
Edey, N.Y., Anna, R409
Edmund, Mass., Mary, BLWt.750-100
Edward, Sgt., Ct., BLWt.5401 iss. 8/10/1789 to Richard Platt
Eleazer, Mass., S12941
Eli, Mass., S18304
Elias, N.C., Sarah, W5773
Elijah, Cont., Ct., Olive,W18569
Elijah, Cont., Va., S17830
Elijah, Mass., S1211
Elisha, Mass., Vt., R410
Elisha, N.C., R 411
Elisha, R.I., S12103
Elisha, R.I., Polly/Molly, W16834
Enoch, Ct., S17250
Ezekiel, Mass., S12044
George, N.C., S17249
Glover, Va., S10351
Henry, Md., BLWt.239-200, Lt. iss. 5/28/1789. No papers
Henry, N.J., Pa., R413
Henry B., S.C., S39171
Huldah, Mass., former wid. of Obediah Trask, S18631; BLWt. 100086-160-55
Isaac, or Jacob Johnson, Cont., N.Y., R415
Isaac, Md., R414
Isaac, Mass., Lois/Louis, BLWt. 16144-160-55
Isaac, N.C., Rebecca, R435
Jacob, Rev.-Indian Wars, S2946

BAKER (continued)
He was pens. for disability; wounded at Battle of Miami, 9/30/1790. Pa. Agency
Jacob, no bounty claim; no pension application. Sur. File 2946
James, Ct., R416
James, Cont., Pa. res., S39958
James, Mass., Sarah, W23501
James, N.C., Elizabeth, W9338; BLWt.13443-160-55
James, Pvt., Pa., BLWt.9054 iss. 12/21/1792
James, S.C., Rhoda, R436
Jeremiah, Mass., R417
Jeremiah, R.I., Sarah, W14265
Jesse/Justus, N.Y., R425
Jesse, S.C., BLWt.304-300-Capt. Iss. 1/4/1790. No papers
Joel, Cont., N.H., Hannah, W1359; BLWt.11167-160-55
John, Cont., Mass., S32668
John, Cont., Mass., Mary, W23486
John, Ga., Va., S39179
John, Md., Pa., S22631
John, Md., War of 1812, R419
John, Sgt., Mass., BLWt.3732 iss. 8/26/1790 to M. Cutler,ass.
John, Mass., S32691
John, Pvt., Mass., BLWt.3773 iss. 2/23/1796 to Jos. Brown, ass.
John, Mass., N.H., R418
John, Mass., N.Y., Vt., S23533
John, Mass., R.I., Abigail Johnson, former wid., R5595
John, Pvt., N.J., BLWt.8094 iss. 9/26/1789
John, Pvt., N.Y., BLWts.6827 & 183-60-55 iss. 8/10/1790 to Stephen Lush, ass.; Elizabeth, W25199
John, N.Y., S23107
John, N.C., S8047
John, Pvt., Pa., BLWt.8995 iss. 6/24/1793 to Philip Stout, ass.
John, Pvt., Pa., BLWt.9036 iss. 1/6/1792
John, Pa., S35774
John, Pa., R420
John, S.C., Chelly, R406
John, Va., S30843
John, Va., R421
John Henry, Pa., S34638
Jonathan, Mass., S44337
Jonathan, Mass., R423
Jonathan, N.J., Hannah, W1210
Joseph, Cont., Mass., S30844
Joseph, Cont., Mass., Elizabeth, W23488
Joseph, Mass., BLWt.129-200, Lt. iss. 2/23/1796 to Marlborough Turner, ass. of Richard Goldsmith Admr. No papers
Joseph, Mass., Monica, W15561
Joseph, N.C., Susanna, W8339
Joseph, S.C., Mary, W9713
Joshua, Ct., S12074
Joshua, Cont., N.H., N.Y., BLWt. 26245-160-55; S12087
Joshua, N.Y., S12033

BAKER (continued)
Josiah, Mass., Lydia, R426
Judah, N.Y., Lydia, W25205; BLWt.2499-160-55
Justus/Jesse, N.Y., R425
Justus, N.Y., Mary/Marcy, R427
Kenelm, Mass., Susannah, W15551
Lewis, Mass., Lois, W3920
Lovel, Cont., Ct., S37715
Lyman, Mass., Catharine, W25216
Malyne/Melyn, N.J., S1397
Michael M., Pa., BLWt.616-100; S46700. Mary Baker, widow of soldier was pensioned as former widow of Andrew McGahee or McGahey, Pa., W23530
Morris, N.Y., S12057
Nahum, Mass., Rhoda, R437
Nathan, Ct., S12118
Nathan, Mass., S44322
Nicholas, Pa., Va., Lucy, W27812
Pardon, R.I., Betsey, W23520
Paul, Mass., R431
Pearse, Pvt., N.Y., BLWt.6800 iss. 10/3/1791 to Philip Hart, ass.
Peter, Cont., Mass., S39178
Peter/Petrus, N.Y., Rachel, R434
Peter, N.Y., Mary, R429
Peter, N.C., Mary, W277
Petrus, See Peter, N.Y.
Philip Horn/Hornbaker, N.J., Pa., S2363
Philip Peter, Va., Elizabeth Dorothy, W5772
Rebecca, Ct., former widow of Nathan Marvin, W18558
Reuben, Mass., S12089
Richard, Cont., Mass., S32692
Richard, Cont., Va. & War of 1812 Francis, R412
Richard Bohun, S.C., BLWt.1221-300; R12281
Robert, Cont., Ct., Sarah, W704; Pvt. Sheldon's Dragoons; BLWts. 286-60-55; 5522 & 255-60-55 iss. 6/24/1793
Robert, Va., S16628
Rufus, Ct., Vt., S16622
Samuel, Ct., N.Y., War of 1812; S9271
Samuel, Cont., Mass., BLWt.713-100 S32681
Samuel, Mass., S29597
Samuel, Mass., Mary, W21638
Samuel, N.C., S39169
Samuel, Va., S10354
Sarah, Va., former widow of Wm. Foster, BLWts. 1462-100; 269-60-55; W2986
Sargeant (or Thomas Sarjent), Mass., S44580
Seth, Ct. Sea Service, S23106
Seth, Mass., Navy, R.I., S6588
Silas, Mass., S36902
Solomon, Green Mt. Boys; Mass., N.Y., Nancy, W5770
Solomon, Indian Spy, Tenn., Va. res. in 1833, R438
Solomon, Mass., S44324
Squire, Cont., Mass., S39168

BAKER (continued)
Stephen, Mass., Prudence Washburn former wid., W25863
Submit, Mass., former wid. of Simeon Shurtliff, W23550
Sylvanus, Mass. Sea Service, Phebe, W14226
Sylvester, N.C., S16618
Theophilus, Mass. Sea Service, S23104
Thoder, Mass. Sea Service, S12037
Thomas, Ga. Sea Service, S15299
Thomas, Pvt., Md., BLWt.10999 iss. 7/18/1794 to Henry Purdy, ass.
Thomas, Mass., S12097
Thomas, Mass., Sarah, W16177
Thomas, N.H., Miriam, BLWt.24617-160-55; W1803
Thomas, N.Y., Molly A., R26255
Thomas, N.C., Molly, BLWt.45593-160-55; R430
Thomas, Privateer, Rev., Navy, 1797-1801, Jane, R1060; Fla. res. of wid. in 1837
Thomas Marshall, Mass. res. Dis. No papers
Thomas Sarjent, Mass. See SARGEANT
Timothy, Mass., S44582
Timothy, Mass., N.Y., Philena, BLWt.26063-160-55; W629
Waterman, R.I., BLWt.26800-160-55; S12092
William, Ct., S44323
William, Mass., Abigail, W14253
William, Mass., Lydia, W23485
William, Mass., Chloe, R407
William, N.J., S2362
William, N.Y., S44581
William, N.C., Buly, R405
William, Pvt., Pa., BLWt.8969 iss. 8/7/1789 to Richard Platt, ass.
William, Va., S12967
Windsor/Buker, Mass., S36453
Wonsley, Md., R439
Ziba, Mass., Milla, BLWt.16268-160-55; R440

BAKUS/BACKUS, Samuel, Ct., S16036

BALANCE/BALLANCE, Leven, N.C.,S6563

BALCAM/BALCOM, Azariah, Ct., S16039
Elias, Ct., S44348
Elias, Pvt., Ct., BLWt.5445 iss. 3/7/1792 to Jonathan Tuttle, ass.

BALCH, Amos, N.C., S2943
Hart, Cont., N.H., S39167
John, Ct., Lucy, W20685
John, N.H., S45520
Joseph, Cont., Ct., BLWt.3641-160-55; S12106
Lydia, Vt., former wid. of Jabez Olmstead, R441
Samuel, Mass., S28996
Stephen Bloomer, Md., S12051
Thomas, Navy, Mass., Privateer, S44338

BALCOM, Azariah, Ct., S16039
Bezaleel, Mass., R.I., Jemima, W21635
Elias, Ct., S44348
Elijah, Mass., Marcy, W23484
John, Mass., S4918
Joseph, Mass., BLWt.117-200, Lt. iss. 4/19/1796 to Jos. Fosdick

BALCOM (continued)
ass. No papers. S32683
Margaret, N.Y., former wid. of Edward Walker, which see
Micah, Mass., BLWt.26453-160-55 S30251
Micah, Mass., Catharine, W16182
Nathaniel, Ct., S22108
BALDEREE, Isaac, K., N.C., Elizabeth, BLWt.39474-160-55; W27543
BALDING, Moses, Pa., See BALDWIN
BALDOCK, Richard, Va., R442
BALDREE, Isaac K., See BALDEREE
BALDRIDGE, John, N.C., Isabella, W5789
Thomas, Pa., R443
BALDRY, Isaac K. See BALDEREE
BALDWIN, Aaron, Ct., Cont., N.Y., S12090
Abel, Ct., Molly, W20677
Abiel/Abial, Ct., Elizabeth, W8351
Abner, Ct., S12126
Asa, Cont., Ct., Dolly, W10372
Ashbel, Ct., S22629
Asil/Azel, Ct., S19196
Benjamin, Ct., Lydia, W16498
Benjamin, N.J., S33256
Benjamin, Va., R19355, Va. Half Pay
Brewin/Brewen, Ct., S12073
Caleb, Ct., Cont., S45517; BLWt. 134-300, Capt. iss. 5/8/1792 No papers
Cornelius, N.Y., S23108
Cornelius, Va., BLWt.255-400, Surgeon. Iss. 8/25/1789. No papers
Daniel, Ct., S12036
Daniel, N.J., BLWt.2515-300, Capt. iss. 7/30/1789. No papers
David, Ct., Ruth, W23524
David, Mass., S32677
David, N.J., S16620
David, N.Y., R444
Desire, former wid. of John Negus/Nigas, Ct. Sea Service, W17228
Edward, N.C., Drusilla, R445
Eleazer, Ct., S2046
Elijah, Cont., Ct., S22103
Elisha, Ct., S44306
Elizabeth, former wid. of Joseph Gorham, Ct., Cont., which see
Enoch, Cont., Mass., S32690
Henry, Cont., Ct., Jane, W17240
Henry, Md., BLWt.245-200, Lt. iss. 8/19/1791. No papers
Hezekiah, N.Y., Abiel, W20656
Ichabod, N.J., Joanna, W473
Isaac, Mass., S22100
Jabez, Ct., Mass., Hannah, W17261
Jabez, Cont., N.H., S39964
Jacob, Mass., N.H., S17827
James, Ct., Sarah, W12241
James, Cont., Ct., S12124
James, Cont., Ct., Nabby, W25203
James, Mass., S4935
Jeduthan, Mass., BLWt.91-500, Col. iss. 4/7/1798 to Lucy Forbes, executrix.
Jesse, N.J., Harriet, BLWt.121-

BALDWIN (continued)
200, Lt. Iss. 8/1789; W887, also recorded as above under Wt. 2517
Joel, Ct., S12067
John, Ct., R447
John, Md., S2364
John, Mass., Esther, W20657
John, Mass., Isabel, W20670
John, N.C., S6565
John, Va., S37733
John, Va., Agness, W1800
John N., N.J., S852
John P., N.J., Mary, W888
Jonathan, Ct., Keziah, W25202
Jonathan, Ct., Submit, W10402; BLWt.26258-160-55
Joseph, Ct., S31530
Joseph, Ct., Rosanna, W17256
Joseph, Mass., Elizabeth, W17255
Joseph, N.C. res. in 1843, Mary, R451
Josiah, Ct., Martha Hill, former widow, W21326
Josiah, Cont., Mass., S39180
Josiah, Cont., N.J., S12079
Levi, Mass., S12091
Levi, Mass., S18702
Linus, N.J., S592
Martin, N.J., Elizabeth, Whiskey Rebellion, War of 1812; BLWt. 79704-160-55; R449
Moses, Pa., BLWt.3814-160-55; W1798
Nahum, N.H., S17256
Nathan, Ct. Sea Service, Avis, W25209
Nathan, Res. Dryden, N.Y., R452
Nathaniel, Ct., S28982
Peleg, Ct., Anna/Anne, W2050
Philemon, Cont., Ct., S18305
Phinehas, Ct., Abigail, W17235
Reuben, Mass., Sarah, W23523
Samuel, Ct., S10335
Samuel, Ct., S12081
Samuel, Cont., Mass., S44308
Samuel, Mass., Green Mt. Boys, S29599
Samuel, Md., S8044
Samuel, N.J., Rhoda, W16831
Seth, Ct., Vt., S44307
Silas, Ct., Dis. No papers
Stephen, Ct., S23111
Stephen, Cont., Mass., S45235
Stephen, N.J., S31539
Theophilus, Ct., Mass., S37719
Thomas, Ct., BLWt.377-200
Thomas, Mass., Vt., Mary, W18553
Thomas, N.H., Margaret D., BLWt. 75108-160-55
Uzal, N.J., S12978
Waterman, Pvt., Ct., BLWt.5431 iss. 2/8/1791
William, Cont., Mass., Sarah, W21624
William Jr., Pvt., Md., BLWts. 10953 & 14092 iss. 1/28/1795 to Francis Sherrard, ass. of Ann Colemore, Admix.
William, Va., S16313
Zachariah, Cont., N.J., BLWt. 1693-100

BALES/BAYLES
Jesse, Va., W8345
BALEY, Abraham, Va., S16319
BALEY/BAYLEY, Daniel, N.Y., S44571
David, Cont., Ct., See BAILEY
Henry, Navy, enl. Pa., res. after Rev. was Del., S31534
John, Ct., N.Y., R454
John, Mass., S12061
Joseph, Pa., S17833
Samuel, S.C., S30258
Stephen, Ct., R392
Stephen, Va., R393
William, N.J., N.Y., Elizabeth, W18570; BLWt.32221-160-55
BALITZ/BALIZTS
George, Cont., Md., Wayne's Indian War; BLWt.1843-100 & 2379-100; S44349
BALKCOM, Elijah, Mass. See BOLCOM
BALKCOM/BALCOM/BOLKCOM, Elijah, Mass., Marcy, W23484
BALL, Aaron, Cont., Va., S37697
Aaron, N.J., S2369
Abner, Mass., War of 1812; Indiana, BLWt.36670-160-55
Abner, N.J., S851
Amos, Md., S2054
Benjamin, Cont. Ct., S12059
Benjamin, Cont., Mass., Huldah, W23515
Benjamin, Sgt., Mass., BLWt.3734
Benjamin, Mass., Mary, W21623
Blackall Wm., Pa., BLWt.207-200 Lt. iss. 7/7/1789. No papers
Burgess, Va., BLWt.252-500, Lt. Col. Commandant, iss. 5/28/1789 No papers
Charles, Mass., S32061
Cornelius, Pvt., N.J., BLWt.8103 iss. 10/2/1789 to Joanna Ball, widow
Daniel, Cont., Mass., Ruth, W23543
Daniel, Mass., Lydia, W15981
Daniel, N.C., Ann, W5768
Daniel, Va., BLWt.271-200, Lt. iss. 1/24/1794 to John Fowler, ass. No papers
David, Va., S37730
Ebenezer, Mass., Phebe, W14232
Edmund/Edmond, N.C., Va., Sarah, W390
Eleazar/Eleazer, Mass., S32685
Eli, Mass., BLWt.3836-160-55; S28997
Elijah, Mass., S19536
Gideon, Cont., Mass., S44587
Hosea, N.C., S2365
Humphrey, Ct., S39176
James, Cont., Mass., Abigail, R456
James, Md., S32107
James, Va., BLWt.1464-200
James, Va., Margaret, W8336
John, Ct., BLWt.143-200 Lt. iss. 2/4/1797. No papers
John, Cont., Mass., Rachel, W23500
John, Mass., S32670
John, Mass., Lydia Conant, former widow, W14526
John, N.J., S850

BALL (continued)
John, N.Y., BLWt.226-200, Lt. iss. 8/2/1793. No papers. Also recorded as BLWt.2613
John, N.Y., Anna, W5767; BLWt. 1197-200
Jonathan, Ct., S44320
Jonathan, Cont., Mass., S44319
Jonathan, Mass., S32686
Jonathan, Mass., Abigail, W16820
Jonathan, N.J., R457
Joseph, Pvt., Mass., BLWt.3716 iss. 3/25/1790
Joseph, Mass., S22102; Sarah Ball wid. of sold. pensioned as former wid. of John Nichols, Mass., which see
Joseph, Mass., S44345
Joshua, N.J., BLWt.1320-100
Joshua, N.C., S6554
Justice, Pvt., N.J., BLWt.8102 iss. 6/11/1789 to Matthias Denman, ass.
Levi, Mass., S39181
Mattice, N.Y., S22628
Nehemiah, N.J., S12946
Osborne, N.C., Mary, R459
Peter, N.Y., S12123
Ruth, former widow of Moses Ware, Mass., R11136
Samuel, Mass., S44586
Samuel, Mass., Hannah, W23518
Samuel, Mass., Dis. No papers
Samuel, N.J., S44321
Silas, Mass., Rhoda Graves, former widow, W3542
Stephen, Va., S17834
Valentine, Va., S16317
Wait, Ct., R460
William, Cont., Va., Elizabeth, W3376; BLWts. 356-60-55 iss. 9/22/1860 & 357-100 iss. 9/22/1807
William, N.J., N.Y., S2354
William, N.Y., S28631
BALLANCE, Leven, See BALANCE
BALLANGER
William, Va., S35179
BALLANTINE, Ebenezer, Mass., S45232; BLWt.127-300 Surgeon, iss. 8/22/1789. No papers
BALLARD, Alexander, N.J. Sea Service; Privateer, S2961
Benoni, Pvt., N.Y., BLWt.6855 iss. 8/26/1790
Benoni, N.Y., S44597
Bland W., Va., also served from 1781-1794; 1st Regt. Ky. Riflemen, War 1812; Elizabeth, W20655; BLWt.13207-160-55; War of 1812, Old War Inv. File 48420, Old War Inv. Ctf. 785
Bristor, Pvt., Mass., BLWt.3720 iss. 10/26/1789
Cader/Kedar, N.C., BLWt.292-300 Capt. iss. 11/7/1796. No papers
Daniel, Ct., Ruth, W474; BLWt. 17702-160-55
Daniel, Mass., R461
Devereaux, N.C., R462
Ebenezer, Pvt., Mass., BLWt.3680 iss. 10/18/1796 to John Coates,

BALLARD (continued)
ass.
Edward, Mass. See BULLARD
Francis, N.C., S6553
Frederick, Mass., S37565
James, Va., S6584; BLWt.36509-160-55
James, Va., S30260
James, Va., & 1786-1794, R463
Jeremiah, N.J., BLWt.180-300 Capt. iss. 6/11/1789. No papers
Jesse, R.I., S44325
John, Cont., Ct., S44596
John, N.J., Mary, R465
John, N.C., R464
John, Va., S37721
Jonathan, Md., S34639
Jonathan, Mass., Betty, W23499
Josiah, Mass., Jane, BLWt.35720-160-55
Kedar, N.C., See CADER BALLARD
Micajah, Va., S44326
Moses, Mass., Ruth Slater, former widow, W6074; BLWt.38546-160-55
Nathan, N.H., S17829
Philip, Mass., S29609
Philip, Va., S9094
Sherebiah, Cont., Mass., S39157
Stephen, Cont., Pa., S39956
Stephen, Mass., Anna/Ann, W3174
Stephen, Pvt., Pa., BLWt.9042 iss. 11/26/1795 to John Shaw, ass
Thomas, S.C., S20283
Uriah, Cont., N.H., S37568
William, Va., Catharine, W25220; BLWt.11164-160-55
William H., Mass., BLWt.94-400 Major. Iss. 3/24/1792. No papers
Wyatt, N.C., S44327
BALLENGER, Edward, S.C., Pleasant, W9720
John, Va., S31543
BALLENTINE, Wm., Pvt., N.Y., BLWt. 6840 iss. 9/22/1790 to Rebecca Slingerland, et al, admx.
BALLERSON/BALLISON
William, Md., S34631
BALLEW, Joseph, N.C., S31541
Richard, N.C., S15305
Robert, N.C., Va., See BALLOW
Stephen/Steven, N.C. Sur. Ctf. 16835
Stephen, N.C., Mary, See BILLUE
BALLIET, Jacob, Pa., Barbara, W5209; BLWt.34266-160-55
BALLINGER, Emanuel, Pa., S39963
BALLISON, Wm., Md., See BALLERSON
BALLON/BALLOU, William, R.I., Mary, W18549
BALLOU, Absalom, R.I., Anna,W20676
Ariel, R.I., S21635
Dutee, R.I., Waity Whipple, former widow, W27501
Edward, R.I., S30253
Jeremiah, Ct., R.I., S23102
Jesse, Mass., R.I., Elizabeth, W15552
Nathaniel, R.I., S12060
Noah, R.I., S21619
Russell, Vt., Bebee, W701
William, R.I., S21620
William, R.I., See BALLON

BALLOW, Charles, Va., Elizabeth, W2905
Nathaniel, R.I., See BALLOU
BALLOW/BALLEW, Robert, N.C., Va., S10350
BALMAIN, Alexander, Va., Lucy, W8116
BALMER, Jacob, Pa., S39950
John, Pa., Va., R466
John, Va., See BARMER
BALMORE, John, Va., See BARMER
BALSLE, John, N.Y., Dis., no papers
BALSLEY, Andrew, N.Y., S12095
Christian, Pa., Ann Elizabeth, W7231
John, N.Y., R467
John, Pa., BLWt.8999-100. No papers
BALTCH, See BALCH
BALTHAZER, Ignatius, Pvt., Pa., BLWt.8966 iss. 5/15/1790 to M. McConnell, ass.
BALTHROP, Augustine, N.C., Holly, W8113; BLWt.26701-160-55
BALTZELL, Charles, Md., BLWt. 238-300-Capt., iss. 3/4/1800. No papers
BALTZER, See BALZAR
BALY, See BALEY
BALYS, See BAYLIS
BALZAR/BALZER/BALTZER, Anthony, Pa., Elizabeth, W3752
BAMPER, Jacob, Cont., Navy; N.Y., Ann, W6100
BANCKER, See BANKER
James, Cont., N.Y., S17831
James, Pvt., N.Y., BLWt.6871 iss. 7/18/1791 to Wm. McKowan, ass.
BANCKSTON/BANKSTON, Elijah, Ga., R478
BANCRAFT, See BANCROFT
BANCROFT
Benjamin, Mass., S19532
Caleb, Cont., Mass., S28995
Ebenezer, Mass., S4928
James, Mass., Sarah, W18550
James, Mass., BLWt.120-200-Lt., iss. 1/29/1790. No papers
John, Cont., Mass., S2965
BANCROFT/BANCRAFT, John, Mass., Anna, W4881
Jonathan, Pvt., Mass., BLWt.3741 iss. 3/25/1790
Jonathan, Mass., S22109
Jonathan, Mass., S29623
Joseph, Mass., S12115
Oliver, Ct., S12080
Robert, Cont., Mass., Abigail, W21637
Thaddeus, Mass., Huldah, W8114, BLWt.15426-160-55
Timothy, Mass., S22632
William, Mass., S12046
William, Mass., S34001
BANDFIELD, James, Md., S45228
BANDY, Thomas, Va., Nancy, W5782
BANE, Ellis, Pa., S23531
BANE/BANES/BAYNES
John, N.C., Susannah, R644

BANESTED, See BONESTEEL
BANFILL, George, Vt., Anna, W17244
BANGHAN/BAUGHAN, Richard, Va., S37724
BANGHART, Barney, Pvt., N.J., BLWt.8137 iss. 6/2/1797 to Abraham Bell, ass.
BANGS, Adnah, Mass., S18694
Barnobas, Mass., Elizabeth, W24640
Joseph, Mass., Sea Service, Desire W24630
Joshua, Mass., Anna Woodbury, former widow, W26625
Nathaniel, Mass., Electa, W14231
Reuben, Cont., Mass., Lucy,W18551
BANISTER, Barzalia, Cont., Mass., Nancy Este, former wid., BLWt. 9060-160-55; W3534. As wid. of Solomon Este, Mass. she rec'd BLWt.61229-160-55
George, Ct., Cont., Pa., S9095
Jason, Vt., S10349
Jesse, Mass., BLWt.10254-160-55
Louis, W25194
Levi, Mass., S44608
Solomon, Mass., S29602
Thomas, Mass., Lydia, W8118; BLWt.12831-160-55
Thomas, Va., S21060
William, Mass., S9809
BANK/BANKS, Joseph, Ct., S12973
BANKER/BANCKER, Flores, N.Y., Martha, R473
Frederick, N.Y., Ellen Elener, W23506; BLWt.18219-160-55
BANKER, John, Mass., S39161
Nicholas, N.Y., Catharine/Caty, R472
Stephen, N.Y., S28637
Stephen, N.Y. res. 1823, R474
William, N.Y., Ruth, W23511
BANKES, Andrew, Pa., S2055
BANKS, Benjamin, Ct., S12954
Benjamin, Pvt., N.Y., BLWt.6845 iss. 7/30/1790 to Edward Cumpston, ass.
Daniel, Ct., S9811
Drury, N.C., R475
Ebenezer, Ct., S12038
Edward, See BRUS
Elijah, Ct., Mabel, W20675
Ezekiel O., Ct., S18303
Gershoon/Gershom, Ct., Ruth, W20669
Hyatt, Ct., S12040
Jacob, Va., S8056
James, Va. Sea Service, Mary, W5762; Va. half pay
John, Cont., N.Y., S35776
John, Cont., Va., Sally, W5763; BLWt.19703-160-55
John, Mass., Abigail, W23502
John, Mass., N.H., Susan, W15557
John, N.J., Mary, W25217; BLWt. 26817-160-55
John, N.Y., Abigail, W16818
Jonathan, Ct., Molly, R476
Joseph, Ct., See BANK
Joseph, Ct., Esther, W20680
Joseph, N.C., S41426
Moses O., Ct., S12035
Moses, Cont., Mass., S37572
Nathan, Ct., Mabel, W17236 ;

BANKS (continued)
BLWt.26131-160-55
Nehemiah, Ct., S12974
Obadiah, Ct., N.Y., S12050
Pelatiah, Cont., Mass., Sarah, W23521
Peter, N.C., S6557
Samuel, Pvt., Md., BLWts.10948 & 11705 iss. 5/4/1797 to James DeBaufree/DeBaufre, ass.
Samuel, N.Y., Charity, W17234
Thomas, Cont., Ct., S44602
William, Mass., Betsey, W23529
William, Va., Elizabeth, W10376; BLWt.13895-160-55
Zachariah, Pvt., Mass., BLWt. 3761 iss. 9/4/1792
BANKSON, John, Pa., Mary, W25210; BLWt.199-300-Capt. iss. 5/19/ 1789. No papers
BANKSTON, Andrew, Ga., Mary Sorrel/ Sorrels/Sorrells, former wid. W8746; BLWt.26785-160-55
Elijah, Ga., BLRej., 63944
Elijah, See BANCKSTON
Thomas, N.C., R477
BANNER, Benjamin, N.C., S6562
Ephraim, N.C., Elizabeth, W3923
Joseph, N.C., Sarah, W9716
BANNERMAN, George, N.C., S8055
BANNET/BENNET, Samuel, Ct., S15747
BANNISTER, Andrew, Mass., S29621
Jesse, See BANISTER
Seth, Mass., BLWt.100-300-Capt. iss. 12/31/1795. No papers
Thomas, Mass., See BANISTER
BANNON, Jeremiah, Pa., Agnes, W10380
Jeremiah, Pvt., Pa., BLWt.9075 iss. 11/5/1789
BANOW, See BARROW
BANQUET, William, Sgt., Pa., BLWt. 8996 iss. 9/4/1789 to Ann Short, admx.
BANTA, Abraham D., N.J., S6575
Barnet/Helebrant, N.Y., Deborah, W18559
BANTA/BONTA, Daniel, N.J., S2090
Hendrick, See BONTA
Henry, Va., R480
Samuel, Pa., R479
BANTHAM, John, Md., S44344, BLWt. 434-100
BANTHAM/BENTHAM, Peregrine, Md., S34636
Perry, Pvt., Md., BLWt.10972 iss. 8/14/1795 to Francis Sherrard, ass.
BANTON, Molly, former wid. of John Smith, Mass., W14258
BAPTIST/BAPTISTE/BATTIST/BETTIS
John, Cont., Mass., Eunice, W24641
John, Pvt., Va., BLWt.11944 iss. 1/20/1796 to --
BARALOW/BARCALOW
Cornelius, Cont., N.J., S45230
BARBARICK, John, Mass. Agency, Dis. No papers
BARBEE, Daniel, Cont., Va., S12951
Elias, Va., S12972
John, Va., Mary, W24626
Joseph, N.C., Sally/Sarah, W23522

BARBEE (continued)
Joshua, Va., S12952
Thomas, Va., BLWt.258-300-Capt. iss. 7/15/1789. No papers
BARBER, Abraham, Ct., Cont., Sarah, W16832
Amaziah, Ct., Cont., S44340
Augustus, R.I., Mich. res. in 1850 R481
Bela, Cont., Ct., S12071
Benjamin, Ct., Lydia, R484
Benjamin, R.I., S17252
Benjamin, R.I., S17254
Daniel, Cont., Ct., S8052
Daniel, R.I., S21631
David, Ct., BLWt.154-150-Ensign, iss. 8/7/1789 to James Noyes Barber, admr. No papers
David, N.Y., S12088
Ebenezer, Mass., BLWt.31896-160-55; S29608
Francis, N.J., BLWt. 111-450
George, Md., Sea Service, S8050
Henry, R.I., R21771
James, Mass., N.Y., S15312
James, R.I., Margaret, W20678
James, Va., Indian Wars. S16042
Jesse, N.J., R482
Jethro, N.H., Molly, W23527
Job, Ct., S15309
Job, Cont., Ct., S12083
Joel, Cont., Ct., S12099
John, Cont., N.H., Miriam, W21639
John, Cont., Pa., S35772
John, Pvt., Hazen's Regt., BLWt. 12761, iss. 3/25/1790
John, Md., R483
John, Mass., S28980
John, N.Y., S29613
John, Pvt., Va.; Lee's Legion; BLWts.11093 & 14073 iss. 4/3/1794
Jonathan, Ct., Abi, W17259
Jonathan, R.I., S21633
Joseph, R.I., S21634
Michael, Cont., Ct., S31531
Moses, Mass., Patty, W14269
Moses, R.I., Sarah, W4125; BLWt. 28610-160-55
Nathan, R.I., S17251
Obadiah, Ct., S15300
Peter, Mass., S16623
Rebecca, former widow of Thomas Simons, Ct., which see, W20679
Reuben, Ct., R485
Reuben, Cont., Ct., Elizabeth, W24624
Reuben, Ct., N.Y., Hannah, W10291; BLWt.11277-160-55
Reynolds, R.I., S21632
Robert, Pvt., Cont. Artillery Crane's, Mass., BLWt.3812 iss. 1/28/1790 to Joseph May, ass.
Robert, Pa., S2044
Samuel, N.J., Charity, W702; BLWt.28601-160-55
Samuel, R.I., R486
Sarah, Mass., former wid. of James Wheeler, which see, W15569
Silas, Sgt., Crane's Cont. Artillery, Mass., BLWt.3821 iss. 6/7/1790 to Silas Barber
Simeon, Ct., S16037

BARBER (continued)
Smith, R.I., S9273
Solomon, Cont., Mass., Deborah, W23494
Stansell, N.C., R20207
Stephen, Ct., S12030
Stephen, N.Y., R487
Thomas, R.I., Elizabeth, W16178
Uriah, Pa., S2950
William, Cont., N.J., Ann Broom/Broome, former wid., BLWt.176-400-Maj. & A.D.C., iss. 8/19/1791. No papers. W18641
William, Pvt., Mass., BLWt.3805 iss. 6/15/1797 to Simon Wyman, ass.
William, N.Y., R.I., Sarah, W16175
William, N.C., See BARLER
William, Va., S6572
William, Va., S10333
Zachariah, Mass., BLWt.2192-160-55 R488
BARBEY, Elijah, Cont., Va., S35180
BARBOUR, Mordecai, Va., S8043
Solomon, Mass., See BARBER
BARBRE, Stansell, See BARBER
BARBUR/BARBER, Mathew, Mass., Mary, W14244
BARCALOW, Cornelius, See BARALOW
BARCE, Josiah, Ct., See BERCE
BARCKERT, Christian, Pa., S5268
BARCKLEY, Robert, Pa. See BARKELY
BARCLAY, Jennet; see Abraham Lufberry, former wid. of; Cont., N.J., N.Y., which see
John, N.C., See BARKLEY
John, Pa., Esther, W680; BLWt. 1041-200, iss. 4/26/1822
Michael, N.Y., Gertrude, W17231
Thomas, Del., S12054
BARCO, John, N.C., S34640
Thomas, N.C., S33253
BARD, John, Ga., BLWt.311-300-Capt. iss. 7/27/1795. No papers
BARDAN, Henry, N.J., S987
BARDEAN, Moses, Cont., Mass.,S12962
BARDEEN, Aaron, Mass., S38528
Stephen, Cont., Mass., S44610
BARDEN, Abraham, Ct., R1448
Benjamin, Mass., S33976
Ebenezer S., Ct., R492
Ichabod, Cont., Mass., S33996
James, Cont., Mass., Sarah,W15983
Lemuel, Mass., S21628
Oliver, former wid. of Benjamin Allen, Mass., R.I., which see
Samuel, Cont., Ct., Mary, W16833
Timothy, Mass., S33979
BARDSLEE/BEARDSLEE
Thaddeus, Ct., S14952
BARDSLEY, William, Ct., Elizabeth, W23584; BLWt. 5507-100-Pvt., iss. 9/14/1792. No papers
BARDWELL, Obadiah, Mass., S15736
Reuben, Cont., Mass., S29603
Samuel, Mass., S30839
Simeon, Mass., Caty/Catharine, BLWt.16264-160-55
BARDWIN, Samuel, Ct., See BURDWIN
BARE, Edward, Cont., N.Y., Margaret, W16825
BARE/BAER, Jacob, Cont., Pa.,

BARE/BAER (continued)
Catharine, R364
BAREITH, John, Cont., Va., See BARETH
BAREMORE, Henry, see BARMORE
Marshal, N.Y., S23113
BARETH/BARRETT/BAREITH
John, Cont., Va., Elizabeth, W5213 BLWt.1660-100
BARGA, Peter/Piter, See BIRCKI
BARGE, Balzer, Pvt., Pa., BLWt. 8983 iss. 11/2/1791 to John McCleland, ass.
BARGENHOFF, Wm., See BERGERHOFF
BARGIS, Jacob, Mass., See BURGESS
BARHAM, Benjamin, Va., S37720
Hartwell, Va., S41418
James, Va., S16614; BLWt.26246-160-55
BARHYDT/BARHEYDT
Jeron/Jerone, N.Y., Cornelia, W25200
Nicholas, N.Y., Susannah, W16819
BARHYT, Daniel, N.J., Dis. No papers
BARHYTE, James, N.Y., S12948
BARKELEW, Runyan, N.J., S854
BARKELOW, James, N.J., S22097
BARKELY/BARCKLEY
Robert, Pa., S2061
BARKER, Abijah, Mass., S23530
Archelaus, Ct. Sea Service, Mary, W17225
Barnabas, Cont., Mass., S18701
Barnabas, Mass., BLWt. 76-100
Benjamin, Mass., S12049
Benjamin, Mass., Dorcas, W23548
Charles, Cont., Va., S45234
Daniel, Cont., Mass., S37573
Daniel, Mass., S10339
Daniel, Mass., S37574
Daniel, Mass., Anna, W18563
David, Ct., Privateer; Sea Service, and Vt., S6573
David, Mass., Sally, W21646
David, Mass., Mary, W24642
David, N.C., S6560
Edward, Va., Elizabeth, R496
Elijah, Mass., S22633
Ephraim, Cont., Mass., Rebecca, W25219; BLWt.279-60-55
Ephraim, Sgt., Mass., BLWts.3774 & 279-60-55 iss. 12/3/1789
Ethan, Ct., S15308
Ezra, Mass., S26993
Ezra, Mass., Sally B., W15564
Francis, Mass., S45515
George, N.C., S2953
George, N.C., Va., S37710
Grace, former wid. of Robert Swan Mass., which see, W14227
Hannaniah, Cont., Ct., S38519
Hezekiah, Cont., R.I., Sarah, W18565
Isaac, R.I., res., Wealthy,R21772
Isaac Bowen, Cont., Mass., Elizabeth, W20662
Jacob, S.C., R497
James, Ct., Lydia, W21628
James, Md., See BARKERS
James, Mass., Catharine, W10306
James, Mass., N.H., S37576
Jesse, Pvt., Mass., BLWt.3671

BARKER (continued)
iss. 2/22/1792 to John Peck, ass.
Jesse, Mass., S29612
Jesse, Mass., Prudence, W21649
John, Cont., Ct., Huldah, W25215
John, Mass., S45514
John, Mass., Phebe, W15563
John, Mass., Prudence, R502
John, N.Y., Margaret, W25189; BLWt.15178-160-55
John, Pvt. "Sappers & Miners" BLWt.12756 iss. 11/18/1794 to Sampson Crosby, ass.
John, Va., Lucy, W8340
Jonas, Mass., R499
Jonathan, Ct., S28636
Jonathan, Mass., N.H., S37571
Joseph, Ct., Susannah, R 504
Josiah, Mass., Navy, S30257
Levi, Cont., N.Y., S12063
Matthias, no service record, Pa. res. in 1823, R500
Nathan, Mass., Mehitable, W25206; BLWt.3956-160-55
Nathaniel, Va., Letitia, W5774
Oliver, Ct., Ruth, W1698
Peleg, R.I., S21636
Peter, Cont., Mass., Sarah, W21642
Phineas, Ct., Privateer, R501
Robert, Mass., Navy, R503
Russell/Russel, Ct., Elizabeth, W23528
Sally, former wid. of David Barker, W21646, which see
Samuel, Ct., S12977
Samuel, Ct., S33990
Samuel, Ct., BLWt.220-300
Samuel, Mass., S37570
Samuel, Pvt., Mass., BLWt.3794 iss. 3/1/1792 to Jos. Brown, ass.
Simeon, Cont., Mass., S33970
Simeon, Drummer, Mass., BLWt. 3727 iss. 8/22/1789 to B. Winchell, ass.
Stephen, Pvt., N.Y., Elizabeth, W10371; BLWts.6859 & 190-60-55 iss. 12/28/1791 to Moses Phillips, ass.
Theodore, Mass., N.H., S22099
Thomas, Cont., Mass., Hannah, W21645
Thomas, Mass., Sea Service,S4938
Timothy, Ct., S16615
William, Ct., Phebe, W24629; BLWt.9467-160-55
William, Cont., Ct., S45223
William, Pvt., Del., BLWt. 10695 iss. 9/2/1789
William, Md., S35775
William, Va., R506
Williams, No service record, Me. res. BLWt.113859-160. Special Act of Congr., approved 6/10/1872
Zebediah, Mass., Susannah, R505
Zenas, N.Y., S12116
BARKERS, James, Md., S2948
BARKHUFF/PERKHOOF/BARKRUFF
Frederick, N.Y., Mary, W16181

BARKLEY, James, N.C., Sarah, W44
John, N.C., S2960
Robert, N.H., See BERKLEY
Robert, N.C., Ellenor, W17252
Samuel, N.Y., Agnes, R508
Thomas, Pa., See BARTLEY
William, S.C., S16314
BARKMAN, Jacob, N.Y., S23528
BARKRUFF, See BARKHUFF
BARKSDALE, Henry Hickerson, Va., Molly, W4636
Samuel, Va., Jemima, W18568
BARKUS, John, Del., BLWt.2050-100, iss. 7/12/1834
BARLEE, Michael, Mass., Navy, S37708
BARLER, William, N.C., Amey/ Naoma/Nodoma, W17232
BARLET, John, Pa., S2057
Paul, Pa., S23524
BARLETT, Jacob, Cont., Pa., Christina, W4882
BARLEYS, James, Pa., S8049
BARLOW, Aaron, Ct., Rebecca, W20665
Abner, Cont. N.H., BLWt.19616-160-55; Eunice, W3919
Abner, Mass., S12085
Christopher, Va., Barbara, W8341
David, Cont., Ct., Lucy, R510
George, Cont., Mass. Sea Service, S33993
John, Ct., S37732; BLWt.1416-100
Joseph, Va., S35773
Lewis, Va., S16619
Moses, N.Y., Sarah, W1209
Nathan, N.H., Matty, W18561
Obed, Mass., Elizabeth, W15558
Samuel, Cont., Ct., S6585
Tempa, former wid. of Jonah Carter, which see
Thomas, Pvt. "in Proctor's Artillery", Pa., BLWt.9044 iss. 7/16/1789 to M. McConnell, ass.
BARMER, John, Va., S8042
BARMORE, Henry, N.Y., Elizabeth, R493; BLWt.31699-160-55
BARN, David, Pvt., Ct., BLWt. 5502 iss. 10/31/1791 to Isaac Brown
BARNABE, Chandler, Ct. See BARNEBE
BARNABY, Jonathan, N.Y., R.I., S28992
BARNACK, John, See BARNHOCK
BARNARD, Benjamin, Mass., Lucy, W17248
Benjamin, Va., S9096
Cyprian, Cont. Navy, Ct., R512
Dan, Ct., S23532
Daniel, Cont., Mass., S37569
Edmund, Mass., Sarah, W12233
Elisha, Mass., Dorcas, W1207; BLWt.9480-166-55
Ezekiel, Mass., Mary, W1804
Grove, Ct., Mary Ann, W17224
John, Ct., BLWt.133-300-Capt., iss. 5/4/1795. No papers
John, Cont., Pa., Elizabeth, W3208
John, Mass., S12940
John, Mass., Martha, W15550. Her first husb., Timothy Bailey, also served.
Jonathan, Cont., Mass., Obedience,

BARNARD (continued)
W392
Jonathan, Mass., Annas, W23542
Joseph, Mass., S33973
Lydia, former wid. of John Babcock, which see
Moses, Ct., Reliance, W4634
Moses, Ct., Hannah, W16817
Nathan, Cont.,Mass., Sarah, W23541
Peter, Va., R19356. Va. half pay
Pharez, Pvt., Ct., BLWt.5478 iss. 7/22/1789
Richard, Pvt., Mass., BLWt.3656 iss. 7/22/1789
Richard, Mass., Abigail, W14224; BLWt.3656-100-Pvt. iss. 7/22/ 1789. No papers
Rufus, Ct., Mary, W3644
Silas, Mass. Navy, Phebe Fillebrown, former wid., W24192
Thomas, Va., See BERNARD
Timothy, Cont., Ct., Phebe, W25214
William, Ct., S12125
William L., Md., S16315
BARNATT, Carter, See BARNETT
BARNEBE/BARNOBE, Chandler, Ct., R.I., Esther, W20661
James, Ct., Ann, W20687
BARNER/BARNES, John, Cont. (French) N.Y. res. & agency, S44313
BARNES, Aaron, Mass., Rebecca, W15562
Abel, Ct., S12055
Abel, Ct., S44317
Abel, Ct., R514
Abraham, Cont., Mass. Margaret, W23512
Abraham, Pvt., Lamb's Artillery N.Y., BLWt.6889 iss. 7/9/1790 to Theodosius Fowler, ass.
Ambrose, Ct., S44316
Amos, Cont., Ct., See BARNS
Amos, Cont., Ct., Elizabeth, W17238
Amos, Sgt. "in the Corps of Invalids", BLWt.12841 iss. 12/12/ 1789 to Theodosius Fowler, ass.
Amos, Cont., N.H., See BARNS
Amos, Pvt., Sheldon's Dragoons, Ct., BLWt.5530 iss. 10/7/1789 to Benjamin Tallmadge, ass. of Samuel McNeil, admr.
Andrew, Dragoon, Va., BLWt.11928 iss. 3/20/1797
Armistead, Va., S37700
Barnet, S.C., R557
Bathsheba, former wid. of Ephraim Parkhurst, Mass., which see
Benjamin, Mass. See BARNS
Benjamin, Mass., S30262
Bingamond, Va., S12970
Caesar, N.H., BLWt.2102-100
Canterbury, Mass., S4924
Charles, S.C., BLWt.11982-100, iss. 3/31/1794. No papers
Chesley/Chesly, N.C., Mary, W4877
Comfort, Mass., Elizabeth, W3924
Corbin/Corban, Mass. Sea Service, Phebe, W14268
Daniel, Ct., S12084
Daniel, Ct., Sarah, R527
Daniel, Cont., R.I., S38527

BARNES (continued)
Daniel, Pvt. "in Sappers & Miners" BLWt.12752 iss. 5/28/1792 to Israel Angell, ass.
David, Ct., S12944
David, N.Y., Dis. No papers
Ebenezer, Mass., Vt., S32106
Elijah, Cont., Mass., Lucy,W20674
Elijah, Md., Catharine, W9717
Elijah, Mass., Margaret, W17237
Eliphalet, Cont., Ct., S37695
Enos, Pvt., Ct., BLWt.5436 iss. 10/7/1789 to Benj. Tallmadge
Enos, Cont., Ct., See BARNS
Freelove, former wid. of Jonathan Seelye, which see
George, Va., S16316
Heartwell/Hartwell, Ct., S44312
Henry, Pvt., N.Y., BLWt.6828 iss. 12/11/1789 to Benj. Brown, ass.
Henry, N.Y., S44314
Israel, Cont., Ct., See BARNS
Ithiel, Ct., Grissel, W23504; BLWt.5447-100. Fifer, Iss. 6/10/1790 to David Knap. No papers
James, Cont., Md., S39968
James, Cont., Va., S39173
James, Md., N.A., Acc. No.874, 050008. Half Pay. Pension file not ident. for this half pay.
James, Md. res. 1822. See BARNS
James, Mass., BLWt.1323-100
James, N.C., S1746
Jared, Ct., See BARNS
Jared, Ct., See BARNS
Joel, Ct., Dolly, See BARNS
John, Ct., Rachel, R525
John, Cont., Ct., See BARNS
John, Cont., French. Served various corps for 27 yrs. Marine in 1814. N.Y. res. & agency. S44313
John, Ct., N.Y., S12105
John, Ct., N.Y., S23110
John, Cont., Va., Milly, W8338
John, Pvt., Del., BLWt.10708 iss. 7/22/1797 to James DeBaufre,ass.
John, Del., Md., R520
John, Mass., Sarah, W23491
John, Mass., Sarah, W23510
John, Pvt., Va., BLWt.11921 iss. 11/12/1791 to John Clingman,ass.
John, no service record. Ga. res. R519
John C., Ct., N.Y., Abigail, W10385
John L. or S., no service record. Springwater, N.Y. res. See S12105 for add. corresp. Pens. Act of 1832. Suspended as found his name not on records as alleged by him.
Jonah, Ct., Abigail, W20692
Jonathan, Drummer, Ct., BLWt.5410 iss. 12/12/1789 to Theodosius Fowler
Jonathan, Ct., S44330
Joseph, Mass., Lydia, W24623
Joshua, Ct., See BARNS
Josiah, Cont., Ct., Olive, W25213
Josiah, Mass., S12120
Lambert, Pvt., Pa., BLWt.8970 iss. 8/7/1789 to Richard Platt, ass.

BARNES (continued)
Lemuel, Mass., S44332
Lemuel, Mass., Dis. No papers
Lovell/Lowell, Cont., Mass., R522
Moses, Ct., S2356
Moses, Pvt. "in the Invalids", BLWt.12843 iss. 11/2/1791 to Jonathan Tuttle, ass.
Nathan, Ct., S15307
Nathan, Mass., S33994
Nehemiah, Pvt., Hazen's Regt., BLWt.12804 iss.1/13/1791 to William Lane, ass.
Nicodemus, Md., R524
Orrange/Orange, Ct., See BARNS
Reuben, Cont., Ct., S12104
Reuben, N.H., S12129
Richard, Pvt., Pa., BLWt.8919 iss. 10/13/1791
Richard, Va., R526
Robert, Pa., See BARNSE
Samuel, Ct., S44318
Samuel, Mass., Pvt., BLWt.3718 iss. 4/1/1790
Samuel, Mass., S12041
Samuel, Pa., S23522
Shadrach, Va., See BARNS
Simeon, Ct., See BARNS
Solomon, Corp., Lamb's Artillery N.Y., BLWt.6888 iss. 9/13/179- to John Smith, ass.
Solomon, Mass., R528
Solomon, N.C., S6569
Thomas, Cont., Ct., Sibel, W4123
Thomas, Cont., Mass., S33987
Thomas, Cont., Mass., S33995
Thomas, Vt., Anna Dunton, former wid., W17732
Thomas, Pvt., Va., BLWt.11910 iss. 5/29/1792 to Francis Graves, ass.
William, Md., S1787
William, Mass., S33977
William, Navy, R.I., N.Y., S44315
William, S.C.,res. at enl. N.C., Elizabeth, W2585; BLWt.58692-160-55
William, Vt., See BARRON
BARNET, Benjamin, N.H., S38523
Daniel, Md., S35777
George, Pa., S45243; Wt. No.9004 iss. 8/29/1793
Hugh, Pvt., Pa., BLWts.8923 & 12794 iss. 8/31/1792 to Allen Power, ass. of James Barnet, admr.
James, Md., Pa., Martha, R535
John, Mass., S44310
John, N.Y., S44309
Joseph, Pa., S6583
Robert, Pa., Margaret, W1211
Simon, Pa. Sea Service, R539
Thomas, S.C., S12971
William, S.C., S30846
William M., N.J., BLWt.177-400-Surgeon. Iss. 9/7/1789 to Isaac Cox Barnet, heir & legal repr. No papers
BARNETT, Ambrose, Va., Sally,W2989
Andrew, N.C., S.C., S1165
Carter, N.C., Mary, W5784; BLWt. 26656-160-55

BARNETT (continued)
Carter, Privateer, N.C., R530
Charles, Va., S8048
David, N.C., S17826
George, Pvt., Pa., BLWt.9004 iss. 8/29/1793 to Casper Iserloan,ass.
Hannah, former wid. of Robert Crouch, Md., which see
Isaac, Va. res., R532
James, Va., Marcey, W391; BLWt. 424-200
James P., N.C., Va., S12963
Jesse, N.C., R533
Joel, Ga., S.C., R534
John, Mass., S44311
John, Pvt., Va., BLWt.11897 iss. 4/21/1796 to James Morrison, ass.
John, Va., Elizabeth, W9718
Joseph, Pa., S22668
Lance, S.C., S39174
Leona, former wid. of Lewis Howell, Va., which see
Michael, Va., Esther, W2051; BLWt.19541-160-55
Moses, Ct., N.Y., S15303
Nathaniel, Ct., R536
Peter, Md., R537
Peter, Va., See BARNARD
Robert, Cont. N.H., BLWt.2131-200
Robert, Va., R538
Sion, N.C., Frances, R531
Thomas, N.C., S8041
William, N.C., Mary, W1532; BLWt.27589-160-55
BARNEY, Asa, Cont., Mass., S44339
Benjamin, Cont. Mass., S44592
Jabez, Mass., BLWt.130-150, Ens. Iss. 3/14/1796. No papers
Jeffrey, N.H., Fila/Filie, R541
John, Mass., See BARNY
Jonathan, Mass., S4941
Joseph, Mass., S12114
Joseph, Mass., Sally, W14242
Joshua, Navy, served 1776 to 1818 Harriet. Old Act, Navy, W79
Luther, Ct., Privateer, Ruth,W4124
Martin, Mass., R.I., S12958
Nathaniel, Cont. Mass. Dis. No papers. BLWt.1888-100
Peleg, Mass., Lucinda, W23539
Prince, Cont. Mass., Mary, W5783; BLWt.2357-160-55
Samuel, Ct., Sea Service, Sarah, W17233
Thomas, Vt., Mabel, W20693
William, Cont. Pa., S20686
William, Mass., Mary, W15675
William, R.I., Sarah, W20686
BARNHACK, John. See BARNHOCK
BARNHARDT/BERNHARDT, George, N.C., Mary, R544
BARNHART, Anna, former wid. of William Hunt, N.J., which see
Cornelius, N.Y., Elizabeth, W8347; BLWt.26580-160-55
Daniel, Pa., BLWt.2066-100.No papers
David, N.Y., Margaret, W12263; BLWt.28587-160-55
George Peter, Pa., S12093
Henry/John Henry, Pa., Maria/ Mary Sophia, W3645

BARNHART (continued)
Jeremiah, N.Y., S12112
John, N.J., See BURNHART
John, Pvt., N.Y., BLWt.6841 iss. 7/30/1790 to Edward Cumpston, ass.
John Christopher, Cont. Pa., Elizabeth, R545
John Henry, Pa., See Henry
Philip, Pa., R546
BARNHEISER, John, Pa., S34637
BARNHILL, Henry, N.C., S6579
James, N.C., Susan, W3751; BLWt. 9419-160-55
John, N.C., S16318
Robert, Pa., R547
Samuel, Pa., S10344
BARNHOCK/BARNHACK/BARNACK, John, No service shown Sarah, R548. Me.res. of dau. in 1846
BARNITZ, Jacob, Pa., Mary, W3066
BARNS, Abraham, Mass. See BARNES
Ambrose, Corp., Ct., BLWt.5444 iss. 1/7/1802 to Ambrose Barns
Amos, Ct., Cont., S44333
Amos, Cont. N.H., Polly, W21640; BLWt.32215-160-55
Bathsheba, former wid. of Ephraim Parkhurst, which see
Benjamin, Ct., Abigail Clapp, former wid., R1957
Benjamin, Mass., S18700
Burrell/Burwell, N.C., S6549
Daniel, Ct., Dis. No papers
Elijah, Ct., S12976
Elisha, Mass., N.H., S12975
Enos, Cont., Ct., Lucy, W20650
Hartwell/Heartwell, Ct. See BARNES
Israel, Cont. Ct., Susanna, W25201
Ithiel, Ct., See BARNES
Jacob, N.Y., S38524
James, Md., R515
James, N.H., Submit Avery, former wid., W15980
James, Va., S1894
Jared, Ct., Silence, W25197
Jared, Ct., R516
Joel, Cont., Ct., Dolly, W3497; BL 3611-160-55
John, Cont., Ct., S2047
John, Md., S22106
Jonathan, Ct., S44603
Jonathan, Ct., See BARNES
Joseph, Mass., See BARNES
Joshua, Ct., S18302
Lemuel, Mass., See BARNES
Lowell/Lovell, See BARNES
Nehemiah, Cont., Ct., S39965
Orrange/Orange, Ct., Olive, W21647
Robert, Pa., See BARNSE
Samuel, Ct., See BARNES
Samuel, Cont., Mass., S37729; BLWt.1745-100
Sarah, former wid. of Joel Bullard, Mass., which see
Shadrach, Va., S30840
Silas, Mass., S29620
Simeon, Ct., S37731
Warner, Cont., Ct., Elizabeth, W25218; BLWt.30611-160-55
William, Pvt., Ct., BLWt.5477 iss. 10/16/1789 to Theodosius Fowler

BARNS (continued)
William, Pa., S39954
William, R.I., S17253
BARNSE, Robert, Cont., Pa., S45240
BARNTHISLER/BARNTHISTLE, Christopher, Pa., Catharine, W2744; BLWt.9492-160-55
BARNUM, Amos, Pvt., Ct., BLWt.5437 iss. 8/1/1795
Amos, Ct., S37707
Daniel, Ct., Hannah, W1123; BLWt. 3812-160-55
Eli, Ct., BLWt.144-200, Lt. iss. 10/12/1789 to Eunice Barnum, no papers
Eliakim, N.Y., R551
Ezbon, Cont., Ct., S12979
Jehiel, Ct., S44334
Josiah, Ct., Abigail, R549
Levi, Ct., R552
Noah, Cont., Ct., S37722
Ruth, former wid. of John North, Mass., which see
Samuel, Pvt., Ct., BLWt.5426 iss. 9/14/1792 to John Stephenson
Samuel, Ct., N.Y., S44335
Seth, Ct., Abigail, W21625
Stephen, Ct., S4917
Stephen, Ct., Green Mt. Boys, S39960
Stephen, Mass., S23114
Thomas, Mass., Anna, R550
Thomas, N.Y., Martha, W5788; BLWt.22358-160-55
Zenas, Ct., BLWt.1074-100
BARNWELL, Edward, S.C., Mary, W8352
James, N.C., See BARNHILL
James, Va., S37727
John, Pa., Jane, W3209
Robert, S.C., S31540
BARNY/BARNEY, John, Mass., Lucy, W1206; BLWt.28603-160-55
BAROB, Andrew, See BEARUP
BARON/BASSETT/BASSO/LEBAROW, Peter, R.I., R604
BAROTT, Hezekiah, Ct., S10353
BARR, Alexander, Cont., Vt. Green Mt. Boys. Rachel Landon, former wid., W20407; BLWt.684-100
David, Pa., S6564
Hugh, Mass., Sarah, W17229
Hugh, N.J., S35771
or O'BARR, Hugh, N.C.,Va., S32110
Isaac, Cont., Va., S41419
James, N.J., S15744
James, N.C., S31537
John, Cont., Pa., S45244
John, Cont., Pa., Mary, W3496
John, Cont., Va., BLWt.284-100, iss. 8/9/1806
John, Pvt., Hazen's Regt., BLWt. 12800 iss. 12/15/17--
John, N.Y., Hannah, W17258; BLWt. 167-150, Ensign, iss. 7/5/1792 to John Gansey, ass. No papers
John, Pa., Patsy/Polly/Martha Hand, former wid., W11217; BLWt. 91087-160-55
Philip/Phillip, Va., S37725
Robert, Pa., S6574
Samuel, Pa., S2366

BARR (continued)
Samuel, Pa., S5262
Thomas, Cont., BLWt.155-200-Capt. & Lt. of Crane's Artillery. Iss. 8/10/1790 to Martha Barr, exec. & heir. Also recorded as above under BLWt.2536
William, Pa., Va., Mary, W2743
William, Pvt., Va., BLWt.11880 iss. 1/7/1793 to Robert Means, ass.
BARRAGE/BARRAGER, Walter, N.Y., See BARRIGER
BARRAGER, John, Pvt., Lamb's Artillery, N.Y., BLWt.6875 iss. 7/16/1790 to P. Van Cortland, ass.
BARRAL, Jacob, Pa., S5267
BARRAM, Fielding, Cont., Va., S36407; BLWt.551-100
BARRELL, James, Cont., Mass., S33998
Noah, Cont., Mass., S33984
William, Pvt., N.J., BLWt.8155 iss. 9/23/1789
BARRET, Bartholomew, See BARRITT
Francis, Va., S12961
Isaac, Md., Lucy, W9341
Joel, Mass., S21062
Jonathan, Pvt., Mass., BLWt.3789 iss. 1/20/1796 to Jos. Fosdick, ass.
Lemuel, Mass., Phebe, W1358; BLWt.32219-160-55
Oliver, Mass., Mary, W20658
Richard, Va., See FRANKS
Simon/Solomon, Fifer, Md., BLWts. 10962, 14152 & 201-60-55 iss. 6/28/1799
Smith, Ct., S29605
Solomon, Md., See Simon
Wait, Pvt., Mass., BLWts.3681 & 28-60-55 iss. 6/24/1793 to J. Stephenson, ass.
William, Va., BLWt.270-300
BARRETT, Abraham, N.Y., S17261
Benjamin, Mass., S12053
Benjamin, Mass., S45231
Bethuel, N.Y., S23103
Elizabeth, former wid. of Wm. Nichols, N.C., which see
Hannah Newell, dau. of Noah Harrod, which see
Henry, Va., S8057
Israel, Mass. & War of 1812, Lucy, W16179
Jacob, Ct., S6576
James, Mass., S37575
James, N.Y., BLWt.163-300-Lt., iss. 5/24/1793. No papers
James, Pa., S46421
Jeremiah, Pvt., Ct., BLWt.5468 iss. 10/16/1789 to Theodosius Fowler
Jeremiah, Ct., S37711
Jeremiah, Cont., Mass., S38520
John, Cont., Va., See BARETH
John, Mass., Susanna, R562
John, Va., R558
Jonathan, Ct., S2049
Jonathan, Md., Sophia, R560
Jonathan, Mass., S30259

BARRETT (continued)
Jonathan, N.H., Submit, R561
Jonathan, Va. Sea Service, Amy, R 3, Va. half pay
Joseph, Ct., See BURRITT
Joseph, S.C., Elizabeth Bennett, BLWt.91059-160-55
Joshua, Sgt., Md., BLWt.10954 iss. 2/7/1790
Lemuel, Mass., Anna, W21647; BLWt.24162-160-55
Lewis, Va., S31533
Mary, former wid. of John Morgan, N.H., which see
Miles, no service record, Rej. BL 7248
Nathaniel, N.H., Mercy, W24627
Nathaniel, N.H., Sybil, W7230; BLWt.9417-160-55
Oliver, Ct., Mass., S4920
Oliver, Cont., Vt., N.Y., Elizabeth, W10384; BLWt.80-200-Lt. of Warner's Regt. Iss. 6/4/1793 No papers
Peter, Pvt., N.Y., BLWt.6792 iss. 7/30/1790 to John W. Wendell, ass.
Reuben, N.Y., Elizabeth, W25211
Reuben, S.C., Thombson, W2583; BLWt.24621-160-55
Richard, Md., S12058
Roger, Cont., Mass., Anna,W21648
Samuel, N.Y., S12052
Samuel, Va., S6590
Sarah, former wid. of Wm. Harper, Va., which see
Solomon, Md., Susan, W703; BLWt. 201-60-55
Thomas, Cont., Mass., Sarah G., W679; BLWt.3869-160-55
Thomas, Mass., R563
Wait, Mass., See BARRITT
William, Ct., S12048
William, N.Y., S12130
William, N.C., S8046
William, No service shown. Va. Agency. Dis. No papers
BARREY, John, Pvt., Ct., BLWt. 5498 iss. 1/14/1799 to Israel Stowell, Jr.
BARRICK, Henry, Md., S8054
Peter, Md., R555
BARRIGER/BARRAGER/BARRAGE/BARRINGER
Walter, N.Y., Margaret, W18572; BLWts.1599-100; 204-60-55
BARRINGER, David, N.Y. See BERRINGER
Paul, N.C., Catharine, R564
Peter, N.Y., S12968
Walter, See BARRIGER
BARRINGTON, Joseph Billings, Pa., Tamar, W9343; BLWt.28504-160-55
BARRITT, Bartholomew, Ct., S44579
Benjamin, Ct., Mass., S18697
Lemuel, Mass., Anna, W21647; BLWt.24162-160-55
Nathaniel, N.H., See BARRETT
Oliver, Ct., Mass., See BARRETT
Wait, Mass., Rebecca, W23532; BLWt.28-60-55
BARRON, Barnaba, N.C., Constance Askew, former wid., W3917

BARRON (continued)
Benjamin, Sgt., Mass., BLWt.3790 iss. 8/18/1797 to Simn. Wyman
Benjamin, Mass., Abigail, W21636; BLWt.67-100
Elias, Mass., No papers
Fielding, Pvt., Va., BLWt.11918 iss. 5/29/1792 to Francis Graves, ass.
James, Va. Sea Service & U.S. Navy Mary A.B., W12264. Va. half pay
John, N.C., Va., Susannah, W2987
Jonathan/Jotham, Cont., Mass., Mehitable, W23505
Jonathan, Mass., S4936
Jonathan, N.H., S28986
Jonathan, N.H., Susannah, W23487; BLWt.38-100
Joseph, Cont., N.H., Magdelaine, W1534; BLWt.34524-160-55
Moses, Mass., S45518
Richard, Va. Sea Service, R5, Va. half pay
Robert, Cont., N.Y., Phebe, W21644
Samuel, Cont., Mass., N.H., S21101
Samuel, Va. Sea Service, R6, Va. half pay
Thomas, N.C., Obedience, R565
William, Navy, R1065, died on voyage to France in 1778
William, N.C., Va., S1788
BARRON/BARNES, William, Vt., S15298
BARRONS, Abraham, Cont., Mass., See BARNES
Marks, R.I., BLWt.2-100, Special Act of 6/4/1842. For special act and other papers, see case of Robert Allen, R.I., BLWt. 1-100
BARROTT, Peter, Va., S41427
Solomon, Md., Susan, W703; BLWt.201-60-55
BARROW, Amos, Pvt., Mass., BLWt. 3730 iss. 10/22/1791 to Ebenezer Kingsley, ass.
Daniel, N.C., Va., S32104
John, N.C., R566
John, N.C., Va., See BARRON
Joseph, Cont., N.H., See BARRON
William, N.C., Susanna, W1533
BARROWS, Aaron, Mass., Mary, W14420
Abiel, Cont., Mass., S44607
Abner, Cont., Mass., Sea Service, S29617
Asa, Mass., S16038
Eleazer, Ct., S23101
Ephraim, Mass., Charlotte, W23551; BLWt.40505-160-55
Ichabod, Mass., Polly, W8110; BLWt.36510-160-55
Isaac, Ct., S17248
Isaac, Ct., S39162
Jacob, Ct., Emela, W2515; BLWt. 32224-160-55
Joseph, Mass., Hannah, W23517
Lemuel, Ct., Abigail, W5780; BLWt.7445-160-55
Moses, Mass., Elizabeth, W18560
Peter, Pvt., R.I., BLWt.2955 iss. 2/11/1800

BARROWS (continued)
Peter, R.I., Elizabeth, W23545
Philbrook, Mass., Privateer. Phebe, W5781; BLWt.13181-160-55
Samuel, Mass., Azubah, W21631
Thomas, Ct., S15297
Thomas, Mass., S12080
William, Cont., Mass., Katharine, W8348
BARRUP, Andrew. See BEARUP
BARRUS, Jeremiah, Cont., Mass., N.H., S10345
Nathan, Cont., Mass., N.H., S44604
Thomas, Ct., See BURRUS
BARRY, Andrew, N.C., Ruth, R569
Bartholomew, Pa., BLWt.8940 iss. 1793
Benjamin, N.H., S18709; BLWt. 3837-160-55
Ebenezer, N.H., S22105
John, Ga., S39163
John, Sgt. "in Proctor's Artillery", Pa., BLWt.9050 iss. 6/29/1789 to M. McConnell, ass.
Jonathan, Mass., S20286
Joshua, Mass., N.H., Eleanor, W16821
Peleg, R.I., See BERRY
Phillip, Pa., S33255
William, Cont. Md., See BERRY
BARSE, Adam, N.Y., R570
BARSTO, Ebenezer, Ct., S15740
BARSTOW, Benjamin, Mass., Susanna, W23495
Job, Ct., N.Y., R571
John, Ct., S12039
Joseph, Mass., S4919
Mary, former wid. of Hugh Cox, Mass., which see
Michael, Ct., S45519
Samuel, Ct., Lucina, W25196; BLWt.10241-160-55
Timothy, Mass., S16629
BARTEE, David, Va., S6586
John, Ind. res., Martha Slater, former wid., BLRej., S330162-1855
BARTEL, Philip, N.Y., See BORTEL
BARTER, Henry, Cont. N.H., Jemima, W23544
Henry, Pvt., N.H., BLWt.2945 iss. 7/21/1789 to Eliph. Ladd & Jonathan Cass, assnes.
John, Pvt., N.H., BLWt.2934 iss. 10/12/1795 to James A. Neal, ass.
John, N.H., S37566
John, no service shown; no serial no., pensioned at N.H. agency. No papers
Pelatiah/Peletiah, N.H., Navy, S37567
BARTH, Nicholas, N.Y., See BORT
BARTH/BAIRD, Stephen, Cont. Pa., S39959; BLWt.178-100
BARTHARICK, Lazarus, Mass., S37699
BARTHE, George, Pa., See BAITH

BARTHOLF/BERTHOLF, Jacobus, Privateer, Mass., R573
BARTHOLOMEW, Abraham, Pvt., Sheldon's Dragoons, Ct., BLWt.5541 iss. 10/7/1789 to Benjamin Talmage
Benjamin, Cont. N.Y., Abigail, W4128
Benjamin, Pa., Rachel, W3228; BLWt.195-300, Capt. Iss. 8/19/1789. No papers
Charles, Ct., Lenda/Belinda, W25195; BLWt.10006-160-55
Daniel, Cont., Pa., S22635
Isaac, Cont., Ct., S44590
Isaac, Pvt., Sheldon's Dragoons, Ct., BLWt.5540 iss. 6/1/1793 to Stephen Thorne
James, Cont., Ct., S12943
John, Pvt., N.Y., BLWt.6771 iss. 7/11/1791
John, N.Y., S44591
John, N.C., Elizabeth, W4880
Jonathan, Ct., S12068
Joseph, Ct., Sina, W9345; BLWt. 61241-160-55
Luther, Cont., Ct., S21625
Moses, Ct., S15314
Oliver, Cont., Ct., S12086
Philip, N.Y., Elizabeth, W23508
Samuel, Ct., Elizabeth, W20651
Samuel, Cont., Mass., S33999
William, Ct., S37717
BARTISS, John, Ct., R575
BARTLE, George, Pvt., Pa., BLWt.9005 iss. 3/29/1791
John, N.Y., R576
BARTLET/BARTLETT
Adonijah, Mass., S29622
Amos, Mass., S12069
Benjamin, N.H., Vt., R577
Christopher, Ct., S10340
Daniel, Ct., S12077
David, Mass., S21063
Elisha, Cont. Mass., Vt., S23100; BLWt.3769-160-55
James, Mass., R582
John, Cont., BLWt.520-100
Joseph, Cont., Mass., S21626
Levi, Ct., N.Y., S12082
Paul, Pa., See BARLET
Philip, Mass., Lydia, R584
Samuel, Ct., S12982
Samuel, Ct., R585
BARTLETT,
Aaron, Cont., Mass., Joanna, W16830
Abraham, Ct., S28629
Asa, R.I., S21055
Benjamin, Mass., S12101
Caleb, Cont., Mass., Elizabeth, W23481
Cornelius, Mass., S33988
Daniel, Mass., BLWt.108-400, Surgeon. Iss. 12/31/1795. No papers
Daniel, Mass., S1633
Daniel, Mass., Deborah, W15570
Ebenezer, Mass., S39957
Ebenezer, N.Y., S32109
Edmund, Va., S17247
Eli, Mass., Mary, W15559

BARTLETT (continued)
Elihu, Mass., Rachel, W14239
Elijah, Mass., S4923
Elisha, Mass., Rebecca, W23531
Elisha, Mass., Sarah, W23549; BLWt.3391-160-55
Elkanah, Mass., Sea Service, R580
Evan, Mass., Hannah, W16099
Hannah, former wid. of James Harlow, Mass., which see
Hastin, N.C., Elizabeth, W4883
Haynes, N.Y., S10336
Isaac/Isaac I., Cont., Ct., Sybel, W517; BLWt.33570-160-55
Jeremiah, N.H., R583
John, Cont., Mass., S33971
John, Cont., Mass., S37563
John, Cont., Va., S39158
John, Cont., Va. Sea Service, S35183
John, Mass., N.H., S16627
Jonathan, Mass., BLWt.1017-100
Joseph, Pvt., Mass., BLWt.3772 iss. 8/31/1790 to Jos. Nye, ass.
Joseph, Mass., Sea Service, Navy, S29611
Joseph, Mass., Hannah, W516; BLWt.34958-160-55
Joseph, N.H., Hannah, W278; BLWt.8380-160-55
Joshua, Mass., S44347
Josiah, Cont., Mass., S1634
Lemuel, Pvt., N.Y., BLWt.6812 iss. 9/27/1790 to Wright Carpenter, ass.
Malachi, Cont. Mass., Mary, W23547; BLWt.26806-160-55
Moses, Mass., S28630
Moses, Mass., Esther, W24628
Moses, Mass., Betsey, R578
Nathaniel, Cont., N.H., S44588
Nathaniel, Cont., N.H., Esther, W5792; BLWt.6252-160-55
Nathaniel, Mass., Vt., Lucy, W20689
Nathaniel, N.H., S23529
Nicholas, Mass., S12076
Nicholas, Mass. Sea Service, Navy, S33986
Otis, Cont., Ct., S10346
Philip, Va. Sea Service, R7, Va. half pay.
Reuben, Cont., Mass., Amy, W24622
Robert, Drummer, Ct., BLWt.5494 iss. 12/3/1789 to Daniel Watrous
Samuel, Mass., R586
Samuel, Mass. Sea Service, R585 1/2
Scipio, Mass., Kate Gilbert, former wid., R4010
Silas, Mass., S18703
Solomon, Cont. Mass., S34000
Solomon, Pvt., Mass., BLWt.3705 iss. 8/24/1790 to B.J. Gilman, ass.
Solomon, Mass., S39170
Solomon, Mass., Jerusha, W20664
Stephen, Cont., Ct., S44589

BARTLETT (continued)
Susanna, former widow of Jonathan Pettingill, which see
Thaddeus, Mass., S30845
Thomas, Mass., S15304
Thomas, N.H., Sarah, R587
William, Cont., Mass., S4940
William, Mass., Lois, W14243
William, Mass., Azubah, W18557; BLWt.5074-160-55
William, Mass. Sea Service, Navy; Tabitha, W14238
William (Berkley), Va., S12964
Wyman/Wiman, Mass., Elizabeth, R579
Zachariah, Pvt., Mass., BLWt. 3652 iss. 8/31/1790 to Joseph Nye
BARTLETT/BARTLET, Zadock, Cont. Mass., Hannah, W23483
BARTLEY, Henry, N.Y., Ann or Nancy, W23483
John, Pvt., Va., BLWt.11957 iss. 7/6/1793 to Francis Graves, assignee
John, Va., S39949
Robert, S.C., S31535
Thomas, Md., S18708
Thomas, Pa., Margaret, R591
Thomas, not Rev. War-Wayne's War 1792-3. Margaret; BLWt.22711-160-55
William, N.C., Sarah, R590
Zilpha, former widow of Wm. Dotson, which see
BARTLIT, Samuel, See BARTLETT
BARTLON, Cornelius, N.J., S23527
BARTMAN, Joseph, Ct., or Mass. Sea Service, War against France, Algiers, War of 1812; R593
BARTO/BARTOE, Morris, N.Y., S44595
Reuben, N.Y., S44594
BARTOE, Morris, Pvt., N.Y., BLWt. 6767 iss. 8/6/1790
BARTOL, Frances, former wid. of Hezekiah Coombs/Combs, which see
BARTOLF/BERTHOLF, Crynes, N.J., S12205
John S., N.J., See BERTOLF
BARTOLL, Samuel, Cont., Pa., S33974
BARTON, Andrew, R.I., BLWt.143-100; claim missing in 1912. Reg. shows "iss. 2/28/1804; not delivered"
Bazaleel, Mass., N.H., S12966
Benjamin, Mass., Mehitable, W15567
Benjamin, S.C., Dorcas, W20683
Benjamin, R.I., S21622
Caleb, Ct., Mass., Elizabeth, W15565
Ebenezer, Mass., Dorothy, W23497
Elisha, Va., S19198
Elkanah, Cont. Ct., Mass., S37712
James, Mass., R594
John, Cont., Mass., S34002
John, Pvt., Mass., BLWts.3651 & 14147 iss. 3/7/1798
John, Mass., Abigail, W23490
John, N.J., S1164
John, N.C., Elizabeth, R12277
Jonathan, Cont., Mass., S44612
Jonathan, Cont., Mass., S45229

BARTON (continued)
Jonathan, Pvt., Mass., BLWt. 3682 iss. 2/9/1793 to P. DeWitt, ass.
Jonathan, Mass., S36908
Joseph, Pvt., Md., BLWt.10949 iss. 2/7/1790
Josiah, Mass., Eunice, W5785 BLWt.39490-160-55. A Jenny Barton, alleged widow of Josiah also applied for pension and B.L. See papers within
Nicholas, Cont., Mass., S12122
Peter, Mass., R596
Roger, N.Y., Sarah, W16828
Rufus, R.I., Prudence, W10387
Ruth, former wid. of Josiah Conant, Ct., which see
Sibley, Mass., Lucretia, W14243
Simon, Pvt., R.I., BLWt.2976 iss. 12/31/1789
Susannah, former wid. of Elijah Bailey, Mass., which see
Timothy S., Cont., Mass., S12100
William, Cont., Ct., Clarissa, W10375; BLWt.19779-160-55
William, Cont. Mass., N.H., Miriam, R595
William, N.J., BLWt.179-300-Capt. iss. 9/7/1790. No papers
William, R.I., Rhoda, W23503; BLWt.83-500 iss. 4/20/1790
BARTOW, John, Cont., Ct., S37718
John, Pvt., Sheldon's Dragoons, Ct., BLWt.5529 iss. 12/10/1789
Jonah, Pvt., N.Y., BLWt.6768 iss. 3/9/1796
Jonah, N.Y., S45245
BARTRAM, Isaac, Cont., Ct., S12110
James, Ct., S12066
Job, Ct., Dis. No papers
Noah, Ct., S12043
BARTTLET/BARTLETT, Solomon, Cont., Mass., S34000
BASCOM, Samuel, Mass., S33975; BLWt.90-100
Urial, Ct., R597
BASEY, William, Cont. See BASY
BASFORD, Benjamin, N.H., S___, Martha Basford, wid. received pension as former wid. of John Bean, N.H., which see
James, Cont., N.Y., S39952
James, Pvt., Pa., BLWt.9033 iss. 3/19/1792 to George Moore, ass.
Martha, N.H., former wid. of John Bean, which see
BASHAM, Obediah/Obadiah. See BASSHAM, Va.
BASHARROW/BUGGAROW, John, Pvt., N.Y., BLWts.6849 & 156-60-55 iss. 3/7/179-, W6849, to Barent V. Benthuysen
BASHAW, John, Cont., Va., S37706
Peter, Va., S2962; BLWt.26359-160-55
BASKERVILLE, John, Va., Milley/Mildred, W3753
Samuel, Va., S45238; BLWt.272-200-Lt., iss. 4/9/1800. No papers.
BASKETT/BASKET, Martin, N.C. &

BASKETT (continued)
Va., Frances, W2990
BASON, Daniel, Pvt., N.Y., BLWt. 6782 iss. 10/11/1790 to Henry Tremper, ass.
BASS, Edward, Cont., Mass., Bathsheba, W24625
Edward, N.C., R599
Edward, Va., S6595
Elijah, N.C. See claim of Benjamin Richardson, W4061, for military history of this soldier
BASS, Foard, Cont., Mass., Rosanna, W4132
Henry, Pvt., N.Y., BLWt.6830 iss. 7/29/1790 to Abm. Handenburg
Henry (or Curtis), N.Y., S40873
James, Va., S1745
John, Va., S6592
Joseph, Ct., Cont., N.Y., See BEARCE
Joseph, Va., Jenney, W5765
Joshua, N.C., Priscilla, R600
Philip, N.C., Patsy, W23482
Richard, N.C., R20324,
Samuel, Cont., Ct. res. in 1802, BLWt.87-100
Samuel, Pvt., Del., BLWt.10703 iss. 5/11/1790
Samuel, Mass., S15737
William, Va., Sarah, W5766
BASSELL, Michael, Pvt. "in the Corps of Invalids", BLWt.12821 iss. 8/6/1790 to Abraham Ten Eyck, ass.
BASSETT, Abel, Ct., S45227
Benjamin, Cont., Mass., Mary, W8349
Caesar, N.Y., Flora, W16827
Jonathan, Cont. Mass., S33974
Samuel, Ct., S15746
Samuel, Mass., S30847
BASSETT, Abraham, Ct., Mary, W17253
Barakiah, Mass., BLWt.93-450-Lt. Col. iss. 4/16/1790. No papers
Benjamin, Pvt., Mass., BLWt.3706 iss. 8/31/1790 to Joseph Nye, ass.
Caleb, Mass., S17255
Cornelius, Mass., Sea Service, Navy, S30255
David, Ct., Sarah, W17241
David, Navy, Maine agency & res. S36905
Edward, Cont., Ct., Damarius/Dammarius, W12234
Hayward, Cont. Mass. See Howard
Howard, Cont. Mass., S38521
Isaac, Ct., S12062
Isaac, Mass., Mahitable, W14249; BLWt.33564-160-55
James, Ct., S17259
James, Mass., Bethiah, W15560
Jedidiah/Jedediah, Mass., S21056
Jeremiah, Mass., Hannah, W14257
John, Mass., Elizabeth, W18567
Joseph, Cont., Mass., S35770
Joseph, Mass., Nancy, R602; BLWt. 43516-160-55

BASSETT (continued)
Joshua, Cont., Ct., Lydia, W21634
Lot, Mass., Deborah, W20660
Nathan, Ct., R603
Nathan, Cont., Mass., S18695
Nathan, Mass., S28634
Nathaniel, Mass., Navy, Bethiah, W15566
Nathaniel, Va., S1895
Peter, R.I., See BARON
Samuel, Mass., N.H., Martha, W16501
Thomas, Mass., Sea Service, Lydia, W14240
William, Pvt., Ct., BLWt.5489 iss. 6/3/1791 to Isaac Bronson
William, Cont., Va., Peggy, W9739
William, R.I., Avis, W16835
Zachariah, Cont. Navy, R.I., S39160
BASSEY, William, Cont., See BASY
BASSHAM/BASHAM, Obadiah/Obediah, Va., S35185
BASSO, Peter, R.I., See BARON
BAST, George, N.C., See BOST
BASTEDO, William, N.J., Pa., Margaret, W3921
BASTEEN, Joseph, Cont., Mass., S36907
BASTIAN, Jacob, Pa., S22630
BASTO/BARSTO, Moses, Pvt., Mass., BLWt.3752 iss. 1/14/1796 to Moses Bairsto
BASTON/BOSTON, Elijah, Cont., Mass. S18327
Jonathan, Mass., See BARTON
Thomas, Mass., S18325
Winthrop, Mass., Hannah, W1538; BLWt.13870-160-55
BASTOW, William, Mass., S38516
BASWELL/BOSWELL, Weldon, Pa., R605
William, N.C., Lydia, W18639
BASY/BASEY/BASSEY, William, Cont., Ky. res. in 1830. S---; BLWt. 1650-100
BASYE/BAYSE, Richard, Va., Nancy, Stallard, Va., former wid., W8755
BATCHELDER, Amos, Mass., Huldah, W23492
Archelaus, Cont., Mass., N.H., S45508
Betsey, former wid. of Robert Littlefield, Mass., which see
David, Cont., N.H., S37564
Dorothy, former wid. of Lawrence Ellis, Mass., which see
Israel, Cont., Mass., Abigail Nye former wid., W15140
James, Pvt. "in the Invalids", BLWt.12824 iss. 3/25/179-
James, Mass. res. Dis. No papers
James, N.H., S45510
John, N.H., Martha, W389; BLWt. 6019-160-55
John P., Pvt., R.I., BLWt.2966 iss. 3/25/179-
Jonathan, Mass., S45511
Jonathan, N.H., R352
Josiah, N.H., S16617
Mark, N.H., S15302
Nathanial, N.H., Mary Bunker former wid., W24634

BATCHELDER (continued)
Phineas, N.H., S16621
Ruppe, R.I., See BACHELLER
Simon, N.H., S17828
Stephen, Cont., N.H., See BACHELDER
William, N.H., Joanna, W2429; BLWt.17596-160-55
William, N.H., See BACHELDER
BATCHELLER/BATCHELER, Jeremiah, Mass., Lydia, W20654
John Prescott, Cont., Mass., S33980
Josiah, Mass., Ruth, W16500
BATCHELLOR/BATCHELOR, Enoch, Mass., S19537
BATCHELLOR/BATCHELOR/BATCHELLER, Joseph, Mass., Sally, W17254; BLWt.33568-160-55
BATCHELOR/BATCHELLOR, Benjamin, Cont., Mass., S45509
Peter, Va., S37704
BATEMAN, Danial, N.J., S948
George, Md., S34635
John, N.Y., BLWt.2626-200-Lt., iss. 7/30/1793. Certified 4/9/1816. No papers
John, Pvt., Va., BLWts.11906 & 14128 iss. 8/8/1795 to Joseph Blackwell, admr.
Joseph, Mass., S18706
Levi, Pa., BLWt.8926
Moses, N.J., S595
Nathan, Md., BLWt.2132-100-iss. 1/27/1836
Susan, former wid. of Wm. Asberry, Va., which see
Thomas, N.C., R606
William, Cont., Md., S32099
William, N.J., S947
William, Pa., S33252
Zadock, Mass., Lucy, W18573
BATES, Aaron, Mass., S29601
Alpheus, Mass., Elizabeth, W20671
Amasa, Mass., Jemima, W15873
Ambrose, Mass., Priscilla, W23537
Archibald, R.I., Hannah, R613; BLWt.39495-160-55
Asa, R.I., S17260
Barnabas/Barnabus, Mass., Sylvia/Silvia, W17246
Barnabas, Mass., R.I., S23109
Benjamin, Cont., Ct., S12148
Benjamin, Mass., Navy, S12045
Benjamin, N.J., S2361
Bennoi, Pvt., R.I., BLWt.2982 iss. 7/20/1791 to Simn. Fishbough, ass.
Benoni, Pvt., R.I., BLWt.2971 iss. 12/31/1789
Benoni, R.I., S38515
Benony, R.I., S39961
Carver, Mass., S41425
Christopher, R.I., S12113
Clement, Mass., S29600
Conrad, Pvt., N.Y., BLWt.6847 iss. 5/14/1793 to Thomas Russell, ass.
Cornelius, Mass., Anna, W14248
Daniel, Mass., N.J., N.Y., R609
Daniel, N.J., S18301
Daniel, R.I., Elizabeth, W23538
David, Cont., BLWt.140-300-Capt.

BATES (continued)
in Col. Seth Warner's Regt. Iss. 8/8/1789 to John Doty, ass. No papers
Doughty/Douty, Mass., Mary, W24633
Eleazer, Ct., S33991
Elias, Ct., S12949
Elisha, Sgt., Mass., BLWt.3674 iss. 8/10/1789 to Richard Platt, ass.
Elisha, Mass., S29619
Ephraim, Va., S2051
Ezra, Ct., S12117
Francis, R.I., S41421
George, Pvt., Pa., BLWt.8984 iss. 2/14/1791 to Alexander Power, ass.
Hickey, N.H. Sea Service, N.Y., R614
Hinsdale, Ct., S16043
Humphrey, N.C., Rachel, W25204, BLWt.27615-160-55
Isaac, res. N.C., S328
Israel, Mass., R615
Issachar, Mass., S2360
Jabez, Mass., Navy, Privateer, S15745
Jacob, Cont., Mass., S33982
Jacob, Fifer, Mass., BLWt.3743 iss. 8/10/1789 to Richard Platt, ass.
Jacob, Mass., S29616
James, Cont. Privateer, R.I., Sarah, W23534
James, Mass., Mary Battles, former widow, W17245
James, Mass., Betsey Switser or Sweetser, former wid., W22349. Her last husband, Phillips Sweetser, Mass. pensioned, S11500.
James, N.C., S2938
James, N.C., Va., S30850
James, Va., Lavina Francis or Levina, W5787; BLWt.26846-160-55
John, Ct., S40738
John, Cont., Mass., S44599; res. Warren County, N.Y.
John, Mass., R----; Res. Otsego County, N.Y.
John, Mass., Abigail, R607
John, R.I., R617
Jonathan, Cont., Mass., S33989
Joseph, Cont., Ct., S34642
Joseph, Mass., Lucy, W23489; BLWt.8008-160-55
Joseph, Mass., N.H., S33985; BLWt.99-300-Capt., iss. 4/16/1790. No papers
Joseph, Pvt., Sheldon's Dragoons Ct., BLWt.5532 iss. 10/16/1789 to Theo. Fowler
Joshua, Mass., Tirzah Hunt, former wid., W15556. Her last husband, Ebenezer Hunt, Mass. pensioned, S29254
Josiah, Cont. Mass., S41422
Lebbeus/Libbeus, Cont., Mass., Melatiah, W1126; BLWt.7300-160-55
Lemuel, Cont., Mass., S20618
Lemuel, Mass., Fairrizina, R612

BATES (continued)
Mory/Mowry, R.I., Hannah, W10379; BLWt.40707-160-55
Moses, Cont., Mass., S41423
Nathaniel, N.H., Abigail Stroud, former wid., BLWt.479-100
Nehemiah, Mass., BLWt.38821-160-55
Noah, Mass., S28984
Oliver, Mass., S44598
Phinehas, Ct., Keziah, R618; BLWt.84508-160-55
Reuben, Mass., R621
Reuben, R.I., Abigail, R608
Robert, Mass., Nabby, W712; BLWt.24918-160-55
Rufus, Cont., Green Mt. Boys, Vt. S22634
Samuel, Ct., Deborah Wright, former wid., W16798; BLWt. 1534-100
Samuel, Cont., Mass., S29598
Samuel, Mass., S38526
Samuel, Mass., Susannah, W23516
Samuel, N.H., S44343
Simeon, Mass., R623
Susanna, former wid. of Moses Orcutt, Mass., which see
Thaddeus, Mass., S12029
Theodore, Mass., Abigail, W25193; BLWt.3991-160-55
Thomas, Mass., S18705
Thomas, Va., S35186
William, Mass., S12047
William, N.C., S32105
William, Va., S35176
William, Va., R623 1/2
Worth, Mass., Hannah, W14235
BATHE, George, Pa., See BAITH
BATHRICK, Jason, Mass., S34579
Stephen, Mass., Patty, W18556; BLWt.2355-160-55
BATHURST, Lawrence, Pa., Rebecca, W4630
BATMAN, Thomas, Md., S35182
BATS, Charles, Pvt., Pa., BLWt. 8920 iss. 7/8/1791 to Simon Fishbaugh, ass.
BATSON/BATTISON, Mardica/Mordecai, Va., S35184
BATTEL/BATTLE, Hezekiah, Mass., Mary, W14264
BATTELLE, Josiah, Mass., S28983
BATTELS/BATTLES, Jared, Mass., S18698
BATTEN, Ebenezer, Cont., Mass., S33997
John, Pvt., Hazen's Regt., BLWt.12803 iss. 1/17/1794
BATTERSBY, John, Pvt., Pa., BLWt.8981 iss. 5/16/1791
Robert, N.Y., BLWt.956-100
BATTERSHELL, Freeman, Va., Nancy, W2913
BATTERSON, Abijah, Ct., S12075
George, Ct., Mary, W17257; BLWt.2356-160-55
James, Ct., Nancy, R624
John, Ct., Sarah, W17239
Joseph, Ct., Rebecca, W23536; BLWt.1404-100
Stephen, Pvt., Ct., BLWt.5452 iss. 8/7/1789 to Richard Platt

BATTERSON (continued)
Stephen, Ct., S40737
William, Ct., R625
BATTERTON/BUTTERTON, Samuel, Cont. Va., S35803
BATTES/BATTIS, John, a Frenchman, Cont., Mass., S33981
BATTESON, James, See BATTERSON
BATTEY, William, R.I., Lucy, W1208; BLWt.26945-160-55
BATTIN, John, Cont., Md., Mary, W4413
BATTIS, John, Cont., Mass., See BATTES
John, Pvt., Mass., BLWt.3711 iss. 3/21/1792 to M. Park, ass.
BATTIST, John, Mass., See BAPTIST
BATTLE, Hezekiah, Mass., See BATTEL
Ithiel, Cont., Mass., Keziah, R626
James, Cont., Mass., S44601
Justus, Cont., Mass., S4939
BATTLES, Asa, Mass., Polly, W24631
Jared, Mass., See BATTELS
John, Cont., Mass., S44600
John, Mass., S39962; BLWt.1222-100
Mary, former wid. of James Bates, Mass., which see
Noel, Va., S12960
Shadrack/Shadrick, Va., S37713
BATTON, Henry, Pa., S31542
BATTS, John, Mass., Rebecca, W14233
BATTSON, Mordecai/Mardica, See BATSON
BAUCH/BOUCK, Johonness/John, N.Y., R1053
BAUER, Frederick, Pa., S2213
BAUGH, Henry, Va., Margaret, W8337
BAUGH/BOUGH, Jacob, Va.; also served in 1774; R627
Joseph, Va., R21837
BAUGHAN, Richard, See BANGHAN
BAUGHMAN, George, Pvt. "in the Artillery", Pa., BLWt.9062 iss. 2/11/1791
BAUGHMAN/BACHMAN, George, Pa., Barbara, W4632
Paul, Cont. Pa., R635
BAUJEAN, Charles, Cont., Mass., Anna, W16824; 16 Rev. ltrs.
BAULDREE, Isaac K. See BALDRY
BAULDWIN/BALDWIN, Edward, N.C., Drusilla, R445
James, no service shown. Elizabeth. Children applied from Hancock Co., Tenn., R628
BAUM, Frederick, N.Y., Margaret, W15833
Frederick, Pa., S6561
John, Md., Mary, W8109; BLWt. 30621-160-55
BAUMAN, Charles, Pvt., Crane's Cont. Artillery, Mass., BLWt. 3822 iss. 12/2/1791 to John Blanchard, ass.
BAUMAN/BAUMANN/BOWMAN/BOARDMAN, Frederick, Cont., Pa., BLWt. 243-100
BAUMAN, Philip, Pa., Magdalena, R629
BAUMANN/BOWMAN, Nicholas, N.Y., R1081

BAUME, Joseph, See DE LA BAUME
BAUMGARDNER, Henry, Pa., See BAUMGARTNER
William, Md., See BOMGARDNER/BUMGARDNER
BAUMGARTEL, Leonard, Cont., Va., See BAUMGARTNER
BAUMGARTEN, Henry, See BAUMGARTNER
BAUMGARTNER
Henry, Cont., Va., S45246; BLWt.1567-100
BAUMGARTNER/BAUMGARDNER, Henry, Pa., S22098
Leonard, Cont., Va., BLWt.1305-100
BAURY DE BELLERIVE/BAURY, Louis, French, Mary, W28025
BAUSE, John, Pa., R631
BAUSHER, Peter, Pa., R632
Philip, Pa., S22096
BAUSMAN, William, Cont., Pa., Elizabeth, W8117
BAUTCHEBY, Joseph, Pvt., Md., BLWt.10996 iss. 4/18/1797 to James DeBaufre, ass.
BAVIDGE, Cortney/Courtney, Mass. See BABBIDGE
BAVOR/BEAVOR, Edward, Cont., N.Y., S35178
BAWCUTT, William, Cont., Va., Sarah, W3498; BLWt.1364-100; BLWt.296-60-55
BAWLING, Charles, Va., See BOWLING
William, Va., See BOWLING
BAWMAN, Sebastian, Cont., BLWt. 168-400-Major in Col. Lamb's Regt. Artillery. Iss. 7/2/1790. No papers
BAXTER, Aaron, Ct., S37714
Aaron, N.Y., S12064
Abigail, former wid. of Ebenezer Wild, Mass., which see
Alexander, Pvt., Mass., BLWt. 3765 iss. 6/2/1795 to Samuel Emery, ass.
Andrew, N.C., Elizabeth, W4635
Benjamin, Cont., Ct., Hannah, R633
Benjamin, Cont., N.H.,Margaret Cutter, former wid, W9401; BLWt.71141-160-55
Cornelius, Mass., S33972
David, Mass., S33983
Ebenezer, Mass., S38517
Edward Willard, Mass., Esther Vose, W15554
Francis, Ct., Dis. No papers
Israel, S.C., R21696
James, Pvt., Pa., BLWt.8956 iss. 7/27/1789 to Richard Platt, ass.
John, Cont., Green Mt. Boys, Mass., Eunice, W10399
John, Cont., Mass., Privateer. Candace, W12262; BLWt.1297-160-55
John, Mass., Reliance, W23496
John, N.Y., S23098
John, N.C., S24898
Malochi, Mass., Rhoda, W20652

BAXTER (continued)
Moses, Mass., R636
Nathan, Ct., R637
Nathan, Cont., Ct., S6594
Nathan, Mass., S28990
Simeon, Ct., Mass., R638
Thomas, Mass., Prudence, R639
William, Ct., Vt., Deborah, W25207
William, Mass., S44606
William, Pa., BLWt.225-150-Ens. iss. 5/14/1793. No papers
William, Va., S6591
BAY, Andrew, N.C., S2940
David, Va., S45237
Robert, Pa., 1812, S2043
BAYARD, Stephen, Pa., BLWt.190-450-Lt. Col., No papers.
BAYLES, David, Pa. or Va., R641
Elias, N.Y., S44584; BLWt.6853-100-Pvt. Name spelled Elias Baylis, iss. 3/7/1792 to B.V. Benthuysen, ass. No papers
Elijah, N.C., Va., & Indian War, S1940
Hezekiah, N.C., Va., S16624
BAYLES/BALES, Jesse, Va., Jane, W8345
BAYLES/BAYLIS, Nehemiah, Cont. N.Y., Rebecca, W4878
BAYLESS, John, Not Rev. War; 1792; see 1812 Fleet Files; BLWt.2283-160-50
Sarah, former wid. of William Dickson, S.C., which see
BAYLEY, Daniel, N.Y., S44571
Dudley, N.H., S16320
Enoch, Mass., Pa., Rep. BLWt.----
Frye, N.H., S41424
Hudson, Mass., Sarah/Sally, W24635
Jacob, N.H., Vt., Mary, W23509
James, Vt., R643
James, Vt., Sally/Sarah Stevens, former wid., W19092. She also was pensioned as widow of her last husband, Otho Stevens, Vt.
John, Vt., R376
Jonas, Mass., S5265
Jonas, Mass., Elizabeth, W14228
Joseph, Corp., Mass., BLWt.3696 iss. 1/28/1790 to J. Patterson, ass.
Joshua, Mass., Sarah, W23533
Joshua, Mass., Vt., S18707
Josiah, Cont. Mass., Mary, W475; BLWt.32214-160-55
Mary, former wid. of Ephraim Eddy, Cont., Mass., Vt., which see
Moses, N.H., Lucinda, BLWt. 105586-160-55
Noah, Pvt., Cont., Mass., Lucy, W2584; BLWt.203-60-55 & 3754-100 iss. 4/1/1790. Endorsed "memo certified for Seth Hyatt" 6/20/1818.
Robert, Va. Sea Service, Nancy,

BAYLEY (continued)
R384
Roger (See David CLARK), Mass., R388
BAYLEY/BAILEY, Samuel, Mass., served until 1785, Elizabeth, W14250
Shuball, Mass., Hannah, W14255
Solomon, N.H., S6618
Thomas, Mass., BLWt.126-200-Lt. iss. 4/16/1792. No papers
Thomas, Navy, Mass. Agency & residence. S33992
Timothy, N.H., Zeruiah, W4127
William, Va., Nancy, W5778
Zadock, Va., S37696; BLWt. 1252-100
BAYLIE, John, Pa., S2060
BAYLIES, Hodijah, Major, Mass., BLWt.96-400 iss. 2/16/1795
BAYLIS, Elias, N.Y., See BAYLES
Elias, Pvt., N.Y., BLWt.6853 iss. 3/7/1792 to B.V. Benthuysen, ass.
Henry, Va., BLWt.491-150
Nehemiah, Cont., N.Y., Rebecca, W4878
William, Pvt., Crane's Cont. Artillery, Mass., BLWt.3829 iss. 3/26/1792 to Francis Graves, ass.
William, Va., S12953
BAYLISS, John, Va., S39175
BAYLISS/BAYLESS, Sarah, former wid. of Wm. Dickson, S.C.,
BAYLOR, George, Cont. Va., Lucy Burwell, former wid., W5966; BLWt.114-500
George, Pa., S39955
Michael, N.J., S2368
Walker, Cont. Va., Dis. No papers
BAYLY/BAYLEY, Jeremiah, R.I., Roby Dorrance, former wid., W19191
Laban, Va. Sea Service, R.I., Va. half pay
Mountjoy, Md., S12094; BLWt. 685-300
BAYNE, John, Va., Sally, W9336; BLWt.26128-160-55
BAYNES, John, N.C., See BANE/BANES
BAYNTON, Jonathon, Mass., See BOYNTON
BAYSE, Richard, Va. See BASYE
BAYTOP, James, Va., S37701
John, Va., R19357; Va. half pay. See N.A. Acc. No.874-050009, John Baytop
BAZIL, Daniel, Pvt., Md., BLWt. 10961 iss. 8/14/1793 to Francis Sherrard, ass.
BAZWELL/BOZZELL, David, N.C., Va., Susan, R645
BAZZELL, John, Va., S37805
BEABOUT, Benjamin, N.J., R646
BEABOUT/BEBOUT, John, N.J., S2069
BEACH, Aaron, Mass., Vt., R648
Adna, Ct., Sarah, W1212; BLWt.16270-160-55
Amos, Pvt., N.Y., BLWt. 6813 iss. 10/10/1791 to Anthony

BEACH (continued)
Maxwell, ass.
Asa, Pvt., Ct., BLWt.5421 iss. 2/5/1790
Asa, Ct., S10362
Asa, N.J., S28638
Ashbel, Ct., S12173
Dan, Ct., Abigail, R649
Daniel, Ct., S12178
Daniel, Ct., Comfort, W17290
David, Cont. Ct., Anna, W15823; BLWt.146-200-Lt. Iss. 6/9/1790 to Ezekiel Moore, ass. No papers
David, Ct., Elizabeth, R650
Edmund, Ct., S10367
Elihu, Ct., Mercy, W4889
Elnathan, Ct., S12162
Ezekiel, Ct., Azubah, W4130
Francis, Ct., Mass. Sea Service, S15323
Israel/Isreal, Ct., S12160
Jabez, Ct., Parthenia, W17279
Jedediah, N.J., Mary, S10371
John, Ct., S12138
John, Ct., Rhoda, W23559
John, Ct., Green Mt. Boys, S12200
John, N.J., Sarah, W838
John H., Ct., Phebe, W18575
Jonathan, Ct., Martha, W5806; BLWt.26392-160-55
Joseph, Ct., Hannah Harrison, former wid., W23187
Julius, Ct., S12182
Lodowick B., Va., R706
Miles, Ct., Sarah, R653
Nathan, Pa., Margaret, W10294; BLWt.57754-160-55
Nathaniel, Pvt., Ct., BLWt.3311 iss. 9/20/1790
Nathaniel, Cont. Ct., Ruth, W21655
Obil/Obiel, Ct., S4264
Reuben, Pvt., Ct., BLWt.5490 iss. 3/20/1790
Reuben, Ct., S46336
Richard Bayse, Va., See BEECH
Robert, Cont. Ct., S16046
Roswell/Rosewell/Rosewill, Ct., S45315; BLWt.15412-160-55
Samuel, Cont., Green Mt. Boys, S38512; BLWt.79-200-Lt. iss. 6/18/1791. No papers
Samuel, Mass., S34005
Stephen, Ct., Vt., S28998
Stephen, Pvt., N.J., BLWts.8001 & 8156, iss. 5/19/1798
Thaddeus (or Mial Camp), Navy, Ct., S37741
Thomas, Ct. Sea Service, S14946
BEACKMAN/BLACKMAR, Holland, Vt., Jerusha Jepherson, former wid. W21459. Her 2nd husband was Jedediah Jepherson, a pensioner, which see
Michael, S.C., S35190
BEACROFT, John, Md., S34645
Lott, Pvt., Va., BLWt.11955 iss. 12/9/1793 to Francis Graves, ass.
BEADLE, Benjamin, Ct., Rhoda, W20705
BEADLES, Edmund, Va., S17842
Joel, Va., S17841
BEADUC, Elias, Pvt., N.J., BLWt.8122 iss. 4/21/1796
BEAGLE/BEEDLE, John, N.Y., Winche, W20699
BEAHAM, James, Pvt., Va., BLWt. 11895 iss. 4/6/1790
BEAIRCE, Levi, Mass., See BEARCE
BEAIRD, Henry, Cont., Pa., See BEARD
BEAKLEEY/BEAKLEY, Christopher, Cont. N.Y., Pa., S12147
BEAKNEY, James, Pa. See BLEAKNEY
BEAL, Azariah, Mass., S12206
Daniel, Cont. Mass., S37587
Daniel, Mass., Celia, W14297
David, Mass., Lydia, W14294
Jairus, Mass., Susannah, W23587
Job, Mass., Elizabeth, W21662
John, Mass., Lydia, W24648; BLWt.3665-100-Pvt., iss. 3/25/1790. No papers
John, Va., Julia, W4893; BLWt.8168-160-55
Joseph, Cont. Mass., S37588
Joseph, Cont. Mass., S39184
Joseph, Pvt., Mass., BLWt.3658 iss. 8/1/1789 to Thomas Cushing, ass.
Joseph, Mass., S15315
Joshua, Mass., S30268
Noah, Cont. Mass., S29629
Obadiah, Mass., Rebekah, W5216
Samuel, Mass., S29006
Sarah, former wid. of Joseph Boyington, which see, Mass.
Shadrach (of Benjamin Cooper), Va., S6596
Shadrach, Va., S6610
Thomas, Mass., S12161
William, Pvt., Va., BLWt.11946 iss. 11/14/1794
Zachariah, N.H., BLWt.1839-300
BEALE, Christopher, Md. See BEALL/BELL
Jonathan, Cont. Mass., S12155
Richard E., Va., Mary E., W1128; BLWt.17873-160-55
Robert, Va., Elizabeth, BLWt. 431-300; see BLWt.263-300
Robert, Va., BLWt.263-300-Capt. iss. 2/15/1794 to Robert Means, ass. No papers
William, Va., S37758
BEALL, Archibald, Va., Milly, W8353
Benjamin, Cont., See BEALS
Christopher, Md., S34649
Lawson, Md., Henrietta, W23575; BLWt.36517-160-55
Lloyd, Md., BLWt.234-300-Capt. iss. 8/13/1796. No papers
Nathaniel, Cont., Va., BLWt. 493-100
Ninian/Ning, Cont. Md., Christina, W9722
Robert, Va., See BEALE
Robert L. Md., S12164
Samuel B., Md., See BELL
Thomas, Md., S45270
William Dent, Md., BLWt.229-400-Maj. iss. 3/2/1795. No papers
BEALLE, Robert, Va. See BEALE
BEALOR, George, Cont., Va., S22640
Jacob, N.C., See BEELER
BEALS, Adam, Mass., S41434
Azariah, Mass., Bathsheba, W5811
Benjamin, Cont., Jane, W1700; BLWt.34522-160-55
Caleb, Mass., Sally, W14277
Caleb, Mass., Dorothy, W14293
Enoch, Mass., S38537
Henry, Pvt., Mass., BLWt.3666 iss. 2/7/1799 to John Duncan, ass.
Isaac, Mass., Lydia, W23553
Jonathan, Mass., S12174
Joshua, Cont. Mass., S34008
Uriah, Cont. Mass., S34019
BEAM, Anthony J., N.J., See BEEM
Conrad, Cont., Md., Jane, W25323; BLWt.175882-160-55
Frederick, Pvt. "in the Artillery Artificers of Pa", BLWt.12851 iss. 2/14/1791
Jacob, Pa., R12436
John, N.J., Sarah, W785
John, Pa., R658
Michael, Va., S2986
BEAM/BEAN, Peter, N.J., S951
BEAMAN, Caesar/Cesar, Ct., S39190
Gideon, Mass., Dolly, W18582
Jonas, Mass., Rebecca, W21659
Joseph, Cont. Mass., N.H., S38536
Josiah, Mass., S30266
Moses, Pa., S2970; BLWt.455-100
Nathaniel, Mass., Thankful, W17273
BEAMAS/BEAMIS, Levi, Mass., R661
BEAMON, Lemuel, Ct., S40741; BLWt.5449 iss. 9/20/1791 to Eleasor Curtiss
BEAMONT, Cesar/Caesar, Ct., See BEAMAN
BEAMONT/BEMENT, Deodate, Cont., Ct., S12334
BEAN, Benjamin, Cont., N.H., Susan, W21661
Benjamin, N.H., S22115
Conrad, Cont. Md., See BEAM
BEAN, Daniel, Cont., N.Y., S45522
Daniel, Md., See BENNETT/BENNING
Daniel, Mass., Margaret, W23571
Daniel, Mass., N.H., S12170
Daniel, Pa., Susannah, W8124; BLWt.67698-160-55
Ebenezer, Cont. Mass., S37581
Ebenezer, Cont., N.H., S38540
Ebenezer, N.H., S6619
Henry H., Md., R663
James, Pa., S22641
James, Va., S30264
Jeremiah, Mass., N.H., Lydia, W15580
Jesse, N.C., S8067
John, Cont. N.H., Martha Basford/Bassford, former wid., W5791; BLWt.19811-160-55. Her late husband, Benjamin Basford, pensioned, which see

BEAN (continued)
John, Md. Dis. No papers
John, N.H., S19358
John, Pvt., N.H., B.L. Rej. 234855-1855
John, Pvt., Va., BLWt.11901 iss. 9/2/1790
Jonathan, Mass., S37585
Jonathan, N.H., Mary Fullington former wid., R3843
Joseph, N.H., S45521
Josiah, N.H., Hannah Blossom, former wid., W24702
Josiah, N.H., Lois, W21650
Leonard, Md. Sea Service, S35189
Nathaniel, Mass., N.H., S44619
Nicholas, Cont. Pa., S32112
Peter, N.J., See BEAM
Phinehas/Phineas, N.H., R664
Richard, N.C., Chinea/Chena, W5813
Richard, Va., S14938
Samuel, Cont., Mass., S37584
Thomas, Ct. Sea Service, Mass., S21065
William, Mass., S28642
William, Mass., Privateer, Sarah, W15575
BEANS, William, Pa., S22117
BEAR, Catherine, former wid. of Lodowick Russell, N.Y., which see
Edward, Pvt., N.Y., BLWt.6869 iss. 9/15/1790 to Abraham Varrick, ass
Jacob, Cont. Pa., See BAER
John, N.J., Mary, R665
BEARCE, Andrew, Cont., N.H., BLWt.2376-100
Benjamin, Mass., S18711
Ebenezer, Cont. Mass., Lydia, W21652
Gideon, Mass., Sea Service, Lucy, W23566
BEARCE, Joseph, Ct., Cont., N.Y. Sea Service, R666
Levi, Cont., Mass., S37582
BEARD, Abijah, Cont. Ct., S28640
Andrew, Ct., Susan, W17288
Christopher, Pa., R667
David, Ct., S12204
Ebenezer, Mass., S17270
Francis, Pa., Va., S2978 (not identical with Francis Baird, W3210)
Frederick, Md., Magdalin, W3379
Henry, Cont., Pa., Elizabeth, R668
Jacob, Va., Rosana, W25224; BLWt. 24989-160-55
James, Va., R669
John, Pa., Indian War 1790-1792, Maty, W631; BLWt.29042-160-55
John, S.C., Mary, R670
Jonathan, Mass., Abigail, W23555; BLWt.36615-160-55
Moses, S.C., Elizabeth, W5818
Nathaniel, Mass., S39183
Olive, former wid. of Asa Laviston/Leaviston, Mass., W14273
Robert, Pa., Va., Sarah, W5217
Robert, Va., S1789
Samuel, Va., S2980
Samuel, Va., Mary, W4131

BEARD (continued)
William, Md., N.C., S2370
William, Md., Pa., R671
William, Mass., Elizabeth W12266; BLWt.3760-160-55
William, N.C., S2979
William, S.C., S2981
BEARDEN, John, S.C., S2991
Richard, S.C., R672
BEARDSEE, Moses, Cont., Ct., R675
BEARDSLEE, Aaron, Ct., Sally, W25237
Abijah, Ct., S17278
Abijah, Ct., b. 1750, d. 1789 Drusilla, W17289
Abijah, Ct., b. 1755, d. 1832 Elizabeth/Betsey B., W8133; BLWt.5475-100-Pvt. Iss. 7/2/1790 to Abijah Beardsley. No papers
Ichabod, Ct. See BEARDSLEY
John, Ct., Margaret, W17265
Joseph, Ct., S14939
Robert Chauncey, Ct., Huldah, W20710; BLWt.26687-160-55
Thaddeus, Ct., S14952
Thomas, Cont., Ct., S12142
BEARDSLEY, Abijah, Pvt., Ct., BLWts.5475 & 131-60-55 iss. 7/2/1790 to Abijah Beardsley
Abijah, Ct. See BEARDSLEE
Benjamin, Ct., Amelia, W24649
David, Ct., Huldah, W25238
Elijah, Ct., S45265
Gershom, Cont., Ct., S44622
Ichabod, Ct., S12995
James, Cont. Ct., Ruth, W1364; BLWt.15180-160-55
John, Ct. See BEARDSLEE
Josiah, Ct., S16631
Moses, Cont., Ct. See BEARDSEE
Salmon Wheeler, Ct., Abigail, W23585
Silas, Ct., Catharine Whitaker former wid., W3370
Whitmore, Ct., Dolly, W24650
William, Pvt., Ct., BLWt.5507 iss. 9/14/1792
William, Ct. See BARDSLEE
BEARES, Judah, Mass. See BEARSE
BEARMOR, Lewis, N.J., S949
BEARS, Foard, Cont., Mass., Rosanna, W4132
James, Service "Col. Warner" res. Ct. Dis. No papers
BEARSE, David, Mass., S30267
Judah, Mass., Rebecca, W14290
Prince, Mass., S29626
BEARSS, Joseph, Ct., S16632
BEARUP, Andrew, N.Y., Magdelene, W16188
John, N.Y., Caty, R676
BEARWART, John, N.Y., Barbara R677
BEASFLEY, Cornelius, Va. See BEAZLEY

BEASELEY (continued)
William, N.C., Elizabeth, W9352 BLWt.51879-160-55
BEASELY, William, N.C., S41432
BEASLEY, Benjamin, Va., Rachel W3757
Jacob, N.C., R680
John, Va., S37748
Smith, Va., S38567
William, N.C. See BEASELEY
William, Pvt., Pa., BLWt.8990 iss. 11/9/1792 to Mary Johnson, admx.
BEASLY, Isham, N.C., See BEESLEY
Leonard/Len, Va., S9276
William, Pvt., Pa., BLWt.8935 iss. 1/12/179- to Sarah Shepperd, ass.
BEASTON, William, N.J., S2985
BEATEMAN, William, Mass. See BEATMAN
BEATH, Archibald, Pvt., N.J., BLWt.8153 iss. 11/9/1791
BEATLEY, Isaac, Mass., S44617
BEATMAN, William, Mass., S44645
BEATTY, Alexander, N.Y., R682
Arthur, N.Y., Elizabeth, W20694
Daniel, N.J., S30851
David, N.C., Isabella, W4894
Erkuries, Pa., BLWt.206-200-Lt. iss. 10/17/1789. No papers
George, N.J., R20325
George, Va., Sarah, W2909. She married two brothers. George, her 1st husb., and John Beatty 2nd, was a Rev. War pensioner. See his claim within.
Henry, Md., Va., S19203
Henry, Pa., R684
James, N.J., Pa., S23540
James, N.C. See BEATY
James, Pa., Va., S2988
James, Pvt., Va., BLWt.11960 iss. 3/4/1796
John, Cont. Pa., Catharine/Kitty, W630; BLWt.5111-160-55
John, Pa., S22644
John, Pa., S39987
John, Pa., See BEATY
John, Va., See George Beatty, widow Sarah. His claim is in file W2909 of Sarah, widow
Joseph, Pa., S35188
Reading, Cont. Pa., Christina, W3126; BLWt.214-400 Surgeon, iss 9/12/1789. No papers
Robert, N.Y., See BEATY
Thomas, Lt., Md., BLWt.246-300 iss. 5/27/1796. No papers
Thomas, Pa., S39986
Walter, Pa., Mary, W5804

BEATTY (continued)
William, Md., BLWt.644-300
William, Pvt., Pa., BLWt. 9059 iss. 3/31/1800
BEATY, Alexander, N.Y., See BEATTY
Andrew, Va., S2989
David, N.C., See BEATTY
Edward, Pa., R683
Hugh, Pa., S2062
James, N.C., S2990
James, Pa., Catharine, W5802
John, N.Y., S9275
John, N.Y., S14937
John, Pa., BLWt.8961-100-Pvt., iss. 7/21/1793. No papers
John, Pa., Jane, W5803; BLWt. 33567-160-55
Joseph, N.Y., S10369
Robert, N.Y., R685
Samuel, Pa., S34646
Thomas, N.C., R686
Walter, Pa., Mary, W5804
William, N.Y., S12194
William, Va., S10357
BEAULIEU, Lewis, See De BEAULIEU
BEAUMONT
Dan, Ct., Lois, W20703
Isaiah, Cont. Ct., S9099
Oliver, Ct., Jane, W1361; BLWt. 2182-160-55
Samuel, Cont. Ct., S37736
William, Ct., BLWt.145-200-Lt., iss. 9/24/1790 to Peleg Sanford, ass. No papers
BEAVEN/BEVEN, Charles, Md., S36414
BEAVER, Adam, Pa., See BIEBER
Benjamin, Pa., S39990
Edward, Pvt. Lamb's Artillery N.Y., BLWt.6884 iss. 10/5/1790
George, Pa., S39985
Jeremiah, N.C., S6603
John, Pa., R20315
John, Pa., See BEEBER
Martin, Md., W34647
Obadiah, Va., See BABER
BEAVERS
John, Va., S30853
Robert, N.J., Catharine, W3756; BLWt.32237-160-55
Samuel, Va., Jane, W4887; BLWt. 29048-160-55
BEAVETT/BEAVERT, John, N.C., Rachel, R688
BEAVOR, Benjamin, Pvt., Pa., BLWt.9000 iss. 11/25/1793 to Casper Iserloan, ass.
Edward, Cont., N.Y., See BAVOR
BEAXTER, Andrew, N.C., See BAXTER
BEAZELEY/BEAZLEY/BEAZELY, James, Va., Mary, W5044
BEAZLE, Leonard/Len, Va. See BEASLY
BEAZLEY, Cornelius, Cont., Va., S34648
Cornelius, Va., R678
Ephraim, Va., S6597
James, Va., See BEAZELEY
BEBEE, Bonarjus, Pvt., N.Y., BLWt.6803 iss. 9/14/1792 to

BEBEE (continued)
Joseph Emerson, ass.
David, Ct., See BEEBE
(or BEEBEE), James, Ct., Mehitable, W10408
Joel, Pvt., Ct., BLWt.5482 iss. 10/26/1789
Samuel, Cont. Mass., S8069
BEBOUT, Daniel, N.J., R689
BEBOUT/BEABOUT, John, N.J., S2069
BECANNON, Philip, French; also War of 1812-N.Y. Mil. R690; BLWt.83890-40-50. Papers in War of 1812 file. N.Y. res. of widow in 1852.
BECHER/BEECHER, John, Cont. Pa., S39982
BECHTEL/BECKTEL, Borick, Pa., S23542
Philip, Md., Pa., S22637
BECK, Andrew, N.C., S14936
George, Pa., Agnes, R691
Jeffrey/Jeoffrey, N.C., S21067
Jesse, Va., Ann, W5805
John, N.C., S8060
John, Va., Rebekah, W3755; BLWt.275-200 Lt., iss. 6/3/1791. No papers
John, Va., Sarah, R692
Jonathan, Mass., N.H., Mary, W15573
Thomas, Md., Ann/Nancy, W8354
Thomas, Navy, N.H., S45524
William, N.C., S2376
BECKCOM, Solomon, Ga. See BECKHAM
BECKENBAUGH/BACKENBAUGH, Catharine W4122; BLWt.27681-160-55
BECKER, Abraham, N.Y., S12994
Barent/Barnet, N.Y., S12193, N.A. Acc. No. 874-050010-Half pay Barent Becker
(or BECKES/BACCHUS), Benjamin Cont., Pa., R695
David D., N.Y., S28639
Henry, N.Y., S22643
Henry, Pa., Catharine, W3646
Jacob, N.Y., S12135
Jacob, N.Y., R693
John, N.Y., Sarah, W16837
John P., N.Y., S23536
John P., N.Y., Margaret, W16187
Martinus, N.Y., Jane, W2431; BLWt.26592-160-55
Philip, N.Y., S12191
William, N.Y., S12188
William, N.Y., S12190
BECKES, Benjamin, Cont. Pa., See BACCHUS
BECKET, Peter, Pvt., Del., BLWt. 10698 iss. 12/28/179- to Wm. Lane, ass.
BECKETT/BECKET, Humphrey, Md. Polly/Mary, W9726
Humphrey, Va., S2066
John, Pa., S15324
BECKEY, Magnus, Cont., Me. Res. in 1820. S37580
BECKFORD, Benjamin, See BICKFORD
Joseph, Mass., R696
BECKHAM, James, Va., S37746
BECKHAM/BECKCOM, Solomon, Ga., Susannah Stacy, R697

BECKHAM (continued)
William, Va., S37738
BECKLER, Daniel, Mass., Elizabeth, W23573
BECKLEY, Daniel, Ct., S12199
Henry, Pa., R20327
Richard, Cont., Ct. res. in 1818, S39188
Solomon, Ct., S31583
Zebedee, Cont. Ct., Elizabeth, W15579; BLWt.26807-160-55
BECKMAN, John R., Mass., N.H., S14940
BECKNEL, Thomas, N.C., S12985; BLWt.61274-160-55
BECKTEL, Berick/Borick, See BECHTEL
George, Cont. Va., S39979
BECKWITH, Abner, Ct., S12158
Amos, Cont. Ct., Susannah, W17299
Benjamin, Md., S2063
David, Cont., Mass., & 1812, S44350
George, Md., Ann/Leonah, W9355; BLWt.91507-160-55
Ichabod, Cont. Mass., S34023
Jesse, Ct., S16633
Job, Ct., S12168
John, Cont. Ct., S28643
Joseph, Ct., S9278
Joseph, Ct., N.Y., Esther, W17826
Lemuel, Ct., S12167
Nathan, Cont. Ct., S39189
Nehemiah, Md. Sea Service,S8062
Niles, Cont. N.H., Jemima, W16503
Phineas/Phinehas, Ct., S40745
Rice, N.Y., Vt., S15321
Roswell, Cont. Ct., S10358
Rufus, Vt., R698
Samuel, Ct., Cont., Sea Service, Polly Tinker, former wid. W25485
Seth, Ct., Esther, W25234
Silas, Ct., N.Y., S32115
Thomas, Ct. Sea Service, S12149
Timothy, Pvt., Ct., BLWt.5458 iss. 11/15/1791
Timothy, Cont., Ct., Lydia, W25226
William, Md., S2071, N.A. Acc. No. 874. See 050011 Half Pay, Wm. Beckwith
BECRAFT, Abraham, N.Y., S14951
BECRAFT, BENAFT, Francis, N.Y., S12192
BEDDLE, Benjamin, Pvt., N.J., BLWt.8121 iss. 6/11/1789 to Benjamin Bonnel, ass.
Moses, Pvt., N.J., BLWt.8118 iss. 2/25/1790 to John Ludlow, ass.
BEDDOW/BEDDO, Thomas, Md., Sarah, W5816
BEDEL, Joshua, N.H., S45523
BEDEL/BADEL, Moody, N.H., Mary, W9349; BLWt.13859-160-55
BEDELL, Abner, N.J., R699
David, Cont. Pa., S17839; BLWt. 1634-100
Isaac, N.J., S15322
BEDEN, Wesson, Mass., S34006
William, Cont. Ct., S44620
William, Corp. "in the Invalids", BLWt.12831 iss. 10/7/1789 to Benj. Tallmadge, ass.

BEDFORD, Stephen, N.J., S2372
BEDIENT, John, Ct., Betsey, W18576
Mordica/Moredcai, Ct., Polly, W9354; BLWt.42882-160-55
BEDINGER, Christopher, Cont. Pa., Mary, W18564
Daniel, Va., Sarah, W8138; BLWt. 2477-50 & BLWt.285-150 Ensign, iss. 8/25/1789. No papers
George Michael, Va., & Indian Wars. Henrietta, W2992
Henry, Va., S8059; BLWt.267-300 Capt. iss. 8/25/1789. No papers
Philip, Pvt., N.Y., BLWt.6833 iss. 1/4/1791
BEDKIN, Henry, Cont., BLWt.319-300-Capt. in Armand's Corp., iss. 10/10/1789. No papers
BEDLAM, William, Pvt. of Invalids, Mass., BLWts.3650 & 12840 iss. 5/12/1796 to Melancthon L. Woolsey, ass.
BEDLE, Francis, Pa., Va., S2375
BEDLO, William, See BEDLAM
BEDLOCK, Benjamin, Pvt., N.J., BLWt.8120 iss. 6/16/1789 to Thomas Coyle, ass.
BEDLON, Matthias, Mass., S19445
BEDSELL, John, See BETSELL/BETSILL
BEDUNAH/BEDUNO, Moses, Cont., Mass., N.H., S44618
BEDWELL, Robert, N.C., S16321
BEDWORTH, William, Pvt. "in the Invalids", BLWt.12827 iss. 12/8/1791 to Sarah Brickell, Executor
BEEBE, Alexander, Cont., Mass., Navy, Sarah, W23572
Allen, Mass., R701
Amon, Ct., Mass., S49302
Asa/Asahel, Cont. Ct., Annanell, W23576; BLWt.1751-100
Asa, Mass., S44613
Asahel/Asa, See Asa BEEBE
Constant, N.Y., S14942
Daniel, Ct., Jane, W21656
David, Ct., S16045
David, Ct., S40746
David, Mass., Esther, R12433
Elizabeth, former wid. of John Young, N.Y., which see
Ezekiel, Mass., S44614
Ezra, N.Y., Naomi, W14295; BLWt.6109-160-55
Gideon, Cont. Mass., S10359
Hopson, Ct., Mass., N.Y., S4262
Jeduthan, Sr., See Richard Jeduthan BEEBE
Joel, Ct., S40742; BLWt.5482-100 Pvt., iss. 10/26/1789. No papers
John, Mass., N.Y., R702
Joseph, Ct., S12997
Lemuel, Ct., S9097
Paul, Cont. Ct., Mary, W17274
Peter, Cont., Ct., Green Mt. Boys, S12157
Peter, N.H., S17843; BLWt.1365-100
Philo, N.Y., Sarah, W20698
Reuben, Ct., S22638
Richard, Ct., Nancy, W2053; BLWt.24608-160-55

BEEBE (continued)
Richard Jeduthan, Ct., Rachel, W5808; BLWt.26330-160-55
Roderick, N.Y., Anne, W16190
Roswell, N.Y., Sarah Frisbee former wid., W16997,3 Rev. ltrs.
Ruel, Ct., S12169
Seba, N.H., Vt., Sarah, W18590
Solomon, Cont. Mass., S38531
Stephen, Pvt., Mass., BLWt. 3731 iss. -/9/1790 to James F. Sebor, ass.
Thaddeus, Ct., Dis.-no papers.
Thomas, N.J., Elizabeth, R704
William, Ct., R705
BEEBE/BEEBEE, Zaccheus, Cont. Ct., S12196
BEEBEE/BEEBE, Comfort, Ct., Lydia, W17268
David, Ct., Sarah, W16838
James, Cont. Ct., Mehitabel, W10408
Joseph, Ct., S17257
BEEBER/BEAVER, John, Pa.,R687
BEECH, Asa, Cont. Ct., S35187
John, N.J., See BEACH
Lodowich B., Va., See BEACH
BEECH/BEACH, Richard Bayse, Va. Mary, R652
BEECHER, John, Cont. Pa., See BECHER
Jonathan, Ct., See BUCHER
Moses, Ct., Privateer, Dorcas R707
Nathan, Ct., N.Y., Lucy, W20707; BLWt.6390-160-55
Wheeler, Ct., S14943
BEEDEL, Thomas, N.H., See BEEDLE
BEEDLE, Henry, Mass., S29000
Jacob, Pvt., N.J., BLWt.8154 iss. 9/29/1790
John, Pvt., N.Y., BLWt.6824 iss. 9/25/1790 to D Hudson & Co., assignees
John, N.Y., See BEAGLE
BEEDLE/BEEDEL, Thomas, N.H., S21637
BEEDY, Rosiah, Pvt., N.H., BLWt. 2926-100 iss. 10/10/1796 to William Woodward; S39185
BEEK, Thomas, Pa., S2065
BEEKARTH, John Frederick, Cont. Pa., S39978
BEEKMAN, Barnard, S.C., BLWt. 301-500-Col., iss. 6/7/1796. No papers
Jerrick, N.Y., See Tjerck BEEKMAN
John, Sgt., N.Y., BLWt.6858 iss. 8/6/1790 to John Lansing, Jr., ass.
Samuel, S.C., Ann, W10410; BLWt. 307-200-Lt., iss. 5/10/1796 to John Stiles, ass. No papers
Tjerck, N.Y., Rachel, W17294; BLWt.161-200-Lt., iss. 10/2/ 1790. No papers
William, N.J., N.C., Sarah, W24644
BEEL, Henry, Mass., S44621
BEELER, George, See BEALER
BEELER/BEALOR, Jacob, N.C., S5277

BEEM/BEAM, Anthony, N.J., S950
BEEM, Daniel, S.C., R709
John, N.J., See BEAM
BEEMAN, Aaron, Mass., S20287
Daniel, Ct., Mass., Green Mt. Boys, Mary, W17295
Ebenezer, N.Y., S39989
Friend, Ct., S12140
Isaac, Ct., S6623
(or BEMAN, Jabez, Mass., BLWt.2118-100
John, Mass., Hannah, W23563
Josiah, N.J., Sarah, W5809
Matthias, Pvt., Ct., BLWt. 5441 iss. 4/15/1796 to Nathaniel Ruggles
Mathias/Matthias, Ct., N.Y., S37755
Samuel, N.Y., See BEMAN
Simon, N.Y., S12145
Tracy, Ct., Polly, W10404; BLWt.26663-160-55
Truman, Ct., N.Y., S23121
William, Ct., See BEMAN
BEEMAS/BEMIS, John, Cont., N.H. BLWt.1481-100
BEEMEN, Moses, Pa., See BEMAN
BEEMON, Lemuel, Ct., See BEAMON
BEEMONT/BEMENT, Benjamin, Ct., S12179
BEEMUS, John, Pvt., Mass., BLWt.3699 iss. 5/1/1792 to D. Quinton, ass.
BEEN, Daniel, Cont.N.Y., See BEAN
Henry, Pvt., Pa., BLWt.9019 iss. 6/29/1789 to M. McConnell, ass.
BEER, James, Pa., S2064
Robert, Pa., S12185
Thomas, Pa., Addy/Adda, W3647; BLWt.9079-160-55
BEEROP, John, N.Y., See BEARUP
BEERS, Daniel, Ct., S12132
David, Ct., S10365
David, Ct., Molly, W25212; BLWt.7055-160-55
Ezra, Ct., S12181
Fanton, Ct., S37750
Gershom, Ct., S18314
Isaac, Ct., S12198
Isaac, Ct., S39182
Jabez, Ct., S12171
James, See BEARS
James, Ct., Ruth, W25330; BLWt.26718-160-55
James, Cont. Ct., Rebecca, W25227; BLWt.81-100
Jerusha, former wid. of Squire Ambler, Cont., which see
Joel, Cont. Ct., Phebe Gardner, former wid., W19482; BLWt.3755-160-55
John, Pvt., Ct., BLWt.5485 iss. 3/10/1796 to Wm. Cogshell
John, Cont. Ct., S14949
Josiah, Ct., Sea Service, S12197
Lewis, Cont. Ct., S31547
Matthew, Ct., Phebe, W8355; BLWt.26317-160-55
Nathan, Ct., S12999
BEERS/BIERS, Nathan, Ct., S15335

BEERS (continued)
Nathan, Lt., Cont. Ct., Mary, W17269; BLWt.147-200 iss. 10/6/1789
Peleg, Pvt., Mass., BLWt.3698 iss. 6/20/1789
Phineas, Ct., S16635. Jerusha Beers, wid. of soldier, received pension as wid. of Squire Ambler, which see
Samuel, Ct., Mass., S17267, Ann Beers, wid. was pensioned as former wid. of Thomas Phillips, Ct., which see
Silas, Ct., S14935
Spencer, R.I., Lillis Wood, former widow, W26116
Zacheriah/Zacchariah, Ct., S4946
BEERWORTH, John, See BEARWART
BEESLEY/BEESLY, Isaac, Va., R710
BEESLEY/BUSLEY/BEASLY, Isham, N.C., S1943; BLWt.17854-160-55
William, N.C., See BEASELEY
BEESON, Edward, N.C., S12984
BEETAM, Jacob, See BEETEM/BEETUM
BEETEM, Adam, Pa., Va., S30270
BEETEM/BEETAM/BEETUM, Jacob, Pa., S2984 & S39976
BEETLEY, Isaac, Pvt., Mass., BLWt. 3782 iss. 8/16/1796
BEETTON, William, Cont. Mass., S39988
BEETUM, Jacob, Pa., See BEETEM
BEGEANT/BAGENT, John, Cont. Va. S37747
William, Cont. Va., S9098
BEGGS, Alexander, N.C., Pa., S32114
Moore, Sgt., Pa., BLWt.8977 iss. 4/6/1790
Moore, Pa., S36405
Thomas, Sgt., Pa., BLWt. 8927 iss. 7/16/1789
BEGLEY/BEGLY, Henry, Va., R711
John, Pvt., S.C., BLWt.11966 iss. 5/2/1794
BEHALL, Casper, Pvt., N.J., BLWt. 8134 iss. 6/16/1789 to Thomas Coyle, ass.
BEHNE, Peter, Pa., See BEHWEY
BEHNEY, Peter, Pa., See BEHWEY
BEHNY, Peter, See BEHWEY
BEHUE, Peter, See BEHWEY
BEHWEY, Peter/George Peter, Pa., Anna Maria, W2907
BEICKNELL/BEICHNELL, Thomas, N.C. Rachel, R12399
BEISS, Peter, N.Y., See BOYCE
BEKER/BICKER, Henry Jr., Pa., BLWt.104-300-Capt., iss. 5/12/1789. No papers
BELANGER, Julian, Cont. Canada, Margaret, W21654
BELCHER, Ann, former wid. of John Carraway, S.C., which see
Bartlet, Va., Alice, W2054
Elisha, Cont. Ct., Lydia, W9725
Jacob, Mass., S29625
Jonathan, Cont., Mass., Sarah, W23557
Joseph, Ct., BLWt.2113-100
Joseph, Mass., Hannah, W23558
Nathan, Ct., Lucy, W17281

BELCHER (continued)
Richard, Mass., S30861
Robert, Va., S39186
Samuel, Cont., Mass., S30273
Supply, Mass., Margaret, W23565
BELDEN, Azor, Ct., Hannah, W8356; BLWt.13737-160-55
Benjamin, Ct., Sylvia, W5819
Bildad, Cont., Ct., S40744
Charles, Ct., S10355
Daniel, Cont., Mass., S16047
David, Ct., R714
Ezekiel Porter, Cont., Ct., Mary, W17280
John, Corp., Ct., BLWt.5407 iss. 10/9/1789 to Esther Heacock, formerly Esther Belden, Admx.
John, Ct., S12137
Joshua, Ct., S15326
Lura, former wid. of Amos Woodruff, which see
Othniel, Cont. Ct., Sarah, W21660
Richard, Cont., Ct., BLWt. 5492-100 iss. 5/18/1790; S40740
Seth, Cont., Ct., Christian, W17266
BELDING, Abraham, Pvt., Ct., BLWt. 5500 iss. 6/26/1789 to James Percival
Abraham, Cont. Ct., Mary, W17285
John, Mass., S30269
Jonathan, Mass., S14950
Jonathan, Mass., S44616
Lura, former wid. of Amos Woodruff which see
Moses, N.H., BLWt.68-200
Othniel, Cont., Ct., See BELDEN
Richard, Corp., Ct., BLWt.5492 iss 5/18/1790 to Theodosius Fowler
Selah, Cont., Mass., Lydia, W1130
Simeon, Ct., BLWt.142-200-Lt. iss 9/1/1789. No papers
BELEW, Solomon, Va., Elinia, W8358
BELFIELD, John, Va., BLWt.254-400-Major. Iss. 12/11/1797. No papers
BELKNAP, Abel, Cont., Mass., S12150
Calvin, Vt., Bathshua/Bathsheba, W5215
Ebenezer, Cont., Mass., S12992
Ebenezer, Mass., Polly, W23580
Ezekiel, N.H., S6615
Francis, Ct., Vt., S31548
Isaac, Cont., N.Y., Susan, W25322
John, N.Y., S45168
John, N.Y., R716
Jonas, Cont., Mass., S36408
Josiah, Mass., S22118
Lois, Mass., former wid. of Eseck Chase, which see
Simeon, Ct., Miniam/Mirriam, R717; BLWt.40931-160-55
Thomas, N.Y., Naomi, W5817; BLWt. 32230-160-55
William, Cont., N.Y., S45167; BLWt 166-200-Lt. Iss. 1/31/1791 to Cornelius Roosa & Peter Curtenius Jr., assnes. No papers
BELL, Abraham/Abram, Ct., S12195
Andrew, Cont., Ct., S12993
Andrew, Pa., Elizabeth, R719

BELL (continued)
Arthur, Pa., S14945
Benjamin, Ct., S38538
Benjamin, N.C., Elizabeth, W3925
Benjamin, Pa., R718
Christopher, Md. See BEALL/BEALE
Daniel, Pvt., Mass., BLWt.3762 iss. 3/25/1790
Daniel, Mass., Hannah, W14299
Daniel, Mass., S15572
Daniel, Va., S30271
Flora, former wid. of Pomp Sherburne, N.H., which see
Frederick Mordaunt, Cont., N.H. Elizabeth Bennett, former wid., W15571; BLWt.738-300 & BLWt. 2269-300
Henry, Cont. Va., BLWt.623-200
Isaac, N.Y., Jemima, R722
Jacob, N.Y., Elizabeth, W17292
James, Ct., S37735
James, Cont., Pa., b.Md., res. N.J., S33257
James, Md., S6607
James, N.C., S2971
James, Pa., Mary, R723
James R., Del., Jane, W3329
Jesse, Ct., S22639
John, Cont., N.Y., S12189
John, Ga., N.C., S.C., S21068
John, Md., S39980
John, Md., Catharine, W9347
John, N.J., S22642
John, Pvt., Pa., BLWt.8971 iss. 7/31/1794
John, Pa., S235357
John, Pa., Margaret, W9348
John, Pa., Va., S22116
John, Va., S12986
John, Va., S16640
John, Va., S30272
John, Va., Dis. No papers
Jonathan, Ct., Agnes, W1362
Jonathan, N.H., S12172
Joseph, Pa., R722 1/2
Joseph, Va., S6608
Josiah, Pvt., N.J., BLWt.8119 iss. 6/11/1789 to Matthias Denman, ass.
Josiah, N.C., S41433
Lawson, Md., See BEALL
Matthew, Pvt., N.Y., BLWt. 6791 iss. 8/4/1790 to Henry Hart,ass.
Matthew, N.Y., Esther, W21658
Nathaniel, N.C., S.C., S32113
Nathaniel, Pa., R724
Ning, See Ninian BEALL
Oliver, Ct., Vt., S23123
Patterson/Paterson, Pa.,S22119
Phineas, Pvt., Armand's Corps, BLWt.12739 iss. 4/19/1796 to Thomas C. Drew, ass.
Phineas, Cont., N.J., Sarah, W20712
Richard, N.C., Candis, W25231; BLWt.28511-160-55
Richard, Va., S8064
Robert, Mass. Sea Service, Navy, Leathhead, S37609
Robert, N.C., BLWt.300-200-Lt. iss. 8/14/1792 to Isaac Cole, ass. No papers

BELL (continued)
Robert, Va., S8065
Samuel, Green Mt. Boys, N.H., Vt., S12146
Samuel, N.C., S6598
Samuel, S.C., Mary, W4892; BLWt.13743-160-55
Samuel, Va., Rebecca, W12267; BLWt.26094-160-55
Samuel B., Md., S37740; BLWt.690-200
Sarah, former wid. of Wm. McCord, Pa., which see
Stephen, Ct., S16636
Thaddeus, Ct., S17274
Thomas, N.C., alive in 1825; S2973
Thomas, N.C., d. in 1825; Jane, R720
Thomas, Va., S2972
Thomas, Va., War of 1812, Ky., S30859 & Old War Inv. File 6630 (1812)
Thomas, Va., R726
Thomas, Va., BLWt.256-300-Capt. Iss. 3/1/1796. No papers. This warrant located in U.S. Mil. Dist. Ohio. Report by phone from General Land Office 5/31/1934
Walter, Ct., Mass., S18712
William, N.H., S45272
William, N.C., Sarah, W446
William, S.C., R727
William, Va., S30855
William, Va., S42617
William M., N.H., BLWt.73-300-Capt. Iss. 7/1790. No papers
BELLAMY, Abner, Mass., S45273
Asa, Ct., S42086
Justus, Ct., S17838
Matthew, Ct., S23117
BELLANGER, Noel, Pvt., Hazen's Regt., BLWt.12765 iss. 1/22/1790 to Benj. Mooers, ass.
BELLAS, Martha, former wid. of Frederick Donkemoyer/Donkeymeyer, N.J., which see
BELLERIVE, Louis Baury de, See Baury DE BELLERIVE
BELLES, Andrew, N.J., W800
BELLESFELT, Peter, Pa., S16048
BELLEVILLE, Nicholas, Cont., French, Ann, R728
BELLINGER, Adam, N.Y., Lena G., W23583
Catharine, former wid. of Richard Marcus Petrie or Hondedrick M. which see
Christian, N.Y., S9277
Frederick, N.Y., S12991
John, N.Y., Ernestine Staring, former wid., W16424. Her first husb., John Meyers, also served in Rev. See papers within
John, N.Y., R730
Julian, Pvt., Hazen's Regt., BLWt.12763 iss. 1/22/1790 to Benjamin Mooers, ass.
Peter P., N.Y., R731 & R732
William, N.Y., S28641
BELLINGTON, Isaac, See BILLINGTON

BELLIS, Andrew, See BELLES
John, N.J., Nellie, R733
BELLNAP, Isaac, See BELKNAP
BELLOS/BELLIS, Adam, N.J., S955
BELLOWS, Charles, Cont., Mass., S22114
Elihu, Cont. Mass., Sarah, W14296; BLWt.488-100
Ezra, Mass., S19205
Isaac, Ct., Mary, W18591 & R739; BLWt.2354-160-55
Isaac, Mass., Dis.--No papers
John, N.Y., S45271
Samuel, Sgt., Sheldon's Dragoons Ct., BLWt.5528 iss. 5/24/1790
Stephen, Mass., Lydia, W23577; BLWt.12738-160-55
Thomas, Ct., N.Y., Vt., Delia, W17284
Timothy, Cont., Mass., S34020
BELMAN, DeWalt, Pa., See BILLMAN
BELNAP/BELKNAP, Calvin, Ct., Bathshua/Bathsheba, W5215
Jesse, Cont., Ct., S2068
BELOTE/BELOTTE, Jonas, Va., S21066; BLWt.30912-160-55
BELSER, Christian, S.C., Mary/Maria, W21651
BELT, John Sprigg, Capt., Md., BLWt.232-300 iss. 5/12/1795; S34644
BELTON, Thomas, N.J., S952
BELTZ/BETTZ, Henry, Cont. Pa., R735
BELUE, Frederick, N.J., R20134
BELVILLE/BELVELL, Samuel, Del., S15317
BELVIN, Aaron, Va., S37759
BEMAN, See BEEMAN, Jabez, Mass.
Moses, Pa., See BEAMAN
Nathan, Cont., Green Mt. Boys, S45266
Samuel, Green Mt. Boys, N.Y., S12152
Simon, N.Y., See BEEMAN
William, Ct., S32111
BEMENSDERFER, John, Pa., Elizabeth, R736
BEMENT/BEEMONT, Benjamin, Ct., S12179
Consider, Mass., S12131
Deodate, See BEAMONT
Ebenezer, Mass., Dis.-No papers
John, Mass., S4943
Phinehas, Mass., S29624
BEMIES/BEMIS, Henry, Mass., N.H., Susanna, W15574
BEMIS, Amasa, Mass., Nancy, W1363; BLWt.36511-160-55
Amos, Mass., Lydia, W23589
Daniel, Cont., Mass., S34004
Daniel, Mass., Martha, W23581
Daniel, Mass., Anne/Ann, W23578; BLWt.11264-160-55
Henry, See BEMIES
Isaac, Cont. Mass., Mary, W20695
Jacob, Mass., S37578
James, Cont. Mass., Lois, W18585
Jeduthan, Cont., Mass., Statira, W17283
Jesse, Mass., Hannah, W23556
John, Cont., Mass., S34013
John, Cont., N.H.; BLWt.1481-100;

BEMIS (continued)
Pension Ctf. 775
John, Mass., Lucy, W23552
John, Mass., Vt., S18312
Jonas, Cont., Mass., Mary, W14279
Jonas, Mass., S34014
Joseph, Mass., Vt., Jemima,W20713
Joshua, Mass., S38535
Josiah, Cont., Mass., Joanna, W18581
Levi, Vt., S32116
Marcy, former wid. of Buckminster White, Mass., which see
Phinehas, Mass., Sarah, W14278, 1775 Journal
Thaddeus, Mass., S35783
BEMISS, Edmund, Cont., Mass., Abigail, R737 and 738
Jonas, Pvt., Mass., BLWt.3735 iss. 2/14/1793
Jonas, N.Y., S18310
Jotham, Corp., R.I., BLWt.2953 iss. 6/15/1789 to Jotham Bemus
BEMUS, Jotham, R.I., Asenath,W8357
BENAFT, Francis, See BECRAFT
BENBROOK/BAINBROOK, Ezekiel, N.C., R397
BENCHLEY/BENCHLY, Arnold, R.I., Betsey, W21653
David, R.I., Abigail, W2430; BLWt.7088-160-55
Joseph, R.I., S12165
BENDER, Daniel, N.C., Ferriba, W889
George, Cont., Mass., S34024
Jacob, Pa., Elizabeth, R739
John, Pa., Margaret, W15581
Lewis, Pa., S39970
BENEDICT, Aaron, Ct., S12133
Aaron, Mass., R740
Abraham, Ct., S10363
Ambro/Ambros/Ambrose, N.Y., S45274
Ambrose, Pvt., N.Y., BLWt.6814 iss. 6/21/1791
Amos, Ct., Mass., Mary, W23568
Benjamin, N.Y., Elizabeth, W16502
Caleb, N.Y., R12435
Daniel, Cont.,res. of heir N.Y., BLWt.714-100
Darius, Ct., S37744
Ebenezer, Ct., S12202
Eleazor, Pvt., Ct., BLWts.5409 & 13947 iss. 12/9/1789 to John Benedict, Admr.
Elias, N.Y., R741
Elisha, Ct., N.Y., S12183
Ezra, Ct., S12144
Gamaliel, Ct., S12983
George, Pvt. "in Proctor's Artillery," Pa., BLWt.9056 iss. 7/9/1789
George, Pa., Susannah, W3331
Isaac, Ct., S17276
Isaac, Mass., N.Y., S12156
James, Ct., S17273
James, Mass., N.Y., Sarah, R742
John, Ct., Cont., Chloe, W23599
John, Ct., Reumah, W17287
Jonah, Ct., Elizabeth, W18587
Jonathan, Ct., Huldah, W23579; BLWt.26709-160-55
Joseph, N.Y., S23535
Joshua, Ct., S23116

BENEDICT (continued)
Levi, Cont. Ct., Elizabeth, W18589
Levi, Pvt., Sheldon's Dragoons,Ct. BLWt.5536 iss. 6/1/1792
Micajah, Mass., N.Y., S12159
Nathaniel, Ct., S17272
Nimrod, Ct., S15316
Noah, Ct., S12987
Noble, Ct., BLWt.1256-300 iss. 9/11/1827
Peter, N.Y., Susannah, W17271
Samuel, Ct., S6625
Thomas, Ct., S21064
Thomas, Mass., S16630
Timothy, N.Y., Phebe, W24655
William, Ct., Ruth, W18578
BENEGER, George, See BENIGER
BENGE, David, N.C., S38530
Obadiah M., N.C., Sarah, R743
BENHAM
Ebenezer, Ct., Elizabeth, W25230
Elihu, Ct., S15748
Isaac, Ct., Cont., S15320
James, Ct., S45247
Jared, Ct., Elizabeth, W17267
John, Ct., Elizabeth, W16836
Joseph, Ct., S17268
Lemuel, Ct., Margaret, W21666
Lyman, Ct., Lois, W25325
Samuel, Ct., S45269
Silas, Ct., BLWt.1295-200
Thomas, Ct., S8068
BENHAM/BONHAM, Zedekiah, N.J., Prudence, W3215; BLWt.56510-160-55
BENIGER/BENEGER/BINEGER, George, Va., R744
BENINGFIELD, Henry, Va., S36413
BENJAMIN, Aaron, Ct., Dorothy, W25223; BLWt.149-200-Lt. Iss. 5/16/1796. No papers
Asa, Ct., S12207
Asa, Ct., Mary, W23586; BLWt. 9489-160-55
Asa, Cont., Mass., Polly, W5797
Barzilla, Cont. Ct., Mass., Mary, W17291
Daniel, Cont., N.Y., S34026
Daniel, Cont., N.Y., Sarah Rice, former wid., W20023
Daniel, Mass., Jane Hutchinson, former wid., W23386. Her other husb., Ephraim Hutchinson, Mass. also served. See papers within
Darius, N.Y., S23122
Ebenezer, N.Y., S12151
James, Ct., Mary Crompton, former widow, W20935
Jesse, Pvt., Ct., BLWt.5417 iss. 5/22/1793 to Ebenezer Farnham
Jesse, Ct., S45275
Joel L., Mass., S29002
John, N.Y. res. Sarah, pensioned as former wid. of Aaron Osborn, N.Y., which see
Jonas, Mass., Polly, W8135; BLWt. 3819-160-55
Jonathan, Mass., S12134
Jonathan, Mass., R746
Jonathan, Pa., S18311
Joseph, Cont., Va., S34643
Josiah, N.Y., R747

BENJAMIN (continued)
Judah, Cont., N.H., & N.Y., S39981
Lucinda, former wid. of Elijah Lawrence, Vt., which see
Phinehas/Phineas, Ct., S45259
Roger, Mass., Elizabeth, R745
Salah B., Mass., S45261
Samuel, Ct., S31546
Samuel, Cont., Mass., Tabitha, W23562; BLWt.112-200-Lt. iss. 4/4/1796. No papers
Samuel, Pvt., N.Y., BLWt.6776 iss. 1/25/1791 to John Hathorn, ass.
Samuel, N.Y., S45260
Sarah, former wid. of Joseph Conklin/Conckling, N.Y., which see
William, Mass., Bulah, W17293
BENNATT, Richard, Va., S6632
BENNER, Christopher, Cont., Mass., S37586
Peter, Mass., Abigail, W23597; BLWt.3675-100-Pvt. Iss. 2/22/1792 to John Peck, ass. No papers. Name spelled "Bennor"
BENNET, Aaron, Ct., R748
Aaron, Pvt., N.J., BLWt.8158 iss. 6/14/1791
Abraham, N.J., S953
Archibald, Pa., R749
Benjamin, Ct., Mercy, W10405
Benjamin, Del., S39969
Brister, Mass., Patience, W24654
Charles, Pvt., N.Y., BLWt.6835 iss. 7/30/1790 to John W. Wendell, ass.
Charles, N.Y., S45248
Cromwell, Ct., Cont., R751
Daniel, N.C., S.C., R752
David, Mass., S10361
Deliverance, Mass., S34021
Ebenezer, N.Y., S12163
Elias, Ct., Lydia, W2908
Elijah, Ct., Cont., Rebecca, W20701
Ezekiel, Cont. Ct., S45253
Frederick, Pvt., Md., BLWt.10963 iss. 5/6/1794
Godfrey, R.I., S21642
Henry, Pvt., N.Y., BLWt.6836 iss. 2/10/1792 to ---. Ctf. 8/15/1814
Henry, N.Y., Harriet, W18585
Henry, R.I., Mahetable/Mehitebell R770
Isaac, N.J., S474
Jacob, Pvt., N.Y., BLWt.6769 iss. 11/11/1791 to Samuel Broome, ass.
Jacob, N.Y., S45250
Jacob, Pa., R758
James, Ct., N.Y., Catharine, W16191; BLWt.150-200-Lt. Iss. 4/9/1791. No papers
James, Navy, R.I., Patience, W17296
Jeremiah, Mass., S14944
Jeremiah, Pvt., N.Y., BLWt.6770 iss. 8/26/1790 to Joseph Wright, ass.
Jesse, Ct., Temperance, W17263
Jesse, Ct., N.Y., S12184
John, Ct., S23119

BENNET (continued)
John, N.J., Pa., S5274
John L., N.J., S954
Joseph, N.H., Sea Service, Mary R767
Joseph, Pvt., N.Y., BLWt.6881 iss. 4/26/1791
Joshua, Ct., Esther, W17298
Matthew, R.I., S45254
Miles, Ct., S12166
Nathan, Ct., S45258
Nathan, Cont., N.Y., Mary M./May M., W9353; BLWt.26267-160-55
Nathan, R.I., Mary, W14281
Oliver, Ct., Pa., Catharine, W4886
Roland/Rowland, Mass., BLWt. 3766 iss. 1797
Rufus, Pvt., Ct., BLWt.5418 iss. to Gentleman who came with Wm. A. Bradley, 3/25/1818
Rufus, Ct., Martha, W3378
Samuel, Ct., S10368
Samuel, Ct., Dis. No papers
Samuel, Ct., See BANNET
Samuel, Cont. Mass., Mary, W23567
Samuel, Cont., R.I., S23124
Samuel, Mass., Vt., S18306
Sarah, former wid. of Samuel Townsend, N.Y., which see
Stephen, Ct., Mary, W2906
Stephen, Ct., Cont., S37760
Stephen, Mass., S34025
Terrence, Pvt., Mass., BLWt.3788 iss. 7/28/1791
Thaddeus, Ct., Martha, W17278
Timothy, Sgt., N.Y., BLWt.6793 iss. 7/16/1790 to Philip Van Cortlandt
William, Ct., S23538
William, R.I., S37743
BENNETT, Aaron, Ct., See BENNITT
Aaron, N.J., S597
Abraham/Abram, N.Y., See BENNITT
Amos/Ames, Ct. Cont., Wealthy, W3377; BLWt.21812-160-55
Andrew, Mass., S36910; BLWt.803-100
Andrew, R.I., Phebe, W18593
Asher, R.I., Mary, W14283
Barnes, N.J., Caty, W18592
Benjamin, Pvt., Ct., BLWt.5400 iss. 5/8/1792 to Amos Muzzey
Benjamin, Ct., S12187
Benjamin, Ct., S22645
Benjamin, Ct., S38529. Betty, his wid. pensioned as former wid. of Walcott Patchen/Patchin, Ct.
Benjamin, Cont., Mass., Elizabeth, W14288
Benjamin, Pa., S12175
Benajah/Bennajah, Mass., S45251
Bettey, former wid. of Wolcott Patchen, which see
Caleb, Ct., Freelove, W18579
Caleb, Vt., Elizabeth, W24645
Caleb P., Del., S35779; BLWt. 227-200-Lt. Iss. 5/30/1789. No papers
Charles, N.C., S21641

BENNETT/BENNITT/BENNET (cont'd)
Daniel, Ct., S37734
Daniel, Ct., Navy, R.I., Delight, W24635
Daniel, Md., S37752
David, Ct., S12201
David, Mass., Martha, W23594
David, N.J., Mary, R769
David, N.Y., Temperance, W5801; BLWt.36612-160-55
David, R.I., Mary, W25364
Ebenezer, Ct., S23118
Ebenezer, Ct., R753
Ebenezer, Mass., Elizabeth King, former wid., R5941
Ebenezer, N.H., Privateer. Sarah, W21665
Eleazer, N.H., S12771
Elias, Pvt., Ct., BLWt.5412 iss. 9/24/1790 to Peleg Sanford
Elias, Ct., See BENNITT
Elisha, Navy, N.Y. res. & agency S45257
Elizabeth, former wid. of Frederick Mordaunt Bell, Cont. N.H., which see
Elizabeth, former wid. of Jos. Barrett, S.C., which see
Ephraim, N.Y., See BENNITT
Eunice, former wid. of Nathaniel Shattuck, Mass., which see
Francis, Mass., Caturah, BLWt. 3968-160-55
George, S.C., R755
Gershom, N.J., N.Y., R756
BENNETT/BENNELL, Hezekiah, R.I., S21638
BENNETT/BENNITT/BENNET
Isaac, Ct., S45249
Isaac, Mass., Abigail, W23595; BLWt.31445-160-55
Isaac, Mass., Catharine, R750
Jabez, Ct., Abigail, W25328
James, Cont., Mass., Mary, W23596
James, Cont. Pa., BLWt.2459-100
James, Sgt. Major, Pa., BLWt. 9035 iss. 4/6/1790
Jedediah, Mass., S45256
Jeremiah, Ct., N.Y., Lois, W23591
Jeremiah, N.J., S45255
Jeremiah, N.Y., Elizabeth, W23590; BLWt.19535-160-55
Jesse, Md., R759
John, Ct., R.I., S23541
John, Cont. Ct., S45252
John, Pvt., Md., BLWt.11012 iss. 5/11/1790
John, Mass., S23115
John, Mass., Sarah, W25324
John, N.J., S37751
John, N.C., R760
John, Pvt., Va., Lee's Legion, BLWts.11898 & 12855 iss. 2/17/1792
Jonas, R.I., S38534
Jordan, Va., Nancy, W2713; BLWt. 31446-160-55
Joseph, Ct., S37742
Joseph, Ct., N.Y., Vt., S21639
Joseph, Cont., Mass., Mary,W15582
Joseph, Mass., S29001

BENNETT/BENNET/BENNITT (continued)
Joseph, Mass., Susannah, W18580, BLWt.26192-160-55
Joseph, N.J., Jane, W2746; BLWt.2302-100
Joseph, R.I., S15318
Joseph, R.I., Esther, W8359; BLWt.26044-160-55
Joseph, R.I., Mary, W20702
Joseph, Va., S1495
Joseph D., R.I., Elizabeth, W25228; BLWt.26710-160-55
Josiah, Ct., S12136
Micajah, R.I., Polly, W23560
Moses, Cont., Mass., S37577
Nathan, Mass., S15325
Peter, N.C., Elizabeth, R754
Phineas, Mass., Hannah, W23569
Reuben, N.C., S18714
Richard, Va., See BENNATT
Richard, Va., S36412
Richard, Va., Margaret, W9350; BLWt.73540-160-55
Roland, Pvt., Mass., BLWt.3766 iss. 8/18/1797 to Simeon Wyman, ass.
Roland, Cont., Mass., S34016
Samuel, Ct., R21769
Samuel, Cont., N.J., S34017
Solomon, N.C., R771
Stephen, Ct., Hannah, W25236
Stephen, Cont., Mass., S41430
Stephen, R.I., S38532
Thomas, Ct., S12143
Thomas, Mass. Sea Service, S12154, see Na Acc. No.874 not half pay
Timothy, N.Y., Martha, W23593
William, Ct., Elizabeth, W25235; BLWt.26061-160-55
William, Mass., Sally, W21663
William, Mass., N.H., S30854
William, N.Y., S5276
William, R.I., BLWt.1590-100
William, Vt., S18307
William, Va., Mary, R768
William (?), son's res. Pittsylvania Co., Va. in 1854. R772
William, Va. Sea Service, R8; Va. half pay
Wolcott, Ct., Joanna, W17264
BENNEVILLE, Daniel, Va., See DE BENNEVILLE
BENNING, Daniel, Md. See BENNETT
BENNINGTON, Job, Cont. Pa., S37753
BENNIT, Josiah, Ct., S12136
BENNITT/BENNETT, Aaron, Ct., S19206
Abram/Abraham, N.Y., S2987
Elias, Ct., S15319
Ephraim, N.Y., S23120
Gershom, N.J., N.Y., R756
Isaac, Ct., S45249
Stephen, Ct., Hannah, W25236
BENNOR, Peter, Pvt., Mass., BLWt.3675 iss. 2/22/1792 to John Peck, ass.
BENOIST, Francis, S.C., R773
BENSELL, George, Pa., Mary, R774

BENSINGER, Daniel, Pa., S22646
BENSLEY/BENCHLEY, David,R.I., Abigail, W2430; BLWt.7088-160-55
BENSON, Abel, Mass., Rhoda, W23574
Asa, Mass., S17269
Barak, Cont. Mass., Sarah, W25329
Charles, R.I., Barsheba, R775
Danson/Daniel, Mass., Phebe, W4891; BLWt.9448-160-55
Elevin, See Levin
Enoch, Va., S31549
Francis, Cont., Mass. Sea Service S34018
Henry, Va.?, Nancy, R779
Ichabod, Cont., Mass., Abigail, W23554
Isaac, Mass., S34022
James, Pa., R778
Jeptha, Mass., Mary, W25332; BLWt.36508-160-55
Joel, N.Y., S23539
John, Cont. Mass., N.Y., S45264
John, Pvt., Del., BLWt.10702 iss. 4/19/179- to Eliz. Benson adminx.
John, Mass., S39971
John, N.C., S8061
John, Pa., Elizabeth, W18584
Jonah, Mass., S4942
Joseph, Md., S12989; BLWt.46942-160-55
Joshua, Mass., BLWt.106-300-Capt. No date of issue. No papers
Levin/Elevin, Del., Rebecca, W329
Levin, Va., Jane, R777
Matthew, N.Y., Johannah, W18577; BLWt.26600-160-55
Perry, Md., S10087; BLWt.236-300-Capt. iss. 5/25/1789 to Perry Benson. No papers
Peter, Mass., S16044
Reuben, Cont. Pa., N.C. res. in 1828. S41435; BLWt.1045-100
Robert, Mass., Dorothy, R776
Robert, N.Y., Dinah, W20708
Seth, Mass., Lydia, W18586
Spencer, Del., S1496
Thomas, N.H. res. Susannah, R---
Thomas, N.C., S8066
William, Va., Sarah, W5218
BENSTEAD, Alexander, Pa., BLWt. 212-200-Lt. Iss. 7/16/1789 to Matthew McConnell. No papers
BENT, Joel, Mass., Mary, W14282
Nathan, Cont. Mass., S45589
Prince, Pvt., R.I., BLWt.2983 iss. 11/4/1794
Prince, R.I., S38541
Silas, Mass., R781
William, Mass., Abigail, R780
BENTALOU, Paul, Cont. BLWt.321-300-Capt. in Pulaski legion. Iss. 6/8/1789. No papers
BENTEY/BEUTEY/BENTY, Francis, French, Ohio res. 1832, R789
BENTHAM, Peregrine, See BANTHAM
BENTHEUSEN/BENTHISEN, William, N.Y. See VAN BENTHUYSEN
BENTLEY, Azel, Ct., S29007
Benjamin, N.Y., Lydia, W20696
Caleb, N.Y., Mary, W16184
Charles, Ct., Cont. Hannah,W14298

BENTLEY (continued)
Efford, Va., S16637
Elisha, Ct., Mass., R.I., R783
(or BENTLY), Ezekiel, R.I., Anna, W10407
George, Ct., Lucy, W17272
George, N.Y., S45263
Gideon, Privateer, R.I., S12177; BLWt.26166-160-55
Henry, Pvt., Pa., BLWt.8925 iss. 7/9/1789
Henry, Pa., S39977
James, Vt., S12153
Jeremiah, Va., S3919
Jesse, Ga., Mary Scott, R785
John, Ct., S45262
John, N.C., R784
John, Pvt., Pa., BLWt.8951 iss. 3/10/1790
William, Pvt., Ct., BLWt.5474 iss. 1/24/1792 to Stephen Thorne
William, Mass., Diana/Drama, W217 BLWt.79534-160-55. She also applied for B.L. for service of former husb., Joseph Paddock, War of 1812, which not allowed. See papers within. B.L. Reg. 102443-55
William, N.Y., S12141
William, Va., S37745; BLWt.266-300-Capt. Iss. 12/12/1794. No papers. Va. half pay.
BENTLY, Thomas, N.C., S8063
BENTON, Abijah, N.H., S45588
Adoniram, Ct., Cont., Betsey, W1360; BLWt.19808-160-55
Bethel, Mass., S12176
Chandler, Ct., BLWt.2430-100
David, Mass., Privateer, Pa., Thankful, W9351; BLWt.67516-160-55
David, N.C., S39195
Elijah, Pvt., Ct., BLWt.5533 iss. 10/14/1796
Elijah/Elisha, Ct., Cont., Sarah, R787
Elkanah, N.C., S41429
Felix, Mass., Tamer, W15577
Jacob, Ct., Sarah, W17276
James, N.C., R786
Job, N.C., S6613
Joel, Ct., Vt., Elizabeth, W20711
John, (?) N.C. Res.; Dis. No papers
Jonas, Cont., Mass., S34012
Jonathan, Ct., S20004
Jonathan, Mass., S29627
Joseph, N.C., S31551
Nathaniel W., Ct., Susannah, W16186
Noah, Ct., Phebe, W18574; BLWt.29037-160-55
Samuel, Ct., Mass., Mary, W5807
Selah, Ct., BLWt.137-300-Capt. iss. 11/19/1792. No papers
Zadock, Ct., Lydia, W3926
Zebulon, Ct., Cont., S34007
BENTSCHOTEN, Ignus, See VAN BENSCHOTEN
BENTY, Francis, See BENTEY

BERCE, Josiah, Ct., Freelove R489
BERCH, William, N.C., Elizabeth, R788
BERDAN, Isaac, N.J., Christiana W518
BERDEEN, Timothy, See BURDEEN
BEREGSON, Joseph, Pvt., Hazen's Regt., BLWt.12796 iss. 2/25/1793 to Benj. Moore, ass.
William, Pvt., Hazen's Regt., BLWt.12798 iss. 2/25/1793 to Benj. Moore, ass.
BEREMAN, Thomas, N.J., S16322
BERGAMYER, Daniel, See BERGMEYER
BERGEN, Christopher, N.J., S10356
BERGERHOFF, Nicholas, Cont., Pa., S42087
William, Cont., Pa., S39967
BERGH, Abraham, N.Y., Lena, W17282
Philip, N.Y., S28999
BERGIN, John, N.H., S45591
BERGMEYER, Daniel, Cont. Pa., Christiana, W1699; BLWt.3983-160-55
BERIS, James, See BIERCE
BERKHAMMER, Henry, Pa., R21768
BERKLEY, George, Va., Sarah, W8130
John, Va., S12990
Robert, N.H., Rhoda, W15578
William, Va., S12964
BERKMIRE, Daniel, See BERGMEYER
BERKSHIRE, Maria, Va., Joshua Prewett, former husband which see
BERLIN, Isaac, Cont. Pa., Maria, W4638; BLWt.55-60-55 & 9027-100
Jacob, Pa., S6624
BERNARD, Benjamin, Va. See BARNARD
John, Cont. Pa., Elizabeth, W3208
Phares, Ct., Huldah, W25229
Thomas, Va., Mary, W5815
Walter, Va., S6634
BERNER, Joseph, N.Y., S12998
BERNETT, John, N.Y., See BARNET
BERNHARDT, George, See BARNHART
BERNHART, Daniel, Pa., S39972; BLWt.2066-100
Henry/John Henry, See BARNHART
BERRAY, Seth, Ct., Anna, W24646; BLWt.30610-160-55
BERRETT, Isaac, Md., Lucy, W9341
BERREY, Samuel, N.H., S12139
BERRIEN, John, N.J., Mary, W5812
BERRINGER, David, N.Y., R791
BERRY, Asahel, Ct., Abigail, W25225
Barnabus, Ct., S12186
Bartholomew, Pvt., Pa., BLWt. 8940 iss. 5/22/1793
Bartholomew, Pa., See BARRY

BERRY (continued)
Benjamin. Pvt., Mass., BLWt. 3755 iss. 12/3/1789
Benjamin, Mass., Hannah, W21657
Benjamin, Mass., Sea Service, Pa. Sea Service, Desire, R794 BLWt.71015-160-55
Benjamin, N.H., S18709; BLWt. 3837-160-55
Benjamin, N.H., Sobriety, W23570; BLWt.2437-100
Benjamin, N.J., Va., S6627
Benjamin, Va., S30857
Bethiah, former wid. of John Allen, Mass., which see
Charles, R.I., S38542
Daniel, N.J., Dorcas, W4637
Edward, Pvt., Md., BLWt.11011 iss. 9/5/1789
Elisha, Mass., R797; BLWt. 9214-160-55
Enoch, N.C., Barbary, W8128; BLWt.26820-160-55
Ephraim, Mass., Polly, R798
Francis, Va., R795
George, Mass., Rhoda, W12269
George, Va., S36411
Jabez, N.Y., Sarah, W16504
James, Cont., Mass., S34003
James, Del., R796
James, Mass. Sea Service, N.H., Betsey, W683; BLWt.26733-160-55
James, Pvt., Pa., BLWt.8938 iss. 7/16/1789
James, Pvt., Pa., BLWt.8945 iss. 7/16/1789 to McConnell, ass.
James, Pa., S37756
James, Pa., S39984
James, Va., Sarah, R799
Jeremiah, Cont., Mass., Betty, W14292
Joel, Va., S30265
John, Cont., N.J., S37757
John, Cont., Pa., S34009
John, Ga., See BARRY
John, N.C., S41428
John, Va., Elizabeth, W5219; BLWt.29001-160-55
John, Va. Dis.-- No papers
Jonathan, Mass., S29630
Joseph, Pvt., Mass., BLWt.3704 iss. 7/22/1789
Joseph, Mass., S45267
Joseph, Mass., Abigail, W24656; BLWt.30587-160-55
Joshua, Mass., N.H., See BARRY
Josiah, Mass., S18710
Josiah, Mass., Elizabeth, W24647
Kellogg, Ct., S17279
Lemuel, Ct., S10360
Levi, N.H., Sally, W20704
Lydford, Cont. Del., S39193
Michael, Pvt. "in the Invalid Regt.", BLWt.12834 iss. 8/19/1791
Nathaniel, Cont., Mass., S36912
Nathaniel, N.H., S17836

BERRY (continued)
Nichols, Mass., S18713
Nicholas, N.Y., Elizabeth, W18583
Peleg, R.I., Mary, W10406
Peletiah, Mass., Nice, W1805; BLWt.19525-160-55
Peter, Cont., Va. res. of son in 1828; BLWt.1422-100
Peter, Pa., S5275
Polly, former wid. of Gideon Garland, N.H., which see
Robert, Md. Sea Service, Lucy, W5796
Robert, N.C., Nancy, W5795
Samuel, Mass., Ruth, W23561
Samuel, N.Y., R20328
Sanford/Sandford, S.C., S1638
Thomas, Mass., S30860
Thomas, Mass., S36911
Thomas, N.H., S17838
Thomas, Pa., S36415
Thomas, Va., S2070
Thomas, Va., S14941
Thomas, Va., Catharine, W24643
Timothy, Cont. Mass., S37579
William Cont. Md., Navy, Hannah, W9724
William, N.J., S34010
William, N.Y., S10366
William, Va., S2371
William, Va., S17266
William, Va., S39187
William, Va., Elizabeth, W5794; BLWt.26133-160-55
William, Va. N.A. Acc. No. 874-050013. No half pay. May be same as William Berry, S2371
Zebulon, Mass., S30852
BERRYHILL, Alexander, S.C., S16639
BERRYMAN, John, Pvt., Md., BLWt. 10941 iss. 6/3/1795 to Francis Sherrard, ass.
BERSIE, Mary former wid. of Philip Carpenter, N.Y., which see
BERTHOLF, Crynes, N.J. See BARTOLF
Henry, N.Y., Anna, R801
Jacobus, Privateer, Mass., R573
BERTIE, John, N.C., Hannah, W8126
BERTOLF, John S., N.J., Susana W5810
BERTOULIN, Joseph, French, R802
BERTRUG, Peter, Va., S18309
BERWICK, John, Pvt. "in the Invalids"; BLWt.12848 iss. 10/6/1794 to William Berwick, admr.
BESANCON, Peter, French, R803
BESARD, John, See BIZZARD
BESIMER, Johannis, N.Y., S45268
BESLY, Sarah, former wid. of Henry Adams, Mass., which see
BESS, Edward, Pa., S39975
BESSE, Ebenezer, Mass., S29628
Jabez, Mass., Sarah, W8127; BLWt.26403-160-55
Joseph, Cont. Mass., S36909
Silas, Mass., Abigail, W14276
BESSENT, John, S.C., S45834
BESSEY, Jabez, See BESSE
BESSOM, Nicholas, Mass., Sea Service, S29005
BESSON, John, N.J., S832
BESSY/BESSEY, Nehemiah, Mass., S14948
BEST, Abraham, Cont., Pa., S48870. No papers
James, Va., Susan, R804
John, N.J., S6602
John, N.C., S6614
John I/John J., N.Y., Christina, W20706
Samuel, Pvt., Pa., Vol., BLRej. 52992-1855
BESTERFIELD, Andrew, Cont. Pa., Elizabeth Wilson, former wid., BLWt.624-100
BETH, Archibald, See BIRTH
BETHAM, Jacob, Pvt., Ct., BLWt. 8929 iss. 2/14/1791 to Alexander Power, ass.
BETHEA, Elisha, N.C., S17840
BETHEL/BETHELL, John Isham, Va., Margaret, W8131, BLWt.30607-160-55
BETO/BETTO, Peter, Cont. S.C., S36409
BETSILL/BEDSELL/BETSELL, John, Cont. Va., S39194
BETSINGER, John, N.Y., R20582
BETTERFIELD/BUTTERFIELD, Oliver, N.H., S12358
BETTERLEY/BETTERLY, Thomas, Mass., Lydia, W20709
William, Cont., Mass., Ann, W3330; BLWt.86035-160-55
BETTERS, John, Pvt., Crane's Contl. Artillery, Mass., BLWt.3826 iss. 12/8/1791
BETTERSON, Naboth, See BETTISON
BETTERSWORTH, Richard, See BETTISWORTH
BETTERTON, Joshua, S.C., S6612
BETTES/BETTIS
Jacob, Md., S39983
Jeremiah, Cont., Mass., S29003
Leonard, Cont., Mass., S34015
Nathaniel, Mass., See BETTIS
BETTESWORTH, Richard, See BETTISWORTH
BETTEY, William, Cont., Mass., Olive, W27362
BETTINEO, Francis, Pvt., Pa., BLWt.8972 iss. 4/3/1794 to Jos. E. Field, ass.
BETTIS, Jacob, Md., See BETTES
John, Mass., See BAPTIST
Nathaniel, Mass., S42085
BETTISON/BETTERSON, Naboth, N.H., S45590
BETTISWORTH/BETTSWORTH, Charles, Va., S32117
Mary, former wid. of Robertson McKinney, Va., which see
BETTISWORTH/BETTESWORTH/ BETTERSWORTH, Richard, Va., S36410
BETTO, Peter, See BETO
BETTON/BITTON, John, Cont., N.H., S45592
BETTS, Aaron, Mass., S16634
BETTS/BIGALOW, Bartlett, Mass., Ann, R805
Charles, Pa., S39973
Daniel, Ct., S17275
David, Pvt., Ct., BLWt.5496 iss. 12/30/1796
David, Ct., S37737
David, Mass., Rhoda, W15876
Hezekiah, Ct., Grace; dau. Juliette; W29929
Isaiah, Ct., S17277
Isaiah, Ct., Hannah, W23592
Jacob, Md., See BETTES
James, Pvt., N.Y., BLWt.6766 iss. 11/26/1791 to Isaac Brooks, ass.
James, N.Y., Vilettee/Viletta, W23598
Joseph, N.J., 1794; War of 1812, R806
Mary, former wid. of William Livingston, N.J., which see
Nathan, N.Y., R807
Peter, Ct., Bathsheba, W25222; BLWt.26569-160-55
Peter, Ct., Cont., Phebe, W20700
Preserved, Mass., Elizabeth, W16840
Reuben, Ct., S14947
Richard, N.Y., R808
Robert, Cont., N.Y., R809
Silas, Ct., R810
Stephen, Ct., Cont., S37749; BLWt.139-300-Capt. Iss. 5/18/1789. No papers
Uriah, Ct., Lucy, W476; BLWt. 27619-160-55
William Maltby, Cont., Ct., R811
Zophar, Ct., S9812
BETTSWORTH, Charles, See BETTISWORTH
BETZ/BELTZ, Henry, Cont., Pa., R735
BETZ, Adam, Pa., R812
Peter, Cont., Pa., Elizabeth, W5814; BLWt.816-160-55
Solomon, Pa., R813
BETZLER, Casper, N.J., R814
BEUBIER/BUBIER, William, Cont., Mass., Navy, R162
BEUTEY, Francis, French, See BENTEY
BEVAN, Philip, N.J., S5271
William, N.C., S6600
BEVANS, Henry, Cont., Ct., S37754
BEVEL, Robert, See BEVILL
BEVEN, Charles, Md., See BEAVEN
BEVENS, Benjamin, Pvt., N.Y., BLWt.6819 iss. 8/4/1790 to Henry Hart, ass.
Benjamin, N.Y., Elizabeth, W16189
BEVER, John, Pa., See BEAVER
BEVERIDGE, Matthew, Mass., Clarissa, W25232; BLWt.28658-160-55
BEVERLY, James, N.H., Margaret, W15576
John, Pa., R815
BEVERS, James, Va., S37739

BEVIER/BOVIER, Conrad, N.Y., Catharine, W25327; BLWt. 30609-160-55
David, N.Y., Sarah, W5820; BLWt.19825-160-55
Elias, N.Y., R816
Jacob J., N.Y., S4263
Philip D., N.Y., BLWt.159-300-Capt. iss. 10/12/1790. No papers
Simon, N.Y., Elizabeth, R817
BEVIERE, Francis, See DEBIERVE
BEVILL/BEVEL, Edward, Va.,S16638
Robert, N.C., Nancy, W2586; BLWt.26140-160-55
BEVINGTON, Thomas, Pa., S39974
BEVINS, Ebenezer, Ct., Cont., Dis. No papers
Hedir, Pvt., Ct., BLWt.5499 iss. 8/23/1790
Wilder, Pa., BLWt.204-200-Lt. Iss. 10/28/1791
BEWEL, Matthew, See BUELL
BEWLEY, George, Md., See BULEY
BEYER, Godlis, Pvt., N.Y., BLWt. 6832 iss. 7/30/1790
BEZARD, John, N.J., See BIZZARD
BIAS, James, Pvt., Md., BLWt. 10976 iss. 6/11/1790
BIBB, Benjamin, Va., Agness, W5821; BLWt.26097-160-55
Henry, Va., S6651
James, Va., S30865
Thomas, Va., S9100
BIBBENS, Benjamin, See BIBBINS
BIBBER, James, Mass., S15749
BIBBIE/BIBBY, Solomon, N.C., S6644
✓ BIBBINS/BIBBENS, Benjamin, Cont. Ct., War of 1812, R819; BLWt.44801-160-55
BIBEE, Thomas, Va., S3002
BIBLE, Adam, Va.,Magdalene, W18596
BICE, Dennis, N.J., S30866
BICKEL/BICKLE, George, Va. or served in 1793. Mary, R821
Jacob, Pa., S2075
John, Pa., S22122
BICKER/BRICKER, Adam, Pa., Rebecca, W2714
Henry, Jr., Pa., See BEKER
Henry, Pa., BLWt.221-500-Col. Iss. 5/11/1789 to Henry Bricker, no papers
Walter, Pa., S45283
BICKERS, Nicholas, Va., S18178
BICKERTON, Elizabeth, former wid. of Alexander James, Pa., which see
BICKFORD, Aaron, N.H., BLWt. 865-100
Andrew, N.H., S49303
Benjamin, Mass., S29009
Benjamin, R.I., BLWt.742-100
Daniel, N.H., Martha, W21671
Dennis, Pvt., N.H., BLWt.2944 iss. 3/25/1790
Dennis, N.H., S49304
Eli, N.H., S18319; BLWt.5455-100-55
John, Cont., N.H., Navy, Elizabeth, W23611

BICKFORD (continued)
John, N.H., S17846
John, N.H., Jemima, W23610
Joseph, Mass., See BECKFORD
Samuel, Cont. N.H., Abigail, W23609
Samuel, Cont., N.H., Jean/Jane, W21673
William, Mass., S29631
BICKHAM, Abner, Ga., S30274
John, Pa., BLWt.188-200
BICKLE, George, Va. See BICKEL
BICKLEY, Charles, Va., S10091
William, Va., S30864
BICKMORE, John, Cont. Mass., S37590
BICKNELL, Abner, Mass., S17845
Amos, Vt., R822
Esau, Md., S34650
(or BICKNALL, Joshua, R.I., Amy, W23606
Josiah, Ct., S37777
Luke, Mass., Olive, W23600
Peter, Mass., Mary, W14309
Thomas, N.C., See BIECKNELL
BIDDIE, John, S.C., S10374
BIDDLE, Elijah, N.C., R824
John, Pvt., Hazen's Regt., BLWt.12773 iss. 6/21/1791 to Pat McGlouchlin
John, Pvt., Pa., BLWt.9011 iss. 3/12/1792
Richard, Pvt., Md., S34651; BLWt.10955 iss. 3/22/1797; no papers
BIDDLECOM, Daniel, Mass., R.I., R825
Richard, Vt., Ruth, W9736
BIDGOOD, Philip, Pvt., Va., BLWt.11902 iss. 2/18/1793 to Robert Means, ass.
Remington, R.I., See BITGOOD
BIDLACK, Benjamin, Cont. Ct., N.J., S39991
BIDLACK/BIDLOCK, Philemon, Ct., Pa., Sarah, W4895; BLWt.26086-160-55
BIDWELL, Allen, Cont., Ct., Anna, W18600
Daniel, N.Y., S32118
Eleazer, Ct., S14955
Elisha, Ct., S12221
John, Ct., Cont., Sarah Potter, former wid., W16684
Ozias, Ct., S37766
Patience, former wid. of Reuben Lamb, Mass., which see
Phineas, Ct., S12220
Samuel, Cont., Ct., Mass., R826
Thomas, Ct., Cont., Elizabeth, W21672
BIEBER/BEAVER, Adam, Pa., S2067
BIECKNELL/BEICKNELL/BICKNELL, Thomas, N.C., Rachel, R12399
BIERCE, Andrew, Cont., N.H., See BEARCE
BIERCE/BERIS, James, Ct., S12209
William, Sgt., Ct., BLWts. 5425 &14154 iss. 1/7/1800
William, Ct., S4265
BIERS, Nathan, Ct., See BEERS
BIFFEL/BIFFLE, Jacob, N.C.,S3003

BIGALOW, Bartlett, See BETTS
BIGBIE/BIGBY, William, Cont., Va. res. in 1828. S46368; BLWt.1457-100
BIGELAR, Nicholas, N.J., S9816
BIGELOW, Abijah, Mass., S16049
Alpheus, Mass., S18719
BIGELOW/BIGLOW, Andrew, Mass., Lydia, W1365; BLWt.10013-160-55
Converse/Convers, Mass., Anna, W14306
Daniel, Mass., Elizabeth, W18602; BLWt.10031-160-55
Daniel, Navy, Mass. res. 1819 R828
Eli, Cont., Ct., S37768
Ephraim, Mass., Mary, W14303
Frederick, Ct., S37767
Humphrey, Mass., Hannah, W14304
Jabez, N.J., S45277
James, Mass., S39997
Joel, Ct., Lucretia, W1535
John, Mass., S18717
Jonas, Mass., Lydia, W14308
Josiah, Ct., See BIGLOW
Moses, Cont., N.J., BLWt.398-100
Noah, Mass., S45276
Samuel, Mass., S34027
Samuel, Mass., Betsey, W14310
Samuel, N.Y., S14957
Sarah, former wid. of Simon Avery, Ct., which see
Simeon, Cont., Mass., S21643
Timothy, Ct., S2074
Timothy, Mass., BLWt.90-500-Col. Iss. 4/1/1790. No papers
Timothy, N.J., Hannah, W3758
William, Mass., Hannah, W27375
BIGFORD, Samuel, N.Y., Anna, W8142; BLWt.26950-160-55
BIGGER, Robert, N.C., Catharine, W9734
BIGGES/BIGGS, Benjamin, Pvt., Md., BLWts.12753 & 14116 iss. 3/25/1795 to John Wright, ass. of Thomas Bigges/Biggs, admr.
BIGGS, Benjamin, Va. & War of 1812. Priscilla, W1366; BLWt. 257-300-Capt. iss. 6/3/1791 6 Rev. War ltrs. in this file
Elija, N.C., R829
Elizabeth, former wid. of John Wilson, Pa., which see
James H., Del., Mary, W16873
John, Cont., Va., S37775
John, Cont., Va., Sarah, W8364; BLWt.1767-100
John, Pa., See BAGGS
John, Va., BLWt.1421-100
Joseph, Va., Mary, R831
Randolph/Randall, Sea Service, Va., Mary, R832
Richard, Pvt., Pa., BLWt.9006 iss. 7/12/1790
Robert, Pa., Jane, W9733
Stephen, Va., R833
William, Va., Nancy, R19360; Va. half pay
BIGHAM, Andrew, N.C., S1639
Joseph, N.C., S6638

BIGHAM (continued)
William, N.C., S1497
BIGLEY/BAGLEY, Winthrop N.H., Maria, W20682; BLWt.30591-160-55
BIGLOW, Andrew, Mass., See BIGELOW
Barna, Mass., Lois, W5826; BLWt. 12825-160-55
BIGLOW/BIGELOW, Josiah, Ct., Lucy, W20716
Noah/Neah, Mass., S12215
Samuel, Sgt., Mass., BLWt.3798 iss. 8/10/1789 to Richard Platt, ass.
Samuel, Mass., S34027
Simeon, Cont., Mass., See BIGELOW
Timothy, Ct., See BIGELOW
BIGNELL, Joseph, Mass. his former wid. rec'd pension as wid. of Daniel Lilly/Lillie, Mass., which see
Thomas, Sgt., Pa., BLWt.8953 iss. 7/27/1789 to Richard Platt, ass.
BIGSBEE, Aaron, Pvt., N.H., BLWt. 2927 iss. 1/28/1790 to James Patterson, ass.
BIGSBY/BIXLY, Jonathan, N.Y., Elizabeth, R880
Solomon, Ct., See BIXBY
BIGWOOD, James, Pvt., Md., BLWt. 10975 iss. 3/11/1791
BILBORY/BILBRY, Nathaniel, Cont., N.C., S.C., S6645
BILBURY/BILBY, Wooldrick/William N.J., S34581; BLWt.8100-100 Pvt. Iss. 12/2/1781. No papers
BILES, Thomas, N.C., Tabitha, W3928
BILES/BOYLE, Thomas, Pa., BLWt. 338-400
BILL, Abiel, Ct., S22648
Azariah, Ct., N.Y., S17283
Benejah, Ct., Privateer, Content, W17308
Daniel, Ct., S15751
Eleazer, Ct., S18316
Elijah, Ct., Cont., Privateer, S12218
Jabez, Cont., Mass., S28645; BLWt.111-200-Lt. Iss. 5/24/1790. No papers
Jonathan, Ct., S12222
Jonathan, Ct., Hannah, R834
Joshua, Ct., Privateer, S17282
Phineas, Ct., Mercy, W16844
Rozzel/Roswell, Ct., S37771
William, Mass., Mary Bliss, W519; BLWt.26329-160-55
BILLEU, Stephen, See BILLUE
BILLHIME, Michael, N.J., Elizabeth R835
BILLIGER/BILLINGER, Michael, N.Y., S12203
BILLING, Samuel, Pvt., Mass., BLWt.3657 iss. 8/10/1789 to Richard Platt, ass.
BILLINGS, Abel, Mass., Elizabeth, W23614
Abraham, Va., R836
Benjamin, Ct., Wealthy, W1702-BLWt.541-160-55
Benjamin, Mass., S12223

BILLINGS (continued)
Ebenezer, Cont., N.H., Mass., Patience, W23603
Elisha, Ct., Lucretia, W17302
Enoch, Cont., Mass., Nancy, W23608
Ephraim/Ephriam, Mass., S29632
Ezekiel, Ct., Cont., Navy, Privateer, R.I., R837
Gideon, Mass., R838
Isaac, N.H., S38548
James, Ct., Cont., S45285
Jasper, N.C., Elizabeth, W10295; BLWt.19508-160-55
Jasper, S.C., R839; BLWt.31700-160-55
Jesse, Mass., S4951
John, Ct., Cont., Vt., Olive, W23601
John S., N.J., Privateer, Phebe, S19909; BLWt.30943-160-55
Jonathan, Mass., Sarah, W18599; BLWt.34526-160-55
Joseph, Ct., Cont., S12210
Leavett, Mass., Anne, W16843
Lemuel, Mass., S12225
Matthew, Ct., Cont., S45282
Nathan, Pvt., R.I., BLWt.2962 iss. 5/28/1792 to Israel Angell
Robert, Mass., BLWt.2104-100
Samuel, Mass., Hannah, W21669
Samuel, R.I., S38544
Silas, Mass., S38547
Stephen, Ct., Anna Dennis, former wid., W25523; BLWt.135-300-Capt. Iss. 10/26/1795 to Joseph Emerson, ass.No papers
Stephen, Mass., N.H., S16644
BILLINGSLEY, John, N.C., S30862
BILLINGSLY, Walter, N.C., R840
BILLINGTON, Elisha, R.I., S38551
Ezekiel, N.J., Esther, W8365; BLWt.32210-160-55
Isaac, Mass., Navy, Rebecca, W23617
John, Mass., S45279
Thomas, R.I., S38545
BILLIP, Henry, Pvt., Md., BLWts. 10952 & 11971 iss.12/22/1794
BILLS, Ebenezer, Cont., Mass., Hannah, W16841
Elisha, N.Y., S12217
John E., Va., Mary, W25243; BLWt.26322-160-55
Judah, Pvt. "in the Invalid Regt.", BLWt.12835 iss. 9/15/1790 to Nicholas Root, ass.
Nathaniel, Cont., Mass., S34029
Sylvanus, Ct., Lydia, W10414; BLWt.36611-160-55
Thomas, Pvt., Lamb's Artillery N.Y., BLWt.6885 iss. 8/4/1790 to Peter De Witt, ass.
William, N.J., S598
William, Va., S39992
BILLUE, Stephen, N.C., Mary, W2745. Pensioned as Billeu & heirs as Ballew
BILLUPS, Thomas, N.C., Sarah, W3927

BILMAN/BELMAN, Dewalt, Pa., S39993
BILSON, William, Cont., N.J., Harriet, W16192
BINDON, Joseph, N.Y., R841
BINER, George, Va., S4266
BINEGER, George, See BENEGER
BING, John, Pvt., Pa., BLWt. 9009 iss. 3/3/1794 to Michael Stiver, ass.
BINGHAM, Aaron, Ct., S45280
Abel, Ct., S37772
Abner, N.H., Privateer, R842
Alvan, Ct., N.H., Elizabeth, W5220
Benjamin, Pvt., Mass., BLWt. 3802 iss. 7/21/1789 to Jonathan Cass, ass.
Benjamin, Va., S2377
Chester, Ct., Mass., S37765
Elias, Ct., Cont., S38543
Gurdon, Ct., S37762
Ithamar, Ct., Hannah, W17301
Jeremiah, Ct., S12211
Jeremiah, Pvt., Mass., BLWt. 3745 iss. 3/25/1790
Jeremiah, Mass., Mary Whipple former wid., W20130
Jeremiah, Vt., S12213
Johnson, Ct., Anna, W18595; BLWt.26556-160-55
Lovina, former wid. of Wm. Wilson, Mass., which see
Maltiah, Ct., Marcy, W21667
Ozias, Ct., S22120
Ripley, N.H., Elizabeth, W23612
Robert, Md. or Va., Elizabeth, R843
Samuel, Ct., S12230
Silas, Ct., Green Mt. Boys, Vt. S2076
Thomas, Ct., S38550
Thomas, Pa., S39998
BINGLEY, Lewis, Va., Elizabeth Nance, former wid. W24325. See claim of her last husb. Zachariah Nance, Va.
William, Pvt., Cont. Artillery Crane's Mass., BLWt.3819 iss. 5/2/1789
BININGER, Isaac, N.Y., Elizabeth W23616
BINKEY, Fridrik, See BINKLEY
BINKLEY, Adam, N.C., S1890
Frederick/Fridrik, N.C., Elizabeth, W4898
BINNEY, Barnabas, Pa., BLWt. 1989-450
BINNS, Thomas, Ct., BLWt.466-100
William, Pvt., Va., BLWt.11939 iss. 7/14/1792 to Robert Means, ass.
BIRCH, Ebenezer, Ct., See BURCH
James, Sgt., N.J., BLWt.8113 iss. 7/7/1789
John, Pa., Jane, W8363; BLWt.26257-160-55
Thomas, Md., Mary, W3380
William, Va., Rebecca, W27940
BIRCHARD, Daniel, Ct., Anna, W1379; BLWt.26920-160-55
Elias, Ct., S12216

BIRCHARD (continued)
Joseph, Ct., R844
Levi, Mass. R845
BIRCHFIELD, Thomas, Pa., S6642
BIRCKI, Peter/Piter, N.Y., Anne/Elizabeth/Elizabeth Ann, W17310
BIRD, Abigail, former wid. of Ralph Pope, Mass., which see
Andrew, Pa., S39994; BLWt. 2134-100
Benjamin, N.C., R21880
Bonner, N.C., S8070
Edmund, Mass., BLWt.983-100. Iss. 3/10/1821
Edmund/Edmond R., Cont. Mass., Eve, W16193
Hardy, N.C., Jerusha, W18597
Henry, Va., See BYRD
Isaac, Cont., N.J.res. in 1828, Gertrude, W1806; BLWt.9537-160-55
John, Mass., Joanna Bunce, former wid., W14429. 3 1776-77 ltrs. in file
John, N.J., S6639
John, R850. Rev. War rej. book shows, Act 1832 res. Pa. No corresp., everything searched 6/19/1911. The pensioner John Bird, N.J., S6639, Act of 1832 was then res. of Kingston Twp. Luzerne Co., Pa. List of rej. pensioners, 1852, p.206, shows suspended pensioner Act 1832, John Bird of Kingston, Luzerne Co., as "Application under Act of 1818 rej. -- no proof of service under this act."
John, S.C., S10372
John, S.C., S39196
Jonathan, Mass., Anna, R852
Joseph, Mass., S19210
Joshua, Va., S36416
Levin, Va. Sea Service, R9, Va. half pay
Nathaniel, Mass., Hannah, R847
Reuben, Cont., N.C., S37776
Robert, Ky. Mil. 1792-3; Wayne's War, Ky. Mil; War of 1812, Ill. Vols.; Black Hawk War; see papers in 1812 Flat files Wt.26786-160-55
Thomas, Cont.,Mass. res. 1818, S34030
Thomas, N.J., Hannah, R848
Thomas, N.C., Jane, BLWt.61001-160-55
Thomas, N.C., See BYRD
BIRDSEY, Ezra, Ct., S14954
BIRDSEYE, Thaddeus, Ct., Helen, W25247; BLWt.10242-160-55
BIRDSONG
John, N.C., R855
William, N.C., Mary, R856
BIRDWELL, Benjamin, N.C., Mary, W218
BIRGE, David, Ct., Cont., S38549
Hosea, Cont., Ct., S12224
James, Ct., S10364
John, Ct., Lucy, W8362; BLWt. 26631-160-55

BIRGE (continued)
John, Ct., Ruhama, W17309; BLWt.9471-160-55
BIRDMIDGHAM, Daniel, Md. See BRUMIGUM
BIRTH/BETH, Archibald, N.J., S39995
BISBE/BISBEE, John, Mass., S30276
BISBEE/BISBE/BISBY, Benjamin, Mass., Milly, W2057; BLWt. 9408-160-55
Charles, Cont., Mass., S16642
Ebenezer, Mass., S18720
Elijah, Mass., Susannah, W27384
Elisha, Cont., Mass., S37589
Elisha, Cont., Mass., Jemima, W18604
George, Mass., Grace, W15583
Gideon, Mass., Elizabeth, R857
Isaac, Mass., Mary, W12294
Jonah, Mass., S18716
Luther, Mass., S14960; BLWt. 14963-160-55
Noah, Mass., S16643
Samuel, Cont., Mass., S34031
BISBY, Benjamin, See BISBEE
Joseph, Ct., S45284
BISCOE, James, Navy, Va. Sea Service, Polly, W8230; BLWt. 13442-160-55
Josiah, Md., Privateer, R859
BISH, Frederick, Va., S8071
BISHOP, Abraham, Ct., Charity, W5822; BLWt.26563-160-55
Austin, Ct., Annah, W17306
Benjamin, N.J., S32119. See N.A. Acc.No.874; 050014. Not half pay claim. Benjamin Bishop
Bennoi, Pvt., R.I., BLWt.2980 iss. 10/10/1791
Benoni, R.I., Elizabeth, W21668
Charles, N.Y., Dis.-- No papers
David, Ct., S6652
Ebenezer, R.I., Lydia, W1213
Elijah, Vt., S23125
Elisha, Va., S30867
Enos, Mass., S29010
Ezekiel, R.I., Mary, W632; BLWt.26283-160-55
Gabriel, Cont., N.Y., Sarah, W25246
Gabriel, Pvt., N.Y., BLWt.6874 iss. 9/24/1791 to Platt Rogers
Golden, Ga., S37763
Henry, Va., Fanny, W5823
Hezekiah, Ct., Polly, W2587; BLWt.50857-160-55
Hooper, Mass., S29008; BLWt. 7054-160-55
Isaac, Mass., S44623
Jacob, Ct., S17280
Jacob, Cont., Md., Mary, W3381; BLWt.15435-160-55
James, Ct., wid. Mary, S16641
James, Ct., Elizabeth, W25241
James, Cont., Mass., S41438
James, N.J., Mary, W18603; BLWt.2183-160-55
James, N.Y., Catharine, W20715
James, Va., S6637
Jared, Ct., Sarah Foot/Foote, former wid., W17915

BISHOP (continued)
Jared, Ct., R860
Jeremiah, Va., S6636
Jesse, Ct., Mass., S41437
Joel, Ct., d.1843; R862
Joel, Ct., Phebe, R864
John, Pvt., Ct., BLWt.5503 iss. 5/6/1793 to John Walden
John, Ct., Sarah, W17303
John, Ct., S45281; BLWt.1667-100
John, Ct., S12219
John, Pvt., Lamb's Artillery, N.Y., BLWt.6877 iss. 7/16/1790 to Philip V. Cortland, ass.
John, Mass., Sally, W2588
John, N.H., R863
John, N.J., BLWt.185-150-Ensign iss. 2/2/17-- (torn) No papers
John, N.Y., S47915
John, S.C., S9279
John, Vt., Esther, W18594
Joseph, Ct., Ruth, W25245; BLWt.10229-160-55
Joseph, R.I., Susanna, R868
Joshua, Cont., N.Y., Hannah, W20719; BLWt.1342
Lawrence, Pa., S1166
Lemuel, Vt., S12228
Levi, Cont., N.Y. res. 1828, Nancy, W25239; BLWt.6876-100
Levi, Vt., S12231
Moses, Ct., Jerusha, W20714
Napthala, Vt., Rebecca, R865
Nathaniel, Ct., BLWt.231-200
Nathaniel, Pvt., Lamb's Artillery N.Y., BLWt.6887 iss. 10/23/1790
Newman, Ct., S29634; BLWt.24614-160-55
Nicholas, S.C., S17847
Paul, Pa., Sarah, R866
Richard, Ct., Mercy, W23613; BLWt.815-160-55
Richard, N.C., Nancy/Ann, W18598
Richard, Pvt., Pa., BLWt.8994 iss. 10/27/1792 to Frederick Molinoux
Richard, Va., S35192
Robert, N.H., S46422
Seth, Ct., S12212
Silvanus/Sylvanus, Mass., S12208; BLWt.3512-160-55
Simeon, Ct., Cont., S19910
Solomon, Mass., S12229
Solomon, Va., S30863
Squier/Squire, Mass., S19544
Stephen, Ct., S37769
Stephen, Cont., Va., S37770
Sylvester, Cont., Mass., Vt., Deborah, W15585
Thalmeno, Ct., BLWt.40-100
Thomas, Ct., Amy, W17305
Thomas, ---, Md. Agency, Dis. No papers
Thomas F., Ct., S14953
Timothy, Ct., S28646
William, N.C., S.C., Elizabeth, W9356
William, S.C., S30275
William, Va., Winney, W4897
William, Va., R869
Wyatt, Va., S14958

BISHOP (continued)
Zadock, Mass., R.I., S15750
Zepheniah/Zephaniah, Mass., S17281
BISON, Charles, Pa., See BISSON
BISSEL, Benjamin, Ct., S12214
BISSELL, Archelaus, N.Y., S37773
Benjamin, Pvt., Ct., BLWt.5454 iss. 10/7/1789 to Benjamin Tallmadge
Benjamin, Ct., S37774
Benjamin, Ct., Elizabeth, W5825
Calvin, Ct., S14956
Daniel, Sgt., Ct., BLWt.5439 iss. 11/9/1789
Daniel, Ct., & U.S. Army until 1821. Deborah, W9735
Daniel, Ct., Theoda, W23604
David, Privateer, R.I., S21644
Ebenezer Fitch, Ct., S18315
Elisha, Ct., Rhoda, W17304
Ezekiel, Ct., S31553
George, Ct., S12227
George, Ct., Lois, R871
Jerijah, Ct., S24064
John, Ct., S---. Ctf. No. 7762
John, Ct., Huldah, R870
John, R.I., Ruth, W14305
Jonathan M., Mass., S18715
Josiah, Ct., S29633
Lemuel, Ct., Sally, W520; BLWt. 26639-160-55
Leveritt, Ct., Cont., Sarah, W25248; BLWt.28540-160-55
Noadiah, Ct., S22647
Oliver, Cont., Mass., S44624
Ozias, Cont., Ct., S37764. He d. 11/16/1822. Wid. Anner, was pensioned as former wid. of Jonathan Miller, Ct.,which see
Return, Ct., S15257
Samuel, Cont., R.I., S38546
Samuel, Cont., R.I., S45278
Thomas, Ct., Eleanor, W12295; BLWt.57522-160-55
BISSON/BISON, Charles, Pa., Elizabeth/Eliza, W10417
BISTORIES/BISTORIUS, Frederick, Not Rev. War, Navy 1799-1803, Pa. res. Old Act Navy Inv. Rej. 170
BISWELL, John, Cont., Va., S35191
John, Pvt., Va., BLWt.11912 iss. 5/2/1794
BITELEY/BITELEE/BITLEY, Henry, N.Y., Elizabeth, W25242
BITELEY/BITTEY, John, N.Y., Martha, R872
BITER/BITHER, Peter, Cont., Mass., S36913
BITGOOD, John, R.I., S14959
BITGOOD/BIDGOOD, Remington, R.I., Affe, W29717
BITHER, Peter, See BITER
BITLEY, Henry, See BITELEY
BITTEY, John, See BITELEY
BITTICKS, John, N.C., Hannah, R874
BITTING, Joseph, Cont., Pa., S2072
BITTLE, Samuel, Pa., S22121
BITTON, John, See BETTON
BITZ, Michael, Pa., S39996
BIVINS, Abner, Cont., Mass., R.I., Hannah, W2432; BLWt. 3759-100

BIVINS (continued
Iss. 1798. No papers. BLWt. 277-60-55
John, Cont., Mass., N.Y., Hannah, R875
William, Del., R876
BIXBE/BIXBY, Benjamin, Mass., R878
BIXBEE, Solomon, See BIXBY
BIXBEY, Aaron, Ct., Mary, R877
BIXBY, Aaron, N.H., S41436
Adonijah, Mass., S19545
Benjamin, Ct., Cont., Mass., S42618
Benjamin, Mass., See BIXBE
Daniel, N.H., S14166
David, Mass., Privateer, Nancy, W16842; BLWt. 7447-160-55
Elias, Ct., Grace, W20718
Jacob, Ct., S49305
Jacob, Mass., Martha, W23602
John, Mass., S34028
Jonathan, Mass., Esther, W21670
Moses, Ct., Mary/Molly, W25240
Nathaniel, Mass., Catharine, W5828; BLWt.813-160-55
Olive, former wid. of Samuel Brown, Mass., which see
Rhoda, former wid. of Edward Downs, Mass., which see
Samson, Mass., S31552
Samuel, Mass., Mary, W18601
Samuel, Mass., N.H., S18317
Solomon, Ct., Lucy, W23607; BLWt.56972-160-55
Thomas, ---. Rhoda, W---. See her former husband, Edward Downs, Mass.
BIXLEY, David, Mass., See BIXBY
Jacob, Mass., See BIXBY
BIXLY, Jonathan, N.Y., See BIGSBY
BIZZARD, John, N.J., R818
BIZZEL/BIZZELL/BIZZILL, Amy, former wid. of Thomas Cole, N.C., which see
BLACHFORD/BLATCHFORD, Uriah, Mass. Sea Service, R935
BLACK, Adam, Pa., Sarah, W3127
Alexander, Va., R881
Benjamin, See SIMMONS, Ct.
Cato, Cont., Mass., Rebecca, W17313
Daniel, Pa., S40006
David, Pvt., N.Y., BLWt.6804 iss. 4/26/1796
David, N.Y., Catharine, W5835
David, N.C., S10393
Ezekiel, N.C., Sarah, W8144
George, Cont., Va., S6659
George, Mass., S44633
George, Mass., Bethia Allen, R882
George, Pa., Jane, W3211
Henry, Cont., Mass., Sally, W15985
Henry, Pa., S2081
Hugh, Md., Sarah, R893
Hugh, Pa., R884
Jacob, Mass., S18722
Jacob, S.C., S9281

BLACK (continued)
James, N.C., S31557
James, Pa., S2077
James, Privateer, S.C., Nancy, W20733
James, Va., R886
Joab, Mass., S37592
John, Ga., Margaret, R890; BLRej. 229010-55
John, Md., Va., born Pa. & lived there later. R887
John, Pvt., N.Y., BLWt.6837 iss. 9/29/1790 to Richard Lush, et al assignees
John, N.C., S9280
John, S.C., S37783
John, S.C., Elizabeth, W9359
John, Va., Milly, R891
Jonathan, Pvt., N.H., BLWt. 2923 iss. 9/2/1789 to Archd. McMullen, ass.
Jonathan, Pa., S5286
Joseph, Mass., BLWt.1395-100
Joseph, Mass., R888
Joseph, N.C., S.C., S21646
Josiah, Mass., S16647
Martin, N.C., S41441
Moses, Mass., S37593
Richard, Del., BLWt.1166-100
Robert, Va., S1167
Rudolph, Md., S30874
Samuel, Md., Va., & Sea Service, R892
Samuel, Mass., S29012
Samuel, R.I., Rebecca Bailey, former wid., W23535
Thomas, Pa., S9103
Thomas, Pa., S22651
William, Cont., Pa., S40007
William, Cont., Pa., S46752
William, Ga., Elizabeth, W9730
William, Pvt., Hazen's Regt., BLWt.12823 iss. 11/29/1799 to John Duncan, ass.
William, Mass., S12241
William, Mass. & 1812, Catharine, W24699; BLWt.19782-160-55
William, N.C., S.C., S32122
William, Pa., S31554
William, Pa., See BLAKE
BLACKARD, Willyoube/Willoughby, N.C., S29638
BLACKBOURN, Clement, Va., S10388
BLACKBURN/BLACKBOURN
Benjamin, ---. Ala. agency & res.; former res. Va. & Tenn., S24916
James, Cont., Tenn. Agency & res. S39197
James, Cont., Md., Va., S42619
James, Pa., S2078
John, Cont., Pa., Elizabeth, W1367; BLWt.34949-160-55
John, ---. Invalid Pens., Pa., 1789-93. No papers
Moses, Pa., S16645
Nathan, N.C., S6654
Samuel, Cont., Md., Pa., S35194
William, Va., S14967
BLACKEMORE, George, Va. See BLACKMORE
BLACKEY, Mark, N.H., Betsey, W24697

BLACKFORD, Anthony, N.J., Hulda Fisher, former wid., W24200
David, Cont., Mass., S34047; BLWt.1802-100
David, N.J., Hannah, W10296 BLWt.26287-160-55
Jacob, N.C., Pa., Margaret, W2058; BLWt.26669-160-55
Nathan, N.J., Rachel, W3648
Samuel, N.J., S2079
BLACKHAM, George, Pvt., Md., BLWt. 10946 iss. 2/7/1790
BLACKINTON/BLACKINGTON, James, Mass., S37595
Peter, R.I., Hepzibah Taft, former wid., W15441
BLACKISTON/BLACKSTONE, John, Ct., S14963
BLACKLEACH, John, Ct., S37786; BLWt.156-200-Lt. Iss. 11/19/ 1793. No papers
BLACKLEDGE, Ichabod, N.J., S36417
BLACKLER, William, Mass., R895
BLACKLEY, Micajah, See RACKLEY
BLACKLY/BLAKELY, Thomas, S.C., S21650
BLACKMAN, Chloe, former wid. of David Hill, Ct., N.Y., which see
Dan, Ct., S45286
Daniel, Ct., Mary, W16848
David, Ct., Cont., S37791
David, S.C., R898
Edward, Ct., Hannah, W25249
Elijah, Cont., Ct., S42622
Elisha, Ct., S2084
Enoch, Ct., Lydia, W2059
Ephriam, Green Mt. Boys, Orpha, R899
George, Mass., Phebe, W14322; BLWt.32207-160-55
Jacob, R.I., See BLACKMAR
James, Ct., Ann, W17312
Joel, N.Y., also War of 1812, Catharine, BLWt.35842-160-55
Jonathan, Ct., S34038
Kemar/Kemer, Mass., Dinah, W23627
Nehemiah, Ct., ---. Wid. Hannah pensioned as former wid. of Asahel Terrell, which see
Phebe, former wid. of Joshua Northrup, Ct., which see
Sampson, Ct., S37787
Samuel, Ct., Cont., S37793
Samuel, Cont., Mass., Abigail, W23630
Samuel, Mass., Jerusha, W23625; BLWt.13418-160-55
Silvanus, R.I., R900
Thomas, Pvt., N.J., BLWt.8150 iss. 9/1/1791
Zachariah, Ct., S45295
Zachariah, Ct., See BLAKEMAN
BLACKMAR, Holland, Vt. See BEACKMAN
Jacob, R.I., Zeruiah, W4133; BLWt.19712-160-55
Silvanus, R.I., See BLACKMAN
Stephen, R.I., S12240

BLACKMARR, John, Ct., See BLACKMORE
BLACKMER, Abner, R.I., Sarah, W18610
Ephriam, Green Mt. Boys, Mass., N.H., Mary Collins, former wid., W16925
Isaac, Mass., N.Y., S5285
James, Mass., R902
John Holland, Mass., R904
Nathaniel, Mass., R905
Polly, former wid. of Frederick Weaver, R.I., which see
Solomon, Mass., S19546
BLACKMORE, George, S.C., Wt.11978-100-Pvt., iss. 8/18/ 1795
George, Va., Sarah, W2558; BLWt.24987-160-55
George D., Cont., Md., Indian Wars 1785-1794. S45898
Isaac, Mass. See BLACKMER
John, Ct., Navy, Silence, W23637
John, Cont., Mass., alive in 1818. S38553
John, Mass., died 1817; BLWt. 1100-100
John, Va., See BLAKEMORE
Thomas, Pvt., Va., BLWt.591-100
Timothy, Vt., S2378
BLACKNALL/BLACKWALL, Thomas, Va. S46023
BLACKNER/BLACKNOR, Godfrey, N.J., S34042; Pvt., N.J. BLWt.8147 iss. 1/14/1791
BLACKNEY, James, Pa., See BLEAKNEY
BLACKSHIRE, Ebenezer, Del., S45995; BLWt.349-100
BLACKSLEE, Caleb, Ct., See BLAKSLEE
BLACKSLE/BLACKSLEE, Samuel, Ct., Vt., S16052
Caleb, Pvt., Ct., BLWt.5446 iss. 11/2/1791 to Jonathan Tuttle
BLACKSLEY/BLAKSLEY/BLAKELEY, Enos, Ct., Dis.---. No papers
BLACKSTON, William, Mass., S30869
BLACKSTONE, John, Ct., See BLACKISTON
John, Pvt., N.J., BLWt.8105 iss. 9/30/1790 to Jos. Halsey, Jr., ass.
John, N.J., Rebecca, W23629
Priticks, ---, Biddy Shilling former wid., R9508. Her 2nd husb., Geo. Shilling, also served
BLACKWALL, Thomas, See BLACKNALL
BLACKWELDER, Charles, N.C., S6658
Isaac, N.C., S6660
BLACKWELL, Abraham, S.C., S18328
Ann, former wid. of Edwin Hull, Va., which see
Benjamin, N.J., Pamelia, W839
David, N.C., Va., S3014
David, Va., S6666
David, Va., Ann, W9358

BLACKWELL (continued)
Elijah, N.J., S801
Hugh, Md., See BLACK
James, N.C., Temperance, W18613
John, N.C., S2083
John, Va., S30873
John, Va., BLWt.264-300. Iss. 2/26/1793. No papers
Joseph, Va., S37781; BLWt.265-300-Capt. Iss. 2/26/1793. No papers
Joseph, Va., Ann, W---. Wid. Ctf. 1191. She was also pensioned as former wid. of Edwin Hull, Va., which see
Robert, Va., died 1837. S34653
Robert, Va., Indian War 1791. Alive in 1855. BLWt.38822-160-55
Thomas, Va., S35193; BLWt.87-300-Capt. Iss. 2/25/1793. Also recorded under W2493. No papers
William, Va., BLWt.1861-300
BLACKWOOD, Atecheson, Sgt. "Proctor's Artillery", Pa., BLWt.9052 iss. 7/27/1789 to Richard Platt, ass.
James, Cont., Mass., Nancy, W21675
John, Pvt., Pa., BLWt.8952 iss. 7/13/1791
Samuel, Sgt. "Proctor's Artillery", Pa., BLWt.9045 iss. 6/ 29/1789 to M. McConnell, ass.
BLADE, Eli, Md., See BLADS
BLADES, John Levy, Md., Sarah Lancaster, former wid., W9502 Her last husb. pens., William Lancaster, Va., which see
BLADS, Eli, Md., R908
BLAIKLEY, William, Va., S46753
BLAIN, Alam, Cont., Ohio res. in 1818; Catharine, W5834; BLWt.5213-160-55
James, N.Y., Pa., Sea Service, Mary, W20734
James, Pa., S2082
James, Va., S35780
Thomas, N.Y., S958
BLAINE, Ephraim, Cont., Pa., Sarah, W1215
BLAIR, Abraham, N.J., S4267
Allen, Va., Mary Ann, W5833
Ezekiel, Mass., Elizabeth Clark, former wid., W23822
James, Cont., N.H., S42621
James, Mass., S23127
James, Mass., S37594
James, N.C., S22125
James, Va., See BLAIN
Joel, Mass., Polly, W18607
John, Cont., BLWt.174-200-Capt. Lt. of Harrison's Artillery. Iss. 9/19/1789 to Archibald Blair, heir and legal repr. Also recorded under BLWt.2538 No papers
John, Cont., Mass., S45296; BLWt.1842-100
John, Mass., S18725
John, N.J., BLWt.1809-200 iss. 2/24/1832 to John Blair, sole devisee. Also invalid pens. No

BLAIR (continued)
papers
John, Pvt., Pa., BLWt.9017 iss. 11/26/179- to John Harper, ass.
John, ---, N.A. Acc. No. 874 050015 half pay. No pension file ident. for this veteran.
John Neal, Va., S37779
Joseph, Pvt., Mass., BLWt.3728 iss. 4/19/1792 to Whit[d] Swift, ass.
Joseph, Mass., Masy/Mercy, W20726
Reuben, Mass., Hannah N., BLWt. 56506-160-55
Reuben, Mass., Susan, W18614
Robert, Pvt., N.J. BLWt.8110 iss. 11/5/1789
Robert, Washington's Life Guard, ----, no papers
Samuel, N.C., S3009
Samuel, N.C., R910
Samuel, Pa., Rebecca, W3067
Samuel, Pa., N.J., S14966
Seth, Mass., S12234
Solomon, Mass., S29637
Thomas, Cont., Pa., S35781
Thomas, Pa., Eleanor, W3068
Thomas, S.C., Jane, W891
Timothy, Mass., S34039
William, Cont., Mass., Elizabeth, W21680
William, N.J., Jane, R909
William, Pa., S21647
BLAISDELL, Daniel, See BLASDEL
Daniel, N.H., S22124
Isaac, N.H., Abagail, W24696; BLWt.19539-160-55
John, N.H., BLWt.2101-100
John, N.H., See BLASDELL
Jonathan, Mass., Elizabeth Coffin, former wid., W23856
Levi, Cont., Mass., N.Y., Mary, W25251; BLWt.26394-160-55
Samuel, Mass., See BLASDEL
BLAKE, Benjamin, Mass., S37591
Christopher, Ct., S45598
David, Ct., S23128
Ebenezer, Sgt., Mass., Chloe, W5836; BLWts.3722 & 8-60-55 iss. 3/25/1790. No papers
Edward, Cont., Mass., Dorcas, W21677; BLWt.680-200
Edward, alias for John Blake Vose, Mass., S14770; BLWt.786-100
Edward, Mass., W18605
Edward, Sgt., Pa., BLWt.8954 iss. 3/10/1790
Eleazer, Mass., S17285
Eleazer, Sgt., Mass., BLWt.3721 iss. 3/25/1790
Elijah, Ct., S14964
Elijah, Cont., N.H., Sarah, W15586
Elijah, N.H., S6671
George, Mass., S30278
George, Mass., See BLACK
George, Va., R911
Henry, Cont., N.H., Molly, W20727
Isaac, N.H., S12242
Jacob, Pvt., Md., BLWt. 10964 iss. 8/14/179- to Francis

BLAKE (continued)
Sherrard, ass.
Jacob, Md., S34654
Jacob, Mass., S18726
James, Cont., Mass., Navy, S34037
James, Cont., N.Y., Nancy, W20724
James, Corp., Hazen's Regt. BLWt. 12781 iss. 10/16/1790 to Waterman Lippett, ass.
James, Mass., Sarah, W23634
James, Navy, Mass., Mary, W24698; her former husb., Wm. Cook, also served in Rev. War.
James, Va., Sarah, W17318
Jason, Cont., Mass., S34033
Jemima, former wid. of Samuel Hart, Cont., Mass., Which see
Jeremiah, Mass., S12250
John, Mass., S28648
John, Mass., Thankful, W23623
John, Mass., Deborah, W24701
John, Navy, Mass., Mercy, W23620
John, N.H., S15753
John, N.H., S16649
John, N.H., Mehitable, W17317
John, N.H., R19631
John, S.C., R913
John P., N.H., Sally, W4899
Jonathan, Mass., S30876
Jonathan, N.H., Judith, W16194
Joseph, Cont., Mass., Hannah, R912
Joshua, N.C., S8074
Josiah, Mass., R.I., Sarah, W4639 ; BLWt.3527-160-55
Michael, Pa., BLWt.8957, iss. 2/5/1794 to Caspar Iserloan, ass. No papers
Nathan, N.H., Molly Tenny, former widow, W16079
Paul, N.H., Abagail, W21676
Philip, Mass., R916
Reuben, Pvt., Ct., BLWt.5422 iss. 8/23/1790
Reuben, Ct., Eunice, W25256 BLWt.2184-160-55
Robert, N.H., Martha, W23635
Seth, Mass., S45599
Thomas, Pvt., Ct., BLWt. 5495 iss. 6/24/1793 to Samuel Emery
Thomas, Cont., Mass., Susanna, W14311
Thomas, N.H., Mary, W14313; BLWt.77-200-Lt. Iss. 4/1/1790 No papers
Thomas, Va., S6657
Thomas, Va., S6662
Timothy, Cont., N.H., S38555
Timothy, Mass., BLWt.2370-100
William, Ct., Sarah Miller, former widow, W10502
William, Mass., Sarah, W18606
William, Pa., S40000
BLAKE/BLACK, William, Pa., BLWt. 222-100
Willing, Mass., S30875
BLAKELEY, Enos, Ct., See BLACKSLEY
Robert, Va., See BLEAKELEY
BLAKELY
Aquilla, Va., S31558
James, Ct., S2085

BLAKELY (continued)
James, S.C., See BLEAKLEY
Obed, Pvt. "in the Artillery Artificers"; BLWt.12816 iss. 8/20/1790
Thomas, S.C., See BLACKLY
William, S.C., S21649
Zealous, Ct., S37789
BLAKEMAN, Zachariah, Ct., Cont., Sarah, W20729
BLAKEMORE, George, Va., S6665
George, Va., See BLACKMORE
BLAKEMORE/BLACKMORE, John, Va., S30871
Thomas, Va., BLWt.591-100
BLAKENEY, James, Pa., See BLEAKNEY
John, N.C., S.C., Nancy, W2716; BLWt. 34506-160-55
John, Pa., BLWt.8936-100 iss. 11/5/1789, or possibly 1798
William, Pa. & Privateer, Va., S40002
BLAKESLE/BLAKESLEY, Abel, Ct., Mary D., W8369; BLWt.26691-160-55
BLAKESLEE, Ambrose, Ct., R907
Eber, Ct. Sea Service, S23129
James, N.Y., S22126
Jesse, Ct., Cont., S37792
Philip, Ct., S38610
Rebecca, former wid. of Henry Hull, Ct., which see
Samuel, Ct., S45293. See BLWt. 25862-160-55 iss. to Rebecca Blakeslee, widow, for his service as Col., War of 1812
Zealous, Ct., See BLAKELEE/BLAKELEY
BLAKESLEY, Abel, See BLAKESLE
Jared, Ct., Rhoda, W20722
Jesse, Pvt., Hazen's Regt., BLWt.12775 iss. 4/11/1792 to Martin Kingsley, ass.
Obed, Ct., See BLAKLEY
BLAKESLY, Enos, Pvt., Ct., BLWt.5420 iss. 12/14/1789 to Richard Platt
BLAKEY, George, Va., Margaret, W8367; BLWt.19802-160-55
William, N.C., R918
BLAKLEY, Aquilla, See BLAKELEY
Jared, Ct., See BLAKESLEY
BLAKLEY/BLAKELY, Moses, Ct., Cont., S12232
Obed, Ct., Cont., Mass., S44629. No half pay. File identifies this man; see N.A. Acc. No.874. 050016 Half Pay Obed Blakley
BLAKNEY, James, Pa. See BLEAKNEY
John, N.C.,S.C., See BLAKENEY
BLAKSLEE, Caleb, Ct., S34304
Jared, Ct., See BLAKESLEY
Nathaniel, Vt., Debbe, W16846
BLAKSLEY, Enos, See BLACKSLEY
BLALACK,
Charles, N.C., S3013; BLWt. 38551-160-55
David, N.C., See BLALOCK

BLALACK (continued)
Thomas, N.C., See BLALOCK
BLALOCK, Charles, See BLALACK
David, N.C., S3011
David, N.C., R919
George Henry, N.C., R20206
Jeremiah, N.C., Lucy, W8368
John, Va., Polly, W1807; BLWt.24979-160-55
Thomas, N.C., Ann, W18615
BLAN, Jesse, Va., S8073
John, N.J., See BLANE
BLANCH, Isaac, N.J., Henrietta, W23632
BLANCHAR, Jedediah, Ct., S14961
BLANCHARD, Aaron, Mass., S38552
Abner, Cont., Mass., S29639
Abner, Cont., N.Y., S40008
Amos, Mass., Lavina, W23636
Andrew, Cont., R920, N.Y. res. in 1828
Andrew, Cont., R.I., S40001
Anthony, N.Y., See BLANCHER
Benjamin, Pvt., R.I., BLWt. 2956 iss. 12/27/1798 to Israel Harris, ass.
Benjamin, R.I., S37782
Caleb, R.I., S21645
Cuff, Mass., See CHAMBERS
Daniel, Mass., Mary Wiggin, former wid., see claim of Wm. Wiggin, Mass.
Daniel, Mass., Mary, W20725
David, N.H., S12237
Elias, Ct., Cont., S12247
Elias, R.I., S44626
Ephraim, Pvt., N.Y., BLWt. 6862 iss. 2/14/1791
Ephraim, N.Y., S44627
Francis, Cont., Mass.,Thankful, W21681; BLWt.3700 iss. 1792 to B. Haskell, ass.
George, Mass., R921
Isaac, Mass., Olive, W15986; BLWt.11252-160-55
Isaac, N.J., S34035
Jacob, Ct., S37784
James, N.H., BLWt.78-200-Lt. Iss. 9/13/1790. No papers
Jedediah, Ct., See BLANCHAR
Jeremiah, Mass., Sarah, W27867; BLWt.3529-160-55
Jeremiah, Mass., R923
John, Cont., Mass., S45290; BLWt.104-300-Capt. Iss. 8/7/1789 to Richard Platt, ass. No papers
John, Mass., S29015
John, Mass., S45291
John, N.H., S29013
John, R.I., Vt., Mary Meyers, former wid., W5397
Jonathan, Mass., S29014
Joseph, Cont., N.H., S41442
Joseph, Mass., S16648
Joseph, Mass., Hannah Cutler, former wid., W22876; BLWt. 8459-160-55. He d. 1810 Ticonderoga, N.Y.
Joseph, N.Y., Mary Ladow,

BLANCHARD (continued)
former wid., BLWt.93556-160-55
Joseph, Pa., S44628
Josiah, Mass., Betsey, W21678
Leban, Pvt., N.J., BLWt.8130 iss. 10/-/--- to Ebenezer Farnham, ass.
Lysias, Mass., S34050
Nathaniel, Cont., Vt., S10385
Nathaniel, Mass., S34045
Nathaniel, Mass., Eunice, W16849
Peter, Cont., Canadian, Martha, W16506
Peter, Pvt., Hazen's Regt., BLWt.12771 iss. 2/4/1790
Reuben, N.H., Mary, W25250
Reuben, R.I., Amy, W18616
Russell, R.I., S15339
Samuel, R.I., Betty, W20731
Seth, Mass., Lydia, W12301; BLWt.34975-160-55
Simeon, Mass., Lois, W16851
Simon, Mass., S34582
Simon, Mass., Jemima, W20732; BLWt.2189-160-55
Solomon, Mass., Navy, S19216
Theophilus, Mass., See BLANCHER
Thomas, Mass., S22652
Timothy, Cont., Mass., S28647
William, Ct., Sarah, W17320
William, Cont., Mass., S30277
William, N.J., Mary, W5839
William, ---, Mass. agency, S46757
BLANCHER/BLANCHARD, Anthony, N.Y., Tamar, W18612
Daniel, Mass., See BLANCHARD
Theophilus, Cont., Sarah, W23622, Mass. res. in 1818
BLANCHET, Thomas, N.C., Elizabeth Lane, former wid., W20395
BLANCHFIELD, James, Pvt., S.C., BLWt.11980 iss. 11/24/1795
BLANCIT, Joel, N.C., Va., S29640
BLANCK/BLANK, Peter, Pa., Catharine, R926
BLAND, James, Pvt., Va., BLWt.11916 iss. 3/26/1792 to Francis Graves, ass.
James, Va., Amy, W5837
BLANDEN, Jonas, Mass., S34044
Samuel, Ct., Mass., S10389
BLANDER, John, N.Y., S6663
BLANDFORD, Clark, Ct., N.J., R927
Richard, Md., See BLANFORD
BLANDIN, Elisha, Cont., Mass., S34041
Francis, Mass., S34049
Jonathan, Ct., Mass., Submit, W1704
BLANDIN/BLANDEN, Lamech, Mass., S32123
BLANDING, Christopher, Mass., Martha, W23631; BLWt.13212-160-55
BLANE, George, Va., Rachael, R929
BLANE/BLAN, John, N.J., Margaret, W10423; BLWt.11410-160-55
BLANEY, John, Pvt., Hazen's Regt., BLWt.12772 iss. 9/2/1789
Samuel, Cont., Mass., Anna, W20723
BLANFORD/BLANDFORD, Joseph, Md., R928
Richard, Md., S10392

BLANK, Cornelius, Pvt., N.Y., BLWts.6788 & 6648 iss. 8/3/1790 to Cornelius Van Dyck, ass.
Cornelius, N.Y., S45294
Peter, Pa., See BLANCK
BLANKENBAKER, Nicholas, Va.,S30872
BLANKENSHIP, Abel, Va., Fanny, R931
Abraham/Abram, Va., Susan, W10425
Benjamin, Cont., Va., S30870
Daniel, Va. See BLANKINSHIP
Henry, Va., S6668
John, Va., S6667
Josiah, Va., S8072
Reuben, Va., S32120
William, Va., R932
Wommock, Va., S34652
BLANKINSHIP, Daniel, Va., S10390
BLANSFORD, Richard, Pvt., Md., BLWt.10945 iss. 8/14/1795 to Francis Sherrard, ass.
BLANTON, Burwell/Burrell, N.C., BLWt.59093-160-55
James, N.C., S6653
Thomas, Va., Scilly, S330
William, Va., Hannah, R933
BLASDEL, Daniel, Mass., Phebe Howard, former wid., W667; BLWt.19820-160-55
John, N.H., Laney, W5841; BLWt.12725-160-55
John, N.H., Dorothy, W21679
Levi, Cont., Mass., N.Y., See BLAISDELL
Samuel, Mass., Dorothy, W1214; BLWt.13882-160-55
BLASDELL, Daniel, N.H., See BLAISDELL
Ezra, N.H., S22123
John, N.H., See BLAISDELL
John, Mass., S29018
Parrit, Cont., Mass., N.H., S38556
Philip, Cont., N.H., Hannah, W17319
Philip, Mass., N.H., S18330; BLWt.26078-160-55
Philip, Pvt., N.H., BLWt.2930 iss. 2/8/1796 to Robt. Fletcher, ass.
William, Mass., S41443
BLASHFIELD, James R., Mass., Sally Davis, former wid., W19139
Ozem, Mass., Bathsheba, W14315
BLATCHFORD, John, Cont., Mass., BLWt.2166-100
John C., Cont., Mass., S37788
Uriah, Mass. See BLACHFORD
BLAUVELT, Abraham, N.J., S2080
Abraham, N.Y., Dis.--- No papers
Abraham P., N.Y., S22654
Cornelius, N.Y., S22650
Frederick, Pvt., N.J., BLWt. 8152 iss. 6/20/1789
Frederick, N.J., Elizabeth, W24700
Harman, N.J., S959
Harmanus, N.Y., S22653
Isaac, N.J., Sarah, R936
Isaac, N.Y., Eleonard/Ellen/Helen Van Houten, former wid., W18204. Her former husband, John Van Houten/Van Houtan, was pensioned, which see.

BLAUVELT (continued)
James J., N.J., N.Y., Rachel, W5838; BLWt.32238-160-55
John A., N.J., S956
John G., N.Y., Ann, W20728
John J./John I., N.Y., S22649
John J., N.Y., Clauche/Clausha, W20721
Maria, former wid. of Paul Powles/Powel Powels, N.J., which see
Richard, N.Y., Sarah, W16845; BLWt.10227-160-55
BLAYLOCK, George Henry, See BLALOCK
BLAZE, Joseph, Pvt., Md., BLWt. 10947 iss. 8/14/1795 to Francis Sherrard, ass.
BLAZEUR, Lawrence, N.Y., S23130
BLEAKLEY, George, Pa., S39999
BLEAKLEY/BLAKELY/BLAKELEY, James, S.C., R917
Robert, Va., Margaret, W279; BLWt.31772-160-55. She also applied for B.L. on acct. of service of 1st husb., John Maloney in 1806. Claim rejected. Papers within.
William, Va., R937
BLEAKNEY, James, Pa., BLWt.2503-100. Also spelled Blackney/Blackny/Blakeney/Blekny/Blakney/Bleckney/Blakney
BLECHER/BLEECHER, Yost, Cont. Pa., S40005
BLECHYNDEN, Charles, Va., S6656
BLECKMAN, Daniel, See BLEEKMAN
BLECKNEY, James, See BLEAKNEY
BLEDSO/BLEDSOE, George, ?, N.Y. agency. S14962
BLEDSOE, Benjamin, N.C., Sarah, R938
George, Ga., See BLEDSO
Jacob, N.C., S3012
James, Va., Judith Forsee, former widow, R3672
John, N.C., Sarah, R939
Lewis, Ga., N.C., Fanney, W17315
Miller, Va., S31556
Thomas, N.C., Margaret, W68
BLEECHER, Yost, See BLECHER
BLEECKER, Leonard, N.Y., S29017; BLWt.158-300-Capt. iss. 6/12/1790. No papers
BLEECKMAN/BLACKMAN/BLECKMAN, Daniel, Ct., Mary, W16848
BLEKNEY, James, See BLEAKNEY
BLESDELL/BLESDILL, Henry, Mass., Mary, W14314
BLETCHER, Jacob, N.C., S39198
BLETHEN, Ichabod, Mass., Elizabeth, R940
BLETHEN/BLITHIN, Increase, Mass. Isabella, W23621
BLEU, Seeley, N.J., See BLEW
BLEUFORD, William, See BLUFORD
BLEVENS/BLEVINS
Daniel, N.C., Va., S31555
James, N.C., Va., S32121
James, Va., See BLEVIN
John, Va., See BLEVINS
Nathan, Va., See BLEVINS
BLEVER, James, Md., See BLEWER
BLEVIN, James, Va., Hannah O., W5221; BLWt.31444-160-55
Samuel, R.I., Dis.---, no papers
BLEVINS, Abraham, N.C., R941
Daniel, N.C., Va., See BLEVENS
Henry, N.C., Catharine, W1703
James, Va., See BLEVENS
John, Va., Sally, R943
Nathan, Va., Lydia, W25253; BLWt.26822-160-55
William, Va., R945
BLEW, Frederick, N.J., R944; not same as Frederick Blue.
Seeley, N.J., Anna, W1369; BLWt.71186-160-55
BLEWER, George, Pa., BLWt.1140-200
James, Md., S10093
BLICK, James, Va., S6664
John, Va., S30868
BLIMBY, William, N.Y., See BLIMLY
BLIMLINE, Charles, See PLEMLINE
BLIMLY, William, N.Y., S12236
BLIN, Simeon, Ct., N.Y., S45292
William, Ct., S41444
BLING, Silas, Mass., See BLINN
BLINN, George, Cont., Mass., R.I., Jane, W1131; BLWts.224-60-55 & 2968-100 iss. 2/22/1792. No papers
Justus, Ct., S37790
Silas, Mass., Triphena, W18608
BLISH, Azubah, former wid. of Joseph Ransom/Ransome, Ct., which see
Ezra, Cont., Ct. res. 1818, S37785
BLISS, Asa, Mass., S19548
Calvin, Mass., S21070
Constant, N.H., Elizabeth Dame, former wid., W14583
Dan, Ct., Eunice, W23626
Daniel, Ct., N.Y., Martha, W10420
David, Ct., Jane, W5829
Ebenezer, Ct., Cont., Lucinda, W5832
Eli, Ct., Cont., S34046
Elijah, Cont., Mass., Rebecca Cheney, former wid., W22744; BLWt.2193-100. Her 2nd husb., Samuel Cheney, also served See papers within
Elijah, Mass., Elizabeth Wolf/Woolf, former wid., R11768. Her last husb., Fred. Wolf/Woolf also served. See papers within
Elijah, Mass., BLWt.574-100
Gains, Mass., S29635
Isaac, Mass., S12246
Isaac, Mass., Hannah, W15587
Isaiah, N.H., S16650
Jacob, Mass., S12249
Jacob, Mass., Mary, R948
James, Ct., Mehitable, W9728; BLWt.814-160-55
John, Ct., R.I., Reliance, W18609
John, Ct., Mary Freeman, former wid., R3781
BLISS (continued)
Jonathan, Navy, R.I. res. & Agency in 1823; S38560
Joseph, Cont., BLWt.123-200. Capt in Col. Crane's Regt. Artillery. Iss. 3/10/1790. No papers
Joshua, Cont., Mass., S38554
Moses, Mass., S29011
Nathan, Mass., Ruth, W3649; BLWt.19901-160-55
Nathan, Mass., Submit, W20730
Nathaniel, Mass., Susan, W26634
Noah, Mass., Elizabeth Ham, former wid., W9472; BLWt.39224-160-55
Polly, former wid. of Edmund Towne, Mass., which see
Reuben, Mass., Ruth, R949
Samuel, Ct., S18329
Samuel, Ct., Elizabeth, W17314
Samuel, Cont., Mass., S34048
Samuel, Mass., S12239
Samuel, N.Y., R950
Theodore, Col. Lamb's Regt. Art., BLWt.169-300-Capt. Iss. 7/9/1790 to Theodosius Fowler ass. No papers. See Heitman's Hist. Reg. & Mass. Archives, Thos. Theodore Bliss.
Thomas Theodore, see Theodore
William, Ct., R.I., S4953
Zenas/Zenas G., Vt., Hannah, R946 Allowed B.L. St.86938-40-50 for service War of 1812, but warrant cancelled. See within. See pension and B.L. claim of Dorcas, wid. of Edmund Whedon, N.Y. She also applied for B.L. as former wid. of Zenas Bliss, War of 1812 which was rejected.
BLITHIN, Increase, See BLETHEN
BLIVEN, Arnold, R.I., Mary, W15753
George, R.I., Vashti, W21682
James, R.I., Dis.-- No papers
BLIVEN/BLIVIN, Nathan, R.I., S21073
William, R.I., S21648
BLIVIN, Nathan, See BLIVEN
BLIVINS, Henry, See BLEVINS
BLIZZARD, Burton, Va., Sarah, W20720
BLOCKMON, Chloe, See BLACKMAN
BLODGET, Admatha, Ct., Mass., S45288
Amos, Cont., Mass., S45594
Artemas/Artomus, Ct., S45287
Artimas, Pvt., Ct., BLWt.5423 iss. 6/1/1793 to Stephen Thorn
BLODGET/BLODGETT, Benjamin, Ct., S16050
Caleb, N.H., BLWt.76-200-Lt. Iss. 4/2/1800 to Sam Blodget, heir
David, Mass., Margaret, W18617
Ebenezer, N.H., Sarah Hickok, former wid., W14913
Isaiah, Mass., Privateer, R952
Jacob, Mass., N.H., S15338
James, Mass., S10391
Jonas, Cont., Mass., S20634
Jonathan, N.H., Parney, W2715; BLWt.26402-160-55

BLODGET (continued)
Joseph, Mass., Lucy, R954
Joshua, Mass., S16051
Ludin/Ludim, Mass., S12238
Nathan, Mass., S12248
Rufus, Mass., S45289
Salmon, Mass., S45593
Samuel, Ct., Abigail, W17316
Samuel, Green Mt. Boys, Vt., S18724
Sardius, Green Mt. Boys, Vt., R21881
Silas, Ct., Mass., S44631
Solomon, Mass., S12244
Thomas, N.H., BLWt.2340-100
William, Mass., S29636
William, ---, BLWt.175-400-Maj. & Aide de Camp. Iss. 11/30/1789. No papers. Also recorded under BLWt.2542
BLODGETT, Abisha, Ct., U.S. Army 1785, S15752
Benjamin, Mass., Hannah Babcock, former wid., W4879
Elijah, Mass., N.H., S38557
Henry, Mass., Abigail, W18611
James, Mass., S34032
Joshua, N.H., Ruth, W16505
BLODGIT, Josiah, N.H., S45595
BLOGGET, Samuel Ct., See BLODGET
BLOGGETT, Benjamin, See BLODGET
BLOOD, Abel, Cont., Mass., S45596
Amos, Cont., Mass., S12243
Asa, N.H., S44632
Caleb, Mass., S34043
David, Cont., Mass., S15258
David, Mass., Jane G., W2516; BLWt.13719-160-55
Edmund/Edmond, Mass., Navy, S21072; BLWt.32206-160-55
Ephraim, N.H., Emeline Gallagher former wid., S46369; BLWt.966-100 & 248-60-55
Isaac, Mass., Lydia, W18619
Israel M., Mass., S23126
John, Mass., Piercy, W890; BLWt. 34966-160-55
Jonas, Cont., Mass., Sarah,W27385
Josiah, Cont., Mass., S34040
Lemuel, Mass., Lucy, W23618
Levi, Mass., S16323
Moses, Mass., S4952
Nathaniel, N.H., S18723
Phineas, Pvt., Mass., BLWts. 3785 & 253-60-55 iss. 2/27/1790. BLWt.3785 to Theos. Fowler, ass.
Phinehas, Mass., Lois Hitchcock, former wid., W3993; BLWt.253-60-55
Reuben, N.H., S34051
Samuel, Mass., S23131
Samuel, Mass., Sally, W16847; BLWt.13860-160-55
Simeon, Cont., Mass., N.H., S49265
Thaddeus, Mass., S12233
Thomas, N.H., S45597
BLOODGOOD, John, N.J., Elizabeth, W23628
BLOOM, Abraham, N.J., Mary, R955

BLOOM (continued)
Albert, N.Y., See BLUM
Daniel, Pa., S40004
Peter, N.J., R956
Peter C., N.Y., S17284
BLOOMER/BLUMER
Gilbert, N.Y., S15337
Stephen, Md., S12051
William, N.Y., S44630
BLOOMFIELD, Aaron, N.J., Keziah, W1536
James, N.J., S2380
Joseph, N.J., Isabella, W10418; BLWt.124-400-Major. Iss. 8/11/ 1789. Also recorded as Wt. 2518. No papers
Nathan, N.J., Betsy, W16195
Thomas, N.J., S957
Thomas, N.J., Ann, R958
BLOOMLY, John, Pvt., Hazen's Regt., BLWt.12746 iss. 3/12/ 1790 to Christian Gross, ass.
BLOON, Solomon, Mass. See MALOON
BLOSS, Joseph, Ct., Cont., S21071
Samuel, Mass., Emilison, W1368
Valentine, Va., S9102
Walter, N.H., Hannah, W21689
William, N.Y., S12251
Zadok, Cont., Ct., R960
BLOSSOM, Benjamin, Cont., Mass., S38559
David, Mass., Sea Service, Privateer, Vt., Rhoda, R961; BLWt. 38823-160-55
Hannah, former wid. of Josiah Bean, N.H., W24702
Peter, Mass., Privateer, Vt., S12235
Rufus, Mass., R.I., R962
BLOUNT, Elisha, Ct., See BLUNT
Frederick, Pvt., N.C., BLWt. 11968 iss. 3/6/1799 to Alisha Thomas, ass.
John, Cont., Mass., See BLUNT
Nathaniel/Natt, Va., See BLUNT
Reading, N.C., BLWt.289-400-Maj. Iss. 12/21/1795. No papers
BLOUNT/BLUNT, William, N.Y.,S10384
BLOWER, Judith, former wid. of Isaac Boynton, N.H., which see
BLOWERS, David, N.Y., S9819
Ephraim, N.Y., S38558; BLWt. 1956-100
John, N.J., S2381
Robert, Pvt., N.J., BLWt.8145 iss. 9/21/179- to John G. Hopper, ass.
Robert, N.J., S34036
Samuel, N.Y., S12245
BLOXSOM, Scarborough, Va. Sea Service, Leah, W5842
BLUE, Adrian, Pvt., Hazen's Regt. BLWt.12813 iss. 6/29/1789 to Matthew McConnell, ass.
David, not Rev. War, N.West Indian War - 1791, res.: Va., Ky., Ind.; O.W. Inv. File No. 6670, also O.W. Inv. File 26011 not used now
David, Va., R964
Frederick, Pa., N.J., S23544
Isaac, N.J., Amey, R963

BLUE (continued)
John, Cont., N.Y. & Braddock's Campaign in 1755, S42620
John, N.C., S6655
John, Pa., S16646
Jonathan, N.H., Jennet, W16100
Michael, N.J., S23543
Peter, Va., Susannah, R965; BLRej.253874-1855
Samuel, N.H., Hannah, W23624
William, Drummer, N.J., BLWt. 8088 iss. --/--/---- to Charles Ellis, ass.
BLUEFORD/BLEUFORD/BLUFFORD
William, Cont., Va., Sarah, W25252
BLUM/BLOOM
Albert, N.Y., Anna Eva, W17321; BLWt.4788-100
John Henry, Pa., S41440
BLUMER, Gilbert, See BLOOMER
BLUNDELL, Absalom, Tenn. res. in 1838, R966
BLUNDIN, John, Cont., Mass.,S40003
William, Drum Major, Hazen's Regt BLWt.12815 iss. 6/20/1789
BLUNDON/BLUNDOM, Elijah, Va., S37778
BLUNK, Andrew, Pa., Mary, R967
BLUNT, Asher, Ct., S29016
BLUNT/BLOUNT, Elisha, Ct., Privateer, Sally, W16850
John, Mass., Sarah, W23619; BLWt.16256-160-55
Jonathan, Cont., Mass., S44634; BLWt.3818 iss. 1799
Jonathan, Matross, Cont. Artillery (Crane's), Mass., BLWt. 3818 iss. 6/22/1799 to Marlbry Turner, ass.
Natt/Nathaniel, Va., S49296
William, Navy, N.H., Privateer, Mary, W23633; BLWt.13438-160-55
William, N.Y., See BLOUNT
William, Va., S42088
BLURTON, Edward, N.C., Rosa, W5223; BLWt.17880-160-55
BLUSH, Joseph, Ct., R969
BLY, Jacob, Va., Catharine, W18618
John, R.I., S18721
John, Va., S37780
Moses, N.H., S14965
Oliver, R.I., S21069
BLYDENBURGH, Keturah, former wid. of Joseph Tooker, N.Y. which see
BLYE, John, Mass., Margaret, W14312
BLYTH, Joseph, N.C., BLWt.290-400-Surgn., iss. 10/20/1791 to Joseph Blyth. No papers
BLYTHE, David, Pa., Elizabeth, W5222
Mary, former wid. of James Bray, N.J.,N.Y., Pa., Which see
BOACHUS/BACCHUS/BACKUS, George N.Y., S39951
BOADLEY, Andrew, N.Y., See BODLEY
BOADLEY/BOWDLEY, John, S.C., R970
BOAN/BONE
George, N.C., S.C., S18326
Lewis, S.C., Mary, R971
BOARD, Cornelius D., N.J., R974
BOARD/BYRD, John, Md., Nancy, R975

BOARD/BOORD, Patrick, Va., Mary, W5854; BLWt.47617-160-55
Philip, N.J., S14979
BOARDMAN, Aaron, Mass., R977
Amos, Ct., S21077
Amos, Cont., Mass., See BORDMAN
Benjamin, Cont., Mass., S16653
Elias, Mass., Hannah, W14323
Elijah, Sgt., Ct., BLWt.5483 iss. 12/14/1789 to Richard Platt
Elijah, Ct., Nancy, W15754
Elijah, Cont., Ct., Mercy, W10433
Elijah, Cont., Ct., Mary Ann, W25262
Frederick, Pa., See BAUMAN
Jehiel, Vt., Salla, W15595
John Howe, Cont., Mass., S6293
Jonas, Ct., Elizabeth, W23649
Jonathan, Ct., S46204
Josiah, Cont., Ct., Susannah, W16854
Moses, Ct., Dis.---. No papers
Nathaniel, Vt., S18730
Samuel Allen, Ct., Catharina, R12576
Seth, Ct., Cont., S36419
Timothy, Ct., Sea Service, S22128
William, Pvt., Mass., BLWt.3750 iss. 5/1/1792
William, Mass., Betsey, W21683
BOARDWINE, Backus, Mass., S34062
BOAS, Henry, Pa., S16053. See N.A. Acc. No. 874-050017. Not half pay. Henry Boas
BOATMAN, Claudius, Pa. res. of heir in 1860, R12556
William, Pa., Va., S8085
BOATWRIGHT, John, Va., S5290
BOAZ, James, Mass., S36921
James, Va., S6694
Meshach, Va., S39205
BOBBETT, Isham, See BOBBITT
William, N.C., Susannah, W9740
William, Va., R979
BOBBITT, Isham, N.C., Elizabeth, W24709
Sherwood, N.C., Sarah, W17328
BOBO, Absalom, S.C., R980
Joseph, Va., R981
BOCK, George, Pa., S3020
Michael, Va., S6679
BOCKOVEN, Jacob, N.J., Elizabeth, W4134
BOCKUS, Jacob, N.Y., Juda, W21692
BODEN, James, N.J., S478
Theodore, Cont., Mass., Hannah, W1537; BLWt.34951-160-55
William, Cont. Mass., Experience, W13428
BODENHAMER, Peter, N.C., Agnes, R982
BODFISH, William, Mass., Abigail, W5849
BODINE, Frederick, Pa., S9105
Isaac, N.Y., S12258
John, Cont., Va., S42624
John, Cont., Va., S42628
John, N.J., Mary, W259
BODLE, Abraham, Pa., BLWt.291-100
BODLEY, Andrew, N.Y., S42605; BLWt.1442-100

BODLEY (continued)
Thomas, Pa., S3038
BODLY, John, S.C., S32128
William, N.Y., S2093
BODRAY, John, Md., See BOUDY
BODWELL, Henry, Mass., Sally, W14337
John, Mass., S40025
William, Corp., Mass., BLWt. 3793 iss. 12/3/1789
William, Mass., S42629
BODWIN, Henry, Pvt., "in Moylan's Dragoons", Pa., BLWt.9029 iss. 11/5/1789
BODY, Robert, Drummer, Md.,BLWt. 11019 iss. 1/17/1793 to John Wright, ass. of Samuel Davis, admr.
BOFFENMEYER, Henry, Pa., R1414
BOGAART, Isaac, N.Y., BLWt. 217-200-Lt. iss. 12/12/1791. No papers. Also recorded as above under BLWt.2577
BOGARDUS, Henry, N.Y., S44636
Henry, N.Y., Mary, W18634; BLWt.3068-160-55
Henry, N.Y., Rachel, R984
Jacob, N.Y., R983
James C., N.Y., Mary, W15878
BOGART, Cornelius, N.J., BLWt.8151-100
Cornelius, N.Y., Sarah, W23650
Henry, N.Y., Prudence, W20750; BLWt.33569-160-55
John, N.Y., S23547
James N., Pvt., N.J., BLWts. 8090 & 13953 iss. 10/22/1791 to -------, N.J.
Nicholas, N.Y., See SISCOW
Nicholas N., R.I., Elsie Van Rensselaer, former wid., W6372; BLWt.1157-300. See case of her other husb., James Van Rensselaer, N.Y.
BOGE, Jeffry A., See BOOGE
BOGERT, David R., N.J., Margaret R., W3502; BLWt.27618-160-55
Henry, N.Y., See BOGART
James/Jacobus, N.J., Elizabeth Suffren, former wid., W17890
John G., N.Y., S22656
Nicholas N., R.I., See BOGART
BOGG, John, Pvt., N.Y.; BLWt. 6773 iss. 7/10/1790 to John Quackinboss, ass.
BOGGE, John, Pvt., N.Y., BLWt. 6809 iss. 9/15/1790 to John S. Hobart, et al, ass.
BOGGS, Alexander, Pa., S14971
David, Pa., S40024
Francis, Va., R985
Jeremiah, Va., R986
John, N.C., Eve, W18627; BLWt. 16262-160-55
Thomas, S.C., Elizabeth, W27895
William, Pa., Elizabeth, R987; BLWt.34547-160-55
BOGGUS, Jeremiah, See BOGGS
BOGLE, Andrew, Pa., Va., Elizabeth, R1107
Joseph, Pa., Va., Margaret, W69
Thomas, Mass., Elizabeth, W24705

BOGLE (continued)
William, Cont., Mass., Lucy, W15590
BOGMAN, Charles, R.I., S38564
BOGS, Samuel, Mass., See BOGUES
BOGUE, Jeffrey A., See BOOGE
Publius V., Ct., S46024
BOGUES, Samuel, Mass., Susannah, W26635
BOHAN, Dennis, Pvt., Hazen's Regt. BLWt.12774 iss. 12/5/1791 to Wm. Thomas, ass.
Joseph, Cont., Poland, S37794
BOHANNON, Ambross, Va., BLWt.280-200-Lt. Iss. 5/29/1792 to Robt. Means, ass. No papers
John, N.J., R988
John, Va., Helen, R989
BOHON, Benjamin, Va., Sarah, W8375
John, Va., S14975
BOHONON, Ananiah, N.H., S38563
Stephen, N.H., Olive, W24713
BOICE, Abraham, Va., See BOYCE
George, Cont., Md., BLWt.163-100
James, Navy, N.H., See BOYCE
James, Pvt., N.Y., BLWt.6821 iss. 9/28/1790 to Bartholomew & Fisher, assnes.
Peter, N.Y., S45304
BOID, George, N.Y., S12274
BOIDRE, Gill, Cont., B.L. Reg.---
BOIES, James, N.H., Betsey, W15599
Joel, Mass., Betsey Treat, former wid., R10690. She was pensioned under Thomas Treat, which see
John, N.H., Mary, W24707; BLWt. 9490-160-55
BOILEAU, Abraham, Cont., N.Y., S44639
Amable, Cont., N.Y. res. 1828, S46349; BLWt.12799-100. Pvt. in Hazen's Regt. Iss. 1/22/1790 to Benj. Mooers, ass. No papers
Pierre, Pvt., Hazen's Regt., BLWt. 12797 iss. 1/22/1790 to Benj. Mooers, ass.
Pierre, Cont., BLWt.313-200-Lt. in Hazen's Regt. Iss. 1/22/1790 to Benj. Moore, ass. No papers. See BOILEAU, Pierre Anable in Heitman's Hist. Reg.
BOIN, Reuben, Va., See BOWEN
BOIS, John, N.H., See BOIES
BOISE, Peter, Pvt., N.Y., BLWt.6775 iss. 11/18/1791 to Ebenezer Farnham, ass.
BOISSEAU, John, Va., S3040
BOLAND, Daniel, Pa., See BOTAN
BOLCOM, Bezaleel, Mass., R.I. See BALCOM
David, Mass., Navy, Mary, W15594
Elijah, Mass., Jemima, W14333, of Falmouth & Norton during Rev. & of Mansfield later.
BOLDER, John, Va., S37597
BOLDEREY, John, Cont., Mass. Sea Service, S35785
BOLDMAN, John, N.Y., Esther, W8149; BLWt.49047-160-55
BOLE, James, Pa., S3023
Thomas, Pa., R12578
BOLEN, John, Va., S1790

BOLENER, Adam, Va., S12267
BOLES, Samuel, Del., Md., Privateer, Nancy, W10444; BLWt. 30615-160-55
Zachariah, Va. See BOWLES
BOLEY, Frederick, Not Rev., French War 1798-1800. Reg. 1396-55, U.S. Navy. Pa. res.
Prestley, Cont., Va., S39204
BOLICK, Casper, N.C.,Mary, W18566
BOLIN, Thomas, N.C., S32126
BOLING, Edmond/Edmon, Va., S39206
BOLING/BOWLING, Jarret, Va., S18324; BLWt.26360-160-55
Jesse, N.C., S14974
BOLKCOM, Elijah, Mass., See BOLCOM
Elijah, Mass., See BALKCOM
BOLLEN, John, N.J., Ann, W11173
BOLLES, Amos, Cont., Mass., R991
Asa, Mass., Keziah, W17331
James, Ct., Cont., S36420
BOLLES/BOWLES, John, Mass., Cynthia; BLWt.67541-160-55
Joseph, Cont., Ct., Betsey, W17327
BOLLING, Joseph, Va., See BOWLING
Robert, Va., S6689
Robert, Va. Sea Service, Clara, R19363; Va. half pay
BOLLINGER, Abraham, Pa., R993
BOLLINGTON, John, Pvt., 1st Regt. of Dragoons, BLWt.12762 iss. 2/4/1793
BOLLZ, Joseph, Va., See BOWLING
BOLSTER, Baruch, Mass., S41449
Isaac, Cont., Mass., Aphia Carey/ Alphia Cary, former wid., W25385
Joel, Mass., Sarah, W18629
Nathan, Mass., S45606
BOLT, Abraham, S.C., Va., S9232
BOLTEN, George, Pvt., N.Y., BLWt.6810 iss. 10/12/1790 to Isaac Bogoart, ass.
BOLTENHOUSE, John, See BOULTENHOUSE
BOLTER, Benjamin, Mass., See BOULTER
Lemuel, Mass., S34660
BOLTON, Aaron, Cont., Mass., S12271
Alexander, N.Y., Sarah, W20752
Benjamin, N.C., S37795
David, Cont., Mass., Hannah, W1705
Ebenezer, Mass., S29645
James, Md., N.C., R994
James, N.Y., Margaret, W16510
John, Mass., BLWt.3685-100-Pvt. iss. 5/6/1797 to H. Newman, ass. No papers
John, Mass., S29649
John, Mass., S34583
John, N.J., BLWt.8095-100-Pvt. iss. 10/27/1796 to Joseph Lewis. No papers
John, N.J., S34064
Joseph, Mass., S34052
Joseph, Mass., Huldah, W23658
Joseph, N.J., BLWt.8108-100-Pvt. Iss. 12/27/1791. No papers

BOLTON (continued)
Joseph, N.Y., S44637
Mathew, N.Y., BLWt.6822-100-Pvt. Iss. 7/6/1790. No papers
Philip, Mass., Bethiah, W14334
Solomon, Cont., Mass., S37596
Spencer, See BOULTON
Timothy, Cont., Mass., S41445
BOLTZ/PULS, John, Pa., R468
BOMAN, John, Va., S18323
BOMAR, John, Va., S2383
BOME, John, S.C. See BONE
BOMGARDNER, David, See BUMGARNER
George, Md., S40022
William, Md., S34657
BONAR, Henry, Pa., S3042
BOND, Adonijah, Mass., S12253
Asa, N.H., Sarah, W18624
Bailey, Mass., S29646
Benjamin, Md., R1000
Benjamin, N.J., R999
Bethuel, Mass., Lydia, W21686
David, Vt., Patty, W23655
Elihu, N.J., Phebe, W10430; BLWt.28612-160-55
Gilbert, Mass., S45601
Israel, Mass., Polly, W21694
Israel, Sgt., Mass., BLWt.3739 iss. 7/20/1789 to Reuben Lilley, ass.
Jacob, Ct., N.J., N.Y., S12273
James, Md., R1001
John, Pvt., Md., BLWt.10950 iss. 8/16/1797 to James DeBaufre, ass.
John, Md., S39199
John, Va., Joannah, W5225; BLWt. 6441-160-55
Jonas, Mass., Eunice, W1132
Joseph, Cont., Mass., Polly, W23648
Joseph, Cont., N.J., Mary, W23657
Joseph, Pvt., "in the Invalids" BLWt.12846 iss. 8/10/1789 to Richard Platt, ass.
Pedee, former wid. of Leonard Proctor, Mass., Sea Service, which see
Phineas, Mass., Navy, S21076
Richard, N.Y., Angelica, R997
Richard, Va., Susannah, W5847
Samuel, Md., R1002
Samuel, Pvt., Mass., BLWt.3688 iss. 3/25/1790
Samuel, Mass., N.H., S45600
Seth, Mass., Amy, R998
Thomas, Cont., BLWt.316-600-Purveyor in Gen. Hosp. Iss. 8/17/1789. No papers
Thomas, Pvt. "in the Invalids" BLWt.12826 iss. 2/14/1791
William, Cont., Mass., S14976
William, N.C., S3027
William, Va., Ann, W5848
William, Va., Ga., Sarah, W8370
Wright, Va., S3028
Wright, Va., Patsey, W3382
BONDY, John, See BOUDY
BONE, Archibald, N.C., S41456
George, N.C., S.C., See BOAN
John, N.C., S14981
John, S.C., S14980
Lewis, S.C., See BOAN
William, N.C., Jemima, R1003

BONES, Rachel, former wid. of Andrew Uhler, Navy, Pa., which see
BONESTALE/BONESTEEL, Philip, N.Y., S12254
BONESTEEL, David, N.Y., Susannah, R470
Henry, N.Y., R1006
Philip, N.Y., See BONESTALE
BONET, Joseph, Sgt., Ct., BLWt. 5433 iss. 2/13/1790 "Certifd. the issue on an application of the Hon. Mr. Tichenor".
BONETT, Joseph, Ct., Cont., Green Mt. Boys, S41450; BLWt.5433-100-Iss. 2/13/1790. No papers
BONEY, Daniel, N.C., S6672
BONFOY, Benamuel, Ct., Concurrence, W17330
Henry, Ct., Cont., S12266
BONHAM, Absalom, N.J., BLWt.182-200 Lt. No papers
Malakiah, Md., BLWt.240-200-Lt. Iss. 2/28/1789. No papers
Zederkiah, See BENHAM
BONKER, Oliver, N.Y. See BOUKER
William, N.Y., See BANKER
BONNEL, Aaron, N.J., Rachel, R1009
Abner, N.J., S18321
Caleb, Gilbert, N.J., Joanna, W777
Paul, Pvt., Pa., BLWt.8998 iss. 6/11/1789 to Matthias Denman, ass.
Paul, Pa. & 17th & 19th U.S. Inf. War of 1812, S42625
BONNELL, Benjamin, Pvt., N.J., BLWt.8161 iss. 10/22/1789 to Samuel Potter, William & John Valentine, admrs. of Obadiah Valentine, dec'd., late ass.
James, Cont., N.J., Elizabeth, W10437; BLWt.178-300-Capt. Iss. 8/14/1789. No papers
John, N.J., S6676
John, Pvt., Lamb's Artillery, N.Y., BLWt.6891 iss. 2/7/1792 to Heil Peck, ass.
Joseph, N.J., S2087
Samuel, Q.M. Sgt., N.J., BLWt. 8112 iss. 4/23/1790
BONNER, John, N.H., Sarah Moors, former wid., W13742
John, N.C., S6681
John, Pa., Jane, W3214
John, Va., S2382
Joseph, Pa., S40021
William, N.C., Elizabeth, W8376
William, Pa., Hannah, W5937
BONNETT, Jacob, Va., S8080
Lewis, Va., S5294
Peter, Va., S5293
BONNEWELL, Thomas, Va. Sea Service R10. Va. half pay
BONNEY, Ezekiel, Mass., S4957
Isaac, Mass., S18733
Joseph, Cont., Mass., Mary, W15588
Silence, former wid. of Clement Drake, Mass., which see
Thomas, Va., S6688
BONNIFIELD, Samuel, Va., R1007
BONNY, Benjamin, Mass., Hannah,

BONNY (continued)
W16857
Isaac, Mass., See BONNEY
John, N.Y., Annatje/Anna, R1010
BONSALL, Benjamin, Pa., S22132
Clement, Pa. Sea Service, R1011
BONDSTED, Frederick, Mass., N.Y., S22659
BONTA, Daniel, N.J., See BANTA
Hendrick/Henry, N.Y., Engeltje/ Angelica, W21704
BONTIN, John, N.C., See BOUTIN
BONWELL, James, Va., S42626
BOOCHER, Abraham, Va., See BOOKER
BOODY, John, Pvt., Md., BLWt. 10986 iss. 2/1/1790
Mary, former wid. of Thomas Burnett, Md., which see
BOOFEE, Thomas, Cont., N.H., S37599
BOOGE, Jeffrey A., Cont., Freedom, W18638. Also BOGUE/BOOGUE/BOGE
Oliver, Ct., Cont., Lucy, W17326
Samuel Cook, Ct., Tryphena, R1013
BOOGUE, Jeffrey A., See BOOGE
BOOKER, Aaron, Mass., S30878
Abraham, Va., Frances, W3651; BLWt.28625-160-55
Daniel, Mass., BLWt.34959-160-55
George, Va., S16054
Gideon, Ga., BLWt.310-300-Capt. Iss. 8/8/1797 to Abraham Baldwin, ass. No papers
Isaiah, Mass., Sarah, W23660
Lewis, Va., BLWt. 8-200
Samuel, Va., Nancy A., W521
Samuel, Va., BLWt. 315-300
Young, Mass., Ann, W17333; BLWt. 13708-160-55
BOOKHOUT, James, N.Y., Margaret, W18628; BLWt.5202-160-55
BOOLES, William, N.C. See BOWLES
BOOM, John, N.Y., S45311
Nicholas, N.Y., S44642
BOOMER, Ephraim, Mass., War of 1812, Abigail, W14325; BLWts. 792-100 & 9-60-55
James, Mass., S18728
Martin, Mass., Sarah, R1014
BOON, Elisha, N.C., S35196
Francis, Mass., R1016
Hawkins, Pa., Jane Fertenbaugh, former wid., W10979
Jesse, N.C., S31562
John, Pvt., N.Y., BLWt.6846 iss. 4/18/1792 to Cornelius Vandyke
John, N.C., Anne, W10445; BLWt. 40913-160-55
John, Pa., S39203
John, Pa., Elizabeth, R1017
John, Pvt. "in Proctor's Artillery", Pa., BLWt.9057 iss. 6/20/1789
Lewis, N.C., S6683
Moses, N.J., S2086
Moses, Pvt. "in the Corps of Artillery Artificers of Pa.", BLWt.12852 iss. 8/7/1789 to Richard Platt, ass.
Raiford/Racford, N.C., Polly, W4900
Ralph, Pa., S3026

BOON (continued)
Samuel, N.C., S.C., See BOONE
Samuel, Pvt., Pa., BLWt.8982 iss. 3/8/1792 to Stephen Murphy, ass.
Thomas, S.C., Mary, W23656
Willis, N.C., S41455
BOONE, Adam, Md., S8075
Deidamia, former wid. of Ezra Davison, Ct., which see
John, Md., S8076
Jonathan, Pa., R9327
Joseph, Sr. Not Rev. Indian War 1790, enl. Ky. Old War Inv. File 26014
Samuel, N.C., S.C., S1168
Squire, S.C., Anna, W8372
BOORAEM, Jacob, N.J., Christiana, W395
BOORD, Patrick, N.J., See BOARD
BOOSE, Cato, R.I., S15342
BOOSWITH, James, Drum Major, N.Y., BLWt.6765 iss.7/24/1790 to John Lawrence, ass.
BOOTEN/BOOTON, Travis, Va., Ruth Kavanaugh, former wid., W9382
BOOTH, Beverly, Va., Mary, W25267; BLWt.28655-160-55
David, Ct., Betsey, W1370; BLWt.26719-160-55
David, N.Y., S36425
Edward/Edwin, Md. Rachel, R1021
Erastus, Ct., S44644
George, Va., S1791
Gideon, Ct., Hannah Lewis, former wid., W26206; BLWt.5378-160-55
Henry, Pvt., Ct., BLWt.5402 iss. 12/2/1791 to Isaac Bronson
Isaac, Ct., S14983
Isaiah, Ct., Cont., Polly, W1809; BLWt.8174-160-55
Isaiah, Mass., Nancy, W17329
James, Va., S30880
James, Va., Caty, R1018
John, Ct., Sarah, R1022
John, S.C., Rebecca, W25258; BLWt.83523-160-55
John, Va., R1020
Lucretia, former wid.of Frederick Chapin, Ct., which see
Nathaniel, Ct., S10381
Peter, Ct., Mass., Mary, W15597
Ruth, former wid. of Isaac Jones, Ct., which see
Samuel, Ct., S12272
Silas, Ct., S14969
Stoten, Mass., Amie/Anne, W18632
Thomas, Ct., S14970
Thomas, Va., S10383
Walter, Ct., Cont., S36422
William, Cont., Mass., BLWt.712-100
William, N.Y., R1023
William, Va. Sea Service, R11, Va. half pay
William, Mass., Elizabeth, W24710
BOOTHWICK, George, See BORTHWICK
BOOTLE, Thomas, Mass., N.C., Martha, W16507
BOOTMAN, Jacob H., See BUTMAN

BOOTMAN (continued)
Nathaniel, Cont., N.H. res. in 1818. S49307
Thomas, N.H., R1025
BOOTON, Travis, Va., See BOOTEN
William, Va., Amelia, W8377
BOOTWRIGHT, Samuel, Va., S6684
BOOTY, Joseph, N.J., Johannah, W23639
BOOZ, Jacob, Pa., S22131
John, Va., S35198
Richard, Va., R1026
BOOZE, John, Pvt., Va., BLWt. 11917 iss. 5/5/1790 to Wm. J. Vreedenburgh, ass.
BOOZER, Jacob, Pa., Christiana, W5864
BOOZMAN, Jesse, N.C., S41447
BORAH, Jacob, Pa., See BORRAH
BORDEN, Benjamin, Ct., R.I., Sarah, R1028
Ebenezer, Mass., Azibah, W21693
Elijah, Cont., Mass. res in 1818, S34584
Gale, R.I., Mary Hopkins, former wid., R5211
Gideon, R.I., S29651
Job, N.J., S2050
John, Navy, Mass., Charlotte, W8176; BLWt.28586-160-55
Joshua, Ct., Betsey, W16855
Josiah, Navy, R.I.,Susannah,W23644
Nathan, N.Y., R1447
Selden, Mass., S45603
Theodore, Cont., Mass. See BODEN
William, R.I., S21075
BORDERS, Christopher, Va., S9104
Peters, Cont., N.C., Esther, W2914; BLWt.15173-160-55
Peter, Va., R1029
BORDINE, James, N.J., S2389
BORDMAN, Amos, Cont., Mass., Mary, W20737
Moses, Pvt. "in the Corps of Invalids", BLWt.12837 iss 12/14/ 1789 to Richard Platt, ass.
BORDWELL, John, Mass. See BODWELL
BORELAND, Thomas, Md., S40010
BOREN, John, Md., R1030
William, S.C., S16652
BORER, Charles, Va., S8082
BORGER, Yost, Pa., S40012
BORING, Isaac, N.C., Phebe, R1031; BLWt.14980-160-55
BORNHEIMER, Jacob, Mass., Mary, W3501
BORRAH, Jacob, Pa., S30883
BORRES, John Proctor, Ct., Lydia, W18636
BORREY, John, Cont., Pa., S40023
BORROWS, John, Cont., N.J., Pa., S22134
BORST, John, N.Y., Christiana, W20736
John J., N.Y., See BUST
Martines, N.Y., Elizabeth, W18630; BLWt.8143-160-55
BORT, Nicholas, N.Y., Sophrona, W16852
BORTEL, Philip, N.Y., Martha/ Patty, R1034
BORTHWICK, George, N.Y., R1024

BORTLE, Andrew, N.Y., Sophia, R26156
Philip, N.Y., See BORTEL
Philip, N.Y., R1035
BOSAN, Nathaniel, Pvt., Mass., BLWt.3778 iss. 5/8/1792 to Ezra Blodget, ass.
BOSHART, Rudolph, S.C., R1036
BOSKERK, Martin, See VAN BUSKIRK
BOSKITT, John, Pvt., Hazen's Regt. BLWt.12779 iss. 7/18/1791 to Henry Pells, ass.
BOSS, Adam, Md., Harriet, W10238; BLWt.79530-160-55
Benjamin, Cont., R.I., S21078
Christian, Pvt., Md., BLWt. 11013 iss. 6/11/1790
Jabez, R.I., Sarah, W16508
John L., R.I., Sarah, W12316
Joseph, N.J., S1095
Richard, N.C., See BASS
BOSSET, Isaac, Ct., S36426
BOST, George, N.C., Hannah, R1038
BOSTAIN, Andrew, N.C., See BOSTIAN
BOSTEAN, Jacob, N.C., See BOSTON
BOSTEYON, Adam, Va., See BOSTON
BOSTIAN, Andrew, N.C., S6680
BOSTICK, Absalom, Va., R1039
Ezra, N.C., Drusilla, W23653
John, N.C., R1040
BOSTIL, Philip, Sgt. "in the Invalids", BLWt.12825 iss. 1/5/1791 to Sarah Bostil, sole executrix
BOSTMAN, Frederick, Pvt. Hazen's Regt., BLWt.12811 iss. 9/11/1792
BOSTON, Adam, Va., Juliet/Julianna W18622
Andrew, N.C., S8078
Christopher, N.C., Elizabeth, W12323; BLWt.30604-160-55
Christopher, Pa., R1041
Elijah, Cont., Mass. See BASTON
Garsham/Gershom, Cont., Mass., Dorcas, W20739
Jacob, N.C., S6675
John, Pvt., N.J., BLWt.8139 iss. 6/17/1789
Jonathan, Mass., See BARTON
Peter, Ct. Sea Service & Mass., Rhoda, W3650
Reuben, Va., S16330
Sawney, Pvt., Ct., BLWt.5419 iss. 9/22/1789 to Erastus Perkins
Shibuel, Mass., S16654
Thomas, Mass., See BASTON
Winthrop, Mass., Hannah, W1538; BLWt.13870-160-55
BOSTWICK, Amos, Cont., Ct., S45312
Andrew, Cont., Ct., S36915
David, Ct., S36418; BLWt.2193-160-55
Doctor, Ct., S2384
Ebenezer, Ct., S42090; BLWt. 32-100
Elisha, Ct., Cont., S10376
Elizur/Eliezer, Ct., S4269
John, Mass., Betsey, W1810; BLWt.6408-160-55
Jonathan, Ct., S14978

BOSTWICK (continued)
Levi, Ct., Anne/Anna, W21699
Medad, Ct., Mary M., R1042; BLWt.34591-160-55
Nathan, Ct., S40009
Oliver, Ct., Dis.---. No papers
Reuben, Ct., S19551
William, N.J., BLWt.153-200-Lt. Iss. 12/23/1799 to Obadiah Bostwick & other sons. Also recorded under BLWt.2524, iss. same date to Obadiah Bostwick, son of Wm. and to Andrew Morrell guardian to Chas. & John, sons of Wm. No papers
BOSWELL, Jesse, Md., Mary, W705; BLWt.11419-160-55
Macher/Machin, Va., R19364; Va. half pay
Reuben, Va. See BOZZELL
Samuel, Pvt., Md., BLWt.10959 iss. 2/1/1790
Thomas, ----, res. Columbus Co., N.C. in 1828; R20330
Weldon, Pa., R605
William, Mass., R1044
William, N.C., Lydia, W18639
William, Pa., R1045
William, R.I., S38565; BLWt.1527-100
BOSWORTH, Allen, Ct., Sarah, R1048 BLWt.50856-160-55
Benjamin, Mass., S15756
Benjamin, Mass., S40013
Benjamin, R.I., Sarah, R1049
Chloe, former wid. of Shubael Wheeler, Mass., which see
Daniel, Ct., Cont., Rachel, W447
Daniel, Cont., Mass., Huldah, W24706
Elisha, Cont., R.I., S18320
Ichabod, Mass. See BOZWORTH
Isaac, Mass., S15758
Jacob, Ct., Cont. S----; BLWt. 1625-100
John, Mass., See BOZWORTH
Jonathan, Cont., Mass., Abigail, W23641
Jonathan, Cont., R.I., S45607
Jonathan, Pa., See BOZORTH
Nathaniel, Ct., Cont., Vt., S38561
Richard, Cont., Mass., S34060
Samuel, R.I., Tabitha, W12315
Sarah, former wid. of Joshua Ford, Mass., which see
Timothy, Privateer, R.I., Nancy, W20738
William, R.I., R1050
Zadock, Mass., See BOZWORTH
BOTAN, Daniel, Pa. Sea Service, Mary Frost, former wid., W791
BOTCHFORD, Aaron, Ct., See BOTSFORD
BOTHEL, James, Mass., N.Y., Mary, W21691
BOTHMAN, Barnhart, N.J., Va., Catharine, W5861
BOTKIN, Thomas, Va., Margaret, W5860
BOTOMOR, Jacob, Cont., Pa., R1557

BOTON, Matthew/Mathias, N.Y., See BOWDEN
BOTSFORD, Aaron, Ct., Comfort, W23654
Clement, Ct., Mary, W20742
Eli, Ct., Polly, W25264
Samuel, Ct., S31560
Simeon, Ct., Esther, R1051
BOTT, Frederick, Va., Martha, W5855
BOTTGER, Andrew, Pvt. Hazen's Regt., BLWt.12766 iss. 5/1/1795
BOTTOM, Abel, Ct. See BOTTUM
Amaziah, Ct., Wealthy, W17322
Asahel/Asel, Ct., See BOTTUM
John, Ct., S46459; BLWt.1396-100
Miles, Va., S21651
BOTTOMER, Jacob, See BOTOMOR
BOTTS, Moses, Va., S16329
Seth, Va., S35195
BOTTUM, Abel, Ct., S45305
Asel/Asahel, Ct., S15341
Darius, Ct., S14982
Jabez L., Ct., S14968
BOUCE, Henry, N.Y., Dis. No papers
BOUCHER, Elizabeth, former wid. of Abraham Cammer, N.Y., which see
Genevieve, former wid. of Felix Victor, Cont., Canada, which see
Richard, Va., S36421
BOUCK, John/Johannes W., N.Y., Maria, R1053
Peter, N.Y., Maria, W18625
BOUDE, Samuel, Pa., BLWt.223-200-Lt. Iss. 2/24/1791 to Thos. Boude, Admr. Also recorded under Wt.2580. No papers
Thomas, BLWt.200-300 iss. 2/24/1791. No papers
BOUDEN, Amos, Mass., S36916
BOUDY, John, Md., Elizabeth, W5858
BOUGE, Samuel Cook, Ct. See BOOGE
BOUGH, Jacob, Va., See BAUGH
John, Pa., Elizabeth, W3070
BOUGHER, Abraham, Va. See BOOKER
BOUGHMAN, John, Del., S31559
BOUGHNER, Sebastian, N.J., R1055
BOUGHTON, Azor, Ct., See BOUTON
Azor, Pvt., Sheldon's Dragoons, Ct.,; BLWt.5537 iss. 2/8/1798 to William Gilleland
Benajah, N.Y., S23133
David, Ct., Dinah, W15755
Eleazer, Ct., S32130
John, Pvt., Ct., BLWt.5505 iss. 4/5/1792
Joseph, Ct., Zesuah, W21698
Matthew, Ct., Cont., N.Y.,S10378
Samuel, N.Y., Lucy Williams, former wid., R11597 1/2
William, N.Y., Mary, R1056
BOUKER, Ithamar, Mass., S45302
John, Mass., Elizabeth, W21697
Oliver, N.Y., R1058
BOULDIN, Wood, Va., Joanna, W18637
BOULTENHOUSE, John, Cont., N.J., S42630

BOULTER, Benjamin, Mass. See BOLTER
Nathanael/NATHANIEL, Mass., S36919
BOULTON, George, N.Y., S45307
Spencer, S.C., R995
BOUMAN/BOWMAN, Adam, N.Y., S10379
BOUND, William, Pvt., N.J., BLWt. 8159 iss. 2/7/1794
BOUNDS, John, Pvt., Mass., BLWt. 3708 iss. 5/8/1792
BOUNEY, Joseph, Va., S35782
BOURN, Ebenezer, Va., S32129
James, Va., S30877
John, Mass., S29642; BLWt.9426-160-55
John, Va., S39200
Moses, Cont., Mass. Huldah, W18623
Nathaniel, Mass. Sea Service, S29647
Shearjashub, Mass., S34054
Shearjashub, R.I., Rachel, W21687
Shubael, Ct., S22655
Zuriel, Mass., S18727
BOURNE, Aaron, R.I., S21652
John, Cont., Me. res. 1832, S30879
John, Va., Mary, W5856
Judith, former wid. of Frederick Zimmerman, Va., which see
BOUSH, Charles S., Va. Sea Service, R12; Va. half pay
Goodrich, Va., R19365; Va. half pay
Robert, Va., R19366; Va. half pay. See N.A. Acc. No.874, 050018 half pay, Robert Boush
BOUTELL, James, Ct., Chloe, W20740
John, Mass., S12261
Joseph, Ct., See BOUTTELL
BOUTIN, John, N.C., R1012
BOUTON, Azor, See BOUGHTON
Benajah, N.Y., See BOUGHTON
David, Pvt., Ct., BLWt.5518 iss. 6/27/1789 to Samuel Hait
George, N.Y., See BOULTON
Moses, N.Y., S23546
Samuel, Ct., Elizabeth, W25271; BLWt.36512-160-55
Samuel, N.Y., See BOUGHTON
Seth, Ct., S12262
Seth, N.Y., R1057
William, Ct., Sarah, W17324
BOUTTELL, Joseph, Cont., N.H., Molly, W893; BLWt.36609-160-55
BOUTWELL, Asa, N.H., S41452
Hepsibah, former wid.of William Brooks, Cont., N.H, which see
John, N.H., S23545
Stephen, S.C., R1061
BOUVET, Lewis, Pvt. Hazen's Regt., BLWt.12764 iss. 2/20/1792 to Benjamin Moore, ass.
BOUY, William, Pvt., N.Y., BLWt. 6852 iss. 7/26/1790 to G.H. Wagenen, ass.
BOVEE, Jacob, N.Y., S23132
Jacob, N.Y., S23135
Nicholas P., N.Y., See BOVIE
Nicholas R., N.Y., S12275
BOVIE, Nicholas P., N.Y., Polly Cole, former wid., W16916, which see. Her other husb. was also a pensioner. See Benjamin Cole, R.I.

BOVIER, Conrad, N.Y., See BEVIER
BOW, Edward, Ct., Ruth, W24776
Samuel, Ct., Mary, W25269
Thadeus, Mass., Mabel, W18840
BOWAN, John, Sgt., Von Heers Dragoons, BLWt.12745 iss. 11/5/1789
BOWARS, Leonard, Md., Rebecca, W49
BOWDEN, Amos, Mass., See BOUDEN
Elias, Va., Celia, W331
Matthias/ Mathew, N.Y., Martha, W258; BLWt.6822-100-Pvt. Iss. 7/6/1790. No papers. See endorsements on Dis. ctf.
Michael, Mass., R1062
Samuel, Mass., S17288
Thomas, Cont., Mass., S34065
William, N.C., S2388
BOWDISH, Joseph, Mass., S41451
BOWDLER, Samuel, Mass., BLWt.871-100
BOWDLEY, John, S.C., See BOADLEY
BOWE, Hannah, former wid. of Jacob Merrill, Mass., R1063
Thadeus, Mass., See BOW
BOWELS, Samuel, Del.,Md. See BOLES
BOWEN, Aaron, Mass., Abigail, W25263; BLWt.3813-160-55
Abraham, Pvt., Md., BLWt.10973 iss. 8/14/1795 to Francis Sherrard, ass.
Andrew, Va., S16324
Asa, Ct., Cont., Mass., S44635
Benjamin, Cont., R.I., S15340
Benjamin, N.C., Mary, W20743
Bracy, Va., S6693
Charles, Va., S16055
Christopher, Cont., Ct., Betsey, W1808; BLWt.26803-160-55
Consider, R.I., Sabra, W18633
Daniel, Privateer, R.I. Sea Service, Mary R., W25261; BLWt. 51878-160-55
Eleazer, R.I., S17290
Elijah, N.C., Sabry, W25259; BLWt.89501-160-55
Elkanah, R.I., S45301
Enoch, N.H., S41453
Ephraim, Cont., R.I., S46643
Isaac, Cont., Mass., Innocent, W4641
Jabez, Mass., Molly, R----
Jacob, Navy, R.I.,Hannah, W23651
Jacob Gibson, Navy, Res. & Agency, Mass., S34061
James, Cont., Md., S34057
James, R.I., S15754
James, R.I., S21074
James, R.I., Ruth, W14332
Jeremiah, Cont., N.H., Mass., S17289
Jeremiah, N.H., Vt., Miriam, W1539
Joel, Ga., R1065
Joel, Mass., S30882
John, Ct., Cont., Abigail, W20751
John, Va., S32124
John, Va., Elizabeth, W5851
John, Va., BLWt.540-200
John P., Va., S6761
Joseph, Cont., Privateer, R.I., S4268
Joseph, Mass., Mary, W15589

BOWEN, Joseph, N.J., R1066
Micajah, Va., S29643
Michael, Mass., Sarah, W23640; BLWt.1264-100
Michael, Pa., Anna, W4136; BLWt.30614-160-55
Nathan, Mass., S5295
Nathan, Mass., Patience, BLWt. 31695-160-55
Obadiah, Cont., Mass., Rose, W21688
Prentice, N.Y., BLWt.162-200-Lt. Iss. 7/16/1790 to Wm. I. Vreedenburgh, ass. of Wm. Tapp, excr. No papers
Reuben, Va., Sarah, W5852
Robert, Pvt., Md., BLWt.10997 iss. 11/29/1790 to Michael Loyd, Admr.
Sabritt, Cont., Md., Elizabeth, W4135
Sabritt, Pvt., "in Moylan's Dragoons", Pa., BLWt.9020 iss. 2/23/1797
Samuel, Mass., S12264
Samuel, Mass., S17287
Samuel, Pvt., N.J., BLWt.8160 iss. 6/27/1791
Samuel, N.J., S22133
Samuel, N.C., Nancy, W12321; BLWt.26672-160-55
Samuel, R.I., S23134
Simeon, Mass., R.I., Elizabeth, W20748
Simeon, R.I., S21653
Stephen, Mass., Priscilla, W18635
Stephen, N.C., Rachel, W5853
Stephen Lewis, Md., S34661
Thomas Bartholomew, Pa., BLWt. 198-300-Capt. Iss. 4/20/1796. No papers
William, Cont., R.I., S45605
William, Mass., S45300
William, R.I., S21654
William, Va., S8081
William, Va., R1067
Zadock, Navy, N.J., Privateer, S960
BOWER, Andrew, Va., See BOWEN
Elis/Ellis, N.J., Martha, W5850
George, N.J., R1068
Jacob, Md., Pa., Anna, W5227
Jacob, Pa., Rebecca, W3212; BLWt.201-300-Capt. Iss. 2/22/1791. No papers
Joel, N.Y., S29020
John, Ct., Catharine, W20747
John, N.J., Sarah, W8379; BLWt. 26007-160-55
John Jacob, Pa., S40014
William, Cont., N.Y., Md. Agency, S34656; BLWt.958-100
BOWERMAN, Peter, Pa., R21697
BOWERS, Alpheus, Ct., S14977
Asa, Mass., Molly, W12313
Balaam, Va., S10096
Benaiah, Ct., S36424
Benjamin, Mass., S29650
Benjamin, Mass., S36918
Benjamin, N.H., Sarah Farmer, former wid., R3442
Ephraim, Corp., Ct., BLWt.5405

BOWERS (continued)
iss. 12/3/1789
Ephraim, Ct., S36423
Ephraim, Mass., Mary, W23646
George, Pvt., Md., BLWt. 10995 iss. 11/5/1789
George, Md., S40017
George, Md., S40018
James, Mass., S----; BLWt.1643-100
James, Pvt., N.J., BLWt.8114 iss. 9/29/1791
James, N.J., S1498
Jerahmeel/Jeremiah, N.H., S45602
Joab, Pvt., Ct., Elizabeth, W8231; BLWts. 5248 & 30-60-55 iss. 4/19/1790
John, Ct., Sarah, R1073
John, Cont., Mass., Abiah, W15591
John, Drummer, N.J., BLWt.8143 iss. 6/11/1789; BLWt.23-60-55
John Brittain, Va., S6674
John D., N.J., Rebecca, W1216; BLWt.23-60-55
Jonathan, Ct., Rebecca, W25265; BLWt.27666-160-55
Jonathan, Mass., Dorcas, W25273
Josiah, Cont., Mass., S18729
Lemuel, N.J., Sally, W17323
Leonard, Md., See BOWARS
Lewis S., N.J., R1072
Michael, N.J., Electa, W9360; BLWt.51880-160-55
Morris, Pvt., Va., BLWt.11923 iss. 7/14/1792 to Robt. Means, ass.
Nehemiah, Mass., Sarah, W23652; BLWt.85062-160-55
Olive, former wid. of John Kelly, Ct., which see
Oliver, Cont., Mass., S44638
Sebastian, Md., S40748
Zepheniah, Ct., S45306
BOWIE, William, Md., R1075
BOWING, Jabish, Cont., N.H., S37598
BOWKER, Antipas, Mass., Miriam/Meriam, W23643
Asa, Mass., Hannah, W21696
Edmund, Cont., Mass., Hannah, W14259
Ezekiel, Mass., S19554
Ishmael, Mass., S29648
John, Cont., Mass., Philinda, W706; BLWt.56509-160-55
John, Mass., S29644
Levi, Mass., Betsey, W5865
Samuel W., Mass., Charlotte, W5866; BLWt.7213-160-55
Silas, N.Y., Amy, W21684
Windsor, Mass., See BUKER
BOWLAND, Thomas, Md. See BORELAND
BOWLES, Benjamin, N.C., S41448
Charles, Cont., Mass., N.H., S44640
Fortune, Pvt., Mass., BLWt. 3669 iss. 12/23/1796 to A. Foster, ass.
George, Va., Betsy, W5046
John, Cont., Deidamia, W394 Ct. res. of wid. in 1838. Also N.J.

BOWLES (continued)
John, Cont., R.I., S45297
John, Mass., See BOLLES
Jonathan, Mass., Tabitha, W18621
Martin, Md., BLWt.2249-100
Matthew, Va., U.S. Army & War of 1812, Nancy, W25270; BLWt. 79533-160-55
Ralph H., Mass., Hannah, W20749; BLWt.115-200-Lt. Iss. 1/12/1799. No papers
Samuel, Del., Md., See BOLES
Sithey, former wid. of Joseph Coleman, Va., which see
Thomas, N.C., Nancy, W5857; BLWt.12577-160-55
Thomas, Va., S8079
William, N.C., Sally, R1076
Zachariah, Va., S39201
BOWLEY, John, N.H., S12263
Presley, Pvt., Va., BLWt.11936 iss. 7/14/1792 to Francis Graves, ass.
BOWLING, Charles, Va., S16041
Edward, Va., S31561
James, Va., Letty M., W5863
Jarret, Va., See BOLING
Jesse, N.C., See BOLING
Joseph, Va., Martha, W25257; BLWt.91514-160-55
Thomas, Va., BLReg.264321-1855
Thomas, Va., Sarah, R1078
William, Va., S16040
William I., Md., S34655
BOWMAN, Abiathar, N.H., Thankful, W21685
Abraham, Va., Sarah, W396; BLWt. 1566-500. Iss. 10/30/1829 to John H. Bowman
Adam, N.Y., See BOUMAN
Andrew, N.J., S34056
Daniel, Va., S3036
Elijah, Cont., Pa., S40020
Elisha, Ct., S22130
Francis, Mass., Susanna, R1082
Frederick, See BAUMAN
Isaac, Va., R19362, Va. half pay
John, Mass., S29641
John, N.C., Eleanor, W397
John, Va., Barsheba, W21; BLWt. 40510-160-55
Luke, N.Y., BLWt.6783 iss. 5/17/1796 to Chauncey Goodrich, ass.
Luke, N.Y., S46488
Mackness, Va., S6691
Margaret, former wid. of Benjamin Garvin, Va., which see
Marshall, N.C., S16651
Nathaniel, N.J., BLWt.23-400
Nicholas, N.Y., See BAUMANN
Philip, Md., S2091
Phineas, Mass; BLWt.105-300-Capt. Iss. 5/7/1790. No papers
Samuel, Cont., N.Y., Dorothy, W27663
Samuel, Mass.; BLt. 114-200-Lt. Iss. 2/25/1792 to Richard Fullerton, ass. No papers
Samuel, N.C., R1118
Shearwood, N.C., S6678
Solomon, Cont., Mass., S34059

BOWMAN (continued)
Sparling, Md., S3048
William, Va., S1640
William, Va., S16328
William, Va., Mary, R1080
BOWND, Obadiah, N.J., S22658
BOWNE, Henry, N.J., Eleanor, W1371; BLWt.26564-160-55
James, N.J., S2385
Thomas, Va.; BLWt.259-300-Capt. Iss. 10/28/1789 to Mathew McConnell, ass. No papers
William, N.J., S34058
BOWRY, Louis, BLReg.243775-1855
BOWSER, James, Va.; BLWt.2001-100
Thomas, Md.; BLWt.2385-100
BOWSHER, Anthony, Pa., S2092
BOWTELL/BOWTELLE, Ebenezer, Cont., Mass., Polly, W14335
BOWTON, Azor, See BOUGHTON
BOWYER, Henry, Cont., Va., Agatha, W5859; BLWt.283-200-Lt. Iss. 12/31/1790. No papers
Michael, Va.; BLWt.288-300-Capt. Iss. 6/24/1796. No papers
Philip, Va., S39202
Thomas, ---, Nancy C., R1083. Widow's res. Va. in 1858
Thomas, Va.: BLWt.268-300-Capt. Iss. 12/31/1795 to Henry Bowyer Actg. Executor. No papers
BOX, Daniel, ----, res. Providence Co., R.I. Dis. No papers
Edward, S.C., Nancy, W25268; BLWt.26455-160-55
Samuel, S.C., S3015
BOXWELL, Joseph, Va., S34659
Robert, Va., S34658
BOY, Jacob, Va., Mary, W8146; BLWt.16276-160-55
BOYCE, Abraham, N.Y., S12259
Abraham, Va., Hannah, W3213
David, Cont., Mass. Sea Service, S30280
George, Mass., Lydia, W23645
James, Navy, N.H., S36920
Jonathan, Mass., BLWt.2072-100
Joseph, Pvt., Pa., BLWt.8988 Iss. 11/27/1794 to Alexander Power, ass.
Peter, N.Y., Abby/Abigail, W20735
Thomas, N.Y., Catharine, W25266; BLWt.817-160-55
William, Pvt., Mass., BLWt.3661 iss. 8/31/1790 to Joseph Nye,ass.
William, N.C., S.C., Elizabeth, W9361
William, Va.; BLWt.82-200-Lt. Iss. 2/3/1800. Also recorded under Wt.2485. No papers
BOYD, Abraham, Pvt., Pa., BLWt. 8946 iss. 7/9/1789
Alexander, Cont., Pa.; BLWt.1470-100. Iss. 2/3/1829. Also Dis. No papers
Alexander, Pvt., N.J., BLWt.8129 iss. 5/7/1790 to John Linn, ass.
Benjamin, Cont., S6690, Md. Agency & res.
Benjamin, Pvt., Md., BLWt.10983 iss. 8/14/1795 to Francis Sherrard, ass.

BOYD (continued)
Daniel, Va., S41454
David, S.C., Va., R1085
Francis, Va., S42627
George, N.Y., S12274
Henry, Pa., & St. Clair's Indian War, S35783
Henry, Va., S2089
Henry, Va., S30884
James, Cont., N.Y., S44641
James, Md., Pa., Flora, R1086
James, N.Y., S12260
James, N.C., S32127; see N.A. Acc. No. 874 050019
James, N.C., Va., S12269
James, Pa., Lydia, W9362; BLWt. 26496-160-55
John, Md., S2088
John, Mass., S19555
John, Pvt., N.J., BLWt.8142 iss. 6/11/1789
John, N.J., S34055. 2 Geo. Washington signatures
John, N.C., Ann, W24708
John, N.C., Mary, R1089
John, N.C., S.C., S41446
John, Pa., S39207
John, Pa., Rebecca, W8371; BLWt.211-200-Capt. Lt. Iss. 2/28/1795. No papers
John, Pa., Mary, R1090
John, Va., R1088
Joseph, Ct., S45299
Patrick, Va., Ann, W5846
Richard, N.Y., S45298
Robert, Pa., S6682
Robert, S.C., Sarah, R1092
Samuel, Mass., S18731
Samuel, N.Y., Mehitable, W20746
Samuel, S.C., Isabella, W9737
Thomas, Md.; BLWt.248-200-Lt. No date of issue. No papers
Thomas, N.Y., S28649
Thomas, N.C., S17286
Thomas, Pa.; BLWt.218-200-Lt. Iss. 2/28/1795 to John Boyd, only surv. brother & heir at law. No papers
Thomas, Pvt., Pa., BLWt.9010 iss. 4/6/1790
William, Ct., Vt., Jennet, W5226
William, Cont., Md., Pa. or Va.? S35197
William, Cont., N.H., Dorcas, W23647
William Pvt., N.Y., BLWt.6842 iss. 7/22/1790 to Thomas Tillotson, ass.
William, N.Y., Getty, W16856
William, N.C., S30881
William, N.C., S45878
William, N.C., R1094
William, Pa., S22127
William, Pa., BLWt.219-200-Lt.
William, S.C., Keziah, W5845; BLWt.19916-160-55
William, Va., S8084
William, not Rev., Indian War, Nancy, Old War Inv. File 46769, Old War Wid. Rej. 20706; File in Rev. War files.

BOYDEN, Amos, Pvt., Mass., BLWt.3701 iss. 8/26/1790 to M. Cutler, ass.
Amos, Mass., S34063
Jacob, Mass., Chloe, W25272; BLWt.36669-160-55
John, Mass., Mary J., W10432; BLWt.13213-160-55
Jonathan, Mass., R1095
Joseph, Mass., S29019
Josiah, Mass., S30279
Josiah, Mass., Lydia, W17332
Justus, Mass., S45308
Thomas, Mass., S34066
BOYDSTUN, Samuel, N.C., Sarah, R1096
William, N.C., Va., S3041
BOYEA/BOYEE, John/John Peter, N.Y., Catherine, W15824
BOYER, Christian, Pa., Julia, W4640
Daniel, Del., Sarah, R1103
Frederick, Cont., Pa., Mary Elizabeth, W3069
Frederick, Pa., Margaret, R1102
Henry, N.J., Pa. Sea Service, S22129
Jane, former wid. of Barent/ Barnt Hartwick, N.J., which see
John, N.Y., Elizabeth, W522; BLWt.28660-160-55
John, S.C., S32125
John Gotlieb, Md., Anna Mary, W8378
John P., Pvt., N.Y., BLWt.6860 iss. 8/24/1790 to Cornelius Glenn et al, assnes
Jonathan, Va., R20194
Lewis, Cont., Va. res. in 1805, S46370; BLWt.187-100
Michael, Cont.; BLWt.237-300-Capt. of the German Regt. Iss. 9/14/1789. No papers
Peter, Cont; BLWt.216-300-Capt. in the German Regt. Iss. 8/8/ 1789. No papers
Peter, Pvt., Pa., BLWt.9065 iss. 1/17/1792 to George Moore, ass.
Peter, Pa., Catherine, R1098
Valentine, N.Y., Elizabeth, R1100
BOYERS, Asamus/Oysel, Pa., Elizabeth, R1099
Jacob, Pa., Va., Margaret, W24703; BLWt.36281-160-55
Lewis, Cont., Va. res. 1805, S46370; BLWt.187-100
Michael, Pa., Va., S3022
Oysel, See Asamus
BOYES, James, N.H., S45604
Robert, N.H., Genet, W16196
Samuel, Mass., Isabella, W23642
BOYINGTON, Andrew, See BOYNTON
Joseph, Cont. Mass., Sarah Beal, former wid. Which see
BOYKIN, Bias, Wid. applied from N.C., Sampson Co. Sarah, R1104
John, N.C., S6551
BOYL, James, Pvt., Md., BLWt. 11021 iss. 1/17/1793 to John Wright, ass. of Edward Blades, Admr.

BOYLAN, Aaron, N.J., Sarah, W10434
James, N.J., R1106
John, N.J., Eleanor, R1105
BOYLE, Andrew, Pa., See BOGLE
Charles, N.Y., Pa., S6677; BLWt. 3989-160-55
Daniel, Pa., S40016
James, N.Y., Mary Howell, former wid., W19812
James, Pa., S40019
John, Pa., S40011
Michel, N.J., Va., See BOYLS
Robert, Pa., S5289
Robert, Va., S15755
Thomas, Pa., BLWt.338-400
BOYLES, Charles, Cont., Va., S35784; BLWt.1455-100
Charles, S.C., R1110
David, Cont., Va., Polly, W12322; BLWt.1456-100; BLWt.309-60-55
George, Cont., N.Y., S45303
James, Pvt., N.Y., BLWt.6774 iss. 8/24/1791 to Wm. Thomson, ass.
Timothy, Del., S42091
Walter, N.Y., S12255
BOYLL, Charles, Cont. Va., See BOYLES
BOYLLS, David, Cont., Va., See BOYLES
BOYLS, Charles, Cont., Va., See BOYLES
Michel, N.J., Va., R1108
BOYLSTON, William, Mass., S12265
BOYNTON, Andrew, Vt., S14972
Bela, Ct., S18322
Caleb, Mass., Phebe, R1113
Daniel, Mass., Hannah Severance, former wid., R9393
David, Mass., S22657
David E., Mass., Bethiah, W16853
Elias, Mass., N.H., Bettee, W23659
Eunice, former wid. of Chester Rogers, Ct., which see
Isaac, N.H., Judith Blower/ Blowers, former wid., W10297; BLWt.61126-160-55
Jewett, Mass., Pamelia, W20745
John, N.H., R1111
Jonathan, Mass., S34053
Joseph, N.H., S36914; BLWt.75-200-Lt. Iss. 8/24/1790 to Benj. Ives Gilman. No papers
Joshua, Mass., Mary, W16509
Moses, Cont., Mass., S12268
Moses, Mass., Lucy, R1112
Pelatiah/Peletiah, Mass., S36917
Richard, N.H., S45608
Solomon, Cont., Mass., S45309
Stephen, Mass., Tabitha Eddy, former wid., W14670. 3 Cont. ltrs. 1776-1777
Thomas, Mass., S4956
BOYT, Jacob B., N.C., S6686
William, N.C., R1115
William, Va., Sally, W5844
BOYTE, William, N.C., R1109
BOZEMAN, John, ----, Miss. res. of claimant, R1117
Peter, S.C., R20332
Ralph, S.C., R1116
BOZORTH, Jonathan, Pa., Mary,R1047

BOZWORTH
Ichabod, Pvt., Mass., BLWt.3763 iss. 9/13/1796 to James Brison, ass.
Ichabod, Mass., Ruth, W15592
John, Mass., Silence, W21695
Richard, Cont., Mass., S34060
Zadok/Zadock, Mass., S12270
BOZZELL/BOSWELL, Reuben, Va., Pa., S8077
BRABROOK, Benjamin, Mass., Betsey Converse, former wid; BLWt. 32208-160-55
Joseph, Mass., Eunice, W23675
BRABSTON, William, Va., Mary May, former wid., W960; BLWt.180-100
BRACCO, Bennett, Md.; BLWt.2167-300
BRACE, Charles, Ct., Perses, R1363
David, Ct., S16658
Elijah, Ct., Catharine, W17339
Jeffery/Jeff Stiles, Ct., S41461
Joseph, Ct., Lois, W25298; BLWt. 34525-160-55
BRACEY, James, Mass., S36938
Thomas, Va., See BRESSIE
BRACHALL, Martin, Cont., Pa., Catharine, W9368; BLWt.100125-160-55
BRACKENRIDGE, Alexander, Va.; BLWt.287-300-Capt. Iss. 4/14/1790. No papers
BRACKET, Cornelius, Pvt., Lamb's Artillery, N.Y., BLWt.6890 iss. 8/20/1790
Hawkins, N.C., Sally, R1121
Hezekiah, Pvt., Ct., BLWts.5520 & 29-60-55 iss. 4/19/1792
John, Mass., Lovina/Lovinia, W404; BLWt.24334-160-55
Joseph, Mass., S18734
Samuel, Mass., Betsey, W14349
Thomas, N.H., Martha Robinson, former wid., R8908
BRACKETT, Benajah, Ct.; BLWt. 962-100
Benjamin, Mass., Susannah, W14401
Daniel, Mass., S44682
Ebenezer, Mass., Rebecca, W20768
Hezekiah, Ct., See BROCKETT
James, Mass., S17852
James, Mass., Mary, W1540
John, Mass., S28655
Joshua, Mass., S29034
Joshua, Mass., S31567
Josiah, Mass., S36939
Lydia, former wid. of John Ross, N.C., which see
Nathan, Mass., S30902
Peter, Mass., Sarah, W23691
Samuel, Mass., S18744
William, Cont., Mass., BLWt.708-100
William, Mass., S30901; BLWt. 34970-160-55
BRACKIN/BRACKEN, William, N.C., R1119
BRACY, Cornelius, Mass., S38576; BLWt.31443-160-55
BRADBERRY, John, Pa., Va., R1122
BRADBURY, Ammeyruhama, Mass., Sarah, W17347

BRADBURY (continued)
Daniel, Pvt., Mass., BLWt.3648 iss. 3/25/1790
Daniel, Pvt., N.H., BLWt.2942 iss. 3/8/1796
Daniel, N.H., S34090
James, Mass., S34073
Moses, Mass., Eunice, W23709
Paul, Mass., S30898
Samuel, Mass., Hannah Yeaton, former wid., W22705
Winthrop, Pvt., Mass., BLWt.3756 iss. 4/5/1796 to Samuel Stone, ass.
BRADEEN, Joseph, Cont., Mass. Sea Service, S34098
Robert, Cont., Mass., S30892
BRADEN, Andrew, N.C., Dorothy, W779
James, Va., R1124
John, Va., S1643
BRADFORD, Andrew, Mass., S4973
Andrew, N.H., Lucy, W23668
Charles, Va.; BLWt.2055-200
David, Cont., Mass., S34100
Elijah, Cont., Mass., S36941
Elisha, Ct., Lucy, W24676
Enoch, Va., Mary, R1126
Ezekiel, Mass., Mary, W23682
Gamaliel, Col., Mass., BLWt. 89-500 iss. 9/5/1789. No papers
Gamaliel, Lt., Mass., BLWt.119-200 iss. 5/17/1790. No papers
George, R.I., Susannah, W21703
Hannah, former wid. of Ephraim Lyon, Ct., which see
Hannah, former wid. of Samuel Freeman, Cont., Mass., which see
Henry, Cont., France, see Jeannerel, Claude Francois, Elizabeth, R1125. Res. 1818, Va.
Israel, Mass., Olive, W12344; BLWt.12583-160-55
James, Cont.; BLWt.170-200-Lt. in Col. Lamb's Regt. Artillery. Iss. 4/17/1795 to Margaret Doyle, admx. No papers
James, Cont., N.J., S40037
James, Mass., S29660
James, N.C., S6716
Joel, Mass., Navy, R.I., S21081
John, N.H., S12318
John Angel, S.C., Mary, R1127
Josiah, Cont., Mass., S34093
Margaret, former wid. of Benjamin Horn, N.J., which see
Nathaniel, Mass., S29654
Noah, Mass., S29656
Oliver, Mass., Sarah, W18657
Peabody, Mass., S29035
Perez, Mass., S4963
Peter, Mass., S15761
Robert, Cont., Mass., S42099; BLWt.103-300-Capt. Iss. 11/28/1789. No papers
Samuel, Cont., N.H., Mary, W16516
Samuel K., Cont., Jane Vermonnet/Vermonet, former wid., W4608; BLWt.1241-200
Susanna, former wid. of Wm. Jones N.C., which see

BRADFORD (continued)
Thomas, Ct., Cont., Philena, W17351
William, N.H., S9824
William, Jr., R.I., BLWt.84-400-Maj. Iss. 5/19/1796. No papers
William, Va., S39240
BRADIE, David, Ga., R1128
BRADISH, Daniel, Mass., S12297; BLWt.26571-160-55
BRADLEY, Aaron, Ct., Cont., S17302
Alexander, Ct., Lydia, W17336
Alling, Ct., Cont., S36447
Aner, Ct., Anna, W17335
Ashbel, Ct., Chloe, W25295; BLWt. 8172-160-55
Augustine/Austin, Va., Franky, W5867
Benjamin, N.H., Judith, W1217; BLWt.14957-160-55
Benjamin, Vt., R1143
Burrel, N.C., S6747
Cornelius, Md., S35798
Daniel, Sgt., Ct., BLWt.5486 iss. 7/21/1789; BLWt.2478 dated 1/11/1853 iss. in lieu of 5486
Daniel, Ct. & U.S. Army until 1802, S36442; BLWt.148-200-Lt. Iss. 3/13/1790. No papers
Daniel, Ct., S36443; BLWt.2478-100
Daniel, Va., S6766
David, Pvt., Ct., BLWt.5513 iss. 6/3/1791 to Isaac Bronson
David, Ct., S34099
David, Mass., N.H., Vt., S44664
David, Mass., N.H., Vt., Bathsheba, R1130
David, Va., Susan, R1132
Dimon, Ct., Beulah, W14380
Eber, Vt., S12324
Eli, Mass., R1133
Elihu, Ct., Sybel, W16864
Elijah, Ct., S15343
Elijah, Ct., Privateer, Esther, W18664
Elisha, Ct., Ann B., R1129
Elisha, Ct., Vt., S12310
Francis, N.C., S6740
Gee, N.C.; BLWt.293-300-Capt. Iss. 1/10/1791. No papers
George W., N.C., Sally, W48
Gilbert, Vt., R21698
Gilead, Ct., Cont., S17293
Hope, Mass., S12308
James, Pvt., Ct., BLWt.5404 iss. 10/22/1792
James, Cont., N.Y.; BLWt.595-100
James, Cont., Pa., S44665
James, N.C., Dolley, W70
James, Pa.; BLWt.975-100
James, Va., S6736
Jehiel, Pvt., Ct., BLWt.5487 iss. 10/7/1789
Jesse, Mass., Bathsheba, R1131; BLWt.16265-160-55
John, Pvt., Mass., BLWt.3749 iss. 12/14/1789 to Richard Platt, ass.
John, Mass., Mary, W5938
John, N.C., S31575
John, Va., S1792
John, Va., S3081

BRADLEY (continued)
Joseph, Ct., Vt., S12347
Joshua, Mass., Mary, W15606
Lemuel, Ct., Lois, S14990
Lemuel, Vt., Mercy Brownson, former wid., R1361
Lent, Mass., Roxada, W1701
Leonard, N.C., R12679
Levi, Mass.; BLWt.109-200-Lt. Iss. 6/2/1795 to Samuel Emory, ass. No papers
Moses, Ct., S23138
Nathan, Ct., Dis.--- No papers
Nathan, Ct., S12301
Nathaniel, Ct., R1138
Philbrick, N.H., S16663
Philip Burr, Ct., Ruth, W21702; BLWt.131-500-Lt. Col. Iss. 5/14/1796. No papers
Reuben, Ct., Mass., R1139
Richard, N.C., Catharine, W896
Robert, Sgt., Pa., BLWt.8985 iss. 7/16/1789 to M. McConnell, ass.
Samuel, Mass., S15763
Samuel, Mass., S21084
Samuel, Vt., Abigail, W17360
Stephen, Ct., Mehitable, W25301
Thadeus/Thaddeus, Ct., Parnal, W5942; BLWt.6394-160-55
Thomas, Ct., R1141
William, N.C., Aspasia, W8399
William, Va., Dis.---No papers
William, Va., S6734
William, Va., Elizabeth, R1135
BRADLY, James, Va., See BRADLEY
Sturgis, Ct., R1140
BRADNER, Andrew, Pvt., N.Y., BLWt.6778 iss. 9/24/1790
BRADSHAW, Benjamin, Va., Fanny, W894
Claibourn/Claburn, Va., Elizabeth, W8394
George, Pa., S34663
James, Ct., Cont., S29023
John, Va., S6738
John, Va., S15760
Jonas, N.C., Elizabeth, W3932
Jonathan, Mass., S38574
Larner, Va., S35200
Nathaniel, Mass., S29026
Robert, Pa., S5297
Robert, Va., S6708
William, Pvt., N.J., BLWt. 8127 iss. 6/20/1789
William, Va., Selah, R1142
BRADSTREET/BRADSTREED, Dudley, Mass., Dis.--- No papers
John, Mass., S17297
BRADT, Cornelius, N.Y., Annatje/ Annatie, W18649
Ephraim, N.Y., Annatje, W16860
Gerret Teunis/Garret Teunis, N.Y., Sarah, R1166
Henry, N.Y., Dis.--- No papers
BRADWELL, Nathaniel/Nathan, S.C., BLWt.1211-200
BRADY, Benjamin, Vt., See BRADLEY
Benjamin, Va., S8107
Christopher, Cont. N.Y., S36438
James, N.C., S8090; BLWt.39477-160-55

BRADY (continued)
James, Va., See BRADEN
John, Pvt., Md., BLWt.10987 iss. 4/18/1794
John, Pvt., Md., BLWt.11110 iss. 12/18/1794 to Henry Purdy, ass.
John, Va., Keziah, W8392
John, Va., Roseman Porter, former wid., R8353. She was pensioned as wid. of John Porter, Va., which see
Joseph, N.C., S32143
Lewis, Pvt., N.Y., BLWt.6806 iss. 4/16/1791 to John Addoms, ass.
Lewis, N.Y., S44681
Luke, "Pvt. in the Invalids", BLWt.12783 iss. 5/23/1795 to James Welch, Execr.
Michael, Pvt., Pa., BLWt.8934 iss. 3/29/1791
Samuel, Pa.; BLWt.197-300-Capt. iss. 1/21/1793. No papers
Thomas, Pvt., Pa., BLWt.9013 iss. 5/26/1794 to Michael Stever, ass.
Thomas, Va., S4271
William, Ga., S.C., S34671
William, Va., S8103
BRAFORD, Robert, Cont., Sarah, W23688
BRAGDEN, Warren, Pvt., Mass., BLWt.3683 iss. 9/10/1789 to H. Newman, ass.
BRAGDON, Aaron, Cont., Mass., S36940
Amos, Mass., Sarah, W1372; BLWt.17734-160-55
Arthur, Cont., Mass., S30903
Daniel, Mass., S36924
Ezekiel, Cont., Mass., S36926
James, Mass., Ruth; BLWt.92010-160-55
John, Mass., S28654
John, Mass., S36937
John, Mass., Dorothy, W23678
Joseph, Mass., Martha, W15605
Samuel, Cont., Mass., Olive, W524; BLWts. 1670-100 & 262-60-55
Solomon, Mass., Susanna, W15990
William, Cont., Mass., Sarah, W24673
BRAGG, Benjamin, Mass., S44679
Benjamin, Pvt., Va., BLWt.11913 iss. 11/14/1794
David, N.C., Elizabeth, R1144
Henry, Sgt., Mass., BLWt.3740 iss. 12/14/1789 to Richard Platt, ass.
Joab, Cont., Mass., Lydia, W24668
John, Mass., S34588
Moses, Mass., Lydia, W18656
Peter, Mass., N.H., S19222
Robert, N.H., Lydia, W14391
Thomas, Mass., Jenny, R1145
William, Cont., Mass., S12346
William, Vt., S18748
William, Va., S1500
William, Va., Cecely, W2517
William, Va., Ruthy, W3764

BRAINARD, Ansel, Ct., War of 1812, Mary, W8768; BLWts. 83430-120-55 & 70805-40-50
Bezaleel, Ct., Lydia, W23671
Church, Ct., See BRAINERD
Daniel, Ct., Privateer, S3099
Elijah, Ct., See BRAINERD
Jabez, Ct., S4968
Mary, former wid. of Moses King, Mass., which see
Othniel, Pvt., Ct., BLWt.5504 iss. 11/19/1789
Othniel, Ct., Cont., S44683
Reuben, N.Y., Hannah, W3763
Seba, Ct., Anna, R1146
Simon, Ct., S17296
Stephen, Ct., Rachel, W20794
BRAINERD, Amos, Ct., Jerisha, W5234; BLWt.27572-160-55
Church, Ct., Navy, N.H.,S29032
Elijah, Ct., S10105
Timothy, Ct., Sarah, W14392
BRAITHWAITE/BRAITHWAIT, William, Md., Catharine, W5934
BRAKE, Abraham, Va., R1147
John, Va., S15762
BRAKEMAN, Lodowick, N.Y., Eve, R1148
BRALEY, Gideon, Mass., S8094
William, N.C., See BRAWLY
BRALY, John, N.C., R1149
BRAMAN, Benjamin, Cont., Mass., BLWt.2315-100
Benjamin, Mass., Anne/Anna, W14363
Daniel, Ct., S12276
Daniel, Ct., S46777
James, Ct., S18746
Joseph, R.I., See BRAYMAN
Silas, Pvt., R.I., BLWt.2972 iss. 12/31/1789
Sylvanus, Ct., Mass., S18743
BRAMBLE, David, Pvt., Md., BLWt. 10958 iss. 8/14/179- to Francis Sherrard, ass.
Hackett/William, Md., Elizabeth, R1151
Robert, Ct., Hannah, W25297
William, See Hackett
William, N.Y., S23550
BRAMBLET, Nancy, former wid. of George Adams, Va., which see
Reuben, Va., S30896
Reuben, Va., R1152
BRAMBLETT, James, Va., S14996
BRAMHALL, Sylvanus/Silvanus, Mass., S45619
BRAN, Jeremiah, Mass., See BRAND
William, N.Y., Margaret, W1219; BLWt.26568-160-55
BRANAGON, George, Pvt., Pa., BLWt.8960 iss. 10/4/1796 to John Stoy, ass.
BRANAMON, Benjamin, Pa., R1158
BRANARD, Ansel, Ct., See BRAINARD
BRANCH, Aholiab, R.I., S38575
Benjamin, Mass., R1153
Burrell, N.C., S6698
Elijah, Cont., Vt., S41460
John, N.C., Elizabeth, W5925; BLWt.11170-160-55
Joseph, Pvt., Ct., BLWt.5516 iss.

BRANCH (continued)
12/5/1791 to Jonathan Groat,Jr.
Olive, Va., S8101
Samuel, Ct., Ruth, W2717; BLWt. 26155-160-55
Thomas, Va., Nancy/Ann, R1154; BLWt.50806-160-55
Walter, Ct., Eunice Snow, former wid., W4076
William, Ct., Lucretia, W1544; BLWts.5413-100 & 73-60-55 iss. 12/16/1793 to John Chadwick
Zephaniah, Cont., Vt., Lucy, W16199
BRAND, Amos, Pvt., Mass., BLWt. 3709 iss. 2/7/1799 to J. Cuncan, ass.
Amos, Mass., S44688
Jeremiah, Mass., Nancy, W25296
William, N.C., S31577
BRANDENBURG, William, Md.,S2405
BRANDENBURGH, Anthony, Va., S8095
BRANDHUFER, Adam, Pa., See BRANTHIFER
BRANDOM, Thomas, Va., Margaret, W4643
BRANDON, Benjamin, N.C., Polly, W4901
Charles, S.C., S3086
Christopher, S.C., S9288
Francis, Va., R1156
John, Pa., Mary, W5946
Josiah, N.C., Rachel, W335
Peter, Va., S35201
Richard, S.C., Agnes/Nancy, W21714
Thomas, Va., See BRANDOM
William, N.C., S3082
William, N.C., Pa., S.C., Jane, W71
BRANDOW, Nicholas, N.Y., R1157
BRANDT, Joachim J., Navy, Pa. res. Dis. No papers
Simeon, R.I., See BRANT
BRANEMAN, Christian, Pa., S16060
BRANHAM, James, Pvt., Va., BLWt. 11954 iss. 7/6/1793 to Francis Graves, ass.
William, Pvt., Va., BLWt.11929 iss. 10/11/1796
William B., Va., Mary, W5939; BLWt.36635-160-55
BRANK, Robert, N.C., S30893
BRANN, Andrew, Cont., Va., BLWt. 207-100
Jeremiah, Va., Sarah, W5933
Joseph, Cont., Va.; BLWt.208-100
William, Sr., Va., S17864
BRANNACK, Levi, Mass., R1159
BRANNAN, Thomas, N.C., S39211
BRANNON, Adam, N.Y., S44686
David, Pa., S2094
John, Pa., S42098
John, Pa., S46480; BLWt.1741-100
John, Pvt., Va., BLWt.11924 iss. 10/5/1791 to Jacob Clingman
Michaël, Pvt., Pa., BLWt.9072 iss. 11/5/1789 to Michael

BRANNON (continued)
Brannon (Wm. Alexander, last name in red ink)
Richard, Pvt., Hazen's Regt., BLWt.12787 iss. 1/11/1796 to Anthony Musegenuny, ass.
Thomas, Pvt.,Va., BLWt.11094 iss. 5/29/1792 to Robt. Means, ass.
BRANSCOM, Charles, Mass., Rebecca, W23662
BRANSFORD, William, Va.; BLWt. 11907-100. Iss. 5/21/1794 to Richard Smyth, ass. No papers
BRANSON, John, Md., S34662
John, Pvt., Md., BLWt.10942 iss. 8/14/1795 to Francis Sherrard, ass.
BRANT, Christian, Pvt., N.Y., BLWt.6839 iss. 9/28/1790 to Bartholomew & Fisher, assnes.
Christian, N.Y., S44689
Christian, N.Y., Hannah, R1374
John, N.J., S42635
John, R.I., S19564
Simeon, R.I., Prudence, W3218; BLWt.26948-160-55
BRANTHIFER, Adam, Pa., Magdalena, W3504
BRANTLEY, Amos, N.C., S38569
BRASBRIDGE, John, See BRASSBRIDGE
BRASFIELD, John, N.C., Sally, W5941; BLWt.5212-160-55
BRASHEARS, Ignatius, Md., S12279
Morris, Md., S3083
Richard, Va., R12756; Va. half pay. N.A. Acc. No. 874. See 050020 Half Pay, Richard Brashears
Samuel, N.C., Margaret, W9370; BLWt.14544-160-55
BRASHER, Henry, N.Y., R1161
John, Ct., N.Y., S16507
John, N.C., R1162
Richard, Va., Susan, R1163
BRASINGTON, Samuel, Cont., Pa., Miriam, W16870
BRASS, Garrit/Garret, Mass., Lucy, W3762
Thomas, Cont., Mass., Sarah, W5048; BLWt.18383-160-55
BRASSBRIDGE, John, N.H., S42102; BLWt.1067-100
BRASSELL, Isaac, N.C. See BRASWELL
BRASSWELL, Jacob, N.C., See BRASWELL
BRASTED, Henry, N.J., Molly,R1164
BRASWELL, Henry, S.C., S17851
Isaac, N.C., R1165
Jacob, N.C., Nancy, W3933; BLWt.81726-160-55
Richard, N.C., Penelope, W4888
Sampson, N.C., Lucretia, W3930
BRATCHER, Charles, Va., S1501
Samuel, N.C., S39227
William, S.C., S39223
BRATT, Garret Teunis/Gerret Teunis, See BRADT
BRATTLE, Dick, Ct., Mass., R1167
William, Mass., Hannah, W10456
BRATTON, Bartholomew, N.Y., Pa., S40036

BRATTON (continued)
James, Pa., S4272
William, Md. Sea Service, R1168
BRATTY, David, N.J. See BREATTY
BRAUGHTON, Joseph, N.C. See BROUGHTON
BRAUSS, Michael, Pa., S3054
BRAWLY, William, N.C., S4961
BRAWN, Daniel, Mass., Dis.--- No papers
BRAXTON, James, Va., Indian War of 1794, Mary, R1169; BLWt. 27080-160-55
BRAY, Andrew, N.J., S856
Daniel, N.J., Mary, W5920
David, N.C., S8106
Elisha C., Va., N.A. Acc. No. 874; 050021. Not half pay. No pension file found for veteran
James, N.J., N.Y., Pa., Mary Blythe, former wid., W3176
John, Cont., N.J., Ellen Kincheloe/Eleanor Kincheloe, former wid., W12026
John, N.J., S2402
John, Va., Elizabeth, W4145; BLWt.89502-160-55
Joseph, Mass., Anna, W23680
Nicholas, Cont., Mass., S36942
Sampson, Ct., S28659
Samuel, Mass., S18147
William, Cont., N.J., N.Y., Pa., S44680
BRAYDON, Solomon, Mass. See BRAGDON
BRAYFORD, Eli, Mass., R20334
BRAYHILL, James, Va., S32136
BRAYMAN, Benjamin, Cont., Mass. See BRAMAN
James, Ct., See BRAMAN
Joseph, R.I., S21673
BRAYNARD, Othniel, Ct., Cont. See BRAINARD
BRAYTON, Borden, Mass., Privateer S21087
Francis, R.I., Amey, W1811; BLWt.26284-160-55
Freeborn, R.I., Mary, W14367
James, ----, Lucy, R----
James Wheaton, Privateer, R.I. Sea Service, Roby, W27389
Thomas, R.I., Patience, W12359
BRAZIL, Byrd, N.C., S31571
BREADLY, John, Pvt., N.J., BLWt. 8128 iss. 1/28/1793
BREADON, John, Pvt., N.Y., BLWt. 6787 iss. 6/15/1792
BREAKBILL, Peter, Md., Pa., Catherine/Katharine, W46
BREARLEY, Joseph, N.J., Rachel, W5944
BREATTY, David, N.J., Mary, BLWt.880-100
BRECHAL, Martin, Cont., Pa., See BRACHALL
BRECHEN, William, N.C., Elizabeth, R1170. Not identical with R1119, Wm. Brackin
BRECK, Daniel, Mass., S23552
Daniel, Mass., Patty, W14379
John, Pvt., Ct., BLWt.5427 iss. 4/26/1793

BRECK (continued)
Jonas, Mass., See BRICK
BRECK/BREEK, Jonathan, Mass., Patience, W23681; BLWt.14520-160-55
BRECKEN, William, N.C., See BRECHEN
BRECKER, Peter, Pa., S40035
BRECKINRIDGE, Robert, Va., S46371; BLWt.273-200-Lt. Iss. 4/14/1790. No papers
BREDEN, Andrew, N.C. See BRADEN
Charles, N.C., Johanna, W334
BREDON, John, Va., See BRADEN
BREECH, Thomas, Pa., R1171
BREED, Allen, N.H., S28658
Ephraim, Mass., R1173
Frederic/Frederick, Cont., Mass., S34104
Jabez, Ct., Sally Wheeler, former wid., W19621; BLWt.1911-160-55
Jesse, Navy, Ct. res. 1819, Cynthia R., R1172
John, Mass., N.H., S12344
Joseph, Ct., Navy, R.I., Mercy, W2751
Joseph, Mass., Anna, W25282; BLWt.7210-160-55
Oliver, Ct., S12298
Stephen, Ct., Esther, W16511
Thomas K., Cont., N.H., Polly, W24675; BLWt.13433-160-55
BREEDEN, Charles, See BREDEN
Enoch, Va., S1747
BREEDING, John, Va., S17862
BREEDLOVE, John, Va., S2102
William, Va., S2392
BREEK, Jonathan, Mass. See BRECK
BREES, Henry, N.J., S12309
James, N.J., Euphemia, W5927
Samuel, N.J., S22143
Timothy, N.J., S42632
BREESE, Garret, N.J., S961
Henry, N.J., S802
John, Pa., R1174
Timothy, Pvt., N.J., BLWt.8116 iss. 2/10/1796
BREETON, William, Mass. See BRITTON
BREEZE, John, Md., Pa., S36429
Stephen, ----, N.J. res., R1175
BREIDEGAN, John, Pa., S2103
BREMAR, Francis, S.C., Eliza E., W1708
BREMER, Lewis, Pvt., Pa., BLWt. 9043 iss. 2/11/1800
BRENDON, Benjamin, See BRANDON
BRENEZE, Catherine, See BRENIZE
BRENNON, John, Pa., S40034
BRENOT, Felix, Pa. See BRUNOT
BRENSINGER, Casper, Pa., R1179
BRENT, John, Pvt., Va., BLWt. 11934 iss. 5/29/1792 to Walter Stewart, ass.
John, Va., Jane, R1176
William, Va., R20335
BRENTON, Adam, Pa., Va., Indian War of 1794, R1178
James, Va., Mary, W2518; BLWt. 26696-160-55
John, Pa., Va., S16059. See N.A. Acc. No. 874; 050022. Not half

BRENTON (continued)
pay. John Brenton
Robert, Va., S16062
William, Pa., Va., S16061
BRESSIE, Thomas, Va., R12763 N.A. Acc. No.874. See 050023 Half Pay, Thomas Bressie
BREST, John, Va., S10420
BRESTON, Edward, Va., R1180
BRETON, William, Mass. See BRITTON
BRETT, Amzi, Mass., S29663
Daniel, Mass., S4959
John, Cont., Mass., S29038
Richard, S.C., See BRITT
William, Mass., R1177
BRETTY, David, N.J. See BREATTY
BREVARD, Alexander, N.C., Capt. res. when pension applied for was Lincoln Co., N.C., Ctf.508. Iss. 8/3/1829 or 8/19. $480 per annum began 5/3/1826. Agent Daniel M. Tooney, Exr. D.10/25/1828. No papers in file as claim was adjudicated in Treas. Dept. See BLWt.294-300
Benjamin, N.C., S3068
Joseph, N.C.; BLWt.299-200-Lt. Iss. 1/12/1799. No papers
Robert, N.C., Nancy, R1181
BREVETT, John, Md; BLWt.241-200-Lt. Iss. 10/16/1789. No papers
BREWER, Abraham, See BROWER, N.J.
Ambrose, N.C., R1182
Barrett, Va., S32131
Benjamin, Pa., S46025
Daniel, Ct., Molly, W25302
Daniel, Ct., Cont., S36435
Daniel, Pvt., "in Moylan's Dragoons", Pa., BLWt.9032 iss. 6/29/178- to M. McConnell, ass.
David, Mass., S4974
Edward, N.C., R1183
Eliab, Mass., S21670
Elijah, Drummer, Mass.,BLWt.3777 iss. 3/4/1790 to Eli^h Mather
Elisha, Cont.,Mass., Martha, W4143
Elisha, Mass., Chloe, W10454; BLWt.17709-160-55
Francis, Mass., R1184
Henry, Cont., Va., S42093; BLWt.1631-100
Henry, N.Y., S42100
Henry, N.C., S39213
Isaac, Mass., Esther, W14366
Isaac, N.C., R1185
James, N.H., S17858
Jesse, N.C., Frankey, W5872
John, Cont., Va., Mary, W3652; BLWt.29460-160-55
John, N.J., S40028
John, N.Y., War of 1812, Mary, W1706
John A., N.J., S5298
Joseph, Mass., R1186
Lois, former wid. of Ebenezer Drake, Ct., which see
Moses, Cont., Mass., S45620
Moses, Cont., Mass., Molly/Mary, W23706
Paul, Pvt., N.J., BLWt.8138 iss. 2/15/1796
Peter, N.Y., S44690

BREWER (continued)
Priscilla, former wid. of Joshua Merritt, Mass., which see
Samuel, Pa., Rebecca, W8401
Solomon, Mass., Rene, W15826
Thomas, N.J., S855
Thomas Stockett, Md., Susanna, W9369; BLWt.3974-160-55
William, N.C., S3085
William, N.C., S41458
William, Va., S30885
BREWINGTON, Joshua, N.C., S8091
BREWSTER, Caleb, Cont., N.Y., S28367; BLWt.172-200-Capt.-Lt. of Col. Lamb's Regt. Artillery Iss. 12/15/1790. No papers
Charles, Vt., Anna, R1187; BLWt. 98554-160-55
Daniel, Mass., Mary Johnson, former wid., R5645
Daniel, Pvt., N.J., BLWt.8149 iss. 7/16/1789
Darius, Ct. Sea Service, S30900
David, Green Mt. Boys, N.Y., Hannah, W16862; BLWt.26132-160-55
Elias, Ct., S15765
Elisha, Cont., Ct., Sarah H., W14394
Frederick, Ct., S15346
Henry, N.Y., S28366
Hezekiah, Ct., Cont., S36439
Hugh, N.C., S.C., S31578
James, Cont.; BLWt.171-200-Lt. Iss. 6/20/1796. No papers
James, N.H., Eleanor, W16097
James, N.Y., Anna, W4642
Jesse, N.Y., S12291
John, Matross, Crane's Cont. Artillery, Mass., BLWt.3820 iss. 10/25/1792
John, N.H., S45616
Joseph, Ct., Cont., Mass., R.I., S12286
Joshua, Mass., S29670
Joshua, Mass., S34071
Justus, Ct., Cont., Joanna, W14354; BLWt.7099-160-55
Lois, former wid. of John Drew, N.H., which see
Morgan, Ct., R1189
Nathan, N.Y., Hannah, W5230; BLWt.29035-160-55
Nathaniel, Ct., See claim of Anna, wid. of Isaac Holmes.
Samuel, N.Y., Sarah S., W523; BLWt.26799-160-55
Sheriff, S.C., S31570
Timothy, Ct., Mass., R1190
William, Mass., S34072
William, N.Y., S3084
William, N.C., S9287
Zadoc, Ct. Sea Service, Lucy, W23685
BREY, Christopher, Pa., S22142
BRIAN, Daniel, Md., S39246
Thomas, Va., Margaret, W5918; BLWt.26487-160-55
BRIANCE, Henry, N.C., S32133
BRIANT, Benjamin, N.J. See BRYANT
Benjamin, Va., See BRYANT
Christian, N.Y., See BRANT

BRIANT, David, Cont., Mass. See BRYANT
David, Mass., Abigail, W23670
Isaac, Mass., Betsey, W23699
Jacob, Ct., Vt., R----
John, N.H., See BRYANT
John, N.J., See BRYANT
William, N.C., See BRYANT
William, Va., See BRYANT
Zachariah, Va., S16326
BRICK, Jonas, Cont., Mass., Judith, W14388
BRICKELL, George, Pa., S5302
BRICKER, Adam, Pa., See BICKER
BRICKETT, Daniel, Mass., S1642
James, Mass., Ruth, W1378; BLWt.30588-160-55
BRICKEY, Peter, Va., Elizabeth, R1192; BLWt.44800-160-55
William, Va., S6751
BRIDDLE, John, ----, Sarah. See Rej. claim Wid. Original No. 45304, War of 1812. She claimed pension for husband's serv. as fife major in the Rev. & alleges he was drafted in Franklin Co., Ky. Claim was rejected on ground he could not have served in Rev. and no evidence of War of 1812 service.
BRIDGE, Benjamin, Cont., N.J., S42094
BRIDGEMAN, Gideon, Ct., Green Mt. Boys, N.H., S15002
Joseph, Pvt., Va., BLWt.11953 iss. 7/6/1793 to Francis Graves, ass.
Thomas, Va., Mary, R12791
BRIDGES, Abraham, Mass., Rebekah; BLWt.43515-160-55
Allen J., N.C., Elizabeth, W8159
Benjamin, N.C., S35199
Benjamin, Va., R1193
Daniel, Pvt., N.H., BLWts.2929 & 351-60-1855 iss. 3/25/1790
Edmund, Mass., S36936
George, N.C., S32139
Hackaliah, Mass., Lydia, W8397
John, Cont., Va., Jane, W4904
John, Pa., R1194
John, Va., S47819
Joseph, N.C., Va., Frances, W4646
Philip, Mass. Sea Service, Hannah, W18662
Ransom, Pvt., Va., BLWt.11925 iss. 10/22/1791 to Jacob Clingman, ass
Ransone, Cont., Va., S39245
Samuel, Ct., Content, W10299; BLWt.31306-160-55
BRIDGET, James, Va., S39208
BRIDGEWATER, Levi, Va. See BRIDGWATER
Samuel, Va., Mary Ann, W9371
William, Va. See BRIDGWATER
BRIDGHAM, John, Cont., Mass.,S18742
Samuel, Cont., Mass., Lucy, W23696
William, Mass., S20293
BRIDGMAN, Elisha, Mass., Sybel, W15600
Erastus, Mass., Rhoda Morgan, former wid., W19888; BLWt.9064-160-55

BRIDGMAN, Isaac, N.H., Theoda, W15989
BRIDGWATER, Levi, Va., Patience, W9752
Samuel, Va., Hannah, R1195
William, Va., S6737
BRIDWELL, Simon, Va., S10417
BRIEN, John, N.C., Margaret, W9747
BRIERLY, George, Md., Mary, R1196
BRIFFAULT, Augustin Louis Guilliaume, Cont., French, BLWt.2321-300
BRIGER, John, Pvt., Hazen's Regt. BLWt.12807 iss. 9/5/1790 to John S. Hobart, Egbert Benson, John McKesser, Ebenezer Hazard & Richard Platt, Executors of Alexander McDougal, ass.
BRIGES, Benjamin N.C. See BRIDGES
BRIGGS, Aaron, Mass., S6701
Abial/Joseph, Ct., R.I., Jane, W20764
Abiezer, R.I., S29671
Abner, Cont., Mass., S29669
Abner, Mass., Sarah, W18655
Abner, Mass., R.I., S28656
Abraham, Cont., R.I., S12287
Aden, Mass., Abigail/Nabby Seavey, former wid., W22177; BLWt.78534-160-55
Amos, R.I., Thankful, W23703
Anderson, R.I., S38573
Anderson/Andrew, Pvt., R.I., BLWt.2959 iss. 12/22/1795 to John Hubbart, ass.
Arnold, Cont., Mass., S34587; BLWt.123-100
Asa, Cont., Green Mt. Boys, Olive, W8158; BLWt.26495-160-55
Asa, Mass., R.I. Sea Service, Vt., S29031
Benjamin, Mass., S30292
Benjamin, R.I., Lydia, W2060; BLWt.26201-160-55
Benjamin, Va., S30889
Burton, Cont., R.I., S38581
Cary/Carey, Mass., R.I., S28650
Daniel, R.I., S38582
Darius, Mass., Elizabeth, W20784
Darius, Mass. Sea Service, Phebe, W21712
David, Mass., S29033
David, Va., Margaret, W2994; BLWt.26717-160-55
Delius, Mass., R1198
Edmund, Cont., Mass., S29652
Elisha, Cont., Mass., S18736
Elisha, Mass., S30291
Elisha, Mass., Deborah, W14399
Enos, Mass., S18740
Ephraim, Cont., Ct., Dilla, R1199
Ephraim, Cont., Ct., Vt., Rhoda, W23710
Ephraim, R.I., Nancy, W24664
Ezra, Ct., S46788
Ezra, Mass., Lydia, W14395
Gideon, Cont., Mass., Abigail, W17349
Henry, Cont., Mass., S44677
Isaac, Cont., Ct., Lucy Ann, W23664

BRIGGS (continued)
Isaac, R.I., S21658
Jabez, Mass., S34105
Jacob, Mass., S34069
Jacob, Mass., S45614
Jacob, Mass., R.I., S34586
Jacob, Res. Washington Co., R.I. Dis. ----. Invalid pension $48 per yr. from 3/4/1789 under Act of 6/7/1785. No papers
James, Ct., S44676
James, Cont., Mass., Sarah, W14345
James, Mass., Privateer, R.I., S.C. Sea Service, S15344
Jeremiah, N.Y., S44678
Jesse, Cont., Mass., Naomi, W24659
Jesse, Mass., Betty, R1197
Job, R.I., S38578
Job, R.I., Sarah, W20790
John (son of Noah), Ct., S12331
John, Ga., Susannah, R1202
John, Pvt., Mass., BLWt.3801 iss. 10/8/1792 to Wm. Thompson, ass.
John, Mass., S44674
John, Mass., Lorania, R1208
John, N.Y., See Jonathan, S44675
John, Pa., Dorothea, R1200
John, Pvt., R.I., BLWt.2961 iss. 2/11/1800
John, R.I., Mary, W23674
Jonathan, Pvt., N.Y., BLWt.6796 iss. 11/27/1790
Jonathan/John, N.Y., S44675
Jonathan, R.I., S38583
Jonathan, R.I., Abigail, W23686
Joseph, Ct., R.I., See Abial
Joseph, Cont., Vt., Patience, W16512
Joseph, Mass., S16058
Joseph, R.I., S21430
Joshua, Ct., Cont., Tryphena, W20753
Joshua, Ct., N.Y., R1203
Leonard, Cont., Mass., S34096
Matthias, N.Y., Margaret, W25288
Michael, Vt., Sarah, R1207
Nathan, N.C., Mary, R1204
Nathaniel, Navy, N.H. agency & res. in 1818, S45615
Owen, Ct., Mass., Margery, W18644
Paul, Mass., R.I., S30899
Paul, R.I., S46789
Perez, Mass., S4960
Phinehas, Mass., S12328
Polly, former wid. of Seth Holcomb, Ct., which see
Richard, Mass., Hannah, W15602
Richard, Privateer, Mass., S.C. Sea Service, Huldah, W10458
Rufus, Mass., N.H., N.Y., S10405
Samuel, Mass., Rebecca, W525; BLWt.10249-160-55
Samuel, Mass., Rachel, W5923; BLWt.16275-160-55
Seth, Mass., Deborah, W20759
Solomon, Cont.; Vt. agency & res. Lydia, W18653
Stephen, Ct., Deborah, W17337
Stephen, Mass., Sarah, W14387
Sweet, R.I., S12303

BRIGGS (continued)
Thomas, R.I., S21660
Tobias, R.I., BLWt.2338-100
William, Ct., S12281
William, Mass., S36925
William, Pa., S34076
William, R.I., S21089
William, R.I., Catharine, W20793
Zephaniah, Ct., S12336
BRIGHAM, Aaron, Mass., Betsey R., W23700; BLWt.6038-160-55
Abel, Mass., S12326
Abraham, Cont., Mass., Emma, W23665
Amariah, Cont., Mass., Sally, W4896; BLWt.24172-160-55
Daniel, Mass., Anne/Anna, W24670; BLWt.12710-160-55
Don C., Ct., Polly, W17350
Edward, Mass., S18331
Elnathan, Ct., S14987
Henry, Cont., Mass., Anna, W23702
Jesse, Mass., Elizabeth, W20758
Joel, Mass., Elizabeth, W20765; BLWt.195-100
John, Mass., Eunice, W14386; BLWt.24612-160-55
John, Mass., Lydia, W23676; BLWt.9194-160-55
Jonas, Mass., Dorcas; BLWt.47904-160-55
Jonathan, Cont., Mass., S22665
Lovell, Mass., Betty, W23712; BLWt.6115-160-55
Mary, former wid. of Elisha Johnson, Ct., which see
Origen, Cont., Mass., Eleanor, W5931; BLWt.1664-300
Paul, Ct., Lydia, W23695
Paul, Mass., Fanny, W15677; BLWt.12721-160-55
Phinehas, Mass., Susanna Sanford, former wid., W19311
Samuel, Cont., Mass. See BRIDGHAM
Stephen, N.H., S12300
Warrin, Cont., Mass., Lucy, W23687; BLWt.26134-160-55
Winslow, Mass., Alice, W25244
BRIGHT, Francis, Va. Sea Service, R16. Half Pay
James, Pvt., Lamb's Artillery, N.Y., BLWt.6879 iss. 11/26/1791
James, Md., Sarah, W402
Joseph, Mass., Hannah, R1209
Levi, Pvt., Del., BLWt.10713 iss. 5/26/1790
Simon, N.C., S6725
Simon, N.C., S9293
Willis, N.C., S41459
Windle/Wyndle, N.J., Va., Barbara, W27861
BRIGHTMAN, Henry, Ct., Mary, W25293
Israel, R.I., S29667
Johnson, N.Y., S12321
Peleg, Mass., S29659
Thomas, Mass., R.I., Rebeckah, W23708
Thomas, R.I., S21657
BRIGHTWELL, Anderson, Va., Nancy, W18643
Charles, Va., S6767
BRIGNOL, Joseph, Mass. This

BRIGNOL (continued)
man's former wid. received pension as wid. of Daniel Lilly/Lillie, Mass. which see
BRILEY/BRILY, John, Md., S42631; BLWt.1790-100
BRILL, Michael, Va., R1212
BRILLIFONT/BULLEFANT, James, Va., S39236
BRIM, Henry, Cont., Pa., S40033
BRIMER, William, N.C., Elizabeth, W336
BRIMHALL, Gideon, Mass., S34107
Joshua, Mass.; BLWt.118-200-Lt. Iss. 2/23/1796 to Joseph Brown, ass. No papers
Sarah, former wid. of Simon Gilman, N.H., which see
Sylvanus, Mass., S29658
Sylvanus, Mass., See BRAMHALL
BRIMIDGHAM, Daniel, Md. See BRUMIGUM
BRIMIGION, Thomas, Cont., Mass., S36922
Thomas, Pvt., Mass., BLWt.3787 iss. 8/26/1796
BRIMLEY, William, N.J., See BRINLEY
BRIMMAGE/BRUMMAGE, John, N.C., S38568
BRIMMER, Isaac, Va., S6762
Joseph, N.C., See BRYMER
BRINCKERHOFF, Henry, N.Y., S12333
BRINCKLY/BRINCKLEY, John, Navy, Mass. res. & agency, S34083
BRINDLEY, Francis, N.Y.; BLWt.165-200-Lt. Iss. 5/27/1793 to Richd. Ryan, ass. of Patience Tisdale, admx. No papers
BRINE/BRYNE, Richard, Mass., S34081
BRINK, Aaron, Cont., N.J., Lena, W5943; BLWt.970-100. Iss. 2/26/1821. Mary,alleged wid. of this soldier received pension. See papers in W4903
Adam, N.Y., Elinda, W25299; BLWt. 5082-160-55
Benjamin, Pa., S5306
George, N.J., S15007
Henry, Cont., N.J., Jemima, W1375; BLWt.5089-160-55
Jacob, N.Y., S15009
John, N.Y., Diana, W15759
John, N.Y., Margaret, W16197
John C., N.Y., Catharine, W20755
Moses, N.J., S15004
Peter, N.Y., S12314
Peter C., N.Y., S12345
BRINKER, Henry, Pa., S5307
Henry, Va., S5305
BRINKERHOFF, Garret, N.J., Margaret W136
James J., N.J., Cornelia, W3766; BLWt.29036-160-55
BRINKLEY, Aaron, Va., Sarah, R1214
William, Va., R1215
BRINLEY, William, N.J., Rachel, W1542
BRINSFIELD, William, Md. res. Dis. ---- No papers
BRINSMADE, Cyrus, Ct., Sally, W2559; BLWt.26611-160-55

BRINSON, Hilary, N.C., Elizabeth, W5231
BRINTNAL, Peter, Mass., S12342
BRISBAN, John, Pa., S40026
John, Pa., R1216
BRISBIN/BRISBON, Elenor/Nella, former wid. of John McCrea, N.Y., which see
BRISCO/BRISCOE, Nathaniel, Ct., S12313
BRISCOE, Henry, Md., S30888
Philip, Md., S6723
Reuben, Va., BLWt.81-300-Capt. Iss. 5/26/1789. Also recorded under Wt.2475. No papers
BRISLER, John, Mass., Esther, W23673
BRISSET, Joseph, Cont., N.Y. res. in 1829, R20452
BRISTALL, John, Ct. See BRISTOLL
BRISTER, Aaron, Va., Betsey, Colored; W17341
John, Pvt., Ct., BLWt.5461 iss. 5/26/1790
John, Ct., Lilly, W20772
BRISTOL, Austin, Ct., R1218
Benjamin, Pvt., Ct., BLWt.5443 iss. 11/2/1791 to Jonathan Tuttle
Benjamin, N.Y., S9292
Bezaleel, Ct., Mary, W20781
David, Ct., S17300
Gideon, Ct., S12323
John, N.Y., R1219
Jonathan G., Ct., S12288
Mary, former wid. of James Dunham, N.J., W5233, which see
Nathaniel, Ct., Cont., S12341
Reuben, Ct., Cont., S12316
Samuel, Vt., S23549
Thomas, Ct. agency, Dis.--- No papers
BRISTOLL, Eli, Ct., S22664
John, Ct., R1217
BRISTOR, Stephen, Ct., S36437
Peter, Pvt., Ct., BLWt.5411 iss. 4/2/1792
BRITAIN, Daniel, N.J See BRITTON
James, Cont., Mass., Martha, W18668
John, Va. Sea Service, See BRITTAIN
BRITBINER, Bernard, Pvt., Hazen's Regt., BLWt.12769 iss. 5/24/1792 to Robert Ross, ass. of Mathias Roland, Admr.
BRITE, Willis, N.C. See BRIGHT
BRITON/BRITTON, Michael, N.C., Nancy, W4905
BRITT, Charles, Ga., S.C., S17850
James, Pvt.,"in the Corps of Sappers & Miners", BLWt.12754 iss. 5/6/1793
John, Md., Pensioned in Me., S36935
John, Pvt., Va., Lee's Legion, BLWt.13968 iss. 11/2/1792 to Robert Means, ass.
Obed, Va., S1499
Richard, S.C., S39226
BRITTAIN, James, Cont., See

BRITTAIN (continued)
BRITAIN
Jeremiah, N.J. See BRITTAN
John, N.C., Mary, R1220
John, Va. Sea Service, R13, Va. Half Pay
Philip, N.C., S39243
William, N.C., S8100
BRITTAN, Daniel, N.J., S34070. Elizabeth Brittan/Britton, wid., was pensioned as former wid. of William Pence, N.J., which see
Jeremiah, N.J., U.S.A., Elizabeth, W15756
Jeremiah, N.J., BLWt.1729-100
Samuel, N.J., Anne, W4146
William, Pvt., Mass., BLWt. 3781 iss. 3/25/1791 to D. Quinton
BRITTEN, John, N.J., Va., S44662
BRITTENHAM, Solomon, Pvt., Md., BLWt.10989 iss. 7/3/1797 to James DeBaufre, ass.
BRITTIN, John, Cont., N.J., S44663
Joseph, N.J., S857
BRITTINGHAM/BRITTINGHAN, Solomon, Md., Leah, W9754; BLWt.96800-160-55
BRITTON, Asa, N.H., Sally, W1541; BLWt.24603-160-55
Claudius, Vt., R1222
Daniel, N.J., d. 3/1834, S2098
Daniel, N.J., d. 1802/3, Charlotte/Catharine, W9750; BLWt. 8096-100-Pvt. iss. 12/20/1791 to Jacob Heller, ass. No papers
James, N.J., S12293
Job, N.H., Abigail, W17338
John, Mass., Jerusha, R1223
John, Pvt., N.J., BLWt.8106 iss. 5/27/1790 to Jeptha Arrison, ass.
John, N.J., S34669
John, Va., S46496; BLWt.999-100
John, Va. Sea Service, See BRITTAIN
Jonathan, Mass., Beulah, W25281
Joseph, Cont., Md., S39221; BLWt.244-200-Lt. Iss. 7/30/1790 No papers. Half Pay Claim, Act July 5, 1832
Joseph, N.J., S34084
Joseph, Pa., Hannah, W3216
Joseph, Va., S8087
Michael, N.C., See BRITON
Nathaniel, Mass., S4972
Samuel, Sgt., N.H., BLWt.2941 iss. 7/30/1790
Samuel, N.H., S28653
Samuel, Pvt., Va., BLWt.11956 iss. 3/16/1792 to Mary Britton, Admx.
William, Cont., N.J., Sarah, R1224
William, Mass., S42097
BRITTON/BRETON/BREETON/BRITTAIN/ BRITTAN, William, Mass., BLWt. 838-100
Zachariah/Zacchariah, Mass., S12320

BRIZEE, Mary, See BERSIE
BRIZENDINE, Bartlett, Va., Nancy, R1225
Leroy, Va., S1941
Reuben, Va., S6754
William, Va., S6752
BROACH, Benoni, Va., Ann, W18646
Charles, Cont., Va., Martha, W5921
BROAD, Amos, Mass., R1226
BROADAWAY, John, S.C., S39218
William, S.C., See BROADWAY
BROADDUS, John, Va., R1227
Pryor, Va., S8109
Reuben, Va., R1228
BROADHEAD, Daniel, N.Y., See BRODHEAD
Garret, N.J., Affy, W2748
Luke, Pa. See BRODHEAD
Samuel, N.Y., See BRODHEAD
BROADRICK, John, Mass., S30293
BROADUS, William, Va., Martha R., W8396; BLWt.1875-200 & Va. Half Pay
BROADWATER, Charles Lewis, Va. Sea Service, Va., S8096
BROADWAY, Samuel, Va., S8086
William, S.C., Mary, W8398; BLWt.30600-160-55
BROADWELL, Jacob, N.J., S2099
BROBST, John, Pa., Catharine, R1229
BROCAS, John, Mass., S21671
BROCAW, Isaac, N.J. See BROKAW
BROCK, Bezzant, N.C., S6722
Francis, Mass., Sarah, W17355; BLWt.24160-160-55
George, Va., R1231
Henry, Va., S36431
Isaac, N.C., S.C., R1230
James, Mass., See Le BROKE
Jesse, N.C., S30887
John, Ct., Cont., See BROCKE
Reuben, N.C., S9285
Sarah, former wid. of Francis Courtney, N.Y., which see
Uriah, Va., S34670; BLWt.1722-100
BROCKE, John, Ct., Cont., Hannah, W20767
BROCKET/BROCKETT, William, S.C., Patsey, W24665
BROCKETT, Giles, Ct., S16661
Hezekiah, Ct., Asenath, W8167; BLWt.29-60-55
Joel, Ct., Elizabeth, W10452
John, Ct., Mass. Navy, S21082
BROCKINTON, John, S.C., S9286
BROCKIT, Isaac, Ct., S36441
BROCKLEBANK, James, Mass., Sarah, W16513
Job, Cont., Mass. res. 1818. S34092
Joseph, Mass., S18332
BROCKMAN, Joseph, Va., S40031
Sarah, former wid. of James Daniel, Va., which see
Thomas, Va., R1233
BROCKUS, John, Va., S39224
BROCKWAY, Asa, Ct., S15350
Benjamin, Cont., Ct., S36428
Enoch, Ct., S12337

BROCKWAY (continued)
Ephraim, Ct., S12278
Gideon, Ct., Tryphena, W20786
John, Ct., Irene, W25280; BLWt.19716-160-55
Martin, N.H., S15348
Pardon, Ct., Jane, W12340; BLWt.40907-160-55
Russell, N.Y., Mary, W16514
Russell, Pvt., N.Y., BLWt.6811 iss. 3/22/1796 to Theodorus Bailey, ass.
Samuel, Mass., R1235
Sarah, former wid. of Isaac Still, which see
Semilius, ----, Bridget Ely, former wid. He was her 1st husb. and died in service. See claim of Abner Ely, Ct.
Zebulon, Ct., S31565
BRODERICK, Absalom, N.J., R1236
William, Pvt., N.J., BLWt.8123 iss. 4/21/1790 to Jonathan Nichols, ass.
BRODHEAD, Daniel, N.Y., Blandina, W23690
Daniel, Pa., S40030; BLWt.1095-200
Daniel, Pa., BLWt.187-500-Col. Iss. 2/15/1790. No papers
Garret, N.J., See BROADHEAD
Luke, Pa., BLWt.222-300-Capt. Iss. 3/26/1793. No papers
Samuel, N.J., N.Y., Dinah, W21715
BRODRICK, William, Cont., N.J., S2396
BROGA, Andrew, Cont., Mass., S34086
BROGNARD, John Baptiste, French, N.J. res. 1823, Mary, R1238
BROILE, Philip, Pa., S44687
BROKAW, Abraham, N.J., Phebe, W18647
George, N.J., Jane, R1232
Isaac, N.J., S602
Isaac, N.J., S803
Jasper, N.J., Catharine, W23663
Peter, N.J., Elizabeth, W3761
Richard, N.J., Rebecca, W401
BROKE, James, Mass. See LeBROKE
BROKS, Shadrach, Mass. See BROOKS
BROMAGEN/BROMIGIN, Jarvis, Va., S30895
BROMLEY, Joshua, Vt., Anna, W15608
Margaret, former wid. of Ralph Falkner, Va., BLWt.514-400
Samuel, Mass., R1239
William, Vt., See BRUMLEY
BROMLY, William, Vt., S22135; b.3/14/1766 at Preston, Ct.; res. at enl. Danby, Rutland Co., Vt.; res. 1813-1836, Clarendon, Vt.
BRONNAN, Adam, N.Y., See BRANNON
BRONNER, Frederick, N.Y., Anna Eve, W477. Her ch. by former husband, Elias Garlach, Pvt. 13th Inf., killed 10/13/1812, rec'd half pay pension, iss. in lieu of B.L., Ctf. No. 899
BRONNON, Lawrence, Pvt., Md., BLWt.10981 iss. 4/28/1791
BRONSON, Asahel, Ct., S12289
Elijah, Ct., See BRUNSON

BRONSON (continued)
Isaac, Ct., Thankful, W10470
Isaac, Cont., Ct., Anne, W5932; BLWt.152-300 to Isaac Brunson Surg'n Mate, Col. Sheldon's Regt. Cavalry. Iss. 7/28/1789 to Richard Smith, ass. No papers
Jabez, Ct., Marilla, W25303
Joel, Ct., See BROWNSON
Joseph, Ct., S12295
Joseph, Ct., Cont., S44685
Michael, Ct., Eunice, W20773
Pheneas/Phinehas, Ct., See BRUNSON
Reuben, Ct., See BROWNSON
Samuel, Ct., S16056
Selah, Ct., Anna, W9367; BLWt. 61329-160-55
Silas, Ct., Sally, W17365
Titus, Ct., Hannah, W17356
BROOCKE/BROOCKS, William, Va. [illegible] See BROOKS
BROOK, Benjamin, Pa., R1240
David, Mass., Waity, W5910
Eleazer, Vt. See BROOKS
George, Va., S39247
John, Va., BLWt.282-200-Lt. Iss. 6/21/1796 to Chs. Croughton. No papers
BROOKBANK, John, Pvt., Md., BLWt. 10943 iss. 8/14/1795 to Francis Sherrard, ass.
BROOKE, Dudley, Va., S3055
Edmund, Va., S46423; BLWt.1097-200
Francis, Va., BLWt.281-200-Lt. No date of iss. No papers. See Francis T. Brooks, Cont., Va.
Francis T., Cont., Va., S8093
George, Pa., S2096
Humphrey, Cont., Va., S6763
Walter, Va., sea service, R14, Va. Half Pay
BROOKER, Benjamin D. (alias CAIN) N.Y., S34080
Isaac, Ct., S29653
Samuel, Ct., Polly, W5945; BLWt. 8151-160-55
Walter, Pvt., N.Y., BLWt.6816 iss. 9/15/1790 to John S. Hobart, ass.
BROOKES, Jonathan, N.C., S6721
BROOKFIELD, Brown, N.J., S2401
Jacob, N.J., Huldah, W478
Job, N.J., S3080
BROOKHOUSE, Rudolph, Pvt., Pa., BLWt.8933 iss. 4/13/1791
BROOKHOUSER, Adam, Pa., Mary, R1241
BROOKINS, Artemas, Mass., Lois, W20754; BLWt.698-100
James, Green Mt. Boys, Vt., Mary, W27386
Reuben, Mass., S44684
William, Mass., N.Y., R1242
BROOKMAN, John, N.Y., Anna, W17353
BROOKOVER, John, Md., Va., S5300
BROOKS, Ahira, Ct., S29037; BLWt. 26700-160-55
Almarin, N.J., S34108; BLWt.186-150-Ens. Iss. 7/7/1789. No papers. Also 1794, Major
Alpheus, Mass., S18738
Amos, Mass., S45617

BROOKS (continued)
Asa, Ct., Betsey, W16198
Austin, Mass., S32141
Azariah, Mass., Vt., S18737
Benjamin, Pvt., Ct., BLWt.5488 iss. 1/17/1793 to Samuel Emery
Benjamin, Md., BLWt.228-400-Maj. Iss. 3/11/1791. No papers
Benjamin, Pvt., Va., BLWt.11892 iss. 10/24/1789
Caleb E., Ct., Jane E., R1244
Charles, Pvt., Pa., BLWts.8918 &11891 iss. 11/5/1789
Charles, Pa., S2404
Charles, Va., Malinda, R1256
Cornelius, Pa., S14997
Daniel, Mass., Susanna, R1260
David, Ct., Jane, W4148
David, Cont., Pa., Maria M., W23711; BLWt.1909-200
David, Va., S1641
Ebenezer, Mass., Ede, W14390
Ebenezer, N.H., Dis. --- No papers
Edward, Mass. Sea Service, R1245
Edward, Mass., Vt., S12302
Eleazer, Vt., Olive, W1812; BLWt. 24433-160-55
Elias, Va., S6768
Elisha, S.C., Nancy, W9741
Elizabeth, former wid. of Joshua Rutledge, Md., which see
Francis, Mass. See SOUCEE
George, S.C., Va., S31574; BLWt. 6382-160-55
George, Va., Barsheba, W18665
Hananlah/Hannaniah, Cont., Mass., S17292
Henry, Va., S16655
Jabez, Ct., Rhoda, W15601
James, Ct., R1249
James, Ct., Cont., Lydia, W3929
James, N.J., S34585; BLWt.2481-100
James, Va., S10418
James, Va., S36430
James, Va., Nancy, R1258
Job, Mass., S15345
Joel, Mass., R1250; BLWt.34579-160-55
John, Ct., S15003
John, Ct., S23557; BLWt.26157-160-55
John, Cont., N.H., Emma, W2519; BLWt.3975-160-55
John, Md., Va., S3056
John, Mass., S10416
John, Mass., S34087
John, Lt.-Col. Commandant, Mass. BLWt.92-500 iss. 3/14/1796
John/John Drury, Mass., R1253
John, N.Y., S23137
John, N.Y., R1251
John, N.Y., Orilla, W10451
John, N.C., S2398
John, N.C., S6732; BLWt.80030-160-55
John, Pvt., Va., BLWt.11958 iss. 6/23/1793 or 5 to Robt. Means, ass.
John, Va., S30897
Jonas, Mass., Rest, W5909; BLWt. 39476-160-55
Jonathan, Mass., S44670

BROOKS (continued)
Joseph, Pvt., Crane's Cont. Artillery, Mass., BLWt.3832 iss. 5/31/1790 to Theodosius Fowler, ass.
Joseph B., Ct., Cont., R1254
Joshua, Mass., S17865; BLWt.1787-100
Joshua, Mass., Sarah, R22013; BLWt.16269-160-55
Joshua, N.Y., R1255
Josiah, Ct., Abigail, W20766
Lemuel, Ct., Hannah, R1248
Levi, Mass., S19568
Littleton, N.C., S1503
Micajah, Ga., S.C., Margaret T., W27694; BLWt.51752-160-55
Michael, N.Y., S28341
Middleton, Va., S31572
Nathan, Pvt., Mass., BLWt.3660 iss. 1/12/1792
Nathan, Mass., S34102
Nathaniel, Mass., Lucy, W17334
Nathaniel, Mass., Deborah, W20756
Nehemiah E., Mass. See ESTABROOK
Nelson, Va., Frances, W5912
Oliver, N.J., S2095
Reuben, Ct., S30294
Reuben, Mass., Anna, W18667
Robert, Va., S10422
Robert, Va., Rhoda, W5913
Samuel, Ct., Elizabeth, R1246
Samuel, Cont., Mass., S36928
Samuel, Pvt., Lamb's Artillery N.Y., BLWt.6892 iss. 5/25/1790
Samuel, Mass., Lucy, W23667; BLWt.19617-160-55
Samuel Lewis, Ct., Cont., S44671
Shadrach, Mass., S12317
Silas, Pvt., Ct., BLWt.5416 iss. 1/28/1792 to Moses Sill
Silas, Ct., S17861
Simon, Mass., Theodosia Root, former wid., W26400; BLWt. 50891-160-55
Solomon, Mass., S29665
Thaddeus, Mass., S44673
Thomas, Ct., Esther, W16871; BLWt.30-100
Thomas, Ct., Surviah/Zurviah, W23701
Thomas, Pvt., N.Y., BLWt.6795 iss. 1/2/1792 to Thos. Brooks, Certif. 4/25/1806
Thomas, N.Y., Dis. ---- No papers
Thomas, N.C., Angelica, R1243
Thomas, N.C., Martha, R1257
Thomas, N.C., Va., S1795
Thomas, Va., S5296
Thomas, ----, N.J. res. 1835, R12671
Timothy, Cont., Mass., Katy, W16859
William, Cont., N.H., Hepsibah Boutwell, former wid., W10446; BLWt.24427-160-55
William, Ga., R1263
William, a Marine, Va. res. at enlistment, R1262
William, Md., N.C., S6717
William, Mass., S17866
William, N.C., S6705

BROOKS (continued)
William, Sgt., Pa., Proctor's Artillery, BLWt.8949 iss. 7/16/1789 to M. McConnell, ass.
William, Va., Nancy/Ann, W5908
William, Va., Nancy, R1259
William, Va., R1264
Zachariah Smith, S.C., S9294
BROOKSHIER, John, N.C., S6726
BROOKSHIRE, Manring/Mannering, N.C., S6707
William, N.C., S6706
BROOM, Ann, former wid. of William Barber, Cont., N.J., which see
Edward, Pvt., S.C., BLWt.11979 iss. 7/13/1795
Isaac, Pa., S40032
John, S.C., S21664
Mason, N.C., S41457
Thomas, Sgt., Va., Col. Lee's Legion, BLWts.11896 & 12854 iss. 10/20/1789
BROOME, John, Va., S42095
BROSIUS/BROSUS, Abraham, Pa., S39248
BROSS, Hermanus, N.J., Ann, W239
BROTHERS, Mathew, Pa., BLWt.9073 Iss. 1789
BROTHERTIN, Thomas, N.C., S6696
William, N.C., S31793
BROTHERTON, John, N.Y., R1265
BROTHWELL, Benjamin, Ct., S14991
Joseph, Fairweather, Ct., Privateer, S15008
Thomas, Ct., Nancy, W5928; BLWt. 26802-160-55
BROUCHER, Christian, Pa., R1269
BROUGH, William, Va., R1267
BROUGHAM, John, N.Y., Margaret, W16861
BROUGHER, Christian, See BROUCHER
BROUGHTON, Bartholomew, Pvt., N.Y., BLWt.6856 iss. 7/16/1790 to Wm. I. Vreedenburg, ass.
Ebenezer, Ct., Lois, W18650
Job, Ga., N.C., Mary, W8395
John, Ct., Hannah, W20769
Joseph, N.C., Polly, W5929; BLWt.36507-160-55
Michael, Ct., Sarah, W18666
Nathan, Pvt., Hazen's Regt., BLWt.12760 iss. 2/27/1790 to Theodosius Fowler, ass.
Thomas, S.C., Mary, W897
BROUILLET, Frances, former wid. of Henry Vanderburgh, N.Y., which see
BROUSE, Michael, Pa. See BRAUSS
BROUWER, Garret, Cont., BLWt. 2571-200-Lt. of Artillery Artificers. Iss. 10/18/1790. No papers
BROVARD, Benjamin, N.C. See BREVARD
BROW, Peter, Cont., Mass.,S34097
BROWDER, Isham, Va., Elizabeth, W1183; BLWt.30598-160-55
Jesse, ---, Polly Penticost, former wid., Va. res. 1844, R8100
BROWER, Abraham, N.Y., Rebecca, W17352
Abraham J. or I., N.J., Maria

BROWER (continued)
W23707; BLWt.26331-160-55
Jacob, Pa., S6724
John, N.Y., S28651
John C., N.Y., S14989
William, N.Y., Mary/Mariah, W5877; BLWt.30605-160-55
BROWN, Aaron, Ct., S6733
Aaron, Ct., S36434
Aaron, N.H., Anna, R1276
Aaron, Va., Nancy, R1332
Abel, Cont., Mass., S45611
Abel, Mass., S12335
Abel, Mass., S34106
Abial, Mass., R.I., S21659
Abigail, former wid. of Thomas Taylor, Mass., which see
Abijah, Mass., Bethiah, W8155; BLWt.17862-160-55
Abraham, Cont., Mass., S34068
Abraham, N.H., Mary, W15988
Adam, N.Y., S22662
Adonijah, N.Y., Eleanor, W25287; BLWt.10303-160-55
Alexander, Pa., S40754
Alexander Crawford, Del., S42634
Amasa, Ct., Mary, R1326
Amasa, Ct., Cont., Jerusha, W17344
Ambrose/Ambrous, Mass., Susannah, W25285; BLWt.13421-160-55
Amos, Cont., S34079. In 1819 he was a res. of Duxbury, Mass., aged 60 yrs.
Amos, Cont., Mass., S36931
Amos, Cont., Mass., Hannah, W23689
Amos, N.H., R1275
Amos, N.C., Elizabeth, W5869; BLWt.26467-160-55
Andrew, Mass., S34110
Andrew, Mass., Rachel, W21713
Andrew, Mass., Rebecca, W9744; BLWt.96062-160-55
Andrew, Pvt., R.I., BLWt.2963 iss. 12/31/1789
Arabia, Va., Elizabeth, W8384
Archibald, S.C., S39249
Archibald, S.C., Mary, W21704
Aris, Va., Joanna, W8386
Arthur, N.C., S39222
Arthur, N.C., Lucy, R1322
Asa, N.Y., S10410
Asa, R.I., S22139. Fraudulent claim, no such soldier. Also see claim of Jotham Ford, Mass.
Asher, Ct., Mary, W25277
Austin, Pvt., Ct., BLWt.5424 iss. 6/20/1795
Austin, Ct., Anne, W23697
Barnabas, Mass., S29036; BLWt. 1902-160-55
Barron/Baron, Mass., S44658; BLWt.1154-100
Basil/Bazel, Va., S9713
Bazil, Md., BLWt.2068-100
Benajah, N.Y., Violetta Dustin, former wid., W21021
Benedict, Cont., R1280. In 1824 was aged 70 yr. and res. of N. Kingston, Washington Co., R.I.
Benjamin, Cont., Mass., S34089

BROWN (continued)
Benjamin, Cont., Mass., S45609
Benjamin, Cont., Mass., Jean, W4142
Benjamin, Mass., S29666
Benjamin, Mass., Hannah, W24669
Benjamin, Mass., N.H., Miriam/ Merriam, W15607
Benjamin, Navy, Susannah, W5051. D. 9/17/1831 at Waldoborough, Lincoln Co., Me.
Benjamin, N.H., 11th U.S. Inf. War of 1812, Betsey, W27388; BLWts. 770-100 (Rev.) & 22981-160-55 (1812).
Benjamin, N.Y., S12307
Benjamin, N.C., S3061
Benjamin, N.C., S16327
Benjamin, N.C., S31564; BLWt. 26295-160-55
Benjamin, N.C. or Pa., R1281
Benjamin, R.I., Patience, W24658
Benjamin A., N.J., Pa. Sea Service Rebecca, W3934
Bernis, Va., Henrietta, R1301
Bridgham, Ct., Mary, W17364
Brightberry, Va., R1282
Caleb, Mass., N.H., S12296
Charles, Pvt., Ct., BLWt.5469 iss. 12/26/1789 to David Knap
Charles, Ct., S18745
Charles, Ct., See Charles F.
Charles, Ct., Cont., R1283
Charles, Ct., R.I., S21663
Charles, Cont., N.H., S12285
Charles, N.Y. See Chas. Frederick
Charles, S.C., Susannah, W21708; BLWt.2137-200
Charles, Va., S35794
Charles, Va., S35797
Charles F., Ct., Lucretia Hilliard former wid., R1321
Charles F., Pvt., N.Y., BLWt.6825 iss. 7/18/1791 to Samuel Smith, ass.
Charles Frederick, N.Y., S44660
Christopher, Ct., Privateer, S10411
Christopher, Cont., Ct., Eunice, W12339; BLWt.35844-160-55
Christopher, R.I., Anna, W20778; BLWt.27616-160-55
Claiborn, Va., Sarah, R1284
Clark, Cont., R.I., S38577
Cornelius, Pvt., Pa., BLWt.8976 iss. 5/21/1792 to Moses Sill, ass.
Cyril, Navy, R.I., S29028
Cyrus, Ct., N.Y., S6759
Daniel, Sgt., Ct., BLWt.5403 iss. 1/22/1790
Daniel, Ct., Cont., S10408
Daniel, Ct., Navy, Lydia, W20787
Daniel, Ct. Sea Service, R1286
Daniel, Cont., Ct., Anna, W20782
Daniel, Pvt., Mass., BLWt.3753 iss. 12/17/1789 to Richard Platt, ass.
Daniel, Mass., S10412
Daniel, Mass., S34078
Daniel, Mass., Betty Russell, former wid., W22129; BLWt.36544-160-55

BROWN (continued)
Daniel, Mass., Chloe, W21710
Daniel, Mass., Sarah, W14402
Daniel, N.H., S17853
Daniel, N.H., Dolly, R12633 1/2; BLWt.71140-160-55
Daniel, N.J., S34074
Daniel, Vt., Sarah, W1373
Daniel, Va., S32132
Daniel, Va., Elizabeth, W5907
David, Ct., S22136
David, Ct., S28353
David, Ct., BLWt.461-100
David, Cont., Mass., S18735
David, Cont., N.Y., S29021
David, Pvt., Mass., BLWt.3695 iss. 8/23/1796 to J. Thomas, ass.
David, Mass., S34077
David, Mass., R1289
David, Mass., Navy, S36934
David, Mass., N.Y., Lydia, W10453
David, N.Y., Rachel, W18642
David, R.I., S29655
David, Va. Sea Service, R15; Va. Half Pay
David E., N.C., S39239
Ebenezer, Ct., S36446
Ebenezer, Ct., S44650
Ebenezer, Ct., Abigail, R1270
Ebenezer, Mass., S29662
Ebenezer, Mass., Abigail, W8382; BLWt.113-200-Lt. Iss. 8/10/1789 to Richard Platt, ass. No papers
Ebenezer, Mass., Lydia, W15610
Ebenezer, N.Y., S12330
Edward, Cont., Mass., BLWt.379-100
Edward, Mass., Susanna, R1345
Edward, Mass. Sea Service, S30283
Edward, N.H., S45612
Edward, Va., R1292
Eleazer, Cont., Vt. res. 1818, S39231
Eli, Ct., S44659
Eli, Ct., Cont., Privateer, S23548
Eliada, N.H., Vt., S18741
Elias, Ct., Cont., S12332
Elias, N.Y., BLWt.6893 iss. 4/21/1792
Elias, R.I., S36440
Eliezer, R.I., S21669
Elihu, Mass., S29668
Elijah, Ct., S44661
Elijah, Cont., Mass., Relief, W18660
Elijah, N.Y., R1293
Elijah, N.C., S2403
Elisha, Cont., R.I., S44654
Elisha, Pvt., Hazen's Regt., BLWt. 12793 iss. 11/28/1792 to Fonde Tufts
Elisha, Mass., Merrill, W18640
Elisha, R.I., Waite, W20776
Elisha, R.I., R1294
Elizabeth, former wid. of William Allen/Allyn, Mass., which see
Elizabeth, former wid. of Walter Hier, N.J., which see
Elkanah, Ct., Cont., S44647
Enoch, Mass., S36927
Enos, N.Y., S22146
Ensley, N.H., S45651

BROWN (continued)
Ephraim, Ct., R1297
Ephraim, Mass., S12329
Ephraim, Mass., S31580
Eseck, R.I., S21672
Eseck, R.I., S21079
Ezekiel, Ct., Ruhannah, W16868
Ezekiel, Mass., S2399; BLWt.107-400-Surgn. Iss. 2/23/1796 to John Coats, ass. No papers
Ezekiel, Pa., S3064
Ezra, Ct., S2391
Ezra, N.J., S34094
Francis, Cont., N.H., S45610
Frederick, Ga., S31576
George, Cont.,Mass., Sally, W18659
George, Pvt., Md., BLWts.10960 & 14123 iss. 6/3/1795 to John Wright, ass. of Wm. Brown, Admr.
George, N.J., S3062
George, N.Y., S44656
George, N.C., Margaret, W25274
George, R.I., S21668
George, Va., S32134
Gershom, Ct.,Cont., Eunice, W14389
Hamilton, S.C., Nancy, W1707
Henry, Cont., Pa., S34665
Henry, N.Y., S36436
Henry, Va., S8098
Henry, Va., S35787
Henry, Va., Elizabeth L., W9365; BLWt.36610-160-55
Henry, Va., Frances, W8380
Holsey, N.Y., R1300
Hubbard, Va., S21666
Humphrey, Ct., Olive, W18648; BLWt.29010-160-55
Humphrey, Ct., R1302
Ichabod, Ct., S28657
Isaac, Ct., Cont., Hannah, W17343
Isaac, Ct., N.Y., R.I., S6745
Isaac, Mass., S29661
Isaac, N.H., S22141
Isaac, N.Y., S12306
Isaac, N.Y., R1303
Isaac, R.I., S21086
Isaac, Va., S39214
Isaac, Va., Esther, W4415
Isaiah, Mass., S17298
Isaiah, N.C., Jane, W72
Isham, Va., S39210
Israel, N.Y., R1304
Issachar, Pa., S8102
Jabez, Ct., Annis, R1278
Jacob, Ct., S39235
Jacob, Cont., Mass., R1305
Jacob, Cont., N.Y., Mercy, W18658
Jacob, Mass., S2394; BLWt.707-100
Jacob, Mass., S30284
Jacob, Mass., S34088
Jacob, Mass., Mary, W24677
Jacob, N.J., S963
Jacob, N.C., Mary/Polly, W2062; BLWt.13750-160-55
Jacob, N.C., S.C., Elizabeth, W333
Jacob, Pa., S2097
Jacob Roberts, Va., BLWt.2389-200
James, Ct., Deborah, W21701
James, Ct., Silence, W3219; BLWt. 347-100
James, Cont., N.H., Anna, W20774
James, Cont., Mass., Mary, W8154;

BROWN (continued)
BLWt.3729 to Samuel Smith, ass. & 22-60-55 iss. 10/3/1791
James, Ga., R1308
James, Mass., S18739
James, Mass., S42096
James, Mass., S44655
James, Mass., Asenath, W23672
James, Mass., Ruth, W35292
James, Mass., Navy, S12282
James, N.H., S17857
James, N.H., S44651
James, N.H., Hannah, W24660
James, N.H., R1307
James, N.C., S6702
James, N.C., S40753
James, Pvt., Pa., BLWt.8947 iss. 7/16/1789
James, Pa., S40750
James, Pa., Rachel, W15879
James, S.C., Livina, W25294; BLWt.39473-160-55
James, S.C., Mary, R1309
James, Va., S3066
James, Va., S6718
James, Va., S15347
James, Va., S36929
James, Va., S39217
James, Va., Martha, W3760
James, Va., Mary, W403
James C., N.Y., R1306
Jedediah, Pvt., Ct., BLWt.5430 iss. 1/28/1790
Jedediah, Ct., Mary, W20763
Jedediah/Jedidiah, Ct., Cont., S36432
Jepthah/Jephtheh, Ct., S12340
Jeremiah, Ct., Anna, W25283; BLWt.6423 -160-55
Jeremiah, Cont., Mass., Abigail, R1271
Jeremiah, Mass., S30886
Jeremiah, Mass., N.H., S12315
Jeremiah, N.H., S15000
Jeremiah/Jeramiah, N.J., N.Y., S22138
Jeremiah, N.C., Jane, W27542
Jeremiah, Va., S6764
Jerusha H., dau. of Samuel Hayward, Ct., which see
Jesse, Mass., Elcey, W23684
Jesse, N.C., S6719
Jesse, R.I., Mary, W5232; BLWt. 26326-160-55
Jesse, Va., S8099
Job, Pvt., N.J., BLWt.8157 iss. 6/11/1789 to Matthias Denman, ass.
John, Ct., S22660
John, Ct., S40749
John, Ct., Elizabeth, W5871
John, Ct., Rebecca, W17357
John, Ct., R1314
John, Ct., N.Y., S12339
John, Cont., Va. res. 1808, BLWt.1367-100
John, Cont., Ct., Phebe, W25284
John, Cont., Del., Mary, W24663
John, Cont., Mass., S34067
John, Cont., Mass., S34103
John, Cont., Mass., S36932
John, Cont., Mass., Mary, W1218;

BROWN (continued)
BLWt.13878-160-55
John, Cont., Mass., Sarah Green, former wid., W16023
John, Cont., N.Y., Mary Ryder, former wid., W27481
John, Cont., Pa., Barbara, W5874
John, Del., S2393
John, Corp., Hazen's Regt., BLWt.12782 iss. 2/14/1791 to Alexander Power, ass.
John, Pvt., "in the Invalids", BLWt.12847 iss. 6/22/179- to Asa Spaulding, ass.
John, Pvt., Lamb's Artillery, N.Y., BLWt.6883 iss. 7/16/1790 to Wm. I. Vreedenburgh, ass.
John, Pvt., Lamb's Artillery, N.Y., BLWt.6867 iss. 9/15/1790 to John S. Hobart, et al assnes.
John, Sgt., Md., BLWt.10944 iss. 11/5/1789
John, Pvt., Md., BLWt.10965 iss. 8/14/1793 to Francis Sherrard, ass.
John, Sgt., Mass., BLWt.3649 iss. 1/26/1790 to John May, ass.
John, Pvt., Mass., BLWt.3687 iss. 7/6/1792 to John Bridges, ass.
John, Mass., S6739
John, Mass., S9718
John, Mass., S12343
John, Mass., S29029
John, Mass., S30289
John, Mass., S34095
John, Mass., Betsey, W24678
John, Mass., Lovina Paine, former wid., W4562
John, Mass., Sarah, BLWt.47968-160-55
John, Mass., BLReg.281-329-1855
John, Mass., N.H., S22137; BLWt. 26364-160-55
John, Mass., R.I., Betsey, W14357
John, Navy, See BROWNE
John, Navy, R.I., S38566
John, N.H., Betsey, W14360
John, N.H., R1313
John, N.H., Vt., Hannah, W5903; BLWt.28599-160-55
John, N.J., S12327
John, N.J., Mary, W5870
John, N.J., Mary, W5902
John, Pvt., N.Y., BLWt.6948 iss. 4/5/1792
John, Pvt., N.Y., BLWt.6850 iss. 4/5/1792
John, Pvt., N.Y., BLWt.6868 iss. 2/7/1792 to Heil Peck, ass.
John, N.Y., S17301
John, N.C., Lucy, W9746
John, N.C., Mildred, W18651
John, N.C., Lucy, R1315
John, Pvt., Pa., BLWt.8967 iss. 5/21/1792 to John P. Schott, ass.
John, Pvt., Pa., BLWt.8975 iss. 9/17/1790 to Joseph Ashton, ass.
John, Pvt., Pa., BLWt.9015 iss. 9/4/1792
John, Pvt., Pa., BLWt.9074 iss.

BROWN (continued)
11/1/1789
John, Pa., S22145
John, R.I., Lois, W14385
John, S.C., S17848
John, S.C., S39242
John, S.C., S45835
John, S.C., Jincey, W5906; BLWt.26845-160-55
John, Vt., Betsey, W17362
John, Va., See claim of Nancy, wid. of Robt. Anderson, Va., W2579. She claims her 1st husb., John Brown, Va. troops who died in Pulaski Co., Ky. in 1811 was a soldier of the Rev.
John, Va., Mary, See John G.
John, Pvt., Va., BLWt.11959 iss. 7/7/1792 to Robt. Means, ass.
John, Va., S1748
John, Va., S6720
John, Va., S6735
John, Va., S6753
John, Va., S30282
John, Va., S34667
John, Va., S39219
John, Va., S39229
John, Va., Ann M., R1277; Acct. No. 874 not 1/2 pay
John, Va., Nancy, R1333; BLWt. 30702-160-55
John G., Va., Mary, W25276; BLWt.21828-160-55
John Matthias, N.Y., S28660
Jonah, Mass., S19567
Jonas, Mass., S17859
Jonas, Sgt., N.Y., BLWt.6793 iss. 6/22/1790 to James Brown, admr. & BLWt.13951
Jonas, N.Y., Sarah Hoyt, former wid., W11332
Jonathan, Pvt., Ct., BLWt.5414 iss. 10/22/1789 to Theodosius Fowler
Jonathan, Ct., S3058
Jonathan, Ct., S17294
Jonathan, Ct., S17295
Jonathan, Ct., S40751
Jonathan, Ct., Esther, W5229; BLWt.12826-160-55
Jonathan, Cont., N.Y., R1316
Jonathan, Mass., Deborah, W24657
Jonathan, Mass., Sarah, W14361
Jonathan, N.Y., Lucy, W16863
Jonathan, R.I., S12312
Joseph, Cont., Mass., Ruth, W21709
Joseph, Cont., Mass., Sarah, W20777
Joseph, Pvt., Mass., BLWt.3748 iss. 11/5/1792 to Jonathan Tuttle, ass.
Joseph, Jr., Pvt., Mass., BLWt. 3837 iss. 7/7/1790
Joseph, Mass., S29027
Joseph, Mass., R1318
Joseph, N.H., S----, res. during Rev. was Keene, N.H., and there in 1832, age 68 yrs.
Joseph, N.H., Lydia, W20783
Joseph, N.H., Weighty, W5875; BLWt.32220-160-55

BROWN (continued)
Joseph, N.H., Elizabeth, R1317
Joseph, N.H., Polly, R1335
Joseph, Pvt., N.Y., BLWt.6807 iss. 9/25/1790 to D. Hudson & Co., ass.
Joseph, N.Y., S12338
Joseph 1st, N.Y., S44652
Joseph, N.Y., Elizabeth, W17340
Joseph, N.Y., Mary, R1327
Joseph, N.C., S17291
Joseph, N.C., S39225
Joseph, N.C., Mary, W3931; BLWt. 2327-100. Iss. 1/22/1844
Joseph, N.C., Jemima Robinson/ Robertson, former wid., W5744; BLWt.5077-160-55
Joseph, Pa., Catharine, W2747
Joseph, Pa., Margaret, W8385
Joseph, Pa., Mary, W25291; BLWt. 26657-160-55
Joseph, Pa., BLWt.191-400-Surgeon. Iss. 1/4/1793 to Joseph Brown. No papers
Joseph, Pa., Va., R1319
Joseph, R.I., Lucretia, W1543; BLWt.26918-160-55
Joseph, R.I., See Joseph T.
Joseph, R.I., Olive, BLWt.1780-100
Joseph, S.C., S12305
Joseph T., R.I., Mary, W20780
Joshua, Del., BLWt.2012-100
Joshua, N.H., S12292
Joshua, R.I., S21661
Josiah, Ct., Cont., S45164
Josiah, Mass., S44646
Josiah, Mass., N.C., N.Y., Va., S2101
Josiah, Pvt., N.H., BLWt.2936 iss. 4/25/1798 to Daniel Gookin, ass.
Josiah, N.H., Mary/Molly, W23692
Jude, Ct., S40029
Jude C., Pvt., Ct., BLWt.5467 iss. 5/22/1790 to John Ramsay
Judith, former wid. of Seth Griffin, Mass., which see
Kingsley, R.I., Mary, W20761
Knight, Mass., Priscilla, W21705
Levi, Pvt., Mass., BLWt.3742 iss. 4/1/1790
Levi, Mass., S42633
Lewis, Va., Clarissa, W399 BLWt.6416-160-55
Libbeus/Lebbeus, Cont., Ct., S36445
Lovinia, former wid. of Jotham Bruce, Mass., which see
Low, Va., S5299
Marcy, former wid. of Oliver Babcock, Ct., Cont., which see
Marlin, N.Y., R6978
Mary, former wid. of John Flint Ct., which see
Mary, former wid. of James Tooly Cont., Mass., Navy, which see
Mathew/Matthew, S.C., S32135
Matthias, N.Y. See John Matthias
Moody, Mass., Lucy, W5900; BLWt. 39475-160-55
Morgan, Cont., N.C., S.C., S3063

BROWN (continued)
Moses, Cont., Mass., Mary, W14400
Moses, N.H., Lydia, W16515
Moses, Vt., S22144
Moses, Va., S1942
Nathan, Ct., S23136
Nathan, Ct., Mass., Philadelphia, W15603; BLWt.36613-160-55
Nathan, Cont., Mass., S23556. Parthena Brown, wid. of soldier was pensioned as former wid. of Ezra Rood, Mass., which see
Nathan, Mass., N.H., S12319
Nathan, Mass., R.I., S6765
Nathan, N.H., S45613
Nathan, N.Y., Tamar/Tama, W8153; BLWt.24767-160-55
Nathaniel, Ct., Abigail, W20757
Nathaniel, Ct., also in Gen. Wayne's Indian War, BLWt.1772-100
Nathaniel, Ct., Cont., S36427
Nathaniel, Pvt., Mass., BLWt.3713 iss. 12/3/1799 to Elnathan Fitch ass.
Nathaniel, Pvt., N.H., BLWt.2925 iss. 1/26/1796 to James A. Neal, ass.
Nathaniel, N.H., Jemima, W21700
Nathaniel, Vt., Abigail, R1274
Nathaniel, see Philip JUDD. Philip Judd's wid. had a husb. Nathaniel Brown, stated to have served in the Rev. War
Neal, Va., Rebecca, W4645
Nehemiah, Ct., N.Y., S17299
Nehemiah, N.H., S20648
Nehemiah, N.Y., S6744
Nicholas, N.H., Molly, W17361
Nicholas, Pvt., N.Y., BLWt.6857 iss. 8/4/1790 to Henry Hart, ass.
Obadiah, Pvt., Ct., BLWt.5415 iss. 12/31/1796
Obadiah, Ct., S44649
Obadiah, Cont., Mass., S14994
Obadiah, Mass., Drusilla, W18645
Obadiah, N.J., S16656
Oliver, Ct., Hannah Winslow, former wid., W1118; BLWt. 5446-160-55
Oliver, Cont., Mass., S8088
Oliver, Mass., S29030
Oliver, Mass., Vt., Esther, W3333
Oliver, N.H., S17855
Othniel, Navy, R.I., Nancy, W1135; BLWt.27620-160-55
Parthena, former wid. of Ezra Rood, Mass., which see
Paten/Peyton, Va., Sally, W707; BLWt.50808-160-55
Patrick, Pa., S34664
Patrick, Va., S16325
Paul, Pvt., Mass., BLWt.3784 iss. 2/15/1797 to Abel Boynton, ass.
Peter, Ct., Mercy Gallup, former wid., W25615. Her last husb. also a pensioner. See case of Nehemiah Gallup, Ct.

BROWN (continued)
Peter, Cont., Pa., Sarah, W16867; BLWt.1686-100
Peter, Pvt., Mass., BLWt.3663 iss. 7/1/1789
Peter, N.H., S12277
Peter, Drummer, N.J., BLWt. 8097 iss. 7/21/1789
Peter, N.Y., S28652
Peter, N.Y., Pa., Elizabeth, W4147
Peter Wyer, Cont., Mass., S36933
Peyton, Va., See Paten
Phenix, R.I., S21088
Philip, R.I., R1334
Phinehas, Mass., Huldah, W5905
Pollard, Va., S21656; BLWt.26243-160-55
Polly, former wid. of William Ingraham, R.I., which see
Purchis/Purchase, Mass., Marcy, R1324
Reuben, Ct., Matilda, W20775
Reuben, Cont., Ct., Ruth, W17359
Richard, Fifer, N.Y., BLWt.6872 iss. 7/26/1790 to G.H.V. Wagennen, ass.
Richard, N.Y., Desire, W18654
Richard, N.C., Ann, W5873; BLWt. 34956-160-55
Richard, N.C., Sarah, W1545
Richard, S.C., Judah, R1320
Robert, Ct., Lorinda, W1374; BLWt.9211-160-55
Robert, Ct., Mary, W20771. 2 Contemp. ltrs. to wife
Robert, Del., S35793
Robert, Mass., S35795
Robert, N.C., S3057
Robert, N.C., S6714
Robert, N.C., Milley, W219
Robert, Pa., Catharine, W4418; BLWt.18700-160-55
Robert, S.C., R1337
Robert, Va., S31569
Robert, Va., R12652; Va. Half Pay. See N.A. Acc. No. 874, 050026 Half Pay. Robt. Brown
Roswell, Mass., S4971
Sampson, Mass., Dis. No papers
Samuel, Pvt., Ct., BLWt.5434 iss. 4/9/1791
Samuel, Ct., S10413
Samuel, Ct., S44653
Samuel, Ct., S12283
Samuel, Ct., Anna, W16866
Samuel, Cont., Mass., S34085
Samuel, Cont., Mass., Mary, W15758; BLWt.938-100
Samuel, Cont., Mass., Patience, W24671
Samuel, Ct., Mass., Vt., S8108
Samuel, Cont., N.H., S34101
Samuel, Cont. Va., S32138; BL Reg. 232630-1855
Samuel, Pvt., Hazen's Regt., BLWt.12759 iss. 6/11/1793 to James Poulson, ass.
Samuel, Pvt., Mass., BLWt.3710 iss. 10/10/1791 to A. Maxwell, ass.
Samuel, Mass., S2395

BROWN (continued)
Samuel, Mass., S19224
Samuel, Mass., S34091
Samuel, Mass., S42636
Samuel, Mass., Bethiah, W27387
Samuel, N.H., R1340
Samuel, N.J., Lucy, W3217
Samuel, N.Y., S6703
Samuel, N.Y., S12311
Samuel, N.Y., S44648
Samuel, N.Y., R1341
Samuel, N.Y., R1343
Samuel, R.I., Amie, W24661
Sanford, Mass., Hannah, W25279
Scip, Pvt., R.I., BLWt.2973 iss. 12/31/1789
Scipio, Cont., R.I., S38584
Sewall, Mass., N.H., S12290
Shearjashub, R.I., See BOURN
Silas, Cont., Mass., S14988
Silas, Mass., S21083
Silas, Mass., S39232
Silas, N.Y., Margaret, W1136; BLWt.29011-160-55
Simeon, Cont., Mass., S34111
Solomon, Ct., Betty, W5901
Solomon, Cont., Mass., S23553
Solomon, Mass., Sally, R1339
Stark, Va., S31566
Stephen, Ct., Lydia, R1323
Stephen, Mass., Margaret Safford, W14350; BLWt.13864-160-55
Stephen, N.J., Phebe, W4417; BLWt.26835-160-55
Stephen, R.I., S21667
Stephen, R.I., S29025
Stephen, Va., S1749
Stukely, R.I., Sarah, W20770
Tarlton, S.C., S21665
Thaddeus, Ct., S44657
Thaddeus, Mass., S29664
Thomas, Pvt., Ct., BLWt.5493 iss. 6/10/1794
Thomas, Ct., Sea Service, S29022
Thomas, Cont., Mass., Esther, W20765
Thomas, Cont., N.Y., S40752
Thomas, Cont., R.I., S12322
Thomas, Cont., Va., S3060
Thomas, Pvt., Md., BLWt.11007 iss. 9/6/1792 to William Power, ass.
Thomas, Mass., Sea Service, Privateer, S19569
Thomas, Navy, N.H., Eunice, W23669
Thomas, N.H., S45652
Thomas, N.H., Hannah, W5904; BLWt. 6405-160-55
Thomas, N.J., Gunboat service guarding coast, R1346
Thomas, N.C., Lucy, W9745
Thomas, Pvt., N.C., BLWt.11964 iss. 4/26/1798 to Street Ashford, ass.
Thomas, N.C., S.C., S3059
Thomas, N.C., Va., Phebe, W8381
Thomas, Pvt., Pa., BLWt.8921 iss. 6/20/1789
Thomas, Pvt., Pa., BLWt.8939 iss. 3/12/1792 to Henderson Wright, Admr.
Thomas, Pvt., Pa., BLWt.9078 iss.

BROWN (continued)
4/2/1792 to John McCleland, Admr.
Thomas, Pvt., R.I., BLWt.2978 iss. 4/20/1790
Thomas, S.C., Mary Ann, R1329
Thomas, Vt., S12325
Thomas, Va., S6750
Thomas, Va., S6769
Thomas, Va., S30890
Thomas, Va., S35790
Thomas C., Va., Mary, W9364; BLWt.26362-160-55
Timothy, Pvt., N.J., BLWt.8117 iss. 2/19/1790
Timothy, N.J., S35786
True, N.H., S17854
Uriah, S.C., S32140
Waldo, Ct., Abigail, W25286
Waller, N.C., S31573
William, Pvt., Armand's Corps., BLWt.12743 iss. 6/2/1791 to Christopher Hofman, ass.
William, Sgt., Ct., BLWt.5432 iss. 8/8/1789
William, Ct., S10406
William/Yellam, Ct. or Mass., Miriam, R1331. He was a Hessian and deserted from the British Army. Died 5/24/1839 at Centreville, Allegany Co., N.Y.
William, Ct., Cont., Sarah, W10469
William, Cont., Ct., Elizabeth Tryon, former wid., W18164
William, Cont., Md., BLWt.230-400-Rev. No papers
William, Cont., Mass., Mary, W20792
William, Cont., N.C., S6697
William, Cont., Pa., Indian War of 1791; Military Serv. 1801-1804, Margaret Carr, former wid., W73 Her other husb. was a pensioner, see William Carr
William, Pvt., Hazen's Regt., BLWt.12778 iss. 3/12/1792 to Cath. Jones, Admx.
William, Pvt., Hazen's Regt., BLWt.12802 iss. 7/26/1791 to Patrick McLaughlin, ass.
William, Mass., Martha/Patty, R1325
William, Mass., R---, b., lived and died in Blandford, Mass.
William, Mass. or Ct., Miriam, R1331. See Claim under Ct. serv.
William, Mass., Elizabeth, W5876
William, Mass., Mary/Marcy, W14383
William, Mass. Sea Service, S22140
William, N.H., S39233; BLWt. 26080-160-55
William, N.H., S45653
William, Pvt., N.J., BLWt.8136 iss. 4/27/1789
William, N.J., S962
William, N.J., S42101
William, N.J., Phebe, W778
William, N.Y., Pa., Mary, R1328
William, N.Y., R1346 1/2
William, N.C., S8092
William, N.C., S31563

BROWN (continued)
William, N.C., Lucretia, W17354
William, N.C., BLWt.1881-100
William, N.C., R1349
William, N.C., S.C., S16664
William, N.C., S.C., Nancy, W5878
William, Pa., S2397
William, Pa., S22661
William, Pa., S40757; BLWt. 1332-100
William, Pa., S46460; BLWt. 2245-100
William, Pa., Mary, W2749
William, Pa., BLWt.2139-200
William, Pa., R1350
William, Pa., Sea Service, S40755
William, Pa., Va., S23551
William, Pvt., R.I., BLWt.2919 iss. 1/26/1790 to James Smith, ass.
William, S.C., S39237
William, Va., S2400
William, Va., S14995
William, Va., S14998
William/William R., Va., S15764
William, Va., S35788
William, Va., S39228
William, Va., Lucy, W5879
William, Va., R1348
William, Ambrose, Va., Mary Grigsby Traverse, R1330
William R., Va. See William
Willis, N.C., S6728
Windsor, Va., BLWt.1816-300
Yellam, Ct. or Mass., See William
Zebedee, Ct., Cont., Rosamond, W23698
Zebulon, Sgt., N.J., BLWt.8124 iss. 3/16/1799 to Abraham Bell, ass.
Zebulon, N.J., Sarah, R1344
Zephaniah, R.I., BLWt.85-300
BROWNE, John, Navy, Dis. No papers Res. Phila. Co., Pa.
BROWNELL, Gardner, Navy, R.I., Ruth, W12360
Gideon, R.I., Phebe, W23704
Giles, Cont., R.I., Navy, S38579
Ichabod, Mass., R.I., S36923
Joseph, R.I., Deborah, W23705
Nathaniel, R.I., Mass., Sarah, W14384; BLWt.28564-160-55
Prince, Mass., Delia, W1376; BLWt.2352-160-55
Robert, Mass., R.I., Judith, W16839
Stephen, R.I., Mary, W25278; BLWt.40903-160-55
Sylvester, Mass., R.I., S21085
Thomas, R.I., R1352
BROWNFIELD, Robert, Cont., S.C., BLWt.306-300
Robert, Pa., R1353
BROWNING, Daniel, Ct., R1354
Daniel, R.I., S21080
Enos, Va., Jane, W9753
Francis, N.C., S6731; BLWt. 26187-160-55
Isaac, Va., R12796; Va. Half Pay. See N.A. Acc. No.874 050027 Half Pay, Isaac Browning

BROWNING (continued)
Jeremiah, Md., R1356
John, R.I., Susannah, W14362
Levi, N.C., S2406
Robert, N.C., Frances, R1355
Samuel, R.I., S12304
William, N.C., R1357
BROWNLEE, Alexander, Cont., BLWt. 2353-150. Va. res. of heir 1845
James, Va., Mary, W12385; BLWt. 3970-160-55
John, Cont., Va., S35799
John, Pa., S39238
Joseph, Pa., Elizabeth Guthrie, former wid., W3245. Also in file pension application by her husb., Wm. Guthrie, Pa., Rev. Not filed by him but forwarded to Pension Bur. in 1847 with this claim.
William, Va., BLWt.2609-200. No papers
BROWNLOW, John, N.C., R1358
BROWNSON, Abraham, Cont., BLWt. 1720-100. N.Y. res. in 1831
Ashbel, Ct., R1359
Elijah, Ct., See BRUNSON
Gideon, Cont., Vt., Disability & pension claim, BLWt.72-200-Major in Warner's Regt. Iss. 2/14/1793. No papers
Gideon, ----, R1360. N.Y. res. of dau.
Isaac, Cont., Ct., S40027
Isaac, Cont., N.H., Green Mt. Boys, Huldah, W23693
Joel, Ct., S15006
Joseph, Ct., See BRONSON
Luman, Ct., S49297
Mercy, former wid. of Lemuel Bradley, Vt., which see
Nathan, Cont., Ga. res of heirs in 1836; BLWt.2154-400
Reuben, Ct., Huldah, W25300
Roger, Pvt., Sheldon's Dragoons Ct., BLWt.5524 iss. 6/26/1789 to James Percival
Samuel, Ct., See BRONSON
Silas, Ct., See BRONSON
BROWNWELL, Prince, Mass., See BROWNELL
Sylvester, Mass., R.I., See BROWNELL
BROYHILL, James, Va. See BRAYHILL
BROYLE, Philip, Pvt., Pa., BLWt. 8937 iss. 2/5/1794 to Casper Iserloan, ass.
BROYLES, Daniel, Va., S1502
Michael, N.C., Va., S3052
BRUCE, Abijah, Mass., Hanah, W16872
Benjamin, Mass., S44691
Benjamin, Va., Milly, R1362
Daniel, Pvt., Mass., BLWt.3747 iss. 1/7/1796 to Calvin Sanger, ass.
George, N.C., S39212
George, Va., S35791
Jesse, Mass., S39209
John, N.J., S6749
Jonas, Cont., Mass., Sarah, W1377

BRUCE (continued)
Joseph, Mass., S12284
Jotham, Cont., Mass., Lovinia Brown, former wid., W17346
Lewis, Mass., Navy, Hannah, W14364; BLWt.13024-160-55
Reuben, Mass., Lucy, W1134; BLWt.26438-160-55
Robert, Md., S34666
Silas, Mass., Louisa, W25289; BLWt.26180-160-55
Simeon, Mass., Esther, W14396
Timothy, Cont., Mass., Matilda, W23679
William, Md., S34668; BLWt. 233-300-Capt. Iss. 9/21/1789 No papers
William, N.C., S30287
William, Va., S3053
BRUCH, Lewis, French troops, Catharine, R1440
BRUEN, Jacobus, N.Y., BLWt.157-400-Lt. Col. Iss. 9/15/1790 No papers
Jeremiah, Cont., BLWt.183-400-Major. Artillery Artificers Iss. 6/21/1790. No papers. Also recorded as BLWt.2560
Peter Bryan, Va. See BRUIN
BRUFF, James, Md. S. disability pension. No papers. BLWt.235-300-Capt. Iss. 11/2/1791
William, Md., BLWt.433-100
BRUGLER, Peter, N.J., R1364
BRUIN, Peter Bryan, Va., S42092; BLWt.2365-400
BRUIS, Robert, N.Y., S22663
BRUIZEE, Wynsen, N.Y., S9284
BRUMBACK, Peter, Cont., Ga., Elizabeth, W8400
Peter, Lee's Legion, BLWt. 11930-100-Pvt. Iss. 4/13/1791 to James Reynolds, ass. No papers
BRUMBLEY, Perry, R.I., S21662
Simeon, R.I., S21090
William, Ct., See BRUMLEY
BRUMBLY, Alas, Ct. See BRUMLEY
Hannah, former wid. of Samuel Cross, Cont., Mass., which see
BRUMBY, Alas, Ct. See BRUMLEY
BRUMER, Anthony, Pvt., Lamb's Artillery, N.Y., BLWt.6866 iss. 9/25/1790 to Abraham Nelson, ass.
BRUMFIELD, Humphrey, Va., S8105
John, S.C., S30894
Robert, Va., R1365
BRUMIGUM, Daniel, Md., BLWt. 1886-100
BRUMLEY, Alas, Ct., Esther, W9748; BLWt.34206-160-55
Hannah, See BRUMBLY
Jesse, R.I., R1367
Simeon, Pvt., N.Y., BLWt.6829 iss. 8/24/1790 to Cath. Bleecker et al assnes.
William, Ct., Mary Hilliard, former wid., W21324
William, Cont., Vt., Faithful, R1366
William, Pvt., N.Y., BLWt.6865

BRUMLEY (continued)
iss. 8/3/1790 to Corns Van Dyck, ass.
BRUMMAGE, John, N.C., See BRIMMAGE
BRUMMAL, Benjamin, Va., S14984
BRUMMET, Thomas, Va., Mary, R1368
BRUMPTON, Robert, Pvt., Pa., BLWt. 9037 iss. 7/18/1791 to Andrew Porter, ass.
BRUNDAGE, Israel, N.Y., Keziah, W238
Jesse, N.Y., Martha, R1369
Nathaniel W., N.J., N.Y., Rebecca, R1370
Solomon, N.J., N.Y., Mary, W20779
BRUNER, Frederick, N.Y., See BRONNER
George, Va., S8097
Jacob, Md., Pa., S35792
Jacob, Md., Margaret, W332
Peter, Pa., S5303
BRUNLY, Perry, R.I. See BRUMBLEY
BRUNNER, Peter, Pa., See BRUNER
Valentine, Md., Elizabeth, W633
BRUNO, Peter, Cont., France, Wayne's campaign against Indians, War of 1812, R1372
BRUNOT, Felix, Pa., Elizabeth Kreider, R1371
BRUNSON, Amos, Cont., Mass., Lucy, W18661; BLWt.3834-160-55
Asa, Ct., S36433
Elijah, Ct., Delia/Deliverance, W17363
Levi, Ct., S2100
Phinehas/Pheneas, Ct., S32137
Stout, Pa., S38572
William, S.C., R1373
William R., S.C., S21655
BRUS/BANKS, Edward, Va., S39172
BRUSH, Alexander, Cont., Vt., Ruth, W15825; BLWt.19606-160-55
Benjamin, Ct., Semantha, W10455
David, N.J., S44666
Eli, Ct., R1375
Eliakim, Pvt., N.Y., BLWt.6799 iss. 7/10/1790 to John Quackinboss, ass.
Gilbert, Ct., S44667
John, N.Y., R1376
John Cicero, Ct., S35789
Jonas, Ct., Tamar, W5924
Josiah, Vt., Betsey, W20789
Nehemiah, not Rev. War, N.W. Indian War, Navy, War with Tripoli, Old War Inv. File No. 28084; no BLWt.
Robert, Ct., N.Y., S23555
Selah, Pvt., N.Y., BLWt.6797 iss. 9/24/1791 to Platt Rogers, ass.
BRUSTER, Elisha, Sheldon's Dragoons, Ct., BLWt.5521 iss. 5/17/1792 to Moses Bissell
James, Va., S38571
Nathan, N.Y., See BREWSTER
Sheriff, S.C., See BREWSTER
BRUTON, Benjamin, N.C., S16665
George, S.C., S30891
BRUTTON, Arthur, Pvt., N.Y., BLWt.6781 iss. 7/30/1790 to Edward Cumpston, ass.

BRYAN, Asa, N.C., Ann, W23666
Barrick, Va., Ann, W2993
Benajah, Ct., Lucy, W17342
Charles, Cont., Md., Catharine, W2750
Charles, Pvt., Pa., BLWt.9021 iss. 12/23/179- to Chas. Bryan
Daniel, N.C., S1172
Edward, Pvt., Pa., Artillery Artificers, BLWts. 8924 & 12849 iss. 9/7/1789
Elijah, Ct., S17860; BLWt.5519 iss. 4/9/1791. No papers
George, N.C., S32142
Hardy, N.C., S6756
Hezekiah, N.C., Mary, W895
James, Del., S5304
James, R.I., S44669; BLWt.1605-100
James, Va., See BRYANS
Jehiel, Ct., Polly, W10450
John, Ct., S12280
John, Pvt., Del., BLWt.10716 iss. 4/8/1797 to James DeBaufre, ass.
John, Cont., Pa. res. of heirs in 1849; BLWt.2441-100
John, N.Y., R1379
John, N.C., Nancy, W5914
John, N.C., See BRIEN
John, Pvt., Pa., BLWt.9055 iss. 7/12/1792
John, Pa., Nancy, W4902; BLWt. 15186-160-55
John, S.C., Lydia, W8388
John, Va., Catharine, W3759
Joseph, Pa., S40758
Luke, Md., R1380
Oliver, Ct., Esther, W20762
Reuben, Va., S41462
Richard, Corp., Mass., BLWt.3760 iss. 1/26/1790 to John May, ass.
Samuel, N.C., Va., Mary, W9366
Seth, See Zephaniah, Va.
Thomas, Pvt.,Hazen's Regt., BLWt.12808 iss. 3/3/1794 to John Kline, ass.
Thomas, Md., S3050
Thomas, Va., See BRIAN
William, N.C., S6699
William, N.C., S8089
William, Pa., BLWt.9008. Iss. 1789
William, Va., S6760
Zephaniah/Seth, Va., Jane, W2061
BRYANS, James, Va., S39244
BRYANT, Abijah, Mass., S20292
Alexander, Mass., S9289
Amasa, Cont., Mass., R.I., S39230
Amos, Cont., Mass., S45618
Benjamin, Mass., Elizabeth, W20788
Benjamin, Pvt., N.J., BLWt.8141 iss. 4/22/1790
Benjamin, N.J., R1381
Benjamin, Va., Nancy, W8389
Billa/Billey/Billy, Mass., S34109
Caleb, Mass., S30286
Charles, Cont., Va., S39216; BLWt. 562-100
Daniel, Mass., Sarah, W24662

BRYANT (continued)
Daniel C., Cont., Mass., War of 1812; Susa, W21706
Daniel D., Ct., Bethiah, W18652
David, Cont., Mass., Elizabeth Cook, former wid., W22807; BLWt. 2691-300-Capt. Iss. 6/10/1797 to Elizabeth Bryant, only child & heir. No papers
David, N.J., S8104
Ebenezer, Ct., S17849
Elias, Mass., Mary, W14393
Fowler, Ct., R1383
Isaac, Mass., See BRIANT
Israel, R.I., S45525
Jacob, Ct., Vt., See BRIANT
Jacob, Pvt., N.J., BLWt.8126 iss. 6/27/1791
Jacob, N.J., Mary, W5917
James, Md., Sea Service, S14993
James, Va., S3051
James, Va., Ruth, S31568; BLWt. 34505-160-55. He rec'd the pension; d. in 1853. Wid. Ruth, granted BL, Act of 1855
Jesse, Pvt., Va., BLWt.11950 iss. 7/6/1793 to Francis Graves, ass.
Jesse, Va., S6695
Jesse, Va., S39241; BLReg. No. 95766-55. BLWt.11950-100-Pvt. Iss. 7/6/1793. No papers
John, Cont., Va. res. 1818, S38570
John, Mass., Almay, W23683; BLWt. 38549-160-55
John, Mass., Tabitha, R1388
John, N.H., Elizabeth Sargeant/ Sergeant, former wid., W22170
John, Pvt., N.J., BLWt.8135 iss. 8/19/1789 to Peter Lott, ass.
John, N.J., BLWt.204-100
John, N.J., Caroline, W8163; BLWt.71-60-55
John, N.C., See BRYAN
John, Va., S12299
John, Va., S35796
John, Va., Mary, W8390
John, Va., Sarah/Sally, W8391
Jonathan, Mass., Va., S34075
Joseph, Mass., S16662
Levi, Mass., Sea Service, Lydia/ Lyda, W23661
Matthew, Pvt., R.I., BLWt.2979 iss. 3/5/1793
Parmenas, Va., Margaret, R1385
Patrick, Mass., Anna, W21707; BLWt.6400-160-55
Peter, Va., S30290
Reuben, Ct., S36444
Robert, N.H., Johanna, W15604
Robert, Va., S6700
Silvanus, Mass., S23534
Solomon, Mass., S29657
Stephen, Cont., S36930
Thomas, N.C., Va., Ruth, W3503; BLWt.8449-160-55
Thomas, Va., S16657
Thomas, Va., S30288
Timothy, Mass., S12294
William, N.C., S16660
William, N.C., S39215
William, N.C., Patience, W5916;

BRYANT (continued)
BLWt.2360-100
William, N.C., Anne Ellen, pensioned as former wid. of James Eaton, which see
William, Va., S39220;BLWt.416-100
William, Va., Mary Ann, W5915; BLWt.49743-160-55
William G., Va., S3049
Zenas, Mass., S30285
BRYCE, John, Cont., BLWt.213-300-Capt. in Col. Thos. Proctor's Regt. Art. Iss. 6/9/1789. No papers
BRYDIA, David, Ct., Green Mt. Boys N.H., S39234
BRYMER, Joseph, N.C., Celia, W5947
BRYNE, Richard, Cont., Mass.,S34081
BRYON, Elijah, Ct., See BRYAN
BRYSON, Andrew, N.C., R1389
Andrew, Pa., S40756
Daniel, N.C., War of 1812, Martha, W5940; BLWt.26981-160-55
John, Pa., R1390
Samuel, N.C., S1644
Samuel, Pa., BLWt.205-200-Lt. Iss. 7/9/1789. No papers
BUBE, Thaddeus, Ct., Dis. No papers
BUBIER, John, Cont., Mass., Hannah, W20820
William, Cont., Mass., See BEUBIER
BUCHANAN, George, S.C., S32147
Henry, Cont., applied Va., S37807
James, Pa., S40765
James, S.C., S37821
John, S.C., BLWt.271-300
Robert, N.J., S37806
Robert, Pa., S40784
Robert, S.C., R12819;S.C. Half Pay appl.of nephews & nieces rejected
Thomas, Cont., Pa., S40770
Thomas, N.C. See BUCHANNAN
William, N.Y., S9827
William, S.C., S21675
William Willis, N.C., Va., R1401
BUCHANNAN, Alexander, N.Y., S40763
James, Pvt., S.C., BLWt.11977 iss. 5/2/1794
John, Md. See BUCHANON
John, Va., BLWt.1959-200
Thomas, N.C., S2105
BUCHANON, John, Md., BLWt.1495-100. Iss. 3/31/1829
John, Pa., Va., S40762
BUCHER, Abraham, Va., See BOOKER
John, Cont., Pa., See BUTCHER
Jonathan, Ct., S36455
Philip Peter, Va., S8128
BUCHLEY, Thomas, Pvt., Md., BLWt. 10994 iss. 12/22/1794 to Henry Purdy, ass.
BUCHTER, Matthias, Pa., S40783
BUCK, Aaron, Cont., N.Y., S9115
Aaron, Sgt., R.I., BLWt.2960 Iss. 3/25/1790
Aaron, R.I., S36458
Abel, Cont., Mass., S39256
Abner, Ct., S44694
Amasa, Ct., S17869
Asaph, Ct., Phebe, W25314; BLWt.26597-160-55
Benton, Ct., S15330

BUCK (continued)
Charles, Va., R1392
Daniel, Mass., S12391
Daniel, Mass., Content, W14432
Ebenezer, Mass., Mary, W23739
Ebenezer, Mass., N.H., S16063
Elijah, Ct., Mass., S12387
Francis, Pvt., Ct., BLWt.5514 iss. 8/7/1789 to Richard Platt
Francis, Cont., Mass., S44695
George, Ct., Agnes, W23737
Henry, Pa., Rachel, R1399
Hepsibeth T., former wid. of John Swift, Ct., N.Y., War of 1812, Which see
Ichabod, N.Y., Sybil, W5971; BLWt.26659-160-55
Isaac, Cont., Mass., S34136
Isaac, Pvt., Crane's Cont. Artillery, Mass., BLWt.3830 iss. 10/12/1790 to Abel Boynton, ass.
Isaac, N.C., S9113
Isaac, Vt., S28662
Israel, N.Y., S23560
Joel, Ct., S44693
John, Del., R1396
John, Mass., Mary, W23750; BLWt.16113-160-55
John, Pa., S32155
John, Pa., S42103
Jonathan, Ct., S3108
Joseph, Mass., S44692
Joseph, BLWt.184-200. Iss. 7/7/17 (last 2 nos. illeg.). No papers. He may have been a Lt. having rec'd 200 acres, and probably of N.J. as on the list of N.J. officers, but rank and corps are dittoed to the officer just above who was a Major of Artillery Artificers and got 400 acres.
Josiah, Ct., R1397
Leonard, Pa., S40764
Levi, Vt., Isabella, R1394
Michael/Michel, Mass., S44696
Moses, Mass., Hannah, W14409
Samuel, Cont., Mass., See AMES
Samuel, Cont., Mass., S23143
Thomas, Ct. Sea Service, S22666
Thomas, Vt., R1463
Thomas, Va., S16672
William, Cont., Mass., S29685
William, Pa., Va., Phebe Christian, former wid., W25411; BLWt.26976-160-55
Zebediah, Ct., S17316
BUCKALAW/BUCKELLEW/BUCKALEW, John, N.J., Sarah, W141
BUCKALOE/BUCKALEW, John, S.C., R1391
BUCKANAN, Henry, Va. See BUCHANAN
BUCKBEE, Ezekiel, N.Y., R1400
Josiah, N.Y., S44697
BUCKELEW, Frederick, N.J., S804
John, N.J., See BUCKALAW
BUCKELL, John, See BUSKILL
BUCKELLEW, John, N.J. See BUCKALAW
BUCKER, Israel H. See BUKER

BUCKER (continued)
Philip Peter, Va. See BUCHER
BUCKERLEW, John, N.J., S858
BUCKET, Humphrey, Pvt., Md., BLWt.10984 iss. 3/11/1791 to Humphrey Bucket
BUCKHANNON, John, Va. See BUCHANNON
BUCKHART, George, Pa. See BURGHART
BUCKHER, George, See BURCKHER
BUCKHOLTS, Peter, S.C., R1465
BUCKHOUT, Jacob, N.Y., Jane, W24689
John, N.Y., Anna, W16201
John, Pvt., Va.,Lee's Legion, BLWts.11899 & 12858 iss. 8/26/1789
BUCKINGHAM, Reuben, Ct., S44708
Stephen, Ct., Polly, W25306; BLWt.87018-160-55
Thomas, Ct., R1403
BUCKLAND, Alexander, Ct., Mass., Lois, R1404
George, Ct., Cont., S23561
Jonathan, Ct., Laura, W25315; BLWt.32240-160-55
Joshua, Ct., S15332
BUCKLEW, Isaac, N.J., R1405
Peter, N.J., Nancy, W8180; BLWt.36279-160-55
BUCKLEY, Abraham, Va., Catharine, R1406
Charles, Navy, Ct., See BULKELEY
Daniel, Cont., Ct., Rhoda, R1407
Daniel, Pvt., Md., BLWt.10998 iss. 1/21/1795 to John Faires, ass.
James, Pvt., Hazen's Regt., BLWt.12767 iss. --/--/----
James, Va., Mary, W339
James, Pvt., Va., Lee's Legion, BLWts.11890 & 14144
Job, Va., Susannah Hinson, former wid., R5042
John, Pvt., Md., BLWt.10966 iss. 7/17/1792 to Mary Buckley, Admx.
Joshua, Va., S42104
Michael, Va., BLWt.176-100
Solomon, Ct., See BECKLEY
BUCKLIN, Rufus, Mass., Privateer, R.I., S22147
BUCKLIP, Charles, Pvt., Md., BLWt.10968 iss. 2/1/1790 to Charles Bucklip
BUCKMAN, Asa, Mass., R1408
Benjamin, Sgt., Mass., BLWt.3693 iss. 5/24/1790
Benjamin, Mass., S32145
Elias, Vt., S15023
Jacob, Mass., R1409
Jeremiah, Mass., Ruth Sanders, former wid., BLWt.44511-160-55
Joses, Mass., Nabby, W24680
Nathan, Cont., Mass., Elizabeth, W25305
Reuben, Mass., N.H. or Vt., Mercy, W2589; BLWt.7098-160-55
Samuel, Mass., S44709
Stephen, Ct., Abigail, W17369
Susannah, former wid. of Asa Colburn, Mass., which see

BUFF
Michael, Md., S31588
BUFFINGTON, David, Va., Margaret, W4906
Preserved, R.I., S5310
Samuel, Mass., S34124; BLWt. 110-200-Lt. Iss. 4/1/1790. No papers
BUFFUM, Samuel, Ct. Sea Service, Mass. Sea Service, S12352
BUFORD, Abraham, Va., S46372; BLWt.251-500-Col. Iss. 5/3/1793. No papers
Jane, former wid. of Thomas Quirk, Va., which see
John, Pvt., Va., BLWt.11937 iss. 7/14/1792 to Francis Graves, ass.
John, Va., S30301
John, Va., Rhoda, W5967
Simeon/Simon, Va., S1180
BUGBEE, Amos, Ct., Martha, W17388
Benjamin, Ct., S36461
Benjamin, Ct., Mehitable, W23722
Elijah, Ct., Sarah, W20802
Edward, Cont., BLWt.312-200-Lt. in Hazen's Regt. Iss. 1/5/1797 to Benjamin Dana, ass. No papers
George, N.Y., S16666
James, Ct., Thirza, W479; BLWt. 28570-160-55
John, Ct., Cont., See BUGBEY
Josiah, N.Y., See BUCKBEE
Lydia, former wid. of Zephaniah Snow, Mass., which see
Nathaniel, N.H., S45621
Peletiah/Pelatiah, Ct., S44698
Pelatiah, Pvt., Sheldon's Dragoons, Ct., BLWt.5535 iss. 12/6/1791 to Stephen Thorn
Peter, Ct., Isabel, W21720; BLWt.7066-160-55
Rufus, Ct., S18751
Sylvester, N.H., Vt., Jemima, R1415
BUGBEY, John, Ct., Cont., Hannah, W17378
BUGEMEYER, Daniel, Cont., Pa. See BERGMEYER
BUGG, William, N.C., Elizabeth, W898
BUHER, Jacob, Va., BLWt.11893-100-Pvt. Iss. 11/5/1789. No papers
BUIE, John, N.C., S.C., R1417
BUKER, Israel H., Cont., Mass., Sally, W25566; BLWts.890-100 &342-60-55 iss. 3/31/1820
Jacob, Pvt., Va., BLWt.11893 iss. 11/5/1789
Windsor, Mass., S36453
Windsor, Mass., BLWt.926-100
Zebulon, Mass., Grace, W23718
BULEY/BEWLEY, George (colored), Md., W27576; BLWt.38345-160-55
BULGER, Daniel, Pvt., Md., BLWt. 10985 iss. 6/11/1790
BULKELEY, Charles, Navy, Ct. & Privateer, 1812, S12349
John, Ct., Cont., S17314
BULKLEY, Abram, Ct. Sea Service, S15331

BUCKMINSTER, Lawson, Mass., Mary, W15760
BUCKNAM, Ebenezer, Mass., Rachel, W14405
Nathan, Cont., Mass. See BUCKMAN
William, Cont., Mass., S34119
BUCKNER, Dorothea B., former wid. of Wm. McWilliams, Va. which see
Thomas, Va., BLWt.269-300-Capt. Iss. 2/27/1796 to Robt. Camp, ass. No papers
William, Va., S37804
William, Va. Sea Service, R17; Va. Half Pay. No file in N.A. Acc. No. 874
BUCKSTAFF, Peter, N.Y. See BURKSTUFF
BUDD (or SAMPSON), Bristol, Ct. Phoebe, W25304; BLWt.24772-160-55
Conkling/Conklin, N.J.,Ruth,W5957
George, N.J., S2407
John, Mass., N.Y., S22670
John, Pa., S3090
John Shivers, S.C., BLWt.2271-200
Nathaniel, N.J., S964
Samuel, N.C., R20171
Samuel, N.C., BLWt.296-300-Capt. Iss. 3/10/1790. No papers
BUDING, Conrad/Conradt, Cont., Pa. res in 1828, BLWt.1268-100
BUDLONG, Benjamin, Ct., N.Y., R.I., S15011
Moses, R.I., Mary A., W23729
Rhodes, R.I., Anna, W23746
Samuel, R.I., Waity, W14423; BLWt.17579-160-55
Stephen, R.I., Isabella, W2064; BLWt.26278-160-55
BUEL, Asa, Ct., Mercy, W21735
Cyrus, N.Y., Sarah, W24690; BLWt.18364-160-55
Ezra, N.Y., S15030
Job, Ct., Cont., Ruth, W17375
Joseph, Cont., Ct., See BUELL
Nathan, Ct., S23558
Phebe, former wid. of Benjamin Thacher/Thatcher, Ct. which see
Solomon, Ct., S17318
Solomon, Ct., Sophia, W18670
BUELL, Daniel, Ct., S22149
David, Ct., S31584
David, Ct., Cont., S12348
Deborah, former wid. of William Kircum/Kirkum, Ct. Which see
Gideon, Ct., Lucy, W2520
Hezekiah, N.Y. res. of children in 1850, Lorinda C., R1411
Isaac, Cont., Ct., S10395
James, Ct., S17305
John, Ct., S12363
John H., Ct., BLWt.136-300-Capt. Iss. 1/25/1791. No papers
Joseph, Cont., Ct., Lucy, W14408
Josiah, Cont., Ct., S44707
Levi, Ct., Vt., S18313
Martin, Ct., Sybil, R1413
Matthew, Ct., Mary, W20810
Oliver, Ct., Elizabeth, W20801
Orange, Ct., R1412
Timothy, Ct., S15013

BULKLEY (continued)
Charles, Navy, Ct. See BULKELEY
Daniel, Cont., Ct., See BUCKLEY
Edward, Ct., Cont., Prudence, W21727; BLWt.138-300-Capt. Iss. 4/20/1791 to Prudence Bulkley, admx. No papers
Eleazer/Eleazar, Ct., Sea Service, S18336
Francis, Ct., Elizabeth, W1221; BLWt.951-160-55
Gershom, Ct., Amelia, W17367
Joseph, Ct., S23141
Joseph, Ct., Grizzle, W20799
Nathan, Ct., Jerusha, W25318; BLWt.24773-160-55
Seth, Ct., Mary Dayton, former wid., W20956
Turney, Ct., Esther, W17371
BULL, Aaron, Cont., Ct., BLWt. 151-200-Lt. Sheldon's Cavalry. Iss. 6/25/1789. No papers
Ambrose, N.C., Elizabeth, R1418
Curtis, Va., S18338
Daniel, Va., S18337
Henry, Cont., Ct., S36459
Jeremiah, Ct., Anne, W17374
John, Ct., Martha, W17377
John, Cont., Mass., S10398
Reuben, Ct., S17307
Thomas, Pa., S2056
Thomas, Va., S32153
William, N.Y., BLWt.160-300-Capt. Iss. 12/15/1790. No papers
BULLARD, Aaron, Cont., Mass., S44720
Asa, Mass., BLWt.116-200-Lt. Iss. 1/28/1790 to Joseph May, ass. No papers
Asa, Mass., S19228
Baruch, Mass., Julitta, W14425
Benjamin, Cont., Mass., S29673
Benjamin, Mass., Hannah, W14430
David, Mass., Elizabeth, R1419
Edward, Mass., Elizabeth, W18570
Elisha, Mass., Rachel, W14433
Ephraim, Mass., see claim of Abigail Bullard pensioned as former wid. of Abijah Richards, Mass.
Isaac, Mass., S2048
Isaac, Mass., S35801
James, N.C., Sarah, W18678
Joel, Mass., Sarah Barns, former wid., W18554
John, Cont., Mass., S34116
John, Cont., Mass., Ruth, W15620
John, Mass., S29050
John, Va., S3103
Joseph, Mass., S30297
Nathan, Mass., S19574
Nathan, Mass., Rebecca, R1421
Thomas, N.C., S6770
BULLEFANT, James, Va., See BRILLIFONT
BULLEN, David, Pvt., Ct., BLWt. 5517 iss. 2/21/1792 to Elijah Austin, ass. of Israel Holt, Admr.
BULLIN, Isaac, Va., Susannah, W5962
BULLMAN, John, Pvt., Crane's Artillery, Mass., BLWt.3833 iss. 8/10/1789 to Richard Platt
BULLOCH, Ebenezer, R.I., S29047
BULLOCK, Charles, N.C., S9108
Comfort, Mass., S12399
Dan, S.C., Jane, W8403
Daniel, Mass., S12383
Daniel, N.C., Mary, R1424
Darius, Mass., Chloe, W23727
David, R.I., Phebe Cole, former wid., W20907
David, Va., Catharine W., W1816
David, Va., Jane, R1422
Elkanah, R.I., R20336
Hawkins, S.C., S31586
Israel, Mass., S22152
James, Va., S8121
John, Md., S22153
Joseph, Va., Martha, R1423
Preserved, Mass., Sarah Yaw, former wid., W20143
Rice, Va., R12822; Va. Half Pay
Simeon, R.I., S21091
William, Mass., Margaret, W23719
William T., Md., Sarah, W9765
BULLY, Benjamin, N.Y., Elizabeth, W709
BULSON, Henry, N.Y., S12373
John, N.Y., S15015
BUMBO, John Henry, Pvt., Pa., BLWt.8989 iss. 3/14/1793 to Gideon Merkle, ass.
BUMFRIES, Morris/Mories, See BUMPUS
BUMFRIES/BUMPFRIES/BUMPHRY, Stephen, Ct., N.Y., Sarah, W8182; BLWt.30623-160-55
BUMGARDNER, Daniel, N.C., S32150
George, Pvt., Md., BLWt.10977 iss. 10/6/1794 to Henry Purdy, ass.
George, Md., See BOMGARDNER
William, Md., See BOMGARDNER
BUMGARNER, David, Va., Catharine, W5968
BUMLEY, James, Va., See BROWNLEE
BUMP, Aaron, N.Y., S12380
Asa, Mass., See BUMPUS
Bethia, former wid. of John Sloan, Cont., N.Y., which see
Isaac, Mass., Molly, W18632; BLReg. 30326-1850
John, Pvt., Ct., BLWt.5406 iss. 1/28/1792 to Moses Sill
John, Ct., Rebecca, W2590
Joseph, N.Y., S15028
Moses, N.Y., Vt., S12362
Sally, former wid. of Philip Lee, Mass., which see
BUMPAS, Abraham, See BUMPUS
Daniel, Mass. See BUMPUS
BUMPASS, Samuel, N.C., R20337
William, Va., Betsey/Elizabeth, W2718
BUMPFRIES, Stephen, See BUMFRIES
BUMPHRIES, Stephen, See BUMFRIES
BUMPHRY, Stephen, See BUMFRIES
BUMPUS, Abraham, Mass., Navy, Elizabeth Cole, former wid., R2124
Asa, Mass., Achsah, W14412; BLWt.912-100
Daniel, Mass., S34128
Edward, Ct., S34112
Joseph, Mass., Lydia, W8406; BLWt.30620-160-55
Joseph, Mass., Abiah, R1427
Mories/Morris, Cont., Mass. res. in 1818, Huldah, W25307
Noah (or PERRY), Mass., Mercy, W20819
Reuben, N.Y., S23562
Shubeal, Mass., S36943
William, Cont., Mass., Hannah, W21726
BUMSTEAD, Joseph, Mass., S4980
BUNAP, John, Ct., See BURNAP
BUNCE, Asa, Ct., W24695
Daniel, Pvt., Mass., BLWt.3668 iss. 5/1/1799 to A. Holbrook, ass.
Daniel, Mass., S44715
Isaiah, Ct., Dis. No papers
Jared, Pvt., Ct., BLWt.5484 iss. 9/1/1790 to Theodosius Fowler
Joanna, former wid. of John Bird, Mass., which see
John, Pvt., Mass., BLWt.3736 iss. 12/3/1792 to Noble Dewey, ass.
Rory, Ct., Elizabeth, W18673
Timothy, Ct., R1428
BUNCH, Jeremiah, S.C., S17867
Richard, Va., S16334
BUNDGE, Michael, Pvt., N.Y., BLWt. 6808 iss. 8/2/1791
BUNDRON, Fransis/Francis, N.C., S21098
BUNDY, Christopher, N.C., S17309
Elisha, Mass., Abigail, W4910; BLWt.30613-160-55
Francis, Pvt., Va., BLWt.11915 iss. 3/26/1792 to Francis Graves, ass.
Francis, Va., S37799
Joshua, Ct., Elizabeth, W20817
Joshua, Pvt. "In the Sappers & Miners", BLWt.12751 iss. 9/9/1790 to James F. Sebor, ass.
BUNEL, John, Ct., Pure, W20825
BUNKER, Benjamin, Navy, Mass., S19575
Bethuel, N.Y., R1429
Elizabeth, former wid. of Thomas Templer, N.Y., W16880
Jonathan, N.H., Elizabeth, R1430
Mary, former wid. of Nathaniel Batchelder, N.H., which see
Richard, Mass., Sea Service, S29677
BUNN, Barnes/Barron, Cont., N.J., S481
John, N.J., S2355
Nathaniel, Cont., Mass., Lydia, W14397
Samuel, Cont., Mass., S44702
Samuel, Pvt., "in the Corps of Artillery Artificers", BLWt. 12818 iss. 2/22/1790 to Theodosius Fowler, ass.
BUNNEL, Amos, Ct., S36460

BUNNEL (continued)
Enos, Ct., Naomi, W17385
Frederick, Ct., S44716
Jehiel, Ct., Statira, R1434
Joel, Ct., S15334
John, Ct., S12382
John, Ct., See BUNEL
Patience, former wid. of Giles Andrews, Ct., which see
BUNNELL, Daniel, Ct., R1432
John, Cont., Va. agency & res., Hannah Byers, former wid. W6222
Joseph, Ct., S10403
Joseph, Ct., S36448
William, Ct., S17317
BUNNER, Rudolph, Pa., BLWt.1984-450-Lt. Col. Pa. Line
BUNPUS/BUMPUS, Frederick/Fredrick N.Y., S2045
BUNT, Ludwick/Ludswick, Pvt., N.Y. BLWt.6772 iss. 5/4/1791 to Maxwell Anthony, ass.
BUNTEN, John, N.H., S15327
BUNTIN, William, Va., Nancy, Wid. Ctf. 34773
BUNTING, Ramoth, N.J., S42637
Solomon, Va., S37800
Thomas, Cont., N.Y., Pa., Susan Wood, former wid., W834
Thomas, Sgt., N.Y., BLWt.6786 iss. 12/11/1789 to Benj. Brown, ass.
William, Va., S37808
BUNTON, Samuel, Pa., Martha, R1435
BUOY, Robert, Va., R1523
BURBAGE, Thomas, S.C., S17868
BURBANK, Benjamin, Mass., R1436
David, N.H., S15021
Eleazer/Eleaser, Mass., Elizabeth W18677; BLWt.11270-160-55
Eleazer, Mass., Mary, W23744
Elijah, Mass., Mehitable, R1437; BLWt.84016-160-55
Eliphalet, Mass., Susannah, W21723
Henry, Mass., R1438
Isaac, Mass., Judith, W17394; BLWt 7078-160-55
Israel, Mass., Ruth, W23713
Joel, Ct., Eunice, W21717
John, Mass., Dorcas, W23715
John, Mass., Navy, N.H., Privateer S19227
Jonathan, Pvt., N.H., BLWt.2921 iss. 4/5/1796 to Samuel Atkinson
Jonathan, N.H., S45654
Josiah, Pvt., N.H., BLWt.2940 iss. 12/12/1792 to Daniel King, ass.
Nathaniel, Cont., N.H., S40774
Samuel, Cont., Mass., Mehetabel/Mehitable, W14415
Samuel, Mass., Eunice Morse, former wid., W17173. 5 1776 ltrs. to his wife.
Thomas, Cont., Mass., Elizabeth, W14431
Wells, N.H., S39255
BURBECK, Henry, Cont., Mass., Lucy E. W10480; BLWt.122-300-Capt. Iss. 12/3/1789. No papers
James, Cont., Mass., S8127
John, Cont., Mass., S34126
Joseph, Cont., Mass. res. 1818,

BURBECK (continued)
S34117
Thomas, Cont., Mass., S34121
BURBRIDGE, George, Va., S30906
John, Pvt., S.C., BLWt.11976 iss. 10/11/1796 to John Cannon, ass.
Lincefield, Va., S30907
BURCH, Benjamin, Md., Chloe, W4137; BLWt.108-60-55
Benjamin, Md., Rebecca, W23743
Daniel, Pa., R1441
Ebenezer, Ct., Phebe, W16204
Edy, Vt., S17303
Francis, Md., S39260
George, Va. Sea Service, R1442
Isaiah, Pvt., N.Y., BLWt.6826 iss. 11/27/1790 to Thomas Sears, ass.
Isaiah, N.Y., S44625
James, N.J., S34133; BLWt.8113-100. Iss. 7/7/1789. No papers
John, Md., Va., Elizabeth, W5238
John, Sgt., N.Y., BLWt.6780 iss. 9/3/1790 to James Hamilton, ass.
John, Pa., See BIRCH
Joseph, Va., Ann J., W12388; BLWt 38842-160-55
Philip, Pvt., N.Y., BLWt.6854 iss. 7/30/1790 to Edward Cumpston, ass.
Thomas, N.Y., S12401
Thomas, N.C., Sarah, W6218
Warren, Pvt., Mass., BLWt.3804 iss. 1/29/1790
William, N.C., Judith, W26976
William, N.C., See BERCH
William, Va., See BIRCH
Zachariah, Md., Mildred, W9759; BLWt.38844-160-55
BURCHAM, David, Pa., R1443
BURCHARD, Jonathan, Cont., Mass., S10399
Joseph, Ct., See BIRCHARD
Nathaniel, N.Y., Mariam/Miriam, W20807
Sabra, former wid. of Hosea Gridley, Ct., which see
William, Pvt., Del., BLWt.10697 iss. 9/2/1789
BURCHEL, Daniel, Va., S39261
BURCHETT, Robert, Va., S10394
William, Va., S1179
BURCHFIELD, John, N.C., Mary, W8175
Meshack, N.C., S16668
Robert, N.C., Elizabeth, R1444
BURCHITT/BURCHETT, John, Va., S30300
BURCHNELL, James, Res. in 1834 Lewis Co., Va., R1445
BURCHDORFF, John, N.Y., S44357
BURCKHER/BUCKHER, George, Pa., S22148
BURD, Benjamin, N.C., R21880
Benjamin, Pa., S40788
David, N.J., R1446
BURDAN, Nathan, N.Y., See BORDEN
BURDEEN/BERDEEN, Timothy, Mass., Molly, W12386; BLWt.1953-100
BURDEN, Abraham, N.J., S44703
Gale, R.I., See BORDEN

BURDEN (continued)
John, Navy, Mass., See BORDEN
Jonathan, Mass., Bilote, W20813
Lucy, former wid. of Samuel Bailey, Mass., which see
Nathaniel, Ct., Mass., S17313
Timothy, Mass., S23142
BURDETT, Jarvis, Va., S16680
BURDGE, Michael, N.Y., S12402
BURDICK, Adam, Mass., R.I., S12370
Elisha, N.Y., S44700; BLWt.6817-100. Iss. 11/17/1791 to Elisha Camp, ass. No papers
Francis, Ct., N.Y., S23144
Gideon/Gidion, Cont., R.I., S38586
Gideon, N.Y., S3107
Hazard, R.I., S9296
Henry, N.Y., S44701; BLWt.932-100
Ichabod, R.I., Mary, W23741
Isaiah, R.I., S14238
James, R.I., Amey, W21722
John, R.I., S8112
Moses, Pvt., Gen. Armand's Legion BLWt.12737 iss. 1/26/1790 to John May, ass.
Peleg, Cont., Mass., R1449
Perry, R.I., S28661
Sylvester, R.I., S12354
Thompson, Cont., R.I., S44699
Walter, R.I., S19925
BURDIN, John, Del., N.Y., S12369
BURDINE, Francis, Pvt., N.Y., BLWt.6802 iss. 9/27/1790 to Jacob Tremper, ass.
James, N.J., See BORDINE
BURDITT, Ebenezer, Mass., Privateer, Ruth, W15614
BURDOO, Silas, Mass., S21099
BURDUE, Nathaniel, Pa., S3104
BURDWIN/BARDWIN, Samuel, Ct., Lois, W20814
BURELLE, John, French troops, Patience Hanna, R1494. Contains 1775 license from city of Marsailles, France to practice medicine on ships
BURFEE/BURPEE, Nathan, Mass., S45657
BURFORD, John, N.C., S15259
Moses, Pvt., N.H., BLWt.2946 iss. 12/23/1799 to Moses Burford
Philip T., N.C., S1646
BURGDOFF/BURGDORFF, Conrad, N.Y., Jerusha, W17391; BLWt.9183-160-55
BURGE, Lothrop, Ct., S12392
Lott, Ct., Mass., Hannah, W20804 BLWt.15163-160-55
BURGER, Jeremiah, N.Y., Maria, R1452
John, Mass., Hannah Knapp, former wid., W16319. Widow's last husb., Samuel Knapp, a pensioner, which see
Nicholas, Va., S30905
Zachariah, N.Y., Elizabeth, W21738
BURGES, Abial, Cont., Mass., Jane, W20816
Michael, Pvt., N.Y., BLWt.6838 iss. 7/16/1790 to W.I. Vreedenburg, ass.

BURGES (continued)
Stephen, Mass., S38588
William, Mass., See BURGISS
BURGESS, Anthony, Mass., Eunice, W26781; BLWt.11181-160-55
Asa, Ct., Cont., Sarah, W20798
Bangs, Mass., Phebe, W20818
Basil, Md., BLWt.243-200-Lt. Iss. 8/2/1797 to Abraham Drake, ass.
Benjamin, Cont., Mass., S40772
David, Mass., S16682
Edward, Md., S37813
Edward, Mass., S36949
Edward, Va., S35806
Ephraim, Ct., S34114
Ichabod, Pvt., Mass., BLWt.3655 iss. 3/23/1797 to M. Turner, ass.
Ichabod, Mass., S34120
Ichabod, Mass., Keziah, W23728
Isaac, N.J., R1450
Jacob, Cont., Mass., Sarah, W21732
James, Cont., S44718
John, Cont., N.Y., S42639
John, Pvt., Lamb's Artillery, N.Y., BLWt.6873 iss. 4/21/1791 to David Quinton, ass.
John, Pvt., Md., BLWt.10987 iss. 8/14/1795 to Francis Sherrard, ass.
John, Mass., S30302
John, N.C., S9295
John, Va., S8113
Jonathan, Pvt., Mass., BLWt. 3714 iss. 2/23/1797 to Benjamin Dana, ass.
Jonathan, Mass., S15769
Joseph, R.I., Lydia, W1815
Joseph, R.I., Freelove, W21721
Joshua, Md., BLWt.242-200-Lt. Iss. 5/10/1800 to Joshua Burgess. No papers
Josias/Josiah, Md., S31589
Michael, N.Y., Hannah, W18674
Nathaniel, Mass., Lucretia, R1451
Ruth, former wid. of James Gunner Va., which see
Seth, Mass., Olive, W16875
Stephen, N.Y., Elizabeth, W17395; BLWt.34523-160-55
Thomas, Mass., Jemima, W5969; BLWt.24615-160-55
William, Va., S37797
BURGET, Lambert, N.Y., Margaret, W1710; BLWt.28588-160-55
Milbury, Mass., N.Y. See BURGHARETT
BURGEY, John, N.C., See AMBURGEY
BURGHARDT, John, Mass., S23139
BURGHARETT, Milbury, Mass., N.Y., Mary, W21730
BURGHART/BURKHART/BUCKHART, George, Pa., R1402
BURGHER, Jeremiah, N.Y. See BURGER
BURGIN, John, N.H., See BERGIN
BURGIS, Achsah, former wid. of John Thayer, Mass., which see
Jacob, Cont., Mass., Sarah, See BURGESS
John, Cont., N.Y., S44704

BURGISS, Bangs, Pvt., Mass., BLWt. 3725 iss. 5/28/1792 to Israel Angell, ass.
John, Pvt., Mass., BLWt.3775 iss. 5/1/1792 to D. Quinton, ass.
Thomas, Mass., See BURGESS
William, Mass., Lucy, W14424
BURGOON, Robert, Md., R1453
BURHANS, Abraham, N.Y., W21725
Edward, N.Y., Bridget, W16878
Tjerck, N.Y., See BURHAUS
BURHAUS, John, Cont., N.Y., Abigail, R1455
Tjerck, N.Y., Catherine, wid., S12379
BURIL, Humphrey, See BURRELL
BURK, Charles, N.C., Sally, W18474
George, Va., S32152
James, Va. Sea Service, S6649
John, Pvt., Hazen's Regt., BLWt. 12758 iss. 8/17/1789
John, Md., Mary, W5952
John, Mass., S40781
John, N.C., S16332
John, Pa., R1459
Jonathan, N.H., S40780
Joseph, Navy, R.I., Hannah, W5949 BLWt.36608-160-55
Joseph, N.C., Mary, S3095; BLWt. 30608-160-55 cancelled; BLWt. 36121-160-55
Joseph, Vt., Abigail, W18686
Josiah, Pvt., Mass., BLWt.3780 iss. 4/7/1792
Martin, Md., S30298
Michael, Va., S1174
Michael, ---- Ky. res. in 1842, R----.
Nathan, Md., S34674
Patrick, Pa., S40782
Peter, N.J., R1460
Robert, N.J., Pa., R1462
Robert, N.C., S3094
Samuel, N.J., Elizabeth, W5950
Samuel, Va., Mary, W2912
Silas, Mass., S46425; BLWt.1721-100
Silvanus, Mass., Achsah, W4414
Thomas, Pa., S40785
Thomas, ---- N.Y. res. of wid. in 1853. Eleanor, R1456
William, Pa., S40789
William, Va., Susanna, W5951
BURKARD, Frederick, Pa., S3105
BURKDOFF, John, Pvt., N.Y., BLWt.6823 iss. 8/4/1790 to Henry Hart, ass.
BURKE, Edmund, Pa., BLWt.192-300-Capt. Iss. 7/11/1797 to Wm. Matthews, ass. of Patrick Edwards & James Scanlon, devisees of Edmund Burke. No papers
Elihu/Elisha, N.C., Siller, W8233; BLWt.36636-160-55
Isham, Ga., S3093
James, Pa., Catharine, W3175
John, N.Y., S28665
John, Pvt., Va., BLWt.11949 iss. 7/6/1793 to Francis Graves, ass.
John, Va., R1458
Joseph, N.H., S45656
Richard, Md., BLWt.1507-100
Richard, Md., Pa., R1461

BURKE (continued)
Robert, Va., Hannah, W9373; BLWt.26474-160-55
Tobias, Pvt., Va., BLWt.11947 iss. 4/6/1793 to Francis Graves, ass.
William, Cont., Va., S37802; BLWt.1353-100
William, Va., S37801
BURKEHART, Jacob, Pa. See BURKHART
BURKES, Samuel, N.C., S16670
BURKET, Frederick, Va., S3102
BURKETT, Uriah, N.C., R20316
BURKHART, George, Pa. See BURGHART
Henry, Va., S8129
Jacob, Pa., S22150
BURKMAR, Thomas, Ct., S36947
BURKS, Edward, Ga., Elizabeth, R1457
Isham, Va., Elizabeth, W9758
Samuel, N.C., See BURKES
BURKSTUFF/BUCKSTAFF, Peter, N.Y., R1466
BURLEIGH, Edward, Mass. Sea Service, N.H., Mary, W21729
Stevens, N.H., Abigal See BURLEY
William, Mass., N.H., S45655
William, N.H., See BURLEY
BURLESON, Rachel, former wid. of Daniel Warner, Mass., which see
BURLEW, Abraham, N.J., Ruth, W3765
BURLEY, Ebenezer, Ct., N.Y., Eunice, W2915
Gordon, N.H., Elizabeth, W23788
Jacob, Ct., S36451
James, Va., See BROWNLEE
Joseph, N.H., S15022
Joseph, Vt., S15328
Stevens, N.H., Abigail, W21736
William, Mass., BLWt.97-300-Capt. Iss. 1/29/1790. No papers
William, N.H., Sarah, W18683
BURLIN, Isaac, Pa. See BERLIN
BURLINGAME, Benedict, R.I., Rachel, W1814
Chandler, R.I., See BURLINGHAM
Christopher, Mass. See BURLINGGAME
Content, former wid. of Elisha Aldrich/Aldrick, Navy, R.I., which see
Daniel, R.I., S40759
David, R.I., S21092
Jeremiah, R.I., Ruth, W16879
John, R.I., R1469
Nathan, R.I., S8118; BLWt. 26123-160-55
Nathan, R.I., See BURLINGGAME
Pardon, R.I., S21093
Solomon, Cont., Mass., Vt., Elizabeth, R1467
Wanton, Vt., S12378
William, Navy, R.I., Eunice, W23745
BURLINGGAME, Christopher, Mass., S9124
Nathan, R.I., Sea Service, Mary, R1468
BURLINGHAM, Chandler, R.I., BLWt. 86-200-Lt. Iss. 12/31/1789. See this name in Heitman, p.134. It may be this officer. Given as Chandler Burlingame.

BURLINGHAM (continued)
Hopkins, R.I., S12400
Nathan, R.I. See BURLINGAME
Pardon, N.Y., Dorcas Remsen/ Remson, former wid., W17526. Her 1st husb., Hamonus/ Harmanus Rutgers, also served. Her 3rd husb. was Abraham Remsen
BURLISON, John, R.I., S40777
BURN, David, N.C., S9299
John, Md., S34672
Thomas, Md., S40787
BURNAM, Andrew, N.H., Elizabeth, W16874; BLWt.11158-160-55
Israel, N.H., S44713
James, Ct., See BURNHAM
Jeremiah, Mass., Mahetable, See BURNHAM
John, Pvt., Ct., BLWt.5509 iss. 3/21/1791 to Josiah Starr
Jonathan, Cont., N.H., S18749
Joshua, Cont., Mass. See BURNHAM
Joshua, N.H., Jemima, S45658 & W23752. Her claim for pension was adjudicated as wid. of Joshua Burnham, Ctf.10889, and these papers are filed under W23752
Wesley/Wesly, Mass., S18750
William, N.H., S18753
Zadock, Mass., S40779
BURNAP, Abijah, Mass., S12359
Edward, Mass., Polly, W23732; BLWt.14977-160-55
Jeriah, Ct., Abigail, W10472; BLWt.26311-160-55
John, Ct., Abigail, W25313; BLWt.24331-160-55
John, Mass., Candace, W23723
John, Vt., Polly, W634; BLWt. 17865-160-55
Joseph, Mass., Mary, W21734
Naomi, former wid. of John Ogden, Mass., which see
BURNELL, Ephraim/Ephriam, Mass., S29675
John, Mass., S36945
Joseph, Cont., Mass., S30299
Samuel, Ct., Sophia, W17390
BURNER, Abraham, Va., Mary, W24693
Daniel, Va., R1471
Jacob, Cont., BLWt.215-300- Capt. in the German Regt. Iss. 6/29/1789 to M. McConnell, ass. No papers
BURNES, Hannah, former wid. of James Hodge, N.Y., which see
James, Pa., Elizabeth, BLWt. 1663-100
Phillip, N.C., S30909
Robert, N.Y., S44705
Samuel, Pa., S40769
Walter, R.I., S38585
BURNET, Aaron, N.J., S805
David, N.J., S859
Ebenezer, Pvt., N.Y., BLWt.6779 iss. 9/3/1790
Edmund, N.J., S3106
James, N.C., Elizabeth, R1472
Robert/Robert R., Cont., N.Y.

BURNET (continued)
agency, Ctf. 303; BLWt.173-200- Lt. Iss. 9/15/1790. No papers
Squire, N.J., S42110
Thomas, N.Y., S15012
William, Cont., BLWt.314-450
BURNETT, Andrew, Navy, R.I., Mass., S21677
Charles Ripley, Mass., Lovina, W23748
Ebenezer, N.Y., Lydia Kitchell, former wid., W470. Her 2nd husb. David Kitchell, N.J., was a pensioner, which see
George, Pvt., Pa., BLWt.8944 iss. 8/31/1791 to Dudley Woodbridge, ass.
Ichabod, N.J., BLWt.2565-400- Maj. & Aide-de-Camp to Gen. Green. Iss. 9/1/1790. No papers
James, Ct., Chloe, W25317
John, Ct., See BURNAP
John, Ga., N.C., Moley, R1473
John, Pvt., Md., BLWt.11905 iss. 8/7/1794 to Henry Purdy, ass.
John, Pvt., N.J., BLWt.8115 iss. 6/22/1790 to Henry Cole, ass.
John, N.Y., S44717
John, Pvt., N.Y., BLWt.6794 iss. 9/25/1790 to D. Hudson & Co., ass. BLWt.209-200-Lt. Iss. 10/12/ 1790. Also recorded as above under BLWt.2570. No papers
John, Va., Sarah, R1475
Joseph, Va., See BARNETT
Joseph, Va., Mabel, W4644
Joshua, Ga., S32154
Richard, Va., R1474
Robert R., Cont. See BURNET
Thomas, Md., Mary Boody, former wid., BLWt.211-100
William, Mass., S30303
William, N.Y., See BURNITT
William, Pvt., N.C., BLWt.11967 iss. 5/18/1797 to Gabriel Holmes, ass.
William, Va., R540
BURNETT/BURNETTE, Williamson, Va., Priscilla, W3383
BURNEY, David, Ga., R1475 1/2
Nichols, Pvt., Pa., BLWt.8968 iss. 8/31/1790 to Dudley Wood- bridge, ass.
Samuel, N.C., Nancy, W9374; BLWt.84039-160-55
BURNHAM, Abner, Ct., S12390
Ammi, Mass., Ruhamah, W21719
Amos, Mass., S29043
Andrew, N.H., See BURNAM
Asa, Ct., Cont., S12371
Asa, N.H., Elizabeth, W15616
Asahel, Ct., S44712; BLWt.447-100
Benjamin, Mass., S22669
Benjamin, N.H., Elizabeth Goss, former wid., W27956; BLWt.45664- 160-55. Her other husb. was pen- sioned, see Samuel Goss, N.H.
Charles, Mass., Sarah, W14426
David, Mass., Martha, W23725; BLWt.50807-160-55
Eben/Ebenezer, Ct., S15766
Ebenezer, Mass., S29676

BURNHAM (continued)
George, N.H., Sarah, W24684
Gurdin, Ct., Cont., Navy, S31585
Isaac, Cont., Mass., S42638
Isaac, Pvt., Mass., BLWt.3746 iss. 3/25/1790
Isaac, Mass., S34134
Isaac, N.C., S9122
Israel, N.H., S44713
Ivey, N.C., R1478
James, Ct., Tamma, W17380
James, Ct., Mehetabel, W20823
James, Cont., Ct., Eunice, W14428
James, Cont., N.H., Abigail, W23736
Jedediah, Ct., R1479
Jeremiah, Mass., Mahetable, W5970; BLWt.3832-160-55
Jeremiah, Mass., Navy, S34130
Jeremiah, Privateer, Mass., S9111
John, Ct., Bridget, W1548
John, Ct., Cont., S18339
John, Cont., Ct., S46822
John, Cont., Mass., S45659; BLWt. 95-400-Maj. Iss. 1/25/1790. No papers
John, Mass., S29045
John, Mass., S42107
John, Mass., Roxanna, W710; BLWt. 6293-160-55
Jonathan, Cont., Mass., Ruth, W20815
Joseph, Ct., S12381
Joseph, Ct., Cont., S17315
Joseph, Corp., Mass., BLWt.3791 iss. 3/25/1790
Joseph, Mass., S24135
Joseph, Pvt., N.H., BLWt.2932 iss. 6/17/1790 to Benj. L. Gilman, ass
Joshua, Ct., R1480
Joshua, Cont., Mass., Ctf.10889. Wid. Jemima Burnam's application for pension was adjudicated as wid. of this Joshua, but should have been as wid. of Joshua Burnam, S45658, so her papers in that claim.
Josiah, Ct., S12386
Josiah, N.Y., S12393
Moses, Pvt., Mass., BLWt.3803 iss. 3/25/1790
Nathan, Ct., S36452
Nathan, Ct., S36457
Nathan, Mass., Mary, R1481; BLWt. 38825-160-55
Oliver, Ct., Cont., S15333
Orrin, Ct., S28664
Pike G., N.H., Polly, W25309
Roger, Ct., S23563
Rufus, Mass., S34125
Solomon, Mass., Anna, BLWt.94504- 160-55
Stephen, Ct., Cont., S36454
Sylvester, Ct., Caroline, W21728
Thomas, Pvt., Mass., BLWts.3795 & 261-60-55 iss. 3/25/1790
Thomas, Mass., Mary, W8404; BLWt. 32204-160-55
Thomas, Mass., Ruth, W2752
Thomas, Mass., Hepsibah, W14416
Thomas, Mass., Vt., Deliverance, W23740

BURNHAM (continued)
Thomas M., Mass., Mary, W14434; BLWt.261-60-55
William, Ct., Mary, W23742
William, Pvt., N.Y., BLWt.6801 iss. 7/24/1790 to John Lawrence, ass.
Wolcott/Woolcott, Ct., Sarah B., W1220; BLWt.16259-160-55
Zadock, Mass., See BURNAM
BURNHART, Daniel, Pa., BLWt.2066-100
John, N.J., S40760
BURNHEATER/BURNHETER, John, Pa., R1482
BURNIE, John, Pa., S40786
BURNIT, Squire, N.J. See BURNET
BURNITT, William, Va., S1645
BURNIX, Fortune, Pvt., Mass., BLWt.3796 iss. 2/29/1792 to Moses Beard
BURNLEY, Garland, Va., BLWt. 1885-300
Henry, Va., S31582
James, Va., See BROWNLEE
BURNS, Alexander, Pvt., Pa., BLWt.8959 iss. 7/10/1789 to Ann O'Brian, ass.
Andrew, Va., S30296
Bryan, Pvt., Va., BLWt.11938 iss. 7/14/1792 to Francis Graves, ass.
Daniel, Ct., Martha, W16519
David, N.Y., S44706
David, N.Y., Anne DeNoyelles/DeNoyelle, former wid., W26778
George, Va., R1483
Hannah, See BURNES
Harvey, Pvt., Hazen's Regt., BLWt.12791 iss. 3/24/1798
Henry, Pvt., Del., BLWt.10717 iss. 7/26/1797 to James De Baufre, ass.
James, N.C., S4979
James, Sr.?, Pvt. "in the Artillery", Pa., BLWt.9048 iss. 11/5/1789
James, Pa., S34673
James, Pa., S35805
James, Pa., R1484
Jeremiah, Va., Elizabeth, W2063; BLWt.40908-160-55
John, Md., See BURN
John, N.H., S45528
John, N.C., S1944
John, N.C., S9118
John, N.C., R1501
John, Pa., S35802
John, Pa., Elizabeth, R1485
John, Pa., BLWt.496-100
John, Va., See BYRNE
John, Va., Lucretia, W9372; BLWt.71127-160-55
John, Va., Ann McKizick, former wid., R6770
Laird, S.C., S3091
Lawrence, Pvt., Pa., BLWt.8950 iss. 2/5/1800
Michael, Pvt., Pa., BLWt.8931 iss. 6/17/179- to Francis Kirkpatrick, ass.
Michael, Va., See BURRUS

BURNS (continued)
Peter, S.C., R20205
Phillip, N.C., S30909
Robert, N.C., S44705
Samuel, Mass., S40778
Samuel, Pa., S40769
Samuel, S.C., Mary, W9757
Thomas, Pvt., Pa., BLWt.8941 iss. 11/15/1791 to Sarah Shepherd, ass.
Walter, R.I., See BURNES
William, Ct., S36462
William, Va., S16669
BURNSIDE, James, Pa., S45996; BLWt.9047-100
John, N.C., S16333
John, Va., BLWt.11894-100. No papers
Jonathan, Cont., Va., S42112; BLWt.2471-100. Iss. 7/2/1852
Robert, N.C., S17304
BURNSIDES, Andrew, S.C., S9300
BURPE. Isaac, Mass., S12356
BURPEE, Ebenezer, Mass., Elizabeth, W18669
Elijah, Mass., Hannah, W24694
Nathan, Mass., See BURFEE
Nathan, Mass., Lucinda, W27391
Nathaniel, Mass., S29680
Nathaniel, Mass., N.H., S12351
BURR, Aaron, Cont., N.J., Eliza B., R12837
Asa, Ct., Malinda, W16202
Cushing, Mass., S29672
Daniel, Cont., Mass., S16679
David, Ct., Sarah Anna, W17373
David, Ct., Jane Sherwood, former wid., R9502
Edmund, Ct., Navy, S37810
Ephraim, Mass., BLWt.128-300-Capt. Iss. 6/22/1799 to Elijah & Calvin Burr, surv. heirs. No papers
Hezekiah, Ct., Mary, W17382
Jabez, Ct., Mary, R1490
Joel, Ct., S12385
Jonathan, Mass., Sarah, W15611
Joseph, Mass., Dolly, W21718
Joshua, R.I., S46829
Levi, Mass., S30252
Nathan, Cont., heir's res. was Mass. in 1818, BLWt.709-100
Nathaniel, Ct., S16667
Roger, Ct., Jane, W20806
Salmon, Ct., Dis. No papers
Semo/Simon/Seymour, Mass., Mary, W23726
Seth, Mass., S29044
Seymour, See Semo
Simeon, Mass., Elizabeth, W18672
Simon, See Semo
Sylvanus, Mass., Sarah, W24686
Thomas, N.Y., R1491
William, Ct., Sarah, W25375; BLWt.15421-160-55. Large file
William, Mass., Nabby, W1549
Zebina, Ct., S16064
BURRAGE, Charles, Va., Catharine, W8342
BURRALL, Jonathan, Ct., S29046; four 1779-80 ltrs. in file
BURRANCE, Robert, Pvt., N.Y.,

BURRANCE (continued)
BLWt.6785 iss. 2/14/1791 to James Hamilton, ass.
BURREL, Zachariah, Pvt., N.J., BLWt.8109 iss. 10/12/1790
BURRELL, Abigail, former wid. of Jonathan Jackson, which see
Benoni, Cont., Mass. See BURRILL
Francis, Va., R1492
Humphrey, Cont., Mass., Molly, W21737
Isaac, Mass., S4976
Jedediah, N.J., S42106
John, Cont., Mass., Elenor/Eleanor, W711; BLWt.26573-160-55
John, Pvt., Mass., BLWt.3676 iss. 5/3/1791 to James Palmer, ass.
John, Mass., S34129
Nathaniel, Mass., S8117
Noah, Pvt., Mass., BLWt.3672 iss. 4/1/1790
Noah, Mass., S17308
Sylvanus, Mass., Mary, W14417
BURRETT, Anthony, Ct., Abigail, W2996; BLWt.34807-160-55
Charles, Pvt., Ct., BLWt.5476 iss. 8/3/1789 to James E. Beech
Israel, Ct., Vt., See BURRITT
BURRIDGE, John, Mass., Lois, W21731
John, Mass., Mary Dodge, former wid., W24075
BURRIGE, John, Pvt., Pa., BLWt. 8922 iss. 7/27/1789 to Richard Platt, ass.
BURRIL/BURWELL, Zachariah, N.J., Martha, W5235
BURRILL, Alden, Mass., S29687
Benjamin, Mass., Esther, W1550
Benoni, Cont., Mass., Lydia, W24691
Ebenezer, Ct., S12395
Ebenezer, Cont., Mass., Mary, W14413
Humphrey, Cont. Mass. See BURRELL
John, Mass., See BURRELL
Joseph, Mass., S29041
Nathaniel, Mass., See BURRELL
Samuel, Mass., Mary, W14418
BURRIS, Elisha, Md. See BURROUGHS
Jacob, Va., See BURRUS
Martin, Va., S32151
Nathenial/Nathaniel, Va., S15026
Solomon, N.C., Judith, W3936
BURRISS, John, Indian War of 1780. See Isaac Wilson, Rev. & Indian War 1785, R11656
BURRITT, Andrew, Ct., R1496
Anthony, Ct., See BURRETT
Charles, Ct., Hannah, W23747
Eben, Ct., Sarah, W17384; BLWt. 82008-160-55
Elihu, Ct., Elizabeth, R1497
Israel, Ct., Vt., S19229
Joseph, Ct., Sally, W21627
Josiah, Ct., Mabel Curtis, former wid., W25463
Nathan, Ct., S17306
Wakeman, Ct., S12942

BURRITT (continued)
William, Ct., Dis. No papers
Zalman, Ct., S16331
BURROS, Thomas, Pvt., N.Y., BLWt. 6784 iss. 9/4/179- to John Suffron, ass.
BURROUGH, Dobson, Va. See BURROW
BURROUGHS, Clarissa, former wid. of Wm. Parrot, N.J., which see
Daniel, N.H., S32144
Eden, N.J., See BURROWES
Elijah, N.H., S42105
Elisha, Md., Margaret P., R1503
George, Va., Jean, R1499
John, N.J., S34132
John, N.J., Rhoda, W841
John, N.Y., S22667
John, ---- Ky. res. in 1839 & 1840, R1500
Josiah, Cont., N.H., S12384
Josiah, Mass., R1502
Matthew, Cont., N.Y., Green Mt. Boys, S44353
Norman, Md., Esther Turner, W3935
Stephen, Ct., S3110
Zebulon, Ct., Hannah, W23751
BURROUS, John Proctor, See BORRES
BURROW, Dobson, Va., S9117
Willey/Willie, N.C., S41466
BURROWES, Eden, N.J., S40766; BLWt.181-200-Lt. Iss. 5/11/1795. No papers
BURROWS, Aaron, Mass., Mary, W14420
Caleb, Ct., Judith, W25311; BLWt.11076-160-55
Elisha, Ct., S28406
Ezekiel, Del., S39259
Giles, Mass., S34113
Hubbard, Ct., Mary, W25316
James, Fifer, N.J., BLWt.8148 iss. 8/10/1789 to Richard Platt, ass.
Jeremiah, Md., S8110
John, Navy, R.I., S44714
John, Pvt., N.J., BLWt.8107 iss. 8/11/1791
John, N.J., BLWt.610-400
Jonathan, Mass., N.H., Elizabeth, W15615
Joseph, Ct., Cont., Mary, W5237
Joseph, Pa., Dis. No papers
Joseph, R.I., S36449
Josiah, Ct., Sarah, W16518
Michael, Va., R1504
Nathan, Ct., Anna Cunningham, former wid., W17674
Nathaniel, Pa., S22151
Paul, Ct., Catharine, W21724
Robert, Ct., S28663; BLWt. 26363-160-55
Samuel, Pvt., Lamb's Artillery, N.Y., BLWt.6886 iss. 7/14/1790 to Richard Platt, ass.
Stephen, Ct., R1032
William, Ct., See BURRUS
William, Ct., Navy, Sarah, R1505
William, Ct., Vt., S12396
William, Cont., Mass., S45527
BURRUS, Jacob, Va., Susannah/Susana, W340
Michael, Va., W8111
Solomon, N.C., Judith, See BURRIS

BURRUS (continued)
Thomas, Ct., Esther, W8402; BLWt.57751-160-55
William, Ct., S19927
BURSEIL, Moses, See BURSIEL
BURSELL, Moses, See BURSIEL
BURSIEL, Moses, Mass., S22671; and S20658
BURT, Aaron, Mass., Hannah, W4907
Aaron, N.Y., R1506
Alven, Mass., S28666
Benjamin, Cont., N.J., Mary, W1137
Calvin, N.Y., R1507
David, Cont., Mass. res. 1818, S34115
Ebenezer, Mass., Ruth, W20809
Edward, Va., R1508
Henry, Cont., N.Y., Susannah, R1512
James, N.Y., S12388
James, Pvt., Hazen's Regt., BLWt. 12805 iss. 3/12/179- to Cath. Jones, Admx.
Joel, Mass., S29678
John, Ct., Eunice, W3653
Moody, Va., R1511
Reuben, Cont., Mass., S34123; BLWt.10307-160-55
Stephen, Mass., S15014
Thomas, N.Y., S23140
BURTCH, Billings, R.I., Jane, W20797
BURTIS, Elizabeth, former wid., of Robert Eldredg, Ct., which see
BURTLESS, William, Pvt., N.J., BLWt.8087 iss. 2/26/1794 to John Cannon, ass.
William, Jr., Pvt., N.J., BLWts. 8089 & 14072 iss. 3/28/1794 to John Cannon, ass. of James Burtless, Admr.
BURTON, Absalom, N.C., Ann, R1515
Asa, Mass., S34118
Benjamin, Pvt., Ct., BLWt.5472 iss. 8/10/1789 to Richard Platt
Benjamin, Cont., Mass., S16677
Benjamin, Green Mt. Boys, Vt., Hannah, W20824
Daniel, Ct., Cont., S12377
David, N.H., S40773
Elijah, Ct., Cont., Vt., S18335
Henry, N.C., Va., S39262
Henry, Vt., Ann, W18676; BLWt. 30594-160-55
Hutchens, Va., R1516
Isaac, Ct., N.Y., Abigail, W2719; BLWt.26393-160-55
Isaac, Pvt., Md., BLWt.11008 iss. 8/14/1795 to Francis Sherrard, ass.
Jacob, Pvt., Del., BLWt.10706 iss. 9/2/1789
James, Ct., Naoma, W24682
James, Va., Elizabeth, S48412; BLWt.1924-300
Jarret/Jarett, Va., R1517
John, N.C., Susanna, W4140
John, R.I., R1519
John, Va., S32140
John, Va., S46831

BURTON (continued)
John, Va., R1518
Jonathan, N.H., Huldah, W15991
Joshua, Md., Pa., Va., S42111
Josiah, N.H., Abigail, W20812
Lewis, Ct., S17310
Marshall, Va., S37251
May, Va., Sarah, W4141
Nathan, Ct., S17311
Richard, Ga., S40761
Richard, Va., S8114
Robert, Va., S6609
Samuel, Va., S39254
Seley/Selah/Othaniel Selah, Ct., S12394
Thomas, Cont., Mass., S15770
Thomas, Va., Dicey, W5236; BLWt.6436-160-55
William, Mass., Chloe, W1709; BLWt.7312-160-55
William, Mass., Shuah, W10473; BLWt.79517-160-55
William, Va., Sarah, W9760
William H., N.C., See William HALLIBERTON
BURTS, Benjamin Robert, N.H., Mary Pattrill, former wid., W26829
BURWELL, Daniel, Ct., Abigail, W17386
Jere, Ct., Cont., Lucy, W17381
Jonathan, Pa., S26561
Lucy, former wid. of George Baylor, Va., which see
Nathaniel, Cont., Va., Martha, W18681; BLWt.260-300-Capt. Iss. 2/13/1798. No papers
Zachariah, N.J., Martha, W5235
Zacharias/Zachariah, N.J., & Gen. Wayne, S42109
BURZETT/BURZETTE, Charles, Cont., Ct., S44356
BUSBY, Isaac, S.C., R1524
James, Cont., Va., Elizabeth, W2995
John, N.C., See BUZBY
Nedom/Needham, S.C., S9114
Robert/Robart, Cont., Va., S30904
William, Cont., Va., R1526
BUSEY, Josiah, Mass., BLWt.125-200-Lt. Iss. 1/22/1799 to Elijah Busey, ass. of heir at law. No papers
BUSH, Abijah, Mass., Mary, W10477
Adam, Va., Margaret, W5960
Alpheus, N.Y., R1528
Charles, Mass., Joana McAdams, former wid., W4545
Charles, Va., Elizabeth, W2911
Conrad, Cont., N.Y. res., S46424; BLWt.6870-100. Iss. 7/11/1791 No papers
Daniel, Mass., S29770
Daniel, Pa., S23559
Dennis, Va., S39253
Drury, Va., Nancy, W8170
Enoch, Va., S3089
Frederick, N.Y., S12397
George, Ct., S15768
George, Cont., Pa., Ann Smyth, W9304; BLWt.1744-300
George, N.Y., S12355

BUSH (continued)
George, Pa., R1530
Henry, N.Y., Beulah, W20808
Henry, Pa., Eve, W4138
Henry, Pa., R1531
Hezekiah, Mass., S12364
Jacob, Va., Margaret, W24685
Jacobus H., N.Y., Hannah, W1546; BLWt.26523-160-55
James, Va., S1176
Japhet, Mass., R1532
John, Pvt., Mass., BLWt.3712 iss. 5/3/1791 to James Palmer, ass.
John, Mass., Eve, W17389
John, N.J., S12353
John, N.Y., Jane, W20822
John, N.C., Susannah Alexander, former wid., W4626
John, Pa., BLWt.196-300
John, S.C., BLWt.247-200-Lt. Iss. 7/3/1797 to heirs. Also recorded under BLWt.2687 iss. same date to Isabella Lacombe in behalf of herself & as ass. of her sister, Martha Nelson, the only surviving children & heirs. No papers
John D., N.Y., Sarah, W21733
Jonathan, Mass., Deborah, W23720
Lewis, Cont., Pa., BLWt.210-400
Peter, N.Y., Sarah, W16985
Richard, R.I., S21676
Rufus, Ct., Cont., S12374
Samuel, Pvt., Ct., BLWt.5510 iss. 6/27/1789 to Smith Weed
Samuel, Ct., S36450
Stephen, Ct., Mass., S12357
William, N.C., BLWt.298-200-Lt. Iss. 8/14/1792 to Isaac Cole, ass. No papers
William, not Rev. War, N.W. Indian War of 1791, Ky. agcy., Old War Invalid File 8122
Zachariah, N.Y., S12376
Ziba, Mass., S34122
BUSHEE, Consider, R.I., Patience, W1547; BLWt.33571-160-55
James, R.I., Deborah, W24683
Jonathan, R.I., Anstis, W20796; BLWt.30606-160-55
Samuel, R.I., Mary, W24687
BUSHER, Moses, S.C., R1534
BUSHES, Jonathan R. See BUSHEE
BUSHEY, Peter, Pvt.,N.Y.,BLWt.6878 iss. 9/29/1790 to O'Beers, Admr.
BUSHMAN, Jacob, Md., R1535
BUSHNELL, Daniel, Ct., S17319
David, Ct., BLWt.141-300-Capt. Iss. 2/3/1800. No papers
Doud, Ct., Privateer, S18752
Elisha, Ct., Lydia, W17368
Ephraim, Ct., S12368
Jason, Ct., S2104
Nathan, Ct., Esther, W17372
Samuel, Md., R1536
BUSHONG, Jacob, Va., S9297
BUSKILL, John, N.W. Indian War, 1790-1795, Hester, Old War Inv. File 8125. Old War Wid. Rej. 12917 & BLWt.11026-160-55
BUSKIRK, Aaron, Va., Ctf. 26833
John, Va., S32148
Lewis, Pa., Sarah, R1537

BUSLEY, Isham, N.C., See BEESLEY
BUSS, Ephraim, Mass., Lydia, W16881
John, Mass., Sarah, W23731
John, Pvt., N.H., BLWt.2935 iss. 8/26/1790 to Manassah Cutler, ass.
Samuel, Mass., Lydia, W15621
BUSSARD, Jacob, Pa., S5308
BUSSELL, Daniel, N.H., Mary, W15624
Isaac, Mass., S36948
Jonathan, Mass., Susan, W17379
Matthew, Va., Sea Service, Fanny, W899; BLWt.36513-160-55
Noah, N.H., Hannah, W17393; BLWt.3821-160-55
William, Va., Sarah, W337; BLWt.13891-160-55
BUSSEY, Benjamin, Mass., Judith, W18685
Cornelius, Va., R1539
Enos, N.Y., S44354
John, Mass., S12367
BUSSING, William, N.Y., Susannah, W23734
BUSSLE, Vincent, Va. See BUSTLE
BUST/BORST, John J., N.Y., R1033
BUSTER, Claudius, Va., Eleanor, W25310; BLWt.48607-160-55
Michael, Va., S1178
BUSTLE, Vincent, Va., Elizabeth, W5963
BUSWELL, Daniel, Mass., Eda, W9763; BLWt.9535-160-55
Elias, Mass., S8126
John, N.H., Lovina, W23721
Noah, N.H., See BUSSELL
Richard, N.H., Anna, W21739; BLWt.3810-160-55
BUTCHER, Benjamin, Mass., S40776
John, Cont., Pa., BLWt.2092-100
Samuel, Va., R1540
Sarah, former wid. of James Wells, Va., which see
BUTIMORE, Jacob, See BOTOMORE
BUTLAND, Jesse, Mass., S29042
Nathan, Mass., S36946
BUTLER, Allin/Allen, Cont., Mass., S12398
Asaph, N.H., Jane, W21716; BLWt.18378-160-55
Azariah, Mass., S29040
Benjamin, Ct., Cont., Lydia, W17376
Benjamin, Corp., "in Gen. Armand's Legion", BLWt.12736 iss. 7/9/1797
Benjamin, N.H., S45530
Benjamin, Va., S3096
Charles, Fifer, Mass., BLWt.3776 iss. 2/19/1800 to Uriah Tracy, ass.
Charles, N.C., S41464
Daniel, Ga., Dis. No papers
David, Pvt., Ct., BLWt.5408 iss. 5/1/1797 to John Duncan
David, Ct., S10397
Easton, Mass., S12366
Edmund/Edmond, Navy, Ala. res. in 1829, R1542
Edward, Pvt., Pa., BLWt.8943 iss.

BUTLER (continued)
1/28/1791 to R. Murthwaite, Admr.
Edward, Pa., BLWt.208-200-Lt. Iss. 2/19/1798. No papers
Eleazer, Ct., R1543
Ephraim G., Mass., Sea Service, Love, R1547
Ezekiel, Pvt., Ct., BLWt. 5508 iss. 12/11/1799
Ezekiel, Ct., Lydia, W17392
Ezra, Ct., Mehitable, W17370
Ezra, N.H., Tryphena, R1555
George, Ct., Mass., S12375
Isaac, Ct., S39257
Israel, Ct., Cont., S44329
Jacob, Va., Sarah, W5954
James, N.Y. res. of heirs 1837, R1545
James, N.C., Agnes, W338
James, Pa., Mary, R1548
James, Va., S16674
Jethro, N.C., S41465
Jethro, S.C., S30908
Joel, Ct., Sea Service, Privateer, R1546
John, Ct., S44328
John, Ct., Patty, W20821
John, Pvt., Mass., BLWt.3684 iss. 12/6/1799 to James ____, ass.
John, Mass., S29049
John, Mass., Mary, W16200
John, Mass., Abigail, W18684
John, Mass., Dorothy, W23717
John, Mass., Sarah, R1553
John, N.C., S21674
John, N.C., S41463
John, Pvt., Pa., BLWt.8980 iss. 3/10/1790 to John Parker, ass.
John, Pa., S46461; BLWt.1505-100
John, Pvt., "Sappers & Miners", BLWt.12755 iss. 7/20/1790 to Lamuel Curray
John, Va., S8115
John, Va., S30295
John, Va., S39263
John, Va., Molly, W5948
John, Va., Mary, W5953
John Osborn, Navy, Mass., S16678; Va. pensioner
Jonathan, Cont., Mass., Lois, W10486
Joseph, Ct., S40775
Joseph, Va., Frances, W3384; BLWt.26951-160-55
Josiah, Ct., Hannah, W16517
Lawrence, Va., BLWt.261-300-Capt. Iss. 5/22/1789. No papers
Mathew/Matthew, Cont., Mass., Anna, W14411
Matthew/Mathew, Ct., S16673
Moses, Mass., Rebecca Crooks, former wid., W10686
Moses, Mass., Mary, W23730
Nace (colored), Md., Mary, R1549
Nathaniel, Mass., Tabitha, W23749
Noble, Md., S8116
Patrick, Pvt., Pa., BLWt.8955 iss. 6/13/1795
Patrick, Pa., S40767
Patrick, Va., S31587
Percival, Pa., BLWt.203-200-Lt. Iss. 3/29/1791. No papers

BUTLER (continued)
Peter, Ct., S37811
Peter, Mass., N.H., S34131
Peter, Va., S20890
Phineas, Mass., S36944
Reuben, Cont., Va., Ann L., W4909
Richard, Md., S39264
Richard, Md., R1551
Richard, Md., BLWt.2407-100
Richard, N.J., S35804
Richard, Pa., BLWt.188-500-Col. Iss. 5/5/1789. No papers
Rufus, Mass., Jane, R1552; BLWt. 6288-160-55
Sarah, former wid. of Richard Jones, N.C., which see
Sarson, Mass., Navy, Susan, W23714
Solomon, Ct., S21095
Solomon, Va., Mary, R1550
Stephen, Pvt., Ct., BLWt.5491 iss. 11/2/1791 to Jonathan Tuttle
Stephen, Ct., S12350
Stephen, Ct., S37796
Stephen, Ct., Cata, W23724
Stephen, Ct., Cont., Phebe, W4908
Thomas, Mass., Margaret, W24692
Thomas, Pa., BLWt.193-300-Capt. Iss. 7/16/1789. No papers
Thomas, Va., S3098
Thomas, Va., S15029
Walter, Pvt., Ct., BLWt.5473 iss. 8/27/1789
Walter, Ct., Hannah, W16520
William, Ct., S12360
William, Cont., Pa., S49198; B.L. Rej.
William, Ga., R1556; BLWt.40509-160-55
William, Mass., S44710
William, Mass., Betsey, R1541
William, N.J., S45314
William, Pvt., Pa., BLWt.9041 iss. 1/8/1795
William, Pvt., Pa., BLWt.9084 iss. 1/25/179- to Butler & Davidson, Admrs.
William, Pa., Ann, W10479
William, Pa., BLWt.189-500-Lt. Col. Commandant. Iss. 11/5/1789 No papers
William, Pvt. "In the Sappers & Miners", BLWt.12757 iss. 8/10/1789 to Richard Platt, ass.
William, S.C., Beheathland/Behethland, W20803
William, Va., S3097
William, Va., S15024
William, Va., S16671
William, Va., S30306
William O., Dis. No papers. See printed list of 1835, Dist. of Columbia, also War of 1812 flat files. No service is given.
Zachariah, Md., N.C., Rachel, Ctf. 13697
Zachariah, Va., Elizabeth, W341; BLWt.26418-160-55
Zebulon, Ct., Phebe, W5955; BLWt.132-500-Col. Iss. 9/15/1791. No papers

BUTMAN, Benjamin, Cont., Mass., S18334
Benjamin, Mass., Rebecca, W24681
Jacob H., Navy, Mass. Hannah, W18671
Thomas, Mass., N.H. See BOOTMAN
William, Mass., Vt., S15025
BUTNAM, Jacob H., See BUTMAN
BUTRAM, William, N.C., S3100
BUTRICK, Oliver, Cont., Mass., S12389
BUTT, Archibald, Md., N.C., S39252
Barruck/Barrach, Md., S39258
Burduck, Md., BLWt.10974-100-Pvt. Iss. 2/3/1796. No papers. Possibly the same as Barruck Butt, S39258
Edward, Md., BLWt.1072-100. The papers in claim of Zachariah Butt are in this file
Jacob, Va., S39250
Thomas, Md., Mary, W8232; BLWt. 10982-100. Iss. 2/1/1790. No papers
Zachariah, Md., BLWt.1073-100. Papers are on file under Edward Butt, BLWt.1072-100
BUTTEN, Jonathan, Ct., S17870
Luke, Pvt., Va., BLWt.11922 iss. 7/14/1792 to Robt. Means, ass.
BUTTERFIELD, Benjamin, Mass., Sarah, W15612
Elijah, Mass., Hannah, W23716; BLWt.24609-160-55
Henry, N.H., Rachel, W23733
Isaac, Mass., Ruth, R1559
Isaac, Pvt., N.H., BLWt.2949 iss. 3/21/1790 to Joseph Davis, ass.
Isaac, N.H., Orpha, W20805
James, Cont., Mass., N.H., N.Y., S44351
Jesse, Mass., S16676
John, Mass., Susannah, W15623
Jonathan, Mass., Vt., R1558
Joseph, Mass., Elizabeth, BLWt.47969-160-55
Nathaniel, Mass., Esther Campbell former wid., W18852
Oliver, N.H., S12358
Peter, N.H., S12365
Philip, Mass., S30305
Reuben, Mass., BLWt.32213-160-55
Robert, N.H., S12372
Samuel, Vt., R1560
William, N.H., Chloe, W25312; BLWt.26726-160-55
BUTTERFOSS, Andrew, N.J., S4982
BUTTERICK, Edward, R.I., S44355
BUTTERS, Benjamin, Mass., Elizabeth, R1561
William, Mass., S29682
BUTTERTON, Samuel, Va. See BATTERTON
BUTTERWORTH, Freelove, former wid. of Joseph Robinson, R.I. which see
John, R.I., S21094
Noah, R.I., S29048
BUTTERY, William, Pa., S37798

BUTTLES, Abijah, See BUTTOLPH
BUTTOLPH, Abijah, Mass., Olive, W14427
George/Georg, Ct., S37809
BUTTON, Benjamin, Ct., S44352
Daniel, Ct., R.I., R1562
Elias, Ct., Mass., S44711
Elijah, Ct., S17312
Isaiah, Ct., R.I., S21096
John, R.I., S38589
Joseph, R.I., S9638
Levin, Pvt., Md., BLWt.10992 iss. 2/1/1790 to Ann Tootle, Admx., James Williams & Joseph Dawson, Admrs. of James Tootle, deceased, late assnes.
Mary, former wid. of Jonathan Hale, Ct., which see
Nathan, R.I., S45313
Newbury, Ct., R1563
Samuel, Ct., S38587
BUTTONSTONE, Philip, Pvt., Pa., BLWt.9034 iss. 6/22/1792 to John W. Godfrey, ass.
BUTTRICK, Edward, Pvt., R.I., BLWt.2952 iss. 5/8/1790 to Theodosius Fowler, ass.
Oliver, Mass., S12361
Tilly, Mass., S29684
BUTTS, Coggeshall, Navy, R.I., S21097
Esaias, Ct., S37803
John, Ct., Susanna Kirkland, former wid., W26724
Josiah, Ct., Lydia, W14414
Josiah, Ct., Eunice, W20800
Seth, Va., R1564
Sherebiah, Ct., S29674
Thomas, Pvt., Hazen's Regt., BLWt.12801 iss. 4/6/1790
Thomas, Mass., S29681
William, Mass., N.Y., Rachel, W16876
BUXTON, Abijah, Pvt., Md., BLWt. 10956 iss. 3/11/1791 to Abijah Buxton
Ebenezer, Mass., Susannah, W18679
Elijah, Pvt., Md., BLWt.10951 iss. 3/11/1791
James, Mass., BLWt.98-300-Capt. Iss. 3/3/1797. No papers
James, Va., Dis. No papers
John, Mass., S34127
John, Pvt., Pa., BLWt.8992 iss. 12/30/1790
Peter, Ct., Susanna, W17383
Stephen, Mass., S29683
William, Mass., S16681
BUYCE, Thomas, N.Y., See BOYCE
BUYERS, George, Pa., S40768
BUYFORD/BAYFORD, Henry, Pvt., N.Y. BLWt.6831 iss. 1/6/1792
BUYS, James, N.Y., R1565
James, N.Y., Leah, W16203
BUZAN, John, Va., S35800
Philip, Va., S30304
BUZBEE, Jacob, S.C., S32149
BUZBY, Jeremiah, S.C., R1566
John, N.C., R1525
Sherod, S.C., R1416
BUZZEL, Andrew, N.H., BLWt. 2313-100

BUZZELL, Henry, N.H., S45529
James, Mass., S16675
Jonathan, N.H., Martha, W16098
Joseph, N.H., S15329
Noah, N.H., See BUSSELL
Solomon, N.H., Susan, BLWt.7067-160-55
BYAM, Jesse, Mass., Sarah, W18688; BLWt.8165-160-55
John, Mass., Sarah, W23753; BLWt.30590-160-55
BYAN, Samuel, Va., See BYLAND
BYARD/BYERD, Godfrey, N.Y., S44721
BYARLEY, Michael, Va., See BYERLY
BYARS, James, Va., See BYERS
Joseph, Pa., See BYERS
Nathan, N.C., Delphy, W6223; BLWt.30601-160-55
BYBEE, Neilly, Va., Mildred, W8184; BLWt.35827-160-55
Pleasant, Va., Mildred, W18687
BYERD, Godfrey, N.Y. See BYARD
BYERLY, Frederick, Pvt., Pa., BLWt. 9038 iss. 6/20/1789
Jacob, Va., Pa., S22672
Michael, Va., S16065
BYERS, Asamus/Oysel, See BOYERS
Ebenezer, Pa., R1568
Hannah, former wid. of John Bunnell, Cont., which see
James, S.C., Sarah, R1569
James, Va., Lovinia, W8407
Joseph, Pa., R1567
Oysel/Asamus, Pa., See BOYERS
William, Md. Sea Service, S8131
William, S.C., S3112
William, Va., S8130
BYINGTON, Andrew, Vt. See BOYNTON
Ebenezer, Ct., S37814
Isaac, Ct., Elizabeth, W1380; BLWt.6413-160-55
John, Ct., S29051
Justus, Ct., Lucy, W23754
Samuel, Ct., Olive, W15625
Zuba/Zuby, former wid. of William Pratt, Ct., which see
BYLAND, Samuel, Va., Mary, W6221; BLWt.26712-160-55
BYLES, Charles, N.C., S3113
BYMER, George, Pvt., Pa., BLWt. 8930 iss. 1/26/179-
BYNUM, Drury, Pvt., N.C., BLWt. 11969 iss. 6/10/1791 to Abisha/Abishai Thomas, ass.
Drury, N.C., S37815
John, Ga., S3111
Tapley, N.C., S15031
BYRAM, Ebenezer, Cont., Mass., S29052
James, Mass., Deborah, W25320; BLWt.12569-160-55
John, N.C., See BYROM
Jonathan, Cont., Mass., S18754
Melzar, Mass., Alice/Else Allen, former wid., W695; BLWt.13867-160-55
Seth, Mass., BLWt.916-100
Susan, former wid. of William Hurt, N.C., which see
BYRD, Andrew, Va., S5311
Baylor, Va., Nancy, R853
Francis, Va., R1573

BYRD (continued)
Francis Otway, Va., Anna, W6219
Henry, Va., S30307, BLWt.28609-160-55
Jesse, N.C., R1574
John, Md., See BOARD
John, Va., S35807
Thomas, N.C., Nancy, W8183; BLWt.56942-160-55
Thomas, Pvt., Va., BLWt.11952 iss. 7/7/1792 to Robert Means, ass.
William, N.C., Va., S12403
William, Va., S39266
BYRN/BYRNE, Lawrence, Pa., Elizabeth, R1576
BYRNE, Abigail, former wid of Steven/Stephen Rogers, Ct., which see
John, Pa., S2408
John, Va., S35808
BYRNE/BURNS, John, Va., S42108
BYRNES, James, Md., Pa., S39267
John, Cont., Pa., Va., Esther, W6224
William, Pvt., Pa., BLWt.9001 iss. 3/21/179- to Robert Thompson
BYRNS, John, See BYRNES
BYROD, Frederick, Pa., S22154
BYROM/BYRON, John, N.C., R1571 combined with file of John, N.C., S30910
BYRUM, Jacob, N.C., S4983
James, Va., S8132
Lawrence, N.C., S9125
BYRUN, Benjamin, N.J., Va., Mary Squire, former wid., R10027
BYUM, Jesse, Mass., See BYAM
BYXBE, Ebenezer, Mass., Hannah, W6220

C

CAAR, Thomas, N.J., See CARR
CABBAGE, Adam, Va., S2111
John, Va., S3134
CABELL
Nicholas, Va., R1577
Samuel J., Va., BLWt.446-450-Lt. Col. iss. 1/21/1796. No papers
CABLE, Abner, Ct., S10438
Jacob, Pvt., Pa., BLWt.9113 iss. 1/20/1797 to Jacob Cable
Nathaniel, Mass., See CORB
CABLES, Zebulon, N.Y., Catharine, W9380
CACKLER, Christian, Pa., S42641
CADE, John, Del., S35815
CADEY, Samuel, Pvt., Ct., BLWt. 5571 iss. 8/20/1790
CADLE, Thomas, N.C., R1579
CADMAN, George, N.Y., Desire, W17592; BLWt.28661-160-55
CADWELL, Aaron, Ct., Mary, W17595
John, Ct., S12442
John, Ct., S44365
Jonathan, Mass., S40042
Phineas, Cont., Ct., S37822; BLWt.16127-160-55
Reuben, Pvt., Ct., BLWt.5639 iss. 10/12/1789 to John P. Wyllys
Reuben, Ct., Rebecca, W18875
Tempy/Tamar, former wid. of Nathaniel Noyes, which see
Theodore, Ct., Lucy, W22738; BLWt. 27627-160-55
CADY, Abijah, Ct., S37818
Abner, Ct., Molly, W17589
Darius, Pvt., Crane's Cont. Artillery, Mass., BLWt.3990 iss. 1/28/1790
David, N.Y., S29053
Ebenezer, N.Y., Chloe, W16524
Elias, R.I., R1580
Elijah, Ct., S31591
Elijah, N.Y., S9149
Elisha, Ct., S10433
Elisha, N.Y., Ruth, W16205
Elizabeth, former wid. of Obadiah Daley, Cont. Ct., which see
Ezra, Ct., S12434
Isaac, Cont., N.H., S39271
Jeremiah, Cont., Mass., S19582
Jeremiah, Mass., S15032
John, Vt., Sarah, W3511; BLWt. 19533-160-55
Jonathan, Ct., S17323
Jonathan, Ct., S18344
Jonathan, Vt., S12427
Luther, Ct., N.Y., S28670
Manasseh, Ct., Navy, Elizabeth, W20838
Nedabiah, Ct., S12436
Palmer, Hazen's Regt., BLWt.494-200-Lt. Iss. 10/12/1790. No papers
Phineas, Pvt., Mass., BLWt.3975 iss. 3/25/1790
Phinehas, Mass., Hannah, W16523
Reuben, Ct., Cont., S44729
Richard, Ct., Allice, W10571; BLWt.26991-160-55

CADY (continued)
Richard, Mass., Lois, BLWt.36244-160-55
Squire, Ct., Cont., Abiah, W1553; BLWt.31891-160-55
Warren, Mass., S44369
William, Ct., Mass., S39276
Zadock, Ct., Lucy, W1714
CAESAR, Jesse, Mass., BLWt.915-100
CAEZAR, Levi (colored), R.I., S39269
CAGLE, Jacob, N.C., Sarah, R1581
CAHAIL, Cornelius, Pvt., Ct., BLWt. 5600 iss. 10/22/1789 to Theodosius Fowler
CAHALL, John, N.Y., S44731
CAHILL, Elisha, Md., R1582
James, Md., S8186
John, Cont., N.J. res. & agency, S34153
John, Pvt., N.Y., BLWt.6911 iss. 11/3/1791 to Richard Colliar ass.
CAHO, Thomas, Pvt., Md., BLWt.11065 iss. 12/18/1794 to Henry Purdy, ass.
CAHOE/KAHOE, Thomas, Md., S34681
CAHOON, Charles, Del., Pa., R1584
CAHOON/COHOON, Gamaliel, Mass., Azuba, W14446
Joel, N.C., Naomi, W8576
CAHOONE, Joseph, R.I., Margaret, W20837; BLWt. 26997-160-55
CAILE, William, N.C., Ruth, W5241; BLWt.42263-160-55
CAILES, John, Va., S8165
CAIN, Benjamin, N.Y., S34080, alias Benjamin D. Brooker, which see
Daniel, Cont. Mass., S34145
David, Cont., Mass. See CANE
Dennis, N.J., S40794
Edward, N.Y., Bethiah, R1585
James, N.C., Mary, W5891
James, N.C., R1586
John, Mass. Sea Service, War of 1812, Mary, R1588; BLWt.77022-160-55
John, Pa. Sea Service, Va., Margaret, R1587
John, S.C., Susannah/Susan, W3510
John, Va., S9307
John, Va., S17873
Michael, S.C., Mary Harris/Harriss former wid., W7665
Nathaniel, N.J., Mary, W843
Nicholas, Cont., S36960
Patrick, S.C., S1185
Peter Warren, N.Y., Angelica, W16525
Samuel, Mass., Jemima, W22723
William, Va., S39286
CAINE, John, N.Y., War of 1812, Sophia, W18849; BLWt.5441-160-55
CAINS, Richard, Va., S35822
CAIRLL, David, N.J. Sea Service, Pa. Sea Service, S34154
CAISEY, John, Va., Mary, See CASEY
CAKE, Lewis, Va., See CLARK
Philip, N.C., See COKE
CALAHAN, Daniel, Pa. See CALLAHAN
CALDER, James, Mass., S21107
CALDER, John, Ga., See CAULDER
Robert, Navy, S34146
William, Ct., Cont., Mass., S44725
William, Sgt., Hazen's Regt., BLWt 12874 iss. 12/12/1789 to Theodosius Fowler, ass.
CALDERWOOD, James, Va., BLWt.407-300-Capt. iss. 10/20/1796 to Adam Calderwood, etc., heirs; also recorded under BLWt.2594 iss.10/20/1796 to Adam Calderwood, heir at law of James Calderwood, subject, nevertheless, to the dower of Rachel Watson, late wid. of James Calderwood. No papers
John, Navy, Mass., S20315
Thomas, Cont., Mass., S36952
CALDWELL, Alexander, Va., R1589
Andrew, enl. res. not shown; BLWt. 363-300- Hospital Mate. Iss. 6/27/1789. No papers. Also recorded as above under BLWt.2506
David, N.C., S21104
George, Va., S3141
James, N.H., S45625
James, N.H., Mary, R1592
James, N.C., Sarah, W4150; BLWt. 26834-160-55
James, Matross, Pa., BLWt.9214 iss. 11/27/1790
James, S.C., S8163
James, Va., Indian War of 1790, Meeke, W9770
John, Mass., N.Y., S44364
John, N.H., S30317
John, N.C., Elizabeth, See COLWELL
John, S.C., Elender, W8580
John, Va., S9146
John, Va., S16344
John, Va., S20328
John T., N.H., Lucy, W10301
Joseph, Cont., Mass., S9151
Joseph, S.C., Tabitha, R1595; BLWt.61335-160-55
Matthew, Pvt., N.Y., BLWt.6978 iss 7/22/1790 to Thos. Tillotson, ass
Medford, Mass., S39277
Moses, Mass., S34144
Philip, N.Y., Nancy, W18861; BLWt. 6979-100-Pvt. Iss. 2/14/1791 to Joseph Caldwell, ass. No papers. BLWt.85-60-55
Robert, N.C., S.C., R1593
Robert, Pa., S35814
Robert, Pa., Mary, W4650
Robert, Pa., BLWt.437-300-Capt. iss. 7/16/1792. No papers
Samuel, N.H., S45662
Samuel, N.C., Elizabeth, W528; BLWt.36661-160-55
Samuel, Va., S32168
Tempy, former wid. of Nathaniel Noyes, R.I., which see
Thomas, Cont., Mass., S34140
Thomas, Pvt., Pa., BLWt.9131 iss. 9/23/179- to John Hoge, ass.
William, Cont., N.H., Vt., S12441
William, Pa., S35821
William Pa., S44732
William, S.C., S1648
William, S.C., S2116
William, S.C., Margaret, W22727;
CALDWELL (continued)
BLWt.17887-160-55
William, Va., S35823
William, Va., Eleanor, W345
CALEB Henry, N.Y., Susan, R1596
CALEF, Ebenezer Winter, Navy, Mass. res. & agency, S34169
James, N.H., R1597
Joseph, N.H., S9127
CALHOON, Andrew, Va., BLWt.12027 iss. 3/2/1799 to John Brahan, ass.
George, Pa., Va., S30914
Hugh, Pa., S34151
John, Mass., S19584
John, S.C., Sarah, W8597
Joseph, N.C., R1599
Samuel, Mass., Lucy, W18854
Samuel, Pa., S2413
CALHOUN, Andrew, Pa., Indian Wars, Anna Maria, R1598
James, Cont., Mass., War of 1812, Isabella, W1140; BLWt.9445-160-55
John, S.C., Violet, W9777
Samuel, Mass., See CALHOON
William, Va., S2113
CALIFF, Stephen, Pvt. "in the invalids", BLWt.12955 iss. 4/2/1790
CALKIN, Eli, Cont., N.Y., Sally, W1139; BLWt.33563-160-55
Moses, Ct., N.Y., S12426
Nathaniel Skiff, Ct., Sea Service, S15034
Solomon, Ct., N.H., Vt., S23568
CALKINS, Daniel, Ct., N.Y., S44374
Darius, Ct., Abigail, W6648
Durkee, Ct. Cea Service, S22156
Elizabeth, former wid. of Silas Winans, Cont., N.Y., which see
Frederick, Navy, Ct., Annis, W5056
James, Ct., Esther, W23778
John, Mass., See CORKINS
Jonathan, Mass., See COLKINS XXXX
Nathaniel, Ct., Lois, W16884
CALL, Alexander, Pa., See CAUL
Ebenezer, Green Mt. Boys, Vt., R1600
Hugh, Va., R1602
John, Ct., Lornhannah, See MC CALL
John, Ct., BLWt.1727-100
John, Mass., S34233
Nathaniel, N.H., S15362
Richard, Cont., Va., BLWt.354-400
Samuel, Mass., Esther, W22718
Silas, N.H., War of 1812, Mary, W16521
Thomas M., Va., See CAUL
William, Privateer, N.C., R1603
CALLAGHAN, John, Pvt., Pa., BLWt. 9095 iss. 6/20/1789
John, Pvt., Pa., BLWt.9225 iss. 11/5/1789
Patrick, Pa., Eve, W3177
Thomas, Cont., N.Y., Nancy, R7299 She was pensioned as former wid. of John Monk, which see
CALLAHAM, David, Va., S16695
CALLAHAN, Daniel, Pa., S40815; BLWt.964-100
Dennis, Md., S42118
Edward, Sgt. "in Proctor's Artillery," Pa., BLWt.9194 iss.

CALLAHAN (continued)
5/20/1793 to Thos. E. Newton, ass.
James, Va., R1604
Joel, N.C., S21110
John, Pvt., Md., BLWt.11109 iss. 1/8/1796 to George Ponsonby, ass.
John, N.C., S2417
Josias, N.C., Elizabeth, S31600; BLWt.71077-160-55
Patrick, Pvt. Pa., BLWt.9156 iss. 3/11/1791
Samuel, Pvt., Md., BLWt.11070 iss. 2/7/1790
Volentine, N.C., R20338
CALLAMOR, Anthony, Pvt., Mass., BLWt.3908 iss. 3/25/1791 to David Quinton, ass.
CALLAWAY, Chesley, Va., S30917
Dudley, Va., S39282
James, Va., Susan, W9771
Lowder, Del., S35810
Micajah, Va., See CALLOWAY
Peter, N.C., Elizabeth, W10564; BLWt.52464-160-55
Samuel, Va., See CALLOWAY
CALLENDER, John, Col. Crane's Regt. of Artillery, BLWt.356-200-Lt. Iss. 3/31/1794. No papers
John, Cont., Md., S40792
Samuel, Cont. Pa., Va., S40814
Silas, Cont. Mass., S34147
Stephen, Mass., R1605
Thomas, N.C., BLWt.482-300-Capt. iss. 8/12/1789. No papers
William, Mass., Catharine F. W., W23774
CALLEY, Edward, Mass., S39275; BLWt.1009-100
Jonathan, Mass., N.H., Elizabeth, W22716
William, Mass., S17878
CALLIHAN, Michael, Pvt., Md., BLWt. 11046 iss. 8/14/1795 to Francis Sherrard, ass.
CALLIS, George, Va., Elizabeth, W14444; BLWt.26637-160-55
William, Va., S16683
William Overton, Lt., Va., Anne, W6645; BLWt.459-200 iss. 11/10/1791. No papers on BLWt. BLWts. 1613 & 2484 iss. for 200 acres same date to William O'Callis.
CALLOWAY, Chesley, Va., See CALLAWAY
James, Va., Susan, See CALLAWAY
Micajah, Va., Franky, W6646; BLWt. 26660-160-55
Samuel, Va., S35813
CALMES, George, Va., S8172
Marquis, Va., S12674
William, Va., S9303
CALNAN, Thomas, N.H., Sarah, R1606
CALVERT, Jonathan, Va., half pay R18
Joseph, Va., half pay, R12980
Spencer, Va., S30312
CALVIN, Ruth, former wid. of George Corwine, N.J., which see
CALVITT, Joseph, Va., half pay, See CALVERT
CALWELL Medford, Pvt., Mass.,

CALWELL (continued)
BLWt.3943 iss. 12/2/1789
CAMBE, James, N.Y., S44372
CAMBELL, Silvanus, Mass., Rhoda, R1642
CAMBRAY, Louis Antoine Jean Baptiste, Comte de, Cont., French, BLWt.2270-450
CAMBRIDGE, John, Cont., R.I., S45666
CAMBRY, James, Pvt., N.Y., BLWt. 6895 iss. 9/13/1791 to Benj. Crosby, ass.
CAMEL, Thomas (colored), Va., R1609
CAMER, Abraham, N.Y., Elizabeth Poucher, former wid. W3593; BLWt.7213-160-55
CAMERON, Alexander, Pa., S6771
Allen, N.C., Isabella, R1610
Charles, Va., Rachel, W6624, 3 Cont. letters in file
James, Va., Ann C, See CAMRON
John, N.C., Jane, W1711
Murdock or Birdie CAMPBELL, N.Y. S46426
CAMM, William, Pvt., Md., BLWt. 11101 iss. 11/29/1790 to Bazil Shaw, Admr.
CAMMACK, John, Va., Nancy, R1612
William, Va., S24944
CAMMELL, John, Pa., See Alice CAMPBELL
CAMMET, Silas, Mass., N.H., Martha, W15630
Thomas, N.H., Billacha, W18866
CAMMETT, Samuel, N.H., S36950
Thomas, Mass., Nabby, W23775
CAMP, Abel, Ct., Cont., S12435
Amos, N.H., S45322
Asa, Mass., N.Y., Sea Service, S22673
Benjamin, Navy, R.I., Privateer, Sarah, W14450; BLWt.27628-160-55 BLWt.34947-160-55
Casper, Cont., Pa., Christiana, W3220
Casper, Pvt. "in Moylan's Dragoons", Pa., BLWt.9191 iss. 2/25/1791 to Charles Colver, ass
Chauncy, Ct., R1613
Edward, N.C., R1614
Elias, Ct., S17326
Ephraim, Ct., S12432
Ezra, Ct., S15033
Israel, Ct., S16689
James, Ct., Elizabeth, R1615
Joel, no res. shown. Dis. No papers
John, Ct., Annis, W23762; BLWt. 31457-160-55
John, Ct., R1616
John, Cont., Ct., S37819
John, Pa., S2418
John, Pa., Margaret, W2177. Her 1st husb., Michael Slauterback was a pensioner, which see
John, Pvt., Sheldon's Dragoons, Ct., BLWt.5651 iss. 9/4/1790
John, Va., S40041
John, Va., R1617
John H., Va., R13000

CAMP (continued)
Joseph, Ga., see War of 1812 under BLWt.40059-80-55 for service in 1796-97
Joseph, Mass., Privateer, R1618
Manoah, Ct., Clarissa, W1818
Matthias, Sgt. "in Proctor's Artillery," Pa. BLWt.9199 iss. 6/29/1789 to M. McConnell, ass.
Mial, Navy, Ct., see Thaddeus BEACH
Morris D., Cont. N.J., S34172
Nicholas, Mass., N.Y., S12446
Polly, former wid. of Isaac Learned, which see
Rejoice, Ct., S16066
Samuel, Ct., S23148
Samuel, Ct., S38590
Samuel G. or J., Ct., R1619
Sharp, Pvt., Ct., or Va., BLWt. 5610-Ct.; BLWt.11996-Va., iss. 11/30/1795 to Timothy Pitkin
Sharp, Ct., S37821
Thomas, Va., Martha, W3938
William, Va., half pay, R13001
CAMPBELL, Abraham, S.C., S21108
Alexander, Cont., Mary, W23781
Alexander, Cont., N.Y., Pa., S40813
Alexander, Pa., Va., Jane, W4648
Andrew, Mass., R1621
Andrew, Navy, Del., Naomi, W20828
Andrew, Pvt., N.Y., BLWt.6929 iss. 12/22/179-
Andrew, N.Y., S34161
Anthony, Va., S9138
Archibald, Ct., S12448
Archibald, N.Y., Eliza, W1138; BLWt.13434-160-55
Archibald, Pa., Jane, W18878
Archibald, Pa., BLWt.435-200 Lt. iss. 7/7/1789 to Thomas Campbell, executor of last will of A.C. No papers
Archibald, S.C., R1622
Archibald, Pvt., Va., BLWt.12021 iss. 2/9/1796 to Robert Camp, ass.
Archibald, Va., Elizabeth, W4647
Archibald, Va., Sarah S., W10572; BLWt.61301-160-55
Archibald, Va., BLWt.421-100
Betsey, former wid. of John Seelye, Ct., which see
Burdie, Pvt., N.Y., BLWt.6963 iss. 1/12/1791 to Wm. I. Vreedenburgh, ass.
Burdie, N.Y., See Murdock CAMERON
Charles, Va., S9136
Charles, Va., S12686
Christopher, N.J., Martha, W3508
Daniel, Mass., Lucy Elliott, former wid., W16113
Daniel, N.H., Ann, W1820; BLWt. 7205-160-55
Daniel, N.C., R1624
Daniel, Pa., application for BL rejected
Daniel Richardson, Mass., Maria, W25389; BLWt.1863-100; BLWt. 56513-60-55
David, Cont., N.H., Rachel,W18859

CAMPBELL, David, N.Y., S24101
David, S.C., Lucinda, R1637
David, Vt., Susan Locke, former wid., BLWt.61127-160-55
David, Va., S1504
David S., Indian Wars 1791-1794. See 1812 flat files
Dennis, Va., BLWt.66-100
Donald, N.Y., BLWt.364-500-Col. Iss. 7/20/1790 to Donald Campbell. Also recorded under BLWt.2507. No papers
Duncan, Pvt., N.Y., BLWt.6968 iss. 11/11/1791 to Samuel Broome, ass.
Duncan, N.Y., Dis.; BLWt.345-200-Lt. in Livingston's Regt. iss. 3/29/1792. Also recorded as above under BLWt.2447. No papers
Duncan, N.C., Barbara, R1625; BLWt.10921-160-55
Duncan, Va., R1626
Ellis, N.J., Nancy, W406
Eneas/Enos, Md.,Elizabeth Ann, R1627
Enos, N.J., S35205
Esther, former wid. of Nathaniel Butterfield, Mass., which see
George, Pvt., N.J., BLWt.8199 iss. 6/11/1789 to Matthias Denman, ass.
George, N.C., S8166
George, N.C., S31590
George, S.C., S10436
George, ---, BLWt.2062-450-Surgeon
Henry, Va., Sarah, W6615
Isaac, Ct., S12406
Jacob, R.I., S29057
James, Cont., Mass., Sabra, W23772
James, Cont., N.H., War of 1812, S29056
James, Del., BLWt.405-200-Lt. Iss. 5/30/1789. No papers
James, Pvt., Mass., BLWt.3851 iss. 4/1/1790
James, Mass., S9134
James, Mass., S15035
James, Mass., Anna, W22728
James, Mass., Prudence, R1640
James, N.H., S10423
James, N.Y., S2110
James, N.C., S1647
James, N.C., S30310
James, N.C., Gennant/Gennett, W344
James, N.C., Isabella, W6619
James, Pa., S9302
James, Pa., Cassandana, W3387; BLWt.422-200-Lt. Iss. 1/29/1790 No papers
James, R.I., Elizabeth, W25393
James, S.C., Indian Wars, Sally, R1644
James, Va., Elizabeth, W25384; BLWt.34507-160-55
James, Va., Dis. No papers
Jeremiah, Mass., S34139
Jeremiah, N.C., S3131
Jeremiah, Pvt., Pa., BLWt.9161 iss. 1/14/1791
Jesse, N.H., Eleanor, W22719
John, Ct., S17321

CAMPBELL (continued
John, Cont., N.Y., Ann W. Hutchings, former wid., R5447
John, Cont., N.Y., Art., BLWt.397-200. Iss. 2/3/1792. No papers
John, Del., Mary, W3178
John, Ga., S42640
John, Pvt., "in the Invalid Regt." BLWt.12933 iss. 6/29/1789 to Matthew McConnell, ass.
John, Pvt., Md., BLWt.11052 iss. 2/28/1794 to Josiah Witter, ass.
John, Md., S30915
John, Mass., S4994. His wid. pensioned as Asenath Campbell, former wid. of James Miller, R.I., which see
John, Mass., S12428
John, Mass., Hannah Mason, former wid., W15064
John, Mass., Hannah, W18864
John, Mass., N.H., Betsey, W23759
John, Mass., N.H., Privateer, S12425
John, N.J., N.Y., Catharine, W20834; BLWt.30698-160-55
John, N.J., Pa., S40816
John, Pvt., N.Y., BLWt.6896 iss. 8/27/1790 to Nicholas Fish, ass.
John, N.Y., S12667
John, N.C., Corah/Cora, W6616
John, N.C., Euphemia, W18860
John, N.C., BLWt.487-200-Lt. Iss. 6/1/1792. No papers
John, Pvt., Pa., BLWt.9103 iss. 4/1/1791
John, Pa., S2112
John, Pa., S9155
John, Pa., Ailce/Elsey, W6618
John, Pa., Mary, W9772; BLWt. 32235-160-55
John, Pa., Elizabeth, R1628
John, Pa., R1635
John, S.C., Va., Sarah, W10579; BLWt.101563-160-55
John, S.C., R1634
John, Va., S3128
John, Va., S9160
John, Va., S35820
John, Va., S35824
John, Va., Sarah, W1713; BLWt. 26821-160-55
John, Va., Frances, W18869
Joseph, Pa., R1636
Joseph, Va., S2414
Joshua, Mass., Hannah, W6622; BLWts.31441-160-55 & 36659-160-55
Kenneth, Pvt., N.Y., BLWt.6975 iss. 7/29/1790 to Ab^{m} Hardenberg, ass.
Kenneth, N.Y., S44726
Lawrence, Va., S30912
Lewis, Pvt., N.J., BLWt.8232 iss. 5/19/1789 to John Campbell
McDonald, N.J., Pa., S2109
Moses, N.J., Catharine, W6623
Noble, Ct., Janet, W16888
Owen, Va., Jemima, W6620
Patrick, N.Y., R1639
Richard, N.C., S.C., Rachel, W343
Richard, Va., BLWt.347-450-Lt.Col.

CAMPBELL (continued)
Iss. 2/22/1799 to heirs; also recorded under BLWt.2500-450-Lt. Col. iss. 2/22/1799 to Joseph, John, Richard, & Jona. Campbell, surviving ch. & heirs.
Robert, Ct., S44373
Robert, Cont., Mass., Sarah, W23767
Robert, Mass., Asenath, R1623
Robert, N.H., S45624
Robert, N.J., S34174; BLWt.8181-100-Pvt. Iss. 8/28/1792. No papers
Robert, N.J., Mary, W3334
Robert, N.Y., S23565
Robert, N.C., S3129
Robert, Pa., Rachel, W3071; BLWt.947-100
Robert, Pa., Martha, W4913
Robert, Va., Katy, W6621
Samuel, Mass., R1643
Samuel, Pa., Mary, W3072
Samuel, Pa., R12939
Solomon, N.C., S39287
Spencer, N.J., Sarah Reynolds, former wid., R8718
Sylvenus, Mass., Rhoba, see CAMBELL
Thomas, Cont., Md., S40040
Thomas, Cont., Pa., S40791
Thomas, Cont., Va., S39294
Thomas, Mass., Rebecca, W25376; BLWt.9414-160-55
Thomas, N.Y., R1646
Thomas, N.C., S8169
Thomas, Pvt., Pa., BLWt.9189 iss. 3/10/1795 to Robert Hunter, ass.
Thomas, Pa., BLWt.413-300-Capt. iss. 7/7/1789. No papers
Thomas, Pa. res., Dis. No papers
Thomas, Va., See CAMEL
Thomas, Va., R1647 & R1648
Walter, N.C., R1649
William, Cont., N.H., Hannah, W23761
William, Cont., N.J., S35826; BLWt.1754-100
William, Cont., Pa., Susan, W3386
William, N.J., S967
William, N.J., S9126
William, N.Y., S12404
William, N.Y., S23145
William, N.C., S32162
William, N.C., R1652
William, Pvt., Pa., BLWt.9195 iss. 2/2/1792
William, Pa., S3130
William, Pa., S42117
William, Pa., Rachel, W9773
William, Pa., Martha, R1638
William, S.C., Elizabeth B., W9774
William, Va., S34675
William, Va., Sarah, W3770
William, Va., U.S.A. in 1799, Susan, W4149; BLWt.1903-300
William, Va., Sarah, W6617
William, Va., Jane, R1632
Winny, former wid. of James Harrison, N.C., which see

CAMPEN, James, N.C., BLWt.485-300-Capt. iss. 4/18/1796. No papers
Joseph, N.C., S8171
CAMPER, John, Va., S9142
Tilman, Va., Dinah, W8573
CAMPERNELL, William, Cont., Mass., S17325
CAMPFIELD, Jabez, Cont., N.J., S34163; BLWt.401-400-Surg. Iss. 9/3/1790. No papers
John, N.J., Apphia, W6937; BLWt. 14527-160-55
Napthali, Pvt., Mass., BLWt.4530 iss. 5/24/1790
Nathaniel, Cont., N.J., S34160
CAMPHIRE, Thomas, Pvt., Md., BLWt.11086 iss. 1/11/1794 or 6 to Joshua Ward, ass.
CAMRON, Alexander, N.Y., S34164
James, Va., Ann C., W3767
William, Va., S8188
CANADA, David, Cont., Ct., Lucy, W25388; BLWt.26313-160-55
CANADAY, John, Va., See CANNADAY
Leroy, Va., S9156
Merriday/Meredith, Va., R1655
Thomas, N.C., Nancy, W3561; BLWt.38506-160-55
CANADY, John, Sea Service, Va., SEE CANNADAY
John, Va., BLWt.2091-100
William, Va., S39272
CANAFAX, William, Va., S19233
CANAHAN, Nathan, Mass. See CARNEHAN
CANDE, Zaccheus, Ct., S29062
CANDEE, Job, Ct., S13036
Nehemiah, Ct., R1656
Samuel, Ct., S17327
CANDEL, Absalom, N.C., Elizabeth, W10589
CANDER, Zacheus, Ct., See CANDE
CANDLE, Absalom, N.C., See CANDEL
CANDLER, William, Va., S9159
CANE, David, Cont., Mass., S36958
Hugh, Md., S34676
James, Pa., See O'KAIN
CANEDY, Noble, Mass., S18760
CANELY, William J., Pa., S23564
CANFIELD, Amon, N.Y., Meribah, W20832
Andrew, Ct., Eunice, R1658
Azariah, Pvt., Ct., BLWt.5601 iss. 2/23/1797 to Ithamar Canfield
Daniel, Cont., Ct., S29696
Daniel, N.Y., Elizabeth, W9768
Dennis, N.Y., Polly, W6636; BLWt.222-160-55 &6956-100
Ebenezer, N.Y., Elizabeth, see below
Ebenezer, N.Y., Polly, W5245; BLWt.35843-160-55. A wid. Elizabeth also allowed pension but dropped from the rolls.
Elijah, Cont., Ct., S2106
Elijah, Cont., N.Y., S45316
Isaiah, Ct., service on Lake Champlain, Anne, W16883. 5 contemp. ltrs. in file
Israel, Cont., Vt., S40801
Israel, N.J., S3142

CANFIELD (continued)
Ithamar, Ct., Betsey, R1657
John, N.Y., S10425
Oliver, Ct., Cont., S23566
Philo, Ct., Mary P., R1659
Samuel, Ct., Cont., S15772
Timothy, Pvt., N.Y., BLWt.6953 iss. 3/16/1792 to Ebenezer Purdy, ass.
Timothy, N.Y., S45317
CANINE, Peter, N.J., S1182
CANION, William, N.J., See CANNION
CANK, Garret, Pvt., Va., Lee's Legion, BLWts.11990 & 12964 iss. 1/19/1792
CANN, Augustine, Md., BLWt.2059-100
John, Pvt., N.Y., BLWt.6989 iss. 11/13/1792 to Heil Peck, ass.
William, Va., R1660
CANNADAY/CANNADY
John, Va., Mary, R1654
John, Va., See CANADY
William, Va., See CANADY
CANNAN, James, N.Y., R1661
John, Pvt., of Invalids, Pa., BLWt.12945 iss. 7/27/1789 to Richard Platt, ass.
CANNDAY, John, Va., Sea Service, S9161
CANNEDAY, Andrew, Pa., See KENEDY
CANNER, Daniel, Cont., Mass., S45321
CANNEY, John, Cont., N.H., Charity, W15993
CANNION, William, N.J., Martha, W842
CANNON, Cornelius, Mass., Mary, W15632
Ebenezer, Cont., Mass., S34137
Ellis, Va., S39284
Furna, N.C., Sarah, R1663
Henry, Va., S8187
Ira, Ct., Mass., Olive, W18855
James, S.C., S16684
James, S.C., S32166
Jesse, Va. Sea Service, R19, Va. half pay
John, S.C., S30309
Luke, Va., S46373; BLWt.462-200-Lt. Iss. 7/5/1799 to James Taylor, ass. No papers
Luke, Va., Sea Service. No papers See Va. State Auditor's Report dated 3/14/1832 on file in Rev. War Claim of Jesse Cannon, R19; not luke Cannon, S46373
Mary, former wid. of John Heminger, Ct., which see
Nancy, former wid. of James McPherson, S.C., W5896
Nathaniel, S.C., S31594
Philip, Mass., Phebe, W18803
Pugh, N.C., S3139
Thomas, N.Y., Abigail, W18867; BLWt.6962-100-Sgt. Iss. 8/30/1790. No papers
William, N.C., Va.?, R1665
William, S.C., S2114
William, Va., R1664
William, Va., Elizabeth, W5897
CANOUS, John, French troops, see John NICHOLS

CANTER, John, Va., S42642
CANTERBURY, John, Va., R1667
Sid, Va. Alias James M. Franklin, which see
CANTINE/CANTON
George, Cont., Mass., Mary, W25380; BLWt.3980 iss. 1789. No papers. BLWt.332-60-55
John, N.Y., Ann, BLWt.52776-160-55
CANTWELL, John, S.C., Va., Jane, R1668
CAPE, John, Va., S30916
CAPELL, John, Mass., Mary, W23768
CAPEN, Abijah, Mass., Rachel, W18876
Ebenezer, Cont.,Mass. res. & agency, S34141
Ebenezer, Pvt., Mass., BLWt.3951 iss. 3/7/1792 to John Heaton
Ebenezer, Mass., S39273
James, Pvt., Mass., BLWt.3904 iss. 10/22/1790 to Richard Platt, ass.
James, Mass., S29686
James, Mass., S29688
James, Mass., S34156
John, Mass., S12431
Purchase, Ct., Theodosia, R1670
Samuel, Cont., Mass., S29064
Samuel, Mass., Lydia, BLWt.19717-160-55
Timothy, Ct., S30313
CAPERON, Ephraim, Mass., Hannah, See CAPRON
CAPERS, Jim (colored), S.C., Milley, R1669
CAPES, William, Va., See COPIS
CAPIN, Thomas, Pvt., Hazen's Regt., BLWt. 12915 iss. 2/10/1797 to Noah Amherst Phelps, ass.
CAPLE, Samuel, Md., R1671
CAPPS, Dempsey, N.C., Sarah, W22735
Greenberry, S.C., See CAPS
Mathew, N.C res. in 1858, Minty, R1673
William, N.C., S6772
William, N.C., Va., S8133
CAPRON, Blandfield, R.I., S29771
Elisha, Mass., S45320
Ephraim, Mass., Hannah, W901; BLWt 9077-160-55
Greene, R.I., S.C., Lydia, W639; BLWt.26071-160-55
Jeremiah, Ct., Jerusha, R1674; BLWt.2453-100
Jonathan, Mass., Lois, W20841
Joseph, R.I., Esther, W638; BLWt. 26170-160-55
Nathan, Mass., N.H., S9128
Seth, Mass., Eunice, W22741
CAPS, Greenbery, S.C., S21105
CAPSHAW, Catharine, former wid. of Johan Sensenbach, Va. which see
CAPWELL, James, R.I., See COPWELL
Jeremiah, R.I., See COPWELL
William, R.I., S28671
CAR, Ebenezer, N.J., Esther, W16890
CARADINE, Thomas, N.C., Pa., Elizabeth, W20836

CARAKER/KARCHER
George, N.C., Francis, W9488; BLWt.26310-160-55
CARAWAY, William, S.C., See CARRAWAY
CARBACH, Peter, Cont., Pa., S16691
CARBEE, Joel, Cont., Mass., Lois, R16102
CARBERRY, Francis, N.J., S40806; BLWt.8218-Pvt. Iss. 12/7/1798. No papers
Henry, Pa., Sybella, See CARBERY
Peter, Md. agency, see CASBURY
CARBERY, Henry, Pa., Sybella, W23776; BLWt.415-300-Capt. Iss. 12/20/1791. No papers
CARBURY, Francis, N.J., See CARBERRY
CARD, Elisha, Ct., Cont., R1676
Jemima, former wid. of George Congdon, R.I., which see
Jonathan, Vt., S12447
Joseph, R.I., Sarah, W20835
Joshua, R.I., S21106
Nathaniel, Mass. Sea Service, War of 1812, S34171
Peleg, Mass., R.I., Vt., S12418
Potter, Pvt., R.I., BLWt.3038 iss. 2/24/1800. No papers. No means of knowing whether this soldier and pensioner, Potter Card, S38595, were the same
Potter, R.I., S38595
Sarah, former wid. of John Frees/Frieze, Mass., which see
Shadrach, R.I., Betsey, W25396; BLWt.26524-160-55
Stephen, R.I., Lydia, W22722
Thomas, Vt., S10430
William, Navy, Privateer, R.I. res. & agency, Abby, W15626
CARDEN, Youen/Edwin, Cont., Va., S8178
CARDER, John, Va., See CORDER
Sanford, Cont., Va., Sarah, W9377; BLWt.36504-160-55
William, Va., S17872
CARDIFF, John, Cont., Pa., Dis. No papers
Thomas, Pvt., Md., BLWt.11125 iss. 2/7/1790
CARDONA, John, Va., BLWt.11998 iss. 2/23/1792
CARDOZO, David N., S.C., Sarah, W20830
CARDWELL, James, Va., Sarah, W2998
Perrin, Va., Elizabeth, W346; BLWt.31447-160-55
Robert, Va., S8179
William, Cont., Va., Famariah, W8590
William, Pvt., Va., BLWt.12017 iss. 5/5/1790 to Wm. I. Vreedenburgh, ass.
Wiltshire, Va., Mary, W6632
CARE, Tunis, Pvt., N.Y., BLWt. 7006 iss. 6/17/1791 to H. Fisher, Admr.
CAREL, John, Ct., S12416
William, Md., See CARROL
CAREY, Absalom, N.Y., Temperance, W17590

CAREY (continued)
Aphia, former wid. of Isaac Bolster, Cont., Mass., which see
Arthur, Pvt., Pa., BLWt.9126 iss. 3/22/1791 to Alex. Power, ass.
Caleb, Mass., Mary, W14445
Ebenezer P., Vt., S15197
Ephraim, Cont., Mass., S12443
Francis, Mass., See COREY
Jabez, Ct., Mary, W25399; BLWt. 18952-160-55, See CARY
James, Pvt., Lamb's Artillery N.Y., BLWt.7010 iss. 8/4/1790 to Peter DeWitt, ass.
John, Ct., See CARY
John, Cont., Pa., S40793
Joseph, Pvt., Mass., BLWt.3870 iss. 9/13/1792
Joshua, Mass., BLWt.845-100
Josiah, Cont., Mass., S34680
Levi, Ct., Cont., S8157; Reg. 317141-1855
Lewis, Pvt., Crane's Cont. Artillery, Mass., BLWt.3987 iss. 12/27/1796
Luther, Cont., Mass., See CARY
Michael, Md., S40039
Simeon, Mass., See COREY
CARGILE, Thomas, N.C., See CARGILL
William, N.C., R1686
CARGILL, David, Mass., S28668
Thomas, N.C., Mourning, W6896; BLWt.33757-160-55
Zachariah, N.Y., Esther, R1685
CARGLE, John, N.C., Va., R1687
CARHART, Jacob, N.Y., S12437
John, N.J., S2419
Robert, N.J., Mary, W3941; BLWt.9415-160-55
Thomas, N.J., S483
Thomas, N.J., Mary, W3768
CARHARTT, John, N.Y., Hannah, W16895
CARICK, Adam, S.C., S18341
CARIES, Peter, N.J., Catharine, W18871; BLWt.26706-160-55
CARIGAN, John, Pvt., Hazen's Regt., BLWt.12920 iss. 12/20/1798
CARIL, David, N.J., See CAIRLL
CARITHERS, Robert, S.C., Mary, W23779
William, S.C., Mary, W6628
CARKHUFF, Henry, N.J., R1688
CARL, Elijah, N.J., S17324
John, Mass., Lois, W23764
CARLE, Ephraim T., N.J., S3121
John, N.J., Sarah, W2523; BLWt.27574-160-55
Joseph, Mass., Margery, See CARLL
CARLETON
Benjamin, Mass., N.H. See CARLTON
David, Mass., S18758
Ebenezer, Cont., N.H., S46428
Ebenezer, Pvt., N.H., BLWt. 3015 iss. 4/13/1796 to John Smith, ass.
Edmund, Mass., Abigail Johnson, former wid., W1295. She was also pensioned for service of

CARLETON (continued)
other husband, Seth Johnson, Ct., which see
Edward, Pa., S40800
Enoch, Cont., N.H., Clarissa, W1222; BLWt.93544-160-55
Ezra, N.H., See CARLTON
Jesse, Mass., Nancy, W16887; BLWt.6013-160-55
John, N.H., S12419
John, Pvt., Pa., BLWt.9141 iss. 6/29/1789 to M. McConnell, ass.
John, Pa., Mary, W3221
Michael, Mass., See CARLTON
Michael, Mass., S29054
Moses, Mass., S29697; BLWt.348-200-Lt. Iss. 8/1/1796 to Benjamin Dana, ass. No papers
Osgood, Corps of Invalids, BLWt. 359-200-Lt. Iss. ---/29/1789. No papers
Peter, Mass., Azubah, W25394; BLWt.34508-160-55.
Samuel, Cont., Mass., Sarah, W22732
Samuel, Mass., S29691
Samuel, Mass., Sarah, See CARLTON
Samuel, Mass., BLWt.360-450-Lt. Col. Iss. 4/11/1796 to Abraham Foster, ass. No papers
Thomas, Cont., Mass., S17874
Timothy, Cont., Mass., S45622
Timothy, Mass., Rebecca, See CARLTON
CARLEY, Albert, N.Y., Hannah, R1694
Jonathan, Cont., Mass., Vt. res. & agency 1818, S38592
Jonathan, Pvt., Crane's Cont. Artillery, Mass., BLWt.3982 iss. 12/2/1791 to Martin Kingsley
Jonathan, N.Y., S23152
Joseph, Pvt., N.Y., BLWt.6898 iss. 12/15/1796 or 1790 to Eliz. Sill and others
Joseph, N.Y., S44371
William, Vt., S15771
CARLILE, Francis, S.C., See CARLISLE
James, S.C., Margaret, W8583; BLWt.61091-160-55
James, P., Va., S30320
William, Mass., Deborah, W23763
William, Pa., S3135
CARLIN, William, Md., Mary, W3937
CARLISLE, Benjamin, Cont., Md., S42115
Daniel, N.H., Lydia, W15629; BLWt.26730-160-55
Francis, S.C., Margaret, W10576
Hosea, S.C., 4th U.S. Inf. in 1802, Margaret, R1697
James, Mass., Sally, W526; BLWt. 36664-160-55
James, S.C., Margaret, See CARLILE
John, Hazen's Regt., BLWt.493-300-Capt. Iss. 4/20/1792 to John Carlisle. No papers
John, Mass., N.H., Abigail, W527; BLWt.29745-160-55
Joseph, Mass., S19230
William, Mass., Lovinah, W27393; BLWt. 17723-160-55

CARLISLE (continued)
William, N.C., Va., Nancy, R1698
CARLL, Ebenezer, Mass., S36957
John, Mass., Mary, W16206
Joseph, Mass., Margery, R1689
William, Mass., S16688
CARLON, William, Pvt., Md., BLWt.11044 iss. 9/2/1789
CARLOW, Daniel, Cont., Mass., S34165
Daniel, Pvt., Mass., BLWt.3922 iss. 5/6/1797 to Marlbry Turner
CARLTON, Ambrose, Ga., N.C., S32160
Benjamin, Mass., S21101
Benjamin, Mass., N.H., R1690
Benoni, Va., S8154
Christopher, Va., Jane, W6638
David, Mass., See CARLETON
David, N.H., Ruth, W15633
David, N.C., S8170
Edward, N.H., S45623
Edward, Pa., See CARLETON
Enoch, Cont., N.H., Clarissa, See CARLETON
Ezra, Pvt., N.H., BLWt.3013 iss. 7/6/1796 to James Witham, ass.
Ezra, N.H., S44730
Humphrey, Va., S9308
John, ----, See CHARLTON
John, Mass., Ann Moore, former wid., W8278; BLWt.9498-160-55
Jonathan, Mass., Eunice, W17594
Kimball, Mass.(?), N.H. Sea Service, Elizabeth, R1691
Lewis, N.C., Va., Elizabeth, R1692
Michael, Mass., S4987
Moses, Mass., See CARLETON
Moses, Mass., Mary, W23760; BLWt.24765-160-55
Richard, Ct., S39280
Samuel, Cont., Mass. See CARLETON
Samuel, Mass., See CARLETON
Samuel, Mass., Sarah, W15631
Thomas, Cont., Mass., See CARLETON
Timothy, Mass., Rebecca, W16891; BLWt.9532-160-55
Woodman, Cont., N.H., Rebecca, W22725; BLWt.34667-160-55
CARLY, Mary, former wid. of Daniel Holt, Mass., which see
Simeon, N.Y., R1695
CARMACK, Cornelius, Va., S2420
John, N.C., Mary, W3772; BLWt. 19817-160-55
John, Va., R21699
William, Va., S9139
CARMAN, Abraham, N.Y., Eve, W23765
Andrew, Pvt., "in Moylan's Dragoons", Pa., BLWt.9183 iss. 10/28/1789 to M. McConnell, ass.
Benjamin, N.J., R1699
Daniel, Pvt., N.J., BLWt.8200 iss. 7/7/1795 to Jonathan Rhea, ass.
Daniel, N.Y., S10434
Henry, N.Y., Dis. No papers
Isaac, N.Y. See CARMER
James, Pvt., Md., BLWts.12870 & 14094 iss. 1/28/1795 to Francis Sherrard, ass. of Nathaniel

CARMAN (continued)
Crawford, Admr
John, Ct., S12409
John, N.Y., Galetta, W16885
John, N.Y., Elizabeth, W16893
John, N.Y., R1702
John, N.C., R1703
John J., N.J., R1705
Mary, former wid. of Samuel Coolidge, Mass., which see
Nathaniel, N.J., Elizabeth, R1707
Samuel, N.J., S965
Samuel, N.Y., Polly, W6904
Thomas, N.J., Nancy, W407; BLWt. 290-60-55
Willet, Pvt., N.Y., BLWt.6950 iss. 11/4/1792 to Wm. Ely, ass.
CARMER, Abraham, N.J., Sarah, W1552 BLWt.8169-100. No papers
Isaac, N.J., S8164
CARMICAL, Duncan, See CARMICHAEL
CARMICHAEL
Duncan, N.C., S41467
John, Pa., S26989
Thomas, Pa., See CARMICLE
CARMICHAL/CARMICKELE, John, Pa., S31595
CARMICLE, Thomas, Pa., S16696
CARMILE, Colothel, Pvt., Md., BLWt. 11093 iss. 11/29/1790 to Michael Loyd, Admr
CARMODY/CARMOODY, John, Pa., Sea Service, S2108
CARN, Catharine, former wid. of John Hurteigh, N.Y. Which see
Daniel, Cont., N.C., S21682
Lewis, S.C., S21681
CARNAGEY, William, Pa., Mary, W5886; BLWt.39227-160-55
CARNAHAN, Andrew, N.C., Sarah, W8577; BLWt.51882-160-55
James, Pa., BLWt.417-300-Capt. iss. 9/26/1792. No papers
Nathan, Mass., Lydia, BLWt.36242-160-55
William, Cont., Pa., See KERNACHAN
William, Pvt., Pa., BLWt.9133 iss. 4/13/1791
CARNALL, Patrick, Va., S8156
CARNAN, James, ----, Phila. res. in 1791, Elizabeth, R1701
Nathaniel, N.J., Elizabeth, See CARMAN
CARNE, John, Southern Hospital, BLWt.503-400-Asst. Apothecary. Iss. 5/3/1793 to Ebenezer Thayer, ass. No papers
CARNER, Anthony, Navy, N.C., Privateer, Catherine, W2753
John, N.C., Elizabeth, See CARNEY
Philip, N.Y., Anna, R1708
CARNES, Ephraim, N.J., S966. Son of Lt. John Carnes
John, Pvt., Va., BLWts.11986 & 12089 iss. 12/13/1791 to Francis Graves, ass.
Joshua, Va., R1709
Matthias, Pvt., N.J., BLWt.8226 iss. 6/20/1789
Patrick, Va., BLWt.2266-300
Philip, N.C., S3117
Robert, Pvt., Md., BLWt.11034

CARNES (continued
iss. 8/14/1795 to Francis Sherrard, ass.
William, Pa., See CARNY
CARNEY, Barnabas, Pvt., Pa., BLWt. 9084 iss. 3/13/179- to James Bennet, ass.
John, N.C., Elizabeth, R1710
John, Pa., Mary E., W6639
John, Va., S16070
Patrick, Cont., Pa., S40795
Patrick, Pvt., Md., BLWts.12872 & 14097 iss. 1/28/1795 to Francis Sherrard, ass. of Elizabeth Cooley, Admx.
Patrick, Pvt., Va., Leo's Legion, BLWts.11995 & 14000 iss. 11/2/1792 to Robert Means, ass.
Thomas, Pvt., Lamb's Artillery later transferred to Corps of Invalids, BLWt.12939 iss. 10/15/1789 to James Reynolds, ass.
Thomas, Pvt., Md., BLWt.11050 iss. 10/14/1795 to Henry Davis, ass.
Thomas, Md., S35203
Thomas, Va., R1711
William, Va., Rosanna, W18874
CARNINE, Andrew, Va., Lydia, See CONINE
Edward, Pvt., N.J., BLWt.8191 iss. 6/11/1789 to Jonathan Dayton, ass.
Jeremiah, Va., BLWt.12010-100-Pvt. iss. 12/27/1794. No papers
Peter, N.J. See CANINE
CARNS, Godfrey, Pa., S46432; BLWt. 241-100
John, N.J., S2115
CARNY, William, Pvt. "in Proctor's Artillery", Pa., BLWt.9211 iss. 7/9/1789
CAROTHERS, James, N.C., S10428
John, N.C., Va. (or Pa.), S8182
John, Pa., S40804
Robert, N.C., See CARROTHERS
Thomas, N.C., S35809
CARPANTER, Philip, N.Y., Mary Bersil, former wid., W14275; BLWt.100550-160-55
CARPENTER, Abel, Cont., R.I., S21680
Abiel, Cont., Mass., S12449
Allen, Ct., Cont., S44307
Amos, Va., Margaret, W5239; BLWt.26301-160-55
Barnard, N.Y., Phebe, R1716
Benjamin, Mass., S19232
Benjamin, N.H., Privateer, S16687
Benjamin, N.Y., Margaret, W25392
Benjamin, N.C., Sarah, W5242
Benjamin, R.I., S21684
Benjamin, Va., S32156
Christopher, Pvt., Va., BLWt. 11994 iss. 4/21/1796 to James Morrison, ass.
Comfort, Ct., S12422
Comfort, Ct., S37823
Daniel, Ct., Cont., S42116
Daniel, Mass., Mary, W18870
David, Ct., S29063
David, Ct., Asubah, W16892

CARPENTER (continued)
David, Va., R1712
Ebenezer, N.H., S16686
Elias, Ct., S21683
Elijah, Ct., Sarah Sargeant, former wid., R9204
Eliphalet, Ct., S23151
Ephraim, Ct., S12670
Esther, former wid. of Clement Stoddard, Ct., which see
Ezra, Cont., Mass., Mary, W15628
Greenwood, Cont., N.H., Hannah, W6630
Hope, N.J., Phebe, W18850
Isaac, N.C., S8168
Isaiah, Ct., S28672
Israel, Ct., S30315
James, N.C., Sarah, R1717
Jeremiah, N.Y., R1713
Jesse, Mass., S9143
Jesse, Va., S9309
John, Ct., S15371
John, Cont., Ky. res. in 1818 and Ind. in 1828, S35812
John, Cont., Mass., S22157
John, Mass., Abigail, W10580; BLWt.39487-160-55
John, R.I., S21102
John, Va., S8160
Jonathan, Mass., Cont., Vt., Olive, W18873
Joseph, Ct., S12411
Joseph, R.I., S12421
Joshua, Cont., Ct., S45319
Lewis, Mass., Mary Ann, W26782
Matthew, N.Y., S23153
Nathan, Mass., R1715
Nathan, N.H., S19231
Nathaniel, Ct., Elfrida, W20839
Nathaniel, N.H., S34148
Nehemiah, N.Y., BLWt.395-150-Ensign. Iss. 1/4/1791. No papers
Phebe, former wid. of Solomon Eaton, Ct., which see
Philip, N.Y., see CARPANTER
Remember, Mass., Phebe Peck, former wid., W26855
Robert, Mass., BLWt.1354-100
Rufus, Mass., Peggy, W20831
Samuel, N.Y., Anna, W641; BLWt. 26087-160-55 & 34509-160-55
Samuel, Va., Peggy, W6631
Simeon, Ct., R1718
Simeon, Mass., S29694
Thomas, N.H., S28667
Thomas, N.J., R1717 1/2
Thomas, N.Y., Martha, W18877; BLWt.28585-160-55
Timothy, Ct., S12675; BLWt.26546-160-55
Timothy, Vt., Polly, W15627; BLWt.6433-160-55
Uriah, Ct., Eliphal, W25379
Warren, N.Y., Jerusha, W16886
William, Sgt., Sheldon's Dragoons Ct., BLWt.5647 iss. 9/24/1790
William, Cont., Ct., S37820
William, Cont., N.H., S10426
William, Mass., S15367
William, Va., Mary, R1714
CARPER, John, Va., S37825
CARQUILE, Wm., N.C., See CARGILE
CARR, Benjamin, R.I., S9312

CARR (continued)
Benjamin, R.I., Mary, W23756
Caleb, R.I., S38594
Clement, Ct., S38597
David, Mass., Mercy Corey, former wid., W23859. Her last husband, Philip Corey was pensioned, which see
Ebenezer, Ct., S45318
Ebenezer, N.J., Esther, See CAR
Ebenezer, R.I., S21685
George, N.C., Va., S16693
Gideon, Va., S3119
Hezekiah, Md., Edith Parsons, W3509; BLWt.563-100
Jacob, Cont., N.H., S12410
James, Cont., N.H., S45560; BLWt.324-400-Major. Iss. 12/31/1799 to James Carr. No papers
James, N.H., See KARR
James, N.J., Julia Ann Clark, former wid., R1721
James, N.Y., Margaret, W16522
James, Pvt., BLWt.11999 iss. 7/7/1792 to Robert Means, ass.
James, Va., S32157
James, Va., S32159
Jesse, Mass., S12408
John, Del., Dis. No papers
John, Md., S35204
John, Md., Margaret Long, former widow, W9507
John, N.J., R1720
John, N.Y., S29055
John, R.I., Mary, W1551; BLWt. 26442-160-55
John, Va., S39274
John Baxter, Mass., Navy, Susannah Grindle, former wid., W23165
John F., Va., S3118
Jonathan, Cont., Mass., Catharine, W1817
Joseph, Mass., Elizabeth, W22724
Joseph, R.I., S9311
Levi, Mass., Betsey, W9378; BLWt. 26610-160-55
Matthew, Pvt., Pa., BLWt.9116 iss. 9/11/1789
Meekins, Va., S8137
Moses, N.C., S8141
Nathan, N.H., Polly, W1223; BLWt.6276-160-55
Peter, N.J., Hester, See KARR
Robert, Ct., S44724
Robert, Cont., N.H., S46027
Robert, N.C., S8778
Robert, Pa., S21678
Robert, R.I., See CARSE
Robert, Va., S16071
Robert R., N.Y., Rej.168347-1855
Samuel, Mass., BLWt.333-400-Major iss. 8/24/1796 to Samuel Tenny, ass. No papers
Samuel, Mass., Mary, W14437
Solomon, N.C., Sarah, W5893
Stephen, S.C., Juliana, W9379
Thomas, Cont., N.H., Bethiah, W16101
Thomas, Cont., N.H., Elizabeth, W23771
Thomas, N.J., S12673

CARR (continued)
Thomas, Va., N.W. Indian War, Anna, R12966; BLWt.92652-160-55
William, Ct., S39289. Margaret Carr, widow of above, received pension as former wid. of Wm. Brown, Cont. Pa., which see
William, Mass., S36953; BLWt.910-100
William, N.H., Ann, W15880
William, N.Y., S12445
William, N.Y., S22674
William, N.Y., S44723
William, N.C., S1896
William, N.C., S8138
William, S.C., See KERR
William, S.C., Elizabeth, R1719
William, Va., S39288
CARRANCE, William, Va., R1738 1/2
CARRAWAY, William, S.C., Elizabeth R1725
CARREGEN, Gilbert, N.Y., S27587
CARREL Aaron, Mass., Sally, W18858
George, Md., S42138
William, N.Y., War of 1812, Naoma W25395; BLWt.33559-160-55
CARRELL, Aaron, Mass., See CARREL
Benjamin, Cont., Mass., Eleanor, W25387; BLWt.12839-160-55
Daniel, N.C., Hannah, R1726
Hardy, N.C., S41469
James, N.C., Rhoda, W6899; BLWt. 86103-160-55
Jesse, Mass., S39268
William, N.J., S44227
CARRICK, Patrick, Va., S35825
CARRICO, Alexander, Mass., S34679
CARRIEL, Daniel, N.C., Hannah, See CARRELL
CARRIER, Amaziah, Cont., Mass., N.Y., S12438
David, Ct., Rebecca, R1727
Hannah, former wid. of Guy Dodd, Ct., which see
John, Ct., S12429
CARRIGAN, Gilbert, N.Y., See CARREGEN
Henry, Pvt., N.J., BLWt.8225 iss. 10/16/1789 to Lewis Bond, ass.
James, N.C., Jane, R1728
Peter, Pa., S40790
William, N.Y., R1729
William, N.C., S8177
CARRIL, Aaron, Mass., See CARREL
Daniel, N.C., See CARRELL
CARRINGER, Martin, Pa., Molly, W6905; BLWt.1259-100
CARRINGTON, Clement, Cont., Va., S46427; BLWt.475-150-Ensign. Iss. 4/18/1796. No papers
Edward, Cont., Va., Eliza/Elizabeth/Jaquelin, W6635; BLWt.465-450-Lt. Col. Iss. 1/29/1790. No papers
George, N.C., S8185
George, Va., BLWt.474-200-Lt. Iss. 1/21/1800. No papers
Gilbert, N.Y., See CARREGEN
Jesse, Ct., Elizabeth Lewes, former wid., W20429
John, N.J., Mary, See CORRINGTON
Joseph, N.J., S34235

CARRINGTON (continued)
Lemuel, Ct., Abigail Rice, former wid., W17538
Mayo, Va., BLWt.450-300-Capt. Iss. 2/22/1799 to Wm. R. Bernard, ass. No papers
Reverius, Ct., Loly Merrick former wid., W9959; BLWt.17577-160-55
Timothy, N.C., Winney, R1730
CARRIS, Peter, N.J., See CARIES
CARRITHERS, William, Pa., R1789
CARROL, Bartholomew, Va., S35827
David, Pvt., N.J., BLWt.8213 iss. 9/8/1789 to Samuel Rutan, ass.
David, N.J., R1732
Dempsey, N.C., S32161
Dennis, Pa., S2117
Ebenezer, Mass., See CARLL
Hardy, N.C., See CARRELL
John, Pvt., Md., BLWt.11091 iss. 2/1/1790
John, Md., S30913
William, Md., S2107
William, N.C., Keziah, W6640
CARROLL, Benjamin, N.C., Nancy, W10587
Berry, Va., S39270
Daniel, Va., S3132
David, Va., S9144
Dennis, N.C., R1724
Dennis, Pa., See CARROL
Jesse, Mass., See CARRELL
John, Md., Isabella Smith, former wid., W6118
John, S.C., R1733
John, Va., Ann, R1731
Joseph, S.C., Martha, W9778
Malachi, Va., S8180
William, Mass., Hannah, W14440
William, N.Y., War of 1812, See CARREL
William, N.C., S----
CARROTHERS, Robert, N.C., S2416
CARRUTH, John, N.C., S3140
Josiah, Cont., Mass., R1735
CARRUTHERS, John, Pa., BLWt.406-200-Lt. Iss. 1/2/1792. No papers
Samuel, N.C., See CARUTHERS
CARSE/CAR, Robert, R.I., Dis.; BLWt.2127-100
CARSEY, John, Ga., S.C., R1736
CARSHAW, Abraham, Pvt., Pa., BLWt.9140 iss. 1/17/1792
CARSON, Alexander, N.C., R1737
Andrew, N.C., S8173
Benjamin, Pa., S40798
Henry, N.C., S1506
James, Del., S36956
James, Pvt., N.Y., BLWt.6912 iss. 8/12/1790 to John D. Coe, ass.
James, N.Y., Maria/Mary, W25381
James, N.C., S1183
John, Harrison's Artillery, BLWt. 366-200-Lt. Iss. 8/4/1789 to John Barnaby, admr.; also recorded under BLWt.2516. No papers.
John, Pvt., Md., BLWt.11040 iss. 1/21/1794
John, N.C., S9132

CARSON (continued)
John, N.C., Hollon, W18862
John, S.C., S35819
John, Va., S32167
Robert, Pa., R2338
Robert, Va., S3207
Samuel, N.Y., S44366
Samuel, Pa., S42113; BLWt.9086-100. Iss. 3/31/1790
Samuel, Pa., See CAUSTIN
Thomas/John Perkins, N.C., Frances, W2640
Thomas, Pvt., Pa., BLWt.9157 iss. 4/22/1798
Thomas, Va., S31596
Walter, N.C., S.C., Mary, R1738
Walter, Pa., S.C., S32165
William, Pa., S40803
William, S.C., S9305
William, S.C., S30319
William, Va., S17877
CARSWELL, Abner, Mass., N.Y., S12450
David, N.Y., Martha, W6634
Joseph, N.H., Lydia, W22737
CART, John, N.C., S.C., S8139
William, Pa., S39281
CARTER, Aaron (colored) Ct., Rachel, W22726; BLWt.5566 iss. 8/23/1790. No papers
Abijah, Mass., Nancy, W22731
Abraham, Va., R1739
Anthony, Cont., N.Y., Mary, W4911
Arnold, Va., S2118
Barnabas, Va., Rebecca, W713; BLWt.26302-160-55
Benjamin, Ct., Phebe, W1715
Benjamin, N.J., S46430; BLWt. 1730-100
Benjamin, N.Y., R1741
Benjamin, N.C., S46541; BLWt. 480-300-Capt. Iss. 7/30/1792. No papers
Benjamin, ---, d. Chatham, N.C. 1831, R1740
Charles, N.C., S31593
Charles, N.C., Lydia, R1752
Charles, Va., S1649
Charles, Va., S3125
Charles, Va., S10435
Daniel, Cont., Ga., N.C., S.C., S3126
Daniel, N.H., Mary, W23758
David, N.H., Dorcas, W15994
David, N.C., Va., S16335
Edward, Pvt., Ct., BLWt.5575 iss. 8/23/1790
Edward, N.H., S36955
Elihu, Cont., Ct., S12420
Elijah, Mass., S44359
Ephraim, N.C., S8152
Evan, Pvt., Ct., BLWt.5564 iss. 8/23/1790
George, N.J., S34173
Gideon, Cont., Mass., S34166
Giles Landon, Ga. Sela, R1766
Hemen, Ct., S44358
Henry, Va., S12684
Henry, Va., Sarah, W3940
Henry, Va., Nancy, W8536
Henry, Va., Ind. Wars 1793-4,

CARTER (continued)
R1744
Hubbard, N.H., Abigail Andrews, former wid., W23454
Hugh, Va., R1745
Hulsey, Va., S8151
Isaac, Mass., Priscilla, W1023
Isaac, N.C., S8147
Isaac, N.C., Charity, W4912
Isham (colored), S.C., S39293
Ithiel, Ct., Cont., Lois, W17591
Jabez, Cont., Mass., N.Y., S44360
Jacob, N.H., S17876
Jacob, N.C., Pa. service in 1774, R1746
James, Cont., Pa., S34150
James, Md., S8148
James, Mass., S29690
James, N.C., S8146
James, N.C., R1747
James, Va., S8145
James, Va., S9162
James, Va., S21109
James, Va., Eleanor, R1743
James M., Va., See James MC CARTER
Jirah, Cont., Ct., S23147
Job, N.J., S34678
Joel, Mass., Sally, R1755
John, Ct., Susanna, W10565
John, Ct., Lucinda, W20840
John, Cont., Ky. res. 1818; S35817
John, Cont., Vt. res. in 1829; BLWt.1545-100
John, Cont., Mass., S40809
John, Cont. Va., Mourning, R1753. See BLRej. 272650-55
John, N.H., S12665
John, N.H., S37816
John, N.J., Mil., Rej.138633-1855
John, N.Y., R1750
John, Pvt., N.C., BLWts.12048 & 12866 iss. 8/14/1792 to Isaac Cole, ass.
John, N.C., Pa., Elizabeth, W10590
John, N.C., R1749
John, Pa., Helena, W3939; BLWt. 10216-160-55
John, S.C., S16336
John, S.C., Elizabeth, W8587; BLWt.34510-160-55
John (d.1815), S.C., War of 1812, Elizabeth, W22721
John, Va., Caroline Co. res.,S9131
John, Va., Bedford Co. res. 1830, S39285
John, Va., Mourning, BLRej. 272650-55
John B., Va., Elizabeth, Ky. res. in 1832, W8588
John Champ, Va., Harrison's Artillery, BLWt.468-300-Capt. Iss. 8/26/1789. No papers
Jonah, Ct., Tempa Barlow, former widow, W10383; BLWt.113036-160-55
Jonas, Mass., S15368
Joseph, Va., S30321
Joseph, Va., Lucy, W6893; BLWt. 1094-100, & 16-60-55
Joshua, Mass., S29695
Josiah, Mass., Prudence, W23773
Josiah, N.C., Mary, W8187, BLWt. 28547-160-55

CARTER (continued)
Landon, N.C., Elizabeth, W900
Landon, Va., S41471
Luke, Pvt., Md., BLWt.11024 iss. 2/7/1790
Martin, Va., S30911
Michael, Mass., Navy, S45665
Moses (colored), N.C., S41470
Nathan, N.H., Sarah, R1754
Ned, Ct., Eunice, W20850, See Edward Carter CHAPPEL
Nicholas, Va., S46431; BLWt.1704-100
Obadiah, Cont., Va., Judith,W8585
Peter, Pvt., Mass., BLWt.3890 iss. 11/29/1796
Philip, N.C., Sarah, W5895
Philip, Va., S1184
Povall, Va., S8149
Reuben, Ct., Elizabeth Moss, former wid., BLWt.571-100
Richard, N.Y., S28669; BLWt. 19608-160-55
Robert, Va., S31598
Rufus, Ct., Cont., S9208
Samuel, Ct., S10437
Samuel, Pvt., Md., BLWt.11119 iss. 4/18/1797 to James DeBaufre ass.
Samuel, S.C., Va., S1505
Sarah, former wid. of Samuel Litchfield, Cont. Mass., which see
Seth, Pa. res. 1833, R1757
Silas, N.J., Mil., Rej.201872-1855
Silas, S.C., R1758
Solomon, Ct., S18340
Stephen, Ct., S12407
Stephen, Cont., Mass., N.H., S44728
Thaddeus, Cont., Mass., S36954
Thomas, Cont., Va., S40038
Thomas, Pa., Margaret, W10556; BLWt.26987-160-55
Thomas, Va., S8150
Thomas, Va., Betsey, W342
Thomas, Va., Half Pay, R12974
Thomas. His widow applied for pension for service of former husband, Thomas Palmer, Va., which see
Uzzial, N.J., S16069
William, Cont., Mass., See CARTTER
William, Pvt., Md., BLWt.11027 iss. 2/7/1790
William II, Pvt., Md., BLWt.11087 iss. 7/8/1797 to James DeBaufre, ass.
William, Mass., S12414
William, N.C., S3127
William, N.C., Va., S9133
William, N.C., Va., Susanna, W3385; BLWt.26952-160-55
William, Pa., S31592
William, Va., Martha, W3773
William, Va., Sarah, W25391; BLWt.89520-160-55
CARTERET, John, Mass., Nancy, W25390; BLWt.14975-160-55
CARTHELL, Pelatiah, See CORTHELL
CARTLEDGE, James, Ga., S8167

CARTLEDGE (continued)
Samuel, Ga., R1790
CARTLING. Gideon, Pvt., N.H., BLWt.3020 iss. 2/22/1792 to John Peck
CARTMILL, Henry, Va., S29692
CARTRIGHT, Cyrus, Ct., Mary, See CARTWRIGHT
Joseph, N.C., S8161
Robert, N.C., Va., Susanna, See CARTWRIGHT
Toney D., Pvt., Mass., BLWt.3906 iss. 1/20/1796 to Joseph Fosdick ass.
CARTTER, William, Cont., Mass., S12440
CARTWRIGHT, Christopher, Cont., Vt., S44368
Cyrus, Ct., Mary, W6627
Jesse, Cont., Va., See Justinian CARTWRIGHT
Joseph, N.C., See CARTRIGHT
Justinian, Cont., Va., S30316
Lemuel, N.C., R1760
Peter, Va., Christiana, R1759
Robert, N.C., or Va., Susanah, R1761
Solomon, N.J., S4993
Thomas, Cont., Mass., BLWt. 2021-300
CARTY, Clark, Ct., Mabel, see Mabel MC CARTY
Daniel, Pvt., N.J., BLWt.8182 iss. 7/27/1795 to James Christie, ass.
Daniel, N.J., S34178
Isaac, N.J., S34159; BLWt.8174-100. Iss. 6/14/1791
James, Pvt., Md., BLWts.12881 & 14112 iss. 2/24/1795 to Francis Sherrard, ass. of Henry Purdy, Admr.
John, Pvt., N.J., BLWt.8179 iss. 7/27/1795 to James Christie, ass.
John, N.J., S34158
John, Pvt., "in the Artillery Artificers of Pa.," BLWt.12956 iss. 2/14/1791 to Alexander Power, ass.
Matthew, Pvt., Md., BLWt.11103 iss. 12/18/1794 to Henry Purdy ass.
Timothy, Mass., BLWt. rejected
CARTZ, Thomas, Pa., See CURTS
CARUTH, Alexander, N.C., Letitia W9767; BLWt.73541-160-55
CARUTHERS, Elizabeth, former wid. of Wm. Richardson, which see
Hugh, N.C., S16697
James, Va., Margaret, W1224
John, S.C., S32163
Samuel, N.C., Hannah, W5244
William, Pa., See CARRITHERS
William, S.C., See CARITHERS
CARVELL, Henry, Mass., See CARVER
CARVER, Aldric, Cont., Ct., res. & agency, S38596
Asa, Ct., S23150
Christian, N.C., Mary, W27516; BLWt.73542-160-55
Christopher, Pa., R1762

CARVER (continued)
Henry, Mass., Mercy Carvell, W22734
Jabez, Mass., Phebe, W22717
James, Va., S1186
John, Mass., S30318
Joseph, Ct., Tabitha, W20829
Nathaniel, Cont., Ct., Lydia, R1763
Richard, Va., S21679
Rufus, Mass., S29059
William, N.C., S8158
CARWILL, Zachariah, Va.,S9310
CARY, Aaron, Cont., Mass.,S34142
Alexander, Ga., R1679
Anson, Ct., S9148
Caleb, Mass., Mary, See CAREY
Christopher, N.H., Vt., Margaret Kelley, former wid., R5847; BLWt.34593-16-55
Hezekiah, Cont., Ct., S39279; BLWt.33561-160-55
Jabez, Ct., Mary, W25399; BLWt. 18952-160-55
John, Ct., S9730; BLWt.578-100
John D., Md., BLWt.445-200-Lt. Iss. 3/4/1800. No papers
Jonathan, Mass., BLWt.352-200-Lt. Iss. 11/6/1795 to Jeremiah Hill, ass. No papers
Jonathan, Mass., S30311
Joseph, Ct., Sarah, W18865
Joseph, Cont., Mass., S12439
Levi, Ct., Cont., see CAREY
Luther, Cont., Mass., S18755
Michael, R.I., S17322
Nathan, Pa., R1681
Oliver, Ct., Cont., S23149
Peter, Cont., Mass., S34149
Recompense, Mass., S9154
Richard, Mass., Mary, W6612
Samuel, Va. State Troops, R13013, Va. half pay. N.A. Act. #874; see 050029
Saul, Md., R1684
Seth, Mass., S39283
Seth, N.Y., Vt. res. at enlistment, R1682
William, Cont., Mass., S34168
William, Va., S10424
CARYL, John, Mass., Eunice Walker former wid., W5163. Her last husband, Benjamin Walker, Mass. was a pensioner, which see.
CASADAY, James, Va., S8176
CASAR, Jesse, Mass., See CAESAR
CASBER, Jonathan, N.J., Pa., Va., S9163
CASBOLT, Robert, Cont., Pa., Polly, W8575; BLWt.31440-160-55
CASBURY, Peter, Md. agency, S12666
CASE, Aaron, Ct., Abigail, R1764
Abel, Ct., Hartford Co. res. in 1833, S12668
Abel, Cont., Ct., Tioga Co., N.Y. res. in 1818, S44362
Abner, Ct., Hannah, W17588
Adam, R.I., Hannah, W1024; BLWt. 26629-160-55
Asahel, Ct., S16068
Ashbel, Ct., Azubah, R1765
Augustus, N.J., S8136

CASE (continued)
Daniel, N.J., Sarah, R1770
Ebenezer, Navy, Mass. res. & Agency, S34167
Enos, N.Y., R1766
Fithen, Ct., Amrilles, W17586
George, Ct., Cont., S3115
Giles, Ct., Dorcas, W17585
Gillam, N.Y., S44363
Hosea, Ct., Cont., Sarah, W17584
Ichabod, Ct., S31602
Isaac, Mass., R.I., S31599
Isaiah, N.J., N.C., S16692
James, Ct., Lydia, R1767
James, Mass., S12405
James, Pa., S16694
John, N.J., Elizabeth, W405
John, Va., R---, for papers see claim of Wm. Case, BLWt.1826-100
John M., Ct., Abigail, W23770; BLWt.26725-160-55
Joseph, N.C., S41472
Joseph Rue, Orange Co., N.Y. res. during service, Elizabeth Lee, former wid., W6247
Lemuel, Ct., Mary, W9766; BLWt. 93530-160-55
Micah, Ct., Mass., S17328
Nathan, Ct., Cont., S22159
Oliver, Ct., Amy, W17587
Reuben, Ct., R1769
Richard, Ct., Mary, W20833; BLWt. 264-100
Roswell, Ct., S38593
Rufus, Ct., Rachel, W3665; BLWt. 9062-160-55
Stephen, N.Y., R1771
Teunis, N.J., S2415
Timothy, Cont., Mass., S35202
William, Ct., Dis. No papers
William, Ct., Cont., S44361
William, Cont., Pa., Va., Rebecca, W1819; BLWt.36667-160-55
William, Va., BLWt.1826-100. The papers in the claim of John Case are within
CASELDINE, John, Md., Indian Wars, War of 1812, R1778; BLWt.77830-40-50 for 1812 service
CASEWELL, Simeon, Mass. See CASWELL
CASEY, Archibald, Del., Hannah, W9381
Archibald, Va., S39292
Charles, Va., S16067
Christopher, S.C., S16685
Edward, R.I., R1774
Edward, Va., S39291
Henry, Sgt., N.J., BLWt.8183 iss. 9/8/1789 to Samuel Rutan, ass.
Jacob, Cont., Pa., Va., Md.; Cols. Rallings & Stephenson, S42114
James, Pvt., N.Y., BLWt.6986 iss. 7/6/1791 to Carlile Pollock, ass.
James, Va., S9158
John, Ct., R.I., Vt., Abigail, W25378; BLWt.85507-160-55
John, Cont., Va., S30308; BLWt. 770-100
John, N.J., Privateer, S40811
John, Pa. res., Dis. No papers
John, Va. agency, Dis. No papers
John, Va., S3123

CASEY (continued)
John, Va., Mary, W29604
Joseph, Pa., S15364
Levi, S.C., R1777
Mary, former wid. of Joseph Allsop, Md., which see
Nicholas, Va., S9152
Robert, Pvt., N.Y., BLWt.6957 iss. 3/29/1792
Robert, N.Y., Rebecca, W22739
Wanton, R.I.,also under St. Clair, 1788, S21686
William, Pvt., Md., BLWt.11063 iss. 10/6/1794 to Henry Purdy, ass.
William, N.C., S.C., S32158
William, N.C., Va., Mary Kersey, W29906 1/2
CASGROVE, Thomas, Pvt., Pa., BLWt. 9145 iss. 7/3/1789
CASH, Bartlett, Va., Elizabeth, W4649
George, Mass., Navy, S34176
James, Mass., Mary, W14439
James, N.C., Ann, W4151
John, Cont., Mass., S28673
John, Va., Lucy, W5894, born 4/5/1757 Amherst Co., Va.; there at enlist. After war lived there then 13 yrs. Bedford Co., Va., then Elbert Co., Ga. & Henry Co. Ga. in 1832.
John, Va., born 2/1/1760 in Amherst Co., Va.; there at enlistment. In 1832 lived Jackson Co., Ga. where he had been 32 yrs. R----.
Lois, former wid. of Zenas Goodrich, Ct., which see
Peter, N.C., S8142
Peter, Va., R1781
Samuel, Mass., S29689
Samuel, Mass., S36959
Warren, Va., S10431
William, Md., S3120
William, Va., Dorothy/Dolly, R1779
CASHIN, David, Va., See CASHON
CASHMAN, Daniel, Cont., Ct. See CUSHMAN
Eliphalet, Ct., See CUSHMAN
Holmes, Cont., Mass., See CUSHMAN
Judith, former wid. of David Austin, Cont., Mass., which see
CASHON, Burrel, Va., S8181
David, Va., Sarah, R1782
Thomas, Va., Tabitha, W5890
CASHWELL, Henry, Va., S9153
William, Va., Betsey, W3771
CASIER, Benjamin, N.J. See COSIER
CASKY, Joseph, Pa., R1776
CASLAR, Richard, N.Y., Margaret, W6637; BLWt.26707-160-55
CASLER, Adam, N.Y., Maria, W18868
Jacob, N.Y., Mary Catharine, R1786
John, N.Y., S12681
Marks, N.Y., R1785
Nicholas, N.Y., S12424
Richard, N.Y., See CASLAR
CASNER, Adam, Pa., S9141
CASON, Cannon, S.C., S21103
Edward, Va., Ann F., W25383; BLWt. 27630-160-55

CASON (continued)
James, Va., S3124
John, N.C., S8174
John, Va., S8184
Thomas, Va., Nancy, W8574
William, S.C., S16338
William, Va., S9157
William, Va., Sarah, R1672
CASS, Daniel, N.H., Abigail, W16894
John, Mass., R1787
Jonathan, N.H., S46350; BLWt.325-300-Capt. Iss. 3/25/1790. No papers
Moses, Ct., Abia Judd, former wid., W20223
Moses, N.H., Mary, W22733; BLWt. 9491-160-55
Theophilus, Pvt., N.H., BLWt.3008 iss. 2/19/1796 to Wm. S. Thom,ass.
Theophilus, Cont., N.H., Susannah, W22729
CASSADA, John, N.Y., Margaret, W16882
CASSADAY, William, Pvt. "in the Artillery", Pa., BLWt.9202 iss. 11/5/1789
CASSADY, Michael, Va., Indian Wars in Ky., Mary, W6643
Peter, Pvt., N.Y., BLWt.6903 iss. 8/23/1790 to Chas. Newkerk, ass.
Thomas, Ga., R1788
CASSE/CASE, Abel, Pvt., Sheldon's Dragoons, Ct., BLWt.5666 iss. 9/4/1789 to Ezekiel Case
CASSEDY, Edward, Pvt., N.Y., BLWt. 7014 iss. 8/30/1790
Michael, Pvt., Mass., BLWt.3860 iss. 5/2/1780
CASSEL, Abram, Md., Catharine, W2916
Ephraim, S.C., R1792
Ralph, N.C., R1791
CASSELL, Andrew, Pvt., Pa., BLWt. 9213 iss. 8/14/1793 to Jasper Iserloan, ass.
CASSELL, James, Navy, Mass., S30314
CASSELMAN, Christian, N.Y., Barbara, See COSLEMAN
John, N.Y., Catharine, W18944
CASSELS, Thomas, N.C., S41473
CASSETTY, Thomas, Va., S3143
CASSETY, John, N.Y., See CASSADA
Thomas, Va., See CASSETTY
CASSIDY, Michael, Va., See CASSADY
Nicholas, N.Y., S40797
CASSIN, Samuel, Pa., See CAUSTIN
CASSITY, Thomas, S.C., R1793
CASSLER, John, N.Y., See CASLER
CASSON, William, Va., See CASON
CASTEEL, Samuel, Pvt., Pa., BLWt. 9221 iss. 8/20/1791
Samuel, Pa., S40808
Zadock, Pa., Sarah, R1795
CASTEN, John, N.Y., S12677
CASTER, Isaac, N.J., See CASTOR
William, N.Y., See CASTOR
CASTERER, John, N.Y., S12423
CASTERLINE, Jacob, N.J., Eunice, W6644
Joseph, N.J., Peninnah, W2522; BLWt.39481-160-55
Loammi, N.J., Charlotte, R1796

CASTILE, Samuel, Pa., See CASTEEL
CASTILLO, James, Pvt., S.C., BLWts.12059 & 12865 iss. 5/2/1794
CASTILLOE, Miles, N.C., Isabella, W10300; BLWt.95167-160-55
CASTINO, Ramon, Mass., S15036
CASTLE, Bazle/Baswell, Va., S15369
Daniel, N.Y., R1798
Gideon, N.Y., Abigail, W16526
Joel, Ct., S8143
John, N.Y., Lydia, W23834
Robert, Va., Charity, W25377; BLWt.3761-160-55
Samuel, N.C., S8144
William, Va., S44226
CASTLEBERRY, William M., Ga., S16337
CASTLEBURY, Mary, N.C., former wid. of Jonas Hill, which see
Paul, Ga., Nancy, W27664; BLWt. 67529-160-55
CASTLEMAN, Christian, Pvt., N.Y., BLWt.6966 iss. 8/11/1790 to John Joseph Pall, ass.
CASTNER, Thomas, N.C., See COSTNER
CASTOR, Isaac, N.J., S40810
Jacob, Pa., S9140
Philip, Pvt., Pa., BLWt.9155 iss. 11/27/179- to Joseph Pall, ass.
Vincent, Md., Hannah, R1800
William, N.Y., Mary, W14448
CASWELL, Abraham, Mass., S34175
Barnabas, Mass., S18759
Elijah, Cont., Mass., S34155
Ezra, Ct., S34177
Jedediah, Mass., Susanna, W23755
Job, Mass., S34677; BLWt.368-100
Job, Mass., BLWt.369-100
John, Mass., S34162
John, Mass., Hannah, W25397
John, Mass., R1801
John, N.C., Va., S3133
Jonathan, Mass., S34157
Joseph, N.H., Lydia, See CARSWELL
Joshua, Cont., Mass., S44228
Julius, Ct., R1802
Lemuel, Cont., Mass., Deliverance W20826
Nathan, N.H., S15366
Ozias, N.H., S22158
Richard, Cont., Mass., S4988
Samuel, Ct., R1803
Samuel, Navy, Mass., S30918
Simeon, Mass., Rachel, W23782
Squire, Cont., Mass., Deborah Harlow, former wid., W7681; BLWt.7440-160-55
William, Sgt., Mass., BLWt.3947 iss. 2/22/1790 to Richard Platt
William, Mass., Hannah Andrews, W18853
Zebulon, Cont., Mass., Navy, S29060
CATCHUM, Hugh, N.C., S16690
CATE, Andrew, N.H., S45664
Elisha, N.H., S18757
Enoch, N.H., S18756
Neal, N.H., Sally, W1381
Robert, N.C., Sarah, W3769
Samuel, N.H., R1804
Samuel W., N.H., S29693
CATEN, Richard, Mass., S44370
CATER, Abraham, N.Y., S12415
Edward, N.H., S45663
John, N.Y., War of 1812, Elizabeth, See KEADER
CATES, Matthew, N.C., Minty, R1806
CATHCART, James Leander, Navy, Pa., S12413
Joseph, S.C., S3136
Thomas, Mass., S23146
CATHEY, Alexander, N.C., Margaret A., R1807
George, N.C., S16699
CATHON, Binwell, N.C., See Burrel CASHON
CATLETT, David, Va., Ann, R1808
George, Va., Sea Service and Va. Half Pay; Lucy, W2524; BLWt.3962-160-55
Peter, Va., Susan, R1809
Thomas, Va., BLWt.2712-300-Capt. Iss. 1/17/1800 to James Taylor, ass. of John Catlett, heir of T.C. No papers
CATLIN, Abel, Ct., Privateer, S3
David, Ct., Cont., S12430
Eli, Ct., Cont., S40812
Elisha, Ct., Roxanna, R1812
Elizabeth, Ct., wid. of Jacob Catlin, former wid. of Simeon Curtiss, which see
Hezekiah, Ct., Sarah, W18851
Isaac, Ct., S12433
Lewis, Ct., Cont., S17320
Nathan, Ct., Abigail, W20827
Phineas, Cont., Sarah, W18872; BLWt.545-100
Putnam, Ct., Mary/Polly, R1810
Putnam, Fife Major, Ct., BLWt. 5619 iss. 7/8/1790
Roswell, Ct., S39278
Simeon, Ct., Cont., S10432
Timothy, Mass., S16074
CATO, Burrel, S.C., R1813
George, Va., R1814
Henry, N.J., R1815
William, Pvt., Md., BLWts.11042 & 14046 iss. 5/30/1793 to John Cato, Admr.
William, S.C., Susan, R1805
CATOR, William, Pvt., N.Y., BLWt. 6946 iss. 9/27/1790 to James Roe, ass.
CATRON, Peter, Va., S15363
CATT, Philip, Pa., Va., S16072
CATTELL, Jonas, N.J., S2421
CATTERLIN, Jonathan, N.J., S12444
CAUGHEY, John, Pa., See COUGHEY
CAUGHRAN, George, Va. See COUGHRAN
CAUGHRON, Joseph, Va. See COUGHREN
CAUL, Alexander, Pa., Hannah, R1601
Thomas M., Va., S18342
CAULDER, John, Ga., S.C., Winewood F., W8578
CAULFIELD/COPFIELD, James, Pvt., N.Y., BLWt.6897 iss. 7/14/1790 to Richard Platt, ass.
CAULK, Jacob, Del., S37824; BLWt. 1781-100
CAULKINS, Darius, Ct. See CALKINS
Joel, Ct., S23567
Roswell, Ct., Eunice, W4915
CAULLIFLOWER, Michael, Md., R1817
CAURUTHERS, Elizabeth, Va., former wid. of Wm. Richardson, which see
CAUSSIN, Samuel, Pa., Hannah, See CAUSTIN
CAUSTEN, Isaac, Cont., N.Y., S8183
CAUSTIN/CAUSSIN, Samuel, Pa., Hannah, R1818
CAVANAUGH, Edward, Pa., S40805
John, Pa., S40802
CAVANCE, Joseph, Pa., See CAVANEE
CAVANDER, Joseph, Va., S35818
CAVANEE, Joseph, Pa., Catharine, W5240; BLWt.36662-160-55
CAVARLY, John, Ct., Caroline, W17593
CAVE, Benjamin, Va., S3116
Reuben, Va., S8140
William, N.C., S12678
CAVELL, Benjamin, Mass., See COVELL
CAVENAH, Thomas, Pvt., Md., BLWts. 12885 & 14113 iss. 3/25/1795 to Francis Sherrard, ass. of Henry Purdy, Admr
CAVENAUGH, Barney, Pvt., Pa., BLWt.9226 iss. 2/21/1791
Garrett, Pvt., Va., BLWt.11989 iss. --/--/----
Patrick, Pa., S40796
CAVENDER, Charles, Cont., Mass., N.H., S17875
John, Del., Md., N.C., Margaret, W9776
Joseph, Va., See CAVANDER
Moses, Pvt., N.Y., BLWt.6907 iss. 9/27/1790 to Jacob Tremper, ass.
William, N.C., Margaret See CAVINDER
CAVENDISH, Alice, Va., former wid. of William McClintic, which see
CAVENNAUGH, John, Pvt., Pa., BLWt. 9129 iss. 9/25/1789
CAVENOUGH, Patrick, Pvt., Md., BLWt.11075 iss. 1/8/1794 to George Ponsonly, ass.
CAVETT, Richard, N.C., R1820
CAVILIER, John, N.J., S34152
CAVIN, John, N.C., Jane, W4916
William, Pa., S40807
CAVINDER, William, N.C., Margaret W6903
CAW, Peter, Pa., S10114
CAWDERY, Samuel, Cont., Ct., See COWDERY
CAWDRY, Edward, Ct., Submit, W23863
Samuel, Cont., Ct., See COUDERY
CAWOOD, Berry, N.C., S37817
CAWTHON, Richard, Va., S8175
CAYCAUX, Joseph, N.Y., Mary, W16889
CAYCE, Ambrose, Va., R1821
CAYEAUX, Peter, Lower Canada res. in 1800
CAYORE, Pierre, Pvt., Hazen's Regt., BLWt.12910 iss. 2/4/1790
CAYWOOD, John, N.J., Catharine, W16528
CAZEY, Ambrose, Va., See CAYCE
CEACE, Michael, Pa., War of 1812 See SEASE

CEASER, Jesse, Mass. See CAESAR
CEASOR, James, Pvt., N.J., BLWt. 8195 iss. 3/8/1800 to James Ceasor
John, Pvt., N.J., BLWt.8198 iss. 3/14/1800 to J. & M. Ceasor, heirs
CEASY, John, Pa., S30919
CEATER, William, N.Y., S45449
CECIL, William, Va., Nancy, R1823
CEESE, Michael, Pa., War of 1812, Rebecca, See SEASE
CELORON, Paul Louis, Cont. (foreign), BLWt. Rejected
CENTER, Jonathan, Cont.,Pa.,S42119
Ruth, N.H., former wid. of Joseph Hart, which see
William, N.C., Elizabeth, See SENTELL
William, 1855 Rejected 197-941
CERSEY, George, N.C. See KEARSEY
CERTAIN, John, N.C., Susanna,R1824
CEVEN, Samuel, Pa., See CEVER
CEVER, Samuel. Pa., R1825
CEZAR, Julius,(colored), N.Y.R1822
Levy, R.I. See CAEZAR
Solomon, R.I., S44375
CHACE, Aquila, Mass. See CHASE
Ebenezer, Mass., Hannah, W17617
Ephraim, Mass., Phebe, W22743
Ezekiel, Mass., S30323
Ezra, R.I., S19592
Grindal, R.I., Lucretia,See CHASE
Isaac, Ct., See CHASE
Isaac, Mass. See CHASE
Isaac, R.I., R1826
Jacob, Mass., S8202
Jared, Cont., Mass., See CHASE
Jerahmeel, Mass. See CHASE
Jeremiah, R.I., S12501
Job, Pvt., Mass., BLWt.3926 iss. 4/26/1795 to Leonard Hinds
John, Pvt., N.Y., BLWt.6967 iss.3/16/1792 to Nathaniel Platt, ass.
John, R.I., S29709
Jonathan, N.H., See CHASE
Lot, Ct., Rhoda, See CHASE
Nathaniel, Drummer, Mass., BLWt. 3877 iss. 8/7/1789 to Anspach & Rogers
Nathaniel L., Mass., Lydia,W14456
Samuel, N.H., S39302
Simeon, Mass., R.I., S15374
Stephen, R.I., Hetty,W1554; BLWt. 27571-160-55
CHADBOURN, Levi, Mass., S20681
Silas, Mass., S36965
Simeon, Mass., Elizabeth, W23789; BLWt.15439-160-55
CHADBOURNE, Scamon, Mass., Polly, W715
CHADD, Samuel, Md., S16339
CHADDAIN, John, Va., Sarah, See CHAUDOIN
CHADDERDEON, Lewis, N.Y., R1827
CHADDOCK, Bowman, Mass., Mercy, W23801
CHADOIN, Andrew, Va., Sarah, W2918
John, Va., Sarah, See CHAUDOIN
CHADSEY, Benjamin, Cont., Rebecca, W10615; BLWt.1497-100
Jabez, R.I., Hannah, W16898

CHADSEY (continued)
Timothy, Jr., Pvt., R.I., BLWt. 3042 iss. 12/31/1789
CHADWELL, Harris, Mass., S12466
William, Mass., Privateer, S19242
CHADWICK, Abijah, Pvt., Mass., BLWt.3948 iss. 8/3/1797 to Joseph Fosdick
Caleb, Mass., Dis. No papers
Elihu, N.J., Rebecca; dau. Susannah, W29888
Isaac, Mass., S29704
James, Ct., BLWt.1458-100
James, Mass., Navy, S36966
John, Cont., Mass., S39307; BLWt. 386-300-Capt. Iss. 7/6/1791, also recorded under BLWt.2585. No papers
John, Navy, Mass. agency & res. S34188
John, N.H., Abigail, W22774; BLWt.10294-160-55
John, N.C., Lucinda, W9385; BLWt.75103-160-55
John, R.I., BLWt.1855-100
Joseph, N.H., S45671
Joshua, Mass., Mary, W16103
Levi, N.J., S42643; BLWt.716-300
Nathan, Ct., Vt., 16709
Richard, Ct., S12690
Sylvanus, Ct., N.Y., Susannah Spear, former wid., R13093
Thomas, Mass., S34190; BLWt. 1547-100
William, Md., S40817
William, Mass., S11997
CHAFE, Joel, Ct., See CHAFFEE
Joseph, Mass., R1829
CHAFEE, Abiel, Ct., Hannah, See CHAFFEE
Calvin, Ct., Ruth, See CHAFFEE
Thomas, Ct., S37833
CHAFFEE, Abiel, Ct., Hannah, W25401
Calvin, Ct., Ruth, W16208
Chester, Ct., Caroline, W17599
Clifford, N.H., Vt., Anna Cobb, former wid., W23847
Comfort, Mass., S39304. His wid., Lucy, was pensioned as former wid. of Reuben Hoit, which see
Ephraim, Mass., S29074
Frederick, Ct., S17881
Joel, Ct., Eleanor, W6909; BLWt. 26046-160-55
Jonathan, Ct., Mass., Olive, W22771
Josiah, Ct., Joanna, W18887; BLWt.3531-160-55
Nathaniel, Mass., S39301
Serrill, Ct., Mass., S18346
Shubal, Corp., R.I., BLWt.3044 iss. 4/20/1790
Thomas, Ct., See CHAFEE
William, Ct., Mary, W17619
CHAFFEN, Eles, N.C., S32172
CHAFFEY, Thomas, Pvt., N.J., BLWt.8221 iss. 6/11/1789 to Matthias Denman, ass.
CHAFFIN, Christopher, Va., Mary Ann, W4919
David, Mass., S12687
David, Mass., S39305

CHAFFIN (continued)
Joseph, Mass., S9172
Samuel, Mass., S22171
Simon, Mass., R20135
Stephen, Mass., S34201
Tilla, Mass., Hannah, W15637; BLWt.28563-160-55
CHAFFY, Thomas, N.J., Sarah, W89
CHALFANT, Achsa, former wid. of James Cotton, which see
Solomon, Cont., Va., See CHALFFIN
Thomas, Pa., Mary, R1829 1/2
CHALFFIN, Solomon, Cont., Va., S9166
CHALKER, Jabez, Ct., Hannah, W20852
Jesse, Ct., Elizabeth, W17596
Moses, Ct., S31604
Oliver, Ct., S17329
Samuel, Ct., Damaras, W23802
CHALLES, Thomas, N.H., Elizabeth, W15640
CHALLIS, Christopher, N.H., S45633
Ephraim, N.H., S45667
Nathaniel, Mass., S45668
Thomas, N.H., S16704
Thomas, N.H., Elizabeth, See CHALLES
CHALMERS, Andrew, Pa., Alice, W4152
James, Md., S8199
CHAMBERLAIN, Aaron, Mass., S36963
Aaron, N.J., S968
Benjamin, Mass., S21687
Benjamin, Mass., S44734
Benjamin, Mass., Mary, W23792; BLWt.11411-160-55
Daniel, N.H., S44384
David, Mass., S44727
Ebenezer, Mass., S39300
Ebenezer, N.H., S39299
Elisha, Mass., Susannah, R1835
Ephraim, Ct., BLWt.372-300-Capt. Iss. 2/6/1797. No papers
Ephraim, Mass., S28679
Ephraim, Mass., S36962
Freegift, Pa., S3151
George, Va. Sea Service, Va. half pay. R23
Henry, N.H., See CHAMBERLIN
James, N.H., S45626
James, Pa., Ann, W2756
Jason, N.H., S45627
Jeremiah, Ct., Sarah, W23790; BLWt.3516-160-55
Joel, Ct., Vt., Lovina, W16903
John, Mass., S19241
John, N.J., S2427
John, Vt., Lydia, W25402
Joseph, Mass., S39303
Joseph S., Ct., S37826
Josiah, Mass., Mary, W17608
Lewis, Mass., Rebecca, W8604
Mary, Cont., Vt., former wid. of Nathaniel W. Seaver, which see
Moses, Mass., S36967
Nathaniel, Mass., S18778; BLWt. 36817-160-55
Nathaniel, Mass., Prudence Tenney, former wid., W15963
Nathaniel, Mass., Huldah Perley, former wid., W21950
Pliney, Ct., Martha, See CHAMBERLIN

CHAMBERLAIN (continued)
Richard, Ct. agency, Dis. No papers
Samuel, Pvt., Ct., BLWt.5603 iss. 3/21/1791 to Daniel & Elijah Boardman
Samuel, Ct., S37841
Seth, Pvt., N.J., BLWt.8204 iss. 12/29/1790
Silas, Mass., Susanna, W23788
Stout, Pa., S2119
Swift, Ct., Mary, W1555; BLWt. 30694-160-55
Theodore, Ct., Fanny, W1226; BLWt.31893-160-55
Theodore, Pvt., Sheldon's Light Horse, BLWt.5567 iss. 6/25/1789
Thomas, Mass., Molly, W14475
Thomas, N.H., Judith, W22767
William, Ct., S44733
Wyatt, Ct., Dinah, W17612
CHAMBERLAINE, George, Va. Sea Service, Va. half pay, R23
CHAMBERLANE, Benjamin, Pvt., Mass. BLWt.3963 iss. 4/1/1790
CHAMBERLAYNE, Byrd, Va. Sea Service & Va. half pay, R22
Edward Pye, Va., Sea Service & Va. half pay. R21
CHAMBERLIN, Aaron, Ct., Wealthy, W27394
Aaron, N.J., See CHAMBERLAIN
Benjamin, Mass., S39306
Benjamin, Mass., See CHAMBERLAIN
Calvin, N.H., S39310
Charles, Vt., S23154
David, Mass., See CHAMBERLAIN
David, N.J., R1832
Elias, N.H., Vt., Eunice, W25413; BLWt.86034-160-55
Ephraim, N.H., Mehitable Spaulding, former wid., W25060
Henry, N.H., S38601
Hinds, N.H., Betsey, R1831
Isaac, Ct., Cont., S45836
Jireh, Ct., S22170
John, Cont., N.J., S806
John, Ga., Va., Milly, W6655
John, Mass., Patience, W14461
John, N.J., See CHAMBERLAIN
John, N.J., R1833
Jonas, Md., BLWt.418-100
Joshua, Mass., S34687
Judah, N.Y., Phebe, S9314; BLWt. 31570-160-55
Leander, Ct., S40826
Moses, Cont., N.H., Vt., Abigail, W4652
Nathaniel, Ct., Rhoda, W14474
Nathaniel, Mass., See CHAMBERLAIN
Phineas, Mass., Rebecca, W1716
Pliny, Ct., Martha, S29708; BLWt. 17724-160-55
Russell, Mass., Loisa, W16896
Samuel, Mass., S44735
William, Ct., See CHAMBERLAIN
William, Mass., S12462
William, N.J., Mary, W6658
CHAMBERS, Alexander, N.C., Va., S32173
Benjamin, Mass., Sally, W1383; BLWt.28543-160-55

CHAMBERS (continued)
Benjamin, Pa., Jane, W10302
Cuff (colored), Mass., Bette, W23810
David, Cont., Va., Isabel, W6657; BLWt. 39479-160-55
David, Mass., S34203
David, N.J., S860
Edward, Md., S34684
George, Pvt., Md., BLWt.11081 iss. 1/8/1796 to George Ponsonby, ass.
James, Cont., N.J., S34199
James, Pvt., N.J., BLWt.8220 iss. 8/6/1790
James, N.J., Elizabeth, W6656
James, Pa., S9171
James, Pa., S34683
James, Pa., BLWt.255-100
James, Pa., BLWt.408-500-Col. Iss. 10/24/1789
James, Pvt., Va., BLWt.12016 iss. 1/3/1794 to John Stockdall, ass.
James, Va., S37838
James, Va., Anne, R1836
John, Cont., Mass., Martha, W16899
John, Pvt., Hazen's Regt., BLWt. 12899 iss. 3/24/179- to George Moore, ass.
John, N.J., S34194
John, Pa., S24106
John, Pa., BLWt.---. See papers in claim of James Chambers, BLWt.255-100
John, Va., S1651
John, Va., S34686
John, Va., S35834
Joseph, Pa., S2120
Leonard, Pvt., N.Y., BLWt.6960 iss. 11/5/1789
Leonard, N.Y., S44748
Matthew, Mass., BLWt.340-300-Capt. Iss. 8/26/1790 to Mannassah Cutler, ass. No papers.
Nathaniel, N.C., S32171
Robert, Cont., Va. S8194
Stephen, Pa., BLWt. 434-300-Capt. Iss. 9/12/1789 to Jasper Yates & Robert Coleman, Executors No papers
William, Ct., S42644
William, N.J., Lydia, W16210
William, N.C., S16078
William, Pvt., Pa., BLWt.9099 iss. 11/26/179- to Wm. Lane, ass.
CHAMP, William, Va., S42120
CHAMPE, John, Cont., Va., Phebe, W4153; BLWt.948-100
CHAMPENOIS, William, N.Y., N.Y. res. & agency, S27615
CHAMPION, Daniel, Cont., Green Mt. Boys, Betsey, W9784; BLWt. 14953-160-55
Elisha, Ct., Phebe, W25406
Epaphroditus, Ct., S16711
Ezra, Ct., Lucy, W6662; BLWt. 110-60-55
Henry, Ct., S12463
John, N.C., Temperance, R1840
Reuben, Ct., S38600
Reuben, Ct., Rhoda H., W9783
Salmon, Ct., R1839

CHAMPION (continued)
Samuel, Ct., Cont., S38604
CHAMPLIN, Adam B., R.I., Henrietta, W10605
Caleb, Ct., S15043
Charles, Ct., Mary, W17614
Elisha, N.Y., R1841
George, Cont., R.I., Lydia, W684; BLWt.26589-160-55
Hugh, Pvt., Md., BLWt.11114 iss. 3/16/1794
James, N.J., N.Y., Sally, R1843
Jeffery, R.I., S15041
Jeffrey, R.I., Lydia, W12721
Jonathan, R.I., S12456
Joseph, R.I., S21693
Nathan, Pvt., Crane's Cont. Artillery, Mass., BLWt.3985 iss. 12/31/1789
Newport, R.I., BLWt.1768-100
Oliver, R.I., Thankful, R1844
Samuel, R.I., S40045
Silas, Ct., Cont., S18347
Silas, R.I., Hannah, R1842
Stephen, Ct., S15040
Stephen, Mass., S21111
Thomas, N.Y., R1845
Thomas, R.I., Charity Sparks, former wid., W13919
William, Ct., Privateer, R.I., S12473
William, R.I., Susannah, W9785
York, Pvt., R.I., BLWt.3046 iss. 11/4/1794 to F.D. Tschiffley, Gen. Land Office Cert. 6/12/1817
York, R.I., S34689
CHAMPNEY, Nathan, QM Sgt., Mass., BLWt.3891 iss. 2/18/1796
Nathan, Mass., S44755
CHANCE, Evens, Ct., Vt., S10441
Fanny, N.J., former wid. of Isaac Fisher, which see
James, Va., S39316
Samuel, N.C., R1846
CHANCELLOR, David, Va., S35833
Julius,Va., Alley Utley, former wid., See CHANSLEY
Thomas, Va., S9176
CHANCLER, Julius, Va., See CHANSLEY
CHANDLER, Abiel, N.H., S45670; BLWt.171-100
Ballard, Mass., S44753
Carter B., Va., S8198
Claiborn, Va., S16341
Daniel, Ct., S13035
Daniel, N.C., Frances, W8597
Daniel, S.C., S32175
David, N.C., R1847
David, Va., Mildred, R1851
Ebenezer, Cont., N.H., S40829
Ezekiel, Mass., S34192
Henry, Mass., Sarah, W20856
Hiel, Mass., S18779
Howard/Howland, Mass., S34183
Isaac, Mass., N.H., S30326
Isaac, N.Y., Betsey Duer, former wid., W25549; BLWt.11175-160-55
Jacob, Ct. Sea Service, Navy, Anna, W14462
James, Mass., N.H., Phebe, W18891
James, N.C., S30927
Jeremiah, Mass., Judith, W22760

CHANDLER (continued)
Joel, Cont., Mass., Deborah Glidden, former wid., W23113; BLWt.811-100
John, Ct., Dis. No papers
John, Cont., Mass. res. S34688
John, Cont., Mass., Hannah, W22766
John, Mass., S30921
John, Mass., Margaret, W27395
John, N.H., Mary, W17604
John, S.C., S10443
John, Va., S30925
Jonathan, Ct., Sea Service, Privateer, R21842
Jonathan, N.J.,N.Y., May, W902
Joseph, Ct., S35206
Joseph, Mass., S30324
Joseph, N.H., S9313
Joseph, N.H., R1850. No papers
Joshua, Mass., Lydia, W6660; BLWt.28569-160-55
Josiah, Cont., Ct., Navy, S22167
Josiah, Mass., Margaret, W20855
Josiah, N.H., S45669
Josiah, N.C., Sarah, W159
Littleton, Va., Susan, W4651
Margaret, former wid. of George Purcell, Va., which see
Martin, Corp., N.J., BLWt.8214 iss. 11/16/1789
Martin, N.J., Meribah, W20853
Matthew, N.Y., S10442
Meshach, S.C., Sally, W10616
Mordecai, Ga., S.C., Elizabeth, R1848
Moses, Mass., Sarah, W22762; BLWt.769-100
Moses, N.H., Mary L., W530; BLWt.27608-160-55
Nathan, Cont., Mass., Lucy, W20858
Nathan, Mass., S11999
Nathaniel, Mass., S30922
Peter, Cont., Mass., N.H., Mercey, W23783
Rachel, Mass., former wid. of Paul Sanborn, which see
Robert, Ct., S40399
Robert, Va., Susannah, W8598
Samuel, Mass., Sarah, W1556; BLWt.16153-160-55
Samuel, Mass., Mary, W18883
Samuel, Pvt., N.J., BLWt.8196 iss. 6/11/1789 to Jonathan Dayton, ass
Samuel, N.Y., Phebe, W18896
Samuel, S.C., Jane, W8599; BLWt. 26446-160-55
Shadrack, S.C., S31606
Silas, Mass., S17336
Simeon, Ct., S15774
Stephen, Mass., S44383
Stephen, Mass., Freelove, W15635
Thomas, Mass., S29699
Thomas, N.C., S39314
Thomas, Va. Sea Service, Va. half pay, R24
William, Mass., Joanna, W14454
William, Va., S35832
William, Va., Sally, R1852
Zebedee, Mass., S30327
CHANDLEY, William, Va., Sarah Lovell, former wid., W5027; BLWt.28619-160-55
CHANEY, Abraham, Va., Nancy, W25412; BLWt.28653-160-55
John, Cont., N.C., S.C., S32177
John, Mass., S36961
John, Mass., Abigail, W23791; BLWt.11257-160-55
Joseph, Cont., Mass., Betsey, See CHENEY
Joseph, Mass., Isabella Stevens, former wid., W25081
Nathaniel, Cont., Mass., Hannah, See CHENEY
CHANNON, Thomas, Pvt., Md., BLWt. 11084 iss. 5/4/1797 to James DeBaufre, ass.
CHANPENOIS, William, N.Y., see CHAMPENOIS
CHANSLEY, Julius, Va., Ally Utly, former wid., W8968; BLWt.40927-160-55
CHANY, Enoch, Mass., S40832
CHAPEL, Daniel, Ct., Anna, W17606
Guy, Ct., Delight, W25407
Isaac, Pvt., Mass., BLWt.3880 iss. 8/22/1789
Jedediah, Ct., Lucy, W17597; BLWt.6287-160-55
Samuel, Ct., Abigail, W23785; BLWt.26525-160-55
Samuel, N.C., Polly/Mary, See CHAPPELL
Stephen, Ct., Lucy, W18880; BLWt.26012-160-55
CHAPELL, Noah, Ct., S40825
Russel, Ct., Dis. No papers
CHAPELON, Peter, Pvt., Hazen's Regt., BLWt.12882 iss. 8/10/ 17-- to Richard Platt, ass.
Peter, Fifer, Hazen's Regt., BLWt.12887 iss. 8/7/1789
CHAPEN, Abijah, Mass., Rachel, See CAPEN
CHAPIN, Abel, Mass., Dorcas, W15642
Adams, Cont., Mass., S5004
Anna, former wid. of Daniel Tidd, Cont., Mass., which see
Asa, Ct., S15775
Benjamin, Va. Sea Service, Va. half pay, R25
Benoni, Mass., S15773
Calvin, Mass., S12451
Calvin, Mass., Vt., Huldah, W20864
Charles, Mass., Mary, R1858
David, Ct., Ruth, W22768; BLWt. 2490-160-55
Elias, Ct., Dimis, W2528; BLWt. 27621-160-55
Enoch, Mass., R1854
Frederick, Ct., Lucretia Booth, former wid., W18626
Gad, Mass., S9167
Gideon, Ct., Lydia, W23799
Ichabod, Ct., S15372
Isaac, Mass., S29700
Japhet, Mass., Lucy, W14458
Jesse, Mass., S12457
Joel, Pvt., Mass., BLWt.3897 iss. 7/7/1797
Joel, Mass., S45997
John, Ct., Mass., French & Indian War, War of 1812, Elizabeth, W10601; BLWt.31438-160-55
CHAPIN (continued)
Jonathan, Mass., Abigail, W22755
Joseph, Pvt., Mass., BLWt.3882 iss. 4/1/1790
Joseph, Mass., S18348
Joseph, Mass., S29710
Joseph, Mass., S44381
Leonard, Pvt., N.Y., BLWt.6988 iss. 11/11/1791 to Samuel Broome, ass.
Levi, Pa., S29698
Lewis, Mass., Esther, W23787
Lucius, Mass., Susan, W6674; BLWt.2188-160-55
Luke, Mass., Elizabeth, W22754 Four 1776 ltrs. in file
Nathan, Mass., Lavina, W23812
Oliver, Ct., Elizabeth, W25408
Oliver, Cont., Mass., Mary, W18897
Paul, Mass., S34182
Paul, Mass., R1859
Peter, Mass., S16079
Phinehas, Ct., Cont., N.H., S12701
Samuel, Mass., Susanna, W6912; BLWt.34942-160-55
Samuel, Mass., R1860
Samuel, Mass., BLWt.1556-200
Samuel, Vt., S16706
Seth, R.I., R1861
Sylvanus, Mass., Martha, W18903
Timothy, Cont., Ct., Tacy, W18890
CHAPLIN, Daniel, Cont., Mass., Mary, W23809
David, Mass., S30926
Ebenezer, Ct., S16075
John, Mass., Sea Service, S29073
John, Mass., S40831
Jonathan, Mass., S44382
Joseph, Mass., S45628
Joseph, Mass., Abigail, W23805
Micah, Cont., N.H., S45629
CHAPLINE, Abraham, Va., Va. half pay, R13134
CHAPMAN, Abner, Ct., Cont., S12464
Albert, N.Y. agency, Ct. res., S27612
Albert, Ct., BLWt.367-400-Major. Iss. 6/6/1797 to Nathaniel Satterlee, ass. No papers
Alcowt, Mass., S34594
Amos, N.Y., Betsey, W20849; BLWt.16272-160-55
Amos, Pa., S35828
Asa, Ct., Elizabeth, W17621
Ashbel, Ct., Lydia, W25404
Barnabas, Mass., Dis. No papers
Benjamin, Md., Va., S1798
Benjamin, Mass., Zilpha, R1881; BLWt.19756-160-55
Benjamin, N.H., R1863
Caleb, Ct., Lydia, W16209
Caleb, Ct., Privateer, S15039
Caleb, Mass., S34682
Ceaser, Pvt., Ct., BLWt.5565 iss. 11/2/1791
Collins, Ct., Mary, W17600
Comfort, Ct., S44377
Constant, Ct., Jemima, W6652
Dan, Ct., Cont., Sea Service, S23571
Daniel, Ct., S12682
Daniel, Mass., N.Y., Keziar,

CHAPMAN (continued)
R1876. Margaret Chapman also applied for pension as widow of Daniel. See papers within.
Daniel, Mass., Sea Service, Privateer, Elizabeth, W23803; BLWt.30691-160-55
Daniel, N.Y., Lucretia, W23794
David, Ct., S22161
Ebenezer, Ct., Mary, W17618
Ebenezer, Mass., S12000
Edmund, Va., S16701
Edward, Ct., S38606
Edward, Ct., N.Y., Rebecca, W14466; BLWt.30612-160-55
Eliakim, Ct., S31603
Elias, Vt., S22676
Elijah, Ct., S37848; BLWt.375-300-Capt. Iss. 5/19/1779 to Elijah Chapman. No papers
Elijah, Ct., S44739; BLWt.627-100
Elijah, Ct., Cont., Esther, W17605
Elisha, N.H., S9168
Elizabeth, Ct., former wid. of Joseph Smith, which see
Erasmus, Va., R1867
Ezekiel, Mass., Jerusha, W16529
Ezekiel, N.Y., S23157
Frederik, Ct., S24107
George, Sgt., Pa., BLWt.9207 iss. 7/9/1789
George, Pa., S40822
George, Va., See Geo. Chapman Jr., War of 1812. Rev. War BLWt.36858-120-55
Heman, N.Y., S16076
Henry H., Md., BLWt.444-200-Lt. Iss. 2/11/1791. No papers
Isaac, Va., Elizabeth Whitaker former wid., W3483; BLWt.10245-160-55
Isaac, Va., R1869
Israel, Vt., Ct., Navy, R1870
Jacob, Va., S19237
James, Ct., S37831. Ellen Turney former wid., was pensioned as former wid. of first husband, Samuel Squires, Ct. which see
James, Ct., S37835
James, Va., R1871
Jason, Ct., Mary, R1877
Jedediah, Ct., S12691
Jehiel, N.Y., R1872
John, Ct., S24108
John, Mass., S29701
John, Mass., S34189; BLWt. 791-100
John, N.C., Leanna, W18895, erroneously called Joseph
John, Va., Lucy B., W905
John, Va., Va. half pay, R13115
John H., Va., S3148
Joseph, Ct., S10445
Joseph, Ct., Cont., S40821; BLWt.377-200-Lt. Iss. 9/24/1790 to Peleg Sanford, ass. No papers
Joseph, N.H., Martha, W22751
Joseph/John, N.C., see John, W18895

CHAPMAN (continued)
Joseph, N.C., S.C., S21691
Joshua, Ct., Lucy, R1874
Joshua, Mass., S17335
Lebbeus, Ct., S37842
Lemuel, Ct., N.Y., S35831
Lemuel, Mass., Sicha Tracy, former wid., W1144
Levi, Mass. Sea Service, N.H., Sarah, W22752
Lydia, Ct., former wid. of Wm. Cochran, W23793, which see
Michael, Ct., S42645
Nahum, Ct., S44376
Nathan, Va., Elizabeth, W6654; BLWt.1589-160-55
Nathaniel, Cont., Mass., Sarah, W22763
Nicholas, N.C., S8193
Noah, N.Y., Mary, W18888
Oliver, Ct., Eunice, R1868
Peter, Mass., Asenath, R1862
Plumb, R.I., Lois, W24830
Reuben, Ct., Dis. No papers
Richard, Ct., S22168
Robert, Ct., Judith, W24844; BLWt.27625-160-55
Robert, S.C., S39313
Rufus, Pvt., R.I., BLWt.3035 iss. 5/16/1794
Rufus, R.I., S44378
Salathiel, Ct., Amy, W4920; BLWt.26440-160-55
Samuel, Pvt., Ct., BLWt.5636 iss. 1/25/1793
Samuel, Ct., S12472
Samuel, Ct., BLWt.1954-100
Shadrach, N.H., Lydia, R1875
Silas, Ct., S37847
Simeon, Ct., R1879
Smith, N.H., S12454
Solomon, Pvt., N.H., BLWt.2988 iss. 1/14/1790 to Ladd, ass. & Cass, ass.
Stephen, Ct., BLWt.186-100
Stephen, N.H., N.Y., Sarah,W15997
Taylor, Ct., S28675
Thomas, Pvt., Ct., BLWt.5584 iss. 10/22/1790
Thomas, Ct., Cont., Mass., Phebe, W25405; BLWt.1903-160-55
Thomas, Pvt., Lee's Legion, BLWts.12892 & 13969 iss. 3/3/1792
Thomas, Va., Nancy, W8605
Thomas, Va., BLWt.1358-100
Timothy, Ct., Avis, W15881
Uriah, N.Y., Rebecca, W6653
Valentine, N.H., S22162
William, Mass., Anna/Amy, W18884
William, N.J., S24105
William, R.I., S44740
William, Va., S2121
William, Va., S41474
Zachariah, Ct., S28677

CHAPPEL, Benjamin, Jr., Pvt., N.Y., BLWt.6927 iss. 9/25/179- to Eliz. Chappel, Admx.
Daniel, Ct., Mary, W2527; BLWt. 26193-160-55
Edward Carter, Ct., Eunice, W20850
Noah, Ct., Lydia, W16530
Roswell, Pvt., Sheldon's Dragoons,

CHAPPEL (continued)
Ct., BLWt.5643 iss. 8/11/1790
Stephen, Ct., Lucy, See CHAPEL
William, Ct., S22677
William, Va., Ruth, W25410; BLWt.82542-160-55

CHAPPELL, Abner, Va., S16707
Amaziah, Ct., S44749
Benjamin, Pvt., N.Y., BLWt.6926 iss. 7/14/179- to Richard Platt, ass.
Benjamin, Va., S38599
Curtis, Ct., Sarah, W17603
Dan, Ct., Experience, W20843
Hicks, S.C., Elizabeth, W22758
Hiram, Ct., S12474
James, Cont., R.I., S19935
John, Va., Mary, W6670
Samuel, N.C., Polly/Mary, W6671
Stephen, Ct., Lydia, W16533
Thomas, Pa., S22163
Thomas, R.I., S12460
William, Ct., Lydia, W4154
William, Va., S9315

CHAPPIL, Samuel, Pvt., Md., BLWt.11089 iss. 6/19/1793

CHAPPLE, Curtis, Pvt., Ct., BLWt.5633 iss. 10/14/1795
John, Ct., Dis. No papers

CHARD, Barce, N.Y., Catharine, W10602; BLWt.51881-160-55
Caleb, Mass., See CHEARD

CHARITY, Charles, Va., S39317; BLWt.2085-100

CHARLES, Thomas, Mass., S29072
Thomas, Pvt., R.I., BLWt.3039 iss. 4/20/1790

CHARLESWORTH, John Miles, N.Y. Margaret, W16532; BLWts. 322-60-55 & 6928-100 iss. 8/30/1790

CHARLEVILLE, Francis, Va., Va. half pay, R13147

CHARLEY, George, Va., Christena W9781

CHARLICK, Henry, N.Y., S23569

CHARLON, Peter, Pvt., Hazen's Regt., BLWt. 12889 iss. 2/20/1792 to Benj. Moore, ass.

CHARLONT, Peter, Can. Dis. No papers

CHARLTON, Charles, Pa., S34193
Francis, Va., Susannah, W3657; BLWt.31894-160-55
Jacob, Va., S3149
John, Md. res. in 1827, R1883. No papers
John, N.J., S3150
John, Va., S2425

CHARNOCK, John, Va., S38598

CHARTER, James, Vt., Phebe; BLWt.84507-160-55

CHARTHIE, Joseph, Cont., N.Y. S40828

CHARTIER, Antonie, Pvt. Hazen's Regt., BLWt.12923 iss. 1/22/179- to Benj. Moore, ass.
Cemaur, N.Y., R20340
John, Pvt., Hazen's Regt., BLWt.12921 iss. 1/22/179- to Benj. Moore, ass.

CHARTIER, John,Mary, Cont., Canada, Sally, W17598
Joseph, Pvt., Hazen's Regt., BLWt. 12909 iss. 2/20/1792 to Benj. Moore, ass.
Joseph, Pvt., Hazen's Regt., BLWt. 12883 iss. 9/14/1789 to James Reynolds, ass.
Peter, Cont., Polly, W23786, Vt. agency and res. in 1818
Peter, Pvt., Hazen's Regt., BLWt. 12884 iss. 2/20/1792 to Benj. Moore, ass.
Samuel, Cont., N.Y., R20449
CHASE, Aaron, Mass., S40824
Abner, N.H., R1884
Amariah, Mass., Aviah, W1558
Aquila, Cont., Mass., S34202
Asa, Mass., Olive, W15639
Baruch, N.H., R21776
Benjamin, Mass., Phebe, W18881
Benjamin, Mass., Alice, W18882
Benjamin, N.H., S36964
Dean, Mass., S23156
Ebenezer, Mass., S16705; BLWt. 26566-160-55
Ebenezer, Mass., S22678
Ebenezer, N.Y., S12468
Enoch, Mass., S34589
Ephraim, Mass., See CHACE
Ephraim, Mass. Sea Service, S19238
Eseck, Mass., Lois Belknap, former widow, W14285
Ezekiel, Cont., Mass., Betsey, W17615
Ezekiel, Mass., R7300. See claim of Samuel Munrow, Mass.
Ezra, R.I., See CHACE
Gadeliah, N.Y., Rebecca, W10607; BLWt.26320-160-55
Gideon, Cont., S37827
Grindal, R.I., Lucretia, W4921
Isaac, Ct., S37849
Isaac, Pvt., Hazen's Regt., BLWt. 12900 iss. 8/23/1790
Isaac, Mass., Sarah, W20861
Isaac, Mass., Lucy, W22760
Isaac, Mass., Lois, W23784
Isaac, R.I., See CHACE
Isaiah, Mass., Navy, S18782
Jacob, Mass., See CHACE
James, Mass., S29070
James, R.I., S18781
James, R.I., Emily, W10603. This woman applied for pension (rejected) as former wid. of Peter Grover, soldier in War of 1812. Her minor children by Peter Grover were pensioned for such service under Ctf. #473. Both cases are in file R14580 of rejected files.
Jared, Cont., Mass., S18345
Jerahmeel, Mass., R.I., Sybel, W18901
Jeremiah, R.I., See CHACE
Joel, Mass., S44738
John, Mass., S34591
John, Mass., Elizabeth, W1142; BLWt.11086-160-55
John, Mass., Mercy, W23811

CHASE (continued)
John, N.H., Lovisa, R1887
Jonathan, N.H., S45673
Jonathan, N.Y., R1886
Joseph, Mass., Polly, W16531
Joseph, N.H., S44737
Joshua, N.H., Mary, W15636
Josiah, N.H., S45634
Lemuel, Mass., Sarah, W6908; BLWt.26426-160-55
Lot, Ct., Rhoda, W20846
Lydia, Mass., former wid. of James Stewart, which see
Mary, Ct., former wid. of Ziba Roberts, which see
Mary, N.H., former wid of John Daniels, which see
Mehitable, Mass., former wid. of Jacob Rowe, which see
Moses, Mass., S34593
Moses, Mass., Elizabeth, W2525
Moses, N.H., S40827
Moses, N.H., Mehitable, W6647; BLWt.7068-160-55
Moses, N.H., Polly, W23798; BLWt.6459-160-55
Nathaniel, Mass., Joanna, W1025; BLWt.14525-160-55
Nathaniel L., Mass. See CHACE
Oliver, Mass., R.I., S16710
Parker, N.H., Polly, W903; BLWt. 16271-160-55
Perley, Cont., Mass., S17879
Reuben, Pvt., Mass., BLWt.3895 iss. 4/2/1792
Reuben, Mass., Polly, R1889
Reuben, Navy, Mass. res & agency, S46885
Richard, R.I., S5000
Robert, N.H., Abigail, W2526; BLWt.798-100
Robert, Pvt., N.Y., BLWt.6948 iss. 5/19/1790 to Platt Smith, ass.
Robert, N.Y., Sarah, W6911; BLWt.26493-160-55
Robert, Va., Sally, W6910; BLWt. 27629-160-55
Samuel, Ct., S19240; BLWt.103392-160-55
Samuel, Mass., S34685
Samuel, Mass., S45674
Samuel, N.H., See CHACE
Samuel, N.H., Molly, W22776; BLWt. 10295-160-55
Samuel, Pa., S40836
Simeon, Mass., R.I., See CHACE
Simeon, N.H., R1892
Solomon, N.H., Vt., Sarah, R1891
Stephen, Mass., Elizabeth, W18879
Stephen, N.H., Hannah, W27928
Stephen, R.I., Hetty, See CHACE
Thomas, Mass., Desire, W22753
Thomas, Navy, N.H., S22169
Timothy, Pvt., Mass., BLWt.3893 iss. 2/27/1790 to Theodosius Fowler
Timothy, Mass., S44736
William, Cont., Mass., S15776
William, N.H., R.I., Rhoda, R1890
CHASEY, John, N.J., S2428
CHASTEEN, James, Cont., Va., Nancy W2917

CHATFIELD, Dan, Ct., S37830
Isaac, Cont., Ct., S12475
Joel, Mass., S44745
John, Ct., S38605
Jonathan, Ct., Dinah, R1894
Jonathan, N.Y., S44744
Josiah, Ct., S37837
Levi, Ct., S37843
CHATHAM, John, Va., S41475
William, Md., R1895
William, Pa., Nancy, W6663; BLWt.13195-160-55
CHATLAND, William, Pvt., Md., BLWt.11071 iss. 4/28/1791
CHATTERDON, Nathaniel, Cont., N.Y., Mary, W15641; BLWt.1576-100
CHATTERTON, Wait, Ct., Privateer, Melinda, W529; BLWt.11096-160-55
CHAUDOIN, John, Va., Sarah, W22745
Lewis, Va., S20892
CHAUNCEY, Nathaniel, W., Ct., S15044
CHAVERS, Anthony, Va., R1889 1/2
CHAVIS, Lazarus, S.C., S9316
CHAVORS, Anthony, Va., See CHAVERS
CHEADLE, Asa, Vt., Sarah, W14464; BLWt.26827-160-55
Elijah, Ct., S11994
CHEANEY, Nathaniel, Mass., S40044
CHEARD, Caleb, Mass., S17333
CHEATHAM, Benjamin, Va., S2429
Bernard, Va., Judith, R1897
Josiah, Va., Lucy, W18889
Stephen, Va., S39308
William, Va., S31607
CHEATWOOD, William, Va., Susannah, R1898
CHEDEL, John, Vt., S21692
CHEEK, Ellis, S.C., S8204
James, N.C., S8190
James, Va., S16708
William, S.C., Sinthia, W1141; BLWt.29742-160-55
CHEENEY, Thomas, Mass., See CHENEY
CHEENY, John, N.H., Judith, former wid. of Michael Sutton, which see
CHEESBROUGH, Elijah, Ct., Thankful, W22748; BLWt.26951-160-55
Lois, Ct., former wid. of Joseph Hilliard, which see
CHEESE, Samuel, Pvt., Ct., BLWt. 5632 iss. 9/16/1796 to Ebenezer Drakely
CHEESEBOROUGH, James, R.I., S28676
CHEESEMAN, Abel, Mass., Mary, R1902
Benjamin, Mass., See CHESMAN
Calvin, Mass., R1901
Thomas, Va. Sea Service, R27, Va. half pay
William; N.J., Lydia, W9386
CHEESMAN, Anson, Mass., Elizabeth Cary, W16900
Stephen, Mass., S34592
Thomas, Va. Sea Service, See CHEESEMAN
Ziba, Mass., Mehitable, R1903
CHEEVER, Abijah, Cont., Mass. Sea Service, S34590; BLWt.1512-300
Bartholomew, Mass., S29702
Ebenezer, Ct., Privateer, S12452
James, Mass., S29707
Joseph, Cont., Mass., Sarah,W22747

CHEEVERS
Samuel, Pvt., Mass., BLWt.3873 iss. 2/27/1790 to Theodosius Fowler
CHELTON, George, Va., S1188
Stephen, Va., S1189
CHENAULT, John, Va., S38602
James, Va., S39296
CHENDWETH, John, Md. See CHENOWETH
CHENEY, Benjamin, Mass., S40818
Daniel, Mass., S9164
Ebenezer, Mass., Lydia, W22773; BLWt.29744-160-55
Ebenezer, Mass., Abigail, BLWt. 34585-160-55
Elias, N.H., Deborah Clifford, former wid., W2531
Elijah, Ct., S37839
Eliphalet, Mass., Mary, W20863
Enoch, Mass., See CHANY
John, Mass., See CHANEY
Jonathan, Mass., S29071
Jonathan D., Cont., Mass., N.H., Lavina, W18898
Joseph, Ct., Rebecca, W20847
Joseph, Ct., Cont., S44754
Joseph, Cont., Mass., Betsey, W20845
Joseph, Mass., S30328
Judith, N.H., former wid. of Michael Sutton, which see
Moses, Mass., S29069
Nathaniel, Cont., Mass., Hannah, W23797; BLWt.26197-160-55
Nathaniel, Cont., Mass., N.H., S45630
Nathaniel, Mass., S12453
Rebecca, Cont., Mass., former wid. of Elijah Bliss,which see
Samuel, Mass., S45631
Samuel, Mass., Rebecca, see former husband, Elijah Bliss
Solomon, Clark, Mass., Molly, W14460
Thomas, Cont., N.H., Mass., Privateer, W17602
Thomas, Mass., Jane, W14470
Waldo, Ct., Priscilla, W20854
William, Ct., Sarah, R1905
William, Mass., S34180
CHENOWETH, John, Md., Mary, W9787; res. at enl. Allegany Co., Md. Died 3/3/1820
John, Va., Mary, W18899
Thomas, Md., Casandra, R1906
CHENULT, John, Va., See CHENAULT
CHENY, Enoch, Mass., See CHANY
CHERDOVOYNE, Anthony, N.Y., R1908
CHERRY, Henry, Cont., N.J., Abigail, W3942
John, Pvt., N.Y., BLWt.6930 iss. 9/15/179- to Wm. Bell, ass.
Joshua, N.C., S32174
Peter, Pa., S39312
Reuben, N.J., R1909
Samuel, N.H., S44746; BLWt.323-300. Capt. Iss. 6/24/1795 to Wm. S. Thom, ass. No papers
William, Va., Va. half pay, R13143; BLWt.2343-300
CHESEBRA, Christopher, Ct., R1900
CHESEBROUGH, Asa, Ct., R1899

CHESEBROUGH (continued)
Elijah, Ct., See CHEESBROUGH
James, R.I., See CHEESEBOROUGH
James, Ct., S38607
Nathaniel, Ct., Cont., S37845
Perez, Ct., S15042
CHESHIER, James, Va., R1910
CHESHIRE, John, Va. Sea Service, Va. half pay, R26
Richard, N.C., Prudence, W25403
CHESIRE, John, Va., See CHESHIRE
CHESLE, Sawyer, N.H., S37829
CHESLEY, Corydon, N.H., S45635
James, Navy, N.H., Elizabeth, W15996
John, N.H., S11996
John, N.Y., Magdalena, W4922; BLWt.14962-160-55
Nathaniel, N.H., Hannah, R1912
Sarah, N.H., former wid. of Winthrop Frost, which see
Sawyer, N.H., See CHESLE
Simon, Mass., Elizabeth, W6667; BLWt.28626-160-55
CHESMAN, Benjamin, Mass., S22163
CHESNEY, Benjamin, Cont., Va., S39297; BLWt.598-100
James M., N.J., S896
Thomas, Pvt., Pa., BLWt.9146 iss. 11/3/1791 to John McChesney, Admr.
CHESNUT, Benjamin, Cont., Va. See CHESNEY
Benjamin, Pa., S22165
Robert, Pvt., Hazen's Regt., BLWt.12906 iss. 7/13/1792 to Robert Ross, ass.
CHESSHER, James, Va., R1911
CHESSHIR, John, Va., S35829
CHESTER, Christopher, Ct., Cont., S40043
David, N.C., R20317
Edward, Pvt., N.J., BLWt.8165 iss. 5/3/1793
Giles, Navy, Ct., Mary, W17611
John, Ct., Navy, S38603
John, N.J., BLWt.95-100
John, N.C., S1897
John, Pa., Mary, W20
CHESTERMAN, William, Va., Frances Thornton, former wid., W5189; See her claim as wid. of William Thornton
CHESTON, John, N.J., Amy, W906
CHEUVRONT, Joseph, Va., Sarah, R1907
CHEVALIER, Anthony, Va., S42646
John, Pvt., N.Y., BLWt.6923 iss. 4/9/1791 to Elisha Camp, ass.
CHEVERS, William, Mass., S44752
CHEW, John, Va. agency, Dis. No papers
Nathaniel, Navy, Md., Margaret M. W9383
Richard, Pvt., N.J., BLWt.8175 iss. 5/26/1790
Richard, ---, Va. res. 1834, R1914
CHEWNING, Robert, Va., R1915
CHEYNEY, Richard, Pa., S40823
CHICHESTER, David, Ct., Mary, W17610
Henry, Ct., S17330

CHICHESTER (continued)
Nathan, Ct., Theodosia, W17607
CHICK, Isaac, Mass., Lydia, W714; BLWt.16118-160-55
James, Cont., Va., S10440
John, Mass., S36971
Nathaniel, Pa., War of 1812, R1916
CHICKERING, John, Mass., Ruth, W22742
Nathaniel, Mass., Esther, W23808
Oliver, Mass., S34181
CHIDESTER, Phinehas, N.J.,Rebecca Pitney, former wid., W1472
William, Ct., Martha, W4918
CHIDSEY, Ephraim, Ct., Hannah, W17620
Isaac, Ct., Lydia, W17601
CHIEVES, Joel, Va., S9178
CHILCOAT, Isaac, N.J., S969
John, Pa., S16702; BLWt.35826-160-55
CHILCOTT, Elihu, Va., Lydia, W6665
Thomas, Pa., BLWt.9193 iss. 6/20/1789. Sgt. In Proctor's Art.
CHILD, Abel, Mass., Polly, R1921
Abiathar, Mass., S19591
Abijah, Cont., Mass., S34184
Amos, Mass., Hannah, W2065; BLWt.11180-160-55, See CHILDS
Cephas, Ct., Cont., S12469
Cromwell, R.I., S22675
Ebenezer, Mass., S12458
Elias, Ct., S31605
Enoch, Mass., S30923
Francis, N.C., Frances, BLWt. 383-300
Isaac, Vt., S21112
Jesse, Ct., R1919
John, Mass., S34200
John, Mass., Mary, R1920
Jonas, Cont., Mass., Anna, W1559; BLWt.21830-160-55
Jonathan, Pvt., Mass., BLWt. 3965 iss. 9/28/1790 to Theodosius Fowler
Lyman, Ct., S21690
Obadiah, Ct., S37832
Penuel, Ct., Sabra, W716
Salmon, N.Y., S21689
Samuel, Mass., Lucy, W23796
Stephen, Ct., Zilpha, W18886
Timothy, Ct., Ama, W20859
Willard, Ct., S10444
William, Mass., S12467
Zachariah, Mass., Lydia, W14455
CHILDERS, Abraham, Va., R1922
David, Ga., S39298
Goldsby/Goolsberry, Va., S30924
Henry, Va., S16340
Isom, N.C., S30928
Jacob, S.C., R1923
Miller, N.C., S37846
Mosby, Va., S42121
Patterson, N.C. or Va., Nancy, See CHILDRESS
Pleasant, N.C., Sarah, R1924
CHILDRESS, Alexander, Cont., Va., Temperance, W10604; BLWt. 24332-160-55

CHILDRESS, Benjamin, Va., R1926
John, N.C., S3146
John, N.C., S31609
John, Va., S2423
Mitchel, N.C., S2426
Patterson, N.C. or Va., Nancy, R1928
Robert, Va., R1929
Thomas, Ga., Va. res., S3147
William, N.C., Martha, W6666
William, N.C., S.C., Charity, R1927
William, Va., Anne, See CHILDREY
CHILDREY, William, Va., Anne, W3775
CHILDS, Abel, Mass., Hannah, W14459
Abram, Mass., S30322
Amos, Cont., Hannah, W2065, b. Mass., Me. res. 1818; BLWt. 11180-160-55
Charles, Sgt., Sheldon's Dragoons, Ct., BLWt.5665 iss. 1/28/1790
George, Corp., Md., BLWt.11039 iss. 5/11/1790
Isaac, Mass., Sarah, W20860
Isaac, N.J., Privateer, Pa., R1918
John, Cont., Mass., Susanna, W22749
Jonas, Cont., Mass., Anna, See CHILD
Jonathan, Mass., Anna, W20857
Penuel, Ct., Sarah, W20842
Reuben, Mass., S29068
Timothy, Cont., Mass., Rachel, W14476
CHILES, Henry, Va., S9175
Hezekiah, N.C., S2424
James, Va., S8200
Thomas, S12703
CHILLSON, John, R.I., BLWt.1908-100
Reuben, Mass., S39295
CHILNER, Christopher, Pvt., N.Y. BLWt.6964 iss. 8/25/1790 to William Kline, ass.
Christopher, N.Y., S44756
CHILSON, Ezra, Mass., Privateer, Pamelia, W6664
Joseph, R.I., S30325
CHILTON, Andrew, Va., Betsey, R1930
John, Va., BLWt.519-300
CHINA, John, S.C., S46593
CHINN, Perry, Va., Elizabeth, W6650
CHIPMAN, Deziah, Mass., former wid. of Sylvester Lincoln, which see
Jesse, Mass., Vt., Mary, W16897
John, Cont., Ct., S46351; BLWt. 376-300-Capt. Iss. 3/3/1797 to Samuel Fitch, ass. No papers
Nathaniel, Ct., S18780
Samuel, Vt., S15038
Thomas, Ct., Cont., S44741
Timothy, Ct., S37834
William, Cont., Mass., Jane, W1382; BLWt.12845-160-55
CHIPS, Morris, N.J., Sarah, W4157
CHISAM, John, S.C., Sarah, R1932
CHISELDON, Edward, Pvt., Pa., BLWt.9223 iss. 9/23/1791 to Samuel Black, ass.
CHISEM, John I., N.Y. See CHISM
CHISHAM, George, Va., Mary, See CHISM
CHISHAM (continued)
James, Va., Catharine, W8595
CHISHOLM, George, Pvt., Va., BLWt.12038 iss. 2/24/1794 to Anthony New, ass.
CHISHOLME, Walter, Va., S9169
CHISM, George, Va., Mary, W8594
John I., N.Y., R1931
CHISMAN, Thomas, Va., See CHEESEMAN
CHITTAM, Aquilla, Md., BLWt.2277-100
John, N.C., S10116
CHITTENDEN, Abraham, Ct., S16703
Asahel, Ct., Anna McFarland, former wid., W25688; BLWt.28539-100-55
Benjamin, Ct., S37836
Calvin, Ct., S17334
Cornelius, Ct., S17880; BLWt. 11279-160-55
Gideon, Pvt., Ct., See CHITTENDON
Gideon, Ct., S42660
James, Ct., S23570
Jared, Ct., Cont., S44742
John, Ct., Cont., S17332
Levi, Ct., Hannah, W17622
Nathan, Ct., S17331
Nathaniel, Mass., Ruth, W13537
Solomon, Ct., Susannah, R1934
Thomas, Cont., Mass., Love, W22757
CHITTENDON, Cornelius, Ct., See CHITTENDEN
Gideon, Pvt., Ct., BLWt.5581, iss. 8/23/1790
Reuben, Ct., S44743
William, Ct., S34197
CHITTIM, John, N.C., See CHITTAM
CHITTINGDON, Jared, Pvt., N.Y., BLWt.6999 iss. 7/20/1791
CHITTINGTON, Jerard, See CHITTENDEN
CHITWOOD, James, S.C., S1751
William, Va., Susannah, See CHEATWOOD
CHIVVIS, William, Cont., S44751
CHOAT, Benjamin, Cont., N.H., Abigail, W22775
Christopher, S.C., S3144
Greenberry, N.C., S32176
Jonathan, Mass., S45672
CHOATE, David, Cont., Mass., Miriam, W18902
David, Mass., S45531
Ebenezer, Mass., Elizabeth, W3658; BLWt.11407-160-55
James, Mass., S11995
Simeon, Cont., Mass., S34187
CHOCKLEY, Thomas, Va., S40819
CHOICE, Tully, Va., Rebecca, W3774
William, Va., Mary, W3656
CHOPMAN, Caleb, Ct., See CHAPMAN
CHOPS, John, Pvt., Ct., BLWt.5609 iss. 1/13/1792
CHRIGER, Philip, N.H., Elizabeth Ryder, former wid., W17583
CHRISMAN, Felix, Pa., See CHRISTMAN
John, Pa. res. in 1843, R1943
Joseph, Va., R1936
CHRISP, John, Va., S3222
CHRIST, Adam, Pa. agency, Dis. No papers
Henry, Pa., R1937
Lawrence/Lorentz, Pa., R1938
CHRIST (continued)
Philip, Pa., S8197
CHRISTAL, Timothy, Pvt., Mass., BLWt.3881 iss. 2/19/1796 to Dan Bartlett, ass.
CHRISTEYANCE, Isaac, N.Y., S28678
CHRISTIAAN, Charles, Pvt., N.Y., BLWt.6981 iss. 9/25/1790 to Abraham Nelson, ass.
CHRISTIAN, Allen, Va., S32170
Andrew, Va., Mary, W8603
Daniel, Pa., S8201
James, Pvt., N.C., BLWts.12055 & 12869 iss. 2/13/1797 to Murdock McKenzie, ass.
James, N.C., Cumberland Co. res. Dis. S12699
James, N.C., Hertford Co. res. Dis. No papers. Applied for pension in 1795.
James, N.C., Wake Co. res. Dis. No papers
John, Mass., S34196
John, N.Y., S12700
John, N.Y., Sarah, W18894; BLWt.902-100-Pvt. Iss. 10/2/1790. No papers
John, N.C., Mary, W6668
John, Va., S12689
John, Va., S15276
Michael, Pvt., Lamb's Artillery N.Y., BLWt.6992 iss. 3/27/1792
Peter, Pvt., Armand's Legion, BLWt.12868 iss. 6/6/1799 to Abraham Bell, ass.
Phebe, Pa., W25411; BLWt.26976-160-55; former wid. of Wm. Buck
Rawleigh C., Cont., Va., Elizabeth, W18892
Robert, Va., S9177
Thomas, Va., Mary, W25409; BLWt.28656-160-55
Valentine, N.J., S2122
Walter, Va., Patsey/Martha, W6669
William, N.Y., Phebe, R1939
William, Va., S35830
William, Va., Mary, W4917, Va. half pay; BLWt.67606-160-55
Zachariah, N.Y., Lydia, W16207
CHRISTIANCE, Isaac, N.Y., S23159
Isaac, N.Y., See CHRISTEYANCE
John, N.Y., S12702
CHRISTIE, James, Pvt., N.J., BLWt.8228 iss. 1/28/1791
James, Pa., BLWt.416-300-Capt. iss. 9/6/1792. No papers
James, Va., Sarah, W9782
John, N.J., Elizabeth, W6673
John, Pvt., Lamb's Artillery N.Y., BLWt.7002 iss. 5/26/1790 to Joseph Johnston, ass.
John, Pa., BLWt.418-300-Capt. iss. 6/26/1792. No papers
John G., N.Y., R1940
Thomas, Va., BLWt.466-400-Surg. Iss. 12/19/1793. No papers
CHRISTLER, David, Va., Elizabeth W8596
Elias, Sgt., Pa., BLWt.9135 iss. 8/7/1789 to Richard Platt, ass.
CHRISTMAN, Felix, Pa., Elizabeth,

CHRISTMAN (continued)
W25400; BLWt.13726-160-55
Frederick, Md., R1942
Jacob, N.Y., S12461
Nicholas, N.Y., S44757
CHRISTMAS, Richard, N.C., S8196
Richard, N.C., S16342
CHRISTOPHER, Andrew/Andrias, Pvt. N.Y., BLWt.6909 iss. 9/15/1790 to John S. Hobart, et al ass.
CHRISTSINGER, John, N.Y., See GREATSINGER
CHRISTY, Daniel, Va., St. Clair's Indian War, War of 1812, R1944
James, Va., R1945 & R1946
William, Corp., Legion of the U.S. "Old War"Invalid Rej.13150
CHRISWELL, Samuel, Pa., S12617
CHROUSHOUR, Nicholas, Va., R2545
CHRYSMAN, Jacob, N.Y., S31608
CHRYSTYANCE, Dorcas, N.Y., W17613 Former wid. of John Davis
CHUBB, David, Vt., Molly, W23807
John, Pvt., Va., BLWt.12042 iss. 7/14/1792 to Robert Means, ass.
Joseph, Ct., S44747
Silas, Mass., Mary, W15638
Thomas, Mass., S34195
William, Cont., Ct. res. of dau. in 1820. BLWt.917-100
CHUBBUCK, Ebenezer, Ct., Lucina, W2919
Levi, Cont., Mass., S45632
Simeon, Cont., Mass., S44385
CHUMBLEY, John, Va., S32169
CHUMLEY, Daniel, Cont., enl. in Va., S3152
CHUN, Silvester, Va., S39314
CHURCH, Alexander, Mass., Patience, W1822
Amasa, Ct., Cont., S12688
Amos, N.C., S8191; BLWt.36647-160-55
Anthony, R.I., S29075
Asa, Sgt., Mass., BLWt.3928 iss. 1/28/1800
Asa, Mass., Rachel, W22746
Benjamin, Mass., S29705
Caleb, Mass., S34179
Caleb, R.I., Mercy, W20844
Charles, Mass., Rebecca, W1717; BLWt.11091-160-55
Charles, Mass., Rachel, W9780; BLWt.8141-160-55
Constant, N.Y., Deborah, W22765
Daniel, Ct., S23155
David, N.Y., R1947
Earl, Mass., S29703
Ebenezer, Ct., Eunice, W3130
Eber, Mass., S34198
Eleazer, Vt., S22160
Elihu, Sgt., Ct., BLWt.5582 iss. 5/18/1790 to Theodosius Fowler
Elihu, Ct., S44379
Fairbanks, Ct., S12470
Gideon, Pvt., Ct., BLWt.5577 iss. 10/18/1791 to Ebenezer Farnham
Gideon, Ct., Abigail, W2755
Gideon, R.I., Hannah S. Pierce,

CHURCH (continued)
former wid., W27690; BLWt. 114125-160-55
Isaac, Mass., S40835
James Cady, Ct., S44380
Joel Winter, Cont., Ct., S28674
John/Jonathan/John J. Ellis/ John J. Elias, Ct., Abigail W1143; BLWt.39493-160-55
John, Ct., Green Mt. Boys, Mass., S15373
John, alias Hogg/Hodges, Cont., N.H., S12455
John, Mass., Susanna, W24843
John, Mass., R1949
John, N.C., Nancy, W3943; BLWt.26751-160-55
John, Pvt., Va., BLWt.12003 iss. 5/29/1792 to Robt. Means, ass.
John J.E., Ct., Abigail, See John CHURCH
Jonathan, Ct., Abigail, See John CHURCH
Jonathan, Mass., Sarah, W14468
Joseph, Ct., Cont., Priscilla, W23806
Joseph, R.I., S21688
Joshua, Cont., Mass., Vt. or N.H., Jane, W6649; BLWt.26616-160-55
Joshua, Cont., R.I., Abigail, W3335
Joshua, N.H., Vt., S40833
Joshua, Vt., Sally, W636; BLWt. 26380-160-55
Nathaniel, Ct., S19933
Nathaniel, N.H., Mary, W20851
Nathaniel, R.I., S23158
Parlly, Ct., R1951
Philemon, Cont., Ct., S42122
Reuben, Cont., N.Y., S40834; BLWt.328-150-Ensign. Iss. 8/7/1789 to Anspack & Rogers, assnes. No papers
Samuel, Ct., S40830
Samuel, Ct., Lydia, R1950
Samuel, Cont., Ct., S39309
Samuel, Mass., S29067
Silas, Mass., S11998
Simeon, Ct., Mass., N.H., S12471
Thomas, Cont., N.Y., S12465
Thomas, Mass., S34204
Thomas, Pa., BLWt.410-400. No papers
Thomas, R.I., Molly, W8600
Uriah, Ct., S34185
Uriah, Ct., S37844
Willard, Ct., S44750
CHURCHELL, Caleb, Mass., S22164; BLWt.785-160-55
CHURCHFIELD, John, Pa., S40821
CHURCHILL, Elijah, QM Sgt., Sheldon's Dragoons, Ct., BLWt. 5661 iss. 10/6/1789 to Theodosius Fowler
Elijah, Cont., Elanor, W14457
Elizabeth, Mass., W22750, former wid. of Joshua Totman, which see
Ephraim, Mass., Silence, W14472
Francis, Mass., Phebe, W20848
Isaac, Mass., Elizabeth, W20862
Isaac, N.Y., S12706

CHURCHILL (continued)
Jabesh, Mass., Merriah, W22761; BLWt.3807-160-55
Jabez, Cont., Mass., S36968
Jacob, Ct., Lillis, W14471
James, Mass., S36970
James, Mass., Priscilla, W22756
John, Ct., Cont., R1952
Jonas, N.Y., S15037
Jonathan, Cont., Mass., S39311
Joseph, Mass., S30920
Joseph, Mass., S34186
Joshua, Mass., S36969
Josiah, Mass., S20330
Moses, Pvt., Ct., BLWt.5618 iss. 3/7/1792 to Jonathan Tuttle
Nathaniel, Ct., Lydia, W22770
Oliver, Ct., Lydia, W2560; BLWt.9433-160-55
Samuel, Ct., R1953
Samuel, Mass., Deborah, W14473
Solomon, Mass., S19239
Stephen, Ct., Mary, W1225
William, Mass., Mary/Polly, W8601; BLWt.50860-160-55
CHUTE, David, Mass., Ruth, R1954
Josiah, Mass., Mary, W24842
Thomas, Mass., Mary, W23800
CHYSMAN, Jacob, N.Y., See CHRYSMAN
CILLEY, Daniel, N.H., S40940
Jonathan, Mass., N.H., Hannah, W18904
Jonathan, N.H., Dorcas, W5246; BLWt.327-200-Lt. Iss. 1/16/1800 to Jona. Cilley. No papers
Joseph, N.H., BLWt.322-500-Col. Iss. 1/16/1800 to Jona. Cilley, heir. No papers
Samuel, Mass., N.H., S12476
Thomas, Mass., S42867
CISCO, Abraham, N.J., Sarah, W12723; BLWt.16255-160-55
CISM, Peter, Margaret, See SCISIM
CISNA, Stephen, Pa., Cont., S42647
CITY/CITTY, Jacob, Md., Elizabeth/ Betsey, W6672
CLABAUGH, Martin, Pa. See CLAUBAUGH
CLACK, Moses, Cont., Va., Ann, W2921; BLWt.12009-100. Iss. 11/26/1792. No papers
Sterling, Va., Mary, W240
CLACKNER, Adam, Pa., S34692
CLAFFLIN, John, Cont., Mass., Henrietta, W20886
CLAFLEN, Allen, Mass., S44792
Comfort, Mass., S34211
Ebenezer, Mass., S34595
Ephraim, Mass., Polly, W409; BLWt.291-60-55
Phinehas, Mass., Hannah, R1955
Timothy, Cont., Mass., S39320
CLAGETT, Horatio, Md., BLWt.3-300
Jane Contee, Cont., Md., W14488, former wid. of Wm. Murdock
CLAGGETT, Samuel, Md., Amie, W6693
CLAGHORN, Joseph, Mass., Navy, S28686
CLAIBORNE, Leonard, Va., Frances, W3388
CLAIBOURN, Richard, Va., BLWt.470-

CLAIBOURN (continued)
200-Lt. Iss. 12/4/1794.No papers
CLAIR, Godfrey, N.J., Nancy, W24829; BLWt.9499-160-55
CLAITT, Isaac, Ga. res in 1828, See CLIATT
CLAMPITT, Govea, N.H., Sarah, W18; BLWt.5075-160-55
CLAMSON, Ezra, N.Y., See CLAWSON
CLANAHAN, John, Pvt., Lamb's Artillery N.Y., BLWts. 7005 & 83-60-55 iss. 7/16/--
Robert, Md., BLWt.11069 iss. 1/21/1795 to John Faires, ass.
Robert, Md., S39319
CLANCEY, John, Pvt., Md., BLWt. 11028 iss. 2/1/1790
John, Md., S42126
Michael, Fifer, Md., BLWt.11048 iss. 2/7/1790
CLANDENNAN, John, N.C., BLWt. 1803-200, See CLENDENMAN
CLANNING, Edward, Navy, R.I., Dorcas, W22785
Henry, Pa. Sea Service, R.I., Sea Service, S21115
CLAP, Caleb, Capt., Cont. Mass., Elizabeth, W27398; BLWt.339-300 iss. 4/1/1790
Eliakim, Cont., Mass., Pamela, W23823
Eliphas, Mass., S17345
Timothy, Mass., Sally, W25422
CLAPP, Abigail, Ct., R1957, former wid. of Benjamin Barns, which see
Adam, N.C., S30937
Asa, Mass., Elizabeth Wendell, W1560
Barnabas, R.I., Ruth, W20875
Benjamin, Mass., Mary, W23828
Caleb, Cont., Mass., See CLAP
Daniel, N.H., Mary Morrill, former wid., W20892; BLWt. 326-200-Lt. Iss. 12/14/1793 to Asa Days, ass. No papers
David, Mass., S12482
Dwelly, Mass., Rachel, W14485
Earl, Cont., Mass., S12490
Ebenezer, Cont., Mass., Elizabeth Smith, former wid., W15357; BLWt.18394-160-55
Elijah, Mass., Martha, W14477
Henry, N.Y., Elizabeth, W22804
Isaac, Mass., S39318
Jacob, N.C., Barbara, W17624
John, Mass., S34213
John, Mass., Polly, W18905
John, R.I., Anna, W20866
Joshua, Mass., Nabby, W22800; BLWt.351-200-Lt. Iss. 4/1/1790 No papers
Leodwick, N.C., S8211
Oliver, Ct., S16718
Paul, Mass., S29078
Roswell, Mass., Vt., Rachel, W20882
Samuel, Ct., Cont., N.H.,S39321
Silas, N.Y., S12505
Simeon, Mass., S5012
Stephen, Cont., Mass., Lydia, W6676; BLWt.71205-160-55

CLAPP (continued)
Timothy, Mass., Sally, See CLAP
CLAPPARD, John, Pvt., S.C., BLWts. 12057 & 12863 iss. 10/7/1795
CLAPPER, George, Pa., Elizabeth, John, N.Y., S15045 & R1958
Valentine, Md., S39325
CLARDY, Thomas, Va., S8216
CLAREY, Daniel, Pvt., Ct., BLWt. 5658 iss. 7/19/1791
CLARIDGE, James, Mass., Navy, Mary, W14495
Levin, Md., BLWt.1779-100
CLARK, Aaron, R.I., Eunice, W14493
Abel, Pvt., Ct., BLWt.5596 iss. 1/3/1799 to Horace Olds
Abel, Ct., Hannah Murray, former wid., W21770
Abel, Ct., Sarah, R13178
Abijah, Mass., S29711
Abraham, Sgt., Ct., BLWt.5624 iss. 9/4/1789 to Ezekiel Case
Abraham, N.Y., Rachel, R2010, S12696
Abraham, N.Y., See Abram CLARK
Abram, Ct., S44776
Abram, N.Y., S44772
Adna, Ct., S8209
Amasa, Ct., S17348
Amos, Pvt., Ct., BLWt.5586 iss. 1/11/1791 to Samuel Emery
Amos, Ct., S23574
Amos, Ct., S37872
Amos, Ct., S44774
Amos, Ct., Hannah, W25419; BLWt.26492-160-55
Amos, Ct., Mass., Sarah, W1229
Amos, Mass., Lydia, W15643
Amos, Mass., Ursula, R2021; BLWt.36243-160-55
Andrew, Ct., Vashti, W480; BLWt.31890-160-55
Andrew, Ct., Anna, W17633
Andrew, Ct., N.Y., Vt., S28687
Anne, N.H., former wid. of Samuel Demerett, which see
Anthony, Md., Va., S3156
Anthony, Mass., Lucinda, W9388; BLWts.260-60-55 & 3-100-55
Arthur, Mass., BLWt.892-100
Arthur, Pvt., N.J., BLWt.8180 iss. 1/5/1790
Asa, Ct., S12504
Asa, Ct., S38611
Asa, Mass., S29714
Augustus, Ct., BLWt.5623 iss. 7/14/1790
Augustus, Ct., Anna, W16211
Barnabas, Ct., BLWt.1451-100
Barnabas, Mass., S19600
Barnabas, Mass., Judith, W14478
Barnabas, Mass., Bethiah, W22777
Benjamin, Ct., S10465
Benjamin, Ct., N.H., Privateer, S12502
Benjamin, Ct., Pa., S41487
Benjamin, Cont., Mass., Mehetabel, W14486
Benjamin, Mass., S34215
Benjamin, Mass., Sarah, W20880
Benjamin, Mass., Betsey, W22787
Benjamin, N.H., S12483
Benjamin, N.H., S23163

CLARK (continued)
Benjamin, N.H., Elizabeth, BLWt.6032-160-55
Benjamin, N.C., S31611
Benjamin, N.C., S.C., S3155
Bennoni, Ct., S12491
Beriah, Ct., S34209
Beriah, Pvt., R.I., BLWt.3034 iss. 6/1/1792
Bunker, N.H., S36980
Burgess, N.C., Rhodey, W2758; BLWt.34972-160-55
Caesar (colored), Ct., S37871
Caleb, Cont., N.H., Lodama, W20876
Caleb, R.I., R1963
Carey, Cont., R.I., S19940, 2nd Lt. 16th U.S. Inf. 1799, U.S. Arty. 1803
Champion, Ct., S16082
Charles, Mass., S15777
Charles Goodwin, Mass., S30939
Chipman, Ct., S9181
Clement, Vt., S42130
Comfort, Ct., Esther, R1973
Cutting, Mass., Lucy, W22795
Cyrenus, Ct., S37808
Daniel, Ct., S12695
Daniel, Ct., S17341
Daniel, Ct., S18354
Daniel, Ct., Cont., S10457
Daniel, Cont., Ct., S23161
Daniel, N.Y., R1966
David, Ct., S17349
David, Ct., Jane, W25424
David, Ct., Sarah, R2015
David, Cont., Mass., Bridget, W23817
David, Cont., N.H., S45636
David, Pvt., Md., BLWts.12875 & 14105 iss. 2/24/1795 to Francis Sherrard, ass. of Elizabeth Coley, Admx.
David, Mass., S34208
David, Mass., S36983; BLWt.527-100
David, Mass., Mehitable, W1719
David (or Roger BAYLEY), Mass., R388
David, Sgt., N.Y., BLWt.6917 iss. 9/28/1790
David, N.C., S30936
David, N.C., Charity, R1964
David, Pvt., Va., BLWt.11997 iss. 4/21/1796 to James Morrison
Dennis, Pa., Va., S2127
Ebenezer, Cont., Mass., Rachel, W9788
Ebenezer, Cont., Mass., Ruth, W15644
Ebenezer, Cont., Mass., N.H., Hannah, W15645
Ebenezer, Mass., S30938
Ebenezer, Mass., S34216
Ebenezer, N.H., Hannah, W22781
Edmund, Va., BLWt.458-200-Lt. No papers
Edward, Cont., N.H., Elizabeth, S38614
Edward, Pvt., Hazen's Regt., BLWt. 12908 iss. 10/16/1789 to Theodosius Fowler, ass.
Edward, N.J., Phebe, W3944; BLWt. 11409-160-55

CLARK (continued)
Edward, Va., S37856
Eleazer, N.H., S36979
Eleazer, N.H., R1971
Elezar, Cont., R.I., S17346
Elias, Ct., S15046
Elias, Ct., N.Y., R1970
Elias, N.J., N.Y., S12479
Elijah, Pvt., Ct., BLWt.5559 iss. 10/16/1789 to Theodosius Fowler
Elijah, Ct., S37867
Elijah, Cont., Mass., Lucy, R1996
Elijah, Md., S37861
Elijah, Mass., Julia, W14498
Elijah, Mass., N.H., Martha, W23825
Elijah, Va., S10448
Eliphalet/Eliphlael, Ct., S44767
Eliphalet, Ct., S12477
Elisha, Ct., Sarah, W17630
Elisha, Cont., Ct., Martha, W718; BLWt.8159-160-55
Elisha, Cont., Green Mt. Boys, Vt., Edna, W23826
Elisha, Sea Service, Mass., R1972
Elizabeth, Cont., Mass., W23822, former wid. of Ezekiel Blair
Elizabeth, Mass., W24828, former wid. of Elisha Prouty
Elliot, Mass., Hannah, W22780
Ephraim, Mass., Navy, N.H., S28680
Ephraim, N.Y., Sarah, W18920
Ethan, N.H., Lucy, R1997
Ezra, Ct., N.Y., R.I., Vt., S18353
Ezra, Cont. Ct., Eunice, W18911
Ezra, Mass., S34206
Ezra, Pvt., N.J., BLWt.8185 iss. 10/8/1795
Field, Va., Mary, R2002
Flavel, Ct., S12481
Francis, Ct., S23165
Francis, N.Y., S23162
Francis, Pa., S41479
Gardner, R.I., S28685
George, Ct., S28683
George, Ct., S37873
George, Ct., Cont., S12489
George, Md., BLWt.1484-100
George, Pvt., Mass., BLWt.3933 iss. 12/9/1797 to John W. Blake, ass.
George, Mass., S12497
George, Pvt., N.Y., BLWt.7007 iss. 4/21/1791
George, N.C., S3157
George, N.C., S32179
George, Pa., R1974
Gershom, Ct., S23575
Gershom, Ct., Lavinia, W20890
Gideon, Ct., Jemima, W17627
Gideon, Mass., S34207
Giles, Ct., Polly, W2592
Greenleaf, Mass., Privateer, Elenor, W14494
Gregory, Mass., Margaret, W2591
Gregory, N.C., Lurany, R1998
Hannah, Mass., W23824, former wid. of William Alld
Hannah, N.H., W6682; BLWt.6014-160-55; former wid. of Richard Clement
Hanson, Mass., S36973
Henry, N.J., S972
Hezekiah, Pvt., Armand's Corps. BLWt.12862 iss. 5/6/1795 to Peter Manuel, ass.
Hezekiah, Ct., Lucy, W6688
Hezekiah Ward/Ward, N.H., Judy, W23829
Ichabod, N.J., S971
Ichabod, N.J., R1977
Ichabod G., Mass., Vt., S22177
Ira, Ct., S37854
Isaac, Ct., S16714
Isaac, Mass., Polly, W6685; BLWt.36241-160-55
Isaac, N.C., S41488; BLWt.191-100
Israel, Ct., Cont., S42139
Israel, Mass., Mary, W14499
Jabez, Ct., S12495
Jabez, Mass., S21695
Jacob, Ct., S10453
Jacob, Mass., Susannah, W14490
Jacob, N.H., S19249
Jacob, N.C., Sarah, W4155
Jacob N., Md., S15379
James, Ct., BLWt.2045-200
James, Ct., Cont., S12514
James, Ct., Cont., S44768
James, Ct., Cont., Jerusha, W20874
James, Md., Barbara McMahon, former wid., W9182
James, Mass., S36976; BLWt.898-100
James, Mass., S44777
James, Mass., S46644
James, Mass., Margaret, W20889
James, N.J., S2123
James, Pvt., N.Y., BLWt.8178 iss. 7/18/1789
James, N.Y., Deborah, W16907
James, N.C., S8207
James, Pa., S2125
James, Pa., S24117
James, S.C., S32181
James, S.C., R1980
James, Va., S3159
James, Va., S18351
James, Va., S30941
James, Va., S35841
James, Va., R1979
James R., N.Y., Hannah, W17636
James W., Ct., Betsey, W20873
Jeptha, Mass., Rhoda, W16904
Jeremiah, Cont., Mass., S44764
Jerome, Ct., Cont., Privateer, Nancy, W4156; BLWt.14510-160-55
Jesse, Ct., Olive, W17632
Jesse, Mass., Sarah, W17631
Jesse, N.H., S44765
Job, Mass., Esther, W14480
Job, R.I., S23572
Job B., R.I., R1984
John, Ct., S12500; BLWt.32223-160-55; b.1762, enl. Lyme, N.Y. res.
John, Ct., S37857, b.1754, res. Washington, Ct.
John, Ct., Phebe, W17629
John, Ct., Sea Service, R1986
John, Ct., Cont., Amy, W14482
John, Ct., Cont., Lucy, W25423
John, Cont., Ct., S44386, b.1753 enl. Mansfield, res. Ashford, Ct., d.1833
John, Cont., Md., Sarah Cochran, former wid., W6741. See also Sarah, wid. of Simon Cochran, Va.
John, Cont., Mass., S18762
John, Cont., Mass., S34698
John, Cont., N.Y., Ruth Randall former wid., W26348; BLWt.83-60-55. She applied for pension and rej. for service of 1st husb., Lemuel Fox, N.Y.
John, Cont., Pa., S41482; BLWt. 3-850. Special Act, 2/20/1819
John, Cont., Va., S17884
John, Del., S41481
John, Md., S46462; BLWt.1336-100
John, Pvt., Mass., BLWt.3855 iss. 11/2/1791 to Titus Street, ass.
John, Sgt., Mass., BLWt.3929 iss. 5/21/1801 to Ab. Halbrook
John, Mass., S15376
John, Mass., S28681
John, Mass., S30329
John, Mass., S41486
John, Mass., Lydia, W22779
John, Mass., Navy, Bethia, W18917
John, N.H., S45639
John, N.H., Sarah, W14497
John, N.H., Hannah, W15761
John, N.H., Elizabeth, W22789; BLWt.137-60-55 & 818-160-55
John, N.H., Sarah, W22793; BLWt. 51877-160-55
John, N.H., Eunice, W23814
John, N.H., Mehitable Morse, former wid., W24011; BLWt. 17730-160-55
John, N.H., Jane, R1982
John, Pvt., N.J., BLWt.8164 iss. 5/31/1790
John, N.J., S2128
John, N.J., S41480
John, Pvt., Lamb's Arty. N.Y., BLWts.7005 & 83-60-55 iss. 7/16/1790 . BLWt.7005 to Wm. L. Vreedenburgh, ass.
John, N.Y., S44763
John, N.Y., Hannah, W15822
John, N.Y., R1988
John, N.Y., R1989
John, N.C., S1898
John, N.C., S42124
John, N.C., Va., Lucy, W10625; BLWt.2495-160-55
John, N.C., Tamar, W10627; BLWt.26390-160-55
John, N.C., S.C., Margaret, R1999
John, Pvt. "in Artillery Artificers of Pa.", BLWt.12958 iss. 6/29/1789 to Matt. McConnell, ass.
John, Pa., Major U.S. Army & Indian Wars, 1791-1794, S41484; BLWt. 419-300-Capt. Iss. 8/19/1789. No papers.
John, Pa., S41485
John, Pa., S42127

CLARK (continued)
John, Pa., Agnes, W4654; BLWt. 9128-100-Pvt. Iss. 12/13/1791 to Gideon Merckle, ass.
John, Pa., Julia Ann, W9789; BLWt.89505-160-55
John, R.I., S28682
John, R.I., R1983
John, Va., S39326
John, Va., Catharine, R1965
John, Va., Mary, R2003
John S., Mass., S12493
Jonas, Ct., Cont., Mass., Sarah, R2016
Jonas, Mass., S29715
Jonas, N.C., S.C., Ann, W1386; BLWt.26462-160-55
Jonathan, Ct., Polly, W9387
Jonathan, Ct., R1992
Jonathan, Ct., R1993
Jonathan, Ct., Martha, R2001
Jonathan, Cont., Mass., S36977
Jonathan, Cont., Mass., S45638
Jonathan, Mass., Hannah, W27396
Jonathan, Mass., N.H., S12512
Jonathan, N.H., S12508, See claim of Hannah Clark, former wid. of Richard Clement, N.H, which see
Jonathan, N.H., S45680
Jonathan, N.C., S2438
Jonathan, Va., BLWt.447-450-Lt. Col. Iss. 12/11/1797. No papers
Joseph, Ct., S17347
Joseph, Ct., S37855
Joseph, Ct., S37858; BLWt.5621-100-Sgt. Iss. 10/12/1790. No papers
Joseph, Ct., Sarah, W20871
Joseph, Ct., Jemima Spelman, former wid., R9969
Joseph, Ct., Mass., Judith, W14479
Joseph, Ct., Mass., Rozina King, former wid., R19377
Joseph, Mass., S34210
Joseph, Mass., S36982
Joseph, Mass., Navy, R.I., S1652
Joseph, N.H., Vt., S12487
Joseph, Pa., Mary, W25418
Joseph, S.C., Ruth, W8608
Joseph, Va., S8208
Joseph C., Ct., Sally, R2018
Joshua, Mass., Sarah, W24831; BLWt.9484-160-55
Joshua, R.I., Wealthy, W22790
Josiah, Cont., Mass., Lucy, W25417
Josiah, Cont., Mass., N.H., Patience, W23820
Josiah, Mass., S18764
Josiah, Mass., R1994
Josiah, N.H., S22172
Josiah, N.H., Pernell, W22803; BLWt.33560-160-55
Judah, Mass., Esther, W18913
Julia Ann, N.J., former wid. of James Carr, R1721
Justus, Mass., S29713
Lamberton, Pvt., Ct., BLWt.5570 iss. 2/26/1794 to Wm. Walter Parson
Lamberton/Lambert, Ct., Martha, W18919

CLARK (continued)
Lawrence, R.I., Hannah, W22784
Lee, N.C., Va., S2431
Lemuel, Mass., See CLARKE
Lemuel, Mass., Susannah, W2757
Lemuel, Mass., Sea Service, Navy & Privateer, S18763
Levi, Ct., S37852
Levi, Ct., Anna, W1146
Lewis, Va., S39324
Lewis, Va., Sally, W6679; BLWt. 34973-160-55
Lydia, Ct., former wid. of Joseph Judson, which see
Lyman, Ct., S37851
Lyman, Mass., Sousana, W15646
Maltiah, Mass., Hannah, W1718
Martin, Ct., BLWts.5549 & 5463 iss. 9/24/1790
Mathew, Mass., S12503
Matthew, Mass., S5011
Matthew, Mass., S44762
Matthew, Va., R2004
Micajah, N.C., S30940
Micajah, Va., Keziah, W6678
Michael, Pvt., Md., BLWt.11060 iss. 11/29/179- to Edward Jenkins, Admr.
Michael, Pvt., Md., BLWt.11095 iss. 8/8/1797 to James DeBaufre ass.
Moses, Ct., S10454
Moses, Ct., Patty, W6684
Moses, Mass., S16712
Moses, Mass., S34699; BLWt.725-100
Moses, Mass., Sarah, W16537
Moses, Mass., Elizabeth, W18914
Moses, R.I., S21696
Nathan, Ct., Miriam, W17635
Nathan, Ct., Ruth, W25420
Nathan, Mass., BLWt.40940-160-55
Nathan, Mass., R.I., S12513
Nathan, N.Y., S12697
Nathaniel, Ct., Sarah, W20879
Nathaniel, Mass., S2433
Nathaniel, Mass., S20687
Nathaniel, N.H., S45637; BLWt. 366-100
Nathaniel, N.C., Louisa, W1387; BLWt.32233-160-55
Nathaniel, S.C., R2007
Nathaniel Saunders, Cont., N.H. S23164
Nicholas, R.I., Barbara, W20872
Noah, Ct., R2008
Noah, N.J., R2007 1/2
Norman, Mass., S16715
Oliver, Ct., Huldah, W717; BLWt. 33758-160-55
Oliver, Ct., Betsey, W23816
Oren, N.H., S38613
Orpha, Mass., former wid. of John Fox, which see
Osborn, N.C., S41489
Patrick, Va., S30932
Paul, Cont., R.I., S17885; BLWt. 941-100
Paul, Mass., Submit, W23821
Peter, Mass., Navy, Betsey/ Elizabeth, W15648
Phebe, Ct., former wid. of Samuel Husted, W16909

CLARK (continued)
Phineas, Mass., Elizabeth, W18915
Reuben, Ct., S12506
Reuben, Ct., Prudence, W10624; BLWt.8171-160-55
Reuben, Ct., Zeruiah, W14483
Reuben, Cont., Mass., S44775
Richard, Mass., R2012
Richard, Mass., R.I., S17344
Richard, N.J., Elizabeth, W10618
Richard, N.Y., S12609
Richard, Va., Va. half pay
Robert, Ct., S37864
Robert, N.H., Hannah, W1823
Robert, Va., S1752
Rodman, Mass., R2013
Roger, Ct., S44773
Roswell, Ct., Susannah, W6681; BLWt.26590-160-55
Roswell, Ct., Dolly, W6686; BLWt.8167-160-55
Rowland, R.I., Sarah, W14469
Rufus, Ct., Lydia, W10621
Rufus, Pvt., Mass., BLWt.3915 iss. 4/1/1790
Salvanus/Sylvanus, Mass., S30330
Samuel, Ct., b. Milford, Ct., S18350
Samuel, Ct., Haddam res. at enl. Susannah, W17626
Samuel, Ct., Middletown res. at enl., Hannah, R1976
Samuel, Ct., Cont., S44771
Samuel, Cont., Mass., b.Sherburn, Mass., S29712
Samuel, Cont., Mass., S34696. His wid. pensioned as former wid. of Thos. Herring, which see
Samuel, Mass., b. & enl. Newton, Mass., S12484
Samuel, Mass., b.& enl. Berwick, Me., S12492
Samuel, Mass., N.H., b. Billerica, Mass., Saloma W., W1385; BLWt.35830-160-55
Samuel, N.H., Shutesbury, Mass. res. at enl., Sarah, W1228
Samuel, Pvt., N.J., BLWt.8212 iss. 6/16/1789 to Thomas Coyle, ass.
Samuel, N.J., enl. at Morristown, N.J., Catharine, W2530
Samuel, N.J., Essex Co. res., Abigail W., R1961
Samuel, N.J., N.Y., Seneca Co. res., S44770
Samuel, N.C., enl. in Burke Co., Margaret, R2000
Samuel, R.I., enl. Hopkinton, R.I., S44759
Samuel, R.I., b.Bellingham, Mass., Cumberland, R.I., res. at enl., also War of 1812, S12496
Samuel, Va., res. & enl. in Augusta Co., S9188; BLWt. 26366-160-55
Samuel Hill, N.H., Comfort Smith, former wid., W22252
Sarah, Ct., former wid. of Miles Dickson, W20881
Sarah, Mass., former wid. of

CLARK (continued)
Thomas Moore, R2017
Selah, Mass., S44769
Seth, Mass., S18355
Seth, Mass., S34697
Seth, Mass., Eleanor, R1969
Shadrack, Va., R2019
Silas, Phila.,Pa. agency, Dis.
Silas, Mass., BLWt.336-300-Capt. Iss. 3/6/1790. No papers
Silvanus, Ct., S17342
Smith, Ct., Jane, R1981
Solomon, Ct., Mahitable, W16536 BLReg.295616-55
Stephen, Ct., S17886
Stephen, N.H., Mary, W15882
Susana Elizabeth, Va., former wid. of John Scott, which see
Sylvanus, Mass., See Salvanus CLARK
Taylor, War of 1812, Lovey Aldrich, ---. This man's wid. m. Caleb Aldrich, which see
Thaddeus, Mass., S44761
Theophilus, Mass., War of 1812, BLWt.47962-160-55.
Theophilus, Mass., Navy, Privateer, S16081
Thomas, Ct., S19247
Thomas, Ct., R.I., Fanny, W22797
Thomas, Pvt., Del., BLWt.10727 iss. 12/28/1791 to Ashton Humphreys, ass.
Thomas, Del., BLWt.2047-100
Thomas, Mass., S36974
Thomas, Pa., S41483
Thomas, S.C., S31610
Thomas, Va., enl. Charlotte Co., S17888
Thomas, Va., War of 1812, Tenn. Militia, Sally, S39327, Tenn. res. in 1820
Thomas, Va., Jane, W2920; BLWt. 2492-160-55
Thomas, Va., Lucy, W18910
Thomasin, Mass., former wid. of Thomas Herring, which see
Timothy, Vt., S28689
Ward/Hezekiah Ward, N.H., Judy, W23829
Waters, Cont., Ct., S38612
Watrous, Cont., Ct., S38612
Wells, Mass., R.I., S9835
William, Ct., S5009
William, Ct., S10458
William, Ct., S16713
William, Ct., S37863
William, Ct., S44758
William, Ct., Eunice Ford, W18906; BLWt.7082-160-55
William, Ct., Anner, W22791
William, Cont., Ct., S44760; BLWt.5642-100. Iss. 4/1/1790 No papers
William, Mass., S17340
William, Mass., S23573
William, Mass., S30332
William, Mass., S34214
William, Mass., S34695
William, Mass., French & Indian War, S46575
William, Mass., Hannah, W14484

CLARK (continued)
William, Mass., Eunice, W14491
William, Mass., R2022
William, N.H., S29080
William, Pvt., N.J., BLWt.8211 iss. 10/4/1796
William, N.J., S973
William, N.J., BLWt.370-200-Lt. Iss. 8/11/1789, also recorded as BLWt.2519. No papers
William, N.Y., Phebe Reeve, former wid., R8682
William, N.C., Ruth, W6680
William, N.C., Elender, R1968
William, Corp., Pa., BLWt.9203 iss. 3/10/1790 to Wm. Clark
William, Pa., S3160
William, Pa., R2023
William, S.C., Sarah, W8606; BLWt.30697-160-55
William, S.C., Rosa, W8610; BLWt.36506-160-55
William, Va., Nancy Ann Andrews, former wid., W1694; BLWt.19723-160-55
William, Va., Barbara, W6683
Zachariah, Pvt., Md., BLWt.11102 iss. 6/11/1790
Zelotes, Ct., S3161

CLARKE (See also CLARK)
Abashaba, former wid. of Noah Parr, N.C., R1960
Abel, Ct., Lois, W1561
Arnold, R.I., Fillee, W17625
Arnold, R.I., Lucy, W17628
Benjamin, Pvt., Ct., BLWt.5553 iss. 12/13/1791
Benjamin, Pvt., Mass., BLWt.3938 iss. 1/7/1796 to Calvin Sanger
Bunker, Pvt., N.H., BLWt.2991 iss. 12/18/1795 to Francis Appleton, ass.
Christopher, Va., Elizabeth, W25426
Edward, R.I., S22176
Elias, R.I., S21699
Ethan, R.I., S21697
George, R.I., Keturah, W22778
Isaac, N.Y., S9317
Isaac Smith, Navy, R.I., Mary, W17634
Joel, Ct., Susannah, W22799; BLWt.1515-100
John, Ct., S37859
John, Cont., Md., S35839
John, Del., R1991
John, Md., S3158
John, Mass., S34700
John, Pvt., N.Y., BLWt.6899 iss. 9/5/1791
John, Pvt., N.Y., BLWt.7009 iss. 3/15/1791
John, S.C., S2439
John, Va., S35842
John, Va., Ann, W8607
John, Va., R1990
John, Va., BLWt.2439-200
Jonathan Dana, N.H., Phebe, R2009
Joseph, Ct., BLWt.383-200-Lt. Iss. 1/29/1790. No papers
Joseph, Va., S30943

CLARKE (continued)
Joshua, Mass., Miriam, W15647
Lemuel, Mass., S17343
Lemuel, Mass., S19599
Norris, Pvt., N.J., BLWt.8168 iss. 4/2/1790 to Josiah Hunt, ass.
Obadiah, Va., Nancy, W8609
Oliver, R.I., BLWt.426-300-Capt. Iss. 4/18/1793. Also recorded under BLWt.2631
Peter, Mass., S34701
Phinehas, Mass., Jemima, W14496
Robert, Va., S8210
Samuel, Pa., S39322
Simeon, R.I., Betsey, W1231
Spencer, Va., Elizabeth/Nancy Elizabeth, W2529; BLWt.3066-160-55
Stephen, Va., S9180
Thomas, Pvt., Md., BLWt.11032 iss. 8/14/1795 to Francis Sherrard, ass.
Thomas, N.C., BLWt.474-500-Col. Iss. 2/23/1795 to John Innes Clarke heir-at-law to his brother, T.C. No papers
Thomas, R.I., Sarah, W23819
Thomas, S.C., S10451; BLWt.45711-160-55
Thomas, Pvt., Va., BLWt.12044 iss. 1/31/1794 to John Stockdale, ass.
Turner, Va., Elizabeth, W3389
Weeden, R.I., Thankful, W14492
Weston, R.I., S40046
William, Md., S8213
William, R.I., Sea Service, Privateer, Mass., Ruth, R2014
William, Va., S16353
William, Va., Hannah, W6687
William Case, R.I., Sarah, W22783

CLARKSON, Constantine, Va., S32180
David, Va., Phebe, W9794; BLWt. 28519-160-55
Matthew, Cont., Mass., BLWt. 2019-400
Randolph, N.J., Catharine, W448

CLARY, Allen, Mass., R21839
Daniel, Cont., S23576
David, Mass., Rhoda, W14487
James, Ct., Cont., N.Y., S44785
John, Va., Sarah, W6691
Phinehas, Mass., S15778
Samuel, Pvt., Ct., BLWt.5657 iss. 4/6/1795
Samuel, Ct., S44791
William, Pvt., Mass., BLWt.3923 iss. 8/11/1790 to Robt. Dunlop

CLASON, Isaac, Ct., Rachel, W10619 BLWt.50859-160-55

CLASPY, John, Va., S30934

CLATON, Zebulon, N.J., Mary, See CLAYTON

CLATTERBUCK, James, Va., S9179
Reuben, Va., Martha, W9796

CLAUBAUGH/CLAUGHBAUGH, Martin, Pa., Margaret, W3222

CLAUNCE, George, N.C., Chloe, See CLONTZ

CLAUSEN, John, Pa. res. 1853, R2025

CLAUSON, Ezra, N.Y., See CLAWSON

CLAUSON (continued)
Jacob, N.Y., R2024
CLAWSON, Ezra, N.Y., S44784
Garret, Va., Kezia, W3776
John, N.J., R13199
CLAXTON, Rosannah, former wid. of Howel Tatum, which see
CLAY, Benjamin, Mass., S36978
Daniel, N.H., S42128
David, N.C., Eva, W6690; BLWt.5001-160-55
Elijah, Va., S32178
George, Pvt., Hazen's Regt., BLWt.12905 iss. 6/20/1789
John, Mass., N.H., S10446
John, Va., Melison, R2029
Matthew, Va., BLWt.456-200-Lt. Iss. 5/20/1797. No papers
Samuel, Mass., S38615
Thomas, Va., S9319
William, Va., Rebecca, W156
CLAYBORN, John, Va., S1945
CLAYBORNE, Leonard, S.C., R1956
CLAYCOMB, Frederick, Va., S16083
CLAYES, Elijah, N.H., BLWt.455-300-Capt., & 2709-300-Capt. No papers
Peter, Cont., Mass., S38609; BLWt.341-300-Capt. Iss. 1/7/1790 to Peter Clays.No papers
CLAYPOLE, Abraham G., Pa., BLWt. 414-300-Capt. Iss. 5/3/1796. No papers
CLAYS, Peter, See CLAYES
CLAYTON, Augustine, S.C., S12693
Coleman, N.C., Jane, W6692; BLWt.17574-160-55
Elijah, N.J., Leah, W3073
Elisha, N.J., Elizabeth, W1145; BLWt.26529-160-55
Henry, N.J., S34212
Henry, Pa., Ann, W4655; BLWt. 3605-160-55
Jehu, N.J., S2432
Job D., N.J., S2434
John, N.J., S613
John, N.J., Rebecca, W3777; BLWt.15167-160-55
John, N.C., S9183
John, S.C., Hannah, R2031
Jonathan, N.J., S16717
Joseph, Va., BLWt.2474-100
Lambert, N.C., Sarah, W4923
Noah, N.J., Elizabeth, R2030
Peter, Pa., Rachel, W20878
Philip, Va., BLWt.460-200-Lt. Iss. 4/6/1792. No papers
Zebulon, N.J., Mary, R2034
CLAYWELL, Shadrack, Cont., Va. S30929
CLEAMONS, Patrick, Pa., S41476
CLEAR, Godfrey, N.J., Nancy, See CLAIR
Philip, N.H., S45677
CLEARWATER, Benjamin, Va., See CLEARWATERS
Jacob, N.Y., S12478
Jacob, N.Y., Sarah, W16906
John, N.Y., Rachel, W23818
Martin, Pvt., N.Y., BLWt.6914 iss. 12/28/1791 to Moses Phillips, ass.

CLEARWATER (continued)
Martin, N.Y., Lea, W20883
Mary, Cont., Pa., former wid. of James Young, W20885
Matthew, N.Y., S10456
CLEARWATERS, Benjamin, Va., Elender, W4925
CLEARY, William, Pvt., Md., BLWt.11035 iss. 9/24/1792
CLEASBY, Joseph, Mass., S45678
Joseph, Mass., Sarah Ambrose, former wid., W15870
Joseph, Mass., BLWt.26465-160-55
CLEAVELAND, Amasa, Mass., S18349
Aquilla, N.H., Mercy Wellman, former wid., R2036; BLWt.2036-100
Benjamin, Cont., R.I., Mass., Sarah, W16903
Chester, Ct., Elizabeth, See CLEAVLAND
Ebenezer, Mass., S34596
Elisha, N.H., Hannah, R2035
Enoch, Cont., Mass., Lydia, W20888
Frederick, Ct., Susannah, W20884
Gardner, Ct., Huldah, W25425; See CLEVELAND
Isaac, Ct., Mamre, W22796
Jacob, Ct., S37860
John, Ct., Sarah, See CLEVELAND
John, N.C., Catharine, W6696
John, Va., Elizabeth, W2999
Johnson, Ct., See CLEVELAND
Joseph, Ct., Cont., S10447
Joseph, Mass., S44781
Joseph, Mass., Jemima, See CLEVELAND
Josiah, Ct., Mass., See CLEVELAND
Josiah, Mass., Delight, See CLEVELAND
Nehemiah, Mass., Hannah, W17616; BLWt.9436-160-55
Nehemiah, Mass., Experience, W22801
Roswell, Mass., S44783
Samuel, Ct., Lucy, See CLEVELAND
Samuel, Mass., Mercy, See CLEVELAND
Silas, Ct., Navy, S12486
Solomon, Ct., Martha, See CLEVELAND
Squier, Ct., See CLEVELAND
Tracy, Ct., S2124
William, Ct., See CLEVELAND
William, Ct., Sarah Converse, former wid., W23836
William, Va., Margaret, W8611
CLEAVENGER, Isaiah, N.J., Catharine, W4653
CLEAVER, Benjamin, Pvt., Md., BLWt.11029 iss. 8/14/1795 to Francis Sherrard, ass.
Benjamin, Va., R2039
William, Va., S30331
CLEAVES, Abraham, Mass., Deborah, W6700; BLWt.61058-160-55
Edmund, Mass., S36975
James, Mass., See CLEVES
Nathaniel, Mass., Mary Porter, former wid., W15624
William, Pvt., Mass., BLWt. 3850 iss. 8/1/1789 to Thomas Cushing, ass.

CLEAVES (continued)
William, Mass., Eleanor, W23804
CLEAVLAND, Chester, Ct., Elizabeth, W20865
Cyrus, Ct., Mary, W20877
Solomon, Mass., See CLEVELAND
CLEER, Peter, Cont., D.C. agency & res., S35835
CLEFFORD, John, N.H., Sarah, W20868
CLEFTON, George, Del., Milly, See CLIFTON
CLELAND, John, Ct., Thankful, W20869
CLEM, John, Md., Susannah, R2040
John, Va., R21840
CLEMANS, John, Va., S2435
CLEMENCE, Ebenezer, Mass., S18765
Joseph, Md., S30933
Peter, Pa., S41478
CLEMENS, Henry, N.J., See CLEMMENS
John, Mass., Polly, See CLEMONS
John, N.C., See CLEMANS
John, Pa., BLWt.312-100
CLEMENT, Charles, Pvt., Md., See CLEMENTS
Christopher, Mass., Hannah, W20870
Edmund, Va., S21698
Isaac, Sgt., Mass., BLWt.3964 iss. 2/27/1790 to Theodosius Fowler
Isaac, Mass., S20976
Isaac, N.H., Dorothy, W18907
Jesse, N.H., R2044
John, N.H., S17883
Lambert, N.Y., Mary, W6695
Moses, Mass., S18761
Nicholas, Pvt., N.Y., BLWt.6974 iss. 7/10/1790 to John Quackinboss, ass.
Peter, Pvt., Pa., See CLEMENTS
Reuben, Mass., Hannah, W20887
Richard, N.H., Hannah Clark, former wid., W6682; BLWt.6014-160-55. See Claim of Jonathan Clark N.H. probably her husband, and her 1st husb., Enoch Noyes, who d.1801 was a Rev. soldier.
Robert, Pvt., Ct., BLWt.5597 iss. 3/7/1792 to Eneas Munson
Simeon, N.H., S17887
Vachel, Va., R21700
CLEMENTS, Aaron, Mass., BLWt. 868-100
Benjamin, Va., Mildred, W1230; BLWt.13427-160-55
Bernard, Cont., Va., See CLEMONS
Charles, Pvt., Md., BLWt.11036 iss. 8/14/1795 to Francis Sherrard, ass.
Charles, Va., S8214
Clement, S.C., S8217
Cornelius, N.C., S8218; BLWt. 7430-160-55
David, N.C., S35840
Gabriel, S.C., Mary, W27592; BLWt.67699-160-55
Henry, Md., BLWt.441-200-Lt. Iss. 3/10/1790. No papers
Jacob, N.Y., S9187
John, Va., S12511
Mace, Va., BLWt.464-400-Surgeon Iss. 5/29/1792. No papers

CLEMENTS (continued)
Peter, Pvt., Pa., BLWt.9176 iss. 4/27/1793 to Alex. Power, ass.
Roger, N.C., Hannah, R2043
Thomas, N.H., S45676
Thomas, Va., Mary, R2045
Timothy, N.H., S45675
William, Mass., S44789
William, Mass., Anna, W16910
William, N.C., S30942
William, N.C., Elizabeth, R2042
CLEMM, William, Pa., Catharine, R2041
CLEMMENS, Henry, N.J., S41477
CLEMMONS, John, Md., N.C., S8215
John, R.I., Phebe, W20891
Richard, R.I., S21114
Thompson, N.C., S1946
CLEMONS, Benjamin, Mass., S12480
Bernard, Cont., Va., Sally, W9792
Edward, Pvt., Mass., BLWt.3913 iss. 8/26/1789
John, Mass., Polly, W20867; BLWt. 5201-160-55
John, Pa., See CLEMENS
Jonathan, Mass., S44790
Patrick, Pa., See CLEAMONS
CLENCY, George, Va., S3164
CLENDENIN, Isaac, N.J., Ann/Mary, R2046
James, Md., S22679
John, Pa., Rebecca, W3223
CLENDENNAN, Adam, Pvt., Pa., BLWt.9105 i-s. 6/24/-- to Francis Kirkpatrick, ass.
John, N.C., BLWt.1803-200
CLENDENNIN, James, Pa., S40837
CLENNY, William, N.C., S32182
CLERNO, Francis, Pvt., Hazen's Regt., BLWt.12878 iss. 8/14/179- to Benjamin Moore, ass.
CLEVEDENCE, John, See CLEVIDENCE
CLEVELAND, Absalom, N.C., S6774
Aquilla, N.H., Mercy Wellman, former wid., R2036
Enoch, Cont., Mass. See CLEAVELAND
Enoch, Pvt., Mass., BLWt.3950 Iss. 12/12/1792 to Daniel King
Ephraim, Mass., BLWt.362-300-Capt. Iss. 3/25/1790. No papers
Gardner, Ct., Huldah, W25425; BLWt.12715-160-55
Henry, Mass., S19248
Ichabod, N.J., Keturah, W6698; BLWt.27626-160-55
Jacob, Pvt., Ct., BLWt.5546 iss. 3/27/1794 to Zephaniah Swift, ass.
John, Ct., Sarah, W16535; BLWt. 2334-150
John, Ct., Mass., S44780
Johnson, Ct., S37862
Joseph, Cont., Mass., Jemima, R2037
Josiah, Ct., S37850
Josiah, Ct., Mass., S44782
Josiah, Mass., Delight, W25421; BLWt.3878-100-Pvt. Iss. 11/3/1791. No papers
Lydia, Mass., R2038, former wid. of Nathan Kinney
Samuel, Ct., Lucy, W720; BLWt.

CLEVELAND (continued)
6040-160-53
Samuel, Mass., Mercy, W6697
Solomon, Ct., Martha, W6699
Solomon, Ct., Hannah, W10617
Solomon, Mass., S44778
Squier, Ct., Cont., Pamelia, W22798
Stephen, Ct., Hannah, W23815
Stephen, Cont., Mass., Vt., S44779
Timothy, Ct., BLWt.442-200-Lt. Iss. 12/31/1795. Also recorded under 2658. No papers
William, Ct., S12494
William, Va., See CLEAVELAND
CLEVENGER, Eden/Eben, Va., S42648
Isaiah, N.J., See CLEAVENGER
CLEVER, Alexander, N.Y., S37853
CLEVES, James, Mass., R2047
CLEVIDENCE, John, Md., Mary, W6689; BLWt.24775-160-55
CLEVINGER, Thomas, Pvt., N.J., BLWt.8170 iss. 4/23/1798 to Abraham Bell, ass.
CLEVLAND, Josiah, Mass., Delight, See CLEVELAND
Samuel, Ct., S15378
CLEWLEY, Isaac, Pvt., Crane's Cont. Artillery, Mass., BLWt. 3981 iss. 7/28/1795 to George Brewer, Jr.
CLEWLY, Isaac, Mass., Abiah, R2048
CLEWS, Thomas, Pvt. "in the Invalids", BLWt.12950 iss. 10/31/1791
CLIATT, Isaac, R20341, Ga. res. in 1828
CLIBORNE, Leonard, Va., Frances, See CLAIBORNE
CLIBOURN, William, Va., Sarah, W10620; BLWt.77535-160-55
CLIFFORD, David, N.H., Mehitable, W1026; BLWt.24774-160-55
Deborah, N.H., W2531; former wid. of Elias Cheney
Isaac, N.H., S10450
John, N.H., Sarah, See CLEFFORD
John, N.J., S970
John, Pa., Elizabeth Cottle, former wid., R19372
Michael, N.C., Elizabeth, W25416; BLWt.26975-160-55
Nathan, Mass., S30931
William, Cont., N.H., S45681
William, Pvt., N.H., BLWt.3022 iss. 1/14/1790 to Ladd & Cass, assignees
Zacharias, Cont., N.H., S18852
CLIFFTON, Thomas, Cont., Md. res., S42125
CLIFT, Adna Winslow, Mass., Bethiah, W22786
Joseph, Pvt., N.Y., BLWt.6921 iss. 10/22/1791 to Asa Ballard, ass.
Lemuel, Ct., BLWt.373-300-Capt. Iss. 9/2/1790. No papers
Willis, Ct., Cont., Mary, W22788; BLWt.368-400-Major. Iss. 6/6/1797 to Nathaniel Satterlee, ass. No papers
CLIFTON, George, Del., Milly, W10632; BLWts. 61-60-55 and

CLIFTON (continued)
1794-100
Joshua, Pvt., Va., BLWt.12035 iss. 11/1/1791 to Wm. Lane, ass.
Joshua, Va., S35836
Thomas, Md., S42125
Whitinton, Del., S35842
Whittington, Pvt., Del., BLWt. 10735 iss. 9/2/1789
William, N.C., Sarah, W3945
CLINCKENBEARD, John, N.C., S30930
CLINE, Andrew, Pa., S12507
Catharine, Pa., W9791; BLWt. 98555-160-55; former wid. of Robert Cuning
Conrad, Pa., S34691
Conrad, Pa., S42123
George, Pvt., Md., BLWt.12880 iss. 5/6/-- to himself
Henry, N.Y., S29079
Jacob, Pvt., N.Y., BLWt.6901 iss. 7/18/1792 to Daniel Baldwin, ass.
Jacob, N.Y., Lydia, W16911
John, Va., S35837
Jonas, N.Y., Caty, R2049
Michael, N.C., Fanny, W6675
William, Md., R2050
William, Pa., S40838
CLINENDEN, James, Pa. See CLENDENNIN
CLINGLER, John, Pa., Catharine, See KLINGLER
CLINKENBEARD, Isaac, Md., Va., S15380
CLINTON, Alexander, Cont., Col. Lamb's Regt. Arty., BLWt.396-200-Lt. Iss. 9/15/1790. No papers
Allen, Ct., S12510; BLWt.34501-160-55
Benjamin, N.J., Elizabeth, W844
Henry, Ct., R2052
Isaac, Ct., S12498
James, N.Y., BLWt.387-850
James, Pvt., Pa., BLWt.9190 iss. 3/10/1795 to Joseph Rigloss, ass.
James, Pa., S34205
James, S.C., S2437
Joseph, Pvt., N.Y., BLWt.6976 iss. 9/15/1790 to John S. Hobart, et al ass.
Joseph B., Ct., Cont., W6832; BLWt.1873-100 & 313-60-55; Margaret More, former widow
Mathew, Pvt., Pa., BLWt.9092 iss. 3/22/1791 to Alexander Power, ass.
Peter, S.C., Frances B., W9390
Richard, S.C., S21113
Thomas, Md., S34693; BLWt.632-100
William, S.C., Violet, R2053
CLIZBE, Joseph, N.J., S29133
CLOBBOGH, Martin, Pa. See CLAUBAUGH
CLOCK, John, Ct., Sarah, W17623
CLODFELTER, George, N. C., See GLATFELDER
CLOES, Charles, Md., Hannah, R2054

CLONTZ, George, N.C., Chloe, W4924
Jeremiah, N.C., S8219
CLOPP, John, Pa., R2055
CLOPTON, Thomas, Va., S9318
Walter, Va., S3165
CLOSE, Abraham, Ct., Mary, W25414
Benjamin, Ct., S27645
Charles, Md., See CLOES
Henry, Pa., S24116
Jesse, N.Y., R2056
Solomon, Ct., S15377
CLOSER, Christopher, Pvt., N.Y., BLWt.6902 iss. 8/3/1790 to Corn[s] Van Dyck, ass.
CLOSS, Charles, Md., See CLOES
CLOSSEN, Zachariah, Pa., S22173
CLOSSER, Christopher, N.Y., S44787
CLOSSON, Nathan, Cont., R.I., S46374; BLWt.2328-100
Nehemiah, Vt., Mary, W18918
CLOTHER, Jesse, Mass., S12488
CLOUD, D. Forest, Ct., Anna, W25415
Ezekiel, Ga., Elizabeth, W6920; BLWt.26643-160-55
Forest, Ct., See D. Forest CLOUD
John, Ga., S.C., S30935
Joseph, Pvt., Hazen's Regt., BLWt.12919 iss. 10/12/1790
Noah, Ga., S.C., Unity, W9389
William, Va., Nancy, W5247; BLWt. 36666-160-55
CLOUGH, Aaron, Cont., N.H., Elizabeth, W23827
Abigail, N.H., W18908, former wid. of Samuel Silver
Abner, N.H., S16716
Benjamin, Cont., Mass., Molly/ Mary, W22792
Benjamin, Mass., S19250
Benjamin, Mass., Joanna, W18916
Benjamin, Pvt., N.Y., BLWt.6961 iss. 10/5/1790
Cornelius, N.H., Mary, W15998
Daniel, Mass., S29077
Daniel, Pvt., N.H., BLWt.2994 iss. 1/26/1796 to James A. Neal, ass.
Daniel, N.H., Ruth Foss, former wid., W21149; BLWt.36763-160-55 She also applied for BLWt. for service of last husb., Benjamin Foss, N.H., which see
David, Mass., S38608
David, N.H., S9185
Gibson, Mass., BLWt.454-150-Ensign. Iss. 2/9/1798 to Addison Richardson, ass. No papers Also recorded under BLWt.2697
Gilman, N.H., S18766
John, Pvt., N.H., Invalids, BLWts.2989 & 12949 iss. 2/22/1792 to John Peck, ass.
John, N.H., S36981
John, N.H., Dolly, W15883
Jonathan, Ct., R2058
Jonathan, Mass., Elizabeth, W14481
Joseph, Mass., S45679
Joseph, N.H., S22174
Noah, Mass., See CLUFF
Obadiah, N.H., Sarah, W18912
Oliver, N.H., Sally, W6701; BLWt.8472-160-55

CLOUGH (continued)
Rhoda, Cont., N.H., former wid. of Elisha Woodbury, which see
Simon, N.H., S22175
William, Mass., S34597
Zaccheus, Corp., N.H., BLWt. 3023 iss. 7/21/1790 to Ladd & Cass, assnes.
CLOUSEN, John, See CLAUSEN
CLOUSER, Mathias, Pvt., Va., Lee's Legion, BLWt.12970 iss. 1/19/1792 to Wm. Lane, ass.
CLOUTIER, Charles, Cont., Canada, S44788
CLOUTMAN, Thomas, Mass., Hepsibah, W1227; BLWt.13879-160-55
CLOWARD, Abraham, Md., Ann, See CLOWERD
CLOWER, Daniel, N.C., S37865; N.A. Acc. No.874, see 050032 Va. half pay
George, Va., S39323
Henry, Va., See CLOYER
Jonathan, Cont., N.C., Mary, W22802
William, N.C., S34690
CLOWERD, Abraham, Md., Ann, W408
CLOWNEY, Samuel, S.C., Elizabeth, W9391
CLOYD, William, Pa., S1799
CLOYER, Henry, Va., S35838
CLUER, Joseph, N.H., Margaret, See MC CLURE
CLUFF, Isaac, Pvt., Ct., BLWt. 5568 iss. 10/7/1789 to Benjamin Tallmadge
Isaac, Ct., S37870
John, Mass., Mehitable, W719
Noah, Mass., S36972
Samuel, Mass., Abigail W6694; BLWt.40935-160-55
CLUM, Adam, N.Y., S28688
CLUMBERG/CLUMBARD/CLUMBRED, Philip, Pa., Catharine Howard, former wid., R5274
CLUMP, Jeremiah, N.Y., R6007
CLUNG, Henry, Va., See KLUNCK
William, Pvt., Va., BLWt.12036 iss. 7/14/1792 to Robert Means, ass.
CLUTCH, John, N.J., S2126
Obediah, Pvt., N.J., BLWt.8167 iss. 9/9/1790 to John Pope, ass.
CLUTE, Bartholomew, N.Y., S12499
Derrick, N.Y., See Garret Derrick CLUTE
Frederick, N.Y., R2063
Garret, N.Y., Batshabe, W16905
Garret Derrick, N.Y., Margaret, W23813
Geradus, N.Y., S23160
Isaac, N.Y., Helen, W16212
Jacob I., N.Y., Mary, W16534
Jacob P., N.Y., S28684
John F., N.Y., Mary, R2065
CLUTTER, Caspar, Md., S5010
Simeon, Md., R21843
William, N.J., R2066
CLUVERIUS, Gibson, Va., Susan Loury, former wid., W8061;

CLUVERIUS (continued)
BLWt.30754-160-55
CLUXTON, Samuel, Ct., S37866
COAKLEY, Robert, Pvt. "in Moylan's Dragoons", Pa., BLWt.9186 iss. 9/19/1791
COAL, Enos, N.J., R2126
Willis, N.C., Ruth, W6936; BLWt.47771-160-55
COALDEN, James, Va., S35846
COALMAN, David, N.J. See COLEMAN
COALTER, Samuel, Pa., S39352
COAN, John, Ct., S31628
Phebe, former wid. of Joseph Hull, Mass., R2068
Samuel, Ct., Cont., Betsey, See CONE
William, Mass., S44793
COANS, Frederick, N.J., R2069
COAS, William, Mass., Privateer, S29729
COATES, Charles, Pvt., Mass., BLWt.3894 iss. 5/24/1790
John, Pa., Dis. No papers
John, Va., S10131
Reuben, Mass., S34245
Robert, Ct., Cont., S12599
William, Va., S8232
William, Va., Susannah, W10675 1/2
COATNEY, James, Va., S3203
Michael, Va., See COURTNEY
COATS, Amos, Ct., Anna, W10643
Benjamin, N.H., S9196
Christopher, N.Y., S12515
Edward, Ct., S15780
John, Mass., S34249
John, Pvt. "in the Artillery Artificers of Pa.," BLWt.12959 iss. 2/14/1791 to Alexander Power, ass.
John, Pa., See COATES
Reuben, Mass., See COATES
Thomas, Ct., Lois Delano, former wid., W22925
William, Va., See Susannah COATES
Zebulon, Mass., N.Y., Privateer, S12591
COBANN, Joseph, Ct., See CORBIN
COBB, Abel, Pvt., Mass., BLWt. 3927 iss. 3/10/1796
Abel, Mass., S43369
Anna, N.H., Vt., former wid. of Clifford Chaffee, W23847
Benjamin, Ct., Azubah, W10661; BLWt.26248-160-55
Benjamin, Mass., S12534
Binney, Mass., S22184
Daniel, Cont., Mass., S45688
Daniel, Mass., S28691
Daniel, R.I., S40048
David, Cont., Mass., S46433; BLWt.331-500-Col. Iss. 4/20/1790. No papers
David, N.C., Catharine, R2071
Ebenezer, Cont., Mass., Elizabeth, W23870
Edward, Mass., Hannah, W23843
Eliphalet, Mass., Lucy, W20917
Ethelred, Indian War, St. Clair's, Old War Inv. file 342

COBB (continued)
Ezekiel, Mass., Nancy Swett, former wid., W22359
Fleming, Va., Indian War, 1793, Sally, BLWt.83776-160-55
Francis, Cont., Mass., Phebe, W22842
George, Cont., Mass., S43386
Gideon, Mass., Mehitable Hovey, former wid., W14923. Her last husband, Dominicus Hovey was pensioned, which see
Henry S., Ct., R2073
Isaac, Mass., S19258
Isaiah, Mass., Lydia, W14572
Jacob, Mass., S15782
James, Mass., Deliverance, W14511
Jeremiah, Mass., BLWt.326-100
John, Ct., Mary, R2076
John, Ct., Mass., S38618; BLWt.537-100
John, Mass., S18767
John, Mass., S18776
John, Mass., S34234
John, N.C., Va., Frances, W20902
John, R.I., S43370; BLWt.1529-100
Joseph, Mass., R2074
Mallatiah, Cont., Mass., Betsey, R2070
Mallatiah/Melatiah, Mass., S45687 BLWt.812-100
Mason, Mass., Anna, W23850
Matthias, N.J., S43338
Melatiah, See Mallatiah
Nathan, Mass., S12556
Nathan, Mass., S43389
Nathaniel, Mass., S30947
Nathaniel, Mass., R1578
Nehemiah, Mass., S18775
Pharoah, N.C., S1657
Phebe, Mass., former wid. of Samuel Talbot, which see
Rowland, Mass., S36990
Salmon, Mass., Bathsheba, W4159; BLWt.56507-160-55
Samuel, Mass., Margaret, R2075
Samuel, Mass., N.H., S12593
Samuel, Va., S17359
Silas, Mass., S29091
Silvanus, Cont., Mass., S36996
Silvanus, Mass., S30944
Simeon, Ct., S38629
Simeon, Mass., N.H., Privateer, S18358
Sylvester, Mass., Vt., S12608
Thomas, N.J., Clara R., W8614; BLWt.10306-160-55
Thomas, R.I., Amey, W23846
William, Mass., Martha, W685; BLWt.5443-160-55
COBBS, John, Va., S15786
Robert, Va., Ann G., W18929
Samuel, Va., BLWt.355-200
COBBY, Salem, Pvt., N.H., BLWt. 2995 iss. 1/28/1790 to James Patterson, ass.
COBEA, John, Pa., BLWt.1224-300
COBIA, Daniel, S.C., Margaret B. Gruber, former wid., W21233
Nicholas, S.C., Ann, W22843
COBLEIGH, Eleazer, Cont., N.H.,

COBLEIGH (continued)
Tabatha, W18925; BLWt.24919-160-55
Reuben, N.H., Lucy, W4929
COBLER, Frederick, N.C., S1654
COBORN, James, Ct., S43401
COBURN, Andrew, Cont., N.H., See COLBURN
Asa, Cont., N.H., S12559
Asa, Mass., BLWt.342-300-Capt. Iss. 4/1/1790. No papers
Daniel, Ct., S34242
Hezekiah, Ct., S15054
Jeptha, Mass., S36986
Jesse, N.C., R2078
John, Pa., S3213
Josiah, Mass., Mary, BLWt. 14976-160-55
Lemuel, Ct., Sarah, W18946; BLWt.34961-160-55
Lydia, Cont., Mass., former wid. of Hugh Mason, which see
Merrill/Morrel, N.H., Abigail, W16106
Moses, Mass., S36993
Moses Bradstreet, Mass., S5018
Nathan, N.H., Phebe, W20921
Nathaniel, Cont., Mass., S40856, enl. in Ct.
Nathaniel, Mass., Mercy, W15654
Phinehas, Mass., Polly, W8190; BLWt.31892-160-55
Primus (colored), Mass., S34703
Saul, Mass., S34223
Titus, Mass., Rosanna, W6734; BLWt.12826-160-55
Zebediah, Cont., S43385
COCHRAN, Benjamin, N.C., Hannah, R2081
Blaney, Pa., S40854
Charles, Pa., R13321
Daniel, Sgt., Del., BLWt.10736 iss. 9/2/1789
Edward, Cont., Sea Service, Pa. res., S40848
Edward, Pvt. "in the Artillery Artificers of Pa.", BLWt.12960 iss. 7/27/178- to Richard Platt, ass.
Elijah, N.H., S15052
James, Md., Ann Mary, W25438; BLWt.14967-160-55
James, Pvt., N.H., BLWt.2987 iss. 11/4/1795 to Joseph Brown
James, N.H., S22694
James, N.H., Sally, W14565
James, Va., Temperance, W6743
James, R2082, Sumner Co., Tenn. res. in 1832
John, Cont., BLWt.1796-100. Vt. res. in 1816
John, Cont., Pa., Sarah, R2083
John, General Hospital; BLWt. 498-850-Director Gen. No papers
John, Navy, Mass., Elizabeth, W16214
John, N.C., S2140
John, N.C., S16720
Joseph, Va., See COUGHREN
Patrick, Sgt., Mass., BLWt.3840 iss. 12/3/1789 to Moses W. Barker, ass.

COCHRAN (continued)
Robert, Pa., S40855
Robert, S.C., S18359
Robert, Vt., Thankful, W4161
Samuel, Cont., Va., Sarah, W280
Samuel, Green Mt. Boys, N.Y., Mary Dutcher, former wid. W16964
Samuel, Pa., Hannah, R2080
Sarah, Va., former wid. of John Clark, which see
Thomas, Ga., Va., S16350
William, Ct., Lydia Chapman, former wid., W23793; BLWt. 27597-160-55
William, Va., S38624
William, Va., Mary, R2083
COCHRANE, Abner, Mass., Elizabeth, W5248
COCHRUN, Simon, Va., Sarah, W--- See Sarah Cochran, former wid. of John Clark, Cont. & Md.
COCK, Charles, Va., S8228
Jacob, N.J., S12595
James, N.Y., Hannah, W15884
John, Va., S3171
COCKE, Anderson, Va., S9232
Charles, Va., Indian Wars, 1774 & 1790, R2086
Colin, Va., BLWt.451-300, Joseph Watkins, ass. No papers
John Catesby, Va. Sea Service, Va. half pay, R28
Nathaniel, Va., Va. half pay, Rebecca, R13415
William, Va., S3187
COCKENBOUGH, John, Pa., S22186
COCKEREL, Peter, Va. See COCKRELL
COCKERHAM, Daniel, N.C., S8241
David, N.C., S8240; BLWt.26828-160-55
COCKERIL, Hanson, Va., Sarah, W4658; BLWt.26828-160-55
COCKEY, Edward, Md., R2088
COCKLE, John, Pvt., Crane's Artillery Mass., BLWt.3986 iss. 6/27/1789
John, Cont., Mass., S45699
COCKLEY, John, Pvt., N.Y., BLWts 6916 & 14027 iss. 10/5/1791 to Samuel Stringer, ass.
John, N.Y., S43382
COCKRAN, Blaney, Pvt., Pa., BLWt.9165 iss. 2/20/1794 to Thomas Denton, ass.
John, Va., S39353
Mathew, Va., S32185
Robert, N.Y., BLWt.389-450-Lt. Col. iss. 8/4/1791. No papers
William, Va., Mary, See COCHRAN
COCKRELL, John, Va., S35854
Peter, Va., S35849
COCKREM, Daniel, N.Y., S34231
Squier/Squire, Cont., N.J., S34225; BLWt.115-100
Thomas, Sgt., Lamb's Artillery N.Y., BLWt.6983 iss. 5/24/1790
COCKRIL, Hanson, Va., Sarah, See COCKERIL
COCKRILL, William, S.C., S39349
COCKRUM, William, Va., S30962
COCKS, Benjamin, Cont., Va., S39351

CODDING, Abijah, Mass., S45704
Robert, Mass., S12578
CODDINGTON, Benjamin, N.J., Privateer, S10468
Enoch, N.J., N.Y., S12560
Robert, N.J., Margaret, W3950
CODE, William, Pvt., N.Y., BLWt. 6954 Iss. 8/23/1796 to Joseph Roberts, ass.
CODER, Henry, Pa., R2091
CODRINGTON, Robert, N.J., See CODDINGTON
CODWISE, Christopher, N.Y., BLWt.392-200-Lt. Iss. 9/1/1790 to Abraham Kilson, ass. of Catherine Codwise, admx. No papers
CODY, James, Mass., R20627, See Lydia APTHORP
John, Mass., Mary, W15651
Joseph, Sgt., Mass., BLWt. 3898 iss. 6/7/1790
Joseph, Mass., Sarah, W15828
Samuel, Mass., S29097
COE, Abner, Ct., S18364
Asher, Ct., Huldah, W17639
Benjamin, Pa., R20342
Ebenezer, Ct., Cont., S2448
Ebenezer, Pa., S40852
Halsted, N.Y., Abby, W3951
Ichabod, Cont., N.Y., Polly, W2593; BLWts. 474-100 & 54-60-55
Jedediah, Ct., S21141
John, Ct., Lois, W23852
John, N.Y., S22700
Peter, N.J., Pa., S3167
Philip, Cont., R2095. Dau. res. in Washington Co., Ohio in 1854
Richard, Md., S12543
Samuel, Ct., S43404
Samuel, N.Y., Sarah, W22831
Samuel W., N.Y., Elizabeth, R2093; BLWt.35845-160-55
Seth, Ct., S18363
Thomas, Ct., S38630
Timothy, Ct., Abigail, W5250
William, Md., S8227
William, N.Y., S46645
Zachariah, Ct., S9195
COELMAN, David, N.J., See COLEMAN
COEN, Edward, Pa., S17356
James, Pa., S2139
COENRADT, Peter, N.Y., See CONRAD
COETRE/COTEREE, Richard, Pvt., N.Y., BLWt.6924 iss. 2/21/1792 to Wm. Campbell, ass.
COFER, George, Va., S15787
Joseph, Va., See COFFER
Reuben, Va., See COFFER
COFF, William, Va., S39347
COFFEE, Anthony, Vt., Abigail, W16922
John, Pvt., Pa., BLWt.9115 iss. 4/6/1790
William, Mass., R21844
COFFEL, James, Pa., S2459
COFFENBERRY, George, Va., See COFFINBERRY
COFFER, Joseph, Va., R2097
COFFER (continued)
Reuben, Va., Gincey, W1027; BLWt.26533-160-55
COFFEY, Benjamin, N.C., S1655
Eli, N.C., R2098
James, Pa., Mary, W410; BLWt. 24986-160-55
Osbourn, Va., Mary, W8612
Reuben, N.C., S46916
COFFIN, Alexander, S.C. Sea Service, Mary, W8617; BLWt. 34935-160-55
Arthur, Pvt., Md., BLWt.11038 iss. 3/11/1791 to Arthur Coffin
Daniel, Mass., R2099
Edmund, Mass., R2100
Elizabeth, Mass., former wid. of Jonathan Blaisdell, which see
Enoch, Mass., Huldah, W14505
Enoch, N.H., S16349
George, Mass., Dolly, W908; BLWt.40916-160-55
Isaac, Ct., Sarah Stiles, former wid., W17876
Isaac, Mass., N.H., S17900
James Josiah, Navy, Mass., S29730
John, Mass., Mary Mooers, former wid., W15080
Lemuel, Cont., Mass., Catharine, W18953
Nathaniel, Mass., S36989
Nicholas, N.H., Lydia, W8189; BLWt.29743-160-55
Obed, Mass., Violet, W14569
Peter, Cont., N.H., Mass., Jane, W1150
Prime (colored), N.H., See Prime LANE
William, Mass. Sea Service, Mary, R2101
COFFINBERRY, George, Va., Elizabeth, W6726; BLWt.26514-160-55
COFFING, Isaac, Ct. See COFFIN
COFFMAN, George, Va., Christina, R2102
Jacob, Md., Chloe, W6943; BLWt. 24766-160-55
Joseph, Va., R2106
COFFROTH, Conrad, Md., S40840
COFREN, Robert, N.H., Sarah, W1388; BLWt.5448-160-55
COGAN, Richard, Pvt., Del., BLWt.10733 iss. 9/2/1789
COGBURN, Henry, N.C., S21711
COGDELL, Francis, R2104. Dau. res. in N.C. in 1854
COGER, Enoch, Cont., Ct., Avis, W16541
Enoch, Pvt., Hazen's Regt., BLWt.12876 iss. 11/19/1792
Joseph, Cont., Ct., BLWt.1889-100
Peter, Va., S10481
COGGESHALL, Gideon, R.I., Mary, W18940
James, Mass., Zilpha Hackett, former wid., W14892
James, R.I., Martha, W18934
Timothy, Mass., Sea Service, Navy, Celia Eddy, former wid., W22998
COGGESHALL (continued)
William, Ct., Sea Service, Eunice, R17658
COGGIN, Robert, N.C., S41492
William, S.C., Cynthia, S8238; BLWt.39206-160-55
COGGLEHONAS, Isaac, Pvt., N.Y., BLWt.7012 iss. 5/14/1793 to Thomas Russell, ass.
COGGSHALL, Christopher, R.I., Anna, W22841
James, Mass., See COGSHALL
COGGSWELL, John, Ct., S12613
COGHILL, James, Va., S35860
Ralph, Va., Mary, See COWGILL
Thomas, Va., S15785
COGSHALL, James, Mass., Zilpha Hackett, former wid., W14892
COGSWELL, Amos, Ct., S24127
Amos, Cont., Mass., S45702; BLWt.343-200-Capt. No papers
Benjamin, Cont., Ct., Mercy, W14523
James, Mass., S30338
Jesse, Ct., S12565
John, Ct., See COGGSWELL
Jonathan, Mass., Elizabeth, W15655
Joseph, N.J., BLWt.2333-100
Mary, Mass., former wid. of Stephen Tambling, which see
Mary, Mass., former wid. of Jonathan Tarbill, which see
Northend, Mass., S18770
Reubin/Reuben, Mass., S43344
Rufus, Mass., S30351; BLWt. 24758-160-55
Samuel, Mass., BLWt.350-200-Lt. Iss. 1/25/1799 to James Fitch Cogswell & Maria Cogswell, only ch. of Samuel (minors). No papers
Thomas, Cont., Mass., Ruth, W16927; BLWt.332-400-Major. Iss. 2/8/1800 to Thomas Cogswell. No papers
William, Ct., S17360
William, Cont., N.H., Judith, W20910; BLWt.1273-300
COHEN, Abraham, S.C., Cecilia Solomons, former wid., R9931
Gershom, S.C., Rebecca, R2108
Moses, S.C., Judith Abrahams, former wid., W21599
COHOON, Gamaliel, Mass., See CAHOON
Joel, N.C., Naomi, W8576
John, Ct., S12705
COIEL/COILE, James, S.C., S31624
COINS, Domini, Pvt., Md., BLWts. 11043 & 14051 iss. 8/24/1793 to Domini Coins
Dominick, Md., S34706
COIT, Benjamin, Ct., Sea Service, Sarah, W10639; BLWt.26047-160-55
Farwell, Ct., Anna, W17669
Isaac, Ct., Ruamy, W14517
Richard, Ct., S12521
COKE, Philip, N.C., Pa., S42651
COKER, Thomas, N.C., S30957
William, Cont., Mass., Navy, Mary, W22849

COLATTER, Jacob, See COLLATTER
COLBATH, Dependance, Pvt., N.H. BLWt.3010 iss. 12/29/1792 to Dudley Woodbridge, ass.
Dependence, N.H., See COLBREATH
George, N.H., S22692
Lemuel, Mass., S29724
COLBERT, John, Cont., Va.,S9212
John William, Md., R2110
COLBETH, Peter, Mass., Hannah, W22819
COLBEY, Christopher, Cont., N.Y., S9207
COLBORN, Robert, N.J., S22691
COLBOURN, Andrew, Cont., N.H., See COLBURN
John, N.H., See COLBURN
Thomas, Cont., N.H., S36995
COLBRATH, William, N.Y., BLWt. 393-200-Lt. Iss. 11/18/1790 No papers
COLBREATH, Dependence, N.H., S17894
Neel, N.C., Martha, R2112
Thomas, N.Y., Susannah, W16921
COLBURN, Andrew, Cont., N.H., R8990, Phebe Root, former wid.; BLWt.329-450-Lt. Col. Iss. 1/16/1790 to Ephraim & Phebe Root, legal reprs. No papers
Asa, Mass., Susannah Buckman, former wid., W16877
Asa, N.H., R2114
Charles, N.H., Anna, W1239; BLWt.9066-160-55
Daniel, Ct., Elizabeth, W17655
Daniel, Cont., Mass., Sarah, W17654
David, Vt., Sarah, R2115
Ebenezer, Mass., S29083
Elizabeth, Mass., former wid. of Joseph Wyman, which see
James, Pvt., Ct., BLWt.5630 iss. 10/7/1789 to Benj. Tallmadge
James, N.H., S45696
John, N.H., Theoda, W23837
Jonathan, Mass., Rachel, W18968
Joseph, Mass., S18772. Widow pensioned for service of former husband; Elizabeth Colburn former wid. of Jonas Wyman, which see
Josiah, Ct., S10475
Josiah, Mass., S29089
Lewis, Mass., S30346
Nathan, Mass., Betty, W22835
Nathan, N.H., Abigail, W15887
Simeon, Mass., Abigail, W22838
Stephen, Mass., Mariam, W16001
Thomas, N.H., See COLBOURN
William, Mass., S20331
Zeruiah, Mass., N.H., former wid. of Simon Stickney, which see
COLBY, Aaron, Mass., Abigail, W14573
Abraham, R.I., Sally Sephton, former wid., W22169
Benjamin, Mass., S19257
Benjamin, N.H., S12611

COLBY (continued)
Daniel, Mass., S22185
Daniel, Pvt., N.H., BLWt.2998 iss. 8/26/1790 to Manassah Cutler, ass.
Daniel, N.H., Sarah, W18956
David, N.H., BLWt.730-100
Eben, N.H., S45684
Ebenezer, Mass., Anna, W22840
Ebenezer, N.H., S29725
Enoch, Mass., N.H., Lydia, W16215
Ezekiel, Vt., S12580
Hezekiah, N.H., BLWt.735-100
Ichabod, Mass., N.H., Ruth, W23766
James, Mass., S30946
Lois, Mass., former wid. of Isaac Sabens, which see
Moses, N.H., S12714
Moses, N.H., Abigail, W15999
Roswell, Cont., N.H., Lydia, W22824
Salem/Salem B., N.H., S38619
Samuel, Cont., Mass., Mary, S20907 1/2
Samuel, Pvt., Mass., BLWt.3971 iss. 4/3/1797 to Ezra King
Samuel, Mass., Sally, W22820
Stephen, N.H., Sally, W18966
Sylvanus, Pvt., Mass., BLWt.3932 iss. 4/3/1797 to Ezra King
Sylvanus, Mass., Dorcas, W22830
Theophilus, Pvt., N.H., BLWts. 2993 & 2985 iss. 11/6/1795 to James A. Neal, ass.
Theophilus, N.H., S45682
Thomas, Cont., N.H., S45683
Thomas, Mass., Dorothy Rogers former wid., W24790
Thomas, Mass., N.H., Lydia, R2116
Thomas, N.H., Eunice, W1721; BLWt.8460-160-55
William, Pvt., N.H., BLWt.3021 iss. 10/15/1792
William, N.H., S43352
COLCHORD, Thomas, N.H. See COLCORD
COLCORD, Eliphalet, N.H., Nancy, W22834
John, Cont., N.H., S45693
John, N.H., Lydia, R2117
Joseph, N.H., Margaret, W1152; BLWt.36505-160-55
Josiah, Mass., N.H., S29081
Thomas, N.H., S45692
COLDON, Redman, See CONDUN
COLDWATER, Philip, Cont., Pa., Margaret, W9804; BLWt.12938-100-Pvt. iss. 6/29/1787 to Matt McConnell, ass. No papers. BLWt.350-60-55
COLDWELL, James, N.C. See CALDWELL
Joseph, S.C., See CALDWELL
Robert, Va., Dis. No papers
COLE, Abel, Mass., Sea Service, S15783
Abijah, Mass., Nancy, W22828; BLWt.8161-160-55
Abner, Ct., Cont., S38631; BLWt. 382-150-Ensign. Iss. 4/15/1800 No papers
Abner, R.I., Lydia, W14518
Abraham, ---, Cecil, R2119, Md.

COLE (continued)
res. in 1845
Amos, Ct., S12594
Amos, Mass., Lucy, W22850
Andrew, Cont., Mass., S5030
Andrew, Pvt., N.J., BLWt.8171 iss. 5/23/1791 to Andrew Cole
Andrew, N.Y., S25583
Asa, Mass., S29090
Azor, N.Y., S10473
Barnabas, Mass., Mehitable, W15762
Barnabas, N.Y., Sarah, W3512
Barnet, Mass., Elizabeth, W25443. She was also pensioned for services of 1st husb., John Cole, Mass., which see
Benjamin, Ct., Jemima, W1236; BLWt.17701-160-55
Benjamin, Pvt., Sheldon's Dragoons, Ct., BLWt.5653 iss. 5/6/1794
Benjamin, Pvt., Ct., BLWt.5561 iss. 4/26/1792
Benjamin, Cont., Ct., Rachel McMurphy, former wid., R6797
Benjamin, Cont., Md., Elizabeth, W3000; BLWt.13441-160-55
Benjamin, Mass., S30948
Benjamin, Mass., BLWt.2310-100
Benjamin, R.I., S21134
Benjamin, R.I., S43387. Polly Cole wid. was pensioned as former wid. of Nicholas P. Bovee, N.Y., which see
Benjamin, R.I., Martha, R2136
Charles, Mass., Esther, W15650
Charles/John, N.C., S41493
Daniel, Ct., Cont., Edith, W22848
Daniel, Mass., Elizabeth, W25441; BLWt.6417-160-55
Daniel, N.Y., Susan, R2145; BLWt. 34619-160-55
Daniel, R.I., Zilpha, W16917
Daniel, Va., S8236
Daniel, Va., S22182
David, Pvt., Ct., BLWt.5602 iss. 12/22/1791 to Peter Fairchild
David, Ct., S38626
David, Pvt., Md., BLWt.1111 iss. 7/26/1797 to James DeBaufre, ass.
David, Pvt., N.Y., BLWt.6915 iss. 11/1/1791 to David Cole
David, N.Y., Mercy, W18957
David, Pvt., Pa., BLWt.9188 iss. 4/19/1792 to Adam Harbison, ass.
Ebenezer, Pvt., Mass., BLWt.3843 iss. 8/1/1789 to Thos. Cushing
Ebenezer, Mass., Elizabeth Leighton, former wid., W21564
Ebenezer, R.I., R2122
Eleazer, Mass., Lucy, W23862
Eli, Cont., Mass., S16733
Eliphalet, Cont., Mass., N.H., Ruth, W14502
Elisha, Ct., Asenath, W18932; BLWt.12758-160-55
Elizabeth, Cont., Md., former wid. of Michael Gilbert, which see
Elizabeth, Mass., Navy, former wid. of Abraham Bumpus, which see
Enos, N.J. See COAL

COLE (continued)
Ephraim, Mass., S39328
Ezekiel, Md., R2127
Fones, R.I., S22686
Francis, N.Y., S43351
Francis, Va., Martha, W8615; BLWt.36660-160-55
Gale, Cont., Mass., N.H., also served in 1798. Cynthia Dennett former wid., W22929. Mary Cole also applied as wid. of Gale Cole & was rejected, R2137
George, Md., S34704
George, N.C., S41491
Gideon, N.J., S9210
Hamlin, Va., S39342
Hendrick, Ct., Phebe, W17644
Henry, Mass., Alethea, W3660
Henry, Mass., Anna, R2118
Henry, N.C., S39359
Hugh, R.I., Dorothy, W23831; BLWt.26281-160-55
Hutchinson, R.I., S21132
Ichabod, R.I., S17353
Isaiah, Cont., Mass., Mary Catharine, W22827
Jabez, Ct., S15053
Jacob, Mass., Huldah, W18930. N.A. Acc. No.874. See 050033 Half Pay, Huldah Cole, wid. of Jacob Cole
Jacob, N.Y., R2128
Jacob, N.Y., R2129
Jacob P., N.Y., S12590
Jacobus, N.Y., S43354
James, Ct., S23171
James, Cont., Mass., S34598
James, Mass., S43373
James, Mass., Lucy, W17641
James, Sea Service, Dis., N.Y. res. in 1794. No papers
James, N.C., S3174
Jesse, Pvt., Mass., BLWt.3957 iss. 6/14/1791 to Anthony Maxwell
Job, Md., S2455
Job, Mass., S18774
John, Ct., Mary, W2068; BLWt. 30595-160-55
John, Cont., N.Y., S43348
John, Cont., N.Y., Olive, W25442
John, Pvt., Md., BLWt.11054 iss. 3/22/1797 to Abijah Holbrook,ass.
John, Md., R2130
John, Mass., Mary, W22851
John, Mass., Lucretia, W23860; also War of 1812
John, Mass., Elizabeth Cole, former wid., W28044. She was also pensioned for service of 2nd husb., Barney Cole, Mass., which see
John, Mass., Rebecca, R2140
John, N.H., Keziah, W23854; also War of 1812
John, N.J., S2135
John, N.Y., Pamela, W6926; BLWt. 26796-160-55
John, Pvt., N.Y., BLWt.6940 iss. 7/16/1790 to Wm. I. Vreedenburgh ass.
John, N.C., See Charles COLE

COLE (continued)
John, N.C., R2131
John, Pa., BLWt.412-200-Lt. Iss. 4/19/1792 to Hester Cole, admx. Also recorded under BLWt.2610 (located in Ohio). No papers
John, R.I., Sarah, W20919
John, Va., S2458
John, Va., S39344
Jonathan, Ct., Lois, W17643
Joseph, Cont., Mass., Chloe, W22813
Joseph, N.Y., R2133
Joseph, R.I., S17354
Joseph, R.I., R2132
Joseph, Va., S8230
Joseph, Va., Sarah, W347
Justin, Mass., Elizabeth, R2125
Landal, R.I., Elizabeth, W12764
Lemuel, Mass., S29720
Levi, Ct., S28694
Levi P., Navy, R.I., Anna Watkins, former wid., W25917
Martin, Pvt., N.C., BLWts.12053 & 12867 iss. 4/14/1795 to Abishai Thomas, ass.
Martin, N.C., S39345
Nathan, Mass., N.H., S12539
Nathan, Mass., R.I., Judith, W18960; BLWt.19536-160-55
Nathaniel, Ct., S15048
Nathaniel, Mass., S15788
Nathaniel, Mass., R2138
Nathaniel, Mass., R.I., S38637
Parker, Mass., S20694
Phebe, former wid. of David Bullock, R.I., which see
Richard, Va., S8229
Robert, Va., Dicey, W18924
Royal, N.Y., R.I., Hannah, W5883; BLWt.27607-160-55
Rufus, Mass., S12538
Samuel, Cont., Ct., S23167
Samuel, Cont., Ct., S10478
Samuel, Cont., Mass., Anna, W10676
Samuel, Md., R2142
Samuel, Mass., S23580
Samuel, Mass., S29082
Samuel, Mass., Sarah, W2436; BLWt.5454-160-55
Samuel, R.I., S21131
Sands, Ct., S31619
Seth, Mass., Celea, R2120
Seth, R.I., S17361
Silas, Pvt., Hazen's Regt., BLWt.12877 iss. 10/4/1789 to Abraham June, ass.
Simeon, Mass., S5028
Sisson, R.I., S23578
Solomon, Ct., Lydia, W1827; BLWt.26797-160-55
Solomon, Mass., Mary Abbot, former wid., W15503
Solomon, N.H., S45690
Solomon, N.C., R2144
Stephen, Mass., Hannah, W20915
Stephen, N.C., S3176
Thankful, Ct., former wid. of Wm. Fancher, which see
Thomas, Ct., Mary, W17637

COLE (continued)
Thomas, Mass., BLWt.353-200-Lt. iss. 4/20/1790. No papers
Thomas, N.C., S39348
Thomas, N.C., Amy Bizzel, former wid., W5824; BLWt.71209-160-55
Thomas, R.I., Anna, W14519
Thomas Herrick, Mass., Susanna, W22856
Tobias, N.H., S40849
Tobias, N.Y., Sarah, R2143
Tunis, N.J., R2147
Tunis, Pvt., N.Y., BLWt.6905 iss. 1/2/1792
Walter King, Va., Sea Service, Sally, R13238, Va. half pay
William, N.Y., Thankful, R2146
William, Va., S39338
William, Va., Mourning, W5884
Willis, N.C., Ruth, W6936; BLWt.47771-160-55. See COAL
Zebulon, Del., BL. Reg.
Zephaniah, Mass., R.I., S12520
COLEBATH, George, See COLBATH
COLEGATE, Asaph, Md., S39341; BLWt.63-60-55
COLEGROVE, Christopher, R.I., S15047
Jeremiah, R.I., Lydia, W24837
Stephen, R.I., Polly, R2151; BLWt.26022-160-55
William, N.Y., Theodasia, R2153
William, R.I., S21120
COLEHAMMER, Andrew, N.Y., S23172
COLEHOOF, Frederick, See KALEHOFF
COLEMAN, Benjamin, N.Y., Hannah, W16918
Benjamin, N.C., BLWt.479-300-Capt. Iss. 7/1/1799 to Isaac Cole, ass. No papers
Charles, S.C., R2155
Charles P., N.C., Fanny, W25435 BLWt.28536-160-55
Daniel, N.J., Mary, W1826; BLWt. 3515-160-55
David, N.J., R2157
Edward (colored), S.C., R2160
Hardy, N.C., Avey, W26
Hawes, Va., S16732
Israel, Pvt., Lamb's Artillery, N.Y., BLWt.7003 iss. 9/25/1790 to Ebenezer Clark, ass.
Jacob, Cont., N.J., S42140
Jacob, Va., S35848; BLWt.1206-200
James, N.H., Dorcas, R2159
James, Pvt., Va., BLWt.12019 iss. 9/26/1792 to James Reynolds, ass.
Job, Mass., Nanny, W14510
Joel, N.Y., S22680
Joel, Va., S42139
John, Ct., S17350
John, Cont., Pa., S40843
John, Ga., S39339
John, N.J., S34222; BLWt.124-100
John, N.J., Mary, R2163
John, N.Y., S43347
John, N.Y., Rachel, W1720
John, Pa., S42132
Joseph, Va., Sithey Bowles,

COLEMAN (continued)
former wid., W9738
Leonard, N.J., Eunice, W9810
Naiad, Va., S42657
Nathan, Ct., Deborah, See COLMAN
Nathaniel, Mass., S3195
Nathaniel, Mass., Elethrar, W15656
Nicholas, Pa., BLWt.436-200-Lt. Iss. 12/8/1792. No papers
Niles, Mass., S43377
Noah, Ct., BLWt.369-400-Surgeon Iss. 3/1/1797. No papers
Richard, Va., BLWt.457-200-Lt. Iss. 1/17/1800 to James Taylor ass. of Francis Coleman, heir. Also recorded under BLWt.2711. No papers
Robert, S.C., Prudence, W23858
Robert, Va., S19255
Robert, Va., Catharine, W8620
Samuel, N.C., R2164
Samuel, Va., BLWt.469-200-Lt. Iss. 1/6/1795 to Robert Means, ass. No papers
Solomon, Mass., See COLMAN
Spencer, Va., S3194
Theophilus, N.C., Keziah, R2162
Thomas, Pa., S23579
Thomas, Va., S16345
Thomas, Va., Lucy, W3002; BLWt. 6383-160-55
Timothy, N.Y., Elizabeth, W15763
Valentine, Pa., R2166
Whitehead, Va., BLWt.467-300-Capt. Iss. 8/8/1792. No papers
William, Cont., Ga., S39337, enl. in Va.
William, N.C., S3196
COLES, Ebenezer, Pvt., Mass., BLWt.3953 iss. 5/17/1792 to Moses Bissell
James, R.I., S21135
Jesse, N.Y., S12523
John, Mass., Ann, W14516
Solomon, Ct., Cont., N.Y., See COWLES
Thomas, Mass., S21713
COLESWORTHY, Nathaniel, Mass., Lydia, W14509
COLEY, Francis, N.C., Va., S3197
Isham, Va., R2167
James, N.C., See COOLEY
Jeffery, N.C., Sally, W4160
Samuel, Cont., N.Y., S43378
William, N.Y., S23166
COLFAX, Jonathan, Ct., Elizabeth, W262
Robert, Ct., S34219
William, Ct., Cont., Esther, R2174; BLWt.378-300-Capt. Iss. 12/9/1796. No papers
COLFIX, Samuel, Vt., S12536
COLGAN, Barney, Pvt., Pa., BLWt. 9087 iss. 4/6/1790
William, Cont., Va., S42652
COLGROVE, Caleb, R.I., S21136
Stephen, R.I., Polly, See COLEGROVE
William, R.I., See COLEGROVE
COLHOON, Jacob, Pvt., N.J.,

COLHOON (continued)
BLWt.8224 iss. 4/24/1792 to Jonathan Philips
COLIER, Joseph, Pvt., Ct., BLWt. 5595 iss. 2/27/1793 to John Stevenson
COLIN, John, Pvt., Md., BLWt.11026 iss. 6/2/1797 to James D. Baufre, ass.
COLIS, Thankful, R.I., former wid. of Pomp Reeves, which see
COLKINS, Jonathan, Pvt., Mass. BLWt.3844 iss. 4/1/1790
Jonathan, Mass., Nancy, W5882
Matthew, N.Y., S12598
COLL, Levi, Ct., See COLE
COLLAMER, Anthony, Mass., Tryphinia W20912
Samuel, Mass., Elizabeth, W18965
COLLAR, David, Pvt., R.I., BLWt. 3041 iss. 5/28/1792 to Israel Angell, ass.
Hezekiah, R.I., S21138
Jason, Mass., See COLLER
John, Cont., S38623; BLWt.5663-100-Pvt. Iss. 9/4/1789 to Ezekiel Case. No papers. Ct. res. in 1818
Phineas, Pvt. "in the Invalids", BLWt.12953 iss. 1/26/1790 to John May, ass.
COLLARD, Abraham, N.Y., Hannah, W18955
Thomas T., Ct., See COLIERD
COLLATER, Jacob, Cont., Pa., S34217
COLLAUGH, Peter, N.J., S2129
COLLEMER, Samuel, Mass., Elizabeth, See COLLAMER
COLLENS, Ambrose, Ct., S17892
COLLER, Jason, Mass., Hannah, W531; BLWt.14764-160-55
Norris, Ct., Cont., S12576
COLLERD, Thomas T., Ct., R13363
COLLESTER, James, Mass., Abigail, W18936
John, Mass., S29718; BLWt.34944-160-55
COLLETT, Isaac, Va., S30964
John, Va., Elizabeth, W3003
COLLEY, Charles, Va., See COLLIE
Charles, Va., S34702
Elizabeth, Mass., Sea Service, Privateer, former wid. of Francis Goss, which see
George, Ct., S18361
Henry, N.Y., Elizabeth, W124
Israel, Mass., Mary Montgomery, former widow, W13741
Mainyard, Va., S38628
Richard, Mass., S29726
William, N.C., R2168
COLLIE, Charles, Va., S9233
COLLIER, Aaron, Va., R2111
James, Pa., Martha, W4162
Joseph, Ct., S43399
Joseph, Pa.; BLWt.420-200
Oliver, Ct., S12555
Richard, Pvt., Lamb's Artillery N.Y., BLWt.6990 iss. 9/24/1790 to Thomas Lawrence, ass.
Richard, N.Y., R2169
William, N.C., S21121
William, Va., S39334

COLLIN, Michael, Pvt., Md., BLWts.12879 & 14106 iss. 2/24/1795 to Francis Sherrard, ass. of Elizabeth Coley, Admx.
COLLINGS, Jeremiah, Va., See COLLINS
William, Cont., See COLLINS
William, Pa., S982
COLLINS, Anthony, N.J., Mary, W6931; BLWt.26337-160-55
Asael, R.I., Sarah, W14525
Asel, R.I., Robe, W20916
Benjamin, Pvt., Mass., BLWt. 3973 iss. 3/25/1790
Benjamin, Mass., S36992
Benjamin, N.Y., S18365
Caleb, N.C., S41490
Chedor, Mass., Sarah, W20905
Daniel, Ct., Eunice, W17648; BLWt.16104-160-55
Daniel, Ct., Cont., Anna, W20899
Daniel, Mass., Olive, W22822
Daniel, Mass., N.H., S29716
Daniel, Navy, R.I., S16726
Daniel, R.I., BLWt.1646-100
Ebenezer, Mass., S42135
Eleazer, R.I., S21708
Eli, N.C., S31615
Elisha, Ct., Mass., Roxa, W10305; BLWt.96060-160-55
Elisha, Va., S10463
George, Va., S8247
Henry, Mass., S12584
Hezekiah, Va., R20343
Isaac, Cont., Mass., Navy, S12527
Jabez, Ct., S16088
Jacob, Pvt., Md., BLWt.11100 iss. 8/7/1794 to Henry Purdy, ass.
Jacob, Md., S34707
James, Pvt., Md., BLWt.14110 iss. 2/24/1795 to Francis Sherrard, ass. of John Colberth, admr.
James, N.J., S34257
James, Pvt., N.Y., BLWt.6942 iss. 9/15/1790 to James Caldwell, ass.
James, N.C., S1653
James, N.C., S8246
James, N.C., Tempey, W6737
James, Pa., S17895
James P., S.C., R2173
Jeffrey, Va., S9192
Jeremiah, Va., R2175
John, Cont., Mass., S10486
John, Cont., Pa., S40844
John, Cont., Va., Margaret, W9813
John, Pvt., Hazen's Regt., BLWt. 12895 iss. 6/20/1789
John, Jr., Pvt., Hazen's Regt. BLWt.12896 iss. 9/2/1797 to John Collins, Jr.
John, Md., S2442
John, Pvt., Md., BLWts.11010 & 11033 iss. 4/19/1797 to James DeBaufre, ass.
John, Mass., Navy, S29732
John, Pvt., N.J., BLWt.8207 iss. 2/25/1790 to John Ludlow, ass.
John, N.Y., Sarah Manning, former wid., R6878
John, N.C., S41496
John, N.C., S.C., Va., Phebe, W6735

COLLINS (continued)
John, Pvt., Pa., BLWt.9125 iss. 2/22/1792
John, R.I., S22183
John, S.C., S8248
John, Va., S9204
John, Va., S39356
John, Va., Jane, W6736
John, Va., R2176
Jonathan, Ct., S23577
Jonathan, S.C., S18771
Joseph, Ga., R2179
Joseph, Mass., S20695
Joseph, Pvt., N.Y., BLWt.6943 iss. 9/16/1796
Joseph, N.Y., Catharine, W18954
Joseph, Pvt., Pa., BLWt.9153 iss. 5/16/1792
Joseph, Pa., S34256
Joseph, Va., S2142
Joshuah, Md., Va., S12530
Josiah, Md., S16730
Josiah, Va., S30336
Lemuel, Cont., Mass., Sea Service, S29084
Levi, N.H., S34708
Lewis, S.C., S21142
Lois, Ct. Green Mt. Boys, Vt., former wid. of Nathaniel Wood, which see
Mary, Green Mt. Boys, Mass., N.H., former wid. of Ephraim Blackmer, which see
Mason, Va., S39355
Molly, Cont., N.Y., former wid. of Stephen Dustin, which see
Moses, Cont., Mass., N.H., Privateer, S12519
Nathaniel, Cont., Ct., S12585
Oliver, Corp. Crane's Continental Artillery, Mass., BLWt. 3988 iss. 1/10/1800
Oliver, Mass., Keturah, W1564
Oliver, R.I., S15055
Philemon, Mass., S29722
Pickering, Mass. Sea Service, Charity, W14566
Ralph C., Va., R2182
Richard, Mass., Mary, R2181
Richard, Pvt., Pa., BLWt.9167 iss. 10/24/1792 to Henry Ridgway, ass.
Robert, Pvt., Pa., BLWt.9192 iss. 3/10/1795 to Robert Hunter, ass.
Samuel, Ct., Betsey, W17645; BLWt.41-100, BLWt.27622-160-55
Samuel, N.H., S16724
Samuel, N.Y., S29098
Samuel, N.C., Martha, W3778
Sarah, Ct., former wid. of Thomas H. Hooker, which see
Shepherd, Del., S2138
Solomon, Mass., S36998
Solomon, Mass., S38634
Solomon, N.C., R2183
Solomon, Pa., S39331
Stephen, Ct., S10484
Stephen, Cont., N.J., St. Clair's Indian War, S34221
Stephen, Pvt., N.J., BLWts.8166 & 12901 iss. 7/7/1795 to Jonathan Rhea, ass.

COLLINS (continued)
Stephen, N.C., S30335
Thaddeus, Mass., Esther, W18931
Thomas, Pvt., Del., BLWt.10721 iss. 10/18/1791
Thomas, Mass., S38636
Thomas, Pa., Leah, R2180
Thomas, Pvt., Pa., BLWt.9123 iss. 6/7/1793 to Philip Stout, ass.
Timothy, Md., Elizabeth, W3186
Tyrannus, Mass. See claim of dau. Clarissa, wid. of John Dudley, Mass.
William, Ct., S32184
William, Ct., S43350
William, Cont., S46463; BLWt. 172-100. N.J. res. in 1802
William, Drum Major, Mass., BLWt.3846 iss. 8/10/1789 to Richard Platt, ass.
William, Mass., S28692
William, Pa., S40845
William, Va., S31613
William, Va., S39354
William Lock, Ct., S36472
COLLINSWORTH, John, Va., S30965
COLLIS, William, Pvt., Md., BLWt. 11031 iss. 8/14/1795 to Francis Sherrard, ass.
COLLISTER, James, Mass. See COLLESTER
COLLOM, Jonathan, Pa., R2184
COLLVER, Samuel, N.J., See CULVER
COLLY, Asa, Pvt., Va., BLWt.12032 iss. 7/14/1792 to Robt. Means, ass.
COLLYER, John, N.C., Va., S16728
Thomas, N.J., S2134
COLMAN, Betty, Mass., former wid. of David Emery, which see
James, N.H., See COLEMAN
John, N.Y., See COLEMAN
John, Pa., See COLEMAN
Nathan, Ct., Deborah, W17652
Solomon, Mass., S21144
Solomon, Mass., S34254
COLN, George, S.C., See CONN
COLOMBE, Louis Ange De La, See DE LA COLOMBE
COLONEY, Isaac, Ct., S12564; BLWt.26464-160-55
COLONNA, Benjamin, Va., S46634
COLONY, Richard, N.H., Dis. No papers
COLQUITT, Ransom, Va., Susanna, W6742
COLSEN, Bolter, See Bolter COLSON
COLSON, Abiah, Mass., Sarah, W20903; BLWt.8004-160-55
Bolter/Bolton, Mass., Sarah, W18941
Christopher, Mass., Patty, W25437; BLWt.1904-160-55
David, Mass., Mary, R13378
Hateevil, Mass., S36987
John, Mass., R13383
Joseph, Pvt., Mass., BLWt.3910 iss. 2/14/1793 to Joseph Jones, ass.
COLSTON, James, N.J., S35850

COLSTON (continued)
Joseph, Pvt., Sheldon's Dragoons Ct., BLWt.5659 iss. 4/15/1796 to Nathaniel Ruggles.
Patrick, Pvt., Pa., BLWt.9122 iss. 2/3/1794 to Alexander Power, ass.
Samuel, Va., BLWt.2294-300
COLT, Jabez, Ct., S9321
John, Ct., Sea Service, S18769
Peter, Ct., Sarah, W5880
COLTER, James, Pvt., Pa., BLWt. 9118 iss. 9/3/1791
James, Pvt., Pa., BLWt.9144 iss. 2/14/1791 to Alexander Power, ass
John, Md., See COULTER
John, Pvt., Pa., BLWt.9181 iss. 2/7/1799 to Abraham Ball, ass.
John, Pa., S34710
John, Pa., BLWt.1467-100
Samuel, Pa. See COALTER
William, Md. See COULTER
COLTMAN, Robert, Pa., BLWt.425-300-Capt. Iss. 3/31/1796. No papers. (Probably COULTMAN, See Heitman's Register)
COLTON, Alpheus, Mass., S34250
Caleb, N.H., See COTTON
Charles, Mass., BLWt.361-300-Capt. Iss. 3/26/1790 to Peter Sevier, ass. No papers
Charles, N.Y., Alethia, W15657
Elihu, Mass., Abigail, W14515
Enoch, Mass., S21145
Frederick, Mass., S34230
Hanan, Mass., Esther, W5249; BLWt.36240-160-55
James, N.J., See COLSTON
John, Mass., Hannah, W18927
Julius, Mass., Sybil, W14512
Mehitable D., Ct., Cont., former wid. of Pownal Deming, which see
Samuel, Ct., Cont., Lois, W17663
Simeon, Cont., Mass., S34251
COLUMBUS, James, Pvt., Ct., BLWt. 5615 iss. 3/12/1792 to Moses Sill
COLVER, David, N.Y., S17358
Nathaniel, Ct., Catherine, W10697; BLWt.92088-160-55
COLVILLE, James, Va., S2465
COLVIN, Benedict, R.I., S21706
Benjamin, Va., S16727
Benoni, R.I., Elizabeth, W12763
David, Mass., R.I., S15387
Edmund, R.I., S21129
George, R.I., Mary, W14562
Henry, Va., S12600
Jacob, Indian War 1792-1794, BLWt.19631-160-55
John, Va., Sarah, W18951
Levi, Vt., Lydia, W23849
Mason, Cont., Va., S9198
Peter, R.I., Mercy, W4659
Philip, R.I., Sarah, W3513
Samuel, Wayne's Indian War, 4th U.S. Inf., enl. in Vt., O.W. Inv. File 26048
COLWELL, Arthur, N.Y., S9205
David, R.I., S21127
John, N.C., Elizabeth, R1590

COLWELL (continued)
John, R.I., S12572
John, Va., See CALDWELL
Stephen, R.I., Martha, W22808
COLYER, Charles, Va., S30967
John, N.C., Va., See COLLYER
John, Va., Grizzy, W8624. Also in N.W. Indian War 1790-1795. Pension based on latter service.
COMBE, Peter, N.Y., See COOMBE
COMBES, William, Va., S35859
COMBLER, Michael, Pvt. "in the Invalids", BLWt.12947 iss. 1/28/1790 to Eliphalet Downer, ass.
COMBS, Anthony, Mass., Lydia, W16000
George, N.C., S41497
Gilbert, N.J., Christiana, W17
Hezekiah, Mass., See COOMBS
Hosea, Mass., S36997
John, Ct., Cont., R2185
John, Cont., Mass., N.H., S---
John, Mass., Dorothy, W1724; BLWt.14522-160-55. Res. of Harpswell, Me. D. 12/1842-43
John, Mass., Eunice S., W1825; BLWt.14503-160-55
John, S.C., S31626
John, Va., S35851
Joseph, Mass., R.I., S19944
Joseph, N.J., S2461
Joshua, Mass., S43357
Lawrence, Pvt., N.J., BLWt.8192 iss. 10/28/1791
Mahlon, Va., See COOMBS
Moses N., Cont., N.J., S2447
Nicholas, N.C., R2186
Robert, Va., S8251
Samuel C., Mass. See COOMBS
William, N.C., See COOMBS
William, Va., See COOMBS
William, Va., Sarah Ann, R2187
COMEE, Oliver, Mass., Elizabeth, W14567
COMEGYS, Cornelius, Md., Catharine, W6718
COMER, Augustine, Va., Catharine/Catreen, W18945
James, N.C., R20350
John, R.I., S17362
John, Va., S17899
Thomas K., R.I., See COOMER
COMES, Azubah, Mass., former wid. of Gad Woodruff, which see
Ebenezer, Ct., R2188
COMFORT, Mariah, N.Y., former wid. of Adam Lair, which see
COMIDINE, Nicholas, Pvt., N.Y., BLWt.6965 iss. 7/28/1790 to Gerrit H.V. Wagenen, ass.
COMING, Gersham, Mass., Rhoda, W14514
COMINGORE, Henery/Henry, Pa., Tiny/Teny, W1391; BLWt.27624-160-55
John, Pa., S1190
COMINGS, Benjamin, N.H., Mary, R2574
Nathaniel, Vt., Sally, See CUMINGS
COMINS, Alexander, Md., Pa., S2133
John, Ct., Cont., S23582
Jonas, Mass., S17363
Stephen, Ct., Cont., S43342
William, Ct., BLWt. 13-100
COMMANS, Robert, Pa., S9259
COMMING, Thomas, Mass., S16084
COMMINGS, Remmington, R.I., Vt., R2575
William, Ct., Rhoada, See CUMMINGS
COMMINS, Harmon, Va., S21701
Jedediah, Ct., Pa., Olive, W17677
Nathan, Mass., N.Y., S3241
Obed, Mass., S23175
William, Ct., BLWt. See COMINS
COMO, Francis, N.H., S45698
COMP, George Adam, Pa., S8235
COMPTON, Archibald, Va., Sally, W18959
Edmund H. Md., S17896; BLWt. 1266-200
George, Pvt., N.J., BLWt.8189 iss. 4/24/179-
George, N.J., S488
James, Md., Frances, W6729
James, Pvt., N.J., BLWt.8193 iss. 2/13/1800
Jeremiah H., Va., Elizabeth, W29
Job, N.J., Mary, W845
Job, N.J., Catharine, R2191
Joseph, N.J., S2144
Lewis, N.J., S2132
Sally, N.J., former wid. of Wm. Hedglen, Which see
Thomas, S.C., R----
COMSTOCK, Aaron, Ct., Ann, W17647
Abner, Ct., S12575
Achilles, Ct., Sarah, W20900
Ansel, Ct., Betsey, W18950; BLWt.32222-160-55
Anson, Ct., S12532
Caleb, Ct., Lucy, W6725
Daniel, Navy, Mass. res. & agency, S34248
David, Ct., S12589
Elisha, Ct., S12570
James, Ct., Amy, W17651
Jason, Ct., Sarah, W17646
John, Ct., Charlotte, W25434
John, Mass., Elizabeth, R2193
Levi, Vt., S15779
Martin L., Ct., S19260
Medad, Mass., S12547
Nathan, Ct., R2194
Oliver, Ct., Cont., Navy, Army, W17660
Samuel, Ct., S36474; BLWt.374-300-Capt. Iss. 1/16/1797. No papers. Wilton Ct., res.
Samuel, Ct., S36475, age 84 in 1818, Saybrook, Ct., res.
Samuel, Ct., Else Scofield, former wid., W22163; BLWt.10029-160-55. D. 12/6/1788 Stamford.
Samuel, Ct., Cont., S22693, enl. Lyme, Ct., at Marlow, N.H. in 1832
Serajah, Ct., Climena Austin, former wid., W16170
Simeon, Ct., S36463
Stephen, Ct., S12573
Theophilus, Ct., S43379
Zachariah, Vt., S9839
CONABLE, Samuel, Mass., Susan, W23873
CONANT, Abel, Cont., Mass., Lydia; BLWt.7057-160-55; W18964
Amos, Mass., S43358
Benjamin, Mass., S16723
Caleb, Mass., S16348
Daniel, Mass., Millicent Wallis, former wid., W25912
Ebenezer, Ct., S29095
Eli, Mass., R2196
Israel, Mass., Sybil, W20922
James, Cont., Mass., S5031
Jeremiah, Mass., Chloe, W8618
John, Mass., S29728
Jonathan, Jr., Mass., S45685
Josiah, Ct., Ruth Barton, former wid., W17260
Luther, Mass., Susannah, W18970
Lydia, Mass., former wid. of John Ball, which see
Peter, Mass., Elizabeth, W14522
Peter, Mass., Jane, W23869
Phineas, Mass., S5017
Rufus, Mass., N.H., S16346
Silvanus/Sylvanus, Ct., Cont., S16737
Simeon, Mass., Betsey, W23838
Solomon, Mass., S45686; BLWt. 942-100
Stephen, Mass., S21146
Sylvanus, Mass., Sylvia, W22837
William, Mass., S34252
CONAWAY, Charles, Md., S16087
John, Pa., Va., R2244
Richard, Va., See CONWAY
Samuel, Md., S22180
CONCA, Peter, N.Y., R2197
CONCKLIN, Edmund, N.Y., See CONKLIN
Isaac, N.Y., S23176
Joseph, N.J., S3201
Joseph, Pvt., N.Y., BLWt.6906 iss. 10/9/1790 to Daniel Concklin, admr.
CONCKLING, Joseph, N.Y., Sarah Benjamin, former widow, BLWt. 36656-160-55
CONDE, Adam, N.Y., Catalina, W16912
CONDEN, Thomas, Pvt., Md., BLWt. 11112 iss. 2/1/1790
CONDERMAN, John, N.Y., Catharine R2366
CONDICT, Abner, N.J., See CONDIT
CONDIT, Abner, N.J., S2452
Benjamin, N.J., S2467
Daniel, N.J., Mary, W449
Japhia, N.J., S975
Joel, N.J., S4645
John, N.J., S2469
Moses, N.J., S3212
Simon, N.J., Elizabeth, W1148; BLWt.24990-160-55
CONDON, James, N.J., S34220
Peter, Pvt., Pa., BLWt.9197 iss. 4/13/1793 to James Bennet, ass.

CONDREY, John, Va., S9214
CONDRY, William, Va., R2198
CONDUN, Redmun/Redman, Pa.,S42658
CONDY, Thomas Hollis, Cont., Mass., S32325; BLWt.346-200-Lt. Iss. 1/29/1790. No papers
CONE, Beriah, Ct., S9237
Daniel, Ct., S17352
Daniel H., Ct., S36473
Elijah, Cont., Judith, W10662; Mass. res., Me. agency
Henry, Ct., Waitstill, W25432
Israel, Pvt., Ct., BLWt.5547 iss. 3/7/1792 to Aaron Camp
Israel, Ct., Cont., S36477
Jared, Ct., N.H., Caroline W., W6952; BLWt.21807-160-55
Jesse, Ct., S36478
Joseph, Ct., Cont., S12569
Joshua, Pvt., Ct., BLWt.5622 iss. 6/26/1789 to James Percival
Joshua, Ct., Sarah, W25428; BLWt.81566-160-55
Joshua, Ct., Cont., Mehitable, W18933
Nathaniel, Cont., Ct., S36476
Noadiah, Ct., Polly, W1030; BLWt.30696-160-55
Oliver, Ct., S12525
Ozias, Ct., S43341; BLWt.1317-100
Reuben, Cont., Ct., Esther Edwards former wid., R3256
Robert, Ct., Sarah, W18961
Samuel, Ct., S36988
Samuel, Ct., Cont., Betsey, W16538
Timothy, Ct., S9197
William, Ct., Cont., S38635
CONERY, Stephen, N.H., S45701
CONEWAY, Cornelius, N.Y., S43353
CONEY, John, Mass., Lovina, W18963
Michael, Pvt., Ct., BLWt.5646 iss. 4/13/1791
CONGAR, Joseph, Ct., S9223
CONGDON, George, R.I., Jemima Card former wid., W9376; BLWt.71200-160-55
Henry, R.I., S22181
Jairis, Pvt., Sheldon's Dragoons, Ct., BLWt.5649 iss. 4/19/1792 to Isaac Bronson
James, R.I., S21712
John, Ct., Cont., S43388
John, R.I., S21137
John, R.I., Mary, W27856
Jonathan, R.I., S21133
Joseph, R.I., Deborah, R2200
Joseph, R.I., BLWt.3049 iss. 1793
Sally, R.I., former wid. of Langworthy Pearce, which see
Stephen, R.I., S21710
Stephen, R.I., Martha Taber, former wid., W22364
CONGER, Benjamin, N.J., Rachel, R2202
Elijah, Ct., S12544
Uzziah, N.Y., R2201
Zenas, Cont., N.J., S12550
CONGERS, Ephraim, S.C. See CONYERS
CONGLETON, Daniel, Md., S34243
Moses, Pa., Mary, W4930; BLWt. 26738-160-55
William, Dis. No papers. Phila.

CONGLETON (continued) agency
CONGROVE, William, Va., S19261
CONICK, John, Mass., See MC CONNICK
CONINE, Andrew, Va., Lydia, W9809
Jeremiah, Cont., Va., S42142
Philip, N.Y., BLWt.391-200-Capt. Lt. Iss. 1/4/1791. No papers
CONK, John, N.J., S2446
CONKEY, Alexander, Mass., S12566
Joshua, Mass., Milicent, W18947
Richard, N.Y., S22689
Robert, Mass., S45585
CONKLIN, Abraham, N.Y., S22699
Benjamin, N.J., Hannah, R2210
Daniel, N.Y., S39360
David, N.Y., R2209
Edmund, N.Y., S43391
Elias, N.J., N.Y., Charlotte, R2206
Francis, N.Y., Hester, W18921
James, N.J., R2211
John, Cont., N.Y., S12553
John, N.J., S2464
John, N.J., S43360
John, N.Y., Susannah, W23845; BLWt.89518-160-55
John, N.Y., Rachel, R2214
John D., N.Y., S12708
John L., N.Y., S43345
Jonathan, N.Y., Agnes, R2204
Joseph, N.J., See CONCKLIN
Joseph, N.Y., Catharine, W15658
Joseph, N.Y., Sarah Benjamin, former wid., BLWt.36656-160-55
Matthew, N.Y., S23586
Nathan, N.Y., Ann, R2205
Samuel, N.Y., Phebe, R2213; BLWt.39482-160-55
Seth, N.Y., S24128
Thomas, N.Y., Sarah Place, former wid., W17456
William, N.Y., Elizabeth, W15885
William, N.Y., Hannah, W16915
William N., N.Y., See CONKLING
CONKLING, John, N.J., S34227
Jonathan S., N.Y., Juliana, W18938
Josiah, N.J., Dis. No papers
Stoddard, N.Y., Juliana, W18939 See Jonathan S. CONKLING
Thomas, N.Y., S12579
William N., N.Y., R2215
CONKWRIGHT, Gerardus, N.Y., See CRONKWRIGHT
CONLEY, Charles, Va., S30333
Jacob, N.Y., S16721
John, Md., R20351
John, N.C., See CONNELLY
Michael, Md., Rebecca, W1240; BLWt.9443-160-55
Neal, N.J., S8243
Patrick, Pa., Margaret, See CONNELLY
Thomas/William, N.J., Indian War, War of 1812, R2218
CONLY, Elizabeth, Mass., former wid. of Ebenezer McKenzie, Which see
John, (not Rev. War) Indian War 1792, O.W. Inv. Rej. file 2220.

CONLY (continued)
Appl. made in Giles Co., Va.
Neill, N.C., R2221
Nicholas, Pa., Mary, R2217
CONN, Benjamin, N.C., R2316. No papers
George, S.C., S17891
James, N.C., S15386
John, Md., N.C., S17890
Jonathan, Cont., Mass., Hannah, W6702; BLWt.130-60-55
Jonathan, Mass.; BLWt.1070-100 An erroneous allowance. See claims of Jonathan Conn and his widow, Hannah
Samuel, N.J., BLWt.334-200-Lt. Iss. 4/30/1792 to John Black, execr. Also recorded under BLWt.2101. No papers
Samuel, Va., S15384
William, N.C., S.C., Elizabeth, W8616
William Y., Md., Va., S15784
CONNALLY, Michael, N.Y., BLWt.394-200-Lt. Iss. 7/12/1790. No papers
CONNAWAY, James, Pvt., Pa., BLWt. 9119 iss. 10/30/1792 to Jane Murthwaite, Admx.
John, N.Y., S40857
CONNEL, Daniel, Ga., S31631
CONNELL, Benoni, Ct., Cont., Soviah W20914
Christopher, N.Y., S22685
Francis, Va., R2223
Terrence, Sgt., Pa., BLWt.9177 iss. 6/29/1789 to M. McConnell, ass.
Thomas, N.C., R2224
CONNELLY, Henry, N.C., Tempy, W8188 BLWt.30599-160-55
Hugh, Cont., Md., S34705; BLWt. 827-100
Hugh, N.Y., S28690
John, Md., S16719
John, N.C., Jane, W20920
John, Va., S30345
John, Va., Mary, W74
Nicholas, Pa., See CONLY
Patrick, Md., See CONNOLLY
Patrick, Pvt., Pa., BLWt.9122 iss. 2/3/1794 to Alexander Power, ass.
Patrick, Pa., Margaret, W9815
Robert, Pa., BLWt.431-300-Capt. Iss. 12/13/1791. No papers
William, Md., Priscilla, W25429
William, Va., BLWt.1967-100
CONNELY, Arthur, Va., Martha, W8626
Nicholas, Pa., Mary, See CONLY
CONNER, Andrew, Pa., Mary, R2230
Arthur, Va., Ellena, W6733
Benjamin, Privateer, N.H., R277
Charles, Pvt., Pa., BLWt.9110 iss. 7/16/1789
Daniel, Ga., Martha, R2228
Daniel, Pvt., Mass., BLWt.3861 iss. 11/15/1792 to Jonathan Tuttle, ass.
Daniel Mass., See CANNER
Daniel, Va., Mary, W1235; BLWt. 17867-160-55
David, Pvt., Md., BLWt.11030 iss.

CONNER (continued)
8/14/1795 to Francis Sherrard, ass.
David, Pa., R2225
Derby, N.C., R2226
Edmund, ---, Pa. res. Dis.
Edward, N.C., S.C., S21123
Eliphalet, N.H., See CONNOR
George, Pa., See CONNOR
Isaac, N.C., S10465
James, Cont., N.C., S8237
James, N.C., S21709
John, Cont., See SHEHEE
John, Cont., Va., BLWt.2380-100
John, Mass., S43394
John, Pvt., Lamb's Artillery, N.Y., BLWt.7008 iss. 9/24/1790 to Thomas Lawrence, ass.
John, N.C., Sarah, W3659
John, Pa., Elizabeth, W25431; BLWts. 331-60-55 & 9101-100-91
John, Pa., See CONNOR
John, Pvt., Pa., BLWt.9101 iss. 3/29/179-
John, Va., See CONNOR
Joseph, Cont., Va., S42137
Joseph, Mass., S34253
Joseph, N.H., Anna, See CONNOR
Lawrence, Va., S35853
Margaret, Pa., former wid. of Samuel Henderson, BLWt.246-100
Matthew, Pvt., Pa., BLWt.9139 iss. 9/4/1789
Maximilian, S.C., Phebe, W75
Michael, Md., BLWt.268-100
Patrick, Drummer, Pa., BLWt. 9158 iss. 7/9/1789 to Pat Conner
Philip, Va., See CONNOR
Philomen, Va., S17364
Samuel, Pa., R2231
Terrence, Va., S35862
William, Md., BLWt.2209-100
William, N.Y., S43346
William, N.C., S30955
William, Va., See CONNOR
Wright, N.C., Ziney, R2222; BLWt.44807-160-55
CONNERLY, William, N.H., S45697
William, Va., S40053
CONNICK, John M. Mass., See MC CONNICK
William, N.H., S45586
CONNITE, Conrad, Pvt., N.Y., BLWt.6937 iss. 7/30/1790 to John J. Gurnee, ass.
CONNOLLY, Charles, Pvt., Del., BLWt.10719 iss. 9/2/1789
George, Va., S16734
James, Pvt., Sheldon's Dragoons, Ct., BLWt.5660 iss. 12/11/1789
James, Ct., S34229
James, Pvt., Pa., BLWt.9147 iss. 10/28/1789 to M. McConnell, ass.
Patrick, Pvt., Del., BLWt.10724 iss. 9/12/1789
Patrick, Md., S35861
Patrick, Pa., See CONNELLY
Timothy, Matross "in the Artillery"

CONNOLLY (continued)
Md., BLWt.11115 iss. 6/14/1796
William, Pvt., Md., BLWt.11123 iss. 2/1/1790
William, Md., Priscilla, See CONNELLY
CONNOR, Benjamin, Privateer, N.H., See CONNER
Eliphalet, N.H., Hannah, W18937
George, Pa., S40839
Hugh, Mass., Pa., S34247
John, Armand's Corps, S35858; BLWt.1977-100. Iss. 11/2/1833. Enl. in Va.
John, Pvt., Del., BLWt.10729 iss. 9/2/1789
John, Mass., See CONNER
John, N.Y., S22179
John, Pvt., Pa., BLWt.9219 iss. 11/5/1789
John, Pa., Elizabeth, See CONNER
Joseph, N.H., Anna, W24838
Michael, Md., See CONNER
Patrick, Pvt., Md., BLWts.12873 & 14102 iss. 2/24/1795 to Francis Sherrard, ass.
Philip, Va., S42134
Terrence, Va., See CONNER
Thurtrim/Tristam, Pvt., N.H., BLWt.3000 iss. 8/26/1790 to Manassah Cutler, ass.
William, N.J., See DOUGHERTY
William, N.Y., See CONNER
William, Va., Va. Half Pay, Rosanna, W22817
CONNOREY, John, Pvt., Va., BLWt. 12030 iss. 11/20/17-- to John Connorey
CONNOVER, John, N.J., See CONOVER
CONOLLY, Robert, ----, Dis. No papers. Pa. res. in 1794
CONOVER, Ann, N.J., former wid. of John Voorhees, which see
Elias, N.J., S12609
Jesse, N.J., S2462
John, Pa., R2234
John M., N.J., Pa., Ann, W907; BLWt.16278-160-55
Levi, N.J., S2471
Samuel, N.Y., S12412
Thomas, N.J., Abigail Cowenhoven, W3074
CONOWAY, Charles, Md., See CONAWAY
CONRAD, Adam, N.J., S2130
Jacob, Pvt., Va., BLWt.11992 iss. 7/20/1792 to Robert Means, ass.
Jacob, Va., See CONROD
Peter, N.Y., Elizabeth, W16543
Philip, Pa., Catharine, R2235
Rachel, N.C., former wid. of David Enoch, which see
CONREY, John, N.Y., S32188
Samuel, Mass., S12522
CONROD, Charles, Pvt., Pa., BLWt.9206 iss. 9/26/1791 to John McCleland, ass.
Jacob, Va., S39361
CONROE, William, N.Y., Ruth, W6732; BLWt.950-160-55
CONROID, John, Pvt., Mass.,

CONROID (continued)
BLWt.3852 iss. 5/14/1794 to Alexander Hunt, ass.
CONROY, James, Pvt., Pa., BLWt. 9170 iss. 4/6/1790
CONRY, Stephen, N.H., See CONERY
CONSELYEA, George, N.Y., S12712
CONSOLVER, John, ----, Va. agency Dis. No papers
CONSTABLE, Garret, N.Y., S45584
William, N.Y., Henricca, W22810
CONSTANTINAN, Nicholas, Cont., N.Y., Charlotte, R2239; BLWt. 1369-100
CONSTANTINE, Edward, Md., Catharine, R2238
Jacob, Mass., Elizabeth, W23842
Nicholas, Cont., N.Y., See CONSTANTINAN
CONTRYMAN, John, N.Y. See COUNTRYMAN
CONVERS, Benjamin, Ct., S12549
John, Mass., Privateer, S17351
Stephen, Ct., See CONVERSE
CONVERSE, Betsey, Mass., former wid. of Benjamin Brabrook, which see
Demon Read, Ct., R2241
Dyer, Ct., S36479
Elisha, Ct., Cont., S12517
Jeremiah, Ct., Mass., R2242
John, Mass., See CONVERS
Jonathan, Ct., Zuruah, W722
Josiah, Mass., Elizabeth, W14506; BLReg.276271-55
Nathaniel, Ct., Abigail, R2240
Sarah, Ct., former wid. of William Cleaveland, which see
Solvin, Ct., Sarah, W25436
Stephen, Ct., Mass., Sarah, W22847
Thomas, Ct., BLWt.371-300-Capt. Iss. 2/14/1791. No papers
CONWAY, Elizabeth, Cont., former wid. of Stephen Hill, which see
Henry, Va., Sarah, W6719
Hugh, Pa., S30951
James, Va., S40050
James, Va., Va. Half Pay, R13351
Jesse, Va., Margaret, W10674
John, Cont., Pa., Esther, R2243
John, N.J., BLWt.400-450-Lt. Col. Iss. 6/11/1789. No papers
John, Pa., Va., See CONAWAY
John, Va., Anna, W8622
Joseph, Va., BLWt.461-200-Lt. Iss. 2/17/1797. No papers
Michael, Pa., S43397
Richard, Va., S16731; BLWt. 26414-160-55
William, S.C., S31623
CONY, Daniel, Mass., S29727
CONYERS, Benjamin, Va., S38625
Ephraim, S.C., S8244
John, Ga., S31617
Straughan, S.C., S18357
Thomas, Pa., S3200
CONYNE, Abraham, N.Y., R2245
Peter, N.Y., S28693
COOK, Aaron, Mass., S36471

COOK (continued)
Aaron, Pa., R2246
Abel, Mass., Mary, W16540
Abiel, Ct., N.Y., Julia Anna, W6704; BLWt.24761-160-55
Abiel, R.I., Anna, W18949
Abraham, Ct., Elizabeth, W3224
Abraham, Pvt., Mass., BLWt.3848 iss. 3/25/1790
Abraham, R.I., S5019
Abram, Mass., Navy, Sarah, W23840; also War of 1812
Amasa, Mass., S23168
Archibald, Ct., S15781
Archibald, Pa., Martha, W9393
Ariel, R.I., Dorcas, W20908
Arthur, R.I., Philena, See COOKE
Asahel, Mass., S12592
Atwater, Ct., Mary, W16914
Benjamin, Ga., S31622
Benjamin, Ga., Va., Catharine, W8628
Benjamin, Md., R2248
Benjamin, Va., Jemima, W8630
Charles, Va., S35857
Christopher, N.C., S2466
Christopher, R.I., S21700
Daniel, Cont., N.H., Indian Wars & 1812, Mehitable, W16104
Daniel, Pvt., N.H., BLWt.3006 iss. 3/25/1790
Daniel, N.H., S45695
Daniel, N.J., Rebekah, W16913
Daniel, Pa., R2251
Darius, Ct., N.Y., Elizabeth, W10672
David, Cont., Mass., S36991; BLWt.355-300-Capt. Iss. 1/26/1790 to John May, ass. No papers
David, Mass., Polly, W17668
David, Mass., Abigail Perkins, former wid., W26862
David, N.J., Alice, W1234; BLWt. 26708-160-55
David, N.J., Mary, W6706
David, R.I., S12528
Dawson, Va. Sea Service, See COOKE
Ebenezer/Ebenezer H., Ct., Jemima, W6929; BLWt.24330-610-55
Ebenezer, Corp., N.H., BLWt.3002 iss. 11/28/1789
Ebenezer, Mass., N.H., S12529
Ebenezer, Mass., N.H., Vt., S21703
Edward, N.C., Ann, W3949
Edward, Pa., Rebecca McGrew, former wid., W3354
Elender, N.C., See LOWRY, John
Eli, Cont., Me. res. & agency, Hannah, W8629; BLWt.256-60-55
Elias, Mass., Abigail, W10655; BLWt.24759-160-55
Elihu, Ct., Lois, W2066
Elihu, Mass., Cynthia, R2250
Elijah, Ct., S29085
Elisha, R.I., S12557
Elizabeth, Cont., Mass., former wid. of David Bryant, which see
Elkanah, Mass., Navy, Privateer, S30341
Ellis, N.J., S34224
Enoch, Mass., S5015

COOK (continued)
Enos, Mass., See COOKE
Ephraim, Pvt., Crane's Cont. Artillery, Mass., BLWt.3984 Iss. 3/26/1792 to John Peck
Ezekiel, Ct., S12526
Ezekiel, N.Y., S38640
Francis, Mass., S22697
George, Ct., R2254
George, Ct., BLWt.655-100
George, Pvt., N.Y., BLWt.6920 iss. 10/12/1790
George, N.C., S31627
George, Pa., Sarah, W640; BLWt. 24776-160-55
Gideon, Ct., Huldah, W20924
Hannah, Mass., former wid. of Phineas Aldrich, which see
Henry, Md., S8234
Henry, N.J., S974
Henry, N.C., S2460
Henry, Pa., S40846
Henry, Va., S3181
Henry Vander/Henry VanDerCook, N.Y. Anna VanNess, former wid., W26615
Isaac, Mass., Emma, W2720; BLWt. 17860-160-55
Isaac, N.C., R2256
Jacob, N.J., R2258
Jacob, Pa., S43396
Jacob, Va., R2257
James, Fifer, Mass., BLWt.3866 iss. 1/26/1790 to John May, ass.
James, N.J., R2260
James, N.Y., S3180
James, Va., S12616
Jesse, Ct., BLWt.385-300-Capt. Iss. 4/23/1798 to Jesse Cook. No papers
Job, N.Y., S15264
Job, R.I., S21119
Job, R.I., R2261
Joel, Corp., Ct., BLWt.5550 iss. 5/17/1790
Joel, Ct., S3182
Joel, Ct., S43392
John, Cont., Mass., Lydia, W22829; BLWts.1078-100 & 166-60-55
John, Pvt., Del., BLWt.10730 iss. -/--/----
John, Pvt., Del., BLWt.10734 iss. 9/2/1795
John, Mass., Privateer, S29096
John, Mass., R2263
John, Pvt., N.H., BLWt.3011 iss. 3/25/1795
John, N.H., S45694
John, N.J., Catharine, W22853
John, Pvt., N.Y., BLWt.6970 iss. 7/30/1790 to Edward Cumpston, ass.
John, N.C., S16343
John, Pa., S1507
John, Pa., S40847
John/John Anthony, Pa., Rachel, R2272
John, R.I., S9200
John, S.C., S39332
John, S.C., S39358
John, Va., Mary, W23865
John Anthony, Pa. See John COOK

COOK (continued)
John Wanton, R.I., S21140
Johnson, Ct., S42141; BLWt. 5572. Iss. 12/6/1791
Jonah, Ct., S19948
Jonathan, Pvt., Del., BLWt. 10731 iss. 11/13/1797 to James DeBaufre, ass.
Jonathan, Mass., Charlotte, W22845
Jonathan, N.Y., S29094
Joseph, Ct., Mercy, R2269
Joseph, Cont., Mass., Navy, S36994
Joseph, Green Mt. Boys, N.Y., Vt., S2136
Joseph, Mass., S34246
Joseph, Mass., R2264
Joseph, R.I., Mercy, W14568
Joshua, Mass., Lucy, R2265; BLWt.36655-160-55
Joshua, N.J., Martha, W6703; BLWt.26276-160-55
Lemuel, Ct., S23173
Lemuel, Cont., Mass., S33258; BLWt.5670-100 (1790), BLWt. 86-60-55. No papers
Levi, Mass., S43380
Levi, Mass., Sarah, W23864
Lewis, Va., S39340
Lucy, Cont., Ct., former wid. of John Priest, which see
Marimon, Ct., S2453; BLWt.26126-160-55
Matthew, Privateer, Va., War of 1812, R2268
Miles, Drummer, Ct., BLWt.5628 iss. 8/23/1790
Miles, Ct., S43366
Moody, Cont., N.H., Mass., S9190
Moses, Ct., S15056
Moses, Ct., R2270
Moses, Pvt., Mass., BLWt.3874 iss. 12/20/1799 to Nehemiah Nelson
Moses, Mass., S43362
Moses B., N.Y., S34711
Nathan, Ct., S36482
Nathan, Mass., Beulah, W14574
Nathan, N.Y., S12542
Nathan, N.Y., R2271
Nathaniel, Ct., Dis. No papers
Nathaniel, Ct., Anise, W17642
Nathaniel, Navy, R.I., S21714
Nicholas, Cont., N.Y., S43372
Nicholas, Pvt., N.Y., BLWt.6900 iss. 7/30/1790 to Edward Cumpston, ass.
Noah, Pa., S3184
Oliver, Ct., Submit, W16929
Oliver, N.H., S21143
Paul, Mass., Rosannah, R2273
Paul, N.H., S38638; BLWt.2016-100
Peter, N.H., Elizabeth, W24957; BLWt.2488-160-55
Peter, Va., Mary, W6705
Pitman C., Mass., S29731
Rains, Ga., BLWt.2161-300
Rebecca, former wid. of Daniel Smith, Md., which see
Reuben, N.C., S10483
Richard, Pvt., Ct., BLWt.5557

COOK (continued)
iss. 3/12/1792
Richard, Ct., S12545
Richard, Ct., S43368
Richard, Pvt., Mass., BLWt. 3902 iss. 9/11/1792
Richard, Mass., S34258
Robert, Mass., Judith, W14575
Robert, N.C., S8233
Robert, N.C., S30963
Roswell, Pvt., Ct., BLWt.5593 iss. 11/30/1795 to Timothy Pitkin
Rudolph, N.Y., Dis. No papers
Rudolph, N.Y., Koch, Hannah, R2255 1/2
Samuel, Ct., S22187
Samuel, Ct., Cont., Mary, W15829
Samuel, Pvt., Mass., BLWt.3887 iss. 8/23/1796 to Joseph Thomas
Samuel, Mass., S15385
Samuel, Surgeon, N.Y., BLWt. 390-400
Sarah, former wid. of Joseph Smead, Mass., which see
Saul, Cont., Mass., S35207
Serad, Ct., S12533
Severinus, N.Y., S12563
Shubael, Ct., Sarah, R2274
Silas, Mass., S30350
Solomon, Mass., S12537
Solomon, Mass., S43375
Solomon, Mass., Elizabeth, W16228
Stephen, Mass., Mary, W14529
Stephen, ---, Sylvia, R2275. Died in Franklin Co., N.Y.,1829
Theodosius, N.C., R2276
Thomas, Pvt., Ct., BLWt.5608 iss. 4/15/1790 to Peter DeWitt
Thomas, Corp., N.H., BLWt.3003 iss. 3/25/1790
Thomas, N.H., Anna Potter, former wid., W21996
Thomas, N.C., S31618
Thomas, N.C., Ann, R2247
Thomas, N.C., Elizabeth, R2253
Thomas, N.C., R2278
Thomas, Va., Martha, W23855
Trueworthy, Ct., S43395
Uriah, N.H., Mary, R2267
Uriah, Ct., R2279
Warren, Pvt., Ct., BLWt.5594 iss. 9/9/1790 to James F. Sebor
Warren, Ct., Cont., Lois, W18926 BLWt.49466-160-55
William, Pvt., Ct., BLWt.5578 iss. 11/15/1791
William, ----, see case of his wid., Mary, who was pensioned as wid. of her 2nd husb., James Blake, Mass. which see
William, Ct., S36467
William, Ct., S38641
William, Ct., S43381; BLWt.1415-100
William, Ct., Asenath, W1723; BLWt.11421-160-55
William, Ct., Keziah, W23871; BLWt.5558-100-Pvt. Iss. 6/26/1795. Cert. 12/4/182? by Wm. M. Stuart. No papers

COOK (continued)
William, Cont., Va., S21147
William, Pvt., Md., BLWt.11055 iss. 2/7/1790
William, Md., R2280
William, Md., Pa., S2141
William, Pvt., Mass., BLWt.3914 iss. 8/10/1789 to Richard Platt, ass.
William, N.J., S24129
William, N.J., Elanor T., W27814; BLWt.12846-160-55
William, N.C., S10480
William, N.C., S31612
William, R.I., Elizabeth, W14528; BLWt.26477-160-55
William, R.I., Ruth, W23835; BLWt.16253-160-55
William, Pvt., Va., BLWt.12018 iss. 8/29/1791
William, Va., S38627
William, Va., Clara, W6708
Thadeus, Pvt., Ct., BLWt.5671 iss. 4/19/1790
Zachariah, Va., S42655
COOKE, Arthur, R.I., Philana, W23832
Dawson, Va. Sea Service, Mildred, W4657
Ebenezer, Pa., S21117
Enos, Mass., S22682
John, Va., S3179
John, Va., Ann, W1232; BLWt.71017-160-55
Lemuel, Pvt., Sheldon's Dragoons Ct., BLWts.5670 & 36-60-55
Noah, Mass., S34599
Samuel, Mass., Mehitabel, W23872
Silvanus, R.I., Martha, W12761
Stephen, N.J., N.Y., S3185
Thomas B., Pa., Elizabeth, W3948; BLWt.439-300-Capt. Iss. 7/10/1797. Also recorded under BLWt. 2652. No papers
William, Cont., Va., See COOK
COOKENTENFER/COOKENDORFER, Michael, Md., S30337
COOKERS, Michael, Va., Elizabeth, W6722
COOKMAN, Henry, Pvt., Mass., BLWt.3901 iss. 8/15/1792 to Samuel Allen, ass.
William, Va., R2281
COOKSEY, Charles, Va., S12540
Zachariah, Va., S17357
COOKSON, Reuben, Mass., S35208
COOL, Henry, N.Y., S44794
Hyman/Wyman, Pvt., Ct., BLWt. 5560 iss. 11/10/1792
Isaac, Pvt., Ct., BLWt.5611 iss. 11/10/1792
John, Mass., Abigail, W12744
COOLBAGH, Peter, N.J., S2129
COOLBAUGH, John, N.J., Mary, W6939; BLWt.26795-160-55
COOLBROTH, Daniel, Mass., Elizabeth/Betsey, W22806
COOLEDGE, Paul, Mass., S9228
Silas, Cont., N.H., Elizabeth, W22825
COOLEY, Aaron, Mass., S45703
Abner, Mass., Maria, W16544

COOLEY, Azariah, Mass., S34232
Charles, Mass., S30347
George, Mass., Penelope, W22846
Gideon, Mass., Dinah, W1824
James, Mass., Mary, W20897
James, N.C., S3188
James, N.C., S.C., S30961
James, Pa., BLWt.9100-100. Iss. 5/5/1791. No papers
Jeffery, N.C., See COLEY
John, N.H., Dorothy, W16229
Justin, Mass., S9221
Luther, Mass., S15389
Owen, Pvt., Hazen's Corps., BLWt.12893 iss. 9/27/179-
Reuben, Ct., S36469
Richard, Md., Rachel, R2283
Roger, Mass., Electa, W1028; BLWt.1115-160-55
Samuel, Cont., BLWt.50-100, N.Y. res. in 1800
Solomon, Mass., Lucy, W18948
Thomas, Ct., Elizabeth, R2282
William, N.Y., Nancy, W6744; BLWt.26376-160-55
COOLIDGE, Daniel, Mass., Beulah, W18928
Joel, Mass., S30348
John, Cont., Mass., S12546
John, Mass., S34603
Joseph, Mass., Mary, W22816
Persis, Ct., N.Y., former wid. of John Allen, which see
Samuel, Mass., Mary Carman, former wid., W23780
Silas, Cont., N.H., Elizabeth, See COOLEDGE
Thomas, Mass., Molly, R13379
William, Mass., S34602
COOMBE, Peter, N.Y., Rachel, W16217
COOMBS, Anthony, Mass., R2284
Asa, Mass., Mary, W1233; BLWt.12841-160-55
Benjamin, Mass., R2285
Hezekiah, Mass., Frances Bartol, former wid., W1124; BLWt.19527-160-55
John, Mass., Dorothy, See COMBS
John, Mass., Charlotte, W22833 Died 4/19/1835
John, N.H., N.Y., Joanna, W22823; BLWt.13703-160-55
John, Va., Nancy, W1828; BLWt. 26793-160-55
Joseph, Mass., Elizabeth, R2286
Joseph, Mass., R.I., See COMBS
Joseph S. Mass., S16735
Mahlon, Va., S42659
Nathan, Mass., Sarah, W23848
Peter, Pvt., N.Y., BLWt.6936 iss. 10/5/1790 to John Tilman, ass.
Samuel C., Mass., Rachel, W22821
William, Mass., S30945
William, Pvt. "in the Invalids", BLWt.12943 iss. 2/16/1797
William, N.C., Michale Staire, former wid., W8757; BLWt.14968-160-55

COOMER, John, Mass., S30958
John, R.I., See COMER
Thomas K., R.I., S21130
William, Mass., BLWt.1622-100
COOMES, John, N.H., Joanna, See COOMBS
COOMS, Samuel C., Mass., See COOMBS
COON, Adam, S.C., Mary, W9800
Anthony, Va., S9213
Bridget, former wid. of Robert Tifft, R.I., which see
Christian, Md., S34712
Conrad, N.Y., S43383
Conrad, S.C., S3177
Daniel, Ct., S12568
Ebenezer, ----, Amy, R2287. Died in Pa. in 1831
Israel, Pvt., Va., Lee's Legion BLWts.11991 & 12965 iss. 9/9/1790 to Israel Coon
Jacob, Pvt., N.Y., BLWt.6925 iss. 8/28/1790 to Tellis Yates, ass.
James, Pvt., Ct., BLWt.5591 iss. 10/22/1792
James, Cont., Warner's Regt., BLWt.381-200-Lt. Iss. 3/18/1790 to Deborah Beach, late Coon. No papers
James, Cont., R.I., Sarah Crandall, former wid., R2439
Jeremiah, N.J., S862
John, Pvt., Ct., BLWt.5617 iss. 2/20/1790 to Solomon Goss
Joseph, Ct., R.I., S12583
Levi, N.J., Margaret, R2289
Matthew, N.Y., S22688
Michael, Va., R2290
Peter, N.Y., Cert. No. 18538
Peter, N.Y., Lydia, See KOONS
COONEY, James, ----, Pa. Agency & res., S3189
James, Pa., BLWt.9148-100. Iss. 7/9/1789. No papers
John, Pvt., Hazen's Regt., BLWt.12918 iss. 8/16/1797 to James DeBaufre, ass.
John, Pvt. "in the Invalids", BLWt.12941 iss. 5/18/1791 to Alexander Power, ass.
John, ----, Dis. No papers
COONROD, John, Pa., S16729
COONS, Abraham, N.Y., S15051
Adam, N.Y., S44229
Frederick, Va., S35844
Jacob, N.Y., R2291
John A., N.Y., R2292
William, N.C., R2294
COOP, Horatio, Md., S3193
COOPER, Abel, Mass., Vt., S18768
Abner, Ct., S22178
Abraham, Pvt., Ct., BLWt.5576 iss. 5/15/1795 to Eneas Munson, Jr., & Kneeland Townsend, assnes.
Abraham, Ct., S36468
Adam, N.C., Elizabeth, W1722; BLWt.24764-160-55
Alexander, Mass., S38639
Alexander, N.C., Mary, W4424
Apollos, Va., BLWt.2258-200
Asa, N.Y., Jemima, W16213

COOPER (continued)
Barnabas, Va., S9201
Benjamin, N.Y., Mary Magoun, former wid., R6829
Benjamin A., Va., S16722
Caleb, Va., S30959
Charles, Pa., S40853; BLWt. 9102-100. Iss. 8/14/1793. No papers
Christopher, Va., Jane, R2298
Christopher, Va., Permelia, R2303; also Indian Wars, 1774-1791
Dabney, Va., Henrietta, R2296
David, N.J., S809
David, N.J., S980
David, N.J., S3191
Eiles, Va., Sarah, W6711
Elijah, N.H., Sarah, W9802
Ephraim, Va., BLWt.1165-100
Ezekiel, Invalid Corps., Mass. BLWt.338-300-Capt. Iss. 3/25/1790. No papers
Frederick, N.C., Pa., Dorothy, W3001
Gasper, N.J., S807
George, Ct., N.Y., Phebe, W2761
George, Pvt., N.H., BLWt.2992 iss. 2/15/1797 to "Boynton ass. of Brown".
Henry, N.Y., S981
Isaac, Cont., Ct., Lydia, W3946
Isaac, Pvt., Lamb's Artillery, N.Y., BLWt.7001 iss. 10/23/1790
Jacob, Mass., S34609
Jacob, N.C., S12604
James, Cont. Pa., res. of son in 1840. BLWt.2278-100
James, Pvt., Del., BLWt.10741 iss. 5/12/1797 to James DeBaufre ass.
James, Pvt., N.J., BLWts.8172 & 12966 iss. --/--/----
James, Mass., S34600
James, N.C., S3192
James, Pa., Sea Service, R2297
James, Va., (colored), S39362
James B., Elizabeth, Cont. Navy, N.J. res. 1812-1854; S47185; Old Act, Navy Rej. Wid. 1124; BLWt. 45547-160-55
John, Pvt., Md., BLWt.11056 iss. 8/8/1791 to James DeBaufre, ass.
John, Pvt., N.H., BLWt.2990 iss. 10/12/1795 to James A. Neal, ass.
John, N.J., Dis. ----. No papers
John, N.J., S618
John, N.J., Prudence, W3952
John, N.J., Polly/Mary, W16926
John, Pvt., N.Y., BLWt.6941 iss. 7/20/1791
John, Pvt., N.Y., BLWt.6949 iss. 12/6/1791 to James Reed, ass.
John, Pvt., N.Y., BLWt.7013 iss. 3/30/1791 to Richard Edwards, Admr.
John, N.Y., S45998
John, N.Y., Lydia, W17659
John, Pa., Hannah, W3780
John, Pa., Ann Barbara, W6715
John, Va., Patsey/Martha, W8633; BLWt.26716-160-55

COOPER (continued)
John, Va., R2300
John Martin, Pa., Mary, R2301
Jonathan, N.H., S45691
Jonathan, Pa., Eleanor, W6714
Joseph, Cont., Mass., S10488
Joseph, Cont., N.Y., S12586
Joseph, Pa., S40851
Leaton/Leighton, Va., S35867
Leonard, Va., Christina, W6712; BLWt.1111-300
Leven, Va., S35866
Martin, Pa., See John Martin
Michael, Pa., Mary, W22857
Moses, Pvt., N.H., BLWt.2997 iss. 3/25/1796
Obediah, N.Y. S15392
Price, Ct., S43349
Richard, N.Y., S42133
Richard, N.C., R2304
Richard, Pvt., Va., BLWt.12005 iss. 5/15/1795 to Robert Means, ass.
Richard, Va., S39357
Robert, N.Y., Elizabeth, W16219
Sally, former wid. of John King, Mass., which see
Samuel, Cont., enl. N.Y., S40841
Samuel, Cont. Mass., S15789; BLWt.358-200-Lt. Iss. 11/17/1789. No papers
Samuel, Mass., S34607
Samuel, Navy, Mass., Margaret, W24834
Samuel, Pa., Jane Johnson, former wid., R5632
Sherman, N.H., Vt., S16725
Sion, N.C., S.C., Mary, R2302
Spencer, Va., BLWt.11985-100-Matross. Iss. 8/27/1800. No papers
Sterling, N.C., S6776
Sterling, Va., S9206; BLWt. 31895-160-55
Tecy/Tacey, Navy, Pa., S12602
Thomas, S.C., S21128
Thomas, Va., S39333
Vincent, Va., R2305
William, Cont., Md., Polly, W8632
William, Mass., R2307
William, N.Y., S12567
William, N.C., S8250
William, Pvt., Va., BLWt.12040 iss. 1/7/1793 to Robert Means, ass.
William, Va., S47186
COOSARD, Valentine, N.J., S2457
COOVERT, Burgum, N.J., See COVERT
Daniel, N.J., See COVERT
Isaac, N.J., S35865
James, Cont., N.Y., See COVERT
COP, Andrew, Pa., S43390
COPE, Barachias/Barakias, Md., Tenn., Mil., Creek War 1814; O.W. Inv. File 336, S21139
COPELAND, Aaron, S.C. See COPLAND
Alexander, S.C., Rebecca, W9395
Amasa, Ct., Cont., S36464
Asa, Pvt., Ct., BLWt.5640 iss. 1/28/1790
Asa, Ct., Abilene, W2594
Asa, Mass., S34604

COPELAND (continued)
Benjamin, S.C., S21122
Cader/Cato, N.C., Nancy, W17665
Elisha, Mass., S21116
Gershom, Mass., S34608
Isaac, Mass., Rebecca, W18938
James, Va., Sarah, W6730
Joel, N.C., See COPLAND
John, N.C., S40052
John, N.C., R2310
John, S.C., See COPLAND
Jonathan, Ct., See COPELIN
Richard, N.C., S39335
Ripley, N.C., See COPLAND
Samuel, Mass., S5029
William, Mass., S5027
William, Pvt., N.Y., BLWts.6944 & 14041 iss. 11/26/1792
William, N.Y., Bethiah, See COPLIN
William, S.C., S17889
COPELIN, Jonathan, Ct., S31616
William, Va., See COPLIN
COPENHAVER, Thomas, Va., R2311
COPES, Parker, Va., S39350
Southy, Va., S42650
COPIS, William, Va., S42136
COPLAND, Aaron, S.C., R2308
Asa, Ct., See COPELAND
Joel, N.C., R2309
John, S.C., S30966
Ripley, N.C., Rachel, W9811
Zacheus, N.C., S2470
COPLAR, Barnabas, Pa., BLWt.628-100
COPLEY, Benjamin, Mass., Hannah, W14520
Daniel, Ct., Cont., S12518
Matthew, Mass., Sea Service,S30342
Samuel, Ct., S18362
COPLIN, Benjamin, S.C. See COPELAND
Benjamin, Va., S10464
William, N.Y., Bethiah, W16218
William, Va., S31629
COPP, Aaron, Dis. ---, Pa., res. in N.H. No papers. Died about 1809
David, N.H., Margaret, W14504. Also served in French & Indian War
Ebenezer, Ct., Deborah, W20911
Ebenezer, N.H. Dis.--- No papers
Joseph, Ct., S43398; BLWt.569-100
Joseph, Cont., Mass., N.H., S45700
Josiah, N.H., Ruth, W4928; BLWt. 26813-160-55
COPPAGE, John, Va., S39363
COPPEDGE, Thomas, Va., S8239
COPPENHAFFER, Michael, Pa., S22690
COPPERNOLL, Adam, N.Y., S28430
Richard, N.Y., Elizabeth, W16542
COPPINGER, Higgins, Va., S40051; BLWt.2494-100
COPPLE, Daniel, Cont., Pa., S42656
Nicholas, Sgt. "in Proctor's Artillery", Pa., BLWt.9208 iss. 6/29/1789 to M. McConnell, ass.
Nicholas, Dis.--- No papers. Phila. agency
COPPS, David, Pvt., N.H., BLWt. 2999 iss. 3/7/1792 to Jonathan Tuttle, ass.
David, N.H., S36470
COPSEY, John, Va., R2313
COPUS, William, Va., S1801
COPWELL, James, R.I., S9329
Jeremiah, R.I., S40049
COQUILLET, Daniel, N.Y., S22698
CORAM, William, Pvt., Va., BLWt. 12007 iss. 3/4/1794
CORBET, Edward, Mass., See CORBITT
Jacob, Md., S35852
Thomas, Pa., See CORBITT
CORBETT, John ---- Va. agency, Dis. No papers
John, Mass., Privateer, Lydia, W14507
John, N.C., Va., Elizabeth, W9806 BLWt.95152-160-55
John, Pvt., "in the Va. line of Invalids", Va., BLWts.11988 & 12942 iss. 5/21/1799
Samuel, Va., See CORBIT
CORBIN, Anderson, Va., Elizabeth, W6739; BLWt.26456-160-55
Asa, Mass., S12596
Clement, Ct., Sabra, W3661; BLWt.9418-160-55
David, Cont., N.Y., Sarah, W1151; BLWt.9496-160-55
Eliphalet, Mass., S36465
Elisha, Cont., Mass., Experience, W27401
Elkanah, Mass., S43384
George, Va., Sarah, W1237; BLWt. 26093-160-55
James, Mass., Lois Sleeper, former wid., W22229
John, See Margaret, below
John, Va., S3202
CORBIN/COBANN, Joseph, Ct., S34601
CORBIN, Joseph, Ct., Mass.,S9323
Joshua, Mass., S12581
Lewis, Va., S30949
Margaret. Not a pension claim, but much corresp. relating to her. See mag. article giving hist. of Margaret Corbin in pens. claim of Deborah Gannett, Mass., S32722. Pensioned by State of Pa.; see p.948, Vol.3, Pa. Archives, 5th Ser. Seh was granted half pay under Resolution of Congress dated 7/6/1779 See Jour. of Cont.Congress, Vol.14, p.805. Said to be first pension granted to a woman.
Nathaniel, Mass., S18773
Peter, Ct., Vilette, W24836; BLWt.13412-160-55
Robert, Va., S8245
Stephen, Mass., Patience, W18923
CORBIT/CORBETT, Samuel, Va., S9202
CORBITT/CORBET, Edward, Mass.,S29721
CORBITT, Joseph, Ct., Hannah, W17661
CORBITT/CORBIT/CORBET, Thomas, Pa., Sarah, W16227
CORDELL, John, Va., Judith, W9814
Stephen, N.C., See CORDILL
CORDER, Benjamin D., Va., S38622
CORDER/CARDER, John, Va., S10121
CORDERY, James, Del., S9266
CORDILL, James, N.C., S30344; N.A. Acc. No.874, No.050034, not Half Pay
Stephen, N.C., Sarah, R2315; N.A. Acc.874, No.050035,not Half Pay
CORE, Henry, Pa., Sarah, W3336
COREN, Benjamin, N.C. See CONN
COREY/CORY, Benedick, Ct., R.I., R2317
COREY/CAREY, Francis, Mass., S34138
COREY, Gideon, R.I., S39330; BLWt.1837-100
Isaac, Cont., Mass., S12588
James, R.I., Vt., S10460
COREY/CORY, Joseph, R.I., Sarah, W22836; BLWt.26277-160-55
Josiah, Mass., Sarah, W17664
Mercy, Mass. See CARR/KARR, David
COREY/CORY, Pardon, R.I., Jemima, W26636
Paris, R.I., Lydia, W1238; BLWt. 34502-160-55
Peleg, R.I., R2319
Philip, Mass., S43405
COREY/CAREY, Simeon, Mass.,S36951
COREY/CORY, Thomas, R.I., Nancy, W4656
Timothy, Mass., Elizabeth, W27909
William, R.I., Martha, W17662
CORIELL/CORRIELL, Elisha, N.J., Nancy, W533; BLWt.26288-160-55
CORK, William, Md., S40850
CORKINS, John, Mass., S38621
CORL, John, N.Y., S15263
Leonard, Pa., S40842
William, N.Y., Maria, W22736
CORLE, Samuel, N.J., S979
CORLESS/CORLISS, Samuel, Cont., N.H., Jane, W23868
Timothy, Cont., Mass., Hannah, W20896
CORLEW, Edward, Vt., S21702
John, N.C., R2323
CORLEY, Abner, S.C., S21707
Austin, Va., S3198
George, Md., S9199
William, Va., S2422
Zaceous, S.C., S16736
CORLIS, Thankful, R.I., W12762; See Pomp REEVES
CORLISS, Bliss, Ct., Phebe, W17650
Elihu, N.H., S16347
CORLISS/CORLESS, Emerson, Cont. Mass., N.H., Mehitable, W24835
CORLISS, Susannah, Vt., W20918. Wid. of Simeon Stevens, which see
Timothy, Mass., See CORLESS
CORLY, Aquila, Va., Mary Ann Turner, former wid., R10757. Her last husb., Joshua Turner, was also a soldier, Md.
CORN, George, Pa., Va., S2143
Jesse, Va., Nancy, W909
John Peter, Va., Elizabeth, W5885
Timothy, Va., Elizabeth, W1147
William, Cont., Pa., Elizabeth, W3131
CORNEIL/CORNIEL, John, Mass., BLWt.16-100
CORNELISON, Conrad, N.C., Susannah, W10660
CORNELISON/CORNENELISON, John, N.Y., Sarah, W16545

CORNELISON (continued)
John, N.C., S35209
CORNELIUS, Charles, Va., S6775
Henry, N.Y., Margaret, W1149; BLWt.3773-160-55
John, Ct. res. in 1821, R2324. No papers
John, N.Y., Cornelia, W24839; BLWt.10-60-55
William, Pvt., Ct., BLWt.5573 iss. 7/11/1789 to Obadiah Walker
CORNELL, Benjamin, R.I., Martha, R2328
Caleb, N.Y., Martha Norton, R7723
Daniel, N.Y., S42654
David, N.Y., S43367
Gidion, R.I., Martha, W20904
Jacob, N.Y., R2327
John, N.Y., R13353
Joseph, Mass., Anne, R2325
Joseph, R.I., S40047
Latham, R.I., Susannah Matteson, former wid., W13684
Oliver, R.I., S17355
Richard, N.Y., S12562
Thurston, Mass., R.I., R2329
William, N.J., S22687
William, N.Y., See CORNWELL
CORNETT, Jesse, Va., S9193
William, Va., Mary, W6723; N.A. Acc. No.874, not half pay
CORNEYLE, Jacob, Va., S12709
CORNIN, Allen, Pvt., Ct., BLWt. 5634 iss. 10/14/1796
CORNING, Allen, Ct., S36480
Bliss, Ct., S22684
Uriah, Ct., Navy, S15262
CORNISH, Gabriel, Mass., Anna, W22852; BLWts.103-60-55 & 3345-100 iss. 12/6/1791
George, Ct., S15058
Jabez, Mass., R2330
Joel, Ct., S12561
John, Mass., S38633
Stephen, Mass., S23169
Theophilus, Pvt., Mass., BLWt. 3859 iss. 1/26/1790 to John Nay, ass.
William, Mass., S30343
CORNS, Joseph, N.J., R13366
CORNUE, Wessel, N.Y., Christina, W1029; BLWt.9070-160-55
CORNWALL, Caleb, Pvt., N.Y., BLWt.6977 iss. 7/9/1790 to Nicholas Fish, ass.
Caleb, N.Y., See CORNELL
David, Pvt., Lamb's Artillery, N.Y., BLWt.6996 iss. 9/15/1790 to Samuel Ellis, ass.
Dectus, Cont., N.Y. See Wm. CORNWELL
Isaac, Ct., S23584
Richard, Ct., BLWt.1586-100
Thomas, N.Y., R2333
CORNWELL, Amos, Ct., R2334
Ashbel, Ct., Privateer, Roxana, W27665; BLWt.15192-160-55
Avery, Del., S31632
Benjamin, Ct., S43393

CORNWELL (continued)
Daniel, Ct., Rachel, W25427; BLWt.7061-160-55
John, Ct., S10485
Nathaniel, Ct., Anna, W17653
Samuel, Ct., Sarah, W23844
William, Cont., Harrison's Artillery, BLWt.11116-100-Pvt. Iss. 9/22/1795. No papers. Name found in old U.S. B.L. Book under Md.
William, Cont., N.Y., S35885; BLWt.6994-100. Iss. to Thomas Russell, ass., 6/24/1793
William, N.J., S24130
William, Va., S21125
COROTHERS, Thomas, Pvt. "in the Artillery Artificers" of Pa., BLWt.12957 iss. 9/26/1791 to John McCleland, ass.
CORPE, Caleb, R.I., Anna, W22809
Philip, Pa., R2325
CORRIGEL/CORRIGIL, John, N.Y., BLWt. 1675-100
CORRINGTON, Archibald, N.J., Mary, R2336
Benjamin, N.J., Hannah, W6724; BLWt.50858-160-55
John, N.J., Mary, W4914; BLWt. 26064-160-55
CORRY, Nicholas, N.C., S.C., S21126
CORSE, John, Del., S35864
CORSER, Mary, N.H., W14503, former wid. of Samuel Downing, which see
CORSON, Abel, Fife Major, N.J., BLWt.8162 iss. 4/27/1799 to Abraham Bell, ass.
Abel, N.J., S34226
David, N.H., Navy, Privateer, S22696
CORT, Martin, N.Y., Ann Eliza, W10304; BLWt.61128-160-55
CORTELYOU/CORTLEYOU, Hendrick, N.J., S863
CORTER, Pvt., N.Y., BLWt.6969 iss. 6/19/179- to Thos. Anderson, ass.
CORTHELL, Pelatiah, Mass., S31597
Robert, Cont., Mass., Pa., Elizabeth, W23861
Sherebiah, Mass., Lydia, W23866
CORTLANDT, Philip, Col., N.H., BLWt.388-500-Col., iss. 7/7/1790
CORTRIGHT, William, N.J., Elizabeth R2341
CORTTIS, Japheth, Ct., Mary, W17649
CORTWRIGHT, David, Pa., R2340
Gideon, Pa., S16086
CORUN, Wm., Cont., Pa. See CORN
CORVIN, John, Va., Indian War, Elizabeth, R2343
CORWEN, Samuel, N.Y., S30953
CORWIN, Amaziah, Ct., S12582
Gersham, Pvt. "in the Invalids", BLWt.12946 iss. 9/25/1790 to Daniel & Wm. Birdsall, assnes.
Gersham/Gershom, Cont., N.Y., Margaret, W18948
Jacob, N.Y., R2345
Joseph, N.J., S3204
Richard, N.J., Pa., S29093
Selah, Ct., Joanna, W22805

CORWINE, George, N.J., Ruth Calvin, former wid., R1607
Samuel, N.J., S978
CORY, Abraham, N.J., S2468
Benjamin, Mass., Ann, W14521
Ebenezer, Cont., Mass., Joanna, W4158
Elnathan, N.J., Sarah, W2760
Gabriel, N.Y., Pa., S23581
Nathan, Mass., Molly, W22839
Oliver, Cont., Mass., S12558; BLWt.11083-160-55
Samuel, Mass., S12535
Samuel, N.J., S9194
Samuel, R.I., Jemima, W20893. She was wid. of Pardon Cory/Corey, brother of Samuel. See claim by her under Pardon Cory
Sheffield, R.I., R2321
Stephen, Mass., S12554
Thomas, R.I., R2322. Not same as Thos. Corey
William, Mass., S30339
William, R.I., Vt., Rachel, W25430; BLWt.34934-160-55
William, R.I., Meribah, R2318
CORYELL, David A., N.J., S29099
Emanuel, Cont., Pa., Frances, W20925
John, Pvt., N.J., BLWt.8205 iss. 6/11/1789 to Jonathan Dayton, ass.
COSART, John, N.J., Susannah, W18958
COSBEY, Sydnor, Pvt., in the Artillery, Va., BLWts.11987 & 12204 iss. 7/6/1793 to Robert Means, ass.
COSBY, Garland, Va., S30334
John, Va., S30340
Zacheus, Va., S8249
COSHAL, Thomas, Pvt., Lamb's Artillery N.Y., BLWt.7000 iss. 9/15/1790 to John S. Hobart, et al, ass.
COSIER, Benjamin, N.J., R1783
COSLEMAN, Christian, N.Y., Barbara/Maria Barbara, W20895
COSNAHAN, Joseph, N.C., S18356
COSPAR, John, Pa., See COSPER
COSPER, John, Pa., Martha, W5061
COSSART, John, Pvt., N.J., BLWt. 8231 iss. 9/29/1790 to John Hale, ass.
COSSELMAN, Pardel, N.Y., S29088
COSSIT, Timothy, Ct., S23170
COSTEN, Stephen, N.C., S6777
COSTIGAN, Francis, N.J., S42653
COSTIGIN, Lewis J., N.J., S43337; BLWt.403-200-Lt. Iss. 2/10/1790. No papers
COSTIN, Ebenezer, N.H., Sally/Sarah Eastman, former wid., R2348; BLReg.202184-1855
COSTNER, Thomas, N.C., W18856
COSTON, Bishop, N.H., S43356
Thomas, N.C., R2349
COTCHELLS, Benjamin, Pvt., Md., BLWts. 12888 & 14115 iss. 3/25/1795 to Francis Sherrard, ass. of Nathaniel Crawford, Admr.

COTES, John, Ct., S10474
COTRELL, James, Va., R2350
COTTELLE, Phillip, Pvt., Lamb's Artillery, N.Y., BLWt.6987 iss. 7/13/179-
COTTEN, George, N.C., R2353
COTTEN, John, S.C., S35845
COTTER, Edward, Sgt. "in Proctor's Artillery", Pa., BLWt.9198 iss. 6/20/1789
COTTERAL, Thomas, Va., See COTTRILL
COTTERELL, Daniel, Pa., Va., R2351
COTTLE, Jedediah/Judiah, Va., BLWt.500-100
Joseph, R2352. Not Rev. War. Generals Harmer's & Wayne's Indian Wars, 1790-1792. Ky. enl. & res.
Peter, Mass., S46028
Robert, Mass., Lydia, W18969; BLWt.572-100
COTTON, Benjamin, Sgt., N.H., BLWt. 3016 iss. 10/30/1789 to Ephraim True, ass.
Benjamin, Cont., N.H., Dolly, W5888
Bibye L., Ct., S12571
Caleb, N.H., S38620
Elias, Navy, Mass. res. & agency, S34606
George, Ensign, Ct., BLWt.380-150, no papers
Henry, Pvt., "in Proctor's Artillery", Pa., BLWt.9200 iss. 7/16/1789 to M. McConnell, ass.
James, N.J., Achsa Chalfant, former wid., R1830
James, Va., Nancy, W6942
John, Cont., Mass., S42649
John, Mass., S38617
Josiah, Mass., S34218
Michael, Mass., S43374
Nathaniel, N.Y. res. in 1820, R2354
Rowland, Ct., Cont., War of 1812, S11170
Samuel, Ct., Navy, R2356
Thadeus, Pvt., Ct., BLWt.5671 iss. 4/19/1790
Thomas, N.C., Priscilla, W6727
Ward, Ct.,Nabby, W22826
William, Ct., S34244
William, Mass., S29723
William, N.H., Ruth, R2355
William, N.H., R2357
William, N.C., S32187
William, Pa., S22695
COTTRELL, Asa, Mass., S29087
Nicholas, Cont., Mass., Lydia, W15652
COTTRILL, John, Va., S39597
Thomas, Va., Nancy, W4165
COUCH, Abraham, Ct., S36481
Amos, Ct., Phebe, W20901
Daniel, Ct., S29086
Ebenezer, Ct., S36483
Ebenezer, Ct., Asenth, W23839; BLWt.27599-160-55
Edward, N.C., Mary, R2359
John, Ct., Lois, W17640
John, Ct., Prudence, W2360

COUCH (continued)
Joseph, Mass., Sarah, W16105
Joshua, Ct., Sea Service, Patty, W17656
Samuel, Ct., Cont., Mass., S29717
Stephen, Ct., Poliphema, W14508
Thomas, Ct., Sarah, W20906
Thomas, Mass., S12524
William (colored), Ct., R2358
William, Mass., S12577
William, Pa., Va., Margaret, R2532
William, S.C., R2361
COUGHEY/CAUGHEY, John, Pa., S35816
COUGHRAN, George, Va.,R1816 & R2362
COUGHREN, Joseph, Va., Prudence, W1712
COULSON, David, Va., S1899
COULTER, Andrew, Pvt., Pa., BLWt. 9162 iss. 10/7/1792
John, Md., S2445; BLWt.274-100
John, Pa., R2364
Martin, N.C., Elizabeth, R2363
Matthew, N.C., S30349
Nathaniel, Cont., Pa., Va., Isabella, W3953; BLWt.556-160-1812. B.L. papers for U.S. Army services.
William, Md., BLWt.1357-100
COUNCE, Nicholas, N.C., S2443
COUNCIL, Jesse, Va., S9191
COUNEY, Michael, Cont., Ct., Mehitable, W16919
COUNT, Abner/Jesse Abner, Pvt., Mass., BLWt.3959 iss. 8/17/1796 to John Kessler
COUNTRYMAN, Conrad, N.Y., Margaret, W16920
Frederick, N.Y., Appolonia, W22855
Jacob, Pvt., N.Y., BLWt.6938 iss. 12/28/1791 to Moses Phillips, ass.
Jacob, N.Y., S43339
John, N.Y., S43359
Nicholas, N.Y., R2367
COUNTZ, Adam, Pvt., N.Y., BLWt. 6958 iss. 10/12/1791
COURSEY, Hampton, Pvt., Md., BLWt. 11053 iss. 3/11/1791
James, Va., Indian disturbances in 1774, Susannah, R2308
COURSON, James, S.C., Lavice/Laveci W9805; BLWt.95168-160-55
Timothy, Mass., N.H., Betsey, W16924
COURT, John, Mass., Privateer, S.C., R2370
COURTER, Henry, N.J., Ann, W18942
Philip, Pvt., N.Y., BLWt.6908 iss. 1/12/1792 to David Weaver, ass.
COURTNER, Anthony, Va., Catharine, W6731
COURTNEY, Cornelius, Pvt., Pa., BLWt.9164 iss. 2/2/1791 to Hannah Courtney, Admx.
Francis, N.Y., Sarah Brock, former wid., W15987
James, Va., S9265. See N.A. Acc. No. 874, 050037, not Half Pay
Luke, Pvt., N.J., BLWt.8209 iss. 8/11/1789
Luke, N.J., Zipporah/Zephorah, W3779

COURTNEY (continued)
Michael, Va., S35863
Samuel, Pvt., Va., BLWt.12037 iss. 7/7/1792 to Robert Means, ass.
Samuel, Va., S39346
Thomas, Md., Catharine, R2371
William, Pvt., Pa., BLWt.9160 iss. 3/17/1791 to Alexander Power, ass.
COURTS, Low, Pa., S46435
Richard H., Md., Eleanor C., W8627
COUS, Jacob, N.Y., S12587
COUSENS, Ebenezer, Mass., S36985
Nathaniel, Mass., S29092
COUSINS, Jacob, Vt., Bethia, R2372
Samuel, Mass., Pamelia, W22814
COUTIER, Charles, Pvt., Hazen's Regt., BLWt.12911 iss. 2/20/1792 to Benj. Moore, ass.
COVALT, Abraham, Pa., Loassa/Louisa Davis, former wid., R2742
COVART, Isaac, N.J., See COOVERT
COVEL, David, Navy, Mass., R2373
Ebenezer, Ct., R.I., S31625
Ebenezer, Mass., S34240
James, Cont., Ct., Margaret, W5251; BLWt.6256-160-55
COVELL, Benjamin, Mass., S43361; BLWt.2307-100
Eliphalet, Ct. Sea Service, Mass. Privateer, S10477
Ephraim, Ct., S12597
Henry, Ct., Mass., S30954
Isaac, Mass., R2375
Jacob, N.Y., Electa, R2376
James, Ct., Lucy, R2377
Richard, Mass., Mercy, W6738
Samuel, Mass., Jerusha, W16930
COVENHOVEN, Abraham, N.J., N.Y., Charlotte Lake, former wid., W12108; BLWt.78023-160-55
Albert, N.J., S34610
Isaac, N.J., N.Y., S12531
Jacob, N.J., S976
Jacob, N.Y., R2379
Lewis, N.J., S861
Robert, Pa., S12574
William, N.Y., Susanna, W20913
COVENHOVER, Peter, N.Y., S28444
Thomas, N.J., R2380
COVENTRY, John, Mate, General Hospital, BLWt.505-300 iss. 11/21/1793
COVERLY, Thomas, Va., S24960; BLWt.406-200
COVERT, Bergun, N.J., Catharine, W6740
Bergun/Burgum, N.J., S3215
Daniel, N.J., S10462
Ellisson, N.J., S977
Jacob, N.J., S808
James, Cont., N.Y., S19254
Jeremiah, Ct., S10466
John, N.Y., Catharine, R2381
Luke, N.J., S23174
Luke P., N.J., Mary, W23830
Peter, N.J., Va., S43340
Thomas, N.J., Jane, W10671
Tunis, Pvt., N.J., BLWt.8206

COVERT (continued)
iss. 12/20/1791 to Jacob Heller, ass.
Tunis, N.J., Catharine Fell, former wid., W7251
Tunis D., N.J., R2383
COVEY, Joseph, N.Y., Amy, R2384; BLWt.44802-160-55
Samuel, N.Y., Va., S3190
COVIL, Abraham, Ct., Mehitable R2378
David, Ct., Sarah, W18952
Ebenezer, Ct., Cont., S15261
Joseph B., Mass., S23178
COVILL, Judah, Cont., Mass., S31621
COVINGTON, John, S.C., Susannah, R2385
Matthew, N.C., S2444
Robert, Va., Amy, W2067; BLWt. 9530-160-55
COWAN, Edward, Lt., Ga., BLWt.491-200-Lt. Iss. 8/20/1799
Isaac, Cont., Mass., Elizabeth, W22815
Isaac, N.Y., R2386
Joseph, N.C., Nancy, W25444; BLWt.28614-160-55
Thomas, N.C., Mary, W18922
William, Mass., N.H., See COWEN
William, Pa., Mary, R2388
COWARD, Joel, S.C., Anna, R2389
Joseph, Cont., N.J. res. & agency, S34255
Samuel, N.J., Elizabeth, R2390
William, Md. Sea Service, Nancy/Ann, R2391
COWDEN, James, Mass., S12548
James, Mass., Persis, W14527
Robert, N.C., S.C., S1656
COWDERY, Ambrose, Ct., S15050
Asa, Ct., S10479
Edward, Ct., Submit, See CAWDRY
Samuel, Cont., Ct., BLWt.132-100
William, Ct., R2392
COWDREY, Benjamin, N.Y., S43343
John, Cont., Mass., S31620
COWDRY, Benjamin, Pvt., N.Y., BLWt.6951 iss. 9/7/1790
Jonathan, Mass., Sarah, W16923
Nathaniel, Mass., Jerusha, W15653
William, Ct., See COWDERY
COWELL, Isaac, N.J., S2131
John, Pa., BLWt.1907-300
Samuel, Ct., S10476
COWEN, David, R.I., S32183
John, Navy, R.I., S43402
Jonathan, R.I., S12541
Joseph, R.I., S12552
William, Mass., N.H., Jane, W23857
William, N.Y., Jane, W18935
William, Pa., S2137. See N.A. Acc. No.874. Not half pay
COWET/COWETT, Ebenezer, Mass., S34236
COWFER, John, Pvt., Sheldon's Dragoons, Ct., BLWt.5644 iss. 10/16/1789 to Theodosius Fowler
COWGILL, Daniel, Va., S3199
Ralph, Va., Mary, W1389; BLWt. 10262-160-55

COWHAWK
James, Pvt., Pa., BLWt.9151 iss. 1/30/1792
COWHERD, Francis, Va., Lucy, W6721; BLWt.452-300-Capt. Iss. 7/5/1799 to James Baylor, ass. No papers
James, Va., S10482
Jonathan, Va., Elizabeth, W8619
COWING, Calvin, Cont., Mass., Dolly Woodward, former wid., W10286; BLWt.96084-160-55
Gathelues, Mass., S34241
Job, Mass., S9209
John, Mass., S12551
COWL, Benjamin, Cont., N.Y., Mahitable/Mehitable/Mahitabel, W723; BLWt.16108-160-55
COWLES, Asa, Mass., N.Y., S12516
Daniel, Pvt., Artillery Artificers, BLWt.12927 iss. 12/6/179- to Stephen Thorn, ass.
Ezekiel, Ct., S12614
Isaac, Ct., S16089
Jabez, Ct., S15057
Nathaniel, Mass., S23585
Noah, Ct., R2394
Phineas, Ct., S23177
Samuel, Ct., R2395
Solomon, Ct., Cont., N.Y., S15049
Thomas, Ct., Tamer, W23851; BLWt.9202-160-55
Timothy, Cont., Mass., Anna, W16546
COWLEY, Robert, S.C., S39336
COWLING, John, Pvt., Mass., BLWt. 3958 iss. 2/25/1791 to Samuel Whiting
COWLS, Adonijah, Mass., S21118
Asa, Ct., S36466
COWNOVER, Garret, N.J., Lydia, R2365
COX, Andrew, Va., S8226
Artemas, Mass., Sally, W17667
Bartlett/Bartlet, Va., Polly, W1562
Benjamin, Mass., S38632
Benjamin, N.Y., Pa., S2463
Benjamin, N.C., S2146
Benjamin, N.C., S2440
Benjamin, Vt., Irene/Irena, W9392
Bray, Navy, Me. res. & agency in 1818; S36984
Caleb, N.C., S30950
Charles, Pvt., N.Y., BLWt.6918 iss. 8/15/1790 to John S. Hobart, ass.
Curd, Va., S3169
Daniel Powell, Del., BLWt.532-300
Ebenezer, Cont., Mass., S15382
Edward, N.C., S3170
George, Vt., S15388
George, Va., S9203
Hugh, Mass., Mary Barstow, former wid., W5790; BLWt.30619-160-55
Isaac, Md., S32186
Isaac, N.J., S9215
Israel, Mass., S29719

COX (continued)
James, Mass., S34237
James, Mass., Mary, W22812
James, Va., S2441
James, Va., Sarah/Sally, R2412
Javan, N.C., Mary, W25433; BLWt. 32209-160-55
John, Cont., N.Y., S43365
John, Pvt., N.Y., BLWt.6931 iss. 7/9/1790 to Theodosius Fowler, ass.
John, N.C., S2454
John, N.C., S6778
John, N.C., S35847
John, N.C., S41495
John, N.C., Va., S21124
John, Va., R2404
John, Va., R2405
John, Va. Sea Service, S8223. See acct no.837-Va. State Navy Va. Half Pay
Joseph, Md., S1800
Joseph, Mass., S34239
Joseph, N.C., S41494
Joseph, Pa., S8224; BLWt.438-200-Lt. iss. 2/14/1791 to Alexander Power, ass. No papers
Joshua, N.C., Mary, R2408
Michael, Pa., S5020
Moses, N.C., Martha, R2407
Nathaniel, Md., R2411
Philip, N.J., S18360
Philip, N.C., Jemima, W22844
Phineas, ---, N.Y. res. in 1794. Dis. No papers
Phinehas, Va., Barbary/Barbara, W3004; BLWt.26798-160-55
Reeves, N.Y., Elizabeth Horton, former wid., W16293
Richard, N.J., BLWt.402-400-Maj. Iss. 6/11/1789. No papers
Richard, N.C., S31630
Robert, Pvt., Ct., BLWt.5554 iss. 6/21/1791
Robert, Ct., S43400
Robert, Pvt., N.Y., BLWt.6913 iss. 7/18/1792 to Baldwin & Shay, ass.
Robert, N.Y., Mary, W23853
Samuel, S.C., S21705
Samuel, Va., S39343
Simon, Pvt., N.Y., BLWt.6922 iss. 7/24/1790 to John Lawrence, ass.
Solomon, N.C., S15383
Solomon, N.C., Mary, R2409
Thomas, Md., S3168
Thomas, N.C., Bethany, R2399
Thomas, Va., Martha, W10303; BLWt.56991-160-55
Tunis, Pa., S22681
William, Cont., N.Y., S43363
William, Pvt., Md., BLWt.11064 iss. 12/22/1794
William, Mass., Mary, R2410
William, N.J., N.Y., Hulda, R2401
William, N.C., S8225
William, N.C., Elizabeth, R2400
William, Pa., Mary, W3179; BLWt. 433-300-Capt. iss. 5/26/1790. No papers
William, S.C., S21704

COX (continued)
William, Pvt., Va., BLWt.12043 iss. 4/12/1792 to Robert Means, ass.
William, Va., S30960
COXE, Bartlett/Bartlet, Va., S24964
COY, Christopher, Md., Elizabeth, W9798
David, Ct., S43364
David, Ct., R2413
Edee, Cont., Ct., S43376
Edu, Pvt., Sheldon's Dragoons Ct., BLWt.5668 iss. 8/23/1790
Elisha, R.I., Mary, W23833
Ephraim, Ct., Rebekah, W17638
John, Mass., Molly, W22854
Joseph, Cont., Capt. Jedediah Waterman & Col. John Durkee, S43371
William, Md., S31614
Willis, Cont., Mass., S34238
COYE, Nehemiah, Ct., Anne, W20909
Vine, Ct., S19262
COYKENDALL/COYKENDOLL, Benjamin, N.J., S12607
Harmon/Harman, N.J., N.Y., Pa., Catharine, W4926
COYLE, Manasseh/Manassah, Pa., Isabella, W2759
Mark, Pvt., Pa., BLWt.9169 iss. 5/15/1790
Mark, Pa., S34709
Patrick, Va., S30952
COZBY, Robert, S.C., S24966
COZENS, Mathew, Pvt., N.Y., BLWt.6947 iss. 10/11/1790
COZZENS, Issachar, R.I., R2414
Richard, R.I., Julia, W9817; BLWt.334-60-55; BLWt.3045-100. Iss. 11/4/1794
CRABB, Abijah, Cont., enl. in N.Y., S43408
Abijah, Pvt., N.Y., BLWt.6984 iss. 10/10/1791 to Anthony Maxwell, ass.
Asa, Ga., R2416
Benjamin, N.C., S39368
Jarrot/Jarrott, N.C., S41499
John, N.C., R2417
CRABROUNE, William de, Navy, Scotland, res. of France in 1832, R78 1/2. See William NICHOLSON
CRABTREE, Abraham, Va., R2418
Isaac, Va., S30972
Jacob, Va., Mary, R2420
James, Va., S32195
John, N.C., R2419
Richard, N.C., Sarah, W8642; BLWt.27623-160-55
William, N.C., Mary, W17689
William, N.C., R2421
CRACRAFT, Charles, Va., BLWt. 61361-160-55; Elizabeth Price former wid., W10228
CRADDICK, Eleazer, N.C., S8252
CRADDOCK, John, N.C., BLWt.478-300-Capt. Iss. 8/14/1792 to Isaac Cole, ass. No papers
Robert, Va., S46436; BLWt.463-200-Lt. Iss. 7/15/1789. No papers
CRADLEBAUGH, William, Va., S30354
CRADY, David, Pvt., Md., BLWt. 11094 iss. 11/29/1790 to James Currie, Admr.
CRAFFORD, Alexander, S.C., S3229
Elijah, Pa., S2148
John, Mass., S38752
James, Mass. Sea Service, See CRAWFORD
CRAFT, Aaron, Cont., Mass., Abigail, W23876
Archillis, N.C., S30357
Benjamin, Ct., Jane, W5258; BLWt.202-60-55
Charles, N.Y., R2423
Ezekiel, N.C., See CROFT
George, Pa., Sarah, R2424
Nathaniel, Pvt., N.Y., BLWt. 6932 iss. 9/2/1790
Samuel, Pvt., Mass., BLWt.3956 iss. 3/25/1790
CRAFTON, Anthony, Va., S16351
James, Va., Frances, W6764
Thomas, Va., Mary, W6763
CRAFTS, Graves, Mass., S17337
Joseph, Cont., Ct., S46352; BLWt.51-100
Reuben, Mass., Henrietta, W23889
Samuel, Ct., Lucy, BLWt.56948-160-55
Samuel, Mass., S28695
Thomas, Mass., Polly, W14537
William, R.I., S39366
CRAGAN, Dennis, Pvt., Md., BLWt. 11120 iss. 9/24/1792
CRAGE, Nathan, Mass., S19618
CRAGIE, Andrew, Cont., Mass. See CRAIGIE
CRAGO, Robert, Pa., See CRAIGO
CRAIG, Abijah, Mass., Sukey, W23890
Alexander, N.C., S.C., S1658
Ann, former wid. of John Cunningham, S.C., which see
Daniel, Sgt., Sheldon's Dragoons, Ct., BLWt.5667 iss. 7/17/1789 to James Reynolds
David, N.H., Elizabeth, W14530
David, N.J., S15268
Elias, Mass., Olive, W22865
Enoch, Cont., Mass., S15791
Frazee, N.J., Rebecca, W17690
Gerard, Pvt., "in the Invalids" BLWt.12944 iss. 2/28/1791
Isaac, Cont., Pa., Amelia, W4660; BLWt.424-400-Maj. Iss. 1/28/1791. No papers
James, N.H., S42143
James, N.J., S864
James, Pa., S2477
James, Pa., BLWt.1359-100
James, S.C., Margaret Miles, former wid., W25711; BLWt.14531-160-55
James, Va., BLWt.428-300-Capt. Iss. 12/5/1794. Also recorded under BLWt.2648. No papers
John, Cont., Pa., S40859; BLWt. 427-300-Capt. Iss. 1/30/1792. No papers
John, Md., S24885; BLWt.286-100
John, Mass., S19268
CRAIG (continued)
John, N.H., S42661
John, N.J., S2149
John, N.J., S15278
John, Pa., S8253
John, S.C., Catharine, W22864; BLWt.26494-160-55
John, S.C., Barbary, R2426
John, Va., S16740
John, Va., Jane, W8638
John Hawkins, Va., Sally S., W6759; BLWt.34967-160-55
Matthew, Pa., BLWt.1360-100
Moses, Pvt., Crane's Cont. Artillery, Mass., BLWt.3991 iss. 3/25/1790
Moses, Mass., S29734
Robert, Cont., Pa., Mary, W8641
Robert, Pa., R2427
Rodrick, N.C., R2428
Samuel, Mass., S17908
Samuel, N.J., Elizabeth, W450
Samuel, Pa., Jane Innis, W348; BLWt.411-300-Capt. Iss. 11/4/1789. No papers
Samuel, Pa., Elizabeth, W3075
Thomas, Md., Elizabeth, W5255; BLWt.1187-100
Thomas, Mass., S12630
Thomas, N.C., S30971
Thomas, Pa., S40861; BLWt.409-500-Col. Iss. 2/27/1792. No papers
Thomas, Pvt., Va., BLWt.11993 iss. 11/5/1789
Thomas, Va., Mary, W3954
William, Md., See CRAIGE
William, Mass., See CRAIGUE
William, Va., S30355
William, Va., Mary, W8639
William, Va., BLWt.1345-100
CRAIGE, Andrew, Cont., Mass., See CRAIGIE
Robert, Pvt., N.H., BLWt.3026 iss. 8/26/1790 to Manassah Cutler, ass.
Thomas, Mass., S12628
William, Md. & Boat Service, S2479
CRAIGEE, William, Pvt., Mass., BLWt.3838 iss. 11/24/1791 to Isaac Bronson, ass.
CRAIGHEAD, Robert, N.C., S352
CRAIGIE, Andrew, Cont., Mass., Elizabeth, W14534; BLWt.500-450-Apothecary. Iss. 12/30/1790. No papers. Wid. erroneously pens. as Cragie. Mass. wrongly reports name on rolls as Craige.
CRAIGO, Robert, Pa., Elizabeth, W25445; BLWt.16280-160-55
CRAIGS, George, Pvt., Md., BLWt. 11099 iss. 11/29/1790 to Thomas McMames, Admr.
CRAIGUE, William, Mass., S22192
CRAIK, James, BLWt.502-500-Physician Gen. Iss. 6/3/1789. No papers
CRAIL, John, Va., Allathea/Allithia, W4426
William, Pvt., Md., BLWt.11068 iss. 1/11/1790 to Joshua Ward, ass.

CRAIN, Amariah, Ct., Tryphena, W17688
Amos, Vt., S12716
Daniel, Ct., Cont., S12713
Ebenezer, Vt., See CRANE
Elisha, Ct., S15266
Joel, N.C., Margaret, W25452; BLWt.45663-160-55
Jonathan, Ct., Sybil, W23882
Roger, Ct., Mass., Sarah, W18981
Silas, S.C., S32190
Stephen, N.C., Mary, W9823
Thomas, Va., S16352
William, N.C., S1753
William, N.C., See CRANE
Zebulon, N.H., Rhoda, W20936
CRALEY, Hugh, Pvt., N.J., BLWt. 8230 iss. 12/28/1789 to John Hollingshead, ass.
CRAM, Benjamin, S17906
Ebenezer, N.H., R----
Ephraim, N.H., S45707
Humphrey, N.H., S39374
John S., Mass., S37000
Samuel, N.H., Susannah, R2433; BLWt.82007-160-55
Samuel, Tilton, N.H., Betty, W22860; BLWt.8471-160-55
Smith, N.H., R2449; BLWt.16137-160-55
Theophilus, Cont., N.H., Mary, R2432
Tristrem/Trustram, Cont., N.H., Anna, W23874
Zebulon, N.H., S22705
CRAMER, Andrew, N.J., S40806
Conrad, N.Y., R2434
David, Cont., Pa. res. of dau. in 1828, BLWt.1310-100
Helfer, Pa., Sophia, W2762
Henry, Ct., Cont., Jemima, R2436
Henry, N.Y., Sarah, W20928
Jacob, Cont. Md., S40867
Jacob, Cont., Pa., BLWt.2507-200
Jacob, N.Y., S12635
John C., N.Y., Christina, W16548
Joseph, N.Y., S43416
Josiah, N.J., Elizabeth, W264
CRAMMER, Andrew, Pvt., N.J., BLWt. 9/9/1790 to John Pope, ass.
CRAMPTON, Jonathan, Ct., Elizabeth H., W1725; BLWt.8453-160-55
Mary, former wid. of James Benjamin, Ct., which see
Thomas, Md., S34719
CRAMTON, Elon, Ct., S10502
CRANDAL, Amherst, R.I., Polly, W23878
Barney, R.I., S21715
Benjamin, R.I., S9244; BLWt. 73599-160-55
Edward, Ct., Cont., S43410
Elijah, Cont., R.I., S39372
Ezekiel, R.I., S28696
Ezra, Ct., S12618
Isaiah, Ct., R.I., S12636
James, R.I., Barbara/Barbary, W5257; BLWt.3971-160-55
Joseph, Cont., R.I., S39375
Joseph, R.I., W9827; BLWt.17728-160-55
Sylvester, Mass., N.Y., S19264

CRANDALL, Abner, R.I., Mary, W18972
Ammariah, Ct., See CRANDOL
Azariah, R.I., Anna, R2437
Cary, R.I., Mehitable, W1390; BLWt.26013-160-55
Christopher, Ct., R.I., S15269
Ethan, R.I., S12620
George, N.Y., R2440
Gideon, Ct., R.I., S15272
Gideon, N.Y., R.I., S12621
Hosea, R.I., Sarah, W27402; BLWt.1308-100
Jesse, R.I., S21151
John, Ct., R2438
Jonathan, R.I., Cynthia, W1566
Joshua, R.I., Mary, W18983
Levi, Mass., S29737
Luke, N.Y., Rachael, W16931
Lydia T., former wid. of Elias D. Trafton, R.I., which see
Peter, R.I., S15267
Richmond, Ct. Sea Service, Lucretia, W20930; BLWt.34962-160-55
Sarah, former wid. of James Coon, Cont., R.I., which see
Simeon, R.I., Catharine, W17691
CRANDEL, Jeremiah, Ct., N.Y., R.I., S10506
CRANDELL, Azel, Ct., S12633
John, Cont., R.I., S38645
CRANDLE, Godfrey, Pvt., N.Y., BLWt. 6945 iss. 5/24/1791 to William Faulker, ass.
CRANDOL, Ammariah, Ct., S16090; BLWt.26081-160-55
CRANE, Aaron, N.J., Tabitha, R2441
Abel, Pvt., Mass., BLWt.3868 iss. 7/22/1789
Abijah, Cont., Mass. Sea Service, Polly, W1241; BLWt.19724-160-55
Asa, N.J., S38644
Benjamin, N.J., Sarah, W10678
Bernice, Mass., R.I., Joanna, W22858
Caleb, N.J., R2442
Curtis, Pvt., Ct., BLWt.5625 iss. 5/7/1792 to Thos. Stanley
Curtis, Ct., Elizabeth, W16547
David, Pvt., Mass., BLWt.3934 iss. 5/24/1797 to Jacob Griggs
David, Mass., S34267
David D., N.J., Martha, W451
Ebenezer, Ct.? or Mass.? R---
Ebenezer/Enezer, Vt., Ruth, R2430
Edmond/Edmund, N.J., R2443
Elihu, Ct., S24134
Elijah, Ct., Susannah, W16223
Elijah, N.J., S2481
Elisha, N.Y., Ruth, W16934
Elizabeth, former wid. of Ozias Hanford, Ct., which see
Enos, Ct., Sophia Williams, former wid., W11832; BLWt.10138-160-55
Henry, Pvt., Md., BLWt.11074, iss. 1/8/1796 to George Ponsonby, ass.
Isaac, N.Y., Anna, W18980; BLWt. 820-160-55
James, Ct., Cont., N.Y., Pa., S23588

CRANE (continued)
James, Va., BLWt.444-300
John, Ct., S43415
John, Ct., Phillis, W8192; BLWt.26324-160-55
John, Cont., Mass., Dis. No papers. BLWt.330-500-Col. Iss. 7/24/1792
John, Mass., BLWt.335-400-Surgn. Iss. 6/9/1797 to Moses Fish, ass. of John Huntingdon Crane, only son & heir-at-law of J.C. No papers
John, Mass., S39373
John, Mass., Lettitia/Letitia, W17687; BLWt.354-200-Lt. Iss. 3/1/1790. No papers
John, N.J., S986
John, N.J., S2147
John, N.J., Mary Cumming, former wid., W4169
John, N.J., Catharine, W23777
John, N.J., Catharine, R2431
John, N.C., S3218
Jonathan, N.J., S34261
Jonathan, N.Y., Bethia, W16224
Jonathan E., N.J., S2478
Joshua, Mass., Polly Fish, former wid., W14716
Lewis, Ga., Sophia, R2450
Mayfield, S.C., S30356
Nathaniel, Pvt., Ct., BLWt.5583 iss. 12/31/1791 to Isaac Bronson
Nathaniel, Ct., S36484
Noah, N.J., R2448
Obadiah, N.J., S985
Peter, Cont., Mass., Elizabeth, W23891
Rufus, Ct., Rachel, W23877
Rufus, Mass., S29736
Samuel, Mass., Experience, R2447
Samuel, N.J., Jane, W9822
Silas, Ct., Clarrissa, R13483; BLWt.85080-160-55
Silas, N.J., Zipporah, W3782
Simeon, Ct., Mass., Anne, W18977
Stephen, Pvt., N.J., BLWt.8190 iss. 11/20/1792
Stephen, N.Y., Jerusha Fuller, former wid., R3831
Timothy, N.Y., S29102
William, N.J., S626
William, N.Y., Dis. No papers
William, N.C., Elizabeth, R2429
William, S.C., S21716
Zadok/Zadock, N.J., R2451
CRANK, Peleg, Pvt., Mass., BLWt. 3790 iss. 2/29/1792 to Moses Beard
CRANMER/CRAMER, John, N.J., Keturah, W3225
CRANNEL, Isaac, N.Y., Maria, W22861
CRANNELL, Martin, N.Y., S15059
CRANS/CRANZ, Philip/Phillip, N.Y., Elizabeth, R2452
CRANSON, Asa, Mass., Zillah, W18971
CRANSTON, Benjamin, R.I. Sea Service, Mary, W14544
John, R.I., S21719
Peleg, R.I., Elizabeth, W16226

CRANSTON (continued)
Peleg, R.I., Mary, W20933; BLWt.30693-160-55
Samuel, Cont., R.I., S23182
Samuel, R.I., Zilpha, W16221
Thomas, R.I., R2453
CRANTZ/GRANTS, Mark, N.Y., Catharine, W6758; BLWts.111-60-55 & 6971-100 iss. 1/4/1791
CRAPO, John, Mass., Linda, W15660; BLWt.36239-160-55
Jonathan, Mass., Celia, W5254
Peter, N.Y., S43414
CRARY, Elias, Vt., R2454
John, N.H., Vt., R2455
Joseph, Ct., Privateer, R.I., Lucy, W22867
Nathan, Ct., Vt., Lydia, R2456
CRASWELL/CRESWELL, Robert, S.C., S21150
CRATLY, Andrew, Pvt., Pa., BLWt. 9107 iss. 7/9/1789. BL card gives last name as CRATTY
CRAVEN, Andrew, Md., S34721
James, S.C., R2457
John, Pa., S22701
Joseph, N.J., S34612
CRAW, David, Ct., S12622
Elias, Ct., See CROW
Jacob, Ct., S12631
Reuben, Pvt., Ct., BLWt.5605 iss. 6/10/1790 to David Knapp
Reuben, Cont., Ct., S38643
CRAWFORD, Alexander, Del., See Alexander Crawford BROWN
Andrew, Pa., See CROFFORD where Mass. service is given
Andrew, Pvt., Pa., BLWt.9196 iss. 6/6/1792
Andrew, Pa., Mary, R2468
Arthur, S.C., S31634
Charles, Pvt., Va., BLWt.12000 iss. 8/20/1791
Daniel, N.Y., Eleanor, W22869
David, Pa., S2152
David, Va., Margaret, W76
Edward, Pa., S12625; BLWt.421-200-Lt. Iss. 10/15/1789. No papers
Eleazer, N.H., Vt., Mary, W1830
Henry, Cont., N.Y. res. 1794. Dis. No papers
Isaac, Mass., Katharine, R2465
Jacob, Md., BLWt.440-200-Lt. Iss. 5/7/1790. No papers
James, Ct., Hannah, W17685
James, Md., S34720
James, Mass., Sea Service, Navy, Martha, W4164
James, N.Y., R2459
James, Pa., R2460
James, S.C., N.C., S3227
James, Va., S1191
Jason, Pvt., Ct., BLWt.5588 iss. 12/14/1793 Ctfd to Hon. Shaw, iss. 4/3/1818 to Silas Pepoon
Jason, Ct., Bethsheba Strowbridge/Strobridge, former wid., W19110. Her other husb., George Strobridge/Strowbridge, also served in Rev. War.

CRAWFORD (continued)
John, Ga., N.C., Rebecca, R2470
John, Ga., N.C., S.C. (born England), S39369
John, Pvt., Mass., BLWt.3952 iss. 4/1/1790
John, Mass., R2462
John, N.Y., S10504
John, N.Y., S15279
John, N.Y., Ann, R13434; BLWt. 110339-160-55. BLReg. 314973-55
John, N.C., S3226
John, Pa., U.S.A. in 1791, S40870; BLWt.423-200-Lt. Iss. 9/22/1791. No papers
John, Pa., Catharine, W2070; BLWt.6296-160-55
John, S.C., B.L. Reg.270805-1855
John, Va., S8256; BLWt.453-200-Lt. Iss. 8/27/1795 to Smith & Ridgeway, assnes. No papers
John, Va., Sarah/Sally, R2472
Joseph, Mass., S29104
Joseph, N.Y., Margaret, R2466
Josiah, Va.?, Sarah, R2473
Moses, Va., Nancy, W910
Nehemiah, Cont., Md., S34718
Patrick, Pvt., Pa., BLWt.9205 iss. 11/5/1789. Note: BLWt.1596 iss. 2/10/1830 to heirs of Wm. Diehl, ass. of Patrick Crawford, in lieu of BLWt.9205
Peter, Cont. (N.J. or Pa.), N.J., S40858
Peter, Va., Hannah, W2765; BLWt. 31887-160-55
Richard, N.J., S984
Richard, N.J., Sea Service, Sarah, R2471
Robert, Pvt., Md., BLWts.12871 & 14095 iss. 1/28/1795 to Francis Sherrard, ass. of Leonard Holt, Admr.
Robert, Pa., S9245
Robert, S.C., born N.Y., S3225
Samuel, Pvt., Pa., BLWt.9097 iss. 3/29/1791
Samuel S., N.Y., S12629
Thomas, Cont., Mass., S30969
Thomas, Pa., Mary, W8644
Thomas, Va., S42147
William, Mass., Sea Service, Martha, W5256
William, Mass., N.H., Vt., S16741 Sally/Silver Crawford, wid. of soldier was pensioned as former wid. of Benjamin Ainsworth, which see
William, Capt., Pa., BLWt.430-300 iss. 9/7/1789
William, Va., BLWt.921-500
William G., N.J., Martha, R2467
CRAWLEY, Charles, S.C. Sea Service Hannah, R2475
James, Mass., Privateer, S34269; BLWt.834-100
Samuel, Va., R13467; Va. Half Pay N.A. Acc.874. See 050039 Half Pay
Thomas, Ga., N.C., Va., Margaret, R2476

CRAWLEY, William Robert, Va., Polly, W1567; BLWt.3606-160-55
CRAWSMAN, James, Mass., S22709
CRAWSON, Samuel, Pvt., N.Y., BLWt.6972 iss. 7/30/1790 to John W. Wendell, ass.
William, Pvt., Mass., BLWt.3884 iss. 6/2/1795 to Edw. Stone Jr., ass.
CRAYCRAFT, Charles, Va., Pa., 1792-1794, Va. 1796; Elizabeth Price, former wid., W10228; BLWt.61361-160-55
CREAMER, Daniel, Md., Va., Sarah R2477
Eleanor, former wid. of William Russwurm, N.C., which see
Francis, Pvt., Pa., BLWt.9168 iss. 9/5/1791
Henry, Ct., Cont., See CRAMER
John, Mass., S30968
John, N.Y., Dis. No papers
CREASEY, John, Va., S37877
CREATON, Pvt., Hazen's Regt., BLWt.12890 iss. 2/25/1792
CRECK, Peter, Pvt., Va., BLWt. 12045 iss. 5/29/1792 to Francis Graves, ass.
CREE, Asa, Cont., Mass., Love, W281; BLWt.6008-160-55
Joseph, Mass., Jane, W23885
Stephen, Mass., Hannah, W14543
CREECH, Richard, Mass., Elizabeth, W23887
CREED, Colby/Colbay, N.C., S32194. See N.A. Acc. No.874, 050040, not half pay
CREEDON, Cornelius, Pvt., Hazen's Regt., BLWt.12903 iss. 9/24/179- to Wm. I. Vreedenburgh, ass.
CREEKBAUM, Phillip, Cont., Md. S40860
CREEL, John, Va., Frances, W534
Solomon, N.Y., R2479
CREELY, Peter, Pvt., N.Y., BLWt. 6997 iss. 11/11/1791 to Samuel Broome, ass.
CREEMER, Jacob, Pa., S35868
James, N.C., S2480
William, N.J., Phebe, W17692; BLWt.116-160-55
CREEPMAN, John, Pvt., Hazen's Regt., BLWt.12891 iss. 2/24/1800 to Jonathan Creepman, heir
CREERY, William, Del., S8258
CREESEY, Benjamin, Pvt., Mass., BLWt.3942 iss. 5/24/1797
CREGER, John, N.J., R2480
CREGO, Abraham, N.Y., S12637
William, N.Y., R2481
CREKENBOOM, Johannes, Pvt., N.Y. BLWt.6955 iss. 9/9/1790 to John G. Gebhard, ass.
CRENSHAW, Daniel, Va., Nancy, R2482
John, Va., S2482
Nathaniel, Va., Unity, W6772
William, Va., S8257
CRESEY, Benjamin, Mass., S37876
CRESS, George, Va. res. & agency, S24983

CRESSEY, Benjamin, N.H., S34260
Jonathan, Cont., Ct., S34262
CRESSON/CRISON, Andrew, N.C., Lucy, W6767
CRESWELL, Andrew, Va., S1948
Charles, Cont., Pa., Isabella, W3515
Henry, S.C., S3232
James, Pa., R2484
Samuel, Va., S35811
CRESY, John, Cont., Mass., S45706
CREVISTON, Jacob, Pa., BLWt.454-100
CREWS, Gideon, Va., S39371
James, Va., S39387
Joseph, Cont., Va., Nancy, W221; BLWt.86018-160-55 & BLReg.244867-55
Joseph, Pvt., Va., BLWt.12025 iss. 1/31/1794 to Francis Graves, ass.
Redman, S.C., S40054
CRIDER, David, Cont., Pa., S40868
CRIER, James, S.C., Martha McGinney former wid., R6720. She also applied for pension as wid. of other husb., James McGinney, S.C. See papers within
CRIHFIELD/CRITCHFIELD, William, Va., S9242
CRILL, John, Pvt., N.J., BLWt.8229 iss. 9/15/1790 to Isaac Mun, ass.
CRILLY, Peter, N.Y., S43438
CRIM, Harmon, Va., S8254
Henry, See Heinrich GREM. His name not Crim in the claim, but inquiries are made for Crim and in N.Y. book he is recorded as "Crim".
CRIPPEN, Alpheus, Mass., Phebe, W15678
Elisha, Pvt., Mass., BLWt. 3481 iss. 12/24/1791
Elisha, Mass.? or Vt.?, Mary R2486
Ichabod, N.Y., Mary, W18982
Joseph, Mass., S10509
Reuben, N.Y., Beulah, W25450; BLWt.19777-160-55
Silas, Ct., N.Y., Elizabeth, W20929
CRIPPS, John, N.J., R2487
CRISE, Barnet, N.Y., S12639
CRISPEL/CRISPELL, Thomas, N.Y., R2488
CRISPIN, Richard, Cont.,Mass., Mehitable Hardwick, former wid., W19674
CRISSEY, Gould, Ct., Eunice, R2483
John, Ct., S19265
Sylvanus, N.Y., Keziah, W16938
CRISSWELL, Richard, Va., S6779
CRIST, David, N.Y., Catharine,R2489
CRISTMAN, Frederick, N.Y., R1941. (Also a Frederick Christman, R1942)
CRISWELL, David, Pa., S30973
CRITCHARD, Benjamin, N.H. See CRITCHET
CRITCHET, Benjamin, N.H.,S42145
CRITCHETT, John P., N.Y., R2490
CRITCHFIELD, John, N.C., R2547
John, Va., S42144

CRITCHFIELD (continued)
Joshua, Md., Va., S2476
Nathaniel, Pa., Va., S2473
William, Pa., S16091
CRITCHLOW, James, Pa., Va., Mary, W6771
CRITTENDEN, Amos, Mass., S29100
Ebenezer, Cont., Mass., S43407
John, Va., R13465; Va. Half Pay
Medad, Mass., BLWt.16142-160-55
Mehitable, former wid. of Jesse Wild, Mass., which see
Richard Hazelwood, Va., Sally, R2491
William, Va., S9268
CRITTENDON, John, Va., BLWt.471-200-Lt. Iss. 4/19/1792. No papers
CRITTENTON, Levi, Mass., S15265
Nathaniel, Cont., Mass., Jerusha, W781
CRITTINGTON, William, Va., S8259
CRITZ, Hamon, Va., Nancy, W6755
CRITZER, Leonard, N.J., S9251. (There is also a Leonard Kretzer)
CROAT, John, N.Y., S43422
CROCE, Philip, N.C., See CROSE
CROCKER, Ansel, Mass., S15273
Anthony, S.C., S9267
Benjamin, Mass. res., Dis. No papers
Benjamin, Mass., S36999
Benjamin, Mass., Hannah, W6761; BLWt.26902-160-55
Bursley/Burseley, Mass., Molly/ Mary L., W14536
David, Ct., Navy, S42146
Dyer, Ct., S22710
Ephraim, N.Y., S22708
George, R.I., S21720
Heman, Mass., Lydia, W14535
James, Ct., Mary, R2492
Jedediah, Mass., Sarah, W6760
Jesse, Va., S17903
John, Ct., S36485
John, Pvt., Md., BLWts.12886 & 14114 iss. 3/25/1795 to Francis Sherrard, ass. of Henry Purdy, Admr.
Jonathan, Mass., Clarissa, W6762; BLWt.26028-160-55
Josiah, Mass., Thankful, W14538
Nathaniel, Mass., BLWt.16273-160-55
Peter, Ct., R2493
Peter, Mass., Hannah, W15662; BLWt.30695-160-55
Richard, Mass., Polly, W14533
Rolon/Roland, Cont., Mass., Navy, S15277
Solomon, S.C., Susan, W9398
Theophilus, Mass., R.I., S12627
Zebulon, Ct., Sarah, W25453; BLWt.26682-160-55. 4 Ltrs. of 1776 in file
CROCKETT, Alexander, N.C. or Va.? Elizabeth, R2496
Anthony, Va., S10492; N.A. Acc. 874-050041, Half Pay
Ephraim, Mass., Rebecca, W23888
Joseph, Va., S46377; N.A. Acc.874-050042, Va.Half Pay; BLWt.365-400 Maj. Iss. 7/15/1789; also record-

CROCKETT (continued)
ed under BLWt.2509. No papers
Robert, Va., S30353
Ruth, former wid. of Samuel Lord, Cont., Mass., which see
Samuel, Cont., Mass., Abigail, W22868; BLWt.14524-160-55
CRODDY/CRODY, John, Va., S9324
CROEL, Joel, N.Y., Elizabeth, W263
CROES, John, N.J., Martha, W241
Joseph, Va., S39386
CROFFORD, Andrew, Mass., S43412
Stephen, Mass., S42662
CROFOOT, Benjamin, N.Y., S23180
Ephraim, Cont., Ct., Lois, W20927
CROFT, Ezekiel, N.C., S16739
Henry, Pvt., N.Y., BLWt.6995 iss. 5/5/1791
James, N.Y., Esther/Hester, W20931
John, Cont., Md., Christian/ Christiana Reisher, former wid., W3457
John, N.Y., S10491; BLWt.26156-160-55
Joseph, Pa., S22188
CROFUT, Elizabeth, former wid. of Lewis Hunt, Ct., which see
John, Ct., R2497
Seth, Ct., Sarah, W22859; BLWt. 26319-160-55
CROGHAN, William, Va., BLWt.448-400-Maj. Iss. 3/4/1799. No papers
CROKER, Jeremiah, Mass., S12619
CROLIUS, William, N.Y., Mary, W10685
CROMBIE, James, N.H., Dis. No papers
William, Sgt., Mass., BLWt.3962 iss. 8/10/1789 to Richard Platt
CROMER, John, Pa., S17338
CROMETT, Jeremiah, Mass., S37875
CROMLY/CROMLEY, Jacob, Pa., Christiana, W2763
CROMMY, Andrew, Pvt., Md., BLWt. 11107 iss. 3/3/1792
CROMWELL, Christopher, N.Y., S23589
Harmanus, N.Y., Catharine, W16222
Hugh, Pvt., Hazen's Regt., BLWt. 12916 iss. 4/19/1791
Joseph, Mass., S37874
Oliver, Pvt., N.J., BLWt.8186 iss. 10/31/1791 to James Finnemore
Oliver, N.J., S34613
Philip, N.Y., Magdalen, R2498
CRONCK, John, Pvt., N.Y., BLWt.6959 iss. 7/30/1790 to Edward Cumpston ass.
CRONE, Henry, Pvt., Pa., BLWt.9088 iss. 9/17/1792 to Alexander Power, ass.
CRONIN, Patrick, N.Y., BLWt.398-150-Ens. Iss. 9/1/1790. No papers
CRONINGER/GRONINGER, Joseph, Pa., Elizabeth, R2499
CRONISTER/MC CRONISTER, James, N.C. S34989
CRONK, Dennis, N.Y., S15061
Garret, Cont., N.J., Susanna, W8635

CRONK (continued)
John, N.Y., Lois, W20926
John, N.Y., R2500
John, Pa., S22702
Matthew, N.J., S2472
CRONKHITE/CRONKITE, Francis, N.Y., S43424
John, N.Y., See CRONK
CRONKITE, Patrick, N.Y., Maria, W16932
CRONKWRIGHT/CONKWRIGHT, Gerardus, N.Y., S15260
CRONMILLER, Martin, Pa., S24135
CRONTS, Michael, N.Y., S32191
CROOK, Andrew, N.H., S15270
Charles, Cont., N.H., S17902
Charles, Va., Nancy, R2502
Eli, Pvt., Crane's Cont. Artillery, Mass., BLWts.3983 & 256-60-55 iss. 9/10/1789 to Henry Newman. (3983 only)
Henry, Va. res., Dis. No papers
Jeremiah, Va., Jane, W8634
Joseph, Ct., S15271
Joseph, Mass., BLWt.349-200-Lt. Iss. 6/26/1789. No papers
Martin, N.Y., S43418
Patience, former wid. of Isaac Swift (Indian), Mass., which see
Thomas, N.H., S12638
CROOKE, John, Va., S30970
CROOKER, Benjamin, Cont,, Mass., Sea Service, S17905
James, Mass., S34264
Joshua, Mass., Ruth, W23875
Noah, Mass., Faith, W18974
Tilden, Mass., Navy, Priscilla, W22862
CROOKS, Henry, Mass., R2503
Michael, Va., R2504
Rebecca, former wid. of Moses Butler, Mass., which see
CROOKSHANKS, John, Va., S39384
CROPPER, James, Va., S39383; BLWt.1254-100
John, Va., Catharine, W3781
CROSBY, Alpheus, N.H., S16738
Charles, Cont., R.I., Mary, W23886
David, Pvt., Ct., BLWt.5614 iss. 2/5/1790
David, Ct., S43413
David, Pa., S12626
Eben, Mass., S20332
Ebenezer, Ct., BLWt.1759-400
Enoch, Ct., N.Y., S10505
Enoch, N.Y.,Rhoda, W18934
James, Md., S17339
Jesse, Pvt., Va., Lee's Legion, BLWt.12961 iss. 5/16/1792 to Jesse Crosby
Joel, Mass., S46376
John, Mass., Mary, W18973
John, N.H., Elizabeth, R2506
John, Va., R2509
Jonathan, Mass., S34265
Joseph, Mass., Sally, W2595
Joseph, N.H., Ruth, R2510; BLWt.40936-160-55
Joshua, Mass., S30358

CROSBY (continued)
Lucy, former wid. of Amos Shed/Shead, Mass., which see
Nathan, Pvt., Mass., BLWt.3871 iss. 5/8/1790 to Jonathan Crosby
Nathan, Mass., S5041
Nelson, Va., pensioned from N.H., S45705
Obadiah, N.Y., R2512
Obed, Ct., Jerusha, W25446
Samuel, Mass., R2513
Sawney, Ct., See Sawney YORK
Simon, Pvt., Ct., BLWt.5607 iss. 1/28/1792 to Moses Sill
Simon, Ct., S43420
Simon, Cont., Mass., Hepzibah, W14542
Sparrow, Mass., S29735
Stephen, Mass., S43423
Stephen, Mass., N.H., S35211
Thomas, Ct., N.Y., Diantha, W3516
Timothy, Mass., S23181
William, Va., S34611
CROSE/CROCE, Philip, Va., S32193
CROSIER, James, Pvt., Md., BLWt. 11073 iss. 2/15/1796
John, Cont., Mass., S43406
John, Pvt., Md., BLWt.11128 iss. 1/28/1793 to John Wright ass. of Andrew Crosier, Admr.
CROSLEY, Jesse, Cont., Pa., BLWt. 1184-200
Moses, Md., Rachel, R2516
Nathan, Pvt., Hazen's Regt., BLWt.12924 iss. 2/25/179- to Benjamin Moore, ass.
Prince, Ct., Caroline, W24833
William, Md., Sarah, R2517
CROSMAN, Asahel, Mass., S21721
Noah, Mass., S5043
Thomas, Ct., Cont., Ct. Sea Service, S12634
CROSS, Abijah, Mass., S18783
Abraham, N.C., S1900
Asahel/Acil, N.C., Temperance, R2523
Caleb, Mass., S19267
Daniel, Pvt., N.H., BLWt.3017 iss. 3/31/1796 to Joseph Davis, ass.
Daniel, Pa., S40869; BLWt.1014-100
David, Cont., N.H., Roba, W4163; BLWt.2493-160-55
Elijah, N.C., S1947
Eunice, former wid. of Isaac Tubbs, Ct., which see
Jacob, N.C., Hannah, W18975
James, Pa., S22704
John, Cont., Mass., Abigail, W18979
John, Cont., Va., S39382
John, Pvt., N.H., BLWts.2996 & 2986 iss. 12/21/1790 to Philip Schuyler, ass.
John, N.H., S18785
John, Pvt. "in the Invalids" BLWt.12952 iss. 1/26/1790 to John May, ass.
John, Pvt., Va., BLWt.12011 iss.

CROSS (continued)
10/26/1795 to John Stockdell,ass.
Joseph, Ct., S39385
Joseph, Ct., Seviah, W16940
Joseph, Cont., Mass., Sally, W23881; BLWt.29746-160-55
Joseph, Md., S46375; BLWt.311-200
Joseph, Pa., Sarah, W25445; BLWt. 82009-160-55
Joshua, Mass., Lydia, W14539
Lemuel, N.Y., R2521
Michael, N.Y., S43419
Moses, Mass., N.H., S45708
Nathan, Mass., S39367
Nero, Ct., S39370
Patrick, Pvt., Pa., BLWt.9106 iss. 6/20/1789
Peleg, R.I., S21717
Reuben, N.Y., Esther, W20934
Robert, Md., Mary Green, former widow, W25651
Samuel, Cont., Mass., Hannah Brumley/Brumbly, former wid., W25275
Samuel, Del., BLWt.2320-100
Samuel, Pa., S2475
Samuel, S.C., Elizabeth, W8636
Solomon, Ct., S21148
Stephen, Ct., Sarah, W23892
Thomas, Cont., N.H., Hannah, W17693; BLWt.26578-160-55
Thomas, N.H., Sarah, BLWt.75049-160-55
Timothy, N.H., S15274
Uriah, Ct., Green Mt. Boys, Mass., S10499
William, Mass., Mary, R2525
William, Mass., N.H., S9239
William, N.Y., Catharine, W16220
William, N.C., Va., S3221
William, Va., R2526
Zachariah, N.C., Easter, R2519
CROSSAN, John, Pa., Gen. Wayne's Army, 1812, U.S. Navy, S40864
CROSSEN, Asa, Pvt., N.H., BLWt. 3007 iss. 9/24/1790 to Peleg Sanford, ass.
CROSSETT, John, Mass., Esther, W9397; BLWt.67615-160-55
CROSSFIELD/CROSFIELD, Timothy Adams, Cont., Mass., N.H., S34263
CROSSLAND, John, S.C., S18784
CROSSMAN, Cyrus, Mass., Uriana/ Urania, R2529
Elijah, Mass., Elizabeth, W1568
Ephraim, Mass., Celia, W20932
Joseph A., Navy, Me. Agency & res., Elizabeth, W1565
Josiah A., Cont., Mass., R.I., S29105
Peleg, Mass., Peggey, W14531
Sarah, former wid. of William Ware, Mass., which see
Simeon, Mass., Navy, S34268
Trobridge, Ct., Phebe, W25448
William, Mass., Eunice, W1829
William, Mass., Vt., S12632
CROSSON, John, Pa., Acksah/ Achsah, W6766
Robert, S.C., Va., S41498
CROSTICK, Edward, Va., S9240

CROSTON/CROSSTON, Gustavus, Va., S39379
CROSWELL, Benjamin, Mass., S34714
James, Navy, R.I., S34713
John, Ct., S22703
CROUCH, Christopher, Ct., S17904
David, Pvt., Ct., BLWt.5574 iss. 6/21/1791
David, Ct., N.Y., Eleanor Wiley, former wid., W18354; BLWt. 33553-160-55
Jesse, Va., R2531
John, Va., S10135
John, Va., S21149
Joseph, Pvt., Md., BLWt.11122 iss. 12/18/1794 to Henry Purdy, ass.
Robert, Cont., Md., Hannah Barnett former wid., S34717; BLWt.49282-160-55
Robert, Trumpeter, Md., BLWts. 11041 & 12962 iss. 1/18/1800
Thomas, Md., R2533
William, Pa., or Va., See COUCH
William, Va., Elizabeth, W27913; BLWt.12823-160-55
William, Va., R----
CROUDUS/CROWDUS, William, Va., Dorotha, W9399
CROUS, Ezekiel, N.Y., Mary, R2536
CROUSE, Christian, Pa., S9243
Elbert, Pvt., N.Y., BLWt.6973 iss. 5/19/1791
John, Md., R2535
Joseph, N.Y., S29101
Leonard, N.Y., Lany, W16935
CROUT, Mathias, Pa., S40863
Matthias, Pvt., Pa., BLWt.9124 iss. 4/12/1799 to John Duncan, ass.
CROUTZ, Henry, N.Y., S23179
CROW, Abraham, N.C., Va., Maria, W9396; BLWt. 75109-160-55
Benjamin, Va., R20353
Christian, Pa., War of 1812, U.S.A., S43417; BLWt.9111-100, & BLWt.19704-160-12
David, Ct., See CRAW
Dennis, Va., S39380
Elias, Ct., R2458
George, Pa., S40862
Jeremiah, N.J., S624
John, Va., Elizabeth, W18978
Robert, Va., S39365
Shubael, Cont., Ct., Huldah, W25447
Shubal, Pvt., Ct., BLWt.5672 iss. 6/14/1791 to Isaac Bronson
Thomas, S.C., Sarah, R2538
William, Va., S32196
CROWDER, John, Pa., BLWt.280-100
Philip, Va., S30974
Sterling, Va., S10496
William, Va., Lucy, R2540; BLWt. 36280-160-55
CROWEL, David, Mass., S15275
David, N.J., Chloe, R2541
Joel, N.Y., See CROEL
Thomas, Mass., Va., R2542
CROWELL, Ebenezer, Mass. Sea

CROWELL (continued)
Service, Phebe, W23879
Edward, Ct., Rachel, W17684
Enoch, Mass., S35210
George, N.C., S8255
Joseph, N.J., S625
Manoah, Mass., S32192
Michael, Mass., Annah, W22870
Samuel, Ct., Jerusha, W4931
Samuel, Ct., Sarah, W25451; BLWt.27631-160-55
Samuel, Pvt., Md., BLWt.11106 iss. 12/18/1794 to Henry Purdy, ass.
Shivrick, Mass., Susanna, W20937
Solomon, Ct., S23587
Sylvanus, N.J., S983
Thomas, Mass., Dis. No papers
CROWER, Rudolph, Pa., Elizabeth, W2764
CROWL, William, Pa., Sally, R2544
CROWLEY, Charles, S.C. Sea Service, Hannah, See CRAWLEY
Darby, Pvt., Md., BLWt.11067 iss. 10/14/1795 to Henry Davis, ass.
David, Pvt., "in the Invalids Corps", BLWt.12936 iss. 9/4/1789
Florence, Cont., Mass., Elizabeth W23884; BLWt.357-200-Lt. Iss. 1/29/1790. No papers
James, Va., S15790
Laurence/Lawrence, Pvt., Pa., BLWts.9089 & 14031 iss. 3/1/1792 to Alexander Power, ass. of Miles Crowley, admr.
Miels, Pa., S40865
Royal/Royall, Mass., S24136; BLWt.7293-160-55
Timothy, Pvt., Pa., BLWt.9224 iss. 2/14/1791 to Alexander Power, ass.
CROWNINSHIELD, Benjamin, Navy, Mass., Privateer, Mary, W24832
William, Mass., S34266
CROWNOVER/CRONOVER/COWNOVER
Daniel, S.C., Va., S32189
Joseph, Va., S1754
CROXALL, Charles, Cont., Pa., S17907; BLWt.2330-300
CROXFORD, Daniel, Mass., Peggy, W8191; BLWt.24432-160-55
John, Mass., Wilmot, W23883
CROXON, Archibald, Del., R2546
CROXTON, Archibald, See CROXON
Carter, Va., S9250; BLWt. 52777-160-55
CROY, Christian, N.Y., S15060
CROZER, John, Pa., S2150
CRUFF, Thomas, R.I., S21718
CRUIDSON, Benjamin, See CRUZAN
CRUISE, John, N.C., See CRUSE
CRUIZE, Walter, Pa., BLWt.432-200-Capt. Iss. 11/27/1794. No papers
CRUM, Adam, Md., Mary, W2069
Adam, N.C., Va., S8260
Annatje/Ann, former wid. of Robert Martin, N.Y., which see
Elias, N.Y., Annatje, R2548. She rec'd pension as former wid. of Robert Martin, N.Y.

CRUM, Henry, N.J., S12623
John, Md., S12624
John, N.Y., Catrina, W16939
Peter, Pa., Elizabeth, W10320; BLWt.47616-160-55
Richard, Cont., Mary, W25454; BLWt.289-60-55. Pa. agency & res. of wid. N.J. res. of soldier 1829
William, Cont., Pa., Martha, W16225
William, Dragoon in Moylan's Regt., Pa., BLWt.9187 iss. 8/11/1790
CRUMB, Arnold, R.I., S39376
CRUMB/SCHOONOVER, Christopher, N.Y., S43421; BLWt.2479-100
CRUMB, Joseph, Ct., Oliviet Tuthill, former wid., W11675; BLWt.99761-160-55
Simeon, R.I., S38642
CRUMBIE, Aron/Aaron, Ct., Mass., S34716
CRUMLOW/CRUMLUFF/CROMLOW, Caleb, Pa., Ann, W3226; BLWt.27606-160-55
CRUMLUFF, Caleb, See CRUMLOW
CRUMLY/CRUMLEY, Thomas, N.C., S31633
CRUMM, Richard, Pvt., Lamb's Artillery, N.Y., BLWts.6985 & 289-60-55 iss. 8/18/1790. Wt.6985 to Joseph Sringtram, ass.
CRUMMELL, Thomas,?, Margaret Dreimer, former wid., R3086. She also claimed pension for service of 2nd husb., Abraham Teller, N.Y.
CRUMMETT/CROMETT, Ebenezer, N.H., Hannah, W16933
James, N.H., S22706
CRUMP, Abner, Va., R13459; N.A. Acc.874-050043, Va. Half Pay
Conrad, N.C., See KRUMP
Joshua, Va., S30352
Thomas, Va., S15394
Thomas, Va., Peggy Logwood, former wid., W8058
CRUMPSTON, Edward, Mass. See CUMPSTON
CRUMPTON, James, Md., See COMPTON
CRUNK, John W., N.C., S38646
CRUSE, John, N.C., Anna, R2552
John, Pa., S22196
CRUTCHER, Anthony, N.C., BLWt.483-200-Lt. Iss. 11/10/1796 to Henry Wiggin, ass. No papers
James, Pa., S39377
John, Va., Sarah, W6773; BLWt. 36663-160-55
William, Va., Elizabeth, R2553
CRUTCHFIELD/CRITCHFIELD, Arthur, N.C., Lucy, R2554
John, N.C., S10498
John, Va., S39381
Stapleton, Va., S9249
CRUTCHLEY, Benjamin, Md., S39378
CRUTCHLOW, James, Pa. See CRITCHLOW
CRUTE, John, Va., S24980; BLWt. 367200
Robert, Va., S9246
CRUTSINGER/KRUTSINGER/CUTSINGER, Solomon, Md., Pa., Katharine, W375
CRUTTENDEN, Timothy, Mass., Lucy,

CRUTTENDEN (continued)
W6769
CRUTTENDON/CRITTENDEN, William S., Cont., Mass., Privateer, Mary, W23880
CRUVER, John, N.Y., S22707
CRUZAN/CRUDSON, Benjamin, Va., S35869
CRYDER, John, Pvt., Va., BLWt. 12015 iss. 7/14/1792 to Robert Means, ass.
CRYE, William, S.C., Sarah, W6757
CRYER, Morgan, S.C., S31635
CRYSEL, Jeremiah, Va., Mary, W4932; BLWt.26843-160-55
CUDDEBACK, Jacob, N.Y., Dinah, W24840
William, N.Y., R2557
William A., N.Y., R2556
CUDDY, James, iron worker, York Co., Pa., res. Pa. at enl., Va. res. at application, Alcy, R2559
CUDWORTH, David, Cont., Mass., Navy, Mercy, W27405
Nathaniel, Cont., Mass., S39394
Samuel, Mass., Betsey Day, former widow, W2075
CUFF, Cato (colored), Ct., S36487
Samson/Sampson, Ct., S34616
CUFFEY/CUFFEE, Charles, Va., Catharine, W9402; BLWt.75038-160-55
CUKSEY/CUCKSEY, William, Ga.,R20354
CULBERTSON, Alexander, Pa., R2560
Josiah, S.C., S16354
Robert, N.C., S21722
William, N.C., See CUTHBERTSON
CULBREATH, Daniel, N.C., R2561
James, Ga., S8271
CULBRETH, Neel, N.C. See COLBREATH
CULL, Hugh, Pvt., Pa., BLWt.9134 iss. 7/16/1789
CULLEN, Daniel, Va., S9260
John, Del., Elizabeth, W6950; BLWt.8442-160-55
CULLENS, John, Va., See CULLINS
CULLEY/CULLY, Armistead, Va., S8270
CULLIN/CULLEN, Charles, Va., S35872
CULLINS, John, Va., S9258
John, Va., Jane, R2562
CULLY, Charles, N.Y., See Charles Cully PRICE
CULP, John, S.C., S21152
CULPEPPER, Joseph, S.C., R2565
Malachi, Ga., R2566
CULTON, Joseph, Va., S16742
CULVER, Aaron, Ct., Phebe, R2569
Abel, Ct., BLWt.2128-100
Abraham, N.J., S24140
Christopher, Ct., S12660
Dan, Mass., Mary, R2567
Daniel, Mass., Abigail, W18989
David, Ct., Cont., Mary, W4933; BLWt.14514-160-55
Eliakim, Ct., S23184
Enoch, Ct., Lucy, W25464
James, Ct., Hannah, W23900
John, Ct., S45713
John, Cont., N.J., Sarah, R2573
Joseph, Mass., S46029
Levin, Del., BLWt.2004-100
Nathaniel/Nathan, Ct., Catharine,

CULVER (continued)
See COLVER
Phinehas, Ct., N.Y., R2571
Reuben, Ct., R2572
Samuel, N.J., Phebe, R1570
Sarah, former wid. of Josiah Atkins, Ct., which see
Solomon, N.Y., S18343
Stephen, Del., BLWt.2003-100
Thomas, Ct., S23185
Timothy, Cont., Ct., S40871
CUMING/CUMMING, John Noble, Lt. Col.-Commdt. N.J., Sarah, W7234; BLWt.399-500 iss. 6/11/1789. No papers on BLWt.
CUMBERFORD, James, Pvt., Pa., BLWt.9212 iss. 1/28/179- to James Bennett, ass.
CUMINGS, James, Mass., S29743
Josiah, Mass., S18366
Nathaniel, Vt., Sally, W9819
CUMINS, John, N.J., S3240
CUMMING, Mary, former wid. of John Crane, N.J., which see
William, N.C., S8265
CUMMINGS, Amos, Mass., S36486
Andrew, Pa., Jane, W911
Asa, Mass., Lydia, W3518
Benjamin, N.H., See COMINGS
Cornelius, Pvt., N.Y., BLWt.6980 iss. 8/3/1790 to Cornelius V. Dyck, ass.
Daniel, Mass., Lydia, W8193; BLWt.11098-160-55
David, Mass., S34618
Ebenezer, N.H., R2576
Elijah, Mass., S29738
Elijah, Mass., S34617
Enoch, N.H., S12651
Isaac, N.Y., S9325
Jacob, Mass., R.I., Hannah, W481; BLWt.9495-160-55
Jacob, N.Y., Mary, W3517
James, Pa., S42667
John, Cont., Md., S39400
John, Mass., S39391; BLWt.960-100
John, Mass., Sarah Alexander, former wid., W21610
John, S.C., R2577
Jonathan, Mass., S45709
Joseph, Mass., S29739
Joseph, Mass., R.I., Vt., Mary, W2766
Joseph, Va., S1659
Josiah, Mass., S29742
Mathew/Matthew, Va., S35870
Noble, Mass., S34270
Oliver, Mass., Phebe, R2578
Rachel, former wid. of Emanuel Wagerman, N.Y., R2579
Richard, Mass., S30976
Samuel, Mass., S34277
Simeon, Ct., Naomi Lilly, former wid., W26217
Thomas, Mass., S35213
Thomas, Mass., Mary, W6751
Thomas, N.C., S6780
Thomas, Pa., Abigail, W2923
Thomas, R.I., Lodema, W5252; BLWt.7302-160-55
William, Ct., S39389
William, Ct., Rhoda, W17671

CUMMINS, Asa, Ct., Catelina, W18992; BLWt.31442-160-55
Asa, N.J., R2580
Benoni, Mass., S30361
Ebenezer, Pvt., N.Y., BLWt.6934 iss. 5/4/1791
Edward, Pvt., Pa., 9093 iss. 6/20/1789
Elijah, Pvt., Mass., BLWt.3920 iss. 1/28/1790 to Eliphalet Downer
Joseph, R.I., Olive, W17678
William, Md.; BLWt.11025-100 No papers
William, N.J., Deborah, W5253; BLWt.67676-160-55
William, R.I., S39395
CUMP, Henry, Va., S15792
CUMPSTON, Edward, Mass., S43409
Mathias, Pvt., Lamb's Artillery, N.Y., BLWt.6998 iss. 9/25/1790 to Abraham Nelson, ass.
CUNDIFF, Isaac, Va., S9252
John, Va., S8272
John, Va., Sally, W8647
CUNE, John, Ct., See MC EWEN
CUNIAS, John, Pvt., Pa., BLWt.9142 10/2/1789
CUNING/CUNNING, Robert, Pa., Catharine Cline, former wid., W9791; BLWt.98555-160-55
CUNINGHAM/CUNNINGHAM
James, S.C., S8273
James, S.C., S21723
James, Va., BLWt.1409-100
CUNNIAS, John, Pa., S43441
CUNNINGHAM, Anna, former wid. of Nathan Burrows, Ct., which see
Ansel/Ansell, Va., S31636
Archibald, Pvt., N.Y., BLWt. 6919 iss. 6/29/1792 to David Hawkins, ass.
Charles, N.Y., S12661
Daniel, Pvt., N.J., BLWt.8203 iss. 8/3/1789 to Wm. I. Vreedenburgh, ass.
David, Pvt., Pa., BLWt.9112 iss. 11/8/1791 to Peter Rodermal, ass.
Deborah, former wid. of Ebenezer Rowe, Mass., which see
Dennis, Pvt., Mass., BLWt.3974 iss. 11/4/1795 to Henry Foye
George, S.C., Mary, W2071
Henry, Cont., Col. Lamb's Art., BLWt.384-200-Lt. Iss. 7/26/1790 No papers
Hugh, N.C., Mary, W9820
Jacob, Va., S9257
James, Pa., S2154. Died 1823
James, Pa., R---, Fayette Co.,Pa.
James, Pa., Sea Service, R---, Westmoreland Co., Pa.
James, Va., S1508
James, Va., S8268
James, Va., S16746
James, Va., See CUNINGHAM
Jeremiah, N.C., Hannah, W6753; BLWt.28546-160-55
John, Ct., S18367
John, Cont., N.Y., Sarah Jones, former wid., W20192
John, Ga., Ann, W6752

CUNNINGHAM (continued)
John, Pvt., N.J., BLWt.8215 iss. 6/16/1789 to Thomas Coyle, ass.
John, N.J., Rebecca Sherman, former wid., W17801. Her former husb., William Sherman, R.I. pensioned.
John, Pvt., Lamb's Artillery, N.Y., BLWt.7004 iss. 8/20/1790 to William Cumming, ass.
John, N.Y., S43440
John, Pa., S9262
John, Pa., S16749
John, S.C., Ann Craig, former wid., R2425
John, Va., S3250
John, Va., Margaret, W10696
Joseph, Pa., Margaret, W2767
Matthew, Pvt., Pa., BLWt.9130 iss. 1/28/179- to Ebenezer Sprout, ass.
Matthew, Va., Elizabeth, R2582
Murrell, Va., S30975
Nathan, Va., Agness, R2581
Nathaniel, Va., Elizabeth, W9821
Patrick, Pa., S43439
Peter, Ct., Mass. Sea Service, Elizabeth, W17672
Peter, Pa., Louisa, W6754
Richard, Pa., S2483
Robert, Ct., Hannah, R2584
Robert/Robert Moore, N.C., Emily M., W1031; BLWt.36665-160-55
Robert, Pvt., Pa., BLWt.9094 iss. 6/30/1794 to Silas Hart, ass.
Samuel, Mass., Sarah, W22884
Samuel, Mass., Privateer, Eunice, R2583
Samuel, Va., R2587
Shubal, N.Y., S43425
Thomas, Cont., N.H.?, S35212. Mass. and Me. res.
Thomas, Va., S42664
Thomas, Va., Phebe, W4166
Timothy, Mass., Navy, S18786
Valentine, Va., S39390
Walter, Va., S9263
William, N.C., S3249
William, Va., S8264; BLWt. 26387-160-55
William, Va., Susan, R2588
William, Va., R13534; Va. Half Pay; BLWt.443-400-Maj. Iss. 3/22/1796. Also recorded under BLWt.2664. No papers
William, Va. Sea Service, R---, Va., Half Pay claim
CUPP, Leonard, Pa., Susannah, W4167
CUPPLES, James, Pa., R2589
CUPPY, John, Va., R2590. Warrant 7954-160-50 iss. for Indian War service 1790-1794. W.O. No. 42522 of Lydia, wid. of John Cuppy, Indian War of 1790-1792
CURBOW/KERBO, Joseph, N.C., S31637
CURD, John, Va., Nancy W., W8645
CURL, John, Pvt., S.C., BLWts. 12058 & 12864 iss. 10/7/1795
CURLE, Jacob, Va., BLWt.2041-100
Richard, Va., BLWt.2040-100
CURLEY, Barney, Pvt., Pa., BLWt. 9090 iss. 7/9/1789
John, Pvt., N.J., BLWt.8223 iss. 9/26/1791 to William Lane, ass.
CURRANCE, William, Va., See CARRANCE
CURRELL, James Va. Sea Service, R31; Va. Half Pay
Nicholas, Mass., Betsey, W14556
CURREY, Hugh, N.C., S8267
John, N.C., S.C., S2484
William, Pvt., Pa., BLWt.9098 iss. 11/11/1794 to Francis Kirkpatrick, ass.
CURRIE, Robert, Pvt., Mass., BLWt.3905 iss. 3/3/1797 to Samuel Fitch
Robert, Mass., Rhoda, W18990
Samuel, Navy, R.I., S12640
CURRIER, Abi, former wid. of Eliphalet Richardson, Mass., which see
Abiah, former wid. of Dudley Sanborn, N.H., which see
Abraham, Mass., S29061
Abraham, N.H., Polly, W20940
Ammi, Vt., Margaret, W25462
Amos, Mass., Hannah, W15888; BLWt.5444-160-55
Asa, Mass., S45714
Assa, Fifer, Mass., BLWt.3865 iss. 3/-/1790
David, Mass., R2593
David, N.H., S17909
Ebenezer, N.H., S45715
Ebenezer, N.H., Mercy, W724; BLWt.14751-160-55
Edward, N.H., Sarah, W22879
Hannah, former wid. of Moses Pigeon, Mass., which see
Henry, Cont., Mass., N.H., Abigail, W16004
John, Mass., Mary, W16005
Jonathan, Mass., N.H., Nancy, W16549
Joseph, Ct., S43426
Joseph, Pvt., Mass., BLWt.3972 iss. 9/21/1790 to Benj. Moers
Moses, N.H., S12650
Richard, N.H., S32197
Samuel, Pvt., Mass., BLWt.3907 iss. 3/25/1790
Samuel, Mass., N.H., S16744
Samuel, Mass., S39396
Samuel, N.H., S3246
Sargent, N.H., S42666
Theophilus, Mass., Elizabeth, W22873
Thomas, N.H., Ednor, W16942
Thomas, N.H., Jane, W22880
William, Mass., Bette, W16002
William, not Rev. War, Wayne's War, 1792-1795, U.S.A. Old War Inv. Rej. File 2594. BLWts. 22930-160-50 (cancelled) & 27408-160-50
Willis, Mass., Sarah, W22886
CURRIN/CURREN, Edward, N.Y., Olive, W4168; BLWt.6933-100 iss. 6/1/1792. BLWt.231-60-55
James, Md., S34724; BLWt.2-100. Iss. 5/5/1803
CURRIN (continued)
Samuel, Pvt., N.Y., BLWt.6939 iss. 9/29/1790
CURRY, Edward, S.C., S15393
James, Pa., S22713
James, Pa., S40872
James, Pa., Martha, R2595
James, Va., S44230; BLWt.449-300-Capt. Iss. 7/28/1790. No papers
James, Va., Ann, W8646
John, Pvt., N.J., BLWts.8187 & 8201 iss. 6/11/1789 to Matthias Denman, ass.
John, N.J., W242, Rhoda Currey
John, N.Y., S12662
John, N.C., S8266
John, Pa., S16748
Prudence, former wid. of William Gay, S.C., which see
Rachel, former wid. of James Halks, Va., which see
Samuel, N.J., Gen. Harmer's N.W. Indian War, S22189
Thomas, Va., S16747
Torrence, Va., R20355
William, N.Y., S49282
CURTICE, Isaac Palmer, N.H., Sarah, W20941
Jacob, N.H., S9255
CURTICE/CURTIS, Lemuel, N.H., S45712
Stephen, Mass., N.H., Bridget, W22872
CURTIS, Abner, Mass., Lydia, W14558
Agur, Ct., Huldah, W25456; BLWt.26316-160-55
Amos, Ct., S36488
Augustine, Ct., N.Y., Lodema/Lodeme, W18988; BLWt.26534-160-55
Benjamin, Ct., Aurelia, W6900; BLWt.9206-160-55
Benjamin, Navy, Mass., S35217
Benjamin, N.J., S628
Bowlin, Cont., Va., Mary, W349; BLWt.2400-100
Caleb, Ct., Catherine, W17682
Caleb, Mass., Susan, W1727; BLWt. 13868-160-55
Charles, Mass., S35214
Chauncey/Chancy, Ct., Cont., Mary, W6746; BLWt.1986-100
Daniel, Pvt., Ct., BLWt.5562 iss. 2/5/1790
Daniel, Ct., Cont., Mary, R2605
Daniel, Cont. Mass., Keziah, W6747; BLWt.39205-160-55
Daniel, Mass., Sally, W14550
David, Ct., Lois, R2603
David, Cont., Mass., S43427
David, Mass., S35210; BLWt.929-100
Ebenezer, Ct., Dis. No papers
Ebenezer, Mass., S5039
Eli, Ct., S37001
Elijah, Ct., S12641
Elisha, Pvt., Mass., BLWt.3869 iss. 1/28/1790
Felix, Ct., S43429
Fielding W., S.C., Charity, W2922
Francis, Pvt., Pa., BLWt.9180 iss. 1/17/1792 to George Moore, ass.
Frederick, Ct., Persis, W17676

CURTIS (continued)
Henry, N.Y., S40873
Hull, Ct., Cont., S18787
Isaac, Ct., S16094
Isaac, Mass., S12652
Isaac, R.I., S36490
Isaac, R.I., BLWt.2339-100. See BLWt.2338-100 of Tobias Briggs. No papers for this warrant.
Jacob, Mass., Mehitable Day, former wid., W22910
James, Ct., Mass., S12659
James, Ct. Sea Service, Sarah, W17679
James, Va., S39393
Jesse, Va. res. 1834, R2601
Joel, Ct., S43428 1/2
Joel, Ct., Sally, W25460; BLWt. 26318-160-55
Joel, Pvt., Mass., BLWt.3842 iss. 4/15/1790 to John Warren, ass.
Joel, Mass., Lydia, S43428
Joel, N.Y., S2153
John, Md., S34725
John, Mass., S34275
John, N.H., S12646
John, Sgt., N.J., BLWt.8163 iss. 1/18/1790
John, Pa., S12645
John, Vt., S17910
John, Va., Dolly, R2599
Jonah/Samuel I, R.I., See Samuel I. CURTIS, R.I.
Jonathan, Pvt., Mass., BLWt. 3919 iss. 2/15/1797 to Joseph Brown, ass.
Jonathan, Mass., S34278
Jonathan, N.H., Eunice, W18986; BLWt.13720-160-55
Jonathan, N.C., S8269
Joseph, Pvt., Mass., BLWt.3872 iss. 9/13/1792
Joseph, Mass., R2600
Joseph, Mass., R2602
Joseph, N.H., Sarah, W25461
Joseph, Vt., Adelia/Delia, W23903
Joshua, Mass., Nancy, W24841
Joshua, N.C., S39392
Jotham, Ct., Elizabeth, W6745; BLWt.33760-160-55
Mabel, former wid. of Josiah Burritt, Ct., which see
Marmaduke, N.J., S40874
Michael, Pvt., Md., BLWt.11088 iss. 12/22/1798 to Elisha Jarrett, ass.
Michael, Md., S39398
Nathan, Mass., BLWt.2150-100
Nehemiah, Mass., Hannah, W16941
Oliver, Mass., Elizabeth, W14554
Peter, N.C., Susanna, W3005
Philip, Cont., Mass., S29740
Richard, N.C., R2606
Robert, Mass., Jane Hammond, former wid., W19748
Robert W., Ct., S28698
Russell, N.C., S12664
Samuel, Ct. Sea Service, Navy, Zippora, W3956
Samuel, Navy, Mass., S4276

CURTIS (continued)
Samuel I./Jonah, R.I., S43433; BLWt.25-100
Sarah, former wid. of Robert Lewis, Ct., which see
Seth, Mass., Lydia, W2072; BLWt. 10251-160-55
Silas, Ct., BLWt.5674 iss. 3/11/1791 to Isaac Bronson
Silas, Cont., Ct., War of 1812, S43436
Simeon, Cont., Mass., S39397
Simeon, Mass., S5035
Solomon, Ct., Mass., N.Y., Hannah, W23895
Solomon, N.Y., S28697
Stephen, Pvt., Mass., BLWt.3885 iss. 8/1/1789 to Thos. Cushing, ass.
Stephen, Mass., S35218
Stephen, Mass., Martha, W23899
Thomas, Cont., Pa., S34620
Thomas, Mass., Anna, W635; BLWt.13005-160-55
Thomas, N.Y., S12655
Thomas, N.C., Mary, W6748
Vinson, Mass., S29745
William, Mass., S34276
William, Mass., Mary, W14551
William, Va., S43430
Zachariah, Mass., Lucinda, W1153; BLWt.340-60-55
Zadock, Ct., Rosy, W17681
Zarah/Zerah, Cont., Ct., Abigail, W282; BLWt.205-60-55 & 5669-100 iss. 10/7/1789. No papers. Her claim for B.L. for service of former husb., Elias Edward/Edwards, War of 1812, was rejected.
CURTISS, Agur, Ct., Mercy, W25465 b.3/28/1755, d. 11/10/1838
Andrew, Ct., N.Y., Eunice, R2597
Asahel, N.Y., S12656
Ebenezer, Ct., S18789
Enoch, Cont., Mass., S36489
Enoch, Pvt. in Invalids, BLWt. 12954 iss. 11/14/1791 to Enoch Curtis
Everard, Ct., S17368
Gideon, Ct., Hannah, W9400; BLWt.5440-160-55
Giles, Lt., Ct., Lucy, W637; BLWt.379-200 iss. 11/10/1789
Giles, Ct., Hannah, W22874; BLWt.26794-160-55
Jacob, Ct., S12657
Joseph, Ct., Lydia, W25457
Lysander, Ct., S17367
Martin, Ct., S22711
Philip, Ct., S12658
Robert, Ct., Clara, W25466; BLWt.40943-160-55
Samuel, Ct., R2608
Simeon, Ct., Elizabeth Catlin, former wid., W10569; BLWt. 14667-160-55
Thomas, Ct. or Mass., Eunice, R2598
Timothy, Ct., Rebecca, W20943
William, Ct., Cont., N.H., Charry, W23902

CURTNEY, Francis, Sgt., N.Y., BLWt.6911 iss. 9/28/1790 to Alexander Robertson, ass.
CURTS, Michael, Pa., S42665
Thomas, Pa., S22714
CURWAIN/CURRIN, Edward, Pvt., N.Y., BLWts.6933 & 231-60-55 iss. 6/1/1792
CUSACH, Christopher, Pvt., Md., BLWt.11090 iss. 10/16/1794 to John Wright, ass.
CUSHING, Abel, Mass., S34619
Adam, Mass., S34272
Azel, Pvt., Mass., BLWt.3876 iss. 10/12/1790 to Richard Platt
Charles, Mass., S21724
Charles, Mass., Hannah, W22871
Daniel, N.H., S17913
Elizabeth, former wid. of Philip Fowler, Cont., Mass.,which see
Er, Cont., Mass., S34273
Ezekiel, Mass., Lydia, W14553
John, Privateer, S.C. Sea Service S16356
Jonathan, Mass., Sea Service, S30362
Joshua, Mass., S34614
Loring, Mass., S35216
Nathaniel, Cont., Mass., Alice, W22887
Nathaniel, Mass., S34727
Nathaniel, Mass., BLWt.337-300-Capt. Iss. 4/1/1790. No papers
Regemmeleck/Regemeleck/Regemmelech, Mass., S34726
Samuel, R.I., BLWt.14142 iss. -/-/---- to Matt Cushing
Seth, Mass., Hannah, W1392; BLWt. 26557-160-55
Thomas, Mass., BLWt.344-200-Lt. Iss. 9/1/1796. No papers
William, Mass., Ruth, W1569
CUSHMAN, Amos, Pvt., N.J., BLWts. 8177 & 14148 iss. 3/13/1798 to William Cushman, heir
Andrew, Mass., S17912
Benjamin, Ct., Cont., Elizabeth, W22883
Benjamin, Mass., S30360
Caleb, Mass., S15793
Caleb, Mass., Abigail, W2073
Charles, Ct., Desire Gates, former wid., W17003
Daniel, Pvt., Ct., BLWt.5655 iss. 4/12/1792
Daniel, Cont., Ct., S23183
David, Cont., Mass., S10510
Eliphalet, Ct., S44389
Ephraim, Cont., Mass., Mary, W23893
Frederic, Ct., Vt., S10512
George, Mass., Navy, Anna, W15664 BLWt.3398-160-55
Gideon, Mass., S28699
Hannah, former wid. of Lemuel Parker, Mass., which see
Holmes, Cont., Mass., S22155
Isaac, Mass., S19271
Isaac, Pa., S8263
Isaiah, Mass., Sarah, W23894
Jacob, Mass., S30359

CUSHMAN (continued)
Joab, Ct., Hannah, W17683
Jonah, Ct., Rachel, W14557
Jonathan, Mass., Elizabeth, W23901
Jonathan, Mass., Navy, Privateer, S29744
Joseph, Ct., Tabitha, W20938; BLWt.14501-160-55
Joseph, Mass., S12647
Joseph, Mass., Margaret/Peggy, W22882
Joshua, Ct., S43437
Joshua, Mass., S16743
Nathaniel, Ct., Hannah, W25459 Papers lost
Nathaniel, Cont., Ct., S38648, Vt. res. in 1818
Obed, Mass., Navy, R.I., S34274
Peres, Mass., Lucina/Lucinda, W536; BLWt.1905-160-55
Robert, Mass., Lucy, W18985
Silvanus, Mass., Sarah, W22878
Solomon, N.H., Vt., Sarah, W17675
William, Mass., S19269
Zachariah, Mass., Saba, W14549
Zebedee, Mass., Navy, Sarah, W22885
CUSICK, Christopher, Md., Mary, W3955
John, Pvt., Pa., BLWt.9138 iss. 7/27/1789 to Richard Platt, ass.
Nicholas, N.Y., S18788; BLWt. 439-200. Name also given as Kayhnatsno/Kaghnatshon/ Kanaghtjoh
CUSSARD, Philip, Pa., S22715
CUSTAR, William, Va., Indian War of 1788, Anna, R2610
CUSTARD, Conrad, Pa., S8262
Isaac, N.J., See CASTOR
Jacob, Va., S16093
CUSTER, Richard, Va., Jane, W6749
CUTHBERT, Benjamin, Cont., N.Y., Privateer, S12654
Daniel Alexander/Alexander/Daniel, Ga., BLWt.2142-300
William, N.Y., S22712
CUTHBERTSON/CULBERTSON, William, N.C., Rachel, W17680
CUTLER, Abel, Mass., Sarah, W14552
Abner, Mass., S43434
Andrew, Pa., S35871
Benjamin, Pvt., Mass., BLWt.3935 iss. 2/26/1799
Charles, Mass. Sea Service, Navy, Polly, W23897
Ebenezer, Mass., Sally, W1242; BLWt.17866-160-55
Ebenezer, Mass., Elizabeth, W14555
Hannah, former wid. of Joseph Blanchard, Mass., which see
Henry, Pvt., Lamb's Artillery, N.Y., BLWt.7011 iss. 7/10/1790 to John Quackinboss, ass.
Hodges, N.H., S12663; BLWt.6251-160-55
Isaac, Mass., Elizabeth, W1726; BLWt.10256-160-55
John, Mass., S16745
Jonathan, Ct., S15794
Joseph, Pvt., Ct., BLWt.5548

CUTLER (continued)
iss. 10/30/1789
Joseph, Ct., S43432
Joseph, Ct., R.I., S12643
Josiah, Mass., S34723
Margaret, former wid. of Benjamin Baxter, Cont., N.H., which see
Nathan, N.Y., S12642
Oliver, Mass., S30362
Seth, Ct., S28700
Tobias, N.H., S45710
William, Cont., N.H., S46085
William, Pvt., N.H., BLWt.3025 iss. 9/11/1795 to William S. Thorn, ass.
William, N.H., Eunice, W16003
CUTRIGHT, John, Va., Rebecca, W6626; BLWt.30692-160-55
Peter, Va., S32164
CUTSINGER, Solomon, Md., Pa., See CRUTSINGER
CUTTER, Abner, Pvt., Mass., BLWt. 3900 iss. 1/19/1792 to Resolve Waddron
Benjamin, Mass., Elizabeth, W18987 BLWt.14668-160-55
Charles, Mass., S29741
Ebenezer, Mass., Mehitable, W18991
Joseph, N.H., S12648
Josiah, Mass., S39388
Moses, N.H., Rachel, W22881
Nathaniel, Mass., S38647
Seth, Cont., Mass., N.H., S18790
Thomas, Mass., Navy, N.H., Betsey W29917 1/2
William, Mass., S34271
William, Mass., Rebecca, W23898
CUTTING, Aaron, Mass., S34615
Benjamin, Mass., S45711
Bille, Ct., S16355; BLWt.26077-160-55
Earl, Mass., S17365
Eliphalet, Mass., Tersey, W20942
Hezekiah, Sgt., Mass., BLWt. 3945 iss. 4/1/1790
Hezekiah, Mass., Sarah Mann, former wid., W17106
John Browne, Cont., S46437; BLWt.650-450. Wash., D.C. res. & Agency; also Va. res.
Jonas, Cont., Mass., War of 1812, S39399
Jonathan, Mass., S19623
Moses, Mass., S10963
Silent/Silas, Mass., S34722
Zebedee, Ct., S12644
CUTTS, William, N.C., S8274
William, Va., Elizabeth, W25458; BLWt.85060-160-55
CUYKENDALL, Martin, N.Y., S12649
CUYZER, Frederick, N.J., BLWt. 289-100
CYILDER, John, Cont., Green Mt. Boys, Vt., Sally, W20944
CYESTER, Henry, Md., S8275
CYPHER, Daniel, Cont., Pa., R2612
Jacob, N.Y., Rachel, W20945
Peter, N.Y., See SYPHER
Peter, Pa., See SIFERT
CYPHERS, Andrew, Pvt., Va., BLWt. 12033 iss. 3/4/1796 & 232-60-55
CYPRUS, Andrew, Va., Hannah,

CYPRUS (continued)
W25468; BLWts.232-60-55 & 12033-100 iss. 3/4/1796. No papers. Name also given as CYPRESS, SYFRITT/SIFRITT
CYRE, Nicholas, Va., Jane, W5064. Jane Cyre was m. before to James Davidson, a sold. of Bedford Co. Va. who d. Campbell Co., Va. 1816/1817
CYRUS, Bartholomew, Va., Phebe, W25467; BLWts.1475-100 & 9327-160-55
Exeter, Ct., S36491

D

DABALL, Benjamin, Ct. See DABOLL
DABBS, John, N.C., S16359
DABNEY, Charles, Va., R13624; N.A. Acc.874-0550044, Va. Half Pay
George, Va., Elizabeth, W3007
John Q., Va., Sarah, W10311; BLWt.61203-160-55
DABOLL, Benjamin, Ct., Prudence, W6991. She was pensioned for services of former husb., Joseph Moxley, Ct. who rec'd pension for dis. & d. 11/10/1815. No papers in his claim
John, Pvt., Ct., BLWt.5705 iss. 11/30/1799 to Abijah Holbrook
John, Ct., S19950. See affidavit in claim of John DABOLL 2nd from John Daboll. It shows this man, the son of John & Abiah, was born 13 Feb. 1751.
John, 2nd, Ct., Cont., Anstis/ Austis, W24033
DACHSTETER, John/Hannes, N.Y., See DOCKSTADER
DACKSTETER, John, N.Y., S31654
DACON, Aaron, N.J., Patience Wilcox, See DEACON
DACON/DAKIN, Jonathan, Del., S39410
DACUS, Nathaniel, Va., S21153
DACY/DAISY, John, Mass., Mehitable, W24853
DADE, Francis, Va., BLWt.606-200-Lt. Iss. 7/5/1799 to Francis Laurence & Polly Dade, the only surv. ch. & heirs (minors). No papers
Isaac, Cont., Va., S.C. Sea Service, Fanny, W19149
DADMUN, Jonathan, Mass., S30373
DAFFRON, John, N.C., R2614
Rody, N.C., Milly, R2613
DAFRON, John, N.C., Sarah, R2615
DAGGER, Peter, Va., S39412
DAGGET, Jacob, Mass., S16098
Reuben, Mass., S29107
Tristram, Mass., Pvt., Mass., BLWt.4050 iss. 1/31/1797 to Benj. Dana
DAGGETT, Abner, Cont., Mass., Mary, W20954
Daniel, Cont., Mass., Sarah, W22901
Darius, Mass., S10531
Elijah, Mass., S34309
Gideon, Mass., S44125
Henry, Ct., Anna, W17709; BLWt.539-200-Lt. Iss. 8/21/ 1789. No papers
Joab, Mass., Chloe, W15669
John, Ct., Vt., S23595
Joseph, Mass., S15064
Joseph, Mass., Mercy/Marcy Hall, former wid., W24386. Her last husb. also a pensioner. See Labon Hall, N.H.
Mayhew/Mahew, Green Mt. Boys, N.Y., S12728
Nathan, Ct. Sea Service, Mass. Sea Service, R21987

DAGGETT (continued)
Samuel, Mass., S34306
Samuel, Mass., Hannah, R2617
Samuel, Mass., R2618; BLWt. 45594-160-55
Silas, Ct. & Mass., Sea Service, Deborah, W22899
Thomas, N.Y., R2619
Tristram, Mass., S35238
Tristram, Pvt., Mass. See DAGGET
William, Mass., Privateer, Lucy, W1729
DAGHL, John, Mass. See DAL
DAHARSH, Philip, See DEHAISH
DAIL, John, N.C., S6783
DAILEY, Bennett, Pa. See DALY
Cornelius, Pa., R2620
David, Ct., Vt., S43445
Dennis, Cont., Va., S30375
Elijah, N.Y., Vt., Jane, W16551
George, Pa., Maria Elizabeth, See DEILY
James, Pvt., Va., BLWt. 12087 iss. 12/13/1791 to Francis Graves, ass.
Jeremiah, Mass., Sea Service, Elizabeth Aylward, See DAYLEY
Jesse, Va., Polly, W6980
John, N.J., S865
John, N.J., Naomi Tongue, former wid., W9523; BLWt.61273-160-55
John, Va., S39414; BLWt.2419-100
Joseph, Pa., Margaret Morrison/ Morison, former wid., BLWts. 900-100
Lonon/London, N.H., Nancy, W5260; BLWt. 140-60-55
Nezer, Mass., S30982
Owen, S.C., R2622
Peter, Pvt., R.I., BLWts.3076 & 3068 iss. 1/12/1796
Robert, N.Y., BLWt.440-100
Solomon, Pvt., R.I., BLWt.3087 iss. 6/17/1794
Vincent, not Rev. War, War of 1791-1793, Anna/Anne, see 1812 files, Old War Wid. Rej. File 13645
DAILLY, Dennis, Pa., S40879
DAILY, Elias, Pa., Polly, R2628
Farrell O'Neill/James Farrell O'Neill, Nancy, W8658
Giles, Ct., S36500
James, Pvt., Ct., BLWt.5687 iss. 3/21/1791 to Josiah Starr
James, Ct., S43465
John, Pvt., Pa., BLWt.9301 iss. 1/19/17-- to Conrad Stringer, ass.
Samuel, Ct. or Mass., S44128
William Johnson/Johnson, Ct., Lydia, W1393; BLWt.7212-160-55
DAIMWOOD, Boston, Va., S3268
DAIN, John, Mass., Elizabeth, W24034
DAINS, Abraham, N.Y., S43463
Asa, Ct., Privateer, Jane, W6960
Castle, ---, S46378; BLWt. 1608-100. Iss. 5/13/1829. Litchfield, Ct. res. at enl.; N.Y. in 1829

DAINS, Ephraim, Pvt., Ct., BLWt.5724 iss. 1/14/1799 to Israel Stowell, Jr.
Ephraim, Cont., Ct., Irene, W4937; BLWt. 16128-160-55
Jesse, Ct., Chloe, R2624
DAKE, Benjamin, R.I., R2625
John M., N.Y., S19272
Oliver, N.Y., Hannah Lapham, former wid., R6159
DAKIN, Elisha, N.Y., Fanny, R2627
Thomas, Mass., S35232
DAL, John, Mass., Elizabeth, W22909. Name also appears as DALL, DEAL, DAGHL & SNOWDEAL
DALBY, William, Va., See Wm. DOLBY
DALE, Abraham, Va., Mary, W8648
Archelaus, Mass., S34314
Campbell, Md., R2630
Henry, Pa., See DEAL
John, Va., Lucy, W725
Richard, Va., Polly, W25515; BLWt.26321-160-55
Samuel, Mass., See DOLE
William, Va., Elizabeth, W9828
DALEY, John, Pvt., N.J., BLWt. 8258 iss. 6/11/1789 to Matthias Denman, ass.
Matthew, Pvt., Md., BLWt.11156 iss. 1/8/1796 to George Ponsonby, ass.
Michael, Pvt., N.J., BLWt.8249 iss. 6/11/1789 to Matthias Denman, ass.
Nathan, N.Y., R2621
Nathaniel, Mass., R2623
Obadiah, Cont., Ct., Elizabeth Cady, former wid., W23757
Silas, N.Y., S43464
DALLABY, Jonathan, Pvt., Sheldon's Dragoons, Ct., BLWt.5718 iss. 10/7/1789 to Benj. Tallmadge
DALLAS, Archibald, N.J., BLWt. 573-200-Capt. Iss. 5/24/1797 to Alex., Chas., & Archibald Dallas, heirs. Also recorded as BLWt.2686. No papers
Robert, Va., Nancy, W6981
DALLIBA/DALLABY/DALIBA, George, Ct., Cont., S43461; BLWt. 943-100
DALMOT, William, Pvt., Hazen's Regt., BLWt.12994 iss. 1/22/ 1790 to Benj. Mooers, ass.
DALRYMPLE, David, Mass., S12719
David, Mass., S22195
Edmund, N.J., S988
James, Mass., See DERUMPLE
Jesse, N.J., S2159
John, N.J., R2633
Thomas, Pa., S22717
DALTON, Pvt., N.Y., BLWt.7024 iss. 2/14/1791 to James Talmadge, ass.
George, Sgt., Pa., BLWt.9329 iss. 6/26/1789 to John Dalton, legal repr.
Isaac, Mass., N.H., Judith, W482; BLWt.15185-160-55
James, Pvt., N.J., BLWt.8273 iss. 2/9/1798

DALTON (continued)
James, N.J., S34297
John, Va., S1755
Mathew, S.C., Mary, W22503
Michael, N.H., S10523
Samuel, N.H., Rachel, W6982; BLWt.35829-160-55
Solomon, Va., Polly/Mary, R2635
Thomas, N.C., Elizabeth, W6983
Valentine Thomas, Va., Caty Shaw, former wid., W3610; BLWt. 39282-160-55. N.A. Acc. 874-050045, Va. Half Pay
William, Pvt., N.J., BLWt.8245 iss. 6/18/1795 to James Christie, ass.
William, N.C., Va., S8295
DALY, Bennett, Pa., S30980
John, Pa., Nancy, W3228
DAMAN, Abraham, Mass., S3269
Edmond/Edmund, Ct., Bethiah, W10313
Edward, Mass., S34303
Luther, Mass., Sea Service, S30368
Noah, Mass., Esther S., W10711; BLWt.36643-160-55
Stephen, Mass., S5325
DAMANS/DAMONS, Abiah, Mass., Lucretia, W22894; BLWt.12735-160-55
DAMARIS, Adam, Pvt., N.J., BLWt. 8240 iss. 4/10/1799 to Abraham Bell, ass.
DAME, Edward, Mass., N.H., Lucy, W20946; BLWt.2349-160-55
Elizabeth, former wid. of Constant Bliss, N.H. Which see
Jonathan, Mass., N.H., Hannah, W20960
Joseph, Mass., S10524
Theodore, N.H., Martha, W16006
DAMERON, Charles, Ga., Polly, W4173; BLWt.2030-160-55
George, Ga., S41501
Joseph, Va., S8310
Martha, former wid. of Christopher Tompkins, Va. Sea Service, which see
DAMMON/DAMON, Isaac, Mass., S29746
DAMON, Benjamin, Mass., S10529
Benjamin, Mass., S18371
Daniel, Mass., S29749
Isaiah, Mass., Mercy, W24847
Jason, Mass., Lucy, W3957
Jedediah, Mass., Jemima, R2637; BLWt.54269-160-55
Joseph, Cont., Mass., S17376
Mary, former wid. of Paulipus Hammond, Mass., W6988; BLWt. 56508-160-55
Oliver, Mass., S10547
Reuben, Mass., S30367
Stephen, Mass., S30370
DAMOND, Peter, Hazen's Regt., BLWt. no number-200-Lt. Iss. 11/16/1791 to Peter Damond, no papers
Peter, Lt., Pa., Moylan's Dragoons, BLWt.9309 iss. 11/16/1791 to Peter Damond.

DAMONS, Gamaliel, Mass. See DEMONS
DAMPEER/DAMPIER, Daniel, Ga., R2639
DAMPH, Frederick, N.Y., S49301
DAN, Abijah, N.Y. See DANN
James, N.Y., S15067
Jonathan, N.Y., S12732
Nathaniel, N.Y., Mary, W17696
Samuel, N.Y., S23590
Squire, Ct., Rhoda, W2439; BLWt.50901-160-55
DANA, Asa, Cont., Mass., S12717
Benjamin, Mass., S47182; BLWt. 523-200-Lt. Iss. 10/26/1789 to himself. No papers
Daniel, N.Y., S2156
David, Ct., S22194
David, Cont., Mass., Rebecca, W24040
Ezra, Cont., Mass., S43467
Joseph, Ct., S28705
Josiah, Cont., Mass., S38657
Luther, Navy, Mass., French War, Lucy, W24042
Stephen, Mass., Eleanor, R2642
DANBAR/DUNBAR, George, N.Y., S10540
DANBERRY, Nicholas, Cont., N.J., S34287
DANBURY, William, Cont., N.J., S34298
DANCE, Ethelred, N.C., Sarah, W19148
Thomas, Va., Sea Service, R2643
DANDRIDGE, John, Cont., Va., Elizabeth, W6993; BLWt.602-300-Capt. Iss. 3/26/1793 to Francis Graver, ass. No papers
DANE, Benjamin, Mass., S5327
DANFIELD, John, Pa., S5314
DANFORD, Joseph, Mass., S22197
Joshua, Pvt., N.H., BLWt.3053 iss. 2/24/1791
Joshua, N.H., S43470
Prince, Pvt., N.Y., BLWt.7044 iss. 2/14/1791
Prince, N.Y., S43472
DANFORTH, Abner, Mass., S35233
Asa, Cont., Mass., Hannah, W16553
Edward, N.H., Mary, W22914
Elijah, Mass.; BLWt.531-300-Capt. Iss. 12/20/1792 to Joseph Brown, admr. No papers
Elkanah, N.H., Molly, W15889
Henry, N.H., Betsey, W22889
Jedediah, N.H., S12722
Jesse, Pvt., "in the Invalid Corps", BLWt.13028 iss. 1/7/1796 to Calvin Sanger, ass.
Job, R.I., S17370
John, Mass., Pvt., BLWt.4056, iss. 3/25/1790
John, Mass., BLWt.2428-100
John, Mass., S34280
Jonathan, Mass., S38650
Joshua, Mass., S28703; BLWt. 174-200
Joshua, Mass., Lydia, W14579
Moses, N.H., Mehitable, W20959
Peter, Mass., S2506
Samuel, Cont., Mass., Sarah,

DANFORTH (continued)
W20950
Thomas, Mass., Mary Ann, W537; BLWt.7215-160-55
Thomas, N.H., S45724
William, N.H., Olive, W16007
DANIEL, Andrew, Pvt., BLWt. 10754 iss. 9/2/1789
Archibald, N.C., S32204
Benjamin W., N.C., S3264
Beverly, Va., S15795
Buckner, Va., S17372
Campbell, Va., Elizabeth, W6985
Christopher, Va., S8294
Ezekiel, S.C., S21729
Frederick, N.C., R2646
James, N.C., See McDANIEL
James, Va., Sarah Brockman, former wid., W10298; BLWt.61184-160-55. She recd. B.L. for service of last husb., Curtis L. Brockman, in War of 1812. See BLWt.70121-120-55
Joab, N.C., See Job
Job, N.C., Elizabeth, R2645
John, N.C., S31638
John, N.C., R2647
John, Va., Elizabeth, W6984
Richard, Va., S8293
Samuel, Va., Mary, R2648
Sion, N.C., Mary, R2653
Spilsby/Spilsbey, Va., S21158
William, Cont., Mass., S34291
William, Va., S3263
William, Va., S32201
William Powell, Va., R2655
DANIELLY, Daniel, ---, Ga. res. in 1782. Dis. No papers
Daniel, N.J., S34307
DANIELS, Adah, former wid of Lemuel Turner, Mass., N.Y., which see
Amariah, Mass., Olive, W4939; BLWt.45662-160-55
Daniel, Ct., S43471
Daniel, Pa., R2650
David, Ct., Lucina, W3959
Eleazer/Eleazar, Mass., Mary/Polly, W1731; BLWt.27633-160-55
Ephraim, N.H., Anna, W16552
Ezekiel, Pvt., Ct., BLWt.5683 iss. 8/23/1790
Ezekiel, Ct., S36498
Ezekiel, Ct., S43454
Henry, Pvt., N.Y., BLWt.7071 iss. 10/1/1791 to John Thompson, ass.
Isaac, N.Y., R13613
Jacob, N.H., Dolly Foss, former wid., W14734
Japheth, Mass., BLWt.516-300-Capt. Iss. 4/1/1790
Jesse, Mass., Pruda, W24851
Job, Ct., Jane, W4662
Job, N.J. S2505
Joel, Mass., Mary, W14598
John, Ct., S38653
John, Cont., Mass., N.H., Mary Chase, former wid., W683
John, Pvt., Mass., BLWt.4039 iss. 12/14/1793 to Samuel Emery
John, Mass., Love, W2598; BLWt. 784-160-55

DANIELS (continued)
John, N.J., N.Y., S16752
John, Privateer, N.C. & Pa., R2651
Jonathan, Ct., R2652
Jonathan, Mass., Sarah, W22891
Jonathan, N.H., S45722
Joseph, Mass., Susanna/Susan, W25518
Joseph, Mass., N.H., S45723
Mary, former wid. of Peter Taft, Mass., which see
Nathan, Ct., S12730
Nathan, Mass., S15797
Nathan, Vt., S46030
Nehemiah, Ct., Elizabeth, W2074
Peletiah, Ct., Huldah, W25513
Reuben, Ct., S36499
Samuel, Ct., S16753
Samuel, Ct., Lydia, W25510; BLWt.11179-160-55
Samuel, Mass., N.H., S23594
Samuel, N.H., Sarah, W19158
Solomon, N.H., S21726
Starling, Mass., Charity, W22924
Thomas, Pvt., N.J., BLWt.8242 iss. 4/27/1799 to Abraham Bell, ass.
Thomas, N.J., Sarah, W6986
DANIELSON, Altamont, Mass., S29112
Calvin, Cont., Mass., S10536
James, N.H., Molly, W14582
Lothario, Mass., See DONALDSON
Luther, Mass., S44123
Timothy, Mass., Abigail, W17704
DANKS, Eliakim, Mass., S30372
John, Va., S30979
Samuel, Mass., Abigail, W24044
Zadok/Zadock, Mass., S30374
DANLEY, James, Cont., Mass., S43457
John, Sgt., Mass., BLWt.4018 iss. 8/10/1789 to Richard Platt
DANN, Abijah, Ct., N.Y., Vt., Anna, R2641; BLWt.40939-160-55
DANNELLY/DANNELLEY, James, Ga., or S.C., R2657
DANNELS, James, N.Y., S15071
DANNER, Frederick, Va., Catharine, R2658
DANNER/TANNER, Jacob, Pa., S39411
DANNOR, David, Md., S32208
DANOVAN, Hannah, former wid. of Thomas Piper, Cont., N.H., which see
DANSDILL, George, N.J., S23596
D'ANTIGNAC, John, Va., Hannah, W4116
DARBE, Asa, Ct., S15396
Jedediah, Ct., Cont., S43455
DARBEE/DARBY, Moses, Ct., Dorothy, W3339
DARBY, Abner, Mass., R2660
Arnold, Pvt., Mass., BLWt.4004 iss. 4/18/1796 to James Baker, admr. of Wm. Quiner, ass.
Benjamin, Ct., Constant, W20979
Benjamin, S.C., S16758
Charles, Mass., Tabitha, W14580
Charles, Fifer, N.Y., BLWt.7021 iss. 11/5/1789 to Chas. Darby

DARBY (continued)
Eliab, Mass., Bethiah, W16948
Elnathan, Mass., Lucy Peterson, former wid., W19982
Ephraim, N.J., BLWt.608-200
John, Mass., Elizabeth, W1573; BLWt.24151-160-55
Joseph, Cont., Mass., Elizabeth Perkins, former wid., W15196. Her 2nd husb., John Hunter, also served, which see
Mehitable, former wid. of Abraham Rugg, Mass., which see
Nathaniel, Va., BLWt.605-200
Richard, Ga., S32203
Samuel, Mass., S15798
Samuel, Mass., Hannah, W22930; BLWt.13014-160-55
Samuel, N.J., S10525
Samuel, N.Y., S12741
Samuel, ---, Preston Co., Va. in 1834, R13662
Squier, Mass., Privateer, R2662
William, Pa., S44124
William, Drummer, N.J., BLWt. 8262 iss. 1/12/1790
DARCEY, John, N.J., BLWt.620-300
DARDEN, George, Ga., S.C., S16757
DARE, Philip, N.J., W6957
DARING/DERING/DEARING, Henry, Va., Barbara, R2898; N.A. Acc. 874-050046, Va. Half Pay
DARKE, William, Va., BLWt.598-500-Lt.Col. Comdt. Iss. 8/25/1780. No papers
DARLEY, Peter, Pvt., R.I., BLWt. 3086 iss. 3/25/1790
DARLIN, David, Mass., Mercy/Marcy, W25519
DARLING, Aaron, Pvt., Mass., BLWt.4013 iss. 3/25/1790
Aaron, Mass., S38654
Benjamin, Ct., S43452
Benjamin, Ct., Mary, W17705
Benjamin, Pvt., Mass., BLWt. 4037 iss. 3/25/1790 to Jere Mason
Benjamin, Mass., S30376
Benjamin, N.Y., S43444
David, Mass., S34279
Ephraim, Pvt., N.Y., BLWt.7063 iss. 8/21/1790 to Abel Belknap, ass.
George, Pa., Elizabeth, See DORLAN
Jacob, ----, Mass. res. at enl., Sarah, R2667
Jewitt B./Jewett B., Cont., Mass., Hannah, W5259
Job, Mass., S34293
John, Mass., S16095
John, Mass., S38652
John, Mass., Annah, W22900
John, N.Y., Rebecca, R2664; BLReg.181597-1855
John, R.I., Levice, W16234
John, Vt., Asenath, W19146
Jonas, Mass., Mary, W14593
Joseph, Mass., S29110
Levi, Cont., Mass., War of 1812, Charlotte, W1831
Moses, N.H., Judith, W24848

DARLING (continued)
Moses, Pvt., N.Y., BLWt.7068 iss. 8/4/1790 to John N. Bleecker, ass.
Oliver, Mass., S19273
Pelatiah, Mass., Phila., R2663
Peter, Mass., Percy, W22902
Peter, R.I., Jerusha, W20951
Richard, Mass., S43456
Samuel, Cont., Mass., R.I., S10518
Samuel, Mass., Priscilla, W24065
Samuel, N.Y., R2665
Samuel, N.Y., R2666
Solomon, N.Y., S22719
Zelek, Mass., S5320
DARLINGTON, John, Pa., Elizabeth, W3132
DARNABY, John, Va., S16360
DARNALL, Adam, Va., W35879
Joseph, N.C., S2515
DARNELL, Cornelius, Pa., Va., S1802
William, N.C., Elizabeth, W6989; BLWt.39204-160-55
DARRACH, John, N.C., S6789
DARRAGH, Charles, Pa., BLWt.1997-200
Daniel, Pa., BLWt.579-200-Lt. Iss. 5/21/1794. No papers
DARRAH, William, Pvt., N.H., BLWts. 305A & 14075 iss. 4/19/1794
DARRIN, Daniel, Ct., N.Y., Martha, W19141; BLWt.26924-160-55
DARRON/DURON, William, Pvt., Crane's Cont. Artillery, Mass., BLWt.4064 iss. 4/29/1794 to Joseph Perkins
DARROW, Ammirias/Ammiras/Ammirus, N.Y., Sarah, W19154; BLWt. 14502-160-55
Benjamin, Ct., S46229; BLWt.1945-100
Benjamin, Ct. Sea Service, Navy, Grace, W24850
Christopher, Ct., Cont., Mass. & N.Y., Bridget, W16554
Daniel, Ct., S36492
Daniel, N.Y., S10526; BLWt.67576-160-55
Ebenezer, Pvt., Ct., BLWt.5720 iss. 11/2/1791 to John Heaton
Ebenezer, Ct., S18369
Ebenezer, Cont., Ct., S15072
George, Mass., Abigail, W22906
George, N.Y., S23189
George, N.Y., R2669
James, Ct., Sarah, W1394
Jedediah, N.Y., Alche, W1570; BLWt.17568-160-55
John, N.Y., Martha, W25511
Nathan, Ct., S15075
Samuel, Ct., S23186
William, Ct., Sally, R2670
Zaccheus, Mass., Chloe, W24032
DARSEY/DARCY/DOSSEY, Joel, Ga., S6788
DARST/DART, Peter, Pa., R2671
DART, Abiel, Cont., N.Y., S12731
Abigail, former wid. of Benjamin Sawyer, N.H., which see
Caleb, Ct., Margaret, W16943
David, Ct., S18368
Dolphin, Ct., S36496

DART (continued)
Elias, Ct., Ruth, R2673
Jonathan/Johnathan, Ct., S17922
Levi, Ct., Elizabeth, W24046
Thomas, Ct., N.H., R2674
DARTEN, Edward, Va., S30983
DARTT, Justus, N.H., Vt., Hannah, W2768
DARWIN, John, S.C., Va., S21155
DASCOMB, Jacob, Mass., S45726
DASKAM, John, Ct., Cont., 1st Canadian, S43453
William, Ct., S36495, Abigail Daskam, wid. of soldier, was pensioned as former wid. of Jonas Weed, Ct., which see
DASKUM, John, Pvt., Ct., BLWt. 5685 iss. 9/20/1790
William, Pvt., Ct., BLWt.5712 iss. 6/27/1789
DATAMER/DETEMER, John, Pa., Dorothea, W3227
DAUB, Dilman, Pa., Nancy, W2535; BLWt.26539-160-55
DAUGHERTY, John, Va., S35898
Patrick, Va., BLWt.12075-100 No papers
William, Pa., S.C., Mary, W3229
DAULTON, Moses, Va., Mary, W8650; BLWt. 5252-160-55
DAVENPORT, Abner, Mass., Eunice, W22907
Addington, Navy, Mass. agency & res., S34294
Adrian, Cont., Md., Va., S35874
Anthony S., Va., S9383
Benjamin, Ct., Elizabeth Judson, former wid., W7948
Caleb, R.I., S34305
Charles, Ct., Mabel, W17706
Claiborn/Claiborne/Clayborn, Va., S35875
David, Ct., Patience, R2682
David, Pvt., Sappers & Miners, BLWt.12977 iss. 4/21/1791 to John Boles, ass.
Eliphalet, Ct., Elizabeth, W16233
Ephraim, Mass., Sarah, W22908
Franklin, N.J., S2508
Henry, N.Y., S28702
Henry, N.Y., R2680
Henry, Va., Ann, R2676
Hezekiah, Ct., BLWt.2329-200
Humphrey, Ct., Cont., Jerusha, W20952
Jacobus, N.Y., S10519; BLWt.34580-160-55
James, Sgt., Mass., BLWt.4052 iss. 8/17/1796
James, Mass., S34304
James, Va., S12725
James, Va., Jane Nelson, former wid., R7591. Her 2nd husb. name was John Nelson, d.1835. They lived in Halifax Co., Va.
Joel, Va., S39413
John, Ct., Mary S., W17711
John, Ct., Polly, W24031
John, Mass., S3271
John, N.Y., Henrietta, R2679
Jonathan, R.I. Dis. No papers

DAVENPORT (continued)
Moses, Mass., S15065
Noah, Ct., Lydia, W22911
Pardon, R.I., Comfort, R2677
Phebe, former wid. of Yale Todd, Cont., Ct., which see
Reuben, Va., S39407
Richard, Cont., enl. in Ct., S43443
Richard, N.Y., Anna, W20953
Richard, Va., S17914
Robert, N.Y., Pa., S8325
Samuel, R.I., S21730
Squire, Ct. See DEVANPORT
Thomas, Ga., BLWt.1904-300
Thomas, Mass., Lydia, W22916
William, Navy, Mass. agency & res., S34290
William, N.Y., R2684
William, N.C., S2507
William, N.C., Comfort, R2678
William, Va., S8309
William, Va., Mary Davis, former wid., W19155
William, Va., Patsey, R2683
DAVERSON, Josiah, Pvt., Mass., BLWt.4015 iss. 12/14/1789 to Richard Platt
DAVES, John, N.C., BLWt.610-300-Capt. Iss. 12/31/1798 or 1788. No papers
DAVID, Azariah, S.C., S2503
Henry, Va., Nancy, R2686
John, Cont., N.Y., Lydia, W6958; BLWt.17570-160-55
Jonathan, N.Y., Lillis, W16230
Michael, Va., S12729
Peter, S.C., S39417
Zebediah, Pa., S2504
DAVIDHISER/DAVIDHEISER, Henry, Pa., Elizabeth, W3391
DAVIDS Solomon, R.I., S38651
DAVIDSON, Abraham, Va., S3272
Alexander, Mass., S35222
Alexander, Pvt., Pa., BLWt.9287 iss. 12/29/1791 to Sarah Shepperd, Admx.
Barnabas, Cont., Mass., S39422; BLWt.1680-100
Benjamin, Pvt., Hazen's Regt., BLWt.12982 iss. 10/9/1792 to Albert Warnick, Admr.
Benjamin, Mass., Molly/Polly, W26659
David, Cont., Va., Maza, W6978; BLWt.1595-100
David, Sgt., Pa., BLWt.92421 iss. 7/9/1789
David, Pa., S45999
Douglas/Douglass, Ct., Cont., Asenath, W19145; BLWt.31287-160-55
Edward, Pvt., Pa., BLWt.9243 iss. 3/10/1795 to John Steward, ass.
Edward, Va., Judith, W3958
Francis, Pa., Elizabeth, R2688
George, S.C., Elizabeth, W283
Giles, Va., S6790
Hezekiah, Ct., R2689
Isaac, Pvt., Ct., BLWt.5689 iss. 4/9/1791
Isaac, Va., S2509

DAVIDSON (continued)
Jacob, N.J., See DAVISON
James, Cont., Pa., S12718
James, Md., S8305
James, Pvt., Pa., BLWt.9234 iss. 6/22/1792 to William Lane, ass.
James, Pa., S9382
James, Pa., Sarah Glenn, former wid., W25635
James, Pa., BLWt.559-400-Surgn. Iss. 10/24/1789. No papers
James, see claim of Nicholas CYRE, Va., Jane, W5074
John, Ct., N.Y., BL Rej.
John, Pvt., "in the Invalid Corps", BLWt.13029 iss. 1/29/1790
John, Md., R20262
John, Md., BLWt.582-400-Major Iss. 9/1/1789. No papers
John, Pvt., Mass., BLWt.4022 iss. 4/14/1795
John, Mass., Anna, W24039
John, N.J., Jane, See DAVISON
John, Pvt., N.Y., BLWt.7039 iss. 7/18/1795 to Henry Pells, ass.
John, N.Y., Elizabeth, W16944
John, N.C., S1758
John, S.C., S31639; BLWt.26173-160-55
John, Va., ----. No papers
John, Va., S8304
Joseph, N.C., Sarah, W4175
Joseph, Va., Mary, W6977
Joseph, Va., R2690 & R2691
Joshua, Cont., Va., S1192
Joshua, Pa., S16099
Josiah, N.C., R2692
Peter, Ct., S15063
Samuel, Mass., S29750
Stephen, Va., S8306
William, N.C., R2696
William, N.C., BLWt.607-450-Lt.Col. Iss. 6/1/1792. No papers
William, Pa., Va., Catharine, W1732
William, Pa., BLWt.1249-300
William, Va., R2695
Zachariah, Ct., Hannah, W17712
DAVIE, Joseph, S.C., R2739 & R2698
Solomon, Mass., Jedidah, W14594
DAVIES, Andrew, N.C., S.C., S3256
Edward E., Navy, N.J. res. & agency, Sarah/Sally, W1154; also see papers within of rejected wid., alleged, Esther/Hetty
Hezekiah, Pa., S2161
Jesse, Va., S8282
John L., N.C., S2496
Marmaduke S., Md., Indian War, Eleanor, W6967; BLWt.26188-160-55
William, Va., S45896
William, Col., Va., BLWt.597-500 Iss. 5/7/1797
DAVIS, Aaron, Cont., Mass., Susannah W22904
Aaron, Sgt., Mass., BLWt.4036 iss. 8/10/1789 to Richard Platt
Aaron, Mass., S15801
Aaron, Mass., Abigail/Nabby, W22915
Abel, Ct., Green Mt. Boys, Vt.

DAVIS (continued)
S12902
Abel, Mass., S29748
Abner, N.H., S10532
Abraham, Cont., Mass., Grace, W14591
Abraham, Mass., S45720
Abraham, Va., Polly, W538; BLWt. 15433-160-55
Adaliah, N.Y., R2699
Allen, Mass., S16750
Allen, Mass., Elizabeth, W25514
Alpheus, Mass., S15398
Amos, Corp., Mass., BLWt.4053 iss. 3/25/1790
Amos, Mass., S34283
Amos, Mass., Hannah, W9829; BLWt.95311-160-55
Amos, N.Y., S12733
Andries, N.Y., S12742
Anthony, Md., S34729
Aquilla, N.H., Abigail, W27927
Aquilla, Va., S35882
Aron/Aaron, N.C., Rebecca, W6968
Asa, Va., S1757
Benaijah, R.I., Welthan/Welthon, W9830
Benet/Benit/Bennett, Mass.,S34310
Benjamin, Mass., S17374
Benjamin, Mass., S17375
Benjamin, Mass., S35230
Benjamin, N.H., S39423
Benjamin, N.H., S17918
Benjamin, N.Y., S23187
Benjamin, N.Y., R2702
Benjamin, N.C., Elizabeth, W3783
Benjamin, Pa., S44127
Benjamin, Va., Lydia, W4172
Burwell, N.C., S8286
Castle, See DAINS
Cato, Pvt., Mass., BLWt.4033 iss. 1/13/1792 to Ezra Blodget
Chapman, Pvt., N.Y., BLWt.7036 iss. 5/25/1791
Chapman, N.Y., S43466
Charles, N.C., S6785
Charles, ---, Va. agency, Dis. No papers
Charles, Va., R13594; Va. Half Pay
Clement, S.C., Elizabeth, W4936
Comfort, Pvt., Mass., BLWt.4100 iss. 7/24/1789
Comfort, Mass., S43468
Conrad, N.J., R2705
Cornelius, Ct., Ruth, W10716; BLWt.31897-160-55
Cornelius, Mass., S29751
Cornelius, Mass., Mary, W19137
Cyrus, Mass., Bridget, W22917
Cyrus, N.C., S41500
Daniel, ---, BLWt.1199-100 by special act of Congress approved 5/20/1826. No papers
Daniel, Ct., S17915
Daniel, Ct., Deborah, W20947
Daniel, Cont., N.Y., Mary, W3519
Daniel, Mass., S22722
Daniel, Mass., Elizabeth, W22920; BLWt.82555-160-55
Daniel, Mass., Ruth, R2762
Daniel, N.J., S40878
Daniel, Pvt., N.Y., BLWts.14037 &

DAVIS (continued)
13003 iss. 6/1/1792
Daniel, Pa., R2707
Daniel, Va., S8287
David, Ct., S23592
David, Cont., N.H., S45717
David, Cont., Pa., S35878; BLWt.252-100
David, Mass., S16754
David, Mass., Polly, W15668
David, Mass., N.H., Hannah, W20957
David, N.H., Sarah, W22888
David, N.J., Hannah, W3662; BLWt.16106-160-55
David, Pvt., N.Y., BLWt.7025 iss. 6/3/1797 to Evander Childs, ass.
David, N.Y., S43473; BLWt.6002-160-55
David, N.C., Jane, W6962
David, Vt., R2710
David, Va., R2711
Dudley, Mass., S44119
Ebenezer, Ct., S34292
Ebenezer, Cont., N.Y., S8279
Ebenezer, Mass., S12737
Ebenezer, Mass., BLWt.524-200-Lt. Iss. 10/11/1792 to Ebenezer Davis. No papers
Edmund, Mass., S21728
Edmund, N.H., S10528
Edmund/Edmond, S.C., Va., Milly/Milley/Mildred, W3393; BLWts. 944-100 & 233-60-55
Edward, N.C., S8284
Eli, Va., R20356
Eliakim, Mass., S15069
Elias, Mass., Lucy, W19150
Elias, N.Y., S43469
Elijah, Ct., S10548
Elijah, Mass., Phebe Whitney, former wid., W25990
Elijah, N.H., Anna, R2700
Elijah, Vt., S22716
Elisha, Ct., Elizabeth, W1730; BLWt.29736-160-55
Elisha, N.H., R2715
Enoch, N.C., R13582
Enos, Md., S35877
Ezekiel, Mass., Sussannah, W14588
Ezra, Cont., Me. agency & res., Abigail, W22905
Ezra, N.Y., S10542
Forrest, Md., S30369
Francis, Va. agency, Dis. No papers
Francis, N.H., S18794
Francis, N.C., S.C., S8290
George, Ct., S22193
George, Ct., Deborah, R2712
George, Pvt., N.J., BLWt. 8270 iss. 5/9/1792
George, N.Y., Jane, W20948
George, N.C., S21154
Gershom, Mass., S32207
Gideon, Mass., S39418
Gilbert, N.Y., S23593
Goldsmith, N.Y., S43458
Hannah, former wid. of Stephen Palmer, Ct., which see
Harman, S.C., BLWt.616-300-Capt. Iss. 5/10/1796 to James

DAVIS (continued)
Kennedy, ass. No papers
Harmy/Harma/Herma, N.H., Mehitable, R2748
Henry, Cont., Mass., N.H., Mary, W19140
Henry, Mass., S34285
Henry, N.J., Anna, W912
Henry, Pvt., N.Y., BLWt.7081 iss. 1/25/1791 to Israel Rogers, ass.
Henry, N.Y., R22164
Henry, N.C., S30981
Henry, Pa., S9381
Henry Babcock, R.I., Mary, W20949
Henry W., Va., Judah, W350
Hezekiah, S.C., S32211
Hugh, Va., S10136
Ichabod, Md., R2724
Increase, Mass., Rachel, W22922
Isaac, Mass., S10550
Isaac, Mass., S35226
Isaac, Mass., Hannah Leighton, former wid., W15018
Isaac, Mass., Rachel, W22890
Isaac, Pvt., N.H., BLWt.3064 iss. 7/22/1790
Isaac, N.H., S43442
Isaac, N.Y., Dis. No papers
Isaac, Pvt., Pa., BLWt.9307 iss. 1/17/1792 to George Moore, ass.
Isaac, Va., S15799
Isham, S.C., Wineford/Winneford, W6970
Israel, Mass., Hannah Dowell, former wid., W14627
Jacob, Ct., Catharine, W19136; BLWt.2-60-55, BLWt.5680-100-Pvt. Iss. 2/25/1790. No papers
Jacob, N.H., Deborah, W24043
Jacob, N.J., S989
Jacob, Va., S17916
James, Ct., S17378
James, Ct., Ruth, W10706; BLWt. 10239-160-55
James, Pvt., Del., BLWt.10743 iss. 9/2/1789
James, Del., S35880
James, Mass., S15073
James, Mass., S18791
James, Mass., S34313
James, Mass., S39401
James, Mass., Eunice Bacon, former wid., W15982
James, Mass., BLWt.522-200-Lt. Iss. 4/1/1790. No papers
James, Mass., N.H., Susannah, R2725
James, N.C., S2498
James, N.C., Mary, R2745
James, S.C., Mary, W8656
James, Va., S8281
James, Va., S8288
James, Va., S12724
James, Va., served in 1744, S16751
James, Va., S38655
James, Va., Susannah, W4171
Jesse, Ct., Mary Gennings, former wid., R3971
Jesse, Mass., R2728
Jesse, N.H., Sarah, R2763

DAVIS (continued)
Jesse, N.C., S2497
Jesse, Va., S12735; BLWt.17583-160-55
Jesse, Va., Nancy, W8652; BLWt. 2325-300
Jesse, Va., Rebecca, R13608; BLWt.50902-160-55
Joel, Mass., S16096
Joel, N.C., Rebecca, W351
John, Ct., S12720
John, Ct., Eunice, W17699
John, Ct., Cont., S39402
John, Ct., Cont., S45716; BLWt. 765-100
John, Cont., N.H., Vt., R2733
John, Cont., N.J., S40881
John, Cont., Pa., S44126; BLWt. 26-60-55
John, Pvt., Md.,BLWt.11170 iss. 1/28/1795 to Francis Sherrard, ass. of Henry Davis, admr.
John, Mass., S29747; BLWt.702-100 Elizabeth Herriden/Hariden alleged wife of sold. was pens'd. as former wid. of Jos. Varriel, which see
John, Mass., S34312
John, Mass., Lucy, W6961; BLWt. 36516-160-55
John, Mass., Mary, W6975
John, Mass., R2732
John, Mass., BLWt.525-200-Lt. Iss. 8/10/1789 to Richard Platt, ass. No papers
John, Navy, N.H., S45718
John, N.H., S17921
John, N.H., Eleanor, W6972; BLWt. 26309-160-55
John, N.H., Deborah, W16231
John, N.J., S34295
John, N.J., S35220
John, N.J., Margaret, W8654
John, Pvt., N.Y., BLWt.7064 iss. 10/7/1796 to Ebenezer Drakley, ass.
John, N.Y., S44121
John, N.Y., Dorcas Chrystyance, former wid., W17613
John, N.Y., BLWt.544-400-Maj. Iss. 6/3/1791 to Perah(?) Davis, admr. No papers
John, N.Y., Rev. War papers in this file were taken from claim of John Davis, N.Y., S44121
John, N.C., Va., S2155
John, N.C., S3259; BLWt.29748-160-55
John, N.C., S6781, b.6/9/1764 in St. Mary's Co., Md. Res. Edgecomb Co., N.C. at enl. Res. after war in Edgecomb, Onslow & Duplin Cos. N.C.
John, N.C., S6787, b. 9/25/1756, Prince Georges Co., Md.; to N.C. with parents when young. Res. at enl. was Orange Co., N.C. In 1833 res. Caswell Co., N.C., formerly part of Orange Co.
John, N.C., Mourning, W19156
John, N.C., Nancy Terry, former wid., R10467
John, Patton's Regt., BLWt.534-450

DAVIS (continued)
Surgn. Iss. 7/23/1791; also recorded as above under BLWt. 2589. No papers
John, Corp., "in Moylan's Regt.", Pa., BLWt.9305 iss. 8/26/179- to James Grey, ass.
John, Pvt., "In Proctor's Artillery", Pa., BLWts.9311 & 26-60-55 iss. 6/29/1789 to M. McConnell, ass.
John, Pa., S16361
John, Pa., S22718
John, Pa., S44117
John, Pa., Sarah, W3338; BLWt. 13447-160-55
John, Pa., Ann, W4934
John, Pa., R2734
John, Pa., BLWt.561-300-Capt. Iss. 8/19/1789. No papers
John, R.I., Theody, W26787; BLWt.3523-160-55
John, S.C., S21725
John, S.C., S37880
John, Va., S16358
John, Va., S30371
John, Va., S31642
John, Va., S35876
John, Va., S39403
John, Va., Nancy, W6959
John, Va., Margaret, W24852; BLWt.819-160-55
John, Va., R2735
John, Va., Mary, R2746
John C., N.Y., S15074
John L., Cont., Mass., Susannah, W1395; BLWt.3607-160-55
John Phelps, Mass., Polly, W19144 BLWt.7089-160-55
John R., Va. Sea Service, R32, Va. Half Pay. No supplemental Half Pay file
Jonas, Mass., S45721
Jonathan, Ct., S36494
Jonathan, Cont., Mass., R2736
Jonathan, Mass., S39419
Jonathan, N.H., S10533
Jonathan, N.H., S12726
Jonathan, N.J., S35873
Jonathan, N.J., S44122
Jonathan, N.C., S17919
Jonathan, N.C., Hannah, R2722
Jonathan, Va., Elizabeth, R2716
Joseph, Ct., Cont., S17373
Joseph, Ct., Mass., Vt., Azubah, W14581
Joseph, Cont., Va., R2738
Joseph, Mass., S15062
Joseph, Mass., wife named Marcy, S34284
Joseph, Mass., Hannah, W15667
Joseph, Mass., Mercy, BLWt. 67579-160-55
Joseph, N.H., S45719
Joseph, N.H., BLWt.2462-100
Joseph, N.J., R2737
Joseph, N.J., Penelope Plunkit/Plunket, former wid., R8291. He d. while prisoner of war.
Joseph, N.Y., S12740
Joseph, N.C., See NOTHERN
Joseph, N.C., S.C., Elizabeth,

DAVIS (continued)
R2717
Joseph, Pa., Rachel, W6965
Joseph, Pa., BLWt.1168-300
Joseph, R.I., Lydia, W14590
Joseph, S.C., S10534
Joseph, Va., S15397
Joseph, Va., S15399
Joseph, Va., S31159
Joseph, Va., BLWt.599-400-Surgn. Iss. 1/31/1794 to Francis Graves, ass. No papers
Joshua, Cont., Mass. agency & res., S38656
Joshua, Mass., S18373
Joshua, Mass., S35221
Joshua, N.H., S29111
Joshua, N.H., Jemima, W6966
Joshua, Pvt., N.Y., BLWt.7041 iss. 7/19/1790 to John Howell, ass.
Joshua, N.Y., Abigail, W17698
Joshua, N.Y., Azubah, R2701
Joshua, N.C., R2741
Joshua, S.C., R2714 1/2
Josiah, Pvt., Ct., BLWt.5692 iss. 5/5/1791 to B. Tallmadge
Josiah, Ct., S---, No papers
Josiah, Ct., Annis F., W20961; BLWt.26658-160-55
Josiah, Mass., S19277
Josiah, Mass. S34311
Josiah, Mass., Ruth, W14595
Josiah, Mass., N.H., S10520
Josiah, N.C., S6786
Kitteridge, Ct., Mass., S10537
Lathrop, Ct., Mary, W20958
Leonard, Va., S12736
Levi, Md., S32210
Levi, Mass., S2502
Levi, Pa. Sea Service, S40876
Levi, Va., S21156
Lewis, Va., S8280
Lewis C., Va., S32199
Llewellyn, Pa., Martha, W3133; BLWt.569-200-Lt. Iss. 8/19/1789. No papers
Loassa/Louisa/Lois, former wid., of Abraham Covalt, Pa., which see
Lodowick, Md., Dolly Ann, R2713
Lois, former wid. of Elihu Judd, Ct., which see
Mary, former wid. of Wm. Davenport Va., which see
Meshack/Mashack/Moshack, N.C., R2747
Methuselah, Pa., S40880
Micah, Mass., S35236
Micajah, Ct., Betsey, R2703
Micajah, N.C., Martha, W6969
Michael, Mass., S35235
Moses, Cont., N.H., S35225
Moses, Mass., S29108
Moses, Mass., Sarah, W19147
Moses, N.J., R2749
Moses, Pa., Rachel, W3392
Nancy, former wid. of Abner Lee, Ct., which see
Nathan, Cont., Ct., Betsa, W19142
Nathan, Mass., S34282
Nathan, Mass., Lucy, W16550
Nathan, N.H., Tryphena, W24037

DAVIS (continued)
Nathan, N.J., Mary, W453
Nathan, N.Y., Dis. No papers
Nathan, N.Y., S27664
Nathaniel, Ct., R2751
Nathaniel, Sgt., Mass., BLWt. 3998 iss. 8/1/1789 to Thomas Cushing
Nathaniel, Pvt., Mass., BLWt. 4006 iss. 8/1/1789 to Thomas Cushing
Nathaniel, Mass., S18370
Nathaniel, N.C., Va., S30366
Nicholas, Mass., S35239
Nicholas, N.J., Pa., Catharine, R2704
Nicholas, R.I., S38649
Nicholas, Va., Mary, W30
Obadiah, N.H., S39409
Patrick, Pvt., N.Y., BLWt.7037 iss. 1/25/1791 to Israel Rogers, ass.
Patrick, N.Y., S43447
Paul, Sgt., Mass., BLWt.4030 iss. 12/20/1799 to Nehemiah Nelson
Paul, Cont., Mass., S43449
Peter, Pvt., Mass., BLWt.4016 iss. 3/25/1790
Peter, Mass., S39420
Peter, Pvt., N.Y., BLWt.7093 iss. 1/25/1791 to Israel Rogers, ass.
Peter, N.Y., S10535
Peter, N.Y., S43448
Peter, Pvt., Pa., BLWt.9253 iss. 8/16/1792 to John Kenoon, ass.
Philamon/Philemon, Md., S31640
Philip, Pa., Hannah, W3337
Phillip, Cont., Mass., Hannah, W22919; BLWt.11189-160-55
Phinehas, N.Y., R2753
Reuben, Va., R20210
Rezin, Md., BLWt.586-300-Capt. No papers
Richard, Md., R2758
Richard, N.Y., S43446
Richard, N.Y., Temperance, W22912; BLWt.7016-100-Pvt. Iss. 7/30/1790. No papers
Richard, Pvt., Lamb's Artillery N.Y., BLWt.7085 iss. 1/25/1791 to Israel Rogers, ass.
Richard, N.C., S41502
Richard, Pa.(?), Sarah, R2764
Richard, Pa., Va., Rebecca, W2438; BLWt.3393-160-55
Richard, Pvt., Va., BLWt.12069 iss. 7/14/1792 to Francis Graves, ass.
Robert, Cont., N.H., Mass., Mary, W14589
Robert, Mass., S19275
Robert, Mass., BLWt.530-300-Capt. iss. 7/24/1792. No papers
Robert, N.C., Loucinda, R2744; BLReg. No. 239514
Robert, S.C., R2760; see BL Reg. 169800-55
Robert, S.C., R2761

DAVIS (continued)
Robert, Va., S2500
Rufus, Navy, Mass. agency & res., S34308
Sally, former wid. of James R. Blashfield, Mass., which see
Sampson, N.C., Ruth, W6964; BLWt.17575-160-55
Samuel, Ct., S9380
Samuel, Ct., Olle, R2752
Samuel, Ct., R.I., Lucy, W17701; BLWt.30700-160-55
Samuel, Pvt. "in the Invalid Corps", BLWt.13027 iss. 4/19/1792 to Jane Murthwaite, admx.
Samuel, Pvt., Md., BLWt.1131 iss. 1/22/1793 to John Wright, ass.
Samuel, Sgt., Md., BLWt.11169 iss. 8/27/1789
Samuel, Md., S34730
Samuel, Drum Major, Mass., BLWt. 4007 iss. 2/22/1790 to Theodosius Fowler
Samuel, Mass., S21727
Samuel, Mass., S28701; BLWt. 828-160-55
Samuel, Mass., S34289
Samuel, Mass., S43451
Samuel, Mass., Betsey, W6963
Samuel, Mass., Mary C., W10310; BLWt.37642-160-55
Samuel, Mass., Ruth, W17702
Samuel, Pvt., N.H., BLWt.3058 iss. 11/6/1795 to James A. Neal, ass.
Samuel, N.H., S16357
Samuel, N.H., S35229
Samuel, N.H., S49289
Samuel, N.H., Martha, W1572; BLWt.51884-160-55
Samuel, N.H., Rachel, R2754
Samuel, Pvt., N.Y., BLWt.7045 iss. 1/25/1791 to Israel Rogers, ass.
Samuel, N.C., S8285
Samuel, N.C., S39406
Samuel, N.C., Nancy, W4938
Samuel, Pa., S40877; BLWt.578-200-Lt. Iss. 4/19/1791 to Alexander Power, ass. No papers
Samuel, Va., S2499
Samuel, Va., S16756
Samuel, Va., S35885
Samuel, Va., S37878
Samuel, Va., Ruth, W2534; BLWt.26528-160-55
Samuel, Va., Jane, W19157
Samuel, Va., Elizabeth, R2718
Samuel Barker, Va., Ann, W1728; BLWt.34532-160-55
Samuel D., Pa., Nancy, R2750; BLWt.40902-160-55
Sanford, Mass., S35224
Septimus, Cont., Pa., S30365
Silas, Ct., Cont., Matilda, W10709
Simon, Mass., Mary, W24041
Simon, N.H., Margaret, W22918
Simon, N.Y., Vt., Mary, W17700
Simon, R.I., Chana Hopkins,

DAVIS (continued)
former wid., W13476
Simon, S.C., S6784; BLWt.11168-160-55
Snead, Ga., N.C.,S.C., S32205
Solomon, Ct., Mary, R2765
Solomon, Mass., Dorcas, W15666
Spencer, Va., Nancy, W5261
Spillman, Pvt., Va., BLWt.12071 iss. 7/20/1792 to Robert Means, ass.
Squier, Mass., S30364
Squire, N.Y., S15076
Stephen, R.I., Priscilla, W14586
Stephen B., Ct., S36497
Surry, S.C., R2766
Thomas, Ct., Abigail, W19152
Thomas, Ct., R2769
Thomas, Ct., R.I., Rebecca, W17703
Thomas, Cont., Va., Indian Wars 1792, Elizabeth, W4935; BLWt. 1453-100
Thomas, Md., Joanna, W6974
Thomas, Mass., S17377
Thomas, Mass., S29109
Thomas, Mass., Lettice, W14596
Thomas, Navy, N.H., S35223
Thomas, N.H., Sally, W24035
Thomas, Pvt., N.J., BLWt.8255 iss. 4/14/1790 to Isaac Willis, Jr., ass.
Thomas, N.J., S34296
Thomas, N.C., S1756
Thomas, N.C., S8289
Thomas, Pa., S23597
Thomas, Pa., S40875
Thomas, S.C., S1509
Thomas, S.C., Nancy, W8655
Thomas, Va., Frances, W539; BLWt.28551-160-55
Thomas, Va., Susannah, W8651
Thomas, Va., Rachel, R2755
Thompson, Pvt., Va., BLWt.12070 iss. 7/20/1792 to Robert Means, ass.
Timothy, Mass., Betty, W24845
Tolaver/Tolliver, Va., S37879
Vachel, S.C., R2770
Valentine, N.Y., Sarah, W19135
Van, Cont., Va. res. of heirs in 1834; BLWt.2044-100
Walter, Va., Mary, W4170
Wells, N.H., Abigail, W22892
Wendle/Wendell, Navy, S19276, Me. res. in 1839. Service in Mass. ship
Willard, Ct., BLWt.67513-160-55
William, Pvt., Ct., BLWt.5710 iss. 3/19/1794
William, Ct., S42668
William, Cont., Va. res. in 1829, BLWt.1536-100
William, Cont., Mass., S35231
William, Cont., Pa., Elizabeth, W2596; BLWt.34981-160-55
William, Cont., Va., S3255
William, Pvt., Md., BLWt.11166 iss. 7/8/1797 to James De Baufre, ass.
William, Md., S32202
William, Md., S34731

DAVIS (continued)
William, Mass., S15068
William, Mass., S34301
William, Mass., S35227
William, Mass., S35228
William, Mass., Elizabeth, W14597
William, Mass., Rebecca, W14601; BLWt.36641-160-55
William, Mass., Margaret, W24045
William, Mass., Navy, Privateer, S17371
William, N.J., S5329
William, N.J., S16097
William, N.J., S34300
William, N.Y., S12721
William, N.Y., S23188
William, N.Y., S35237
William, N.Y., S43450
William, N.Y., R2774
William, N.C., S8291
William, N.C., S31158
William, N.C., Anna, W8657; BLWt.49037-160-55
William, Pa., S40882; BLWt.1459-100
William, R.I., S44120
William, R.I., Lucy, W19151
William, R.I., Penelope, W22895
William, R.I., Elizabeth, W22903
William, S.C., S31641
William, S.C., Martha, W8653
William, Va., S2160
William, Va., S3257
William, Va., S8277
William, Va., S10521
William, Va., S12738
William, Va., S15796
William, Va., S35884
William, Va., Mary, W284; BLWt.333-60-55
William, Va., Benedicta, W6973
William, Va., Jane, W10309
William F.R., Md., S3258
William S., N.Y., S8278
Winthrop, Cont., N.H., Sarah, W22898; BLWt.3759-160-55
Zachariah, Pa., S1660
Zebulon, Mass., S18795
DAVISE, John, Va. Sea Service, Amy, W19138
DAVISON, Benjamin, Ct., Cont., Mass., Roxy, W16946
Daniel, Cont., Mass., S39421
Daniel, Mass., S18792
Daniel, Mass., S20719
Ezra, Ct., Deidamia Boone, former wid., W25260
Jacob, N.J., S34299
James, N.J., S631
John, Ct., S32209
John, Ct., Mass., Lydia, W14600
John, N.J., S629
John, N.J., Jane, W847
Joseph, Ct., W25517
Paul, Ct., Sally, W20962
Samuel, Va., R2694
Susannah, former wid. of Benjamin Weaver, R.I., which see
Thomas, Ct., S15066
William, N.J., Catharine, W452
DAVISSON, Josiah, Va., S8301
Josiah, Va., S8307

DAVOL, William, R.I., Elizabeth, W14576
DAWES, John, Mass., Dolly, W27853; BLWt.31403-160-55
DAWKINS, Charles, Md., Elizabeth, W4174
John, N.C., Susannah, W6992; BLWt.24768-160-55
Joseph, S.C., Drusilla, W8665
DAWLEY, Daniel, R.I., Elizabeth, W24038
Michael, R.I., S21157
Nathan, R.I., Elizabeth, W14592
DAWS, Cato (colored), Mass., BLWt.99-100
Thomas, Mass., Rebecca, W22893
DAWSON, Anthony, Pa., Mary, R2777
Benjamin, Cont., Va., S39405
Christopher, Va., Lydia, W2721; BLWt.27632-160-55
Daniel, Pvt., N.Y., BLWt.7056 iss. 8/2/1791 to Samuel B. Webb, ass.
Ezra, Pvt., Mass., BLWt.4059 iss. 1/28/1790 to Eliphalet Downer
Francis, Pvt., Va., BLWt.12085 iss. 4/15/1792 to Francis Graves, ass.
Henry, Va., S10549
Henry, Va., BLWt.601-200-Lt. Iss. 4/21/1796 to James Morrison, ass. No papers
James, Cont., N.C. or S.C., Jane Ford, former wid., S9657; BLWt. 112143-160-55
James, Va., S44116
Jeremiah, Va., Nancy Agnes, R2778
John, Pvt., Md., BLWt.11133 iss. 1/8/1796 to Geo. Ponsonby, ass.
John, Pa., S8296
John, Va., S32206
Jonas, S.C., R2776
Joseph, Md., S34733
Peter P., Del., R2779, Indian Wars 1792-1795
Titus, Ct., S15070
William, Cont., Pa., S35883
William, Ga., N.C., S.C., S17920
William, Md., S34732
William, Sgt., Pa., BLWt.9263 iss. 6/29/1789 to M. McConnell, ass.
DAY, Aaron, N.J., BLWt.1454-200. Iss. 12/31/1829. See BLWt.1849-200 iss. 5/21/1832 to the grandchildren of said soldier
Aaron, N.J., BLWt.1849-200. Iss. 5/21/1832. See BLWt.1454-200 which was fraudulently obtained on this man's services.
Aaron, N.Y., S43462
Abraham, Mass., Mary, W22921
Amos, N.J., Martha, W4176; BLWt. 250-60-55 & 8237-100, iss. 6/11/1789. No papers
Anthony, Vt., Hannah, W17697
Artemas, N.J., Bethany, W4661
Asa, Mass., N.Y., Mary, W6955; BLWt.13416-160-55
Betsey, former wid. of Samuel Cudworth, Mass., which see
Comfort, Ct., Esther, W16232
Daniel, Md., Margaret, R2789

DAY (continued)
Daniel, Mass., Ambrey, W10308
Daniel, N.H., S16759
David, Sgt., Mass., BLWt.4017 iss. 4/1/1790
David, Mass., S47188
David, Mass., War of 1812, Susannah, W15665. Cert. 593 iss. in lieu of B.L., by which Harvey Clap, guardian of Chloe Day, a minor, only child of David Day, relinquished claim to the military B.L. to which her father would have been entitled if he had served the term of his engagement in the army, and in lieu thereof accpted 5 yrs. Half Pay.
Edward, Va., S32200
Edward, Va., R2781
Elijah, Mass., Mary Wilcox, former wid., W22666; BLWt.526-200-Lt. iss. 10/15/1789. No papers
Ezekiel, Pa., S12727
Francis, Ga., N.C., Jane, W6956
Heman, Mass., S5326
Henson, Va., Rosanna, R2782
Isaac, Cont., Ct., Sarah, W6954; BLWt.11-60-55; BLWt.5716-100-Pvt. Iss. 2/23/1797. No papers
James, Md., Sarah, W10713; BLWt. 101193-160-55
James, Va., R2784
Jediah/Jedediah, Mass., S29106
Jehial, N.J., S3254
Jeremiah, Mass., S18372
Jeremiah, Pvt., N.J., BLWt.8271 iss. 6/16/1789 to Thomas Coyle, ass.
Jeremiah, N.J., S42669
Jesse, Mass., Mary, W2597; BLWt.9487-160-55
Joel, Mass., Martha, W14577
John, Ct., Annis, W17694
John, Md., R2787
John, Mass., S22720
John, Mass., S29113
John, N.J., Rebecca, W117
John, Pvt. "Lamb's Artillery," N.Y., BLWt.7079 iss. 12/2/1789
John, Pvt., Pa., BLWt.9273 iss. 1/19/1792 to Peter Rathermal, ass.
John, Va., S3252; BLReg. 335101-55
John, Va., Rebecca, W3006; BLWt. 26338-160-55
John, Va., Joanna, W4177; BLWt. 56990-160-55
Jonathan, Pvt., Sheldon's Dragoons, Ct., BLWt.5729 iss. 12/26/1789 to David Knap
Jonathan, Cont., Mass., Eunice, W16945
Joseph, Sgt., Ct., BLWt.5702 iss. 2/5/1790
Joseph, Ga., R2788
Joseph, Ga., BLWt.2175-300
Joseph, Mass., Susannah/Susan, W8649; BLWt.31427-160-55
Joshua, Mass., S34286
Justin, Mass., Rhoda, W19153

DAY (continued)
Levi, Mass., S17917
Lewis, Mass., S2157
Lewis, Mass., N.Y., S43459
Luke, Capt., Mass., BLWt.517-300 iss. 10/15/1789
Mehitable, former wid. of Jacob Curtis, Mass., which see
Moses, Cont., Pa., or N.J., Joanna, W782
Moses, N.J., S42148
Moses, Pvt., Pa., BLWt.9290 iss. 5/13/1793
Nathaniel, Cont., Mass., S35234
Nathaniel, Mass., Rachel, W22923; BLWt.2031-160-55
Nehemiah, N.J., Phebe, W846
Noah, Ct., S23591
Philip, N.C., Mary, W915
Ransom, Va., Catharine B., R2790
Robert, Mass., S34302
Russell, Ct., Anna, R2780
Samuel, Ct., Cont., S10530
Samuel, Mass., Sally, W1571
Samuel, Mass., BLWt.532-200-Lt. Iss. 6/21/1797 to Marlbry Turner, ass.; also marked Cert. to Steph. Phelps, 6/27/1818. No papers
Solomon, Ct., S22721
Thomas, Ct., Susannah, W17695
Thomas, Mass., S34288
Timothy, N.H., Vt., Judith, W22913
Westbrook, Ct., S39404
William, Mass., Lucretia French, former wid., R3796
William, N.J., R13650
William, S.C., S16755
William, Va., S39408
William, Va., S39416
Zebina, Cont., Vt., S12739
DAYHOFF, George P., Pa., R2792
DAYLE, London, Pvt., N.H., BLWts. 3065 & 140-60-55 iss. 10/27/1792
DAYLEY/DAILEY, Jeremiah, Mass. Sea Service, Elizabeth Aylward, former wid., W15723
Robert, N.Y., BLWt.440-100
DAYTON, Andrew, Ct., Jerusha, W17708
Benjamin, Ct., S17369
Bennet Benj., Pvt., Sappers & Miners, BLWt.12978 iss. 12/5/1789
David, Ct., Elizabeth, R2793
Elias, N.J., BLWt.556-850-Brig. Gen. Iss. 6/11/1789. No papers
Ephraim, Ct., Mary, W10707; BLWt.91508-160-55
Frederic/Frederick, N.Y., S43460
Frederick, Pvt., N.Y., BLWt.7075 iss. 11/16/1791 to Marton O'Reilly, ass.
Henry, R.I., Mary, W24036
Jonah, Ct., S13691
Jonathan, N.J., Susan, W6994; BLWt.555-300-Capt. Iss. 6/11/1789. No papers.
Joseph, N.Y., S28704
Mary, former wid. of Seth Bulkley Ct., which see
Nathan, N.Y., S8298

DAYTON (continued)
Nathaniel, Ct., S10527
Samuel, Ct., Naomi, W20955
DAZEY/DASEY, Jesse, Del., R2795
Thomas, Del., S35881
DEACON, Aaron, Pvt., N.J., BLWt. 8266 iss. 5/25/1797 to Enoch Conger, Jr., ass.
Aaron, N.J., Patience Wilcox, former wid., W510
DEACONS, Jonathan, Cont., R.I., Mass., S34322
William Pvt., Hazen's Regt., BLWt.13009 iss. 4/8/1794
DEADERICK/DEADRICK, David, Va., Margaret, W3521; BLWt.43880-160-55
DEAGLE/DEAGLES/DEGLE, Absalom, Va., R2796
DEAGUE, Mathias, Pa., S3277
DEAK/DEAKE, William G., N.Y., S12764
DEAKE/DAKE, Immanuel, N.Y., S16105
DEAKENS, James, Va. See DEAKINS
DEAKINS, James, Va., Martha, W9833; BLWt.28627-160-55
Thomas, Pvt., Md., BLWt.11154 iss. 12/22/1794
William, Cont., Md., S38659
DEAL, George, Pvt., Cont., Mass. Mary, W726; BLWt.5722-100 iss. 5/24/1797 to James Davenport; BLWt.211-60-55
George, Md., S2171
Henry, Pa., R2631
Jacob, N.C., S8313; BLWt.26154-160-55
John, Mass., Elizabeth, See DAL
DEAL/TEAL/DHIEL/DIEHL/DIEL, Samuel, Pa., Isabella, W6253
DEALE, Daniel, Pa., See DEALL
Thomas, Va., R2797; BLWt.34582-160-55
DEALL/DEALE/DEAL, Daniel, Pa., Catharine, W6999; BLWt.36640-160-55
DEAMER, Philip, Pa., S5345
DEAN, Aaron, Ct., S9384; BLWt.28523-160-55
Abiathar, Mass., Wealthy Nichols former wid., R7660
Abiezar, Mass., Mary, W14616; 4 Cont. ltrs. in file
Abraham, N.Y., Zilphia, R2811
Abram, Mass., R.I., Molly, W24049
Archelaus, Mass., S21733
Archibald/Ashbel, Cont., N.Y., Rachel, W20965
Ashbell, Pvt., Lamb's Artillery, N.Y., BLWt.7089 iss. 4/27/1792 to Timothy Benedict, ass.
Benaiah, Mass., Temperance, W14614
Benjamin, Cont., Ct. was daughter's res. in 1833; BLWt.1988-100
Benjamin, Mass., Mary, W16107
Benjamin, N.J., S35888
David, Ct., S39424
David, Ct., Mary, W1246; BLWt. 26489-160-55
David, N.J., Phebe, W10735

DEAN (continued)
David, N.Y., S29118
Ebenezer, Ct., N.Y., S31647
Ebenezer, Mass., Jane, W10724; BLWt.26792-160-55
Edmund, Mass., Rebecca C. Lawrence, former wid., W1437
Elijah, Ct., Anna, W19162; BLWt.3766-160-55
Enos, Ct., Vt., S15400
Enos, Mass., S30378
Enos, Mass., Lydia Wilde, former wid., W27504; BLWt.19503-160-55
Ephraim, Va., R13698; Va. Half Pay
Gideon, Mass., R.I., S28706
Gilbert, N.Y., Mary, R2803
Hoptill/Hopstill, Ct., former wid. of Ephraim Johnson, Ct. which see
Isaac, N.Y., S43480
Jabez, N.Y., Hannah, W1244; BLWt.29735-160-55
Jacob, N.J., Lydia, W6997
James, N.H., Dis. No papers
James, Pvt., N.Y., BLWt.7033 iss. 9/16/1796 to Ebenezer Drakley, ass.
James/Benjamin, N.Y., Eunice, R2798
James, Privateer, Mass., R2799
James L., Ct., S22200; BLWt. 56505-160-55
Jeremiah, Mass., S18800
Jesse, Mass., S30384
Job, Cont., Mass., S23598
Joel, Ct., Mass., S15083
John, Ct., Martha, W17714
John, Cont., Mass., S18797
John, Cont., Va., S39427; BLWt.2186-100
John, Md., Privateer, Sea Service, S16100
John, N.J., S812
John, N.Y., Mary, W16555
John, N.Y., R2802
John, Pa., S12751
John, Pa., Jane, R2800
John, Pvt., Va., BLWts.12029 &12065 iss. 5/29/1792 to Francis Graves, ass.
Jonathan, Ct., S43487
Joseph, Mass., S10557
Joseph, Pvt., N.J., BLWt.8247 iss. 8/7/1789 to Richard Platt, ass.
Joshua, Va., Tabitha, R2810
Josiah, R.I., S36506
Lemuel, Mass., S30382
Lemuel, N.H., Dis. No papers
Levi, Pvt., Ct., BLWt.5685 iss. 9/24/1790 to James F. Sebor
Michael, Va., S36503
Moses, N.C., Rachel, W4664
Nathaniel, Mass., S5334
Nathaniel, N.J., S810
Nehemiah, N.J., S866
Noble, Md., R2805
Obed, Mass., S18376
Philip, Mass., Abigail,

DEAN (continued)
BLWt.32205-160-55
Philip, N.C., Mary, W19165
Phineas/Phinehas, Cont., Ct., Ruth, W25527; BLWt.17576-160-55
Phinehas E./Phineas E., Mass., S30383
Reuben, Ct., Roxalana, W17713
Reuben, Ct., Lucretia, W25524
Richard, N.C., S38658
Richard, N.C., S.C., S16761
Robert, Md., S34742
Samuel, Ct., N.Y., Hannah, W25520; BLWt.71027-160-55
Samuel, Mass., S29116
Samuel, Mass., S34324
Samuel, Pvt., N.Y., BLWt.7062 iss. 9/15/1790 to Wm. Bell, ass.
Samuel, N.Y., S43497
Samuel, Pa., Mary, W10722; BLWt. 576-300-Capt. Iss. 5/27/1791 No papers
Samuel, Pa., R2806
Samuel, S.C., R2807
Samuel, Va., R2808
Seth, Mass. Sea Service, S10561
Seth, Mass., Ruth, W5262; BLWt. 10255-160-55
Seth, Mass., Edene, W14617
Silas, Mass., S15088
Stewart, N.Y., Sea Service, R2809
Susanna, former wid. of Joseph Ingalls, Mass., which see
Susanna, former wid. of Vincent Glass, Va., which see
Thomas, Cont., N.H., S34323
Thomas, Mass., Privateer, Martha, W14611
Thomas, S.C., Sarah, W27602; BLWt.15156-160-55
Timothy, N.Y., R.I., S21734
Walter, Mass., BLWt.519-300-Capt. Iss. 8/22/1789. No papers
William, Cont., Ct. res., N.Y. agency, Anna, W20977
William, Mass., Olive, W19167
William, Pvt., N.J., BLWt. 8250 iss. 7/22/1789 to Josiah Hunt, ass.
William, Pvt., Pa., BLWt.9268 iss. 4/19/1791
William W., N.Y., S12760
Zebediah, Mass., S29757
Zimey, Mass., S43488
DEANE,Isaac, Pvt., N.Y., BLWt. 7022 iss. 1/19/1792 to Resolve Waldron, ass.
John, Pvt., N.Y., BLWt.7074 iss. 9/8/1790 to William Jackson, ass.
John, Va., S16760
John, Va., Betsey, W6998
Samuel, Mass., S3274
William, Cont., Mass., Susanna, W16008
DeANGELIS, Paschal Charles Joseph, Ct., Sea Service, Privateer, Elizabeth, W17715
DEAR, John, Pvt. "in Proctor's Artillery", Pa., BLWt.9310

DEAR (continued)
iss. 7/27/1789 to Richard Platt, ass.
Jonathan, Ct., S34740
DEARBORN, Abraham, Navy, N.H., S18796
Asa, N.H., Anna, W19164
Henry, N.H., S46354; BLWt.507-500-Lt.Col. Cmdt. Iss. 8/24/1790 to Benjamin Ives Gilman, ass. No papers
James, N.H., R2813
John, Mass., R2815
John, N.H., Anna, W20974; BLWt.3530-160-55
Joseph, N.H., S10560
Joseph, N.H., S15401
Josiah, N.H., Susanna, W16009
Levi, N.H., S18798
Nathaniel, N.H., S12745
Nathaniel, N.H., Hannah, W16010
Shearborn/Sherburn, N.H., Susan, R2817; BLWt.40917-160-55
Shubael, N.H., Ruth, W22934
Simon, N.H., S35246
DEARMAN, George, N.J., R2818
DEARMOND, Michael, Pa., S42155
DEART/DART, Ebenezer, Cont., Ct., Hannah, W1243; BLWt. 10305-160-55
DEARWART/DOARWART, Martin, Pa., R2820
DEARWELL, Margaret, former wid. of Patrick Sullivan, N.J., which see
DEATH, Patience, former wid. of Robert Potter, which see
DEATLY/DEATLEY, James, Va., S10139
DEATS, Henry, N.J., S2165
John, N.J., S12759
DEAVER, Aquila, Pvt., Md., BLWt. 11150 iss. 8/7/1794 to Henry Purdy, ass.
Aquila, Md., S34737
John, Md., Sarah, R2822
Miscal, Md., S34738
William, Md., S12754; N.A. Acc.874-050047, not Half Pay
William, Va., S6791
DEAVOURS, Rachel, wid. of George Deavours & former wid. of John Watkins, S.C., which see
DeBEAULIEU, Lewis, Armand's Corps, BLWt.640-200-Lt. Iss. 6/15/1793. No papers. See BEAULIEU, Louis de, Heitman's Reg., p.95
DeBEER, Francis Suza, Mass., BLWt.508-300-Surgn.Mate. See DEBIEVRE
DEBELL, Alexander, Cont., N.H., Betty Taylor, former wid., W22382; BLWt.31326-160-55. Her 2nd husb., Eliphalet Taylor, a pensioner, which see
deBELLERIVE, Louis Baury, Cont. French, See BAURY de BELLERIVE, Louis
deBENNEVILLE, Daniel, Va., BLWt. 562-400-Surgn. Iss. 1/21/1795. Also recorded under BLWt.2649.

deBENNEVILLE (continued)
No papers
deBERT, Clauduis, Gen. Armand's Legionary Corps, BLWt.635-300-Capt. Iss. 10/14/1789. No papers
DeBESSE, Joshua, Cont., Mass., Privateer, S15803
DEBORD, Charlotte, former wid. of Isham Dickeson, N.C., which see
DEBOW, Frederick, N.C., Rachel, W7005
Garret, not Rev. War, N.J., Militia, Whiskey Insurrection, Elizabeth, BLWt.63685-160-55. No claim for pension
John, N.J., Catharine,W19161
DEBRULER/DEBRULAR, John, Md.,S35890
deCALLA, Theodore, Cont., N.H., see DeKELLEY
Theodore, Pvt., Hazen's Regt., BLWt.13011 iss. 8/11/1795
deCAMBRAY/CAMBRAY, Louis Antoine Jean Baptiste, Comte, Cont., French, BLWt.2270-450
DeCAMP, Enoch, N.J., Elizabeth, R2824
Ezekiel, N.J., Rachel, W7009
John, N.J., Elizabeth, W2536
Mathias, N.Y. res. No papers
Morris, Cont., N.J. See Morris D. CAMP
DECILVA/DESILVA, William, Mass., Hannah, BLWt.817-100
DECK, Henry, N.Y., S8314. He d. in 1802, wid. Hannah
John, N.C., R2826
Michael, Va., Susannah, W22935
DECKER, Abraham, Cont., Pa., S15405
Abraham, Pa., S5332
Adam, Pa., S43494; BLWt.1862-100
Andrew, N.Y., Mary, R2833
Benjamin, Pa., S42670
Christopher, N.Y., enl. Pa., S43496; BLWt.7043-100. Iss. 1/25/1791. No papers
Elias, N.J., R2827
Ephraim, N.Y., Mary, W20982
Evert, N.Y., R2828
George, N.Y., S30381
George, N.Y., S44135
Henry, N.Y., R2829
Isaac, Pa., S10553
Jacob, Cont., N.Y., S10563
Jacob, Pa., S22206
James, N.Y., R3110
James, N.Y., R22236
John, N.Y., S44142
John, Va., S30380
John C., N.Y., R2830
Martin, N.Y., S43475
Martiness, N.Y., Mary Middaugh, former wid., R7158
Matthew, N.Y., R2834
Michael, N.Y., BLWt.1572-100
Michael, Pa., Indian Wars 1792-1795,1796, War of 1812, R2835
Peter, N.Y., S15091
Peter, N.Y., R2836
Peter, Pa., BLWt.2599-300-Capt. Iss. 12/24/1791 to Jacob Decker ass. of George Decker, admr. No papers

DECKER (continued)
Petrus, N.Y., S15077
Samuel, Cont., Va., S35893
Samuel, N.J., Sarah, W16954; BLWts. 490-100 & 9446-160-55
Samuel, ---, Jane, R---, N.Y. res. of widow
Thomas, Mass., S35243
William, Mass., S17927
William, Va., S12750
DECKIRTT, John, Jacob, Pa., R2831
DECLERK, Abraham, Pvt., N.Y., BLWt.7054 iss. 9/28/1790 to William Sloo, ass
DECOASTER, Jonathan, Pvt., Mass., BLWt.4040 iss. 12/3/1789 to Moses W. Barker
DECOINE/DECOIN, Edward, Cont., N.Y., Elizabeth, W10314; BLWt.61336-160-55
DECOURCY/DECOURSEY, William, N.C., Elizabeth, W8665 1/2
deCOUTURES, Jacques Delahair, Cont., French (?)
DEDIER, John, Pa., S42671
DEDMAN/DEADMAN, Samuel, Va., S35887
DEDMAN, William, Mass., Mary, W14610
DEDMON, Mark, N.C., Hannah, W3960
DEE/DOE/DAW, John, N.H., R2997
DEEDS, George, Va., Mary, W10734
George M., N.J., Phebe, W2537
Peter, Pa., S40925
DEEKER, Christopher, Pvt., N.Y., BLWt.7043 iss. 1/25/1791
Martin, Pvt., N.Y., BLWt.7042 iss. 1/25/1791
DEEM, Adam, Pa., S10522
Jacob, Pa., R2838
DEEMER, Peter, Pa., S6792
DEEN, Benjamin, Va., S44130
Julius, Ga., S39436
Micajah, N.J., Cornelia Ann, W20964
DEER, Martin, Va., S8311
DEES/DEESE, Joel, N.C., R2841
DEETS, Adam, Va., Mary Stiles, former wid., W598
DEFEVER/LEVEVER, John, Va., Nancy, W1834; BLWt.31432-160-55
DEFFENDERFER/DIFFENDERFER, Jacob, Pa., BLWt.61148-160-55
DEFFENDORF, Henry, N.Y., BLWt. 2614-200-Lt. Iss. 7/31/1793. No papers
deFLEURY/FLEURY, Louis Tessidre, Cont., France, BLWt.1352-400
DEFNALL/DEFLENN, David, N.C., S37887
DeFORD, Thomas, Md., S2514
DeFOREST, Abel, Ct., S15086
Abraham, N.J., S5331
Ebenezer, Ct., N.Y., S31643
Gideon, Ct., Hannah, R2842
Mary, former wid. of Thos. W. Ruland, Ct., which see
Mills, Ct., S13046
Philip, N.Y., S12770
Reuben, Ct., N.Y., S17380
Samuel, Ct., Mary, W16559

DeFOREST (continued)
Samuel, Ct., BLWt.538-200-Lt. Iss. 6/3/1780. No papers
William, N.Y., S28712
DEFRANCE/DEFANCE, John, Pa., Martha, W728; BLWt.26624-160-55
DEFREEST/DEFORREST, David M., N.Y., Rachel, W16560
DEGALES, Michael, Pvt., Mass., BLWt.4027 iss. 1/17/1793 to Samuel Emery
DeGARMO, Matthew, N.Y., S23599
DeGARNIO, Matthew, See DeGARMO
DeGOLYER, James, N.Y., S44141
Joseph, N.Y., S12744
DeGRAAF, Isaac, N.Y., S23193
John, N.Y., See DeGRAF
DeGRAF, John, N.Y., S15090, b. 8/17/1754
DeGRAFF, John, N.Y., R2846, b. 2/7/1756 in Kings Co., N.Y.; in 1832 res. in Florida, Montgomery Co., N.Y.; d. 3/19/1833
Michael, N.Y., Jane, R2844
DEGRAFFENRIED/DEGRAFFENREED, Vincent, Va., Martha Green, R2845
DeGRAFT, John, N.Y., S28711, b.1760 Schenectady, N.Y.; Res. in 1832 was Camillus, Onondaga Co., N.Y.; d.2/22/1838
DEGRAW, Luke, N.Y., S23191
DeGROAT, John, Cont., N.Y., S18378
DeGROOT, Cornelius, N.Y., Maria/Mary, W19543
Jacob, N.J., S811
William, N.J., Ann, W417
DEGROTE, John, Pvt., Lamb's Artillery, N.Y., BLWt.7073 iss. 8/20/1790 to Wm. Cumming, ass.
DEGROVE, John, Qtrmaster Sgt., Crane's Cont. Artillery, Mass. BLWt.4060 iss. 10/16/1789 to Benj. Harris
DEHAISH/DEHARSH/DAHARSH, Philip, N.Y., S22730
DEHARSH, Philip, See DEHAISH
DEHART, Abraham, Pvt., Pa., BLWt.9245 iss. 5/15/1792
Abraham, Pa., S39426
Cornelius, N.J., S12769; BLWt.26350-160-55
Cyrus/Cyrus D., N.J., S5426; BLWt.557-300-Capt. Iss. 7/9/1790. No papers
James, N.J., Ann, W7006
Samuel, Pa., S35892
Winant, N.J., S813
DEHAVEN, Edward, Pa., S35891
Isaac, Cont., Va., S8318
DEHM, William, Pa., S5344
DEHOUSE, Edward, Va., Polly, W8664
DEHUFF, Abraham, Pa., BLWt.575-300-Capt. Iss. 7/13/1795. No papers
John, Cont., Pa., S2164

DEILEY/DEILI, Daniel, Pa., S42156
DEILY, George, Pa., Maria Elizabeth, W3520
Philip, Pa., S5340
DEINOR, Jacob, Va., BLWt.2194-100
DEIS, John, Cont., N.Y., Pa., S42149
DEISKY/DEASKY/DESKY, Leiman/Leaman/Leeman, N.J., S35886
DeKalb, John, Cont., Bavaria, See KALB
DeKAY, Charles, Va. Sea Service, R34. Acc. No. 837-Va. State Navy, U.S. File, Va. Half Pay
DeKELLEY, Theodore, Cont., N.H., Naomi, R5832
DEKLAMAN, Charles, Va. R13678; Va. Half Pay
DEKLANMAN, Charles, See DEKLAMAN
de la BAUME/BAUME, Joseph, Cont. French, R2856
de la COLOMBE, Louis Ange, Cont. French, BLWt.2292-300. Iss. 11/11/1842
DELAMARTER/DILAMATER/DELAMEATER
John, N.Y., Elizabeth, R2849
DELAMATER, Isaac, N.Y., Abigail, W20980
John, Pvt., N.Y., BLWt.7069 iss. 9/24/1791 to Platt Rogers, ass.
John S., N.Y., S43493
Samuel, N.Y., S12749
DELAMETER, Johannis, N.Y., Elizabeth, W17719
DeLANCEY, Abraham, N.Y., S43474
DELAND, Jacob, Mass., S43495
DELANEY/DULANY, Benjamin, Va., S2527
DELANO, Aaron, Ct., Cont., Mass., Anna, W19171
Alpheus, Mass., Peggy, W22932
Amaziah, Mass., Betsey Leighton former wid., W2817; BLWt. 12561-160-55
Isaac, Mass., Elizabeth W., W19160
Jabez, Mass., S35245
Jepthah, Cont., Mass., Sarah, W7008; BLWt.39485-160-55
Jesse, Mass., Margaret, W19159
Jonathan, Ct., S39429
Jonathan, Mass., Ruth, W22926
Lois, former wid. of Thomas Coats, Ct., which see
Malachi, Mass., S5342
Nathan, N.Y., S15093
Oliver, Mass., Mary, W10736
Philip, Mass., S34321
Philip, Mass., Sarah, W14607
Reuben, Mass., S5341
Seth, Mass., S15802
Susanna, former wid. of Ephraim Everson, Mass., which see
Thomas, Ct., N.Y., S23194
Thomas, Mass., R2852
DELANOY, Ellen, see claim of Abraham Ressequie, Ct. & Richard Hill, Mass. She was the former wid. of each.
John, N.Y., R2854
DELANY, John, Md., S46438; BLWt.

DELANY (continued)
1343-100
Martin, Pa., S39425; BLWt. 1056-100
DELAP, Henry, Va., S6793
James, N.J., S32215
DELAPLAINE, James, Va., BLWt. 600-200-Lt. Iss. 6/29/1789
DeLAVAN, Daniel, N.Y., S43483
DELAVAN, John, N.Y., Martha, W15764
John, Pa., Barbara, R2855
Nathaniel, N.Y., Mary Nelson, former wid., W17396
DELAY, Nathan, Cont., Mass., S35241
DELEAN/DELAN, Daniel, N.H., R2850
DELEMATTER, Henry/Hendrick, N.Y., R13726
DELEMORE, Robert, N.J. See ELMORE
DELESDERNIER, Lewis Frederick, Mass., Sophia, W4941; BLWt.17563-160-55
DELEWAY/DELAWAY, John, N.H., S39437
DELEZENNE/DELEZEN, Christopher/ Joseph, Corps of Engrs., Mary, W10725; BLWt.633-300 iss. 8/7/ 1789 to Richard Platt, ass.
DELIFORCE, Joseph, Va., Catharine, R2848
DeLIGNEY, Peter, Pa., S34743
DELINE, Uriah/Ryer, N.Y., Mary, W25531; BLWt.32228-160-55
DELINGER/DELLINGER, Frederick, Cont., Pa., Mary Ann, W24048
DELISLE, John, Pvt., Hazen's Regt., BLWt.12983 iss. 10/12/ 1790
DELLARIDGE, Jacob, Pvt., Hazen's Regt., BLWt.12997 iss. 7/6/ 1791 to Anthony Musegening, ass.
DELLINGER, Christian, Va., R2857
John, N.C., Barbara, W19180
DeLOMANGNE, Jean Baptiste, Cont. France, See LOMAGNE
DELONG, Daniel, N.Y., S10556
Francis, N.C., S34741; BLWt. 33761-160-55
John, Pa., S43498
Joseph, Cont., N.Y., Nancy, W27517. Alleged wid., Mary, also applied for pension and was rejected. See papers within
DELOZEAR, Asa, Va., BLWt.12080-100-Pvt. Iss. 7/9/1794. No papers
DELZELL, William, Pa., S43478
DEMAN, Isaac, N.Y., S10555
DEMANDER, James, R.I., BLWt. 3078-100-Pvt. Iss. 5/22/1790 to John Ramsey, ass. No papers
DeMARAINVILLE/DeMARIANVILLE, Charles, R.I., S42152
DEMARAY, David, N.Y., R2859
DeMARCELLIN, Anthony, Pa. See MARCELLIN
DEMAREE, John, Va., Jane, W7004; BLWt.26098-160-55
DeMARESQUELLE, Lewis Ansart, Cont., French, Catharine, See ANSART
DEMAREST, John, N.J., Anna, W455
John, N.J., R2860

DEMAREST (continued)
Peter, N.J., Sally, W27879; BLWt.32236-160-55
Peter D., N.J., S990
Philip, N.J., S29114
Samuel, N.J., S15081
DEMARY, Ezekiel, N.H., BLWt. 3071-100-Pvt. Iss. 2/3/1792 to Nathan White, ass.
Ezekiel, N.H., R2863
Thomas, N.H., Rebecca, W16108
DEMASS/DUMAS/DUMASS, Peter, Cont., Mass., Mary, W21012; BLWt.1617-100
DeMASTERS, Edward, Va., See MASTERS
James, S.C., Va., Mary, R2861
John, Va., Martha, W3394
DEMELT, Barnet, N.J., S31646
deMERANVILLE, Simeon, Mass., S15403
DEMEREST, Gilliam, N.J., Bridget, W16952
DEMERETT, Samuel, N.H., Anne Clark, BLWt.67553-160-55
DEMERITT, Daniel, N.H., Sarah, BLWt.16138-160-55
Robert, N.H., S17925
DEMING, Alpheus, N.H., S17383
Andres, Cont., Mass., Hannah, W16235
Andrew, Crane's Cont. Artillery, Mass., BLWt.4070-100-Pvt. Iss. 10/31/1791. No papers
Benjamin, Mass., S18799
Chauncey, ?, Steuben Co., N.Y. res. in 1834, R2864
Daniel, Mass., N.Y., S15092
David, Ct., Ann, W2599; BLWt. 14961-160-55
David, N.Y., R2865
Davis, Ct., Elizabeth Ann, See DEMMING
Edmund, Ct., Bethiah, See DAMAN
Elijah, Ct., Lucy, W17717
Gideon, Ct., Mass., S10552
James, Ct., R2866
John, Ct., b.1749; Elizabeth, W14606
John, N.Y., Ann, W16556
Jonathan, Ct., S39428; BLWt. 745-100
Julius, Ct., S17381
Pownal, Ct., Cont., Mehitable D. Colton, former wid., W20894; BLWt.8463-160-55. BLWt.537-200-Lt. Iss. 4/22/1796 to Mehitable Deming, admix. marked "entered 22nd Feb., 1815".
Prosper, Mass., S9844
Simeon, Mass., R2867
Simeon, N.Y., Mary, W22928
Solomon, Mass., S3275
Stephen, Ct., S37883
Theron, Ct., S31648
Wait, Ct., Ruth Morey, former wid., W17135
William, Mass., S46032
Zebulon, N.Y., R2868
DEMINT/DEMENT, Jarret, Pa., S30984
DeMIRE, John, N.Y., W19170

DEMLER, Henry, Col. Lamb's Regt. of Artillery; BLWt.552-200-Lt. Iss. 10/12/1790 to David Brooks & Richard Platt, exs. No papers
DEMMING, Andrew, See DEMING
Davis, Ct., Elizabeth Ann, W17716
Stephen, Pvt., Ct., BLWt.5719 iss. 4/11/1792 to Jonas Prentice
Thomas, Ct., See DENNISON
DEMMON, Amos, Mass. See DEMMONS
Jason, Mass., Lucy, See DAMON
John, Nichola's Regt. of Invalids, BLWt.13025. Iss. 6/20/1789. No papers
Thomas, Ct., R2880 , See DENNISON
DEMMONS, Amos, Mass., BLWt.4011-100-Pvt. Iss. 4/19/1792 to Isaac Bronson. No papers. See "Mass. Soldiers & Sailors".
DEMONEY, Henry, N.J., Mary, W20976
DEMONS, Gamaliel, Mass., Helena, W24030
DEMOREST, Peter, N.Y., S15082
DEMOSS, Andrew, Va., R2869
John, Va., Lucy, W9832; BLWt. 60-100
Peter, Va., S10558
DEMOTT, Isaac, N.Y., R2870
Peter, N.J., Mary, W1733; BLWt. 36503-160-55
Richard, N.Y., S44140
William, Cont., N.Y., S43492
William, Lamb's Art. N.Y., BLWt.7087-Fifer. Iss. 8/14/1790
DEMOUNT, Hanyost, See DEMOUT
DEMOUT, Hanyost/John Joseph, N.Y. Sarah Fisher, former wid., W25579
DEMPSEY, Charles, Pa., BLWt.9246-100-Pvt. Iss. 7/9/1789
David C., Va., Peggy, W727
Dennis, Del., Mary, W3076; BLWt. 918-100
John, Va., S34744
Richard, Del., S34327
Sampson, Pa., BLWt.9274-100-Pvt. Iss. 7/18/1793 to Wm. Ripton, ass.
Sampson, Pa., S39432
Thomas, N.Y., Mary, W1574
Thomas, Pa., BLWt.9326-100. Iss. 6/20/1789. No papers
Timothy, Pa., BLWt.9262-100-Pvt. Iss. 7/9/1789. No papers
DENBO, Cornelius, N.H., S22723
DENEAN, William, N.J., BLWt.8272-100-Fifer. Iss. 9/12/1789
DENEEN, James, N.J., S2162
DENEGER, George, N.Y., S44136
DENER, George Frederick, S.C., Christiana, W8667; BLWt.24168-160 -55
DENGES, Henry, Pa., R2871
DENHAM, Benajah, R.I., S30379
David, N.C., Fanny, W27540; BLWt. 56853-160-55
Harden/Hardin, N.C., S30985
DENIGHT, James, N.J., S34317
DENIKE, Davis, N.J., S2172
Samuel, N.J., S635
DENIO, Aaron, Mass., Vt., S15404
Frederick, Mass., S12748

DENISON, Abigail, former wid. of Asa Gillet, Ct., R4032
Amos, Ct., S39438
Avery, Ct., Prudence, W20984
Bebee/Beebe, Ct., S9328
Chauncy, Ct. See DENNISON
Daniel, Ct., Lucy, W17718
David, Ct., Vt., S5335
Elizabeth, former wid. of Wm. Jones, N.Y., which see
George, Ct., S10551
George, Ct., S12768
Gilbert, Ct., S15805
Henry, Ct., Cont., Navy, Mary, W15890
James, Ct., S37881
James P., Ct., S15079
Jedediah, Ct., S15084
Joseph, Cont., Ct., S10564
Nathan, Ct. Sea Service, S22203
Robert, Mass., S29754
Samuel, Ct., R2878
DENISTON, Daniel, N.Y., See DENNISTON
DENKINS/DINKINS, Joshua, N.C., S3278
DENMAN, Matthias, N.J., S2512
DENMARK, Burnardus/Barnardus, Ct., N.J., S43482
John, Pa., BLWt.9295-100-Pvt. Iss. 7/9/1789. No papers
DENNARD, John, S.C., R2872
DENNESTON, James, Mass., See DENNISON
DENNET/DENNETT, Ebenezer, Mass., S18375
Joseph, Cont., Mass., Sarah, W22931
Shuah, former wid. of Stephen Ferguson, Mass., which see
DENNETT, Cynthia, former wid. of Gale/Gail Cole, Cont., Mass., N.H., which see
John, N.H., BLWt.510-300-Capt. Iss. 9/9/1789. No papers
Rebecca, former wid. of John Holland, Mass., which see
DENNEY, Elijah, N.C., S2513; BLWt.15174-160-55
James, Pa., S22728
John, Va., R2875
DENNING, Elijah, Ct., BLWt.5698-100-Pvt. Iss. 4/8/1797 to John Steel
Jona, Ct., BLWt.5688 iss. 9/13/1796
William, Cont., Pa., S42150
DENNIS, Adonijah, Mass., S29752
Andrew, Pa., S44129
Anna, former wid. of Stephen Billings, Ct., which see
Benjamin, Mass., Navy, S34318
Daniel, Pa., BLWt.1682-200
Edward, Md., S30377
Enos, N.J., S35242
Henry, ?, res. Worcester Co., Md. in 1852, R2876
Jacob, Pa., S34735
James, Mass., Eunice, W686; BLWt.32229-160-55
James, Pa., R13707
John, ?, Mass. agency, Dis. No papers

DENNIS (continued)
John, Cont., Mass., Abigail W20973
John, N.J., Sarah, W8196; BLWt. 26790-160-55
John, Lamb's Art., N.Y., BLWt. 7077-100-Pvt. Iss. 7/10/1790 to John Quackinboss, ass.
Jonas, Mass., Sea Service, S17382
Josiah, Md., R2877
Lydia, former wid. of William Pritchard, Mass., which see
Michael, Pa., BLWt.9321. Iss. 7/13/1789. No papers
Minard, N.Y., Elizabeth, W16558
Moses, Mass., Sarah, W15891
Myndut, N.Y., BLWt.7018-100-Pvt. Iss. 6/6/1791 to Alven Purdy, ass.
Philip, N.Y., Anna, W20966
Philip, Pa., Susanna, W9406; BLWt.2235-100
Reuben, N.J., R13708
Samuel, Mass., Anna, W20968
Thomas, R.I., Lydia, W20971
William, Cont., Va., S39433; BLWt.1792-100
William, Va., See William Dennis HAMPTON
DENNISON, Chauncy, Ct., Sarah, W24055
David, Mass., S29755
Henry, Ct., Mary, See DENISON
Isaac, Mass., Sarah, W24056
James, Cont., Mass., S43485; BLWt.1558-100
Prince, Ct., Dis. No papers
Thomas, Ct., R2880
William Ct., BLWt.5679-Cpl. Iss. 9/26/1789
DENNISS, Russell, Ct., S15804
Samuel, Navy, Ct. agency & res., S37884
DENNISSON, Andrew, Pa., S2168
Christopher, N.Y., S22207
Matthew, Cont., N.Y., Margaret, W16561
DENNISTON, Daniel, N.Y., Elizabeth, W19168; BLWt.549-200-Lt. Iss. 6/22/1790. No papers
George I. or J., N.Y., Margaret W10723; BLWt.547-200-Lt. Iss. 9/2/1790. No papers
James, Pa., BLWt.9324-100. Iss. 4/23/1793. No papers
John, ?, N.J. agency., Dis. No papers
Matthew, Crane's Cont. Arty. Mass., BLWt.4066. Iss. 4/11/1795. No papers
Thomas, N.Y., BLWt.7030-100. Iss. 11/16/1791. No papers
William, N.J., Pa., Elizabeth, W2924
DENNY, Abraham, N.C., R2882
Absalom, Ct., Bethia, W20969
Charles, N.Y., S32213
David, Pa., Martha/Patty, W9834; BLWt.97058-160-55. 4 Cont. documents
Ebenezer, Pa., BLWt.565-200-Lt. Iss. 10/17/1789. No papers

DENNY (continued)
Elijah, N.C., See DENNEY
Henry, N.J., S28710
Isaac, Mass., Grace D. Sargent, former wid., R----. She was pensioned as wid. of other husb., John Sargent. Mass., which see
Joseph, N.C., S8323
Peter, Pvt., N.Y., BLWt.7031 iss. 12/15/1790 to Thomas Scott, admr.
Richard, N.Y., S16001
Robert, Md., BLWt.589-200-Lt. Iss. 9/1/1789. No papers
Samuel, Va., S32212
Walter, Pa., R2879
William, Va. & 1790-91, Mary, R13730; BLRej. 315946
DENOON, John, Md., S44133; BLWt.11135-100. Iss. 3/11/1791. No papers
DeNOYELLES/DeNOYELLE, Ann, former wid. of David Burns, N.Y., which see
DENSLOW, Benjamin, Ct., S27671
Eli, Ct., Polly, W25528; BLWt. 104-60-55
Elijah, Ct., S15087
Martin, Lt., Ct., Roxavene Wright, former wid., W6593; BLWts.3191-160-55 & 540-200 iss. --/26/1790
DENSMOOR, Samuel, N.H., Mary, See DINSMOOR
DENSMORE, John, Mass., S45727
Samuel, Mass., See DINSMORE
Thomas, Ct., Hannah, W2601
Thomas, Mass., See DINSMORE
DENSON, John, Md., BLWt.11136-100. Iss. 9/13/1799 to Asahel Phelps, ass.
Benjamin, N.C., R2887
John, N.C., Va. Sea Service, S3279
Thomas, S.C., R13729
DENT, George, Md., S12755
John, Md., Eleanor, W9403
John, Va., Margaret, W4663
DENTON, Amos, N.Y., S44139
Daniel, Ct., S43486; BLWt. 1747-100
David, Va., Rachael/Rachel, W8662
John, N.C., Va.?, Mary, W352
John, Va., S41503
John, Va., R2888
Thankful, former wid. of John Winn, Cont., which see
William, Va., S39431
DENTZLER, Christian, Pa., Margaret, W3134
DENWOOD, Levin, Md., BLWt.583-400-Surg. Iss. 6/4/1789. No papers
DEO, Elias, N.Y., S9326
DEON, Jabez, N.Y., See DEAN
DEOPERVINE/TAPERVINE, John, N.Y., S39439
DEP, Hannah, former wid. of Joshua Simmons, N.Y., which see

DEPEW, Abraham, N.Y., Catharine, W19169
Cornelius, N.Y., S15080
David, N.J., Mary, See DEPUE
Hannah, former wid. of Amos Kniffen, N.Y., which see
Henry, N.Y., BLWt.7023-100. Iss. 7/9/1790 to Elias Benjamin, ass.
Henry, N.Y., S43484
Isaac, N.Y., See DEPUY
Isaac, Va., R2892
John, N.Y., R2890
DEPOISTER/DEPOYSTER, John, Del., S32214
DePONTGIBAUT, See PONTIGBEAU in Heitman's Reg., p.445; BLWt.637-300-Capt. & Aide-de-Camp. Iss. 10/20/1798. No papers. Also noted as "Certified & returned to Secy. of the Treas., the 24th Oct. 1837".
DEPOY, Christopher, Va., S2166
DEPP, William, Va., S2511
DEPRIEST, Randolph, S.C., Amy, R2987
Robert, Va., Patsey, R2986
William, N.C., S8319
DEPUE, David, N.J., R2891
Henry, ?, N.J. res. during Rev. War, R2893
John, N.Y., S44134
DEPUTRON, William, Cont., R.I., S34325
DEPUY, Aaron, Pa., S5333
Benjamin, N.Y., S31645
Cornelius, N.Y., S29115
Isaac, N.Y., Catharine, W2769
James, N.Y., R2894
James, N.Y., R2895
John, N.Y., S23195
John, N.Y., S23196
Moses, N.Y., Hellena, W19203
DEQUISE, Charles, See DUZUA
DERBY, Benjamin, Ct., See DARBY
Benjamin, Ct., Esther, W26207
Charles, Mass., Tabitha, See DARBY
Edward, Mass., S43479
John, Mass., See DARBY
Jonathan, N.H., Vt., Sarah, W16950
Samuel, Mass., Hannah, See DARBY
Samuel, Mass., BLWt.515-400-Maj. Iss. 1/10/1797 to Allen Crocker ass. No papers
Simeon, N.H., Vt., S16363
DEREMIAH, John, Va., S36504
DEREVAUX, Francis, Hazen's Regt. BLWt.12989-100. Iss. 8/7/1789. No papers
DeREVERE, Cornelius, N.Y., Sarah, W24057
DERING, Henry, Va., See DARING
DERMONT, Stephen, Ct., BLWt.5701-Sgt. Iss. 10/16/1789 to Theodosius Fowler. No papers
DERMOTT, Richard, Pvt., N.Y., BLWt.7027 iss. 7/26/1791
DERONDE, John, N.Y., See RONDE
deROSENTHAL, Gustavus H., Pa.
deROSENTHAL (continued)
See Gustavus H. HENDERSON
DERR, Christian, Pa. See DORR
John, Cont., Pa., S12762
John, Pa., S22205
Matthias, Pa., Elizabeth, W4940
DERREBERRY, Andrew, N.C., See DERRYBERRY
DERRICK, Ephraim, Ct., Elizabeth, W25529
James, N.J., BLWt.766-100
John, Pa., R2899
Thomas, Del., BLWt.2163-100. Warrant No.2163 was lost & Warrant No. 2183 iss.
DERRINGTON, William, Md., See DUNNINGTON
DERROUGH, John, Va., S44137
DERRY, John, Mass., Rebecca, W14604
Peter, Mass., S39434
DERRYBERRY, Andrew, N.C., Sarah, W10312
DERSHUM, Ludwig, Pa., S2167
DERUMPLE, James, Mass., Azeba/ Azuba, W24846
Robert, Pa., BLWt.9260-100. Iss. 4/6/1790. No papers
DERUSSY, Thomas, Navy, French, Madeline Beissiere, W20975
DeSt.MARIA, LeVacher, S.C., BLWt. 615-300-Capt. Iss. 6/4/1792 to David Cay, ass. See Heitman's p.348. No papers
DeSAUSSURE, Louis, S.C., BLWt. 1585-200
DESBROW, Henry, Ct. See DISBROW
Joshua, Ct., See DISBROW
Justus, Ct., See DISBROW
DESEARN, Frederick, N.C. See DESERN
de SEGOND, James, Cont., See SEGOND
DESERN, Frederick, N.C., S38660 BLWt.119-100
DESHASURE/DESHAZER/DESHAZURE, Henry, Ga., S.C., b. Va., S16362
DeSHAY, William, N.J., S28709
DESHAZO, William, Va., Jane, W1832; BLWt.29739-160-55
DESHLER, Charles, Pa., S22204
DESHON, James, Mass., Catharine, W24052; BLWt.7070-160-55
Moses, Mass., S29753
DESILVIA, William, Mass. See DECILVA
DESKINS, Daniel, Va., S36501
DESKY, Leaman, N.J., BLWt. 8241-100. Iss. 7/24/1796
Leeman/Leiman/Leamon, N.J., See DEISKY/DEASKY
DESMOND, John, Invalid Regt., BLWt.13018-100. Iss. 3/19/ 1792 to John Snell, ass.
DeSPAIN, Peter/SPAIN, Peter D., Va., S14559; BLWt.39229-160-55
DESPERITT, Henry, Pa., BLWt.9328-100. Iss. 3/11/1791
DETEMER, John, Pa. See DATAMER
DETTER, Michael, Invalid Regt., BLWt.13021-100. Iss. 8/13/1789 No papers
DETWILER, John, Pa., See DUTWEILER
DEUEL/DUEL/DEWEL, Benjamin, N.Y., Hannah, W8666
DEUSENBERY/DEUSENBURY/DUSENBERRY, William, Cont., N.J. agency & res., S10554
DEUSENBURY/DUSENBURY, Gabriel, N.Y., Elizabeth, W22927; BLWt.26374-160-55
DEUSLER, John, N.Y., Catharine, See DUESLER
DeVALTZ, Peter, N.Y., BLWt.7052-100. Iss. 7/20/1790 to Edward Compston, ass. No papers
DeVANBRUN, John LeVacher, Md. See Le VACHER de VANBRUN
DEVANE, James, N.C., S8317
John, N.C., Ann Julan, W3961
Thomas, N.C., Helen, R2901
DEVANEY, Jenkins, N.C., Alice, R2902
DEVANPORT, Squire, Ct., S44118
DEVAUN/DEVON, James, Md., S44132
DEVAUR/DEVOIR/DEVORE, Luke, N.J., S35240; BLWt.160-100
DEVEAUX, Peter, Ga., S37886
DEVENEY, Daniel, Pa., S22724
John, Pa., S42154
DEVENIX/DEVEREX, William, Md. S34736
DEVENS, John, N.J., S34320
DEVENY, Aaron, N.C., S8321
John, Pa., BLWt.9275-100. Iss. 7/9/1789. Notation on file "Not delivered".
DEVER, Patrick, Pa., BLWt.9314-100. Iss. 8/31/1790 to D. Woodbridge, ass.
DEVERAUX, John, Cont., Mass., N.Y., S15402
DEVEREUX, Benjamin P., Mass., Elizabeth, W14605
DEVERICKS/DEVERICK, John, Va., Mary, W7007
DEVERS, James, Va., S17924
DEVETT/DEWITT, John, Crane's Cont. Art., Mass., BLWt. 4068. Iss. 8/1/1796 to Joseph Fosdick
DEVIANCE/DEORANCE, John H., N.Y., BLWt.7059. Iss. 4/6/ 1793 to Uriah Lewis, ass.
DEVIEZE, Abraham, Pa., R2904
DEVIN, Robert, Va., Nancy, W3395; BLWt.13745-160-55
William, Md., Mary, R2906
DEVINE, Hugh, Pa., No papers
DEVINNEY/DEVINY, James, Pa., S2169
DEVINS, John, N.J., BLWt.8233-100. Iss. 5/27/1790 to Jeptha Arrison, ass.
DEVLIN, James, S.C., S39435
DEVOE, Anthony, N.Y., S10562
David, N.Y., S10559
Henry, N.Y., S22726
Isaac, N.Y., Getty, W28975. She was pensioned as former wid. of 1st husb., John D. Schronton/Schonton, N.Y. Mil., War of 1812, Old War

DEVOE (continued)
Wid. File 10727. See papers within. See BLWt.48149-80-50 for War of 1812 serv. of 1st husb.
Jeremiah, Cont., N.Y., S43477
Jeremiah, Va., Lee's Corps, BLWt.12068 & 13038-Pvt. Iss. 7/2/1790
John, N.J., Hellen, W20972; BLWt.26559-160-55 & 39493-160-55 iss. and cancelled.
John, N.Y., S23190
William, N.Y., S22729
William, N.Y., Harriet/Hannah, R2908
DEVOIR, Isaac, Va., BLWt.12066-100 iss. 5/12/1792 to James Morrison, adr.
Luke, N.J., See DEVAUR
DEVOL, Jonathan, R.I., S44131
DEVON, James, Md. See DEVAUN
DEVONS, Leonard, N.J., S2173
DEVOR/DEVORE, David, Pa., R20357
DEVORE, Cornelius, Pa., S34319
Elijah, Pa., R2907
John, N.J., S34328
Luke, N.J., See DEVAUR
DEW, John, N.C., Nancy, W2722. Her 1st husb., John Wright, N.C. also served. See papers within
Thomas, Va., R2909
DEWALL/DUVALL, Thomas, Md., S34315
DEWALT, Michael, Pa., Va., S43489
DEWALTZ, Peter, N.Y. See WALTZ
DEWEES, Isaac, Navy, Pa., S35889
Samuel, Pa., Julia Ann, W9405; BLWt.267-60-55 & 9296-100-Fifer. Iss. 6/28/1799, to Abrm. Bell, ass. No papers
DEWEESE/DEWESE/DEWISE, Hezekiah, N.C., Annis, W7014
DEWETT, George, Md., BLWt.11147-100. Iss. 1/11/1796 to Joshua Ward, ass.
DEWEY, Abijah, Ct., S22725
Abraham, Ct., Cont., S12746
Alpheus, Ct., Lydia, W24050; BLWt.26685-160-55
Andrew, Ct., Betsy Stone, former wid., R10210
Barzilla, Vt., S22199
Daniel, Ct., S17926
Darius, Ct., Jerusha, W1833; BLWt.3802-160-55
David, Ct., Cont., R.I., R2911
Ebenezer, N.H., Vt., S19282
Elias, Mass., R2912
Elijah, Mass., Hannah, W19166
Enos, Ct., R2913
Ezra, Mass., Freelove, R2914
Gideon, Mass., Eunice, W1155; BLWt.19809-160-55
Isaac, Ct., S17379
Jeremiah, Ct., Mass., Vt., S21732
John, Mass., BLWt.4012-100. Iss. 12/18/1789
John Woodward, Ct., Emma, W25530; BLWt.34531-160-55

DEWEY, Josiah, Ct., Lydia, W20981
Martin, N.H., S12767
Oliver, Mass., S8322
Peleg, Ct., S22727
Russell, Mass., S34739
Samuel, Mass., Edith, W25526; BLWt.24763-160-55
Samuel, N.Y., Vt., S9327
Silas, Ct., S15085
Silas, Mass., Sally, R2918
Thomas, Vt., Charity, W19172
Timothy, N.H., S39430
DEWING, Elijah, Cont., Mass., S17384
John, Mass., S29758
Nathan, Mass., S34734
DEWITT, Aaron, N.J., Mary, W456
Abraham, N.Y., Anna, W25525; BLWt.28615-160-55
Abraham, Pa., S31644
Cornelius Depuy, N.Y., Margaret, W19173; BLWt.16112-160-55
Egbert/Egbert D., See WITT
Francis, N.Y., R2919
Garrit/Garret, Ct., Elizabeth, W25522
Jacob, Ct., Martha, W20970
Jacobus, N.Y., S12758
Johannis, N.Y., Annatie, W16951
John, Lamb's Arty., N.Y., BLWt. 7090. Iss. 8/26/1790 to Wm. J. Vreedenburgh, ass. No papers
John, N.Y., S34316
John, N.Y., Mary, W16949
John A., N.Y., Elizabeth, W10730; BLWt.29737-160-55
John C., N.Y., S9846
Martin, S.C., R13728
Moses, N.J., R2921
Nancy, former wid. of George Kelly, Va., which see
Paul, Pa., Elizabeth, W3663; BLWt.26256-160-55
Peter, Md., Va., S30986
Simeon, Cont., N.Y. agcy. S15095
William, N.Y., S12763
William, Pa., S43476
William, Pa., Elizabeth, W729; BLWt.26609-160-55
DEWOLF, Benjamin, Ct., Navy, S43490
Daniel, Ct., S29117
Daniel, Ct., Hannah, W1245; BLWt.14507-160-55
Edward, Ct., Privateer, S15089
John, Privateer, R.I., Sea Service, Ruth, W2476; BLWt. 28634-160-55
Joseph, Ct., S3280
Levi/Levy, Ct., Huldah, See De WOOLF
Peter, Ct., S18377
Samuel, Ct., Susannah, W20978
Seth, Ct., Hannah, See D'WOLF
Stephen, Ct., Privateer, U.S. Navy, Abigail, W2600
DeWOLFE, Elisha, Cont., Ct., S29756
Matthew, Mass., R2924
DeWOOLF, Levi/Levy, Ct., Huldah, W25521; BLWt.3519-160-55
DEWS, William, Va., S8312

DEXTER, Abigail, former wid. of Aaron French, Ct., which see
Benjamin, R.I., Phebe, W14609
Benjamin G., R.I., Mary, W20967
Caleb, Vt., Lucy, W22933
Daniel S., Capt., R.I., S15406; BLWt.513-300 iss. 4/20/1796
David, Mass., S22198
Elisha, Cont., Mass., S30385
Elisha, R.I., Susan, W7011; BLWt.26332-160-55
Eseck, R.I., BLWt.3075-Sgt. Maj. Iss. 4/20/1790
George, R.I., S21735
John, Ct., S23192
John Singer, R.I., BLWt.512-400-Maj. Iss. 4/20/1790. No papers
Joseph, Mass., Mary, W14603
Joseph, R.I., BLWt.3077. Iss. 9/13/1791. No papers
Nathan, Ct., S37889
Nathan, R.I., S18374
Nathaniel Balch, Lucy, R2926, Mass. res. in 1781
Robert, Pa., BLWt.9286-100. Iss. 2/7/1792 to Rosanna Manning, admx.
Stephen, R.I., S21159
Thomas, Cont., Mass., N.Y., S44138
Thomas, Mass., S35244
Thomas, R. I., S37888
Warham, Ct., R---
William, Mass., Betsy Lowe, former wid., W3146
William, R.I., S43481
DEY, Daniel, N.J., S12743
John, N.J., Rebecca, See DAY
John, N.J., Mary, W454
Josiah, N.J., S630
Peter, N.J., S15078
Samuel, Va., S6782
Sarah, former wid. of John Freeman, N.J., which see
William, N.J., Margaret, W913
DEYER, Emanuel, Pa., S22201
DEYGERT/DYGERT, Severenus/Selvenus, N.Y., S23208; b.11/23/1760, res. at enl. Palatine, N.Y.; res. in 1833 Wheeler, Steuben Co., N.Y.
DEYMONT, Hanjost, Pvt., N.Y., BLWt.7053 iss. 11/18/1790
DEYO, Abraham, N.Y., Bridget, W16236
Elias, N.Y., See DEO
Hugh, N.Y., Catharine, W20963
DHIEL, Samuel, Pa. See DEAL
DIAL, Jeremiah, S.C., Ann, W914
Martin, S.C., R13777
DIALL/DIAL, Daniel, N.C., S.C., S41506. See N.A. Acc. No.874-050048. Not Half Pay
DIAMOND, John, S.C., S30991
William, Cont., Mass., Rebecca, W22941; BLWt.24163-160-55
William, N.Y., BLWt.7049-100 Iss. 7/10/1790 to C.C. Elmendorph, ass. No papers
DIAS/DICE/DIES/DYCE, George (colored), Md., S42161; BLWt. 618-100

DIBBEL, Asa, Cont., Vt., Lois, W19176
DIBBLE, Abraham, Ct., R2928
Benjamin, Ct., S15098
Daniel, Ct., Susanna, W17723
Hezekiah, N.Y., Betty, W7021
Israel, Ct., S20337
John, Ct., S15097
Moses, Ct., See DIBOL
DIBLE, John, Ct. See DIBBLE
DIBOL, Moses, Ct.,Elizabeth, W27931
DIBRELL, Anthony, Va., Wilmuth/Wilmouth, W3398
Charles, Va., S21160
DIBRILL, Charles, Va. See DIBRELL
DICK, Alexander, Va., R13751. Va. Half Pay. See N.A. Acc. No. 874-050050. Half Pay
Charles, S.C., Rebecca, W10739
Henry, N.Y., Lenah, W1734; BLWt. 17571-160-55
Jacob, Cont., Pa., Mary, W9407; BLWt.13010-100. Iss. 9/9/1799 No papers
Jacob, Pa., S23601
John, S.C., Margaret, W8668
John, Vt., R2930
DICKASON, Samuel, Pa., Elizabeth, W285. See. N.A. Acc. No. 874-050049. Not Half Pay
DICKEN, Ephraim, Va., S30989
John, Va., Polly/Mary, W1836; BLWt.26595-160-55
Joseph, Va., S3287
Richard, Va., Elizabeth, W4179
William, N.C., Elizabeth, W8197; BLWt.24985-160-55
DICKENS, Arnold, N.Y., Rachel, W17720
James, N.Y., S42160
Thomas, N.C., S41509
William, N.Y., BLWt.7051 iss. 5/19/1790 to Peter Smith, ass. No papers
William, N.Y., S43502
DICKENSON, Edward, Md., S34745
Elijah, Va., S6796
Griffeth, Ga., Va., S20896
Nathaniel, Ct., Lucy, W25540
Simeon, Mass., S30987
DICKERMAN, Enoch, Mass., Rhoda, W9410; BLWt.29740-160-55
John, Vt., Thankful, W7024; BLWt.24905-160-55
Joseph, N.Y., Mary Giddings, former wid., W4205
Peter, Mass., S34746
DICKERSON, Abraham, N.Y., BLWt. 7017-Sgt. Iss. 6/17/1790. No paper
Abraham, N.Y., S12780
Benjamin, Cont., N.Y., S27691 Wounded & carried to Fairfield, Ct.; also married there
Bradock, N.Y., S28714
Charles, Va., Nancy. See DICKINSON
David, N.Y., BLWt.7028-100. Iss. 1/5/1791. No papers
David, N.Y., S44145
John, Cont., Del., Catharine, See DICKINSON

DICKERSON (continued)
Kinzer, Pa., R2933
Moses, N.J., S867
Nathaniel, N.Y., Sarah, W20986
Robert, Va., S46335; BLWt.1385-100
Solomon, Md., S30990
Thomas, Pa., S44148
Walter, N.J., Sarah, W25543; BLWt.32324-160-55
DICKESON, Isham, N.C., Charlotte, Debord, former wid., R2823
DICKEY, Adam, Cont., N.H., Jennett/Jane, R2934
Charles, Pa., S42158
David, Ga., N.C., S.C., S6798
David, N.C., S2522
Ebenezer, N.C., Mary,W8669
Eleazer, Mass., S35249
Elias, Mass., N.H., Jennett, W20990
James, Mass., N.H., Mary M., W1156; BLWt.17893-160-55
James, N.H., BLWt.3063-100 Iss. 3/25/1790. No papers
James, N.H., Lydia, W1735; BLWt.56504-160-55
Jesse, N.H., R2935
John, N.C., Elizabeth, W3962
John, Pa., S22211
Matthew, N.H., Mary, W16562
Moses, Pa., S8331
Peter, Ct., S23600
Robert, Pa., Va., S2174
Robert, Pa., S30988
Thomas, Pa., S2175
William, Cont., N.H., Sarah, W22945; b. 1/1755 Londonderry, Rockingham Co., N.H. and res. there at enl. In 1832 had lived over 40 yrs. in Hillsboro, N.H. & d. there 8/9/1842
William, N.H., S45729. Res. in Londonderry, N.H. during Rev. War. Res. 1820 in Francestown, Hillsboro, N.H., age 72 yrs. D. 10/31/1825
DICKIN, Joseph N., Va., R2948
DICKINS, Arnold, N.Y., Rachel, See DICKENS
Trustum, R.I., S17388
DICKINSON, Aaron, Mass., R2937
Asahel, Ct., Lucy, W19179
Cesar, Mass., See BAILEY
Charles, N.Y., S28713
Charles, N.Y., S29119
Charles, Va., Nancy, R2940
Consider, Mass., Esther, BLWt.56860-160-55
Cotton, Mass., Olive, W24856
David, Ct., Sybil, W17725
David, Mass., R2936
Ebenezer, Mass., S18801
Edmund B., Va., BLWt.523-400-Maj. Iss. 1/14/1792 to Robt. Gibbons & Agnes R. Wills, heirs. Also recorded as above under BLWt. 2562, except words "legal reprs. are used instead of "heirs". No papers
Elijah, Ga., S39443

DICKINSON (continued)
Elijah, Mass., Jerusha, W14623
Francis, Mass., Olive, W19175
Friend, Ct., S44147
George, Md., S4277
Gideon/Gidion, N.Y., S39440
Ichabod, Ct., N.Y., S17385
Isaac, N.J., See DICKISSON
James, Mass., Priscilla, W14622
Jesse, Ct., S42157
Joel, Mass., Eunice, W22946
John, Cont., Del., Catherine, W7026; BLWt.32232-160-55
John, Mass., S10566
John, N.Y., S12776
John, Pa., N.J., S991
John, Va., R2938
Jonathan, Mass., S29120
Josiah, Ct., Lucy, W24062
Levi, Ct., Privateer, Bethiah, W14619
Lydia, former wid. of Timothy Rose, Mass., which see
Nathaniel, Ct., See DICKENSON
Oliver, Ct., Anna, W17726
Ozias, Ct., Mary, W17721
Rebecca, former wid. of Joshua McMaster, Mass., which see
Reuben, Mass., Ruth, W26660
Samuel, Ct., Hannah, W16955
Samuel, Mass., S30386
Seth, Mass., S10574
Silvanus, Cont., Ct., Mary, W17724
Simeon, Ct., Privateer, S17386
Simeon, Mass., See DICKENSON
Solomon, Ct., Elizabeth, W1736
Solomon, Mass., S19283
Thomas, Mass., N.Y., S18379
Thomas, Va., Ann, W4178
Thomas, Va., Jemima, W27891; BLWt.14672-160-55
Timothy, Mass., Margarett, W14624
Varsel, N.Y., S44149
Vicarious, Va., S39442
Wait Still, Ct., BLWt.5699-100 Iss. 3/11/1791 to Isaac Bronson. No papers
Waitstill, Ct., Cont., S17928
William, Va., S8332
William, Va., Mary, R2939
DICKISON, Isaac, N.J., BLWt.8260-100. Iss. 4/24/1795. No papers
Nathaniel, N.C., S3289
DICKISSON, Isaac, N.J., Margaret, W3397
DICKMAN, John, Mass., Phebe, R2941
Richard, Lamb's Arty. N.Y., BLWt. 7083. Iss. 6/3/1789. No papers
DICKS, David, Ct., S43500
George, Pa., BLWt.9277-100. Iss. 6/28/1792. No papers
Isaac, Va., S34748
John, Va., S16762
DICKSON, Benjamin, N.Y., S22210
James, N.Y., S22208
James, S.C., Hannah, R2942
Jesse, N.C., S.C., S2521
Joel, N.C., S41508
John, N.C., Mary, W25541
John, Pa., BLWt.9315-Sgt. in

DICKSON (continued)
Proctor's Arty. Iss. 7/31/1789 to M. McConnell, ass. No papers
John, Va., S41507
Jonas, Mass., S35248
Joseph, Ct., Cont., Mercy, W22939
Joseph, Cont., N.C., S41505; BLWt.1103-100
Joseph, Md., R2944
Josiah, Va., S16765
Miles, Ct., Sarah Clark, former wid., W20881
Robert, N.Y., Ruth Young, former wid., R13762
Thomas, Ct., W1397
Thomas, N.C., Ann, W3963
Thomas, Pa., R2945
William, Mass., Rachel, W19177
William, N.Y., Sarah, W22940
William, N.C., S3288
William, Pa., See DIXON
William, S.C., Sarah Bayliss/Bayless, former wid., W328
DICTRICK, Peter, Pa., BLWt.595-150-Ens. Iss. 7/22/1791 to David Dictrick. No papers
DIDDEY, Jeremiah, Pa., BLWt.9308-Pvt. "in Moylan's Dragoons". Iss. 10/28/1789 to M. McConnell ass.
DIDDLE, John, Va., S5349
DIDDLESTON, Thomas, Va., S35894
DIDO, Franz/Francis, Pa., Eleanor, W7017; see N.A. Acc. No.874-050053. Not Half Pay.
DIDSON, Benjamin, Cont., Mass., Polly, W2602
Seth, Mass., Privateer, Bridget, W22947
DIEFENDORFF, Jacob H., N.Y., S10567
John, N.Y., Catharine, See DUFENDORF
John Jacob, N.Y., S12772
DIEFFENDERFER, David, Pa., S3291
DIEFFENDORPH, Jacob, N.Y., Dis. No papers
DIEHL, Jacob, Pa. See DIRL
Samuel, Pa., Isabella, See DEAL
DIEL, Samuel, Pa., See DEAL
DIES, George, Md., S42161; See DIAS
DIETER, John, Pa., Magdalena, W3180
DIETRICH/DITRICH, Georg/George, Pa., S42167
DIETRICK, Michael, Mate in General Hosp., BLWt.621-300 iss. 10/9/1789
DIETZ, Adam, N.Y., Margaret, R2847
Johan Jost/John Joseph, N.Y., S45837
DIFFEE, John, N.C., R2949
DIFFENDERFER, Jacob, Pa., See DEFFENDERFER
Peter, Md., Pa., S12771
DIFFORN, John, N.C. See DAFFRON
DIGBY, Simon, Pa., BLWt.9266-100. Iss. 3/10/1795 to Robt. Hunter, ass. No papers
DIGGERS, Derbrick, S.C., BLWt.

DIGGERS (continued)
12098, 12993-100. Iss. 11/24/1795 No papers
DIGGES, Dudley, Sr., Va., S8328; See N.A. Acc. No. 874-05001. Half Pay
Edward, Va., See DIGGS
William, Va., S8327
DIGGINS, Martin, Ct., Lydia P., W540; BLWt.9187-160-55
DIGGS, Edward, Va., R13760; Va. Half Pay. See N.A. Acc. No.874-050052. Half Pay.
John, Va., Dolly, R2950
William, Cont., Mass. See DIX
William, Va., See DIGGES
DIKE, Adin, N.H., Vt., S15411
Benjamin, Mass., Susannah, W3523
Calvin, N.H., Vt., S15410
Daniel, Jr., Mass., BLWt.4025-100. Iss. 12/12/1792 to Daniel King. No papers
Daniel, Mass., S39449
Daniel, Mass., Molly, R2951
Henry, Va., S44146
Jonathan, Mass., Abigail, W24859
Nathan, Cont., N.Y., S44144
Nicholas, Mass., Joanna, W22943
Samuel, Vt., S21170, BLWt.5456-160-55
William, Ct., S10572
DIKEMAN, Daniel, Ct., S15408
Eliphalet, Ct., Huldah, W25542; BLWt.7056-160-55
Frederick/Frederic, Ct., Cont., S39447
Hezekiah, Ct., Esther, W25545
Levi, Ct., Rebecca, W24857
DIKINS, Richard, N.Y., Mercy, W19143
DILAMATER, John, N.Y. See DELAMARTER
DILDAY, Amos, N.C., S6794
Joseph, Va., (?), S6795
DILDINE, Jonathan, N.C., Nancy, W1396; BLWt.26677-160-55
DILKS, Samuel, N.J., Nancy, R2952
DILL, Archibald, N.C., S3285
Daniel, Mass., Mary, W27419; BLWt.19819-160-55
George, Cont., German, S21736
James, Pa., BLWt.593-200-Lt. Iss. 12/24/1794 to Thomas Dill, admr. No papers
John, Cont., N.Y., S10569
John, N.C., S8326
Lemuel, Cont., Mass., Milcah, W19178; BLWt.699-100
Nicholas, Lamb's Arty., N.Y., BLWt.7080 iss. 7/16/1790 to John Daniel, ass. No papers
Reynolds/Runnells, N.C., Va., Evaline, R2953; BLWt.34598-160-55
Richard, N.C., S3273
Thomas, Mass., S34747
Thomas, Pa., S42166
DILLARD, Benjamin, Va., S1803
James, N.C., Sarah, W7020
James, S.C., S6797
James, Va., Jane, W7019
John, N.C., S3286

DILLARD (continued)
John, Va., S31649
John, Va., Keturah, W19174; BLWt.2487-100
DILLE, David, Va., & 1793-94, Mary, W7018
DILLEBER, John, Ct., S12747
DILLEN, Benjamin, Va., S8329
Henry, Va., S45891
DILLENBACH, Andrew, N.Y., Catharine Zielley, former wid., R2955. Her 2nd husb., Capt. John Zielley, also served.
DILLENTAGH, Henry, N.J., See DILLENTASH
DILLENTASH, Henry, N.J., Dinah, R2957
DILLENTUSH, Henry, See DILLENTASH
DILLEY, Ephraim, N.J., S18380
DILLINGHAM, Benjamin, ?, Ct. res. in 1819; R---
Elisha, Mass., S38661
Elizabeth, former wid. of John Pettingill, Cont., Mass. which see
John, Cont., Mass., R.I., S35247 d.1819.
John, Mass., S15815, living 1832
Joshua, Mass., Navy, Marcy,W24059
Lemuel, Navy, Mass., or Me.,S29760
Nathan, Mass., S29759
Paul, Mass., Hannah, W19181
DILLMAN, Andrew/Andres, Pa., Barbary, W7022
William, Pa., BLWt.9264-100. Iss. 10/7/1791. No papers
DILLON, Richard, N.C., Privateer, R2959
Thomas, Va., S31650
DILLOW, Peter, Va., R2958
DILS, Peter, N.J., War of 1812, Abigail, R2960; BLWt.73384-160-55 for 1812 service
DILTS, Peter, N.J. See DILS
William, N.J., S868
DIMAN, David, Mass., S34750
DIMICK, Elias, Ct., S21737
Jeduthan, Ct., S37890
Joseph, Ct., S39448
Samuel, Ct., S16364
Shubael, Ct., Mass., R2962
DIMMICK, Amasa, Ct., Matilda, W3396
Benjamin, Ct., S43501; BLWt.541-200-Lt. Iss. 9/4/1789. No papers
Benjamin, Ct., Miriam Raymond, former wid., W18787; BLWt. 27576-160-55
Braddock, Mass., Susan D., W642; BLWt.13742-160-55
Edward, Ct., Esther, W4427
John, Ct., S12775
Joseph, Sheldon's Dragoons, Ct., BLWt.5727-100. Iss. 9/1/1790 to Theodosius Fowler, no papers
Moors, Mass., S15407
Peter, Ct., S23197
Shubel/Shubael, N.Y., S16763
Simeon, Ct., Priscilla, W4942
Sylvanus, Mass., S15096
DIMOCK, David, Ct., Cont., Vt.

DIMOCK (continued)
S5347
Joseph, Ct., Fanny, W22942
DIMON, William, R.I., S21161
DIMOND, Benjamin, R.I., S21738
Elizabeth, former wid. of Francis Moore, R.I., which see
Isaac, Cont., N.H., S12774
Israel, Mass., Abigail, W16109
Reuben, N.H., Mary, R2964
DINAH, James, Ct., BLWt.5711-100 Iss. 3/7/1792 to Jonas Prentice
DINE, John, N.J., R2964 1/2
DINER, James, Ct., S37891
DINGEE, Elijah, N.Y., S17387
DINGHAM, Abraham, N.Y., S43503
DINGLEY, John, Ct., BLWt.5715-100. Iss. 10/22/1789 to Theodosius Fowler
Levi, Mass., Hannah, W22948
DINGMAN, Abraham, N.Y., BLWt.7058-100. Iss. 2/12/1795 to Stephen Lush, ass. No papers
Andrew, N.J., Pa., S22731
Gerardus, N.Y., S46224
Gerrardus, N.Y., BLWt.7066-100 Iss. 1/25/1791. No papers
Peter, N.J., S16103
Rudolphus, N.Y., S10570
DINGUID, George, Va., S5348
DINKINS, Joshua, N.C. See DENKINS
DINNING, David, N.C., S30992
DINSDELL, Joshua, Mass., BLWt. 711-100
DINSMOOR, Samuel, N.H., Mary, W20988
DINSMORE, Abraham, Mass., N.H., S12777
Elijah, N.H., S8333. Pvt.,son of Capt.
Elijah, N.H., R---, Capt.
John, Mass., See DENSMORE
Samuel, Mass., Dorothy, W1575
Thomas, Mass., S45728; BLWt. 1910-100
DINTURFF, Philip, Pa., S10568
DINWIDDIE, John, Va., Sarah, W8671
DIONNE, Germain, Cont., Canadian, BLWt.2489-200
DIPPER, John, Mass., Sarah Roundey former wid., See DUPAR
DIRGIN, John, Cont., Mass., See DURGIN
DIRL, Jacob, Pa., S22209
DISBROW, Asa, Ct., S9385
Henry, Ct., Hannah, W9408; BLWt. 11260-160-55
John D., N.J., Susannah, W7023
Joshua, Ct., S37882
Justus, Ct., S37885
Simon, Ct., Philana, W17722; BLWt.821-160-55
DISHAROON, John, N.C., Elizabeth Townson/Townsen, former wid., W9524
DISHMAN, James, Va., BLWt.12074-100 Iss. 4/8/1796 to Wm. Taylor, Henry Bowyer, & Thos. Scott, assnes. No papers
James, Cont., Va., Privateer, Jane W9409

DISHMAN (continued)
William, Privateer, Va., Sally, R2965
DISHON, Lewis, N.C., Privateer, Elizabeth, R2966
DISKILL, Nathaniel, N.Y., BLWt. 7078-100. Iss. 2/3/1792 to Nathan White, ass. No papers
DISMUKES, Paul, Va., S3290
DISPAIN, Benjamin, N.C., Lucy, W8670
DITCHER, Robert, N.Y., S42163
DITERICK, Balsar, Pa., S2520
DITMAN, Godfrey, Hazen's Regt., BLWt.13012-100. Iss. 11/9/1793. No papers
DITRICH, George/Georg, Pa., S42167
DITSON, Samuel, Mass., Mary, W15892
Seth, Mass., Privateer, See DIDSON
Thomas, Mass., S34749
DITTO, Francis/Franz, Pa., Eleanor, See DIDO
DITTY, John, Pa., Mary Ann, W265
DITZLER, Peter, Pa., S16102
DIVIN, James, Va., S16365
DIVINE, John, N.Y., Sarah, W20985
Thomas, Del., Jemima, R2968
DIX, Benjamin, Ct., BLWt.5706-Cpl. Iss. 10/7/1789 to Benj. Tallmadge. No papers
Benjamin, Ct., S39446
Jonathan, Cont., Mass., Amy, W24058
Joseph, Mass., S44071
Nathan, Mass., BLWt.518-300-Capt. Iss. 8/31/1790 to Dudley Woodbridge, ass. No papers
Samuel, Ct., Sarah Willson, former wid., W18414
Thomas, Cont., Va., Sarah, W7016; BLWt.254-200
Thomas, Va., BLWt.603-200-Lt. Iss. 12/13/1791 to Francis Graves, ass. No papers
William, Cont., Mass., Abigail Diggs, W24858
William, Va., Rebecca, R2970
DIXON, Alexander, Vt., Anna, W10741; BLWt.40507-160-55
Amos, Ct., S23602; BLWt. 26588-160-55
Anthony Tucker, Va., R13772. Va. Half Pay.
Charles, N.C., BLWt.613-200-Lt. Iss. 1/14/1797 to Jesse Franklin, ass. No papers
Curtis, Mass., Lydia, W15830
David, Ct., S43499; BLWt. 5700-100-Pvt. Iss. 2/28/1794
Elizabeth, former wid. of James Floyd, N.H., which see
George, Cont., Va., S16764
George, Md., BLWt.11141-100 Iss. 8/16/1797 to James De Baufre, ass. No papers
George, Va., S38662

DIXON, Henry, Md., Henrietta Mickum, former wid., W23988
Jacob, Pa., BLWt.9299-100. Iss. 11/5/1789. No papers
Jacob, Pa., S42164
James, Ct., BLWt.5695-100. Iss. 2/26/1793. No papers
James, Cont., Pa., S42165
James, Hazen's Regt., BLWt. 13004-100. Iss. 2/14/179-
James, S.C., Hannah, See DICKSON
Jared, Ct., S39441
Jeremiah, N.C., S10565
John, Cont., Ct., BLWt.1021-100
John, Md., BLWt.11134-100. Iss. 2/14/1797. No papers
John, Md., R20318
John, Pa., Dragoon in Moylan's Regt., BLWt.9302. Iss. 6/20/1789. No papers
John, Pa., Elizabeth, W9835
John, Va. See DICKSON
Joseph, Ct., Cont. See DICKSON
Joseph, Cont., N.H. See DICKSON
Marshall, N.Y., S10142
Nathaniel, Va., S8330
Patrick, Pa., Pvt. In Proctor's Arty., BLWt.9320 iss. 7/27/1789 to Richard Platt, ass. No papers
Patrick, Pa., S42159
Patrick, Pa., Mary, R2973
Peter, Va., S32694
Robert, R.I., BLWt.3079-100. Iss. 12/31/1789. No papers
Sanky, Pa., Ann, W784; BLWt. 26519-160-55 & 567-200-Lt. Iss. 3/10/1790
Thomas, Cont., Amy; N.Y. res. & agcy., W5263
Thomas, Lamb's Arty., N.Y., BLWt. 7082-100. Iss. 9/27/1790
Thomas, Pa., R2945. See DICKSON
Thomas, Va., S30387
Tilman, N.C., BLWt.611-300-Capt. Iss. 7/11/1791 to Abisha Thomas, ass. No papers
Wayne, N.C., BLWt.614-200-Lt. Iss. 11/22/1791. No papers
William, Cont., Va., S16104; BLWt.1147-100
William, Del., R2972
William, Md., Pvt. "in the Artillery,"BLWt.11167. Iss. 6/11 1790. No papers
William, N.C., Sarah, W3522; BLWt.31431-160-55
William, Pa., Pvt. "in Proctor's Arty.", BLWt.9323 iss. 7/9/1789
William, Pa., S42162
Wynne, N.C., S46000
DIXSON, John, Ct., Jane, W25544
Patrick, Pa., See DIXON
Robert, Ct., S10571
DOACK, Robert, Pa., S22214
DOAK, Benjamin, Mass. Sea Service, Sarah, W24068
Michael, Mass., Deliverance Porter, former wid., W18776
DOAN, Josiah, Ct., Lois, W16239
Richard, Ct. See DONE
DOANE, Amos, Mass., R.I. Sea Service, Abigail, W8672;

DOANE (continued)
BLWt.9463-160-55
Hezekiah, Mass., Mary, W22954
Joel, Ct., Jemima, W3525;
BLWt.6108-160-55
Martha, former wid. of Jason
Allen, Mass., which see
Oliver, Ct. Sea Service, Mass.,
S20339
Prince, Navy, Mass., Sabrina,
R2975
Seth, Mass., Privateer, S18381
DOAR, Henry, Mass., R2977
John, Cont., Mass., Rebecca,
W22962
DOARWART, Martin, See DEARWART
DOBBIN, James, Pa., S22732
John, Cont., N.H., Sarah, W4943
DOBBINGS, James, Md. Sea Service,
Pa., Indian Wars, War of 1812,
R2979
DOBBINS, David, N.C., S.C., S1805
James, S.C., Nancy, W3964
James, S.C., Catharine, W25534;
BLWt.31429-160-55. He d. in Me.
and married in Nova Scotia.
John, Pa., Elizabeth, W3784
DOBBS, Chesley, N.C., Va., Hannah,
W917
Jarvis, N.Y., Elizabeth, R2980
John, N.Y. See DOP
Nathan, Cont., Va., S16370
Nathaniel, 1st Regt. of Dragoons,
BLWt.12999 & 14132. Iss. 8/7/
1795. No papers
DOBEL, John, Cont., Mass., Navy,
S15100
DOBEY, John, N.C., S31652
DOBKINS, Jacob, Va., S3305
DOBSON, George, Pa., Va., R2983
Henry, Md., BLWt.592-300-Capt.
Iss. 8/4/1789 to Adam Dobson,
Admr. No papers
Jessey, ?, N.C. res. 1780,
Avverilla, R2982
John, Pvt., Md., BLWt.11165 iss.
1/8/1796 to Geo. Ponsonby, ass.
John, N.Y., BLWt.7019-100. Iss.
9/3/1790. From Vols. 2-4 of
"Land Wts. iss. Prior to 1800",
which are regs. of BLWts. iss.
to non-com. officers & Pvts.
under Congr. resolutions of 9/16/
1776 & subsequent dates. Other
records relative to the appli-
cations for Wts. appear to have
been destroyed in the War Dept.
fire of 11/9/1800. Information
concerning Wts. surrendered to
the Fed. Gov. is to be found in
General Land Office records in
N.A.
John, N.Y., S34756
John, N.Y., S43504
John, Va., S8348
Joseph, N.C., Mary, W19187
Richard, Va., S9386
Robert, Va. Sea Service, R36, Va.
Half Pay. See N.A. Acc. No. 837-
Va. State Navy, YS file
Thomas, Pa., BLWt.631-100
DOCKER, John, N.Y. See DECKER

DOCKHAM, James, N.H., Hannah,
W24067; BLWt.968-100 & 142-
60-55
DOCKSTADER, George, N.Y.,
Barbara/Baraba, W16563
John/Hannes, N.Y., S29121
John, N.Y., W31654
John Nicholas, N.Y., Darcus/
Turkye, R2984
Leonard, N.Y., Nancy, W16241
DOCKUM, James, N.H., Polly,
W7037
William, Crane's Cont. Arty.
Mass., BLWt.4071 iss. 1/26/
1790 to John May. No papers
DOD, Daniel, N.Y., S43505
DODD, Abel, Navy, S15812. Mo.
agency and res.
Abijah, N.J., S2179
Bishop, Ct., S37894
David, N.C., S38670
Ebenezer, N.J., S16367
Eli, Del., BLWt.2026-100
Guy, Ct., Hannah Currier,
former wid., W10573
Isaac, N.Y., Ann, W7027; BLWt.
26488-160-55
Jesse, N.C., S39453
John, Ct. res. in 1843, Anna,
R2989
John, Ct., Hannah Mansfield,
former wid., W17092
John, Mass., Hannah Hubbard,
former wid., W14957
John, N.J., S22736
Matthias, N.J., Sarah Harrison,
former wid., W853
Moses, N.J., S2177
Robert, N.C., S41510
Stephen, Mass., Eleanor, W24066
Thomas, Va., Anna, R2990
Timothy, Ct., Susannah, W20991
Timothy, N.J., S34331
William, N.C., S3292
William, S.C., Frances, W22956
DODDRIDGE, Jacob, Cont., Pa.,
S42180
DODDS, Margaret, former wid. of
Thomas Kirkpatrick, which see
Zachariah, N.Y., S9849
DODGE, Abner, Cont., Mass.,
Elizabeth, W22953
Abraham, Mass., S34759
Abraham, Mass., R2992
Amos, Mass., S43516
Benjamin, Ct., Tabitha, W16956
Billy, Mass., Frances, W14639
Brewer, N.H., Anna, W7028;
BLWt.32234-160-55
Caleb, N.H., Elizabeth, R2993
Daniel, Ct., Irena Hubbs, for-
mer wid., W8963
Ebenezer, Mass., S18804
Ebenezer, Mass., Eunice, W16240
Edward, Mass., S10578
Elihu, Ct., Lucretia, W17730
Francis, Mass., S43515; BLWt.
1042-100
Henry, N.Y., BLWt.546-200-Lt.
Iss. 8/22/1791. No papers
Ira, Ct., S8335
Isaac, Mass., S9850

DODGE, Israel, Ct., BLWt.5713-100.
Iss. 1/28/1790. No papers
Israel, Cont., Mass., S34763
Joel, Ct., S15099
John, Mass., S29762
John, Mass., Lucy, W22949
John, Mass., Privateer, Lucy,
R2994
John, N.H., Jane, W22950
John, R.I., Sally, W4184; BLWt.
234-60-55
John Thorn, Mass., S10582
Levi, Mass., S43513; BLWt.520-200-
Lt. Iss. 5/2/1789. No papers
Lucy, former wid. of Silas Adams,
Mass., which see
Mary, former wid. of John Burridge
Mass., which see
Nathaniel, Mass., S29123
Nathaniel, N.H., Privateer, R2995
Nathaniel, N.Y., S19284
Nathaniel Brown, Mass., S39454
Nicholas, N.H., Elizabeth, W24070
Paul, Cont., Mass., S35260
Phineas/Phinehas, Mass., S12790
Reuben, Ct., Dolly/Dorothy, W20994
Reuben, Mass. Sea Service, Eliza-
beth, W20996
Richard, N.Y., BLWt.7046-100. Iss.
5/3/1793 to Abel H. Smith, ass.
No papers
Richard, N.Y., S46379
Robert, Mass., S45730
Rufus, Mass., S12793
Samuel, Mass., S34758
Samuel, N.Y., BLWt.548-200-Lt.
Iss. 2/23/1792. No papers
Samuel, N.Y., BLWt.550-150-Ens.
Iss. 2/14/1791. No papers
Shadrack/Shadrach, N.H., S43509
Simon, Mass., S45641
Thadeus, Mass., S5359
Thomas, Mass., S15413
Thomas, Mass., Sally, W10316;
BLWt.94540-160-55
Thomas, Mass., Sea Service,
Mehitable, W13093; BLWt.12828-
160-55
Thomas, N.H., S43517
William, Ct., S43512
William, Cont., Mass., S34752
William, Mass., BLWt.4057-100.
Iss. 1/5/1797 to Benj. Dana.
No papers
William, N.Y., S16767
DODSON, Caleb, Va., R2996
George, Va., Lucy, BLWt.51883-160-
55
John, N.C., Va., S2518
Michael, Md., S42173
Thomas, N.C., BLRej. 160888-1855
Thomas, Pa., S39459
William, Va., S30994
DOE, David, N.H., BLWt.3074-100.
Iss. 7/7/1791 to B. Swartwout,
ass. No papers
James, Mass., Olive, W24073
John, N.H. See DEE
Samson/Sampson, Mass., S35261
Simon, Cont., Mass., N.H.,W22963
DOEBLER, Abraham, Pa. & 1794, Mary,
W4429; BLWt.13448-160-55

DOEKUM, Benjamin, N.H., BLWt. 3072. Iss. 8/26/1790 to Manassah Cutler, ass. No papers
DOELITTLE, Joel, Ct., BLWt.5709-100. Iss. 5/22/1793 to Ebenezer Farnham. No papers
DOGAN, Jeremiah J.,Va., S32219 BLWt.26367-160-55
Lovel H., Va., S1196
DOGGETT, Richard, S.C. (?), Va., BLWt.1983-300
Samuel, Mass., See DAGGETT
DOGHERTY, Patrick, Va., Dis. No papers
DOHERTY, George, N.C., Mary, R3000; BLWt.343-400. Iss. 4/7/1807 to Mary Doherty & others
George, N.C., Va., also served in 1774, S1807
John, Pa., See DOUGHERTY
John, Va., See DAUGHERTY
DOKE, Immanuel, N.Y. See DEAKE
DOLAHIDE, Francis, N.C., S32220
DOLAND, John, Va., Susannah, W7040; BLWt.26872-160-55
DOLANE, George, Pa. See DORLAN
DOLBEAR, Benjamin, Mass., S35262
James, Mass., Mary, W14636
DOLBEE, Jonathan, R.I., S43507
Pardon, Mass., Rhoda, W19186
DOLBEER, Jesse, N.J., Mary, W91
DOLBY, William, Va., S25033
DOLE, Amos, Mass., Matilda, W22966; BLWt.3526-160-55
Benjamin, N.H., S43514
Campbell, Md., See DALE
David, Mass., S29125
Enoch, Cont., Mass., Molly, W14634
James, Ct., Cont., N.Y., S43518; BLWt.542-200-Lt. Iss. 12/1/1789. No papers
Jeremiah, Mass., Abigail, W14599
Lemuel, Cont., Mass., Rebecca, W22961
Richard, Mass., S35253
Samuel, Mass., S45725
DOLHAGIN, Fredrick, N.Y., S43506
DOLIBER, Thomas, Mass., S34754
Thomas, Mass., Sarah, W22955
DOLIN, Michael, Pa., S42178
DOLISON, John, Mass., BLWt.4044-100. Iss. 8/10/1789 to Richard Platt. No papers
DOLL, Christian, Cont., N.J., See DULL
Henry, Pa., S42182
John, Pa., S5363
Martin, Pa., Elizabeth, W2770
DOLLAR, Elijah, N.C., Rebecca, W17729
James, N.C., Mary, W25535; BLWt.26005-160-55
Jonathan, N.C., S9330
William, N.C., S8355
William, Va., Ruth, W22965
DOLLAWAY, Andrew, N.Y., Hannah, W16238
DOLLERHIDE, John, N.C., R3001
DOLLERSON, John, Mass., Esther, W16958
DOLLEY, John, N.C., S6802
DOLLIF, Richard, N.H., Tamasia/Tamma, See DOLLOFF
Noah, N.H., See DOLLOF
DOLLINGER, John, Pa., S15101
DOLLINS, Presley, Va., S1806
DOLLIVER, Joseph, R.I., Abigail, W16959
Peter, Mass., S35250
William, Cont., Mass., Elizabeth, W24071
DOLLOF, Noah, Cont., N.H., S35251
DOLLOFF, Daniel, N.H., Mercy, W8198; BLWt.6281-160-55
John, N.H., BLWt.3069-100-Pvt. Iss. 7/21/1789 to Ladd & Cass, ass. No papers
Richard, N.H., Tamasain/Tamma, W22957
Thomas, N.H., Alsa, W20999
DOLPH, Stephen, Ct., S35897
DOLSBURY, Lyles, Va., S17929
DOLSON, John, Pa., S12788
DOLTON, John, Lamb's Arty. N.Y. BLWt.7091-100-Sgt. Iss. 7/16/1790 to Wm. J. Vreedenburgh, ass.
DOMINE, David Spencer, See HOWLAND
DOMINEY, Andrew, S.C., Margaret, W9412
DOMINICK, Henry, S.C., S9329
Phebe, former wid. of Jacob M. Vermilia, N.Y., which see
DONAHAY, James, ?, Pa. res., R3002
DONAHO, James, Cont., Del., See DONOHO
DONALD, William, Pa. See DONNALD
DONALDSON, James, N.J., BLWt.8236-100-Pvt. Iss. 11/24/1791. No papers
John, N.J., BLWt.8238. No papers
John, Pa., S42181
Lothario, Mass., Hannah, W7042; BLWt.31434-160-55
Robert, N.C., See DONELSON
William, N.J., Susanna, W4665
William, N.C., S31653
DONALLY, Patrick, Va., See DONNALLY
Thomas, Cont., N.Y. See DONNELLY
DONALSON, James, N.J., S34329
Matthew, Mass. See DONELSON
Robert, N.C., See DONELSON
DONATHAN, Elijah, Ga., Rachael, R3004
DONAVAN, James, Pa., BLWt.9285-100-Pvt. Iss. 4/30/1793 to Alexander Power, ass. No papers
DONAWAY, Charles, Va., R3010
William, Pa., See DONOWAY
DONE, Richard, Ct., S43510
Thomas, N.Y., S27705
DONELSON, Matthew, Mass., S5358
Robert, N.C., Margaret, W7041
DONEVAN, Timothy, Pa., Sarah, BLWt.260-100
DONEY, William, N.Y., S15102
DONITA, Francis, Privateer, Cont. N.Y., S23603
DONKEMOYER, Frederick, N.J., Martha Bellas, former wid., W2055
DONKIN, Daniel, Va. See DUNIKIN
DONLEY, Stephen, Cont., Pa. S23203
DONNALD, William, Pa., S22734
DONNALLY, Patrick, Va., R3007
DONNAM, Charles, See DUNNOM
DONNAN, Andrew, N.Y., Grissal/Gracie Tannahill, former wid., W26503
DONNAVAN, John, N.Y., BLWt.7032 Iss. 9/15/1790 to John S. Hobart, et all, assnes.
DONNELL, Andrew, N.C., S8347
Daniel, N.C., S8351
George, N.C., S3294
John, N.C., Elizabeth, W4180
John, Pa., Sarah, W19182
Jotham, Mass., S35255
Nathaniel, Cont., Pa., S42176; BLWt.527-300-Capt. Iss. 3/4/1791. No papers
Obadiah, Cont., Mass., Navy, Abigail, W24870
William, N.C., S3293
DONNELLS, David, Ct., BLWt.5690 Iss. 10/22/1792. No papers
DONNELLY, Barney, Pa., BLWt. 9313-100-Pvt. Iss. 6/7/1793 to James Bennet, ass. No papers
Daniel, N.J., BLWt.8248-100-Pvt. Iss. 4/23/1798 to Abraham Bell, ass. No papers
John, Pa., S42179
Robert, Ct., R3008
Thomas, Cont., N.Y., S23201
DONNISON, William, R.I., S30388
DONNOLLY, John, Va., BLWt.12091-100-Pvt. Iss. 7/20/1792 to Robert Means, ass. No papers
DONOHO, James, Cont., Del., S35900; BLWt.183-100. No papers
Joseph, Md., BLWt.11160-100-Pvt. Iss. 3/11/1791. No papers
Robert, ?, Ky. res. in 1848, Sally, R3009
Thomas, N.C., Keziah, W9838; BLWt.608-400-Maj. Iss. 5/3/1796 No papers
DONOHOO, Elizabeth, former wid., of Jacob Murray, Pa., which see
DONOHUE, John, Pa., BLWt.9288-100-Pvt. Iss. 6/28/1793 to John Wheeler, ass. No papers
Patrick, Pa., BLWt.9293-100-Pvt. Iss. 6/28/1793, to John Wheeler, ass.
DONOWAY, Charles, Va. See DONAWAY
William, Pa., R3011
DOOEY, Peter, Pa., S2181
DOOLEY, Jacob, Va., Nancy, W1837, BLWt.13721-160-55
DOOLITTLE, Benjamin, Ct., Sarah, R3015
Benjamin, Mass., R3013
Charles, Ct., S12796
David, Ct., N.Y., Ann Elizabeth, W25537; BLWt.35832-160-55
Eber, Ct., Mary, W26974; BLWt. 26686-160-55. Her 2nd husb. was pensioned. See Obed Doolittle.
Ezra, Ct., Sarah, R3016
George, Pvt., Ct., BLWt.5677 iss. 11/18/1790
George, Ct., Grace, R3014
John, Ct., Hannah, W19194
Joseph, Cont., Ct. res., S37893
Nathaniel, N.Y., S23198

DOOLITTLE (continued
Obed, Ct., S16766. See also Eber Doolittle, Ct.
Reuben, N.Y., Mary, W19188
Thomas, Ct., R3017
Uri, Ct., S10577
DOOR, Henry, Mass., See DOAR
John, Cont., Mass., See DOAR
DOP, John, N.Y., R3018
DOPS, John, N.Y., See DOP
DORAN, Abraham, N.Y. See DORN
Alexander, N.J., S12784
James, Pa., BLWt.9276-100-Pvt. Iss. 9/4/1789. No papers
Myles, Mass., S34753
Patrick, Md., BLWt.11158. Iss. 8/4/1789. No papers
Polly, former wid. of William White, Va., which see
Terence, Va., S39457
DORANCE, Roby, former wid. of Jeremiah Bayley, R.I. Which see
DORAND, Richard, Vt., S12792
DORCH, William, Md., S35896
DORCHESTER, Cont., Ct., Anna, W19190
Reuben, Ct., S10576
Stephen, Ct., See DORCKESTER
DORCKESTER, Stephen, Ct., Abigail, W19192
DORE, Benaiah/Beniah, Mass., Mary, W10745; BLWt.11401-160-55. He d. 2/1854
Benaiah, N.H., BLWt.17580-160-55. He d. 3/1856
Jonathan, Mass., Navy, N.H., S10581
DOREMUS, David, N.J., Leah Westervelt, former wid., R11353
DORESHE, Anthony, N.Y., BLWt.7029-100-Pvt. Iss. 1/12/1791 to William J. Vreedenburgh, Admr.
DOREY, James, Cont., N.Y., S45323
James, Pvt., Sappers & Miners, BLWt.12980 iss. 1/21/1792
DORGIN, John, Md. & Boat Service, S8352
DORIN, Miles, Mass., BLWt.4041-100-Pvt. Iss. 3/25/1796 to Peter Swier
DORLAN, George, Pa., Elizabeth, R3020
DORLAND, Lambert/Lombart, Pa., S42171
Lombart, Pa. See Lambert
Peter, N.J., Margaret, W131
DORMAN, David, Ct., Mabel, R3021
Gersham, Sheldon's Dragoons, Ct. BLWt.5721-100-Pvt. Iss. 9/15/1790 to Nicholas Root
Gorshom, Cont., Sharon, Ct. res. Dis. No papers
Israel, Cont., Mass., S30993
John, Mass., S35263
Ludwig, Pa., S42175
Timothy, Mass. Sea Service, Deborah, W15670
DORMIRE, Anna, former wid. of William Ewen, Va. which see
DORN, Abraham, N.Y., Polly, W24077; BLWt.9544-160-55

DORN (continued)
George, Pa., See THORN
John, N.Y., BLWt.7067. Iss. 1/5/1791. No papers
DORNBAUCH, John, Pa., Anna Maria, S42174
DOROTHY, Charles, N.Y., N.Y., S39460; BLWt.1344-100
DORR, Christian, Pa., S42153
Edward, Mass., S29124
Edward, R.I., Judith, R3024
Elisha, Ct., R3023
Melcher, N.C., See TAR
Samuel, Arty. Artificers, Ct., BLWt.5678 & 13015-100-Pvt. Iss. 2/3/1800
Samuel, Cont., Ct., Abigail, W14632
William, Mass., Jane, W24074
DORRAH, Arthur, Mass., N.H., S22213
DORRANCE, David, Ct., Cont., S45331 BLWt.535-300-Capt. Iss. 3/5/1793 to Samuel Darrance, ass. This Wt. iss. under "Darrance". No papers
DORRIS, William, N.J., Eleanor, W916
DORSEY, Bazel, Md., BLWt.161-100
Daniel, Md., S45324
James, Cont., Mass., S45325
James, Crane's Cont. Arty. Mass.; BLWt.4061-100-Cpl. Iss. 12/14/1789 to Richard Platt
John, N.Y., Sarah, See DOSSEY
Leaven, Md., R3026
Matthew, Pa., BLWt.9251-100-Pvt. Iss. 7/20/1791. No papers
Nicholas, Md., Rachel, W9411
Richard, Md., BLWt.584-300-Capt. Iss. 1/19/1793. No papers
DORTCH, Abel, Va., S32221
William, Md., See DORCH
DORTON, Benjamin, Cont., S.C., R20358
Henry, Va., S5362
DORVILL, John, Pa., S32218
DOSHER, Peter, Va., Alley, W22951; BLWt.75004-160-55
DOSS, John, Va., S5350
John, Va., S38669
William, Va., Nancy, W9404; BLWt.80029-160-55
DOSSETT, Thomas, S.C., S37892
DOSSEY, John, N.Y., Sarah,W25533; BLWts.251-60-55 & 5-100-55
DOTA, John, Ct., N.Y., S12791
DOTEN, Edward, Mass., S34760
Ephraim, Mass., See DOTON
Lemuel, Mass., Phebe Warren, former wid., W14115. Her other husb. was pensioned. See Benjamin Warren, Mass.
Samuel, Mass. Sea Service, Lydia W25532; BLWt.13436-160-55
Silas, Mass., R3027
DOTEY, Daniel, Ct., Talatha/Talitha, W22952
James, Mass., S34755
DOTON, Ephraim, Mass., S45731
DOTSON, Esau, N.C., S6800
Richard, Va., S5364

DOTSON (continued)
William, N.C., Zilpha Bartley, former wid., R592
DOTTER, Samuel Solomon, Pa., S22735
DOTTY, Moses, Mass., See DOTY
DOTY, Asa, Cont., Mass., S42673
Azariah, N.C., S1804
Benjamin, Ct., S45327
Benjamin, N.Y., Abeline, W20998
Cornelius, N.Y., R3029
Danforth, Ct., Sarah, W19193
Daniel, N.J., Elizabeth, W243
Elias, N.Y., R3030
Ellis, Mass., S45410
Ezra, Mass., S42183
Gilbert, N.Y., R3031
Isaac, Mass., N.Y., S23200
Isaac, Pvt., N.J., BLWt.8234-100-Pvt. Iss. 8/11/1795
Isaac, N.J., S45329
Isaac, Lamb's Arty., N.Y., BLWt. 7072-100-Pvt. Iss. 4/25/1792. No papers
Isaac, N.C., S38668
Jacob, N.J., Aulchy/Alchy, W10753; BLWt.30772-160-55
James, N.J., S3299
Jerathmeel, Cont., Mass., Navy, also War of 1812, S39450; BLWt. 15166-160-55
John, Ct., S12781
John, Mass., Dorcas, W8199; BLWt. 287-60-55
Jonathan, N.J., S5356
Joseph, Ct., Mary, R3034
Joseph, Mass., Susannah, W14626
Joseph, N.J., S992
Joseph, N.Y., Rhoda, R3035
Levi, N.J., Pa., R3033
Moses, Mass., S45328
Nathaniel, Cont., Mass. See DOUGHTY
Nathaniel, N.J., S2176
Nathaniel, N.J., Jane, R3032. See N.A. Acc. No. 874-050054. Not Half Pay
Peter, N.J., S18382
Samuel, Ct., N.Y., S45326
Samuel, Pa. Regt. Arty., BLWt. 571-200-Capt.-Lt. Iss. 3/10/1790 to Alex. Power, ass. No papers
William, Ct., S10584
Zebulon, N.J., Jane Jewell, former wid., W7889; BLWt.26956-160-55
DOUBERMAN, Henry, Pa. See DOWBERMAN
DOUBLEDAY, Ammi, Ct., Lois, R3037
Asahel, Ct., S18803
Benjamin, Cont., Mass., Mary, BLWt.1829-100
Jacob, Ct., R3036
Joseph, Ct., S39458
Joseph, Ct., Lucy, W14625
Seth, Ct., S10580
DOUD, Benjamin, Ct., S21739
Chandler, Mass., S42672
Ezekiel, Mass., Ruth, W13099
Isaac, Cont., Mass., N.Y., Eleanor Ketchum, former wid., W26171
Jesse, Cont., Green Mt. Boys, Rebecca, W1737
Richard, Sheldon's Dragoons, Ct., BLWt.5717-100-Pvt. Iss. 6/25/

DOUD (continued)
1789. No papers
Richard, Cont., Ct., Rebecca Wilcox, former wid., W22641
Samuel, Ct., R3038
Samuel Miles, Vt., Huldy, W4183
Solomon, Ct., S38663; BLWt.419-100
William, Ct., Hannah, W19183
DOUDEEN, Thomas, Va., Mary,See DOWDEN
DOUDEL, Jacob, Pa., S10583
DOUDLE, William, Cont., Md. See DOWDLE
DOUDON, Clementius, See DOWDON
DOUGAL, Thomas, Cont., Ct., Ann Page/Paige, former wid., W17417
DOUGALL, Thomas, Sheldon's Dragoons Ct., BLWt.5723-100-Pvt. Iss. 10/7/1789 to Benj. Tallmadge. No papers
DOUGAN, James, N.C., S3306
John, N.C., Martha, W9836; BLWt. 31428-160-55
DOUGE, Peter, N.C., S41511
DOUGHERTY, Andrew, Pa.,Sarah, W2078
Anthony, N.J., BLWt.8265-100-Pvt. Iss. 7/16/1789 to Thomas Coyle, ass. No papers
Barney, Pvt., Pa., BLWts.9236 & 13023 iss. 2/25/1793
Charles, N.J., BLWt.8275-100-Pvt. Iss. 7/16/1789 to Thomas Coyle, ass. No papers
George, Pa., Fifer in the Arty. BLWt.9318-100. Iss. 6/20/1789. No papers
George, Pa., S39456
Henry, ?, Pa. agency & res., S12799
Hugh, Hazen's Regt., BLWt.12991-100-Pvt. Iss. 9/2/1789. No papers
James, Cont., Pa., S42170
James, Pa., BLWt.9257-100-Pvt. Iss. 9/29/1792 to Wm. Lane, ass. No papers
James, Pa., BLWt.9270-100-Pvt. Iss. 11/29/179-
James, Pa., BLWt.9271. Iss. 10/8/1789. Notation: Wt. No. 1202, new series, iss. in lieu of it in favor of the heirs.
James, Pa., BLWt.1202-100
James, Va. State Navy, R13659; Va. Half Pay. See N.A. Acc. No. 837. YS File.
John, Pa., S12779
John, Pa., S.C. res., S39461
John, Pa., S42169
John, Pa., R2999
Michael, Del., BLWt.10749. Iss. 9/2/1789 to Mary Dougherty, admx. No papers
Michael, R.I., BLWt.3085-100-Pvt. Iss. 4/15/1790. No papers
Mordecai C., Pa., R3039
Peter, N.J., BLWt.8259-100-Pvt. Iss. 6/11/1789 to Jonathan Dayton, ass. No papers
Robert, ?, Pa. res. 1852, R3040
Samuel, Mass., Mary Pratt, former wid., W13833
William, N.J., R3041

DOUGHERTY (continued)
William, N.Y., BLWt.7055-100-Pvt. Iss. 8/3/1790 to Cornelius Van Dyck, ass. No papers
William, N.Y., S34333
William, N.C., Mary, W10315
William, Pa., S42674
William, Pa., Lydia, W4182
William, Pa., S.C. See DAUGHERTY
William, Va., S16369
DOUGHTEN, William, Va., S32217
DOUGHTY, Benjamin, Mass., S44796
Christopher, N.J., S3300
Elias, N.Y., S45330
Ichabod, Mass., S35252
Jacob, Pa., S34332
James, Cont., Mass., Ruth, W24063
James, Mass., S16770
John, N.Y. Arty., BLWt.551-300-Capt. Iss. 1/10/1791. No papers
Joseph, Mass., S17930
Linton, N.J., S993
Nathaniel, Cont., Mass., S35257; BLWt.61092-160-55
Samuel, Ct., BLWt.5697-100-Pvt. Iss. 4/11/1792 to Martin Kingsley. No papers
Skilman, N.J., Hannah, W24064
Stephen, Mass., R5051
Thomas, Pa., S519
DOUGLAS, David, Ct., S10579
Mary, former wid. of Nathaniel Gatchell, Mass., Which see
Peleg, N.Y., R3048
Thomas, Pa. Arty.; BLWt.570-300-Capt. Iss. 3/29/1791 to Wm. Kidd & Jas. Montgomery, admrs. No papers
Thomas, S.C., S37895
DOUGLASS, Alexander, Cont., Mass., N.H., S19285
Alexander, N.J., S994
Andrew, Va., S42168
Barnard, Mass., Betsey, W541; BLWt.5449-160-55
Charles, R.I., Mercy, W20993
David, Mass., R.I., See DUGLAS
David, Pa., R3043
Edward, N.C., S3297
Ephraim, Pa., S6804
George, N.Y., BLWt.7020-100-Pvt. Iss. 8/12/1790 to John D. Coe, ass. No papers
James, Ct., S46033
James, Ct., Elizabeth, R3045
James, N.Y., BLWt.7060-100-Pvt. Iss. 8/31/1790 to Samuel Smith, ass. No papers
James, N.Y., Sarah, W20992
John, Cont., Mass., Hannah, W22959
John, Cont., Pa., S2180
John, Mass., S35259
John, Mass., Mehitable Picher, former wid., W10901
John, Mass., Lydia, R3047
John, N.C., See DUGLESS
John, Va., Mary, W7032
Joseph, Ct., Hannah, R3046
Joseph, R.I., Abigail, W14637
Nathaniel, Ct., S45333
Phinehas, Mass., S45768
Randall, S.C., S43508

DOUGLASS (continued)
Richard, Ct., Lucy, W730; BLWt. 536-300-Capt. Iss. 1/28/1790
Robert, Cont., Pa., enl. in Del. Elizabeth, W3524; BLWt.17585-160-55
Robert, Md., S8353
Robert, Mass. Sea Service, S17931
Robert, Va., S1510
Sarah, former wid. of Lebbeus Harris, Ct., which see
Skeen, Ct., Lorilla, W4619; BLWt. 18019-160-55. See Skene Douglass SACKET
Thomas, N.C., S3296
Thomas, S.C., BLWts.12097 & 12981-Pvt. Iss. 9/28/1796 to John Young, ass. No papers
Thomas, Va., Elizabeth Weymouth, former wid., W9885; BLWt.87047-160-55
William, N.Y., W10833; BLWt. Rej. See claim of Catharine, wid. of Wm. Oakley; also pens. as former wid. of Wm. Douglass
William, N.C., BLWts.12094 & 12996-Pvt. Iss. 11/10/1796 to Henry Wiggin, ass. No papers
William, N.C., S38667
DOUGLESS, John, Pa., S22217
DOUTHIT, Silas, Va., S16368
DOVE, Richard, M., S17391
Thomas, Cont., Va., S1661; BLWt. 2090-100
William, Va., S8336
DOVENBERGER, Jacob, Pa., S43511
DOVER, Andrew, Pa., S42172; BLWt. 572-200-Lt. Iss. 2/14/1791 to Alexander Power, ass. No papers
Francis J., N.C., S.C., R3052
John, Pa., S42177
Joshua, Ga., R3053
DOVIN, John, Del., BLWt.10756-100-Pvt. Iss. 9/27/1791 to George Walton, ass. No papers
DOW, Alexander, Art. Artificers, BLWt.521-300-Capt. Iss. 2/14/1791. Also recorded under BLWt. 2553. No papers
Alexander, N.Y., BLWt.554-200-Lt. Iss. 8/4/1791. No papers
Benjamin, N.H., S18793
Benjamin, N.H., Ruth, W16564
Ebenezer, N.H., Mary, W15893
Fulcurd, N.Y., S39452
Henry, Mass., S35258
Henry, N.J., Keziah, W411
Jabez, N.H., Anna, W14629
Jesse, Mass., Phebe, W16242
John, Mass., Mehitable Hancock, former wid., W14846
John, N.H., Rebecca, R2775; BLWt.6261-160-55
Jonathan, N.H., S22215
Joseph, Mass. Sea Service, N.H., Rhoda, W22964
Levi, N.H., Elizabeth, R3054; BLWt.38826-160-55
Moses, Mass., S23604
Nathan, Ct., S23202
Nathan, Mass., S45642
Nathaniel, N.H., S22212

DOW (continued)
Polly, former wid. of Benj. Libbey, Navy, Mass., which see
Rebecca, former wid. of Nathaniel Everett, Mass., which see
Robert, Mass., Susannah, W14631
Salmon, N.H., Vt., S16366
Samuel, Mass., S29761
Samuel, Mass., Eunice, W14630
Simeon, Mass., BLWt.85059-160-55
Stephen, N.H., S16768
Thomas, N.H., Elizabeth, R3056
Volker, N.Y., BLWt.7048-100-Pvt. Iss. 4/19/1791 to James Roe, ass. No papers
Zebulon, N.H., S22733
DOWBERMAN, Henry, Cont., Pa., S39453
DOWD, Connor/Conner, N.C., Hannah W3664; BLWt.31425-160-55
Daniel, Ct., R.I., S12789
John, N.C., R13793
Moses, Ct., Abigail Smith, former wid. See papers in claim of Elijah Smith, Navy, Mass.
DOWDEN, James, Md., S30996
Thomas, Va., Mary, W4181
DOWDERMAN, Jacob, Pa., Sabrina, W3399
DOWDLE, William, Cont., Md., S34764; BLWt.2259-100
DOWDNEY, Samuel, N.J., BLWt.8253-Sgt. Iss. 5/31/1790. No papers
DOWDON, Clementius, Md., Pa., S30995
DOWE, William, Cont., N.H., R.I., Vt., S21740
DOWEL, James, N.C., BLWt.118-100
John, N.C., S.C., R3059
DOWELL, Elijah, Va., Lucy, R3060
George, N.C., S.C., Va., S32222
Hannah, former wid. of Israel Davis, Mass., which see
Major, Va., R3061
Richard, Md., N.C., Va., Mary, W7035
DOWEN, Francis, Mass., Nelly, R3062
DOWER, James, Ct., S21741
DOWERS, Conrad, Cont., Pa., Mary, W9839
Edward, N.J., S2178
Jacob, Pa., S16371
DOWLAN, George, N.Y., BLWt.7065-100-Pvt. Iss. 9/10/1790 to George Dowlan. No papers
DOWLAND, John, Va., BLWt.12076-100-Pvt. Iss. 7/20/1792 to Robert Means, ass. No papers
DOWLER, George, N.Y., Mary, W16957
DOWLEY, Joseph, Mass., BLWt. 4049-Pvt. Iss. 10/3/1791 to Richard Platt. No papers
DOWLF, Ellis, Mass., S35256
DOWLING, Andrew, N.Y., BLWt. 7088. Iss. 10/3/1791 to Phineas Knapp, ass. No papers
Andrew, Cont., N.Y., Catharine McDougal, former wid., W17113
James, Md., Va., S8346
James, Pa., S10575
DOWN, Jabez, Ct., S45643
John, Mass., S34761
DOWNE, Francis, Mass., See DOWEN
Nathaniel Holmes, Mass. Sea Service, Polly H., W22958
Samuel, Mass., Eunice, W17727
DOWNER, Avery, ?, Ct. res., R3063
Cushman, Vt., S21162
Eliphalet, Navy, Mass. res. in 1795. Dis. No papers
Elisha, Ct., Cont., S12786
James, Ct., See DOWER
Jason, Ct., Vt., S16769
Joseph, N.H., Vt., S15412
Zaccheus/Zacheus, Ct., Vt., S12782
DOWNES, Jesse, Mass., Naomi, W24072
William, Md., BLWt.11137-100-Pvt. Iss. 8/9/1797 to James DeBaufre, ass. No papers
DOWNEY, James, N.C., R3064
James, Md., BLWt.11139-100-Pvt. Iss. 4/28/1791. No papers
John, Pa., S1195
Patrick, Md., N.C., S8350
Patrick, Pa., BLWt.9297. Iss. 8/6/1792 to Alex. Power, ass. No papers
Samuel, Va., S12778
Thomas, Pa., S35895
DOWNIE, Alexander, Md., S38666
DOWNING, Daniel, Ct., S15414
Daniel, N.H., BLWt.715-100
David, Mass., BLWt.4019. Iss. 9/16/1791 to Joseph Morrill, admr. No papers
Francis, Md., Henrietta, W8674
George R., N.H., BLWt.3059-Sgt. Iss. 3/25/1790. No papers
George R., N.H., S45640
James, N.C., Sarah, W25536
John, Ct., S39451
John, Cont., Mass., Eunice, W2603; BLWt.13858-160-55
John, Mass., Ruth, W2077; BLWt.9184-160-55
Jonathan, Ct., Cont., Huldah, W24868
Jonathan, Mass., Susannah, W1838; BLWt.8441-160-55
Jonathan, N.H., Alice, W16011; BLWt.3052-100 iss. 4/25/1798 to Daniel Gookins, ass.
Lawrence, Hazen's Regt., BLWt. 12992-100-Pvt. Iss. 7/13/1791 No papers.
Lucy, former wid. of Barzillai Hines, N.H., which see
Moses, Mass., S34757
Palfry/Palfray, Mass., S34762; BLWt.3997-100-Pvt. Iss. 10/13/1791 to Asa Spaulding
Phineas, Ct., S31651. This sold. m. Polly Young, wid. of Robt. Young, which see
Richard, N.C., Polly, W19185
Samuel, Cont., Mass., Lucy, W1157; BLWt.15171-160-55
Samuel, Md., S35899
Samuel, N.H., S40055; BLWt.293-60-55 & 3067-100-Pvt. Iss.
DOWNING (continued)
3/22/1796 to Nathan Preston, ass.
Samuel, N.H., Mary Corsier, former wid., W14503
Stephen, Ct., Privateer, S29122
DOWNMAN, Rawleigh, Ga., Va., BLWt. 1917-300
DOWNS, Aaron, Mass., S17390
Benjamin, Mass., Mary, W21002
David, Ct., S17392
Edward, Mass., Rhoda Bixby, former wid., W15984. Her 2nd husb., Thomas Bixby also served. See papers within.
Elijah, Ct., Ruth, W10755
Gersham, N.H., S22216
Jabez, Ct., See DOWN
James, Ct., BLWt.5704-100-Pvt. Iss. 9/20/1790. No papers
James, Ct., S38664
Jesse, Mass., Naomi, See DOWNES
John, Ct., BLWt.5703 iss. 9/20/1790. No papers
John, Ct., Dis. No papers
John, Pa., Dis. No papers
Jonathan, S.C., Sarah, W21000
Joseph, Ct., S12785
Michael, Md., Margaret McCaw, former wid., R6614
Nathaniel, Ct., S15813
Noah, N.H., S45332
Paul, Cont., Mass., Lydia, W24076
Robert, Del., Pamelia, W8673; BLWt.1053-100
Thomas, N.C., S.C., S8337
Zepheniah, N.H., BLWt.3062-100-Pvt. Iss. 1/28/1790 to James Patterson, ass. No papers
DOWNUM, Speakman/Speekman, N.C., Esther, W128
DOWNY, John, Pvt., Md., BLWt.11139 iss. 4/28/1791
DOWREY, Joe, Mass., S36493
DOWS, Eleazer, Mass., Linda/Malinda W19184; BLWt.3993-160-55
Joseph, Mass., S17393
DOWSE, Eleazer, Mass., Mary, W14633
Joseph, Mass., S17394
DOWSETT, Amos, Ct., Mary, W17728
DOWTIN, John, N.C., S6801
DOXEY, Jeremiah, Va. Sea Service, S3303
DOXSTATER, Peter, See DOXTATOR
DOXTATOR, Honyere, N.Y., Indian, See TEWA-HON-GAR-AH-KEN, Honyere
Honyost, N.Y., Indian, See TE-WA-HON-GAR-AH-KEN, Honyost
Peter, N.Y., S23199
DOYAL, John, Pa., See DYAL
DOYEN, Daniel, N.H., S12794
Jacob, N.H., Mercy Hibbert, former wid., W27513. See papers within claim of contesting wid., Mary Doyen, rejected
Samuel, N.H., R3069
DOYLE, Daniel, S.C., See DOYLEY
Edward, S.C., S32216
Henry, Hazen's Regt., BLWt.13005-Sgt. Iss. 9/2/1789. No papers
Henry, Pa., S34330
James, Md., BLWt.11140-100-Pvt.

DOYLE (continued)
Iss. 10/14/1795 to Henry Davis, ass. No papers
James, Mass., S35254
John, Md., S38665
John, Pa., BLWt.2452-300
John, Va., BLWt.12092 iss. 4/12/1792 to Francis Graves, ass. No papers
Jotham, Mass., Huldah, W24069
Michael, Mass., S18802
Morris, Pa., BLWt.9252-100-Pvt. Iss. 2/19/1792. No papers
Robert, Va. Lee's Legion, BLWts. 12072 & 13993-Pvt. Iss. 11/2/1792 to Robt. Means, ass. No papers
Thomas, Pa., BLWt.9249-100-Pvt. Iss. 11/25/1793 to Casper Iserloan, ass. No papers
Thomas, Pa., BLWt.563-200-Lt. No papers
Thomas, ?, Pa. agcy., Dis. Capt. No papers
DOYLEY, Daniel, S.C., BLWt.617-200-Lt. Iss. 4/14/1794 to Standish Forde, ass. No papers
DOZIER, Peter, Va. See DOSHER
Richard, Va., S8349
DRAKE, Abial, Ct., N.Y., Anna, R3071
Abiel, Ct., S38674
Abraham, N.H., Anna, W1398; BLWt.34595-160-55
Adam, Mass., S5365
Albertain, N.C. See Albrittian
Albrittian/Albertain, N.C., Ruth, W8676
Benjamin, N.Y., S2182
Clement, Mass., Silence Bonney, former wid., W14336; BLWt.8150-160-55
Cornelius, N.J., BLWt.8244-100-Pvt. Iss. 4/5/1793. No papers
Cornelius, N.J., S45336
David G., N.Y., S23606
Ebenezer, Ct., BLWt.5684-100-Pvt. Iss. 6/12/1797 to Wm. Woodward. No papers
Ebenezer, Ct., Lois Brewer, former wid., W20791
Ebenezer, Mass., S35264
Elihu, Ct., S38673
Elijah, N.Y., Phebe, W16243
Elijah, Pa., Abigail, W3665; BLWt.26666-160-55
Ephraim, N.H., S16771
Gideon, Ct., Annah, W14643
Isaac, N.J., Pa., R3072
Jacob, N.J., S637
James, N.H., Hannah, W21006
James, N.J., BLWt.8257-100. Iss. 5/7/1790. No papers
James, N.Y., Charity, W7043; BLWt.26851-160-55
Jasper, N.Y., S12801
Jeremiah, N.J., Sarah, W16961
Jeremiah, N.Y., Phebe, W19196
John, Mass., Molly, W24078
John, N.H., S17933
Joseph, Md., S9387
Joshua, ?, N.J. res. 1777, 1778,

DRAKE (continued)
1779, R3075
Joshua, Cont., N.Y., 579-200-Lt., BLWt.553-200-Lt. Iss. 9/8/1790 to Samuel Drake, ass. & marked "Certified to Land Office on the 30th day of Jan. 1837 that Wt. No.579, New Series, had iss. to the heir of Lt. J. Drake." No papers
Josiah, Mass., Julia Ann, W25538; BLWt.50900-160-55
Josiah, N.Y., S10587
Lemuel, Ct., S31655
Lory/Lowry, Ct., Sarah, R3078; BLWt.43879-160-55
Lot, Mass., S29763
Margaret, former wid. of Humphrey Hubbard, Mass., which see
Melzer/Melzor, Mass., Chloe, W24875
Michael, Cont., Mass., Privateer, Sarah, W22970
Moses, Ct., Abigail, W17731
Nicholas, N.J., S34334
Noah, Ct., S12802
Noah, Mass., S45334
Oliver, Cont., Mass., Navy, S35265
Oliver, Mass., Ruth, W21003
Perez, Mass., S44795
Peter, Cont., N.J., S2185
Peter, N.J., BLWt.8256-100-Pvt. Iss. 5/7/1790 to John Linn, ass. No papers
Phinehas, Ct., S31657
Richard, N.Y., S29127
Richard, N.C., Louisa, W3788
Ridly, Va., S9388
Seth, Mass., S45335
Simon, N.H., Tamson, W22969
Thomas, Va., Catharine, W5264
Uriah, N.Y., Ruth, R3077
William, Cont., N.Y., S42186; BLWt.7084-100 iss. 11/8/1791. No papers
William, Mass., S29767
William, N.C., S8375
William, Va., Anna, W8675
DRALLE, John, Armand's Legion, BLWt.12975-100-Pvt. Iss. 1/19/1792. No papers.
DRALLY, John, Cont., Mass., S42184
DRAPER, James, S.C., Va., Obediance W3786
Jonathan, Mass., N.H., S2184
Joshua, Mass., S10586
Josiah, Mass., Keziah, W14642
Nathan, Mass., Hannah, R3079
Nathaniel, Mass., S29764
Nathaniel, Mass., Ann, W19195
Robert, Va., S38672
Samuel, Mass., S23605
Samuel, Mass., Privateer, S17389
Simeon, Mass., Catharine C., W2441; BLWt.24760-160-55
William, Mass., S34765
DRATT, John, N.Y., R3080
DRAUGHT, Richard, See DROUGHT
DREAHR, George, Pa., S22738
DREHER, George, See DREAHR
Godfried, Pa., Christina, W8873

DREIMER, Margaret, former wid. of Thomas Crummell, which see
DRENEN/DRENNEN, William, Pa., Va., S15816
DRENNAN, Hugh, Pa., Margaret, W1843
James A., Pa., Martha, W3527
DRENNEN, Thomas, Pa., S3308
DRENNING, William, Pa., S22737
DRESSER, Aaron, S29765
Daniel, Mass., Susanah, W19197
Elijah, Mass., Sarah, W22971
Jonathan, Mass., Elizabeth, W22972
Joseph, Mass., S31656
Levi, Mass., S17934
Moses, Privateer, Mass., S5366
Richard, Mass., S35267
DRESSNER, John, Pvt., Von Heer's Corps, BLWt.12976-100. Iss. 7/13/1792 to John Snell, ass. of John Sapp, admr. of John Dressner
DREW, Andrew, N.H., S22219
Benjamin, Mass., S29126
Comfort, former wid. of Noah Smith Mass., which see
Ezra, Vt., R3082
Francis Adam, N.H., Hannah Atwood, former wid., W25373
Isaac, Mass. Sea Service, Navy, Weltha, W14640. 6 Cont. documents
Isaac, N.Y., S10585
Job, Mass., Thankful Delano, W21005
John, N.H., Lois Brewster/McDuffee former w., R6696
John, Va., BLWt.981-100
Joshua, N.C., S6803
Mary, former wid. of Matthias Parcell, N.J., which see
Oliver, N.Y., S45337
Samuel, Ct., Green Mt. Boys, Mass. N.H., N.Y., S45338
Samuel, Mass., S35266; BLWt.582-100
Samuel, Mass., S39462
Samuel, N.Y., S28716
Seth, Mass., BLWt.514-400. No papers
Solomon, N.C., Franky, W27541; BLWt.34948-160-55
Stephen, Mass., Jerusha, W24080
Thomas C., N.H., S22739
Thomas H., Va., R13852. Va. Half Pay
William, N.Y., S23204
William, Vt., R3084
DREWRY, John, Va., Martha Griffin, former wid., R4314
Richard, Va., Jemima, R3085; BLWt.34620-160-55
DRIGGS, Israel, Cont., Mass., or Ct., S37897
DRING, Nathaniel, Navy, R.I., Susannah, W20479
DRINKARD, John, Va., Lucy, R3087
DRINKWATER, Daniel, Mass., Navy, Rebecca, R3088; BLWt.17595-160-55
DRISCALL, William, Cont., R.I., Elizabeth, See DRISKILL
DRISCOLL, Asa, Navy, Ct. agcy & res., S37896
Jeremiah, Mass., S34766
DRISKELL, Jeremiah, Md., BLWt.

DRISKELL (continued)
11142-100-Pvt. Iss. 2/1/1790. No papers
Joseph, 3rd Regt. Arty., Col. Crane's Mass., BLWt.529-200-Lt. Iss. 5/30/1789. No papers
DRISKILL, David, N.C., Agnes, W22974
Jeremiah, Mass., BLWt.4038-100-Pvt. Iss. 3/25/1790. No papers
Timothy, Cont., Pa., S45348
William, Cont., R.I., Elizabeth, R3089
DRIVER, Francis, Va., S35901
James, Md., BLWt.11161-100-Pvt. Iss. 12/18/1794 to Henry Purdy ass. No papers
Jasper, Pa., BLWt.9289-100-Pvt. Iss. 12/22/1791 to John Kern, ass. No papers
Stephen, Mass., S34767
DRODY, Samuel, Mass., Sarah, W14641
DROLINER, Frederick, See DRULLINGER
DRONE, William, Cont., Va., Susannah, W3785
DROUGHT, Richard, N.H., S42675
DROWN, Caleb, R.I., S38671
Daniel, R.I., Freelove, R3090
Frederick, Mass., Martha, R3091
Jonathan, Cont., Mass., Sarah, W27408
Jonathan J., R.I., S17932
Moses, Mass., died 1812, Louisa Gray, former wid., R13857
Moses, Mass., died 1825, S47316
Samuel, R.I., Lydia, W21004; BLWt.2526-100
Solomon, N.H., S45645
Solomon, R.I., Betsey, W8201
Stephen, Mass., S45838
Thomas, N.H., R3092
DROWNE, Philip, R.I., BLWt.3083; iss. 1/15/1800. No papers
DROWT, Robert, N.H., Susanna, W16110
DRUIN, Samuel, Va., S16772
DRULLINGER, Frederick, N.J., S16106
DRUM, Christopher, N.J., S42185
Philip, N.C., Mary, W2079; BLWt.26271-160-55
Philip, Pa., S22218
Robert, N.J., Amy, R3093
DRUMBAR, Henry, Pa., Frances, R3094
DRUMHELLER, George, Va., R3095
Leonard, Va., Annie/Anna, W5265 BLWt.26960-160-55
DRUMMOND, John, Va., S8376
John, Va., BLWt.2347-100
Joshua, Va., Mary, W7045
Peter, Pa., Mary, R3096; BLWt.1994-200
William, Cont., N.J., R20359
DRURY, Eleazer, Mass., Elizabeth, W7044; BLWt.26864-160-55
Henry, N.C., Mary, R3096 1/2
Leonard, Md., S2183
Luther, Vt., Rhoda, W19163; BLWt.11183-160-55

DRURY (continued)
Michael, ?, res. Somerset Co., Pa., Dis. No papers
Thomas, Mass., Privateer, S15817
William, Del., BLWt.10755-100-Pvt. Iss. 9/2/1789. No papers
William, Mass., Hannah, W1247; BLWt.30699-160-55
DRY, Jacob, N.C., R3097
DRYDEN, Artemas, Mass., S29763
DUBA, John, N.Y., S45349
DUBEE, John, Hazen's Regt., BLWt. 13002-Pvt. Iss. 7/14/1789. No papers
DUBOIS, Barent, N.Y., S15105
Benjamin C., N.Y., S12816
Gerrit/Garret, N.Y., Sarah, W20995
James, N.Y., Jane, R3099
John, N.Y., S45339
John, N.Y., Hannah, W2771; BLWt. 254-60-55 & 7034-100. Iss. 10/12/1790
Lewis, N.Y., BLWt.7061-100-Pvt. Iss. 7/18/1791 to William Ely, ass. No papers
Martin, N.Y., S29129
Nathaniel, N.Y., S45441
Samuel, N.Y., R3100
DUBOISE, Stephen, S.C., S3311
DUBOSE, Peter, S.C., S21163
DUBOYS, Lewis, N.Y., S45340; BLWt. 560-500-Col. Iss. 6/6/1794. Also recorded under BLWt.2643. No papers
DUCAS, Joseph, Hazen's Regt., BLWt. 12985-100-Pvt. Iss. 10/12/1790
DUCIT, John, Ct., See DUSETT
DUCK, Jacob, Cont., Pa., S12806
Philip, Pa., Elizabeth, W3230
DUCKER, John, Va., S15409
DUCKWORTH, John, N.C., S6805
DUCLOS, Francis, N.J., Navy, S22220
DUCOIN, John, Ga., BLWt.2260-300
DUDDEROW, John, Md., Catharine, R2947
DUDLEY, Ambrose, N.C., See DUDLY
Benajah, Ct., S12824
Daniel, Mass., Lucy, W14651
Daniel, N.H., Anna, W16966
Eber/Ebor, Ct., Hannah, W21016
Freeworthy/Trueworthy, Mass., S45648; BLWt.863-100. Alive 1818.
George, N.C., S41514
Guilford, N.C., Anna Bland, W8681
Harman, Ct., S27737
Henry, Va., R13891; Va. Half Pay
Isaac, Ct., Anne, R3101
Jared, Ct., Anna, W17737
Jeremiah, Mass., N.H., S28717
John, Mass., Anna, W413; BLWt. 26576-160-55
John, Mass., Clarissa, R3102; BLWt 54425-160-55. She also applied for pension for services of father, Tyrannus Collins. See papers within
John, N.H., S32225
John, Va. Sea Service, R35. Va. Half Pay
Medad, Ct., R3104
Nathan, Cont., Mass., Sylvia,

DUDLEY (continued)
W918; BLWt.11414-160-55
Nathan, Mass., S17397
Nathaniel, N.H., Harriet, BLWt. 34823-160-55
Paul, Mass., Dorothy, W21020
Peter, Mass., Elizabeth Walker, former wid., W25873
Roswell, Ct., S10592
Samuel, Ct., Privateer, S6806
Stephen, N.H., Polly/Molly, W22977
Thomas, Ct., BLWt.5696-Pvt. Iss. 6/26/1789 to Peleg Sanford. No papers
Thomas, Ct., S22222
Thomas, N.C., BLWt.612-200-Lt. Iss. 2/2/1797 to Amos Johnston, ass. No papers
Trueworthy, Mass. See Freeworthy
Trueworthy/Worthy, N.H., War of 1812; Sarah, W22980. Died in 1814-1815
William, N.C., R3105
DUDLY, Ambrose, N.C., S1949
DUDUIT/DUDWIT/DUIDWIT, William, Indian War 1792-5, not Rev. War Zier, Old War Wid. Rej. File 13903; BLWt.21470-160-55
DUE, James, Md., S34771
Peter, Pa., See DOOEY
DUEL, Benjamin, N.Y. See DEUEL
DUER, Betsy, former wid. of Isaac Chandler, N.Y. Which see
DUESLAR, Marcus, N.Y. See DUSLER
DUESLER, Jacob, N.Y., See DUSLER
John, N.Y., Catharine, W16244
DUEY, Emanuel, Pa., S2170
DUFAN/DUFAU, Michael, Cont., S46380
DUFAU, Michael, See DUFAN
DUFAULT, Michael, Hazen's Regt. BLWt.13000-100-Pvt. Iss. 8/14/1792 to Benj. Moore, ass. No papers
DUFENDORF, John, N.Y., Catharine, W24061
DUFF, Henry, Del., BLWt.581-300-Capt. Iss. 9/12/1789 to Thos. Duff, admr. No papers
Hugh Eliott, Pa., R3106
James, Pa., S42680
John, Va., S30390
DUFFEE, Thomas, Md., Bridget, W3787
DUFFEL, Thomas, N.C., Lurany/Luvany, W1738; BLWt.32218-160-55
DUFFEY, James, Pa., BLWt.9281-100-Pvt. Iss. 6/9/1789 to M. McConnell, ass. No papers
James, Va., BLWt.12064-100-Pvt. Iss. 11/5/1789. No papers
DUFFIELD, Abraham, Va., S9389
Anthony, S.C., BLWts. 12096 & 12979. Iss. 5/2/1794
Felix, Pa., BLWt.9303. Iss. 6/10/1794 to Silas Hart, ass. No papers
John, Cont., Surg. in Crane's Art. Mass., U.S. Hosp. Dept. in 1778 in Phila., Margaretta, W4185;

DUFFIELD (continued)
BLWt.528-400-Surg. Iss. 5/9/1789
DUFFY, James, Sgt.,Hazen's Regt., BLWt.12994 iss. 6/20/1789
DUFRENCE, Joseph, Pvt., Hazen's Regt., BLWt.12987 iss. 2/20/1792 to Benj. Moore, ass.
DUGAN, Abraham, Md., BLWt.11162-100-Pvt. Iss. 11/29/1790 to Lawrence Brannan, Admr. No papers
Charles, Pvt., Pa., BLWt.9259 iss. 6/28/1793 to Samuel King, ass.
Daniel, N.J., Catharine, W7059; BLWt.36642-160-55
Henry, Pa., S42686
Hugh, Wayne's War 1792-5, not Rev. War; Md. res., Pension appl. Ky., Old War Rej. 3107
John, N.C., See DOUGAN
William, Mass., BLWt.4046-100-Cpl. Iss. 11/26/1790 to John May. No papers
William, N.J., S42678
DUGGANS, William, Mass., Elizabeth, See DUGGINS
DUGAR, Robert, Va., S39465
DUGAW, Peter, Cont., Canadian, See LEUCAW
DUGGAR, William, N.C., R3109
DUGGER, John, Va., Frances, W7062
Julius, N.C., Indian War 1788, R3108
DUGGINS, William, Mass., Mary, W22979
William, Mass., Elizabeth, W24082; BLWt.24-60-55
DUGLAS, David, Mass., R.I, S5355
DUGLESS, Edward, N.C., S3297
John, N.C., S2517
DUGUID, John, Pa., BLWt.1159-200
DuHAMMELL, John B., Pa., BLWt. 9283-100-Pvt. Iss. 5/28/1790. For papers, see Anthony de MARCELLIN, Pa.
DUICK, Timothy, Pvt., Ga., Mil., Reg. 273482-1855
DUKE, Clevears, Va., S39471
Hardeman, N.C., Elizabeth, W783
Harden/Hardin, Va., S8357
Henry, Va., Susannah, W9415; BLWt.101228-160-55
James, N.C., S8358
John, Cont., Pa., Sally, W9841
Matthew, Va., S1199
William, N.C., S6808
William, N.C., Va., S8356
DUKES, Isaac, Md., Privateer, Elizabeth, R3111
DULA, William, Va., R3112
DULANEY, Zachariah, Va., Mary, W3789
DULANY, Benjamin, Va. See DELANEY
DULEY, Philip, N.Y., S12822
DULIN, John, Pa., Sarah, W10765
John, Va., S39468
DULL, Caspar, Pa., R3114
Christian, Cont., N.J., S42688
William, Pa., BLWt.9261-100-Pvt. Iss. 3/19/1792 to George Steinmetz, ass. No papers
DUM, Peter, Cont., Pa. res. 1785, Catharine, See THUM

DUMARESQUE, Ebenezer, Mass.,S45352
DUMAS, Peter, See DeMASS
DUMBLETON, John, N.Y. See DUMBOLTON
DUMBOLTON, John, N.Y., Ruth, R3115
DUMFEE, Cornelius, N.H., See DUNFEE
DUMMER, Jeremiah, Mass., S30997
Richard, Mass., S15820
Stephen, Ct., R3116
DUMOND, John H., N.Y., Catharine, R3117
DUMONT, John, N.J., S2531
DUN, Henry, N.Y., R3118
DUNAVANT, Josiah, Va., S18384
DUNAVENT, Frederick, ?, Va. res. in 1841, R3120
DUNAWAY, Samuel, Va., S2530
DUNBAR, Abner, Mass., S5367
Amos, Mass., S37899
Amos, Mass., Rachel, W22982
Amos, N.Y., S22223; BLWt.31433-160-55
Daniel, Mass., R.I., Phillipa, W24088
David, Cont., Mass., Elizabeth, W22981
Elijah, Mass., S30999
Enoch, Cont., Mass., R.I., S17396
George, N.Y., See DANBAR
Jacob, Mass., S31001
Jeremiah, Mass., R3121
Jesse, Cont., Mass., Sarah, W15672
Joel, Ct., S43525
John, Cont., Mass., S12817; BLWt. 26085-160-55
Jonathan, Va., S19286
Joseph, Cont., Ct. res. 1794, Dis. No papers
Joshua, colored, Mass., Privateer, Lydia, W19198
Josiah, Mass., Martha/Patty, W5266 BLWt.13893-160-55
Lucy, former wid. of Moses Sampson, Mass., which see
Melzar, Mass., Nabby, W14657
Miles, Ct., Tryphosa, W16962
Nathaniel, Mass., S29769
Nehemiah, Mass., BLWt.4008-Pvt. Iss. 6/1/1792. No papers
Nehemiah, Mass., S46381
Obed, Mass., S18805
Peter, Mass., Relief, W22976
Peter, Mass., S29768
Robert, Ct., S39463
Samuel, colored, Mass., N.Y., S15106
Samuel, Vt., BLReg.286310-55
Thomas, Ct. Sea Service, R.I., Eunice, W24081; BLWt.29039-160-55
Thomas, S.C., Mary Shackelford, former wid., W3879; BLWt.2371-200
Thomas, Va., S30998
William, N.Y., BLWt.7035-Pvt. Iss. 10/1/1791. No papers
William, N.Y., BLWt.7038-Pvt. Iss. 10/3/1791 to Isaac Brooks, ass. No papers
William, N.Y., S34770
William, Va., S2163
DUNBER, Ebenezer, Mass., S34776
DUNCAN, Alexander, Pa., S42187
Archibald, Va., Hannah, W8679
Benjamin, N.C., Mary, W7052

DUNCAN (continued)
Charles, Va., Margaret/Peggy, W22973
Christopher, Va., R20198
David, N.H., Sea Service, S45646
Elijah, N.C., S3309
Francis, Mass., S34773
Gabriel, Va., S10588
George, N.C., S41513
George, Va., Elizabeth, W9845
James, Cont., res. 1818 Huntingdon Ct., Pa., S42681
James, Cont., Pa., Pa. res. & agcy., S47181; BLWt.626-300-Capt. Iss. 9/22/1789
James, N.Y., BLWt.7070-Pvt. Iss. 10/10/1791 to Anthony Maxwell, ass. No papers
James, Pa., S2187
James, Pa., Margaret, W3400
James, Va., S37901
Jared, Ct., Dolly, R3122
Jesse, N.C., S16774
John, Mass., S27738
John, N.H., Betsy, W1841; BLWt. 7206-160-55
John, S.C., Ann, R3125
John, Va., S8373
John, Va., Margaret, W353
John, Va., Lydia, R3126
Joseph, Md., Va., S30389
Joseph, Va., S1809
Minrod, Va., Hannah, W2925
Robert, Md., BLWt.11146-100-Pvt. Iss. 10/14/1795 to Henry Davis, ass. No papers
Robert, Md., S42188
Robert, N.C., S21167
Samuel, Cont., Va., S12812
Samuel, Va., R3128
Simeon, Mass., S12827
Thomas, N.Y., BLWt.7026-100-Pvt. Iss. 7/7/1790. No papers
Thomas, ?,N.Y. res. Dis. No papers
Thomas, Va., Rhoda, W1577
William, N.C., Sarah, W21015
DUNCKLE, Nicholas, N.Y., S21164
DUNCOMBE, Edward, Ct., Anna, W25553
DUNCOST, Joseph, BLWt.12986-Pvt. in Hazen's Regt. Iss. 10/12/1790. No papers
DUNDY, Samuel, BLWts.9237 & 14135-Pvt. in Pa. Arty. Iss. 8/26/1795 to Eliz. Knight, late Dundy, admx. No papers
DUNFEE, Cornelius, N.H., S35274
DUNFIELD, Henry, N.J., BLWt.8264-100-Pvt. Iss. 9/29/1790 to Thos. L. Vickers, ass. No papers
DUNFORD, William, Va. Sea Service, R37. Va. Half Pay. No papers
DUNGAN, Thomas, Pa., BLWt.566-200-Lt. Iss. 10/17/1789. No papers
DUNHAM, Abishai, Mass., Privateer, S15107
Ammi, Mass., S35272
Asa, Mass., Me., War of 1812; Lydia, W10764
Azariah, N.J., S995
Calvin, Mass., S10591
Cornelius, Ct., S12828
Cornelius, Mass. Sea Service, Lydia, R3133

DUNHAM (continued)
Daniel, Ct., S43523; BLWt.10235-160-55
David, Mass., S42684
Ebenezer, Cont., Mass., S39470
Ebenezer, N.Y., S22744
Edward, Mass., N.Y., Mary, W1158
Elijah, Mass., S34782
Elisha, Ct., Mehitable, W25546
Enoch, N.J., Jemima, W7054; BLWt. 3513-160-55
Ephraim, Mass., S43522
George, Mass., Paitence, W14645
Gershom, Ct., Marcy, W21013
Gideon, Ct., Privateer, Anna, W16565
Hannah, former wid. of John Lawrence, Ct., which see
Holtum/Holtom, N.Y., S43521
Jacob, N.J., Sarah, W7055; BLWt. 36558-160-55
James, Ct., Cont., S31658
James, Mass., R3131
James, N.J., Mary Bristol, former wid., W5233; BLWt.27610-160-55
Jehu, N.J., S870
Jeremiah, Mass., BLWt.4009-100-Pvt. Iss. 6/1/1792. No papers
Jeremiah, Mass., S43524
Jesse, Mass., R3132
John, Mass., BLWt.4021-100-Pvt. Iss. 10/20/1789 to John Holmes. No papers
John, N.J., S2158
Joseph, Mass., S34777
Joseph, R.I., S12831
Manassah, Mass., BLWt.4003-100-Pvt. Iss. 12/2/1791 to Martin Kingsley. No papers
Moses, Cont., Mass., S16773
Nathaniel, N.J., BLWt.8274-100-Pvt. Iss. 7/16/1789. No papers
Obadiah, Vt., Lois, W24865
Philomen, Mass., BLWt.4026-100-Pvt. Iss. 9/13/1792 to Henry Newman. No papers
Richardson, Mass., Phebe, W1840; BLWt.310-60-55
Robert/Robart, Mass., S34777
Salathiel, Ct., Lucy, W19202
Samuel, Ct., Asenath Turner, former wid., W27795; BLWt. 114388-160-55
Samuel, Cont., Ct., Dolly, S45346
Samuel, Mass., Elizabeth, W14654
Samuel, Mass., Mary, R3134
Samuel, N.Y., Martha, W2772
Solomon, Mass., N.H., S15416
Stephen, Ct., S12804
Timothy, Mass., Lydia, W19207
William, Mass., Experience, W21007
DUNIKIN/DONKIN, Daniel, Va., S38675
DUNING, Edmund, Ct., S15819
DUNKAN, Edward, N.C., S17395
DUNKESON/DUNKINSON, Thomas, Va., Lucretia, W8680
DUNKIN, Anthony, Va., S1808
Isaac, Md., BLWt.11138-100-Pvt. Iss. 1/8/1796 to George Ponsonby ass. No papers
DUNKLE, Francis, N.Y., R3130

DUNKLE (continued)
George/Johann George, N.Y., Elizabeth, W24086
DUNKLEBERGER, Peter, Pa., S2529
DUNKLEY, John, Va., Tabitha, W5267
Moses, Va., S9331
DUNLAP, Andrew, Invalid Regt., BLWt.13016-100-Pvt. Iss. 3/27/1793. No papers
Andrew, N.Y., S19287
Berias, Sheldon's Dragoons, Ct., BLWt.5728-100-Pvt. Iss. 4/1/1790 No papers
George, Mass., S34774
James, Cont., Mass., Elizabeth, R3136
James, N.H., BLWt.3070 iss. 10/12/1795 to James A. Neal, ass. No papers
James, Pa., S35904
John, Cont., Mass., Dorcas, W22978
John, Pa., Elizabeth, R3137
Joseph, N.J., R3138
Joseph, Va., S38676
Robert, N.J., S8374
Samuel, Cont., Mass., S42679
Samuel, S.C., S3310
Samuel, Va., S39466
Sarah, former wid. of John McLaughlin, Navy, which see
Thomas, N.Y., S45345
William, Pa., S15415
William, S.C., Margaret, W2723
William, S.C., Nancy, R3139
DUNLAVY, Francis, Pa., Va., S2526
DUNLEVY, Patrick, N.J., BLWt.8267 Iss. 6/11/1789 to Jonathan Dayton, ass. No papers
DUNMORE, Jane, former wid. of James Merrill, Ct., which see
DUNN, Aaron, N.Y., S32223
Abner M., Cont., Pa., Priscilla, W9842; BLWt.564-200-Lt. Iss. 9/7/1790. No papers
Alexander, N.Y., BLWt.7015-100-Pvt. Iss. 7/6/1790 to Frederick Shober, ass. No papers
Alexander, N.C., R3142
Alexander, Pa, S31002
Andrew, Va., S43519
Cary, Cont., N.Y., S12823. 8 Cont. documents in file
Christopher, Mass., S17936
Duncan, Mass., Vt., S42685
George, S.C., S41515
Henry, N.Y., See DUN
Isaac, N.J., S869
Isaac, Va., S43520
Isaac Budd, Pa., Abbey, W21022; BLWt.2224-300
James, Mass., Rachel, W14652
James, N.J., Priscilla, W7049
James, Pa., Elizabeth, W19199
James, Va., BLWts.12067 & 12703-Pvt. Iss. 12/16/1795. No papers
James, Va., S8359
James T., N.J., Eleanor, W732; BLWt.26587-160-55
Jane, former wid. of Robert McConnell, Pa., which see
Jeremiah, N.J., Sarah, W412
Joel, N.J., Rachel, W919

DUNN (continued)
John, Mass., Mary, W14646; BLWt. 21813-160-55
John, N.Y., S10593
John, Pa., BLWt.9254-100-Pvt. Iss. 8/9/1796 to John Brown, ass. No papers
John, Va., S35903
John, Va., R3144
Joseph, N.C., S12811
Joshua, Mass., S35271
Joshua, Va., S39467
Josiah, ?, res., sometime, in Ga., R3145
Martin, Va., R3146
Moses, N.J., S2523
Nahum, N.J., Elizabeth, W7051
Nicholas, N.C., S8360
Philip, N.J., S22224
Richard, Va., Elizabeth, R3143
Robert, N.J., R20196
Samuel, Ct., N.J., Barbara, W7048; BLWt.26927-160-55
Silas, N.C., R3147
Thomas, Pa., Peggy, W21024
Thomas, Va., S16373
Thomas P., N.J., BLWt.8254-100-Pvt. Iss. 5/7/1790 to John Linn, ass. No papers
Timothy, Ct., Mehitable, W1249; BLWt.11176-160-55
William, Md., S35273
William, Mass., S34783
William, N.J., BLWt.8252. Iss. 6/20/1789. No papers
William, Va., b. England, Catharine, W286
DUNNAVANT, William, Va., S8365
DUNNAVON, John, Pa., BLWt.9247-100-Pvt. Iss. 6/29/1789 to M. McConnell, ass. No papers
DUNNAWAY, Thomas, Va., Gen. St. Clair's & Wayne's Indian Wars, R3149
DUNNELL, John, Mass., Polly/Mary, W1576
DUNNELLS, David, Mass., Avis, W15673
DUNNING, Abel, Vt., Maria, W21010
Abram, Vt., Tryphena, R3152
Butler, Md., See MARLOW
David, Ct., S15103
David, Mass., Elizabeth, W26661
Dennis, Md., BLWt.11132-100-Drummer. Iss. 2/1/1790. No papers
Dennis, Md., S42676
Ebenezer, N.Y., S12826
Ebenezer, N.Y., Martha, W21008
Elizabeth, former wid. of Wm. Hunt, Mass., which see
Ephraim, Mass., R20362
James, Ct., Cont., N.Y., S12830
John, Mass., S22740
John, Mass., S31000
Josiah, Ct., N.Y., Vt., S23207
Luther, Ct., R3151
Michael/Mitchell, Capt. Cont., N.Y., Hannah, W16245. On comm. his name written Mitchell instead of Michael. BLWt.511-200-Lt. in Lt.Col. Seth Warner's Regt. Iss. 8/8/1789 to John

DUNNING (continued)
Doty, ass. BLWts. 543-300-Capt. & 2597-300-Capt. in Warner's Regt. iss. 11/28/1791 to John Thompson, ass.
Stephen, Mass., S12832
DUNNINGTON, William, Md., Martha/ Patsey Swiney/Swinney, W27409; BLWt.1091-100; BLWt.38545-160-55
DUNNOM, Charles, Cont., Md., R20361
DUNOVAN, Hannah, former wid. of Thomas Piper, Cont., N.H., which see
DUNPHEY, James, Cont., N.H., S3312
DUNSCOMB, Edward, N.Y., Mary, W19206; BLWt.545-300-Capt. Iss. 6/22/1790. No papers
Samuel, Pvt., Pa., BLWt.9282-100 iss. 3/12/1792 to Moses Sill, ass.
DUNSETT, Cato (colored), Mass., Azube, W14659
DUNSICK, Prince, Mass., Hannah, See BAILEY
DUNSMOOR, James, N.C., Jane, W7058; BLWt.32231-160-55
John, Mass., Sarah, W21017
DUNSMORE, John, Mass., Phebe, W17733
DUNSTER, Jason, Mass., Polly/ Mary, W16012; BLWt.3640-160-55
Peter, Md., BLWt.11172-100-Pvt. Iss. 9/12/1792 to John Wright, ass. of Sarah Mantle, admx. No papers
DUNSTON, Almon, Va., Alice, W731; BLWt.12729-160-55
John, Mass., S45343
DUNTEN, Joseph, Mass., S23607
DUNTLIN/DUNTLEN, Nathaniel, Cont., Mass., Sarah, W24862; BLWt.888-100
DUNTON, Anna, former wid. of Thomas Barnes, Vt., which see
David, Mass., S45342
Isaac, Mass., Bulah, W14644
James, Mass., BLWt.4000-100-Pvt. Iss. 3/14/1791 to David Quinton No papers
James, Mass., Sally, W3528
Levi, Mass., S34781
Samuel, Mass., Mary, W14647
Silas, Mass., S30391
William, Mass., Vt., Mary, W19200
William, Navy, Pa. res. in 1794. Dis. No papers
DUNWELL, Stephen, Ct., S2188
William, Ct., S34772
DUNWORTH, George, Ct., Abigail W. W9416; BLWt.26314-160-55
DUPAR/DIPPER, John, Mass., Sarah Roundey, former wid., W13858. See claim of other husb., Joseph Roundey, Mass.
DUPEE, John, Mass., Deborah, W7056; BLWt.15160-160-55
DUPERE, Baptist John, Hazen's Regt., BLWt.12984-100-Pvt. Iss. 10/12/1790. No papers
DUPILLE, Antoine, Cont., enl. in

DUPILLE (continued)
Va., res. in Md., S34769
DUPLESSE, Henry, Hazen's Regt., BLWt.12988-100-Pvt. Iss. 10/ 12/1790. No papers
DUPLEX, Prince (colored), Ct., Lement, W16963
DuPONCEAU, Peter Stephen, Cont., S5371; BLWt.638-300-Capt. & Aide-de-Camp. Iss. 1/21/1794
DUPORTAIL, Louis Le Begne, Cont. French, BLWt.2293-1100. No papers
DUPPELLE, Antoiene, Hazen's Regt. BLWt.13001-100-Pvt. Iss. 10/ 12/1790. No papers
DUPREE, Jeremiah, Va., R3155
William, Pvt., Ba., B.L. Rej. 281092-1855
DUPUY, John, Va., Mary, W7060
Moses, N.Y., Hellena, See DEPUY
William, Ga., S12821
DURAND, Alexander, Ct., Elizabeth, W21014
Andrew, Ct., S2528
Ebenezer, Ct., Polly, W25547; BLWt.13202-160-55
Eleazer, Ct., S45354
Fisk/Fish, Ct., S12807
Isaac, Ct., S19961
John, Ct., S37898
John, Navy, Ct. agcy. & res., S37900
Joseph, Ct., N.Y., S12829
Lemuel, Ct., Catharine, W1248
Samuel, Ct., Susanna, W17734
William, Ct. Sea Service, Mary, W25552
DURANT, Allen, Cont., Mass., Parthenia, W21018
David, Mass., S18386
Ephraim, Cont., Mass., BLWt. 787-100
Isaac, Mass., S34780
Joshua, Mass., N.H., S18806
Thomas, Mass., Elizabeth, W14650
William, Mass., Mary, W14655
DURDEN, Mills, N.C., Polly, W17736
DURDIN, John, N.C., S6807
DURELL, Benjamin, Mass., S35270
David, Mass., S20341
Peter, Mass., S35268
DURFEE, Abner, R.I., See claim of his wid., Nancy Durfee, who was allowed pension as former wid. of David Gray, R.I.
Benjamin, Mass., S29128
Earl, R.I., R21680
Joseph, Mass., Elizabeth, W9414. She was also pensioned as former wid. of 1st husb., Eleazer Nichols, Mass., which see
Lemuel, R.I., Prudence, W19204
Nancy, former wid. of David Gray, R.I., which see
Richard, R.I., S21165
Robert, R.I., S21166
Thomas, R.I., Mary, W24084
Walter, Vt., Anna, W21009
DURFEY, Ebenezer, Ct., Abigail, W2080; BLWt.13187-160-55
Elijah, Ct., Elizabeth, R3156

DURFEY (continued)
John, Ct., Privateer, Mary, W21011
Joseph, Ct., Experience, See DURPHY
DURGEY, Moses, Vt., See DURKEE
DURGIN, Henry, N.H., BLWt.2103-100
John, Cont., Mass., S18807
John, N.H., S45647
Joseph, N.H., S8370
Josiah, N.H., & War of 1812; Hannah, W21023
Richard, N.H., S12814
DURHAM, Asa, Mass., S12820
Charnel, S.C., Nancy, W9418
James, Va., S35902 & S8367
James, N.C., Va., Martha, W8371; BLWt.81501-160-55
John, N.C., S42677
John, Va., S31003
Joseph, N.C., R3158
Mastin, N.C., S1197
Mathew, N.C., S32224
Samuel, Va., R3135
Samuel Davis, Va., Isbel, W7053
Simeon, Ct., S10595
Stephen, N.Y., BLWt.7057-100-Pvt. Iss. 7/30/1790 to Edward Compston, ass. No papers
Stephen, N.Y., S45347
William, Md., Anna/Ann, W4186; See also Wm. Durham
William, Md. R3160. See also William Durham
DURKEE, Asahel/Asel, Ct., Sarah, W19201; BLWt.9453-160-55
Benjamin, Ct., Cont., S39473; BLWt.420-300
Daniel, Ct., S22742
Ebe, Ct., S2524. See BLWt.100834- of Jemima, wid of John Durkee, brother of Ebe.
John, Ct., d. 1838, son of Capt. Joseph Durkee, Jemima, BLWt. 100834-160-55
John, Ct., Cont., BLWt.533-300-Capt. Iss. 7/7/1791. Has papers on file. Son of Col. John Durkee
John, Ct., Cont., BLWt.580-500-Col. Iss. 4/12/1812. He d. 5/30/ 1782
John, N.H., S16372
Lydius, N.Y., S22741
Moses, Vt., S23205
Moses, Vt., Eunice, W21019
Nathan, N.Y., S22743; also Cont. service
Nathan, Green Mt. Boys, N.H., Phebe, W22975; BLWt.3756-160-55
Nathaniel, Ct., Cont., Melinda, W25548; BLWt.19729-160-55
Phineas, Ct., BLWt.606-100
Robert, Ct., BLWt.432-300
Sally/Sarah, former wid. of Walter Tiffany, Cont., Ct., which see
Solomon, Ct., Cont., S42682
William, Ct., S18385
DURNALL, John, See DURNELL
DURNELL, John, ?, Pa. agcy. & res. S12813
DURNEY, Philip, Pa., Elizabeth, W2081

DURON, William, Cont., Mass., Ruth, W24863
DUROSETT, Samuel, Va., S34778
DURPHY, Joseph, Ct., Experience, W1839; BLWt.6415-160-55
DURRELL, Thomas, Mass., Mary, R3163
DURRETT, Claburn/Claiborne, Va., S39569
DURRINGTON, Walter, Md., R3180
DURYEA, Charles, N.J., S4278
DURYEE, John, N.J., S5368
DUSENBERRY, William, Cont., N.Y. agcy. & res., See DEUSENBERRY
DUSENBERY, Moses, N.Y., Sarah,R3164
DUSENBURY, Gabriel, N.Y. See DEUSENBURY
John, N.Y., S45353
DUSET, John, Ct., BLWt.5707-100-Pvt. Iss. 2/22/1790 to Theodosius Fowler. No papers
DUSETT, John, Ct., S45351
DUSINBERY, William, N.J., S8372
DUSKY, John, Del., S42687
DUSLER, Jacob, N.Y., Marthalain/Mathlin, R3165;BLWt.34584-160-55
Marcus, N.Y., S10589
DUSTIN, Amos, Mass., S2186
Ebenezer, N.H., Susan, R3167
John, Mass., Sarah, W15671
Moody, N.H., BLWt.509-300-Capt. Iss. 3/25/1790. No papers
Moses, N.H., S10590
Moses, N.H., BLWt.10-300-Capt.
Parley, N.H., R3166
Stephen, Cont.,Mass., N.H., Molly Collins, former wid., W18962
Violetta, former wid. of Benajah Brown, N.Y., which see
Zacheus, N.H., Mary, W1578; BLWt. 9450-160-55
DUTAIL, John, Pvt. "in Arty.", Pa. BLWt.9317-100 iss. 1/6/1791
DUTCH, Jeremiah, N.H., Mary Kenniston, former wid., W15918
John, Mass., BLWt.4032-100-Pvt. Iss. 9/26/1791 to William Lane
DUTCHER, Abraham, N.Y., S45350
Barnard, N.Y., BLWt.7050-100-Pvt. Iss. 10/4/1792. No papers
Barnet, N.Y., Charity, R3168
Cornelius, N.Y., Mary, R3169
Henry, N.Y., S42683
Jacob, Mass., N.Y., S12825
Mary, former wid. of Samuel Cochran, N.Y., which see
Simeon, N.Y., S10594
Solomon, Mass., N.Y., S15104
William, N.Y., Catharine, W15831. Son Daniel
DUTRICK, Lewis (Baron), Gen. Armand's Legionary Corps, BLWt.626-300-Capt. Iss. 10/10/1789. No papers. See Uechritz, Louis Augustus de, (Baron), or Uttricht, in Heitman's Register, p.553
DUTTIN, William, Mass., BLWt.4045-100-Sgt. Iss. 4/19/1790 to John Bush. No papers
DUTTON, Abel, Mass., N.H., Susannah, W24864
Amasa, Ct., Elizabeth, W1399
Asa, Cont., Ct., S39464

DUTTON (continued)
Asa, Mass., Vt., S12818
Ephraim, Mass., S39472
John, N.H., S45732
Joseph, Ct., Mary, W25551
Nancy, former wid. of Thomas O'Bryan, Mass., which see
Oliver, Ct., Ruth, W24861
Oliver, Ct., Cont., Mass., Phebe, S18383; BLWt.9437-160-55. Her former husb., Stephen Powers, Mass., was pensioned, which see
Richard, Mass., Elizabeth, W24860
Thomas, Ct., R3170
Thomas, Mass., N.H., S17935
Timothy, Mass., BLWt.4042-100-Pvt Iss. 3/25/1790. No papers
Timothy, Mass., S34775
Titus, Ct., Cont., S45344
William, Mass., S12819; BLWt. 4045-100-Sgt. Iss. 4/19/1790 to John Bush
William, Mass., Susanna Parker, former wid., W16052
DUTTROE, Jacob, Md. See claim of James Winchester
DUTWEILER, John, Pa., Barbara, W3401; BLWt.26791-160-55
DUTWILER, John, See DUTWEILER
DUTY, Moses, N.H., BLWt.33-100
William, N.H., Polly, W24083
William, Lt., N.H., B.L. Rej. 217364-1855
DUVAL, Daniel, Va., Maria, W5069
Jemima, former wid. of Caleb Hazle, Md., which see
William, Va., S8362
DUVALL, Benjamin, of Elisha, Md., S34768
Edward, Md., BLWt.590-200-Lt. Iss. 4/11/1799 to Benj. & Gabrl. Duvall, Susannah Hodges, Delilah & Sarah Duvall & the issue of Elizabeth Duvall, vis., Judson Clarke, Wm. Russel Clarke, & Benj. Duvall Clarke, the only surviving heirs of E.D. No papers
George, Md., BLWt.12998 & 14098-Pvt. Iss. 1/28/1795 to Francis Sherrard, ass. of Samuel Thompson, admr. No papers
Isaac, Md., BLWt.574-200-Lt. Iss. 4/11/1799. Same as Edward Duvall, above
Joseph, Md., S35906
Joseph, Md., Mary, W9417
Lewis, S.C., R3181
Richard, Md., BLWt.11148-100-Pvt. Iss. 8/18/1792. No papers
Samuel, Md., S35905
Thomas, Md. See DEWALL
DUYO, Abraham, N.Y. See DEYO
DUZUA, Charles, French, R2896
DWELLY, Allen, Mass., S35275
Jeremiah, R.I., Elizabeth,W24089
John, Navy, Mass., Deborah, W17738; BLWt.26605-160-55
Joseph, Mass., Ruth, W10770
Pearce, Mass., Rose, W22985
DWIGHT, Alpheus, Ct., Fanny, W25554; BLWt.29738-160-55
Henry W., Mass., Abigail/Abby,

DWIGHT (continued)
W14661
Timothy, Cont., Ct., Mary, W21025
DWINEL, Aaron, Mass., R3172
Archelaus, Mass., S40056
Solomon, Mass., Hannah, W14660
DWINELL, Amos, Cont., Mass., N.H., S12834
Henry, Mass., Lydia, W21026
Jonathan, Mass., N.H., S9851
DWINNELL, John, Mass., Rachel, W22984
Thomas, Mass., Sarah, W16967
DWIRE, Thomas, Md., R13913
D'WOLF, Seth, Ct., Hannah, W2562; BLWt.26504-160-55
DYAL, John, Pa., Christina, W2082
DYALL, Margaret, former wid. of John Fisher, N.J., which see
DYAR, Ebenezer, Ct., R3177
Elisha, N.C., S31659
James, Mass., S19288
DYCH, Mathias, Md., BLWt.11145-100-Pvt. Iss. 10/6/1794 to Henry Purdy, ass. No papers
Peter, Md., Va., S42689
DYCHE, Charles, Va., S1950
John, Va., S12833
DYCKMAN, Benjamin, N.Y. S13815
Richard, N.Y., S45355
William, N.Y., S29130
William N., N.Y., Rebecca, W24371
DYCUS, Edward, N.C., S.C., S3314
DYE, George, S.C., R13919
John, N.J., See DAY
John, N.J., Elizabeth, R3173
John, Pa., Ruth, W7064
Jonathan, Va., BLWt.2226-200
William, Va., Sarah Reynolds, former wid., R8719
DYER, Amherst, Cont., R.I., Cynthia, W19208
Anthony, R.I., Sarah, W21027
Bela, Mass., Ruth, W14662
Benjamin, Ct., Ann Mills, former wid., W18520
Benjamin, Mass., Hannah, W24090
Bickford, Mass., S35276
Caleb, Mass., S17398
Charles, Mass. Sea Service, Bethiah, W21028
Charles, R.I., R3175
Charles, Va., R3176
Edward, Md., BLWt.620-300
Edward, N.H., Elizabeth, R3178; BLWt.53680-160-55
Eliab, Mass. See DYRE
Elisha, N.C., See DYAR
Elkanah, Mass., Catharine/Caturah, BLWt.32212-160-55
Ephraim, Mass., Hannah, W24872
Esek, R.I., S21169
Francis, Va., S39476
George, Md., BLWt.11153-100-Pvt. Iss. 1/11/1796 to Joshua Ward, ass. No papers
Henry, R.I., S12835
Ichabod, Mass., S39474
Isaac, Mass., Abigail, W1400
Isaac, Mass., Mary, W24873; BLWt.399-100

DYER (continued)
James, Mass., Mary, W16968
James, Mass., S21168
John, Mass., Tenn. res. 1836, S2189
Jonathan, Md., S25046
Jonathan, R.I., S28718
Joseph, Hazen's Regt., BLWt. 12990-100-Pvt. Iss. 4/26/1791. No papers
Joseph, Ct., Charlotte, W25555; BLWt.9203-160-55
Joseph, Mass., BLWt.4028-100-Pvt. Iss. 1/6/1797. No papers
Joseph, Mass., Eunice, W10776
Joseph, Pa., See DYRE
Lemuel, Mass., Sally, W24874
Manoah, N.C., Va., S2532
Mark, Mass., Martha, W24092
Moses, Mass., S45733
Paul, Mass., Sarah, W24093
Robert, Mass., Mariam, W24091
Samuel, R.I., Waite, W24094
Samuel, Va., S8378
Solomon, Mass., Mary, W14663
Solomon, Mass., Isabella Nickerson, former wid., R7669
Stephen, R.I. Sea Service, S18808
Thomas, Mass., Sibbil, W17739; BLWt.4035-100-Pvt. Iss. 6/28/1797 to Benjamin Dana
Walter, Lt., Md., S42690; BLWt. 587-200. Iss. 11/14/1791
DYGART, Jost, N.Y., Marillis Torkey, former wid., R26546
Orpha, former wid. of Solomon Welch, Ct., which see
DYGERT, Peter, N.Y., S10596
Safrinus/Soverinus, N.Y., S10598 B. 9/15/1766; res. at enl. Herkimer Co., N.Y.; 1845 res. London Dist. of Upper Canada, where he d. 11/10/1849
Selvenus/Severinus, N.Y., See DEYGERT
William, N.Y., Anna, R3179
DYKE, Charles, Va. See DYCHE
Henry, Va., See DIKE
John, Va. See DYCHE
DYKEMAN, Benjamin, N.Y., S10597
DYRE, Eliab, Mass., S23608
Joseph, Pa., S22225
DYSART, James, ?, Dis. No papers
John, N.C., S3315
DYSON, John, Va., S12836
Robert, Va., S39475
Thomas A., Md., BLWt.588-200-Lt. Iss. 9/21/1789. No papers

E

EABS, Emanuel, Pvt., Md., BLWt. 11197-100. Iss. 12/31/179-
EACKER, Jacob, N.Y. See EAKER
Nicholas, N.Y., Barbara, W22988
EADES, Charles, Va., Sarah, R3241
Joseph, N.Y., BLWt.7102-100-Pvt. Iss. 8/3/1790 to Cornelius Van Dyck, ass. No papers
EADS, Charles, Va., living in 1833, S30392
Henry, Md., S32226
EAGER, Archibald, See EDGAR
George, N.H., S3316
Haran/Haron, Mass., S34791
James, N.Y., Esther, W643; BLWt.11055-160-55
Noah, Mass., Sarah, W14668
Oliver, Mass., Seraphina, W24103
Zerubbable, Cont., Mass., Hannah Smith, former wid., W21039
EAGGLESONE, Asa, R.I., Content, W22994
EAGIN, John, Pa., BLWt.9347-100-Fifer. Iss. 7/9/1789. No papers
EAGINS, Joshua, N.Y., BLWt.7100-100-Pvt. Iss. 12/5/1791 to Richard Oliver, ass. No papers
EAGLE, William, Va., S39480
EAGLES, Michael, Cont., Mass., Sarah, W24329; BLWt.1805-100
EAGLETON, Isaac, R.I., Comfort Sawyer, former wid., R9232
EAKER, George, N.Y., See EKER
Jacob, N.Y., Margaret/Margareth, W16566
Nicholas, N.Y., See EACKER
EAKIN, Samuel, N.C., S3317
William, N.C., R3183
William, S.C., Elizabeth, W3530
William, Va., R3184
EAKINS, Gabriel, Va., S16775
John, Pa., See AIKEN
EALY, John, Ga., S2191
EAMES, Charles, Cont., Mass., Olive, W24122
Ebenezer, Mass., S35279
Gershom/Gusham, Mass., S8386
James, Mass., S9852
James, Mass., Ruth, W24102
Jonathan, Cont., Mass., S34816
Jonathan, Mass., Mehitable, W24118; BLWt.7072-160-55
Jotham, Mass., Eusebia, W22996; BLWt.24770-160-55
Mark, Mass., Anna, W24104
Nathan, Mass., See EMES
Phinehas, Mass., R3185
Samuel, Mass., S34784
Samuel, Mass., Thankful, W1401; BLWt.822-160-55
EANES, Edward, Va., R3186
EANSTEAD, Henry, See ANSTEAD
EARDEN, Martin, Pa., Elizabeth, W3402; BLWt.26655-160-55
EAREL, James, Pa., S34790
EARENFIGHT, Jacob, Cont., Ohio res. & agcy, S42691
EARHART, John, N.J., Margaret, R3187
EARICK, Henry, N.J. Eleanor, R3188
EARL, Cornelius, N.Y. See EARLS
Doming, R.I., S16776
Ebenezer J., Mass., BLWt.4075-100-Pvt. Iss. 3/25/1790. No papers
Henry, N.J., R3189
Israel, N.J., S34143
Joel, Mass., S22227
John, N.J., Keturah, W112
John, R.I., Deborah, W13116
Joseph, N.Y., S12844
Morris, N.J., Elizabeth/Elesabeth, W849
Moses, N.Y., S12417
Robert, Mass., S21172
Stephen, Navy, Mass., Priscilla, W21035
EARLE, David, Vt., S22226
John, Mass., Eunice, W24097
John, N.J., S996
John, R.I., Priscilla, W22993
Jonathan, N.Y., See EARLL
Samuel, S.C., S21174
Samuel, Va., Tabitha, W7065
William, Navy, Martha who res. Mass. in 1837, R1162
William, Pa., Sarah, W3231
EARLL, Jonathan, N.Y., S22745
Robert, Cont., N.Y., R3193
Watson, N.Y., R3194
EARLS, Cornelius, N.Y., Mary, W21030; BLWt.26469-160-55
Joseph, N.Y. & Sea Service, R3195
EARLY, Jeremiah, Va., Rachel, R3191
Patrick, Pvt., N.J., BLWt.8277-100 iss. 4/21/1790 to Jonathan Nichols, ass.
EARLYWINE, Daniel, Va., BLWt.1649-100
EARNEST, Felix, N.C., Sally, W7066; BLWt.31771-160-55
George, Va., Katharine, W4666
EARNHART, George, N.C., R3196
EARP, Abednego, Va.,Susannah, W3529
Edward, N.C., S41468
Josiah, Md., S31004
EARTH, Samuel, R.I. See EATHFORTH
EARTHMAN, Isaac, N.C., S21173
EARTINHOUSIN, Conrad, Va., R3199
EASLAND, James, N.Y., Deborah, W2724
John, Mass., Sally, W25557; BLWt. 61057-160-55
EASLY, Daniel, Va., S6810
EASON, Cyrus, Mass., BLWt.4099-100-Fifer. Iss. 2/22/1790 to Richard Platt. No papers
Jacob, N.C., S41516
John, Mass., S23211
Moses, N.C., Bashoba, R3198
Samuel, Va., Nancy, R3197
EASOR/EASER, Aaron, Del., S35907
EAST, Isham, Va., Mary, W19209
James, Va., Martha, W5070
John, Mass., S38677
EASTABROOKS, Aaron, R.I., S21742
EASTEN/EASTON, Obadiah, Ct., S21171
EASTER, John, Md., S18389
Michael, N.C., Barbara See EASTOR
EASTERBROOK, Benjamin, Mass.S12840
EASTERBROOKS, Abel, N.H. Ruth,

EASTERBROOKS (continued)
W22995
Benjamin, R.I., R3200
EASTERLING, William, N.C., S.C., R14028
EASTES, Brizele/Brazel, Ga., N.C., S.C., See ESTES
Elisha, Va., Molly, W9419
EASTIN, Philip, Va., Sarah, W9420; BLWt.621-200
William, Cont., Va., S39479
EASTLICK, Alexander, N.J., S45361
EASTMAN, Asahel, Ct., Mary, W19210
Benjamin, Mass., Anna, W287; BLWt. 24914-160-55
Charles, Mass., S2533
Clark, Ct., Betsey, W9421; BLWt. 36638-160-55
Daniel, Mass., S18390
Daniel, Mass., S31006
Daniel, Mass., Hannah, W14665
Deliverance, Ct., S8389
Dorothy, former wid. of William Forrest, N.H., which see
Ebenezer, N.H., Susannah, W21043
Edmund, N.H., Hannah, W7125; BLWt.31898-160-55
Edward, N.H., BLWt.3092-100-Pvt. Iss. 3/25/1790. No papers
Eli, Ct., Vt., S18810
Henry, N.H., Eleanor, W1250
Jacob, N.H., BLWt.3089-100-Pvt. Iss. 3/30/1798 to Jacob Eastman No papers
Jacob, N.H., Mary, W3667
Jacob, N.H., Abigail, R3202
James, N.H., S10603
James, N.H., Sarah, W5040
James, N.H., Olive, W21042
John, N.H., Elizabeth, W1251; BLWt.17566-160-55
John, N.H., Joanna, W14669
John, N.H., Judith, R3204
Jonathan, N.H., Vt., Phebe, W21041
Joseph, Ct., Elizabeth, W7107; BLWt.26434-160-55
Josiah, N.H., Dorothy, W21031
Nathaniel, Ct., N.H., Ruth, W22992
Obadiah, Cont., Mass., S45735
Peaslee/Peasley, N.H., Mary, W4187
Peter, Mass., R3206
Peter, Mass., N.H., R3205
Samuel, Cont., N.H., S39478
Samuel, N.H., S8384
Sarah, former wid. of Ebenezer Costin, N.H., which see
Simeon, N.H., Anna, W21044
Thomas, Cont., N.H., S8383
William, N.H., S45734
Zachariah, Mass., S35278
Zachariah, Mass., BLWt.733-100
EASTON, Ahimaaz/Ahimaz, Mass., Maria, W19213; BLWt.8469-160-55
Ashbel, BLWt.13054-100-Pvt. "in the Corps of Arty. Artificers" iss. 9/4/1789. No papers
Ashbel/Ashbell, Cont., Mass. res. & agcy., S17938
Eliphalet, Ct., Dis. No papers
Giles, Cont.,Ct., Anna, W22997

EASTON (continued)
Giles, Md., S10633
Henry, N.Y., BLWt.7105-100-Pvt. Iss. 10/12/1790 to Elkanah Watson, ass. No papers
Henry, N.Y., S37903
James, Cont., Mass., Dis. No papers
Julian, Ct., S37902; BLWt.1209-100
Moses, N.J., S46356; BLWt.156-100
Obadiah, R.I., See EASTEN
Richard, Md. Sea Service, Pa., S22746
Samuel, Ct., Dis. No papers
Samuel, N.J., BLWt.8286-100-Pvt. Iss. 2/6/1790. No papers
Samuel, N.J., S46439
Sarah, former wid. of John Jordan, Md., which see
Theophilus, R.I., S15109
EASTOR, Michael, N.C., Barbara, W18857
EASTWICK, John, Pa., S35908
EASTWOOD, Daniel, N.Y., S15108
Isreal, Ga., b. N.C., S31660
John, N.Y., S28719
EATER, Christopher, N.C. See EATON
EATHFORTH, John, Mass. Sea Service R.I., Mary, W24099
Samuel, Mass., R.I., Elizabeth, W24100
EATINGER, Jacob, Pa., Mary Ann, See ETTINGER
EATON, Abiathar/Abiather, Mass., S45360
Abigail, former wid. of Ashbel Merrill, Ct. W16970
Abijah, Cont., Mass., N.H., Elizabeth, W5268
Abijah, Mass., S8382
Abither, Mass., BLWt.4080-100-Pvt. Iss. 5/31/1790 to Theodosius Fowler. No papers
Abram/Abraham, Cont., Mass., Mary, W24096
Alexander, N.H., Edna, W16246
Aron, Pa., S10634
Benjamin, Ct., Cont., N.J., War of 1812, S45359
Benjamin, Mass., Mary, W16969
Benjamin, Mass., Lydia, W22989
Benjamin, Mass., BLWt.655-200-Lt. Iss. 4/22/1796. No papers
Benjamin, N.H., S10599
Benjamin, N.H., S12841
Benjamin, N.J., BLWt.8292. Iss. 9/24/1791 to Resolve Waldron, ass. No papers
Betsy, former wid. of Ichabod Swain, N.H., which see
Brigham, Mass., S45356
Christopher, N.C., Susan, R3214
Cyrel/Cyril, Ct., S32227
Daniel, Ct., Nancy, W19211
David, N.H., S16777
Ebenezer, Ct., Lois, W21038
Ebenezer, Ct., Mass., R.I., Polly, W7067
Ebenezer, Mass., S18387
Ebenezer, N.H., S17937

EATON (continued)
Eleazer, N.Y., S12838
Eliab, Mass., Lucretia, W22987
Elijah, N.Y., Deliverance, R3208
Enoch, Vt., Abigail, W19212; BLWt.9519-160-55
Ephraim, Ct., Mass., N.Y., S45357
Eunice, former wid. of Joseph Walker, Ct., W17740
Ezra, Cont., Mass., S23210
Hannah, former wid. of David Lowed, Mass., which see
Henry, Pa., BLWt.9341-100-Pvt. Iss. 6/20/1789. No papers
Henry, Pa., S35909
Isaiah, Mass., S18388
Israel, Mass., S4995
James, Ct., Eleanor, W21037
James, Ct., Anna, W25556
James, N.H., Sarah, W27754; BLWt.15417-160-55
James, N.C., S.C., Anne Ellen Bryant, former wid., W18663. Her last husb., Wm. Bryant, also a soldier. See within
John, Cont., N.H., Phebe, W21029
John, Mass., Mehitable, W21032
John, N.H., S10600
Jonathan, N.H., Sarah, W22991; BLWt.1334-100
Joseph, Cont., Pa., See EATTON
Joseph, Mass., S30393
Joseph, Mass., R3209
Joseph, N.H., S10604
Joseph, N.C., b.Pa., S31005
Joseph True, N.H., Mehitable, W24101
Josiah, Ct., S12839
Lemuel, Mass., Sarah, W21033
Levi, Mass., N.H., S16778
Lot, Cont., Mass., S45358
Luther, Ct., Sally, W21034
Luther, Mass., Mary, W10940; BLWt.39488-160-55
Maverick, Ct., S18809
Moses, Mass., Esther, W22986
Nathan, Ct., S15821
Nathaniel, Mass., S34787
Nathaniel, Mass., S34788
Nathaniel, Mass., R3211
Nathaniel, ---, also War of 1812, Susannah, R3215. Her res. W. Springfield, Mass., in 1836
Origen, Mass., BLWt.4078-100-Pvt. Iss. 1/23(?)/1799
Origen, Mass., S47183
Pearson, Mass., S34789
Pinkethman, N.C., BLWt.653-400-Maj. Iss. 3/14/1800 to John Eaton, heir. No papers. Also recorded under BLWt.2713
Samuel, Ct., S12837
Samuel, Cont., Mass., S35277
Samuel, Mass., S29131
Samuel, Mass., Sarah, W24095; BLWt.3610-160-55
Samuel, N.H., Lydia, R3210
Samuel, N.H., R3212
Samuel, N.H., R3213
Samuel, N.H., Vt., S39477
Solomon, Ct., Phebe Carpenter,

EATON (continued)
former wid., W8591; BLWt.30597-160-55
Stephen, Ct., S23209
Sylvanus/Salvanus, Mass., N.H., Abigail, W14666
Timothy, Mass., S34785
Uriah, Cont., Mass., Eunice Rebecca, W17741
William, Cont., Mass., Nancy, W3666; BLWt.10250-160-55. Died 5/7/1852
William, Cont., Mass., Sarah, W8203; BLWt.14978-160-55. Died 7/11/1838.
William, Cont., Mass., Abigail, W22990. Died 11/30/1841
William, Cont., Mass., N.H., S16374. B. 1757 Saybrook, Rockingham Co., N.H.; d. 9/31/1835 at Sanbornton, Strafford Co., N.H.
William, Mass., Betsy, R3207. B. 1755 at Seabrook, N.H.; d. 10/11/1837. Res. Sanbornton, N.H.
EATTON, Joseph, Cont., Pa., S3318
EAVANS, Wiggin, N.H., Sea Service, Mary, See EVANS
EBB, Emanuel, Cont., Md., S34792
EBBS, Emanuel, See EBB
EBERHARD, John, Ct., BLWt.5737-100-Pvt. Iss. 9/24/1790. No papers
EBERHART, Jacob, N.C., S31661
EBERLY, Henry, Pa., R3216
EBERT, Henry, Pvt. in Hazen's Regt. BLWts. 12722 & 13042 iss. 7/7/1789. No papers
EBET, William, Mass., See EBIT
EBIT, William, Mass., Rosannah, W8204; BLWts. 842-100 & 2025-160 (sic)-55
EBLEN, Samuel, Va., S32228
EBLING, John, Pa., BLWt.9345-100-Pvt. Iss. 7/27/1789 to Richard Platt, ass. No papers
EBNER, Casper, Cont., Pa. See ABNER
Jasper, Pa., "Drummer in Proctor's Arty.," BLWt.9357 iss. 7/27/1789 to Richard, Platt, ass.
EBRIGHT, Philip, Pa., S3319
ECCLES, John, Drummer, N.J., BLWt. 8288. Iss. 2/25/1790
John, N.C., Jane W., W7072; BLWt. 9423-160-55
ECCLESTON, David, Ct., Catharine, W19217
Isaac, R.I., Comfort Sawyer, former wid., See EAGLETON
Joseph, Ct., R.I., See EGLESTON
ECHERT, John/Johannes, N.Y., S22747
ECKART, John, Pa., Elisabeth, W2926
ECKELBARNER, Joseph, Va., See EICHELBERGER
ECKELS, Arthur, Pa., S42694
ECKER, Johannes, N.Y., Elizabeth, R3182
ECKERSON, Cornelius, N.J., S997
Cornelius, N.Y., Catharine, W16971
John, N.Y., See ACKERSON
Teunis, N.Y., Charity, W19215
ECKERT, Jeremiah, N.Y., R3237; BLWt.49048-160-55. His wife was

ECKERT (continued)
Marie (Mareitje). Nancy was allowed B.L. on his service erroneously. Her papers should not have been in this claim. She evidently was wid. of another Jeremiah Eckert.
Stephen, N.Y., S45362
ECKLAR, John, N.Y., See ACKLAR
ECKLE, Philip, Md., R3238
ECKLER, Christopher, N.Y., R3239
Henry, N.Y. & War of 1812, S10605; BLWt.24610-160-55
Peter, N.Y., Hannah, R3217; BLWt. 53754-160-55
ECKLEY, Abraham, Pa., Maria Salome R3240
ECKOLS, William, N.C., S41517
ECTOR, Samuel, N.C., Susannah, W19216
EDDINGS, William, N.C., Va., S3226
EDDINGTON, Jonathan, Pa., R3219
EDDINS, Samuel, Va., BLWt.683-300-Capt. Iss. 8/10/1795. No papers
William, S.C., S32230
EDDLEMAN, Leonard, Md. See EDLEMAN
Peter, N.C., S30398; BLWt.529-160-55
Peter, N.C., See EDLEMAN
EDDY, Abisha, Mass., S17402
Apollos/Appollos, Mass., Martha, W16111
Asa, Ct., Rebecca, W25561; BLWt. 26789-160-55
Barnard, R.I., Julia G., W10942
Benjamin, R.I., Sally, W10945
Bryant, Mass., S22748
Caleb, R.I., S39485
Celia, former wid. of Timothy Coggeshall, Mass., which see
David, R.I., Cynthia, W21052
Ebenezer, Mass., S34795; BLWt. 1022-100
Edmund, Mass., S18811
Elijah, Mass., S8392
Elkanah, R.I., Mary, W21051
Ephraim, Cont., Mass., Vt., Mary Bayley, former wid., W20691
Esek, R.I., R3221
Gilbert, Ct., Privateer, 1812, Prudence, W25560. See BLWt. 15046-160-55 for serv. of above soldier as Brig. Gen. N.Y. Mil. from 9/1 to 19, 1814
James, N.H., BLWt.3091-100-Pvt. Iss. 10/10/1796 to Thes. Woodward, ass. No papers
James, Vt., S18813
Jesse, Mass., S10612
Joanna, former wid. of William Haskins, Mass., which see
John, Navy, R.I., Sarah Walker, former wid., W14105
Joshua, Capt., Mass., Lydia P., W21048; BLWt.656-300 iss. 11/4/1794 to Samuel Emery, ass.
Josiah, Pvt., Mass., BLWt.4088 iss. 3/30/1796 to Peter Swier
Josiah, Mass., S34796
Josiah, Green Mt. Boys, Vt., Hannah, R3222
Levi, Ct., Rhoda, W21046

EDDY (continued)
Lippitt, R.I., S17400
Loved, Mass., S34799
Michael, Mass., Phebe, W24107
Noah, R.I., S10611
Oliver, R.I., Sarah, R3226
Olney, R.I., R3225
Reuben, Mass., S6811
Samuel, Mass., S30396
Samuel, Mass., S45370
Samuel, Mass., Sally, W19221
Samuel, Mass., Mary, W21047
Samuel, N.J., S998
Sarah, Ct., Cont., W21045, former wid. of Samuel Waterous
Seth, Ct., S39483
Seth, Mass., S18812
Tabitha, Mass., W14670, former wid. of Stephen Boynton
Thomas, Mass., Elizabeth, W24109
Willard, Navy, R.I., S12851
William, Cont., Mass., R.I., S10616
William, Mass., Olive King, W26721
William R., Mass., Philenda/Philinda, W4188; BLWt.36514-160-55
EDEGH, Jacob, N.Y., Dis. No papers See one Jacob C. Ittig, both in Col. Bellinger's Regt.
EDELEN, Clement, Md., Lucy Ammons, former wid., W20606; BLWt.101431-160-55
EDELMAN, see EDLEMAN
EDENFIELD, David, S.C., Elizabeth, W10944; BLWt.34272-160-55
EDENS, Alexander, S.C. or Va., Mary, R3229
Elias, S.C., Nancy Ann Green, former wid., W11092; BLWt.102089-160-55
Jacob, N.C., R3228
John, N.C., Margaret, W4945; BLWt.40914-160-55
John, S.C., S35911
EDER, Anthony, Ct., Cont., Phillis, See NEEDAR
EDERBAUGH, See Peter RADUBACH
EDERINGTON, James, S.C., R3230
EDES, Collins, Mass., S34798
James, Hazen's Regt., BLWt. 13050-100-Pvt. Iss. 7/22/1791
John, Corps of Arty. Artificers, BLWt.13053-100-Pvt. Iss. 8/10/1789 to Richard Platt, ass. No papers
Jonathan, N.H., S45737
Samuel, Mass., Mary, R3231; BLWt. 44804-160-55
Thomas, Mass., BLWt.4098-100-Pvt. Iss. 11/2/1795 to Joseph Fosdick. No papers
Thomas, Mass., N.Y., S15822
EDGAR, Archibald, N.J., Catharine, W850
David, Cont., N.J., S34336; BLWt. 664-300-Capt. Iss. 8/4/1790. No papers
David, Pa., BLWt.9344-100-Pvt. Iss. 3/5/1799 to Geo. Taylor, Jr., ass. No papers
David, Pa., S42697

EDGAR (continued)
James, Pa., Mary, W2927
James, Pa., Elizabeth, W9422; BLWt.3868-160-55
John, Pa., S30395
Thomas, Navy, Ct., S37905
EDGCOMB, Gilbert, Mass., Lucy, W19218
Jabez, Ct., S37906
James, Mass., Anna, W24108
Samuel, Ct., Privateer, S20743
EDGE, John, N.C., R3232
John, Va., Nancy, W4946; BLWt. 11408-160-55
EDGECOMB, Roger, Ct., Cont., Navy, S10615
Samuel, Ct., Dis. No papers
EDGERLY, James, N.H., S45368
John, N.Y., BLWt.7104-100-Pvt. Iss. 12/28/1791. No papers
Joshua, Cont., N.H., S45736
Josiah, N.H., S17399
Richard, N.H., Abigail, W24106
EDGERTON, Abel, Ct., Cont., S10613
Ariel, Ct., Cont., Privateer, S18816
David, Ct., Sea Service & Privateer, S15110
Ebenezer, Ct., S37904
Ebenezer, Jr., Cont., Ct., S34793
Edward, Pa., Prudence, W7086
James, Ct., Privateer, S18391
Jediah, Ct., Sarah, R3235
Jedidiah, Ct., Vt., S21743
Lydia, former wid. of John Babcock, Ct., which see
Roger, Ct., Cont., Betsey, W19219
EDGMAN, William, N.C., S1810
EDICH, Conrat/Conrad, Cont., N.Y., See ITTIG
EDICK, Conrad, N.Y., Elizabeth, W2084; BLWt.28558-160-55
George, N.Y., S12854
EDIE, John, Pa., BLWt.2373-200
EDINBURG, Sewell, Va., R13947, Va. Half Pay, N.A. Acc. No. 874-050055, Half Pay
EDLEMAN, Leonard, Md., S30397
Michael, Md., S38678
Peter, N.C., Dica, W7085; BLWt. 26399-160-55
EDMAN, See EDMOND
EDMESTER, See EDMINSTER
EDMESTON, Thomas, Pa., S31007
EDMINSTER, Noah, Mass., Sea Service, Sarah, W7084; BLWt. 9497-160-55
EDMISTER, Zebedee, Mass., S16375
EDMINSTON, Samuel, Cont., Md. See EDMISTON
Samuel, Md., BLWt.674-200-Lt. Iss. 1/23/1792. No papers
EDMISTEN, William, N.C., Va., R3243
EDMISTON, Hugh, N.J., Margaret, R3242
Samuel, Cont., Pa. res., BLWt. 62-450
EDMOND, Andrew, Ct., Esther, R3247

EDMOND (continued)
George, Cont., Ct., Abigail, W17744
Samuel, N.J., S16779
William, Ct., S20742
EDMONDS, Andrew, Ct., Elizabeth, R3248
Benjamin, Cont., Mass., S45366
Daniel, Va., S8394
Ebenezer, Mass. See EDMUNDS
Esther, former wid. of Peter Rose, Ct., Cont., which see
George, N.Y., R13951
Jacob, N.J., S34335
John, Cont., Mass. See EDMUNDS
John, Mass., Sarah, W21049
Jonathan, N.H., Catharine, W16112
Samuel, N.Y., War of 1812, Lydia, W15894
EDMONDSON, Benjamin, Va., R13953, Va. Half Pay, N.A. Acc. No. 874-050056, Half Pay
Edmond, Va., Jane, W19223
William, N.C., Mary, R3246
EDMONSON, John, S.C., S32229
William, Pa., S2192
EDMONSTON, James, N.Y., S12850
EDMUNDS, Asa, Mass., Eunice, W23001
Ebenezer, Mass., Mary, W24105; BLWt.27635-160-55
Eliphalet, Cont., R.I., Vt., S16781
James, Vt., S12853
John, Cont., Mass., Experience, W2773; BLWt.10220-160-55
Thomas, Va., BLWt.997-200
William, R.I., BLWt.3096-100-Pvt. Iss. 7/6/1796 to William Woodward, ass. No papers
William, Cont., R.I., S45367
EDMUNDSON, William, N.C., S6813
EDNEY, Robert, N.C., Mary, R3249; BLWt.91506-160-55
EDSALL, James, N.J., Mary, W920
Richard, N.J., Jemima, W7074
EDSON, Amasa, Mass., S23609
Benjamin, Ct., Anne, W19220; BLWt.39494-160-55
Benjamin, Mass., Sarah, R3252
Caleb, Mass., Mehitable, R3251
Caleb, Mass., N.H., S29775
David, Mass., Lydia, R3250
Ebenezer, Mass., S34794
Eliab, Ct., S15419
James, Mass., S45369
Josiah, Ct., S39486
Lydia, former wid. of Timothy Harrington, Ct., which see
Nathan, Ct., S39482
Peter, Mass., BLWt.1340-100
Samuel, Mass., BLWt.4083-100-Sgt. Iss. 10/10/1796 to Wm. Woodward
Samuel, Mass., S39484
Seth, Ct., Cont., S10614
Seth, Mass., S29772
Thomas, Mass., S8393
EDWARD, David, Va., Ailcey, W7081
Michael, Pa., Elizabeth, R3255
Spencer, Va., Elizabeth, W7078
EDWARDS, Abel, Ct., Sarah, W17745
Abraham, Navy, Mass. agcy. & res., S34800
Andrew, N.C., S3320
Andrew, S.C., Phebe, R3262
Benjamin, Mass., S45364
Benjamin, N.C., Sabra, W3790; BLWt.34273-160-55
Benjamin, Va., S8397
Benjamin A., Mass., S45363
Brown, N.C., S35910
Charles, N.C., Jane Jackson, former wid., W20162
Charles, Pa., BLWt.1297-100. No papers
Christopher, R.I., S10608
Clark, Ct., R.I., Catharine, W14671
Daniel, Ct., Hannah, W17743
Daniel, Ct., Privateer, S8395
Daniel, R.I., Lois, W2083
David, N.C., S6812
Ebenezer, Navy, Mass. agcy. & res., S34797
Edmond, Va., BLWt.12105 & 14077-100-Pvt. Iss. 5/27/1794
Edward, Mass., BLWt.4095-100-Pvt. Iss. 3/30/1796 to Peter Zwier. No papers
Edward, Mass., also War of 1812, Jane, W7079
Edward, Mass., B.L. Rej. 297128-1855
Eli, Mass., S29774
Elisha, Mass., S30394
Enoch, Pa., Frances, W3135
Esther, former wid. of Reuben Cone, Cont., Ct., which see
Evan, Cont., Pa., Catharine, W10943; BLWt.1205-400
Fletcher, S.C., Mary Scaggs, former wid., R9250
George, Va., S12856
George, Va., Elizabeth, W8684
Henry, N.C., S45839
Hezekiah, Ct., S16780
Isaac, Ct., Mary, W25558; BLWt. 26586-160-55
Jabez, Ct., S10607
Jacob, N.J., Abigail, W1579
Jacob, Va., S10609
Jasper, Pa., Betsey, R3253
Jesse, Pvt., N.J., BLWt.8291 iss. 9/4/1789 to David Whitehead, ass.
Jesse, Pa., Va., S17401; BLWt. 34960-160-55
John, Cont., N.H., Mary, W14675
John, Md., BLWt.11195-Pvt. Iss. 8/14/1797 to James De Baufre, ass. No papers
John, Mass., S18815
John, N.J., BLWt.8278. No papers
John, N.Y., S12852
John, N.C., S10610
John, N.C., R3258
John, Pa., Mary, W8685; BLWt.882-100
John, Va., S31662
John, Va., Ruth, W19222
John, Va., Frances, R3257
John S., Mass., S10606; BLWt. 26001-160-55
Jonathan, Ct., Mass., S42696; BLWt.5746-100

EDWARDS (continued)
Joseph, N.J., S34337
Joseph, N.C., R3259
Joseph, R.I., Olive, W21050
Joseph, Va., R3260
Joseph, Va., R13943
Joshua, Mass., S35282
Joshua, Navy, Pa., S3321
LeRoy, Va., BLWt.677-300-Capt.
Mercy/Marcy, former wid. of Joel Judd, Ct., which see
Moses, N.C., Mary, W25559; BLWt. 31423-160-55
Nathaniel, Ct., S44797; BLWt. 659-200-Lt. Iss. 12/14/1792 to Nathaniel Edwards
Nathaniel, Mass., S35280
Newit/Newett, Va., S39481
Nicholas, R.I., Marcy, W22999
Oliver, Mass., Rachel, W14672
Oliver, Mass., Sarah, W23003
Paul, R.I., Rachel, W16567
Perry, R.I., BLWt.3098-100-Pvt. Iss. 12/31/1789. No papers
Perry, R.I., Rhoda, W4667
Peter, Va., S8398
Reuben, N.C., S16376
Robert, Mass., BLWt.4092-100-Pvt. Iss. 1/29/1790. No papers
Robert, N.C., Nancy, W77
Samuel, Ct., S12855
Samuel, Mass., S18814
Samuel, Mass., S29773
Simon, N.C., Sally, R3264
Solomon, Va., Sarah, W7080
Stephen, Mass., S35281
Stokes, N.C., R3265
Thomas, Cont., Mass., Polly, W1252 BLWt.650-200-Lt. Iss. 10/26/1789. No papers
Thomas, Green Mt. Boys, Vt., Matilda, W16973
Thomas, Md., S42695
Thomas, R.I., Temperance, W23000
Thomas, Va., Martha, W7076
Thomas, Va., b. Pa., S3327
Timothy, Mass., S29776
William, N.C., Rebecca, R3263
William, R.I., BLWt.1756-100
William, Va., S3322
EDY, Samuel, Mass. See EDDY
EELLS, Daniel, Ct., R3267
Edward, Ct., Abigail, BLWt.102-300
Jeremiah, Ct., S44798
John, Ct., S29132
John, Ct., R3268
John, Mass., Vt., Polly, W7071; BLWt.31901-160-55
Samuel, Ct. See ELLES
Waterman, Mass., Vt., Abigail, R3266
EFFINGER, John Ignatius/Ignaz, Cont., Pa., Barbara, W7087; BLWt.136-60-55 & 244-100
EFLAND, John, N.C., S6814
EFNER, Joseph, N.Y., S29777
Wilhelmus, N.Y., S23610
EGBERT, John, N.J., Hannah, W7089
Thomas, N.J., S999
EGBERTS, Anthony, Cont., N.Y., Eve, W21054; BLWt.15193-160-55
V. Jacob, Gen. Hosp., BLWt.691-

EGBERTS (continued)
200-Surg. Mate. Iss. 7/20/1797 to Anthony Egberts, ex. No papers
EGERTON, Ariel, Ct. See EDGERTON
Benjamin, N.C., Ivireller, W8686
Lydia, former wid. of John Babcock Ct., which see
EGGELSTON, Timothy, Ct., Cont., S42698
EGGERS, Landrine, N.Y., N.C., S6815
EGGERT, John, Mass., S2193
EGGLESONE, Asa, R.I. See EAGGLESONE
EGGLESTON, Azariah, Cont., Mass., Sarah, W483; BLWts. 26673-160-55 & 651-200-Lt. Iss. 7/22/1789
Benedict, Ct., S38694; BLWt.6381-160-55
David, Ct., BLWt.5736-100-Pvt. Iss 8/7/1789 to Richard Platt. No papers
Eliab, Cont., N.Y., Lucy, W2774
James, Ct., Cont., See EGLESTON
John, Md., BLWt.671-400-Maj. Dated 4/18/1794. No papers
Joseph, Cont., Va., Judith C., W8687; BLWt.675-400-Maj. Iss. 8/10/1789 to Richard Platt, ass. No papers
Moses, Mass. See EGLESTON
Samuel, Ct., R3270
Samuel, Mass., S10617
Timothy, Cont.,Ct. See EGGELSTON
EGGNER, Peter P., N.Y., S23611
EGGS, Samuel, N.Y., BLWt.7108-100-Pvt. Iss. 4/1/1790 to Edmund Ogden, ass. No papers
EGLES, Michael, See EAGLES
EGLESTON, Azariah, Mass. See EGGLESTON
Benedict, Ct. See EGGLESTON
Elijah, Mass., Bernice McKinstry former wid., R6769
Gershom/Garshom, Ct., Avis, W1739
James, Ct., Cont., Jemima, W17747
John, Mass., S34801
Joseph, Ct., R.I., Elizabeth, W17748
Moses, Mass., Margaret, W4947; BLWt.34990-160-55
EGMONS, Lott, N.J., Mary, W7090; BLWt.29051-160-55
EGNER, Matthias/Mathias, N.C., S21745
EGNEW, George, S.C. See AGNEW
EGOLF, Michael, Pa., S22749
EGOLFF, Henry, Pa., S23612
EHLE, Anthony, N.Y., Angelica, R3271
Harmanus/Harmanes, N.Y., R3276
Peter, N.Y., Catharine, W17750
Peter H., N.Y., S23212
William, N.Y., S44799
EHLER, Christian, Pa., Margaret, W3403
Michael, Pa., S16377
EHRENZELLER, Jacob, Cont., Pa., S2194
EICHELBERGER, Barnett, Pa., BL Rej.
George, Pa., S3328
Joseph, N.C., Pa., Va.,

EICHELBERGER (continued)
Christina, R3272 1/2
Martin, Cont., Pa., Elizabeth, W9423
EICKHOLS, John, Pa., S42699; BLWt.2108-100
EIDSON, James, S.C., S17939
Shelton, Va., S32231
EIGABROAT, Peter, N.Y., S11287
EIGENBRODT/EYGANBROADT, George, N.Y., Catharine, W21055
EIGHMEY/EIGHMAY, Daniel, N.Y., R3274
EIKELBERGER, John, Md., Pa., Mary, W9424
EINSTED, Henry, See ANSTEAD
EIRWIN, David, N.C., Lydia, R3369
EISAMAN, Christian, Pa., S23725
EISELL, John, Md., S34802
EISENBURGH, Charity, former wid. of Uriah Johnson/Johnston, N.Y., which see
EISENHART, George, Pa., R3275
EISENHAUER, Frederic, Pa., Anna Rodes/Roads, former wid., R8927
Philip, Pa., S39764
EITTINGER, Jacob, Pa. See ETTINGER
EKEHEART, Frederick A./John, See HEART
EKER, George, N.Y., S10602
EKKER, Johannes, N.Y. See ECKER
EKSTEIN, David, Pvt. in Hazen's Regt. BLWt.13044. Iss. 7/6/1791 to Anthony Musegenning, ass. No papers. Notation: David Ekstein is found in Von Heer's Regt. The above must be wrong.
ELA, David, N.H. See ELLA
Samuel, Cont., Mass., S45744
ELAM, Alexander, ?, R3277
Godfrey, Va., S10452
Solomon H., Va., S17940
ELBERT, John L., Gen. Hosp., Md. BLWt.2157-150 & 645-300-Surg. Mate. Iss. 9/22/1791, also recorded under BLWt.2593. No papers
Samuel, Ga., BLWt.1230-500
ELBERTSON, William, N.Y. agcy. Invalid. No papers
ELDEN, Gibeon, Mass., S28721
ELDER, Andrew, Va., R3278
Claiborne, Va., S39489
Ephraim, Va., Martha Moore, former wid., W7471. N.A. Acc. No. 874-050057, Half Pay. Her last husb., Mark Moore/More also served in Rev. War
John, Pa., S23616
John, Pa., Mary, W24117
Joseph, N.Y., Margaret, W24111
Joshua, Mass., S29139
Robert, ---, war unknown, S.C. agcy. to Ky. agcy., Old War Inv. File 8406
Robert, Va., S12865
ELDERKIN, Elisha, Ct. Sea Service Mary, W17758
ELDRED, John, Ct., Cont., S42705
Judah, Ct., S6817
Robert, R.I., S21746

ELDRED (continued)
Samuel, Lt., Cont., Mass., S42702
BLWt.649-200 iss. 4/12/1792 to
Silas Pepoon, ass. No papers on
BLWt. Name recorded as Eldridge
Samuel, Cont., R.I., See ELDRIDGE
ELDREDG, Robert, Ct., Elizabeth
Burtis, former wid., R1513
ELDREDGE, Ebenezer, Mass., S29779
Edward, Mass., R3281
Elisha, Ct., Cynthia, W23007
James, Ct., S22231
John, Ct., S37911
Jonathan, Ct., S39487
Joseph, Ct., S23213
Joseph, Ct., Rhoda, W17756
William, Mass., Sea Service, S18817
ELDRIDGE, Daniel, ---, R.I. res.
1794, Dis. No papers
Daniel, Mass., Phebe, W24116
Elisha, Ct., See ELDREDGE
Elisha, Ct., Mass., R3282
Hannah, former wid. of Daniel
Littlefield, Mass., which see
Henry, Ct.,R.I., Elizabeth, W23004
Jeremiah, Crane's Arty., Mass.;
BLWt.4106-100-Pvt. Iss. 12/31/
1789. No papers
Jeremiah, Mass., S44805
John, N.J., Rebecca, W7100
John, R.I., Huldah, W16248
Joseph, Cont., Mass., S44814
Samuel, Cont.,R.I., Rebecca,W24113
Simeon, N.C., S3333
William, Mass., Sea Service, See
ELDREDGE
William, Pvt., Sheldon's Dragoons
Ct., BLWt.5753 iss. 9/1/1790
William, N.Y., S23613
William C., Cont., N.Y. res. &
agcy., S47184
Zoeth, Ct., Bethiah, R3280
ELEY, William, Ct., S42706
ELGAR, Thomas, Mass., Azubah
Perkins, former wid., W13809
ELGIN, Gustavus, Va., b. Md.,
S8412
Samuel, Md., S16783
Walter, Va., b. Md., S9548
ELHOLM, George C. Augustus,
Pulaski's Corps; BLWt.692-300-
Capt. Iss. 1/6/1792. No papers
ELIOT, Francis, Mass., Nancy,
W2538; BLWt.221-60-55
Gideon, N.Y., Hannah, W4189;
BLWt.31899-160-55
John, Mass., Rebekah/Rebecca,
W7098
John, Pvt., Mass., BLRej.
242070-1855
John, N.H., Rachel, W14678
Oliver, N.H., S10626
Samuel, Cont., See ELLIOTT
William, Cont., Mass. See ELLIOT
ELIOTT, Arthur, S.C. See ELLIOTT
ELITHORP, Samuel, Ct., Cont.,
Amy, W21064
ELKIN, James, Va., Martha, W8803
Joshua, S.C., S10624
ELKINS, Johnson, S.C., S39494
Jonathan, N.H., Vt., Eunice,
W1159

ELKINS (continued
Joseph, Cont.,Mass.,N.W., S45740
Joshua, N.C., Martha, W17755;
BLWt.36639-160-55
Richard, S.C., S2535
Samuel, N.H., S45741
Shadrick, N.C., R3280
William, Md., BLWt.11186-100-Pvt.
Iss. 8/9/1797 to James DeBaufre,
ass. No papers
William, Md., S42703
ELLA, David, N.H., S45743
ELLAM, See ELMS
ELLEDGE, Abraham, S.C., S10625
Abram, N.C., R13966
Jacob, N.C., S1511
ELLEM, Leonard, See HELMS
ELLENDER, Joshua, Pvt., N.J.,BLWt.
8289 iss. 6/16/1789 to Thomas
Coyle, ass.
ELLENWOOD, Benjamin, N.H. See
ELLINWOOD
Hananiah, Mass., S15112
Ralph, N.H., Susannah, W21057
Samuel, Mass., Sarah, W19227
ELLER, John, N.Y., Elizabeth,
W21059; BLWt.17569-160-55
John McKor/Melker, N.C., S6819
ELLERY, Nathaniel, Mass., Priva-
teer, Sarah, W19228
William, Mass., BLWt.4807-100-
Drummer. Iss. 6/4/1789. No
papers
ELLES, Samuel, Cont., Ct., S37912
ELLET, Robert, N.C., Mary Ann,
W4948; BLWt.10011-160-55
ELLETT, Zachariah, N.C., b. N.C.,
R3287
ELLEY, Edward, Va., S8403
ELLINGTON, Daniel, N.C., Sarah,
W3966
David, N.C., Va., b. Md., S37908
David M., Va., R3288
ELLINGWOOD, John, Mass., S34809
William, Mass., S29781
ELLINWOOD, Benjamin, Cont., N.H.,
S42700
ELLIOT, Archibald, N.Y.,BLWt.7097-
100-Pvt. Iss. 7/16/1790 to Wm.
J. Vreedenburgh, ass. No papers
Benjamin, N.Y., S9853
Daniel, N.Y., S22750
Francis, Mass. See ELIOT
Francis, N.Y., BLWt.7107-100-Pvt.
Iss. 9/9/1790 to G. Patterson,
et al, assnes. No papers
George, Ct., Percy, W25612
George, Mass., Eleanor, W16972;
BLWt.1153-100
Jacob, Mass., S31010
Jacob, N.H., Martha, W1580
Jedediah, Cont., N.H., S16785
John, Cont.,Mass.,N.H.,Mary,W16114
John, Md., BLWt.11189-100-Pvt.
Iss. 11/29/1790 to Thomas
McManus, admr. No papers
John, N.Y., & War of 1812, Nelly,
R3320; BLWt.662-300-Surg. Mate.
Iss. 8/14/1792. No papers to BLWt.
John, N.C., b. N.C., S8411
John, Pa.? or Md.?, S22751
John, Pa., S23615

ELLIOT (continued)
John, Pa., S42701
Joseph, Mass., Joanna, W14677
Micajah, N.Y., S22752
Nathaniel, Cont., R.I., S38679
Oliver, N.H. See ELIOT
Richard, Mass., S12857
Thomas, Md., BLWt.11191-100-
Pvt. Iss. 11/29/179? to Thomas
McManus, admr. No papers
William, Cont., Mass., S45742
William, Pa., Mary/Polly, R3303
ELLIOTT, Abraham, N.C., R3289
Alexander, Va. Sea Service, son
of George, S31008
Arthur, S.C., Mary, R3300
Barnard, S.C., Catharine, W4432,
BLWt.1213-100
Benjamin, Pa., R3293
Bradford W., organization not
shown, Utah res. See N.A. Acc.
No. 874-050059. Not Half Pay.
No pension file for him.
Ezekiel, N.H., R3295
Francis, Mass., See ELIOT
Francis, N.Y., S43526
George, Va. Sea Service, R38.
See N.A. Acc. No. 837. Va.
State Navy, YS File, Va. Half
Pay
Henry, Ct., R3296
John, Cont., N.H., S16784
John, Md., S25056
John, Md., Sarah, W9426
John, Mass., S15823
John, Mass. See ELIOT
John, N.C., b. Va., S32232
John, R.I., S19962
John, Va., S8410
Jonathan, N.Y., R3299
Joseph, N.Y., Pa., S8409
Lucy, former wid. of Daniel
Campbell, Mass., which see
Reuben, Va., Mary Horner, for-
mer wid., W10122; BLWt.67531-
160-55
Richard, Cont., Ct., S12864
Robert, Md., Martha, W10951;
BLWt.28639-160-55
Robert, Va., Elizabeth, W3404;
BLWt.1900-160-55
Samuel, Cont., Mass. res., Mary,
W8691; BLWt.5751-100-Pvt. Iss.
3/25/1790. No papers. BLWt.
25-60-55. Papers in pension
claim.
Samuel, Md., R3306
Samuel, Mass., Achsah/Axah, W3668;
BLWt.14701-160-55
Samuel, Va., Winifred, W19225
Thomas, Ct., S31664
Thomas, Md., S34803
Thomas, Md., S34805; BLWt.1300-100
Thomas, Md., Abigail, W4190; BL
Rej.
Thomas, Mass., S12863
Thomas, Va., S39490
Thomas, Va., Elizabeth, R3294
William, Sheldon's Dragoons, Ct.,
BLWt.5750-160-Pvt. Iss. 3/25/
1790. No papers
William, Cont., Va., Elizabeth,
W7097

ELLIOTT (continued)
William, Mass., Sarah, W14676
William, N.Y., S12861
William, Pa., b. Pa., S16378
William, Pa., R20364
William, S.C., Phoebe, W8690
William, S.C., b. Pa., res. during Rev. N.C., Miriam, R3301
William, Va., b. in Accomack Co. Va., Arzele/Anzele, W4668
William, Va., Sarah, R3307
ELLIS, Aaron, Mass., See ALLIS
Abel, Mass., S29778
Abner S., Va. See N.A. Acc. No. 874-050058. Not Half Pay. No pension file found for him
Abraham, Pa., Va., S16109
Absalom, N.C., S41519
Asa, Mass., S29138
Atkins, Mass., Elizabeth, W2604
Augustus, R.I., Desire, W21063
Benjamin, Mass., S16107
Benjamin, Mass., N.H., S46499; BLWt.644-300-Capt. Iss. 6/2/1796 to Jos. Thomas, ass. No papers
Benjamin, Va., R3310 1/2
Carpenter, Ct., BLWt.5732-100-Pvt. Iss. 9/1/1790 to Theodosius Fowler. No papers
Charles, Mass., Fanny, W7094
Charles, Mass., Lucia, W14680
Daniel, N.J., S35912
David, Cont., Mass., S10622
David, Del., BLWt.2010-100
Dudley, Va., S2195
Ebenezer, Cont., Mass., Hannah, W21065
Ebenezer, Mass., S10619
Edward, N.H., Olive, W23009
Ephraim, Mass., S3330
Ephraim, N.C., S.C., S3331
Ezekiel, Mass., S29782
Ezekiel, Mass., S44806
Freeman, Mass., Sarah, W24114
Gamaliel, Mass., S39488
Henry, Md., b. Ireland, S22229
Isaac, Pa., b. Md., Ann, W10013
Jacob, Mass., Latitia, W1402
James, Va., S39492
Jeremiah, Pa., Va., b. Md., R3313
Jesse, Pa., Va., b. Md., S8402
Joel, Mass., S17403
John, Md, b. Md., S10620
John, Mass., Lois, W687; BLWt. 15164-160-55
John, Mass., Vt., Anna, W10014; BLWt.9420-160-55
John, N.H., R3315
John, N.Y., BLWt.7099-100-Pvt. Iss. 6/12/1792 to William Kline, ass. No papers
John, N.C., BLWt.12111 & 13041-Pvt. Iss. 10/11/1796 to John Cannon, ass. No papers
John, N.C., S32233
John, N.C., Lucy, R3316
John, Old War Inv. File, 27753; Wayne's War; BLWt.13665-160-55
John, Va., S32234
Joseph, Mass., Sarah, W1581
Joseph, N.H., S45738

ELLIS (continued)
Joseph, Pa., S22230
Joseph, S.C., b. N.C., Elizabeth, R3311
Lawrence, Mass., Dorothy Batchelder, former wid., W25186; BLWt. 90032-160-55
Leonard, Pa., Va., b. Md., Jane, W8689
Lyman, Mass., Sylvia, W7093; BLWt.10014-160-55
Marvel, Mass., Cynthia, W16250
Mary, former wid. of David Farrington, Mass., which see
Michael, Md., S6818
Nathan, Ct., Phebe, W17752
Nathan, Md., R3317
Nathan, Mass., S10627
Nichols, R.I., R3318
Paul, Mass., d. 1827; Rebecca, W23010
Paul, Mass., d. in battle 1778, BLWt.2344-300
Phenix Carpenter, Ct., Cont., S17941
Reuben, decd., Pa., BLWt.9349 & 13960 "Pvt. in the Artillery." Iss. 9/5/1791 to Hannah Ellis, Extx. No papers
Richard, Mass., R3321
Robert, N.H., Mariam/Miriam, W23005; BLWt.720-100
Robert, N.C., S41518
Robert, S.C., b. Va., S26084
Samuel, Mass., Mary, W23008; BLWt.36515-160-55
Samuel, N.C., S30400
Samuel, Pa., S8400
Shadrack, N.C., S31666
Stephen, Ct., Rebekah, W6716
Stephen, Va., Sally, R3322
Thomas, Md., BLWt.11183-100-Pvt. Iss. 12/21/1791. No papers
Thomas, Md., S34806
Walter, N.C., Mary, W4431
William, Ct., Sea Service, S28720
William, Cont., Fla. res. 1852, R20319
William, Va., Elizabeth, W7092
ELLISON, Charles, N.C., b. N.C., Massy, W354; BLWt.26867-160-55
David, Pa., Va., pensioned in N.Y., S44807
James, Va., b. N.J., S6821
John, N.Y., BLWt.7109-100-Pvt. Iss. 8/12/1790 to Samuel Coe, ass. No papers
John, Va., b. N.J., S3334
John, Va., b. Pa., S6820
John, Va., b. N.J., R3285
Robert, N.Y., BLWt.7096-100-Pvt. Iss. 8/26/1790 to Joseph Wright, ass. No papers
William, Mass., Rachel, BLWt. 54268-160-55
ELLITHORP, Azariah, Ct., S10618
Samuel, Ct. See ELITHORP
ELLMES, Benjamin, Mass., Elizabeth R3320
ELLMORE, Frederick Wm., Pa., Anna Martha/Hannah, R3325
Nathan, ---, N.J. res. 1833,R3323

ELLS, Samuel, Ct., BLWt.5747-100-Pvt. Iss. 1/25/1790. No papers
ELLSWORTH, Anthony, Mass., S12859
George, N.Y., Sarah, W19226
Job, Ct., Huldah A., W7103; BLWt. 9078-160-55
John, Ct., b. Mass., S2196
John, Ct., N.H., R.I., S9854
John, N.Y., Elizabeth, W16974
John, N.Y., R3333
Jonathan, Mass., Esther, W2725; BLWt.19726-160-55
Jonathan, Mass., Anna Kimball, former wid., W15919
Mary, former wid. of Wm. Gillespie Cont., Ct., which see
Moses, Ct., BLWt.5745-100-Pvt. Iss. 1/28/1792 to Moses Sill. No papers
Moses, Ct., S37909
Thomas, Mass., Lucy, W14682
William, N.Y., Barbara, W10952; BLWt.26628-160-55
ELLWOOD, Joseph, Ct., Naomi, W21058
Nathan, Ct., Abigail, W15765
Peter, N.Y., Peggy, W16568
ELLY, Michael, Pa., S34804
ELLYS, Stephen, Arty. Artificers, Ct., BLWts. 5740 & 13052-100-Pvt. Iss. 3/3/1797 to Samuel Fitch, ass. No papers
ELMENDORF, Conradt, N.Y., S12860
John, N.Y., S10623
ELMENDORPH, Cornelius J., N.Y., S12858
Jonathan, N.Y., S10621
ELMER, Ebenezer, N.J., S4280; BLWt. 663-400-Surgn. Dated 4/21/1790. No papers
Elijah, Ct., R3328
Elijah, N.H., Vt., S16110
Joel, Ct., Zillah, W24112
Joseph, Ct., Ruth, W19224
Moses/Moses G., N.J., S2197; BLWt.665-300-Surgn. Mate. Iss. to John Hole, ass. No papers
Samuel, Ct., S31665
Stephen, Ct., S23617
ELMES, Eliphalet, Mass., Chloe, W21062
ELMORE, Daniel, Ct., Elizabeth, W21060
Daniel, Pa., BLWt.9359-100-Pvt. Iss. 4/29/1794 to Francis Kirkpatrick, ass. No papers
Joel, Ct., S30399
John, N.C., Va., b. Va., S31009
John, Va., S39491
Matrom, Va., R3326
Matthias, S.C., b. N.C., R13965
Peter, N.C., b. Va., R3327
Robert, N.J., S42704
Thomas, Va., Patsey, W7095
William, N.C., S8414
ELMS, Charles, N.C., S8413
ELSBURY/ELLSBURY, Jacob, N.C., b. Md., Mary, W10016
ELSEY, Thomas, Va., b. Md.,S8404
ELSTON, Benjamin, N.J., Elizabeth, W9425; BLWt.29032-160-55
Jonathan, N.J., S16782
Samuel, N.J., Charity, W7099

ELSTON (continued)
Spencer, N.J., R3331
ELSWORTH, Benjamin, Ct., S37910
Benjamin, N.Y., S29134
David, R.I., S23614
Eliphalet, Cont., Ct., War of 1812, Jemima, R3332
Israel, Cont., Green Mt. Boys, Vt., See Israel Elsworth HOLLIDAY
John, N.Y., S8407
Peter, N.Y., BLWt.660-200-Capt.-Lt. Iss. 1/4/1791. No papers
William, Pvt., Mass., BLWt.4001 & 4074 iss. 3/25/1790. No papers
ELTER, John, Pa., b. Pa., moved to Va., S6816
ELTINGE, Thomas, N.Y. & Sea Service Rosina, W16569
ELTOM, Thomas, Pa., b. England, S22228
ELTON, Anthony, Pa., b. Ireland, moved to Pa., S.C., Ga., R3335
Bradley, Ct., Grace, W17751
ELWELL, Ebenezer, Ct., S43527
Elias, Mass., S29780
Jabez, Mass., Thankful, W17754
John, Mass., Judith, W23006
John, Mass., Abigail, R3336
Robert, Mass., S34810
Samuel, Mass., Privateer, Elizabeth, W21061
Thomas, Cont., Va.; Md. res., moved to Ohio, Elizabeth, W7096; BLWt.695-100-Pvt.
Zebulon, Mass., S34807
ELWOOD, Abijah, Ct., Susan, W25562
Abram, Ct., S44803
Isaac, ?, N.Y. res. Dis. No papers
Isaac, Ct., S44804
Stephen, Ct., Betty, W17757
Thomas, Navy, Ct. agcy. & res., S37907
ELY, Abner, Ct., Sea Service, Bridget, W21056. Her 1st husb., Senilius Brockway, d. in service.
Andrew, Cont., Ct., S44801
Daniel, Ct., S31663
Darius, Mass., S18392
Enoch, Mass., S29136
Gabriel, Ct., Eunice, W2775
Gad, Cont., BLWt.5748-100-Pvt. Iss. 1/11/1790. No papers
Gurdon, Ct., S17404
Jabez, Ct., S44802
Jacob, Ct., S15111
John, Ct., S3329
John Edwards, Mass., S34808
Joseph, Mass., S29137
Jube, Mass., S29135
Moses, N.J., Rebecca, W921
Simeon, Mass., Margaret, W17753
Wells, Ct., S44800
William, Va., S39493
ELZEY, William, Va., Sarah, W3531
EMBERSON, William, Pa., S34338
EMBICK, Christopher, Pa., Anna Maria, W9427
EMBLY, Samuel, N.J., BLWt.8284-100-Pvt. Iss. 9/7/1790 to Wm. Barton, ass. No papers
EMERICK, Elizabeth, former wid. of John Shulter, N.Y., which see

EMERICK (continued)
Philip, S23618
Wilhelmus/Withelmus, N.Y., S10630
EMERSON, Amos, N.H., S45745
Benjamin, Mass., Eunice, W19229
Catharine, former wid. of John Skinner, Ct., which see
Charles, Cont., N.H., S45746
Elias, Mass., Phebe, W24121
Enoch, Mass., N.H., Vt., S18393
Ephraim, Mass., Ann/Anna, W10956
Henry, N.C., S21747
Henry, Va., Nancy, W4949
James, Md., b. Md., R3339
James, Mass., S34812
John, Cont., Mass., Phebe, W24126
John, Mass., Keene, N.H. res. 1820. No number
John, Mass., N.H., Keziah, W23014
John, N.H., Mary, W15896
John, Va., War of 1812, Catharine W8694; BLWt.1611-200
Jonathan, Cont., N.H., Mass., N.H., S42707
Jonathan, Cont., N.H., Mary, W17759
Jonathan, Mass., R3342
Joseph, Ct., R3343
Joseph, Mass., S2536
Joseph, Mass., Rebecca, W14685
Mark, Mass., S17942
Michael, Mass., Elizabeth, W21066
Nathaniel, Ct., Mary, W21068
Nathaniel, Mass., Deborah Poland, former wid., W15266. She was wid. of Abner Poland, which see
Nehemiah, Mass., S34815; BLWt. 647-300-Capt. Iss. 10/18/1796 to John Coates, ass.
Parker, Mass., Rebecca, W21067
Peter, N.H., Esther, W21070; BLWt.31422-160-55
Ralph, N.H., Alice Fletcher, former wid., W24215
Samuel, Cont., N.H., Mass., Mary Sargeant, former wid., R9203
Samuel, Mass., S29141
Samuel, Mass., N.H., Abigail, W733; BLWt.3616-160-55
Samuel Moody, Mass., Elizabeth, W25611
Smith, N.H., Hannah, W16013
Stephen, Ct., S22754
Thomas, Mass., BLWt.4079-100-Pvt. Iss. 11/4/1795 to Joseph Brown, no papers
Thomas, Cont., Mass., Ruth, W24125
William, Mass., Sea Service, Lydia, W1253; BLWt.17562-160-55
William, N.H., ?, Papers found in claim of Daniel Smith, R9826.
William, R.I., Hannah Tower, former wid., W14025
EMERTON, Ephraim, Cont., Mass., S34813
Thomas, Mass., Privateer, S12869
EMERY, Abraham/Abram, See HEMBREE
Daniel, N.H., S35284
Daniel, N.H., S45747
David, Cont., Mass., Abigail, W24123
David, Mass., Betty Colman, former wid., R2154

EMERY (continued)
Eliphalet, N.H., Lois, W15895
Ephraim, Mass., Mary, W14684; BLWt.654-200-Lt. Iss. 3/25/1790. No papers
George, Va., See EMREY
Isaac, Mass., S20346
Jacob, Cont., Mass., Huldah, W24119
James, Mass., S29143
James, Mass., S31011
Jesse, Mass., BLWt.4101-100-Pvt. Iss. 3/25/1790. No papers
Jesse, Cont., Mass., Ruth, W23012
Job, Cont., Mass., S29783
Joel, N.H., S10628
John, Mass., Ruth, W14686
John, Mass., Deborah, W23011; BLWt.7306-160-55
John, Mass., Mercy, R3347
Joshua, Cont., Mass., Abigail, W2605; BLWt.11415-160-55
Levi, Mass., BLWt.9540-160-55
Nathaniel, Mass., S35283
Noah, N.H., Lucy, BLWt.44512-160-55
Peter, Cont., Va., N.J., Mary, R3346
Ralph, Mass., S35285
Rama, N.H., S45748
Samuel, Mass., Hannah, W7104
Shem, Mass. See EMORY
Stephen, Mass., S31012
Thomas, N.H., Mary, W21069
William, N.H., S17943
William, N.C., Lucy, W7107; BLWt.13904-160-55
EMES, Alexander, Mass., Beriah M., W23013; BLWt.19614-160-55
Charles, Cont., Mass. See EAMES
Jonathan, Mass., See EAMES
Joseph, Ct., See AMES
Luther, Mass., S34817
Nathan, Mass., BLWt.17851-160-55
Worsley, Arty. Pa., BLWt.669-300-Capt. Iss. 4/5/1791. No papers
EMETT, William, Ga., b. N.C., S32237
EMMEL, George, Pa., b. Germany, Martha, W786
EMMERSON, George, N.H., Betsey/Betty, W16014
Henry, N.C., Nancy, See EMERSON
Nathaniel, Ct., BLWt.5735-100-Pvt. Iss. 10/22/1792. No papers
Reuben, Va., b. Va., S30401
William, Mass. Sea Service, Lydia, See EMERSON
EMMERT, Frederick, Pa., Barbara, R3345
George, Cont., Va., S38680
EMMERTON, James, N.J., BLWt.96-100. No papers
EMMES, Joshua, Mass., S16108
Nathaniel, Mass., Rebecca, W24124
EMMITT, John, Md., Margaret B., W8692
EMMONS, Arthur, Ct. See EMONS
Daniel Spencer, Ct., Luna, W17760
James, Va., Sarah, W7108
John, N.H., S45749

EMMONS (continued)
John, N.J., S12870
John, Va., BLWt.12104-100-Pvt. Iss. 11/12/1791 to John Clingman, ass. No papers
John, Va., S46440
Jonathan, Ct., Privateer, S22755
Jonathan, Mass., Lydia, W14687
Joseph, Mass., BLWt.4084-100-Pvt. Iss. 1/29/1790. No papers
Noah, N.H., S12868
Pendleton, Mass., S29142
Peter, Va., S39495
Phinehas/Phineas, See EMONS
Samuel, Ct., Sarah, W7101; BLWt. 26995-160-55
Solomon, Ct., S22753
Solomon, Vt., Prudence, W25613
EMONS, Arthur, Ct., S29140
Phineas/Phinehas, Ct., N.Y., Keziah, W21071
EMORY, Gideon, Md., Anna L., W3669
John, Mass. See EMERY
Shem/Shim, Mass., Martha, W4433; BLWt.825-160-55
William, Cont., Md. agcy. & res., S34811
EMPIE, John F., N.Y., S10629; BLWt.526-160-55
EMREY, George, Va., S32236
ENCHES, Jesse, R.I., S21181
ENDECOTT, Moses, N.C., b. N.J., Wellmett, R3348; BLWt.44803-160-55
ENDERKIN, Francis, See ANTRICAN
ENDERS, Jacob, N.Y., S12872
John, N.Y., Elizabeth, W19230
ENDICOTT, Samuel, Cont., Mass., S4281
ENDSLEY, John, N.C., Deborah, R3349
ENGAL, George, Pa., S2537
ENGART, Benjamin, See ENYART
ENGELHAUPT/ENGLEHOPT, John, Pa., Eva Barbara, W2776
ENGLAND,John, Va., Mary, W5270
John, Va., b. in Pa., R3350
Joseph, N.C., S2541
William, N.C., S.C., S10631
ENGLE, Adam, Pa., S1811
Andrew, Pa., Genet, R3351
George, Pa. See ENGAL
Jacob, Pa., S23619
John, Va., S38861
Michael, Pa., S2538
ENGLER, David, N.J., R3353
Leonard, Pa., S22232
ENGLIS, Andrew, Mass., Rachel, W23015; BLWt.648-300-Capt. Iss. 8/11/1795. No papers
ENGLISH, Charles, Cont., Va. res. of bro. in 1828, BLWt.1379-100
Charles, Va., S39498
James, Cont., N.J., Hannah, W97
James, N.Y., For service see papers in claim of John Morris Foght, Cont. & N.Y.
James, Pa., BLWt.9339-100-Pvt. Iss. 3/26/1792 to Thomas Knight, admr. No papers
James, Pa., S12873
James, Pa., Jame, W3232; BLWt. 965-100

ENGLISH (continued)
John, N.Y., S22756
John, Pa., S42710
John, Va., BLWt.181-100. No papers
Michael, Pa., BLWt.9342-100-Pvt. Iss. 3/10/1795 to John Jones, ass. No papers
Robert, Cont., N.Y., S10632
Robert, Md., Pa., Va., R3354
Robert, N.J., S2540
Samuel, N.Y., Catharine, W16976; BLWt.661-200-Lt. Iss. 7/7/1791. No papers
William, N.H., S43528; BLWt. 1957-100
William, N.Y., R3355
William, Pa., S8421
William, Va., S3336
William, Va., Adria Kemp, former wid., W7970
ENGLISHER, John, Crane's Cont. Arty., Mass., BLWt.4102-100-Pvt. Iss. 6/15/1797 to Simeon Wyman. No papers
ENGLY, Timothy, Mass., Levina, W14693
ENGRAM, Timothy, Mass., Priscilla, W14691
ENLOE, Potter, S.C., Nancy, W11912; BLWt.34586-160-55
ENLOW, Deason, S.C., S39496
ENNIS, Abraham, R.I., S21180
Enoch, Md., BLWt.11180-100-Pvt. Iss. 9/5/1789. No papers
Henry, N.Y., BLWt.7101-100-Pvt. Iss. 9/15/1790 to John S. Hobart et al, assnes. No papers
John, Md., BLWt.1867-100. No papers
John, Pa., See INNIS
Leonard, Md., Jane, W9429; BLWt. 199-60-55
Paul, R.I., Hannah, W21072
Richard, Hazen's Regt., BLWt. 13048-100-Pvt. Iss. 7/13/1792 to Robert Ross, ass. No papers
William, R.I., Avis, W7110; BLWt. 646-200-Lt. Iss. 2/12/1799 to Wm. Ennis. No papers
ENNOS, Francis, Pa., BLWt.9346-100-Pvt. Iss. 3/25/1797 to Mary Ennos exts. for uses mentioned in will
ENO, Isaac, Ct., Vt., R3356
Levi, Ct., S31667
Reuben, Ct., Lois, W25564
William, Ct., BLWt.5738-100-Pvt. Iss. 3/30/1798. No papers
ENOCH, David, N.C., Rachel Conrad, former wid., R2236
ENOCHS, Enoch, Pa., Va., 1774, 1792 1793 & 1794, R3357
ENOS, Alexander, Ct., S15113
David, Ct., S37914
David, Ct., S39497
Elisha, Ct., Sarah, W16252
Erasmus, Ct., Anna, R3358
Joseph, R.I., Thankful, W16977; BLWt.27634-160-55
Matthias/Mathias, Ct. Sea Service, R.I., Anna, W16251
Olive, former wid. of Joseph

ENOS (continued)
Holcomb, Cont., Ct., which see
Roger, Ct., Jerusha, W24127
ENSIGN, Daniel, Ct., Elizabeth, W10957
Eliphalet, Ct., S12874
James, Ct., S37913
Otis, Ct., Hannah, W9428; BLWt. 6431-160-55
Rhoda, former wid. of John Ford, Mass., which see
ENSLEY, George, Pa., Elizabeth, W4669; BLWt.16120-160-55
ENSMINGAR, Joshua, Va., b. Md., R3360
ENSMINGER, Henry, N.J., S42709
John, See ENTSMINGER
ENSWORTH, Jesse, Ct., S15114
John, Ct., Mary, W17761
ENT, Daniel, Sr., Pa., S3335
ENTREKIN, Thomas, N.C., S.C., b. Pa., Mary, W7112
William, S.C., b. Pa., Sarah, W3532; BLWt.26272-160-55
ENTROT, Henry, Mass., BLWt.4096-100-Pvt. Iss. 4/20/1798. BLWt. 282-60-55. No papers
ENTROTT, Henry, Mass., Hannah, W4191; BLWt.282-60-55
ENTSMINGER, John, Va., S42708
ENYART/ENGART, Benjamin, N.J., S2539
EOFF, Isaac, S.C., b. N.J., Margaret, R3362
EOLLY, Michael, Pa. See ELLY
EPES/EPPES, William, Va., BLWt. 360-200
EPHLAND, David, N.C., S32239
EPLEY, John, Pa., S21182
EPLY, Jacob, N.Y. See his record in claim of Peter Suits who m. his wid., Elizabeth.
John, Pa., S42711
EPPERLY, George, Md., b. Pa., S32238
EPPERSON, Francis, Va., S37915
John, Va., Alcey, See APPERSON
Samuel, Va., BLWt.12102-100-Pvt. Iss. 11/17/1794. No papers
Thomas, N.C., S4282
Thomas, Va., Martha, W7113
Thompson, Va., Mary, See EPPOSON
William, N.C., See APPERSON
EPPES, Peter, Va., S8424
Richard, Va., S38681
William, Va. See EPES
EPPOSON, Thompson, N.C., Va., Mary, W7115
EPPS, John, Va., S8423
Moses, Va., S6822
EPTON, Benjamin, N.Y., BLWts. 7095 & 7901-100-Pvt. Iss. 12/10/1789 to C.F. Weissenfels, ass. No papers
ERB, Henry, Pa., S23620
Jacob, Pa., S8425
Jacob, Pa., Elizabeth, W3181
ERDMAN, Andrew, Pa., Susannah, W3533
Yost, Pa., Barbara, R3363
ERICKSON, Michael, See ERRICKSON

ERNEST, Christian, Armand's Corps, BLWt.13040-100-Pvt. Iss. 5/20/1793. No papers
ERP, Erasmus, Md., R3364
ERRICKSON, Michael, Cont., N.J., Ann, W16253
Thomas, N.J., S640
ERSKINE, Christopher, N.H., Freelove, R3365
David, Mass., Privateer, S29784
John, Mass., N.H., Phebe, W17763; BLWt.27598-160-55
ERVIN, Charles, Pa., S35913
Henry, Pa., See ERWIN
James, Md., Sarah, W9430; BLWt. 11192-100 iss. 2/1/1790
John, N.J., S871
ERVINE, James, Crane's Cont. Arty. Mass., BLWt.4105-100-Corp. Iss. 7/16/1789. No papers
ERWIN, David, N.H., Isabella/Isabel, W21074
David, N.C., Lydia, See EIRWIN
Henry, Pa., Mary/Maria, W2085
Jacob, --?--, Phila., Pa. agcy., Dis. No papers
James, Md., BLWt.11192-100-Pvt. Iss. 2/1/1790. No papers
James, N.Y., BLWt.7106-100-Pvt. Iss. 8/9/1796 to John Broom, ass. No papers
James, N.Y., S44808
James, Pa. See IRVIN
James, Pa., Frances, W7117; BLWt.1099-200
John, N.H., Sarah, W21075
John, N.Y., BLWt.7098-100-Pvt. Iss. 9/1/1790 to James McLaughlin ass. No papers
John, N.Y., Martha, W21073
John, N.C., S1512
Joseph, Pa., BLWt.1161-300
Peter, N.J., Sarah, W7116; BLWt. 2028-100
Richard, N.C., Nancy, W922
William, Cont., N.Y., S43529
William, N.J., BLWt.8280-100-Pvt. Iss. 6/11/1789 to Matthias Denman, ass. No papers
William, N.J., BLWt.8283-100-Sgt. Iss. 3/12/1790. No papers
William, N.J., BLWt.8285-100-Pvt. Iss. 11/16/1791 to Adam Nutt, ass. No papers
William, N.J., S41520
William, N.C., S6823
ESCHLEMAN, Abraham, Pa., b. Switzerland, S22757
ESHOM, John, Del., BLWt.2033-100
ESKRIDGE, George, Va., S8428
George, Va., Elizabeth, W8693
Malachi, Va., R21701
William, Va., Elizabeth, W4192; BLWt.505-200
ESLAND, John, Mass. See EASLAND
ESLER, Conrad/Coonrad, N.J., S34339
John, N.J., S2542
ESMOND, Isaiah, N.Y., R3370
ESPEY, James, N.C., b. Pa., S31668
Samuel, N.C., b. Pa., S6824
ESPY, George, Pa., S23621
John, N.C., S31669
ESQUIRE, Henry, See SQUIRE or WINCKLEBLACK
ESSELSTYN, Jacob, N.Y., S29144
ESSER, Jacob, Pa., Mary Ann, W3405
ESSICK, Jacob, Pa., R3371
ESSIG, Joseph, N.C., S8434
ESSOP, Samuel, Pa., BLWt.9356-100-Pvt. Iss. 3/14/1793. No papers
ESTABROOK, John, Mass., S34818
Nathan, Mass., S43530
Nathan, Mass., S43531
Nehemiah, Ct., S44809
Nehemiah, Mass., S34786; BLWt. 982-100
ESTABROOKS, Warren, R.I., S10601
ESTE, Solomon, Mass., Nancy, BLWt.61229-160-55. She was allowed pension & BL as the former wid. of Barzila Banister, Mass., which see
ESTELL/ESTILL, William, Cont., N.Y., S35914; BLWt.1798-100
ESTEN, John, R.I., S21183
ESTERBROOK, Joel, Mass., S8433
ESTERLING, William, N.C., S.C. See EASTERLING
ESTES, Abraham, Va., S12878
Abraham, Va., Nelly, W7119
Brazel/Brizele, Ga., N.C., S.C., R3201
Elijah, Va., S39499
Elizabeth, former wid. of Paul Thayer, Mass., which see
George, N.C., Va., S18394; BLWt.26130-160-55
John, N.C., Eliza, W17764
John, Va., S3338
John, Va., S8429
Lyddal, Va., R3372
Rowland, Va., Elisabeth M. W1740
Thomas, Va., Cynthia, W1160; BLWt.26461-160-55
ESTEY, Moses, N.J., S3339
ESTILL, Samuel, Va., S12876
Wallis, Va., S1759
ESTY, Edward, Mass., S19290
ETCHBERGER, William, Pa., Magdalena, W3791
Wolfgang, Md., S35287
ETCHENSON, William, Md., Mary, R3373
ETCHISON, Edmond, N.C., b. Md., S8436
ETHELL, Anthony, Va., S6825
Benjamin, Va., S35286
Henry, Va., R3374
ETHEREDGE, Joel, N.C., R3375
ETHERIDGE, John, N.C., R3376
ETHERINGTON, John, Va., Susan, W4670
ETHRIDGE, Stephen, N.H., Jane, W21076; BLWt.26734-160-55
ETTER, John, Va., S46542; BLWt. 1502-100
ETTICK, George J., Ct., N.Y., S10635
ETTING, Henry, N.Y., Catharine
ETTING (continued)
W24110
John, N.Y., Cornelia, W19231
ETTINGER, Jacob, Pa., Mary Ann, W5269
ETZ, William, N.Y., S28722
EUBANK, Achilles, Va., Nancy, W27743
Daniel, N.C., R3379
John, Cont., Va., Elizabeth Fogg, former wid., W7298
John, Va., Sarah, W19232
John, Va., Katharine, R3378
Joseph, Va., R3380
Royal, Va., S39500
EURE, Uriah, N.C. See URE
EUSTACE, John, Va., Dinah Lee, former wid., W4014
John, Va., BLWt.682-300-Capt. Iss. 1/27/1800 to William Eustace, heir
EUSTIS, Abraham, Cont., Mass., Margaret, W19233
Jacob, Mass., S35288
William, Cont., Mass., Caroline L. W3535; BLWt.501-160-55 & 690-450-Surgn. Gen. Hosp. Iss. 10/26/1789. No papers
William, Mass., S31013
EVANS, Abel, Pa., S41521
Abiather, Ct., BLWt.5739-100-Sgt. Iss. 10/16/1789 to Theodosius Fowler, ass. No papers
Abiather/Abiathar, Ct., Mary, W21080
Allen, Ct., BLWt.5744-100-Pvt. Iss. 11/2/1791 to Titus Street. No papers
Andrew, Mass., S43532
Andrew, N.C., Va., Elizabeth, W10019
Andrew, Va., S3341. See N.A. Acc. No. 874-050060. Not Half Pay
Anthony, Pa., BLWt.9360-100-Fife Maj. Iss. 11/5/1789. No papers
Anthony, Pa., S42713
Ardin, Va., S1812
Asa, Mass., Elizabeth, W3670; BLWt.14756-160-55
Batte, Va., S39502
Benjamin, Cont., Mass., Thankfull W24131
Benjamin, R.I., S10636
Benjamin, Stacy, Ct., Sybil, S22759; BLWt.6268-160-55
Charles, Va., Elcy/Alcy/Alice, W7123
Cornelius, N.C., S3340
Cotton, Daniel, Ct., S23623
Daniel, Ct., Sarah, W17766
David, Ct., S12887
David, R.I., Roba, W19235; BLWt.6457-160-55
Edward, Md., BLWt.11179-100-Pvt. Iss. 9/12/1792 to John Wright, ass. of Wm. Evans, admr.
Edward, Md., BLWt.11190-100-Pvt. Iss. 6/11/179? to Samuel Johnston, ass. No papers
Edward, N.Y., S8437
Edward, Va., Elizabeth, R3382; BLWt.43878-160-55

EVANS (continued)
Eldad, N.H., S12882
Elijah, Md., BLWt.673-300-Capt. Iss. 5/25/1789. No papers
Elisha, N.C., S6830
Evan, Pa., Susannah, W7124
Ezekiel, Arty. Artificers, Pa., BLWt.13057-100 iss. 3/21/1791 to Samuel Horton, admr.
George, Mass., Lois, W14697
George, Pa., S42715
George, S.C., BLWt.2197-200. No papers
Gilbert/Gettrel, Del., Polly, W7122; BLWt.26857-160-55
Guilford, R.I., Elizabeth, W5271; BLWt.826-160-55
Henry, Mass., Sarah, W14700
Henry, Va., S8441
Hooper, Md., Frances/Fanny, W2928
Isaac, Ct., S44813
Israel, Cont., N.H., N.Y., Huldah, W23016
James, Pa., BLWt.9340-100-Pvt. Iss. 10/3/1792 to Peter Snider, ass. No papers
James, Va., S39501
James Pratt, Mass., S29145
Jenkin, Del., BLWt.10759-100-Pvt. Iss. 12/6/1797. No papers
Jesse, Va., S15826 & Va. Half Pay Claim, Act of July 5, 1832. N.A. Acc. No. 874-050061. Half Pay
Jesse, Va., Unicy, R3409
John, Md., BLWt.11194-100-Pvt. Iss. 2/1/179?
John, Md., S12886
John, N.H., S10639
John, N.H., S18395
John, N.H., Vt., S10638
John, N.J., S41525
John, N.C., S2200
John, N.C., R3388
John, Pa., BLWt.9358-100-Pvt. Iss. 4/18/1796. No papers
John, Pa., S42714
John, Va., BLWt.12101-100-Pvt. Iss. 10/26/1795 to John Stackdell, ass. No papers
John, Va., S8444
John, Va., Mary, W1582; BLWt. 27000-160-55
Joseph, Mass., S35292
Joseph, N.H., Vt., S38684
Joseph, N.Y., BLWt.7103-100-Pvt. Iss. 8/4/1790 to Henry Hart, ass. No papers
Joseph, res. Caledonia, Mo. N.A. Acc. No. 874-050062. Half Pay. No pension file for this man.
Joseph, Va., S35289
Josiah, Ct., BLWt.5734-100-Pvt. Iss. 10/16/1789 to Theodosius Fowler, ass. No papers
Josiah, Ct., S43533
Lemuel, N.H., BLWt.2085-160-55
Leonard, Mass., Lovina, W1254; BLWt.827-160-55
Lewis, Navy, Mass. agcy. and res., S34820
Moses, Ct., BLWt.5743-100-Pvt.

EVANS (continued)
Iss. 5/18/1790 to Theodosius Fowler. No papers
Moses, Ct., Thirza, W7121
Moses, N.Y., Vt., S38685
Nancy, former wid. of Joseph Bacon, Mass., which see
Nathan, Mass., Martha Alexander, former wid., W16810
Nathaniel, Mass., S23622
Nathaniel, Mass., S35293
Obadiah, N.J., S34341
Owen, S.C., Agnes, W10965
Perry, Md., S39503; BLWt.417-100
Peter, Va., Ann, W14695
Philip, N.C., Gracy, W5272; BLWt. 19727-160-55
Randol/Randall, Ct., N.H., S12879
Reese, Pa., Ruth Graff, former wid., R4173
Reuben, N.C., S41524
Robert, Pa., R3391
Sampson, Pa., Va., S8440
Samuel, ---, d. Onondaga Co., N.Y. 1832, R3392
Samuel, Cont., N.C., Peggy, W7126; BLWt.35824-160-55
Samuel, Mass., N.Y., Rhoda, W25563
Samuel, N.C., S6827
Seth, Mass., R.I., Vt., R3393
Sherebiah, Mass., Crane's Cont. Arty., BLWt.4103-100-Pvt. Iss. 2/27/1790 to Theodosius Fowler.
Sherebiah, Mass., S44277
Silas, Mass., Melescent, W21079
Simeon, Mass., S45751
Thomas, Pvt., Md., BLWt.11176 iss. 2/1/1790
Thomas, Md., S34821
Thomas, Mass., Sea Service, Privateer, S21185
Thomas, N.C., BLWt.685-300-Capt. Iss. 9/12/1789. No papers
Thomas, Va., Jane, W923
Walter, Md., R3395
Wiggin, Mass., N.H. Sea Service, Mary, W24130
William, ---, Md. agcy. Dis. No papers
William, Ct., N.Y., S12880
William, Ga., b. Va., S31670
William, Mass., Ann, W4193; BLWt.14523-160-55
William, Mass., R3397
William, Mass., R.I., Merribah, W14698
William, N.Y., R20365
William, R.I. Sea Service, R3398
William, Va., S8445
William, Va., S10640
William, Va., S25069; BLWt.681-200-Lt. Iss. 4/26/1798. No papers
Zachariah, Md., S30403
Zechariah/Zachariah, N.C., S30402
EVARTS, Ezra, Ct., Lorrain, W21078
Reuben, Ct., S23624
Stephen, Ct., S44811
EVELAND, Daniel, N.J., S2198
Peter, N.J., S22233
EVELETH, Aaron, Mass., S30405
Isaac, Mass., Deborah, W2374
James, Mass., Sarah Rollins,

EVELETH (continued)
former wid., W7142; BLWt.38564-160-55
John, Mass., Patience, W1255
Joseph, Cont., Mass., Elizabeth, W288
Sarah, former wid. of John Wentworth, Mass., which see
EVELITH, Zimri, Mass., BLWt.4094-100-Pvt. Iss. 3/26/1796 to Peter Swier. No papers
EVELT, Daniel, Ct., BLWt.5741-100-Pvt. Iss. 9/20/1790. No papers
EVENS, Allen, Ct., S37916
Barnabas, Cont., R.I., Elizabeth, W8695
Benjamin, Mass., S31014
Joseph, N.Y., Hannah, W24129
Nathan, Mass., N.Y., S43536
EVEREST, Benjamin, Cont., BLWt. 1031-100. Papers
Benjamin, Cont., Vt., S38683
Daniel, Ct., Eunice, W21082
Elisha, Ct., S43534
EVERETT, Abner, Pa., Susannah Smith, former wid., W6087 She m. Robt. Smith from whom she separated & resumed the name of Everett
Eleazer, Mass., Lucy, W23018; BLWt.11405-160-55
Jeremiah, Navy, Ct., Maria, W21081 BLWt.26585-160-55
John, N.C., R3403
John, Va., S16786
Josiah, Cont., Mass., S35290
Levi, Mass., S45750
Nathaniel, Mass., Rebecca Dow, former wid., R3055
Peletiah, Cont., Mass., S34819; BLWt.652-200-Lt. Iss. 12/31/1795. Name spelled Everette. No papers
Richard Clair, Mass., Persis, W23017
Samuel, Marine Service, Md., S2543
William, Va., S3342
EVERHARD, Frederick, Pa., Rebecca, R3401
EVERHART, George, Pa. Sea Service, S6826
John, Pa., S2201
John, Pa., S41522
Lawrence, Cont., Md., Anne Mary, S25068 and W9431
Peter, N.C., Mary, W7128
Philip, Pa., BLWt.9338-100-Pvt. Iss. 11/5/1789. On file, not delivered
EVERINGHAM, William, N.J., S34343
EVERIT, Ebe, Ct., S15417
Oliver, Ct., BLWt.5733-100-Piper. Iss. 12/14/1789 to Richard Platt. Also BLWt.265-60-55
EVERITH, Sarah, former wid. of John Wentworth. See EVELETH
EVERITT, Abner, Ct., S15827
Andrew, Ct., S12884
Daniel, Ct., S22758
Daniel, Mass., S44812
Eliphalet, Ct., Rhoda, W19234
John, N.J., N.Y., S12883
John, Pa., S34340

EVERITT (continued)
John, N.C., Sarah, R3404
Joseph, N.C., Lettice, R3402
Nathaniel, N.C., S6829
Oliver, Ct., Mary, W1583; BLWt.265-60-55
Robert, Va., S38682
Susanna, former wid. of Alpheus Morgan, Mass., which see
Thomas, N.C., b. Md., S6828
EVERLY, George, Pa., BLWt.9351-100-Pvt. Iss. 2/26/1791. No papers
John, Md., Va., R3405
Michael, Pa., Sarah, W3233
Michael, Pa., Catharine Markley, former wid., W4537; BLWt.667-200-Lt. iss. 3/11/1791. No papers
Simeon, Va., b. Md., S8446
EVERMAN, Christian, Pa., BLWt. 9348-100-Pvt. Iss. 11/8/1791 to Peter Rodermell, ass. No papers
EVERS, Andrew, Pa., S22760
EVERSOLE, Peter, Pa., S46231; BLWt.9343-100-Pvt. Iss. 2/21/1793
EVERSON, Adam, N.Y., Dorothy, W19236
Ephraim, Mass. Sea Service, Susanna Delano, former wid., W14608
George R., Pa., S41523
John, N.Y., Jane, W17767
Joseph, Mass., S30404
Levi, Mass., Eunice, W14702
Samuel, Mass.,Sea Service, S30406
EVERTON, Benjamin, Cont., Mass., Lucinda, W14701; BLWt.2473-100
Thomas, Mass., S2202
Zephaniah/Zepheniah, Mass.,S35291
EVERTS/EVARTS, Daniel, Ct., N.Y., S10637
Eber, Ct., Cont., Green Mt. Boys, S12881
Edward, Vt., R3407
Nathaniel, Ct., Mary, W21077
Solomon, Ct., S12888
Stephen, Cont., Ct., S27768
EVERY, Thomas, Pa., BLWt.9352-100-Pvt. Iss. 9/26/1791 to John M. Cleland, ass. No papers
EVETT, John, N.C., R3408
EVIG, Christian, Pa., S2199
EVINGHAM, Stacey, Va., Lee's Legion, BLWt.12103-100-Pvt. Iss. 6/7/1790 to George Painter, ass. BLWt.13059. No papers
EVINS, Benoni, Ct., S43535
David, Va., S32695
John, N.C., Va., R3387
EVRITT, James, Del., S34342
EWELL, Charles, Va., War of 1812, Maria D., W9432; BLWt. 1850-300 Va. Half Pay. BLWt.17591-160-55 N.A. Acc. No. 874-050063
Thomas, Va., R14052; Va. Half Pay N.A. Acc. No. 874-050064
Thomas Winder, Va., R---; BLWt. 2497-300; Va. half pay
EWEN/EWING, Timothy, N.J., or N.Y., Sarah, R3416
William, Va., Anna Dormire, former wid., R3022
EWER, Jonathan, Mass., S35294

EWER (continued)
Paul, Mass., S12891
Prince, Mass., BLWt.2008-100
EWERS, Rufus, N.H., S19291
EWING, Alexander, N.C., Sarah, W1584; BLWt.36637-160-55
Alexander, Pa., Jane, R3413
Alexander, Pa., S8448
Alexander, Va., Sally, W152
David, Hazen's Regt., BLWt. 13049-100-Pvt. Iss. 11/12/179- to Timothy Kelly, ass. No papers
George, N.J., S35916
George, Va., Margaret, W9
James, Pa., R3412
James, Pa., S2203
James, Vt., Naomi, W15832
John, Va. Sea Service, Mary, R3415
John, Va., S31015
William, Pa., S22234
William, Pa., S8447
William, Pa., S35915
EXLINE, John, Va., S42716
EYERS, Samuel, N.H., S19646
EYLER, Jacob, Pa., S8451
Jonas, Pa., Anna Regina/Rachel, W9433
EYMAN, Henry, Pa., S8450
EYSTER, George, Pa., S2204
EZELL, Balaam, Va., S31016
Timothy, N.C., S38686

F

FACKENTHALL, Michael, Pa., S2206
FACKS, See FAKS
FACTOR, John, N.Y., BLWt.7116-100-Fifer. Iss. 7/16/1790 to Wm. J. Vreedenburgh, ass. No papers
FACUNDUS, Abraham, Mass., S34828
FADDEN, John, Mass., Catharine, W21084
FADE, John, Pa., S34834
FAGAN, Henry, N.J., S34344
Mary, former wid. of Famous Mortimer, Cont. Va.,which see
Michael, Pa., S35922
William, N.Y., Invalids Regt., BLWt.7128-100-Pvt. & BLWt. 13102. Iss. 7/30/1790 to Edward Compston, ass. No papers
William, Pa., BLWt.9379-100-Pvt. Iss. 3/1/1792 to Cath. Fagan, admx. No papers
FAGG, Joel, Md., S2205
FAGIN, Henry, N.J., BLWt.8307-100-Pvt. Iss. 10/17/1791 to William Lloyd, ass. No papers
FAGUNDAS, George Ferdinand, Pa., Mary, W3234
FAIDO, Absalom, Md., BLWt.11238-100-Pvt. Iss. 1/11/1796 to Joshua Ward, ass. No papers
FAIL, Dixon, S.C., S6833
Frances, former wid. of William Grimes, N.C., which see
FAILING, Jacob J., N.Y., Nancy, W21092
John D., N.Y., Elizabeth, W19242
John J., N.Y., S10646
Peter, N.Y., See FALING
Philip, N.Y., Margaret, W19237
FAIN, Ebenezer, Ga., N.C., Va., b. Pa., Mary, R3421
William, Va., R3422
FAINTER, Martin, Va., S19292
FAIR, Barnabas, N.C., S12895
John, Pa., See FEHR
FAIRBANK, Benjamin, Mass., S34825
Calvin, Mass., S15421
Cyrus, Mass., S5381
Ephraim, Mass., Prudence, W17892
George, Mass., S1662
James, Mass., S5379
John, Mass., BLWt.4162-100-Pvt. Iss. 4/5/1796 to Oliver Ashley
John, Mass., S35299
Jonathan, Mass., S34824
Jotham, Mass., Beulah, W19238
Levi, Mass., Eunice, W14706
Luther, Mass., S21749
Pearley, Mass., Tabitha, R3424
William, Mass., S29148
FAIRBANKS, Abel, Mass., S12896
Asa, Mass., Julitta/Juletta, W19245
Asa, Mass., Hepzibah, W23025; BLWt.15416-160-55
Elijah, Mass., S18821
John, Mass., S29789
John, Jr., Mass., Fanny, W21098
Nathaniel, Mass., Lydia, W23020; BLWt.13714-160-55
Oliver, Mass., S39511

FAIRBANKS (continued)
Samuel, Ct., S16788
William, Cont., Mass., S18818
William, R.I., Judith, R3423
FAIRBROTHER, Francis, Md., BLWt. 11210-100-Pvt. Iss. 2/1/1790
Francis, Md., Patience, W8804
Richard, Cont., Mass., S18820; BLWt.4146-100. Iss. 4/15/ 1800 to Abijah Holbrook
William, Mass., S34835
FAIRCHILD, Aaron, Mass., S12899
Abel, Ct., S12892
Abijah, Cont., N.J., Pa., S13000
Abijah, N.C., Violate, R3428
Abina/Abind/Abiud, N.C., S15420
Abraham, N.J., Phebe, W787
Affiah, former wid. of Noadiah Holcomb, Mass., which see
Benjamin, N.J., N.Y., Marcy, W16981
Clement, Ct., Jerusha, W1741
Ephraim, Ct., Mary, W2929
Gilbert, Ct., S15116
James, Ct., Mary, W21093
James, N.Y., S10651
John, Ct., N.Y., S10641
Joseph, Ct., S43542
Nathan, Ct., Sarah, W25568
Nathaniel, N.J., N.Y., Elizabeth, W19240
Peter, Ct., BLWt.5758-100-Pvt. Iss. 12/3/1796 to Nathaniel Ruggles. No papers
Peter, Ct., S38688
Peter, Ct., Rachel, W7248
Peter, N.J., S4283
Stephen, N.Y., Elizabeth, W1403; BLWt.26275-160-55
FAIRE, Jonathan, Va., S38691
FAIRFIELD, Edward, N.H., Elizabeth Kimball, former wid., W21522
John, Mass., Hannah, W25570
Peter, Ct., See FAIRCHILD
Samuel, Mass., Anna, W21102
Thaddeus, Mass., S30409
William, Cont., Mass., Polly, W23019
FAIRLEY, Jonathan, Mass., See FARLEY
FAIRLIE, James, N.Y., S17945; BLWt.733-200-Lt. Iss. 1/13/1791
FAIRMAN, Daniel, Ct., S12894
John, Cont., Mass. agcy., S34827
Roswill/Roswell, Ct., Anna, W645 BLWt.26372-160-55
FAIRWEATHER, Samuel, Pvt., Ct., BLWt.5757 iss. 9/20/1790
Samuel, Ct., See FAYERWEATHER
FAITH, Abraham, Pa., S42189
FAITHALL, Robert, Va., BLWt.12125-100-Pvt. Iss. 5/29/1792 to Robert Means, ass. No papers
FAITHFULL, William, Va., BLWt.12139 -100-Pvt. Iss. 6/10/1792 to Abishai Thom, ass.
FAKNER, John, Pa., See FALKNER
FAKS, Philip, Pa., R3417
FALCH, Benjamin, N.H., Sarah, W4671
Jabez, N.H., Patience, W23026

FALCH (continued)
Nicholas, N.H. See FELCH
FALCONBURY, Jacob, N.C., S16789
FALES, Aaron Clark, Mass., Hepzibah, W14705
James, Cont., Mass., Keziah, W14737
John, R.I., Martha, W21091
Jonathan, Cont., Mass., Betsey, W14709; BLWt.34283-160-55
Jonathan, R.I., S21189
Nathaniel, R.I., Elizabeth, W24173
Samuel, Mass., See FOWLE
Samuel, Mass., War of 1812, Abigail, S34822; BLWt.32216-160-55
FALING, Peter, N.Y. See FAILING
FALKENBURY, Levi, N.Y., S10652
FALKNER, David, N.C., S3346
Hardy, N.C., Mary, R3466
Henry, Va., See FOLKNER
John, Pa., S42721
Ralph, Va., Margaret Bromley, former wid., BLWt.514-400
Robert, Mass., Phebe Hanford, former wid., W19669; BLWt. 2026-160-55
FALL, Aaron, N.H., S17410
George, Cont., N.H., Dorcas, W735; BLWt.771-100
Hatevil/Henry Hatevil, Cont., Mass., Sarah, W19250
Joshua, Mass., Betsey, BLWt. 61230-160-55
Joshua, N.H., BLWt.3103-100-Pvt. Iss. 12/31/1794. No papers
Samuel, Mass., BLWt.4175-100-Pvt. Iss. 11/6/1795 to James A. Neal. No papers
Samuel, Mass., Judith, W16571
FALLEN, John H., See FALLIN
FALLIN, John, Md., BLWt.11198-100-Pvt. Iss. 5/11/1790. No papers
John H., Va., S10642
FALLIS, Isaac, Pa., Elizabeth, W3671; BLWt.2018-100
FALLS, John, Mass. Sea Service, Flora, R3430
John, Pa., Sarah, W924
William, N.C., S6834
FALWELL/FALLWELL, James, Va., Elizabeth, W7247; BLWt. 31902-160-55
FAMBROUGH, Thomas, Va., Caron H./Keronhappoch Ward, former wid., R19380
FAME, John, Va. See FRAM
FANCHER, Abraham, N.Y., S22762
Isaac, Va., S42719; BLWt.1786-100
James, Va., See FENESHER
John, N.Y., S23625
Rufus, Ct., S43540
Squire, N.Y., S27770
William, Ct., Thankful Cole, former wid., W22811
William, N.Y., Lucy, W4950
FANDRE, Thomas, Va., S8455
Vachel, Va., Agnes A., W1407; BLWt.28631-160-55
FANE, Charles, N.C., S3343

FANN, John, Mass., BLWt.4127-100-Pvt. Iss. 12/30/1796 to Able Boynton
John, Mass., S45754
FANNEY, John, N.C., Ann, W4194
FANNING, Asa, Ct., Jerusha, W19247; BLWt.34996-160-55
Charles, Ct., S13001; BLWt.723-200-Lt. Iss. 12/24/1799 to William Wells, ass.
Frederick, Ct., BLWt.5777-100-QM Sgt. Iss. 8/21/1789. No papers
James, N.J., BLWt.8300-100-Pvt. Iss. 6/11/1789 to Matthias Denman ass.
James, N.J., Susanna, W3406
John, Ct., Abigail, W1585
Jonathan, Ct. Sea Service, Navy, S23214
Nathaniel, Navy, U.S. Navy up to 1805; Elizabeth Palmer, former wid., Old Act Navy, W424
Thomas, Ct., BLWt.5771-100-Pvt. Iss. 7/2/1790. No papers
Thomas, Ct., Cont., Susannah, W17891
William, Mass., BL Reg.
FANON, James, N.J. See FANNING
FANSHAR, James, Va. See FENESHER
FANT, George, Va., S35301
FANTRESS, Valentine, Va., Sarah/ Sally, W3008
FANVER, Frederick, N.J., S1000
George, N.J. See FAUVER
FARAR/FARRAR, Abel, Va., S17947
Field, S.C. See FARRAR
Leonard, N.C.,Va. See FARRAR
FARBER, Daniel, N.J., R3432
FARDEN, Mary, former wid. of John Lonass, Cont. Md., which see
FARE, Edmund, Va., Priscilla, W2726
Jacob, Pa., R3434
Jonathan, Va. See FAIRE
FARENCE, Henry, Cont., Md., S39508
FAREWELL, Isaac, N.H., BLWt.694-300-Capt. Iss. 4/1/1796. No papers
James, Pa., S41529
FARGESON, Larkin, Va., S35923
FARGO, Ezekiel, Ct., Mass., S10650
Samuel, Ct., Hannah, W24178
Timothy, Ct., Betsey, W25569
William, Ct., BLWt.5754. Iss. 1/21/1794 to Samuel Prentice, ass. No papers
William, Ct., Polly, W19241
FARGUSON, Abraham, Va., S16379
FARIAR, John, Mass. See FARRIER
FARINGTON, Abner, Mass., S35297
Frederick, Mass. See FARRINGTON
Ithamar, Mass., S29149
Samuel, Cont., Mass., Privateer, S16787
FARIS, Alexander, S.C., b. Pa., S3344
Elijah, Va., Martha, W7239; BLWt.29004-160-55
Gilbord, N.Y., See FERRIS
Isham, Va., R3452

FARIS (continued)
Martin, Va., S8452; BLWt.29747-160-55
Moses, Va., S31019
Thomas, Va., S30407
William, Mass. Sea Service, Navy, Frances, W24182
William, Va., Margaret, W7238; BLWt.29734-160-55
William, Va., R3457
FARISS, Jacob, Va., S8453
William, Ga. res. in 1833, R3456
FARLEY, Benjamin, Mass., Polly, W14708
Benjamin, Mass., N.H., Susanna, W7243; BLWt.19611-160-55
Jabez, Mass., Susanna S., W24172
Jonathan, Mass., S43544; BLWt.1668-100
Obediah, Va., R3437
Robert, Mass. Sea Service, Susanna K., W19251
Samuel, Mass., S43541
Stephen, Va., Mary, W78
Thomas, Va., Patty/Patsey, W7244
William, Mass., N.H., Elizabeth, R6707
FARLOW, Huldah, former wid. of Joseph Moger, Ct., which see
FARMAN, Jacob, Vt., Lois, W24170
Nathan, N.J., See FURMAN
FARMBROUGH, William, Va., R3438
FARMER, Aaron, Mass., BLWt.318-100
Benjamin, Mass., S10648
Benjamin, Mass., Sarah, W24179
Benjamin, Va., Ermine, W7242
David, Cont., N.H., S45756
Ezekiel, S.C., S16112
Henry W., Mass., Sybil, W16980
James, N.J., S39504
Jesse, Cont., Va. res. of heirs in 1828, BLWt.1349-100. Iss. 8/4/1828
John, Mass., Sarah, W16115
John, Mass., Lydia, R3440
John, S.C., S21191
Lewis, Pa., BLWt.751-450-Lt. Col. Iss. 7/30/1789. No papers
Ludowick, Va., Elizabeth, W19244
Matthew, Va., S16790
Nathan, Cont., Va. res. of heirs in 1828; BLWt.1348-100. Iss. 8/4/1828
Nathaniel, Md., S35917
Oliver, Cont., Mass., N.H., S17409
Oliver, Mass., Hannah, W21096
Richard, Md., R3441
Samuel, Tamer, R3443
Sarah, former wid. of Benj. Bowers, N.H., which see
Shadrack, S.C., S21190
Thomas, Ct., S43546; BLWt.722-200-Lt. Iss. 10/7/1789. No papers
William, Mass., BLWt.789-100
William, N.C., S35919
FARNAM, Benjamin, Cont., Ct., Ann Giffin, former wid., R4305
Eben, N.H., Lydia, W17893
Elijah, Ct., S10643
Eliphalet, Ct. See FARNAN
John, Ct., Mary, W5273

FARNAM (continued)
John, Mass., Navy, S44816
Jonathan, Mass., BLWt.4122-100-Pvt. Iss. 4/20/1797 to Daniel Aiken. No papers
Jonathan, Cont., Mass., Dorcas, W24231
Joseph, N.H., See FARNUM
Joshua, Cont., Mass. See FARNUM
Levi, Cont., Ct., Dorcas Taylor, former wid., W16752. Her 2nd husb., Ebenezer Perry, Ct. or Mass., also served. See papers within. Her 3rd husb. and last, was pensioned. See Thos. Taylor, Ct.
Peter, Ct., See FARNUM
Peter, Ct., Sylvia, W25571
Ralph, Mass. See FARNHAM
Rufus, Ct., Navy, Priscilla, W10973; BLWt.26181-160-55
Zebediah, Ct., Cont., S38689
FARNAN, Eliphalet, Ct., Hannah, W24175
FARNEY, George, N.J., S34346
FARNHAM, Abial, Ct., Chloe, W21089
Bezaleel/Bazaleel, Ct., S40058
David, Mass., Abigail, W21100
Eliphalet, Ct. See FARNAN
John, N.H., BLWt.3100-100-Pvt. Iss. 1/26/1798 to James Smith, ass. No papers
Jonathan, Cont., See FARNAM
Jonathan, Mass., S35296
Joseph, Ct., S13003
Joseph, N.H. See FARNUM
Joshua, Cont., Mass. See FARNUM
Levi, Ct. See FARNAM
Nathaniel, N.H., S35300
Ralph, Mass., S31018; BLWt.9451-160-55
Reuben, Cont., N.Y. Agcy. & res. S43549
Rufus, Ct. See FARNAM
Thomas, Ct., Cont., S17408
FARNSHIELD, William, Pa., S34838
FARNSLER, Henry, Pa., S15829
FARNSWORTH, Amos, Mass., S29791
Daniel, N.J., S16113
Ebenezer, Cont., Mass., S39510
Ebenezer, N.Y., See FARNWORTH
Edmund, Mass., BLWt.4163-100-Pvt. Iss. 3/25/1790. No papers
Edmund/Edmand, Mass., Hannah, W10969; BLWt.36762-160-55
Edmund/Edmond, N.H., S13410
Harbour, Mass., Lucy, W16015
Isaac, Mass., S17407
Jonathan, Mass., S21748
Jonathan, Mass., S39506
Joseph, Mass., S39505
Levi, Mass., S34823
Manassah, Mass., S39507
Moses, N.H., Ruhamah, W7249
Oliver, Mass., S26997
Oliver, N.H., S15115
Robert, Mass., Mass. Sea Service, Bridget, W23023
Samuel, Mass., N.H., Anna, W19253
Thomas, Mass., S22236
William, Mass., BLWt.4131-100-

FARNSWORTH (continued)
Sgt. Iss. 4/1/1790. No papers
William, Mass., S28723
William, Mass., Abigail, W24180
Zacheus, Mass., Hannah, W23021
FARNUM, Amos, Mass., Lydia, BLWt.19902-160-55
Benjamin, Mass., S5375
Eben, N.H. See FARNAM
Ebenezer, N.H., S45755
Elijah, Ct. See FARNAM
Elisha, Mass., S18397
Israel, Mass., S45532
John, Ct., BLWt.5779-100-Pvt. Iss. 4/1/1795 to Benj. Talmadge. No papers
John, Ct., See FARNAM
Joseph, N.H., S16791
Joseph, N.H., Edith, R3444; BLWt.36657-160-55
Joshua, Cont., Mass., S15422
Peter, Ct., S17405
Peter, Mass., Hannah, W21087
Rufus, Ct. See FARNAM
Samuel, N.H., Sarah, W16982
Simeon, Mass., S31671
FARNWORTH, Ebenezer, N.Y., S28724
FARQUHER, James, Md., Betsey, R3445
FARR, Archibald, N.Y., S12898
Francis, Mass., Sarah, W14712
Nathaniel, N.H., S16111
Robert, Pa., Polly Jarvis, former wid., W8223; BLWt.49032-160-55
Salmon, Mass., Vt., S31673
Thomas, N.H., Sarah, W23022
William, Mass., S34837
William, S.C., Elizabeth Taleavo, W21094
FARRA, Samuel, N.C., Pa., Privateer, S31022
FARRABY, Richard, Md., BLWt.11230-100-Pvt. Iss. 11/29/1790 to James Ryon, Admr. No papers
FARRAGUT, George, Navy, R1172
FARRAND, Bethuel, N.J., Rhoda, W17894
Enos, N.J., S2207
Jarad, Cont., Vt., S15423; BLWt.26127-160-55
Joseph, Ct., Vt., S18396
Phinehas, N.J., Jemima, W851
William, Vt., S15828
FARRAR, Abigail, former wid. of Samuel Sherman, Mass. which see
Asa, Cont., Mass., Dorinda, W7241
Charles, Mass., Polly, W14707
Ephraim, Mass., Lavina/Lovina, W14710
Field, S.C., BLWt.70-800
Francis, Va., S31672
Isaac, Mass., Hannah, W24176
John, Mass., S43537
Joseph, Mass., Mary, R3447
Leonard, N.C., Va., S17406
Matthew, Va., R3448
Nathaniel, N.C., S8458
Stephen, Va., Elizabeth, W7240; BLWt.28654-160-55
Thomas, S.C., R3449
William, N.C., Amy, W3968

FARRARE, Emanuel, Md., BLWt. 11233-100-Pvt. Iss. 2/7/1790. No papers
FARRELL, Isaac, Va., S35920
James, Va., BLWt.339-100. Iss. 3/11/1807
John, Md., R3450
Thomas, Mass., BLWt.4141-100-Pvt. Iss. 5/10/1799 to Allen Crocker. No papers
William, N.C. See FERRELL
William, Pa., BLWt.9407-100-Pvt. Iss. 3/29/1791. No papers
William, Pa. See FERRELL
William, Va., BLWt.12122-100-Pvt. Iss. 4/13/1791 to James Reynolds, ass. No papers
FARREN, John, Mass., S35295
FARRES, Charles, Va. See FARRIS
FARRIER, John, Cont., Mass., S45753
FARRIN, Richard, Mass. See FERRIN
FARRINGTON, Aaron, Mass., BLWt. 4115-100-Pvt. Iss. 3/31/1790 to Theodosius Fowler. No papers
Aaron, Mass., S34832
Abner, Mass. See FARINGTON
David, Mass., Mary Ellis, former wid., W14679
Ebenezer, Mass., S10653
Elijah, Cont., Mass., Elizabeth, W19248; BLWt.28596-160-55
Eliphalet, Mass., BLWt.4114-100-Pvt. Iss. 8/10/1789 to Richard Platt. No papers
Eliphalet, Mass., Jemima, W21083
Frederick, Mass., Judy, W10972; BLWt.34998-160-55
George/George Lyon, Mass., Rhoda, W734; BLWt.3999-160-55
Henry, Mass., Sally, W2086
James, N.Y., Lamb's Art., BLWt. 7131-100-Pvt. Iss. 11/11/1791 to Samuel Broome, ass. No papers
John, Mass., S20354
Jonathan, Mass., Freelove, W24171
Josiah, Mass., BLWt.4182-100-Pvt. Iss. 3/26/1792 to George Bliarm (or Blevin/Blivin). No papers
Lewis, Mass., S21188
March, Cont., Mass., S44815
Matthew, Mass., S34829
Nathaniel, Mass., Elizabeth, W21085
Samuel, Cont., Mass., Privateer, S16787
Thomas, Cont., Mass., Jerusha, W16984
William, Mass., S29786
FARRIS, Caleb, S.C. See FERIS
Charles, Va., R3451
Elijah, Va., See FARIS
James, Mass., Betsey/Elizabeth, W24169
James, Va., R3452
John, Va., R3455
Jonathan, N.Y., S12897
Nancy, former wid. of Richard Gentry, Va., which see
Nathan, Va., also 1786, Polly Fitzgerald, former wid., R14085 Va. Half Pay

FARRIS (continued)
William, Ga. res. See FARISS
William, Mass., Martha, W644; BLWt.36765-160-55
William, Va., See FARIS
William, Va., See FARIS
FARROW, Abraham, N.J., BLWt. 8320-100-Pvt. Iss. 6/27/1791. No papers.
Ezekiel, Cont., Mass., Boat service on Lake Champlain, Miriam, W23045
Jesse, S.C., S38687
John, Cont., Mass., Sea Service, S31020
John, S.C., S21193
Landon, S.C., Rachel, W21088
Seth, Mass., R3458
Thomas, N.C., S.C., S17946
FARWELL, David, Mass., S29146
Eleazer, Mass., S29785
Isaac, Ct., Vt., S12893
Joseph, Mass., S29147
Josiah, N.H., S41530
Leonard, Mass., S43548
Thomas, Ct., S34831
FASSET, Adonijah, Ct., Anna, R3459
Asa, Mass., S43547
FASSETT, Hetty, former wid. of John Durham Alvey, which see
John, Md., S34826
Jonathan, Mass., S19807
Joshua, Mass., BLWt.4177-100-Pvt. Iss. 4/19/1790 to John Bush. No papers
Richard, Mass., S29150
Robert, N.C. See FAUCETT
FAST, Christian, Pa., Va., Anna Barbara, W4195; BLWt.26389-160-55
FASY, John, Pa., S2235
FATE, Samuel, Pa., S35921
FATZINGER, Henry, Pa., S22761
FAUBER, Peter, Pa., S8454
FAUCETT, John, Pa., S32240
Robert, N.C., S.C. State Navy, S41528; BLWt.193-100
FAUDRE, Vachel, Va. See FANDRE
FAUGHEY, William, Pa., BLWt. 9377-100-Pvt., BLWt.14076. Iss. 4/23/1794 to Thomas Campbell, Admr. No papers
FAULCONER, James, Va., S31021
Joseph, Va., Frances, W8805
Samuel, Va., S5376
FAULKENBERRY, David, S.C., S3350
FAULKNER, Aaron, Ct., BLWt.5769-100-Pvt. Iss. 3/9/1796 to Wm. Armstrong, Admr. No papers
Ammi, Mass., S34833
Caleb, Ct., Martha, W19239
James, Va. See FAULCONER
John, Mass., S29787
Jonas, Mass., Eunice S., W23024
Peter, Cont., N.J., S35918; BLWt.740-150-Ens. Iss. 7/28/1790. No papers
Robert, Mass. See FALKNER
Robert, Pa., S42717
Thomas, Ct., R3467
William, N.Y., S27774

FAULKNER (continued)
William, Pa., S42720
FAUN, George, Va. See FANT
FAUNCE, Ansell, Mass., Hope, W21097
Thomas, Mass., S34836
FAUNTLEROY, Griffin, Va., BL 300 acres. No papers
Henry, Va., BLWt.1087-300
Moore, 4th Regt. Dragoons, BLWt.741-400-Maj. Iss. 3/21/1795 to Peter Manifold, Admr. No papers
Robert, Va., S5380
FAUROT, James, N.Y., S6832
FAUSBROOK, John, See FOSBROOK
FAUST, Gosper, S.C. See Jasper
Jasper/Gosper, S.C., Esther, R3468
John, Pa., S41527
Philip, Pa., S22763
FAUSY, John, Pa., See FASY
FAUVER, Frederick, N.J. See FANVER
George, N.J., Elizabeth, W3967
FAUX/FOX/FEUX, Patrick, Pa., Rebecca, W27525
FAVERTY, Joseph, Va., R3469
FAVOUR, Samuel, Mass., S29788
FAW, Matthias, Pa., BLWt.9373-100-Pvt. Iss. 5/22/1790. No papers
FAWCETT, Obediah, Va., Ann, R3470
FAWLKES, James, Va. See FOWLKES
FAWN, William, N.C., Elizabeth, W7237; BLWt.771-300-Capt. Iss. 2/8/1798. No papers
FAWNS, John, Va., See FONS
FAWVER, Henry, N.J., S34345; BLWt. 128-100. Iss. 2/25/1804
FAXON, Allen, Mass., Margaret, W21090
Asaph, Cont., Mass., Rachel, W24209
Caleb, Mass., Lydia, W1844
Elisha, Mass., Sarah, W14703
Francis, Cont., Mass., Dorcas, W19246; BLWt.6118-160-55
Jacob A., Mass., S43539
James, Mass., Susan Hills, former wid., W1429
John, Mass., Lydia, W24174
Samuel, Mass., Priscilla, W24177; BLWt.2024-160-55
FAY, Aaron, Mass., Abigail, W21095
Asa, Mass., S38692
Barnabas, Mass., Chloe, W21099
Francis, Mass., Visa, W24181
Heman, Mass., Martha, W19243
Hezekiah, Mass., Patty, W21101; BLWt.8183-160-55
John, Ct., S43543
John, Cont., Mass., S45752
John, Mass., S5377
Joseph, N.H., Sarah, W16983
Joseph, N.H., BLWt.902-150
Levi, Mass., S10645
Levi, Mass., S29790
Moses, Ct., Mary, W21086
Moses, Mass., S39509
Nathan, Ct., Vt., Mary, R3471
Paul, Mass., R3472
Sherebiah, Ct., Mass., S10647
Silas, Mass., S31017

FAY (continued)
Thomas, Mass., S34839
Thomas, Mass., Sea Service, S18819
Timothy, Ct., Cont., Mass., Sarah How, former wid., W13469
William, Ct., S43538
FAYERWEATHER, Samuel, Ct., S37917
FAYHATT, William, Navy, N.H., S10649
FAYRER, William, Artificers, Pa., BLWts. 9367 & 13104. Iss. 12/12/1797. No papers
FAYSSOUX, Peter, Cont., S.C., BLWt.1976-450
FEAGAN, Daniel, Va., Violet, R3473
James, Pa., BLWt.9392-100-Pvt. Iss. 8/8/1796. No papers
FEAGANS, William, Va., R20366
FEAR, Edmund, Va. See FEARS
FEARER, Charles, Va. See FIERER
FEARS, Edmond/Edmund, Va., R3474
Thomas, Va., S6835
William, Cont., Mass., Patience, W24213
FEARSON, Joseph, Md., Elizabeth, W24186; BLWt.2089-100
FEASTER, Henry, ---, N.J. res. in 1834, R14115
FEATHER, Isaac, Pa., S2208
Jacob, Pa., Mary, W7255; BLWt. 2023-160-55
John, N.J., Mary, W3236
FEATHERGILL, Joseph, Mass., BLWt. 4179-100-Pvt. Iss. 7/8/1797 to Sol. Wolcott, Jr. No papers
Joseph, Mass., S34844
FEATHERHOOF, Mathias, Pa., R3477
FEATHERLEY, John, N.Y., S43550
FEATHERLY, Henry, N.Y., Polly, W2727
John, N.Y., BLWt.7113-100-Pvt. Iss. 8/23/1790 to Charles Newkerk, ass. No papers
John, N.Y., S10658
Thomas, N.Y., BLWt.7114-100-Pvt. Iss. 8/23/1790 to Charles Newkerk, ass. No papers
Thomas, N.Y., See FETHERLY
FEAZLE, John, Va., S4284
FEBIGER, Christian, Va., BLWt. 760-500-Col. Iss. 5/5/1789. No papers
FEDERA, Jacob, Pa., BLWt.9368-100-Pvt. Iss. 3/27/1799 to Abraham Bell, ass. No papers
FEE, John, Pa., Jane, R3479
Michael, Pa., Rebecca, W10020
FEELY, Alexander, Va., Elizabeth, R3480
John, Va., R3481
FEERO, Peter, Ct., S16792
FEETER/VETTER, William, N.Y., S13013
FEETZ, Henry, Crane's Cont. Art. Mass., BLWt.4193-100-Pvt. Iss. 11/21/1791 to David Quinton. No papers
FEGAN, Garrett, Pa., BLWt.9394-100-Cpl. Iss. 7/16/1789 to M. McConnell, ass. No papers
John, N.J., S22765
FEGELY, John, Pa., S2213
FEGINS, James, Va., Mary, W4952; BLWt.1602-100
John, Va., BLWt.12126-100-Pvt. Iss. 7/20/1792 to Robert Means, ass. No papers
FEHR, John, Pa., Eva, S3482
FEHRE, John, Va., S39513
FEIMSTER, William, N.C., Jerusha, W1745; BLWt.19774-160-55
FEITH, John, Mass., BLWt.4156-100-Pvt. Iss. 2/11/1791. No papers
John, Mass., S37925
FELCH, Jabez, N.H. See FALCH
Nathan, Mass., Sally, W542; BLWt.7443-160-55
Nicholas, N.H., Sarah, W24183
FELIX, Peter, Pa., S42191
FELKER, George, Pa., See GODFREY
Joseph, Cont., enl. N.H., S35302
FELKINS, John, Va., S39517
FELL, Catharine, former wid. of Tunis Covert, N.J., which see
Henry, Pa., S6837
FELLER, Peter Rocky, Cont., N.J. See ROCKAFELLAR
FELLOWS, Abial, Ct., N.Y., Dorcas, W25576; BLWt.92023-160-55
Ezekiel, N.H., Ann, W24185
Isaac, Ct., S13006
Jacob, N.Y., Barbara, R3485
John, Mass., S22767
John, N.H., Prudence, W14715
John, N.H., Lois, W21110; BLWt.36645-160-55
Jonathan, Cont., N.H., S10656
Jonathan, N.H., S10657
Joseph, N.H., S16380
Joseph, N.H., Molly, W21112
Josiah, N.H., S22766
Moses, N.H., Sarah, W23030; BLWt.5375-160-55
Nathan, N.H., S39519
Parker, Mass., S42722
Rosel, Ct., Molly, W17899
Samuel, Ct., S34840
Sarah, former wid. of Benj. Fenn, Ct., which see
Tobias, ---, BLWt.13078-100-Pvt. Iss. 9/29/1792. No papers
Varney, Ct., Anna, W23027
William, Cont., Mass., Aliff, W19256
Willis, Cont., Mass., S35303
FELLYAW/FELYAW, Stephen, N.C., S8467
FELMOTT, Dorus, Md., Martha, W3969; BLWt.7304-160-55
FELPS, Thomas, Ga. See PHELPS
FELT, Eliphalet, Mass., Lone, W21108
Jonathan, Mass., BLWt.704-300-Capt. Iss. 4/1/1790. No papers
Joseph, Cont., Mass., S10659
Joseph, Cont., N.H., S45759
Joseph, Mass., S34842
Lemuel, Mass., S5385
Samuel, Cont., Mass., Naomi, W23031
FELTER, John, N.Y., Martha, W21106
Peter, ---, N.Y. res. 1794, Dis.
FELTER (continued)
No papers
Sarah, former wid. of Thomas Onderdonk, N.Y., which see
Tunis, N.Y., R3522
FELTHOUSEN, John, N.Y., S23627
FELTON, Benjamin, Cont., Mass., S34846
Daniel, Cont., Mass.,Mary, W19259
Matthias, Mass., S10663
Stephen, Mass., Sarah, W14713
FELTS, Allen, Va., Martha, R3487
Christopher, Md., BLWt.11199-100-Pvt. Iss. 2/7/1790. No papers
Frederick, Va., S8464
Rowland/Roland, N.C., S2546
FELTY, Arnest, Pa., Rosina/Rose Anna, W3237
Henry, Pa., BLWt.9375-100-Pvt. Iss. 8/22/1791 to John McCleland, ass. No papers
Henry, Pa., Anna Maria, W3077
FELYAW, Stephen, See FELLYAW
FEMISTER, William, See FEIMSTER
FENDERSON, John, Cont., Mass., S35305
Pelatiah, Mass., S28725
William, Mass., Sea Service, R3488
FENDLEY, William, Va., Frances, W7258; BLWt.26056-160-55
FENDLY, John, N.J., S38693
FENDRER, Frederick, Va., S8462
FENES, Daniel, R.I., BLWt.3124-100-Pvt. Iss. 11/30/1799 to Abij. Holbrook, ass. No papers
FENESHER, James, Va., Indian War of 1789, R3738
FENIMORE, Jonathan, Cont., Pa., S34347
Samuel, N.J., R20367
FENLY, Uz, S.C., R3557
FENN, Benjamin, Ct., S13011
Benjamin, Ct., Sarah Fellows, former wid., W17898
Daniel, Ct., S37918
David, Ct., R3490
Edward, Ct., Cont., S13012
John, Ct., S2545
John, Va., Sarah, W2087; BLWt. 31425-160-55
Thomas, Ct., S13010
Thomas, Va., BLWt.767-200-Lt. Iss. 5/21/1794 to Richard Smyth, ass. No papers
Titus, Ct., R3491
FENNAN, Simon, Hazen's Regt., BLWt.13087-100-Pvt. Iss. 7/13/1789. No papers
FENNEGAN, Christopher, Pa., BLWt. 13087-100-Pvt. Iss. 7/13/1789. No papers
FENNEL, Joseph, N.C., S2547
FENNELL, John, Va., Lee's Legion, BLWt.12136 & 14125-Pvt. Iss. 8/3/1795. No papers
Morris/Morice, N.C.,Penelope,W7257
Nicholas, N.C., Margaret, W3970
Patrick, Pa., BLWt.9371-100-Pvt. Iss. 6/20/1789. No papers
Stephen, Md., S43553; BLWt.11200. Iss. in 1791. No papers

FENNER, Arthur, R.I., S43554
Arthur, R.I., Lydia, W21105
Benjamin, R.I., Mary, R14113
Daniel, R.I., BLWt.151-100
Jeremiah, R.I., S21750
John, Pa., S15424
Joseph, R.I., Ruth, W17345
Pardon, R.I., S21194
Richard, N.C., Ann, W789; BLWt. 772-200-Lt. Iss. 5/17/1796. No papers
Richard, R.I., S21751
Robert, N.C., BLWt.770-300-Capt. Iss. 6/28/1792. No papers
Stephen, R.I., Mary, W21109
FENNIMORE, Samuel, See FENIMORE
FENNO, Ephraim, Col. Lamb's Art. Regt., N.Y., BLWt.737-200-Lt. Iss. 5/14/1794. No papers
Joseph, Mass., Margaret, W21107; BLWt.8012-160-55
Joseph, Va., S34811
Oliver, Mass., BLWt.914-100
FENSTERMACHER, John, Pa., R3524
FENT, Matthew, Pa., BLWt.9412-100-Sgt. Iss. 4/21/1800 to Matt. Fent. No papers
FENTON, Adonijah, Ct., S23217
Asa, Ct., S31674
Benjamin, Mass., R3492
Bethuel, Mass., S13008
Daniel, Mass., N.Y., S15117
Elijah, Ct., S10662
Gamaliel, Ct., Elizabeth, W4951; BLWt.26089-160-55
John, Ct., Lucy Scott, former wid., W26957
John, N.J., N.Y., R3494; BLWt. 1627-100
John, Pa., S530
John, Va., R21884
Jonathan/Jotham, Lamb's Art., N.Y., BLWt.7139-100-Pvt. Iss. 10/23/1790. No papers
Jonathan, Ct. Sea Service, Rosalinda, R3496
Joseph, Mass., BLWt.134-200. Iss. 2/28/1804 to Sally Fenton
Joseph, Pa., S10655
Jotham, Ct., S37919
Nathaniel, Ct., S13014
Nathaniel, Ct., S18398
Samuel, Mass., See FINTON
Solomon, Ct., S13007
Solomon, Ct., Cont., children, W17120
William, Pa., S43552
FENTRESS, James, N.C., S3356
Valentine, Va., See FANTRESS
FENWICK, Richard, Md., Ann, R3497
William, Md. Sea Service, S16381
FERBUSH, William, Va., Sally Stewart, former wid., W5180; BLWt.26530-160-55
William, Va., W7300, Barbara, See FORBES
FERDINAND, Joseph, Navy, Mass. Agcy. & res., S34843
FERDON, John, N.Y., BLWt.7111-100-Pvt. Iss. 9/15/1790 to John S. Hobart et al, assnes. No papers
FERDONE, Abraham, N.J., Magdalen, W7254
FEREBEE, Samuel, N.C., S8466
FEREE, Joseph, Hazen's Regt., BLWt.13071-100-Pvt. Iss. 2/23/1792. No papers
FERGASON, See FERGUSON
FERGO, Thomas, Ct., S29152
William, Ct., See FARGO
FERGUS, Francis, Pa., R3498
James, N.C., BLWt.769-400-Surg. Iss. 8/1/1794. No papers
James, Pa., S.C., Susan, W25573; BLWt.40919-160-55
John, S.C., Milly, W8807; BLWt. 28509-160-55
FERGUSON, Abraham, N.Y. See FORGASON
Alexander, N.Y., R3499
Amy, former wid. of Moses Haight, N.Y., which see
Andrew (colored), Va., S32243; BLWt.26016-160-55
Caleb, N.Y., S19293; BLWt.13007-160-55
Daniel, Ct., R3500
David, Va., S35925
Ebenezer, Pa., S22237
Edmond/Edmund, Va., Elizabeth, R3501
Isaac, N.Y., R3503
James, Mass., Hannah Robinson, former wid., W4576
James, N.Y., BLWt.7118-100-Pvt. Iss. 4/27/1792 to Timothy Benedict, ass. No papers
James, N.Y., Betsey, W19257
James, Va., S31675
John, Mass., BLWt.4032-100-Pvt. Iss. 3/3/1792, to Jane Ferguson, Admx. No papers
John, Mass., N.H., S13104
John, Mass., N.H. See FURGUSON
John, N.Y., See FORGERSON
John, N.C., Va. See FORGUSON
John, Pa., Martha, W21103
John, S.C., R3504
John, Va., S1814
Joseph, Hazen's Regt., BLWt. 13074-100-Pvt. Iss. 7/10/1789 to Ann O'Brian, late Ann Ferguson, the wid.
Joshua, Va., S16793
Josias/Josiah, Pa., Mary G., W7261
Larkin, Va., See FORGESON
Lewis, Va., S32241
Moses, S.C., S17411
Robert, Mass., Jane, BLWt.54231-160-55
Robert, Va., Lee's Legion, BLWt. 12128-100-Pvt. Iss. 12/15/1791. No papers
Robert, Va., S39512
Robert, Va., Besheba, W7262; BLWt.19751-160-55
Samuel, Ct. See FURGESON
Samuel, Cont., Pa., S35924
Solomon, Mass., S29792
Stephen, Mass., Shuah Dennet, former wid., W22936
Thomas, N.J., BLWt.8923-100-Pvt.
FERGUSON (continued)
Iss. 11/1/1792 to Hannah Ferguson, Admx.
Thomas, N.Y., S13101
William, Col. Proctor's 4th Regt. of Art., BLWt.748-300-Capt. Iss. 6/4/1789. No papers
William, Cont., Pa., Elizabeth, W2777
William, N.H., Betty, W21111; BLWt.8470-160-55
William, Pa., BLWt.9390-100-Pvt. Iss. 5/9/1791. No papers
William, Pa., S35927
William, Pa., S45757
William, Va., Judah/Judeth, W7263; BLWt.26900-160-55
FERGUSSON, John, Md., Catharine, W8808
Moses, Va., S8461
Thomas, Pa., S31023
William, Cont., Va., S39516
FERIER, Charles, Va. See FIERER
FERIN, Zebulon, Ct., S21752
FERIOLE, Alexander, See FERRIOL
FERIS, Caleb, S.C., S1813
Isaac, S.C., S3352
FERNALD, Dennis, Cont., Mass., Elizabeth, W24184
Hercules, Mass., S20360
Joshua, Cont., Mass., S45758
Nicholas, Mass., S35333
Rendal/Randall, N.H., R3510
Tobias, Mass., S35304
Tobias, Mass., BLWt.847-450
FERO, Peter, N.Y., R3511
FERQUHER, James, Md. See FARQUHAR
FERRAL, John, Pa., S39514
FERRALL, Michael, Pa., BLWt. 9381-100-Pvt. Iss. 5/16/1791 to John M. Taylor. No papers
Patrick, Pa., BLWt.9369-100-Pvt. Iss. 7/9/1789. No papers
Zepheniah, Va., BLWt.13062 & 14130. Iss. 10/13/1795. No papers
FERRAN, Moses, N.H. See FERREN
FERRE, Moses, Ct., Cont., Jerusha, W19255
Solomon, Mass., S30410
FERREL, James, N.C., Tabitha, W23029
James S., Va., S7697
John, N.J., BLWt.8324-100-Pvt. Iss. 5/26/1790. No papers
John, Pa., S3554
FERRELL, Gabriel, N.C., Nancy, R3514
John, N.C., S6836
John, N.C., Elizabeth, R3512
Micajah, N.C., S31676
Robert, Va., Lee's Legion, BLWt. 12123 & 13108-Sgt. Iss. 3/6/1790. No papers
William, Md., BLWt.11226-100-Pvt. Iss. 2/1/179?. No papers
William, N.C., S3355
William, N.C., S6831
William, N.C., BLWt.2402-200
William, Pa., S42192
William, S.C., Va., S13015

FERREN, Jonathan, pens. in Me., S35926
Moses, Mass., N.H., Jane, W7256; BLWt.305-60-55
FERRICK, Michael, Pa., S42190
FERRIE, John, Mass., S34845
FERRILL, John, N.J., S34348
Smith, N.C., S1513
Zephaniah, Cont., Va., S35928
FERRIN, Jonathan, Cont., Mass., N.H., Hannah, W16986
Moses, N.H., BLWt.3108-100-Pvt. Iss. 8/24/1790 to Benj. Ives Gilman, ass. No papers. BLWt.305-60-55
Richard, Mass., S35646
Zebulon, R.I., See FERIN
FERRINGTON, Elijah, Cont., Mass., See FARRINGTON
FERRIOL, Alexander, Hazen's Regt. BLWt.782-200-Lt. Iss. 2/20/1792 to Benj. Moore, ass. No papers. See FERIOLE, Alexander, in Heitman's Hist. Reg., p.225. There is also a Pvt. Alexander Ferrioll in same Regt. See S43557.
Joseph, Hazen's Regt., BLWt. 13082-100-Pvt. Iss. 9/21/1790 to Benj. Moers, ass. No papers
FERRIOLE, Alexander, Hazen's Regt. BLWt.13072-100-Pvt. Iss. 7/26/1790. No papers
FERRIOLL, Alexander, Cont., N.Y., S43551
FERRIS, Coenradt, N.Y., b. in Germany, S10654
Ezra, Cont., N.Y., Charity, W16987
Gilbert, N.Y., R3515
Gould, Ct., S28726
Jeremiah, Ct., Nancy, W17897
John, N.Y., S8465
John, N.Y., Susan, W17896
John A., Cont., N.Y., Freelove, W7252; BLWt.2029-160-55
Jonah, Ct., Anne, W25572
Jonathan, N.Y., See FARRIS
Joshua, N.Y., S10660
Oliver, Ct., Sea Service, Abigail, W16254
Peter, Lamb's Art., N.Y., BLWt. 7143-100-Pvt. Iss. 4/9/1791. No papers
Ransford Avery, Ct., S20751
Richard, N.Y., Catharine, W25574; BLWt.18012-160-55
Samuel, N.Y., S23216
Squire, Vt., War of 1812, R3518
Sylvanus, N.Y., Lydia, W2088; BLWt.9473-160-55
Thomas, N.Y., Mary Ann, W23028
FERRY, Charles, Mass., BLWt. 4143-100-Pvt. Iss. 5/1/1792 to David Quinton. No papers
Charles, Mass., Eunice Holt, former wid., W23331
Daniel, Del., Pa. Sea Service, R3519
Eliphalet, Ct., Mercy, W21104
James, Mass., R10463
Thaddeus, Mass., S18399
FERRYMAN, Stephen, Va., S39515
FERST, John Adam, N.J., R3558
FERTENBAUGH, Jane, former wid. of Hawkins Boon, Pa., which see
FERVER, Henry, N.J. See FAWVER
FESEMIRE, John, Pa., Catharine, W3235
FESMIRE, John, See FESEMIRE
FESSENDEN, Benjamin, Jr., Mass., BLWt.4165-100-Pvt. Iss. 10/18/1796 to John Coates. No papers
Ebenezer, Cont., Mass., S20361
John, Mass., BLWt.4166-100-Pvt. Iss. 2/27/1790 to Theodosius Fowler. No papers
John, Mass., Eunice, W14714
Joseph, Mass., Sea Service, Mary Kelly, former wid., W14992
Peter, Mass., Tabitha, W19258; BLWt.28512-160-55
Samuel, Mass., Sarah, R3521
FESTER, Jacob, N.Y., R3520
FETHERLY, Thomas, N.Y., Jane, R3478
FETNER, Aberhart, Cont., S.C., S19294
FETTER, Jacob, Pa. See FEATHERS
FETTERHOFF, Baltzer/Balson, Pa., R3523
FETTERLY, Thomas, N.Y. See FETHERLY
FETTY, George, N.J., S22764
FETZER, Jacob, Pa., S41532
Joachim, Va., S39518
FEUX, Patrick. See FAUX
FEWER, Henry, N.J. See FAWVER
FIBES, Daniel, Mass. See FOBES
FICK, David, Capt.-Lt. Artillery, Pa., Rebecca; BLWt.750-200 iss. 1/15/1790 to the Legal Repr. & Exectrx. of said Fick, Margaret Thurston, formerly Margaret Fick. No papers
FICKET, Vinson, Mass., S35932
FICKETT, John, Mass., Lucy,W23064
Nathaniel, Mass., S36509
Zebulon, Mass., Mary, W7274; BLWt.36764-160-55
FICKLE, Benjamin, Md., S8478; BLWt.197-200
FICKLIN, John, Va., S35938
FIDDIS, Hugh E., Ct. Sea Service, Navy, R3525; BLWt.75105-160-55
FIDDLER, John, N.J. See FIDLER
FIDLER, John, N.S., S2552
John, N.Y., S32246
FIEALDS, John, Mass. See FIELDS
FIELD, Abiezer, Mass., S18400
Ansel, N.C., Martha, W10021
Barzillai, Mass., S30418
Benjamin, N.J., S46035
Benjamin, Va., Mildred, W3009; R14149. See N.A. Acc. No.874-050067, Va. Half Pay
Daniel, Mass., S5386
Daniel, Mass., Rachel, W24202
Daniel, R.I., Zipporah, W21114
David, Ct., R3256
David, R.I., Mary, W21113
Dennis, N.J., Sicke, W8810; BLWt. 26858-160-55
Ebenezer, Navy, Mass., Mary
FIELD (continued)
Pratt, former wid., W15224. Her last husb., Samuel Pratt, served in Mass. troops in Rev. War.
Edward, Ct., BLWt.5787-100-Pvt. Iss. 2/24/1800 to Obadiah Sprague
Elisha, Vt., R3527
Ephraim, Mass., Ruby, W23032
Hendrick, N.J., S873
Henry, Va., Suky/Sucky, W8811
Ichabod, Ct., S16800
James, Ct., Anna/Anna Hurd, W25582
James, Mass., S34853
James, R.I., Rebecca, W24201
Jeremiah B., N.J., S872
Jeremiah R., N.J., Jane, W7268
Joarab, Ct., R3528
John, Mass., S17953; BLWt.2492-100, BLWt. 311-60-55
John, Mass., Lucy, W13164
John, Mass., Privateer, Vt.,S13017
John, N.C., Rahab, W1161; BLWt. 34274-160-55
John, Pa., R20368
John, Va., S35937
John, B., N.J., S643
Joshua, N.H., S21753
Lemuel, Mass., S5393
Lemuel, R.I., S21196
Lewis, Va., S30413
Lydia, Vt. See Amasa POWERS
Pardon, Ct., S43555
Pardon, R.I. Sea Service, R3531
Reuben, Va., Frances, W8812; BLWt. 763-300-Capt. Iss. 4/2/1790. No papers
Richard R., N.J., S642
Samuel, Ct., Huldah, W17907
Samuel, Mass., S15830
Seth, Mass., Martha, W10023; BLWt. 8383-160-55
Theophilus, Va. Sea Service, R60. See N.A. Acc. No.837,Va. Half Pay
Thomas, R.I., S21198
William, N.C., See FIELDS
Zebulon, Mass., S29794
FIELDER, Dennis, Va., S8476
George, Va., S35935
John, Va., R3533
FIELDING, Ebenezer, N.H., S45766
Eppa, Va., BLWt.12134 & 14056-Pvt. Iss. 4/3/1794 to Francis Walker, ass. No papers
Eppa, Cont., Va., Mary Ann, W7272
FIELDS, Bartholomew, N.C., S10670
Edmond, Ct., BLWt.5756-100-Sgt. Iss. 5/17/1790. No papers
Edmond, Ct., S37920
George, Ct., BLWt.5782-100-Pvt. Iss. 2/14/1793. No papers
George, Ct., S43356
George, Md., BLWt.11216-100-Pvt. Iss. 2/3/1792. No papers
George, Md., S34851
John, Ct., S13018
John, Mass., S45765
John, N.J., Privateer, S8472
John, N.C., S8471
John, N.C., Mary, W3971
John, N.C., R3529
Joseph, Md., S35933
Lucy, former wid. of Isaac Wood,

FIELDS (continued)
N.C., which see
Robert, Mass., S17951; BLWt.2465-100, & 280-60-55
Simon, Va., S42723
Thomas, Navy, Mass., S31026
William, N.C., Elizabeth, S25088; BLWt.36652-160-55
William, Va., S30416
FIENDLEY, John, N.J., Rhoda, BLWt. 979-100
FIERER, Charles, Va., R22811. See N.A. Acc. No. 874, Va. Half Pay
FIERO, Abraham, N.Y., Sarah, W19264 BLWt.10223-160-55
Peter, N.Y., Polly, W21118
Stephen, N.Y., Catrena/Catharine, W16257
FIERS, William, Va., S30414
FIETS, John, Pa., BLWt.9386-100-Pvt. Iss. 8/7/1789 to Richard Platt, ass. No papers
FIFE, William, Va., Margaret, W7265
FIFER, George, Pa., S17949
Jacob, Cont., Md., N.C., Va., Katharine, R3534
FIFIELD, Abraham, N.H., S10669
Benjamin, N.H., Susanna, W1742; BLWt.14988-160-55
Edward, N.H., See FAIRFIELD
John, Crane's Cont. Art., Mass., BLWt.4195-100-Pvt. Iss. 3/10/1810 to John Fifield. No papers
John, Cont., Mass., Phebe, W24197
John, Navy, N.H., Hannah Proale/Proal, former wid., W17500
Joseph, N.H., Anna, W16016
Mark, N.H., Deborah, W21123
Moses, N.H., Lucy, W23034; BLWt.36650-160-55
Winthrop, N.H., Navy, S10672
FIGELY, Peter, Md. See FIGLA
FIGGINS, James, See FEGINS
William, Va., R3536
FIGHT, Conrad, N.C., Elizabeth, W3973
John, Mass. See FEITH
FIGLA, Peter, Md., S8468
FILE, Samuel, Cont., Mass., Esther, W23033
FILER, Orris, Ct., S23632
Thomas, Mass., S23219
FILES, Adam J., S.C., S13026
Ebenezer, Mass., S28729
Jeremiah, S.C., S13025
John, S.C., S32245
William, Mass., S29796
FILKINS, Isaac, N.Y., R3538
FILLEBERT, Antoine, Hazen's Regt. BLWt.13080-100-Pvt. Iss. 8/14/1792 to Benj. Moore, ass. No papers
FILLEBROWN, Calvin, Mass., Catey, W24188
James, Mass., S18822
John, Mass., S5389
Phebe, former wid. of Silas Barnard, Mass., Navy, R24192
Thomas, Mass., S29153
Thomas, Mass., Sarah, W2090; BLWt.8007-160-55
FILLER, Frederick, Cont., Md.

FILLER (continued)
Catharine Hanker, former wid., W4692
Peter, Pa., Catharine Howry, former wid., R5303
FILLEY, Mark, Ct., BLWt.5768-100-Pvt. Iss. 11/2/1791 to Titus Street. No papers
Mark, Ct., Elinor, W17901
Moses, Ct., S13016
Remembrance, Ct., Cont., Hannah, W17903; BLWt.193-60-55, BLWt. 5817-100. Iss. 4/21/1791. No papers
Sylvanus, Ct., Jemima, W17906
FILLMORE, Cyrus, Ct., N.Y., Jemima, R3539
Henry, Ct., S28538
FILLOW, Adams, Ct. See PHILO
Isaac, Ct., S17416
FILLY, See FILLEY
FILMORE, George, Mass., Sarah, W21124
FINCH, Abigail, former wid. of Isaac Smith, Mass., which see
Abraham, Ct., S28727
Amos, Green Mt. Boys, N.Y., S13022
Casar/Ceaser, R.I., BLWt.3-100-Spec. Act of 6/4/1842. See Robert Allen, R.I., BLWt.1-100 Spec. Act of 6/4/1842
Elnathan, N.Y., Elizabeth, W7267; BLWt.3996-160-55
Ezra, Ct., R3541
Isaac, Ct., BLWt.5801-100-Fifer. Iss. 6/19/1790. No papers
Isham, N.C., S41538
James, N.Y., S13021
James, Pa., BLWt.9370-100-Pvt. Iss. 8/29/1793 to Caspar Iserloan, ass. No papers
Jeremiah, Ct., S37923
Jeremiah, Ct., S43560
John, N.Y., Martha, W21119
John, Pa., BLWt.9416-100-Pvt. Iss. 7/16/1789 to M. McConnell, ass. No papers
Jonathan, Ct., BLWt.5805-100-Pvt. Iss. 10/22/1789 to Theodosius Fowler. No papers
Jonathan, Ct., S37924
Jonathan, N.Y., Jemima, W16572
Joseph, Md., S35934
Nathaniel, N.Y., Keziah, R3542
Reuben, N.Y., Anna, W24198
Samuel, Ct., N.Y., Polly, R3543
Silvanus, N.Y., S10665
Stephen, Ct., Mindwell, W24187
Timothy, Ct., R3544
William, Ct., S3359
William, Ct., N.Y., S22768
William, Va., S31677
FINCHER, James, N.C., S31678
FINCHLEY, George, Ct., Sarah, W19261 & S43557
FINCK, Andrew, N.Y., S43563; BLWt.729-300-Capt. Iss. 10/9/1790. No papers
David, Pa., BLWt.9387-100-Pvt. Iss. 2/14/1791 to Alexander

FINCK (continued)
Power, ass. No papers
Jonathan, N.Y., See FINCH
William, N.Y. See FINK
FINDALL, James, N.C. See TINDAL
FINDELY, John, N.J. See FIENDLEY
FINDER, Frederick, Va., S25089
FINDLEY, David, Pa., Jennett/Janet, W25577
George, N.C., Nancy, W7273; BLWt.34280-160-55
John, N.J. See FIENDLEY
John, N.C., S6843
Paul, Ga., S.C., W9440
Robert, N.J., BLWt.8299-100-Pvt. Iss. 3/10/1790 to soldier
Samuel, N.C., Va., R14183
FINDLY, William, N.J., S34350
FINE, Andrew, N.Y., S43561
Peter, Md., S2209
FINFROCK, Andrew, Pa., Barbara, W2779
Andrew Peter, Pa., Anna Margaret, W8205
FINIGAN, Patrick, Va., BLWt.555-100
FINK, Andrew, N.Y. See FINCK
Christian, N.Y., S13034
Daniel, Va., S31027
David, Pa., S42194
David, Pa., Catharine, W3239
George, Pa., R14172
John, N.Y., S28728
John or Hans Finkanover, N.Y. R3549
Michael, Pa., S41536
Michael, Pa., R3552
William, N.Y., S23218
FINKANOVER, Hans, N.Y.See John FINK
FINKS, Mark, Va., R3551
FINLAY, Robert, N.J. See FINDLEY
FINLEY, Andrew, Pa., R20369; BLWt.528-200
Archibald, Va., Margaret, R3554
Charles, N.Y., S43562
Charles, N.C., S6845
Ebenezer, Md., BLWt.2287-200
James Edwards Burr, Mass., Mary, W8815; BLWt.714-400-Surg. Iss. 4/1/1790. No papers
James, N.C., S6838
John, N.J., Elizabeth, W788
John, Pa., S31025; BLWt.745-300-Capt. Iss. 10/24/1789. No papers
John, Pa., R3553
John, S.C., Sally, W1257
John H., Pa., BLWt.2038-200
Joseph Lewis, Pa., Jane, W8814; BLWt.743-300-Capt. Iss. 4/6/1791. No papers
Paul, S.C., See FINDLEY
Robert, Va., S16797
Samuel, Mass., BLWt.715-400-Surg. Iss. 3/5/1790. No papers
Samuel, N.C., R3556
Samuel, Va., Mary, W10026; BLWt. 761-400-Maj. Iss. 1/5/1796. No papers
William, Md., Nancy, R3555
William, N.J., BLWt.8314-100-Pvt. Iss. 8/5/1789. No papers

FINLEY (continued)
William, N.J. See FINDLY
FINLY, Daniel, Md., S41534
FINN, Peter, Md., N.C., S32244
Thomas, Va., Lee's Legion, BLWt. 12124-100-Pvt. Iss. 9/24/1789 to Mary Finn, wid., BLWt.13945
William, Va. See FAIN
FINNAGAN, Patrick, See FINIGAN
FINNELL, Charles, Va., S16799
FINNEY, Bethuel, Mass., S34856
Eleazer, Ct., S17415
John, Pa., S9101
John, Pa., Sarah, W10025
John L., not Rev. War, Sgt. Maj. U.S.A. 1799, Phila. Agcy., Old War Inv. File 9872
Jonathan, Ct., Cont., Mass., Sarah, W19262; BLWt.34594-160-55
Joseph, Ct., See PHINNEY
Josiah, Ct., S15280
Lazarus, Pa., S13032
Lewis, Mass., S34849
Nathan, Mass., Urana/Uriana, W24193
Reuben, Va., BLWt.12135-100-Pvt. Iss. 2/22/1799 to Jonathan Jones, ass. No papers
Reuben, Va., Elizabeth, W10024
Robert, S.C., S37926
Roger, Pa., BLWt.9374-100-Pvt. Iss. 12/3/1792 to Patrick Brien, ass. No papers
Samuel, Mass., S39522
Sylvester, Ct., N.Y., S16114
Thomas, N.C., BLWt.773-200-Lt. Iss. 11/25/1796 to Hardy Murfree, ass. No papers
Walter, Pa., BLWt.746-300-Capt. Iss. 7/30/1791. No papers
FINNIE, William, Va., R14175. Va. Half Pay.
FINNIGIN, Patrick. See FINIGAN
FINT, Philip, Va., S42718
FINTON, Benjamin, Mass. See FENTON
John, N.J., N.Y., See FENTON
Samuel, Mass., Isabella, W3672
FIPPS, John, Mass., S34860
FIRER, Charles, Va. See FIERER
FIRING, George, Pa., S41531
FIRKINS, Peter, Pa., S34349
FIRMAN, Gabriel, N.Y., BLWt. 1684-100
Jacob, Vt. See FARMAN
Nathan, N.Y., Jemima, R3855
FIRNHAM, John, Mass., S38697
FIROR, Henry/Heney, Md., S8470
FISBOCK, Jacob, N.Y., S15118
FISCHER, William, Va., BLWt.12129-100-Pvt. Iss. 5/2/1794. No papers
FISCUS, Abraham, Pa., Catharine, W2778
Adam, N.C., Va., S16115
FISEMIRE, John, Pa. See FESEMIRE
FISH, Aaron, Ct., Navy, S10673
Abner, N.Y., S43559
Artemas/Artamas, R.I., S21754
Caleb, N.Y., S23623
Daniel, Mass., R.I., Rebecca, W24190

FISH (continued)
David, Ct., S13019
David, Mass., S35306
Elihu, Privateer, R.I., R3576
Elisha, R.I., Elizabeth, R3559
Ephraim, N.Y., S3357
Esther, former wid. of John Ladd, Ct., which see
Isaac, Mass., Deborah, W14721
Isaac, Mass., Privateer, Mary Whitney, former wid., W26007
Jacob, Mass., S18823
John, Ct., See FISK
John, Mass., N.H., S13027
John, Pa., S6840
Jonathan, Cont., Mass., S44820
Jonathan, Mass., R.I. Sea Service, Lillis, W21115
Joseph, N.Y., Martha, W2089
Lemuel, Navy, Mass. Agcy. & res., S34854; BLWt.26415-160-55
Levi, Mass., R3560
Moses, Ct., S13029
Nathan, Mass., S34861
Nathaniel, Mass., S17414
Nicholas, N.Y., Elizabeth, W8809; BLWt.727-400-Maj. Iss. 8/9/1790 No papers
Pardon, N.Y., S22769
Seberry, N.Y., S29797
Simeon, N.H., S35308
Sylvanus, Mass., Lucretia, W13161 BLWt.53679-160-55
Thomas, Mass., S29798
Thomas, Mass., Ursula, W13163
Thomas, N.J., Mary, W25578; BLWt. 27637-160-55
FISHBACK, Jacob, Va., Hannah, R3562
John, Cont., Va., Patty, R3563
FISHBOURN, Benjamin, Pa., BLWt. 2206-300
FISHBURN, Ludwig, Pa., R3564
Philip, Pa., Anna Maria, W4434
FISHER, Aaron, Mass., S30417
Aaron, Mass., Rachel, W14717
Aaron, Mass., Lucy, W19267
Abijah, Cont., Mass., S34858
Abner, Mass., S22238
Asa, Mass., S15832
Asahel, Ct., Anna, W19263
Azubah, former wid. of Ebenezer Melendy, Mass., which see
Benjamin, Va., S39520
Charles, N.Y., S23628
Cyrus, Mass., S34850
David, Mass., Lois, W7269; BLWt. 9493-160-55
David, Mass., Mehetable, W23039
David, N.J., BLWt.8294-100-Pvt. Iss. 5/26/1790. No papers
David, N.J., S34351
David, N.Y., S43588
Ebenezer, Cont., Mass., Sarah, W23037
Ebenezer, Mass., S8473
Ebenezer, Mass., S19659
Eleazer, Mass., Susanna, W14722
Elias, Va., Sarah, W26789
Elijah, Mass., S35307
Frederick, Va., S20364
George, Pa., BLWt.9415-100-Pvt. Iss. 1/4/1792 to A. Kassler, ass. No papers

FISHER (continued)
George, Pa., S23631
George, S.C. Sea Service, S46036
George, Va., R3568
Henry, Md., BLWt.11237-100-Pvt. Iss. 2/1/1790. No papers
Henry, Cont., Md., S41535
Henry, Pa., BLWt.9395-100-Pvt. Iss. 6/20/1789. No papers
Henry/John Henry, Pa., Mary, W3792
Henry, Pa., Happy, R26119
Huldah, former wid. of Anthony Blackford, N.J., which see
Ichabod, Mass., Rhoda, W24195
Isaac, N.J., Fanny Chance, former wid., W10598; BLWt.105513-160-55
Isaac, Va., S39524
Israel, Mass., Hannah, W14723
Jabez Pond, Mass., Fanny, W25581 BLWt.24152-160-55
Jacob, Mass., S28730
Jacob, N.J., S2212
Jacob, Pa., S----
Jacob, Va., S15120
Jacob, Va., Catharine, R3565
James, Md., Nancy, W7271
James, Pa., BLWt.9393-100-Pvt. Iss. 7/25/1793. No papers
James, Va., Mass. res., R3569
Jason, Mass., S34857
Jeremiah, Ct., Sabra, W7270; BLWt.11424-160-55
John, Ct., S13020
John, Md., Sea Service, S2211
John, N.J., Sarah, W925
John, N.J., R3570
John, N.J., Wayne's War 1795, Margaret Dyall, former wid., W10318; BLWt.95039-160-55. Reg. 45823-50
John, N.C., S.C., Lucinda, W25580; BLWt.31418-160-55
John, Pa., S23630
John, R.I., BLWt.3122-100-Pvt. Iss. 5/11/1792 to Ezra Blodget No papers
John, Va., S2210
John B., not Rev. War; N.W. Indian & War of 1812, Juliet, Old War Inv. File 8479; Old War Wid. Rej. 20155; Wid Orig. 31209; BLWt.26257-160-55
John H., N.J., S2550
John Henry, Pa. See Henry
Joseph, Md., S34848
Josiah, Mass., S13033
Leonard, Mass., BLWt.4152-100-Pvt. Iss. 9/22/1792 to John Peck. No papers
Leonard, Mass., S34855
Lewis, Mass., Rebecca, W14720; BLWt.29732-160-55
Maddox, Va., R3571
Matthias, Pa., S22239
Michael, Pa., S5392
Nathaniel, N.Y., Jinne/Jinney W16573
Obed, Mass., S29793
Peter, N.J., BLWt.8326-100-Pvt. Iss. 11/26/1796. No papers

FISHER (continued)
Peter, N.J., Mary, W10985
Peter, Pa., R3573
Peter, Va., R14157
Philip, Md., Margaret, W3972
Polly, former wid. of Joshua Crane, Mass., which see
Sally, former wid. of Benjamin Howard, N.H., which see
Samuel, Md., BLWt.11212-100-Pvt. Iss. 10/14/1795 to Henry Davis, ass. No papers
Sarah, former wid. of Hanyost/ John Joseph Dement, N.Y., Which see
Seth, R.I., BLWt.3128-100-Pvt. Iss. 2/11/1800 to Theodore Foster, ass. No papers
Seth, R.I., S38696
Thomas, Mass., BLWt.4138-100-Pvt. Iss. 9/13/1792 to Jonathan Jenks. No papers
Thomas, Mass., S10671
Thomas, N.Y., Jane, W21121
Thomas, Va., BLWt.12130-100-Pvt. Iss. 3/26/1792 to Frances Groves, ass. No papers
Thomas, Va., S3360
Thomas, Va., BLWt.2071-100
Timothy, Ct., S38695
Timothy, Mass., S44821
Timothy, Mass., Dorcas, W2539; BLWt.34281-160-55
William, N.J., S814
William, Va., Sarah, W8813; BLWt.3532-160-55
Zachariah, Pa., Margaret, R3572; BLWt.91503-160-55
FISHLEY, George, N.H., Privateer, S45764
FISK, Abijah, Ct., Sea Service, Mass., S5394
Abner, Mass., S15119
Abner, Mass., Hannah, W24191
Aurelia, former wid. of Nathaniel Stowell, Ct., which see
Benjamin, Mass., Sprout's Regt. BLWt.4124-100-Pvt. Iss. 4/15/ 1796 to Samuel Atkinson. No papers
Cato, N.H., BLWt.3104-100-Pvt. Iss. 3/25/1790. No papers
Cato, colored, N.H., Elsa, W14719
Daniel, Mass., Beulah, W14718; BLWt.12816-160-55
Daniel, R.I., Anna, W17904
David, Mass., Prudence, W1845
David, N.H., S45763
Eleazer, N.H., S16795
Elisha, Mass., Hannah Plimpton, BLWt.47990-160-55
Ephraim, Cont., N.H., S45762
Jacob, Mass., S19660
James, Ct., Mass., S21199
James, Mass., Azubah King, former wid., W20343; BLWt.7305-160-55
John, Ct., Eunice, W17900
John, Cont., Vt., Green Mt. Boys, Irena, R3577
John, Navy, R.I., S31024

FISK (continued)
John, Vt., Orange, W19266
Jonathan, Ct., Mehitable, R3578
Joseph, Mass., Elizabeth, W1256; BLWt.686-400
Moses, Mass., Betsey, W19260
Nathan, Mass., Ruth, W21117
Nathan, Mass., Abigail, R3575
Nathan, N.H., R3579
Noah, R.I., S21197
Robert, Mass., Elizabeth, W9438; BLWt.2332-100
Samuel, Ct., R3580
Samuel, Mass., Lydia, BLWt.75104; 160-55
Seberry, N.Y. See FISH
Simeon, Mass., Elizabeth, W24194
Stephen, Mass., S22240
Thomas, Cont., Mass., S44819
Zedekiah, Cont., Mass., S30412
FISKE, David, Mass., Navy, Ruth, W10983; BLWt.6273-160-55
Nathan, Mass., S30415
Squire, R.I., Amey, W21120
FISLAR/FISLER, John, N.J., Gen. Harmer's Indian War, S32247
FISLER, Jacob, N.J., S2551
John, N.J. See FISLAR
Leonard, N.J., S2549
FISS, Henry, Pa., Catharine, W3238
Jacob, Pa., BLWt.1134-200
FISTER, George, Pa., S23629
FITCH, Andrew, Ct., Abigail, W21116; BLWt.721-300-Capt. Iss. 8/7/1789. No papers
Asa, N.Y., S15121
Cordilla, Ct., Joanna Walker, former wid., W18263; BLWt. 31740-160-55
Daniel, Ct., S37922; BLWt.38-60-55 & 5760-100. Iss. 12/6/1791 to Stephen Horn.
Darius, Ct., Lydia, W1162; BLWt. 17587-160-55
Elnathan, Ct., S45134
Ephraim, Sheldon's Dragoons, Ct. BLWt.5819-100-Pvt. Iss. 5/17/ 1792 to Moses Bissell. No papers
Giles, Ct., S13408
Hannah, former wid. of Robert Williams, Ct., which see
Henry, Va., War of 1812, R14170
James, Ct., Esther, W17905
James, Ct., Vt., R3582
James P., Ct., BLWt.5828-100-Pvt. Iss. 12/6/1791 to Stephen Thorn, ass. of Daniel Fitch. No papers
Jesse, Ct., S10668
John, Ct., S10664
John, Ct., S13028
John, Ct., S13030
John, Mass. See FEITH
John, Va., Barbara, W1586
Joseph, N.Y., Cataline Kelsey, former wid., W20312
Luther, Ct., Privateer, S16794
Moses, Mass., Dis. ---No papers
Nathaniel, Ct., Caty, W23035
Nathaniel, Cont., Ct. agcy. & res., Abigail, W21122
Prentice, Ct., BLWt.5778-100-Cpl. Iss. 5/10/1798 to John

FITCH (continued)
Allen. No papers
Prentice, Ct., S44818
Rosel W./Roswell W., N.Y., S13031
Rufus, Ct., Cont., S44817
Thaddeus/Thadeus, Mass., S34862
Timothy, Mass., Abigail, W24199
Walter, Mass., S16801
William, Ct., Mary, W19265
William, Ct., Sea Service, Elizabeth, W16990
FITCHETT, Joshua, Va., S16798
FITCHPATRICK, Anthony, Va., R3588
James, Va. See FITZPATRICK
FITE, John, N.J., S1901
Leonard, N.J., Peggy/Margareth, W790; BLWt.26409-160-55
FITHIAN, Isaac, N.J., S4285
FITSGERRALD, George, Va. See FITZGERALD
FITSIMMINS, John, Pa., S13023
FITTS, John, Cont., N.C., Mary D. W9439; BLWt.75039-160-55
Richard, N.H., Dorothy, W16255
Samuel, Mass., S17412
FITZ, Abraham, R.I., Abigail, W24189. Wid. also applied for pension for service of 1st husb., John Morgan, which see
Robert W., Va., S8475
FITZGARREL, Thomas, Va., Indian Campaign 1790; R3586
FITZGERALD, Bartlett Hawkins, Cont., Va.,S9562; BLWt.515-100
Benjamin, Md., BLWt.11203-100-Sgt. Iss. 6/20/1789. No papers
Benjamin, Md., S35931
Benjamin Hawkins, Cont., Va., S13308; BLWt.552-100
Charles, Md., S17950; BLWt.1338-100
Daniel, Va. See FITZJARRELL
David, Cont., Mass., S35929
Edward, Pa., BLWt.9396-100-Pvt. Iss. 12/22/1794 to Henry Purdy, ass. No papers
George, Va., S37921
George, Va., S39523
Harvey, Va., Elizabeth, W7278
Henry, Ct., BLWt.5774-100-Pvt. Iss. 5/16/1794 to William Davis, ass. of Benj. Marble, Admr. No papers
Henry, Pa., S42724
James, Md., S35930
James, Va., BLWt.1436-100
John, Cont., Mass., Sophia,W24203
John, Md., BLWt.11239-100-Pvt. Iss. 5/1/1792. No papers
John, Pa., BLWt.9397-100-Pvt. Iss. 7/21/1795. No papers
John, N.Y., Sarah, W16256
John, Va., BLWt.764-300-Capt. Iss. 7/14/1792 to Robt. Means, ass. No papers
Maurice, Navy, Pa. agcy. & res., S41537
Nicholas, Md., S34852
Patrick, Pa., S42193
Polly, former wid. of Nathan Ferris, Va. Also 1786. Which see
Thomas, N.Y., BLWt.7117-100-Pvt.

FITZGERALD (continued)
Iss. 4/19/1791 to Moses Hatfield, Admr.
William, Md., S16796
William, Mass., S29795
William, Va., S30411
FITZGERRALD, Joseph, not Rev. War; Wayne's Indian War, res. Va. & Ind.; BLWt.14554-160-55
FITZGIBBONS, James, N.Y., R3587; BLWt.1591-100
FITZHUGH, Daniel, Cont., Va., S8474
Peregrine, Cont. Va., Elizabeth C., W16989; BLWt.762-300-Capt. Iss. 6/2/1790. No papers
William, Cont., Va., S17948; BLWt.768-150-Cornet. Iss. 9/16/1789, noted "Certified by N. Cutting, 5/9/1820". No papers
FITZIMMONS, John, ---, Phila. Agcy., Dis. ---. No papers
FITZJARRELL, Daniel, Va., S31028
James, Va., R3585
FITZPATRICK, Edward, N.C., Polly F., W1988. See Edward F. PATRICK
James, Va., S32696; BLWt.937-100
John, N.C., Sarah, W7276; BLWt. 3635-160-55
Nathan, Md., S8469
Peter, Corps of Invalids, N.Y., BLWt.13098-100-Sgt. Iss. 2/14/1791 to Alex. Power, ass. No papers
FITZIMMINS, John, Pa. See FITSIMMONS
FITZSIMMONS, Thomas, Pa., Susannah, R3589
Thomas, Va., S17952; BLWt.1635-100. Iss. 6/12/1830
William, Va., S22770
FIVEASH, Peter, Va. Sea Service, R39, Va. Half Pay
FIX, Henry, Pa., Anna Lovis, W8087
Philip, Va., Margaret, W7264
FLACH, Mathias, Cont., Pa. res., S10995
FLACK, James, N.C., Nancy, W1587; BLWt.34548-160-55
James, N.C., Pa. See FLOCK
James, Pa., S5407
Mathias, Cont. See FLACH
FLAGG, Abijah, Ct., Thankful, W17909
Asa, N.H., S35939
Azubah, former wid. of Rowland Lawrence, Mass., which see
Benjamin, Mass., Hannah, W14733
Ebenezer, Mass., S38698
Ebenezer, R.I., BLWt.698-400-Maj. Iss. 3/27/1790 to Elizabeth Flagg, Admx. Also recorded as BLWt.2546
Eleazer, Mass., Patty, W24205
Elijah, Mass., S10679
Gershom, Mass., S10674
Henry Collins, Cont., S.C., Rachel, W10996; BLWt.775-400-

FLAGG (continued)
Surg. Iss. 2/25/1800. No papers
Hiram, Mass., S29154
Isaac, N.H., S31029
Jonathan, Ct., Christiana, W14726
Jonathan, Mass., S30420
Josiah, Mass., S15835
Nathaniel, Mass., S5402
Peter, N.Y., Roxy/Roxana Lee, former wid., W12099; BLWt.6025-160-55. In German "Flock" and pronounced "Flogh" as stated in claim.
Samuel A., Mass., S35316
William, Mass., S23220, Elizabeth Flagg, wid. of Wm., was pensioned as former wid. of Jonas Smith, Mass., which see
FLAKE, George, Pa., Enl. Md., S42725
John, N.J., BLWt.8302-100-Pvt. Iss. 7/9/1790 to Peter Anspach, ass. No papers
FLAMMING, James, Mass., S35313; BLWt.664-100
FLANAGAN, Ebenezer, N.J., Va., R3595
William, Del., BLWt.10763-100-Pvt. Iss. 3/21/1792 to Peter Rose, ass. No papers
William, N.C.,Sarah, W5275
FLANBURGH, John, N.Y. See FLANSBURGH
FLANDERS, Abner, N.H., S9887
Daniel, Mass., N.H., Anna, W14727
David, N.H., S45760
Dennis A., N.Y., S15123
Ezekiel, N.H., S21756
Henry, N.Y., S13037
Jacob, Mass., S38699
Jacob, N.H., S35946; BLWt.2030-100
Jacob, N.H., BLWt.449-100
Jacob, N.Y., Catharine, W16258
John, Mass., S35315
John, Mass., S38704
John, Va., S10675
Joseph, N.H., Hannah, BLWt.47965-160-55
Josiah, N.H., Deborah, W21126
Levi, Cont., Mass., Mary, W23043
Moses, N.H., Gartrude, W7289; BLWt.7065-160-55
Nathaniel, N.H., Mary, R3597
Onesiphous/Seth, N.H., Sally, W24211
Philip, N.H., S35314
Seth, N.H. See Onesiphous
Stephen, Cont., Mass., N.H., S10680
FLANIGAN, Henry, Md., Lydia, W10030
FLANNAGAN, David, N.C. See FLENNIKEN
FLANNAGAN, Timothy, Pa., BLWt. 9388-100-Pvt. Iss. 7/16/1789. No papers
FLANNAGEN, Dennis, Md., BLWt.11232-100-Pvt. Iss. 11/9/1789. No papers
FLANNEGAN, Daniel, N.Y., Dis. ---. No papers
Henry, Md., See FLANIGAN
William, N.C. See FLANAGAN

FLANSBURGH, Anthony, N.Y. See FLAUSBURGH
David, N.Y., R3600
John, N.Y., R3594
Mathews, N.Y., BLWt.14664-160-55
Richard, N.Y. See FLAUSBURGH
William F., N.Y., S29155
FLANSBURY, David, N.Y. See FLANSBURGH
FLARIDY, John, Pa., S39527
FLASH, Lewis, Md., BLWt.11235-100-Pvt. Iss. 1/11/1796 to Joshua Ward, ass. No papers
FLATFORD, Thomas, Va., Chloe, W10029
FLATHERS, Edward, Va., S17418
FLATT, Andrew, Pa., S5403
John, Pa., R3602
FLAUGH, Mathias, See FLACH
FLAUSBURGH, Anthony, N.Y., Susannah, W24204; BLWt.17567-160-55
Richard, N.Y., R3601
FLECK, Christopher, Va., R3603
George, Pa. See FLAKE
James, N.C., Pa., S15430
Peter, Pa. See FLOK
FLEECE, John, Cont., Va., S35945; BLWt.1696-100
FLEEHART, Massy, Pa., S42727. See also FLEUHART
FLEEHARTY, Stephen, Md., S39529
FLEEMAN, Thomas, Va., S39525
FLEENOR, Michael, Va., Sally, W7288
FLEET, John, Va., R14208; Va. Half Pay, N.A. Acc. No. 874. See 050066
FLEETWOOD, Isaac, Va., S35942
Johnson, Del., BLWts.10764 & 14139-100-Pvt. Iss. 10/15/1795 to Abigail Fleetwood, Admx.
Thomas, Crane's Cont. Art., Mass., BLWt.4194-100-Pvt. Iss. 10/26/1795 to Edward Stowe
FLEISHER, Jacob, Navy, Pa., S.C., Sea Service, S2214
FLEK, George, Pa. See FLAKE
Peter, Pa., S42196
FLEMING, Allison, N.C., S6857
Asa, N.Y., Catharine, W24207
Benaiah, Del., S31679
Benoni, Ct., Louisa, W19288
Charles, N.C. See FLEMMING
George, Col. Lamb's Art. Regt., BLWt.736-300-Capt. Iss. 5/10/1790. No papers
Jacob, N.J., R14194. Heir also claims for service of Samuel F. Allen, Capt., N.J. See papers within
James, Md., Mary M./Polly, R3605; BLReg. 304715-55
James, Mass. See FLAMMING
James, N.C., Mary, W646; BLWt. 12733-160-55
Jeremiah, N.J., Heyttje Sparling, former wid., R9961
John, N.J., BLWt.8312-100-Pvt. Iss. 12/29/1791 to Archibald Shaw, Admr.
John, Va., BLWt.12137-100-Pvt.

FLEMING (continued)
Iss. 5/5/1790 to Wm. J. Vreedenburgh, ass. Also BLWt. 347-60-55
John, Va. See FLEMMING
John, Va., BLWt.409-400
Michael, N.Y., S34352
Mitchel, N.C., S16810
Peter, Pa., Va., Nancy, R3606
Robert, Pa., S42726
Robert, S.C., Martha, W7283
Samuel, Ga., S32248
Samuel, N.C., S1952
Thomas, Md., R3607
Thomas, Va., BL.---
William, Mass., Nancy, W15898
William, N.C., S.C., S32250
William, Va., BLWts.12132 & 13986-100-Pvt. Iss. 9/4/1792 to Andrew Dunscomb, ass. No papers
FLEMISTER, Lewis, Va., BLWt.12127-100-Pvt. Iss. 3/19/1794. No papers
Lewis, Cont., prob. Va., Washington's Life Guards, Ellender, W5274. Ga. agcy. & res.
FLEMMING, Benoni, Ct. See FLEMING
Charles, N.C., Elizabeth, W3974
James, Mass., See FLAMMING
James, N.C. See FLEMING
James, N.C., Jane, W8819
Jeremiah, N.J., BLWt.8304-100-Pvt. Iss. 8/14/1789. No papers
John, Va., Elizabeth, W7284; BLWt. 347-60-55. BLWt.12137-100. Iss. 5/5/1790. No papers
Michael, N.Y., BLWt.7132-100-Pvt. Iss. 5/19/1791 to John Tappen, ass. No papers
Robert, S.C. See FLEMING
FLENNIKEN, David, N.C., S10154
FLESHER, Adam, Va., Indian Wars 1782-1792, Elizabeth, S18403; BLWt.47338-160-55
FLESHMAN, Moses, Va., S8484
FLETCHER, Alice, former wid. of Ralph Emerson, N.H., which see
Archelaus, Mass., S44822
Benjamin, Ct., BLWt.5824-100-Pvt. Iss. 7/25/1799 to Abijah Holbrook. No papers
Benjamin, Cont., Mass., S28732
Charles, Mass., Sarah, W16574
Daniel, Mass., S21201
David, Lamb's Art., N.Y., BLWt. 7136-100-Pvt. Iss. 4/27/1792 to Timothy Benedict, ass. No papers
Ebenezer, N.H., Mary, W25598; BLWt.2095-160-55
George, Va., S13038
Gideon, N.H., BLWt.874-100
Isaac, Mass., S38701
Isma, Va., S8482
James, Cont., Va., S35941
James, Mass., S29800
James, Mass., Catharine, W19290; BLWt.11087-160-55
James, N.Y., BLWt.7129-100-Pvt. Iss. 9/28/1790 to Alexander Robertson, ass. No papers
James, N.Y., S44823
James, Vt., R3610

FLETCHER (continued)
James, Va., S16811
Jeremiah, Mass., S28731
John, Ct., BLWt.5762-100-Pvt. Iss. 1/20/1797. No papers
John, Cont., Mass., S22771
John, Mass., S13039
John, Mass., Elizabeth, W23041
John, N.Y., BLWt.7135-100-Pvt. Iss. 9/1/1791 to John W. Watkins, ass. No papers
John, S.C., S45841; BLWt.26452-160-55
John, Va., S35940
Jonathan, Mass., Rebecca, W15679; BLWt.31904-160-55
Joseph, Pa., BLWt.9406-100-Pvt. Iss. 6/29/1789 to M. McConnell, ass. No papers
Joshua, Mass., S5405
Josiah, Mass., S29801
Levi, Mass., Phebe, W14725
Luke, Mass., S44824
Mary, former wid. of Nathaniel Foster, Mass., which see
Nathan, Mass., S35312
Nathan, Va., Mary, W7286
Oliver, Mass., S44826
Peter, Mass., Sarah, W15899
Philip, Md., S35310
Reuben, N.C., S5408
Richard, Va., S8481
Samuel, Mass., N.H., Elizabeth Annar/Hannah, W24208
Sherebiah, Mass., Marian, W1163; BLWt.19752-160-55
Silas, Vt., Avice, R3608
Simeon, N.H., S8490
Simon, Pa., BLWt.9410-100-Q.M. Sgt. Iss. 11/5/1789. No papers
Simon, Pa., S41539
Solomon, Mass., Abigail, W16259
Stephen, Va., BLWt.12120-100-Pvt. "in the Dragoons." Iss. 5/5/1790 to Wm. J. Vreedenburgh, ass. No papers
Stephen, Va., Mary, W7285
Thomas, Va., S1514
Thomas, Va., S8483
Thomas, Va., S8486
William, N.J., BLWt.8325-100-Pvt. Iss. 5/26/1790. No papers
William, N.C., S32249
FLEUHART, Massy, Hazen's Regt., BLWt.13085-100-Pvt. Iss. 5/1/1792. No papers, but see FLEEHART, Massy, Pa.
FLEURY, Louis Tessidre, Cont., France, BLWt.1352-400
FLEWELLEN, William, N.C. See FLEWELLIN
FLEWELLIN, William, N.C., S3366
FLICK, Martin, N.Y., BLWt.7125-100-Pvt. Iss. 7/26/1796. No papers
FLIN, Daniel, Va., S39526
Thomas, Va., Mary, W17908
FLING, Abel, Ct., Susanna, W24214
James, Va., S8489
John, Mass., BLWt.218-100
Lemuel, Ct., Sarah, R3611
Patrick, Cont. See O'FLYNG

FLING (continued)
William, Pa., S3364
FLINN, Benjamin, N.J., S8487
John, N.J., BLWt.8318-100-Pvt. Iss. 7/2/1790 to Israel Smith, ass. No papers
John, N.Y., R3612
John, N.C., W4953
Thomas, Del., BLWt.10768-100-Pvt. Iss. 9/2/1789 to James Tilton, ass. No papers
William, Va., Nancy, W8818
FLINNER, Henry, N.J., BLWt.8315-100-Pvt. Iss. 10/17/1789 to John Pope, ass. No papers
FLINT, Aaron, Ct., S15124
Asel/Asael, Ct., Sea Service, Sally, W25597; BLWt.3823-160-55
Austin, Mass., S19662
Benjamin, Mass., S5409
Benjamin, Mass., BLWt.4183-100-Pvt. Iss. 2/27/1790 to Theodosius Fowler. No papers
Benjamin, Mass., S45761
Benjamin, Mass., Rebecca, W14731
Charles, Mass., Betsey, W27907
Daniel, Ct., S38703
Daniel, Mass., Priscilla, W14728
Davis, Ct., Lucy, W16991
Ebenezer, Mass., BLWt.4184-100-Pvt. Iss. 11/4/1795 to Joseph Brown. No papers
Ebenezer, Mass., W14730
Edmond/Edmund, Mass., S30419
Edward, Mass., Betsey, W23042
Henry, Mass., S35309
Jabez, Ct., S10681
Jacob, N.H., S22772
James, Ct., BLWt.5755-100-Sgt. Iss. 1/27/1790 to Daniel Segor. No papers
James/James L., Ct., Jerusha, W17911
James, Ct., R3613
John, Ct., Cont., Mary Brown, former wid., W20785
John, Md., R3614
John, Mass., Phebe, W19285
John, Mass., Betty, W21127
Jonas, Mass., S13040
Jonathan, Ct., S15834
Joshua, Cont., Ct., Sarah, W17910
Luke, Ct., S42195
Margaret, former wid. of John Hillery, N.H., which see
Martha, former wid. of Thomas Kinsman, Mass., which see
Nathaniel, Ct., S38702
Nathaniel, Cont., Mass., Nabby/Abigail, W7282; BLWt.24161-160-55
Robert, N.Y., S23221
Thomas, Mass., S35311
Thomas, Mass. Sea Service, Navy, S36334
Tilly, Mass., S5411
William, Mass., Mehitable, W14724
Zacheus, Ct., Sarah, W16260
FLIPPEN, Joseph, Va., S8485
FLIPPIN, Joseph, See FLIPPEN
Robert, Va., Sarah R., W25596;

FLIPPIN (continued)
BLWt.43873-160-55
FLIPSE, Harmanus, N.Y., S10676
FLISHER, George, Pa., R3567
FLOCK, Mathias, Cont. See FLACH
FLOOD, Alexander, Cont., N.Y., S44828
Amos, N.H., Polly, W21125; BLWt. 34278-160-55
Henry, Mass., Jemima, W7279
James, Mass., Susanna, W23040
Jonathan, N.H., BLWt.3113-100-Pvt. Iss. 4/5/1796 to Samuel Stone, ass. No papers
Joseph, Mass., S44827
Joseph, Pvt., N.H., BLReg. 316233-1855
Noah, Va., Sarah, R3615
Richard, N.H., S37927
Stephen, Mass., BLWt.4110-100-Sgt. Iss. 1/26/1790 to John May. No papers
William, Va., S42728
FLORA, Abijah, Va., R3616
Jacob, Md., BLWt.11204-100-Pvt. Iss. 12/24/1791. No papers
Lazarus, N.C., Winnifred, W3975
FLORANCE, William, Va. See FLORENCE
FLORENCE, Thomas, Mass., S34863
William, Va., Sarah, W7291
William, Va., Elizabeth, W25599; BLWt.34279-160-55
FLORY, John, Mass., BLWt.4155-100-Pvt. Iss.4/14/1790. No papers
Lazarus, N.C. See FLORA
Peter, Pa., S42197
FLOURNOY, Jacob, Va., S8492
James, Va., R3617; BLWt.36606-160-55
FLOWER, Abdiel, Ct., S46361
Isaac, Ct., Bathsheba, BLReg. 37252-55. See B.L. files
Thomas, Pa., S35944; BLWt. 1201-100
Zephon, Ct., Cont., S6856; BLWt. 5825-100. Iss. 4/26/1792. BLWt. 3-60-55
FLOWERS, Abdiel, Ct., BLWt.5808-100-Pvt. Iss. 5/8/1792 to Amos Muzzy. No papers
Absalom, Va., S8494
John, Va., Sarah, R3619
Rowland, Va., Ann/Anna, W12
Thomas, N.J., S22773
William, N.J., S34353
FLOYD, Abraham, S.C., S32251
Andrew, N.C., S21757
Benjamin, R.I., Martha, W14729
Ebenezer, Mass., BLWt.709-150-Ensign. Iss. 3/1/1799. Presented certificate 10/7/1816 or 1806. No papers
George, Va., S13041
Henry, Va., R14982 1/2; Va. Half Pay
Henry F., Va., S39528
Henry H., Va., S31030
James, N.H., Elizabeth Dixon, former wid., W22944
John, N.C., S.C., Va., Nancy, W8817; BLWt.24999-160-55

FLOYD (continued)
John, Va., S8493
John, Va., S15122
Josiah, Va., Mary, W7281
Matthew, Va., S18402
Orson, N.C., R3620
Perry, Va., S38700; BLWt.2087-100
Thomas, N.C., BLReg. 91911-1855
William, Mass., S34864
William, Va., S2553
FLOYED, William, Mass., Patience, W14732
FLUD, William, Va. See FLOOD
FLUE, William, Pa., R3621
FLUHART, Stephen, Md., BLWt.11220-100-Sgt. Iss. 6/11/1790. No papers. But see FLEEHARTY, Stephen, Md.
FLUKER, George, N.C., S10678
John, Ga., S16382
FLY, John, Cont., Mass., Molly, W24206
William, Mass., S18401
FLYN, John, N.C. See FLINN
Thomas, Del., Md., S35943
FLYNN, Daniel, Va. See FLIN
Jacob, Mass., Abigail W. Gooden former wid., W1414
Michael, Ct., Fanny, W24212
Simon, Pa., S42198
Thomas, Va. See FLIN
FLYNT, Levi, Mass., S17417
FOARD, Bille, Mass. See FOORD
Hezekiah, Md., S47187; BLWt. 758-200-Lt. Iss. 8/4/1789. No papers
Jonathan, Ct. See FORD
FOAT/FOOT. Not plainly written.
Isaac, N.Y., Lamb's Art., BLWt. 7142-100-Corp. Iss. 10/12/1789. No papers
FOBES, Daniel, Mass., S28735
Edward, Mass., Eunice, W14735
Ezra, Mass., Mary, W19274
John, Mass., S13062
John, R.I., Rosinda, R3646
Jonah, Mass., S35325
Jotham, Mass., S6855
Lemuel, Mass., Anne, W7301
Nathan, Ct., S2218
Robert, Mass., Abiah, W21130
Simon, Ct., Mass., S16119
FOCHT, George, Pa., S23634
FODDRELL, Charles, Va. See FODRELL
FODRELL, Charles, Va., Mary, W7317; BLWt.38343-160-55
FOG, Joseph, Cont., N.C. res. & agcy., S41545
FOGAT, John, Va. See FUGAT
FOGELSONG, Henry, Hazen's Regt. BLWt.13076-100-Pvt. Iss. 6/20/1789. No papers
FOGG, Aaron, Mass., S35323
Abigail, former wid. of Lemuel Raymond, Mass., which see
Caleb, Mass., N.H., Olive, W23048
Charles, Mass., S35317
Daniel, N.H., Susanna, W14748; BLWt.11266-160-55
Elizabeth, former wid. of John Eubank, Va., which see

FOGG (continued)
George, Mass., S29159
James, Va., S3367
Jeremiah, Cont., N.H., Lydia, W16116; BLWt.696-300-Capt. Iss. 5/25/1790. No papers
Jeremiah, N.H., S10698
Jonathan, N.H., S10695
Jonathan, N.H., Sarah, W16261
Moses, Mass., Hannah, W23056
Samuel, N.H., Hannah, W21136
Samuel, N.H., Ruth, W24224
Stephen, N.H., Mary, W3538; BLWt.35000-160-55
FOGGERSON, Francis, Va., S8502
FOGGETT, Richard, Md., S8498
FOGHT, George, Pa. See VOGHT
John Morris, Cont., N.Y., S46382; R3623; BLWt.1491-200. Wid. also applied for pension for service of former husb., James English/Inglis, N.Y. See papers within
FOGLE, George, Von Heer's Corps, BLWt.13068-100-Pvt. Iss. 2/14/1791 to Alex. Power, ass. No papers
FOGLER, Simon, Cont., Md. res. in 1794. Dis. No papers
FOLCK, Daniel, Pa., S15836
FOLEY, John, Va., N.Y. State in 1832, R3624
Mason, S.C., Caty, W7314
FOLGER, Thomas, N.Y., S10697
FOLIARD, John, N.Y., BLWt.7112-100-Pvt. Iss. 10/1/1790 to Abraham Nelson, ass. No papers
FOLK, Simon, Pa., S22241
William, N.C., S.C., R3626
William, Pa., R3625
FOLKER, Chloe, former wid. of Wm. Russell, Ct., which see
Ebenezer, Ct., S37938
FOLKNER, Abraham, Privateer, Pa. R3627
Ezekiel, N.C., S3374
Henry, Va., R3429
Thomas, N.C., S4289
FOLLANSBEE, James, Mass., Sarah, W14739
Nathan, N.H., Ann, W24652
Nehemiah, Mass., S17960
William, N.H., Eleanor, W16118
FOLLENSBEE, James, N.H., War of 1812, Sarah Foster, former wid., R3694
John, N.H., S10694
FOLLET, Benjamin, N.H., S13045
Samuel, Mass., N.H., S30422
Thomas, Mass., Mary, W14744
William, R.I., S21203
FOLLETT, Philip, Cont., Mass., Navy, Privateer, Sarah Reynolds, former wid., W24751
Robert, Ct., S8509
FOLLIARD, John, N.Y., S44850
FOLLOCK, Adam, N.Y., Lany/Magdalena, W25828; BLWt.31759-160-55
FOLS, Conrad, N.Y., Catharine, W24218
Georg, N.Y., S13055

FOLSOM, Asa, N.H., Mary, W7318; BLWt.26422-160-55
Jeremiah, N.H., Olive, W16117
John, Cont., Mass., S35319
John, N.H., Mary, W17913
Jonathan, N.H., BLWt.3114-100-Pvt. Iss. 7/21/1789 to Ladd & Cass, assnes. No papers
Levi, N.H., R3629
Moses, Cont., N.H., S31031
Thomas, N.H., R3630
FOLTS, Conrad, N.Y., Catharine, W24218
George, N.Y. See FOLS
Honyost/John Joseph, N.Y., S27800
John Joseph, Pvt., N.Y., BL Reg. 216616-1855
FOLTZ, Conrad, N.Y. See FOLTS
George, Pa., S41541
John Jost, N.Y. Honyost FOLTS
Joshua, Va., S13054
FONDA, Abraham, N.Y., S10686
Abraham D., N.Y., Hendreke, W16576
Douw J. or I., N.Y., BLWt.735-150-Ens. Iss. 6/1/1792. No papers
Dowee, N.Y., R3631
Eldert/Eldred, N.Y., S28734
Jacob, N.Y., S10687
Jacob Glen, N.Y., R3632; BLWt. 45661-160-55
Jellis A., N.Y., S10684
Jellis J., N.Y., S49266
John, N.Y., BLWt.734-150-Ensign. Iss. 10/12/1790. No papers
John, N.Y., Angelica, W23046
FONDEY, Douw, N.Y. See FONDA
John, N.Y. See FONDA
FONES, John, R.I., ---. Discharge Cert. of John Fones/Foney/Tones/Toney; name not clear; of the R.I. Regt. showing 6 yrs.,2 mos., 10 days service, signed by G. Washington, dated 6/15/1783, is on file and locked up for safe keeping. No pension or B.L. for said soldier. A. Wilson.
John, Va. See FONS
William, R.I., wid. Dorcas, W25595 BLWt.27600-160-55
FONEY, John, R.I., See FONES
FONS, John, Va., Elizabeth, W25595; BLWt.29733-160-55
FONTAINE, Moses, Va., Elizabeth, W5076
William, Va., Ann, W7319; BLWt. 1949-450. Va. Half Pay
FOOR, John C., N.Y., BLWt.7121-100-Pvt. Iss. 10/11/1790 to Henry Tremper, ass.; BLWt.177-60-55. No papers
FOORD, Bille/William, Cont., Mass., Lucina, W10999
Charles, Mass. See FORD
Hezekiah, Ct., S45538
Jonathan, Ct. See FORD
Joseph, N.H., Ester, W23049
Nathaniel, Mass. See FORD
Sanbun, Cont., See Sanburn FORD
FOOS, Mathias, Cont., Pa. res.,

FOOS (continued)
S42200
FOOSHEE, Elijah, N.C., R3635
John, N.C., S8511
FOOT, Abraham, Ct., Abby, R14246
Amos, Ct., S13069
Beeri, Ct., S13074
Bronson, Ct., Thankful, W21144
Daniel, Vt., S22244
Darius, Ct., N.Y., S17957
Ebenezer/Ebenezer E., Ct., N.Y., S44841
Elihu, Ct. Sea Service, S15838
Ezra, Ct., BLWt.5770-100-Pvt. Iss. 6/24/1795 to Eneas Munson. No papers
Ezra, Ct., Mercy Parson/Parsons former wid., W19962
Freeman, Mass., Vt., Bathsheba, W25584; BLWt.89517-160-55
George, N.C., Lucretia, W10032
Heli, Ct., Sea Service, Ruth, W21142
Isaac, Cont., Ct., S44839
Jacob, Ct., Lucy, R3641
Jehiel, Mass., Lucretia, W1589; BLWt.1549-100
Jesse, Cont., Ct., S29157
John, Mass., N.Y., R3639
Joseph, Mass., S44840; BLWt. 281-60-55
Martin, Vt., Anna, W25589; BLWt. 31420-160-55
Prudence, former wid. of James Knowles, Ct., Navy, which see
Robert, Sarah, Mass. res. She was pensioned as former wid. of her other husb., Church Mendall/Mendell, Mass., which see
Rowel, Mass., Sarah, R3642
Samuel, Mass., BLWt.4185-100-Pvt. Iss. 3/25/1790. No papers
Samuel, Mass., Sally, W21131
Sarah, former wid. of Jared Bishop, Ct., which see
Simeon, N.Y., S23635
Susannah, former wid. of Benj. Johnson, Ct., which see
Timothy, Ct., S17958
FOOTE, Ambrose, Ct., S13059
Asahel, Mass., S13044
Ebenezer, Ct., Privateer, Matilda, W25583; BLWt.34276-160-55
Fenner/Fener, Mass., S13065
Hannah, former wid. of Robert Kimberly, Ct., which see
Isaac, N.H., Privateer, S17955; BLWt.13430-160-55
John, Ct., R3640
Robert, See claim of Church Mendell/Mendall, Mass.
Stephen, Ct., Hannah, W17912
FOPLESS, John, Del., BLWt.10766-100-Pvt. Iss. 9/2/1789. No papers
John, Del., BLWt.2024-100
FORBES, Aaron, Mass., S44848
Alexander, Va., S2559
Alexander, Va., Judith, W10998; BLWt.26642-160-55

FORBES (continued)
Charles, Mass., Susanna, W24221
Daniel, Pa., Dis. No papers
Ebenezer, Mass., Eunice, BLWt. 47963-160-55
Edward, Mass., S38705
Eli, Ct., S15837
Elisha, Ct., S27801
Hugh, Pa., S2215
James, Mass., BLWt.4153-100-Pvt. Iss. 7/7/1797. No papers
James, Lamb's Art., N.Y., BLWt. 7134-100-Sgt. Iss. 8/24/1790 to Glenn & Barent, and to the estate of Paris, admrs. assnes. No papers
James, N.Y., S44847
John, Ct., S15427
John, Ct., Cont., BLWt.1298-100
John, Mass., S19666
John, Mass., Elizabeth, R3643
John, N.Y., Abiah, W16992
John, N.Y., Nancy Shippey, former wid., R9517
John, N.C., See FORBIS
John, R.I. See FOBES
John, S.C., Rebecca, R3645
Jonathan, Mass., Jane, W14738
Joseph, S.C., S6849
Jotham, Mass. See FOBES
Levi, Ct., Sarah, W21133
Nathan, Mass., S42201
Nicholas, N.Y., Sarah, R3647
Samuel, Cont., Mass., Martha, W25588; BLWt.19537-160-55
Thomas, Md., also served in 1794, Catharine, R14250
William, Mass., Lucy, W1744
William, Pa., S5410
William, S.C., Margaret, R3644
William, Va. See FERBUSH
William, Va., Barbara, W7300
FORBIS, John, N.C., S.C., Mary, W25591; BLWt.26083-160-55
Joseph, S.C. See FORBES
FORBS, Aaron, Mass. See FORBES
James, Ct., S37928
FORBURK, Alexander, N.Y., BLWt. 7122-100-Pvt. Iss. 9/15/1790 to John S. Hobart et al, assnes.
FORBUS, Hugh, N.C., S6853
John, N.Y., Nancy Shippey, former wid., See FORBES
FORBUSH, Bartholomew, N.Y., Catharine, W16994
David, Mass., S34882; Dorcas, wid. of above soldier who remarried Isaac Lovering, rec'd pension as former wid. of Jacob Lufkin, Mass. See papers in said claim. Her husb. Isaac Lovering also pensioned, Mass.
Ebenezer, Mass., See FORBES
James, Mass., Eunice, W24226
John, N.Y., Nancy Shippey, former wid., See FORBES
Nicholas, N.Y., See FORBES
Rufus, Mass., Mary, W24228
William, Del., BLWt.10765-100-Pvt. Iss. 4/12/179?. No papers
FORCE, Amariah, Mass., S34880
Benjamin, N.Y., R3649

FORCE (continued)
David, N.Y., BLWt.7130-100-Pvt. Iss. 5/21/1791 to James Brebner, ass. No papers
Ebenezer, Ct., S34873
Henry, Hazen's Regt., BLWt.13075-100-Pvt. Iss. 6/3/1791. No papers
Henry, Cont., N.J., S44845
James, N.J., BLWt.79501-160-55
Jeremiah, Mass., Sally, W7236; BLWt.18203-160-55
Jesse, Va. See FOREE
Joseph, N.J., BLWt.8317-100-Pvt. Iss. 6/11/1789 to Matthiss Denman ass. No papers
Joseph, N.J., S34358
Joseph, Va., S37939
Peter, N.C., S31036
Silas, Va., R3650
Timothy, N.Y., BLWt.7119-100-Pvt. Iss. 7/16/1790 to Wm. J. Vreedenburgh, ass. No papers
William, N.J., S44846
FORD, Abel, Mass., R.I., S44843
Abel, N.Y., S10688
Abijah, R.I., BLWt.3123-100-Pvt. Iss. 12/1/1789 to Wm. Albertson, ass. No papers
Abijah, R.I., R3652
Alexander, Md., S16806
Alexander, Pa., BLWt.9402-100-Pvt. Iss. 7/30/1793 to Francis Kirkpatrick, ass. No papers
Alexander, Pa., Martha, W9445
Amos, Ct., S15428
Amos, Ct., S37936
Amos, Ct., Eunice, W25585; BLWt. 26167-160-55
Andrew, Mass., S5398
Asher, N.Y., Jane, W7296; BLWt. 17725-160-55
Benjamin, Ct., S44842
Benjamin, Cont., N.J. res. in 1818, S34355
Benjamin, Md., Mary, R3658
Benjamin, Md., BLWt.1133-450 Iss. 9/20/1825
Benjamin, Pvt. in "Lee's Legion" "Pa. Quota", BLWt.9366 & 13107. Iss. 4/27/1799 to Ab M. Bell, ass. No papers
Caleb, Mass., Rachel, W23051; BLWt.19828-160-55
Charles, Mass., Sally, W1404; BLWt.31903-160-55
Chilion, Col. Lamb's Art. Regt. BLWt.738-200-Lt. Iss. 8/4/1790. No papers
Christopher, Pa., S18405
Dabney, Va., S39531
David, Del., BLWt.10770-100-Pvt. Iss. 6/26/1797. No papers
David, N.J., S42202
Elisha, S.C., Sarah, W8821
Hezekiah, Md. See FOARD
Isaac, Ct., BLWt.5804-100-Pvt. Iss. 9/16/1796 to Ebenezer Drakley. No papers
Isaac, N.Y., S42203
Isaiah, Vt., R3654
Jacob, N.Y., S13050
Jacob, --- Mo. res. in 1834, R3655

FORD (continued)
James, N.H., Dis. No papers
James, Va., Lucy, W8820
Jane, former wid. of James Dawson, Cont. S.C., which see
Jesse, Va., S31035
John, Ct., Anna, W14743
John, Md., S39532
John, Mass., S34878
John, Mass., Rhoda Ensign, former wid., W16975
John, N.C., BLWt.2143-200
John, Pa., Esther/Easther, R3653
John, Va., Elizabeth, W11000
John Morrison, Mass. or R.I., Privateer, Ct., R3656
Jonathan, Ct., S23222
Jonathan, Ct., S44844
Jonathan, Ct., BLWt.1498-100
Joseph, Md., S34867
Joseph, N.H., Esther Richards, W23049
Joseph, N.C., S15429
Joshua, Ga., S3368
Joshua, Mass., Sarah Bosworth, former wid., W5862; BLWt.38843-160-55
Jotham, Mass., S10683
Lewis, Va., Anne/Ann, W24223
Lot, Del., BLWt.2002-100
Loyd, Md., S2555
Mahlon, N.J. & U.S.A., Sophia B., W24227; BLWt.697-200-Lt. Iss. 8/4/1790. Also recorded under BLWt.2526. No papers
Martin, Ct., BLWt.5813-100-Pvt. Iss. 12/24/1796. No papers
Martin, Ct., S37932
Matthew, Ct., BLWt.5772-100-Pvt. Iss. 2/5/1790. No papers
Miles, Mass., Susannah, W23054
Morgan, Pa., R3659
Nathan, Ct., S2557
Nathan, Vt., Betsey, W24216
Nathaniel, Ct., S13049
Nathaniel, Mass., Lydia, W24217
Noah, Mass., Abigail, R3651
Phinehas, Ct., S37929
Prince, Mass., S10691
Richard, R.I., S22246
Sanbun/Sonburn, Cont., N.Y. res. in 1819, S13052; BLWt.498-100
Stephen, Ct., S16807
Stephen, N.J., Pa. Sea Service, R3661
Sybel, Vt., former wid. of Abel Wright, which see
Thomas, Mass., S34871
Thomas, Mass., S34881
Thomas, N.J., Hopeful, W4435
Tobias, S.C., BLWt.2375-150
William, Md., S31034
William, N.C., S2558
William, Pa., BLWt.9404-100-Pvt. Iss. 5/7/1794 to Christian Hubbard. No papers
William, Va., S8506
FORDHAM, Nathan, Ct. Sea Service, N.Y., S6848
FORDICE, John, N.J., BLWt.8313-100-Pvt. Iss. 6/16/1789 to Thos. Coyle, ass. No papers

FORDON, James, N.J., BLWt.8309-100-Pvt. Iss. 5/3/1791. No papers
FORDYCE, Henry, N.J., S32256
James, N.J., S17961
FOREE, Jesse, Va., S31039
FOREHAND, David, N.C., S6850
James, N.C., R3633
John, Cont., Va., Rebecca, W7316
FOREMAN, Alexander, Pa., S26998
Jacob, Pa., S32254
Leonard, Md., Ann C., W10036; BLWt.26972-160-55
Miles, N.Y., S23638
Peter, Pa., S22242
William, Md., BLWt.11209-100-Pvt. Iss., no date, to P. Read & I. Johnson, admrs. Note, same warrant no. recorded as iss. for service of Moses Foster, Pvt., Md. Line, no date of iss., no ass. named.
William, Md., BLWt.11219-100-iss. 2/27/1793
FOREST, James, N.C., S1663
John, Mass., See FORIST
Robert, Con., N.H., Elizabeth, W19278; BLWt.7086-160-55
FORESTER, John Dogens, Va., Mary, R3668
Robert, Va., S1517
William, Va., S10156
FORGASON, Abraham, N.Y., Polly, W4197
Daniel, Ct. See FERGUSON
Gilbert, N.Y., S6851
James, N.C., R3664
William, N.Y., S23224
FORGERSON, John, N.Y., S5384
FORGISON, John, N.Y., Mary, W4954
FORGUERAN, Peter, Va., Grace, W8824
FORGUS, John, Pa., Mary, W458
FORGUSON, John, N.C., Va., Bethany/Bethena, W10777; BLWt. 26925-160-55
FORGY, Hugh, Pa., S31037
FORIST, John, Mass., S34868; BLWt.1562-100
FORISTELL, John, Mass., Lydia, R3666
FORISTER, John, See FORISTELL
FORKER, Samuel, N.J., S815
FORMAN, Aaron, Md., Pa., Va., S8507
Jonathan, N.J., Martha, W457
Jonathan, N.J., BLWt.739-450-Lt. Col. Iss. 6/11/1789. No papers
Lewis, Va., S4679
Miles, N.Y. See FOREMAN
Thomas M., Cont., Md., Pa., Martha B., W5276
Tunis, N.J., S646
FORMBY, Nathan, Va.,Tabitha,W3794
FORNEY, Abraham, N.C., Martha/ Rachel, W3976; BLWt.28507-160-55
Dennis, Ct., BLWt.5794-100-Pvt. Iss. 12/24/1796. No papers
Peter, N.C., Nancy, W4955
FORNS, Edmund, S.C., Edith, W9446
FORQUERAN, Peter, See FORGUERAN

FORRAT, Henry, Pa. See FRATT
FORRAY, Jacob, Pa. See FORREY
FORRESDALE, Stafford, Md., BLWt. 11211-100-Pvt. Iss. 5/11/1790 No papers
FORREST, Andrew, Pa., BLWt.754-300-Capt. Iss. 3/16/1790. No papers
David, Mass., Abigail, W7311
Ebenezer, Mass., Hannah, W24232
George, Cont., Va., S39538
James, N.C. See FOREST
John, Mass. See FORIST
Robert, N.H. See FOREST
Samuel, Mass., S34877
Uriah, Md., Rebecca, W24225; BLWt.756-450-Lt. Col. Iss. 9/13/1799. No papers
William, Cont., N.H., S13070
William, Mass., BLWt.4144-100-Pvt. Iss. 4/7/1792 to Stephen Thomass. Cert. by Mr. Taylor 3/12/1829 & sent to Gen. Land Office
William, N.H., Dorothy Eastman, former wid., W21040
William, N.C., S8512
FORRESTALL, Joseph, Mass. See FORRISTALL
FORRESTER, James, N.C., S6854
John, S.C., R22015
John, Va., S35948
Peter, Pa., R3669
Solomon, S.C., R3670
Stephen, N.C., S1902
FORREY, Jacob, Pa., S16117
FORRIS, Peter, Ct., Mary/Morry; W19281; BLWt.1331-100. Iss. 5/21/1828 to this soldier. BLWt.53-60-55
FORRIST, David, Mass. See FORREST
Ebenezer, Mass. See FORREST
FORRISTALL, Joseph, Mass., Hannah, W22832
FORRISTER, John Dogens, Va. See FORESTER
Robert, Va. See FORESTER
FORSEE, Charles, Va. See FORSIE
Judith, former wid. of James Bledsoe, Va., which see
William, Va., S31038
FORSETT, Robert, N.C. See FAUCETT
FORSHY, Thomas, Pa., S3376
FORSIE, Charles, Cont., Va., Rebecca H., W11001; BLWt. 26903-160-55
FORSTER, David, Ct. See FOSTER
Joseph, Mass., S13058
Joseph, Mass., See FOSTER
Thomas, Cont., Va., Mary/Polly, W647; BLWt.36501-160-55
FORSYTH, Hugh, N.C., Nancy, W7315
John, Pa., S16121
Joseph, S.C., Va., S23636
Latham, Ct., Abigail, W2442; BLWt.26049-160-55
Robert, Cont., Va., R14237; Va. Half Pay
William, Ct., Prudence, W11007
FORT, Albert, S.C., S6847
Benjamin, N.J., S32257
Daniel, N.Y., Leah, W15766

FORT (continued)
Jacob, N.Y., Angelica/Anna, R3674
John, N.Y., R3675
Nicholas, N.Y., R3676
Sherwood, N.C., S8499
Thomas, N.J., S13073
Turner, N.C., Elizabeth, W7295
FORTENER, Peter, Pa., S34356
FORTETENOR, Peter, Pa. See FORTENER
FORTNER, Benjamin, N.J., Margaret, W9447
Emanuel Ford, N.C., S32258
Ezekiel, N.C. See FOLKNER
FORTUNE, Gardiner, Va. See Garner
Garner/Gardiner, Va., Lucy, W24233
John, Va., Nancy, W7309
Richard, Ct., S37933
William, Md., S3373
William, Md., R20370
William, Va., S8513
FOSBROOK, John, Pa., S35949; BLWt.1676-100
FOSCUE, Frederick, N.C., Privateer, S2562
FOSDICK, James, Ct., BLWt.5776-100-Pvt. Iss. 5/7/1792 to Thomas Stanley. No papers.
James, Ct., S38707
John, Mass., N.Y., R3677
Thomas U., Cont., Ct., BLWt. 1239-150
William, Ct., R3678
FOSGATE, Ezekiel, Mass., R3679
FOSGOOD, Ebenezer, N.H., BLWt.3102-100-Pvt. Iss. 3/25/1790. No papers
FOSHA, Reuben, N.Y., Fanny, W7312
FOSHET/FOSKET, Ephraim, Mass., S29803
FOSKET, Ephraim, Mass. See FOSHET
FOSS, Benjamin, N.H., Ruth, S10696 BLRej. --. She was pensioned as former wid. of 1st husb., Daniel Clough, N.H., which see
Dolly, former wid. of Jacob Daniels, N.H., which see
Ebenezer, N.H., S13057
Elias, Mass., Anna, W4198
George, Mass., Mary Robinson, former wid., W22093
George, N.H., S22776
George, N.H., Jane, W737; BLWt. 539-160-55
Isaiah, N.H., S29156
James, Mass., S18824
Jeremiah, N.H., S13063
John, Mass., Susanna, W23052
John, N.H., BLWt.3107-100-Pvt. Iss. 3/25/1790. No papers
John, N.H., S8515
Joseph, Mass., S35947
Nathaniel, Cont., N.H., S45339
Nathaniel, N.H., S22775
Zachariah, Mass., S16805
FOSSETT, Robert, N.C. See FAUCETT
Robert, Pa., BLWt.9372-100-Pvt. Iss. 6/29/1789 to M. McConnell, ass. No papers
FOSTER, Abel, Cont., Mass., Mary, W19277; BLWt.5109-160-55

FOSTER (continued)
Abial/Abiel, Mass., S45534
Abner, Mass., Betsey, W23050
Abner, Va., Judy, W8823
Abraham, Mass., S34869
Achilles, Va., Margarett, R3689
Alexander, Pa., S32252
Alpheus, Ct., Esther, W21129
Amos, Mass., S17959
Andrew, Mass., S45533
Anna, former wid. of John Poppino, N.Y., which see
Anthony, N.C., Va., S2561
Asa, Ct., N.Y., Sarah, W5277
Asa, N.H., S22243
Asa, N.H., Sarah M., R3681; BLWt.101214-160-55
Benen/Benan, Mass., Deborah, W23047
Benjamin, Ct., S37931
Benjamin, Vt., S5421
Caleb, N.Y., Rachel, W25593
Catharine, former wid. of John Portman, Pa., which see
Cato, Mass., BLWt.4118-100-Pvt. Iss. 5/8/1792 to Ezra Blodget No papers
Chauncey, Cont., Ct., Charlotte, W17917
Cosby, Cont., Va., Susan, W3010; BLWts. 292-100 & 31419-160-55
Daniel, Mass., S9891
Daniel, Mass., S29805
Daniel, Mass., N.H., Vt., Submit, W19276
Daniel, N.H., Mary, W21134
David, Ct., S44835
David, Cont., Mass., S34875
David, Mass., Anna, W19272; BLWt.2092-160-55
David, Mass., R.I., S35320
Edmund, Va., Martha, W3795
Edward, Ct., S37935
Edward, Mass., S30421
Elisha, Mass., BLWt.710-150-Ensign. Iss. 4/15/1790 to John Warren, ass. No papers
Elizabeth, former wid. of Samuel Warren, Mass. Which see
Ephraim, Cont., Pa. or N.J., Rachel Thompson, former wid., W1512
Ephraim, N.H., S42729
Erastus, Mass., Chloe, W19283; BLWt.17601-160-55
Ezekiel, Mass., Chloe, W13200
Ezra, Mass., Abigail/Nabby, W4199; BLWt.63163-160-55
Faith, former wid. of John O. Waterman, Ct., R3684
George, R.I., S21758
George, Va., BLWts.12131 & 13970-100-Pvt. Iss. 6/19/1793 No papers
George, Va., R3685
Gershom, Mass., S44836
Gideon, Mass., Mary, W738; BLWt.1309-160-55
Giles, Ct., S13051
Hackaliah, Mass., S27806
Henry, Va., Esther, W25586; BLWt.45712-160-55

FOSTER (continued)
Ichabod, N.J., BLWt.8305-100-Pvt. Iss. 4/21/1790 to Matthias Denman, ass. No papers
Isaac, Ct., Esther, R3683
Jacob, Ct., Susanna, W24219
James, Md., b. Ireland, S8501
James, N.H., Hannah, W19284
James, Pa., S39536
James, Va., S8503
James, Va., Nancy McClure, former wid., W7409
Jeremiah, Mass., N.H., S45535
Jeremiah, N.J., BLWt.8297-100-Pvt. Iss. 5/26/1790. No papers
Jesse, Ct., S37934
Job, Va., S2216
Joel, Va., Mary, W11008; BLWt. 77533-160-55 iss. 11/19/1789. No papers
John, Ct., BLWt.5775-100-Pvt. Iss. 11/19/1789. No papers
John, Ct., Chaplain in War of 1812, S13047
John, Ct., Pruella, R3692
John, Ct., N.Y., S17962
John, Cont., Mass., R.I., Sally, W7302; BLWt.14657-160-55
John, Mass., Anna, W10034
John, Mass., R3686
John, Mass., Vt., S16118
John, Lamb's Art., N.Y., BLWt. 7141. Iss. 7/16/1790 to Wm. J. Vreedenburgh, ass. No papers
John, N.Y., S44837
John, N.Y., Susannah, W21128
John, Pa., S23637
John, Va., S1515
John, Va., S8504
John, Va., S35950
John, Va., Sydney, R3696
John Hardin, Va., Martha, W3793 BLWt.589-150
Jonathan, Mass., S35321
Jonathan, Mass., Rachel, W14740
Jonathan, Mass., N.H., Sarah, W1258; BLWt.19601-160-55
Jonathan, Mass., N.H., Mercy, W14742
Jonathan, N.H., S22247
Jonathan, N.J., BLWt.1973-100
Jonathan, Pa., Elizabeth, W24230
Joseph, Ct., Mass., S16802
Joseph, Ct., Mass., Vt., Dolly, W736; BLWt.9043-160-55
Joseph, Mass., BLWt.4160-100-Sgt. Iss. 12/10/1789. No papers
Joseph, Mass. See FORSTER
Joseph, Mass., S29804
Joshua, Va., Mary, W21139
Jude, ?, Mass. Agcy. Invalid. No papers
Larkin, Va., Polly, W7306; BLWt. 34999-160-55
Lemuel, Mass., Dolly/Dolley, W7304
Leonard, Mass., S34872
Luna, Mass., Lydia, W1405; BLWt. 9452-160-55
Mark, Md., BLWt.11213-100-Pvt. Iss. 10/10/1799 to Asahel Phelps, ass. No papers

FOSTER (continued)
Michael, Pa., Sarah, W5275 1/2; BLWt.27638-160-55
Moses, Md., BLWt.11209-100-Pvt. Iss., no date. Note-Same Wt. No. recorded as iss. for service of Wm. Foreman, Pvt.-Md. Line
Moses, Mass., Mary, W14747
Nathan, N.H., Abigail, W14736
Nathan, N.H., BLWt.2405-100
Nathaniel, Mass., S19295
Nathaniel, Mass., S34866
Nathaniel, Mass., Mary Fletcher, former wid., W19287
Nathaniel, N.J., Pa., Va., S16803
Nathaniel, N.Y., S44838
Nathaniel, Va., S32253
Parker, Cont., Mass., S35326
Parla, Mass., S8508
Peter, Ct., BLWt.5767-100-Pvt. Iss. 12/14/1789 to Richard Platt. No papers
Peter, Ct., Tommy, W14745
Peter, Ct., Sea Service, R3691
Peter, Sea Service Va., S46443; BLWt.1770-200 & Va. Half Pay
Richard, Mass., S45536
Rigby, Md., BLWt.11222-100-Pvt. Iss. 4/11/179? to James De-Baufre, ass. No papers
Robert, Pa., S2220
Robert, Va., Elizabeth, W19270
Rufus, Cont., Mass., Susanna, W1743
Samuel, Ct., S13043
Samuel, Mass., Mary, W21132; BLWt.17581-160-55
Samuel, Mass., R.I., S35318
Samuel, N.H., Tabitha, W21870
Samuel, N.Y., Phebe, W17920; BLWt.8010-160-55
Samuel, R.I., Waity, W21145
Samuel, S.C., Barbara, W7303
Samuel, Va. ?, R3693
Samuel S., Ct. Sea Service, Privateer, S13071
Sarah, former wid. of James Follensbee, N.H., War of 1812, which see
Saul, Ct., S16808
Simeon, N.H., S39533
Smith, Mass., S34870
Stephen, Mass., Diadema/Diadama, W10035; BLWt.18207-160-55
Thomas, Cont., Pa., S39537
Thomas, Pvt., Mass., BLWt.4181-100 iss. 1/28/1790
Thomas, Mass., BLWt.706-200-Lt. Iss. 3/25/1790. No papers
Thomas, Mass., Susan S/Susanna, W19291
Thomas, N.Y., Hannah, W24222
Thomas, N.Y., R4004
Thomas, Pa., Barbara, W2780
Thomas, R.I., Esther, W2781
Thomas, Va. See FORSTER
Timothy, Ct., Desire, W16577
Timothy, Mass., Rachel, W27412
Vincent, N.Y., Jemima, W24220; BLWt.28616-160-55

FOSTER (continued)
Wareham, Ct., Cont., Lucretia, R3688
William, Cont.,N.Y., Phebe,W19282
William, Cont., Va., Sarah Baker, former wid., W2986; BLWts.1462-100 & 260-60-55
William, Md., BLWts.13061 & 14118-100-Pvt. Iss. 5/1/1795 to Francis Sherrard, ass. of James Smith, admr. No papers
William, Mass., S19664
William, Mass., S46543; BLWt.1552-100
William, N.H., Betsey, W21141
William, N.Y., Susannah, R3695
William, R.I., BLWt.3116-100-Pvt. Iss. 2/24/1800. No papers
William, R.I., R3697
William, Va., S38706
William, Va., S39534
William, Va., Nancy, W4674
FOULK, John Peter, Pa. or Va., Privateer, also Navy, R3698
FOULKES, William, Va. See FOWLKES
FOULKROD, Jacob, Pa., Mary, W4436; BLWt.26923-160-55
FOUNDER, John, Pa., R3699
FOUNTAIN, John, ---, Ct. agcy., Dis. No papers
Solomon, N.C., S41544
Stephen, Mass., S42199
FOURT, Henry, N.J., S874
Thomas, N.J., See FORT
FOUSHEE, George, Va., S8505
William, Va.,R14233; Va. Half Pay
FOUST, Jacob, Pa., S2560
FOWL, Curtis, Mass., BLWt.4171-100-Pvt. Iss. 11/30/1799 to Abijah Holbrook. No papers
FOWLE, Curtis, Mass., S34929
John, Cont., Mass., S34876
John, Cont., Mass., Privateer, Lois, W19271
John, Mass., S34874
Phinehas, R.I., S35322
Samuel, Mass., S3701
FOWLER, ?, Me. res., Susanna,R3719
Abiathar, Ct., Asenath, W14746
Abner, N.H., Mary, W16017
Amos, Ct., S15839
Amos, Ct., Rebecca, W17914
Benjamin, R.I., Dis. No papers
Caleb, Ct., Olive Pratt, former wid., W4057
Daniel, Ct., S10685
David, N.J., BLWt.8319-100-Pvt. Iss. 6/11/1789 to Matthias Denman, ass. No papers
Ebenezer, Ct., S10689
Edward, Ct., BLWt.5798-100-Pvt. Iss. 8/17/1790. No papers
Elexis, Md., Rachel, R3712
Eli, Ct., R3702
Elisha A., Ct., Mary, R3710
George, N.Y., Privateer, Mass., R.I., War of 1812, Betsey, W25587; BLWt.2091-160-55
Isaac, N.Y., R.I., Susan, R3718; BLWt.56785-160-55
Jacob, Mass., S45537
Jesse, Mass., S34879

FOWLER (continued)
John, Ct., Anna, W17919
John, Mass., Mary, W24229
John, N.C., S16809
John, Va., S31033
John L., N.Y., R3706
Jonathan, Ct., Cont., S41542
Jonathan, N.Y., S23639
Joseph, Md., BLWt.11205-100-Pvt. Iss. 2/1/1790. No papers
Joseph, N.J., BLWt.8310-100-Pvt. Iss. 5/26/1790. No papers
Joseph, N.J., S34354
Joseph, Va., S39530; BLWt.1370-100
Joshua, Md., S16120
Lewis, N.Y., Hannah, R3703
Matthew, Mass., Sarah, R3717
Medad, Mass., R3711
Nathaniel, Ct., Ruth, R3713
Nathaniel, Mass., Nanna, W14741
Patrick, Pa., BLWt.9382-100-Pvt. Iss. 4/7/1795 to John Nicholson ass. No papers
Philip, Cont., Mass., Elizabeth Cushing, former wid., W23896
Philip, N.H., BLWt.3109-100-Drum Major. Iss. 3/25/1790. Official Note: "No. 3109 is iss. as Mass., recorded N.H." No papers
Reuben, Ct., S44851
Robert, Mass., S29158
Robert, N.J., See WARDELL
Sadoc, Md., S3714
Samuel, Ct. Sea Service, R3715
Samuel, S.C., S17954
Sherwood, Va., S1516
Silas, Ct., S13072
Theodosius, N.Y., Maria, W16575; BLWt.728-300-Capt. Iss. 7/9/1790. No papers
Theophilus, Ct., Sarah, W17916
William, N.C., Lucy, R3709
William, S.C., Hannah, R3704
FOWLES, Benjamin, Mass., BLWt. 4116-100-Pvt. Iss. 3/25/1790. No papers
John, Mass., BLWt.701-300-Capt. Iss. 4/18/1796 to Jeremiah Mason, ass. No papers
FOWLKES, James, Va., S8457
Josiah, Va., S16804
William, Va., Sally, W19273
FOWLS, Samuel, Mass. See FOWLE
FOX, Aaron, Ct., Lydia, W4437
Abigail, former wid. of Joseph Williams, N.H., which see
Adam, Md., R3721
Allyn/Allen, Ct., Chloe, W19275; BLWt.1315-100
Amon, Ct., R3722
Amos, Ct., Jemima, W11009
Amos, Ct., Mary, W25590
Andrew, Pa., Catharine, W7293
Andrew, Von Heer's Corps, BLWt. 13066-100-Pvt. Iss. 3/30/1791
Appleton, Ct., R3723
Asa, Ct., BLWt.5810-100-Pvt. Iss. 1/28/1790 to William Walter Parsons. No papers
Bachus, Ct., BLWt.5764-100-Pvt. Iss. 12/3/1789 to Daniel Watrous, ass. No papers

FOX (continued)
Chrispus, Mass., Susannah, W11004
Christopher W., N.Y., S10682
Consider, N.Y., S16116
Daniel, N.C., Elizabeth, W9443
David, Ct., S2217
David, Ct., S23223
David, Pa., War of 1812, Maria Elizabeth, W3340; BLWt.16635-160-55
David, Von Heer's Corps, BLWt. 13064-100-Pvt. Iss. 4/26/1791 to Charles Colver, ass. No papers
Ebenezer, Ct., S13066
Ebenezer, Ct., S39539
Ebenezer, Mass., Sea Service, Anna, W19269
Edward, N.H., Anna, W16993
Elijah, Cont., Ct., S22774
Elisha, Ct., S22777
Elisha, Ct., Cont., S10693
Eunice, former wid. of Marshall Palmer, Ct., which see
Ezekiel, Ct., Susan, W25592
Francis, N.C., S41543
Gatus/Gater, N.C., R3725
Isaac, Ct., S37937
Israel, Ct., S4288
Jabez, Ct., S13053
Jacob, Ct., S17956
Jacob/Jacob McCoy, Ct., S44829; BLWt.725-200-Lt. Iss. 4/5/1793 to Reuben Murray, ass. No papers
Jacob, Cont., Ohio Agcy., S49271
Jacob, Pa., S9888
Jacob, Von Heer's Corps, BLWt. 13067-100-Pvt. Iss. 1/12/1792 to Michael Bright, ass. No papers
Jacob McCoy, Ct. See Jacob
Jedediah/Jedidiah, Ct., S44830
Jeremiah, Cont., Mass., S13076
Jesse, Ct., Ruth, R3732
Joel, Ct., W4673
Joel, Mass., Hannah, W19280; BLWt.29730-160-55
John, Ct., Louisa, W2091; BLWt. 7203-160-55
John, Ct., Cont., S15426
John, Mass., Sarah W., W21146
John, Mass., Orpha Clark, former wid., W23055
John, N.H., Susan, W414; BLWt. 34997-160-55
John, N.C., Virlintia, R3734
John, S.C. Sea Service, S2219
John, Va., S41540
Joseph, Cont., Mass., S44833; BLWt.700-300-Capt. Iss. 2/11/1800. Cert. 6/9/1815. No papers
Joseph, N.J., BLWt.8311-100-Pvt. Iss. 6/16/1789 to Thomas Coyle, ass. No papers
Joseph, N.J., S34357
Joseph, Pa., Va., Elsey, W7292; BLWt.2351-160-55; Not half pay, see acct. No. 874-050069
Lemuel, Ct., Prudence, W11018
Lemuel, N.Y., Ruth Randall, former wid., R3733
Matthew, S.C., R3729
Matthias, Pa., R3728
Nathaniel, N.H., BLWt.1555-100

FOX (continued)
Nathaniel, Capt., Va., BLWt.705-300 iss. 7/21/1797 & BLWt.2676; S39535; Va. Half Pay
Patrick, Pa. See FAUX
Peter, Ct., S22245
Peter, N.J., BLWt.8301-100-Pvt. Iss. 3/10/1790. No papers
Peter, N.J., Amy, W1259
Peter/Peter W., N.Y., Maria, W7294; BLWt.9468-160-55
Reuben, Ct., S32255
Robert, Ct., BLWt.2177-100
Roswell, Ct., Martha Hall, former wid., W17051
Samuel, Ct., BLWt.5761-100-Pvt. Iss. 2/22/1790 to Theodosius Fowler. No papers
Samuel, Ct., S44832
Samuel, Ct., S44834
Silas, N.H., BLWt.3112-100-Pvt. Iss. 10/30/1789 to Ephraim True, ass. No papers
Silas, N.H., S45540
Simeon, Ct., S44831
Sinkler, Cont., N.H., S18404
Stephen, Ct. & Harmon's Indian War (1790), Mary, W10031
Thomas, Ct., S13048
Thomas, Ct., Chloe, W3673
Thomas, Mass., S37930
Thomas, Va., R14268; Va. Half Pay
Thomas, Va., BLWt.765-300-Capt. Iss. 7/17/1800. No papers
Titus, N.C., Elizabeth, R3724
Uriah, N.H., S13042
Variah, Ct., BLWt.5818-100-Pvt. Iss. 2/5/1790. No papers
Vaniah/Venia, Ct., Cont., S9335
William, Ct., Cont., S9334
William, Pa., BLWt.9384-100-Pvt. Iss. 6/29/1789 to M. McConnell, ass. No papers
William P., ?, N.Y. res., Dis. No papers
William W., N.Y., S10690
FOXWORTHY, John, Va., S31032
William, Va., Clarissa, W8825
FOY, James, N.H., S35324
Jane, former wid. of Henry Jamar, Pa., which see
John, Mass., S29802
John, N.J., BLWt.8306-100-Pvt. Iss. 2/25/1790 to John Ludlow, ass. No papers
John, N.J., R---
Moses, Mass. See FOYE
FOYE, Moses, Mass., S4287
FRADENBURGH, John, N.Y., S44858
Peter, N.Y., S44859
FRAIL, Zerviah, former wid. of Andrew Allard, Mass. Which see
FRAILEY, John, Pa., S23641
FRAKER, Philip, Mass., Abigail, W11020; BLWt.24434-160-55
FRALEY, James, Va., R3736
FRALIGH, Valentine, N.Y. See FRELIGH
FRAM, John, Va., S41526
FRANCE, Adam, N.Y., Margaret, W23061; BLWt.71201-160-55
Jacob, N.Y., Maria, R3737

FRANCE (continued)
John, Va., Catharine, W7327
Peter, Cont., Md. or Va.?, Elizabeth, W7328
Wilhelmus, N.Y., Anna, W19295
FRANCES, David, Ct., Anna, W21148
FRANCHER, James, Va. See FENESHER
FRANCIS, Aaron, Mass., S13097
Aaron, Mass., S34888
Alexander, Md., BLWt.11206-100-Pvt. Iss. 6/11/1790 to Alexander Francis. No papers
Charles, Mass., BLWt.4170-100-Pvt. Iss. 3/10/1795 to Sampson Crosby. No papers
Charles, Pa., S41550
David, Ct. See FRANCES
Ebenezer, Mass., BLWt.719-500-Col. Iss. 7/8/1789 to Judith Francis, legal repr. No papers
Elijah, Ct., Jane, W25610
George, Cont., Pa., S42204
George, Pa., BLWt.9364-100-Sgt. Iss. 4/6/1790. "On file, not delivered." No papers
Henry, N.Y. See Francis HENDRICKS
Henry, Va., R3739
Jacob (colored), Cont., Mass., N.J., Mary, W459
James, Ct., S15841
James, Ct., Mary, R3743
James, Ct., Sarah, R3747
James, Cont., Ct., S37942
James, Pa., See FRANCISS
Job, Ct. See FRANSSES
John/John Baptiste, Navy, b. France, d. Mass., Polly, W14756
John, Md., BLWt.11214-100-Pvt. Iss. 5/8/1790. No papers
John, Mass., BLWt.4142-100-Pvt. Iss. 11/4/1794. No papers
John, Mass., S34887
John, Va., R3741
John, Va., Nancy, R3746
Jonathan, Mass., BLWt.4161-100-Pvt. Iss. 12/14/1789 to Richard Platt. No papers
Jonathan, Mass., S43575
Joseph, S.C., S31041
Justus, Ct., Abi North, former wid., W10822
Loring, Mass., R3742
Malachi, Va., Mary, R3744
Micajah, Va., R3745
Robert, Ct., Lydia Deming, W25606; BLWt.2496-160-55
Robert, Mass., S17420
Samuel, Mass., Vt., S5412
Samuel, S.C., S39543
Thomas, Mass., S34885; BLWt.699-300-Capt. Iss. 4/18/1796 to Jere Mason, ass. No papers
Thomas, Mass., S44868
Thomas, Pa., S17965
Titus, Ct., S16813
William, Ct., S37944
William, Cont., Va., S39542
William, N.J., BLWt.8295-100-Pvt. Iss. 8/16/1792 to James Rhea, ass. No papers
William, Art. Artificers of Pa., BLWt.13015-Pvt. Iss. 10/15/1789

FRANCIS (continued)
No papers
FRANCISCO, Abraham, N.J., Sarah, W12723; BLWt.16255-160-55
Cornelius, N.Y., Anna, W16998
Henry, Cont., S44864
John, Not Rev. War-N.J. Mil.-Whiskey Insurrection; Louisa, BLWt.77315-160-55. No claim for pension
John, N.Y., S13095
Levi, N.Y., S10706
Michael, N.Y. See FRANSISCO
Peter, Va., War of 1812, Mary B., W11021; BLWt.8002-160-55
FRANCISCUS, Jacob, Pa., Abigail, W14755
FRANCISS, James, Pa., Hannah, W1592; BLWt.26274-160-55
FRANCK, Johann Adam, N.Y., Juliana, R3749
FRANCOIS, Anthony, Ct., R7765 See Anthony F. O'Cain
Jacob, Mass., BLWt.4180-100-Pvt. Iss. 3/25/1790. No papers
FRANCONI, Harriet, former wid. of Zebediah Ward, N.J., which see
FRANCOUR, John, Armand's Corps, BLWt.13063-100-Pvt. Iss. 6/20/1789. No papers
FRANCUM, Francis, S.C., S39552
FRANEY, James, Pa., BLWt.9401-100-Pvt. Iss. 7/26/1792 to Adam Harbison, ass.
FRANK, Adam, N.Y., Catharine, W16996
Andrew, R.I., S21207
George, Pa., R3750
Henry, Cont., enl. N.Y., S10700
Henry, N.Y., S39544
James, Mass., S29809
John, N.Y., S23644
John Baptiste, Pa. See FRANCIS
Joshua, Ct., S37945
Michael, N.Y., BLWt.7115-100-Pvt. Iss. 12/15/1790. No papers
Michael, N.Y., Catharine, W24247
Thomas, Mass., Hannah, W23067
William, R.I., BLWt.3127-100-Pvt. Iss. 6/18/1795 to Samuel Emery, ass. No papers
FRANKFORT, Henry, Pa., S41548
FRANKLIN, Abel, Ct., S37948
Abel, Mass., R3753
Absalom, Va., Margaret, W8830
Arnold, Pa., Lucinda, R3757
Benjamin, Mass., Olive, W14759
Dean, Mass., S13096
Elisha, R.I., S34360
Ezra, Ct., S16812
Hannah, former wid. of James Radford, Va., which see
Henry, Va., S38713
James, N.H., S10710
James M., alias Sid Canterbury, Va., S31040
Jehiel/Jeile, Ct., S44863
John, Mass., R3755
John, N.C., S.C., R3756
John, Va., BLWt.12121-100-Pvt.

FRANKLIN (continued)
Iss. 4/13/1791 to James Reynolds, ass. No papers.
John 2nd, Va., BLWt.12133-100-Pvt. Iss. 4/13/1791 to James Reynolds, ass. No papers
John, Va., S35952
John, Va., S39541
John, Va., Agness, W3796
John, Va., Ann, W19294
Jonathan, Mass., N.H., R.I., S10709
Joseph, Va., Elizabeth, W10041
Joshua, R.I., Luramy/Lurana, W21152; BLWt.28607-160-55
Lewis, N.C., Va., S8519
Mordecai, N.C., R3759
Moses, Vt., Hannah, W7337; BLWt. 26620-160-55
Nathan, N.Y., Sally, W8207; BLWt.9458-160-55
Reuben, Va., S13082
Richard, Md., BLWt.2322-100
Samuel, Ct., BLWt.5786-100-Pvt. Iss. 10/31/1791 to Isaac Bronson. No papers
Samuel, Ct., S37940
Samuel, Pa., BLWt.9365-100-Pvt. Iss. 6/13/1792 to James Rhea, ass. No papers
Samuel, Va., S6860
Squire, R.I., S21206
Stephen, N.C., Va., S15432
Thomas, Va., Letitia, W1590; BLWt.26959-160-55
Thomas P., Va., S8517
William, Mass., BLWt.4147-100-Pvt. Iss. 3/1/1792 to Joseph Brown. No papers
Willson, Ct., BLWt.5822-100-Pvt. Iss. 6/11/1799 to Sylvester Fuller. No papers
FRANKLYN, Edward, Corps of Invalids, BLWt.13097-100-Sgt. Iss. 5/24/1791 to Alexandria Tuntz, ass. No papers
FRANKS, David S., Aid-de-Camp, BLWt.400-Maj. Iss. 7/28/1789. No papers
Henry, Pa., S8522
Henry, Pa., Christiana/Christina, W4956
Isaac, Cont., Mass., N.Y., S41549
John, Sheldon's Dragoons, Ct., BLWt.5823-100-Pvt. Iss. 10/7/1789 to Benj. Tallmadge. No papers
John, Ct., Mass., S34884
John, N.Y., S44867
Marshall, S.C., S10703
Richard/Barret, Va., W2223
Samuel, S.C., Polly, W21160; BLWt.35849-160-55
FRANS, Conrad/Counradt, N.Y., Salome, S44862 & W17927
FRANSEWAY, Anthony, Ct. See Anthony F. O'CAIN
FRANSISCO, Henry, Vt. See FRANCISCO
Michael, N.Y., S13088
FRANSSES, Job, Ct., S13084; BLWt.26395-160-55

FRANSUOI, Anthony, See Anthony F. O'CAIN
FRANTS, Counradt, See Conrad FRANS
FRANTZ, Adam, Pa., S8521
Conradt, N.Y., BLWt.7123-100-Pvt. Iss. 12/15/1790. No papers
Counradt, See Conrad FRANS
FRAPWELL, William, Pa., BLWt.9400-100-Pvt. Iss. 1/26/1792 to Stephen Loudon, ass. No papers
FRARY, Eleazer, Mass., S17424
Julius C., Mass., Navy, S44866
Nathaniel, Mass., S29808
Phineas, Mass., Rhoda, W14761
Seth, Ct. See FRERY
FRASAR, Benjamin, Pa., BLWt.402-100
FRASER, Daniel, Mass., Polly, R3760
John, Va., S13080
William, Pa., Jane, R3761
FRASEUR, John, Va., Phebe, W8829
FRASHER, Frederick, Va., Elizabeth, R3762
FRASHUR, Andrew, N.Y., S13079
FRASHURE, Micager, Va. See FRAZEUR
FRASIER, Charles, Mass. See FRAZER
FRASUER, John, Va. See FRASEUR
FRATT, Henry, Pa., Rebecca, W7325
FRAWNEY, John, decd., Md., BLWt. 11202-100-Pvt. Iss. 8/8/1792 to Charles Robeson, admr. No papers
FRAYER, David, N.Y., S23226
FRAZAR, James, N.C., Privateer, R3764
FRAZEE, Jonas, N.J., Sarah, W10038; BLWt.14985-160-55
Matthias, N.J., S816
Zebedee, N.J., S34359
FRAZER, Benjamin, Pa. See FRASAR
Charles, Cont., Mass., Tabithe, W13211; BLWt.403-100 & 63-100
Christian, N.J., S2563
Duncan, Corps of Invalids, BLWt. 13096-100-Sgt. Iss. 1/5/1791. No papers
George, N.J., BLWt.8328-100-Pvt. Iss. 6/16/1789 to Aaron Ogden, ass. No papers
James, N.C., See FRAZAR
Jeremiah, N.Y., S13093
John, Ga., Lenah Middaugh, former wid., W3284; BLWt.19803-160-55. See Rev. claim of Henry C.T. Middaugh of Pike Co., Pa., who d. 8/4/1836
John, Ga. See FRAZIER
John, Ga., R3766
John, Lt., Ga. Rej.241203-1855
John, Va. See FRASER
John, Va., S17964
Lowell, N.C. See Sowell FRAZER
Robert, ---, Pa. agcy. Dis. no papers
Samuel, Cont., See FRAZIER
Samuel, Hazen's Regt., BLWt. 13086-100-Pvt. Iss. 1/24/1792 to Wm. Thomas, ass. No papers
Sowell/Lowell, N.C., Sarah, R3767; BLWt.44910-160-55
FRAZEUR, Micager,Va., Susan,W3407
FRAZIER, Alexander, Del., Pa., Privateer, S1815
Andrew, S.C., S21208

FRAZIER (continued)
Daniel, Mass. See FRASER
Henry, Md., BLWt.11225-100-Pvt. Iss. 10/14/179? to Henry Davis, ass. No papers
James, Md. Sea Service, S23225
James, S.C., S21209
James A., R.I., Lucy, W21156
Jeremiah, N.Y., BLWt.7137 & 14058-100-Pvt. Iss. 3/20/1794. No papers
John, Ga., Mary, W24241; BLWt. 2015-200
John, Va. See FRAZER
John, Va.?, Hannah, R3765
Levin, Md., Sea Service, Elizabeth, W9436
Lowell, N.C. See FRAZER
Robert, Ct., BLWt.5773 & 13940-100-Pvt. Iss. 8/10/1789 to Richard Platt, ass. No papers
Samuel, Cont., Md. agcy. & res. in 1839, Penelope, W25608
Simon, Sheldon's Dragoons, Ct., BLWt.5821-100-Pvt. Iss. 8/6/1790 to J.V. Renssellar. No papers
Sowell, N.C. See FRAZER
Thomas, N.C. Sea Service, Elizabeth, W341; BLWt.44513-160-55
William, Md., Henrietta M., W3797
William, Va., S17966
FREAM, William, Md., S10699
FREANEY, James, Pa. See FRANEY
FREAR, Abraham, N.Y., R3769
FREAS, John, N.J., R3770
FREAZE, Martin, Pa., Elizabeth, W2782
FREBBELL, John, Pa., BLWt.9383-100-Pvt. Iss. 8/19/1789 to John Phillips, Exec.
FREDENBURGH, Elias, See FREEDENBURG
James, N.Y., S43568
John, N.Y. See FRADENBURGH
Peter, N.Y., See FRADENBURGH
FREDERICK, Felix, N.C., Catharine, W10040
Francis, N.Y., S23643
Jacob, Pa., Mary, S2092
John, N.Y., BLWt.7126-100-Pvt. Iss. 9/3/1790. No papers
Joseph, Navy, Mass., Privateer, b. in Lisbon, Jerusha, W24243
Michael, Pa., S41552
Rachel, former wid. of Winthrop Peavey, N.H., which see
Sebastian, Pa., Mary, R3771
FREEBORN, George, Cont., Pa. res. of son in 1828; BLWt.1402-100
Henry, R.I., Mary, R3772
FREEBUSH, Matthew, N.Y., BLWt. 7110-100-Pvt. Iss. 9/9/1790 to Wm. Henderson, ass. No papers
FREEDENBURG, Elias, N.Y., R3804
FREEDOM, Cato, Ct., S44849
Dick (colored), Ct., BLWt.590-100
Jack, Ct., BLWt.5795-100-Pvt. Iss. 9/15/1790 to Nickls Root. No papers
Ned, Ct., BLWt.5766-100-Pvt. Iss. 7/12/1792. No papers
Ned, Ct., S37946

FREEHOLD, William, Va., S42730
FREELAND, Abraham, Navy, Privateer, S.C. Sea Service, N.J. res. & agcy.- transferred to N.Y., S44865
Abraham, N.J., S1002
Agnes, former wid. John Ray, N.C., which see
Garrett, N.J., S22778
John, N.J. See VREELAND
John, Privateer, Md., R3773
Joseph, Mass., Judith, W19299
Michael, Pa. See VREELAND
Robert, N.J., N.Y., S2224
William, Mass., S18407
FREELOVE, David, Mass., S13077
FREEMAN, Aaron, N.C., Judith, W8833
Abial, Mass., S17421
Abney, Va., See Dabney
Alden, Mass., Priscilla, R3783
Alexander, N.J., R3775
Andrew, Ct., Elizabeth, W21149
Andrew, Mass., S34883
Artillo (colored), Mass., S44853
Asher, Mass., S34890
Benjamin, ---, Phila. res. & agcy., S9893
Benjamin, Mass., Silvia, W14750
Benjamin, Mass., Hannah, W21159
Benjamin, N.J., S23642
Call, Ct., BLWt.5789-100-Pvt. Iss. 11/26/1792. No papers
Call (colored), Ct., S36513
Caser/Casar (colored), Ct., S43567
Castor, Ct., BLWt.5815-100-Pvt. Iss. 12/20/1797 to Kneeland Townsend. No papers
Cato, Mass., BLWt.4158-100-Pvt. Iss. 4/20/1790. No papers. See O.W.I. file 44849
Charles, R.I., BLWt.3115-100-Pvt. Iss. 6/24/1794 to Brazillai Bowen, ass. No papers
Charles, R.I., S38711
Chatham (colored), Ct., S36524
Coldrup, Va., S37941
Constant, Crane's Art., BLWt. 717-300-Capt. Iss. 7/9/1797 to Constant Freeman. No papers
Cuff, Ct., BLWt.5791-100-Pvt. Iss. 11/2/1791 to Jonathan Tuttle. No papers
Cuff, Ct., S36522
Cuff (colored), Ct., Amelia, W19298
Cuffee/Cuff, Ct., BLWt.5811-100-Pvt. Iss. 4/1/1790. No papers
Cyrus, N.J., S3379
Dabney/Abney, Va., R3778
Dan, N.H., S30427
Daniel, Ct., S45543
Daniel, Mass., Sally, W14751
Daniel, Mass. See FREMAIN
Daniel, N.C., S31681
David, Ct., BLWt.5796-100-Pvt. Iss. 9/23/1791 to Isaac Bronson. No papers
David, Ct., S36511
Devonshire (colored), Ct. Cont.

FREEMAN (continued)
S36519
Doss (colored), Mass., Sarah, W14760; BLWt.1981-100
Edmund, Vt., S18825
Eli, Mass., Vt., Sarah, R3784
Elijah, N.Y., Pernel, W24240; BLWt.27569-160-55
Elisha, Mass., S29806
Elisha, N.Y., S44854
Enoch, Ct., Sarah, W21157
Ezra, N.H., Vt., R3779
Fortune, Mass., BLWt.4189-100-Pvt. Iss. 1/29/1790. No papers
Fortune (colored), Cont., Mass. S43572
Francis, Md., BLWt.11228-100-Pvt. iss. 11/26/1792. No papers
Francis, Md., S35951
Frank, Ct., BLWt.5793-100-Pvt. Iss. 12/24/1796. No papers
Haskell, Mass., S35327
Henry, N.J., S2565
Henry, N.J., Privateer, S875
Howell, N.C., Hannah, W19296; BLWt.51885-160-55
Israel, N.J., R3776
Jack, Ct. See Jack ROWLAND
James, Ct., S36518
James, Ct., S38708
James Paine, Cont., Mass., Deborah, W14749
James, Mass., S34892
Jehiel, N.J., S647
Jeremiah, Art. Pa., BLWt.749-300-Capt. Iss. 5/18/1791 to Alexander Power, ass. No papers
Jethro (colored), Ct., S36520
Job, Mass., Louisa, W21150
Joel, No claim for pension, Indian Wars 1795-1799, Ga. res. in 1853. Reg. No. 43325-50
John, Ct., S36517
John, ---, Ga. res., Catharine, R3777
John, Mass., S18410
John, Mass., S34889
John, Mass., S35330
John, Mass., Lydia, W8834; BLWt. 9065-160-55
John, Mass., Prudence, W23060; BLWts.939-100 & 179-60-55
John, N.J., Sarah Dey, former wid. W848
John, N.C., S1760
John, N.C., Frances, W8832; BLWt. 31424-160-55
John, Va., Phebe, W3798
John, Va., Rebecca, W9437
Jonathan, N.H., Sarah, W3785
Jonathan, N.J., S2221
Joseph, Ct., Cont., S39548; BLWt.1540-100
Joseph, N.J., S648
Juba/Jube, Ct., BLWt.5785-100-Pvt. Iss. 3/30/1790. No papers
Mary, former wid. of John Bliss, Ct., which see
Michael, N.C., S30426
Nathan, Mass., S2566
Nathan, N.C., BLWt.121-100
Obadiah, N.Y., BLWt.7127-100-Pvt. Iss. 8/3/1790 to Cornelius V.

FREEMAN (continued)
Dyck, ass. No papers
Pearson, Cont., Mass., Rebecca, W24246; BLWt.26810-160-55
Peleg, Ct., Privateer, R3782
Peter, Ct., BLWt.5784-100-Pvt. Iss. 10/7/1789 to Benjamin Tallmadge. No papers
Peter, Ct., S36516
Peter, 2nd, (colored), Cont., Ct., R.I., S36521
Philemon, Ct., BLWt.5799-100-Pvt. Iss. 9/24/1790 to Peleg Sanford. No papers
Philemon, Ct., S36523
Philip, N.J. See FREEMEN
Philip/Phillip, Va., S39540
Phoebe, former wid. of London Wallace/Wallis, Ct., which see
Plymouth, Ct., BLWt.5806-100-Pvt. Iss. 5/8/1793. No papers
Plymouth, Ct., S44852
Primas, Ct., BLWt.5802-100-Pvt. Iss. 4/15/1796 to Nathaniel Ruggles. No papers
Prince, Ct., BLWt.5807-100-Pvt. Iss. 5/6/1791. No papers
Prince (colored), Ct., Cont., S39549
Providence, Ct., Azuba, W739; BLWt.31307-160-55
Reuben, Mass., Bethiah, W24238
Richard, Cont., N.Y., Hannah, W19300
Roger, Ct., S43574
Rufus, N.H., S8518
Salisbury, R.I., Rhoda, W8206; BLWt.178-60-55 & 3117-100
Sampson, Navy, Mass., S17419
Samuel, Ct., Jemima, W17926; BLWt.1413-100
Samuel, Cont., Mass. Hannah Bradford, former wid., W24666
Samuel, N.J., S4290
Samuel, N.C., BLWt.190-100
Samuel, S.C., S9336
Samuel, Va., S8529
Sharper, Mass., S34891
Solomon, Mass., N.Y., S8530
Stephen, N.Y., S43573
Stephen, Va., BLWt.2393-100
Thomas, Ct., BLWt.5765-100-Pvt. Iss. 9/7/1795 to Eneas Munson. No papers
Thomas, R.I., Bathsheba, W289; BLWt.34275-160-55
Thomas, Vt., S22251
Thomas D., Mass., BLWt.995-200
Timothy, Mass., Va., Mary Ann, W17923
William, Ct., S13085
William, Ct. See COUCH
William, Cont., Va., S39547
William, N.C., Mary, W10042
William, Va., R3786
FREEMEN, Phillip/Philip, N.J., S2564
FREEMOULT, Robert, Corps of Invalids, BLWt.13099-100-Sgt. Iss. 179? to Eliza Freemoult, admx.

FREEMOYER, David, N.Y., R20137
FREEMYER, John, N.Y. See FRYMIRE
FREER, John J., N.Y., Margaret, W15767
Peter, N.Y., S43566
Solomon, S.C., Elizabeth, W8826; BLWt.31426-160-55
FREES, John, Mass. See FRIEZE
FREESE, Jacob, Mass., Saray, W2606
Martin, Moylan's Dragoons, Pa., BLWt.9403-100-Pvt. Iss. 1/13/1796. No papers
FREETHEY, Joseph, Mass., Elizabeth, W23059; BLWt.34950-160-55. She also applied for B.L. in acct. of services of her son Joseph, War of 1812, rejected. See papers within.
FREEZE, Gordon, N.H., S45542
Jacob, Mass. See FREESE
FREIDLEY, Ludwick, Pa. See FRIDLEY
FRELIGH, Joseph, N.Y., BLWt.732-200
Valentine, N.Y., Marie, W16995
FRENCH, Aaron, Ct., Abigail Dexter, former wid., W22937
Abel, Cont., Ct., S13087
Abner, N.Y., BLWt.730-300-Capt. Iss. 8/30/1790
Adonijah, Mass., Mary, W14754
Anderson, N.J., S31680
Asa, Mass., S5416
Asa, Mass., Mary, W16580
Asa, Mass., Sarah, W24236
Benjamin, N.H., Mary, R3797
Benjamin, Va., Catharine, W7330; BLWt.34815-160-55
Charles, Cont., Mass., Privateer, R3788
Christopher, Mass., S13094
Cromwell/Comewell/Commel/Cummel, Ct., Elizabeth, R3790
Daniel, Mass., Sarah, W24244
Daniel, N.J., S41551
Daniel, Va., Ann, R14291; BLReg. 308673-1855
David, Mass., BLWt.4172-100-Sgt. Iss. 1/18/1800 to Peter Millington. No papers
David, Mass., S43565
David, Mass., N.H., Hannah, W7334; BLWt.11400-160-55
David, N.Y., S13086
Ebenezer, Ct., Mass., N.Y., S13090
Ebenezer, Mass., S43569
Ebenezer, N.H., S15845
Edward, Mass., Mary, W7332; BLWt.12817-160-55
Elijah, Ensign, Mass., Susannah W24234; BLWt.711-150 iss. 12/12/1792 to Daniel King, ass. No papers on BLWt.
Elkanah, Mass., Patience, W7333; BLWt.9528-160-55
Ezekiel, N.H., Phebe, W21158
Francis, Ct., Sylvia, W17925
Gideon, Mass., S29160
Isaac, Mass., Hepzibah, W21153; BLWt.28608-160-55
Jacob, Mass., Esther, W16578
Jacob, Mass., Mary, W24245; BLWt.957-100

FRENCH (continued)
James, Ct., S1200
James, N.J., R3792
James R., Ct., S15844
Jeremiah, N.J., S43570
John, Mass., BLWt.4130-100-Pvt. Iss. 3/16/1795 to Gideon Brockway. No papers
John, Mass., S17422
John, Mass., N.H., Nancy, W23068
John, N.Y., R3794
John, Va., Dolly, R3795
Jonas, Mass., S15125
Jonathan, Ct. Sea Service, S28737
Jonathan, Cont., Mass., S38712
Jonathan, Cont., Mass., Elizabeth, W25609; BLWt.353-60-55
Jonathan, Mass., Elizabeth, W14752
Jonathan, Mass., Mary, W484; BLWt. 36760-160-55
Jonathan, N.Y., S8516
Joseph, Mass., S10707
Joseph, Mass., S18826
Joseph, Mass., Nabby Whiting, former wid., W15475
Joseph, N.H., Polly, W23070
Joseph, N.Y., S9900
Joseph, Va., Judah, W79
Joshua, Mass., S29811
Jotham, Mass., S39550
Lafford/Lifford, S.C., Elizabeth, W7329; BLWt.44514-160-55
Lemuel, Mass., BLWt.4125-100-Pvt. Iss. 5/31/1790 to Theodosius Fowler. No papers
Lemuel, Mass., S39546
Levi, Cont., Ct., BLWt.5826 iss. 1792. Correspondence
Lifford, S.C. See Lafford
Lucretia, former wid. of Wm. Day, Mass., which see
Moses, Cont., Mass., N.H., S22250
Nathan, Mass., Mary, W1846; BLWt. 26606-160-55
Nathaniel, Cont., Mass., S34886
Nathaniel, Cont., Mass., Joanna, W1408
Nathaniel H., Ct., S18827
Nehemiah, Mass., or N.H., Submit, W21147
Nicholas, Mass., Rachel, W16581
Noah, N.J., Joanna, W21151
Obadiah, N.H., S18828
Offen/Orphin, N.H., Susannah, W16579
Orphin, N.H., See Offen
Richard, Va., S35955
Roger, Mass., Achsah, W19297
Samuel, Ct., S16814 (son of John, b. 1753, d.1833)
Samuel, Ct., S36515 (son of Jehiel, d. 1836 or 7)
Samuel, Mass., S29810
Samuel, Mass., Lucy, W21154
Samuel, Mass., R.I., Mary, W24239
Samuel, N.H., Tamson, W21155; BLWt.2378-100
Samuel, N.Y., S29163
Seba, Mass., Mary/Molly, W4201
Silas, Mass., Molly, W14757
Silas, Mass., N.H., S21212

FRENCH (continued)
Silvanus, Mass., Azubah, W24235
Simon, Mass., Betsey, W3539
Tertius, Mass., Juliana, W17922
Thomas, Cont., N.H., Mass., S45541
Thomas, Mass., S18409
Thomas, Mass., N.H., Pa., S18406
Thomas, N.C., S1518
Truman, Ct., BLWt.5780-100-Pvt. Iss. 3/12/1792 to John Blanchard. No papers
Truman, Ct., S36512
William, Cont., Lucy Smith, former wid., W3609; BLWt.1200-100
William, Cont., Mass., S17423
William, Mass., S3377
William, Mass., N.H., Sarah, W24237
William, Pa., S18411
William, Va., S37943
Zenas, Mass., S30424
FRENEAU, Philip, N.J., Pa. Sea Service, Privateer, Eleanor, W23069
FRENISTER, William, N.C. See FEIMSTER
FRERY, Seth, Ct., S29517
FRESH, Stephen, Md., BLWt.11227-100-Pvt. Iss. 6/8/1797 to James DeBaufre, ass. No papers
FRESHOUR, John, Va., Margaret, W7607; BLWt.29046-160-55
FRETTS, Valentine, Va. See FRITTS
FRETWELL, Richard, Va., S16384
FREUTTLE, Jonathan, See FRICKLE
FREY, John, N.Y., S27820
John, Pa., R3801
John, Va., R3819
Peter, Pa., S13083
Philip, Pa., Anna Margaretta, W3079
Philip Martin, S.C., Nancy, W9435
FREYER, Henry, Pa. See FRYER
FREYMIRE, John, N.Y. See FRYMIRE
FRIAR, Abraham, N.Y. See FREAR
FRIATT, Robert, Va., S32558
FRICK, Jacob, N.C., Elizabeth, W23063
FRICKER, Eve, former wid. of John Zweier, Pa., which see
George, Von Heer's Corps, BLWt. 13069-100-Pvt. Iss. 7/3/1795. No papers
Peter, Cont., Pa. & Indian Wars, S41546
Peter, Von Heer's Corps, BLWt. 13065-100-Pvt. Iss. 8/31/1790 to Dudley Woodbridge, ass.
FRICKLAN, Robert, N.J., BLWt. 8298-100-Pvt. Iss. 11/21/1791 No papers
FRIDAY, Conrad/Cownrad, N.Y., S43564
Conradt, N.Y., BLWt.7124-100-Pvt. Iss. 9/20/1790
FRIDENBURG, Elias, See FREEDENBURG
FRIDLE, Jonathan, See TRICKLE
FRIDLEY, Ludwick, Pa., S22248
FRIEDENBURG, Elias, See FREEDENBURG
FRIEDLY, Ludwick, See FRIDLEY
FRIEND, Gabriel, Md., R3805

FRIEND (continued)
Nathaniel, Mass., Mary, W697
FRIERSON, John, S.C., BLWt. 2096-200
FRIES, Peter, Pa., S23640
FRIESS, Martin, Pa. See FREAZE
FRIEZE, John, Mass., Sarah Card, former wid., W22720
FRINK, Amos, R.I., Lydia, W25607; BLWt.165-60-55 & 3120-100
Isaac, Ct., S10705
Jabish/Jabesh/Jabez, Ct., S28736
John, Mass., S32700
Nathan, Ct., Clarissa, W24251
Nathaniel Lothrop, Ct., Rebecca Gilbert, former wid., W25623
Samuel, Mass., S32701; BLWt. 712-150-Ensign. Iss. 5/6/1789 No papers
Thomas, Ct., BLWt.1506-100
Thomas, Mass., S43571
Willard, Mass., Betsey, W19292; BLWt.9044-160-55
FRISBEE, Jonah, Mass., S35956
Joseph, Ct., Diantha, R3806; BLReg. 288492-1855
Sarah, former wid. of Roswell Beebe, N.Y., which see
Thomas, N.Y., Abigail, W4200; BLWt.9435-160-55
FRISBIE, Abraham, Ct., Olive, W3341
Asahel, Ct., S10708
David, Ct., R3807
Ichabod C., Ct., S15842
Israel, Ct., Esther, R3808
Jacob, Ct., Dis. No papers
John, Ct., Rachel, W17921
Jonah, Mass., BLWt.718-200-Lt. Iss. 10/1/1791 to Thaddeaus Frisbie, admr. No papers
Josiah, Ct., Sea Service, S17425
Luman, Ct. Art. Artificers, BLWt.5763 & 13092-100-Pvt. Iss. 2/5/1790. No papers
Luman, Cont., Ohio res. & agcy., W5078
Luther, Cont., Ct., S42731. Sally Frisby/Frisbie, wid of above sold. was pensioned on acct. of service of 1st husb., Elizur/Eleazer Talcott, which see
Noah, Ct., S23227
Philemon, Ct., Rhoda, R3809
Reuben, Ct., S36514
Thadeus, Mass., BLWt.4107-100-Pvt. Iss. 8/22/1789. No papers
FRISBY, Reuben, Ct., BLWt.5792-100-Pvt. Iss. 8/23/1790. No papers
FRISON, Peter, Hazen's Regt., BLWt.13083-100-Pvt. Iss. 8/14/1792 to Benj. Moore, ass. No papers
FRISSELL, John, Ct. See FRIZZLE
FRITH, Valentine, See FRITTS
FRITTER, Moses, Va., S1201
FRITTS, George, N.C., S6864
John, N.C., S10701
Valentine/Volentine, Va., S42732

FRITZ, Balzer, Pa., S22249
FRITZINGER, John, Pa., Catharine, R3800
FRIZEL, Earl, Mass. & some later war, R3811
Nathan, S.C., S3380
FRIZZLE, Elisha, Mass., Dis. No papers
John, Ct., Cont., Martha, W19293; BLWt.11268-160-55
FROENELL, John, Mass. See FURNELL
FROGGET, William, Va., S16383
FROHOCK, Thomas, N.H., Catharine Leavitt, former wid., W24498
FROMLEY, Thomas, Md., BLWt.11224-100-Pvt. Iss. 1/8/179? to Geo. Ponsonby, ass. No papers
FRONABARGER, John, See FRONEBARGER
FRONEBARGER, John, N.C., Barbara, BLWt.86036-160-55
FROST, Aaron/Aron, Cont., Mass., S44857
Amos, Ct., BLWt.5790-100-Pvt. Iss. 8/27/1796 to Joseph Whitton. No papers
And Snow, Va., S7570
Charles, Mass., R3812
Daniel, Mass., Hannah, R3814
David, Mass., Mary, W4957
Elisha, Mass., S29807
Elliot, Mass., S29161
Fredrick/Frederick, Mass., S22253
George Pepperill/Pepperell, Cont. N.H., S44856; BLWt.1616-300
Gideon, Mass., R3813
Ichabod, Mass., S44855
Jacob, Mass., S19670
James, Mass., S33261
James, N.C., Isabella, R3815
John, Mass., S13089
John, Navy, N.H., S35331
John, N.J., Pa.?, Mary, W7324
Joseph, ---, Mass. res. 1795, Dis. No papers
Joseph, Ct., S29164
Joseph, Mass., BLWt.4164-100-Pvt. Iss. 6/12/1797 to Joseph Fosdick. No papers
Joseph, Mass., S39551
Joseph, Va., Anna, W23066
Mark, Mass., Hannah, W24242
Mary, former wid. of Daniel Boton/Boland, Pa. Sea Service, which see
Micajah, Va., S31043
Moses, Mass., Lucy, W23058
Nathaniel, Mass., Sarah, W24248; BLWt.727-100
Nathaniel, Navy, S32699
Nathaniel, N.H., BLWt.2198-100
Oliver, Mass., Sarah Russell, former wid., R9106
Richard, Mass., BLWt.4167-100-Pvt. Iss. 5/8/1792 to Benj. Haskell. No papers
Richard, Mass., Rachel, W13212
Samuel, Cont., Mass., S35953
Samuel, Jr., Mass., BLWt.703-300-Capt. Iss. 10/18/1796 to John Coates, ass. No papers
Solomon, Ct., R3816
Stephen, Navy, N.H., S35328

FROST (continued)
Thomas, N.Y., Abigail, W7323; BLWt.26584-160-55
William, Cont., Mass., Elizabeth, W24250
Winthrop, N.H., Sarah Chesley, former wid., W15995; BLWt. 8005-160-55
Zephaniah/Zepheniah, Mass., S18408
FROTHINGHAM, Benjamin, Mass., BLWt.716-300-Capt. Iss. 12/14/1790. No papers
Ebenezer, Ct., Cont., BLWt. 1229-200
Samuel, Ct., S46253
Thomas, Cont., Mass., Elizabeth, W23065
Thomas, Mass., Sarah Sawyer, former wid., W18999
FRUCHMAN, Elias, See FRUTCHMAN
FRUITS, George, see War of 1812 files. W.O.34228 alleged service in Capt. Kirkwood Pa. Co. Rev. War & Indian Wars 1787, 1790, 1795. Ky. & Pa. Troops & War of 1812. d. 8/6/1876 in the 114th yr. of age
FRUTCHMAN, Elias, Pa., S42045
FRY, Allen, R.I., S10704
Andrew, R.I., S21760
Benjamin, ---, Ga. agcy. Dis. No papers
Benjamin, R.I., Esther Stone, former wid., W25160
Benjamin, R.I. Sea Service, S17426
Benjamin, Va., Ann, R3818
Christopher, N.Y., S10702
Conrad, Cont., Pa., Elizabeth, W3674
Gabriel, Va., S38710
Henry, Cont., Sarah, W3240; BLWt.4191-100-Pvt. in Crane's Art. Iss. 11/1/1791 to Geo. Walton, ass. No papers
Jacob, Cont., Pa., S41547
Joseph, R.I., S21759
Joshua, Va., S37947
Lawrence, Pa., Mary, W1260; BLWt.14971-160-55
Nathan, Ga., S39545
Nicholas, Cont., enl. in Md., Margaret, W1591
Nicholas, N.C., S6859
Peleg, Ct., R.I., Barbara, W17924
Philip, Pa. See FREY
Rhodes, Mass., Joanna, W9434
Rozier, Mass., S44861
William A., Va., S30425
Windsor, R.I., BLWt.3126-100-Pvt. iss. 12/31/1789. No papers
Windsor/Winsor (colored), R.I., S38709
FRYE, Benjamin, Mass., S33260
Ebenezer, N.H., S35329
Frederick, Mass., S44860; BLWt. 708-150-Ensign. Iss. 7/1/1796. No papers
Isaac, N.H., BLWt.695-300-Capt.

FRYE (continued)
Iss. 8/26/1790 to Manassah Cutler, ass. No papers
John, Mass., S32702
John, Mass., R3820
Joshua, Mass., S33259
Lucy, former wid. of Perez Wright, Mass., which see
Nathaniel, Mass., Dolly, W13213; BLWt.707-200-Lt. Iss. 11/13/1789. No papers
Nicholas, Md. See FRY
Peter, Mass., S30423
Richard, Mass., BLWt.4145-100-Pvt. Iss. 3/12/1792 to John Blanchard. No papers
Theophilus, Mass., Lucy, W24249
FRYER, Charles, Lamb's Art., N.Y., BLWt.7140-100-Pvt. Iss. 11/2/1791 to Susannah Fryer, Admx. No papers
Henry, Pa., Anna Maria, R3822
Isaac W., N.Y., R3823
John, Va., S6866
Mercy, former wid. of Daniel True, N.H., which see
FRYMIRE, John, N.Y., R3802
FUCHS, Jacob, Pa., See FOX
FUDGE, Solomon, S.C., Elizabeth, R3824
FUGAT, John, Va., S3369
FUGATE, James, Va., S15846
Jeremiah, Va., S10717
Jonathan, Va. & Indian War 1791, R3925
Randall F./Randal, Va., Eleanor, W1261; BLWt.27636-160-55
FUHR, John C., N.Y., Elizabeth, W7342; BLWt.177-60-55
FULBRIGHT, Jacob, N.C., R3826
FULCHER, Richard, Va., S30428
FULER, John C. See FUHR
FULFORD, James, N.C., Rebecca, W4352
John, ---, Ct. res. Dis. No papers
John, Corps of Invalids, BLWt. 13095-100-Sgt. Iss. 10/30/1789 No papers
Stephen, N.C., Lovisa, W1849
FULFORDS, John, Ct. Dis. No papers
FULHAM, Charles, Md., BLWt.11028-100-Pvt. Iss. 3/22/1791 to Abijah Holbrook, ass. No papers
Charles/Charles B., Md., S42734
George, Md., Dis. No papers
John, Md., BLWt.11223-100-Pvt. Iss. 1/8/179? to Geo. Ponsonby, ass. No papers
FULK, David, Va., S39554
William, Pa. See FOLK
FULKERSON, Caleb, N.J., Deborah, W17935; BLWt.513-160-55
Henry, N.J., S1003
John, N.J., b.1759, d.1834; Catharine, W3078
John, N.J., b.1754, d.1835; Margaret, W8836
Joseph, N.J., Privateer, S42207
William, N.J., S34362
FULKINSON, John, N.J., S8534

FULKISON, John, Va., S1817
FULLAM, Jacob, Mass., S46037
Oliver, Cont., Mass., Betsey, W24252
FULLER, Aaron, Mass., Mary, W2443; BLWt.17857-160-55
Abiah, Mass., Susannah, W25604; BLWt.8189-160-55
Abijah, Ct., Cont., Abigail, W17928
Abraham, Ct., R14329
Abraham, Mass., S21762
Alexander, N.C., S8537
Amasa, Cont., Mass., S22254
Andrew, Mass., BLWt.4173-100-Pvt. Iss. 1/16/1793 to Samuel Emery. No papers
Andrew, Mass., Hannah, W24253
Arthur, N.C., S9337
Asa, Ct., Abigail, W24258
Azariah, Mass., S35957
Bartholomew, Cont., Mass., S21761
Barzillai, Mass., Mary, W24255; BLWt.529-100
Benajah, Ct., Catharine, W4675
Benjamin, Ct., Clarissa, W1746; BLWt.26626-160-55
Benjamin, Ct., Polly, W21163
Benjamin, Mass., S38714
Benjamin, N.H., S18831
Benjamin, N.Y., S13098
Benjamin, N.Y., Mary, W15768; BLWt.14757-160-55
Consider, Mass., Ruth, W4959
Daniel, Ct., Sarah, W19302
Daniel, Cont., Mass., Anna W., W1847; BLWt.6404-160-55
Daniel, Mass., S18830
Daniel, Mass., N.H., S9903
Daniel, N.Y., S22781
Darius, Ct., S22782
David, Ct., Eunice, W17931
David, N.H., War of 1812, Orinda, W17930; BLWt.31209-160-55
David, N.Y., Sarah, W290; BLWt. 9474-160-55
Dayton, Ct., S29166
Diadama, former wid. of John Stewart, Vt., which see
Ebenezer, Ct., Juan Fernandis, W21162
Ebenezer, Mass., S29813
Ebenezer, N.Y., R3829
Edward, Ct., S36528
Edward, Mass., S10711
Eleazer, Ct., S32707
Eleazer, Ct., Mass., Rachel, W14762
Eleazer, Mass., S32703
Eli, Ct., S36527
Eliphalet, Mass., B.L. Rej.
Elisha, Cont., Mass., S10716
Elisha, Navy, Mass., Eleanor, W19303
Elizabeth, former wid. of Sampson Henderson, Va., which see
Elkanah, Mass., Jerusha, W25602; BLWt.13730-160-55. Widow's 1st husb. also served in Rev. War. See claim of Stephen Crane, N.Y.
Enoch, Mass., Lydia, W23072

FULLER (continued)
Enoch, ---, N.H. res., Sarah, R---
Ephraim, Mass., Abigail, W24259
Ezekiel, Cont., Mass., Mary, W14763
Ezra, Ct., Cont., S36526
George, N.C., S38715
Gershom, N.Y., S13106
Ichabod, Mass., Martha, R3838
Ignatius, Mass., R3830; BLWt. 11182-160-55
Isaac, Ct., Mass., Elizabeth, W11029; BLWt.24155-160-55
Isaac, Mass., S36529
Isaac, N.Y., S8536
Isaiah, Cont., Mass., S32706
Israel, Ct., See Tuller
Jacob, Mass., Sarah Goodale, former wid., R4102
James, Ct., Cont., S36525
James, Invalid Corps, BLWt. 13103-100-Pvt. Iss. 9/11/1792. No papers
James, Mass., Ct. res. at enl., S2226
James, Mass., S23646
James, Mass., S29812
Jason, Mass., Catharine, W24256
Job, Mass., R3832
John, Ct., S13115
John, Ct., S31684
John, Ct., Wealthy, W17929
John, Ct., R3834
John, Ct., Cont., S43580
John, Cont., Mass., S32704
John, Cont., Mass., S43578
John, Mass., BLWt.4176-100-Pvt. Iss. 1/5/1791. No papers
John, Mass., S39556; BLWt.702-300-Capt. Iss. 8/10/1789 to Richard Platt, ass. No papers
John, N.H., Betsey, W16999
John, R.I., Chloe, W24261
John, S.C., Braddock's Expedition, R3835
John, Vt., S16122
Johnson, Privateer, R.I., R3836
Jonathan, Ct., N.H., S36530
Jonathan, Mass., S29815
Jonathan, Mass., Annah/Anna, W24257
Jonathan, N.Y., S10713
Joseph, Cont., Mass., Phebe, W25600; BLWts.905-100 & 98564-160-55
Joseph, Mass., BLWt.4140-100-Pvt. Iss. 4/12/1790 to Stephen Thomas. No papers
Joseph, Mass., S29814
Joseph, Mass., S42206
Joseph, Mass., Vt., Eunice, W14767
Joseph, Va., S41555
Joshua, Ct., S43579
Josiah, Ct., S16815
Josiah, Cont., Mass., S32705
Josiah, Cont., Mass., S43576
Josiah, Mass., S32708
Josiah, Mass., Eleanor, W13225
Lemuel, Ct., Cont., Polly, W648; BLWt.26490-160-55
Lemuel, Mass., BLWt.4157-100-Pvt.

FULLER (continued)
Iss. 4/1/1790. No papers
Littleton, N.C., S31683
Lot, Mass., S13109
Luther, Ct., Mass., R3837
Mary, former wid. of: 1st, Josiah Fuller; 2nd, Robert Simpson, N.Y. which see
Matthias, Pa. Sea Service, R3839
Meshack/Meshac, Ga., Bethany, W4958
Nathan, Ct., S17427
Nathan, Ct., Hannah, W19301
Nathan, Mass., S32709
Nathaniel, Crane's Cont. Art., Mass., BLWt.4192-100-Sgt. Iss. 12/7/1789. No papers
Nathaniel, Mass., Hannah, W24262; BLWt.15159-160-55
Noah, Ct., Lucy, W23073
Noah, Mass., S13100
Noah, Navy, Mass. res. & agcy., Jerusha, W14764
Peter, Mass., S13103
Peter, N.Y., BLWt.7138-100-Pvt. Iss. 2/21/1792 to Moses Fuller, ass. No papers
Robert, Mass., S35322; BLWt.530-100
Rufus, Mass., Hannah, W16262
Samuel, Ct., Lydia, W17932
Samuel, Ct., Mary, W25603
Samuel, Cont., Ct., N.H., S44869
Samuel, Mass., S22780
Samuel, Mass., BLWt.828-100
Samuel, N.H., Polly, W1848
Seth, Cont., Mass., S39555
Shubael, Ct., R3841
Simeon, Mass., BLWt.4135-100-Pvt. Iss. 9/10/1789 to Henry Newman. No papers
Simeon, Mass., S13107
Stephen, Ga., S37949
Stephen, Mass., S20766. Res. Walpole at enl. N.H. agcy.
Stephen, Mass., S29165. Enl. at Munson, Mass. In 1832 was at Brimfield, Mass.
Stephen, Mass., S43577
Stephen, Lydia, W24254
Thaddeus, Mass., S42205
Theodore, N.H., S17967
Thomas, Cont., Mass., S39553
Thomas, N.H., BLWt.3099-100-Pvt. Iss. 1/28/1790 to James Patterson, ass. No papers
Thomas, N.H., S45544
Timothy, Ct., Hannah Hayes/Hays former wid., W17974. Her 2nd husb., Benj. Hays/Hayes also served. See papers within
Titus, Mass., Christiana Jonah, former wid., W21501
Varsell, N.Y., Mary, W15769
William, Cont., Mass., R.I., S42733
William, Mass., Lucy, W17933
Witt, Mass., Deborah, R3827
FULLERTON, Arunah, Mass., Lillis Hackett, former wid., W19702
Benjamin, N.C., See TUTTERTON

FULLERTON (continued)
James, N.H., S13099
John, Cont., Mass. Sea Service, Sarah, W24263
John, Pa., S10714
Richard, Pa., BLWt.747-200-Lt. Iss. 8/19/1789. No papers
Samuel, Mass., Persis, R3842
Thomas, Pa., Hannah, W3408
FULLILOVE, Anthony, Va., S31045
FULLINGTON, Arunah, Mass. See FULLERTON
Ezekiel, Cont., N.H., Jane, W24260
Mary, former wid. of Jonathan Bean, N.H., which see
FULLOM, Oliver. See FULLAM
FULLONTON, Ezekiel, See FULLINGTON
FULLTON, James B. See FULTON
FULLUM, Oliver, See FULLAM
FULLWOOD, William, S.C., S18829
FULMER, Casper, Armand's Corp.,BLWt 13060-100. Iss. 3/10/1791. No papers
Casper, Cont., Pa., Mary, W4676
George, N.Y., BLWt.7133-100-Pvt. Iss. 4/21/1791 to Hendrick Kyser, ass. No papers
Jacob, N.Y., Margaret, R3844
Jacob, S.C., Elizabeth, W7343; BLWt.34818-160-55
John, Cont., Pa., War of 1812, Mary, R3845
FULMORE, Joseph, Pa., S10667
FULNER, Jacob, S.C. See FULMER
FULP, Michael, N.C., Phebe, W10043
Peter, N.C., Elizabeth, W5278
FULPER, William, N.J., S34361
FULTON, Andrew, Va., (?), Elizabeth, R3848
David, N.C., S8539
James, Pa., S22779
James, Va., R3849
James B., Md., Anastasia, W8835
Jesse, Pa., S23645
John, N.Y., BLWt.7120-100-Pvt. Iss. 9/15/1790 to Wm. Bell, ass. No papers
Robert, Crane's Cont. Art., Mass., BLWt.4197-100-Sgt. Iss. 1/26/1790 to John May. No papers
Robert, Va., S8532
Samuel, Pa., Catharine, W2783
Samuel, Pa., R3850
Thomas, Va., R3851 & R14317
FULTZ, Conrad, N.Y. See FOLTS
Frederick, ---, Res. Chester Co., Pa. Dis. No papers
Joshua, Va. See FOLTZ
FUND, Nicholas, Hazen's Regt., BLWt.13081-100-Pvt. Iss. 3/1/1792. No papers
FUNDERBUCK, John, S.C., b. N.C., S31682
FUNK, George, Md., S41553
Henry, Va., Elizabeth, W23075
Martin, Pa., S8533
FUQUA, Joseph, Va., Celia, W7345
FURBECK, John, Cont., Ct., S13108
FURBEE, Caleb, Del., Mary, W740; BLWt.26096-160-55
FURBEN, Thomas, N.H. See FURBER
FURBER, Joshua, N.H., Betsey,W17934
Mary, former wid. of Pierce Powers Navy, N.H., which see
Richard, N.H., S10712
Thomas, N.H., Elizabeth, W23071
FURBISH, Benjamin, See FURBUSH
William, Va. See FERBUSH
FURBUSH, Aaron, Mass., Katherine, W14765
Benjamin, N.H., Lydia, W23074; BLWt.12559-160-55
Simeon, Mass., Rachel, W17895
William, Va. See FORBES
FURGASON, Andrew, Va. See FERGUSON
James, N.C., S1816
Robert, Va. See FERGUSON
FURGESON, Lotty, former wid. of Benj. Scott, Md., which see
Samuel, Ct., S29151
FURGURSON, Isaac, Va., Nancy, R3506
FURGUS, John, See FERGUS
FURGUSON, Abraham, N.Y. See FORGASON
George, Va., R3502
John, Md. See FERGUSSON
John, Mass., N.H. See FERGUSON
John, alias John WILSON, Mass., N.H., Mary, W25575; BLWt.14528-160-55
John, Pa., BLWt.14032-100-Pvt. Iss. 3/3/1792 to Jane Furguson, Admx. No papers
Thomas, See FERGUSON
William, See FERGUSON
FURGUSSON, William, Col. Proctor's 4th Reg. of Art., BLWt.748-300-Capt. Iss. 6/4/1789. No papers
FURMAN, Abraham, Cont., N.Y., S10715
Benjamin, N.J., R3854
John, N.Y., BLWt.731-200-Lt. Iss. 6/9/1791. No papers
Joshua, N.J., Sarah, W543; BLWt. 26640-160-55
Nathan, N.J., S2544
Nathan, N.Y., Jemima, R3855
Nowell, N.Y., S18412
FURNALD, Amos, N.H., S8538
Nicholas, Mass. See FERNALD
FURNELL, John, Mass., S41554
FURNESS, Emanuel, R.I., BLWt. 3129-100-Pvt. Iss. 8/19/1791 to Mary Furness, Admx. No papers
William, Cont., Mass. See FURNISS
William, Navy, Sea Service, D.C. Agcy. & res., S35958
FURNICE, Anthony, Mass., Sea Service, Privateer, Sarah, W21161
FURNISH, James, Va., Nancy, W7341; BLWt.26291-160-55
Thomas, Cont., Va., S13105
FURNISS, Benjamin, Cont., Mass., S13102
William, Cont., Mass., Sybel/Sybil, W10045; BLWt.26033-160-55
FURR, Enoch, Va., Sarah, W11030
Henry, N.C. See FURRER
FURRAR, John, Mass. See FARRAR
FURRER, Henry, N.C., Catharine,
FURRER (continued)
W1262; BLWt.26033-160-55
FURRONER, Edward, Md., BLWt.11229-100-Pvt. Iss. 7/9/1799. No papers
FURTOR, David, N.J., BLWt.8321-100-Pvt. Iss. 6/11/1789 to Jonathan Dayton, ass. No papers
FUSON, William, Va., S4291
FUSSELL, William, Ga., N.C., S31046
FYLER, John, Ct., Asenath, W2379; BLWt.26014-160-55
John, Ct., Ruth, W17936
FYSEL, William, Ga., N.C. See FUSSELL

G

GABBARD, Jacob, N.C., S30431
GABBERT, George, N.C., S31047
Michael, Va., S13123
GABEAU, Anthony, S.C., Elizabeth, W21170
GABEL, Joseph, W., Pa., S31052
GABHART, George, N.C., S31047
GABLE, Henry, Pa., BLWt.9501-100-Pvt. Iss. 9/20/1791. No papers
Joseph W., Pa., S31052
Peter, Pa., BLWt.9432-100-Pvt. Iss. 6/13/1792 to George Gilbert, admr. No papers
GABRIEL, James, N.C., S2571
GABY, George, Mass., S39564
GADCOMB, William, R.I., Amey Aldis, former wid., W15517; BLWt.36629-160-55
GADD, Thomas, Md., BLWt.11260-100-Pvt. Iss. 5/1/1792. No papers
Thomas, Md., S25549
Thomas, Md., S31050
William, Pa., S2231
GADDE/GADDY, Joseph, Va., Peggy, W8209; BLWt.2494-160-55
GADDIS, Henry, Va., S23652
Thomas, Pa., Va., S4292
GADDY, Bartholomew, Va., Martha, W7494; BLWt.31465-160-55
Joseph, Va. See GADDE
GADSDEN, Thomas, S.C., BLWt. 288-300
GAFF, James, R.I., S17432
GAFFETT, John, N.H., BLWt.3130-100-Fifer, Iss. 11/10/1789. No papers
GAFFIT, John, Fifer, N.H., Catharine, W11264; BLWt.3130
GAFFORD, Joseph, Va., Mary, W7505
GAGE, Aaron, Ga., S2229
Abel, Cont., N.H., S45548
Abijah, Mass., S29169
Alden, N.Y., Hannah, W21172
Amos, Cont., N.H., Mass., Privateer, Lois, W24271
Anthony, Mass., Sally, BLWt. 101744-160-55
Asa, Cont., Mass., Mary, W19489 BLWt.31907-160-55
Daniel, N.H., BLWt.3138-100-Sgt. Iss. 12/6/1799 to James Manuel, ass. No papers
Daniel, N.H., S31048
David, Mass., S23229
David, N.H., Elizabeth, W14777
Dolly, former wid. of Jacob Russell, N.H., which see
Ebenezer, Mass., S32712
George, Vt., R3858
Isaac, Cont., Mass., BLWt.2237-200
James, N.C., S32262
John, Cont., N.H., S29820
John, Mass., Mary, W1747; BLWt. 6260-160-55
John, N.H., paid to son John, W16019
John, N.J., S15582
John, N.Y., BLWt.7186-100-Pvt.

GAGE (continued)
Iss. 11/27/1790 to Thomas Sears, ass. No papers
Jonathan, Cont., Mass., S13114
Jonathan, Mass., S32713
Moses, Ct., R3861
Nathaniel, Mass., N.Y., S13117
Phineas, Cont., Mass., N.H., S10757
Reuben, Mass., S3387
Thaddeus, Ct., Judith, R3860
Thadeus/Thaddeus, Mass., S16820
William, Mass., Rhoda, W14775
Zenas, Mass., S32714
GAGER, Samuel R., Ct., Lucretia, W7493; BLWt.26045-160-55
GAILER, William, Navy, N.Y., S15130
GAINE, William, ---, Mass. res. Dis. No papers
GAINER, Edward, N.Y., R3862
Hugh, Md., BLWt.11274-100-Pvt. Iss. 2/7/1790. No papers
GAINES, Ambrose, Va., Mary, W224
Henry, Va., Catherine/Kayty, R3864
James, Mass., BLWt.4206-100-Pvt. Iss. 2/11/1797 to Calvin Sanger No papers
James, Mass., S39563
James, Va., Carey, W25652; BLWt. 28548-160-55
Josiah, Mass. See GAINS
Levi, S.C., R3865
Richard, Va., S8546
Richard, Va., R3866
Robert, Va., Ann, R3863
Thomas, Va., S38721
Thomas, Va., Catharine L., W11048; BLWt.26505-160-55
William, Va., S31687
William Fleming, Va., BLWt.880-300 -Capt. Iss. 2/13/1800 to John Marshall. No papers
GAINS, Henry, Va., Catherine, R3864
Josiah, Mass., Jane, W13239; BLWt.91558-160-55
Jude, Ct., Anner, W17004
William, Mass. See GAINE
GAITER, Henry, Pa., BLWt.9492-100-Pvt. in Art. Iss. 12/27/1789 to Richard Platt, ass. No papers
GAITHER, Benjamin, Md., BLWt.2290-100
Greenberry, Md., Anna, W8840
Henry, Md., BLWt.854-300-Capt. Iss. 4/4/1792. No papers
GAITSKILL, Henry, Pvt., Va., BLRej. 230096-1855
William, Mass., S35338
GALBRAITH, Alexander, Pa., S41558
GALBRATH, James, ---, Pa. agcy., S----. No papers
GALBREATH, Alexander, Pa., BLWt. 9474-100-Drummer. Iss. 7/16/1789. No papers
Josiah, Pa., BLWt.9440-100-Corp. Iss. 6/20/1789. No papers
William, Pa., Va., Phebe, W23093
GALE, Abraham, Mass., Abigail, R3867
Asa, N.H., S22256

GALE (continued)
Bethia, former wid. of Josiah Locke, N.H., which see
Betty, former wid. of Edward Newton, Mass., which see
Daniel, Mass., Esther, W14768
Daniel, Mass., N.H., S18414
Daniel, N.H., Rhoda, W16264
Edmund, Mass., BLWt.4213-100-Sgt. Iss. 12/23/1796. No papers
Edmund, Mass., S32723
Eli, Vt., S18835
Henry, Mass., S44873
Henry, Mass., R3869
Jesse, Mass., BLWt.4297-100-Pvt. Iss. 12/9/1799 to Enoch Gale, Levi Gale, Lucretia Gale, Joel Fairbanks & Mary Fairbanks, heirs of Jesse. No papers
John, Md., BLWt.422-300
John Carte, N.H., Huldah, W16265
Jonathan, Mass., Susanna, W649; BLWt.58693-160-55
Jonathan, Mass., R3870
Joseph, N.J., BLWt.8359-100-Pvt. Iss. 7/11/1791. No papers
Joseph, N.J., S34370
Joseph, N.J., Hannah, S34895, R---
Matthias, Va., Joice, W7491
Paul, Mass., S39562
Richard, N.Y., S16816
Robert F., Va., S31053
Samuel, Mass., Sea Service, Martha, W14770
GALL, George, Va., S2569
Jack, N.Y., BLWt.7163-100-Pvt. Iss. 7/10/1790 to John Quackinboss, ass. No papers
GALLAGHER, Daniel, Pa., BLWt. 9473-100-Pvt. iss. 1/30/1792. No papers
Emeline, former wid. of Ephraim Blood, N.H., which see
Francis, See GALLAHER
John, Md., See GALLEGHER
GALLHER, Ebenezer, N.J., Mary, W7508
Francis, ---, Pa. agcy. & res., S10170
GALLAMORE, John, N.C., & Cont., Rachel, W10051; BLWt.61149-160-55
GALLASPEE, William, N.Y., BLWt. 7181-100-Sgt. Iss. 7/16/1790 to Wm. J. Vreedenburgh, ass. No papers
GALLAWAY, Benjamin, Va., S39559
Terry, Va., Nancy, W4202
GALLEGHER, John, Md., S39561
GALLENDIN, Jacob, Pa., S23653
GALLEY, Elizabeth, former wid. of Daniel G. Rogers, N.Y., which see
Peter, Pa., BLWt.2447-100
GALLIGER, Abraham, N.J., BLWt. 8351-100-Pvt. Iss. 6/11/1789 to Jonathan Dayton, ass. No papers
GALLIMORE, Abraham, Va., Sarah, R3875
GALLION, Gilbert, Md., R3876
GALLOP, Enos, Mass., S29818
Isaac, N.C., S41560
John, Ct., S10721

GALLOP (continued)
Nathaniel, R.I., Vt., R3879
William, Mass., S27842
GALLOWAY, Benjamin, Va. See GALLAWAY
James, Cont., Pa., Jane, W8841
James, Pa., Va., S2232
John, Va., Elizabeth, W9448
John, Va., R3877
Marshall, Md., S38718
Peter, Ct., BLWt.6284-100-Pvt. Iss. 6/14/1790. No papers
Peter, S.C., R3878
GALLUCIA, Daniel, Mass. See GALLUSHIA
GALLUP, Amos, Ct., S13116
Andrew, Ct., S17430
Benadam, Ct., Mary, BLWt.24441-160-55
Ezra, Ct., S29168
George, Ct., Freelove Kinne, former wid., W21532
Isaac, Ct., Cont., Anna Williams, former wid., W26032
Joseph, Ct., S15137
Joseph, Cont., R.I., Rachel, W741
Levi, Ct., S8544
Nehemiah, Ct., S13110, Mary Gallup, wid. of soldier was pensioned as former wid. of Peter Brown, which see (Ct.)
Prudence, former wid. of Phinehas Killam, Green Mt. Boys, Vt., which see
Robert, Ct., S23651; BLWt.28531-160-55
Rufus, Mass., S13118
William, Ct., S15581
GALLUSHA, Daniel, Mass. See GALUSHIA
GALPIN, Abel, Mass., S31685
Amos, Ct., Cont., S13129
Daniel, Cont., Ct., S13113; BLWt.253-100
Jehiel, Ct., Lucy, Morgan, former wid., W17161
Samuel, Ct., S15132
GALT, John Minson, Va., R14353; Va. Half Pay, N.A.Acc. No. 874. See 05070
GALUSHA, Abiram, Ct., S43583. See claim of Joseph GREGORY, R4300
Jacob, Ct., Dinah, W24270
Samuel, N.H., Vt., S44155
Sarah, former wid. of Joseph Gregory, Mass., which see
Thomas, Ct., Mass., Vt.,S23648
GALUSHIA, Daniel, Mass., Elizabeth, W4961; BLWt.19830-160-55
GALVIN, John, Pa., Proctor's Art., BLWt.9505-100-Pvt. Iss. 6/29/1789 to M. McConnell, ass. No papers
GALWAY, Robert, Cont., Pa. agcy. & res., S41559
GALWORTH, Gabriel, Md., S8549
GAMAGE, Joshua, Mass., Hannah, R3882; BLWt.45595-160-55
Samuel, Mass., Navy, Polly/Mary, W16266
William, N.C., Charity, R3883
GAMBEE, John, Pa., R3884
GAMBEL, John, Mass., S22255
Joseph, Mass., S44156; BLWt. 335-100
GAMBELL, James, N.Y., S16125
GAMBER, John, Pa., S22787
GAMBERTON, Charles, N.J., Mary, W21173
GAMBILL, Martin, N.C. See GAMBRILL
Thomas, Va. See GAMBLE
GAMBLE, Abraham, Md., BLWt. 2341-100
Archibald, N.H., Abigail, W8210; BLWt.31905-160-55
David, Va., Pa., 1774, S32264
George, Mass., BLWt.839-100
George, Pa., Va., S10720
James, N.Y., See GAMBELL
James, Pa., Art., BLWt.841-200-Lt. Iss. 5/27/1791 to James Gamble. No papers
Jehu, S.C., BLWts.12173 & 13119-100-Pvt. Iss. 6/24/1795. No papers
Robert, Pvt., S.C., BLWts.12172 & 13118 iss. 6/24/1795
Robert, Va., BLWt.869-300-Capt. Iss. 9/18/1789. No papers
Samuel, Pa., R3886
Thomas, Va., S38717
William, N.J., S10722
GAMBLIN, Joshua, N.C., Mary, W11039; BLWt.34984-160-55
GAMBLING, James, N.C., Mary, W460
GAMBRILL, Martin, N.C., Nancy, W7504; BLWt.24169-160-55
GAME, Jacob, Md., BLWt.11268-100-Pvt. Iss. 7/9/1799. No papers
GAMEL, James, Cont., N.Y., Nancy, W19491
GAMELL, William, Mass. See GARNELL
GAMMAGE, Joshua, See GAMAGE
William, N.C. See GAMAGE
GAMMAR, Joseph, Cont., France, R4183; Tenn. res. in 1833
GAMMELL, William, See GARNELL
GAMMON, Benjamin, Mass., S32716
David, Mass., S20372
Harris, Va., S3389
Jesse, N.C., Sarah, W1 (evidently 1st wid. pension)
Joseph, Mass., S29822
Joshua, Mass., S29819
Moses, Mass., S28738
Samuel, Mass., Susanna, W23085
Susanna, former wid. of Tobias Ricker, N.H., which see
GAMMONS, John, Mass., S32719
GAMMUT, Paul, R.I., Vt., S15133
GAMWELL, James, Mass., Polly, W11263; BLWt.175-60-55
GAN, Nathan, N.C., Va., S1820; BLWt.50893-160-55
GANAWAY, Robert, Va. See GANNAWAY
GANDEE, Uriah, Cont., Pa., R3890
GANDER, Jacob, Pa., S2570
GANDY, Brinkley, N.C., R4185
David, N.J., S1004
Enoch, N.J., Rachel, W4963; BLWt.27667-160-55
Uriah, Pa. See GANDEE
GANES, Henry, Va. See GAINES
GANEY, William, N.C., S6880
GANGWER, Andrew, Pa., S22258
George, Pa., S23654
GANGWOIR, George, Pa. See GANGWER
GANN, Nathan, N.C., See GAN
Samuel, N.C., S9664
Thomas, N.C., S3388
GANNAWAY, Gregory, Va., R3893
Robert, Va., Lucy, W5082
GANNETT, Deborah, alias Robert Shurtleff, Mass., S32722
Joseph, Mass., S28739
GANNON, Joseph, Pa., R3895
William, N.J., N.Y., S49299
William, N.C., b. Ireland, S32259
GANO, Daniel, Cont., N.Y., Jemima, W4962; BLWt.53678-160-55
GANONG, Reuben, N.Y., Elizabeth, W21177
GANOUNG, Moses, See GENUNG
Reuben, N.Y. See GANONG
GANSEVOORT, Leonard, N.Y., R3898
Peter, N.Y., BLWt.824-500-Col. Iss. 9/27/1790. No papers
GANSEY, Seth, Ct., S39565; BLWt. 897-100
GANSON, Nathan, Mass., Rebecca, W17937
GANTT, Erasmus, Md., S10727
GAPEN, Stephen, Pa., S8545
GARABRANT, Garabrant N., N.J., Elizabeth, W852
GARBER, Christian, Pa., Anna, R3899
GARBERICH, John, Pa., See N.A. Acc. No. 874-050071, Not Half Pay. No pension file found for him in Rev. War files. See Old War Inv. File 10164, John Garberick, Pvt., Capt. Frazier 3rd U.S. Art., res. in 1827 was Dauphin Co., Pa.
GARD, Daniel, N.J., Hannah, W420; BLWt.8340-100-Pvt.
GARDEN, Alexander, Cont., S.C., BLWt.1825-200
Andrew, N.Y., S41564
GARDENER, Elijah, Mass. See GARDNER
GARDENIER, Andrew, N.Y. See GARDNER
Gilbert, N.Y., Catharine, W23092
John, Ct., N.Y., R3903
Samuel, ---, N.Y. res. S----. No papers
GARDINEAR, Andries. See GARDNER
GARDINEER, John, N.Y., R3900
GARDINEIR, Jacob, N.Y., S47145
GARDINER, Amos, R.I., Abigail, W13240
Benjamin, Mass. See GARDNER
Benjamin, R.I., S21766
Benoni, N.Y., S44153
Elizabeth, former wid. of Ezekiel Tinker, Ct., which see
Charles, Mass. See GARDNER
Christopher, R.I., See GARDNER
David, Ct. See GARDNER
Elizabeth, Ct. See Ezekiel TINKER

GARDINER (continued)
Gideon, R.I. See
Jacob, Mass., BLWt.4224-100-Pvt. Iss. 12/22/1792 to John Peck. No papers
James, N.J. See GARNER
John, Navy, N.Y., S3386
John, N.J. See Jane TRAPP, former wid.
John, R.I., S21215
Nicholas, N.Y., Rachel, W17002
Phebe, former wid. of Joel Beers, which see
Richard, R.I. See GARDNER
Sherman, Ct. See GARDNER
Silas, R.I., See GARDNER
William, R.I. See GARDNER
GARDINIER, Abraham, N.Y., S29171
Gilbert, N.Y. See GARDENIER
John, Ct., N.Y. See GARDENIER
Nicholas, N.Y., Rachael, R3904 (not same as Nicholas Gardiner)
GARDNER, Abel, Mass., Mary, W7501; BLWt.6257-160-55
Abiel, R.I., S13183
Abijah, Ct., BLWt.5843-100-Pvt. Iss. 3/14/1793. No papers
Abijah, Ct., S44154
Andrew, Mass., S18413
Andris, N.Y., BLWt.7161-100-Pvt. Iss. 7/30/1790 to Edward Cumpston, ass. No papers
Andrew/Andris, N.Y., S44152
Anna, former wid. of John Howe, Vt., which see
Benjamin, Mass., Sarah, W14771
Benjamin, N.Y., Lucy, R3911
Benjamin, R.I., S21765
Benjamin, R.I. See GARDINER
Benoni, N.Y., BLWt.7203-100-Pvt. Iss. 2/14/1791 to Elisha Evans, ass. No papers
Benoni, N.Y. See GARDINER
Caleb, Mass., S32710
Caleb, Mass., Mary, W7497
Carswell, Cont., Mass., Elizabeth, W1409
Charles, Mass., BLWts.4204 & 4363-100-Pvt. Iss. 7/3/1795 to Edward Stowe. No papers
Charles, Mass., S35339
Christopher, Del., R3907
Christopher, N.H., S15580
Christopher, R.I., Elizabeth, W17938
Cornelius, N.J., S34366
David, Ct., Surrender Cert. 1002. He d. 6/22/1821
David, Ct., Fanny, W1850; BLWt.31909-160-55. He d. 1/11/1835
David, Mass., Elizabeth, W14774
David/Henry, Mass. Sea Service, Navy, Privateer, Lovina, W24272
Elias, N.C., S6875
Elijah, Mass., S35334
Elijah, Mass., S44157

GARDNER (continued)
Ezekiel, Cont., Mass., Betsey, W17001
Francis W., R.I., Waity, W23087
George, Va., S2228
George Utter, R.I., BL rejected. His son, Sharper Utter Gardner. See also BLWt.619-100
Gideon, R.I., S10747
Gilbert, N.Y., BLWt.7180-100-Pvt. Iss. 10/12/1790 to Stephen Hogeboom, ass. No papers
Henry/David, Mass. See David GARDNER
Isaac, Ct., Esther, W7499; BLWt. 26788-160-55
Isaac, Mass., Sarah, W24267
Isaac, Mass., Mary, W21165; BLWt. 986-100
Jack/John Slade, Mass., Mary, W1593
Jacob, Mass., Deborah, W14769
James, Cont. Art., parents of N.Y., after Rev. War lived N.C., BLWt.668-200
James, N.J., Elizabeth, W267
James, N.J., N.Y., R3909
James, N.C., R3908
James, Pa., S41561
James, R.I., Mary, W742; BLWt. 26090-160-55
James, R.I., Abigail, W21174
Jesse, N.Y., BLWt.7164-100-Pvt. No papers
Jesse, N.Y., Martha, W3409
John, Cont., Mass., Navy, S36531
John, Md., S35963
John, N.J., S22261
John, N.J., Jane Trapp, former wid., W2278; BLWt.3767-160-55
John, N.J., Elizabeth, W23091
John, N.C., R20372
John, N.C., S.C., S6877
John, Pa., S31686
John, R.I., S21215
John, Va., pensioned in Mass., Cynthia, W7498; BLWt.36754-160-55
Jonathan, Ct., S17429
Jonathan, Mass., S44150
Jonathan, Mass., Sarah, W23086
Joseph, N.J., Sarah, W246; BLWt. 61218-160-55
Josiah, Mass., S13126
Jotham, N.J., S31051
Nathan, R.I., S28740
Nathaniel B., N.Y., S15131
Peregrine, Sappers & Miners, BLWt.13114-100-Pvt. Iss. 7/18/1791. No papers
Perez, Mass., Silence, W14776
Phebe, Ct., former wid of Joel Beers, which see
Richard, R.I., S10728
Samuel, Mass., Nabby, W14772
Samuel, N.Y., BLWt.7174-100-Pvt. Iss. 7/30/1790 to Edward Cumpston, ass. No papers
Samuel, N.Y., S35336
Samuel, S.C., See GARNER
Sarah Ann, former wid. of Benoni Hall, R.I., which see

GARDNER (continued)
Seth, Mass., Eunice, W21169
Sharper Utter (colored), R.I., BLWt.619-100
Sherman, Ct., S5176
Silas, R.I., S10724
Stephen C., R.I., R3912
Thomas, Ct., Esther, W16020
Thomas, Cont., N.J., Phebe, W7500; BLWt.31-60-55
Thomas, Mass., BLWt.4271-100-Sgt. Iss. 5/24/1790. No papers
Thomas, Mass., Sally, W21164
Thomas, Va., S8548
Townsend S./Townshend S., Mass., Thankful, W19490
William, Ct., BLWt.5859-100-Pvt. Iss. 10/1/1789. No papers
William, Ct., Margaret, W1750; BLWt.8387-160-55
William, Ct., Hannah, W25618
William, R.I., S23649
William, R.I., Abigail, W21176
GAREE, Christopher, Crane's Cont. Art., Mass., BLWt.4282-100-Pvt. Iss. 8/19/1786 to Peter Lott. No papers
GARET, Henry, Pa. See GEHRET
GARETT, John, N.Y. See GARRETT
GAREY, Benjamin, Mass., Sally, W19481
Gilbert, Ct., Nancy/Anna, R3961
Seth, Mass., S43582
William, N.J., S2574
GARFIELD, Jesse, Mass., S43586
John, Mass., S29167
Joseph, Mass., S18834
Nathaniel, Mass., Eunice, W19487; BLWt.13866-160-55
Reuben, Mass., S32718
Samuel, Mass., S16385
Thaddeus, Mass., Mary, W24269
GARGIS, Job, N.C., S8547
GARIS, Valentine, Pa., Charlotte, R3913
GARLAND, Christopher, Va., Mary, R3915; BLWt.41932-160-55
Edward, Va., Sarah, W7506
Elisha, N.C., Lucy, W926
George, Lamb's Art., N.Y.,BLWt. 7200-100-Pvt. Iss. 10/12/1790. No papers.
Gideon, N.H., Polly Berry, former wid., W21664
Henry, N.C., R3914
Humphrey, N.C., S38716
Jacob, Cont., N.H., Abigail, W24273
James, Cont., N.H., Mehitable, W26202
John, N.H., See GARLIN
John, N.H., Mary, W16119
John, N.C., Susannah, W3011 BLWt.17897-160-55
Moses, Mass., S17969
Peter, Va., BLWt.524-300
Richard, N.H., S17970
Thomas, Navy, N.H., Hannah, W15901
GARLIN, John, N.H., S45549
GARLINGHOUSE, Benjamin, N.J., BLWt.8331-100-Pvt. Iss.

GARLINGHOUSE (continued)
1/5/1792. No papers
Benjamin, N.J., S44879
GARLINGTON, Christopher, S.C., Va., S6874
GARLOCH, Adam, See GARLOUGH
GARLOCK, Adam, See GARLOUGH
Adam, N.Y., R3917
Jacob, N.Y., S13119
GARLOUGH, Adam, N.Y., S23228
GARMAN, William, Pa., S10178
GARNAR, Thomas, Pa., See GARNEAR
GARNEAR, Thomas, Cont., Pa., S34368
GARNELL, William, Mass., S17431
GARNER, Andrew, N.Y., S15127
Charles, Va., S37950
Henry, N.C., R3919
James, Md., N.Y., S34363
James, Va., Lucy, W7495
John, Cont., Va., S39557
John, Cont., Va., Matilda, W8208 & S25099
John, Va., Lee's Legion, BLWt. 12148-100-Pvt. Iss. 4/13/1791 to James Reynolds, ass. No papers
John F., N.C., S1821
Joseph, Va., Sarah, W7496
Peter, Pa., BLWt.9494-100-Pvt. Iss. 6/17/178?, to Mary Ripely, Admx. No papers
Samuel, S.C., S38720
Sturdey, N.C., Va., S16819
William, Va. Lee's Legion, BLWt. 12147-100-Pvt. Iss. 4/13/1791 to James Reynolds, ass. No papers
GARNET, Alexander, Mass., Ruth, W14773
GARNETT, Benjamin, Cont., BLWt. 328-200. D. in Md. prior to 1807
Calvin, Mass., BLWt.4230-100-Pvt. Iss. 4/8/1797 to Marlbry Turner. No papers
Daniel, Mass., S5337; BLWt.1060-100
Henry, Va., R14340; Va. Half Pay
John, Cont., N.Y., Elizabeth, W19484
John, N.Y., BLWt.7193-100-Pvt. Iss. 5/3/1791 to Samuel Gale, ass. No papers
John, Va., S31055
Laban, Navy, Mass., R3920
GARNEY, Thomas, Mass., Sea Service, Margaret, W21178
GARNS, Anthony, N.C., S38723
GARNSEY, Chauncey, Ct., S13120
David, Ct., S22785
David, N.H., S22783
Joel, Ct., S15136
Samuel, Ct., S13111
GARRABRANTS, Garabrant N. See GARABRANT
GARRARD, William, S.C., S32263
William, Va., S13122
GARRATT, Benjamin, N.Y., BLReg. 225612-55
GARRELL, John, Va., Nancy/Ann

GARRELL (continued)
W7874
GARRET, Abigail, former wid. of Gideon Scofield, Ct., which see
Abraham, Pa., BLWt.9466-100-Pvt. Iss. 7/22/1793 to Philip Stout, ass. No papers
Samuel, N.Y., BLWt.7189 & 13955-100-Pvt. Iss. 5/5/1791 to Mary Garret, Admx. No papers
William, N.C., S.C., S6879
GARRETSON, Jacob, N.J., Pa. Sea Service, Melicent/Milicent, W10050
John, S.C., S35962
Richard, N.J., Nelly, W33
GARRETT, Alexander, Pa., Dis. No papers
Andrew, Mass., S33262; BLWt. 797-200-Lt. Iss. 4/16/1790
David, S.C., S38719
Edward, S.C., R21702
Elisha, Ct., BLWt.5844-100-Pvt. Iss. 9/7/1790. No papers
Francis, Ct., S16124
Henry, Va., S1664
John, Ct., BLWt.5848-100-Pvt. Iss. 9/24/1790 to James F. Sebor. No papers
John, Ct., S22786
John, Ct., S43581
John, N.Y., Stasha, W19486
John, Va. See GARROTT
John Catlett, S.C., Elizabeth, W10046
Robert, Pa., BLWt.9464-100-Drummer. Iss. 6/29/1789 to M. McConnell, ass. No papers
Robert, Va. See GARROTT
Robert, Va., R3925
Stephen, ---, Va. res. of wid. in 1841, Martha, R3924
Thomas, S.C., S38722
William, S.C. See GARRARD
GARRIGUES, John, N.J., S2573
GARRIS, Bedford, N.C., S6876
Sikes, N.C., S13130
GARRISH, Joseph, N.J., S649
GARRISHAM, James, Pa., BLWt. 9489-100-Pvt. Iss. 5/2/1798. No papers
GARRISON, Aaron, N.J., S2572
Abraham, N.J., S34367
Abraham, N.J., Jane, W4960
Abraham, N.Y., BLWt.7172-100-Pvt. Iss. 9/3/1790 to James Harrison, ass. No papers
Abraham, N.Y., S13127
Abraham, N.Y., S44151
Abraham, N.Y., Elizabeth, W16583
Abraham, Va., R3927
Abram H./Abraham H., N.J., S2230
Benjamin, N.J.; BLWt.8336-100-Pvt. Iss. 12/27/1798. No papers
Benjamin, N.J., S42737
Benjamin, Pa., S5170
Bennet, N.J., BLWt.8349-100-Pvt. Iss. 6/2/1797 to Jonathan Wayman, ass. No papers
Bennet/Benet, N.J., S34369
Dennis, N.Y., S15135
Isaac, Pa., BLWt.9450-100-Pvt.

GARRISON (continued)
Iss. 2/14/1791 to Alexander Power, ass. No papers
James, N.C., S16123; BLWt.13203-160-55
James, N.C., S32260
Joel, N.J., S32261
John, N.Y., BLWt.7155-100-Pvt. Iss. 9/9/1790 to Joseph Allison, Jr.,ass. No papers
John, N.Y., S10718
John, N.Y., S41563
John, N.Y., R3929
Jonah, N.J., Mary, W108
Joseph, N.J., BLWt.8348-100-Pvt. Iss. 6/11/1789 to Matthias Denman, ass. No papers
Leonard, Pa., Rebecca, W7503
Matthias/Mathias, N.J., S34894
Peter, N.Y., BLWt.7202-100-Pvt. Iss. 1/5/1791 to Abm. Garrison Admr. No papers
Richard, ---, N.Y., Agcy. Dis. No papers
Samuel, N.C., S31049
Samuel, Va., Mary, R3930
Silas, N.J., BLWt.8335-100-Pvt. Iss. 7/7/1789. No papers
Stephen, N.C., S46444
Thomas, Lamb's Art., N.Y., BLWt.7199-100-Pvt. Iss. 5/23/1789. No papers
William, Mass., BLWt.4208-100-Pvt. Iss. 1/24/1793. No papers
GARISS, Henry, N.C., S5173
GARRISSON, John, S.C., S3384
GARRIT/GARRITT, John, Cont., Ct., S44159
GARROTT, David, S.C. See GARRETT
John, Va., S35961
Robert, Va., S31054
Thomas, N.C., Margaret, W19488
Thomas, Va., Joanna, R3926
GARROUTTE, Michael, Sea Service, N.Y. res., Rej. 3931
GARTEN, Nathaniel, Va. See GARTER
GARTER, Nathaniel, Va., S10719
GARTH, John, Va., S31056
GARTHRITE, John, See GARTHWAIT
GARTHWAIT, John, N.J., S34365
GARTSEE, John, Crane's Cont. Art., Mass., BLWt.4285-100-Corp. Iss. 5/2/1789. No papers
John, Mass., S44878
GARVEN, Isaac, Va. See GARVIN
GARVEY, Bartholomew, Pa., Eleanor, W23078; BLWt.1652-100
Francis, N.Y., Amy, W2094
Job, Va., Elizabeth, W8839
John, Pa., S41565
Thomas, N.C. See GORVEY
GARVIN, Benjamin, Va., Margaret Bowman, former wid., R1079
Ephraim, N.H., War of 1812, Mary, W24265; BLWt.27185-160-55. 11th Inf., War of 1812
Henry, Pa., BLWt.9434-100-Pvt. Iss. 7/9/1789. No papers
Isaac, Va., Jane, W8837
Thomas, Pa., BLWt.9481-100-Pvt. in Moylan's Dragoons, BLWt. 9481. Iss. 11/5/1789. No papers

GARVIN (continued)
Thomas, Va., R3932
GARY, Elisha, Mass., S44874
Eneas, Ct., S13128
Jonas, Mass., Polly, W23094
Josiah, Cont., Ct., S37003
Moses, Mass., S33263
Peter, Cont., Pa., Catharine, W3675; BLWt.361-100. Iss. 10/15/1807
Richard, Md., R3933
Seth, Mass. See GAREY
Thomas, Mass., BLWt.1294-100
GASAWAY, Thomas, N.C. See GAZAWAY
GASCHET, Levi, See GASSETT
GASKILL, Abraham, N.J., BLWt. 2395-100
William, N.J., BLWt.8365-100-Pvt. Iss. 3/16/1796 to Henry Ridgeway, ass. No papers
GASKIN, Joseph, Crane's Cont. Art., Mass., BLWt.4279-100-Pvt. Iss. 6/1/1790 to John Warren. No papers
GASKINS, Herman, N.C., S13124
Jesse, Va., S39560
Thomas, Va., BLWt.867-450-Lt. Col. Iss. 5/29/1792 to Robt. Means, ass. No papers
GASPAR, Peter, See GASPER
GASPENSON, John, N.C., S1818
GASPER, Peter, N.Y., BLWt.7188-100-Pvt. Iss. 2/14/1791. No papers.
Peter, N.Y., S43585
GASS, Henry, Pa., BLWt.9431-100-Pvt. Iss. 4/6/1790 to Henry Gass. No papers
John, N.C., Betsey, W7492; BLWt. 12575-160-55
Patrick (see 1812 files), Old War Inv. File 25097. He served between Rev. War & 1812, and in War of 1812
GASSAWAY, Henry, Md., BLWt.859-200-Lt. Iss. 7/28/1790. No papers
James, Va., Elizabeth, W11044; BLWt.40016-160-55
John, Md., Elizabeth, W8842; BLWt.853-300-Capt. Iss. 6/19/1789. Assigned by Wm. Ball to Rob Pollard. No papers
Nicholas, Md., BLWt.862-200-Lt. Iss. 2/25/1800 to Richard Gassaway. No papers
Samuel, Md., Nancy, B.L. Rej. 93393-55
GASSETT, John, Mass., S32717
Levi, Mass., Vashti, W23081
GASSOWAY, James, See GASSAWAY
GAST, Matthias/Mathias, Pa., S22259
GASTER, Jacob, N.C., S6871; BLWt.26410-160-55
GASTON, Daniel, N.J., Nancy, W11037
Hugh, S.C., S10729
James, S.C., Catharine, W23082
John, S.C., Janet, W30007

GASTON (continued)
Joseph, S.C., Jane, W22089; BLWt.18015-160-55
William, S.C., S32265
GATCHELL, Benjamin, Mass., S35335
Jeremiah, Mass. Sea Service, Privateer, War of 1812, Elizabeth, W21175; BLWt.7071-160-55
Nathaniel, Mass., Mary Douglas, former wid., W5068; BLWt.101134-160-55
Samuel H., Mass., S34893
William, Mass. See GATHELL
Zachariah, Cont., Mass., Mary Goodale, former wid., W16263
GATES, Adam, Pa., BLWt.9445-100-Pvt. Iss. 3/14/1792 to Moses Sill, ass. No papers
Amos, Mass., S45545
Asa, Ct., R.I., S21214
Asa, Mass., Fanny, W14696
Caleb, R.I., R3940
Cyrus, Ct., R.I., S22262
Daniel, Ct., R3871
Desire, former wid. of Charles Cushman, Ct., which see
Edward, Navy, Mass. agcy. & res. S32711
Ezra, Ct., N.Y., S10726
Ezra, Cont., N.H., Vt., S15129; Wt. 13128-100 iss. 3/8/1796
Freeman, Ct., S42735
George, Mass., S10725
Henry, Mass., S5179
Horatio, Va., BLWt.863-1100. No papers
James, Ct., Polly, W23083
James O., Cont., Mass., Phebe, W16582
Jehiel, Ct., S44875
John, Mass., S18832
John, N.Y., Gertrude, W11041
John, N.C., R3943
John, Pa., S5172
John, Va., S1819
Jonas, Mass., S40885
Jonathan, Mass., Hannah, W14778
Jonathan, Mass., Zerviah, W19492
Joseph, Ct., Mary, W4203
Lemuel, Crane's Cont. Art., Mass. BLWt.4290-100-Sgt. Iss. 3/25/1790. No papers
Lucy, former wid. of Bezeliel Mack, Cont., N.Y., which see
Luther, Ct., Ann, W21168
Marvin, Ct., S15138
Micah, Mass., S29817; BLWt.11418-160-55
Nathan, Ct., S21764
Nathaniel, Navy, Ct., S41562
Nehemiah, Ct., Ruth, W25614
Nehemiah, N.Y., S21753
Oldham, Mass., Deborah, W19493
Oliver, Ct., Sea Service, Jemima, R3941
Oliver, Mass., S30430
Paul, Mass., S15128
Peter, Mass., S32724
Samuel, Ct., S18833
Samuel, Mass., S22257
Samuel, Mass., Susannah, W15900

GATES (continued)
BLWt.6258-160-55
Silas, Mass., S23647
Silvanus/Sylvanus, Mass., S6872
Simon, Mass., S29170
Solomon, Mass., S30429
Stephen, Ct., Dis. No papers
Stephen, N.Y., R3946
Thomas, Ct., Rachel, W11040
Timothy, Mass., Susannah, R3947
William, Ct., S43584
William, Md., Sarah, W5279
William, Mass., S29821
William, Va., Liddy, W19485
Zebulon Waterman, Ct., Alice, R3939
GATEWOOD, Dudley, N.C., S6873
Edmund, Va., S6870
James, R3948
John, Va., S13121
John, Va., Nancy, W415
William, Va., S8551
William, Va., S17968
GATHELL, William, Mass., Elizabeth, W1164; BLWt.12712-160-55
GATLIFF, Charles, Va., Rachel, R3949
GATLIN, Edward, Navy, Va. agcy. & res., S39558
Jesse, N.C., Elizabeth, W10047
GATTIN, Jesse, N.C. See GATLIN
GATTIS, Alexander, N.C., Rosanna, W688; BLWt.13200-160-55
James, N.C., S3385
GATTY, John, N.Y., Sarah, R3951
GAUDINIER, Jacob, N.Y., S15583
GAUDY, Ephraim, N.C., S.C., S17971
GAUF, John, Pa., S41557
GAUL, John F., Pa., S22260
GAULDEN, William T., Va., Malissa, W7509; BLWt.26787-160-55
GAULDING, William T. See GAULDEN
GAULEY, John, Pvt. Cont., Canadian & Hazen's Regt., S46358; BLWt.14/100 iss 5/13/1803 to Tappan Webster
GAULT, James, Mass., S15134
John, N.H., S32715
Matthew, N.H., Mary, R3950; BLWt.6452-160-55
Robert, S.C., Phebe, W25616; BLWt.19773-160-55
GAULTNEY, Nathan, See GWALTNEY
GAUNEY, Timothy, N.C., S3383
GAUSS, Benjamin, N.Y., S13125
GAUYD, William, See GOUYD
GAVETT, Samuel, Mass., S34364
GAVIN, John, Md. See John MORGAN
John, N.J., BLWt.8344-100-Pvt. Iss. 3/19/1792. No papers
GAVIT, Edward, ---, res. Providence, R.I., S----. No papers
John, R.I., Desire, W21167
Sanford, R.I., Hannah, W21166
GAW, Chambers, Pa., R3952
GAY, Allen, N.C., Anna, W1033; BLWt.26060-160-55
Asahel, Ct., Temperance, W17940

GAY (continued)
Ebenezer, Mass., Hannah, W21171
Edward, Ct., S13172
Henry, Md., R3954
James, Mass., Elizabeth, W25617; BLWt. 89503-160-55
James, Sr., Va., S2568
Jason, Ct., S44871
Jeremiah, Mass., Lydia, W23084
John, Cont., Mass., S45547
John, Mass., BLWt.4246-100-Pvt. Iss. 7/24/1792. No papers
John, N.Y., S10723
Jonathan, Mass., BLWt.4272-100-Corp. Iss. 5/24/1790. No papers
Jonathan, Mass., S44870
Joseph, Mass., BLWt.4274-100-Pvt. Iss. 5/24/1790 to Jonathan Gay, heir & legal repr. of Joseph Gay, dec'd. No papers.
Lewis, Mass., Mary, W23076
Richard, Ct., S16817
Stephen, Mass., S32721
Thomas, Cont., Mass. res., S32720
William, Mass., Catharine, R3953
William, N.C., S45842
William, S.C., Prudence Curry, former wid., W22875
Zerobabel, N.C., Selah, W7490; BLWt.3675-160-55
GAYLARD, Levi, Ct., Cont., S4293
GAYLE, Mathias, Va., S16818
Matthias, Va., See GALE
Thomas, Va., Susannah, R3955
GAYLOR, William, Navy, N.Y., See GAILER
GAYLORD, Ambrose, Ct., BLWt.5839-100-Pvt. Iss. 1/5/1792. No papers
Ambrose, Ct., Eleanor, W4677; BLWt.290-100
Chauncy, Ct., S13112
Deodate, Ct., S17433
Eleazer, Ct., Sylvia, W17941
Elijah, Ct., S15139; BLWt.9465-160-55
Hezekiah, Cont., Mass., W23088
Jedidiah/Jedediah, Ct., S22784
Joel, Ct., Mass., S46357; BLWt. 374-100
John, Ct., Charlotte, W17005
John, Mass., Jannet, W4678
Jonathan, Ct., S44876
Jonathan, Ct., Navy, S42736
Joseph, Ct., S15848
Josiah, Ct., Mary Ann, W19483
Justus, Ct., Lucretia, W3342
Lemuel, Ct., R3958
Levi, Ct., See GAYLARD
Robert, Mass., Patience, W24268
GAZAWAY, Thomas, N.C., Va., Jane, R3959
GAZETTE, John, Mass., See GASSETT
GAZLAY, Jonathan, N.Y., S23650
GEAN, Sherod, N.C., R3960
GEAR, George, Ct., S36534
GEAREY, Gilbert, See GAREY
GEARHART, Jacob, N.J., S3392
GEARING, Edward, Mass., Molly, W14781
GEARON, Thomas, N.J., Sea

GEARON (continued)
Service from Phila., Barbarie, W461
GEARY, David, Cont., Mass., Sarah, W14779
Ichabod, Mass., S32725
Jonathan, Mass., BLWt.4250-100-Sgt. Iss. 3/25/1790. No papers
Jonathan, Mass. See GERREY
Joshua, Mass., S38724
Reuben, Mass., Joanna Green, former wid., W14816
GEASEY, Henry, Md., S8554
GEBHART, John, Md., Phebe, W10054; BLWt.96097-160-55
GEDDES, Joseph, Pa., S41569
GEDDING, Samuel, See GODDING
GEDDINS, John, Ct., Achsah, W25624
GEE, David, N.Y., BLWt.7146-100-Pvt. Iss. 10/22/1791 to Asa Ballard, ass. No papers
David, N.Y., Polly, W3241
Ebenezer, Mass., Olive Branch, W4679
Ezekiel, N.Y., S44880; BLWt.1468-100
John, N.Y., S43589; BLWt.7165-100; BLWt.214-60-55
John, N.Y., S43592
Joseph, Md., Belinda, W9449
Moses, N.Y., BLWt.7166-100-Pvt. Iss. 1/2/1792. No papers
Moses, N.Y., Phebe, W5280
Parker, Va., R3964
Richard, Md., BLWt.11276-100-Pvt. Iss. 11/29/1790 to Bazil Shaw, Admr. No papers
Richard, Va., Mary, W8843
Thomas, Q.M. Sgt., Lamb's Art. N.Y., BLWt.7157 iss. 12/15/1790 & BLWt.8067
GEER, Allyn, Ct., Mass., S17972
Amos, Ct., S23230
Asa, Ct., S41571
Benajah, Ct., S43588
Charles, N.H., Elizabeth, W19544
David, Ct., R3965
Ebenezer Stoel, Ct., Catharine/Catherine, W1265; BLWt.31910-160-55
Elihu, Ct., Eleanor, W21180
Ezra, Mass., Abigail, W5085
George, Ct., S17434
George, N.H., Vt., Honor, W23097
Gurdon, Cont., Ct., S42738
Jedediah, Ct., S42741
John, Ct., Onnah, W14782
Michael, Crane's Cont. Art., Mass., BLWt.4288-100-Pvt. Iss. 12/30/1790. No papers
Nathan, Ct., S16126
Nathaniel, Ct., S15849
Richard, Ct., S13132
Robert, Ct., S13131
Roger, Ct., S8552
Walter, N.H., S35965
GEERS, Benjamin, N.Y., BLWt.7179-100-Pvt. Iss. 2/14/1791. No papers
Benjamin, N.Y., S44158
GEERY, John, Pa., S2233
GEESLER, John, N.Y., R4394

GEESLIN, Charles, N.C., S37951
GEHAN, Peter, Pa., BLWt.9435-100-Corp. Iss. 6/10/1789. No papers
GEHRET, Henry, Pa., Christina, R3967
Henry, Pa., Elizabeth, R3968
GEIB, Henry, Pa. See GEIP
GEIER, Andrew, Pa. See GEYER
GEIGER, Henry, Pa., S29172
Jacob, Pa., See GRIGNER
Jacob, S.C., Dorothy, W2728; BLWt.34282-160-55
John L., Pa., S22876
GEIP, Henry, Pa., Anna Catharine, W4439; BLWt.31436-160-55
GEISE, Jeremiah, Pa., S41568
GEISENCEDER, Martin, See KISENCEDERS
GEISENSIEDER, Martin, See KISENCEDERS
GEISSINGER, John, Pa., R3969
GELAT, George, R.I., S22788
John, Mass., R.I., Keziah, W19496
GELDEN, Isaac, N.C., W17943
GELLER, George, Pa., S41570
GELSON, Matthew, Lamb's Art. N.Y., BLWt.7201-100-Pvt. Iss. 9/25/1790 to Nehemh. Rockwell. No papers
GELSTON, William, N.J., N.Y., Asenath, W17942
GELWICKS, Nicholas, Pa., Anna Maria, W3184
GENAT, Thomas, Va., See GINNETT
GENNINGS, Eliphalet, See JENNINGS
Mary, former wid. of Jesse David, Ct., which see
William, Mass., R.I., See JENNINGS
GENT, Charles, Ga., S1903
George, Crane's Cont. Art., Mass., BLWt.4278-100-Pvt. Iss. 6/29/1789. No papers
Jessee/Jesse, N.C., Mary Ann, W7510
GENTER, John H., N.Y., S43591
GENTHER, John H., Cont., France, Mary, R3973
GENTHNER, Andrew, Mass., S31688
GENTREY, Claiborn, N.C., S3391
GENTRY, David, Va., Sarah, W7511; BLWt.31908-160-55
Gaddis, Va., Patsey, W7512
George, Va., S6885; BLWt.26177-160-55
James, Cont., Va., S8555
Meshack, N.C., R3974
Richard, S.C., b. Va., Justina/Jestin, W8844; BLWt.26713-160-55
Richard, Va., Nancy Farris, former wid., W10976; BLWt.81502-160-55
William, Cont., Va., S39566
GENTZERMAN, John, Pa., Eve Ann, W2784
GENUNG, Cornelius, N.J., Jemima, R3975
Jacob, N.J., BLWt.8333 & 8452-100-Pvt. Iss. 6/16/1789 to Thomas Coyle, ass. No papers

GENUNG (continued)
Jacob, N.J., S34371
Moses, N.J., R3897
GEOGHEGAN, Anthony, Md., Ann, W4964; BLWt.1269-100
John, Md., S35964
GEOHEGAN, Anthony, See GEOGHEGAN
GEORGE, Amos, Ct., S43593
Austin, N.H., Lydia, W16585
Benjamin, Cont., N.H., Abigail, R3976
Breton, N.C., See BRITTON
Britton/Breton, N.C., S38725; BLWt.1326-100
David, N.H., R39568
Edward, S.C., BLWts.12175 & 13120-100-Pvt. Iss. 10/15/1795. No papers
Francis, Mass., Tabitha, W7514; BLWt.10222-160-55
James, S.C., Elizabeth H., see file of her former husb., David Hamilton, S.C.
Jesse, Va., S4295
Jesse, Va. Sea Service, R51; Va. Half Pay. See N.A. Acc. No. 837. Va. State Navy YS file
John, Ct., BLWt.5861-100-Pvt. Iss. 12/12/1794 to William Richards, ass. No papers
John, Cont., Mass., Margaret, W23090; BLWt.805-200-Capt.-Lt. Iss. 4/18/1796 to Jeremiah Mason, ass. No papers
John, N.H., S45551
John, N.J., BLWt.8343-100-Pvt. Iss. 6/11/1789 to Matthias Denman, ass. No papers
John, N.J., BLWt.8364-100-Pvt. Iss. 6/6/1797 to William Holmes, heir. No papers
John, N.J., S16386
John, Pvt., Pa., BLWt.9504 iss. 7/27/1789 to Richard Platt, ass. S17974
John, Pa., R3976 1/2
John, R.I., Bridget, W13248
Jorden, Va., S1202
Joseph, Va., Margaret, W7515
Lewis, Mass., Alice Stevens, former wid., W25080
Mathew, Pa., S5191
Michael, N.H., Hannah, W24274; BLWt.777-100
Moses, BLWt.13146-100-Pvt. "in the Invalids". Iss. 3/22/1790 to Nathan Preston, ass. No papers
Moses S., N.H., S39569
Prince, Ct., BLWt.5883-100-Pvt. Iss. 2/7/1799 to John Duncan. No papers
Prince, Ct., S43594
Reuben, Va., S39567
Robert, Va., R14396; Va. Half Pay. N.A.Acc. No. 874. See 050072
Samuel, Mass., N.H., S16822
Samuel, N.H., S15140
Southy, Md., BLWt.11278-100-Pvt. Iss. 11/29/1790 to John Robins, Admr. No papers
Thomas, Mass., Hannah, W14780

GEORGE (continued)
Thomas, N.H., Joanna, W23095
Thomas, Va., S16821
William/William Augustus, Pa., S41572; BLWt.484-100
William, Va., S3390
William, Va., Nancy, R3977
William, Va., R20373
William, Va. Sea Service, R14395; Va. Half Pay
GEORGES, Gideon, Mass., BLWt. 4241-100-Pvt. Iss. 3/18/1790. No papers
GEORGIA, Simon, Ct., BLWt. 1289-100
GEPHART, John, Md. See GEBHART
GERALD, Gamaliel, Mass., Jemima, W25619
Thomas, Cont., Ct., BLWt.1034-100
GERARD, Charles, N.C., Elizabeth Hunter, former wid., W3999; BLWt. 884-200-Lt. Iss. 6/1/1792
John, Cont., Va., S42740
GEREN, Solomon, N.C., Eleanor, W80
GERHART, Peter, Pa., S5180
GERKINS, Zachariah, N.C. See GHERKINS
GERLACH, George, ---, Pa. Agcy. & res., S10179
GERLACK, George. See GERLACH
GERLOCK, John, ---, Phila., Pa. pensioner-invalid. No papers
GERMAN, Charles, Ct. See JARMAN
James, N.Y., Elizabeth, W25620
William, Va., BLWts.13125 & 14048-100-Pvt. Iss. 6/27/ 1793. No papers
GERMOND, Jacob, Mass., S43587
GEROCK, Samuel, Md., S6884
GEROLMAN, Henry, N.Y., S43590
GEROULD, Samuel, Mass., Azubah, W23000
GERRALDS, Thomas, Cont., Ct. See GERALD
GERRARD, Charles, See GERARD
John, Cont., Va. See GERARD
GERREY, Jonathan, Mass., Hepsibah, W14783
GERRILLS, John, Mass., S42739
GERRISH, Edward, Md., S34897
John, Mass., S29173
Thomas, N.H., S45550
Timothy, Navy, N.H., Mass. Sea Service, S17975
GERRY, Nathan, Mass., Martha, W19494
GERVOIR, John, Hazen's Regt., BLWt.13121-100-Pvt. Iss. 2/25/ 1793 to Benj. Moore, ass. No papers
GERWAS, John, N.Y. See JERVIS
GETCHEL, Zachariah. See GATCHELL
GETCHELL, Abel, Mass., BLWt.844-100
Benjamin, Mass. See GATCHELL
Jeremiah, Mass., S18415
Joseph, Mass. See GITCHELL
Nathaniel, Mass., Elizabeth, R3979
Seth, Cont., Mass., Sarah, R3980
William, Mass. See GATHELL
GETCHER, John, Pa., Von Herr's

GETCHER (continued)
Corps, BLWt.13112-100-Pvt. Iss. 2/25/1791 to Charles Colver, ass. No papers
GETMAN, Conrad, N.Y., W19497
Peter, N.Y., Anna Elizabeth, W16267
Peter, N.Y., Elizabeth, W19495
Thomas, N.Y., Elizabeth, W16584
GETTING, George, Pa., BLWt.9457-100-Pvt. Iss. 7/27/1789 to Richard Platt, ass. No papers
GETTYS, Joseph, Pa. See GEDDES
GETZ, John, Pa., S22263
GEVANDIN, John, See GEVEDANN
GEVEDANN, John, Va.,Mary, W8845
GEVIDON, John, Va. See GEVEDANN
GEVIN, Thomas, Va. See GIVIN
GEWGAW, Peter, See LEUCAW
GEYER, Andrew, Pa., Maria Barbara, R3981
George, Mass., BLWt.4234-100-Pvt. Iss. 2/23/1797 to Benj. Dana. No papers
George, Cont., Mass., S32726
John, Cont., Va. See KEGER
John, Pa. See GIER
GHADEN, Joseph, Ct., Cont., S36548
GHERKINS, Zachariah, N.C., S45843
GHOLSON, William, Va., S35966
William, Va., R4097
GHORMLEY, Joseph, Pa., S16130
GIARD, Gabriel, See TZOR
GIBB, William, Pa., BLWt.9471-100-Sgt. Iss. 7/9/1789. No papers
GIBBES, William Hasell, S.C.,S9339
GIBBNY, George, Pa., S2234
GIBBON, James, Pa., S13138; BLWt. 1538-500
GIBBONEY, Alexander, Cont., Pa., Ann, R3982
GIBBONS, Bildad/Beldad, Mass., S29826
GIBBONS, David, Pa., BLWt.9513-100-Pvt. Iss. 11/5/1789. No papers
Isaac, Cont., Pa., Mary, W4204; BLWt.2282-100
James, Pa., BLWt.9437-100-Pvt. Iss. 6/20/1789. No papers
James, Pa., BLWt.9458-100-Pvt. Iss. 10/25/1792. No papers
John, Del., S35967
John, N.Y., BLWt.7168-100-Pvt. Iss. 9/15/1790 to John S. Hobart et al, assnes. No papers
Peter, Cont., Mass., S43595
Timothy, Mass., S13142
GIBBS, Benjamin, Mass., S29825
Benjamin, Mass., Chloe, R3983
Benjamin, S.C., Elizabeth, W8847
Caleb, Cont., Mass., Catharine, W24277; BLWt.792-400-Maj. Iss. 5/19/1789. No papers
Churchill, Va., S46002; BLWt. 1694-100. Va. Half Pay. N.A. Acc. No. 874. See 050073
Cornelius, Mass., S39582
David, Ct., S13141
David, N.H., S39583
Edward, Va., S13149
Eldad, Ct., S29176

GIBBS (continued)
Elijah, Mass., Hepsibah, W14785; BLWt.1590-160-55
Elisha, Mass., N.H., S28741
Elizabeth, former wid. of Abram Smith, N.J., which see
Frederick, Mass., S44160
Gershom, Ct., Cont., S15144
Harod, Va., Anna, W17947. See N.A. Acc. No. 050074 Not Half Pay, but papers relating to above pension file, W17947 of Harod Gibbs, wid. Anna
Isaac, Mass., N.H., S18416
Ithamar, Ct., S44161
Jabez, Mass., Mehitable, W2541; BLWt.7432-160-55
James, Cont., Mass., N.H., Abigail, W27414
James, Mass., BLWt.4202-100-Pvt. Iss. 1/26/1790 to James Smith, no papers
James, Va. Sea Service, S16825
John, Mass., BLWt.4251-100-Drummer. Iss. 1/26/1790 to John May. No papers
John, N.C., S8556
John, N.C., Va., Hannah, W2729
John, R.I., S46038
Joseph, Mass., S29824
Joseph, N.Y., S22264
Joshua, Mass., Hannah, R3987
Joshua, N.H., S41579
Josiah, Mass., Lucy, W4681; BLWt.10021-160-55
Julius, Va., Caty, W10055
Luman, Vt., S13169
Mary, former wid. of Ephraim Sampson, Mass., which see
Moore, Ct., Cont., BLWt.5890-100-Pvt. Iss. 12/14/1796 to Nathaniel Smith.
Moore, Ct., Cont., Patience, S36546 & W25628
Pelatiah, Mass., S15854
Peter, Ct., BLWt.5869-100-Pvt. Iss. 1/16/1796 to Aneas Munson. No papers
Philo, Ct., Lois, W7518; BLWt. 19524-160-55
Samuel, Ct., Julia F., W7519; BLWt.822-200-Lt. Iss. 7/27/1789. No papers
Samuel, Cont., Ct., Caty, W689; BLWt.29731-160-55
Shadrach, S.C., S10740
Simeon, Ct., N.Y., Esther, W17008
Simeon, N.Y., S36541
Solomon, Ct., S17439
Solomon, Vt., S22267
Spencer, Ct., S36542
Stephen, Cont., Ct., Ruth, R3989
Stephen, Mass., Mehitable, W23108
Sylvanus, Ct., Betsy, W24276
Thomas, Mass., S39586
Thomas, Mass., Temperance, W14789
Thomas, N.H., S43598
William, Ct., S13145
William, Va., S42746
William, Va., Nancy, W1034; BLWt. 12732-160-55
William Hasell, S.C. See GIBBES

GIBBS (continued)
Zenas, Mass., R3990
GIBERSON, James, N.J., R3991
John, N.J., S2235
Joseph, N.J., R3992
GIBHART, Adam, Md., Sarah M., W4206; BLWt.40910-160-55. See B.L. claim allowed heirs of Adam Kephart, 2nd Md. Regt., Wt. 2404-100
GIBSON, Alexander, Pa., S13146
Bellingsby/Billingsby, Va., S1761
Charles, N.C., S41575
Charles, N.C., R3995
Elisha, N.C., S31062
Erasmus, Va., S21767
George, Va., Abigail, W8852
George, Va., BLWt.1985-500
Gideon, Pa., Abigail, R3993
Henry, N.H. See GIPSON
Henry, Pa., BLWt.9507-100-Pvt. Iss. 6/9/1794 to Gideon Merkle, ass. No papers
Jacob, N.C., S10744
Jacob, Va., Mary, R3998
James, Cont., Mass., S13167
James, Mass., S35343
James, N.H., Isabell, W23105
James, N.J., BLWt.8346-100-Sgt. Iss. 6/17/1789. No papers
James, N.J., S43600
James, Pa., BLWt.786-300-Capt. Also recorded as BLWt.2552-300-Capt. Iss. 4/2/1791. No papers
Joel, N.C., S35968
John, Md., S38729
John, Mass., S39578
John, Mass., See GILSON
John S., Mass., N.H., N.Y., S31690
John, N.Y., Margaret, W23101
John, N.C., S3395
John, N.C., Va.(?), S31065
John, R.I., S34899
John, Va., S8572
John, Va., S9338
John, Va., S13153
John, Va., S31060
John, Va., S41578; BLWt.865-500-Col. Iss. 10/24/1789. No papers
John, Va., Dorcas, W25627; BLWt. 82543-160-55
John, Va., R3996
John, Jr., Va., BLWt.874-150-Ensign. Iss. 10/24/1789. No papers.
John, Va. Sea Service, R52; Va. Half Pay. See N.A. Acc. No.837-Va. State Navy. YS file
John Blaney, Not Rev. War; Wayne's War & War of 1812, res. Pa. & Ohio. Old War Inv. Rej. File 14453. Wts. 45570-80-50 & 43964-80-55
John S., Va., N.H.(?), Pa., R3997
Jonathan, Md., BLWt.858-300-Capt.
Joseph, N.C., b. Ireland, S8562
Miles, Va., Margaret Nunnaly/

GIBSON (continued)
Nunnelley, former wid., R7742. See this woman's claim as wid. of Israel Nunnelley/Nunnaly, Va.
Nicholas, Va., S8559
Robert, Va., Sinah, W8851; BLWt. 1970-160-55
Roger, Ct., S29827
Samuel, Ga., R3999
Samuel, Mass. See GILSON
Samuel, Va., Elizabeth, W9450; BLWt.27639-160-55
Solomon, N.H., N.Y. See GILSON
Thaddeus, Cont., Mass., S45555
Thomas, Cont., Va., S39573
Thomas, Mass., Relief, W21184
Thomas, N.J., BLWt.8345-100-Pvt. Iss. 1/29/1793. No papers
Thomas, N.C., S8560
Wilbourne, N.C., R4000
William, Cont., N.H., Mass., S43602
William, Mass., Abigail, R3994
William, N.C., S38728
William, N.C., R4001
William, Va., S8561
GIDDEMAN, John, Pvt., N.J., BLWt.8354 iss. 2/10/1792
GIDDEN, Richard, S.C. See GIDEON
GIDDINGS, Benjamin, Ct., Affiah, W17946
Isaac, Mass., S19296
Isaac, Mass., S29175
John, Ct. See GEDDINS
John, Mass., Nabby, W23096
Joseph, Ct., Mary, W25625
Joseph, Ct., Cont., N.Y., S10736
Joshua, Ct., S3396
Mary, former wid. of Joseph Dickerman, N.Y., which see
Niles, Ct., S10738
Peggy, former wid. of Peletiah Warren, N.H., which see
Thomas, Ct., Anna, W1410; BLWt. 29021-160-55
GIDEON, George, Cont., Pa., S41576
Jacob, Cont., Pa., S13144
Peter, Md., S6887
Richard, S.C., Elizabeth, R4002
GIDLEY, Jasper M., N.Y., Hannah, W17012
GIER, John, Pa., S41567
GIESECKAS, Diederick William, Armand's Legion, BLWt.13110-100-Sgt. Iss. 9/10/1789 to Charles Bush, ass. No papers
GIFFEN, Ezra, Ct., N.J. See GRIFFEN
GIFFIN, Ann, former wid. of Benj. Farnam, Ct., Cont., which see
Simon, Ct., Cont., S36543; BLWt. 5873. Iss. 10/7/1789 to Benj. Tallmadge
Stephen, Pa., Mary, W7584
GIFFINS, Joshua, N.J., BLWt.8363-100-Pvt. Iss. 8/31/1791. No papers
Joshua, N.J., Margaret, W113
GIFFORD, Absalom, Ct., S13134
Elihu, R.I., S21226
Elisha, N.Y., Polly, W1842; BLWt.26036-160-55
Gideon, Privateer, R.I. Sea

GIFFORD (continued)
Service, S21227
Gideon, R.I., Betsey, W3676; BLWt.11423-160-55
Ichabod, Mass., BLWt.2017-100
James, Mass., S10734
Jeremiah, Ct., Sally, W1411
John, N.Y., S10737
Jonathan, R.I., BLWt.3155-100-Pvt. Iss. 5/30/1791. No papers
Lewis, Mass., S15501
Lot, Mass., S10742
William, Ct., R.I., S2236
William, N.Y., S41580
GIFT, John Nicholas, N.C., Regina, R4005
GIGO, Francis, Hazen's Regt., BLWt.13132-100-Pvt. Iss. 8/6/1792 to Elmer Cushing, admr. No papers
Francis, Cont., Canadian, Eliza W21182
GIGUET, Louis Nicholas, Mass., Mary, R4006
GILAM, Robert, S.C. See GILLAM
GILBERT, Allen, Sheldon's Dragoons, Ct., BLWt.5888-100-Pvt. Iss. 5/5/1791 to Benjamin Talmadge. No papers
Allen, Ct., S44162
Amos, Mass., Margaret, W16271
Asa, Ct., Cont., Mary, W17944
Asahel, Cont., Ct., S32268
Benjamin, Ct., Cont., S13139
Benjamin, Cont., Mass., Mary S., W19498; BLWt.796-200-Lt. Iss. 2/5/1794. No papers
Benjamin, N.Y., BLWt.1533-200
Benjamin, Va., Nancy, R4013
Burr, Ct., BLWt.5829-100-Pvt. Iss. 4/26/1792. No papers
Burr, Ct., Clarissa Turney, former wid., W18165
Butler, Ct., Cont., W43607
Charles, N.C., S31057
Daniel, N.Y., S13133
David, Ct., Molly, W25621
Ebenezer, Ct., BLWt.5846-100-Pvt. Iss. 2/15/1797. No papers
Ebenezer, Ct., S36539
Ebenezer, Ct., Ruth, W17945
Ebenezer, Navy, Ct., S27
Elam, Mass., S39585
Eleanor, former wid. of Richard Skinner, Mass. Sea Service, which see
Gardner, Ct., Cont., Mary, W13265; BLWt.91126-160-55
Gershom, Ct., S10743
Heber, Ct., Lucina, W4966
Henry, Mass., S32728
Hooker, Ct., S13136
Isaac, Ct., S13137
James, N.C. See GILBIRT
Jedediah, Ct., BLWt.5847-100-Pvt. Iss. 1/28/1790. No papers
Jesse, Ct., BLWt.5867-100-Pvt. Iss. 12/30/1796. No papers
Jesse, Ct., S36544
Jesse, N.Y., S22790
Joel, Mass., Esther, W14787
Joel, Mass., Ruth, W24279

GILBERT (continued)
John, O.W. Inv. File 10184. N.W. Indian War. Pa. res.
John, Ct., BLWt.5850-100-Pvt. Iss. 4/26/1792. No papers
John, Ct., S15585
John, Ct., Elizabeth, W16268
John, Mass. See GILLBERT
John, ?, Lansdown, Leeds Co., Upper Canada address when he applied for pension, R4008
John, N.Y., BLWt.7148-100-Cpl. Iss. 9/25/1790 to John Thompson, ass. No papers
Jonas, Mass., S30433
Jonathan, Mass., Hannah, W17010
Jonathan, Mass., Susannah/Susey W19499
Joseph, Ct., S43605
Joseph, Ct., Cont., Miriam, W23112
Joseph, Cont., Va., Md.(?), S40059
Joseph, Mass., Vt., Jemima, W17007
Joseph, N.Y., R4009
Josiah, Mass., Mary, R4012
Kate, former wid. of Scipio Bartlett, Mass. Which see
Lemuel, Ct., Amorillis, W21185
Lewis, Ct., S22265
Lewis, Mass., Naomi, W14786
Michael, Cont.,Md., Elizabeth Cole, former wid., W3947
Moses, Ct., BLWt.5831-100-Sgt. Iss. 7/31/1789. No papers
Moses, Ct., S15145
Nathan, Ct., S17440
Obadiah, Ct., S39579
Rebecca, former wid. of Nathaniel Lothrop Frink, Ct., which see
Reuben, Mass., S13147
Samuel, Ct., S16127
Samuel, Mass., S16828
Samuel, Mass., Hannah, W21181
Samuel, N.Y., S43606; BLWt.43-60-55
Samuel, Va., S8569
Seth, N.Y., BLWt.7169-100-Pvt. Iss. 10/20/1790. No papers
Sewel, Vt., S3394
Simeon, Mass., Sarah, W19504
Solomon, Cont., Ct., Thankful, W17009
Stephen, N.Y., S23655
Stephen, Pa., BLWt.9478-100-Pvt. Iss. 10/21/1791 to John Klein, ass. No papers
Stephen, Pa., S41574
Stephen, Pa., Pamelia, W3182
Susannah, former wid. of William L. Moore, Pa. which see
Thaddeus, Ct., S43596
Thaddeus, Mass., S32727
Theodore, Ct., Mass., S10739
Theodore, Cont., Ct., S43601
Thomas, Ct., S31689
Thomas, Cont., Mass., Hannah, W1748; BLWt.651-100
Thomas, Mass., Hannah, W19509
Timothy, N.Y., Hannah, R4014

GILBERT (continued)
Truman, Ct., S18417
William, Ct., Hope, W24275
William, N.Y., BLWt.7154-100-Pvt. Iss. 9/25/1790 to Abrm. M. Nelson, ass. No papers
William, N.C., S31693
William, Pa., BLWt.9479-100-Pvt. Iss. 5/26/1794 to Michael Stever, ass. No papers
GILBIRT, James, N.C., S31691
GILBREATH, Thomas, Pa., S38727
GILBY, Henry, Md., BLWt.11254-100-Pvt. Iss. 3/11/179?
Thomas, Pa., BLWt.9430-100-Pvt. Iss. 6/29/1789 to M. McConnell ass. No papers
GILCHRIST, George, Va., BLWt. 868-400-Maj. Iss. 8/24/1789 to George Gilchrist
James, Pa., Elizabeth, W25622; BLWt.91125-160-55
James, Pa., BLWt.838-200-Lt. Iss. 9/16/1789 to Robert Gilchrist, heir & legal repr. No papers
John, Pa., Eleanor/Ellen, R4015
Richard, Mass., N.H., S16826
Robert, Mass., Chloe, W23107
Samuel, Cont. See GILLCHRIST
William, N.Y., BLWt.7160-100-Pvt. Iss. 4/19/1791 to Moses Hetfield admr. No papers
GILDER, Daniel, Va. See GUILDER
Reuben, Del., BLWt.849-400-Surgn. Iss. 5/19/1789. No papers
GILDERSLEAVE, Benjamin, N.J., S877
GILDERSLEEVE, Finch/Fitch, N.Y., Polly, W23109; BLWt.831-200-Lt. Iss. 9/13/1791. No papers
Fitch, N.Y. See Finch
GILE, Asa, Mass., Nancy, W25626; BLWt.984-100 & 176-60-55
Benjamin, N.H., Hulda, W1749 BLWt.11193-160-55
Henry, N.Y. See GUILE
Ray, N.J., R4017
GILES, Aquila, Cont., Md., N.Y. Agcy. & res., S43597; BLWt. 852-400-Maj. or Aid-de-Camp of Md. Iss. 9/22/1789. No papers
Ebenezer, Mass., S39577
George, N.C., Va., S8558
James, Mass., N.Y., S13148
John, Mass., Mary, W23102
John, Mass., Mary, W27413; BLWt.24171-160-55
John, N.C., Martha, W7522; BLWt.9274-160-55
Joseph, N.H., S35346
Josiah, Va., Patsey, W3799
Samuel, Cont., Mass., N.Y., Laurana, W19503
Samuel, Mass., S36545
Thomas, Ct., S15141
GILGO, Fabin, N.C., S41573
GILHAM, Thomas, Md., BLWt.11264-100-Pvt. Iss. 10/14/1795 to Henry Davis, ass. No papers
GILKEY, James, Mass., S35342
Samuel, S.C., Elizabeth, R4019
William, Mass., S13140

GILKIE, Samuel, See GILKEY
GILL, Amos, Mass., Mehitable, W23103
Benajah, Cont., Del., Mary, W416 BLWt.259-60-55
Daniel, Cont., Md., S42745
Erasmus, Moylan's Dragoons, BLWt. 839-300-Capt. Iss. 8/27/1795 to Smith & Ridgeway, assnes. No papers
George, S.C., b. N.J., S21229
George, S.C., d. Tenn., S38726
Henry, N.Y., See GUILE
Hugh, Md., Mary, R4022
James, S.C., b. N.J., Mary, R4023
John, Armand's Legion, BLWt.13111-100-Pvt. Iss. 9/24/1791 to John McCleland, ass. No papers
John, Ct., S39576
John, Pa., Jane, R4020
John, Va., Lettice, W7520
Jones, Va., S10185
Joshua, Mass., BLWt.17-100
Michael, Mass., S31063
Moses, Md., Va., S16823
Obadiah, Cont., Mass., Anna, W19507; BLWt.24616-160-55
Robert, S.C., b. Pa., R4024
Samuel, Ct., R4025
Samuel, Va., Ruth, W8882; BLWt. 2337-300
Thomas, S.C., b. N.J., d. Ill., S31061
Thomas, S.C., b. Pa., Rebecca, W3978
William, Mass., S39572
William, N.C., R4026
William, Pa., S2237
William, Va., Mary, W7521
GILLAM, Ezekiel, N.J., S10741
Jonathan, Pa., Va. See GILLUM
Robert, S.C., W8848
GILLASPI, Joseph, N.Y., BLWt. 7194-100-Pvt. Iss. 1/25/1791 & 97-60-55
GILLASPIE, David, N.C., See GILLESPIE
Jacob, Va., S3398
John, S.C., Holly, W27593; BLWt. 26596-160-55
William, N.J. See GILLESPY
William, Va., Margaret, W7531
GILLASPY, William, N.J. See GILLESPY
GILLASS, Arthur, Pa., BLWt.9495-100-Pvt. Iss. 3/16/1799. No papers
GILLBERT, Gardner. See GILBERT
John, Mass., Polly, W19508
GILLCHREST, Samuel, Cont., Me. agcy & res., S35344
GILLEGAN, Thomas, Mass., BLWt. 4253-100-Pvt. Iss. 1/11/1797. No papers
GILLELAND, Daniel, N.J., Mary, W5281
GILLEN, Hugh, Va., BLWt.1852-100
Thomas, Cont., Md., pensioned N.Y. State, S43603; BLWt. 1597-100
Thomas, Md., BL Rej.
GILLES, Joseph, Mass., S21225
GILLESON, James, S.C. See GILLISON
John, Va. See GILLISON
GILLESPIE, Allen, N.C., S21230
Andrew, N.Y., S10732
Daniel, S.C., S31692
David, N.C., Mary, R4031
George, Va., S13150
James, N.C., S16827
John, Cont., Del., S41581
John, Hazen's Regt., BLWt.13122-100-Pvt. Iss. 4/2/1792. No papers
John, N.Y., Sarah, W17006
Joseph, Cont., War of 1812, Anna Hyatt, former wid., W7857; BLWt. 97-60-55
William, Cont., Ct., Mary Ellsworth, former wid., W16249
William, S.C., S32267
William, Va., R4030
GILLESPY, James, N.C. See GILLESPIE
William, N.J., S41582
William, Va. See GILLASPIE
GILLET, Adna, Ct., R4033
Alpheus/Alphius, Cont., Ct., S41577
Asa, Ct., Abigail Denison, former wid., R4032
Asa, Cont., Ct., S34898
Benjamin, Ct., Privateer, S15143
Benoni, Ct., Polly, W2607; BLWt. 29022-160-55
Benoni, Ct., Phebe, W25630
Elijah, Ct. See GILLIT
Ephraim, Ct., S36538
Isaac, Ct., S17978
Jabez, Ct., N.H., Hannah, W19501
Jeremiah, Ct., S36535
Jeremiah, Ct., S45554
Joel, Ct., S36540
John, Ct., BLWt.5830-100-Pvt. Iss. 3/6/1796. No papers
John, Ct., Mary, R4034; S36537
Joseph, Ct., S15850
Joseph, Ct., Parcey, W7524; BLWt.9546-160-55
Luther, Ct., S6890
Nathan/Nathaniel, Ct., S42744
Noadiah, Mass., Hannah, W16269
Othniel, Ct., S36536
Reuben, Ct., S21228 , missing
Rufus, Ct., Ellen, W17948
Samuel, Ct., S22789
Simon, N.H., S39581
Stephen, Ct., Cont., S13143
William, Ct., Mass., Abigail, W2930
GILLETT, Benjamin, Cont., Ct. res., BLWt.437-100
John, Ct., Mercy Hoar, former wid., W18035
Jonathan, Ct., S15851
Reuben, Ct., Cont., R20374
GILLETTE, Benoni, Ct. See GILLET
GILLEY, Francis, N.C., R4035
Richard, Va., S8568
GILLHAM, Isaac, S.C., S32270
Jacob, S.C., S3397
John, S.C., S32269
GILLIAM, Archelaus/Achels, Va.
GILLIAM (continued)
S8567
John, N.C., S6889
John, Va., Mary, W5282
John, Va., Elizabeth, W8849; BLWt.39228-160-55
Jourdan, Va., R4037
Robert, S.C. See GILLAM
GILLIGAN, Thomas, Mass., S43604
GILLIHAN, Clammans/Clemmans/Clement, Va., Nancy/Ann, W8850; BLWt.1027-100
William, S.C., Va., S38731
GILLILAN, James, Pa., Va., S15852
GILLILAND, Daniel, N.J. See GILLELAND
James, Pa., Va., S15852
William, Ga., S.C., Susan, W7533; BLWt.28640-160-55
GILLINGWATER, James, Va., S39570; BLWt.6418-160-55
GILLIS, Alexander, N.Y., R4038
Arthur, Pa., S42742
John, Crane's Cont. Art., Mass., BLWt.4281-100-Sgt. Iss. 8/10/1789 to Richard Platt. No papers
John, N.Y., S10733
GILLISON, James, S.C., Jane, W10061
John, Va., Sarah Alexander,W7530; BLWt.870-300-Capt. Iss. 7/5/1799 to James Taylor, ass. No papers. Name also recorded as Gilleson
GILLIT, Asa, Cont. See GILLET
Elijah, Ct., S17436
Jeremiah, Ct. See GILLET
Rufus, Ct. See GILLET
GILLMAN, Charles, N.J., Mercy/Macy, W17013
Samuel, Pa. See GILMORE
GILLMOR, Daniel, Mass., Nabby, W14788
Samuel, Mass., Reuhma/Reumah, W23106; BLWt.9462-160-55
GILLMORE, Adam, Mass., S15853
John, Mass. See GILMORE
GILLOCK, John/Samuel, Va., S35969
Samuel, Va. See John
GILLON, Alexander, S.C., Sea Service, Ann, W25629
John, N.C., Jane, W7523; BLWt. 26445-160-55
GILLPATRICK, James, Mass., S29177
Joseph, Mass., Alice, W8853
Joshua, Mass., S31059
Nathaniel, Mass., S29178
Nathaniel, Mass. See GILPATRICK
GILLS, John, Va., S17976
William, Va. See GILL
GILLSON, Daniel, Mass., Rachel, W744
GILLUM, John, Va. See GILLIAM
John, Va. See GILLIAM
Jonathan, Pa., Va., S16824
Jourdan, Va. See GILLIAM
William, N.C., Wilkes Co. res., Mary, R4036 1/2
GILMAN, Andrew, Cont., N.H., S8566
Anthony (colored), Cont., Mass., N.H., S32729
Benjamin, N.H., Sally, W16270

GILMAN (continued)
Benjamin, N.H., Elizabeth, BLWt. 34622-160-55
Caleb, N.H., S10735
Calvin, Ct., Hannah, W19506
Charles, N.J. See GILLMAN
Daniel, Mass., Mehitable/ Mahitable, W16120
Dudley, N.H., Molly, W23104
Edmund, Va., S8565
Ezekiel, Cont., N.H., S35347
Ezekiel, Cont., N.H., Betsey, W23111; BLWt.3144-100-Pvt. Iss. 3/14/1793 to Benj. Bailey, ass. No papers
James, Cont., N.H., S9909
Jeremiah, Cont., Mass., N.H., S45552
Jeremiah, N.H., Sally, W1267; BLWt.26670-160-55
John, Cont., N.H., S45553
John, N.H., R4041
John, Va., S39574
Jonathan, N.H., Keziah, W24278
Joseph, Cont., Md. res. in 1811, S34900; BLWt.576-100
Joseph, N.H., BLWt.3139-100-Pvt. Iss. 3/25/1790. No papers
Joseph, N.H., War of 1812, Sarah, R4042
Joshua, N.H., S13135
Moses, N.H., Sarah, W16586
Nathaniel, N.H., Sarah, W17011
Nicholas, N.H., BLWt.784-300- Capt. Iss. 8/14/1789. No papers
Peter, N.H., S17980
Peter, N.H., Martha, W23110
Philip, Pa., Clarinda, R4040
Samuel Thing, Cont., N.H., Sarah, W19500
Simon, N.H., Sarah Brimhall, former wid., W15609
Simon, N.H., Tabitha, W15903
Stephen, N.H., Dorothy/Dolly, W21183; BLWt.6430-160-55
William, N.H., Anna, R4039
GILMOR, Thomas, Cont., N.H. See GILMORE
GILMORE, Alexander, Va., Rebecca, W10056
Charles, N.J., N.Y., Jane, W7526; BLWt.26333-160-55
Daniel, Mass. See GILLMOR
Daniel, Va., Rhoda, W1268; BLWt. 123-60-55
David, Mass., Mary, R4046; BLWt. 43877-160-55
David, Mass., Vt., S15142
George, N.C., Va., S13151
Huriah, Va., S32266
James, Mass., Navy, N.H., Elizabeth, W1269
James, N.C., Mary, W4207
James, N.C., Easter, W4680
John, Mass., S13152
John, Mass., S22266
John, Mass., Ruth, W291; BLWt. 13215-160-55
John, N.C., b. Pa., S10745
John, Art. Artificers of Pa., BLWt.13147-100-Pvt. Iss. 4/26/ 1791 to Alexander Power, ass.

GILMORE (continued)
of Dorothy Gilmore, admx. No papers
John, Va., S8570
Joseph, S.C., Elizabeth, W355
Robert, Mass., S36547
Samuel, Mass., See GILLMOR
Samuel, Pa., Dis. No papers
Thomas, Cont., N.H., S39575
Thomas, Pa., Elizabeth, R4044
William, Cont., Mass., N.Y., S8571
William, N.Y., BLWt.1285-100
GILMOUR, James, Va. & Indian Wars 1764 and 1774, S30432
GILPATRICK, Joseph, See GILLPATRICK
Nathaniel, Mass., S35345
GILPIN, Benjamin, Md., S13155
Israel, Del., S4297
Joseph, Del. Sea Service, S4296
William, Md., S39571
GILREATH, Alexander, N.C., S8564
William, N.C., S6888
GILSON, Daniel, Mass. See GILLSON
David, N.H., Polly, W10060; BLWt. 43872-160-55
Eleaser, Ct., BLWt.5862-100-Pvt. Iss. 9/15/1790 to Nicholas Root. No papers
Eleazer, Ct., S17973
Eleazer, Mass., S29174
Jacob, Ct., BLWt.5863-100-Pvt. Iss. 1/25/1796. No papers
Jacob, Ct., S39584
John, Mass., Abigail, W2540
Joseph, Mass., BLWt.4244-100- Pvt. Iss. 11/24/1791 to Isaac Bronson. No papers
Nathaniel, Mass., BLWt.4236-100- Pvt. Iss. 4/5/1796 to Oliver Ashley. No papers
Nathaniel, Mass., S45556
Peter, Mass., Sea Service, Lucinda, W11054; BLWt.40924- 160-55
Peter, Mass., S23232
Ruth, former wid. of Matthew Pierce, Mass., which see
Samuel, Mass., Rhoda, W19502
Solomon, Mass., Tamar, W14784
Solomon, N.H., Vt., Dolly, W19510; BLWt.11090-160-55
GILTNER, Francis, Pa., R4048
GILWAY, Robert, Cont. See GALWAY
GINDALL, John, Mass., BLWt.4249- 100-Sgt. Iss. 1/28/1790 to Joseph May. No papers
GINDER, Jacob, Cont., Pa. res., BLWt.2431-100
GINGER, Henry, Pa., S31064
GININGS, Abel, Mass., S29926
GINNETT, Thomas, Va., S39619
GINNINGS, William, Va., R4050
GIPSON, Charles, N.C. See GIBSON
Henry, N.H., S43599
Jacob, Va. See GIBSON
William, N.C., S17437
William, N.C. See GIBSON
GIRARDEAU, John, Ga., S17979. He also entered service in S.C., N.C. & Va., but troops not designated & cannot be identi-

GIRARDEAU (continued)
fied as given names of most of his officers are missing.
GIRDLER, James, Pa., BLWt.9508- 100-Pvt. Iss. 3/14/1799. No papers
James, Pa., S35994
GIROUX, Jean Baptiste, Cont., N.Y. See Baptiste JERO
GISH, Sany, former wid. of James Murry, which see
GIST, John, Md., BLWt.857-300- Capt. Iss. 12/16/1799 to John Gist. No papers
Joseph, N.C., Elizabeth, W7517
Mordecai, Cont., Md., BLWt. 108-850
Nathaniel, Cont., BLWt.1874-500
Thomas, N.C., S1762
GITCHEL, Zebulon, N.H., S23231
GITCHELL, Joseph, Mass., Sally, W23098
GITLING, William, Cont., Pa., see GITTING
GITSINGER, Adam, S.C., Franzine, W8880
GITTING, William, Cont, Pa., BLWt.196-150
GIVEN, John, Mass., S28742
Robert, Mass., BLWt.798-200-Lt. Iss. 2/23/1796 to John Coates, ass. No papers
William, N.J., R4053
GIVENS, James, N.C., S1879
Patrick, Pa., S38730
Robert, N.C., Va., Martha, R4054
Robert, Va., S13168
Samuel, N.C., S.C., Lucinda, W743
William, Va., S31058
GIVIN, John, Va. See GWIN
William, N.J. See GIVEN
GIVOURD, John, N.Y. See JERVIS
GLADDEN, Azariah, Ct., Navy, S29828
John, Pa., BLWt.9506-100-Pvt. Iss. 7/13/1789. No papers
Solomon, Va., S23656
GLADDING, James, Mass., Annar, W19511
Jedediah, Ct., Elizabeth, W25634
Nathaniel, R.I., Phebe, W24281
William, R.I., S38732
GLADHILL, Eli, N.J., BLWt.8339- 100-Pvt. Iss. 2/29/1789. No papers
Ely, N.J., Dis. No papers
GLADING, Jedediah, See GLADDING
Joseph, Ct. See GHADEN
GLADSON, William, Md., S34372
GLANDEN, Major, N.C., S41583
GLANN, John, N.Y., Jane, R4055
GLANTON, John, S.C., Elizabeth, W927
GLASCO, Caleb, N.C. See GLASCOW
GLASCOCK, Robert, Va. See GLASSCOCK
Thomas, Va., BLWt.877-200-Lt. Iss. 6/23/1796. No papers
GLASCOW, Caleb, N.C., R4056 1/2
GLASGO, William, Md., Elizabeth, W25632; BLWt.8178-160-55
GLASGOW, Caleb, N.C. See GLASCOW

GLASGOW (continued)
Cornelius, N.C., S1905
James, Pa., Jane, W25633; BLWt.39478-160-55
Lemuel, N.C., Alsey, R4056
Richard, N.C., Nancy/Ann, W7536; BLWt.36756-160-55
Robert, Va., R4057
GLASON, Patrick, See GLEASON
GLASS, Alexander, Ct., Jemima, W15770
Charles, Va., Nancy, W3410
Consider, Mass., Martha, W928; BLWt.824-160-55
George, Pa., S8575
Henry Vincent/Vincent, Va. See Vincent GLASS
James, Pa., S.C., S32272
John, Mass., S32730
John, Mass., S32733
John, Mass., S37005
Levi, N.C., S10749; BLWt.71212-150-55
Lucy, former wid. of Benjamin Pierce, Mass., which see
Michael, Md., Va., S16830
Seraiah, Mass., S32735
Vincent/Henry/Henry Vincent, Va., Susanna Dean, former wid., R4059; BLWt.296011-55
GLASSCOCK, Robert, Va., Nancy Howell/Howel or Weatherman/Wetherman, former wid., W11311; BLWt.90042-160-55
GLASSCOW, Caleb, N.C. See GLASCOW
GLASSES, Silas, Ct., BLWt.5879-100-Pvt. Iss. 9/20/1790. No papers
GLASSMIRE, Jacob, Pvt., Pa., BLWt.9459 iss. 10/28/1791
GLASSMYER, Jacob, Pa., S39587
GLATFELDER, George, N.C., S8220
GLAUTZ, Johannes/John, Pa., S3432
GLAZE, Thomas, N.C., Milly, W5283; BLWt.36614-160-55
Thomas, S.C., S10748
GLAZEBROOK, Julius, Va., S16831
GLAZER, Aaron, Mass. See GLAZIER
GLAZIER, Aaron, Mass., BLWt.4252-100-Pvt. Iss. 9/1/1790 to Theodosius Fowler. No papers
Aaron, Mass., S39593
Benjamin, Mass., S39592
Ebenezer, Mass., S44163
Eliphalet, Ct., Rachel, R4060
John, Ct., BLWt.5868-100-Pvt. Iss. 10/7/1789 to Benj. Tallmadge. No papers
John, Ct., Hannah, W4208
Jonathan, Mass., Zubah, W14790
Oliver, Mass., S29829; BLWt.9055-160-55
William, Mass., Lucena, W1852; BLWt.36758-160-55
GLEAN, Anthony, N.Y. & Sea Service, S23657
GLEASON, Benjamin, Ct., Cont., S39589; BLWt.642-100
Benjamin, Mass., Sarah, W9451; BLWt.71108-160-55
Benjamin, Mass., Deborah, W14794
Caleb, Mass. See GLEEZEN
Daniel, Mass. See GLEZEN

GLEASON (continued)
Ebenezer, Mass., S15146
James, Ct., Lovina, W24280
John, Ct., S31694
John, Mass., S32724
Joseph, Ct., N.Y., Elizabeth, W17949
Moses, Mass., R4061
Patrick, Cont., Va., S39590; BLWt.293-100
Phinehas, Mass., Margaret, W13277. D. 1809. Not identical with Phinehas Glezen
Thomas, Cont., Mass., S32732
Thomas, Mass., Dis. No papers
Thomas, Mass., S39591
Timothy, Navy, N.H. See GLEESON
William, Mass., BLWt.4235-100-Pvt. Iss. 1/6/1792. No papers
William, Mass., S32737
Windsor, N.H., Dis. No papers
GLEDDEN, William, Cont., N.H., Abigail, W16588
GLEESON, Timothy, Navy, N.H., Eleanor, W23114
GLEEZEN, Caleb, Mass., Barbara, W745
GLEN, Andrew, Pa., S30434
John, Cont., Pa., S38733
Robert, N.Y., BLWt.7182-100-Pvt. Iss. 6/9/1791 to William Thompson, ass. No papers
Thomas, N.J., BLWt.8360-100-Pvt. Iss. 4/5/1793 to John Potter, ass. No papers
GLENCER, John, Pa., Anna Margaretta, W3080; BLWt.2094-100
GLENDY, William, Pa., S39588
GLENN, Andrew, Pa. See GLEN
Bernard, Va., R14477; Va. Half Pay. See N.A. Acc. No. 874-050075 Half Pay
Hugh, Pa., BLWt.634-100
James, N.J., BLWt.8352-100-Pvt. Iss. 2/28/1791 to S. & Rosanna McCoy, admrs. No papers
James, N.C., S21768
James, Pa., S4298
John, Cont., Pa. See GLEN
John, Va., R4063
Sarah, former wid. of James Davidson, Pa., which see
GLENNEY, Isaac, Cont., Ct., Mass. Sarah, W17015
William, Ct. See GLENNY
GLENNY, Isaac, Mass., BLWt.4258-100-Sgt. Iss. 3/25/1790. No papers
William, Ct., Mary, W17950; BLWt.815-200-Lt. Iss. 8/5/1789 No papers
GLENTWORTH, George, Gen. Hosp., BLWt.808-450-Surgn. Iss. 5/9/1791. Also recorded as BLWt. 2584. No papers
James, Pa., S10186; BLWt.836-200-Lt. Iss. 8/14/1789. No papers
GLENTZER, John, Pa. See GLENCER
GLESEN, Benjamin, See GLEASON
GLESON, Caleb, Pvt., Mass., BLWt.4229 iss. 7/6/1791 to

GLESON (continued)
Silas Pepoon
GLESSINGER, John, Pa. See GRETSINGER
GLEZEN, Daniel, Mass., Hannah, W21186
Phinehas, Mass., S23233. Living in 1832
GLIDDEN, Andrew, Mass., S18837
Arnold, Cont., Mass., Hannah, W1594
David, Mass., N.H., Sarah, W19512
Deborah, former wid. of Joel Chandler, Cont. Mass., which see
Gideon, Cont., N.H., S37004
John, Cont., N.H., Abigail, W16587
William, Cont., N.H. See GLEDDEN
GLIDEWELL, Robert, Va., R4065
William, Va., S32271
GLINES, Benjamin, N.H., War of 1812, R4066
Eli, Cont., N.H., Polly, W25631
Israel, N.H., Margaret, W1851
Israel, N.H., Mary, W19513
John, N.H., Sarah Hutchins, former wid., W23356
Nathaniel, N.H., BLWt.3135-100-Pvt. Iss. 8/8/1793 to Samuel Finney, ass.
Nathaniel, N.H., Elizabeth, W24282
Robert, N.H., R4069 1/2
William, N.H., S45557; BLWt. 5374-160-55
GLINN, John, Va., S13166
GLISAN, Thomas, Md., BLWt.11284-100-Pvt. Iss. 12/18/1799. No papers
GLISSON, James, N.C., R4067
GLODE, John, Mass., S32731
Samuel, Mass., R6420. See Samuel Glode LONG
GLONINGER, John, Pa., Catharine, W2785
GLONTZ, John, Pa. See GLAUTZ
GLORY, William, Md., BLWt.11257-100-Pvt. Iss. 1/8/1796 to Geo. Ponsonby, ass. No papers
GLOSTER, James, See GLOUCESTER
GLOUCESTER, James, Va., S8578
GLOVER, Alexander, Mass., Nancy, W21187
Amos, Del., R4068
Barbara, former wid. of John Smith, S.C., which see
Benjamin, N.C., Va., S16829
Caesar, Mass., S32738
Chesley, Va., Mary, R4072
Edmund, Mass., Margaret, W14793
Ezekiel, N.Y., R4071
James, Cont., Pa., S6891
John, Cont., Mass., BLWt.763-850
John, N.H., S10746
John, N.C., S38734
Jonathan, Cont., Mass., S19681
Joseph, Va., Celia, W7534; BLWt.61056-160-55
Lemuel, Ct., BLWt.5892-100-Pvt.

GOINES, Levi, See GAINES
GOING, Daniel, Va., S38744
Edward, N.C., S6899
Jonathan, Mass., S13179
Sherard, Va., Susannah, W7545
William, Va., Mary, W7546; BLWt. 26870-160-55
GOINGS, William, Va., Elizabeth, W930
GOLD, Jabez, Mass. See GOULD
Joseph, Mass., S36557
Noah M., Ct. See GOULD
Seth, N.H., BLWt.3137-100-Pvt. Iss. 11/9/1792 to Wm. Hyde, ass. No papers
Tolcut, Navy, N.Y. res. & agcy. S44168
William, Md., BLWt.11263-100-Pvt. Iss. 5/12/1797 to James DeBaufre, ass. No papers
GOLDEN, Andrew, S.C., War of 1812, R14523
David, N.J., Deborah, W7553
Silas, Mass., BLWt.4233-100-Pvt. Iss. 12/16/1793 to Asa Baldwin. No papers
William, Pa., BLWt.9462-100-Drummer. Iss. 6/20/1789. No papers
Windsor, Mass. See Winsor GOOLDEN
GOLDER, Archibald, Md., Sarah, W9453
GOLDING, Amos, N.Y., Betsey, W21189
Reuben, S.C., S21770
William, Va., S31069
GOLDSBERRY, Charles, Md., War of 1812, Anne, W9459; BLWt.647-100, BLWt.337-60-55
John, Va., S2242
GOLDSBOROUGH, Charles, See GOLDSBERRY
William, Md., BLWt.860-200-Lt. No papers
GOLDSBURY, Mark, See Mack GOOLSBERRY
GOLDSBY, Elizabeth, former wid. of James Langham, Va. which see
GOLDSMITH, James, Ct., BLWt.5838-100-Pvt. Iss. 9/23/1789. No papers
James, Ct., S22794
Jeremiah, Cont., N.Y., S44167
Jeremiah, Mass., S29834
John, S.C., S31699
John, Va., S35974
Joseph, Ct., BLWt.5878-100-Pvt. Iss. 9/23/1789. No papers
Josiah, N.J., S13170
Pelatiah M., Mass. See Pelatiah McGOLDSMITH
Thomas, Md., BLWt.2399-20
William, Ct., BLWt.5858-100-Pvt. Iss. 9/23/1789. No papers
Zaccheus, Cont., Mass., S32746
GOLDTHWAIT, James, Mass., S32744
Philip, Ct., BLWt.5891-100-Pvt. Iss. 3/7/1798 to Thomas G. Thornton. No papers
Philip, Cont., Mass., Martha, W24299
Samuel, Mass., Thankful W., BLWt.11406
Timothy, Cont., Mass., S29831;

GOLDTHWAIT (continued)
BLWt.6005-160-55
GOLDY, John, N.J., BLWt.8327-100-Sgt. Iss. 10/17/1789 to John Pope, ass. No papers
John, N.J., Mary, W3081
Nicholas, N.J., S34373
GOLEAR, William, See GAILER
GOLENTINE, Abraham, See GOLLINTINE
GOLIGHTLY, David, S.C., S18888
GOLLADAY, Joseph, See GOLLODAY
GOLLENTINE, Abraham, See GOLLINTINE
GOLLINTINE, Abraham, Va., W3540; BLWt.96074-160-55
GOLLODAY, Joseph, Va., Mary, W7555
GOLLYHORN, Solomon, Va., S6907
GOLSAN, Lewis, S.C., Elizabeth, R4096
GOMBARE, John, Md., S25111
GONSALUS, James, N.J., S23234
GONSALVA, John, See GONSOLVE
GONSOLVE, John R.I., S21771
GONTER, John, Cont., Pa., Elizabeth, W11059; BLWt.7-60-55 & 234-100
GOOCH, James, Navy, N.H. res., S22268
Jedediah, Cont., Mass., Mary, W23116
John, Mass., S39606
Rowland, N.C. See GOUCH
GOOD, Jacob, Pa., Catharine,R4104
James, Mass., See GOUD
John, Crane's Cont. Art., Mass., BLWt.4289-100-Pvt. Iss. 11/6/1795 to Jeremiah Hill. No papers
Solomon, N.C., S6897
William, N.C., Va., Mary, W1413; BLWt.13749-160-55
GOODALE, Benjamin, N.Y., BLWt. 7190-100-Pvt. Iss. 8/12/1790 to Cornelius Glen, ass. No papers
Chester, Ct., Asenath, W19522; BLWt.26983-160-55
Ebenezer, Ct., Jerusha, W4967
Ebenezer, Mass., S29832
Ebenezer, Mass., Betsey, W21190
Eli, Mass., Mary Ann, W16272
Elijah, Mass., Elizabeth, R4100
Ezekiel, N.H., S43609
Isaac, Mass., Electa, W8860; BLWt.6386-160-55
Mary, former wid. of Zachariah Gatchell, Cont., Mass., which see
Nathan, Mass., BLWt.4221-100-Fifer. Iss. 7/25/1799 to Abijah Holbrook. No papers
Nathan, Mass., S44165
Nathan, Mass., BLWt.794-300-Capt., iss. 1/20/1790. No papers
Samuel, Mass., S32742
Sarah, former wid. of Jacob Fuller, Mass., which see
Zachariah, Mass., S37019
GOODALL, Alvin/Alvan, Ct., Cont., Alice Potter, former wid., W18769
Ezekiel, N.H., See GOODALE

GOODALL (continued)
Jacob, Ct., S45562
James, N.Y., BLWt.7158-100-Pvt. Iss. 7/20/1790 to Samuel Curray, ass. No papers
James, N.Y., S43624
John, Va., Sally/Sarah, W5284; BLWt.87006-160-55
Richard, Va., S15861
Silas, Ct., Cont., S36559; BLWt. 813-200-Lt. No papers
GOODCOURAGE, John, N.Y., BLWt. 7175-100-Pvt. Iss. 12/28/1791 to Cornelius Vandyck, ass. No papers
John, N.Y., Sally, W17955
GOODDELL, Jabez, Ct., Peninah, W14800
GOODE, Edmund, Va., Sarah, W3801
John, Va., S30443
Richard, N.C., Rebecca, W8855
Thomas, Va., S38742
William, Md., S6904
William, Va., S8581
GOODELL, Alvan, Ct. See Alvin GOODALL
Amos, Mass., Susannah, W25641
Asa, Ct., S15865
Asenath, former wid. of John Lovejoy, Vt. Which see
Elijah, N.Y., Lydia, W16021
Ezra, Ct., S43608
Jabez, Ct. See GOODDELL
Jacob, Ct., See GOODALL
James, Mass., Eunice, W11067
Josiah, Cont., Mass., S13156
Silas, Cont., Ct., S36559; BLWt.813-200-Lt. Iss. 5/13/1796. Soldier's named spelled Goodall
William, Mass., S42209
GOODEN, Abigail, W1414, former wid. of Jacob Flynn, Mass., which see
George, N.Y., S44881
James, Md. See GOODING
Lewis, Va. See GOODIN
GOODENOUGH, Adino, Mass., N.H., Rebecca, W21200
Calvin, N.H., BLWt.3132-100-Pvt. Iss. 3/26/1796 to Peter Sweir, ass. No papers
David, Mass., N.H., Vt., Abigail, W17953
Ebenezer, Mass., S38739
Ephraim, Pvt., Invalids, BLWt. 13145 iss. 2/27/1790 to Theodosius Fowler, ass.
Isaac, Mass., S32752
Salmon, Green Mt. Boys, Vt., R4105
GOODENOW, Daniel, Mass., S22272
David, Mass., Abigail, W14795
Eliab, Mass., Jemima/Mima, W19525
Ephraim, Mass., S32743
Isaac, Mass. See GOODENOUGH
John, Mass., S2239
Nahun, N.H. See GOODNOW
William, Mass., Phebe, W19524
GOODFAITH, David, Ct., BLWt.5885-100-Pvt. Iss. 9/24/179? to James F. Sebor. No papers

GOODFAITH (continued)
David, Ct., S36553
David, Ct., See GOODHARD
GOODHARD, David, Ct., R4106
GOODHUE, Joseph, Mass., Vt., R4108
Josiah, N.H., Elizabeth, R4107; BLWt.61275-160-55
Phineas, Cont., Mass. or N.H., Hannah, W14806
GOODIN, Isaac, Pa., S2240
Lewis, Va., Charlotte, W2608; BLWt.15447-160-55
GOODING, David, ?, Ann/Anna, R4109 Va. res. of wid. in 1855
James, Md., W3343
Jonathan, Cont., Mass., R4110
Richard, Mass., Anna/Ann, W2097; BLWt.3995-160-55
Thaddeus, Mass., S45563
GOODKINS, Samuel, Ct., BLWt.5887-100-Pvt. Iss. 8/27/1790 (or 1796?) to Joseph Whitton, no papers
GOODLETT, John, S.C., S9340
William, S.C., Nancy, W8857
GOODLOE, Henry, Va., S35975
GOODMAN, Ansel, Va., S13175
Elihu, Mass., S31068
Elizabeth, former wid. of Wm. Pollard, S.C., which see
Henry, S.C., S3399
Horsley, Va., Elizabeth/Betsey, R4111
Jacob, N.C., S1206; BLWt.26416-160-55
John, N.Y., R4112
Joseph, Va., Nancy, W3411; BLWt. 10243-160-55
Moses, Ct., Cont., S36550
Richard, Ct., Cont., S13165
Thomas, Va., BLWt.12157-100-Pvt. Iss. 5/11/1792 to Robert Means, ass. No papers
Thomas, Va., S17981
GOODNER, Conrad, N.C., Elizabeth, R4113
GOODNIGHT, Christopher, Diannah, W9458; BLWt.75005-160-55
Henry, N.C., S38743
GOODNO, Calvin, N.H., S38737
GOODNOUGH, Calvin, See GOODNO
GOODNOW, Abner, Mass., Esther, W2563
Eben, Mass., S13158
Eli, Mass., S44882
Eliab, Mass. See GOODENOW
John, Mass., S30439; BLWt.11265-160-55
Nahun, N.H., S15862
GOODOWN, Jacob V., Ga., S31701
GOODRICH, Abel, Ct., S13181
Abner, Ct., Cont., S42754
Allen, Ct., S18418
Bethuel, Ct., S38740; BLWt.5833-100-Pvt. Iss. 4/19/1790. No papers
Charles, Mass., Ann, W19516
Crafts, Ct., R4115
Daniel, Mass., BLWt.1548-100
David, Ct., Penelope Hillyer, former wid., R5026. Her 2nd husb., Elijah Hubbard, and her

GOODRICH (continued)
3rd husb., James Hillyer, also served in Rev. War.
David, Ct., Cont., S10760
Elisha, Ct., S43612
George, Ct., S32755
Gideon, Ct., S10753
Gilbert, Mass., Sarah, W21199
Hezekiah, Vt., S18839
Ichabod, Ct., BLWt.5886-100-Pvt. Iss. 8/15/1792 to George Wells. No papers
Ichabod, Ct., S36556
Isaac, Ct., Electa, R4116; BLWt.21835-160-55
Isaac, Ct., Cont., Sarah, W17016
Jacob, Mass., S28745
James, Ct., Ct. Sea Service, Privateer, S15864
Jared, Ct., BLWt.5849-100-Pvt. Iss. 8/15/1792 to John & George Wills/Wells. No papers
Jared, Cont., Ct., Deborah, W17954
John, Ct., Cont., Mabel, W24292
John, Ct., Cont., BLWt.1607-100
John, Va., S1763
John H., Ct., Mary, W4682
Joshua, Mass. See GOODRIDGE
Josiah, Vt., Lucy, W7554; BLWt. 33566-160-55
Levi, Ct., Cont., Julia Ann,R4118
Micah, Ct., S15858
Michael, Ct., S43628
Nathan, Ct., S32276
Noah, Mass., BLWt.4205-100-Pvt. Iss. 4/21/1794. No papers
Noah, Mass., Martha, W21204
Ozias, Ct. See Ozius GOODRIDGE
Roswel/Roswell, Ct., S31696
Roswell, Ct., Cont., S13182
Samuel, Mass., S43610
Simeon, Ct., S21772
Simeon, Ct., R4119
Solomon P., Ct., Anna, W2095
Stephen, Ct., Cont., S38735
Thomas, Mass., S13164
Thomas, Mass. See GOODRIDGE
William, BLWt.13115-100-Pvt. "in the Sappers & Miners". Iss. 9/6/1791. No papers
William, Ct., Phebe, W17019
Zenas, Ct., Lois Cash, former wid., R1780
Zenas, Mass., Mary, W21202
GOODRICK, John, Ct. See GOODRICH
GOODRIDGE, Abijah, Mass., S5201
Asael, Mass., S9911
Benjamin, Mass., S37008
Daniel, Mass. See GOODRICH
Ezekiel, Mass., BLWt.809-200-Lt. Iss. 3/23/1797 to Benjamin Dana ass. of Bernard Goodridge, only son & heir of E.G. No papers
Francis, Mass., S18841
John, Mass., S30438
Joseph, Mass., Dis. No papers
Joshua, Mass., Sally, W21195
Oliver, Mass., S21769
Ozius, Ct., BLWt.821-150-Ensign Iss. 8/10/1789 to Richard Platt, ass. No papers
Samuel, Mass., S32749

GOODRIDGE (continued)
Samuel, Mass. See GOODRICH
Thomas, Mass., Betsey, W17020
William, Mass., Elizabeth,W23124
GOODRUM, Bennet, Va., Sarah/Sally, R4120
John, Va., S8589
GOODSELL, Ephraim, Ct., Navy, S29182
Isaac, Ct., Elizabeth Webster, former wid., BLWt.40502-160-55
John, Ct., Abigail, W17952
Rachel, former wid. of William Bailey, Ct., which see
Samuel, Ct., Abigail, W21192
Thomas, Ct., S10756
GOODSEY, William, Va. See GODSEY
GOODSON, Benjamin, S.C., Dorothy, W7550; BLWt.28637-160-55
Joshua, N.C., S.C., S2578
Thomas, S.C., S9342
Thomas, Va., S6901
William, R.I., Anna Sprague, former wid., R10008, BLWt.3157-100-Pvt. Iss. 8/7/1789 to Richard Platt, ass. No papers
William, Va., S30440
GOODSPEED, Elijah, Mass., Privateer, R4122
Elisha, Mass., Esther, W545; BLWt.9457-160-55
Nathaniel, Ct., Mass., N.H., Abigail, W23117
Sympson, R.I., Marcy, W2786; BLWt.26825-160-55
GOODWILL, John, Mass., Sally, R4123
GOODWIN, Aaron, Navy, Mass., & probably N.H., S37020
Adam, Mass., S19301
Amaziah, N.H., S29179; BLWt. 24752-160-55
Amos, Va., Elizabeth, W2096; BLWt.29726-160-55
Amos W., Mass., Eunice, W24298
Benjamin, Mass., S46039
Benjamin, Mass. and probably N.H., S18840
Benjamin, Va., S34903
Daniel, N.H., S10755
David, S.C., Nancy, W650; BLWt.28562-160-55
Elijah, Cont., Vt., S38736
Francis, Pa., Va., R4126
Francis L.B., Mass., BLWt.803-300-Surgn's. Mate. Iss. 4/9/1790. No papers
George, Mass., S37022; BLWt. 19725-160-55
George, N.Y., BLWt.7159-100-Pvt. Iss. 9/27/1790. No papers
Hezekiah, Ct., BLWt.5852-100-Pvt. Iss. 12/5/1791 to Martin Kingsley. No papers
Hezekiah, Ct., Polly, W27873
Huldah, former wid. of Abel Merrill, Mass., which see
Jacob, Mass., S37014
James, N.H., Mary, W14804
John, Mass., Sarah, W7551; BLWt. 19758-160-55
John, N.C., b. Va., S6900
John, N.C., S6908

GOODWIN (continued)
John, Pa., Rachel, W3136
John, Va., S8587
Joseph, Ct., S29180
Joseph, Mass., S29833
Joseph, Mass., Mary, W23126
Julius Coleman, Va., S1207
Lemuel/Lemel, N.C., S8588
Levi, Ct., S17442
Mary, former wid. of Robert Wright, Va., which see
Moses, Ct., S13157
Nathaniel, Ct., R4130
Nehemiah, Mass., R4131
Paul, Cont., Mass., S37010
Reuben, Mass., S18419
Reuben, Mass., Ruth, W24284; BLWt.34545-160-55
Richard, Mass. See GOODING
Robison, N.C., S6894
Samuel, N.H., S16387
Seth, Ct., Mahitable, W1412; BLWt.28557-160-55
Simeon, Cont., Mass., Mary, W24293
Solomon, Ct., Ann, W24283
Theophilus, N.C., S37954
Thomas, Mass., S2241
Thomas, Mass., S32750
Thomas, Va., S13176
Uriah, Cont., Mass., Esther, W2098; BLWt.17879-160-55
Uriah, Mass., Abigail, W24288
Wiley, N.C., S37952
William, Mass., S32740
William, N.Y., BLWt.7183-100-Pvt. Iss. 8/18/1790 to Joseph Stringham, ass. No papers
William, S.C., Grace, W8861
Zebedee, Cont., Ct., Caroline, W21198
GOODWYN, David, Va., R4125
William, S.C., R4134
GOODY, Lambert, Md., BLWt.11277-100-Pvt. Iss. 12/22/1794 to Henry Purdy, ass. No papers
GOODYEAR, Edward, Ct., BLWt.5853-100-Pvt. Iss. 3/7/1792 to Jonathan Tuttle. No papers
Edward, Ct., S43623
George, Pa., S22270
Stephen, Ct., S16832
Theophilus, Ct., Dis. No papers
GOOGINS, David, Mass., Mary, W24297
Stephen, Cont., Mass., S37011
GOOKIN, Daniel, Mass., N.H., S17985; BLWt.785-200-Lt. Iss. 1/4/1793. No papers
GOOKINS, Samuel, Ct., Polly, W10064
GOOLD, Alexander, See GOULD
Daniel, Mass., S37006
Ebenezer, Mass. See GOULD
James, Ct., Mary, W17022
James, N.H., S8231
James, N.H., S45561
John, Ct., R.I., S16128
John, Mass., Margaret, W23125
John, Vt., Nancy, W19517; BLWt. 26379-160-55
Joseph, Mass., Lydia, W23123

GOOLD (continued)
Seth, Mass., N.H.,Vt. See GOULD
Simeon, N.H., S43618
William, N.H., Mehitable, W24296
William, N.Y., See GOULD
William, Vt., Abigail, W19518; BLWt.27640-160-55
GOOLDEN, Winsor/Windsor, Mass., Ruby, W1167; BLWt.29729-160-55
GOOLSBERRY, Mack/Mark, Va., S35976; BLWt.1084-100
GOOSELY, George, Va. Sea Service, R55, Va. Half Pay. See N.A. Acc. No. 837, YS File
James, Va., R14483, Va. Half Pay
GORDAN, Bernard, N.J. See GORDON
Lawrence, Va. See Laurance GORDON
GORDARD, Lewis, Navy, France, R4103, N.Y. res. See GODARD
GORDEN, Abner, Va. See GORDON
Alexander, S.C., R20375
Ambus, Cont., Va. See Ambrose GORDON
Caleb, Mass. See GORDON
Charles, N.C., S45881
Eliphalet, N.J., S43621
James, N.C., b. Md., Mary, W3979
John, Pa., S2577
John, Pa., S39603
John, Va., Mary, W8858
Robert, Hazen's Regt., Canadian, BLWt.13127-100-Pvt. Iss. 5/16/1792 to Jacob Miller, Admr. Notation: "Cert. of issuing this Warrant given 5/14/1814."
GORDIN, Isaac, N.C., Va., S9341
GORDON, Abel, N.H., S16835
Abner, Va., Elizabeth, W8859; BLWt.56503-160-55
Albion, Va., Elizabeth, W7548
Alexander, Ct., Privateer, R4137
Alexander, S.C. See GORDEN
Ambrose/Ambus, Cont., Va., BLWt. 539-200
Anna, former wid. of Wm. Herrick N.Y., which see
Archibald, Md., Pa., S34904
Archibald, N.J., Siche, W7547
Barnard, N.J., BLWt.8356-100-Pvt. Iss. 3/16/1790. No papers
Benjamin, Cont., Res. Belmont, Me. in 1818, S37009
Benjamin, N.C., S32274
Bernard/Bernadus, N.J., S42753
Caleb, Mass., Miriam, W23122
Chapman, N.C., Charity, W356; BLWt.11066-160-55
Charles, Va., S41585
Daniel, Md., R4140
Daniel, Pa., BLWt.9453-100-Pvt. Iss. 4/19/1791. No papers
David, N.J., BLWt.8361-100-Pvt. Iss. 9/8/1789 to Samuel Rutan, ass. No papers
David, N.J., S2576
David, N.J., S43617
Eliphalet, N.H. See GORDEN
Eliphalet, N.H., BLWt.1054-100. Soldier was dead in 1822. This claim allowed on service of Eliphalet Gorden, S43631, who was living in 1836.

GORDON (continued)
George, Ct., Cont., S39599
James, Cont., N.H., Mass., S37015
James, N.H., S43629
James, Va., S37953
James F., N.C., S32278
Jesse, Ga., N.C., Nancy, W13280
John, Md., BLWt.11266-100-Pvt. Iss. 6/11/1790. No papers
John, Mass., S19300
John, Mass., Susannah/Susan, W19515
John, N.H., Jane, W14803
John, Pa. See GORDEN
John, Pa., S42751
John, Pa., Sarah, W3412
John, Pa., BLWt.2031-100
John, Va. See GORDEN
Joseph, Mass., N.H., Dorothy/Dolly, W1751; BLWt.2009-100
Joseph, Pa., S43616
Josiah, N.H., S29838
Josiah, N.H., Jane, W23119
Kenneth, N.J., S10752
Laurance/Lawrence, Va., S31071
Lyddal, S.C., Va., S31700
Lydia, former wid. of John James, Mass., which see
Nathaniel, Mass., Alletha/Allethea, W25637; BLWt.29727-160-55
Peter, Hazen's Regt., Canadian, BLWt.13124-100-Pvt. Iss. 1/23/1790. No papers
Peter, N.J., S28743
Richard, N.C., Ga., S3404
Robert, Pa., S39604
Robert, Pa., Mary, W1853; BLWt.34985-160-55
Samuel, Ct., S43614
Samuel, S.C., S30441
Solomon, N.C., S41584
Thomas, Del., BLWt.10774-100-Pvt. Iss. 9/2/1789. No papers
Thomas, Pa., Mary, W2932
Timothy, Mass., N.H., S29181
Timothy, N.J., Allthe, W17017
William, Cont., Mass., S32745
William, Cont., N.H., Hannah, W15905
William, N.H., BLWt.3143-100-Sgt. Iss. 3/25/1790. No papers
William, N.C., b. Md., S3403
Zebulon, N.H., Anna, R4139; BLWt.19513-160-55
GORE, Avery, Pa., R4142
Eleazar/Ealeazor/Eleazer, S.C. S35978
John, Cont., Va. See GOARE
John, Pa. & Ct., S22793
Joseph, Cont., Mass., S32741
Notley, Ga., N.C., S31070
Obadiah, Ct., S39601; BLWt. 817-200-Lt. Iss. 2/22/1791. No papers
Samuel, Pa. & Ct., Sarah, W3242
Thomas, Del., BLWt.10771-100-Drummer. Iss. 9/7/1789 to Wm. J. Vredenburgh, ass. No papers
Thomas, S.C., S38746
GORHAM, Daniel, Ct., Cont., S13159

GORHAM (continued)
George, Cont., Ct., S13161
George, Mass., S32748
John, Mass., S30437; BLWt.1905-100
John, Mass., Thankful, W19523
Joseph, Cont., Ct., Elizabeth Baldwin, former wid., W17247
Joseph, Mass., S32754
Joseph, Lamb's Art., N.Y., BLWt.7196-100-Pvt. Iss. 10/23/1790. No papers
Josiah, Mass., Martha, W1165; BLWt. 1965-100. Iss. 9/9/1833; BLWt.138-60-55
Nathan, Ct., Sea Service, S15150
Nehemiah, Ct., S36552; BLWt.814-200-Lt. Iss. 2/25/1800 to Jonas Stanbury. No papers
Phinehas, N.Y., S36555
Seth, Ct., S15587
Seth, Ct., Lovisa, W9457; BLWt. 26199-160-55
Silas, Mass., Cynthia, W25642
GORIN, John, Va., Indian War & War of 1812, Elizabeth, W25643; BLWts. 65448-120-55 & 65991-40-50, allowed on services in War of 1812.
GORLAND, John, N.C. See GARLAND
GORMAN, Archibald, Pa., S1204
John, Md., BLWt.11255-100-Pvt. Iss. 5/11/179?. No papers
John, Pa., (?), R4144
Joseph, Pa., S34374; BLWt.1244-150-Ensign
Lawrence, Pa., BLWt.9436-100-Pvt. Iss. 7/27/1789 to Richard Platt, ass. No papers
GORRELL, John, Pa., BLWt.9454-100-Pvt. Iss. 8/14/1793 to Jasper Iserloan, ass. No papers
John, Pa., S35970
GORSAGE, John, N.C., S2579
GORSLINE, Samuel N.Y., S43615
GORTON, Benjamin, Cont., Ct., S13154
Benjamin, R.I., S21235
Hezekiah, R.I., R4145
John, R.I., Phebe, W13285
Joseph, Ct., S31698
Prosper, R.I., S38741
Samuel, R.I., S23237
Slaid, R.I., Mary, W21191
William, R.I., Sarah Greene/Green, former wid., W24317
GORVEY, Thomas, N.C., S41556
GORY, Thomas, Mass. See GARY
GOSA, James Wallace, S.C., Elizabeth Ann, R25446
GOSELIN, Lewis, Col. Hazen's Regt., Canadian, BLWt.886-200-Lt. Iss. 9/21/1790 to Benj. Moers, ass. No papers. See Louis Gossalin in Heitman's Reg., p.254
GOSLEE, Solomon, Ct., Cont., S31697
GOSLEY, Solomon. See GOSLEE
GOSLIN, Lewis, Moses Hazen's Regt., S43613
GOSLINE, Samuel. See GORSLINE
GOSLING, George, S.C., See GOSSLING
Samuel, N.J., S817
GOSNELL, Benjamin, Va., Dorcas, W11060; BLWt.36757-160-55
George, Pa., Eleanor Kramer, former wid., W5016
GOSNER, Peter, Pa., BLWt.834-300-Capt. Iss. 8/31/1792 to William Lane, ass. of Dan Gosner, Admr. No papers
GOSS, Abraham, Pa., S22792
Andrew, Ct., S32747
Comfort, Mass., Dorcas, W16589
Ebenezer, Cont., Pa., S16129
Ebenezer H., Cont., N.H., S37021
Ephraim, Cont., N.H., Anah, W17023; BLWt.1971-160-55
Ephraim, Mass., Ruth, W21193; BLWt.35828-160-55
Francis, Mass., Sea Service, Privateer, Elizabeth Colley, former wid., W14559
Jacob, N.C., S8579
John, Mass., N.H., Catharine, W21194
John A., N.H., S45560
Jonathan, Mass., R.I., S32275
Oliver, N.Y., Vt., Rachel, W19526
Phillip/Philip, N.H., S5200
Richard, Mass., Hannah, W14807
Samuel, N.H., S47179
William, Navy, Mass., Privateer, Susan, R4148
GOSSARD, Rufus, See GODARD
GOSSELIN, Clement, Cont., Canada, Catharine, W16655; BLWt.885-300-Capt. Iss. 1/22/1790. No papers
Louis, See Lewis GOSELIN
GOSSET, John, Va., S42750
GOSSETT, William, Va., S6905
GOSSLER, Philip, Pa., Mary, W4443
GOSSLING, George, S.C., Elizabeth Powers, former wid., W10230; BLWt.56971-160-55
GOSSOM, Joseph, Mass., S32757
GOSWICK, Nicholas, N.C., R4149
GOTAN, Henry, See GOTMAN
GOTHAM, Edward, N.H., BLWt.3152-100-Fifer. Iss. 8/10/1789 to Richard Platt, ass. No papers
Henry, See GOTMAN
GOTMAN, Henry, Cont., N.H., enl. in Mass., Betsey, W1753; BLWt. 6444-160-55
GOTT, Abi, former wid. of Josiah West, Mass., which see
John, N.Y., Sarah, W25636; BLWt.19761-160-55
Joshua, Mass., S29837
Robert, N.C., R4150
Story, N.Y., Polly, W23129
GOUCH, Joseph, See GOUGE
Rowland, N.C., Milley, W7541
GOUD, James, Mass., Nancy, W4151; BLWt.31789-160-55
Lazarus, Mass., Rahannas, R4152
GOUDELOCK, Davis, S.C., S21236
GOUGE, Hannah, former wid. of Edward McCollum, N.H. which see
GOUGE (continued)
Joseph, N.C., S.C., Rosa R4156; BLWt.18368-160-55
Phebe, former wid. of Eli Smith, Ct., which see
GOUGER, Henry, N.C., Catherine, R4157
GOUGH, Ignatius, Va., S1205
John Baptist, Md., S16833
GOULD, Abraham, Mass., S32756
Alexander, Mass., Navy, Betsey, W7542; BLWt.36750-160-55
Amos, Mass., S13174
Asa, Mass., S13177
Asa, Mass., Sally, W2542; BLWt. 17878-160-55
Asa, Mass., N.Y., Betsey, W15749
Benjamin, Cont., Vt. Green Mt. Boys, S43622
Benjamin, Cont., Mass., S19682
Benjamin, Mass., Mary, W15904
Benjamin, Mass., Eusebia, W21197
Cabaralzaman, Mass. See Camaralsaman
Camaralsaman/Cabarlzaman, Mass., S33265
Daniel, Cont., Mass., Ann M., W1166; BLWt.6443-160-55
Daniel, Mass., S29839
Daniel, Mass., See GOOLD
Daniel, N.J., S22269
David, Mass., S5199
Ebenezer, Mass., Mille, W14799
Ebenezer, Mass., Anna, W23118
Ebenezer Brewster, Mass., Beulah, W14802
Edmond/Edmund, Mass., S23238
Eli, Mass., S33264
Elijah, Mass., Lucinda, W19527
Elijah, N.H., Freelove, W5285; BLWt.19771-160-55
Isaac, Mass., S13162
Jabez, Cont., Mass., R.I., Esther, W23127
Jacob, N.H., S38738
Jeremiah, Cont., N.H., S45559
Jesse, Mass., Polly, W3800
John, Ct., S39605
John, Mass., S20775
John, Mass. See GOOLD
John, Mass., Mary/Molly, W24289
John, N.J., S1005
John, N.Y., S10754
John, R.I., BLWt.3162-100-Pvt. Iss. 11/26/1791. Note in book: "Served to the end of the war and rec'd the gratuity. See Rolls"
John, R.I., BLWt.2318-100
Jonas, Cont., Mass., S37007
Jonathan, Mass., Lydia, W24286
Joseph, Mass. See GOOLD
Joseph, Mass., S8583
Joseph, Mass., R4160
Josiah, N.J., S1006
Levi, Pa., BLWt.9484-100-Dragoon Iss. 1/13/1800 to Abijah Holbrook, ass. No papers
Moriah, Mass., Lucy, W23120
Nathan, Ct., Navy, Patience, W17957
Noah, Mass., S43620

GOULD (continued)
Noah M., Ct., Mass., S37013
Oliver, Mass., Sarah, W21203
Peter, Mass., Margaret, W19519
Phebe, former wid. of Silas Roso/Rosier/Rosury, Mass., which see
Robert, N.J., Hester, W1270; BLWt.36538-160-55
Samuel, Ct., Sarah, W21201
Samuel, Mass., Catharine, W1415
Samuel, Mass., Ruth, W14797
Sarah, former wid. of Joshua Hinckley, Cont., N.Y., which see
Seth, Mass. (?), N.H., Vt., Submit, R4162. She was pensioned on acct. of service of her 1st husb., James Williams, Mass., which see
Silas, Ct., Mass., S37023
Simeon, N.H., See GOOLD
Stephen, Mass., N.H., S8582
Submit, Mass., wid. of Seth, which see
Thomas, Cont., Ct., S22271
Timothy, N.J., Jemima Vreeland, former wid., W6376; BLWt.38514-160-55
Tobias, Mass., Rhoda Wagg, former wid., W22502. Her last husb. was a pensioner. See James Wagg, Cont., Mass.
Willard, Ct., Cont., Mass., S13180
William, Ct., BLWt.5864-100-Pvt. Iss. 4/6/1790. No papers
William, Ct., S42752
William, Md., Sarah, W9454
William, Mass., S43611
William, N.H., S45558
William, N.H., See GOOLD
William, N.J., S2575
William, N.Y., Sarah, R4161
William, Vt., See GOOLD
GOULDMAN, Francis, Va., S39595
GOULDSBOROUGH, William, Md., BLWt.860-200-Lt. Iss. 5/15/1789. No papers. See William Goldsborough in Heitman's Reg.
GOURLEY, Thomas, Pa., R4163
GOURTHLEY, William, Lamb's Art., N.Y., BLWt.7191-100-Pvt. Iss. 9/3/1790 to John Brown, ass. No papers
GOUTCHES, Abraham, N.Y.(?), Rachel, R4164
GOUYD, William, R4390
GOVE, Ebenezer, N.H., S15439
Jacob, Mass., Martha, W23130
John, Cont., Lois, W23115
Levi, Mass., N.H., S17984
GOWAN, Ezekiel, Mass. See GOWEN
Francis, Pa., BLWt.9426-100-Pvt. Iss. 9/4/1789. No papers
Hugh, Pa., BLWt.9463-100-Pvt. Iss. 3/4/1791. No papers
Hugh, Pa., S46198
GOWDY, Alexander, Ct., S10750
Hill, Ct., Roxana, W17951
John, Ct., S31066
Samuel, Ct., S15151

GOWELL, Benjamin, Mass., Susanna, W24294
GOWEN, Ezekiel, Mass., Navy, Lucy, W14796; BLWt.28566-160-55
Francis, Pa., S34902
Frederick, Va. See GOEN
Jacob, Va., S32273
John, Cont., Mass., Mary, W23128; BLWt.2348-160-55
William, Mass., Elizabeth, R4166
Zephaniah, Va., R4165
GOWENS, Charles, Va., S31072; BLWt.26106-160-55
GOWER, Abel, N.C., Elizabeth, W7552
George, Pa., S22791
Matthew, N.C., R4168
GOWIN, William, Mass., See GOWEN
GOWING, Jabez, Mass., Sarah, W14805
GOWNS, Edward, Mass. See McGOWNS
GOYNE, James, S.C., S30442
GRAAF, John, Pa. See GAUF
GRACE, Aaron, Pa., BLWt.9483-100-Pvt. "in Moylan's Dragoons." Iss. 7/30/1789. Certified by N. Cutting, 12/19/1820
Benjamin, N.H., S44169
Charles B., N.H., S13218
George, Pa., BLWt.9482-100-Pvt. "in Moylan's Dragoons". Iss. 8/5/1789 to John Baldwin, ass. Notation: "Cert. by N. Cutting, Dec. 12th, 1820".
Jacob, Pa., S39629
James, N.Y., BLWt.7171-100-Pvt. Iss. 9/15/1790 to John S. Hobart, et al, ass. No papers
John, Mass., Dis. No papers
John, Mass., S17988
John, N.J., S34375; BLWt.1925-100
John, N.C., Nancy, W7582
John, Pa., BLWt.9486-100-Dragoon. Iss. 10/27/1791. No papers
Joseph, Mass., Mara, R4171
Lawrence, N.Y., Elizabeth, W16276
Manuel, Mass., S29184
Newell, Mass., R4172
Patrick, Cont., Mass., Huldah, W24311
Richard, Md., R14603
William, Md., Lydia, W10067
GRACEY, John, N.J. See GRACE
Matthew, N.J., BLWt.8357-100-Pvt. Iss. 2/10/1792. No papers
Robert, N.C., S.C., S8635
GRACY, John, N.C. See GREACEY
GRADDY, Susan, former wid. of John McQuady, Va., which see
GRADY, William, Va., S39617
GRAEFF, Frederick, Pa., Margaretta W3082
GRAFF, John, Mass., BLWt.4219-100-Pvt. Iss. 9/9/1790 to Elizabeth Graff, wid. No papers
Philip, N.Y., Deborah, W23154
Ruth, former wid. of Reese Evans, Pa., which see
Samuel, Pa., Susannah, W7566
GRAFFAM, Enoch, Mass., S37038
Increase, Mass., Elenor, W24310

GRAFFAM, Uriah, Mass., R4176
GRAFFUM, Ephraim, Mass., Sarah, W23151
GRAFORD, John, Pa. See CRAWFORD
GRAFT, Philip, Pa., b. N.J., S15164
GRAFTON, John, Va., W5391, Jinny Moody, former wid.
Joseph, R.I., R4177
GRAGG, George, N.H., S38768
Henry, S.C., S10773
Isaac, N.H., Hannah, W25647
Samuel, Mass., Rachel, W23163; BLWt.9061-160-55
Samuel, Va. See GREGG
William, Va., Nancy, W7570; BLWt.26833-160-55
GRAHAM, Amos, Va., S13204
Andrew, S.C., Frances, W81
Ann, former wid. of William Hixt/Hext, S.C., which see
Arthur, N.C., Mourning Scull, former wid., W4068; BLWt. 2090-160-55
Charles, N.Y., BLWt.827-300-Capt. Iss. 10/12/1790. No papers
Charles, N.C., S3424
Christopher, Va., R4178
Daniel, Pa., S39615
Duncan, Va., R14599
Francis, Pa., S8622
George, N.J., S22796
Gershom, Mass., Esther, W14813
Henry, Pa., S23673
Hugh, Del. & Crawford's Indian Expedition, S23670
Isaac Gilbert, Mass., S3420; BLWt.807-300-Surgn. Mate. Iss. 6/25/1789. No papers
Isaac, N.C., See GRAYHAM
James, N.Y., S28751
James, N.C., S8623
James, Pa., S29192
James, Pa., Elizabeth, W1168; BLWt.26190-160-55
James, S.C., S21786
Jesse, Ct., BLWt.5836-100-Pvt. Iss. 12/30/1790. No papers
Jesse, Ct., Elizabeth, W25663
Jesse, Mass., Anna, W19552
John, Ct., S42755
John, Cont., N.Y., S17986; BLWt.825-400-Major. Iss. 1/4/1791. No papers
John, Md., BLWt.11246-100-Pvt. Iss. 1/8/1796 to Geo. Ponsonby ass. No papers
John, Mass., S22799
John, N.C., S3422
John, N.C., b. Pa., S6936
John, Pa., BLWt.9449-100-Pvt. Iss. 10/28/1791. No papers
John, Pa. See GRIMES
Joseph, N.C., S6937
Martha, former wid. of John Lee, Md., which see
Michael, Pa., Va., S8621
Moses, Md., BLWt.11275-100-Pvt. Iss. 6/11/1795 to Samuel Johnston, ass. No papers
Oliver, Ct., S22797
Robert, N.Y., Mary Thom, former wid., R10566

GRAHAM (continued)
Roswell, N.Y., S13215; BLWt. 12837-160-55
Sally, former wid. of Robert Stark, Va., which see
Stafford, N.C., Elizabeth, W8872
Stephen, ---? ---, Va. res., BLWt.2288-300
Thomas, Cont., Va., S31081
Thomas, Pa., S39620
Walter, Va., R14600; Va. Half Pay
William, Ct., S13222
William, Cont., Mass., S44172
William, Mass., BLWt.4210-100-Pvt. Iss. 12/13/1790 to Augustus Blanchard. No papers
William, Mass., N.H., Mary, W10068
William, N.J., BLWts.8330 & 8388-100-Corp. Iss. 1/1/1793 to Jane Shelfox, Admx. No papers
William, N.C., S8624
William, N.C., R4182
William, N.C., Va., S3423
William, Pa., Frances, W2787
William, Pa., R4180
William, Pa., Indian service under Wayne, R4181
William, Va., S16135
William, Va., S38767
GRAHAMS, Adam, Pa. See GRIMES
GRAIMS, Adam, Pa. See GRIMES
GRAINGER, Zaccheus, See GRENGER
GRAMLIN, Adam, Pa., Cont., S2246
GRAMMAR, Joseph, See GAMMAR
GRAMMER, Jacob, N.C., S3430
GRAMPS, Henry, N.Y., Nancy, W16273
John P., N.Y., Nancy, W17959
GRAMS, Adam, Pa. See GRIMES
GRANBERY/GRANBERRY, Thomas, N.C., S41592
GRANBY, Richard, N.Y., R4184
GRANDA, Asa, Mass., BLWt.4273-100-Pvt. Iss. 6/1/1793 to Stephen Thomas. Notation: "Cert. by Mr. Taylor 12 Mar. 1829 and sent to G.L.O."
GRANDALL, Daniel, N.H. See GRENDELL
GRANDEY, Asa, Mass., N.H., Sarah, R4187
Bezaleel, N.H., S44170
Edmund, Ct., S38772
GRANDISON, Simeon, Cont., Mass. S32776
GRANDT, Charles H. See GRANT
GRANDY, John, N.H., Rachel, R4186
Reuben, Mass., BLWt.4256-100-Pvt. Iss. 7/22/1796 to James A. Neal, ass. No papers
GRANE, Philip, N.C., Mourning, R4188
GRANGER, Bildad, Ct., S36561
Daniel, Mass., S17452
Ebenezer, Ct., Patience, W1169
Frederick, Cont., Mass., S32769 BLWt.7-100
Ithamar, Ct., Jemima, W14812
Jacob, Cont., Ct., Esther, R4189; BLWt.5895-100-Pvt. Iss. 1/28/1792 to Moses Sill. No papers
John, Ct., Certif. No. 19334

GRANGER (continued)
John, Crane's Cont. Art., Mass., BLWt.4292-100-Pvt. Iss. 5/31/1790 to Theodosius Fowler. No papers.
John, Mass., Rebecca, W27417
John, N.Y., BLWt.7162-100-Pvt. Iss. 2/14/1791 to Alexander Alexander, ass. No papers
Justin, Mass., S8626
Lydia, former wid. of Josiah Myers, N.Y., which see
Moses, Ct., Lucy, W15907
Moses, Ct., Vt., R4190
Sebe/Seba, Mass., Molly, W1755
Thaddeus, Mass., Julia, BLWt. 49472-160-55
Thomas, Mass., S16131; BLWt.4214-100. Iss. 4/2/1792. No papers
GRANNES, Jared, Ct., Privateer, S31704
GRANNIS, David, Ct., Clarissa, W24302
Elle, Ct., S17449
Robert, Ct., R4192
Samuel, Cont., Ct. agcy. & res., Charity Irion/Tryon/Trion, W26154
GRANNISS, Enos, Ct., Cont., S39613; BLWt.818-300-Lt. of Art. Artificiers. Iss. 3/10/1796 under name of Eneas Granniss & also recorded under BLWt.2663. No papers
GRANT, Aaron, Ct., Lucy, W17967
Alexander, S.C., S3407
Amos, Mass. Sea Service, Privateer, R4193
Andrew, Ct., S18847
Azariah, Ct., BLWt.5881-100-Pvt. Iss. 5/7/1792 to Thomas Stanley. No papers
Azariah, Ct., S38775
Benjamin, N.H., Sarah Smith, former wid., W24986. Her other husb. was also a pensioner. See case of Frederick Smith, Vt. S---
Benjamin, R.I., S17446
Benoni/Benony, Cont., N.Y., Catharine, W1855; BLWt.820-200-Lt. Iss. 6/18/1789. No papers
Beriah, R.I., Elizabeth, W21227
Charles H., Cont., Mass., Abigail W19530; BLWt.1228-100
Daniel, N.H., BLWt.807-100
Daniel, Va., S35985
David, Ct., S15870
David, N.C., S38766
Edward, Mass., BLWt.4270-100-Sgt. Iss. 3/2/1790. No papers
Edward, N.H., S37029; BLWt.867-100
Elihu, Ct., R4194
Elisha, N.C., S41587
Elnathan, Ct., S13193
George, N.J., BLWt.8341-100-Pvt. Iss. 3/5/1793. No papers
Gideon, Ct., S36565
Gilbert, R.I., S38749
Gustavus, Ct., Phebe, W2101;

GRANT (continued)
BLWt.9204-160-55
Hamilton, Ct., Privateer, Lucy, W1417; BLWt.3521-160-55
Hezekiah, Ct., S30446
Isaac, Ct., R4195
Isaac, N.C., R4196
Isaac, Va., S4305
James, Ct., S38759
Jehu, Ct., R4197
Jesse, Ct., Dis. No papers. BLWt.823-300-Capt. Iss. 2/18/1793. No papers
John, Cont., Navy, Mass., S37026
John, N.H., Dorothy, W14817
John, N.J., Pa., S31077
John, N.Y., Eunice, W14821
John, N.C., S6930
John, N.C., R4198
Jonathan, Va., S42758
Joseph, N.H., S44178
Joseph, N.C., S31713
Joshua, Mass., Abigail, W23143
Martin, Mass., S37034
Oliver, Ct., Hannah, W25126
Patience, former wid. of John Rankins, Cont., Mass. Which see
Peter, Mass. Sea Service, N.H., S16841
Reuben, Ct., Anna, W21228
Reuben, Timothy Bedel's Regt., N.H., Vt. Mil., S16395
Richard, R.I., BLWt.3165-100-Pvt. Iss. 1/15/1800 to Wm. S. Brown, ass. of Bliss, ass. No papers
Robert, Va., Susannah, W8212; BLWt.36751-160-55
Roswel/Roswell, Ct., S15161
Roswell, Ct., S31710
Samuel, Mass., R4199
Samuel, Pvt., N.H., BLWt.3150 iss. 3/25/1790
Samuel, N.H., Abigail, W23135
Samuel, R.I., BLWt.3153-100-Pvt. Iss. 6/20/1789. No papers
Silas, Mass., S31715
Thomas, Ct., S8605
Thomas, Cont., Mass., Lydia, W19547
Thomas, Mass., Elizabeth, W24304
Thomas, Pa., Deborah, W11083
Thomas, ---? ---, Ga. res. of wid. in 1857, Martha H., BLWt. 58691-160-55
Vincent, N.J., N.Y., R4200
William, Ct., Mass. Sea Service, Polly, W19531
William, Md., BLWt.11286-100-Pvt. Iss. 3/11/1791. No papers
William, Mass., S29190
William, N.H., S37027
William, S.C., Mary, W1757; BLWt.26273-160-55
William, Va., S42760
GRANTHAM, Henry, Md., BLWts.13123 & 14109-100-Pvt. Iss. 2/24/1795 to Francis Sherrard, ass. of Henry Reding, Admr. No papers
Nathan, N.C., S31716
Richard, N.C., S.C., Frances,

GRANTHAM (continued)
W418; BLWt.34546-160-55
GRANTS, Mark, N.Y. See CRANTZ
GRAPES, Philip, N.H., Elizabeth Ryder, former wid., W17583
GRASS, Frederick, Va., S39607
Peter, Va., S8599
GRASTY, James George, Va., Rutha, R4902
John, S.C., Lucy, R4201
GRATECLASS, Gilbert, N.J., BLWt. 8830-100-Corp. Iss. 2/15/1790. No papers
GRATER, Francis, Cont., Mass., S10771
GRATESINGER, John, See GREATSINGER
GRATON, Crary, N.Y. See GRATTON
James, Mass., R21885
Thomas, Mass., Becca, W14824; BLWt.14973-160-55
GRATT, Nicholas, Pa., S8602
GRATTON, Crary, N.Y., Anna, W17966 BLWt.27601-160-55
Thomas, Mass., S21773
GRATZINGER, Peter, Pa., BLWt. 9498-100-Pvt. Iss. 12/28/1793 to Christian Hubbard, ass. No papers
GRAUL, Jacob, Pa., Susanna, R4204; BLWt.44909-160-55
GRAUTZ, Henry, See CROUTZ
GRAVATT, John, N.J., S8633
John, Va., Judith, W7605
GRAVE, John, Ct., Hannah, W25661
Timothy, Ct., S31705
GRAVES, Abner, Mass., S33267
Allen, Mass., S39632
Amos, Ct., Mass., Hannah, W7579; BLWt.26067-160-55
Anna, former wid. of John Hutchins N.Y., Vt., which see
Asa, Cont., Mass., Roxenena, W11085; BLWt.802-150-Ensign. Iss. 4/1790. No papers
Asa, Mass., Almena, W7577
Asahel, Ct., R4205
Bela, Ct., S9344
Benjamin, Ct., Cont., Sarah, W4972; BLWt.157-60-55; BLWt. 5870-100. Iss. 12/9/1796 to William Gilliland. No papers
Boston, N.C., b. Pa., Sarah, R4213
Chauncey/Chancy, Vt., S15869
Constant, R.I., Comfort Knight, former wid., W13594
Daniel, Mass., S13185
Daniel, Mass., Mary, W14826
David, N.Y., S22278
David, Va., S8597
Ebenezer, Mass., BLWt.4223-100-Pvt. Iss. 5/24/1790. No papers
Ebenezer, Mass., S44884
Edmund, N.C., S37955
Elijah, Ct., S8596
Elijah, Ct., S44173
Eliphalet, Mass., S13190
Francis, N.C., BLWt.883-200-Lt. Iss. 1/26/1796 to Peter Butt Oran, ass. of Henry Banks
Gideon, Mass., Crane's Regt., BLWt.4283-100-Sgt. Iss. 4/1/1790. No papers
Gideon, Cont., Mass., S32767
Gideon, Mass., S44883
Gideon, Mass., S46442
Gilbert, Ct., BLWt.5880-100-Pvt. Iss. 5/1/1797 to John Duncan. No papers
Gilbert, Ct., Elizabeth, W25649
Hobart, Ct., S28746
James, Mass., S13209
James, S.C., Massey, W21232
James, Va., S13212
Jedediah, N.Y., Polly, W23147
Jesse, Vt., Ruth, W21231
Job, Mass., S31074
John, Ct. See GRAVE
John, Mass., S17451
John, Va., BLWt.12155-100-Pvt. Iss. 7/14/1792 to Robert Means ass. No papers
John, Va. Lydia, W3014; BLWt. 26574-160-55
John, Va., Mary A., W7580
Jonathan, Mass., S43644
Joseph, Cont., Mass., Densey, W5288; BLWt.17894-160-55
Josiah, Ct., S29842
Josiah, Mass., War of 1812, Mary, W7578; BLWt.36748-160-55
Julius, Mass., Roxe, BLWt.96593-160-55
Levi, Mass., Lydia, W7581; BLWt. 13217-160-55
Lewis, N.Y., Elizabeth, W17030
Lewis, N.C., S.C., R4207
Nathaniel, Vt., R4209
Noadiah, N.Y., R4210
Oliver, Mass., Abigail, W2100
Peter, Ct., S43640
Philip, Md., R4211
Ralph, Va., Jane, W2102; BLWt. 40933-160-55
Ralph, Va., R14569; Va. Half Pay
Reuben, Mass., S8595
Reuben, Mass., S17450
Reuben, Va., S3408
Rhoda, former wid. of Silas Ball Mass., which see
Richard, S.C., S8598
Samuel, Cont., Mass., Mary, R4208
Samuel, Mass., R4212
Selah, Mass., S32778
Seth, Ct., Elizabeth, W21222
Simeon, Ct., S43641
Stephen, Mass., S38757
Thadeus, Ct., Mass., S16134
Thomas, N.C., Sarah, R4214
Thomas, Va., S16839
Thomas, Va., Marley P., W1418; BLWt.26898-160-55
Timothy, Ct., S15162
Timothy, Ct., See GRAVE
Whitney, Ct., S15159
William, Cont., Va., S37957
William, Mass., S23240
William, Mass., Sea Service, R4215
William, Vt., S10774
William, Va., R14570; Va. Half Pay. N.A. Acc. No.874-050077
William, Va. State Navy, Va. Half Pay. See N.A. Acc. No. 837. YS File
GRAVEY, James, Md., BLWt.11250-100-Pvt. Iss. 4/8/1797 to James DeBaufre, ass. No papers
GRAVIT, John, Va., S31083
GRAWBARGAR, Henry, N.Y., R4216
GRAY, Aaron, Cont., Mass., S37030
Alexander, Cont., Pa., S39618; BLWt.425-100
Alexander, Mass., S18845
Amos, Ct., Dis. No papers
Amos, Mass., Vt., S29846
Andrew, N.Y., Catharine/Catharina, W21221
Andrew, Pa., Mary, W21218
Anna, former wid. of Abel Rice, N.H.,Vt., which see
Benjamin, Md., BLWts.11252 & 12252-100-Pvt. Iss. 1/4/1794. No papers
Brevity, Mass., BLWt.800-100
Cato, Mass., See DUNSETT
Charles, R.I., BLWt.3156-100-Pvt. Iss. 5/28/1792. No papers
Daniel, Ct., R4219
Daniel, Mass., Tabitha, W21224
Daniel, N.J., S2248
Daniel, N.J., N.Y., S9913
Daniel, Va., Lee's Legion, BLWt. 12153-100-Pvt. Iss. 10/8/1792 to James Reynolds, ass. No papers
Daniel, Va., S39621
David, Mass., S38776
David, Mass., R---
David, Pa., S32282
David, R.I., Nancy Durfee, former wid., W14649. She also applied for pension on acct. of service of her last husb., Abner Durfee. See papers within
Dominicus, Mass., Sarah, W19548; BLWt.7058-100-55
Ebenezer, Ct., BLWt.812-450-Lt. Col. No date of issue. No papers
Ebenezer, Mass., S21774
Elijah, Md., S8593
Elijah, Mass., Anna, W1854; BLWt.19605-160-55
Eliphalet, Ct., Lydia, R4223
Elliot, Mass., S30447
Francis, Cont., Va., Eleanor, W7575; BLWt.873-200-Lt. Iss. 6/24/1793 to Joseph Higbee, ass. No papers
Frazier, Del., BLWt.10775-100-Pvt. Iss. 9/2/1789. No papers
Frazier, Del., Elizabeth, W2099
Frederick, S.C., S21779
Gabriel, Va., S8590
George, Cont., Va., S35989
Henry, N.J., BLWt.8342-100-Pvt. Iss. 6/11/1789 to Matthias Denman, ass. No papers
Henry, N.J., S34378
Henry, S.C., S38750
Hugh, Mass., BLWt.810-200-Lt. Iss. 1/27/1795 to James Gray, bro. & heir of H.G. No papers

GRAY (continued)
Ichabod, Mass., R4300 1/2
Isaac, N.J., Anna/Ann, W3541
Jabesh, Ct., S43643
Jacob, N.J., BLWt.8337-100-Pvt. Iss. 3/19/1790. No papers
Jacob, N.J., Elizabeth, W462
Jacob, N.C., S.C., S31709
James, Ct., BLWt.5841-100-Pvt. Iss. 10/22/1789 to Theodosius Fowler. No papers
James, Ct., Cont., N.Y., S2245
James, Del., S39626
James, Md., BLWt.1302-100
James, Mass., S23668
James, Mass., S42761
James, N.H., S45567
James, N.Y., S43645
James, N.C., S6928
James, N.C., S8594
James, Pa., S42759
James, Va., S17987
James, Va., Elizabeth, W7573; BLWt.19516-160-55
James, Va. Sea Service, R50, Va. Half Pay. See N.A. Acc. 837 Va. State Navy, YS File
James W., Md., BLWt.856-300-Capt. Iss. 5/29/1794 to Elizabeth Gray, admx. No papers
Joel, Mass., S44179
Joel, Pa., Cont., S39616
John, Ga., Elizabeth, W419; BLWt.56568-160-55
John, Green Mt. Boys, N.Y., S13197
John, Md., BLWt.11279-100-Pvt. Iss. 3/22/1797 to Abijah Holbrook, ass. No papers
John, Mass., S37040
John, Mass., N.Y., Margaret, W24306
John, Mass., Sea Service, Sally, W7572
John, N.H., S45566
John, N.Y., Mary, W16278
John, N.Y., R4221
John, N.C., S3409
John, Pa., BLWt.9515-100-Pvt. Iss. 12/22/1794. No papers
John, Pa., also Indian Wars in 1785 & 1792, S23669
John, R.I., Elizabeth, W13334
John, Va., S1464
John, Va., Nancy Walters, former wid., W6395; BLWt.14659-160-55
Joseph, Ct., Eunice, W21226
Joseph, Ct., Mass., Lydia, W21225
Joseph, Mass., S13210
Joseph, Mass., S39622
Joseph, N.H., Chloe, W16022
Joseph, N.J., S1007
Joseph, Pa., Phebe, W4685
Joseph, Va., S1822
Joseph, Va., S16390
Joshua, Mass., BLWt.4260-100-Sgt. Iss. 8/10/1789 to Richard Platt, No papers
Joshua, Mass., Sarah, W24303; BLWt.39207-160-55
Josiah, N.J., S876

GRAY (continued)
Louisa, former wid. of Moses Drown, Mass., which see
Lynch, Cont., Md., S34908
Maria, former wid. of David Shannon, Cont., N.J., which see
Matthew, Mass., S29187
Morton/Moulton, N.C., Ann, W10066; BLWt.19542-160-55
Moulton, N.C. See Morton
Nathan, Pa., BLWt.9425-100-Pvt. Iss. 6/20/1789. No papers
Nathaniel, N.Y., S16132
Peter, S.C., BLWt.126-300
Presley, Va., Indian Wars, Ky. Mil. to 1815, R4226
Richard, Va., R4227
Robert, Mass., S18846
Robert, Mass., S45569
Robert, N.Y., R4229
Robert, Pa., Mary, W4446; BLWt.36749-160-55
Robert, Va., R4228
Samuel, Ct., Abigail Hadley, former wid., R4415
Samuel, Ct., Cont., N.Y., S43638
Samuel, Cont., Ct., S13188
Samuel, Md., BLWt.11249-100-Pvt. Iss. 7/17/1797 to Abraham Jarritt, ass. No papers
Samuel, N.J., BLWt.8350-100-Pvt. Iss. 6/11/1789 to Jonathan Dayton, ass. No papers
Samuel, N.Y., S13221
Samuel, N.C., Rachel, W7574
Samuel, Pa., BLWt.845-200-Lt. Iss. 3/5/1792 to Robert Connally, Admr. No papers
Samuel, Va., Leah, W8864
Shared, N.C., S31707
Silas, N.Y., S43637; BLWt.828-300 Capt. Iss. 8/23/1790 to Caleb Sweet, ass. No papers
Solomon, N.H., S45568
Thomas, Mass., S32768
Thomas, N.Y., BLWt.7153-100-Pvt. Iss. 8/2/1790 to Joseph Arthur, ass. No papers
Thomas, N.Y., S43636
Thomas, N.C., Nancy, W3981
Thomas, S.C., R20510
William, Cont., BLWt.1486-200
William, Mass., BLWt.4238-100-Pvt. Iss. 12/23/1796 to Abraham Foster. No papers
William, Mass., Sarah Hill, former wid., W19768
William, N.C., S31079
William, N.C., S41586
William, N.C., Ann, W7576
William, N.C., Va., S3410
William, Pa., BLWt.9433-100-Sgt. Iss. 4/6/1790. No papers
William, Pa., Mary, W3243; BLWt. 835-300-Capt. Iss. 2/7/1792 to Samuel Nicholson, ass. No papers
William, Pa., Va., S2253
William, S.C., R4232
William, Va., Susanna, R4300 3/4

GRAY (continued)
Willis, N.C., Elizabeth, W19554
GRAYBILL, Philip, See GUIBLE
GRAYDON, Alexander, Pa., S39623; BLWt.806-300-Capt. Iss. 1/5/1791, also recorded under BLWt.2576. No papers
GRAYHAM, Isaac, N.C., S3421
GRAYSON, John/William John, S.C. Susan Joyner, former wid., W21474; BLWt.1179-200
William, Cont., Ky. res. of son in 1836, BLWt.1366-500
William John, See John
GREACEY, John, N.C., Rachel, W357
GREAFFE, Frederick, Von Heer's Corps, BLWt.13113-100-Pvt. Iss. 1/12/1796 to Fred. Greaffe. No papers
GREANLEAF, John, See GREENLEAF
GREAR, Thomas, N.C., Pa., b. Ireland, S8553
GREASHAM, David, See GRESHAM
GREAT, David, Va., See GREATS
GREATHOUSE, John, Pa., S8630
GREATON, John, Cont., Mass., BLWt.791-850-Brig. Gen. Iss. 8/10/1789 to Richard Platt, ass. of Sarah Greaton, admx. on estate of John Greaton, no papers
John, W., Mass., BLWt.801-200-Lt. Iss. 3/10/1794 to Samuel Emery, ass. No papers
Richard, Mass., BLWt.800-150-Ensign. Iss. 8/10/1789 to Samuel Emery, ass. No papers
GREATS, David, Va., S38747
GREATSINGER, John, N.Y., R4233
GREDY, Thomas, Pvt., N.Y., BLWt. 7167 iss. 10/12/1790 to Isaac Hoasbrouck, ass.
GREEGOR, Cato, Pvt., Mass., BLWts.4211 & 134-60-55 iss. 11/27/1797. BLWt.4211 to John Duncan
GREELEY, Joseph, N.H., S23239
Noah, N.H., Hannah, W23153
GREELY, Enoch, Cont., N.H., Dorothy, W24314
John, N.H., S43646
Jonathan, Cont., Mass., Rhoda, W14819
Matthew, N.H., Abigail, W16121
Nicholas, Mass., Mary, W15906
GREEN, Aaron, Mass., Lydia, W13333
Abel, Ct., S43642
Abner, Ct., S17448
Allen, Mass., Vt., S18420
Allen, R.I., S21792
Amasa, Cont., Ct., Lurena, W4684
Amos, Ct., Lavina, W25646
Amos, Md., BLWt.11269-100-Pvt. Iss. 10/14/1795 to Henry Davis, ass. No papers
Amos, Mass., S29844
Andrew, Not Rev., Gen. Harman's Indian War, 1790, applied in Ky., Old War Inv. File 8608
Andrew, Va., S37958

GREEN (continued)
Arthur, N.C., R4238
Asa, Mass., Phebe, W546; BLWt. 34547-160-55
Asa, Mass., Martha, R4239
Asahel, Ct., Grace, W17962
Benjamin, Mass., S37024
Benjamin, Mass., Prudence, W14822; BLWt.17560-160-55
Benjamin, Va., b. N.J., S4302
Benjamin, Va., R4240
Beriah, Vt., Anna, W23152
Bradbury, N.H., BLWt.3133-100-Pvt. Iss. 11/28/1789. No papers
Bradbury, N.H., S45571
Bradbury, N.H., Jemima, W19556; BLWt.7060-160-55
Caleb, Ct., Rebecca, W21206
Cato, R.I., BLWt.3159-100-Pvt. Iss. 12/31/1789. No papers
Chafey/Chaffey, Mass., R.I., Diana, W2611; BLWt.6442-160-55
Charles, Va., S10207
Charles, Va., S35991
Clement/Clemens/Clemenus, Cont., Md. res., BLWt.2423-100
Cleophas, Cont., Mass., S32763
Coggeshall, R.I., S4301
Cuff, R.I., BLWt.3160-160-Pvt. Iss. 5/4/1791. No papers
Daniel, Mass., BLWt.4222-100-Fifer. Iss. 8/1/1789 to Thomas Cushing. No papers
Daniel, Mass., S18426
Daniel, Mass., S37035, BLWt. 18386-160-55
Daniel, Mass., S43630
Daniel, N.Y., Mary, W16277
David, Va., S6913
Dexter, R.I., Mary, W2610
Dorastus, Ct., S36564
Drewry, S.C., R4246
Duty, Mass., S4300
Ebenezer, Ct., S13217
Ebenezer, N.H., BLWt.1324-300
Ebenezer, N.Y., Priscilla, W23164
Edward, N.Y., R.I., S13208
Edward J., R.I., S15163
Eleazer, Mass., Lucy, W21217
Elezer/Eleazer, Ct., S44885
Elias, Mass., S22276
Elijah, Va., S37961
Eliphalet, Mass., S32760
Elisha, S.C., R4248
Ezra, Ct., Amy, W17965
Ezra, Cont., Navy, N.H., S4303
Fortunatus, Va., S15155
Francis, Mass., S46003; BLWt. 793-300-Capt. Iss. 9/13/1792 to Henry Newman, ass. No papers
Francis, Mass., Lucy, W23155
Gabriel, Va., also served in 1797, Sarah Anne, W23136, Va. Half Pay, BLWt.872-200-Lt. Iss. 1/17/1800. No papers
George, ---, enl. in Va., Pd. at S.C. agcy, S6912
George, N.C., S2580
George, N.C., R4254
Gerard, Va., Verlinda, W3012
Gideon, Ct., R4255

GREEN (continued)
Henry, Ct., Cont., S13187
Henry, Md., Priscilla, W23145; BLWt.11256-100. Iss. 1/8/1796 to Geo. Ponsonby, ass. No papers
Henry, Md., Elizabeth, W25657
Henry, Mass., Betsey, W11081; BLWt.19733-160-55
Henry, Va., R4255 1/2
Irijah, Mass., S39630
Isaac, Cont., N.Y., S13213
Isaac, Mass., S5215
Isaac, Mass., S39628
Isaac, Mass., Elizabeth, W19546
Isaac, Mass., Anna, W24309
Jabez, Mass., R.I., Abigail, W19528
Jack (colored), Ct., N.Y., S43631
Jacob, Ct., S44176
James, Ct., S10770
James, Ct., Sarah, W25644; BLWt. 36502-160-55
James, N.H., R4256
James, N.Y., S13184
James (colored), N.Y., See WEEKS
James, R.I., S39610
James, Va. Sea Service, Frances, W7563
James W., N.C., BLWt.2261-400
Jehiel, N.Y., Esther, W7556
Jeremiah, Mass., Martha, W21209
Jeremiah, N.C., S6916
Jesse, N.C., Mary, W11084; BLWt. 49031-160-55
Joanna, former wid. of Reuben Geary, Mass., which see
Joel, Ct., R4257. No papers--in 1877
Joel, Mass., Irene, W24307
John, Ct., S23659
John, Ct., See Jack Green
John, Ct., Esther, R4251
John, Cont. (?), Mass. res., Waitstill, R4278
John, Cont., Va. res. of children in 1828, BLWt.1435-100
John, Cont., Pa., Elizabeth Taylor, former wid., W11590; BLWt.91121-160-55
John, Green Mt. Boys, Mass., N.Y., Sarah, W3982
John, Md., S13216
John, Mass., BLWt.4231-100-Pvt. Iss. 10/26/1789. No papers
John, Mass., S32766
John, Mass., S42756
John, Mass., Sarah Adams, former wid., W15510
John, Mass., Elizabeth, R4249
John, N.Y., BLWt.7145-100-Pvt. Iss. 8/12/1790 to John D. Coe, ass. No papers
John, N.Y., Jane, W2612
John, N.Y., R4258
John, N.Y., & Wayne's War, S36562
John, N.C., S6917
John, N.C., Hannah, W19540
John, Pa., S35990
John, Pa., (?), R4259
John, R.I., S23667
John, R.I., Amelia, W25664; BLWt. 26705-160-55

GREEN (continued)
John, Pa.(?), BLWt.13116-100-Pvt. "in the Sappers & Miners." Iss. 6/29/1789 to Matt McConnell, ass. No papers
John, S.C., S6914
John, Vt., Anna, W8869
John, Va., S37960
John, Va., Elizabeth, W8870
John, Va., BLWt.866-500. No papers
John Hayes/Hase, Del., S36010
John Morley, R.I., BLWt.788-200-Lt. Iss. 6/30/1790. No papers
Jonas, Mass., Dis. No papers
Jonathan, Cont., Mass., S10769
Jonathan, Mass., S37031
Jonathan, N.H., Mary French, W23159
Jonathan, R.I., Anne/Anna, R4236
Joseph, Ct., Cont., Mass., Vt., Jerusha Morey, former wid. W17148
Joseph, Mass., Susanna, W19555
Joseph, Mass., Hannah Hill, former wid., W23282
Joseph (colored), Mass., Sarah, W27415
Joseph, Navy, N.H., S37044
Joseph, N.H., BLWt.3136-100-Pvt. Iss. 8/26/1790 to Manasseh Cutler, ass. No papers
Joseph, N.H., S45572
Joseph, N.J., Anna, W485
Joseph, N.Y., R4281
Joseph, Pa., S8611
Joseph, Va., S37959
Josiah, Ct., Susannah Holbrook, former wid., W21395
Josiah, Va., BLWt.12158-100-Pvt. Iss. 4/12/1792 to Francis Graves, ass. No papers
Levi, Mass., S29183
Lewis, Va., S31080
Lodowick, R.I., S23660
Malachi, R.I., S8612
Mark, Mass., S45570
Mary, former wid. of Robert Cross, Md., which see
Meshack, N.C., Susannah, W25658 BLWt.50898-160-55
Morris, N.Y., Elizabeth, R4250
Nancy Ann, former wid. of Elias Edens, S.C., which see
Nathan/Nathaniel, Mass., Sarah, W23139
Nathan, Mass., R4266
Nathan, N.C., S3412
Noah, Ct., S29840
Obadiah/Obideah, Ct., S18422
Obadiah, N.Y., R4268
Othniel, R.I., Elizabeth, W17027
Paul, Md., S10767
Peleg, R.I., S18421
Peter, N.Y., BLWt.7149-100-Pvt. Iss. 7/20/1797 to James Reed, ass. No papers
Peter (colored), N.Y., S32772
Phebe, former wid. of Charles Headle, Mass., which see
Phineas, Mass., R4272
Pierson, N.J., BLWt.8332-100-Pvt. Iss. 3/27/1797. No papers
Pierson, N.J., S34377

GREEN (continued)
Prince (colored), R.I., S38754 (Not same as Robt. or Prince Green, S33268)
Reuben, R.I., S23664
Rhoda, former wid. of Abel Nutting, Mass., which see
Richard, N.H., BLWt.3141-100-Pvt. Iss. 8/26/1796 to Joshua Pickering, ass. No papers
Richard, N.H., Mary, W16280
Robert, Cont., Va., S35992; BLWt.640-100
Robert, Md., Elizabeth, W10065
Robert/Prince (colored), R.I., S33268
Robert, Va., Frances, W8866; BLWt.365-200
Roswell, Ct., S28749; BLWt. 9403-160-55
Russel, Mass., Patience, W21219
Sampson/Samson, enl. in France, Va. res. in 1832, R4274
Samuel, Ct., BLWt.5884-100-Pvt. Iss. 3/1/1796. No papers
Samuel, Ct., S13196
Samuel, Ct., Tamazen, W21223
Samuel, Ct., Polly, W25662; BLWt.8179-160-55
Samuel, Mass., Abigail, W14814
Samuel, Mass., Olive, R4269
Samuel, N.Y., BLWt.7197-100-Pvt. Iss. 7/6/1791 to Carlile Pollock, ass. No papers
Samuel, N.Y., R4276
Samuel, R.I., S23658
Samuel, Va., R4275
Samuel B., Va., R14649; Va. Half Pay. N.A. Acc. 874. See 050078 Samuel "Ball" Green
Sarah, former wid. of John Brown, N.H., which see
Sebra, former wid. of Stephen Harrington, Ct., which see
Silas, N.Y., Lydia, W17031
Simeon, Va. See Simon
Simon, Mass., Deborah, W14825
Simon/Simeon, Va., S10766
Simon, Va., S35987
Stephen, N.Y., S23242
Stephen, Va., BLWt.13153-100-Pvt. Iss. 5/15/1799, to Stephen Green. No papers
Thomas, Mass., Mary, R4264
Thomas, N.Y., S13202
Thomas, R.I., Mary, R4282
Thomas, Va., S31702
Thomas, Va., S32279
Timothy, Ct., Jane, W21207
Timothy, Mass., BLWt.4226-100-Pvt. Iss. 4/5/1796 to Oliver Ashley. No papers
Timothy, Mass., BLWt.4232-100-Pvt. Iss. 10/26/1789. No papers
Timothy, Mass., Prudence, W3344
Timothy, N.Y., BLWt.7185-100-Pvt. Iss. 8/3/1790 to Cornelius V. Dyck, ass. No papers
Timothy, N.Y., S43633
Timothy, R.I., Catharine, W23133
Uzziah, Mass., S21776
Wardwell, Ct., R.I., Esther,W23161

GREEN (continued)
Warwick, Mass., Mary, W19535
Willard, Ct., S13198
William, Cont., Mass., Elizabeth, W23157; BLWt.19602-160-55
William, Ga., R4279
William, Md., S13220
William, Mass., Abigail, W19542
William, N.J., S878
William, N.J., Phebe, R4271
William, N.Y., Catalyntje, W17024
William, N.C., S3413
William, N.C., Kezziah, W7557
William, S.C., Biddy, W9460; BLWt.47554-160-55
William, S.C., Va., Betsy, W24319
William, Va., Lucy, W8868
William R., N.J., Elizabeth,W7560
Zeeb, Mass., Sarah, W21211
GREENAWALT, John Philip. See Philip Philip/John Philip, Pa., Catharine R4288
GREENE, Amos, R.I., Alse, W21214
Benjamin, Ct., R.I., S21783
Benjamin, R.I., Sarah, W13314
Cato (colored), Cont., R.I.,S38753
Charles, R.I., S38755
Christopher, R.I., BLWt.798-500-Col.
Cuff, Cont., R.I., S38758
Daniel, N.Y., Lydia, W13326; BLWt.26638-160-55
David, R.I., S21245
George, R.I., S8610
Henry, R.I., Marcy, W23132
Jabez, Ct., R.I., S13189
James, R.I., S21789
James, R.I., S22795; BLWt.31421-160-55
James, R.I., S44181
James, Va., S8606
Job, R.I., S13194
John, Mass., BLWt.799-200-Lt. Iss. 8/10/1789 to Richard Platt, ass. No papers
John, R.I., Ruth, W17026
John, Va., Johanna, W4216
John G., R.I., R4260
Joseph, R.I., Patience, W21229
McKeen, Ga., N.C., S.C., Frances, W7561; BLWt.11275-160-55
Mancer/Mansier, R.I., S44175
Nathaniel, Mass., BLWt.4220-100-Sgt. Iss. 8/7/1789 to Anspach & Rogers. No papers
Nathaniel, R.I., BLWt.787-1100-Maj. Gen. Iss. 12/22/1795 to Catharine Green, Extx. No papers
Peter, R.I., BLWt.3166-100-Pvt. Iss. 12/31/1789. No papers
Peter, R.I., S13223
Phillip/Philip, R.I., S21791
Richard, Mass., S32777
Sarah, R.I., W7559, former wid. of Jonathan Remington
Sarah, former wid. of Wm. Gorton, R.I., which see
Stephen, R.I., S21781
Stephen, R.I., S21787
William, R.I., S21784
William, R.I., S38756
William, Va., Elizabeth, W25645;

GREENE (continued)
BLWt.36282-160-55
William, R.I., Esther, W13328
Zachariah, Ct., Cont., S28747; BLWt.13732-160-55
GREENELSH, Edward, Va., S5209
GREENEWALT, Nicholas, Pa., Mary, W2103; BLWt.26985-160-55
GREENFIELD, Charles, N.H., S45575
Enos, Cont., S44177, enl. New London, Ct.
James, Ct., S13192
Lydia, former wid. of James Stone, N.H., which see
William, Ct., Cont., Green Mt. Boys, Prudence, R4283
GREENING, James, Va., Sarah, W10071
Nehemiah, Va., S38762
GREENLAND, James, Pa., BLWt.9511-100-Pvt. Iss. 3/4/1792. No papers
James, Pa., S39611; BLWt.689-100
GREENLAW, John, Mass., Lucy, W23141
GREENLEAF, Benjamin, Mass., S37041
Caleb, Mass., S29188
Daniel, Mass., Mary, R4286
David, N.H., S45767
Ebenezer, Mass., R4284
Enoch, Mass., BLWt.4254-100-Pvt. Iss. 4/3/1797 to Ezra King. No papers
Enoch, Mass. See GREENLEAFE
Israel, Mass., S39608
John, Mass., Annah, W19534
Nathan, N.H., BLWt.3147-100-Corp. Iss. 3/25/1790. No papers
Nathan, N.H., Mary, W23158
Stephen, Vt., R4287
William, Cont., Mass., S32775; BLWt.795-200-Lt. Iss. 10/18/1796 to John Coates, ass. No papers
GREENLEAFE, Enoch, Mass., S37039
GREENMAN, Gideon, R.I., S21785
Jeremiah, R.I., Mary, W23146; BLWt.789-200-Lt. Iss. 3/9/1790. No papers
Job, --- Dis. No papers
John, Mass., S28750
John, R.I., Anna, W24305; BLWt. 28580-160-55
GREENNELL, Owen, R.I., S21788
GREENOLD, Amasa, Ct., BLWt.5876-100-Pvt. Iss. 9/29/1790 to Cornelius Williams. No papers
William, Ct., S29843
GREENOUGH, John, Mass., S32785
Jonathan, Mass., S37042
Manuel, Mass., S32761
Susan, former wid. of James Shirley, Mass.,N.H., which see
William, Crane's Cont. Art., Mass., BLWt.4284-100-Pvt. Iss. 1/28/1790 to Eliphalet Downer, no papers
William, N.H., S8613
GREENSLET, Benjamin, Ct., Martha, W25659
John, Cont., Ct. res. 1820, S36563
GREENSLIT, Joel, Ct., Cont., S10765
John, Ct., Saloma, W9465; BLWt. 34327-160-55
John, Cont., See GRENSLET
GREENTREE, Benjamin, See MARSHAL

GREENWALD, Abraham, Cont., Pa., S39609; BLWt.426-100
Jacob, Pa., S2250
GREENWAY, George, Va., R20376
William, Va., S1907
GREENWELL, Ignatus, Md., S16836
John, Md., S31076
GREENWILL, Bennet, Md., S16391
GREENWOOD, Aaron, Mass., S32762
Abel, Mass., Sally, W24318
Bartlee, Cont., Va., Nancy, W3013; BLWt.10259-160-55
Enoch, Mass., S32773
James, Md., BLWt.11243-100-Pvt. Iss. 12/18/1794 to Henry Purdy, ass. No papers
John, Md., BLWt.11272-100-Pvt. Iss. 12/17/1799 to Asahel Phelps, no papers
Joseph, Del., Md., S13225
Moses, Mass., Abigail, W19550
Philip, Md., Sarah, R4289
Thomas, Mass., Deborah, W21216
GREER, Henry, Pa., BLWt.842-200. No papers
James, Cont., Pa., see GRIER
James, Mass., N.H., Sarah, W23149
James, S.C., Sarah, R4277
John, S.C., R4290
Matthew, N.H., BLWt.3134-100-Pvt. Iss. 8/12/1795 to Sampson Crosby, ass. No papers
Meshack, N.C. See GREEN
Moses, Ga., N.C. See GRIER
Moses, Pa., S34906
Moses, Va., S8609
Richard, Pa., S.C., b. Pa., S3416
Samuel, Pa., S38769
Walter, N.C., Va., b. Pa., S3415
GREGER, Cato, Mass. See GRIGER
GREGG, David, Ct., Mass., N.H., S15590
David, N.H., Sally, BLWt.47665-160-55
David, N.Y., BLWt.7170-100-Corp. Iss. 7/7/1791 to R. & Wm. Gregg, admrs. No papers
Hezekiah, N.Y., S34379
Isaac, N.H. See GRAGG
James, N.Y., Mary, W17025; BLWt. 826-300-Capt. Iss. 7/3/1790 to Nathan Brewster, admr. No papers
James, N.C., Rachel, R4334
John, Cont., N.H., S13201
John, Pa., Margaret, W4970; BLWt. 1322-200; BLReg.80761-1855
Mary L, former wid. of Robert Livingston, N.H., which see
Matthew, Va., S35981
Peter, Cont., Va. agcy. & res., S38764
Robert, Pa., BLWt.9441-100-Pvt. Iss. 5/7/1794 to Sam. King, admr. No papers
Samuel, Va., S16840
Thomas, N.Y., BLWt.7177-100-Pvt. Iss. 11/11/1791 to Samuel Broome, ass. No papers
GREGGOR, Cato, Mass. See GRIGER
GREGGS, Ephraim, See GRIGGS

GREGGS (continued)
Robert, N.C. See GRIGGS
GREGORY, Abram/Abraham, N.C., Chasey, W7600; BLWt.8443-160-55
Asahel, Mass., S23674
Bry, N.C., S2249
Christian, Pa., S38761
Daniel, Ct., S17453
Ebenezer B., N.J. R4291
Elias, Ct., Cont., Elizabeth, W17960
Elisha, Mass., Abagail, W13329
Elnathan, Ct., S29841
Esbon, Mass., S29189
Ezra, Ct., Huldah, W4971; BLWt. 15197-160-55
George, N.C., Sarah, R4299
George, Va., S38763
Isaac, N.C., S38771
Isaac, Va., R4293
Jabez, Ct., Mercy, W21213
James, Ct., S17445
James, N.C., Va., b. England, Eleanor, R4292
John, Hazen's Regt., Can., BLWt. 13126-100-Pvt. Iss. 3/1/1797
John, Ct., Jerusha, W1419
John, Cont., Pa., S39624
John, Md., BLWt.11247-100-Pvt. Iss. 6/11/1790. No papers
John, N.J., R4294
John, Pa., S23671
John, Va., Barbara, W8875
John, Va., BLWt.2627-200-Lt. Iss. 2/14/1793 to Richmond Terrell/Terrill, guardian to John Mumford Gregory, son & heir. No papers
Joseph, Ct., Deborah, W1596
Joseph, Mass., Sarah Galusha, former wid. R4300. Her 3rd husb. also served. See Abiram Galusha, Ct.
Joshua, N.Y., S8625
Josiah, Ct., Ellen, W24308
Matthew, Ct., S46360; BLWt.819-200-Lt. Iss. 12/5/1799
Moses, Ct., Abigail, W25655
Nathan, Ct., S13214
Nathaniel, Ct., R4296
Nehemiah, Ct., N.Y., S22803
Richard, Va., S31712
Samuel, Ct., Charity, W17970
Samuel, N.Y., R4298
Samuel, Va. & Indian War, R4297
Sarah, Mass. See claim of Joseph Gregory, wid. Sarah Galusha
Silas, Ct., Sarah, W25653
Spittsby/Spillsby, Va., S10775
Stephen, Ct., S22274
Stephen, Ct., Cont., S13191
Thomas, Cont., Mass., S44182
Thomas, Cont., Va., Sally,W8876
Thomas, N.C., S41588
Thomas, N.C., S41589
Thomas, Va., Elizabeth, W7599
Uriah, Ct., N.Y., S15157
Walter, Va., S37966
William, Ct., S29191
William, Mass., Mella, R4295; BLWt.43517-160-55

GREGORY (continued)
William, N.C., S1666
William, N.C., Margaret, W19539
William, Pa., BLWt.9467-100-Pvt. Iss. 12/22/1794 to Henry Purdy, ass. No papers
GREINDER, Martin, Pa., Ann, R4334; BLWt.30703-160-55
GREIR, James, Cont. See GRIER
GREM, Heinrich, N.Y., S23244
GREMBS, Henry, N.Y. See GRAMPS
GREMMER, Jacob, N.C. See GRAMMER
GRENDELL, Daniel, N.H., Elizabeth, W23138
GRENELL, Amasa, Ct., S43650
Michael, Ct., S2251; BLWt.26451-160-55
GRENGER, Zaccheus, Cont., N.Y., S13206
GRENINGER, Henry, Pa., S10764
GRENNELL, Owen, R.I. See GREENNELL
William, Ct. See GRINNELL
GRESHAM, David, S.C., b. Va., S16393
George, Ga., Elizabeth, W2933
James, N.C., Jane, W4969; BLWt.26832-160-55
Littlebury, N.C., S16394
Moses, N.C., See GRISHAM
Robert, Not Rev. War; Indian War 1791; Old War Inv. File 427
GRESHOM, Richard, See GRISSUM
GRETSINGER, John, Pa.,BLWt.1961-100
GREY, Ichabod, Mass. See GRAY
Isaac, N.J., See GRAY
GRIBBENS, John, Pa. See GRIBBON
GRIBBON, John, Pa., Margaret, W4965; BLWt.26548-160-55
GRIBLE, Philip, Pa. See GUIBLE
GRICE, Thomas, S.C., R4301
William, N.C., b. N.C., S6934
GRIDER, Henry, Va., Elizabeth, W8874
Jacob, N.C., Elizabeth, W3980; BLWt.11262-160-55
Jacob, Va., R4302
John, N.C., Isabel, W358; BLWt. 28529-160-55
Michael, Pa. See GRINDER
Valentine, N.C. See GRYDER
GRIDLEY, Asahel, Ct., Chloe, W15771
Ashbel, Cont., Ct., Jemima,W17961
Elijah, Ct., Abigail Eliza, W4968; BLWt.29725-160-55
Elisha, Ct., Lois, W19545
Hannah (2), R4304, former wid. of Henry Wentworth
Horea/Hosea, Ct., BLWt.5835-100-Pvt. Iss. 11/2/1791 to John Heaton. No papers
Hosea, Ct., Sabra Burchard, former wid., W15992
John, Cont., S43639; BLWt.804-200-Capt.-Lt. Iss. 1/20/1790 to John May, ass. No papers
John, Cont., Mass., Anna, W23137
Obediah, Ct., Elizabeth, W16274
Richard, Cont., Mass., BLWt. 2029-500
Seth, Ct., S15588

GRIDLEY (continued)
Silas, Ct., S4304
Theodore, Ct., Amy, W5287; BLWt. 11281-160-55
Thomas, Ct., S29186
GRIDSBY, Benjamin, Va., S1208
GRIER, Charles, Armand's Corps., BLWt.897-300-Surgn. Mate. Iss. 9/16/1791 to Sarah Grier, Admx. No papers
Charles, Va., R14616; Va. Half Pay. N.A. Acc. No. 874-050080
James, Cont., Pa., Mary, W1595; BLWt.833-400-Maj. Iss. 5/18/1789. No papers
John, N.C., S1906
John, Pa., BLWt.9424-100-Pvt. Iss. 7/9/1789. No papers
John, S.C. See GREER
Moses, Ga., N.C., b. Pa., S32281
Thomas, N.C., Susannah, W7567
GRIFEN, Thomas, Mass., N.H., Anne, W14815
GRIFFEN, Ezra, Ct., N.J., S16136
GRIFFETH, Ellis, Mass., S23241
Nathan, Mass., S34905
GRIFFEY, Zachariah, Va., S42757
GRIFFIN, Amos, Md., S41590
Andrew, Mass., Sally, R4316
Benjamin, Mass., S32763
Benjamin, Mass., Mary, W9464; BLWt.31906-160-55
Benjamin, N.Y., BLWt.7152-100-Pvt. Iss. 6/10/1793 to B. Fisher, ass. No papers
Benjamin, N.Y., Phebe, W23150
Charles, Md., Rebecca, W4445
Corbin, Va. Sea Service, R56, Va. Half Pay. See Acc. No. 837 Va. State Navy-YS File
Cornelius, N.Y., R4306
Daniel, N.Y., S37036
David, Pa., BLWt.9444-100-Pvt. Iss. 5/21/1792 to John P. Schott, ass. No papers
Edward, ---, Ga. agcy. S13224
Elijah, Va., R4307
Ezra, Ct. See GRIFFEN
Gideon, S.C., Patience, W8877
Gordon, Pa., S35982
James, Mass., Elizabeth, R4308
James, N.C., Sarah, W7586
James, Va., S47201
James, Va., R4311
Jeremiah, N.H., BLWt.3146-100-Pvt. Iss. 8/19/1795 to James A. Neal, ass. No papers
Jeremiah, N.H., S45574
Jesse, Cont., S.C., S38760
Joel, Ct., R4319
John, Ct., S37037
John, N.C., Jane, R4312
John, Va., Cynthia, W3677; BLWt.264-160-55
John, Va., Susannah, W23142
Jonathan, N.H., Hannah, W16275
Joseph, Ct., Cont., S8615
Joseph, Cont., N.Y., S2581
Joseph, N.H., S21780
Joseph, N.C., Mary, R4315; BLWt.44872-160-55
Joseph, S.C., S21247; BLWt.50899-

GRIFFIN (continued)
160-55
Joshua, N.Y., Margaret, W7583; BLWt.7147-100. Iss. 9/4/1798. No papers
Joshua, N.Y., R4313
Kirkland, Navy. See Kirtland
Kirtland/Kirkland, Navy, Privateer, N.Y. res. & agcy., S43647
Lewis, Va., S21248
Martha, former wid. of John Drewry, Va., which see
Martin, Ct., Anna, W21210
Morgan, S.C., S18844
Moses, Md., S1764
Nathan, Md., S8619
Nathaniel, Mass., Sarah Howe, former wid., W24443
Nathaniel, N.H., S10772
Obadiah, Va., S8614
Philip, R.I., S38774
Ralph, S.C., S16389
Reuben, Va., S35993
Richard, N.C., S.C., S6919
Robert, N.J., R20138
Samuel, Ct., S23666
Samuel, Ga., Elizabeth, R4309
Samuel, N.H., Sophia Atwood, former wid., W20637
Samuel R., N.Y., S22802
Seth, Mass., Judith Brown, former wid., W23677
Sherrod, Cont., Va., S13219
Stephen, Pa. See GIFFIN
Theophilus, N.H., Sarah, W23162
Thomas, Ct., Polly, W19537; BLWt.26598-160-55
Thomas, Mass., Anne, W14815
Thomas, N.C., S6923
William, Ct., BLWt.5857-100-Pvt. Iss. 3/21/1791 to Josiah Starr. No papers
William, Md., R4318
William, S.C., S13205
William, Va., Nancy, W24313
Zachariah, Va., Clara, W7585; BLWt.61261-160-55
GRIFFING, David, N.Y., S31711
Samuel, N.Y. See GRIFFIN
Stephen, Ct., N.Y., Elizabeth, W19549; BLWt.9542-160-55
GRIFFIS, Abner, N.Y., S13199
James, N.Y., R4321
John G., N.J., S.C., R4322
Reubin, Va., Sarah, W7601
Southward, R.I., S21244
Stephen, N.Y., S15160
William, N.Y., S29185
William, S.C., Cortney, R4320
William, S.C., R4323
GRIFFITH, Barnabas, Mass., S32765
Charles, Md., BLWt.11285-100-Pvt. Iss. 12/22/1794 to Henry Purdy, ass. No papers
Chisholm, Md., S15866
Daniel, Mass. See David GRIFFITH
David/Daniel, Mass., Elizabeth, W9462
Eli, Ct., N.Y., R4324
Elijah, Md., Eunice, W4215
Elisha, Md., S2583
Elisha, Md., S10192

GRIFFITH (continued)
Evan, Pa., S8618
George, Ct., S43648
Isaac, N.C., S6918; BLWt.34954-160-55
Jeremiah, Ct., N.Y., Mary, W19532
John, N.J., S2584
John, N.C., S3425
John, Pa., BLWt.9456-100-Pvt. Iss. 5/6/1791. No papers
John, Pa., S39625
John, R.I., S38748
Joseph, Va., S3426
Joseph, Va., Polly, W7589
Levi, N.J., BLWt.8328-100-Pvt. Iss. 4/10/1799 to Abraham Bell, ass. No papers
Levi, Pa., S39614; BLWt.837-200-Lt. Iss. 2/13/1797
Lucy, former wid. of Ebenezer Hitchcock, Ct., which see
Nathan, Md., S8616
Philemon, Md., S8617
Samuel, Md., Ruth, W4214
Samuel J., N.Y., S3427
Thomas, N.J., Pa. & Va., Mary, W4213
Thomas, Lamb's Art., N.Y., BLWt. 7192-100-Pvt. Iss. 9/15/1790 to John S. Hobart, et al, ass. No papers
Thomas, N.Y., Vt., S22663
William, N.Y., S13195
William, N.Y. See GRIFFIS
William, Pa., BLWt.9427-100-Pvt. Iss. 4/18/1791. No papers
William, Pa., S22273
William, Va., Susannah, R4326
Zaddock, Md., S6921
GRIFFITHS, Abraham, Pa., Anna Maria, W7587
James, N.Y., See GRIFFIS
Paul, R.I., S22798; BLWt.18381-160-55
Sarah, former wid. of John Jefferies, Pa., which see
GRIFY, John, Pa. See GRIFFITH
GRIGER, Cato (Delaware Indian), Mass., Rachel (white woman), W2731; BLWt.134-60-55
GRIGG, Henry, Ct., Elizabeth, W11087
Josiah, Va., S6932
Lewis, Va., S3417
Matthew, Va. See GREGG
GRIGGS, Benjamin, N.J., S879
Charles, N.C., S6933
Daniel, N.J., BLWt.8358-100-Pvt. Iss. 9/29/1790 to Thomas L. Vickers, ass. No papers
Ephraim, Ct., Hannah, W16024
George, Va., BLWt.12163-100-Pvt. Iss. 1/7/1793 to Robert Means, ass. No papers
John, N.J., Mary, W16279
Joseph, Ct., S30445
Robert, N.C., S3418
Samuel, Mass., Beulah, R4327
Simeon, ---, Vt. res., Letty, R4328; BLWt.8018-160-55
William, Mass., BLWt.4225-100-

GRIGGS (continued)
Pvt. Iss. 2/16/1799 to John Pond. No papers
William, N.J., BLWt.8329-100-Pvt. Iss. 6/22/1791. No papers
GRIGNER, Jacob, Pa., S39612
GRIGSBY, Aaron, Navy, S2582
Benjamin, Va. See GRIDSBY
Moses, Va., Abigail, W10069; BLWt.29728-160-55
GRILL, Thomas, N.Y., S43634
Thomas, N.Y., BLWt.7156-100-Pvt. Iss. 2/21/1792 to Wm. Campbell, ass. No papers
GRIM, Jacob, Pa., S2243
John, Va., S8628
Peter, Va., S37963
GRIMBS, Henry, N.Y. See GRAMPS
GRIMES, Abraham, Ct., Mass., S13200
Adam, Pa., Elizabeth, R4330
Andrew, Mass., S38765
James, Va., S2244
James, Va., S17455
John, Pa., BLWt.9510-100-Pvt. Iss. 7/2/1790. No papers
John, Pa., S3414
John, Pa., S22801
John, Va., Nancy, W931
Joseph, Ct., Jemima, W21234
Leonard, Pa., S35984
William, N.C., Frances Fail, former wid., W19249; BLWt. 67609-160-55
William, N.C., Beady, R4331
William, S.C., R4332
William, Va., S35980
GRIMKE, John Faucheraud, S.C., Mary, W11088; BLWt.888-450-Lt. Col.
GRIMMER, Jacob, See GRAMMER
Thomas, N.C., Mary, W4974
GRIMMIT, Josiah, Va., S3428
GRIMSLEY, George, N.C., R4333
Joseph, Va., S3429
Thomas, Va., S37956
GRIMSON, Samuel, Pa., Sarah, W3244; BLWt.2444-100
GRINARD, Paul, Md., BLWt.11270-100-Pvt. Iss. 6/7/1798 to Elisha Jarrett, ass. No papers
GRINDELL, Daniel, N.H. See GRENDELL
GRINDER, Martin, Pa. See GREINDER
Michael, Pa., R4303
GRINDLE, Susannah, former wid. of John Baxter Carr, Mass. which see
William, Cont., R.I., Eunice, W23144
GRINDSTAFF, Jacob, N.C., S31075
Michael, N.C., S35995
GRINER, John M. See GRIVER
Peter, N.J., S16837
GRING, David, Pa., S8603
GRINIELL, William, Ct. See GRINNELL
GRINNEL, Jethro, R.I., Catharine, R4336
GRINNELL, Bailey, Navy, R.I., S15868
George, R.I., S43635
Jonathan, R.I., Martha, R4337
Richard, Navy, Mass. res. & agcy.

GRINNELL (continued)
S32759
Robert, R.I., S21782
Royal, R.I., Hannah, W24301; BLWt.17906-160-55
William, Ct., S29843
William, R.I., S10763
William B., Ct., Sarah, W17968
William G., R.I., Experience, W24315
Wise, Ct., S45573
GRINSELY, William, N.Y., BLWt. 7184-100-Pvt. Iss. 11/5/1791 to Henry Adam Vrooman, ass. No papers
GRINSHAW, William, Hazen's Regt. (Canadian), BLWt.13129-100-Fifer. Iss. 3/25/179?
GRINSTAFF, Michael,See GRINDSTAFF
GRINSTEAD, John, Va., S35988
John, Va., R4338
William, Va., S15867
GRINTER, John, Va., S36560
GRISHAM, James, N.C. See GRESHAM
Jeremiah, ---, La. res. in 1853; R4339
John, Va., S21790
Moses, S.C., S21246
GRISSUM, Richard, N.C. res. & agcy., S10205
GRIST, Benjamin, N.C., Catharine, W1170
Jacob, Pa., R4341
GRISWOLD, Aaron, Ct., Polly, W747
Abel, Ct., S17447
Adonijah, Vt., Mary, R4347
Alexander, Ct., R4342
Andrew, Ct., Anna, W17963; BLWt. 1068-200
Andrew, Ct., Eunice, W21205
Asa, Ct., S37028
Benjamin, Mass., S38773
Constant, Ct., S16133
Daniel, Ct., Mass., Nancy, W11086; BLWt.40938-160-55
David, N.Y., Jane, W1754; BLWt. 11085-160-55
David, Vt., Ruby, W19538
Ebenezer, Cont., S37025 (enl. at Castleton,Vt.,served in Col. Moses Hazen's "Congress Regt.", Ct. res.
Eber, Hazen's Regt., BLWt.13117-100-Pvt. Iss. 10/22/1789 to Theodosius Fowler, ass. No papers
Edmund, Ct., Jane, W7608; BLWt. 508-160-55
Edward, Ct., Asenath, W19553
Elihu, Ct. Sea Service, R1204
Elijah, Ct., S37032
Elijah, Ct., Lydia, W25650
Elizabeth, former wid. of Samuel Sweet, R.I., which see
Francis, Ct., S23245
George, Ct., BLWt.5840-100-Pvt. Iss. 2/20/1790 to Solomon Goss, no papers
George, Ct., S17456
George, Ct., S31703
Gilbert, N.H., BLWt.3148-100-Pvt. Iss. 3/25/1790. No papers
Jabez, N.Y., S43651

GRISWOLD (continued)
Janna, Cont., Ct., Lucy, W21220
Joel, Ct., S31708
John, Ct., Vashta, W9466; BLWt. 2346-160-55
John, Ct., Lydia, W25654; BLWt. 10237-160-55
John, Ct., R4345
John, Mass., Elizabeth, R4344
Joseph, Ct., S43652
Joseph, Ct., Mehitable, W14811
Midian, Cont., Ct., Annis, R4343
Moses, Ct., BLWt.5874-100-Sgt. Iss. 2/5/1790. No papers
Nathaniel, Ct., S31706
Samuel, Ct., Hannah, W21230; BLWt.336-100 & 235-60-55
Samuel, Ct., R4348
Samuel, Vt., S18842
Selah, Ct., Cont., S17454
Simeon, Ct., Cont., S13092
Solomon, Ct., S15589
Sylvanus, Ct., Mary/Maria, W25648
Zenas, Ct., S15158
GRITE, William, N.Y., BLWt.7176-100-Pvt. Iss. 9/28/1790 to John Maley, ass. No papers
GRITTON, John, Pa., S13203
GRIVER, John M., Ga., R4349
GROAT, Abraham S., N.Y., S13186
Henry, Cont., N.Y., Sophia, W17028
Isaac, N.Y. See GROOT
John, N.Y., Sarah, R4364
Nicholas, N.Y., Esther, W4212; BLWt.15190-160-55
Peter, N.Y., S10768
William, N.Y., Catharine, W19529
GROAVES, Michael, Pa., Catharine, R4350
GROCE, Alexander, Pa., BLWt.9469-100-Pvt. Iss. 2/25/1791 to Charles Culver, ass. No papers
George, Mass., Elizabeth, W27416
GROESBECK, Hugh, N.Y., S23665
Peter W., N.Y., Alida, R4351
GROESBEECK, Gerrit I., N.Y., R4352
GROESSEL, John, Va., S37967
GROGAN, Patrick, Va., S41593
GROGEN, John, N.Y., BLWt.7151-100-Pvt. Iss. 7/10/1790 to C.C. Elmandorph, ass. No papers
Patrick, Va. See GROGAN
GROMETH, Jacob, German Regt., BLWt.861-200-Lt. Iss. 9/14/1789 to Mich I. Boyer, admr. No papers
GRONINGER, Joseph, See CRONINGER
GRONT, Silas, Mass. See GRANT
GROOM, George, Art. Artificiers, BLWt.13138-100-Sgt. Iss. 8/10/1789 to Richard Platt, ass. No papers
Major, Va., S31073
GROOMS, Abraham, Va., S3419
John, Pa., Sea Service, S2247
Jonathan, ---, b. England, S19305, Enl. in Va. & Va. res.
Levi, Va., BLWt.1937-200

GROOT, Derick, Mass., S23661
Derick C., N.Y., S23243
Isaac, N.Y., S8604
Simon A., N.Y., Rebecca, W23140
GROOVER, Peter, N.C., S31717
GROSCOST, Daniel, Pa., S8629
Jacob, Pa., S8632
GROSE, Philip, Pa., S13226
Samuel, Ct. See GROSS
GROSECLOSE, Peter, Pa., Elizabeth R4354
GROSH, Michael, Md., S37964
GROSS, Alexander, Mass., S33266
Benjamin, Mass., S18424
David, N.H., Sally, W23148; BLWt.12843-160-55
David, N.C., S30444
Elisha, Cont., Mass., Deborah, W14820; BLWt.177-100
George, Mass. See GROUSE
George, Mass. See GROCE
John, Ct., Susannah, W21212
John, Pa., S6931
John, R.I., Hannah, W21208
Jonah, Ct., S32774
Nicholas, Pa., S4355
Peter, N.Y., BLWt.7198-100-Pvt. Iss. 7/6/1791 to Wm. W. Morris, ass. No papers
Peter, Cont., N.Y., S43649
Samuel, Ct., S49283
Thomas, Ct., S4356
Thomas, Va., Sally, R4357
GROSSCROSS, John, Pa., S8631
GROSSCUP, Paul, Pa., Sybilla, R4358
GROSVENOR, Asa, Ct., S10762
Betsey/Elizabeth, former wid. of Joseph Hunt, Mass., which see
Joshua, Ct., S15156
Lemuel, Ct., S15154
Polly, former wid. of Elihu Mather, which see
Thomas, Ct., R4361
Thomas, Ct., Cont., S37033; BLWt.811-500-Lt.Col. Cmdt. Iss. 1/28/1790. No papers
GROTE, William, N.Y., BLWt.7187-100-Pvt. Iss. 2/14/1791 to Alexander Alexander, ass. No papers
William, N.Y. See GROAT
GROTECLASS, Gilbert, N.J., S46225
GROTON, Prosper, R.I., BLWt.3161-100-Pvt. Iss. 1/28/1790. No papers
GROUARD, Peter, N.H. Sea Service, also on sea up to and during War of 1812, S22275
GROUSE, George, Mass., S37043
GROUT, Abel, Mass., S18423
Amasa, N.H., S22280
Elias, Mass., S29845
Elihu, Vt., S18843
Hilkiah, N.Y., S23672
Joel, Cont., Mass., Asenah/Asenath, W14818
Jonathan, N.H., Lydia, BLWt. 49471-160-55
Nathan, Mass., Mary, W14827
Silas, Mass., Susannah, W14810
William, Mass., S17989

GROUT (continued)
William, Mass., Amy, W7568
GROVE, David, Md., S34907
George, Pa., R4365
John, N.H., BLWt.3140-100-Pvt. Iss. 7/21/1789 to Ladd & Cass, no papers
John, N.J., S880
John, Pa., S37965
John, Pa., Margaret Ann, W1756
Jonas, Va., S41591
Michael, Pa. See GROAVES
Peter, Pa., Sarah, W2788
Philip, Pa., S22277
Samuel, N.J., Alcha, W7565
Wendell/Windle, Pa., Jane, W4210; BLWt.18379-160-55
Windle, Pa. See Wendell
GROVENER, Polly, former wid. of Elihu Mather, Ct., which see
GROVER, Amasa, Ct., S38751
Amaziah, Ct., N.H., Joanna, W746; BLWt.9520-160-55
Benjamin, Ct., BLWt.5834-100-Pvt. Iss. 11/2/1791 to Titus Street. No papers
Benjamin, Mass., BLWt.4239-100-Pvt. Iss. 11/30/1799 to Abijah Holbrook. No papers
Benjamin, Mass., S32770
Benjamin, Mass., R4368
Daniel, Ct., R4369
David, Cont., Mass., Martha, W24316
Ebenezer, Ct., N.Y., Mary, W17964
Eleazer, Cont., Mass., Vt.,S28748
Hannah, former wid. of James Mills, Cont., Mass.,N.H. which see
Isaiah, Mass., Elizabeth, W3183
Jabez, Ct., Jerusha, W7604; BLWt.27641-160-55
Jacob, Ct., BLWt.748-100
Jacob, Cont., Vt., S38777
Jedediah, Mass., Elizabeth, W23131
Jonathan M., Md., S31082
Joseph, Ct., Cont., S39631
Luther, Ct., S21777
Nehemiah, N.Y., S23662
Peter, ---, Ct. res. in 1789, Diadama, R14578
Phineas, Ct., BLWt.816-200-Lt. iss 4/18/1796 to Thomas Lloyd, ass. to Jabin Strong & Ruth Strong, admrs. No papers
Stephen, Ct., Mary, W268
GROVES, Isaac, Md., BLWt.11248-100-Pvt. Iss. 1/8/1796 to Geo. Ponsonby, ass. No papers
John, Invalid Corps., BLWt.13139-100-Pvt. Iss. 3/3/1791. No papers
Robert, N.J., Elizabeth, W88
Stephen, Pa., b. England, S31714
Thomas, Va., Mildred, W4211; BLWt.2409-100
William, Md., BLWt.11253-100-Pvt. Iss. 4/17/1792 to Ann Dugan, Admx. No papers
William, Md., Mary, W9461
GROVESNOR, Richard, Pa., S35983
GROVIER, Isaiah, See GROVER
GROW, Ambrose, Ct., Vt., Amy,

GROW (continued)
W1416; BLWt.26560-160-55
David, Ct., Martha, W2609; BLWt. 6285-160-55
Ebenezer, Ct., Cont., S36566; BLWt.1426-100
John, Ct., S13211
Peter, Mass., S18425
GROWNHART, John, N.Y., S43632
GRUB, Darius, Va., S16838
John, N.Y., S34376
GRUBB, Jacob, Pa., S40061
Peter, Pa., Sarah Hoyt, former wid., W4993; BLWts. 17703-160-55 & 36724-160-55
GRUBBS, Hensley, Va., BLWt.12165-100-Pvt. Iss. 3/26/1792 to Francis Graves, ass. No papers
Hensley, Va., S37962
John, Va., Sarah, R4371
Nathan, Va., S8600
Philip, Not Rev. War. Harmar's War of 1790, Pa. res.; Old War Rej. 4372
GRUBER, Margaret, former wid. of Daniel Cobi, S.C., which see
Philip, S.C., S21778
Valentine, Cont., Pa., S39627
GRUMMON, Ebenezer, N.Y., Johanah, W16591
Ephraim, N.Y., Rachel, W17029
GRUMON, Moses, Ct., R4373
GRUNDY, Edmund, Ct. See GRANDEY
GRUNEWALD, Nicholas, See GREENEWALT
GRUNNWALD, Abraham, See GREENWALD
GRUNNWALT, Jacob, Pa. See GREENWALD
GRUSH, Thomas, N.H., S32771
GRUVER, John, Pa., R4374
GRYDER, Martin, N.C., S31078
Valentine, N.C., Mary, W11082; BLWt.19544-160-55
GRYMES, George, Cont., Va., BLWt.1939-100
GUARD, Daniel, See GARD
GUARTNEY, Michael, Va., S8637
GUBTAIL, Thomas, Mass., Lydia, W21235
GUDGEON, Robert, R.I., Elizabeth, BLWt.741-100
William, Md., R4375
GUDGER, William, N.C., Martha, W15772
GUELLOW, Francis, Mass., S33272
GUERNSEY, Southmayd, Ct., R3921
GUESS, Benjamin, N.C., S32283
George, Pa., Ctf. 4770
Henry, S.C., Sophia, W7609
Joseph, N.C., Constance, W8878
GUEST, Albert, Pa., BLWt.9428-100-Pvt. Iss. 4/6/1795. No papers
James, Pa., S3431
John, Cont., Mass., S37046
Moses, N.C., Eleandor/Eleanor, W11072; BLWt.15436-100-55
Richard, Md., S8639
William, N.C., Anna, W21239

GUEY, John, Va., R4377
GUFFIN, Andrew, N.Y., S13236
GUFFEY, James, Pa., S31718
GUFFY, Alexander, Pa., Ann, W3015
GUGEL, David, Ga., R4378
GUI, John, Va. See GUEY
GUIBLE, Philip, Pa., BLWt.2398-100
GUICE, John, Md., Va., Elizabeth, W4686
GUILD, Abner, Mass., Sarah, W14832
Amos, Mass., S29194
Ebenezer, Mass., Molly, W21236
Elias, Mass., S29847
Jacob, Mass., Chloe, W14835
Jesse, Mass., S18850
John, Mass., S15434
Joseph, Mass., Martha, W14831; BLWt.701-60-55
Napthali, Mass., R.I., S13229
Oliver, Mass., Anna, W24322
Richard, Ct., Eleanor Rice, W1420 BLWt.15444-160-55
Richard, Mass., Zillah, BLWt.18377-160-55
Samuel, Cont., Mass., S29848
Samuel, Mass., Mittee, W14829
Samuel, Mass., Betsey, W25666; BLWt.34544-160-55
GUILDBRAND, Renne, Hazen's Regt., BLWt.13131-100-Pvt. Iss. 8/14/1792 to Benj. Moore, ass. No papers
GUILDER, Daniel, Va., Mary, W4217; BLWt.8162-160-55
GUILE, Abraham, Ct., Cont., Deborah, W1421
Asa, Mass. See GILE
Henry, N.Y., Zillah, W19560
Joseph, N.Y., R4379
Nathan, Mass., Eunice, W17971; BLWt.2274-100
GUILFORD, John, Mass., S37048
John, Mass., Sarah, W1597
Joseph, N.C., S8640
Samuel, Mass., Elizabeth, W14833
Simeon, Mass., Rheuhamah, W11073
Timothy, Mass., Salley, W21238
GULL, John, Va., S35998
William, Va., S6942
GUILLAM, John, Pa., Art. Artificer BLWt.13150-100-Pvt. Iss. 7/28/1789 to Richard Smith, ass.
GUILMAT, Francis, Hazen's Regt., BLWt.887-200-Lt. Iss. 1/22/1790 to Benj. Mooers, ass. No papers
GUILTNER, Francis, See GILTNER
GUIN, William, Pa., R4380
GUINN, Andrew, Va., S37970
Thomas, S.C. See Thomas C. HOLMES
GUION, Isaac, Cont., N.Y., S44992; BLWt.832-200-Lt. Iss. 5/18/1790
GUISE, John, Md. See GUICE
GUIZA, John, Md. See GUICE
GULDY, Nicholas, See GOLDY
GULICK, Abraham, N.J., S13233
Abraham J., N.J., Sarah, W792
Cornelius, N.J., R4381
Ferdinand, N.J., Va., S2586
James, N.J., Elizabeth, W7611; BLWt.27604-160-55
John, N.J., S818

GULICK (continued)
Nicholas, N.J., Elizabeth, W25665; BLWt.26378-160-55
Peter, N.J., S881
GULLET, Reece/Reese, Va., R4383
GULLEY, John, N.C. See GULLY
John, Va., S2585
Richard, Va., S38781
GULLICK, Margaret R., former wid. of Moses Henry/Hendry, N.C., which see
GULLION, Jeremiah, Pa., Va., Isabella, W8879
John O., Pa., S36567
Robert, Pa., S16396
GULLIVER, Lemuel, Mass., S5219
Reuben, Mass., S29849; BLWt.7100-160-55
GULLY, John, N.C., Ann, W19557; BLWt.16125-160-55
GUM, Shepherd, Va., R4384
GUMP, Frederick, N.J., R4385
Frederick, Pa., S2255
GUMPF, Christopher, Pa., S22806
GUN, James, Va., BLWt.659-300
GUNBY, John, Md., BLWt.851-500-Col. Iss. 9/8/1789. No papers
GUNDEWAY, Richard, Mass., Betty W24320
GUNDY, Jacob, Pa., S32284
GUNION, Hugh, Pa., R4388
GUNISON, Samuel, Va., S35996
GUNN, Aaron, Mass., Betsy, W17972
Abel, Ct., Cont., S44887
Alexander, Mass., S33270
Alexander, N.C., Bedy Oak, R4386
Asahel, Mass., Submit, W14828
Daniel, Mass., S44886
Daniel, N.C., Susan, W7614
Eli, Mass., Sibbel, W14836
Elisha, Mass., R4387
Gabriel, N.C., Alsey, W7613
James, Va., BLWt.659-300
John, Md., S2256
Moses, Mass., S31085
Noble, Mass., Lucy, W3983
Salmon, Mass., S31084
Starling, Cont., Va., S6941
GUNNELL, John, Cont., Va., S40062
John, Va. See GUNNILL
William, Cont., S.C. res. in 1818, Martha, W1172; BLWt.11184-160-55
GUNNELS, William, Va., BLWt.12149-100-Pvt. Iss. 12/2/1793. Notation "Certified to the Gen. Land Office, 24 Sept. 1830"
GUNNER, James, Va., Ruth Burgess, former wid., W5959; BLWt.39496-160-55
Peter, Pa., BLWt.9493-100-Pvt. Iss. 6/7/1793 to Christian Hubbart, ass. No papers
GUNNILL, John, Va., BLWt.12150-100-Pvt. No papers
GUNNISON, Josiah, N.H., S17991
GUNSALUS, Daniel, N.Y., S44889
Richard, Pa., S23246
GUNSALUSS, Henry, N.J., N.Y.,

GUNSALUSS (continued)
S8643
GUNSAULA, John, N.J., Pa., S2254
GUNSAULD, John, See GUNSAULA
GUNSAULIS, James, N.Y., S16397; See N.A. Acct. No. 847-050076; Not Half Pay
GUNSOLLEY, Benjamin, N.Y., R4389
GUNSTON, James, N.C., S6939
GUNTER, Benjamin, N.C., Elizabeth, W19558
Charles, S.C., Elizabeth, W27550; BLWt.18028-160-55
Henry, S.C., S38778
Joel, N.C., S38780
John, Pa., Elizabeth, W9467; BLWt.16130-160-55
John, Sea Service, Va., S38779
GUPTAIL, John, Mass., R4391
GURGANIS, David, N.C., Rebecca, R4392
GURGANUS, Reuben, N.C., S8638
GURLEY, Isham, N.C., R4393
Jeremiah, N.C., S13231
Joseph, N.C., Mary, W4973
GURNEE, Francis, N.Y., S13232
GURNEY, Asa, Ct., Sarah, W7616; BLWt.9416-160-55
Asa, Mass., S18849
Bazaliel, Ct., S44993
Benjamin, Mass., Thankful, W14837
David, Mass., Jane, W14834
Eliab, Mass., Sarah, W23167
Francis, Pa., Mary, W3678
George, Mass., S29193
Jacob, Mass., S20375
Jonathan, Mass., S37047
Joseph, Mass., S18848
Joseph P., Mass., S17435
Lemuel, Mass. & Navy, Susan, W1171; BLWt.10012-160-55
Levi, Mass., Rebecca, W7615; BLWt.18876-160-55
Zachariah, Mass., Nohitable, W14830
GUSHEE, Elijah, Mass., Phebe, W8838
Samuel, Mass., Rachel, W1271; BLWt.34945-160-55
GUSHERT, Detrick, Pa., S22804
GUSTENE, Joel, Ct., Ann Taylor, W23166
GUSTIN, Amos, Pa., S41595
Benajah, N.J., Eleanor, W7610
Jesse, Mass., BLWt.2229-100
Josiah, N.H., Margaret, W19556; BLWt.19772-160-55
Thomas, Mass., S37045
GUSTINE, Edward, Ct., S13234
Elisha, Cont., N.H., S13228
Joel, Ct. See GUSTENE
GUTH, John G., N.Y., BLWt.7173-100-Pvt. Iss. 4/18/1791. No papers
GUTHERIE, George, Lt., Pa., Moylan's Light Horse, BLWt.840-220 iss. 5/25/1792 to Peter Manifold, ass.
GUTHERY, David, Va. See GUTTRY
James, N.C., S21793
John, Pa., S41594

GUTHERY (continued)
William, Pa., S35997
William, Pa. See GUTHRIE
GUTHREY, Benjamin, Va., R21672
David, Va. See GUTTRY
Francis, N.C. See GUTHRIE
John, Md., Va., S37968; BLWt. 691-100. Iss. 4/21/1818
John, Va., S8642
GUTHRIE, Abraham, N.Y., S44888
Christian, N.Y., BLWt.1915-100
Elizabeth, former wid. of Joseph Brownlee, Pa., which see
Francis, N.C., R4395
Frederick, N.C., R4396
George, Pa., BLWt.840-200-Lt. Iss. to Peter Manifold, ass. No papers
Henry, N.C., Nancy, W4975, BLWt.36753-160-55
James, Ct., Mehitable, W25667
James, N.C. See GUTHERY
James, Pa., Va. & Indian Wars, Eunice, W9468
John, N.C., S10776
John/John Pollard, Va., Eliza, W5286
John, Va., BLWt.691-100
Joseph, Mass., BLWt.4203-100-Pvt. Iss. 4/21/1794 to Joseph Guthrie. No papers
Joseph, Mass., S46383
Nathaniel, Va., See GUTTRY
Robert, S.C., Mary, W293
William, Del., BLWt.10772 & 13941-100-Pvt. Iss. 9/2/1789 to Thomas McGuire, admr. No papers
William, Pa., S40063
William, Pa. See Joseph BROWNLEE, Pa.
GUTHRY, John, Va. See GUTHRIE
William, Pa. See GUTHERY
GUTRICH, Nathan, Ct. See GOODRICH
GUTRY, John, N.C., R4398
GUTTERSON, William, Mass., Mary, W24321
GUTTRICK, Christian, N.Y. See GUTHRIE
GUTTRY, David, Va., Mary, R4397; BLWt.45671-160-55
Nathaniel, Va., S13235
GUY, James, N.C., Sarah, R4399
John, N.J., S34380
John, N.Y., S13230
John, Va. See GUEY
Jonathan, Pa., S40060
William, N.Y., R.I., Phebe, W19559
William, Va., Abigail, S17969
GUYANT, Luke, BLWt.5889-100-Pvt. in Sheldon's Dragoons, Ct.; Iss. 9/24/1790 to James F. Sebor. No papers
Luke, Ct., Cont., S17990
GUYER, John, See KEGER
GUYERS, James, Mass., BLWt.4209-100-Pvt. Iss. 1/28/1790 to Joseph May. No papers
GUYGER, George, Pa., BLWt.1135-200
GUYLE, Abraham, See GUILE
GUYNISS, Benjamin, N.J., S34381
GUYNN, William, Pa., S22805

GUYTON, Aaron, S.C., Margaret, W21237; BLWt.36605-160-55
Moses, S.C., Nancy, R4400
GWALTNEY, Nathan, S.C., S41596
GWIN, Andrew, Va. See GUINN
Edward, N.C., Rachel, R4401
Jesse, Ga., Va., S8645
John, N.C., S3393
John, Va., Mary, W7618
Thomas, Va., S42208
William, N.C., Hannah, R4402
GWINN, John (dec'd), Md., BLWt. 11262-100-Pvt. Iss. 7/14/1795 to Wm. Marbury, ass. of David Lawler, admr.
John, Md., Julia, W3802; BLWt. 1494-100
Samuel, Va., S17992
Thomas, S.C. see Thomas C. HOLMES
GWINNUP, George, N.J., Margaret, W7619; BLWt.8334-100-Sgt. Iss. 11/17/1796
GWINUP, George, See GWINNUP
GWYN, Humphry/Humphrey, Va., S37969
GWYNN, John, Md. See GWINN

H

HAAS, Christian, Pa., b. Germany, S5478
Henry, N.J., R4727
Jacob, Pa., Ann, R4404
John, N.J., S1012
John Peter, Pa., Eve; BLWt.61130-160-55
HABERSHAM, John, Ga., BLWt.1226-400
HABURN, Wm., N.Y., BLWt.7265-100-Pvt. Iss. 10/9/1790. No papers
HACKADAY, William, See HOCKADAY
HACKATHORN/HACKEDORN
David, Pa., S22820
HACKELBANDER, Joseph, See EICHELBERGER
HACKER, John. Not Rev. War, N.W. Indian War, Tenn. res. at enl. Old War Inv. Rej. File 21027
HACKET, Charles, N.H., R4407
Daniel, N.H., Hannah, W19739
Ezekiel, Mass., S37078
George, Mass., S15873
John, Va., Pvt., BLWt.12235-100 Iss. 1/31/1794 to John Stockdell, ass.
Joshua, Pvt., N.J., BLWt.8406. Iss. 6/9/1795
Judah, N.H., S37067
Zilpha, Mass., W14892, former wid. of James Cogshall, which see
HACKETT, Allen, N.H., Sally, W7691; BLWt.30785-160-55
Edward, Mass., S13254
Elijah, Mass., S37074
John, Mass., Polly, W21282
John, Va., S37979
Joshua, N.J., S34389
Josiah, Mass., R.I., S13284
Lillis, Mass., Arunah Fullerton/Fullington, former wid., see FULLERTON
Zebedee, Mass., S15438
HACKLEY, John, Lt., Va., BLWt.1077-200. Iss. 4/2/1790
HACKNEY, George, N.Y. See HAKNEY
George, N.Y., Mary, W17036
John, Del., Jane V., W7727; BLWt. 1516-100
Joseph, Cont., N.Y., Margaret, W1600; BLWt.10246-160-55
Joseph, N.C., S6973
Richard, Va., S6971
Robert, Va., R4408
Samuel, Va., S36001
Thomas, Va., S2281
William, Lamb's Art., N.Y.; BLWt. 7285-100-Pvt. Iss. 6/24/1790 to Elkanah Watson, ass. No papers
HACKWORTH, Austin, Va., R4410
John, Va., Mary, R4411
Thomas, Va., S31115; BLWt.36726-160-55
William, Va., Dorothy, W3415
HADAR/HARDAR, William, N.J.,S2270
HADCOCK, Daniel, N.Y., S21258
HADDEN, Elisha, N.C., Va., R4412
Thomas, N.J., Mary, R4413
William, Ga., Mary, W7697; BLWt. 43503-160-55
HADDEY, John, N.J. See HEADDY

HADDON, George, Va., S45893
HADDOX, William, Va., S8694
HADEN, Anthony/Anthony D., Va., S18013; BLWt.2158-100
Anthony, Va., R4418
Jeremiah, Va., Ann, W2107; BLWt.1647-100
John, Md., BLWt.11335-100-Pvt. Iss. 1/8/1796 to George Ponsonby, ass. No papers
John, N.J. See HAYDON
William, Cont., Mass. See HAYDEN
HADER, Nehemiah, Md., BLWt.11327-100-Pvt. Iss. 2/1/1790. No papers
HADGER, Robert, N.Y., S13239
HADLEY, Abijah, N.H., Abigail, R4414
Benjamin, Mass., S32814
Ebenezer, Mass., Phebe, W14845
Enos, Mass., N.H., S10807
Frederick, N.J., N.Y., Catharine, R4416
George, N.Y., Margaret, W1598; BLWt.26501-160-55
Isaac, N.Y., S44902
Jacob, N.H., S18854
Jonathan, N.H., Vt., Resign, W15910
Joseph, Mass., BLWt.4421-100-Pvt. Iss. 5/1/1792 to David Quinton. No papers
Joseph, N.H., S44903
Joseph, N.Y., Abigail, W2615; BLWt.5442-160-55. Her 1st husb., Samuel Gray, also served, which see
Joshua, N.C., BLWt.1096-300-Capt. Iss. 2/21/1791 to Abisha Thomas, ass. No papers.
Josiah, Mass., R4417
Moses, N.J. See HADLY
Stephen, N.J., N.Y., S13263
Thomas, Mass., S32815
William, N.Y., Grace, W14856
HADLOCK, James, N.Y., S22817
Samuel, Ct., Cont., Navy, Sarah, W25757; BLWt.860-800
Samuel, N.Y., S22808
Thomas, Ct., Lovina, W487; BLWt. 28589-160-55
HADLOOCK, Josiah, Mass., S29200
HADLY, James, Pa., Rhoda, W16288
Moses, N.J., S41626
William, R.I., S13369
HADON, See HADEN
HADSALL/HADSDELL, Elijah, Ct., R.I., Anna, W1859; BLWt. 5070-160-55
HAELEY, Hugh, N.J., See HEALEY
HAFFERNAN/HEFFERNAN, Hugh, Pa., Catherine, R4419
HAGADORN, Jacob, N.Y., R4420
William, N.Y. See HAGEDORN
HAGAMAN, Henry, N.J., Lydia, R4421; BLWt.13198-160-55
James, Va., S13313
Joseph, N.J. See HAGEMAN
HAGAN, Charles, Va., S36008
Francis, Va. See HAGINS
James, Md., S36003
Peter, "in the Sappers & Miners, BLWt.13162-100-Pvt. Iss. 7/9/1789 to Peter Hagan. No papers
Raphael/Ralph, Md., Rebecca, W8907
HAGANY, Cornelius, Del., BLWt. 1971-100
HAGAR, Aaron, Mass. See HAGER
David, Mass., S38804
Ezekiel, Mass., See HAGER
John, Cont. See HAGEY
John, Mass. See HAGER
Simon/Simeon, N.C., S8686
Simon, N.C., See HAGER
HAGARTY, Robert, ---, N.J. res. of heir in 1853, Rachel, R14867
HAGEDORN, William, N.Y., Mary, W2110; BLWt.10017-160-55
HAGEMAN, Aaron, N.J., S819
Barnet, Pa., R4426
Henry, N.J. See HAGAMAN
John, Pa. See HEGEMAN
Joseph, N.J., Alledy, W214
William, N.Y., R4422
HAGENS, Edmund, Mass., S16865
Walter, Mass., S15878
HAGER, Aaron, Mass., Rachel, W19708
Abram, Mass., S34404
Benjamin, Mass., S34382
Ezekiel, Mass., Esther, W23248
Henry, N.Y., S10809
John, Mass., S29857
John, Mass., Bathsheba Alexander, former wid., W16808. Her last husb., Jonathan S. Alexander, N.Y., also served, which see
John, Pa., S2284
Joseph, N.Y., Nancy, W25748
Simon, N.C., Elizabeth, R4424
Stephen, Mass., Elizabeth, W27959
HAGERMAN, Barnet, See HAGEMAN
Henry, N.J., See HAGAMAN
James, Pa., S39664
James, Va. See HAGAMAN
Ruliff, N.J., Catherine/Catharine Stout, former wid., W506
HAGERTY, George, Md., BLWt.11365-100-Pvt. Iss. 11/29/1790 to James Curren, admr. No papers
John, N.J., BLWt.8385-100-Pvt. Iss. 6/16/1789 to Thomas Coyle, ass. No papers
John, N.J., Va., Mary, W7702
Nicholas, Va., BLWt.12181-100-Pvt. Iss. 7/14/1792 to Robert Means, ass. No papers
HAGEY, Adam, Pa., R4427
John, Cont., French, Catharine, R4428
HAGGARD, David, Va., R4429
Henry, Va., S13316
James, Va., S31109
William, N.C., Va., S31090
HAGGERTY, Patrick, Va., BLWt. 12229-100-Pvt. Iss. 5/2/1794. No papers
William, Pa., S36574
HAGGET, Abner, Mass., S10782
HAGGETT, Benjamin, ---, Maine res. in 1818, R4430
Jesse, Mass., S44916
HAGGINS, Henry, Pa., S5433
HAGIE, John, See HAGEY
HAGINS, Francis, Va., S36007
William, N.C., S30459
HAGLE, John, Va., S8669
HAGOOD, Benjamin, N.C., Mary, R4789
Jesse, N.C., Elizabeth, R4432
HAGUE, John, Cont., French, See HAGEY
HAHN, George, Md., S8683
Henry, Pa., R4433
Henry, Pa., See HORN
John, Pa., Catharine, W3249
Michael, Md., Pa., Nancy, R5109
Paul, Md., R4434
Valentine, Pa., S13297
HAIGHT, Moses, N.Y., Amy Ferguson, former wid., R3853
Samuel J., N.Y., S13267
William, Navy, N.J., S884
HAIGLER, Jacob, S.C., S21797
HAIL, Garshom/Gershom, Ct., S22283
Simon, Va. See HAILE
William, not Rev. War, N.W. Indian War 1797; O.W.I. 24608
HAILE, Barnard, R.I., S17464
Joseph, N.C., S38814
Simon, Va., R4435
HAILES, Silas, N.C., S.C., Spicy, W27546; BLWts.26702-160-55 & 35848-160-55
HAILEY, Anthony, Va., S41624
Barnabas/Barnaby, Va., S30477
George, N.J., BLWt.8404-100-Pvt. Iss. 10/17/1789 to John Pope, ass. Also BLWt.220-60-55. No papers
George, N.J. See HALEY
Joseph, Va., Mary, W7686
HAIN, Frederick, Pa., R4436
Henry, Md. See HAYNE
John, Pa., See HANES
Philip, Pa., S23685
HAINE, Frederick, Pa.,See HAIN
HAINER, William, N.H. See HANER
HAINES, Aaron, Mass. See HAYNES
Abraham, N.J., R4437
Christopher, Va., See HAINS
Daniel, N.J., BLWt.8366-100. Iss. 1789
Evan, Ga., Charity, W8897
Henry, N.Y., R4440
Jacob, N.Y., Anna, R4438
John, Ct., S13240
John, Lamb's Art., N.Y., BLWt. 7240-100-Pvt. Iss. 7/10/1790 to John Quackinboss, ass. No papers
John, Pa., S2266
John, Pa., See HANES
Jonathan, Pa., Va., b. Pa., R14821
Nathan, N.H., Hannah, W19736
Peter, Va. See HAINS
Samuel, Mass., S37095
Samuel, N.H., S13342
Simeon, Cont., N.H. See HAINS
Simeon, N.H., Eunice, W21281

HAINES (continued)
Simon, N.H., Phebe, W23255
Thomas, N.H., Hannah, W23217; BLWt.5072-160-55
Walter, N.H., Rachel, W23176
William, N.J., Barbara Ann, R4439
HAINS, Benjamin, N.Y., Sophia, W4693; BLReg.312065, 10/3/1855
Christopher, Va., Tallitha, W8896
George, Va. See HAYNES
John, N.Y., See HANES
Nathan, N.H., See HAINES
Peter, Cont., Va., S38008
Richard, Va. See HAYNES
Samuel, Mass., See HAINES
Simeon, Cont., N.H., Welthea, W24412
HAIR, Daniel, Va., S5493
David, N.C., S6978
John, Mass., S32798
John, Pa., S2593
John, Pa., S4325
John, Va., S17469
Robert, N.C., S9567
HAIRBOLT, Adam, Pa., BLWt.9607-100-Pvt. Date & person to whom iss. not shown. No papers
HAIRHOLD, John, Hazen's Regt., BLWt.13167-100-Pvt. Iss. 9/10/1789. No papers
HAIRRIS, John C. Va. See HARRIS
HAIRSTON, James, S.C., R4442
HAISLIP, John, Va., Catharine, W11232; BLWt.28527-160-55
Laban, Md. or N.C., Rebecca Peace, former wid., R8024
HAISTEN, John, Va., Nancy, W7704
HAIT, Joel, Ct. See Joel HOYT.
Joseph, Ct. See Joseph HOYT
Minnah, N.Y. See HYATT
Samuel, Ct., S46004; BLWt.967-200-Lt. Iss. 6/27/1789
Samuel, Ct., Cont. See HOYT
Stephen, Mass., Enl. in Ct., S37056
HAKES, Caleb, Ct., R.I., S23247
George, Ct., Cont., R.I., S44911
Jesse, N.Y., War of 1812, Esther W19704
John, Mass., N.Y., S5483
Jonathan, Ct., Cont., R.I., S23255
HAKET, John, Mass. See HACKETT
HAKNEY, George, N.Y., S44914
HALBERT, William, Cont., Va. res. in 1813, BLWt.607-100
HALBROOKS, George, N.C., R5120
HALDEMAN, Christopher, Pa. See HALDERMAN
HALDERMAN, Christopher, Pa., R4445; BLWt.36524-160-55
HALDRIDGE, Jehiel, N.H. See HOLDRIDGE
HALE, Aaron, Cont., Ct., N.Y., Hannah, W17041; BLWt.1203-200 iss. 1/26/1827
Amon, Md., Mary, W227
Amos, Mass., Elizabeth, W23245
Asa, Mass., N.H., Vt., S18862
Benjamin, Mass., Mercy, W7622; BLWt.36723-160-55

HALE (continued)
Calvin, Mass., S10804
Daniel, Mass., S16855
Ebenezer, Ct., Theda, W17986
Eleazer, Mass. See HEALD
Francis, Mass., Olive, W23213; BLWt.26029-160-55
Gershom, Ct. See Garshom HAIL
Israel, Mass., Esther, W23254
James, R.I., S29852
John, N.H., Vt., S18002
John, N.Y., S13276
John, Pa., BLWt.9566-100-Corp. Iss. 8/7/1789 to Richard Platt, ass. No papers
John, Va., S1765
Jonathan, Ct., S21257
Jonathan, Ct., Mary Button, former wid., W17387
Joseph, Mass., Dis. No papers
Joseph, N.H., Martha, W23184
Leonard, Va., S5488
Mary, former wid. of Wm. Parker, N.H., which see
Matthew, Ct., Ruth, W25749
Mordecai, Cont., N.Y., Catharine, W19744; BLWt.950-300-Surgn. Mate Iss. 10/23/1790. Also recorded as BLWt.2573. No papers
Nathan, Cont., N.H., Abigail, W23178
Nathan, Md., S4311
Nicholas, N.C., S4313
Oliver, Mass., Elizabeth N., W2108 BLWt.12709-160-55
Reuben, Ct., BLWt.5944-100-Pvt. Iss. 1/7/1800 to Uriah Tracey. No papers
Reuben, Ct., S44898
Richard, Md., R4448
Samuel, N.H., S47214
Silas, Mass., S13279
Simon, Va. See HAILE
Thomas, Ct., S44899
Thomas, N.C., S.C., S37975
William, N.H., Esther, W4485; BLWt.8006-160-55
William, N.C., S1522
William, Va., S37982
Zachariah, Mass., Navy, See HALL
HALEMAN, Tandy, See HOLEMAN
HALES, Isaiah, N.C., S1824
HALEY, Ambrose, Va., S8689
Anthony, Va. See HAILEY
Barnaby, Va. See Barnabas HAILEY
Benjamin, Va., S31114
David, S.C., Va., R4451
George, N.J., Clemence, W8215; BLWt.220-60-55
George, Va., BLWt.12212-100-Pvt. Iss. 3/31/1794. No papers
James, Va., S4316
John, Md., S10213
Joseph, Mass., Jemima, W23210
Lewis, Va., S5487
Morris, Pa., S36005
Pleasent, Va., Mary, W25192; BLWt.29057-160-55
Randall, Va., S13318
Richard, Mass., S37088
Samuel, N.H., Martha, W16593

HALEY (continued)
Thomas, Md., S41625
HALFPENNY, Isaac, Va., BLWt.12191-100. Iss. 11/5/1789. No papers
John, Cont., N.H. See HATHPENNY
Thomas, N.J., BLWts.8338 & 8368-100-Pvt. Iss. 10/31/1789. No papers
Thomas, N.J., Ursilla/Ursula, W856
HALINSDOFF, William, Cont., Md. res. in 1812, BLWt.599-100
HALKERSTONE, Robert, Md., S34917; BLWt.1053-200-Lt. Iss. 9/21/1789 to Robt. Hulkuston. No papers Name spelled Halkuston
HALKS, James, Va., Rachel Curry, former wid., W10307
HALKUSTON, Robert. See HALKERSTONE
HALL, Aaron, Ct., S13330
Aaron, Ct., Em, W16286
Aaron, Mass., S46206
Abigail, former wid. of John Morrison, N.H., which see
Abner, Ct., S13273
Abner, Mass., BLWt.4322-100-Pvt. Iss. 5/9/1797 to Simeon Wyman. No papers
Abner, Mass., S21794
Abner, Mass., S32805
Alexander, N.C., S8691
Alpheus, Ct., Marcy, W19717
Ammie R., Cont., Mass., S45577
Amos, Ct., S18015; BLWt.5928-100 Iss. 8/23/1790. No papers
Amos, Ct., Phebe, W16289
Anan, Ct., Comfort, W21250
Andrew, Ct., S13258
Andrew, Ct., S13335
Ann, former wid. of Wm. McElwain, Mass., which see
Anthony, N.C., Va., Ruth, W1764; BLWt.26425-160-55
Asa, Ct., Elizabeth, R4460
Asa, Cont., Ct., S44892
Asa, Mass., Elenor, W13344
Asa, N.Y., S6945
Asahel, Ct., R4455
Baxter, Mass., S29861
Benajah, Ct., Ruth, W17980
Benajah, N.Y., S22814
Benjamin, Cont., N.H., S44895
Benjamin, Cont., R.I., S13259
Benjamin, Mass., Eleanor, W13403
Benjamin, R.I., S32295
Benjamin, R.I., R5362 1/2
Benoni, R.I., Sarah Ann Gardner, former wid., W13242
Caleb, Ct., S13292
Caleb, Mass., N.H., S17999
Calvin, Mass., S20382
Calvin, Mass., Mercy, W19712
Casa, Del., BLWt.10784-100-Pvt. Iss. 9/2/1789. No papers
Ceasar, Corp of Invalids, BLWt. 13231-100-Pvt. Iss. 9/2/1789. No papers
Charles, Cont., Mass., S37089
Charles, R.I., S13274
Christopher, Ct., N.Y., Sarah Benedict, former wid., W27521; BLWt.8155-160-55. Her other husb., James Benedict, Mass.,

HALL (continued)
N.Y., also a pensioner, which see
Clarissa, former wid. of Solomon Pinto, Ct., which see
Clement, N.C., S38790; BLWt.1095-300-Capt. Iss. 8/6/1789. No papers
Daniel, Ct., S30472
Daniel, Ct., Cont., S10789
Daniel, Mass., S44896
Daniel, N.H., Vt., Sally, W23199
Daniel, S.C., Susanna, W21267
David, Ct., S37084
David, Ct., Ann, W17053
David, Del., BLWt.1038-500-Col. Iss. 9/2/1789 to David Hall. No papers
David, Mass., Abigail, W14840
David, N.H., S44410
David, N.H., Lydia, W21251
David, N.J., Hannah, W7640
David, N.C., S1823
David, N.C., 1828. No papers
David, Pa., S36572
David, Sappers & Miners, BLWt. 13161-100-Pvt. Iss. 9/6/1792. No papers
David, Va., S37989
Docia, see James MAIDEN, Va.
Dorcus, former wid. of Simon Reno, N.Y., which see
Ebenezer, Ct., S31721
Ebenezer, Mass., Mary, W14838
Ebenezer, N.H., S18016
Ebenezer L., Mass., Lydia, W23212; BLWt.3817-160-55
Edward, N.H., Sarah, W23247
Edward, N.C., S32294
Edward, Va., S16147
Edward, Va., Milly, W3017
Edward, Va., R20511
Elias, Mass., S38787
Elias, Vt., S18861
Elihu/Ellehu, Ct., S29210
Elihu, Md., Gertrude/Charity, W9469
Elijah, Cont., N.H., Lois, W14849
Elisha, Ct., S13249
Elisha, Mass., Asenath, W21272
Elisha, Mass., R4459
Elkanah, Mass., Mehitable, W14884
Enoch, Ct., Esther, W25762
Enoch, Cont., Mass., Miriam, W23231
Enoch, Mass., S18856
Enoch, Mass., S32306
Enos, Ct., S10806
Ephraim, Ct., Mass., S13238
Ephraim, Mass., Hannah, W14880
Farnham, Mass., Sarah, W14850
Frederick, Md., R7569
Gad, Ct., S23679
George, N.J., R4462
George, R.I., Mercy, W17049
George, Va., Jane, W7643; BLWt.36734-160-55
Hananiah, Mass., N.H., S13277
Henry, Mass., S18855
Henry, N.H., S18430

HALL (continued)
Hezekiah, Cont., Ct., S16138
Hiland, Ct., Cont., Hannah Hubbard, former wid., W23371
Hiram, Ct., BLWt.2352-100
Hudson, See Hall HUDSON, S.C.
Ignatius, N.C., R4464
Isaac, Mass., S17461
Isaac, Mass., Sarah, W653; BLWt.26593-160-55
Isaac, Mass., Martha, BLWt. 40706-160-55
Isaac, Mass., Privateer, S18005
Isaac, R.I., S21259
Isaiah, R.I., R4465
Isham, Va., Zuriah, W7638
Jabez, Mass., Tryphena, W23237; BLWt.6012-160-55
Jacob, Mass., N.H., S18863
Jacob, N.H., Mary, W13356
Jacob, N.J., S34909
James, Ct., S10784
James, Cont., Mass., S32786; BLWt. 5-200
James, Ga., S.C., b. Va., Elizabeth, W25741; BLWt.87048-160-55
James, Mass., S38805
James, Mass., Privateer, Sarah, R4486
James, N.H., ---. No papers. Act of 1828 adjudicated at Treas. Dept.
James, N.H., Elizabeth, W16592
James, N.H., Huldah, W16025
James, N.H., Vt., R4468
James, N.J., Elizabeth, W96
James, N.Y., BLWt.7272-100-Pvt. Iss. 8/12/1791 to Cornelius Glenn, ass. No papers
James, N.Y., S44894
James, N.C., Edea, R4458
James, R.I., BLWt.3232-100-Pvt. Iss. 12/29/1794 to Ephraim Cutler. No papers
James, R.I., applied for pension in Miss., S46005
James, Va., S5492
James, Va., S6946
James, Va., Margaret, R4478
Jeremiah, R.I., S13340
Jesse, Ct., Mass., S5432
Jesse, N.Y., S8666
Jesse, N.C., S.C., Hannah, W21258; BLWt.24754-160-55
Joanna, former wid. of Samuel Willard, N.H., which see
Job, Mass., Martha, W2104; BLWt.782-100
Job, Mass., Abigail, W14843
John, Ct., Damaris, W24400
John, Ct., N.Y., Sarah, W16282
John, Ct., R.I., S2588
John, Md., BLWt.11305-100-Pvt. Iss. 1/21/1795 to John Faires, ass. No papers
John, Md., N.C., b. Md., S1210
John, Mass., S5424
John, Mass., S9561
John, Mass., S32816
John, Mass., S44890
John, Mass., Dilla, W7641;

HALL (continued)
BLWt.11192-160-55
John, Mass., Hannah, W23250
John, Mass., R4470
John, Navy, Pa., R4474
John, N.H., S37082
John, N.H., BLWt.821-100
John, N.J., S2267
John, N.Y., S13334
John, N.Y., BLWt.1492-100
John, N.C., S30451
John, N.C., S41621
John, N.C., Polly, W23236; BLWt.6121-160-55
John, N.C., Hetty, R14699
John, N.C., R22017
John, Pa., R4470 1/2
John, R.I., R4471
John, S.C., b. Ireland, S2590
John, Vt., R4472
John, Va., BLWt.12198-100-Pvt. Iss. 1/6/1791. No papers
John, Va., S2259
John, Va., S2589
John, Va., S5482
John, Va., S5490
John, Va., S31106
John, Va., Elizabeth, W3413
John, Va., S9558
John, Va., BLReg.252708-1855
John B., Ct., S10814
Jonathan, Ct., S29866
Jonathan, Cont., Mass., Abigail, W23230
Jonathan, Mass., Marcy, W24416; BLWt.6428-160-55
Jonathan, N.Y., BLWt.5937-100-Pvt. Iss. 8/23/1790. No papers
Joseph, Md., BLWt.11292-100-Pvt. Iss. 6/8/1797 to James DeBaufre No papers
Joseph, N.H., BLWt.3188-100-Pvt. Iss. 6/17/1790 to Benj. S. Gilman, ass. No papers
Joseph, N.H., S37069
Joseph, Pa., S16146
Joseph, R.I., Vt., S44897
Joseph, Va., S13302
Joseph, Va., S37983
Joshua, Ct., Rhoda, W17050
Josiah, Mass., S29865; BLWt. 12820-160-55
Josiah, Mass., Mary, W19725; BLWt.8456-160-55
Josiah, N.J., Abigail, W855
Josias Carvel, Md., BLWt.1044-500
Jotham, Ct., S44964
Jude, N.H., BLWt.3189-100-Pvt. Iss. 7/21/1789 to Ladd & Cass, assnes. No papers
Jude, N.H., Rhoda, W23238
Justus, N.Y., Susan, W7642; BLWt.30781-160-55
Laban, N.H., S48852
Lebbeus, R.I., R4476
Lemuel, Ct., BLWt.6001-100-Pvt. Iss. 3/29/1792 to Joel Rice. No papers
Levi, Ct., S10818
Levi, Ct., Cont., Mass., R.I., S16850
Levi, Mass., Jane, W23235

HALL (continued)
Levi, Vt., Grace, W19743
London, R.I., BLWt.3234-100-Pvt. Iss. 12/31/1789. No papers
Lot, Navy, Mass., Polly, W19751
Luther, Mass., Elizabeth, W23200
Lydia, former wid. of Israel Meade, Mass., which see
Lyman/Lymon, Ct., Charity, W17983
Lyman, Mass., S29858
Lyman, R.I., Phebe, W5289; BLWt. 26689-160-55
Martha, former wid. of Gamaliel Parker, Ct., which see
Martha, former wid. of Roswell Fox, Ct., which see
Mary, former wid. of George Humphrey, Cont. Va., which see
Mary, former wid. of Basil Newton, Md., which see
Mercy, former wid. of Joseph Daggett, Mass., which see
Moses, Ct., BLWt.5912-100-Pvt. Iss. 3/29/1792 to Joel Rice. No papers
Moses, Ct., Lucy, W23193
Moses, Ct., Rebecca, R4484
Moses, Cont., N.H. res. 1818, S45579
Moses, Cont., Mass., Olive, W19723; BLWt.531-160-55
Moses, Mass., S4326
Moses, N.C., Nancy, W10105; BLWt.112981-160-55
Moses, Vt., R4479
Moses R., Ct., R4480
Nathan, Va., S6943
Nathaniel, Ct., Elizabeth, W7637 BLWt.28606-160-55
Nathaniel, Ct., Cont., S44891
Nathaniel, N.H., R4481
Nathaniel, Vt., Belinda, W2105
Nicholas, N.H., Mary, W15773; BLWt.1015-100
Noah, Mass., Privateer, S16849
Obed, Cont., Mass., Eliza Odell, former wid., W2327; BLWt.6435-160-55
Oliver, Mass., BLWt.4424-100-Fifer. Iss. 8/12/1789. No papers
Percival, Cont., Mass., S32817
Peter, Ct., Cont., Vt., S13268
Peter L., N.J., S16856
Phebe, former wid. of Alexander Torrence, Mass., which see
Primus (colored), Cont., Mass., (or Primus TRASK), Ann, W751; BLWt.26340-160-55
Rebecca, former wid. of James Mills, N.Y., which see
Recompence, Cont., Vt., Phebe, R4482
Reuben, Cont., Pa., S2591
Reuben, N.H., S45578
Rhodes, R.I., S29206
Richard, Cont., Mass., S45580
Richard, Md., BLWt.1801-100
Richard, Mass., BLWt.34963-160-55
Richard, Pa., Phebe, R4483
Robert, Ct., S37079

HALL (continued)
Robert, Cont., Va., S16403
Robert, Mass., BLWt.4373-100-Pvt. Iss. 4/21/1796. No papers
Robert, Mass., S44893
Robert, N.C., S2258
Robert, N.C., Mary, R4492
Robert, Va. Sea Service, R40. Va. Half Pay. See Accession No. 837-Va.State Navy- YS File
Samuel, Ct., BLWt.5908-100-Pvt. Iss. 3/16/1792 to Lee Hall, exec. No papers
Samuel, Pvt., Ct., BLWt.6005-100 Iss. 3/16/1792 to Lee Hall, ass.
Samuel, Ct., Lucy, W19673
Samuel, Ct., Esther, W21260
Samuel, Cont., Mass., BLWt.385-100
Samuel, N.C., Letitia, R4477
Seburt/Seabert, Md., R4487
Seth, Ct., S10812
Silas, N.Y., S29201
Silas, R.I., S21799
Silvanus/Sylvanus, Cont., Mass., S44398
Solomon, N.C., S21802
Stephen, Ct., S37058
Stephen, Ct., BLWt.1193-300
Stephen, Cont., N.H., S38798; BLWt.3776-160-55
Stephen, Mass., S29875
Stephen, Mass., S32793
Stephen, Mass., Sea Service, R4488
Stephen, N.Y., Elizabeth, W19678
Talmage, Ct., BLWt.1232-200
Thomas, Ct., BLWt.5931-100. Iss. 7/14/1789. No papers
Thomas, Cont., N.H., S44399
Thomas, Mass., Priscilla, W24418
Thomas, N.H., BLWt.3202-100-Pvt. Iss. 5/27/1797 to Christopher S. Thorn, ass. No papers
Thomas, N.C., S1829
Thomas, Pa., Amy, W1857; BLWt. 26522-160-55
Thomas, R.I., S47219
Thomas, Va., S13339
Thomas, Va., S16862
Thomas, Va., Ann, R4453
Timothy, Cont., N.H., Anna/Ann, W19693
Timothy, Mass., S30
Timothy, Mass., S39647
Timothy, Mass., S44455
Timothy, Va., S5469
Titus, Ct., Cont., Olive, W21283
Wildman, Ct., S13344
William, Art. Artificiers, BLWt. 13203-100-Pvt. Iss. 12/3/1789. No papers
William, Ct., R.I., S23248
William, Cont., Mass., Mary Page former wid., W19956
William, Cont., Va., Urcilla, W8884
William, Del., Elizabeth, W7639
William, Mass., S37096
William, Mass., S44184
William, Mass., R4490 1/2
William, N.Y., Annatie, W15834
William, N.Y., Rebecca, W25758;

HALL (continued)
BLWt.41452-160-55
William, N.Y., R4491
William, N.C., S2592
William, N.C., S13306
William, N.C., R21886
William, N.C., S.C., b. Pa., S31089
William, N.C., Va., S16859
William, Pa., S5434
William, Pa., Sarah, W10072
William, S.C., S32305
William, S.C. Sea Service, Ann/Anna, W21255
William, Va., S5475
William, Va., S6944
William, Va., S16142
William, Va., S37974
William, Va., R20121
Zachariah, Mass., Navy, Mary Smith, former wid., R9806

HALLADAY, Eli, Ct., S2605
Job, Mass. See HOLLIDAY
John, N.C., S41627
Jonah, Mass., Patience, W19665
Roger, Ct., S31723

HALLAM, John, Ct., S13283
Robert, Ct., Lydia, W19731

HALLAWAY, Thomas, N.C. See HALLOWAY

HALLECK, Hannah, former wid. of John Shutts, N.Y., which see

HALLET, Elisha, Mass. Sea Service, Mass., S15879
George, N.Y., Betsey Wetherell, former wid., W16782
Solomon, Mass., S29873
Thomas, Ct., BLWt.5910-100-Pvt. Iss. 5/6/1791. No papers
Thomas, Ct., Cont., S37064
William, N.Y., S44915

HALLETT, Barnabas, Cont., Mass., Bethiah, W19687
Benjamin, Mass., Navy, S10803
Jonah, Cont., Pa., Isabella, W3248; BLWt.1024-100-Lt. Iss. 10/12/1790. No papers
Jonathan, N.Y., Martha, W3083; BLWt.984-300-Capt. Iss. 10/20/1790. No papers
Solomon, N.Y., Eleanor, W656; BLWt.9464-160-55

HALLEY, Henry S., Va., R4493

HALLIBERTON, William H., N.C., S9121

HALLIDAY, Eli, Ct. See HALLADAY
Jonah, Mass. See HALLADAY

HALLING, Solomon, Cont., N.C. res. in 1820, BLWt.54-450

HALLMAN, George, Pa., S39646

HALLOCK, Daniel, N.Y., S10788
John, N.Y., R4495
Joseph, Cont., N.Y., Sarah, W19682; BLWt.213-60-55
Moses, Mass., S29876
William, Ct., Ruth, W25754

HALLOMS, James, S.C. See HOLMES

HALLOW, Richard P., Ct. See Richard PENHOLLOW

HALLOWAY, George, Va. See HOLLOWAY
John, Mass. See HOLLOWAY

HALLOWAY (continued)
Nathaniel, Mass. See HOLLOWAY
Taylor, S.C. See HOLLOWAY
William, Cont., Mass., Mary, W23343
HALLOWELL, Henry, Mass., S32800
HALLOWS, James, S.C. See HOLMES
HALLSTED, John, Ct., S44908
Richard, Ct., S44909;BLWt.205-100
HALLY, Timothy, Pa., R4494
HALSEY, Abraham, N.Y., BLWt. 7229-100-Pvt. Iss. 4/26/1791 to Henry Ludlam, ass. No papers
Henry, N.C., S2597
Isaac, Art. Artificiers, BLWt. 13206-100-Pvt. Iss. 8/8/1791 to Wm. Boyd, ass. No papers
Isaac, N.J., Sarah, W7701
Job, N.Y., R4496
John, N.J., S22813
Luther, N.J., S44921; BLWt.999-200-Lt. Iss. 6/11/1789
Malachi, N.C., S2598
Matthew, N.Y., S10781
Philip, Ct., N.Y., S16845
Stephen, Ct., N.Y., Hamutal, W24413
Sylvanus, N.Y., S13298
Thomas, N.Y., BLWt.7225-100-Pvt. Iss. 4/16/1791 to Henry Ludlam, ass. No papers
William, Cont., N.J., Rachel, R4497
Zephaniah, Cont., N.Y., Rebecca, W28008
HALSTEAD, Edward, N.Y., S2633
Jacob, N.Y., Charity, W1177; BLWt.26645-160-55
John, Ct., BLWt.5919-100-Pvt. Iss. 7/27/1789. No papers
John, N.J., S2271
Joseph, Ct., S10811
Joseph, Lamb's Artillery, N.Y., BLWt.7300-100-Pvt. Iss. 12/4/1790 to Anthony Maxwell, ass. No papers
Richard, Ct. See HALLSTED
Samuel, N.Y., Pa., R5179
HALSTED, Matthias, N.J., S34386
Richard, Ct. See HALLSTED
Thomas, N.Y., S13338
Timothy, N.Y., R4499
HALTOM, Joseph, N.C., Mary, W25782
HALTZZAPPLE, Zachariah, N.Y., BLWt.7211-100-Pvt. Iss. 12/9/1791 to Philip Rockefeller, ass. No papers
HALY, Pleasant, Va. See Pleasent HALEY
HAM, Benjamin, N.H., S8655
Drury, Va., Maria Perkins, former wid., W27678
Elizabeth, former wid. of Noah BLiss, Mass., which see
Ephraim, N.H., Elizabeth, W23209; BLWt.6110-160-55
Ichabod, N.H., Sea Service, R4500
John, N.Y., BLWt.3196-100-Pvt. Iss. 4/25/1798 to Daniel Gookin. BLWt.112-60-55. Notation: Two men of this name - one killed. No papers.

HAM (continued)
John, N.H., S18004
John, N.H., Mary, W1599; BLWt. 112-60-55
John, N.H., BLWt.2214-100
John, S.C., Phebe, R4501
Joseph, Mass., Margaret Staples, former wid., W27489
Nathaniel, Mass., S32285
William, S.C., R20209
HAMAR, James, N.J., S41618
HAMBEL, Robert, Va., R4502
HAMBILTON, Thomas, N.C. See HAMBLETON
HAMBIN, David, Mass. See HAMLIN
HAMBLE, Robert, Va. See HAMBEL
HAMBLEN, Job, Va. See HAMBLIN
Prince, Mass., S37077
Samuel, Mass., See HAMLIN
HAMBLET, Jonathan, Mass., S32790
Phinehas/Phineas, Cont., N.H., S44407
William, Mass., N.H., S---
HAMBLETON, James, S.C., S6983
Thomas, N.C., S32301
William, N.J., R4503
HAMBLIN, Bazalael, Corp., Invalids, BLWt.13224 iss. 1/26/1790 to John May, ass.
Daniel, Mass., S18851
James, Ct. See HAMLIN
Job, Va., Eleanor, W10085
John, Cont., Ct., S18428
John, Mass., S23250
Joseph, Ct. See HAMLIN
Levi, Ct., S41617
Pierce Dant, Va., b. Md., S2264
Thomas, S.C. See HAMLIN
Zaccheas/Zacchias, N.Y., S11171
HAMBLING, Reuben, Mass., BLWt. 4321-100-Pvt. Iss. 3/23/1797 to Marlbry Turner. No papers
HAMBLY, Peleg, R.I., Abigail, W21257
HAMBRICK, David, Cont., BLWt. 604-100
HAMBRIGHT, Frederick, N.C., Mary, R4504
Henry, Pa., S4321
John, N.C., Nancy, W932
HAMBY, William, N.C., S1909
HAMER, James, N.J., BLWt.8393-100-Pvt. Iss. 2/11/1800 to Philemon Thomas, ass. No papers
HAMERSLY, Andrew, See HAMMERSLY
John, Pa., Sally/Sarah, W421
HAMES, John, S.C., S16409; BLWt.16277-160-55
Samuel, Ct. See HAWES
William, S.C., Elizabeth, R4506
HAMESTREET, Isaac, N.Y., Mary, W17058; BLWt.3540-160-55. See N.A. Acc. No. 874-050081. Not Half Pay
HAMILL, Ebenezer, Pa., R4508
Hugh, Pa., Jane, W7695
Robert, Pa., Jane, W1173; BLWt. 26538-160-55
HAMILTON, Abner, Va., S31105
Adam, Pa., S32796

HAMILTON (continued)
Alexander, N.Y. res. Col. & Aid de Camp to the Commander in Chief. Elizabeth (Schuyler), W13402; BLWt.2279-450. Iss. 2/20/1840, in lieu of lost Wt. No. 622. Contains true copy of Hamilton's will & names his children. File contains true copy of the Reformed Protestant Dutch Church in city of Albany, 1780. In addition to record of A. Hamilton's marriage, it shows "1780 Dec. 17, John Shultis & Margarita Jacobs"
Alexander, Va., S9556
Andrew, N.J., S39636
Andrew, S.C., S18000
Asa, Mass., S46446
Benjamin, N.J., S34383
Benjamin, Pa., S16400
Benjamin, Va., S31111
Charles, Del., S41614
Charles, Mass., R4511
Charles, N.C., Hannah, R4512
Charles, Va., Margaret, R4519
Cumberland, Pa., BLWt.9541-100-Pvt. Iss. 7/9/1789. No papers
Daniel, Mass., Keziah, W19729
Daniel, Pa., S2280
David, Ct., Cont., S23678
David, N.C., Susan, R4521
David, S.C., S17998
David, S.C., S21804
David, S.C., Elizabeth H. George, former wid., W10053. Her 2nd husb., James George also served in Rev. War.
Edward, Md., BLWt.1054-200-Lt. Iss. 3/10/1790. No papers
Eliakim, Mass., S13242
Eliphalet, Mass., S32779
Frederick, R.I., S21810
George, Md., BLWt.11318-100-Pvt. Iss. 7/18/1793 to Wm. Ripton, ass. No papers
George, Md., BLWt.1046-300-Capt. Iss. 8/4/1789. No papers
Hosea, N.Y., Ann Spencer, former wid., R9974
James, Ct., Jemima, W2111; BLWt. 28597-160-55
James, N.J., Sarah, W793
James, N.J., R4514
James, N.C., Jane, W155
James, N.C., Martha, W2732; BLWt.30782-160-55
James, ---, S.C. agcy. No papers
Jameš, Pa., S31098
James, Pa., S45887
James, Pa., BLWt.1010-400-Maj. No papers
James, Va., b. Pa., S1214
James, Va., S4320
James, Va., S25128
James, Va., Rebecca, W24403
James, Va., BLWt.1080-200-Lt. Iss. 5/19/1797 to George Mathews, ass. No papers
James, Va., Dis. No papers
John, Md., S18010; BLWt.1613-100
John, Md., BLWt.1058-200-Lt.

HAMILTON (continued)
John, Mass., S15880; BLWt.11071-160-55
John, Mass., Catharine, W19730
John, N.H., Jane, W24384
John, N.C., b. Pa., R4516
John, Pa., BLWt.9587-100-Pvt. Iss. 1/26/1795. No papers
John, Pa., BLWt.9603-100-Pvt. Iss. 4/17/1793 to Ebenezer Hogg, ass. No papers
John, Pa., S39653
John, Pa., S39654
John, Pa., b. Md., Deborah, W1759
John, Pa., R4515
John, S.C., S37981
John, S.C., BLWt.1106-200-Lt. Iss. 6/4/1792 to David Cay, ass. No papers
John, Va., S1209
John, Va. See HAMMILTON
John Agnew, Md., Margaret, W9478; BLWt.1047-300-Capt. Iss. 5/25/1789. No papers
Jonathan, Mass., S37066
Jonathan, Pa., Indian War 1793; Martha, R4520
Joseph, Mass., S38793
Joseph, Mass., Martha/Marthe, W7670; BLWt.34540-160-55
Joseph, N.C., R4517
Joshua, Ct., Mary, W21263
Joshua, N.C., Va., S2608
Nathan, Mass., Abigail, R4509
Reuben, Mass., Elizabeth, W7669
Reuben, Mass., BLWt.1742-100
Richard, N.H., Mary, W9058; BLWt.26570-160-55
Richard, Pa., S5431
Robert, Mass., Margaret, W21268
Robert, Pa., Ann, W5293
Robert, Pa., Anna, W7668; BLWt. 83513-160-55
Samuel, Ct., Wealthy, W2794
Samuel, Md., BLWt.11344-100-Pvt. Iss. 11/29/1790 to John Smith, Admr. No papers
Silas, Mass., BLWt.4396-100-Pvt. Iss. 12/9/1799 to Dwight Foster, guardian to Leonard Hamilton & Silas Hamilton, minor ch. & heirs of Silas.
Silas, Mass., S6984
Thomas, N.J., BLWt.8405-100-Pvt. Iss. 11/5/1791. No papers
Thomas, N.C., S6982
Thomas, N.C., See HAMBLETON
Thomas, N.C., S.C., b. Pa., S21267
Thomas, Pa., BLWt.9524-100-Pvt. Iss. 12/21/1791 to Adam Harbison, ass. No papers
Thomas, Pa., BLWt.9601-100-Pvt. Iss. 7/17/1792 to Ebenezer Hogg, ass. Memo: Cert. of this Wt. sent to the Hon. Wm. Wallace dated 17th Dec. 1817
Thomas, Pa., Catharine, W3084
Thomas, S.C., S30470
Thomas, S.C., Va., R4522
Thomas, Va., Anna, W7671

HAMILTON (continued)
Thomas, Va., R14776; Va. Half Pay. N.A. Acc. No. 874-050082 Half Pay.
William, Mass., S28752
William, Mass., S39650
William, Mass., Beulah, W14868
William, N.J., Abigail, W94
William, N.Y., R4523
William, Pa., S22818
William, Pa., Magdalena, W5294
William, Va., BLWt.12231-100-Pvt. Iss. 8/8/1796 to John Verell, ass. No papers
William, Va., Ruth, W9059
William, Va., Isabel, R4513
HAMISTON, Jared, Ct., BLWt. 6003-100-Pvt. Iss. 3/21/1794 to Eneas Munson, ass. of John Peck, Admr. No papers
HAMLEN, Levi, Cont., Ct., Mary, W23168, BLWt.13440-160-55
Nathaniel, N.J., S2603
Seth L., Mass., Jerusha, W23174
HAMLET, Hezekiah, N.H., R4524
HAMLETT, John, N.C., S13311
William P., Va., S13305
HAMLIN, Africa, Mass., Susanna, W23222; BLWt.933-150-Ensign. Iss. 4/19/1792 to John Peck, ass. No papers
America, Mass., Mary, W11244; BLWt.89516-160-55
Amos, N.Y., S28755
Asa, Mass., Hannah, W19690
Benjamin, Ct., S10815
Cornelius, Ct., S37050
David, Mass., S22807
Elisha, Ct., S10816
Europe, Mass., S44406
James, Ct., S29196
John, Ct., Cont., Privateer, Caroline, W17985
John, Cont., Ct., Lucy, W23219
John, Mass., S18869
John, N.J., S17465
John, N.C., S15443
Joseph, Ct., Rhoda, W9057; BLWt.26684-160-55
Mark, Ct., S23680
Samuel, Mass., Hannah, W19691
Seth, Mass. See HAMLEN
Thomas, S.C., Sarah, W8910
William, Ct., S37068
HAMLINTON, Daniel, Mass. See HAMILTON
William, Mass. See HAMILTON
HAMM, John, N.C., S31095
John, N.C., Va., Happy, W2935
Mordecai, N.C., Rebecca, W4976
HAMMAN, Abraham, Va., Charity, W10088
John, N.Y. See HAMMOND
HAMME, Christian, Pa., Anna Maria, W2790
HAMMEL, Frederick, Pa. See HUMMEL
Hugh, Pa., See HAMILL
HAMMELL, Robert, Pa. See HAMILL
HAMMER, George, Md., S32291
Henry, Va., Mary, W7652
Palser, Pa., Va., S6950

HAMMER (continued)
Peter, Pa., Sarah Rice, former wid., W5699
HAMMERLY, James, Pa., Judith, W7705; BLWt.26068-160-55
HAMMERSLY, Andrew, Not Rev. War, N.W. Indian War, 1792-1795, enl. in Pa., O.W. Inv. Rej. File 14902; BLWt.9017-160-50
James, Pa. See HAMMERLY
HAMMET, Caleb, R.I., S44913
HAMMETT, George, Va., S8693
William, Ga., R4528
HAMMILL, William, N.Y., S10794
HAMMILTON, John, Va., S36568
HAMMOCK, John, Va., S2601
Martin, Va., R4529
William, N.C., S15442
HAMMON, John, N.C., S9559
John, N.C., R4542
Peter, Mass. See HAMMOND
Philip, Va., S30452
Thomas, Va., S10791
HAMMOND, Abijah, Mass., BLWt. 939-200-Lt. Iss. 2/27/1800. No papers
Abner, Ga., S.C., Sarah, W25753; BLWt.3533-160-55
Abram G., Cont., N.Y., R4530
Absalom, N.C. See HAMMONS
Daniel, N.Y., R4531
David, Ct., Phebe, W11243; BLWt.67686-160-55
David, N.H., BLWt.3184-100-Pvt. Iss. 3/25/1790. No papers
David, N.H., Hannah, W23252
David, Pa., BLWt.1007-200-Lt. Iss. 12/21/1790. No papers
Elijah, Mass., BLWt.4366-100-Sgt. Iss. 4/1/1790. No papers
Elisha, Mass., S10819
Experience, Mass., S32808
Gardner, Navy, Mass. res. & agcy., S32795
George, N.C., b. Va., R4553
Gideon, Mass., S29863
Gideon, R.I., Sarah, R4540
Hinsdel, Mass., Lucy, W21252
Isaac, Ct., Cont., Dorcas, R4532
Isaac, N.C., Dicey, W7654
Isaac, Va., S4327
Isabel, former wid. of Ebenezer Whittemore, Mass., which see
James, Md., BLWt.11359-100-Corp. in the Artillery. Iss. 9/5/1789. No papers
Jane, former wid. of Robert Courtis/Curtis, Mass., which see
Jason, Ct., Mary, W16287
Job, Cont., S.C., S36569
John, N.Y., Blandina, W23228; BLWt.693-100
John, R.I., S21260
Joshua, Mass., Olive, W21269; BLWt.84013-160-55
Joshua, S.C., b. Va., S21803
Lewis, Va., R4535
Moses, Mass., Abigail, W23173
Noah, Mass., S10783
Obadiah, N.C., S2263
Paul, Cont., N.Y., R4536
Paulipus, Mass., Mary Damon, former wid., W6988; BLWt.56508-160-

HAMMOND (continued)
55
Peter, Md. See HAWMAN
Peter, Mass., BLWt.4349-100-Pvt. Iss. 11/2/1791 to Jonathan Tuttle. No papers
Peter, Mass., Eleanor Olds, former wid., W19937
Prince, R.I., BLWt.3287-100-Pvt. Iss. 12/31/1789. No papers
Raleigh, N.C., Margaret, W11237; BLWt.81067-160-55
Robert, Ct., Ruamah, R4539
Roger, Mass., R4537
Samuel, S.C., Va., S21807
Shubal/Shubel, Mass., Anna, W21296
Staats, N.Y., ---. No papers
Stephen, Navy, R.I., S10800; BLWt.51886-160-55
Susannah, former wid. of Philip Prater, which see
Thomas, Ct., S18865
Thomas, Md., W4224
Thomas, Mass., Esther, W14844
Thomas, N.J., S882
Thomas, Pa., BLWt.9634-100-Pvt. Iss. 9/19/1799 to Abraham Bell, ass. No papers
Thomas, Pa., S44910
Titus, Ct., Charity, W7653; BLWt.26058-160-55
HAMMONDS, John, N.C., S8654; BLWt.34955-160-55
John, Va., S31094
Peter, N.C., Va., S30461
HAMMONS, Absalom, N.C., S5497
Benjamin, N.C., Sarah, W4978; BLWt.19509-160-55
Edmund/Edmond, Mass., S17995
John, Va., R26146
Joseph, Va., Martha, R4544
HAMNER, Henry, Va., Sarah, W8912
John, Va., Mary, W10081
HAMON, William, not Rev. War; Wayne's War, Pa. res.; Old War Rej. 4543
HAMPTON, Joel, N.C., Hanah, R4547
John, Art. Artificiers, BLWt. 13232-100-Pvt. Iss. 11/1/1792 No papers
John, Cont., Pa., R4548
John, S.C., Joyce, W7700
John, Va., BLWt.12206-100-Pvt. Iss. 7/20/1792 to Robt. Means, ass. No papers
Preston, Va., Eliza, R4546
Thomas, Va., S16842
Wade, S.C., Reg. Army, War of 1812, Mary, W10078; BLWt.92093-160-55
William, Va., Hannah, W424; BLWt. 40015-160-55
William Dennis, Cont., Va., S37990
HAMRICK, Benjamin, Va., S5472
David, Cont. See HAMBRICK
David, Cont., Va., Lettis/Lettice, W5292
Gilson, Va., R4550
Henry, Pa., S39659
Siars/Siras, Va., S18009
HAMRICKHOUSE, Peter, See

HAMRICKHOUSE (continued)
HUMRICKHOUSE
HAMSAN, William, Pa. See HAMSON
HAMSHER, Adam, Pa., S22307
HAMSON, Edson, Mass., S44920
Henry, Mass., Hannah, W13362
John, Mass., Elizabeth, W14889
William, Pa., S39652
HAMSTEAD, Robert, N.J., BLWt. 8374-100-Sgt. Iss. 4/21/1790. No papers
HAMTRAMCK, John F., N.Y., BLWt. 983-300-Capt. Iss. 8/4/1791. No papers
HAN, David, Pa., S34918
HANBY, Jonathan, Va., Sarah, W4687
HANCE, John, Mass., BLWt.4306-100-Pvt. Iss. 8/1/1789 to Thomas Cushing. No papers
John, N.J., BLWt.8401-100-Pvt. Iss. 12/15/1789 to John Hance. No papers
HANCHET, Jonah, Ct., S9568
HANCHETT, Ezra, Ct., S13291
HANCKETT, Ezra, See HANCHETT
HANCKS, Abraham, Va. See HANKS
HANCOCK, Austin, Va., S5499
Belcher, Cont., Mass., Ann, W14857
Benjamin, Va., Susannah, W5291; BLWt.35836-160-55
Bennet, Va., BLWt.1629-100; iss. 6/8/1829
Celia, former wid. of Joshua Temmons, which see
Cullop, N.J. See Cutlope
Cutlope, N.J., S22281
Edward, Va., Jane, W7648
Elias, Mass., S19318
Elihu, Ct., BLWt.1760-100
Isaiah, N.C., S30449
James, Va., S5495
John, N.C., Hannah, W10086; BLWt.87014-160-55
John, N.C., R4551
John Lane, R.I., Hannah, W5094
Joseph, N.C., Mary B., W359
Joseph, Pa., S36573
Levi, Mass., S15437
Martin, N.C., S2260
Mehitabel, former wid. of John Dow, Mass., which see
Moses, Mass., Wealthy, W14875
Nathan, Ct., Phebe, W19706
Nathan, Mass., Sarah, W24379
Samuel, Ga., N.C., S.C., S8687
Samuel, Va., Ann, W---. See papers in claim of child of this woman by her former husband, Jacob Moon, Va.
Stephen, Md., BLWt.11332-100-Pvt. Iss. 10/5/1792. No papers
Stephen, Va., S1955
Thomas, "Artillery Artificiers of Pa.", BLWt.13233. Iss. 7/2/1791. No papers
Thomas, Mass., S32784
Thomas, Mass., BLWt.56947-160-55
William, Mass., S32780
William, Mass., Elizabeth, W24404
William, Va., S21265

HANCOCK (continued)
William, Va., R4552
HANCOX, Edward, S16843
HAND, Aaron, N.J., Phebe, W651
Abraham, Cont., N.Y., S41613
Christopher, Va., S6951
Darius, Mass., Elizabeth, W19740
David, N.J., Prudence, R4555; BLWt.61337-160-55
David, N.Y., S23256
Edmond, Ct., Huldah, W27775
Edward, Pa., BLWt.1005-850-Brig. Gen. Iss. 5/5/1789. No papers
Ichabod, Ct., S31722
Ira, N.H., Mehitable, W19722
Jeremiah, N.J. Sea Service, R4554
John, Va., Jane A., W3016
Joseph, Mass., S13299
Joseph, N.C., Keziah, W7625
Josiah, Cont., N.Y., S13337
Patsey/Polly, former wid. of John Barr, Pa., which see
Recompence/Remembrance, N.J. Sea Service, R4556
Remembrance, See Recompense
Robert, N.C., R4557
Samuel, N.C., S.C., Mary, W10
Uriah, N.C., R4558
HANDCOCK, John, N.C. See HANCOCK
HANDELL, John, N.Y., S39660
HANDERHAM, Edward, See UNDERHAND
HANDERSON, Gideon, Mass., Abigail, W21241
Timothy, Mass., S10779
HANDFORD, Ebenezer, See HANFORD
Timothy, Ct., BLWt.5966-100-Pvt. Iss. 4/27/1792. No papers
HANDLEY, Charles, Mass., S13331
George, Ga., BLWt.1255-300
Richard, N.J., Sarah, W7696
HANDLIN, Matthias, N.J., Anna, W4218
Patrick, Pa. See HANLIN
Stephen, Pa., S38794
HANDLY, Handy, Md., S16401
Samuel, N.C., Va., b. Pa., S1911
HANDY, Benjamin, Mass., Sea Service, Navy, Lucy, W23244
Charles, Mass., Mary, W14842
Ebenezer, R.I., Sally, W4981; BLWt.26627-160-55
Edward, Mass., Mary, W19668
Elnathan, Mass., S37052
Gamaliel, Mass., BLWt.4420-100-Pvt. Iss. 1/26/1790 to John May. No papers
Gamaliel, Mass., S32791
George, Md., BLWt.1061-300-Capt. Iss. 3/1/1801. No papers
John, R.I., Frances, W8899
John Lawson, Del., S36002
Joseph, Mass., Ruth, W21299
Levi, Mass., Ruth, W14893; BLWt.21809-160-55
Levin, Md., Nancy, W9475
Nathaniel, Ct., Martha, R4560
Russell, Mass., S38783; BLWt. 753-100
Samuel, Ct., BLWt.5948-100-QM Sgt. Iss. 7/14/1789 to himself. Wt. returned to Gen. Land Office 6/23/1827

HANDY (continued)
Samuel, Mass., S32811
Sethel, Mass., BLWt.4319-100-Pvt. Iss. 1/26/1790 to John May. No papers
Silas, Mass., Lois, W14859
Thomas, Mass., S32812
Thomas, Pa., Sarah, R4561
William, Cont., Ct., Martha, W23241
William, Mass., Love, BLWt.45710-160-55
HANER, William, N.Y., S10808
HANES, Benjamin, Va., S2587
John, N.Y., Eve, R4562
John, Pa., Elizabeth, W7261; BLWt.487-100
John, Va., S37985
Nathan, N.H. See HAINES
HANEY, Barney, Md., BLWt.11322-100-Pvt. Iss. 1/11/1796 to Joshua Ward, ass. No papers
Charles, Pa., Va., S8661
Daniel, Mass., S16860
David, Pa., S36570; BLWt.1152-100
David, Pa. See HENEY
Francis, Va., S32292
Henry, Pa., BLWt.9555-100-Pvt. Iss. 6/17/1793 to Francis Kirkpatrick, ass. No papers
James, Va., S8679
John, Md., BLWt.11297-100-Pvt. Iss. 1/8/1796 to Geo. Ponsonby, ass. No papers
John, Md., S25133, S37976, S37894
John, Pa., Rebecca, R4577
Michael, Va., BLWt.12183-100-Pvt. Iss. 11/5/1789. No papers
Robert, N.C., S.C., Va., Elizabeth, R4563
William, Md., Susanna, W9049
William, Va., Elizabeth, W11258
HANFORD, Ebenezer, Ct., S31720
Levi, Ct., S23676
Matthew, Ct., Elizabeth, W21288
Ozias, Ct., Elizabeth Crane, former wid., W25449
Phebe, former wid. of Robert Falkner, Mass., which see
HANGARA, Gabriel, "Invalids", BLWt.13215-100-Pvt. Iss. 9/4/1789. No papers
HANGER, George, Va., R4565
HANKER, Catharine, former wid. of Frederick Filler, Md., which see
HANKERSON, William, N.Y., R.I., S37092
HANKINS, Abraham, Va., Sally, W363
George, Va., S31102
James, Va., S1521
John, Va., S16404
Zachariah, See Zackariah HAWKINS
HANKINSON, Joseph, N.J., S5435
HANKS, Abner, Va., S31719
Abraham, Va., Lucy, R4569
Benjamin, Cont., Mass., Anna, W21300
Ebenezer, Mass., Abigail, W7620; BLWt.948-160-55
Elijah, Ct., Mary, W4688
Epaphroditus, N.C., R4567

HANKS (continued)
James, N.C., R4568
Levi, Mass., Chloe, W1860
Richard, N.C., R4570
Thomas, Va., R4571
William, Cont., Mass., S13246
HANDLEY, James, N.Y., BLWt. 7226-100-Pvt. Iss. 9/13/179- No papers
HANLIN, Matthias, N.J. See HANDLIN
Patrick, Pa., BLWt.9585-100-Pvt. Iss. 12/17/1795. No papers
Patrick, Pa., Margaret, W10077
HANLON, James, Va., S37994
Marmaduke, Pa., BLWt.9542-100-Pvt. Iss. 6/29/1789 to M. McConnell, ass. No papers
HANLY, Handy, Md. See HANDLY
Russell, Mass. See HANDY
HANMER, Francis, N.Y., BLWt. 989-200-Lt. Iss. 9/28/1790. No papers
Lanson, Cont., Mass., Abigail Adams, former wid., W20569
HANMOR, Jabez, N.Y., Anna Maria, W655; BLWt.503-160-55
HANMORE, David, Cont., N.Y., S44919
Moses, N.Y., BLWt.7297-100-Pvt. Iss. 12/15/1791. No papers
HANNA, Adam, Pa. or Va., Nancy, R4575
John, Cont., Va., S41607
John, Del., BLWt.10790-100-Pvt. Iss. 9/2/1789. No papers
John, Del., Pa., S36009
John, Hazen's Regt., BLWt.13176-100-Pvt. Iss. 11/22/1797. No papers
John, Pa., b. Scotland, S15166
John, Pa., S36006; BLWt.936-100
Joseph, Va., b. Md., R4576
Robert, Md., S22823
Robert, Pa., S22284
Robert, S.C., S22290
Robert, S.C., Elizabeth, R4574
William, Md. See HANNON
HANNAFORD, Thomas, Cont., N.C., S18003
HANNAH, Andrew, N.C., Jane, W794
David, Va., R4573
James, Ct., Cont., S43653
John, Cont., Pa., S39634
HANNAMAN, William, Va., S32299
HANNAN, Esom, Cont., Va., Mary, W7644
Thomas, Va., Sea Service, R4578
HANNESS, William, Cont., N.Y., Margaret, W19699
HANNEWELL, William, See HUNNEWELL
HANNEY, John, Pa. See HANEY
HANNIS, Henry, N.Y., Va., S32288
HANNON, John, Md., BLWt.11300-100-Pvt. Iss. 8/8/1797 to James DeBaufre. No papers
Thomas, Va. See HANNAN
William, Md., R4579
William, Pa., BLWt.9623-100-Pvt. Iss. 2/4/1791. No papers
HANNOR, John, N.C., Sally, BLWt. 36221-160-55
HANNUM, Moses, Mass., Jerusha,

HANNUM (continued)
W15726
Seth, Mass., Anne, W24408
William, Mass., Mercy, W17033
HANOR, Philip, N.Y., Ann Maria, W16285
HANS, James, Mass., S37090
William, Mass., BLWt.4309-100-Pvt. Iss. 2/22/1792 to John Peck. No papers
William, Mass., S37085
HANSARD, William, Va., R4580
HANSBROUGH, John, Va., Fanny, W2614; BLWt.26531-160-55
William, Va., Sarah, W3808; BLWt.28518-160-55
HANSCOM, Aaron, Mass., Lydia, W21244
Humphrey, Mass., S28756
John, Cont., Mass., S37075
John, Mass., S37076
Mark, Mass., Eleanor Worcester, former wid., W26119
Moses, Mass., Mary, W23175; BLWt.12844-160-55
Nathan, Mass., S29197
Nathaniel, Mass., S37072
Reuben, Mass., Alice, W24399
Robert, Mass., S35401
Stephen, Mass., Hannah, W24401
Uriah, N.H., Hannah, R4581; BLWt.14545-160-55
HANSCOMB, Gideon, Cont., Mass., Mehitable, W25751
HANSCOME, Jeremiah, Mass., Abigail Jordan, former wid., W7926
HANSDON, Allen, N.Y. See HERNSDON
HANSE, Cornelius, Lamb's Art., N.Y., BLWt.7282-100-Pvt. Iss. 10/9/1790 to Michael Meyers, ass. No papers
HANSECUM, Robert, See HANSCOM
HANSEL, Michael, See HENSEL
HANSELL, Anthony, N.J., S1009
Charles Frederick, Pa., Margaret, R4582
George, "Invalids", BLWt.13211-100-Pvt. Iss. 3/31/1794. No papers
HANSEN, Dirk, Cont., N.Y., Helen Linn, former wid., W16726, BLWt.981-300-Capt. Iss. 7/13/1790. Name recorded as Dirck Hanson. No papers
HANSFORD, Cary H., Va., R14850; Va. Half Pay
Charles, Privateer, Va., S16402
William, Va., BLWt.12188-100-Pvt. Iss. 5/9/1797 to Daniel Vertner, ass. No papers
William, Va., S36004
HANSIUM, Robert,See HANSCOM
HANSLEY, Robert, N.C., S4323
HANSON, Anthony, N.H., BLWt. 3207-100-Pvt. Iss. 3/25/1790. No papers
Charles, Cont., N.H., Zilpha, W4226; BLWt.3757-160-55
Christopher, Ct., S37059
Dirck, Cont., N.Y. See HANSEN
Isaac, Md., BLWt.1059-200-Lt.

HANSON (continued)
Iss. 9/5/1789 to Keziah Clark, Admx. No papers
Isaac, Navy, N.H., Mary, W2616; BLWt.13190-160-55
Isaac, N.H., Sarah, W23328
John, Lee's Legion, BLWt. 13242-100-Pvt. Iss. 9/2/1789. No papers
John, N.Y., Mary, W17045
Jonathan, Mass., Lydia, W8909; BLWt.79531-160-55
Nathan, N.H., S13303
Samuel, Md., Mary, W14878
Samuel, Md., BLWt.1050-200-Lt. Iss. 2/25/1796. No papers
William, Ct. See HENSON
William, Md., BLWt.1055-200-Lt. Iss. 10/4/1797 to Robert Gover, ass. No papers
HANSPAN, Cutlip, Md., S34913
HANTSEL, Charles Frederick, Pa. See HANSELL
HANWAY, Samuel, Va., Sea Service, R4583
HANYER, Charity, former wid. of Mordecai Mott, N.Y., which see
HAPGOOD, Thomas, Mass., Hannah, W14871
HAPPAL, Adam, N.Y., Alice, R4584
HAPPER, William, N.C., S37995
HAPPES, Michael, Pa., S23686
HAPPY, John George, N.Y., Barbara, W17047
HAPTINSTALL, Abraham, See HAPTONSTALL
HAPTONSTALL, Abraham, N.Y., S32302
HARADEN, John, Vt., Betsey, W23256
HARADON, John, Mass., S38784
HARALSON, Herndon, N.C., S1828
Paul, N.C., Mary, W1763; BLWt. 28638-160-55
HARAMAN, David, Md., S9560
HARBAUGH, Jacob, Va., S39663
HARBERSON, William, Pa. See HARBISON
HARBERT, Edward, Va., S15448
John, ---, Va. res. in 1834, R4585
Samuel, Va., S15447
William, Va., See HARBIT
HARBESON, John, Not Rev. War, Old War Inv. File 10215
Thomas, Pa., BLWt.9592-100-Pvt. Iss. 9/26/1791 to George Harbeson, Admr. No papers
William, Pa. See HARBISON
HARBINSON, George, S.C., R4586
Robert, Pa. See HARBISON
William, N.C., Sarah, W7706
HARBISON, David, Pa., S31733
Francis, Pa., Catherine, W4982
James, S.C., Jane, W17039; BLWt.114166-160-55
James, Va., War of 1812, Rachel, W7707; BLWt.71190-160-55
John, Va., S38788
Robert, Pa., S18434
William, Pa., Jane, W25747; BLWt.26653-160-55

HARBIT, William, Va., Enlisted & married in Pa., Margaret, R7673
HARBOLT, Adam, Pa., S39662
HARBOR, John Nicholas, N.H., BLWt.3206-100-Pvt. Iss. 3/26/1796 to Peter Seveir/Swier. No papers
Michael, Hazen's Regt., BLWt. 13192-100-Sgt. Iss. 2/20/1792 to Benj. Moore, ass. No papers
HARBORN, Joseph, Pa. Sea Service, R4587
HARBOUR, Noah, Va., S8673
HARCOURT, John, N.Y., R4589
HARDAR, William, N.J. See HADAR
HARDAWAY, Joseph, Va., S2607
Rebecca, former wid of Littleberry Mason, Va., which see
HARDCHY, John, See HARTCHY
HARDEE, Abraham, N.C. See HARDIE
Thomas, N.C., Dicey, R4590
William, N.C., Nancy, W9054
HARDEN, James, N.C., R4592
John, N.Y., See HARDER
John, N.C., See HARDIN
Lewis, N.C., See HARDIN
Reuben, Mass., See HARDIN
Richard, Pa., Dis. No papers
Richard, Pa. See HARDIN
Samuel, Mass., S32787
HARDENBERG, Abraham, N.Y., BLWt. 985-200-Lt. Iss. 7/29/1790. No papers
John L., N.Y., BLWt.986-200-Lt. No papers
HARDENBROOK, Lodwick, N.J., S16858
HARDER, John, N.Y., Elizabeth, R4591
Peter, N.Y., Eve, R4595
HARDESTY, Francis, Pa., b. Md., S8684, (entered service as sub. for John Hardesty, b. 9/2/1763 on eastern shore of Md.)
Hezekiah, Pa., S32296
Obadiah, Pa., S46362
Richard, Cont., Pa., S17468
HARDEY, Isaiah, N.H., Sarah, W21138
HARDICK, John, N.Y., Polly, W19672
HARDIE, Abraham, N.C., R4597
HARDIMAN, John, N.C. See HARDMAN
HARDIN, Benjamin, N.C., S32293
Benjamin, Va., S31100
Henry, N.C., S31732
James, Ct., S44194
John, N.C., Nancy, R4599
John, Pa., b. Va., S2274
Joseph, N.C., S13322
Lewis, N.C., S38799
Mark, Pa., Susanna, W423
Reuben, Mass., Rebecca, R4600
Richard, Pa., S41604
Samuel, Mass. See HARDEN
Samuel, Pa., R4593
Thomas, Cont., Del., S8685
Thomas, Va., Ann, W8916
Thomas, Va., R4594
William, Md., S18427
HARDING, Abiel, Mass., S13261
Abijah, Mass., S32785
Abraham, Mass., S19695
Abraham, N.Y., R4601

HARDING (continued)
Cornelius, Mass., Mary, W19749
David, Mass., S37086
Ede, Pa., S32287
Ephraim, Ct., Susan, W17054
George, Ct., Martha, R4602
George, Va., S17220
Henry, Pa., Hannah Atwater, former wid., W16815
Henry, Va., S16145
Hezekiah, Mass., S37091
Israel, Ct., BLWt.5920-100-Pvt. Iss. 7/13/1792. No papers
Israel, Ct., Lydia, W2791
Jeremiah, Ct., S13286
John, N.J., S34387; BLWt.534-100
Joshua, Mass., Jemima, W24388
Nathan, Mass., Sea Service, S29851
Nathaniel, Mass., Sea Service, R4603
Oliver, Cont., N.Y., Cloey, W19711
Oliver, N.Y., BLWt.7301-100-Pvt. Iss. 1/31/1792. No papers
Robert, Va., Elizabeth, W7679
Samuel, Mass., S46040
Seth, Mass., Phebe, W23224
Stephen, Mass., S5453
Thomas, Md., BLWt.11309-100-Pvt. Iss. 10/14/1795 to Henry Davis, ass. No papers
Thomas, Pa., Sarah, W10079
Vachel, Md., Mary, W1601
William, R.I., S21261
HARDISON, Benjamin, Mass., Jane, W226; BLWt.79518-160-55
James, N.C., S1827
James, N.C., Lucretia, R4596
Stephen, Mass., S37087
HARDIST, John G., Pa., BLWt.9638-100-Pvt. Iss. 5/5/1794 to Alexander Power, ass. No papers
HARDISTY, Obadiah, Pa., BLWt.9644-100-Pvt. Iss. 10/26/1791. No papers
HARDMAN, Henry, Md., BLWt.1045-400-Maj. Iss. 6/11/1790. No papers
John, Va., S2606
Michael, N.J., S34388
HARDWICK, George, Va., S8674
Mehitabel, former wid. of Richard Crispin, Cont., Mass., which see
HARDY, Abraham, Pa., BLWt.9558-100-Pvt. Iss. 2/21/1793 to Gideon Merkle, ass. No papers
Andrew, Va., R4603 1/2
Arnold, Md., Barbara, R4604 1/2
Benjamin, Cont., enl. in Mass., S38810
Benjamin, Mass., S13321
Benjamin, N.Y., BLWt.7284-100-Pvt. Iss. 7/18/1791 to Jedediah Sanger, ass. No papers
Daniel, Mass., S38809
Elias, Md., Cassandra/Casandra, W4451; BLWt.35833-160-55
Elijah, Pa., BLWt.9458-100-Corp. Iss. 10/20/1789 to Peter Smith, ass. No papers

HARDY (continued)
Henry, Mass., Rachel, W14886
Isaac, Mass., N.H., Lydia, W21297; BLWt.10260-160-55
Isaiah, N.H. See HARDEY
Jacob, R.I., BLWt.3219-100-Pvt. Iss. 4/20/1790. No papers
Jesse, Mass., Abigail, W23183
John, Cont., Va., S16140
John, Va., BLWt.12215-100-Pvt. Iss. 11/12/1791 to John Clingman, ass. No papers
Jonas, Mass., S16852
Joshua, Cont., Mass., Lucy, W21277
Moody, Mass., S17460
Nathaniel, Ct., S41598
Noah, N.H., Sarah, W15911
Pary, N.H., S18436
Phinehas/Phineas, N.H., S13319
Samuel, Mass., Judith, W19747
Thomas, Cont., N.H., Lucy, W17034
Thomas, Va., Martha, W361; BLWt. 28554-160-55
William, Mass., Hannah, W23251; BLWt.24996-160-55
William, R.I., S44192
HARDYEAR, Elijah, See HARGER
HARDYMAN, John, Va., Sea Service, R14719; see N.A. Acc. No. 874-050083, Va. Infantry. See N.A. Acc. 837, YS File, Va. State Navy
HARE, John, Pvt., Mass., BLWt. 4386 iss. 1/12/1792 to Ezra Blodget
Michael, Pa., S39645; BLWt.441-100
Richard, Va., S8697
Robert, Mass., Mary, W19670
Thomas, Md., S44188
HARENDEN, Reuben, R.I., See HERENDEEN
HARFORD, Ephraim, N.Y., Ruth,W19738
Peter, N.Y., Eunice, W17991
HARGAN, Michael, Pa., Elizabeth, W8906
HARGASS, Abraham, See HARGIS
HARGATE, Peter, N.C. See HERGET
HARGER, Elijah, Ct., R4605
HARGES, John, Va. See HARGUS
HARGILL, William, Navy, R.I., Elizabeth, R4606
HARGIS, Abraham, N.C., Elizabeth, W4480
Thomas, N.C., b. Va., S8663
William, N.C., Elizabeth, W82
HARGRAVE, Hezekiah, Va. See HARGROVE
John, N.C., See HARGROVE
John, S.C., S32297
William, N.C., S37980; BLWt. 835-200
HARGROVE, Alexander, S.C., S6972
Bennett, Va., R4608
Hezekiah, Va., S5481
John, N.C., S37978
HARGUS, John, Va., S35382
HARIDEN, Elizabeth, former wid. of Joseph Varriel, Cont., Mass., which see
HARIMAN, Jacob, N.J., Sarah, W10101; BLWt.67681-160-55
HARING, Abraham G., N.J., S29203

HARING (continued)
David P., N.J., Tryntie, W24395
Garret F., N.J., Sarah, W7663
John A., N.J., S6980
John D., N.J., Jane, W16594
John F., N.J., Jamima, W7662
HARINGTON, Elisha, Mass., W19698
Nathaniel, R.I., S13290
HARKER, Abraham, N.J., BLWt.8403-100-Pvt. Iss. 7/22/1796 to Peter Footman, ass. No papers
HARKERADER, John, Pa., S13323
HARKERIDER, John, See HARKERADER
HARKESHIMER, John, Va., S34912
HARKISHIMER, John, See HARKESHIMER
HARKNESS, James, Mass., Elizabeth, W21243
John, Cont., N.H., Elizabeth, W23253; BLWt.34267-160-55
John, Mass., S2269
HARKSTON, William, R.I., Candace Johnson, former wid., W20206
HARLAN, George, Va., Catharine, W8918
Jonathan, Pa., R4610
Razen R./Rezin R., Va., R4609
HARLESS, Daniel, Va., R4611
Ferdenen, Va., R4612
Philip, Va., R4613
HARLESTON, Isaac, S.C., BLWt.1800-400
HARLEY, Benjamin, Cont., Mass. res. of dau. or sister in 1821; BLWt. 991-100
Solomon, Mass., S33279
Thomas, Ct., N.Y., Mary, W17059
HARLON, Jonathan, See HARLAN
HARLOW, Ansel, Mass., S30463
Asa, Mass., Elizabeth, W19735
Bartlett, Va., Lucy, W8913
Deborah, former wid. of Squire Caswell, Cont. Mass., which see
Ellis, Mass. Sea Service, Sarah, W14881
George, Va., Susan, W8915; BLWt. 27603-160-55
James, Cont., Mass., Hannah Bartlett, former wid., R581
James, Mass., Phebe, W19716
James, Mass. Sea Service, Sarah, W24417
John, Mass., Eliza, BLWt.17598-160-55
John, Va., S13309
Josiah, Cont., Mass., Privateer, Olive, W23195
Lewis, Mass., BLWt.840-100
Michael, Va., Lucy, W8914
Nathaniel, Mass., Mary, W17988
Nathaniel, Va., S37988
Robert, Mass., Charity, W23182; BLWt.6429-160-55
Silvanus/Sylvanus, Mass., S29213
Thomas, S.C., R4615
William, Mass., S13289
HARMAN, Charles, Va., Piercy, W7645; BLWt.31280-160-55
Conrad, Pa., S41611
Edward, Del., BLWt.10779-100-Pvt. Iss. 9/2/1789. No papers
Edward, Md., BLWt.11311-100-Pvt. Iss. 7/9/1800 to Asahel Phelps,

HARMAN (continued)
ass. "Presented for certification 9/30/1816 by M. Nourse". No papers
Elijah, Mass. See HARMON
George, Pa., R4616
George, Va., BLWt.1361-100
Jacob, Pa., Elizabeth, W4689
Jacob, Pa., R4621
Jacob, Pa., R14846
Jaques, Ct., BLWt.969-150-Ensign. Iss. 5/26/1790. No papers. No Ct. officer of this name located in printed records. Probably Jacques Harmon, see Ct. Archives
John, Cont. See HERRMAN
John, Pa., S23251
Lazarus, Md., S34911
Martin, Mass., See HARMON
Samuel, Cont., Mass. See HARMON
Thomas, Mass. See HARMON
William, Cont.,Mass. See HARMON
HARMANY, Jacob, Pa. See HERMANY
HARMAR, Francis J., Mass., BLWt. 4307-100-Pvt. Iss. 1/26/1790 to John May. No papers
Josiah, Pa., Sarah, W3246; BLWt. 1009-450-Lt. Col. Iss. 10/17/1789
Lazarus, Md., BLWt.11353-100-Pvt. Iss. 7/9/1800 to Asahel Phelps. "Presented for certification 30th Sept. 1816 by M. Nourse." No papers
HARMON, Abner, Cont., Mass., Sarah, W1278; BLWt.34542-160-55
Adam, N.C., Va., Barbara, W754; BLWt.34541-160-55
Alpheus, Green Mt. Boys, N.Y., Vt., R4618
Charles, Va. See HARMAN
Conrad, Pa. See HARMAN
Edward, Del., S36000
Elijah, Mass., Rebecca, R4622 1/2
Jacob, Pa., See HARMAN
Jacob, Va., served in 1774, R4620
Jacques, Ct. See Jaques HARMAN
Jehiel, Ct., Betsey E., W25759; BLWt.26615-160-55
Joel, Mass., S18868
John, Mass., S13247
John, N.C., b. Va., Mary, W2795; BLWt.1307-160-55
John, Pa., R4545
John, Va., S1825
John, Va., S18006
Joseph, Ct., R4622
Josiah, Mass., S37073
Lazarus, Md., S34911
Martin, Mass., S39644
Moses, Mass., Sarah, W23215
Oliver, Vt., S16143
Pelatiah, Cont., Mass., Sarah, W547; BLWt.24440-160-55
Samuel, Cont., Mass., S37071
Seth, Green Mt. Boys, Vt., S15441
Thomas, Cont., Mass., S16863
William, Cont., Mass., Mehitable, W4220; BLWt.11254-160-55
William, Va., Elizabeth, W7647; BLWt.26989-160-55

HARMONY, Nicholas, Pa., Ann/ Anna, W19728
HARN, James, BLWt.13163-100-Pvt. "in the Sappers & Miners." Iss. 4/5/1796 to Oliver Ashley, ass. No papers
HARNDEN, Benjamin, Mass., Hannah, W27420
Richard, Mass., S29195
HARNE, Christian, Hazen's Regt., BLWt.13181-100-Pvt. Iss. 2/28/ 1794 to Christian Harne. No papers
HARNEST, John, Va., Margaret, W7682
Patrick, See HARTNEY
HARNEY, Selby, N.C., BLWt.1093- 500-Col. Iss. 8/6/1789. No papers
HARNUCK, Abraham, Pa., BLWt. 9552-100-Pvt. Iss. 11/17/179? to Michael Stever, ass. No papers
HARP, Frederick, Pa., Catharine Herb, W7624
Joseph, N.C., Sylvia, R4624
Sampson, N.C., Sarah, R4623
HARPER, Adam, Va., S30453
Alexander, N.Y., Elizabeth, R4626
Daniel, Md. Sea Service, Navy, S39637
Daniel, N.H., Mary, W4221
Ebenezer, Pa., S31728
Godfrey, Ct., S29202
Henry, Pa., BLWt.9533-100-Pvt. Iss. 6/29/1789 to M. McConnell, ass. No papers
Henry, Va., S19315
James, N.Y., BLWt.7209-100-Pvt. Iss. 7/16/1790 to William J. Vreedenburgh, ass. No papers
James, Pa., Eve, W1862; BLWt. 12850-160-55
James, Va., R14859, Va. Half Pay
James, Va., BLWt.2148-200 & Rejected Va. Half Pay
Jeduthan, N.C., Gizael, W19734
Jesse, Va., S10790
John, N.H., S16848
John, N.H., R4627
John, N.C., S8657
John, N.C., Sarah, W4977
John, Pa., S36012
John, Pa., BLWt.1015-200-Lt. Iss. 4/24/1794. No papers
John, Va., S30454
John, Va., R21782
John W., Va., S2599
Joseph, Del., Md., & War of 1812 Hetty, W9056
Joseph, ---, on N.Y. list, Dis. No papers
Joseph, Md., S---. This man's wid. Eleanor, was pensioned as former wid. of James Ryan, Md. Which see
Josiah, Va., S1953
Lewis L., S.C., R4628
Nathan, Md., BLWt.11314-100-Pvt. Iss. 6/13/1794. No papers
Nathan, N.C., S31091
Richard, N.C., S1908
Samuel, Md., BLWt.11299-100-Pvt. Iss. 1/11/1796 to Joshua Ward, ass. No papers

HARPER (continued)
Samuel, Pvt., Pa., BLReg.81866- 1855
Samuel A., Md., S34910
Thomas, Del., BLWt.10788-100. Iss. 9/2/1789. No papers
Thomas, Pa., BLWt.9581-100-Pvt. Iss. 1/16/1797 to Daniel Wheaton, ass. No papers
Thomas, Pa., S32304
Thomas, Pa., S38789
William, Md., Bethala, W3679; BLWt.7303-160-55, cancelled & duplicate Wt. iss. 10/4/1858
William, N.C., R4630
William, Pa., S41608
William, Pa., Mary, R4629
William, Va., Sarah Barrett, former wid., R559
William, Va., R4631
HARPHAM, Robert, Md., BLWt. 11339-100-Pvt. Iss. 3/31/1797 to James DeBaufre, ass. No papers
HARPLE, John, Pa., Mary/Maria/ Maricha, W3138
HARPOLE, Adam, Va., R4632
HARPOOLE, Henry, Pa., BLWt. 9536-100-Pvt. Iss. 6/20/1789 No papers
HARPS, Manon, Va., Sarah, R4625
HARRADON, John, Mass. See HARADON
John, Mass., BLWt.135-100. Iss. 2/28/1804. Not delivered. Claim missing in 1912
HARRALD, Jeremiah, See HARROLD
HARRALL, Wm., Va. See HORRALL
HARRAR, Daniel, Pa., S6974
HARRARD, John, N.C., R4633
HARRAU, Jacob, See HORRAUF
HARREL, Thomas, Pa., BLWt.9568- 100-Pvt. Iss. 1/11/1791. No papers
HARRELL, George, Va., S2596
Henry B., Md. See HORRELL
Joel, N.C., Va., R4635
John, Md. See HORRELL
John, N.C., S6976
John, Va., S9557
Josiah, N.C., S8690
Kidder, N.C., S6963
Reuben, Va., Rebecca, W8926
Simon, Va., Lydia, W8895; BLWt.30769-160-55
HARRENDEN, Reuben, See HERENDEEN
HARRIER, William, Pa., R4636
HARRILL, James, N.C., R4634
HARRIMAN, Joab, Mass., Hannah, W23221
Joseph, Mass., N.H., S13350
Levi, N.H., R4637
Moses, Mass., S44404
Simon, Mass., Elizabeth, W23188
HARRINDEEN, Ephraim, R.I., Sarah, W23203
HARRINGER, William, Pa., R4645
HARRINGTON, Abiel, Mass., S37070
Abraham, Ct., Privateer, R.I., Electa, W1602
Abram/Abraham, N.Y., S28754
Ahab, Cont.,Mass., R.I.,

HARRINGTON (continued)
Phebe, W16598
Allen, Cont., Mass., Elizabeth, W2617; BLWt.61288-160-55
Ammi, Mass., BLWt.4390-100-Pvt. Iss. 3/25/1790. No papers
Andrew, Ct., S37051
Anna, former wid. of Elijah Porter, Ct., which see
Anthony, Md. & Sea Service, W31108
Asa, Mass., Asenath, W17055; BLWt. 751-100
Benjamin, Sheldon's Dragoons, Ct., BLWt.6000-100-Pvt. Iss. 8/26/ 1790 to Manassah Cutler. No papers
Benjamin, Ct. See HERINGTON
Benjamin, Ct. See HERRINGTON
Caleb, Mass., Sarah, W13401
Daniel, Mass., Relief, W14854
David, R.I., Waity, R4644
Drury, N.C., S6979
Ebenezer, Cont., Mass., Martha, W16281
Ebenezer, Cont., Mass., Lucretia, W17040
Eber, Ct., R.I., Susannah, W23229
Edward, Mass., Susanna/Susan, W14848
Elisha, Ct., BLWt.5907-100-Pvt. Iss. 10/31/1791 to Isaac Bronson. No papers
Elisha, Mass., Betsey, W19698
Ephraim, Mass., Abigail, W21293
Hannah, former wid. of Oliver Kendall, Mass., which see
Isaac, Navy, R.I., R4639
Israel, R.I., Rhoda Shelly/ Shelley, former wid., W19026
James, Mass., S32801
James, R.I., Hannah, W11227; BLWt.7314-160-55
James, R.I., Mary, W19680
Job, R.I., Meriba, W21292
John, Mass., S36014
John, N.Y., R4640
John, R.I., Pernilepa, W13363
Jonathan, Mass., S29850
Joshua, Mass., Sarah, W14888
Joshua, N.H., S15436
Josiah, R.I. See HERRINTON
Lemuel, Mass., Eleanor, W19692
Levi, Mass., S13332
Loammi, Mass., Sarah, W19737
Micah, Mass., S30462
Nathan, Mass., Elizabeth, W24402
Nathaniel, R.I. See HARINGTON
Noah, Mass., S17458
Noah, Mass., S33275
Parley, Ct., S44183
Peter, Md., R4642
Priscilla, former wid. of James Shovel, Mass., which see
Randall, R.I., S21805
Sally, former wid. of Simon Rice, Mass., which see
Samson, R.I., See HERRINGTON
Samuel, Ct., S44195; BLWt.953-100
Samuel, Mass., S32789
Samuel, Mass., Anna, W24420
Simeon, Mass., Hannah, W23202
Stephen, Ct., Sebra Green, former

HARRINGTON (continued)
wid., W19541; BLWt.128-160-55
Thomas, Mass., S5430
Timothy, Ct., Lydia Edson, former wid., W17742
Uriah, Mass., Martha, W2543; BLWt.11078-160-55
William, Ct., Elizabeth, W19726 BLWt.33741-160-55
William, Cont., Mass., Comfort, W16596
William, Md., BLWt.2095-100
William, Mass., S29855
HARRIOT, Israel, N.Y., BLWt.7292-100-Pvt. Iss. 3/15/1791. No papers
Reuben, Cont., Pa., Ann, W24396
HARRIOTT, Ephraim, N.J., Mary, W7687
Israel, Cont., N.Y., S23249
Samuel, N.J., S44409
HARRIS, Abiel, Mass., Silence, W10083; BLWt.56854-160-55
Abigail, former wid. of Aaron Witham, Mass., which see
Abijah, N.Y., S32286
Abraham, N.J., R4646
Amos, Ct., BLWt.5979-100-Pvt. Iss. 4/20/1796. No papers
Amos, Mass., Isabella, W21242
Andrew, Armand's Corps, BLWt. 13157-100-Pvt. Iss. 10/--/ 1789 to Theodosius Fowler, ass. No papers
Andrew, Ct., Elizabeth, W27423
Arthur, Md., BLWt.1271-200
Asa, Ct., Navy, Vt., Rachel, W19667
Benjamin, Mass., S38816
Benjamin, N.C., Bethana/ Bethena, W5295
Benjamin, N.C., Charlotte, W11211; BLWt.36739-160-55
Benjamin, Va., Mary, W7664
Benjamin, Va., Rutha, R4652
Benton, Md., BLWt.11362-100-Pvt. Iss. 12/22/1794 to Henry Purdy, ass. No papers
Brantly, N.C., Elizabeth, W19727
Charles, Mass., S37065
Charles, Pa., R4648
Cyrus, Va., S37977
Daniel, Ct., S10797
Daniel, Cont., Mass., Judith, W13397
Daniel, Cont., Va., Pa., S36575
Daniel, Mass., S29877
Daniel, Mass., S38820
David, Ct., S37062
David, Mass., S44393
David, N.Y., R4650
David, Va., S38796
Ebenezer, Ct., R4651
Edward, ---, Elizabeth, R---
Edward, N.C., Mary, R4663
Edward, N.C., Martha, R4683
Edward, S.C., Clarissa, R4649
Edward, Va., S37992
Edwin, N.C., S4307
Ezekiel, N.Y., S9914
Ezekiel, N.Y., Elizabeth, W17978
Fanny P., former wid. of Levi

HARRIS (continued)
Arnold, Ct., which see
Fieldman, Va., S8668
George, N.J., S1008
George, Pa., BLWt.9636-100-Pvt. Iss. 4/9/1791. No papers
Goodman, N.C., S38801
Henry, Cont., Va., S37986
Henry, Md., BLWt.11364-100-Pvt. Iss. 5/12/1797 to James DeBaufre, ass. No papers
Henry, N.Y., BLWt.7218-100-Pvt. Iss. 9/27/1790 to Jacob Tremper, ass. No papers
Henry, Lamb's Art., N.Y., BLWt. 7303-100-Pvt. Iss. 6/19/1790 No papers
Henry, N.Y., S44189
Henry, Va., S16399
Herbert, N.C., Polly, R4669
Hugh, N.C., Elizabeth, W25743; BLWt.24915-160-55
Isom/Isham, Va., R4654
Israel, Green Mt. Boys, Mass., S6952
Jacob, N.J., S2594
Jacob, N.J., BLWt.1002-400-Surgn.
James, Cont., N.J., S44186
James, N.J., R4656
James, Lamb's Art., N.Y., BLWt. 7280-100-Pvt. Iss. 1/1/1793 to Thos. Russell, ass. No papers
James, N.Y., R4658
James (colored), N.C., Keziah, W11223; BLWt.31703-160-55
James, N.C., R4659
James, N.C., Va., Elizabeth, R4653
James, R.I., S21255
James, Va., BLWt.12214-100-Pvt. Iss. 10/22/1791 to Jacob Clingman, ass. No papers
James, Va., S31726
James, Va., S37996
James, Va., S38006
James, Va., Patte, W8892
James, Va., R4657
James, Va., Mary, R4666
Jason, Ct., Elizabeth Annis, former wid., W23443
Jedediah/Jedidiah, Ct., S16844
Jesse, N.C., Judah, W1277; BLWt. 19728-160-55
Jesse, N.C., R4655
John, Ct., S10787
John, Ct., S37049
John, Ct., Martha, W2112
John, Ct., Cont., BLWt.1608-200
John, Cont., Mass., Navy & Privateer, Mary C., W19679
John, Cont., Va., Rebecca, W1422; BLWt.2297-200
John, Del., Pa., Eleanor, W2936
John, Mass., Phebe, W1276; BLWt. 24771-160-55
John, Mass., Lydia, W25744; BLWt.26644-160-55
John, Mass., Mary Smith, former wid., W26478; BLWt.89504-160-55
John, N.C., S30476
John, N.C., Jane, W21247

HARRIS (continued)
John, N.C., R4660
John, N.C., R4661
John, Pa., BLWt.9564-100-Pvt. Iss. 3/12/1792. No papers
John, Pa., BLWt.9600-100-Pvt. Iss. 1/17/1792 to George Moore, ass. No papers
John, Pa., BLWt.9628-100-Bombardier. Iss. 4/15/1796. No papers
John, Pa., S39643
John, Pa., S39657
John, Pa., BLWt.1428-300 (cancelled); BLWt.2413-300
John, Privateer, Va., Sea Service R41; Va. half pay
John, S.C., R4662
John, S.C., Va., S21808
John, Va., S5491
John, Va., S37997
John, Va., S37998
John, Va., S37999
John, Va., S38001
John, Va., Martha, W24391; BLWt. 31466-160-55
John C., Va., S6953
Jonathan, Cont., Mass., Ann, W14869; BLWt.14541-160-55
Jonathan, N.H., Rachel, W16122
Jonathan, N.C., Margaret, W4979
Jordan, Va., BLWt.1083-150-Ensign Iss. 4/2/1796 to Joseph Fenwick, ass. No papers
Joseph, ---, N.Y. Agcy. Dis. No papers
Joseph, Ct., Anna, R4647
Joseph, N.H., Martha, W14847
Joseph, N.C., Elizabeth, W2793
Joseph, Pa., S44391
Joshua, Mass., N.Y., Vt., S22822
Joshua, N.Y., S22809
Joshua, Va., Martha, R4685
Justus, N.Y., Jemima, W15909
Lebbeus, Ct., Sarah Douglass, former wid., R3049
Luda, Mass., S32783
Luke, Mass., Leah, W19713
Mary, former wid. of Michael Cain, S.C., which see
Mason, Mass., S29207
Matthew, Ga., S31730
Moses, Mass., Betsey Seabury, former wid., W22176
Moses, N.Y., S13295
Moses, S.C., S17996
Nathaniel, Va., S5456
Nathaniel, Va., S37971
Nelson, N.C., Elizabeth, R4668
Nicholas, N.J., S5440
Oliver, Cont., Mass., Mehitable, R4664
Oliver, Mass., Relief, W19710
Oliver, R.I., Mary Ann, W9473; BLWt.2084-160-55
Overton, Va., S31107
Paul, Ct., S31719
Pearly, Ct., Aby, W21287
Peter, Mass., Rachel, R4670
Philip, Ct., Cont., Anna, W25755; BLWt.26553-160-55
Richard, Md., R4671
Richard, Va., S13315

HARRIS (continued)
Richmond, N.C., Polly, W8891; BLWt.26305-160-55
Robert, Ct., Lucretia, W10076
Robert, N.C., Lucy, W23240
Robert, Pa., BLWt.1173-300
Robert Hood, N.C. See Robin Hood
Robin, N.C., Tabitha, R4672
Robin Hood/Robert Hood, N.C., Jemima, R4665
Salathiel, N.Y., S21795
Samuel, Pa., BLWt.9595-100-Pvt. Iss. 12/16/1793 to Casper Iserloan, ass. No papers
Samuel, Va., S10813
Sherrod/Sherwood, N.C., Martha, W3984; BLWt.10300-160-55
Sherwood, N.C.
Simeon, Va., S15871
Simon, Va., Rebecca, R4684; BL Reg. 82807-55
Solomon, N.H., BLWt.3192-100-Pvt. Iss. 2/22/1792 to John Peck, ass. No papers
Squire, Cont., N.Y., Mary, W3989
Stephen, Mass., BLWt.996-100
Stephen, N.C., Polly, W3804
Stephen, R.I., S21811
Susanna, former wid. of Caleb Joy, Mass., which see
Thomas, Ct., Cont., Elizabeth, W21270
Thomas, Md., Nancy, R4686
Thomas, N.C., S13312
Thomas, N.C., Pa., S4308
Thomas, R.I., S38815
Thomas, Va., S36576
Thomas, Va., S38002
Thomas, Va., Mary, W3414
Walter, Cont., Ct., Jane A., W2106; BLWt.30787-160-55
William, Ct., BLWt.5904-100-Corp. Iss. 10/22/1789 to Theodosius Fowler. No papers
William, Ct., Mary, W23226; S38811
William, Cont., Mass., N.H., S44390
William, Mass., BLWt.4403-100-Pvt. Iss. 4/11/1792. No papers
William, Mass., BLWt.4404-100-Pvt. Iss. 6/25/1799 to Jeremiah Hill. No papers
William, Mass., Mary, W23226, Ctf. No. 7523. Her claim placed with Wm. Harris, S38811, Aug. 1937, where it belongs. MHF
William, Mass., S29214
William, Mass., S32794
William, Mass., S32799
William, Mass., S44392
William, N.J., Martha, W486
William, N.Y., BLWt.7259-100-Pvt. Iss. 10/10/1791 to Anthony Maxwell, ass. No papers
William, N.Y., Rachel, W17052
William, N.Y., Cynthia, W19696
William, N.Y., R4673
William, N.C., S5441; BLWt.13716-160-55
William, Pa., BLWt.9596-100-Pvt. Iss. 12/13/1791. No papers
William, Pa., S2276

HARRIS (continued)
William, Va., S5489
William, Va., S6954
William, Va., S6956
William, Va., S8696
William, Va., S13314
William, Va., S18435
William, Va., S25132
William, Va., S30458
William, Va., S41616
William, Va., Diana, W4222
William, Va., Keziah, W8890
William, Va., Lydia, W8893
Winans, N.J., Hannah, W3544; BLWt.30777-160-55
HARRISON, Aaron, N.J., S1010
Abijah, N.J., S2272
Abraham, N.J., S2273
Alexander, Va., BLWt.1884-100
Answorth, Va., R14755
Anthony Alexander, Va., S32303
Barzillai/Barzillia, N.C., R4675
Battle, Va., BLWt.2374-200
Benjamin, Md., S10786
Benjamin, N.C., Charity, W5296
Burditt, Va., S8667
Charles, 1st Regt. Artillery in the service of the U.S. BLWt. 1063-500-Col. Iss. 8/10/1789 to Richard Platt, ass. No papers
Daniel, Ct., S15165
David, N.J., S1011
David, Va., R4677
Dempsey/Demsey, N.C., S41623
Elisha, Md., BLWt.965-300-Surgn. Mate. Iss. 5/30/1793. Also recorded under BLWt.2632. No papers
Ezekiel, Va., Sarah, W23211
Gideon, N.C., S2602
Hannah, former wid. of Joseph Beach, Ct., which see
Henry, Va., Charlotte, W748
Ichabod, Not Rev. War, N.J. Mil. Whiskey Insurrection, Elizabeth O.W. Wid. Rej. File 20140, BLWt.48620-160-55
Isaac, N.J., Mary, W98
Isham, N.C., Amy, W10089
Jairus, Ct., S37081
James, N.C., Winny Campbell, former wid., R1653
James, Va., b. Md., S4309
James, Va., S5496
James, Va., Mary, W548
James, Va., BLWt.2355-200
Jesse, N.C., S41620
Job, N.J., Lydia, W4690; BLWt. 26423-160-55
John, Ga., Rosanna, W3988
John, N.J., R4679
John, N.C., S41601
John, Pa., Rachel, R4682
John, Va., Lee's Legion, BLWts. 12182 & 13241-100-Sgt. Iss. 3/19/1790. No papers
John, Va., S5471
John, Va., BLWt.1075-200
Joseph, Md., S38818
Joseph, N.J., S2275
Joseph, N.C., Mary Ann, R4676
Joseph, Va., Mary, W8917; BLWt.

HARRISON (continued)
34539-160-55
Justus, Ct., Sea Service, Sarah, W19742
Kinsey, Md., Sarah, W9053
Lawrence, Va., Mary, W4223; BLWt. 1074-200-Lt. Iss. 4/30/1793
Lemuel, Ct., R4680; BLWt.31644-160-55
Matthew, N.J., Sarah, W19695
Moses, N.J., S657
Nathan, Ct., S13343
Nathaniel, N.C., S1667
Nathaniel, N.C., Jemima, R4678
Newbegin, N.C., Catharine Smith, former wid., W16412
Reuben, N.C., R4687
Reuben, Va., Mary, W7689
Richard, Ga., N.C., Va., Mary, W3807; BLWt.2359-160-55
Richard, Va., R14762, Va. Half Pay. See N.A. Acc. No. 874-050086 Half Pay Richard Harrison
Robert, R.I., BLWt.3220-100-Pvt. Iss. 5/28/1792 to Israel Angell, ass. No papers
Robert, R.I., Betsey/Elizabeth, W17056
Robert Hanson, Cont., Va., BLWt.1700-450
Sarah, former wid. of Mathias Dodd, N.J., which see
Silas, Cont., Ct., S13281
Solomon, Ct., S16137
Stephen, Ct., Mass., N.H., Vt., S18433
Theodore, Ct., Cont., S13251
Thomas, Md., BLWt.11288-100-Pvt. Iss. 3/11/1791. No papers
Thomas, N.J., S883
Thomas, N.J., S13264
Thomas, N.Y., S8646
Thomas, N.C., b. Md., Nancy, W360
William, Md., S38782
William, N.J., Martha, W4449
William, N.C., S41599
William, N.C., Elvira, W463; BLWt.507-200
William, Pa. or Va., Sarah Springer, former wid., R10017. See papers in claim of Uriah Springer, Va.
William, S.C., R4688
William, Va., Mary A./Molly A., W657; BLWt.34543-160-55
William, Va., Sina/Lina, W4481; BLWt.3977-160-55
William B., Va., BLWt.1091-150-Ensign. Iss. 6/18/1793. No papers
Zephaniah, Va., R4689
Zepheniah, Va., R4690
HARRISS, William, Va., R4674
Wooten, Va., Frances, W23186
HARRISSON, Richard, N.C., Rachel, W2934
HARROD, Noah, Cont., Mass., Eusebia, W29930
William, Pa., Va., S16398
HARROFF, Jacob, Pa. See HORRAUF Lewis, Pa., R4692

HARROLD, Jeremiah, S.C., S17467
HARRON, Thomas, Pa., Sarah Higbee, former wid., W7741; BLWt.36731-160-55
HARROW, Jacob, Va., S5480
HARROWF, Jacob, Pa. See HORRAUF
HARRY, Charles, Pa., S16139
John, Pa. See HARRIS
John, R.I., S38786
Richard, Md., Rachel, W24407
HARSHFIELD, Henry, See HASHFIELD
HARSIN, Garret, N.Y., Sea Service, Elizabeth, W10082
HART, Aaron, Ct., Sarah, W19707
Aaron, R.I., S13260
Absalom, N.J., Susan, W425
Adam, N.C., S46576; BLWt.1469-100. Iss. 2/3/1829 for himself through Hon.A.H. Sheppard
Anthony, Va., S5494
Ard, Ct., Lucy, W8894; BLWt. 949-160-55
Asa, Mass., Lois, W1761
Asher, N.J., S2283
Benjamin, Ct., S37080
Betsy, former wid. of Amariah Winchester, Mass., which see
Bliss, Ct., Silva/Sylvia, W7630
Charles, N.C., S16406
Christopher, Md., S23684
Cyrus D., N.J. See DE HART
Daniel, N.J., Prudence, W95
Daniel, N.Y., S13293
Ebenezer, Mass., BLWt.4367-100-Pvt. Iss. 4/11/1796 to Abraham Foster. No papers
Ebenezer, Mass., S19325
Ebenezer, Mass., Polly, W14852
Ebenezer, N.J., Permillia, R4698
Edward, N.J., Nancy, W7628
Elias, Ct., Cont., S17462
Elisha, Ct., S44408
Frederick A., Ct. See HEART
George, Pa., BLWt.9532-100-Pvt. Iss. 7/8/1791 to Simon Fishbaugh, ass. No papers
George, Pa., S39658
George, R.I., S13333
Gilbert, Ct., N.H., S13304
Henry, N.Y., Anna Eva, W21246
Henry, S.C., Martha, R4699
Hezekiah, Ct., S15167
Hosea, Ct., R4696
Ithurel, Ct., S15872
Jacob, Mass., S32781
Jacob, Mass., S35389
Jacob D., Pa., BLWt.594-150-Ensign. Iss. 11/18/1795 to Wm. D. Hart, admr. Also recorded under BLWt.955. No papers
James, Ct., S10793
James, Cont., Mass., S35390
James, N.C., b. Pa., S9555
Job, Ct., S44196
John, Ct., S36011
John, Ct. See Frederick A. HEART
John, Cont., Ct., S37054
John, Cont., Mass., S3546; BLWt. 937-400-Surgn. Iss. 4/22/1797. No papers.
John, Md. Sea Service, S47241

HART (continued)
John, N.H., S29217
John, N.C., b. Pa., S13320
John, S.C., Mary, W3805; BLWt. 1108-200-Lt. Iss. 5/10/1796 to John Shtis(?), ass. No papers
John, Va., S32300
John R., N.J., S2282
Joseph, S.C., S18860; BLWt. 15189-160-55
Josiah, N.H., Ruth Center, former wid.; BLWt.54424-160-55
Lent, Ct., S13257
Lewis, Cont., Ct. res. in 1810, BLWt.497-100
Martin, Ct., S5438
Martin, Pa., BLWt.9550-160-Pvt. Iss. 3/10/1790. No papers
Martin, Pa., S39655
Munson, Ct., S13252
Nicholas, Cont., R.I., S39651; BLWt.443-100
Nicholas, Pa., BLWt.9613-100-Pvt. Iss. 4/21/1792. No papers
Nicholas, Pa., S39642
Oliver, S.C., BLWt.2331-300
Patrick, N.J., BLWt.8399-100-Pvt. Iss. 3/25/1790. No papers
Peleg, Ct., Hannah, W17990
Pharo/Pharoah, Ct., S34392
Phinehas/Phineas, Mass., S37061
Reuben, Ct., Ruth, W19721
Robert, Va., BLWt.12216-100-Pvt. Iss. 12/13/1791 to Francis Groves, ass. No papers
Robert, Va., Dis. No papers
Samuel, Ct., Dis. No papers
Samuel, Ct., Patience, W1176; BLWt.9472-160-55
Samuel, Cont., Mass., Jemima Blake, former wid., W23638; BLWt.30589-160-55
Samuel, N.J., Mary, W7627
Samuel, N.J., Miriam, R4700
Samuel, N.C., S41619
Sanford, R.I., Hannah, W21266
Selah, Ct., S17471
Selah, Ct. See HEART
Seth, Mass., Molly, W19701
Stephen, Ct., BLWt.2372-100
Stephen, N.J., S2257
Thomas, Ct., S13325
Thomas, Ct., Mary, W17982
Thomas, N.Y., BLWt.7270-100-Pvt. Iss. 8/4/1791 to himself. No papers
Titus, Ct., S13282
William, Lamb's Artillery, N.Y., BLWt.7304-100-Pvt. Iss. 7/13/1790 to Dirck Von Ingen, ass. No papers
William, Pa., Elizabeth, R4695
Zachariah, Cont., N.Y., S15445
HARTCHELL, John, See HARTCHY
HARTCHY, John, Cont., Mass., Catharine, W4980
HARTER, Adam, N.Y., BLWt.7256-100-Pvt. Iss. 1/5/1791. No papers
Adam, N.Y., Elizabeth, W16283
Lawrence Philip, N.Y., R4701

HARTER (continued)
Lewis, Va., S39649
Nicholas, N.Y., S23253
HARTESFIELD, John, See HARTSFIELD
HARTGROVE, Howell, Va., S8678
HARTHORN, James, Pa., S2279
HARTKIE, John, Armand's Corps. BLWt.13156-100-Pvt. Iss. 9/12/1789. No papers
HARTLESS, Peter, Va., S5470
William, Va., S5498
HARTLEY, Daniel, Va., S36571
Laban, N.C., S21269
HARTLINE, Jacob, Cont., enl. in Va., S39640
HARTMAN, Adam/Hans (John) Adam, N.Y., S22811
Adam, Pa., S23687
Christopher, N.J., Mary, W4219
George, Cont., Pvt. in Hazen's Regt., BLWt.242-100. Iss. 4/18/1806. No papers
George, N.J., Elizabeth, W2789
Hans (John) Adam, See Adam
Jacob, Pa., Margaret, W4450
John (Hans) Adam, N.Y. See Adam
John, Pa., S15281
John, Pa., Christina, W7680
Michael, Cont., Md., Elizabeth, W3680
Michael, Md., BLWt.11349-100-Pvt. Iss. 1/8/1796 to Geo. Ponsonby, ass. No papers
Peter, Hazen's Regt., BLWt. 13199-100-Pvt. Iss. 2/22/1791. No papers
Philip, Pa., S9595
HARTNEY, Patrick, ---, Pa. Agcy. & res., S10235
HARTON, Howell, ---, N.C. & Tenn. agencies, O.W.I. File No.20377
HARTSFIELD, John, N.C., Mary, W3985
John, N.C., Peggy, W4482
HARTSHORN, Aaron, Mass., Zeruah, W19694; BLWt.57642-160-55
Andrew, Mass., R4703
Catharine, former wid. of Burrows Norris, N.J., which see
David, Mass., S30455
Hezekiah, Ct., Mary, W19733
Jacob, R.I., Lucy, W15912
James, N.H., Martha Weston, former wid., W14117
Jeremiah, Mass., S29870
Jeremiah, Mass., S30471
Jesse, Mass., S30467
John, Md., Agnes Williams, former wid., W4393; BLWt.2383-200
John, Mass., Catharine, W14867
Joshua, Ct., Huldah, W21279
Oliver, Ct., Hannah, W21256
Silas, Mass., Betsey, W14866
HARTSHORNE, Keziah, former wid. of Ezra Towne, Cont., N.H., which see
Richard, N.J., Catharine, W103
Thomas, Mass., BLWt.920-300-Capt. Iss. 1/29/1790. No papers
HARTSON, Hezekiah, Ct. See HARTSHORN
HARTSTOCK, Valentine, Pa., BLWt.

HARTSTOCK (continued)
9583-100-Pvt. Iss. 6/29/1789 to M. McConnell, ass. No papers
HARTUNG, Christopher, Pa., S22810
HARTWELL, Asael Josiah, Mass., R4704
Benjamin, Mass., Merriel, W23196
Daniel, Cont., Mass., Mehitable, W24393
Edward, Mass., S31087
Ephraim, Mass., S18857
Isaac, Mass., Abihail, W21289; BLWt.9410-160-55
John, Cont., Mass., S44917
Nathan, Mass., Sally, W3803
Oliver, Ct., S44187
Oliver, Mass., S35393
Samuel, Ct., R4705
Samuel, Mass., S10817
Samuel, Mass., Mary, W14841
Solomon, Mass., S13329
Thomas, N.Y., S13301
HARTWICK, Barent/Barnt, N.J., Jane Boyer, former wid., W840; BLWt.9072-160-55
John, Cont., N.Y., Sarah, W21249
John, Lamb's Art., N.Y., BLWt. 7306-100-Drum Major. Iss. 7/20/179- to Hercules Heron, ass. No papers
Lawrence, N.Y., Martha, W25358; BLWt.268-60-55
HARTZELL, Jacob, Pa., Margaret, R14891; BLWt.26040-160-55
HARVEST, John Adams, N.H., S35386
HARVEY, Anna, former wid. of Joseph Stewart, Ct., which see
Archibald, N.H., S38807
Archibald, Pa., Elizabeth, R4708
Barnet, N.H., R4707
Charles, Md., BLWt.11315-100-Pvt. Iss. 11/1/1797 to Elisha Jarrot, ass. No papers
David, Mass., Abigail, W19675; BLWt.24920-160-55
David, N.C., Margaret, R4712
Edward, R.I., BLWt.3229-100-Pvt. Iss. 12/31/1789. No papers
Edward, R.I., S38785
Edward, Va., S41606
Elisha, Cont., N.Y., S32804; BLWt.992-200-Lt. Iss. 3/28/1791. No papers
Ezra, Ct., BLWt.5975-100-Pvt. Iss. 2/5/1790. No papers
George, Pa., BLWt.9543-100-Pvt. Iss. 8/17/1789. No papers
James, N.H., BLWt.3193-100-Pvt. Iss. 4/25/1798 to Daniel Gookin ass. No papers
James, N.H., Sarah, W11215
Joel, S.C., b. Va., R4709
John, Mass., BLWt.4395-100-Pvt. Iss. 3/30/1796 to Peter Swier. No papers
John, Mass., S44190
John, N.H., BLWt.902-200-Lt. Iss. 3/25/1790. No papers
John, N.C., S10830
John, N.C., S16851
John, N.C., Comfort, W249

HARVEY (continued)
John, Pa., S18001
John, Pa., BLWt.9538-100. No papers
John, Va., Nancy, R4714
Jonathan, Ct., S13270
Jonathan, Mass., Welthea, W21253
Joseph, Mass., R.I., Susannah, W17977; BLWt.24922-160-55
Joseph, Va., Lucy, R4711
Kimber, N.H., Mary, W17979
Levi, N.H., R4710
Mary, former wid. of Jonathan Joice/Joyce, Mass., which see
Matthew, Cont., Md., Magdalen, W19681
Matthew, Va., Lee's Legion, BLWt. 13237. Iss. 4/9/1796. No papers
Moses, Mass., N.Y., Abigail, W7683; BLWt.26328-160-55
Nathan, Ct., S13272
Norment/Norman, Va., S38005
Paul, Mass., Hannah, W3545; BLWt. 6283-160-55
Robert, Ct., Asenath, R4706
Samuel, ---, Phila. agcy. Dis. No papers
Silas, R.I., S10778
Thomas, Ct., S13288
Thomas, Mass., R4716
Thomas, Mass., N.H., S44402
Thomas, N.H., BLWt.3180-100-Sgt. Iss. 7/28/1796 to Jeremiah Mason, ass. No papers
Thomas, N.H., BLWt.3197-100-Pvt. Iss. 9/13/1792 to Jonathan Jenks. No papers
Thomas, N.H., S18008
Thomas, Va., S5474
Thomas, Va., Mary/Polly, R4715
Timothy, N.H., S44403
William, Ct., Sea Service, Jane, W4225
William, alleged Capt. of Cont. Line, Rev. War, Rejected No. 247558, Can No. 1776, Bundle No. 15 Claimant & heir of Md.
William, Mass., S29205
William, Mass., Elizabeth Parker former wid., R7944
William, N.Y., BLWt.7257-100-Pvt. Iss. 7/22/1790 to Thomas Tillotson, ass. No papers
William, N.C., S4362
Zadock, Md., S34919
HARVICK, Jacob, N.C., S32298
HARVILLE, William, Va., Oney/Omey/Naoma, R4717
HARVIN, Edward, Md., S18014
HARVY, George, Ct., Mass., R.I. Philena, W1037
Jonathan, Mass., S32806
HARWARD, James, N.C. See HARWOOD
John, N.C. See HARRARD
HARWELL, Andrew, Va., S31104
Lowden, Cont., N.C., S.C., R4718
William, Va. See HARVILLE
HARWICK, Hannah, former wid. of Joseph Passage, N.Y., which see
Jacob, N.C., See HARVICK
HARWOOD, Daniel, Mass., S18431

HARWOOD (continued)
Ebenezer, Mass., S39648
Ezra, Mass., Anne, W24414
Francis, Mass., Lucinda, BLWt. 9478-160-55
Gershom, Cont., Mass., Susannah, W24387
Jacob, Mass., Lydia, W14870
James, N.C., Rachel, W11231; BLWt.39225-160-55
Jesse, Mass., BLWt.4418-100-Pvt. Iss. 2/5/1790. No papers
Jesse, Mass., S37063
John, Cont., N.H., S44405
John, Mass., S32782
John, Navy, R.I. agcy. & res., S38808
Jonathan, Mass., S32810
Marville, Mass., Polly, W13390
Oliver, Mass., Fear, W21248
Osborn S., Md., S8677
Peter, Mass., Betsy, W14851
Thomas, N.J., S39641; BLWt. 861-100
Thomas, Lamb's Art., N.Y., BLWt. 7281-100-Pvt. Iss. 9/15/1790 to John S. Hobart, et al, ass. No papers
HASBROUCK, Benjamin J., N.Y., R4719
Solomon, N.Y., S13243
HASE, David, N.H., S16405
Robert, N.H., S18853
HASELIAK, Jacob, Md. See HAVELY
HASELTINE, James, Mass. See HAZELTINE
John, Mass., N.H., S41603
Jonas, Mass., See HAZELTINE
Joseph, Mass., Martha, W19684; BLWt.19519-160-55
Richard, Mass. See HAZELTINE
Thomas, Cont., Vt. See HAZELTINE
Thomas, Hazen's Regt., BLWt.13166-100-Corp. Iss. 2/13/1790. No papers
William, Mass., N.H., Eunice, W19697
HASELTON, John, N.H. See HAZELTON
William, N.H. See HASELTINE
HASEY, Ebenezer, Mass., S16853
John, Mass., S38803
John, Mass., R4720
William, Mehitable/Hitty Johnson, former wid., Mass., W26800
HASFORD, Daniel, See HOSFORD
HASHFIELD, Henry, Pa., Elizabeth, W1608; BLWt.26932-160-55
HASILTINE, Jonathan, N.H. See HAZLETON
HASKALL, Moses, Mass., Susannah, W749
HASKEL, Nathaniel, Mass. See HASKILL
HASKELL, Benjamin, Cont., Mass., S32807
Benjamin, Mass., Sarah, W13400
Benjamin, Mass., Sarah, W23206
Caleb, Mass., Ednah, W19676
Charles, Mass., S38817
Comfort, R.I. See HASKILL
David, Ct. & Cont., Mass., N.H. Mary, W7650; BLWt.16110-160-55

HASKELL (continued)
Ebenezer, Mass., R4721
Elnathan, Cont., Mass., U.S.A. in 1787, Charlotte, W21254; BLWt.914-300-Capt. Iss. 1/29/1790. No papers
Henry, Mass., BLWt.972-450-Lt. Col. Iss. 6/7/1793. Also recorded under BLWt.2634. No papers
Jacob, Ct., Diantha, W21298
Job, Mass., S10777
Job, Mass., N.H., S18866
John, Ct., S21809
John, Mass., S44191
John, Mass., Mary, W24397
Jonathan, Mass., BLWt.929-200-Lt. Iss. 4/20/1790. No papers
Joseph, Mass., S29869
Josiah, Mass., S44193
Josiah, Mass., Rebekeh/Rebecca, W652; BLWt.26179-160-55
Josiah, Mass., Abigail, W9051
Moses, Mass. See HASKALL
Moses, Mass., Hannah, W24382
Noah, Mass., Sarah, R4723
Philip, Cont., Mass., S29872
Prince, Mass., Leah, W7651
Roger, Mass., Mary, W14853
Samuel, Cont., Mass., S13253
Samuel, R.I., S6322
Simeon, Cont., Mass., Sally, W422; BLWt.34284-160-55
Solomon, Mass., S31112
Stephen, Ct., Mass., S29859
Stephen, Mass., Rebecca, W23177
Ward, Mass., Sarah, W23214
William, Mass., S15876
William, Mass., S35394
Zebulon, Mass., Susannah, W23181; BLWt.5377-160-55
HASKET, John, N.C., S4317
HASKEW, John, S.C., S9350
HASKILL, Comfort, R.I., Lepha, W21261; BLWt.26664-160-55
Josiah, Mass., See HASKELL
Moses, Cont., Mass., S41610
Nathaniel, Mass., S23252
HASKIN, Abraham, Ct., Mass., S44923
Asahel, Mass., S34914
Enoch, Mass., S28758
Isaac H., Mass., R4724
HASKINS, Aaron, Va., S18437
Abner, Mass., Joanna, W24415
Benjamin, Ct., Mass., Mary, R21635; BLWt.31697-160-55
Eli, Mass., R.I., Rhoda, W23239; BLWt.29045-160-55
Elijah, Mass., S30464
Enoch, Mass., See HASKIN
Henry, Mass., S29211
Jacob, Mass., Mercy, W21276
Jacob, Mass., Mary, W23171
James, N.C., Ann, W19732
John, Pa., BLWt.9574-100-Pvt. Iss. 12/16/1793 to Casper Iserloan, ass. No papers
Joshua, Cont., Mass., S30456
Lemuel, N.Y., S31725
Nathan, Mass., See HOSKINS
Nathaniel, Mass., Hopestill,W17046

HASKINS (continued)
Preserved, Mass., R.I., See HOSKINS
Richard, Vt., S22288
William, Mass., Joanna Eddy, former wid., W14674
William, Mass., Susanna, W21240
HASLET, Kenley, Del., See Kinlar HAZELET
Robert, Pa., S39661
Samuel, Pa., Nancy, W4377; BLWt. 33730-160-55
HASLETINE, Jonas, Mass., See HAZELTINE
HASLIP, Richard B., Md., BLWt. 11296-100-Pvt. Iss. 3/11/1791. No papers
HASS, Henry, N.J., See HAAS
Ludwick, Pa., BLWt.9561-100-Pvt. Iss. 7/17/1794 to Robert Ross, ass. No papers
Robert, N.Y., Eleanor, W23204
HASSELL, Benjamin, N.C., Mary, R4728
Joseph, N.C., S41602
HASSELTINE, John, Mass., Rebecca, W19666
HASSELTON, David, See HESSELTINE
HASTIN, Absalom, Va., Martha, W962
William, Va., Amey, W3986
HASTINGS, Abijah, Cont., Mass., S32803
Amos, Mass., Elizabeth/Betsey, R4729
Benjamin, Mass., S15435
Charles, Cont., Mass., S5425
David, Mass., S29856
Elihu, Mass., S28757
Eliphalet, Mass., S32788
James, N.H., Sarah, W16159
John, Cont., Mass., S32792; BLWt. 919-300-Capt. Iss. 8/6/1792. No papers
John, Mass., S32809
John, Mass., R.I., S18432
John, Pa., BLWt.9591-100-Pvt. Iss. 6/24/1793 to Francis Kirkpatrick, ass. No papers
John, Pa., S34384
Jonas, Mass., S19694
Jonas, Mass., S31101
Jonathan, Mass., Nancy, W21278
Josiah, Mass., R4731
Levi, Mass., Phebe, W21280
Moses, Mass., S21796
Moses, Mass., Rebecca, R4732
Nevenson, Mass., Lucretia, W19750
Oliver, Mass., S13266
Oliver, Mass., Dorothy, W23197
Robert, Del., S38800
Samuel, Mass., S30460
Sylvanus/Salvenus, N.H., Elizabeth, W17992
Thaddeus, N.H., R4733
Theophilus, Mass., Betsey, W14863
Timothy, Mass., BLWt.4316-100-Pvt. Iss. 8/8/1793 to Samuel Tinney. No papers
Timothy, Mass., Hannah, R4730
Walter, Mass., BLWt.936-400-Surgn. Iss. 3/20/1800. No papers
William, N.H., Dis. No papers

HASTINGS (continued)
Zachariah, Va., S6975
Zacheus, Mass., Mary, W23227
HASTY, Archibald, Del., S31116
Clement, Va., S38003
David, Mass., Susanna, W23220
James, Va., Christian, W1174; BLWt.26904-160-55
John, Va., Rebecca, W8919
Samuel, Mass., N.H., S32290
William, Cont., Mass., S17993
HASZARD, Thomas, Mass., S29213
HATCH, Abiel, Cont., Mass., S13256
Adrian, N.H., Vt., Sally, W24394
Alexander, N.C., Va., S8648
Anthony Eames, Mass., Bethiah, W13379
Asa, Ct., N.H., Ruthamah, W752; BLWt.26958-160-55
Asa, Mass., Jane, W24392
Asa, N.H., R4735
Benjamin, N.Y., S5473
Caleb, Mass., Sally, W756; BLWt. 16109-160-55
Dan, Ct., Lucy Northrup, former wid., W19922
David, Mass., S20383
Ebenezer, Mass., Dimis/Dimmis, W15681
Ebenezer, N.Y., R4736
Ede, Ct., S44918
Eliakim, Mass., S35388
Elihu, Mass., S31113
Elijah, Mass., S35392
Estes, Navy (Land service?), Vt. agcy. & res., S39656
Ezekiel, Mass., S18859
Gideon, Mass., Ann, W23198
Gilbert, Ct., Martha, W225; BLWt.9521-160-55
Harris, Mass., Deborah, W19752
Heman, Ct., S34393
Ichabod, Cont., Ct., S38813
Isaac, Ct., Polly, W17993; BLWt.26194-160-55
Jeremiah, Mass., S18007; BLWt. 1394-100
John, Ct., S13250
Joseph, Ct., S37057
Joseph, Mass., BLWt.4412-100-Pvt. Iss. 12/12/1797 to Iobod Hatch (probably Ichabod Hatch) No papers
Joseph, Mass., S33273
Josiah, Ct., S5437
Josiah, Mass., Martha, W14874; BLWt.11194-160-55
Josiah, N.H., Molly, W24389
Lewis, Mass., S29198
Luther, Navy, Mass., S29204
Mary, former wid. of Thomas Murray, Mass., which see
Mason, N.H., Vt., Mittee, R4738
Micah, Mass., S39635
Moses, Ct., BLWt.5963-100-Pvt. Iss. 11/5/1795. No papers
Moses, Ct., Cont., Abigail, W25745
Moses, Mass., BLWt.16147-160-55
Nathan, Ct., N.H., S13278
Nathan, Mass., S21798
Oliver, Ct., Cont., N.Y., Phebe, W21137

HATCH (continued)
Phillips, Mass., S18858
Prince, Mass., Navy, S13275
Prince, Mass. Sea Service, S17994
Samuel, Cont., S35391
Samuel, Mass., S29199
Samuel, N.Y., Elizabeth, R4737
Samuel, R.I., Phebe, W755; BLWt. 5004-160-55
Seth, Mass., S30473
Shubel/Shubael, Mass., S33286
Silence, former wid. of Sylvanus Raymond, Mass., which see
Silvanus/Sylvanus, Mass., S29216
Simeon, Mass., Jemima, W23216
Thomas, N.H., S10798
Timothy, Ct., S13296
Timothy, Cont., Ct., Lucinda, W2109
Timothy, Mass., S18438
Walter, Mass., S29860
William, Ct., Mass., S13237
Zaccheus/Zachariah, Mass., Mary, W7674
Zachariah, Mass. See Zaccheus
HATCHER, Benjamin, S.C., Lucy, W21275
Daniel, Va., Mary, W7675
Henry, Va., S13326
John, Va., Nancy, W7677
Samuel, Va., S13324
Seth, Va., S5479
Timothy, N.C., R4739
William, S.C., S31727
William, Va., BLWt.12192-100-Pvt. Iss. 7/6/1793 to Robert Means, ass. No papers
William, Va., S41622
HATCHETT, Edward, Va., S13310
HATCHMAN, John, Pa., S33278
HATFIELD, Aaron, N.J., S13245
Elias, N.J., Ann, W4694
Joseph, Va., Rachel, W5; BLWt. 26158-160-55
Mason, Mass., Azubah, W25750; BLWt.5106-160-55
Peter, N.Y., R4740
Richard, N.Y., Mary, W16597
HATHAWAY, Abial, Mass. See HATHEWAY
Abner, Mass., S44185
Abraham, Mass., S17457
Alfred, Vt., Rebecca, R4747
Arthur, Mass., S33291
Arthur, Mass., Esther, W21291
Benoni, N.J., S538
Ebenezer, Ct., S23675
Eleazer, Mass., Anna, W13399
Elisha, R.I., Susannah, W27422; BLWt.26692-160-55
Ephraim, Mass., S16864
Erastus, Vt. See HATHEWAY
Guilford, Ct., S13287
Isaac, Mass., Elizabeth, R4743
Jabez, Mass., Navy, Hannah, W1175; BLWt.31468-160-55
James, R.I., Mary, W1858; BLWt. 12722-160-55
Jeremiah, R.I., S29864
Job (colored), Mass., BLWt. 1931-100
Joel, Mass. See HATHEWAY

HATHAWAY (continued)
John, Mass. Sea Service, S29853
John, Va., R4745
Joseph, Mass., Sarah, W19754; BLWt.31469-160-55
Joshua, Vt. & War of 1812-N.Y., Mary, W8216; BLWts.3869-40-50 & 61547-120-55
Josiah, Mass., Tryphena, W14879
Levi, Mass., See HATHWAY
Nathan, Mass., S9348
Peleg, Mass., Mercy, R4746
Peter, Mass., Betsey, W14865
Philip, Mass., S31088
Richard, Pa., Abigail, W3137
Robert, R.I., S8692
Samuel, Mass., Sarah, R4748
Seth, Mass., Tryphena, W15680
Shadrack, N.J., Martha, BLWt. 154-100
Shadrack, Vt., Jael, W19720
Silas, Mass., Navy, R.I., Charlotte, W21294; BLWt.9529-160-55
Theophilus, N.J. See HATHEWAY
Thomas, Mass., S44904
Timothy, Mass., S29854
HATHCOCK, Holiday, N.C. See HETHCOCK
HATHERLY, Thomas, Mass., S33289
HATHEWAY, Abial, Mass. Sea Service, R4742
Arthur, Mass. See HATHAWAY
Erastus, Vt., Anna, W19741
Joel, Mass., S31086
John, Ct., Cont., Mass., N.Y., S13271
Theophilus, N.J., S34385
HATHORN, Nathaniel, Mass., S31099
Silas, Mass., Lucy, R4749
William, Pa., S38004
HATHPENNY, John, Cont., N.H., S35387; BLWt.633-100
HATHWAY, Levi, Mass., S19972
Zenas/Zenus, Ct., S44905; BLWt. 5923-100-Pvt. Iss. 7/24/1789 No papers
HATLER, Michael, Va., S31117
HATMAKER, Malachi, N.C., Mary, R4750
HATTER, John, Pa., S9570
HATTON, Basil, Ga., Md., S8665
Henry, Va., Hannah, R4751
Reuben, Va., S17466
William, Cont., S36577
HATZ, John, Pa., S22285
HAUCK, George M., Md., S18012
Nicholas, N.C. See HOUK
HAUGE, Christian, Pa., BLWt. 9565-100-Pvt. Iss. 3/12/1792 to Moses Sill, ass. No papers
HAUGHAWOUT, Lifferd, N.J., Hannah, R4752
HAUGHT, Peter, Va., Sarah, S6981; BLWt.71143-160-55
HAUGHTON, Lebbeus, Ct., S37094
HAUKINS, James, Va. See HANKINS
HAULEY, Nathan, Ct. See HAWLEY
HAUPT, John Matthias, Cont., Mass., Catharine, W3806; BLWt.869-100
Philip, Pa., Margaret, R5205

HAUSE, Leonard, Pa., S39638
HAUSER, Henry, Pa., Christena, R4753; BLWt.45668-160-55
Jacob, N.Y., R4754
Ludwig, Pa. See Ludwick HOUSER
HAUSMAN, Conrad, Pa., BLWt.9575-100-Pvt. Iss. 1/31/1800 to Mary Hausman, heir. No papers
Paul/Poal, N.Y. & Pa., R20378
HAUTZ, Baltzer, Pa., S2619
HAUVER, Andrew, N.Y., R4755
HAVELASH, Michael, N.Y., BLWt. 7217-100-Pvt. Iss. 8/27/1790 to Nicholas Fish, ass. No papers
HAVELY, Jacob, Cont., enl. in Md., Elizabeth, W8902
HAVEN, Elias, Mass., BLWt.925-100
John, Mass., BLWt.4329-100-Pvt. Iss. 12/13/1796. No papers
John, Mass., Abigail, W21274
Silas, Mass., BLWt.4313-100-Pvt. Iss. 1/27/1797 to James Millan No papers
William, see claim of soldier's wid., Lucy, who was pensioned as former wid. of John Shepard, Mass.
HAVENS, Cornelius, Ct., S37093
Daniel, Vt., S19324
James, Mass., S38812; BLWt.92-100
John, Ct., Mary, W25760; BLWt. 11258-160-55
John, R.I., Elizabeth, W7694; BLWt.26198-160-55
Joseph, N.Y., BLWt.7261-100-Pvt. Iss. 7/30/1790 to John W. Wendell, ass. No papers
Joseph, N.Y., Martha, W19719
Joseph, Vt., R4757
Nathaniel, Mass., S10795
Peleg, Ct., R.I., S9349
Peter, N.Y., BLWt.7235-100-Pvt. Iss. 3/29/1791 to James Roose-Velt, ass. No papers
Peter, N.Y., S34915
Robert, Green Mt. Boys, R.I., Vt., S21800
Samuel, Vt., Olive, W21259
William, N.Y., BLWt.7233-100-Pvt. Iss. 3/29/1791 to James Roosevelt, ass. No papers
William, N.Y., Theodosia, R4758
HAVEY, Daniel, Vt. See HOVEY
HAVILAND, Isaac, N.Y., R4759
John, N.Y., S10799
HAVLICH, Melhoir, See Melchoir HEFFLISH
HAWA, Nicholas, See HAWWAWAS
HAWBEARD, Thomas, See HAWSBEARD
HAWE, William, Md., S38795
HAWES, Abijah, Mass., S29871
Asa, Mass., BLWt.4371-100-Pvt. Iss. 6/29/1792 to Stephen Thorn. No papers
Benjamin, Ct. See HAWS
Christopher, Pa., BLWt.9598-100-Pvt. Iss. 12/22/1794 to Henry Purdy, ass. No papers
David, Mass., Hannah, W7655; BLWt.15445-160-55
Elijah, Mass., S13265

HAWES (continued)
Ezekiel, N.C., Bethany, R4760
George, Mass., Nancy, W659; BLWt.10020-160-55
Jason, Mass., Molly, W24421
Joel, Mass., S5436
John, Mass., S5429
Jonathan, Mass., S36013
Joseph, Mass., S30468
Joseph, Mass., S35396
Matthias, Mass., Sarah, W23223
Pelatiah, Mass., BLWt.4369-100-Pvt. Iss. 4/2/1792. No papers
Pelatiah, Mass., S33285
Robert, Mass., S33290
Samuel, Ct., Jemima, W24411
Samuel, Va., BLWt.1066-450-Lt. Col. Iss. 7/5/1799 to Elizabeth Buckner, late Hawes, Mary Buckner, late Hawes, Charlotte Buckner, late Hawes, Elliott Hawes, Richard Hawes, & Walker Hawes, only surviving heirs of of S.H. No papers. Located in U.S. Military Dist. of Ohio. (Not near Dayton). Reported by telephone from Gen. Land Office June 1940. MHF
Thomas, Mass., Navy, S18867
Thomas, Va., Susannah, W1766
Zenas, Ct. See HOWES
HAWGERDON, John, N.Y., Dis. No papers
HAWK, Isaac, Va., S9571
Jacob, Md., Va., Peggy/Margaret, W362; BLWt.36738-160-55
James, Pa., Va., S2278
HAWKE, Michael, Md., BLWt.11354-100-Pvt. Iss. 2/7/1790. No papers
HAWKENBERRY, John, N.J., S39633
HAWKES, Jotham, N.Y. See HAWKS
Thomas, Va. See HAWKS
HAWKEY, Henry, N.Y., BLWt.7212-100-Pvt. Iss. 4/29/1793 to Wm. Hawkey, admr. No papers
HAWKINS, Abraham, Vt., S13235
Amaziah, Ct., S23254
Bartlett, Cont., Va. See Bartlett H. FITZGERALD
Benjamin, Cont., Va., See Benj. Hawkins FITZGERALD
Benjamin, R.I., S21263
Benoni, R.I., S38802
Catharine, former wid. of Wm. Steelman, N.C., which see
Christopher, N.Y., S10802
Darius, R.I., S21801
David, Ct., Sea Service, R.I., Sarah, W21264
David, N.Y., S22815
David, N.Y., Sarah, W19709
Ebenezer, Ct., S29208
Elisha, Va., S31103
Ephraim, N.C., Ann, W3987; BLWt.13903-160-55
George, Va., See HANKINS
Giles, Va., S1211
Henry, Md., BLWt.1057-200-Lt. No papers
Hezebiah, R.I., BLWt.3221-100-Pvt. Iss. 5/28/1792. No papers
Isaac, Ct., Anna, W17987

HAWKINS (continued)
Isaac, N.Y., Elizabeth, R4761
James, Ct., N.Y., Nancy, W19746
James, Cont., Va., S37991
James, N.Y., S16846
James, Va., Jane, W8886
Jeremiah, Pa., Nancy, W8885; BLWt.51753-160-55
Job, Ct., Hannah, W19714
John, N.C., S16857
John, R.I., Sea Service, Nancy Mann/Man, former wid., W21753; BLWt.27570-160-55
John, Va., S5451
John H., Hazen's Regt., BLWt. 13198-100-Sgt. Maj. Iss. 7/2/1790. No papers
Joseph, Ct., BLWt.5978-100-Pvt. Iss. 8/23/1790. No papers
Joseph, Ct., Vt., S23689
Joseph, Mass., Navy, Abigail, R7760
Joseph, N.C., S4322
Joseph, R.I., S10801
Joshua, Va., Susan, W9055
Laban, Va., Catharine, W7659
Moses, Ct., S23683
Moses, Va., BLWt.1449-300; BLWt. 1847-300
Nathan, Va., S30457
Philemon, N.C., S6957
Phillip/Philip, Md., S41612
Reuben, Va., Rebecca, W8887
Rodolphus, Ct., Tryphena, W11230
Samuel, Ct., Hannah, W13387
Samuel/Samuel B., Mass., Pharaba, W1604
Samuel, N.Y., S24201
Stephen, N.Y., Mary, W19700
Stephen, R.I., S21262
Thomas, N.Y., Nancy, W2792
Thomas, S.C., S10796
Thomas, Va., S4310
Uriah, R.I., S32289
William, Ct., BLWt.5898-100-Sgt. Iss. 6/30/1790 to James Davenport. No papers
William, Ct., N.Y., S44900
William, Mass., BLWt.4338-100-Pvt. Iss. 8/22/1789. No papers
William, R.I., S21264
William, Va., S6960
Zachariah, N.J., S656
Zachariah, N.Y., S44901
Zopher, N.Y., S46261
HAWKINSBURY, John, See HAWKENBERRY
HAWKLEY, James, N.H., BLWt.3176-100-Pvt. Iss. 3/25/1790. No papers
James, N.H., Betsey, W21271; BLWt.5008-160-55
HAWKS, Ephraim, Mass., Elizabeth, R4766
Frederick, Va., S31734
Henry, Mass., Dis. No papers
Jotham, N.Y., Mary, W25756; BLWt.9441-160-55
Phebe, Mass. see John WINTER
Reuben, Mass., Silence, R4768
Thomas, Va., Margaret, W7658
William, Ct., R4769
William, Mass., Sarah, W11224
HAWLEY, Abel, Ct., S9346

HAWLEY (continued)
Abel, Ct., Sarah, W11245; BLWt. 26992-160-55
Abraham, Ct., BLWt.5940-100-Sgt. Iss. 3/15/1790. No papers
Abraham, Ct., S28753
Chapman, N.Y., Vt., S29209
Daniel, Cont., Ct., S6970
Ebenezer, Ct., Lucy, W1760; BLWt.26511-160-55
Ebenezer Rice, Ct., Cont., S9572
Edmund, N.Y., Lucy, W17981
Elijah, Ct., S16847
Elisha, Ct., Charity, W11251; BLWt.26508-160-55
Francis, Va., Sarah, W163
Gad, Ct., S10805
Gideon, Sheldon's Cavalry, Ct., BLWt.973-200-Lt. Iss. 1/18/1791 to Sam Penfield, admr. No papers
Henry, N.J., S13241
Hezekiah, Ct., BLWt.5945-100-Pvt. Iss. 4/27/1792 to Zalmon Sanford. No papers
Hezekiah, Ct., Anne, W17989
Israel, Ct., S17470
James, Ct., Martha, W19705
Joseph, Ct., S19686
Joseph C., Mass., See HOLLY
Joseph C., Ct., S44906
Liverius, Ct., Anne, W19715
Nathan, Ct., BLWt.5959-100-Corp. Iss. 3/15/1790. No papers
Nathan, Ct., S20779
Nathan, Ct., Ruamy, W7656
Nero, Ct., S20784
Ozias, Ct., Sarah, W4484
Peter, Va., S13328
Philo, Cont., Vt., Green Mt. Boys, R4770; BLWt.45670-160-55
Robert, Ct., Mary Elizabeth, W17984
Salmon, Ct. See Solomon
Samuel, Ct. Sea Service & Mass., & boat service on Lake Champlain, Lucy, W21295
Samuel, Mass., S34916
Seth, Ct., S33277
Solomon/Salmon, Ct., R4771
Theodosia, former wid. of Hooker Low, Mass., which see
Thomas, Ct., Mary, W7657; BLWt. 26652-160-55
Thomas, Ct., Keziah, W25761
Zadok/Zadock, Ct., S44907
HAWLY, Rawleigh, See HOLLEY
HAWMAN, Peter, Md., Elizabeth, W9474
HAWN, Henry, Pa. See HORN
HAWS, Benjamin, Ct., Mass., Sarah, W24410
HAWSBEARD, Thomas, Pa., S41609
HAWSEY, John, Cont., Mass., R4773
HAWSON, Thomas, Md., BLWt.11291-100-Pvt. Iss. 1/11/1796 to Joshua Ward, ass. No papers
HAWSY, John, See HAWSEY
HAWTHORN, John, N.C., R4775
John, S.C., b. Ireland, S31097
Joseph, S.C., Frances, R4774
Robert, S.C., b. Ireland, Mary,

HAWTHORN (continued)
W23326. Her former husb., Robert McClary, also served. See papers within
HAWWAWAS, Nicholas (Indian), Mass., S17997. He was also called Nicholas Hawa, Nicholas Ovas, Joseph Nicholas, Joseph Nicholas Hawwawas, Capt. Nichols, Nicholas Howwahwas. These names may also refer to his father.
HAY, Abram, N.C., Susannah Bachelor former wid., W17262
Alexander, N.Y., S10792
Conrad, N.Y., R4791
Daniel, Mass., S33274
David, N.J., Margaret, W7632
Isaac, N.C., R4779
Joseph, Va., R14714; Va. Half Pay, N.A. Acc. No. 874-050087. Half Pay. Joseph Hay
Priscilla, former wid. of James Sheppard, Va., which see
Samuel, Pa., Jane, W23233; BLWt. 1008-450-Lt. Col. Iss. 11/4/1789. No papers
Samuel, Pa., Elizabeth, R4778
Thomas, Va., S31096
Udney, Cont., N.Y. res. of heirs in 1827; BLWt.1258-450
William, Cont., Mass., Betsy, W19753
William, N.C., S8670
William, R.I., BLWt.144-100. Iss. 2/28/1804 to Israel Angell. No papers
HAYARD, Jacob, Mass., S13436
HAYCOCK, Daniel, N.J., S35999
John, N.Y., BLWt.7263-100-Pvt. Iss. 7/16/1790 to Daniel Shew, ass. No papers
HAYCRAFT, Samuel, Va., Margaret, W8904
HAYDEN, Abel, Mass. Sea Service, Lydia, W24380
Allyn, Ct. See HEYDON
Asa, Mass., Anna, W2733; BLWt. 15161-160-55
Benjamin, Va. See HAYDON
Charles, Ct., Cont., Molly, W23243
Daniel, Ct., Zerviah, W21262
Daniel, Mass., S33293
Daniel, Mass., S44922
David, Mass., S29862
Delight, former wid. of Elisha Litchfield, Mass., which see
Ebenezer, Mass., Sally Reupke/Rupkee, former wid., W5757; BLWt.11263-160-55
Ebenezer, Mass., Anna, W13357
Ezra, Ct., Olive, R4781
Ezra, Mass., S33284
Jacob, Ct., S43654
Jacob, Mass., S33281
James, R.I., BLWts.3214 & 14156-100-Pvt. Iss. 2/24/1800 to John Tarp, Guardian of Phebe Hayden, in trust for her as heir
Jeremiah, N.J., Sarah, W854
Jeremiah, Va., See HADEN
Jesse, Mass., S13300

HAYDEN (continued)
Joel, Mass., Jemima, W14864
John, N.J. See HAYDON
Jonathan, Mass., Lydia, W23234; BLWt.7307-160-55
Josiah, Cont., Mass., S35384
Levi, Mass., S33276
Lewis, Mass., S33283
Moses, Cont., Mass., S33288
Nathaniel,Cont.,Mass.,Sea Service Mary, W1275; BLWt.8164-160-55
Samuel, Ct., S16144
Samuel, Mass., R4782
Silas, Cont., Mass., S43655
William, Cont., Mass., Elizabeth, W24390
William, Mass., S29867
William, Mass., Deborah Wild, former wid., W15490
Ziba, Mass., S30475
HAYDON, Benjamin, Va., S37972
James, Va., S30466
Jeremiah, Va., See HADEN
John, N.J., Mary, W1861; BLWt. 26095-160-55
John, Va., S37993
Peleg, Mass., BLWt.4382-100-Sgt. Iss. 12/3/1789 to Moses W. Barker. No papers
HAYES, Aaron, N.H., Phebe, W25742
Abraham, N.Y., S22816
Amos, Ct., S10810
Amos M., N.H., Privateer, S20381
Benjamin, Ct.,BLWt.5916-100-Pvt. Iss. 11/2/1791 to John Heaton
Benjamin, Ct., Alathea, W21285
Benjamin, Ct., Hannah. See case of her former husb., Timothy Fuller, Ct.
Dudley, Ct., Beda, W17975; BLWt.3815-160-55
Elijah, Ct., S13280
Enoch, Ct., Louisa, W11252; BLWt.28577-160-55
Enoch, N.H., S8688
George, N.C., S1668
George S., N.H., S16407
Henry, Va., S30455; BLWt.36607-160-55
Henry, Va., Mary, W14
Hezekiah, Ct., S37055
James, Cont., Pa., R4785
James, Mass., S10780
James, Navy, Mass., S33287
Jesse, Ct., N.Y., S15168
Joanna, former wid. of Elisha Thomas, N.H., which see
John, N.Y., also after 1790 under St. Clair, Olive, W23179
John, N.C., S21268
John, S.C., Mary, W21245; BLWt. 24166-160-55
John, Va., BLWt.12199-100-Pvt. Iss. 12/13/1791 to Francis Graves, ass. No papers
John Hawkins, Md. See HAYS
Jonathan, Cont., Mass., Hannah, W19685
Joseph, Ct., Cont., Privateer, S13327
Levi, Ct., S4328
Nathaniel, Cont., N.H., S44400

HAYES (continued)
Nathaniel, N.Y., S10820
Obadiah, Ct., Ahinoanna/Ahinoam, W17973
Oliver, Ct. See HAYS
Richard, N.H., Lydia, W23249
Robert, N.J., Eunice, W269
Samuel, Ct., Eunice, R4784
Seth, Ct., Cont., Mass., Mehetable, W23207
Solomon, N.H., Lois, W23192
Thomas, N.H., S22287
Thomas, N.C., S41600
Thomas, Va., Judith Langdon, former wid., W20375 & Va. Half Pay, N.A. Acc. 874-050084
William Cont., N.H., S44401
William, Va., BLWt.12226-100-Pvt. Iss. 5/8/1794. No papers
Zebedee, Mass., R.I., S9915
Zenas, Ct., See HAYS
HAYFORD, Daniel, Mass., Molly, W24385
Ira, Ct., Sarah Wheeler, W660; BLWt.31569-160-55
Nathaniel, Cont., Mass., Philena, W7676; BLWt.8158-160-55
William, Mass., S29215
HAYGOOD, Benjamin, N.C. See HAGOOD
William, N.C., S4314
HAYLES, Chapman, N.C., S2595
HAYLEY, Daniel, Va., S38007
HAYMAN, Henry, Ga., R4798
HAYMOND, Edward, Pa., Va., S38009
HAYNE, Henry, Md., Sarah, R14892
HAYNES, Aaron, Cont., Mass., S30448
Aaron, Cont., Mass., BLWt.1731-300-Iss. 4/29/1831. Also BLWt. 944-300-Capt. Iss. 3/5/1793 to Matthias Mossman, admr. No papers
Aaron, Mass., BLWt.4383-100-Sgt. Iss. 2/27/1790 to Theodosius Fowler. No papers
Abel, Mass., Abigail, W23205
Alexander, N.C., S1519
Benjamin, N.Y. See HAINS
Christian, N.Y., R20139
Christopher, N.C., Frances, W4227
David, Pa., S8652
Elisha, N.H., S16854
Ephraim, Mass., S35383
George, Cont., Va., S38791
James, Mass., S33280
James, Mass., S35399
James, Va., S1910
James, Va., Sally/Sarah, W2938
John, N.Y., See HAYNS
John, N.C., Margaret, W27
John, Va., S5460
Jonas, Cont., Mass., S18852
Jonathan, Ct., BLWt.5970-100-Pvt. Iss. 2/5/1790. No papers
Jonathan, Vt., Dis. No papers
Joshua, Mass., Dis. No papers
Margere, former wid. of Lovell/Lovewell Hurd, Ct., which see
Mathias, Mass., Mary, W23169
Perley, Mass., S35385

HAYNES (continued)
Reuben, Mass., S30474
Richard, Va., S32307
Thomas, N.Y., BLWt.7279-100-Pvt. Iss. 8/12/1790 to Cornelius Glenn, ass. No papers
William, Va., BLWt.12184-100-Pvt. Iss. 7/6/1793 to Francis Graves, ass. Also recorded under BLWt. 13975
HAYNIE, Ezekiel, Md., BLWt.743-400
William, N.C., Ann, W7693
William, Va., S37987
HAYNS, John, N.Y., Hannah, W17044
Joseph, N.C., S1954
HAYS, Aaron, Ct., S9345
Archibald, Pa., BLWt.9625-100-Pvt. Iss. 5/6/1793 to Joseph Henszey, admr. No papers
Asa, Ct., S37060
Asa, "in the Invalids", BLWt. 13213-100-Pvt. Iss. 9/1/1790 to Theodosius Fowler, ass. No papers
Benajah, Ct., Cont., S9565
Benjamin, Ct., Hannah, see case of widow's former husb., Timothy Fuller, Ct.
Benjamin, Ct., See HAYES
Benjamin, N.Y., R4790
David, N.J., Pa., S2268
David, N.C., S6949
Dudley, Ct., See HAYES
Edmund, S.C., Martha, W7634; BLWt.29749-160-55
Ezekiel, Ct., S31724
George, Pa., Sarah, W2937
George, S.C., Sarah, W7635
Henry, Va. See HAYES
Henry, Va.(?), See HAYES
Israel, Mass., S15874
James, Pa., Sea Service, S23681
James, S.C., R4787
John, N.J., Elizabeth, W7633
John, N.Y., See HAYES
John, N.C., Mary, R4794
John, N.C., Va., S16408
John, Pa., S31093
John, S.C., See HAYES
John, S.C., Martha, R4793
John, Va., Mary/Polly, W1272; BLWt.14982-160-55
John, Va., BLWt.1068-400-Major Iss. 8/24/1789. No papers
John, Md., Teresa, W2544; BLWt. 24333-160-55
Jonathan, Cont., Mass. See HAYES
Joseph, N.J., S9566
Joshua, N.C., R4792
Michael, N.J., BLWts.8369 & 13635-100-Pvt. Iss. 5/24/1797. No papers.
Moses, N.J., R4794 & R4795
Obadiah, Ct., See HAYES
Oliver, Ct., S2262
Pliney/Pliny, Mass., Ann, R14702
Robert, N.C., S38792; BLWt.1098-200-Lt. Iss. 2/12/1795. No papers
Samuel, Md., R4788
Seth, Ct., See HAYES
Stephen, N.J., S1013

HAYS (continued)
Thomas, Md., S31110
Thomas, N.Y., BLWt.7308-100-Pvt. Iss. 3/30/1791 to Richard Edwards, Admr. No papers
Thomas, Va. See HAYES
William, N.J., S655
William, N.C., S37973
William, Pa., BLWt.389-100
William, Va., S38797
William, Va., Elizabeth, R4783
Zenas, Ct., Sarah, W25752; BLWt.71154-160-55
HAYSE, David, N.H. See HASE
John, Va. See HAYS
HAYSLET, Thomas, Va., S38010
HAYT, Stephen, Ct., Hannah, W16290
Stephen, Mass. See HAIT
HAYWARD, Barzilla, Mass., BLWt. 4379-100-Pvt. Iss. 4/1/1790. No papers
Benjamin, Cont., Mass. See HEYWOOD
Benjamin, Mass., Hannah Williams, former wid., W19649
Daniel, Mass., Mary, W24383
David, Mass., See HOWARD
Ebenezer, Ct., S13248
Edmund, Mass., Susanna, W23180
Ephraim, N.J., BLWt.8391-100. Iss. 6/2/1797 to Abraham, ass.
Ephraim, N.J., Deborah, W2613; BLWt.230-60-55
Isaiah, Mass., S35395
Jacob, Vt. See HAYWOOD
James, Mass., S30469
James, Mass., S44912
John, Mass., Anna, W1274; BLWt. 14666-160-55
Joshua, Mass., S32802
Joshua, N.H. See HOWARD
Lemuel, Cont., Mass., Sally, W3543
Levi, Mass., S16141
Nathaniel, Mass., S18429
Samuel, Ct., Sarah, W29934; BLWt. 29061-160-55. His dau. Jerusha H. Brown was pensioned under Spec. Act for her father's Rev. War services, dropped from said roll, and then pensioned under Spec. Act for the Civil War service of husb., Edward M. Brown, Lt. Col., 8th Vt. Vol. Inf. All papers relating to Civil War pension are in the admitted files under Wid's Ctf.608657. She had not been reported dead on 9/10/1910.
Samuel, Mass., Bethial/Bethiah, W19745
Seth, Mass., S29868
Simeon, Ct., Hannah, W14882
Simeon, Mass., S23677
Simeon, Mass., Hepsibah, W21290
Simeon, N.J., Sarah, R4800
Solomon, Cont., Mass., S21266
Solomon, Mass., S41628
Stephen, Mass., S13294
Stephen, Mass., Ruth, W23185
Waldo, Mass., S5443
William, Mass., Nancy, R4801

HAYWARD (continued)
Ziba, Mass., S13336
HAYWOOD, Benjamin, Cont., Mass., See HEYWOOD
Eleazer, N.H., Tobitha, W16026
Jacob, Vt., Esther, W21273; BLWt.26786-160-55
Jesse, Mass., Sarah, W18489
John, Mass., See HEYWOOD
Josiah, Mass., Margaret, W654; BLWt.24907-160-55
Lemuel, Mass., S29878
Paul, Mass., Amity, W24422
Samuel, Mass., S29874
William, Mass., BLWt.4397-100-Sgt. Iss. 5/31/1790 to Theodosius Fowler, ass. No papers
William, N.H., Dorety, W16123
HAYWORD, Daniel, Mass. See HAYWARD
HAZARD, Charles, N.J., S34390
George W., R.I., S21806
Jason, H.H. See HAZZARD
John, R.I., Sarah, W1864
Levi, Mass., S44397
London (colored), R.I., S17463
Martin, Pvt., Va., BLReg. 167666-1855
Peter, R.I., BLWt.3235-100-Pvt. Iss. 1/28/1790. No papers
Pharaoh, R.I., See HAZERD
Richard "in the Invalids", BLWt. 13226-100-Pvt. Iss. 12/31/1798. No papers
Sampson, R.I., BLWt.3236-100-Pvt. Iss. 12/31/1789. No papers
Stephen F., R.I., BLWt.3223-100-Pvt. Iss. 11/30/1799 to Abijah Holbrook, ass. No papers
Stewart, Ct., N.Y., S13262
Thomas, Mass., See HASZARD
Thomas S., Navy, R.I., Margaret, R4803
HAZEL, Elisha, ---, Margaret, R4808. Va. res. of son in 1854
HAZELET, Kinlar/Kenley, Del., BLWt.575-100
HAZELHURST, John, Pa., BLWt.9637-100-Pvt. Iss. 9/26/1791. No papers
HAZELTINE, Benjamin, Mass., Abigail, W19703; BLWt.30767-160-55
Elijah, Mass., S33292
James, Mass., Hannah, R4810
John, Mass., See HASSELTINE
Jonas, Mass., S23688
Prince (colored), Mass., S32282; BLWt.922-100
Richard, Cont., Mass., Jane, W24398
Richard, Cont., Mass. See HAZELTON
Thomas, Cont., Vt., Ruth, W19677; BLWt.13166-100-Corp. Iss. 2/13/1790
Thomas, Mass., Sarah, W19671
William, N.H., S44394
William, N.H., See HASELTINE
HAZELTON, Abraham, N.J., BLWt. 8395-100-Pvt. Iss. 5/30/1791. No papers

HAZELTON (continued)
John, N.H., Polly, W16595
Jonathan, N.H., See HAZLETON
Nathaniel, N.H., See HAZLETON
Richard, Cont., Mass., S44395
Solomon, N.H., BLWt.3198-100-Pvt. Iss. 3/25/1790. No papers
Solomon, N.H., S466447
HAZELWOOD, Benjamin, Va., R4811
HAZEN, Abraham, N.J., Levinah/Levina, W248
Andrew, Ct., Polly, W23170
Hezekiah, N.H., Vt., Sarah, W14885
Jacob, Ct., Cont., S17459
Jacob, Mass., S35397
Moses, Cont., N.Y. res. & agcy. Charlotte, W27620; BLWt.1118-500-Col. Iss. 12/27/1798
Solomon, N.H., Vt., Sarah, W1765; BLWt.31272-160-55
HAZERD, Pharaoh, R.I., Rej. B.L.
HAZLE, Caleb, Md., Jemima Duval, former wid., R3171
Elisha, ?, See HAZEL
HAZLET, John, Del., BLWt.1041-500-Col. Iss. 9/2/1789 to Wm. Killen, executor. No papers
HAZLETINE, James, See HAZELTINE
John, Mass. See HASSELTINE
HAZLETON, Jonathan, N.H., Mariam, W23194
Nathaniel, N.H., S44396
Prince, Mass., See HAZELTINE
HAZLETT, Robert, N.J., R4809
Robert, Pa., See HASLET
HAZLEWOOD, Luke, Va., Nancy, W9477; BLWt.67515-160-55
HAZZARD, Arthur, Del., S41615
Cord, Del., S20389
James, Mass., N.H., Betty, W23218; BLWt.19781-160-55
Jason, N.H., Nancy, W7703; BLWt.82538-160-55
Pharaoh, R.I. See HAZERD
Thomas, N.Y., R4805
William, S.C., BLWt.1238-200
HEAD, Britin, N.J., N.Y., Mahatable W25768; BLWt.2498-160-55
Daniel, N.H., Druzilla, W21312; BLWt.16140-160-55
Fobes, R.I., R4813
Henry, N.Y., S29221
James, N.H., S18439
James, S.C., R4814
James W., Navy, Mass., S19326; BLWt.26401-160-55
John, Cont., Md., S39680; BLWt.1384-100
John, Md., BLWt.11298-100-Pvt. Iss. 7/9/1800 to Asahel Phelps. No papers
John, N.H., BLWt.3171 & 3567-100-Pvt. Iss. 12/28/1796 to Christopher S. Thom, ass. No papers
John, N.H., S43665
John Stromatt, S.C., S6995
Joseph, R.I., S13380
Lovit, R.I., S23690
Moses, N.H., S35404

HEAD (continued)
Richard, N.C., S13365
Richard M., Cont., S.C. res. Charlotte, W9060; BLWt.1119-200-Lt. Iss. 6/10/1794. No papers
Robert, N.C., R4815
William Beckwith, Md., R21695
HEADDY, John, N.J., Jane, R4817
HEADEN, William, S.C., S31120
HEADERICK, Peter, See HEADRICK
HEADING, Marcus, N.Y., R4816
HEADLE, Charles, Mass., Phebe Green, former wid., R4270
HEADLEY, Jacob, N.J., S22295
James, N.J., S16150
John, N.J., See HEADDY
John T., N.J., Catherine, W427
Joseph, N.J., S4359
Stephen, N.J., S2300
William, R.I., See HADLY
HEADLY, Carey, N.J., Mary, W4741
HEADMAN, William, N.Y., Pa., R4818
HEADON, Delight, former wid. of Elisha Litchfield, Mass., which see
HEADRICK, Frances, N.C., Margaret, R4842
Peter, N.C., Prudence, W11288; BLWt.75050-160-55
HEADY, Daniel, Ct., Mary, W25764
Jacob, N.C., S2288
HEAGAN, John, Mass., Elizabeth; BLWt.61248-160-55
Patrick, Pa., S4357
HEAKSLEY, James, N.Y., BLWt.7267-100-Drummer. Iss. 7/29/1790 to John McMillen, ass. No papers
HEAL, John, Mass., Lydia, BLWt. 36742-160-55
HEALD, Amos, N.H., R4820
Asa, Mass., Jerusha, W15835
Benjamin, Mass., Rebecca, R4821; BLWt.61249-160-55
Eleazar, Mass., Elizabeth, R4825
Ephraim, Mass., Sarah/Sara, W21314
Oliver, Cont., Mass., Esther, W23262
Thomas, Mass., S18872
Timothy, Mass., Nabby, BLWt. 40335-160-55
HEALEA, Thomas, Md. See HALEY
HEALEY, Comfort, Vt., S21812
Eliphaz, Mass., Lucy, W24431
Hugh, N.J., S36578
Samuel, Va. Sea Service, R42. Va. Half Pay. See N.A. Acc. No. 837-Va. State Navy, YS File
HEALY, George, Ct., Mass., Bethia, W17065
John, Ct., S23691
John, Mass., S39670
Lemuel, Mass., Dolly, W14897
Paul, R.I., Mary, W13424
Stephen, Mass., S13366
Thomas, Md., See HALEY
Thomas, R.I., S15882
William, Va., BLWt.12201-100-Pvt. Iss. 5/29/1792 to Francis Graves
HEAPE, Archibald, Md., S8701
John, Md., S8700
HEARALD, William, N.Y., Anna,

HEARALD (continued)
W19758
HEARD, Amos, Mass., Mary, R4823
Isaac, Ct., See HURD
James, Cont., N.J. res. in 1818; S540; BLWt.1003-300-Capt. Iss. 8/27/1789 to John Brown, ass. No papers
James, Cont., Elizabeth, W23263
John, Cont., N.J. res. in 1818, S34395; BLWt.1023-300-Capt. Iss. 6/11/1789. No papers
John, Va., S8709
John G., Ga., R4822
Nathaniel, Mass., S29883
Richard, Ga., Elizabeth, W4229
Richard, Mass., S4347
Robert, Ct., Cont. See HURD
Tristram, N.H., S29224
William, Mass., Thirza, W7712; BLWt.10032-160-55
HEARICK, Hezekiah, Ct., Mass., S10828
HEARL, John, Mass., S20392
HEARN, Daniel, Mass., Elizabeth, W17064
Drury, N.C., Karen/Keren, W3548; BLWt.17888-160-55
Ephraim, Va., S38020
John, S.C., S4338
HEARNE, Ebenezer, N.C., S6997
James, N.C., S41631
HEARSEY, David, Mass., S32823
Ezekiel, Mass., S30481
James, Mass., S31121
John, Mass., S17474
Jonathan, Mass., S33349
Noah, Mass., S29879
Peter, Mass., S33295
William, Mass., S33296
Zadok/Zadock, Mass., S31122
HEART, Frederick A./John, Ct., Sally, W1603; BLWt.1912-100. Iss. 2/4/1833. Soldier was called by surnames of Acart, Ekeheart, Acheheart, Akeheart, also John Frederick Martin Akehart, etc.
Job, Ct. See HART
John, Ct., BLWt.968-150-Ensign. Iss. 8/22/1798. No papers
Jonathan, Ct., BLWt.955-300-Capt. Iss. 9/7/1790. No papers
Reuben, Ct., S41633
Selah, Ct., Ruth, W21286
HEATH, Aaron, Ct., Mass., Rhoda, W13440
Abiel, N.H., S22298
Augustine, N.C., Sarah, W3417
Benjamin, Cont., N.H., Dolly, W23273
Benjamin, Hazen's Regt., BLWt. 13164-100-Pvt. Iss. 9/21/1790 to Benj. Moers, ass. No papers
Benjamin, Mass., S28761
Daniel, Cont., Mass., N.H., S44413
Daniel, N.H., Tryphena, W2547; BLWt.21825-160-55
Daniel, N.Y., Azubah, W7711; BLWt.40013-160-55
Dearborn, N.H., Mary, W8217;

HEATH (continued)
BLWt.13018-160-55
Elias, Mass., BLWt.4368-100-Corp. Iss. 7/21/1789 to Jonathan Cass. No papers
Elias, Mass., Olive Mason, former wid., W17094
Enoch, N.H., Elizabeth, W23268; BLWt.6299-160-55
Isaac, Mass., S18871
Isaac, N.H., S23259
James, N.H., S22297
James, N.H., Vt., Mercy/Marcy, W24426
Jesse, N.H., S39676
John, Ct., Cont., S23693
John, "in the Invalids", BLWt. 13223-100-Corp. Iss. 5/17/1790. No papers
John, Mass., Dis. No papers
John, Mass., N.H., S16868
Jonathan, Cont., N.H., S38821
Jonathan, R.I., Rebecca, W21302
Joseph, Mass., Patience, W17996
Josiah, N.Y., S13347
Peleg, Ct., BLWt.957-200-Lt. Iss. 2/5/1790. No papers
Peleg, R.I., Annar, W24428
Reuben, N.H., Cont., S10823
Richard, Mass., Abigail, W1279; BLWt.12822-160-55
Richard, N.J., S820
Richard, Jr., N.J., S1014
Richard, N.C., R4827
Samuel, Mass., N.H., Sarah, W19764
Samuel, Mass., N.H., R4828
Samuel, N.H., S44412
Samuel C., Ct., BLWt.5942-100-Pvt. Iss. 3/3/1797 to Samuel Fitch. No papers
Samuel C., Ct., Leah, R21311
Simon, N.H., R4829
Sterling/Starling, N.H., Elizabeth, W21303; BLWt.3210-100. Iss. 2/1/1799 to Wm. S. Thom, ass.
Thomas, Ct., S46041
Thomas, Ct., Polly, W24423
William, Ct., S29219
William, Ct., Mary, W17997
William, Cont., Mass., BLWt. 908-1100-Maj. Gen. Iss. 7/3/1789 to Wm. Heath. No papers
William, N.H., S39666; BLWt. 1674-100
William, N.H., R4831; BLWt. 1709-100. Iss. 2/20/1831
William, N.C., Sally, W27670; BLWt.30773-160-55
William, Va., S10829
Zebadiah, Green Mt. Boys or Vt. R4832
HEATHCOCK, James, N.C., S2613
HEATON, Charles, Hazen's Regt., BLWt.13172-100-Pvt. Iss. 12/6/1791 to Stephen Thorn, ass. No papers
Charles, Ct., Cont. See HAYDEN
Ebenezer, ---, born N.J., res. Pa., Va., Ind. R4834
James, Cont., Md., Elizabeth,

HEATON (continued)
W7716
James, Hazen's Regt., BLWt.13183-100-Pvt. Iss. 4/19/1791. No papers
John, Va.(?), Not Rev. War. BL Reg. 167760-1855
Orange, Vt., R4833
HEATOR, Elias, N.J., R4835
HEAVENER, Christopher, Pa.,S31123
HEAVILOW, Reuben, See HEVELO
HEAVNER, Charles, Mass. See HEBNER
Christopher, Pa. See HEAVENER
HEBARD, Arminda, Cont., W4985. See Obadiah PHELPS, Cont.
Asa, Ct., S32824
Diah, Ct., Zerviah/Zeviah, W21306
Jabez, Ct., S18442
Jedediah, Ct., S43666
Ozias, Ct., Mary, W7722; BLWt. 26783-160-55
Samuel, Lamb's Artillery, N.Y., BLWt.7291-100-Pvt. Iss. 6/20/1795. No papers
Uriah, Ct., S43686
Vine Timothy, Ct. See HIBBARD
HEBB, William, Cont., Va. S38022
HEBBARD, Ebenezer, Ct., S15170
Jacob, Mass., S32821
Joseph, Ct., Lydia, W23260; BLWt.26703-160-55
Ozias, Ct. See HEBARD
Rufus, Ct., S10840
HEBBERD, Bushnell, Ct., Rebecca/Rebekah, W11290
Ebenezer, Ct., S13412
Jacob, Mass., Elizabeth, W21309
John, Mass., S35409
Jonathan, Pa., S35407
Oliver, Mass., Elizabeth, W19800
HEBERLY, Frederick, Md. S39665
HEBERT, Paul, Cont., Canadian, Angelique, W23264. One Paul Hubert of same regt. was allowed BLWt.13170, but no proof of identity
HEBLINGER, Peter, See KEBLINGER
HEBNER, Charles, Mass., S16869; BLWt.19755-160-55
HEBRON, William, N.Y., Dis. No papers
HECK, Youst, Pa., S38019
HECKMAN, Adam, Pa., Elizabeth, W3085
George, Pa., S39668
HECKTOR, Monday, Mass., Lucy, W13441
HECOCK, Aaron, Ct., S16867
HECOX, Elihu, Mass., Sabrina Wheeler, former wid., W18395
Samuel, Cont., Ct., Lucema, W1036; BLWt.5174-160-55
Truman, Ct., S2304
HECTOR, Monday, See HECKTOR
William, Mass., S32822
HED, John, N.H., See HEAD
HEDDELSON, William, See HEDDLESON
HEDDEN, Betsey, former wid. of Samuel Sears, N.J., which see
David, N.Y., S1016
James, N.J., S4360

HEDDEN (continued)
Job, N.J., S23694
Jonas, N.J., S886
Obediah, N.J., S2306
Simon, N.J., Pa., S2308
Zadock, N.J., Frances S., W1424; BLWt.26509-160-55
Zephaniah, N.J., S1017
HEDDINGS, William, Pa., R4836
HEDDLESON, William, Pa., Elizabeth, W5107; BLWt.26015-160-55
HEDDRICK, Francis, See HEADRICK
HEDERICK, Peter, See HEADRICK
HEDGCOCK, Thomas, See HITCHCOCK
HEDGE, Asa, Mass., Miriam, R5082
Isaac, Mass., Thankful, W19766
William, Md., BLWt.11348-100-Pvt. Iss. 6/8/1797 to James DeBaufre, ass. No papers
HEDGEPETH, Abraham, N.C., S6989
HEDGER, Edward, N.Y., S13378
Stephen, Va., R21644
Thomas, Va., S32314
William, N.Y., S10824
HEDGES, Benjamin, N.J., S2609
Christopher, N.Y., Hannah, R4838
Eleazer, N.Y., S13352
Elijah, Not Rev., Va. Rangers 1791. Old War Inv. File 4342
Gilbert, N.J., Margaret, W7721
Henry, Ct., R4839
Joseph, N.J., S34394
Reuben, Mass., Hannoh, W19759
Robert, Va., Mary, W11327; BLWt.31276-160-55
HEDGLEN, William, N.J., Sally Compton, former wid., W6728; BLWt.28621-160-55
HEDGPETH, John, N.C., S2610
HEDLEY, Moses, N.J., BLWt.8411-100-Pvt. Iss. 5/31/1790. No papers
HEDREIK, William, Pa., S4355
HEDRICK, Henry, Va., R4841
John, Pa. See HETRICH
Peter, N.C., See HEADRICK
HEELY, Timothy, Mass., Sarah, R4844
HEEMSTRAT, Philip, See HEMSTRAT
HEERINGTON, Daniel, See HERRINGTON
HEERMAN, Friedrick W., Mass., S13356
HEERMANCE, Andrew, See HERMANCE
Simon, N.Y., R4914
HEETER, George, Md., S16410
HEETH, Samuel, Mass., See HEATH
HEFFELFINGER, Philip, Pa., S5503
HEFFEMAN, Hugh, Pa., BLWt.9579-100-Sgt. Iss. 6/20/1789. No papers
HEFFERLIN, John, Va., S38012
HEFFERMAN, Stephen, R.I., S21815
Thomas, Pa., BLWt.9647-100-Pvt. Iss. 6/29/1791
HEFFERNAN, Hugh, Pa. See HAFFERNAN
HEFFINGTON, Archibald, Va. Sea Service, R4970
HEFFLEBOWER, Jacob, Pa., S5501
HEFFLER, John, Pa., S23695
HEFFLINGER, George, Pa., BLWt. 9528-100-Pvt. Iss. 12/1791. No papers

HEFFLISH, Melchoir/Melhoir, N.Y., S39674
HEFFNER, Jacob, Cont., Md., Elizabeth, W2546; BLWt.67701-160-55
Valentine, Pa. See HEFNER
HEFLER, John, Pa., See HEFFLER
HEFLEY, Jacob, Md. See HAVELY
HEFNER, Valentine, Pa., b. Ger., R4846
HEGAMAN, John, N.J., S659
HEGEMAN, John, Pa., S22821
HEGERMAN, James, Pa. See HAGERMAN
HEGIN, Edward, Pa., S39669
HEIDLER, Joshua, See HIDLER
HEIFNER, Jacob, See HEFFNER
HEILER, George, See HILLER, John George
HEIMER, Daniel, Cont., Pa., BLWt.1999-100
John, Pa., R4845
HEIN, Conrad, Pa., See HINE
HEINISH, George, Pa., R4847
HEISAM, John, N.Y., S39672
HEISER, George, Pa., ---
HEITRICK, Jacob, Pa., S2313
HEIVILL, John, See HIWILL
HEIZER, John, Va., R4848
HEKTOR, Monday, See HECKTOR
HELIKER, John, N.Y., S16149
HELLAM, Leonard, Va. See HELMS
HELLEN, John, Pa., See HELLER
HELLER, Frederick, Pa., Hannah, R4849
John, Pa., S8702
John, Pa., S39671
John, Pa., S39685
HELM, Daniel, N.Y., S13379
George, Cont., Va., S38824
John, N.C., Va., Anna, W3811
John, Pa., BLWt.1035-300-Capt. Iss. 2/15/1790. No papers
Leonard, Va., See HELMS
Leonard, Va., R14982; Va. Half Pay
Samuel, N.J., S4356
Samuel, N.J., S10825
Simon, N.Y., R4850
HELMAGE, John, Ct., S43667
HELME, James, R.I., R4852
Niles, R.I., S13357
Peleg, R.I., BLWt.3213-100-Pvt. Iss. 2/27/1790 to Theo. Fowler. No papers
Peleg, R.I., Huldah, W14899
Samuel, R.I., R4851
William, R.I., S38822
HELMER, Adam/Adam Frederick, N.Y., Anna, W17067
George, N.Y., S27971
John, N.Y., BLWt.7269-100-Pvt. Iss. 8/10/1790 to Stephen Lusk, ass. No papers
John, N.Y., S22827
John F., N.Y., Margaret, W7718
John G., N.Y., S13348
John William, Pa., S34920
Philip, N.Y., S43671
HELMERHASON, H.F. See HELMERSHAUSON
HELMERSHAUSON, Henry F., Cont., Mass., S35403
HELMES, William, N.J., BLWt. 994-300-Capt. Iss. 6/11/1789 to Mathias Denman, ass. No papers
HELMICK, John, Pa., Catharine, W10094; BLWt.61202-160-55
Nicholas, Va., Sarah, W489; BLWt.36736-160-55
HELMS, Leonard, Va., S38021; BLWt.573-100.
HELMSTORFF, William, See HALINSDOFF
HELMUT, John H., Mass., BLWt. 4409-100-Pvt. Iss. 9/10/1789 to Charles Bush. No papers
HELP, Ludwick, Pa., BLWt.9627-100-Pvt. Iss. 11/5/1789. No papers
Ludwick, Pa., Mary Ann, W3185
HELPHINSTINE, Philip, Va., Rebecca, W8930
HELSINGER, Michael, N.Y., S23692
HELSLEY, Jacob, Pa., S5511
HELTON, Abraham, N.C. See Abram
Abram/Abraham, N.C., S4353
Abram, Va., R4853
Peter, N.C., R4854
HEMBREE, Abraham/Abram, S.C., S38823
Drewry, S.C., R4855
HEMENWAY, David, Mass., Polly, W24424
Ebenezer, Mass., Ruth, W23271
Elias, Mass., Molly, W23266; BLWt.30786-160-55
Jeffry, Mass., Hepsibah, W19757
Jonathan, Mass., S32818
Peter, Mass., Dis. No papers
Phinehas, N.H., S43666
Rufus, Mass., S43662
Thaddeus, Mass., R4859
HEMINGER, John, Ct., Mary Cannon, former wid., W23769; BLWt. 67543-160-55
John, Pa. See HIMINGER
HEMINGWAY, David, Mass. See HEMENWAY
Enos, Ct., S10827
Isaac, Mass., R4858
Jacob, Ct., S10677
James, Mass., BLWt.2222-100
Thaddeus, Mass. See HEMENWAY
HEMINWAY, Samuel, Mass., S18440
HEMMENWAY, Asa, Mass., S18870
David, Mass. See HEMENWAY
Ebenezer, Mass. See HEMENWAY
Peter, Mass. See HEMENWAY
HEMMEWAY, Peter, See HEMENWAY
HEMPFIELD, Joseph, Hazen's Regt. BLWt.13189-100-Pvt. Iss. 8/27/?. No papers
HEMPHILL, James, N.H., Ruth, W1427; BLWt.31277-160-55
James, S.C., b. Ireland, S21277
Joseph, Lee's Legion, Va., BLWt.13239-100-Pvt. Iss. 10/20/1789. No papers
Joseph, Va., S38825
HEMPLEMAN, George, Pa., R4860
HEMPSTEAD, Samuel, Navy, Ct. res. in 1794. Dis. No papers
Stephen, Ct., S24612
HEMPSTEAD (continued)
Thomas, N.Y., R4862
HEMPSTED, Nathaniel, Ct., Elizabeth, W14902
Nathaniel, N.Y., R4861
HEMSTEAD, Nathaniel, Ct. See HEMPSTED
HEMSTRAT, Philip, N.Y., S23257
HEMSTROUGHT, David, Cont., N.Y., S13371
HENDEE, Caleb, Ct., Cont., S13349
HENDER, Frederick, N.Y., BLWt. 7276-100-Pvt. Iss. 2/21/1792 to Augustus Sacket, ass. No papers
Thomas, Ct. See HENDOR
HENDERLITER, Michael, Pa., S38016
HENDERSHOT, Abraham, N.J., R4863
John, Pa., S9574
HENDERSON, Alexander, N.Y., Margaret, W23269
Alexander, Pa., BLWt.9544-100-Pvt. Iss. 12/22/1794 to Henry Purdee, ass. No papers
Andrew, N.H., R4864
Andrew, N.C., R4865
Andrew, Pa., BLWt.1020-200-Lt. Iss. 1/14/1795. No papers
Archibald, ---, Ga. res., R4866
Benjamin, Cont., Mass., Navy, Mary, W24427
Benjamin, Md. & Sea Service, S31119
Benjamin, Mass., S29222
Daniel, Cont., Vt. res. 1808, BLWt.2023-100
David, Ct., S43658
David, Cont., Del., Sarah, W4228; BLWt.506-160-55
David, Va., S17476
David, Va., R4867
David, Va. Sea Service, S5506
Edward, Va., S15885
Ezekiel, N.C., S6994
George, S.C. See Charles TEULON
George Lewis, Pa., R4870
Gustavus H., Pa., BLWt.1029-300-Surgn. Mate. Iss. 5/24/1791 to John Henderson, admr. No papers See Heitman's Hist. Reg., p.474 John Rose, which states John Rose's proper name was Baron Gustavus H. de Rosenthal & that he was appointed as Surgn's Mate under name of Gustavus Henderson
Henry, Pa., BLWt.9527-100-Pvt. Iss. 7/6/1791 to John McCleland, ass. No papers
Henry, Va., Nancy, R4875
Isaac, N.J., Elizabeth, W933
James, Md., N.C., S8708
James, N.Y., Vt., S16148
John, Del., S22296
John, N.H., Mary, R4874
John, N.C., R4871
John, S.C., Martha, W4984
John, S.C., Elizabeth, R4869
John, Va., S38014
John, Va., Jemima, W10103
Jonathan, Mass., Privateer, R.I., Eleanor, W3809
Joseph, Ct., S43661

HENDERSON (continued)
Joseph, Mass., N.H., S39675
Joseph, Pa., S22291
Joseph, Va., R4872
Margaret, former wid. of James A. Wilson, Pa., which see
Matthew, Pa., BLWt.1031-300-Capt. Iss. 4/23/1796 to Wm. Henderson, admr. No papers
Meshack, N.C., S4332
Pleasant, N.C., S1912
Robert, N.C., S.C., Mary, S31738; BLWt.17706-160-55
Robert, Va., S31736
Sampson, Va., Elizabeth Fuller, former wid., W7339; BLWt.39230-160-55
Samuel, Mass., N.H., S18873
Samuel, N.J., Ann, R14951
Samuel, N.Y., BLWt.7248-100-Pvt. Iss. 7/20/1790 to Samuel Curray, ass. No papers
Samuel, N.C., S.C., S9351
Samuel, Pa., Margaret Conner, former wid., BLWt.246-100
Thomas, Cont., N.J., Rachel, W426
Thomas, Pa., R4877
Thomas, S.C., Elizabeth, W10102
William, Mass., Elizabeth, W21304 BLWt.107-100
William, N.J., S39683
William, N.C., BLWts.12253 & 13171-100-Pvt. Iss. 9/28/1796 to John Young, ass. No papers
William, Pa., S32313
William, Pa., BLWt.1011-300-Capt. Iss. 10/15/1789. No papers
William, S.C., BLWt.1102-450-Lt. Col. Iss. 7/23/1790. No papers
William, Va., S---. Dorcas Henderson, wid. of above sold., was pensioned as former wid. of John Towers, Va., which see
William, Va., Nancy, W228; BLWt. 30779-160-55
William, Va., R14952; Va. Half Pay
William, Va. & War of 1812, Eleanor/Elendor, R4868
Wilson, S.C., R4878
Zoath, N.H., BLWt.2301-100
HENDLEY, William, Mass., S33294
HENDOR, Thomas, Ct., Sally, W17994
HENDRAKE, Andrew, Cont., Ct., S39667
HENDRICK, Abijah, Mass., S30479
Coe, Ct., Navy, S18441
Daniel, Va., S8706
Elijah, Va., Nancy, W10104
Joseph, Mass., Sarah, W4881
Moses, Mass., S46042
Obediah, Ga., S38017
HENDRICKS, Albert, Cont., Md., N.C., Margaret, W83
Daniel, Ct., BLWt.5922-100-Pvt. Iss. 12/3/1789. No papers
Francis, N.Y., R4879
Hannah, former wid. of Thomas Middleton, N.J., which see
Hillary, N.C., S7000
John, Va., R4882
Moses, Va., also served in 1794,

HENDRICKS (continued)
Nelly, W2545; BLWt.36730-160-55 cancelled, BLWt.5078-160-55
Philip, N.Y., R4880
Solomon, Va. See HENDRIX
William M., N.J., S2303
Zachariah, Va., S38018
HENDRICKSON, Benjamin, N.J., Phebe, R4884
Daniel, N.J., S1018
Hendrick, N.J., Francinka, W661
Henry, N.Y., Elizabeth, W19767
James, N.J., S885
Moses, Md. & Sea Service, S32312
Oke/Okey, N.J., R4883
Peter, N.J., S2614
Peter, N.Y., S29223
William, Md., S2301
HENDRIKSON, Cornelius, N.Y., BLWt.7268-100-Pvt. Iss. 9/27/1790 to Abr'm Oothoudt, ass. No papers
HENDRIX, David, Ct., S37098
John, Va. See HENDRICKS
Nathaniel, Ct., S38015
Solomon, Va., S4352
HENDRIXEN, Isaac, N.C., S8703
HENDRON, William, Va., BLWt. 12207-100-Pvt. "in the Artillery". Iss. 7/6/1793 to Robert Means, ass. No papers
HENDRY, David, N.Y., Selina, W3990
Moses, N.C. See Henry GULLICK
Samuel, N.J., S4361; BLWt.996-300-Capt. Iss. 7/20/1790. No papers
HENDRYX, Isaiah, Mass., Esther, W21305
Nathaniel, N.Y., S32309
HENDY, John, Pa., S13381
HENEBERGER, John, Pa., S22824
HENECKER, Henry, Cont., Pa. res. of dau. in 1828, BLWt.1350-100
HENEGAN, Coonrod, See HENEGAR
HENEGAR, Coonrod, N.C., S38011
HENERY, Francis, Pa., S39679
Joseph, N.C. See HENRY
HENESY, John, Pa., S39681
HENEY, David, Pa., See HANEY
David, Pa., BLWt.427-100
HENFIELD, John, Mass., S19700
HENING, John, Cont., Pa., S39677
HENKSON, John, N.H. See HINKSON
HENLEY, Henry, N.H., S44416
Michael, Pa., BLWts.9442 & 9526-100-Pvt. Iss. 2/23/1792. No papers
Samuel, Mass., BLWt.911-300-Capt. Iss. 10/16/1789. No papers
Thomas, ---, BLWt.938-400-Major & Aide de Camp. Iss. 4/6/1790 to Samuel Henley, legal repr. Also recorded under BLWt.2482. No papers
William, N.J., See HURLEY
HENLY, David, Mass., BLWt.942-500-Col. Iss. 8/7/1789 to Richard Platt, ass. No papers
Henry, Pa., BLWt.1018-200-Lt. Iss. 10/28/1789 to Matthew McConnell, ass. No papers
Hezekiah, Va., R4885

HENLY (continued)
Hugh, Pa., BLWt.9525-100-Pvt. Iss. 8/19/1789 to Richard Murthwaite, ass. No papers
HENMAN, Isaac, Ct. See HINMAN
Samuel, Ct., BLWt.5938-100-Pvt. Iss. 11/27/1790. No papers
HENMON, Weight, Ct. See HINMAN
HENNAGIN, Joseph, See HENNEGIN
HENNARD, Robert, See HENWOOD
HENNECKER, Henry, See HENECKER
HENNEGIN, Joseph, Cont., N.Y., Rhoda, W10097
HENNEN, Matthew, Pa., S22828
Thomas, Del., S39678
HENNESEY, John, BLWt.7234-100-Pvt. Iss. 1/25/1791 to Levy Ellis, ass. No papers
HENNEY, Joseph, Mass., S4345
HENNIGAN, John, Md. See HENNIGAR
HENNIGAR, John, Md., S15884
HENNING, Adam, Pa., R4886
Conrad, Pa., R4887
George, Pa., BLWt.9584-100-Pvt. Iss. 6/24/1793 to Philip Stout, ass. No papers
George, Pa., N.J.(?), S39673
HENNION, Cornelius, N.J., Harriet Ramsey, former wid., W17506
HENNIS, Benjamin, Md., S35402
HENNISON, William, See HENNUSSEY
HENNON, Abel, Del., S39682
Thomas, Del., See HENNEN
HENNUSSEY, William, Cont., Pa., BLWt.159-100
HENRY, Adam, Mass., S13351
Andrew, Mass., S29882
Barzilla, Ct., BLWt.5924-100-Pvt. Iss. 12/21/1789. No papers
Benjamin, Navy, R.I., Ruth, W7715
David, N.Y., S23260
David, N.C., Margaret, R4895
David, Va., S2287
Enoch F., N.Y., R4889
Francis, Mass., S17475
Francis, N.Y., See HENDRICKS
Francis, Pa. See HENERY
George, Pa., BLWt.9588-100-Pvt. Iss. 1/29/1790. No papers
Hugh, N.Y., Mary, W17063
Hugh, Va., S2611
Jacob, Pa., S35405
James, Mass., S10821
James, S.C., b. Pa., Elizabeth, W428
James, Va., S16871
John, Ct., Fanny, W19763
John, Ct., Esther, R4890
John, Cont., Pa., Rosanna, W4892
John, Hazen's Regt., BLWt.13177-100-Pvt. Iss. 9/23/1791. No papers
John, N.Y., R4891
John, N.C., See HINREY
John, N.C., S.C., S10826
John, Pa., S2285
John, S.C., S6992

HENRY (continued)
John, Va., S1524
John, Va., S1767
Joseph, N.J., R4893
Joseph, N.C., S8705
Joseph, N.C., Mary, W7714
Joseph, N.C., Mary, W10096
Josiah, Mass., Abigail, W24429
Malcolm, N.C., S.C., S16866
Michael, Mass., S32820
Moses, N.C., Margaret Gullick, former wid., R4382
Moses, Va., S5508
Nathaniel, N.Y., Mary, W19761
Nicholas, Pa., S5505
Patrick, Va., R4898 (alleged by his dau. to have been a Col. from Hanover Co., Va.)
Peter, N.J., S22300
Philip, Pa., BLWt.9549-100-Pvt. Iss. 3/12/1791. No papers
Robert, N.Y., R4899
Robert, Pa., Va., S1830
Robert R., Cont., N.H., Mary, W10325; BLWt.900-400-Surgn. Iss. 9/23/1789. No papers
Samuel, N.H., Esther, W1865; BLWt.26196-160-55
Samuel, Pa., R4901
Samuel, R.I., S21814
Silas, Mass., S32825
Thomas, R.I., Anna, W21308
Wells/Wills, N.Y., Elizabeth, W21313
William, Ct., BLWts.5915 & 14050-100-Pvt. Iss. 7/18/1793 to James Henry, admr. No papers
William, Pa., Va., S6999
William, Va., Elizabeth, W364
Wills, N.Y. See Wells
HENSEL, George, Va., S6990
Michael, Va., Barbara, W7717
William, Pa., S2307
HENSEY, Andrew, Ct., Sarah, W8922
HENSHAW, Benjamin, Ct., Elsa/Sarah, W21307
John, R.I., Susanna, W23258
Mary, former wid. of Isaac Howard, Mass., which see
Thomas, Mass., Meriam/Miriam, W11283; BLWt.18004-160-55
William, Ct., Wt.962-200. No papers
William, Mass., Mary, R4903
William, Va., BLWt.12194-100-Pvt. Iss. 7/6/1793 to Francis Graves, ass. No papers
HENSLEY, Samuel, Va., S21278
HENSON, Daniel, Cont., Va., Fariba, W3991
Elijah, Va., Fanny, W1767; BLWt. 26671-160-55
Jesse, N.C., R4906
Jesse, Va., Polly, W8921
John, N.C., Va., Jane, W21301; BLWt.34933-160-55
Joseph, Pa., BLWt.9645-100-Pvt. Iss. 3/14/1800 to Joseph Henson. No papers
Paul, N.C., Elizabeth, W9480; BLWt.67700-160-55

HENSON (continued)
Richard, N.C., R4909
Robert, S.C., Va., R4902
William, Ct.,S43669; BLWt.1446-100
William, N.C., Anne/Ann, W8923; BLWt.34932-160-55
William, N.C., R4910
William, Va., S41629
William, Va., Sivilly, W3416; BLWt.6450-160-55
HENTHORN, Philip, Va., BLWt.556-100
HENTZE, Frederick, Cont., Va., Margaret, W3251; BLWt.307-100
HENTZEL, Michael, Va. See HENSEL
HENUSSEY, William, See HENNUSSEY
HENWOOD, Robert, Cont., Md., Rebecca, W934; BLWt.674-100
HENZE, Frederick, See HENTZE
HEPBURN, Peter, Ct. Pvt.; BLWt. 14043-100 iss. 12/29/1792 to Peter Hepburn, Admr. Ctfied by N. Cutting 1/9/1822. Also BLWt. 5897-100
HEPPARD, William, N.J., S13370
HEPPEL, Adam, N.Y., See HAPPAL
HEPPENER, John, N.J., S43656
HERALD, Henry, N.Y., S34396
William, N.Y. See HEARALD
HERALSON, Herndon, See HARALSON
HERB, Frederick, Pa. See HARP
HERBERT, Charles, Navy, Mass., Molly Parker, former wid., W15175
James, N.H., S15449
James, N.J., Mary, W7720
Jeremiah, Md., Mary, W9061
John, Pvt., Mass., BLReg.212482-1855
Josiah, Va., S31124
Pasco, Va. Sea Service, R43, Va. Half Pay. See N.A. Acc.837-Va. State Navy, Pascow Herbert, YS File. Va. Half Pay.
Samuel, N.J., S1015
Stewart, Pa., Susan, W3252; BLWt. 1021-200-Lt. Iss. 5/28/1789. No papers
Thomas, N.J., S18443
Thomas, N.J., R4912
Thomas, Va. Sea Service, R15006; Va. Half Pay
HERBEST, Peter, See HERBST
HERBISON, Francis, See HARBISON
HERBST, Peter, Pa., S23696
HERD, Eleazer, N.H. See HURD
HERDER, Lawrence Philip, See HARTER
HEREFORD, John, Va., Sarah, W1425; BLWt.28613-160-55
HERENDEEN, Hezekiah, R.I., S37097
Reuben, R.I., Dorothy, W23261
HERGET, Peter, N.C., S31092
HERICK, Daniel, Ct. See HERRICK
Ebenezer, Mass., See HERRICK
Richard, Mass., See HERRICK
HERIN, Gersham, N.J., S22299
Isaac, S.C., Ann, W10098
William, Va., S8704
HERING, Henry, Pa. See HERRING
Jesse, N.C., See HERRING
Ludwing/Lewis, Pa., Anna Maria, R4924
HERINGTON, Benjamin, Ct., S32813
HERMAN, Frederick W., See HEERMAN

HERMAN (continued)
George, Pa., See HARMAN
John, Cont., See HEERMAN
John, Von Heer's Corps, BLWt. 13160-100-Pvt. Iss. 5/29/1792 to Nathaniel Grimes, ass. No papers
HERMANCE, Andrew, N.Y., Maria Ten Broeck, former wid., W18116
John, N.Y., S13376
HERMANNI, John, Pa., R4915
HERMANY, Jacob, Pa., Christina, W2797
HERN, Thomas, Va. See HERNDON
HERNDEN, Reuben, Va., Frances, W11275
HERNDON, Edward, Va., S5509, d. Mar. 5, 1845
Edward, Va., S30478 & Va. Half Pay. d. Spotsylvania Co., Va., Nov. 1837
George, N.C., S13373
James, ---, Mary, ---, Christian Co., Ky. res. in 1845
James, N.C., Mary M., W9479; BLWt.31437-160-55
James, Va., S1669, missing
John, Va., Judith, W8925
Joseph, N.C., b. N.C., S31740
Thomas, Va., Mary, W8924
William, Va., S9575
William, Va., Susan, R4856
HEROD, Ezra, Mass., BLWt.4334-100-Pvt. Iss. 12/23/1796 to Abraham Foster, No papers
Ezra, Mass., Anne, W24414
John, Md., Indian Wars, R4917
Joseph, Pa., R4918
William, Va., S2286
HERRAL, Reuben, Va. See HARRELL
HERRELL, Joel, N.C. See HARRELL
HERRENDEEN, Hezekiah, See HERENDEEN
Thomas, R.I., R4876
HERRICK, Abel, Ct., R4919
Andrew, Mass., S32827
Asa, Mass., S32828
Charles, Mass., S44415
Daniel, Ct., Olive, W25765
Daniel, N.Y., S5504
Daniel, N.Y., R4920; BLReg.25142-1855
Ebenezer, Mass., S44925
Ebenezer, Mass., Abigail, W2113; BLWt.11097-160-55
Edmund, Mass., Mehitable, W24432
Edward, Mass., Mary, W16027
Elijah, Mass., Hannah, W19760
Elijah, N.Y., S13372
Ephriam, Ct., Navy, S13346
Ephraim, N.Y., S10822
Hezekiah, Mass., See HEARICK
Israel, Ct., Ruth, W17061
Jacob, Mass., S32310
James, N.Y., R4922
John, Ct., BLWt.5901-100-Pvt. Iss. 7/26/1794 to Stephen Thorne, ass. of Sam. How, admr. No papers
John, Ct., Avis Howe, former wid., W21387
John, Mass., BLWt.4305 & 4263-100-Pvt. Iss. 12/2/1791 to

HERRICK (continued)
John Blanchard. No papers
John, Mass., Anna Nash, former wid., W21832
Jonathan, N.Y., S22825
Joseph, Ct., S13368
Joseph, N.H., S44414
Joshua, Mass., S32819
Josiah, Mass., Fanny, W7723; BLWt.17714-160-55
Lemuel, Ct., Lucy, W19756
Libeus, Ct., S41634
Martin, R.I., Sarah, W5101
Nathan, N.Y., Priscilla, R4923
Nehemiah, Mass., Elizabeth, R4921
Richard, Mass., Sea Service, Betsey, W1605; BLWt.44843-160-55
Robert, Ct., Alice, Wb11287; BLWt. 855-100
Simeon, Ct., S13375
Stephen, Cont., Ct., Rebecca, W27784
William, N.Y., Anna Gordon, former wid., R4138
Zebulon, Mass., BLWt.4401-100-Pvt. Iss. 7/22/1789. No papers
HERRIDEN, Elizabeth, former wid. of Joseph Varriel, Cont., Mass. which see
Joseph, Mass., S22829
HERRIMAN, Jacob, See HARIMAN
Jonathan, Mass., S44924
Joseph, Mass., N.H. See HARRIMAN
William, Mass., BLWt.4416-100-Sgt. Iss. 3/25/1790. No papers
HERRIN, Benjamin, N.Y., See HERRING
Daniel, Mass., S31118
Isaac, S.C. See HERIN
John, S.C., b. N.C., S13377
Patience, former wid. of Levi Odom, N.C., which see
Thomas, Mass., See HERRING
HERRING, Benjamin, N.Y., Catharine W23257; BLWt.991-150-Ens. Iss. 7/16/1790. Wm. J. Vreedenburgh, ass. Name recorded as Herrin. No papers
Christian, Pa., S5500
George, Va., S1215
Henry, Pa., R4925
Isaac, S.C., See HERIN
Jacob, N.Y., BLWt.7222-100-Pvt. Iss. 9/24/1790 to Thomas Lawrence, ass. No papers
James, Va., Judy, W11276
Jesse, N.C., Enomey/Enomy/Naoma, W7725; BLWt.40909-160-55
Lemuel, Mass., Sarah, W13414
Lewis, Pa. See Ludwig HERING
Patrick, Pa., BLWt.9529-100-Pvt. Iss. 11/26/1795 to Christian Hubbard, ass. No papers
Pellatiah, Mass., Katherine, W14898
Thomas, Mass., Thomasin Clark, former wid., W18909; BLWt.833-100. Her last husb. was pensioned. See Samuel Clark, Mass.
HERRINGTON, Abraham, Ct. See HARRINGTON
Anna, former wid. of Elijah

HERRINGTON (continued)
Porter, Ct., which see
Anthony, Md. See HARRINGTON
Benjamin, Ct., R4638
Bezelah/Bezeleh, R.I., S44927
Daniel, Md., Pa., Mary, W7729
David, R.I., See HARRINGTON
Eber, Ct., R.I., See HARRINGTON
Isaac, N.C., S41630
Jacob, Pa., BLWt.438-100
John, Ct., N.Y., S28759
John, N.Y., See HARRINGTON
Jonathan, R.I., Patience, R4641
Joseph, Mass., S32826
Josiah, R.I., See HERRINTON
Peter, Mass., S13374
Samson, R.I., Vt., R4643
HERRINTON, Josiah, R.I., Louisa, W1866; BLWt.26282-160-55
William, R.I., Freelove, W24430
HERRMAN, John, Cont., Hazen's Regt., BLWt.13191-100-Sgt. Iss. 9/19/1799 to Abraham Bell, ass. No papers
HERRON, Allan, N.C., S7001
David, Va., S4337
Isaac, S.C., See HERIN
John, Ct., S37099
John, N.Y., S9916
John, N.Y. res. in 1826, Deborah Newel, former wid., R7616
Thomas, Pa. See HARRON
HERSEY, John, Mass. See HEARSEY
Jonathan, Mass., See HEARSEY
Peter, Mass. See HEARSEY
HERSHEY, Jacob, Pa., Margaret, W3139
HERTER, Lawrence, N.Y. See HARTER
Philip, N.Y., S28760
HERTZ, Conrad, Flying Camp, Pa., S22293
HERTZBERG, George, Von Heer's Corps., BLWt.13159-100-Corp. Iss. 8/9/179?. No papers
HERVEY, Benjamin, Mass., N.Y., S10832
Jonathan, Mass., See HARVEY
Paul, Mass. See HARVEY
HESCOCK, Samuel, Mass., S15450
HESELTON, Joseph, N.H., Elizabeth, W23270
HESS, Christian, N.Y., Elizabeth, W17068
Conrad, N.Y., R4927
Daniel, N.Y., S22826
George, Pa., Barbara, W3418
Han Jost/John Joseph, N.Y., S44926
Hezekiah, Va., S8707
Jacob, Pa. See HUSS
Johannis/John, N.Y. No papers. Invalid pensioner, res. unknown, N.Y. Agcy., $12 per annum. Probably Arm of Rev.
John Joseph, N.Y. See Han Jost
Michael, N.Y., S13353
Peter Martin/Martin Peter, N.J., Mary, R4928
HESSELTINE, David, N.H., S39639
John, Mass. See HASSELTINE
HESSER, Frederick, Pa., S22292
HESTER, Abraham, N.C., S21813
Benjamin, N.C., S6998

HESTER (continued)
Charles, S.C., R4930
Farel/Ferrel, Md., N.C., S32315
Joseph, N.C., Elizabeth, W19762
Robert, N.C., S31737
Thomas, N.C., S6991
Zachariah, N.C., S7002
HESTON, Edward, Pa., Sarah, W3681
Thomas, Pa., Hannah, W3250
HESUM, John, N.Y., BLWt.7236-100-Pvt. Iss. 1/6/1791. No papers
HETFIELD, Daniel, N.J., Sarah, W144
Stephen, N.J., Elizabeth, W2734; BLWt.345-60-55
HETH, Henry, Va., BLWt.1070-300-Capt. Iss. 8/29/1791. No papers
John, Va., BLWt.1081-200-Lt. Iss. 8/22/1789. No papers
William, N.H. See HEATH
William, Va., BLWt.1064-500-Col. Iss. 2/9/1798. No papers
HETHCOCK, Holiday, N.C., R4812
HETHERLY, Thomas, Va., S2612
HETRICK, John, Pa., Susanna, R4843
HEUSTEN, William, Mass. See HUESTEN
HEVELO, Reuben, Del., S31739
HEVENOR, Charles, See HEBNER
HEWELL, William, Va., Susannah, R4931; Reg. 92407-55
Wyatt, Va., S32308
HEWES, Benjamin, Mass., Hannah, W1426
Benjamin, Mass., Jemima, W17995
Daniel, Cont., Mass., Privateer, S13359
George, R.T., Mass., Privateer, Ct. & R.I., S13367
Joseph, N.H., See HEWS
Samuel, N.H., Betsey, W23259
William, N.H., S32311; BLWt.7052-160-55
HEWET, Gideon, N.Y., S22294
William, N.H., BLWt.3174-100-Pvt. Iss. 10/2/1795 to James A. Neal, ass. No papers
HEWETT, Alice Rogers, former wid. of Josiah Rogers, Ct. which see
Andrew, Ct., See HEWIT
Bartimeus, Mass., Anna, W25767
Charles, Crane's Cont. Art., Mass. BLWt.4442-100-Pvt. Iss. 1/13/1792 to Heil Peck. No papers
Ebenezer, N.C., S41632
Elisha, Cont., Ct., S16151
Elkanah, N.Y. See HEWIT
Ephraim, Mass., See HEWIT
John, Mass., R4934
Patrick, Va., S4350
Richard, Ct. See HEWITT
Sterry, Ct., R.I., S13354
Thomas, Mass., S17473
William, N.H., See HEWIT
HEWINS, Joseph, Mass., N.Y., S29884
HEWIT, Andrew, Ct., Julia, W27860
Arthur, N.Y., R4933
Asa, Cont., Vt., Green Mt. Boys, S43657
Edward, Ct. See Edmund HEWITT
Elkanah, Ct., Desire, W1280; BLWt.26930-160-55
Ephraim, Mass., Susannah, R4937

HEWIT (continued)
Gershom, Ct., Green Mt. Boys, S31735
John, Ct., S43660
John, Va., Margaret, W2618; BLWt.26545-160-55
Joseph, Ct., S43659
Nathaniel, R.I., S19328
Randal, Ct., S43664
Richard, Ct., S23258; BLWt.26032-160-55
William, N.H., Sarah, W23267; BLWt.3174-100-Pvt. Iss. 10/12/1795 to Jas. S. Neal, ass.
HEWITT, Bartimeus, Mass. See HEWETT
Caleb, Pa., BLWt.1280-100
Daniel, Ct., Sarah, R4930
Ebenezer, N.C., See HEWETT
Edmund/Edward, Ct., N.Y., Hannah, W15774
Elisha, Cont. Ct., See HEWETT
Henry, Ct., S29218
Israel, Ct., Sally, W2796
James, Md., BLWt.2125-100
James, N.Y., S13358
John, N.C., See HUITT
John, N.C., R4935
Lewis, Ct., Sea Service, Charlotte W17066
Richard, Ct., Cont., Experience, W16599
Robert, Ct., Abigail, W3683; BLWt.5251-160-55
Shamgar, N.J., Letter of Marque, R4932
Simeon, Ct., Mehala, W25766
Thomas, Ct., Sea Service, R4939
HEWLETT, Aaron, Ct., Cynthia, W19831; BLWt.18365-160-55
Asa, Mass. See HULET
HEWS, Alpheus, N.J., Va., S2299
James, Va. See HUGHES
Joseph, N.H., Cynthia, W4983; BLWt.17876-160-55
Samuel, N.H., See HEWES
HEXT, William, S.C. See HIXT
HEYDECKER, John Anthony, S.C., b. Ger., S32317
HEYDON, Allyn/Allen, Ct., S29220
David, Ct., S43668
HEYER, Jacob, N.J., BLWt.1000-150. No papers
Jacob, N.Y., BLWt.7262-100-Pvt. Iss. 8/11/1790 to Robert Dunlap ass. No papers
HEYSHAM, David, Va., Elizabeth, W3810; BLWt.24995-160-55
HEYWARD, Caleb, Mass., BLWt.4314-100-Pvt. Iss. 4/3/1792. No papers
HEYWOOD, Benjamin, Cont., Mass., Mehitable/Mehetabel, W19688; BLWt.918-300-Capt. Iss. 4/1/1790
Eleazer, N.H., See HAYWOOD
John, Mass., Hannah Lamson, former wid., W15300; BLWt.34810-160-55
Nathaniel, Mass., S29880
HEZELTON, Joseph, See HESELTON
HIATT, Asa, Md., R4943
Minnah, N.Y. See HYATT
Shadrack, Md., S13361

HIBBARD
Aaron, Ct., Sarah, W16602
Andrew, Ct., Ruth, W19774
Andrew, Ct., BLWt.1488-100
Arminda, former wid. of Obadiah Phelps, which see
David, Ct., Cont., S10835
Ebenezer, Ct. See HEBBERD
Ebenezer, Ct. See HEBBARD
Israel, Cont.,Mass., Abigail,R4944
Jacob, Mass. See HEBBERD
Joseph, Ct. See HEBBARD
Joseph, Cont., Mass., Dorothy, W23291
Rufus, Ct., See HEBBARD
Silas, Ct. See HUBBARD
Thomas, N.H., Lucy Sandborn/Sanborn, former wid., W15311
Timothy, Ct., S44422
Timothy, Ct., Abigail Noble, former wid., W19931
Uriah, Ct. See HEBARD
Vine Timothy, Ct., Dorcas, W662; BLWt.24755-160-55
William, Ct., S13400. Arminda Hebbard/Hibbard, wid. of sold. was pensioned as former wid. of Obadiah Phelps, Cont., which see
HIBBEN, John, War of 1812, BLRej. 273759-55, Barbary. See Nicholas Starnes, Va.
HIBBERD, Oliver, Mass. See HEBBERD
HIBBERT, Jonathan, Pa. See HEBBERD
Joseph, Mass. See HIBBARD
Mercy, former wid. of Jacob Doyen, N.H., which see
HIBBIN, John, War of 1812, See HIBBEN
HICE, George, Pa., S22423
HICHBERGER, Adam, Hazen's Regt., BLWt.13186-100-Pvt. Iss. 4/9/1793. No papers
HICHCOX, Asher, Pvt., Ct., BLWt. 5958 iss. 2/9/1793 to Peter DeWitt
HICHMAN, Salsbury, Pvt., Mass., BLWt.4408 iss. 3/26/1792 to John Peck
HICK, Joshua, Mass., S23697
HICKCOX, Amelia, former wid. of Robert Wilson, N.Y., which see
Amos, Ct., R4957
Asher, Ct., S46384
Elihu, Mass. See HECOX
Giles, N.Y., Mass., S2311
HICKEL, Samuel, Va. See HICKLE
HICKENS, John, Md., BLWt.11295-100-Pvt. Iss. 2/7/1790. No papers
HICKES, Jesse, N.C. See HICKS
HICKEY, Daniel, ---, Me. res. & agcy., S19703
Daniel, Pa., Jane, W7744
David, Pa., Dis. No papers
George, N.Y., Catherine, W18009
James, Va., Elizabeth, R4946
John, N.Y., R4945
HICKLE, Lewis, Va., R4947
Samuel, Va., Elizabeth, W7743

HICKLEY, Thomas, Pa., BLWt.9593-100-Pvt. Iss. 8/10/1792 to Evander Childs, ass. No papers
HICKLIN, Jonathan, Pvt. Ky., BLWt. 90121-120-55
HICKMAN, Adam, Pa., S38030
Adam, Va., S5540
Benjamin, N.C., Judith, W366
Edwin, Sr., N.C., S8712; BLWt. 15411-160-55
Francis, Pa., Va., S16876
Henry, Md., R20379
Isaac, N.J., R4950
Jacob, Del., S32318
Jacob, N.C., S41643
James, Va., S31130
James, Va., Elizabeth, W1768; BLWt.15155-160-55
Joel, Va., S13391
John, N.C., S31127
John, N.C., Elizabeth, W7745
John B., Va., S18445
Michael, Ct., R20514
Samuel, Md.,S.C., See HICKMON
Solsbury, Mass. See HITCHMAN, Salisbury
Sotha, Va., S5516
Thomas, Cont., N.J., R21703
Thomas, N.C., S4371
William, N.C., S16877
William, Va., Rebecca B., R4953
HICKMON, Samuel, Md., S.C.,S9581
Theophilus, N.C., R4954
HICKOCK, Ichabod, Mass. See HICOK
HICKOK, Asa, Ct., Esther, W2798
Benjamin, Vt., Rebecca, R4958
Daniel, Ct., S13402
Darius, Ct., Lucinda Miles, former wid., W18521
Durlin, Mass., Betsey, W4988
Ebenezer, Ct., S5541
Nathaniel, Ct., S2316
Samuel, See HICOCK
Sarah, former wid. of Ebenezer Blodget, N.H., which see
HICKOX, David, Ct., See HICOCK
Ebenezer, Ct., S2617
James, Ct., Hannah, W18011
Stephen, Mass., S29891
HICKS, Abraham, Navy, R.I., Mary, R21329
Benjamin, N.H., S44421
Benjamin, N.Y., S--- (Ctf. No. 349); BLWt.982-300-Capt. Iss. 6/9/1791. No papers
Benjamin, N.Y., R4959
Daniel, N.Y., S47267
Daniel, R.I., S21285
Daniel, S.C., S5533; BLWt.26266-160-55
David, R.I., S38831
David, S.C., R5063
Dempsey, ---, R4960. Ind. res. in 1834. Rej. book states rejected on acct. of desertion. Papers in the case of Dempsey Hicks of Ind. were sent to the Hon. E.A. Hannegan on 2/26/1834, by J.L. Edwards, Comm. of Pensions, & since that time have not been held in this office.
Durfee, Navy, R.I., S43680

HICKS (continued)
Gabriel, Mass., R4961
Gershom, Pa., BLWt.9570-100-Pvt. Iss. 4/20/1796. No papers
Harris, N.C., Temperance, W4989
Henry, Va., R4962
Isaac, Ga., BLWt.1113-300-Capt. Iss. 3/12/1794. No papers
Isaac, N.C., S38024
Jacob, N.Y., BLWt.7224-100-Pvt. Iss. 3/25/1791 to David Quinton, ass. No papers
Jacob, N.Y., Polly, W23290
James, Mass., S19332
Jesse, N.C., Zelvira, W25773; BLWt.17871-160-55
Joel, Va., S4365
John, Ct., S13406
John, Cont., Mass., S19706
John, N.C., Elizabeth, W4695
John, Va., S1527
John, Va., S7018
John, Va., S41638
Joseph, N.Y., Julia Ann, W11297
Josiah, Mass., Susannah, R4965
Mary, former wid. of Solomon Whitlow, N.C., which see
Meshach, Va., Elizabeth, BL Reg. 226005-55. No pension claim
Micajah, N.C., Mary, W7738
Miles, Va., Maria, W758; BLWt. 26785-160-55
Nathan, Mass., S30485
Samuel, Ct., Cont., S18446
Samuel, Mass., S28762
Samuel, N.J., S34400
Samuel, R.I., S17480
Sarah, former wid. of Reuben Woodmancy, R.I., which see
Simeon, Mass., N.H., Vt., S16152
Solomon, S.C., S31128
Stephen, Mass., See HIX
Thomas, N.Y., R4966
William, Cont., Va., S38027
William, Md., BLWt.11342-100-Pvt. Iss. 11/29/1790 to Christian Boss, admr. No papers
William, N.Y., Phoebe, R4964
William, Va., S7016
William, Va., S35410
William, Va., Mary, W8931
Zechariah/Zachariah, Mass., S29889
HICOCK, David, Ct., S41637
Samuel, Ct., Cont., S43673
HICOK, David, Ct. See HICOCK
Ichabod, Mass., S32838
Samuel, Mass., R4956
HICXSON, Matthew, N.J., S18022
HIDDEN, Samuel, Mass., Sea Service, Elizabeth Story, former wid., W27774
HIDE, Agur, Ct., S36610
Jesse, N.C., R4968
John, Md., BLWt.11319-100-Pvt. Iss. 7/31/1797 to James DeBaufre, ass. No papers
Thaddeus, Mass. See HYDE
William, N.C., S9601
HIDECKER, John Anthony, See HEYDECKER
HIDEN, William, Va. See HYDEN
HIDLER, Joshua, Pa., R4969
HIER, Hendrick, N.J., Sarah, W7731
Jacob, N.Y., S44202
Walter, N.J., Elizabeth Brown, former wid., W147
HIESTER, Joseph, Pa., S5532
HIFFINGTON, Archibald, Va. See HEFFINGTON
HIGBEE, Edward, N.J., Sarah, R4971
Elnathan, Mass., N.Y., Abigail, W19784
Hendrick, N.J., S43676
Sarah, former wid. of Thomas Harron, Pa., which see
HIGBEY, Samuel, N.Y., BLWt.7228-100-Pvt. Iss. 9/25/1790 to Daniel W. Birdsall, ass. No papers
HIGBY, Nathaniel, Ct., Nancy,R4972
Samuel, Ct., Hannah, W11301
HIGDEN, Joseph, Not Rev. War, Whiskey Rebellion & Wayne's War-1795, Old War Inv. Rej. 21040. Enl. Md. Pension application-Ky.
HIGDON, Charles, Va. Sea Service, S5538
Daniel, N.C., Mary, W25769; BLWt. 3774-160-55
Joseph, Cont., Md., Margaret, W8935
Leonard, N.C., Susannah, R4975
Philip, N.C., S10839
HIGGANS, Daniel, Va., S17482, not same as S5527, Daniel Higgins
HIGGASON, Samuel, Va., S4370
Thomas, Va., S13393
HIGGENS, Phillip, Mass. See HIGGINS
HIGGIBOTHAM, Jacob, Va. See HIGGINBOTHAM
HIGGINBOTHAM, Benjamin, Va., S5542
Jacob, Va., R4977
James, Va., R15097. Va. Half Pay
William, Va., S46448
HIGGINS, Ananias, N.C., R4979
Andrew, Del., S39686
Benjamin, Ct., Jane, W16600
Benjamin, Mass., S33300; BLWt. 767-100
Cornelius, Ct., Cont., Esther, W21325
Daniel, Va."& later Wars", S5527 Not same as Daniel Higgans
Daniel, Va. see HIGGANS
Ebenezer, Ct., Mary, R21320
Eleazer, Mass., Lurania, W19786
Hawes, Ct., S16873
Henry, Mass., S21283
Henry, S.C., R4978
Ichabod, Mass., S39690
Isaac, Ct., N.Y., Hannah, W19773; BLWt.35839-160-55
James, N.J., Rebecca, W270
James, Pa., BLWt.9556-100-Pvt. Iss. 2/21/1793 to Gideon Merkle, ass. No papers
James, Va., BLWt.975-300-Capt. Iss. 11/27/1794. Also recorded as BLWt.2647. No papers
John, Va., Mary, W365
Joseph, Ct., BLWt.971-300-Surg. Mate. Iss. 12/13/1796. No papers
HIGGINS (continued)
Josiah, Mass., S32832
Moses, N.Y., Elizabeth, W18002
Nathaniel, Cont., Mass., S43685
Nathaniel, N.Y., BLWt.7287-100-Pvt. Iss. 10/10/1791 to Anthony Maxwell, ass. No paper
Peter, Va., BLWt.1076-200-Lt. Iss. 4/5/1796. No papers
Philip, Mass., Mary, W23277
Solomon, Mass., Sea Service, S18448
Thomas, N.Y., Abigail, W19783
Timothy, Ct., S37109
Timothy, Cont., Mass., Susannah, R4982
William, Ct., BLWt.963-200-Lt. Iss. 5/17/1796 to Wm. Higgins. No papers
William, Va., S16155
HIGGS, Henry, Md., BLWt.11355-100 Pvt. Iss. 2/1/1790. No papers
John, N.C., R4983
Samuel, N.Y., S44199
HIGH, Gardner, Va., N.C., Rachel, W19778
George, Pa., S23701
Jacob, Va., S32322
John, Va., R4985
HIGHBAUGH, George, Ga., R20512
HIGHNOTE, Philip, Ga., Agness, W10108
HIGHSMITH, Moses, N.C., Esther, W7752
HIGHT, George, Cont., Va., Lovia, W19769
John N., N.J., S31743
Matthew, Va., S8715
Patrick, Va., S4988
Robert, N.C., Mary, R4987
Thomas, Va., S32321
HIGHTOWER, Joshua, S.C., Va., S10834
HIGLEY, Brewster, Ct., Vt., Naomi, W7742
Nathaniel, Ct. see HIGBY
Obed, Ct., Cont., S17481
Roswell, Ct., N.Y., S13411
Seba, Mass., N.Y., Bethiah, W1179; BLWt.19765-160-55
Seth, Cont., N.Y., Lucy, W18005
HIGHNIGHT, James, N.C., Va., S16153
HIGNOTE, Philip, See HIGHNOTE
HILAND, Amasa, Mass., Prudence, W23287
HILBERT, John, Armand's Corps, BLWt.13155-100-Pvt. Iss. 3/22/1797 to Abijah Holbrook, ass. No papers
William, Mass., S33297
HILBORN, Robert, Mass., Lucy, W23293
HILDRETH, Abel, Mass., Haldah, W21322
Abijah, Mass.,N.H., See HILDRITH
Ephraim, N.H., R4989
Jeremiah, Mass., Abigail, W19776
Jesse, N.H., S33305
Jonathan, Mass., S33298
Jonathan, N.J., Amanda Lyon,

HILDRETH (continued)
former wid., W10209; BLWt. 87049-160-55
Martin, N.H., Zilpha, W18007
Reuben, Cont., N.H., S43674
Simeon, N.H., S10836
William, Mass., Mary, W7747; BLWt. 36238-160-55 & 930-200-Lt. Iss. 12/15/1796. No papers
HILDRITH, Abijah, Mass., N.H., S13362
Ephraim, N.H., BLWt.3179-100-Pvt. Iss. 4/5/1796 to Samuel Stone. No papers
HILDTIBRANT, Charles, Pvt., N.J., BLReg.280017-1855
HILER, Henry, Cont.,Pa. See HILGER
Jacob, Mass., Sea Service, Navy, Grace, W19781
John, Va. (?), Jane, ---
HILES, Conrad/Coonrod, Pa.,S39692
John, Va., S31125
HILEY, Abraham, Pa., S31744
John, Mass., S37108
HILFORD, Matthew, Del., BLWt. 10783-100-Pvt. Iss. 8/4/1789 to Benjamin Toland, exer. of Adam Toland, dec'd, ass. No papers
HILGER, Andrew, Hazen's Regt., BLWt.13187-100-Pvt. Iss. 6/24/1793 to Edward Osborn, ass. No papers
Henry, Cont., Pa., S39688; BLWt. 257-100
HILGERT, Peter, Pa. See HILYARD
HILHARD, Thurston, Art. Artificiers, Ct., BLWts.5913 & 13201-100-Pvt. Iss. 10/25/1796 No papers
HILIARD, Joseph, Va. See HILLIARD
HILL, Aaron, Mass., Katharine, W21315
Abner, Ct., S37100
Abraham, Mass., Ruth, W18015; BLWt.17731-160-55
Abraham, N.C., S.C., S7015
Abram, Ct., Lydia, W25770; BLWt.9429-160-55
Abram, N.C., S15890
Adam, Pa., BLWt.9551-100-Pvt. Iss. 5/15/179?. No papers
Alexander, Pa., BLWt.9611-100-Pvt. Iss. 8/7/1795 to James Decorcy, ass. No papers
Alexander, Pa., R4991
Alpheus, Mass., Martha, W13454
Amasa, N.Y., S9578
Ambrose, Mass., Lucy, W21338
Andrew, Mass., R4992
Asa, Cont., Mass., Privateer, Sarah, W24433
Asa, N.Y., S44198
Bartholomew, Mass., S13399
Baylor, Va., BLWt.249-300-Capt. Iss. 5/3/1800. Also recorded under BLWts.2716 & 940. No papers
Benajah, Ct., S23699
Benajah, Mass., S41635
Benjamin, Mass., S22305
Benjamin, N.C., R4993
Benjamin, R.I., Hannah, W23280

HILL (continued)
Benjamin Benoni, See Benoni
Benoni/Benjamin Benoni, Cont., N.H. & U.S. Navy 'til 1820, Ruby Willson/Wilson, former wid. W6529; BLWt.38335-160-55
Bernard, Mass., S29225
Caleb, N.Y., S4376
Caleb, R.I., Sarah, W21337
Christopher, Navy, R.I., S38828
Clem/Clement, Va., Mary, W10106
Cyrus, Mass., Relief, W2548
Daniel, Ct., BLWt.5911-100-Pvt. Iss. 11/24/1791 to Isaac Bronson. No papers
Daniel, Ct., Cont., See HILLS
Daniel, Cont., Mass., S28763
Daniel, Mass., S10841
Daniel, Mass., Alice, W19775
Daniel, N.J., Mary, W18008
Daniel, N.C., S1670
David, Ct., N.Y., Chloe Blackman/Blockmon, former wid., R15052
David, Ga., Polly Worldley, former wid., R11867
David, Mass., S31129
David, Mass., Parnell, W18012
Ebenezer, Ct., See Primus
Ebenezer, Ct., S43691; BLWt. 1691-100
Ebenezer, N.H., Sally, W25776; BLWt.44515-160-55
Edmond E., N.Y., BLWt.7283-100-Pvt. Iss. 2/24/1791 to Shadwick Mead, ass. No papers
Edmund E., Mass., N.Y., S33306
Eleazer, N.Y., See HILLS
Elijah, Ct., Esther, W13457
Elisha, Mass., S43682
Erastus, Ct., S43675
Frederick, Cont., Pa., b. Ger., Elizabeth, W7736
Frederick, Pa., S35408
Frederick/Fridrick, Pa., S47702
George, Cont., Ct. res. & agcy., Elizabeth Conway, former wid., W18885
George, Cont., Va., Hannah, W4987 BLWt.614-100
George, Va., BLWt.12178 & 13236-100-Pvt. Iss. 6/19/1793. No papers
George, Va., S41642
Hannah, former wid. of Joseph Green, Mass., which see
Henry, Ct., S15455
Henry, Md., Hester, W14907
Henry, N.H., R4999
Henry, N.Y., BLWt.7247-100-Pvt. Iss. 8/3/1790 to Cornelius Van Dyck, ass. No papers
Henry, N.Y., Nelly, W23279
Henry, Pa., Rachel, W2800
Henry, Va., S41639
Hermon, Md., S30482
Humphrey, Va., S5530
Ichabod, Cont., Ct., Anna, W2549; BLWt.2353-160-55
Ichabod, Mass., BLWt.4359-100-Pvt. Iss. 5/5/1794. No papers
Isaac, Ct. & French & Indian War, S31747

HILL (continued)
Isaac, N.C., Nancy, W3812
Isaac, N.C., R5001
Isaac, R.I., S21286
Israel, Mass., War of 1812, Lydia, W21323
Jacob, Pa., BLWt.9523-100-Pvt. Iss. 5/3/1792. No papers
Jacob, R.I., R5002
James, Md., S9579
James, Mass., S5515
James, Mass., Rebeckah, W15682
James, Mass., Sarah Staples, former wid., BLWt.36547-160-55
James, N.C., Anne, W3815
James, R.I., See HILLS
James, R.I., See HITT
James, Va., S38029
Jedediah, Ct., Abigail, W23274; BLWt.26491-160-55
Jeremiah, Cont., Mass., S35406
Jeremiah, Mass., BLWt.922-200-Lt. Iss. 1/4/1794. No papers
Jesse, Mass., S13389
Joel, Mass., S15451
Joel, N.C., Anne/Anna, W23288; BLWt.28636-160-55
John, Ct., Rhoda, W11302
John, Cont., BLWt.663-100
John, Cont., Mass., S19333
John, Cont., Va., Nancy, W3814
John, Md., S34921
John, Mass., S13401
John, Mass., S18444
John, Mass., S33299
John, N.Y., S43683
John, N.C., S13383
John, N.C., (son of Abraham), Huldah, W18014
John, N.C., R21669
John, N.C., BLWt.1100-200-Lt. Iss. 2/7/1798 to Gabriel Holmes, ass. No papers
John/John P., N.C., Creek War & War of 1812, S2615
John, Pa., BLWt.9612-100-Pvt. Iss. 3/17/1791 to Alexander Power, ass. No papers
John, Pa., Maria/Mary, W2799
John, Pa., Elizabeth, W5298
John, R.I., S21816
John, S.C., Savory, R5012
John, Va., S5536
John, Va., S38026
John, Va., Mary, W19770
John B., Navy, N.H., S44418
John P., N.C. See John Hill
John S., Del., Martha D., R5004
Jonas, N.C., Mary Castlebury, former wid., R1799
Jonathan, Mass., BLWt.4339-100-Pvt. Iss. 2/23/1797 to William Blanchard. No papers
Jonathan, Mass., Anna, W14911
Jonathan, Mass., Rosilla, W16291
Jonathan, N.H., BLWt.3201-100-Pvt. Iss. 3/25/1790. No papers
Jonathan, N.H., Sarah, W14910
Jonathan, R.I., S38830
Joseph, BLWt.13204-100-Pvt."In the Artillery Artificiers". Iss. 4/14/1790 to Wm. Wells,

HILL (continued)
ass. No papers
Joseph, Cont., N.Y. res. & agcy., S47276
Joseph, Cont., Mass., S33303
Joseph, Mass., S32830
Joseph, N.C., Sarah, R5010
Joseph, Pa., S23702
Joshua, N.C., S7017
Joshua, N.C., b. Va., R5003
Josiah, Ct., R.I., Ellen, W13456
Leonard, Mass., S32833
Levi, R.I., S22303
Lydia, former wid. of Joseph Tupper, Mass., which see
Martha, former wid. of Josiah Baldwin, Ct., which see
Moses, Mass., S16415
Nathaniel, Mass., S38826
Nicholas, N.Y., Sarah, W11294; BLWt.7260-100-Pvt. Iss. 8/3/1790 to Cornelius V. Dyck, ass. & BLWt.321-60-55
Nicholas D., N.H., S18821
Noah, Mass., S29890
Obadiah, Lamb's Artillery, N.Y. BLWt.7299-100-Pvt. Iss. 10/7/1789. No papers
Parker, Mass., Elizabeth, R21799
Peleg, Ct., Mary, W23281
Peter, Cont., Mass., Susanna, W27428
Philemon, Ct., BLWt.961-200-Lt. Iss. 7/14/1789 to himself. Wt. via G.L. Office returned to ditto 6/23/1827. No papers
Philip, Md., BLWt.1051-200-Lt. Iss. 9/24/1792. No papers
Primus/Ebenezer (colored), Ct., S43677
Reuben, Ct., R5007
Reuben, Navy, Mass., Catharine, W23292
Reuben, N.Y., War of 1812, S22831; BLWt.30625-160-55
Reuben, N.C., S31742; BLWt. 26342-160-55
Richard, Mass., Invalid Corps, BLWt.4310 & 13228-100-Pvt. Iss. 4/18/1798 to Christopher S. Thorn, ass. No papers
Richard, Mass., S39687
Richard, Mass., Ellen Delanoy, former wid., R2853. She was pensioned as former wid. of Abraham Ressequie, Ct., which see
Richard, N.C., Esther, R4996
Richard, N.C., Rebecca, R5006
Richard, Va., S5528
Richard, Va., R5008
Robert, Mass., Jane, W15775
Robert, N.H., R5009
Robert, N.Y., S13364
Robert, N.C., S7012
Robert, Va., S13390
Robert, Va., S38833
Roswell, Md., N.C., Sarah, R5011
Samuel, Del., or Md., N.C., Va., S9577
Samuel, Mass., BLWt.4342-100-Pvt. Iss. 3/26/1796 to Peter

HILL (continued)
Swier. No papers
Samuel, Mass., S32835
Samuel, Mass., Anna, W14908
Samuel, Mass., Olive, W19785
Samuel, Mass., N.H., S13387
Samuel, Navy, Mass., Rebecca, W21317
Sarah, former wid. of William Gray, Mass., which see
Simeon, Mass., S5539
Simon, Va., S41644
Smith, Va. See Hill SMITH
Solomon, Mass., S19705
Solomon, N.Y., S18023
Stephen, Pa., R5013
Stukley/Stukely, R.I., Sarah, W21318
Thomas, Ct., S43678
Thomas, Cont., Mass., Ruth Stubbs, former wid., W25090
Thomas, Mass., BLWt.4425-100-Pvt. Iss. 2/22/1790 to Richard Platt. No papers
Thomas, Mass., S29885
Thomas, N.H., S22301
Thomas, N.J., Charity, W935
Thomas, N.Y., S43672; BLWt. 1283-100
Thomas, N.C., Elizabeth, W663; BLWt.35825-160-55
Thomas, N.C., Catharine, W1606
Thomas, R.I., S37101
Thomas, S.C., S31131
Thomas, Va., BLWt.1067-400-Major
Thomas, Va., BLWt.1429-100. Iss. 12/6/1828 to James Hill, brother
Uri, Ct., Mass., S19331
Uriah, N.Y., S43681
Whitney, Mass., Rachel, W14914
Willey, N.H., R5015
William, Md., BLWt.11321-100-Pvt. Iss. 11/1/1791 to William Lane, ass. No papers
William, Mass., S32831; BLWt.673-100
William, Navy, Boston, Mass. res. in 1818, S32836
William, N.H., Lucy, W17069; BLWt.2182-100
William, N.Y., Abigail, W13447
William, N.C., b. Va., R5016
William, Va., BLWt.12241-100-Pvt. Iss. 1/3/1793 to Robert Means, ass. No papers
William, Va., S5529
William, Va., S5531
William, Va., Anna, W2939
William, Pvt., Va., BLReg.288611-1855
Zimri, Ct., S27996
HILLAN, James, N.C., S38028
HILLARD, Azariah, Ct., S13386
David, N.Y., S13392
John, Ct., S37102
Jonathan, R.I. See HILLIARD
Sarah, former wid. of John Steele Ct., which see
William, Cont., Ct., Hannah, W18010
HILLARY, Ashburn/Ausburn, Md., Elenore, W8219; BLWt.26633-160-55

HILLARY (continued)
Christopher, Ga., BLWt.1243-200
Rignal, Md., BLWt.1659-200
HILLBURN, John, S.C., S31745
HILLEBRANT, Henry, N.J., BLWt. 8408-100-Pvt. Iss. 1/19/1798 to Abraham Bell, ass. No papers
HILLEN, George, N.C., S.C., S7006
HILLER, Edward, Mass., R5019
John George/George, Cont., Pa., S2305
Thomas, Mass. Sea Service, Navy, S29894
Timothy, Ct., Mass., S10833
HILLERY, John, N.H., Margaret Flint, former wid., W19286; BLWt.6037-160-55
Rignal, Md. See HILLARY
HILLHOUSE, William, S.C., S7008
HILLIARD, Azariah, Ct. See HILLARD
Barnabas, Ct., Martha, W7749; BLWt.27669-160-55
Daniel, Ct. See HILYARD
John, Cont.,Va., Elizabeth, W7748
Jonathan, R.I., Susannah, W23283
Joseph, Ct., Lois Cheesbrough, former wid., W16901
Joseph, Va., S38033; BLWt.993-100
Lucretia, former wid. of Charles F. Brown, Ct., which see
Luther, N.H., S17478
Mary, former wid. of Wm. Brumley/Brumbley, Ct., which see
Peter, Pa. See HILYARD
Thomas, N.C., S9576
Thurston, Ct., Dis. No papers
William, Cont., Ct. See HILLARD
HILLIKER, Nicholas, N.Y., Rachel, W18006
HILLIS, Samuel, N.C., S2314
HILLMAN, Benjamin, --, Mass. res., Mary, R---
Benjamin, Pa., Mary, R5022
James, Pa., 1784-1785 & War of 1812, R5020
John, Pa., R5021
Samuel, N.J., Mary A., W3813; BLWt.26448-160-55
William, Md., BLWt.11323-100-Pvt. Iss. 8/27/1789. No papers
William, Md., Sally, W4230
HILLMON, William, Pa., BLWt.9563-100-Pvt. Iss. 5/21/1792 to Moses Sill, ass. No papers
HILLOCK, Robert, Mass., BLWt.4303-100-Pvt. Iss. 11/27/1797 to John Duncan, ass. No papers
HILLS, Asahel, Cont., Ct., S38829
Daniel, Ct., Cont., S10838
Ebenezer, Ct., BLWt.974-300-Capt. Iss. 6/14/1790. No papers. See his commissions in claim of his son Ebenezer, Jr., Ct., N.Y.
Ebenezer, Jr., Ct., N.Y., Rev. & 1786, Mary, W7735
Ebenezer, N.H., Hannah, W19777
Eleazer, N.Y., S5537
Frederick, N.Y., Dis. No papers
Guy, Ct., S13405
Jacob, Ct., S18447
James, Mass., S21284
John, Mass., R.I., Mehitable,

HILLS (continued)
W19787
John, N.H., Mary, W16028
John, N.C., S16413
Joseph, Ct., S17477
Joseph, Ct., S37107
Nathan, Ct., BLWt.5899-100-Pvt. Iss. 9/1/1790 to Theodosius Fowler. No papers
Nathan, Ct., R5018
Nathaniel, Mass., S30483
Nathaniel/Samuel, N.H., S44419
Samuel, Ct., S13407
Samuel, N.H., See Nathaniel
Seth, Ct., Karine, W19779
Solomon, N.Y. See HILL
Stephen, Cont., See George HILL, Cont., Ct.
Stephen, Mass., S44420
Susan, former wid. of James Faxon, N.H., which see
Thomas, Mass., S29226
Thomas, Mass., N.H., S15452
William, Mass., N.H., S19334
Zimry, Ct., Mille, W3992
HILLSINGER, Elias, N.Y., R5024
Michael, N.Y., See HELSINGER
HILLSMAN, Jose, Va. See Joseph
Joseph/Jose, Va., Elizabeth, W7854; BLWt.36729-160-55
HILLYARD, Daniel, Ct. See HILYARD
HILLYER, Andrew, Ct., also served in British Army, Lucy, W8933; BLWt.17720-160-55
Asa, Ct., S37105
David, Corps of Invalids, BLWt. 13207-100-QM Sgt. Iss. 8/4/1789 to Matt. McConnell, ass. No papers
James, N.J., S2318
James, --, Penelope, --. No papers. See case of her former husb., David Goodrich, Ct.
Pliny, Ct., Jane, R5025
Seth, Ct., Sibil, W4496
Theodore, Ct., S37104
William, N.J., Mary, W92
HILMAN, Thomas, N.J., S32320
William, Md. See HILLMAN
HILMERHAUSEN, Frederick Hendrick See HELMERSHAUSON, Henry F.
HILSABECK, Jacob, N.C., S7013
HILSEY, Joseph, N.J., BLWt.8377-100-Pvt. Iss. 5/28/1790. No papers
HILSINGER, Jacob, N.Y., S22830
HILTEN, Jacob W., See HILTON
HILTON, Andrew, Md., S32316
Derick/Derrick/Richard, N.Y., Maria, W3550; BLWt.14965-160-55
Dudley, N.H., S19335
Ebenezer, Cont., Mass., S18018
Ebenezer, Mass., Abigail/Abby, W23289
Edward, Mass., Mary, W23278
Edward, Va., S2312
Hale, Mass., Elizabeth, W2564; BLWt.13880-160-55
Isaac, Mass., Privateer, S18019
Jacob W., N.Y., Mary, W19788

HILTON (continued)
James, N.Y., S13395
James, N.C., S30484
John, Del., Lydia, W9062
John, N.H., BLWt.3190-100-Pvt. Iss. 6/12/1792 to Wm. Kline, ass. No papers
John Pike, N.H., Love, W21316
Jonathan, N.Y., Catharine, W21335
Joseph, Cont., Mass., S15887
Joseph, N.H., Anna, W1863
Morral/Morrill, R.I., Lydia, W23285
Richard, N.Y., S13403
Richard, N.Y., See Derick HILTON
Richard, N.Y., R20513
Samuel, Mass., Susan, BLWt. 104272-160-55
Susannah, former wid. of George Mason, Mass., which see
William, Cont., Mass., N.H. & Navy, Anne, W7750, b. New Market, N.H. & d. at Cornville, Somerset Co., Me., 1/22/1841
William, Mass., Hannah, W1181; BLWt.3396-160-55, b. Wiscasset, Me., d. 7/14/1846
William, N.H., W16124. He resided at Salisbury, N.H., during Rev. & d. at Schenectady, N.Y. 9/1/1792
HILTS, George/George N., N.Y., BLWt.15181-160-55
John, N.Y., Susanna, W24434
Lawrence, N.Y., S9352
HILTSDORPH, John, Pa., BLWt.9546-100-Pvt. Iss. 6/7/1790. No papers
HILTY, Conrad, Lamb's Art., N.Y., BLWt.7286-100-Pvt. Iss. 9/15/1790 No papers
HILYARD, Daniel, Ct., Sea Service, Rebecca, W23294; BLWt.10230-160-55
Jonathan, N.H., S44423
Joshua, Ct., Sea Service, Elizabeth, W549; BLWt.31273-160-55
Minor, Ct., Vt., S22302
Peter, Pa., Elizabeth, S2317
Peter, S.C., S18020
HIMELWRIGHT, John, Pa., Catharine, W19771
HIMINGER, John, Pa., Mary, W3547
HIMROD, Aaron, Pa., Isabella, R5028
Andrew, Pa., S2616
HINTING, Jonathan, See HUNTTING
HIN, Philip, Pa. See HAIN
HINARD, Michael, N.Y., S13384
HINCHER, Isaac, Ct., Marcy/Mary, W19780
Josiah, Mass., See HINSHAW
HINCKLEY, Abner, Mass., S30487
David, Ct., S13388
Ebenezer, Ct., BLWt.5941-100-Pvt. Iss. 2/5/1790. No papers
Ebenezer, Ct., S13397
Gershom, Ct., N.Y., Prudence, W25771
Gillet, Ct., Typhena/Tryphena, W5297; BLWt.14669-160-55
Heman, Mass., Lydia, W21321
Ichabod, Ct., BLWt.951-300-Capt. Iss. 10/16/1789 to Theodosius

HINCKLEY (continued)
Fowler, ass. No papers
Jared, Ct., S19338
John, Ct., Rachel, W691; BLWt. 17895-160-55
Joshua, Cont., N.Y., Sarah Gould, former wid., W4683; BLWt.208-60-55
Joshua, Cont., N.Y., R5029
Nehemiah, Mass. See HINKLEY
Nymphas, Mass., Chloe, W21330
Prince, Mass., Eunice, W14906
Samuel, Mass., S5513
Samuel, Mass., See HINKLEY
Seth, Mass., Genet Mayo, former wid., W23931
Silvanus, Mass., S29887
Wiat/Wiatt, Ct., S13360
HIND, John, Va., S39693; BLWt. 2173-100
HINDE, Dennis, N.J., S34398
HINDES, John, Pvt., N.J., BLReg.230092-1855
Joseph, N.J., BLWt.8390-100-Pvt. Iss. 2/25/1790. No papers
HINDMAN, James, Pa., S22306
HINDS, Abijah, Mass., Dis. No papers
Bartlett/Bartlet, Mass., S39691
Benjamin, Mass., Anna, W750; BLWt.7308-160-55
David, Mass., BLWt.4301-100-Sgt. Iss. 8/10/1789 to Richard Platt. No papers
Esau, N.J., S2309
Hardy, N.C., See HYNES
Isaac, N.J., R5030
James, Va., Sarah, W27658
Jesse, Mass., Martha, W18013
John, Mass., Elizabeth, W7730; BLWt.21810-160-55
John, N.J., BLWt.8410-100-Pvt. Iss. 4/22/1790. No papers
John, S.C., Martha, W25772; BLWt.4301-160-55
Nimrod, Mass., Betsey, W1281; BLWt.1594-160-55
Samuel, Cont., N.J., Mary/Polly, W25778; BLWt.252-60-55 & 26572-160-55
Seth, Mass., S43688
HINE, Benjamin, Ct., S28764
Conrad, Pa., S39695
Ebenezer, Pvt., Ct., BLReg. 26713-1855
Hezekiah, Cont., Ct., S37106
Hollingsworth, Ct., S31741
Newton, Ct., Mary, R5031
Richard, Mass., Abiah, W23284
Samuel, Ct., S16874
Titus, Ct., BLWt.5969-100-Pvt. Iss. 3/29/1792. No papers
Titus, Ct., See HINES
HINEMAN, Henry, Cont., Pa. See HINESMAN
HINES, Barzillai, N.H., Lucy Downing, former wid., W14628
Hardy, N.C. See HYNES
Henry, Va., S38023
Jacobas, Md., S16411
James, Va., BLWt.12243-100-Pvt.

HINES (continued)
Iss. 1/7/1793 to Robert Means, ass. No papers
James, Va., S38832
James, Va., See HINDS
John, S.C., See HINDS
Richard, R.I., S32834
Samuel, Art. Artificiers, BLWt. 13200-100-Pvt. Iss. 2/22/179? to John Peck, ass. No papers. Also BLWt.252-60-55
Titus, Ct., S37103
William, Va., Sally, W294
HINESMAN, Henry, Cont., Pa., Charity, W3549; BLWt.73598-160-55
HINEY, George, Pa., Mary, W1282; BLWt.26084-160-55
Jacob, Pa., BLWt.9630-100-Pvt. "in Proctor's Artillery." Iss. 8/7/1789 to Richard Platt, ass. No papers
HINK, John, Pa., BLWt.9582-100-Pvt. Iss. 1/15/1796 to Alexander Power, ass. No papers
HINKLE, Casper, N.C., S16875
Henry, Va., S29886
Nathan, Pa., S32319
HINKLEY, Benjamin, Ct., Puanna, W18000
Edmund, Mass., Mary, W25338
Heman, Mass. See HINCKLEY
Josiah, N.Y., S15169
Nathaniel, Mass., S4377
Nehemiah, Mass., Edith, W23295; BLWt.3830-160-55
Philip, Mass., S32829
Samuel, Mass., See HINCKLEY
Samuel, Mass., S29227
Samuel, Mass., R21767
Seth, Mass., S29228
Seth, Mass., S36579
Shubel, Mass., S29888
Thomas, Mass., Mary, W23286; BLWt.9069-160-55
HINKSON, John, Not Rev., N.W. Indian War 1792-1794, Old War Inv. File No. 25568
John, N.H., Anna, W18004
Samuel, Cont., Mass., N.H., S39697
HINMAN, Benjamin, Ct., Cont., Anna, W23364; BLWt.21602-160-55
Enoch, Ct., S30486
Ephraim, Ct., Sylvania, W17999
Husted, Ct., Mercy, W17998
Isaac, Ct., Martha, W4986; BLWt.5452-160-55
Joel, Ct., Sarah, W21332; BLWt. 30771-160-55
Jonas, Ct., Caty, R5035
Lewis, Ct., N.Y., Lucy, W18001
Samuel, Ct., BLWt.5983-100-Pvt. Iss. 1/30/1790. No papers
Samuel, Ct., Elizabeth, W21334
Thomas, N.Y., Vt., Rhoda, W18003
Timothy, Ct., Phebe, W1607; BLWt.14765-160-55
Wait/Weight, Ct., Eunice, BLWt. 52615-160-55
HINREY, John, N.C., S4351

HINSDALE, Abel, Ct., S13363
Elias, Ct., R5037
Elisha, Ct., S41640
Jacob, Ct., Sarah, R5038
HINSHAW, Josiah, Mass., Sarah, W24425
HINSLEY, Thomas, N.C., S31746
HINSON, Charles, N.C., S7014
Daniel, Va. See HENSON
John, S.C., R5039
Lazerous, N.C., S16412
Martin, N.C., R5040
Moses, N.C., R5041
Susannah, former wid. of Job Buckley, Va., which see
HINTON, Lewis (colored), Sea Service, Va., S10831
HIOTT, Joseph, S.C., S21817
HIPP, John, N.C., R4911
Valentine, N.C., Margaret, R5043
HIPPARD, William, N.J. See HEPPARD
HIPPLE, Conrad, Pa., S22832
John, Pa., S4373
Lawrence, Pa., S4368
HIPSHER, Andrew, Va., S9580
HISCOCK, Richard, Mass., Sarah, W16292
HISCOX, Clarke, R.I., S46044
Edward, R.I., S17479
Ephraim, R.I., S38827
HISE, Conrad, N.C., Sophia, W4453
George, N.C., R5044
Jacob, N.C., R5045
Leonard, Va., S8713
HISEL, Frederick, Va., S41641
Thomas, Va. See HISLE
HISER, John, Pa., Sarah, W8932
HISLE, Benjamin, Va., S38025
Samuel, Va., S31132
Thomas, Va., Nancy, R5046
HISOR, Adam, Mass., BLWt.4389-100-Pvt. Iss. 4/20/1797 to Daniel Aiken. No papers
HISSEY, William, Md., Sophia, R4929
HISTED, Thaddeus, N.Y., S2315
HITCH, Gillis, Del., R5049
HITCHCOCK, Aaron, Mass., S29893
Aaron, Mass., Mary, W14905
Abel, Ct., BLWt.5955-100-Pvt. Iss. 6/20/1795. No papers
Abel, Ct., Mary, W21327
Abijah, Mass., Anna, W1769; BLWt. 17573-160-55
Abraham, Cont., N.Y., S16154
Ashbel, Ct., S13398
Brampton, Cont., Va. res. of wid. in 1846, Elizabeth Pritchard, former wid., R8489
Brampton, N.Y., BLWt.7298-100-Pvt. Iss. 9/28/1790 to Bartholomew & Fisher, assnes. No papers
Chileob, N.Y., S16872
Daniel, Ct., BLWt.5918-100-Pvt. Iss. 2/24/1795 to Eneas Munson, Jr. No papers
Daniel, Ct., Lydia, W1180; BLWt. 15422-160-55
Ebenezer, Ct., Lucy Griffith, former wid., W7588
Eli, Mass., S9918
Eliada, Mass., Esther, W25777

HITCHCOCK (continued)
Elida, Mass., BLWt.4304-100-Pvt. Iss. 10/26/1789 to Theodosius Fowler. No papers
Gad, Mass., S1831
Gains, Mass., S19339
Ichabod, Ct., Lucy, W11293; BLWt. 95681-160-55. Wid. was also allowed pension as wid. of Charles Tuttle, former husb.,who d. in service in War of 1812.
Ira, Cont., Ct., Hannah, W23276
Isaac, Md. Sea Service, R5054
Jared, Ct., BLWt.5903-100-Pvt. Iss. 6/20/1795. No papers
Jared, Ct., Irene, W16601
Joel, N.Y., Elizabeth, R5052
John, Cont., Ct., Lucy Manley, former wid., W9929
John L., Ct., Eunice, R5053
Jonathan, Ct., S7009
Jonathan, Mass., Molly, W21328
Joshua, N.C., S31126
Lemuel, Ct., S43679
Levi, Ct., BLWt.5943-100-Pvt. Iss. 11/2/1791 to Jonathan Tuttle. No papers
Levi, Ct., S10837
Levi, Ct., Mary, W8936
Lois, former wid. of Phinehas Blood, Mass., which see
Luke, Cont., Mass., Elizabeth, W25774
Luke, Mass., S13409
Luke, Mass., S33302
Luther, Mass., S29892
Lyman, Ct., Cont., Md., S43687
Merick, Mass., Abigail, W14912
Moses, S.C., R5056
Nathaniel, Mass., S39689
Oliver, Mass., S23698
Phinehas, Mass., S43690
Reuben, Mass., S30488
Samuel, Ct., S13404
Samuel, Cont., Ct.,BLWt.1185-100
Samuel, N.Y., BLWt.7215-100-Pvt. Iss. 7/10/1790 to John Quackinboss, ass. No papers
Samuel, N.Y., S43684
Thomas, S.C., R5057
HITCHENS, Major, Del., S36017
HITCHERICK, Philip, Pa.,BLWt.9578-100-Pvt. Iss. 6/28/1793 to John Wheeler, ass. No papers
HITCHINGS, Nathaniel, Mass.,S33301
Thomas, Mass., Ruth, R5059
HITCHINS, Caleb, Del., BLWt.10780-100-Pvt. Iss. 4/15/1799. No papers
Major, Del., BLWt.10777-100-Pvt. Iss. 4/15/1799. No papers
Nathan, Mass., S32837
HITCHMAN, Salisbury/Solsbury, Mass., S33304
HITE, Abraham, Va., S46385; BLWt. 1071-300-Capt. Iss. 7/28/1790. No papers
Christopher, Cont., Pa., BLWt. 308-100
Conrad, Pa., S13396
George, Cont., Va., Deborah,

HITE (continued)
W5105; BLWt.1089-200-Lt. Iss. 3/6/1790. No papers
Isaac, Va., S8714; BLWt.189-200
Jacob, Va., S16414
James, N.J., Pa., R5060
Julius, Cont., Va., S18024; BLWt.12223-100-Pvt. Iss. 5/8/1794
Mathias/Matthias, Va., S38031
HITES, John, Cont., France, R5062
HITT, Dennis, N.Y., Abigail, W23275
James, R.I., S44197
Malinda, former wid. of Francis Kendall, which see
Peter, Va., Hannah, W7732
HITTY, Conrat, See Conrad ITTIG
HIWELL, John, See HIWILL
HIWILL, John, Cont., Mass., BLWt.227-200
HIX, Daniel, Mass., S15454
David, S.C., See HICKS
Farthing, Va., S5534
Stephen, Mass., R.I., S13394
William, Va. See HICKS
William, Va. See HICKS
HIXON, Amos, N.J., S1019
Elijah, Va., S41636
Isaac, Mass., Persis, BLWt.56946-160-55
James, Va., See HIXSON
John, N.J., S38032
Joseph, Mass., S39698
Sarah, former wid. of Joseph Wolcott, Ct., which see
HIXSON, Elijah, Va. See HIXON
Elkanah, Mass., S39694. Sarah Hixon/Hixson wid. of sold. was pensioned as former wid. of Joseph Wolcott/Wolcutt, Ct., which see
James, Cont., Va., Mary, W757; BLWt.26385-160-55
James, N.J., S4375
Jonathan, N.J., S34399
Matthew, N.J., See HICXSON
HIXT, William, S.C., Ann Graham, former wid., W7593; BLWt.2179-300
HOADLEY, Culpeper, Ct., S17492; BLWt.11397-160-55
Ebenezer, Ct., S37122
Silas, Ct., Privateer, S13355
Thomas, Mass., S39700
HOADLY, Ebenezer, Ct., BLWt. 5967-100-Pvt. Iss. 2/10/1797. No papers
Philo, Ct., S2624
Samuel, Ct., BLWt.5902-100-Pvt. Iss. 12/18/1795 to Eneas Munson Jr., ass. No papers
HOAG, Ebenezer, N.H., S44432
Hussey, N.H., Abigail, W13499
Polly, former wid. of Samuel Walker, N.H., which see
HOAGLAND, Derrick, N.J., Pa., Va., Catharine, W7806
James, N.J., See HOGELAND
John, Cont., N.C. agcy & res., Mahala, W272; BLWt.118-60-55
John, N.J., S43694
John, N.J., Anne, W464
HOAGLAND, John, N.J., R5064
John, N.Y. See HOOGLAND
John, Pa., R5065
Joseph, Pa., See HOGELAND
Richard, N.J., S888
Tunis, N.J., S1023
HOAK, Frederick, N.Y., Margaret, W18022
HOAR, Benjamin, Mass. See Benjamin WHITNEY
Braddock, Mass., Charity, W1285
Edmund, Mass., BLWt.4354-100-Sgt. Iss. 7/20/1789 to Reuben Lilley. No papers
Edmund, Mass., Azubah, W21352
Leonard, Mass., S29229
Leonard, Mass., Lydia, R5067
Mercy, former wid. of John Gillette, Ct., which see
Peter, Mass., Marcy, W14948
HOARD, David, N.Y., Lydia, W16298
Isaac, Mass., S10857
Jonathan, Mass., Charlotte,W19755
Samuel, N.Y., R5069
Samuel, Va., S30491
Simeon, N.Y., S16156
Thomas, Va., BLWt.1073-300-Capt. Iss. 12/13/1791 to Frances Graves, ass. No papers
HOARE, Leonard, Mass., S43692
HOAŚMAN, Poal, See Paul HOUSMAN
HOBACK, Philip, Pa., BLWt.9443-100-Pvt. Iss. 2/23/1792. No papers
HOBART, Edmund, Mass., S13439
Elijah, Mass., Polly, BLWt.85075-160-55
Isaac, N.H., S44436
Jacob, N.H., S44435
Jeremiah, Mass., Rebecca, W18033
John, Ct., BLWt.966-200-Lt. Iss. 7/6/1795 to Eneas Munson, Jr., ass. No papers
John, Mass., S15464
John, N.H., Huldah, W14937
Jonas, N.H., S35416
Jonathan, Mass., N.H., S10844
Joseph, N.H. See HOBERT
Joshua, Mass., Sarah, W14946
Leonard, Mass. See HOAR
Mason, Ct., S17487
Nathaniel, Mass., S29241
Nathaniel, Mass., Hannah, W23341
Noah, Cont., Mass., S29897
Solomon, Cont., N.H., Nancy, W759 BLWt.6033-160-55
William, Mass., Dolly, R5070
William, N.H., S41661
HOBAUGH, Philip, Pa., Christeny, W10125; BLWt.212-100
HOBBS, Benjamin, Cont., Mass., S33322
Benjamin, Cont., Mass. & War of 1812, S32846
Benjamin, Mass., BLWt.4346-100-Sgt. Iss. 4/1/1790. No papers
Elisha, N.J., Va., S38043
Ezekiel, Va., Elizabeth, W8940; BLWt.26632-160-55
George, Mass., S17494
James, Md., R5072
James, N.H., Sarah, W21362
HOBBS (continued)
Job, Va., S32328; BLWt.91042-160-55
John, Mass., S32843
Jonathan, Ga., Margaree, R5075
Joseph, N.H., S44429
Josiah, Mass., Polly, W23334
Morrell, Mass., S35436
Robert, S.C., Mary, W5300
Thomas, Mass., Abigail, W23332; BLWt.3643-160-55
Thomas, Va., S1672. Res. at enl. Hertford Co., N.C.
William, N.C., S7034
HOBBY, Hezekiah, Ct., S17488
John, Mass., BLWt.913-300
Thomas, Ct., Dis. No papers. BLWt.1543-450
William, Mass., S35418
HOBERT, Joseph, N.H., S43697, BLWt.34-100
Leonard, Mass. See HOAR
HOBOUGH, Philip, Pa. See HOBAUGH
HOBSON, Jeremiah, Cont., Mass., S44444
Lawson, Va., S2626
Moses, Mass., Sarah, W21407
William, Mass., S35417
William, Va., Elizabeth, W7793
HOCHKISS, Truman/Trueman, Ct., Ruth, W18064
HOCHSTRASSER, Baltes/Baltus, N.Y., R5079
Paul I., N.Y., S13434
HOCKADAY, Philip, Va., BLWt. 2217-200
William, N.C., Anna, R4405
HOCKINGBERY, Harman, N.J.,S22836
HOCKLEY, James, See HAWKLEY
HODG, Philo, See HODGE
HODGDON, Caleb, Mass., S18038
Hanson, N.H., Mary, W23308
Jeremiah, Mass., S35429
John, N.H., BLWt.3211-100-Pvt. Iss. 7/22/1796 to James A. Neal, ass. No papers
John, N.H., S39722
Joseph, Cont., N.H., S18035
Joseph, N.H., Sarah, W23314
Phinehas, N.H., S44424
Samuel, Cont., Pa., Mary, W3420
HODGE, Abraham, N.Y., BLWt.7249-100-Pvt. Iss. 8/4/1790 to Henry Hart, ass. No papers
Abraham, N.Y., S43700
Abraham, N.Y., Prudence, W15837
Alexander, N.H., Anna Temple, former wid., W22386. Her husb., Enos Temple, also a pensioner, which see
Alexander, N.C., S8737
Asahel, Ct., S43702; BLWt.954-300-Capt. Iss. 5/8/1792 to Amos Muzzy, ass. No papers
Asahel, Ct., Martha, R5080; BLWt. 43876-160-55
Benjamin, Ct., Privateer, R5081
Benjamin, Ct., R.I., S39720
Benjamin, S.C., Nancy, W10115
David, Ct., BLWt.5981-100-Pvt. Iss. 10/9/1789. No papers

HODGE (continued)
David, Ct., Cont., S44201
Edmond, N.C., See HODGES
George, N.C., Elizabeth, W4234; BLWt.26698-160-55
James, N.Y., Hannah Burns/Burnes former wid., W10476; BLWt.344-60-55
John, Cont., N.H., See John CHURCH
John, --, N.J. res., Dis. No papers
John, S.C., S21825
Levi, Ct., Navy, S33320
Philo, Ct., Cont., Lucy, W24447
Thomas, Cont., Ct., S44426
William, N.H., See HOGG
William, S.C., b. Pa., Ann, W4233
HODGEDON, Jeremiah, See HODGDON
HODGEMAN, Nathan, N.H. See HODGMAN
Thomas, Mass., See HODGMAN
HODGES, Abednego, Va., S38037
Benjamin, R.I., S21823
Daniel, N.Y., Elizabeth, W23306; BLWt.47615-160-55
David, Cont., Mass., N.H., Lydia, W21359
Edmund, N.C., S1528
Elijah, Mass., S15891
Eliphalet, Mass., R.I., Vt., S13438
Ephraim, Mass., R.I., S13442
Ezra, Cont., Mass., R.I., S35423
Isaac, Mass., S10853
Isaac, N.Y., Anna, W10116
James, Mass., Mary, W19825
James, N.Y., Sea Service, Abigail R5084
James, S.C., Nancy, W7776; BLWt. 36727-160-55
Jesse, Va., S31143
Jesse, Va., R5087
Job, Ct., S37123
John, Mass., Abigail, W14939
John, S.C., b. Va. ,Frances,W10117
Joseph, N.C., Sarah, W3995; BLWt. 14989-160-55
Joseph, N.C., R5088
Josiah, Mass., Tabitha, W23319
Leonard, Ct., Sarah, W19815; BLWt.11092-160-55
Nathaniel, Mass., S29913
Philemon, N.C., S32326
Robert, Va. See HEDGES
Rufus, Mass., S10870
Samuel, N.Y., Rebecca, R5089
Seth, Vt., Margaret, W21389; BLWt.9522-160-55
Timothy, Mass., Privateer, R.I., Deborah, W1287; BLWt.14516-160-55
William, Mass., S29901
William, N.C., S21826
William, S.C., R5090
William, Va., S18031; BLWt. 2188-100
William, Va., Amelia, R5086
Willis, N.C., b. Va., Lucy, W7775
Zebulon, Mass., S22837
HODGGETS, Emanuel, Mass., S32845
HODGIN, Joseph, Ga., R5091
HODGINS, Samuel, --, BLWt.13219-

HODGINS (continued)
100-Pvt. "in the Invalid Corps". Iss. 9/3/179? to Edith McKee, Admx. No papers
HODGKIN, Ambrose, Ct., S17493
Jonas, Mass., N.H., Vt., Anna, W25796; BLWt.26059-160-55
HODGKINS, Hezekiah, Mass., Lydia, W21380
Jacob, Mass., Martha, W14916
John, Mass., S22311
John, Mass., Abigail, W23311
John, Mass., BLWt.1033-100
Joseph, Cont., Mass., S32864
Joseph, Mass., BLWt.4426-100-Pvt. Iss. 3/16/1792. No papers
Nathaniel, Ct., S23261
Samuel, Md., Lydia, R5092; BLWt. 44806-160-55
Samuel, Mass. See HODSKINGS
Thomas, Ct., Cont., Tryphena, W23352
Thomas, Cont., Mass., Martha, W23349
Thomas, Mass., S35427
Thomas, Mass., Abigail, W13498
Timothy, Cont., Mass., Eunice, W21382
William, Cont., N.H., Ruth, W14936
HODGMAN, Abel, Mass., N.H., S46045
Asa, Mass., Sibil, W19818
John, Mass., Mehitable, W9066
Joseph, Cont., N.H., S39716
Joseph, N.H., BLWt.3172-100-Pvt. Iss. 9/30/1792. No papers
Nathan, Mass., N.H., Lydia, R5083
Thomas, Mass., Rebecca, W21333
Zacheus, N.H., Eunice, W25797
HODSDON, Benjamin, Mass., S35430
Jacob, Mass., S44445
Samuel, N.H., Anna, W23322
Stephen, Mass., S35398
HODSKINGS, Samuel, Mass., Anna, W671; BLWt.31281-160-55
HODSKINS, Jonas, See HODGKIN
HOEVENBERGH, Henry V., N.Y., Hester, W16607
HOEY, Benjamin, Col. Proctor's Regt. of Art., BLWt.941-200-Lt. Iss. 8/10/1789 to Richard Platt, ass. No papers
HOFF, Henry, Pa., S22313
Isaac, N.J., S4408
Jacob, Pa., S39712
John, N.J. See HUFF
Nicholas, N.J., S28023
William, N.Y., S13452
William, N.Y., S44200
HOFFAINS, Adam, Cont., Mass., S33307
HOFFLER, William, Va., S38047; BLWt.2162-300
HOFFMAN, Ambros/Ambrose, Va., S16420
Andrew, N.Y., BLWt.7271-100-Pvt. Iss. 12/11/1789 to Benj. Brown, ass. No papers
Cornelius, Pa., S39709
George, Hazen's Regt., BLWt. 13180-100-Pvt. Iss. ---. No papers
Henry, Pa., Mary, W10127

HOFFMAN (continued)
Henry, Pa., Elizabeth, R5096; BLWt.2135-100
Henry, Privateer, R.I., S13463
Herman, Mass., R5098
John, N.J., See HUFMAN
John, N.Y., BLWt.7219-100-Pvt. Iss. 6/15/1792 to Thomas Walker, Admr. Also Wt. 13193. No papers
John, Pa., S10855
John, Va., S8735
Ludwick/Ludwig, Pa., Catharine, W2801
Philip, Va., R5099
Reuben, Va. See HUFFMAN
William, N.J. See HUFFMAN
HOFFMIRE, Samuel, N.J., S4403
HOFFNAGLE, George, See HOOFNOGGLE
HOFFNER, Martin, N.C., S8727
HOFFORD, Malachi, R.I., S32323
HOFFSES, Christian, See HOFFSES
HOFFSTADER, Christian, N.Y., S43693
HOFMAN, Christian, Pa., S39752. Not same as Christian Hoofman, S38042
Evert, N.Y., S13440
HOFNER, Nicholas, N.C., Christiana W3994; BLWt.27668-160-55
HOFSTALAR, George, N.C., S15176
HOGABOOM, Peter, N.Y., Dis. No papers
HOGAN, Benoni, Cont., Ct.,W19802
Cardell, N.C., S10849
David, N.C., R5101
David, S.C., S38837
Dennis, R.I., BLWt.3233-100-Pvt. Iss. 7/26/1792 to Samuel Emery. No papers
Edmond, N.C., S1671
John, Mass., S39719
John, N.Y., BLWt.7208-100-Pvt. Iss. 10/7/1790 to Noadiah Crammer, ass. No papers
Pat, N.Y., S43699
Prosser, N.C., S36592
Roger, Md., BLWt.11306-100-Pvt. Iss. 11/1/1797 to Elisha Jarrett ass. No papers
William, Navy, Mass., Salome, W23330
William, S.C., S21287
HOGE, John, Pa., S23710; BLWt. 2630-200-Lt. Iss. 4/23/1793. No papers
HOGEBOME, John, N.Y., S13427
HOGEBOOM, James, N.Y., S13457
John, N.Y., See HOGEBOME
Peter C., N.Y., S23266
Richard C., N.Y., R5103
HOGEKEYS, Samuel, S.C., BLWt. 12254 & 13158-100-Pvt. Iss. 9/14/1796. No papers
HOGELAND, Abraham, N.J., S28766
Derrick, Va., See HOAGLAND
James, N.J., S8723
Jeronimus, See HOOGLAND
John, Pa. See HOAGLAND
Joseph, N.J., Ann, W25789; BLWt. 26852-160-55
HOGENKAMP, Martines/Martinus,

HOGENKAMP (continued)
N.J., Sophia, W23307
HOGG, Abner, N.H., S44433; BLWt. 5217-160-55
Alexander, Mass. See Alexander CHURCH
Elisha, N.C., Patty, W19808
James, Md., S39715
John, Cont., N.H. See John CHURCH
John, Va., Susannah, W7763
John, Va., R5105
Samuel, S.C., Eleanor, W7762
Samuel, Va., S38845; BLWt.1072-300-Capt. Iss. 5/7/1793 to Francis Graves, ass. No papers
Thomas, N.C., BLWt.104-100
Thomas, Va., S5566
William, N.H., S44434
William, N.H., Lydia, W936; BLWt. 13739-160-55
William, Va., S38040
HOGGANS, Thomas, Va., BLWt.12225-100-Pvt. Iss. 5/2/1794. No papers
HOGGARD, John, N.C., Penelope, R4804
HOGGE, James, Pa., S39699
HOGH, Gideon, N.C., S38846
HOGHSTRASEN, Baltes, See HOCHSTRASSER, Battes
HOGHTALING, James, See HOUGHTALIN
HOGINS, Abram, N.C., S4380
Benoni, Sheldon's Horse, Ct., BLWt.5995-100-Pvt. Iss. 11/6/1789. No papers
HOGLE, Nicholas, N.Y., R5106
HOGUE, Andrew, N.C., Alley, R5108
HOGWOOD, Benjamin, See HAGOOD
HOHNE, Christopher, Md., also Md. Mil., War of 1812, Mary, R5110; War of 1812 BLWt.832-40-50, 73513-40-50, & 1516-80-55
HOISINGTON, Bliss, Vt., Phoebe, W24406
Ebenezer, Green Mt. Boys, Vt., S23711
Elias, Cont., Vt., Mary/Molly, W21393
Isaac, N.H., S39738
Veline/Velina, Vt., S29242
Vespasian/Vespation, Vt., Hannah, R5236
HOIT, Benjamin, N.H., S39733
Benjamin, N.H., Sarah, W14919
Benjamin, N.H., Privateer, S8720
David, Ct., Vt., Sarah, W23301
Elisha, Cont., Mass., W19826
Elisha, Crane's Cont. Art., Mass. BLWt.4444-100-Pvt. Iss. 1/7/1796 to Calvin Sanger. No papers
Ephraim, N.H., S43701
Jeremiah, Green Mt. Boys, Mass., Vt., S18881
John Millet, Mass., Catharine, W23309
Joseph, N.H., S13418
Mary, former wid. of Andrew L. Stone, Ct., which see
Nathan, Ct., S13426
Nathan, Mass., No papers. File must have been lost prior to 1870. "The records of this office show that Nathan Hoit was a Lt. in the Mass. Line, War of the Rev. Allowed pension on acct of this service, under Act of 3/18/1818, at which time he was about 62 yrs., and a res. of Strafford Co., N.H. He d. 1/6/1820. Date & place of birth are not given, nor any data in regard to his family." An inquiry to Commr. of Pensions from Henry D. Warren, Kendall Green, Mass., Asst. Secy. of Soc. of Cincinnati, State of N.H., dated 9/16/1927 states place of res. was Moultonborough(?), Strafford Co., N.H.
Nathan, N.H., BLWt.3199-100-Pvt. Iss. 12/24/1799 to Jonathan Case, ass. No papers
Nathan, N.H., S44437
Nehemiah, Mass., See HOYT
Reuben, Mass., Lucy Chaffee, former wid., W17609. Her last husb. was pensioned, see Comfort Chaffee, Mass.
Richard, Cont., Mass., S44438
Robert, Mass., See HOYT
Silas, N.Y. See HOYT
Simeon, N.H., See HOYT
Stephen, N.H. See HOITT
Warren, Ct., Mary, W25782; BLWt. 10238-160-55
HOITT, Stephen, N.H., S22839
HOLADAY, William, N.Y., S23704
HOLAM, Samuel, Pa., S41647
HOLAND, Joseph. See HOLLAND
HOLBEN, Lorentz, Pa., S22309
HOLBERT, Aaron, Va., S18028
HOLBROOK, Abel, Ct., Hannah, W11343 BLWt.31274-160-55
Abel, Mass., Elizabeth Kingsbury, former wid., W26718
Amariah, Mass., Molly, W13495
Amos, Mass., S1768
Amos, N.H., Vt., Lydia, W21398
Caleb, Mass., Sarah, W1771; BLWt. 9048-160-55
Caleb, N.C., Drusilla, R5116
Calvin, Ct., S10873
Daniel, Cont., Mass., S5544
Darius, Mass., Olive, W14945
David, Cont., Mass., S32847; BLWt. 915-300-Capt. Iss. 4/1/1790. No papers
David, Mass., S23709
David, Mass., Judith, R5118
David, N.H., Hepsibah/Hepsibeth, W3552; BLWt.26565-160-55
Ebenezer, Ct., S21820
Edy, Va., Charity, W7796
Elijah, Mass., Abigail, W24439
Elizabeth, former wid. of Josiah Stites, Mass., which see
Henry, Mass., S29908
Ichabod, Cont., Mass., S32852
James, Mass., S21299
Jesse, Va., S31756
John, Mass., S29238
John, Mass., S32324
John, Mass., Sarah, W16603

HOLBROOK (continued)
Jonathan, Mass., Sarah, W21361
Miriam, former wid. of Elisha Allen, Mass., which see
Nathan, Cont., Mass., Susanna, W18063; BLWt.921-200-Lt. Iss. 1/4/1790. No papers
Nathaniel, Ct., Allice, W18061
Nathaniel, Mass., S33310
Peter, Mass., S29233
Peter, Mass., Mary, W21408
Reuben, Mass., S43695
Richard, N.H., R5119
Samuel, Navy, N.H., Martha, W16605
Seth, Mass., S15173
Seth, Mass., S21295
Silas, Mass., S35415
Silas, Mass., Tirzah, W7797
Silas, Mass., Betsey, R5114
Susannah, former wid. of Josiah Green, Ct., which see
Sylvanus, Mass., Lucy, W21373
Thomas, Mass., Sarah, W21374
William, N.C., Aggia, R5113
HOLBROOKS, George, N.C. See HALBROOKS
HOLBURTON, William, Ct., Eunice, W21346
HOLCOMB, Abel, Ct., Elizabeth, W18034
Abner, Ct., S13433
Abram, Ct., S17489
Asahel, Ct., S37112
Asahel, Ct., Hannah, W7795. Wid. allowed BL for service of her 3rd husb., Jacob Holcomb, which see
Azariah, Mass., Christiana, W21403 BLWt.71142-160-55
Beriah, N.Y., Lucretia, R5130
Dose, Ct., S29910
Ebenezer, Ct., Chloe, W25794
Elijah, Sheldon's Dragoons, Ct., BLWt.6002-100-Pvt. Iss. 9/1/1790 to Theodosius Fowler. No papers
Elijah, Ct., S32853
Elijah, Cont., Ct., Mary, W21353
Elijah, N.J., Pa., S41654
Ezekiel, Ct., Susannah, W21358
Jacob, Ct., Hannah, BLWt.47422-160-55. Wid. allowed pension for service of former husb., Asahel Holcomb, which see
James, Mass., R5128
Joel, Ct., Sarah, W3685
John, Ct., S31751
John, Va., Dis. No papers
John G., Ct., S37116
Jonathan, Mass., Hannah, W1609; BLWt.28572-160-55
Jordan, S.C., b. N.C., S31731
Joseph, Sheldon's Dragoons, Ct., BLWt.5996-100-Pvt. Iss. 2/22/1790 to Theodosius Fowler. No papers
Joseph, Ct., S30489
Joseph, Cont., Ct., Olive Enos, former wid., W17762
Levi, Ct., S21818
Luther, Ct., Sally, R5134
Nahum, Ct., S16879
Noah, Ct., R5131

HOLCOMB (continued)
Noadiah, Mass., Afiah Fairchild/ Fairchilds, former wid., R3433
Obed, Ct., Indian War 1783 & 1784, Elizabeth Worden/Wordin, former wid., R11866
Peter, Ct., S15175
Phinehas, Ct., S10862
Richard, N.J., S1020
Roger, Ct., Mass., R5133
Seth, Ct., Polly Briggs, former wid., R1206
Sherwood, S.C.,b. N.C.,Jane,W7794
Timothy, Ct., S15892
HOLCOMBE, Increase, Ct.,Mary,W18017
Philemon, Va., S4399
HOLDAWAY, Henry, Va. See HOLDWAY
HOLDEN, Aaron, Mass., BLWt.910-300-Capt. Iss. 2/25/1791 to Samuel Whiting, ass. No papers
Abel, Mass., S43703
Abraham, Mass., S43696
Abraham, N.H., S18454
Amos, Ct. See HOLDIN
Asa, Mass., S44439
Asa, Mass., Mary, W25788; BLWt. 3192-160-55
Benjamin, Mass., Elizabeth, W13471
Benjamin, Mass., Abigail, W21376
Benjamin, Mass., R5121; BLWt.979-450-Lt. Col. Iss. 2/9/1795 to Addison Richardson, ass. Also recorded as BLWt.2695. No papers
Daniel, Cont., Mass., Statira, W672; BLWt.80-100
Daniel, Mass., Dorothy, W14924
Darius, Mass., S43698
Ebenezer Mitchel, Mass., Hepsebeth W21356
Ephraim, Cont.,Mass.,N.H., S23712
Henry, N.J See HOLDREN
Isaac, Cont., R.I., S39732
James, Mass., S22838
James, N.C., R5122
Job, N.C., R5125
John, Cont., Mass., S18874
John, Cont., Mass., S33323; BLWt. 927-200-Lt. Iss. 5/1/1792 to David Quinton, ass. No papers
John, Cont., R.I., S38838; BLWt. 904-300-Capt. Iss. 12/31/1789. No papers
John, BLWt.13220-100-Pvt. "in the Invalids", iss. 12/14/1789 to Richard Platt, ass. No papers
John, Mass., BLWt.4308-100-Pvt. Iss. 3/25/1790 to Ezra Lunt. No papers
John, Mass., S35437
John, Mass., Mary, W23299
Jonas, Mass., Sarah, W18039; BLWt. 5003-160-55
Joseph, Mass., S47287; BLWt.877-100. Jemima Holden, wid. of above sold. rec'd pension as former wid. of Samuel Marsh, Mass., which see
Kemp, Md., BLWt.2268-100
Lemuel, Mass., S44440
Levi, Cont., Mass., S34406; BLWt. 928-200-Lt. Iss. 5/31/1790 to Theophilus Fowler,ass. No papers

HOLDEN (continued)
Nathan, Mass., Abigail, W24455
Nathaniel, N.H., Hannah, W2446; BLWt.24917-160-55
Nehemiah, Mass., S41646
Oliver, Navy, Mass., S29899. "Unofficial information: This man composed the hymn 'Coronation'."
Phinehas, Mass., Susan Mansur, former wid., W9919; BLWt.105037-160-55
Richard S., Mass., S41662
Robert, Mass., S32850
Samuel, Mass., BLWt.4378-100-Sgt. Iss. 1/28/1790. No papers
Samuel, Mass., S35438
Sarah, former wid. of Jacob Reed, Mass., which see
Sartell, Mass., S7038
Thomas, Mass., BLWt.4447-100-Pvt. Iss. 2/25/1791 to Samuel Whitney No papers
Thomas, R.I., S29898
Thomas, R.I., Phebe, W24449
Timothy, Cont., N.H., Catharine, W7774; BLWt.16114-160-55
HOLDER, Daniel, Va., Ruth, W9064
Jacob, Pa., S39703
James, Va., S8736
John, Md., BLWt.11336-100-Pvt. Iss. 2/7/1790. No papers
Kemp, Md. See HOLDEN
HOLDERMAN, John, Va. See HULLDERMAN
HOLDIN, Amos, Ct., S32851
HOLDMAN, Tandy, Va. See HOLEMAN
HOLDREN, Henry, N.J., BLWt.8371-100-Pvt. Iss. 6/14/1791. No papers
Henry, N.J., Elizabeth, W25783
HOLDRIDGE, Amasa, N.Y., S45382
Ephraim, R.I., S39730
Hezekiah, Ct., BLWt.947-450-Lt. Col. Iss. 3/28/1797. No papers
Jehiel, N.H., S38806
John, Mass., S45383; BLWt.923-200-Lt. Iss. 8/22/1789. No papers
Robert, Ct., S37124; BLWt.12720-160-55
Rufus, Ct., Hannah, W18053
HOLDSTON, Thomas, See HOLSTEN
William, Del., BLWt.10792-100-Pvt. Iss. 12/28/179? to Wm. Lane, ass. No papers
HOLDWAY, Henry, Va., Eleanor Anderson, W18028
Timothy, N.C., S2630
HOLE, Daniel, N.J., Va., S32331
James, Hazen's Regt., BLWt.13178-100-Pvt. Iss. 1/27/1790. No papers
James, Cont., N.Y., S45371
John, Cont. See John LOCH
HOLECOMB, Richard, See HOLCOMB
HOLEMAN, George, Va. See HOLMAN
Isaac, N.C., See HOLMAN
Tandy, Va., Betsey/Elizabeth, W25793; BLWt.2502-100; BLWt. 325-60-55
Yancy, Va., S8719
HOLENBAKE, Ephraim, Mass., R4450

HOLGATE, Cornelius, Pa., Mary, R5135
William, Pa., S39702
HOLIDAY, Daniel, S.C. See HOLLADAY
HOLINSDOFF, William, See HALINSDOFF
HOLLINSHEAD, James, Pa., S2631
HOLISTER, Nathan, Ct., Cont., S4406
HOLLADAY, Amos, Ct., S10858
Benjamin, S.C., Va., S31136
Daniel, S.C., S10867
John, N.C. See HALLADAY
Moses, Pa. (?), Va.(?), Elizabeth, R5136
Stephen, Va., S15459
Zacharias, Va., S31141
HOLLANBECK, Ruth, former wid. of William Scott, N.Y., which see
HOLLAND, Charles, Md. & War of 1812 Sarah, W1611
Charles, S.C., S7027
Drury, Cont., Va., Sarah, W3419
Edward, Md., Mary, W27851; BLWt. 11287-100. Iss. 9/5/1789
Ephraim, Mass., Eunice, W24453
Henry, N.C., S31759
Hugh, S.C., S38038
Isaac, Md., BLWt.11289-100-Drummer. Iss. 2/7/1790. No papers
Isaac, Md., S34928
Ivory, Mass., S45392; BLWt.926-200-Lt. Iss. 4/1/1790. No papers
Jacob, Cont., Md., Mary, R5141
Jacob, S.C., b. Md., S10866
James, Cont., N.C., Zilphia, W7800; BLWt.8447-160-55
Joab, Mass., S32840
John, N.C., Mary, R5142
John, Sea Service, Mass., Rebecca Dennett, former wid., R2874
John, S.C., Jane, R5139
John H., N.Y., BLWt.7293-100-Pvt. Iss. 2/23/1792 to Timothy Pettee, ass. No papers
John T., Cont., Md., S34923
Jonas M., Va., Theodocia, W8944
Joseph, Ct., S5567
Joseph, Ct., S29240
Joseph, Md., S34924
Joseph, Mass., S18884
Joseph, Mass., Polly, W23345; BLWt.27584-160-55
Martha, former wid. of Caleb Knapp, Cont., N.Y., which see
Park, Mass., S18449; BLWt.931-200-Lt. Iss. 4/1/1790. No papers
Reuben, Mass., S39727
Thomas, Del., BLWt.1042-300-Capt. Iss. 9/27/1789 to James Armstrong, Admr. No papers
Thomas, N.J., BLWt.8378-100-Pvt. Iss. 4/23/1798 to Abraham Bell, ass. No papers
Thomas, N.J., Ann, W2941
Thomas, N.C., R5144
Thomas, S.C., S32327
Thomas, Va., S17222
William, Md. See HOLLIN
William, N.C., Margaret, W4698
HOLLAWAY, Thomas, Va., S5562
HOLLEMS, William, S.C., Hannah,

HOLLEMS (continued)
W27864. Res. of Spartanburgh Dist., enl. 7/4/1777, b. Halifax Co., Va., 11/29/1760/61. Moved to Spartanburgh when 10 or 12 yrs. of age. D. 11/10/1848
HOLLENBEAK, John, Ct., Esther, W23353
HOLLENBECK, Abraham, Mass., Margaret, R5145; BLWt.17719-160-55
Jacob, N.Y., BLWt.7213-100-Pvt. Iss. 10/11/1790 to Oliver Trowbridge, ass. No papers
Jacob, N.Y., Margery, W19807
Ruth, former wid. of Wm. Scutt, N.Y., which see
HOLLER, John, Pa., R5146
HOLLES, Stephen, Cont., Mass., See HOLLIS
HOLLET, George, N.Y., See HALLET
HOLLEY, Abraham, Ct., BLWt.5952-100-Pvt. Iss. 6/27/1789 to Samuel Hait. No papers
Benjamin, R.I., S23269
Elijah, Ct., Mass., R.I., S32857
Francis, N.C., Martha Thompson former wid., R10549. Her 2nd husb. was pensioned, see Electious Thompson, Md.
George, Mass., S45387
Henry, N.Y. See HAWLEY
John, Ct., BLWt.5914-100-Pvt. Iss. 3/18/1790. No papers. Also BLWt.13950
John, Ct., S37111
John, Cont., R.I., Hannah, W16295
John, N.C., S21302
Jonathan, Mass., S23705
Joseph, Ct., S45386
Joseph, Ct., Dorothy, W18037
Joseph, Mass., Mary, W14951
Rawleigh, Cont., Va., S38034
Robert, Ct., Hannah, W21391
Samuel, N.Y., BLWt.7206-100-Pvt. Iss. 10/10/1791 to Ebenezer Owen ass. No papers
Stephen, Ct., S21819
William H., Mass., Hannah, W21390
HOLLIDAY, Amos, Ct. See HOLLADAY
Benjamin, S.C. See HOLLADAY
Daniel, S.C., See HOLLADAY
Israel Elsworth, Cont., Green Mt. Boys, Vt., S10856
James, Pa., S7025
James, Pa., BLWt.1017-200-Lt. Iss. 2/11/1800 to John Holliday & other heirs. Also recorded as BLWt.2699-200-Lt. Iss. 2/11/1800 to John Holliday, Wm. Holliday, Ruth w. of Jas. Somerville & Mary w. of Wm. Galbraith, heirs. No papers
James, ? Va. res. of heirs in 1855, R5147
Job, Mass., R5148
John, Cont., Pa., S39706
John, Md., BLWt.11369-100-Pvt. Iss. 11/26/1792 to Clayton Colwell, Admr. No papers
John, Va., S4378
Robert, Md., S45391

HOLLIDAY (continued)
Samuel, Pa., Sarah, R15136
William, Ga., R5149
William, N.Y. See HOLADAY
HOLLIDAYOKE, Daniel, Md., Anna, W9483
HOLLIMAN, James, N.C., S9590
HOLLIN, William, Md., Lavinia/Lovey, W9065; BLWt.28628-160-55
HOLLINGSHEAD, Benjamin, N.C., S16883
Sarah, former wid. of Mordecai Morgan, Pa., which see
Thomas, N.C., Mary, R5151
HOLLINGSWORTH, Elias, S.C., R5152
Henry, N.C., S8729
Jacob, Pa., R5153
Stephen, N.C., S8726
Zebedee/Zebulon, N.C., Elizabeth, W5301
HOLLINS, William, S.C. See HOLLEMS
HOLLINSHEAD, Sarah, Pa. See HOLLINGSHEAD
HOLLIS, Adam, Mass., Susannah, W7799
Barnabus, Cont., Mass., Huldah Penniman/Pennyman/Peniman, former wid., W21928; BLWt.2192-100
David, Mass., S32856
Elijah, Mass., S45395
James, N.C., S21290
James, N.C., Va., R5154
John, Pa., S35435
John, N.C., S46642
John, S.C., S21827
Richard, Mass., Sarah, W23347
Samuel, Mass., BLWt.4324-100-Pvt. Iss. 2/23/1796 to Joseph Brown
Samuel, Mass., BLWt.584-100
Stephen, Mass., Abigail, W23310; BLWt.4352-100
William, S.C., S10845
HOLLISTER, Asa, N.Y., S13425
Asahel, Ct., Elizabeth, W7803
Ashbel, Ct., Cont., S15461
David, Ct., Sarah, W21347
David, Ct., Hope, W21409; BLWt. 26704-160-55
Elijah, Ct., S22315
Elijah S., Mass., Lucy, W25791
Ephraim, Mass., S13460
Innett, Ct., Vt., S10846
Jesse, Cont., Mass., Clarissa, S39736; BLWt.916-300-Capt. Iss. 9/30/1791. No papers
John, N.J., R5157
Joseph, Ct., Navy, S16880
Josiah, Ct., Cont., S31748
Josiah, Ct., N.Y., R5158
Lucy, former wid. of Gideon Noble, Ct., which see
Nathan, Ct. See HOLISTER
Smith, Mass., N.Y., S13461
HOLLOMAN, Kinchen, N.C., R20383
HOLLOMS, James, S.C. See HOLMES
HOLLOW, Richard P. See PENHOLLOW
HOLLOWAY, Benjamin, R.I., S5546
Billy, Va., S38844
David, Mass., Lois, W19823
George, Va., S30450
James, Va., R20382; BLWt.1715-200
John, Mass., Elizabeth, W18050

HOLLOWAY (continued)
John, N.C., Rebecca, W271
John, Pa., Dis. No papers
Levi, Md., S32332
Nathaniel, Mass., Hannah, W21365
Taylor, S.C., S6966, res. at enl. Dinwiddie, Va.
Thomas, N.C., Lydia, BLWt.91502-160-55
William, Cont., Mass. See HALLOWAY
HOLLOWELL, Miles, N.C., Ann, W8951
HOLLY, Abraham, Ct., S37110
Abraham, Ct., S37114
Benjamin, S.C., Priscilla, W8941
David, Mass., S15171
Jacob/Jesse, N.C., Winnifred/Winford, W21388; BLWt.26420-160-55
Jesse, N.C., See Jacob
John, Ct., Tammey, W21396
John, Va., S9588
Joseph, Mass., Lucinda, W21400
Nathan, Mass., S23703
Osborn, N.C., S7021
Samuel, N.Y., Deborah, W8942
Silas, N.Y., Esther, W24437
Stephen, Ct., Deborah, W21354
HOLMAN, Edward, Mass., Martha, R5164
Eliphalet, Mass., S29230
Eliphalet, Mass., S41655
George, Pa., See HALLMAN
George, Pa., BLWt.9606-100-Pvt. Iss. 7/29/1794. No papers
George, Va., Indian War 1787, War of 1812, S17496; BLWt. 26265-160-55. Ky. res.
Isaac, N.C., Lilles/Lillis, W4235; BLWt.29003-160-55
Isaac, N.C., S.C., S4401
Jacob, S.C., R5165
John, Mass., S13437
John, Va., S8738
John, Va., S31753
Jonathan, Mass., Susanna, W24451
Nathaniel, Mass., Abigail, W19820
Richard, Va., S31133
Samuel, Mass., Betsey, W7786; BLWt.13193-160-55
Stephen, Mass., S18883
Thomas, Ct., Mass., Mary, W7787; BLWt.26955-160-55
Thomas, N.J., S5525
HOLMES, Abijah, N.Y., S13455
Anthony, N.J., S662
Azel, Vt., R5166
Barchlay/Bartlett, Va., S34926
Bartlett, Va., See Barchlay
Benjamin, Va. agcy., Dis. No papers. This vet. recorded as Benjamin Hoomes in Agcy. book. In Rept. of Secy. of War, 1835, name recorded as Benjamin Holmes. See Benjamin Hoomes, BLWt.977-300-Capt., which may relate to same indiv.
Cornelius, Mass., S30494
David, Ct., S33309
David, N.Y., S31752
David, Va., BLWt.1084-400-Surgn. Iss. 3/14/1796. No papers
Ebenezer, Ct., Abigail, W18058

HOLMES (continued)
Ebenezer, Cont., N.Y., R.I., S18885
Edward, Ct., Mass., S13423
Eliphalet, Ct., S10859
Eliphalet, Mass., Amey, W24441
Elisha, Ct., S15178
Ezra, Ct., Cont., Mass., S13421
George, Mass., Rachel, W23298
Gershom, Mass., S29902
Hannah, former wid. of Abner Woodin/Wooden. Mass., which see
Hardy, N.C., BLWt.1099-200-Lt. Iss. 5/31/1798. No papers
Isaac, Mass., BLWt.4327-100-Pvt. Iss. 11/28/1789. No papers
Isaac, Mass., Anna, W7769
Isaac, Va., R15233, Va. Half Pay
Jabez, N.Y., S23262
James, Ct., Rhoda J., W25780; BLWt.13886-160-55
James, Cont., Pa., Jane, W2802
James, N.J., S29234
James, N.C., Esther, W4697
James, N.C., R5170
James, S.C., R5171
James, Va., Sarah, W7768
Jedediah, N.Y., Hannah, W7772 BLWt.34979-160-55
John, Cont., Ct., Rachel, W21386
John, Cont., N.Y., Catee, W18031
John, Mass., S18878
John, Mass., Esther, W9063; BLWt. 17896-160-55
John, N.H., Polly, W1283; BLWt. 3965-160-55
John, N.J., BLWt.995-300-Capt. Iss. 7/7/1789. No papers
John, N.Y., BLWt.7231-100-Pvt. Iss. 9/29/1790 to Wm. Tilford, ass. No papers
John, N.C., R5173
John, Pa., BLWt.9648-100-Pvt. Iss. 1/21/1793 to Alexander Power, ass. of James Bennet, Admr. No papers
John G., N.J., R5172
Jonathan, Cont., Mass., Mercy, W23335; BLWt.560-100
Jonathan, N.H., Mary, W24438
Jonathan, N.J., BLWt.997-300-Capt. Iss. 6/11/1789. No papers
Jonathan, N.Y., S17221
Jonathan, N.Y., Sarah, W21348
Joshua, Ct., Lucretia, R5176
Lazarus, N.H., Mary, W21337
Lemuel, Ct., S13459
Lemuel, Cont., Mass., N.H., S39731
Lemuel, N.H., Abigail, W25784; BLWt.35838-160-55
Levi, Ct., S37117
Mather, Mass., Silence, W24440
Moses, N.Y., Betsey, W23320
Nathaniel, Cont., Ct., S45380
Nathaniel, Mass., S45381
Nathaniel, Mass., Jerusha, W13502
Nathaniel, N.J. & Sea Service, R5177
Oliver, Mass., Lydia, W21366
Orsamus, Green Mt. Boys, Vt., S2621
Philip, Mass., BLWt.4337-100-Pvt.

HOLMES (continued)
Iss. 3/26/1796 to Peter Swier. No papers
Robert, Mass., BLWt.4302-100-Pvt. Iss. 9/26/1791. No papers
Robert, Mass., S32863
Robert, N.C., Pa., Marjory, W84
Rozel/Roswell, N.Y., S13445
Samuel, Ct., S45389
Samuel, Cont., Mass., Pamila, W16604
Samuel, Mass., Invalid Corps, BLWt.13229-100-Pvt. Iss. 2/--/1790 to Theodosius Fowler, ass. No papers
Samuel, Mass., Mary, W1610; BLWt.8381-160-55
Samuel, Mass., Hannah, W14950
Samuel, N.J., S661
Samuel, N.Y., Vt., Sallena/Salina, W18066; BLWt.31279-160-55
Seth, Ct., Rhoda, W7770; BLWt. 61310-160-55
Seth, Mass., S41645
Silas, Ct., Cont., Louisa Palmer, former wid., W8282
Simeon, Ct., BLWt.5951-100-Pvt. Iss. 4/21/1794. No papers
Simeon, Ct., S31754
Stephen, N.Y., Rebecca, W18042
Stephen, Vt., Lydia, W7771; BLWt.47772-160-55
Sylvester/Selvester, Mass., BLWt. 795-100
Thomas, Ct., BLWt. 5953-100-Sgt. Iss. 5/8/1790. No papers
Thomas, Cont., Ct., S13466
Thomas, Mass., S31137
Thomas, N.H., S44425
Thomas, N.Y., BLWt.7220-100-Pvt. Iss. 9/15/1790 to Wm. Bell, ass. No papers
Thomas, N.Y., Anna, W21343
Thomas, S.C., b. England, S31758
Thomas C./Thomas Gwinn/Guinn, S.C., R5178
Titus, Ct., S18880
William, Mass., Sibel, W14931
William, Mass., Judith Goss, BLWt.21824-160-55
William, N.J., Mary, W429
William, N.J., BLWts.8370 & 14141-100-Pvt. Iss. 3/21/1796. No papers
Zachariah, Mass., See Zacheus
Zacheus/Zaccheus/Zachariah, Mass. S32849; BLWt.816-100
Zebulon, Mass., Rachel, W19813
HOLMS, John, Ct., Cont.,See HOLMES
HOLMSTOFF, William, See HALINSDOFF
HOLOBORD, Azariah, N.Y., S13435
HOLOMBACH, John, Ct. See HOLLENBEAK
HOLOWAY, Samuel, Mass., BLWt.4406-100-Pvt. Iss. 5/31/1790
HOLSAPPLE, John, N.Y., Hannah, W18048; BLWt.9425-160-55
Nicholas, N.Y., S10871
William, N.Y., R5200
HOLSART, John, N.J., Mary, W3684
HOLSHART, John, See HOLSART
HOLSON, William, Va., S9587

HOLSONBAKE, Derrick, S.C., Mary, W9067; BLWt.11271-160-55
HOLSTED, John, See HALLSTED
Timothy, Ct., S2625
HOLSTEN, Thomas, Del., S36018
HOLSTON, William, R.I., BLWt. 3226-100-Pvt. Iss. 12/31/1789 to Thomas Howland. No papers
HOLT, Abel, Mass., Eunice, W14942
Abiel, Mass., Lydia, W21342
Asa, Mass., Vt., R5180
Benjamin, R.I., Edith, W13423
Charles, N.C., Martha, W7756
Clabourn/Claibourn, Va., S38835
Daniel, Mass., Mary Carly, former wid., W14438
Darius, Mass., S35413
David, Cont., N.H. res. 1819, S13416
Ebenezer, Ct., Elizabeth, W25790
Ephraim, Mass., Jerusha, W1867; BLWt.30775-160-55
Eunice, former wid. of Charles Ferry, Mass., which see
Evan, Pa., BLWt.9537-100-Pvt. Iss. 11/5/1796. No papers
Evan, Pa., BLWt.1569-100-Pvt. No papers
Evan, Pa., S41653
Featherstone/Fetherston, N.C., R5181
Francis, N.C., R5182
George, Ct., S10875
George, Cont., Mass., S44427
George, N.C., S7024
Isaac, Cont., Mass., S34402
James, Mass., Olive, W19799
James, N.C., S9585
James, Va., BLWt.453-200
Jesse, Ct., S37121
Jesse, Mass., Dis. No papers
Joel, N.H., Polly, W21394; BLWt.11404-160-55
John, Mass., Lydia, W23340
John, Va., R5183
John Hunter, Va., BLWt.2121-300
Jonathan, Ct., Anna, W21360
Jonathan, Mass., Patty, W23342
Jonathan, Mass., Mary, W24457
Joseph, Mass., Mary, W21406
Joseph, Va., R15187; Va. Half Pay
Joshua, Mass., Hannah, W21375
Jotham, Mass., Lydia, W18059; BLWt.16274-160-55
Leonard, Md., BLWt.11328-100-Pvt. Iss. 2/7/1790. No papers
Nathan, N.H., Susannah, W15913
Nathaniel, R.I., Nabby, W18019
Nicholas, Mass., R5186
Obadiah, N.H., Susanna Micels/Michaels, former wid., W26269; BLWt.17859-160-55
Peter, Ct., BLWt.5985-100-Pvt. Iss. 12/31/1789. No papers
Reuben, N.C., S4387
Reuben, Va., BLWt.1412-100
Samuel, Ct., Navy, Margaret, W3141
Shadrach, N.C., Martha, R5185
Silas, Ct., BLWt.1774-200
Silas, Mass., S44937
Thomas, Pa., S4400

HOLT (continued)
Thomas, Va., R5187
Thomas, Va., BLWt.1069-300-Capt. Iss. 2/22/1799 to Joseph Walkins & Wm. R. Bernard, assnes. No papers
Valentine, Mass., R5188
William, Mass., S18456
William, Mass., S36019
William, Mass., Elizabeth, W18029
William, Mass., Esther F., W23191; BLWt.6397-160-55. See Wm. Holt, S36019, should have been combined with this case.
HOLTEN, Jonathan, N.H., Dis. No papers
HOLTON, Arad, Vt., Eunice, W5290; BLWt.13186-160-55
David, N.C., S13419
Elisha, Ct., Lydia, W7801
John, Pa., S41651
HOLTSLANDER, Adam F., N.Y., Pa., S5564
HOLTZ, John, Cont., Va., S38013
HOLTZAPPLE, Zachariah, N.Y., S44941
HOLTZER, Jacob, Pa. See HOLTZINGER
HOLTZINGER, Jacob, Pa., Barbara, W3203
HOLTZMAN, Jacob, Pa. See HOLZEMAN
HOLYFIELD, Valentine, N.C., Susannah, W19822
HOLZEMAN, Jacob, Pa., S22310
HOMAN, Eber, N.J., S4405
Edward, Mass., Sarah, W14918
John, Mass., Sea Service, Navy, Sarah, W19821
John, N.J., S2627
John, N.Y., Cleo, W21402
Joseph, Mass., Sea Service, S33318
Joseph, N.H., Sarah, W23323
Thomas, Mass., Sea Service, Tobitha, R5189
HOMANS, John, Cont., Mass., Sally, W3554
HOMER, Jacob, Mass. Sea Service, Elizabeth Wellington, former wid., W22556
Stephen, Mass., Thankful, W14925; BLWt.10310-160-55
Titus, Mass., S38834
HOMES, James, Md., BLWt.11347-100-Pvt. Iss. 3/27/1792 to John Wright, ass. No papers
Thomas, N.H., BLWt.3181-100-Pvt. Iss. 4/24/1800. No papers
HOMINGWAY, Jonathan, Mass., BLWt. 4320-100-Pvt. Iss. 1/17/1791. No papers
HOMISTON, Daniel, See HUMMISTON
HOMMEL, Harmanus, See HUMMEL
Peter, N.Y., Rachel, W16296
HOMMER, Jacob, Md., S5545
HOMSHER, Adam, Pa. See HAMSHER
HON, Henry, Pa. See HORN
HONE, Christopher, See HOHNE
HONEA, Tobias, N.C., S31761
HONEY, Accillis, See John A.
Daniel, N.J., N.Y. See HOWEY
John A./Accillis, S38842
HONEYMAN, William, Cont., Pa., BLWt.285-200
HONEYWELL, Isaiah, Green Mt. Boys, Mass., S29236
John, N.Y., BLWt.7278-100-Pvt. Iss. 7/28/1790 to G.H.V. Wagennen, ass. No papers
Matthias, Ct., N.Y., Esther, W19809; BLWt.26897-160-55
Rice, Green Mt. Boys, Mass., N.Y., R5191
William, N.J., R5192
HONNELL, David, N.J., R5193
HONSON, Aurt, N.Y., Mariam, W9481; BLWt.34988-160-55
HOOD, Aaron, N.H., S44430
Amos, Mass., Phebe, W14934
Andrew, N.C., S7030
Benjamin Landon, Mass., S18455
Charles, N.C., S41659
Daniel, Mass., S35424
Edward, Md., S34922
George, Cont., Va., Catharine, W8939; BLWts.1487-100 & 105-60-55
Jacob/John, Pa., S38841
James, Md., Kitty, W3816
John, Mass., S13465
John, Mass., Ruth, W19814
John, N.C., b. Del., S15468
John, Pa., See Jacob
John, S.C., N.C. res. at enl., S1534
John, S.C., b. Va., S7031
Joseph, Cont., Mass., Dorcas, W21401
Lazarus, Pvt., S.C., BLReg. 87482-1855
Martha, former wid. of Ebenezer Preble, Mass., which see
Morgan, N.C., S4389
Reuben, N.C., S8728
Richard, Mass., S32844
Robert, Mass., S35428
Samuel, Mass., S29895
Samuel, Mass., S30225
Thomas, Cont., Va., S38039
Thomas, N.C., S21289
Thomas, N.C., Va., S4379
Thomas, Va., BLWt.12220-100-Sgt. Major. Iss. 5/5/1790 to Wm. J. Vreedenburgh, ass. No papers
William, N.C., Catharine, W25781; BLWt.26978-160-55
William, Va., S35414
HOOF, James, Va., BLWt.12177-100-Pvt. Iss. 4/22/1794. No papers
Samuel, Pa., R5195
HOOFENBERGH, Henry, See HOEVENBERGH
HOOFMAN, Christian, Pa., S38042 Not same as Christian Hofman, S39752
HOOFNAGLE, George, See HORFNAGGLE
HOOFSES, Christian, Cont., Mass., Margaret, W23302
HOOGLAND, Jeronimus, Cont., N.Y., BLWt.541-300
Johanis, N.J., S34407
John, N.Y., Susannah, R5066
William, Pa., BLWt.9619-100-Pvt. "in the Dragoons." Iss. 2/28/1795 to Wm. Hoogland. No papers
HOOK, Frederick, Md., R5196
George, N.C. See HOOKE
HOOK (continued)
James, Va., S39713
Joseph, Md., Ann, W669
Nicholas, N.C. See HOUK
Stephen, Md., S8733
William, Del., BLWt.10789-100-Pvt. Iss. 7/9/1799. No papers
William, Va., Mary, W7755
Willoughby, N.C., S1533
HOOKE, George, N.C., Jane, W10112
HOOKER, Amos, Mass., Hannah,W27429
Benjamin, Mass., S32858
Brainard, Ct., Molly, W16297
Daniel, Ct., S31760
Gilbert, Ct., Mass., N.Y., S9353
Increase M., Vt., R5197
Ira, Cont., Ct., S15180
Israel, N.H., S44942
James, Ct., BLWt.5962-100-Corp. Iss. 3/8/17--. No papers
James, Ct., S39735
James, Ct., Mary, W25800
James G., Va., S4386
John, N.C., S.C.(?), Va.(?), R20384
John, Va., R5198
Martin, Ct., S9919
Philip, Cont.,R.I., Mass., Privateer, Hannah, W19819
Roger, Ct., S37120
Ruel/Reuel, Mass., Vt., S23267
Simeon, Mass., S13464
Thomas, Ct., Mary, W19804; BLWt. 8169-160-55
Thomas H., Ct., Sarah Collins, former wid., W24442
William, Ct., Vt., R5199
William, Cont.,Ct., Hannah,W21349
William, Mass., S33317
William, N.C., Jerusha, W10119
Zeban, Cont., Mass. See Zibeon
Zibeon/Zeban, Cont., Mass.,S33321; BLWt.925-200-Lt. Iss. 11/6/1795 to Jeremiah Hill, ass. No papers. Name recorded as Zeban Hooker
HOOKS, William, Va., S38035
HOOMES, Benjamin, Va., BLWt.977-300-Capt. See Benjamin Holmes (Dis.) which may relate to same individual
HOOPER, Abraham, Md., S34927
Absalom, S.C., Ga., Sarah, W7813; BLWt.19510-160-55
Betsy, former wid. of Reuben Hubbard, Mass., which see
Casper, Navy, Me. res. & agcy., S35420
Daniel, N.H., Hannah, W21341. She was pensioned as Hannah Hooper, but it is stated in claim by one Ephraim Tibbetts that after Hooper's death she m. Samuel Jones
David, Mass., Rachel, W23318
Ennis, N.C., S1833
Jacob R., N.Y., BLWt.7275-100-Pvt. Iss. 1/4/1791. No papers
James, N.J., S34408
James, Va., Elizabeth, W4457
James, Va., Mary Ann, W25792; BLWt.4-100-55 & 263-60-55
Jesse, Ga., S1913

HOOPER (continued)
Obadiah, Va., Sarah, W9482; BLWt.26811-160-55
Richard B., Va., S16418
Robert, Pa., BLWt.1034-200-Lt. Iss. 5/27/1791. No papers
Sarah, former wid. of Abijah Tarbox, Mass., which see
William, Mass., Sea Service, S18452
Zalmon A., Mass., R5201
HOOPLE, John, N.Y., Eleanor, R5202
HOOPS, Adam, Md., S18030; BLWt. 350-300
HOORNBECK, Abraham, N.Y., S31755
Jacob D., N.Y., Maria, W18044
HOOS, Hendrick, Mass., Sally,W25798
Mathias, N.Y., S13454
Nicholas, N.Y., S23263
HOOSE, Hendrick, Mass., BLWt.4343-100-Pvt. Iss. 2/23/1796 to Abel Boynton. No papers
HOOTEN, Elijah, N.C., S4388
HOOTON, John, Mass., S29911
HOOVEN, Henry, Pa., S39708
HOOVER, Anthony, Pa., Mary, W4459
Henry, Pa., See HOOVEN
Henry, Va., Lucretia, W1772; BLWt. 27642-160-55
Jacob, Pa. See HUBER
Jacob, Pa., Jane, W7805
Jacob, Va., S10842
John, N.Y., R5203
John, Pa., S4402
John, Pa., S18027
John/John George, Pa., b. Ger., Barbara, W4991
John Michael, Pa., Anna Barbara, W8220; BLWt.26784-160-55
Lawrence, Va., S13424
Michael, Va., S5560
Thomas, Va., S18029
HOPE, Benjamin, Va., Elizabeth, W1612
John, Va., S18033
Philip, Pa. See HAUPT
Ralph, Md., BLWt.11345-100-Pvt. Iss. 1/25/1796 to Samuel Johnston, ass. No papers
William, Md., BLWt.11346-100-Pvt. Iss. 2/1/1790. No papers
William, S.C., S1956
HOPEWELL, John, Va., S36591
HOPKINS, Archibald, Va., Margaret, W3686
Barnet, R.I., S21822
Benjamin, Cont., Vt., BLWt.1039-200
Braddock, Mass. See Lawrence
Caleb, Mass., S18876
Caleb, N.J., Ruth, R5213
Chana, former wid. of Simon Davis, R.I., which see
Charles, Ct., S37119
Consider, Ct., S13443
Daniel, N.C., S41660
Daniel, R.I., R5207
David, Cont., Md., S34925; BLWts. 1190-300 & 1087-400-Maj. of Dragoons. Iss. 7/29/1790. No papers

HOPKINS (continued)
David, Pa., S13307
David, S.C., BLWt.2216-300
Dennis, N.C., R5208
Driver, Pa., BLWts. 9280 & 9540-100-Pvt. Iss. 5/21/1792 to John P. Schott, ass. No papers
Ebenezer, Vt., Rachel, W7781
Elisha, Ct., BLWt.956-300-Capt. Iss. 8/9/1798. No papers
Ephraim, R.I., S21300
Ezekiel, R.I., S21301
Francis, Md., BLWt.11304-100-Pvt. Iss. 3/11/1791. No papers
Frederick, Ct., Susan, R5215; BLWt.45961-160-55
Frederick, N.Y., Lucy, BLWt. 103823-160-55
Garner, Cont., N.Y., Polly,W8945
George, Cont., Ct., Rachel, W18068
Giles, Mass., Thankful D., R5216
Isaac, N.C., S7043
Isaac, R.I., S21824
James, Cont., Vt. res. in 1770, BLWt.2466-100
James, Mass., Reliance, W14930
James, N.C., R5209
James, Pa., BLWt.9618-100-Sgt. "in the Dragoons". Iss. 8/26/1789 to James Gray, ass. No papers
James, R.I., BLWt.3225-100-Pvt. Iss. 5/28/1792. No papers
James, Va., S41650
James, Va., Mary, W3553
Jesse, N.C., Polly, W665; BLWt. 26905-160-55
John, Ct., Mass., S13447
John, Mass., Phebe Smith, former wid.; W22234; BLWt.33766-160-55
John, Mass., BLWt.136-100. Claim missing in 1912. Reg. shows "Iss. to Nehemiah Nelson, 2/28/1804. Not delivered." No papers
John, Mass., Privateer, S32854
John, Pa., BLWt.9557-100-Pvt. Iss. 2/21/1793 to Gideon Merkle, ass. No papers
Jonathan, N.Y., S46046
Joseph, Mass., Patty, W7782; BLWt. 34270-160-55
Lawrence/Braddock, Mass., Mary, R5212
Levi, Mass., Elizabeth, W11330; BLWt.26139-160-55
Mary, former wid. of Gale Borden/Burden, R.I., which see
Moses, Mass., S10854
Oliver, R.I., Susanna, W18045
Peleg, R.I., Elizabeth, W23336
Peter, ---, Me. res. Dis. No papers
Peter, R.I., Hannah, W1286; BLWt. 26690-160-55
Rhoderick, Cont., Ct., S44929
Richard, Mass., BLWt.4385-100-Pvt. Iss. 5/15/1790 to R. Hopkins. No papers
Richard, Mass., Ruth, R5214
Richard, R.I., S38840
Robert, Ct., Pa., Elizabeth,W8946

HOPKINS (continued)
Robert, N.Y., Catherine, R5206
Robert, S.C., S44928
Samuel, Va., BLWt.1065-450-Lt. Col. Iss. 8/10/1789 to Richard Platt, ass. No papers
Seth, Cont., Mass., S29903
Solomon, Mass., S35421
Solomon, Navy, Me. res. & agcy., S35422
Stephen, Mass., Mary, W18036
Theophilus, Cont., Mass., W23350
Thomas, Md., S18026
Tibbits F./Tippits, R.I., BLWt. 302-100
Timothy, Ct., Phebe, W4238
Timothy, Mass., Rebecca, W18060
Timothy, R.I., Sarah, W21384; BLWt.43502-160-55
Tippits, R.I., See Tibbits F.
Wait/Wate/Weight, Cont., Vt., BLWt.1115-300
Weight, See Wait
William, N.H., S8722
William, N.C., Va., S7033
William, Pa., BLWt.9617-100-Dragoon. Iss. 6/20/1789. No papers
William, Va., S31140
Zaphas/Zopher, N.Y., BLWt.7246-100-Pvt. Iss. 10/22/1791 to Asa Ballard, ass. No papers
HOPKINSON, Caleb, Mass., S17223
David, N.H., S39724
HOPPER, Abram A., N.J., Elizabeth, W251; BLWt.91124-160-55
Andrew, N.J., Maria, W857
Garret A., N.J., Catharine, R5219
Harmon/Harman, N.C., Sarah, W252
John, N.J.,S34409; BLWt.1001-150-Ensign. Iss. 4/14/1790. No papers
John, N.C., Catharine, W7785; BLWt.31275-160-55
John, Va., BLWt.12208-100-Pvt. Iss. 7/6/179? to Robert Means, ass. No papers
John A., N.J., Mary, R5220
John I., N.J., S1021
Lambert, N.Y., Lovica, W7784
Moses, N.C. See Moses EDWARDS
Peter, N.Y., BLWt.7241-100-Pvt. Iss. 8/12/1790 to Thomas Rossell, ass. No papers
Peter, N.Y., Delilah, W23346
Rinard, N.J., N.Y., S1022
Thomas, S.C., R5222
William, N.C. See HAPPER
William, N.C., R5221
HOPPIN, John, Cont.,Mass., S33316
Mary, former wid. of Joseph Whitney, R.I., which see
HOPPIS, Adam, Pa., S7040
HOPPS, Edward/Jeremy, R.I., Esther, W10111
HOPSEGAR, Paulus, N.J., BLWt.8387-100-Pvt. Iss. 7/30/1789. No papers
HOPSEKER, Powles, N.J. res., Dis. No papers
HOPSON, Benjamin, N.C., R5223
Rew, Ct., Sarah, R5224
William, N.C., S7004
William, Va., S30497

HOPWOOD, William, Va., S2324
HORAN, Moses, N.J., BLWt.8389-100-Pvt. Iss. 2/10/1792. No papers
Patrick, N.Y., R5229
HORBIN, Joshua, Md., N.C., S4390
HORD, Elizabeth, former wid. of Robert Scott, Va., which see
HORDER, William, Pa., S39705
HORE, Peter, Mass., See HOAR
HOREN, Patrick, N.Y. See HORAN
HORFNOGGLE, George, Cont., Pa., S39714; BLWt.2501-100. Name also given as Hoofnogle, Huffnagle, Hoffnagle & Hufnogle
HORLESS, Daniel, See HARLESS
Ferdenen, See HARLESS
Philip, Va. See HARLESS
HORN, Aaron, Va., R5225
Abraham, Pa., S39718
Andrew, Cont., N.H., Dorcas, W11314; BLWt.2361-160-55
Benjamin, N.H., Ruth, W21364
Benjamin, N.J., Margaret Bradford, former wid., W400; BLWt. 21829-160-55
Christopher, Cont., Va., Elizabeth, W664; BLWt.34931-160-55
Daniel, N.H., BLWt.3182-100-Pvt. Iss. 3/25/1790. No papers
Daniel, N.H., Deborah, R5227
Ebenezer, Cont., N.H., S8721
Ebenezer, Cont., N.H., Hannah, W21379
Frederick, Hazen's Regt., BLWt. 13182-100-Pvt. Iss. 7/30/1792 to Casper Camp, ass. No papers
Frederick, Pa., S2321
Frederick, Pa., Mary, W4494
George, N.H., S15460
George, Va., S4407
Henry, Cont., Pa., b. Ger., S5535
Henry, Pa., Christena, R5226
Ichabod, N.H., S44431
Jacob, Cont., N.Y. agcy. & res. S44940; BLWt.1898-100
James, N.J., Susan Myers, former wid., W185
Jeremiah, N.C., or Va., Mary, W3555; BLWt.26676-160-55
Jonathan, Cont., Navy, N.H., S35434
Joseph, Pa., S2620
Joshua, N.C., Micha, R5228
Matthias, Va., Susan, W10110
Nathan, N.C., R5232
Patrick, N.Y. See HORAN
Phanton, N.Y., BLWt.7210-100-Pvt. Iss. 7/30/1790 to Edward Cumpston,ass. No papers
Ralph R., N.Y., Va., Sea Service, S38046
Robert, N.C., S7023
William, Pa., R5230
HORNBAKER, Philip, See Philip Horn BAKER
HORNBECK, Abraham, Va., Hannah, W10120
Matthew, N.Y., R5231
Peter, N.Y., S15179
Samuel, N.Y., S10872
Samuel, Va.,Susan/Susanna, W8950

HORNBLOWER, Joseph, N.J., BLWt. 8386-100-Pvt. Iss. 9/8/1789 to Samuel Rutan, ass. No papers
HORNE, Henry C., Mass., BLWt. 4407-100-Pvt. Iss. 2/3/1792 to Nathan White, Admr. No papers
Joab, N.C., S45844
Nicholas, N.C., S4395
HORNEFORD, Andrew, N.J., BLWt. 8400-100-Pvt. Iss. 6/25/1793. No papers
HORNER, Francis, N.Y., BLWt. 7296-100-Pvt. Iss. 7/18/1791 to Richard Platt, ass. No papers
George, N.C., Priscilla, W3996
Isaac, N.J., Zilpha, R5233
John, Pa., BLWt.9571-100-Pvt. Iss. 12/14/1791. No papers
Mary, former wid. of Reuben Elliott, Va., which see
Thomas, N.C., S8682
HORNEY, William, Md., BLWt.11302-100-Pvt. Iss. 3/24/179? to James DeBaufre, ass. No papers
HORRALL, William, Va., S17472
HORROUF, Jacob, Pa., S8647
HORRELL, Henry B., Md., R5234
James, Va., S2322
John, Md., Martha, W7798; BLWt. 1316-100
HORSAM, Ebenezer, Cont., Mass., S22314; BLWt.886-100
Timothy, Mass. See HORSOM
HORSE, Valentine, Pa., S39711
HORSEFIELD, Thomas, Va., BLWt. 12180. Iss. 1789
HORSELEY, James, Va., S36590
HORSEWELL, Ephraim, R.I., BLWt. 3227-100-Corp. Iss. 1/15/1800. No papers
Philip, R.I., S21821
HORSFIELD, Thomas, See HORSEFIELD
HORSFORD, John, ---, Ct. res., Dis. No papers
Joseph, N.Y., BLWt.7214-100-Pvt. Iss. 5/21/1791. No papers
Samuel, Mass., S44935
HORSINGTON, Vespatian, See HOISINGTON
HORSKINS, Zebulon, See HOSKINS
HORSLEY, James, Va., S30490
Richard, N.C., Va., S9354
Rowland, Va., R5235
Samuel, Mass., Mary, W14947
HORSOM, Benjamin, See HORSUM
Ebenezer, Ct. See HORSAM
Jacob, N.H., S35431
Jonathan, Mass., N.H., S16884
Samuel, Mass., Navy, S31134
Timothy, Mass., Judith, R5237
HORSUM, Benjamin, Mass., Dorcas, W21371
David, Cont., Mass., Navy, N.H. S31142
Ebenezer, See HORSAM
HORSWELL, Ephraim, R.I., Ruth, W24444
Nathaniel, R.I., S13431
HORT, Levi, N.H., BLWt.3186-100-Pvt. Iss. 8/26/1790 to Mannassah Cutler, ass. No papers

HORTH, Francis, Mass., Vt., Anna, S22835
HORTON, Abel, R.I., Vt., S10876
Abram/Abraham, N.C., b. Pa., Ditha/Aditha, W7778; BLWt.40011-160-55
Barnabas, Cont., Mass., Mary, W23296
Benjamin, Mass., S32855
Benjamin, N.Y., Anna, R5238
Christopher, Ct., BLWt.5960-Corp. Iss. 9/2/1789. No papers
Daniel, N.J., Martha, W7780
Daniel, N.C., S1834
David, N.J., S2319
Elisha, Cont., Mass., Marilla, W11333; BLWt. 5-10-55 & 935-150-Ensign. Iss. 2/25/1796
Elizabeth, former wid. of Reeves Cox, N.Y., which see
Enoch, Mass., Bathsheba, W14921
George, Pa., b. Dutchess Co., N.Y., S29232
Henry, Ct., Cont., S41652
Isaac, Mass., S10850
Isaac, Mass., Polly, R19526
Isaac, N.C., S16419
James, Cont., Ct., S44930
James, Mass., S13450
Jason, N.Y., Mary, R5241
Jeremiah, N.Y., S13429
John, N.J., Mary, R5242
John, N.C., Va., b. N.Y. State, Nancy, W367; BLWt.26854-160-55. (Marriage bond gives wife's name as Agnes)
John, R.I., Vt., Mercy, W19806
John Payton, Va., S2320
Joseph, Cont., Va., Mary, W7777; BLWt.34271-160-55
Josiah, Cont., Mass., S44931
Josiah, Mass., BLWt.4336-100-Pvt. Iss. 4/1/1790. No papers
Lemuel, Mass., S20405
Nathan, N.J., Elizabeth, W7779
Robert, Va., Jaley, R5239
Rufus, Mass. Sea Service, Abigail, W23316; BLWt.79532-160-55
Samuel, Cont., U.S. Inf. in 1800; Adah, W4700; BLWt.26931-160-55. Res. Canandaigua, N.Y. in 1818
Samuel, Mass., Mary, W13492
Samuel, N.Y., S15172
Samuel, Va., BLWt.12179-100-Pvt. Iss. 5/21/1794 to Richard Smyth, ass. No papers
Samuel, Va., Jane, W7809; BLWt. 27670-160-55
Sarah, former wid. of Abner Perry, N.C., which see
Thomas, N.Y., Hepsibeth, W19824
Thomas, S.C., b. Va., Orender/Orander, W670; BLWt.3969-160-55
William, N.Y., Vt., S13446
Zephaniah, N.J., Jany, W3997; BLWt.35847-160-55
HORTWICK, Barnabas/Barnt, N.J., Dorotha, W7814; BLWt.8384-100 Iss. 1792; BLWt.122-60-55
Barnt, See Barnabas
Matthias, N.J., BLWt.8372-100-

HORTWICK (continued)
Pvt. Iss. 2/10/1792. No papers
HOSBROOK, George, N.Y., BLWt. 7239-100-Pvt. Iss. 9/15/1790 to Wm. Bell, ass. No papers
HOSEA, John, Mass., S33312
HOSECK, William, See HOSICK
HOSER, John, N.Y. See HOSIER
HOSFORD, Daniel, Mass., S22289
Joseph, N.Y., S44934
Samuel, N.Y., S13430
HOSHAL, Jesse, Cont., Md., Mary, W4236
HOSICK, William, Va., S44932
HOSIER, John, N.Y., S44933. He d. 4/18/1822
John, N.Y., Phebe, R5243. He d. 6/11/1830.
Samuel, Va., R5244
HOSKINS, Achilis, Va., S1218
Asa, Ct., Kitty Adams, former wid., W25366
Ashbel, Ct., Rachel, W5302
Benoni, Mass., Vt., R5245
Cornelius, Mass., S41648
David, Ct., S23708
Eli, Mass., R.I. See HASKINS
Elijah, Ct., S5568
Isaac, Pa., BLWt.9610-100-Pvt. Iss. 9/25/1792. No papers
James, Va., S1219
John, Ct., S21298
John, Pa., S39707
Nathan, Mass., Lydia, W17037
Noah, Mass., BLWt.4345-100-Pvt. Iss. 6/20/1795. No papers
Preserved, Mass., R.I., S30498
Randall/Randal, Md., S36584
Robert G., S.C., b. England, R5246
Thomas, Va., S38044
Timothy, Ct., Rhoda, W21344
Timothy, Mass., R.I., S18036
Zebulon, Ct., BLWt.5933-100-Pvt. Iss. 9/4/1781 to Ezekiel Case. No papers
Zebulon, Ct., Kezia, W18026
Zipporah, former wid. of Timothy How, N.Y., which see
HOSKINSON, Basil, Va., Eleanor, W753; BLWt.30780-160-55
Charles, Md., S30493
Isaiah/Isaaih, Va., S16157
Josiah, Cont., enl. Md., S41649
HOSLER, Michael, Pa., Christiana, R5095
HOSLEY, John, Navy, Mass., Eliza-beth/Elizabeth R., W11340; BLWt.57652-160-55
Sampson, Mass., S13444
HOSMAN, Joseph, Del., BLWt.1039-200-Lt. Iss. 6/6/1794 to Wm. D. Brown, ass. No papers
HOSMAR, John, Ct., BLWt.5930-100-Pvt. Iss. 12/4/1789 to Richard Platt. No papers
HOSMER, Ashbel, Ct., Polly, R5248
Daniel, Mass., S29244
David, Ct., Sarah, W668; BLWt. 30784-160-55
Graves, Ct., Navy, S44938
John, Ct., S45390

HOSMER (continued)
John, Mass., S17483
Prentice, Ct., BLWt.959-200-Lt. Iss. 12/12/1789 to Theodosius Fowler, ass. of Elizabeth Horner, Admx. No papers
Prosper, Ct., Catharine, W23339
Reuben, N.H., BLWt.3183-100-Pvt. Iss. 3/25/1790. No papers
Samuel, Mass., Sarah, W19683; BLWt.30776-160-55
Timothy, Ct., BLWt.970-400-Surgn. Iss. 2/15/1799 to Timothy Hosmer No papers
HOSTETTER, Ulrick, Pa., S5563
HOSTINGS, Ebenezer, N.Y., BLWt. 7302-100-Pvt. Iss. 7/30/1790 to Edward Cumpston, ass. No papers
HOSTION, Jacob, N.C. See BOSTON
HOSTON, Henry, Ct. See HORTON
HOSUM, Jonathan, Mass. See HORSOM
HOTCHKIS, Thebus, Ct., R5249
HOTCHKISS, Abraham, Ct., Rosette, W18057
Ambrose, Ct., Lucretia, W23321
Asahel, Ct., Ruhamah, W25787; BLWt.30770-160-55
Eben, Ct., S36582
Eldad, Ct., Privateer, S13242
Elihu, Ct., Sally, W21397
Elijah, Ct., S10864
Ezekiel, Cont., Ct., S36585
Harris, Ct., Navy, S2632
Ira, Ct., S36581
Isaac, Ct., Ann, W18021
Isaac, Ct., Cont., Olive, W18032
Jared, Ct., Betsey, W368
Jeremiah, Ct., Mabel, W24450; Rej. B.L.
Joseph, Ct., Temperance, W18051
Josiah, Ct., Asenath, W18030; BLWt.30768-160-55
Levi, Ct., Susannah, W18054
Lodowick/Lodwick/Ladwick, Ct., S36583
Medad, Cont., Ct., S36586
Prince, Ct., BLWt.5909-100-Pvt. Iss. 3/3/1795 to Thomas S. Cornwell. No papers
Reuben, Ct., Thankful, W18062
Roswell, Ct., S13453
Samuel, Ct., S10877
Samuel, Ct., Chloe, W7811; BLWt.8154-160-55
Samuel, Ct., Chloe, W18047
Simeon, Ct., S10868
Stephen, Ct., Tamar, W18040
Titus, Ct., Mass. Sea Service, Rachel, W18049
Trueman, Ct. See Truman HOCHKISS
HOTMAN, George, N.J., BLWt.8379-100-Pvt. Iss. 8/24/1793. No papers
HOUCHIN, Charles, Va., R5250
HOUCHING, Bernard, Va., S38048
HOUCHINS, Edward, Va., Nancy, W11318
Francis, Va., R5251
HOUCKE, Nicholas, See HOUK
HOUDIN, Michael Gabriel, Mass., BLWt.917-300-Capt. Iss. 10/23/1790. No papers

HOUGE, James, Pa. See HOGGE
HOUGH, Azel, Ct., R5253
Bede, former wid. of Baldwin Woodruff, Cont., Ct., which see
Bernard, Va., S9589
Daniel, N.H., Lydia, W16029
David, Ct., N.Y., Abigail, R5252
Elijah, Mass., S44936
Erastus, Ct., S13456
Jabez, Ct., Eunice, W21357
Joel, Ct., S17495
John, Ct., Susannah, W15685
John, N.C., Elizabeth, W1183; BLWt.11153-160-55
John, Va., S7026
Moses, N.J., S31156
Samuel, Cont., Ct., S36580
Walter, Ct., Martha, W3687
William, Va., S8724
Zephaniah, N.Y., Sabra, W18065
HOUGHLAND, John, Lee's Legion, Va., BLWt.13240-100-Pvt. Iss. 6/7/1790 to John Houghland. Also BLWt.118-60-55. No papers
HOUGHTALIN, James, N.Y., Naily, W18067; BLWt.14958-160-55
HOUGHTON, Aaron, N.J., S32330
Abel, Mass., Relief, W20154; BLWt.16107-160-55
Abijah, Mass., S20799
Adonijah, Mass., Jane, W21399
Darius, Mass., N.H., Sibbell/Sybil, W23325; BLWt.17721-160-55
Ebenezer, Mass., Vt., Hadassah, W18025
Edward, N.H., S32841
Elijah, Mass., S29907
Elijah, Mass., Vt., S18450
Elisha, Mass., S39725
Ephraim, Ct., Mary, W2550; BLWt. 26829-160-55
Ephraim, Mass., Polly, W1284; BLWt.14984-160-55
Jonas, Mass., S29906
Jonas, Mass., Phebe, W15683; BLWt.7588-160-55
Jonathan, ----, Vt. res., Dis. No papers
Jonathan, Mass., S35412
Nathaniel, Mass., Annah, W4992
Nathaniel, Mass., Esther, W14933
Robert, Mass., S10851
Rufus, Mass. & War of 1812, Mary, R5256
Samuel, Mass., Sarah, W21405
Shevah, Mass., S13449
Silas, Mass., N.H., N.Y., S---
Silas, ---, N.Y. res. 1791, Hannah, ----. See her claim as former wid. of Samuel Wessels/Wessells, N.J.
Simeon, Mass., S45393
William, N.J., Margaret, W19816; BLWt.26558-160-55
Zarah, Mass., Eleanor, W14922; BLWt.19720-160-55
HOUGTON, Ebenezer, See HOUGHTON
HOUK, Michael, N.C., S32329
Nicholas, N.C., Sarah, R5257
Tobias, N.J., Rachel, W15685
HOULT, Lewis, Pa., BLWt.9609-100-Pvt. Iss. 7/16/1789. No papers

HOUNSLER, Charles, Va., S4394
HOUSE, Abner, Ct., R5259
Adam, Va. (son of Matthias), Hannah, R5260
Andrew, Pa., Hannah, W27893; BLWt.34538-160-55
Andrew, Pa., R5261
Benjamin, Ct., S18032
Christian, N.Y., BLWt.13174-100-Pvt. Iss. 3/21/1794. Also BLWt. 14069. No papers
Christian, N.Y., Huldah, W7759; BLWt.24909-160-55
Cornelius, Lamb's Art., N.Y., BLWt.7282-100-Pvt. Iss. 10/9/1790 to Michael Meyers, ass. No papers
Cornelius, N.Y., S45384
Eleazer, Ct., R5262
Eleazar, Ct., Cont., S10847
Elias, N.C., S24216
George, Sheldon's Dragoons, Ct. BLWt.5987-100-Corp. Iss. 4/14/1790 to Wm. Wells. No papers
George, Cont., Ct., Mary, W23317
George, N.Y., S19340
George, Pa., S39701
George, Va., S2622
Henry, N.Y., BLWt.7242-100-Pvt. Iss. 6/29/1790. No papers
Henry, N.Y., S45385
Henry, N.Y., Nancy, W21383
Jacob, N.Y., BLWt.14068-100-Pvt. Iss. 3/21/1794. No papers
Jacob, N.Y., Anna Eva, R15176
Joel, Ct., Cont., Lois, W18023; BLWt.2482-100
John, Sheldon's Dragoons, Ct., BLWt.5988-100-Corp. Iss. 4/14/1790 to Wm. Wells. No papers
John, Cont., Ct., Esther, W18041
John, N.H., Susanna, W21377
John, N.Y., BLWt.7273-100-Pvt. Iss. 8/18/1790. No papers
John, N.Y., Margaret, W1182
John, N.Y., Mary/Jane Maria, W25785
John, Va., born Md., R5264
Joseph, Mass., S39726
Levi, Pa., Va., R5265
Michael, Pa., S34930
Nathaniel, Cont., Mass., S35432
Nicholas, N.Y., Catharine, W18046
Peter C., N.Y., War of 1812, Anna, W23305, R15237;BLWt.21826-160-55
William, N.Y., S22834
HOUSEHOLDER, Jacob, Pa., BLWt. 9576-100-Pvt. Iss. 10/2/1789 to John Cunias, ass. No papers
HOUSEMAN, Thomas, Pa., BLWts. 11333 & 9534-100-Pvt. Iss. 12/28/1791 to Eleanor Halley, ass. No papers
HOUSER, Andrew, S.C., S21829
George, N.C., Magdalena, W10118
Jacob, N.Y., See HAUSER
John, N.C., Hannah Shamel, former wid., W9650
Ludwick/Ludwig, Pa., S2623
HOUSEWORTH, Henry, N.Y., S15462
HOUSLER, David, N.J., Isabel, R5266

HOUSLEY, John, Md., BLWt.11307-100-Pvt. Iss. 10/14/179? to Henry Davis, ass.
John, Md., S38036
Robert, Va. See HOUSLY
HOUSLY, John, Va. See OWSLEY
Robert, Va., Lydia Ann, R5267
HOUSTEN, Elijah, Del., BLWt. 1814-100
HOUSTON, Archibald, N.C., born Pa., Rosanna, W295
David, Mass., Martha, W14917
Hugh, N.C., Martha, W8928
Isaac, Mass., N.H., Ruth, W23303
James, Ga., BLWt.1231-450
James, N.C. See HUSTON
James, N.C., Asenath, W13500
James, S.C., S21288
James, Va., S1914
John, N.C., S2323
John, N.C., Va., S1832
John, S.C., Mary, W3817
Peter, N.C., (?), R5268
Purnell, Del., Pa., S15467
Samuel, Cont., N.H., Sarah, W23300
Samuel, S.C., b. N.C., Martha, W7810
William, Mass. See HUESTEN
William, Va., S1835
HOUSTOUN, James, Ga. See HOUSTON
HOUTS, Jacob, Cont., Pa., Barbara W3265
HOUTZ, Beltzer, Pa. See Baltzer HAUTZ
HOUZE, Samuel, S.C., S7035
HOVER, Anthony, Pa., BLWt.9621-100-Proctor's Art. Iss. 7/16/1789 to M. McConnell, ass. No papers
John, Pa., BLWt.9577-100-Pvt. Iss. 1/12/179? to Barnard Slanch, ass. No papers
John George, Pa. See John HOOVER
Samuel, Pa., R15140
HOVEY, Amos, Mass., Deborah, R5269
Azel, Ct., Lucy, W1770; BLWt. 39223-160-55
Daniel, Vt., Beulah, W26967; BLWt.3800-160-55
David, Mass., S13420
Dominicus, Mass., S32859; BLWt. 943-200-Lt. Iss. 3/23/1797 to Marlby Turner, ass. His wid. Mehitable Tripp Hovey was pensioned as former wid. of Gideon Cobb, Mass., which see
Dudley, Ct., S18451
Ezra, Mass., BLWt.4353-100-Pvt. Iss. 5/6/1797 to Marbry Turner, ass of Dominicus Hovey, heir of Ezra Hovey. No papers
Ivory, Ct., Mass., S32842
Jacob, Ct., S45394
Josiah, Mass., Elizabeth, W10080; BLWt.2362-160-55
Mehitable Tripp, former wid. of Gideon Cobb, Mass., which see
Nathaniel, Ct., Betsey Mason, former wid., W21778
Roger, Ct., Martha, R5270
Samuel, Ct., S46641

HOVEY (continued)
Samuel, Mass., Navy, Mercy, R5271
William, Ct., Lucinda, W4995
Zaccheus, Ct., S18882
HOW, Aaron, Cont., Mass., N.H., Betsey, W18038; BLWt.11251-160-55
Alvin, Mass., Mary, W19805
Antipass, N.H., Joanna, R5289
Caleb, N.H., S46647
Daniel, Mass., Lucy, W14928
David, Cont., Mass., S29912
David, Mass., S32862
David, Mass., Sally, W11316; BLWt.19610-160-55
David, Mass., Vt., R5287
David, N.Y., S23706
Ebenezer, Mass. See HOWE
Eli, Mass. See HOWE
Ephraim, N.H., S10843
Farnum, Mass., S29245
Fortunatus, Cont., Mass., Sarah, W24446
Isaac, Mass., BLWt.4332-100-Corp. Iss. 2/27/1790 to Theodosius Fowler. No papers
Isaac, Mass. See HOWE
Israel, Ct. See HOWE
Janzaniah/Jaczaniah, Mass., Lois, W1430
John, Cont., Va., Gen. Wayne's Indian Campaign of 1794, enl. in Md., Rachel, W10113
John, Mass., Molly, W14940
John, N.Y., Phebe, W16284
John W., Va., See HOWE
Jonathan, Mass., N.H., S18453
Jonathan, N.H., S18034
Joseph, Cont., N.H., S39728; BLWt.2358-100
Libbeus, N.Y., Anna, W21392
Molly, former wid. of Micah Ross, Mass., which see
Moses, Cont., See HOWE
Nathan, Ct., S15466
Peter, Cont., N.H. See HOWE
Peter, Vt. See HOWE
Reuben, Mass. See HOWE
Reuben, Mass., Vt., Susanna, W24436
Samuel, Mass., S10848
Sarah, former wid. of Timothy Fay, Ct.,Cont.,Mass. Which see
Timothy, N.Y., Zipporah Haskins, former wid., R5247
HOWARD, Aaron, Mass., S15893
Abraham, Mass., Marcy, W23348
Adam, Cont., Mass., S23707
Adam, Va., S8716
Allen, N.C., S8730
Amos, Mass., Navy, Mary, W14915
Amos, N.H., S20407
Andrew, Mass., Clarissa, W7792
Barzillai, Mass., Hannah Parmenter former wid., W34401; BL Rej.---. She was pensioned for service of her last husb., Levi Parmenter, Mass., which see
Benjamin, Ct., Cont., Freelove, W18055
Benjamin, Mass., BLWt.4394-100-Pvt. Iss. 4/1/1790. No papers
Benjamin, Mass., S13414

HOWARD (continued)
Benjamin, Mass., S15458
Benjamin, N.H., S44443
Benjamin, N.H., Sally Fisher, former wid., W10992; BLWt. 102201-160-55
Benjamin, N.C., S31138
Benjamin, Va., R5273
Beriah, Mass., S29231
Betsy, former wid. of Job Stacey, Mass., which see
Brooks, Vt., S29904; BLWt.28533-160-55
Calvin, Mass., S5549
Catharine, former wid. of Philip Clumberg, Pa., which see
Claiborne, Va., S8731
Daniel, R.I., Dorothy, W21350
Darius, Ct., Vt., Susan, W27713; BLWt.26030-160-55. She was former wid. of Asher Warner who was killed in battle in War of 1812. See papers within.
David, Mass., Abigail, W19801
Edward, Crane's Cont. Artillery, Mass., BLWt.4433-100-Pvt. Iss. 1/28/1790 to Joseph May. No papers
Edward, Mass., S29243
Edward, Mass., S32860
Elisha, Mass., Vt., R5275
Enoch, Cont., Mass., N.H., S18037
Enos, N.Y., Martha, W18027
Ezekiel, Mass., S33314
Ezekiel, N.C., S21828
Gordon, Pa., Va., S41657
Hardy, N.C., S8732
Henry, Mass., Anna, W16125
Henry, N.C., R5277
Henry, R.I., S45378
Henry, Va., Isabella, W8948
Hezekiah, N.J., R5278
Ichabod, Cont., R.I., Mary, W24452. He d. July 1818
Ichabod, R.I., BLWt.4-100-Special Act of 6/4/1842. He d. prior to Jan. 1818
Isaac, Mass., Mary Henshaw, former wid., W13415
Jacob, Mass. See HAYARD
James, Ct., Sarah, W18094
James, Mass., S33311
James, N.Y., Va., Rhoda, W10123; BLWt.86051-160-55
James, R.I., S38839
James, S.C., Va., S20406
James, Va., S9563
James, Va., S31139
James, Va., S38045
Jeremiah, Ct., Sally, W18043
Job, Mass., Hannah, W11319
John, Ct., S41658
John, Cont., N.H., Lydia, W16030
John, Ga., Margaret, R5281
John, Md., Margaret, W3551
John, Md., Mary, R5283
John, Mass., BLWt.4351-100-Fife Major. Iss. 11/7/1796. No papers
John, Mass., S29246
John, R.I., Mary, W2114; BLWt. 6026-160-55
John, R.I., Lydia, W21369

HOWARD (continued)
John, S.C., Nancy, W3556; BLWt. 26355-160-55
John, Va., R5280
John Day, Navy, Privateer, Mass., Lucy, W24456
John E., Md., BLWt.1043-500-Col. Iss. 10/18/1796. No papers
John Walker, Md., R5279
Jonas, Mass., S30492
Jonathan, Mass., Beulah, W14935
Joseph, Mass., S28768
Joseph, Mass., S13244
Joseph, Mass., Eunice, W24454
Joshua, Mass., Lydia, W13491
Joshua, N.H., S16416
Josiah, Cont., Mass., Mary,W18018 BLWt.3534-160-55
Oliver, Mass., S18877
Oliver, Mass., S18879
Peter, Va., Dis. No papers
Peter, Va., S4404
Phebe, former wid. of Daniel Blasdel/Blasdell/Blaisdell, Mass. which see
Pitman, Cont., Mass., S44441
Ruth E., former wid. of Reuben Shearman/Sherman, R.I., Vt., which see
Samuel, Cont., N.H., S4442
Samuel, Mass., S35426
Samuel, Mass. See HAYWARD
Samuel, Pa., S7036
Silas, Mass., S15282
Silas, Mass., S32839
Simeon, Ct., See HAYWARD
Simeon, Mass., S45377
Solomon, Ct., Cont., Vt., Anna, W7789
Solomon, N.C., S31757
Stephen, Md., Elizabeth, W8949
Stephen, Mass. See HAYWARD
Thaddeus, Mass., S17485
Theophilus, Mass., Bathsheba, W18016
Thomas, Mass., Ctf.1133. Papers in pension application of Lydia Howard were removed from this jacket, as her claim was erroneously adjudicated as the wid. of this Thomas instead of as wid. of her husb., Thomas Howard, S13467. Papers were placed with that claim 3/28/1933
Thomas, Mass., S32865; BLWt.583-100
Thomas, Mass., S45379
Thomas, Pa., Rhoda, W4237; BLWt. 26695-160-55
Thomas, R.I., Lydia, S13467 & W7788
Thomas, Va., S45796
Uriah, N.H., Vt., Lydia, W23313
William, Ct., S15463
William, Ct., Lucy, W4699; BLWt. 2027-160-55
William, R.I., Hopey, W19810
William, S.C., N.C., S7042
Wilson, N.C., S7032
Zachariah, Mass., Patty, W24448; BLWt.30778-160-55
HOWD, Benjamin, Ct., S20793

HOWD (continued)
Daniel, Ct., Johannah, W11329
HOWDEN, Alexander, R.I., S39717
HOWDERSHELL, Lawrence, Va., S19341
HOWE, Abner, Mass., BLWt.4377-100-Pvt. Iss. 9/9/1790 to James F. Sebor. No papers
Abner, Mass., Nancy, W19789
Amasa, Mass., Polly, W7767; BLWt. 15443-160-55
Asa, Ct., Priscilla, W2552; BLWt. 9526-160-55
Avis, former wid. of John Herrick, Ct., which see
Azor, Mass., Ruth, W15497
Bezaleel, N.H., Catharine, R5286; BLWt.901-200-Lt. Iss. 2/24/1790. No papers
Cato, Mass., Lucy Rogers, former wid., W2354; BLWt.12829-160-55
Daniel, Md., Cont., S7041
Daniel, Mass., S39729
Daniel, Mass., See HOW
Daniel, Va., S5565
Darius, Mass., S45372
David, Ct., Phebe, R5290
David, Mass., See HOW
David, N.H., BLWt.3167-100-Pvt. Iss. 4/5/1796 to Oliver Ashley, ass. No papers
David, N.H., Lucy, W21363
David, S.C., S13422
Ebenezer, Mass., Sarah, W7766; BLWt.17870-160-55
Ebenezer, Mass., Hannah, W21367
Ebenezer, Mass., R21705
Eli, Mass., Polly, W21340
Elijah, N.H., BLWt.3175-100-Drummer. Iss. 3/25/1790. No papers
Ezekiel, Mass., S29239
Fortunatus, Cont., Mass. See HOW
Francis, Mass., S31135
Gardner, Mass., S22317
Hezekiah, Mass., S45374
Isaac, Mass., Lois, W24435
Israel, Ct., Hannah, W25795
Jacob, Cont., Mass., Betty, W23312
Jacob, Pa., R5288
James, Va., Margaret, W7765; BLWt.26608-160-55
Jazaniah, Ct., Mary, W21381
Jazariah, BLWt.13173 & 13272-100-Pvt. "in the Invalid Corps". Iss. 5/1/1797 to John Duncan, ass. No papers
Jazariah, BLWt.13222-100-Pvt. "in the Invalids." Iss. 4/5/1792 to Alexander Catlin, ass. No papers
Jesse, N.Y., Mary, W19798
Joel, Mass., Mary, W21372
Joel, Mass., Esther, W25799; BLWt. 15410-160-55
John, Md. See HOW
John, Mass., S39737
John, Mass., See HOW
John 2nd, N.J., S34403
John, N.Y., BLWt.7221-100-Pvt. Iss. 3/16/1792 to Nathaniel Platt, ass. No papers
John, N.Y. See HOW

HOWE (continued)
John, Vt., Anna Gardner, former wid., W1032; BLWt.34980-160-55
John W., Va., Mary Ann, W8938
Jonathan, Mass., S29896
Jonathan, N.H. See HOW
Joseph, Ct., S45373
Joseph, Mass., BLWt.4398-100-Sgt. Iss. 3/17/1794. No papers
Joseph, Mass., S45376
Micah, Mass., Persis, W2551; BLWt.9210-160-55
Moses, Cont., Mass., Mary, W14922
Moses, Mass., S45375
Nathan, Mass., S29905
Oliver, N.Y., S45581
Perley, Green Mt. Boys, Mass., S10863
Peter, Cont., N.H., S44428
Peter, Vt., S2325
Reuben, Mass., Elizabeth, W25779; BLWt.26866-160-55
Robert, N.C., BLWt.856-1100-Maj. Gen. commanded N.C. troops as Col. at Battle of Greatbridge in 1775; later appt'd Maj. Gen. in U.S. service, commanded a Div. in the main Army 1778-1779 & 1790. Served as member of the Court Martial held for trial of Gen. Chas. Lee in 1778, commanded the expedition against Verplanck's Point at time that Stoney Point was attacked & carried by Gen. Wayne. D. in 1786. M. Sarah ---, and had son Robt. On 2/23/1820 Wt. No.856 for 1100 acres of BL was iss. for the benefit of son Robt. Howe of Brunswick Co., N.C., & other heirs, names not given. It is stated that Robt. Howe was the only male heir of sold. An inquiry dated 7/13/1829 from Samuel W. Hankins, Rm.606, 2061 Broadway, N.Y.C. states in 1822 Govt. granted land in Henry Co., Tenn. to Maj. Gen. Robt. Howe for his Rev. services. File shows Gen. Howe's son, Robt.,in 1820 appt'd. Samuel Hankins his lawful atty. to obtain title to this land.
Salah/Selah, N.H.,Elizabeth,W10114
Samuel, Cont.,N.H.,Judith, W18020
Sarah, former wid. of Nathaniel Griffin, Mass., which see
Selah, N.H., BLWt.3208-100-Pvt. Iss. 5/8/1792 to Benj./Peter Haskell. No papers
Simon, Mass., S39721; BLWt.1204-100
Solomon, Mass., S10852
Squier/Squire, Ct., Phebe, W21351
Squire, R.I., Martha, W16294
Thomas, N.H., Betsey, R5285; BLWt.34814-160-55
Tilly/Tilley, Mass. or N.H.(?), Susannah, R5291
Timothy, Mass., S45388
Timothy, N.Y., S23264
Titus, N.Y., S15174
William, Mass., BLWt.4393-100-Pvt.

HOWE (continued)
Iss. 2/3/1792 to Nathan White. No papers
William, Mass., S35411
William, Pa., BLWt.9631-100-Corp. Iss. 7/16/1789. No papers
William, Pa., S39710
Zadok/Zadock, Ct., Cont., S32866
HOWEL, Charles, Va., S5561
Daniel, Va., b. Pa., S13413
Isaac, Cont., Pa., R5295
John, N.C., Mary, W5297
John, N.C., Va., R5296
Lewis, Va., Leona Barnett, former wid., W9719
Nicholas, Ct., BLWt.1517-100
HOWELL, Aaron, N.Y., S44939; BLWt.7255-100. Iss. 9/25/1790. No papers
Arthur, N.J., Leah, W14944
Benjamin, N.Y., S28765
Benjamin, N.C., S4396
David, Va., Rebecca, R5299
Edward, N.Y., S17486
Ezekiel, Cont., Pa., Elizabeth, W3086; BLWt.1025-200-Lt. Iss. 8/19/1789. No papers
George, N.Y., BLWt.7223-100-Sgt. Iss. 10/12/1790. No papers
George, N.Y., S45396
Henry, N.C., Jane, W795
Hopkin/Hopkins, Ga., S31749
Jeremiah, N.J., S2629
John, N.J., Eleanor, W666; BLWt. 998-300-Capt. Iss. 6/11/1789 to Israel Ludlow, ass. No papers
John, N.C., BLWt.12251 & 13169. Iss. 4/21/1798. No papers
John, N.C., S2628
Jonathan, N.J., BLWt.8375-100-Pvt. Iss. 6/28/1789
Jonathan, N.J., S35419
Jonathan, Va., S2326
Mary, former wid. of James Boyle N.Y., which see
Matthew, N.Y., R5298
Miles, Va., S9586
Nancy, former wid. of Robert Glasscock, Va., which see
Philip, N.C., Mary, W937
Reuben, Va., S2327
Samuel, Md., S30496
Seth, N.Y., BLWt.7230-100-Pvt. Iss. 1/5/1791. No papers
Silas, Mass., S29900
Silas, N.J., Hannah, R5294. This was filed & jacketed as Stephen Howell until 4/17/1934. MMHF
Thomas, Pa., BLWt.9530-100-Pvt. Iss. 1/27/1790 to Ebenezer Sprout, ass. No papers
Thomas, S.C., R20385
Thomas, Va., R5300
William, Ct. Sea Service, Mass. Sea Service, Privateer, S18039
William, Cont., Pa., Va., S39723
William, N.J., S34405
William, N.J., Pa., S7037
William, Va., S2328
William E., N.J., R6302
HOWERTON, James, Va., S38836
William, Va., S15469

HOWES, Abner, Mass., Bethia, W14929
Benjamin, Ct., S30499
Elkanah, Mass., Desire, W13501
Eunice, former wid. of Grove Pomroy, Mass., which see
Isaiah, Mass., R.I., S29909
John, Ct. See HOWS
Lemuel, Mass., Jerusha, W23344
Lott, Crane's Cont. Art., Mass., BLWt.4435-100-Sgt. Iss. 5/14/1789. No papers
Noah, Mass., S18875
Simeon, Mass., N.H., S16417
Sylvanus, Mass., Sarah, W23208; BLWt.24431-160-55
Zachariah, Mass., S30495
Zenas, Ct., S37053
HOWEY, Daniel, N.J., N.Y., Jane, R5190
George, N.C., S8725
HOWLAND, Abraham, Mass., S28767. See N.A. Acc. No. 874-050088. Not Half Pay.
Benjamin, Mass., Lydia, W14920
Caleb, R.I., Vt., S22316
Consider, Mass., S13458
Consider, Mass., S29237; BLWt. 11059-160-55
David Spencer/Spencer/Domine, R.I., Phebe Spencer, W22290
Fortune, Mass., S32861; BLWt. 849-100
James, Mass., Sarah, W7812; BLWt.8144-160-55
John, R.I., S21830
Joseph, Ct., S39734
Joseph, Mass., S22840
Joseph, Mass., S29235
Obadiah, Cont., N.Y., S10861
Seth, Mass., Mary, BLWt.13008-160-55
Shove, Mass., Elizabeth, W19811
William, R.I., S13451
HOWLE, William, Ga.,S.C., S21303
HOWLETT, William, Navy, Vt., Martha, R5305
HOWLITT, William, Ga., Elizabeth, R5304
HOWRY, Catharine, former wid. of Peter Filler, Pa., which see
HOWS, John, Ct., Lucy, R5293
HOWWAHWAS, Nicholas, See HAWWAWAS
HOXEY, Peleg, See HOXIE
HOXIE, Peleg, R.I., S45397
HOXSIE, Benjamin, R.I., R5306
HOXWORTH, Edward, Pa., S22308
HOY, Thomas, Va. See HAY
HOYD, Frederick, Pa., Elizabeth, W4456
HOYER, Jacob, Pa., S8718
HOYLES, John, N.C., Cynthia, R5307
HOYT, Abraham, N.H., R5308
Benjamin, N.H., Sarah, W14919
Daniel, Ct., S16881
Daniel, Ct., Sarah Treadwell, former wid., W18155. She was also pensioned as wid. of Daniel Treadwell, Ct.,which see
David, Ct., Vt., Sarah, W23301

HOYT (continued)
David, Pvt., Mass., BLWt.4445 & 4453 iss. 3/25/1790
David, Mass., S33319
David, Mass., Merriam, W23351
Ebenezer, Ct., S16882
Ebenezer, Ct., S36588
Ebenezer, Mass., Sarah, W23315
Eleazer, Ct., Cont., Clarissa, W4990; BLWt.24993-160-55
Elijah, Mass., S36589
Enoch, N.H., S38843
Enoch, N.Y., Ruth, W21404
Ephraim, N.H., S43701
Ezekiel, Ct., S13448
Gilbert, N.Y., S17490
Henry, N.Y., BLWt.7207-100-Pvt. Iss. 9/3/1790. No papers
James, Ct., Sally, W11342; BLWt. 51755-160-55
Jared, Cont., Ct., Mary, R5311; BLWt.5991-100. Iss. 1789
Jesse, Ct., Lydia, W21370
Joel, Cont., Ct., Abigail W21378
John, Ct., Ruth, W25786
John, Mass., S13415
John Millet, Mass., Catharine, W23309
Jonathan, Ct., S10869
Jonathan, Ct., S13428
Jonathan, Mass., Sarah, W14927
Jonathan, Mass., R5310
Joseph, Ct., S36587; BLWt.946-450-Lt. Col. Iss. 12/14/1789. No papers. Name recorded as Hait
Joseph, Ct., Hannah Weed, former wid., R11273
Joseph, N.H., Anna, W21345
Levi, N.H., Hannah, W19817
Moses, Ct., S10860
Moses, Mass., S33313
Moses, Mass., S33315
Nathan, Ct., R5312
Nathaniel, Ct., S31750
Nathaniel, N.Y., S23268
Nehemiah, Green Mt. Boys, Mass., Chloe, R5112
Nicholas S., N.H., N.Y., S2618
Reuben, N.H., Dorothy, W16606
Richard, Mass., S44438
Robert, Mass., S32848
Robert, Mass., Persis, W7757; BLWt.34986-160-55
Samuel, Ct., S17491
Samuel, Ct., Cont., Hannah, W11328; BLWt.953-300-Capt. Iss. 6/27/1789. No papers
Samuel, N.H., BLWt.3168-100-Pvt. Iss. 3/25/1790. No papers
Sarah, former wid. of Jonas Brown, N.Y., which see
Sarah, former wid. of Peter Grubb, Pa., which see
Seth, Cont., Mass., Catharine, W2940
Silas, N.Y., S10865
Silas, N.Y., Amy, W21410
Simeon, Mass., N.H., Miriam, W23304
Sylvanus, N.Y., Anna, W15914
Thomas, N.H., S22312
Walter, Ct., Grace, W18052

HOYT (continued)
Warren, Ct., Mary, W25782; BLWt.10238-160-55
William, Ct., Anna, W11338
William, Ct., Anna, R5309
William, Cont., Ct., S15177
William, Mass., Elizabeth, W14941
William, N.Y., S23265
HUBARD, Richard, Mass. See HUBBARD
HUBART, Casper, Pa. See HUBERT
Joseph, N.H. See HOBERT
HUBBARD, Abel, Ct., Cont., S38851
Abijah, Cont., Ct., S44962; BLWt. 5986-100-Pvt. Iss. 12/14/1792. No papers
Abner, Ct., BLWt.5927-100-Pvt. Iss. 10/31/1791. No papers
Abner, Ct., Esther, W19846
Abner, Cont., Mass., Catharine, W23381
Abner, Mass., BLWt.4350-100-Pvt. Iss. 2/14/1791. No papers
Anna/Hannah, former wid. of Samuel Palmer, Navy, N.H., which see
Asa, Ct., S2333
Bathsheba, former wid. of Zebulon Mygatt, Ct., which see
Benjamin, Mass., Abigail, R5313
Benjamin, Va., Martha, W19782
Caleb, Mass., Lucretia, W14956
Charles, Va. Sea Service, Lucy, W19834
Daniel, Cont., Mass., Lucy, W23382
Daniel, Mass., Mary, W19792
David, Ct., S17504
David S., Mass., Rebecca, W1869; BLWt.11082-160-55
Dimond, Mass., Phebe, W23370
Elihu, Ct., Martha, W16610
Elijah, ---, Penelope Hillyer, former wid. ---. See case of her former husb., David Goodrick, Ct.
Elijah, Ct., Abigail, W21425
Eliphalet, N.J., BLWt.8397-100-Pvt. Iss. 6/11/1789 to Matthew Denman, ass. No papers
Elisha, Ct., Cont., S18457
Elizabeth, former wid. of Titus Mershon, N.J., which see
Eppa, Va., Cont., S35450
Ezekiel, N.Y., Mary, R5315
Francis, Mass., Ruth, W7831; BLWt.28659-160-55
George, Ct., BLWt.5956-100-Pvt. Iss. 4/5/1796 to Oliver Ashley. No papers
George, Ct., S44451
George, Ct., Emily, W7828; BLWt. 26536-160-55
Hannah, former wid. of John Dodd, Mass., which see
Henry, N.Y., S22848
Hezekiah, Ct., BLWt.964-200-Lt. Iss. 11/9/1789. No papers
Humphrey, Mass., Margaret Drake, former wid., W25539
Israel, Mass., S18458
Jedidiah/Jedediah, Ct., S10897
Joel, Ct., Cont., Privateer, S10886

HUBBARD (continued)
Joel, Mass., S19348
John, Ct., S5593
John, Ct., S23715
John, Cont., Mass., Susanna, W21430; BLWt.101795-160-55
John, Mass., Patience, W551; BLWt.8157-160-55
John, N.H., R5314
John, N.Y., BLWt.7232-100-Pvt. Iss. 1/5/1792 to John Gansey, ass. No papers
John, N.Y., S45399
John, N.C., Milley, W19841
Jonas, Ct., BLWt.5934-100-Pvt. Iss. 9/4/1789 to Ezekiel Case. No papers
Jonas, Ct., S38858
Jonathan, Mass., S31146
Joseph, Va., S7048
Josiah, Ct., Cont., Mary, W19847
Levi, Mass., Mary, W23369
Lucretia W., former wid. of John R. Watrous, Ct., which see
Miles, Crane's Cont. Art., Mass., BLWt.4438-100-Pvt. Iss. 2/22/1792 to John Peck. No papers
Moses, Mass., Ann, W1288; BLWt. 11081-160-55
Nathan, Mass., S45400
Nathaniel, Cont., Mass., S19350
Nathaniel, Cont., Mass., Hannah, W19838
Nehemiah, Ct., Cont., S10882
Noadiah, Mass., S44963
Peter, S.C., S31154
Philip, Mass., Mehitable, W23357
Reuben, Mass., Betsy Hooper, former wid., W23333
Richard, ---, BLWt.13221-100-Pvt. "in the Invalids." Iss. 4/19/1791 to James Geary, ass.
Richard, Mass., Sarah, W23380; BLWt.31278-160-55
Robert, Ct., Phebe Skeel, former wid., R9629
Samuel, Mass., S45398
Selah, Cont., Tryphena, W1290; BLWt.10304-160-55
Seth, Cont., Mass., S21305
Silas, Ct., Dis. No papers
Thomas, Ct. See HUBBART
Thomas, Va., S17227
Titus, Cont., Ct., S5572
William, Mass., S29914
William, N.C., b. Va., S21310, BLWt.36728-160-55
William, Va., Letitia, W7830
HUBBART, John, R.I., BLWt.906-200-Lt. Iss. 5/18/1792 to John Blanchard, ass. No papers
Joseph, N.H. See HOBERT
Philip, Ct., Ambrillis, W19843
Thomas, Ct., Silence, W15916
HUBBEL, Gideon, Ct., S31763
Ithamar, N.Y., S17226
HUBBELL, Aaron, Ct., Sarah, W11360
Aaron, Vt., Lucinda, W1871; BLWt. 13748-160-55
Abijah, Ct., S10890
Abijah, N.Y., Betsey, W1291; BLWt.26300-160-55
Amos, Ct., Lucy, W18073

HUBBELL (continued)
David, Ct., Abiah, W18075
David, Ct., Elizabeth, W19849
David, Cont., Mass., S18889
Ezbon, Ct., S44943
Gershom, Ct., Sarah, R5316 1/2
Gershom/Gersham, N.Y., S2642
Hezekiah B., N.J., R5317
Isaac, Ct., N.Y., S36601
Isaac, Col. Lamb's Regt., BLWt. 976-200-Capt.-Lt. Iss. 8/2/1790 to Oliver Beers, Admr. No papers
Jesse, N.Y., Elizabeth Shepard, former wid., W19016
John, Mass., S39745
John, N.J., BLWt.8380-100-Pvt. Iss. 1/29/1794. No papers
John, N.J., Mary, W9484
Lemuel, Vt., S5591
Richard, Cont., N.Y., S30500
Salmon, Ct., S36604; BLWt.960-200-Lt. Iss. 6/16/1789. No papers
Samuel, Ct., Mary, W18076
Seth, Ct., Salome, W2115; BLWt. 1500-100 & BLWt.67677-160-55
Sillemon/Sillimon, Ct., Polly, W1774; BLWt.26869-160-55
Thaddeus, Ct., S13482
William, Ct., Cont., Margaret, W8952
HUBBERT, Anthony, Pa., Mary, W3142
Christian, Pa., S39754
HUBBILL, Ezbon, Ct., BLWt.5950-100-Pvt. Iss. 2/27/1793 to Alexander Power. No papers
HUBBLE, Isaac, N.Y., BLWt.7250-100-Pvt. Iss. 9/28/1790 to McAulay & Brown, ass. No papers
HUBBS, Alexander, N.Y., S13487
David, N.J., S34413
Irena, former wid. of Daniel Dodge Ct., which see
Jacob, Md., Va., also served 1785-1793, S16421
John, S.C., Mary, W1035; BLWt. 26933-160-55
Samuel, N.Y., S13497
HUBER, Andrew, Pa., S2641
Christian, Pa., S22322
George, Pa., S39743
Henry, N.Y., Elizabeth, W23355
Henry, Pa., R5318
Jacob, Pa., S5543
John George, Pa. See John HOOVER
HUBERT, Casper, Pa., Magdalena, W3254
Frederick, Cont., Pa. See HUBNER
Paul, Cont., Canadian, BLWt.13170-100-Pvt. Iss. 10/12/1790. Res. in 1800-Lower Canada. One Angelique, wid. of Paul Hebert of same Regt. was allowed pension, which see, but no proof of identity.
Peter, Hazen's Regt., Canadian, R5319
HUBLEY, Adam, Pa., BLWt.1151-500
Bernard, Cont., Pa., Elizabeth Perkinpine, former wid., W2850; BLWt.1027-300-Capt. Iss. 5/14/1790. No papers
Frederick, Pa., S39750
HUBNER, Frederick, Cont., Pa., Catharine, W3088; BLWt.1319-100
HUBPERT, Casper, Pa. See HUBERT
HUCANS, Abiah, Md. See Abia HUKILL
HUCHERSON, Solomon, N.H., Susannah, W21417
HUCHINS, Jacob, Mass., S4414
HUCKABY, Philip/Phillip, N.C., S31766
HUCKINS, Israel, N.H., Ruth, W16127
Jonathan, N.H., R5320
HUCKSTEP, Charles, Va., S9596
HUDCHINS, William, See HUDGENS
HUDDLESON, William, Pa. See HEDDLESON
HUDDLESTON, Robert, Va., S20894
HUDELSON, William, N.J., Ann, R5323
HUDGALLE, Nicholas, N.Y., BLWt.7216-100-Pvt. Iss. 3/30/1793 to Thos. Russell, ass. No papers
HUDGEN, Anthony, Va., S10883
HUDGENS, Ambrose, N.C., Hannah, R5321
Ambrose, S.C., S18888
William, N.C., R5322
HUDGEONS, Samuel, Va., S1957
HUDGIN, Kemp, Va., Joice, W19842
HUDGINS, Ambrose, S.C. See HUDGENS
Anthony, Va., See HUDGEN
Hugh, Va., S10884
James F., Va., S8740
John, N.C., Nancy, W7835
John, N.C., Ruth/Rutha Murphy, former wid., R7515
Samuel, Va. See HUDGEONS
William, S.C. See HUDGENS
HUDLAR, John, N.C., Nellie Messer former wid., W8450
HUDLY, John, Va., R15345; Va. Half Pay
HUDNALL, John, Va., Frances M., W25806; BLWt.34817-160-55
Thomas, Cont., Va., S41664; BLWt. 12197-100. Iss. 10/6/1792 to Thomas Newton, ass. No papers
HUDNUT, Richard, N.J., Grace, R5324
HUDSON, Abraham, N.J., S44949
Benjamin, Va., Jemima, W8956
Benoney/Benoni, Cont., R.I.,S44950
Brooks, N.H., Vt., S22846
Charles, Va., S5576
Charles, Va., S8743
Daniel, Mass., R.I., Ruth Reed, former wid., W17520
David, S.C., Va., S31767
Edward, N.Y., Sophia, W15915
Edward, S.C., R5328
Eli, Mass., Sarah, W14961
Elijah, Cont., Mass., Elizabeth, R5329
Elisha, Mass., Susannah, R5339
Enos, Mass., BLWt.4400-100-Pvt. Iss. 1/25/1799 to Abel Boynton. No papers
Enos, Mass., S45403
Hall/Hudson HALL, S.C., R4463
Hall, Va., R5331
Henry, Del., BLWt.10778-100-Pvt. Iss. 10/10/1799 to Asahel Phelps, ass. No papers
Isaac, N.C., R5332
HUDSON (continued)
James, Md. Sea Service. Applied for pension in Mass., R5333
James, N.C., S38852
James, N.C., R5334
James, Va., R5338
John, Cont., Mass., S38848
John, Cont., Pa., Judy, W8958; BLWt.11278-160-55
John, Mass., BLWt.4355-100-Corp. Iss. 3/25/1790. No papers
John, N.J., N.Y., S22844
John, N.Y., BLWt.7252-100-Pvt. Iss. 5/3/1791 to James Brebner, ass. No papers
John, N.Y., S41665
John, N.C., S41674
John, Va., War of 1812, Ann, W3422; BLWt.12240-100
John, Va., Elizabeth, R5330
John, Va., R5336
John, Va., Mary, R15350; Va. Half Pay
Joseph, Va., Ann, R5325
Joshua, Ct., Celia, R5326
Joshua, Va., R5093
Obadiah, Ct., N.Y., R5337
Peter, Va., S5596
Rush, Cont., Va., S38064; BLWt. 1948-100
Rush, Va., BLWt.1432-100
Samuel, Pvt., Mass., BLWt.4380 iss. 3/26/1796 to Peter Sivier
Samuel, Mass., S32877
Samuel, N.H., S13483
Samuel, R.I., Lydia, W21418
Samuel, S.C., S34931
Seth, Mass., S38847
Stephen, Mass., S33327
Thomas, Md., S36020
Thomas, Crane's Cont. Art., Mass., BLWt.4434-100-Pvt. Iss. 8/1/1796 to Joseph Fosdick. No papers
Thomas, Va., S2330
Thomas, Va., Dorothy, W7832
Timothy, Cont., Mass., Jane, W23376
Vincent, Va., Mildred, W7833
William, Del., BLWt.10785-100-Pvt. Iss. 10/10/1799 to Asahel Phelps, ass. No papers
William, Mass., R5340
William, Va., BLWt.1346-200
HUDSPETH, Carter, N.C., S7058
HUEBNER, Frederick, Cont., Pa. See HUBNER
HUEIT, Philip, N.C. See HUIET
HUES, James, N.C., Rachel, R5342
HUESTEN, William, Mass., S30480
HUEY, James, S.C., b. Va., S31148
John, Pa., S31151
Lewis, N.C., S31150
Robert, N.J., R5344
HUFACRE, George, Va., S1826
HUFF, Benjamin, N.J., S39746
Daniel, Cont., Mass., S35442
Daniel, Mass., S29247
Isaac, N.J., Ann, W16301
Israel, Mass., S20411
Jacob, Pa. See HOFF
James, Va., S13476

HUFF (continued)
John, Mass., N.H., S18890
John, N.J., Martha, W4232
John, Va., S5590; BLWt.87034-160-55
Moses, Cont., Mass., Navy, S18461
Peter, Md., S9597
Peter, N.J., S10896
Richard, N.J., S23719
Stephen, Va., S18045
HUFFMAN, Christian, Pa. See HOFMAN
Cornelius, Pa., BLWt.9545-100-Pvt. Iss. 12/2/1791 to John Myer, ass. No papers
Daniel, N.Y., S23713
Henry, Va., S5580
John, Va., Lucretia, W10132
Joseph, Va., Elizabeth, W7826
Philip, Va., BLWt.2289-200
Phillip, Va., Elizabeth, R5347
Reuben, Va., Catharine, W7827
William, N.J., Mary, W938
William, N.J., Jane, W939; BLWt. 26583-160-55
HUFFNAGLE, George, Cont., Pa. See HORFNOGGLE
Michael, Pa., Catherine/Catharine, W3087
HUFMAN, John, N.J., S887
Philip, Va. See HOFFMAN
HUFNAGEL, Christian, N.Y., S23714
Christian, Pa., S2600
HUFNOGLE, George, Cont., Pa. See HORFNOGGLE
HUGAN, John, N.Y., Sarah Nash, former wid., R7559
HUGELEY, Charles, Va., S31157
HUGER, Benjamin, S.C., BLWt.1817-400
Isaac, S.C., BLWt.1101-850-Brig. Gen. Iss. 3/31/1796 to Joseph Hardy, ass. No papers
HUGG, Isaac, Ct., S13492
HUGGANS, Robert, N.Y. See HUGGINS
HUGGET, John, Va., Mildred, W19794
HUGGINS, Benjamin, S.C., BLWt. 2306-150
James, N.C., S46449
John, S.C., S38855
Robert, N.Y., S23276
Robert, N.C., R5348
Samuel, S.C., S18044
William, S.C., Nancy, W9485
Zenas, Mass., Senah, W23366
HUGH, John, Vt., Abigail, W3558; BLWt.57648-160-55
Moses, N.J. See HOUGH
HUGHAN, John, N.Y. See HUGAN
HUGHE, George, N.C., S21306
HUGHES, Absolom/Absolam, Va.,S31149
Andrew, N.C., Nancy, W25805; BLWt.36737-160-55
Benjamin, Va., S3079
David, N.C., S2637, from Pa. to N.C. in 1777
Edward, Va., S5574
Elias, Va., son of Thomas, S8747
Francis, N.C., b. Va., S3075
Gabriel, Va., Mary, W19836, son of Gabriel and Ann
George, R.I., BLWt.3230-100-Pvt.

HUGHES (continued)
Iss. 5/28/1792 to Israel Angall. No papers
Greenberry, Pa., BLWt.1033-200-Lt. Iss. 6/1/1796. No papers
Henry, Va., BLWt.1082-150-Ens. Iss. 9/24/1795. No papers
James, Cont., Md., S39751
James, N.C., Sarah, W3818
James, Pa., BLWt.9531 & 13168-100-Pvt. Iss. 8/10/1795. No papers
James, Pa., BLWt.9597-100-Pvt. Iss. 12/16/1793 to Casper Iserloan, ass. No papers
James, Va., S7046
James, Va., Nancy, R5350; BLWt.36537-160-55
Jasper, Col. White's Regt. of Cavalry, Va.; BLWt.1090-150-Cornet. Iss. 8/10/1789 to Richard Platt, ass. No papers
Jesse, Va., S9594
John, Cont., Va., Ann, W18082; BLWt.1086-300-Capt. Iss. 8/10/1789 to Richard Platt, ass.
John, Md., S5594
John, Md., b. Ireland, Hannah, W3821
John, N.H., Mehitable, W14962
John, N.C., Esther, W8954
John, N.C., War of 1812, Nancy E., R15282
John, Pa., S39753
John, Pa., BLWt.1013-200-Capt. Lt. Iss. 1/29/1790. No papers
John, Pa., BLWt.1016-200-Lt. Iss. 7/16/1789. No papers
John, Va., S30501
John, Va., See HUGHS
Jonathan, Va., S9591
Joseph, Md., Va., S17228
Joseph, N.H., Cynthia, See HEWS
Joseph, S.C., S7047
Joseph, S.C., S31764
Margaret, former wid. of Moses McCurdy, Cont., Pa., which see
Parley, Cont., Ct., Mary, W11361; BLWt.43511-160-55
Peter, Va., See HUGHS
Richard, N.H., S44452
Robert, Mass., BLWt.4312-100-Pvt. Iss. 3/15/1800. No papers
Robert, N.J., Susannah, W7824
Robert, Va., R5355
Samuel, Va., R5356
Stephen, Va., Tabitha, R5352
Thomas, Cont., R.I., Welthian, W23373; BLWt.903-300-Capt. Iss. 12/31/1789
Thomas, N.Y., S45405
Thomas, Va., S5589
Thomas, Va., Indian War 1784-1795, R5357
William, Ct., Cont., S36599
William, N.C., Sarah, See HUGHS
William, N.C., Va., Nancy, R5354
William, Pa., BLWt.9614-100-Pvt. Iss. 12/20/1791 to Wm. Lane, ass. No papers
William, Va., Sarah, W7825
HUGHEY, George, N.C., See HUGHE

HUGHEY, John, Pa., S22324
HUGHLETT, William, Va., S38055
William, T., N.C., Mary, W4996
HUGHS, Francis/Francis Alexander, Va., S38059
Henry, Va., S41669
Henry, Va., Kasia, R5353
John, N.C., also St. Clair's Defeat, S1536
John, Vt., See HUGH
John, Va., See HUGHES
John, Va., d. 1815, R15270; Va. Half Pay
John, Va., BLWt.1390-100
Peter, N.C., Va., Lucy, W7823
William, N.C., b. S.C., Sarah, W7822
William, S.C., b. Md., S21311
William, Va., Mary, W8964
HUGHSON, Robert, N.J., R5360
HUGO, Thomas B., Md., Elizabeth Amos, former wid., W9328; BLWt. 1049-300-Capt. Iss. 8/4/1787. No papers
HUGON, Thomas B., See HUGO
HUIET, Philip, N.C., R5341
HUITT, John, N.C., Elizabeth,W3682
HUKELL, Daniel, Md. See HUKINS
HUKILL, Abia/Abiah, Md., S35439
Daniel, Md. See HUKINS
HUKINS, Abiah, Lee's Legion, Va. BLWt.13238-100-Pvt. Iss. 2/11/1800 to Philemon Thomas, ass. No papers
Daniel, Md., S36608
HULBARD, Hannah, former wid. of Hiland Hall, Ct., which see
HULBERT, Aaron, N.Y., BLWt.7274-100-Pvt. Iss. 12/10/1790. No papers
Amos, Ct., S15896
Daniel, Ct., See HULBUT
Elijah, Ct., Ruth, W19845
Ephraim, N.J., S2643
Gideon, Ct., Sarah, W18087
Simeon, Mass., S44944
Thaddeus, Mass. See HURLBURT, Thadeus
Timothy, Ct. See HURLBUT
HULBURD, Eliphalet, Ct. See HURLBERT
Hannah, Ct., See Hiland HALL
HULBURT, Gideon, Ct. See HULBERT
Thomas, Ct., Eunice, W21422
Timothy, Ct. See HURLBUT
HULBURTON, William, Ct. See HOLBURTON
HULBUT, Daniel, Cont., Ct., S44454
HULET, Aaron, Ct. See HEWLETT
Asa, Mass., Polly, R5362; BLWt. 84049-160-55
James M., Va., S36606
John, Md., BLWt.11313-100-Pvt. Iss. 4/14/1794. No papers
John, Mass., Hannah, W7843; BLWt.36735-160-55
John, N.J. See HULIT
Nehemiah, Mass., S23275
Phinehas, Ct., S34932
Seth, Ct., S29249
Sylvanus/Silvanus, Mass., S41672

HULETT, Charles, N.J., S9592
Daniel, Ct., Vt., S18864
Joseph, Mass., S18887
Thomas, Mass., R4940
HULFISH, John, N.J., Mary, W2553
HULICK, Derrick, N.J., S29252
John, N.J., Mary, W9048
HULING, Andrew, Va., S5584
Augustus, R.I., S23718
John, N.Y., S10898
John, Vt., S46637
Jonathan, Va., S2332
HULINGS, John, Pa., BLWt.1030-400-Maj. Iss. 3/8/1791. No papers
HULIT, George, N.J., Nancy, W430
John, N.J., Deborah, W132
HULL, Abner, Ct., S2335
Agrippa, Mass., Margaret, W760; BLWt.4326-100-iss. in 1789. No papers. BLWt.32-60-55
Asa, Mass., S44968
Asahel, Ct., S16159
Benjamin, Ct., S13510
Chester, Sheldon's Dragoons, Ct. BLWt.5989-100-Corp. Iss. 10/7/1789 to Benj. Tallmadge. No papers
Chester, Cont., Ct., S44965
Daniel, N.C., b. N.J., Mary, R5363 1/2
David, Ct., BLWt.5972-100-Pvt. Iss. 12/5/1796. No papers
David, Ct., S22843
David, Ct., S32871
David, Ct., Abigail, W19795; BLWt.5925-100. Iss. 10/7/1789. BLWt.161-60-55
Edwin, Va., Ann Blackwell, former wid., W14316; BLWt.2367-300. She was also pensioned as wid. of Joseph Blackwell, Va.
Eli, Ct., BLWt.5935-100-Pvt. Iss. 4/2/1798. No papers
Eli, Ct., S18041
Eli, Ct., Sally, W26663; BLWt. 6114-160-55
Eliakim, Ct., Rachel, W19840
Eliakum, Ct., BLWt.5973-100-Pvt. Iss. 9/23/1791 to Isaac Bronson No papers
Elias, R.I., S22318
Ezra, Ct., Mary, W8959
Fleet, Mass., BLWt.4357-100-Pvt. Iss. 1/28/1790. No papers
George, Ct., S44967
George, Va., S13317
Henry, Ct., Rebecca Blakeslee, former wid., W3332; BLWt.2470-100. She m. 1st Henry Hull; 2nd John Pearson, 3rd Samuel Blakeslee
Henry, Va., Elizabeth, W1432; BLWt.10016-160-55
Hezekiah, N.Y., Lucy, W16299
Isaac, N.J., S9599
Isaac, N.Y., S13499
Isaac, Va., S2634
Israel, N.H., Lydia McLaughlin, former wid., W15074
James, N.J., S1027
James, W., Mass., S33325

HULL (continued)
Jehiel, Ct., Rachel, W25813; BLWt.18022-160-55
Jeremiah, Ct., Phebe, W19718
Jeremiah, Mass., BLWt.4300-100-Sgt. Iss. 7/22/1790. No papers
Jeremiah, Mass., Tamer, W7817
John/Jonathan, Ct., BLWt.5957-Corp. Iss. 5/18/1790 to Theodosius Fowler. No papers
John, Cont., R.I., Elizabeth, W21427
John, Md., BLWt.11303-100-Pvt. Iss. 1/8/179? to George Ponsonby, ass. No papers
John, N.H., pensioned from Va., Catharine, W3822
John, Pa., S2636
Joseph, Ct., S23272
Joseph, Ct., Cont., Freelove, W7815; BLWts.15199-160-55 & 980-200-Lt. Iss. 2/20/1791. No papers
Joseph, Mass., Phebe Coan, former wid., R2068
Joseph, S.C., S3070
Josia/Josiah, Ct., Mehitable, W16608
Josiah, Mass., S44969
Justus, N.Y. See HALL
Mary, former wid. of George Humphrey, Cont., Va., which see
Peleg, R.I., S21832
Pomeroy, Cont., Mass., Polly, W22532
Prince, Ct., S36596
Ruth, former wid. of William Lurvey, Mass., which see
Samuel, Ct., BLWt.5982-100-Pvt. Iss. 8/23/1790. No papers
Samuel, Ct., S13496
Samuel, Ct., S44966
Samuel, Ct., Mabel, W21284
Samuel, N.Y., BLWt.7237 & 14146-100-Pvt. Iss. 7/13/1797. No papers
Samuel, N.Y., Dis. No papers
Solomon, N.J., S2635
Stephen, ---, Ct. agcy., d. 1803; Dis. No papers
Stephen, Cont., N.Y., S13495
Thomas, Mass., BLWt.4360-100-Pvt. Iss. 1/23/1799. No papers
Wakeman, Ct., Esther, W7816
Wakerman, Ct., BLWt.5932-100-Pvt. Iss. 4/3/1794 to Joseph Coles Field. No papers
Warren, Mass., S22841
William, Mass., BLWt.909-450-Lt. Col. Iss. 10/26/1789. No papers
Zalmon, Ct., S15472
Zephaniah, Cont., Ct., Rachel, W25801; BLWt.521-100
HULLDERMAN, John, Va., R5365
HULLFISH, John, See HULFISH
HULLINGER, Daniel, Pa., S2329
HULME, George, Va., S---, Margaret Hulme, wid of sold., applied for pension as former wid. of Anthony Sharp/Sharpe, N.C., which see
HULS, James, Va., Martha, R5367

HULSE, Jacob, N.Y., S32335
James, Va., S41666
Mathias/Matthias, N.J., Elizabeth, W253
HULSHART, John, N.J., Margaret, W940
HULSIZER, Christopher, N.J., S34411
Valentine, N.J., R5368
HULSLANDER, John, N.Y., S22842
HULTS, Stephen, Ct., N.Y., S10880
HUM, Henry, Pa., S2331
HUMAN, Alexander, N.C., Elizabeth, W7849; BLWt.11156-160-55
HUMASON, Joel, Ct., Ann, W4244
HUMASTON, Abraham, Ct., R5369
Jesse, Ct., Abi, W25809
HUMBEL, Robert, Pa., S13481
HUMBLE, Michael, Va., S13473
HUME, John, Pa., S23717
John, Pa., S31765
HUMES, Josiah, Mass., S32878
Stephen, Mass., S30503
HUMFRES, John, Va., S31145
HUMISTON, Daniel, See HUMMISTON
David, Ct., S17225
HUMMEL, Elijah, N.J., S2277
Frederick, Pa., S22286
Harmanus, N.Y., Maria, W18085
Henry, Pa., S39740
Peter, N.Y., See HOMMEL
HUMMELS, John George, Pa., Christiana, R5370
HUMMISTON, Daniel, Cont., Ct., BLWt.305-100
HUMPHEYS, David,Pa. See HUMPHREYS
HUMPHLET, Thomas, Va. Sea Service, R-45. See N.A. Acc. No. 837-Va. State Navy - YS File, Va. Half Pay
HUMPHREES, Samuel, Va., Ailsey, W8955
HUMPHRES, Aleiander, Del., R5371
HUMPHREY, Alexander, N.Y., BLWt. 7238-100-Pvt. Iss. 5/27/1795 to Samuel Humphrey. No papers
Asahel, Cont., Ct., Prudence, W21424
Benjamin, Mass., S32879
Benjamin, Va., Elizabeth, W4245
Charity, former wid. of Lodywick Vandemark, N.Y., which see
Charles, N.Y., S13503
Ebenezer, Mass., S29916
Elijah, Va., S38066
George, N.Y., Mercy, W19830
George, Va., Mary, W369
Hugh, Mass., S10879
Israel, Ct., BLWt.1500-100
Jacob, Pa., Jane, W4999; BLWt. 1012-300-Capt. Iss. 8/19/1789. No papers
James, Mass., Deborah, W14959
James, N.H., Jane, W16128
Jesse, Mass., S35456
Joel, Ct., Amelia, W4246; BLWt. 13413-160-55
John, Cont., Va., Margaret, W7841
John, Mass., Hannah, W1870
John, N.Y., BLWt.7227-100-Pvt. Iss. 9/7/1790 to John Folsom, ass. No papers
John, Pa., BLWt.1026-200-Lt.

HUMPHREY (continued)
Iss. 8/19/1789. No papers
John, R.I., Elizabeth, W24461
Jonathan, Va., S5583
Joseph, N.C., R5374
Levi, Ct., Polly, W2619
Merrit/Merritt, Va., Mary, W5303; BLWt.26896-160-55. See N.A. Acc. No. 874-050089. Not Half Pay
Nathaniel, R.I., S44957
Noah, Ct., Hannah, W18099
Oliver, N.Y., S13485
Peter, N.Y., R5376
Phebe Ann, former wid. of Alexander McKay, N.Y., which see
Robert, Mass., S13469
Robert, Pa., S5582
Roswell, Ct., Elizabeth, W4998
Samuel, Cont., Ct., S28771
Tower, Mass., BLWt.4362-100-Pvt. Iss. 2/21/1800. No papers
William, R.I., Lydia, W24459; BLWt.1306-300
William, Va., R5377
HUMPHREYS, Alexander, Del., See HUMPHRES
Amos, Mass., Martha, W19796
David, N.C., Martha, W9047
David, Pa., S33849
Ebenezer, Mass., S18040
Elijah, Ct., Cont., Anna, W18092 BLWt.952-300-Capt. Iss. 2/5/1800 to Anna Humphreys & John Humphreys, Admrs. in trust for the heirs & legal reprs. of E.H. No papers
George, Cont., Va., Mary Hull, former wid., W761; BLWt.1401-100. BLWt.60-60-55
James, Ct., Abiah, W19829
James, Mass., S13509
James, N.Y., BLWt.7245-100-Pvt. Iss. 1/5/1791. No papers
John, Md., S8741
John, N.Y., S44958
John, Va. See HUMFRES
Lot, Ct., S31762
Reuben, Va., Martha, W3557
Robert, Pa., BLWt.9539-100-Pvt. Iss. 9/26/1791 to John McCleland, ass. No papers
Royal, Mass., S19349
Solomon, Ct., S17498
William, N.J., R5380
William, S.C., Frances, W4000
William, Va., S21307
HUMPHRIES, Absolem/Absalom, S.C., Barthena/Berthena, W2942
David, Ct., BLWt.948-450-Lt. Col. Iss. 2/28/1795
Elisha, Va., Susan, R5382; BLWt. 57643-160-55
Joseph, Pa., S41670; BLWt.935-100
Robert, Va., Esther, W1613; BLWt. 36725-160-55
HUMPHRY, Abraham, Ct., S23273
Amos, R.I., Sally, W21421
Asa, Mass., S33328
James, N.Y., S28769
John, Mass., Melatiah, W21412
John, Pa., S8744
Nathaniel, Ct., Cont., S36594
HUMPHRY (continued)
Samuel, N.Y., S44956
Timothy, Cont., Ct., Rhoda, W18070
HUMPHRYS, Jacob, Va., S41667
HUMPTON, Richard, Pa., BLWt.1006-500-Col. Iss. 1/18/1791. No papers
HUMRICKHOUSE, Peter, Pa., Mary, W27514
HUNDLEY, Cy, See Josiah
John, Va., S31152
Joshua, Va., S38063
Josiah/Cy, Va., Ann, W7844
Nehemiah, Va., R5385
Noah, Crane's Cont. Art., Mass., BLWt.4432-100-Pvt. Iss. 8/31/1790 to Dudley Woodbridge. No papers
HUNDLY, Joseph, Va., S5581
HUNEWELL, Richard, Cont., R.I., Nabby, W23362
HUNGERFOOT, James, See HUNGERFORD
HUNGERFORD, Elijah, Ct., S13494
Green, Ct., S46048
James, Ct., S15182
James, Ct., S44946
James, Va., S38856
Jehiel, Ct., S13489
John P., Va., S5586
Joseph, Ct., S13285
Lemuel, Ct., S16160
Levi, N.Y., Ann, R5387
Mary, former wid. of Ashbel Upson, Ct., Cont., which see
Robert/Robart, Ct., Olive, W19793
Thomas, Va., BLWt.934-200-Lt.
Uriel, Ct., Hannah, W18090
HUNGERMAN, Nicholas, Pa., BLWt. 9650-100-Pvt. Iss. 3/5/1792 to Curtis Lewis, Admr. No papers
HUNKINS, John, N.H., Polly, W1868
Robert, Mass., Abigail, W16609
HUNN, Derrick, Cont., N.Y., Anna, W18069
Samuel, Ct., S13508
HUNNEWELL, Benjamin, Mass., Phebe, W22367
Jonathan, Cont., Mass., S29919
Richard, Cont.,R.I. See HUNEWELL
Thomas, Mass., S35452
William, Mass., Nancy, R5388
William, Navy, Mass., Rebecca, W23172
HUNSDON, Allen, N.Y., Elizabeth, W24381
HUNSUCKER, Abram, N.C., S5258
HUNT, Abijah, Cont., N.J., Privateer, S.C. Sea Service, pensioned in N.Y., S23271
Abner, Mass., Dimmus, W19833; BLWt.11173-160-55
Abraham, N.C., Va., S15471
Anthony, Mass., S18459
Benjamin, Crane's Cont. Art., Mass., BLWt.4441-100-Pvt. Iss. 1/26/1790 to John May. No papers
Benjamin, U.S. Navy, Eunice, Mass. res. of wid. in 1831, R1241
Benjamin, Va., R5389
Benoni, Mass., Lydia Reeves, former wid., W26364; BLWt.83522-160-55
HUNT (continued)
Benoni, R.I., S44954
Berry, Va., S7059
Caleb, N.H., Dis. No papers
Catharine, former wid. of Ezra Allen, Ct., Mass., which see
Charles, Ct., Sea Service, S9920 BLWt.6379-160-55
Daniel, Cont., Ct., S39749
Daniel, N.H., Hannah, W8222; BLWt. 40014-160-55
Daniel, N.C., S7049
David, Mass., Sarah, W3421
David, N.H., S44955; BLWt.296-100
David, N.C., S41671
Davis, N.J., Jerusha, W25803
Ebenezer, Mass., S29254. His wid. was pensioned as Tirzah Hunt, former wid. of Joshua Bates, Mass., which see
Ebenezer, Mass., Clarissa, W1185; BLWt.15408-160-55
Edward, Mass., BLWt.4318-100-Pvt. Iss. 1/26/1790 to John May. No papers
Elijah, Pa., Mary, W27433
Elisha, N.C., S13486
Elvin, N.H., S9355
Enoch, Mass., Sylvia, W13517
Enoch, N.H., S44453
Ephraim, Mass., Vashti, W24463
Ephraim, Mass., BLWt.924-200-Lt. No papers
Ephraim, Mass., Rhoda, BLWt.34928-160-55
Ephraim, N.H., Mary, R5392; BLWt. 21831-160-55
Esli, N.C., Va., S7054
George, N.H., Mary, W23374; BLReg. 294323-55
George, R.I., S10889
Gideon, Mass., S18891
Henry W., Mass., Sally, W4240
Howell, N.C., Nancy, R5396
Humphry/Humphrey, N.H., Peggy, W23375; BLWt.10228-160-55
Ichabod, Cont., Mass., S35455
Isaac, Ct., S17499
Isaac, Mass., S18892
Isaiah, Mass., S32874
Israel, Mass., S10895
Israel, N.J., S1024
Israel, N.J., R5393
Jacob, Cont., Mass., Hannah, W4241
Jacob, Md., S38061
Jacob, N.J., Ann/Nancy, W4997
Jacob, Pa., S23721
James, Md., BLWt.11350-100-Pvt. Iss. 5/4/1797 to James DeBaufre ass. No papers
James, Md., S41663
James, N.J., S2604
James, N.J., Catharine, W7821; BLWt.10028-160-55
James, S.C., b. N.C., R5394
James, Va., S38062
James, Va., Christiana, W942
James, Va., Rhoda, W19832
Jane, former wid. of Jonathan Pitman, N.J., which see
Jeremiah, R.I., S21833

HUNT (continued)
Joel, Ct., Cont., S36605
John, Cont., Mass., S18460
John, Mass., S13506
John, Mass., S29251
John, Mass., S31153
John, Mass., Hannah, W10129; BLWt.24175-160-55
John,/Joshua, N.Y., BLWt.7244-100-Pvt. Iss. 8/18/1790 to Joseph Stringham, ass. No papers
John, N.C., S38053
Jonas, Mass., Anna, W18072
Jonathan, Cont., Mass., S5578
Jonathan, Mass., S31144
Jonathan, N.C., S18048
Joseph, Mass., Betsey Grosvenor, former wid., W21215
Joseph, Mass., Elizabeth, R5391
Joseph, Mass., Bulah, BLWt. 19529-160-55
Joseph, N.Y., BLWt.7289-100-Pvt. Iss. 6/6/1791. No papers
Josiah, Cont., N.J., Hester, W2554
Josiah, N.J., BLWt.8367-100-Pvt. Iss. 7/22/1789. No papers
Josiah, Pa., & Gen. Wayne's Ind. War, Bethia, W1289
Julius, Va., Mary, W3819
Laban, Mass., Sarah, R5397
Lewis, Ct., Elizabeth Crofut, former wid., W17686
Little B./Littleberry, Va., S18047
Littleton, Va., Ga.?, N.C., Sarah, W3820
Lot, Mass., S32868
Lydia, former wid. of Stephen Wheeler, N.Y., which see
Matthew, Mass., Winefred, W14960
Moses, N.H., Hannah/Ruth, W24460
Nathan, Mass., S10881
Nathaniel, Mass., BLWt.4374-100-Pvt. Iss. 3/25/1790. No papers
Nathaniel, Mass., Hannah Linfield, former wid., W13633
Noah, Mass., S32869
Oliver, Mass., S35454
Oliver, N.J., S2638
Peter, Cont., Mass., S46047
Peter, Cont., N.Y., Hannah, W16302
Peter, Mass., Privateer, S18462
Philip, Cont., N.H., Anna, W14954
Richard, Mass., S39747
Richard, N.J., Rhoda, W7820; BLWt.36740-160-55
Richard, Va., Winifred, W8953
Russell, Ct., S13474
Russell/Russel, Ct., Hester, W25810
Sampson R., Ct., S37125
Samuel, Mass., S22319
Samuel, Mass., Lydia F., W296; BLWt.9182-160-55
Samuel, N.C., Susannah, BLWt. 107997-160-55
Samuel, Va., S25168
Sarah, former wid. of John Millet, Mass., which see
Seth, Mass., Abigail Richardson, former wid., W11143
Seth, Mass., Sally True, former wid., W22448

HUNT (continued)
Thomas, Md., S3072
Thomas, Mass., BLWt.912-300-Capt. Iss. 10/26/1789. No papers
Thomas, N.H., BLWt.3191-100-Pvt. Iss. 8/11/1790 to Robert Dunlap. No papers
Thomas, N.H., S36593
Thomas, N.Y., Jerusha, W18083; W18083; BLWt.987-200-Lt. Iss. 7/18/1791. No papers
Timothy, Mass., Hannah S., W1428
Varnel, N.J., S1026
Walter, Ct., S44953
William, Ct., Mass., N.Y., Mary, W7819
William, Cont., Mass., S32875
William, Cont., Vt., Dis.
William, Mass., S10878
William, Mass., Elizabeth Dunning, former wid., W24087
William, N.J., Anna Barnhart, former wid., R542
William, N.Y., Nicena, W8221; BLWts. 2495-100 & 145-60-55
William, N.C., b. Va., S7051
William, Pa., Nancy, W25802
William, Pa., BLWt.913-100
William, R.I., Betsey, W24462
Wilson, N.J., S30502
Wilson, N.C., Margaret, W4242; BLWt.34968-160-55
Zaccheus, N.H., BLWt.3169-100-Pvt. Iss. 3/25/1790. No papers
Zacheus, N.H., Miriam/Meriam, W14958
Zebulon, N.H., S38857
HUNTER, Alexander, Mass., Navy, S33326
Alexander, Va., S5575
Andrew, Va., S17500
Austin, Va., S15899
Benjamin, Cont., Pa. res. in 1828, S---; BLWt.1377-100
Benjamin, Cont., N.Y., Pa., S41673
Daniel, Ct., R5400
David, Mass., S44951
Dempsey, S.C., Kathrine, R5399
Elizabeth, former wid. of Seth Jackson, Ct., which see
Elizabeth, former wid. of Chas. Gerrard, N.C., which see
Francis, Va., S13472
Francis, Va., R5401
George, Cont., Pa., Phebe, W23361
Henry, N.C., S7057
Humphrey, N.C., S.C., Jane, W3998
Jacob, Va., Elizabeth, W9046; BLWt.46181-160-55
James, ---, BLWt.13209-100-Pvt. "in the Invalids." Iss. 2/20/1794 to Francis Kirkpatrick, ass. No papers
James, N.Y., S44952
John, Mass., Dis. No papers
John, Navy, Mass., R5402. Elizabeth Perkins, who m. John

HUNTER (continued)
Hunter for her 2nd husb. was pensioned as former wid. of Joseph Darby, Cont., Mass., which see
John, Pa., S23720
John, Pa., S32334
John, Pa., Martha, R5405
John, S.C., R5403
John, Va., S15897
John, Va., Ann, W432
John, Va., Ruth, W8957; BLWt. 29002-160-55
John, Va., R5404
John W., S.C., Ga., res. at enl. Lincoln Co., N.C., S10899
Jonathan, Mass., S15181
Jonathan, N.Y., S39739
Joseph, Ct., S32873
Moses, N.Y., Elizabeth Rundle, former wid., R9072
Nathaniel, Ct., N.Y., Sarah, W19835; BLWt.26031-160-55
Patrick, Pa., Va., S17501
Rachel, former wid. of Charles Nuttle, Pa. Sea Service, which see
Robert, Cont., Navy, N.Y., S13513; BLWt.993-200-Lt. Iss. 9/29/1790
Robert, Pa., Ann, W3424; BLWt. 26954-160-55
Robert, R.I., BLWt.907-150-Ens. Iss. 4/25/1791. No papers
Robert, S.C., S41678
Samuel, N.C., Elizabeth, W941
Thomas, Navy, res. Hadley, Mass. in 1818, W32876
Thomas, N.C., S.C., S2639
Thomas, N.C., S.C., S4411
Thomas Nash, See Thomas NASH, Mass.
William, Green Mt. Boys, Vt., Mary, W19827
William, Mass., S15894; BLWt. 13218-160-55
William, Pa., BLWt.9559-100-Pvt. Iss. 6/18/1789. No papers
William, S.C., R5406
HUNTING, Amos, Mass., S29920
Asa, Mass., S29917
Converse, Mass., R5408
Israel, Mass., S17502
Jonathan, Mass. See HUNTTING
Moses, Mass., S5569
HUNTINGDON, John S., Ct. See HUNTINGTON
HUNTINGTON, Andrew, Ct., S23716
Andrew, Ct., Hannah A., W21429
Azariah, Ct., S10888
Christopher, Ct., Eunice, W7853; BLWt.57526-160-55
Ebenezer, Ct., Cont., S36595; BLWt. 949-450-Lt. Col. Iss. 10/13/1789. No papers
Elisha, Ct., S44959
Hezekiah/Hesekiah, Ct., Cont., S15475
Hiram, Ct., S23722
Jedediah, Ct., BLWt.945-850-Brig. Gen. iss. 10/26/1791. No papers

HUNTINGTON (continued)
Jeremiah, Green Mt. Boys, N.Y., R5409
John, Ct., Rebecca, W18081
John S., Cont., Ct., Katurah, W19844
Joseph, Ct., Susannah, W19839
Joseph, N.H., S22845
Roger, Ct., S10901
Roger, Ct., Cont., S44449
Samuel, Ct., S23274
Theophilus, Ct., S44960
Thomas, Ct., Cont., S44961
Wightman, Ct., R5411
William, Ct., S13490
William, Mass., S32870
Ziba, N.H., R5412
HUNTLEY, Abner, Ct., Cont., S13480
Adriel, Ct., Lucy Stedman, former wid., R10092
Andrew, Ct., Zelinda, R5413; BLWt.85067-160-55
Elihu, Ct., Naomi, W19791
Elisha, N.H., Clarissa, W21411
Ezekiel, Ct., S13511
Hoel (his mark), Ct., S18043
Jabez, Ct., S36600
Jehiel, Ct., N.Y., S10894
Jonathan, Ct., S18893
Moses, Ct., S21308
Reuben, Cont., Ct., S13501
Rufus, Ct., S45404
Solomon, Ct., Abigail A., W27854 BLWt.7438-160-55
Thomas, N.Y., BLWt.7205-100-Pvt. Iss. 7/23/1792 to Eliphalet Seaman, ass. No papers
Thomas, N.Y., S36603
Zadock, Ct., S23270
HUNTLY, Dan, Ct., R5414
Martin, Ct., R5415
Reynold, Ct., R5416
HUNTON, Thomas, Va. Sea Service, R44, Va. Half Pay
HUNTOON, Aaron, Cont., N.H.,S44450
Amos T., N.H., R5418
Caleb, N.H., Juda, W16031
Charles, Cont., Mass., Susannah, W23354
Charles, N.H., S17497
John, N.H., Susannah, W23379; BLWt.3604-160-55
Jonathan, Mass., Hannah, W23378
Joseph, N.H., R5419
Moses, N.H., S13470
Philbrick, N.H., See Thomas P.
Reuben, Cont., N.H., Mary, W25808; BLWt.8446-160-55
Thomas P/Philbrick, N.H., Elizabeth, R5417
HUNTRESS, Jonathan, N.H., BLWt. 2285-100
Joshua Lang, Navy, N.H., Anna, W21413
HUNTSLEY, Nicholas, Mass., S5588
HUNTSMAN, John, Va., Betsey, R5420
HUNTTING, Jonathan, Mass., S13385
HUPP, Philip, Va., Mary, W4239
HUPPELL, Adam, N.Y., Alice, R4584
HURD, Aaron, Mass., Abigail, R5429
Abijah, Ct., S44947

HURD (continued)
Adam, Ct., Vt., S18463
Benjamin, Ct., S10885
Cooley, Ct., Sarah, W431; BLWt.26432-160-55
Crippen/Crippin, Ct., Elizabeth, W24458
Daniel, Vt., Lucinda, W21419
David, Ct., BLWt.5968-100-Pvt. Iss. 10/7/1789 to Benjamin Tallmadge. No papers
David, Ct., S20804
David, N.Y., S34410
Ebenezer, Cont., N.H., Mass., Abigail, W21416
Eleazer, N.H., S5510
Elijah, Ct., Polly, W1773
Elnathan, Ct., Cont., S13505
Graham, Ct., Love, W23242
Isaac, Ct., Mary, W1184
Isaac, Mass., S1769
Jacob, Ct., S17505; BLWt. 13021-160-55
John, Jr., Mass., BLWt.932-150-Ensign. Iss. 10/26/1789 to John Hurd, Legal Repr. of J.H. No papers
Lewis, Ct., S18886
Lovell/Lovewell, Ct., Margere Haynes, former wid., W25763
Mead/Mede, Ct., S29250
Philo, Ct., S36597
Robert, Ct., Cont., Olive, W18095
Robert Lane, Vt., S29918; BLWt. 14986-160-55
Roswell, Ct., R5431
Stephen, N.H., Betsey, W18080
Thomas, Mass., Navy, S13498
Uzzel, Cont., N.H., S13484
Wilson, Ct., S17506
Zadok/Zadock, N.H., S25585
HURDELL, Lawrence, See HURDLE
HURDLE, Laurence/Lawrence, Md., Nancy, W2157; BLWt. 1-60-55
Robert, Md., Susan, W7845
HURLBERT, Daniel, Mass., R5425
Eliphalet, Ct., Mehitabel, W18093
John, Ct., See HURLBUT
John, R.I., Hannah, W19837; BLWt.17572-160-55
Josiah, Mass., N.H., Vt., Hannah C., W1431; BLWt. 19766-160-55
Silas, Ct., Sarah, W18074
HURLBRETT, George, Ct., BLWt. 978-300 & 2680-300
HURLBUD, Lucius, Ct., BLWt.5906-100-Pvt. Iss. 5/18/1790 to Theodosius Fowler. No papers
HURLBURT, Abiram, Ct., Cont., See HURLBUT
Asher, Ct., Ama/Amy/Anna, W16126
John, Ct., Sarah, R5426
Jubilee A., Cont., Ct., Polly/Molly, W21423
Matthias, Ct., Clemence, W21426
Shadrach/Shadrack, Ct., Cont., S29915
Stephen, Ct., R5427

HURLBURT (continued)
Susanna, former wid. of Ebenezer McGregory, Mass., which see
Thadeus/Thaddeus, Mass., S32867
Thomas, Ct. See HULBURT
Wait, Ct., BLWt.5939-100-Pvt. Iss. 7/12/1793 to Reuben Murray No papers
HURLBUT, Abiram, Ct., Cont., S10887
Alfred, Ct., BLWt.5817-100-Pvt. Iss. 9/1/1790 to Theodosius Fowler. No papers
Amos, Ct., S15896
Asahel, Vt., R5422
Bartholomew, Ct., R5424
Christopher, R.I., Elizabeth, W16303
David, Ct., S45401
Elisha, Mass., Hannah, W7848; BLWt.9188-160-55
John, Ct., Cont., Judith, W16612
John, R.I., See HURLBERT
Jonathan, Mass., S45402
Oliver/Alvin, Ct., BLWt.5905-100-Pvt. Iss. 6/9/1796 to Timothy Pitkin, Jr. No papers
Raphael, Ct., BLWt.6004-100-Pvt. Iss. 6/25/1789 to R. Hurbut. No papers
Seymour, Ct., S13500
Simeon, Mass. See HULBERT
Stephen, Ct., d. 4/30/1807, Abigail, W25812
Stephen, Ct. See HURLBURT
Timothy, Ct., Cont., Olive, W25807; BLWt.2028-160-55
Wait, Ct., S39757
William, Cont., Pa., S36602
HURLBUTT, Alfred, Ct., Lydia, W25804
Daniel, Ct., Esther, W18077
George, Ct., BLWt.978-300-Capt. Iss. 3/3/1797 to Ann Welsh, Devisee. Also recorded as BLWt.2650. No papers. See George HURLBRETT
Gideon, Ct., S36598
Sarah C., dau. of Elijah Weeks, Mass., which see
HURLEHOY, John, Ct. See HURLEROY
HURLEROY, John, Ct., BLWt.270-1-10
HURLEY, Arthur, N.Y., BLWt.7254-100-Pvt. Iss. 3/25/1791 to Wm. Ball, ass. No papers
Cornelius, Va., S41677
David, N.C., S38051
John, Mass., S33329
John, N.C., BLWts.12248 & 13165-100-Pvt. Iss. 5/18/1797 to Gabriel Holmes, ass. No papers
John, Pa., Rebecca, W3423
Joseph, N.C., S38050
Joshua, N.C., S7053
Matthew, Va., BLWt.12187-100-Pvt. Iss. 11/5/1789. No papers
Nehemiah, Del., Hannah, R5428
William, N.J., Rhoda, W25811; BLWt.53676-160-55
HURLY, Salem, Md. & Navy, S10893
HURST, Harman/Harmon, S.C., S21309

HURST (continued)
Henry, Va., S30504, d. 11/2/1844
Henry, Va., d. 11/29/1834, Mary Ann, R5433
Henry, ---, Va. agcy. Dis. No papers
Richard, Va., S9593
Samuel, Md., S34933
William, Pa., S31155
HURT, Benjamin, Va., Mary S., W27878;
Francis, Va., Margaret, R5436
James, Va., S38850
West, Va., S38067
William, N.C., Susan Byram, former wid., R1572
William, Va., S15473
Zachariah, Va., Frances, R5434
HURTEIGH, John, N.Y., BLWt.7251-100-Pvt. Iss. 7/8/1791. No papers
John, N.Y., Catharine Carn, former widow, W25382
HUSBANDS, James, Del., BLWt.10787-100-Sgt. Iss. 9/2/1789 to James Husbands. No papers
James, Del., S38058
William, N.C., S31768
HUSE, Isaac, Cont., Mass., S10900
John, Mass., Privateer, S10892
Samuel, Cont., Mass., S32872
Samuel, N.H., S18046
William, Mass., N.H., Rachael, W23365
HUSPRAN, Aron, N.Y., BLWt.7264-100-Pvt. Iss. 10/12/1790 to Asa Byram, Admr. No papers
HUSS, Jacob, Pa., Elizabeth, R5437
HUSSTEAD, Moses, Va., S9600
HUSTEAD, Robert, Pa., Sarah, W2804
HUSTED, David, N.Y., S29248
Hosea, N.J., S34412
John, N.J., S34414
Jonathan, N.Y., Mary, R5438
Nathaniel, Ct., Ruth, W18089
Reuben, N.J., Ruth, W465
Samuel, Ct., Phebe Clark, former wid., W16909
Thaddeus, Ct., N.Y., S16158
HUSTLER, Thomas, ---, N.Y. res. & agcy., S28036
HUSTON, Alexander, Cont., Pa., BLWt.1217-200
Daniel, Pa., S7055
Hugh, Cont., res. in Ohio, S41679
Hugh, N.C. See HOUSTON
James, N.Y., R5440
James, N.C., S8717
James, Pa., Mary, W273
James, Va., Anne, W2803
John, Mass., S35444
Philip, Md., S39741; BLWt.857-100
Samuel, Mass., R5441
William, Ct., Elizabeth, W7847
William, Pa., S41675
William, Pa., BLWt.1019-200-Lt. Iss. 12/7/1791 to Susannah Taylor, late Susannah Huston, wid. of W.H., in trust for herself & ch., legal heirs No papers

HUTCH, John, N.J., BLWt.8396-100-Pvt. Iss. 8/19/1791. No papers
HUTCHENS, Charles, Mass., Hannah, W16611
James, Cont., Mass., N.H. res. at enl., Susanna, W23377; BLWt. 10258-160-55
Jonathan, Va., R5449
Noah, Mass., S13507
William, Md. See HUTCHESON
HUTCHERSON, James, S.C., See HUTCHINSON
James, Va., S9598
John, Va., S5579
William, Va., S38054
HUTCHESON, Thomas, Md., S5454
William, Md., R5456
William, Va., R5443
HUTCHINGS, Ann W., former wid. of John Campbell, N.Y., which see
Boswell, Va., S5587
Eastman, Mass., S35446
Gabriel, N.J., S41668
Jacob, N.Y., S13479
John, N.H., S35453
John, N.C. See HUDGINS
Moses, Va., S8742
Thomas, Mass., Esther, W23372
William, Mass., S22320; BLWt. 2022-160-55
William, N.J., S2334
HUTCHINS, Amasa, Ct., Hannah, W19790
Amos, N.H., R5446
Benjamin, Mass., Nancy, W23359
Benjamin, Mass., Navy, S35449
Bulkley, N.H., S13512
Edmund/Edmond, N.H., S35447
Edward, N.C., S38052
Enoch, Cont., Mass., Mary, W23368
Gabriel, N.J., BLWt.8392-100-Pvt. Iss. 9/8/1789 to Samuel Rutan, ass. No papers
Hezekiah, Mass., S33324
Hollis, Mass., Elizabeth, W4243
Jacob, Mass. See HUCHINS
James, N.C., Ann, W19828; BLWt. 26264-160-55
John, N.J., BLWt.1004-200-Lt. Iss. 3/17/1791. No papers
John, N.Y., Vt., Ann Graves, former wid., W19533
John, Pa., BLWt.9535-100-Pvt. Iss. 12/7/1790. No papers
John Church, Ct., Irene, R5448
Joseph, Mass., Sally, R5450
Levi, Cont., Mass., S35445
Levi, Cont., N.H., R.I., S44447; BLWt.1901-160-55
Moses, Mass., S15470
Moses, Mass., S18042
Moses, N.H., BLWt.3170-100-Pvt. Iss. 1/6/1797 to Richard Speers ass. No papers
Nathan, Ct., Vt., Lois, W1614; BLWt.10236-160-55
Nathaniel, Cont., N.H., S35441; BLWt.531-300-Capt.
Samuel, Vt., Betsey Mehurin, former wid., W21794

HUTCHINS (continued)
Sarah, former wid. of John Glines, N.H., which see
Shubael, Ct., Avis, W21428
Simeon, Mass., S35443
Simon, N.H., S22323
Solomon, Mass., Navy, S10891
Thomas, Cont., Mass., Abigail, W21414
Thomas, N.C., Sarah, W7836
William, Cont., Mass., N.H., S44446
William, N.H., S15474
William, Vt., Mary, W8960; BLWt.31467-160-55
Zadoc, Ct., S13478
HUTCHINSON, Abijah, Ct., Cont., S13491
Amos, Ct., Lucy, W18088
Asa, N.H., Eunice, W23384; BLWt.26594-160-55
Dudley, N.H., Mehitable, W23358
Ebenezer, N.Y., BLWt.1022-300-Surgn. Mate. Iss. 12/22/1791 to Wm. H. Cook, Admr. Also recorded as BLWt.2598. No papers
Eleazer, Ct., Huldah, W18079
Elisha, N.H., Elizabeth, W19797
Elizabeth, former wid. of George Snead, Va., which see
Ephraim, Mass., ----. See case of soldier's wid., Jane Hutchinson, who was pensioned as former wid. of Daniel Benjamin, Mass.
Israel, Mass., S29253
Israel, N.H., Jane, W23385; BLWt. 24756-160-55
James, S.C., Elizabeth, W50
Jerome, Vt., Content, W14955; BLWt.24605-160-55
Job, Ct., S13493
John, Ct., Mary Adams, former wid., W20571
John, Ct., Tryphena, R5455
John, Ct., Vt., S22321
John, Cont., Pa., Mary, W4701
John, Pa. See HUTCHISON
John, Vt., S13502
John, Va., Margaret, R5452
Jonathan, Ct. See HUTCHISON
Joseph, Va. See HUTCHISON
Levi, N.H., S44448
Nehemiah, Cont., N.H., Mary, W23360
Peter, Cont., Va., Sarah, W3019; BLWt.3755-160-55
Samuel, Ct., R5453
Samuel, Cont., Mass., S35451
Samuel, Cont., N.H., S39756
Samuel, Mass., S38854
Samuel, Mass., Hannah, W16300
Stephen, Mass., S35448
Stephen, Va., S38853
Thomas, Md. See HUTCHESON
Thomas, N.H., S39755
Thomas, Va., S38065
Timothy, Mass., Prudence, W21415
William, Pa., BLWt.9605-100-Pvt. Iss. 9/15/1789 to James Leonard, ass. No papers
HUTCHISON, Cornelius, Pa. S39744

HUTCHISON, David, Cont., Va., S17224
Drury, Va., S7056
James, S.C. See HUTCHINSON
John, Pa., S44945
John, Pa., See HUTCHINSON
John, Sr., Va., S5585
Jonathan, Ct., S17503
Joseph, Va., W7838; BLWt. 26100-160-55
Peter, Cont., Va. See HUTCHINSON
Samuel, N.C., S.C., S21831
Samuel, Va., Polly, R5442
Thomas, Va. See HUTCHINSON
William, Del., Pa., S5570
William, N.C., S.C., Catharine, W10133
William, Va., R5457
HUTINACK, Francis, Ct., S13488
HUTS, Jacob, Va. See HUTTS
HUTSON, James, N.C. See HUDSON
Thomas, Pa., S5447
William, Va., S35440
HUTT, Gerard, Va., S5592
John, Va., S17507
Preston, Del., BLWt.10786-100-Pvt. Iss. 3/20/1800 to Preston Hutt. No papers
HUTTEN, George, Cont., Pa., S41676
HUTTO, Henry, S.C., S38057
HUTTON, Christopher, N.Y., S28770; BLWt.990-200-Lt. Iss. 10/25/1790. No papers
George, Pa. See HUTTEN
James, Md., BLWt.1974-100
James, Pa., BLWt.9572-100-Pvt. Iss. 7/16/1789. No papers
James, Pa., S39742
James, Va., S31147
John, N.Y., Elizabeth, W18071
Timothy, N.Y., S1025
Timothy, N.Y., Elizabeth, W18086
William, Md., BLWt.11360-100-Corp. Iss. 2/27/1799 to James DeBaufre, ass. No papers
William, N.Y., S13475
William, R.I., BLWt.3231-100-Sgt. Iss. 12/31/1799. No papers
HUTTS, Jacob, Va., BLWt.1347-100
Leonard, Va., Sally, W550; BLWt. 12563-160-55
HUVEY, Lewis, N.C. See HUEY
HUXFORD, Cornelius, Mass., R5460
John, Ct., S13504
HUXLEY, James, N.Y., S44948
HUY, John, Pa., Margareth, W3247
HUYCK, William, Ct., Pa., S22847
HUYLER, John/John G., N.J., War of 1812, Phebe, W1775
HUZZEY, James, Mass., Susanna, W18091; BLWt.7092-160-55
HYAR, John, Cont., Pa.; BLWt. 9622-100. Iss. 1789. No papers See John HYER
HYAT, Abraham, N.Y., BLWt.988-200-Lt. Iss. 5/5/1791. No papers
HYATT, Abraham, Ct., N.Y., Privateer, Anna, W16613
Alvan, Ct., S18049
Alvin, Lamb's Art., N.Y., BLWt. 7290-100-Pvt. Iss. 11/27/1790

HYATT (continued)
to Anne Lacey, Admr.
Anna, former wid. of Joseph Gillespie, Cont., which see
Asa, Md. See HIATT
Byaley, N.Y., Eunice, W19851
Ezekiel, N.Y., Rebecca, W28007
Hezekiah, Ct., R5461
Isaac, Ct., Esther, W18098
John, N.Y., Rachel, W5001; BLWt. 71187-160-55
John Vance, Del., BLWt.1040-200-Lt. Iss. 5/13/1789. No papers
Minnah, N.Y., Rachel Sutphin/Sutfin, former wid., W25174; BLWt.7243-100-Pvt. Iss. 1/2/1796 to Elijah Snow, ass. No papers. BLWt.19-60-55
Samuel, Ct., Cont., Judy/Judia, W15776
Stephen, Ct., Eunice, W25818
William, N.Y., R5462
HYDE, Agur, Ct., See HIDE
Alexander, Ct., S36609
Andrew, Ct., S15477
Azel, Ct., BLWt.5900-100-Pvt. Iss. 3/30/1793. No papers
Azel, Ct., S46464
Azel, Ct., Arethusa, W25817
Benjamin, Ct., S13515
Clark, Ct., S45407
Ebenezer, Ct., S13516
Elihu, Ct., Hannah, W25814
Elijah, Ct., Cont., S5597
Elisha, Ct., Abigail, W25815
Ephraim, Vt., Rebecca, W19850; BLWt.36288-160-55
Gershom, Cont., Mass., Catharine, W24464
Ichabod, Ct., R.I., S15476
Irvine, Va., Mary, R5464
James, Ct., BLWt.958-200-Lt. Iss. 10/22/1789 to Theodosius Fowler, ass. No papers
James, Ct., Cont., Eunice, W5000; BLWt.258-60-55
Jedediah, Ct., S39759
Jedidiah, Ct., Elizabeth, W25816
Joel, Ct., S13514
John, Ct., S10902
John, Mass., Azubah, W13522
John, Mass., Olive, W18097
Jonathan, Ct., S23723
Joseph, Ct., R5463
Joseph, Ct. Sea Service, Betsey, W1186
Joseph, Mass., Susannah, W18096
Joshua, Mass., Sally, W27866
Moses, Ct., Sarah, W5465
Oliver, Ct., S45406
Phineas, Navy, Ct., S32
Sarah, former wid. of David Kent, N.J., which see
Thaddeus, Mass., Elizabeth, W19765
Theophilus, Mass., BLWt.4415-100-Pvt. Iss. 10/18/1791 to Ebenezer Farnham. No papers
Thomas, N.Y., BLWt.7260-100-Pvt. Iss. 9/25/1790 to James Mapes, ass. No papers
William, N.C. See HIDE
Zenas, Vt., S21834

HYDEN, William, Va., Martha, W11370 BLWt.26033-160-55
HYER, Alexander, N.Y., BLWt.7253-100-Pvt. Iss. 10/11/1790 to Henry Tremper, ass. No papers
Conrad, Mass., S35457; BLWt.28520-160-55
Jacob, N.J. See HEYER
John, N.J., S1028
John, Pa., BLWt.9622-100-Sgt. in Proctor's Art. Iss. 8/12/1789. No papers
HYLAND, Amasa, Mass. See HILAND
Henry, N.J., S34415
Samuel, Mass., S32880
William, Cont., Mass., S15900
HYLE, Conrad, N.Y., BLWt.7309-100-Pvt. Iss. 6/6/1791 to Joseph Bindon, Admr. No papers
HYLTON, Nathaniel N., Va., R5467
HYMER, Daniel, Cont., Pa. See HELMER
HYNES, Hardy, N.C., R5468
HYNSON, Richard, N.C. See HENSON
HYRE, Jacob, Va., Elizabeth, W7856
HYRNE, Edmund Massingbird, S.C., BLWt.1478-100
HYSEL, Frederick, Va. See HISEL
HYSLOP, Levin, Va., Susan, W7858

I

IAMS, John Frederick, Md., Mary, W434
Thomas, Md., S8751
ICE, Adam, Va., R5470
Andrew, Va., S32336
ICKES, Nicholas, Pa. See IKASS
IDDINGS, William, Pa., S22849
IDE, Israel, Mass., Martha, W21431
Jacob, Mass., S17508
James, Mass., S45408
Jesse, Vt., Lucy, W9333; BLWt. 56852-160-55
John, Mass., Anna, W14965
Joseph, R.I., S21835
Nathan, Mass., Mary, W14964
Nathaniel, Mass., Lydia, W21432
Nehemiah, Mass., Mary, W3257
Oliver, Mass., S18464
Reuben, Mass., Polly, W1187; BLWt.13741-160-55
IDEL, Conard, Pa. See Conrad IDLE
IDEN, John, Va., b. Pa., S2302
IDLE, Barney, Pa., S39760
Conrad/Conard, Pa., Catharine, W3256
John, Pa., R5472
IDOL, Jacob, N.C., Cloy, W7859; BLWt.26839-160-55
John, Pa. See IDLE
IHLER, Jona, Pa. See EYLER
IHRIG, Abraham, N.C., S7062
IIAMS, John Frederick, Md. See IAMS
Thomas, Md. See IAMS
IJAMS, Vachell, Md., N.C., S32337
IKASS, Nicholas, Pa., R5471
ILER, Philip (dec'd), Pa., BLWt. 13270-100-Pvt. Iss. 5/29/1792 to George Hess & Margaret Hess, Admrs. No papers
ILES, Samuel, Md., R5474
William, N.C., Va., R5475
ILMER, Frederick Wilhelm, Pa. See ELLMORE
ILMORE, Frederick Wilhelm, See ELLMORE
ILSLEY, Isaiah, Cont., Mass., S32881
IMESON, John, Md., S34934
IMHOFF, Frederick, See IMHOOF
IMHOOF, Frederick, Cont., Pa., S38068; BLWt.492-100
IMLAY, David, N.J., Abigail, W145
Isaac, N.J., Mary, W466
IMMAN, Henry, Pa. See INNMAN
IMMEL, Leonard, Pa., S22826
IMPSON, Henry, N.J., Pa., S33332 BLWt.9701-100-Pvt. Iss. 6/24/1793 to Thos. Russell, ass. No papers
INCELL, John, N.J., BLWt.2354-100
INGALLS, Amos, N.H., Mary, W21435
Anna, former wid. of Nathan Lovell, Mass., which see
Caleb, N.H., Vt., Mary, R5476
Daniel, Mass., S29256
Ebenezer, N.H., S16161
Edmund, Cont., Mass., S18894
Elihu, Mass., N.Y., Mary, W20156

INGALLS (continued)
Isaiah, Mass., Phebe, W26664
Israel, N.H., Hannah Nichols, former wid., W21850
Jacob, Cont., Mass., S13517
James, Crane's Cont., Art., Mass., BLWt.4499-100-Pvt. Iss. 2/22/1790 to Richard Platt. No papers
Joseph, Mass., Susanna Dean, former wid., W14615
Joseph, Mass., Lucy, W14966
Luther, Ct., S44972; BLWt.26079-160-55
Moses, Cont., Mass., Susannah, W21437
Nathan, Mass., Lydia, W26811
Phineas, Cont., Mass., Elizabeth, W26153; BLWt.9470-160-55
Solomon, Mass., S23724
Stephen, Mass., Sarah, W20157
INGALS, Israel, N.H., S9740
James, Cont., Mass., S32882
James, N.Y., Abigail, W23455
Joseph, Green Mt. Boys, Mass., S9739
Nathaniel, Mass., S32883
INGALSBE, John, Mass., S22850
INGELL, Jonathan, Mass., S30506
Zadock, Cont., Mass., Privateer, S18895
INGERSOL, George, Crane's Art., Mass., BLWt.1132-200-Lt. Iss. 1/29/1790. No papers
Samuel, Mass., BLWt.4476-100-Pvt. Iss. 10/12/1790 to Asa Spaulding No papers
INGERSOLL, Abraham, Mass., S33330
Andrew, Mass., S33331
Artemadores, Mass., S39767
Briggs, Ct., Abigail, W1188; BLWt.9438-160-55
Ebenezer, Mass., Margaret, W20155
Francis, Mass., Rachel, W21434
John, Ct., S10904
John, Mass., Sea Service, Elizabeth, R5479
John, N.J., Privateer, R4425
John, N.Y., Mary, W1874; BLWt. 26241-160-55
Jonathan, Mass., S21837
Moses, Mass., Lovine, R5478
Nathaniel, Mass., Sarah, W21436
Peter, Mass., R20192
Philip, N.Y., S46648
Rosannah, former wid. of Abraham Parker, Ct., which see
Thomas, Mass., R5477
Zebulon, Mass., Mary Woodbury, former wid., W26123; BLWt.51761-160-55
INGERSON, John, N.Y. See INGERSOLL
Richard, N.H., S35459
INGERSULL, John, N.J. See INGERSOLL
INGHAM, Daniel, Ct., S29255
David, Ct., S35458
Holladay, Ct., S45409
Isaac, Ct., Lucy, W16305
Joseph, N.J., Privateer, R5480
Samuel, Cont., Ct., Zillah, W297; BLWt.34285-160-55
Solomon, Ct., Cont.,Molly, W13527

INGHAM (continued)
Thomas, Va. See INGRAM
INGLE, Henry, Va., R5481
John, Va. See ENGLE
Michael, Va., S38860
INGLEDOE, Thomas, Pa., BLWt.9678-100-Pvt. Iss. 10/?/179? to Paul Libo, Admr. No papers
INGLEE, Ebenezer, Mass., Elizabeth Otis, W7860; BLWt.40017-160-55
INGLES, John, N.C., BLWt.1172-300-Capt. Iss. 2/8/1790. No papers
INGLESS, William, N.H. See ENGLISH
INGLEY, Joseph/Josiah, Ct., BLWt. 6008-100-Pvt. Iss. 7/15/1790 to Wm. Moore. No papers
INGLIS, James, N.Y., for service see papers in claim of John Morris Foght, Cont., N.Y.
William, Md., BLWt.11381-100-Pvt. Iss. 5/11/1790. No papers
William, N.H. See ENGLISH
INGLISH, John, Va., BLWt.181-100
INGOLS, Amos, N.H. See INGALLS
INGRAHAM, Amos, Ct., S44971
Benjamin, Mass., S38862
David, Mass., Lydia, W20158
Hezekiah, Ct., Mary, W26150; BLWt.6266-160-55
Holladay, Ct. See INGHAM
James, Ct., S17509
Job, Mass., Lucy, W26665
John, Mass., S18465
Jonathan, Ct., Mass., S30505 See N.A. Acc. No.874-050090 - Not Half Pay
Samuel, Ct., S22325
Simeon, Ct., S21838
William, R.I., Polly Brown, former wid., W14372
William, R.I., Esther, W26790
William, Va., b. N.C., S21314
INGRAM, Andrew, Va., b. N.C.,S32338
Edwin, N.C., b. Va., S9741
Jedediah, Mass., R5482
Jeremiah, Va., S15184
John, Mass., S10903
John, S.C., Ruth, R5483
Philip, Mass., S13518
Sally, former wid. of Nahor Norris, N.C., which see
Samuel, N.C., b. Va., son of John, R5485
Sarah, former wid. of Lemuel Thorowgood, Va., which see
Thomas, Va., S4419
INHERSTON, Robert, Crane's Cont. Art., Mass., BLWt.4494-100-Pvt. Iss. 2/23/1796. No papers
INLO, Thomas, Va., R5488
INLOE, Potter, S.C. See ENLOE
INLOW, John, S.C., S38859
Potter, S.C. See ENLOE
INMAN, Aaron, S.C., R5489
Abraham, R.I., Cynthia, W1873
Asa, R.I., S21836
Elisha, R.I., Joanna, W13528
Rufus, Mass., S41680
INNALLY, Patrick, N.J., BLWts. 8418 & 8587-100-Pvt. Iss. 5/4/1791 to Wm. Barton, ass. No papers

INNERS, Jacob, See INNOIS
INNIS, James, Pa., Isabella, BLWt.77005-160-55
John, Md., See ENNIS
Polly, R20294. See John ENNIS, Md.
INNMAN, Henry, Pa., S5601
INNOIS, Jacob, Pa., Mary, W3688
INSCOE, William, Va., S11363
INSKEEP, John, N.J., Sarah, W4703
INSLEE, Martha, former wid. of Benjamin Marshall, Pa., which see
IOR, Gabriel, Canadian, See TZOR
IPOCK, Samuel, N.C., S9742
IRBY, David, Va., S5602
Douglass/Douglas, Va., S38069
John, S.C., Va., Anne, W5003
William, Va., R5492
IRELAND, Dayton, N.J., S1029
James, N.C., Nancy, R5494
John, Md., BLWt.11403-100-Pvt. Iss. 2/7/1790. No papers
John, Pa., Elizabeth, W2116
Joseph, N.J., R5493
IRELY, John, Pa., R5495
IRESON, John, Mass., Sarah, W13529
IRICK, Abraham, N.C. See IHRIG
John, Hazen's Regt., BLWt.13257-100-Pvt. Iss. 9/6/1792. No papers
IRION, Charity, former wid. of Samuel Grannis, Cont., which see
IRISH, Isaac, Mass., Anna, R5496
Nathaniel, Artillery Artificers, BLWt.1133-300. Also BLWt.2591-300
Thomas, Mass., S20412
William, Mass., Sarah, W24724
IRON, Robert, Not Rev., Va., Indian Wars 1790-1795. BLWt.27032-160-50. No claim for pension
IRONS, Garret, N.J., Hester, W2377
Jeremiah, R.I., S21315
John, Md., BLWt.11407-100-Pvt. Iss. 3/11/1791. No papers
IRVIN, Andrew, Va., Elizabeth, W9045
Edward, Pa., S5598
Hannah, former wid. of Thomas Whitlow, Va., which see
James, Md. See ERVIN
James, Pa. See IRWIN
James, Pa., Margaret, W4704
James, S.C., Rebecca, W2117
William, Pa., Nancy, See case of wid's. former husb., William Smith, N.C.
William, Va., S44975
IRVINE, Andrew, Pa., BLWt.1150-300-Capt. Iss. 7/29/1798 to Wm. & James Irvine, Execrs. of the last will & testament of A.I. No papers
James, Va., S4422
James, Va., S36611
John, Pa., S39761
John, (d. 1835), Pa., S39762
John, Va., S39763
Mathew/Matthew, Cont., S.C. res. in 1807, BLWt.342-400
William, Pa., BLWt.1146-850-

IRVINE (continued)
Brig. Gen. Iss. 5/18/1789. No papers
William, Va., S16422
IRWIN, Ezekiel, Pa., S16162
Francis, Pa., S5497
Henry, N.C., BLWt.504-450
Henry, Pa. See ERWIN
James, Mass., S41681
James, Pa., S9743
James, Pa., Margaret, W3689
John, Pa., R5498
John, Pa., BLWt.1148-300-Capt. No papers
John, Va. See IRVINE
Nathaniel, Pa., S4418
Robert, Mass., S32884
Thomas, N.C., S.C., S9356
Thomas H., S.C., S31164
ISAACS, Isaac, Ct., Chloe Wilcox, former wid., W6541
Samuel, N.C., S.C., b. Va., S5600
ISABEL, James, N.C. See ISBELL
ISAPISA, George, Pa. BLWt.974-100
ISBELL, Benjamin, Va., S9358
Christopher, Va., S9357
Daniel, Va., Franka Tilley, former wid., W9856
Elizabeth, former wid. of James King, N.C., which see
Garner, Ct., Mary, W20160
Henry, Va., S9359
Henry, Va., S35461
James, N.C.(?), Va.(?), Polly, W7863; BLWt.26782-160-55
Joel, Ct., Mary, R5500
Pendleton, Cont., Va., Margaret, W5308; BLWt.34930-160-55
Thomas, Va., Discretion, W7862
ISELEY, Coonrod, N.C. See AEISLA
ISELY, Philip, N.C., Mary, W26149; BLWt.84011-160-55
ISEMAN, Christian, Pa. See EISAMAN
Michael, Pa., S22327
ISENHOUR, Phillip, Pa., See EISENHAUER
ISEPISA, George, Pa., BLWt.974-100
ISHAM, Daniel, Ct., S15592. Hannah Isham, wid. of above sold. was pensioned as former wid. of Joseph Nichols, N.H., which see
George G./George F., Ct., S41682
Hannah, N.H., See Joseph NICHOLS
Isaac, Ct., Faith, R5491
Jehiel/Jehial, Ct., S39766
Jirah, Ct., S18466
John, Ct., Cont., Lois, W16304
Joshua, Ct., BLWt.6006-100-Sgt. Iss. 3/25/1790. No papers
Joshua, Ct., Martha, W26791
William, Ct., BLWt.6010-100-Pvt. Iss. 8/25/1796 to James A. Neal. No papers
William, Ct., S39765
ISHMAEL, Benjamin, Cont., Pa., S35460
ISLEY, Philip, N.C. See ISELY
ISNER, Henry, ---, R5501, Va. res. in 1834

ISNER (continued)
Thomas, Va., R5502
ISOFISE, George, Pa. See ISEPISA
ISOM, Elijah, Va., R5503
ISRAEL, John, N.C., S17510
John, Va., S44973
ISSLEY, Coorod, N.C. See AEISLA
ITNEUER, Daniel, Md., S9744
ITNISE, Daniel, Md. See ITNEUER
ITTERLY, Jacob, Pa., R5504
ITTICK, Jacob C., N.Y. See ITTIG
ITTIG, Conrat/Conrad, Cont., N.Y. Nancy, W1776; BLWt.135-60-55; BLWt.7286-100 Iss. 9/15/1790. No papers
Jacob C., N.Y., Catharine, W26155
IVENS, Solomon, N.J., Catharine, W858; BLWt.8437-100-Pvt. Iss. 9/7/1790 to Wm. Barton, ass.
IVERS, Samuel, Mass., S32885
IVERY, James, N.Y. See IVORY
IVES, Amasa, Mass., S23277
Amos, Ct., S15186
Charles, Ct., S13519
Ichabod, Ct., S18050
James, N.C., BLWts. 12285 & 13252-100-Pvt. Iss. 8/14/1792 to Isaac Cole, ass. No papers
Joel, ---, Ct. agcy. Dis. No papers
John, Ct., Cont., S44974
John P., N.C., S9745
Lent, Ct., S28048
Lent, Ct., Vt., Mary, W26812
Levi, Ct., S15187
Phineas, Ct., Martha, W20161
Sarah, former wid. of Asa White, Mass., which see
Thomas, N.C., S20899
Thomas, Va., S38863
IVESTER, George, Pa., S5599
IVEY, Adam, S.C., b. N.C., R5507
Curtis, N.C., BLWt.1174-200-Lt.
David, N.C., Nancy, W26156; BLWt.35823-160-55
Elijah, S.C., S15188; BLWt.67525-160-55
John, N.C., Mourning, R5505
IVIE, Anselem/Anslem, Va., S38070
IVINGTON, Jeremiah, Md., S34936
IVINS, John, N.C., S1766
IVORY, James/Jacobus, N.Y., Sarah, W21433
IVY, David, Va., S4417
Henry, N.C., Jane, W433
William, Va. Sea Service, R46; Va. Half Pay
IZABEL, Augustine, Hazen's Regt., BLWt.13254-100-Pvt. Iss. 10/12/1790. No papers
IZAMENT, Peter, Hazen's Regt., BLWt.13251-100-Pvt. Iss. 2/20/1792 to Peter Izament, ass. No papers. BLWt.13251 also recorded being iss. for John James' service, to Elizabeth James, Executrix on 2/29/1792
IZELEY, Philip, N.C. See ISELY

J

JABINE, John, N.Y., BLWt.7316-100-Pvt. Iss. 9/28/1790 to Bartholomew & Fisher, assnes. No papers
JACK, James, N.C., b. Pa., S8750
James, Va., S2644
John, Ct., Hannah, W20167
John, Pa., Nancy, W4706; BLWt. 31282-160-55
Matthew, Pa., Nancy, W2807; BLWt.2483-300
Robert, Mass., S36619
Thomas, Pa., Jane, W4705
JACKLIN, Ebenezer, Ct., S32891
JACKMAN, Benjamin, Cont., Mass., S32886
Enoch, Mass., Privateer, Hannah, W26793
Joseph, Va., R5508
Richard, Mass., Martha, W1876; BLWt.12713-160-55
Richard, Mass., Abigail, W10143; BLWt.33557-160-55
Richard, Mass., R5523
Samuel, Cont., N.H., Hannah, W762
JACKO, William, Va. See JACO
JACKSON, Aaron, Mass., Sarah, W16129
Abednego, Md., S10909
Alexander, Pa., S4435
Amasa, Cont., Mass., Mary, W1190; BLWt.8464-160-55 & BLWt. 1125-150-Ensign. Iss. 9/30/1789. No papers
Andrew, Va., R5510
Anthony, ---, Pa. agcy., Dis. No papers
Archibald, Ct., Cont., R.I., S13521
Asa, Mass., S32888
Asa, N.H., Mary, W7878; BLWt. 13889-160-55
Barnabas, Mass., S35465
Bartholomew, Mass., S29257
Benjamin, Cont., Ct., Sabrina, W26157
Benjamin, N.J., S4430
Benjamin, N.C., S21317
Caleb, Cont., Mass., S13523
Charles, N.J., Privateer, R5513
Churchwell, N.C., S4432
Daniel, Ct., S36615
Daniel, Ct., Sea Service, S17512
Daniel, Cont., Mass., S32894; BLWt.1130-200-Lt. Iss. 4/18/1796 to Jeremiah, Mason, ass. No papers
Daniel, N.J., Sarah, W26639; BLWt. 39218-160-55
David, ---, Paid at Phila., Pa., Dis. No papers
David, Ct., S45412
David, Ct., Olive, W20170
David, Cont., Pa., Susan, W3258
David, Mass., BLWt.4483-100-Pvt. Iss. 1/26/1790 to John May. No papers
David, Mass., Miriam, R5521
David, N.C., Margaret, R5518
Drury, Va., S38075

JACKSON (continued)
Ebenezer, Cont., Mass., S32892
Ebenezer, Col. Crane's Regt. of Art., BLWt.1129-200-Lt. Iss. 9/12/1789. No papers
Ebenezer, N.Y., Lois, BLWt. 40503-160-55
Ebenezer, Vt., Abigail Keys, W7885
Edward, S.C., Mary, W2119
Eleazer, N.H., Olive, W435; BLWt.7090-160-55
Eli, Mass., S36618
Elias, Ct., R.I., Agnes/Nancy, W4002
Enoch, N.Y., S9361
Ephraim, Mass., Phebe, W763; BLWt.10004-160-55
Ephraim, Mass., Hannah, W14967
Francis, N.Y., BLWt.7330-100-Pvt. Iss. 2/14/1791 to Jereh Van Ranselar, atty. No papers
Francis, Va., S13525
George, Va., S36613
George, Va., R15396. Va. Half Pay
Hannibal, N.Y., Rachel, W21441
Henry, Mass., Sarah, W26666
Henry, Mass., BLWt.1120-500-Col. Iss. 1/29/1790. No papers
Henry, Va., S5609
Isaac, Mass., S18052
Isaac, Pa., S46451; BLWt.549-100 (The BL jacket of Joseph Jackson, BLWt.550-100 is also in this file)
Isaac, Va., BLWts.12259 & 14060-100-Pvt. Iss. 2/10/1794 to Francis Graves, ass. No papers
Isaac, Va., S38072
Isaac, Va., Winifred, W944
Jacob, Crane's Cont. Art., Mass., BLWt.4501-100-Corp. Iss. 1/28/1790 to Joseph May. No papers
James, Md., BLWt.11376-100-Pvt. Iss. 2/7/1790. No papers
James, Md., S41690
James, Mass., Dorothy, W16308
James, N.Y., Sarah, R5528
James, N.C., S38077
James, Pa., BLWt.9677-100-Pvt. Iss. 7/9/1789. No papers
James, Va., BLWt.12262-100-Sgt. "in the Dragoons". Iss. 5/5/179- to Wm. J. Vreedenburgh, ass. No papers
James, Va., S38071
Jane, former wid. of Charles Edwards, N.C., which see
Jeremiah, Mass., Sally, W20172
Jeremiah, Mass., BLWt.1134-150-Ens. Iss. 9/14/1792 to John Stephenson, ass. No papers
Jeremiah, Pa., BLWt.1149-300-Capt. Iss. 6/25/1789. No papers
Jesse, N.C., Elizabeth, R5515
John, Ct., BLWt.6021-100-Pvt. Iss. 5/14/1790 to Benj. Tallmadge. No papers
John, Ct., S22851
John, Ct., Delight, W21445
John, Del., S36021; BLWt.2106-100

JACKSON (continued)
John, Md., BLWt.11384-100-Pvt. Iss. 3/11/1791. No papers
John, Mass., Ruth, W2120; BLWt. 51756-160-55
John, N.Y., Eleanor, R5514
John, Pa. Sea Service, S2647
John, S.C., Ann, R5511
John, Va., Katharine/Catharine, W3425; BLWt.36219-160-55
John/John E., Va., Jane, W3823; BLWt.36721-160-55
John, Va., Mary F., R5519
John C., Va., S2648
Jonas, Cont., Mass., S32895
Jonathan, Cont., Mass., Hannah, W21440
Jonathan, Mass., Abigail Burrell, former wid., W3654
Jonathan, Va., S1836
Jonathan, Va., Mary, W15
Joseph, Ct., S10907
Joseph, Cont., Mass., U.S. Navy, S35464
Joseph, Cont., N.H?, Mass. & Me. res., S36621
Joseph, Mass., S32893
Joseph, Mass., Rebecca, W21450
Joseph, N.H., Martha, W16307
Joseph, N.C., b. Pa., Margaret, W370
Joseph, Pa., S41687; BLWt.550-100. For B.L. jacket see claim of Isaac Jackson, BLWt.549-100
Joseph, Va., Charlotte, W7884; BLWt.39217-160-55
Joshua, Mass., Eleanor, W7882
Joshua J., N.Y., Susanna, W7881
Josiah/Josias, N.C., Sarah, W9074
Josiah, Va., Sarah, W9332; BLWt. 73543-160-55
Lyman, Mass., N.Y., Deidamia, W2806
Mark, S.C., b. Va., S1675
Matthew, Ct., Cont., Mass., Jane, W10142
Matthew, Va., R5520
Michael, Ct., Deborah, W16033
Michael, Mass., Dis. BLWt.1121-500-Col. Iss. 5/9/1796. No papers
Michael, Mass., BLWt.1124-200-Lt. Iss. 5/9/1796. No papers
Michael, N.Y., S44985
Moses, Cont., Mass., Sarah, W21444
Moses, Va., Christiana, W9073
Nathan, Mass., BLWt.4461-100-Pvt. Iss. 2/22/1792 to John Peck. No papers
Nathan, Mass., BLWt.4478-100-Pvt. Iss. 7/22/1789. No papers
Nathan, Mass., S39770
Nathaniel, Mass., S36620
Obadiah, Va., S4434
Oliver, Cont., Mass., S32889
Patton/Pattin, N.Y., S45411; BLWt.1145-200-Lt. Iss. 7/8/1790
Peter, Md., BLWt.1900-100
Peter, Pa., S5611
Philip, Va., Ann, W11931; BLWt. 30774-160-55
Pomp, Mass., BLWt.4450 & 4423-100-Pvt. Iss. 12/9/1796 to Pomp

JACKSON (continued)
Jackson. No papers
Reuben, Mass., Sally, R5527
Reuben, Va., BLWt.12276-100-Pvt. Iss. 12/13/1791 to Francis Graves, ass. No papers
Reuben, Va., S38074
Richard, N.J., BLWt.8442-100-Sgt. Iss. 3/24/1790. No papers
Richard, N.J., S41683
Robert, Ct., R.I., S9994
Robert, Mass., S4456
Samuel, Ct., BLWt.1167-100
Samuel, Ga., Elizabeth, W945, See N.A. Acct. No. 874-050091 Not Half Pay
Samuel, Mass., Mercy, W7879; BLWt.30763-160-55
Samuel, N.C., Judith, W4001
Samuel, N.C., Hannah, W5004
Samuel, N.C., Jane, R5517
Samuel, Va., Vashti, R5529
Seth, Sheldon's Dragoons, Ct., BLWt.6044-100-Pvt. Iss. 9/24/1790 to James F. Sebor. No papers
Seth, Ct., Elizabeth Hunter, former wid., W10131; BLWt. 5447-160-55
Simon, Mass., BLWt.1122-300-Capt. Iss. 3/21/1796. No papers
Solomon, N.C., S16424
Stephen, Cont., Mass., Vt., S41685
Stephen, N.C., S.C., Nancy, R5522
Thomas, Cont., Mass.res. of heirs in 1836, BLWt.2141-300
Thomas, Mass., S29922
Thomas, N.Y., BLWt.7312-100-Pvt. Iss. 9/10/1790 to Justus Banks, ass. No papers
Thomas, S.C., b. England, S5608
Thomas, S.C., b. Va., S31166
Thomas Tredwell, Sheldon's Regt. Ct., BLWt.1139-200-Lt. Iss. 8/20/1789. No papers
William, Md., Jemima, W7883
William, Md., Pa., Va., S38079; BLWt.1791-100
William, N.Y., Sophia, W4707; BLWt.174-60-55
William, N.C., S4433
William, N.C., Sarah, W21448
William, Pa., S31769
William, S.C., b. Pa., Elizabeth W., W9072; BLWt.1176-300-Capt. Iss. 2/17/1798. No papers
William, Va., S1676
William, Va., S4431
William, Va.,(a free man of color), Nicey, W7877
JACKWAY, Daniel, Ct. See JAKWAYS
JACKWAYS, Joseph, R.I. See JAQUAYS
William, Ct. See JACQUES
JACO, William, Va., S36612
JACOB, John Jeremiah, Md., Susan J., W11930; BLWt.1405-200; BLWt.15431-160-55
JACOBI, Michael, Pa., BLWt.9692-100-Pvt. Iss. 3/29/179- to Barnard Slauch, ass. No papers

JACOBI (continued)
Philip, Pa., BLWt.9680-100-Pvt. Iss. 2/8/1791 to Alexander Power, ass. No papers
JACOBS, Abel, N.Y., BLWt.7337-100-Pvt. Iss. 4/9/1791 to James Wadsworth, ass. No papers
Asa, Ct., R.I., Phebe, W9070; BLWt.21819-160-55
Asahel/Ashael, Ct., S15478
Benjamin, N.C., S38073
Cornelius, Cont., N.Y., Elizabeth W20163
David, N.H., Molly, W14970
David, Pa., BLWt.9676-100-Pvt. Iss. 4/1/1790. No papers
David, Pa., S38865
Edward G., Md., N.C., S1540
Eli, Mass., Anna, W11934; BLWt. 14665-160-55. She also rec'd pension on acct. of former husb. Cornelius McClease, Pvt., 23rd U.S. Inf., War of 1812. See papers within
Enoch, Ct., Lois, R5532
Esop, Mass., BLWt.4474-100-Pvt. Iss. 7/21/1789 to Eliphalet Ladd & Jonathan Cass. No papers
Ezekiel, Ct., S10908
Francis, Cont., N.Y., Catherine, R5533
George, Cont., Mass., Hepsibah, W26668; BLWt.1450-200
Gershom, Ct., Mary, W16309
Henry, Md., BLWt.2124-100
Isaac, Mass., BLWt.4486-100-Corp., Iss. 3/2/1790. No papers
Isaiah, Mass., S39771
James, Pa., S39773
Jesse, Md., BLWt.11396-100-Pvt. Iss. 7/22/1797 to James DeBaufre, ass. No papers
John, Cont., Mass., S18467
John, Cont., Mass., S35463
John, Cont., Va., Ann, W9071; BLWt.41581-160-55
John, Mass., BLWt.4467-100-Pvt. Iss. 11/2/1795 to Joseph Fosdick. No papers
John, Mass., Ruby, W21438
John, N.J., Nancy, W1189; BLWt. 229-60-55
John, N.Y., BLWt.7314-100-Sgt. Iss. 9/25/1790 to John Bristol, ass. No papers
John, N.Y., Anna, W15838
John, Pa., S22328
John, Pa., S41689
John, Pa., Eliza, W2805
John, Va., Sarah, W9069
John Jeremiah, Md. See JACOB
Jonathan, Pa., Dorothy, W3345
Joseph, N.C., Lucy, W7875
Lemuel, Mass., Sarah, W14973
Lewis, N.Y., S18897
Nathaniel, Ct.(?), R.I., S13520
Nathaniel C./Nathaniel, Mass., S39769; BLWt.18393-160-55
Peter, Pa., Elizabeth, W7876; BLWt.38505-160-55
Primus (colored), Mass., Dinah, W21446
Primus, N.C., S41688

JACOBS (continued)
Rebecca, former wid. of Wm. Alexander , N.H. res.,which see
Roley, Va., S36617
Samuel, Va., Lydia, W11921; BLWt. 82006-160-55
Simeon, Mass., Sarah, W20164
Uriah, Cont., N.Y., Elizabeth, W21442
Whitman, Cont., Mass., Hannah, W16614
William, Ct., S23278
William, Md., S2289
William, Va., S36614
William, Va., R5536
Zachariah, N.C., Sally, W5304; BLWt.71037-160-55
JACOBY, Margaret, Pa. See Andrew Kiefer
Nicholas, Cont., Pa., BLWt.278-100
Nicholas, Pa., Barbara, W3346
Philip, Pa. See Pfillib YACOBI
JACOCKS, Gershom, Ct. See JACOBS
Joshua, Ct. See JACOX
JACOX, Bowers, N.Y., S13524
Joshua, Ct., S45432
JACQUE, Louis, Hazen's Regt., BLWt.13256-100-Pvt. Iss. 2/20/1792 to Benj. Moore, ass. No papers
JACQUES, Daniel, Mass., Hannah, W14969
Nathan, Navy, R.I. See JAQUAYS
Richard, Cont., Mass., S35466
William, Ct. See JAKWAYS
William, Ct., Ann, W2118
JACQUETT, Peter, Del. See JAQUETT
JACQAYS, Robert, Ct., Dis. No papers
JAGGAR, Abraham, N.Y., S31770
JAGGARS, Jeremiah, S.C., Nancy, R5544
Nathan, S.C., Va., S32339
JAGGERS, Jeremiah, ---, N.J. res. of dau. in 1881, R20314
JAGGOR, Abraham, N.Y. See JAGGAR
JAKWAYS, Daniel, Ct., N.Y., Olive, W20166
William, Ct., S5612
JAMAR, Henry, Pa., Jane Foy, former wid., R3735
JAMEISON, James, S.C. See JAMIESON
JAMERSON, Robert, Va., S16885 1/2
JAMES, Aaron, Pa., S1538
Abner, N.C., S7065
Alexander, Pa. Sea Service, Elizabeth Bickerton, former wid. R820
Amos, Ct., Mass., R.I., Phebe, W1615
Ann, former wid. of Matthew Lewis, Va. Sea Service, which see
David, N.J., BLWt.8422-100-Sgt. Iss. 7/12/1792. No papers
David, N.J., S889
David, Va., S1674
Ebenezer, N.Y., BLWt.7320-100-Corp. Iss. 7/9/1790 to Nathaniel Scribner, ass. No papers

JAMES (continued)
Ebenezer, N.Y., S44982
Edward, Pa., Margaret, W3187
Elisha, Cont., Mass., S30507
George, R.I., S17511
Henry, N.Y., R5545
Isaac, Va., S18053
Jabez, N.H., Sally, W7867; BLWt.56970-160-55
Jamaica (colored), Mass., S44984
James, N.C., S7063
Jeffery, Ct., S36616
Jehiel, N.J., Elizabeth, W130
Jeremiah, N.C., Rebecca, W467
John, Cont., Mass., Lydia Gordon, former wid., W11066
John, Hazen's Regt., BLWt.13251-100-Pvt. Iss. 2/29/1792 to Elizabeth James, Executrix. No papers BLWt.13251 recorded as being iss. 2/20/1792 to Peter Izament, Pvt., Hazen's Regt.
John, Hazen's Regt., BLWt.13259-100-Pvt. Iss. 2/29/1792 to Elizabeth James, Admx. No papers
John, N.J. See JEMES
John, N.Y., Fanny, W9068
John, S.C., S18051
Jonathan, Pa., S4429
Joseph, R.I., Elizabeth, W21449
Joseph, Va., S35462
Joseph Rogers, N.C., S32340
Joshua, N.C., S20895
Michael, Va. Sea Service, R47, Va. Half Pay. See N.A. Acct. No.837-Va. State Navy--YS File
Nathan, Pa., S4428
Nicholas, Pa., S5547
Paul, Ct., S44983
Rhoda, former wid. of Billy Trowbridge, Ct., which see
Richard, Mass. Sea Service, R5548
Robert, N.J., Ann, W4461
Rollings, S.C., S2018
Ruth, former wid. of Nathaniel Chittenden, Mass., which see
Shaderick/Shederick, N.C., Theny, S18896; BLWt.36556-160-55
Silas, R.I., Phebe, W24728
Thomas, Md., S16423
Thomas, Mass., S29921
Thomas, Mass., Sarah, W14972
Thomas, N.J., BLWt.8421-100-Pvt. Iss. 5/7/1800 to Wm. Duncan. No papers
Thomas, N.J., Ann, W7868
William, Ct., Lovisa, W20168
William, Mass., Mary, W13535
William, N.J., BLWt.34581-160-55
William, N.C., Mary, W2943
William, Pa., S5604
William, Va., Frances, W1875; BLWt.26965-160-55
William, Va., R5550

JAMESON, Adam, Md., BLWt.1162-200-Lt. Iss. 5/25/1789. No papers
Charles, Mass., Ruth, W7869; BLWt.5105-160-55
David, N.J., BLWt.8423-100-Pvt. Iss. 6/21/1797 to Abraham Bell, ass. No papers
David, Va., S5607

JAMESON (continued)
David, Va., S31167
Esther, former wid. of Samuel Marshall, Mass., which see
George, Va. See JEMERSON
Hugh, N.H. See JAMISON
John, Cont., Va., R15404, Va. Half Pay, & BLWt.1164-450-Lt. Col. of Col. Sheldon's Cav. Regt. Iss. 8/10/1789 to Richard Platt, ass. No papers
John, Va., S4427
John, Va., Nancy, 5552
Samuel, Cont., Ct. See JAMESSON
Thomas, N.H., S23726
William, Va., S13527

JAMESSON, Samuel, Cont., Ct., Rosanna, W16032

JAMIESON, James, S.C., S21839
John, Cont., Va. See JAMESON
Joseph, S.C., S9360
Samuel, Va., Margaret, W5112

JAMISON, Adam, Md., BLWt.11389-100-Pvt. Iss. 10/14/1795 to Henry Davis, ass. No papers
Esther, Mass. See Samuel MARSHALL
Francis, Cont., Pa., S41686
Hugh, N.H., Margaret, W21439
John, N.J., S31165
John, N.C., S1673
John, Pa., S39772
John, Pa., Nancy, W21447
Richard, Pa., BLWt.9656-100-Pvt. Iss. 3/?/1794. No papers
Robert, Va. See JAMERSON
Samuel, Cont. Ct. See JAMESSON
Samuel, Pa., Margaret, W4460
William, N.C., S8749

JANES, Benjamin, Va., S1959
David, Mass., S38078
Elijah, Cont., Mass., Phebe, W21443; BLWt.1140-200-Lt. Iss. 12/15/1791. No papers
Jonathan, Mass., S38864
Peleg Cheney, Mass., Martha, R5553
Seth, Ct., S28772
Thomas, Mass., Ruth, W27919
William, Mass., S29923

JANIS, Jean Baptiste, Va. & Indian Wars, S15901 & Va. Half Pay

JANNEY, Thomas, Pa., BLWt.1155-200. No paper

JANSEN, Benjamin, N.Y., S13522
Blandina, former wid. of Jacobus Rosekrans, N.Y., which see
Cornelius T./J., N.Y., Christiana Low/Chrystian Louw, former wid., W16333; BLWt.1142-300-Capt. Iss. 9/1/1791. No papers
Matthew H., N.Y., Judith/Judica, W16306

JANSON, Johannes, N.Y. See YANSON

JAPSON, William, Mass., Keziah, W26795

JAQUA, Asahel, N.Y., S44981
Gamaliel, Ct., Eleanor, W7888; BLWt.26826-160-55
Simon, Vt., Ruth, R5539

JAQUAS, Nathan, R.I., S38866

JAQUAYS, Joseph, R.I., Navy, Hope, W20171

JAQUAYS (continued)
Nathan, Navy, R.I. & French & Indian War, Hannah, W26667

JAQUES, Daniel, Mass. See JACQUES
Nathan, Mass., S32887
Parker, Mass., S21316
Samuel, Mass., Eunice, W20165
Samuel, N.J. & Whiskey Insurrection 1794; Rachel, R5542; BL Rejected 273375-55
William, Ct., BLWt.6023-100-Pvt. Iss. 1/5/1792. No papers

JAQUET, Daniel, See John Daniel
John Daniel/Daniel, Cont., Md., Margaret, W27879 1/2

JAQUETT, Peter, Del., S46500, BLWt.1160-300-Capt. Iss. 5/30/1789. No papers

JAQUINS, John, Mass., S44980

JAQUISH, John, N.Y., S44979; BLWt.931-100

JAQUITH, Ebenezer, Mass., S10906
Samuel, Mass., Lois/Louis, W21451

JARDON, John, N.Y., S28779

JARED, Joseph, Va., S1539

JARMAN, Azariah, N.J., S1001
Charles, Ct. & Cont., Betsey, W20169
Emory, N.C., R5555
William, Cont., Va., W4003

JARRARD, Benjamin, Ct., R5556

JARREL, Solomon, Va., S38076

JARRELL, John, Va. See GARRELL
William, Va., Elizabeth, R5557

JARRETT, Andrew, Pa., BLWt.9704-100-Pvt. in Proctor's Art. Iss. 7/7/1789. No papers

JARVINS, Daniel, Md., BLWt.11387-100-Pvt. Iss. 2/1/1790. No papers

JARVIS, Bill, N.Y., S5605
Edward, Mass. Sea Service, S32890
Edward, N.C., Mary, W7871
Elisha, Md., Drucilla, W11929
Field, Va., S5606
Henry, Ct., R5559
John, Md., Ann, W9331
John, Mass., S44978
Joseph, Mass., Abigail, R5558
Polly, former wid. of Robert Farr Pa., which see
Robert, N.H., S44977
Solomon, Md., R5560
Thomas, N.C., S2649

JASPER, William, S.C., BLWt. 2272-100

JAY, David, N.Y., Polly, W3241
Joseph, N.J., S46661
Martha, former wid. of Alexander Lawson Smith, Md., which see

JAYCOX, Joshua, Ct. See JACOX

JAYNE, Samuel, N.Y., Eleanor, W7870; BLWt.26010-160-55

JEAN, Nathan, N.C., S41692
Philip, N.C., b. Va., Sarah,W3824
Sherod, N.C. See GEAN
William, N.C., S7071

JEANNEREL, Claude Francois/Henry Bradford, Cont., France, Elizabeth, R1125; BLWt.20476-160-12 for service 20th U.S. Inf., War of 1812

JEANNRET, Elias, N.C., S8758
JEFF, Robert, Pa., BLWt.9705-100-Pvt. Iss. 8/31/1790 to Dudley Woodbridge, ass. No papers
JEFFERDS, Samuel, Crane's Art. Wt.1131-200-Lt. No papers
Samuel M., Mass., S20417
JEFFEREYS, William, R.I. See JEFFERS
JEFFERIES, John, S.C., S18055
William, Va., BLWt.12266-100-Pvt. Iss. 4/8/1794. No papers Also BLWt.275-60-55
William, Va., S16886
JEFFERS, Allen, S.C., S1770
Anna, former wid. of James Snow, Mass., which see
Berry, S.C., Hannah/Joannis, W10145
Gawin, Va. See Gowin JEFFRIES
George, Ct., Martha, R5562
Jacob, Md., Ann, R5561
John, Ct., BLWt.6016-100-Sgt. Iss. 1/29/1790. No papers
John, N.Y. See JEFFRIES
John, Va. See JEFFREYS
Joseph, Mass., S44990
Samuel, S.C., R5563
William, R.I., S38867
JEFFERSON, Justinian, Md., S30508
JEFFERY, Charles, Ct., S13539
Francis, N.J., See JEFFREY
Garret/Garrett, N.J., S1030
Humphrey, N.J. See JEFFREY
JEFFERYS, Henry, N.J., R5567
JEFFORD, Elizabeth, former wid. of Thomas White, S.C., which see
JEFFORDS, William, Mass., S47339
JEFFRESS, Thomas, Va., Mary C., R5565
JEFFREY, Drewry/Dreury, N.C., S7067
Francis, N.J., Elizabeth, W946 BLWt.35820-160-55
Humphrey, N.J., Ann Martha, W21458
John, Pa., U.S. Navy, Demaries/Demarias, W4708
JEFFREYS, John, N.J. See JEFFRYES
John, Va., S8754
John, Va., Delilah, W26158; BLWt. 26840-160-55
William, Va., S18470
JEFFRIES, Alexander, Va., S8755
Gowin/Gawin, Va., S32341
Isaac, Va., BLWt.1151-150-Ensign. Iss. 1/29/1799 to Rd Jeffries & other heirs. Also recorded under BLWt.2703 iss. 1/29/1799 to Richard Jeffries the only surviving heir. No papers
Jacob, Md. See JEFFERS
John, N.Y., S44989; BLWt.7323-100 Iss. 9/2/1790 to John Quackinboss ass.
John, Pa., Sarah Griffith/Griffiths, former wid., W9463; BLWt.2191-100
John, S.C. See JEFFERIES
John, Va., S16888
Reuben, Va., Anne, W20178
Samuel, S.C. See JEFFERS

JEFFRIES (continued)
William, R.I. See JEFFERS
William, Va., Nancy, W9076; BLWt.275-60-55
JEFFRYES, John, N.J., S4440
JEFFRYS, Thomas, Va. See JEFFRESS
JEFFS, Thomas, Mass., BLWt.862-100
JELLIFF, James, Ct., S17514. His wid., Eunice, was pensioned on acct. of services of her former husb., John Lockwood, which see
JELLY, Joseph, Hazen's Regt., BLWt.13255-100-Pvt. Iss. 10/12/1790. No papers
JEMERSON, George, Va., Elener, R5551
JEMES, John, N.J., S5603
JEMISON, David, Pa., Indian War-1791, S2290
John, Va., S36623
JEMMISON, Matthew, Invalid Corps. BLWt.13268-100-Pvt. Iss. 10/29/1794 to Sampson Crosby, ass.
JENCKES, George, R.I. See JENKS
Jedediah, See JENKS
Joseph, R.I., Lydia, W26701
JENCKS, Boomer, R.I., S15902
Dickinson, N.Y., Susannah, W20177
John, Ct. See JENKS
Lory, R.I., S13538
Nicholas, R.I., Betsey, W20176
Samuel, R.I., Abigail, W11936
JENIFER, Daniel, Md., BLWt.1082-450
JENINGS, Abraham, Ct. See JENNINGS
Esbon, Ct. See JENNINGS
William, Va. See JENNINGS
JENISON, Joseph Brooks, Mass., S44986
Robert, Mass., Hannah, W14977
William, Mass., Judith, W14975
JENKINS, Aaron, N.C., S7069
Abraham, N.C., Elizabeth, W20180
Alvan, Mass., S18898
Anthony, Va., S16426
Benjamin, Mass., N.H., Hannah, W1292; BLWt.1593-160-55
Benjamin, R.I., BLWt.588-100
Caleb, Va., S8757
Calvin, Ct., BLWt.6019-100-Pvt. Iss. 2/3/1794 to Benjamin Sandford. No papers
Calvin, Ct. See JINKINS
Calvin, Mass., S18899
Charles, Va., BLWt.12273-100-Pvt. Iss. 7/14/1792 to Robert Means, ass. No papers
Charles, Va., S41693
David, Mass., S44459
Edward, Va., Mary AnnR5573
Enoch, Mass., S39776; BLWt.332-100
Ezekiel, Va., S16163
Gideon, Mass., Mercy, W26700
Isaac, Md., BLWt.14064-100-Pvt. Iss. 3/1/1794 to Edward Jenkins, Admr. No papers
James, N.J., Hannah, W20179; BLWt.8444-100. Iss. 6/29/1789. No papers
James, S.C., S18054
James, S.C., Hannah, R5569
Job, Va., Elizabeth, W26806
Joel, Mass., Elizabeth, W16616;

JENKINS (continued)
BLWt.1123-200-Lt. Iss. 8/10/1789 to Richard Platt, ass. No papers
John, Ct., Bethiah, W7895; BLWt. 448-200
John, Cont., Va., S36632; BLWt. 2174-100
John, Cont., Va., BL Rej.
John, Cont., Va., BLRej.
John, Mass., Abigail, R5568
John, Navy, N.H. See JUNKINS
John, S.C., S31776
John, S.C., Sarah, W21457
John, Va., S16425
John, Va., Mary, W7894; BLWt. 28646-160-55
Joseph, Md., BLWt.11383-100-Pvt. Iss. 10/14/1795 to Henry Davis, ass. No papers
Joseph, Mass., S13532
Joseph, Mass., S13536
Joseph, Mass., R5571
Josiah, Cont., Mass., Prudence, W26703
Lemuel, Mass., S29258
Lemuel, Mass., Hannah, W11944
Lewis, N.C., S31771
Lewis, N.C., R5572
Nathaniel, Mass., S18901
Nathaniel, N.Y., S16164
Obadiah, Mass., S44460
Philip, Md., Sarah, W9486
Reuben, Va., R5574
Richard, Va., Jemima, W7893; BLWt.87087-160-55 (This man sometimes called Jaw Dick Jenkins)
Samuel, Ct., S44461; BLWt.2203-100
Samuel, Mass., Thankful, W1434
Stephen, Cont., Vt., Lydia, W21456
Thomas, Md., S10915
Thomas, N.C., S2651
William, Md., BLWt.11390-100-Pvt. Iss. 12/28/1791 to Wm. Lane, ass. No papers
William, Mass., S29925
William, Pa. See JENKINSON
William, S.C., S31774
William, S.C., S38080
William, Va., S7070
William, Va., Keziah, W2944
William, Va., BLReg.335774-1855
Zaccheus/Zacheus, Mass., S29924
JENKINSON, William, Cont., Pa., S7068
JENKS, Adam, R.I., S2291
Anthony, R.I., Laura, W11940; BLWt.1845-100 & 326-60-55
George, R.I., Ruth, W13539
Jacob, R.I., S18471
Jedediah, R.I., S21318
John/John S., Ct., S39775; BLWt. 1821-100
Levi, R.I., Hannah, W10144; BLWt.61231-160-55
Nicholas, R.I. See JENCKS
Prince, R.I., BLWt.3253-100-Pvt. Iss. 1/28/1790. No papers
Thomas, Mass., BLWt.4458-100-Pvt. Iss. 4/21/1794. No papers

JENNE, Aaron, Vt., Abigail, W21460; BLWt.14754-160-55
Ebenezer, Mass., N.H. See JENNINGS
Prince, Mass., S38868
Seth, Mass., S13530
JENNERSON, Moses, Mass., Sarah, W21453
Robert, Mass., BLWt.4469-100-Pvt. Iss. 2/29/1792 to Moses Beard. No papers
JENNESS, Job, N.H., BLWt.758-100
John, N.H., Temperance, W26705
JENNIFER, Daniel, Md. See JENIFER
JENNINGS, Aaron, Ct., S13535
Abijah, Ct., Eleanor, W26669
Abner, Mass., Betsey, W26159; BLWt.26532-160-55. Wid., Betsey, married 1st Andrew Fordham, War of 1812 sold. on whose service she rec'd BLWt.87502-160-55
Abraham, Ct., Charity, W21455
Benjamin, Mass., S32899
Benjamin, Pa. See JINNINGS
Burritt, Navy, Ct., S36625
Daniel, Ct., S36628
Ebenezer, Mass., N.H., Dorcas, W20175
Edmund, Va., S4439
Edward, Pa., BLWt.9657-100. Iss. 5/16/1793. No papers
Eliphalet, Ct., S18468
Eliphalet, Mass., S35469
Esbon, Ct., S41695; BLWt.2208-100
George, Md., BLWt.11399-100-Pvt. Iss. 12/18/1794 to Henry Purdy, ass. No papers
James, N.C., Va., Hannah, W7897; BLWt.27580-160-55
James, S.C., S36630
John, Pvt., Mass., BLWt.4457 iss. 3/25/1790
John, N.H., BLWt.3247-100-Pvt. Iss. 1/28/1790 to James Patterson ass. No papers
John, Va., b. England, S13529
John, Va Sea Service, R48; Va. Half Pay. See N.A. Acc. No. 837. Va. State Navy - YS File
Jonathan, Sheldon's Dragoons, Ct. BLWt.6041-100-Pvt. Iss. 3/5/1790 No papers
Jonathan, Ct., S39778
Jonathan, Cont., Ct., S38871
Jonathan, Mass., Mary, W27435
Jonathan Shery, N.Y., Mary, W15777
Joseph, Mass., S45416
Joseph, Mass., Sarah, W1433
Joshua, Ct., Sarah, W20181
Justus, Ct., S44987
Nathan, Cont., Ct., S31775
Nathan B., Ct., Ann/Nancy, R5577
Noah, Ct., S23727
Peter, Ct., Sarah, W24746; BLWt. 30766-160-55
Peter, R.I., S4436
Royal, Va., S1541
Solomon, N.Y., BLWt.7332-100-Pvt. Iss. 7/9/1790 to Nathaniel Scribner, ass. No papers
Solomon, N.Y., Polly, W10147
Stephen, N.H., S38869

JENNINGS (continued)
Thomas, N.C., S41694
Thomas, Pa., BLWt.9708-100-Drummer in Proctor's Art. Iss. 7/27/1789 to Richard Platt, ass. No papers
William, Ct., S13537
William, Ct., S36622
William, Mass., R.I., S18469
William, N.J., S10910
William, Va., Polly, W27144
William, Va., R15422; Va. Half Pay. See N.A. Acc. No. 874-050092. Also papers in N.A. Acc.837-Va. State Navy.-YS File
William, Va. Sea Service, S5615
JENNISON, Moses, Mass. See JENNERSON
Samuel, Mass., S36631
William, Cont., Mass., Navy, Mary, W14974
William, Mass. See JENISON
JENNISS, Job., N.H. See JENNESS
JENVILLE, Alexis, Pvt., Hazen's Regt.; BLWt.13250-100. Iss. 2/20/1792 to Benjamin Moore, ass.
JEPHERSON, Aaron, R.I., Deborah, W27436; BLWt.15407-160-55
Jedediah, Mass., Navy, S32898. Wid., Jerusha, was former wid. of Holland Blackmar, Vt., which see
Jerusha, Vt. See Holland BLACKMAR
John, Mass., Mary, W14976; BLWt. 26436-160-55
Joseph, Mass., Navy, Ruth, W26794
JEPSON, David, Cont., Mass.,S39779
John, Mass., S32900
Joseph, Mass. See JIPSON
William, Mass. See JAPSON
JERALDS, Thomas, Cont., Ct., See GERALD
JERALEMON, Nicholas, See JORALEMON
JERAULD, James, R.I., Eleanor, W2121
JEREMIAH, John, N.Y., S44988
JEREMY, Edward, R.I. See Edward HOPPS
JERKINS, Zachariah, N.C. See GHERKINS
JERMAIN, Henry, Pa., BLWt.9710-100 -Pvt. Iss. 4/26/1791. No papers
JERNIGAN, George, N.C., S8756
JERO, Baptiste/Jean Baptiste, Cont. N.Y., Hippolite, R5580
JEROHMAN, James, N.Y., Dis. --
JEROM, Robert, Ct. res., Dis. No papers
JEROME, David, Ct., S36627
Levi, Mass., S9921
Thomas, Ct., S17513
JERRALD, Hugh Pugh, S.C., S41691
JERRELL, Ezekiel, N.Y., BLWt.7338-100-Pvt. Iss. 1/3/1792 to George Knox, Admr. No papers
JERVIS, John, N.Y., Hannah/Anne, W15778
JESEPH, Joseph, Mass., S32915
JESS, Samuel, Cont., N.J. res. in 1806; BLWt.309-100
JESSE, William, Va., Elizabeth,

JESSE (continued)
W3825
JESSEE, Thomas, Va., R5581
JESSUP, Ebenezer, Ct., Rebecca, R5582
Jonathan, Cont., N.Y. City res. in 1818, Ct. in 1820; S36626
JESTER, Daniel, Del. See JESTOR
James T., N.C., S2650
Nimrod, N.C., Mary, W27599; BLWt.31783-160-55
JESTOR, Daniel, Del., S31773
JESUP, Joseph, Ct., Eunice, W16310
JETER, Dudley, N.C., R5584
Fielding, Va., S36629
James, S.C., S21840
Littleton, Va., Jane, W9077
JETT, William, Va., S16885
William Storke, Va., S5614
JEWEL, Ephraim, Mass., S15479
John, N.Y., S13531
Seth, Cont., N.J., S39777
William, N.J., S22329
William, N.J., S33333
JEWELL, Benjamen/Benjamin, Mass., S38870
Daniel, N.H., S10912
David, N.H., Molly, W26699
Elisha, N.J., S13533
Elisha, Va., Mildred, W7890
George, N.Y., R5585
Hubbard, N.J., BLWt.8425 & 13952-100
James, N.H., S10911
Jane, former wid. of Zebalon Doty, N.J., which see
John, Mass., S35467
John, N.H., Mary, W26702; BLWt. 704-100; BLWt.237-60-55
John M., Mass., S45413
Jonathan, Mass., S45414
Jonathan, Va., R5586
Joseph, Cont., N.Y., S15480
Samuel, Mass., S16887
Seth, N.J., BLWt.8419-100-Pvt. Iss. 9/29/1790 to John Hole, ass. No papers
William, Mass., S39780
William, N.C., S1837
William, Va., Mary, W11946; BLWt. 82174-160-55
JEWETT, Alpheus, Ct., N.Y., Abigail, W24734
Benjamin, Mass., S44457
Caleb, Ct. -- No papers, Invalid pensioner
David, Mass., BLWt.4452-100-Fifer Iss. 7/22/1789. No papers
David, Mass., S32896
David, Mass., Ruth, R5590
David, N.H., Mary, W26704
Ebenezer, Mass., N.H., Polly.R5589
Enoch, Cont., Mass., S44458
Epes, Mass., Invalid Corps, BLWts.4464 & 13269-100-Pvt. Iss. 2/5/1790. No papers
Epes, Mass., S32901
Frederick, Vt., Else, W20174; BLWt.10225-160-55
James, Mass., S18056
James, Mass., Lydia, R5588

JEWETT (continued)
Jedediah, Mass., S10913
Jedediah, N.H., Elizabeth, R5587
Jeremiah, Mass., Temperance, BLWt.13001-160-55
John, Mass., S31772
John, N.Y., Prudence, W20182; BLWt.26711-160-55
Jonathan, N.H., Sarah, W21461
Joseph, Ct., Rachel, W21454
Joseph, Mass., Sarah, W26805
Joseph M., Ct., S4438
Moses, Mass., S35468
Nathan H., Ct., S13541
Nathaniel, Mass., S22852
Noah, N.H., S20416
Oliver, Cont., Mass., S32897
Samuel, Mass., S10914
Thomas, N.Y., S13540
William, --; See Philip JUDD
Zebulon, Ct., N.Y., Vt., S18900
JEWITT, Alpheus, Ct. See JEWETT
Benjamin, Mass., BLWt.4487-100-Musician. Iss. 3/14/1793 to Benjamin Bailey. No papers
John, N.Y. See JEWETT
JIGNEY, John, Pa., BLWt.9666-100-Pvt. Iss. 1/25/1791 to Richard Murchwaite, Admr. No papers
JILES, Thomas, Sheldon's Dragoons Ct., BLWt.6043-100-Pvt. Iss. 2/25/1791 to Samuel Whiting. No papers
JILLSON, David, N.H., Vt., S21319
Nathan, R.I., Susanna, W13543
Oliver, Mass., Mass. Sea Service Navy, Nancy, W26670
JINCKS, Benjamin, Cont., R.I., S44991
JINKINS, Absalom, Va., S5616
Anthony, Va. See JENKINS
Calvin, Ct., S36624
James, S.C. See JENKINS
Joel, Mass. See JENKINS
JINKS, Thomas, N.C., S41696
JINNEY, Aaron, Vt. See JENNE
JINNINGS, Abel, Mass. See GININGS
Benjamin, Pa., Rhoda, W7896
James, N.C. See JENNINGS
JIPSON, Joseph, Mass., S5613
JOB, Daniel, Md., R21887
Enoch, Va., Sarah, W1193
John, N.J., BLWt.8439-100-Pvt. Iss. 5/29/1790. No papers
John, N.J., BLWt.8450-100-Pvt. Iss. 4/17/1794. No papers
Peter, N.J., Ann Mount, former wid., R7471
Richard, N.J., BLWt.8431-100-Drum Major. Iss. 11/10/179? No papers
Robert, Cont., N.J., Elizabeth, W7899
Samuel, N.J., BLWt.8449-100-Pvt. Iss. 2/10/1792
JOBE, Enoch, Va. See JOB
JOBS, Richard, N.J., S39792
JOEL, Richard, Mass., BLWt.4462-100-Pvt. Iss. 12/31/1793 to Samuel Emery. No papers
Richard, Cont., Mass., Betty,

JOEL (continued)
W26680
JOHN, Elhanan, Va., Catharine, W3260
Thomas, Md., S34943
William, Pa., Isabella, R5591
JOHNES, Elias, Mass. See JONES
Michael, N.J. See JONES
Timothy, N.J., Abigail, W468
JOHNS, George, Va., S36025
Jacob, Navy, Del., Elizabeth, W1192
James, Va., Mary, R5593
John, S.C., R5592
Samuel, Mass., S32918
Stephen, Mass., S10926
Thomas, Va., S41707
Zachariah, Va., R5594
JOHNSON, Abel, Mass., Vt., Susannah Streeter, former wid., R10262; BLWt.237424-1855
Abel, N.C., Ann, R5600
Abigail, former wid. of John Baker, R.I., which see
Abner, Ct., Anna, W21481
Abner, N.C., Nancy, R5649
Abraham, Ct., BLWt.6032-100-Pvt. Iss. 9/29/1790. No papers
Abraham, Ct., S36650
Abraham, N.J., S13552
Abraham, N.Y., S43729
Abraham, S.C., S38099
Abraham, Va., S16427
Abram, N.C., S8770
Absalom, Md., S15484
Adam, N.H., Mary, R5644
Adrian, N.J., S3336
Alexander, N.C., Esther, W5034
Alexander, N.C., Franky, R15508
Alexander, Va., Jane, R5631
Amos, Ct., S13575; BLWt.26779-160-55
Amos, Ct., Lucene/Luceny, W21473
Amos, Mass., S32916
Andrew, N.H., War of 1812, Catharine, W7936; BLWt.3241-100. Iss. 1/26/1796 to James L. Neal, ass. No papers. BLWt.71774-40-50 & 117-60-5
Andrew, N.J., S45422; BLWt.8420-100-Pvt. Iss. 9/18/1799 to Mahlon Dickerson. No papers
Andrew, N.J., Pa., Indian Wars 1791-1797, S15905
Andrew, N.C., R5599
Ann, former wid. of Joseph Stout Navy, N.J., which see
Archibald, Md., S34938; BLWt. 1388-100
Arthur, Va., Lucy, W10152
Asa, Mass., S20420
Asa, Mass. See JONSON
Azel, Mass., S2658
Bailey, Va., Hannah, W4006
Barnabas, N.C., S4448
Barney, N.J., S33345
Barny/Barney, Md., S39783
Benedict, Md., BLWt.11404-100-Pvt. Iss. 2/1/1790. No papers
Benjamin, Ct., BLWt.6015-100-Pvt. Iss. 4/12/1792 to Stephen Thorne. No papers

JOHNSON (continued)
Benjamin, Ct., Susannah Foot, former wid., W7299
Benjamin, Cont., N.J., Ann, W4467
Benjamin, Md., BLWt.11378-100-Pvt. Iss. 3/11/1791. No papers
Benjamin, Md., Elizabeth Price, former wid., W27761
Benjamin, Mass., R.I., S32917
Benjamin, N.H., BLWt.3242-100-Pvt. Iss. 4/15/1796 to Joseph Cannon, ass. No papers
Benjamin, N.H., Priscilla, W1191
Benjamin, N.J., S1033
Benjamin, N.C., Charity, W13; BLWt.44545-160-55
Benjamin, Va., Phebe, R5651
Benjamin, Va., Rebecca, R5652; BLReg. 291229-1855; see Benjamin Johnson, R5674
Benjamin, Va., R5674
Benoni, Ct., S13578
Bristol/Briston, Ct., Vira, W20207; BLWt.1592-160-55
Bulkley, Mass., S43721
Caleb, Ct., Naomi, W26802
Caleb, Ga., S7081
Caleb, Mass., Elizabeth, W21490
Caleb, N.J., Esther, W4251
Calvin, Ct., Sally, W20205; BLWt.31282-160-55
Candace, former wid. of Wm. Harkston, R.I., which see
Catharine, former wid. of Nathan Spicer, N.Y., which see
Cave, Va., S8767
Charles, Cont., N.H., S43714
Charles, Md., S35470
Charles, Va., S5643
Christopher, N.J., S2670
Clabourn, Va., S16892
Comfort, Artillery Artificiers BLWt.13262-100-Pvt. Iss. 12/6/1791 to Stephen Thorn, ass. No papers
Comfort, Cont., Mass., S10917
Constant, Ct., Thankful, R5668
Daniel, Ct., S46051
Daniel, Ct., Cont., S45423
Daniel, Cont., Ct., S36644
Daniel, Mass., Lois, W20203
Daniel, N.H., Jane, W2735; BLWt.9199-160-55
Daniel, N.Y., BLWt.7328-100-Pvt. Iss. 7/10/1790 to John Quackinboss, ass. No papers
Daniel, Pa., S33341
David, Ct., Eunice, W15779
David, Ct., Mary, W21463
David, Ct., Cont., S13547
David, Cont., Mass., S30517
David, Cont., N.Y., S43722; BLWt. 7334-100-Corp. Iss. 6/8/1789. No papers
David, Mass., Prudence, W20200
David, Mass., Mary, W26677
David, Mass., Sea Service, S18902
David, N.H., Mary, W21465
David, N.J., S13555
David, Pa., Catharine, W5009
David, Va., S5641

JOHNSON (continued)
David, Va., S32349
Dennis, Mass., S36658
Dilmus/Dalmath/Dillamus, Va., Nancy, S2662
Ebenezer, Ct., S13570
Ebenezer, Ct., S17519
Ebenezer, Ct.,(son of John), Elizabeth, W1294; BLWt.30765-160-55
Ebenezer, Mass., Eleanor, W21476; BLWt.658-100
Ebenezer, Pa., R5608
Ebenezer, R.I., S21322
Edmond, Va., S30509
Edward, Ct., S13572
Edward, Ct., R5609
Edward, Md. & U.S. Navy 1786-1799, R5612 1/2 & Old Act Navy Inv. File 833
Edward, Mass., BLWt.4451-100-Sgt. Iss. 7/31/1798 to Zeb[e] Douglass. No papers
Edward, Mass., S45424
Edward, Mass., Relief, W26698
Elias, Ct., S29263
Elijah, Ct., S44463
Elijah, Mass., S13589
Elijah, Mass., R---
Elijah, N.C., S18060
Eliphalet, Ct., R5611
Elisha, Ct., S29933
Elisha, Ct., Mary Brigham, former wid., W17348
Elisha, Ct., Cont., S45425
Elisha, Mass., S18472
Elisha Edwards, S.C., S38885
Ellis, Va., Mary, W7941; BLWt. 267 67-160-55
Enos, Va., Levinia, W11959; BLWt.26160-160-55
Ephraim, Ct., Hoptill/Hopstill/Hopestill Dean, former wid., W16237
Ephraim, Cont., Mass., S44464
Ezekiel, R.I., Rosanna, W437
Fenn, Ct., Rebecca, W20212
Francis, S.C., Margaret Miller, former wid., W21805
George, N.J., S33339
George, N.Y., S43713. See case of Geo. Johnstone, same state and number
George, N.C., Va., S7096
George, ---, Frances, widow's res. Tenn., R5612
George, Va., S23731
Gideon, Ct., S17515
Gideon, N.C., S4456
Gideon, Va. See JOHNSTON
Giles, Va., S38090
Hardy, N.C., S16428
Hardy, Va.(?), R5616
Harmon, Mass., Demaris, W10157
Henry, Ct., Huldah, R5619
Henry, Cont., N.J., Sarah, R5660
Henry, Del., R5618
Henry, Mass., Betsey, W15780
Henry, N.J., R5617
Henson, Va., S16171; BLWt.26778-160-55
Hezekiah, Ct. & War of 1812,

JOHNSON (continued)
N.Y., S19353
Howell, Va., Holly, W4468; BLWt. 26766-160-55
Hugh, Pa., BLWt.9698-100-Pvt. Iss. 7/16/1789. No papers
Hugh, Pa., S36641
Ichabod, Ct., S10928
Ichabod, Mass., Sarah, W14982
Ira, Mass., BLWt.4484-100-Pvt. Iss. 4/1/1790. No papers
Isaac, Ct., BLWt.6012-100-Pvt. Iss. 7/14/1789. No papers
Isaac, Ct., S10920
Isaac, Ct., Lucy, W20209
Isaac, Ct., Rebekah, W20211
Isaac, Mass., S30515
Isaac, Mass., S32928
Isaac, Mass., Dinah, W21479
Isaac, Mass. Sea Service, S28774
Isaac, N.H., S32927
Isaac, N.J., BLWt.8424-100-Pvt. Iss. 4/23/1790 to Joseph Meeker, ass. No papers
Isaac, N.J., Agnes, R5598
Isaac, N.Y., Hannah, R5615
Isaac, N.C., Privateer, S5645
Isaac, Pa., Va., S36642
Isaac, R.I., Elizabeth, W21464
Isaac, Va., S21326
Isaiah, Ct., S13581
Israel, Ct., BLWt.6007-100-Pvt. Iss. 6/21/1791. No papers
Israel, Ct., S43726
Israel, Ct., Huldah, W26681
Ithamar, Mass., BLWt.4459-100-Pvt. Iss. 8/30/1790. No papers
Jacob, ---, Va. res., Dis. No papers
Jacob, Cont., Ct., Mass. Sea Service, R5623
Jacob, Cont., N.Y., Isaac Baker, R415
Jacob, Mass., Esther, W20210; BLWt.4481-100-Corp. Iss. 10/12/1789. No papers
Jacob, Mass., Rachel, W26676
Jacob, N.J., Sarah, W796
Jacob, N.J., R---
Jacob, N.J., N.Y., S2660
Jacob, N.C., Nancy, R5622
Jacob, Pa., S22332
Jacob, S.C., BLWt.12290 & 13246-100-Pvt. Iss. 9/28/1796 to John Young, ass. No papers
Jacob, S.C., S13579
Jacob, Va., Dis. No papers
James, Sheldon's Dragoons, Ct., BLWt.6038-100-Q.M. Sgt. Iss. 10/7/1789 to Benjamin Tallmadge
James, Ct., S43720
James, Ct., S45417
James, Ct., Phebe, W26163; BLWt. 39212-160-55
James, Cont., Ct., S13557
James, Cont., N.H., Hannah, W21494
James, Cont., Va., S36664; BLWt.1963-100
James, Mass., Hannah, W26697; he d. in 1814
James, Mass., R5630

JOHNSON (continued)
James, Mass., Rebeccah, R5653
James, Mass., N.H., Anna, W1436; BLWt.10296-160-55
James, Mass., Sea Service, Hannah P., W2122; BLWt.14670-160-55. He d. 2/10/1838
James, N.J., S1031
James, N.J., S29260
James, N.J., Elizabeth, W142
James, N.J., R5629
James, N.C., Delila, R5607
James, Pa., Mary, S38906; BLWt. 1719-100
James, Pa., Sarah, W9089; BLWt. 2363-160-55
James, S.C., Mary, W9088
James, Va., BLWt.12257-100-Pvt. Iss. 4/16/1794. No papers
James, Va., S15904
James, Va., S16891
James, Va. See JOHNSTON
James, Va., S35471
James, Va., S36636
James, Va., Esther, W7934
James, Va., R5628
Jane, former wid. of Samuel Cooper, Pa., which see
Jared, R.I., Rebecca, W14983
Jedediah, Ct., Lucy, W7943; BLWt.27671-160-55
Jedidiah/Jedediah, Vt., Elizabeth, W26679
Jeremiah, N.H., S39789
Jeremiah, N.Y., Sarah, R5661
Jesse, Cont., N.C., S38884
Jesse, Mass., Sarah, W21478
Job, R.I., S23281
John, Ct., S36027
John, Ct., S38877
John, Ct., Mary, W7933
John, Ct., Abigail, W20198
John, Ct., Clarissa, W27621; BLWt.7439-160-55
John, Cont., Va. res. of son in 1828; BLWt.1362-100
John, Cont., Mass., S32914
John, Cont., N.C., S.C., R5635
John, Cont., Va., S38082
John, Cont., Va., R5634
John, Md., Elizabeth Mahoney, former wid., W4278
John, Mass., BLWt.4456-100-Pvt. Iss. 7/14/1796. No papers
John, Mass., BLWt.4472-100-Pvt. Iss. 4/18/1796 to Jere Mason. No papers
John, Mass., BLWt.4475-100-Pvt. Iss. 1/28/1790 to Joseph May. No papers
John, Mass., S10931
John, Mass., S45419
John, Mass., Lydia, W8226; BLWt.26397-160-55
John, Mass., Lydia, W14979
John, Mass., Abigail, W21488
John, Mass., Anna Tibbetts/Tibbets, former wid., W26533; BLWt.215-60-55
John, Mass., Jane, W26809
John, Mass., BLWt.802-100
John, Mass., Navy, S33338

JOHNSON (continued)
John, N.H., Sally, W21491
John, N.J., BLWt.8434-100-Sgt. Iss. 5/25/1790. No papers
John, N.J., BLWt.8443-100-Pvt. Iss. 5/26/1790 to Joshua Mersereau
John, N.J., S2665
John, N.J., S23730
John, N.J., Anna Maria, W20197
John, N.J., N.Y., S13580
John, Lamb's Art., N.Y., BLWt. 7318-100-Pvt. Iss. 9/1/1791 to John W. Watkins, ass. BLWt. 7535. No papers
John, N.Y., S5646
John, N.Y., S43723
John, N.Y., Hannah, W26692
John, N.Y., Caty, R5604
John, N.Y., BLWt.1143-300-Capt. Iss. 9/29/1790. No papers
John, N.C., S30512
John, N.C., ---. These papers were taken from claim of Tabitha, wid. of John M. Johnson or Moses Johnson, N.C., R5666. There is a difference in services as well as in names, and discrepancies in other things are so many that the two claims cannot be the same man F.W. 9/26/1911. On 4/27/1836 he made affidavit & he was then a res. of Pickins Co., Ala., aged about 74 years.
John, N.C., Rosannah, W5011
John, Va.,S32345; BLWt.26351-160-55
John, Va., S35480
John, Va., S36026
John, Va., Elizabeth, W9086
John A., Navy, R.I., S38880
John B., Va., BLWt.1167-300-Capt. Iss. 7/3/1799 to Robt. Camp, ass. No papers
John H., Ga., S.C., Sarah, W4464
John Jacob, N.J., S23734
John M./Moses, N.C., Tabitha, R5666
John R., N.J., S666
Jonah, Mass., Mary, W15686; BLWt. 26439-160-55
Jonas, Mass., S32904
Jonathan, Ct., BLWt.1136-450-Lt. Col. Iss. 1/19/1789. No papers
Jonathan, Cont., N.H., Rhoda, W20199
Jonathan, Mass., S32906
Jonathan, Mass., S36660
Jonathan, Mass., Annis, W15781
Jonathan, Mass., Elizabeth, W21495
Jonathan, N.Y., Elizabeth Lane, former wid., R6120. See other husb., William Lane, N.Y.
Jonathan, S.C., S31779
Joseph, ---, Md. res. of wid. in 1855, Elizabeth, BLWt.36520-160-55
Joseph, Ct., R5637
Joseph, Ct., Cont., S13550
Joseph, Ct., Cont., BLWt.1277-100
Joseph, Cont., N.H., Polly,W26689

JOHNSON (continued)
Joseph, Cont., Va., Elizabeth Williamson, former wid., R11631
Joseph, Md., BLWt.11377-100-Pvt. Iss. 2/28/1795. No papers
Joseph, Md., S46091
Joseph, Mass., BLWt.4490-100-Pvt. Iss. 1/19/1792 to Resolve Waldron. No papers
Joseph, Mass., S16895
Joseph, N.J., S2659
Joseph, N.J., Mary, W7937; BLWt. 15423-160-55
Joseph, N.J., Martha, W7938
Joseph, N.Y., Grace, W16313
Joseph/Thomas Rosekrans, N.Y., R5636
Joseph, N.C., S7085
Joseph, N.C., S7093
Joseph, Pa., S35481
Joseph, Pa., R5639
Joseph, Va., S31782
Joseph Payne, Va., S38095
Joshua, Mass., Martha, W13552
Joshua, N.H., S21323; BLWt.2365-160-55
Josiah, Ct., S16893
Josiah, Ct., N.Y., R5641
Josiah, Va., Susan, R5665
Jotham, Mass., Eunice, W21497
Justus, Ct., S13566
Lawrence, Ct., Grace, W20202
Lawrence/Anthony McLean, N.Y., Margaret, W764; BLWt.13725-160-55
Lebeus/Lebius/Libeus, Mass., S43711
Levi, Ct., Ruth, W1777; BLWt. 9231-160-55
Lewis, N.J., BLWt.8417-100-Pvt. Iss. 4/11/1792. No papers
Libeus, Mass. See Lebeus
Luther, Mass., S13562
Mary, former wid. of Daniel Brewster, Mass., which see
Mehitable/Hitty, former wid. of Wm. Hasey, Mass., which see
Micah, Va., R5648
Miles, Ct., S22855
Moses, Mass., Vt., S16897
Moses, N.J., S13551
Moses, N.C., Nancy, W153
Moses, N.C., Rebecca, R5654
Moses, N.C., Tabitha, See John M.
Moses, Va., S36024
Nahum, Va., S7079
Nathan, Mass., S10922
Nathan, Mass., S32929
Nathan, Mass., Mary, W26675
Nathaniel, Ct., S45418
Nathaniel, Ct., Rebekah, W11979
Nathaniel, Ct., Sarah, R5662
Nathaniel, Cont., Mass., S32926
Nathaniel, Mass., S32905
Nathaniel, Mass., S32920
Nathaniel, N.C., S1841
Nicholas, N.Y., BLWt.7333-100-Pvt. Iss. 7/10/1790 to John Quackinboss, ass. No papers
Obadiah, Mass., Azubah, W21467
Obadiah, Va., Mary, R5646
Orange, Mass., S45421

JOHNSON (continued)
Orringh, Mass., BLWt.4455-100-Pvt. Iss. 7/6/1796 to Wm. Woodward, ass. No papers
Othniel, N.J., S41709
Ozias, Cont., Mass., S22338
Peleg, R.I., S38881
Peter, Cont., N.J., S38886; BLWts.2042-100 & 52-60-55
Peter, Mass., S32930
Peter, N.H., Dis. No papers
Peter, N.Y., S36643; BLWt.1263-100
Pheneas/Pinchas, Ct., BLWt.6017-100-Pvt. Iss. 12/15/1795 to Eneas Munson, Jr. No papers
Philemon, Vt., S2667
Philip, Cont., Va., S36657
Philip, Jr., N.H., BLWt.3240-100-Pvt. Iss. 5/25/1795 to Joseph Brown, ass. No papers
Philip, N.Y., Susannah, W11982; BLWt.102113-160-55
Phineas, Mass., S16429
Phinehas, Ct., S36639
Reuben, Ct., S16167
Reuben, N.C., Nancy, W10156
Reynolds, Ct., S13544; BLWt. 26472-160-55
Rhoda, former wid. of Benjamin Thompson, Mass., which see
Richard, Cont., Ala. res. & agcy. Frances, W11956
Richard, Md., R5657
Richard, Mass., S29928
Richard, Va., BLWt.12275-100-Pvt. Iss. 4/13/1791 to James Reynolds, ass. No papers
Richard, Va., S2664
Richard, Va., S8766
Richard, Va., S16896
Robert, ---, N.Y. Res. Dis. No papers
Robert, N.C., b. Pa., Elizabeth, W371
Robert, Jr., Pa., BLWt.9707-100-Pvt. Iss. 2/4/1793 to Alexander Power, ass. No papers
Robert, Pa., S5637
Robert, Va., S1838
Roland, Va., S21846
Rufus, Ct., S13576
Rufus, Ct., Mass., Mary, W5647
Rufus, Mass., S13545
Rufus, R.I., Vt., S13546
Samuel, Hazen's Regt., BLWt. 13249-100-Pvt. Iss. 3/28/1797. No papers
Samuel, Ct., S13569
Samuel, Ct., S15481
Samuel, Ct., S43710
Samuel, Ct., R5655
Samuel, Ct., R5659
Samuel, Ct., BLWt.1141-400-Major. Iss. 7/23/1789 to Samuel Johnson. No papers
Samuel, Cont., N.Y. res. & agcy. S45420
Samuel, Cont., N.Y., Elizabeth, W16619
Samuel, Mass., S18475
Samuel, Navy, Mass., Privateer, S32908

JOHNSON (continued)
Samuel, N.H., S44462
Samuel, N.H., Betsey, W16312
Samuel, N.J., S1032
Samuel, N.J., Mary, W20208; BLWt.27643-160-55
Samuel, N.Y., BLWt.7322-100-Pvt. Iss. 8/10/1790 to John Warren, ass. No papers
Samuel, N.Y., S23280
Samuel, N.C., Mary, W5012
Samuel, N.C., Va., b. Pa., S16430
Samuel, Pa., BLWt.9694-100-Pvt. Iss. 7/9/1789. No papers
Samuel, Vt., S18907
Samuel, Va., Patsey, W7939
Seth, Ct., Abigail, W1295
Seth, Cont., Mass., Mary, W14980; BLWt.15409-160-55
Seth, Mass., S9922
Shadrach, Ct., Hannah, W20201
Shepherd, N.Y., Dis. No papers
Shubal, Ct., BLWt.6018-100-Pvt. Iss. 4/11/1792 to Jonas Prentice No papers
Silas, Ct., S5636
Silas, Va., BLWt.12277-100-Pvt. Iss. 6/29/1793 to John Spencer, ass. No papers
Silas, Va., S41705
Solomon, Ct., BLWt.430-100
Solomon, N.C., Rachel, W20204
Solomon, N.C., R---
Solomon, Va., R5664
Stephen, Ct., S10919
Stephen, Ct., Cont., Persis, W21487
Stephen, Mass., S18909
Stephen, Mass., S29261
Stephen W., Ct., Sea Service, Navy, W28776
Sylvester, R.I., S21321
Teresha/Terisha, Va., R5667
Theodata, Ct., Ruth, W26672
Thias, Mass., S43709
Thomas, Md., S13553
Thomas, Md., Margery, W13555
Thomas, Mass., S36661; BLWt. 940-100
Thomas, N.H., Abigail, R5596
Thomas, N.J., S33334
Thomas, N.J., S33337
Thomas, N.J., Abigail, W7940; BLWt.12847-160-55
Thomas, N.C., S41698
Thomas, Pa., BLWt.9687-100-Pvt. Iss. 5/26/1794 to Michael Stever, ass. No papers
Thomas, Pa., Dis. No papers
Thomas, Pa., S38882
Thomas, Pa., S41708
Thomas, Va., S18064
Thomas, Va., S31177
Thomas, Va., S38100
Timothy, Ct., S22853
Timothy, Cont., Ct., S36645
Timothy, Cont., Mass., Betsey, W16618
Timothy, Mass., Sarah, W16620
Timothy, Mass., Chloe, R5605
Turner, Ct., S43724

JOHNSON (continued)
Uriah, Mass., Betsey, W1194; BLWt.11151-160-55
Uriah, N.Y., Charity Eisenburgh/ Eisenburg, former wid., W16247
Uzal, Ct., R.I., Mehitable, W26161
William, Pvt., Ct., BLWt.6035 iss. 8/23/1790
William, Ct., S8761
William, Ct., S36635
William, Ct., S36651
William, Ct., Hadassah, W5305; BLWt.30762-160-55
William, Ct., Anna White, former wid., W27500; BLWt.102200-160-55
William, Cont., N.Y. res., S45426 BLWt.1128-200-Capt. Iss. 7/7/ 1791. No papers
William, Cont., Mass., S10925
William, Cont., Mass., S13563
William, Cont., Va., d.1833, Elizabeth, W7932
William, Ga., R5669
William, Md., S41704
William, Mass., BLWt.4463-100- Pvt. Iss. 12/22/1791 to Silas Pepoon. No papers
William, Mass., S29934
William, Mass., S36659
William, Mass., S39786
William, Mass., Zady, W5010; BLWt.26433-160-55 & 36228-160-55
William, Mass., Lucy, W14978; BLWt.30764-160-55
William, Navy, Ct., S36634
William, N.H., Rhoda, W16035
William, N.J., S18678
William, N.J., R5670
William, N.Y., BLWt.7321-100-Pvt. Iss. 4/19/1791 to Moses Hetfield ass. No papers
William, N.Y., S48926
William, N.Y., Catharine, W20213
William, N.C., S7088
William, N.C., b. Va., S7095
William, N.C., b. Va., S8764
William, N.C., S15189
William, N.C., Va., b. Va., S2661
William, Pa., S5644
William, Pa., S33340
William, R.I., S21842
William, S.C., b. N.C., S10918
William, Vt., R5671
William, Va., S1226
William, Va., S13583
William, Va., S30510
William, Va., S46050
William, Va., Nancy, W24
William, Va., Margaretta, W10151
William, Va., Nancy/Alsey, R5650
William, Va., R5672
William, Va., R5673, enl. King William Co., Va., d. 1826/27
William E., Va. Sea Service, R49; See N.A. Acc. No. 837-Va. State Navy - YS File Half Pay
Windsor, N.J., S43725; BLWt.8438-100-Pvt. Iss. 5/21/1794. No papers
Zachariah, N.C., S32344
Zopher, Va., S1840

JOHNSTON, Andrew, H.H., BLWt.3241-100-Pvt. Iss. 1/26/1796 to James A. Neal, ass. No papers. & BLWt. 117-60-55. No papers
Andrew, N.J., S668
Andrew, Pa., BLWt.1152-200-Lt. Iss. 7/7/1789. No papers
Archibald, Va., S38091
Benjamin, Cont., Ct., Clarissa, W1435; BLWt.26781-160-55
Benjamin, Md., R5602
Cato, Pa., BLWt.9665-100-Pvt. Iss. 4/10/1793 to Philip Stout, ass. No papers
Crawford, N.C., Sally, W21486; BLWt.1284-100
Daniel, Pa., BLWt.9663-100-Pvt. Iss. 11/26/1795 to Christian Hubbard, ass. No papers
David, Mass. Sea Service, N.H., R5675
David, Lamb's Art., N.Y., BLWt. 7334-100-Corp. Iss. 6/8/1789. No papers
David, N.C., S13587
Drewry/Drury, N.C., Rhoda, R5656
Eleanor, former wid. of Alexander McKay, Cont., N.Y., which see
Francis, Md., BLWt.346-100
Francis, N.C., Hannah, S13585 & R5614
Francis, Pa., BLWt.1148-500-Col. Iss. 7/3/1789. No papers
Frederick, S.C., Eda, W4004
George, N.J., BLWt.8441-100-Pvt. Iss. 1/1/1793. No papers
George, N.Y., S43713. See George JOHNSTONE, same state & number
George, Va., S38088
Gideon, Va., S38089 N.A. Acc. No. 874-050093; Half Pay
Henry, Ct., BLWt.6011-100-Pvt. Iss. 10/22/1789 to Theodosius Fowler. No papers
Henry, Mass., Polly, W14981
Henry, N.J., BLWt.8416-100-Pvt. Iss. 2/11/1800 to Abraham Bell, ass. No papers
Hugh, Pa., S39790
Isaac, Pa., BLWt.7336 & 9661-100-Pvt. Iss. 3/2/1792 to Thomas Shaw, ass. No papers
Isaac, Pa., Va. See JOHNSON
James, Ga., S36633
James, Mass., Sea Service, R5626
James, N.J., S4454
James, N.Y., BLWt.1144-200-Lt. Iss. 9/15/1790 to John Sloss Hobart, Egbert Benton, John McKesson, Ebenezer Howard, & Richard Platt, executors of the estate of Alex. McDougall, ass. No papers
James, N.C., S16168
James, Pa., S2298
James, Pa., S2666
James, Pa., S16165
James, Pa., S23732
James, Pa., Betsey, W21462
James, Pa., R5627
James, S.C., S21843
James, Va., S1225; BLWt.34964-

JOHNSTON (continued)
160-55
James, Va., S5640
James, Va., Ann, W7935; BLWt. 1735-100
James, Va., Joice, W7945; BLWt. 121-60-55 & 12271-100
John, Del., BLWt.10794-100-Pvt. Iss. 1/25/179? to George Stout, ass. No papers
John, Mass., S39785
John, Navy, Ct., Ruth, W26673
John, N.J., S36646; BLWt.1735-100
John, N.J., S39793
John, N.J., S43712
John, N.J., BLWt.8434-100-Sgt.
John, N.J., BLWt.8443-100-Pvt. No papers
John, N.Y., S29927
John, Pa., BLWt.9667-100-Pvt. Iss. 11/12/1791. No papers
John, Pa., BLWt.9681-100-Pvt. Iss. 10/24/177? to Owen McCarthy Admr. No papers
John, Pa., S22336
John, Pa., R5633
John, S.C., Martha, W7942
John, Va., S1958
John, Va., b. Ireland, S8763
John, Va., S31168
Jonas, N.C., Esther, W21470
Joseph, ---, Phila. agcy. Dis. No papers
Joseph, Corps of Invalids, BLWt. 13263-100-Sgt. Iss. 9/4/1789. No papers
Joseph, Mass., Charlotte Badger, former wid., W4126
Joseph, N.J., BLWt.969-100
Joseph, N.C., Nancy, W5033
Joseph, Pa., BLWt.9682-100-Pvt. Iss. 2/19/180?. No papers
Joseph, Va., S36654
Lancelot, N.C., Zerniah/Zerviah, W5114
Lewis, N.J., BLWt.8429-100-Pvt. Iss. 8/21/1789 to Elias Dayton & Son, assnes. No papers
Lewis, N.J., S890
Lewis, N.C., R5643
Lewis, Va., R5642
Martin, Va., Nancy, W436
Michael, N.H., Sarah, W20216
Nathaniel, N.C. See JOHNSON
Nicholas, Md., S34942
Peleg, R.I., BLWt.3250-100-Pvt. Iss. 12/31/1789. No papers
Peter, Cont., Va., Anne B., W27629; BLWt.1171-200-Lt. Iss. 9/9/1789 to Henry Lee, execr. of the last will & testament of Alexander Skinner, dec'd., late ass. No papers
Peter, N.J., S667
Richard, Cont., Va., S5639
Richard, N.Y., R5678
Richard, Va., S38873
Robert, Cont., Pa., S38872
Robert, Gen. Hospital, BLWt. 1178-450-Physician & Surgn. Iss. 10/15/1789. No papers
Robert, N.C., S7092

JOHNSTON (continued)
Robert, N.C., S.C., S15482
Robert, Pa., BLWt.9706-100-Pvt. "in Proctor's Artillery". Iss. 7/27/1789 to Richard Platt, ass. No papers
Robert, S.C., S36637
Robert, Vt., Hepzibah, W21483. Also an affidavit of this wid. in claim W24566 of Betsey, wid. of Nehemiah Lovewell
Samuel, N.J., BLWt.8446-100-Pvt. Iss. 8/26/1789 to James Gray, ass. No papers
Samuel, N.Y., Elizabeth, W20217
Samuel, R.I., S43719
Samuel, Va., S18066
Samuel C., N.J., Margaret, W20215
Solomon, S.C., S34944; BL Rej.
Stephen, Va., BLWt.12279-100-Pvt. Iss. 5/11/1793 to John Stockdale ass. ("This man's name is Stockdale & Stockdell elsewhere in the old book. MHP.")
Thomas, Cont., Pa., Sarah, W10158
Thomas, Va., Rachel, W254
William, Cont., Mass., S39791
William, Del., Ann, BLWt.2086-100
William, N.J., BLWt.8435-100-Pvt. Iss. 5/21/1799 to Abraham Bell, ass. No paper
William, N.J., S13567
William, N.J., Sarah, R5680
William, N.Y., S10923
William, Pa. "Corps of Invalids," BLWt.9658 & 13265-100-Pvt. Iss. 12/18/1799 to David Morgan, ass. No papers
William, Pa., S39795
William, Pa., Sidney, W4250
William, Pa., Margaret, R5677
William, S.C., S18062
William, Va., S31780
William, Va., BLWt.1166-300-Capt. Iss. 7/5/1799 to James Taylor, ass. No papers
Windsor, N.J., BLWt.8438-100-Pvt. Iss. 5/21/1794. No papers
Witter, N.Y., S23729
JOHNSTONE, George, N.Y., S43713
Peter, Pa., S---. He enl. for 3 yrs. in fall of 1776 with Capt. John Wilson, Col. Brodhead's 8th Pa. Regt. In 1779 he transferred to Capt. Samuel Brady's Co. of Riflemen & discharged at end of 3 yrs. by Lt. Col. Bayard. He was pensioned as a Pvt. at $80 per annum, on Cert. No. 938 which iss. 9/30/1829. In 1832 he resided in Monongalia Co., Va. & d. 9/6/1840.
JOHONNOT, Gabriel, Cont., Mass., S36666
Oliver, Mass. Sea Service, Privateer, S29929
Prince, Mass., S18057
William, Cont., Mass. res. in 1833 BLWt.2231-400
JOICE, Jonathan, Mass., Mary Harvey former wid., R4713
JOINER, Benjamin, N.C., BLWts.12283

JOINER (continued)
& 13248-100-Pvt. Iss. 5/18/1797 to Gabriel Holmes, ass. No papers
Hepsibah, former wid. of Janner Sutlief, Ct., which see
Jonathan, Ga., Elizabeth, W300
Michael, Cont., Navy, Pa. res. & agcy., S7078
Moses, Va. See JOYNER
Nathan, N.C., R5684
Thomas, N.C., S7090
JOLIFF, Eunice, former wid. of John Lockwood, Ct., which see
JOLLEY, Boling, Va., R5686, b. Dinwiddie Co., Va. M. in Chatham Co., N.C.,in 1842 res. of Morgan Co., Ill.
Lewis, N.J., S1034
Wilson, S.C. See JOLLY
JOLLY, Henry, Pa., S41710
John, S.C., Sarah Savage, former wid., W9276
Joseph, S.C., Elizabeth, R5687
Mayberry, Pa., BLWt.1157-300-Capt. Iss. 5/12/1796 to Chas. Jolly, Admr. in trust for the heirs of said M.J. No papers
William, Ct., Desire, W20196
Wilson, S.C., Mary, R5688
JOLLYWOOD, John, N.Y. See JERVIS
JONAH, Christiana, former wid. of Titus Fuller, Mass., which see
Jacob, Mass., S32910
JONAS, Jeremiah, See JONES
John, N.J., Md. res., Dis., BLWt.593-100. No papers
JONCE, Henry, Pa., R5689
JONES, Aaron, Md., BLWt.11391-100-Pvt. Iss. 2/1/1790. No papers
Aaron, Md., S34937, enl. in Talbot Co., Md. In 1818 was res. of Dorchester Co., Md., age 58 years
Abel, Del., or Md., Pa., Margaret, R5723, enl. in New Castle, Del., d. 9/1/1831
Abel, Mass., Lucinda, W13554, enl. in Holden, Worcester Co., Mass. In 1818, aged 59 yrs. & res. of Winchendon, Worcester Co., Mass.; d. there 8/29/1836
Abraham, N.J., S2294, b. 11/25/1752 in Maurice River Twp., Cumberland Co., N.J. res. there at enl. and in 1832
Abraham, Va., S46452; BLWt.1893-100. In 1832 aged 71 yrs. & res. of Buckingham Co., Va.
Abraham P., Ga., S38087. In 1819 aged 66 yrs. & res. of Wilkes Co., Ga., d. 1/28/1831. Wife's name was Ann.
Albridgton, Va., BLWt.359-200. In 1807 a res. of Southampton Co., Va.
Alexander, N.J., BLWt.8432-100-Pvt. Iss. 3/10/1790. No papers
Alexander, N.J., S33335, enl.

JONES (continued)
at Deerfield, N.J. In 1818 aged 59 yrs. & res. of Pitts Grove, Salem Co., N.J. Wife Anna
Alexander, Va., S34939. In 1820 aged 60 yrs. Res. Prince Georges Co., Md. Wife Mary
Allen G., Mass. See Goodspeed JONES
Ambrose, Cont., Va., Martha, W9083 b. 8/10/1756, enl. in Augusta Co., Va. In 1821 res. Floyd Co., Ky., d. 6/12/1833
Ambrose, N.J., BLWt.8447-100-Pvt. Iss. 6/16/1789 to Thos. Coyle, ass. No papers
Amos, Ct., Lydia, W20183; b.1/17/1748, res. at enl. Colchester, Mass.; res. in 1832, Rush, Monroe Co., N.Y., d. 9/10/1840
Amos, Mass.,S35473, b. Lunenburg, Mass. In 1818 aged 57 yrs., res. Unity, Kennebec Co.,Me. Wife Mary
Amos, Mass., Azubah, W13560; b. 6/21/1755 Weston, Middlesex Co., Mass., res. there at enl. In 1832 res. Lincoln, Middlesex Co., Mass.; d. 4/24/1836
Armstrong, Pvt., N.J., BLWt.8430 iss. 12/23/1790 to Silas Condist, ass.
Asa, Ct., S13558, enl. at Plainfield, Ct. In 1818 aged 60 yrs.; res. Chagrin, Cuyahoga Co., Ohio. In 1825 res. Henrietta, Monroe Co., N.Y. In 1837 res. Hebron, Tolland Co., Ct.
Asa, Ct., N.Y., S13568, b. 5/15/1740 at Saybrook, Ct.; res. at enl. Horseneck, Ct.; res. in 1832, Green, Chenango Co., N.Y.; d. 11/26/1832
Asa, Mass., S13584,enl. at Lunenburg, Mass. In 1819, res. Groton, Middlesex Co., Mass., in 1820 aged 61 yrs., res. Rindge, Cheshire Co., N.H., wife Mary
Asal, N.J., BLWt.8415-100-Q.M. Sgt. Iss. 4/4/1798. No papers
Asaph, Ct., Hannah, W1293; BLWt. 17704-160-55; b.9/11/1758 Preston, New London Co.,Ct. res. there at enl.;d. 3/31/1836-37 at Kingston, Luzerne Co., Pa.
Augustus, Ct., S18059, b. 8/11/1752 at Saybrook, Middlesex Co., there at enl. and in 1832
Barnabas, Cont., Mass., S38878. In 1820 aged 74 yrs. & res. of Providence, R.I.
Benjamin, Ct., S13565; b. 1764 at White Plains, N.Y.; res. at enl. Norwalk, Ct.; in 1832 res. Preble, Cortland Co., N.Y.
Benjamin, Ct., S45428, res. Coventry, Windham Co., Ct. prior to 1799. In 1825, aged 68 yrs., res. Coventry, Chenango Co.,N.Y.
Benjamin, Cont., Mass., S45430 In 1820 aged 84 yrs., res.Attica Genesee Co., N.Y. Wife Susanna
Benjamin, Del., BLWt.10795-100-

JONES (continued)
Pvt. Iss. 3/31/1797 to James DeBaufre, ass. No papers
Benjamin, Mass., Sarah, W1877, BLWt.9189-160-55; res. at enl. Taunton, Mass.; in 1837 aged 81 yrs., res. Turner, Oxford Co., Me.; d. 2/7/1838 at Turner
Benjamin, N.J., Rachel, W4465; b. 1/11/1754 in Kingwood Twp., Hunterdon Co., N.J. In 1833 res. of West Buffalo Twp., Union Co., Pa.; d. 12/11/1836
Benjamin, N.Y., Pa., S2295; b. 6/9/1763 at Goshen, N.Y.; res. during Rev., Luzerne Co., Pa. & Goshen, N.Y.; res. in 1832, Concord Twp., Champaign Co., Ohio
Benjamin, N.C. or S.C., Susannah, R5746; res. at enl. S.C.; d. Franklin Co., Tenn., 5/14/1815 or 1817
Benjamin, N.C., Va., S7076; b. 3/28/1754 in King William Co., Va.; lived there at 1st enl.; res. in 1832, Stokes Co., N.C.
Benjamin, Pa., S5626; b. 10/10/1757 in Harford Co., Md. & res. there at enl., but enl. at Peachbottom Twp., York Co., Pa. and lived there in 1847.
Benjamin, R.I. Sea Service, S38874. In 1820 aged 75 yrs. & res. of Providence, R.I.
Benjamin, S.C., S31172; b. 1760 or 1761 in Spartanburg Co., S.C. & res. there at enl.; in 1832 res. of Hickman Co., Ky.
Benjamin, Va. See JANES
Benjamin, Va., Elizabeth, R5699; res. at enl. Orange Co., Va.; d. 12/27/1820.
Berryman, Va., S5632; b. 1757 in Amherst Co., Va.; res. at enl. Augusta Co., Va.; res. in 1832, Greenbrier Co., Va.
Brereton, N.C., Martha Diana, W20193; b. 7/12/1755; res. at enl. Granville Co., N.C.; d. there 12/17/1810
Britain/Britton, N.C., Rhoda, R5739; enl. in Pitt Co., N.C. & res. there in 1818, then 57 yrs. old; d. 4/17/1847
Cadwallader, Cont., N.C. res. of son in 1838; BLWt.2308-
Cadwallader, S.C., Va., S1543; b. Lunenburg Co., Va. in 1745; res. at enl. Charlotte Co., Va. res. in 1832, Wilson Co.,Tenn.
Charles, Cont., Vt., Betsey, W21482; BLWt.12736-160-55; res. during Rev. Rehobeth, Mass. & Putney, Windham Co., Vt.; in 1823, aged 67 yrs. & res. of Providence, R.I.; in 1827 res. De Ruyter, Madison Co., N.Y.; d. 3/26/1836
Charles, Md., BLWt.11388-100-Pvt. Iss. 2/1/1790

JONES (continued)
Charles, N.C., S8759; b. Bertie Co., N.C.; res. at enl. Sampson Co., N.C.; there in 1832, aged about 90 years
Charles, N.C., Patsy, R5733, m. in Cleveland Co., N.C. In 1855 had been dead about 25 yrs.
Charles, S.C.,Nancy, R5731; m. in Laurens Dist., S.C.; d. 2/1/1822
Charles, Va., S36647, enl. in Bedford Co., Va. In 1819, res. Adair Co., Ky., aged 76 yrs.,d. 1840
Charles, Va., BLWt.1169-200-Lt. Iss. 2/24/1797 to John McKim, ass. No papers
Charles, Va. Sea Service, R50. Va. Half Pay. See N.A. Acct. No. 837 - Va. State Navy -YS File; d. 1/1/1810
Churchill, Cont., Va., BLWt.304-300. In 180-, res. of Chatham
Consider, Mass., S32913; enl. from Pelham, Mass. In 1818 aged 78 yrs.; res. Middleborough, Plymouth Co., Mass.
Cooper, N.C., R5694, res. Washington Co.,N.C.; d. 10/1797
Cornelius, Mass., Sea Service, Privateers, S31169; b. 1/30/1762 in Taunton, Bristol Co., Mass.; there at enl. In 1832 res. of Turner, Oxford Co., Me.
Cornelius, N.Y., S13564; b. 1759 at Warwick, Orange Co., N.Y.; res. there at enl. & in 1832; d. 3/26/1841
Cotter, Md., S34946; BLWt.2250-100. In 1818 aged 60 yrs. & res. Worcester Co., Md.; in 1820, aged 57 yrs., res. Somerset Co., Md. Wife Nancy
Crocker/Croker, Ct., S41702; enl. in Wyoming Valley, Pa. In 1818, aged 70 yrs., res. Plymouth, Luzerne Co., Pa.; in 1820, res. Delaware Co., Ohio; d. 12/27/1839
Daniel, Ct., Cont., S2297; b. 2/3/1757 at New London, Ct.; enl. at Lebanon, New London, Ct. In 1832 res. Morris Co., N.J.; d. 12/22/1847
Daniel, Cont., Ct., S45429. In 1824, aged 68 yrs., wife Caty; in 1823 res. Stevenstown, N.Y.
Daniel, N.Y., R5695; b. 12/29/1766; in 1833 res. Haverstraw, N.Y.
Daniel, N.C., S1915; b. 3/1757; res. at enl. Orange Co., N.C.; res. in 1832 Hawkins Co., Tenn.
Daniel, N.C., BLWt.506-300; res. Granville Co., N.C.
Darling, N.C., Nancy, W7922; BLWt.26674-160-55; b. 1764 in Wake Co., N.C., res. at enl. on frontiers in what was later Carter Co., Tenn; in 1834 res. of Washington Co., Tenn., d. there 10/9/1848

JONES (continued)
David, Ct., BLWt.6033-100-Pvt. Iss. 10/10/1791 to John Leinberger. No papers
David, Ct., S28777; b. 1751 in Colchester, Hartford Co., Ct. & res. there at enl.,in 1832 res. of Blenheim, Schoharie Co., N.Y.
David, Cont., Mass., Elizabeth, W5116. In 1818 aged 70 yrs., res. North Yarmouth, Cumberland Co., Me. D. there 3/27/1822
David, Ga., R5697. B. 3/2/1749 in Chester Co., Pa., res. at enl. Richmond Co., Ga. Res.in 1832, Meriwether Co., Ga.
David, Md., S8769. B. near Patuxent River in Prince Georges Co., Md. Res. there at enl. & in 1832, then 67 yrs. old
David, N.Y., S13586. B. 10/6/1762 at Fishkill, Dutchess Co., N.Y., & res. there at enl. In 1832 res. of Warwick, Orange Co., N.Y. D. 6/9/1833, wid. Margaret
David, N.C., S2653. B. 2/17/1763 in Dobbs Co., N.C. Res. there at enl.(it was later Greene Co.) In 1833 res. Knox Co., Tenn.
David, Va., S1677. B. 1/26/1755. Enl. in Louisa Co., Va. In 1832 res. Robertson Co., Tenn.
David, Va., S17517; B. 1/--/1761 Pittsylvania Co., Va.; res. at enl. Henry Co., Va.; res. in 1833 Cooper Co., Mo. See N.A. Acc. No. 874-050094. Not Half Pay
David, Va., Rebecca, W10150. B. 1759 in King George Co., Va. Res. at enl. in what was later called Kanawha Co., Va. After Rev. lived Nelson Co., Ky. & Jefferson Co., Ind. D. there 5/6/1835
Dennis, Md., Eleanor, W2126. Enl. at Hagerstown, Washington Co., Md.;in 1825 aged 67 yrs. & res. Greene Co., Pa. D. 3/16/1839
Diodate Pratt, Ct., S36649. In 1824 aged 61 yrs. res. of Hamden, New Haven Co., Ct. See also Pratt Jones
Eaton, Cont., Ct., Mary, W20187 Enl. at Litchfield, Ct. & res. there in 1819, aged 58 yrs. D. there 1/5/1838
Ebenezer, Mass., S5634. B. 1763 at Sandwich, Mass. Res. there at enl. In 1832 res. Cincinnatus, Cortland Co., N.Y.
Ebenezer, N.Y., Sarah, R5743. Enl. in Dutchess Co., N.Y. D. 1/2/1840 in Malahide Twp., Elgen Co., Canada
Edmond, See Zebulon COLE, Del., Rej. B.L.
Edmond, N.C., S7086. Enl. in Orange Co., N.C. In 1833 res. of Chatham Co., N.C., aged 83 yrs.
Edward, Mass., Judith Leavitt, former wid., W24511; BLWt.3809-160-55. Res. at enl. Taunton, Mass. Res. after Rev., Littleborough (Leeds), Kennebec Co., Me. & died there 4/8/1814
Edward, Va., BLWt.12278-100-Pvt. Iss. 5/11/1792 to Francis Graves, ass. No papers
Edward, Va., S5622. B. N.C.,res. at enl. Washington Co., Va. In 1832 aged 75 yrs. res. Sumner Co., Tenn.
Edward, Va., S45872. B. 4/7/1759 in Richmond Co., Va. In 1832 res. Stokes Co., N.C.
Edward, Va., Frances, W7908. Lived in Caroline Co., Va. & d. there in 1807
Eli, Mass., Anna, W26678. Res. during Rev., Waltham, Mass., D. 5/9/1811 at Lincoln, Middlesex Co., Mass.
Elias, Mass., Chloe, W1040; BLWt. 15428-160-55. See N.A. Acc. No. 874-050094. Not Half Pay. Res. at enl. Sherburne, Middlesex Co., Mass. Res. in 1839, Harrisburgh, Lewis Co., N.Y. D. 3/4/1843 at Wardsbury, Windham Co., Vt.
Elijah, Mass., Patience, W26807. Native of Wrentham, Mass. & res. there during Rev. D. 7/1808 in Bremen, Penobscot Co., Me.
Elijah, Mass., Deborah Pierce, former wid., R8234. B. Vienna, Dorchester Co., Md. Res. at enl. Wellfleet, Barnstable Co., Mass. and drowned in the harbor at Wellfleet, 1/12/1791.
Elijah, Va., S8762. Res. at enl. Nansemond Co., Va. Was there in 1833, aged 72 yrs.
Elisha, Cont. Va., S5633. Res. at enl. Hanover Co., Va. In 1832 res. Pittsylvania Co., Va., aged about 70 yrs.
Elisha, N.C., S7084. B. 2/20/1761 in Dobbs Co. (later Wayne Co.), N.C. Res. at enl. Duplin Co., N.C. Was there in 1832. D. 3/24/1840
Elkanah, Ct., S16170. B. 4/28/1761 at Hebron, Ct. Res. during service Hebron & Colchester, Ct. Res. after Rev. in N.Y. & Mass. In 1830 res. Painesville Twp., Geauga Co., Ohio
Enoch, N.J., S821. Res. at enl. Gloucester Co., N.J. In 1832 aged 74 yrs. & res. Upper Freehold Twp., Monmouth Co., N.J.
Epaphras, Cont., Ct., S16889. B. 2/10/1764. Enl. at Hartford, Ct. Res. in 1832, Providence, Floyd Co., Ind.
Ephraim, Ct., Anna, W2620. B. 3/23/1758 in Norwalk, Ct., res. during Rev., New Canaan & Brookfield, Ct. In 1832 res. Stamford, Fairfield Co., Ct. D. 10/15/1837
Ethel, Ct., S22854. B. 1765 in Preston, Ct. Res. during Rev. Preston & Salisbury, Ct. Res. in 1832 Great Barrington, Berkshire Co., Mass., and in 1834, Canaan, Wayne Co., Pa.
Evans, N.Y., BLWt.7317-100-Pvt. Iss. 10/11/1790 to Lewis Graham, ass. No papers
Ezekiel, Ct., S28778. B. 11/1760 at Colchester, Ct. Res. there at enl. Res. in 1832, Oneida Co., N.Y.
Ezekiel, Mass., BLWt.4466-100-Pvt.Iss. 12/6/1791 to Stephen Thorn. No papers
Ezekiel, Mass., S19361. B. 11/11/1758 at Holliston, Mass. Res. at enl. Milford & Mendon, Worcester Co., Mass. Res. in 1832 Milford, Mass.
Ezekiel, Mass., Hannah, W21466. In 1818 aged 64 and res. Whitehall, Washington Co., N.Y. Died 10/10/1833
Ezekiel, N.C., Rosannah, W5005. B. 4/3/1764. Res. of N.C., d. 11/1/1825
Ezra, Ct., R15464. B. at Saybrook, New London Co., Ct. in 1762. Res. at enl. Canaan, Litchfield Co., Ct. Res. in 1832, Phelps, Ontario Co., N.Y.
Ezra, N.Y., Elizabeth, W20189. Res. at enl. Dutchess Co., N.Y. Res. in 1818 at Sempronius, Cayuga Co., N.Y., aged 60 yrs. D. 1 or 2 Jan. 1833 at Locke, Cayuga Co., N.Y.
Fowler, N.C., R5701. B. 9/22/1758 in Granville Co., N.C. & always lived there to 1832.
Francis (see Zebulon COLE, Del., BL Rej.)
Francis, N.C., S8768. B. Wake Co., N.C. Res. there at enl. Res. after Rev. Chatham Co., N.C. D. 2/23/1844 in Orange Co., N.C., aged about 86 yrs.
Francis, N.C., S36653. In 1818 res. Wake Co., N.C. In 1839 res. Wayne Co., Ind.
Francis, Pa., BLWt.9686-100-Pvt. Iss. 9/7/1789. No papers
Freeman, N.C., Christian/Christina W7900. B. 1763 in Brunswick Co., Va. Res. at enl. Rutherford Co., N.C. Res. in 1833, Pickens Co., Ala. D. there 8/26/1835
Gabriel, N.C., S36652. Enl. in Surry Co., N.C. In 1818, aged 92 yrs. & res. Floyd Co., Ky. D. 3/1832
George, Ct., Lucretia, W21484. B. 3/15/1755 in Hartford, Ct. Res. at enl. & in 1832, Harwinton Litchfield Co., Ct. D. 2/7/1841
George, Pa., Siche, R5745. In 1828 res. Terre Haute, Vigo Co., Ind. D. in N.Y. 3/11/1835
George, Va., S4455. B. 11/17/1762

JONES (continued)
in Fauquier Co., Va. Res.Fauquier & Culpeper Co., Va. Res.1832, Pike Twp., Madison Co., Ohio
George, Va., S38888. In 1826, aged 80 yrs. & res. Williamson Co., Tenn.
George, Va., Sarah, W7923. Enl. in King George Co., Va., res. of Stafford Co., Va. D. 10/12/1810
George, Va., Mary, W9082. B. 10/4/1753 or 1757 in Prince William Co., Va. Res. at enl. Fauquier Co., Va. Res. in 1833, Henry Co., Ky. D. 2/9/1835
Gideon, Cont., Mass., Lydia, W20194. In 1818 aged 64 yrs. & res. West Springfield, Hampden Co., Mass. D. 1/3/1824
Gideon, Mass., BLWt.4471-100-Corp. Iss. 4/1/1790. No papers
Giles, Mass., S33346. Enl. in N.Y. In 1818 aged 75 yrs. & res. Burlington Co., N.J.
Godfrey, Hazen's Regt., BLWt. 13260-100-Pvt. Iss. 4/19/1792 to Conrad Feger, ass. of Robert Copeland, Admr. No papers
Goodspeed/Allen G., Mass., BLWt. 43875-160-55. B. Barnstable, Barnstable Co., Mass., res. there at enl. & in 1855 then 92 yrs. old, son of Isaac
Gray, Va., Elizabeth, W3690; BLWt. 33731-160-55. B. Sussex Co., Va., res. there at enl. In 1833, aged 73 yrs. & res. Bedford Co., Va. D. 6/13/1848
Griffen, N.Y., BLWt.7324-100-Pvt. Iss. 5/4/1791 to Samuel Loudon, ass. No papers
Griffin, N.Y., Meraby, W21480. In 1818 aged 53 & res. Orange, Saratoga Co., N.Y. D. 4/6/1836 at Halfmoon, Saratoga Co., N.Y.
Hannah, wid. of Daniel Hooper, N.H., which see
Hardy/Hardie/Hardee, N.C., S41699 Enl. in Jones Co., N.C. In 1818 aged 58 yrs. & res. Lenoir Co., N.C.
Harris, Ct., S36655. Enl. at New Haven, Ct. In 1820 aged 86 yrs. & res. Litchfield Co., Ct.
Harrison, Va., S25603. B. 1758. Enl. in Cumberland Co., Va. Res. Va. & Ga. In 1836 res. Marshall Co., Miss. D. 1/12/1841
Henry, Ga., Va., R5704. B. 1762 in Dinwiddie Co., Va. Res. at enl. Brunswick Co., Va. Res. in 1839, Barbour Co., Ala.
Henry, Mass., R5703. Res. at enl. Whately, Mass., res. about 1833, New London Co., Ct.
Henry, Va., Rachel, W4249; b. 12/7/1751 King George Co., Va.; Res. at enl. Fauquier Co., Va. Res. in 1833, Hardy Co., Va.; d. 2/6/1838
Henry, Va., Cassandra, R5692; BLWt.33558-160-55. Res. of Floyd

JONES (continued)
Co., Va. & d. there 10/1829/1831
Herman, N.Y., S43706. Enl. in N.Y. In 1826 aged 66 yrs. & res. Herkimer Co., N.Y.
Hezekiah, N.J., Hannah, R5702. B. 10/26/1762. Res. at enl. Alexandria, Hunterdon Co., N.J. D. 4/12/1818 in Hunterdon Co.
Horatio, Pa., S23728. B. 1763 at Great Valley, Chester Co., Pa. Res. at enl. Old Fort Littleton, Bedford Co., Pa. Res. in 1834, Geneseo, Livingston Co., N.Y.
Hugh, Crane's Cont. Art., Mass., BLWt.4496-100-Pvt. Iss. 1/12/1791. No papers
Income, Mass., R.I., S18905. B. 6/16/1757 at Dighton, Bristol Co., Mass. Enl. Swanzey, Bristol Co.,Mass. Res. in 1832 Brattleboro, Windham Co., Vt.
Isaac, Ct., S18058. B. 3/8/1755 at Colchester, New London Co., Ct & res. there at enl. After Rev. res. Hampshire Co., Mass. In 1832 res. Lebanon, New London Co., Ct.
Isaac, Ct., Ruth Booth, former wid., W20741. B. 8/3/1764 in Stratford, Fairfield Co., Ct. & res. there until death 8/6/1793
Isaac, Cont., Ct., Mass., S10921 Enl. at Worcester, Mass. & Bolton, Ct. In 1818 aged 62 yrs. & res. Columbus, Chenango Co., N.Y. Wife Sarah
Isaac, Mass., S28773. B. 7/29/1758 at Falmouth, Me. Res. at enl. Topsham, Me. Res. in 1833 Bowdoin, Lincoln Co., Me.
Isaac, N.J., BLWt.8427-100-Pvt. Iss. 12/20/1792 to Ezekiel Day, Admr. No papers
Isaac, N.Y., Anna, W21469. Enl. at Dover, Dutchess Co., N.Y. & res. there in 1818. D. 5/28/1834 at Kent, Litchfield Co., Ct.
Isaac, N.C., Va., S31777. B. 3/30/1761 in N.J. Res. during Rev., Frederick Co., Va. & Guilford Co., N.C. Res. in 1836 Telfair Co., Ga. Had resided also in Jefferson & Wilkinson Cos., Ga.
Israel, Mass., S15486; BLWt.15200-160-55. B. 1761 in Raynham, Bristol Co., Mass. In 1832 res. of Halifax, Windham Co., Vt.
Israel, Mass., S18906. B. 10/11/1761 in Ipswich, Essex Co., Mass. Res. at enl. Shapleigh, Me. Res. in 1832, Highgate, Franklin Co., Vt.
Issachar, Ct., Eleanor, W21472. Res. at enl. Somers, Tolland Co., Ct. D. 12/1/1823
Jacob, N.Y., BLWt.7315-100-Pvt. Iss. 1/16/1792 to Abraham Jones, admr. No papers
Jacob, N.Y., Hannah, W20184

JONES (continued)
B. 2/1759. Res. Orange Co., N.Y. D. 5/4/1839
Jacob, N.C., S9363. Enl. in Bute Co., N.C. In 1820 aged 67 yrs., res. Pendleton Dist., S.C., wife Martha. In 1833 res. Pickens Dist., S.C.
Jacob, Pa., Abigail, R5690. Res. at enl. Westmoreland Co., Pa. D. 5/10/1831 at Weathersfield, Trumbull Co., Ohio
James, Cont., BLWt.1141-100. No papers
James, Cont., Mass., Huldah, W26696; b. 5/15/1756; enl. at Cambridge, Mass. In 1818 res. Chateaugay, Franklin Co., N.Y.; d. 1/--/1829, Mt. Vernon, Me.
James, Cont., Pa., S32925. Res. at enl. Marblehead, Mass. In 1820, aged 57 yrs. & res. Boston, Mass. Wife Mehitable
James, Cont., Va., S45890; BLWt. 1876-100. Enl. at Fredericksburg, Va. In 1818 aged 57 yrs. res. of Stafford Co., Va. Wife Molly
James, Md., S22333. Enl. at Annapolis, Md. In 1834 res. of Kingston, Luzerne Co., Pa. Age 74 yrs
James, Md., BLWt.1894-100. D. 1819
James, N.H., BLWt.3243-100-Pvt. Iss. 10/31/1789. No papers
James, N.J., BLWt.854-100-Pvt. Iss. 7/19/1790. No papers
James, N.Y., BLWt.7331-100-Pvt. Iss. 7/30/1790 to John W. Wendell ass. No papers
James, N.Y., Catharine, W21468. B. 7/22/1754, son of Henry. Res. at enl. Stephentown (little Hoosick), Rensselaer Co., N.Y., and d. there 7/26/1803
James, N.C., S31170. B. 1760 in York Co., Pa. Res. at enl. Rowan Co., N.C. Res. in 1833 Daviess Co., Ky.
James, N.C., S41700. Enl. in Newbern, N.C. In 1820, aged 65 yrs. & res. Carteret Co., N.C.
James, N.C., S41701. In 1821 aged 60 yrs. & res. Halifax Co., N.C.
James, N.C., S.C., R5706. B. 1753 in Charlotte Co., Va. Res. during Rev. Ninety Six District, S.C. & Washington Co., N.C. In 1834, res. Butler Co., Ky.
James, Pa., S31173. B. 9/9/1764 or 1766, in York Co., Pa. Res. at enl. Northumberland Co., Pa. Res. in 1833, Scott Co., Ky.
James, Pa., BLWt.1153-400-Surgn. Iss. 5/30/1789. No papers
James, S.C., S1839. Res. at enl. Kershaw District, S.C. In 1832 aged 77 yrs. & res. Marion Co., Tenn.
James, Va., S2656. B. 6/17/1752. Enl. from Powhatan Co., Va. In 1832 res. of Robertson Co., Tenn.
James, Va. S5624. B.7/1/1749. Always lived King William Co., Va.

JONES (continued)

James, Va., S35472. B. Dublin, Ireland. In 1820 aged about 76 years. & res. Warren Co., Ky.

James, Va., S45873. B. 4/20/1758 in Fauquier Co., Va. Res. in 1832, Culpeper Co., Va.

James, Va., Sarah, W5008; BLWt. 1591-160-55. B. 1762 in Charles Co., Md. Res. at enl. Fairfax Co., Va. Res. in 1833, Tyler Co., Va. D. 11/10/1850 in Ritchie Co., Va.

James, Va., Mary, W7917. B. 11/16/1760 in Prince William Co., Va. Res. at enl. Fauquier Co., Va. Res. in 1832 Monroe Co., Va. D. 3/16/1849

James, Va., Sally, W26165; BLWt. 57645-160-55. Res. during Rev., Amherst Co., & Montgomery Co., Va. In 1832 aged 72 yrs. & res. Wayne Co., Ky. D. there 1/10/1844

James, Va., Catharine, R5693; BLWt.33534-160-55. D. 1/28/1841 in Orange Co., Va.

James Morris, Pa., BLWt.1242-200 Res. of Philadelphia Co., Pa.

Jason, Md., S----. B. 1757 in Anne Arundel Co., Md. Was there at enl. and in 1832. D. 2/7/1838 Elizabeth Jones, wid. of above sold. rec'd pension as former wid. of John Thompson, Md., which see

Jasper, Ct., BLWt.6020-100-Pvt. Iss. 9/29/1790 to George Smith. No papers

Jeremiah/Jonas, Mass., S32924. In 1818 aged 63 yrs. & res. of Plymouth Co., Mass. In 1820 res. of Norfolk Co., Mass.

Jeremiah, S.C., S18061. B. 12/27/1759 in Orangeburg Dist., S.C. and res. there in 1833

Jesse, N.Y., R5709. B. 1767 in Reading, Hunterdon Co., N.J. Res. at enl. Duanesburg, Albany Co., N.Y. Res. in 1832 Tompkins Co., N.Y. Res. in 1834 Steuben Co., N.Y.

Jesse, N.C., S---. B. 12/1758 in Duplin Co., N.C. & res. there at enl. After Rev. res. in Horry District, S.C. Res. in 1833, Montgomery Co., N.C.

Jesse, N.C., Sarah E., R5744. Enl. from Wilmington District, N.C. Res. of Surry Co. & Cumberland Co., N.C. D. 3/1833 in Davie Co., N.C.

Jesse, Va., S38086. Enl. in Caroline Co., Va. & res. there in 1818, aged about 80 yrs.

Jethro, Mass., S32921, enl. at Blandford, Hampden Co., Mass. & res. there in 1818, age 85 yrs.

Joel, Ct., Cont., Mass., S43730. In 1820 aged over 68 yrs. & res. of Whitehall, Washington Co., N.Y., wife Sarah

JONES (continued)

Joel, Mass., Rhoda, W3691. Born 7/7/1764 at Charlton, Worcester Co., Mass. D. 8/11/1845 in Crawford Co., Pa.

Joel, Va., BLWts.12256 & 12667-100-Pvt. Iss. 7/14/1792 to Robert Means, ass. No papers

John, Ct., S13573. Res. at enl. Fairfield, Ct., In 1832, aged 83 yrs. & res. Walton, Delaware Co., N.Y.

John, Ct., S31781. B. 1/4/1762 at Saybrook, Middlesex Co., Ct. Lived there up to 1832

John, Ct., N.Y., S43727. Born 12/1757. Res. at enl. Danbury, Ct. In 1820 res. York, Genesee Co., N.Y. Wife Esther

John, Cont., Mass., S32911. In 1820 aged 60 yrs. & res. of Rehoboth, Bristol Co., Mass.

John, Hazen's Regt., BLWt.13253-100-Pvt. Iss. 11/4/1791. No papers

John, Hazen's Regt., BLWt.13261-100-QM Sgt. Iss. 2/10/1797. No papers

John (deceased), Md., BLWt.11380-100-Pvt. Iss. 11/29/1790 to John Jones, Admr. No papers

John (of Benjamin), Md., R5712. B. 2/11/1757 at Wetipquin, Somerset Co., Md. There at enl. In 1833 res. of Nanticoke, Somerset Co., Md.

John, Md., R5713. B. 9/4/1755 in Dorchester Co., Md. Res. of Dorchester Co., Md. & d. there 2/5/1848

John, Mass., BLWt.4470-100-Pvt. Iss. 1/16/1793 to Samuel Emery. No papers

John, Crane's Cont. Art., Mass., BLWt.4498-100-Pvt. Iss. 2/18/1793 to Wm. Ashley, ass. No papers

John, Mass., S13560. B. 6/25/1764 at Braintree, Mass. & res. there at enl. In 1832 res. Columbia Co., N.Y.

John, Mass., S22335. B. 1757 in Plymouth, Mass. Res. at enl. Halifax, Plymouth Co., Mass. In 1830 res. of Winchester, Cheshire Co., N.H.

John, Mass., S31783. B. 8/20/1757 at Cape Elizabeth, Me. Res. at enl. Brunswick, Me. In 1833 res. of Westbrook, Cumberland Co., Me.

John, Mass., S36665. B. Newfoundland. In 1818 res. Bowdoin, Lincoln Co., Me.

John, N.H., BLWt.3248-100-Pvt. Iss. 9/13/1792 to Jonathan Jenks. No papers

John, N.J., R5710. Born Burlington Co., N.J. In 1838 about 80 yrs. old and res. Varick, Seneca Co., N.Y.

JONES (continued)

John, N.Y., S32350. B. 6/22/1752 in Albany, N.Y. Res. at enl. New Baltimore, Albany Co. (Greene Co.), N.Y.

John, N.Y., W20188. B. in Philipstown, Dutchess Co., N.Y. Res. at enl. Cortland Manor, Westchester Co., N.Y. In 1832 aged 71 yrs. & res. of Spencer, Tioga Co., N.Y. D. 12/5/1844

John, N.C., S13542. B. 5/29/1759 in Orange Co., N.C. Res. at enl. Guilford Co., N.C. Res. in 1832 Morgan Co., Ala.

John, N.C., Mary, W373. B. Brunswick Co., Va. Res. at enl. Rutherford Co., N.C. Res. in 1832 Marion Co., Tenn. aged 73 or 74 yrs. D. 11/23/1839 or 1841

John, N.C., Va., R5714. B. 4/3/1746 in Morris Co., East Jersey. Res. at enl. Henry Co., Va. Res. in 1832 Grayson Co., Va.

John, N.C. War of 1812, R5719; BLWt.35719-160-55. B. 3/1761 in Henry Co., Va. Res. during Rev. Surry Co., N.C. Res. during War of 1812, Spartanburg, S.C. Res. in 1852 Washington Co., Tenn.

John, Pa., BLWt.9659-100-Pvt. Iss. 1/18/1791 to Cath. Shiney, Admr. No papers

John, Pa., S2293. B. 8/10/1756 in Scotts Plains, N.J. Res. at enl. Allegany Co., Pa. Res. in 1833 Clinton Co., Ohio

John, Pa., R5711. B. 6/15/1747 at Philadelphia, Pa. Enl. in Lancaster Co., Pa. Res. in 1834 Philadelphia, Pa.

John, S.C., S7089. B. 3/19/1756 in Marion District, S.C. & res. there at enl. In 1834 res. Marion Co., S.C. In 1842 res. Robeson Co., N.C.

John, S.C., R5717. D. 6/4/1842 in Columbia Co., Ga.

John, Va., BLWt.12255-100-Pvt. Iss. 7/17/1792 to Robert Means ass. No papers

John, Va., BLWt.12261-100-Pvt. Iss. 7/30/179- to Richard Smyth, ass. No papers

John, Va., S1678. B. 5/8/1750 in Albemarle Co., Va. & res. there at enl. In 1833 res. Maury Co., Tenn. D. 9/16/1841

John, Va. S5629. B. in Spotsylvania Co., Va. Res. at enl. Orange Co., Va. Res. in 1833, Madison Co., Va.

John, Va., S5631. B. 1758 in Culpeper Co., Va. Res. at enl. & in 1832, Halifax Co., Va. D. 3/17/1838

John, Va., S31171. B. 2/1/1760 in Albemarle Co., Va. Res. at enl. Amherst Co., Va. Res. in 1832 Calloway Co., Ky.

John, Va., S31174. B. 9/3/1763 in Brunswick Co., Va. Res. in

JONES (continued)
1834 Garrard Co., Ky. D.2/6/1838
John, Va.,S38085. Enl. in King George Co.,Va. In 1819 aged 83 yrs. & res. of Caroline Co., Va.
John, Va.,R5715. B. Dinwiddie Co., Va. & always lived there up to 1832, then about 76 yrs. old.
John, Va., R5716, b. 2/1758. Res. at enl. & in 1835, Mecklenburg Co., Va.
John, Va., Susan, W299. In 1823 aged 65 yrs. res. of Albemarle Co., Va. & d. there 7/15/1849
John, Va., Mary, W372. B. 1762 in St. Mary's Co., Md. Res. at enl. Botetourt Co., Va. Res. in 1834 Claiborn Co., Tenn. D. 2/10/1842
John, Va., Jane, W9084; BLWt.38552-160-55. B. 6/3/1769. D. 5/17/1840 in Nelson Co., Ky.
John, Va., Leah, W10149; BLWt. 96588-160-55. In 1829 aged 77 yrs. & res. of Lincoln Co., Tenn. D. there 12/23/1831.
John, Va., also Dunmore's War in 1774, Frances, W7920. B. 2/2/1755 in Culpeper Co., Va. Res. during Rev., Greenbrier Co., Va. Res. in 1833 Kanawha Co., Va.
John, Va., Indian Campaigns in Ky. 1783-84, R5718. B. 2/20/1762 in Roan Co., N.C. Res. at enl. in what was later Woodford Co., Ky. In 1847 res. Bath Co., Ky.
John Courts, Md., Dorothy H. Storer, former wid., W25166; BLWt.1161-300-Capt. Iss. 2/26/1794. He d. 5/20/1802
Jonathan, Mass., S10916. B. 7/26/1748 at Dracut, Middlesex Co., Mass. & enl. there. In 1832 res. of Reading, Windsor Co., Vt.
Jonathan, Mass., Abigail, W16130. B. 11/16/1757 in Wilmington, Mass. Res. at enl. Woburn, Middlesex Co., Mass. D. 9/4/1839 at Milford, N.H.
Jonathan, N.C., S31778. Res. at enl. Onslow Co., N.C. In 1834 aged 77 yrs. & res. Laurens Co., Ga.
Jonathan, S.C., Elizabeth, W231. Res. at enl. Chester District, S.C. & d. there 8/4/1835
Joseph, Ct., S45845. In 1818 aged 68 yrs. & res. Norfolk, Litchfield Co., Ct.
Joseph, Cont. (N.J.?), S36667. In 1822 aged 69 yrs. & res. St. Clair Co., Ill.
Joseph, Cont., R.I., Mass.,S41703 Enl. in 1779 at Harvard, Worcester Co., Mass. In 1820 aged 65 yrs. & res. Richland Co., Ohio
Joseph, Md., BLWt.11395-100-Pvt. Iss. 12/18/1794 to Henry Purdy, ass. No papers
Joseph, Mass., S13561. B. 1757 in Norton, Bristol Co., Mass. Res. at enl. New Marlboro, Berkshire Co., Mass. Res. in 1833 Vernon, Oneida Co., N.Y.
Joseph, Mass., S13582. B. 1752 in Saybrook, Ct. Res. at enl.Stockbridge, Berkshire Co., Mass. In 1832 res. Newark, Tioga Co., N.Y.
Joseph, N.J., BLWt.8433-100-Sgt. Iss. 7/7/1789. No papers
Joseph, N.Y., BLWt.7327-100-Pvt. Iss. 8/18/1790 to Joseph Stringham, ass. No papers
Joseph, N.C., Va., S2652. B. 7/6/1758 or 1759 in N.J. Res. during Rev., Burke Co., N.C. & Culpeper Co., Va. Res. in 1832, Giles Co., Tenn.
Joseph, Pa., BLWt.9703-100-Pvt. Iss. 6/24/1793 to James Humphrys, ass. No papers
Joseph, Pa. & Indian War, Mary, R5725. Res.of Pa. D. 1/24/1814 in Symmes Twp., Hamilton Co., Ohio
Joseph, Va., Joanna, W943. Enl. in Hampshire Co., Va. In 1824 aged 69 yrs. & res. Greene Co., Tenn. & d. there 4/22/1826
Joseph, Va., Sarah, W9079. B.5/8/1751 in Caroline Co., Va. Res. during Rev., Caroline Co. & New Kent Co., Va. Res. in 1832, Owen Co., Ky. D. 12/5/1837
Joshua, Md., S31175. Res. at enl. Harford Co., Md. In 1832 aged 73 yrs. & res. Clarke Co., Ky., wife Araminta.
Joshua, Mass., Sarah, W16617. Res. of Dracut, Mass. & New Boston, Hillsborough Co., N.H. D. 1/11/1830
Joshua, Mass., Dorothy, W26684. In 1818 aged 60 yrs. & res. of Durham, Cumberland Co., Me. D. 2/14/1836
Joshua, Pa., S5628. B. 8/1760 in Bucks Co., Pa. Res. at enl. Philadelphia Co., Pa. Res. in 1832 Harrison Co., Va.
Joshua, Va., Mary, R5726. B. 4/25/1761. Res. at enl. Northumberland Co., Va. Res. in 1833 Grant Co., Ky. D. 1/6/1844
Josiah, Cont., Mass., S544. Enl. in Bristol Co., Mass. After Rev. res. in R.I. In 1844 aged 88 yrs. & res. Mercer Co., N.J.
Josiah, Mass., S29264. B. 3/1/1754 in Middleborough, Plymouth Co., Mass. Was there at enl. In 1833 res. Dalton, Berkshire Co., Mass.
Josiah, Mass., BL Rej. & Dis. Res. of Sandwich, Barnstable Co., Mass. D. in Maine 2/23/1826
Josiah, N.J., BLWts.8426 & 9660-100-Pvt. Iss. 12/21/1791. No papers
Josiah, N.C., S18065. B. 1/26/1756 Res. at enl. Wintin, N.C. Since Rev. res. in S.C., Ga. & Ala. In 1828 res. Washington Co., Fla.
Josiah, N.C., Va., R5722; b. 1752 in Cumberland Co., Va. Res. during Rev. in Va. & Rutherford Co., N.C. Res. in 1833, Anderson District, S.C.
Lazarus, Cont., Mass., Betsey, W21475. B. Kittery, Me. In 1818 aged 64 yrs. & res. North Hill, Somerset Co., Me. D. 11/1/1836
Lazarus, N.C., Keziah, W26796. Enl. in Pasquotank Co., N.C. D. 6/17/1814 Hawkins Co., Tenn.
Lewellin/Lewellen, Va., Catharine W7906. In 1820 aged 60 yrs. & res. Campbell Co., Va. D. 10/30/1821
Lewis, Cont., Mass., S32919. In 1820 aged 65 yrs. & res. Roxbury, Norfolk Co., Mass.
Lewis, Va. Sea Service, Milly, W7904. Res. of Lancaster Co., Va. D. 2/1800
Lucretia, former wid. of Elijah Smith, N.J., Va. Which see
Matthew, N.C., R5728. B. 12/9/1754. Enl. in Cumberland Co., N.C. In 1837 res. of Robeson Co., N.C.
Matthew, N.C., R5729. B. 8/29/1760 in Isle of Wight Co., Va. Res. at enl. Franklin Co., N.C. Res. in 1832 Putnam Co., Ga.
Matthew, Va., S32348. B. 3/18/1758 in Nottoway Parish, Southhampton Co., Va. & res. there at enl. In 1833 res. of Wayne Twp., Owen Co., Ind. D. 1/18/1837
Michael, N.J., S33343. Enl. at Pompton Plains, N.J. In 1818 aged about 65 yrs. & res. Hunterdon Co., N.J.
Moris/Morris, Ct., Cont., S13571. Enl. at New London, of Madison, Ct. In 1820 aged 64 yrs. & res. of Guilford, New Haven Co., Ct.
Morton, Va., Frankey, W7903. B. 8/10/1747 in Orange Co., Va. & res. there at enl. In 1832 res. of Franklin Co., Tenn. D. 11/8/1841
Moses, N.C., S8752; BLWt.57644-160-55. B. Granville Co., N.C. & res. there at enl. In 1855 aged 93 yrs. & res. of Orange Co., N.C.
Moses, N.C., S32347. B. 9/1762 in Isle of Wight Co., Va. Res. at enl. Gates Co., N.C. Res. in 1832 Franklin Co., Ill.
Moses, Va., Sarah, W5113. Enl. in Caroline Co., Va. & res. there. D. about 1826
Musgrove, N.C., S7094. B. 10/30/1761 in Bladen Co., N.C. Always lived there up to 1832
Nathan, N.C., or S.C., Jane, R5707. Enl. in Duplin Co., N.C. D. in Bladen Co. about 1829
Nathaniel, S.C., Rebecca, W7918; BLWt.26447-160-55. B. Wake Co., N.C. Res. at enl. S.C. In 1833

JONES (continued)
aged 80 yrs. & res. of Kershaw District, S.C. D. 5/6/1846
Neals/Nelce, Md., S36023. In 1818 aged over 70 yrs. & res. Pencader Hundred, New Castle Co., Del.
Nehemiah, Mass., Anna, W26808. B. 6/17/1760 in Norton, Bristol Co., Mass. Res. during Rev. Norton & New Marlborough, Mass. Res. in 1832, Westmoreland, Oneida Co., N.Y. D. 12/19/1838
Nelce, Md. See Neals
Nelsey, Md., BLWt.11379-100-Pvt. Iss. 1/18/1793. No papers
Nicholas, Md., S8771. B. 1751. Res. at enl. Harford, Baltimore Co., Md. In 1832 res. Allegany Co., Md. D. 6/7/1835
Nicholas, N.C., S7083. B. 1758 in Del. Res. at enl. Rowan Co., N.C. Res. in 1832 Iredell Co., N.C.
Nicholas, Va., S16169. B. 11/14/1762 in Caroline Co., Va. & res. there at enl. In 1832 res. of Clarke Co., Ky.
Nicholas, Va., Amarella, W7907. B. 7/3/1760. Res. at enl. Amherst Co., Va. D. Rockbridge Co., Va., 4/7/1831 (or 1834).
Noah, Mass., S23735. Res. at enl. Worcester, Mass. Res. in 1832 Shoreham, Addison Co., Vt., aged 73
Oliver, Ct., Hannah, W20185. B. 10/13/1764 at Hebron, Tolland Co., Ct. There at enl. & in 1832. D. 10/23/1835
Oliver, Cont., Mass., Vt. Susannah, W26671. In 1818 aged 60 yrs. & res. Guilford, Windham Co., Vt. D. 12/24/1832
Peregrine, Cont., Pa., Ann, W298; BLWt.26850-160-55. Enl. in Northampton Co., Pa. In 1818 age 61, res. of Kingston, Luzerne Co., Pa. D. 9/28/1845
Peter, Pa., BLWt.1980-200. Of Philadelphia Co., Pa.
Peter, Va., S8772. Enl. in Dinwiddie Co., Va. In 1818 aged 70 yrs. & res. Warren Co., N.C. D. 2/10/1833
Philip, Ct., R5734. B. 12/10/1759, at Ridgefield, Ct. Res. at enl. Norwalk, Ct. Res. in 1832 Brandon Rutland Co., Vt.
Philip, Cont., Md., S36029, & 34941. In 1820 aged 62 yrs. & res. in District of Columbia & Prince Georges Co., Md.
Philip, Pa., S39782. In 1820 aged 80 yrs. & res. Chester Co., Pa.
Philip, Va., S32342. Enl. at Amelia C.H., Va. In 1832 aged about 70 yrs. & res. Logan Co., Ky.
Phillip, Md., BLWt.165-100. In 1797 res. of Calvert Co., Md.
Phillip, N.C., BLWt.2123-200

JONES (continued)
Phineas/Phinehas, Ct., S43707. In 1818 aged 58 yrs. & res. Columbia Twp., Bedford Co., Pa. In 1820 res. Cato, Cayuga Co., N.Y.
Phinehas, Mass., S5623. B. 2/17/1762 in Charlton, Worcester Co., Mass. & res. there at enl. In 1832 res. of Spencer, Worcester Co., Mass.
Phinehas/Phineas, Mass., Mary, W13556. Res. at enl. Greenfield, Hampshire or Franklin Co., Mass. D. 10/25/1806
Pratt, Ct., BLWt.6030-100-Pvt. Iss. 9/24/1790 to James F. Sebor No papers. See Diodate Pratt Jones, Ct.
Pratt, Ct. See Diodate Pratt Jones
Reuben, Ct., S2292. B. 5/1763 in Preston, New London Co., Ct. & res. there at enl. In 1832 res. Plymouth Twp., Luzerne Co., Pa.
Reuben, Ct., R5737. B. 10/11/1759 at Wallingford, New Haven Co., Ct. & res. there at enl. & in 1832
Reuben, S.C., R5738. B. 1766, Craven Co., S.C. & res. there at enl. In 1832 res. Tuscaloosa Co., Ala.
Richard, Cont., Ct. See Richard L.
Richard, Cont., Pa., S38081. Enl. at York, Pa. In 1820 aged 80 yrs. & res. Harrison Co., Va.
Richard, Cont., Va., S38097. In 1818 aged 80 yrs. & res. of Chesterfield Co., Va.
Richard, Cont., Va., Sarah, W2123 Res. at enl. Charlotte Co., Va. In 1824 aged 63 yrs. & res. Rutherford Co., Tenn. D. there 6/2/1835
Richard, Md., Susannah, W20190. B. 2/2/1757. Res. at enl. Prince Georges Co., Md. D. 4/18/1821 at Hopewell, Ontario Co., N.Y.
Richard, N.C., Mary, W26799. B. 6/8/1766 in Guilford Co., N.C. & res. there at enl. In 1832 res. of Sumner Co., Tenn. D. 8/14/1837
Richard, N.C., Sarah Butler, former wid., R1554. D. 4/15/1805 in Wilkinson Co., Miss.
Richard, S.C., Rebecca, W9081; b. in Edgefield Dist., S.C. & res. there in 1832; d. 7/19/1838
Richard, Va., BLWt.12260-100-Pvt. Iss. 4/12/179- to Francis Groves, ass. No papers
Richard, Va., BLWt.12280-100-Pvt. Iss. 10/17/1791. No papers
Richard, Va.; no action taken. These papers were filed originally in Richard Jones, Cont., Va., S38097, but do not appear to belong there as he did not serve as herein stated. Papers consist of affidavit dated

JONES (continued)
10/1/1847 by John Jones of Madison Co., Va. (Witness to oath gives S.C.), aged 83 yrs. stating that his brother, Richard Jones, m. Mildred Row, that the said Richard Jones was first what was then termed "a minute man" and that he went to Gwins Island & afterward he enlisted for the term of 3 yrs. under Abram Bluford/Buford, & that after said Richard Jones had served out the term his enl. under Buford he afterwards enl. for duration of the war - recollects seeing him while in the service & knowing that sd Richard Jones was a regular soldier
Richard, Va., S2654; b. 5/9/1745, Essex Co., Va. Res. at enl. Brunswick Co., Va. & Henry Co., Va.,res. in 1832 Barren Co., Ky.
Richard, Va., S4441; b. Amelia Co. Va. 5/5/1763. Res. at enl. Charlotte Co., Va., after Rev. in Ga. Res. in 1832 Giles Co., Tenn.
Richard, Va., S4444; b. 1748 in Wales, res. at enl. Rockbridge Co., Va. Res.in 1832, Weakley Co., Tenn.
Richard L., Cont., Ct., Elizabeth W765; BLWt.5439-160-55; b. 5/15/1767; enl. in Ct., m. in N.Y. In 1830 res. of Gallia Co., Ohio. D. 7/23/1852 in Albany, Floyd Co., Ind.
Robert, Pa., S36028; BLWt.1109-100; & 167-60-55. Enl. at Little York, Pa. In 1820 aged 52 yrs. res. Mercer Co., Ky.
Samuel, Ct., Tabitha, W26685; BLWt.6396-160-55; b. 12/3/1759 at Lebanon, Ct. & res. there at enl. In 1832 res. Pompey, Onondaga Co., N.Y. D. 6/26/1847
Samuel, Ct., Cont., Mercy, W21485 Res. at enl. & until death, Saybrook (Westbrook), Middlesex Co. Ct. D. 12/1/1827
Samuel, Ct., Cont., R.I., S13559; b. 1757 at Stonington, Ct. & res. there at enl. In 1832 res. Rensselaer Co., N.Y.
Samuel, Ct., N.Y., S23283; b. 5/15/1752 (O.S.) at Wallingford, Ct. Res. during Rev. Cornwall, Litchfield Co., Ct. & Canaan (New Lebanon), Columbia Co., N.Y. there in 1833 then called New Lebanon.
Samuel, Cont., Ct., S28775, b. at. Litchfield, Ct. & res. there at enl. In 1832 aged 72 yrs. & res. Chenango Co., N.Y.; d. 2/17/1840
Samuel, Cont., Mass., Mehitable, W24757; BLWt.4454-100; b. at Somersworth, N.H. Enl. at Berwick, Mass. (Me.) In 1818 res. Gardiner, Me. D. 4/29/1821
Samuel, Cont., Vt., S43708; enl.

JONES (continued)
at Poultney, Vt. In 1825 aged 65 yrs. Res. Washington Co., N.Y. Wife Hannah
Samuel, Cont., Va., Patsey, W3826 Enl. at Petersburg, Va. Res. of Amelia Co., Va. D. 6/6/1816
Samuel, Mass., BLWt.4449-100-Pvt. Iss. 9/26/1791 to Wm. Lane. No papers
Samuel, Mass., S13574; b. 1761 in Waltham, Mass. Res. at enl. & in 1832 Leominster, Worcester Co., Mass.
Samuel, Mass., S30516; b. Hopkinton, Middlesex Co., Mass. Res. in 1832, Sudbury, Middlesex Co., Mass., aged 73 yrs.
Samuel, N.J., S28065; b. 3/6/1759 In 1786 res. Elizabethtown, N.J. In 1824 res. of New York City.
Samuel, N.Y., BLWt.7313-100-Pvt. Iss. 7/30/1790 to Edward Cumpston, ass. No papers
Samuel, N.Y., Elizabeth, W26164. Enl. at Schenectady, N.Y. In 1820 aged 59 yrs. & res. of Thompson, Sullivan Co., N.Y. D. 10/8/1849 in Orange Co., N.Y.
Samuel, N.C., Elizabeth, W230; d. 10/1831 in Maury Co., Tenn.
Samuel, N.C., BLWt.1173-300-Capt. Iss. 8/14/1792 to Isaac Cole, ass. of Kilby & Richard Jones, admrs. to the estate of S.J. No papers
Samuel, Pa., R5742; b. 1754 in Amity Twp., Berks Co., Pa. & res. there at enl. In 1833 res. Logan Twp., Centre Co., Pa.
Samuel, S.C., S21844; res. at enl. & in 1833, Kershaw Dist., S.C., aged 70 yrs. in 1833
Samuel, Va., S13554; b. 9/23/1756, probably a res. of Dinwiddie Co., Va. In 1832 res. of Christian Co., Ky.
Samuel, Va., S41706; BLWt.1848-100; b. 7/1762, enl. at Winchester, Va. In 1818 res. Brown Co., Ohio
Samuel L., Ct., Elizabeth, R5700 B. 8/20/1766 at Groton, Ct. & res. there at enl. D. 10/3/1803 probably in New York City.
Samuel P., Mass., BLWt.4477-100-Pvt. Iss. 2/23/1796 to Joseph Brown. No papers
Samuel Payne, Mass., Pamelia, W21496. In 1818 aged 59 yrs. & res. Scituate, Plymouth Co., Mass.; d. 5/1/1819
Samuel Z., Pa., S18477; b. 1/30/1759 in Gloucester Co., N.J. Res. at enl. Cumberland Co.,Pa. Res. in 1832, Lewis Co., Va. & d. there 4/16/1846
Sarah, former wid. of John Cunningham, Cont., N.Y., which see
Seth, Mass., N.Y., Vt., Esther Kountz, former wid., W12055; BLWt.91501-160-55; b. 9/28/1755; d. 9/10/1824 in Meigs Co., Ohio
Seth, N.Y., BLWt.7325-100-Pvt. Iss. 12/15/1790 to Alexander Galloway, ass. No papers
Seth, N.Y., S45427. In 1820 aged 70 yrs. & res. N.Y. City
Silas, Mass., S21845; b. 8/27/1762. Res. at enl. Greenwich, Hampshire Co., Mass. Res. in 1832, Pawlet, Rutland Co., Vt.
Silas, Mass., Sarah, W5007. Enl. at Great Barrington, Berkshire Co., Mass. In 1832 aged 70 yrs. & res. Fowler Twp., Trumbull Co., Ohio. D. 4/8/1841 there.
Silas, N.Y., R.I., Mercy, W15782 B. 4/26/1760 at East Greenwich, R.I. & res. there at enl. In 1832 res. Berlin, Rensselaer Co., N.Y. D. 10/14/1832
Simeon, Ct., S16894; b. 9/18/1762 in Preston, New London Co., Ct. & there at enl., and in 1832
Simpson, Cont., Mass., S32907. In 1776 aged 21 yrs. & res. of Medway, Mass.; was there in 1818
Solomon, Cont., Ct., S32903; enl. at Roxbury, Mass. In 1818 aged 64 yrs. & res. Lenox, Berkshire Co., Mass.
Solomon, Cont., Ga., N.C., S38083 Enl. in 1776 in Va. In 1827 aged 66 yrs. Res. McIntosh Co., Ga. Wife Nancy
Solomon, Md., Eliza, W9080; d. 11/30/1830, probably in Baltimore, Md.
Solomon, Mass., S35475. In 1820 aged 61 yrs. res. of Raymond, Me.
Solomon, Mass., Joanna, W5006; BLWt.1135-150-Ens. Iss. 8/27/1792 to Benj. Whitcomb, ass. In 1782 res. of Charlton, Mass., In 1820 aged 68 yrs. & res. Delaware Co., Ohio; d. 2/9/1822
Squire, Ct., BLWt.6042-100-Pvt. Iss. 7/25/1799 to Abijah Holbrook No papers
Squire, Cont., Ct., Polly, W21471; b. 8/31/1753. In 1818 res. Gaines-ville, Genessee Co., N.Y., d. 5/4/1835 at Otto, Cattaraugus Co. N.Y.
Stephen, Ct., S43728. In 1825 aged 60 yrs. & res. Kent, Litchfield Co., Ct. In 1828 res. Dutchess Co N.Y.
Stephen, Cont., Va., Mary, W7916; b. Dinwiddie Co., Va., res. at enl. & in 1833, Bedford Co., Va. D. 1/3/1834
Stephen, Mass.,S29930; b.9/2/1760 at Holliston, Worcester Co.,Mass. Res. & enl. Uxbridge, Worcester Co.,Mass. Res. after Rev. in Me. & Vt. In 1832 res. of Pelham, Hampshire Co., Mass.
Stephen, Mass., Navy, Mehitable, W776; b. 4/6/1762 in Berwick, York Co., Me. & res. there at enl. In 1832 res. of Waterbury, Washington Co., Vt. D.3/1/1846
Stephen, N.J., S15903; res. at enl. Newark, Essex Co., N.J. In 1837 res. of Caldwell Co., Mo., aged 74 yrs. Also res. in Ind. & Ill.
Stephen, N.Y., S33344; b. in Dutchess Co., N.Y., enl. near Poughkeepsie, N.Y. In 1819 res. Newark, Essex Co., N.J.
Stephen, N.C., S38092; b.8/19/1750 in St. Mary's Co.,Md. Res. during Rev. Granville & Surry Cos., N.C. In 1834 res. Harlan Co., Ky.
Strother, Cont., Va., BLWt.2442-300-Capt. Iss. 5/2/1791. Served 1776-1783 in Col. Gist's Regt. D. prior to 1791. His heirs, Wm. Strother Jones, Frances L. Burton James F. Jones, Francis B. Jones, Beverly Jones, Marshall Jones, & Martha Jones, were in Frederick Co., Va. in 1849
Sylvester, Mass., Privateer,S18903 b. 1760 at Taunton, Mass. & res. there at enl. In 1832 res. Fayette, Kennebec Co., Me.
Taverner, Va., S5627, b. 1755 in Culpeper Co., Va. & res. there at enl. and in 1832 in that part which became Madison Co., Va.
Thomas, Ct., Cont., S43716. Res. of Pomfret, Ct. In 1818, aged 67 yrs. res. Middlefield, Otsego Co., N.Y.
Thomas, Cont., Mass., S32923. Res. at enl. Brookfield, Mass. In 1818 aged 63 yrs. & res. New Marlborough, Berkshire Co., Mass. Wife Lydia in 1829
Thomas, Cont., Mass., S35474. In 1818 aged 62 yrs. & res. of Wells, York Co., Me.
Thomas, Cont., Va., Elizabeth, W3020; BLWt.1648-100 & 228-60-55 Enl. in Prince William Co., Va. In 1818 aged 68 yrs. & res. Shelby Co., Ky. D. 10/3/1833
Thomas, Del., R5748. In 1850 res. Ohio. Probably in Belmont Co.
Thomas, Md., BLWt.11374-100-Pvt. Iss. 6/2/1794
Thomas, Md., BLWt.11375-100-Pvt. Iss. 11/29/1790 to John Jones, admr. No papers
Thomas, Md., BLWt.11400-100-Pvt. Iss. 1/21/1792. No papers
Thomas, Md., S2655; b. 1/26/1756 in Washington Co., Md. & res. there at enl. Res. after Rev. in Pa. & Ky. Res. in 1832 Clermont Co., Ohio
Thomas, Md., S34940. In 1820 aged 66 yrs. & res. of Anne Arundel Co., Md.
Thomas, Md., S38093. In 1820 aged 63 yrs., res. Hancock Co., Ga.

JONES (continued)
Thomas, Md., Elizabeth, W9487. Res. at enl. Prince Georges Co. Md. D. 1/1/1813
Thomas, Md., Elizabeth, W26797, res. Montgomery Co., Md. Died about 1824
Thomas, Md., R20304. Res. at enl. Charles Co., Md. In 1833 res. of Prince George's Co., Md. aged 78 yrs.
Thomas, Md., N.C., Va., S8760; b. 1/1/1752 in Frederick Co., Md. Enl. Frederick Co., Md. & Randolph Co., N.C. In 1833 res. of Randolph Co., N.C.
Thomas, Mass., S44465; res. at enl. Hardwick, Mass. In 1818, aged 74 yrs. & res. of Antrim, Hillsborough Co., N.H.
Thomas, N.H., S36663. In 1823 aged 82 yrs. & res. Union, Lincoln Co., Me. D. 2/6/1835
Thomas, N.H., S38879. In 1818 aged 88 yrs. & res. Waterbury, Washington Co., Vt.
Thomas, N.Y., BLWt.7311-100-Pvt. Iss. 9/10/1790 to William Henderson, ass. No papers
Thomas, N.Y., BLWt.7329-100-Pvt. Iss. 5/4/1791 to Sam. Loudon. No papers
Thomas, N.Y., S39794. Enl. at Fishkill, N.Y. In 1820 aged about 61 yrs. & res. Allegheny Co., Pa. Wife ---
Thomas, N.Y., S43718. Enl. at Oswego, Dutchess Co., N.Y. In 1818 aged about 75 yrs. & res. New Paltz, Ulster Co., N.Y.
Thomas, N.C., Milly, W7919; b. 6/13/1760. Res. of Caswell Co., N.C. Moved in 1794 to Laurens Dist., S.C. where he d. 5/1/1826
Thomas, N.C., Mary/Polly, R5735 After Rev. res. in Charlotte Co., Va. & Gallatin Co., Ky. D. in Bartholomew Co., Ind. 6/12/1832
Thomas, N.C., R5750; b. 11/5/1753 in Baltimore, Md., res. at enl. Chatham Co., N.C. Res. in 1833 Weakley Co., Tenn.
Thomas, N.C., Va., S7077; b. 5/4/1763 in Amelia Co., Va. Res. there at enl. In 1832 res. Stokes Co., N.C. & was there since 1781
Thomas, Pa., BLWt.9669-100-Pvt. Iss. 7/27/1789 to Richard Platt, ass. No papers
Thomas, Pa., R5747; b. 2/4/1754 in York Co., Pa., res. there at enl. and in 1844
Thomas, Va., BLWt.12258-100-Pvt. Iss. 4/13/1791 to James Reynolds ass. Also BLWt.228-60-55. No papers
Thomas, Va., S4453; b. 3/1751 in S.C. Res. during Rev., Charlotte Co., Va. & Halifax Co., Va. Res.

JONES (continued)
in 1832, Madison Twp., Jackson Co., Ohio
Thomas, Va., S5630; b. 9/10/1755 Caroline Co., Va. & res. there at enl. In 1833 res. Spotsylvania Co., Va. D. 12/16/1844
Thomas, Va., S36656. Enl. in Amherst Co., Va. In 1818 aged 73 yrs. & res. Mercer Co., Ky. In 1832 res. Putnam Co., Ind.
Thomas, Va., S46053; b. 3/6/1757. Res. at enl. Frederick Co., Va. Res. in 1832, Bourbon Co., Ky.
Thomas, Va., Susannah/Susan, W43; BLWt.26429-160-55; b. 1762 in Loudoun Co., Va. Res. during Rev. Fauquier Co. & Henry Co., Va. Res. in 1832 Sullivan Co., Tenn. D. 7/25/1842
Thomas, Va., Lavinia, W7901; b. Amherst Co., Va. Res. at enl. Henry or Henrico Co., Va. In 1832 res. Greenbrier Co., Va., aged 84 yrs.; d. 8/26/1839
Thomas, Va., Catharine, W7905; res. at enl. in that part of Amherst Co., Va. that was later Nelson Co. In 1832 aged 77 yrs. & res. Nelson Co., Va. where he d. 7/8/1835
Thomas C., Ga., S.C., Margaret, W26160; BLWt.41291-160-55, BLWt. 26365-160-55 cancelled, b. 6/19/1765 in S.C. Res. at enl. Edgefield Dist., S.C. & Ga. in 1783. Res. in 1834, Blount Co., Ala. & d. there 2/5/1856
Tim, Va., S18063. In 1833 aged 86 yrs. & res. York Co., Va.
Timothy, Ct., Lydia, W20186. Res. at enl. Cheshire, New Haven Co., Ct. Res. also Plymouth, Litchfield Co., Ct. D. 7/25/1810 in Litchfield Co., Ct.
Timothy, Mass., S29262; b. 1762 in Worcester, Mass. & res. there at enl. In 1832 res. Springfield, Hampden Co., Mass.
Uriah, R.I., R5752, b. 8/13/1761 in Smithfield, R.I. Res. at enl. & in 1832, Cumberland, Providence Co., R.I. D. 12/1845 in Providence, R.I.
Vincent, S.C., S32343; b. 1762 in N.C. Res. at enl. Fairfield Co., S.C. After Rev. in Ga., N.C., Tenn. In 1832 res. of Shelby Co., Ala.
Westwood A., N.C., S21325; b. 1764 Res. at enl. Granville Co., N.C. Res. 1832 Haywood Co., Tenn.
William, Ct., BLWt.6022-100-Pvt. Iss. 8/15/1792 to George Wells. No papers
William, Ct., S13577; b. 1/8/1764 in Stonington, Ct. & res. there at enl. After Rev. res. in Vt. In 1833 res. Madison Co., N.Y. D. 1/19/1835
William, Ct., S36640. In 1819 aged 57 yrs. & res. New Haven,Ct.

JONES (continued)
William, Ct., S38875, enl. at Stamford, Ct. In 1818 aged 58 yrs. & res. Middlebury, Addison Co., Vt.
William, Ct., S39784. Enl. at Killingsworth, Ct. In 1818 aged 55 yrs. res. Putnam, Washington Co., N.Y. In 1820 res. Benson, Rutland Co., Vt.
William, Ct., Sea Service, Dis. No papers; res. Norwich Ct., & Nova Scotia.
William, Cont., Ct., S43715. Enl. at Weathersfield, Ct. In 1818 aged 60 yrs. & res. Amsterdam, Montgomery Co., N.Y.
William, Cont., Va., S5727. Enl. at Petersburg, Va. In 1827 aged 65 yrs. res. Pittsylvania Co., Va. D. 12/15/1833
William, Md., BLWt.11372-100-Pvt. Iss. 9/24/1792. No papers
William, Md., BLWt.11397-100-Pvt. Iss. 2/3/1792. No papers
William, Md., BLWts.13258 & 14117-100-Pvt. Iss. 4/14/1795 to Francis Sherrard, ass. of Nehemiah Jones, admr. No papers
William, Md., Margaret, W4248, enl. & res. in Talbot Co., Md., d. 11/1822
William/William N., Md., Mary Tillett, former wid., W6292; BLWt.13899-160-55; enl. at Annapolis, Md. In 1819 aged 56 yrs. Res. Fairfax Co., Va., d. 3/26/1829
William, Md., R5754. Enl. at Hagerstown, Md. In 1833 res. Scrubgrass Twp., Venango Co., Pa.
William, Md., R5755; b. 6/13/1760 in Somerset Co., Md. & res. there at enl. and in 1851
William, Md., R5756; b. 10/16/1756 in Caroline Co., Md. & res. there at enl. and in 1836
William, Md., Ind. War of 1792, Elizabeth, W4005; res. at enl. Dorchester Co., Md., d. 11/1834
William, Mass., Polly, R5736; b. 12/24/1758 in Westfield, Hampshire Co., Mass. Res. at enl. Great Barrington, Berkshire Co., Mass. Res. in 1833, Chesterfield, Essex Co., N.Y. D. 8/14/1853 at Bridport, Addison Co., Vt.
William, Mass., Susannah, BLWt. 19625-160-55. He was son of Wm. Enl. at Lunenburg, Worcester Co., Mass. Res. there & d. there 5/15/1854
William, N.H., Abigail, W16034; res. at enl. Hillsboro, N.H. In 1818 aged 73 yrs. & res. Windsor, Hillsborough Co., N.H., d. at Windsor 4/1/1833
William, N.J., BLWt.8440-100-Pvt. Iss. 7/30/1789. No papers
William, N.J., S33342. In 1819 aged 64 yrs. & res. of Woodbridge Middlesex Co., N.J.

JONES (continued)
William, N.J., R5758, b. 3/13/1744 in Bucks Co., Pa.; res. at enl. Sussex Co., N.J., res. in 1834, Sangamon Co., Ill.
William, N.Y., S9362; b. 1748 in Sussex Co., N.J., wife Mercy. Res. of Hardwick, Sussex Co., N.J. & Owego, Pa.; d. 1/1/1833 at Scarborough, Canada West
William, N.Y., Elizabeth Denison former wid., W20983. BLWt.5103-160-55; son of Henry. Res. at enl. Stephentown, Rensselaer Co., N.Y. D. there 3/22/1788
William, N.C., S4442. Vol. in Caswell Co., N.C. Res. in 1832 Smith Co., Tenn. D. 3/27/1836
William, N.C., S8765; b. in 1758 Brunswick Co., Va. Enl. Franklin Co., N.C.,was there in 1832
William, N.C., Susanna Bradford, former wid., W5935. Res. of Orange & Anson Cos., N.C., d. 4/27/1798 in Burke Co., N.C.
William, N.C., R5757; b. Va. 1755 Enl. Guilford Co., N.C. Was in Carroll Co., Tenn. in 1836
William, Pa., BLWt.9679-100-Pvt. Iss. 2/5/1792 to Sarah Shepperd, ass. No papers
William, Pa., Catharine, W2124; BLWt.39216-160-55; b. Little York, York Co., Pa. 1764. Res. at enl. Westmoreland Co., Pa. Res. in 1834, Allegheny Co., Pa. & d. there 9/17/1836
William, R.I., S32922. In 1819 aged 63 yrs. res. of Seekonk, Bristol Co., R.I.
William, S.C., BLWts.12287 & 13244-100-Pvt. Iss. 6/24/1795 No papers
William, S.C., Va., Ann Parker, former wid., R7934; res. of Amherst Co., Va. & Sumter Dist., S.C. D. 2/12/1809
William, Va., BLWt.12264-100-Pvt. Iss. 4/13/1791 to James Reynolds, ass. No papers
William, Va., BLWt.12274-100-Pvt. in Lee's Legion. Iss. 11/2/1792 to Robt. Means, ass. No papers
William, Va., S13549; b. 3/3/1759 in Frederick Co., Va. In 1832 res. of Hickman Co., Ky.
William, Va., S16172; BLWt. 78030-160-55; s. of Wm., b. 1761/1762 in Md. Res. at enl. Montgomery Co., Va., res. in 1851, Clermont Co., Ohio
William, Va., S16890, b. in Albemarle Co., Va. & res. there at enl. In 1833, aged 77, res. Boone Co., Mo.
William, Va., S35482. In 1825 aged 75 yrs. & res. of Casey Co., Ky.
William, Va., Mary, W4463; BLWt.26780-160-55; b. 12/13/1759 in Fauquier Co., Va. & res. there at enl. In 1832 res. Perry Co., Ohio and d. there 7/24/1834
William, Va., Dorothy, R5698; b. about 1760 in Henrico Co., Va. & enl. from there. D. 1/1/1835 in Yancy Co., N.C.
William, Va., Martha, R5724; d. 11/12/1828 in Halifax Co. Va.
William, Ga., Va., Milly/Emilia, W11950; BLWt.9197-160-55; enl. in Va. In 1829 aged 70 yrs. & res. of Jasper Co., Ga. Died 2/20/1841
William C., Ct., S18473; b. 5/9/1760 in Enfield, Ct. Res. at enl. Lebanon, Windham Co., Ct. After Rev. res. Herkimer Co., N.Y. In 1832 res. Trumbull Co., Ohio. D. there in 1840
Williamson, Va., S17516; b. ca. 1759 in Essex Co., Va.; res. at enl. Caroline Co., Va., res. after Rev. Ky., res. in 1832 Morgan Co., Ind.
Zebulon, N.Y., Mary, W20195; b. 3/19/1747 in Summers, Hartford Co., Ct. Res. at enl. Little Hoosick, N.Y. In 1833 res. Cornwall, Addison Co., Vt. D. 11/25/1836
Zimri, N.Y., S16166; b. 11/1/1764 in Farmington, Ct., res. at enl. Crompond, Westchester Co., N.Y. Res. in 1832 Greene Co., N.Y.

JONGST, Peter, Pa. See JUNGST

JONSON, Asa, Mass., S32902
James, Ct., Phebe, W26163

JOPLING, Thomas, Va., Mary/Molly, W7927

JORALEMON, Nicholas, N.Y., S23279

JORDAN, Abigail, former wid. of Jeremiah Hancome/Hanscomb, Mass., which see
Abner, Cont., Mass., Hannah, W26688
Abraham, Mass., S35477
Adam, N.Y., Nancy Margaret, R5771
Barak, R.I., Zeniah/Zetruiah Vorce, former wid., R10965
Benjamin, R.I. See JORDEN
Caleb, N.C., BLWt.12281 & 13247-100-Pvt. Iss. 4/21/1798 to Thomas Creesy & Hardy Murfree, assnes. No papers
Charles, Ga., Frances, R5761
Daniel, S.C., BLWts.12288 & 13245-100-Pvt. Iss. 7/13/1795. No papers
David, Mass., S35479
Dempsy/Dempsey, Ga., Sarah, W4462
Dominicus, Mass., Sea Service, R5772
Edmond/Edmund, R.I., Elizabeth, W13562
Eleazer, N.H., S44466
Elijah, Mass., S35478
Elisha, Privateer, Mass., R5762
Experience, former wid. of Charles Wilson, Mass., which see

JORDAN (continued)
Fountain, N.C., S38084; BLWt. 2349-100
Frederick, N.J., BLWt.8414-100-Pvt. Iss. 2/14/1791. No papers
Freeman, Va., S5618
George, Va., S31176
Henry, Cont., Pa., R5763
Henry, Va., S38887
Hezekiah, Mass., S36662
Hezekiah, N.C., Martha, R5766
Hugh, Md., S5619
Humphrey, Mass., Joanna, W26694; BLWt.2364-160-55
Ignatius, Mass., Sally, W2125; BLWt.24329-160-55
James, Ct., BLWt.6039-100-Pvt. Iss. 2/22/1790 to Theodosius Fowler. No papers
James, Mass., Lydia, W26690
James, Mass., Hannah, W26691
James, N.J., Margaret, W8225
James, S.C., b. Pa., S32346
Jesse, Cont., Mass., Hannah, W26693; BLWt.11394-160-55
John, Ct. Cont. See John Jordan KENEA
John, Cont., Md., Sarah Easton, former wid., W24098; BLWt.1510-150
John, Cont., Pa. See JORDEN
John, Cont., Pa., Catharine, W3426; BLWt.1165-300. Iss. 2/14/1791. No papers
John, Ga. or Va.?, Winnifred, W29726. Dau. Mary Newton
John, Md., S34945
John, Mass., S29265
John, Mass., Jane, R5764
John, N.Y. See John YORDAN
John, N.Y. See JARDON
John, Va., S38098; BLWt.1127-300-Capt. Iss. 5/7/1793 to Francis Graves, ass. Also recorded under BLWt.3550. No papers
Josiah, Mass., S23339
Lemuel, Mass., R5765
Michael, N.J., S39781
Peter, Va., Susannah, W9091
Richard, N.J., BLWt.8453-100-Pvt. Iss. 6/11/1789 to Matthias Denman, ass. No papers
Richard, N.C., S7087
Robert, Mass., Priscilla G. Ramsbottom, former wid., W24726
Robert, N.Y., N.J., b. Pa., S23733
Samuel, Ga., Margaret, W8224; BLWt.29335-160-55
Samuel, Mass., S29932
Samuel, Pa., S5617
Sharshall, Va., Efferilla, W9090
Solomon, Mass., S39788
Solomon, Mass., Sarah, W26674
Stephen, Ct., Mary, W20220
Thomas, Mass., S36668
Thomas, N.Y., See JURDEN
Thomas, N.C., Tabitha, R5767
Thomas, Pa., Rebecca, W10159; BLWt.96085-160-55
Thomas, Pa., R5768

JORDAN (continued)
Thomas, Va., Anna, R5759
Timothy, Cont., Mass., S19354
William, Mass., S36638
William, N.C., R5770 & R5773
William, Va., S8774
William, Va., S10929
JORDEN, Benjamin, R.I., Mary, W21493; BLWt.21808-160-55
Ebenezer, R.I. See JORDON
George, Va. See JORDAN
John, Ct., Cont. See John J. KENEA
John, Cont., Pa., S38883
John, N.J., S2671
Philip, R.I., S22334
Samuel, Pa. See JORDAN
JORDON, David, Mass., S32909
Ebenezer, R.I., S21841
Edmund, R.I. See Edmond JORDAN
Hezekiah, Mass. See JORDAN
Humphrey, Mass. See JORDAN
Ignatius, Mass. See JORDAN
James, Pa. See JORDAN
Jesse, Cont., Mass. See JORDAN
John, Cont., Pa. See JORDEN
John, Pa., BLWt.9688-100-Pvt. Iss. 11/23/1791 to John Hoge, ass. No papers
Robert, S.C., S18910
Thomas, N.Y. See JURDEN
William, Va., S5620
JOSE/JOSS, John, Mass., Abigail, R5774
JOSEPH, William, Md., R5775
JOSIAH, James, Navy, Elizabeth, W3259. Pa. agcy. & res. in 1818
JOSLEN, John. See JOSLIN
Reuben, Ct., Mary, W20219
JOSLIN, Darius, Mass., Sybil, W3827
David, Ct., S13543
David, Mass., Becca, W21492
Hezekiah, Mass., S15326
John, Mass., Sarah, W21489
John, R.I., Almy, W7928; BLWt. 26443-160-55
John, R.I., Deborah, W13551
Joseph, Ct., R.I., S17518
Nathaniel, Mass., S15483
Peter, Mass., Sarah, W16131
Reuben, Ct. See JOSLEN
Zebediah, Mass., Hannah, W14971
JOSLYN, Reuben. See JOSLEN
JOSS, John, Mass. See JOSE
JOSSELYN, Francis, Mass., Mary, W14968
Jabez, Mass., S43717
John, Mass., S30514
Joseph, Mass., Deborah, W13561
Nathaniel, Mass., Mercy, W2565; BLWt.12000-160-55
JOSTIN, George, Ct. See JUSTIN
JOTHAM, Calvin. See JOTHAN
Luther (colored), Cont.,Mass., Rhoda Watson,former wid., W9911; BLWt.100391-160-55
JOTHAN, Calvin, Mass., S35476
JOUETT, Matthew, Va., BLWt.1126-300; BLWt.2510-300
JOURDAN, Fountain, See JORDAN
Humphrey, Mass. See JORDAN
JOURDEN, Dempsy, Ga. See Dempsey JORDAN
Edmond/Edmund, Mass. See JURDEN
JOY, Abiathar/Abiather, Vt., S13556
Amos, N.Y., Vt., S18904
Anna, former wid. of Clement Minor, Ct., which see
Benjamin, Ct., S40888
Caleb, Mass., Susanna Harris, former wid., W14883
David, Mass., BLWt.696-100
Ebenezer, Ct., N.H., Vt., S22337
Francis, Pa., BLWt.9689-100-Pvt. Iss. 6/10/1794 to Daniel Stever ass. No papers
Gershom, Mass., S39787
Jacob, Mass., R5777
James, N.J. See MONJOY
Jedediah, Mass., S30513
Jesse, Mass., S29931
Joseph, Mass., N.Y., Sea Service, S18908
Micah, Mass., S40887
Nathaniel, Mass., Sarah, W26683
Nehemiah, Mass., Hannah, W26162
Richard, Va., S25182
Samuel, Mass., Lydia, W26695
Samuel, Mass., N.Y., Sarah, R5778
JOYAL, John B., N.Y., S15485
JOYCE, Alfred, Mass., BLWt.4460-100-Corp. Iss. 3/25/1790. No papers
Alfred, Mass., Abigail, W16311
Charles, Pa., BLWt.9699-100-Pvt. Iss. 12/3/1792 to Alexander Power, ass. of Mary Johnson, Admr. No papers
David, Ct., N.Y., S13548
George, N.C., Va., S30511
Jonathan, Mass. See JOICE
Michael, Pa., BLWt.9685-100-Pvt. Iss. 7/7/1792 to Samuel Mans, ass. of Daniel Fortis, Admr. No papers
William, Md., BLWt.11392-100-Pvt. Iss. 1/8/1796 to Geo. Ponsonby, ass. No papers
JOYNER, Benjamin, Ga., N.C., R5779
Eli, N.C., Drucilla, W7925
Jonathan, Ga. See JOINER
Joshua, Va., Sarah, W7924; BLWt. 26092-160-55
Moses, Va., Honor, R5683
Nathan, N.C. See JOINER
Susan, former wid. of John Grayson, S.C., which see
William, S.C., S20419
JOYNES, Levin, Va., BLWt.1163-500-Lt. Col. Iss. 11/24/1792 No papers
JUCKETT, Elijah, Mass., Ann, W21503; BLWt.1560-100
JUDD, Abia, former wid. of Moses Cass, Ct., which see
Alexander, Ct., BLWt.6029-100-Pvt. Iss. 9/15/1790 to Nicholas Root
Anthony, Ct., S23282
Arunah/Aruna, Mass., Sarah,W4252
JUDD (continued)
Balmarine, Ct., S31784
Calvin, Ct., Mary, W26801
Dan, Ct., S13590
Demas, Ct., S10932
Eben W., Ct., Lydia, W26706
Elias, Ct., Cont., S17520
Elihu, Ct., Lois Davis, former wid., R2743
Freeman, Ct., Cont., Deborah, W21500
Isaac, Ct., R5781
James, Ct., Esther, W20222
Jehiel, Ct., S20816
Job, Ct., Mary, W10160; BLWt. 26116-160-55
Joel, Ct., Marcy/Mercy Edwards, former wid., W17746
John, Sheldon's Dragoons, Ct., BLWt.6045-100-Pvt. Iss. 10/7/1789 to Benj. Tallmadge. No papers
John, Cont., Ct., Hannah, W26707
Levi, Ct., S18067
Nathan, Ct., S44467
Oliver, Mass., Tryphena, W21502
Ozias, Mass., Dis. No papers
Philip, ---, Mary Parkhurst, former wid., R7957. She also m. Nathaniel Brown, Wm. Jewett & John Parkhurst, all of whom are alleged to have served in the Rev.
Reuben, Ct., R5782
Reuben, Mass., S41712
Samuel, Ct., Phebe Waters, former wid., R11184. It is alleged her other husb., Oliver Waters, also served in the Rev. War. See papers within.
Solomon, Ct., S23736
Stephen, Ct., Sarah, W21499
Thomas, Ct., S31785
Walter, Ct., Margaret, W20221
William, Ct., S19724
William, Ct., BLWt.1137-300-Capt. Iss. 7/1/1790. No papers
JUDKINS, Benjamin, Cont., N.H., S18911
Jacob, N.H., S35483
Jonathan, Cont., N.H., S35485
Philip, N.H., S35484
Samuel, N.H., BLWt.3238-100-Drummer. Iss. 3/25/1790. No papers
Samuel, N.H., BLWt.3245-100-Pvt. Iss. 4/15/1796 to Joseph Cannon ass. No papers
Samuel, N.H., Elizabeth, W1778
Samuel, N.H., W7949
Samuel, N.H., Mary, W26708
JUDSON, Aaron, Ct., S17522
Agur, Ct., S15594
David, Ct., Elizabeth, W21504 & 1738-300-Capt. Iss. 10/17/1789. No papers
Elizabeth, former wid. of Benjamin Davenport, which see
John B., Ct., Hepsy, R5784
Joseph, Ct., Lydia Clark, former wid., W22782
Lemuel, Ct., S17521

JUDSON (continued)
Nathaniel, Ct., S13592
Nehemiah, Ct., Cont., S16899
Phineas, Ct., Cont., S13591
Solomon, Ct., S29266
Stiles, Ct., Naomi, W21498
JUDY, John, Pa., S4462
JULIEN, Isaac, Pa., S46054
JULIN, Isaac, Pa. See JULIEN
JUMP, Amos, Ct., N.Y., S23284
Gilbert, N.Y., R5785
John, Pa., S31178
William, N.Y., Bethiah, W20225
JUMPER, Daniel, Cont., Mass., Mary, W26810
JUMPS, Gilbert, N.Y. See JUMP
JUMPT, William, Pa., Margaret Sturgeon, former wid., R10287
JUNE, Abraham, N.Y., Jane, R5786 Wiancha/Lavinia June also applied for pension as wid. of sold. See papers within
Benjamin, N.Y., S23285
Israel, Cont., Ct., S36670
Joel, Ct., R5787
Joshua, Vt., Sarah, W16314
Reuben, Ct., Mary, W2555
Seth, Ct., Hannah, W20224
Thomas, Mass. See JONES
Zabud, Cont., N.Y. S45431
JUNG, Johannes, N.Y., Elizabeth, W20147
JUNGKURTH, Frederick, Pa., Barbara, R5788. Also given as Yonker/Yunker/Younker
JUNGST, Peter, Pa., S8000
JUNIOR, Anthony, Va., R5789
JUNKINS, John, Navy, N.H., Hannah, W1616; BLWt.6018-160-55
JUPITER, Silas, N.Y., BLWt.7319-100-Pvt. Iss. 4/26/1791 to Alexander Zuntz, ass.
JURDEN, Edmond/Edmund, Mass., S32931
Thomas, N.Y., Nancy, W21477
JUSTICE, David, N.C., Susanna, W7947
George, Va., S38889
Jacob, Pa., BLWt.9673-100-Pvt. Iss. 4/5/1790. No papers
Jacob, Pa., Elizabeth/Elisabeth, W3089
James, Pa., S16898
Jesse, Armand's Corps; BLWt. 13243-100-Pvt. Iss. 6/18/1799. No papers
John, S.C., Amy, W9092
Peter, Pa., S22856; BLWt.407-100
Richard, Va., S8775
Robert, Pa., S41711
Simeon, S.C., b. Va., Delpha, W7946; BLWt.36722-160-55
Thomas, N.C., S1842
Walcut, Ct. See Walcut JUSTIN
JUSTIN, Charles, Ct., S36669; BLWt.1172-100
George, Ct., Lucy, W20226
Gershom, Ct., Navy, Susannah, R5791
Walcut/Walcote, Ct., S45433
JUSTUS, Moses, N.C., Va., S32351

K

KACHLEIN, Peter, Pa., Elizabeth, W2945
KACHLINE, Abraham, Pa., S22304
KADER, Adam, N.Y., Nancy, W26167
John, N.Y., BLWt.7350-100-Pvt. Iss. 8/23/1790 to Charles Newkerk, ass. No papers. Also BLWt.127-60-55
KAGHNATSHON, Nicholas, N.Y. See CUSICK
KAHIKTOTOW, Cornelius (Indian), BLWt.1200-200-Lt. Iss. 3/8/1792 Also recorded under BLWt.2605. No papers
KAHM, Michael, Pa., Elizabeth, W7951; BLWt.26537-160-55
KAHOE, Thomas, Md. See CAHOE
KAIN, Edward, Md., S25195; BLWt.225-100
Edward, N.J. See KEAN
John, Pa., BLWt.9740-100-Pvt. Iss. 8/6/1792 to Manus Kain, Admr. No papers
John, Pa., BLWt.9781-100-Pvt. Iss. 9/3/1792 to Alexander Power, ass. No papers
John, ---, BLWt.13282-100-Pvt. "in the Sappers & Miners." Iss. 8/10/1789 to Richard Platt, ass. No papers
Thomas, Va., BLWt.12298-100-Pvt. Iss. 5/29/1792 to Francis Graves, ass. No papers
KALB, John de, Cont., (Bavaria), BLWt.1002-1100
KALDER, Johannes, N.Y., Peter Nella, W20289
KALEHOFF, Frederick, Pa., S23737
KALLAM, Luther, Ct., R.I., S13594
KALLOCH, Findley, Mass. See KELLOCK
KAMP, Andrew, Pa., S2674
David, Pa., S2675
KAMPER, Tilman, Va. See CAMPER
KANADAY, John, Va. See CANNADAY
KANADY, Andrew, Pa. See KENNEDY
KANAGHTJOH, Nicholas. See CUSICK
KANE, James, Pa., S45434
Patrick, Cont., Navy, Pa. agcy. S39797
Peter Warren, N.Y. See CAIN
KANEDAY, William, Ct. See KENNEDY
KANISTON, David, N.H. See KINNASTON
KANN, Peter, Pa., Elizabeth, W2809
William, Cont., Pa. See CORN
KANNADY, John, N.C. See KENNEDY
KANNON, Oreashy, N.C., S4464
KANOUSE, John, French, S23823
KAPLE, John, Ct., S13593
KAPPES, George, Pa., S40065
KAPPLINGER, Christley, Va., b. in Pa., S8776
KARACHER, George, N.C. See KARCHER
KARAKER, George. See KARCHER
KARAKIN, John, Pa., S2681
KARAKIR, George. See KARCHER
KARCHER, George, N.C., Frances, W9488; BLWt.26310-160-55
KARIKER, George. See KARCHER

KARNEY, Gilbart/Gilbert, Pa., S3347
KARR, David, Mass., See CARR
Henry, ---, Ga. res., Dis. No papers
James, N.H., S45661
James, N.C., Mary, W9093
James, Pa., S2673
James, Va., See KERR
Jonathan, Cont., Mass., See CARR
Peter, N.J., Hester, W5892
Walter, N.J., Naomi, W7950
William, S.C., See KERR
KARREN, Barney, Va., S15906
KARSH, George, Hazen's Regt., BLWt.13293-100-Pvt. Iss. 5/9/179?. No papers
KASLER, Adam, N.Y. See CASLER
Nicholas, N.Y., Delia, W21505
KASSELMAN, John S., N.Y., S10934
KASTOR, Jacob, Pa. See CASTOR
KATTON, John, Cont., N.Y. res. in 1800, BLWt.52-100
KATZEMEYER, Ludwig, Pa., R5797
KAUFFMAN, George, Va. See COFFMAN
KAUFMANN, John, Md., Va., R5798
KAULL, John, Cont., Ct., R5800
KAUP, Peter, Pa., S2678
KAUSLER, John, Pa., S8777
KAUTZ, Thomas, Pa., S7098
KAUTZMAN, John Valentine, Va. Sea Service, R59. Va. Half Pay. See N.A. Acc. No.837-Va. State Navy-John V. Kautzman-Y.S. File
KAVAN, James, Mass., S35486
KAVANAUGH, Ruth, former wid. of Travis Booton, Va., which see
KAY, James, Va., S31179
Robert, Va., BLWt.1211-200-Lt. Iss. 7/18/1791 to John Inskeep, ass. No papers
KAYHNATSHO, Nicholas. See CUSICK
KAYKENDALL, Mathew, See KUYKENDALL
KAYSER, Jacob, Md. See KEYSER
KEA, Charles, Va., S39039
Henry, N.C., S8783
KEACH, Seth, R.I., Waity, W21514
KEADER, John, N.Y., War of 1812, Elizabeth, W26949; BLWt.7350-100. Iss. in 1790; BLWt.127-60-55
KEAMEN, Nicholas, Pa., BLWt.9761-100-Pvt. Iss. 4/7/1792. No papers
KEAN, Dennis, Pa., S39802
Edward, Md. See KAIN
Edward, N.J., S33348
James, Pa., S22342
Michael, Pa., BLWt.9725-100-Pvt. Iss. 12/29/1791 to Mary Kean, Admx. No papers
KEARN, Michael, Ct. See KERN
KEARNEY, Edward, Del., S15495
KEARNS, Godfrey, Pa. See KERNS
Michael, Va., BLWt.12291-100-Pvt. Iss. 5/12/1792 to James Morrison Admr. No papers
Thomas, Md., BLWt.11413 & 14035-100-Pvt. Iss. 5/8/1792 to John Davidson, Admr. No papers
William, Hazen's Regt., BLWt. 13284-100-Pvt. Iss. 6/27/1789. No papers

KEARSEY, George, N.C., R5801
John, Pa., BLWt.9765-100-Pvt. Iss. 6/20/1789. No papers
KEARSLEY, Samuel, Pa., S1962
KEARSLICK, Abraham, S.C., R20387
KEASEY, John, Pa., S39801
KEATES, Thomas, Md., S38109
KEATH, Cornelius/Cornelious, Mass., Lydia, W26744
William, Va.,Mary McInlin, former wid., W26150; BLWt.36646-160-55
KEATING, ---, BLWt.13305-100-Pvt. "in the Invalids." Iss. 5/15/1791. No papers
Thomas, Lamb's Art., N.Y., BLWt. 7370-100-Pvt. Iss. 8/27/1792 to Evander Childs, ass. No papers
KEATLEY, Christopher, Pa., Esther, R5802
KEATON, Cornelius, N.Y. See KEATOR
John, Pa., BLWt.9723-100-Pvt. Iss. 10/28/1789 to M. McConnell, ass. No papers
John C., N.Y. See KEATOR
Zacharia James, Va., R5803
KEATOR, Cornelius, N.Y., S16174
Eunice, former wid. of Josiah Patchin, Ct., which see
Jacob N., N.Y., S13607
John C., N.Y., Rebecca, W26174
William, N.Y. See CEATER
KEBLINGER, Adam, Va. See KEEBLINGER
Jacob, Mass. See KIBLINGER
Peter, Pa., S39684
KEE, Joseph, See KIES
Stewart, Mass. See Steward KEY
KEEBLE, William, Va., Mary, W1880; BLWt.14518-160-55
KEEBLINGER, Adam, Va., Elizabeth, W1618
KEECH, James, N.Y., R5805
Jeremiah, R.I., Rachel, W21516
Job, R.I., S21329
John J.S., S36671
KEEDER, Adam, N.Y., BLWt.7352-100-Pvt. Iss. 2/21/1792 to William Campbell, ass. No papers
KEEFER, Frederick, Pa., Anna Maria W3348
KEEL, Simon, N.C., Penelope, W10164 BLWt.71018-160-55
KEELAN, James, Md., S38110
KEELAND, James, Md., BLWt.11410-100-Pvt. Iss. 1/11/1796 to Joshua Ward, ass. No papers
John, Pa., BLWt.9727-100-Pvt. Iss. 11/5/1789. No papers
Thomas, Pa., BLWt.9739-100-Pvt. Iss. 6/17/1794 to Henry Hipple, ass. No papers
KEELE, Richard, N.C., Va., S1977
KEELER, Aaron, Ct., Gloriana Olmsted/Olmstead, former wid., W21867; BLWt.1191-150-Ens. Iss. 8/17/1790. No papers
Aaron, Ct., Chloe, R5806
Aaron, Mass., S40890
David, Ct., S16904
David, Ct., S45442
Ebenezer, Ct., Lucy, W3261
Ebenezer, Mass., R5807
Edward, Cont., N.J., S33350
KEELER, Elijah, Mass., S23288
Frederick, N.Y., BLWt.7345-100-Pvt. Iss. 5/7/1795. No papers
Frederick, N.Y., Margaret, W16318
Henry, Ct., Vt., Martha Miller, former wid.,W7452; BLWt.355-60-55
Hezekiah, Ct., BLWt.6061-100-Pvt. Iss. 1/27/1796. No papers
Hezekiah, Ct., Mercy, W12005
Isaac, Ct., S45440; BLWt.1188-200-Lt. Iss. 5/9/1789. No papers
Isaac, Ct., Deborah, W20314
Isaac, Ct.,Cont., Catharine,W26178
Isaiah, Cont., N.Y., S13625
James, N.Y., R5808
Jeremiah, Ct., Cont., S45441; BLWt.6052-100-Pvt. Iss. 1/16/1797
John, N.Y., S5555
Levi, Ct., Dorcas, W20294
Lewis, Ct., S4471
Matthew, Ct., Ruth, R5809
Nathan, Ct., Huldah, W20302
Nathaniel, N.Y., Ann, W9492; BLWt.24906-160-55
Nehemiah, Ct., S15494
Philip, Ct., S15493
Samuel, Ct., BLWt.201-300
Thaddeus, Ct., BLWt.1187-200-Lt. Iss. 1/16/1797. No papers
Thomas, Ct., BLWt.639-100
Thomas, N.J., BLWt.8456-100-Pvt. Iss. 4/23/1798 to Abraham Bell, ass. No papers
Thomas, N.J. See KEELOR
Uriah, Pvt., Ct., BLWt.6070 iss. 4/12/1792 to Stephen Thorn
Uriah, Ct., Lydia, R5810
KEELEY, Joseph, Pa. See KEELY
KEELING, Edmund, Va., R5812
Robert, Mass., BLWt.4515-100-Pvt. Iss. 5/24/1790 to Benj. Prescott. No papers
KEELOR, Thomas, N.J., S41721
KEELS, Daniel, S.C., S18071
KEELY, Joseph, Pa., R5811
KEEMLE, John, Cont., Va., S5652
KEEN, Abram, Va., S11710
Andrew, Pa., S22343
Benjamin, Mass., S18479
Edward, N.J. See KEAN
Isaac, Mass., S35498
Isaiah, Mass., Lydia, W13567
Jacob, Mass., Hannah, BLWt. 3982-160-55
Jacob, N.J., BLWt.8468-100-Pvt. Iss. 3/30/1796 to Hannah Keen, Admx. No papers
James, Mass., S35496
Jesse, Mass., S29935
John, Mass., Priscilla, W24742
John, N.C., Elizabeth, W7959
John, Va., BLWt.12294-100-Pvt. Iss. 7/7/1792 to Robert Means, ass. No papers
John, Va., S37127
Joshua, Mass., Lydia, W21517
Meshack, Cont., Mass., S16902
Michael, Md., BLWt.11430-100-Pvt. Iss. 1/11/1796 to Joshua Ward, ass. No papers
Tubal, Mass., Navy, S32941
William, N.C., S41715
KEENE, Lawrence, Pa., BLWt.1235-300
Samuel Y., Md., BLWt.213-300. No papers found. Old BL Reg. shows: Surgn. Mate - Warrant iss. 9/5/1805. Delivered to T. Worthington
William, Mass., Celana/Celena, W26746
KEENEY, Ashbel, Ct., Sarah, W20300
Ethel, Ct., R5813
James, Ct., Anne, W20326
Richard, Ct., S13620
Thomas, Ct., S9366
William, Ct., S18072
KEENON, Nicholas, Pa., BLWt.9760-100-Pvt. Iss. 8/15/1792 to John Keenon, Admr. No papers
KEEP, Jabez, Mass., S32937
Jabez, Mass., Lydia, W20298
James, Va., BLWt.12297-100-Pvt. Iss. 7/3/1795. No papers
James, Va., S39804
John, Mass.?, Abigail, W9094
Stephen, Mass., S29939
KEEPHEART, Adam, Md. See KEPHART
KEEPER, Thomas, N.J., S5653
KEES, Daniel, Pa., BLWt.9743-100-Pvt. Iss. 8/14/1793 to Jasper Iserloan, ass. No papers
Philip, Pa., Catharine, W7957; BLWt.2488-100; BLWt.75-60-55
KEET, Jonathan, Mass., Dolly, W14990; BLWt.12703-160-55
KEETER, Jacob (Indian), Mass., BLWt.1928-100
James, (Indian), Mass., Mercy, W32942; BLWt.1929-100
John, Mass., S45448
KEETH, John, S.C. See KEITH
KEETON, David, Va., S2685
Isaac, N.C., Margaret, W9097
John, Va., S13614; BLWt.26475-160-55
KEEVER, James, S.C. See KEVER
John, Md., Mary, R5814; BLWt. 61232-160-55
KEFFER, Joseph, Pa., R5815
KEGER, John, Cont., Va., S38118; BLWt.2013-100
KEHELA, Christopher, N.C., Polly, W3693
KEHL, Jacob, Pa., Catharine, W2811
KEHR, David, Pa., S32359
KEIBLER, George, Pa. See KIEBLER
KEIFER, Frederick, Pa. See KEEFER
KEIPHART, George, Cont., Md., S36673
KEISER, George, N.C., Elizabeth, W7997
Jacob, Pa., R5817
John, Mass., S15910
John, Pa., Elizabeth, R5816
Lewis, Pa. See KEIZER
KEISINGER, Andrew, Va., R5818
KEISLING, John, Pa., S16434
KEISON, John, Mass. See KEISER
KEISTER, Peter, Pa., R5819
KEITH, Alexander, Va., S36672
Asa, Mass., S10943
Barak, Ct., S13613
Caleb, Mass., Molly, W1619
Daniel, Va., S38115
David, Mass., S32943

KEITH (continued)
Grendal/Grindell, Mass., S40892
Ichabod, Cont., Mass., S10938
Isaac, Mass., S32939
Isaiah, Mass., Sarah, W26741
James, Cont., Mass., Anna, W27437
James, N.Y., S5650
Jane, former wid. of John McGaughey/McGoughey, N.C., S.C., which see
Japheth, Mass., BLWt.4511-100-Pvt. Iss. 5/6/1793. No papers
John, Ct., Mass., S44479
John, Mass., S29273
John, S.C., Va., Nancy Smith, former wid., W11478; BLWt.17892-160-55
Peter, Ct., S45447
Reuel/Ruel, Mass., S18913
Simeon, Mass., S21848
Thomas, Va., Judith, W5119
Unite, Mass., Sarah, W15687
William, Va. See KEATH
KEIZER, Lewis, Pa. Ann Elizabeth/Anna Elizabeth, W4709
KELAN, James, Md. See KEELAN
KELCEY, Giles, N.H. See KELSEY
KELCH, John, N.Y., Susan, R5824
Leonard, N.C., Va., R5823
Philip, N.Y., S45446
KELEY, Benjamin, N.Y., BLWt. 7344-100-Pvt. Iss. 5/29/1793 to Bartholomew & Fisher, assnes. No papers
KELHAM, William, Mass., Ann/Anna, W14984
KELHNER, Matthias, Pa., Maria, W5013
KELKNER, Henry, Pa., S38114
KELL, Christopher, See KILL
James, N.C., S32357
Robert, N.C., S32355
KELLAM, Housten/Houston, Va., Elizabeth, W4254
Spencer, Va., Margaret, W1178; BLWt.95517-160-55
KELLAR, Conrad, Pa., Catharine, R5826
George, Pa., BLWt.9769-100-Art. Iss. 4/16/1795. No papers
John, Pa., S4465
KELLEE, Jeremiah M., Ct.,S15911
KELLER, Abraham, Va., R15580; Va. Half Pay. N.A. Acc. No. 874-050096
Adam, Pa., BLWt.1202-200-Lt. Iss. 3/19/1792 to George Moore, ass. No papers
Conrad, Pa., S46310; BLWt.1969-100
Devault/Devalt, S.C., S32358
Francis, Pa., BLWt.9784-100-Pvt. Iss. 6/29/1789 to M. McConnell, ass. No papers
Frederick, Pa., S39808
George, Cont., Pa., Margaret, W3090
George, Pa., Elizabeth, W4470; BLWt.18727-160-55
George, Va., S5649
George, Va., Sophia, R5827 He d. in March 1844
George, Va. R5528. He died

KELLER (continued)
between 10/19 & 11/7/1836
Jacob, Pa., Catharine, W3347
Jacob, Pa., Elizabeth, R5829
John, N.Y., Catharine, W692; BLWt.100-60-55
Simon, Pa., S22857
KELLEY, Charles, Ct., S45445
Charles, N.C., Nancy, W948
David, N.H., S10939
David, N.Y., R5839
Dudley, N.H., R5830
Elias, Pa., S16175
George, Pa., BLWt.9763-100-Pvt. Iss. 3/19/1792 to George Moore, ass. No papers
Griffin, Northwest Indian War 1790-1794, Old War Inv. 23483; O.W. Wid. Rej. 15571, War of 1812, Sally
James, Va., S16433
James, Va., Elizabeth, R5841
Jared, N.J., Mary, W114
Jeremiah, N.Y., S29267
John, Mass., Molly, W20291
John, Pa., BLWt.9719-100-Pvt. Iss. March 1791. No papers
John, S.C., Mary, W21521
John, Va., S41717
John, Va., Ann, W9095
Jonathan, N.H. See KILLEY
Joshua, Md., R21706
Lloyd, S.C., S31790
Margaret, former wid. of Christopher Cary, N.H., which see
Mathew, Md., BLWt.11412-100-Pvt. Iss. 12/23/1795 to George Ponsonby
Mathew, Md., BLWt.11421-100-Pvt. Iss. 12/1795. No papers
Micajah, Mass., N.H., S18073
Moses, Md., S8786
Oliver, Cont., N.J., S41724
Robert, N.Y. See KELLY
Stephen, Mass., Mary, W26739
Timothy, Hazen's Regt., BLWt. 13288-100-Pvt. Iss. 6/17/1799 to Abraham Bell, ass. No papers
William, Cont., Va., Lucinda Whitmond/Whitman, former wid., W25993; BLWt.43528-160-55
William, Md., Martha, R5831
William, Pa., S39809
William, Va., Sally, S13595; BLWt.34666-160-55
William, Va., R5833
KELLICUT, Thomas, Mass., Mary, W8004; BLWt.30761-160-55
KELLOBRUE, Lawrence,See KILLEBREW
KELLOCH, David, Mass., Mary, W7976; BLWt.9432-160-55
Mathew/Matthew, Mass., Navy, S35493
KELLOCK, Findley, Mass., Hannah, W3563; BLWt.52472-160-55
KELLOG, Enoch, Ct., BLWt.6072-100-Pvt. Iss. 3/24/1790. No papers
Josiah/Joseph? (in pencil), Ct. BLWt.6056-100-Pvt. Iss. 8/27/1782. No papers

KELLOG (continued)
Preserved, Vt., S23289
Solomon, Ct., BLWt.6055-100-Pvt. Iss. 8/27/1792. No papers
William, Ct., BLWt.6060-100-Pvt. Iss. 8/27/1792. No papers
KELLOGG, Aaron, Navy, Mass., S32933
Amos, Cont., Vt., Lucretia, W20315
Benjamin, Mass., S13627
Daniel, Ct., S10944
Ebenezer, Mass., S29270
Eldad, Ct., Mass., Elizabeth, W7977; BLWt.523-160-55
Elijah, Ct., S23738
Elijah, Ct., Mass., S13599
Elijah, Mass., Eunice, W26740
Eliphalet, N.Y., S2692
Enoch, Ct., S45439
Enos, Mass., S18476
Ezekiel, Mass., S13601
Ezra, Mass., S30520
Helmont, Ct., S21847
Horace/Horrace, Ct., S45437
Jason, Mass., S45438
John, Mass., S29272
Joseph, Mass., S45435
Josiah, Ct., S41722
Josiah, Mass., Jerusha, W26738
Levi, N.Y., S13609
Loomis, Mass., Perses, W1039; BLWt.26396-160-55
Martin, Ct., S10940
Martin, Mass., S2691
Medad, Ct., Mass., S15492
Nathaniel, Cont., Mass., N.Y., S13597
Nathaniel, Mass., War of 1812, Betsey, W5307; BLWt.11420-160-55
Noah, Ct., S45436
Phineas, Ct., S42774
Phinehas, Mass., S---. His wid., Mabel Kellogg, applied for pension as former wid. of Elijah Andrews, Ct., which see
Pliny, Cont., Mass., S13612
Pliny/Pliney, Mass., S41718
Samuel, Ct., S39806
Seth, Mass., S42776
Silas, Mass., S29271
Solomon, Ct., Cont., S40896
Stephen, Ct., Dis. No papers
Stephen, Ct., Lydia, W21506
Stephen, Mass., S29269
Thomas, Mass., S13619
Titus, Mass., S40889
William, Pa., S42775
KELLON, Edward, Pa., BLWt.9734-100-Pvt. Iss. 4/11/1791. No papers
KELLOW, William, Md., BLWt.1934-100
KELLUM, Reuben, N.Y., BLWt.7361-100-Pvt. Iss. 1/11/1792. No papers
KELLY, Abraham, N.J., S23744
Abraham, S.C., S38891
Andrew, S.C., R5837
Anthony, Mass., S13616
Beal, Va., S15490
Benjamin, N.C., R5838

KELLY (continued)
Carpenter, N.J., Hester Van Saun, former wid., W877
Craig, Ct., Sibbel, W20304
David, Hazen's Regt., BLWt. 13287-100-Pvt. Iss. 7/12/1792. No papers
David, Md., BLWt.11409-100-Pvt. Iss. 3/22/1797 to Abijah Holbrook, ass. No papers
David, N.Y., BLWt.7362-100-Pvt. Iss. 1/25/1791 to Elihu Marvin, ass. No papers
David, N.Y., Mary, W11993
David, R.I., S21328
Dennis, Del., Elizabeth, W947
Edmond, N.Y., BLWt.7343-100-Pvt. Iss. 11/9/1789 to James Reynolds, ass.No papers
Edmond, N.C., S.C., Va., R5840
Edmund, N.Y., Lovina/Lavinia, W26748
Edward, Mass. See CALLEY
Edward, Pa., BLWt.9735-100-Pvt. Iss. 11/12/1789 to Mary Doyle, ass. No papers
Eleazer, R.I., Mercy, W20319
George, N.Y., Elizabeth, W20303
George, Va., Nancy Dewitt, former wid., R2922
Giles, S.C., S31788
Henry, Lee's Legion, Va., BLWts. 13292 & 13574-100-Pvt. Iss. 9/2/1789. No papers
Henry, N.C., Mary, W20290
Jacob, Ga., Jane, R5843
James, Cont., S.C., S1544
James, Pv., Md., BLWt.11414 iss. 2/1/1790
James, Pa., S39799
James, Va., S16903
James, Va., Catharine, W7969
Jeremiah M., Ct. See KELLEE
John, Ct., Olive Bowers, former wid., W393
John, N.J., R5844
John, Lamb's Art., N.Y., BLWt. 7372-100-Pvt. Iss. 5/14/1790 to Jer[h] Osborn, ass. No papers
John, N.C., S35489
John, Pa., BLWt.9717-100-Pvt. Iss. 3/10/1790 to John Kelly.
John, Pa., BLWt.9771-100-Pvt. Iss. 6/27/1791. No papers
John, S.C., R5845
John, Va., S36674
John O., see John O'KELLY, R.I.
Jonathan, N.H., BLWt.3255-100-Pvt. Iss. 8/26/1790 to Manassah Cutler, ass. No papers
Joseph, Mass., S35492
Joseph, N.J., War of 1812, R5846
Joshua, Mass., S35497
Joshua, N.Y., BLWt.7339-100-Pvt. Iss. 7/29/1790 to Nathaniel Scribner, ass. No papers
Joshua, N.Y., S45444
Keelan, Pa., BLWt.9733-100-Pvt. Iss. 12/22/1794 to Henry Purdy
Magdalina, former wid. of Martin Reese, N.Y., which see
Mary, former wid. of Joseph

KELLY (continued)
Fessenden, Mass., which see
Maurice, Mass., S32935
Nathaniel, N.H., S4472
Nathaniel, N.H., Sally/Sarah, W21520
Oliver, Cont., N.J., See KELLEY
Patrick, N.J., BLWt.8470-100-Pvt. Iss. 10/16/1789 to Benj. Harris, ass. No papers
Patrick, Pa., S5647
Patrick, Pa., BLWt.2110-100
Peter, S.C., b. Ireland, S32352
Richard, Va., S1680
Robert, N.Y., BLWt.7348-100-Pvt. Iss. 2/7/179- to Wm. Thorne, ass. No papers
Robert, N.Y., Elizabeth, W20306
Samuel, Md., S38112
Samuel, Pa., S2686
Stephen, R.I., S13605
Thady/Thaddy, Va., R15579. Va. Half Pay. N.A. Acc. No. 874-050097
Thomas, Pa., BLWt.9756-100-Pvt. Iss. 8/5/1789 to John Baldwin
Thomas, Pa., BLWt.9762-100-Pvt. Iss. 8/6/1792 to Alex. Power
Thomas, Pa., Ellen, W9096; BLWt.959-100
Thomas, Va., S36031
Timothy, Mass., Joanna, W12017
Timothy, Pa., BLWt.9718-100-Pvt. Iss. 11/9/1791. No papers
William, Mass., S45443
William, N.H., Sarah, W26749
William, N.C., S.C., b. S.C., Elizabeth, W7
William, Pa., BLWt.9731-100-Pvt. Iss. 12/13/1791 to Gideon Merkle
William, Pa., BLWt.9738-100-Pvt. Iss. 5/16/1792. No papers
William, Pa., BLWt.9775-100-Pvt. Iss. 8/7/1789 to Richard Platt
William, Pa., BLWt.9776-100-Pvt. Iss. 4/19/1792. No papers
William, Pa., S2689
William, Pa., S33353
William, Pa., Jane, W3692
William, Va., b. Pa., Sarah, W10165
William, Va., BLWt.1947-100
KELP, Andrew, Pa., BLWt.9751-100-Pvt. Iss. 6/11/1793 to Casper Iserloan, ass. No papers
KELSEY, Benjamin, Ct., S36676
Cataline, former wid. of Joseph Fitch, N.Y., which see
Ezra, Ct., S15491
Giles, N.H., Dis. No papers
Giles, N.H., S40897
Heth/Heath, Ct., S13611
Hugh, S.C., Margaret, R5850
Joel, Ct., S16432; BLWt.26777-160-55
John, Ct., Lucy, W20301
John, N.Y., S13610
Merry Seymour, Ct., R.I.(?), Sarah, R5852
Noah, Ct., BLWt.6062-100-Pvt.

KELSEY (continued)
Iss. 8/16/1790. No papers
Noah, Ct., Margaret, R5851
Reuben, Ct., S10937
Samuel, Ct., S13622
Seymour, Ct., R.I., See Merry Seymour
Stephen, Ct., Lois, W26168
Thomas, N.Y., S2687
Zachariah, N.H., S44478
KELSIMERE, Francis, Md., S41716
KELSO, Alexander, N.C., S.C., b. Va., Margaret, W9493
David, N.Y., Ann, W26175
James, Va., S18068
John, N.Y., Elizabeth, W26752
John, Pa., BLWt.9715-100-Sgt. Iss. 11/5/1789. No papers
John, Pa., Mary, W4469
Samuel, S.C., Lucy, R5853
Thomas, Md., Penelope, W9099
KELSON, George, Md., BLWt.11427-100-Pvt. Iss. 2/1/1790. No papers
KELSY, Samuel, Ct. See KELSEY
KELTLINGER, Adam, Va. See KEEBLINGER
KELTON, Amos, Mass., S10942
Edward, Mass., Hannah, W13575
John, Mass., Rachel, W21512
Thomas, Mass. See KILTON
KELTY, James, Md. See KILTY
John, Pa., Margaret, W15917
KELTZ, Nicholas, N.Y., BLWt.7357-100-Pvt. Iss. 4/2/1793 to Henry Platner, ass. No papers
KEMBLE, Hazadiah, Mass., BLWt.4529-100-Pvt. Iss. 9/10/1789 to Henry Newman. No papers
Peter, N.J., R5925
Peter, N.Y., Elizabeth, W20311
KEMISTON, James, Cont., N.H., See KENISTON
KEMMERER, Frederick, Pa., S40068
KEMP, Adria, former wid. of Wm. English, Va., which see
Asa, Mass., Alice, W14995
Benjamin, N.H., S10941
Dudley, Cont., Mass., Abigail, W26755; BLWt.90-60-55
Ebenezer, Mass., S35495
Elijah, Mass., N.H., Sarah, W26747
James, Va., R15581. Va. Half Pay. N.A. Acc. No. 874-050098
John, N.H., R5854
Jonas, Mass., S32938
Jonas, Mass., W21508
Joseph, Mass., S32944
Reuben, N.H., S36675
Reuben, Va., S16901
Simeon, Cont., Mass., Tryphena, W16621
Thomas, Cont., N.H., S44475
Thomas, Va., R15582
William, Ga., S.C., R5856
William, Mass., BLWt.901-100
William, Va., BLWt.12293-100-Pvt. Iss. 12/12/1791 to Francis Graves, ass. No papers
KEMPER, Charles, Va., Susannah, W20292
Daniel, Cont., N.J., N.Y.,S2693

KEMPER (continued)
Jacob, N.J., BLWt.1329-200
John, Cont., N.Y., Pa. Sea Service, S13621
KEMPFIELD, Napthali, Mass., BLWt. 4530-100-Pvt. Iss. 5/24/1790. No papers
KEMPLIN, William, Pa., Elizabeth, W7971; BLWt.38511-160-55
KEMPTON, Oliver, Mass., BLWt.884-100
Rufus, Mass., N.H., Vt., See KIMPTON
Samuel, Cont., Mass., N.H., Catharine, W13578
KENADY, Jesse, Va. See KENNEDY
KENAID, Elizabeth, former wid. of Solomon Todd, N.H., which see
KENAN, Roger, Pa., BLWt.9721-100-Pvt. Iss. 2/14/179- to Alexander Power, ass.No. papers
KENARDA, John, N.C. See KENNEDY
KENCH, Thomas, Cont., Mass., S35499
KENDAL, Clayton, Cont., N.Y.,S33352
Isaac, Ct., Rachel, W12007
Isaac, Cont., Mass., Mary, W14994
Joshua, Ct., S13615
KENDALL, Aaron/Aron, Md., S31180
Aaron, Va., S15909
Asa, Mass., S29936
Benjamin, Mass., Elizabeth, W14996
Benjamin, Va., Elizabeth, R5857
Chever/Cheever, Mass., S31786
Custis, Va., BLWt.1209-300-Capt. Iss. 6/26/1789. No papers
Ebenezer, Ct., Elizabeth, R5930
Eleazer, Mass., S22340
Ephraim, Mass., Experience, R5858; BLWt.34812-160-55
Francis, Va., Malinda Hitt, former wid., W25775; BLWt.2360-160-55
George, Va., R5859
Isaac, Mass., S21330
Jacob, Mass., S15489
James, Hazen's Regt., BLWt.13286-100-Drummer. Iss. 8/3/1789, to Wm. J. Vredenburgh, ass. No papers
Jeremiah, Va., S23743
John, Ct., BLWt.6067-100-Sgt. Iss. 8/25/1789. No papers
John, Ct., Cont., S39812
Joshua, Mass., S44472
Joshua, Mass., Beulah, W20295
Nathan, Mass., S30519
Nathan, N.H., S10936
Noah, Mass., Joanna, W14987
Oliver, Mass., BLWt.4541-100-Pvt. Iss. 3/25/1790. No papers
Oliver, Mass., Hannah Harrington, former wid., W14890
Peter, Vt., S13628
Peter, Va., Nancy, R5860
Reuben, Mass., BLWt.4527-100-Pvt. Iss. 2/25/1791 to Samuel Whitney
Reuben, Mass., S44471
Thomas, Mass., S10935
Timothy, Mass., Lucy, W14991
Timothy, Mass., Eunice, W21509; BLWt.3524-160-55
William, Mass., S18912

KENDALL (continued)
William, Mass., Abigail, W26753; BLWt.2345-160-55
KENDLE, William, S.C., Elizabeth, W7978; BLWt.29025-160-55
KENDRICK, Abel, S.C., R5861
Benjamin, Va., Frankey, W9098
Benoni, Va., S36030
Daniel, N.H., S16870
Daniel, Va., Winifred, W9491
Heth, Vt., S16176
Isham, N.C., Elizabeth, R5862
Jacob, Va., R5863
John, --, Invalid pensioner - No papers --Savannah, Ga. agcy.
John, Mass., Dolly, W26754
Oliver, Cont., Mass., S44473
Samuel, N.H., S23740
William, Va., S31182
William, Va., Fanny, W26743
KENEA, John Jordan, Ct., Cont., Obedience, W26177
KENEDA, William, Va., S4468
KENEDAY, Thomas, N.C. See CANADAY
KENEDY, William, Ct. See KENNEDY
William, S.C., S2695
KENERSON, John, Mass. See KINERSON
KENESON, Joseph, N.H. See KENISON
KENEY, John, Mass., R26216
Richard, Ct. See KEENEY
KENFIELD, Erastus, See KENTFIELD
Noah, Mass., S29938
KENISON, Job, N.H., BLWt.737-100
Joseph, N.H., S40895; BLWt.784-100
KENISSON, Ebenezer, N.H., Betsey W21310
KENISTON, David, N.H., S9364. B. at New Market, N.H. & res. there at enl. In 1832 aged 75 yrs & res. of Sandwich, d. 11/9/1841
James, Cont., Mass., N.H., S8785
James, N.H., BLWt.3261-100-Pvt. Iss. 7/21/1789 to Ladd & Cass. No papers
Job, N.H., See KENISON
John, Mass. See KINERSON
Josiah, N.H., Anna, W14993
KENISTONE, Mary, former wid. of Jeremiah Dutch, N.H.,which see
KENMOURE, John, S.C., S21850
KENNADAY, Joseph, Va., S31181
KENNADY, John, Va. See CANNADAY
KENNAHORN, William, Va., Delany, W26642; BLWt.8175-160-55
KENNAN, Isaac, Mass., S16173
KENNARD, Benjamin, Pa., S38892
John, Md., See KINNARD
John, N.J., S41723
Joseph, Pa., BLWt.9753-100-Pvt. Iss. 1/5/1792 to Stephen Loudon, ass. No papers
Joseph, Pa. See KINNARD
Timothy, Mass., S19365
KENNEDA/KENNADA, John, N.Y., R5866
KENNEDAY, Sherwood, N.C., b. Va. S8779
Thomas, N.C. See CANNADAY
KENNEDY, Andrew, N.C., Rachel, W161
Andrew, Pa., S41713; BLWt.89-100

KENNEDY (continued)
Charles, Va., S13617
David, N.C., S8782
David, S.C., Keziah, W7972
David, Va., Jane, W7973
Dennis, Pa., BLWt.9737-100-Pvt. Iss. 6/20/1789. No papers
Hugh, Ct., R.I., S42777
Isaac, N.C., S13602
James, Cont., N.H., Me. res., S35488
James, Md., S38893
James, Mass., S23739
James, S.C., Mary Eliza, W490; BLWt.1216-200-Lt. Iss. 5/10/1796. No papers
James, Va., R15594. Va. Half Pay. See N.A. Acc. No. 874-050099
Jesse, Va., Susan Alfred, former wid., R93. She also applied for pension of her other husb., Thomas Alfred, Sea Service & Va., see papers within
John, N.Y., BLWt.7353-100-Pvt. Iss. 7/28/1790 to G.H.V. Wagenen,
John, N.Y., Hannah, W15839
John, N.C., Cherry, W10170
John, Pa., S23742
John, Privateer, Mass., N.H. res. & agcy. S20006
John, Va., S38890
John, Va. See CANADY
Joseph, Ct., Agnes, W20329
Joseph, N.C., Va., S13600
Joseph, Va. See KENNADAY
Patrick, N.H., Mary, W20293
Robert, Ct., N.Y., Eunice, R5868
Samuel, N.Y., Catharine, W20317
Samuel, Pa., BLWt.1199-300-Capt. Iss. 7/24/1789 to John Pinkerton, ass. No papers
Seth, Ct., Cont., Mass., & Navy, S31789
Thomas, Md., BLWt.294-100
Thomas, N.Y., b. Ireland, Dorothy, W16316
Thomas, N.C., S31185
Thomas, Pa., Navy, R5867
Thomas, S.C., Sarah, W10167
William, Ct., Mary, W15783
William, Va. See KENEDA
William, Va., S38117
KENNELLY, John, Cont., N.Y., S42778; BLWt.13289-100-Pvt. Iss. 2/14/1791 to Edward Savage, ass.
KENNELY, John, Pvt. Hazen's Regt. BLWt.13289 iss. 2/14/1791 to Edward Savage, ass.
KENNER, Jonathan, N.Y. See KINNER
Rodham, Va., Va. Sea Service, S1228
KENNERLEY, Samuel, Va., S16900
KENNERLY, Thomas, Va., S1843
William, Va., S8781
KENNEY, Abijah, Mass., S18477
Amos, Mass., S40066
Amos, N.Y. See KINNEY
Archelaus, Mass. See KINNEY
Benjamin, Mass., Lydia, W301; BLWt.13709-160-55

KENNEY (continued)
Edward D., Pa. See John
Israel, Mass., S35490
Jesse, Mass. See KINNEY
Jesse, Mass., R15611
John, Cont., N.H., Betsey, W21515
John/Edward D., Pa., S35487
Lyman, Ct., Dis.
Samuel, S.C., BLWts.12304 & 13283-100-Pvt. Iss. 10/15/1795
Thomas, Mass., Hannah, W26745; BLWt.6393-160-55
William, Mass., S40899
William, S.C., R5871
KENNIBROUGH, James. See KINNEBROUGH
KENNICUTT, Luther, Cont., N.Y., R20389
KENNISON, Ebenezer, N.H. See KENISSON
Joseph, N.H. See KENISON
KENNISTON, David, N.H. See KINNASTON
Job, N.H. See KENISON
Josiah, N.H. See KENISTON
Mary, N.H. See Jeremiah DUTCH
KENNON, Oreashy, N.C. See KANNON
Richard, Va., BLWt.2298-300
William, Va. See CANNON
KENNY, Benjamin, Mass., Elizabeth, W23265
Daniel, Pa., S37126
David, Mass., BLWt.4540-100-Pvt. Iss. 1/26/1790 to John May. No papers
David, Mass., S32932
Jacob, N.J., S46453
Neal, Pa., BLWt.9755-100-Pvt. Iss. 6/24/179- to James Humphreys, ass. No papers
Richard, Va. See KINNEY
Samuel, Cont., Mass., Elizabeth, W20296
Samuel, Mass., S18478
Samuel, N.Y., BLWt.1203-200-Lt. Iss. 5/31/1791 to Charles Weir, Admr. No papers
KENSAUL, John, N.C. See KINSAUL
KENSEY, William, Pa. See KINSEY
KENSOR, Michael, Va. See KINSER
KENSYL, Frederick, Pa. See KINSELL
KENT, Abel, Cont., Mass., S16431
Absalom, Pa., S8784
Alexander, Va., S38113
Bela, Cont., Ct., Lucretia, W7962
Benjamin, Mass., R5872
Cato (colored), Ct., Beulah, W26169
Charles, Ct., S13618
Dan, Vt., Betsy, W21519
Daniel, Va., R15583, Va. Half Pay
Darius, Ct., S31791
David, N.J., Sarah Hyde, former wid., W13521; BLWt.10183-160-55. Her last husb., Abel Hyde, served in War of 1812.
Ebenezer, Cont., Mass., Dis. No papers
Ebenezer, N.H., War of 1812, W29940
Elihu, Ct., Elizabeth, W26172
Ezekiel, Mass., S13596
Ichabod, Mass., Abigail, W21513

KENT (continued)
Isaac, Md., BLWt.11425-100-Pvt. Iss. 8/4/1789. No papers
Isaac, Md., S41725
Jacob, Ct., R20388
Jacob, N.J., S688
Jacob, N.Y., Huldah, R5873
James, N.J., Catharine, W20313
Job, N.H., S8780
John, Ct., Mary, W3559; BLWt. 8354-160-55
John, Mass., Betsey, W26757
John, N.H., S44476; BLWt.701-100
John, Vt., Mary, W4253
John, Va., Susan, R5875
Jonas, N.J., BLWt.8464-100-Pvt. Iss. 1/28/1790. No papers
Jonathan K., Ct., S31792
Joseph, Ct., S42764
Joseph, R.I., Sabra, W7961; BLWt.17718-160-55
Levi, N.C., S41714
Moses, Vt., R5874
Nathaniel, Cont., Mass., Abigail, W14986; BLWt.3399-160-55
Peter, Va., Sarah Ann, W85
Phineas, N.J., Sarah, W469
Richard, Mass., S5654
Robert, Va., Sarah, W27875
Samuel, Ct., Mary, W5306
Thomas, Md., S23741
Thomas, N.Y., S42773
Thomas, Va., S4466
Titus (colored), Ct., BLWt. 1665-100
William, Mass., Hannah, W14985
William, Pa., S2684
KENTFIELD, Aseph/Asaph, Mass., BLWt.15-100
David, Mass., S29937
Ebenezer, Mass., S41726
Erastus, Mass., S32940; BLWt. 31284-160-55
KENTNER, John P., Ct., R5876
KENTON, Simon, S41719. Famous Ky. scout b. 4/3/1755 in Va. Explored Ky. region in 1771. Served in Lord Dunmore's War in 1774. In Rev., served as a spy & messenger, was Gen. Geo. Rogers Clark on many expeditions and to Kaskaskia. Taken prisoner by indians in Sept. 1778, escaped following July & returned to Ky., & continued to serve under Gen. Clark in 1780 & 1782. Returned to Va. in 1783 for a short time, then back to Ky. on active service on the frontier, was with Gen. Wayne in 1st campaign of 1793. Left service after treaty of Greenville in 1795. Was Brig. Gen. of Volunteers in War of 1812. Granted pension by Special Act of Congress, fecctive 1/1/1829, then living in Ohio. He d. 4/29/1836.
KENWORTHY, Mary, former wid. of Abraham Meriam, Mass., which see
KENYON, Alexander, See KINYON

KENYON (continued)
Amos, R.I. See KINYON
Caleb, R.I., Martha, W21518
Clark, R.I. See KINYON
David, R.I., See KINYON
Griffin, N.Y. See KINYON
James, R.I., S21851
John, R.I., S23286
Joseph, R.I., Hezediah, R5878
Joseph, R.I. See KINYON
Lodowick, R.I., Hannah, W26750
Moses, R.I. See KINYON
Payne, Ct., S42767
Thomas W., R.I. See KINYON
Thurston/Thruston, R.I., S13598
William, R.I. See KINYON
Zephrah, former wid. of Wm. Prentice, which see
KEPHART, Adam, Md., BLWt.2404-100. See claim, W4206 in which Adam Gibhart stated he was the only sold. of that name in the 2nd Md. Regt.
George, Md. See KEIPHART
Henry, Va. See KIPHART
Martin, Md., S41727
KEPLER, George P., Pa. See KESSLER
Samuel, Pa., Susanna, R5881
KEPLINGER, Peter, See KEBLINGER
KEPP, Amos, N.Y., BLWt.7354-100-Pvt. Iss. 9/8/1790. No papers
KEPPS, Jacob, Va., Elizabeth, W7993; BLWt.35835-160-55
KERBAUGH, David, Pa., S39800
KERBO, Joseph, N.C. See CURBOW
KERBOUGH, David, See KERBAUGH
KERBY, Archibald, S.C., S21852
Christopher, N.C., S32356
Hezekiah, R.I. See KIRBY
Jesse, Va., Sophia, W9489
Leonard T., Va., S31183
Stephen, N.Y. See KIRBY
William, N.C., S4470
William, Va., Elizabeth, W7998; BLWt.17717-160-55
KERCHEVAL, John, Cont., Va., Jane, W3023
John, Va., Elizabeth, W9490; BLWt.38507-160-55
William, Va., R5882
KERCHNER, Michael, Md. See KIRSHNER
KERKER, John, Art. Artificers, BLWt.13299-100-Pvt. Iss. 6/4/1790. No papers
KERN, John, N.Y., S13604
Michael, Ct., N.Y., Mary, W7964
Michael, Pa., S5648
William, Pa., S4463
KERNACHAN, William, Cont., Pa., S39803
KERNALS, William, Md. See KERNELL
KERNELL, William, Md., S38108
KERNER, John, Pa., S39807
Philip, N.Y. See CARNER
KERNES, William, Va., Sarah, W7965; BLWt.38512-160-55
KERNEY, John, Va., R15613. Va. Half Pay
KERNINE, Eder, N.J., S33351
KERNON, Francis, Crane's Cont. Art., Mass., BLWt.4547-100-Pvt.

KERNON (continued)
Iss. 1/28/1790 to Joseph May.
KERNS, Godfrey, Pa. See CARNS
William, Cont., N.Y., Susannah, W20297
William, Va. See KERNES
KERR, Andrew, S.C., S21327
Daniel, N.C., Elizabeth, W7963
Daniel, Pa., BLWt.660-100
David, S.C., Sarah, R5890
David, Va., S31186
David, Va., S38111
Henry, Ga. res. See KARR
James, N.C. See KARR
James, Pa., S13624
James, Va., Ruth, R5888
John, N.J., S31184
John, N.J. See CARR
John, Pa., S39811
Joseph, ---, Dis. No papers. N.C. & S.C. agencies
Joseph, N.J., R5886
Joseph, N.C., S4469
Mark, N.Y., BLWt.7360-100-Pvt. Iss. 1/25/1791 to John Wisner, ass. No papers
Nathaniel, N.C., Margaret, R5887
Robert, Ct., S31793
Robert, N.C., See CARR
Thomas, N.J. See CARR
William, Ct., BLWts.6048 & 5638-100-Pvt. Iss. 11/19/1789. No papers
William, N.C.,R5892
William, Pa., Margaret, W3560
William, S.C. See CARR
William, S.C., b. Pa., R5891
KERRICK, Benjamin H.Md.,S46386; BLWt.11429-100-Fifer. Iss. 9/25/1789 to Benjamin H. Kerrick
KERRY, Barney, Va. See KARREN
KERSCHE, George, Pa., S39810
KERSEY, Edward, Md., BLWt.11420-100-Pvt. Iss. 12/23/1795 to Geo. Ponsonby, ass. No papers
James, N.C., S8788
John, Va., S1679
John, Va., S5507
John, Va., S16435
Stephen, S.C., Nancy, W9101
Williams, N.J., BLWt.1196-200-Lt. Iss. 4/21/1790. No papers
William, N.C., Va. See CASEY
KERSHAW, Mitchell, Del., BLWt. 10803-100-Pvt. Iss. 4/15/1799. No papers
KERSHNER, Michael, See KIRSHNER
KERSTELLER, George, Pa., S40067
KESLER, George Peter, See KESSLER
Jacob, N.C., Pa., S2688
Joseph, N.Y., S42763
KESLING, Teter. See Ditrich KISLING
KESNER, Jacob Va. See KISNER
KESSEBACK, Oswald, Pvt., Pa. Art. Artificers, BLWt.9716 & 13308. Iss. 8/31/1791
KESSELBACH, Oswald, Pa. res. Dis. No papers
KESSLAR, Adam, N.Y. See CASLER
KESSLER, George Peter, Pa., Elizabeth, W2127 (wrongly pensioned as Kepler)

KESSLER (continued)
John, Navy, Pa. Agcy. & res.,S5550
KESTED, Henry, N.J., Maria, W26173; BLWt.26575-160-55
KESTER, Joseph, Va., S2690
Peter, Pa., S2683
KESTERSON, John, Va., S4467
KESTLER, Frederick, Pa., Va.,S16177
KESTOR, Jacob, Pa. See CASTOR
KETCHAM, Benjamin, N.Y., S24239
Ezra, Ct., S42768
John, Pa., S39805
Joseph, N.Y., Charity, W16317
Samuel, N.Y., S42762
Solomon, N.J., Mary, W438
Solomon, Privateer, N.Y. & War of 1812, S13626
KETCHUM, Azariah, N.Y., Elizabeth, W16315
Eleanor, former wid. of Isaac Doud, Cont., Mass., N.Y., which see
Ephraim, N.Y., Jemima, W26176; BLWt.26554-160-55
Ezra, Ct., BLWt.6051-100-Pvt. Iss. 3/21/1791 to Josiah Starr. No papers
John, N.Y., BLWt.7369-100-Pvt. Iss. 2/21/1792 to John Hathorn, ass. No papers
John, N.Y., Phebe Shaw, former wid., W4584
Joseph, Mass., BLWt. Rej. 226418, Act of 1855
Joseph, N.Y., BLWt.7368-100-Pvt. Iss. 1/25/1791. No papers
Joseph, Mass., or N.Y., Sally/Mary, R5894
Joshua, Cont., N.Y., R5893. BLWt.7374-100-Pvt. Iss. 9/1/1790
Nathaniel, N.Y., Pully, W20310
Samuel, N.Y., Sarah, W1195; BLWt. 29052-160-55
KETH, John, Mass. See KEITH
KETNER, Francis, N.C. See KITNER
KETTELL, Andrew, Mass., Eleanor, W13568
Jonathan, Mass., Mary, W1617
Joseph, Mass., S32936
Samuel, Mass., BLWt.4528-100-Pvt. Iss. 5/9/1797 to Andrew Kettell & Sarah Kettell, only heirs of Samuel Kettell
KETTEMAN, Daniel, Va., S15908
KETTERAGE, Thomas, Mass., BLWt. 4517-100-Pvt. Iss. 2/23/1796 to Joseph Brown. No papers
KETTLE, Daniel, Md., BLWt.11426-100-Pvt. Iss. 4/19/1793. No papers
George, --, BLWt.13303-100-Pvt. "in the Invalids Corps." Iss. 7/27/1789 to Richard Platt, ass. No papers
Joseph, N.J., BLWt.8460-100-Pvt. Iss. 7/17/1797 to Abraham Bell, ass. No papers
Thomas, Ct., BLWt.6050-100-Pvt. Iss. 9/11/1792. No papers
KEVER, James, S.C., Jane, W10166; BLWt.26977-160-55

KEY, Bingham, --, R35694. Seems to have applied for pension & his claim rejected. No papers in his application found. His name not on old Rejected Reg. of Rev. War claims, & not on printed list of 1852 Rejected & Suspended claims. See data in regard to him in pension claim of his bro., Wm. Key, R5895, from which this rejected file number above was obtained.
George, Va., Susannah, W10162
Henry, Va., S38116
John, Va., Fathy, W10163; BLWt.67535-160-55
Price, Cont., Va., Sarah, W3021; BLWt.31285-160-55
Prudence, former wid. of Daniel Putman, S.C., which see
Steward/Stewart, Mass., Sarah, W7956
Tandy, Va., S18069
William, Va., Sea Service, Elizabeth, R5895
William B., Va., S31787
KEYER, John, Cont., Va. See KEGER
KEYES, Abner, N.H., S44470
Charles, Mass., S42769
Daniel, Ct., Cont., See KEYS
Daniel, Mass., S41720
David, Ct. Sea Service, S13623
Ebenezer, Mass., Jemima, W26742
Eli, Mass., BLWt.4531-100-Pvt. Iss. 3/25/1790. No papers
Elias, Ct., N.H., Vt., S15912
Elias, Mass., Elizabeth, W2810
Ezekiel, N.H., S44468
Ezra, Mass., Hannah, W20316
Gurish, Mass., Betsey Salters, former wid., W7161
Israel, Mass., Dolly, W14989
John, Ct., Cont., S42766
John, Mass., S40894
Joseph Annis, Mass. See KEYS
Marshal/Marshall, Ct., S42771
Nathaniel, Mass., Olive, W14988
Oren, Mass., S32934
Peter, N.H., N.Y., S13608
Sampson, Ct., Mass., S13606
Silas, Mass., N.H., S9365
Solomon, Mass., Thankful, W26756
Stephen, N.H., S44469
Thomas, Mass., S40893
KEYS, Daniel, Ct., Cont., Abigail, W20309
Daniel, Mass., BLWt.4522-100-Pvt. Iss. 6/7/1797. No papers
Ebenezer, Ct., R5897
James, Va., S15907
Joseph Annis, Mass., Eleanor, R5898
Marshall, Ct. See Marshal KEYES
Matthew, Va., S1681
Philip, Pa. See KEES
William, Md., BLWt.11417 & 10798-100-Pvt. Iss. 1/30/1792 to Wm. Lane, ass. No papers
William, Va., S18070
KEYSACKER, George, Va., R5899
KEYSER, Andrew, Sr., Va., S5651

KEYSER (continued)
Edward, N.Y., S42772
George, Pa., BLWt.9768-100-Dragoon. Iss. 6/26/1789
Henry, Navy, Pa. res. & agcy., 39798
Jacob, Cont., Md., Pamelia, W7952
John, Pa. See KEISER
Micahel J. or I., N.Y., R5900
Nicholas, N.J. See KISER
Reuben, N.H., See KEZER
William, Va., Kesiah/Keziah, W3427
KEYT, John, Cont., Md., N.J., S32354
KEZER, David, Cont., Mass., S35491
Moses, Cont., Mass., S44474
Reuben, N.H., Lydia, W20308
KIBBE, David, Mass., S42794
Edward, Mass., Mary, W26736
Elijah, Ct., Hannah, W26729
Fredrick/Frederick, Ct., S15499
Isaac, Mass., Lucy, R5903; BLWt. 81066-160-55
Jedidiah/Jedediah, Ct., S15595
John, Mass., S29944
Lemuel, Ct., Love, W21530
Phillip/Philip, Ct., S13640
KIBBEE, Israel, Ct., Ruth, W20336
Mehitable, former wid. of Elijah Parker, Mass., which see
Stephen, Mass., S32951
Thomas, Mass. See KIBBEY
KIBBER, George, Pa. See KIEBLER
KIBBEY, Abigail, former wid. of Benj. Packard, Mass., which see
Jacob, Mass., Abiline, W1198; BLWt.6036-160-55
Philip W./Phillip W., Ct.,S44480
Thomas, Mass., Elizabeth, W1038; BLWt.8192-160-55
KIBBIE, Mehitable, Mass. See Elijah PARKER, Mass.
KIBBY, Abigail, Mass., See Benj. PACKARD
Isaac, Mass. See KIBBE
Joseph, Md., R5905
KIBHART, Adam, Md. See GIBHART
KIBLER, George, Pa. See KIEBLER
John, Md., Mary, W5014; BLWt.30753-160-55
KIBLING, John, Mass., S18915
KIBLINGER, Adam, Va. See KEEBLINGER
Jacob, Mass., Sarah, W20299
KICKBERGER, Adam, Hazen's Regt. BLWt.13295-100-Pvt. Date & to whom not shown. Has notation "Has had a patent."
KICKELAND, Heinrich, Mass., See Henry KNEELAND
KIDD, Alexander, N.Y., BLWt.7367-100-Pvt. Iss. 10/12/1790 to Isaac Bogoart, ass. No papers
Alexander, N.Y. & War of 1812, Coziah Ann, W20333
Benjamin, Va., R5906
Charles, Del., BLWt.1206-200-Lt. Iss. 5/31/1797 to Jesse Green. No papers
George, Va., R5907

KIDD (continued)
James, Va., b. N.C., S18481
James H., Va., b. Va., S16436
John, Md., BLWt.11416-100-Pvt. Iss. 8/3/1797 to James DeBaufre ass. No papers
Robert, Va., S32367
William, Va., S31796
KIDDER, Benjamin, Pa., BLWt.9777-100-Drummer. Iss. 7/13/1789. No papers
Daniel, N.H., Elizabeth Williams former wid., W18450
Ephraim, N.Y., S13652
John, Mass., S9368
John, Mass., S18482
John, Mass., Hannah, W20339
John, N.Y., War of 1812, See KEADER
Jonas, N.H., S13653
Phinehas, Mass., Hannah, W26720
Reuben, N.H., Rachel, W27519; BLWt.1872-100. After she was deserted by her husb., Reuben Kidder, she was illegally m. to Edmund Moor. Phoebe Kidder also applied for pension as wid. of Reuben & was rejected (R5910). See papers within.
Wilder, Cont., N.Y., S42765
KIDDS, John, N.C., Catharine, R5908
KIDNEY, Jonathan, N.Y., S14295
KIDWELL, Elijah, N.C., S13643
John, N.C., S13638
Jonathan, N.C., S2706
Mathew, Md., S30523
KIEBLER, George, Pa., S39816
KIEFER, Andrew, Pa., Margaret Jacoby, former wid., R5537
William, N.Y., S13660
KIERSTEAD, Wilhelmus, N.Y., S22864
KIES, Joseph, Green Mt. Boys, N.H., Mary, W20352
KIESINGER, Andrew, Va. See KEISINGER
KIESLING, John, Pa. See KEISLING
KIFF, John, N.Y., S23751
KIHER, George, N.C. See KEISER
KIKER, George, N.C. See KEISER
KILANDER, Philip, N.J., S32363
KILBERN, Henry, Va., Indian War in 1786, R5912
KILBEY, Phillip W., Ct. See KIBBEY
KILBON, John, Cont. See KILBORNE
Stephen, Mass., S19366
KILBORN, Araunah/Arannah, Ct., S13649
Calvin, Mass., Susan, W767; BLWt.5451-160-55
Elisha, Mass., Jemima, R5913
James, Ct., Elizabeth, W20340
James, Mass., S40903
John, Cont., Mass., S35508
Simon, Ct., Eunice, W20328
KILBORNE, John, Cont., Deborah, W20354. N.Y. agcy. & res. in 1818
KILBOURN, Ashbel, Ct., Dis. No papers

KILBOURN (continued)
Benjamin, Cont., Pa., Diana, W7999
John, Sheldon's Dragoons, Ct., BLWt.6075-100-Pvt. Iss. 10/22/1789 to Theodosius Fowler, No papers
Samuel, Ct., S36679
William, Mass., S40902
Zacheus, N.Y., BLWt.7359-100-Pvt. Iss. 7/22/1790 to Thos. Tillotson, ass. No papers
KILBOURNE, Eliphas, Ct., N.H., Polly, W20346
KILBUN, John, Cont. See KILBORNE
KILBURN, Benjamin, Pa. See KILBOURN
Charles, Mass., BLWt.4506-100-Pvt. Iss. 8/22/1789. No papers
Charles, Mass., S42795
Eliphalet/Eliphelat, Cont., Mass. S44481
Henry, Va. & Indian War of 1786. See KILBERN
John, Cont. See KILBORNE
John, Mass., Mary, W13576
Rosewell, Sheldon's Dragoons, Ct. BLWt.6076-100-Pvt. Iss. 6/21/1791 to Stephen Thorn. No papers
KILBY, Christopher A., Cont., Ct., S36678
John, Ct., S31798
John, Md. Sea Service, Navy, S38119
John, Pa., BLWt.9741-100-Corp. Iss. 6/20/1789. No papers
KILE, John, Mass., BLWt.4537-100-Pvt. Iss. 5/22/1790 to John Ramsay. No papers
KILGORE, Charles, Va., S699
Charles, Va., b. N.C., Avarilla, W7994; BLWt.44506-160-55
James, Mass., S35506
John, Cont., Mass. See KILLGORE
KILGOUR, Trueworthy, Mass.,S35507
KILHAM, Thomas, Mass., Mary, R5914
KILL, Christopher, Lamb's Art., N.Y., BLWt.7375-100-Pvt. Iss. 4/21/1791 to Hendrick Kyser, ass. No papers
Christopher, Cont., N.Y., Polly, W16036
KILLAM, Daniel, Mass., Rebecca, W27865; BLWt.9208-160-55
Ephraim, N.J., Pa., S5556
Joseph, Mass., BLWt.1182-300-Capt. Iss. 8/7/1789 to Richard Platt, ass. No papers
Nathaniel, Vt., R5915
Phinehas, Green Mt. Boys, Vt., Prudence Gallup, former wid., W24266
KILLEBREW, Kinchan, N.C., S1844
Larrance/Lawrence, N.C., Elizabeth, W24816
KILLECUTT, Thomas, Mass. See KELLICUT
KILLEGAN, James, Md., BLWt.11431-100-Pvt. Iss. 12/22/1794 to Henry Purdy, ass. No papers
KILLEY, David, Mass., R.I.,S18920

KILLEY (continued)
Jonathan, N.H., S44477
Levi, Mass., S30522
Stephen, Mass. See KELLEY
William, Va. See KELLEY
KILLGORE, John, Cont., Mass., Abigail, W7995; BLWt.34927-160-55
Joseph, Mass., S35509
KILLICUTT, Thomas, Mass., See KELLICUT
KILLIN, John, Pa., Rachel, W3694; BLWt.80032-160-55
KILLING, John, Pa. See KILLIN
KILLINGER, George, Pa., R5919
Jacob, Mass., See KIBLINGER
KILLION, Jacob, N.C., b. N.C., after Rev. lived for a time in Va., S32362
John, N.C., R5916
John, N.C., Becky, R5918
KILLOGH, Samuel, N.C., Pa., S7114
KILLOM, Daniel, Mass. See KILLAM
Thomas, Mass., S10956
KILLOUGH, Samuel, Ga., S.C., S4475
Samuel, N.C., Pa. See KILLOGH
KILLPATRICK, Robert, S.C., S7112
KILLSA, James, Cont., Mass., Lydia, W26722
KILLMER, Maria, former wid. of Conrad Rossman, N.Y., which see
KILPATRICK, Alexander, Pa., Susannah, R5920
Spencer, S.C., S38894
William, Pa. See KIRKPATRICK
KILS/KILTS, Conrat/Conrad, N.Y., S13658
Peter N., Mass. See KILTS
KILTON, Benjamin, Mass., S31191
Edward, Mass., Hannah, W13575
Jonathan, Mass., Margaret, W26719
Thomas, Mass., S22859
KILTS, Conrad, N.Y. See Conrat KILS
Conrad N., N.Y., S11826
Peter N., N.Y., S13629
KILTY, James, Md., S33359
John, Cont., Md., Catharine, W26183; BLWt.1212-300-Capt. Iss. 4/21/1796
William, Md., BLWt.1207-400-Surgn. Iss. 12/21/1792. No papers
KIMBAL, Abraham T., Ct., BLWt. 6050-100-Pvt. Iss. 8/23/1790. No papers
Samuel, N.H., S22346
KIMBALL, Aaron, Mass., S30525
Abel, N.H., S4478
Abner, Mass., Marcy, W12040; BLWt.19512-160-55
Abraham, Mass., Susannah, W12041; BLWt.36649-160-55
Abraham, N.H., S20017
Abraham T., Ct., Sarah, W26180
Amos, Mass., S39821
Andrew, Cont., N.H., S41728
Anna, former wid. of Jonathan Ellsworth, Mass., which see
Benjamin, Ct., S13631

KIMBALL (continued)
Benjamin, Mass., S29278
Benjamin, Mass., S32946
Benjamin, Mass., Navy, N.H., S18480
Boyce, Mass., S32952
Caleb, Mass., Elizabeth, W26728
Charles, Ct., Jerusha, W21527
Daniel, Cont., Mass., S10950
Daniel, N.H., S44484
Daniel, N.H., Hannah, W15001
David, Cont., Mass., S35505
David, Mass., Lydia, W16132
Edmund, Mass., S29277
Elizabeth, former wid. of Edward Fairfield, N.H., which see
Ezra, Mass., S44483
Hezediah, Mass., S35504
Isaac, Ct., S32954
Jared, Ct., S41730
Jedediah, Ct., Eunice, W26735
Jesse, Ct., Indian War, R5921
Jesse, Ct., Privateer, S13639
Joab, Mass., Betsey, W1780
John, Ct., S42792
John, Mass., BLWt.4525-100-Sgt. Iss. 8/10/1789 to Richard Platt. No papers
John, Privateer, R.I., S13657
Jonathan, Mass., S32947
Jonathan, N.H., R5922
Joseph, Ct., Mass., Ede, W10176
Joseph, Mass., S35500
Joseph, Mass., Lucy, W26714
Joshua, Mass., Hannah, W13587
Lebeus/Libbeus, Ct., S16179
Moses, Cont., N.H., S35501
Moses, N.H., Jemima, W4256
Nathan, Mass., Lydia, W26723
Nathaniel, Mass., Sally, W26726
Oliver, N.H., Mary, W26731
Phinehas, R.I., Rebecca Rice, former wid., R8754
Richard, Ct., S39814
Richard, Mass., S32949
Richard, Mass., Lucy, W1779
Rufus, Cont., Mass., Lucy, W26712
Samuel, Ct., R.I. See KIMBELL
Samuel, Mass., S42796
Samuel, Mass., Mary, W13577
Samuel, Mass., Sea Service, Polly, W26734
Samuel, N.H. See KIMBAL
Sargeant, N.H., Betsey, W552; BLWt.8473-160-55
Simeon, Mass., S29276
Thomas, Mass., Sea Service,S30526
Thomas, N.H., BLWt.3256-100-Pvt. Iss. 3/25/1790. No papers
Thomas, N.H., Dis. No papers
Timothy, N.H., War of 1812, Abigail, W21533
William, Crane's Cont. Art., Mass., BLWt.4543-100-Pvt. Iss. 7/30/1792 to David Quinton. No papers
William, Mass., S29275
William, Mass., S32950
William, Mass., Bethiah, W21526
Wills, N.H., Mercy, W21525
KIMBELL, Samuel, Ct., R.I., S21853

KIMBELL (continued)
Timothy, N.H., BLWt.3263-100-Pvt. Iss. 4/1/1790 to John May, ass. No papers
KIMBERLY, Ezra, Ct., R5924
Ora, Ct., BLRej. 238256, Act of 3/3/1855. No pension claim
Robert, Ct., Hannah Foote, former wid., R3638
KIMBLE, Caleb, N.J., S33361
Eliphalett, Crane's Cont. Art., Mass., BLWt.4545-100-Fifer. Iss. 1/26/1790 to John May. No papers
Hansell, Crane's Cont. Art., Mass., BLWt.4546-100-Drummer. Iss. 1/26/1790 to John May. No papers
Jacob, N.J., Va., Mary, W10178; BLWt.94033-160-55
Nathan, N.J., BLWt.536-100
Peter, N.J. See KEMBLE
Peter, N.J., R5926
Peter, N.Y. See KEMBLE
Robert, Va., S38896
Walter, N.J., Pa., R5923
KIMBRELL, Thomas, S.C., Va., R5927
KIMMER, Nicholas, Pa., Sarah, W10179
KIMMEY, James, Del., BLWt.10801-100-Pvt. Iss. 9/2/1789. No papers
KIMMY, Isaac, Va., Margaret, R5977
KIMPTON, Rufus, Mass., N.H., Vt., Abigail, W26737
Samuel, Cont., Mass., N.H. See KEMPTON
KINARD, John, S.C. See KINNARD
Joseph, Pa., S36681
KINCADE, Reuben, Mass., S37128
William, N.Y., S40900; BLWt.333-100
KINCAID, Andrew, Pa., BLWt.9767-100-Dragoon. Iss. 3/3/1790. No papers
James, N.C., S7109
James, S.C., b. Ireland, R5929
James, Va., S16907
John, Cont., Md. res. of heirs in 1836; BLWt.2144-100
John, Mass., Privateer & 4th U.S. Inf. War of 1812, Invalid File 20423, BLWt.14846-160-12. No claim for Rev. War service.
John, Pa., BLWt.9764-100-Pvt. Iss. 8/22/1799. No papers
John, Pa. See KINKAID
John, S.C., b. Pa., Anna, W12029; BLWt.26398-160-55
John, Va., S19367
John, Va., Alice, W3428; BLWt. 38513-160-55
Joseph, Va., R15697; Va. Half Pay
Robert, N.C., Elizabeth, W26186; BLWt.13206-160-55
Robert, Va., Rebecca, W10177; BLWt.84019-160-55
KINCH, William, Ct., Ruth, W21529
KINCHELOE, Ellen, former wid. of John Bray, N.J., which see
Thomas W., Va., Nancy, W1620
KINCHLOE, Eleanor, N.J. See John

KINCHLOE (continued)
Bray
KINDAL, Ebenezer, Ct. See KENDALL
KINDALL, Clayton, Pa. See KENDAL
John, Ct. See KENDALL
Joshua, Mass. See KENDALL
KINDER, Peter, Va., Margaret, R5931
Philip/Phillip, Pa., S40069
KINDLE, Clayton, Pa. See KENDAL
William, Va., S2705
KINDLER, John, Cont., Mass. See SHINDLER
KINDRED, Thomas, Va., S4476
William, Va., S13636
KINDRICK, John, Ga., b. Md., Mary, W4255; BLWt.38509-160-55
John, Va., R5933
KINERSON, John, Mass., Betsey, W20307
KINESMAN, John Henry, Del.,S22862
KINEY, James, Ct. See KEENEY
KING, Aaron, N.Y., Harriet, R5947
Abraham H., N.J., S1035
Alexander, Del., Pa., S39822
Amos, Mass., S10954
Andrew, Va., Sally, W374
Anthony, N.J., BLWt.8457-100-Pvt. Iss. 6/16/1789 to Aaron Ogden, ass. No papers
Anthony, N.J., BLWt.8462-100-Corp. Iss. 10/22/1789 to Samuel Potter, Wm. Valentine & Jonathan Valentine, Admrs. of Obadiah Valentine, decd., late ass.
Anthony, N.J., Mary, W7989
Anthony, N.C., Mary, W439
Apollos/Apollas, Mass., Mary, W20325
Arthur, N.C., R5934
Asa, Mass., Thankful, BLWt. 43881-160-55
Asaph, Cont., Mass., S17523
Aury, N.J., S695
Azubah, former wid. of James Fisk, Mass., which see
Baxter, N.C., Ellen, W20321
Benjamin, Ct., S4767
Benjamin, Hazen's Regt., BLWt. 13291-100-Pvt. Iss. 8/6/1792. No papers
Benjamin, R.I., BLWt.831-100
Caleb, Mass., S42790
Charles, --, BLWts.13294 & 13707-Pvt. "in the Invalids." Iss. 7/9/1794 to Samuel Emery, ass. No papers
Charles, Mass., S32957
Charles, Mass., Va., S2700
Charles, N.C., Elizabeth, R5940
Charles, Va., Rebecca, W20334
Clement, N.Y., R.I., Mary, W24849
Constant Victor, N.J., Odah, W7990
Cornelius, Va., S17527
Cushing, Mass., Eliza, W10172; BLWt.58689-160-55
Daniel, N.H., R.I., S18918
David, N.J., S13655
David, N.J., R5938
David, N.C., S46055

KING (continued)
David, N.C., Nelly, W20347
David, N.C., S.C., b. Scotland, S7107
Ebenezer, Mass., S13661
Edward, N.C., Feely, R5942
Edward, N.C., S.C., S38895
Eli, Ct., BLWt.6069-100-Pvt. Iss. 3/30/1792. No papers
Eli, Ct., Chloe Strong, former wid., W16746
Elias, Mass., Vt., S18483
Elihu, Mass., S32956
Eliphalet, Cont., Ct., Silence, W20338
Elisha, Va., BLWt.324-200. Iss. 2/14/1807. Delivered to L. Goodwyn
Elizabeth, former wid. of Ebenezer Bennett, Mass., which see
Esau, Ct., S23750
Ezra, Mass., BLWt.4532-100-Pvt. Iss. 4/3/1797. No papers
Francis, Md., Mary, W26715
Francis, Pa., BLWt.9736-100-Pvt. Iss. 1/17/1792 to Wm. Thomas, ass. No papers
Francis, Pa., S39815
Francis, S.C., Sally, W9495; BLWt.73526-160-55
Francis, S.C., Isabella, W21523
George, Cont., Va., Mary, R5960
George, Md., Susannah, W7980; BLWt.38515-160-55
George, Mass., Lucy, W20337
George, R.I., S42791
George, S.C.?, R5945
George, Va., S31189
George, Va., Mary, W2736
George H., Mass., S10949
Gerrard, Va., Kesiah C., W7984
Godfrey, R.I., S17528
Henry, Md., R1262
Henry, Mass., Anne/Anna, W20353
Henry, Mass., R5948
Henry, Va., S8792
Hugh, N.C., S.C., b. Scotland, S32365
Ichabod, Ct., Cont., S40901
Ichabod, Cont., Mass., Mary, W26727
Isaac, Md., S42789
Isaac, Mass., S29942
Isaac, Mass., BLWt.47967-160-55
Isaac, Privateer, R.I., R5949
Jacob, Pa., R5950
Jacob, Va., Elizabeth, W7988; BLWt.26041-160-55
James, Ct., S13654
James, Del., R5952
James, N.H., S22860
James, N.C., b. Va., S4477
James, N.C., Elizabeth Isbell former wid., W10139
James, R.I., BLWt.1546-100
James, Va., S31794
Jeremiah, Md., N.J. res., S36032
Jesse, R.I., S21332
Jesse, Va., S5559
John, Ct., Jane, W20349

KING (continued)
John, Cont., Del., R5956; BLWt. 1951-100
John, Del., R---
John, Md., BLWt.11423-100-Pvt. Iss. 4/28/1791. No papers
John, Md., S5553
John, Mass., S10948
John, Mass., Sally Cooper, former wid., W2561; BLWt.34946-160-55
John, Mass., Sarah, W12021; BLWt.20922-160-55
John, N.H., Susannah Pownall, former wid., R8417
John, N.Y., BLWt.7358-100-Pvt. Iss. 8/3/1790 to Cornelius V. Dyck, ass. No papers
John, N.C., Polly/Mary, R5962
John, N.C., Pa., S2701
John, Pa., BLWt.9766-100-Dragoon. Iss. 2/4/1791. No papers
John, Pa., S30521
John, S.C., S32366
John, S.C., R5957
John, Va., Eleanor, W7986; BLWt. 26694-160-55
John, Va., Sarah, W9100
John, Va.(?), Catharine, R5936
John G., Pa., Jane, R5953
Jonah, Ct., Mass., S16908
Jonas, Mass., Abigail, W14998
Jonathan, Cont., Mass. res. in 1824, S33354
Jonathan, Pa., S13645
Joseph, Ct., S42786
Joseph, Mass., S32958
Joseph, Mass., S42793
Joseph, N.J., BLWt.1186-200-Adjt. Iss. --/17/1789. Also recorded as above under BLWt. 2535. No papers
Joseph, N.J., BLWt.8461-100-Pvt. Iss. 6/16/1792. No papers
Joseph, N.J., S39818
Joseph, N.J., BLWt.2046-100
Joseph, Pa., Sarah, W12028; BLWt.108973-160-55
Joshua, Cont., Ct., S13632; BLWt.1192-200-Lt. Iss. 8/26/1789
Josiah, Mass., BLWt.4508-100-Pvt. Iss. 1/22/1796 to Josiah King
Josiah, Cont., Mass., Miriam, W26713
Josiah, Cont., Mass., BLWt.1992-100
Julian/Julius, Va., S38120
Julius, Va. See Julian
Lemuel, Ct., Jane, W26179
Lemuel, Mass., S32945
Leonard, N.Y., S42783
Luther, Mass., S21333
Miles, Va., Martha, W20342
Moses, Mass., Mary Brainard, former wid., W24672
Nancy, former wid. of Jesse Tucker, Va., which see
Nathan, Mass., Sea Service, Prudence, W13588
Nathan, N.C., S7105

KING (continued)
Nathaniel, Mass., Rebecca, W16037
Nathaniel, Va., S10248
Olive, former wid. of Wm. Eddy, Mass., which see
Parks, N.C., R5963
Patrick, Mass., BLWt.4521-100-Pvt. Iss. 6/12/1797. No papers
Peter, Mass., S29945; BLWt.9213-160-55
Peter, N.C., Jane, W7981
Philip, N.Y., BLWt.7355-100-Pvt. Iss. 8/4/1791. No papers
Philip, Va., Nancy, R5961
Philip, Von Heer's Dragoons, BLWt.13279-100-Pvt. Iss. 3/15/1797 to Philip King. No papers
Phillip, N.Y., Rebecca, W12038; BLWt.12835-160-55
Ralph, Del., Indian Wars 1891-2, Pa., R5964
Ralph, R.I., Mary, W27439
Reuben, N.Y., S10946
Reuben, N.Y., S27035
Richard, N.C., S.C., Rachel, W7985; BLWt.26980-160-55
Robert, N.C., R5966
Robert, Pa., Elizabeth, W4710
Robert, Pa., R5965
Rozina, former wid. of Joseph Clark, Ct., Mass., which see
Sabrit, Va., Jerusha, W9253
Samuel, Ct., Betsey, R21531
Simeon, Mass., Achsah, W232; BLWt.24916-160-55
Solomon, N.Y., S13637
Stephen, Mass., Mehitable, W15000
Stephen, Mass., Hannah, W20344
Stephen, Mass., Azubah, R5935
Stephen, R.I., Elizabeth, W2813
Stephen, Va., S5551
Theodore, Ct., Lydia, W24854
Thomas, Md., BLWt.11411-100-Pvt. Iss. 9/12/1792. No papers
Thomas, Md., S34948
Thomas, N.C., Elizabeth, W26185; BLWt.13017-160-55
Thomas, N.C., Pa., S45883
Thomas, S.C., S31795
Vincent, N.C., Margaret, W4007
William, Cont., R.I., S42785
William, Cont., Va., S38121
William, Md., BLWt.11418-100-Pvt. Iss. 5/4/1797 to James DeBaufre, ass. No papers
William, Mass., Susannah Pierce, former wid., W15208
William, Mass., N.H., Catharine, W7983; BLWt.21817-160-55
William, N.Y., S29274
William, N.Y., S42788
William, N.C., S21335
William, N.C., Sarah, W20332
William, Pa., Ann, W3091
William, Va., S30524
William, Va., S32364
William, Va., Mary, W7982
Zebulon, Mass., BLWt.1183-300-Capt. Iss. 12/31/1789. No papers

KINGLAY, Savil, R.I. See KINGSLY

KINGMAN, Alexander, Mass., S41731

KINGMAN (continued)
Benjamin, Cont., Mass., Martha, W21534
Edward, Mass., BLWt.1824-150
Eliab, Crane's Cont., Art., Mass., BLWt.4544-100-Pvt. Iss. 1/24/1797. No papers
Eliab, Cont., Mass., Ann, W9496. S.C. res.
Isaac, Mass., S18917
James, Mass., Releaf, W14999
Loring, Mass., BLWt.4539-100-Pvt. Iss. 8/17/1796. No papers
Loring, Mass., S33948
Thomas, Mass., N.J., S1037

KINGORE, William, Va., S38122

KINGRAM, Alexander, See KINGMAN

KINGSBERY, Asa, Ct., S13644
Jabez, Ct., S17525

KINGSBURY, Aaron, Mass., BLWt. 4513-100-Pvt. Iss. 3/26/1792 to John Peck. No papers
Aaron, Mass., S32953
Andrew, Ct., Mary, W20327
Asa, Mass., S29946
Benjamin, Mass., S32955
Daniel, Ct., Martha, W20324
Eliphalet, Mass., S29948
Elizabeth, former wid. of Abel Holbrook, Mass., which see
Jacob, Ct., Sally P., W1881; BLWt.1190-150-Ens. Iss. 9/12/1789. No papers
John, Cont., Mass., S37129
John, N.C., BLWt.1208-300
Joseph, Ct., S17524
Joseph, Ct., S36680
Joseph, Mass., S2707
Joseph, Mass., Sally, BLWt. 97009-160-55
Lemuel, Mass., S41729
Nathan, Mass., S18914
Nathaniel, Mass., S21331
Oliver, Ct., Sally, W16038; BLWt.6254-160-55
Samuel, Cont., N.H., S36677
Samuel, Mass., Sophia, W15002
Sanford, Ct., Vt., S2708
Solomon, Mass., Keziah, W27438; BLWt.30760-160-55
Thomas, Ct., Esther, R5967
Thomas, Cont., N.Y., S42781
Tilley, Ct., Mass., Anna Seymour, former wid., W19342

KINGSLEY, Aaron, Ct., Sarah, W1781
Alpheus, Ct., R5968
Alpheus, N.H., S37132
Asahel, Ct., R5969
Benjamin, Mass., S29941
Elias, Cont., Mass., Vt., Abigail W26184; BLWt.86031-160-55
Elijah, Mass., S29949
Hezekiah, Cont., Ct., Rhoda, W26181
Jabez, Ct., S13651
James, Ct., BLWt.6057-100-Pvt. Iss. 8/31/1790 to Dudley Woodbridge. No papers
Jonathan, Ct., S13641
Jonathan, N.H., S22858
Martin, Mass., S23746
Rufus, Ct., S13659

KINGSLEY (continued)
Thaddeus, Mass., S13650
Timothy, Mass., S18916
Uriah, Navy, Mass., S10955
Wareham, Ct., War of 1812, R5971
William, Ct., Deborah, W768; BLWt.24994-160-55
Zephaniah, Mass., S22344

KINGSLY, Savil/Sawill, R.I., Ann, W20323

KINGSTON, John, Va., Eleanor, W1513

KINGTON, John, Va. See KINGSTON

KINKADE, Robert, Pa. Sea Service, Va., Mary, W9102

KINKAID, John, Pa., S22345

KINKEAD, Joseph, Va. See KINCAID
Thomas, Va., S5997

KINLEY, Benjamin, Va., BLWt. 2457-200

KINNAN, Edward, N.J., R5972
Joseph, N.J., Mary, W8000
Peter, N.J., S9923

KINNARD, David, Va., S5557
John, Cont., Md., Mary Moore, former wid., BLWt.464-100
John, S.C., b. Pa., S13646
John, S.C., b. Ireland, S32360
Joseph, Pa. See KINARD
Joseph, Pa., Mary, R5974

KINNASTON, David, N.H., S35494; BLWt.903-100. In 1819 & 1828, res. of Boothbay, Lincoln Co., Me.

KINNE, Amos, N.Y. See KINNEY
Asa, Ct., N.Y., R.I. See KINNEY
Freelove, former wid. of George Gallup, Ct., which see
Jesse, N.Y., S10945
Lyman, Ct. See KENNEY
Samuel, Ct., W1197; BLWt.26599-160-55

KINNEAIR, John, N.C., S8793

KINNEBROUGH, James, N.J., S33360

KINNER, Jeremiah, N.Y., S13656
Jonathan, N.Y., S37131; BLWt. 7349-100-Pvt. Iss. 10/23/1790. Name spelled Kenner. No papers

KINNEY, Abraham, Col. Sheldon's Regt. Light Dragoons, Ct.; BLWt.1197-200-Lt. Iss. --/22/1790. No papers
Amos, N.Y., Hannah, W26730; BLWt.3825-160-55
Archelaus, Mass., Dis. --
Asa, Ct., N.Y., R.I., Polly, W26710
Daniel, Cont., Ct., S42779
Daniel, Pa., S35503
David, N.J., S22898
David, N.J., Elizabeth, R5975
Jacob, N.J., BLWt.8459-100-Pvt. Iss. 6/11/1789 to Matthias Denman, ass. No papers
Jacob, Pa., S22861
James, Ct. See KEENEY
Jesse, Mass., Hannah Newton, former wid., W20341
John, N.H., BLWt.3265-100-Pvt. Iss. 4/19(?)/1792 to John

KINNEY (continued)
Peck. No papers
John, N.J., S33357
John, Pa., S16180
Jonas, Ct., R5976
Joseph, Ct., Sea Service, N.H., S22863
Josiah, Mass., Lydia, W20331
Lawrence, Ct., S42787
Nathan, Mass., Lydia Cleveland, former wid., R2038
Paley, Ct. See Parley
Parley, Ct., S29943
Peter, N.J., S822
Peter, Pa. See MC KINNEY
Richard, Va., Susan, W10175; BLWt.2415-100
Samuel, Ct. See KINNE
Seth, Ct., Cont., Vt., Hannah, W20330
Stephen, Ct., R.I., S2704
Thomas, Mass., S40898
William, Mass., See KENNEY
KINNICUT, Elizabeth, former wid. of John O'Kelly/Kelly, R.I., which see
KINNICUTT, Edward, R.I., R5978
Hezekiah, R.I., Lydia, W26716
KINNIN, Anthony, N.C., Christiana, W8002; BLWt.29337-160-55
KINNISON, David, Mass., War of 1812, S42782; BLWt.14607-160-55. He swore in 1818 that he was 56 yrs. old, then a res. of Sodus, Ontario Co., N.Y. In 1820 he swore that he was 79 yrs. old, then a res. of Gates, Genesee Co., N.Y. He d. 2/24/1852
Jacob, Va., S16905
KINNISTON, David, Mass. See KINNISON
Job, N.H. See KENISON
John, Art. Artificers of Pa., BLWt.13310-100-Pvt. Iss. 1/25/1791. No papers
KINNY, Charles, N.Y., BLWt.7351-100-Pvt. Iss. 5/18/1791 to Ebenezer Clark, ass. No papers
Samuel, Ct. See KINNE
KINSAUL, John, N.C., S8790
KINSELL, Frederick, Pa., BLWt. 544-100
KINSER, Michael, Va., Elizabeth, W8001
KINSEY, Courtland, N.J., R5980
David, Md., S39820
James, N.J., BLWt.8469-100-Pvt. Iss. 6/27/1791. No papers
William, Pa., Catharine, R5970
KINSLEY, Azel, Mass., Patty, W26717; BLWt.12706-160-55
Benjamin, Mass. See KINGSLEY
Daniel, Mass., S16906
Daniel, Vt., Lucy, W15688
Jonathan, R.I., S21854
KINSMAN, Jeremiah, Mass., Lydia, W12039; BLWt.17707-160-55
Thomas, Mass., Martha Flint, former wid., W24210
William, Mass., Anna, W26732
KINT, James, N.J. See KENT
KINTER, John, Pa., Isabella, W2128
KINTZ, Lewis, Pa., Lehna, W2812
KINYON, Alexander, R.I., Ruth, W21507
Amos, R.I., Lydia, W13580
Arnold, R.I., S21855
Caleb, R.I., See KENYON
Clark, R.I., Mary, R5879
David, R.I., R5877
Elijah, R.I., Penelope, W20351
Griffin, N.Y., S42770
John, R.I. See KENYON
Joseph, R.I., BLWt.380-100
Moses, R.I., S21849
Oliver, R.I., S10953
Roger, R.I., S38898
Samuel, R.I., Elizabeth, W27560
Thomas W., R.I., S23747
William, R.I., Mercy Lawton, former wid., W274
KIP, James, N.Y., R5982
James, N.Y., R5983
Peter, Cont., N.Y., Margaret, W3262
William, R.I., BLWt.3268-100-Pvt. Iss. 12/1/1793 to Ichabod Ward. No papers
KIPHART, Henry, Va., S31190
KIPP, Amos, N.Y., S33358
Peter, Lamb's Art., N.Y., BLWt. 7373-100-Pvt. Iss. 9/15/1790 to John S. Hobart et all, ass. No papers
William, R.I., Jane, W9494
KIPPERS, John, Va., S15914
KIPPS, Jacob, Va. See KEPPS
Michael, Va., Catharine, R5984
KIPS, Jacob, Va. See KEPPS
KIRBY, Archibald, S.C. See KERBY
Ephraim, R.I., BLWt.1194-150-Ensign. Iss. 10/17/1789. No papers
Hezekiah, R.I., S29268
Isaac, N.J., Phebe, W1196
John, Va., S35502; BLWt.61287-160-55
Stephen, N.Y., S23287
William, Va. See KERBY
KIRCKWOOD, David, Md. See KIRKWOOD
KIRCUM, William, See KIRKUM
KIRK, George, N.Y., BLWt.7363-100-Pvt. Iss. 8/30/1790 to Simon Veeder, ass. No papers
James, Pa., S39817; BLWt.9732-100. Iss. 1790
James, Va., Mahala, W10171; BLWt.26411-160-55
Jemima, former wid. of Daniel McCarty, Va., which see
John, ---, Tenn. Agcy. & res. in 1820, S697
John, Md., R5989
John, Va., S5558
John, Va., S39819
Robert, Cont., Va., S35511; BLWt.1214-200-Lt. Iss. 1/21/1790. No papers
Thomas, Ct., S37130
Thomas, Md., S31188
Thomas, Va., Nancy, W7992
KIRK (continued)
William, Md., Prudence, W20320
KIRKAM, John, Ct., BLWt.6065-100-Pvt. Iss. 12/1/1789 to Richard Platt. No papers
William, Ct., BLWt.6068-100-Drummer. Iss. 7/14/1789. No papers
KIRKENDALL, Samuel, N.J., S550
KIRKHAM, Joseph, Ga., R20392
Michael, Va., S31187
Samuel, Ct., S42780
KIRKLAND, Gideon, N.H. See KIRTLAND
Jabez, Ct., Eunice, W14997
John, Cont., Va., S13634
Joshua, Ct., Privateer, R5991
Robert, S.C., R20391
Susanna, former wid. of John Butts, Ct., which see
William, S.C., S32361
KIRKPATRICK, Abraham, Va., BLWt. 1210-300-Capt.
David, Cont., res. Wilmington, Del. in 1818, S36033; BLWt. 1195-200-Lt. Iss. 5/30/1789. No papers
Isaac, Pa., Nancy, W4472; BLWt.34269-160-55
James, N.J., BLWt.8466-100-Pvt. Iss. 9/11/1792 to James Kirkpatrick. No papers
James, N.J., Keziah, W4008
James, Pa., R5992
James, S.C., S38897
James, Va., BLWt.12300-100-Pvt. Iss. 12/13/1791 to Francis Graves, ass. No papers
John, S.C., Elizabeth, W9497
Robert, S.C., S1845
Robert, S.C., Martha, R5993
Samuel, N.J., BLWt.8458-100-Pvt. Iss. 9/2/1789 to Daniel Thompson, ass. No papers
Spencer, S.C. See KILPATRICK
Thomas, S.C., Margaret Dodds, former wid., R2991
William, Pa., Mary, W3695
KIRKUM, Benjamin, Ct., BLWt. 6071-100-Pvt. Iss. 7/14/1789. No papers. (Certified to the Gen. Ld. Office on 5/29/1832)
Philemon, Ct., S2703
Samuel, Sheldon's Dragoons, Ct., BLWt.6074-100-Pvt. Iss. 5/7/1792 to Thomas Stanley. No papers
William, Ct., Cont., Deborah Buell, former wid., W20795
KIRKWOOD, David, Md., Margaret, W29916 1/2
Robert, Del., BLWt.1102-300. Iss. to heir of BLWt.1205 (old series)
KIRRES, Peter, N.J., See CARIES
KIRSCH, Georg, Pa. See George KERSCHE
KIRSH, George, Pa. See KERSCHE
KIRSHNER, Michael, Cont., Md., S34947
KIRST, George, Pa. See KERSCHE
KIRTLAND, Charles, Pa., S13648

KIRTLAND (continued)
Daniel, Ct., Lovisa, W20348
Elizur, Ct., R5994
Gideon, N.H., Sally, W20345; BLWt.1304 & 17722-160-55
Jabez, Ct. See KIRKLAND
John, Ct., S23748
Martin, Ct., S10947
Martin, Ct., BLWt.1085-300
Nathan, Ct., S17526
KISBY, Richard, Md., S25204
KISE, Peter, Cont. (foreign) N.J. res., S33355
KISENCEDERS, Martin, Cont., Va., S39823; BLWt.2416-100
KISER, Jacob, Pa. See KEISER
Nicholas, N.J., R5902
KISLING, Va., Ditrich/Teter, S16178
Jacob, Va., S5554
KISNER, Jacob, Va., S45886
William, N.Y., S13642
KISSENGER, Charles, Pa. See KISSINGER
KISSINGER, Adam, Pa., S9367
Charles, Pa., BLWt.202-100
KISTWHITE, Henry, Hazen's Regt., BLWt.13290-100-Pvt. Iss. 8/20/1789. No papers
KITCHEL, James, N.J., S1036
Lydia, former wid. of Ebenezer Burnett, N.Y., which see
Phebe, former wid. of Wm. Willis, N.J., which see
Phineas, N.J., R5996
KITCHELL, David, N.J., S2702. His. wid., Lydia Kitchell, was pensioned as former wid. of Ebenezer Burnett, N.Y., which see
KITCHEN, Benjamin, N.C., Lavica Nicholson, former wid., W31797; BLWt.47613-160-55
Daniel, Va., Molly, W8005
James, Va., S31192
James, Va., Jane, R5997
John, S.C., S34949
John, Va., Mary, W2737
Thomas, Va., R5998
KITCHENS, Zachary, S.C., R5999
KITE, John, Va., S21334
KITFIELD, William, Cont., Mass., Sally, W26733
KITLER, John, Mass. See KITLEY
KITLEY, John, Mass., S35510; BLWt.2410-100
William, Mass., BLWt.4518-100-Pvt. Iss. 2/14/1795. No papers
William, Mass., S42784
KITNER, Francis, N.C., Elizabeth, W20322
KITTEL, Edmund, R.I., Patience, W20335
KITTERIDGE, Zephaniah, N.H. See KITTREDGE
KITTLE, Abraham, Cont., Md., Sea Service, S33356
Abraham, N.Y., R6002
Andrew, Mass., BLWt.4512-100-Pvt. Iss. 4/8/1797 to Simeon Wyman. No papers
Daniel, N.Y., Sarah, W21528

KITTLE (continued)
Henry, N.Y., S10951
Jacob, Pa., also 1792, S13630
Joseph, Cont., enl. in N.J., Sarah, W491
KITTREDGE, Francis, Mass., S29947
Joshua, Mass., N.H., S15498
Solomon, N.H., S44482
Thomas, Mass., Susanna, W3562
Zephaniah, N.H., Elizabeth, W26711
KITTS, Charles, Pa., BLWt.9772-100-Pvt. Iss. 3/2/1792 to Alexander Power, ass. No papers
John, N.Y., R6001
John, Pa., S23745
KIYON, Thurston. See KENYON
KIZOR, Edward, N.Y., BLWt.7342-100-Pvt. Iss. 12/28/1791 to Moses Phillips, ass. No papers
Joseph, N.Y., BLWt.7341-100-Pvt. Iss. 3/31/1793 to Thos. Russell ass. No papers
KLECKNER, Christian, Pa., BLWt. 1185-150-Ensign. Iss. 6/6/1795 to Catharine Kleckner, Admx. Also recorded as BLWt.429. No papers
KLEECKMAN, Frederick, N.Y. See KLICKMAN
KLETCKNER, Christian, Pa. See KLECKNER
KLICKMAN, Frederick, N.Y., Mary, R6003
KLINE, Conrad, Pa., BLWt.9744-100-Pvt. Iss. 8/6/1792 to Gideon Merkle, ass. No papers
Gabriel, Pa. See KLYNE
Jacob, N.J., S4479
Jacob, N.Y., Lucy, W26188; BLWt. 24997-160-55
John, N.J., Elizabeth, W26758
John, Pvt., Von Heer's Dragoons BLWt.13280 iss. 7/16/1789 to Matt McConnell, ass.
John Nicholas, Pa., S8796
Nicholas, Pa., Margaret, W3093
Peter, Pa., S22347
Philip, Va., Elizabeth, R6004
Samuel, Pa., S23290
KLINEDINST, Christian, Pa., S7115
KLINEDIRST, Christian, See KLINEDINST
KLINESMITH, Andrew, Pa., Md., Barbara, W2815
KLINGER, Philip, Pa., S8798
Philip, Pa., BLWt.2051-100
KLINGINSMITH, Jacob, Pa., R6005
KLINGLER, John, Pa., Catharine, W4009
KLUMP, Augustine, See KLUMPH
KLUMPH, Augustine, N.Y., R6006
Jeremiah, N.Y. See CLUMP
KLUNCK, Henry, Va., S39824
KLYNE, Gabriel, Pa., Dorothea/ Dorothy, W3092
KNAP, Charles, Cont., Ct., S37141
Daniel, Mass., Hannah, W15784
Elijah, Ct., S27049
Ephraim, Mass., S13672
Hezekiah, Ct., Mary, W20364
John, Ct., S10958

KNAP (continued)
Moses, Mass., BLWt.1181-400-Major Iss. 4/1/1790. No papers
Philip, Mass., Lydia, W15004
Samuel, N.Y., R6014
William, Vt., S5657
KNAPP, Abiel, Mass., S27050
Abijah, Mass., S32960
Benjamin, Ct., Hannah, W1296; BLWt.14761-160-55. See her claim as former wid. of Zebulon Moses, Vt.
Benjamin, N.Y., S13674
Benjamin, N.Y., S34950
Caleb, N.Y., BLWt.7340-100-Pvt. Iss. 10/10/1791. No papers
Caleb, Cont., N.Y., Martha Holland, former wid., W21368
Ebenezer, Ct., Mass. Sea Service, S37140
Edward, Mass., Susannah, W13593
Edward, Mass., Esther Skeel, former wid., W24979
Eleazer, Ct., S40906
Elijah, Ct., BLWt.6053-100-Pvt. Iss. 11/11/1791. No papers
Isaac, Ct., Cont., S13673
Jabez, Mass., Hannah, W20367
Jacob, Ct., Mary, W20362
James, Ct., BLWt.1513-100
James, N.Y., BLWt.7347-100-Pvt. Iss. 11/27/179-. No papers
James, N.Y., S42800
Jared, Ct., BLWt.6054-100-Pvt. Iss. 2/1/1797 to Jared Knapp
Jared, Ct., Catharine, W1621
Joel, Mass., S16183
Joel, N.Y. See Joseph KNAPP
John, Ct., S13665
John, Ct., Sally/Sarah, W26189; BLWt.28593-160-55
John, Cont., N.Y., S23292
John, Va., S41735
John Ross, See John ROSS, N.Y.
Jonas, Mass., BLWt.4510-100-Pvt. & 13961. Iss. 9/6/1791 to Isaac Brooks, ass. No papers
Jonathan, Mass., S29952
Jonathan, N.Y., Mary, W15921
Joseph, Mass., Eunice, W20363
Joseph/Joel, N.Y., Margaret, R6011
Joshua, Ct., Lodema, W5015; BLWt. 1189-150-Ens. Iss. 6/25/1789.
Joshua, Pa., S8802
Josiah, N.Y., S13666
Lathrop, Mass., S44486
Lebbeus, N.Y., S23293
Lemuel, Ct., S22865
Lothrop, Mass., BLWt.4516-100-Pvt. Iss. 11/29/1792 to Tiverell Tufts. No papers
Moses, Mass., Margaret, W24867
Moses, N.Y., S13675
Nathan, Ct., S10959
Peter, Ct., Sarah, W20366
Samuel, Ct., Cont., enl. in Ct., S42801. Hannah, his. wid., was pensioned as former wid. of John Burger, Mass., which see
Samuel, N.Y., BLWt.7371-100-Pvt. Iss. 4/2/1792 to David Hubby, Jr. ass. No papers
Samuel, Pa., S18923

KNAPP (continued)
Shadrick, N.Y., R21888
Solomon, Ct., Rosanna, W20358
Titus, Ct., S16909
Uzal, Ct., S16182, BLWt.6066-100-Sgt. Iss. 6/27/1789 to Uzal Knapp.
William, Ct., S16910
William, N.Y., R6015
KNECHT, Jacob, Pa., R6016
KNEELAND, Aaron, Mass., Hannah, W26763
Abraham, Mass., R6018
Benjamin, N.Y., S13669
Henry/Heinrich, Mass., Nancy Moulton, former wid., W568. Her other husb., Stephen Moulton, Ct., was also pensioned, which see
Ichabod, N.Y., S42804
Jesse, Cont., Ct., S42802
John, Mass., Navy, S23753
Jonathan, Ct., Mary Wood, former wid., W18360
Samuel, Ct., S42798
Seth, Art. Artificiers, BLWt. 13300-100-Pvt. Iss. 9/10/1790. No papers
Seth R., Cont., Ct. agcy. & res., Eunice, W20369
KNEP, George, Pa., S2711
KNICK, William, Md., Flora, W9104
KNICKERBACOR, Samuel, Ct., Judith, S13662; BLWt.43504-160-55
KNICKERBOCKER, Harmonus/Harmanus, Mass., S44236
Philip, N.Y., Hannah, R6020
KNIERBECKER, Herman, Mass., BLWt. 4509-100-Pvt. Iss. 4/21/1796. No papers
KNIESHERN, Christian, N.Y.,S5659
KNIESTCARN, Annatje, former wid. of Denier Relja/Dernier Relyea, N.Y., which see
KNIFFEN, Amos, N.Y., Hannah Depew former wid., W24053
Amos, N.Y. See SNIFFING
John, N.Y. See SNIFFEN
KNIFFIN, Amos, N.Y., S13671
John, N.Y., Rachel, W12046; BLWt.28584-160-55
Thomas, N.Y. See SNIFFIN
KNIFFING, Amos, N.Y. See SNIFFING
KNIGHT, Abraham, N.H., Hannah, W21536; BLWt.29023-160-55 --- (name not shown). Wid. Catharine. See N.A. Acc. No.874-050100 Not Half Pay. No pension file found
Absalom, N.C., S4483
Artemas, Cont., Mass., S16438
Austin, Va., Elizabeth, W8010
Barzillai/Barzillah, R.I., Eleanor W13592
Benjamin, Cont., N.H., Sarah/ Sally, W26760
Benjamin, Navy, R.I., S38899
Carter, Mass., S10961
Charles, Ct., R6022
Christopher, --, Va. res. in 1835, R6023
Comfort, former wid. of Constant Graves, R.I., which see

KNIGHT (continued)
Daniel, Mass., S37133
Daniel, Mass., Esther, W26770
Daniel, Navy, wid., res. in N.H. in 1838, Elizabeth, W21539; BLWt.6039-160-55
David, R.I., S21856
Elijah, Ct., BLWt.6047-100-Pvt. Iss. 9/4/1789 to Ezekiel Case. No papers
Elijah, Ct., S41732
Elijah, Mass., S44489
Elijah, Mass., Vt., S10960
Elisha, N.C., S31801
Ephraim, Mass., S44490
Henry, Va., S7124
Howard, Pa., BLWt.9770-100-Pvt. in the Art. Iss. 10/10/1792 to Alexander Power, ass. No papers
Israel, R.I., S21857
Jacob, Md., BLWt.11415-100-Pvt. Iss. 1/18/1796 to George Ponsonby, ass. No papers
Jacob, Md., S41733
Jacob, Mass., Mary, W26761
James, Cont., Navy, Pa., Margaret W27510
James, N.Y., S23752
James, Va., Elizabeth, W2946
Joel, Mass., Vt., Esther, W20360
John, Cont., Mass., N.H., Abigail, W16039
John, Mass., BLWt.4507-100-Pvt. Iss. 2/22/1792 to John Peck. No papers
John, Mass., S27045
John, Mass., S37135
John, N.C., S1992
John, N.C., Sarah, R6030
John, S.C., R6026
John, Vt., S15916
John, Va., Polly, W12051; BLWt. 238-300
Jonathan, Ct., Anna/Ann, W3024; BLWt.56-300
Jonathan, Cont., Mass., S18074
Jonathan, Mass., S8787
Jonathan, Mass., S29954
Jonathan, Mass., Sarah, W26768
Jonathan, Navy, R.I., Elizabeth W26765
Jonathan, R.I., Sarah, W13597
Joseph, Cont., Mass., Hannah, W26759
Joseph, Mass., S---, His wid., Bathsheba was pensioned as former wid. of Jeremiah Mitchell, Mass., which see. Also rec'd pension due her dec'd husb., above. All papers in W26767.
Joseph, Mass., S37138
Joseph, Mass., Abigail, W21538
Josiah, Ct., S13664
Mark, Mass., Polly, W26762
Michael, Pa., BLWt.9742-100-Corp. Iss. 6/20/1789. No papers
Miles, N.C., BLWt.12302 & 13285-100-Sgt. Iss. 9/6/1796 to John Blakely, ass. of John Macauslan, ass. No papers

KNIGHT (continued)
Moses, N.H., Abiah, W20368
Moses, N.C., S.C., b. Va., R6028
Moses, S.C., Marian H., W10182; BLWt.24988-160-55
Nathaniel, Cont., Mass., S30527
Nathaniel, Navy, Mass.?, R563
Night, S.C., S31194
Oliver, R.I., Sarah/Sally, W21540; BLWt.16121-160-55
Peter, Va., S5660
Phinehas, Ct., S32959
Richard, R.I., Lillis, W13591
Robert, R.I., Elizabeth, W13598
Samuel, Navy, R.I., Mary, W769; BLWt.10018-160-55
Silas, Mass., S19371
Stephen, Mass., Elizabeth, W20370
Thomas, N.J., N.Y., Elizabeth, W20357
Uriah, Cont., Mass., Lydia Sears, former wid., W13885
William, Cont., Mass., Lydia, W24855
William, Mass., S21336
William, Mass., Susannah, W21420
William, N.C., Sea Service, Phebe, W24866
William, N.Y., BLWt.7346-100-Pvt. Iss. 6/22/179-. No papers
William, N.Y., S42797
William, N.C., S31800
William, N.C., R6031
William, Va., Mary, W8009; BLWt.43510-160-55
Zachariah, Mass., S37134
KNIGHTEN, Thomas, S.C., Va., S32368
William, Va., S38123
KNIGHTER, William, Va. See KNIGHTEN
KNIPE, Henry, Pa., S5658
KNIPPING, Frederick, Pa., BLWt. 9745-100-Pvt. Iss. 5/26/1794 to Michael Stever, ass. No papers
KNISKERN, David, N.Y., R6035
KNITTLE, Adam, Pa., S2712
Frederick, Pa., S10952
KNOCK, Drisco, Mass. See NOCK
KNOLTON, Joshua, Mass. See KNOWLTON
KNOTT, Abraham, Ct. See NOTT
Ignatious, Md., S4481
James, Md., BLWt.11419-100-Pvt. Iss. 2/1/1790. No papers
KNOULTON, Nathan, Mass., S29955; BLWt.14800-160-55
KNOUTS, Jacob, N.Y., Elizabeth, R6036
KNOWELS, Ezekiel, N.H., S29950
KNOWER, Thomas, Mass., Ann, W15003
KNOWLES, Amos, N.H., Dorothy/ Dorotha, W16133
Charles, Crane's Art., BLWt. 1193-300-Capt. Iss. 4/13/1792 Also recorded under BLWt.2557 No papers
Daniel, R.I., S17529
Ezekiel, N.H. See KNOWELS
Ezekiel, N.H., S44487

KNOWLES (continued)
Isaac, Cont., Mass., Prudence, W26769
James, Ct., Cont., Martha, W4258; BLWt.13301-100. Iss. 3/10/1790. No papers
James, Ct., Navy, Prudence Foot, former wid., W14036
John, Sheldon's Dragoons, Ct., BLWt.6077-100-Pvt. Iss. 12/14/1789 to Richard Platt. No papers
John, Cont., Ct., Heppy/Hepzibah, W20356
John, N.H., S8799
John, N.H., S18921
John, N.H., Lydia, W21535
John, N.C., Dis. No papers
John, Pa., R6038
Robert, Del., BLWt.10805-100-Pvt. Iss. 5/26/1790. No papers
Sarah, former wid. of John Nute, N.H., which see
Seth, Ct., S42799
Seth, Mass., BLWt.4523-100-Pvt. Iss. 1/28/1790 to Eliphalet Downer. No papers
Simon, BLWt.3254-100-Pvt. Iss. 8/26/1796 to Joshua Pickering, ass.
Simon, N.H., S44488
Simon, Cont., N.H., Lydia, W26764; BLWt.12-60-55
Walker, Ct., S23294
William, Va., Mary, W4257
KNOWLTON, Abraham, Cont., Mass., S49295
Abraham, Mass., S32961
Andrew, Cont., Me. Agcy., S37139
Christopher, Pa., War of 1812, R6041
Daniel, Mass., Abigail Rockwood, former wid., W26401
Ephraim, N.Y., S13667
Frederick, Ct., Cont., Mass., S13670
Grant, S.C., Frances, W10185
John, Mass., S44491
John, Mass., Dorcas, W16622
John, N.Y., S13668
Jonathan, Cont., Mass., Hannah, W20359
Joseph, Mass., S29956
Joseph, Mass., Betsey, W20355
Joshua, Mass., Betsey, R6040
Malachi, Mass., Abigail, R6039
Nathan, Mass., S29953
Nathan, Mass. See KNOULTON
Nathaniel, Ct., S23291
Nehemiah, Mass., S29951
Robert, Cont., Mass., War of 1812, S41734
Robert, Mass., S44485
Stephen, Ct., Deidamia, W6261; BLWt.13426-160-55
Stephen, Mass., S31193
Thomas, Ct., S31803; BLWt.3952-160-55
Thomas, Ct., Cont., BLWt.1149-450
Thomas, Mass., Hannah, W12045; BLWt.54195-160-55

KNOWS, John, French. See NICHOLS
KNOWZE, John, Mass., S40907
KNOX, Benjamin, N.C., S8800
David, Mass., BLWt.4533-100-Pvt. Iss. 4/1/1790. No papers
David, Mass., S37136
David, Mass., S42803
George, N.H., S40904
George, Pa., S2709
George, Pa., Catharine, W15785
Henry, Commanding the Art., BLWt.1180-1100-Maj. Gen. Iss. 1/29/1790. No papers
Hugh, S.C., Janet, W10180
James, Cont., Mass., Lydia, W20361
James, N.C., S7126
James, R.I., Nancy, W21537
James, Va., BLWt.1832-400
John, Cont., Del., S16439
John, Md., BLWt.11424-100-Pvt. Iss. 4/6/1797 to James De-Baufre, ass. No papers
John, Mass., S29279
John, Mass., S37137
John, N.H., S10957
John, N.Y., Mary, W15920
John, S.C., Elizabeth, W10181
Jonathan, Cont., Mass. See NOCKS
Joseph, N.C., S4480
Mathew, Pa., BLWt.508-200
Nathan, Mass., Polly, W2621; BLWt.28565-160-55
Robert, N.C., b. Ireland, S8803
Robert, N.C., Mary, R6043
Robert, S.C., b. Ireland, Milley W26190; BLWt.26714-160-55
Samuel, N.C., b. Pa., S31802
Samuel, S.C., Catharine, W302
Samuel, S.C., Agnes, W8008
Silvanus, N.H. See Sylvanus NOCKE
Timothy, N.H., Molly, W15727
William, N.H., Anna, R6042
William, Pa., BLWt.1201-200-Lt. Iss. 8/19/1791. No papers
William, S.C., S38900
KOCH, Adam, Cont., Pa., S39828; BLWt.1618-100
Adam, Pa., S4484; BLWt.1160-100
Adam, Pa., Dis. No papers
Rudolph, N.Y. See COOK
KOCHENDERFFER, John, Pa., S23754
KOCHENOUR, Jacob, Pa. See KOUCHENOUR
KOCK, Adam, Pa. See KOCH
Henry, Von Heer's Dragoons, Pa., BLWt.13281-100-Pvt. Iss. 7/8/1791 to Simon Fisbaugh, ass. No papers
KOEHLER, Michael, Pa., R6048
KOEN, John, N.C., S8804
KOENIG, Christopher, N.Y., S13677
Johannes, N.Y., Mariah, R6047
KOFFMAN, Daniel. See COFFMAN
KOHLER, Valentine, Pa., Magdalena R6049
KOKEN, Peter, Cont., Pa., Mary, W3264
KOKOGAI, Samuel, Cont., enl. in Pa., S39827

KOLB, Abraham C., Pa., R6050
Jehu, S.C., Angelina, W8011; BLWt.38510-160-55
Peter, S.C., S31799
Thomas, S.C., S38901
KOLLOCK, Cornelius, Mass., S21337
Ebenezer, Mass., S29957
Shepard, Cont., N.J. res. in 1818, Susan, W3143
KONKLE, Lawrence, Pa., S22341
KONNIGHT, Conrad, N.Y., N.J. Agcy., Ctf. 253
KOOKEN, Peter, Pa. See KOKEN
KOON, Christian, Cont., Pa., S547
Christian, Md. See COON
Jacob, N.Y., S16911
John, N.Y. See John A. COONS
Peter, N.Y. See KOONS
Philip, Va., R6053
KOONCE, Philip, N.C., S4485
KOONS, Jacob, N.Y. See COONS
Lawrance, Pa., Mary, R6054
Peter, N.Y., Lydia, R2266
Peter, N.Y., R6055
KOONTS, John, N.C., S7118
KOONTZ, Phillip, Va., S5661
KOPP, Ludwig/Ludovic, Pa., Elizabeth, W2129
KORNER, Philip, N.Y. See CARNER
KORTRIGHT, Lawrence, N.Y., S13676
KOSCIUSZKO, Thaddeus, ---, BLWt. 1219-500-Col. Iss. 8/23/1797 No papers
KOUCHENOUR, Jacob, Pa., R15730
KOUGH, Adam, Pa., S39825
Ludwick, Pa., BLWt.9752-100-Pvt. Iss. 6/9/1794 to Gideon Merkle, ass. No papers
KOUGHER, Daniel, Pa., S39704
KOUNTZ, Esther, former wid. of Seth Jones, Mass., N.Y., which see
KOVELER, Adam, Pa., S39826
KOYLE, Ephraim, See KYLE
KRACH, Gottlieb, N.Y. See KRACK
KRACK, Gotlieb, N.Y., BLWt.7356-100 Pvt. Iss. 8/23/1790 to Charles Newkerk, ass. No papers
Gottlieb, N.Y., Elizabeth, W26771
KRAFT, William, Cont., Pa., Catharine, W9499
KRAM, Simeon, N.Y. See KROM
KRAMER, Eleanor, former wid. of Wm. Russwurm, N.C., which see
Eleanor, former wid. of George Gosnell, Pa., which see
KRAMPS, Henry, N.Y. See GRAMPS
KRAUSE, David, Pa., Regina, W3266
KREAGER?, Jacob, N.J., S5664
KREBS, George, Pa., Catharine, W3094
KREGER, George, N.C., Sally, W3696; BLWt.26262-160-55
KREGOR, George, N.C. See KREGER
KREIS, Peter, Cont., Md., Mary, W2947
KREMBS, Henry, N.Y. See GRAMPS
KREMER, Conrad, Cont., Pa., S19372
John, Pa., S7120
KREMMINGER, Fredrick, N.C.,

KREMMINGER (continued)
Catharine, R6063
KRENER, Jacob, Pa., S33362
KREPS, George, Pa. See KREBS
KRESS, John, N.J., R6057
KRETZER, Leonard, N.Y., Elizabeth, W21541
KREWSON, Simon, Pa., S22867
KRICK, Jacob, Pa., R6058
KRIDER, Jacob, Pa., Harriet, W10186; BLWt.73583-160-55
KRIES, Peter, Pa. See KREIS
KRIM, John, N.J., Pa., Phebe, W26182; BLWt.38508-160-55
KRIMINGER, Frederick, N.C. See KREMMINGER
KRING, Lodwick/Lodowick, N.Y., S10962
KRISER, John, Mass., R20393
KRISS, Conrad, Pa., Mary, W3697
KRIZER, John, Mass. See KRISER
KROAN, John, Pa., S22348
KROESEN, Garret, Pa., S22866
Isaac, Va., S5663
KROM, Benjamin A., N.Y., S13678
Cornelius, N.Y., S13679
Cornelius, N.Y., Maria, W20372
Jacob D., N.Y., R6059
John G., N.Y., Janatje, W66623
Peter, N.Y. See KROUM
Simeon, N.Y., Anna, W16320
KRONKHITE, David, N.Y., R6060
John, N.Y., BLWt.7365-100-Pvt. Iss. 9/3/1790. No papers
Patrick, N.Y., BLWt.7366-100-Pvt. Iss. 9/3/1790. No papers
KROUM, Peter, N.Y., S13680
KROUS, Leonard, N.Y. See CROUSE
KROWS, Leonard, N.Y., S16181
KRUG, Philip/Phillip, Cont., Pa., Mary, W3263
KRUGH, Philipp, Cont., Pa. See Philip KRUG
KRUM, Hendrick W., N.Y., Jane, W20371
KRUMBINE, Peter, Pa., S23756
KRUMP, Conrad, N.C., S6599
KRUTSINGER, Solomon, Md., Pa., See CRUTSINGER
KRYSHER, Simon, Pa., S23755
KRYTSAR, John, Va., S38902
KUDER, Elias, Pa. No claim. See Valentine KUTER
Valentine, Pa. See KUTER
KUGEL, John, Md., S15190
KUHL, Casper, ---, Pa. res., Dis. No papers
KUHNS, Daniel, Pa. See KUNTZ
George, Pa., Susan, W4473; BLWt.26654-160-55
Michael, Pa., Julian/Julia Ann, W3564
KUMPS, George, Pa., S2676
KUNSMAN, George, Pa., S41736
KUNTZ, Christian, Von Heer's Dragoons, Pa., BLWt.13278-100-Trumpeter. Iss. 8/7/1789. No papers
Daniel, Pa., R6062
Henry, Pa., BLWt.9750-100-Pvt. Iss. 5/16/1791 to John M. Taylor, ass. No papers

KUNTZ (continued)
John, Pa., S2713
KUPP, Ludwic, Pa. See Ludwig KOPP
KURAU, Michael G., N.Y. See KURAW
KURAW, Michael G., N.Y., S42663
KURTZ, John, Pa., S5665
Michael, Pa., BLWt.375-100
KUSTER, Jacob, Pa., S22349
KUTER, Elias, Pa. See KUDER
Valentine, Pa., S5655
KUTZ, Peter, Pa., S2714
KUYKENDALL, Mathew, N.C., S.C., S30518
Wilhelmus, N.Y., S23295
KYCENCEDER, Martin, Cont., Va. See KISENCEDERS
KYES, Nathaniel, Mass., See KEYES
KYLE, Anna, former wid. of Mathias Mauk, Va., which see
Ephraim, N.H., R6065
Thomas, Pa., S2716
KYLEFUSS, Esther, former wid. of James Rose, N.Y., which see
KYMES, Coonrod, Va., R5928
KYNION, Joseph, R.I. See KINYON
KYRK, William, N.Y., Jane, R6067
KYTLE, Jacob, N.C., S21338
KYZER, Frederick, Md., R6061

L

LAAR, Jacob, Pa., R20321
LABAR, Cornelia, former wid. of John Van Etten, Pa., which see
Daniel, Pa., S49308
Henry, Pa., R6068
Melekiah/Melakiah, Pa., S42816
LABAREE, James, Mass., Mercy, W24485
LABARON, William, Mass., S40914
LABARRON, Francis, Mass. See LE BARRON
LABBE, Joseph, Hazen's Regt., BLWt.13360-100-Pvt. Iss. 10/12/1790. No papers
LABBEREE, Peter, Mass. See LABREE
LABE, Francis, Cont. No claim for pension or BL for this sold., all records checked, but his discharge cert. was found (with Gen. Washington's signature cut out) in a bundle of papers prior to the adoption of the flat filing method. Papers show he was a Sgt. in Hazen's Regt., served 5 yrs. 6 mos., was discharged 6/22/1783.
Joseph, Cont., Canadian, Mary Ursule, W20387. See claim of Joseph Labo and reports relative to Canadian Regt. in file of John Gauley.
LABO, Joseph, S46534. See also claim of Joseph Labe, above.
LABONTE, John Baptist, N.Y.R20450
Peter, N.Y., R20453
LABONY, Peter, Mass. Sea Service, Privateer, See LABREE
LABOREY, Peter, See LABREE
LABOUTE, John Baptist, N.Y. See LABONTE
LABREE, Peter, Mass. Sea Service, Privateer, R6069
LACEY, Burrall, N.C., BLWt.12334 & 13322-100-Pvt. Iss. 12/11/1797 to Seth Peebles. No papers
Isaac J., Ct., S46501
Jacob, N.J., BLWt.8494-100-Pvt. Iss. 9/29/1790 to John Hole, ass. No papers
John, N.C., S41750
Josiah, Ct., Dis. No papers here, but see Am. State Papers, Class 9, Claims pp. 65, 115.
Thomas, N.J. See LACY
LACHANCE, Antoine, Cont., Canadian, Mass., Sea Service, Sarah, W24475; BLWt.26895-160-55
LACHENAUER, George, N.C., S9371
LACHENOUR, Jacob, N.C., S7129
LACHLER, John George, Hazen's Regt., BLWt.13344-100-Pvt. Iss. 8/7/1789 to Richard Platt, ass. No papers
LACKEY, Adam, Va., Catharine, W8030
Andrew, Cont., Mass., S32966
George, N.C., b. Ireland, S8820
Henry, Pa., Mary, R6073
Hugh, N.Y., BLWt.7413-100-Pvt. Iss. 8/30/1790. No papers

LACKEY (continued)
Isaac, Mass., S40924
James, Lamb's Art., N.Y., BLWt. 7424-100-Pvt. Iss. 9/15/1790 to John S. Hobart et al, assnes. No papers
John, N.C., Elizabeth, W20376
Phillip, Pa., BLWt.9795-100-Pvt. Iss. 8/9/1792. No papers
Robert, Pa., BLWt.9822-100-Pvt. Iss. 7/16/1789. No papers
Robert, Pa., Mary, W2948
Thomas, N.C., b. Ireland, Margaret, W20373; BLWt.10019-160-55
Thomas, N.C., Jane, W21557
Thomas, Va., Elizabeth, W8023
William, N.C., S.C., b. Ireland; to Pa., to N.C., Elizabeth, W1622
LACKLAND, John, Va., S13962
LACKY, Andrew, Va., S30533
LACORN, John, Pa., BLWt.9857-100-Pvt. Iss. 7/7 or 17/1789 to Richard Platt, ass. No papers
LACOST, Francis, N.J., BLWts. 8472 & 13343-100-Pvt. Iss. 1/5/1792.
LACOUNT, Samuel, Mass., S20034
LA CROIX, Michael, Hazen's Regt. BLWt.13368-100-Pvt. Iss. 10/12/1790. No papers
LACY, Elijah, Va., Frankey, W10189
Ephraim, Mass., Mehitable, R6071
Isaac, N.Y., Ellen, W3095
Jacob, N.J., S4498
Jacob, N.J., S33368
Mathew, Va., Susanna, W8077
Samuel, Cont., N.J., S41745
Thomas, N.J., Elizabeth, W8028
William, S.C., b. N.C., S21342
Zachariah, Ct., Betty, W20405
LAD, Elisha, Ct., R6076
LADD, Amasa, Ct., Elizabeth Miller, former wid., W26263
Asa, N.H., S13695
Benjamin, Cont., Mass., S37142
Cyrus, Ct., Amy, W20411
David, N.H., BLWt.3283-100-Pvt. Iss. 12/17/1795 to Wm. S. Thorn, ass. No papers
Elisha, Ct., See LAD
Ezekiel, N.H., S17534
James, N.H., Vt., Hannah, W15006
John, Ct., Esther Fish, former wid., W13162; BLWt.8388-160-55
John, Mass., S29281
John, Mass., S37153
Jonathan, N.H., Sarah, W20396
Joseph, N.H., Sally, W20397
Joseph, N.C., Mary, W3565; BLWt. 85009-160-55
Nathaniel, Mass., Miriam, R6078 BLWt.31448-160-55
Oliver, Ct., S21343
Thaddeus, Mass., Hannah, W21562
William, R.I., S42823
William, Va., W8079
LADEW, John, Cont., N.Y., Mary, W20393
LADIEU, Rachel, former wid. of Benedict Tew, R.I., which see
LADIG, Peter, Pa., S4499
LADNER, Robert, N.J., Elizabeth, W9110
LADOW, John, Cont., N.Y., See LADEW
Mary, former wid. of Joseph Blanchard, N.Y., which see
LADUE, Ambrose, N.Y., BLWt.7427-100-Pvt. Iss. 9/24/1791 to Platt Rogers, ass. No papers
LADY, Philip/Phillip, Va., b. Pa., S30529
LAFAR, Joseph, S.C., Catharine, W21556
LAFERTY, John, N.Y. See LAFFERTY
LAFEVER, Minard, N.J. See LEFEVER
LAFFERTY, Edward, Pa., BLWt.9800-100-Pvt. Iss. 7/9/1789. No papers
John, N.Y., BLWt.7396-100-Pvt. Iss. 9/15/1790 to John S. Hobart et al, assnes. No papers
John, N.Y., S35516
John, N.C., S42813
LAFFOON, James, Ga., Va., S13694
Nathaniel, Va., S8813
LAFLAN, John, Ct., S37601
LAFLECHE, John, Armand's Corps, BLWt.13320-100-Pvt. Iss. 2/11/1800. No papers
LAFLEN, Abraham, Ct., S40923
Charles, Ct., S28785
LAFLER, John, Cont., Green Mt. Boys, N.Y., Jemima, W5122
LAFLIN, Samuel, Ct., Mass., S42825
LAFO, Mary, former wid. of Jacob White, Va., which see
LAFON, Isaac, Cont., Pa. See LEVAN
Richard, Va., Anna, W1785; BLWt.75063-160-55
LA FOND, Peter Simon, N.Y., Maria Loisa/Maria Louisa, W20388
LAFONG, Isaac, Cont., Pa. See LEVAN
Mary, Va. See Jacob WHITE
LAFOU, Richard, Va. See LAFON
LAFOY, James, N.C., S10971
Mary, Va. See Jacob WHITE
LAFRAMBOIS, James, N.Y., S42826
Nicholas, Hazen's Regt., BLWt. 13336-100-Pvt. Iss. 1/22/1790 to Benj. Mooers, ass. No papers
LAGORE, John, Cont., Pa. See LEGORE
LAHEE, William, N.J., BLWt.8499-100-Pvt. Iss. 1/14/1791. No papers
LAHEY, John, Del., S40908
LAHMAN, Christian, Pa., Rosina, R6084
LAIB, John, Cont., Pa. res., BLWt. 949-100
LAIDLEY, Thomas, Pa., Sea Service, S15596
LAIGHTON, James, Navy, N.H.,S44506
LAIN, Charles, Va., Sarah/Sally, W26193; BLWt.26750-160-55
Eleazer, Mass., Henrietta, W13605
Gisborn/Gisborne, Va., S4496
Jacob, N.J., S707
Jacob, N.Y. See LANE
Joseph, Va. See LANE
Joseph, Va., Sarah, W5123
LAINE, Henry, N.J., Mary, R6128
LAINE (continued)
Jacob, N.J. See LAIN
LAING, Thomas, Navy, R.I. Agcy. & res., S38907
LAINHART, Isaac, Va., S30532
LAIR, Adam, N.Y., Mariah Comfort, former wid., R2189
LAIRD, John, Pa. See LARD
Joseph, Mass., R6085
Nathaniel, Pa., Agnes, W950
Richard, Cont., N.J., Lucy, W8078
Robert, S.C., S32369
LAITEN, Richard, Mass., R21785
LA JENNESS, Prudent, Canadian, N.Y. res., R6086
LAKE, Asa, Vt., Chloe, R6087
Charlotte, former wid. of Abraham Covenhoven, N.J, N.Y., which see
Daniel, Ct., son of Matthew, Polly, W12071
Daniel, Cont., N.H., Hepzibah, W15017
Daniel, R.I., Hannah, W20389
David, Ct., R6088
David, R.I., S21340
Elizabeth Q., former wid. of John Pryor, Va., which see
Elnathan, Mass., R.I., S31200
Enos, Mass., N.H., S10964
George, N.J., S1040
Gideon, R.I., Ruth, W20398
Giles, R.I., S21341
Henry, N.H., S15917
Henry, N.Y., S10974
James, Mass. Sea Service, Privateers, Mehitable, R6091; BLWt.61242-160-55
Jeremiah, Mass., S42808
John, Cont., Mass., S37146
John, N.J., S4486
John, N.J., Mary, W99
John, N.Y., S9924
Jonathan, N.H., Lucy, S40918; BLWt.49242-160-55. She was pensioned as former wid. of Hezekiah Wheeler, N.H., which see
Pardon, R.I., Ruth, W24471; BLWt.13002-160-55
Peter, N.Y., Hannah, W26199; BLWt.26776-160-55
Phineas, Ct., Dis. No original papers, but corresp. in file, based on List of Pensioners (1835), Vol.1, Fairfield Co., Ct. Pension Roll, p. 3 indicates that Phineas Lake served as a Pvt., was discharged from the Invalid Corps on 1/4/1783, and granted pension effec. 1/5/1783. At one time res. of Chittenden Co., Vt. & later res. of Fairfield, Ct. Files contain an inquiry dated 1/22/1917 from Edra Lake, Atchison, Kan.,which states Phineas Lake b. 5/1736, m. Elizabeth Stilson 10/17/17-- and had Curtis, Susannah, Mary & Daniel, & lived Shelburne Twp. where he

LAKE (continued)
died in 1819, aged 83, having served in both the French & Indian War & Rev. War. There are no N.A. official rec. confirming or denying this assertion.
Reuben, Ct., S35515; BLWt.546-100
Roger, Ct., S42809
William, Ct., Mary, W26191; BLWt. 11177-160-55
LAKEMAN, James F., Mass., S32965
John, Mass., S32962
Nathaniel, Mass., Elizabeth, W15015
Samuel, Mass., Abigail, W24484
Sarah, former wid. of Isaac Setchell, Mass., which see
Thomas, Mass., Rachel Roach, former wid., W22109; BLWt.2100-100
LAKEN, Oliver, Mass., S44496
LAKIN, David, Mass., S5321
Robinson, Mass., S29958
Simeon, Mass., N.H., Lois, W15922
William, N.H., S42815
Winslow, Mass., Esther, W24495
LALLEN, Michael, Md., S33367
LAM, David, Ct., Navy, See LAMB
John, N.C., Comfort, R6094
LAMA, William, Pa., S41749
LAMAN, Cornelius, Mass., S13702
John, Mass., Diadama, R6092
LAMAR, Marion, Pa., BLWt.2323-400
William, Md., S46388; BLWt.1293-300-Capt. Iss. 2/11/1800
LAMASTER, Joseph, Va. See LEMASTER
LAMB, Abner, N.C., BLWt.1314-200-Lt. Iss. 5/25/1792. No papers
Arthur, N.Y., BLWt.7377-100-Pvt. Iss. 3/16/1792 to Nathaniel Pratt, ass. No papers
Asa, Ct., Cont., S10970
Benjamin, Ct., Mass., S40915
Benjamin, Mass., S10973
Daniel, Mass., S32963
David, Ct., Navy, Anna, W20410
David, Cont., N.Y., Pa., S22875
David, Mass., Sylvania Arnold, former wid., W25355; BLWt. 15405-160-55
Edmund, Cont., Vt., Rebecca, W24489
Frederick, S.C., BLWt.12337 & 13321-100-Pvt. Iss. 6/27/1795. No papers
George, Hazen's Regt., BLWt.13354-100-Pvt. Iss. 3/29/179?. No papers
George, Mass., S35514
Gibbs, N.C., BLWt.12335 & 13324-100-Pvt. Iss. 8/14/1792 to Isaac Cole, ass. No papers
Gideon, N.C., BLWt.1310-500-Lt. Col. Iss. 5/25/1792 to Abner Lamb, Executor. No papers
Hiel, N.Y., See Jehiel
Isaac, N.Y., BLWt.14036-100-Pvt. Iss. 5/16/1792 to Job Mead, Admr. No papers
Israel, Mass., S22869
Jacob, Md., Indian War, R5747
James, Mass., S18931

LAMB (continued)
James, Mass., S22870
James, N.H. & French & Indian War, Judith, W21550
Jehiel/Hiel, N.Y., Huldah, W16626
John, 2nd Regt. Art., BLWt.1259-500-Col. Iss. 8/20/1790. No papers
John, Mass., Susannah, W15013
John, N.C. See LAM
Joseph, Ct., Mass., W9105; BLWt. 19762-160-55
Joseph, N.Y., Martha, W21561
Joseph, Pa., BLWt.9794-100-Pvt. Iss. 8/7/1789 to Richard Platt, ass. No papers
Joseph, Pa., BLWt.9847-100-Pvt. Iss. 2/27/1793. No papers
Joshua, Md., Sarah Windham, former wid., W9168. She was also pensioned as wid. of Thomas Windham, Md., which see
Nahum, Cont., Mass., Lucinda, W8022; BLWt.38517-160-55
Nathaniel, Mass., S22352
Peter, Mass., S40916
Reuben, Mass., Patience Bidwell former wid., W17307
Robert, Mass., Catharine, W15007
Samuel, Mass., Asenath, W20414
Silas, Cont., Ct., Jane, W20399
Thomas, Mass., Rosanna, W15010
Thomas, Va., S30531
William, Mass., R6095
LAMBART, Samuel, Mass. See LAMBERT
Zacchews/Zaccheus, R.I., BLWt. 4608-100-Pvt. Iss. 4/16/1790. No papers
LAMBAUGH, Joseph, Va., S8816
LAMBERSON, David, N.J., S1042
Laurence, N.J., Christena, W8020
Thomas, N.J., S1043
LAMBERSTON, Simon, N.Y., BLWt.7395-100-Pvt. Iss. 9/28/1790 to Alexander Robertson, ass. No papers
LAMBERT, Abraham, Armand's Corp., BLWt.13315-100-Pvt. Iss. 11/11/1791 to Samuel Broome, ass. No papers
Abraham, N.Y., S42810
Charles, Va., Nancy, W8021
Christian, Md. See Christopher
Christopher/Christian, Md., R6096
Cornelius, N.Y., S13687
David, Ct., Lois, W20377
Elizabeth, former wid. of Edward Williams, N.C., which see
George, N.Y., R6098
George, Va., S8810
Henry, Mass., Hannah, W27440
Jacob, Pa., S23298
James, N.J., Hannah, W859
James, Va., served in 1774 against Indians, Jane, R6099
John, N.Y., BLWt.7419-100-Pvt. Iss. 9/6/1791
John, N.C., S41753
John, S.C., S16445, b. Albemarle Co., Va.,res. at enl. Bedford Co., Va.
John, Va., Rachel, W9111; BLWt.

LAMBERT (continued)
17586-160-55
Jonathan, Mass., Hannah, BLWt. 31308-160-55
Mathias/Matthias, Va., Elizabeth, W1784
Meredith, Va., R6100
Peter, N.Y., Cont., S22868
Samuel, Mass., Navy Privateer, Mary, W20418; BLWt.34844-160-55
Samuel, N.J., Elizabeth, W3566
William, N.Y., S13690
Zaccheus, R.I., BLWts.3292 & 4608-100-Pvt. Iss. 4/16/1790. No papers
LAMBERTON, James, Mass., S17533
Obed, Ct., S44493
LAMBERTSON, Simon, N.Y.,Laura,R6101
LAMBETH, Moses, N.C., S4512
LAMBKIN, John, Va. See LAMKIN
LAMBLY, Philip, N.C., Elizabeth, W4712
LAMBRECHT, Daniel, Pa., S8815
LAMBRIGHT, John, Pa., Mary, R6102
LAMKIN, John, Va., Mary, W8018
Sampson, Va., R20395
LAMLEY, Philip, N.C. See LAMBLY
LAMMA, William, Pa. See LAMA
LAMMAS, Dyre, Navy, Mass., S37150
LAMME, Nathan, Va., S46454; BLWt. 1851-300
Samuel, Va., Agness, R6103
LAMON, Moses, N.Y., S13710
Robert, N.C., Pa., b. Ireland, S16916
LAMOND, Archibald, Mass., Mary, W20413
LAMONT, Archibald, N.Y., R6093
John, Cont., Mass., N.Y., S41746
John, Mass., S37154
William, N.Y., Mary, W1782; BLWt.3535-160-55
LAMOREUX, Peter, N.Y. See LOMEREAUX
LAMOTT, George, Mass., BLWt. 4560-100-Corp. Iss. 8/10/1789 to Richard Platt. No papers
LAMPER, Benjamin, N.H., S44494
LAMPHAER, Abel, Ct., S16440
LAMPHAR, Samuel, N.Y., S5671
LAMPHEAR, Daniel, R.I., R6106
Roswell, Ct., Elizabeth, W21544. Not same as Roswell Lanfair
Shubael, Mass. See LANPHEAR
LAMPHER, Paul, R.I. See LANPHER
LAMPHERE, Fitch, Ct. See LANPHERE
LAMPHIER, Amos, Ct., N.Y., S13698
Benjamin, N.Y., S22351
James, Ct. Sea Service, Navy, Grace, W26197
Jedediah, Ct., Elizabeth/Betsey, W20381
Roswell, Ct. See LAMPHEAR
LAMPHIRE, Fitch, Ct. See LANPHERE
LAMPIER, Francis, N.Y., BLWt.7398-100-Pvt. Iss. 9/15/1790 to John

LAMPIER (continued)
S. Hobart, et al, assnes. No papers
LAMPKIN, John, Va. See LAMKIN
LAMPMAN, Jacob, N.Y., S13715
Peter, ---, N.Y. res., Dis. No papers here, but see Peter Lampman on Report of Secy. of War 1835, Invalid Pensioners on the roll of the N.Y. agcy., res. not ascertained.
LAMPREY, Daniel, N.H., Abigail, W492; BLWt.33743-160-55
LAMPSON, Benjamin, Ct. See LAMSON
David, Ct. See LAMSON
Hannah, former wid. of John Heywood, Mass., which see
Joseph, Mass. See LAMSON
Samuel, Mass. See LAMSON
Thomas, N.J. See LAMSON
William, Mass., Martha, W20382
LAMSON, Benjamin, Ct., Mary, W16323
Daniel, Mass., Anna, W10190; BLWt.3520-160-55
David, Ct., Polly, W7163; BLWt.18390-160-55
Ebenezer, Ct., Martha, W4262; BLWt.38518-160-55
Hannah, Mass. See John HEYWOOD
Jonathan, Mass., BLWt.4588-160-Pvt. Iss. 12/12/1792 to Daniel King.
Jonathan, N.H., S11352
Joseph, Mass., Sarah, W16040; BLWt.10007-160-55
Nathan, Mass., BLWt.4561-100-Pvt. Iss. 9/14/1792 to John Stephenson
Nathan, Mass., BLWt.167-100
Samuel, Mass., Mariam/Miriam, R6107
Thomas, Mass., Anna M., W20402
Thomas, N.J., N.Y., S4516
LAMUNYON, Philip, R.I., S28783
Thomas, R.I., Lydia, W2566
LANABEE, John, N.H., BLWt.3273-100-Pvt. Iss. 3/25/1791 to David Quinton, ass. No papers
LANCASTER, Daniel, Mass. See David
David, Mass., R6108. Name erroneously rec. as Daniel by adjudicator of claim
Ebenezer, N.H., Betsey/Elizabeth, W24470
Ezekiel, Cont., Mass., Sarah, W24478
Henry, N.C., S7131
John, Mass., Mary, W8241; BLWt. 53667-160-55
Joseph, Mass., S37156
Samuel, Mass., S21339
Sarah, former wid. of John Levy Blades, Md., which see
Thomas, Mass., S40912
Thomas, Va., BLReg.180089-1855
William, Va., S16912. His wid., Sarah, was pensioned as former wid. of John Levy Blades, Md., which see
LANCER, Abraham, Pa., S40071
LANCET, John Sr.(?) or La(?),

LANCET (continued)
N.Y., BLWt.7399-100-Pvt. Iss. 8/3/1790 to Cornelius V. Dyck, ass. No papers
LANCEY, Samuel, Mass., Elizabeth, W24493
LANCHESTER, Thomas, Mass. See LANCASTER
LANCISTUS, Jacob, Pa., S36035
LANCKTON, Matthias R., Ct., Sea Service, Mass., Margaret, R6110
LAND, John, Va., Nightingale, R6112
Lamon, N.C., Willy, W20401
Lewis, Va., Obedience, W26200; BLWt.31784-160-55
Moses, Va., S36037
Reuben, N.C., S7135
LANDALE, Charles, Va. See LANGSDON
LANDEE, John, N.H., BLWt.3289-100-Pvt. Iss. 1/13/1794. No papers
LANDEN, Benjamin, N.J., BLWt.8490-100-Pvt. Iss. 3/24/1790 to Benj. Case, ass. No papers
Benjamin, N.J. See LANDON
William, Pa., BLWt.9819-100-Pvt. Iss. 7/12/1792 to Sophia Walker, admx. No papers
LANDER, Charles, Va., S31198
Nathaniel, Va., S30536
Peter, N.J., S22871
LANDERDALE, William, Va. See LAUDERDALE
LANDERKIN, Daniel, Cont., Mass. Navy, Lydia, W8240
LANDERS, Aqrilla, Mass., S13697
Asael, Mass., Mercy, W15009
Ebenezer, Mass., Olive, W21551
Ebenezer, N.Y., Mahittabel, W16628
George, Mass., BLWt.4602-100-Pvt. Iss. 3/25/1790
John, N.C., Va., b. N.C., S16444
Joseph, Mass., S13712
Thomas, Va., Nancy, W3831; BLWt. 31288-160-55
LANDES, David, Pa., BLWt.460-100
LANDIS, David, S46544
Jacob, Cont., Pa., Sarah, W4475
Roger, Md., BLWt.11432-100-Pvt. Iss. 3/21/1792. No papers
LANDMAN, Newman, Cont., Va., S41737
LANDNER, Peter, N.J. See LANDER
LANDON, Benjamin, N.J., S33365; BLWt.8490-100. Iss. 3/24/1790
Ebenezer, Ct., S13706
Edward, N.J., Tryphena, W5311
James, Ct., S15505
James, N.J., S41738
Laban, Cont., N.J., N.Y., Elizabeth/Betsy Gilless, W3096 BLWt.8481-100. Iss. 12/8/1794
Nathaniel, N.J., N.Y., Pa., S22873
Rachel, former wid. of Alexander Barr, Cont., Vt., which see
Rufus, Ct., S13682
Thomas, N.J., R6116
LANDRES, Kimbrow, Va., Keziah, W1623

LANDRES (continued)
Thomas, Va. See LANDERS
LANDRUM, James, Va., Mary, W800
Thomas, N.C., S1546
Thomas, Va., S31811
Thomas, Va., S35512
Thomas, Va. Sea Service, R61; Va. Half Pay. See N.A. Acc. No. 837, Va. State Navy-YS File
LANDS, Ephraim, Va., Polly, W4066
Lewis, Va. See LAND
LANE, Abial, Mass., S42817
Abraham, N.J., S1044
Abraham/Abram, N.J., S1045
Alexander, N.Y., Abigail, W2130; BLWt.26069-160-55
Allice, former wid. of Moses Abbot, Mass., N.Y., which see
Aquilla, N.C., Va., Agnes, R6116
Asaph, Mass., S15504
Benjamin, Mass., S18932
Caleb, Mass., S15921
Caleb, Mass., S29961
Charles, Ga., N.C., Indian Wars, R6118
Cornelius, N.J., Elizabeth, W16625
Dan, Ct., S31808
Daniel, N.C., Winneford, W26195; BLWt.83506-160-55
David, Mass., S17532
Davis, --, Rejected book gives res. at Ga., Elizabeth, R6119
Derick/Derrick, N.J., S46387;BLWt. 1271-300-Capt. Iss. 12/21/1795
Drury, Va., Carolina Matilda, W8015
Ebenezer, Mass., 21st U.S. Inf. War of 1812, Catharine, W26194; BLWt. 4571-100. Iss. 4/1/1790. BLWt.328-60-55
Eleazer, Mass. See LAIN
Elizabeth, former wid. of Thomas Blanchet, N.C., which see
Ezekiel, N.J., N.Y., Pa., S23760 and S4491
Francis, Mass., S37144
George, Mass., BLWt.4599-100-Sgt. Iss. 3/25/1790. No papers
George, N.Y., Abby, W12068
George, N.Y., Hannah, R6121
Gilbert, N.J., Rebecca, W3828
Gilbert, N.Y., S13714
Hendrick, N.J., S4494
Henry, N.J., S1041
Henry, Va., R6122
Hezekiah, Mass., S13693
Isaac, Mass., S18930
Isaac, Mass., S42824; BLWt.20-100
Isaac, N.C., Va., Sarah, R6137; BLWt.34621-160-55
Isham, Va., S13705
Jabez, Ct., S31807
Jabez, Cont., Mass., S37143; BLWt.1243-300-Capt. Iss. 12/14/1790. No papers
Jacob, N.J., R6125. Was living in 1833. Widow's name Jane.
Jacob, N.Y., R6123
Jacob, N.C., S41751
James, N.H., Sarah, W16624
James, Pa., BLWt.9846-100-Pvt.

LANE (continued)
Iss. 5/3/1791. No papers
James, Va., S35517
James, Va., Temperance, W8026; BLWt.26818-160-55
James, Va., Rachel, R6133
Job, Mass., Dis. No papers here, but see American State Papers, Class IX, Claims, pp.63,111,162
John, Ct., Cont., Va., S38129
John, Cont., Mass., Hannah, W20378
John, Cont., N.J., Phoebe/Phoebus, R6132; BLWt.1062-100
John, Mass., Elizabeth, W24477
John, N.H., S4497
John, Pa., S2042
John, Va., S41740
John, Va., Margaret/Margret, W27146
Jonathan, N.H., Mary/Molly, R6129; BLWt.34811-160-55
Joseph, Ct., R6126
Joseph, Ct., N.Y., S4495
Joseph, Ga., BLWt.1325-400-Maj. Iss. 9/15/1790 or 1791. No papers
Joseph, N.Y., Hilliche, W26772
Joseph, Va., Rebecca, W1783
Joshua, N.Y., S8808
Larkin, Va., S16442
Leavitt, Mass., S30535
Matthias, N.J., S23297
Michael, N.J., BLWt.8498-100-Pvt. Iss. 6/11/1789 to Jonathan Dayton, ass. No papers
Michael, N.J., S42806
Mordecai, Pa., S41739
Nathan, N.Y., Martha, R6127
Nathaniel, Ct., Melicent, W12060; BLWt.3796-100-55
Nathaniel, N.Y., R6130
Owen, Md., R6131
Prime/Primus (colored), N.H., S44499
Richard, Va., R6136
Samuel, Cont., Mass., Ruth, W21545; BLWt.26195-160-55
Samuel, Mass., S29284
Samuel, N.H., S15503
Samuel, Pa., R11983
Thomas, Va., R6138
Tidence, N.C., Mary, W377
Timothy, Pa., BLWt.9842-100-Corp. --Art. Iss. 10/8/1789. No papers
Turner, Va., S1916
William, Cont., Mass., Maria/Mary, W20392; BLWt.21-100
William, Mass., Sarah, W20408; BLWt.29053-160-55
William, N.J., N.Y., S10965
William, N.Y., S13711
William, N.Y., Elizabeth, S42812
William, N.C., Elizabeth, W20409 BLWt.26697-160-55
William, N.C., R6140
William, Va., S38124
LANEEY, Thomas, N.H. See LANEY
LANEY, John, Va., S18486
Thomas, Cont., N.H., S44498
William, Va., S13684
LANFAIR, Leonard, Mass., S31201

LANFAIR (continued)
Roswell, Ct., Sea Service, S30538
LANFEAR, Ezra, Mass., S9925
LANG, Benjamin, Mass., Elizabeth, W15011
Francis, Md., Susannah/Susan, W10188; BLWt.343-60-55
John, Mass. Sea Service, N.H., S29282
John H., French Army, R6142
Samuel, N.H., Sukey, R6432
William, N.H., N.H. Sea Service, S15502
William, Pa., Mary, W4260
LANGDON, Benjamin, N.Y., BLWt. 7386-100-Pvt. Iss. 9/17/1790 to Jacob Tremper, ass. No papers
Benjamin, N.Y., S41741
James, N.C., Catherine, BLWt. 52778-160-55
John, N.Y., S29960
John, N.Y., S42821
John W., Mass., S18487
Judith, former wid. of Thomas Hays, Va., which see
Lewis, Mass., Submit, W4261
Martin, Mass., S23759
Paul, Cont., Mass., Mary, W16322
Philip, Cont., Ct., S35513
Seth, Mass., R6143
LANGFIT, Philip, Cont., Va., S38126
LANGFITT, Francis, Cont., Va., S38131
LANGFORD, Jonathan, R.I., S37152
LANGHAM, Elias, Cont., Va., S41747; BLWt.1309-200-Lt. Iss. 8/10/1789 to Richard Platt, ass. No papers
James, Va., Elizabeth Goldsby, former wid., W11070; BLWt.84041-160-55
Joshua, ---, Va. res. in 1836, R6146
LANGLEE, Thomas, Cont. ---, native of N.J., Ohio res. in 1829, R20394
LANGLEY, Benjamin, Mass. See LONGLEY
Benjamin, N.H., Betsey, W15924
David, N.H., S44497
Elnathan, N.J., BLWt.8503-100-Pvt. Iss. 4/27/1799 to Abraham Bell, ass. No papers
John, N.J., BLWt.8502-100-Pvt. Iss. 4/10/1799 to Abraham Bell, ass. No papers
Miles, N.C., S7132
Shadrack, N.C., S4518
William, Cont., Va., Lucy, R6147
Winthrop, N.H., S22874
LANGLY, James, N.C., b. Va., S31813
John, S.C., S4502
LANGMAID, John, N.H., R6148
LANGSDALE, Charles, Va. See LANGSDON
LANGSDEN, Charles, Va., BLWt. 12314-100-Pvt. Iss. 3/22/1790. No papers
William, Va., BLWt.12315-100-

LANGSDEN (continued)
Pvt. Iss. 4/22/1794. No papers
LANGSDON, Charles, Va., Edith, W441
LANGSFORD, William, Mass., BLWt. 4558-100-Pvt. Iss. 1/28/1790 to Joseph May. No papers
LANGSTAFF, Henry, N.J., Hannah, W440
James, N.J., S705
John, N.J., S706
LANGSTON, William, N.C., R6149
LANGTON, Daniel, Ct., S32370
LANGWORTHY, Joseph, R.I. See LONGWORTHY
Southcote, R.I., BLWt.3295-100-Pvt. Iss. 12/31/1789. No papers
Stephen, Ct., BLWt.6096-100-Pvt. Iss. 9/14/1789 to Ezekiel Case. No papers
William, Mass., S38906; BLWt. 1052-100
LANHAM, Abel, N.C., Sarah, W1297; BLWt.26105-160-55
Greenberry, Va., Catharine, R6151
John, Md., S25073
Thomas, Md., S30534
LANIER, Lewis, N.C., Va., R6153
LANING, David, N.J., Mary, W3830
James, N.J., R6154
Ralph, N.J., Rebecca, W3829
LANKFORD, Elijah, Md., S34953
William, Va., S8823
LANMAN, James, S.C., S31812
Thomas, Cont., Mass., Naomi, W24490
LANNING, John, N.C., b. N.J., Sarah, W4711
Ralph, N.J. See LANING
LANNUM, Joseph, Va., S1846
LANPHEAR, Shubael, Mass., Elizabeth, W20379
LANPHER, Paul, R.I., Elizabeth, W20400; BLWt.31290-160-55
LANPHERE, Fitch, Ct., Jerusha, W27145
LANPHESE, Shubael, Mass. See LANPHEAR
LANPHIER, Paul, R.I. See LANPHER
LANS, Jacob, Pa., S22350
LANSDALE, Isaac, Del., S18933
Thomas, Md., Cornelia, W13604; BLWt.1227-400
LANSERT, Abraham, Pa. See LANCER
LANSING, Abraham G., N.Y., Susanna, W15840
Abraham H., N.Y., Hannah, R6155
Cornelius, N.Y., S29280
Garret J., N.Y. See LANSINGH
Garret I., N.Y., Sarah, W20391
Garrett, N.Y. See Gerrit G.
Gerrit G./Garrett, N.Y., S42811; BLWt.1265-150-Ensign. Iss. 1/22/1791. No papers
Henry, N.Y., Dolly, W20423; BLWt.30757-160-55
Jacob John, N.Y., Jane, W16325
Jane, former wid. of Evert Van Den Bergh, N.Y., which see

LANSING (continued)
John A., N.Y., Elizabeth, W16627
LANSINGH, Garret I., N.Y., S28784
LANTER, Jacob, Va., Mary, W10191
Peter, Va., Hannah, W9114; BLWt.40005-160-55
Thomas, Va., S31199
LAP, John, Ct., R9200 (to Baltimore; to Bedford Co., Pa.; to Monongalia Co., Va., later called Preston Co.)
LAPE, George, N.Y., R6158
LAPHAM, Asa, Mass., S30528
Caleb, Mass., Sarah, R6160
Hannah, former wid. of Oliver Dake, N.Y., which see
Isaac, Mass., S28782
James, R.I., Jemima, W21555
Lemuel, Mass., Lydia, W15016; BLWt.13873-160-55
Molly/Mary, former wid. of Charles Tuels, Mass., which see
LAPIERRE, Thomas, Hazen's Regt., BLWt.13359-100-Pvt. Iss. 12/4/1789 to James Reynolds, ass. No papers
LAPISH, John, N.H., BLWt.3278-100-Pvt. Iss. 4/15/1796 to James McGregore, ass. No papers
John, N.H., Dis. -- No papers here,but see Amer. State Papers, Class IX, Claims, p. 160
LAPIUS, Abraham, N.Y., S15284
LAPPIN, Paul, Md., BLWt.11434-100-Pvt. Iss. 1/8/1796 to George Ponsonby, ass. No papers
LAPRADE, John, Va., S5666
LAPSLEY, Samuel, Cont., Va., Margaret Lyle, former wid., W9149; BLWt.1301-300-Capt. Iss. 10/29/1792 to Sally Woods Lapsley, heir at law. No papers
LAPUSE, Jacque, Pvt., Hazen's Regt., BLWt.13357 iss. 8/10/1789 to Richard Platt, ass.
LAQUIR, John, N.C., S7130
LARA, James, Cont., Mass., Mary/Molly, W24488
LARABEE, Eleazer, Cont., Green Mt. Boys, S8807
Elias, N.Y. See LARRABEE
Jacob, Mass. See LARRABEE
John, Cont., Mass., S41743
Jonathan, Mass., BLWt.4553-100-Pvt. Iss. 5/9/1797 to Jeremiah Hill. No papers
Jonathan, Mass., S31202
Nathaniel, Mass., Sarah, W24476
Seth, Ct., Sally, W20404
William, N.H. See LARRABEE
LARABY, Seth, Ct. See LARABEE
LARASON, Thomas, N.J., S45879
LARAWAY, Isaac, N.Y., S8806; BLWt.1588-160-55 (living in 1855)
Isaac, N.Y., Sarah, W24491. (He d. in 1828)
Jacob, N.Y. See LARRAWAY
Philip, Mass. See LARWAY
LARCKOM, Paul, Mass. See LARCOM
LARCOM, Paul, Mass., Comfort, W5021

LARD, John, Pa., S33366
Robert, S.C., b. Pa., S32369
Samuel, N.J., Rachel, W9500; BLWt.28618-160-55
LARENCE, Isaac, Md., N.C., S.C., S32373
LAREW, Abraham, --, N.J. res., R6161
Abraham, Va., S41742
James, N.J., S4513
LARGE, John, N.J., Nancy, R6162
Joseph, N.C., b. Va., Mary, R6163
Thomas, N.C., Milly, R6164
William, N.C., Nancy, R6165
LARGENT, James, N.C., S.C., S8824
James, Va., S3857
Nelson, Va., R6166
LARIBEE, Seth, Ct. See LARABEE
LARIMORE, James, N.C., Leaner, W5312; BLWt.26421-160-55
LARKCOM, Paul, Mass. See LARCOM
LARKEN, John, Mass. See LARKIN
LARKIN, Abigail, former wid. of Thomas Adams, R.I.,which see
Covil/Covel, R.I., BLWt.28-100
David, R.I., Sarah C., W770; BLWt.28620-160-55
Edward, Pa., BLWt.9789 & 14083-100-Pvt. Iss. 8/4/1794. No papers
Ephraim, Mass., S5668
James, Va., S38130
Jesse, R.I., S38903
John, Mass., S31203
John, R.I., Mary, W20386
John, R.I., Patience, W21553
Joseph, Ct., Vt., Hannah, W24497
Joseph, Mass., S18924
Joshua, Ct., S16914
Levi, Mass., S13689
Lorin, Ct., Mass., Vt., S13716
Oliver, Mass. See LAKEN
Thomas W., R.I., Marcy, W2132
LARKINS, Benjamin, N.C., S8821
Francis, Hazen's Regt., BLWt. 13333-100-Pvt. Iss. 4/19/1792 to Conrad Feger, ass. of Peter Gutham, admr. No papers
James, Cont., enl. in Md., res. in Ohio, Catharine, R6167
James, Pa., BLWt.9837. Iss. 3/10/1795. No papers
Presley, Va., 1791-1810-1815, R6168
William, Md., BLWt.11453-100-Pvt. Iss. 1/8/1796 to Geo. Ponsonby
LARMON, Jacob, Pa. See LAUMAN
LARMONT, John, Mass., BLWt. 1244-300-Capt. Iss. 4/12/1790. No papers
LARNARD, Moses, Mass., Sally, W24465
Samuel, Mass., S29959
LARNED, Abel, N.H., S40917
Abijah, Cont., N.H., Anna, W8016
John, Mass., S15918
Simon, Mass., BLWt.1233-300-Capt. Iss. 8/22/1789 to

LARNED (continued)
Simon Larned
Sylvanus, N.H., Vt. See LEARNED
Thomas, Ct., Mass., Hannah, W13608; BLWt.10219-160-55
William, R.I., Sarah, R21542
LARNER, Edward, Pa., BLWt.9804-100-Pvt. Iss. 6/20/1789. No papers
Robert, Pa., BLWt.9829-100-Pvt. Iss. 7/12/1792. No papers
LA ROCHELLE, Michael, Armand's Corps, BLWt.13323-100-Pvt. Iss. 5/13/179-. No papers
LAROSE, Jacob, Cont., Pa., S16441
LAROW, Abraham, See LAREW
LARRABE, Richard, Mass., BLWt. 4555-100-Pvt. Iss. 11/21/1791. No papers
LARRABEE, Benjamin, Mass., Ann, W13603
Elias, N.Y., Cornelia, W20403
Isaac, Mass., S37602
Jacob, Mass., Sarah, W8239; BLWt.26815-160-55
John, Cont., Mass. See LARABEE
John, Cont., N.H., S42820
Jonathan, Mass. See LARABEE
Jonathan, Mass., Margaret, W21546
Joseph, Mass., Lydia, W15012
Lebbeus, Ct., Mary, W1882
Nathaniel, Mass. See LARABEE
Richard, Cont., Mass., Ruth, W20406
Samuel, Cont., Mass., S18076
Samuel, Mass., S18926
Samuel, Mass., Betsey, W26773
Seth, Ct. See LARABEE
Stephen, Mass., S18928
Theophilus, Ct., S40909
Thomas, Cont., Mass., Bathsheba, W21543
William, N.H., Ama/Ame/Amy/Anna, W20420
LARRABY, Elias, N.Y., BLWt.7387-100-Pvt. Iss. 7/30/1790 to Edward Cumpston, ass. No papers
LARRANCE, John, Va., Baheathaland, W5310; BLWts. 1493 & 13414-160-55
Rodham, Va., S31195
LARRAWAY, Isaac, N.Y. See LARAWAY
Jacob, N.Y., Elizabeth, W20427; BLWt.3835-160-55
LARRIMORE, Hugh, N.C., S16913
James, N.C. See LARIMORE
LARROWE, Peter, Va. See LERUE
LARRY, Michael, Pa., S37147
LARUE, Abraham. See LAREW
Henry, N.Y., Betsey, W8017; BLWt.26240-160-55
Peter, Va. See LERUE
LARWAY, Philip, Mass., Ruth, W12062; BLWt.809-100
LARY, Daniel, Cont., N.H. res. in 1819, S44495
Daniel, Cont., N.H., Lydia, W8024; BLWt.33742-160-55
John, Va., S8812
LARYMORE, Thomas, Md., BLWt.11449-100-Pvt. Iss. 2/1/1790. No papers

LASAMBERT, Antoine, Hazen's Regt., BLWt.13338-100-Pvt. Iss. 10/12/1790. No papers
LASATER, Abner, N.C., S7134
Hezekiah, N.C., R6172
William, N.C., Rebecca, W4010
LASDELL, Asa, Mass., S37148
LASELL, Josiah, Ct., Lydia, W20380
LASETER, James, Ga., See LASSITER
LASH, Adam, N.J., Pa., R6173. Act of 1818-Indiana Agcy. Ref. to ltr. dated 6/18/1824 to James Delaney from Pension Bur. which shows claim was rejected, presumably returned to veteran. Name found on Suspended & Rejected Book. DAR Library records contain copy of application made in Bartholomew Co., Ind. on 3/24/1824 under the Act of 3/18/1818, according to Miss Martha Lou Houston. Service in upper left hand corner was taken from that application.
Peter, N.J., Susannah, W12066; BLWt.28617-160-55
LASHBROOKS, William, Ct., Zeriah, W24466; BLWt.1376-100; BLWt. 330-60-55
LASHELLS, George, N.J., S4520
LASHER, Anna, former wid. of Christian Leather/Ledder/Leder, N.Y., which see
LASHLEY, Barnabus/Barney, N.C., S8819
Edmun/Edmund, Ga., Delilah, W8014
George, Md., S31814
George, Md., S34951
Howell, N.C., Va. See LESLY, Howel.
William, N.C., Amy, W20425
LASKEY, William, Mass., Sea Service, Navy, W29286
LASLEY, John, N.C., S38904
John, Va., S30687
LASLIE, Alexander, N.H. See LESLIE
LASOUCH, Lewis, Hazen's Regt., BLWt.13345-100-Pvt. Iss. 8/14/1792 to Benj. Moore, ass. No papers
LASSEL, Asa, Mass. See LASDELL
LASSELL, Caleb, Mass., S37603
LASSITER, Elijah, N.C., S9369
Hardy, N.C., S4514
James, Ga., Elizabeth, W4259
LASSLY, John, Mass., enl. N.Y., S42822
LASTER, Thomas, Pa., S41748
LATCH, Jacob, Pa., Jane, W2131
LATHAM, Amos, Ct., S36683
Arthur, Cont., Mass., S18075
Christopher, Ct., Sabra, W8031; BLWt.12564-160-55
James, Mass., Susannah, W20421
Jesper, Ct., S13707
John, Ct., S32967
John, Va., S8811
Joseph, Ct., S16915
Joseph, Cont., R.I., S13696
Noah, N.C., Polly, W5018
Phinehas/Phineas, N.C., S41752

LATHAM (continued)
Samuel, N.Y., S13703
Samuel, N.C., R6175
William, Ct., S13688
LATHERS, Christian, N.Y. See LEATHER
Ezekiel, Pvt., N.Y., BLWt.7408 iss. 2/21/1792 to Augustus Sacket,
LATHISER, Hartman, See LEITHEIZER
LATHROP, Barnabas, Cont., Mass., See LOTHROP
Daniel, Ct., R6179
David, Ct., Anne, W4509
Dixwell, Ct., S17531
Elias, Ct., Dorcas, R6180; BLWt.53753-160-55
Elisha, Ct., S18925
George, Mass. See LOTHROP
Isaac, N.Y., R6181
Job, Ct. See Primus
Joseph, Mass., Martha, R6182
Joshua, Ct., Betsey, W15786
Josiah, Cont., N.Y., Dorcas, W26201; BLWt.15442-160-55
Oliver, Ct., S18484
Samuel, Ct., Lois, W16134
Sluman/Slaman, N.H., Katharine, W16135
Solomon, Mass., S18485
LATIMER, Charles, Ct., R6177
George, Ct. See LATTIMORE
George, Ct., Louisa L., W12061; BLWt.30755-160-55
Henry, Gen. Hosp., BLWt.1331-450-Physician & Surgn. Iss. 1/6/1792. No papers
James, Pa., Va. See LATTEMER
Jehiel, Ct. See LATTIMER
Levi, Sheldon's Dragoons, Ct., BLWt.6132-100-Pvt. Iss. 12/14/1789 to Richard Platt. No papers
Solomon, Ct., S31806
William, Pa., S40073
William, Va., Elizabeth, W26192
Witherel, Ct., S31809
LATIMORE, Benjamin, N.Y., S13683
Richard, Md., R6178
LATNAR, Nicholas. See LATNER
LATNER, Nicholas, S.C., S38905
LATORATTE, Peter, N.J. See LA TOURETTE
LATOUR, Anthony, Mass., S42814
LA TOURATTE, Daniel, N.J. See LA TURRETT
LA TOURETTE, Peter, N.J., Margaret, W4011
LA TOURNEAU, Joseph, Hazen's Regt., BLWt.13339-100-Pvt. Iss. 10/12/1790. No papers
LATOURRETTE, Cornelius, N.J., S1038
John, Whiskey Insurrection 1794, Wt.63197-160-55
LATTELOFF, Henry, Von Heer's Regt., BLWt.13325-100-Pvt. Iss. 7/8/1791 to Simon Fishbaugh, ass.
LATTEMER, James, Pa., Va., R6176
LATTIMER, Jehiel, Ct., S37600
John, N.J., S4507
LATTIMORE, Cyrus, Ct., BLWt.6091-100-Pvt. Iss. 10/16/1789 to Theodosius Fowler. No papers

LATTIMORE (continued)
George, Ct., S13701
Richard, Pa., BLWt.9848-100-Pvt. "in the Art." Iss. 6/20/1789. No papers
William, Pa. See LATIMER
LATTIN, Richard, Cont., Green Mt. Boys, Vt., Keziah, W24482
LATURE, Harman, Pa., S4501
LA TURRETT, Daniel, N.J., S33364
LAUARAY, Isaac, N.Y. See LARAWAY
LAUCK, Peter, Va. See LAUK
LAUDEN, William, Pa., BLWt.9819-100-Pvt. Iss. 7/12/1792 to Sophia Walker, Admx. No papers
LAUDERDALE, William, Va., b. Md., S4505
LAUER, John, N.Y. See LOWER
Philip, Pa., Dis. No papers
LAUGH, Andrew, Pa. See Andrew LOSHE
Johannes Andrus, See Andrew LOSHE
LAUGHEAD, Benjamin, Pa., S7128
LAUGHLIN, Dennis O., Pa., See O'LAUGHLIN
James, ?, Iowa & Ore. res. See N.A. Acc. No. 874-050102. Not Half Pay. No pension file found
James, S.C., Rachel, R6184
Thomas, N.C., Va., Elizabeth, W9112
Thomas, Va., S36682
LAUGHREY, Michael, Pa., BLWt. 9792-100-Pvt. Iss. 7/9/1789. No papers
William, Pa., Margaret, R6185
LAUGHTON, David, Vt., S10968
Jacob, Mass., Esther, W24468; BLWt.9459-160-55
James, Mass., S29283
LAUK, Peter, Va., Emily, R6183
LAUKS, Henry, Pa., S22872
LAUMAN, Jacob, Cont., Pa., S13686; BLWt.28605-160-55
Philip, Pa., S40072
LAUMOY, John Baptist Joseph de, Engineers, BLWt.1334-500-Col. Iss. 2/6/1795. No papers
LAURANCE, Abraham, N.J., R6191
Amos, Mass., S31804
Jacob, Pa. See LAWRENCE
LAURAWAY, Isaac, N.Y. See LARAWAY
LAURENCE, Benjamin, N.Y., See LAWRENCE
Claborn/Claiborn, N.C., R6196
Ferdinand, Md. See LORENTZ
Isaac, Mass. See LAWRANCE
Jacob, N.C. See LOWRANCE
John, N.C., S31805
Jonathan Hampton, N.J., R6193
Joseph, N.C. See LAWRENCE
Joseph, Va. See LAWRENCE
Rowland, Mass. R3592, Azubah Flagg, former wid.
Thomas, Mass. See LAWRENCE
Thomas, N.Y., Catharine Simpkins, former wid., W2632; BLWt.26988-160-55
Thomas, Va. See LAWRENCE
Wendel, Md. See LAWRENTZ
LAURENS, John, S.C., BLWt.781-450

LAUSCH, Henry, Pa., S4515
LAUSSETT, See Henry LAUSCH
LAUTEN, Jacob, Va. See LANTER
LAVALLEY, William, R.I. See LEVALLEY
LAVANBERGER, George, Pa., S5673
LAVARNWAY, Tousant/Toussant, --, N.Y. res. in 1843, R6186
LAVELLE, Antoine, Hazen's Regt. BLWt.13346-100-Pvt. Iss. 2/20/1792 to Benj. Moore, ass. No papers
LAVELY, Jacob, Md., S34952
LAVENDER, Charles, Va.,Lucy, W8025
Hugh, S.C., S10972
William, Va., Sarah, W8080
LAVERI, Richard, Art. Artificers of Pa., BLWt.13390-100-Pvt. Iss. 3/10/1790. No papers
LAVERING, Wickard, Pa., BLWt. 9807-100-Pvt. Iss. 8/9/1791 to Joseph & Benj. Lavering, Execrs. No papers
LAVERSWYLER, Thomas, Pa., BLWt. 1284-150-Ensign. Iss. 3/10/1790 to Mary Laverswyler, Acting Executrix. No papers
LAVERY, John, Pa., S40077
LAVIGNE, Jacque, Hazen's Regt. BLWt.13367-100-Pvt. Iss. 2/20/1792 to Benj. Moore, ass. No papers.
LAVISTON, Asa, Mass., Olive Beard, former wid., W14273
LAVOIX, Lewis, Hazen's Regt., BLWt.13337-100-Pvt. Iss. 8/20/1789. No papers
LAVOKE, Augustus, Cont., N.Y. See LEVAKE
LAW, Barton, Pa., S8817
Henry, Va., S31196
James, Mass., S32968
Jesse, Va., Mary/Polly, R6188
John, Ct., Lydia, W16324
John, Va., S8809
Joseph, Ct., Cont., Dulana, W21549
Nathan, Ct., Eunice, W20385
Reuben, Mass., Ruth, W8019; BLWt.9440-160-55
Richard, Navy, Ct. Agcy. & res., S13699
William, Md., S36036
LAWERY, William, Mass. See LURVEY
LAWHORN, William, N.C., S4506
LAWIER, John Adam, Pa. See LAWYER
LAWLER, Jacob, N.C., R6190
Nicholas, Va., S32372
LAWLESS, Augustine/Austin, Va., Sally, W2950
John, Va., Mary, W9109
LAWMAN, Jacob, Pa. See LAUMAN
LAWRANCE, Abraham, N.J. See LAURANCE
Claiborn, N.C. See Claborn LAURENCE
Daniel, Mass. See LAWRENCE
Isaac, Mass., Mary, W24487; BLWt.3528-160-55
James, Va., S21858
John, Ct. See LAWRENCE

LAWRANCE (continued)
Joseph, Mass. See LAWRENCE
Joshua, Mass., S40919
Samuel, N.Y., S23758
Thomas, Mass. See LAWRENCE
William, Md., Rachel, W5309; BLWts.338-60-55; 6-100-55
LAWRENCE, Abigail, former wid. of Edward Sutton, Ct., which see
Abraham, N.J. See LAURANCE
Absolam, Va., S40910
Amos, Cont., N.Y., Sabra, W20374
Amos, Mass., See LAURANCE
Amos, R.I., S40074
Benjamin, N.Y., BLWt.7376-100-Pvt. Iss. 8/10/1790 to John Warren, ass. No papers
Benjamin, N.Y., Mary Parker, W20394
Benjamin, S.C., Rachel, W21547
Daniel, Mass., Elizabeth, W15923
Daniel, Mass., BLWt.585-100
Daniel, R.I., Margaret, R6195
David, Ct., Marven, W26196
Ebenezer, Mass., S29285
Edward, Mass., Ct., Elizabeth, W24481
Elihu, Cont., Mass., Tamar, W21560
Elijah, Ct., BLWt.6098-100-Pvt. Iss. 2/22/1792 to John Peck. No papers
Elijah, Vt., Lucinda Benjamin, former wid., W2712
Ephraim, Mass., Sarah, BLWt. 49262-160-55
George, N.Y., S4517
Isaac, Md., N.C., S.C., See LARENCE
Isaac, Mass., See LAWRANCE
Jacob, N.Y., BLWt.7394-100-Pvt. Iss. 3/6/1792 to Michael Connolly, ass. No papers
Jacob, Pa., S4521
James, Ct., S40921
James, Va. See LAWRANCE
John, Ct., Hannah Dunham, former wid., W26662
John, Ct., Cont., Sarah, W5017; BLWt.120-60-55
John, Mass., S17530
John, Mass., S28781
John, Mass., S32964
John, Mass., S40922
John, N.Y., S28786
John, N.C., Angelina Mary, W5020
John, Pa., BLWt.1285-300-Capt. Iss. 2/15/1790. No papers
John, R.I., BLWt.3294-100-Sgt. Iss. 6/30/1789. No papers
John, R.I., S37151
John, Va. See LARRANCE
Jonathan, Col. Wm. Malcolm's Regt., N.Y., BLWt.1269-200-Lt. Iss. 6/2/1789. No papers
Jonathan, Ct., S10966
Jonathan, S.C., Sarah, W9115
Jonathan H., N.J., See LAURENCE
Joseph, Mass., Anna, W15014

LAWRENCE (continued)
Joseph, N.C., Lucretia, R6194
Joseph, Va., N.C., S31810
Joshua, Mass. See LAWRANCE
Josiah, Mass., S30537
Josiah, Vt., Huldah, W8029; BLWt.19520-160-55
Levi, Mass., S40911
Levi, Vt., S9370
Michael, N.C. See LORANCE
Nathaniel, N.C., BLWt.1315-200-Lt. Iss. 2/28/1791. No papers
Nicholas, Mass.,, S46207; BLWt. 19705-160-55
Oliver, N.H., S11764
Oliver, N.Y., S23757
Rebecca C., former wid. of Edmund Dean, Mass., which see
Richard, Cont., Ct., S42807
Richard, N.Y., S8814
Robert, Pa., S33363
Rogers, Mass., Navy, Privateer, S18927
Rowland, Mass., Azubah Flagg, former wid., R3592
Samuel, Cont., Mass., Susanna, W21554
Samuel, N.Y. See LAWRANCE
Silas, Mass., Susanna, W15008
Thomas, Mass., Sarah, W20415; BLWt.38527-160-55
Thomas, Mass., Anna, W24472
Thomas, N.J., Elizabeth, W8027
Thomas, N.Y. See LAURENCE
Thomas, Va., S31205
William, Cont., N.H., Submit, W24474
William, Md.,S38128;BLWt.1968-100
William, Md. See LAWRENCE
William, N.Y., S38125
William, N.Y., Elizabeth, W20390
William, Privateer, Mass., S37145
LAWRENTZ, Wendel, Md., W9113; BLWt.78517-160-55
LAWREY, Giles, Va., S5670
LAWS, David, N.C., b. Va., Martha, W5125
Henry, Md. See LOAR
John, Va., S41754
Josiah, S.C., S1847
William, Md., BLWt.11451-100-Pvt. Iss. 9/24/1799 to William Laws. No papers
LAWSON, Benjamin, Va., S38127
Benjamin, Va., BLWt.1225-200
Claiborne Whitehead, Va., BLWt. 1460-300
David, Ct., Sarah, W233; BLWt. 1906-160-55
David, N.C., Elizabeth, R6200
Drewry, Va., R6201
Ebenezer, Ct., S15597
Hugh, Ga., Dis. No papers here, but see Am. State Papers, Class 9 -- Claims, p.169
Isaac, N.Y., R6202
Jacob, Cont., N.Y., Mary, W20426; BLWt.51751-160-55
Jacob, Va., Polly, W86
James, N.Y., Pa., R6203
James, Pa., S40076
James, Va., S30530
John, Cont., S46502; BLWt.1697-100

LAWSON (continued)
John, N.C., Anna, R6199
John, Va., Frances, W376
Lawrence, N.Y., Phebe, W20422
Mormon, Va., Elva, W9501; BLWt. 39226-160-55
Moses, N.C., Elizabeth, W5019; BLWt.34512-160-55
Nathan/Nathaniel, Va., S31197
Randolph, N.C., R6205
Reuben, Va., S1547
Samuel, Ct., S13708
Samuel, N.Y., S13700
Thomas, N.C., S44492
William, N.C., S10969
William, Va., S32374
LAWTON, Benjamin, R.I., S21859
Israel, Mass., S13681
John, Mass., S42818
John, R.I., W26777
Mercy, former wid. of William Kenyon/Kinyon, R.I., which see
Robert, Va. See LORTON
Thomas, R.I., Sally Miller, former wid., W24154; BLWt.77512-160-55
William, Mass., BLWt.1242-300-Surgn's. Mate. No papers here, but see Heitman's Hist. Reg. of Officers of the Cont. Army, 1775-1783 (1914 ed.), p.343
William, R.I., Sarah, R6207
LAWYER, Abraham, N.Y., S23296
Christopher, N.Y., BLWt.7382-100-Pvt. Iss. 12/9/1791 to Philip Rockefetter, ass. No papers
David, N.Y., R6210
Jacob, N.Y., Anna, R6209
Johannes J., N.Y., Angelica, R6208
Johannes L., N.Y. See John L.
John Adam, Pa., Eve Margarett, R6211
John L./Johannes L., N.Y., Pension never granted, apparently because inquiries about this person were consistently misfiled with those of Johannes J. Lawyer, N.Y., R6208, from which file these papers were taken in setting up this file.
Lawrence, N.Y., R6212
Peter, Pa., S40913
LAY, Asa, Ct., Sarah, W20412; BLWt.1253-300-Capt. Iss. 7/7/1792 to Jonas Prentice, ass. No papers
Edward, Ct., Patty, W20383; BLWt.27586-160-55
John, Ct., S37149
Lee, Ct., Dis. No papers here, but see Am. State Papers, Class 9, Claims, p.141
Richard, Ct., BLWt.6105-100-Corp. Iss. 2/5/1790. No papers
Thomas, N.C., Polly, W10187
William, N.C., R6213
LAYER, John Adam, Pa. See LAWYER
LAYFIELD, Josiah, ---, Ga. res., BLRej. 95875-55
Timothy, Del., BLWt.10811-100-Pvt. Iss. 9/2/1789. No papers
LAYLAND, William, Va., BLWt. 381-100
LAYMAN, Henry, Pa., Eve, W3099
Jacob, Va., S4504
John, N.C., Nancy, Rej.144874-55
Robert, Mass., Sarah, BLWt.78038-160-55
Samuel, Pa. See LEHMANN
William, Md., S34954
LAYNE, Anthony, Va., S8822
Robert, Va., S4489
Samuel, Va., S4493
LAYTON, John, Va., R15775; Va. Half Pay
Thomas, Pa., S32371
William, N.Y., R6218
William H., Del., Md., S16443
LAZADEL, Calvin, Cont., Mass., See LAZDELL
LAZARUS, Frederick, Pa., BLWt.9832-100-Pvt. Iss. 8/10/1795 to Frederick Lazarus. No file.
Frederick, Pa., Elizabeth, W2814
Marks, S.C., Rachel, W21558
LAZDELL, Calvin, Cont., Mass., Sarah, W20417; BLWt.3976-160-55
LAZEAR, Hyatt, Va., R6219
LAZEIR, John, Md. See LAZER
LAZELL, Calvin, Cont., Mass. See LAZDELL
Isaac, Cont., Mass., Jane, W20416
Joshua, Mass., Susannah, W2738
Joshua, Mass., Levina, W21548
Luther, Cont., Mass., S30539
Nathan, Cont., Mass., Deborah, W24496
William, Mass., S42819
LAZENBY, Joshua, Md., S---. His application submitted to this Bureau 12/15/1927 to be filed for the sake of posterity, and not for the purpose of obtaining any pension, the original application was partially prepared & dated in 1832 but was never completed. See corres. in file
Samuel, Md., S13704
LAZER, John, Md., S40075
LAZIER, John, Md. See LAZER
LEA, Major, N.C., S1549
Owen, N.C., Elizabeth, R6221
LEACH, Abner, N.J., S8844
Andrew, Va., Mary, W24521
Anna, former wid. of Jonathan Somes, Mass., which see
Benjamin, Mass., Sarah, W16042
Benjamin, N.H.; BLWt.3279-100-Pvt. Iss. 8/26/1790 to Manasseh Cutler, ass. No papers
Benjamin, N.H., S37166
Benjamin, N.H. See STEVENS
Benjamin, N.H., S44240
Burdett, Va., Judith, W3567; BLWt.38519-160-55
Caleb, Cont., Mass., S13738
Christopher, Lamb's Art., N.Y., BLWt.7432-100-Pvt. Iss. 9/7/1790 to Isaac Trowbridge, ass. No papers
Ephraim, Mass., N.Y., S13747
Ezekiel, Mass., S32971
LEACH (continued)
George, Mass., S32975
George, Mass., S37162
George, Va., Ann, W27584; BLWt. 3764-160-55
Hezekiah, Ct., BLWt.6133-100-Pvt. Iss. 11/2/1791 to Cyprian Webster No papers
Hezekiah, Ct., Cont., S49298
James, Ct., S37606
James, Ct., Sibbel, W24500
James, Va., Elizabeth, W5313; BLWt.78-100
Jedediah, Ct.,Cont., Phebe,W20428
John, Mass., S31213
John, Pa., R15859
Joseph, Cont., Mass., Elizabeth, W20448
Joseph, S.C., Martha, R6222
Joshua, Md., Priscilla, W1786
Lewis, Pvt., Ct., BLWt.6082 iss. 6/29/1791 to ---
Lewis, Ct., S38909
Mark, Mass., S37165
Micah, Cont., Mass., S42846
Moses, Mass., Miriam, W10193; BLWt.61240-160-55
Oliver, R.I., S21864
Samuel, Mass., N.H., S19374
Silas, Mass., S44239
Thomas, Va., S8837
William, Mass., Polly, W21570
William, N.C. See LEECH
Zemus, Mass., BLWt.4596-100-Pvt. Iss. 3/12/1793 to Samuel Emery
LEADBETTER, Increase, Navy, Mass. S37164
LEADER, Frederick, Pa., Susannah, W4478
Henry, Hazen's Regt., BLWt.13365-100-Pvt. Iss. 3/29/1792. No papers
LEAFEVOUR, William, Mass., S34959
LEAGUE, Edmond/Edmund, Va., Mary, W378
James, Va., S38134
LEAHER, Peter, Mass. See LEHR
LEAK, James, N.C., S31822
John M., Va., S1550
Walter, N.C., S7136
LEAKE, Henry, Md. See LEEKE
William, Va., S8843
LEALAND, Barak, Mass., S29964
Jeremiah, Mass., Elizabeth,W24517
John, N.H., S32970
LEAMAN, Ephream, N.J., S1050
Samuel, Mass., BLWt.815-150
LEAMING, David, Ct., Debby, R6223
LEANT, Moses, N.Y. See LENT
LEANY, Daniel, Va., S40937
LEAP, John, Pa., R6225
LEAR, Conrad, Va., S31210
George, Va., BLWt.12327-100-Pvt. Iss. 12/9/1793 to Francis Graves, ass. No papers
Joseph, N.H., Mercy, R6226
Samuel, N.H., BLWt.3288-100-Pvt. Iss. 1/26/1790 to James A. Neal, ass. No papers
Samuel, N.H., S9928
Samuel, N.H., S44507
William, Va., Hannah, W3833

LEARD, John, S.C., S21862
William, Va., S40936
LEARMONTH, John, Del., R6227; BLWt.1289-300-Capt. Iss. 9/2/1789
LEARNED, Abijah, N.H. See LARNED
Benjamin, Crane's Cont. Art., Mass., BLWt.4624-100-Pvt. Iss. 7/6/1796 to Daniel Jackson. No papers
Benjamin, Mass., S32977
Daniel, Mass., S32979
Ebenezer, Mass., Dis. No papers here, but see Am. State Papers, Class 9, Claims, pp.63,111,140
Isaac, Mass., Polly Camp, former wid., W9375; BLWt.75030-160-55
James, N.H., Vt., Theodaty, former wid., remarried Ebenezer Learned, R6228
Jonas, Mass., S32985
Samuel, Mass., Abigail, W20468
Silvanus, Mass., S32974
Sylvanus, Mass., BLWt.4572-100-Pvt. Iss. 12/9/1799 to Dwight Foster. No papers
Sylvanus, N.H., Vt., Sally, W15021; BLWt.18392-160-55
LEAROCK, John, Mass., S32976
LEARY, Dennis, Del.; BLWt.10808-100-Corp., Invalid, & BLWt. 13381. Iss. 9/2/1789. No papers
William, N.Y., Harriet, W8246
William, Pa., BLWt.9827-100-Pvt. Iss. 6/6/1792 to Alexander Power, ass. No paper
William, Pa., S40934
LEAS, John, Pa., Sophia, W2133
LEASE, John, Not Rev. War; U.S. Army 1794-1797, O.W. Inv. R. File 15839
LEASON, Jesse, Ct., S37608
Job, Ct., S37614; BLWt.1272-100
LEASSON, George, Mass. See LESSON
LEASURE, Abraham, Pa., Jane, W3568; BLWt.26650-160-55
John, Pa., War of 1792, S22356
Joseph, R.I. See LESEUR
LEATHE, Elijah, Mass., S29294
LEATHER, Christian, N.Y., Anna Lasher, former wid., W20384; BLWt.12717-160-55
LEATHERBY, David, Mass., BLWt. 4589-100-Pvt. Iss. 8/19/1795 to Eneas Munson, Jr. No papers
LEATHERER, Paul, Va. See LEATHERS
LEATHERMAN, Francis, Pa., S23764
Jacob, Pa., R6231
Michael, Md., Pa., S36684
LEATHERS, Enoch, N.H. & War of 1812; S37618; BLWt.15437-160-12, War of 1812
John, N.Y., W20452
Jonathan, N.H., S44508
Joseph, Ct., S18077
Joseph, N.H., S16451
Levi, N.H., Sarah, W772; BLWt. 9195-160-55
Moses, N.C., Sally, R6230
Paul, Va., S16450
LEATHHEAD/BELL, Robert, Mass. Sea Service, Navy, S37609

LEATON, Benjamin, Va. See LEETON
LEAVENS, Hezekiah, Ct., S13740
Jedediah, Ct., Vt., S16919
John (Noah), N.H., BLWt.3274-100-Pvt. Iss. 3/25/1790. No papers
Joseph, Cont., Regt. raised in Mass., N.Y. res. after Rev. War, S42833
Noah, N.H., S42832
LEAVENSWORTH, Nathan, Mass., BLWt. 1230-300-Surgeon's Mate. He is rec. in Heitman's Hist. Reg. as Nathaniel Leavenworth & in Mass. Archives as Nathan Leavensworth & Nathaniel Leavenworth.
LEAVENWORTH, Edmund, Ct., R6232
Eli, Ct., Sarah, BLWt.641-400
Nathan, Mass., See LEAVENSWORTH
Nathaniel, Mass. See Nathan LEAVENSWORTH
LEAVER, William, N.H., S37607
LEAVESLEY, Thomas, S.C., R6233
LEAVETT, Edward, N.H. See LEAVITT
LEAVISTAN, Asa, Mass. See LAVISTON
LEAVIT, Amos, N.H., S23761
David, Mass., S42860
Nehemiah, N.H., BLWt.3271-100-Pvt. Iss. 3/14/1793 to Benj. Bailey, ass. No papers
LEAVITT, Andrew, Mass., N.H., S10976
Benjamin, Mass., S44504
Catharine, former wid. of Thomas Frohock, N.H., which see
David, Mass., BLWt.4551-100-Pvt. Iss. 7/12/1790. No papers
Edward, N.H., Abigail, W9128; BLWt.226-60-55
James, N.H., R44505
John, N.H., R6234
Jonathan, Cont., N.H., S44502
Joseph, Cont., N.H., Polly, W24532
Joseph, R.I., S29292
Joseph, Vt., S23766
Josiah, N.H.; his wid. Sally, was pensioned as former wid. of John Light, Cont., Mass., N.H. & Privateer, which see
Judith, former wid. of Edward Jones, Mass., which see
Levi, N.H., S22357
Nathaniel, Cont., N.H., Mary, W24529; BLWt.1249-200-Lt. Iss. 7/7/1797 to Nath'l Leavitt. Also recorded as above under BLWt.2689. No papers
Nehemiah, N.H., S44503
Samuel, N.H., Polly, W21565; BLWt.6403-160-55
Simon, N.H., S10984
Thomas, N.H., Mary, W24514
Wadleigh, Mass., S21861
William, Cont., Mass., N.H., Betsey/Elizabeth, W24501; BLWt.11072-160-55
LEAY, William, Va., S38910
LEAYCRAFT, George, Col. Lamb's Art. Regt., BLWt.1266-200-Lt. Iss. 7/14/1790 to Richard Platt, ass. No papers

LEAYCRAFT (continued)
Willett, N.Y., R6336
William, Col. Lamb's Art. Regt.; BLWt.1267-200-Lt. Iss. 7/6/1790 No papers
LEBARON, Peter, Mass., N.H. See BARON
LEBARRON, Francis, Mass., S18938 BLWt.17852-160-55
John, Mass., S12078
Solomon, Ct., Zada, W9126; BLWt. 27673-160-55
LEBER, Jacob, N.Y. See LEPPER
Nicholas, Pa., S4535
LEBKICHER, Michael, Pa., S4536
LEBO, Henry, Cont., Pa., Sarah, W3349
LeBOSQUET, John, Mass., S30281
LeBRETT, Charles, Ct., Cont. R.I., S32997
LeBROKE, James, Mass., Sally, W24524
LECAT, Levin, Del., BLWt.10819-100-Pvt. Iss. 5/26/1790. No papers
Mitchael, Del., BLWt.10806-100-Corp. Iss. 5/26/1790. No papers
LECATT, Mitchell, Del., S36040
LECE, Seth, Mass. See LUCE
LECKE, Nicholas, Navy, Md. res. & agcy., S34957
LECKIE, William, Va., Elizabeth, W25
LECOSTE, Francis, Cont., N.Y., S42834
LeCOUNT, John, Pa., BLWt.9857-100-Pvt. Iss. 4/14/1791. No papers
LECROY, Job, N.J., S16449
LEDBETTER, Coleman, N.C., Elizabeth, R6236; BLWt.47513-160-55
Richard, N.C., Va., Elizabeth, W26204; BLWt.29049-160-55
Rowland, N.C., R6237
LEDDER, Christian, N.Y. See LEATHER
LEDDICK, Philip, Pa. See LITTIG
LEDER, Christian, See LEATHER
LEDFORD, Peter, N.C., S7146
William, N.C., R6238
LEDGET, James, Mass., S40932
LEDLEE, James, Pa., S38133
LEDLIE, Andrew, Pa., BLWt.1281-400-Surgn. Iss. 8/26/1789. No papers
LEDNUM, John, N.C., S7142
LEDWIDGE, William, Va. res. in 1818, Rebekah, R6239
LEDYARD, Charles, Ct., S21347
Isaac, Hosp. Dept., BLWt.1333-400-Asst. Purveyor. Iss. 4/9/1791. No papers
Joseph, Pa. See LITCHARD.
Robert, Mass., S4543
LEE, Abial/Abiel, Mass., S44500
Abner, Ct., Nancy Davis, former wid., W16947
Abner, Ct., BLWt.42-100
Abner, Mass., S42852
Abner, Va., Sally, R6257; BLWt. Rej. 225536-1855
Andrew, Ct., S13748

LEE (continued)
Andrew, Ga., S.C., b. Ga., R6241
Andrew, Hazen's Regt., BLWt.1330-200-Lt. Iss. 12/31/1787. No papers
Burwell, S.C., Elizabeth, W9119; BLWt.27674-160-55
Catharine G., dau. of Wm. Rosser, Va., Elizabeth, which see
Charles, Mass., Rhoda, W5467
Dan, Ct., Cont., S37157
Daniel, Mass., S40933; BLWt.1229-300-Capt. Iss. 6/28/1792 to Martin Kingsley, ass. No papers
Daniel, Mass., Hannah, W2622; BLWt.84-60-55
Daniel, N.Y., BLWt.7414-100-Pvt. Iss. 8/30/1790. No papers
Daniel, N.Y., S38136
David, Ct., S18940
David, Ct., Fanny, W2449; BLWt. 21816-160-55
David, Va., R6244
David, Va., Indian War in 1784; Mary, R6256
Dudley, Md., BLWt.2445-100
Ebenezer, Ct., N.J., S42829
Eber, Ct., S13729; BLWt.26107-160-55
Edward, Mass., BLWt. 6-100
Edward, N.J., BLWt.4567 & 8475-100-Pvt. Iss. 12/21/1792. No papers
Elisha, Cont., Ct., S10977
Elizabeth, former wid. of Joseph Rue Case, N.Y., which see
Elliott, S.C., Lucinda, W10194
Elon, Vt., Peggy, W20446
Ezra, Ct., Cont., S37613
George, Del., Mary, W26209; BLWt.21814-160-55
Henry, Lee's Legion, Va., BLWt. 1299-500-Lt. Col. commanding. Iss. 7/3/1789 (See BL Reg., prior to 1800, Vol. 5, for list of officers of Lee's Legion)
Henry, N.C., b. Va., S8833
Isaac, Mass., Rachel, W20463; BLWt. 28538-160-55
Israel, Ct., N.Y., S10981
Israel, N.J., S23767
James, ----, Pa. agcy., S---. Dis. pension. No papers here, but data in the file suppled by interested inquirors appears to tentatively identify him. See also Heitman's Hist. Reg.; Pa. Archives, 5th Ser., Vol. 4, p.566 & Report of Secy. of War (1835), list of Invalid Pensioners paid at Phila. agcy.
James, Cont., Va., Keziah, R6250
James, N.Y., Elizabeth, R6246
James, N.C., S.C., b. N.C., S7145
James, N.C., Elizabeth, W4013
James, Va., S8828
James, Va., S41762
James, Va. Sea Service, Mary, W5466
Jeptha/Jepther, Cont., N.Y.,

LEE (continued)
Esther, W5315; BLWt.7422-100. Iss. 4/9/1791 to the sold. BLWt.173-60-55
John, Ct. & War of 1812, Bridget, W674; BLWt.6275-160-55
John, Cont., Va., S17538
John, Md., Martha Graham, former wid., W4477; BLWt.11459-100. Iss. 6/3/1795, BLWt. 295-60-55. Wid. pensioned as Martha Lee, alias Graham.
John, N.J., S4523
John, N.J., Margaret, R6254
John, N.Y., Ester/Esther, R6248
John, N.C., BLWt.12331-100-Pvt. Iss. 1/3/1800 to Sol. P. Goodrich, ass. No papers
John, N.C., S7144
John, N.C., R6251
John, S.C., b. S.C., son of Wm., S9372
John, Va., S31208
John, Va., Agness, W380
Jonathan, Ct., Mindwell, W20434 BLWt.6454-160-55
Jonathan, N.Y., Hester, W10192; BLWt.67585-160-55
Joseph, Ct., S18078
Joseph, Mass., S32973
Joseph, N.J., Pa., Eleanor, R6245
Joseph, N.Y., BLWt.7430-100-Pvt. "in Art." Iss. 2/7/1792. No papers
Joseph, N.C., Milly, W20440
Joseph, N.C., S.C., R6252
Joshua, Ga., b. N.C., S31209
Josiah, Mass., S32981
Lemuel, N.C., R6253
Levi, Ct., S37167
Levi, R.I., S21345
Ludwell, Va., S8829
Lyman, N.Y., R20397
Mary, former wid. of Gooding Packard, Mass., which see
Matthew, Ct., S37605
Miles, Ct., Fanny, R6249
Moses, Mass., BLWt.4554-100-Pvt. Iss. 6/21/1791. No papers
Nathan, N.H., S44501
Noah, Cont., Hazen's Regt., Ct. & Vt. res., S18939; BLWt.1329-300-Capt. Iss. 4/25/1794
Owen, N.C. See LEA
Parker H., Md., Mary; W26210; BLWt.61002-160-55
Paul, N.J., Eunice, W20451
Peter, Del., BLWt.10815-100-Pvt. Iss. 3/31/1797 to James DeBaufre, ass. No papers
Peter, Del. See MERCELL
Philip, Mass., Sally Bump, former wid., W27901; BLWt.75051-160-55
Philip Richard Francis, Va., BLWt.2366-300. No papers but see Heitman's Hist. Reg.
Richard, N.J., S4526
Roxy, former wid. of Peter Flagg, N.Y., which see
Samuel, Ct., BLWt.6120-100-Pvt.

LEE (continued)
Iss. 1/27/1796 to Hezekiah Keeler. No papers
Samuel, Ct., S42837
Samuel, Ct., Eliza, W26203; BLWt.19714-160-55
Samuel, Ct., Betsey, R6242
Samuel, Mass., Mary, W8039; BLWt.19763-160-55
Samuel, Mass., Lydia Attwood, former wid., W15719
Samuel, Va., S38138
Seth, ---, res. Orange Co., N.Y. in 1782, Mary, R6255
Silas, Mass., R6258
Sinah, former wid. of John Eustace, Va., which see
Solomon, Mass., Rebecca, W9118
Solomon J., Mass., Sally, BLReg.166726-1855
Thomas, Ct., Theodocia, W20437
Thomas, Navy, N.J. res. & agcy. S33371
Thomas, N.J., S4522
Thomas, N.C., S41764
Thomas, ----, BLWt.2608-300-Capt. Iss. 4/4/1792. His name also written opposite BLWt.1254, but a mark drawn through that Wt. No. & no date of issue given. No State to which service was rendered is given under either Wt. No.; the file contains inquiries, unresolved,from persons claiming a Thos. Lee was born in or served in Rev. in N.Y.,Va., Tenn. or Ct.
Timothy, Ct., S15600
Westbrook, N.C., S7143
William, Ct. & War of 1812, S31820
William, Cont., Ct., S13735; BLWt. 1748-100
William, Md., BLWt.11446-100-Pvt. Iss. 12/22/1794 to Henry Purdy, ass. No papers
William, Md., BLWt.2450-100
William, Mass., S31212
William, Mass. Sea Service, Anstis BLWt.41549-160-55
William, N.H., S11172
William, N.J., Abigail, W20465
William, N.Y., BLWt.7392-100-Pvt. Iss. 8/26/1790 to Wm. McKown, ass. No papers
William, N.Y., Sarah, W20454
William, Sgt., Maj., Pa., BLWt. 9852 iss. 11/5/1789
William, Pa., S41755
William, Va. See LEAY
William, Va., Drusilla, W9117
William C., Md., S41757
William H., Ct., Phebe, W20445
William H., N.Y., Abigail, W24504
Zachariah, Va., R6260
Zebulon, Ct., Cont., Pa., Margaret W1624; BLWt.16122-160-55
LEECH, Archibald, Pa., S40935
Burdett, Va. See LEACH
Ebenezer, Cont., N.Y. res. in 1800, BLWt.24-100
James, Pa., BLWt.9851-100-Pvt. Iss. 3/29/1791. No papers
John, Pa. See LEACH
Joseph, S.C. See LEACH

LEECH (continued)
Micah, Cont., Mass. See LEACH
Stephen, Ct., R6261
Thomas, Not Rev. War, O.W. Rej. File 21099, Wayne's Indian War 1792-1794, Ohio res., BLWt. 12777-160-50
William, Ct., S37616
William, N.C., S4528
LEEDER, George, Pa., S23763
LEEDOM, Thomas, Pa., S4578
LEEDS, Abram, Ct., S15191
James, N.J., S31817
Jeremiah, N.J., Millsent/ Milisent, S5686; BLWt.40018-160-55
Nathan, Mass. & Shay's Rebellion in 1787, Elizabeth, W21567
Nathaniel, Mass., S40931
Robert, N.J., S18489
Thomas, Mass., Mary, W15019
William, Ct. Sea Service, Dis. No papers here, but see Am. State Papers, Class 9, Claims, pp. 61, 112, 142
LEEK, Abraham, N.Y., Priscilla, W20450
William, Va., S42853
LEEKE, Henry, Md., S34955
Nicholas, Navy, See LECKE
LEEMAN, Daniel, Mass., S37617
Daniel, Mass., Martha, W24519
George, N.J., BLWt.8476-100-Pvt. Iss. 6/18/1795 to James Christie, ass. No papers
Martha Matilda, former wid. of Dennis O'Laughlin, Pa., which see
Samuel, Mass., S18936
Samuel, Mass. See LEAMAN
William, Mass., R6278
LEEPER, James, N.C., S31819
John, Pa., Catharine Ramsey, former wid., R8573
Matthew, N.C., Margaret, W26205; BLWt.34838-160-55
LEET, Allen, Ct., Asenath, R6265; BL Reg. 243732-55
Luther, Ct., Sybil, W20467
Miles, Ct., R6266
Richard, Navy, Ct., S38908
William, Pa., b. N.J., R6267
LEETON, Benjamin, Va., S41756
LEFACE, John, Foreign Troops, See LEFOE
LEFAE, John, See LEFOE
LEFAVOUR, John, Mass., Abigail, W21569
LEFCEY, Shadrach, Va., S41765
LEFEVER, Isaac, N.C., S.C., b. N.J., S13726
Minard, N.J., S41744
Napthale, Pvt. N.J., BLWt.8489 iss. 6/11/1789 to Matthias Deuison, ass.
LEFEVOUR, William, Mass. See LEAFEVOUR
LEFFAR, John, N.J., S23769
LEFFERTS, Esther, former wid. of Samuel Thorn, N.Y., which see
Zilpha, former wid. of Isaac Stateser, N.J., which see
LEFFLAR, John, N.Y. See LAFLER
LEFLER, George, Va., S35522
LEFOE, John, Foreign Troops, R6269. N.C. res. in 1818. See Claim of Mary Lafoy, former wid.of Jacob White, Va.
LEFOY, Abraham, N.Y., S42841
John, N.Y., R6270
LEFRAIS, Peter, Hazen's Regt., BLWt.13361-100-Pvt. Iss. 10/ 12/1790. No papers
LEFTLER, Uriah, N.C., R6271
LEFTTER, Uriah, See LEFTLER
LEFTWICH, Augustine/Augustus, Va., S11364
Joel, Va., S8830
LEFTWITCH, Augusta. See Augustine LEFTWICH
LEFTYEAR, Uriah, See LEFTLER
LEGARE, Isaac, S.C., Mary, R6272
James, S.C., Mary W., W9123; BLWt.1319-200-Lt. Iss. 6/4/ 1792 to David Cay, ass. No papers
Solomon, S.C., S21860
William, N.J., Eleanor/Ellen, W471
LEGEER, William, N.J., BLWt.8496-100-Pvt. Iss. 12/9/1789 to Jonathan Dayton, ass. No papers
William, N.J., See LEGARE
LEGERE, William, See LEGARE
LEGG, David, Cont., Mass., S32989
David, Mass., S13722
Edward, Md., BLWt.11469-100-Pvt. Iss. 6/11/1790. No papers
Joel, Mass., S28787
John, Mass., S42828
John, Va., S41758
Moses, Mass., Mary, W24508
Nathan, Mass., S42854
Reuben, Mass., S42849
William, Va.,----. Heir's application under Act of 1832 filed 4/20/1840. All papers in this jacket were found in Rev. War pension claim of Joseph Bobo, Va., R981. No record has been found of any action taken in this claim. William LEGG, formerly of Prince William Co., Va. but later a resident of Culpeper Co., Va., enl. from Dumfries, Va., about 10/1/ 1780, and d. 7/22/1833, leaving no wid. and 3 children.
LEGGETT, Abraham, N.Y., S42859; BLWt.1264-200-Lt. Iss. 9/6/ 1791. No papers
William, Pvt., Mass., BLReg. 268189-1885
LEGON, William, Va., S1998
LEGORE, John, Cont., Pa., S35521
LEGRAND, Paulina, former wid. of Edmund Read, Va., which see
LEGRO, David, Mass., N.H., Betty, W26774
LeGROSS, Francis, Mass., BLWt. 4552 & 4247-100-Pvt. Iss.
LEGROSS (continued)
2/15/1797 to Jos. Brown
LEGROW, Joseph, Mass., S37620
LEGUE, Edmund, Va. See Edmond LEAGUE
LEHA, John, Pvt., Del., Wt.10807-100. Iss. 4/28/1800
LEHBERG, John Henry, Va. See LeMOUNTAIN
LEHEU, David, Va., See LEHEW
LEHEW, David, Va., S22355
LEHMAN, Anthony/Antony, Pa., Catharine, W3430
Christian, Pa. See LAHMAN
LEHMANN, Samuel, Pa., Elizabeth, R6338
LEHR, Peter, Mass., Catharine, W24520
LEHRIG, Georg, Pa. See George LENOX
LEIB, Jonas, N.C., Ann Christina, W1883; BLWt.26842-100-55
Nicholas, Pa., S40083
LEIBENGOOD, Jacob, See LIBENGOOD
LEIBERT, Philip, Cont., Hazen's Regt., BLWt.1332-300-Capt. Iss. 12/28/1799. No papers
LEIBLEY, Andrew, Pa., Elizabeth, W3432
LEIBY, George, Pa., S4541
John, ---, Phila. agcy. Dis.
Matthias, Pa., R6273
LEIDEY, Samuel, Pa., Va., S5681
LEIGH, Joseph, N.C. See LEE
Samuel, N.J., S1049
LEIGHTEN, Joseph, Mass., N.H., S18072
LEIGHTHISER, George, Cont., Pa. See LEITHAEUSER
LEIGHTON, Aaron, Cont., N.H., Mary/Molly, W16630
Betsey, former wid. of Amaziah Delano, Mass., which see
Elizabeth, former wid. of Ebenezer Cole, Mass., which see
Ephraim, Mass., S18937
George, N.H., Deborah, R6274
Hannah, former wid. of Isaac Davis, Mass., which see
Jacob, N.H., Mary, W16136
James, Navy, N.H. See LAIGHTON
Jedediah, N.H., S8840
Joseph, Mass., N.H., See LEIGHTEN
Reuben, Mass., Sally, W9122; BLWt.30756-160-55
Robert, Mass., Navy, N.H., S16917
Tobias, Mass., S37619
Valentine, N.H., BLWt.2364-100
LEINTZ, Martin, Hazen's Regt., BLWt.13370-100-Pvt. Iss. 9/ 15/1790 to John S. Hobart, Egbert Benson, John McKessen, E. Hazard & Richard Platt, Execrs. of Alexander McDougall ass. No papers
LEIPS, Philip, Md. See Philip SMITH
LEISNOR, George. See LEISSNER
LEISSNER, George, Mass., S37171;

LEISSNER (continued)
BLWt.4573, iss. 1796
LEISTER, Joshua, Md., BLWt. 11436-100-Pvt. Iss. 9/5/1789. No papers
LEISURE, Gideon, Mass. See LESURE
LEIT, Lewis, Von Heer's Regt., Pa., BLWt.13326-100-Pvt. Iss. 7/14/1789 to Lewis Leit or List
LEITCH, Andrew, Va., BLWt.1251-400-Major. Iss. 7/5/1799 to James Taylor, ass. of James Frisbee Leitch, the only surviving son & heir. Also recorded as above under BLWt. 2708. No papers
LEITENSDORFER, John Eugene, -- Warrant, no number, for 320 acres. Special Act. of 2/6/1805. This special warrant was for his services as a Col. in the forces of the U.S. in Egypt and on the coast of Africa (1804-1805). It was delivered to "himself" 2/11/1805. This info appears on the Reg. of B.L. Wts. for the War of the Revolution, entered on "L" on line between Wt. 2092 & 2093.
LEITHAEUSER, George, Cont., Pa., Catharine, W5318; BLWt.314-100
LEITHEIZER, Hartman, Pa., also served until 1800; Elizabeth, W3429; BLWt.27605-160-55
LEITZ, Henry, Pa. See LUTZ
LELAND, David W., Mass., S32983
Ebenezer, Mass., Milly, W13618
Francis, Pa., BLWt.397-100
Henry, Mass., S20435
Jeremiah, Mass. See LEALAND
John, Cont., N.J., S36039
Joseph, Mass., S46389; BLWt. 1236-200-Lt. Iss. 5/29/1797 to Joseph Leland. No papers
Joshua, Mass., Waitstill, R6276
Oliver, Mass., Abigail, W15027
Patrick, Armand's Corps, BLWt. 13316-100-Pvt. Iss. 11/5/1789. No papers
Samuel, Mass., Sally, W9125; BLWt.24173-160-55
Thomas, Cont., Mass., Lydia, W20441
Thomas, Mass., Anna B., W8085
Timothy, Mass., S30543
LEMAN, Ebenezer, Mass., Navy, Elizabeth, W15317
Matthias S., Pa. See LEMON
Nathaniel, N.H., S15508
LEMANS, Archibald, N.Y. See LAMONT
LEMASTER, Hugh, Md., Mary, W2951
Joseph, Va., W797
Martha, former wid. of Josiah Tanner, S.C., which see
LEMASTERS, Benjamin, Va., S18490
LEMAY, John, Va., S7147
LEMEN, William S., Pa., Agness, W1200
LEMIN, James, Pa., BLWt.1288-200-Lt.
LEMING, David, Ct., See LEAMING
LEMINGTON, Thomas, See LENNINGTON
LEMMAN, Alexander, N.Y. See LEMMON
LEMMON, Alexander, N.Y., S41761
David, See LEMON
Francis, Cont., Mass., BLWt.1757-100
Jacob, Md., Va., Jane, W3698; BLWt.26990-160-55
John, Pa. See LEMON
John, Pa. See LEMON
Moses, Md., R6283
Samuel, Mass., S5678
LEMMOND, William, N.C., Ann Walker former wid., R6280. Her last husb., Andrew Walker, was a Rev. War sold. but did not apply.
LEMMONDS, Alexander, N.C. See LEMONDS
LEMMONS, John, Va., Mary, R6281
LEMMONTON, Timothy, Pa. See LENNONTON
LEMON, Archibald, N.Y. See LAMONT
David, ---, Elizabeth Peel, former wid., R8075. Widow's res. was Ala. in 1857. Mar. in Orange Co., N.C. in 1795
George, Va., S38137
James, Pa., R6282
John, Md. Sea Service, Pa., S40080
John, Pa., S40081; BLWt.950-100
John, Pa., Martha, W3025
Matthias S., Pa. & War of 1812, R6277. His wid., Mary Lemon, was allowed BLWt.100469-160-55 for his services as Lt. Col., N.Y. Militia, War of 1812.
Robert, N.C. See LAMON
Samuel, Va., BLWt.12307-100-Pvt. Iss. 3/10/1790. No papers
William, N.Y., BLWt.7431-100-Pvt. Iss. 1/13/1792 to John Blanchard, ass. No papers
William S., Pa. See LEMEN
LEMOND, William, Pa., S41759
LEMONDS, Alexander, N.C., S8831; BLWt.8378-160-55
Robert, N.C., S8832
LEMONS, John, R.I., BLWt.149-100
LEMONT, David, Mass., S29965
Sarah, former wid. of Consider Turner, Mass., which see
Thomas, Mass., Abigail, W673; BLWt.34829-160-55
Thomas, Mass., Lucy Mallett, former wid., W23923
LEMOREUX, Peter, N.Y. See LOMEREAUX
Le MOUNTAIN, John Henry, Va., S32376
LEMRICK, Patrick, Pa. See LIMERICK
LENARDSON, John T., N.Y., Sarah, R6294
LENDALL, John, Mass., Anna, W20459
L'ENFANT, Charles Peter, Engineers, BLWt.1335-300-Capt. Iss. 11/30/1789. No papers
LENHART, Philip, Pa., S23768
LENINGTON, Thomas, N.Y. See LENNINGTON
LENNAN, Thomas, Mass. See LINNEN
LENNINGTON, Thomas, Cont., N.Y., Sarah, W20439
LENNONTON, Timothy, Pa., S9749
LENOIR, William, N.C., b. Va., S7137
LENOX, Charles, Va., S25629
George/Georg, Pa., S40938
James, Md., S34960
LENSS, William Frederick, N.Y., R6300
LENT, Elias, N.Y., S42830
Hendrick, N.Y. See Henry
Henry, N.Y., Catharine, R6285
Hercules, N.Y., BLWt.7403-100-Pvt. Iss. 7/22/1790 to Thomas Tillotson, ass. No papers
Hermanus, Cont., N.Y., S13717
Hindrich, N.Y., S9927
Isaac, N.Y., S13736
Isaac, N.Y., S42843
Isaac, N.Y., R6287
Jacob, Cont., N.Y., S13739
Jacob, Cont., N.Y., S42861; BLWt.630-100
Jacob, N.Y., Belinda, W8244; BLWt.50943-160-55
John, N.Y., S23762
Moses, N.Y., BLWt.7397-100-Pvt. Iss. 7/22/1790 to Thomas Tillotson, ass. No papers
Moses, N.Y., Phebe, R6224
Philip, N.Y., S42827
William, Va., S10983
LENTZ, Benjamin, N.C., S.C., Rosena, W379
Henry, N.C., S31815
LEONARD, Adam, Pa., BLWt.9814-100-Pvt. Iss. 6/29/1789 to M. McConnell, ass. No papers
Amos, Mass., Marcy, W20462
Archippus, Mass., Asenath, W24507
Asa, Ct., Cont., Olive, W24518
Barnabas, Mass. See Barney
Barney/Barnabas, Mass., Phebe, W24512
Benajah, Ct., Mary, W20436
Caleb, Mass., S29291
Cuff, Mass., S32982; BLWt. 1044-100
Daniel, Mass., Phebe, W24502
David, N.J., N.Y., S13731
David, N.Y., R6290
Ebenezer, Mass., Abigail, R6288
Edward, N.Y., BLWt.7378-100-Pvt. Iss. 7/6/1791 to Carlile Pollock, ass. No papers
Elias, Pa., S4542
Elijah, Mass., Hannah, W24505
Elisha, Mass., S13733
Enoch, Mass., S40928
Enoch, Mass., N.Y., Mary, W16629; BLWt.5211-160-55
Ephraim, Cont., Mass., S32992
Ezekiel, Mass., Rhoda, W2816
Ezra, Mass., Elizabeth, W13617
Frederick, Va., S38911
George, Cont., Va. agcy. & res., Susanna, W3834
George, Mass., S40930
George, Pa., Catharine, W8250;

LEONARD (continued)
BLWt.38529-160-55
Henry, N.Y., S29288
Isaac, ---, applied in Pa. R---
Jacob, Cont., Mass., Mary, W15023
BLWt.1237-150-Ens. Iss. 3/7/1798.
No papers
Jacob, N.C., S7141
James, Del., BLWt.10809-100-Pvt.
Iss. 9/2/1789. No papers
James, Del., Md., S34956
James, Pa., Elizabeth, W5465
John, Mass., Betsey, R6289; BLWt.
11276-160-55
John, N.J., S33370
John, Pa., BLWt.9798-100-Pvt.
Iss. 6/29/1789 to M. McConnell,
ass. No papers
John, Va., Edy, W1625
Joseph, Md., Mary, R6293
Josiah, Mass., Lurany/Lurana,
W24523
Justin, Mass., Theodosia, W20458;
BLWt.13735-160-55
Lot, N.J., Pa., Frances, R6291
Michael, Va., S30542
Moses, Mass., S13749
Nathan B., Mass., Anstus/Antris,
W21568; BLWt.19502-160-55
Nathaniel, Cont., N.J., Esther,
W24513
Nathaniel, Mass., S13744
Nathaniel, N.J., BLWt.1272-300-
Capt. Iss. 6/11/1789. No papers
Nehemiah, Mass., S18488
Noah, Mass., Mehitable, W20457
Patrick, Ct., Pa., S36038
Patrick, Pa., BLWt.4843-100-Pvt.
"in the Artillery". Iss. 11/5/
1798. No papers
Patrick, Proctor's Art., Pa.,
BLWt.9843-100-Pvt. Iss. 11/5/1789
The land claimed on this warrant
was located in the U.S. Military
Dist. of Ohio
Phinehas, Mass., Content, W1199
Richard, Pa., BLWt.9806-100-Pvt.
Iss. 11/19/1789 to John Baldwin
ass. No papers
Robert, N.Y., BLWt.7404-100-Pvt.
Iss. 10/1/1792. No papers
Robert, N.Y., Naomi, W24511
Robert, Va., BLWt.12320-100-Pvt.
Iss. 5/29/1792 to Robert Means,
ass. No papers
Rowland, Mass., Lucy, W13619
Samuel, Cont., N.J., S554
Samuel, Mass., S29293
Seth, Cont., Mass., S32986
Silas, Ct., Mass., S31818
Silas, N.J., S10978
Simeon, Cont., Mass., S40929
Solomon, Ct., Cont., Mass.,
Sarah, W20466
Solomon, Mass., S31206
Stephen, N.J., S42831
Sylvanus, N.H., Vt. See LEARNED
Thomas, N.J., Esther, W3098
Timothy, Cont., Mass., Mary,
W24503
William, Mass., BLWt.4580-100-
Pvt. Iss. 8/22/1789 to Moses

LEONARD (continued)
Ashley. No papers
William, N.J., S35519
William, N.C., Priscilla D.,
W26212; BLWt.26424-160-55
Zephaniah, Sappers & Miners,
BLWt.13328-100-Sgt. Iss. 8/6/
1789. No papers
Ziba/Zeba, Mass., S29963
LEONARDSON, John T. See LENARDSON
LEPER, Jacob, N.Y. See LEPPER
LEPHERD, John, N.Y., BLWt.7389-100-
Pvt. Iss. 8/6/1790 to Abraham
Ten Eyck, ass. No papers
LEPPER, Frederick, N.Y., Mary,
W20447
Jacob, N.Y., Angelica, W1300;
BLWt.33744-160-55
John, N.Y., Mary, W8043; BLWt.
26261-160-55
John, N.Y., Margaret, W20433
Wyant/Wynant, N.Y., S10980
LEPPINWILL, Reuben, Mass. See
LIPENWELL
LEPSE, John, Pa. See LIPSE
LEQUEER, John, N.J., Martha/
Marcia, R6524
LEQUER, Abraham, N.Y. See LEQUIRE
LEQUIER, John, N.J. See LEQUEER
LEQUIRE, Abraham, N.Y., Mary,
R6525
LERAY, John, Ct., Bridget, W12104;
BLWt.27644-160-55
LEROY, George, Pa., BLWt.1277-200-
Lt. Iss. 5/28/1790. No papers
John, Ct. See LERAY
LEROYE, Simon, N.Y., S13730
LERROW, John, Ct., BLWt.6119-100-
Pvt. Iss. 2/5/1790. No papers
LERUE, Peter, Va., R6171
LERVEY, Jacob, Mass., S37163
LESEUR, Joseph, R.I., S13720
LESH, Philip, Cont., Pa., Margaret
W3267
LESLEY, Peter, N.C., S4540
Samuel, ---, Pa. res. in 1816,
Sarah, R6296
William, N.C., S31821
LESLIE, Alexander, Cont., N.H.,
S40927
Alexander, Va., S4539
John, Pa., BLWt.9817-100-Pvt. Iss.
8/31/1790 to D. Woodbridge, ass.
No papers
William, Pa., S22354
LESLY, Howel/Howell, N.C., Va.,
S8825
Thomas, S.C., Mary, W381
LESNITT, Francis, Pa., Rachel,
W8247
L'ESPERANCE, Joseph, Hazen's Regt.
BLWt.13366-100-Fifer. Iss.
2/4/1790. No papers
LESSIG, David, Pa., Magdalene,
W8041
LESSLEY, John, Pa., S38139
LESSON, George, Mass., S32969
LESTER, Alexander, Va., S4538
Asa, Ct., S16921
Ebenezer, Cont., Ct., S37615
Elihu, Ct., Cont., S20041
Francis, Cont., Mass., S32972;

LESTER (continued)
BLWt.1551-100
Guy, Cont., R.I., Cynthia, W20456
Guy/Gay, N.Y., BLWt.7433-100-
Pvt. Iss. 12/15/1790 to Ebenezer
Foote, ass. No papers
Jeremiah, Ct., S13743
John, N.Y., S42844
Joshua, Ct., S17535
Nathan, Ct., BLWt.6084-100-Pvt.
Iss. 10/1789 to Theodosius
Fowler. No papers
Nathan, Ct., S32991
Thomas, Va., S35518
William, Va., R6298
LESTRE, Francis, Cont., Mass.
See LESTER
LESUER, John, Mass., S42857;
BLWt.184-150
William, Mass., S33373
LESUEUR, Martel/Martil, Va.,
Elizabeth, W8035
LESURE, Gideon, Mass., BLWt.
4584-100-Pvt. Iss. 2/24/1800.
No papers
Gideon, Mass., Rhoda, W24499
John, Mass. See LESUER
Levi, Mass., S32990
Samuel, Mass., Hannah, W24528;
BLWt.9477-160-55
LETCH, William, Mass., S49306
LETCHWORTH, Benjamin, Va., S16918
LETFORD, Robert, Pa., BLWt.9805-
100-Drummer. Iss. 3/10/1790.
No papers
LETSON, John, N.J., S708
William, R.I., S13719
LETT, James, N.C., S38912
LETTICE, James, N.J., S10982
LETTS, Abraham, N.Y., Abigail,
W20449
Francis, N.J., S1046
John, N.J., S42847
LEUCAW, Peter, Cont., Canadian,
R6299
LeVACHER, de St. Maria, S.C.
See LeVacher De ST. MARIA
Le VACHER de VANBRUN, John, Md.,
Ann, W10010
LEVAGUE, Augustus, Cont., N.Y.,
See LEVAKE
LEVAKE, Augustus/Augustine, Cont.
N.Y., S40920
LEVALLEY, Cook, R.I., S14426
Peleg, R.I., S13742
William, R.I., Phebe, W24483
LEVAN, Isaac, Cont., Pa., R6301
LEVAND, Isaac, See LEVAN
LEVAQUE, Augustus. See LEVAKE
LEVARNWAY, Toussant. See LAVARNWAY
LeVASCHE de St. Marie, S.C. See
LeVacher De ST. MARIA
LEVENS, Henry, Va., S32375
LEVENSTON, David, Md., W3614
LEVEQUE, Augustus, See LEVAKE
LEVERETT, Thomas, Ga., Mary G.,
W4264
LEVERICK, Gabriel, N.Y., S42851
LEVERING, Jacob, Pa., BLWt.325-100
John, Pa., R6302
Joseph, Pa., Abigail, R6480
LEVERINGHOUSE, Christian, Pa.,

LEVERINGHOUSE (continued)
BLWt.9830-100-Pvt. Iss. 10/13/1791. No papers
LEVI, Alexander, Md., BLWt.11460-100-Pvt. Iss. 11/29/1790 to John Thornton, Admr. No papers
Isaac, Va., Mary, W773
Judah/Judas, Va., Mary, W8037
Rice, Va., Priscilla, W5314; BLWt.26906-160-55. No papers
LEVICK, Caleb, Lee's Legion, Va. BLWt.13395-100-Pvt. Iss. 11/18/1791. No papers
Robert, Cont., Del., Priscilla, W1299; BLWt.129-100
LEVINGSTON, James, N.Y., BLWt. 1260-500-Col. Iss. 4/21/1791. No papers (this is a file)
LEVINS, James, Ga., R7607
LEVINUS, Thomas, N.Y., Levina/Lovina, W20430
LEVISEY, George, Va., Nancy, R6304
LEVISTON, David, Mass., BLWt. 4590-100-Pvt. Iss. 1/26/1790 to James Smith. No papers
David, Mass., S46455
LEVISTONE, David, Md. See LEVENSTON
LEVIT, David, Mass. See LEAVIT
LEVY, Rice, Va. See LEVI
LEW, Barzillai, Mass., Dinah,W20461
LEWALLEN, Richard, Va., Parazeda/Parasida, W26211; BLWt.34923-160-55
LEWES, Elizabeth, Ct. See LEWIS
LEWIN, John, Md., BLWt.11461-100-Pvt. Iss. 1/11/1796 to Joshua Ward, ass. No papers
Thomas, R.I., S31211
LEWIS, Aaron, N.C., S16922
Abel, Ct., S16920
Abel, Ct., S22358
Abel, Ct., S37160
Abel, Ct. Sea Service, R6306
Abiah, former wid. of Reuben Nichols, Ct., which see
Abijah, Ct., S37161
Abijah, Mass., Betty, W24527
Abner, Mass., S16446
Abraham, Ct., S29287
Abraham, Pa., R6307
Abraham, Pa., BLWt.1283-100-Lt.
Ambrose, Va., Sea Service, S36041
Amos, N.C., S41767
Andrew, Ct., S13724
Andrew, Ct., S17536
Andrew, Mass., Mary, W15020
Andrew, ---, Va. res. Dis. No papers
Andrew, Va., Margaret, W3431
Andrew, Va., R6308
Archelaus, Mass., S16923
Asa, Armand's Corps, BLWt.13314-100-Pvt. Iss. 2/1790 to Theodosius Fowler, ass. No papers
Asa, R.I., BLWt.3291-100-Pvt. Iss. 11/30/1799 to Abijah Holbrook, ass. No papers
Augustus, Ct., S17541
Augustus, Ct., S28789
Augustus J., R.I., S21863
Avery, N.Y., S42856

LEWIS (continued)
Axom, S.C., S16924
Basil/Bazzel, Ct., S46230
Benjamin, Ct., Cont., Polly, W675; BLWt.6291-160-55
Benjamin, Mass., Sarah, W15024
Benjamin, N.J., BLWt.483-100
Benjamin, Pa., S13746
Beriah, R.I., S10975
Caleb, R.I., Nancy Parsons, former wid., W17422
Charles, N.C., Elizabeth, W4012
Charles, Pa., BLWt.9838-100-Pvt. Iss. 6/9/1794 to Gideon Merkle ass. No papers
Chauncey, Ct., S37168; BLWt. 1278-100; BLWt.13-60-55
Christopher, N.Y., S23300
Daniel, Md., N.C., S4531
Daniel, Pvt., Md., or S.C., BLReg. 249820-1855
Daniel, Mass., S42848
Daniel, N.J., Rebecca, R15828; BLReg. 310018-1855
Daniel, Va., BLWt.12305-100-Pvt. Iss. 5/16/1791. No papers
Darius, Mass., S29290
David, Ct., Dis. No papers here but see Am. State Papers, Class IX, Claims, p. 118
David, Va., Mary, R6323
Dyer, Mass., S42845
Ebenezer, Ct. ---. No papers in field since 1870
Ebenezer, Ct., R6310
Ebenezer, Ct., R6311
Edward, Cont., N.J., Nancy, W8042
Eleazer, Ct., Catharine, W20442
Eleazer, Ct., R.I., Thankful, W12107
Eleazer, Mass., S18934
Eli, Cont., Mass., S23770
Elijah, Ct., Cont., S13745
Elijah, N.Y., S22353
Elijah, R.I., BLWt.1685-300
Elisha, Ct., Sarah, W24525
Elisha, Navy, S32993
Elisha, N.C., S34961
Elizabeth, former wid. of Jesse Carrington, Ct., which see
Emanuel, Crane's Cont. Art. Mass., BLWt.4620-100-Pvt. Iss. 6/22/1791 to Margt. Lewis, Admx. No papers
Enoch, R.I., Privateer, S21344
Ephraim, Pa., S5684; BLWt. 79520-160-55
Ezekiel, Pa., S4533
Feabus/Fabius, Va., S38135
Frances, former wid. of William Palmer, Ga., which see
Francis, Ct., Sarah, W20435
George, Ga., R6314
George, Md., N.W. Indian War, R21100
George, Mass., S30540
George, Va., Elizabeth Summers former wid., W7218; BLWts.26967-160-55 & 10897-160-55
Gilbert, N.Y., S9926
Hannah, former wid. of Gideon

LEWIS (continued)
Booth, Ct., which see
Henry, N.Y., S27085
Henry, N.Y., S42850
Henry, Pa., S4532
Henry, Sea Service, Va., Polly, R6326
Herbert, Va., S4529
Isaac, Ct., S15922
Isaac, Cont., Ct., S42835
Isaac, Mass., S17537
Isaac, Mass., S32978
Isaac, N.Y., Hannah, W2134
Isaac, Pa., S9748
Jabez, Ct., BLWt.6107-100-Pvt. Iss. 3/11/1791 to Isaac Bronson. No papers
Jabez/Jabish, Ct., S37169
Jabez, Ct., S42838
Jacob, Ct., Eunice, W20453
Jacob, Mass., Abigail Winter, former wid., W16087
Jacob, N.J., S40079
Jacob, N.J., Mary, R6324
Jacob, N.Y., R6316
Jacob, Va., Mary, W8044
James, Cont., Vt., Green Mt. Boys, S44238
James, Cont., Va., S35520
James, Mass., Hannah, W24522
James, N.H., S42840
James, Lamb's Art., N.Y., BLWt. 7434 & 7603-100-Pvt. Iss. 8/12/1790 to John D. Coe, ass. No papers
James, N.C., Ann, W5022
James, N.C., S.C., b. N.C., S8841
James, Va., Mary C., W303; BLWt. 3067-160-55
Jehu, Pa., S22879
Jesse, Va., S5680
Job, Mass., S32987
Joel, N.C., Miriam Crabb, former wid., W780
John, Ct., Mass., S10979
John, Cont., Mass., S42842
John, Md., R6319
John, Mass., Anna, W15028
John, Mass., Mary, R 6325
John, Mass., BLWt.1247-200-Lt. Iss. 11/28/1789 to Asa Spalding, ass. No papers
John, N.H., Abigail, W24510
John, N.J., Phebe, W8040
John, N.J., Elizabeth, W10195; BLWt.61331-160-55
John, N.C., Sarah, R6328
John, Va., BLWt.12324-100-Pvt. Iss. 12/9/1793 to Francis Graves, ass. No papers
John, Va., S10249
John, Va., S16448
John, Va., Ann Berry, W3832
John, Va., BLWt.1864-300. Iss. 7/18/1832
John S., N.Y., R6320
Jonas, Mass., Susanna, W16041
Jonas, Mass., Pa., Lucy, W20432; BLWt.17881-160-55
Jonathan, Md., BLWt.11443-100-Pvt. Iss. 2/7/1790. No papers

LEWIS (continued)
Jonathan, Mass., S22359
Jonathan, Mass., Betsey, W20464
Joseph, Ct., S13721
Joseph, Ct., Cont., Esther, W20455
Joseph, Mass., BLWt.4565-100-Pvt. Iss. 3/25/1790. No papers
Joseph, Mass., Mehitable, W2818; BLWt.43507-160-55
Joseph, Mass., R6321
Joseph, N.H., or Vt., Green Mt. Boys, S4534
Joseph, N.Y., BLWt.7406-100-Pvt. Iss. 8/3/1790 to Cornelius Van Dyck, ass. No papers
Joseph, N.Y., S42855
Joseph, Pa., S41760
Joseph B., S.C., Tabitha, R19780
Josiah, Mass., Martha, W24506
Justus, Cont., Ct., Polly, W1298; BLWt.14506-160-55
Lazarus, N.C., R6322
Lemuel, Mass., S13718
Lewis, Va., Sarah, W3097
Lockard, N.Y. See LUSE
Lockhard, N.Y., BLWt.7412-100-Pvt. Iss. 9/15/1790 to John S. Hobart et al, ass. No papers
Marsh/March, Mass., S32980
Martin, Ct., S28788
Matthew, Va. Sea Service, Ann James, former wid., W7909
Messenger, Ct., S31207
Morgan, N.Y., S16447
Morgan, N.C., S41766
Naboth, Sheldon's Horse, Ct., BLWt.6128-100-Corp. Iss. 6/25/1789. No papers
Naboth, Cont., Ct., Phebe, W27810
Nathan, Ct., Cont., S13737
Nathan, Cont., Mass., Hannah Pratt former wid., W20000
Nathan, Mass., S37159
Nathaniel, Ct., S17540
Nathaniel, Ct., S20844
Nathaniel, Ct., Abigail, W15022
Nathaniel, Mass. Sea Service, Lucy, W24530; BLWt.12818-160-55
Oliver, Ct., S4530
Peter, Ct., Cont., Patience Post, former wid., W17463
Phebe, former wid. of James Lyons, N.Y., which see
Philo, Ct. Sea Service, Charity, W20469
Reuben, N.Y., S13723
Richard, Md., BLWt.11468-100-Pvt. Iss. 7/31/1797 to James DeBaufre ass. No papers
Richard, Mass., S18935
Richard, N.J., S40082
Robert, Ct., Cont., Sarah Curtis, former wid., W20939
Roger, Ct., S37611
Ruel, Va., S8826
Ruth, former wid. of Aaron Phelps Ct., which see
Samuel, Ct., S1047
Samuel, Ct., S37604
Samuel, Mass., S42839
Samuel, N.J., Va., S1048

LEWIS (continued)
Samuel, N.Y., S42836; BLWt.1263-200-Lt. Iss. 8/9/1790
Samuel, Pa., BLWt.9823-100-Pvt. Iss. 7/16/1789. No papers
Samuel, Pa., S40939
Samuel, Pa., S41763
Samuel, R.I., Elizabeth, R6312
Sarah, former wid. of Stephen Seward, Ct., which see
Seth, Ct., Rhoda, R6327
Simeon, R.I., R6331
Solomon, N.C., Catharine, R6309
Solomon, R.I., S13727
Spencer, Va., R9978
Stephen, Ct., S15506
Stephen, R.I., S21865
Stephen, Sappers & Miners, BLWt. 13329-100-Sgt. Iss. 3/14/1792. No papers
Thomas, N.C., S7139
Thomas, Va., S7138
Thomas, Va., Sarah, W8032; BLWt. 27672-160-55
Thomas, Va., Hannah, W9124
Thomas, Va., Sarah Ann Stewart, former wid., W10263; BLWt. 26625-160-55
Timothy, Mass., S13732; BLWt. 54236-160-55
Valentine, Ct., S37170
Valentine, Ct., Sally, W20431
Wait, Ct., BLWt.6126-100-Pvt. Iss. 10/7/1789 to Benj. Tallmadge. No papers
Wait, Ct., S42858
Walker, Ct., Sarah, R6330
Wilford, N.C. & War of 1812. See Lewis WILFORD
William, Ct., S40926
William, Ct., Cont., S13725
William, Cont., Md., Mary, W4263
William, Mass., R32984
William, Mass., Hannah, W771; BLWt.26848-160-55
William, Mass., Elizabeth, R6313
William, Mass., R6332
William, N.Y., Margaret, W20443
William, N.Y., R6333
William, N.C., S8842
William, N.C., R6334
William, R.I., S22878
William, S.C., R6335
William, Lee's Legion, Va., BLWts.12308 & 13957-100-Pvt. Iss. 6/16/1791. No papers
William, Lee's Legion, Va., BLWt. 12323-100-Pvt. Iss. 11/12/1791 to John Clingman, ass. No papers
William, Va., S7148
William, Va., S8827
William, Va. Sea Service, R62. Va. Half Pay
William, Va., BLWt.1300-400-Major Iss. 8/10/1789 to Richard Platt, ass. No papers
Willis, N.C., S41768
LEWTER, Hardy, N.C., S8839
LEYHEW, David, Va. See LEHEW
LEYLAND, William, N.J., R6337
LEYMAN, Samuel, Pa. See LEHMANN
L'HOMMEDIEU, Samuel, N.Y., R15145
LIBBEE, Allison, Mass., Sarah Small, former wid., W2249. Her

LIBBEE (continued)
other husb. was pensioned. See claim of Daniel Small, Mass.
Bennett, N.H., S17545
Francis, Mass. See LIBBY
Robert, Cont., Mass., Rebecca, W24563
Samuel, N.H., Mahitable, W21575
LIBBEY, Benjamin, Mass., Sarah, W24543
Benjamin, Navy, Mass., Polly Dow, former wid., W22967
Benjamin, N.H., See LIBBY
David, Mass., Abigail, W24541
Ephraim, Cont., N.H., Judith, W21572
George, Mass., S16929
James, Mass., Hannah, W24546
James, N.H., S44510
John, Mass. Sea Service, S33000
Joseph, Mass., S28793
Josiah, Mass., S20441
Josiah, Mass., Sarah, W24558
Nathan, Mass., Ruth, W24567
Nathaniel, Mass., N.H., Abigail, W26218; BLWt.40915-160-55
Samuel, Navy, N.H., S37178
Susanna, former wid. of George McAlpin, N.H., which see
LIBBY, Allison, Mass. See LIBBEE
Benjamin, Mass., S37633
Benjamin, Navy, Mass. See LIBBEY
Benjamin, N.H., S18081
Dominicus, Mass., Dorothy, W24515
Edward, Mass., Elizabeth, W24537
Eliakim, Mass., S16927
Ezriah, Mass., S37177
Francis, Mass., S28791
Harvey/Meserve, Mass., Polly, W1438; BLWt.6284-160-55
Isaac, Mass., Abigail, W24542
James, Mass., S37628
Jonathan, Mass., Abigail, W24557
Jotham, Mass., S37634
Luke, Mass., Dolly, W24539
Luke, N.H., S44509
Mark, Mass., S38790
Reuben, Mass., S37175
Reuben, Mass., Mercy/Marcy, W24551
Richard H., Mass., S37630
Robert, Cont., Mass. See LIBBEE
Robert, Mass., S29297
Samuel, Mass., Abigail, W24538; BLWt.6119-160-55
Seth, Mass., Lydia, W21574
Simeon, Mass., S37632
Solomon, Cont., Mass., Sally, W24561
Thomas, Cont., Maine agcy. & res. in 1818, Mary; W26219; BLWt.34921-160-55
William, Cont., Mass., S16928
William, Mass., BLWt.19754-160-55
Zebulon, Cont., Mass., Lydia, W24556
LIBELL, Guillame, Hazen's Regt., BLWt.13341-100-Pvt. Iss. 10/12/1790. No papers
LIBENGOOD, Jacob, Pa., Margaret, W8253; BLWt.82540-160-55
LIBERTY, Cuff, Ct., BLWt.

LIBERTY (continued)
6110-100-Pvt. Iss. 9/15/1789. No papers
James, Ct., BLWt.6125-100-Pvt. Iss. 4/19/1796 to James A. Neale. No papers
Pomp (colored), Ct.,BLWt.1761-100
Sharp (colored), Ct., Lucy Mix, former wid., R7286
LIBEY, David, Mass., See LIBBEY
LIBLEY, Andrew, Pa. See LEIBLEY
LICK, Thomas, Pa., BLWt.9824-100-Pvt. Iss. 2/11/1800 to Philemon Thomas, ass. No papers
LICOTE, John, Hazen's Regt., BLWt. 13342-100-Pvt. Iss. 2/25/1792 to Benj. Moore, Admr. No papers
LIDDELL, Moses, S.C., Elizabeth Haney, former wid., W7698
William, S.C., Ruth, W3835
LIDDICK, Philip, Pa. See LITTIG
LIDDLE, George, S.C., BLWt.1317-300-Capt. Iss. 4/22/1800 to heirs James & Geo. Washington Liddle. No papers
Robert, N.J., S4554
Robert, N.J., Rebecca, W952
LIDDY, Matthew, Pa., S40093
LIDGEARD, Joseph, Pa. See LITCHARD
LIDY, Simon, Pa., Barbara, R6339
LIERLY, Zachariah, N.C., S32389
LIESNER, George, Mass., BLWt.4573-100-Pvt. Iss. 2/23/1796 to Joseph Brown. No papers
LIEUZADDER, Abraham, Va., Leah, W24554
LIFRAGE, William, S.C., R6340
LIGET, John, Va., S31816
LIGGETT, Thomas, See LIGGIT
LIGGINS, William, Cont., Pa., S41769; BLWt.501-100
LIGGIT, Thomas, Cont., Pa., S7155; BLWt.303-100
LIGHT, John, Cont., Mass., N.H., Privateer, Sally Leavitt, former wid., W21563. Her last husb., Josiah Leavitt, N.H., also served in Rev. War. See papers within
John, Cont.,N.J., Catharine, W5322
John, N.Y., BLWt.7393-100-Pvt. Iss. 10/3/1791 to Isaac Brooks, ass. No papers
John, N.Y., S42872
John, N.C., S4549
Prince, N.H., S44511
Vachal, Va., S1551
LIGHTALL, Abraham, N.Y., Katherine, W10197
James, N.Y., BLWt.7401-100-Pvt. Iss. 10/4/1790 to John Prince, ass. No papers
Lancaster, N.Y., BLWt.7402-100-Pvt. Iss. 2/29/1792. No papers
LIGHTBODY, Gabriel, N.Y., S28794
LIGHTBURN, Richard, Va. Sea Service R63, Va. Half Pay
LIGHTCAP, Samuel, Pa., S5691
LIGHTFOOT, Philip, Cont., Va., BLWt.2220-200
Tapley, Va., S4558
LIGHTHALL, Abraham, N.Y. See LIGHTALL

LIGHTHALL (continued)
Abraham J., N.Y., Catharine, W16631
Francis, Cont., N.Y., Sarah, W20470
George, N.Y., S13341
James N., N.Y., S42870
John, N.Y., Nancy, W20484; BLWt. 218-60-55
Nicholas, N.Y., S9929
William, Cont., N.Y., S42862; BLWt.1223-200-Lt. Iss. 8/8/1781 to John Doty, ass. No papers
LIGHTHART, Barnabas, N.Y., S13756
LIGHTNER, John Michael, Pa., Anna Margaret, W9133; BLWt.40006-160-55
LIGON, Blackman, Va., Elizabeth, W9132
John, Va., S4555
Joseph, Va., S132
William, Va. See LEGON
William, Va., S13764
LIGWELL, John, Crane's Regt., Mass., BLWt.1241-200-Lt. Iss. 7/13/1790 to John Ligwell. No papers
LIKE, Henry, N.Y., S42868
LIKENS, Andrew, N.J., Pa., S41776
George, Pa., S40089
LIKES, John, N.J. See LIPES
LILBURN, Andrew, Va., S4562
LILE, Jackson, N.C., Elizabeth, W116; BLWt.26662-160-55
LILES, David, N.C., b. Va., S1848
David, N.C., b. Va., S4544
Ephram, S.C. See Ephraim LISLES
John, Ga., S47930
John, S.C., Nancy, W151
LILLARD, John, Va., S8860
LILLEY, Anna S., former wid. of Asa Waterman, Ct., which see
Benjamin, Ct., Mary, W20488
Benjamin, Cont., Mass., War of 1812, S37624; BLWt.322-100
Benjamin, Sappers & Miners, BLWt.13330-100-Sgt. Iss. 3/25/1791 to David Quinton, ass. No papers
Emmons, Mass. See LILLIE
John, Ct., S40092
Joseph, Navy, Mass. agcy. & res., Hannah, W21579
Reuben, Ct. See LILLIE
Reubin, Mass., BLWt.1235-200-Lt. Iss. 7/20/1789. No papers
LILLEYCRAFT, John, Pa., BLWt. 9799-100-Corp. Iss. 8/7/1789 to Richard Platt, ass. No papers
LILLIBRIDGE, Gardner, R.I., S11400
Gideon, R.I., S17544
Thomas, R.I., Alice, W20472
LILLIE, Amariah, Ct., S38914
Daniel, Mass. Sea Service. See LILLY
Ebenezer, Ct., Cont., Jerusha, W20474
Elijah, Ct., S22362
Elisha, Ct., S15509
Emmons, Mass., Susanna, W1884;

LILLIE (continued)
BLWt.19521-160-55
John, Cont., Mass. & U.S.A. Elizabeth, R6345; BLWt.1240-300-Capt. Iss. 5/30/1796
Jonathan, Ct., S6342
Joseph, Ct., S42864
Nathan, Ct., Mass., S13759
Reuben, Ct., S42873
LILLISTON, William, Va., S38141
LILLY, Abner, Ct., Sybil Upton, former wid., W15809
Bethuel, Mass., S18946
Daniel, Mass. Sea Service, Rebecca, W15031. Her other husb., Joseph Bignell/Brignol was a sold., Mass. in Rev. War
Naomi, former wid. of Simeon Cummings, Ct., which see
Thomas, Mass., Dis. No papers
William, Va., R6343
LILLYBRIDGE, Thomas, R.I. See LILLIBRIDGE
LIMAS, Prince, R.I., BLWt.3293-100-Pvt. Iss. 3/27/1790 to Mary Limas, heir. No papers
LIMBACKER, John, N.Y., BLWt. 7405-100-Pvt. Iss. 1/25/1791 to A. Helme, ass. No papers
LIMBOCKER, John, N.Y., Lovinia, W5024
LIMBRICK, Christopher, R.I., BLWt.146-100. Claim missing in 1912. Shows "Iss. to Barzillai Brown, admr., 2/28/1804. Not delivered. Rank-Drummer."
LIMERICK, Patrick, Pa., S41772
LIMING, Job, N.J., S8867
Samuel, Va., S46390
LIN, John, Ga. See LINN
LINAKIN, Joseph, Mass. See LINEKEN
LINCH, William, Md. See LYNCH
LINCOLN, Abiathar/Abierther, Mass., S29296
Amasa, R.I., Elizabeth, W20477
Anna, former wid. of Timothy Smith, Mass., which see
Asa, Mass., Meletiah, W12133; BLWt.43509-160-55
Benjamin, Mass., BLWt.1226-11-Maj. Gen. Iss. 10/26/1789. No papers
Caleb, Cont., pensioned in Mass., S32999; BLWt.963-100
Daniel, Mass., Abigail, W20476
David, Invalid Corps, BLWt.13384-100-Pvt. Iss. 9/10/1789 to Henry Newman, ass.
David, Mass., S32996
Elijah, Cont., Ct., BLWt.2077-100
Elijah, not Rev. War; Wayne's Indian War 1792-1795, Old War Inv. Rej. 15880. No BLWt. found. B. in Mass. Enl. in Vt. Res. after service, Ohio, Ky. & Tenn.
Elisha, Ct., Rhuama, W20475
Elisha, Mass., Cont., S37173
Ephraim, Mass., Lucy, W1557; BLWt.21815-160-55
Ezekiel, Mass., Jane, W20490
Israel, Mass., S29966

LINCOLN (continued)
Jacob, Mass., S30544
Jacob, Va., Dorcas, R6347
Jairus, Mass., Rachel, W15032
James, Mass., S32995
James, Mass., Abigail, W15029
James, Mass., Rhoda, W20478
Jerome, Mass., Elizabeth, W20471
John, Cont., Mass., Polly, W24535
John, Mass., S37181
John, Mass., S44512
John, Pa., S4556
Joseph, Cont., Mass. Sea Service, Susannah, W24534
Joseph, Mass., BLWt.4559-100-Sgt. Iss. 4/1790. No papers
Lot, Mass., Sally, W20482
Lovid, Cont., Mass., Betsey, W1440; BLWt.133746-160-55
Luther, Crane's Cont. Art., Mass. BLWt.4622-100-Pvt. Iss. 9/23/1791 to Isaac Bronson. No papers
Luther, Cont., Mass., res. of Ct., S37623
Macey, Mass., Relief, R6351
Michael, Pa., S5696
Mitchel, Mass., S10993
Nathan, Ct., Eunice, W20494
Nathaniel, Mass., S5693
Nedabiah, Mass., Sarah, W20473; BLWt.15414-160-55
Oliver, Cont., Mass., Ruth, W21576
Otis, Mass., S42865
Royal, Mass., Sea Service, Jerusha W21573
Rufus, Mass., Lydia, W13634; BLWt. 990-300
Samuel, Ct. See LINKON
Sherman/Shermon, Mass., S15924
Simeon, Cont., Ct., S37626
Sylvester, Mass., Deziah Chapman, former wid., W18900
Thomas, Mass., S21348
LIND, John, Pa. See LYN
LINDEN, Michael, Pa., BLWt.9813-100-Pvt. Iss. 3/2/1792 to Alexander Power, ass. No papers.
LINDENBERGER, John, Cont., Pa., Dorcas, W8045
LINDENSMITH, George, Pa., S40084
LINDER, John, N.C., Jane, R6352
LINDERMAN, Cornelius, N.Y., S10990
John, N.Y., Mary, W676; BLWt. 26329-160-55
LINDERSMITH, George, Pa., BLWt. 9788-100-Pvt. Iss. 12/21/1791. No papers
LINDEY, Jacob, Cont., Pa., S40091
LINDLEY, David, Cont., Mass. See LINDSLEY
LINDLY/LINDLEY, Caleb, N.J., S23301
Moses, N.J., S36685
LINDOLPH, George, N.Y., S10991
LINDSAY, David, Mass., Mary, W20487; BLWt.2414-100. Iss. 2/19/1847
James, Va., S6353
John, Ga., Dis. No papers
John, Pa., S4550
Laban, N.C. See LINDSEY
Lewis, Va., S8862
Mungo, Pa., S40087

LINDSAY (continued)
Samuel, Pa., Dis. No papers
William, Pa., Clarissa, W553; BLWt.28649-160-55
LINDSEY, Abraham, Va., S36043
Benjamin, N.C., Abigail, R6354
Benjamin, S.C., S18082
Daniel, Mass., S32994
David, Ct., BLWt.854-100
David, N.C., S7154
David, Pa., S40090
David, Pa., Sarah, R6356
Felix, Ct., S37627
Hezekiah, Va., S41770
Hugh, Cont., N.Y., Dolly, W20493
James, Mass., S37621
James, N.C., S10992
James, Va., Priscilla Thomas, former wid., W25476; BLWt.44933-160-55
John, Md., Pa., S30545
John, Pa., R6355
Laban, N.C., S7153
Moses, S.C., S4551
Peter, Va., BLWt.12328-100-Pvt. Iss. 12/9/1793 to Francis Graves, ass. No papers
Robert, Cont., Mass., See LINSEY
Samuel, R.I., Parmelia, W21581
Stephen, Ct., S23771
Walter, N.C. See LINDZEY
Walter, Pa., Mary, W8048
William, R.I., Catharine, W27441
LINDSLEY, Brainard, Ct., S13762
David, Ct. See LINDSEY
David, Cont. (sold. was from Liverpool, England), Hannah, W20477 1/2; BLWt.2433-100
David, N.J., S710
Eleazer, N.J., BLWt.1274-450-Lt. Col. Iss. 6/11/1789 to John Ludlow, ass. No papers
Joseph, Cont., N.J. agcy. & res. S33374
Solomon, Ct. See LINSLY
LINDSLY, Daniel, Ct. See LINSLEY
Ephraim, N.J., Martha, W860
LINDZEY, Walter, N.C., Catharine, W4017; BLWt.25000-160-55
LINE, Adam, Va., S7513
Jacob, Pa., R----
John, N.J., S4547
John, Va., S18491
Joseph, Va., Mary Magdalen, R6359
Serring, N.J., S40086
LINEBOCH, Joseph, Pa., S40085
LINEKEN, Joseph, Mass., S37631
LINER, Christopher, Va., Ann, W3699; BLWt.45713-160-55
LINES, Abel, Ct., Arma, W12130
Abraham, Ct., Sarah, W26214
Anthony, N.J., S4546
Benjamin, Ct., S13752
Ebenezer, Ct., BLWt.6100-100-Pvt. Iss. 10/12/1789. No papers
Ebenezer, Ct., Mercy, W2819
Francis, Mass., BLWt.2185-100
John, Ct., BLWt.6086-100-Pvt. Iss. 12/3/1789 to Daniel Watrous

LINES (continued)
John, Ct., S37622
John, Ct., Judith, W26775
Rufus, Ct., Tamer, W2820
Searing, N.J., BLWt.8488-100-Pvt. Iss. 6/11/1789 to Jonathan Dayton, ass. No papers
William, Mass., BLWt.4557-100-Pvt. Iss. 8/8/1793 to John Blanchard. No papers
LINEWEAVER, Jacob, Va., Margaret W5325
LINFIELD, Hannah, former wid. of Nathaniel Hunt, Mass., which see
LINGAN, James M., Md., BLWt.1294-300-Capt. Iss. 3/19/1792. No papers
Thomas, Md., S34962
LINGENFELTER, Michael, Md., S32379
LINGO, Henry, Pa., BLWt.9854-100-Pvt. Iss. 7/10/1790. No papers
Henry, Pa., S41771
William, Del., BLWt.10810-100-Pvt. Iss. 4/19/1777 to James DeBaufre, ass. No papers
William, Del., S38913
LINGRELL, Nehemiah, Md., S36044
LINING, Charles, S.C., BLWt. 1316-300-Capt. Iss. 1/15/1799. No papers
LINK, Adam, Pa. or Va., S1771; BLWt.26343-160-55
Michael, N.C., R6360
LINKON, John, Ct., Weightstill; W24555
Nathaniel, Ct., S17546
Oliver, Cont., Mass. See LINCOLN
Samuel, Ct., S40941
LINKHORN, John, Cont., Mass. See LINCOLN
LINLEY, John, N.Y. See LINNET
LINN, Adam, Pa., Ann, W5023
Dewald, Pa., Elizabeth, W9505; BLWt.34925-160-55
Helen, former wid. of Dirk Hansen, N.Y., which see
James, Ct., Vt., Abigail, R6361
James, Pa., S5695
John, Ga., Rachel, R6362
John, Mass., S37182
John R., Cont., Pa. See LYNN
Patrick, Pa., S36688
William, S.C., S38915
LINNAN, Thomas, Mass. See LINNEN
LINNEBAUCH, Joseph, Pa. See LINEBOCH
LINNEGAR, John, N.Y., BLWt.7407-100-Pvt. Iss. 7/7/1791 to John Ditrick et al, assnes. No papers
LINNEL, Joseph, Mass., R.I., S4557
LINNELL, Elkanah, Mass., S33001
Josiah, Mass. Sea Service, S32998
Samuel, Mass., Susannah, W5319
Uriah, Cont., Mass., S42866
LINNEN, Thomas, Mass., S18080
LINNER, John. See LINNET

LINNET, John, N.Y., R6363. See John LINNEGAR, N.Y., above
LINNIGER, John, N.Y. See LINNET
LINNING, John, N.Y. See LINNET
LINNIT, John, N.Y. See LINNET
LINOR, Philip, Va. See LYNOR
LINSABAUGH, Adam, See SINSABAUGH
LINSCOTT, Theodore, Mass., S37629 BLWt.296-100
LINSCUTT, Samuel, Cont., Mass., S41775
LINSEY, Daniel, Mass., BLWt.4582-100-Pvt. Iss. 12/3/1789 to Moses W. Barker. No papers
Daniel, Mass. See LINDSEY
Robert, Cont., Mass., Esther Salisbury, former wid., W24876; BLWt.82-60-55
Samuel, N.H., S40942
Solomon. See LINSLY
Walter, N.C. See LINDZEY
Walter, Pa. See LINDSEY
LINSLEY, Daniel, Ct., Hannah, W20486
James, Ct., Sarah, W20479
Stephen, Ct., Deborah, W677; BLWt.28571-160-55
LINSLY, Abiel, Ct., Anna, R6366
Obed, Ct., Privateer, R6358
Simeon, Ct., S4553
Solomon, Ct., Lucy, W4266
LINT, Isaac, N.Y., N.C., S8865
Joseph, Pa., Mary, W3144
LINTNER, Peter, Pa., S3912
LINTON, George, Md., BLWt.11462-100-Pvt. Iss. 1/8/1796 to Geo. Ponsonby, ass. No papers
Isaac, Md., S5690
John, N.C., B. Md., S13760
Joseph, Cont., Pa., Jane, W9504; BLWt.2204-100
Joseph, N.C., S19727
Thomas, N.C., S7152
William T/William S., N.C., Mary Ann, W8046
LINTS, Jacob, N.Y., S8863
LINUS, Robert, Ct., S13750
LINVILL, William, Ga., Mary, W5321
LINWOOD, John, N.J., BLWt.8491-100-Pvt. Iss. 7/24/1790. No papers
LION, Jacob, Va. See LYON
LIPE, Jonas, N.C. See LEIB
Leonard, N.C., S32381
LIPEHITE, John, Hazen's Regt., BLWt.13372-100-Pvt. Iss. 2/9/1793. No papers
John, Pa., Cont., S33377
LIPENWELL, Reuben, Mass., S15507
LIPES, John, N.J., Sarah, W4015; BLWt.129-60-55 & 8485-100-Pvt. Iss. 12/20/1791
LIPFORD, Anthony P., Va., Elizabeth, W2623; BLWt.26906-160-55
Henry, Va., S8861
John, Va., S8866
LIPKEY, Henry, Pa., S40094
LIPKY, Henry, Pa., BLWt.9849-100-Pvt. "in the Artillery". Iss. 11/11/1791. No papers
LIPP, John, Md., S8864
LIPPARD, William, S.C. See LIPPERD
LIPPENCOTT, William, N.J., Amelia, W24562
LIPPENCUT, Jacob, N.J., S33376
LIPPERD, William, S.C., Mary, W10199; BLWt.26066-160-55
LIPPETT, Christopher, R.I. See LIPPITT
Moses, R.I. See LIPPITT
Moses, R.I. See LIPPITT
Thomas, R.I. See LIPPITT
LIPPINCOTT, Eneas, N.J., R6373
Samuel, N.J., S4559
LIPPITT, Charles, R.I., S21866
Christopher, R.I., Waity, W24548
Moses, R.I., S21349
Moses, R.I., S31823
Thomas, R.I., Waite, W12128; BLWt.30759-160-55
LIPSCOMB, Ambrose, Va., Winny, W8252
Archibald, Va., Dorothy, W951; BLWt.5076-160-55. She also applied for pension on account of services of her 1st husb., Thomas Lipscomb, Va. Troops, and he was brother of her 2nd husb., Archibald Lipscomb
Benoni, Va., S38140
Henry, Va., BLWt.12325-100-Pvt. Iss. 5/11/1792 to Francis Graves, ass. No papers
James, Invalid Corps, BLWt. 13383-100-Pvt. Iss. 4/19/1791. No papers
John, Cont., Va., Elizabeth, W5323
Richard, Va., Mary, W8254; BLWt. 43508-160-55
Thomas, Va. See Archibald LIPSCOMB, Va.
Yancy, Va., N.A. Acc. No. 874-050103. Half Pay. No pension file for this veteran.
LIPSE, John, Pa., R6375
LISCOM, Samuel, N.Y., Bethany, R6376
LISCOMB, Darius, Cont., Ct., Sarah, W774; BLWt.26607-160-55
Nehemiah, Ct., S18942
Thomas, Ct., S18943
LISCOMBE, John, R.I., Abigail, W21571
LISET, Lewis, Cont., Mass. See LISOTE
LISH, Peter, Pa. See LISK
LISK, John, N.J. See LUSK
John, N.J., Mary, R6377
John, Va., S41773
Jonathan, N.J., BLWt.8501-100-Pvt. Iss. 6/11/1789 to Matthias Denman, ass. No papers
Peter, Pa., BLWt.458-100
LISLES, Ephraim/Ephram, S.C., Margaret,W8051;BLWt.11155-160-55
LISLEY, Samuel. See LESLEY
LISONBIE, Charles, S.C., S21346
LISOTE, Lewis, Cont., Mass., Mary, W24533
LISOTTE, Lewis, Hazen's Regt., BLWt.13340-100-Pvt. Iss. 1/22/
LISOTTE (continued) 1790 to Benj. Mooers, ass. No papers
LIST, Jacob, N.Y., S31214
John, N.Y., BLWt.7420-100-Pvt. Iss. 10/12/1790 to Isaac Bogaart, ass. No papers
John, N.Y., S35523
Lewis, Cont., BLWt.13326-100. Iss. 1789
LISTER, Thomas, Va. See LESTER
William, Md., S32377
LISTON, Thomas, S.C., BLWt.1320-200-Lt. Iss. 3/16/1792 to John Linn, guardian to Esther Liston, dau. of Thos. Liston. No papers
LISWELL, Thomas, Mass., BLWt.4575-100-Pvt. Iss. 12/4/1789 to Richard Platt. No papers
Thomas, Mass., War of 1812, Susanna, R6379
LITCH, William, Mass. See LETCH
LITCHARD, Joseph, Pa., S22363
LITCHFIELD, Caleb, Mass., S13751. N.A. Acc. No. 874-050104. Not Half Pay
Eleazer, Ct., S13753
Elisha, Cont., res. of heir was Vt. in 1821, BLWt.1012-100
Elisha, Mass., Delight Headon/Hayden, former wid., W17062
Francis, Mass., S30546
James, Ct., Lucretia, W16329; BLWt.48-100
John, Mass., Sarah, W15030
Noah, Cont., Mass., Mabel, W24553
Samuel, Cont., Mass., Sarah Carter, former wid., W22730
LITCHFORD, Arthur, Va., S7156
LITHGOW, Arthur, Mass., Martha, W15341
LITLE, Alexander, Pa., S4552
Archibald, N.C., See LYTLE
William, N.C. See Will LYTLE
LITTEL, Ebenezer, Ct., S----. Hannah, wid. of this sold., was pensioned as former wid. of Jonathan Badglet, N.J., which see
LITTELL, James, Pa. & 1774, S34963
Matthias, Pa. See LITTLE
Nathaniel, N.J., Catharine, R6381
William, Cont., Pa., S40944
LITTERAL, Richard, Cont., Va., Jane, W26220; BLWt.521-160-55
LITTIG, Philip, Pa., Catharine, W20460
LITTLE, Alexander, Pa. See LITLE
Benjamin, N.H., Persis H., BLWt. 17726-160-55
Benjamin, N.J., BLWt.8477-100-Pvt. Iss. 6/11/1789 to Matthias Denman, ass. No papers
Benoni, N.Y., S33378
Christy, N.J., Rachel, W2135
Daniel, N.H., S22360
Eleazer, Art. Artificers, BLWt. 1224-200-Lt. Iss. 6/21/1790. Also recorded as above under BLWt.2561. No papers.
Enos, dec'd, N.J., BLWts.8474 &

LITTLE (continued)
13944. Iss. 9/25/1789 to Lewis Little, legal repr. No papers
Ephraim, Sheldon's Horse, Ct., BLWt.6130-100-Corp. Iss. 11/24/1789. No papers
Friend, N.H., S10986
George, Mass. Sea Service, Rachel, W21578
George, N.H., Mehitable, W1439
George, Pa., Elizabeth, R6382
Henry, Cont., R.I., S42871
Jacob, N.J., BLWt.8473-100-Pvt. Iss. 7/20/1795. No papers
Jacob, N.C., R6383
James, Ct., Rosetta, W8256; BLWt.49049-160-55
James, Cont., S42869
James, Lamb's Art., N.Y., BLWt.7425-100-Sgt. Iss. 9/15/1790 to John S. Hobart et al, assnes. No papers
James, Pa. See LITTELL
John, Ct., Sarah, W26216
John, Mass., War of 1812, Mary Sprowl, former wid., W25061; BLWt.67616-160-55
John, N.Y., Dis. No papers here but see Am. State Papers, Class IX, Claims, p. 93
Joseph, Mass., N.H., S44513
Luther, Mass. Sea Service, S18945
Matthias, Pa., S40095
Michael, Md., S40945
Nancy, former wid. of Nathaniel Abbe, Ct., which see
Nathaniel, Mass., R6385
Nathaniel, N.J., See LITTELL
Noah, N.J., S711
Philip S., Del., Sarah, W4016
Samuel, Ct., R6386
Stephen, Cont., R.I., S13754
Thomas, Cont., Pa., Jane, W3268; BLWt.80-60-55
William, Ct., S37179
LITTLEBRIDGE, Thomas, R.I. See LILLIBRIDGE
LITTLEFIELD, Aaron, Mass., Meribah, W20483
Abraham, Mass., Susannw, W24536
Asa, Mass., R6387
Benjamin, Mass., S19375
Benjamin, Mass., Hannah, W24560
Daniel, Mass., S29295
Daniel, Mass., Hannah Eldridge/Eldrige, former wid., W24115. Wid's. 2nd husb., Amos Eldrige served in a Privateer.
David, Mass., Hannah, W24547
Edmond, Mass., Dorothy, W24540
Elijah, Mass., S16926
Ephraim, Mass., S28792
Joel, Mass., Joanna, W24564
John, Mass., Miriam, W24552
Johnson, Mass., S37174
Joseph, Mass., Abigail, W26213; BLWt.1587-160-55
Josiah, Cont., Mass., S42863
Jotham, Mass., S37180
Moses, Cont., Mass., Sarah, W5320 BLWt.28657-160-55

LIVINGSTON (continued)
Isaac, Ct., S37625
James, N.Y. See LEVINGSTON
John, Va., Rachel, R6393
Justice, Va. Sea Service, R64. Va. Half Pay. See N.A. Acc. No. 837, Va. State Navy, YS File
Richard, Cont., N.Y., Special BLWt. for 640 A. Canadian Refugee
Robert, Cont., Md.?, S42874. N.Y. res. & agcy.
Robert, Md., BLWt.11437 & 12466-100-Pvt. Iss. 9/6/1792 to Abraham Bell, ass. No papers
Robert, Md., BLWt.11466. Iss. 9/6/1792 to Abrm. Bell, ass. Note on card: "Mr. Flatequal, Interior Dept. Archives, furnished me name of this sold. It is not on old Wt. Book under this Wt. No. 11466 MMH Finch"
Robert, N.H., BLWt.3269-100-Pvt. Iss. 10/12/1795 to James A. Neal, ass. No papers
Robert, N.H., S46222
Robert, N.H., Mary L. Gregg, former wid., W24549. Sold. d. 1816
Robert H., Lt., Cont., N.Y., Catharine R., W3100; BLWt.1268-200 iss. 7/18/1791
Samuel, N.C. or Va.(?), Phebe, W8050
William, Cont., N.J., Mary Betts, former wid., W25321
William, Mass., Sea Service, S18083
LLOYD, Bateman, N.J., Abigail, W20551
Benjamin, S.C., Mary, W8052; BLWt.2391-200
David, N.J., BLWt.8492-100-Pvt. Iss. 9/8/1789 to Samuel Rutan, ass. No papers
David, Pa., S4590
Edward, S.C., BLWt.2007-200
George E., Va., S41777
James, N.Y., S37197
James, Pa. Art., BLWt.1279-200-Capt.-Lt. Iss. 1/29/1790 to John Hodge & Alexander Addison, assnes. No papers
John, Pa., S40951
Joseph, N.J., S46456; BLWt.8479-100. Iss. 8/7/1789
Joseph, Va., S36050
Martin, Mass. Sea Service, Navy, S5697
Michael, Md., BLWt.11455-100-Pvt. Iss. 2/1/1790 to James Williams, ass. No papers
Peter, Pa., BLWt.9808-100-Pvt. Iss. 12/13/1792 to Richard Murthwaite, admin. No papers
Richard, Gen. Hazen's Regt., BLWt.1328-300-Capt. Iss. 8/2/1790. No papers
Samuel, N.C., S32382
Thomas, Md., Mary, W4672
William, N.J., Rachel, W1626; BLWt.26449-160-55
William, N.C., Hannah, W4018
William, Va., S36049

LITTLEFIELD (continued)
Nathaniel, Cont., Mass., Rebecca, W20485
Noah M., Mass., S37172; BLWt. 1227-450-Lt. Col. Iss. 9/11/1795 to Wm. S. Thom, ass. No papers
Richard, Mass., Navy, Anna, W24559
Robert, Mass., Betsey Batchelder, former wid., W15553; BLWt.61262-160-55
Simeon, Vt., S13758
Timothy, Mass., S37176
William, S.C., S4560
LITTLEHALE, Ezra, Mass., Lydia, W16632
LITTLEJOHN, John, N.C., S32380
LITTLEPAGE, John, Cont., Va.?, Amy, S36042; BLWt.2037-100
John Carter, Va., S7151
LITTLETON, Charles, S.C., b. Va., Elizabeth, W8255; BLWt.43506-160-55
Savage, S.C., b. Del., S32378
William, N.C., S38142
LITTREL, Richard, Cont., Va. See LITTERAL
LITTS, Hendrick, N.Y., S13755
LITZENBERG, George, Pa., R6388
LITZINGER, Henry, Md., S34964
LIVASAY, George, Va. See LEVISEY
LIVELY, Andrew, Pa. See LEIBLEY
Cotrel, Va. See Godrell
Godrell/Goodwill/Cotrel, Cont., Va., Sarah, R6389
Goodwill, See Godrell
Thomas, Va., (colored), S38144
LIVENBERG, Frederick, Pa., S40943
LIVERMORE, Braddyll, Mass., S5692
Daniel, Cont., N.H., Sarah, W21580; BLWt.1220-300-Capt. Iss. 2/19/1796 to Wm. S. Thom, ass. No papers
David, Mass., Sally, W20481
Elisha, Mass., S10994
Isaac, Mass., S10988
Isaac, Mass., S13757
Josiah, Mass., S10985
Silas, Mass., Abigail, R6390
Solomon, Mass., Lois, W26776
LIVESAY, George, Va. See LEVISEY
LIVINGOOD, Peter, Va., S4561
LIVINGSTON, Abraham, N.Y., BLWt. 1262-300-Capt. Iss. 4/21/1791. No papers
Beekman, N.Y., R6391
Benjamin, Mass., Margaret, R6392
Daniel, Pa., S22361
David, Md. See LEVENSTON
David, Pa., S41774
Gilbert James, N.Y., S10989
Henry, N.Y., Jane M., W16328
Henry, N.C., S.C., b. Ireland, Mary, W8049; BLWt.134924-160-55
Henry, Va., Susannah, R6394
Henry Beekman, N.Y., Margaret Beekman, dau., W3145; BLWt. 1117-450. He d. 11/6/1831
Henry Brockholst, Cont., N.J., Catharine, W9506. He d. 3/10/or 18/1823

LOAR, Henry, Md., S41779; BLWt. 1393-100. Iss. 10/23/1828
LOARDON, George, See LOORDON
LOATWELL, Ephraim, Ct., BLWt. 6109-100-Pvt. Iss. 6/14/1791 to Isaac Bronson. No papers
LOBDELL, Isaac, Mass., S16452
Jacob, N.Y., S13787
Joseph, N.Y., S13797
Josiah, Ct., S17552
LOCEY, Abraham, See LOSEY
Jesse, N.J. See LOSEY
LOCH, Jacob, Pa., Nancy, R6397
John, Cont., French, R6396. Res. at enl. Pa., res. in 1834 in Va.
Samuel, N.H., BLWt.3275-100-Pvt. Iss. 9/11/1795 to Wm. S. Thom. No papers
LOCHARY, William, See LAUGHREY
LOCHMAN, Charles, S.C., BLWt. 1323-300-Surgeon's Mate. Iss. 3/2/1791.
John, Cont., S.C., S45901; BLWt.1225-300-Surgeon's Mate. Iss. 3/2/1791. Also recorded as above under BLWt.2582. No papers
LOCHREY, Michael, Pa., Nancy, W20530
LOCHRIDGE, James, S.C., b. Va., Ann, W472
John, Va., S31218
LOCK, Ayres, Mass., Lydia, W2136
Benjamin, Mass., S18492
Benjamin, Mass., Anna, W16332
Charles, Va., S1683
Edward, N.H., Betty, W16137
Elisha, N.H., Mehitable, W20502
Francis, Cont., N.H., S44519
Henry, Hazen's Regt., BLWt.13332-100-Pvt. Iss. 5/1/1799 to Abijah Holbrook, ass. No papers
James, Mass., Sarah, W15040
James, N.C., Anna, W5026
James, Va., S31220
John, Cont., N.Y., Mercy/Mersey, W8257; BLWt.312-60-55
John, N.C., S41782
Jonas, Mass., S33010
Jonathan, Mass., Lucy, W16634
Jonathan, N.H., Alice, W24578
Moses, N.H., BLWt.736-100
Philip, N.J., BLWt.8509-100-Pvt. Iss. 6/11/1789 to Jonathan Dayton, ass. No papers
Philip, N.J., Eunice, W4271
Richard, N.H., S44518
Richard, Va., S21351
Thomas, Mass., Abigail, W15043
Timothy, N.H. See LOCKWOOD
William, Cont., Pa., S40100
William, Mass., Margaret, W16633
LOCKARD, Philip, Va., Margaret, W3836; BLWt.15432-160-55
William, Va., S38152
LOCKART, Aaron, Pa., S38146
LOCKE, Eben/Ebenezer, Vt., BLWt.9518-160-55
Ebenezer, Mass., d. in 1796, Molly/Mary, W3269
Elijah, N.H., S13796

LOCKE (continued)
Frederic/Frederick, Mass., Lucy, W5025; BLWt.6278-160-55
James, N.C., See LOCK
John, Mass., S22367
Joseph, Mass., S5705
Joseph, Va., S38150
Josiah, Mass., N.H., Bethis Gale, former wid., W23080
Sarah, former wid. of John Wallace, S.C., which see
Simon, N.H., Mary, W21583; BLWt. 6270-160-55
Simon, N.H., Lydia, W24581
Susan, former wid. of David Campbell, Vt., which see
William, Va., S8857
LOCKERMAN, Jacob, N.C., S8854
LOCKERT, John, Pa., S40096
LOCKET, Benjamin, Va., BLWt. 12311-100-Pvt. Iss. 2/10/1796 to Anthony New, ass. No papers
LOCKETT, Benjamin, Cont., Va., S41780
Edmund/Edmond, Va., Sally, W8064
James, N.C., Va., S9374
Royall, Va., S6799
LOCKHART, John, Sr., N.C., S8850
John, S.C., Prudence, W384
John, Va., BLWt.12306-100-Pvt. Iss. 11/5/1789. No papers
Tabitha, former wid. of John Armstrong, Pa., which see
William, Va., BLWt.12310-100-Pvt. Iss. 5/29/1792 to Walter Stewart, ass. No papers
LOCKHEART, James, Va., S38151
William, Pa., R6400
LOCKLING, Jonathan, Cont., Vt., R6401
LOCKMAN, John, Pa., Catharine, W11513
Matthias, Pa., S40949
Vincent, ---, Christena, R15900 Wid. res., Ind. in 1860
LOCKRIDGE, James, S.C. See LOCHRIDGE
John, Va. See LOCHRIDGE
LOCKS, Moses, N.H. See LOCK
LOCKWOOD, Betsey, dau., Ct. See Joseph MATHER
Charles, Ct., Betsey/Elizabeth, W26225
David, Ct., S16453
David, Ct., S37642
David, Ct., Hannah, W20491
David, Cont., Ct., Sarah, W26223
David, Navy, N.Y., Rebecca, W5030
David, N.Y., S11001
Drake, Ct., S17548
Ebenezer, Ct., Ann, W8262; BLWt. 34926-160-55
Enos, Ct., Sarah, W20499
George, Ct., R6403
Gideon, Ct., Lydia, R21786
Gilbert/Guilbert, N.Y., S23305
Henry, Ct., S23302
Isaac, Ct., S17553
Isaac, Ct., Anor, W20500
Isaac, N.Y., S42891
Israel, Ct., N.Y., S13777

LOCKWOOD (continued)
James, Ct., S17554
James, Ct., Anna, R6402
Jared, Ct., Cont., Betsey/ Elizabeth, W16639
Jesse, N.Y., R6404
Job, N.Y., Irena, W20531
John, Ct., Eunice Jeliff/ Jolliff, former wid., W26166. Her last husb. was a pensioner; see James Jelliff
John, N.Y., S42876
Joseph, Vt., Lydia, W24570; BLWt.3070-160-55
Lambert, Ct., Elizabeth, W20514
Messenger, Ct., Sarah, W8062
Nathan, Ct., Mary, W776; BLWt. 26141-160-55. He d. 9/26/1841
Nathan, N.Y., Rhoda, W20524. He d. 1/12/1840
Noah, Ct., S13778
Reuben, Ct., Mary, W21586
Reuben, Ct., R6405
Samuel, Del., S13789
Samuel, N.Y., Betty Marshall, former wid., W17105
Timothy, Navy, N.Y., Esther Miller, former wid., R7186. She m. 1st, Jeremiah Mead; m. 2nd, Timothy Lockwood; m. 3rd, Levi Miller
Timothy, N.H., Mary, W21585; BLWt.2178-100
William, Ct., Jemima, W20521
William, Mass., S37635
LOCUS, Valentine, N.C., Rachael, W20497
LODDER, William, N.Y., BLWt.7381-100-Pvt. Iss. 4/6/1791 to Theodosius Fowler & Co., ass. No papers
LODEN, James, Va., Susan, R6406
William, Va., BLWt.12317-100-Pvt. Iss. 5/29/1792 to Francis Graves, ass. No papers
LODER, Daniel, N.J., S32884
Daniel, N.Y., BLWt.7388-100-Pvt. Iss. 8/26/1790. No papers
Jacob, Ct., S31825
John, N.Y., S22881
Zenos, N.J., Barbara, W3837
LODGE, Benjamin, Pa., BLWt.1276-200-Lt.
Lewis, N.C., Martha, R6407
LODOWICK, Thomas, N.Y., S11538
LOER, Henry, Md. See LOAR
LOFFMAN, Benjamin, Md., BLWt. 11456-100-Pvt. Iss. 1/8/1796 to George Ponsonby, ass. No papers
LOFTIN, Ezekel, N.C., 1771-1775, R6408
LOFTIS, Solomon, N.C., Margaret, R6409
LOFTON, Thomas, N.C., S.C., S17114
LOFTY, William, Va., S4571
LOGAN, Alexander, Pa., Elizabeth/ Eliza, W2821
Alexander, Va., S8845
Andrew, S.C., b. N.C., S9375; BLWt.38528-160-55
David, Pa., Elizabeth, W2952

LOGAN (continued)
Drury, N.C. See LOGIN
James, N.J., S13794
James, N.J., S31216
James, Not Rev. War service, 1792. Res. at enl. Pa., R6410
John, N.J., Christiana/Christena, W1788; BLWt.26894-160-55
John, Pa., S8855
John, Pa., S47821
John, Va. See LOGGINS
Joseph, N.C. See LOGIN
Patrick, Va., enl. in Fayette Co., Pa., S41778
Philip, N.C., S38155
Samuel, N.Y., S42884; BLWt.1261-400-Major. Iss. 9/7/1790
Samuel, Pa., S4570
Timothy, Va., Sarah, W3700. Kentucky res.
William, N.J., BLWt.8480-100-Pvt. Iss. 9/21/1789. No papers
William, N.C., S.C., S18955
William, S.C., S32385
William, Va., S31219
LOGEE, Caleb, R.I., Rachel, W13650
Moses, N.H., BLWt.2099-100
LOGEN, David, Pa. See LOGAN
LOGGINS, John, Va., R6414
LOGHRY, Michael, Pa., Nancy, W20530
LOGIN, Drury, N.C., Sarah, W5464
Joseph, N.C., Va., R6413
LOGSDON, Edward, Md., S8320
James V., Va., also 1784-1790 Indian Wars, S30547
LOGUE, Adam, Pa., R6415
Richard, Md., R6416
Thomas, Pa., R6417
William, Md. Sea Service, W1441; BLWt.26057-160-55
LOGWOOD, Peggy, former wid. of Thomas Crump, Va., which see
LOHNAR, John, S.C. See LOHNER
LOHNER, John, S.C., S21869
LOHNES, Adam, N.Y., Elizabeth, W24585; BLWt.26065-160-55
LOHR, Baltzer, Pa., Elizabeth, W9137
Joseph, Pa., S8849
Peter, Md., S5699
LOKEY, William, Md. Sea Service, R6418
LOKNER, Henry, Cont. (daughter's res. Pa. in 1829),BLWt.1531-100
LOLLAR, Daniel, Mass., Dis. No papers
LOLLER, Michael, Md., BLWt.11439-100-Pvt. Iss. 12/23/1795 to George Ponsonby, ass. No papers
LOMACK, William, N.C., S41783
LOMAGNE, John Baptiste de, Cont. France, BLWt.1003-400
LOMAS, Jacob, N.Y., BLWt.7385-100-Pvt. Iss. 9/8/1790. No papers
LOMAX, John, Md., S34966
William, N.C., Tabitha, W5028; BLWt.34833-160-55
LOMBARD, Butler, Mass., S37636
Caleb, Mass. See LUMBARD
Jedediah, Mass. & War of 1812, S18095

LOMBARD (continued)
John, Mass., S15598
John, Mass., S29970
Jonathan, Mass., Azenath/Asenath, W15041
Justin, Ct., Elizabeth, W2556; BLWt.26002-160-55
Nathaniel, Cont., Mass. See LUMBORD
Solomon, Ct., S13769
Stephen, Mass., S13783
Thomas, Mass., Hannah, W24586; BLWt.17861-160-55. He d. 1/1/1837
Thomas, Mass., Hannah, W24589. He d. 12/29/1834
LOMEREAUX, Peter, N.Y., R6284
LOMIS, Jacob, N.Y. See LOOMIS
Samuel, Ct., BLWt.6081-100-Pvt. Iss. 10/31/1791. No papers
LOMORAUX, Peter, See LOMEREAUX
LONAS, George, Va., S8848
LONASS, John, Cont., Md., Mary Fardin/Farden, former wid., W19252
LONDON, Charles, Ct., BLWt.6095-100-Pvt. Iss. 8/23/1790. (A BLWt. with this same no. was iss. for service of Samuel Hall of Ct. Line, also, on 3/16/1792, to Lee Hall, Execr.
Eliel, Ct., BLWt.6122-100-Pvt. Iss. 9/9/1790 to James F. Sebor
LONG, Adam, N.Y., R6421
Alexander, Pa., S22365
Anderson, N.C., Va., S17549
Andrew, Pa., Susan, W3147
Andrew, Pa., Jemima, W8063; BLWt.40504-160-55
Benjamin, N.C., S8851
Benjamin, Pa., S40101
Benjamin, Va., S8846
Benjamin, Va., S32383
Daniel, Va., S13773
David, Mass., S23304
David, N.C., S.C., Mary, W2
Elial, Pa., S22884
Enoch, Mass., N.H., Molly, W16138
Gasper, N.C., S7161
George, Navy, N.H., Sea Service, S18087
George, N.J., BLWt.8482-100-Pvt. Iss. 2/14/1791 to Alexander Power, ass. No papers
George, Pa., Isabel, W9139; BLWt. 26619-160-55
George, Va., S4564
Gideon, Pa., Hannah, W3270
Henry, N.C., R6427
Henry, Va., S1849
Jacob, Pa., Mary, W3434; BLWt. 26186-160-55
Jacob, Pa., Va., Eve, W1790; BLWt.26907-160-55
James, N.C., Sea Service, R6428
James, S.C., Margery, W9509
Job, Mass., BLWt.4563-100-Pvt. Iss. 8/7/1789 to Peter Anspach. No papers.
John, Cont., Va., Mary, W5029

LONG (continued)
John, Md., BLWt.11445-100-Pvt. Iss. 7/17/1797 to Abrm. Jarritt, ass. No papers
John, Md., Nancy, W9508
John, Mass., Esther, W3569
John, N.C., Frances, R6426
John, N.C., R6429
John, Va., S25233
John, Va., S36047
John, Va., Amey, W3433
John, Va., Delilah, W10200
John Phillip, Pa., S38147
Jonathan, Md., Pa., Nancy, W383
Joseph, BLWt.13380-100-Pvt. "in the Invalid Corps." Iss. 11/8/1791 to Judith Long, Admx. No papers
Joseph, Md., Elizabeth, W10201
Joseph, Mass., S18091
Joseph, Mass., Phebe, W15033; BLWt.4583-100. Iss. 8/26/1790. BLWt.219-60-55
Joseph, Pa., Christina, W2137
Josiah, Mass., Mary Smith, former wid., R9801
Levi, Ct., Martha, W2138; BLWt. 1965-160-55
Levi, Cont., Va. res. in 1819, BLWt.924-100
Margaret, former wid. of John Carr, Md., which see
Mathias, Va., Mary, R6430
Matthew, Pa., S7160
Moses, Mass., S23773
Nathaniel, Cont., Mass., Elizabeth, W20515
Nicholas, Va., S31222
Nicholas, Va., Margaret, W953
Paul, N.H., S44516
Peter, Pa., Christina, R6422; BLWt.36746-160-55
Reuben, N.C., S.C., R6431
Reuben, Va., S46457; BLWt. 480-200
Richard, N.J., BLWt.8417-100-Pvt. Iss. 8/27/1792 to Ebenezer Hogg, ass. No papers
Richard, Va., S4565
Robert, Ct., BLWt.6102-100-Pvt. Iss. 11/15/1792. No papers
Robert, Mass., S13775
Robert, S.C., b. Ireland, S7157
Robert, ---, N.Y. agcy. Dis. No papers here
Samuel Glode/Samuel GLODE/ Samuel LONGUN, Mass., Abigail, R6420
Stephen, Ct., S22370
Stephen, Cont., Mass., S33011
Stephen, Mass., Nancy, W15036
Ware, Va., Elizabeth, R6425
William, Ct. Sea Service, Mass., S29967; BLWt.26296-160-55
William, N.C., S18953; BLWt. 1734-100; BLWt.191-60-55
William, Pa., S22882
William, Va., S18088
LONGBY, James, Cont., Mass., See LONGLEY
Nathaniel, Mass., See LONGLEY

LONGCOR, William, N.J., S13786
LONGDON, John, Cont., Va., BLWt. 423-100
LONGEDYCK, Cornelius, N.Y., S13767
LONGEST, John, Va., R6433
Richard, Va., S38149
LONGFELLOW, Samuel, Cont., N.H., Mary, W24590
William, Cont., Mass., Privateer, Sarah, W16638
LONGHAL, Jacob, N.J., BLWt.8487-100-Pvt. Iss. 6/11/1789 to Jonathan Dayton, ass. No papers
LONGLEY, Asa, Mass., S28795
Benjamin, Mass., Mary, W24486
Edmund, Mass., S30551
Eli, Mass., Mary, W24480
Ezekiel, Mass., S22371
James, Cont., Mass., S19728
Jonathan, Mass., S37637
Joseph, Mass., S33004
Nathaniel, Mass., S11007
Rhoda, former wid. of Nathan Taylor, N.H., which see
William, Va., Mary, R6435
Zachariah, Mass., S37640
LONGSTREET, Aaron, N.J., R6431 1/2
Elias, N.J., Rebecca White, former wid., W2504; BLWt.1228-300-Capt. Iss. 1/4/1793 to Rebecca Longstreet & Hendrick Voorhees, Admrs. Also recorded as above under BLWt.2633
LONGSTRETH, John, Pa., Indian War 1794-5, S23778
Martin, Pa., Jane, W12153; BLWt. 79034-160-55
Philip, Cont., Md. & Pa., also served in 1764 & 1774, Salome, W12144
LONGUN, Samuel,Mass. See Samuel Glode LONG
LONGWELL, Stephen, Ct., Jane, W4268
William, Md., Pa., Rachel, R6436
LONGWORTH, William, Va., R6437
LONGWORTHY, Joseph, R.I., Lois, W20523
Southcoot, ---, R.I. Agcy. Dis. No papers here
LONGYEAR, William, N.Y., Bridget, W20508
LONLEY, Jonathan, Mass. See LONGLEY
LONSTRETH, John, Pa. See LONGSTRETH
LOOFBORROW, Isaac, N.Y., S42893
LOOFBOURROW, David, N.J., S23776
LOOK, Cheney/Cheeney, Mass., Navy, S13779
Elijah, Mass., S11003
James, Mass., S22883
John, Mass., Jane, W20534
Jonathan, Mass., S10997
LOOKEBEE, David, N.C., Charity, R6439
LOOKER, Eleazer, N.J., S891
John, N.J. See Johnson LOOKER
Johnson/John, N.J., Elizabeth, W1791
Nathaniel, N.J., Hannah, W954
Othniel, N.J., S32386
LOOKINBEE, David, N.C. See LOOKEBEE
LOOMIS, Abner, Ct., Zilpha, W1363

LOOMIS (continued)
Amasa, Cont., Ct. W24595
Andrew, Green Mt. Boys, Mass., S13771
Asa, Ct., S4568
Benaiah, Mass., S11005
Benjamin, Ct., R6441
Benjamin, Cont., Ct., Chloe, W20511
Brigadier, Sheldon's Dragoons, Ct., BLWt.6134-100-Pvt. Iss. 10/7/1789 to Benj. Tallmadge. No papers
Dan, Ct., Sarah, W20520
Daniel, Ct., R6442
Dick, Ct., BLWt.6088-100-Pvt. Iss. 3/22/1798. No papers
Dyre, See LAMMAS
Eleazer, Ct., Mary, W15035
Elijah, Ct., Rachel, W26221
Epaphras, Ct., S13791
Ezra, Ct., S23772
Ezra, Mass., S15192
Gamaliel, Ct., R6444
George, Ct., Deborah, W3701; BLWt.26830-160-55
Hannah, former wid. of Charles Webster, Ct., which see
Hezekiah, Ct., Else, W15042
Isaiah, Ct., Sarah, W8054; BLWt.33745-160-55
Israel, Ct., S23777
Israel, Cont., enl. in Mass., Hannah, W9141; BLWt.4615-100-Sgt. Date of issuance not recorded. No papers
Jacob, Ct., S46203
Jacob, Ct., Thankful, W15037
Jacob, Mass., Union Whitney former wid., W25982
Jacob, N.Y., S42889
Jerome, Ct., N.H., Vt., Elizabeth, W1627; BLWt.17727-160-55
Jesse, Mass., Lydia, W15038
John, Ct., Mary, W775; BLWt. 26892-160-55
John, Ct., Mass., S23774
Joseph, Cont., Ct., S18947; BLWt.6131-100-1790. No papers. BLWt.76-60-55
Lebbeus/Libbeus, Ct., Cont., S28796; BLWt.1256-200-Lt. Iss. 4/20/1790. No papers
Martin, Ct., R6446
Oliver, Ct., S13770
Oliver, Ct., Cont., S13781
Roger, R.I., S37186
Roswell, Ct., S23775
Samuel, Ct., Betsey, W20527
Samuel, N.Y., S13780
Samuel, R.I., S42894
Simon, Ct., Molly, W20518
Simon, Ct., Cont., S17550
Simon, Cont., Ct., Martha, W15925
Thaddeus, Ct., R6447
Thomas, Ct., Cont., S17551
Uriah, Mass., R6449
LOOMISS, Amasa, Cont., Ct., Ruth, W24595
LOONEY, John, S.C., S1553
LOORDON, George, Navy, Pa., Privateer, S13792

LOPE, John, Mass., BLWt.4564-100-Pvt. Iss. 5/9/1797 to Simeon Wyman. No papers
LOPER, Abraham, N.J., S40097
LOPES, Isaac, N.J., S42892
LOPEZ, Isaac. See LOPES
LORAH, Jacob, Pa., S4574
LORAIN, John, Pa., S40098
LORANCE, Jacob, See LOWRANCE
Michael, N.C., Esther, W382
William, N.C., S31217
LORD, Aaron, Mass., S5703
Abner, Ct., BLWt.6124-100-Pvt. Iss. 2/5/1790. No papers
Abner, Ct., S37645
Amey, former wid. of Edward Mead, Ct., which see
Andrew, Md., S34965
Asa, Ct., S29298; BLWt.26412-160-55
Asa, Mass., S18956
Benjamin, Mass., S45885
Daniel, Ct., Anna, W26222: BLWt.537-160-55
Daniel, Cont., Mass., Hannah, W24573
Daniel, Mass., S44514
Daniel, Mass., Mary, W24582
Daniel, N.H., S37639
David, Ct., Hannah, R6452
David, Mass., S33012
Dominicus, Mass., Mary, W1789; BLWt.3644-160-55
Elias, Mass., Navy, Elizabeth, W21582
Elijah, Ct., BLWt.6121-100-Pvt. Iss. 2/5/1790. No papers
Elijah, Ct., S37188
Eliphalet, Ct., Cont., S42890
Eliphalet, Cont., N.H., Abigail, W24574
Elisha, Mass., S37638
Frederick, Ct., S15599
George, ---, Ct. res., Dis. No papers here, but see Am. State Papers, Class 9, Claims, pp.66 & 115. This George Lord is listed as a Pvt. in Capt. Wright's Co., a res. of East Windsor, Ct., who was wounded at Greenwich in the back of his neck and small of his back, not found in the rosters of Ct. Line.
Henry, Md., Amelia, W9138; BLWt. 3979-160-55
Ichabod, Mass., S29968
Ichabod, Mass., Lydia, W24587
Ichabod, N.J., S5701
Jabez, Ct., BLWt.6118-100-Pvt. Iss. 8/23/1790. No papers
James, Ct., BLWt.1257-200-Lt. Iss. 4/23/1800 to Damaris Lester & others. No papers.
James, Cont., Mass., S37641
James, Mass., S19379
Jeremiah, Ct., S37644
Jeremiah, Ct., Tryphena, W20513
Jeremiah, "the Invalids," BLWt. 13385-100-Sgt. Iss. 11/18/1789. No papers
Jeremiah, Mass., BLWt.1239-150-Ensign. Iss. 4/19/1792 to John

LORD (continued)
Peck, ass. No papers
John, Ct., S15510
John, Mass., Charity, W24588
Jonathan, N.Y., S42897
Joseph, Ct., S18094
Joseph, Ct., Caroline, W20517; BLWt.17872-160-55
Joseph, Mass., Lucy, W24577
Joseph, N.H., Olive, W24569
Levin, Md., BLWt.11438-100-Pvt. Iss. 7/9/1799. No papers
Mercy, former wid. of Jonathan Whaley, Ct., which see
Nathan, Mass., S17547
Philip, Mass., Elizabeth, W20510
Richard, Mass., S29301
Robert, Mass., S29971
Robinson, Va., Nancy, W5326
Roger, Mass., BLWt.4606-100-Pvt. Iss. 3/17/1795 to Evander Childs. No papers.
Samuel, Ct., Mary, W24572; BLWt. 15198-160-55
Samuel, Cont., Mass., Ruth Crocket/Crockett, former wid., W22866; BLWt.17594-160-55
Samuel, Cont., Mass., Tryphena, W24568
Samuel, Mass., N.H., Mary, W26224; BLWt.19609-160-55
Simeon, Cont., Mass., Polly, W20526; BLWt.894-300
Simon, Mass., Elizabeth, W24591
Theophilus, Ct., S37187
Thomas, N.H., S8853
Timothy, Ct., N.Y., S42898
Wentworth, Mass., S37192
William, Ct., Chloe, W20501; BLWt.1255-200-Lt. Iss. 1/29/1793 to Jonas Prentice, ass. No papers
William, Ct., Anna, W20509
William, Mass., S22369
William, Mass., BLWt.866-100
LORDEN, George, Pa., BLWt.9815-100-Pvt. Iss. 1/20/1789. No papers. See George Loordon, Pa.
LORE, Joseph, Pa. See LOHR
Michael, Md., S5708
LOREE, Ephraim, N.J., BLWt. 1248-300-Surgeon's Mate. Iss. 3/25/1797. Also recorded as above under BLWt.2681. No papers
Job, N.J., S2657
LORENTZ, Ferdinand, Md., Elizabeth, W9140
Joseph, Pa., S40948
Wendel, Md. See LAWRENTZ
LORGAIN, Francis, S.C., BLWt. 12336. Not a file. No papers
LORING, Benjamin, N.Y., BLWt. 7426-100-Pvt. Iss. 9/28/1790 to Bartholomew & Fisher, assnes. No papers
Benjamin, Cont., N.Y., S9930
Daniel, Mass., S33013
David, Mass., S18950
Ephraim, N.J. See LOREE
Jacob, Mass., Lydia, W20506

LORING (continued)
John, Mass., Mary, W20516
Jonathan, Mass., S15511
Joseph, Cont., Ct. res., Dis. No papers here, but see pp.63 & 111 of Am. State Papers, Class 9, Claims, which shows him as a Lt. in Col. Knox's Art., Mass., who was disabled in Dec. 1775, his res. in 1782 at Boston, dis. consisted of a very diseased arm, occasioned by the smallpox, which he had while a prisoner at N.Y.
Joseph, Mass., Ann, W13642
Joseph, Navy, res. Mass., S33002
Joshua, Mass., Hannah, W21588
Nathaniel, Mass., S29969
Richard, Mass., S33003
Samuel, R.I., S10995
Simeon, Mass., Rebecca, W13646
Solomon, Mass., S11004; BLWt. 19827-160-55
LORION, Ferman/Forman, Cont., N.Y. agcy. & res., S46006; BLWt.1581-100
LORTON, Robert, Va., Tabitha, R6454
LOSE, George, Pa., S22368
LOSEE, Abraham, N.J., S33014
John, N.Y., S13772
LOSELTON, Ferman, Cont. See LORION
LOSEY, Abraham, Cont., N.Y., Sena, W9142; BLWts.1186-100 & 273-60-55
Jesse, N.J., BLWt.8500-100-Pvt. Iss. 6/16/1789 to Thomas Coyle, ass. No papers
Jesse, N.J., Zilpha/Zilpah, W1787
Moses, N.J., S16257
William, N.J., S16454
LOSHE, Andrew, Pa., R6198. Name also appears as Andrew Laugh, Johannes Andrus Laugh, George Lough, John Lough & George Loyh
LOSHIER, Peter, Lee's Legion, BLWt.13394-100-Pvt. Iss. 4/10/1790. No papers
LOSLEY, James, N.Y., R6457
LOT, Jeremiah, Pa., BLWt.9834-100-Trumpeter. Iss. 4/24/1799. No papers
Levi, Lee's Legion, BLWt.13393-100-Pvt. Iss. 5/15/1792 to Eleanor Johnson, Admx. No papers
LOTHROP, Barnabas, Cont., Mass., Rachel, W10203; BLWt.51887-160-55
Daniel, Mass., S15926
George, Mass., S29962
Jacob, Mass., S31221
John, Mass., S5702
John, Mass., Lydia Reed, former wid., W5672; BLWt.13184-160-55
Joseph, Mass. See LATHROP
Josiah, N.Y. See LATHROP
Nathan, Mass., Phebe, W20419; BLWt.43505-160-55

LOTHROP (continued)
Samuel, Ct., BLWt.6080-100-Pvt. Iss. 12/14/1793. No papers
LOTT, Jacob, N.J., S5709
Jeremiah, Cont., Pa., S33380
John, N.J., S4566
John, N.J., S11006
John, Va., S18089
Nicholas, Pa., Anna Maria, W3148
Philip Jacob, Pa., S40947
Zephaniah, Pa., Else, R6458
LOTZ, Henry, S.C. Sea Service, S40950
LOUCKS, Adam A., N.Y., Magdalena, W16637
Andrew/Antreas, N.Y., R6459
Dietrich, N.Y. See Richard
George, N.Y., S13793
Henry, N.Y., S45899
Jeremiah, N.Y., Magdalene, W20512
Peter H., N.Y., S11008
Richard/Dietrich, N.Y., R6461
William, Pa., Margaret, R6462
LOUD, Benjamin, Cont., N.H., S37196
David, Mass., S5711; BLWt.13214-160-55
Eliphalet, Mass., Anna, W20505
Silvenos/Silvanus, Mass., S30550
William, Mass., Sarah C., W12143; BLWt.40007-160-55
LOUDABACK/LOWDEBACK, John Heinrich, N.Y., S42896
LOUDEN, Stephen, Pa., BLWt.9826-100-Sgt. Iss. 2/14/1791 to Alexander Power, ass. No papers
LOUDERBACK, John, Armand's Corps. BLWt.13317-100-Pvt. Iss. 7/20/1792 to Abraham Sheridan, ass. of John Gish, Admr. No papers
LOUDON, Archibald, Pa., S4573
John, N.Y., S22880
William, Ct., Eunice, W4270
LOUES, George M., N.Y. See LOUIS
LOUGEE, John, N.H., Molly, W21589; BLWt.31289-160-55; BLWt.35834-160-55
Jonathan, Mass., S40953
Moses, N.H. See LOGEE
LOUGH, George, Pa. See Andrew LOSHE
John, Pa. See Andrew LOSHE
LOUGHMAN, James, Armand's Corps, BLWt.13318-100-Pvt. Iss. 12/28/1791 to Wm. Lane, ass. No papers
LOUGHREY, William, Pa. See LAUGHREY
Isaac, N.Y. See Isaac LOOFBORROW
LOUGHRY, William, N.C., Susan, W8263; BLWt.14674-160-55
LOUIS, George M., N.Y., Christina, W20522
LOUMPKIN, Dickeson, Pa., Va. See LUMPKIN
LOUNDSBURY, David, Ct., BLWt.6112-100-Pvt. Iss. 11/2/1791 to Titus Street. No papers
Linus, Ct., Prudence, W20492
LOUNSBERRY, Nathan Munn, Ct., Cont., Sarah W., W10204; BLWt. 510-160-55
Samuel, N.J. See LOWNSBURY
Walter, N.J., BLWt.8484-100-Pvt.

LOUNSBERRY (continued)
Iss. 3/17/1791. No papers
LOUNSBERY, Stephen, N.Y., W20533
LOUNSBURY, Epenetus, N.Y., S11002
Jacob, Ct., R6464
Jarius/Jarias, Ct., Amelia, W20495
Linus, Ct. See LOUNDSBURY
Walker, N.J. See LOWNSBURY
LOUREY, Simeon, S.C. See LOWREY
LOURY, Daniel, Pa., S36686
Susan, former wid. of Gibson Cluverius, Va., which see
LOUTS, Jacob, Va., S4567
LOUW, John I., N.Y. See LOW
LOUX, Hendrick, N.Y., BLWt.7418-100-Pvt. Iss. 9/6/1791. No papers
LOVE, Charles, Md., BLWt.11435-100-Pvt. Iss. 4/18/1797 to James DeBaufre, ass.
Charles, N.C., R6466
Charles, Va., enl. in Phila., S36046
David, Md., BLWt.11440-100-Pvt. Iss. 5/4/1797 to James DeBaufre, ass. No papers
David, Md., S18948
Davis, N.Y., BLWt.7417-100-Pvt. Iss. 11/1/1791. No papers
Edmond, N.C., S4563
Elias, Va., S18092
Henry, ---, Phila. agcy., S9680; d.1809
Henry, Va., S8856
Hezekiah, S.C., Nancy, W12148
James, Va., S21350
John, Ga., Louisa, R21476
John, (deceased), Md., BLWt. 11458-100-Pvt. Iss. 7/18/1794 to Henry Purdy, Admr. No papers
John, N.C., b. Va., S8852
John, Pa., S30548
John, Pa., R6467
John, R.I., R6468
Mark, S.C., S36045
Robert, Mass., Dolly, W234
Robert, N.C., S18093
Robert, Va., S8858
Samuel, N.C., S.C., b. S.C., S9376
Thomas, N.C., S36048
Thomas, Va., b. Ireland, Rosanna W8055
William, Mass., S42877; BLWt.1550-100
William, N.J., Dis. No papers here but see pp. 103 & 172, Am. State Papers, Class 9, Claims. Shows Wm. Love, Q.M. Sgt., 3rd Jersey Regt., rec'd a rupture at the battle of Monmouth, while in the actual line of his duty, enl. 3/22/1777; dis. 6/3/1779. Res. Phila.
William, S.C., Rachel, W956
William, S.C., BLWt.1245-200-Lt Iss. 6/21/1794. Also recorded as above under BLWt.2644. No papers
William, Va., BLWt.12312-100-Pvt. Iss. 5/29/1792 to Francis Graves, ass. No papers
William, Va., Winford, R6469

LOVEGROVE, Hampton, Cont., Vt. res. in 1835, R6470
LOVEJOY, Abner, Mass., BLWt. 4601-100-Pvt. Iss. 10/7/1789 to Benj. Tallmadge. No papers
Abner, Mass., S42899
Andrew, N.Y., S13790
Asa, Mass., S13768
Asa, N.H., Lydia, W16139
Daniel, N.H., Vt., Lorenze, W24576
Francis, N.H., BLWt.976-100
Henry, N.H., S10996
Isaac, R.I., S33009
Jacob, N.H., Elizabeth, R6473
Jesse, Navy, Mass., Sarah, W15045
John, Ct., Anna, R6471
John, Vt., Asnath Goodell, former wid., W24291
Joshua, N.H., R6474
Mary, former wid. of Abraham VanDoren, N,J., which see
Nathan, Ct., N.Y., S42885
Obadiah, Lt., Mass., S18952; BLWt.1231-200 iss. 10/7/1789 to Abner Lovejoy, ass.
Samuel, Cont., Mass., Elizabeth, W24565
Samuel, Mass., Esther, R6472
LOVEL, Nehemiah, Vt. See LOVEWELL
William, N.C., R6476
LOVELACE, Elias, N.C., Anne, W9143
Gershom, N.J., S18954
Philip, Va., Ann, W12145; BLWt.26541-160-55
Vachel, N.C., Margaret, W9144
LOVELADY, Thomas, N.C., S.C., Va., Nancy, W8065
LOVELAND, Abner, Ct., Privateer, S45876
Amos, Ct., Jemima, W8090
Charles, Ct., Mary, W9146; BLWt. 11941-100 & 294-60-55
Daniel, Ct., BLWt.6085-100-Pvt. Iss. 11/24/1791 to Isaac Bronson
Daniel, Ct., Mehitabel, W20528
Frederick, Mass., S41781
George, Mass., Thankful Fanny, W20504
Isaac, Ct., Judah, W8059
James, Ct., Mary, W20496
John, Ct., S13776
Levi, Ct., Esther, W9145
Nathan, Ct., S42887
Thomas "the Invalids," BLWt.13387-100-Pvt. Iss. 4/14/1790 to Wm. Wells, ass. No papers
Trueman, Navy, Ct. res & agcy., S37189
LOVELESS, David, Mass., S40102; BLWt.77510-160-55
George, Va., S4575
Joshua, Mass., S42895
Philip, Va. See LOVELACE
LOVELIFF, Lot, N.J., BLWt.8506-100-Pvt. Iss. 11/16/1791 to Adam Nutt, ass. No papers
LOVELL, Caleb, Mass., Ruth, W15044
David, Mass., S31824
Ezra, Mass., Mary, W13643
James, Cont., Mass., S18949; BLWt.

LOVELL (continued)
1308-200-Lt. Iss. 5/18/1795. No papers.
Jonathan, Mass., Hannah, W16330
Joshua, Ct., R6477
Joshua, Cont., Mass., S10998
Josiah, Mass., S37191
Nathan, Mass., Anna Ingalls, former wid., W26151
Robert, Navy, Vt. See LOVEWELL
Samuel, Mass., Olive, W13639
Sarah, former wid. of William Chanley, Va., which see
LOVELY, John, Sappers & Miners, BLWt.13327-100-Sgt. Iss. 6/29/1789 to Matt. McConnell, ass. No papers
William L., Va., BLWt.1302-300-Capt. Iss. 6/17/1790 to David Jones, ass. No papers
LOVEN, Isaac, N.C., R6478
James, Va., S4572
LOVERIDGE, William, Ct., Lucinda, R6479; BLWt.38841-160-55
LOVERIN, Samuel, N.H. See LOVRIEN
Simeon, N.H., S21868
LOVERING, Benjamin, Mass., N.H., Patience, W21587
Ebenezer, N.H., S18084
Isaac, Mass., S33015; BLWt.793-100. Dorcas Lovering, wid. of above sold., rec'd pension as the former wid. of Jacob Lufkin, Mass. which see. Her husb., David Forbush, Mass. also pensioned.
Jesse, Mass., S23303
John, N.H., S18085
Nathaniel, N.H., Jerusla, W24593; BLWt.11416-160-55
Richard, N.H., Anna, W15039
Samuel, Mass., BLWt.4566-100-Pvt. Iss. 1/7/1796 to Calvin Sanger. No papers
Samuel, Mass., S40952
Theophilus, N.H., BLWt.3285-100-Pvt. Iss. 7/21/1789 to Ladd & Cass, assnes. No papers
Theophilus, N.H., S10999
Thomas, N.H., S18086
LOVERN, Christopher, Va., S38148
Richard, Va., Frances, W8089
LOVETT, Ebenezer, Mass., S33006
John, N.H., S37643
John, N.Y., BLWt.7379-100-Pvt. Iss. 9/15/1790 to John S. Hobart et al, assnes. No papers
John, N.C., R20398
Joseph, Ct. See Josephus
Joseph, Va., Sarah, W26804
Josephus/Joseph, Ct., Elizabeth, W21584
Moses, Mass., S33007
Samuel, Ct., S40099
LOVEWELL, Nehemiah, Vt., Betsey, W24566
Robert, Navy, Vt., War of 1812, Polly, W15689; BLWt.30758-160-55
Zacheus, Vt., R6482
LOVILL, Robert. See LOVEWELL
LOVILLION, Firmin, Hazen's Regt., BLWt.13356-100-Pvt. Iss. 8/14/

LOVILLION (continued)
1792 to Benj. Moore, ass. No papers
LOVING, Christopher, S.C., S38153
Richard, Va., Mary, W8033
LOVINS, Isaac, N.C., See LOVEN
LOVIS, John, Mass. Sea Service, S44515
LOVJOY, Daniel, N.H., Vt. See LOVEJOY
LOVLESS, David, Mass. See LOVELESS
LOVRIEN, Samuel, N.H., S44517
LOVRING, Nathaniel. See LOVERING
LOW, Aaron, Mass., S29300
Abraham, N.J., S28797
Abraham, N.Y., S13784
Alexander, N.J., S1052
Asa, Mass., S44521
Bazel, See Basil LOWE
Bezaleel, Cont., Mass., S37185
Christiana, former wid. of Cornelius Jansen, N.Y., which see
Cornelius D., N.J., S1053
Cornelius P., N.Y., Pa., Johanna, W24580
David, Mass., Hannah Eaton, former wid., W21036
Dennis, Cont., Md. See LOWE
Henry, Md., Eleanor/Ellen, W8259; BLWt.8454-160-55
Hooker, Cont., Mass., Theodosia Howley, W8900
Jacob, Cont., Mass., S44520
Jacob, Cont., Mass., Mary, W24584
Jacob G., N.Y., Catharine, W20532
John, Cont., Mass., S37184
John, Mass., S33008
John, Mass., Elizabeth, W15034
John, N.Y., R6485
John, N.C., S38916
John, Privateer, Mass., S20048
John I., N.Y., Jane, W20507
Jonathan, Sgt. Artillery Artificers, BLWt.13375 iss. 1/28/179- to Joseph May, ass.
Jonathan, Cont., Mass., S37183
Jonathan, Mass., Remember/Remembrance, W9135
Lawrence, Pvt., Mass., BLWt. 4607 iss. 3/25/1790
Lott, S.C., R6486
Mary, N.J. See Abraham VAN DOREN
Obadiah, Mass., Abigail, R6483
Peter, N.Y. See LOWN
Philip, Ga. See LOWE
Phineas, Mass., S37195
Ralph, N.C., R6487
Robert, Mass., S29299
Samuel, Mass., Abigail, W24594
Samuel, Mass., Art., War of 1812 Lydia, W16334; BLWt.15475-160-12
Simon, Cont., N.H., S11000
Stephen, Va. See LOWE
Thomas, Mass., S40946
Thomas, Navy, R.I., Molly, W13645
Wilson, Mass., S42880
LOWDEBACK, John. See LOUDABACK
LOWDEN, William, Ct. See LOUDEN
William, N.J., W12149

LOWDEN (continued)
William, Drum Major, N.Y., BLWt. 7400 iss. 8/3/1790 to Cornelius V. Dyck, ass.
LOWE, Abraham, Mass., Charlotte, W13638
Abraham D., N.Y., S13782
Basil/Bazel, Cont., Md., Trecy, W9136; BLWt.2252
Betsey, former wid. of Wm. Dexter, Mass., which see
Daniel, Mass., Tlice, W16635
Dennis, Cont., Md., S38917; BLWt. 2253
Gilbert D., N.J., S5710
Henry, Md. See LOW
James, Pvt., Del., BLWt.10817 iss. 5/1/1797 to James DeBaufre, ass.
John, Md., S8859
John Tolson, Lt., Md., Susannah, W24575; BLWt.1297-200 iss. 2/28/1795
Nathan, N.C., S7163
Nehemiah, Md., R6489
Peter, See LOWN
Philip, Ga., BLWt.1797-400
Stephen, Va., R6189
Thomas, Va., Mary, R6488
William, N.C., S13795
William, S.C. See LOVE
LOWELL, Barnard, Mass., BLWt.4600-100-Pvt. Iss. 3/25/1790. No papers
Barnard/Bernard, N.H., Sarah Mirick, former wid., W16140
Benjamin, Mass., S37194; BLWt. 911-100
Ebenezer, Jr., Mass., BLWt.1250-100-Ens. Iss. 8/21/1789 to Ebenezer Lowell, legal repr. of E.L., Jr. No papers
Enoch, Mass., Mary, W24592
Ezra, Mass., S30549
Isaac, N.H., Amy/Ama, R6490
Jacob, Mass., Jane/Janne, R6491
John, Mass., S18493
John, Mass., Elizabeth Reed/Read, W2166
Paul, Mass., Elizabeth Stanwood, W24596
Peter, N.H., S13785
Samuel, Cont., N.H., Olive O., W16636
Thomas, Mass., S37193; BLWt.79579-160-55
Timothy, Mass., S42878
William, Mass., Dis. No papers here, but see p. 139, Am. State Papers, Class 9, Claims. Wm. Lowell, Sgt., Col. James Freye's Regt., N.H. Militia, wounded by a musket ball, shot through his body, June 17, 1775, Bunker's Hill, res. Warner, N.H.
William, N.H., Abiah, W20529
LOWENBERY, Frederick, Pa. See LIVENBERG
LOWENSTEIN, David, Md. See LEVENSTON
LOWER, George, Pa., R6493
John, N.Y., Magdalena, W21590

LOWING, William, R.I., Anna Vaughn, former wid., W18184
LOWMAN, Peter, N.Y., BLWt.7411-100-Pvt. Iss. 2/14/1791 to Jer'h. Von Ranselar, atty. No papers
Philip, Pa., BLWt., 9810-100-Pvt. Iss. 11/27/1794 to Alexander Power, ass. No papers
LOWN, Peter, N.Y., Elizabeth, W8053
LOWNDSBURY, David, See LOWNSBURY
LOWNSBERRY, William, Ct., R6465
LOWNSBERY, Henry, N.Y., S13774
LOWNSBURY, David, Ct., S33005
Samuel, N.J., S22364
Walker, N.J., S33379
LOWRANCE, Jacob, N.C., S1682
LOWREY, James, Ct., R6494
John, N.C., Elender Cook, former wid., W6709
Levi, S.C., Ga., Martha, W8091
Simeon, N.C., S.C., S31826
Thomas, Va. See LOWRY
William, Pa., S22366
LOWRY, Jacob, Md., Pa., S13765
John, Hazen's Regt., BLWt.13353-100-Pvt. Iss. 12/2/1791 to Alexander Power, ass.
John, N.C., S31215
John, Va., S5698
Michael, Md., Pa. & Whiskey Insurrection 1794, S22372
Samuel, N.C., R6495
Susan, former wid. of Gibson Cluverius, Va., which see
Thomas, N.C., Sarah, W8060
Thomas, Va., Nancy, W2139; BLWt. 13444-160-55
Thornton, Va., Ann, W8088
LOWTHER, Joel, Va., Nancy, W4269; BLWt.26844-160-55
LOY, John, N.C., b. Pa., R6498
LOYD, James, Va., S38154
Jarrett, N.C., R6499
John, Va., S8847
Nicholas, N.C., S4569
Owen, ---, R6500
Robin/Indian ROBIN, Va., R6501
Samuel, Ct., Cont., S13788
William, Cont., Va., S38145
William, N.C. See LLOYD
LOYDE, George, Va., Elizabeth Armstrong, W8086
LOYER, Christopher, N.Y., S42882
LOYH, George, Pa. See Andrew LOSHE
LOZEAR, Henry, Cont., Mass., N.J. S42881
LOZELL, Isaac, Cont., Mass., See LAZELL
LOZIER, Abraham, N.Y., Jane, W20498
Helebrant, Cont., N.J., Elizabeth, W16331
Hillebrand, Va., Lee's Legion, BLWt.13392-100-Pvt. Iss. 2/2/1790. No papers
Jacob, N.J., Va., Christiana, W24579
John, N.J., Sarah, W20525
Oliver, Lamb's Art., N.Y., BLWt. 7421-100-Pvt. Iss. 7/17/1790.

LOZIER (continued)
No papers
Peter, Cont., N.J., S42886
LUALLEN, Richard, Va. See LEWALLEN
LUCADO, Isaac, Va., S38869
LUCAS, Abijah, Mass., Ruth, S30554; BLWt. 84040-160-55
Abram, Pa., S6503
Amaziah, Ct., S13798
Asahel, Mass., S41786
Barnabas, Mass., Betty, W20543
Basil, Md., S18097
Bela, Mass., S33019
Consider, Mass., Jane, W20538
Daniel, Mass., R6504
Edmund, Mass., S13807
Elisha, Mass., Rebecca, W24606
Ephriam, Mass., Azubah, W13653
Francis, Va., S36687
George, Pa., S7166
Ichabod, Ct., S44203
Isaac, Mass., BLWt.4603-100-Pvt. Iss. 1/1790. No papers
Isaac, Mass., S46391
Israel, Ct., N.Y., Mabel, W10205; BLWt.56943-160-55
James, N.H., Sally, W16335
James, N.H., Anne S./Nancy,W27442
James, Va., Mary, W12163
Joel, Va., R6506
John, Ga., BLWt.2215-300
John, Md., BLWt.11457-100-Pvt. Iss. 12/23/1795 to Geo. Ponsonby, ass. No papers
John, Md., S34967
John, Md., S36052
John, N.H., S13804
John, Pa., S4584
John, S.C., S11010
John, Va., Mary, W5468
Nathaniel, Va., Sarah, W442; BLWt.1234-300-Capt. Iss. 2/28/1794. Also recorded as above under Wt. 2636. No papers
Parker, Va., S8868
Randolph, N.C., Nancy, W8265; BLWt.34922-160-55
Samuel, Ct., BLWt.6093-100-Pvt. Iss. 7/6/1791. No papers
Samuel, Ct., Abigail, R6502; BLWt.1539-100
Samuel, Mass., Jemima, W13651
Simon, N.J., S4576
Thomas, Ct., Abigail, W26227
Thomas, Cont., Navy, Va., S40103
William, Ct., S28798
William, Md., Va., Mary, W20535
William, Mass., S30556
William, N.Y., S31223
William, N.C., R6509
William, Va., S38158
William, Va., R6507
LUCE, Abijah, Mass., Mary, W27443
Abner, Mass., Milison, W13652
Barzilla, R.I., Rhoda, W24611; BLWt.34848-160-55
Benjamin, Mass., Damaris, W8069
David, Mass., S33017
Ebenezer, Mass., Jane, R6512; B.L. Reg.23 1132-55. See statement as to wid. Mercy Luce in report from Treas. Dept. as to

LUCE (continued)
payment of arrears
Ephraim, Vt., S13805
Israel, N.Y., Apphia, R6510
Ivory, Vt., S13799
John, Navy, Mass., Hepsibah, W20546
Jonathan, Ct., BLWt.6123-100-Pvt. Iss. 5/19/1797 to Jonathan Luce. No papers
Jonathan, Ct., Parnel, W20544
Jonathan, Mass., Vt., S22374
Lamuel, Mass., Mehitable, W24605
Lucy, former wid. of David McClure, Ct., which see
Luke, Ct., S31827
Malachi, Mass., Anna, W15047
Mercy, Mass., R6512. See claim of Ebenezer Luce, with wid. Jane
Nathaniel, Ct., Hannah, W26226
Rowland, Mass., Navy, S33020
Samuel, Mass. Sea Service, Navy, S33018
Samuel, Mass., See Lamuel
Seth, Mass., S37198
Timothy, Ct., S37646
Uriah, Ct., S13802
Zimri, Mass., S13801
LUCHES, Henry, Crane's Cont., Art. Mass., BLWt.4610-100-Pvt. Iss.5/8/1792 to Benj.Haskell. No papers
LUCK, John, Va., S13635
LUCKENBACK, Adam, Pa., R6513
LUCKETT, David, Md., BLWt.1086-200
Samuel, Md., S36051
Thomas H., Md., BLWt.653-400
LUCKEY, Hugh, N.C., b. Pa., S4580
Robert, N.C., S38157
LUCKIE, William, N.C., S7165
LUCUS, Samuel, Ct. See LUCAS
William, Va., R6508
LUDDEN, Benjamin, Mass., S18957
Enos, Mass., Sarah, W24597
Samuel, Mass., S29304
Silvanus/Sylvanus, Mass., S29303
LUDDINGTON, Eliphalet, Ct. See Eliphelet LUDINGTON
Lemuel, Ct., S41785
LUDDON, Daniel, Mass., S13808
LUDEMAN, John, "the Invalids", BLWt.13388-100-Pvt. Iss. 5/11/1790. No papers
LUDEMANN, John William, Va., R15955 Va. Half Pay
LUDENTON, Jesse, Ct., S18098
LUDINGTON, Daniel, Mass., Naomi, W27444
Eliphelet/Eliphalat, Ct., S31828
Jesse, Ct. See LUDENTON
Jude, Mass., S30552
Lemuel, Ct. See LUDDINGTON
Stephen, Ct., Betsey, W1628; BLWt.26651-160-55
William, Ct., S22885
LUDLAM, Daniel, N.Y.,BLWt.7391-100-Pvt. Iss. 4/28/1791. No papers
John, N.Y., BLWt.7390-100-Pvt. Iss. 4/14/1792. No papers
LUDLOW, Sarah C., former wid. of David Van Horne, Cont., N.Y., which see
Stephen, "the Invalids", BLWt.

LUDLOW (continued)
13386-100-Pvt. Iss. 6/22/1791 No papers.
LUDLUM, Jacob, N.J., Margaret, W957
LUDWICK, Jacob, Pa., Mary, R6514
John Martin, Cont., Pa. res., Elizabeth, W5031
Warner, Pa., BLWt.9790-100. Iss. 8/8/1796. No papers
LUFBERRY, Abraham, Cont., N.J., N.Y., Jennett Barclay, former wid., W12235. BLWt.8483, iss. 1800, & BLWt.24604-160-55
LUFFKIN, Jacob, Mass., BLWt. 4570-100-Pvt. Iss. 11/7/1796 to Joseph Thomas. No papers
Levi, N.H. See LUFKIN
LUFFMAN, John, N.C. See LUFMAN
LUFKIN, Benjamin, Mass., Sea Service, N.H., Sarah E., W8068; BLWt.38516-160-55
Isaac, Mass., S33016
Jacob, Mass., Dorcas, W13644. Her 3rd husb., David Forbash, Mass., was pensioned, which see. Her 4th and last husb. was also pensioned, see claim of Isaac Lovering, Mass.
Levi, N.H., BLWt.3280-100-Pvt. Iss. 10/30/1789 to Ephraim True, ass. No papers
Levi, N.H., Elizabeth, W24604
Moses, Cont., Mass., Martha, W12162
Samuel, Mass., Sarah, W21593
LUFMAN, John, N.C., S42901
LUGAR, Adam, Cont., N.C., first enl. in Pa., Margaret, W8066
LUGG, Elizabeth, former wid. of Frederick Warneck, Va., which see
LUICKS, Antreas, N.Y. See Andrew LOUCKS
LUKE, Andrew, N.Y., BLWt.7415-100-Pvt. Iss. 5/3/1791 to James Palmer, ass. No papers
John, N.J., S4582
Solomon, N.Y., S13800
Thomas, Pa., R6516
LUKER, David, N.J., S22373
LUKRE, David. See LUKER
LULL, Abner, Mass., Anna, R6517
Asa, Vt., Abigail, W21594
David, Mass., Mary, W20541
Joseph, Vt., Deborah, R6518
William, N.Y., Charlotte, R6519; BLWt.40937-160-55
LUM, Israel, N.J., S4579
John C., N.J., S4548
LUMBARD, Aaron, Mass., Lucy, W15409
Caleb, Mass., Hannah, W24613
David, Mass., S30553
David, Vt., S16455
Jedediah, Mass. & War of 1812, See LOMBARD
John, Mass., S15512
Nathaniel, Cont., Mass. See LUMBORD
Samuel, Mass., Mercy, W20539
Thomas, Mass., Anna, W15690

LUMBLEY, William, Va., S32000
LUMBORD, Nathaniel, Cont., Mass., Ruth, W24583
LUMEREAUX, Joseph, N.Y., S5715
LUMIS, Oliver, Ct., Cont., See LOOMIS
LUMKIN, Moore, Va. See LUMPKIN
LUMLEY, Samuel, N.J., BLWt.8478-100-Pvt. Iss. 6/22/1792. No papers
LUMM, Jesse, Va., S8872
LUMMIS, Joseph, N.J., S41784
LUMOREAUX, Peter, See LOMEREAUX
LUMPKIN, Dickeson, Pa., Va., R6521
Joseph, Va., S8870
Mary, former wid. of John Williams, N.C., which see
Moore, Va., Catharine, W8264; BLWt.12566-160-55
Philip, Va., Nancy Rogers, former wid., W10245; BLWt.93548-160-55
Wilson, Va., S38156
LUMSDEN, Charles, Va., Patty, W8067
John, Va., S8871
LUNA, Peter, Va., S1554
LUND, Jesse, N.H., Sarah/Sally, W20537
John, N.H., Hannah, W15046
Stephen, N.H., S18096
LUNG, Joseph, Ct., BLWt.6097-100-Pvt. Iss. 3/9/1791 to Samuel Smith. No papers
Joseph, Ct., S42902
LUNSFORD, Elisha, N.C., S.C., Eve Mary, R6522
Mason, Va., S32387
Rodham, Va., S13803
LUNT, Amos, Mass., S31224
Daniel, Mass., S31225
Daniel, Mass., Eunice, W24599; BLWt.1232-300-Capt. Iss. 12/22/1798 to Peleg Wadsworth. No papers
Daniel, N.H., S37199
Ezra, Mass., BLWt.2296-300
Henry, Navy, Mass., Sarah, W13654
James, Mass., BLWt.1292-200
Job, Mass., BLWt.1964-100
Micajah, Mass., Privateer, Mary/Marah, W24603; BLWt.34952-160-55
Moses, Mass., Sarah, W24609
Oliver, Mass., BLWt.4605-100-Pvt. Iss. 3/25/1790. No papers
Paul, Mass., Hannah, W15048
Richard, Navy (daughters res. Mass. in 1837), R1286
Sarah, former wid. of Moses Whittier, which see
Thomas, Mass., BLWt.4586-100-Pvt. Iss. 3/25/1790. No papers
Thomas, Mass., S33023
Timothy, Cont., N.H., S33022
William, R.I., S21353
LUNTER, Peter, Va. See LANTER
LUPARDUS, William, N.J., S1039
LUQUEER, John, N.J. See LEQUEER
LUQUER, Abraham, N.Y. See LEQUIRE
LUQUIER, John, N.J. See LEQUEER
LURTY, John, Va. Sea Service, R65, Va. Half Pay
LURVEY, Moses, Mass., S41222
William, Mass., Ruth Hull, former wid., R5364
LUSCOMB, Robert, Mass., Sarah, W20536
LUSCOMBE, Francis, Mass., S5716
Samuel, Mass., S22887
LUSE, Francis, N.J., BLWt.1273-150-Ensign. Iss. 12/9/1789. No papers
Lockard, N.Y., Mary, W3350
Nathan, N.J., Damaris, W8070
LUSH, John, N.Y., BLWt.7380-100-Pvt. Iss. 9/7/1796 to John Folsom, ass.
Philip, Cont., Pa. See LESH
Stephen, N.Y., Lydia, W15926
William, Privateer, Md., R6526
LUSHBAUGH, Henry, Pa., S40104
LUSHER, John, Md., R6527
LUSK, Hugh, Va., S25637
Jacob, N.Y., S29302
John, N.J. & Wayne's War, S38919
John, N.Y., Caty, W21591
John, Pa., S22886
Joseph, N.C., Va., S4581
Michael, N.Y., Elizabeth, W20542
Patrick, ---, Res. Lycoming Co., Pa. Invalid. No papers
Samuel, N.C., S4583
Samuel, N.C., Elizabeth, W8092; BLWt.11051-160-55
William, Pa., BLWt.1275-300-Capt. Iss. 7/16/1787. No papers
LUSTER, John, N.Y., BLWt.7384-100-Pvt. Iss. 1/5/1791 to William Radelift, ass. No papers
LUSTOR, John, N.Y. See LESTER
LUTES, Henry, Md., See LUTZ
LUTHER, Aaron, Mass., S17555
Amos, R.I., Sally, W678; BLWt. 24910-160-55
Benjamin, Mass., S30557
Benjamin, R.I., Waity, W13655
Caleb, R.I., Molly, W24601
Cromwell, Ct., S42903
Eber, Mass., S29305
Eddy, Mass., Charity, R6530
Elisha, Ct., Cont., Lucy, W12164; BLWt.24903-160-55
Elizabeth, former wid. of Nathan Munro, R.I., which see
Ellis, Cont., Ct., S30555
Ezra, R.I., R6531
Frederick, R.I., S21354
George, Md., Elizabeth, W10207
Hezekiah, Mass., R6532
Jacob, Md., R6533
James, Mass., R.I., Mary, W20545
James, R.I., S21871
John, Hazen's Regt., BLWt.13334-100-Drummer. Iss. 12/31/1789. No papers
John, N.Y., Elizabeth, W24598
Josiah, R.I., Priscilla, W24600
Levi, Ct., Cont., S11009
Martin, Cont., Ct., S42900
Martin, R.I., Rachel, W21592
Michael, Md., Mary, W4721
Peleg, Mass., BLWt.77-100
Peleg, R.I., Mary, W24607
Stephen, Mass., Navy, R.I., Mary, W24610
Theophilus, Mass., R.I., Zilpha, W24612
Thomas, R.I., S21870
Thomas S., R.I., S21352
Wheaton, Mass., R.I., S17556
LUTS, John, N.Y. See LUTZ
LUTTERELL, Michael, Va., S32021
LUTTRELL, James, Va., R6535
Nathan, Va., R6536
Rodham, Va., Sea Service, Frances, W10206; BLWt.71057-160-55
LUTZ, Henry, Md., Mary, R6538
Henry, Pa., S4537
John, N.Y., Elizabeth, R6537
LUYSTER, John P., N.J., Anna, W255
LUZADER, Aaron, N.J., Pa., R6539
LYALL, Thomas, N.J., BLWt.8486-100-Sgt. Iss. 8/7/1789 to Peter Anspach, ass. No papers
LYBEA, John, N.Y., BLWt.7410-100-Pvt. Iss. 7/12/1792 to Joseph Purdy, ass. No papers
LYBERGER, Nicholas, Pa., Christina W8075
LYBROOK, Henry, Va., R10368
John, Va., R6540
LYDSTON, Roby, Mass., Olive, W21595
William, Mass., S29973
LYE, Joseph, Cont., Mass., Anna, W24619
LYERLY, Zachariah, N.C. See LIERLY
LYFORD, Fifield, N.H., Judith K., W8072
Nathaniel, N.H., Privateer, R6541
Thomas, Cont., N.H., BLWt.1913-200
LYLE, Jacob, N.J., R6542
Margaret, former wid. of Samuel Lapsley, Cont., Va., which see
LYLES, Richard, Md., R6543
Thomas, Md., R6544
LYMAN, Asa, Ct., Sea Service, Mary, W26228
Benjamin, Mass., Mary, W4871
Benjamin, Vt., S28799
Cornelius, Mass., BLWt.1238-150-Ens. Iss. 12/2/1789. No papers
Dan, Ct., Hannah, W1792; BLWt. 24921-160-55
Daniel, R.I., S46458
Daniel, R.I., BLWt.1252-400-Maj. & Aid-de-Camp. Iss. 12/31/1789. No papers
Eleazer, Vt., S15514
Elihu, Cont., Mass., S33024; BLWt.1246-200-Lt. Iss. 2/10/1792. No papers
Elisha, Ct., Abigail, W8267; BLWt.17712-160-55
Ezekiel, Ct., Cont., Mabel, W12169
Francis, Ct., S16456
Giles, Mass., S30558
Giles, Mass., Mary, W8074
Isaac, Vt., Laura D., W3352

LYMAN (continued)
John, Ct., BLWt.6094-100-Pvt. Iss. 11/23/1798 to Timothy Andrews, ass. "The original Wt. presented by J.W. Bates, Esq. at this office - 4th June, 1832."
John, Ct., S13809
John, Ct., S42904
John, Cont., N.H., S15513
Jonathan, Ct., Sarah, R6545
Joshua, Mass., Sarah, BLWt.12727-160-55
Josiah, Cont., Mass., S33026
Richard, Ct., Mehitable, W2808
Richard, Ct., Philomela, W24616
Samuel, Ct., S11012
Simeon, Ct., Joannah, W20548
Thomas, Mass., S5718
LYN, John, Pa., S8874
LYNAH, Edward, S.C., S18959
LYNAM, Andrew, Va., Betsey, W9148
LYNCH, David, Pa., R6546
Elijah, Va., Rose, W5032
Henry, Va., Sally, W10210; BLWt. 43529-160-55
Hugh, Md., S34968
John, Md., BLWt.1292-400-Major. Iss. 5/27/1794. No papers
John, Md., BLWt.11441-100-Pvt. Iss. 1/13/1792 to Wm. Lane, ass. No papers
John, Mass., S40955
John, N.Y., Mary, R6548
John, Pa., BLWt.9791-100-Pvt. Iss. 7/16/1789 to M. McConnell, ass. No papers
Joshua, Mass., S22888
Joshua, N.C., S41790
Michael, Pa., S40107
Patrick, Md., Va., Martha, W8071
Peter, Pa. & Indian Wars, S41787
Stephen, Pa., R6549
Thomas, Md., S34969
William, Md., BLWt.11465-100-Pvt. Iss. 5/1/1797. No papers
William, Md., Margaret, R6547
William, N.J., BLWt.8510-100-Pvt. Iss. 10/17/1789 to John Pope, ass. No papers
William, N.Y., BLWt.7409-100-Pvt. Iss. 7/20/1790 to Samuel Curray, ass. No papers
LYND, John, N.Y., Huldah, W20549
LYNDE, Benjamin, Cont., Mass., Hannah, W24620
Cornelius, Ct., Green Mt. Boys, Mass., Rebecca, W20489
Jonathan, Mass., Molly, W16336
LYNDSLEY, Joseph, Cont. See LINDSLEY
LYNE, David, Ct. See LYNES
David, Ct., S11013
Ignatius, Mass., Lydia, W24621
LYNN, David, Ct., S32388
David, Md., Mary, W9151; BLWt. 1295-300-Capt. Iss. 2/1/1790. No papers
Dewalt, Pa. See LINN
George, N.Y. See LINDOLPH
Israel, N.C., Mary, W9150

LYNN (continued)
James, N.C., S13817
John, Ct., Cont., S11011
John, Md., BLWt.1298-200-Lt. Iss. 5/1/1792. No papers
John R., Cont., Pa., Jane, dau. Mary Jane, W29933; BLWt.9835-100. Iss. 11/5/1789. No papers. BLWt. 306-60-55 & 78039-160-55
Michael, Cont., Col. Proctor's Art., Pa., BLWt.2207-100. Iss. 4/3/1838. Pa. res. of heirs in 1838.
Patrick, Pa. See LINN
Robert, "the Invalid Corps", BLWt.13379-100-Pvt. Iss. 12/13/1792 to Frederick Molineaux, ass. No papers
Ruth, former wid. of Artemas Willard, Mass., which see
Sarah, former wid. of John Turner, Ct., N.Y., which see
William, Ct., BLWt.1763-200
William F., N.C., S4586
LYNOR, Philip, Va., S38143
LYNOTT, Thomas, Sea Service, Del., R6551
LYON, Abraham, N.J., S41788
Abraham, N.J., BLWt.1221-300-Capt. Iss. 12/24/1789. Also recorded as above under BLWt.2527. No papers
Alvan, N.Y., R6552
Amanda, former wid. of Jonathan Hildreth, N.J., which see
Asa, Ct., BLWt.1869-200
Benjamin, Mass., Elizabeth, W27445
Benjamin, N.J., S23780
Benjamin, Pa., S40105
Daniel, N.Y., R6553
David, N.J., S892
Ebenezer, Ct., Chloe, W24615
Ebenezer, Crane's Cont. Art., Mass., BLWt.4617-100-Pvt. Iss. 4/3/1797 to John Jack. No papers
Ebenezer, Mass., S44522
Edward, N.H., S40956. His pension suspended. See his affidavit in claim of Jonathan Lyon, wid. Lucy
Edward, Va., S38920
Eleazer, Mass., Dorcas, W13656
Enos, N.J., Naomi, W24614
Ephraim, Ct., Hannah Bradford, former wid., W17366
Gideon, Ct., R6555
Henry, Ct., BLWt.6092-100-Pvt. Iss 1/28/1790. No papers
Henry, Cont., N.J., Joanna, W958; BLWt.24439-160-55
Hezekiah, Ct., R6557
Israel, N.Y., S9931
Jacob, Cont., Va., S41789
Jacob, Mass., Jerusha, W21596
Jacob, ---, Pa. res., R---. See papers in jacket on file under Jacob LINE, R---
James, Cont., N.J., S4588
James, N.Y., S23779
James, Va., S38159
Jediah, N.J., S40106
Jesse, Ct. See Jose
Job, Ct., S17557
John, Del., Mary, W3351
John, Mass., Sarah, W24617

LYON (continued)
John, N.J., R6558
John, Pa., Mary, R---
John, Va. Sea Service, R66. Va. Half Pay. See N.A. Acc. No. 837, Va. State Navy, YS File
Jonas, N.J., S33381
Jonathan, Mass., S19384
Jonathan, N.H., Lucy, R6561
Jose/Jesse, Ct., Lois Morris, former wid., W26273
Joseph, Ct., S23306
Joseph, N.J., S1054
Joshua, Ct., S13811
Kimberly, Mass., R6560
Lemuel, Mass., Lydia, W24618
London, Mass., See ATIS
Matthew, Cont., Green Mt. Boys, Vt., S36689. When allowed pension in 1818 he was res. of Caldwell Co., Ky. On 6/28/1820 he stated he was 70 yrs. 11 mos. and 16 days old. In 1775 he was in Col. Ethan Allen's Regt. of Green Mt. Boys in the first expedition to Canada, was at the capture of Fort Ticonderoga & the battle of St. John. On his return he was appointed adj. of a Militia Co. Commissioned 7/19/1776, 2nd Lt. in Col. Seth Warner's Cont. Regt.. Commissioned 7/14/1777 paymaster in the same Regt. & was at the siege and surrender of Burgoyne at Saratoga. In 1778, he was appointed Paymaster Gen. of the Vt. Troops, in 1779 he was appointed Capt. of a Vt. Co. On 11/12/1781 he was commissioned Col. of the "16th Regt. of the Militia of Vt."
Moses, Cont., N.J., Catharine, W29993
Moses, N.Y., S13812
Nathan, Ct., S13816
Nathaniel, N.J., Marcy, W9510
Nehemiah Web, Ct., S15928; BLWt. 26052-160-55
Noah, Ct., Mary, W16640
Robert, Pa., S40108
Samuel, N.H., Vt., S46092; BLWt. 3270-100. Iss. 8/7/1819.
Samuel, N.Y. See LYONS
Samuel, N.Y., R6562
Stephen, Ct., Abigail, W20547
Stephen, Hazen's Regt., BLWt. 13349-100-Pvt. Iss. 10/27/1792. No papers
Stephen, N.J., S4589
Thomas, Ct., Eunice, W12172
Thomas, Cont., Green Mt. Boys, S9687; BLWt.1222-200-Lt. Iss. 8/1/1789 to Anspach & Rogers, ass. No papers
Thomas, Cont., Mass., S33025
Thomas, Mass., S13814
Thomas, N.Y., S21872
William, Ct., Sarah, W21597
William, N.C., b. Va., S8875
William, N.C., S31829
William, Va., Frances, R6554

LYONS, Barnabas, N.J., R6563
Edward, Pa., BLWt.9796-100-Pvt. Iss. 3/10/1790 to Alexander Power, ass. No papers
Hannah, Cont., Mass. See John RUSSELL
Hosea, N.Y., S23308
James, N.Y., Phebe Lewis, former wid., W26208; BLWt.14755-160-55
John, Va. Sea Service, See LYON
Joseph, Green Mt. Boys, Vt., S4587
Joseph, N.Y., R6559
Josiah, Mass., BLWt.4569-100-Pvt. Iss. 10/3/1791. No papers
Michael, N.Y., Mary, W20550
Moses, Pa., BLWt.9811-100-Pvt. Iss. 5/30/1791. No papers
Samuel, Del., S9378
Samuel, N.Y., Elizabeth, W1793. He d. 1819
William, N.J., BLWt.8507-100-Pvt. Iss. 12/7/1797. No papers
William, N.J., S33382
William, Pa., Sea Service, S4585
LYPORT, Jacob, N.Y., S13813
LYTLE, Andrew, N.Y., BLWt.36743-160-55
Andrew, Pa., Margaret, W3271; BLWt.1278-200-Lt. Iss. 7/27/1789 to Richard Platt, ass. No papers
Archibald, N.C., BLWt.84-500 & Rej. File 20322, in which papers are forged.
James, Cont., N.Y., Mary, R6384
Robert, N.Y., Esther Norway, former wid., W4043
Robert, Pa., S16457
Thomas, Pa., BLWt.9836-100-Dragoon. Iss. 11/26/1793 to Francis Kirkpatrick, ass. No papers
Will/William, N.C., S46228; BLWt. 1312-300-Capt. Iss. 6/10/1792 to William Litle. No papers
William, N.Y., S13810
LYTTLE, Robert, N.Y. See LYTLE
Thomas, N.C., S8873

M

MAABE, John, N.C., See MAIB
MAAG, Henry, Pa., S40116
MAAR, Patrick, Ct. See MEARA
MAB, Thomas, N.Y., R6564
MABAN, John, N.C., S1686
MABB, John, N.Y., Seneth, W18466; BLWt.40041-160-55
MABE, John, N.C., See MAIB
MABEN, Henry, S.C., Jennett, R6566
James, Va., BLWt.12-300
MABERRY, Benjamin, N.C., S38926
MABEUF, Baptiste, N.Y., S46533; BLWt.1580-100
MABIE, Cornelius, N.Y., S13825
MABIN, John, N.C. See MABAN
MABLEY, William S. See MOBLEY
MABON, James, Va. See MABEN
MABRY, Braxton, Va., R6569
Daniel, S.C., Louisa, R6570
David, N.C., Jeane, W17072
John, Cont., N.C., S13832
Mathew, Va., S7174
Reps, Ga., S41809
MAC AFEE, Benjamin, N.J., Rachel, W1980; BLWt.6399-160-55
MACAY, John, Mass., S42922
MACCOUN, James, Va., S36068
MAC COY, Alexander, Pa., S9021
MACDILL/MC DILL, David, S.C., S2753
MACE, Abraham, Mass., Reuel, W26248
Andrew, Mass., N.H., S17566
Isaac, Va., S8995
John, Va., S13847
Joseph, Pa., S5725
MACHAR, Patrick, Md. See MACHER
MACHER, Patrick, Md., R6571
MACHIN, Thomas, Cont., N.Y., Susan, W17081; BLWt.1401-300-Capt. Iss. 6/11/1791. No papers
MACHRELL, James, Va., BLWt.12382-100-Pvt. Iss. 10/6/1792 to Thomas Newton, ass. No papers
MACK, Abner, Ct., BLWt.6136-100-Pvt. Iss. 8/10/1795 to Thomas Joslin. No papers
Abner, Ct., Anne/Anna, W16641
Andrew, Ct., S17569
Archibald, Mass., N.H., Vt., S18962
Benjamin, Ct., S40958
Betsey, former wid. of Jabez Alexander, Mass., N.H., which see
Bezeleel/Bezeliel, Cont., N.Y., Lucy Gates, former wid., W11043; BLWt.114-60-55 & 7525-100-Pvt.
David, Ct., S40967
Gurdon, Ct., S23782
Hezekiah, Ct., S13843
James, Mass., Margaret, W18482
Jeremiah, Ct., Cont., Mass. & N.H., S42923
Jesse, N.Y., Lanah, W25675; BLWt.31296-160-55
Joel, Ct., Susannah, W20234
John, N.H., S40975
John, N.Y., Sarah, W9901; BLWt.

MACK (continued)
9142-160-55
Joseph, N.H., S42927
Josiah, Ct., Mary, W17103
Nehemiah, Ct., Caroline, R6572
Philip, Pa., S23807
Ralph, Ct., S29313
Richard, Ct., Betty, W9910; BLWt.1447-100
Zebulon, Ct., Mary, W15691
MACKALL, Benjamin, Md., Rebecca, W2953
MACKANEY, James, N.Y. See MAC KENNY
MACKAY, Daniel, Pa. See MC COY
Thomas, Md. See MACKEY
Walter, Va., Catherine Arthur, former wid., R270
William, S.C., Nancy, W6; BLWt.61199-160-55
MACKE/MACKIE, Samuel, N.C., Mary, W7385
MACKEE, Andrew, Ct., Diantha, W5364; BLWt.38536-160-55
MACKEL, Jacob P., N.Y., Elizabeth, W1301
MacKENLY/McKINLEY, John, N.C., S38184
MACKENNY, James, N.Y., Mary, W19858
MACKENTIER, Eli, Mass., R6573
MACKENTIRE, Benjamin, Mass., S29978
MACKENZIE, Philip, N.Y., Susannah, W24143
MACKEON, John, Pa. See MC KEOWEN
MACKER, Charles, Mass. See MAKER
MACKEY, Alexander, N.Y., Elizabeth, W17091
Daniel, Pa., BLWt.9987-100-Pvt. Iss. 7/8/1791 to Simon Fishbaugh, ass. No papers
James, N.C., S16940
James, Pa., BLWt.1467-200-Lt. Iss. 3/24/1794. No papers
Thomas, Md., S38169
Thomas, S.C., S21357
MACKIE, Samuel, N.C. See MACKE
MACKINTIRE, Rufus, R.I. See MC INTYRE
MACKINTOSH/McINTOSH, Peter, Cont., Mass., S29979
MACKNET, Charles, Pa., S22381
MACKNEY, James, N.Y. See MACKENNY
MACKY, Robert, Va., Anna E., W1041
MACLAIN, John, N.Y., S40127
MACLAUGHLIN, Thomas, N.H., S33385
MACLEAN, William, N.C., Mary D., W3572; BLWt.1207-300
MACLEMORE, John, N.C., b. Va., S4202
MACLURG, Walter, Va., R66117, Va. Half Pay. See N.A. Acc. No. 837 Va. State Navy, Walter McClurg, Y.S. File
MACMIHIN, Jeremiah, N.J., Susanna, BLWt.370-100
MACOMBER, Abiathar, Mass., S33061
Ebenezer, R.I., S42949; BLWt. 1346-300-Capt. Iss. 4/20/1790.
Elijah, Mass., S17571
Ephraim, R.I., S21362
Job, Mass., S40961
John, R.I., BLWt.3340-100-Sgt.

MACOMBER (continued)
Iss. 1/19/1798. No papers
John, R.I., S22375; BLWt.1400-100
Jonathan, Mass., S42931
Jonathan, R.I., Rebecca, R6575
Josiah, Mass., S33044
Lemuel, Mass., S33042
Rufus, Mass., R6576
Samuel, Mass., S21365
Seth, Mass., S33049
Southworth, Mass., Hannah, W9173; BLWt.16124-160-55
William, Mass., S29314
William, Mass., R6577
Zenas, Mass., Hannah, R6574
MACPHERSON, Daniel, N.Y., R6809; BLRej. 165952-55, Amy
John, Navy, Pa., S9771
MACUMBER, John, R.I., See MACOMBER
MADDAN, Michael, Mass. See MADDEN
MADDEN, David, Ga., b. Md., S31835
David, Mass., S13818
John, Mass., BLWt.4711-100-Sgt. Iss. 3/25/1790. No papers
John, Cont., Mass., S37221
Joseph, Md., See MADDIN
Michael, Mass., Esther, W4539; BLWt.26499-160-55
Thomas, Pa., BLWt.217-100
William, Va., Jane, W9902; BLWt. 26908-160-55. See N.A. Acc. No. 874-050106. Not Half Pay
MADDER, Martin, Va., BLWt.12378-100-Pvt. Iss. 11/5/1789. No papers
MADDIN, John, Mass., BLWt.4703-100-Pvt. Iss. 8/10/1789 to Richard Platt. No papers
Joseph, Md., S31237
Thomas, Pa. See MADDEN
William, Md., BLWt.11538-100-Pvt. Iss. 11/1/1796 to Joshua Ward, ass. No papers
MADDING, Chapness, Va., S4184
MADDIS, John, Pa., BLWt.10069-100-Pvt. Iss. 1/8/1796 to Barnard Markle, ass. No papers
MADDOCK, Henry, Mass., R.I., S37208
MADDOCKS, Caleb, Mass., Sea Service, R6824
Samuel, Mass., S37211, BLWt.829-160-55
MADDON, Joseph, Pa. See MADON
Michael, Pa., BLWt.9920-100-Pvt. Iss. 7/16/1789 to M. McConnell, ass. No papers
Thomas, Pa. See MADDEN
MADDOX, Jacob, Va., S1556
John, Va., S30565
John, Va., S38183
Matthew, Va., S38181
Notley, Va., BLWt.12392-100-Pvt. Iss. 1/6/1795 to Robert Means, ass. No papers
Sherwood, Va., Elizabeth, W2823
Wilson, Va., Delilah, W8413
MADEIRA, Michael, Pa., Ann Elizabeth, R6825
Nicholas, Pa., R21708
MADERA, Casper, Pa., Margareth, W7706

MADERA (continued)
Christian, Cont., Pa., S38180
Samuel, Pa., BLWt.9872-100-Pvt. Iss. 12/14/1791. No papers
MADGE, Jared, N.Y., S11122
MADISON, Ambrose, Va., S31229
Gabriel, Va., Mira, W8418, Va. Half Pay
William, Cont., Va., War of 1812, Nancy, W9944; BLWt.2205-200
William, Va., S5724
MADOH, Solomon, N.J. See Sollomon MIDDAUGH
MADON, Joseph, Pa., S40128
MAECK, Frederick, Mass., Abigail, BLWt.33556-160-55
MAER, Henry, Cont., Pa., S33038
MAEYER, John, Cont., Va., S38954
MAFFET, David, Navy, Pa. agcy. & res., S40126
Enoch, Mass. See MOFFAT
MAFFETT, John, Pa., S31238
MAFFIT, Robert, Pa., See MOSCAT
MAFFITT, William, Va., S36063
MAGAR, James, Mass., S40979
MAGARVEY, Francis, Pa., S13848
MAGAW, John, Pa., Margaret,W7428
Robert, Pa. See McGAW
William, Pa.,S5046;BLWt.1446-400-Surgn. Iss. 9/1/1789. No papers
MAGDEN, Robert, N.C. See MAYDEN
MAGEE, James, Cont.,Del. See McGEE
James, N.C., Va., S1555
John, N.J., Martha, W1045
John, N.Y., Rachel, W18465
Patrick, Cont. See McGEE
Peter, N.Y., S41804, BLWt.1395-200-Lt. Iss. 3/8/1794. No papers
Ralph, Va., S13894
Samuel, N.Y., Elizabeth, W1302; BLWt.30934-160-55
William, N.H. See McGEE
William, N.J., BLWt.8580-100-Pvt. Iss. 7/2/1791. No papers
MAGERS, Thomas, N.C. See MAJORS
MAGERT, Henry, Va., S1850
MAGIE, John, N.Y., Sarah, W23924; BLWt.26236-160-55
MAGILL, Andrew, N.C., R6826
Charles, Va., Mary B., W5336
James, Va., Mary, R6827
John, Va., S31230
MAGIN, Charles, Md., S41812
MAGINNIS, Daniel, Pa. & U.S.Army 1812,S46323;BLWt.1834-100 for Rev.;BLWt.11697-160-55 for 1812
MAGIRA, Peter, Ct. See MAGUIRA
MAGLAUGHLIN, Andrew, Pa., S5737
MAGOON, Alex., N.H., Hannah, W2404
Edward, N.H., S40962
John, Mass., War of 1812, R6828
Joseph, N.H., S13881
Joshua, Mass., Elizabeth, W9175; BLWt.57650-160-55
Josiah, N.H., S16938
MAGOUN, Joshua, Mass. See MAGOON
Mary, former wid. of Benj. Cooper N.Y., which see
MAGRAW, Christopher, Md., BLWt. 4626 & 11475-100-Drummer. Iss. 2/1/1790. No papers
MAGREGORY, John, See MEGREGORY

MAGRUDER, Nathaniel Beale, Md., S34973
Norman Bruce, Md., Nancy, W9542
MAGUIRA, Peter, Ct., Ruth, R6830
MAGUIRE, Hugh, N.Y., S11017
MAGUS, Pomp (colored), Cont., Mass., S33059
MAGWIER, Allegany. See MC GUIRE
MAHAFFEY, Samuel, Pa., S2759
MAHAN, James, N.C., Va., also in 1774, S17563
Patrick, N.Y., BLWt.7498-100-Pvt. Iss. 8/24/1790 to Cath. Bleecker et al, assnes. No papers
Samuel, Mass., S11020
MAHANA, John, Mass., S41811
MAHANES, Tapley, Va., S7187
MAHANY, James, Pa., S40121
MAHAR, Patrick, Ct. See MEARA
MAHER, Patrick, Md., R6831
MAHEW, James, Mass. See MAYHEW
Richard, N.J., S40111
William, Mass., BLWt.611-100
MAHL, Frederick, Pa.,Pvtr. S33035
MAHOLLAND, John, N.C., Lucy, R6832
MAHOLM, Samuel, Pa., S5061
MAHON, John, Pa., BLWt.1434-200-Lt. Iss. 10/1/1792 to Flahavan & Wilcox, Admrs. No papers
MAHONE, Archelaus, Va., Magdalina, R6833
MAHONEY, former wid. of John Johnson, Md., which see
James, Pa., BLWt.9957-100-Pvt. Iss. 3/4/1791. No papers
James, Va., BLWt.12377-100-Pvt. Iss. 5/9/1797 to Daniel Vertner
James, Va., S36056
Simon, ---, Mary, Rejected 44666. Rejected on ground of no evidence of service. Res. of wid. in 1888, LaCrosse, Wis.
MAHONY, Daniel, Pa., S40110
Edward, Md., S34970
James, Pa. See MAHANY
Michael, Md., R6835
Timothy, R.I., Huldah, W21747
MAHORNEY, Benjamin, Cont., Va., S32393
Thomas, Va., S38166
MAHURIN, Jonathan, Mass., S13837
MAHY, William, N.Y., R6836
MAIB, John, N.C., Lucy/Lucinda, W4726; BLWt.59092-160-55
MAID, Thomas, Va. See MEAD
MAIDEN, James, Va., Docia Hall, former wid., W5098
Laurence, N.C., S7190
MAIGHER, Richard, Mass., W18490
MAIL, Wilmore, Va., S38171
MAILLETT, Baptiste, Hazen's Regt. BLWt.13452-100-Pvt. Iss. 7/22/1799 to Abraham Bell, ass. No papers
MAIN, Amos, Mass., S31841
Chloe, former wid. of David Smith, N.Y., which see
David, Ct., S16937
Ezekiel, Ct., S22893
Henry, Ct., Hannah Wells, former wid., W22567
Henry, Md., S41806

MAIN (continued)
Peres, Ct., S2720
Philip, Va., S13850
Rufus, Ct., R.I., S17561
William, Ct., R.I., S9392; BLWt. 8021-160-55
MAINARD, James, N.C. See MANARD
MAINE, Rufus, Ct. See MAIN
Stephen, Ct., S13865
William, Ct., R.I., See MAIN
MAINER, Josiah, N.C. See MAINOR
MAINERD, James, N.C. See MANARD
MAINES, George, Va., S36080
William, Mass. See MAINS
MAINOR, Josiah, N.C., S41801
MAINS, Francis, Va., BLWt.12345-100-Pvt. Iss. 7/14/1792 to Robt. Means, ass. No papers
Samuel, Md. or Va.?, R6837
Samuel, N.C., S38163
William, Mass., Sarah Mathews, former wid., W9912; BLWt. 100020-160-55
William, Pa., S2721
MAIRS, Elias, N.C., S.C., S2719
MAITRE, John, N.Y., BLWt.7504-100-Pvt. Iss. 11/10/1791 to Isaac Trowbridge, ass. No papers
MAJOR, Alexander, Md., S31239
George, Vt., S13879
Robert, N.C., S2002
Samuel, Va., Nancy, W8417; BLWt.31293-160-55
William, Va., S15602
MAJORS, Benjamin, S.C., S32392
Humphery, Va., S5723
James, Va., BLWt.12399-100-Pvt. Iss. 3/4/1796. No papers
John, Md., Va., S11026
John, N.C., S16944
Thomas, N.C., S30564; BLWt.18210-160-55
MAJORY, John, Mass., S45733
MAKEMSON, John, S.C., Mary, W7407; BLWt.29336-160-55
Thomas, Pa., R20191
MAKEPEACE, Isaac, Mass., Anna, W13681; BLWt.4000-160-55
Jason, Mass., S40960
Seth, Mass., Lydia, W4541
William, Mass., S30568
MAKER, Borden/Burden, Mass., S23041; BLWt.1058-100
Burden, Mass. See Borden
Charles, Mass., Elizabeth, BLWt. 21823-160-55
Joseph, Ct. See MEEKER
Seth, Mass., Chloe, R6838
MAKINS, Samuel, Navy, Mass., Sarah, W4487
MALABY, John, N.C., S1772
Thomas, N.J., Rachel, W493
MALARY, David, Ct., R6840
David, Ct., Sea Service, R6841
MALATT, Abraham, N.J., BLWt. 8569-100-Pvt. Iss. 8/11/1789 to Matthias Denman, ass. No papers
Abraham, N.J., S2738. In the Rev. War pension claim of Mary, wid. of Wm. Holmes, N.J.

MALATT (continued)
W429, there is evidence of about this man's age, family, etc.
MALBEUF, Baptiste, N.Y. See MABEUF
MALBONE, Godfrey, R.I., Dorcas, W17078
MALCOLM, Henry, Navy, Pa., S5048. Surgeon.
William, Cont., BLWt.1404-500-Col. commanding one of the 16 additional Regts. Iss. 7/9/1790. No papers
MALCOM, Henry, Navy, See MALCOLM
James, Va. State Navy. R68, Va. Half Pay. See N.A. Acc. No. 837-Va. State Navy, YS file
John, Mass., Sea Service, Mary, R6839; BLWt.21834-160-55
William, Cont. See MALCOLM
MALCOME, Hugh, Md., S34420
MALCOMSON, John, S.C. See MAKEMSON
MALES, John, Md., S38168
MALETT, Lewis, Ct. See MALLETT
MALICK, John, N.J., S7177
John, N.J., S13868
MALKEMSON, John, S.C. See MAKEMSON
MALLARD, John, Mass., Polly, W21759
Lawson, N.C., S5051
Thomas, Mass., S33063
William, N.H. See MALLEN
MALLARY, Amos, Ct., BLWt.6163-100-Pvt. Iss. 10/17/1796 to Daniel Hitchcock, ass. No papers
Johin/John, Va., R6846. Born 5/15/1761. Res. at enl. Brunswick Co., Va. Res. in 1839 Hawkins Co., Tenn.
John, See Johin
Nathaniel, Green Mt. Boys, Mass., N.Y. See MALLEROY
Philip, Va., BLWt.1502-300
MALLBIE, Benjamin, Ct., S2752
MALLEN, William, N.H., Miriam, W2403
MALLEROY, Nathaniel, Green Mt. Boys, Mass., N.Y., R6842
MALLERY, David, Cont., Ct., Susannah, W4274; BLWt.26375-160-55
John, Va., S16931. Res. at enl. Orange Co., Va. Res. in 1833, Limestone Co., Ala, aged 74 yrs.
Levi, ---, Ct. res., R6847
Samuel, Ct., S23312
Truman, Ct., Olive, W2824
MALLESON, Benjamin, Ct. See MALLISON
MALLET, Francis, French, Mass. res. in 1832 & 1833, R6849
John, Ct., S16936
Michael, Privateer, Mass., R6850
Miles, Ct., S17560
Thomas, N.C., R6851
William, Mass., Deborah, W9930
MALLETT, Lewis, Ct., Anne, W21760
Lucy, former wid. of Thomas Lemont

MALLETT (continued)
Mass., which see
MALLIHAN, John, ---, Va. res. in 1834, R6852
MALLISON, Benjamin, Ct., S37209
Ezra, Ct., S19731
Roswell, Ct. See MATTISON
MALLON, James, Mass., R6853
MALLONY, Nathaniel, Ct. See MALLORY
MALLORD, Thomas, See MALLARD
MALLORY,
Aaron, Ct., Huldah, W305; BLWt. 26459-160-55
Asa, Ct., Sea Service, S15515
Benajah, Ct., S15930
Benajah, Vt., War of 1812, Sally, W9927; BLWt.26325-160-55
Billy, Va., Catharine L., W2826
Dan (Negro), Ct., Alice, W25678; BLWt.57646-160-55
David, Ct., Sea Service, See MALARY
David, Cont., Ct. See MALLERY
Gideon, Ct., S5727
Jacob, Ct., Sarah, W555; BLWt. 26623-160-55
James, Ct., Nancy, W18477
John, Va., S38161. Enl. in Hanover Co., Va. B. ca. 1761. Res. of Goochland Co., Va. in 1818, aged 57 yrs., wife Elizabeth
John, Va., Elizabeth, W3436. Born 7/14/1755 in Hanover Co., Va. always lived there, d. 1833. In 1840, wid. Elizabeth (Duke) Mallory, res. of Hanover Co., aged 70 yrs.
John, Va., R6845. B. 3/1/1759 in Orange Co., Va. Res. at enl. Louisa Co., Va. After Rev. War moved to Ga. Res. of Benton Co., Ala., in 1835
Lemuel, Ct., Rebecca, W6785
Levi, Ct. See MALLERY
Nathaniel, Ct., Sarah, W2650; BLWt.1389-100 & 126-60-55
Roger, Va., S1684
Samuel, Ct., R6848
Simeon, Ct., R6843
William, Va., S1688
William, Va. See Billy
MALLOW, George, Va., S2735
Henry, Va., S45892
MALLUGAN, John, N.C., S4186
MALONE, Andrew, Md. See MELOAN
Cornelius, S.C., S31834
Deloney, N.C., S2736
Francis, Pa., S16942
Hugh, Md., S38167
John, Cont., Ct. See MELONEY
John, Cont., Pa. See MELONE
John, N.Y., Dis. No papers here but see Am. State Papers, Class IX, Claims, p.94, which shows he was a Pvt. in Col. Willett's Co.; in Feb., 1783 he had his feet frozen and lost some of his toes at "Connajorharrie"
John, Va., S36076
Thomas, Md., S38929
William, Md., BLWt.11556-100-Pvt.

MALONE (continued)
Iss. 7/14/1795 to Wm. Marbury, ass. of Elizabeth Malone, Admx.
William, S.C., S31832
MALONEY, Archibald, Pa., Rachel, W2219; BLWt.1707-100 & 158-60-55
Daniel, Mass. Sea Service, R6854
John, Mass., S42909
MALONY, Lamb's Art., N.Y., BLWt. 7524-100-Pvt. Iss. 9/13/1790 tc Jonas Prentice, ass. No papers
Robert, Va., S31240
William, Pa., BLWt.9876-100-Pvt. Iss. 2/9/179?. No papers
MALOON, Abel, Mass. See Abraham MELOON
Abraham, See MELOON
Josiah, Mass., N.H., Hannah, W24137
Solomon, Mass., Sally, W23921; BLWt.908-100 & 335-60-55
MALORY, Gill, Vt., S11035
Jacob, Ct. See MALLORY
Samuel, Ct. See MALLERY
MALOTT, Dory/Theodore, Md., S2737
John, Md., Elizabeth, W3839
Theodore, Md. See Dory
Thomas, Md., S5059
MALOY, James, Pa. See MELOY
John, N.Y. See MELOY
MALPASS, James, N.C., S9399
MALPUS, Ezekiel, S.C., BLWts. 12424 & 13398-100-Pvt. Iss. 11/20/1794. No papers
MALSINGER, Daniel, N.C., R7145
MALT, Moses, Va., R6856
MALTBIE, Benjamin, Ct. See MALLBIE
Zacheus/Zaccheus, Ct., Jerusha, W27448
MALTSAR, Benjamin, Lee's Legion, Va., BLWts.12353 & 13537-100-Pvt. Iss. 9/2/1789 to Benjamin Maltsar. No papers
MAN, Aaron, R.I., Grace S., W26245
Abel, Va., S32396
David, Mass. See MANN
MANAN, John, Del., Pa., Nancy, W7399
MANARD, James, N.C., Chaney, W10212; BLWt.61200-160-55
MANCHESTER, Abraham, R.I., Anna, W21761; BLWt.19626-160-55
Barzilla, R.I., Abigail, W13687
Edward, R.I., Esther, W18475
Elias, N.Y., S11040
Gideon, R.I., S21876
Giles, R.I., Margaret, W13679
Israel, R.I., Nabby, W20228
James, R.I., R6858
Jeremiah, R.I., Phebe, W12401
Job, R.I., Anna, W13671
Job, R.I., W26244
John, R.I., S5055
John, R.I., Mary, W20233
John, R.I., Mary, W21752
Joseph, R.I., S21878
Joseph, R.I., Hannah, W19859; BLWt.27582-160-55
Nathaniel, R.I., S21361
Stephen, R.I., S42908
Thomas, Navy, R.I., Elizabeth, W20231

MANDAGO, Jeremiah, N.Y. See MANDIGO
MANDELL, Moses, Mass., Abigail, W15062
MANDERS, Henry, Va., BLWt.12407-100-Pvt. Iss. 7/5/1794 to Robt. Means, ass. No papers
MANDERVILLE, Matthew, N.Y., S13836
MANDEVILL, James, N.Y., S13834
John, N.Y., S28800
MANDEVILLE, Giles, N.J. See Yelles
Henry H., N.J., S2757
Henry W., N.J., S2758
Jacob, N.Y., S23311
John, N.Y., Sarah, W17085
Yelles/Giles, N.J., R6860
MANDIGO, Jeremiah, Cont., N.Y., S23786
Judah, N.Y., Sarah B., R6861
MANEBACK, William, Cont., Pa., Catharine, W3435
MANEELY, William, Pa. See McNEELY
MANERS, John, N.J., S2740
MANESS, Ambroes, N.C., R6862
MANEY, Martin, N.C., Va., Keziah, W7398
MANGUM, John, S.C.,b. Va., S16939
MANHART, John, Cont., N.Y., Rebecca W25672; BLWt.82004-160-55
MANIER, David, Va. See MINEAR
MANIFOLD, John, N.H., BLWt.3324-100-Pvt. Iss. 3/25/1790. No papers
MANIS, Seth, N.C., S2739
MANK, Andrew/Henry, Va., S1852
Henry, Indian War of 1774, Va., N.C., R6863
Henry, Va., See Andrew
Mathias, Va. See MAUK
MANKER, William, Va. Indian War of 1790, Sarah, W9942; BLWt. 73506-160-55
MANKINS, William, Md., S2751
MANLEY, Ancil, Va., W959; BLWt. 29024-160-55
John, Cont., Md., Susanna, W5339, BLWt.13525-100-Corp. in Lee's Legion, Va. Iss. 12/2/1799. BLWt.39-60-55
John, Mass. Sea Service. Dis. No papers here but see Am. State Papers, Class IX, pp.59 & 109.
John, Navy, N.Y., S9394
Lucy, former wid. of John Hitchcock, Ct., which see
Micajah, Va., S13824
William, Md., BLWt.11505-100-Pvt. Iss. 9/24/1792. No papers
William, Vt., Elizabeth, W20236
MANLOVE, William, Del., S41813
MANLY, Daniel, Mass., R6864
George, Va., R6865
Jesse, Md., R6866
John, See John MEANLY
Moses, N.C., S41796
Nathan, Vt., R6868
MANN, Abel, R.I., Sarah, W23925
Abiathar, Mass., Jerusha, W17079
Abraham, N.J., S726
Alice, former wid. of Reuben Spencer, N.H., which see
Amos, Mass., Mary, W23927

MANN (continued)
Amos, N.J., Ellsa, BLWt.86060-160-55
Andrew, Ct., S16934
Andrew, R.I., R6871
Andrew Wyer, Mass., R6869
Benjamin, Cont., N.H., S42907
Benjamin, Mass., Hannah, W21758
Benjamin, Va., S36067
Bille, Cont., Mass., S18495
Daniel, Md., BLWt.11503-100-Pvt. Iss. 3/1/1791. No papers
Daniel, R.I., Phebe, W21766
David, Mass., S13864
David, Mass., Sarah, W23930
Ebenezer, Mass., S19729
Ebenezer, Mass., Mary, W9914
Ebenezer, Mass., Sally, W15052
Ebenezer, Va., S38927
Elias, Mass., S33036
Elisha, Ct., Cont., N.J., Sarah, W4544
Francis, N.C., Va., S13826
George, Mass., BLWt.4680-100-Sgt. Iss. 5/31/1790 to Theodosius Fowler. No papers
George, Mass., Susanna, W26242
Henry, N.J., BLWt.8562-100-Pvt. Iss. 7/11/1791. No papers
Isaiah, Del., R6872
Jabez, Ct., Ruhamah, W4540
Jabez, Mass., Elizabeth, W18468
James, Cont., Mass., S13838
James, N.Y., S29318
Jesse, R.I., S11025
John, Mass., N.H., Persia, W2400, BLWt.15195-160-55
John, ---, Pa. res. in 1853, Mary, R6873
Joseph, Ct., S16932
Joseph, Cont., Vt., S44530
Joseph, Mass., S18109
Joseph, Mass., S33034
Joseph, Mass., Mehitable, W26233
Joseph, Va., Ann, R6870
Joshua, Mass., Molly, W15050
Josiah, Mass., S33060
Levi, Cont., Mass., Patience, W24138
Nancy, former wid. of John Hawkins R.I. Sea Service, which see
Nathan, Mass., Polly, W9908, BLWt.8386-160-55
Nathan, N.H., Martha, W21775
Nathan, N.C., S7183
Nathanel, Mass., R6875
Obadiah, Cont., Mass., S44531
Oliver, Mass., S2717
Peter, Va., Martha, W18481
Robert, Va., S38922
Rufus, Mass., Sybil, W18469
Sarah, former wid. of Hezekiah Cutting, Mass., which see
Thomas, Ga., S.C., Sarah, R6876 BLWt.77545-160-55
Timothy, Mass., S21359
Willard, Mass., Vt., Mary, R6874
William, Md., BLWt.11481-100-Pvt. Iss. 7/17/1792. No papers
William, Mass., S5050
William, Mass., S42906
William, Va., Mary, W7383

MANNAN, John, Del., Pa. See MANAN
John, Va., Letitia/Lettice, W9538
MANNERBACK, William, Cont., Pa. See MANEBECK
MANNERING, Andrew, Cont., Del. See MANRING
Jordon, Del., N.C., S2741
MANNING, Andrew, Ct., S16935
Benjamin, N.J., S23783
Benjamin, N.J., Bersheba, W1048; BLWt.26860-160-55
Christopher, Pa., BLWt.10012-100-Corp. Iss. 7/27/1789 to Richard Platt, ass. No papers
Cyrus, Ct., Mary, W17082
Dan, Ct., Lydia, W17099
David, Mass., Anna, W26247
Davis, Va., S16941
Diah, Ct., BLWt.6157-100-Pvt. Iss. 10/--/1789 to Theodosius Fowler. No papers
Diah/Dyer, Ct., Anna, W25673
Dyer, Ct. See Diah
Eliphalet, N.H., BLWt.3298-100-Corp. Iss. 1/28/1790 to James Patterson, ass. No papers
Eliphalet/Eliphelet, N.H., S33046
Henry, Md., S38173
Increase, Ct., S13880
Isaac, Cont., Mass., Sarah, W21742 BLWt.4630-100 & 147-60-55
Isaac, N.J., Rosanna, W7400
Israel, Mass., S33043
James, Crane's Cont. Art., Mass., BLWt.4728-100-Fifer. Iss. 1/26/1790 to John May. No papers
John, Cont., Mass., S33056
John, Del., Pa. See MANAN
John, Mass., N.H., S44537
John, N.H., BLWt.3302-100-Pvt. Iss. 1/28/1790 to James Patterson ass. No papers
John, N.J., Sarah, W961
John, N.Y., S34422
John, N.C., R6877
Jordon, Del., N.C. See MANNERING
Joseph, Ct., S15518
Joseph, R.I., BLWt.3344-100-Pvt. Iss. 1/18/1797 to Sylvester Fuller
Lawrence, Lee's Legion, S.C., BLWt.1457-200
Luther, Ct., Sarah, W3573
Nathaniel, Ct., Matilda, W19864
Peter, Mass., S29311
Phinehas/Phineas, Mass., Abigail, W19863; BLWts.4642-100 & 186-60-55
Rockwell, Ct., Sarah, W25670
Samuel, Ct., BLWt.1050-100
Samuel, Mass., S33027
Sarah, former wid. of John Collins, N.Y., which see
Seabury, Ct., S13866
Thomas, Ct., S2742
Thomas, N.J., BLWt.8530-100-Sgt. Iss. 9/8/1789 to Samuel Rutan, ass. No papers
Thomas, N.Y., S16933
William, Ct., S40980
William, Ct., S41814
William, Mass., Mary, W2654;

MANNING (continued)
BLWt.28641-160-55
William T., Mass., Betsy, W15058; BLWt.785-100
MANNON, Henry, Va., S16187
John, Va. See MANNAN
MANO, Ferdinand, Sea Service, Tenn. res. in 1822, R6879
MANRING, Andrew, Cont., Del., BLWt.72-100
MANROSE, Elijah, Ct., BLWt.6158-100-Pvt. Iss. 4/8/1797 to George Steel. No papers
Elijah, Ct. See MONROSE
MANROW, Asahel, Mass., N.Y., R6880
Joseph, Ct., N.Y., S11024
Noah, Ct., R6881
MANSELL, Joseph, Mass., S20452
MANSFIELD, Charles, Ct., S44539; BLWt.43-100
Daniel, Invalid Regt., BLWt.13512-100-Pvt. Iss. 5/17/1790
Daniel, ---, Ct. res. Dis. No papers
Ebenezer, Cont., Ct., Polly, W18484
Epes, Mass., Sarah, W26240
George, Va., BLWt.12376-100-Pvt. Iss. 12/9/1793 to Francis Graves, ass.
George, Va., S38182
Hannah, Ct. See John DODD
Henry, Md., BLWt.11530-100-Pvt. Iss. 12/23/1795 to George Ponsonby, ass. No papers
Henry, Mass. Sea Service, R6882
James M., Pa., S37205
John, Ct., S37217, BLWt.1382-200-Lt. Iss. 5/17/1790. No papers
John, Mass., S33062
Jonathan, Ct., Mass., Martha, W18471
Joseph, Ct., S37216
Joseph, Ct., R6883
Nathan, Ct., Anna, W20240
Richard, Ct., S37210
Robert, Va., S7185
Samuel, Md., Charity, W4275
Samuel, Mass., Mary, W23905
Thomas, Md., Md. Sea Service, Anna, W7404
Thomas, Va., R6884
William, Md., Kersiah, W10211; BLWt.88030-160-55
William, Mass., R6885
MANSHIP, Henry, Del., BLWt.10847. Iss. 9/2/1789. No papers
MANSIZE, Simon, Mass. Sea Service, R6886
MANSON, David, Pa., S2755
Frederick, Mass., Anna, W15061
John, Mass., BLWt.4710. Iss. 2/22/1792 to John Peck. No papers
John, Mass., Sea Service, Privateer, Elizabeth Richardson, former wid., W22076; BLWt.56945-160-55
John, Pa., BLWt.9999. Iss. 8/14/1793 to Jasper Iserloan, ass. No papers
Nehemiah, Mass., Sea Service, Mercy, W2312; BLWt.38533-160-55

MANSON (continued)
Thomas, Mass., S18106
William, S.C., Mary, W8423
MANSTERSTOCK, Johannes, N.Y., S13856
MANSUR, Susan, former wid. of Phinehas Holden, Mass., which see
MANTER, Alden, Mass., Polly, W18488
MANTLE, George, Md., BLWt.11495. Iss. 8/8/1794 to Christopher Cusack, ass. No papers
MANTLO, John, Va. See MATLO
MANTON, Edward, R.I., Catherine, W13665
Jeremiah, R.I., S21363
MANTZ, Peter, Md., Catherine, W26238
MANTZER, Japat, Pa., Polly, W9541
MANUAL, Paul, Pa., BLWt.10,026. Iss. 3/31/1795 to Simon Rigby, ass. No papers
MANUEL, Christopher, N.C., S7182
Jesse, N.C., S41808
Nicholas, N.C., Milly, R6887
MANVILLE, David, Ct., R6888
Simeon, Ct., Electa, R6889
MAPEL, Benjamin, See MAPLE
Stephen, N.J., Mary, W9904
MAPENBURG, Alexander, See MASSENBURG
MAPES, George E., N.Y., Experience R6890
James, N.Y., S23310
John, N.J., Cont., N.J., S34421; BLWt.13529-100
John, N.Y., S13831
Joseph, N.J., S2718
Phinehas, N.Y., BLWt.7493. Iss. 5/9/1791 to D. Howell, ass. Certified 2/7/1826. No papers
William, N.J., BLWt.8560. Iss. 12/27/1790. No papers
William, N.J., S42914
William, N.Y., S13873
MAPHET, Robert, Ohio res., R16079
MAPLE, Benjamin, N.J., R6891
Stephen, N.J., See MAPEL
William, N.J., S22380
MAPLES, Joshua, Ct., S13859
Josiah, Ct., S11014
Marmaduke, N.C., S41802
William, Ct., S29317
MAPP, John, S.C., Mary, W3840
MAPS, Frederick, N.J., BLWt.8517. Iss. 10/17/1789 to James Reynolds, ass. No papers
Frederick, N.J., Sibyl, W862
MARBLE, Aaron, Mass., Rebecca, W26237
Coker, Navy, Rhoda, R6894, Me. res. of wid. in 1853
Ebenezer, Mass., Navy, also 21st U.S. Inf., War of 1812, Sarah, W23912; BLWt.43518-160-55. Old War Wid. File 7387; BLWt.21058-12
Ephraim, Cont., Mass., S42934
Henry, Mass., S19730; BLWt.1362-200-Lt. Iss. 4/1/1790. No papers
Isaiah, N.Y., R6893
Jabez, Mass., Mary, W15060
John, Cont., Navy, N.H., S37201

MARBLE (continued)
John, N.H. See MARVELL
John, Cont., Vt., Phebe, W20232
Jonathan, Mass., S40957
Joseph, Mass., Lydia, W15063
Joseph, Mass., N.Y., Susan, R6895
Sampson, N.Y., Vt., Sarah Babcock former wid., W15874
Samuel, Mass., War of 1812, Mehitable/Mehitabel, W10214; BLWt.15182-160-55
Thomas, Ct., R6896
Thomas, Mass., Jane, W15053; BLWt. 8177-160-55
MARBURY, Joseph, Md., BLWt.1486-300-Capt. Iss. 3/10/1790. No papers
Leonard, Ga., Ann, W27446
Leonard, Ga., N.C., b. Md., R6892
MARCAN, William, See MAREAN
MARCELLIN/DE MARCELLIN, Anthony de, Pa.; BLWt.568-200-Lt. Iss. 5/20/1789.
MARCELLUS, Garret, N.Y. See MARSELES
John, N.Y. See MERSELLUS
MARCH, Charles, Cont., Md., S40122; BLWt.13463-100
Henry, N.H., S11022
James, Mass., Sally, W9932; BLWt. 90044-160-55
John, Va., R6900
Lydia, former wid. of John Smith, Mass., which see
Nathaniel, Mass., Elizabeth, W13677
Silas, Mass. See MARSH
William, Mass., BLWt.4686. Iss. 11/5/1792 to William March. No papers
MARCHANT, Gurdon, Cont., Ct., Hannah, W20239
Joel, Ct., Molly, W9928; BLWt. 26724-160-55
John, Ct., Cont., Tabitha, W17088
John, Mass., S37215
Joseph, Ct., Mary, W25679; BLWt. BLWt.29040-160-55
William, Mass., Hannah, R6902
MARCHANTS, Joseph, Mass., S33039
MARCHENT, Jabez, Cont. Mass., S33029
MARCKER, Andrew C., Pa., S40109, Pa., BLWt.13519-100 Corp., Art. Artificers of Pa. Iss. 8/21/1789.
MARCKLE, Charles, See MARKLE
MARCLE, Henry, See MARKLE
MARCUM, Arthur, See MARKUM
Josiah, Va., S8999
Richard, N.C., Ann, W3841
Thomas, N.C., b. Va., Fanny, W9540
MARCY, Alfred, Ct., S13869
Alvan, Ct., S13860
Chester, Mass., Vt., S21874
Gardner/Gardener, Mass., Elizabeth, W18467; BLWt.57753-160-55
Samuel, N.H., Priscilla, W26231
Stephen, N.H., Vt., S23784
MARDEN, James, N.H., S44534; BLWt. 864-100

MARDEN (continued)
Moses, N.H. See MARTIN
Stephen, N.H., Anne, W15927
William, Mass., S23781
MARDERS, John, Va., S18500
MARDIN, Edward, N.H., Vt., Chloe, W2221; BLWt.151-60-55 & 3321-100
Thomas, N.J. See MARTIN
MARDIS, William, Va., Elizabeth, W8410
MAREAN, Samuel, Mass., Bathsheba, W13682; BLWt.13219-160-55
William, Mass., Sibbel, W15065
MARENUS, John, N.Y. res., R6903
William, N.Y. See MORENUS
MARESQUELLE, Lewis Ansart de, See Lewis ANSART
MAREY, Caesar, Mass., BLWt.4651. Iss. 4/13/1792. No papers
MARGERRY, Jonathan, N.H., S37202
MARHAR, Patrick, See MAHER
MARICK, John, Va., S11371
MARINE, Charles, Del., BLWt. 10849. Iss. 12/14/1793. No papers
MARINER, Gilbert, Del., BLWt. 10828. Iss. 9/2/1789. No papers
MARINUS, David, N.J., Effy Ackerman, former wid., W385
Thomas, N.Y., Mary, W26229; BLWt.7442-160-55
MARION, Francis, S.C., BLWt. 2199-500
John F., N.C., S.C., S2747
Samuel, Va., S4180
MARIQUART, Jacob, See MARRIQUART
MARIS, Alexander, See MARS
MARITT, Stephen, See MERRITT
MARIUS, Jacob, N.Y., Lamb's Art., BLWt.7527. Iss. 9/8/1790. No papers
Sylvester, N.J., N.Y., S13839
MARK, Joseph, Ct. See claim of Silas Bailey, R.I.
MARKAM, Lewis, See MARKHAM
MARKEL, Jacob P. See MACKEL
MARKELL, Peter, N.Y., Elizabeth/Elisabeth, W7388
MARKER, Andrew, Art. Artificers of Pa. BLWt.13519. Iss. 8/21/1789. No papers
Andrew, See MARCKER
William, See MANKER
MARKHAM, Ambrose, Mass., BLWt. 4690. Iss. 9/1/1790 to Theodosius Fowler. No papers
Ambrose, Mass., S34419
Ambrose, Mass., Elizabeth, W9925
Asa, Mass., S13840
Dan, Ct., R6904
Hannah, former wid. of Timothy Rogers, Ct., which see
Isaac, Ct., Cont., Cynthia, W17073
James, Va. State Navy, R72. Va. Half Pay. See N.A. Acc. No. 837-Va. State Navy, James Markham, U.S. file Va. Half Pay
Jeremiah, Ct., S20860
John, Ct., S11034

MARKHAM (continued
John, Va., S5726
Joseph, Ct., S44538
Lewis, Va., Margaret, W25669; BLWt.39213-160-55
Nathaniel, Cont., Ct., Hannah, R6905. She was pensioned as former wid. of Timothy Rogers, Ct., which see
Stephen, Cont. Mass., Dorothy, W20238
Thomas, Va., Nelly, W7389
MARKLAND, Edward, Navy, Alice, Md. agcy. & res., W4019
John, Pa., S46392; BLWt.1432-200. No papers
MARKLE, Charles, Armands Corps. BLWt.1385-300-Capt. Iss. 9/18/1789. Also recorded as above under BLWt.2537. No papers
Christian, Pa., S2748
Henry, N.Y., Polly, W19877
Jacob P., See MACKEL
MARKLEY, Catharine, former wid. of Michael Everly, Pa., which see
MARKS, Abisha, Hazen's Regt., BLWt.13477. Iss. 8/27/1792. No papers
Edward, Va., S11015
George, N.Y., S42918
Isaiah, Va., R16055, Va. Half Pay BLWt.1655-300
Jacob, Pa., S40124
Jesse, Cont., Mass., Vt., S40959
John, See Johannes MARX, Cont. Pa.
John, Md., S36059
John, Va., Lucy, W4542
Joseph, Ct., See claim of Silas Bailey, R.I.
Samuel, Cont., Mass., Abigail, W21748
MARKUM, Arthur, Va., Anna, R6907
MARL, James, Md. See MARLE
MARLAR, John, N.C., b. Va., S9400
MARLATT, Abraham, Cont., Va., Ann, W21771
Peter, N.J., S38177
MARLE, James, Md., R6908
MARLER, Joseph, S.C., Sarah, R6394
MARLEY, Henry, N.C., R6909
MARLIN/Marlin BROWN/Marlin ROORBACK (colored), N.Y., R6978
MARLOW, Butler, Md., S34974
MARNEY, Amos, Va., Sarah, W1046; BLWt.34830-160-55
Lewis, Jr., Hazen's Regt., BLWt. 13448. Iss. 1/22/1790 to Benj. Mooers, ass. No papers
Louis, Cont., N.Y., S42924
MARONEY, Alexander, N.Y., S42925; BLWt.17708-160-55
Philip, Md., Martha, R6911
MARONY, Alexander, See MARONEY
Horence, N.Y., BLWt.7481. Iss. 8/19/1791 to Jonas Addoms, ass. No papers
MARR, James, Mass., S37213
John, N.C., S41798
John, Va., R6912
William, Md., Airey, W3838
MARRETT, Larose/Rosey, Va., S38176
Rosey, Va. See Larose

MARRETT (continued)
Stephen, N.C. See MERRITT
MARRICAL, Anthony, N.Y. See MIRACLE
MARRICLE, Henry, See MARKLE
MARRINER, Nicholas, N.H., S44536
MARRION, Bartholomew, N.C., b. Va., S7178
MARRIQUART/MARIQUART, Jacob, N.Y. S22892
MARRY, Mark, See MURRAY
MARS, Alexander, Va., R7087
MARSBOURNE, Daniel, See MARSHBURN
MARSDEN, George, Cont., Mass., Wilmot, W17110
Humphrey, N.Y., BLWt.7495. Iss. 9/15/1790 to John S. Hobart, et all, assnes. No papers
John, See MASDEN
MARSELES, Garret, N.Y., Charlotte, W1444. BLWt.141-60-55
MARSELUS, Garret, N.Y., BLWt.13406 & 14070. Iss. 3/21/1794. No papers
John, N.Y., Catharine, W26232
MARSH, Aaron, Mass., Sarah, W13678
Allen, Ct. See Allyn
Allyn/Allen, Ct., Mabel, W26243
Amariah, Mass., Lois, W21757
Amos, Mass., S29316
Ashbel, Ct., R6915
Benjamin, Md., BLWt.11474. Iss. 2/1/1790. No papers
Benjamin, Mass., R6916
Casper, Pa., S22386
Charles, N.J., S1055
Daniel, Mass., Rhoda, W18472; BLWt.739-100
Daniel, N.H., Jane, W3570; BLWt. 11399-160-55
David, Ct., R6917
David, Pa., S40112
David, Va., R6918
Duty, Cont., Mass., Rhoda, W26234
Edmund, Ct., S11019
Eleazer, Vt., S2723
Elizabeth, former wid. of Bartholomew Moulton, Mass., Sea Service, Navy, which see
Enos, Mass., S29310
Henry, N.C., Va., Phereby, W9531; BLWt.26161-160-55
Jacob, Mass., N.H., S18102
Jasper, Ct., Mass., S42912
Jesse, Mass., S15936
Job, Ct., Salome, W17096
John, Ct., BLWt.6185. Iss. 3/17/1792 to Aaron Camp. No papers
John, Ct., S11036
John, Ct., S31836
John, Md., Va., R6922
John, Mass., S11037
John, Mass., S17573
John, N.J., Catharine, W134
John, N.Y., BLWt.1397-150-Ens. Iss. 2/14/1791 to Jeremiah Van Renselaer, esq., Atty. of J.M. No papers
John/Johannus, Pa., R6899
John, Pa., Eliza, R6919
John L., Ct., S23309

MARSH (continued)
Jonathan, Mass., Hannah, W17107
Jonathan, N.H., Betsey, W21764, BLWt.26889-160-55
Joseph, Mass., Zipporah, W15057
Joseph, Mass., Mary, W19852
Joseph, N.H., S23788
Joseph, N.H., S44532
Joseph C., Mass., S13842
Joshua, Md., Temperance, R6924
Lot, Mass., Lydia, W18483
Mercy, former wid. of William C. Rhoades, N.H., which see
Nathan, Mass., Sarah, W16341
Noah, N.H., Hannah, W21763
Obed, Mass., S42921
Peter, N.Y., Dorothy, W19856
Reuben, Cont., Mass., S13875
Reuben, Mass., Lydia, W27449
Robert, Ct., BLWt.6196. Iss. 6/6/1789. No papers
Robert, Va. See MURSH
Roswell, Ct., Huldah, W4273; BLWt.6279-160-55
Samuel, Cont., Mass., Lucretia, W20227
Samuel, Mass., Mary, W17089
Samuel, Mass., Jemima Holden, former wid., W19803. Her other husb. was pensioned, Ill. claim Joseph Holden, Mass., which see
Samuel, Mass., Vt., S16943
Samuel, N.J., BLWt.8548. Iss. 6/16/1789 to Thomas Coyle, ass. No papers
Samuel, N.J., N.W. Indian Wars, W36065
Silas, Ct., Mary, W1977, BLWt. 26582-160-55
Silas, Mass., S43732
Silas, Mass., Deliverance, W21744
Simeon, N.J., Jane, R6921
Stephen, Mass., Lucy, W5332; BLWt.30752-160-55
Stephen, N.H., S31830
Sybil, former wid. of John Medcalf, Mass., which see
Thomas, Va., S38174
William, Mass., S33045
William, N.J., See MASH
William, N.J., Mary, R6925
William, N.C., S7186
William, Pa., Elizabeth, W9171
William, Vt., S21873
Zebulon, Mass., R6926
MARSHAL, Benjamin, Cont., Pa., enl. in Md., Mary, W4020
Simeon/Simion, N.Y., S43731
MARSHALL, Aaron, Del., S36060
Abel, Mass., S22894
Amon, N.Y., S13862
Antipas, Cont., Mass., Navy, S11018
Benjamin, Mass., S37214
Benjamin, Pa., Martha Inslee, former wid., BLWt.1163-200
Benjamin, Va., S5728
Benjamin, Va., b. Md., S7176
Benjamin, Va., b. Md., Elizabeth, W4279
Betty, former wid. of Samuel Lockwood, N.Y., which see

MARSHALL (continued)
Caleb, N.H., Vt., Zeruiah, W18486
Christopher, BLWt.1353-300-Capt. Iss. 1/29/1790. No papers
Daniel, N.Y., S13861
Daniel, Va., R6928
David, Mass., Abigail, W2825
David, Pa., BLWt.9956. Iss. 7/27/1789 to Richard Platt, ass. No papers
David, Pa., Margaret, W3571; BLWt. 1440-200-Lt. Iss. 8/3/1792 to himself
Dixon, N.C., Lucy, S38921; BLWt. 1535-200-Lt. Iss. 5/3/1800 and W18493
Eliakim, Ct., Anna, W17095
Elihu, N.Y., BLWt.1391-300-Capt. Iss. 9/4/1790 to Garrit T. Van Waggener, ass. No papers
Elijah, Ct., S36053
Elisha, Ct., Mary, W17109
Enos, N.Y., BLWt.3838-160-55
Ezekiel, Va., S2743
Francis, Va., Sarah, W6793; BLWt. 31331-160-55
George, Pa., B.L.R.
George, Va., Rachel, W304
Gideon, N.H., Abigail, W15928
Hezekiah, Md., Athe, W25668; BLWt.26498-160-55
Humphrey, Va., S31234 & Va. Half Pay, N.A. Acc. No. 874-050108 Half Pay, Humphrey Marshall
Isaac, Mass., S11016
Isaac, Mass., R6929
Isaac, Va., Mary, W3842
Jacob, Mass., S31228
James, Mass., Joanna, W15054
James, Va. (Capt. and d. 1788), Va. Half Pay
James, Va., Patience, W7390. Alive in 1850
James M., Va., S7173 & Va. Half Pay. N.A. Acc. No. 874-050109 Half Pay, James M. Marshall. Alive in 1832
Jenepher/Jenifer, Va. Sea Service, R70, Va. Half Pay. See. N.A. Acc. No. 837. Va. State Navy Jenifer Marshall, Y.S. File Va. Half Pay
Jesse/Jessy, Va., Nancy, W5350
Joel, Ct., R6931
John, Cont., N.H., Mass. Navy of Rev. & War of 1812, Sarah, W23929
John, Hazen's Regt., BLWt.13472. Iss. 8/24/1790 to Glenn & Bleecker, Admrs. of Isaac Paris, ass. No papers
John, Pa., BLWts.9874 & 13942. Iss. 9/4/1789 to Ann Short formerly the wife and now the legal repr. No papers
John, Pa., S41797
John, Pa., Mary Magdalene, R6932, BLWt.81532-160-55
John, Pa., BLWt.1422-300-Capt. Iss. 1/12/1791. No papers
John, Va., S5731
John, Va., S38162
Joseph, Ct., R.I., S13819
Joseph, Cont., Mass., S33064

MARSHALL (continued)
Joseph, Va. Sea Service, R69. Va. Half Pay. See N.A. Acc. No. 837 Va. State Navy, Y.S. file, Va. Half Pay
Michael, Indian Wars, res. of heir Perry Co., Pa. in 1854, R6933
Moses, Mass., Hannah, W13675
Nathaniel, Mass., S17572
Perez, Ct., Dolly, W19857
Preserved, Ct., Ruth, W2313; BLWt.34977-160-55
Purnell, See MARSHELL
Rebecca, former wid. of William Miller, Pa., which see
Richard, Cont., Va., Keziah, W7391; BLWt.12367 iss. 3/4/1796. Also BLWt.961-100 & 314-60-55. No papers
Robert, Md. In Indian defeat under Wayne, Nancy, W2141; BLWt.38531-160-55
Robert, Mass., N.H., S18100
Robert, N.Y., 7459. Iss. 9/15/1790 to John S. Hobart, et al, assnes. No papers.
Samuel, Mass., Esther Jamison/Jameson, former wid., W9075; BLWt.3827-160-55
Samuel, Mass., Sybil/Sybel, W15051
Samuel, Mass., Navy, W44535
Samuel, Pa., BLWt.10092. Iss. 5/7/1794 to Christian Hubbard, ass. No papers
Samuel, Va., S8997
Samuel B., Ct., S36069
Sylvanus, Ct., S13853
Thomas, Cont., Ct., Freelove, W25734
Thomas, Md., S8992
Thomas, Mass., Mary, W17071; BLWt. 34920-160-55
Thomas, Mass., BLWt.1348-500-Col. Iss. 1/28/1797. No papers
Thomas, N.Y., BLWt.7512. Iss. 6/24/1793 to Thos. Russell, ass. No papers
Thomas, Pa., BLWt.9890. Iss. 10/24/1792 to John Peters, ass. No papers
Thomas, Va., S---
Thomas, Va., d.3/4/1817, R16057, Va. Half Pay. See N.A. Acc., p.74, 050110, Va. Half Pay
Timothy, Mass., S5057
William, Cont., BLWt.2336-100
MARSHAMMER, Sebastian, See MERSHEIMER
MARSHBURN, Daniel, N.C., Delpha, R6913
MARSHELL, Purnell, N.C., S7191
MARSON, George, See MASON
MARSTON, Abraham, N.H., S13823
Asa, N.H., S16461
David, Mass., Navy, S33037
David, Mass., N.H., S18105, b. North Hampton, N.H., aged 60 in 1818. Res. at enl. Epping, N.H., res. 1819 & 1832 was Monmouth, Me.
David, N.H., Mary, b. in Northhampton, N.H., 2/5/1756, res.

MARSTON (continued)
there at enl., d. at Parsonfield, Me., 1/30/1835, W23098
James, N.H., & U.S.A., Gen. Wayne's Legion, S36071
John, Mass., S30559
John, N.H., S13830
John, N.H., S15519
John, Va., R16031, Va. Half Pay; BLWt.2223-200. See N.A. Acc. No. 870 No. 050 M, Half Pay, John Marston
Joseph P., N.H., S29974
Levi, N.H., Privateer, Abigail, W21769; BLWt.9063-160-55
Matthias, N.H., Sarah, W21767
Nathaniel, Cont., N.H., Jane, W23918
Samuel, N.H., Sarah, W15056
Samuel, N.H., Hepzibah, W17108
Samuel, N.H., Rhoda, W23916
Theodore, Cont., N.H., S37203
Thomas, N.H., S18099
MARTAIN, James, N.J. See MARTIN
Lewis, Pa., See MARTIN
Robert, Md., See MARTIN
MARTEN, John, N.H., See MARTIN
MARTENUS, Cornelius, See MARTINUS
Goddard, Ct., S36062
MARTERSON, Philip, Md., BLWts. 11476 & 11584. Iss. 3/11/1791 to Philip Marterson, No papers
MARTHER, Abner, See MATHER
MARTIN, Aaron, Mass., BLWt.4660. Iss. 3/25/1790. No papers
Aaron, R.I., S40974
Abel, Mass., S5058
Absolam, N.J., BLWt.1408-300-Capt. Iss. 9/10/1790. No papers
Absolam/Absalom, N.C., 41800
Adam, Va., Mary, R6961
Albro, R.I., S33055
Alexander, Art. Artificers of Pa., BLWt.13520. Iss. 5/3/1791 to Andrew Porter, ass. of Robert Martin, Admr. No papers
Alexander, N.J., N.Y. Sea Service, Privateer, S2725
Alexander, Pa., Madgalen, W4276
Amasa, Ct., S18494
Amasa, Ct., N.Y., Sarah, W1630; BLWt.14964-160-55
Amos, Mass., S5056
Amos, Mass., N.H., S44526
Andrew, Ct., S18101
Andrew, N.C., S11029
Ann, former wid. of Adam Vigal/Vicall, Md., which see
Anthony, R.I., Susannah, R6972
Arthur, Hazen's Regt., BLWt.13465. Iss. 6/12/1795 to John Hassell, ass. No papers
Asa, Ct., S13858
Ashbel, Ct., S18499
Azariah, Va., Lucy, W554
Balsar/Balser, Pa., Eve Catharine, W2955
Baptist/Baptiste, Cont., N.Y., N.Y. agcy. & res., S18960; BLWt.13451-100
Benjamin, N.H., Vt., S22376
Benjamin, R.I., S17565

MARTIN (continued)
Benjamin, Va., Anna, R6936
Benjamin, Va., Nancy, R6965
Charles, Ct., Privateers, R.I., Mary, W1978; BLWt.26175-160-55
Charles, Cont., Foreign, Res. Pa. in 1816; BLWt.670-200
Christopher, N.H., S40972
Claudius, Pa., S40971
Comfort, Mass., S33057
Cornelius, N.Y. res. of Wid. in 1853, Tamar, R6974
Daniel, N.J., Eve, W2401; BLWt. 4-60-55, & 8557-100
Daniel, R.I., Bethial/Bethiah, W17104
David, Sheldon's Cavalry, Ct., BLWt.6228. Iss. 12/11/1789. Cert. 7/12/1815. No papers
David, Ct., S22382
David, Mass., S37206
David, S.C., Margaret, W9533
David, Va., R6939
David Williams, Cont., res. Phila. at enl. & N.J. in 1820, S41345
Ebenezer, Mass., S13877
Edward, Cont., N.H., Susannah, W26249
Edward, S.C., Mary, W21746
Eleazer, N.H., Mehitable, W24133
Elizabeth, former wid. of Thomas Morris, S.C., which see
Elizabeth, former wid. of John Archer, Va. Sea Service, which see
Ennalls, Pa., S8880
Ephraim, Mass., S40978
Ephraim, N.J., BLWt.1423-500-Col. Iss. 4/2/1790. Also recorded as above under BLWt.2544. No papers
Ephraim, N.J., S31840
Ephraim, Vt., R6943
Francis, Hazen's Regt., BLWt.13249 Iss. 2/4/1790. No papers
Francis, Jr., Hazen's Regt., BLWt. 13430. Iss. 9/21/1790 to Benjamin Moers, ass. No papers
George, Tenn. res., R6496
George, Ct., S41794
George, Mass., S40981
George, Pa., Mary, BLWt.442-100
George, S.C., Alsey, W24132
George, Va., Mary, W4543
George, Va., Elizabeth, R6941
Gershom, N.J., Sarah, W7395
Gershom, N.J., Elizabeth, R6940
Gideon, Va., S31232
Henry, N.C., S41791
Henry, Pa., S8990
Hudson, Va., S7175
Hudson, Va., Jane, W7394 & Va. Half Pay
Hugh, Pa., BLWt.2309-400
Ichabod, N.H., BLWt.1514-100
Isaac, Ct., S16186
Isaac, Mass., S13835
Jacob, Md. Indian War 1758, BLReg. 13706 Act of 9/28/1850
Jacob, Md., S8998
Jacob, Mass., S41795

MARTIN (continued)
Jacob, Mass., Catherine, R6937
Jacob, N.C., S7172
Jacob, Pa., S22385
James, Mass., S33032
James, N.J., Mary, W3438
James, N.J., BLWt.1016-100
James, N.C., S38164
James, N.C., b. N.J., Martha, W4728; BLWt.13425-160-55
James, N.C., Rachel, R6968
James, Pa., S38170
James, R.I., S40977
James, S.C.(?), Martha, ----
James, S.C., S9391, b. in Va.
James, S.C., S31833, b. Ireland
James, S.C., BLWt.1524-400
James, Va., Nancy, R6966
James, Va. Sea Service, R71, Va. Half Pay
James, Va., Indian Wars, S31236
James Nathaniel, N.C., R6948
Jeremiah, S.C., Margaret, BLWt. 91123-160-55
Jesse, Mass., N.H., S18961
Jesse, N.C., R6949
Jirah, Mass., Hannah Cross, W26230
Job, Va., S18496
John, Ct., S42910
John, Cont., Catharine, Md.,S40123
John, Cont., Md., Barbara Ann, W4277
John, Cont., Mass., Lydia, W24135
John, Cont. Va., S36074
John, Ga., S.C., S16459, b. S.C.
John, Md., BLWt.1736-100
John, Mass., Rachael, W26235. M. Rachel Cobb 1785.
John, Mass., R6953. In 1821 wife Anna, age 58 yrs.
John, N.H., S40965
John, N.H., S42911
John, N.J., S---- -- (Cert. 7190)
John, N.J., Sarah, W5338
John, Lamb's Art., N.Y., BLWt. 7517. Iss. 7/28/1790 to G.H.V. Wagenen, ass. No papers
John, N.C., Nancy, W4722
John, Pa., R6951
John, Pa., R6955
John, S.C., S15935
John, S.C. S38165
John, S.C., Eliza Sadler, former wid., W9642
John, Va., BLWts.12341 & 13389 Iss. 11/15/1791. No papers
John, Va., BLWt.12389. Iss. 5/8/1794. No papers
John, Va., S18104
John, Va., S30563
John, Va., Mary, W1443
John, Va., R6954
John O.F., Va., S30569
John Peter, S.C., Isabella Inness, R6956
Jonathan, Mass., S44525
Joseph, Ct., S13863
Joseph, Ct., S36061
Joseph, Ct., Anna, W17101
Joseph, Ct., Lovina, W20241
Joseph/Polland, Cont., Can., Mary A., W27971

MARTIN (continued)
Joseph, French, N.C., Va., b. in France, Telitha, R6957
Joseph, Pvt., Hazen's Regt., BLWt.13431. Iss. 2/4/1790. No papers
Joseph, N.J., Martha, R6960
Joseph, S.C., Joannah, R6950
Joseph, Va., Patsey, W9532
Joseph P., Ct. Cont., Lucy, W1629 BLWt.13410-100 iss. 4/20/1797. BLWt.209-60-55. No papers
Joshua, Ct., Elizabeth, W18464, BLWt.6255-160-55
Joshua, N.C., S41793
Josiah/Josias, N.C., Mary, W1047
Josiah, Va., BLWt.12369. Iss. 3/26/179? to Francis Groves, ass. No papers
Josiah, Va., Sarah, W18485
Kinchen, Va., Chloe, W5337
Levi, Pa., S2731
Lewis, Ct., BLWt.6202. Iss. 8/3/1789 to Wm. J. Vredenburgh, ass. No papers
Lewis, Pa., b. N.J., Elizabeth, W4538
Louis Daniel, S.C., BLWt.173-300
Luther, Ct., S42932
Luther, R.I., Elizabeth, W27447
Martin, S.C., Dicy, W9170
Matt, Ga., S.C., Va., S2726
Merrick/Merick, N.J., Tabitha, W179; BLWt.26679-160-55
Moses, Armond's Corp., BLWt.1431-200-Lt. Iss. 12/20/1790. Also recorded as above under BLWt.2575. No papers.
Moses, Mass., R6964
Moses, N.H., Miriam, W15055
Moses, N.J., Isabel S., W25676; BLWt.9536-160-55
Moses, N.C., Ann, W8415
Nathan, Ct., Martha, W26239
Nathan, N.H., Hannah, W23904
Nathaniel, Mass., S44524; BLWt. 757-100
Nathaniel, N.H., S29977
Nathaniel, N.H., R6967
Nathaniel, N.J., Elsy, W7393
Nathaniel, Vt., Anna, W20230
Nathaniel Ford, Ct., Naomi, W2142; BLWt.6028-160-55
Obediah, N.C., Winneford, R6976
Oliver, Mass., S33047
Patrick, Pa., S40115
Peter, Mass., Elizabeth, W13676
Peter, Mass., Hannah, W26236
Peter, N.J. See Peter Martin HESS
Peter, Pa., S40970
Peter, Pa., BLWt.1477-200-Lt. Iss. 1/20/1791. No papers
Philip, Md., S34971
Pleasant, Va., S2729
Reuben, Ct., Sally, W1906; BLWt. 21838-160-55
Reuben, N.H., S22377
Reuben, N.J., S8989
Rhodeham, N.C., Jane, W9907
Richard, Mass., S13841
Richard, N.C., Frances, R6944
Richard, Pa., S5721

MARTIN (continued)
Robert, Cont. Mass., S37212
Robert, Md., Nancy, W9535
Robert, Mass., N.H., S13822
Robert, N.Y., Annatje/Ann Crum, former wid., W27515. BLWt.12718-160-55. Her 2nd husb., Elias Crum, also served in the Rev. War, N.Y., which see
Robert, N.C., S2732
Robert, N.C., Elizabeth, W1907
Robert, Pa., BLWt.1436-200-Lt. Iss. 7/27/1789 to Richard Platt, ass. No papers
Roger, Pa., S2733
Salathiel, N.C., Mary, W1044; BLWt.61263-160-55
Samuel, Ct., S22383
Samuel, Md., R6971
Samuel, N.H., S44523
Samuel, N.J., Rebecca, W7392
Samuel, N.C., b. Ireland, S9003
Samuel, N.C., Jennet, R15990
Samuel, S.C., S2727
Samuel, Va., S2728
Scott, Va. See Samuel S. SCRUGGS
Seth, Mass., S15933
Seth, N.H., Elizabeth Read, former wid., BLWt.82005-160-55
Solomon, Cont., Mass., S40966
Stephen, Ct., Bethiah, W16337
Thomas, Ct., S2730
Thomas, Mass., BLWt.4692. Iss. 3/25/1790. No papers
Thomas, N.J., S18964
Thomas, N.Y., S13876
Thomas, N.Y., Kesiah, W18487
Thomas, N.C., Sabra, W21740
Thomas, Pa., Mary, W3272
Thomas, Va., BLWt.236-300
Thomas N., Mass., S40964
William, Armand's Corps, BLWt. 13397. Iss. 6/9/1789. No papers
William, Ct., BLWt.6201. Iss. 5/1/1797 to John Duncan, ass. No papers
William, Sheldon's Dragoons, Ct. BLWt.6222. Iss. 12/11/1789. No papers
William, Cont., N.J., Jane, W9937; BLWt.113541-160-55
William, Ga., R6975
William, Mass., N.H., S42917
William, N.J., BLWt.8536. Iss. 3/29/1792. No papers
William, N.J., Margaret, W863
William, N.J., Susannah, W20237
William, N.C., S32395
William, Pa., S40117
William, Pa., BLWt.1450-300-Capt. Iss. 12/20/1797. No papers
William, S.C., S38930
William, Vt., S9396. See N.A. Acc. No. 874-050112 - Not Half Pay, William Martin
William, Va., BLWt.12350. Iss. 12/31/1791 to Benjamin Mifflin, ass. No papers
William, Va., S5736
William, Va., S21355
William, Va., S36070

MARTIN (continued)
William, Va., Lititia, W5327
William, Va., Patsey, W5342, BLWt.5080-160-55
William, Va.; BLWt.1463-100
Zachariah, N.C., S11032
MARTINDALE, Ebenezer, Mass., Lydia, W17074
James, S.C., Mary, R6979
John, Md. Agcy. No papers
John, Mass., BLWt.4655. Iss. 4/1/1790 to John May. No papers
Samuel, Del., N.C., S8878
Stephen, Mass., Huldah, W24134
Uriah, Mass., S31231
William, S.C., R6980
MARTINE, Daniel, N.Y., S22890
Daniel, N.Y., R6981
William, N.Y., Elizabeth, W19853
MARTINUS, Cornelius, N.J., R6982
MARTLING, Abraham, Cont., N.Y., Fanny, W18473
Abraham B., N.Y., S----
Daniel, N.C., N.Y. res., R6983
Deliverance, Haven's Regt., BLWt. 13436. Iss. 8/22/1791 to Richard Smith, ass. No papers
MATRICK, Quorck, Mass., S11039
MARTS, William, N.J., S2724
MARTTING, Abraham B., See MARTLING
MARTZ, George, Pa., S22378
MARVELL, Francis, Mass., BLWt.4695 Iss. 4/27/1792. No papers
John, Mass., Privateer, Sarah, W21765
MARVEN, Richard, Navy, R.I., S38924
MARVIN, Abraham, Ct., Mary, R6985
Benjamin, Ct., Urania Pamela, W6786; BLWt.26207-160-55
Benjamin, N.Y., S40963
David, Ct., S15520
David, Ct., R6984
John C., Navy, Ct., Clarissa, W18480; BLWt.26026-160-55
Jonathan, Ct., S15601
Joseph, Ct., S15516
Mathew, Ct., BLWt.1061-100
Matthew, N.Y., S42920
Nathan, Ct., Rebecca Baker, former wid., W18558
Ozias, Ct., Althea, W1885; BLWt. 29054-160-55
Richard, Navy, R.I., See MARVEN
Samuel, Ct., N.Y., R6986
Seth, N.Y., Hannah, W17098
MARX, Johannes/John MARKS, Cont. Pa., S40114
William, Pa., S40968
MASDEN, John, Pa., Elizabeth, R6914
MASE, Samuel, N.J., BLWt.8513. Iss. 6/11/1789 to Jonathan Dayton, ass. No papers
Samuel, N.J., S34418
MASENGILL, Henry, See MASSENGILL
MASH, David, See MARSH
Samuel, See MARSH
William, N.J., S2722
MASHLER, Adam, See MUSHLER
MASON, Aaron, Mass., R16101
Aaron, R.I., S33050
Abel, Mass., S18498
Adam, Va., S8996

MASON (continued)
Alexander, R.I., S17570
Andrew, N.J., BLWt.8512. Iss. 7/17/1789. No papers
Arthur, Md., S36058
Ashbel, Ct., S42916; BLWt.2251-100
Betsey, former wid. of Nathaniel Hovey, Ct., which see
Broadstreet, N.H., S37207; BLWt. 998-100
Caleb, Md., BLWt.1494-150. Iss. 5/8/1790 to Issacher Mason, Admr. No papers
Caleb, N.C., S1917
Calvert, Md., S8956
Daniel, Mass., S31233
Daniel, Mass., Ruth, W16642
David, Crane's Art., BLWt.1366-200-Lt. Iss. 2/12/1796. No papers
David, Mass., R6991
David, Va., R6990
Ebenezer, Mass., Hannah, W1442; BLWt.17597-160-55
Ebenezer, Mass., Sally, R6992; BLWt.14542-160-55
Edward, Sgt. Major, N.H., BLWt. 3329. Iss. 12/21/1790. No papers
Edward, N.H., S11038
Edward, R.I., Sarah, W21756
Edward, Va., b. England, S4181
Elijah, Cont., Mass., S17559
Elijah, Vt., Electa, W1043; BLWt. 16129-160-55
Elisha, Cont., Ct., S13882; BLWt. 7202-160-55
Elisha, Mass., Sarah, W19862
Elnathan, Ct., Mary, W15842
George, Mass., Susannah Hilton, former wid., R7003
George, Pa., S33053
George, Va., R6995
Hannah, former wid. of John Campbell, Mass., which see
Henry, Ct., Ama, W17097
Hugh, Cont., Mass., Lydia Coburn, former wid., W10642; BLWt.103981-160-55
Isaac, Ct., Sarah, W17084
Isaac, N.Y., & War of 1812, Margaret, W6799; BLWt.52460-160-55
Issacher, Md., BLWt.11491. Iss. 5/8/1790. No papers
James, Cont., Ct., S42919
James, Cont., N.Y., S36064
James, Md., BLWt.11472. Iss. 5/11/1790. No papers
James, R.I., S21364
Jeremiah, N.Y., R6996
John, Ga., S9390, enl. in Mecklenburg Co., Va.
John, Mass., Lucy, W23922
John, N.H., Betsey, R6987
John, N.H., Prudence, R6999
John, N.Y., Chloe, W18479
Jonathan, Ct., Navy, N.H., Deborah, W21773
Jonathan, Navy, R.I., Mary, W17077
Jonathan, N.H., S44527
Joseph, Ct., S36079
Joseph, Cont. Mass., S13820

MASON (continued)
Joseph, Mass., S31227
Joseph, Va., S30562
Lemuel B., Cont., N.H., War of 1812, S44528; BLWt.1342-200-Lt. Iss. 11/28/1789. No papers
Levi, Hazen's Regt., BLWt.13438. Iss. 2/23/1797 to Josiah Starr. No papers
Littleberry, Va. Rebecca Hardaway, former wid., W23190
Luther, Ct., Hepsibah/Hephsibeth, W9172
Mathew, Green Mt. Boys, Mass., S13867
Michael, Cont., Mass., S28804
Michael, Md., S8876
Moses, N.H., Eunice, W23913
Nathan, Mass., S9000
Nathaniel, Cont., Mass., Phebe, W20242; BLWt.1758-100
Nathaniel, Mass., R6997
Noah, Cont. Mass., Lucretia, W23910
Olive, former wid. of Elias Heath, Mass., which see
Pardon, Mass., Elizabeth, W2626
Patrick, N.C., S41810
Paul, Mass., Elizabeth, W21743
Peter, Ga., S38172
Peter, Md., R6998
Peter, Va., S32394
Philip, N.C., S8994
Robert, Ct., R7000
Robert, Cont., Mass., Phebe, W8414; BLWt.12830-160-55
Robert, N.H., S44529
Robert, Va., R7001
Rufus, Cont. Mass., S28803
Simeon, Mass., S29975
Simeon, N.H., Abigail, W21755
Smith, Va., S7180
Thomas, Del., BLWt.10825. Iss. 4/19/1792. No papers
Thomas, Del., S36691
Thomas, Md., BLWt.1482-300-Capt. Iss. 5/24/1792. No papers
Thomas, N.Y., BLWt.7458. Iss. 7/16/1790 to W.I. Vreedenburgh, ass. No papers
Thomas, N.C., Elizabeth, R6993
Thomas, S.C., S41792
Tilley/Tilly, Mass., S29308
William, Hazen's Regt., BLWt. 13449. Iss. 1/19/1790. No papers
William, Pa., S40120
William, Va., Mary, W6792; BLWt. 26466-160-55
MASSAY, John, See MASSEY
MASSENBURG, Alexander, Va., R16060
Va. Half Pay-See N.A. Acc. No. 837-Va. State Navy, Alexander Massenburg, Y.S. File, Va. Half Pay
MASSENGILL, Henry, N.C., Elizabeth, W25681; BLWt.26430-160-55
Michael, N.C., S1687
MASSEY, Alston S., S.C., b. Va., Emeline, R7004; BLWt.87024-160-55
Caleb, Va., Sarah, W3437
Edmond, Va., S16462

MASSEY (continued)
Elias, N.C., Elizabeth, W5328; BLWt.53752-160-55
Ezekiel, N.J. Sea Service, Esther W5330; BLWt.26189-160-55
Henry, Md., Frances, W5343; BLWt. 27677-160-55
Henry, N.C., S1919
Henry, S.C., b. Va., S18103
Jesse, Del., S34975
John, Cont. Mass., N.H., Martha Phelps, former wid., W6641; BLWt.2350-100
John, N.C., Mary, W4021
John, N.C., Lydia, W4724
John, Va., S1918
John, Va., Susannah, R7008
John, Va., BLWt.2076-150
Joseph, N.C., Bathia, R7005
Lovell, Va., Rejected B.L.335497 Act 3/3/1855
Thomas, Va., BLWt.12360, iss. 1/31/179- to John Stockdell, ass. No papers
Thomas, Va. See MASSIE
William, Va., R7007 & R7009
MASSIE, John, Cont. Mass. See MASSEY
John, Va., Judith, W9931
Thomas, Va., S31235
Thomas, Va., Sally, W7403, Va. Half Pay
MASSURY, Joseph, R.I., BLWt.1347-200-Lt. Iss. 4/20/1790. No papers
MASSY, Charles, Va., Elizabeth, W9536
Jacob, N.C., Katharine, R7006
MAST, Jacob, Pa., R7010
MASTEN, Abraham, N.Y., S29312
Ezekiel, N.Y., R7013
Jacob, Mass., S13833
Jacob, N.Y., S28802
Matthew, N.Y., Elizabeth, W2220, BLWt.15191-160-55
MASTERMAN, James, Mass., Sea Service, S15931
MASTERS, Clement, N.J., S13855
Clement, N.J., S40118
Edward, Mass., BLWt.4636. Iss. 8/10/1789 to Richard Platt. No papers
Edward, Mass., S33033
Edward D., Va., Sally, W2651; BLWt.1995-100 & 14979-160-55
Enoch, N.C., S2749
James, Ct., Esther, W23907
John, N.J., BLWt.8585. Iss. 12/30/1796. No papers
John, N.J., S34417
John, Va., S36057
John, Va., See DEMASTERS
Jonathan, N.Y., BLWt.7466. Iss. 7/16/1790 to Wm. I. Vreedenburgh, ass. No papers
Nothy, S.C., Mary, W5365; BLWt. 24170-160-55
Stephen, N.J., Judith, W5340; BLWt.8516-100 & 185-60-55
Thomas, Va., Elizabeth, W13688; BLWt.17891-160-55

MASTERS (continued)
William, N.J., Mary, W5344
MASTERSON, James, N.C., Margaret, W8422
John, Pa., S16460
Patrick, Va., Mary, R7012
MASTICK, Benjamin, Mass., Cynthia, W7397
MASTIN, Abraham, See MASTEN
Cornelius, N.Y., See MARTIN
Ezekiel, N.Y., S28801
John, N.H. See MARSTON
MASTON, Jacob, See MASTEN
MASUERE, Peter, Navy, N.H., S44996
MATEER, William Paul, See William PALMITER
MATHENY, William, N.C., S1999
MATHER, Abner, Cont., Deborah, N.Y. res. of sold. in 1818, W2822; BLWt.6029-160-55
Eleazer, Ct., S2744
Elihu, Ct., BLWt.6192. Iss. 3/1/1790. No papers
Elihu, Ct., Polly Grovener/Grosvenor, former wid., R4360
Increase, Ct., Hepzibah, W25674
Joseph, Ct., S15929
Joseph, Ct., Sarah. Dau. Betsey Lockwood., W29696
Joseph, Ct., Navy, S13878
Nathaniel, Ct., S13872
Phinehas, Vt., Huldah, W24136
Reuben, Ct., S29306
Samuel, Ct., S33
Samuel, Ct., S13871
Samuel, Ct., S17568
Silvanus/Sylvanus, Ct., Caroline, W21774
Stephen, Ct., Elizabeth, W16344
Thomas, N.H., See MATHES
Timothy, Ct., BLWt.1711-400
MATHERS, William, Pa., S30566
William H., Ga., S45846
MATHES, Thomas, N.H., Sally, W21768; BLWt. 3327-100. Iss. 11/28/1789. BLWt.160-60-55
MATHESON, Daniel, See MATTESON
MATHEW, Isaac, Va., S9001
MATHEWS, Abner, Mass., Lydia, W15066
Amos V., Ct., Delila, W9537; BLWt.75006-160-55
Asahel, Mass., S11023
Benjamin, Cont., R.I., S42930
Benjamin, S.C., Mary, W21749
Benjamin, Va., S32391
Charles, Mass., R7018
Daniel, Cont., N.H., Navy, S37222
Daniel, N.H., Mary, W27892; BLWt.2303-100 & 106-60-55
Ebenezer, N.H., S42933; BLWt. 700-100
George, S.C., Mary G., W21750
Gideon, Ct., R7019
Henry, R.I., BLWt.3350-100. Iss. 11/4/1794
Hugh, N.H., Mary Sampson, former wid., W11377; BLWt.81014-160-55
Hugh, N.C., R7020

MATHEWS (continued)
Isaac, S.C. See MATTHEWS
James, Ct., Sea Service, Mass.? Desire/Desiah, W23909
James, N.J., Mary, W17087; BLWt. 8533-100-Pvt. Iss. 6/16/1789 to Thomas Coyle, ass. No papers
James, Va., R7021
John, Mass., S37220
John, N.H., Sally, W21772
John, N.J., S893
John, N.C., S31839
John, S.C., R7025
John B., S.C., R20401
Joseph, N.H., Lucy, W2680; BLWt. 39484-160-55
Moses, Ct., S17558
Peter H., Pa., Rebecca, W5334; BLWt.31294-160-55
Philip, S.C., R7031
Philip, Va., S5729
Richard, Pa., Martha, R7028
Samuel, Va., S5732
Sarah, former wid. of William Mains, Mass., which see
Thomas, Va., Molly, W17076 & R16019; Va. Half Pay
Timothy, Mass., Lois, W15068; BLWt.30909-160-55
William, Ct., S33031
William, Pa., S9004
William, Pa., S41805
William, Va., Nancy, W5131
MATHEWSON, Charles, R.I., S16458
Daniel, R.I., S23785
Elisha, Ct., Elizabeth, W3437 (See Ct. Men In Rev., p.266. Res."Westmoreland Co., Ct.".) (Location in Wyoming Valley, Pa.)
John, R.I., Lydia, W13686
Joseph, R.I., Betty, W13680
Joseph, R.I., R7033
Nicholas, R.I., Abigail, W21751
Richard, R.I., S21877
William, R.I. See MATTHEWSON
MATHIAS, James, Md., S40119
MATHIOT, George, Pa. Sea Service, Ruth, W4486; BLWt.28553-160-55
MATHIS, Eleanor, former wid. of John McLaughlin, N.C., which see
Joseph, ---, R7015, S.C. res. of son in 1854
MATKINS, John, Md., S7181
MATLACK, Isaac, N.J., Mary Pedrick, former wid., R8073
Jacob, N.J., S2756; BLWt.26518-160-55
MATLO, John, Va., S15934
MATLOCK, Jacob, See MATLACK
John, N.C., Mary, W4723
Nathaniel, N.C., Martha, W8409
Richard, See MEDLOCK
Zachariah, Va., Lucy, W8420
MATOON, Ebenezer, See MATTOON
MATSINGER, Adam, Pa., S23739
MATSON, John, Ct., S18963
Joseph, Dis. No papers. Ct. Agcy. See Ct. Historical Soc. Collections, Vol. 8, p.265 under heading of Pensioners-Half Pay.
MATTERSON, Philip, Md., BLWt.11548 Iss. 3/11/1791. No papers

MATTESON, Allen, R.I., S22891
Benjamin, Green Mt. Boys, Vt. See MATTISON
Benjamin, R.I., S21360
Caleb, Mass., S42929
Daniel, R.I., Dorcas, W13689
David, Ct., S40129
David, Vt., Sarah, W17086
Hezekiah, Ct., Elizabeth, W17090
James, Vt., Thankful, W16343
Jonathan, R.I., Katherine, W10213; BLWt.86026-160-55
Joshua, R.I. See MATTISON
Obadiah, R.I., Phebe, W21777
Philip, Vt., Sally, W18492
Rufus, R.I., Rhoda, W13666
Samuel, Vt., Hannah, W21776; BLWt.11178-160-55
Stephen, Mass., S21875
Susannah, former wid. of Latham Cornell, R.I., which see
Thomas, R.I., R7037
William, Ct., S9395; BLWt.3990-160-55
MATTHAY, Frederick, See MATTHEY
MATTHEWS, Atkins, Mass., Sarah, W15067
Caleb, R.I., Orpha, W23928
Daniel, Mass., S42915
David, Cont., Pa., S13854
Elisha, Mass., S18497
Francis, Md., S38178
Garret, N.J., S17564
George, Va., S38179
George, Va., BLWt.1497-500-Col. Iss. 8/7/1789. No papers. (Located in what is now Morrow & Knox Cos., Ohio)
Gilbert, N.C., S41803; BLReg. 313786-1855
Giles, N.C., S8993
Hardy, N.C., S2746
Henry, R.I., BLWt.3350 & 3345. Iss. 11/4/1794. No papers
Isaac, S.C., b. Va., S31843
Jabez, Mass., N.H., N.Y., Lovisa/Lovice, W17093
James, N.J., BLWt.8533. Iss. 6/16/1789 to Thomas Coyle, ass. No papers
James/John, N.Y., R7022
James, N.C., S41818
James, Pa., BLWt.9895. Iss. 4/27/1792. No papers
Jeremiah, N.C., Sarah, W4488
Jesse, Ct., S36075
Jesse, Va., S5735
John, Res. Md. No papers
John, Cont., Ct., S36077; BLWt. 321-100
John, Mass., S37204
John, N.H., BLWt.3315. Iss. 3/25/1790. No papers
John, N.J. See MATHEWS
John, N.Y. See James
John, N.C., Mary, W4725; BLWt. 17885-160-55
John, N.C., R7024
John, Pa., BLWt.9970. Iss. 2/14/1791 to Alexander Power, ass. of Murtoch Sulliven, Admr. No papers

MATTHEWS (continued)
John, Va., R7023
Joseph, Va., S7179
Josiah, Mass., Thankful, W26246
Littleberry/Littlebury, Va., R7027
Nathaniel, Mass., Mercy, R7029
Peter, N.Y., BLWt.7444. Iss. 5/14/1793 to Thomas Russell, ass.
Thomas, Ct., S13857
Thomas, N.H., BLWt.3327 & 160-60-55. Iss. 11/28/1789. See Thomas Mathes, W21758. No papers
Thomas, Va., R7032
William, Ct., BLWt.6154. Iss. 8/21/1789. No papers
William, Md., BLWt.11487. Iss. 1/25/1790. No papers
William, Mass., S33028
William, N.C., b. Va., S31842; BLWt.30911-160-55
William, Va., S2745
MATTHEWSON, Elisha, Ct., BLWt.6138. Iss. 1/5/1792. No papers
William, R.I., Tabitha, W16338
MATTHEY, Frederick, Pa., R7034
MATTHIS, Arthur, N.C., S9397
MATTICE, Joseph, N.Y., R7036
Laurence/Lawrence, N.Y. res., R7035
MATTINGLY, James, Va., Elizabeth, W36055
John, Va., Dykeander, W5346
John B., Ky. res. of heir in 1853, R---.
MATTISON, Benjamin, Green Mt. Boys, Vt., Lois, W17100
Dyer, R.I., S5734
Job, Cont., R.I., Lucy, W20229
Jonathan, See MATTESON
Joshua, R.I., R7038
Roswell, Ct., Elizabeth, W9913
Samuel, N.Y., BLWt.7540. Iss. 3/30/1791 to Richard Edwards, ass. No papers
Samuel, Vt. See MATTESON
William, Ct. See MATTESON
MATTOCKS, Peter, Pa., R7040
Richard, Pa., b. Va., S16185
MATTOON, Abel, Cont., Mass., S42913
Ebenezer, Mass., H.H., S30567
John, N.Y., Chloe, W16339
Sylvanus/Silvanus, Mass., Thankful Mabel, W2402; BLWt.7073-160-55
MATTOX, John, Va., BLWt.12374-100-Pvt. Iss. 7/14/1792. No papers
Margaret, former wid. of Frederick Reeger, Cont., Pa., which see
MAUD, William, Pa., BLWt.9894. Iss. 5/1/1792 to Christian Hubbard, ass. of James Matthews, Admr. No papers
MAUK, Andrew, Va. See MANK
Henry, See MANK
Mathias, Va., Anna Kyle, former wid., R6064
MAULEY, Elijah, Ct., S36078
MAUPIN, Cornelius, Va., R7041
Daniel, Va., S5733
Daniel, Va., Margaret, W556; BLWt. 26486-160-55
Gabriel, Va., R16058. Va. Half Pay
Thomas, Va., Ann/Anna, W7402

MAUPIN (continued)
Thomas, Va., Margaret, W9920; BLWt.40708-160-55
William, Va., S13851
MAURER, John, Pa., Elizabeth, W5133
Peter, Pa., S2750
MAURY, Abraham, Va., S5730
William, Va., S2000
MAUS, Matthew, Pa., BLWt.1063-400
MAUSTERSTOCK, Johannes, See MANSTERSTOCK
MAUZY, Peter, Va., S11031
William, Va., S16184
MAVEN, James, See MABEN
MAXAM, Adonijah, Ct., N.Y., Catherine, W5345; BLWt. Rej.
MAXCY, Joel, Va., Betsey Ann, W5331; BLWt.26968-160-55
Horatio, Va., son of John, R7043
MAXEY, John, Va., S8991
John, Va., Ann, W5351; BLWt. 40002-160-55
William, Va., son of Radford, Nancy, W8412
MAXFIELD, David, R.I., S38925
Dudley, Mass., S29309
Edward, Ct., BLWt.6230. Iss. 9/18/1789. No papers
Edward, Ct., Mary, W17070
John, Mass., Rhoda, W15059
Joseph, Mass., S36066; BLWt. 1645-100
Justin, Mass., R20402
Richard, Mass., S22384
Robert, Mass., N.H., S37218
William, Mass., Isabella, W23914
William, Va., BLWt.12409. Iss. 5/11/1792 to Francis Graves, ass. No papers
MAXHOM, Lemuel, Mass., S36073
MAXIM, William, Pa., BLWt.9908. Iss. 2/28/1797 to Philip Shrader, ass. No papers
MAXON, Asa, R.I. See MAXSON
John, N.J. See MAXSON
John, R.I., See MAXSON
Matthew, R.I., Fanny, W21741
Nathan, R.I. See MAXSON
Silas, Ct., S11028
Torry/Torrey, R.I., S13844
MAXSEN, Zaccheus, R.I., S42905
MAXSON, Asa, R.I., S22889, Mary, wid. of above sold. was pensioned as former wid. of George Potter, R.I., which see
Clark/Clarke, R.I., Nancy, R7044
Joel, R.I., S13852
John, N.J., Leah, W1042
John, R.I., Sarah, W13674
Nathan, R.I., S13870
Phinehas, Cont., R.I., S28805
Stephen, R.I., S42926
MAXWELL, Adam, Elizabeth, Pa.,S5064
Anthony, Cont., N.Y., Eve, W21762; BLWts.30941-160-55 & 1394-200-Lt. Iss. 8/2/1792. No papers
Cornelius, N.Y., BLWt.7473. Iss. 7/22/1790. No papers
David, Sea Service, Mass., Abigail R7045
Hugh, Cont., Mass., Dis. See Am. State Papers, Class 9, p.150,

MAXWELL (continued)
which shows that Hugh Maxwell served under Col. Prescott; was wounded by a musket ball in his right shoulder at Bunker Hill, 6/17/1775. Res. Heath, Mass. Served in Militia & received his commutation as Lt. Col.(evidence complete). BLWt.1350-450-Lt. Col. Iss. 2/6/1795. No papers
James, Md., BLWt.11523 iss. 12/13/1792 to Frederick Mollineux, ass. No papers
James, ?, Esther, R7047, wid's. res. Tenn. in 1845
James, N.H., S44997
James, N.J., Ann, W2828, BLWt. 1501-300
James, Pa., BLWt.10098. Iss. 3/19/1797. No papers
James, Pa., S9932; BLWt.2280-100
James, Pa., S40113
James, Va. Sea Service, R73. Va. Half Pay. See N.A. Acc. No. 837, Va. State Navy, James Maxwell Y.S. file. Va. Half Pay
John, Md., BLWt.11519. Iss. 2/1/1790. No papers
John, Md., Pa., S41817
John, N.C., S1685
John, S.C., S21358, b. Ireland
Josiah, Ga., BLWt.2448-200
Nathaniel, Pa., Esther, W5132
Thomas, Cont. ?, R7048, Ind. res.
Thompson, Cont., N.H., also in French & Indian War & in War of 1812, S7168
William, Del., BLWts.10827 & 10884. Iss. 9/2/1789 to Wm. Maxwell (see note on Wm. Maxwell Wt. 10833, Del. Service. No papers
William, Del., BLWt.10833. Iss. 9/2/1789. No papers
William, Del., S34972
William, Mass., Anna, W6787; BLWt.9539-160-55
William, N.C., Delby, W5329; BLWt.35846-160-55
William, N.C., Elizabeth, R7046
MAY, Abram, Va., S17562
Andrew, N.J., BLWt.8553. Iss. 8/17/1789. No papers
Beckam/Beckom/Beckman, Ga., R7049
Beckman, Ga. See Beckam
Benjamin, R.I., R7050
Cassimore, Pa., S1851
Charles, Pa. or Va., Mary, R7055
David, Va., R7052
Edmond/Edmund, Va., S38923
Eleazer, Mass., S11021
George, Pa., R7053
George, Va., S38928
Humphrey, Va., Susannah, W8408
John, Cont., Mass., S23787
John, Mass., BLWt.4701. Iss. 5/16/1796. No papers
John, Mass., Hepsibah, W23917
John, N.C., S36690
John, N.C., Va., Elizabeth, W18476
John, Pa., R20400
John, Vt., S40973

MAY (continued)
John, Va., Charity, R7051
John, Va., Sarah, R7056
Joseph, Ct., Rebecca, W21745
Levi, Mass., Deborah, W26241
Ludwick, N.C., S7169
Luke, Cont., Mass., Sarah/Sally, W23911
Mary, former wid. of Wm. Brabston, Va., which see.
Nathaniel, Mass., Betsy, W6775; BLWt.19785-160-55
Oliver, Mass., S5049
Rufus, Mass., Eunice, W23906
Stephen, Ct., S40976
Theodore, Mass., Elizabeth, W16340
Thomas, Ct., S40969
Thomas, Mass., Navy, Eunice, W16342
Thomas, N.C., S21356
Thomas, N.C., R7057
Thomas, Va., BLWt.12364. Iss. 3/26/1792 to Francis Graves, ass. No papers
Thomas, Va., S38175
William, N.C., Susannah, W861
William, Pa., BLWts.9873 & 13445. Iss. 5/5/1791. No papers
William, Va., Rhoda, W5335
MAYBEE, David, N.Y., R7058
MAYBERRY, Frederick, Va., R6567
George, Va., S11030
John, Art. Artificers, BLWt.13476. Iss. 4/29/1793. No papers
John, Mass., S18965
Richard, Mass., BLWt.1371-300-Capt Iss. 4/12/1790. No papers
Thomas, Mass. See MAYBERY
Thomas, Von Heer's Dragoons "Invalid". BLWt.13503. Iss. 3/31/1791. No papers
William, Cont., Enl. in N.J., S41807
William, Cont., Navy, Enl. in Pa., S41819
William, Mass., BLWt.4671. Iss. 11/10/1792 to Moses Beard. No papers
William, Mass., Rebecca, W1631
MAYBERY, Thomas, Mass., Sarah, W2641. BLWt.30937-160-55
MAYBIN, Mathew, S.C., b. Ireland, S7171
MAYBRY, Richard, Mass., BLWt.4666. Iss. 4/19/1792 to John Peck. No papers
MAYBURRY, William, Pa., BLWt.10077. Iss. 7/18/179? to Andrew Porter, ass. No papers
William, Jr., Pvt., Pa., BLWt. 10080. Iss. 7/18/1791 to Andrew Porter, ass. No papers
MAYDEN, Robert, N.C., Margaret, W17075
MAYE, William, N.C., S7188
MAYER, Hanhendrick, See Henry MYERS
Jacob, Pa., S34416
John, Cont., Md., R7476
John, See MAEYER
Mathias, Cont., BLWt.1407-100. Pa. res. of heir in 1828

MAYER (continued)
Peter, Pa., Mary, W2653; BLWt.6272-160-55
MAYES, Benjamin. See MAYS
Samuel, S.C., Mary, W2140
William, Va., S41799
MAYFIELD, Abraham, N.C., R7060
Elijah, Va., S2754
Micajah, Va., S36692
Samuel, S.C., b. N.C., S16930
MAYHEW, Charity, former wid. of Silas Alden, Mass., which see
David, N.J., Ann, W3273
Elisha, Cont., Ct., Eunice, W8421
Freeborn, Mass., Hannah, W19861
James, Mass., S37219; BLWt.872-100
John, Mass., S29976
John, Va., S9401
Peter V., N.H., S44998
William, Mass., See MAHEW
William, N.C., S7184
MAYHUE, James, Mass. See MAYHEW
MAYHUGH, Jonathan, Md., S36054
MAYLIN, Jacob, Pa., Jane, W3206
MAYNADIER, Henry, Md., S9002
MAYNARD, Abel, Cont., Mass.,S44995
Anthony, Hazen's Regt., BLWt.13428 Iss. 1/22/1790 to Benj. Mooers, ass. No papers
Banister, Mass., S33054
Benjamin, Mass., Martha, W13667
Calvin, Mass., S30560
Christopher, See MINARD
Ebenezer, Ct., S13874
Elisha B., N.Y., R7063
Israel, Mass., S9398
Jabez, Ct., Cont., Navy, S36072
James, Ct., S17567
James, N.C. See MANARD
John, Ct., S13829
John, Mass., S33048; BLWt.1360-200-Lt. Iss. 7/8/1797. No papers
Jonathan, Mass., S33052; BLWt. 1351-300-Capt. Iss. 7/8/1797. No papers
Joseph, Mass., Elizabeth, W2222; BLWt.4698-100 & 17-60-55
Joshua, Mass., S33030
Lebbeus/Libbeus, Ct., S13821
Nathan, Mass., R7064
Needham, Mass., S13849
Peter, Mass., BLWt.4683. Iss. 7/22/1789. No papers
Peter, Mass., S33051
Richard, Va., S13828
Timothy, Mass., BLWt.43874-160-55
William, Mass., BLWt.1369-200-Lt. Iss. 12/30/1796 to John Wright, Jr., ass. No papers
Winslow, Mass., R7065
Zebediah, See MINARD
MAYNER, Henry, N.C., Catharine, W8268
Richard T., Va., R22014
MAYNOR, Henry, N.C. See MAYNER
MAYO, Benjamin, Va., Judith, W5341; BLWt.28578-160-55
Genet, former wid. of Seth Hinckley, Mass., which see
Isaac, Ct., Mass., Hannah, W23920

MAYO (continued)
Issachar/Isachar, Cont., Mass., S44994
John, N.C., S31838
Joshua, Mass., S37200
Stephen, Va., Rebecca, W25680; BLWt.17884-160-55. (Next to the last surv. pensioned wid. of Revolutionary sold. D.3/6/1904)
MAYPS, John, See MAPES
MAYRANT, John, Navy, S.C. Sea Service, S32390
MAYS, Abraham, N.Y. or Pa., R7067
Benjamin, Va., Leutitia/Lutitia, R7054. See N.A. Acc. No. 874-050113 - Not Half Pay, Benjamin Mays
William, Va. Sea Service, Children of, W18491
MAYSE, Charles, Va., S8879
MAZARETT, John, Va., R16059. Va. Half Pay. N.A. Acc. No. 874. See 050114. Half Pay John Mazarett/Majaret
MAZE, Abraham, See MAYS
James, Va., R7066
Thomas, S.C., Mary, R7069
MAZYCK, Daniel, S.C., BLWt.1543-300-Capt. Iss. 5/10/1796 to John Stites, ass. No papers
Stephen, S.C., Mary, W9174; BLWt.1546-200-Lt. Iss. 12/31/1796
McA, Eliezer, S.C., R6578
McADAM, Joanna, former wid. of Charles Bush, Mass., which see
John, Pa., S2761
John, S.C., b. Ireland, Sarah, W2649; BLWt.26206-160-55
John, Va., BLWt.1088-300
McADAMS, John, N.C., S2762
Joseph, N.C., S33081
Joseph, N.C., Margaret, R6579
William, N.C., S33083
McADDAM, Joseph, N.C. See McADAMS
McADEN, John, N.C., Elizabeth, R6580
McADOW, Andrew, Md., S9020
James, N.C., b. N.C., S2760
John, Md., R6581
McAFEE, Mathew/Matthew, Pa., S36697; BLWt.10095 iss. 1789
Matthew, See Mathew
McAFFERTY, Charles, R.I., BLWt. 3343-100-Pvt. Iss. 2/24/1800
McAFFERY, John, See McCAFFERY
McAIN/McCAIN, John, N.C., Mary, W9543
McALEXANDER, Alexander, Va., Martha, W5359
McALISTER, John, N.C., Sarah, W1887; BLWt.17590-160-55
John, Pa., BLWt.10010-100-Pvt. Iss. 3/29/1791. No papers
Joseph, Va., S31241
Richard, Cont., Mass., Sarah, W2147; BLWt.2179-160-55
William, N.Y., Eleanor, W24142; BLWt.7454-100. Iss. 5/5/1791 to R.V. Howenburgh, ass. No papers
McALLASTER, Benjamin, Mass., N.H., S33073
McALLESTER, Daniel, Va., S31245
McALLISTER, Abdiel, Pa., BLWt. 1452-200-Lt. Iss. 3/14/1794 to Richard McAllister, admr. Also recorded as above under BLWt.2637. No papers
Andrew, S.C., Elizabeth, R6602; BLWt.34665-160-55
James, Pa., R6583
John, N.C. See McCALLISTER
John, Pa., BLWt.9994-100-Pvt. Iss. 7/9/1789. Certified 4/18/1806
John, Pa. See McCALLISTER
Joseph, Va., See McALISTER
Richard, Mass., N.H. See McALISTER
William, Md., Henrietta, W801; BLWt.35822-160-55
William, N.Y. See McALISTER
McALPIN, George, N.H., Susanna Libbey, former wid., W16327; BLWt.825-100
McALPINE, John, N.Y., R6584
McAMIS, Thomas, Va. See McCAMISH
McANALLY, David, Va., Nancy, W966
John, Crane's Cont. Art., Mass., BLWt.4740-100-Pvt. Iss. 1/28/1790 to Eliphalet Downer. No papers
McANELLY, Peter, Va., S16467
McARTHER, Alexander, N.Y., BLWt. 1405-200-Lt. Iss. 12/15/1790 to Thomas McFarran, admr. No papers
Daniel, Pa., R6585
McARTHUR, Alexander, N.Y., Margaret, W17124
Peter, N.Y., Christian/Christiana, W23934
McATEE, Samuel, Md., S36087
Walter, Md., S31845
McATINNEY, Thomas, See McATINNY
McATINNY, Thomas, Pa., S36109
McAULEY, Daniel, Cont., Pd. at N.C. agcy., S18971
Daniel, Hazen's Regt., BLWt. 13466-100-Pvt. Iss. 5/8/1794. No papers
McAWAY, Christopher, Md., BLWt. 162-100
McBANE, Daniel, N.C., Sarah, W4735; BLWt.1541-100
Robert, N.C. See MEBANE
McBARNEY, Thomas, S25654. War service unknown, but list of invalid pensioners of Fayette Co., Ky. printed in 1835 shows Thomas McBarney, Pvt., 1st Regt. Price's Levies, pensioned from 3/4/1789 under Act of June 7, 1785
McBEE, Isaac, N.C., R6587
Israel, Va., res. at enl., N.C., S2784; BLWt.26413-160-55
Silas, S.C., b. Va., S7202
McBOY, James, Pa., BLWt.10128-100-Pvt. Iss. 3/2/179? to Thomas Campbell, admr. No papers
McBRAYER, Hugh, Va., R6588
McBRIDE, Alexander, Cont., Pa., S26261
McBRIDE (continued)
Archibald, ---, Phila. agcy. Dis. No papers
Hugh, Pa., Indian Wars, Mary, W9544; BLWt.77519-160-55
Hugh, Va., R6589
Isaiah/Josiah, N.C., S7206
James, N.C., b. Ireland, S4192
James, Pa., S22896
John, Cont., N.J., S823
John, N.C., b. Pa., S4193
John, N.C., Eleanor, W4730
John, S.C., Frances Anderson, former wid., W9330
Josiah, N.C. See Isaiah
Peter, Pa., BLWt.9974-100-Pvt. Iss. 6/20/1789. No papers
Peter, Pa., S40131
Robert, Pa., BLWt.1701-200. Iss. 12/24/1830
Roger, Del., S41846; BLWt.219-100
Stephen, Va., R6591
William, Va., S9425
McBROOM, Andrew, N.C., S7205
McBURNEY, James, N.J., BLWt.8583-100-Pvt. Iss. 2/10/1790 to Wm. Dayton, ass. No papers
James, N.J., S41839
McCABE, Hugh, Va., S2005
John, Del., BLWt.2027-100
McCADDAMES, John See McADAMS
McCAFFERY, James, N.J., S34425
John, Mass. Sea Service, Navy, Elizabeth Stanford, former wid., R---; BLWt.8375-160-55. This man's wid. pensioned as Elizabeth, wid. of John Stanford, Mass., which see
McCAFFREY, John, See McCAFFERY
McCAIN, Hance, Va., R6594
Hugh, N.C. or S.C., Isabel, R6593
Hugh, ---, Va. res. in 1834, R6596
John, N.C. See McAIN
William, N.Y., Va., Charlotte, R6592
McCAJAKIN, Francis, N.C. See ANTRICAN
McCALEB, Alexander, N.Y., S18969
McCALEY, Edward, Pa., BLWt.10101-100-Pvt. Iss. 7/16/1789. Certified 4/18/1806
McCALISTER, Daniel, Va. See McALLESTER
McCALL, Daniel, N.C., Catharine, W4734
David, N.C., S.C., S18966
George, S.C., R6598
John, Ct., Loruhamah, R6599
John, N.C., S17579
John, S.C., Grizzell, W9545
William, N.C., Elizabeth, R6597
McCALLA, Andrew, Pa., S16473
John, Cont., Md., Margaret, W1450
Thomas, Pa., BLWt.1448-400
McCALLEY, Hugh, N.Y., BLWt.7482-100-Pvt. Iss. 7/30/1790 to Edward Cumpston, ass. No papers
James, N.H., Isabella, W15929
James, Va., S36095
McCALLISTER, Alexander, Pa., R6601
Andrew, S.C. See McALLISTER
James, Md., S34992

McCALLISTER (continued)
John, N.C., S36111
John, Pa., S33387
William, Md. See McALLISTER
McCALLON, James, S.C., S2779
McCALLY, Campbell, Va. See McCAULEY
McCALPIN, George, N.H. See McALPIN
McCAM, John, N.J., R6610
McCAMISH, Thomas, Va., Jinny/Jenny, W6805, BLWt.12574-160-55
McCAMMON, James, S.C., Mary, R6604
Mathew, S.C., S17578
McCAMONT, Isaac, Pa., S2778
McCAMPBELL, Andrew, Va., Mary, R6607
James, Va., Martha, R6606
Solomon, Va., S1694
McCAN, Patrick, Pa., S18502
McCANCE, David, S.C., S16464
McCANDLESS, John, Cont., Va., Jane, W8441
John, N.C., S2777
McCANLASS, John, N.C., S1695
McCANLEY, John, Cont., Pa. See McCAULEY
McCANN, Daniel, Pa., BLWt.9959-100-Pvt. Iss. 3/21/1794 to Daniel McCann. No papers
Daniel, Pa., S40139
Hugh, See McCAIN
James, Pa., Jane, R6609
John, Md., BLWt.11522-100-Pvt. Iss. 12/18/1794 to Henry Purdy, ass. No papers
John, S.C., Va., Biddy, W5361; BLWt.29050-160-55
Michael, Md., BLWt.11482-100-Pvt. Iss. 2/1/1790. No papers
Michael, Md., S34993
Neal, Del., BLWt.10835-100-Pvt. Iss. 12/10/1799 to Alexander McBeath, guardian to Joseph Kirkwood & Mary Kirkwood, ch. of Robert Kirkwood, ass. No papers
Patrick, Not Rev. War, N.W. Indian War 1791-Pa., Mich., Elizabeth, Old War Inv. File 25669. BLWts. 85432-40-50, 54695-80-50, and 35756-80-55
McCANNE, John, N.C., BLWt.883-200
McCANNON, Christopher, Va., BLWt. 12373-100-Pvt. Iss. 5/17/1792 to Robert Means
Christopher, Va., Dis. No papers here but see pp.122 & 164, Am. State Papers, Claims, Class 9, which shows him as Sgt.-Major, in Col. Campbell's Va. Regt., wounded at the battle of Guilford by a musket ball while in the service of the U.S., which wound has almost deprived him of the use of his left arm, wounded 3/15/1781 at Guilford. There are no master rolls of the Va. line for 1781, whereby to ascertain the fact. He was dead before 12/30/1794.
McCANT, James, Va., Elizabeth, W1909
McCANTS, Ann, former wid. of Archibald Scott, S.C., which see
McCAR, John, Pa., S40143
McCARAHER, James, Invalid Corp., BLWt.13508-100-Pvt. Iss. 7/9/1789. No papers
McCARGO, Radford, Va., S16955
Stephen, Va., BLWt.2200-100
McCARMICK, George, Va., S36105 Va. Half Pay
McCARMISH, Thomas, Va. See McCAMISH
McCARNEY, Peter, Va., BLWt.12344-100-Pvt. Iss. 11/5/1789. No papers. Was alive in 1833
McCARNISH, Thomas, See McCAMISH
McCARROL, John, Pa. See McCARROLL
John, Pa., Keziah, W7418; BLWt. 2195-100. This sold. died in 1828
McCARROLL, John, Pa., S2782
McCARTER, Charles, Navy, Pa., Rachel, W3103
James, S.C., S13890
James, Va., S7216
John, Cont., Del., Agnes, W3843
Robert, N.Y., S9429
William, S.C., Isabella, W4736
McCARTHY, John, N.H., S42941
John, Pa., BLWt.10083-100-Pvt. "in the Artillery". Iss. 2/14/1791 to Andrew Power, ass. No papers
Moses, N.Y., R6611
Owen, Pa., BLWt.10078-100-Pvt. Iss. 6/4/1789. No papers
McCARTNEY, Dennis, Pa., BLWt.10047-100-Pvt. Iss. 5/9/1791. No papers
Henry, Pa., S40991
James, Pa., S2772
Jeremiah, N.C., S42947
John, N.C., S31847
Peter, Va., BLWt.2184-100
McCARTY, Andrew, Pa., S38194
Clark, Ct., Mabel, W20248
Daniel, Ct., R6612
Daniel, Cont., Pa., Letitia, W4546
Daniel, Mass., S42939
Daniel, Va., Mary, W8275; BLWt. 11165-160-55
Daniel, Va., Jemima Kirk, former wid., R5988
Dennis, N.Y., BLWt.7469-100-Pvt. Iss. 7/22/1790 to Thomas Tillotson, ass. No papers
Dennis, Pa., BLWt.10067-100-Pvt. Iss. 7/26/1791. No papers
Dennis, Pa., S22388
Francis, N.J., R6613
Michael, S.C., b. S.C., S11049
Philip, Pa., Polly, W3278
Richard, Pa., BLWt.9984-100-Pvt. Iss. 3/24/1792. No papers
Thomas, N.Y., S42938
Thomas, Pa., S23794
Thomas, Va., Ann, W8424
McCARY, Richard, Va., S38187
McCASELTON, Samuel, Pa., BLWt. 9986-100-Pvt. Iss. 5/12/1795 to Alexander Power, ass. of Solomon Sell, acting Executor
McCASKEY, Daniel, Pa., R6657
McCASKILL, Kenneth, N.C., S7197
McCASKREY, Samuel A., See McCOSKRY
William, Cont., Pa., See McCOSKRY
McCASLAND, John, Pa., Va., also under St. Clair, 1791. S4197
McCASLAND (continued)
William, Pa., Eleanor, W21790
McCASLIN, Alexander, Cont., Mass., Abigail, W6801; BLWt.17905-160-55
Patrick, Pa., BLWt.9938-100-Pvt. Iss. 4/7/1795 to John Nicholson, ass. No papers.
McCASTIN, Alexander, See McCASLIN
McCAULEY, Campbell, Va., Mary, W8444
Edward, Invalids Corps, BLWt. 13413-100-Pvt. Iss. 12/21/1789 to Edward Eastham, ass. No papers
James, N.Y., S33391; BLWt.1752-100
John, Cont., Pa., S34997
John, Va., S7207
Mathew, N.C., Martha, W17121
Nathaniel, N.H., BLWt.1345-200-Lt. Iss. 3/26/1792 to John McCauley, admr. No papers
Thomas, Va., S31248
McCAULLEY, Florence, N.H., BLWt. 3309-100-Pvt. Iss. 5/27/1797 to Christopher S. Thorn, ass. No papers
McCAUSLAND, Andrew, Va., S5751
Andrew, Va., S38199
Henry, Cont., Mass., Abiah, W26252
James, R.I., Mary, W23942
McCAW, James, S.C., S18117
Margaret, former wid. of Michael Downs, Md., which see
McCAWLEY, Campbell, Va. See McCAULEY
James, N.Y. See McCAULEY
John, N.Y., BLWt.7470-100-Pvt. Iss. 4/21/1791 to Cornelius Davenport, ass. No papers
McCAY, Alexander, N.Y. See McKAY
Daniel, Mass., R16202; BLWt.229-200
Eliezer, S.C. See McA
John, Md., BLWt.11516-100-Pvt. Iss. 8/14/1797 to James DeBaufre, ass. No papers
John, Md. See McKAY
John, Md., S40132; BLWt.1491-200-Lt. Iss. 8/4/1789. No papers
John, Mass., See McCOY
Neal, Pa., Rachel, W4733
Peter, Invalid Regt., BLWt.13511-100-Pvt. Iss. 12/14/1789 to Richard Platt, ass. No papers
McCEMMON, Mathew, See McCAMMON
McCHAN, John, Md., S34995
McCHANNING, John, N.Y. See McCLANNING
McCHARNING, John, See McCLANNING
McCHESNEY, James, N.J. See CHESNEY
John, N.Y., Abigail, W19867
John, Pa., S25272
Robert, N.J., S612
Walter, N.Y., Chloe, BLWt.67543-160-55
McCHISICK, Rachel, former wid. of John Morris, Va., which see
McCHRISTY, James, Va., S36094
Michael, Pa., BLWt.10099-100-Pvt. Iss. 11/5/1789 to Michael McChristy
McCLAIN, Abijah, Pa., Va., Lydia, W7408; BLWt.17584-160-55

McCLAIN (continued)
Alexander, Pa. See McLAIN
Daniel, Pa., Nancy, W9183
John, Navy, Md. Sea Service, S34990
John, N.C., S31853
John, Pa., Va., b. N.J., S2775
John, S.C., R6616
John, Va. See McLAIN
Laughlin, Va. See McLAIN
Samuel, Mass., S37223
William, Cont., Md., enl. in Md., S41838
McCLALON, Joseph, Va., S31846
McCLANAHAN, Alexander, Va., Sarah, R6617; BLWt.47511-160-55
Mordecai, N.J., S18506
Thomas, Cont., Va., Indian Wars-1793, Tabitha, W1052; BLWt. 33771-160-55
William, Va., S5742
McCLANE, Samuel, See McCLEAN
McCLANNING, John, N.Y., Mary, W18893
McCLAREY, William, Mass., BLWt. 4654-100-Sgt. Major. Iss. 3/25/1790. No papers
McCLARREN, Daniel, See McLARREN
McCLARY, Andrew, N.C., Elizabeth, W7417
James, Cont., Mass., S19732
Michael, Cont., N.H., Sarah, W17115
Robert, S.C. See Robert HAWTHORN
McCLASKEY, Joseph, S.C., Mary, W1449
McCLEAN, Alexander, Pa., S13898
Alexander, Pa. See McLAIN
Andrew, Pa., S2803
Angus, "Sappers & Miners," BLWt. 13416-100-Pvt. Iss. 8/20/1790 No papers
Jacob, Pa., S40997
James, Pa., BLWt.9919-100-Pvt. Iss. 6/17/1793 to Francis Kirkpatrick, ass. No papers
John, N.J., S1057
Moses, Pa., BLWt.2403-300
Neal, N.Y., BLWt.7439-100-Pvt. Iss. 9/27/1790 to Jacob Tremper, ass. No papers
Neal/Neil, N.Y., Sarah, W20249
Samuel, Pa., Sarah, R6781
Thomas, Pa., BLWt.9931-100-Pvt. Iss. 6/11/1795. No papers
McCLEASE, Cornelius, War of 1812, See Eli JACOBS, Rev. War., Mass.
McCLELAND, Daniel, N.C., Pa., S31246
Hugh, Cont., Pa. See McCLELLAND
John, Pa., Anna Maria, W2833
McCLELLAN, Archibald, ---, S.C. res. in 1846, R6621
David, Pa., BLWt.9930-100-Pvt. Iss. 8/7/1789 to Richard Platt, ass. No papers
James, ----, Pa. res. of heir in 1853, R6618
James, Pa., S2764
John, Mass. See McLELLAN
John, N.H., S37225
John, Pa., BLWt.10035-100-Pvt.

McCLELLAN (continued)
Iss. 4/6/1790. No papers
John, Pa., Jennet, R6619
John, Pa., BLWt.1420-300. Iss. 3/25/1796. No papers
Joseph, Pa., Kezia, W3101
Joseph, Va. See McCLALON
Malcolm, N.C., S5070
Samuel, Ct., Nancy, W2224
McCLELLAND, Alexander, Pa., R6620
Cary, Pa., S9006
David, Pa., S34994
George, Pa., S2766
Hugh, Cont., Pa., S41834; BLWt. 1116-100
James, Pa., Sarah, W2315; BLWt. 11069-160-55
Robert, Pa., S2765
Thomas, Cont., N.C., Pa., S2763
McCLEMAN, John, Va., S25267
McCLENAHAN, Alexander, Va. See McCLANAHAN
McCLENATHAN, Charles, Pa. See McLENAHAN
McCLENDON, Shadrack, S.C., S36695
McCLENNAN, William, Crane's Cont. Art., Mass., BLWt.4736-100-Pvt. Iss. 10/8/1790. No papers
McCLENNEN, William, Cont., Mass. Sarah, W19871
McCLERAN, Daniel, N.C., S41836
McCLERRON, Thomas, Pa., BLWt. 10049-100-Pvt. Iss. 12/21/1791. No papers
McCLESKEY, James, N.C., S.C., Va., S16475
Joseph, S.C. See McCLASKEY
McCLEWER, Richard, N.C., b. Pa. S9428
McCLINTIC, William, Va., Alice Cavendish, former wid., R1819
McCLINTICK, Joseph, Va., R6623
McCLINTOCK, Alexander, Pa., BLWt. 1476-200-Lt. Iss. 5/14/1791 to Sarah McClintock, Admx. No papers
Hugh, Pa., S16468
James, Mass., Eleanor, W15071
John, N.H., S33071
Joseph, Mass., Rebecca, W20244
Samuel, Va., R6624
McCLORKEN, Thomas, See McCLURKEN
McCLOSKEY, Joseph, See McCLASKEY
Samuel A. See McCOSKRY
William, See McCOSKRY
McCLOSKRY, Samuel A. See McCASKRY
William, See McCOSKRY
McCLOSKY, Neal, Pa., BLWt.9884-100-Pvt. Iss. 2/12/1794 to Gideon Merkle, ass. No papers
McCLOUCHAN, Robert, N.Y., S9945
McCLOUD, Anguish, Mass., S18970
George, Pa. See McLEOD
John, Cont., N.Y. agcy. & res., Resign, W1445
John, Lamb's Art., N.Y., BLWt. 7528-100-Pvt. Iss. 9/28/1790 to Alexander Robertson, ass. No papers
John, Va., S13883

McCLOUD (continued)
Samuel, Cont., N.H., S41820
McCLUER, David, Cont., N.H., Martha, W21785
Hugh, S.C. See McCLURE
James, N.H., See McLUER
John, Mass., N.H., Hannah, W21783; BLWt.17882-160-55
John, N.C., Nancy, W25692
John, S.C., b. Ireland, S18112
William, Pa. & Wayne's Army, Margaret, W9548
McCLUNG, Archibald, Va., S9010
James, Pa., S16196
John, S.C., Nancy, W1446; BLWt. 38522-160-55
Matthew, Pa., Jane, W9984
Samuel, Md., R6626
William, Va., R6628
McCLUNIE, Michael, Pa., S41845
McCLURE, Alexander, Va., S30575
Andrew, N.J., Mary, W307
David, Ct., Lucy Luce, former wid., W12166
Hugh, Pa., R6629
Hugh, S.C., Jane, W21789
James, Cont., Mass., Mehitable, W16043
James, N.H., Elizabeth Powers, former wid., W17475
James, Pa., Art., BLWt.1449-300-Capt. Iss. 8/20/1789. No papers
John, N.J., S2774
John, N.C. See McCLUER
John, Pa., BLWt.10094-100-Sgt. Iss. 11/5/1789. No papers
John, S.C. See McCLUER
John, Va., Indian War 1786-1789, War of 1812, R6632
Joseph, N.H., Margaret, W17111
Nancy, former wid. of James Foster, Va., which see
Robert, N.H., Martha, W21784
Samuel, Va., S33079
Thomas, Va., Janet, W8429
William, N.C., BLWt.130-400
William, Pa., Tabitha, W9969; BLWt.30938-160-55
William, Pa., Jane Wilson, former wid., R6630
William, Pa., Wayne's Army, See McCLUER
William, S.C., S21366
William, Va., War of 1812, Mary Surber, former wid., R10313
McCLURG, James, Va., N.A. Acc. No.874-050115. Half Pay. No pension file found for this officer (surgeon)
John, S.C. See McCLUNG
Robert, Cont., Mass., N.H., S41859
Samuel, Cont., N.H. See McCLOUD
McCLURKEN, Thomas, S.C., Elizabeth, W21792
McCLURKIN, Matthew, S.C., S32403
McCLUSKIN, Matthew, See McCLURKIN
McCOBB, Samuel, Mass., R20577
McCOLGEN, John, Hazen's Regt., BLWt.13457-100-Pvt. Iss. 8/19/1791. No papers
McCOLLISTER, James, Md. See

McCOLLISTER (continued)
McCALLISTER
James, N.J., R6634
Reuben, Cont., N.H., S40992
McCOLLOCH, Abraham, Va., S15534
McCOLLOCK, John, See McCULLOCK
Joseph, Pa., Elizabeth, W2146
McCOLLOM, Daniel, Md., BLWt.11537-100-Pvt. Iss. 1/11/1796 to Joshua Ward, ass. No papers
David, N.J., S40996
McCOLLOUGH, Joseph, N.J., Sarah, R6672
McCOLLUCK, Robert, See McCULLOCK
McCOLLUM, Cornelius, N.J., S2767
Daniel, N.C., b. N.J., S7213
Edward, N.Y., enl. in 1774, Hannah Gouge, former wid., R4155
James, N.C., R6636
John, Cont., N.J., Pa., S2769; BLWt.2111-200
John, N.J., BLWt.8551-100-Pvt. Iss. 9/30/1791. No papers
Patrick, N.J., S2768
Reuben, N.Y., BLWt.7515-100-Pvt. Iss. 7/16/1790. No papers
Thomas, N.Y., S9971
McCOLM, Samuel, N.Y., BLWt.7494-100-Pvt. Iss. 5/5/1791 No papers
McCOMAS, Aaron, Md., R6638
John, Va., Catharine, W18496
McCOMB, John, N.J., Dis. No papers here. Am. State Papers, Class IX, p.96 shows a John McComb; Pvt. 2nd N.J. Regt., res. Bernard's town, enl. 12/15/1776; disabled 1777 at Short Hills, discharged 10/1777. He lost sight of the right eye by the smallpox, which he caught in the natural way in the summer of 1777, when down on the lines near the place called Short Hills; was removed to the hospital in Mendhams; that he was transferred to the corps of invalids, where he continued to serve as invalid until 7/1783, when he was discharged by General Lincoln.
Robert, N.C., Margaret, R6639
William, Pa., Rebecca, W7413
William, Va., S16198
McCOMBER, Reuben, R.I., BLWt.3352-100-Pvt. Iss. 12/14/1789 to Richard Platt. No papers
McCOMBS, John, Invalids, BLWt.13494-100-Pvt. Iss. 2/24/1791. No papers
McCONAGHY, John, Del., W40133
McCONGHEY, John, Va. See McCONIHEY
McCONDRAY, William, R.I., BLWt. 13407 & 14087-100-Pvt. Iss. 11/4/1794. No papers
McCONEHY, John, Del. See McCONAGHY
McCONIHEY, John, Va., S16953
McCONKEY, David, Md., R6744
McCONN, James, ---, Phila. agcy., Invalid. No papers
McCONNAHY, John, Del. See McCONAGHY
McCONNALLY, Hugh, N.Y., BLWt.7483-100-Fifer. Iss. 4/9/1791. No papers
McCONNEL, Francis, N.J., b. in Ireland, Mary, W3846
Hugh, N.Y., S42955
James, N.C., S11047
John, Cont., N.J. res., BL?
John, Mass., N.H., ---. This cannot be placed with any claim but see claim of John McConnell who served as Jonathan Tyler, S42561
Samuel, Navy, Vt. agcy. & res. in 1818. S41827; enl. in 1777 as an ordinary seaman on the ship Raleigh of 32 guns, commanded by Capt. Thos. Thompson, in the naval service of the U.S. to serve for a cruise--sailed from Portsmouth to Barbary Coast and West Indies--took one prize--served 9 mos.-discharged at Boston
McCONNELEY, John, Va. See McCONIHEY
McCONNELL, Abram, Va., Rosanna, R6643
Benjamin, N.C., Jane, BLWt.36745-160-55
Charles, Pa., BLWt.9921-100-Corp. Iss. 7/27/1789 to Richard Platt, ass. No papers
Hugh, Va., R6641
James, N.J., BLWt.8514-100-Pvt. Iss. 7/9/1789. No papers
John, Cont., Green Mt. Boys, See Jonathan TYLER
John, N.J., R6642
John, N.C., Mary, W9193; BLWt. 30932-160-55
John, Pa., Nancy, W3102
Jonathan, Cont., Green Mt. Boys, Nelly, W25685; BLWt.95516-160-55
Jonathan, Cont., Green Mt. Boys & 1812, S40989
Manual, Ga., S.C., S2773
Matthew, Invalid Regt., BLWt.1454-100-Capt. Iss. 6/29/1789. No papers. Heitman gives this man's name as Nathan.
Robert, Cont., Pa., Jane Dunn, former wid., W7050; BLWt.276-300
Samuel, Md., S34984
Stephen, N.Y., Vt., R6644
William, N.Y., Pa., S40134; BLWt. 7506-100
William, Pa., BLWt.9989-100-Sgt. Iss. 6/23/1789. No papers
McCONNICK, John/John M., Cont., Mass., S43355
McCOOL, John, S.C., Jane, W9546
William, Pa., R6645
McCORD, John, N.Y., Sarah, W19870
John, S.C., b. Va., R6646
Josiah, Pa., BLWt.9988-100-Pvt. Iss. 8/7/1789 to Richard Platt, ass. No papers
Samuel, Va., BLWt.12349-100-Pvt. Iss. 5/29/1792 to Robert Means, ass. No papers
Thomas, Pa., BLWt.9903-100-Pvt. Iss. 3/31/1795 to Abm. Foster, ass. No papers
William, Pa., Sarah Bell, former wid., W25221; BLWt.26164-160-55
McCORD (continued)
William, Va., S16194
McCORKEL, James, N.C., R6647
Robert, Va., S9430
McCORKLE, Archibald, N.C., S9431
Archibald, S.C., S2771
Samuel, Va., S30956
McCORMACK, Adam, Va., BLWt.12406-100-Pvt. Iss. 7/14/179? to Robert Means, ass. No papers
Benjamin, Ga., S31844
James, Armand's Corps, BLWt.13399-100-Pvt. Iss. 5/16/1793. No papers
James, Mass., S37231
Joseph, Va., See McCORMICK
Thomas, Ga., S31857
William, Va., also Indian Wars 1791 & 1792, Nancy, R6648
McCORMICK, Archibald, Vt., Susan, W24140
Charles, Pa., Dis. No papers here, but see Am. State Papers, Class IX, Claims, p.99. Charles McCormick, Pvt., 2nd Pa. Regt., wounded in his left leg by a musket ball while in the actual line of his duty, in an engagement at Germantown; he has had no established place of res. in any town, city or county, but wandered about the country, having been employed as an express rider, etc. Wounded 10/4/1777. Discharged 1/1778
David, Pa., Sally/Sarah, W19868
Dennis, N.J., S23313
Francis, Va., S2783
George, Va. See McCARMICK
Hugh, Pa., Rebecca, W8437; BLWt. 846-100
James, Mass., BLWt.4661-100-Pvt. Iss. 3/16/1797 to Joseph Fosdick. No papers
James, Pa., S8881
James, S.C., R6649
John, Cont., N.H., Vt., S11043
John, Md., Pa., R6651
John, N.Y., BLWt.7486-100-Pvt. Iss. 9/15/1790 to John S. Hobart et al, ass. No papers
John, Pa., BLWt.9882-100-Pvt. Iss. 7/9/1789. No papers
John, Pa., R6652
John, Pa., Va., Catharine, W9557; BLWt.33748-160-55
Joseph, Ga., N.C.?, S32405
Joseph, Va., R6648 1/2
Patrick, Pa., BLWt.9924-100-Iss. 6/29/1789 to M. McConnell, ass. No papers
Robert, N.C., S4198
Seth, Pa., R6655
Timothy, Pa., BLWt.10036-100-Pvt. Iss. 2/4/1793 to George Stout, ass. No papers
William, Pa., Grissil, W2834
William, Va. See McCORMACK
McCORTLEY, Michael, Pa., BLWt. 9902-100-Pvt. Iss. 4/26/1792. No papers
McCOSKEY, Samuel A. See McCOSKRY

McCOSKEY (continued)
William, Cont., Pa. See McCOSKRY
McCOSKRY, Samuel A., Cont., Pa. Alison, W8425; BLWt.1458-400-Surgn. Iss. 7/26/1789, under name of McCoskey. No papers
William, Cont., Pa., Felicity, R6658; BLWt.1628-300
McCOSKY, John, Pa., BLWt.10017-100-Pvt. Iss. 3/14/1793 to Gideon Merkle, ass. No papers
McCULLOUGH, James, N.C., S30570
McCOUN, Alexander, Pa. See McCOWN
McCOWAN, James, Va., S36101
John, Pa., BLWt.1822-300
Patrick, Pa., S38195
McCOWN, Alexander, Pa., Susanna/Susan, W3027
McCOY, Alexander, N.Y., BLWt. 7477-100-Pvt. Iss. 9/24/1790 to D. Howell, ass. No papers
Alexander, Pa., S9021. Alive in Brown Co., Ohio in 1834. See MacCOY
Alexander, Pa., Catharine, W4023 He d. 1829, res. Brown Co., Ohio
Angus, Pa., S22390
Barnabas, Mass., W15796, Mary Reed, former wid. Her 2nd husb., Francis Ryan, Mass., also served in the Rev. War
Charles, Pa., S40130
Charles, Pa., S40999
Daniel, N.H., BLWt.3305-100-Pvt. Iss. 8/26/1790 to Manassah Cutler, ass. No papers
Daniel, N.Y., R6662
Daniel, Pa., S40985
Daniel, Pa., Jane, W965
Daniel, Pa., Nancy, W2959
Daniel, Va., S4195
Daniel, Va., S36083
Eneas, Va., BLWt.12343-100-Pvt. Iss. 5/12/1792 to Jas. Morrison, Admr. No papers
Ephraim, Ct., Sarah, W4024
James, N.Y., BLWt.7489-100-Pvt. Iss. 11/17/1791 to Elisha Camp, ass. No papers
John, Ct., Betsey, W2407; BLWt. 19731-160-55
John, Md. See McCAY
John, Crane's Cont. Art., Mass., BLWt.4725-100-Pvt. Iss. 8/10/1789 to Richard Platt. No papers
John, Crane's Cont. Art., Mass., BLWt.4731-100-Pvt. Iss. 8/11/1790 to Robert Dunlap. No papers
John, Mass., S33074
John, Navy, R.I., res. at enl. N.H., Comfort & Betsey, contesting widows, R6661; BLReg.319065-55
John, N.C., S4190
John, Va., Indian War 1786, R6663
Jonathan, N.H., BLWt.3314-100-Pvt. Iss. 6/26/1790 to James Smith, ass. No papers
Jonathan, N.H., S45003
Michael, Pa., BLWt.9898-100-Pvt.

McCOY (continued)
Iss. 4/22/1793. No papers
Paul, N.H., BLWt.3326-100-Pvt. Iss. 7/12/1793 to Reuben Murray, ass. No papers
Paul, N.H., S33075
Redden, S.C., b. S.C., S7198
Reuben, Pa., BLWt.10089-100-Pvt. "in the Artillery". Iss. 1/23/179? to James Bennet, ass. No papers
Robert, N.C., Margary, W1053
Robert, Va., S16197
Roderick, Pa., BLWt.9963-100-Corp. Iss. 7/16/1789. No papers
Samuel, Va., S38196
Stephen, N.H., BLWt.3306-100-Pvt. Iss. 1/26/1790 to James Smith. No papers
Stephen, N.H., Rachel, W2408
William, Cont., Va., Susan, W9991; BLWt.10287-160-55
William, N.Y., S23316
William, Pa., BLWt.2093-100
William, Va., S36098
McCRACKEN, Gilbert, Rev. ---, War of 1812 Del., R16172
James, Cont., Md., Mary, W9191; BLWt.36197-160-55
James, S.C., Mary, W7416
John, Pa., S40987
Joseph, N.Y., S27176
Philip, "Sappers & Miners", BLWt.13414-100-Pvt. Iss. 7/24/1790. No papers
William, N.Y., Mary, W9192; BLWt. 13884-160-55
William, Pa., R6665
William, Pa., BLWt.1447-200-Lt. Iss. 12/24/1792. Also recorded as above under BLWt.2625. No papers
McCRACKIN, Philip, Ct., R6666
McCRACKMAN, Gilbert. See McCRACKEN
McCRADY, Robert, Pa. See McCREADY
McCRAKEN, William, N.Y. See McCRACKEN
McCRARY, Archibald, N.C. See McCREVY
Hugh, N.C., b. Ireland, S46254
John, Va., S16947
McCRAVEY, John, Va. See McCRARY
McCRAVY, Archibald, See McCREVY
McCRAW, Francis, Va., BLWt.12372-100-Pvt. Iss. 5/11/1792 to Francis Graves, ass. No papers
Francis, Cont., Va., Sally, W7410; BLWt.73-100
Francis, Va., Mary H., W2406; son of Francis
McCRAY, Philip, N.J. See McCREA
McCREA, Griffith J., See McREY
John, N.Y., Elenor Brisbine/Nella Brisbon, former wid., W20005
Philip, N.J., BLWt.320-100
Stephen, Gen. Hosp., BLWt.1379-450-Physician & Surgn. Iss. 12/15/1790. Also recorded as above under BLWt.2533. No

McCREA (continued)
papers
McCREADY, Daniel, Pa., S46058
Robert, Pa., S5747
McCREARY, Archibald, N.C. See McCREVY
George, Pa., S8883
John, N.Y. See McCREERY
John, Pa., S25276
McCREAVY, Archibald, N.C. See McCREVY
McCREERY, Alexander, N.Y., S13883
John, N.Y., R6668
Robert, N.Y., Esther, R6669
McCREIGHT, Robert, S.C., b. in Ireland, S21881
McCRERY, Archibald, See McCREVY
McCREVY, Archibald, N.C., Jane, W8434
McCRISTY, James, Va. See McCHRISTY
McCRONISTER, James, See McCROSKEY
McCRORY, James, N.C., BLWt.2276-150
John, N.C., Catharine, W25689; BLWt.18389-160-55
McCROSKEY, John, Va., S2781
John, Va., Margaret, R6656
McCROSKY, James, Va., S11050
John, Va. See McCROSKEY
McCROSSON, Patrick, Pa., BLWt. 9899-100-Pvt. Iss. 4/6/1790 to Patrick McCrosson. No papers
McCRUM, Michael, Lee's Legion, Va. BLWt.13527-100-Pvt. Iss. 3/27/1793. No papers
William, Pa., S22389
McCUBBIN, James, N.C. See pension claim of his wid. Mary, on account of service of her last husb., John Dicken, N.C., Mary
Nicholas, N.C., b. Va., Nancy, W3574
McCUE, James, N.Y., Angelica, W24146
McCUFF, Pomp, Ct., S36084
McCUIN, Patrick, Va. See McEWING
McCUISTIN, Thomas, N.C., S8885
McCULLA, Alexander, N.J., BLWt. 475-100
John, N.J., BLWt.8561-100-Pvt. Iss. 10/17/1789 to John Pope, ass. No papers
McCULLAM, John, Cont., N.J., Pa., See McCOLLUM
McCULLAR, William, Mass., Chloe, W5363
McCULLEN, Bryan, N.C., S9018
McCULLER, Alexander, Ga., S4196
McCULLERS, John, N.C., S.C., Elizabeth, W4729
Matthew, N.C., Sarah, W7415
William, N.C., S16469
McCULLEY, John, N.J., S34423
McCULLOCH, Alexander, Ga. See McCULLER
James, Mass., Sarah, W15069
John, Va. See McCULLOCK
Joseph, Mass., BLWt.4669-100-Pvt. Iss. 2/27/1790 to Theodosius Fowler. No papers
Robert, Sheldon's Dragoons, Ct., BLWt.6223-100-Pvt. Iss.

McCULLOCH (continued)
5/31/1793. No papers
Robert, Mass., S13893; BLWt. 7446-160-55
Robert, N.C., Ann, W18502
Roger, Invalids Corps, BLWt.13482-100-Pvt. Iss. 7/14/1790 to Richard Platt, ass. No papers
William, Va., S38936
McCULLOCK, Duncan, N.C., S7203
James, N.C., S7201
James, N.C., See McCOULLOUGH
John, N.C., Nancy, R6671
John, Va., S7204; BLWt.47666-160-55
Joseph, Mass., S33076
Joseph, Pa. See McCOLLOCK
McCULLOH, John, Pa., Anna, W4489
McCULLOUGH, James, Va., S36106
John, N.C., Pa., S32404
John, N.C., Constant, W9558
Joseph, See McCOLLOCK
Robert, Ct., S41833
Robert, Pa., Dis. No papers here, but see Am. State Papers, Class IX, Claims, p.103. Robert McCullough, pvt., res. York Co., Pa., disabled 10/1778, at Shamungo & Germantown, wounded in an action with the savages in his left arm at Shamungo, in the Western Territory; also wounded in the left leg at the battle of Germantown
William, Md., S36085
William, N.J., S18504
McCULLUCK, Robert, See McCULLOCH
McCULLUM, James, Va. or Pa., S30579
McCULLY, George, Pa., U.S.A., Ann, W7411; BLWt.1426-300-Capt. Iss. 11/5/1789. No papers
McCUMBER, Abiathar, Mass. See MACOMBER
John, Mass., Philadelphia, R6673
McCUMSEY, Robert, Pa., S2776
McCUNE, John, S.C., S38940
Joseph, Pa., S.C., S16465
Peter, Va., Christiana, W7412
Samuel, Va., S11042
Thomas, Pa., S16193
McCURDY, Alexander, Pa., S40144
Archibald, N.C., Elizabeth, W741 BLWt.26427-160-55
James, Pa., BLWt.9877-100-Pvt. Iss. 7/16/1789. No papers
James, Pa., S7214
John, N.H., S45004
John, Pa., S31855
Moses, Cont., Pa., Margaret Hughes, former wid., W4702; BLWt.283-100
Patrick, Del., BLWt.10824-100-Pvt. Iss. 9/2/1789. No papers
Robert, Pa., BLWt.9878-100-Pvt. Iss. 12/20/1791 to George Walton, ass. No papers
Robert, Pa., S41851
William, Pa., BLWt.1421-300-Capt.
McCUTCHAN, John, Va., S13886
John, Va., S21369

McCUTCHAN (continued)
William, Va., Jean, W1888
McCUTCHEN, Frederick, N.H., S13884
George, Mass., S42948
John, S.C., S32406
McDADE, James, Va., S38193
John, Va., S31856
William, N.J., BLWt.8590-100-Pvt. Iss. 7/15/1789. No papers
McDANAL, John, S.C., R6674
McDANIEL, Ananias, Cont., N.Y., S28810
Archibald, N.C., b. N.C., R6676
Arthur, N.C., Elizabeth, W4732; BLWt.2461-100
Clement/Clemant, Va., Elizabeth, W7419
Edward, S.C., Elizabeth, W9189
George, N.C., S36099
Henry, Va., Hannah, R6678
James, Mass., Susanna, W23949; BLWt.1049-100
James, N.C., b. N.C., S9432
James, N.C., Ann, W8447; BLWt. 1585-160-55
James, Va., also Indian Spy in 1790-1792, R6680
John, Mass., S33069
John, Mass., Elizabeth, S47465 & R6688
John, N.J., See McDONALD
John, N.Y., Barshaba, W18498
John, N.C., Margaret, R6681
John, S.C., See McDANAL
John, Va., Elizabeth, W3845
John, Va., See McDONOUGH
Mathias, Va., S2796
Patrick, Pa., S41861
Randel, S.C., S32402
Thomas, N.C., S38192
Valentine, Pa., Sarah, W25691; BLWt.58688-160-55
Walter, Md., S18505
William, Md., R6683
William, N.H., Hannah, R6679
William, Va. R6684
McDAVIS, Rice, N.C., Rachel E., R6685
McDEARMAN, Thomas, S.C., S32401
Thomas, Va., S5749
McDERMENT, Joseph, N.C., S16472
McDERMID, Francis, Va. See McDURMID
McDERMOT, Cornelius, N.J., BLWt. 8532-100-Pvt. Iss. 6/11/1789 to Jonathan Dayton, ass. No papers
Cornelius, N.Y., BLWt.7507-100-Pvt. Iss. 7/2/1790 to John Hunter, ass. No papers
McDERMOTT, Daniel, Pa., S22900
Joseph, Pa., S22902
McDERMUT, James, Pa., S9014; BLWt.26082-160-55
McDILL, John, S.C., S21879
McDOLE, John, Pa., Mary, R6687
McDONALD, Alexander, Pa., BLWts. 9885 & 14029-100-Pvt. Iss. 1/21/1791 to Murtough Sullivan, Admr. No papers
Archibald, Pa., BLWt.9868-100-Pvt. Iss. 9/6/1791. No papers

McDONALD (continued)
Archibald, Pa., S8889 1/2
Archibald, S.C., BLWts.12427 & 13401-100-Pvt. Iss. 10/7/1795. No papers
Archibald, Va., S38190
Arthur, N.C., Elizabeth, BLWt. 2461-100
Benjamin, N.J., BLWt.8593-100-Pvt. Iss. 2/20/1790. No papers
Charles, Ct., BLWt.6164-100-Pvt. Iss. 1/6/1797. No papers
Charles, Ct., S42963
Charles, Cont., Va., Ohio res. & agcy., W7421; BLWt.2438-100
Daniel, Del., Dis. No papers here, but see Am. State Papers, Class IX, Claims, p.128. Daniel McDonald, corp., Capt.Jaquet's Co., Del. Regt., res. Newcastle Co., Del., enl. 4/1777 for the war, discharged 9/1778, wounded 10/4/1777 at Germantown. Wounded in his leg in the action of Germantown, which crippled him, and rendered him incapable of maintaining himself, being 71 yrs. old.
Daniel, Hazen's Regt., BLWt.13447-100-Pvt. Iss. 10/22/1792. No papers
Daniel, S.C., Elizabeth, W7422; BLWt.11185-160-55
Donald, N.Y., S27177
Donald, Pa., S9426
Edward, N.Y., Content Allen, former wid., W17204
Edward, Pa., S7209
Edward, Va., BLWt.12347-100-Pvt. Iss. 5/29/1792 to Robert Means, ass. No papers
Finlay, N.C., S41828
Francis, Pa., BLWt.9928-100-Pvt. Iss. 7/16/1789. No papers
Francis, Pa. See McDONNALD
George, Hazen's Regt., BLWt.13458-100-Pvt. Iss. 6/9/1791 to James DeBaufre, ass. No papers
Godfrey, Invalid Corps; BLWt. 13491-100-Pvt. Iss. 10/3/1791. No papers
Hugh, N.C., S41837
Hugh, S.C., Rebecca, W8438
James, Ct., BLWt.6186-100-Pvt. Iss. 9/24/1790 to James F. Sebor, ass. No papers
James, Ct., Abigail Russell, former wid., R9095
James, Ct., N.Y., S13902
James, Cont., S.C., Md., Sarah, W4025
James, Mass., See McDANIEL
James, N.J., BLWt.8584-100-Pvt. Iss. 12/27/1791. No papers
James, N.Y., Lamb's Art., BLWt. 7526-100-Pvt. Iss. 9/15/1790 to John S. Hobart, et al, assnes. No papers
James, N.C., b. Md., S18111
James, N.C., b. N.C., Sarah, W7424; BLWt.28561-160-55
John, Cont., N.J., S33393

McDONALD (continued)
John, Invalid Regt., BLWt.13509-100-Pvt. Iss. 11/29/1791 to Elias Cole, Executor. No papers
John, Md., S38932
John, Mass., BLWt.4634-100-Pvt. Iss. 4/2/1793. No papers
John, Mass., S----
John, Mass., S22392
John, Mass. See McDANIEL
John, N.J., Pvt., BLWt.8521-100. Iss. 12/7/1789.
John, N.C., b. Scotland, Isabella, W6814
John, N.C. See McDANIEL
John, Pa., BLWt.9893-100-Pvt. Iss. 2/14/1791. No papers
John, Pa., BLWt.10019-100-Pvt. Iss. 4/26/1791. No papers
John, S.C., S18115
John, Va., S16951
John, Va., Mary, W9186; BLWt. 73544-160-55
John, Va. See McDONOUGH
Joseph, Pa., S23791
Malcolm, Pa., BLWt.9939-100-Pvt. Iss. 10/4/1792 to Alexander Power, ass. of Henry Apker, Admr. No papers
Malcolm, Privateer, Pa., S9699
Michael, Pa., BLWt.9975-100-Pvt. Iss. 6/29/1789 to M. McConnell, ass. No papers
Michael, Pa., Diana, W3844
Pelatiah, Cont., Mass., Dorcas, W23932
Peter, Va., Catharine, W9554
Robert, Pa., BLWt.9901-100-Pvt. Iss. 1/15/1793. No papers
Robert, Pa., See McDONNELL
Robert, Pa., Mary, W3703
Terence, Va., S38191
William, Ct., Md., Privateer & Navy (1813), S34978
William, Cont., N.J., Martha, W6806
William, Del., R6689
William, Lee's Legion, BLWt. 13528-100-Pvt. Iss. 2/19/1790. No papers
William, Pa., BLWt.9869-100-Pvt. Iss. 6/20/1789. No papers
William, Pa., BLWt.9880 & 13959-100-Pvt. Iss. 10/28/1791 to Wm. Leonard & Elanor Leonard, Admrs. No papers
William, Pa., BLWt.10020-100-Pvt. Iss. 3/15/1790 to Rebecca Mc-Donald, legal repr. No papers
McDONEL, Robert, Pa. See McDONNELL
McDONIELD, Joseph, Pa., S33065
McDONNALD, Francis, Pa., S40988
James, Md., BLWt.11529-100-Pvt. Iss. 12/23/1795 to George Ponsonby, ass. No papers
John, Va., See McDONALD
McDONNELL, Robert, Pa., S33396
McDONOUGH, Andrew, N.C., S2795
Hugh, Pa., S2794
John, Mass. See McDANIEL
John, Va., R6690
Redmont, Va., S41852
McDORMAN, Daniel, Va., BLWt.2381-100
David, Va., S---. No papers
McDORMOD, John, Pa., BLWt.10057-100-Pvt. Iss. 5/8/1792. No papers
McDOUGAL, Alexander, S.C., S30576
Catharine, former wid of Andrew Dowling, Cont., N.Y., which see
Daniel, Invalid Regt., BLWt.13516-100-Pvt. Iss. 3/12/1793 to Wm. Ashley, ass. No papers
John, N.Y., S42957
Joseph, Md., R6693
McDOUGALL, Alexander, N.Y., S29320
Alexander, N.Y., BLWt.1388-1100-Maj.Gen. Iss. 9/15/1790 to John Sloss Hobart, Egbert Benson, Jno. McKesson, Ebenezer Hazan & Richard Platt, Exrs. No papers
Stephen, N.Y., BLWt.1389-400-Major Iss. 10/22/1790 to John Lawrence, legal repr. of Elizabeth Lawrence dec'd, who was sister and legal repr. of S. McD. No papers
McDOUGLE, Alexander, Md., S2792
McDOUMAN, David, Va., BLWt.12404-100-Pvt. Iss. 7/7/1792 to Robert Means, ass. No papers
McDOW, Thomas, S.C., b. S.C., S9427
McDOWEL, James, N.Y., S11055
John, Md., N.C., Sarah, W7423; BLWt.38502-160-55
McDOWELL, Alexander, Pa., S36097
Andrew, N.J., Jane, W7420; BLWt. 8153-160-55
Daniel, N.Y., Martha, W3705; BLWt. 30933-160-55
Daniel, Va., S1231
Hugh, Md., BLWt.11549-100-Pvt.Iss. 7/9/1794. No papers
James, Pa., S47832
James, Pa., Elizabeth, R21676
James, S.C., Mary Ann, R6695
James, Va., Mary, W8430
John, Pa., S40995
John, Pa., S41830
John, Pa. See McDOLE
John, Pa., BLWt.1444-400-Surgn. Iss. 4/3/1798. No papers
John, Va., Jane, S30578; BLWt. 1749-200
John, Va., R6694
Michael, Va., S1690
Robert, Ga., N.C., S.C., S16471
Thomas, Md., BLWts.11479 & 12539-100-Pvt. Iss. 9/26/1792. No papers
Thomas, Md., BLWt.11539-100-Pvt. Iss. 9/26/1792. No papers
Thomas, Md., res. at enl. Chester Co., Pa., Mary, W2957
William, Pa., BLWt.1433-200-Lt. Iss. 5/4/1791. No papers
William, Va., S30580
McDOWLE, Thomas, Crane's Cont. Art., Mass., BLWt.4735 iss. 4/18/1796 to Jeremiah Mason. No papers
McDUFF, Daniel, S.C., S155; BLWt. 1620-300
McDUFFE, Randell, N.J., BLWt.8582-
McDUFFE (continued)
100-Pvt. Iss. 12/28/1789 to John Hollingshead, ass. No papers
McDUFFEE, Lois, former wid. of John Drew, N.H., which see
McDUFFEY, Archibald, N.J., BLWt. 8566-100-Pvt. Iss. 11/5/1798 to Archibald McDuffey. No papers
Randle, N.J., S34424
McDUFFIE, John, N.H., Elizabeth, W21781
McDUGAL, Hugh, R.I., BLWt.6-100-Special Act 6/4/1842. For special act & other papers, see case of Robert Allen, R.I., BLWt.1-100, Special Act June 4, 1842
McDURMID, Francis, Va., Margaret, R6686
McELCARR, John, Pa. See McCAR
McELDERY, John, Pa., Ann, W8431
McELDUFF, Daniel, S.C., S---. These papers were found in the Rev. War claim of Daniel McDuff, S.C., S155
McELERY, William, Mass., BLWt. 137-100
McELEVAIN, William, Mass., Ann Hall, former wid., S23953
McELHANNON, John, Pa. See McELHENON
McELHANY, John, Va., R16313
Samuel, S.C., b. Va., Elizabeth, W12455
McELHATTON, William, Cont., Pa., See McHATTON
McELHENEY, William, S.C., b. Va., R6697
McELHENNEY, Stephen, S.C., b. Va., S21368
McELHENON, John, Pa., S31850
McELHERRON, James, Cont., Mass., S28809
McELHOSE, Samuel, Pa., R6698
McELNAY, John, Pa., S2788
McELREAVY, Hugh, Pa., Pvt., BLWt. 10041-100. Iss. 3/11/1799
Hugh, Pa., BLWt.10041-100-Pvt. Iss. 3/11/1799. No papers. There is no way from records of this office to determine whether Wt. No.393 iss. in 1808 to Hugh McElrevy/McElvery and the one above, No. 10041, were to the same man. Mr. Robb of General Land Office said No. 393 was never taken up, but No. 10041 was patented. There is no way to tell whether either of these warrants was issued on account of the service of Hugh McElrevy/McRevy, S40135
McELREVY, Hugh, Pa., S40135
Hugh, Pa. See McELVERY
McELROY, Daniel, Pa., S38938
James, Cont., N.Y., S8882
James, Pa., S34976
James, S.C., S2786
John, N.C. See McKLEROY
John, Pa., BLWt.9980-100-Fife Major. Iss. 7/9/1789 to John McElroy. No papers
John, Pa., S16192

McELROY (continued)
John, Pa., Catharine, W1979
Micajah, N.C., S2785
Thomas, Pa., R6699
McELVAIN, John, Pa., BLWt.10011-100-Pvt. Iss. 6/10/1794 to Daniel Stever, ass. No papers
McELVEEN, William, S.C., S21880
McELVENE, John, S.C. See McILVAIN
McELVERY, Hugh, Pa., BLWt.393-100
McELWAIN, William, Mass. See McELEVAIN
McELWEE, James, S.C., Va., Rhoda, W9553
McELYEA, Patrick, N.C., Va., S2789
William, N.C., Frances, S33084; BLWt.47903-160-55
McENALLY, Matthew, Pa., BLWt.9900-100-Pvt. Iss. 12/30/1790. No papers
McENERMY, Patrick, Pa., BLWt.10021-100-Pvt. Iss. 6/12/1795 to John Hassell, ass. No papers
McENTEE, Barney, N.Y. See McINTIRE
McENTIRE, Daniel, Pa., BLWt.10033-100-Pvt. Iss. 1/17/1792 to George Moore, ass. Dinah McEntire, Admx.
David, Pa., S34986
Jacob, Cont., Mass., S45000
John, Ga., S38189
John, Va., S38935
William, Pa., S36693
McENTYRE, John, N.J., S33392
McEUEN, James, Pa., BLWt.9973-100-Pvt. Iss. 1/28/1795. No papers
John, N.J., BLWt.1410-150-Ensign Iss. 10/9/1790. No papers
McEUIN, Patrick, See McEWING
McEVER, Angus, Pa., Catharine, W5355; BLWt.299-100
James, Mass., Louisa, W23936
McEVERS, Daniel, N.Y., S42942
McEWEN, Duncan, N.Y., Martha, W17117
Francis, Pa. See McQUOWN
Henry, Pa., Elizabeth, W3275
James, Pa., R6700
John, Ct., S11056
John, N.J. See McEUEN
Peter, Mass., Sarah, W15070
McEWING, Patrick, Va., Polly, R16267
McFADDEN, Alexander, N.C., S8887
Connelly, N.J. See McFADEN
Edward, S.C., S2790
John, Md., S5755
John, Md., S7193
John, Pa., S23626
McFADEN, Connelly, N.J., Pa., S41863
McFADON, James, Md., BLWt.1079-200
McFALL, Cornelius, Va., S5753
Patrick, N.Y., Christina, W18497
Paul, Invalids Corps, BLWt.13483-100-Pvt. Iss. 8/4/1790 to Henry Hart, ass. No papers
Thomas, Pa., S40145
McFALLS, Arthur, N.C., Enezy/Emzay, W9187; BLWt.40926-160-55
John, N.C., Martha, W968
McFAREN, William, Cont., N.Y., Elizabeth, R6711

McFARLAND, Andrew, Pa. See McFARLANE
Anna, former wid. of Asahel Chittenden, Ct., which see
Benjamin, Mass., S29321
Ebenezer, Mass., Elizabeth, R6702
Elijah, Mass. See McFARLIN
Ephraim, Mass., R6703
Jacob, N.C., Pa., Jane, W967; BLWt.53675-160-55
James, Mass., S11046
James, Mass., S33390
James, Mass. See McFARLIN
James, N.H., S11053
James, N.Y., Margaret, W20245
James, Pa., BLWt.10008-100-Pvt. Iss. 10/31/1795 to Barnard Merkle, ass. No papers
John, Mass., R6705
Joseph, Cont., N.H., S42946
Moses, Cont., Mass., BLWt.1854-300 & Invalid pensioner
Robert, Va., S2004
Solomon, Mass., Deborah Welsh, former wid., W15469. Her husb., John Welsh, also served in the Rev. War. See papers within
Walter, Green Mt. Boys, Mass., Sarah, W14704
Walter, Pa., S41835
William, Mass., S18503
William, Mass., Lydia, W23944
William, N.Y., R6706
McFARLANE, Andrew, Pa., BLWt.1559-200
James, Mass. See McFARLIN
James, Pa., BLWt.1428-100-Lt. Iss. 4/6/1790. No papers
John, N.J., BLWt.8523-100-Pvt. Iss. 6/20/1789. No papers
John, N.Y., BLWt.7485-100-Pvt. Iss. 8/3/1790 to Cornelius Van Dyck, ass. No papers
McFARLEN, Ephraim, See McFARLAND
McFARLIN, Elijah, Mass., Sarah, W23948
George, S.C., b. Ireland, S18119
James, Mass., S37229
Solomon, Mass., S37233
William, Mass., N.H. See FARLEY
McFARLING, Andrew, Cont., N.Y., S23314
John Bennett, Va., S36086
McFARRAN, Samuel, Va. See McFERRAN
McFARREN, John, Pa., Jane, W2316
Samuel, Pa., BLWt.1459-200-Lt. Iss. 4/5/1794 to Margaret McFarren, Admr. Also recorded as above under BLWt.2460. No papers
William, Cont., N.Y. See McFAREN
McFARSON, William, N.H., R6708
McFATRICK, Daniel, Pa., S40998
John, S.C., Elizabeth, W9556
McFATRIDGE, Daniel, Pa., BLWt. 9914-100-Pvt. Iss. 6/3/1791. No papers
McFAULS, Arthur, See McFALLS
McFEE, Malcom, Md., R6709
McFEELY, William, Pa., S33394
McFERRAN, Samuel, Va., S1691
McFERREN, John, Va., R6712

McFERREN (continued)
Samuel, Va. See McFARREN
William, Va., b. Pa., S2791
McFERRIN, Archibald, S.C., R6710
William, Va. See McFERREN
McFERSON, John, N.H., Agnes, W15692
McGAFFEY, Andrew, N.H., Hannah, W26254
Andrew, N.H., BLWt.37-100
McGAFFY, Neal, N.H., BLWt.1340-200-Lt. Iss. 4/5/1792. No papers
McGAHEE, Andrew, Pa., Mary Baker, former wid., W23530; BLWt.2498-100. Her last husb. also served and pensioned. See Michael M. Baker, Pa.
McGAHEY, John, Invalids Corps, BLWt.13485-100-Pvt. Iss. 9/6/1791. No papers
William, Pa., S36696; BLWt.1004-100. Iss. 12/6/1821. Res. Ohio in 1821
McGANNON, Darby, Cont., Va., S36104
McGARITY, William, S.C., R6713
McGARRICHE, Edward, N.Y., BLWt. 7516-100-Pvt. Iss. 8/3/1790 to Cornelius V. Dyck, ass. No papers
McGARY, Neil, Pa., BLWt.10006-100-Pvt. Iss. 6/13/1792 to Alexander Power, ass. Also BLWt.320-60-55
McGLATHERY, Isaac, Pa., See McGLOTHERY
McGAUGHEY, John, ---, Pa. agcy. Dis. No papers
John, N.C. or S.C., Jane Keith, former wid., R5820
William, Del., BLWt.10830-100-Pvt. Iss. 9/2/1789. No papers
McGAUGHY, Samuel, N.C., Jane, W9981
McGAVOCK, Hugh, Va., S16948 & Va. Half Pay. N.A. Acc. No. 874. See 050116
McGAW, John, Pa. See MAGAW
Robert, Pa., BLWt.1412-500-Col. Iss. 7/16/1789
William, Pa., S22895
William, S.C., Mary, W4291
McGEARY, Neal, See McGERRY
McGEE, Charles, Md., S34979
Daniel, Pa., Arty., BLWt.10081-100-Pvt. Iss. 1/4/1789. No papers
Daniel, Pa., S33389
David, Mass., R6716
Harmon, Va. See Herman
Herman, Va., S7194
James, Cont., Del., Margaret, W2954
James, Del., BLWt.10840-100-Pvt. Iss. 4/7/1792. No papers
James, N.J., Mary, W7427
James, Pa., BLWt.1382-100
James C., Pa., S31250
John, N.J., S1230
John, Va., Esther, R6717
Levin, Del., BLWt.2130-100
Neil, Cont., Mass., Susannah Ryan/Ryon, former wid., W22139; BLWt.36533-160-55
Patrick, Cont., Zadia, W9184; BLWt.40003-160-55
Patrick, Hazen's Regt., BLWt. 13418-100-Pvt. Iss. 9/11/1792 to

McGEE (continued)
Sarah McGee, Admx. No papers
Ralph, Va. See MAGEE
Robert, Pa., BLWt.9954-100-Pvt. Iss. 12/16/179? to William Burgess, Admr. No papers
Robert, Pa., Dis. No papers
Samuel, Va., S31249
Thomas, Ga., N.C., S4194. Res. in Va. at enl., but first enlisted in Balt., Md. under Capt. Templeton & Col. Brown
Thomas, N.J., S5752
Thomas, N.C., S5071
Thomas, N.C., Amy, R6715
Thomas, Pa., S38202
William, Md., S34980; BLWt. 1355-100
William, N.H., S41840
McGEHE, William, Va., S32399
McGEORGE, Thomas, Va., S2801
William, Va., S38201
McGERRY, Neal, Cont., Pa., W8276; BLWt.320-60-55
McGHEE, William, Md. See McGEE
William, N.C., S33068
McGHOGGAN, Alexander, Pa., Jane, W2681
McGILL, James, Pa., BLWt.10104-100-Pvt. Iss. 4/21/17?? to James Morrison, ass. No papers
James, Pa., Indian War, War of 1812, Sarah, W8428
John, Invalid Corps, BLWt.13502-100-Pvt. Iss. 4/7/1795 to John Nicholson, ass. No papers
John, Pa., BLWt.10084-100-Pvt. in the Art. Iss. 7/16/1789 to M. McConnell, ass. No papers
John, Pa., S4189
Robert, N.J., S16946
William, Mass., Martha, W23952
McGILTON, William, Pa., BLWt. 10009-100-Sgt. Iss. 3/10/1790 No papers
McGINNEY, James, See James CRIER
McGINNIS, Andrew, Va., Anna, W8426
Arthur, Lamb's Art., N.Y., BLWt. 7522-100-Pvt. Iss. 1/11/1791 to Joseph Hugg, Admr. No papers
Jacob, N.Y., R6721
James, Pa., S5740
James, Pa. See McGUINNES
John, Pa., BLWt.10024-100-Pvt. Iss. 10/15/1791 to John Godfrey, ass. No papers
John, Pa., BLWt.10053-100-Pvt. Iss. 4/6/1790. No papers
William, Pa., S41855
McGLASSON, John, Va., Nancy, W8440
Matthew, Va., S15530
McGLATHERY, Isaac, Pa., Rachel, W3149
McGLAUCHLIN, Charles, N.J., BLWt. 472-100. No papers
McGLAUGHLIN, Patrick, Hazen's Regt. BLWt.13460-100-Pvt. Iss.3/10/1790
McGLOCHLIN, William, Md., BLWt. 11488-100-Pvt. Iss. 9/24/1789 to Wm. McGlochlin. No papers
McGLOCKLIN, John, N.J., BLWt.8556-100-Pvt. Iss. 4/3/1797. No papers
McGLOTHLIN, John, N.C. See McLAUGHLIN
McGLOUCHLIN, Charles, N.J. See McGLAUCHLIN
McGLOUGHLIN, Charles, N.J. See McGLAUCHLIN
Hugh, Va. See McLOUGHLIN
John, Va., Anne, W18494
McGOHAN, Mark, Pa. & Indian Wars 1786 & 1790, S36100
McGOLDSMITH, Pelatiah, Mass.,S36114
McGONIGLE, George, N.J., BLWt.8591-100-Pvt. Iss. 6/11/1789 to Matthias Denman, ass. No papers
McGONNAGLE, John, Del., BLWt.10845-100-Pvt. Iss. 9/2/1789. No papers
McGOODWIN, Daniel, N.C., S.C., Jane, W9555; BLWt.38540-160-55
McGOOGIN, Alexander, Pa. See McGHOGGAN
McGORAGHEY, Edward, N.Y., Mary, W21196
John, N.Y., Margaret, W23935; BLWt 26468-100-55
McGOUGHEY, John, N.C. See McGAUGHEY
McGOURKEY, Edward, N.Y. See McGORAGHEY
McGOWAN, Jeremiah, N.Y., BLWt.7449-100-Pvt. Iss. 12/15/1790 to Robert Fowt, ass. No papers
John, Cont., Pa., Mary, W17123; BLWt.1453-300-Capt. Iss. 4/7/1795 to John Nicholson, ass. No papers
Robert, Pa., Mary, W8445
William, S.C., S1692
McGOWN, Stephen, N.Y., Margaret, R6723
McGOWNS, Edward, Mass., Susannah, W1304; BLWt.11392-160-55
McGRAGORY, Joel, Ct. See MEGREGORY
McGRAW, Christopher, Md., S36096
Daniel, N.Y., S9947
John, N.Y., S11051
McGREGGER, James, Pa. See McGRIGGER
McGREGOR, Alexander, N.Y., S21370
David, N.H., S42959; BLWt.1339-300-Capt. Iss. 1/4/1799. Name spelled McGregore. No papers
John, Ct., Cont., S38937; BLWt. 1377-300-Capt. Iss. 2/20/1800. Certified 7/17/1815. No papers
McGREGORE, David, N.H. See McGREGOR
McGREGORY, Ebenezer, Mass., Susanna Hurlburt, former wid., W14963
Joel, Ct. See MEGREGORY
McGREW, Rebecca, former wid. of Edward Cook, Pa., S3354
Thomas, S.C., b. Pa., S13895
McGRIGGER, James, Pa., S5741
McGUIER, Luke, N.Y., See McGUYER
McGUIGAN, Michael, BLWt.7511-100-Pvt. Iss. 9/16/1791 to Matthew Watson, ass.
Michael, N.Y., Nancy, W17144
McGUIGAR, Michael, N.Y. See McGUIGAN
McGUIN, Samuel, N.H., S45001
McGUINNES, James, Pa., S41850
McGUIRE, Allegany/Aleygane, Va.,
McGUIRE (continued)
S2797
Andrew, Invalid Regt., BLWt. 13510-100-Pvt. Iss. 5/16/1797. No papers
Andrew, Pa., BLWt.10105-100-Pvt. Iss. 12/10/1790. No papers
Barney, Pa., Jane, W3276
Charles, Pa., S41831
Daniel, N.J., N.Y., S16476
Elijah, S.C., Everet, W8274
James, Va., Indian Wars, S13896
John, Pa., BLWt.9927-100-Pvt. Iss. 6/29/1789 to M. McConnell, ass. No papers
John, Pa., Va., S34426
John, S.C., R6728
John, Va., S31244
Joseph, Va., S13892
Matthew, Pa. Arty., BLWt.1451-200-Capt. Lt. Iss. 3/10/1790 to Alexander Power, ass. No papers
Merry, S.C., R22752
Patrick, N.C., S7211
Peter, Ct., See MAGUIRA
Peter, Md., BLWt.11526-100-Pvt. Iss. 11/1/1797 to Elisha Jarrett, ass. No papers
Richard, N.C., Eleanor, R6727
Thomas, Del., BLWt.10821-100-Sgt. Iss. 9/2/1789. No papers
Thomas, N.C., Jane, W4292
William, Cont., Va., Disability pension. BLWt.1522-200-Lt. Iss. 8/5/1789. No papers
William, Va., S5746
McGUOWN, Francis, See McQUOWN
McGURKEY, Edward, N.Y. See McGORAGHEY
McGUY, Bennet, Va., BLWt.12394-100-Pvt. Iss. 2/24/1794 to Anthony New, ass. No papers
McGUYER, Luke, N.Y., Mary, W17119
McHAFFEY, James, Pa., BLWt.9952-100-Pvt. Iss. 10/19/1789. No papers
Oliver, S.C., S38941
McHANEY, Terry, Ga., S38185
McHARG, Archibald, S.C., S33066
McHARGUE, William, N.C., Sarah, R6731
McHARY, Archibald, S.C. See McHARG
McHATTON, Alexander, Pa. See McILHATTON
John, Pa., S36091. See also Am. State Papers, Class IX, p.803
William, Cont., Pa., Dis. No papers; BLWt.1455-200-Lt. Iss. 2/14/1791 under name of Wm. McElhatton, Invalid Corps. No papers here. See Am. State Papers, Class IX, pp.75, 145
McHENRY, Charles, Pa., BLWt.1460-300-Capt. Iss. 5/9/1791. No papers
Isaac, Va., R6732
James, Md. (?), BLWt.1480-400-Maj.
James, N.C., S31243
John, N.Y., Pa., S11041

Mc HENRY (continued)
Richard, Pa., S41824
Robert, Pa., S41849
Thomas, Pa., Mary, W3353
William, not Rev. War, Wayne's War 1792-1795; BLWt.20429-160-50
McHEW, Charity, former wid. of Silas Alden, which see
McHONE, Archibald, Va., R6733
Daniel, N.J., BLWt.8544-100-Pvt. Iss. 8/10/1795 to James Christie, ass. No papers
McHUGH, John, Cont., N.Y., S42945
McILGAR, John, Pa. See McCAR
McILHANEY, John, Va. See McELHANY
McILHANY, Felix, Pa., S41848
James, Va. See McILHENY
James, Va., Margaret, R6734
McILHATTON, Alexander, Pa., S17577
John, Pa. See McHATTON
McILHENNY, James, S.C., S31242
McILHENY, James, Va., S38188
McILNEY, John, Not Rev. War, Wayne's Indian War, Pa., O.W. Inv. Reg. File, 16311; BLWt.16808-160-50
McILRATH, Andrew, N.J., Alice, W25686, BLWt.13894-160-55
McILROY, William, N.J., S2787
McILVAIN, George, Pa., R6735
Goine, N.Y., Jane, R6736
James, N.H., Nancy, W1886
John, Cont., Mass., S18113
John, S.C., Elizabeth, W21786
William, Cont., Mass., N.H., S11045
McILVAINE, Ebenezer, N.H., Hannah, W495; BLWt.14660-160-55
Thomas, Pa., BLWt.9886-100-Pvt. iss. 6/20/1789
Thomas, Pa., BLWt.10130-100-Pvt. Iss. 3/2/17?? to Thomas Campbell Admr. No papers
McILVAN, George, Pa. See McILVAIN
James, N.H. See McILVAIN
McILVIN, George, Pa. See McILVAIN
McINLIN, Mary, former wid. of William Keath, Va., which see
McINNALLEY, Patrick, N.J., BLWts. 8418 & 8587-100-Pvt. Iss. 5/4/1791 to Wm. Barton, ass. No papers
McINNIS, Daniel, N.C., R21889
McINTEE, Barney, N.Y. See McINTIRE
McINTIER, William, Mass. See McINTIRE
McINTIRE, Andrew, N.H., Margaret, R6738
Andrew, Pa., S9019
Barney, N.Y., Rebecca, W23933; BLWt.97533-160-55
Benjamin, Mass. See MacKENTIRE
Elijah, Mass., S31247
Ely, Mass., Sabra, W557; BLWt. 19816-160-55
Hugh, Pa., Mary, R6739
Jacob, Mass., See McENTIRE
James, Cont., Va. res of heirs in 1828; BLWt.1431-100
Jeremiah, Mass., Eunice, BLWt. 47964-160-55
John, Cont., Mass., S23793
John, N.H., S41000
John, Pa., S2802

McINTIRE (continued)
John, Pa., Catharine, W3702; BLWt.3526-160-55
Joseph, N.J., S33395
Phineas/Phinehas, Cont., Mass., Lydia, W26250
Robert, Va., S5743
Simeon, R.I., Mary, W24141
Thomas, Pa., S41854
Thomas, Pa., BLWt.1441-300-Capt. Iss. 2/28/1795. No papers
William, Cont., Va., S36113
William, Mass., Catharine, W9185; BLWt.38521-160-55
William, Mass., Abigail Parker, former wid., W21919
William, Pa., BLWt.9997-100-Pvt. Iss. 7/16/1789 to M. McConnell
William, Pa., BLWt.10050-100-Pvt. Iss. 10/27/1792 to John Cahill, Admr. No papers
McINTOSH, Alexander, N.Y., R6473 1/2
Alexander, Va., BLWt.12342-100-Pvt. Iss. 6/20/1789. No papers
Archibald, Mass., S33077
Charles, N.C., Candace/Candis, W3704
Francis, Va., R6741 1/2
Gideon, Mass., Mehitable, W13701
Jeremiah, Mass., Susannah, W13700
John, Ga., BLWt.1550-500-Lt. Col. Commandant. Iss. 4/14/1799 to John Wright, ass. No papers
John, Mass., S28808
John, N.Y., BLWt.7478-100-Pvt. Iss. 7/30/1790 to Edward Cumpston, ass. No papers
John, N.Y., S13900
Lachlin, Ga., BLWt.1549-850-Brig. Gen. Iss. 3/13/1800. No papers
Lacklen, Ga., BLWt.1344-200-Lt. Iss. 6/6/1796. Also recorded as above under BLWt.1657. No papers
Murdock, N.C., Nancy, W560; BLWt. 34832-160-55
Peter, Mass., See MacKINTOSH
Samuel, R.I., Mary, W13691
Thomas, Cont., Va., S30573
Thomas, N.C., S1563
Timothy, Ct., S42936
William, Cont., S.C., S9424
William, Ga., BLWt.1552-300-Capt. Iss. 4/14/1799 to John Wright, ass. No papers
William, Va., BLWt.12380-100-Pvt. Iss. 5/5/1790 to Wm. J. Vreedenburg, ass. No papers
William, Va., Dis. No papers
William, Va., S47469
McINTYRE, Barney, See McINTIRE
Ely, Mass. See McINTIRE
Henry, Ct., Jane Ann, W25684; BLWt.1880-100
Rufus, R.I., S42956
William, Mass., See McINTIRE
McISAACKS, Isaac, Pa., S44541
McIVER, Angus, Pa. See McEVER
McJUNKIN, Daniel, S.C., Jane, W9190
Joseph, S.C., S18118
McJUTTY, Samuel, Pa. See McQUIETY

McKAFFERTY, Joseph, N.J., R6742
McKAIMY, Francis, N.C., S1853
McKAMEY, John, S.C., Mary, R6743
McKAMY, James, Va., S2811
McKANNON, Christopher, Va. See McCANNON
McKARNY, James, Va. See McKAMY
McKAY, Alexander, Cont., N.Y., Eleanor Johnston, former wid., W20214
Alexander, N.Y., Phebe Ann Humphrey/Humphreys, former wid., W19848
Alexander, N.C., Jane, W8427
Edward, N.C., S9016
James, Md., S16199
John, Md., S34991
Neal, Pa., S22899
Robert, N.C., Jeanette, R6745
Robert, Va., S16956
William, N.C., Nancy, W7429
McKEAN, Alexander, N.H., S16474
Hugh, N.H. See McKEEN
Samuel, See McKEEN
William, Pa., S33397
McKEDY, Thomas, See McKIDDY
McKEE, Alexander, N.C., S7200
Andrew, Pa., BLWt.10,000-100-Pvt. Iss. 12/17/1795 to Christian Hubbard, ass. No papers
Andrew, Pa., Mary, W3277
Eliezer, S.C., See McA
Gavin/Guian/Guion, Pa., S36112
George, Pa., S22901
Guion, See Gavin
James, Pa., BLWt.10085-100-Pvt. Iss. 11/17/1794 to Michael Stever, ass. No papers
James, Va., S16954
John, Pa., Mary, W8271
John, Pa., Elizabeth, W1910; BLWt.26715-160-55; also Indian War service.
John, S.C., Margaret, W8446; BLWt.3775-160-55
Mary, former wid. of Abraham Anthony, ---, which see
Neil, Cont., Mass. See McGEE
Robert, Ct., Elizabeth, W20250
Samuel, Not Rev. War, Indian War 1792-1794, Old War Inv. File 25290
Samuel, Pa., S41853
Samuel, Va., S30574
William, N.Y., Va.?, R6748
William, N.C., Mary, W18500
William, Pa., S41825
McKEEL, Thomas, Md., S34977
McKEEN, Hugh, N.H., Mary, W19866
John, N.H., S15531
Samuel, N.Y., S27161 & S28806
Thomas, Pa., S41826
McKEEVER, Angus. See McEVER
James, S.C. See KEVER
McKEITHAN, John, N.C., S41841
McKELLIP, Archibald. See McKILLEP
McKELLUPS, Samuel, Cont., N.H., S41001
McKELVEY, Thomas, Pa., BLWt. 9932-100-Pvt. Iss. 5/5/1791. No papers
William, Pa., S41844

McKELVY
William, S.C., b. Ireland, Mary,W3
McKEMY, Samuel, Va., Sarah, W126
McKENDRICK, Archibald, Pa., BLWt. 9904-100-Pvt. Iss. 12/9/1795 to Francis Kirkpatrick, ass.
McKENDRY, William, Mass., BLWt. BLWt.1341-200-Lt. Iss. 10/18/ 1796 to Wm. Hall, ass. Also recorded as above under BLWt.1184. No papers
McKENNAN, William, Del., Elizabeth, W3104; BLWt.1471-300-Capt. Iss. 5/30/1789. No papers
McKENNEY, Abner, Mass., Sarah, W23954
Charles, Va., S16477
Isaac, Mass., S37234
John, S.C., S31848
Jonathan, Mass., S20458
Joseph, Mass., Elizabeth, W23943
Moses, Mass., Lucy Waterhouse, former wid., W25910. Her 1st husb. was Thomas McKenney, Mass., which see
Thomas, Mass., Lucy Waterhouse, former wid., R11180. Her 2nd husb. was Moses McKenney, Mass., which see
Tully, Va. See McKINNEY
William, Mass., See McKENNY
McKENNON, John, S.C., Elizabeth, R6751
McKENNY, William, Mass., Miriam, W24144
McKENSEY, Joshua, Cont., Md., BLWt.11513-100. Iss. 1/15/1793. No papers
McKENT, James, Va. See McCANT
McKENZIE, Alexander, N.Y., Catharine, W19869
Alexander, S.C., Sarah, R6754; BLReg.241205-1855
Alexander, Va., BLWt.12358-100-Pvt. Iss. 11/26/1792. No papers
Alexander, Va. See McKINZIE
Ebenezer, Mass., Elizabeth Conly, former wid., W16216
Jesse, See McKINZEY
John, N.C., S.C., Va., Martha, W1049
John, Pa., Helen, W2832
Moses, Cont., Md. See McKINSEY
William, N.C., BLWt.12421 & 13404-100-Pvt. Iss. 6/10/1791 to Abishai Thomas, ass. No papers
William, N.C., R6755
McKEOWEN, John, Pa. S41823 & S34996
McKESSACK, William, Pa., See McKISSACK
McKETHAN, Neill, N.C., R6756
McKEW, John, N.Y., BLWt.7531-100-Pvt. Iss. 7/16/1790 to Wm. J. Vreedenburgh, ass. No papers
McKEY, Alexander, N.Y., Elizabeth, R6749
Bennett, Va., S38197
William, Capt., Pa., BLWt.1424-300 iss. 7/7/1789
William, S.C. See MacKAY
McKIDDY, Thomas, S.C., Catharine, R6757
McKIE, Daniel, Va., Frances/Fanny, R6750; BLWt.49264-160-55
James, N.Y., Elizabeth, W21788
McKILLEP, Archibald, N.Y., S13891
McKILLIN, Edward, Pa., BLWt. 10002-100-Pvt. Iss. 3/29/1791 to Edward McKillin. No papers
McKILLIP, Alexander, N.Y. See McCALEB
McKILLOP, Abraham, N.Y., BLWt.7537-100-Pvt. Iss. 2/14/1791 to Edward Savage, ass. No papers
McKILLUP, Robert, Pa., BLWt.10126-100-Pvt. Iss. 11/28/179? to Alexander Powers, ass. of Ann McKillup, Admx. No papers
McKIM, Alexander, Md., Catharine Sarah, R6758; BLWt.56952-160-55
James, Pa., S41847
McKIMMINS, John, Pa., BLWt.9879-100-Corp. Iss. 3/10/1790. No papers
McKINLEY, Alexander, Pa., BLWt. 9955-100-Pvt. Iss. 12/22/1794 to Henry Purdy, ass. No papers
Alexander, Pa., BLWt.9977-100-Pvt. Iss. 3/19/1790. No papers
Archibald, N.Y., S42960; BLWt. 692-100
Charles, N.C., Jennet/Janet, R6759
David, Pa., S2812
James, Cont., Pa., S41829
John, Cont., Ct., or N.H., Sarah, W16644
John, Navy, Del. res. & agcy., S36089
John, N.C. See MacKENLY
John, Pa., BLWt.9965-100-Pvt. Iss. 3/10/1790. No papers
John, Pa., BLWt.10034-100-Pvt. Iss. 3/2/1792 to Alexander McKinley, Admr. No papers
Peter, Pa., BLWt.9967-100-Pvt. Iss. 3/2/1799. No papers
Robert, Pa., BLWt.2107-100
William, Md., BLWt.11555-100-Pvt. Iss. 12/24/1794 to John Wright, ass of Benj. Smith, Admr. No papers
McKINNEY, Andrew, Cont., Pa., S42961; BLWt.967-100
Charles, N.Y., BLWt.7442-100-Sgt. Iss. 6/17/1790 to Peter Hughes, ass. No papers
Charles, N.Y., BLWt.7450-100-Pvt. Iss. 6/17/1790 to Peter Hughes, ass. No papers
Charles, Va., S31852
Daniel, ----, N.Y. res. of claimant, R6763
David, N.J. See KINNEY
David, Va., Margaret, R6766
Dennis/Denis, Va., S36110
John, N.J., S33383
John, N.C., R6764
John, Pa., BLWt.10113-100-Pvt. Iss. 4/2/1791. No papers
John, Pa., S---, Ctf.196; BLWt. 1438-200-Lt. Iss. 2/4/1795. No papers
John, Pa., S33386
John, Pa., S41858
McKINNEY (continued)
John, S.C., Va., Wayne's War, Hannah, W558
John, Va., BLWt.12385-100-Pvt. Iss. 3/26/1792 to Francis Graves, ass. No papers
John, Va. (1774), Polley, R6768
Nevin, Va., Sarah, W7431
Peter, Pa., S39813; BLWt.9778-100, iss. 1789
Robert, Mass., Margaret, W26253
Robert, Pa., See McKINLEY
Robertson/Robert, Va., Mary Bettisworth, former wid., R873
Thomas, Va., S36088
Timothy, S.C., S36103
Tully, Va., Mary, R6752
William, Ga., Va., S16470
William, Mass. See McKENNEY
William, N.C., S9017; BLWt.26891-160-55
McKINNON, John, S.C. See McKENNON
Lathlin, Pa., R6753
McKINNY, Michael, Va., R6767
McKINSEY, Alexander, Va. See McKINZIE
Ebenezer, Mass., BLWt.4628-100-Sgt. Iss. 9/2/1789 to Richard Platt. No papers
George, Ct., Anna, W2226; BLWt. 1418-100
Jesse, Pvt., Md., BLWt.11512 iss. 4/8/1796
John, Ct., Dis. No papers here, but see Am. State Papers, Class IX, Claims, pp. 66, 115
John, Ct., Dis. No papers
Moses, Cont., Md., Sarah, W288; BLWt.11514-100. Iss. 4/8/1796. No paper
McKINSTER, Paul, Sheldon's Dragoons, Ct., BLWt.6227-100-Pvt. Iss. 9/1/1790 to Theodosius Fowler, ass. No papers
McKINSTERY, Paul, Ct., S42952
McKINSTRY, Amos, Mass., S40986
Bernice, former wid. of Elijah Egleston, Mass., which see
John, Mass., Dis. No papers here. Am. State Papers, Class IX, Claims, pp.157, 401 show a Capt. John McKinstrey of N.Y.
McKINZEY, James, Navy, Pa. res. & agcy., S41856
Jesse, Cont., Md., Catharine, W7432; BLWt.11512-100. Iss. 4/8/1796.
McKINZIE, Alexander, Va., Tabitha B., W8439
Isaac, Va., S30571
John, Lamb's Art., N.Y., BLWt. 7532-100-Pvt. Iss. 9/27/1790 to Andrew Stockholm, ass. No papers
John, Pa. See McKENZIE
Philip, N.Y. See MacKENZIE
McKIRTH, Thomas, N.H., S40983
McKISICK, Daniel, N.C., Jane, W26251. See also Am. State Papers, Class IX, Claims, p.168. Capt. Daniel McKissick of Lincoln Co., N.C.

McKISSACK, Thomas, N.C., S164
William, Pa., S33398; BLWt.1137-300
McKISSICK, James, Pa., S23792
James, Pa., S34985
Rachel, former wid. of John Morris, Va., which see
McKITRICK, John, Va. See McKITTRICK
McKITTRICK, John, Sr., Va., S13647
McKIZICK, Ann, former wid. of John Burns, Va., which see
McKLEROY, John, N.C., Mary, W8272
McKNIGHT, Adam, Mass., Mercy, W559; BLWt.26088-160-55
Andrew, N.C., Elizabeth, R6773
Benjamin, Va., S38186
Bennet, Mass. See McNITT
Charles, Gen. Hosp., BLWt.1565-450-Physician & Surgn. Iss. 9/25/1790. No papers
David, Pa., Eleanor, W10215; BLWt. 1439-200-Lt. Iss. 7/16/1789. No papers
Dennis, Pa.?, Invalid pensioner.
Eli, Va., S2710
John, Md., BLWts.11477 & 11743-100-Pvt. Iss. 1/28/1795 to Francis Sherrard, ass. of Wm. Smith, Admr. No papers
John, Md., S41860; BLRej. According to Am. State Papers, Class IX,Claims, p.395, John McKnight, Pvt., 4th Md. Regt., was on 1/6/1794 iss. Certificate of registered debt No. 4704, for 160.65, with interest commencing 8/1/1780. On a claim,barred by the statutes of limitation which was adjusted & allowed under the Act of March 27, 1792, "An Act providing for the settlement of claims of persons under particular circumstances barred by limitations heretofore established".
Malcom, Cont. See McNIGHT
Michael, Va., BLWt.12401-100-Pvt. Iss. 3/1/1793. No papers
Michael, Va., S38200
Robert, Mass., Navy, Elizabeth, W18499
Thomas, Ct., S15500
William, S.C., b. N.C., S32407
McKNNEY, William, See McKENNY
McKONKEY, David, Md. See McCONKEY
McKOWEN, John, Invalids Regt., BLWt.13487-100-Pvt. Iss. 4/7/1793 to John Nicholson, ass. No papers
McKOWN, James, Va., Phebe, W7430
McKOY, Alexander, N.C. See McKAY
James, Va., S5750
John, Navy, R.I. See McCOY
Neil, Mass., S42951
Robert, Md., S11044
McKREE, Griffith John, N.C. See McREY
McLACHLAN, Colin, Cont., N.J., Elizabeth, W25687; BLWt.346-60-55 & 13435-100. Iss. 9/4/1796
McLAEN, Alexander, N.C., S17575

McLAEN (continued)
Daniel, Pa. See McCLAIN
McLAIN, Alexander, Pa., Margaret, W3274
Charles, Pa., S41857
George, N.C., Rebecca, W21793
Henry, Va., S7196
John, N.C. See McCLAIN
John, S.C., See McCLAIN
John, Va., S5744
Joseph, N.C., S38805
Joshua, Md., Elizabeth, R6775
Laughlin, Va., BLWt.12346. Iss. 11/5/1789
Thomas, N.J., S38933
Thomas, Pa. See McLEAN
Thomas, Va., S31851
Uriah, Cont., Mass., Elizabeth Sharp, former wid., W6023; BLWt.1726-100
McLANAHAN, Charles, Pa. See McLENAHAN
Thomas, Va. See McCLANAHAN
McLANE, Alexander, N.C. See McLAEN
Allen, Lee's Legion, Va., BLWt. 1474-300-Capt.
Benjamin, Del., S36090
Charles, Pa. See McLAIN
Daniel, Crane's Art., Mass., BLWt.1365-200-Lt. Iss. 10/27/1789 to Joseph Crocker, Admr. for the Estate of Job Sumner late ass. of D. McLane. No papers
Enoch, Md., BLWt.1970-100
Hugh, N.J., BLWt.8579-100-Pvt. Iss. 1/23/1792 to John Morris, Jr., Admr. No papers
Ichabod, Mass., S37232
John, Mass., S18114
John, N.Y., BLWt.7505-100-Sgt. Iss. 10/12/1790. No papers
John, Lamb's Art., N.Y., BLWt. 7533-100-Pvt. Iss. 9/28/1790 to Bartholomew & Fisher, assnes.
Joseph, N.C. See McLAIN
Joshua, Md. See McLAIN
Laughlin, Pvt., Va., BLWt.12346 iss. 11/5/1789
Uriah, Cont., Mass. See McLAIN
McLARDY, Alexander, Va., S36092
McLARREN, Daniel, Va., R6776
McLAUGHLEN, Charles, N.J., BLWt. 8568-100-Pvt. Iss. 8/19/1789 to Peter Lott, ass. No papers
McLAUGHLIN, Hugh, N.J., BLWt.8573-100-Pvt. Iss. 12/27/1791. No papers
Jacob, N.C., Mary, R6778
James, Mass., N.H., S11048
James, N.H., Sarah, BLWt.59096-160-55
James, Pa., Elizabeth, R6777
John, Navy, Pa. res. of wid. in 1843, Sarah Dunlap, former wid., R3140
John, N.H., BLWt.3304-100-Pvt. Iss. 3/25/1790. No papers
John, N.Y., S42950
John, N.C., Eleanor Mathis, former wid., W174
John, N.C., W7436; BLWt.84064-160-55

McLAUGHLIN (continued)
John, N.C., Pa., b. Pa., S7212
John, Pa., S9009
John, Va., S34987
John, Va. See McGLOUGHLIN
Lydia, former wid. of Israel Hull, N.H., which see
Owen, Hazen's Regt., BLWt.13439-100-Pvt. Iss. 2/25/1792. No papers
Owen, Mass., BLWt.4644-100-Pvt. Iss. 10/26/1789. No papers
Robert, Pa., S40146
Stephen, N.C., Nancy, W963
William, Mass., Hannah, W23947
William, N.H., Catharine, W25683; BLWt.10311-160-55
William, Va., S18121
McLAURINE, James, Va., R6780
William, Va., S9015
McLEAN, Anthony, N.Y. See Lawrence JOHNSON
Archibald, Pa., BLWt.9945-100-Pvt. Iss. 6/8/1790. No papers
Arthur, Md., S8884
Charles, Pa., BLWt.10074-100-Pvt. Iss. 2/14/1791. No papers
Daniel, Pa. See McCLAIN
George, N.C. See McLAIN
Henry, Ct., BLWt.6176-100-Pvt. Iss. 10/22/1792
Jacob, Ct., BLWt.6166-100-Pvt. Iss. 10/22/1792. No papers
Jacob, Ct., S40993
Jacob, Pa., BLWt.9929-100-Pvt. Iss. 1/5/1796. No papers
James, Ct., S31854
James, Pa., BLWt.9953-100-Pvt. Iss. 7/20/1799. No papers
John, Ct., BLWt.1942-100
John, N.Y., BLWt.7479-100-Pvt. Iss. 8/6/1790 to Jerh Van Renselar, ass. No papers
John, N.Y., S42962
John, N.Y., Maria, W17122
John, Pa., BLWt.1456-200-Lt. Iss. 4/7/1795 to John Nicholson, ass. No papers
John, Pa., S13899
Neil, N.Y. See McCLEAN
Thomas, Hazen's Regt., BLWt.13459-100-Pvt. Iss. 1/5/1796. No papers
Thomas, Pa., S38939
Uriah, Cont. Mass. See McCAIN
McLEARY, Michael, N.C., S8886
McLELLAN, Daniel, N.C., S7208
John, Mass., S18120
John, N.H. See McCLELLAN
Prince (colored), Navy, Me. agcy. & res., S37228
McLELLAN, William, Mass., Jane, W23946
McLEMONE, John, N.C. see MacLEMORE
McLENAHAN, Charles, Pa., Elizabeth, W2960
McLENDON, Shadrack, See McCLENDON
McLEOD, Alexander, Cont., N.Y., S11052
George, Pa., S33388
John, Pa., S40984
Robert, Md., S34988

McLEOD (continued)
Robert, N.C., S2804
William, N.C., S33082; BLWt.7053-160-55
McLEROY, Andrew, N.C., Phebe, R6783
Reuben, N.C., Christiania, W5360
McLOUGHLIN, Hugh, Va., Agnes Wiley, former wid., W6537
McLOUTH, John, Mass., R.I., Sarah, W7435
Lawrence, Mass., R.I., Wealthy/Weltha, W15930
Lewis, Mass., S30581
McLUCAS, John, Mass., Margaret Welch, former wid., W25950
McLUER, James, N.H., Mary, W23945
McLURE, Abdiel, Pa., Mary, W7434
Andrew, N.J., BLWt.8554-100-Pvt. Iss. 1/14/1791. No papers
Andrew, N.J. See McCLURE
James, N.J., BLWt.8592-100-Pvt. Iss. 5/9/1792. No papers
Robert, N.H. See McCLURE
Thomas, N.C., S8889
William, N.J., S22391
McLUSKY, William, S.C., S1693
McMACHON, Charles, Pa., S34983
McMAHAN, Abner, N.J., S41832
Andrew, Cont., Va., S38931
Archibald, N.C., Ann, W21779
Barbara, former wid. of James Clark, Md., which see
Constantine, Pa., R6784
Daniel, Cont., Me. agcy., S37224
John, S.C., Mary, W23938
John, Va., S2808
John, Va., S18110
Joseph, Mass., S37226
Joseph, Va., Mary, W23941; BLWt.38530-160-55
Redman, S.C., R6785
Robert, Pa., R6787
Robert, Va., Nancy, R16357
William, Va., Rebecca, R6786
McMAHON, Andrew, Va., BLWt.12340-100-Sgt. Iss. 2/15/1799. No papers
Barbara, Md. See James CLARK
Daniel, N.C., S4199
John, Pa., S41842
Peter, Pa., BLWt.10072-100-Pvt. Iss. 6/8/1789. No papers
Peter, S.C., Susannah, W21782
Peter, Va., S34981
Robert, Pa. See McMAHAN
William, Va. See McMAHAN
McMAMUS, John, Pa., BLWt.9889-100-Pvt. Iss. 2/14/1791 to Alexander Power, ass. No papers
McMAN, James, Mass., BLWt.54423-160-55
McMANIS, Christopher, N.J. See McMANUS
Joseph, Pa., R6788
McMANNERS, Daniel, Mass., Betsey, W494; BLWt.12560-160-55
John, Ct., Lucy, W306; BLWt.3963-160-55
John, Mass. See McMANNUS
William, Va., R6789
McMANNIS, Charles, Pa., Va., S2807

McMANNIS (continued)
Charles, Va., S36107
John, Va., S17574
Kenny, N.J., BLWt.8565-100-Pvt. Iss. 6/11/1789 to Matthias Denman, ass. No papers
Moses, N.J., S29322
McMANNUS, Daniel, Mass. See McMANNERS
John, Mass., Elizabeth, W23940
McMANUS, Charles, S.C., R6790; BLWt.38840-160-55
Christopher, N.J., S42940; BLWt. 1589-100
McMARTIN, John, N.Y., S28807
McMASTER, Hugh, N.Y., Martha, W16645
James, N.Y., S23315
James, Pa., S7189
John, Mass., Sarah B., BLWt. 56859-160-55
Joshua, Mass., Rebecca Dickinsen former wid., W1835; BLWt.9212-160-55
William, S.C., R21675
McMASTER, Alexander, N.Y., BLWt. 7514-100-Pvt. Iss. 10/15/1789 to James Reynolds
Andrew, N.C., Sarah, R6792
Edward, Pa., Rhoda, W2831
Isaac, Mass., R6791
James, Cont., Mass., S23790
Michael, Va., S36093
McMATH, Daniel, Pa., S41843
McMEANS, James, Va., R6793
McMECHAN, Alexander, N.Y., Margaret, W17112, BLWt.27646-160-55
McMECHEN, Charles, Pa. See McMACHON
McMECKIN, Robert, Pa. See McMEEKIN
Robert, Va., Martha, W8442
McMEINS, James, Va. See McMEANS
McMENNAMY, Alexander, N.C., S4201
William, N.C., S9013
McMENNES, William, N.Y., S43734
McMICHAEL, Daniel, N.Y., S13885
James, Mass., S29319
James, Pa., BLWt.1437-200-Lt. Iss. 9/12/1787. No papers
John, N.Y., S13889
McMICKIN, Robert, Va. See McMEEKIN
McMILLAN, Daniel, S.C., S32397
James, S.C., Rachel, W9559
John, N.J., BLWt.8537-100-Pvt. Iss. 12/16/1799 to Jonas Crane, ass. No papers
John, N.J., Nancy, W7425
John, Pa. See McMULLEN
Joseph, Va. See McMILLIAN
Robert, Pa., S18501
Samuel, Cont., Md., Mass., Esther, W1908; BLWt.26849-160-55
Thomas, Va., Mary, W2830
William, Md., S2806
McMILLEN, Charles, N.J., BLWt. 8525-100-Pvt. Iss. 9/30/1791. No papers
Daniel, Md., Jane, W6800
James, N.H. See McMULLEN

McMILLEN (continued)
James, N.J., Jane, R6794
John, Cont., Mass. See McMULLEN
John, Pa., S5739
Joseph, Mass. Sea Service, Navy, R.I., S42937
Joseph, S.C., S4200
Robert, Pa., Mary, W7426
Thomas, Pa., S13897
McMILLIAN, Joseph, Va., S18116; BLWt.47425-160-55
McMILLIN, Daniel, Md. See McMILLEN
McMILLION, John, Va., S16463; BLWt.28535-160-55
Joseph, Va. See McMILLIAN
William, Mass., Elizabeth, W24145
McMILLON, John, Va. See McMILLION
Rowley/Rawley, Ga., S16945
McMINN, Nancy, former wid. of Willoughby Williams, N.C., which see
Robert, Md., S1559
McMITCHELL, John, Crane's Cont. Art., Mass., BLWt.4722-100-Fife Major. Iss. 8/11/1790 to Robert Dunlap. No papers
McMONAGILL, Charles, Va., Lee's Legion, BLWts.12351 & 13522-100-Corp. Iss. 9/2/1789. No papers
McMULIN, William, Pa., S42964
McMULLAN, Michael, Pa., S40142
McMULLEN, Alexander, Md., S38198
Daniel, Pa., BLWt.10093-100-Corp. "in the Artillery". Iss. 4/16/1790
Daniel James, Pa., S9007
James, N.H., BLWt.59094-160-55
John, Cont., Mass., Sarah, W19865; BLWt.18-100
John, N.C., Margaret, W4287
John, Pa., BLWt.9883-100-Pvt. Iss. 7/9/1789. No papers
John, Pa., S40147; BLWt.245-100
Michael, Pa., BLWt.9888-100-Pvt. Iss. 3/9/1799. No papers
Michael, Pa. See MULLEN
Neil, Pa., S41864
Rawley, Ga. See Rowley McMILLON
William, Del., S40148
William, Pa., BLWt.10064-100-Corp. Iss. 1/18/1800 to Peter Eyster, ass. No papers
William, Pa. See McMULIN
McMULLIN, Archibald, Mass., S37227
Hugh, Md., BLWt.11501-100-Sgt. Iss. 2/1/1790. No papers
John, N.C. See McMULLEN
McMURDY, John, Pa., S40136
McMURFEY, Saunders, N.H., S45002
McMURPHY, George, N.H., S42943
John, N.H., War of 1812, d. in service, Sarah, W17118
Peter, Mass., Sarah, W23951
Rachel, former wid. of Benjamin Cole, Cont., Ct., which see
McMURRAY, William, Pa., S.C., Sea Service, S41862
McMURRY, John, S.C., Margaret, W4290; BLWt.28502-160-55
Samuel, N.H., Elizabeth, R6798
William, S.C., S36694

McMURTRY, John, Pa. & Privateer, Margaret, W1448
McMURTY, John, See McMURTRY
McMUTREY, Thomas, N.J., BLWt. 8572-100-Pvt. Iss. 6/11/1789 to Matthias Denman, ass. No papers
McMYERS, Andrew, N.J., BLWt.1364-300-Capt. Iss. 6/11/1789 to Mary McMyers, heir & repr. Also recorded as above under BLWt. 2505. No papers
McNABB, Charles, Md., S36082
David, N.C., Elizabeth, W7438
John, S.C., S16466
McNAIR, Angus, Hazen's Regt., BLWt. 13405 & 13563-100-Pvt. Iss. 10/26/1789. No papers
Archibald, Cont., Pa., S---; BLWt. 1640-100
John, Pa., BLWt.9949-100-Pvt. Iss. 4/16/1790. No papers
Robert, Cont., Pa., S16949
Robert, R.I. See McNEIR
McNALLY, John, Mass., S42954
McNAMAR, Peter/Patrick, Mass. See McNEMARA
McNAMARA, Darby, Md.,BLWt.11498-100-Pvt. Iss. 9/5/1789. No papers
John, Cont., Mass., S40982
John, Hazen's Regt., BLWt.13441-100-Sgt. Iss. 10/7/1789 to Benj. Tallmadge. No papers
Patrick/Peter, Mass. See McNEMARA
McNAMEE, William, N.Y., Abigail, R6799; BLWt.47510-160-55
McNARY, Hugh, N.C., S33067
Martin, Ct., S42953
McNATT, James, N.C., Ferebe, W4286
John, Del., S2809
John, S.C., Lucretia, W2655; BLWt.1968-160-55
McNAUGHTEN, Alexander, N.Y.,S13887
McNEAL, Charles, N.Y., BLWt.7451-100-Pvt. Iss. 7/10/1790 to C.E. Elmendorph, ass. No papers
Daniel, N.H., Abigail, W17116
Henry, Cont., Mass., BLWt.2238-100
Henry, N.Y., S42935
John, N.Y., S42944
Neal, N.Y. See Niel McNIEL
Thomas, N.H., BLWt.3335-100-Pvt. Iss. 12/12/1795. No papers
William, N.H., Martha, R6803
McNEALE, James, See NEALE
McNEAR, Robert, R.I. See McNEIR
McNEARY, Martin, Ct. See McNARY
McNEEL, Robert, Pa. See McNEELY
McNEELY, David, Va., S35524
David, Va., Rebecca, W1051
John, N.C., S7261
Robert, Pa., Nancy A., R6801
Simeon, N.J., BLWt.8543-100-Pvt. Iss. 3/13/1790. No papers
William, Pa., Jane, W2956
McNEES, James, S.C., R6802
Robert, S.C., S7192
McNEESE, John, N.C., BLWt.2147-300
Robert, S.C. See McNEES
McNEIL, Hector, N.C., Isabella, W4285. He was b. 1752/1753;

McNEIL (continued)
d. 9/8/1842. See claim of Hector McNEILL, W18501
Jacob, Va., S5745
John, Mass., N.H., Lucy, W21780
Joseph, Mass., BLWt.1374-300-Capt. Iss. 4/11/1792 to Martin Kingsley
Neil, N.Y. See Niel McNIEL
William, N.H. See McNEAL
McNEILL, Archibald/Archebald, Mass., S30572
Archibald, N.C., Effy, W25690; BLWt.8467-160-55
Daniel, N.H. See McNIEL
Daniel, N.C., Isabella, W4026
Hector, N.C., Ayles, W18501. He d. 7/28/1830
John C., N.H., Hannah, W20246
Lauchlin, N.C., Mary, W7437
Malcolm, N.C., Nancy, W18495
Thomas, N.H., S40994
McNEILY, John, BLWt.8552-100-Pvt. Iss. 2/14/1791. No papers
McNEIR, Robert, R.I., S15285
McNELLY, Henry, Mass., S21367
John, Md., BLWt.11527-100-Pvt. Iss. 12/18/1794 to Henry Purdy, ass. No papers
Michael, Va., S38943
McNEMAR, George, See McNERNAR
McNEMARA, Peter/Patrick, Mass., S33072; BLWt.661-100
McNERNAR, George, ---, Va. res. in 1834; R6807
McNESS, Sally, former wid. of Lewis Saxton, S.C., which see
McNICKLE, John, Va. Sea Service, R74. Va. Half Pay. See N.A. Acc. No. 837-Va. State Navy-YS File
McNIEL, Daniel, N.H., Privateer, Sarah, R6806
Henry, Ct., Nancy, W2143
Niel, N.Y., S22897
McNIGHT, Malcom, Cont., N.J. res. & agcy., S33384
McNISH, Alexander, N.Y., Sarah, W23937 & S28094
McNITT, Adam, Mass. See McKNIGHT
Barnard/Bennet, Mass., Elizabeth, W20247
John, Mass., Patty, W16355
John, N.Y., S11054
McNULTY, John, Ct., S28594
McNUTT, Andrew, N.Y., S42958
John, N.Y. See McNITT
McQUADE, John, Pa., BLWt.10070-100-Dragoon. Iss. 6/28/1799 to Abraham Bell, ass. No papers
McQUADY, John, Va., Susan, W7603
McQUAY, John, N.J., BLWt.8529-100-Pvt. Iss. 11/9/1792. No papers
John, N.J. See MUGWAY
William, Va. See McQUIE
McQUEEN, Alexander, Va., S5075
John, N.C., S30577
Joshua, Pa., Va., S36102, BLWt. 1883-100
Thomas, Va., S33080
William, Ct., Sea Service, Tryphena Palmer, former wid.,W17424

McQUIDDY, John, Va. See McQUADY
McQUIE, William, Va., S16952
McQUIETY, Samuel, Pa., Va., R6812
McQUILLEN, James, Pa., BLWt.9993-100-Pvt. Iss. 2/14/1791 to Alexander Power, ass. No papers
McQUIN, John, N.C. See McQUEEN
McQUINN, John, Va., S40141
McQUINNY, Thomas, Md., S34982
McQUITTY, Samuel, See McQUIETY
McQUOWN, Francis, Pa., R6730
John, Va., S41821
McREA, Griffith John, N.C. See McREY
William, N.W., Indian War 1790-1795. Old War Wid. 8443 Wid. Mary. Filed in Rev. War Files. Also War of 1812
McREE, Griffith John, See McREY
William, Pa., S5754
McREVY, Hugh, Pa. See McELREVY
McREY, Griffith John, N.C., Ann, W4731; BLWt.1529-400-Major. Iss. 12/21/1791 to Abishai Thomas, ass. Name spelled McREA. No papers
McREYNOLDS, Joseph, N.C., S33070
McRIE, Griffith John, See McREY
McRIGHT, Matthew, S.C., R6774
McROBERTS, David, Pa., S38934
James, Pa., Va., Mary, W2225; BLWt.26888-160-55
John, Vt., Lucy, W4022
John, Va., R8872
McSHANE, Robert, N.J., R6813
McSOUTCHEON, George, Mass., BLWt.4668-100-Pvt. Iss. 12/21/1790. No papers
McSPADDEN, Archibald, Va. See McSPEDEN
Samuel, Va., S4203
McSPEDDIN, Thomas, Va., S2813
McSPEDEN, Archibald, Va., S4204
McSWAIN, Edward, Va., BLWt.12393-100-Pvt. Iss. 5/29/1792 to Robt. Means, ass. No papers
William, N.C., Elizabeth, W2409; BLWt.6449-160-55
McSWINE, George, Pa., BLWt.9923-100-Pvt. Iss. 6/27/1791. No papers
George, Pa., S40140
McTEER, William, N.J., S1056
McUIN, Patrick, Va. See McEWING
McVANY, Christopher, Va., Mary, S15533
McVAUGH, Jacob, Pa., S7215
John, Pa., Mary, R6815
McVAY, Benjamin, Pa., Elizabeth, W2405; BLWt.26191-160-55
Daniel, Va., S36108
David, S.C., R6816
Eli, N.C., Mildred, W964; BLWt. 2273-100
Hugh, N.C., S.C., S15286
McVENARS, George, See McNERNAR
McVEY, Benjamin, Pa. See McVAY
McVICKERS, Archibald, Pa., BLWt. 10032-100-Pvt. Iss. 6/10/1794 to Silas Hart, ass. No papers
McWAIN, Andrew, Mass., S18968
William, Mass. See

McWAIN (continued)
Hall McELEVAIN
McWATERS, John, S.C., Priscilla, R6817
McWETHEY, Silas, N.Y., S41822
McWHIRTER, James, N.C., R6818
James, S.C., S7199
McWHORTER, Aaron, N.C., S4596
George, N.C., S.C., S9011
Henry, N.J., N.Y., Pa., S7210
John, S.C., b. N.C., S32400
John, S.C., Elizabeth, W9560
McWHORTOR, Robert, Pa., S16195
McWILLIAM, Stephen, Del., BLWt. 1473-200-Lt. Iss. 9/2/1789. No papers
McWILLIAMS, James, Cont., Va. res. in 1834; BLWt.2022-100
James, N.Y., R6821
James, N.C., Va., Martha, W3026
James, S.C., R6822
John, Va., S9005
Joshua, Va. Sea Service, R75, Va. Half Pay
Samuel, Pa., Jane, BLReg.87098-Act of 9/28/1850
William, Pa., Mary, W4289
William, Va., Dorothea B. Buckner, former wid., R1410
McWITHEY, James, N.Y., Vt.,S32398
Silas, N.Y. See McWETHEY
McWOOD, Joseph, Ct., BLWt.6150-100-Pvt. Iss. 6/20/1798. No papers
McWRIGHT, Matthew, S.C. See McRIGHT
MEACH, Elijah, See MEECH
Jacob, See MEECH
Thomas, See MEECH
Timothy, Ann Williams, former wid., R11563
MEACHAM, Abraham, Mass., Vt., Lydia, W17131
Elijah, Ct., Frances, W2318; BLWt.518-160-55
Isaac, Mass., Vt., Lucy, W17083
Jeremiah, Ct., Cont., Chloe, W23963
Jonathan, Mass., S30583
Joseph, N.C., S11062
Richard B., N.C., R7071
Simeon, Mass., Lydia, W2413; BLWt.19627-160-55
MEACHEM, John, Mass., BLWt.4717. Iss. 4/1/1790 to John May
MEACHUM, Ichabod, Cont., Mass., Navy, S38204
MEAD, Abijah, Mass., S18507
Abraham, Ct., No claim
Amos, Green Mt. Boys, Vt., S13903
Andrew, Ct., Amah, W25700
Benjamin, Mass., S30582
Benjamin, Mass., Susannah, W4284
Calvin, Ct., N.Y., S17580
Daniel, N.Y., R7072
David, Ct., N.Y. & Sea Service, Sarah, W19875
David, N.Y., S9975
Ebenezer, Ct., N.Y., S13919
Edward, Ct., Mary, W25694
Edward, Ct., Amy Lord, former

MEAD (continued)
wid., R6450
Eli, Ct., R7073
Eli, Pa., R7074
Enos, Ct., Prudence, W19874
Giles, N.J., BLWt.1406-300-Capt. Iss. 1/26/1790. No papers
Henry, Vt., Mary, BLWt.49470-160-55
Isaiah, N.Y., R7075
Israel, Ct., S13907
Israel, Mass., S29980
Israel, Mass., Vt., S2814
James, Md., Mary, W3847; BLWt. 2434-100
James, N.Y., Abiah, W1911
Jasper, Ct., Elizabeth, W9956
Jasper, Ct., R7076
Jeremiah, Ct., S36119
John, Ct., Elizabeth, W19872
John, N.Y., S32409
John, Sgt., Va., BLWt.12359. Iss. 5/5/1790 to Wm. I. Vreedenburgh, ass. No papers
John, Va., S36125
John, Va., S38210
Jonathan, Lamb's Arty., N.Y., BLWt.7457 & 8068. Iss. 9/10/1790. No papers
Joseph, Ct., S11066
Jotham, Ct., S22903
Levi, Ct., Abigail, W9958
Levi, Mass., Betsey, W21787
Lewis, N.Y., Sarah, W26258
Minor, Va., Jane, W5369; BLWt. 2187-160-55
Moses, Mass., Lizzy, W16646
Peter, Ct., S15938
Reuben, Ct., S16188
Samuel, Fifer, Ct., BLWt.6172. Iss. 6/26/1790. No papers
Samuel, Ct., Cont., Lois, W17134
Samuel, Md., R7077
Silas, Cont., N.Y., S13910
Smith, Ct., S22904
Stephen, N.Y., Elizabeth, W17132
Stephen, Vt., Dorothy, W4740
Thaddeus, Ct., S17584
Thomas, Ct., Ellen, W9952; BLWt. 26458-160-55
Thomas, Va., Sarah, W9561
Tilly, Mass., S33400
Truman, Cont., Vt., S42968
Uriah, Ct., Betty, W1305; BLWt. 1775-100
William, N.J., S31860
William, N.Y., S42967
William, N.Y., Hannah, W16345
William, Va., S38942
Zaccheus, Ct., Deborah, W25699
Zelek, N.Y., R7080
MEADE, Everard, Va., BLWt.2063-300
Israel, Mass., Lydia Hall, former wid., W17057
Thornton, Va., Mary, W18506
William, N.C., b. Va., S19394
MEADEARIS, John, See MEDEARIS
MEADEN, Andrew, N.C., S4188
MEADER, Daniel Meservy, Mass., Jerusha, W23959
Francis, Mass., S37241

MEADERIS, John, See MEDEARIS
MEADERS, Daniel, N.C., S1699
MEADOR, Benjamin, Va., S9405
Isham, Va., Martha, W25697; BLWt.40693-160-55
Joel, Va., Sally, W7445
Jonas, Va., R7081
MEADOW, Josiah, Va., S7225
MEADOWS, Francis, Va., Frances, W5367
Israel, Va., Barbara, W8451
Jacob, Va., S9412
James, N.C., Jane, R7082
James, Va., S8895
John, Ga., N.C., b. N.C.,S7221
William, Va., R16416
MEADS, James, N.J., BLWt.8567. Iss. 1/28/1790. No papers
James, N.J., S34428
MEAGHER, Richard, See MAIGHER
MEAIRS, Alexander, See MARS
MEAKER, Ephraim, Cont., Ct., Comfort, W16643
MEAKINS, Bennett, Md., BLWt. 2210-100
MEALER, James, N.C., Sally, W27921
MEALEY, James, Va., S9408
MEALLY, Charles, N.C., R7083
MEAN, Robert, Va. res., R7084
MEANLY, John, Ga., BLWt.1577-200
John, Va., Philadelphia, W9948; BLWt.30942-160-55
MEANS, George, Mass., Hannah, W23968
Hugh, Pa., Rosanna, W3279; BLWt. 2032-150
James, Mass., S37245; BLWt.79-300
John,, Ky. res., R7086
Philip, See MAIN
Robert, N.J., S17583
Robert, Pa., S22393
Thomas, Mass., S37236
Thomas, Mass., S37242
Thomas, Pa., BLWt.9922. Iss. 2/23/1797. No papers
William, S.C., Susan, W5368; BLWt. 28635-160-55
MEARA, Patrick, Ct., BLWt.269-100
MEARES, Joel, N.C., S2816
MEARS, Alexander, See MARS
Daniel, Navy, Mass., S33096
Hilary/Hillary, Va., S18508
Joel, N.C. See MEARES
John, Mass., S33094
Oliver, Mass., Lydia Strong, former wid., W4814
Russell, Mass., S33090
Samuel, Mass., S33095
William, Mass., S33089
MEASLES, Cader/Cadar/Kader, N.C., R7088
Kader. See Cader
MEBANE, John, N.C., S9403
Robert, N.C., BLWt.1435-55-Lt. Col. Iss. 2/21/1791 to Wm. Mibane, brother & heir-at-law. Also recorded as above under BLWt.2578. No orig. papers
MEDACK, Emanuel, N.J. See MEDAK
MEDAH, Stephen. See MEDAR
MEDAK, Emanuel, N.J., Leah, W9563

MEDAR, Stephen, N.H., S45006; BLWt.772-100
MEDARIS, Massey C., N.C., S9410
MEDBERY, Benjamin, R.I. See MEDBURY
John, Cont., Mass., S33085; BLWt.1373-200-Lt. Iss. 4/20/1790
MEDBURY, Abel, Mass., S15287
Benjamin, R.I., Martha, W20252
Ebenezer, Cont., Mass., Elizabeth, W26255
John, Cont., Mass. See MEDBERY
Joseph, R.I., S13918
MEDCALF, Ebenezer, Ct., Silence, W17128
John, Mass., Sybil Marsh, former wid., W19860
John, Va. See MEDKIFF
MEDDACK, Emanuel, See MEDACK
Frederick, See MITTAG
MEDDAUGH, Daniel, N.J., S16190
MEDDOCK, Moses, N.J., S41870
MEDEARIS, John, N.C., b. Va., S2823; BLWt.1466-300-Capt. Iss. 5/16/1797 to John Porter. Name recorded as Medeasis. No papers
John Washington, See John
MEDEAST, John, See MEDEARIS
MEDER, Stephen, See MEDAR
MEDFORD, James, N.C., S9411
MEDKIFF, John, Va., Mary, W3852
MEDLAR, Boston, Md., BLWt.11494. Iss. 5/12/1800 to Asahel Phelps, ass. No papers
Boston, Md., S38212
MEDLER, Christopher, N.Y., BLWt. 7518. Iss. 7/22/1793 to Philip Stout, ass. No papers
MEDLEY, Bryant, N.C., S8894
John, Va., S1698
William Glover/William GLOVER Md., R7089
MEDLIN, Bradley, N.C., S2817
John, N.C., Nancy, R7090
Shadrach, N.C., S41869
MEDLOCK, Nathaniel, See MATLOCK
Richard, N.C., Mary, W25701; BLWt.30925-160-55
MEDOWS, Francis, See MEADOWS
MEE, Thomas, Md., BLWt.164-100
MEECH, Elijah, Mass., S33091
Elisha, Ct., Mass., Desire,W23950
Jacob, Ct., Privateer, R.I., S15524
Thomas, Ct., BLWt.1712-100. Iss. 3/1/1831
Timothy, See MEACH
MEECHUM, Philip, Ct., S21372
MEED, Jason, Mass., S33092
Stephen, Mass., S9409
MEEDER, Daniel Meservy, See MEADER
Stephen, See MEDAR
MEEDS, Cato, Ct., S41866
MEEK, Abner, N.J., Pa., R7093
Alexander, Va., b. Md., S7218; BLWt.34827-160-55
Bazil, Va., b. Md., S15521
Jacob, Pa., Va., b. Md., S16480
John, Md. Agcy., Disabled; pensioned from 3/4/1789, rate of $40 per annum, Act of 6/7/1785. No papers

MEEK (continued)
Samuel, d. Va., Elizabeth, R7094
MEEKER, Caleb, N.J., Susan, W7443
Cory/Carey, N.J., S22394
David, Not Rev. War, N.J. Mil. Whiskey Insurrection, BLWt.63819-160-55. No claim for pension
Hezekiah, Ct., BLWt.6170. Iss. 9/6/1792. No papers
Ichabod, Ct., N.Y., S13912
John, N.J., S2815
John, N.J., S5087
Jonas, N.J., R7096
Jonathan, N.Y., S23795
Joseph, Ct., S15517
Michael, Cont., N.J., Hannah, W4738; BLWts.8519-100 & 124-60-55
Michael, N.J., Mary, W149
Obed, N.J., Elizabeth, W5370; BLWt.34918-160-55
Robert, N.Y., Catharine, W4027
Solomon, N.Y., BLWt.7484. Iss. 7/30/1790 to Edward Cumpston
Timothy, N.J., Sarah, W7442
Uzal, Cont., N.Y., Privateer (of Pa.), Elizabeth, W969; BLWt. 1409-200-Lt. Iss. 8/26/1789. No papers
MEEKS, Austin, Va., S38211
Britain, N.C., S16478
John, Va., S38207
MEERS, Moses, N.C., S30587
MEESE, Baltzer, Pa., S40152
MEFFORD, Jacob, Md., Eleanor, W9562
John, Va., R7097
William, Md. & Privateer, R7098
MEGAHON, Michael, Pa., S34427
MEGAW, John, Pa., R7099
MEGGS, Richard, Pa., S40151
MEGNAULT, Basil, See MIGNAULT
MEGREGORY, Joel, Ct., S45009; BLWt.6604-160-55
John, Ct., Cont., S11027
MEHAFFEY, John, Pa., S17582
MEHAFFY, Oliver, See McHAFFEY
MEHREN, Jonathan, Mass., S33097
MEHUREN, Isaac, Mass., Mary, R7100
MEHURIN, Betsey, former wid. of Samuel Hutchins, Vt., which see
Jonathan, Mass. See MAHURIN
Jonathan, Mass. See MEHREN
MEIER, Isaac, Pa., R7107
John, See MOYER
MEIGS, Abel, Ct., Deborah, W2410; BLWt.9406-160-55
Abner, Ct., N.H., R7102
Benjamin S., Mass., S41005
Daniel B., Va., Esther, W6818; BLWt.24430-160-55
John, Ct., Cont., Elizabeth, W20255; BLWt.1385-200-Lt. Iss. 11/19/1789. No papers
Nathan, Ct., BLWt.6165. Iss. 7/14/1789. No papers
Nathan, Ct., Mabel, W17126
Phinehas/Phineas, Ct., S42965
Return Jonathan, Ct., BLWt.1376-500-Col. Iss. 5/20/1791
Simeon, Ct., BLWt.44-100
Stephen, Ct., BLWt.6212. Iss. 5/1/1797 to John Duncan, ass.

MEIGS (continued)
Stephen, Ct., S36122
MEISSIENHEIMER, Peter, N.C., b. Pa., S32408
MEKER, Jonathan, N.Y. See MEEKER
MELAM, John, See MILAM
MELCOY, John, Mass., S33088
MELDOLL, Moses, See MANDELL
MELDRUM, John, Mass., S37243
MELENDY, Ebenezer, Mass., Azubah Fisher, former wid., W23036; BLWt.6298-160-55
James, Mass., S19733
John, Mass., S15603
Thomas, Cont., N.H., S13917
MELICK, Henry, N.J., R7103
John, N.J., Mary, W4283; BLWt. 33770-160-55
MELLEM, Mathew/Matthew, N.H., S42970
MELLEN, David, Mass., Mary, BLWt. 34941-160-55
Gilbert, Mass., R7104
John, Mass., R7105
John, N.H., S18973
Joshua, Mass., Rebecca H., W13720
Thomas, Cont., Vt. res. in 1819, S41004
William, Mass., Lucretia, W18505
MELLENGER, Phillip, Pa., or Indian Wars, R7106
MELLER, Casbar, N.Y. See MILLER
MELLETT, Zebulon, R.I. See MILLET
MELLIN, Aitchison/Atchison, Pa., S42974
MELLINGER, Phillip, See MELLENGER
MELLISH, Henry, Sgt., Mass., BLWt. 4653. Iss. 5/31/1790. No papers
Samuel, Mass., BLWt.1361-200-Lt. Iss. 4/10/179? to John Peck
MELLON, Richard, Pa., BLWt.10051. Iss. 8/31/1790 to Dudley Woodbridge
Samuel, Pa., Susanna, W2836
William, See MELLEN
MELLOTT, Benjamin, Pa., S2822
MELLOY, Andrew, S.C., S38945
MELLUS, Daniel, Pvt., Crane's Cont. Arty., Mass., BLWt. 4723. Iss. 11/4/1794 to Samuel Emery. No papers
MELOAN, Andrew, Md., Rachel, W27972
MELONE, Andrew, Md. See MELOAN
John, Cont., Pa., Sarah, W2827; BLWt.353-100
MELONEY, John, Cont., Ct., 30th U.S. Inf. (1812), Betsey, W6820; BLWt.19694-160-55
MELOON, Abel, See Abraham
Abraham /Abel MALOON, Mass., R7108
Enoch, Mass., Mary, W16649
MELOY, James, Pa., res. Md., R7109
John, N.Y., Susannah, R7110
MELROSS, William, Ct., Cynthia, R7111
MELROY, Bartholomew, Vt., Kezia, W4029
MELSOM, James, N.J., S34429
MELSON, Charles, Va., S38209
Samuel, S.C., S18124
William S., Pa. Sea Service, Privateer, S.C., R7112

MELSOPS, Thomas, N.C., Barsheba, R7173
MELTON, Benjamin, N.C., Elizabeth, W2227; BLWt.26773-160-55
Charles, Va., S36123
Isham, Va., S38944
Jonathan, N.C., S41867
Pearce W., Va., S11065
Robert, S.C., BLReg.25452-1855
Thomas, Va., S36116
William, N.C., S36117
William, S.C., Rebecca, W25703; BLWt.30939-160-55
MELTZ, Frederick, N.C., R7113
MELVEN, George, Pa. See MELVIN
James, Matross, Mass., BLWt.4629 Md., BLWt.14143. Iss. 9/5/1796
Samuel, Mass., Sarah, W19876
MELVILL, James, Pa., BLWt.9935. Iss. 8/13/1789. No papers
Thomas, Mass., S5086
MELVIN, Aliard, Md., BLWt.11531. Iss. 11/29/1790 to John Blair, Admr.
David, Mass., S37240
George, Ga., Martha Mathews/ Martha M., W4491; BLWt.175-300
James, Mass., S33099
John, Cont., Mass., S37244; BLWt.899-100
John, N.C., R7114
Jonathan, Mass., S13915
Peter, Md., BLWt.11532. Iss. 7/26/1797 to James DeBaufre, ass.
MELZARD, George, Mass., S33087
John, Cont., R.I., S33093
MENALLY, Michael, See McNELLY
MENDALL, Church, Mass., Sarah Foot/Foote, former wid., W1588, BLWt.36759-160-55. Her last husb., Robert Foot/Foote, also served in the Rev. War
John, Mass., Sarah Weeks, former wid., W15473
MENDELL, Church, Mass. See MENDALL
MENDENHALL, Joseph, Pa., S23803
Nathan, N.C.,S.C., b. Pa., S7219
MENDUM, William, Navy, Mass., Anna, W26259
MENEFEE, Henry, Va., Mary, W18504
Spencer, Va., S16191
MENELY, Jesse, N.J., S41868
MENEMA, Daniel, N.Y., BLWt.1398-400-Surgn. Iss. 7/6/1790. No papers
MENICH, George, See MINING
MENIS, Fredrick, N.C. See MENIUS
John, Pa., Nancy, R7116
MENIUS, Frederick/Fredrick, N.C., Rosanna, W3848; BLWt.36222-160-55
MENTER, Barker, See MINTER
Naomi, former wid. of Nathaniel Williams, Ct., which see
MENTGER, Christian, Pa., BLWt. 9892. Iss. 12/13/1791. No papers
MENTGES, Francis, Pa., BLWt.1415-450-Lt. Col. Iss. 4/7/1795 to John Nicholson, ass. No papers
MENTOR, Thomas, Ct., S42973
MENTZER, Japat, See MANTZER
MENZIES, Samuel P. See MINZIES

MERANDA, Samuel, See MIRANDA
MERCELL, Peter, Cont., N.J., Elizabeth, W184
MERCER, Hugh, Va., BLWt.1527-850-Brig. Gen. Iss. 7/15/1791 to William, John, Hugh, and George Mercer, and Lucy Patten, the only surviving ch. of H.M. No papers
Isaac, Va. Sea Service, R76, Va. Half Pay
Jacob, Ga., S31862
James, See MURCER
John, N.J., R7117
John, N.J., BLWt.1411-300-Capt. Iss. 7/15/1789. No papers
John, See MUSSER
MERCEREAU, Francis, Mass., S34430
John, See MERSEREAU
MERCHANT, Gurdon, See MARCHANT
Thomas, Ct., S36126
MERCY, John, See MASSEY
MEREDETH, David, Va., Elizabeth, R7118
MEREDITH, Henry, N.C., b. Md., S9402
James, Va., Mericha/Merica, W3849
Jesse, Va., S38205
John W. See MERIDETH
Peter, Crane's Cont. Arty., Mass. BLWt.4738. Iss. 9/7/1789. No papers
Samuel, Cont. Del., Mary, W9565
Samuel, Va. Lee's Legion, BLWts. 12354 & 13539. Iss. 9/2/1789. No papers
Thomas, Pa., S40153
William, Cont., S46393; BLWt.1519-300-Capt. of Va. Iss. 2/18/1793 to Francis Graves, ass. Name spelled Meridith. No papers
MEREWETHER, James, Va. See MERIWETHER
Valentine, Va., Priscilla, W8454; BLWt.26099-160-55
William, See MERIWETHER
MERIAM, Abraham, Mass., Mary Kenworthy, former wid., W26170; BLWt.3804-160-55
David, Mass., S22396
Ezra, Cont., Mass., N.H., Susannah, W16044
Jesse, Mass., S30586
John, Mass., S30584
John, Mass., S42972
John, N.H., S18974
Joseph, Mass., S31252
Josiah, Mass., S30585
Timothy, Mass., Huldah, W15077
MERICAL, Henry, See MARKLE
MERICK, Luther, Ct., S31859
MERIDETH, Jesse, See MEREDITH
John W., Del., Vt., Elizabeth, W4737; BLWt.27676-160-55
Samuel, See MEREDITH
William, See MEREDITH
MERIFIELD, Ithamar, Ct., S29324
John, Va., R7119
MERILE, Samuel, N.Y., BLWt.7510 Iss. 9/27/1790 to James Roe, ass. No papers
MERIT, Jeremiah, N.Y., R7138

MERITHEW, William, Mass., Navy, R.I., Sarah, W20251
MERITT, Ezekiel, Mass., Sarah, W23955; BLWt.826-100
James, N.C., S21883
Stephen, See MERRIT
MERIWETHER, James, Va., R16407; Va. Half Pay. BLWt.1509-200-Lt. Drags. Iss. 7/28/1790. Cert. by Sec. of War 2/5/1806. Name spelled Merriwether. No papers
James, Va., R16407 1/2, Va. Half Pay
Thomas, Va., BLWt.1920-400
William, Va., S47954, & Va. Half Pay
MERKEL, George, Pa., S9407
MERLIS, Clement, Hazen's Regt., BLWt.13456. Iss. 4/5/1793. No papers
MERO, Amariah, Cont., Mass., Susannah, W23961
Josiah, Mass., S29982
MERONEY, Philip, See MARONEY
MEROW, David, See MORROW
MERREL, Samuel, See MERRILL
MERRELL, Andrew, N.J., S31253
Ashbel, Ct., Abigail Eaton, former wid., W16970
Benjamin, N.C., S.C., b. N.J., S8891
Caleb, Mass. See MERRILL
Charles, See MERRILL
Daniel, Ct., Mercy Wilcox, former wid., W18451
Daniel, Mass. See MERRILL
Daniel/Dan, N.C., b. N.J., S7222
John, N.J., N.Y., R7129
John, N.C., S7223
Moses, Cont., N.H., Eunice, W21796
Nathaniel, Ct., S36115; BLWt. 6141-100. Iss. 10/7/1789 to Benjamin Tallmadge. No papers
Roger, Ct., Cont., S23318
Simeon, N.Y., S9406
Solomon, Ct. See MERRILL
William, Ct., S11064
MERRELLS, Reuben, Ct., S34998
MERRET, Jeremiah, See MERIT
Stephen, N.C. See MERRITT
MERRETT, Asa, Mass., Disabled - See Am. State Papers, Class 9, pp. 59 & 109 under name of Asa Merritt. He lost the sight of his eyes by inoculation of the smallpox, 1777.
MERRIAM, Aaron, Ct., R7122
Abraham, Mass., Hannah, W15078
Amasa, Ct., S23317
Asaph, S13911
Christopher, Ct., S16959
Edmund, Ct., BLWt.6167. Iss. 8/23/1790. No papers
Ephraim, Ct., BLWt.6171. Iss. 8/23/1790. No papers
Ephraim, Ct., S36121
Ichabod, Ct., Desire, W15787
Isaac, Mass., S13906
John, See MERIAM
Jonathan, Mass., S21371

MERRIAM (continued)
Joseph, See MERIAM
Marshall, Ct., S2818
Timothy, Mass., Huldah, W15077
MERRIAN, Marshall, See MERRIAM
MERRICK, Constant, Mass., S13908
John, Cont., Mass., S31861
Loly, Ct., former wid. of Reverius Carrington, which see
Luther, See MERICK
Noah, Mass., Delphia S., R7123; BLWt.77511-160-55
Peter, Mass., S36120
Samuel F., Mass., S1773
Stephen W., Mass. Sea Service, Privateer, R7124
William Levitt, Md., S8892
MERRICLE, Henry, See MARKLE
Samuel, N.Y., S43735
MERRIFIELD, Abraham, Mass., Bethiah, W23960
Asaph, Mass., Mercy, W21797
Ithamar, See MERIFIELD
Jonathan, Mass., Hanah, W17125
Robert, Mass., Rebecca, R7120
MERRIL, Aaron, Ct., S42971
Abel, N.H., BLWt.3337. Iss. 3/25/1790 to Ruth Merril, Repr. No papers
Roger, Mass., N.H., Dorothy, W23969, BLWt.38537-160-55
MERRILL, Aaron, Ct., Cont., S36698
Aaron, Mass., S16958
Abel, Mass., Huldah Goodwin, former wid., W4442; BLWt.14526-160-55
Abner, Mass., Betsey, W24148
Amos, Mass., S29981
Andrew, N.J. See MERRELL
Annis, Mass., S11058
Asa, Mass., S43025
Benjamin, Mass., S20082
Caleb, Mass., Sarah, W4547; BLWt. 1633-100 & 5203-160-55
Charles, res. N.C., Elizabeth, R7126
Daniel, Ct. See MERRELL
Daniel, Mass., S17581
Daniel, Mass., Mary, W23966
Daniel, N.H., S16957
David, Mass., Martha, W21795; BLWt.14535-160-55
David, N.H., Polly/Molly, W25695
Dudley, N.H., Mary, W16045
Enoch, Mass., N.H., S11057
Frederick, N.Y., Sarah, R7132
Hosea, Mass., S5085
Humphrey, Jr., Mass., Hannah, W24147
Ichabod, Ct., Sarah, W17130
Jacob, Mass., S31251
Jacob, Mass., Abigail, W561; BLWt.13009-160-55
Jacob, Mass., Hannah Bowe, former wid., R1063
James, Ct., Jane Dunmore, former wid., W10769
James, Mass., S15937
Jesse, Cont., Mass., S40150
John, Mass., S16960
John, Mass., S37235
John, Mass., Mehitable, W13722

MERRILL (continued)
John, N.H., S13904
John, N.H., Sally/Sarah, W16648
John, N.H., Sarah, W18503
John, N.C., S7220
John, N.C. See MERRELL
Jonathan, Ct., S23796
Levi, Mass., Jerusha, W23957
Mary, former wid. of Daniel Clapp, N.H., which see
Mead/Medad, Ct., S42969; BLWt. 665-100
Moses, Mass., S18975
Moses, Mass., Elizabeth, W8449; BLWt.3955-160-55
Moses, Mass., Jane, W24149
Moses, N.H. See MERRELL
Nathan, Mass., S9404
Nathan, Mass., S18123
Nathan, Mass., Mary S., W2317
Nathaniel, Ct., BLWt.6141. Iss. 10/7/1789 to Benjamin Tallmadge. No papers
Nathaniel, See MERRELL
Nathaniel, Cont., N.H., S41865
Nathaniel, N.H., S45008
Nehemiah, N.H., BLWt.3308. Iss. 2/12/1796 to James A. Neal, ass. No papers
Nehemiah, N.H., Jenney/Jenne, W9177
Noah, Ct., Zulina, W23964
Phinehas, Ct., Anna, W18509; BLWt.3798-160-55
Phinehas/Phineas, Cont., Mass., S45005
Roger, Ct. See MERRELL
Samuel, Ct., Artemetia, W20254
Samuel, Mass., S21373
Samuel, Mass., S29325
Simon, Cont., N.H., S22905
Solomon, Ct., Jerusha, R7127
Stephen, Mass., S41003
Thomas, Ct., R7133
MERRILLS, Ephah, Ct., R7134
MERRILS, Ezekiel, Mass., S11060
Jeptha, Ct., S11059
Noah, Ct., S5759
Samuel, Ct. See MERRILL
MERRIMAN, Asaph, Ct. See MERRIAM
Charles, Ct., Anna, W18507
Elisha, Ct., Chloe, R7135
Francis, Va., Martha, W157
George, Ct., S13913
George, Ct., Catharine, W17129
Israel, Ct. See MERRIMOM
Josiah, Cont., Ct., Lydia, W16647
Marcus, Ct., Privateer, S13921
Moses, Ct., Lois, W18508
Samuel S., Vt., S21882
MERRIMON, Israel, Ct., S11067
MERRIS, John, See MENIS
MERRIT, Ezekiel, See MERITT
Stephen, N.C., Dicey, W25693; BLWt.36198-160-55
Thomas, N.C., S1233
MERRITT, Aaron, Mass., R7137
Amos, Mass., S19395
Amos, Mass., Lydia, BLWt.40794
Archelaus, Va., S36124
Asa, See MERRETT
Consider, Mass., Sarah, W21798

MERRITT (continued)
Daniel, Mass., S29323
Daniel, N.C., Mary, W6817; BLWt. 26444-160-55
Daniel, N.C., Nancy, W7441
Ebenezer, Ct., Hannah, W17127
Isaac, Mass., Molly, W17133
Jacob, N.C., Jane, W4739
Jeremiah, See MERIT
John, Mass., S33098
Jonathan, Mass., Mary, W26256
Joshua, Mass., Priscilla Brewer, former wid., W21711
Levi, N.J., S38208
Major, Va., BLWt.12368. Iss. 5/7/1793 to Francis Graves, ass. No papers
Major, Va., S38213
Nathaniel, Mass., Hepsibah, W4028
Noah, Mass., Eunice, W26257
Reuben, Ct., Mary, R7139
Samuel, Va., S38206
Shadrach, N.C., S7226
Stephen, N.C., Margaret/Peggy, R7140
Thomas, N.Y., Anna, W2835
William, Mass., S37239
William, Lamb's Arty., N.Y., BLWt.7530. Iss. 10/11/1790 to Asa Rice, ass. No papers
William, N.C., S2821
MERRIWETHER, David, Va., BLWt.1511-200-Lt. Iss. 6/19/1795. No papers
James, See MERIWETHER
Thomas, See MERIWETHER
Valentine, See MEREWETHER
MERROW, David, See MORROW
Joshua, N.H., BLWt.756-200
William, Cont. Mass., Margaret, W29901 1/2
MERRY, Cornelius, Ct., S16479
Jacob O., N.C., S4592
John, Mass., S13920
Jonathan, Navy, Mass., S33086
Philip, Va., Rose, W7440
Samuel, See MERY
MERRYFIELD, William, N.Y., R7121
MERRYMAN, Josiah, Corp., Sheldon's Dragoons, Ct., BLWt.6220. Iss. 1/11/1790. No papers
Luke, Md., Elizabeth, W2648; BLWt.40690-160-55
Thomas, Va., S38203
MERSELLUS, John I., N.Y., R6897
MERSEREAU, John, N.J., Barbara, W17137. Sold. d. 2/21/1820. Uncle of John L. & Joshua
John L., Cont., N.J. & N.Y., S7217. Sold. d. 5/1841
Joshua, Cont., N.Y., Sea Service, & Va., S7224; BLWt.3792-160-55
MERSEY, John, See MASSEY
MERSHEIMER, Sebastian, Pa., Ann Catharine, R7141
MERSHEMER, Boston, Pa., BLWt. 10037. Iss. 8/23/1791. No papers
MERSHIMER, Sebastian, Pa. See MERSHEIMER
MERSHON, Andrew, N.J., Mary, W563
Henry, N.J., S1058
Joab. N.J., S13914

MERSHON (continued)
Titus, N.J., Elizabeth Hubbard, former wid., W10137
William, N.J., S824
MERWIN, Andrew, Ct., Rhoda, W6819
Nathan, Ct., Mary, W4282
MERY, Samuel, Mass., S42966
MERYDITH, Samuel, See MEREDITH
MERYMAN, William, N.C., R7136
MESER, William, Invalids, BLWt. 13514. Iss. 11/18/179? to Sampson Crosby, ass. No papers
MESEROL, Peter, N.J., S894
MESEROLL, Abraham, N.J., S730
Charles, N.J., S11068
MESERVE, Gideon, See MESERVEY
Nathaniel, Cont., Mass., S37237
Solomon, Mass., S37238
William, Mass., Zeporah, W802; BLWt.9196-160-55
MESERVEY, Gideon, Mass., Elizabeth, W23958
MESERVIE, William, See MESERVE
MESLER, John, N.J., R7143
Peter, N.J., Martha, W180; BLWt.26286-170-55
Simon, N.J., Esther, R7142
MESSENGER, Abner, Ct., S9022
Bille, Cont., Mass., Hannah, W9179; BLWt.6387-160-55
Joel, R.I. See MESSINGER
John, Cont., Mass., Lucy, W562; BLWt.8148-160-55
Lemuel, Ct., Abigail, W9957
Reuben, Ct., S36118
MESSER, Christian, Pa., S9023
Dudley, Arty. Artificers, BLWt.13474. Iss. 9/7/1790 to Isaac Trobridge, ass. No papers
Ebenezer, Mass., S45007
George, Pa., BLWt.10100. Iss. 1/12/1791. No papers
James, Mass., Achsah, W15079
Jeremiah, N.C., S8893
John, See MUSSER
Jonathan, Mass., Betsey, W25698
Nelly, former wid. of John Hudler, N.C., which see
Stephen, Mass., R7146
Thomas, N.H., Lydia, W19873
Timothy, Vt., R7147
MESSEROLL, Peter, See MESEROL
MESSERSMITH, Jacob, Pa., Susannah, W9954
Peter, Pa., BLWt.10029. Iss. 6/20/1789. No papers
MESSERVE, William, See MESERVE
MESSHEW, Jesse, S.C., S15523
MESSINGER, Joel, Mass., S42975
MESSLER, Cornelius, N.J., S5088
Simon, See MESLER
METCALF, Benjamin, Cont., Mass., Catharine, W5366; BLWt.28581-160-55
Dan, Ct., Jedidah, W3281
Danza, Ga., N.C., Mary, W4280
Ebenezer, Ct., S18125
Ebenezer, See MEDCALF
Elias, Mass., S41002; BLWt. 26249-160-55
Ezekiel, Mass., Eunice, W15075
James, Mass., S17585

METCALF (continued)
John, Mass. See MEDCALF
Luke, Ct., Nabby, W25702; BLWt.520-160-55
Luke, Mass., N.H., Melatiah, W25696
Luther, Mass., Hannah, W2412; BLWt.17593-160-55
Moses, Mass., Mary Glover, former wid., R4073
Philemon, Mass., Hannah, W9180; BLWt.31292-160-55
Philip, Mass., Anna, W15076
Samuel, Ct., S16189
Samuel, Mass., Betsey, W6822; BLWt.19710-160-55
Timothy, Cont., Mass., Ruth, W23965; BLWt.19709-160-55
Titus, Mass., Rebecca, W2411; BLWt.13871-160-55
Vachel, Va., R7148
Walter, Va., BLWt.410-100
Warner, Ga., N.C., Elizabeth,W4281
William, N.Y., BLWt.7437. Iss. 9/27/1790 to Andrew Stockholm, ass. No papers
William, N.C., S2820
William H., Mass., S15522
METCALFE, Samuel, Mass., S13916
METEER, William Paul, See William PALMITEER
METHANY, William, Cont., Va.,S18122
METHEANY, Luke, Cont., Va., Elender R7149
METTINGER, Jacob, See MYTENGER
METZ, John, Pa., S40149; BLWt. 9870. Iss. 1791
METZGER, Jacob, Pa., S8890
MEYER, Frederick, N.Y., Gertrude, R7533
Jacob, Pa., S11061
John, N.Y., See MYER
John, Pa., S9039
John, Pa. See MOYER
Peter, Pa., Salome, W3440; BLWt. 26004-160-55
Theobald/Daybold Moyer, N.Y., Margaret, W15789
MEYERS, Henry, See MYERS
John, Cont., Mary, R7543, wid's. res. N.Y. in 1844
Nicholas, See MYERS
MIBANE, Robert, See MEBANE
MICALL, Samuel, See MITCHELL
MICELS, Susanna, N.H. See Obadiah HOLT
MICHAEL, Andrew, French Army, Anna/Hannah, R7150
Jacob, Pa., Catharine, R7152
John, Pa., BLWt.10091. Iss. 3/3 1795 to William Ripton, ass.
John, Pa., S40165
MICHAELS, Susanna, former wid. of Obadiah Holt, N.H., which see
MICHALS, William, Mass., Esther, W17144
MICHELL, Reaps, See MITCHELL
MICHELLER, Jacob, N.C., Mary, W25706; BLWt.26979-160-55
MICHIE, George, Va., son of James Michie, R7153
MICHUM, Collin, See MITCHUM

MICK, Philip, See MACK
Philip, Pa., S40155
MICKER, Uzal, See MEEKER
MICKLE, Carl, N.Y., Catrina, R7154
John, See MITCHELL
Reuben, N.J., War of 1812, Elizabeth, W4493; BLWt.1639-100
MICKUM, Henrietta, former wid. of Henry Dixon, Md., which see
MICLES, Susanna, former wid. of Obadiah Holt, N.H., which see
MICOU, Henry, Va., S38218
MIDAGH, Moses, See MEDDOCK
MIDCAP, John, Va., R7155
MIDDAUGH, Adonijah, N.Y., R7157
Cornelius, N.Y., R7156
Henry C.T., Pa., S7234. See Rev. War pension claim of Lenah Middough/Middaugh, former wid. of John Frazer, Ga., W3284, and wid of Henry C. Middaugh of Pike Co., Pa., who d. 8/4/1836
Jasper, N.Y., Pa., R7160
Lenah, See John FRAZER, Ga.
Mary, former wid. of Martiness Decker, N.Y., which see
Sollomon/Solomon, N.J., S23323
MIDDILTOWN, Peter, See MIDDLETOWN
MIDDLEBROOK, John, Ct., Abigail, W804
John, Va., Lucy, W3443; BLWt. 565-100 & 38535-160-55
Oliver, Navy, Ct., R7159
MIDDLESWART, Jacob, Pa., Va., Jane, W4034
MIDDLESWORTH, John V., N.J., S895
MIDDLETON, Basil, Va., Mary, W18522 BLWt.358-450-Surgn.
Benjamin, N.Y., S43001
Christopher, Ct., BLWt.6148. Iss. 11/15/1791. No papers
Elijah, Indian War 1794; BLWt. 45215-80-50; BLWt.38581-80-55
John, Del., BLWt.10836. Iss. 9/13/1793. No papers
John, Lee's Legion, BLWt.2705-150
John, Va., S2847
John, Va., Eleanor, W7464; BLWt. 28594-160-55
Joseph, N.J., BLWt.8559. Iss. 6/14/1791. No papers
Samuel, Mass., BLWt.4663. Iss. 3/25/1790. No papers
Theodore, Md., S11075
Thomas, N.J., Hannah Hendricks, former wid., W7728
MIDDLETOWN, Peter, Ct., S36140; BLWt.31-100
MIDDOUGH, Henry C.T. See MIDDAUGH
John, Pa. See MIDDUGH
Lenah, former wid. of John Frazer, Ga., which see
MIDDUGH, John, Pa., S23806
MIDETON, John, See MIDDLETON
MIDKIFF, Isaiah, N.C., Va., S1700
John, See MEDKIFF
MIDLAR, Christopher, N.Y., Mary Townsend, former wid., W16447
MIEL, Charles, Ct., S28812
MIERS, Alburtus, See MYERS
Daniel, N.Y., S13933
Jacob, See MYERS

MIFFLIN, Jonathan, Pa., S7233
MIGATE, Jonathan, See MYGATT
MIGHEL, Moses, N.H., Elizabeth, W23970
MIGHELL, Asahel, Mass., BLWt.4707. Iss. 8/27/1792 to Amos Murrey. No papers
Thomas, Mass., R7161
MIGHLES, Thomas, Mass., BLWt.4713. Iss. 6/7/1798 to Wm. Woodward, ass of the heirs of Thomas Mighles. No papers
MIGHT, John, S.C., Keranhappock, W4548
MIGNAULT, Basil, N.Y., R20405
MIGNEAULT, Josette/Josephte, former wid. of Charles Racine, Cont., Canada, which see
MIKESELL, Jacob, Md., S16202
MIKLE, John, See MITCHELL
MILAM, John, Va., Polly, W9951
Jordan, Va., Mary, W25709; BLWt.82517-160-55
Rush, Va., S7943
MILBOURN, Andrew, Va., S2845
Nicholas, Corp., Md., BLWt.11478 Iss. 10/20/1789. No papers
Thomas, Va., S2846
MILBURN, Andrew, Va. See MILBOURN
Nicholas, Md., S35003
William, Va., Bertha, W51; BLWt. 26856-160-55
MILEHAM, Joseph, Pa., BLWt.9960 Iss. 8/7/1789 to Richard Pratt, ass. No papers
William, Pa., S41878
MILES, Benajah, N.Y., S29329
Benjamin, N.C., R7164
Caleb, Ct., S40157
Charles, S.C., R21890
Charles, Va., Patty, W8455
Daniel, Ct., S16962
Edward, Md., S11069
Elnathan, Lamb's Artillery, N.Y. BLWt.7529. Iss. 7/16/1790 to John Miles, Admr. No papers
Ephraim, Mass.,Vt.,Zeruiah,W21810
Hardy, S.C., R7166
Isaac, Ct., Mary, W9566
Isaac, Ct., Martha, W19879; BLWt. 26500-160-55
Isaac (decd.), Artillery Artificer of Pa., BLWt.13521. Iss. 3/5/1792 to Elizabeth Leibeck, Extx. No papers
Jacob, N.C., b. Md., S2006
James, Ct., BLWt.6159. Iss. 9/9/1790 to James F. Sebor. No papers
Jesse, Ct., R7167
Jesse, S.C., b. N.C., S21886
Jesse, Va., b. Md., S1235
Joab, Mass., S19734
Joel, Mass., S45013
John, Capt., Cont., Ct. res., S36128; BLWt.1402-200-Capt. Iss. 10/23/1790
John, Md., S2827
John, Md., S36138
John, N.C., S21376
John, Va., S38219
John, Va., Mary, W2682; BLWt.

MILES (continued)
13902-160-55
John, Va., Polly, W9567
Joshua, Md., Jane, W9196
Leonard, S.C., Mary, W1453
Lucinda, former wid. of Darius Hickok, Ct., which see
Margaret, former wid. of James Craig, S.C., which see
Michael, Va., Mary, W8456
Moses, See MIGHEL
Narby, See Nasby MILLS
Samuel, Ct., Sea Service, S15526
Simon, Ct. See Timon
Thomas, Md., BLWt.11484-14119. Iss. 5/1/1795 to Francis Sherrard ass. of James Smith, Admr. No papers
Thomas, Mass., R7169
Thomas, N.C., b. Va., Ann, W8457
Thomas, N.C., b. Va., R7168
Thomas, Va., b. Md., S15939
Timon/Simon, Ct., Mercy, W17141
William, Cont., Mass., Sarah, W23980; BLWt.19767-160-55
William, Md., R7170
William, N.Y., S28813
William, Pa., S22400
William, Va., S36142
MILEY, Jacob, Cont., Pa., Margaret W3280
MILFORD, John, S.C., S21885
Thomas, N.C., S.C., b. Ireland, S21375
William, S.C., Grizzella, W8277; BLWt.61305-160-55
MILIGAN, Joseph, See Josep MILLIGN
MILIKIN, Isaac, See MILLIKIN
MILING, William, See MILLING
MILIRONS, William, Va., S38222
MILKOLLIN, Jonathan, Cont., Va. S16971 (or MILLHOLLIN)
MILLAN, Richard, Mass., Disabled. See Am. State Papers, Class 9 pages 62 & 129 under name of Richard Millan. Disabled by hardships & fatigue which occasioned an incurable sore on his leg
Thomas, Mass., S13929
MILLAR, Caspar, Pvt., N.Y., BLWt. 7508. Iss. 8/24/1790 to Glenn & Beecher, Admrs. No papers
Christian, Pa., BLWt.364-100
George, Va., S16486
John, Cont., Ct. res. See MILLER
Mordecai/Mordica, S.C., S16972
William, R.I., BLWt.1896-100
MILLARD, Joseph, Ct., Hannah, W25705
Leavitt/Levitt, Cont., Ct.,S13935
London, Ct., S13926
Nathan Horton, See MILLER
Nathaniel, N.Y., Mary, W17139
Noah, R.I., S21379
Robert, N.Y., S9978
Samuel, R.I., Sarah, W6826; BLWt.53674-160-55
Sarah, former wid. of John White, Ct., which see
Stephen, N.Y., R.I., S22908
MILLBANK, John, Va., Mary, R7163

MILLBURN, William, See MILBURN
MILLEGAN, John, Va., BLWt.12383 Iss. 5/9/1797 to Daniel Vertner, ass. No papers
MILLEN, James, Mass., BLWt.1349-500-Col. Iss. 4/1/1790. No papers
James, N.H. See McMULLEN
John, See McMULLEN
John, Mass. See MELLEN
William, Mass., S18979
William, S.C. See MILLING
MILLENER, Alexander, See MARONY
MILLER, Aaron, Mass., R7174
Aaron John, Mass., S1855
Abner, Ct., Ruth, W20259
Abner, N.Y., Sarah, W496; BLWt. 26510-160-55
Adam, N.Y., S11073
Adam, N.C., S.C., Elizabeth, W5372
Adam, S.C., BLWts.12428 & 13402. Iss. 8/27/1795 to Wendell Zerban, ass. No papers
Alexander, N.Y., S23320
Alexander Leitch, Quartermasters Dept., N.Y., Margaret Tiers, former wid., W18143
Amos, N.Y., S23321
Andrew, Va., R7176
Asa, Mass., S37246
Barney, Va., S16973
Benjamin, Ct., S36146
Benjamin, Mass., S29326. BLWt. 40680-160-55
Benjamin, N.Y., BLWt.7452. Iss. 3/6/1792. No papers
Benjamin, N.Y., S42976
Benjamin, Va., R7178
Caleb, Ct., Cont., S18976; BLWt. 13479-100. Iss. 10/22/1789 to Theodocius Fowler, ass. No papers
Caleb, R.I., S43736
Caspar/Casbar/Casper, See MELLER
Catharine, former wid. of John Shell, N.C., which see
Charles, Ct., Cont., S36132; BLWt.1381-200-Lt. Iss. 6/3/1791 to Isaac Bronson, ass. No papers
Charles, Pa., BLWt.9990. Iss. 6/29/1789 to M. McConnell, ass. No papers
Christian, Cont. Pa., Pa. Sea Service, S40156
Christian, Pa., BLWt.10007. Iss. 10/21/179? to John Klein, ass. No papers
Christian, Pa., Anna, S41881
Christian, Pa., Mary, W3150
Christian, Pa. See MILLAR
Christian, Va., Catharine, W18515
Clark, N.J., Sarah, W1054
Conrad, Pa., BLWt.9913. Iss. 3/12/1792 to Robt. Ross, ass.No papers
Conrad, Pa., S9416, b. 1757 in Northampton Co., later Lehigh Co.
Conrad, Pa., S40166. Enl. at Fredericktown, Md. In 1818, res. Beaver Co., Pa., age 66 yrs.
Conrad, Pa., R7180, b. 1754 in York Co., Pa. enl. there, and there in 1834
Conrad, Pa., Margaret, R7215, res. during Rev. Kensington, Phila.

MILLER (continued)
Co., Pa., d. 1/1/1815
Consider, R.I., S38948
Cornelius, N.Y., Elizabeth,W16652
Cyrus, Mass., Sarah, BLWt.34816-160-55
Daniel, Ct., R7181
Daniel, N.Y., S23804
Daniel, N.C., Anna, R7177
Daniel, Pa., Esther, R7185
Daniel, R.I., S42994
Daniel, R.I., Mary Sawyer, former wid., W12918
Daniel, Va., S5762
Daniel, Va., Barbara, W18512
David, N.H., Phebe, W18519; BLWt. 17864-160-55
David, N.C., Nancy, W4032
David, R.I., BLWt.3342. Iss. 6/7/1790. No papers
David, Va., Ann, W18516; BLWt. 1328-200, and Va. Half Pay
David B., Ct., Adah, W16651
Dyonisius, N.Y., R7182
Ebenezer, Ct., Sarah, W1306
Edward, Ct., BLWt.6191. Iss. 11/15/1791. No papers
Edward, Ct., S13942
Edward, Va., S16484
Edward, Va., Rebecca, W9571
Eleazer, Mass., N.Y., S13936
Eleazer, N.J., Hannah, W2319
Eliakim, Mass., Rhoda, R7221
Elisha, Mass., Bethiah, W13723
Elisha, N.Y., BLWt.7462. Iss. 10/20/1790. No papers
Elizabeth, former wid. of Amasa Ladd, Ct., which see
Enoch, N.J., Keziah, W1452
Ephraim, Mass., S29327
Esther, former wid. of Timothy Lockwood, Navy, N.Y., which see
Farah, N.H., BLWt.3336. Iss. 3/25/1790. No papers
Farrar, Cont. N.H., S45012
Francis, N.C., Jane, W23984
Francis, Pa., BLWt.603-100
Francis, Va., BLWt.12356. Iss. 10/22/1791 to Jacob Clingman, ass. No papers
Francis, Va., Elizabeth, W8459
Francis, Va., Overilla Owens, former wid., W19951
Frank, Mass., S31863
Frederic/Frederick, Va., S30589
Frederick, Mass., Elizabeth, W23974
Frederick, N.J., BLWt.8588. Iss. 9/28/1790. No papers
Frederick, N.C., Rhoda, W9996, BLWt.30940-160-55
Frederick, Pa., Susan/Susannah, W3576; BLWt.26024-160-55
Frederick, Va., S2831
Fredrick, N.C., Margaret, W8460
Gavin, Pa., BLWt.10046. Iss. 6/20/1789. No papers
George, Cont., Md., Pa., Va., S35001
George, Md., Pa., S22401
George, Md., Pa., Judith, W9570
George, Mass., Mary, W25712;

MILLER (continued)
BLWt.6286-160-55
George, N.C., Eleanor, W4293
George, Pa., S7235
George, Pa., R7189
George, Pa., R7190
George, Pa., R7191, also served 1787 & 1791. Res. almost always same as Geo. Miller, R7190
George, Va. See MILLAR
Giles, N.Y., S23322
Godfried/Godfred, Cont., Pa., Mary, W2961
Helen, R7192
Henry, Cont., N.Y., & Pa., R---
Henry, Cont., Pa., S41879
Henry, Mass., BLWt.4691. Iss. 7/15/1789 to Daniel De LaVan. No papers.
Henry, Mass., N.Y., Judah Roberson, former wid., R8886
Henry, N.Y., R7194
Henry, N.C., Martha, W5377; BLWt.2469-100
Henry, N.C., Pernina, W25707; BLWt.34809-160-55
Henry, Pa., BLWt.10038. Iss. 1/8/1793 to Cath. Miller, Admx. No papers
Henry, Pa., BLWt.10117. Iss. 11/4/? to Michael Stever, ass. No papers
Henry, Pa., Eve, W2838
Henry, Pa., Mary Magdalene, W3283
Henry, Pa., Mary Ann, W7458
Henry, Pa., R7193
Henry, Pa., R7195
Henry, Pa., R7197
Henry, Pa., Va., S2830
Henry, Va., S16481
Henry, Va., R7196
Ichabod, N.J., Joanna, W2646; BLWt.30927-160-55
Increase, N.Y., Freelove, R7188
Isaac, Mass., S15528
Isaac, Mass., Hannah, W7455
Isaac, Pa., BLWt.10102. Iss. 11/5/1789. No papers
Isaac, Pa., R7198
Jacob, Tenn, res., R7202
Jacob, Cont., Pa., S41880
Jacob, Cont., Pa., Nancy, W3105
Jacob, Cont., Pa., Elizabeth, W3708; BLWt.14252-160-55
Jacob, Mass., Mercy, W15082
Jacob, Mass., Phebe, R7219
Jacob, N.C., S7229
Jacob, N.C., Barbara, W4033; BLWt.46879-160-55
Jacob, Not Rev., Gen. St. Clair's Indian War 1791, res. at enl. Md. Old War Inv. Rej. No. 16443
Jacob, Pa., R7199
Jacob, Va., S31258
Jacob, Va., Margaret, W9569, BLWt. 13717-160-55
Jacob, Va., R7200
Jacob P., N.Y., S13923
Jacobus, N.Y., Barbary, W23990
James, Mass., S13941
James, Mass., Mercy, W16046
James, Mass., Sarah, W26270

MILLER (continued)
James, N.Y., Elizabeth, W19881
James, Pa., Elizabeth, W7457. Another woman, named Mary, applied for pension as wid. of this soldier.
James, R.I., S11089
James, R.I., Asenath Campbell former wid., W15634. Her last husb. was pensioned, John Campbell, Mass., which see
James, S.C., S2828
James, Va., b. Md., S4210
James, Va., S38230
Jason, N.Y., S23325
Javan, Va., BLWt.1871-200
Jeremiah, Mass., BLWt.1352-300-Capt. Iss. 8/22/1789 to Ebenezer Williams, Jeremiah Miller, Eleazer Miller, Admrs. on the estate of J.M. No papers
Jeremiah, Pa., S5760
Jeremiah, Pa., Mary, W2837
Jeremiah C., N.Y., Elizabeth, W21806. BLWt.1461-150, Ens. Iss. 12/30/1796. Also recorded as above under BLWt.2667 & 1463-150 Ens. No date of issue. Wm. Radcliffe, Jr., ass. Also recorded under BLWt.2669. No papers
Jeremiah Jacob, N.Y., S22907
Jesse, N.Y., S42980
Job, Mass., Sarah, W27451
Johannes/John, N.Y., Eve, W16650
John, Ct., Privateer, b. 1756 at Lynn, Ct., R7209
John, Cont., BLWt.1621-100. Ct. res. of heir in 1830
John, Cont., Pa., b. 1761, S11072
John, Cont., Pa., b. 1743, S40158
John, Cont., Pa., b. 1751, S40164
John, Hazen's Regt., BLWt.13469. Iss. 6/27/1791. No papers
John, Md., b. 1765, Mary, W47
John, Md., Eleanor/Elenor, W2647. B. 1762 or 1763
John, Md., Mary Ann, W9197
John, Md., Rosanna, W9199
John, Md., BL Reg. 257556
John, Mass., S37247
John, Mass., Hannah, W19882; BLWt.11174-160-55
John, N.J., BLWt.8571. Iss. 1/12/1790. No papers
John, N.J., Sarah, W16653
John, N.Y., BLWt.7448. Iss. 7/10/1790 to John Quackenboss, ass. No papers
John, N.Y., S28128
John, N.Y., S42990
John, N.Y., b. 1750, S43000
John, N.Y., b. Ger. 12/1749, S44540
John, N.Y. See Johannes
John/Johannes, N.Y., Anna Dorothea W18511
John, N.Y., Elizabeth, W24152
John, N.Y., Leah, R7212
John, N.Y., BLWt.2126-100
John, N.C., b. 1763, S9415
John, N.C., d. 1808, Jane, R7204
John, Pa., 10131. Iss. 3/2/1792 to

MILLER (continued)
Thomas Campbell, Admr. No papers
John, Pa., b. 1755, d. 1838, S5757
John, Pa., S16974
John, Pa., S22398
John, Pa., also in 1791, S31255
John, Pa., S40154
John, Pa., d. 1820, Susan, W3151
John, Pa., R7207
John, Pa., b. 1760, R7210
John, Pa., BLWt.2583-300. No papers
John, Pa., BLWt.10110-100. Iss. 11/5/1789 to John Miller
John, R.I., Zerviah Peckham, former wid., W21949
John, S.C., b. 1766/1767, S1702
John, S.C., S38950
John, S.C., Mary, W3706
John, Va., b. 1761, S1921
John, Va., b. 1759, S9026
John, Va., b. 1754, S36136
John, Va., b. Ger. 1750, S38223
John, Va., b. 1761, d.1848, Lucy, W5380; BLWt.14517-160-55
John, Va., d.1832 in Tenn., Eve, R7187
John, Va., d. 1808, Jane, R7203
John, Va., d. 1855 in Ohio, R7208
John A., Cont., N.J., Indian War, U.S. Army, S16965
John A., Va., R7211
John Christine, Ct., Roxalana, W25708
John H., Va., S2829
John P., N.Y., S11082
John Peter, Cont., Pa., Ann Elizabeth, W5149; BLWt.2490-100
John Volchmen, R.I., War of 1812, Mary, W4742; BLWt.26957-160-55
Jonathan, Ct., BLWt.6152. Iss. 5/18/1790 to Theodosius Fowler. No papers
Jonathan, Ct., S20447
Jonathan, Ct., Cont., Anner Bissel, former wid., W23605. Her other husb., Ozias Bissell, Ct., was pensioned, which see
Jonathan, N.Y., Lydia, Rej.197-051
Joseph, Mass., BLWt.1363-200-Lt. Iss. 7/31/1792. No papers
Joseph, N.J., BLWt.8589. Iss. 12/10/1789. No papers
Joseph, N.J., S825
Joseph, Va., S13943
Josiah, R.I., Thankful, W21811
Josias, Md., S40160
Laura, former wid. of John Redington, Ct., which see
Lawrence, Va., S31257
Lemuel, Mass., Cont., Anne/Anna, W23989
Leonard, Cont., Mass., Sarah, R7223
Leonard, N.C., S13940
Levi, Cont., Green Mt. Boys, Vt., S13937
Lewis, Va., S38225
Ludwick, Pa., S22402
Luke, N.J., S1059
Margaret, former wid. of Francis Johnson/Johnston, S.C., which see

MILLER (continued)
Martha K., former wid. of Henry Keeler, Ct., N.H., which see
Martin, Cont., Pa., S41875
Martin, Md., R7213
Martin, N.C., Elizabeth, W7453; BLWt.33747-160-55
Martin, Pa., S7236
Martin, Pa., S41874
Martin, Pa., R7214
Matthew, N.H., R7216
Michael, French, Ohio res., R7217
Michael, Md., Margaret, BLReg. or Wt.?
Michael, Pa., Elizabeth, R7183; BLWt.86149-160-55
Michael, Va., S33103
Mordica/Mordecai, See MILLAR
Nathan, R.I., S21889
Nathan Horton, Mass., R.I., Martha W21809; BLWt.13424-160-55
Nathaniel, Mass., S42998
Nathaniel, N.Y., Anna, W17142; BLWt.3997-160-55
Nelson, R.I., S21378
Nicholas, Ct., N.Y., Elsa, W3442
Nicholas, Cont., Pa., S36137
Nicholas, Pa., BLWt.1136-300
Nichols, Hazen's Regt., BLWt. 13470. Iss. 3/11/1791. No papers
Noah, Mass., S23800
Noah, N.J., S36129
Paul, N.J., Elizabeth, R7184
Peleg, N.Y., Phebe, W18518
Peter, Cont., Pa., S41876
Peter, N.J., N.Y., Mary, W7456
Peter, N.Y., S23798
Peter, N.Y., Catharine, W19878
Peter, N.Y., R7218
Peter, Pa., S23805
Philip, Cont., Va., Lois, W3707; BLWt.40691-160-55
Philip, N.Y., R7220
Philip, N.C., S7230
Philip, Not Rev. War, Pa. Mil., Wayne's War, 1791. No claim for pension. BLWts.75102-40-50 & 79598-120-55
Philip, Pa., Barbara, W4549
Rebecca, former wid. of Joshua Minor, Ct., which see
Richard, N.C., S23808
Robert, Cont., N.H., Mary, W18523
Robert, Del., BLWt.10826. Iss. 9/2/1789 to Samuel Ireland, Admr. No papers
Robert, S.C., Annis, W5376
Robert, Va., S47514
Robert, Va., Jane, R7205
Roswel/Roswell, Ct., Betsey G., W5375; BLWt.26613-160-55
Sally, former wid. of Thomas Lawton, R.I., which see
Samuel, Md., S15940
Samuel, Crane's Cont. Art., Mass., BLWt.4733. Iss. 2/22/1792 to John Peck. No papers
Samuel, Mass., S33109
Samuel, N.H., Betsey, W19880
Samuel, N.J., S42995
Samuel, N.Y., S23326

MILLER (continued)
Samuel, N.Y., S28109
Samuel, Pa., BLWt.1104-300. Iss. 2/7/1825
Sarah, former wid. of William Blake, Ct., which see
Sebastian T., Pa., R7224
Shadrack, Mass., Martha, R7225; BLWt.17713-160-55
Smith, Mass., S42999; BLWt.157-100
Solomon, Mass., S18980
Stephen, Cont., Mass., Jemima, W3444; BLWt.19612-160-55
Thaddeus, N.Y., S23801
Thaddeus, Vt., S18509
Thomas, Mass., R7226
Thomas, N.Y., BLWt.7480. Iss. 9/9/1790 to Mary V. Schaaick, Exr. No papers
Thomas, N.Y., S43003
Thomas, Va., b. Md., Ann, W7454; BLWt.1510-200-Lt. Iss. 12/19/1791 to Daniel Parker, ass. No papers
Valentine, Pa., S40163
Valentine, Va., R7227
William, Cont., Ct., S23324
William, Cont., N.Y., S11085
William, Del., BLWt.10848. Iss. 2/11/1800 to Philemon Thomas, ass. No papers
William, Mass., S42986
William, N.H., S2832
William, N.Y., R7228
William, N.C., S7228
William, N.C., S25689
William, N.C., Va., R7229
William, Pa., Elizabeth, W2839
William, Pa., Margaret, W3282
William, Pa., Rebecca Marshall/Marshel, former wid., W9539
William, Pa., BLWt.2088-300
William, Pa., Va., S16203
William, R.I., See MILLAR
William, S.C., R20181
William, Va., S5764
William, Va., BLWt.1520-200-Lt. Iss. 7/5/1799 to Henry Garnet, Extr. to the last will & testament of Wm. Miller for the uses & purposes of said will. No papers
William C., N.Y., Christina, W17146
William Heath, Va., Joanna, W7451
Zephaniah, N.Y., R7230

MILLERD, Abiather, Mass., R7231
John, R.I., Eunice, W20256
Nathan Horton, See MILLER
Nathaniel, See MILLARD
Samuel, R.I., R.I. Sea Service, S21887

MILLES, Jacob, N.Y., R7232

MILLET, Benjamin, R.I., S38946
John, Mass., Sarah Hunt, former wid., W23363
John, N.H., Lydia, W970; BLWt. 3615-160-55
Thomas, Mass., R7234
Thomas, Navy, Me. Agcy. & res. S37248
Zebulon, R.I., S33111

MILLETT, Abraham, Mass., BLWt. 4708. Iss. 2/22/1799. No papers
Andrew Jonathan, Ct., R7233; res. in N.Y.
James, Mass., S29983
Nathaniel, Mass., S33113
MILLEWAY, Isaac, Del., Susan, S38227; BLWt.1998-100
MILLFORD, Jacob, Md., BLWt.11483. Iss. 1/8/179? to George Ponsonby, ass. No papers
MILLICAN, Andrew, N.C., Lettice, R7235
James, N.C., S31260
Thomas, Ga., N.C., Mary, R7236
MILLIGAN, David, Pa., Mary, W24155
Hugh, Pa., S38232
James, Pa., BLWt.1430-200-Lt. Iss. 5/25/1796. No papers
John, Pa., Va., b. Ireland, S13939
John, Va., S36130
Moses, S.C., Lucy, R7237
MILLIGN, Josep/Joseph, Pa., S16483
MILLIKAN, William, Mass., S17586
MILLIKEN, Abner, Mass., Anna, W23979
Benjamin, Mass., Lydia, W26266
James, N.C., Va., S3609
John, Mass., Christiana, W7465
Joshua, Mass., Margaret, W26267
Josiah, Mass., Sally/Sarah, W1055; BLWt.38503-160-55
Lemuel, Cont., Mass., S16963
Samuel, Mass., R7238
Samuel, N.H., Mary, W17140
MILLIKER, Abner, Mass. See MILLIKEN
MILLIKIN, Daniel, Mass., BLWt. 1936-100
Isaac, Cont., Mass., Sarah, W23982
Joel, Cont., Mass., Elizabeth, W8461; BLWt.1907-160-55
MILLIMAN, Briant, Mass., Susan, R7239
George, R.I., Vt., S42993
MILLIN, Richard, See MILLIAN
MILLINER, Nicholas, See MILLNER
MILLING, Hugh, S.C., S46394, BLWt. 272-300
William, S.C., Jane, R7240; BLWt. 56784-160-55
MILLINGTON, Peter, Vt., Anne, R7241
Samuel, Ct., Christina, W17145
MILLION, John, See McMULLEN
John, Va., R7242
MILLIWAY, Isaac, See MILLEWAY
MILLNER, Luke, Va., S31259
Nicholas, Pa., Hannah, W3028
MILLOTT, Farrell, Lamb's Art., N.Y., BLWt.7521. Iss. 9/24/1790 to Thos. Laurence, ass. No papers
MILLOWAY, Isaac, See MILLEWAY
MILLS, Aaron, Ct., Mass., S13927
Alexander, Ct., BLWt.6195. Iss. 6/27/1789. No papers
Alexander, Ct., S36147
Alexander, N.Y., BLWt.7472. Iss. 7/28/1790 to G.H.V. Wagenen, ass. No papers
Amasa, Ct., Cont., S36148
Andrew, N.Y., BLWt.7456. Iss. 3/16/1792 to Elias Newman, ass. No papers
Andrew, N.Y., R7244
Andrew, Pa., Catharine, W2150
Ann, former wid. of Benjamin Dyer, Ct., which see
Benjamin, Mass., Sarah, W23971
Benjamin, N.C., BLWt.1465-300-Capt. Iss. 12/1/1796. Also recorded as above under BLWt.2670. No papers
Cephas, Mass., Hannah, W2624
Constantine, Ct., Philecta/Philicta, W2151
Cornelius, N.J., S35435
Edward, N.J., S34434
Elias, Ct., S22399
Elijah, Ct., Huldah, W17147; BLWt.9205-160-55
Elijah, Md., S2825
Francis, Va., S38229
Frederick, Cont., Pa., Eve, R7245
Gabriel, Ct., S36131
George, Ct., S43002
George, Mass., BLWt.4689. Iss. 5/6/1793. No papers
George, Mass., Martha, W23981
George, Va., Lydia, W7449
Handy/Hardy, N.C., S33100
Hezekiah, Mass., Elizabeth,W26261
Isaac, Lee's Legion, BLWt.13530. Iss. 3/5/1792. No papers
James, Cont., Mass., N.H., Hannah Grover, former wid., W23134
James, Mass., BLWt.4681. Iss. 3/25/1790. No papers
James, Mass., S11071
James, N.Y., Rebecca Hall, former wid., W17048
James, N.C., BLWt.1533-300-Capt. Iss. 3/2/1799 to Wm. & Benj. Mills, heirs at law. No papers
James, Va., Nancy, R7247; BLWt. 73537-160-55
Jedediah, Ct., Sarah, R7249
Jedediah, N.J., BLWt.8527. Iss. 2/1/1790. No papers
Jesse, N.C., Sarah, W7448
John, Art. Artificers, BLWt. 13475. Iss. 4/19/1792 to Isaac Bronson, ass. No papers
John, Ct., S36139
John, Ct., S36158
John, Ct., S42978
John, Cont., N.Y., S40161
John, Mass., BLWt.1354-300-Capt. Iss. 4/20/1790. No papers
John, Navy, N.H., Sally, W15080
John, N.H., Keziah. No pension nor BL claim. It is an application for half pay
John, N.H., Margaret, W21804
John, N.H., Vt., S13925
John, N.Y., BLWt.7513. Iss. 8/20/1790. No papers
John, N.C., see claim of his wid., Frances Mills, who was pensioned as former wid. of Benjamin Smith, N.C.
John, N.C., S7231
John/John Ripley, S.C., S9024

MILLS (continued)
John, S.C., Mary, W9194
John, Va., Sarah, W4550
John, Va., Ruth, W5378; BLWt. 1512-200-Lt. Iss. 10/26/1791. No papers
Jonathan, N.Y., S23799
Joseph, Ct., S36151, Ann Beers, former wid., was pensioned as former wid. of her 1st husb., Thos. Phillips, Ct., which see
Joseph, N.H., BLWt.1343-200-Lt. Iss. 1/16/1800. No papers
Josiah, Mass., BLWt.4684. Iss. 9/21/1792 to Samuel Emery. No papers
Josiah, Mass., S40159
Kanah, Ct., R7246
Menan/Menam, Va., S31256
Morgan, N.J., BLWt.8550. Iss. 5/9/1792. No papers
Morgan, N.J., S46545
Moses, Va., Keron Happoch/Keron Happoct, W3853
Naaman, N.C., S9417
Nasby, N.C., erroneously pensioned as Narby Miles, S9025
Peter, Cont., N.Y., S36153
Philip, Mass., S16961; BLWt. 61003-160-55
Reuben, Mass., R7248
Richard, N.J., BLWt.8534. Iss. 7/7/1789 to John Crawford, ass. No papers
Richard, N.J., Sally, W140
Samuel, Ct., S28107
Samuel, Cont., Mass., S18977; BLWt.2020-100
Samuel, Cont., Mass., d. 3/8/1830, Jane, W23973; BLWt.34513-160-55
Samuel, N.H., Priscilla, W7450; BLWt.17863-160-55
Samuel, N.J., N.Y., S42984
Samuel F., Ct., S13938; BLWt. 26016-160-55
Solomon, N.Y., S42989
Solomon, N.Y., Mary, W18514; BLWt.11075-160-55
Stephen, Ct., S16201
Stephen, Mass., S23319
Thomas, N.H., R7250
Thomas, Va., S33101
Thomas, Va., also 1791-1793, S16200
Timothy, N.J., S2826
Walter, Cont., Vt. res. in 1817, BLWt.1728-100
William, Md., R7251
William, Mass., S19737
William, Mass., BLWt.1357-300-Capt. Iss. 2/29/1792. No papers
William, Pa., S41873
Wyatt, Va., Sally, W5381
Zachariah, Md., S35000
Zachariah, Va., Mary, W9195; BLWt.71135-160-55
Zebulon, N.Y., R7252
MILLSAPS, Thomas, See MELSOPS
MILLSON, James, Md., S34432
MILLWEE, James, S.C., Margaret, R7254

MILNER, Amos, Va., Indian War, R7252 1/2
Luke, See MILLNER
Nicholas, See MILLNER
MILOY, John R., Mass., Enl. in N.J., pensioned in Va., S38224
MILSAPS, Nancy, former wid. of Belfield Wood, N.C., which see
MILSOCK, Augustus, Pa., BLWt. 10058. Iss. 1/17/1792 to George Moore, ass. No papers
MILSOM, James, N.J., BLWt.8524. Iss. 5/26/1790. No papers
MILSPAUGH, Christian, Cont., N.Y. or N.J., S42992
MILSTEAD, John, Md.,Elizabeth, W5371; BLWts.11551 & 102-60-55. Iss. 3/11/1791. No papers
Zelus, Va., S1857
MILTEAR, William, Va., S16966
MILTIMORE, Daniel, N.H., Agnes, W16047
MILTON, Benjamin, See MELTON
Catharine, former wid. of John Nelson, Md., which see
Elijah, Cont., Va., S30588
John, Ga., BLWt.323-300
Nathaniel, N.C., S1703
Robert, Mass., S33104
Robert, Mass., S33112
Thomas, See MELTON
William, Mass., BLWt.4658. Iss. 8/30/1792 to Wm. Thompson. No papers
William, Mass., S42987
MILUM, Jordan, See MILAM
MILWEE, William, S.C., Martha, W9200
MIMS, Robert, Va., S30590
MINARD, Amos, Ct., S33106
Christopher, Cont., Ct., Lucretia, W21801
William, Ct., Susannah, W9201; BLWt.24327-160-55
Zebediah, Ct., Cont., Anna, R7062
MINCLEAR, Herman, N.Y., S11074
MINDENHALL, Joseph, See MENDENHALL
MINDIN, John, See MUNDIN
MINEAR, David, Va., S15932
MINER, Aaron, Ct., Hannah, R7256
Amos, Ct., Mary, W16346
Anderson, Ct., Mass., S21884
Benjamin, N.J., S18981
Charles, Ct., Rachael, W21808; BLWt.19906-160-55
Christopher, Ct., Cont., S42991
Clement, Ct., BLWt.6217. Iss. 5/8/1797 to George Steel, ass. No papers
Clement, Ct., Cont., Anna Joy former wid., W26682
David, Ct., S11083
David, Ct., Lydia, W7463
Ebenezer, Ct., Rhoda, W17143
Elihu, See MINOR
Elnathan, Ct., BLWt.6203. Iss. 9/20/1790.No papers
Elnathan, Ct., S41871
Ephraim, Ct., Thankful, W24153; BLWt.26238-160-55
Ephraim, Mass. See MINOR
Ichabod, Ct., S5765;BLWt.31295-

MINER (continued)
160-55
Isaac, R.I., S21377
James, Ct., S13932
James, Ct., S23802
James, Ct., Esther, W23977
John, Ct., S9414
John, Pa. See MINOR
Jonathan, Ct. See MINOR
Richard, Mass., S13944
Richardson, Ct., Sally, W2414; BLWt.9482-160-55
Seth, Cont., Ct., S36152
Simeon, Ct., R.I., S14857
Stephen/Steven, Ct., Mary, W25710
Stephen, Navy, Ct., S36134
Sylvester, Ct., S42985; BLWt.652-100
Timothy, Ct., Mary/Polly, BLWt. 34822-160-55
William, Ct., Privateer, S13930
William, N.H., Hepzibah, W23985; BLWt.7448-160-55
MINES, Peter, Va., S38214
MINGAN, Joseph, See MINGIN
MINGEN, Joseph, N.J., BLWt.8577. Iss. 9/9/1790 to John Pope, ass. No papers
MINGENS, Moses, N.Y., BLWt.7501. Iss. 9/4/1790 to Samuel Wood, ass. No papers
MINGIN, Joseph, N.J., Catharine, W2321
MINGUS, Hieronimus, N.Y., S41008
Moses, N.Y., S41006
MINICH, George, See MINING
MINICK, Hendrick, N.Y., BLWt.7496 Iss. 9/3/1790. No papers
MINIHAM, Michael, Mass., BLWt. 4662. Iss. 6/10/1790 to David Knap. No papers
MINING, George, Pa., R7115
MINIX, Margaret, former wid. of Andrew Pitman, Va., which see
MINK, John C., Mass., S31254; BLWt.30908-160-55
Paul, Mass., S18126
Valentine, Mass., S37251
MINKLER, Cornelius, N.Y., Caroline, W1451
MINNEAR, Abraham, See MINNIEAR
MINNIEAR, Abraham, Pa., S16969
MINNIS, Calohill, Va., BLWt.1507-300-Capt. Iss. 7/14/1792 to Robt. Means, ass. No papers
Francis, Va., BLWt.1525-300-Capt. Iss. 11/17/1791 to George Chandler, ass. No papers
Holman, Va., BLWt.1506-300-Capt. Iss. 7/5/1794 to Robt. Means, ass. Calohill Minnis, Extr. to the estate of H.M. No papers
John, N.C., b. Va., S9413
John, Pa. See MENIS
John, Va., BLWt.12397. Iss. 7/14/1792 to Robt. Means, ass. No papers
MINNIX, Margaret. See Andrew PITMAN
MINNS, Joseph, See MINZES
MINOR, Clement, Ct. See MINER
Elihu, Ct., S36135

MINOR (continued)
Ephraim, Mass., Elizabeth Axtell former wid., W23480
Esther, former wid. of Daniel Applegate, N.J., which see
Jacob, Va., S36143
James, Ct. See MINER
Jeremiah, Va., S2843
John, Pa., S2840
Jonathan, Ct., S36157
Joseph, Ct., Cont., S13934
Joseph, Va., Mary, R7260
Joshua, Ct., Rebecca Miller, former wid., W15081
Larkin, Va., S36150
Nathan W., Ct., BLWt.6155. Iss. 2/7/1799 to John Duncan. No papers
Peter, Va., BLWt.344-300
Philip, Ct., R7262
Reuben, Va., Mary, R7261
Richardson, Ct. See MINER
Thomas, Va., Nancy, W4494
Thomas, Va., Elizabeth, W5374; BLWt.1679-300. Va. Half Pay. See N.A. Acc. No.874, No. 050177, Half Pay, Thomas Minor
Threesivelus, Va., S16968
Titus, Ct., S36133
Vivion, Va., Elizabeth, W23992
William, Ct. See MINARD
William, N.H. See MINER
William, Va., S11070
MINOTT, Jonathan, Mass., S19735
MINTER, Barker, Va., BLWt.2187-100
John, Pa., S9027
John, Va., Johanna, W18513
MINTHORN, William, N.J., BLWt. 127-100
MINTON, Ebenezer, Cont., Va., S38949; BLWt.12361-100. Iss. 12/27/1794. No papers
John, Va., S36156
John, Va., Jane, R7263
MINTUN, John, N.J., Rebecca, W9203
MINUET, Peter, Ct., S36159
MINZES, Joseph, N.C., W2148
MINZIES, Samuel P., Va., Hannah, W25713; BLWt.30926-160-55
MINZS, Joseph, N.C. See MINZES
MIRACLE, Anthony, N.Y., Polly, W26268
MIRANDA, Samuel, Pa., S15527
MIRES, John, N.C., S35002
Michael, N.J., Sarah, W10216; BLWt.56783-160-55
Peter, Pa., S41911
MIRICK, Sarah, former wid. of Barnard/Bernard Lowell, N.H., which see
William, See MYRICK
MISENER, Godfrey, Hazen's Regt. BLWt.13421. Iss. 12/23/1795. No papers
MISERVA, William, Mass. See MESERVE
MISSINGER, Joel, See MESSINGER
MITCHEL, Barnabas, Ct., BLWt. 6206. Iss. 5/15/1790 to Barnabas Mitchell. No papers

MITCHEL (continued)
David, Cont., Ct., S42981
Elisha, Cont., Ct. res., Mary, BLWt.512-100
James, N.C., Margaret, R7280
John, Cont., Va., b. Eng.,S5761
John Benjamin, Ct., Jemina, W15693
Joseph, Ct. Sea Service, R7278
Nash, Mass., S42979
Oliver, Ct., Anna, W1632; BLWt. 26683-160-55
Richard, N.J., S34431
Samuel, Cont., Mass., N.H., Peggy, W26262
Thomas, Mass., R.I., S11084
Thomas, N.J., S34433
Thomas, R.I., Elizabeth, W23975
William, Ct., S13928
William, Mass., See MICHALS
MITCHELL, Aaron, Md., BLWt.11502. Iss. 3/11/1791. No papers
Abel, Md. Sea Service, R7264
Abner, Mass., BLWt.4650. Iss. 11/4/1794 to Samuel Emery. No papers
Abner, Cont., Mass., Jenny,W15084
Abraham, N.C., S33102
Adam, Va., R7265
Alexander, N.J., BLWt.1407-300-Capt. Iss. 11/5/1789, but also marked "on file, not delivered". No papers
Amasa, fifer, Mass., BLWt.4647. Iss. 1/13/1799. No papers
Amasa, Mass., S36699
Archelaus, Va., S38226
Benjamin, Mass., Sea Service, S18982
Bradford, Mass., R7267
Caleb, Cont., Mass., S45011
Charles, Md., S47519
Charles, Va., Sea Service,S31261
Cheney/Chaney, Ga., S38228
Cuff, See Cuff ASHPORT
Daniel, Ct., Ruth, R7282
Darius, R.I., Anna, R7266; BLWt. 75110-160-55
David, N.C., Ann, W7460
Day, Mass., S29328
Edward, N.J., S34436
Edward, N.Y., BLWt.7491. Iss. 9/9/1790 to Wm. Henderson, ass. No papers
Edward, Va., Ann/Nancy, W23991
Elijah, N.C., S2838
Eliphaz, Mass., S33105; BLWt. 829-100
Elizabeth, former wid. of Wm. Samways, S.C., which see
Ensign, N.Y., R7271
Flud, S.C., S16970
Francis, N.H., S33108
George, Ct., Lucy, W21807; BLWt.38534-160-55
George, N.C., S21883
George, N.C., Penny, W4031
George, Va., Elizabeth, W9574
Henry, Va., S5768
Hiram, Navy, Pa., S36144
Ichabod, Ct., S41007
Isaac, Pvt., Cont., N.H., War of 1812, N.Y., Jane, W24150; BLWt.

MITCHELL (continued)
10119-40-50 & 3303-100. Iss. 3/16/1792 to ____, Rev. War; BLWt.10759-120-55, War of 1812
Isaac, Md., BLWt.11550. Iss. 2/11/1800 to Philemon Thomas, ass. No papers
Isaac, Md., BLWt.2257-100
Isaac, N.H., BLWt.3303. Iss. 3/16/1792. No papers
Isham, N.C., Mary, W18510
Jacob, N.C., S38217
James, Mass., N.H., R7272
James, Navy, Va., & in 1802, R671
James, N.J., N.Y., Lydia, W23976; BLWt.30930-160-55
James, N.C., S1854
James, Pa., BLWt.10014. Iss. 8/29/1795. No papers
James, Pa., S2839
James, Pa., S41872
James, Pa., S41877
James, S.C., BLWt.2105-300
James, Va., S2836
James, Va., Elizabeth, R7270
James Mills, Mass., S37249
Jeremiah, Mass., Bathsheba Knight, former wid., W26767. She also received pension due her last husb. Joseph Knight, Mass. All papers in same file
Jesse, N.C., Va., b. Va., S7232
Job, Mass., Sarah, W23972
John, Cont., Mass., S37250
John, Cont., Mass., & U.S. Navy, Old Act Navy, S1063
John, Cont., Pa., S33114
John, Cont., Va. See MITCHEL
John, Ga., BLWt.2464-200
John, Md., BLWt.1484-300-Capt. Iss. 9/25/1789. No papers
John, Mass., BLWt.4625. Iss. 11/17/1791 to Geo. Chandler. No papers
John, Mass., BLWt.4699. Iss. 8/21/1789 to John Mitchell. No papers
John, Mass., S40162
John, Mass., R7273
John, N.H., BLWt.3318. Iss. 3/25/1800 to Dan Titcomb. No papers
John, N.H., Abigail, W16048
John, N.J., R7274
John, N.J., N.Y., Sarah, W21800
John, N.Y., BLWt.7463. Iss. 1/5/1792 to Elisha Payne, ass. No papers
John, N.C., S1856
John, Pa., S22397
John, Pa., R7275
John, Va., S5763
John, Va., S5767
John, Va., b. N.C., S16485
John B., Ct., BLWt.6175. Iss. 10/7/1789 to Benj. Tallmadge, ass. No papers
John B., Pa., b. England, R7276
Joseph, Ct., N.Y., R20404
Joseph, Mass., N.H., R7277
Joseph, N.Y., S42996; BLWt.853-100
Joseph, Pa., R7279
Joshua, Mass., Tamma, W24151

MITCHELL (continued)
Josiah, Cont., Mass., Eunice, W23987
Margaret, former wid. of Samuel Abbey, Ct., which see
Mark, Va., S38947
Martin M., N.Y., S42997
Michael, Hazen's Regt., BLWt. 13444. Iss. 2/6/179? to Eleanor Tate, ass. No papers
Nathan, Mass., Rachel, W9997
Nathaniel, Cont., Del., Va., BLWt. 1868-400
Nathaniel, Mass., Alies/Alice, W21803; BLWt.29056-160-55
Nathaniel, Pa., S9418
Nathaniel, Pa., Nancy, W3850
Nazareth, N.C., S8897
Reaps, Va., BLWt.2335-100
Reuben, Ga., Ann, W5373
Reuben, Mass., Anna, W26265
Richard, Md., BLWt.11520. Iss. 3/11/1791. No papers
Richard, Mass., S16964
Richard, Va., S1234
Robert, Mass., Mary, W15083
Robert, Pa., BLWt.9996. Iss. 5/9/1791. No papers
Robert, Va., Letitia, W3441
Robert, Va., Eve, W7459
Rotheas, Mass., Hepzibah, W17168
Samuel, Mass., War 1812, Catherine W10512; BLWt.729-100 & 225-60-55
Samuel, N.Y., BLWt.852-100
Samuel, Pa., S2837
Samuel, Pvt. in the Sappers & Miners. BLWt.13415. Iss. 3/3/1790 to Lucas Morgan, Exec. No papers
Samuel, Va., Margaret C., W3851
Samuel, Va., Malinda, W4030
Samuel, Va., R7283
Solomon, Md., N.C., b. Md., S4222
Solomon, S.C.,b. N.C.,Nancy, W181
Stephen, Mass., BLWt.4656. Iss. 3/25/1790. No papers
Stephen, Mass., S33110
Thomas, R.I., BLWt.462-100
Thomas, R.I., Sea Service, Sarah, W13728
Thomas, Va., S38231
Thomas, Va. State Navy, S5766
Timothy, Mass., Malinda, W803; BLWt.848-100
William, Md., BLWt.11480 & 14063 Iss. 2/11/1794. No papers
William, Mass., Ann, R---(no no.)
William, N.H., Susanna, W26264
William, N.Y., S11087
William, N.C., S4221
William, N.C., Rachel, R7281
William, drummer, Pa., BLWt.9946 Iss. 6/20/1789. No papers
William, Pa., S2835
William, S.C., b. Va., Eleanor, W5379; BLWt.38520-160-55
William, Va., S16967
William, Va., S21374
William, Va., S38216
William, Va., S38221
William, Va., Chloe, R7269
Zephaniah, Ct., Cont., S36155
MITCHELLOR, Jacob, See MICHELLER

MITCHEN, Benjamin, Va., Isabella, R7284
MITCHIAM, Collin, See MITCHUM
MITCHUM, Collin, S.C., S38215
MITMAN, Charles, Pa., Barbara, W3355
MITSCO, Conrod/John, N.J., S40207 BLWt.8576-100-Pvt. Iss. 12/12/1791. No papers
John, See Conrod MITSCO
MITTAG, Frederick, Md., S34999
MITTS, John, Cont. Ct. See SMITH
MIX, Amos, Ct., Clarinda, W7447; BLWt.6189-100. Iss. 6/20/1795. No papers
Amos, Mass., S23797
Benjamin, Ct., Cont., Esther, W19884
Eldad, Ct., Mary, W20258
Elisha, Ct., BLWt.6160. Iss. 1/28/1792 to Moses Sill. No papers
Elisha, Ct., S42977
Elisha, Ct., Anna/Amna, W21799
Elisha, Ct., R7285
Enos, Ct., S36141
Jesse, Ct., Polly, W20257
John, Ct., S13945; BLWt.1384-200-Lt. Iss. 4/26/1791. No papers
Josiah, Ct., S2824
Levi, Ct., Eunice, W19883
Lucy, former wid. of Sharp Liberty, Ct., which see
Peter, Ct., BLWt.6214. Iss. 12/15/1789. No papers
Rufus, Sheldon's Dragoons, Ct., BLWt.6233. Iss. 12/3/1795. No papers
Rufus, Ct., S42982
Samuel, Ct., Roxina, W23986
Stephen, N.Y., BLWt.7538. Iss. 10/10/1791 to Anthony Maxwell, ass. No papers
Timothy, Ct., S17587
Timothy, Cont., Ct. res., aged 80 yrs. in 1820. S36154; BLWt. 1386-200-Lt. Iss. 9/24/1790 to Peleg Sanford, ass. No papers
MIXER, Samuel, Mass., S13931
MIXTER, Daniel, Mass., Esther, W23978
Timothy, Mass., S33107
MIZE, Shepherd, Va., R7287
William, Ct., BLWt.6145. Iss. 2/5/1790. No papers
William, Ct., S42983
MIZELL, William, N.C., S7227
MIZNER, Henry, Pa., S16482
MOAST, John, Cont., Pa., also served in 1791, Elizabeth, W3575; BLWt.26377-160-55
MOBB, Jesse, N.C., R20406
MOBLEY, Clement/CLEMENT, S.C., S31866
Isaiah, S.C., S31864
Micajah, S.C., R7289
William, S.C., Frances, R7288
William Stewart, N.C., R6568
MODERELL, Adam, Va., S31869
MODEWELL, John, Pa. (?) Invalid Pensioner. No papers
MODGLIN, Truman, N.C., Mary Ann, W1057
MOE, Jacob, N.Y., R7290
MOFFAT, Alexander, Cont., N.Y., S41903
Enoch, Mass., Hannah, R7292
Lewis, N.Y. See MOFFETT
MOFFATT, Mathew, Ct. See MOFFITT, Matthew
MOFFETT, Jesse, Va., Elizabeth, W3466
Joseph, Mass., BLWt.4718. Iss. 3/25/1790. No papers
Lewis, Mass., Philothela, R7294
Zebulon, Mass., N.H., S43044
MOFFIT, Eli, R.I., S43035
MOFFITT, Bazaleel, Mass., S43042
Judah, Mass., S13969
Matthew, Ct., S36160
Robert, N.C., Catharine, R7293
William, See MAFFITT
MOGER, Joseph, Ct., Huldah Farlow, former wid., W25567
MOHER, James, Ct., BLWt.6143. Iss. 2/5/1790. No papers
MOHO, Jeremiah (colored), Cont., Mass., BLWt.1991-100
MOHON, John, N.C., S5781
MOIRES, Peter, See MYERS
MOIRS, Elias, See MAIRS
MOISON, Michael, Hazen's Regt., BLWt.13422. Iss. 2/25/1793 to Benj. Moore, Admr. No papers
MOLER, Gasper, Va., S2874
Joseph, Ga., Md., S9033
MOLL, Isaac, N.Y., Agnes, BLWt. 75064-160-55
James A., N.Y., R---(no no.)
MOLLEHON, John, See MOLLIHON
MOLLIHON, John, Va. res. in 1835, R7295
MOLLY ("Capt. Molly"), see Margaret CORBIN
MOLOHON, Patrick, Md., BLWt.11536. Iss. 11/29/1790 to Wm. Bruff, Admr. No papers
MOLOTT, John, Pa., S22404
MOLSBEY, William, Va.(?) or Pa.(?) Nancy, W1061
MOLTEN, Michael, Cont., Navy, R.I. Dolly, W12515
MOLTHROP, John, Ct. See MOTTHROP
MOLTON, Aaron, Mass., BLWt.4664. Iss. 3/25/1790. No papers
MOLTRUP, Moses, See MOULTROUP
MOMIE, Jacob, Pa., R7306
MONCKS, Daniel, R.I., BLWt.3341. Iss. 12/31/1789. No papers
MONDAY, Aaron, Va. See MUNDAY
Edward, Va., BLWt.12370. Iss. 12/13/1791 to Francis Graves, ass. No papers
John, Md. See MONDY
Peter, See MUNDIN
Thomas, Pa., S2873
William, N.C., S.C., Mary, W25733; BLWt.84063-160-55
MONDEN, William, N.C., R7297
MONDLE, George, See MUNDLE
MONDY, John, Md., Rosanah/Rosanna, R7296
MONELL, James, Cont., N.Y.?, R7395
MONEY, John, N.C., S7248
MONFORT, Peter, N.J., Mary, W183
MONGOR, Jonathan, Ct., Cont., S43018
MONIER, John, N.Y., S21385
MONJOY, James, N.J., S35006; BLWt.2467-100
MONK, Christopher, Mass., S11093
Elias, Mass., S29990
George, Mass., S30607
James, See MUNK
John, N.Y., Nancy, W25727; BLWt. 86044-160-55. Her claim as former wid. of Thomas Callaghan, N.Y., was rejected, which see
John, N.C., S16490
Joseph, Va., S38237
MONRO, John, Ct., S31865
John, Ct. See MUNRO
MONROE, Abel, Mass., N.Y., S23809
Abraham, Mass., S11118
Alexander, Cont., Va., S16984
Amos, See MUNROE
George, Va., S7241
George, Va., S46060
George, Va., BLWt.1523-100-Surgn. Iss. 5/30/1789. No papers
Isaac, Ct., See MUNROE
Isaac, Mass., S13999
James, Cont., Va., 5th Pres. of U.S., W26271
John, Mass., See MUNROW
John, Va., S31267
John, Va., Rachael, W8468
Joseph, See MANROW
Joshua, Navy, Ct., Privateer, S9980
Josiah, Mass., BLWt.4657. Iss. 10/12/1789. No papers
Josiah, Mass., Catherine, W16348
Lemuel, Mass., S29334
Spencer, Va., S8900
William, Ct., S11112. In claim of his bro., Isaac Munroe, S43048 this William signs "Munroe".
William, Va., S5784
MONROSE, Elijah, Ct., Martha, W25735
MONSON, Ephraim, See MUNSON
John, See MANSON
Theophilus, Ct., Sarah, BLWt. 185-300
MONTACUE, Peter, See MONTAGUE
MONTAGUE, John, Mass., S29984
John, Mass., Sibel/Sybel, W21823
Jotham/Jonathan, Ct., S36171
Medad, Mass., S31263
Nathaniel, Vt., S11092
Peter, Va., S39239
Rice D., Va., Ann, W2416; BLWt. 30935-160-55
Richard, Va. Sea Service, R77, Va. Half Pay
Rufus, Vt., Catharine, W26279
Seth, Ct., BLWt.6204. Iss. 12/12/1789 to Theodosius Fowler, ass. No papers
Seth, Ct., Cont., S33133
Thomas, Va., S5775
William, Mass., S17595
William, Mass., Persis, W27454
MONTATH, Samuel, N.C. See MONTEATH
MONTAWNEY, Isaac, N.Y., S2879

MONTEATH, Samuel, N.C., Margaret, W4745
MONTEITH, Henry, Pa., R7479 1/2
MONTEY, James, Cont., N.Y.,S43017
MONTFORT, Benjamin, Mass., BLWt. 4646. Iss. 7/12/1797. No papers
Joseph, N.C., BLWt.1531-300-Capt. Iss. 8/6/1789. No papers
Peter, See MONFORT
MONTGOMERY, Alexander, Cont., Mass., R.I., S13985
Alexander, Md., Lydia, W566
Alexander, S.C., S21890; BLWt. 31696-160-55
Alexander, Va., S36172
Burnet, N.J., S2878
David, N.C., Margaret, W4039
Ezekiel, N.Y., Mary, W24165
Henry, Cont., N.H., S13976
Hugh, Mass., Betsey, W13740
Hugh, N.H., Vt., Hannah, R7493
Hugh, Va., S38245
Hugh, Va., War of 1812, S35525, R7318 (these cases were consolidated 12/1939)
James, N.Y., Margaret, W17155
James, Pa., BLWt.9881. Iss. 2/14/1791. No papers
James, Pa., Helena, W101
James, Va., R16521, Va. Half Pay, N.A. Acc. No.874, see 05118 Half Pay James Montgomery
John, Cont., Pa., S18984
John, Cont., Pa., S40177
John, Md. Sea Service, Va., S8901
John, Mass., Julia Ann, R7319; BLWt.7311-160-55
John, N.C., S9042
John, Not Rev. War, Gen. Wayne's Army 1794, Old War Inv. File 25699
John, Pa., BLWt.9978. Iss. 4/6/1790. No papers
John, Pa., BLWt.10071. Iss. 3/21/1792. No papers
John, Va., S30593
John, Va., S33124
John, Va., Nancy Pritchet, former wid., W980; BLWt.15175-160-55
John, Va., R16522, Va. Half Pay
Jonathan, N.C., Zillah, W3579
Josiah, Ct., Mass., R.I., Ruth, W15097
Mary, former wid. of Israel Colley Mass., which see
Mitchell L.K., Pa., Rebecca, W5142
Richard, Pa., Elizabeth, W7485; BLWt.26383-160-55
Robert, N.C., R7316
Samuel, Pa., BLWt.1425-300-Capt. Iss. 7/16/1789. No papers
Thomas, Pa., Va., Francis, W8474; BLWt.17729-160-55
William, N.C., S2008
William, Pa., BLWt.10129. Iss. 3/8/1792 to Robert Connelly, Admr. No papers
William, Va., S16981
MONTH, Ambrose, Va., Daphne, W7477 BLWt.26159-160-55
MONTI, Cloud, See MONTY
MONTIETH, Henry, Pa. See MONTEITH
MONTIGUE, Jonathan, See Jotham/ Jonathan MONTAGUE
MONTOUR, John (an Indian), BLWt. 1572-300 Capt. Iss. 10/24/1789. No papers. Also BLWt.301-300, an Indian Capt. Iss. 12/18/1806 to Montgomery Montour. No papers
MONTROSE, Elijah, See MONROSE
MONTROSS, Abraham, N.Y., S13987
MONTY, Amable, Cont., N.Y.,S43012
Amable, Hazen's Regt., BLWt.13432 Iss. 1/5/1799 to John Duncan, ass. No papers
Claud, Hazen's Regt., BLWt.13424. Iss. 2/4/1790. No papers
Cloud/Claud, Cont., N.H., S41017
Enfant, Hazen's Regt., BLWt. 13433. Iss. 10/12/1790. No papers
Francis, Cont., N.Y. res. in 1794, Dis. BLWt.1393-200-Lt. Iss. 1/22/1790 to Benj. Moers, ass. No papers. See Am. State Papers, Class 9, pages 94 & 403. (Father of Francis Monty, R7317)
Francis, Cont., N.Y. res. in 1818, R7317
Francis, Hazen's Regt., BLWt.13425 Iss. 1/22/1790 to Benj. Moers, ass. No papers
Francis, Jr., Hazen's Regt., BLWt. 13427. Iss. 9/21/1790 to Benj. Moores, ass. No papers
Jaque, Hazen's Regt., BLWt.13420. Iss. 1/22/1790 to Benj. Moers, ass. No papers
John, Cont., N.Y., S43006; BLWt. 81556-160-55
Joseph, Cont., N.Y., Mary, W5384, BLWt.13473-100. Iss. 1/22/1790. BLWt.172-60-55
Placed, Pvt., Hazen's Regt., BLWt. 13434-100. Iss. 1/22/1790 to Benj. Mooers, ass.
Placid, Cont., N.Y., Susan, W2228
MOODEY, Alexander, Pa., S41891
MOODY, Abner, N.H., Martha, W16142
Andrew, Col. Lamb's Art. Regt., BLWt.1399-300-Capt. Iss. 7/29/1790 to Margaret Moody, exec. No papers
Banks, Va. agcy., Dis. No papers
Benjamin, Del., BLWt.10841. Iss. 4/3/1799. No papers
Benjamin, Mass., S22916
Clement, Cont., N.H., S45016
Daniel, Mass., Lucy, W24002
Edmund/Edmond, Va., Sarah, W25726; BLWt.85081-160-55
Edward, N.H., S15943
Edward, Va., Fanny/Frances, W2156; BLWt.19523-160-55
Enoch, Mass., S29332
George, Mass., BLWt.4645. Iss. 3/30/1798. No papers
George, Mass., Rebecca, W24158
Gideon W., Ct., BLWt.6169. Iss. 1/13/1796 to Andrew Cathcart, ass. No papers
Gideon W., Ct., S41014
Jinnie, former wid. of John Grafton, Va., which see
Joel, N.C., Ann, R7301
MOODY (continued)
John, Mass., S28816
John, Mass., Hannah, W20261
John, Pa., R7303
Joseph, Mass., Bridget, W4552
Joshua, Mass., Rebecca, W24159
Josiah, N.H., S22408
Lemuel, Mass., Emma. W2684
Lydia, former wid. of William Story/Storey, Mass., which see
Nathaniel P., Mass., S41888
Samuel, N.H., S18990
Thomas, N.C., S41892
Thomas, Va., Selah, W25732; BLWt.40506-160-55
Thomas, Va., R7304
William, Pa., BLWt.9962. Iss. 5/19/1794 to Henry Hipple, ass. No papers
William, Va., BLWt.12400. Iss. 7/5/1794 to Robert Means, ass. No papers
William, Va., S38233
William, Va., S38246
MOOERS, Benjamin, Cont., N.Y., S23815; BLWt.1562-200-Lt. Iss. 10/14/1789. Name spelled Moores No papers
David, Mass., S18994
Mary, former wid. of John Coffin, Mass., which see
Peter, See MOORES
Samuel, N.J., R7305
MOOMEY, Jacob, See MOMIE
MOOMY, John, See MUMMY
MOON, Jacob, Va., Ann Hancock, former wid., W4691. See papers in claim of this woman who was pensioned for service of her last husb., Samuel Hancock, Va.
James, Pa., BLWt.9950. Iss. 1/15/1796. No papers
James, Pa., S41900
Paul, Ct., S43028
Peleg, R.I., S38953
MOONEY, Artis/Artist, Pa., S22405
Barnet, N.J., BLWt.8511. Iss. 6/22/1789. No papers
Barnet, Cont., N.J., S46009
Briant/Bryant, Ga. or Va., Margaret, R7310
Dennis, Pa. Sea Service, S40182
Henry, Pa., BLWt.9948. Iss. 6/10/1794 to Silas Hart, ass. No papers
John, N.J., BLWt.8545. Iss. 6/16/1789 to Thomas Coyle, ass. No papers
John, N.C., Mary, R7309; BLWt. 31788-160-55
Martin, Va., S38234
Nicholas, N.J., Charlotte, W1457
Pero, R.I., BLWt.3351. Iss. 12/31/1789. No papers
Peter, Crane's Cont. Arty., Mass. BLWt.4730. Iss. 1/26/1790 to John May. No papers
Richard, Va., Milly, W3855
William, N.Y., BLWt.7460. Iss. 9/15/1790 to Platt Smith, ass. No papers

MOONEY (continued)
William, N.C., S41885
MOONY, William, N.Y., S43004
MOOR, Benjamin, Cont., N.H., Apphia, W26276
Benjamin, N.J., S727
Daniel, Cont., N.H., S45026
Elias, Mass., Huldah, W23994; BLWt.14508-160-55
Goff, N.H., Betsey, W7470; BLWt.14760-160-55
James, Mass., Lucy, W25724; BLWt.3537-160-55
James, N.Y., Isabella, W4498
James, Pa., R7328
John, Mass., S41020
John, Mass., Hannah, W16347
John, N.H., Lucy, W17169
John, S.C., Jane, W4035; BLWt.19540-160-55
Joseph, Mass., S40169
Josiah, Mass., S45027
Luther, Mass., S32120
Moses, N.H., Miriam, W4744; BLWt.26890-160-55
Nathan, Mass., S30606
Peres, Mass., S43013
Phinehas, Mass., S30596
Rachel, former wife of Reuben Kidder, N.H., which see. She was illegally married to Edmund Moor after having been deserted by husb., Reuben Kidder
Robert, N.Y., S43036
Samuel, Mass., S41012
Samuel, Mass., Eunice, W8279; BLWt.38526-160-55
Thomas, Mass., S5100
Thomas, N.Y., S43027
Thomas, S.C., S2850
William, N.C. Agcy., Dis. See Am. State Papers, Class 9, pp. 166 & 397. Wounded in knee, in line of duty at Eutaw Springs, S.C.
William, N.H., S11094
William, N.H., S23327
William, N.H., Elizabeth, R7321; BLWt.14534-160-55
MOORE, Abigail, former wid. of Peter Reilly, Pa., which see
Abraham, Md., Va., S2856
Abraham, Mass., S18989
Abraham, Pa., S2855
Alexander, N.C., S9423
Alexander, Va., S5773
Alexander, Va., S41893
Alexander, Va., Mary, R7346
Alexander C., Md., S11091
Aligah/Elijah, N.J., S2852
Amos L., Va., Ann, W5145
Andrew, Pa., S41902
Andrew, Pa., Va., R7313; BLReg. 139857-1855
Andrew, Va., Sarah, W1454; BLWt. 38539-160-55
Ann, former wid. of John Carlton, Mass., which see
Apollos/Apollas, Mass., Debby, W2324; BLWt.19732-160-55
Asa, Va. res., R7314
Asa, Ct., S23817
Asa, Md., Elizabeth, W3030, See

MOORE (continued)
N.A. Acc.874-050119. Not Half Pay
Benjamin, Pa., Magdalena, R7345
Burt, S.C., Mary, W2155
Calvin, Mass., Susanna, W15102
Charles, N.C., S30599
Charles, N.C., Martha, W24005
Christopher, R.I.(?), N.H., BLWts. 3348 & 3338. Iss. 8/6/1790 to Manassah Cutler. No papers
Christopher, R.I., Dis. See Am. State Papers Class 9, p.118, which shows that Christopher Moore suffered rheumatic complaints contracted in the Service.
Daniel, N.J., S16208
Daniel, N.C., S7249
David, Cont., Va., Nancy, R7349; BLReg. 316256-1855
David, N.Y., S43005
David, N.C., Keziah Pritchett, former wid., R8493; BLWt.5651-160-55
David, See MORE
David, Va., S16980
David, Va., Jane, W1456
Ebenezer, Mass., Mary, W10523; BLWt.24159-160-55
Ebenezer, R.I., S43038
Edmund, Mass., Persis, W21813
Edward, Mass., S37255
Edward, Mass., Lucy, W15099 BLWt.11064-160-55
Elijah, N.J., See Aligah
Elijah, N.J., S38244
Elijah, N.C., Susan, W7469; BLWt. 1534-300-Capt. Iss. 1/7/1797 to Nathaniel Macon, ass. No papers
Elisha, Ct., Hannah, W20263
Elizabeth, former wid. of Moses Powers, Vt., which see
Elkins, N.H., BLWt.731-100
Enoch, Md., S5785
Ephraim, Cont., N.H., Susannah, W21814; BLWt.27645-160-55
Ephraim, Del., R7322
Ephraim, Mass., N.H., S15536
Ezekiel, N.H., Mary, BLWt.56949-160-55
Ezra, N.H., N.Y., S11096
Forbus, Sheldon's Dragoons, Ct., BLWt.6226. Iss. 5/29/1790
Francis, Ga., BLWt.1081-400-Major
Francis, R.I., Sea Service, Elizabeth Dimond, former wid., W14620
Frederick, N.Y., BLWt.7475. Iss. 7/28/1790 to G.H.V. Wagenen, ass. No papers
George, Md., S33116
George, N.H., Lois Spaulding, former wid., W6152. BLWt.96618-160-55
George, N.H., Miriam, W15843
George, N.C., S21382
George, Va., S17593
Grove, Ct., S18992
Henry, Gen. Hosp., BLWt.1566-300-Surgeon's Mate. Iss. 7/28/1791 to James H. Kip, ass. of Catherine Moore, excutx. of the

MOORE (continued)
estate of H. Moore. No papers
Henry, N.J., BLWt.8578. Iss. 1/28/1791. No papers
Henry, N.C., b. Pa., S2851
Henry, S.C., S46010; BLWt.273-200
Hiram, Ct., R7326
Hugh, N.H., S45028
Hugh, S.C., Sarah, W8473
Isaac, Cont., N.Y. res., S43030
Isaac, Cont., Mass., S28817
Isaac, Del., S16491
Isaac, Mass., S13954
Jacob, Mass., N.H., Dorcas, R7311
Jacob, Va., S40167
Jacob, A., N.Y., R7354 1/2
James, Ga. res., R7330
James, Ct., S43032
James, Cont., Pa., Mary, W972
James, Del., BLWt.1472-300-Capt. Iss. 5/26/1790. No papers
James, Pvt. of Arty., Md., BLWt. 11544. Iss. 6/11/1790 to James Moore. No papers
James, N.H., BLWt.3322. Iss. 3/25/1790. No papers
James, N.H., Margaret, W15098
James, N.H., Mary, W15103
James, N.H., Abigail, W16049
James, N.H., Margaret, W17158
James, N.H., Ann Witherspoon, former wid., W22648
James, N.J., Abigail, W1060
James, N.Y., BLWt.7534. Iss. 7/7/1791 to John Moore, Admr. No papers
James, N.C., S1705
James, N.C., S8899
James, N.C., S37263
James, N.C., R7334
James, N.C., BLWt.1536-200-Lt. Iss. 3/6/1798 to Thomas Fitzgerald, ass. No papers
James, Not Rev., N.W. Indian War, Pa. agcy., Old War Indian File, 4228
James, Pa., Amy, S41897, R7312; BLWt.667-100
James, Pa., R7331
James, Pa., BLWt.718-100
James, Pa., BLWt.1419-400-Major. Iss. 6/3/1790. No papers
James, S.C. See MORE
James, S.C., R7335
James, Va., S4227
James, Va., S11104
James, Va., S30592
James, Va., R7332
James L., Cont., N.Y., Pa., Mary, W18532; BLWt.30936-100-55
Jesse, N.J., Hannah, W1307; BLWt. 24459-160-55
Jesse, Pa., BLWt.719-100
Jesse, Va., S38242
Joel Forbus, Cont., Ct., Rosanna, W17164
John, killed in battle of Guilford W---
John, Ct., S41011
John, Md., BLWt.11518. Iss. 3/16/1793 to John Moore. No papers
John, Md., Mary, W4037; BLWt.

MOORE (continued)
11493-100. Iss. 2/1/1790. No papers
John, Crane's Cont. Arty., Mass., BLWt.4737. Iss. 9/10/1789 to Henry Newman. No papers
John, Mass., Ruth, W21829
John, Mass., Anna, W23993
John, N.H. See MOOR
John, N.H., Esther, R7323
John, N.J., BLWt.8558. Iss. 8/11/1789 to Matthias Denman, ass. No papers
John, N.J., BLWt.8574. Iss. 6/2/1797 to Abraham Bell, ass. No papers
John, N.J., S22090
John, N.J., S34438
John, N.J., R7336
John, N.Y., Fifer, BLWt.7465. Iss. 8/6/1790 to Abm. Ten Eyck, ass. No papers
John, N.Y., BLWt.7468. Iss. 10/12/1790 to Stephen Hogeboom, ass. No papers
John, N.Y., S40168
John, N.Y., S43029
John, N.Y., S43033
John, N.C., b. Va., S18133
John, N.C., b. N.C., S21384
John, N.C., Elenor, W40
John, N.C., Mary J., W2417; BLWt. 17869-160-55
John, N.C., Mary, W7472
John, N.C., Sally, W8464
John, N.C., R7337
John, N.C., Mildred Lucas, R7340 & R7348
John, Pa., BLWt.9985. Iss. 3/7/1793 to James Humphreys, ass. No papers
John, Pa., Nancy, W1915; BLWt. 726-100.
John, Pa., R16561
John, Pa., Va., S11106
John, S.C., Ruth, W9205
John, S.C., Elizabeth, W9206
John, Va. Sea Service, R78. Va. Half Pay (see also claim 78 1/2 John Moore, Va. Sea Service. See N.A. Acc. No. 837 Va. State Navy John Moore, YS File, Accomac Co. Va. Va. Half Pay)
John, Va. Sea Service, R 78 1/2. See above R78
John Weeks, N.H., BLWt.790-100
Jonathan, Cont., N.J., N.Y., Elizabeth, W4743; BLWt.8595-100 Iss. 1789. No papers. BLWt.349-60-55
Jonathan, Mass., S29988
Jonathan, Mass., Lydia, W6833; BLWt.28567-160-55
Jonathan, Mass., Elizabeth, W15090
Joseph, Ct., S33118
Joseph, Ct. Mil., Alcinia, Rejected 84545
Joseph, Cont., N.H., Elizabeth, W21820
Joseph, Mass. See MOOR
Joseph, N.J., BLWt.8540. Iss. 11/24/1791. No papers
Joseph, N.J., S1063
Joseph, N.J., S9041
Joseph, N.J., S34437
Joseph, N.J., S36177
Joshua, Mass., S37253
Josiah, Mass., S18134
Josiah, N.H., R7342
Judah, Mass., Beulah, W6830; BLWt.34965-160-55
Justus, Mass., Elizabeth, W19887
Kerby, Mass., Ruth, W18539; BLWt.1964-160-55
King, Cont., N.Y., S43031
King, Bombardier, Crane's Cont. Arty., Mass., BLWt.4734. Iss. 4/26/1798. No papers
Lambeth, Va., R7343
Lawson, Mass., S22409
Margaret, former wid. of Joseph B. Clinton, Ct., which see
Mark, see Martha Moore
Martha, Va., former wid. of Ephraim Elder, which see
Mary, Md., former wid. of John Kinnard/Kennard, Md., BLWt. 464-100
Matthew, Md., BLWt.11489. Iss. 2/7/1790. No papers
Michael, Va., S36165
Moses, N.C., Nancy, R7350
Nathaniel, Mass., S18513
Nicholas, Va., S36179
Nicholas Ruxton, Md., Sarah, W26275
Obadiah, N.C., Winney, R7358
Paul, N.Y., BLReg.27107-1855
Pelatiah, Cont., Mass., Elizabeth, W24003
Peter, Ct. See MORE
Peter, Va., Margaret, W25716, BLWt.11159-160-55 & Va. Half Pay. See N.A. Acc. No. 874-050120 Va. Half Pay. Peter Moore
Philander, Ct., S36162
Phineas, N.J., Deborah, W3577
Ralph, Hazen's Regt., BLWt.13446 Iss. 6/21/1791 to Patrick McGlaughlin. No papers
Randolph, N.C., Elizabeth, W52
Rescarrick, N.J., Sarah, W7473
Reuben, Cont., Mass., Henrietta, W24017; BLWt.3973-160-55
Reuben, Md., S35005
Reuben, N.Y., S13963
Reuben, Va., Elizabeth W., W8466
Richard, N.Y., BLWt.7487. Iss. 6/14/179- to Anthony Maxwell. No papers
Richard, N.C., Maddlen, R7344
Richard, Pa., S43037
Robert, N.H., R7353
Robert, N.C., S2857
Robert, N.C., Elizabeth, W4036
Robert, Pa., S2854
Robert, Va., S5790
Robert, Va., R7352
Roderick, Ct., Mary, W9578
Rufus, Mass., S18991
Rufus, Mass., N.J., Rachel, W18535 BLWt.19769-160-55
Sampson, N.H., S13961
Samuel, Mass., S22403
Samuel, N.J., S23814
Samuel, N.C., Nancy, W2656; BLWt.31291-160-55
Samuel, Pa., Jane, W3107; BLWt. 1148-300
Samuel, Va., S16983
Sewall, Mass., Mehitabel, R7347
Silas, R.I., S17597
Simeon, Ct., S40181
Simeon, N.C., S41960
Stephen, Va. Sea Service, Catharine, W9577
Thomas, Cont., Mass., BLWt.2377-100
Thomas, Pvt. In the Invalids, BLWt.13500. Iss. 3/10/1790. No papers
Thomas, Mass., BLWt.4637. Iss. 5/8/1792 to Ezra Bladgett. No papers
Thomas, Mass., S2853
Thomas, Mass., Mary, W15093
Thomas, Mass., Mary, W18540
Thomas, Mass., Sarah Clark, former wid., R2017
Thomas, N.Y., BLWt.7497. Iss. 7/17/1791 to Ebenezer Foote, ass. No papers
Thomas, N.Y. See MORE
Thomas, N.C., S1858
Thomas, Pa., BLWt.9964. Iss. 6/10/1794 to Daniel Stever, ass. No papers
Thomas, Pa., S4226
Thomas, Pa., Hannah, W3356
Thomas, Pa., Va.,Indian War under Gen. Wayne, S36169
Thomas, S.C., BLWt.12426 & 13400. Iss. 10/31/1795 to Barnard Merkle, ass. No papers
Thomas, S.C., b. Ireland, S21387
Thomas, Va., BLWt.12348. Iss. 2/23/1792. No papers
Thomas, Va., S33137
Thomas, Va., Elizabeth, W564
Thomas, Va., Sarah, W5388
Thomas, Va., Tabitha, W5390
Thomas L., Md., R7355
Thomas Lloyd, Pa., Rebecca & Sarah contesting wids., R7351; BLWt.1417-400-Major. Iss. 5/22/1789. No papers
Timothy, Mass., S11108
Tobias, Pa., S9030
Usher, N.Y., S11097
William, Cont., Mass., Patty, W26588; BLWt.1356-300-Capt. Iss. 4/3/1797 to John Jack, ass. No papers
William, Cont., Pa., S18983
William, Md., BLWt.11496. Iss. 5/11/179?. No papers
William, Md., BLWt.11506. Iss. 5/29/1790 to James Moore, Admr. No papers
William, Mass., S13982

MOORE (continued)
William, Mass., S22913
William, Mass., BLWt.1367-200-Lt. Iss. 2/2/1791. No papers
William, N.H. See MOOR
William, N.H., Margaret, W21816
William, N.J., Mary, W4296; BLWt.8539-100. Iss. 5/8/1794 & 329-60-55. No papers
William, N.Y., Elizabeth, W15788
William, N.C. Dis. See Am. State Papers Class 9, p.106, which shows this man was wounded in the articulation of the knee, while in actual line of duty at the action of Eutaw Springs, S.C., 9/8/1781
William, N.C., S183
William, N.C., b. Pa., S7250
William, N.C., R7357
William, N.C., b. Va., S17592
William, N.C., Margaret, W5389
William, N.C., Va., b. Va.,S2858
William, N.C., Va., b. Md., Ann, W2152; BLWt.26485-160-55
William, Pa., S41882; BLWt.1427-200-Lt. Iss. 2/5/1794. No papers
William, Pa., Jane, W25718; BLWt. 34919-160-55
William, S.C., b. N.C., S21391
William, Va., S5787
William, Va., S16982
William, Va., S25312
William, Va., S36166
William, Va., Dianna, R7315
William Daniel, Va., S38241
William L., Pa., War of 1812, Susannah Gilbert, former wid., W27679
Wilson, Va., S31262
Zachariah, Md., S18987; BLWt. 517-100
Zedekiah, Md., BLWt.1493-150-Ens. No date of issue. No papers
MOOREHEAD, Charles, Va., Lee's Legion, BLWts.12355 & 13964. Iss. 2/18/1793 to Robt. Means, ass. No papers
MOOREHOUSE, David, Ct., BLWt.6188. Iss. 9/20/1790. No papers
Jacob, N.J., BLWt.8575. Iss. 8/4/1791. No papers
MOORES, Benjamin, See MOOERS
David, Mass., Navy, S37262
John, N.J., R7339
Peter, N.H., Mary, W23997
Samuel, See MOOERS
MOORHEAD, William, S.C., S18127
MOORHOUSE, Samuel, See MOREHOUSE
MOORLAND, Charles, See MORELAND
Thomas, Va., S2876
MOORMAN, Robert, Va., R7359
MOORS, Abraham, Mass., S45024
John, Mass. See MOOR
Jonathan, Cont., Mass., Relief, W24010
Joseph, Mass., S22914
Joseph, Mass., Margaret, W24015
Samuel, N.H., S16977
Sarah, former wid. of John Bonner, N.H., which see

MOORS (continued)
Timothy, Mass., Sarah B., W1981
William, Mass. See MORRS
MOOSKENUG, Henry, Pa., S47526
MOOSLY, Samuel, N.C., R7361 & S33117. Consolidated 6/16/1930
MOPHET, Robert, See MAPHET
MORAN, William, N.C., Delila, W17167
MORAND, Charles, Hazen's Regt., BLWt.13453. Iss. 10/12/1790. No papers
Francis, Hazen's Regt., BLWt. 13450. Iss. 8/14/1792 to Benj. Moore, ass. No papers
MORARITY, Dennis, Pa., BLWt.9979 Iss. 3/4/1794 to Daniel Stever, ass. No papers
MORCHESON, John, See MURCHESON
MORDAH, William, N.C., Agnes, R7504
MORDEN, Edward, See MARDIN
MORE, David, R.I., Keziah, W1458; BLWt.26370-160-55
James, S.C., R7329
John, N.C. res. in 1788, R7338
John, Mass. See MOORE
John, N.Y., BLWt.1813-100
King, See MOORE
Margaret, See MOORE
Martha, See Ephraim Elder, Va.
Peter, Cont. N.Y., Ct., R20408
Thomas, Mass. See MOORE
Thomas, N.Y., Rachel, W2657; BLWt.3959-160-55
Thomas, Va., See MOORE
MORECRAFT, John, Pa., R7363
MOREDOCK, Elisha, See MURDOCK
MOREHEAD, Charles, Cont., S46363
John, Va., S30600
William, S.C., See MOORHEAD
MOREHOUSE, Aaron, Ct., S13972
Abraham, Ct., S13988
Benjamin, N.J., Phebe, W2637
David, Ct., Dis. See Am. State Papers Class 9, pp. 66 & 116 which show David Moorehouse contracted a rheumatic disorder through fatigue while in service. P.116 shows the name spelled Morehouse
David, Ct., Tryphena, W20265
David, Ct., Rebecca, R7365
David, N.J. or N.Y., Sarah, R7367
Gershom, Ct., S11116; BLWt.34851-160-55
Grummon, Ct., S13955
Isaac, Cont., N.Y., S13983
Jacob, N.J., S35004
Peter, Ct., Phebe, W21812
Samuel, Ct., Mary, W25722
Samuel, Ct., Anner, W25723
Samuel, N.Y., R7366
Simeon, N.J., Rebecca, W7484
Stephen, Ct., S17598
Stephen, Ct., N.Y., S29330
Thaddeus/Thadeus, Ct., Anne, W5393; BLWt.7093-160-55
Thomas, Ct., S17596
William, Ct., Ann, W17172
MORELAND, Charles, Va., S1920

MORELAND (continued)
Dudley/Dudly, Va., Elizabeth, R7368
Hugh, Pa., BLWt.9966. Iss. 6/30/1794 to Silas Hart, ass. No papers
John, Cont., Va., S40170
Moses, Pa., BLWt.9909. Iss. 5/9/1795. No papers
Moses, Pa., S22411
Philip, Md., R7370
Vincent, Md. or Va., Mary, R7369
William, N.H., S45014
MORELL, Nathaniel, N.H., Lydia, W26274
MORELY, Dimick, Ct. See MORLEY
MOREMAN, Thomas, Md., Rachel, R7351
MORENUS, William, N.Y., Margaret, W25717; BLWt.53673-160-55
MOREWISE, Jacob, N.Y., BLWt.7441. Iss. 9/9/1790 to Ezekiel Crane, ass. No papers
MOREY, Benjamin, Mass., S45019
Benoni, Cont., Mass., S41018
Caesar, Mass., S38951
Cesar, Mass., BLWt.4670. Iss. 1/28/1790. No papers
Charles, Mass., S22911
David, N.Y., Abigail, R7372
Ephraim, Ct., N.H., S19402
Gideon, R.I., Nancy, W19885
Isaac, Cont., Mass., S45018
Israel, Mass., Privateer, Sarah, W21826
Israel, N.H., Margaret, W20260
James, Mass., Rachel, R21996
Jerusha, former wid. of Joseph Green, Ct., Cont., Mass., Vt. Which see
John, Mass., See MORY
Jonathan, Cont., Mass., S33126
Jonathan, Mass., BLWt.4673. Iss. 6/20/1789. No papers
Lewis, See MORY
Nathaniel, Mass., S13980
Nathaniel, Mass., S29992
Peter, Va., S1568, pensioned as MOWRY
Robert, Ct., S17591
Robert, Navy, R.I., S17599
Ruth, former wid. of Wait Deming, Ct., which see
Samuel, N.H., Sarah, W3580
Silas, Mass., Eunice, W23998
Silas, N.Y., Elizabeth, W9208
Thomas, Mass., R7373
MORFIT, Henry Pitner, Pa. Hannah/Henrietta, W24020; BLWt.2232-200
MORFORD, Daniel, N.J., S16209
John, N.J., S2877
John, N.J., R7374
Noah, N.J., S23811
Stephen, N.J., S1064
MORGAN, Abel, Pa., Elizabeth, W2840
Abner, Mass., Almira Morgan & Maria A. Saulisbury, daus.,W29670
Alpheus, Mass., Navy, Susanna Everitt, former wid., W16570
Andrew, Mass., S29333
Asa, Ga., S31870
Asahel/Ashel, Ct., S9032
Asher, Ct., S13974

MORGAN (continued)
Benjamin, Mass., Phebe Safford, former wid., R9139; BLWt.1370-300-Surgn's. Mate. Iss. 1/25/1796 to Henry G. Gardner. No papers. She was allowed BL as the wid. of her last husb., Samuel Safford, Vt., War of Rev., BLWt.94503-160-55
Benjamin, Vt., S11110
Benjamin, Va., S2860
Benjamin, Va., Ann, W3854
Caleb, Vt., Rosanna, W18537
Charles, N.J., BLWt.8538. Iss. 3/30/1790. No papers
Charles, Va., BLWt.12352-100. Iss. 4/6/1790. No papers
Daniel, Ct., BLWt.6141. Iss. 8/23/1790. No papers
Daniel, Ct., S36163
Daniel, Cont., Va., BLWt.1496-850-Brig. Gen. Iss. 8/25/1789. No papers. BLReg.336254-55
Daniel, Mass., Navy, S15535
Daniel, N.J., S13979
David, Ct., S16976
David, Md., BLWt.1191-200
David, N.H., BLWt.3323. Iss. 11/3/1796 to Benjamin Dana, ass. No papers
Ebenezer, Ct., Cont., Olive, W17178
Edward, Mass., S43020
Elijah, Cont., Mass., War of 1812, Patty, R7387
Enoch, Mass., Mercy Sherman, former wid., W19349; BLWt. 19915-160-55
Enoch, Pa., Susannah, W3288; BLWt.1156-200
Ephraim, Ct., Elizabeth, W2625; BLWt.8468-160-55
Erastus, Mass., S30602; BLWt. 34943-160-55
Evan, Pa., Va., S11098
George, Pa., Jane, W1635; BLWt. 9958-100. BLWt.153-60-55
Haynes, Va., Mary, W17157
Henry, N.C., Va., Susan, W3709
Isaac, Mass., R7377
Israel, Mass., S33127
Jacob, Mass., Sarah/Sally, W5143; BLWt.34978-160-55
James, Ct., S20887
James, Cont., Mass., S33129
James, Mass. Sea Service, R7378
James, N.J., Ann, W182; BLWt. 3514-160-55
James, N.C., S7251
James, N.C., Naomi, W25729; BLWt.94517-160-55
James, Pa., Va., S33138
James, S.C., b. Va., S1704
James, Va., Ann, W7468
Jesse, Ct., S5099
Jesse, Ct., S5770
John/Joseph, Ct., BLWt.6135. Iss. 4/13/1798. No papers
John, Ct., Privateer, S17588
John, Md., BLWt.11542. Iss. 1/24/1794. No papers
John, Md., S1238

MORGAN (continued)
John Gavin, Md., R7379
John, Mass., S16207
John, Mass., Abigail Fitz, former wid., R3584. Wid. allowed pension for services of her 2nd husb., Abraham Fitz, R.I., which see
John, N.H., BLWt.3300. Iss. 2/22/1792 to John Peck ass. No papers
John, N.H., Mary Barrett, former wid., W16826. B. Pasquetank Co., N.C.
John, N.C., S7243
John, N.C., Ruth, W18528
John, N.C., Va., S21383
John, Pa., BLWt.1470-300-Capt. Iss. 10/11/1792 to Thomas Flahavan, admr. No papers
John, Pa., BLWt.9943. Iss. 2/21/1793 to Abraham Sheridan, ass. No papers
John, Pa., S38956
John, Va., S5777
John, Va., Sarah, W25725; BLWt. 27675-160-55
John, Va., BLWt.2049-150
Jonas, Va., Susannah, W7480
Jonathan, Ct., Esther, R7375
Jonathan, Ct., R7380
Jonathan, Mass., Elizabeth Shumway former wid., W24941
Jonathan, N.H., BLWt.3319. Iss. 3/30/1798 to John Payne. No papers
Jonathan, N.H., S37256
Jonathan, N.H., R7381
Joseph, Ct., Mabel, W20266
Joseph, Ct., Hannah, W26281; BLWt. 6135-100-Sgt. Iss. 4/13/1798. No papers
Joseph, French, French Sea Service R7382
Joseph, N.Y., Mary, W18527; BLWt. 7461-100-Pvt. Iss. 10/20/1790. No papers
Joseph, Pvt. in Art., Pa., BLWt. 10088. Iss. 3/5/1793. No papers
Joshua, Ct., Wealthy/Welthy, W16658
Lott, Ct., Keziah, W17174
Lucy, former wid. of Jehiel Galpin Ct., which see
Mordecai, Pa., Sarah Hollinshead/Hollingshead, former wid., W3523; BLWt.1170-200
Morgan, Va., S31265
Nathan, Ct., Abigail, W17165
Nathan, N.C., b. Md., Naomi, W18529
Nathan, Va., S16985
Nicholas, Ct., Phebe, W10532; BLWt.6267-160-55
Orman, N.C., R7385
Parker, Cont., N.H., Mass., Betsey W16657
Pelatiah, Mass., S40179
Philip, Ga., Patsey, R7386
Raleigh/Rawleigh, not Rev. War, Wayne's N.W. Indian War 1791; Va. res., Elizabeth, Old War Wid.

MORGAN (continued)
File 10531. BLWt.12346-160-55
Reece, Va., Mary, W4297
Reuben, N.H., Mary D., W4295; BLWt.18222-160-55
Rhoda, former wid. of Erastus Bridgman, Mass., which see
Richard, N.C., S.C., S7238
Robert, Md., R7388
Robert, N.C., Mary, R7384
Samuel, N.J., BLWt.8522. Iss. 5/5/1791 to Sam. Morgan. No papers
Seth, Ct., Desire, W17156
Simon, Va., Elizabeth, W8475; BLWt.1500-300-Capt. Iss. 4/16/1794. No papers
Skiff, Cont., N.Y., S41010
Theophilus, N.C., Nancy, R16544
Thomas, Md., S2859
Thomas, N.C., Va., S2862
Thomas, Pa., Hannah, R7376
Thomas, Va., S2861
Timothy, Ct., R7390
Valentine, N.C., S1567
William, Ct., Lucy, S13970 & R7383
William, Mass., S13991
William, Mass., Hannah, W15085
William, N.Y., Invalid, BLWt. 7464 & 13515. Iss. 6/15/1792 to William Shelt/Shett, admr. No papers
William, N.C., S9034
William, N.C., S41886
William, N.C., S41895
William, Va., S5782
William, Va., S7246
William, Va., S18985; BLWt.1944-100
William A., Ct., Cont., Sarah, W1308; BLWt.6437-160-55
Zackquil, Pa., Va., Sina/Cina, W1912
MORGERT, Peter, Va., b.N.J., S4591
MORILL, Nathaniel, See MORRILL
MORIN, Edward, Va., S16489
MORING, John, Va., S7239
MORIS, John, N.C., See MORRIS
Thomas, N.C., Va. See MORRIS
MORISON, David, Mass., S18988
Hugh, N.Y. See MORRISON
Margaret, former wid. of Joseph Dailey, Pa., which see
Morris, N.C. See MORRISON
Moses, Mass. See MORRISON
William, Cont., Ct. See MORRISON
MORISSON, Daniel, N.Y., Rebecca, W17163
MORLAND, William, See MORELAND
MORLATT, Peter, See MARLATT
MORLEY, Abner, Mass., S13968
Daniel, Ct., BLWt.6199. Iss. 9/1/1790 to Theodosius Fowler, ass.
Daniel, Ct., S40180
David, Mass., Hannah, W15091
Demick, Ct., S13992
Derick, Mass., S5788
Ebenezer, Mass., Prudence, R7392
Elijah, See MAULEY

MORLEY (continued)
Ezekiel. Mass. See Ezkiel
Ezkiel, Mass., Rachel, R7393
Isaac, Mass., S40184
John, Cont., Ct., S40176
Thomas, Ct., S18511
MORLING, William, N.H., Drummer, BLWt.3311. Iss. 3/25/1790. No papers
MORONEY, Joseph, N.Y., BLWt.7520. Iss. 4/19/1791 to David Quinton, ass. No papers
MORPHIS, John, N.C., S41884
MORRELL, Benjamin, N.J., S2871
Isaac, N.Y., S43023
Jesse, N.Y., Hester, R7398
John, N.Y., S43034
John, Va., R7396
Joseph, N.Y., S28819; BLWt.1396-150-Ensign. Iss. 9/15/1790. No papers
Richard, Mass., Ruth, R7397
Samuel, N.H., d. 10/7/1834. Disabled. See Am. State Papers, Class 9, p.137 which shows sold. wounded 6/17/1775 at Bunker's Hill by a musket ball, which entering his thigh passed through and came out near his groin.
Thomas, N.J., S2872
Thomas, N.C., S4241
William, N.Y., BLWt.7503-100. Iss. 7/15/1790 to John Hathorn, ass. No papers
MORRIL, Judah H., Mass., BLWt.4712. Iss. 6/3/1789. No papers
MORRILL, Abraham, N.H., R7394
Amos, Mass., S21390
Amos, N.H., BLWt.1337-400-Major Iss. 2/11/1800. No papers
David, N.H., Anna, W16659
Hebard, N.H., S21381
Isaac, N.Y., BLWt.7440. Iss. 4/9/1791. No papers
Israel, Mass., S29335
Jacob, Cont., Me. res. in 1818, S37254
Jeremiah, Mass., S18993
John, N.H., Abigail, W21818; BLWt.879-100 & 6259-160-55
John, N.H., Hannah, W23999
John, N.Y., BLWt.7445. Iss. 4/9/1791. No papers
Jonathan, Mass., S29331
Joseph, Mass., S22412
Joseph, N.H., R7399
Joshua, Mass., S18517
Levi, N.H., Elizabeth, W24016
Lydia, former wid. of Joseph White, N.H., which see
Mary, former wid. of Daniel Clapp, N.H., which see
Nathaniel, N.H., Sally, W9210; BLWt.28644-160-55
Nathaniel, N.H. See MORELL
Richard, See MORRELL
Samuel, Mass., Elizabeth, W19900
Samuel, N.H., d. 11/23/1825, Sarah, W17160
Sargent, Cont., N.H., S11090
William, Mass., S45017

MORRILL (continued)
William, Mass., Sea Service, S21388
MORRIS, Abel, Pa., BLWt.1464-200-Lt. Iss. 5/16/1791 to Catharine Morris, Admx. No papers
Amos, Va., S7244
Andrew, Ct. Sea Service, Lucretia, W1984
Bazil, Va., S5103
Benjamin, Pa., BLWt.1568-150
Benjamin, Va., S2863
Charles, Ct., Sarah, W9207; BLWt. 26054-160-55
Chester, Mass., S13962; BLWt. 57647-160-55
Cornelius, Md., S40175
Daniel, N.Y. agcy., S43040
Daniel, Cont., Pa., Privateer, Anna, R7416
Daniel, N.J., BLWt.8528. Iss. 12/28/1789 to John Pope, ass. No papers
Daniel, N.J., Deborah, W4495
Daniel, N.C., Nancy, W12494; BLWt. 34123-160-55
David, Ct., S44542
David, Ct., Mary, W25728
David H., Pa., Indian Wars 1790 & 1792. S9038; BLWt.9982-100. Iss. 6/20/1789. No papers
Dennis, N.J., S1062
Edmund, Ct. Sea Service, S17590
Edmund, N.Y., BLWt.7509. Iss. 8/10/1790 to Abraham Salisbury, ass. No papers
Edward, Del., BLWt.10834. Iss. 5/12/1797 to James DeBaufre, ass. No papers
Elisha, N.J., S728
Elizabeth, former wid. of David Watkins, Mass., which see
George, N.C., Sarah, R7411
George, Pa., S41894; BLWt.330-100
George, Pa., b. N.J., Dunmore's War 1774, R7403
George, Va., Mary, W27804; BLWt. 53757-160-55
Isaac, Va., BLWt.12398. Iss. 7/15/1789. No papers
Isaac, Va., S13965
Jacob, Cont., N.Y., Sophia, W2322. BLWt.6269-160-55
Jacob, N.J., S33122
James, Ct., S16204
James, Ct., Rhoda F. Wheeler, former wid., W2035; BLWt.1378-300-Capt. Iss.
James, Cont., Mass., Hannah, W15095
James, Md., S41883
James, N.J., Lydia, W864
James, Va., S2865
James, Va., BLReg.298867-1855
Jesse, N.C., S38236
John, Ct., S13957
John, Cont., Md., S9420
John, Del., R7406
John, Gen. Armand's Legion, BLWt.1568-400-Surgn. Iss. 1/29/1790. No papers
John, N.Y., S11120

MORRIS (continued)
John, N.C., S31868
John, N.C., R7405
John, Pa., Nancy, W3106
John, Va., BLWt.12387. Iss. 10/22/1791 to Jacob Clingman, ass.
John, Va., S38235
John, Va., Lucy, W18530
John, Va., Rachel McChisich/McKissick, former wid., R6772
John, Va., R16548
John, Von Heer's Corps, BLWt. 13409. Iss. 9/27/1792. No papers
Jonathan, Md., S41896; BLWt.1483-300-Capt. Iss. 12/11/1795. No papers
Jonathan, Pa., S7247
Jonathan Ford, N.J., Margaret S., W135
Joseph, Md., R7412
Joseph, Morgan's Riflemen & N.J., BLWt.2539-400-Major. See the record of Jonathan Ford Morris, W135, who was heir & legal repr. of this man.
Lester, Va., S2003
Lewis, Cont., N.Y., Ann, W17149; BLWt.1390-400-Major. Iss. 2/13/1796. No papers
Lewis R., N.Y., R21997
Lois, former wid. of Jose/Jesse Lyon, Ct., which see
Micajah, Va., Sally, W4038; BLWt. 34917-160-55
Nathaniel, Cont., Va., S31871
Nathaniel G., Va., S36178; BLWt. 1526-300-Capt. Iss. 2/11/1800 to Philemon Thomas, ass. No papers
Neal, Md., BLWt.11528. Iss. 5/1/1797 to James DeBaufre, ass. No papers
Philip, Cont., R.I., S28815
Reuben, Va., S9036
Robert, Ct., Cont., S43019
Robert, N.Y., BLWt.7539. Iss. 12/2/1791 to John Blanchard, ass. No papers
Samuel, Va., BLWt.214-100
Stayton, Del., BLWt.10844. Iss. 10/11/1791. No papers
Stephen, N.J., S9031
Stephen, N.C., R7413
Thomas, Ga., R16555. Ga. Half Pay
Thomas, N.J., S30597
Thomas, N.C., R7409
Thomas, N.C., Va., Susan, W8465; BLWt.28526-160-55
Thomas, Pa., R7408
Thomas, S.C., Elizabeth Martin, former wid., R6942
Thomas, Va., S41015
Travis, N.C., Va., S33123
William, Cont., Mass., killed in St. Clair's defeat, 1793, Rhoda, W21824
William, Md., S9040
William, Mass., BLWt.4685. Iss. 12/3/1789. No papers
William, Mass., Navy, S37261
William, N.J., Privateer, S1061
William, N.J., Martha, W10520;

MORRIS (continued)
BLWt.26384-160-55
William, N.C., S7252
William, N.C., Betsey, W5147
William, Pa., S22406
William, Pa., S40173
William W., Cont., N.Y. res., S43041; BLWt.1403-200-Lt. Iss. 5/13/1789. No papers
Zadock/Zadoc, Del., S38247
Zadock, Del., BLWt.10846 iss. 9/2/1789. No papers
Zephaniah, N.J., R7410
MORRISON, Abraham/Abram, N.H., S33128
Alexander, N.H., Rebecca, R7425
Andrew, Va., native of N.Y., R7414
Benjamin, Mass., S45021
Daniel, Cont., Pa. See MORRIS
Daniel, N.Y. See MORISSON
David, N.H., Mary, W18531
David, N.H., Margaret, R7423
David, N.Y., BLWt.7443. Iss. 1/4/1792. No papers
Edward, Mass., R7417
Edward, Pa., BLWt.10106. Iss. 9/28/1792 to John B. Schatt, ass. No papers
Ephraim, N.Y., Lucretia, W18534; BLWt.26254-160-55
Ezra, Ga., S13956
Hugh, N.Y., R7419
Hugh, Va., S36180
Isaac, N.J., BLWt.1368-300-Capt. Iss. 6/3/1791. No papers
James, Ct., S13971
James, N.H., S29338
James, N.J., BLWt.8549. Iss. 6/20/1789. No papers
James, N.Y., S43043
James, N.Y., R7420
James, Pa., S23816
James, Pa., Esther, W8467; BLWt. 1443-150-Ensign. Iss. 11/5/1789. No papers
James, Va., S2869
James, Va., S31269
James, Va., See MORRISTON
James, Va., R7421
John, Ga., BLWt.2256-200
John, N.H., S11095
John, N.H., Abigail Hall, former wid., W15096
John, N.H., Mercy Prescott, former wid., W15217
John, N.H., R7422
John, N.C., b. Pa., S2867
John, N.C., Sarah, W17171
John, Not Rev., Old War Wid., Rej. 20759, Wayne's War, Pa. res., Mary M. ----
John, Pa.,BLWt.10065-100. Iss.1790
John, Va., S45874
John, Va., Polly, R7424
Jonathan, N.H., S16978
Jonathan, N.C., Esther, W6831; BLWt.17710-160-55
Joseph, Va., S31268
Larkin, Pvt. in the Invalids, BLWt. 13498. Iss. 9/4/1789. Cert. by N. Cutting, 12/12/1820. No papers

MORRISON (continued)
Margaret, former wid. of Joseph Dailey, Pa., BLWt.900-100
Michael, Pa., BLWt.9983 iss. 8/7/1789 to Richard Platt, ass. No papers
Morris, N.C., S2868
Moses, Cont., Me. res., S37252
Patrick, N.C., Ann, R7415
Richard, N.Y., BLWt.7502. Iss. 7/24/1790 to John Lawrence, ass. No papers
Richard, N.Y., S43022
Robert, N.H., Anna, W16350
Robert, N.H., R7427
Roderick, Ct., S16205
Samuel, Mass., S18131
Samuel, Mass., S43737
Samuel, N.H., BLWt.3299. Iss. 3/25/1790. No papers
Samuel, N.H., S45020
Samuel, N.H., Susa, R7429
Samuel, Pa., BLWt.1442-200-Lt. Iss. 8/31/1792 to Alexander Power, ass. of Peter Summers, admr. of the estate of S.M. No papers
Samuel, Va., R7428
William, Cont., Ct., Margaret, W1058; BLWt.6229-100 & 93-60-55
William, Mass., S16979
William, N.C., Rachel, W1455
William, N.C., R7430
MORRISS, Claiborne, Va., S5776
Edward, N.C., Elizabeth C., R7401
John, S.C., R7407
Stayton, Del., S36164
William, N.C., S2864
MORRISSON, Edward, Va., S5780
MORRISTON, James, Va., S40183
MORROW, David, Mass., Esther, W16050
David, S.C., S7253
Hugh, S.C., S7254
John, Pa., S16206
John, Pa., S33121
John, S.C., Mary, W9209
Joseph, S.C., S21892
Joshua, N.H., BLWt.756-200
Patrick, N.Y., BLWt.7523. Iss. 9/15/1790 to William Bell, ass. No papers
Richard, Pa., R7433
Robert, N.C., Elizabeth, R7431
Robert, Va., BLWt.1508-300-Capt. Iss. 7/5/1799 to James Taylor, ass. of David Morrow, the only surviving bro. & heir of R.M. No papers
Samuel, N.C., Lydia, W7482
Samuel, S.C., S15288
Samuel, S.C., b. Md., Janet/Jannett, W21825
Thomas, Pa., S36176
William, Pvt. in the Invalids, BLWt.13499. Iss. 3/10/1790 to Sarah McMurry, admr. No papers
William, S.C., b. Ireland, S18128
MORRS, William, Mass., Lydia, W24009
MORS, Alexander, Va., S38240
Ebenezer, N.Y., S43015

MORS (continued)
Enos, See MORSE
Mark, Mass., S36700
Rufus, See MORSE
MORSE, Aaron, Ct., BLWt.6151. Iss. 11/9/1791 to Benj. Butler. No papers
Abiel, Ct., Lucy, W10217; BLWt. 26114-160-55
Abner, Mass., Betsey, W18524; BLWt.11269-160-55
Alexander, Va. See MORS
Amos, Mass., S33134
Anthony, Mass., Susa/Susannah, W24160
Artemus, Mass. See Artimas MOSS
Asaph, Mass., Cynthia/Cinthe, W2229; BLWt.8022-160-55
Benjamin, Cont., Mass., Nancy, W16141
Benjamin, Mass., S33135
Benjamin, Mass., Deborah, W19886
Benjamin, Mass., Molly, W23995
Benjamin, N.H., BLWt.3331. Iss. 3/25/1790. No papers
Benjamin, N.H., S45023
Betsey, former wid. of Joseph Winter, Mass., which see
Charles, Ct., Anna, W23996; BLWt. 26237-160-55
Chester, Cont., Mass. res. in 1818, S33132
Cornelius, Mass., Miriam, W1914; BLWt.3866-160-55
Daniel, Mass., S18986
Daniel, Mass., Polly, W26272
Daniel, N.H., S18516
Daniel, N.H., BLWt.1037-100
Darby, See MOSS
David, Ct., See MORSS
David, Mass., S17589
David, Mass., R7438
Ebenezer, Cont., Mass., S29985
Ebenezer, Mass., S15538
Ebenezer, Va., S38243
Elihu, Ct., S23812
Elijah, Mass., S22410
Elijah, Mass., Mary, W7467
Elijah, N.H., Disabled. See Am. State Papers, Class 9, p.136. This sold. afflicted with a nervous inflammatory disorder which deprived him for some time of the use of his reason; which has ever since totally incapacitated him for labor, in consequence of wading a river (encumbered with floating ice) in obedience to his commanding officer. This occurred in 10/1777, battle of Battenkiln River
Eliphalet, Mass., S29989
Enoch, Mass., See MORSS
Enos, Mass., Anna, W20264
Eunice, former wid. of Samuel Burbank, Mass., which see
Isaac, Ct., S23813
Isaac, Mass., S16975
Isaac, N.H., S37260
Jacob, N.H., Thankful, S37257
James, Ct., S43039
James, Ct., R.I., Bethiah, W24156

MORSE (continued)
Jedediah, Ct., R7440
Jeremiah, Mass., S13966
Jesse, Mass., Mercy/Marcy, W21827
Joel, Cont., Mass., Abigail, W15086
John, Ct., N.H., Anne, W24019
John, Mass., S30605
John, Mass., S33130
John, Mass., S43014
John, Mass., Leonice, W27871; BLWt.17856-160-55
John, N.H., S15941
John, N.H., Hannah, W24004
Jonathan, Mass., Sarah, W24013
Jonathan, Mass., N.H., Fanny, W567; BLWt.30931-160-55
Jonathan, N.H., Thankful, W18525
Joseph, Cont., Mass., S21389
Joseph, Cont., Mass., S33131
Joseph, Cont., Mass., Mary, W24001
Joseph, Cont., Mass., Hannah, W25731
Joseph, Mass., S22917
Joseph, Mass., S29337
Joseph, Mass., Annah, R7436
Joseph, Mass., Tabitha, R7442
Josiah, Mass., S37258
Josiah, Mass., Emma, W18533
Levi, Mass., S19403
Levi, Mass., Abigail, W24008; BLWt.6112-160-55
Levi, Mass., Mary, W24018
Mark, Mass., S33125 (not same as Mark Mors, S36700)
Mehitable, former wid. of John Clark, N.H., which see
Micah, N.H., S13975
Moses, Ct., S18510
Moses, Vt., Lydia, W25720
Nancy, former wid. of Joseph Seagrave, Mass., which see
Nathan, Mass., S29336
Nathan, Mass., Abigail, BLWt. 36744-160-55
Obadiah, Cont., Mass., S41899
Obadiah, Mass., War 1812, Inv. File 20093 (1812) Rejected Rev. Claim 7441
Obadiah/Obed, Mass., Joanna,W26278
Obadiah, Mass., Ann, R7435
Obed, Mass. See Obadiah
Ozias, Mass., Lucy, W19889
Peter, Crane's Cont. Army, Mass., BLWt.4724. Iss. 10/3/1791. No papers
Philip, Cont., Mass., N.H., S18132
Philip, N.J., BLWt.8520. Iss. 7/14/1796. No papers
Rufus, Ct., Rebecca, W20262
Samuel, Cont., Mass., S45025
Samuel, Mass., S13990
Samuel, Mass., Sarah, W17159
Samuel, Mass., Thankful, W19854
Samuel, N.H., S9029
Seth, Mass., S16210
Seth, Mass., Polly, W1059; BLWt. 31311-160-55
Simeon, Mass., S5097
Solomon, Mass., Mary Snow, former wid., W15364

MORSE (continued)
Stephen, Cont., Mass., S45022
Stephen, Mass., N.H., Sarah, W17162
Stephen, N.Y., Sarah, W3289
Thomas, Mass., S30595
Timothy, Mass., Nabby/Abigail, W24014; BLWt.11426-160-55
William, Mass., Mary, W17153
William, Mass., Sarah, W2658; BLWt.34957-160-55
MORSEMAN, Oliver, Mass., S7242
MORSHOMER, Sebastian, See MERSHEIMER
MORSMAN, Timothy, Mass., R7443
MORSS, David, Ct., Sarah, W1982; BLWt.26775-160-55
Edmund, Crane's Cont. Art., Mass., BLWt.4726. Iss. 1/28/1790 to Joseph May. No papers
Enoch, Mass., Happy, W24162; BLWt.83526-160-55
MORTIMER, Famous, Cont., Va., Mary Fagan, former wid., R3418
James, Cont., N.Y., S5774
MORTO, Henry, Cont., Mass., S33119
MORTON, Abner, Cont., Mass.,S33136
Alexander, Ct., Ruth, R24157
Archibald, Md., S36170
Benjamin, Mass., Electa, W15092
David, Mass., S43007
David, S.C., S21380
David Elvil, Mass., Mary/Polly, W24166
Ebenezer, Mass., Hannah, R7446
Edward, Va., S5778
Ezra, Mass., S30591
Hezekiah, Va., BLWt.69-300
Isaac, Mass., Mary, W10535; BLWt.57651-160-55
James, Mass., S28818
James, Mass., Abigail, R7445
James, Va., S9035; BLWt.1514-200-Lt. Iss. 4/26/1798. No papers
Joel, Mass., S13973
John, Mass., Abagail, W27452
John, Mass., R7447
Josiah, Mass., S30601
Josiah, Va., S8898
Levi/Livy, Mass., S5098
Livy, Mass. See Levi
Olive Charlotte, former wid. of Peter Tuman, N.Y., which see
Oliver, Mass., Mass. Sea Service, Melinda, W1913; BLWt.67611-160-55
Samuel, Md., R7449
Samuel, Va., S38238
Samuel Gillet, Mass., Judith, W15087
Seth, Mass., Priscilla, R7448
Silas, Mass., S46395; BLWt.1359-200-Lt. Iss. 1/24/1800. No papers
Simeon, Mass., Elizabeth, W---
Thomas, Cont., Mass., Lydia, W5333 BLWt.34828-160-55
Thomas, Pa., Va., S32411
William, Va., S2007
MORVIES, Daniel, N.Y. See MOWRIS
MORY, Abial, R.I. See MOWRY
John, Mass., War of 1812, Martha T., W24006

MORY (continued)
Lewis, Navy, Pa., Elizabeth, W3286
Uriah, See MOWRY
MOSBY, Hezekiah, See MOSLEY
John & Littleberry, Sr. See claim of Wade MOSBY
Joseph, N.C., S15539
Littleberry, Ga., Va., BLWt. 64-300
Robert, Va., Susanna, W7478; BLWt.2382-200
Wade, Va., Susannah, W3856
William, Va., Dianna, W8469; BLWt.1612-100
MOSCAT, Robert, Pa., Dis. See Am. State Papers, Class 9, p.98. He was wounded at Morristown 1/13/1777 by a fall from his horse; the horse fell upon him, and afterwards kicked him in such a manner as to disable him from doing any business of a laborious kind.
MOSELEY, Arthur, Va., S7240
Arthur, Va., Sally, W7481; BLWt. 26542-160-55
Benjamin, Cont., Va., Mary, W5387; BLWt.2436-200
Benjamin, Va., BLWt.1932-200
David, See MORLEY
James, S.C., b. Va., S9421; BLWt. 40688-160-55
Joseph, Va., S21891
Leonard, Va., S36173
Peter, Va., S9037
Robert, See MOSLEY
Thomas, Mass., S13981
Thomas, Va., S15357
William, Va., Nancy, W5385; BLWt. 1189-400
MOSELY, Catharine, former wid. of Aaron Rollins, N.H., which see
Cyphax, Ct., BLWt.6146. Iss. 4/14/1790 to William Wells. No papers
James, See MOZLEY
Joseph, Mass. See MOSLEY
Samuel, N.C., S33117 & R7361
MOSER, Christian, Pa., S22912
Francis, See MOSIER
George, Cont., Pa., See MOSSER
George, Pa., Margaret, W1983
Henry, Cont., Pa. agcy. & res., S41901
Jacob, Cont., Md., Elizabeth Williams, former wid., W9164
John, Pa., S5102
Joseph, Ct., BLWt.6178. Iss. 1/30/1790. No papers
Michael, Cont., Md., Catharine, R7450
Michael, Pa., R7451
Paul, Pa., S5797
Samuel, Jr., Pa., BLWt.10039. Iss. 12/12/1797. No papers
William, N.Y. See MOSHER
MOSES, Abraham, Mass., S41019
Ashbel, Ct., Esther, W17170
Daniel, Mass., S37259
Daniel, N.H., Sea Service, Polly, W18538

MOSES (continued)
Enam, Cont., Ct., Catharine, W20267
Ezekiel, Ct., Eunice, W4551
John, Mass., Polly/Mary, W18526
Joshua, N.C., S30594
Josiah, Mass., N.Y., Martha, W2323; BLWt.17858-160-55
Martin, Ct., Lydia, W1633
Seba, Ct., S13989
Shubel, Ct., Elizabeth, W17151
Zebulon, Vt., Hannah Knapp, former wid., R6009. She was pensioned as wid. of her other husb., Benjamin Knapp, Ct., which see
MOSHER, Aaron, R.I., S18512
David, N.Y., S13993
David, N.Y., S28814
Ebenezer, See MOSIER
Jabez, N.Y., Maria, W5392; BLWt.24901-160-55
James, Cont., Mass., Elizabeth, W7476; BLWt.6292-160-55
Jeremiah, Cont., Mass., Susanna, W7475
Joel, Ct., S36167
John, Cont., Mass., S43024
John, Mass., BLWt.1177-200.
Joseph, N.Y. S13977
Josiah, Mass., S13978
Reuben, N.J., N.Y., S34439
Stephen, Ct., S36168
Thomas, N.Y., Cornelia, W17152
William, N.Y., S13994
William, R.I., R7453
MOSHIER, Ebenezer, See MOSIER
Joel, Ct., BLWt.6213. Iss. 1/30/1790. No papers
John, Mass., See MOSHER
MOSHIR, John, Mass. See MOSHER
MOSHURE, Thomas, N.Y. See MOSHER
MOSIER, Abraham, N.C., S1859
Daniel, Mass. Sea Service, Elizabeth, R7454
Ebenezer, Mass., Jane, W21822
Francis, Md., N.C., Mary, W25719; BLWt.57649-160-55
Tobias, N.C., S16487
William, See MOSHER
MOSLEY, Hezekiah, Va., S13959
John, N.C., R7455
Joseph, Mass., Lois, W565; BLWt.13885-160-55; BL Reg. 322915-55
Robert, Pa., S36174
Thomas, Va. See MOSELEY
MOSMAN, Aaron, Cont., Mass., S18514
Ezra, Mass., S30604
Jesse, Cont., Mass., S41009
Timothy, See MORSMAN
MOSS, Artimas/Artemas, Cont., Mass., Mary, W17150
Benoni, Ct., BLWt.6208. Iss. 10/7/1789 to Benjamin Tallmadge, ass. No papers
Benoni, Ct., Sarah, W25714
Daniel, Ct., S40174; BLWt.810-100
Darby, Ct., R7434

MOSS (continued)
David, N.Y., BLWt.7438. Iss. 4/28/1791. No papers
David, N.Y., Lydia, W18536
Elizabeth, former wid. of Reuben Carter, Ct., which see
Gilbert, S.C., R7457
Henry, Va., BLWt.1504-300-Capt. Iss. 5/29/1792 to Walter Stewart ass. No papers
Isaac, Mass., S40171
Isaiah, Ct.,BLWt.6179. Iss.9/24/1798 to Linus Moss,,ass.No papers
Isaiah, Ct., S43738
James, Va., S18515
John, Ct., Vt., Mary, W25730; BLWt.38538-160-55
John, N.C., S11114
John, Va., S16488
Joseph, Cont., Mass. See MORSE
Joseph, N.C., Nelly, W9204
Levi, Ct., Martha, W17166
Linus, Ct., BLWt.6200. Iss. 9/24/1798. No papers
Moses, Va., S30598
Philip, Cont., N.J., S43016
Reuben, Ct., Esther Tyler, former wid., W6329; BLWt.94-100
Samuel, Va., S8988
Simeon, Mass., N.Y., Paulina, W2415; BLWt.28592-160-55
Solomon, Ct.,Cont.,Mass., S41890
Thomas, Ct., Lucy, R7459
Wilkins, Va. res., R7460
Zeally, Cont., Va., Jenny, W24164
MOSSER, George, Cont., Pa., S41887 BLWt.1877-100
John, Va., S5786
MOSSHER, John, Mass. See MOSHER
MOSSMAN, Jesse, See MOSMAN
MOSSOM, David, Va., R16608, Va. Half Pay
MOSSUM, David. See MOSSOM
MOST, John, See MOAST
MOTE, Levi, Ga., S.C., S7245
MOTES, James, S.C. S38955
MOTHERAL, Samuel, N.C., b. Pa., Sarah, W971
MOTHERSHEAD, Nathaniel, Va., Ruth, W8472
MOTT, Benjamin, N.C., BLWt.12411 & 13403. Iss. 6/10/1791 to Abishal Thames, ass. No papers
Benjamin, N.C., S46327
Ebenezer, N.Y., Mary, W16654; BLWt.1392-200-Lt. Iss. 3/9/1791 No papers
Edgerton/Edgton, N.C., Rhoda, W7466; BLWt.1619-100
Eunice, former wid. of Henry Williams, Ct., which see
Ezekiel, Cont., Enl. in N.Y., Jane, R7463
Gershom, N.Y., BLWt.1400-300-Capt. Iss. 7/7/1791 to Elizabeth Mott, admr. No papers
Jacob, N.Y., R7462
John, Cont., Vt., Mary, W4294
John, N.J., BLWt.1372-300-Capt. Iss. 7/13/1797 to James Mott, ass. Also recorded as above under BLWt.2523. No papers
Joseph, N.Y., Clarinda, W15104

MOTT (continued)
Lent, Ct., R7464
Lyman, Ct., Cont., Rebecca, W15100
Mordecai, N.Y., Charity Hanyer, former wid., W17035
Noah, N.Y., BLWt.7447. Iss. 8/10/1790 to John Robert, ass. No papers
Noah, N.Y., S43008
Samuel, Ct., S43011
Samuel, N.Y., BLWt.7474. Iss. 10/12/1790. No papers
Samuel, N.Y., S40178
Samuel, Pvt. in Sappers & Miners; BLWt.13412. Iss. 10/7/1789 to Benjamin Talmage, ass. No papers
Thomas, N.J., Polly, W16349; BLWt.2425-100
MOTTE, Charles, S.C., BLWt.629-400
Isaac, S.C., Mary, W21819
MOTTHROP, John, Ct., Cont., S36081
MOUL, Jacob, N.Y., Catharine, W20268
John, N.Y., S11113
MOULTHROP, Reuben, Ct., Hannah, W17177
MOULTON, Bartholomew, Mass., Sea Service, Navy, Elizabeth Marsh, former wid., R6920
Daniel, Cont., Mass., Mary, R7466
Daniel, Mass., S31264
Daniel, N.H., S18130
David, N.H., S31266
David, N.H., Dorothy, W2154
Edward Brown, Cont., N.H., S18129
Gurdon, Ct., S43010
James, N.H., S43009
Job, N.H., Anna, W16656
John, Mass., S5101
John Mobbs, N.H., Anna/Anne, W16143
Jonathan, N.H., S11107
Jonathan, N.H., Hannah, W15094
Joseph, Mass., S29991
Joseph, N.H., Sarah, R16650; BLWt.92109-160-55
Joshua, Mass., Mary, R7467
Lydia, former wid. of William Platt, N.Y., which see
Michael, See MOLTEN
Nathaniel, Cont., N.H., S41013
Nathaniel, N.H., BLWt.3301. Iss. 7/21/1789 to Ladd & Cass, assnes. No papers
Noah, N.H., Priscilla, W7483; BLWt.16116-160-55
Phinehas, Mass., R7468
Reuben, N.H., S13967
Salmon, Cont., Ct., S23810
Samuel, N.H., R7469
Sarah, N.H., former wid. of Elisha Thomas, which see
Simeon, N.H., Sally, W1916; BLWt.17564-160-55
Solomon, Mass., Prudence, W17179
Stephen, Ct., Cont., Mass., S49278 BLWt.3958-160-55. His wid., Nancy was pensioned for the service of her former husb., Henry Kneeland, Mass., which see

MOULTON (continued)
William, Ct., Cont., N.Y., S43026; BLWt.1380-300-Capt. Iss. 8/8/1789 to John Doty, ass. No papers
William, Mass., S13984
William, N.H., BLWt.3334. Iss. 2/22/1799 to John Paine. No papers
William, N.H., S45015
MOULTRIE, William, S.C., BLWt. 1538-1100-Maj. Gen. Iss. 6/4/1792 to David Cay, ass. No papers
MOULTROUP, Moses, Ct., Mary, W5383; BLWt.35837-160-55
MOUNT, Adam D., N.Y., R7470
Ann, N.J., former wid. of Peter Job, N.J., which see
Ezekiel, N.J., Va., S11117
George, N.J., BLWt.8518. Iss. 10/28/1791. No papers
Hezekiah, N.J., Mary, W1056
Jesse, N.J., S1060
John, N.J., Elizabeth, W17175
John, N.J., Elizabeth, W18470
Joseph, N.J., S898
Mather. See Matthias
Matthew, See Matthias
Matthias, Va., Dinah, W8470; BLWt.33749-160-55
Moses, N.J., Catherine, W7474
Richard, N.C., S43021
Samuel, N.J., S2870
Timothy, N.J., Deborah, R7472
MOUNTFORD, Daniel, See MOUNTFORT
MOUNTFORT, Daniel, Mass., Elizabeth, W24007
Ebenezer, Mass., S29986
Joseph, Mass. Sea Service, Navy, S30603
MOUNTJOY, Alvin, Va., Mary, W8471
John, Va., S36175; BLWt.1355-300 Capt. Iss. 2/26/1793. Also recorded as above under BLWt.2492 No papers
MONTOUR, John, an Indian. BLWt. 1572-300 & 301-300
MOUNTS, Thomas, Pa., S17594
MOUNTY, John D., Art. Artificers of Pa., BLWt.13524. Iss. 6/29/1789 to Matt McConnell, ass. No papers
MOUR, George, N.Y., S27210
Jacob, N.Y., Helen, W17176
MOURER, Nicholas, Pa., R7473
MOUREY, Christian, Pa.,BLWt.10109 Iss. 11/5/1789. No papers
MOURHOUSE, David, See MOREHOUSE
MOURIS, Daniel, N.Y., S22910 See also Daniel MOWRIS
Peter, N.Y. See MOWRIS
MOURNING, Christopher, Mo. & N.C. res. & Agcy., S24746
MOUSER, Jacob, Pa., BLWt.1462-300-Capt. Iss. 7/25/1796. No papers
MOUTRY, Joseph, N.C., Va., Lucy, R7474
MOWER, Conrad, N.Y., S11109
John, Mass., S15942

MOWER (continued)
Peter, N.Y., Magdalena/Ellena, W2683; BLWt.13728-160-55
Samuel, Mass., S29987
MOWERS, John, N.Y., R7475
MOWHOCK, Peter, Ct., BLWt. Iss. 5/18/1790 to Theodosius Fowler
MOWLAN, Richard, Md., Rachel, W3285
MOWREY, Reuben B., Ct., Mass., S2875
MOWRIS, Daniel, N.Y., S27196 & S22910
Peter, N.Y., Elizabeth, W19901
MOWRY, Abel, R.I., S21893, b. Smithfield, R.I., 2/13/1758. Res. there at enl. & in 1839
Abial, R.I., Tabitha/Tabatha, W21815; BLWt.16103-160-55
Daniel, R.I., S21894
Henry, R.I., Thankful, W27453
Jeremiah, R.I., S21386
John, R.I. res., Dis. No papers D. 8/2/1816
Jonathan, R.I., S21895
Pero, R.I., S38952 (colored)
Peter, See MOREY
Reuben B., Ct. SEE MOWREY
Uriah, R.I., Susannah, W13744
William, R.I., Susannah, W13744
Zebedee, R.I.,Mercy/Marcy,W21821
MOXLEY, George, Cont., Pa., Elizabeth, W3029; BLWt.2342-100
Jeremiah, Va., Hannah Stringfellow former wid., R10269
Joseph, Ct. See claim, W6991, of Prudence, wid. of Benj. Daboll, who was first pensioned as the former wid. of Joseph Moxley
Rhodam/Rhoadham/Rodeham, Va., BLWt.597-200
MOY, Gardner, N.C., S41815
MOYER, Adam, See MYERS
Christopher, N.Y., S11119
Daybold/Theobald, See MEYER
George, Ct., Sea Service, Mass. Sea Service, S18135
Jacob, Pa., S41889
Jacob, Pa., Elizabeth, W2153; BLWt.91122-160-55
Jacob, Pa., BLWt.1654-100
John, Cont., Md. See MAYER
John, Cont., Md., Catharine, R7532
John, Pa., BLWt.10003. Iss. 5/19/1794 to Daniel Stever, ass. No papers
John, Pa., R7541
John Jacob, N.Y., S13960
Leonard, Pa., S41898
Lodowick, N.Y., S11115
Michael, Va., S18107
Nicholas, Pa., S22407
Peter, See MAYER
MOYERS, Adam, Va., R7477
Elias, S.C., R7478
Frederick, Pa., S22915
John, See MEYER
Peter, Pa., S1860
MOYLAN, Stephen, 4th Regt., Light Dragoons, BLWt.1413-500-Col. Iss. 9/7/1789. No papers
MOZE, James, See MAZE

MOZINGO, George, Va., S5783
MOZLEY, James, Va., Martha, W25721; BLWt.31297-160-55
MUCHEMORE, James, N.H., S45030
MUCKELHOSE, Samuel, See McELHOSE
MUCKELROY, John, See McKLEROY
MUCKLEVAINE, Tunis, Va., S9043
MUDD, Bennett, Md., Ann, W26283
Jeremiah, Md., Barbara, W9212
Richard, Md., Mary, W8476
MUDGE, Abraham, Ct., Phebe, W15694
Jared, See MADGE
John, Mass., S29341
MUDGET, David, N.H., S35007
John, Cont., N.H., Tabitha, W24168
Thomas, N.H., Hannah, R7480
MUGFORD, John, Mass., S37266
William, Navy, Mass. res. & agcy., Ruth, W10544; BLWt.26437-160-55
MUGWAY, John, N.J., S34445
MUHLENBERG, Peter, Va., BLWt.1495-850. Brig. Gen. Iss. 5/18/1789. No papers
MUIR, Francis, Cont., Va., Md. Sea Service, BLWt.237-300
John, N.J., S2880
Thomas, Md., S8902
MUIRHEAD, Henry, Va., S30609
MUIRHEID, Jonathan, N.J., S899
MULBERRY, John, Va., Elizabeth, W9584
MULFORD, Benjamin, Cont., N.J., S34446
Matthew, N.Y., S5800
MULHERIN, John, S.C., Elizabeth, W9585
MULIKEN, Benjamin, Mass., S23330
MULKINS, Mary, former wid. of Joseph Robins, Ct., which see
MULL, Isaac, See MOLL
MULLEN, Anthony, Cont., Va., Sarah, W8280; BLWt.198-60-55 & 11-100
Jacob, Pa., R7482
James, N.H., See MULLIN
Michael, Pa., S40194
Patrick, Pa., BLWt.9891. Iss. 7/2/1791. No papers
Philip, N.Y., Elizabeth, W25740; BLWt.34852-160-55
William, N.C. See MULLINS
William, Pa., BLWt.9874. Iss. 9/26/1789. No papers
William, Pa., S40193
MULLENER, Moses, N.Y., BLWt.7453. Iss. 3/17/1792. No papers
MULLENS, John, Va., Nancy, W3032; BLWt.34839-160-55
Joseph, Va. See MULLINS
Joshua, Va., Anna, W25671; BLWt. 26635-160-55
William, Va., R7489
MULLER, Henry, N.Y., BLWt.7471; Iss. 7/20/1790 to Samuel Curray, ass. No papers
Jacob, Pa. See MILLER
Jeremiah C., See MILLER
MULLET, George, Pvt. "in the Invalids", BLWt.13493. Iss. 12/8/1792 to Margaret Mullet, Admx. No papers

MULLET (continued)
Lewis, See MALLETT
Robert, Mass., S33139
Thomas, Mass., Elizabeth, W16660
MULLICAN, Isaac, Mass. See MULLIKEN
Lewis, Md. See MULLIKIN
MULLIKEN, Edward, Mass., S29340; BLWt.19757-160-55
Isaac, Mass., S1775
MULLIKIN, John, Va., S35529
Lewis, Md., Susannah T., W18545
MULLIN, James, N.H., S33401
Philip, N.Y. See MULLEN
William, N.Y., BLWt.7436. Iss. 9/9/1790 to Leonard Fisher, ass. No papers
MULLINER, Moses, N.J., S34447
Moses, N.Y., S43050
MULLINGS, James, Va., S10251
James, Va. See MULLINS
MULLINS, Ambrus, Va., R7484
Anthony, See MULLEN
Bud, N.C., R7485
Charles, N.C., S30610
Clement, N.C., R7486
Flower, N.C., S1557
Gabrel/Gabriel, Va., S30608
James, Va. See MULLINGS
James, Va., Mary, R7488
John, Va. See MULLENS
Joseph, Va., S4248
Joshua, Va. See MULLENS
Malone, N.C., Elizabeth, W5396
Matthew, Va., S31271
Stephen, Va., Dorcas, W10546
William, N.C., Sarah, R7483
William, Va. See MULLENS
MULLOY, Hugh, Mass., Sea Service, S15540
Martin, Hazen's Regt., BLWt. 13462. Iss. 5/7/1790. No papers
MULROONEY, Alexander, See MARONY
MULROW, Francis, Hazen's Regt., BLWt.13467. Iss. 1/22/1790 to Benjamin Mooers, ass. No papers
MULTER, Jacob, N.Y., S43046
MULVANEY, Patrick, Pa., BLWt.9915. Iss. 2/14/1791 to Alexander Power, ass. No papers
MULVENEY, John, Pa., BLWt.10031. Iss. 9/15/1791 to John Mulveney. No papers
MULWEE, John, N.C., S7256
MUMFORD, David, N.J., BLWt.8555. Iss. 10/20/1790 to Israel Ludlow, ass. No papers
Henry, Ct., Mass., S11125
MUMMY, Christopher, Va., S4247
John, Md., R16627
MUMY, Jacob, See MOMIE
MUN, Asa, Ct., S11123
David, Ct., Lois, W17191
MUNCREEFF, Joseph, Navy, Mass. res. & agcy., Sarah Ann, W10540; BLWts.26859-160-55 & 39209-160-55
MUNCRIFF, Charles, Mass., Navy, Hannah Yates, former wid., W22160
MUNDAY, Aaron, Va., Ann, W1634; BLWt.26386-160-55
Benjamin H., Va., S10250

MUNDAY (continued)
Jeremiah, Va., Chloe/Cloe, W2636; BLWt.17886-160-55
Jonathan, Va., S5795
Levi, N.J. See MUNDY
Martin, N.J., S2888
Samuel, Va., S38248
Thomas, Pa., BLWt.9944. Iss. 9/6/1791. No papers
William, N.Y., Leah, W24027
William, N.C., S.C. See MONDAY
MUNDELL, Abner, Pa., S22395
John, Va., R7490
MUNDEN, James, N.Y., BLWt.7455. Iss. 9/15/1790 to John S. Hobart et al, assnes. No papers
MUNDIN, John, Pvt. "in the Invalids", BLWt.13504. Iss. 2/14/1791. No papers
John, N.Y., S43054
John, Jr., Pvt. "in the Invalids", BLWt.13505. Iss. 2/14/1791. No papers
Peter, Cont., N.Y., Peggy, W5153. BLWt.605-100 & 19920-160-55
MUNDLE, George, Md., S41904
John, Va. See MUNDELL
MUNDY, Gabriel, N.J., S900
John Michel/Michael, Mass., S42988
Levi, N.J., S2889
Peter, See MUNDIN
Samuel, N.J., S729
William, N.C. See MONDAY
MUNFORD, James H., Va., Elizabeth R., W8478; BLWt.51758-160-55
William Green, Va., R16697, Va. Half Pay
MUNGEE, William, Mass., S40189
MUNGER, Bela, Cont., Ct., S43047
Billy, Ct., Deborah, W15931
Cyrus, Mass., S29996
Daniel, Ct., BLWt.6190. Iss. 4/12/1792 to Stephen Thorn, ass. No papers
Daniel, Mass., S13996
Eber, Ct., S15541
Elias, Ct., S18996
Ichabod, Mass., S19405
Jehiel, Ct., S31875
Joseph, Mass., Hannah, W17186
Lyman, Ct., Eunice, W18544
Nathan, Mass., Lovisa, W19903
Samuel, Mass., S33143
Timothy, Ct., Loraine, W16352
Timothy, N.Y., Naomi, W17190
William, Mass. See MUNGEE
MUNK, James, N.C., S41905
MUNKS, William, Pa., Rachel, W2149
MUNN, Calvin, Mass., BLWt.4675. Iss. 7/20/1789 to Reuben Libby. No papers
Calvin, Mass., S29994
David, N.J., S1065
Elisha, Mass., S31270
Francis, R.I., S5062
Gideon, Ct., R7491
James, Md., Va., R7492
Jeremy, Mass., Sarah, W15109
Joseph, Mass., S13997
Joseph, Not Rev. War, N.J. Mil., Whiskey Insurrection. BLWt.

MUNN (continued)
63820-160-55. No claim for pension.
Justice/Justus, Sheldon's Dragoons Ct., BLWt.6225. Iss. 1/28/1790. No papers
Sally, former wid. of Michael Thorinton/Thornton, Mass., which see
MUNNERLYN, Benjamin, S.C., Ann, W8479
Loftus R., S.C., S18136
MUNRO, Edward, R.I., S21392
John, Ct., Susannah, W25738
John L., R.I., S29995
Joseph, Mass., Sarah, W15108
Joseph, Privateer, R.I., S17600
Josiah, Ct., S11105
Josiah, N.H., BLWt.1338-300-Capt. Iss. 4/17/1792. No papers
Leonard, Cont., Ct., S40188
Nathan, R.I., Elizabeth Luther, former wid., W24608
Nathaniel, R.I., S21393
Walter, Cont., N.Y., R7494
MUNROE, Abijah, Mass., S37264
Alexander, N.Y., BLWt.7476. Iss. 8/3/1790 to Cornelius V. Dyck, ass. No papers
Alexander, N.Y., S43052
Amos, Mass., S33142
Andrew, Mass., R7495
Benjamin, Mass., Susannah, W15106
Daniel, Ct., BLWt.6177. Iss. 3/21/1791 to D. & E. Boardman, assnes. No papers
Daniel, Ct., BLWt.2424-100
Daniel, Mass., Abigail, W15107
Edmund, Mass., BLWt.1375-300-Capt. Iss. 2/23/1796 to Malborough Turner, ass. of Rebecca Monroe, Admx. to the estate of Edmund Munroe. No papers
Henry, Mass., S33145
Isaac, Ct., W43048. Bro. William signs his own application and is pensioned Monroe
Isaac, Mass. See MONROE
Jedediah, Mass., Sarah, W15105
John, Ct., S43055; BLWt.1219-100
Jonathan, Mass., Sally, BLWt. 14538-160-55
Joseph, Ct., S36182
Joseph, Mass., Rhoda, W18542
Josiah, See MONROE
Malcolm, N.C., S7257
Samuel, See ROWE
Shubael, Mass., R.I.(?), R7496
Solomon, Mass., S33141
Timothy, Mass., S5109
William, Ct. See MONROE
William H., Va., S9433
MUNROW, Briant, Md., S34444
Hugh, Mass., S37267
John, Mass., Hannah, W24022; BLWt.30929-160-55
Lemuel, Mass., Asenath/Arseneth, W4553
Samuel, Mass., R7300. Sold. served under the name of Ezekiel Chase
MUNSEL, Benjamin, Ct., R7497
MUNSELL, Alpheus, Ct., Eunice,

MUNSELL (continued)
W17187
Calkins, Ct., S11124
Elisha, Mass., Dis. See Am. State Papers, Class 9, p.150. Wounded by a ball, which passed through his left wrist at Saratoga, July or August 1775
Hezekiah, Ct., Irena, W17184
Levi, Ct., Lucretia, W1917
Thomas L., Vt., also served in War of 1812, S18520; BLWt. 26381-160-55
MUNSON, Almond/Almon, Ct., S41909
Elisha, Ct., Mabel, W17183
Eneas, Ct., Cont., S34. BLWt. 1387-300, Surgn's Mate. Iss. 6/31/1791. No papers
Ephraim, Ct., Deborah, W26260
Ezra, Hazen's Regt., BLWt.13437. Iss. 11/24/1791 to Samuel W. Pomeroy & Co., assnes. No papers
Isaac, Ct., S40187
John, N.Y., Vt., Mary, R7498
Jonathan, Ct., Sally, W308; BLWt.26680-160-55
Josiah, N.J., Miriam, R7499
Lent, Drummer, Ct., BLWt.6168. Iss. 10/7/1789 to Benjamin Tallmadge, ass. No papers
Medad, Ct., S17601
Moses, Ct., S47547
Orange, Ct., S43045. BLWt.6139-100. Iss. 1789. No papers. BLWt.133-60-55
Samuel, Ct., Pa., Martha, W19902
Stephen, Ct., Elizabeth, W13749
Theophilus, See MONSON
Thomas E., Ct., S36181
Uzal, N.J., S34443
Wait, Ct., S13995
William, Hazen's Regt., Ct., BLWt.1564-300-Capt. Iss. 2/27/1797. No papers
Wilmot, Ct., Privateer, R7501
MURCER, James, N.C., S.C., R7502
MURCH, James, Mass., S29997
Lydia, former wid. of John Smith, Mass., which see
Mathias/Matthias, Mass., S37265
William, Mass., S18519
MURCHESON/MORCHESON, John, Va., R7362
MURCHIE, Robert, Mass., S33144
MURDACH, James, N.C., Margaret, R7507
MURDAH, William, See MORDAH
MURDAUGH, William, N.C. See MORDAH
MURDEN, Mary, former wid. of Anthony Murphy, Md., Va., which see
MURDOCH, Benjamin, Md., S9046
Edmund, Mass., BLWt.4694. Iss. 1/26/1790 to John May. No papers
William, Cont., Md., Jane Conttee Clagett, former wid., W14488; BLWt.263-150. Bounty Land claim missing in 1912. Regt. shows "Cornet, Armand's Legion". Wt. iss. to Addison Murdock, 4/25/

MURDOCH (continued)
1806 and delivered to same.
William, See MORDAH
William, S.C., S31873
MURDOCHS, John, Va., Margaret, W9582
MURDOCK, Andrew, N.C., Margaret, W17180
Asahel, Green Mountain Boys, Vt., S2886
Benjamin, Cont., Mass., S18995
Daniel, Ct., Lurana, W18541
Edward, Mass., S43051
Elisha, Ct., R7506
Elisha, Mass., S29993
James, Cont., Mass., Bathshes/Bersheba, R7505
James, N.J., Hannah, W4040
James, N.Y., Mary, W17188
James, N.C. See MURDACH
Jonathan, Ct., Lucretia, W20269
Robert, Pa., Ann, W4041
Swansey/Swanzy, Mass., S33402
William, See MORDAH
MURDOUGH, Robert, Pa. See MURDOCK
Thomas, N.H., S45029
MURE, Robert, Pa., S34440
MURET, Charles, Pvt. in Arty., BLWt.11546. Iss. 5/11/1790. No papers
MURFREE, George, Va., S38252
Hardy, N.C., BLWt.1528-450-Lt.Col. Iss. 8/6/1789. No papers
MURPHEY, Bartholomew, N.C., Anna, R7508
Charles, Va., S38251
Daniel, Md., BLWt.11497. Iss. 3/24/1797 to James DeBaufre, ass. No papers
Edward, Va., S1569
Gabriel, Va. res. in 1818, Clarissa, R7509
James, Cont., Del., BLWt.10832. Iss. 9/2/1789. No papers. See papers in claim of Richard Murphey, BLWt.2065-100
James, Cont., Pa., Elizabeth, W25739; BLWt.187-60-55
James, Sgt., Del., BLWt.10832-100. Iss. 9/2/1789.
James, N.C., S9047
James, N.C., Sarah, W24167
James, Pa., BLWt.9925. Also BLWt. 187-60-55. Iss. 8/10/1789 to Richard Platt, ass. No papers
James, Pa., S35528
James, Va., S25317
John, N.C., Mary, W1460
John, Pa., S2887
John, Va., b. Ireland, S5798
John, Va., S40191. BLWt.564-100
John, Sr., S.C., S7260
Joseph, Cont., Del., BLRej. See papers in claim of Richard Murphy, BLWt.2065-100
Leander, Va., S11126
Richard, Cont., Del., BLWt.2065-100
Richard, N.C., S9436
Thomas, Md., BLWt.11486. Iss. 2/7/1790. No papers

MURPHEY (continued)
William, Del., BLWt.10839. Iss. 9/2/1789. No papers
MURPHREY, George, See MURFREE
MURPHY, Andrew, Del. & Lee's Legion. BLWts.10822 & 13535. Iss. 8/16/1797 to James DeBaufre, ass. No papers
Anthony, Md., Va., Mary Murden, former wid., R7503
Arthur, N.C., S.C.(?), S31872
Barney, Pa., Dis. See Am. State Papers, Class 9, p.100. Received a wound at the Battle of Monmouth 6/28/1779 on the elbow of his right arm from the splinter of the carriage of a piece of artillery; that the said wound disqualifies him in a great degree from labor which requires the raising of the arms. No papers
Charles, Md., BLWt.11521. Iss. 11/29/1790 to John Thornton, Admr. No papers
Christopher, Pa., BLWt.9992. Iss. 10/28/1789 to M. McConnell, ass. No papers.
Daniel, N.J., S34442
Daniel, N.C., S1861
Gabriel, Cont., Va., S33531
George, Mass., Hannah, W24024; BLWt.12707-160-55
Henry, N.Y., Anna, W18543; BLWt. 17875-160-55
Hezekiah, Md., Sary, W5395; BLWt.26974-160-55
Hugh, N.C., S.C., S9044
James, Md., BLWt.105-100
James, Mass., S36183
James, N.C., Jane, R7512; BLWt. 45714-160-55
James, Va. See MURPHEY
James Jeffrey, Va., S35532
John, N.Y., BLWt.7335 & 7446. Iss. 2/28/1791 to John Carpenter, ass. No papers
John, Cont., N.Y., Phebe, W25736; BLWt.26431-160-55
John, N.Y., S43053
John, Pa. See MURPHEY
John, Pa., Barbara, W3152
John, Pa., Elizabeth, W3290
John, Pa., Ruth, W3581
John, Va., S13998
John, Va., R7514
Joseph, Va., Sarah, W25737; BLWt. 26636-160-55
Lawrence, Pvt. in the Invalids Regt., BLWt.13507. Iss. 2/24/1794. No papers
Martin, R.I., Mary, W17189
Martin, Va., BLWt.12384. Iss. 7/14/179? to Robt. Means, ass. No papers
Michael, Va., BLWt.1425-100
Milan, Mass., S33146
Owen, Va., S41908
Patrick, Va., BLWt.1430-100. Iss. 12/6/1828
Pierce, Navy, Me. res. & agcy., S36702
Ruth/Rutha, former wid. of John

MURPHY (continued)
Hudgins, N.C., which see
Samuel, Va., S22413
Smith, R.I., S21896
Thomas, Cont., Navy, N.H., S29339
Thomas, Pa., BLWt.10042. Iss. 6/11/1795. No papers
Thomas, Pa., S36701
Timothy, N.Y., Mary, R16668
William, N.C., S16986
William, N.C., Va., Rachel, W9580
MURRAH, Joshua, N.C., S.C., Lucy, W1063
MURRAY, Abraham, Ct., BLWt.6215. Iss. 10/--/1789 to Theodosius Fowler, ass. No papers
Alexander, Mass., S41024
Alexander, N.Y., S11121
Amasa, Ct., S36184
Andrew, N.Y., Janet, W26282
Barnabas, N.C., S30611
Barnabas, Pa., S43056
Benjamin, Ct., Lucretia, W24021
Benjamin, Mass., BLWt.4720. Iss. 3/12/1793 to Samuel Emery. No papers
Charles, Pa., Va., S38249
Daniel, N.Y., Elizabeth, R7519
Daniel, Pa., Hannah, W17182
David/David William, Cont., N.Y. res. in 1818, Sarah, R7525
David, Hazen's Regt., BLWt.13419 Iss. 6/24/1797 to John Duncan, ass. No papers
David William, See David
Elihu, Cont., Mass., Lydia, R7518
Elijah, Mass., BLWt.4627. Iss. 7/22/1789. No papers
Francis, Pa., BLWt.1418-400-Major. Iss. 4/12/1791. No papers See an affidavit by this man in Rev. War claim of John Fenton.
Hannah, former wid. of Abel Clark Ct., which see
Ichabod, Ct., S43049
Jack, Ga. Sea Service, R7520
James, Cont., Pa., S41910
James, Md., BLWt.2324-100
James, N.H., Lucy, R7521
James, N.Y., BLWt.7499. Iss. 3/2/1792 to Ichabod Rogers, ass. No papers
James, Pa., Ann, W4746 (Colonel)
James, S.C., S1922
James, Va., Susannah, R7526
Jasper, Ct., S1400
Jeremiah, Pa., BLWt.9911. Iss. 3/10/1795 to Simon Rigby, ass. No papers
Jeremiah, Pa., S41023
John, Ct., Cont., S41022
John, Cont., N.Y., Martha, W17185
John, Pvt., in the Invalids, BLWt.13484. Iss. 6/11/1790. No papers
John, Mass., Sarah, W13750
John, Pa., BLWt.9976. Iss. 1/23/1793 to John Hoge, ass. No paper
John, Pa., S34441
John, Pa., BLWt.1414-450-Lt.Col. Iss. 4/5/1791. No papers

MURRAY (continued)
John B., S.C., Rosana, W24025
Mark, N.C., R7523
Mark, Va., R7522
Patrick, Pa., BLWt.9971. Iss. 7/9/1789. No papers
Reuben, Va. res. in 1838, R7524
Richard, Va., S38253
Solomon, See MURRY
Stephen, Ct., S23329
Thomas, Mass., Mary Hatch,former wid., W23232; BLWt.15441-160-55
Thomas, Pa., S35530
Thomas, Pa., S41907; BLWt.1313-100
Thomas, Va., S31874
William, Mass., Elizabeth, W24023; BLWt.35850-160-55
William, N.J., S40185
William, N.Y., BLWt.7488. Iss. 8/4/1791. No papers
William, N.Y., S43059
William, Pa., BLWt.9906. Iss. 7/27/1789 to Richard Platt, ass. No papers
William, Pa., BLWt.9916. Iss. 12/22/1794 to Henry Purdy, ass. No papers
William, Pa., BLWt.9981. Iss. 7/14/1790 to Richard Platt, ass. No papers
MURREL, Merritt, N.C., S9045
William, N.J., S2884
MURRELL, Benjamin, N.C., Va., Mary, R7527
George, N.C. See MURRILL
Mark, See MURRAY
Samuel, Va., Susannah, W3031
MURREY, Daniel, Pa., BLWt.9933. Iss. 12/22/1794 to Henry Purdy, ass. No papers
David, or David William, See MURRAY
David William, See MURRAY
MURRILL, George, N.C., Nancy, W10219; BLWt.40904-160-55
Mark, See MURRAY
MURROW, Thomas, Pa., BLWt.10122. Iss. 4/26/1791. No papers
MURRY, Amasa, Ct., See MURRAY
Daniel, Va., BLWt.1575-100
Jacob, Pa., Elizabeth Donohoo, former wid., W9837
James, wid's. res. Va. in 1858. Sary Gish, former wid., R4052
James, N.J., S35527
James, Pa. See MURRAY
Jeremiah, Pa. See MURRAY
John, Ct., See MURRAY
John, Lamb's Art., N.Y., BLWt. 7356. Iss. 5/19/1790 to Platt Smith, ass. No papers
John B., S.C. See MURRAY
Mark, N.C. See MURRAY
Mark, Va. See MURRAY
Matthew, Md., S40186
Nathan, Mass., N.Y., S41906
Neal, Cont., Pa., S40192
Robert, See MURE
Sarah, former wid. of William Piatt, N.J., which see
Solomon, Ct., S43058
Thomas, Pa. See MURRAY

MURSH, Robert, Va., Elizabeth, W8416
MURTHWAIT, Richard, Sgt. in the Invalid Regt., BLWt.13489. Iss. 6/29/1789 to Matt McConnell, ass. No papers
MURTIS, Stephen, N.J., BLWt.8542. Iss. 1/14/1791. No papers
MURTLE, Benjamin, Va., S5799
MURVIN, Patrick, Va., S1239
MUSCHERT, John Christian, French, Paris res., Catharine, W7529
MUSE, Fauntley, Pa., Margaret, W8480; BLWt.26831-160-55
George, Va., S35526
Richard, Va., S30612
Thomas, S.C., Elizabeth, W21830
Walker, Md., BLWt.1485-300-Capt. Iss. 12/31/1789 to Walker Muse. No papers
MUSER, Paul, See MOSER
MUSGRAVE, John, Md., S18518
Samuel, Pa., Elizabeth, W9211
MUSGROVE, Samuel, Va., Elizabeth, W9583
William, Va., S40190
MUSH, Robert, Va., BLWt.12408. Iss. 7/14/1792 to Robert Means, ass. No papers
MUSHALLEE, Peter, See MERCELL
MUSHLER, Adam, Md., Catharine, W3153
MUSICK, David, N.C., Capt. in War of 1812, S16988
Thomas R., N.C., S.C., Va.,S16987
MUSKETNUSS, Adam, Pa., S41021
MUSSELWHITE, Milbea, N.C., S7258
Nathan, N.C., S7255
MUSSER, John, Pa., Barbara, R7530
John, Va. See MOSSER
MUSSEROLL, Abraham, See MESEROLL
MUSTAIN, Avery, Va., Mary, W7488
MUTERSPAW, Philip, Cont., Md., Pa., S9435
MUTH, Jacob, Von Heer's Corps, BLWt.13408. Iss. 9/4/1795. No papers
MUXAM, Reuben, Mass., S33140
MUXSUM, John, Mass., S7259
MUZZY, Amos, Mass., Sarah, W16351
Benoni, Mass., Lucy, W1459; BLWt.31310-160-55
Joseph, N.H., Anna, W2841
Nathan, Mass., S2885
Robert, Cont., Mass., S43057. See N.A. Acc. No.874-050121. Not Half Pay Robert Muzzy
MYAT, John Baptist, Pa., S34448
MYER, Abraham, N.Y., Anna, W16353
Adam, Mass., BLWt.4696. Iss. 5/31/1790 to Theodosius Fowler. No papers
Cornelius, N.Y., Maria, W19906
Ephraim, N.Y., Jane, W20272
Frederick, N.Y. See MEYER
Henry, N.Y., d. 6/17/1813, Anna, W20270
John, Cont., Md. See MOYER
John, Cont., Va. See MAEYER
John, N.Y., Elizabeth, S8903
John, N.Y., S11127
John, N.Y., Catharine, W17193

MYER (continued)
Moses, N.Y., S14002
Peter L., N.Y., S14001
Samuel, N.Y., S23331; BLWt.26354-160-55
Stephen, N.Y., Hellena/Helen, W.21831
Teunis, N.Y., Cornelia, W18547
William, N.Y., Rachel, W18548
MYERS, Adam, Mass., S43061
Adam, Pa., Mary, W10552
Alburtus, N.J., Anna, W27973
Andrew, N.Y., S9981
Andrew, Pa., Elizabeth, W5155; BLWt.30910-160-55
Christian, Md., BLWt.1487-300-Capt. Iss. 5/25/1789
Christopher, Md., S2890
Conrad, Cont., Pa., Elizabeth, W2962
Cornelius, N.J., S826
Cornelius, N.Y., Eleanor, R7537
Frederick, N.Y. See MEYER
Gideon, R.I., S33148
Henry, Ct., or N.Y., R7538
Henry, N.J., R7539
Henry, N.Y., BLWt.7500. Iss. 1/24/1792 to Stephen Thorne, ass. No papers
Henry,/Hanhendrick, N.Y., Anna, W17195
Henry, Pa., b. Va., S31876
Henry, Pa., Eleanor, W7489
Henry, Pa., Susannah, R7544
Jacob, N.C., S35533
John, Md., S2892
John, Md., Pa., S----
John, N.J., S1066
John, N.J., S29342
John, N.Y. See John BELLINGER
John, N.Y., Susannah, W19905
John, N.Y., Mary, W20271
John, N.Y., Anna/Anne, W24028
John, Pa., BLWt.10030. Iss. 4/9/1794 to Christian Hubbart, ass. No papers
John, Pa. See MOYER
John, Pa., R7542
John, Pa., Calharin Null, former wid., R7737
Josiah, Ct., N.Y., Lydia Granger, former wid., W17032
Lawrence, Md., BLWt.1096-200
Mary, former wid. of John Blanchard, R.I., which see
Michael, N.Y., Catherine, W16661
Nicholas, N.Y., Cornelia, W18546
Peter, N.C., R20407
Peter, Pa., BLWt.9907. Iss. 6/10/1794 to Silas Hart, ass. No papers
Peter, Pa., S2819
Peter, Pa. See MIRES
Philip, Md., Martha, W4554
Philip, N.Y., Margaret, W17196
Susan, former wid. of James Horn, N.J., which see
Thomas, N.C., S1862
William, Md., Pa. Sea Service, See MYRES
MYGATT, Elisha, Ct., S36185; BLWt.265-100

MYGATT (continued)
Jonathan, Ct., Cont., Prudence, W17194
Zebulon, Ct., Bathsheba Hubbard, former wid., W18078
MYNARD, Lemuel, Ct., S43060
MYNEER, Jacob, Mass., BLWt.4709. Iss. 8/10/1790 to Richard Platt No papers
MYNGOS, Moses, See MINGUS
MYRECK, Samuel, See MYRICK
MYRES, John, N.J. See MYERS
John, N.Y., See MYERS
William, Md., Pa. Sea Service, R7545
MYRICK, Bezaleel, Mass., Sarah, W19904
Francis, N.C., R7547
John, Mass., S33147
John, Mass., d. 1813, R.B.L.
Joseph, Cont., Mass., S9048
Joseph, Mass., S22414
Joshua, N.Y., S9982
Matthew, N.C., S2894
Moses, N.C., S9437
Samuel, Cont., Mass., Martha, W24029; BLWt.1358-200-Lt. Iss. 1/28/1790 to Eliphalt Downer, ass. Name spelled Myreck. No papers
William, Mass., Rebeckah, W10553 BLWt.80064-160-55
MYTENGER, Jacob, Von Heer's Corp of Cavalry, BLWt.1569-200-Lt. Iss. 6/29/1789 to Matthew McConnell, ass. No papers. This officer's name appears in Heitman's Hist. Reg. as Mytinger & Mettinger
MYTINGER, Jacob, See MYTENGER

N

NABB, Joseph, Md., BLWt.11563. Iss. 9/13/1799 to Asahel Phelps, ass. No papers
NABORS, Nathan, Va., S35534. See N.A. Acc. No.874-050123, Not Half Pay. Nathan "Neighbors"
NACE, George, Pa., BLWt.10143. Iss. 6/20/1789. No papers
NADEAU, Basil/Basile/Baszell, Cont., N.Y., S43063
NAFEE, Garret, N.Y., BLWt.7550. Iss. 9/24/1791 to Resolve Waldron, ass. No papers
Garrit, N.Y., S34449
NAGEL/Nagle, Philip, Cont., Pa., S41912
Philip, Pa., Mary, W2963
NAGLE, Christian, Pa., BLWt. 10158. Iss. 4/11/1791. No papers
George, Pa., BLWt.1290-500
Henry, Pa., Catharine, W9213; BLWt.10161-100. Iss. 1/2/1796
Jacob, Navy, Pa., Privateer, S16492
Peter, Pa., S23818
Philip, Pa. See NAGEL
Philip, Pa., Mary, See NAGEL
Richard, Md., S40195
NAI/NEU, Peter, Pa., Anne Maria, R7550
NAIL, John, See NEILL
Mathew, See NEAL
Reuben, Ga., S31877
NAILER, William, Md., BLWt. 11562. Iss. 1/8/1796 to Geo. Ponsonby, ass. No papers
NAILOR, Isaac, Cont., Enl. in Md., S35535
Joshua, Md., S41914
NAILS, John, Ct., BLWt.6247. Iss. 12/12/1789 to Theodosius Fowler, ass. No papers
John, Ct., Sally, W20274
NALL, Nicholas, N.C., Mary, R7552
Richard, N.C., Mary, W5401; BLWt.61055-160-55
NANCE, Elizabeth, former wid. of Lewis Bingley, Va., which see
Frederick, Va., Maria, W186; BLWt.14505-160-55
James, Va., S17166
Peter, S.C., R7553
Sherwood, N.C., S21394
William M., Va., Elizabeth, W5402
Zachariah, Cont., Va., S31272. See pension claim of his wid., Elizabeth Nance. She was allowed pension as former wid. of Lewis Bingley, Va., which see. Much family data on file in this claim
NANNY, David, N.Y., Anna, W26570; BLWt.26871-160-55
NANTZ, Frederick, Va. See NANCE
NAPIER, William P., Va., S15944
NARAMORE, Asa, See NAROMORE
Joseph, Mass., S18998

NARMIR, John H., N.Y., S43062
NAROMORE, Asa, Mass., Sally, W5399; BLWt.30917-160-55
NARRAMORE, Asa, See NAROMORE
John, S.C., S4598
NASH, Abner, Mass., Sally, W1309; BLWt.7080-160-55
Anna, former wid. of John Herrick, Mass., which see
Benjamin, Cont., Mass., S33149
Benjamin, Privateer, Mass., BLWt.13188-160-55
Caleb, Mass., S41026
Daniel, Ct., S11130
Ephraim, Mass., Hannah, W15695
Francis, N.C., BLWt.1602-850. Brig. Gen. Iss. 1/24/1797 to Sarah Waddell only dau. & heir-at-law of F.N. No papers
Griffin, N.C. res. in 1844, R7557
Jacob, Mass., S18138; BLWt.13435-160-55
Jacob, Mass., S29998
James, Mass., S45031
James, Mass., Anna, W24326
Job, Cont., Mass., Nancy, W5403; BLWt.8180-160-55
Joel, Ct., S9983
John, Mass., S22918
John, Mass., S23332
John, N.Y., S14003
John, Va., S38254
John, Va., Elizabeth, R7555
Jonathan, Ct., Eunice, W10778
Jonathan, Mass., S31273
Jonathan, Mass., Lydia, W8482
Joseph, Ct., S29344
Joseph, Mass., S29343
Luke, Cont., Mass., S33150
Michael, N.C., S.C., Nancy, W4042
Moses, Mass., Rachel, W15113
Noah, Ct., Ann, W26568; BLWt. 34976-160-55
Peter (colored), Lydia, Ct., R7558
Samuel, Mass., Navy, S18521
Sarah, former wid. of John Hughan/Hugan, N.Y., which see
Silas, Ct., Hannah Tyrer, former wid., W608; BLWt.28545-160-55
Thomas, Mass./Thomas Nash HUNTER, S41913
Thomas, Mass., Betty, W15111
Timothy, Mass., S18997
William, N.C., b. Va., S4597. See N.A. Acc. No.874-050122. Not Half Pay, William Nash.
William, Pa., Sarah, R7560
NASON, Benjamin, Mass., S22415
David, Mass., Abigail Weaver, former wid., W22573
Edward, Cont., Mass., Polly, W2325; BLWt.3394-160-55
Jacob, Mass., Ruth, W26569
John, Mass., S14005
John, Mass., S28822
Jonathan, Mass., S37268
Joshua, Mass., Betty, W24324
Nathaniel, Mass., S36703; Lost BLWt.895-200; BLWt.2401-200. Iss. 8/22/1846 in behalf of

NASON (continued)
Asenath Canney, Special Act of Congress
Stephen, Mass., Navy, S45032
Willaby, Mass., Mary, W15112
NATION, Daniel, Pa., BLWt.10164. Iss. 3/8/1792 to Robert Connoll, Adm. No papers
Joseph, N.C., Jereter, W5398
NAUGHTON, Solomon, N.Y., S21987
NAVE, John, Not Rev. War, Indian War 1791; BLWt.42628-160-55
NAY, John, Va., S11128
John Jacob/Jacob, Va., S9438
Samuel, N.H., S18137. See N.H. Agcy. Book & list of pensions of Rockingham Co., N.H., printed in 1835. Sold. was a Pvt. N.H. Mil. Age 72 yr. Annual pension $32.99. Ctf. No.832 iss. 10/19/1832 under Act of 7 June 1832.
Samuel, N.H., Mercy, R7561
Samuel, Va., R7563
NAYLOR, Joshua, Md. See NAILOR
NAYSON, Jonathan, Mass. See NASON
Nathaniel, Mass. See NASON
NEAGLE, Morris, Md., BLWt.11564. Iss. 12/22/1794 to Henry Purdy ass. No papers
Richard, See NAGLE
NEAGLES, Michael, See EAGLES
NEAGUS, Benjamin, R.I., Cynthia, W5413; BLWt.40702-160-55
NEAL, Andrew, Mass., S41921
Andrew, N.H., Eleanor, W21839
Basil, Va., Indian disturbances before & after Rev., Sarah H.; BLWt.81555-160-55
Benjamin, Va., Delilah, W10220; BLWt.56951-160-55
Charles, Cont., Va., Ann, W9587
George, See O'NEAL
James, S.C., Sarah, W26574; BLWt.13010-160-55
James, Va., S38257
John, Md., N.J., Margaret Smith, former wid., W19054
John, N.H., S36704
John, S.C., R7565
John, Va., S5810
John, See NEIL
Jonathan, Mass., S29999
Joseph, Mass., S30000
Joseph, N.H., S11132
Joshua, N.H., S45034
Matthew, Ga., N.C., S.C., b. Va., S14004
Micajah, Va., Mildred/Milly, R7579
Samuel, Mass., Mary, W16144
Silence, former wid. of John Shaw, Mass., which see
Stephen, N.C., Rebecca, W6837; BLWt.14658-160-55
Thomas, Ct., Res. Pa., Hannah Wallace, former wid., W18269; BLWt.6235-100-Sgt. Iss. 7/8/1789
Thomas, Mass., Deborah, W25834
Thomas, N.J., BLWt.8596. Iss. 7/30/1791 to Andrew Porter, ass. No papers

NEAL (continued)
Thomas, Va., Elizabeth, W5407; BLWt.30919-160-55
Walter, Mass., N.H., S19409
William, Ct., S4599
Zephaniah, Va., S1863
NEALE, James, Cont., Mass., Mary, W13759; BLWt.1406-100. She was also pensioned as the former wid. of John Atkinson, Cont., Mass., which see
NEALEY, Andrew, N.H., S18528
Joseph, N.H., S45033
NEALLEY, Joseph, N.H. See NEALEY
NEALLY, Joseph, N.H., BLWt.3364. Iss. 5/27/1797? to Christopher S. Thorn, ass. No papers
NEALY, John, Ga., S.C., S31880
NEAR, Carl/Charles, N.Y., Catharine, W19913
Charles, N.Y., S11137
John, Pa., S38261
NEARING, Henry, Ct., Jane, W6839
John, Ct., S43071
Joseph, Ct., Julia, W6840; BLWt.26205-160-55
NEASE, George, N.C., Molly, R7570
Martin, N.C., b. Pa., S1776
NEDEAU, Baszill, See NADEAU
NEDSON, James, Ct., S36188
NEEDAR/EDER, Anthony/Toney Cont., Ct., Phillis, W7073; BLWt.19813-160-55
NEEDER, Henry, Hazen's Regt., BLWt.13548; iss. 6/28/1799 to Abraham Bell, ass. No papers
NEEDHAM, Benjamin, Mass., S23821
Daniel, Mass., S30614
Francis, Mass., S14007
Jeremiah, Mass., Ruth, R7571; BLWt.53751-160-55
John, Cont., Mass., S43070; BLWt.2392-100
John, Mass., Mary, W21840; BLWt.6111-160-55
Stearns, Mass., Hannah, BLWt. 18202-160-55
William A., Md. Agcy. Dis. No papers. See Am. State Papers Class 9, p.403, which shows this man was a Sgt. in the 4th Md. Regt. Ctf. dated 8/27/1794
NEEF, William, Mass., BLWt.4767 Iss. 8/31/1790 to Dudley Woodbridge. No papers
NEEL, John, N.C., b. Ireland, S1865
William, Va., S15945
NEELE, Andrew, N.H., S8917
NEELEY, Joseph, N.C., S31879
NEELY, Abraham, Cont., N.Y., Hannah, W25833; BLWt.1583-300-Capt. Iss. 9/30/1790. No papers
David, Hazen's Regt., BLWt.13545; iss. 4/26/1791. No papers
George, S.C., S4613
Jacob, N.C., S7264
John, N.Y., Margaret, W5408; BLWt.38524-160-55

NEELY (continued)
John, Pa., Nancy, W1064
John, S.C., S11140
John, Va., Sally, W26573; BLWts. 26513-160-55, 34916-160-55 cancelled
Robert, S.C., Jane, W5410
Samuel, Not Rev. War, Gen. Wayne 1792-1795. Pa. Agcy. Old War file 5822
NEER, Charles, N.Y., See Carl NEAR
NEESE, George, N.C., S7268
Lawrence, N.Y., S14008
Peter, Md., Pa., R7572
NEEVE, Daniel, Va., Mary, W8484
NEFF. Jacob, N.J., S4603
Oliver, Ct., R7573
NEFIES, Peter, See NEVIUS
NEGLES, Michael, See EAGLES
NEGRO, Caesar, See SHELTON
Caesar, See CLARK
Cato, See KENT
NEGUS, Benjamin, R.I., See NEAGUS
Isaac, R.I., S21395
John, Ct., Sea Service, Desire Baldwin, former wid., W17228
John, Vt., Lydia, W17397
Noles/Knowles, R.I., Sarah, W24333; BLWt.18026-160-55
Thomas, Mass. Sea Service, R.I. R7574
NEICELY, Samuel K. See NICELY
NEIDER, Henry/Henery, Cont., Pa., S41919
NEIGHBORS, Benjamin, S.C., b. Va., S19000
Nathan, Va., N.A. Acc. No.874-050123. Half Pay. See pension file of Nathan Nabors
NEIL, Daniel, Md., BLWt.11571. Iss. 3/11/1791. No papers
Daniel, N.J., BLWt.1804-300
Daniel, Va., BLWt.12438. Iss. 2/18/1793 to Robt. Means, ass. No papers
John, Va., Martha, W19918
Nicholas, Pa., BLWt.10147. Iss. 7/27/1789 to Richard Platt, ass. No papers
NEILL, Andrew, N.C., Mary, R7580
Gilbrath, N.C., Martha, W17400
James, N.C., S38256
James, Pa., BLWt.10150. Iss. 1/10/1799. No papers
James, Pa., S41918
John, N.C., Cynthia, R7578
Lewis, Va., S31276
NEILSON, Allen, N.Y. See NELSON
Andrew, Pa., BLWt.10154. Iss. 9/7/1789. No papers
John, N.J., S4607
John, N.Y. See NELSON
Joseph, Pa., S41920
NEITHERHOUSE, Daniel, Pa., BLWt. 10142. Iss. 3/2/1792 to Adam Harbison, ass. No papers
NEITZ, Philip, Pa., S4610
NELLES, William, N.Y., S5825
NELLIS, George, N.Y., Elizabeth, W21834
George H., N.Y., R7581
Henry W., N.Y. Dis. See Am.

NELLIS (continued)
State Papers. Class 9, p.94 which shows this sold. was wounded in 1776 in the breast by accident, while acting as a bugleman in exercising. Res. Palatine
John D., N.Y., R7582
John L., N.Y., S23820
Joseph, N.Y., S14017
William, N.Y., See NELLES
William, N.Y., Mary, R7583
NELMES, John E., N.C., S1864
NELMS, Charles, Cont., Va., S7262
NELSON, Abraham, N.C., Jennett, W865
Alexander, Va., S38259
Allen, N.Y., S43068; BLWt.7547-100. Iss. 12/15/1790, name spelled Neilson. No papers
Andrew, See NILSON
Benjamin, N.Y.(?), Vt.(?), S21396
Daniel, Navy, Me. Agcy. & res., Polly, W21841
David, Mass., S18526
Edward, N.C., S7266
Edward, N.C., R7587
Eli, N.Y., S28823
Enoch, Va., b. Pa., R7588
Francis, N.Y., S43067
George, Mass., Navy & Privateer, S14012
George, N.C., R21891
Giles, N.C., S7263
Hanse, N.C., Delila, W1462; BLWt.61198-160-55
Henry, Mass., BLWt.2057-200
James, Cont., Va., S5809
James, S.C., b. N.C., Margaret, W9588
Jane, former wid. of James Davenport, Va., which see
Jarrott, Va., S38959
John, Cont. Arty., BLWt.7554-100. Iss. 8/11/1790 to Dudley Woodbridge, ass. Also BLWt. 9555, Ky. Agcy.
John, Ct., N.Y., Amy, W24340
John, Cont., Va., Nancy, W5414; N.A. Acc. No. 874-050124 Half Pay
John, Md., BLWt.11568. Iss. 12/18/1794 to Henry Purdy, ass. No papers
John, Md., Catharine Milton, former wid., W7462
John, Md., BLWt.1592-200-Lt. Iss. 1/31/1795 to Joseph Nelson, Admr. Also recorded as above under BLWt.2650. No papers
John, Mass., S23334
John, N.C., S1707
John, N.C., Lucy, W53
John, N.C., R20131, see BLWt. 1601-400
John, N.C., BLWt.1601-400-Maj. Iss. to Alexander Nelson, ass. No papers
John, Pa., N.W. Indian War of 1790; S4601

NELSON (continued)
John, Va., b. 1757, S35537; BLWt.1598-300-Capt. Iss. 9/4/1792 to Andrew Duncomb, ass. No papers
John, Va., Sarah, S38958
John, Va., Ruth, W8486; BLWt. 13204-160-55
Joseph, N.H., Mary, W24338
Joseph, Va., S32413
Mary, former wid. of Nathaniel Delavan, N.Y., which see
Moses, Cont., Mass., S41030
Moses, N.Y., Dolly, R7586
Moses, N.C., S4616
Moses, N.C., Va., b. Pa., Catharine, R7585; BLWt.40925-160-55
Nathan, Mass., S18524
Paul, N.Y., Hannah, W19914
Paul, N.Y., Vt., S14016
Philip, Cont., Mass., S23819
Reuben, N.Y., S14009
Robert, See NILLSON
Roger, Cont., Md., Eliza, W1310; BLWt.1600-200-Lt. Iss. 12/23/1790. No papers
Samuel, N.C., S8916
Thomas, Crane's Cont. Arty., Mass., BLWt.4775. Iss. 5/20/1789. No papers
Thomas, N.H., Vt., S29345
Thomas, Lamb's Arty., N.Y., BLWt.7553. Iss. 9/9/1790 to Patterson, et al, ass. No papers
Thomas, S.C., b. N.C., R7592
Thomas, Va., R7593
William, Cont., Mass., Sea Service, S19004
William, Cont., Pa., S41917
William, N.Y., Eunice, R7589
William, N.C., S4615
William, N.W. Indian War. Sarah. Old War Inv. File No. 48225; Old War Wid. File 10803
William, Pa., S5820
William, S.C., R7594
William, S.C., R7595
William, Va., Mary, W21838
NEPHEW, Mathias, N.J., S22920
NESBET, Robert. See NESBIT
NESBETT, John, N.C., Ctf. No. 19516 Act of 1832. See 1835 list Dickson Co., Tenn. Case could not be found under any spelling when searched 9 May 1940
NESBIT, Henry, Del., BLWt.10855. Iss. 4/21/1791. No papers
Robert, N.J., S5826
NESLER, John, N.J. See NESTLER
NESMITH, Benjamin, N.H., S7544
James, N.H., S17603
James, N.H., S45035
NESSLE, Conrod/Conrad, N.Y., Lovina/Levina, R7597
John, N.Y., R7598
NESTELL, George, Lamb's Art., N.Y. BLWt.7551; iss. 10/4/1790 to Meyndert Ten Eyk, ass. No papers

NESTELL (continued)
Martin, N.Y. See NESTLE
NESTER, Frederick, N.C., S1572
Michael, N.J., S902
NESTILL, Peter, Col. Lamb's Arty. BLWt.1587-200-Lt. Iss. 9/9/1790 to Leonard Fisher, ass. No papers
NESTLE, Gotlieb, N.Y., Dis. No papers. See Am. State Papers, Class 9, p.94, which shows this sold's. res. as Palatine and that he was wounded, 1777, in his eye by the oversetting of a baggage wagon on a march.
Martin, N.Y., Catharine, W16354
NESTLER, John, N.J., S40196; BLWt.1542-100
NESTOR, John, N.J., BLWt.8603. Iss. 3/6/1797. No papers
John, N.J., Phebe, W15932
NESTY, John, N.J. See NESTOR
NETHERLAND, Benjamin, Ga., Va., Theodocia, W8487
NETHERTON, John, Va., Rebecca, W5416; BLWt.43519-160-55
NETTERFIELD, William, Pa., Mary, W569
NETTLE, Abraham, Va., Mary, W5406
NETTLES, William, S.C., b. Va., Amelia, R7599
NETTLETON, Benajah, Ct., R7601
Caleb, Ct., Lois, W2659
John, Ct., S14020
Josiah, Ct., S36187
Nathan, Ct., S11133
William, Ct., Zillah, W17399
NEU, Peter See NAI
NEUFVILLE, William, S.C., BLWt. 2056-400
NEVEL, Henry, Pa., S41916
John, N.J., R7605
NEVELL, John, Cont., See NEWELL
NEVENS, David, See NEVINS
James, Mass., Joanna, R7603
NEVES, Daniel, See NEEVE
William, Md., Va., R7604
William, Va., S4600
NEVET, John, Md. See NEVITT
NEVIL, Thomas, Va., S1573
NEVILL, James, Va., S38260
Jesse, N.C., S.C., b. Va., S21899
John, Va., S5827
John, Va., BLWt.1595-500-Col. Iss. 1/13/1800. No papers
Presley, Va., BLWt.1596-300-Capt. Iss. 3/31/1796. No papers
Yelvaton, N.C., S4614; BLWt. 26344-160-55
NEVILS, George, Va., Sarah, R7606
NEVINS, David, Ct., Cont., S14010
David, N.H., BLWt.824-100
Garret/Garett, N.J., S35010
John, N.J., R7608
NEVITT, John, Md., S41924; BLWt. 1035-100
Joseph, Md., S11136
NEVIUS, Peter, N.J., S561
NEW, Christopher, Pa., S40201

NEW (continued)
George W., Va., S30613
Jacob, Va., Mary, W8483
James, Mass., Anna, W13758
James L., Va., S16211
John, Mass., BLWt.4760. Iss. 1/9/1794 to Alexander Power. No papers
John, Mass., S18999
John, Va., Lucinda, R7610
Thomas, Va., S38258
William, N.C., S7267
William, N.C., Frances, W10802; BLWt.52779-160-55
William, Va., S5815
NEWALL, Calvin, Mass. See NEWHALL
NEWAN, Nehemiah, Pa., Cathrine, BLWt.1662-100. May be same as S43073
NEWANS, Nehemiah, Pa., See N.Y. 1818, S43073
NEWBEGIN, George, Mass., War of 1812, S19408
NEWBERREY, William, N.J., S4602
NEWBERRY, Amasa, Ct., S11131
James, Pa. See NEWBURY
NEWBERT, Christopher, Mass. See NEWBITT
NEWBIGGEN, George, See NEWBEGIN
NEWBITT, Christopher, Mass., Jane, R7611
NEWBURY, James, Pa., Sarah, W5412
Jeremiah, Ct., S43072
John, Mass., Lucy, R7613
Stedman, Ct., S14021
NEWBY, Francis, N.C., S41923
John, Pa., BLWt.10162. Iss. 7/6/1798. No papers
John, Va., S31275
Levi, Va., S7265
Matthew, N.C., BLWt.12439 & 13550. Iss. 14/8/1792 to Isaac Cole, ass. No papers
Thomas, Va., S5812
NEWCOMB, Azariah, Ct., R7614
Bethuel, Ct., Mabel, W26572
Bryant, Mass., S14014
Charles, Cont., Mass., Jerusha, W19910
Eleazer, Ct., S36186
Ethan, N.J., S18523
James, Mass., S19003
James, N.Y., W21835
Jeremiah, Mass., S11139
John, Mass., S17604
Julius, See NUCUM
Kinner, N.Y., BLWt.7546. Iss. 2/21/1792 to Wm. Campbell, ass. No papers
Kinner, N.Y., Olive, W5405
Lemuel, Mass., S33153
Lemuel, Mass., Lucy, W15121
Luther, Ct., Mass., Privateer, S18527
Simon, N.Y., S15542
Solomon, Va., BLWt.12437. Iss. 7/14/1792 to Robt. Means, ass. No papers
Solomon, See NUKUM
Thomas, Ct., Navy, Sylvia, R7615; BLWt.8388-160-55

NEWCOME, Samuel, Pa., S40200
NEWCOMER, Peter, Pa., S32412
NEWEL, Deborah, former wid. of John Herron, N.Y. res. 1826; which see
William, Del. See NEWIL
NEWELL, Benjamin, R.I., S4606
Catharine, former wid. of Stephen Saddor, Cont., N.Y., which see
Daniel, Ct., Nancy, W24328
Daniel, Cont., Mass., S15543
David, N.C., Ann, W19907
Ebenezer, Ct., S43066
James, Mass., Mary, W2326
James, N.J., S4611
John, Cont., Res. Pa. in 1818, Susannah, W10805; BLWt.3763-160-55 & 781-160-55
John, Mass., S14013
John, Pa., BLWt.10152. Iss. 8/7/1795 to James Decorcey, ass. No papers
Jonas, Pvt., Mass., BLWt.4748 iss. 2/24/1800 to Abigail O'Brian. No papers
Joseph, Cont., Mass., N.Y., R.I., Navy, S21898
Joseph, Mass., Ruth, W15116
Joseph, Mass., Ana, W15124
Lydia, former wid. of Ezekiel Williams, Ct., which see
Mark, Ct., S36190
Nathaniel, Ct., S14011
Norman, Cont., Ct., S40199
Riverius/Reverius, Cont., Enl. in Ct., Abigail, W805; BLWt. 34859-160-55
Robert, Ct., Cont., Lydia, W19917; BLWt.34915-160-55
Samuel, Mass., S5115
Samuel, Va., Jane, R7617
Seth, Ct., R7618
Stephen, Mass., S29347
Stephen, Mass., S30001
Theodore, Ct., Hannah, W5417; BLWt.14671-160-55
Thomas, Va., S5813
NEWELLE, Samuel, Va. See NEWELL
Thomas, R.I., BLWt.147-100
NEWENS, Nehemiah, Pa. See NEWANS
NEWHALL, Calley, Mass., S30616
Calvin, Mass., S33152; BLWt. 688-100
Daniel, Mass., S30002
Daniel Allen Breed, Mass., Sarah, W15123
Elisha, Mass., Privateer, Rebecca, W21833
Ezra, Mass., BLWt.1574-450-Lt. Col. Iss. 5/18/1790. No papers
James, Mass., S30617
James, Mass. See NEWELL
Joshua, Ct., Cont., Navy, S36189
Josiah, Mass., S45036
Oliver, Mass., S18522
Onesimus, Mass., Navy, S22416
Timothy, Navy, Mass., S11138
William, Mass., Elizabeth, W15117
NEWHOUSE, Anthony, Pa., S40204
Eleanor, former wid. of Van

NEWHOUSE (continued)
Swearingen, Pa., which see
NEWIL, William, Del., S40203
NEWKEY, James, R.I., S17605
NEWKIRK, Charles, N.Y., Old Second Regt., BLWt.1586-200-Capt.-Lt. Iss. 7/23/1790. No papers
Cornelius, N.Y., S14006
Garret/Garrett, N.Y., Rachel, W24339
Henry, N.Y., R7622
Jacob, N.Y., S5811
Jacob, N.Y., Caty, W19912
John, N.Y., S11134
John, N.Y., S23333
William I., N.Y., R7623
NEWKUN, Solomon, See NUKUM
NEWLAND, David, Mass., S43064
Harrod, Pa., S16494
Israel, Cont., Mass., S43065
Jabez, Mass., R.I., Lydia, W19908; BLWt.2489-160-55
John, Va., BLWt.12436. Iss. 2/18/1793 to Robt. Means, ass. No papers
John, Va., S40197
Joseph, Mass., N.Y., S46061
Mathias/Matthew, Cont., Res. Pa., S46396; BLWt.1441-100
Matthew, See Mathias
NEWLUN, William, Va., R7624
NEWMAN, Abner, Va., S38255
Abraham, Ct., N.Y., Lucinda, W24332
Austin, S.C., Elizabeth, R7625
Ebenezer, Cont., Mass., Sally, W24336
Edmund, Va., S1571; BLWt.26352-160-55
Edmund, Va., Mary, W9214
Ezekiel, N.Y., S19407
George, Cont., Va., S5814
Isaac, N.Y., S11135
Jacob, Pa., S2010
Jacob, Pa., S4604
James, N.Y., R7627
John, Cont., Md., S25329
John, Ga., S1299
John, Md., S35008
John, Mass., BLWt.4751. Iss. 3/7/1792. No papers
John, Mass., Deborah, W21836; BLWt.1638-100
Jonathan, Ct., Lucy, W5418; BLWt.44507-160-55
Jonathan, Mass., Elizabeth, W24327
Jonathan, N.Y., S40202
Joseph, Mass., N.Y., Elizabeth, R7626
Joseph, Va., BLWt.12435. Iss. 7/14/1792 to Robt. Means, ass.; no papers
Joseph, Va., S46546
Joshua, Md. See NEWNAM
Josiah, Mass., Abigail, W24335; BLWt.6395-160-55
Nathan, Mass., S5116
Owen, Va., BLWt.12429. Iss. 11/5/1789. No papers
Owen, Va., R7630
Reubin/Reuben, N.C., Sabra,

NEWMAN (continued)
W10812; BLWt.19921-160-55
Rufus, Ct., Polly, W1461
Samuel, Mass., BLWt.837-100. Iss. 12/24/1819
Thomas, Md., BLWt.11558. Iss. 1/8/1796 to George Ponsonby, ass.
Thomas, Fifer, Mass., BLWt.4753. Iss. 8/14/1789. No papers
Thomas, N.H., S41915
Thomas, N.C., BLWt. Reg.229580 Act 3/3/1855. No pension claim
Walter, Pa., Elizabeth, W2230
William, Cont., N.H., S41029
William, N.J., BLWt.8602. Iss. 6/11/1789 to Mathias Denman, ass. No papers
Zadoc, Ct., S15544
NEWMANN, Philip, Cont., Pa., S5114
NEWNAM, Joshua, Md., R7631
NEWPORT, Abraham, Mass., S33151
Dan, Mass., BLWt.4761. Iss. 1/23/1799 to Thomas Hull, ass. No papers
NEWSAM, Jacob, N.C. See NEWSOM
William, Va. See NEWSUM
NEWSOM, Jacob, Va., Lucy/Polly, W4749
John, Va., also served 1789-93, R7632
Randolph, N.C., S14019
NEWSOME, William, Va., S5808
NEWSON, Hardy, N.C., Mary Pearce, former wid., W10225
NEWSUM, William, Va., S4612
NEWTON, Abraham, N.C., S4605
Asahel/Versalle/Verselly, Ct., W15696
Basil, Md., Mary Hall, former wid., W10074
Benjamin, Mass., N.Y., S14015
Benjamin, N.C., S16493
Benjamin, N.C., Nancy, W21837
Calvin, Mass., Betsey, W19909
Daniel, Mass., Elizabeth, W19915
David, Ct., R7633
David, Mass., Dis. No papers. See Am. State Papers, Class 9, p.136, which shows this man disabled 9/1776, near N.Y. He was overcome by the heat in retreating to Haarlem Hghts. near N.Y. which occasioned universal weakness in all his limbs.
Ebenezer, Mass., Sally, W15122
Edward, Mass., Betty Gale, former wid., BLWt.61264-160-55
Edward, N.C., R20410
Elias, Ct., Alice, W4298
Ephraim, Mass., Abigail (Nabby) W17398
Francis, Cont., Mass., Eleanor, W15118
Gideon, Mass., S22417
Gideon, Mass., Vt. res. 1819, S41027
Hananiah, Cont., Mass., S40198
Hannah, former wid. of Jesse Kinney/Kenney, Mass., which see
Henry, Va., S20893

NEWTON (continued)
Hezekiah, Mass., S19740
Israel, Ct., S19002. BLWt.1963-160-55
Ithamar, Cont., Mass., Elizabeth, W20275
James, Ct., S22919
Jason, Mass., Susannah, W1985
Jeremiah, Mass., S30615
Joel, Ct., S23336
John, Ct., S17602
John, Md., S35009
John, Mass., S19005
John, Mass., Abigail, W9589. See N.A. Acc. No.874-050125. Not Half Pay, John Newton
Jonah, Mass., S43069
Joseph, Ga., N.C., Ann, R7635
Josiah, Mass., Elizabeth Rice, former wid., W27477
Marshall, Mass., Lydia, W19911
Mary, dau. of John Jordan, Ga. or Va., wife's name Winnifred, see John Jordan, Ga.
Moses, Mass., S31274
Moses, Mass., Elizabeth, W24330
Moses, S.C., BLWt.12440 & 13543. Iss. 5/26/1794. No papers
Paul, Cont., Mass., S5117
Robert, N.C., S30618
Samuel, Mass., S23335
Samuel, Mass., S41028
Samuel, Mass., S41922
Samuel, Mass., Sarah, W20276
Shadrach, Mass., Mary, W19916
Silas, Mass., Lovina, W15119
Silas, N.J., BLWt.8598. Iss. 9/7/1790 to Wm. Barton, ass. No papers
Simon, Mass., The discharge cft. of Corp. Simon Newton of the 5th Mass. Regt. showing 3 yrs. service, signed Ezra Newhall, Lt. Col., dated at Soldiers Fortune 1/1/1780 is on file but there is no claim for said sold. Said discharge is locked up for safe keeping.
Stephen, Mass., Susanna, W15120
Thomas, N.J., BLWt.8601. Iss. 11/16/1791 to Adam Nutt, ass. No papers
Timothy, Mass., Vt., Abigail, W24334
Timothy, N.H., BLWt.3354. Iss. 3/25/1790. No papers
William, Md., BLWt.11559. Iss. 6/11/1790. No papers
William, N.J., S903
William, N.C., Margaret, R7636
William, Va., Martha, R7637
NEX, Overton, See PEONIX
NEY, Christopher, See NEW
NIBARGER, Christian, Va., S16212
NIBLACH, John, N.J., Dis. No papers. See Am. State Papers, Class 9, p.100 which shows this sold. was wounded in the head in an action with the enemy at Rye, State of N.Y. on 10/20/1776; by means of which wound he has lost the sight of an eye,

NIBLACH (continued)
and part of the skull bone, which has so far injured him as to prevent his supporting himself and family by manual labor.
NIBLET, William, Md., BLWt.11566. Iss. 6/10/1789. No papers
William, Md., S35011
NICCOLS, William, N.C. See NICHOLS
NICE, John, Pa., BLWt.1590-300-Capt. Iss. 4/3/1799. No papers
Magnus, R.I., BLWt.3367. Iss. 1/5/1791. No papers
William, Pa., S40205
NICELY, Jacob, Va., S46335
Samuel K., Va., S15946
NICHELS, Joel, N.C., S5120
John, Mass., S31277
Josiah, N.Y. See NICHOLS
NICHLESTON, James, See NICKLESTON
NICHOL, Daniel, Ct., S11141
John, See NICKLE
NICHOLAS, Christian, See NICHOLS
George, Pa., S4618
Henry, Pa., Mary Magdalene, R7641
John, French, See NICHOLS
John, N.Y., R7640
John, Va., S5829
John, Va., S46397 & Va. Half Pay, BLWt.1386-300
Jonathan, Cont., N.J., S35014
Joseph, See HAWWAWAS, an Indian
Lewis, Commanding the Corp. of Invalids. BLWt.1588-500-Col. Iss. 2/27/1790. No papers. This officer's correct name is NICOLA. See all reference books.
Stephen, N.Y., BLWt.7545. Iss. 2/14/1791 to James Talmadge, ass. No papers
William, Pa., Hannah, W4751
NICHOLDS, John, See NICHOLS
NICHOLES, Leaven, Pa., Va., b. in Md., S9440
NICHOLLS, Daniel, Ct. See NICHOL
John, Mass., S41031
Nehemiah, Del. See NICKOLLS
Samuel, Del. See NICKOLLS
NICHOLS, Aaron, N.H., Sarah, W21842
Adam, Cont., Mass., N.H., S35538
Alpheus, Mass., S33160
Ambrose, Mass., Sarah, R7659
Andrew, N.H., S35015
Asa, Mass., S15947
Bela, Cont. Mass., Dorcas, W24343; BLWt.3639-160-55
Benjamin, Cont., Mass., Sea Service, Rebecca, W15128
Benjamin, N.J., N.Y., R7650
Caleb, Mass., Lydia, W15126
See HAWWAWAS, Capt. (an Indian), Nicholas
Charles, Va., BLWt.12433. Iss. 2/15/1799. No papers
Charles, Va., S38264
Christian, Pa., Susannah, W2842
Daniel, Ct., S36191
Daniel, Ct., Esther, W17402

NICHOLS (continued)
Daniel, Ct., R7643
David, Mass., S22419
David, R.I., Mary, W24342
Ebenezer, Ct., Martha, W2231
Ebenezer, Mass., Elizabeth, BLWt.56856-160-55
Eleazer, Mass., Betsey, W21843
Eleazer, Mass., Elizabeth Durfee, former wid., W27509. She was also pensioned on acct. of services of her last husb., Joseph Durfee, Mass., which see
Eli, Ct., S14024
Eli, Ct., S43076
Eli, Lamb's Arty., N.Y., BLWt. 7556. Iss. 7/16/1790 to William I. Vreedenburgh, ass. No papers
Elnathan, Ct. & Vt. res. Dis. No papers
Ely, Ct., Cont., S22418
Enos, Ct., S14025
Ephraim, Ct., S23340
Fortunatus, Mass., S30621
George, R.I., Susan/Susanna, W26575
Hannah, former wid. of Israel Ingalls, N.H., which see
Hugh, Hazen's Regt., BLWt. Iss. 11/26/1795 to Christian Hubbard, ass. No papers
Humphrey/Humphry, Cont., N.H., Ruth, W24351
Humphrey, Mass., Margaret, W21844, BLWt.3525-160-55
Isaac, Cont., Mass., Dorcas, W24350
Isaac, Cont., N.Y., Elizabeth, W1986; BLWt.19904-160-55
Isaac, N.H., BLWt.1579-200 Lt. Iss. 11/19/1792 to Abijah Bond, ass. of Wm. Hyde, ass. of I.N. No papers
James, Ct., R7645
James, Ct., Navy, R.I., S40206
Jesse, Ct., S11142
Jesse, Mass., Betty, W15127
Jesse, N.Y., S11143
Joel, N.C. See NICHELS
John, Ct., S23338
John, Ct., Mary, W2685
John, Cont., Mass., N.H., Esther, W24349
John, French, Pa. Agcy. & res., S23823. Name also spelled Canous/Kanouse & Nicholas
John, Mass. See NICHELS
John, Mass., Elizabeth, W15125
John, Mass., Sarah Ball, former wid., W23526. Her second husb. was also pensioned. See Joseph Bull, Mass.
John, Mass., R7646
John, Mass., Phebe, R7657
John, N.H., BLWt.3361. Iss. 3/25/1790. No papers
John, N.H., S23337
John, N.Y., BLWt.7544. Iss. 5/3/1791 to James Brebner, ass. No papers
John, N.C., R7648

NICHOLS (continued)
John, Va., BLWt.1474-100
Jonas, Mass., S23824
Jonathan, Ct., Cont., S39829
Jonathan, Mass., Prudence, S5121; BLWt.84065-160-55
Jonathan, Mass., S33159
Jonathan, N.H., Phene (Sacket) W16662
Jonathan, N.J., BLWt.8605. Iss. 6/11/1789 to Matthias Denman, ass. No papers
Jonathan, N.J., S40211
Joseph, Ct., Nancy, R7655
Joseph, Mass., Thankful, W30009
Joseph, N.H., Hannah Isham, former wid., W20159. Her 2nd husb., Daniel Isham, Ct., was pensioned which see
Joseph, N.C., Elizabeth, R7644
Joshua, Mass., S33158
Joshua, N.C., S32414
Josiah, N.Y., Sarah, W5421
Josiah, N.Y., Nancy Ann, R7656
Julius, N.C., R7661
Levi, Mass., R7653
Mansfield, Cont., Ct., S41032
Martin, R.I., S23339
Moses, Del., BLWt.10852. Iss. 1/13/1792 to William Lane, ass. No papers
Moses, Mass., S30622
Nathan, Mass., S43080
Nathaniel, Mass., Zebiah, W21845
Nathaniel, R.I., Mehitable, W24348 BLWt.26602-160-55
Noah, Ct., Cont., N.H., Abigail, W21847
Peter, Mass., Molly, W21846
Philip, Ct., Abiah, W17403
Reuben, Ct., Abiah Lewis, former wid., W21566
Reuben, R.I., S14023
Richard, Pa., S7271
Robert, Ct., Cont., S40209
Samuel, Ct., Sibbel, W5419; BLWts.6239-100 & 182-160-55
Samuel, Mass., Navy, S37269
Samuel, R.I., Mary, W24346
Samuel, Vt., S14022
Silvanus, Ct., S14027
Simeon, N.Y., BLWt.47989-160-55
Stiles, Ct., Phebe, W26576
Thaddeus, N.H., Vt., S18529
Thomas, Cont., Mass., S33157
Thomas, Cont., Mass., Bathsheba, W24347
Thomas, Mass., S23822
Thomas, Mass., Dolly, W19921
Timothy, N.H., R20105
Wealthy, former wid. of Abiathar Dean, Mass., which see
William, Ct., S17607
William, Mass., S22420
William, Mass., S43075
William, N.J. See NICKELS
William, N.C., Elizabeth Barrett, former wid., W10381; BLWt.80033-160-55. Name also appears as Niccols/Nickol
William, N.C., Anna, W19919
William, N.C., Martha, R7654

NICHOLS (continued)
William, Pa., R7649
William, S.C., Reg. 233729-1855
Willibe, N.C., Va., b. N.C., S32415
Zadok/Zadock, Cont., Mass., Calista, W19920
Zepaniah, Va., b. Md., S9439
NICHOLSON, Boling, N.C., R7662
Charles, N.Y., Mary, R7664
Francis, Ct., BLWt.6242. Iss. 4/14/1790 to William Wells, ass. No papers
Francis, Ct., Rachel Weston, former wid., W6454
George C., N.Y., BLWt.1582-400-Maj. Iss. 10/5/1791 to Wm. Gilliland, admr. No papers
Henry, Md., BLWt.11561. Iss. 2/7/1790. No papers
Henry W., Va., R16768. Va. Half Pay. N.A. Acc. No.874-050126 Half Pay Henry W. Nicholson
James, See NICKLESTON
Jesse, Va., S5832
John, Md., BLWt.11569. Iss. 11/29/1790 or 1796 to Daniel Bulger, Admr. No papers
John, Md., BLWt.2362-100
John, N.J., Caty, W4750
John, N.C., S31882; BLWt.26113-160-55
John, Pa., BLWt.10153. Iss. 4/6/1790. No papers
John, Pa., S40208
Lavica, former wid. of Benjamin Kitchen, N.C., which see
Robert, N.C., S38263
Robert, Va., Elizabeth, W5422 & Va. Half Pay. N.A. Acc. No.874-050127 Half Pay Robert Nicolson/Nicholson
Thomas, Cont., Mass., S33155
William, Pa., BLWt.10145. Iss. 7/7/1789. No papers
William, Pa., S16989
William Beard, Cont. R.I., Sea Service, Marvel, W24345; BLWt. 30914-160-55
NICK, Henry, Pa., BLWts.10144 & 14065. Iss. 3/5/1794 to Eve Nick, Admx. No papers
John, Crane's Cont. Arty., Mass. BLWt.4778. Iss. 10/28/1791. No papers
Richard, Mass., Sea Service, Mary, W15130
William, Md. See KNICK
NICKALS, Simeon, N.Y. See NICHOLS
NICKEL, William, Pa., S22421
NICKELL, Isaac, Va., R7647
NICKELS, William, Cont., N.J., S40210
William, Mass., Hannah Redington former wid., W2695
NICKELSON, John, Md. See NICHOLSON
Luke, Mass., S37270
NICKEN, Richard, Navy, Va., S5830
NICKENS, James, Va., S38262
Malachi, N.C., S41925
NICKERSON, Daniel, R.I., S43078
Ebenezer, Mass., R7667

NICKERSON (continued)
Edward, Mass., Sarah, W17401; BLWts.22-100 & 6424-160-55
Enos, Mass., Deborah, W13770
Hezekiah, N.Y. See Issacher
Isabella, former wid. of Solomon Dyer, Mass., which see
Issacher/Hezekiah, N.Y., Jane, W2418; BLWt.38523-160-55
James, Mass., Azubah Snow, former wid., W15363
John, Mass., Deborah, W25837
Jonathan, Ct., S28824
Luke, Mass. See NICKELSON
Moses, Mass., S36706
Paul, Mass., S36705
Reuben, Cont., Mass., Lois, W24341
Salathiel/Salathel, Mass., S30003
Stephen, Mass., Levina, W26579; BLWt.28517-160-55
Uriah, Mass., Patience, W21849
NICKINS, James, Va. See NICKENS
NICKLE, Isaac, Va. See NICKELL
John, Md., S35013
NICKLESTON, James, N.C., S8918; BLWt.7295-160-55
NICKLISSON, Israel, N.Y., Mary, W15129
NICKOL, William N.C. See NICHOLS
NICKOLLS, Nehemiah, Del., BLWt. 2079-100
Samuel, Del., BLWt.2078-100
NICKOLS, John, See NICHOLS
Joshua, Mass. See NICHOLS
William/Joseph WEED, Cont., Mass., Sarah, W5420; BLWt. 8147-160-55
Zadock, Cont., Mass. See NICHOLS
NICOLA, Lewis, See NICHOLAS
NICOLAS, James, Pvt. "in the Invalids", BLWt.13555. Iss. 2/27/1790. No papers
NICOLLS, Simon, N.Y., Dis. No papers. See Am. State Papers, Class 9, p.94. He was injured 6/1776. Had his thigh broken by a baggage wagon going over him, on a march.
Simon, N.Y., S43077
NICOLS, William, Pa. See NICHOLS
NICOLSON, Robert, Va. See NICHOLSON
William/William Nicolson de CRABOURNE, Navy, Scotland, R78 1/2
NIECE, Peter, See NEESE
NIEL, Gilbrath, See NEILL
Thomas, Ct., BLWt.6235. Iss. 7/8/1789. No papers
NIELE, Andrew, See NEELE
NIELL, John, N.C., b. Ireland, R7567
NIGH, Andrew, See NYE
Jacob, Pa., S31881
NIGHBERGER, Christian, See NIBARGER
NIGHT, Jacob, See NIGH
John, Va., R7672
NIGHTINGALE, Samuel, Mass., S33156

NIGHTINGALE (continued)
Timothy, Mass., S21398
NIGIS, William, Mass., BLWt.4768 Iss. 8/4/1790 to Moses Barker. No papers.
NIGUS, John, See NEGUS
NILES, Dan, Ct., S21397
David, Mass., BLWt.4770. Iss. 5/23/1795 to Samuel Rogers. No papers
David, Vt., S16213
Elisha, Ct., Naomi, W26577
Elisha, Mass., Lucy, W24344
Enoch, N.Y., S14026
Ephraim, Mass., S15546
Gaius, N.H., BLWt.3358. Iss. 2/16/1795. No papers
Gaius/Gains, N.H., Percy, W2320; BLWt.30916-160-55
Jehiel, Ct., S43074
Jeremiah, Cont., Mass., Abigail, W10817
John, Mass., Olive, W21848
Nathan, N.Y., S19008
Nathaniel, Ct., S36193
Nathaniel, Mass., Hannah, R7674
Peter, Mass., S15547
Robert, Ct. Sea Service, Privateer, S36194
Robert, R.I., S5828
Samuel, Mass., Lovina, W1463; BLWt.13733-160-55
Stephen, N.Y., R7673
William, Ct., S19006
NILLSON, Robert, N.C., Mary, W26571
NILSON, Andrew, Va., b. Pa., S31878
Edward, Pa., BLWt.10149. Iss. 6/10/1794 to Silas Hart, ass. No papers
NIMBLETT, Robert, Mass., S33154
NIMOCKS, Richard, Mass., Zerviah, R7675
NIMOX, Richard, Mass. See NIMOCKS
NIMS, Daniel, Mass., Lydia, BLWt.15401-160-55
Ebenezer, Mass., S30619
Eliakim, N.H., S11144
NINEMASTER, Michael, N.J., S827
NINNOUGH, Neil, N.J., BLWt.8597. Iss. 7/25/1789. No papers
NIPPER, George, Va., S38265
NIPPLE, Frederick, Pa., S22921
NISBET, Alexander, Pa., S22422
NISBETT, Robert, S.C., S4617
NISBITT, Joseph, N.Y., BLWt.7548 Iss. 8/28/1790 to Christopher Yates, ass. No papers
NITHERCUT, William, N.C., S35539
NITHINGTON, Jeremiah, See IVINGTON
NIVEN, Daniel, N.Y., BLWt.1585-300-Capt. Iss. 9/23/1790. No papers
NIVERSON, John, N.J., Sarah, R7676
NIVINGTON, Jeremiah, See IVINGTON
NIX, Edward, S.C. res. of wid. in 1854, Martha, R7677
George, Ga., S7269
James, S.C., R16495
John, S.C., S31683

NIX (continued)
John, Va., S30620
NIXON, Absalom, Cont., N.C., Edith, W3033
Andrew, Va., BLWt.2281-300
George, Del., S8919
Isaac, N.J., S35012
James, N.J., BLWt.8599. Iss. 10/17/1789 to John Pope, ass. No papers
John, Cont., Mass., Dis. No papers See Am. State Papers, Class 9, p.140. Rank Col. Wounded by a ball in his testicles whereby he was subjected to pain in his groin, and weakness in the lower limbs. Disabled 6/17/1776. Bunker Hill. Also recorded as Brig. Gen.
John, Va., S38960
Joseph, Cont., Mass., Nancy W., W20277; BLWt.19812-160-55
Richard, N.J., Dorothea, W5423
Robert, N.C., BLWts.13551 & 14131 Iss. 8/11/1795. No papers
Stephen, S.C., Martha, R7678
Thomas, Mass., S19007
Thomas, Mass., BLWt.1573-500-Col. Iss. 4/1/1790. No papers
William, N.J., Mary, W806
NOAKES, George, Va., R7679
NOBEL, Tahan, Cont., Green Mt. Boys, Mass. res. & Agcy., S33166
NOBLE, Abigail, former wid. of Timothy Hibbard, Ct., which see
Amos, Mass., S30007
Anthony, Mass., BLWt.4749. Iss. 3/14/1793 to Benj. Bailey. No papers
Anthony, Mass., S36709
Benjamin Eager. See Eager
Caleb, Mass., BLWt.1578-200-Lt. Iss. 5/8/1792 to Amos Muzzy, ass. No papers
Eager/Benjamin Eager, Mass., Molly, W13774
Elihu, Mass., S18531
Elijah, Ct., S36198
Gideon, Ct. "Invalids", BLWts. 6241 & 13553. Iss. 8/23/1796. No papers
Gideon, Ct., Lucy Hollister, former wid., W24445; BLWt.38532-160-55
Goodman, Ct., Sarah, R7681
Isaac, Mass., BLWt.4756. Iss. 2/24/1800. No papers
Jacob, Mass., Eunice, W21853; BLWt.12704-160-55
James, Mass., S19009
James, Va., S16991
John, Del., Jemima, W21856; BLWt. 10298-160-55
John, Mass., S21900
John, Mass., S45037
Luke, Cont., Vt., S14032
Lyman, Ct., Boat service on Lake Champlain. Elizabeth Whiting, former wid., W22613. Elizabeth Whiting applied for B.L. because of service of Wm. Whiting, which

NOBLE (continued)
see
Mark, Mass., BLWt.4750. Iss. 5/28/1792 to Israel Angell. No papers
Medad, Mass., Lydia, W24356
Nathan, Ct., S43092
Oliver, Mass., S11148
Paul, Mass., Hannah, W26584
Silas, Mass., Lucy, W19923
Stephen, N.H., BLWt.3365. Iss. 12/14/1793 to John Peck, ass. No papers
Stephen, Mass. Sea Service, N.H., S31884
Tahan, See NOBEL
Timothy, Mass., Sally, R7680
William, Ct., S43093
William, Mass., S23341
William, N.C., S38962
William, Pa., N.W. Indian 1791, Elizabeth, W4555
NOBLES, Azer, Ct., S4620
Hezekiah, N.C., Elsey/Elcey, W6844
Isaac, Mass., S38967
John, N.C., S8922
Jonathon, Cont., Mass., S33167
Lewis, S.C., Zelpha, W13771
Lewis Sanders/Sanders, S.C., R7683
Roswell, Ct., Anna, R7682
Sanders, See Lewis Sanders
William, S.C., S18142
NOBLET, Thomas, Pa., Ann, BLWt. 49469-160-55
NOBLIT, Samuel, Pa., S7273
NOCHS, Silvanus, N.H. See Sylvanus NOCKE
NOCK, Drisco, Mass., N.H., S18140
Jonathan, N.H. See NOCKS
NOCKE, Sylvanus/Silvanus, Cont., Mass., N.H., Hannah, W21855
NOCKS, Jonathan, Cont., Mass., N.H., Betty, W25838
NOE, Amos, N.J., S1089
James, N.J., S35016
John, Navy, Pa., S43087
Lewis, See NOWE
Marsh, N.J., S733
NOEL, Taylor, Va., S1240
Thomas, Va., S31278
NOELL, Richard, Cont., Va., Mary, W1465
NOESTEL, George, N.Y., Elizabeth W16664
NOLAND, James, N.C., Va., b. Md. Barbara, W9202
Jesse, N.C., S14039
Ledstone, N.C., S16992
Mathew, Va., R7684
William, S.C. See NOLEN
NOLEN, Ezekiel, Cont., Va., S9443
Shadrach, Ga., S.C., b. Va., S4622
William, S.C., 1795 to Va. & Ky. S30623. BLWt.39214-160-54
NOLF, George, Pa., Susanna, W3188
NOLIN, James, S.C., b. Va., S1708
John, Md., R7685
NOLOM, John, See NOLTER

NOLTE, John, See NOLTER
NOLTER, John, Cont., Pa., R7738; BLWt.249-100
NOLTON, John, See NOLTER
NOLTON, Nathan, Mass., Amittai, W24358
Robert, N.Y., S7272
NONEMACKER, James, Pa., R7686
NOONEY, James, Ct., Sarah, R7687
NOORSTRANT, Johannes/John, N.Y., Maria, R7688
NOOSTSTRANT, See NOORSTRANT
NORCROSS, Benjamin, N.J., BLWt. 8600. Iss. 9/10/1790 to John Norcross, Admr. No papers
John, Pa., S27257
NORCUT, Ephraim, Mass., S5122
Zenas, Mass., S5123
NORDYKE, Benajah, Ga., R7691
NORFLEET, Nathaniel, Va., R7692
NORGET, Dennis, Hazen's Regt., BLWt.13542. Iss. 8/3/1789 to Wm. I. Vreedenburgh, ass. No papers
NORK, Jonathan, N.H. See NOCKS
NORKETT, Dennis, Cont., N.Y., S43085
NORMAN, Basil, Md., BLWt.11565 Iss. 1/11/1796 to Joshua Ward, ass. No papers
Bazabeel/Bazebeel, Md., Fortune, W5429
Bazeleel, See Bazabeel
Benjamin, N.J., Hannah, W1065
John, Ct., Sea Service, R.I., S30006
John, Del., S32416
John, Mass., S36707
Joseph, Pa., S5833
Obediah/Obadiah, N.J., Margaret, W1636
Richard, S.C., R7695
Thomas, Va., Frances, W26580; BLWt.19917-160-55
William, Va., son of John, Hannah, W26583; BLWt.33772-160-55
NORRIS, Abner, N.C., Va., S1575
Andrew, N.H., R7696
Arnold/Arnald, Md., Elizabeth, W3710
Benjamin, N.H., S14038
Bethuel, N.J., S4619
Bezaleel, Va., Dragoons, BLWt. 12431. Iss. 5/5/1790 to Wm. I. Vreedenburgh, ass. No papers
Burrows, N.J., Catharine Hartshorn /Hartshorne, former wid., W143
Eliphalet, Cont., N.H., Huldah, W2158
George, Cont., N.J., S35017; BLWt. 1576-200-Lt. Iss. 10/12/1791 to John McCleland, ass. Also recorded as above under BLWt.2554. No papers
Henry, Navy, Ct., Desire, W17407
Jacob, Md., BLWt.1236-200
James, N.H., BLWt.3362. Iss. 3/25/1790. No papers
James, Cont., N.H., Ruth, W21857
John, Ct., Ruth, R7705
John, N.J., S14033

NORRIS (continued)
John, N.C., R7700
John, Va., Mary, W19930
Jonathan, N.H., Sobriety, W19924
Moses, N.H., Rachel, W19929; BLWt.5453-160-55
Nahor, N.C., Sally Ingram, former wid., R5484
Nathan, Mass., Jedidah, R7699
Patrick, S.C., S15198
Patrick, S.C., R7703
Peter, N.J., S4623
Richard, N.C., R7704
Samuel, Ct. Sea Service, Mass., Lucy, W13772
Samuel, Cont., Mass., N.H., Betsey, W15131
Samuel, N.H., Sally, R7706; BLWt. 3363-100. No papers
Shadrach, N.J., Sarah, W16357
Theophilus, N.H., S22426
Thomas, Ct. Sea Service, Sarah, W3445
William, N.C., S38963
William, N.C., Nancy, R7702
William, Va., S4621
William, Va., Elizabeth, R7697
Ziba, N.J., Cont., S4625
NORSTRANT, Johannes, See NOORSTRANT, John
NORSWORTHY, James, N.C., S38961
NORTH, Abi, former wid. of Justus Francis, which see
Abijah, Ct., Cont., Sarah, W2232; BLWt.28632-160-55
Anthony, Va., Martha, W5426
Caleb, Pa., S46389; BLWt.1589-450-Lt. Col. Iss. 8/19/1789. No papers
Daniel, Mass., BLWt.4765. Iss. 6/5/1789 to Edmund Fowle. No papers
Daniel, Mass., Marcy, W15132
George, Pa., Eliza, W5425; BLWt. 26025-160-55 & 1591-200-Lt. Iss. 8/19/1789. No papers
John, Mass., Ruth Barnum, former wid., W17226
John, S.C., R7707
Levi, Ct., Cont., S14041
Robert, N.Y., R7708
Samuel, Crane's Cont. Art., Mass., BLWt.4777. Iss. 8/10/1789 to Richard Platt. No papers
Seth, Ct., S36197
Simeon, Ct., S23342
Thomas, Va., S9442
William, Cont., Mass., S28829; BLWt.1575-300-Capt. Iss. 2/10/1795
William, Pvt., N.J., BLReg.216494-1855
NORTHALL, William, N.J., R7710
John, Ct. See NORTHUM
Jonathan, Ct., S14030
Samuel, Ct., Cont., S14034
NORTHAMMER, Jacob, Pa., R7711
NORTHCRAFT, Edward, Md., S8920
NORTHCUT, Francis, Ga., S21401
NORTHERN, Reuben, Va., S31279
Solomon, N.C., S38965
NORTHEY, David, Mass., Hannah, R7712
Eliphalet, Mass., Abigail, W21851
NORTHGATE, Abraham, Mass., BLWt. 4754. Iss. 6/22/1792 to Benj. Haskell. No papers
NORTHROP, Abijah, N.Y., Elizabeth Smith, former wid., R9719
Amos, Ct., S22424
Andrew, Ct., Clarina, W17410
David, N.Y., Abigail, W21852
Elijah, Ct., S36199
Gideon, Ct., Cont., S22922
Heth, Ct., Ann, W17408; BLWt. 26733-160-55
Isaac, Ct., BLWt.6244. Iss. 8/21/1789. No papers
Isaac, Ct., S36196
Joshua, Ct., Phoebe Blackman, former wid., W10419
Lemuel, Ct., S18530
Nathaniel, N.Y., R7713
NORTHRUP, David, R.I. See NORTHUP
Elija/Elijah, Mass., S43091
Ichabod, R.I. See NORTHUP
Joseph, Ct., Cont., S23826
Lucy, former wid. of Dan Hatch, Ct., which see
Stephen, Ct., N.Y., Rhoda, R7715
Willson, Ct., S43082
NORTHUM, Asa, Ct., Mass., S5834
John, Ct., S14040
Samuel, Ct. See NORTHAM
NORTHUP, David, R.I., S15549
Henry, Cont., R.I. Agcy., S38968
Henry, R.I., S21402
Ichabod, Pvt., R.I., BLWt.3368-100. Iss. 12/31/1789
Ichabod, R.I., Marcy, W20279
John, R.I., S21399
Nicholas, R.I., S21902
Stephen, Navy, R.I., S38970
Stukely, R.I., S38966
Sylvester/Silvester, R.I., S38964
Thomas, Mass., S14031
William, R.I., Waty, W5430; BLWt. 40715-160-55
Zebulon, R.I., S21901
NORTHWARE, George, N.Y., BLWt. 7549. Iss. 8/10/1790 to Stephen Lush, ass. No papers
NORTHWAY, George, Ct., S15548
Ozias, Ct., Sarah, W2419; BLWt. 27647-160-55
Zenas, Mass., Abigail, W2233; BLWt.21805-160-55
NORTHWEAR, George, See NOTEWIRE
NORTON, Aaron, N.Y. res. of heir in 1853, Martha, R----
Abel, Ct., Lucy, W17404
Abel, Ct., N.Y., S14042
Abraham, Ct., BLWt.6240. Iss. 7/14/1787. No papers
Abraham, Ct., S46429
Alexander, Va., Mary, R7725
Ambrose, Ct., BLWt.6237. Iss. 12/24/1789. No papers
Ambrose, Ct., Bethiah, W16356
Amos, Mass., N.H., Hannah, W2420; BLWt.13012-160-55
Azel/Asahel, Miss., S43089
Benjamin, Ct., Elsey. W2234;
NORTON (continued)
BLWt.1581-200-Lt. Iss. 10/16/1789 to Theodosius Fowler, ass. No papers
Benjamin, Ct., Ajubah, W4299
Benjamin, Mass., R.I., Betsey Babbett/Babbitt, former wid., W14256. Her other husb., Abijah Babbett/Babbitt, also served in the Rev. War
Charles, Ct., S28825
Christopher, N.Y., S11149
David, Ct., Lois, W16663
David, Ct., N.Y., S14036
Eber, Ct., R17717
Elias, Ct., S4624
Elihu, Mass., R7718
Elijah, Ct., Rebecca, W20278
Elijah, Mass., S41033
Elijah, Mass., R.I., Mary, W21854
Elnathan, Ct., Dis. No papers. See Am. State Papers, Class 9, p.153. This sold. wounded by a musket ball passing through his body, which occasionally caused delirium. Disabled 7/4/1779 at New Haven.
Elnathan, Ct., Ruth, W19926
Elon, Ct., BLWt.6238. Iss. 12/24/1789. No papers
Elon, Ct., S43090
Freeman, Navy, Mass., Privateer, Betsey, W10824
George, Md., S38969
George, N.Y., BLWt.7542. Iss. 9/23/1790. No papers
George, N.Y., S43088
Giles, Ct., S23952; BLWt.28524-160-55
Henry, Pa., BLWt.10148. Iss. 8/5/1796. No papers
Isaac, Ct., R7719
Isham, N.C., S7275
Jabez, Ct., BLWt.6246. Iss. 8/20/1796 to Asa Spaulding, ass. No papers
Jabez, Ct., S36195
James, Hazen's Regt., BLWt.13547. Iss. 1/11/1791. No papers
James, Pa., S40212
James, Va., Indian Wars 1786-1791, S38266; BLWt.38501-160-55
Jared, Ct., Sarah, W26585
John, Ct., Lucretia, W15134
John, Mass., S30004
John, Pa., S34451
John, Va., R7720
Jonathan, Ct., S14028
Joseph, Ct., S11146
Joseph, Mass., S28828
Joseph, Vt., Mary, W24355
Josiah, Mass., S37271
Josiah, N.Y., R7721
Levi, Ct., R7722
Maria, former wid. of Aaron Van Vliet, N.Y., which see
Martha, former wid. of Caleb Cornwall/Cornell, N.Y., which see
Martin, Vt., S22425
Nathan, Ct., Experience, W17405
Nathaniel, Mass., Hannah, W1464; BLWt.10252-160-55

NORTON (continued)
Nathaniel, Navy Privateer, Mass. S18141
Nathaniel, N.Y., S43084; BLWt. 1584-300-Capt. Iss. 9/17/1792. No papers
Noah, Mass., S32417
Noah, Mass., Love, W13776
Noah W., Ct., S17608
Obed, Mass., Navy, S30005
Oliver, Ct., Martha, R7724
Oliver, Ct., Susanna, R7726; BLReg.292115-1855
Ozias, Ct., S16990
Ozias, Ct., S17609
Patrick, Pa., BLWt.10141-100.Pvt. Iss. 6/20/1789. No papers
Rufus, Ct., BLWt.6236-100-Sgt. Iss. 7/14/1789. No papers
Samuel, Ct., Phebe, W26582
Samuel, N.H., S32418
Seba, Ct., N.Y., Margaret, W19927
Selah, Ct., Anne/Anna, W17409
Stephen, Mass., S16214
Stephen, Mass., S36708
Thode, N.Y., S5837
William, Ct., S43083
William, Hazen's Regt., BLWt.13546 Iss. 11/20/179?. No papers
William, Mass., Hannah, W27908
William, Pa., S40214
William, Pa., Jane, W4556
Zadock/Zadok, Ct., Vt., Anna, W19928
Zerah/Zera, Vt., Elizabeth, W1889; BLWt.26649-160-55
NORVEL, Enos, N.C., Elizabeth, W5428
NORVELL, George, Cont., Va., S38267
Henry Holdcraft, Va., S9441
Hugh H., Va., Margaret, R7716
Lipscomb, Va., S5835; BLWt.1599-200-Lt. Iss. 10/26/1795. No papers. Name spelled Norvel
NORVIL, George, Arty. Artificers, BLWt.13549. Iss. 4/11/1792. No papers
NORVILL, Enos, N.C. or Md.? See NORVEL
NORWAY, Esther, former wid. of Robert Lytle, N.Y., which see
NORWELL, Henry, Navy, Privateer, S19741
Hugh, See NORVELL
NORWOOD, Charles, Va., S35540
David, Mass., Elizabeth, W15729
Francis, N.H., S11147
George, N.C., S31885
John, N.C., Susannah, W4300
John, N.C., Clary, R7729
Moses, Cont., Mass., Abigail Brooks, W24359
Nathan, Mass., S33164; BLWt. 814-100
Stephen, Mass., Anna, R7728
Thomas, S.C., b. Va., S21400
NOSTRANT, Isaac, N.Y., Mary/ Polly, R10881
Johannes/John, See NOORSTRANT
NOTEWIRE, George, N.Y., Huldah, W19925
NOTHERN/DAVIS, Joseph, N.C., S7274
NOTHEY, David, Mass. See NORTHEY
NOTT, Abraham, Cont., Ct., Abigail, W10821
Epaphras, Ct., Cont., S14035
Hezekiah, Sheldon's Dragoons, Ct., BLWt.6243. Iss. 4/19/ 1790 to Gideon Goff, Ann Goff & Lydia Nott, heirs-at-law. No papers
Thomas, N.H., Green Mt. Boys, S5836
NOTTINGHAM, Stephen, N.Y., Ann, W15790
Thomas, N.Y., S43081
William, N.Y., R7732
NOURSE, James, Pvt. "in the Invalids". BLWt.13556. Iss. 12/23/1796 to James Nourse. No papers
James, Mass., Elizabeth, W15133
Joseph, Cont., D.C. Agcy. & res., Maria L., W24161
William, Navy, S.C. Sea Service, Rebecca P., W6845; BLWt.34836-160-55
NOWE, Lewis, N.Y., BLWt.7541. Iss. 9/3/1790. No papers
Lewis, N.Y., S34450
NOWEL, Josiah, N.C., S38971
NOWELL, James, Md., S25331; BLWt. 643-100
Jonathan, Cont., Mass., S37273
Mark, Mass., Navy, S28827
Paul, Mass., S37272
Samuel, Privateer, Mass., S45038
Zachariah, Mass., S28826
NOWLAN, John, N.J., S1088
John, Pa., S40213
NOWLAND, John, Pa., BLWt.10156. Iss. 11/10/1791 to John McClelland, ass. No papers
NOWLEN, James, Va. res. of wid., Ursula, R7733
John, N.J. See NOWLAN
NOWLIN, James, Va. See NOWLEN
NOYCE, Dudley, Mass., BLWt.4752 Iss. 3/1/1792 to Joseph Brown. No papers
NOYES, Aaron, Mass., S29349
Bela, Cont., Mass., Elizabeth, W24354
David, Mass., S29350
Dudly/Dudley, Cont., Mass., Sally, W24352; BLWt.6282-160-55
Eliphalet, Mass., BLWt.4773. Iss. 8/24/1796 to Benjamin Dana. No papers
Eliphalet, Cont., Mass., S33162
Gersham/Gershom, Vt., S14037
Isaac, N.H., S18139
John, Ct., BLWt.1580-400-Surg. Iss. 5/29/1789 to John Noyes. No papers
John, Mass., Zibeah/Zibiah/ Zebial, W24353
Jonathan, Mass., BLWt.4771. Iss. 12/3/1789. No papers
Jonathan, Mass., S23825
Joseph, Mass., S33165
Joseph, R.I., S15948
NOYES (continued)
Matthew, Mass., S29351
Moses, Mass., Nabby/Abigail, W24357
Nathaniel, R.I., Tempy Cadwell/ Tamar Caldwell, former wid., W25386
Oliver, R.I., Eunice, R7734
Olivor/Oliver, N.H., S8921
Samuel, Mass., N.H., R7736
Sanford/Santford, Privateer, R.I., Martha, W26581; BLWt. 24701-160-55
Silas, Mass., S33161
Simeon, Cont., Mass., S33163
Timothy, Mass., S20489
Wadleigh, Mass., BLWt.1808-200
William, N.Y., BLWt.7543. Iss. 7/16/1790 to Philip V. Cortlandt, Admr. No papers
William, Privateer, R.I., Mary, W10823; BLWt.59211-160-55
NOYS, Eliphalet, Cont., Mass., See NOYES
NUCKOLLS, Richard, Va., S4627
NUCOM, Solomon, Va. See NUKUM
NUCUM, Julius, Va., S38957
NUDD, Samuel, N.H., Hannah, W15138
William, N.H., S11151
NUGEN, John, Ct., BLWt.2242-100, and S----
NUGENT, John, Ct., Elizabeth, W26586
NUGEON, John, Ct. See NUGENT
NUKUM, Solomon, Va., Susannah, W973; BLWt.19708-160-55
NULFF, George, See NOLF
NULL, Catharin, former wid. of John Myers, Pa., which see
NULTON, John, See NOLTER
NUMAN, Joseph, See NEWMAN
NUN, Thomas, Va., S1576
NUNALLY, Daniel, Va., R7740
NUNELEY, Henry, Va., S4626
NUNGESSER, John George, Pa., Catharine, R7739
NUNLEY, John, Cont., Va., BLWt.1-100
NUNN, Thomas, Va., S5842
Wharton, Va., Elizabeth, W974
William, N.C., Elizabeth, W17411
NUNNALLY, Daniel, Va. See NUNALLY
John, Va., Suckey, W5432
Moses, Va., R21847
Obadiah, Va., Elizabeth, W4301
William, Va., S5844
NUNNALY, Israel, Va. See NUNNELLEY
NUNNELEE, Edward, Va., Mary A., W176; BLWt.34914-160-55. she was also pensioned as former wid. of Nathaniel Sunderland, Pvt. 39th U.S. Inf. Papers inside
James F., Va., Jane, R16796
NUNNELLEY, Israel, Va., Margaret, R7741. See her claim as former wid. of Miles Gibson, Va.
NUNNELLY, Edward, See NUNNELEE
NUNNERY, Amos, N.C., S8923
NUNNILEE, James, See NUNNELEE
NURSE, Aaron, Cont., Mass., S33168

NURSE (continued)
Lawson, Mass., S30008
Rogers, Mass., S30009
NURSS, Caleb, Mass., Vt., S22427
Daniel, Mass., S5127
Timothy, Mass., Experience, W15136
NUTE, John, N.H., Sarah Knowles, former wid., W26766
Jotham, N.H., BLWt.3357. Iss. 8/26/1796 to Joshua Pickering, ass. No papers
Jotham, N.H., Sarah, W24360
Samuel, Cont., N.H., Sarah, W16051
NUTING, Joseph, Mass., BLWt.4772. Iss. 2/27/1790 to Theodosius Fowler. No papers
NUTMIRE, Hendrick, Sheldon's Dragoons, Ct., BLWt.6248. Iss. 4/2/1793. No papers
NUTT, John, Mass., N.H., R7743
Rhodam, Va. res. in 1834, R7745
William, N.H., Lucy, W10829; BLWt.40717-160-55
William, N.H., Mary, R7744
NUTTER, Anthony, N.H., S18143
Christopher, Va., Rebecca, W5434; BLWt.26388-160-55
David, Del., Elizabeth, R7746
Ebenezer, N.H., S11152
John, N.H., S11150
John, N.J., S43094
Mark, N.H., BLWt.3356. Iss. 11/28/1789. No papers
Robert, Del., Sarah Nutter, former wid., R7747
NUTTING, Abel, Mass., Rhoda Green former wid., W25656; BLWt. 24157-160-55
Amos, Mass., S33171
Daniel, Mass., Molly, W15135
Ebenezer, Cont., Mass., S33170
Eleazar/Eleazer, Mass., S41034
Elijah, Mass., Susanna, W15139
Jacob, Cont., Mass., S33169
John, Mass., S41926
John, Mass., Catharine, W2421; BLWt.30915-160-55
John, Mass., Sea Service, Jane, W26587
Jonathan, Mass., Susannah, W15137
Samuel, Mass., Sarah Tarbell, former wid., W2378; BLWt.10023-160-55. Her last husb., William Tarbell, Mass., was pensioned, which see
Thomas, Mass., Patty, W21858
NUTTLE, Charles, Pa. Sea Service, Rachel Hunter, former wid., W3255
NYE, Abigail, former wid. of Israel Batchelder, Mass., which see
Andrew, Pa., Hester, W3154
Caleb, Mass., Abigail, W17413
Daniel, Ct., S21903
David, Ct., S18532
Ebenezer, Mass., Lucy, W15141
Elias, Mass., S14044
Elijah, Ct., R7748
Elisha, Mass., S30011
Elnathan, Mass., S14043
Ichabod, Mass., S9444
John, Mass., S33174
Jonathan, Ct., Deodama, W17412

NYE (continued)
Jonathan, Mass., S30010
Joseph, Mass., BLWt.4764-100-Pvt. Iss. 4/19/1792 to Whitfield Swift. No papers
Joseph, Mass., S33173
Nathan, Cont., Mass., S21403
Seth, Mass., N.Y., S7276
Solomon, Ct., Mary, W9607; BLWt. 26345-160-55. She rec'd BL on account of service of her former husb., Samuel Woods, Mass., which see
Thomas, Mass., Mary, W21861
William, Mass., S33172
William, Mass., R7749

O

OADHAM, George S., Va., Jane, R7784
OAK, Calvin, Mass., Lucretia, W19932
Nathaniel, Mass., Susan, W25398
Nathaniel, Mass., N.H., S18534
OAKES, Daniel, Mass. See OAKS
Ephraim, N.Y., S14045
John, Md.?, Mass., Pa.?, Rebecca, R7761
John, Mass., R7760
Joshua, Cont., Mass., S36711
Nathaniel, Mass. See OAK
OAKIE, Martin, N.Y., Magdalene, W26589
OAKLEY, Erasmus, Ga., Rhoda, W5437; Res. at enl. & after Rev., Cumberland Co., Va.
George, Va., Sea Service, Susannah W5438
Gilbert, Ct., Eleanor, W26590
James, N.Y., Auley, W19933
James, Va., S4628
Jared, N.Y., R7757
John, Ct., BLWt.6250. Iss. 10/10/1791. No papers
John, Ct., Catharine, W19934
John, N.J., S34452
John, N.Y., BLWt.7558. Iss. 9/15/1790 to John Hobart, et al, assnes. No papers
Jonathan, N.Y., Mary, W5436; BLWt.7560-100 & 159-60-55
Miles, Ct., S18533
Thomas, Lamb's Arty., N.Y., BLWt.7578. Iss. 10/10/1791 to John Oakley, Admr. No papers
William, N.Y., Catharine, W10833; BLWt.8187-160-55. She was also pensioned as wid. of Wm. Douglas, N.Y. See papers inside; also Rej. BL application for William Douglass
William, R.I., S38972
OAKMAN, Constant Forbes, Mass., Rachel, W15142; BLWt.26865-160-55
Samuel, R.I., S33176
OAKS, Daniel, Mass., Deborah D., W26591; BLWt.16146-160-55
Isaac, Va., S14046
John, Boat Service on Lake Champlain, N.H., Thankful, R7762
John, Cont., Mass., Abigail, R7758
John, Mass., BLWt.1982-100
Nathaniel, Mass. See OAK
OAKSMAN, Samuel, R.I., BLWt.3371. Iss. 5/3/1792 to M. Oaksman, Admx. No papers
OAR, Baltus, See ORE
OARD, William, Md., Va., S16496
OATES, Richard Wyatt, N.C., Elizabeth, R7764
OATLEY, Joseph, R.I., Mary, W21862
O'BANNON, Andrew, Va., Mary, R16821. Va. Half Pay
Benjamin, Ga., S31886
Benjamin, Va., S4629
Thomas, Va., S5851
O'BANYON, William, See O'BRYAN

OBAR, Robert, N.C., S38973
O'BARR, Hugh, See BARR
OBART, John, N.J., Mary, W4752; BLWt.3517-160-55
OBDIKE, William, N.J., S34453
OBEAR, Samuel, Mass., Abigail, W26592
OBER, Richard, Cont., Mass., S33175
OBERT, Henry, N.J., S45900
John, N.J. See OBART
OBLENIS, Garret, N.Y., Vrouche, W24361 & S27262
Peter, N.Y., Mary, W16665
OBLINGER, John, Pa., Susanna, W2235; BLWt.26512-160-55
O'BRIAN, Daniel, See O'BRINE
Daniel, Pa., BLWt.10175. Iss. 6/30/1789 to Ann O'Brian, wid. No papers
Dennis, Md., S38274
Dennis, Pvt., Sappers & Miners, BLWt.13561 iss. 7/27/1789 to Richard Platt, ass.
James, Armand's Dragoons, BLWt. 13557. Iss. 5/3/1791. No papers
John, Mass., Abigail, W1311; BLWt.38504-160-55
John, N.Y., BLWt.7568. Iss. 7/30/1790 to Edward Cumpston, ass. No papers
Michael, See O'BRYAN
Patrick, N.J., BLWt.8617. Iss. 9/1/1789. No papers
Philip, Pvt. in the Invalids. BLWt.13568. Iss. 5/7/179? to John Nicholson, ass. No papers
Philip, Md., BLWt.11582. Iss. 2/28/1791. No papers
Thomas, N.Y., BLWt.7564. Iss. 9/15/1790 to John S. Hobart, ass. No papers
William, Mass., Anna, W15757
O'BRIANT, Jesse, S.C., Joyce, W1637; BLWt.16119-160-55
O'BRIEN, Andrew, Cont., Pa., S40216
John, N.J., BLWt.8615. Iss. 6/11/1789 to Nathaniel Denman, ass. No papers
John Sconodoh, N.Y., War of 1812, R16808
Richard, Va. Sea Service, Elizabeth Maria, R7751 & Va. Half Pay
William, Mass. See O'BRIAN
William, R.I., S22923
O'BRINE, Daniel, Cont., Martha, W1638; Enl. in Md., pensioned in Vt., BLWt.8377-160-55
O'BRION, John, Mass. See O'BRIAN
O'BRYAN, Michael, Va., S38974
Thomas, Mass., Nancy Dutton, former wid., W16965
Thomas, N.Y., BLWt.7569. Iss. 10/5/1790. No papers
Tillotson, N.Y., Mary, W2422; BLWt.34840-160-55
William, N.C., S7277
William, Pa., BLWt.10173. Iss. 1/28/1791. No papers
O'BRYEN, Tillotson, See O'BRYAN

O'CAIN, Anthony F.(Francois), Ct., R7765
O'CALLIS, William Overton, See CALLIS
OCCOMAN, Sarah, former wid. of Abraham Savage, Mass., which see
OCKERMAN, Christopher, See ACKERMAN
OCKINGTON, Thomas, Mass., Mary, W24362
O'CONNER, Michael, Md., S35018
Thomas, Md., S35541
ODALL, John, N.H., S11153
ODAM, Aaron, N.C., S38975
Uriah, Va., R7810
O'DANIEL, John, Md., Va., Sarah, W5441
ODEL, John, Vt., Catharine, W5440; BLWt.30920-160-55
ODELL, Aaron, Mass., S43095
Abraham, N.Y., Christina, W24363
Abraham, Va., Mary, W1066
Amos, N.Y., S23343
Eliza, former wid. of Obed Hall, Mass., which see
Isaac, Ct., Grizel, W21863
Jacob, N.Y., S23344
Jeremiah, Va., S8905
John, N.Y., S28830
Jonathan, N.Y., Catharine, W16358
Nathan, Ct., S17610
Reuben, Pa., Va., R20175
Richard, N.Y., S43098; BLWt.26112-160-55
Warren, N.Y. See ODLE
William, Ct., Sea Service, S14048
William, N.Y., S23827; BLWt.11079-160-55
ODER, Joseph, Va., S16497
ODHAM, Uriah, Va. See ODAM
ODIL, John, S.C., b. N.C., S38271
ODIORNE, Samuel, Navy, Me., S36710
Samuel, N.H., BLWt.3374. Iss. 11/4/1789. No papers
ODLE, Jacob, N.Y., Rev. War Files; Margaret, BL Register 234532-55
Richard, N.Y. See ODELL
Samuel, Mass., BLWt.4783. Iss. 5/8/1792 to Ezra Blodget. No papers
Warren, Cont., N.Y., Anna, W4302
ODOM, Archibald, N.C. or S.C., Elizabeth, R7766
Daniel, S.C., Elizabeth, R7767
George S., See OADHAM
Jacob, N.C., S16994
James, N.C., S7278
Jethro, N.C., S8904
Levi, N.C., Patience Herrin, former wid., W10093; BLWt.81013-160-55
Sion, N.C., S.C., S21035
Willis, N.C., S.C., S16993
O'DONAGHY, Patrick, N.Y., Agness, W20997
ODONE, James, N.C. See ODOM
O'DONOHY, Patrick, N.Y., BLWt. 7574. Iss. 9/28/1790 to Alexander Robertson, ass. No papers
O'DORNEN, Murty, See O'DORNER
O'DORNER, Murty, Pa., S40215
ODUM, Seybert, Ga. Agcy., Dis. No papers

O'FARRELL, Dennis, See O'FERRELL
O'FERRELL, Dennis, Va., S25072
OFFICER, James, Pa., S31280
OFFUTT, Jessee, S.C., Obedience, R7769
Nathaniel, S.C., S31887
O'FLAHERTY, John, N.J., BLWt.8618 Iss. 4/20/1792. No papers
O'FLING, See O'FLYNG
O'FLYNG, Patrick, Cont., N.H., War of 1812, S35542. Rejected BL Claim of 1812. For family hist., etc. consult Wid. Ctf. 16785 of Edmund O'Flyng, Pvt. U.S. Inf. War of 1812. Also see Claim for BL allowed on account of services of Lt. Patrick O'Flyng, War of 1812, 23rd W.S. Inf. who d. 11/1/1815. Wt. 3 for 480 A., Act of 4/14/1816. (No orig. papers in this claim)
OGDEN, Aaron, N.J., S19013; BLWt. 1610-300-Capt. Iss. 6/11/1789. No papers
Barne/Barney, N.J., S38279; BLWt.773-200
Benjamin, N.J., S31281
Daniel, N.Y., BLWt.7563. Iss. 7/30/1792. No papers
David, Ct., Sally, W17414
David, N.Y., BLWt.7581. Iss. 7/13/1792. No papers
David, N.Y., Susannah, W24364
Edmond, Ct., Navy, Sebal, R7777
Eliakim, N.J., BLWt.8607. Iss. 6/20/1789. No papers
Gilbert, N.Y., R7770
James, N.J., Ruth, R7772
Jedediah, N.J., S32419
John, Mass., Naomi Burnap, former wid., W15618
John, N.Y., BLWt.7559. Iss. 8/26/1790 to Elijah Rose, ass. No papers
Jonathan, N.Y., S11154
Joseph, Ct., S38277
Joseph, N.J., S11155
Ludlow, N.J., Comfort, W187
Matthias, N.J., BLWt.1609-500-Col. Iss. 6/11/1789. No papers
Nathaniel, Cont., N.J., BLWt. 1281-100
Nathaniel, N.J., S34454
Noah, N.J., BLWt.8010. Iss. 6/11/1789 to Matthias Denman, ass. No papers
Obadiah, N.Y., Martha, R7771; BLWt.45715-160-55
Samuel, N.J., S38273
Stephen, N.Y., Va., S7775
Stephen D., N.J., R7776
Sturges/Sturgess, Ct., S14049
OGEN, Thomas, Va., BLWt.12444. Iss. 3/1/1794. No papers
OGG, James, R.I., BLWt.3369. Iss. 5/16/1791 to Deborah May, Admx. No papers
OGILBY, George, Pa., BLWt.10185 Iss. 6/25/1794 to Gideon Merkle, ass. No papers

OGILVIE, Kimbrough, N.C., S14050
OGLE, Benjamin, Va., R7778
OGLESBY, Elisha, Va., S1866
Jesse, Va., Celia, W1987; BLWt.28523-160-55
Richard, Va. res. of wid. in 1812, Susan, R7779
O'GULLION, John B. See GULLION
O'HARA, Francis, Pa., Nancy, BLWt.233-100
George, N.J., Elizabeth, W5442
John, Md., Susan, W9215
John, Va., S25340
Joseph, Pa., Mary, BLWt.224-100
Patrick, Pa., BLWt.10184. Iss. 4/3/1794 to John Phillips, ass. No papers
OHARRA, Joseph, Pa. See O'HARA
O'HARRO, Francis, Pa. See O'HARA
OHE, John, N.J. See OHL
OHL, Henry, Pa., S2030
John, Pa., S22428
OHLEN, Henry G., N.Y., BLWt.7570 Iss. 8/26/1790 to Wm. Carr, ass. No papers
Henry G., N.Y., Cathrina, S43100 & W19935
OHMET, John, Pa., S40218
O'KAIN, James, Pa., BLWt.319-100
O'KEEFFE, Daniel, Pa., S43101
O'KEIFF, Daniel, See O'KEEFFE
O'KELLY, John/ John O. KELLY, R.I., Elizabeth Kinnicut, former wid., W13579
OKERSON, Nicholas, N.J. See OKESON
OKESON, Nicholas, N.J., S7279
OKIE, Martin, See OAKIE
O'KIEF, Daniel, See O'KEEFFE
O'LAUGHLIN, Dennis/Dennis O. LAUGHLINN, Pa., Martha Matilda Leeman, former wid., W8249; BLWt.12576-160-55
OLCOTT, Isaac, Ct., S31890
Jared, Ct., S47577
Jonathan, Ct., S16996
OLDEN, Thomas, Cont., N.J., Pa., S23828
OLDFELD, William, N.Y., S5128
OLDFIELD, William, See OLDFELD
OLDHAM, Conway, Va., BLWt.503-300
Edward, Md., BLWt.1110-300
George, N.C., S21906
George S. See OADHAM
Isaac, Va., Winnifred, R7785
Jacob, Md., S8908
James, Pa., R7783
John, Md., Ann, W5443
John, Mass., S33404
John, N.C., Annis, W8492
Richard, N.C., S14053
Richard, N.C., Patsey, W6887; BLWt.49241-160-55
Richard, Va., S40220
OLDIS, Robert, Pa., S40221
OLDNER, Joshua, Va. Sea Service, R80, Va. Half Pay
OLDS, Aaron, Ct., BLWt.6257. Iss. 6/29/1792 to Stephen Thorn, ass. No papers
Aaron, Ct., S41035

OLDS (continued)
Daniel, Ct., Lois, W4557
Ebenezer, Ct., BLWt.6259. Iss. 5/1/1797 to John Duncan, ass. No papers
Ebenezer, Cont., Ct., S43099
Eleanor, former wid. of Peter Hammond/Hammon, Mass., which see
George, Green Mt. Boys, Vt., S14052
Gershom, Cont., Vt., S43096
Gilbert, Cont., Mass., S40223
Hannah, former wid. of Thomas Stephenson, Ct., which see
Horace, Mass., S43097
Jasper, Vt. See OLES
John, Ct., Cont., S43102
Marcay, former wid. of John Steward/Stewart/Stuart, Mass., which see
Reuben, Mass., S30624
OLDWINE, Barnard, Pa., BLWt. 10170. Iss. 7/13/1789. No papers
Barney, Pa., BLWt.10187. Iss. 2/12/1795 to Barnard Oldwine. No papers
Barney/Barny, Pa., S35019
Charles, Pa., BLWt.10186. Iss. 12/11/1793 to Alexander Power, ass. No papers
Charles, Pa., S35020
OLENDORPH, Leonard, N.Y., BLWt. 7565. Iss. 2/14/1791 to John Maley, ass. No papers
OLER, Henry, Va., 1774, R7786
OLES, Jasper, Vt., Lydia, W5445
OLEST, John, See Han Jost HESS
OLIN, Caleb, Vt., S16997
OLINGER, Jacob, Va., R7787
OLIPHANT, Andrew, Pa., S40222
David, Deputy Director General of Hospitals in the Southern Dept., BLWt.1620-500. Iss. 12/31/1789. No papers
William, N.Y., Catharine, W2168; BLWt.7573-100 & 46-60-55
OLIS, Boston, S.C. See OLLIS
OLIVE, John, N.C. or S.C., R7788
OLIVER, Alexander, Cont., Mass., S44387; BLWt.1607-150. Ensign. Iss. 9/14/1792 to John Stephenson, ass. No papers
Alva, Va., S8907
Benjamin, N.C., S11156
David, Mass., Mary, W24367
Douglas, Va., Katharine, W1466
George, N.C., S8906
Henry, Mass., S16995
James, N.C., Susannah, W5444
James, S.C., S32421
James, Va., S38269
James B., Mass., S19011
Jilson, Va., S21405
John, Mass., S29353
John, Mass., S31284
John, Mass., S33405
John, Mass., S33406
John, N.Y., R7790
John, N.C., S31888

OLIVER (continued)
John, Va., S5859
John, Va., S11159
John, Va., Elizabeth, W2686; BLWt.9186-160-55
Jonathan, Cont., Mass., S17611
Nicholas/Nichols, Cont., N.J., S43741
Nicholas, Mass., S37274
Nicholas, Va., Lee's Legion, BLWts.12446 & 13573. Iss. 9/10/1790. No papers
Peter, S.C., S21904
Rhesa, N.C., S32420
Richard, Cont., N.Y., Catharine, W15791
Richard, N.C., S31282
Richard, Not Rev. War, Wayne's War, Md. res., Pa., Ind. Old War Inv. Rej.16838; BLWt.4395-160-55
Richard, Pa., BLWt.10181. Iss. 8/12/1793 to James Beagley, ass. No papers
Robert, Cont., Va., R7792
Robert, Mass., BLWt.1606-400-Maj. Iss. 4/1/1790. No papers
Russel, Mass., S33407
Samuel, Del., S38270
Samuel, N.J., R7794
Samuel, Va., R7793
Stephen, Pa., Polly Gracy, W9610; BLWt.44508-160-55
Thomas, N.Y., Keziah, W21865
Thomas, Va., Eleanor, W26593; BLWt.11163-160-55
Tilson, S.C., Claim missing when searched 5/23/1939. Report of Sec. of War shows Pvt. Tilson Oliver, $30 p/a, S.C. Mil.; placed on pension roll 5/18/1833. Pension commenced 3/4/1831. Age 79 yrs.. Pickens Dist., S.C. Agcy. Book shows on the S.C. list Pen. Cft. No. 12679
William, Cont., Mass., Rebecca, W24368
William, Md., S7280
William, Mass., BLWt.4786. Iss. 3/25/1790. No papers
William, Mass., S31283
William, Mass., Mary, W15144
William, N.J., Dis. No papers. See Am. State Papers, Class 9, p.169, 1st Lt., Essex Co., Mil., wounded by a musket ball in the elbow of his right arm, 6/26/1781 at Rahway Meadow. Res. Elizabethtown.
OLIVIA, Lawrence, Hazen's Regt., See Lorant OLVIE
OLLER, Henry, Va. See OLER
OLLIFF, John, N.C. See OLIVE
OLLIS, Boston, S.C., Barbary, R7796
OLLIVER, James, N.C. See OLIVER
William, Cont., Mass. See OLIVER
OLMSTEAD, Ashbel, Ct., S23346
Daniel, Ct., Rosanna, W19936
Gamaliel, Ct., Cont., Elizabeth, W5435; BLWt.30918-160-55
Isaac, Ct., Sarah, W26595
Jabez, Vt., Lydia Balch, former

OLMSTEAD (continued)
wid., R441
James, Ct., BLWt.1608-200. Lt. Iss. 9/1/1790 to Theodosius Fowler, ass. No papers
James, Ct., d. 9/21/1811; Mary, R7799
Joseph, Mass., R7800
Oliver, Ct., Cont., Mercy, W26594
Prince, Mass., S33403
Roger, Ct., S5858
Timothy, N.H., Susanna, W15976
OLMSTED, Benjamin, Ct., Content, W20280
Ebenezer, Ct., Esther, W9611
Francis, Ct., Cont., S40224
Gloriana, former wid. of Aaron Keeler, Ct., which see
James, Ct., b. 4/5/1755, d. 1/4/1841 in N.Y., S5857
John, Ct., R7803
John Bates, Ct., d. 1819; Theodosha/Adosha, R7801
Joseph, Ct., S11157
Matthew/Mathew, Ct., S14054
Nehemiah, Ct., N.Y., S43739
Reuben, N.Y., S14051
Stephen, Mass., Jerusha, R7802
Timothy, Ct., S43740
OLNEY, Amos, See ONEY
Coggeshal, R.I., BLWt.1605-400-Maj. Iss. 4/20/1790. No papers
Elisha, R.I., Dinah, W21866
Esek, R.I., S11158
Gideon, R.I., S21905
James, R.I., Olive, W24365
Jeremiah, Cont., R.I., Sally, W24366; BLWt.1604-500. Lt. Col. Commd. Iss. 4/20/1790. No papers
Lucretia, former wid. of Joseph Mosley, Mass., contesting wid.
Peter, Ct., Tabitha, W21864
Stephen, R.I., S46399
William, Mass., R7804
OLP, John, N.J., Mary, R7805, BLWt.47512-160-55
OLVIE, Lorant, Hazen's Regt., BLWt.1622-300: Capt. Iss. 3/7/1794. No papers. Heitman's Hist. Reg. gives his name as Olivia, Lawrence
OMACK, Thomas, N.J., BLWt.8609. Iss. 6/11/1789 to Matthias Denman, ass. No papers
OMANS, Thomas, Mass., Polly, W807; BLWt.7296-160-55
OMENS, Thomas, Mass. See OMANS
OMEY, John, Mass., S33414
OMOHUNDRO, James, Va., S5860
ONAIR/McNAIR, Angus, Hazen's Regt., BLWts.13405 & 13563. Iss. 10/26/1789. No papers
ONDERDIRK, Frederick, N.Y., S28831
ONDERDONK, Andres/Andries, N.Y. Mary, W15844
Daniel, N.Y., Maria, W21869
Garret, N.Y., S23830
Jacob, N.Y., Anne Remsen, former wid., W17525
James, N.Y., Rachel, R16843
John, N.Y., R7806

ONDERDONK (continued)
Thomas, N.Y., Sarah Felter, former wid., W19254
ONDERKARK, Frederick, See ONDERDIRK
ONDERKIRK, See ONDERDIRK
John, N.Y., S5861
John, N.Y., S28834
O'NEAL, Basil, Va., Indian disturbances before & after Rev., Sarah H., BLWt.81555-160-55. No papers
Christopher, Pa., BLWt.10177. Iss. 8/7/1795 to James Decorcy, ass. No papers
Con, See Conrad O'NEIL
Daniel, Pa., BLWt.10183. Iss. 12/22/1794 to Henry Purdy, ass. No papers
Ferdinand, Cont., Va., R16846. Va. Half Pay. BLWt.1617-300-Capt. Iss. 7/7/1797. No papers
Ferrel, See Ferrell O'Neill DAILY
George, Va., Elizabeth, W2843
Hamilton, Del., BLWt.10859. Iss. 5/26/1790 to George Bacon, Admr. No papers
Henry, N.J., BLWt.8606. Iss. 3/22/1797. No papers
James, Del., BLWt.10858. Iss. 7/9/1799 to Samuel and Elizabeth O'Neal, only heirs. No papers
James, Pa., BLWt.10172. Iss. 3/5/1793. No papers
James, Pa., BLWt.10178. Iss. 8/7/1789 to Richard Platt, ass. No papers
John, Md., Pa., S38272
John, N.J., BLWt.8611. Iss. 5/7/1790 to John Linn, ass. No papers
John, N.J. Sarah, See O'NEIL
John, N.J. Margaret, See O'NEIL
John, Pa., BLWt.10169. Iss. 4/16/1796 to Thomas Espy & William McFarland, Admrs. No papers
John, Va., S32422
Lementation, N.C., R7754
Neal, N.J., BLWt.8619. Iss. 6/17/1789 to John Jacob Faesch, ass. No papers
Patrick, N.C., Mary, R7755
Richard, Pa., BLWt.10171. Iss. 7/9/1789 to William Wallace, ass. No papers
William, Del., S31891
O'NEALE, Constantine/Constantia, Pa., Catharine, W5446
ONEAR, Angus, Pa., S40217. See also Angus ONAIR
O'NEEL, John, See O'NEIL
ONEIAL, John, See O'NEIL
O'NEIL, Conrad/Con., N.J., S34455
Constantine, See O'NEALE
Darius, Va., Mary, W5448
Ferrill, Va., Art., BLWt.12445 Iss. 7/16/1793. No papers
Henry, Navy, Pa. res. of son in 1852, Sarah, R7753
Henry, N.J., S--- Cert. No. 13924. Pa. res.

O'NEIL (continued)
John, N.J., Sarah, W3109
John, N.J., Margaret, W20281
Patrick, N.C., Catharine, W4044
Walter, N.C., Va., b. Ireland, S7281
ONEY, Amos, R.I., R7807
Joseph, Va., S8909
William, Va., S18147; BLWt. 26250-160-55
O'NIEL, Darius, See O'NEIL
George, Va. See O'NEAL
ONION, David, Mass., Caroline, W13781
Juliet, former wid. of William Pendergast, Md., which see
Tabitha, former wid. of Samuel Foster, N.H., which see
ONIONS, John, Md., BLWt.11578. Iss. 8/27/1792. No papers
ONTHANK, William, Mass., S33410
OOLEY, David, Va., R7808
OSTERHOUT, Isaac, N.Y., BLWt. 7562. Iss. 7/30/1790 to Edward Cumpston, ass. No papers
Peter, N.Y., BLWt.6910. Iss. 6/15/1792. No papers
OPPELL, Rachel, former wid. of Jasper Steymets, N.Y., which see
O'QUIN, John, N.C., Rhoda/Rhody, W5449
O'QUINN, Daniel, Md., BLWt.11580. Iss. 11/29/1790 to Elias Hardry, Admr. No papers
ORAM, Cooper, Md., Pa., Abagail, W5452
Darby, Navy, N.J., R.I., S1067
Henry, Va., S38380
Robert, Del., BLWt.10856. Iss. 9/2/1789. No papers
Spedden, See OREM
ORCHARD, Catrina, former wid. of Moses Stiles, N.Y., which see
ORCHEAD, Thomas, Pa., Sarah, W5454
ORCOTT, James, See ORCUTT
William, See ORCUTT
ORCUTT, Caleb, Sgt. "in the Invalids", BLWt.13570 iss. 3/25/1790. No papers
David, Ct. Agcy. Dis. No papers
Elisha, Cont., Mass., Sally, W24371
Ephraim, Cont., Mass., Ruth, W24372
Ephraim, Mass., Abiah, W15145
James, N.Y., Deborah, W21872
John, Ct., S15949
Micah, Mass., Navy, S19012
Moses, Mass., Susannah Bates, former wid., W10394; BLWt. 39486-160-55
Samuel, Mass., S30625
Samuel, Mass., S43757
Samuel, N.H., Alice, R16852
Seth, Mass., BLWt.4779. Iss. 9/8/1792. No papers
Solomon, Ct., Cont., S41037
Stephen, Ct., Mary, W26598; BLWt.8450-160-55

ORCUTT (continued
William, Ct., S4632
William, Cont., Mass., Lucy, W24374
William, Mass., S41036
ORDWAY, John, Mass., Sarah, W21874
Peter, Mass., S22924
Samuel, N.H., S22429
ORE, Baltus, N.Y., S43750
Jacob, N.Y., S14059
OREAR, Daniel, N.C., Va., S31892
Daniel, Va., S7376
John, Va., S31285
OREM, Spedden, Md. Sea Service, R7809
ORENDORF, Christian, Md., S38281
ORGAN, Cornelius, Cont., Va., Rachel, R16856
Isaac, Cont., Mass. See ORGIN
Isaac, Drummer, Mass., BLWts. 4782 & 3613. Iss. 8/10/1789 to Richard Platt. No papers
John, Cont., Pa., Sold. slain at siege of York; BLWt.1029-100
John, Pa., BLWt.10176. Iss. 12/5/1795. No papers
John, Pa., Catharine, W6770. Sold. d. 8/4/1813
Matthew, Cont., Pa., S40226
Matthew, Pa., BLWt.10168. Iss. 1/23/1796. No papers
ORGEN, Dennis, Mass., Lois, W19939
ORGIN, Isaac, Cont., Mass., Elizabeth, W24370
O'RIAN, John, Mass., S36712
O'RIEN, Joseph, Pa., BLWt.10190. Iss. 3/31/1795 to Simon Rigby, ass. No papers
O'RION, John, Mass. See O'RIAN
ORISH, James, Va., BLWt.12443. Iss. 4/14/1792 to Robt. Means, ass. No papers
ORLOP, Frederick, N.Y., Hannah, W21871
William, N.Y., Elizabeth, R16855
ORME, Charles, Md., S35543; BLWt. 896-100
Moses, Md., S8913
ORMES, Charles, Md. See ORME
ORMOND, William, Md. Dis. No papers. See Am. State Papers Class 9, p.127. Wounded at Monmouth in the rt. hand by a musket ball, which has deprived him of the use of his fingers, and in a great measure disabled him from obtaining a livelihood.
ORMS, Jonathan, Ct., Privateer, Lura/Laura, W5632; BLWt.18200-160-55
ORMSBE, Ebenezer, Ct., R.I., Experience, W21873; BLWt.7076-160-55
ORMSBEE, Elisha, Mass., R.I., S15194
Ezra, R.I., S21404
Isaac, R.I., S28833
Jacob, Mass., Ruth Pierce, former wid., W17451
Joseph, Mass., S43756
ORMSBY, Amos, Ct., BLWt.6251. Iss.

ORMSBY (continued)
2/20/1790 to Solomon Goss, ass. No papers
Amos, Pa., S43755
Elijah, Ct., S14060
John, See ARMSBURY
Joseph, N.H., S14056
Stephen, Ct., S45039
ORN, James, Mass., S45040
Joseph, Cont., Mass., Elizabeth, R7812 1/2
ORNDORFF, Christian, See ORENDORF
ORNE, James, Mass., S33409
John, Mass., Sea Service, Sarah, W26597
ORNER, Mardin/Martin, Pa., S23829
Martin, See Mardin
Michael, See ORNOR
ORNOR, Michael, Pa., Dis. No papers. See Am. State Papers, Class 9, p.98. Wounded in the actual line of his duty, being on the bullock guard, the day previous to the Augusta, an armed ship of war in the service of Great Britain, was blown up in the Delaware River. He made a slip with his foot by which he fell, and one of the wagons in the service of the U.S. went over him, by which his hip was put out of place, and he was otherwise much injured.
O'ROARK, David, Va., Jane, W5450
O'ROUKE, James, See REEWARK
ORR, Alexander, Ct., Mass., S34456
Alexander, Cont., Mass. Sea Service, Deborah Ames, former wid., W23437
Baltis, N.Y., BLWt.7577. Iss. 8/4/1790 to Henry Hart, ass. No papers
Daniel, N.Y., BLWt.7561.Iss. 4/21/1791 to Oliver Bostwick, ass. No papers
Daniel, N.C., R7813
James, Cont., Mass., Polly, W24369
James, N.C., b. Pa., S7282
James, N.C., S38976
Jehu, N.C., Jane B., W5453; BLWt.36604-160-55
John, Md., Pa., Elizabeth, R16849
John, N.J., BLWt.8616. Iss. 6/22/1789. No papers
John, N.J., BLWt.1612-200-Lt. Iss. 5/28/1791. No papers
John, Pa., BLWt.10179. Iss. 6/20/1789. No papers
Joseph, Pa., S40225
Joshua, Va., S1577
Robert, Pa., b. Ireland, S4631
Thomas, Cont., Pa., S43754
Thomas, Hazen's Regt., BLWt. 13565. Iss. 7/16/1789. No papers
Thomas, Pa., R7816
William, N.Y., BLWt.7572. Iss. 9/28/1790 to Bartholomew & Fisher, assnes. No papers
William, N.Y., Hoppy, W19941

ORSBON, Isaac, Ct., Mass., Edna, W26602; BLWt.28579-160-55
Richard, See OSBORN
ORSBURNE, Samuel, Va., S40227; BLWt.12442. Iss. 1789. 100 A.
ORSER, Abraham, N.Y., Phebe, W19940
Jonas. See ORSOR
ORSMAN, Benjamin, N.J., S34457
ORSOR, Jonas, N.Y., S14058
ORTAN, William, Del., BLWt. 1987-100
ORTON, Azariah, Ct., S11161
Azariah, Mass., S19742
Darius, Ct., S14055. See N.A. Acc. No.874-050128. Not Half Pay
Eliada, Ct., S41933
Lemuel, Sheldon's Dragoons, Ct., BLWt.6258. Iss. 10/7/1789 to Benj. Tallmadge, ass.
Lemuel, Cont., Ct., Sibbel, W4753
ORVIS, Ambrose, Mass., S29354
David, Ct., Green Mt. Boys, S14057
Gershom, Mass., N.Y., Asenath, R16854
Roger, Ct., S43751
Samuel, Ct., Caroline, W25359
ORWIG, George, Pa., S4633
Henry, Pa., S4636
OSBON, John, Ct. See OSBORN
OSBORN, Aaron, N.Y., Sarah Benjamin, former wid., W4558. BLWt.30622-160-55. Her last husb., John Benjamin, also served in Rev. War.
Abijah, Ct., R7821
Abner, N.J., S23831
Abraham, Ct., N.Y., Privateer, S14061
Abraham, N.J., Elizabeth, W5457
Abraham, N.Y., S29356
Alexander, N.C., Eleanor, BLWt. 40711-160-55
Bennet, N.C., Rebecca, W26603; BLWt.15448-160-55
Daniel, N.Y., S43745
David, Mass., BLWt.4791. Iss. 5/8/1792 to Benj. Haskell. No papers
Ebenezer, Ct., S15550
Edward, Ct., Elizabeth, W20282
Eli, Ct., S43743
Eliada, Ct., Abigail, W1639
Ephraim, Cont., Vt., R7817
Ephraim, Mass., S14064
Ethan, Ct., S4635; BLWt.34953-160-55
Ezekiel, Ct., Lucretia, W26600; BLWt.5205-160-55
Ezra, Ct., Abigail, W15147
Henry, Mass., Sea Service, Betsey, W15148
Isaac, Ct., Mass., See ORSBON
Isaac, Mass., S11162
Jacob, Ct., S29355
James, Mass., N.Y., S14063
Jedediah, N.J., S43746
Jeremiah, Ct., S31894
Jeremiah, Cont., Ct. Agcy. &

OSBORN (continued)
res. in 1818, S38278
Jeremiah, Lamb's Art., N.Y., BLWt.7580. Iss. 5/14/1790. No papers
Joel, Mass., Theda, W16359
John, Ct., S33408
John, Ct., Jerusha, W21875
John, Ct., Rhoda, W21877
John, Mass., S30626
John, Va., S9446
John, Va., S32423
Jonathan, Va., S8912
Joseph, N.J., Rosanna, W5456; BLWt.81-60-55
Joshua, Ct., Diana, W4559
Josiah, Ct., N.Y., S4638
Levi, Ct., S14065
Luke, N.J., S43744
Naboth, Ct., Mass., Susanna, W21878
Nathan, Ct., S23347
Nathan, Ct. res., Cont., S11164
Nathaniel, Ct., Elizabeth, R16862
Nehemiah, N.J., Mary, W188; BLWt.26285-160-55
Richard, Mass., S33412
Roswell, Vt., R7819
Samuel, Ct., Elizabeth, W6862; BLWt.28611-160-55. Wid. later m. Moses L. Pendell after whose death said pension was renewed.
Shadrach, Ct., Cont., Aletta/Alletta, W21879
Stephen, N.J., S11166
Stephen, N.Y., Grizzle, W17416
Thomas, Cont., Ct., Lovisa, W17415
White, Ct., Cont., S14066
William, Ct., Sarah H. Taylor, former wid., R10431. Her other husb. was pensioned on account of disability contracted in service of War of 1812. See Wm. B. Taylor, S6202
William, Mass., Dorcas, W15792
William, N.C., Elizabeth, W4303; BLWt.80035-160-55
Zebedee, Ct., S30012
Zerah, Va., R16861
OSBORNE, Abel, Ct., Annah, W20285
Claibourne, Va., S5866
Henry, N.J., S1071
James, Mass., S29357
John, Navy, See OSBOURNE
John B., N.J., S1069
Jonathan H., N.J., S1068
Joseph, Ct., S23348
Michael, See OSBOURNE
Nathaniel, Sappers & Miners, BLWt. 13560. Iss. 3/16/1790. No papers
Robert, N.C., Jane, W892
Samuel, Ct., S7284
Samuel, Va., BLWt.12442. Iss. 11/5/1789 to Samuel Osborne. No papers
Samuel, Va. See ORSBURNE
Stephen, Cont., Ct., Apame, W9216; 18380-160-55
Thomas, Mass., Pa.(?), Sea Service(?), Navy (?), S33413
Thomas, S.C., Catharine, W9217

OSBOURN, James, Pa. See OSBURN
Jesse, N.C., S41930
Simeon, Mass., BLWt.4780. Iss. 8/10/1789 to Richard Platt. No papers
OSBOURNE, Hugh, Navy, Mass.?, Zuba/Zaba, W6889
John, Navy, Mass.?, S35022
Michael, Cont., Mass., Navy, Judith, W24375
Nathaniel, N.J., S38977
Thomas, See OSBORNE
OSBURN, Aaron, N.Y., BLWt.7571. Iss. 1/5/1791 to Veeder & Alexander. No papers
Aaron, N.Y. See OSBORN
Ephraim, Va., R7822
James, Pa., S40229
John, Md., BLWt.11576 & 11784. Iss. 6/11/1795 to Samuel Johnson, ass. No papers
Samuel, N.Y., S14062
Thomas, Mass., BLWt.4781. Iss. 11/3/1791. No papers
Thomas, N.J., S1070
OSBURNE, Hugh, Navy, Mass. See OSBOURNE
Jesse, N.C. See OSBOURN
Joseph, N.J., BLWt. 8613 iss. 3/27/1799 to Wm. Garrison, ass. and 81-60-55. No papers
Luke, N.J., BLWt.8622. Iss. 6/16/1789 to Thomas Coyle, ass. No papers
Samuel, Va. See ORSBURNE
OSGOOD, Asa, Cont., Mass., Hannah W27894
Asa, Mass., BLWt.4789. Iss. 7/6/1792 to James Witham. No papers
Christopher, Mass., S37275
David, Mass., S45041
Ebenezer, N.H., Anna, W21881
Jeremiah, See OZGOOD
John, N.H., S8911
Josiah, Ct., Cont., S19415
Josiah, Mass., Elizabeth, W19948
Nathan, Mass., S41932
Nathan, Mass., Hepzabah/Hepsibah W2660
Oliver, N.H., Mary, W2328; BLWt. 40678-160-55
Phineas, Mass., BLWt.4787. Iss. 3/25/1790. No papers
Sally, former wid. of Dudley G. Adams, N.H., which see
Samuel, Mass., S33411
Thomas, N.H., BLWt.3372. Iss. 3/25/1790. No papers
Thomas, N.H., S41931
O'SHEALS, Jethro, S.C., S18144
John, S.C., S18146
OSHER, Joseph, Mass., Elizabeth, W21882
O'SHIELDS, Jethro, See O'SHEALS
OSMAN, Benijah, Sgt., N.J., BLWt. 8612 iss. 2/3/1790
Charles, Va., b. N.J., S4634
John, Md., S43747
OSMUN, Benjamin, N.J., BLWt.1611-200-Lt. Iss. 4/21/1790. No papers

OSMUN (continued)
John, N.J., BLWt.8620. Iss. 6/26/1789. No papers
John, N.J., S34458
John, Lamb's Art., N.Y., BLWt. 7579. Iss. 9/15/1790 to John S. Hobart, et al. No papers
OSSEY, Francis, Hazen's Regt., BLWt.13562. Iss. 8/3/1789. No papers
OSTEEN, David, N.C., S4637
Solomon, N.C., S9447
OSTEN, Henry, Md., BLWt.11581. Iss. 11/29/1790 to James Moore, Admr. No papers
OSTERHOUDT, Elias, N.Y., Catharine, W19949
Henry, N.Y., Sarah, W19943
Henry T., N.Y., Mariah, W26601, BLWt.53671-160-55
Kryn, N.Y., Jane, W19944
Tunis, N.Y., Marytie, W19947
William, N.Y., S11165
OSTERHOURT, Peter, N.Y., BLWt.6910. Iss. 6/15/1792. No papers
OSTERHOUT, Isaac, N.Y., S43758
OSTERMAN, Christian, N.Y., Elizabeth, W21876
OSTRANDER, Adam, N.Y., S43759
Andrew, N.Y., Jane, R16868
Henry, N.Y., Patty, W16667
Henry, N.Y., Mary, W20284
John, N.Y., Catharine, W15748
John A., N.Y., Sarah, W20283
Moses, N.Y., Clarissa, W19945
Peter, N.Y., BLWt.7576. Iss. 7/30/1790 to Edward Cumpston, ass. No papers
Peter, N.Y., Christina, W19946
Peter W., N.Y., Catharine, W21880 BLWt.10302-160-55
Teunis, N.Y., S11163
Thomas, N.Y., Elizabeth, W19942; BLWt.1619-200-Lt. Iss. 12/6/1792. Also recorded under BLWt. 2615 as above. No papers
William, N.Y., Maria, S22925
OSTRONDER, Andrew, See OSTRANDER
OSYER, Joseph, See OSHER
OTAAWIGHTON, John, Capt., Indian BLWt.1614-300 iss. 3/8/1792. Also see BLWt.2603
OTIS, Anna, former wid. of Stephen Thayer, Mass., which see
Barnabas, Ct., Cont., S9612
Edward, Ct., S32425
Elijah, N.H., S11167
Isaac, Mass., S43748
Jacob, Mass., S14067
James, Mass., S30627
James, Navy, Ct. Agcy. & res., S38276
John, Mass., S17612
John, N.H., S43749
John T., Ct., S16998
Joseph, Ct., BLWt.6256. Iss. 9/24/1790. No papers
Joseph, Ct., S27276. See Am. State Papers, Class 9, p.153, which shows on list of applicants for invalid pensions from Ct. Joseph Otis, Pvt., Col. Zebu-

OTIS (continued)
lon Butler's Regt. afterwards transferred to Col. Webb's Regt., enl. 1/1/1777 for the war, on the rolls in 1780. Wounded by a musket ball which entered and remained lodged in his thigh,2/1781 at Morrisiana. See also invalid pensioners of New Haven Co., Ct. printed in 1835.
Paul, Mass., N.H., S45042
Richard, Cont., Ct., S45043
OTT, Adam, Pa., S35021
Emanuel, Pa., R7826
Jacob, Pa., R7827
John, S.C., S18145
Peter, Mass., Beulah, W21884
OTTERSON, Hugh, Va., S40230
James, N.H., S16498
Samuel, S.C., S25344, Inv. file No. & S32424; claims placed together
OTTINGER, Christopher, Pa., Elizabeth, W3584; BLWt.80027-160-55
John, Pa., R7828
OTTO, Bodo, Hosp., BLWt.1621-450-Physician & Surg. Iss. 10/8/1794 to Margaret & John Otto, Exrs. of the last will & test. of Bodo Otto. No papers
Francis, N.Y., S16216
John A., Cont., Pa., S5133
Thomas, Hazen's Regt., BLWt. 13566. Iss. 5/20/1795. No papers
OUDERKIRK, Myndert, N.Y., BLWt. 7575. Iss. 9/27/1790. No papers
Peter, N.Y., S22926
Tacarus, See Takel
Takel/Tacarus, N.Y., Maria, W19938
OUGHELTREE, Daniel, N.J., R7829
OUR, Searchman, Va., Mary, R16873
OURANDT, John Detrich, See AURANDT
OURHAND, Dedrich, See John AURANDT
OURS, Searchman, See OUR
OURY, Adam, Pa., Mary, W2964
OUSBY, Thomas, S.C., BLWt.2455-200
OUSLEY, John, Va. See OWSLEY
Robert, See HOUSLY
OUSTED, George, N.J., R7830
OUSTERHOUDT, John, N.Y., R7831
OUT, John, N.Y., R7832
Matthias, N.Y., S9448
OUTHOUSE, Peter, Md., BLWt.11573; iss. 12/23/1795 to George Ponsonby, ass. No papers
Peter, Md., S46400
OUTLAW, Bentley, S.C., Martha, R7833
James, N.C., S41929
OUTTERBRIDGE, Stephen, Md., R7834
OUTWATER, Daniel, N.Y., Nelly, W15933
OVAITT, William, Ct., Sarah, W24376
OVAS, Nicholas, See HAWWAWAS
OVELMAN, George, Md., S8914
OVER, Jacob, See HOOVER
John, Pa., H7835
OVERBAGH, Isaac, N.Y., S16215
Jeremiah, N.Y., War of 1812, Sarah R16875; BLWt.27174-160-12
John, N.Y., Anna, W20286

OVERBAGH (continued)
Peter, N.Y., Catharine, R16874
OVERBY, William, N.C., S4641
OVERCREEK, Joseph, Md., BLWt.11574 iss. 1/8/1796 to George Ponsonby ass. No papers
OVERHISER, Conrad, N.Y., R7836
OVERLEY, Henry, Mo. & Va. res. & Agcy. S24303
OVERLIN, William, Va., Lititia W9612
OVERLINE, William, Va., R20172; BLWt.1466-100
OVERLOCK, Charles, Mass., S16999
OVERMAN, Henry, Pa., BLWt.10189 iss. 4/7/1795 to John Nicholson ass. No papers
OVERNTON, James, N.C., S41927
OVEROCKER, Adam, N.Y., Patience, W2329; BLWt.7091-160-55
John Wandall. See Wendal
Wendal/John Wandall, N.Y., Anny, W20287
OVERSTREET, Henry, Va., S14069
John, Va., S40231
Thomas, Va., Zillah, W8498
Thomas, Va., Fanny, W26604
OVERTON, Eli, N.C., Milla, W5458; BLWt.35821-160-55
James, See OVERNTON
John, Va., BLWt.1615-300-Capt. Iss. 1/19/1792. No papers
Jonathan, N.C., S8915
Justus, N.Y., S23349
Samuel, N.C., S41928
Samuel, Va., S16499
Seth, Ct., Privateer, R7839
Thomas, Ct., S36201
Thomas, Va., BLWt.1616-300-Capt. Iss. 12/31/1796 to William B. Grove, ass. No papers
OVIATT, Ebenezer, Ct., Eunice, W21885
Ebenezer, Mass., S43752
Nathan, Ct. See OVIUTT
Samuel, Cont., Ct., Murdell/Mindwell, W10846
William, See OVAITT
OVIT, Ebenezer, Ct. See OVIATT
Job, Ct., S38275
OVIUTT, Nathan, Ct., S14068
OVUTT, William, Ct., BLWt.6255, iss. 6/27/1789. No papers
OWAN, Thomas, N.C. See OWENS
OWANS, Thomas, See OWENS
OWEN, Alvan/Alven/Alvin, Ct., S43753
Alvan, Ct., R7840
Bailey, N.C., Polly, W3711; BLWt.26289-160-55
Benjamin C., Mass., S14074; BLWt.26268-160-55
Daniel, Ct., Cont., Lydia, W18478
Daniel, N.Y., S43761
David, N.J., Margaret, W3857; BLWt.36220-160-55
David, N.Y., Martha, W24378
David, N.C., Winefred, R16881
Elezer/Eleazer, Ct., Cont., S30628
Elijah, Ct., S30013
Elijah, Ct., Lydia, W13787

OWEN (continued)
Elisha, Mass., N.Y., R7841
Elisha, Vt., S14072
Elisha, Va., Elizabeth, W4560
Ephraim, N.Y. res., R7842
Frederick, Ct., S43762
Frederick, N.C., S21907
Frederick, Va., S1578
Gideon, Ct., Nancy, W20288
Harraway, Va., Elizabeth, W5463; BLWt.26404-160-55
Hugh, Mass., S31286
James, N.Y., S14071
James, S.C., Va., S5134
John, Ct., Lydia, W10221
John, N.C., R20421
John, N.C., S.C., b. N.C. or Va., Martha, R16884
John, Va., Dorothy, W5461; BLWt. 40694-160-55
John, Va., R7843
John, Va., R7844
Jonathan, Mass., N.Y., S14070
Jonathan, Mass., R.I., S43763
Jonathan, R.I., BLWt.3370 iss. 5/28/1792 to Israel Angell, ass. No papers
Joseph, Mass., Susanna, W4045
Joseph, Mass., N.Y., S28832
Mowbray/Mowberry/Mawberry, N.Y., Mary, W19950
Peter, Va., R7845
Philip, Mass., S28835
Samuel, Ct., Cont., Mass. & Vt., S11168
Shadrach, N.C., Mary, W5459
Thaddeus, Ct. Cont., Abigail, R16877
Thomas, Mass., BLWt.977-100
Timothy, N.H., S22430
William, Mass., BLWt.4785, iss. 10/18/1796 to William Hall. No papers
William, Mass., Lucy, W24377
William, N.C., Sally, R16883
William, Pa., S40232
William, Va., Tabitha, W8494
OWENBY, James, See OWNBEY
OWENS, Averilla, former wid. of Francis Miller, Va., which see
Bailey, See OWEN
Barnard, N.C., R7847
Benjamin, S.C., b. N.C., R7846
Charles, Va., Sarah, W10847
Daniel, N.Y., BLWt.7566. Iss. 1/5/1791 to William Radclift, ass. No papers
David, See OWEN
Edmund, N.C., b. Md., R7843
George, Md., S14073
James, S.C., Va. See OWEN
James Hooper, Mass., Navy, Elizabeth Stockwell, former wid., W15401
John, Ct. See OWEN
John, Hazen's Regt., & Invalids, BLWt.13567, iss. 8/1/1791 to Abraham Wayne & James Justice, Admrs. No papers
John, Va. See OWEN
John, Va., R7849

OWENS (continued)
Joseph, Cont., Md., S36200; BLWt.9-100
Mabery, N.Y., BLWt.7557 iss. 10/7/1790 to Anning Owens, ass. No papers
Mason, Va., S32426
Mowbray, See OWEN
Robert, Navy, Pa., Catherine, W3108
Stephen, Md., Nancy, W8281; BLWts. 11575-100 & 200-60-55
Thomas, N.C., Elizabeth, R16882. Name also appears as OWEN,OWAN & OWANS
Thomas, Pa., S38978
Timothy, N.H. See OWEN
Uriah, N.Y., Elizabeth, W5460, BLWt.7567-100 iss. 5/9/1796. No papers
Vincent, Va., S4639
William, N.C., b. Va., S9450
William, Va., res. Pa. at enl., S4640
William, Va., S16500
William, Va., Nancy, W8493
OWER, Searchman. See OUR
OWING, Alvin, Ct., BLWt.6254 iss. 6/9/1796 to Timothy Pitkin, ass. No papers
OWINGS, Richard, S.C., b. Md., S9449
OWL, Robert, Va., BLWt.12448. Iss. 10/21/1791 to Elias Parker, ass. No papers
OWLS, Robert, Va., S36713
OWNBEY, James, N.C., Joannah, W3712
OWNY, John, See OMEY
OWREY, Adam, See OURY
George, Pa., S17613
OWSLEY, John, Va., Charity, R16894
Thomas, See WOOSLEY
Thomas, Va., S35544
OX, Michael, Pa., BLWt.10192 iss. 9/26/179? to John McCleland, ass. No papers
Peter, Va., S40233
OXER, Christopher, Pa., Catharine, R16895
George, Va., R7851
OXX, Peter, Von Heer's Dragoons, BLWt.13559 iss. 10/28/1789 to Matt. McConnell, ass. No papers
OYSTER, John, Pa., Susan, R7851 1/2
OYZER, Joseph, See OSHER
OZBURN, Robert, See OSBORNE
OZGOOD, Jeremiah, Ct., S7283; BLWt.18014-160-55
OZIER, Joseph, See OSHER
OZMUN, Abraham, N.Y., R16897
OZMUND, Abraham, See OZMUN

P

PACE, Jesse, Va., Frances, W4305
Joel, Va., Mary, W21917
John, Va., Margaret, W3586; BLWt.101562-160-55
Michael, N.J., S40610
Newsom/Nusum, Va., Mary, W5496
Robert, Va., S15954
PACHARD, Shepherd, See Shepard PACKARD
PACK, William, Md., Phebe, R7852
William, N.J., Jane, W1467
PACKARD, Abisha, Mass., Rebecca, W26813
Adin, Mass., Keziah, W15159
Anna, former wid. of David Thayer, Mass., which see
Artemisia, former wid. of Joel Simmons, Mass., which see
Asa, Mass., S29371
Asahel, Ct., N.H., Vt., Priscilla, W1312; BLWt.26228-160-55
Benjamin, Mass., Abigail Kibby/Kibbey/Kibbee, former wid., W9103; BLWt.9071-160-55
Caleb, Mass., R.I., S19018
Daniel, Mass., BLWt.4877, iss. 9/10/1789 to Henry Newman. No papers
Daniel, Mass., S36720
David, Mass., S14095
Edward, Mass., Prudence, BLWt. 34825-160-55
Elijah, Cont., Mass., Thankful, W26836
Gooding, Mass., Mary Lee, former wid., W20444; BLWt.7434-160-55
Hezekiah, Cont., Mass., S20501
Ichabod, Mass., S17005
James, Mass., S36719
James, Mass., Freelove, W13797
Jedediah, Mass., Mehitable, W2162; BLWt.10022-160-55
Job, Mass., S18152
John, Ct., BLWt.6328, iss. 2/22/1799. No papers
Jonathan, Mass., S36722
Joshua, Mass., S33417
Levi, Mass., Martha, W18692; BLWt.6414-160-55
Luke, Mass., S29366
Mark, Mass., S11192
Nehemiah, Sheldon's Dragoons Ct., BLWt.6347, iss. 10/7/1789 to Benj. Tallmadge, ass. No papers
Nehemiah, Ct., S43787
Nehemiah, Drummer, Mass., BLWt. 4851, iss. 2/23/1796
Nehemiah, Mass., S36715
Nehemiah, Mass., Lucy, W26833
Oliver, Mass., Relief, W15166
Oliver, Mass., Mercy, W21904
Philip, Mass., Lucinda, W2330
Richards/Richard, Mass., Sarah/Sally, W21836
Robert, N.H., Elizabeth, W26840
Seth, Cont., Mass., Lois, W15160
Shepard/Shepherd, Mass., S5876
PACKER, Eldredge, Ct., Sabrina, W21888

PACKER (continued)
Henry, Cont., Mass., S18538
Jacob, N.J., Sarah, W10854; BLWt.19822-160-55
John, Ct., S38291
John, Ct., Hannah, W26284
John, N.J., S3635
John, N.J., Va., S17627
PACKHARD, Caleb, Mass., R.I., See PACKARD
PACKHURST, Jonathan, N.H. See PARKHURST
Samuel, Mass. See PARKHURST
PADDER, John, N.Y., BLWt.7585 iss. 9/15/1790 to John Hobart, et al, assnes. No papers
PADDLEFORD, Zachariah, See PADELFORD
PADDOCK, Apollos, Mass., R.I. Polly, W2642; BLWt.8452-160-55
Gains, Cont., Mass., Polly, W26850
Henry, N.Y., R7854
John, N.Y., S14076
Nathan, N.Y., Sarah, R7857
Peter, N.Y., R7856
PADELFORD, Benjamin, Mass., Sylvia, W17426
James, Mass., Abigail, W15176
Zachariah, Mass., Navy, Privateer, Lydia, W26285; BLWt. 45667-160-55
PADGETT, John, N.C., Elizabeth, W2331; BLWt.31563-160-55
Thomas, N.J., S1074
PAFFORD, William, N.C., Haney/Bethany, W5483; BLWts.2406-100 & 169-60-55
PAGAN, David, Va., Mary, W5499
PAGE, Abel, Ct., BLWt.6265 & 13578 iss. 5/14/1790 to Benj. Talmadge, ass. No papers
Abijah, Mass., S23350
Abner, N.J., R7860
Abraham, N.H., Dorothy, W26817
Amos, Mass., S23364
Amos, Mass., Elizabeth, W18697
Amos, Mass., R7861
Ann, former wid. of Thomas Dougal, Cont., Ct., which see
Benjamin, Navy, R.I., S3629
Benjamin, N.H., Mary, W5489
Benoni, R.I., Abigail, R7859
Caleb, Cont., Mass., Keziah, W26815
Carter, Va., Lucy, W2161
Chase, N.H., S36724
Coffin, N.H., Betty, W21896
Daniel, Mass., S36723
Daniel, N.H., Ann, W26845; BLWt. 9409-160-55
David, N.H., BLWt.3404, iss. 3/25/1790. No papers
David, N.H., S41940
David, N.H., S45050
Ebenezer, Mass., Rebecca, W8501; BLWt.31567-160-55
Edmund, Ct., Sarah, R7873
Edward, N.H., S37282
Elias, Ct., S23356

PAGE (continued)
Elijah, N.H., S28839
Enoch, Mass., N.H., Elice, W26605
Enoch, N.H., Isabel, R7865
Foster, Mass. See PAIGE
Gad, Ct., Abigail, W17418
Hannah, former wid. of Isaac Van Norman, N.Y., which see
Isaac, Cont., Mass., N.H., S11195
Isaac, Mass., S33426
James, Pa., BLWt.10200, iss. 6/29/1789 to M. McConnell, ass. No papers
Jared, Ct., R7871 1/2
Job, Navy, R.I. Agcy. & res., S38988
Job, N.H., S16502
John, Ct., S41936
John, Mass., S30639
John, Mass., Mary, W13790
John, N.C., S7286
Jonathan, Mass., S34462
Jonathan, Vt., Patience, R7871
Jose, Mass., S46328
Joseph, Ct., Sea Service, R7866
Joseph, Mass., S33416
Joss, Mass., BLWt.4860, iss. 1/26/1790 to John May. No papers
Leme, N.H. See Leme PAIGE
Leonard, Va., S11201
Luther, Ct., BLWt.6261 iss. 4/9/1791. No papers
Luther, Ct., S46329
Luther, Ct., Rachel, R7872
Mary, former wid. of Wm. Hall, Ct., Mass., which see
Moses, Cont., Mass., S41935
Moses, Cont., N.H., S45051; BLWt.1626-200-Lt. Iss. 12/17/1795 to William Thom, ass. No papers
Moses, N.H., R7870
Nathan, Mass., S18535
Nathan, Mass., S41938
Parker, Mass., Eunice, W18705
Philip, Cont., N.H., Mass., Hannah, W21900
Phinehas, Ct., Zeruiah, W18725
Phinehas, Cont., N.H., S45049
Phinehas, Mass., Hannah, W21902
Reuben, N.H., Elizabeth, W18708
Richard, Va., Elizabeth, R7868
Samuel, Mass., Elizabeth Walker, former wid., W14116
Samuel, Mass., Rebecca, W27456
Simon, Crane's Cont. Arty., Mass., BLWt.4887 iss. 12/30/1796 to Evander Childs. No papers
Solomon, N.C., Mary, R7863
Stephen, R.I., S21911
Thomas, Mass., Polly, W6846; BLWt.26612-160-55
Timothy, Ct. See PAIGE
Timothy, N.J., Mary, R7869
Titus, Ct., S23836
William, Mass., S37285
William, Navy, R.I., Elizabeth, W26819
William, N.H., Sarah, W26844
William, N.H., Patience, BLWt. 44509-160-55

PAGETT, Frederick, Va., S8930
PAIGE, Ann, See Thomas DOUGAL, Cont., Ct.
Foster, Mass., Amital/Amity, W15168; BLWt.13422-160-55
Jonathan, Vt. See PAGE
Leme, N.H., Polly Robinson, former wid., W2005
Timothy, Ct., S11186
PAIN, Charles, Mass., S41937
John, Del., S8924
John, R.I., Frances, W6847; BLWt.34857-160-55
Richard, N.H., S21408
Robert, Mass., S43793
Samuel Royal, R.I., R.I. Sea Service, S21413
PAINE, Abel, Mass., R.I., Vt., S15956
Benjamin, Mass., N.Y., R.I., S3623
Benjamin, R.I., Anna, W21897
Benoni, R.I., Martha, W26820
Charles, Mass., BLWt.4841 iss. 2/13/1795 to Abner Stow. No papers
Charles, Mass., S33418
Charles, N.C., Va., S4643
David, N.Y., S14085
Ebenezer, Mass., Rachel, R7875; BLWt.14960-160-55
Edmund, N.C., Va., S3624
Edward, Ct. See PAYNE
Edward, R.I., Margaret, W21894; BLWt.1307-100
Eleazer, Ct. See PAYNE
Eli, Ct., S14093
Francis, Col. Seth Warner's Regt. BLWt.1627-200-Lt. Iss. 8/7/1789 to Anspach & Rodgers, ass. No papers
George, Va., S38980
Isaac, Ct., S36208
Jabez, Mass., Sea Service, S19020
Jesse, Mass., S21915
Joel, Mass., Azubah, R7874
John, Cont., N.H. Green Mt. Boys, See PAYNE
John, Mass., S45058
John, Mass., Rhoda, W18713
Joseph, Mass., S33415
Joseph, Mass., Auley, W19963
Joseph, R.I., BLWt.3416 iss. 6/30/1789. No papers
Lovina, former wid. of John Brown, Mass., which see
Miller, Mass., S41051
Nathaniel, Mass., R7877
Noah, N.H., Polly, W26834
Oliver, R.I., Abigail, W21890
Peleg, Mass., S15951
Rufus, N.Y., S14096
Samuel, N.H., N.Y., S14094
Silvanus, Mass., Susannah, W15156
Simon, R.I., S21910
Stephen, R.I., Elthiah, W21923
Thomas, Ct., Elizabeth, R7876
Thomas, Mass., Anna, W21927
Thomas, N.Y., R.I., Huldah, W18720 BLWt.13729-160-55
William, Md., S40240

PAINE (continued)
William, Mass. See PAYNE
William, Proctor's Arty., Pa., BLWt.10234 iss. 6/29/1789 to M. McConnell. No papers
Zebediah, Mass., Sarah, R7878
PAINTER, Deliverance, Ct., S15567
Edward, N.Y., BLWt.7621 iss. 1/5/1791 to Jonothan Shepherd, ass. No papers
Elisha, Ct., BLWt.1603-400
George, Va., Lee's Legions, BLWt. 12452 & 13634, iss. 1/7/1790. No papers
George, Va., Rebecca H., W8507; BLWt.26768-160-55
Henry, Cont., Md., Sarah, W5470; BLWt.6024-160-55
John, N.C., S32432
John, Pa., Catharine, W3110
Joseph, N.C., S32430
Melcher, Md., Mary, W9226
Thomas, Ct., Sea Service, Privateer, S18536
PAITSELL, Jacob, Pa., Mary, W3858; BLWt.24982-160-55
PALATINE, Cash, Ct., BLWt.6331, iss. 8/7/1789. No papers
PALE, Matthew, See PATE
PALLETT, John, Va., Sarah, W5492
PALMANTEER, Isaac, See PALMATEER
PALMAR, John, N.H. See PALMER
PALMATEER, Abraham, N.Y., S23352
Isaac, N.Y., S43784
John Dorman, N.Y., R7889
William, N.Y., Mary Ann, W26290; BLWt.27648-160-55
PALMATER, John, N.Y., BLWt.7594 iss. 6/30/1790 to Edward Cumpston, ass.
John, N.Y., S19015
PALMATIER, Isaac, N.Y., BLWt.7610 iss. 9/24/1791 to Resolve Waldron, ass. No papers
Isaac, N.Y., Nelly, W18731
PALMER, Aaron, Ct., Mary, R7895
Abiah, N.Y., S14082
Abraham, Ct., S43768
Adin, R.I., Lois, W19965
Amaziah, Navy, N.Y., Rebecca, W26827
Amos, N.Y., Catharine, R7882
Andrew, Pa., BLWt.10219 iss. 5/16/1791. No papers
Benedict, R.I., S21908
Benjamin, Ct., S17616
Benjamin, Ct., S31895
Benjamin, Ct., Sarah, R7907
Benjamin, Cont., Mass., Sybbel, W18717
Benjamin, Va., S38289
Bezaleel, Mass., S36714
Chilion, Cont., Ct., Lydia, W26294
Chilleab, Ct., Mary, W10865; BLWt.11162-160-55
Daniel, Mass. res. of son 1836, R7884
Daniel, Ct., Privateer, S7298
Daniel, Va., S7291
David, Ct., Anne, W18709
David, Mass., Phebe Slaton, former

PALMER (continued)
wid., W19043
Ebenezer, N.H., Dolly/Dorothy, W18721
Edmond, Va., S7295
Edward, Ct., Delia, W18695
Elias, N.Y., Mercy S., W6850; BLWt.36555-160-55
Elijah, Ct., Sea Service, Polly, R7885; BLWt.33533-160-55
Elisha, Ct., Eunice, W26287; BLWt.36561-160-55
Elisha, Va., S5874
Elizabeth, former wid. of Nathaniel Fanning, Navy, U.S. Navy up to 1805, Old Acc. Navy, which see
Elkannah/Elkany, R.I., Emblem/Emblen, W21889
Ephraim, Ct., N.Y., S8940
Ezekiel, Mass., Thankful, W5502; BLWt.10253-160-55
Fones, R.I., S21909
George, Ct., S16221
George, Ct., Hannah, W17419
George, Ct., Privateer, R7887
George M., Md., Mary, W4561; BLWt.1755-100. Name also appears as Parmer, Paulmer, Paulmore, Palmore.
Henry, Ct., N.Y., S14102
Humphrey, Ct., Eunice, W4756; BLWt.24151-160-55
Ichabod, N.H., S17614
Isaac, Ct., Hannah, W21909
Isaac, Mass., S14111
Isaac, Va., S31293
James, Ct., Navy, Privateer, Palmela, W19969
James, Mass., S16220
James, N.H., S11188
James, N.H., Eunice A., W2159
James, Va., S7293
Jared, Ct., Cont., S23358; BLWts.6330-100 & 164-60-55
Jared, N.Y., Jane, W21913
Jenkins, Cont., Mass., S37289; BLWt.1439-100
Jesse, Ct., N.Y., Abigail, W18707
Jesse, N.C., Elizabeth, W5482; BLWt.50895-160-55
Job, R.I., BLWt.3418, iss. 1/23/1796 to Henry G. Gardner. No papers
Job, R.I., S38983
Job, S.C., S21917
Joel, Ct., S38979
John, Ct., S11189
John, Ct., S43807
John, Ga., Susanna, W309
John, Hazen's Regt., BLWt.13591 iss. 3/21/1792 to Samuel Maus, ass. of Adam Kuntz, Adm. No papers
John, Mass., S11209
John, Mass., S37281
John, N.H., S41050
John, N.Y., Olive, W5501; BLWt. 24912-160-55
John, R.I., Elizabeth, W2334;

PALMER (continued)
BLWt.31305-160-55
John, S.C., S17004
John, S.C., Mary, R7896
John, Va., S8928. See N.A. Acc. No. 874. No. 05129. Not half pay
John Stoddard, R.I., Margaret, W26847
Jonah, Cont., Ct., S41049
Jonothan, Ct., Bounty Land, No papers
Joseph, Armand's Corps. BLWt. 13575 iss. 9/7/1790 to Joseph Ashton, ass. No papers
Joseph, Ct., Eunice, W13793; BLWt.6274-160-55
Joseph, N.J., Christian, W3714; BLWt.27679-160-55
Joseph, Va., S31289
Joseph Pearce, Mass., Elizabeth, W19975
Joshua, Mass., S14079
Joshua, S.C., b. Va., S21912
Lazarus, Ct., Rachel, W19952
Levi, Ct., Sarah, W16368
Louisa, former wid. of Silas Holmes, Ct., Cont., which see
Marshall, Ct., Eunice Fox, former wid., W17918
Michael, Md., BLWts.13603 & 14108, iss. 2/24/1795 to Francis Sherrard, ass. of Henry Redding, Admr. No papers
Michael, Md., R7899
Milo, Ct., R7897
Nathan, Ct., R20422
Nathan, Cont., enl. in Ct., S43767
Nathaniel, Cont., Mass., Sarah, W26816
Nathaniel, N.Y., R7902
Nathaniel, R.I., S38984
Nehemiah, Ct., Privateer, Anna S. W9227; BLWt.29012-160-55
Noah, N.Y., Tirzah, R7904; BLWt. 45716-160-55
Noah, R.I., Betsey, W27615; BLWt. 24902-160-55
Ozias/Osias, Ct., Mass., S7294
Parrum/Param, Ct., S36204
Philip/Phillip, N.J., S34459
Reuben, Ct., S14091
Richard, N.J., BLWt.8640 iss. 9/8/1789 to Samuel Rutan, ass. No papers
Samuel, Ct., Cft. No. 28163
Samuel, Ct., S43769
Samuel, Ct., Thankful, W17420
Samuel, Mass., Dorcas, R7906
Samuel, Navy, N.H., Anna/Hannah Hubbard, former wid., W23383
Seth, Ct., Deborah, W21911
Simon, N.H., Phebe, W1641
Smith, Ct., S36205
Solomon, N.Y., S23353
Stephen, Ct., Hannah Davis, former wid., R2721
Stephen, N.Y., S14098
Stephen, R.I., S15952
Thomas, Ct., S36202
Thomas/Thomas Kinne, Ct.,

PALMER (continued)
Margaret, W27925
Thomas, Ct., Cont., N.Y., S16217
Thomas, Cont., Va., S3651
Thomas, Md., Sarah, R7908
Thomas, Mass., S43808
Thomas, Navy, N.H., S45054
Thomas, Va. Sea Service, Judith Carter, former wid., R1751. Her last husb., Thomas Carter, also served in the Rev. War
Thomas Kinne, Ct. See Thomas
Timothy, Cont., Mass., S33433
Tryphena, former wid. of William McQueen, Ct., Sea Service, which see
William, Ct., R7911
William, Ga., Va., Frances Lewis, former wid., W8083
William, N.C., S7287
William, Va., See PARMER
William, Va., R7912
Wyatt, Ct., S23357
Zadock, Mass.; BLWt.4801 iss. 8/22/1789 to Benj. Winchell. No papers
Zadock, see John SMITH, Mass., Jane
Zuer Shadock, Mass., R7913
PALMERTON, John, See PALMETON
PALMES, Andrew, Ct., Cont., Navy, Sarah, W21887
Samuel, Ct., S36206
PALMETER, Benjamin, Cont., N.Y., See PARMENTER
Phoebe Maria, dau., Jonathan Woolley, Mass., N.H., which see
PALMETIER, William, Hazen's Regt. BLWt.13595. Iss. 7/20/1791 to James Hullet, ass. No papers
PALMETON, Benjamin, See PARMENTER
John, Cont., N.Y., Green Mt. Boys, Elizabeth, W19964
PALMETTER, Jesse, Ct., Cont., S43775
PALMITEER, William/William Paul Meteer/William Paul Mateer, Pa., S40242
PALMITER, John, Ct., Anna/Anne, W5474
Jonathan, Ct., R.I., S11180
Joshua, R.I., S4642
Paul, N.J., Ct., S17624
Phinehas, Ct., R.I., War of 1812, S5870
William, Ct., R.I. See PALMITTER
PALMITTER, Joseph, R.I., S14077
William, Ct., R.I., S43765
PALMORE, George M. See PALMER
Jonathan, N.Y., BLWt.7584, iss. 8/9/1790. No papers
William, Ga. See PALMER
PAMPELLY, Bennett, See PUMPILLY
PAMPHILLION, Thomas, Navy, Md. Agcy., & res., S35026
PAMPHLIN, William, Va. See PAMPLIN
PAMPLIN, William, Va., S3653
PANDER, Thomas, N.C., Nancy, W21906
PANGBINE, Moses, Ct., BLWt.6268 Iss. 1/18/1800. No papers
PANGBORN, Joseph, N.J., S34464

PANGBURN, Adonijah, Ct., S38290
John, N.Y.; BLWt.7596 iss. 10/12/1790 to Isaac Bogaart, ass. No papers
John E., N.Y., Nancy, W19968
Peter, N.J., Maria, R7917
Richard, N.Y., S22929
Samuel, Cont., N.Y., S43778
William, N.Y., BLWt.7656, iss. 2/14/1791 to Stephen N. Bayard, ass. No papers
William, N.Y., S35023
Zillah, former wid. of Asa Baker, Ct., Cont., Vt., which see
PANNELL, Benjamin, Va., S3650
PANTER, Adam, Va., S1923
George, Va., See PAINTER
John, N.C., See PAINTER
PAPPEE, Robert, Von Heer's Corps, BLWt.13576 iss. 10/28/1789. No papers
PARCE, Caleb, Mass., R.I., S43833
PARCEL, Thomas, N.J., Elizabeth, W4048
PARCELL, Anthony, N.J., BLWt.8629 iss. 5/9/1792. No papers
Matthias, N.J., Mary Drew, former wid., W3965; BLWt.34596-160-55
PARCHER, George, Mass., S37280
Henry, N.C., S18148
PARCHMENT, Peter, See PERCHMENT
PARDEE, Aaron, Cont., Mass., S45993; BLWt.1656-200-Lt. Iss. 3/20 or 25 or 26, 1790. No papers
Abijah, Ct., Rosanna, W21908
Chandler, Ct., S20905
Charles, Ct., S14087
Daniel, Ct., Sea Service, S17615
Eli, Ct., S23365
James, Ct., Elizabeth, R7918
John, N.Y., Hannah, W18719
John, N.Y., R7919
Joseph, Ct., Sarah, R7921
Lemuel, Ct., S43800
Nathaniel, Ct., S43795
Silas, N.Y., Abigail, W16367
Thomas, Ct., N.Y., Susanna, W3293 BLWt.26739-160-55
PARDO, Joseph, Proctor's Arty., Pa., BLWt.10233 iss. 2/14/1791. No papers
PARDOE, Joseph, Pa., S34461
PARDUE, Lilliston, S.C., Sarah, W5491; BLWt.7299-160-55
William, Ga., R7923
PARDY, Nathaniel, Ct., BLWt.6327, iss. 9/7/? No papers
Samuel, N.Y., Joanna, W5488; BLWt.38572-160-55
PARE, Johannes, See John PERRY
PARENT, William, N.J., Amy, W1067
PARHAM, Drury, N.C., S9452
Kennon, N.C., R7924
Thomas, N.C., Sarah, W809; BLWt. 31568-160-55
Thomas, N.C., Agness, W5524
PARIS, James, N.C., Polly, R7925
Robert, N.C., also served in 1774, R7926
Robert, Va., S31287

PARIS (continued)
William, N.C., Sarah, W10222
PARISH, Charles, N.C., R7929
Cyprian, N.Y. See PARRISH
Ephraim, Mass., Eunice, W18712
Frederick, Va., S5881
Jacob, Cont. See PARRISH
James, Va., Mary, W4046
John, N.Y., S23359
John, N.C., Elizabeth, R7930
John, R.I., Hannah, W8283
John, Va., Rebecca, W5478
Moses, Va., S38286
Roswell, Ct., Eunice, W1918 BLWt.9428-160-55
Stephen, S.C., Theodosia, W2423 BLWt.28505-160-55
William, Va., S35548
PARK, Amaziah, Ct., Mass., Sabra/Sabrey, W2688
Daniel, N.J., S3630
Ebenezer, Ct., S14109
Ezra, Cont., Ct., Anna, W16362
Isaac, Ct. See PARKE
John, Ct. See PARKE
John, Cont., Mass., Lucy, W15155
Jonas, Cont., Ct. Sea Service, Rachel, W19966
Joshua, Mass., S33424
Matthias, Mass., S29360
Oliver, Mass., Lydia. W19976
Samuel, S.C., S32428
Thomas, Ct. See PARKS
Thomas, Ct., R7932
Thomas, Mass., S33423
William, Mass., S19017
William, Mass., Eunice, W15150
PARKE, Caleb, Mass., Ruth, W26824
Daniel, Ct., S7296
Isaac, Ct., Mary, W21895
Jacob, Cont., Mass., S33435
John, Ct., S43789
John, Ct., BLWt.7-100 iss. 8/29/1866
John, Va., b. Md., S17002
Robert, Mass., Ruth, R7970
Thomas, Ct., See PARKS
Zebulon, N.J., S3641
PARKER, Aaron, Mass., S18150
Aaron, Mass., Jerusha, W26822; BLWt.9059-160-55
Aaron, Mass., Navy, Privateer, S15953; BLWt.31553-160-55
Abel, Ct., Lydia, W18706; BLWt.15165-160-55
Abigail, former wid. of Wm. McIntire, Mass., which see
Abijah, Mass., BLWt.4796 iss. 8/26/1790 to M. Cutler. No papers
Abraham, Ct., BLWt.6323 iss. 7/22/1789. No papers
Abraham, Ct., Rosannah Ingersoll former wid., W5002
Abraham, Mass., S30635
Abraham, N.C., S3640
Abram/Abraham, Pa., S31290
Alexander/Elexander, Mass., R.I. Bethiah, R7938
Alexander, Pa., BLWt.1705-300-Capt. Iss. 7/26/1789. No papers
Alexander, Va., BLWt.1740-300-Capt. Iss. 8/10/1789 to

PARKER (continued)
Richard Platt, ass. No papers
Alexander, Va., S38288
Alexander, Va. res., R---
Amasa, N.H., S43791; BLWt.768-100
Amos, Ct., S43766
Amos, Ct., Polly, W26848
Amos, Sappers & Miners, BLWt. 13577, iss. 11/2/1791 to Jonathan Tuttle, ass. No papers
Andress, N.Y., S8939
Ann, former wid. of William Jones, S.C., Va., which see
Asa, Ct., S23354
Asa, N.H., 19416
Asaph, Ct., S7300
Ashael, Ct., R7935
Barnabas/Barnabus, Mass., S37277
Benjamin, Ct., Lorinda, W16360
Benjamin, Ct., R7937
Benjamin, Mass., BLWt.1646-200-Lt. Iss. 6/9/1790. No papers
Benjamin, Mass., Hannah, W13791; BLWt.9479-160-55
Benjamin, Mass., Susannah, W15149
Benjamin, Mass., Elizabeth, W15152
Benjamin, Mass., Lois, W16669
Benjamin, Mass., Rebecca, W21924
Benjamin, Va., S46062
Benjamin Woods, Navy, N.H.,S45044
Cader, See Kader
Caleb, Mass., Thankful, W18699
Charles, Mass., R.I., S15551
Dan, Mass., S23834
Dan, Mass., S44583
Daniel, Cont., Mass., Catharine, W189
Daniel, Mass., S33430
Daniel, Mass., S37283
Daniel, Mass., Sarah, W26842
Daniel, N.H., S11204
Daniel, N.C., R7939
David, Mass., S29369
David, Mass., S30638
David, Mass., Betsey, W570; BLWt. 26886-160-55
Ebenezer, Mass., S30015
Ebenezer, N.Y., BLWt.7593 iss. 10/7/1789 to Benj. Tallmadge, ass. No papers
Ebenezer, Vt., S14101
Edmund, Cont., N.Y., S38294
Edmund, Mass., S28836
Edmund, Lamb's Arty., N.Y., BLWt. 7646, iss. 10/23/1790
Edward, Ct., S14103
Edward, N.Y., BLWt.7615. Iss. 8/3/1790 to Cornelius V. Dyck, ass. No papers
Edward, Va., S31292
Eleazer, Mass., S37288
Elias, Cont., Mass., Mary, W15165 BLWt.1647-200-Lt. Iss. 7/16/1790 No papers
Elijah, Ct., Cont., R7943
Elijah, Cont., Mass., Priscilla, R7951
Elijah, Mass., Mehitable Kibbee/Kibbie, former wid., R5904
Elisha, Ct., S5145
Elisha, Ct., S31288

PARKER (continued)
Elisha, Ct., S.C., S11354
Elisha, Cont., Mass., S45045
Elisha, Mass., R7941
Elisha, N.Y., BLWt.7614; Iss. 8/3 1790 to Cornelius V. Dyck, ass. No papers
Elisha, N.C., S11211
Elizabeth, former wid. of William Harvey, Mass., which see
Ephraim, Mass., Hannah, W4304; BLWt.13182-160-55
Ezra, Mass., S29364
Francis, N.Y., R.I., S11194
Free G./Freegrove, Mass., S32436
Freegrove, See Free G.
Gamaliel, Ct., Martha Hall, former wid., W17038; BLWt.6307-100-Pvt. Iss. 9/2/1791 to Jon^a. Tuttle, ass. No papers
George, Mass., S33425
George, N.J., S1072
Gershom, N.J., BLWt.8662. Iss. 9/11/1789. No papers
Humphrey, N.C., S7285
Imla, Navy, Mass., Hannah, W18723
Isaac, Ct., BLWt.6319. Iss. 6/1/1793 to Stephen Thorn, ass. No papers
Isaac, Ct., Anna, W16365
Isaac, Ct., Esther, W19967
Isaac, Ct., Susannah, R7954
Isaac, Mass., S33422
Isaac, N.Y., S23835
Jackson, N.Y., BLWt.7651. Iss. 5/1/1792 to David Ruinton, ass. No papers
Jacob, Ct., S17006
Jacob, Cont., Mass., S33431
James, Ct., S14106
James, Ct., S21409
James, Mass., BLWt.4844. Iss. 12/29/1792. No papers
James, N.Y., BLWt.7629. Iss. 10/9/1792 to Veeder & Alexander, ass.
James, N.Y., S43770
James, Pa., Rachel, W3587
James, R.I., Miriam, W1920
James, S.C., Jane, R7947
James, Va., Rebecca, W6853
Jesse, Mass., BLWt.4865. Iss. 4/1/1790. No papers
Jesse, Mass., S33440
Jesse, Mass., Hannah, W18724
Jesse, Va., S11217
John, Ct., S38982
John, Ct., S43792; BLWt.112-100
John, Ct., Mass., Elizabeth, W18722
John, Ct., R.I., Vt., S14105
John, Cont., R.I., Mass., Joanna, W21901
John, Mass., S11181
John, Mass., Elizabeth, W26818; BLWt.6406-160-55
John, Mass., Anne, W26837
John, N.C., Rhoda, W10856; BLWt. 24437-160-55
John, Not Rev. War, Indian War 1791, Ky. Mil., Old War Inv.

PARKER (continued)
File 26332
John, Pa., BLWt.10207. Iss. 3/10/1790. No papers
John, Pa., Julian, W3190
John, Pa., Charity, W3588
John, Pa., Va., S14081
John, S.C., S21414
John, Va., b. Md., S32435
Jonas, Mass., Susannah, W15158
Jonathan, Ct., S41039
Jonathan, Cont., Mass., N.H., S45046
Jonathan, Cont., Mass., N.H., Emma/Anna, W5500; BLWt.7444-160-55
Jonathan, R.I., S38987
Joseph, Ct., Hannah, W18704
Joseph, Ct., Cont., N.H., S14107
Joseph, Ct., Vt., Sarah, R7952
Joseph, Cont., Vt., S43772
Joseph, Mass., BLWt.4834. Iss. 11/29/1792 to Samuel Emery. No papers
Joseph, Mass., S43788
Joseph, N.J., S1073
Joseph, Pa., S8927
Joseph, Pa., S40241
Joseph, Va., S38285
Joseph U., Cont., Mass., S43796
Joshua, Mass., Elizabeth, W18696; BLWt.12819-160-55
Josiah, Cont., Mass., S15955; BLWt.6006-160-55
Josiah, Cont., Mass., Susannah, W21915
Josiah, Mass., S29368
Jotham, Ct., Sarah, W19957
Kader/Cader, N.C., BLWt.1028-200
Kedar, N.C., S3636
Kedar/Kidar, N.C., S7299
Kidar, See Kedar
Lemuel, Mass., Hannah Cushman, former wid., W17670
Leonard, Mass., Abigail, BLWt. 16260-160-55
Levi, Ct., S14083
Levi, Ct., Eunice, W4754; BLWt. 34858-160-55
Levi, Mass., S45047; BLWt.1645-200-Lt. Iss. 10/13/1791 to William Allis, ass. No papers
Levi, Mass., Jemima, W21892
Levi, Mass., Mary, W21914
Michael, N.Y., Rachel Shepherd, former wid., R9492
Molly, former wid. of Charles Herbert, Navy, Mass., which see
Nahum, Mass., S11200
Nathan, Ct., Eunice, W24879; BLWts. 1661-100 & 146-60-55
Nathaniel, Ct., BLWt.6262 & Wt. No. 146-60-55. Iss. 10/16/1789. Wt.146 to Theodosius Fowler, ass. No papers
Nathaniel, Mass., Navy, Patience Wood, former wid., W15499. Her last husb., Coolidge P. Wood, was a Rev. soldier
Nehemiah, Mass., S5137
Oliver, Mass., Lydia, W21907

PARKER (continued)
Paul, R.I., Phille, W13792
Peter, Cont., Mass., Brigget/Bridget, W26839
Peter, N.C., S3638
Peter, R.I., Mary, W26291; BLWt.30913-160-55
Peter, Vt., S29358
Philemon, Cont., Mass., S41045
Phinehas, Ct., S9984
Reuben, N.H., Lydia, R7949
Richard, Va., BLWt.525-500
Richard, Va. Sea Service, R81, Va. Half Pay. See N.A. Acc. No. 837, Va. State Navy, Richard Parker, Y.S. file, Va. Half Pay
Richard J./or I., N.Y., BLWt. 7631 iss. 8/10/1790 to John Warren, ass. No papers
Richard J., N.Y., S43801
Robert, Cont., Mass., Betsy, W2638
Robert, Cont., Pa., Mary, W3448; BLWt.1714-200-Capt.-Lt. Iss. 4/10/1790. No papers
Robert, Mass., S33434
Robert, N.H., Rebekah, W26814
Samuel, res. Ct., Dis. See Am. State Papers, Class 9, p.61. He was wounded by a cannon ball, which shot away the rim of his belly, about 2 inches; expedition on R.I.
Samuel, Ct., S18541
Samuel, Ct., Mass., S11190
Samuel, Cont., N.H., S45048
Samuel, Crane's Cont. Arty., Mass., BLWt.4884. Iss. 4/15/1796 to Bradley Richards. No papers
Samuel, Mass., S19019
Samuel, N.H., S21913
Silas, Cont., Mass., S41041
Silas, Mass., Sea Service, Privateer, Mary, W17621; BLWt.61004-160-55
Simeon, Mass., Thankful, W19974; BLWt.30921-160-55
Simon, Mass., Susannah, W18729
Solomon, N.H., Vt., S11183
Stephen, Ct., S17625
Stephen, Mass., Mercy/Marcy, W15169
Stephen, N.H., S41044
Stiles, Mass., S40245
Susanna, former wid. of William Dutton, Mass., which see
Thaddeus, Mass., S43798
Thomas, Cont., N.H., Betty, W26838
Thomas, N.H., Lucretia, W18728
Thomas, R.I., Luranah, W12583
Thomas, Va., BLWt.1741-300-Capt. Iss. 8/10/1789 to Richard Platt, ass. No papers. See also BLWt. 1742
Thomas, Va., BLWt.1742-300-Capt. No date of issue and only the following N.B. Mr. Moore informs us that this Wt. was located at the Treasury 12/24/1802. No papers
Thomas, Va., S1243
Thomas, Va., S1709

PARKER (continued)
Thomas, Va., S38287
Timothy, Ct., BLWt.259-100
Timothy, N.C., S3637
William, Ct., Ruth, W19954
William, Mass., S11216
William, Mass., S12959
William, Mass., S33419
William, Mass., S33432
William, Mass., Sarah, W1640; BLWt.9058-160-55
William, Mass., Elizabeth, W26846
William, Mass., Navy, Susannah, W19973
William, N.H., Mary Hale, former wid., W8213
William, N.C., Va., b. Va., S8936
William, Pa., R7955
William, R.I., d. 10/10/1841, S43773
William, R.I., d. 12/30/1833, S43797
William, Va., Mary, R7950
William H., Va. Sea Service, R82, Va. Half Pay. See N.A. Acc. No. 837-Va. State Navy, Wm. H. Parker Y.S. File, Va. Half Pay
Wyatt, Va., Nancy, W573
Wyman, Ct., BLWts.6320 & 6329. Iss. 7/19/1798 to Wyman Parker. No papers
Wyman, Ct., Cont., Marcy/Mercy, W15793
PARKERS, George, Pa., BLWt.10203. Iss. 8/7/1789 to Richard Platt, ass. No papers
PARKERSON, Jacob, Cont., N.C., Va., b. Va., S31902
James, Va., BLWt.1246; iss. 5/8/1794. No papers
PARKES, David, N.Y., S22928
Ebenezer, Ct., Janette, W2425; BLWt.16111-160-55
George, N.C. See PARKS
Solomon, Va. See PARKS
PARKHILL, David, Mass., Vt., Dorcas W15170
James, Pa., S23832
PARKHURST, Abraham, Ct., Cont., S34465
Alpheus, Mass., Phebe, W19972
Azel, Ct., S21916
Benjamin, Vt., S19421
David, Cont., Ct., Susannah, W24878; BLWts.6348-100-1790 & 155-60-55
Ephraim, Mass., Bathsheba Barnes/Barns, former wid., W21632
George, Mass., BLWt.4807. Iss. 3/25/1790. No papers
George, Mass., Rebecca, R7960
George, Mass., N.H., S37290
John, See Philip JUDD
John, Mass., S46200
John, N.J., Letitia, W4757
Jonathan, Mass., S33427
Jonathan, N.H. & War of 1812, S14080
Leonard, Mass., Hannah, BLWt. 47988-160-55
Moses, Mass.,S38293;BLWt.140-100
Nathan, N.H., Sarah/Sally, W21920

PARKHURST (continued)
Parle, Vt., R7958
Phinehas, Vt., S17620
Pierce, Ct., Sea Service, Cont., S15554
Samuel, Mass., Anna, W2333; BLWt. 31572-160-55
Samuel, N.H., Vt., enl. from Mass. Rachel, W18716
Solomon, Ct., S34463
PARKINS, Nathan, See PERKINS
PARKINSON, Aaron, N.J., S14104
Henry, N.H., S45055
John, Md., BLWt.1782-100
Reuben, N.J., R7962
Silvanus/Sylvanus, Cont., N.J., S28840
Thomas, Md., Elizabeth, W5475
PARKISON, Daniel, Pa., S18542
Thomas, Md. See PARKINSON
PARKMAN, Daniel, Mass., S36717
Ebenezer, Mass., S33442
Thomas, Cont., N.Y. res. & Agcy. Hannah, W18690; BLWt.870-100
PARKS, Aaron, Ct., BLWt.6333. Iss. 4/12/1792 to Stephen Thorn, ass. No papers
Aaron, Ct., S43809
Aaron, Cont., Mass., Lucinda, W9590; BLWt.96076-160-55
Andrew, Va. res. in 1834, R7964
Asa, Mass., S43803
Benjamin, N.C., S31897
David, Ct., S43804
David, N.Y. See PARKES
Eleazer, Mass., Elizabeth, W15162
Frederick, Ct., BLWt.755-100
George, N.C., Catharine, W27457; BLWt.53670-160-55
Henry, N.C., S31898
Hugh, N.C., Elizabeth, W9591
Hugh, N.C., Mary, R7967
Jacob, N.Y., S9985
James, N.C., S17000
James, N.C., Nancy, R7968
John, Phila. Pa. Agcy., Dis., BLWt.13623-100. Iss. 7/27/1789 to Richard, Platt, ass. Pvt. in the Invalids Regt.
John, Ct., BLWt.6260. Iss. 1/6/1797. No papers
John, Hazen's Regt., BLWt.13597. Iss. 7/14/1790 to Richard Platt, ass. No papers
John, Mass., S19422
John, Va., Ann, R7972
Jonas, Mass., Eunice, W15154
Jonathan, Mass., S30632
Joseph, Cont., Green Mt. Boys, Mass., S43805
Josiah, Mass., Bulah, W18715
Leonard, Mass., S5144
Michael, N.H., S3634
Nathan, Mass., Mary, W5483
Peter, N.C., S35546
Reuben, Ct., BLWt.6326. Iss. 9/22/1789 to Frederick Fanning, ass. No papers
Robert, Ct., Martha, W18710
Robert, Mass. See PARKE
Rufus, Ct., Lucy, W26288

PARKS (continued)
Samuel, Mass., S21914
Samuel, N.Y., S32434
Samuel, N.C., b. Va., S8937
Smith, N.Y., R7971
Solomon, Va., Nancy, W5486; BLWt.412-100
Thomas, Ct., enl. in Pa., Abigail, W2845
Thomas, Cont., Pa., Ann, R7965
William, Va., S11202
PARLEY, James, Mass., War of 1812, Prudence, W2424; BLWt.12570-160-55
PARLIN, Eleazer, Mass., S37291
Nathan, Mass., S17007
PARMALEE, Bani, See PARMELE
Jeremiah, Ct., S41048
Phinehas, See PARMELEE
PARMELE, Bani, Ct., Charity, W6852 BLWt.31565-160-55
Charles, Ct., Cont., S11184
Constant, Ct., Hannah, W5473; BLWt.6021-160-55
Giles, Ct., S14097
James, Ct., Lydia, W5481; BLWt. 30701-160-55
Jeremiah, Ct. See PARMALEE
Joel, Ct., Sarah, W15172
Luther, See PARMLEE
Thomas, Ct., S28142
PARMELEE, Hiel, Ct., S14088
James, Ct., S15950
Phinehas, Ct., Rachael, W18718
PARMELL, Joel, See PAMELE
PARMENTER, Abel, Mass., S30633
Abel, Mass., Mindwell, W26851
Benjamin, Cont., N.Y., Green Mt. Boys, Abigail, W21899. Also given as PALMETON/PALMETER/PARMERTER/PARMETREE
Caleb, Mass., Elizabeth, W2687
Ebenezer, Mass., S30640
Ephraim, Mass., S33428
Isaac, Mass., Lydia, W18694
Jacob, Mass., Lois, W18711
Joel, Mass., Zilpah, R7973
Jonas, Mass., Hannah, R7974
Levi, Cont., Mass., Hannah, W5477; BLWt.40703-160-55. She also applied for bounty land on acct. of service of her other husb., Barzillai Howard, Mass., which see
Levi, Mass., S19744
Luther, Mass., Elizabeth, W1919; BLWt.3966-160-55
Nathaniel, Mass., Mary, W2238; BLWt.9209-160-55
Oliver, Mass., S23360
Peter, Mass., S30631
Solomon, Cont., Mass., S21412
Thomas, Mass., Mary, W10859; BLWt.514-160-55
PARMER, Adin, See BALMER
George M., See PALMER
William, Va., Sarah, W5476
PARMERLY, Isaac, Sheldon's Dragoons Ct., BLWt.6336. Iss. 9/30/1790 to Joseph Halsey, Jr. ass. No papers

PARMERTER, Benjamin, See PARMENTER
PARMETAR, Abraham, Mass., S40235; BLWt.1071-100
PARMETER, Nathan, Mass., S5872
Thomas, Mass. See PARMENTER
PARMETREE, Benjamin, See PARMENTER
PARMINTER, Ephraim, See PARMENTER
Oliver, Mass. See PARMENTER
Solomon, Cont., Mass. See PARMENTER
PARMLEE, Luther, Cont., Ct., BLWt.337-100
PARMLY, John, N.C., Elizabeth Smith, former wid., S30637; BLWt.36619-160-55
PARMOR, Charles, Md., Isabella Stewart, former wid., W3585
PARNELL, Benjamin, Cont., Mass., S33436
Joseph, Va., S38283
Stephen, Md., R7976
PARR, Arthur, S.C., S16219
Benjamin, N.J., Martha D., W5497
Isaiah, N.Y., S41939
James, Pa., BLWt.1701-400-Major
Jesse, N.J., S736
John, N.J., S17617
Mathias, N.Y., BLWt.7590. Iss. 4/21/1791 to Moses Smith, ass. No papers
Mathias, N.Y., S46402
Matthias, N.J., S17001
Moses, N.Y., S18149
Moses, R.I., Mary, W26825
Noah, N.C., BLWt.13588 & 14153. Iss. 1/3/1800 to Solomon P. Goodrich. No papers
Noah, N.C., Abashaba Clarke, former wid., R1960
PARRAS, Anthony, Lamb's Arty. N.Y., BLWt.7636. Iss. 8/30/1790 to Simon Veeder, ass. No papers
Anthony, N.Y., S43771
PARRELL, Hugh, Va., S19417
PARRET, Joseph, Va. & 1812. Anna/Ann, W4108; BLWt.1578-200 (Rev.) BLWt.88366-120-55 (1812)
Samuel, Va., S17619
PARRIOTT, Christopher, Md., Martha, W18714
PARRIS, Gabriel, Cont., Pa., Sarah, R7927
Josiah, Mass., Sarah, W10223
Samuel, Cont., Mass., Sea Service, S11210
Samuel, Mass., S21406
PARRISH, Charles, N.C. See PARISH
Claiborne/Claibourne, N.C.,S7297
Cyprian, N.Y., S29363
Daniel, N.Y., Ruth Williams, former wid., W18446
Ebenezer, Mass., Va., S22431
Edward, Md., Clemency, W808; BLWt.504-160-55
Eliphas, Ct., Jerusha Cory, former wid., W1563; BLWt.10313-160-55
Ephraim, See PARISH
Humphrey, N.C., Va., S7301
Jacob, Cont., Res. N.Y. in 1809.

PARRISH (continued)
BLWt.617-100
Jeremiah, Ct., S11215
John, R.I. See PARISH
Nathan, Mass., S40236
Nathaniel, Va., Martha, R7931
Nehemiah, Ct., Privateer, S12128
Oliver, Ct., S9451
Robert, Ga., S3657
Roswell, See PARISH
Silas, N.Y., Elizabeth, R7928
Stephen, S.C. See PARISH
Thomas, N.C., S1868
PARRIT, Silas, N.J. See PARROT
PARROT, Adoniram, N.J., BLWt.8635 Iss. 8/14/1789
Adoniram, N.J., S43776
Christopher, Md. See PARRIOTT
John, Ct., BLWt.6267. Iss. 3/31/1796 to Joseph Davis, ass. No papers
Reuben, Va., S7292
Samuel, Va. See PARRET
Silas, N.J., S34460; BLWt.1694-200-Lt. Iss. 6/11/1789 to Matthias Darman, ass. No papers
William, N.J., Catharine, W2463
William, N.J., Clarissa Burroughs former wid., W5965; BLWt.7074-160-55
PARROTT, Christopher, See PARRIOTT
Esther, former wid. of Jonathan Wakeley/Wakelee, Ct., which see
John, Ct., S38284
John, Va., S8932
Joseph, Va. See PARRET
Lewis, Va., S45897
Mastin, Ct., S18537
Thomas, S.C., S21918
William, Va., S10253
PARRY, Caleb, Pa., BLWt.1857-450-Lt. Col.
John, N.C., Jane, W975; BLWt. 27581-160-55
Joseph, Mass., S41062
PARSEL, Swain/Swaine, N.J., S34466
PARSELL, Peter, N.J., S11213
PARSELS, Thomas, N.Y., S23355
PARSHALL, David, N.Y., Pa., Sarah, W18689; BLWt.26887-160-55
Israel, N.Y., Pa., R7978
James, N.Y., Ct., S43799; BLWt. 1690-100
John, N.Y., S14084
PARSHELL, David, N.Y., Pa. See PARSHALL
PARSHLEY, George, N.H., Merabah, W5487
Richard, Mass., Anna, R7979
Samuel, N.H., S46052
Thomas, N.H. See PARSLEY
PARSIVEL, Stephen, Green Mt. Boys, Vt., S18539
PARSLEY, George, See PARSHLEY
Thomas, N.H., Olive, W16673
PARSON, George, Pa., R8245
PARSONS, Abner/Antres/Anstres, Mass., BLWt.13004-160-55
Abraham, Ct., S14110
Abraham, N.H., S11212
Abraham, N.J., Leonora, W10852 BLWt.34527-160-55

PARSONS (continued)
Amos, Mass., S21410
Andrew, Mass., S41047
Anna, former wid. of John Sleathe, Cont., Va., which see
Bartholomew, Ct., S33429
Charles, N.Y., BLWt.1680-300-Capt. Iss. 12/15/1790. No papers
Daniel, Ct., S11208
Daniel, Del., S35025
David, Ct., BLWt.232-100
David, Ct., BLWt.1667-300-Capt. Iss. 12/5/1795. No papers
Ebenezer, Mass., S43781
Ebenezer, Mass., Nabby, W26830
Eldad, Mass., Cynthia, W2236
Elezer, Mass., Judith, W26828; BLWt.3808-160-55
Eli, Ct., Huldah, W3111
Eli, Cont., N.Y. Agcy., S43782
George, Cont., Va., S38991
Gideon, Mass., S14100
Harmon, N.J., S40234
Israel, Mass., S18540
Jabez, Ct., S3644
James, Va., S40239
Jesse, Ct., S38282
Job, Mass., BLWt.832-100
John, Ct., S31900
John, Ct., Sarah, W18698
John, Ct., Cont., Mass., S11185
John, Mass., S30014
John, N.H., S11214
John, N.J., S3643
John, N.Y., R7982
John, Pa., BLWt.10208. Iss. 7/27/1789 to Richard Platt, ass. No papers
Jonathan, Mass., Molly, W15151
Joseph, Ct., S11207
Joseph, N.H., Privateer, Mary, W15934
Joseph, N.C., Nancy, W4047
Joseph, Va., S8942
Joseph Jabez, See PEARSONS
Josiah, Mass., Sea Service (?) S36721
Justin, Mass., Vt., Prudence L., W2661; BLWt.34902-160-55
Lemuel, Ct., Mass., S33438
Mercy, former wid. of Ezra Foot, Ct., which see
Moses, Mass., Elizabeth, W15171
Nancy, former wid. of Caleb Lewis, R.I., which see
Nathan, Mass., Susannah, W21921, BLWts.3828-160-55 & 1662-150-Ensign. Iss. 5/23/1797 to Marlbry Turner, ass. No papers
Nathaniel, N.H., S37286
Nehemiah, Mass., S33437
Osborn, Ct., S40243; BLWt.1089-100
Philip, Mass., S33439
Samuel, Fifer, Ct., BLWt.6266. Iss. 4/15/1790 to Peter DeWitt, ass. No papers
Samuel, Ct., S35024
Samuel, Cont., Ct., S15552
Samuel, Cont., Mass., N.Y. res. in 1818, Elizabeth, W2237; BLWt.7645 & 171-60-55 iss. 10/12/1790
Samuel, N.J., Mary, W5493

PARSONS (continued)
Samuel H., Ct., BLWt.1665-1100-Maj. Gen. Iss. 8/23/1790. No papers
Seth, Mass., S29359
Silas, Mass., Sarah, W26841
Solomon, Ct., S4646
Solomon, Mass., S5883
Sylvanus, Mass., Mary, W15157; BLWt.11267-160-55
Theodosius, Cont., Mass. res. & Agcy., S33441
Thomas, Va., S14075
Thomas, Va., S38990
William, Ct., S14090
William, Mass., BLWt.4833. Iss. 4/19/1790 to John Bush. No papers
William, Mass. See PEARSON
William, Cont., Va., R16965. Va. Half Pay. BLWt.1752-300-Capt. 3rd Regt. of Dragoons. Iss. 8/27/1795 to Smith & Ridgeway, assnes. No papers
Williams, Va. R---, (taken from William Parsons, R7981)
William, Va., Catharine, R7981
William E., Ct. See PEARSON
PARTEE, Edmund, N.C., R7983
PARTER, Robert, N.C., R8352
PARTLOW, Benjamin, Va., S5871
Orman, N.H./ R.I., Elizabeth, R7984
PARTRIDGE, Abel, Mass., BLWt.4875 Iss. 4/3/1797 to John Jack. No papers
Amariah, Cont., Mass., S45056; BLWt.1746-100
Amos, Mass., N.H., Sally, W26831
Asa, Ct., Anna, W16053. See. N.A. Acct. No. 874-050130. Not Half Pay Asa Partridge
Calvin, See case of sold's. wid. Mary, who was pensioned as the former wid. of Ichabod Alden, Mass., Cont.
David, Cont., Mass., Mary, W21918
James, Ct., Amy, W16668
Jane, former wid. of Joseph Plimpton, Mass., which see
Jasper, Vt., Martha, W5484; BLWt. 9042-160-55
Nathan, Mass., Anne, W26826
Ozias, Mass., Ziporah/Zipporah, W19970
Samuel, Ct., Anna, W15164
Samuel, Mass., S5141
Stephen, Ct., Sarah, W17423
Timothy, Mass., Jennett Winslow, former wid., S21411; BLWt.31774-160-55
PASCHAL, George, Cont., S.C., Agnes, W4306; BLWt.8466-160-55
PASCO, John, Mass., BLWt.4821. Iss. 4/11/1792 to Martin Kingsley, No papers
Jonathan, Ct., S5140
Jonathan, Mass., S36209
PASKO, Ezra, Mass., R7987
John, Mass., Abigail, W19953
PASLAY, Thomas, Va., Winifred, W8506
PASLEY, Robert, S.C., Elizabeth, R7988
Thomas, Va. See PASLAY
PASMORE, Joseph, Mass., Lucy, W17421
PASS, Holloway, N.C., S7289
PASSAGE, George, N.Y., R7989
Joseph, N.Y., Hannah Hardwick, former wid., W17043
PASSMORE, David, N.C., b. Pa., S1924
PASTEUR, John, Va. Sea Service, R83 Va. Half Pay. See N.A. Acc. No. 837. Va. State Navy, John Pasteur Y.S. File. Va. Half Pay
PASTEURS, Thomas, N.C., BLWt.1758-200-Lt. Iss. 3/3/1791. No papers
PASTLEY, John, See PEASLEY
PATCH, Ephraim, Mass., Mary, W18726 BLWt.27649-160-55
George, Mass., BLWt.4867. Iss. 8/1/1789 to Thos. Cushing. No papers
George, Mass., Sarah, W15163
Isaac, Mass., S33420
James, Mass., S30016
John, Mass., BLWt.4812. Iss. 8/26/1796. No papers
John, Mass., S36716
John, Mass., Betsy Reynolds, former wid., W20016
Jonathan, Mass., R7990
Joseph, Mass., Mary C., W4755; BLWt.13863-160-55
Reuben, Mass., BLWt.4837. Iss. 3/25/1790. No papers
Reuben, Cont., Mass., Mary, W21922
Samuel, Mass., N.H., R7991
William, Ct., S11196
PATCHEN, Azor, Ct., Abigail, W6854; BLWts. 1378-100 & 37-60-55
Daniel, Ct., S14089
Ebenezer, Ct., Sarah, W16672
William, Ct., R7993
Wolcott, Ct., Betty Bennett, former wid., W25326; BLWt.278-60-55. Her other husb., Benjamin Bennett/Bennet, Ct., was also a pensioner, which see
Elijah, Ct., Cont., S36207
Freegift, Ct., N.Y., Molly, W21910
Isaac, Ct., Rebekah, W17425
Isaac, N.Y., Sally, W18702
Jacob, Ct., S38986
Josiah, Ct., Eunice Keator, former wid., W21510
Samuel, Cont., N.Y., S23361
Squire, N.Y., S29361
Walter, N.Y., Sarah, W26289; BLWt.33750-160-55
Zebulon, N.Y., Polly, BLWt.61360-160-55
PATCHON, Woolcot, Ct., BLWt.6297 & Wt.278-60-55. Iss. 9/6/1792. No papers. See Wolcott PATCHEN
PATE, Matthew, Va., Drusilla, W5490
PATEE, Edmund, Mass., Elizabeth, W5480
Eliphalet, Mass., S19021
James, P., Mass., N.H., S11193
PATEE (continued)
John, See PATY
William, Mass., N.H., S29367
PATEETE, Edward, S.C., Martha, W10853
PATERSON, John, Cont., Mass., Elizabeth, W16670; BLWt.1632-850-Brig. Gen. Iss. 7/22/1789. No papers
Jonathan, Mass., S43764
Samuel, N.H. See PATTERSON
Thomas, N.J., S34467
William, Hazen's Regt., BLWt. 13602. Iss. 7/26/1791 to Patrick McLaughlin, ass. No papers
William, Mass. See PATTISON
PATISON, Michael, See PATTERSON
PATMOR, Henry, N.Y., S14092
PATRICK, Abel, Ct., R7995
Charles, S.C., Isabella, W8508
Ebenezer, See PATTRICK
Edward F/Edward Fitzpatrick, N.C., Polly F., W1988
Ezekiel, N.C., War of 1812, R7996
George, Pa., BLWt.10210. Iss. 6/10/1794 to Silas Hart, ass. No papers
Jacob, Ct., Privateer, Sarah, W19960; BLWt.24992-160-55
James, Ct., R.I., Temperance, R7988
James, Va., S1241
John, Mass., S41043
Joshua, See PATTRICK
Ralph, Ct., S28837
Reuben, Mass., S5875
Robert, Pa., S16218
Robert, S.C., Rosanna, W21925
William, Mass., BLWt.1678-300. No papers
William, N.C., R7999
William, Va., S5882
PATRIDGE, Abel, Mass., S33421
Asa, Ct. See PARTRIDGE
David, Cont., Mass. See PARTRIDGE
John, Pa., BLWt.10202. Iss. 7/9/1789. No papers
John, Pa., S40238
Timothy, Mass. See PARTRIDGE
PATTEE, Asa, N.H., Mehitable I., W16364
John, Mass., R8372
Moses, Cont., Mass., S45057
Richard, N.H., Phebe, W15167
PATTEN, Asa, Ct., S19743
Benjamin, Mass., S37278
Benoni, Cont., Mass., Sea Service Edith, W16361
David, Mass., N.H., Mary, W18703
Edward, N.Y., S43779
James, Mass., BLWt.4857. Iss. 7/20/1797 to Ezra King. No papers
James, See Edward UNDERHAND, Mass.
James, N.H., BLWt.3405. Iss. 3/25/1790. No papers
James, Pa., S30629
John, Ct., S19745; BLWt.7294-60-55
John, Del., BLWt.1725-400-Maj.
John, Mass. See PATTIN
John, Mass.,N.H.,Hannah, W18701

PATTEN (continued)
John, N.C., BLWt.194-500-Col. Iss. 9/4/1804 to Hans Patten & Ann Cambrelling, the only ch. & heirs of sd. John Patten
Jonathan, N.H., Abigail, W26843
Joseph, N.C., S3632
Nathaniel, Mass., N.H., S37284
Robert, N.C. See PATTON
Thomas, Arty. Artificer, BLWt. 2551-300
Thomas, Ct., Mary, W13795
Thomas, Mass., Sarah, W13796
Thomas, N.J., S828
Thomas, N.C., S32429
William, Ct., Cont., Abigail, W26293
William, N.H., S16501
PATTENGELL, Jacob, Ct., S43780
PATTERSON, Adam, Cont., N.H., Mary, W26821
Alexander, N.H., S31295
Alexander, N.H., BLWt.859-100. See papers in claim of George Patterson, BLWt.858-100
Alexander, Pa., Margaret, W4563; BLWt.1720-300-Capt. Iss. 2/28/1793. No papers
Alexander, S.C., Ga., b. Ireland, S7288
Andrew, Cont., Pa., Margaret, W2844
Ansel, Ct., Polly, W6855; BLWt. 10015-160-55
Benjamin, Pa., Sarah, R8010
Ebenezer, Mass., S14078
Francis, N.C., R20184
George, N.H., BLWt.858-100. The papers in the claim of Alexander Patterson, BLWt.859-100 are in this file
Hezekiah, N.Y., BLWt.7583. Iss. 2/14/1791 to Steward Dean, ass. No papers
Hezekiah, N.Y., S43802
Isaac, N.H., S45052
Jacob, N.Y., S11182
James, Ct., BLWt.6294. Iss. 11/2/1796 to Asa Spaulding, ass. No papers
James, Cont., Pa., Mary, W26823
James, N.Y., BLWt.7617. Iss. 10/9/1790. No papers
James, N.Y., BLWt.7628. Iss. 6/24/1790 to Elkanah Watson, ass.
James, N.Y. See PATTISON
James, N.C., b. 7/5/1758 Va., d. 12/3/1838 in Shelby Co., Ill., Sarah, W10861; BLWt.30924-160-55
James, (?) N.C., Elizabeth, R8001
James, N.C., Va., b. Pa., S8926
James, Pa., S23837
James, Pa., R8002
John, Cont., Mass. See PATERSON
John, Ga., N.C., S.C., S17626
John, N.H., Ky. pensioner, S35549
John, Lamb's Arty., N.Y., BLWt. 7638. Iss. 9/29/1790. No papers
John, N.Y., S43783
John, N.C., S30634
John, N.C., Ann, R8000
John, N.C., b. Pa., R8005

PATTERSON (continued)
John, Pa., Sarah, W3155
John, Pa., R8004
John, Pa., BLWt.1587-300
John, Va., Elizabeth, W8003
Jonathan, Cont., N.Y., S43774
Jonathan, Mass. See PATERSON
Jonathan, N.Y., BLWt.13599. Iss. 6/28/1790. No papers
Joseph, N.H., S26330
Joseph, Vt., S23362
Michael, N.Y., Nelly, W21912.
Peter, N.J., R8007
Peter, N.J., R8008
Poindexter, Va., S8935
Reuben, Mass. See PATTISON
Robert, N.J., b. 1743, m. 1774 d. 1824, Amy, W3189
Robert, Drummer in Arty., Pa., BLWt.10229. Iss. 6/20/1789. No papers
Robert, Pa., b. 1761, Va. Living in Steuben Co., N.Y., 1833. R8009
Robert, Va., S31903
Samuel, Cont., N.H., S41046
Sherman, Ct. and on galleys in North River, Huldah, W19959
Thomas, Md., Dinah, W9228
Thomas, Md., BLWt.1276-100
Thomas, Mass. See PATTISON
Thomas, N.Y., Sarah/Sally, W2190
Thomas, Pa., b. Ireland, Sarah, W8284; BLWt.31560-160-55
Thomas, Va., S8933
Tilman/Tilmon, N.C., S41942
William, Cont., Ct., Lois, W1869
William, Md., Abigail, W8509
William, Mass., Sea Service, Privateer, Mary, R8006
William, N.Y., BLWt.7608. Iss. 1/3/1797 to Wm. Patterson. No papers
William, N.Y., S28838
William, Pa., S32427
William, Va., S3648
William, Va., S35545
William, Va., R8011
PATTESON, Robert, S.C., b. Pa., S3654
Thomas, Va., S2011
PATTIE, William, Va., S10252
PATTILLO, William, Va., S30630
PATTIN, John, Cont., Mass., S36718
PATTINGELL, Joseph, Mass., S33452
PATTISON, David, Mass., N.Y., Chloe, W19961
James, N.Y., S43806
John, Va., See PATTERSON
Michael, N.Y. See PATTERSON
Reuben, Mass., S8925
Robert, See PATTESON
Sundarland, Cont., Ct., S43786
Thomas, Md. See PATTERSON
Thomas, Mass., S14099
William, Ct., Mass., Wealthy, W15153
William, Mass., N.Y., S31896
PATTON, Alexander, Va., S38981

PATTON (continued)
Christopher, Ct., Mass., S8662
David, Mass., N.H., See PATTEN
David, S.C., S18151
George, Va., Sarah, W4049
Isaac, Mass., S31899
Jacob, S.C., S17618
Jacob, Va., S1777
James, Pa., BLWt.10225. Iss.3/5/1795 to Thomas Patton, Admr. No papers
James, Pa. See PATTEN
John, Pa., BLWt.10213. Iss. 10/28/1789 to M. McConnell, ass. No papers
John, Pa. (not identical with R8012), S8931
John, Pa., Sarah, W40237
John, Pa., Margaret, W3447
John, S.C., Mary, W162
John, Va., (not identical with S8931), R8012
Matthew, Md., S31294
Matthew, S.C., S18153
Richard, Pvt. in the Invalids. BLWt.13630. Iss. 10/12/1790 to Richard Platt, ass. No papers
Robert, N.C., Elizabeth, W4758
Robert, Pa., BLWt.1706-300-Capt. Iss. 3/30/1792. No papers
Samuel, Cont., Md., S31901
Samuel, N.C., S8934
Thomas, N.C. See PATTEN
William, Md., S11218
William, N.C., b. Pa., Jane, W4307; BLWt.38576-160-55
William, Pa., S23363
PATTRICK, Ebenezer, N.Y., Nancy E., W6849; BLWt.29055-160-55
Joshua, Ct., N.Y. & Mich. Vols. War of 1812, S32431; Old War Invalid File 26333, War of 1812. All papers in this file.
PATTRILL, Mary, former wid. of Benjamin Robert Burts, N.H., which see
PATTS, David, Cont., Mass., Navvy, W15173
James, Cont., Mass., S45064 Pensioned as PELTS
PATY, John, Mass., S33855
PAUGH, Young, See PEUGH
PAUL, Arthur, N.Y., Lucretia, W19974; BLWts.7616-100-1790 & 6-60-55
Benjamin, Cont., N.J., Bethenia, W148
Christopher, Pa., R8013
David, Mass., S37279
Ebenezer, Mass., R.I., S17622
Edward, Va., BLWt.12450. Iss. 1789
Edward P., Va., R8014
Frederick, See POWELL
George S./George, Va., Elizabeth W5471
Hugh, Mass., S43790; BLWt.1897-100
James, Ct., Zeruah, W26835
James, N.J., S45582; BLWt.1693-200-Lt. Iss. 4/22/1794. No papers
James, Va., R8015
Jeremiah, Mass., Hannah, BLWt. 3642-160-55

PAUL (continued)
Joseph, Pa. See POWEL
Kiles, Ct., Abigail, W572; BLWt. 82541-100-55
Richard, N.J., R8016
Robert, Hazen's Regt., BLWt.13610 Iss. 1/22/179? to Benj. Mooers, ass. No papers
Thomas, Md., Catharine, W9225
William, Mass., BLWt.4852. Iss. 6/2/1795 to Samuel Emery. No papers
William, N.Y., S38292
PAULDING, John, N.Y. No pension. No bounty land. One of Andre's captors. D. 2/18/1818
John, N.Y., S22927
Peter, N.Y., Jane, W26832
William, N.Y., Elizabeth, W16366
PAULENT, Amable, Hazen's Regt. BLWt.13607. Iss. 9/21/1790 to Benjamin Mooers, ass. No papers
Antoine, Cont.(Canada).See PAULIN
PAULETT, Richard, Va., BLWt.1940-200, S----
PAULEY, Wm., Va., Margaret, W10233
PAULHAMUS, Abraham, N.J., Sarah W3292
PAULIER, Clement,Hazen's Regt. BLWt 13604. Iss. 2/4/1790. No papers
PAULIN, Antoine, Cont. (Canada) Theotist, W16671; BLWt.1767-300-Capt. whose name is spelled PAULENT. Iss. 9/21/1790 to Benj. Mooers, ass. No papers
PAULING, Henry, N.Y. See PAWLING
PAULINT, Amiable,Cont.,N.Y., S43777
PAULK, Ammi, Ct., S11199
Ephraim, Ct., Eunice, W18727
PAULL, Benjamin, Mass., Charlotte W571; BLWt.14540-60-55
James, Mass., Jemima, W15174
James, Pa., Va., S3631
John, Mass., Hannah, W21926
Samuel, Mass., S17623
PAULLING, William, S.C., S21407
PAULMER, George M., See PALMER
PAULMORE, George M., See PALMER
PAVEY, Samuel, N.C., R8017
PAWLEY, William, S.C. See PAULEY
PAWLING, Albert, Cont.,N.Y., S19016
Henry, N.Y., S43785; BLWt.1682--300-Capt. Iss. 2/14/1791
PAWNS, James, N.C., b. Va., Elizabeth, W3589
PAXTON, Samuel, Va., S11206
Thomas, Va., S30636
William, Va., S5873
PAYLOR, William, Va., S41941
PAYN, Ebenezer L., Mass. See PAYNE
Noah, N.Y., Vt., S23351
Stephen, Ct., Sea Service, S41040
PAYNE, Augustine, Va., Catharine, W10850
Benjamin, N.Y., S11197
Charles, N.C., Va. See PAINE
Ebenezer L., Mass., Keziah, R8022
Edward, Ct., S3625. He married Lovina Rovey, former wid. of John Brown, Mass., which see
Eleazer, Ct., Aurel, R8021
George, Va. See PAINE
Isaac, N.Y., S11203

PAYNE (continued)
John, Cont., N.H., Green Mt. Boys, Esther, W5472; BLWt.33752-160-55
John, Cont., Va., Ann/Anna, W5495
John, Mass., S17008
John, Va., BLWt.12475. Iss. 2/18/1793 to Robert Means, ass. No papers
John, Va., S3627
Joseph, R.I., S41042
Joseph, Va., Ann, W18693
Josias, Va., BLWt.1747-150-Ensign Iss. 3/26/1792 to Francis Graves, ass. of Wm. Payne, Admr. No papers
Ledford, Va., Jane, S1242; BLWt. 97540-160-55
Moses, N.C., S11191
Nehemiah, N.C., S32433
Richard, Va., BLWt.12460. Iss. 5/8/1794. No papers
Richard, Va., S8929
Rufus, Ct., S28841
Rufus, Ct., S36203
Solomon, Ct., Cont., Mary, W2160
Tarleton, Va., BLWt.1737-300-Capt. Iss. 3/26/1792 to Francis Graves, ass. No papers
Thomas, Ga., BLWt.1764-200-Lt. Iss. 1/28/1797 to Thomas F. Scott. No papers
Thomas, Va., BLWt.1739-300-Capt. Iss. 3/26/1792 to Francis Graves, ass. No papers
Thomas, Va., S7290
William, Ct., S11198
William, Mass., Pamela, W10858
William, S.C., S11187
William, Va., S8938
William, Va., S8938 1/2
PAYNTER, Nathaniel, Del., R8018
PAYNTON, William, N.J., S3645
PAYSON, Asa, Mass., S29362
David, Mass., Nancy, W26849
Edward, Mass., Eunice, R8019
Ephraim, Mass., S37292
George, Mass., S29370
Samuel, Cont., Mass., S37287; d. 6/19/1819
Samuel, Mass., Sarah, W5498; BLWt.26745-160-55
PAYTON, Henry, Va., S8943
Lewis, Va., S17003
William, Va., Catharine, R8020
Yelverton, Va., S31291
PEABBLES, William W., Mass., S31297
PEABODY, Amos, Mass., Rachel, W18746
Andrew, Mass., Privateer, W22438
Bimsley, Mass., Betty, W15179
Dudley, Mass., R8023
Ebenezer, Mass., Sarah, W18745
Francis, Mass., S33453
John, Mass., Molly, W3716
John, Mass., Lydia, W21955
Jonathan, Mass., Lucy, W18742
Joseph, Mass., Dis. No papers. See Am. State Papers, Vol. 9, pp.59, 110, & 162. This sold.

PEABODY (continued)
was wounded by a musket ball, which entered his right side and passed through his body, 6/29/1777 between Fort Edward and Fort Miller. Enl. 4/15/1777, dis. April 1780
Moses, Mass., S21416
Phinehas, Mass., S14150
Samuel, Mass., Abigail, W15186; BLWt.18214-160-55
Seth, Mass., S36729; BLWt.13581-Pvt. Sappers & Miners. Iss. 4/6/1796 to Benjamin Silsbee, ass. No papers
Stephen, Mass., Anna, W15178
Thomas, Mass., S33461
Thomas, N.H., S45068
PEACE, John, Md., S38996
John, Va., S38299
Joseph, Va., Elizabeth Bishop, W3861
Rebecca, former wid. of Laban Haislip, Md., which see
PEACH, John, Cont., Mass., Sea Service, Mary, W18750
William, Mass., S19030
PEACHEY, Benjamin, N.J., S35552
PEACOCK, Abraham, N.C., S21422
Archibald, N.C., R8026
Hugh, N.Y., BLWt.1688-200-Lt. Iss. 5/14/1792. No papers
Isum/Isham, N.C., Lydia, W8513; BLWt.58687-160-55
James, Mass., N.H., Sarah, W26300; BLWt.34850-160-55
Neal, Md., BLWt.11601. Iss. 2/7/1790. No papers
Neal, Md., S40247
Richard, N.Y., S5907
Thomas, Pa., BLWt.10197. Iss. 5/26/1794 to Michael Stever, ass. No papers
Uriah, N.C., Zilphia, W18744
PEADRICK, Joseph, N.H., BLWt. 3401. Iss. 4/22/1796 to R. Fletcher, ass. No papers
PEAGAN, Joseph, Ct., S33459
PEAK, Abel, Va. See PECK
Christophel, See PEEK
James, Pa., BLWt.10193. Iss. 8/27/179?. No papers
Jesse, Pvt., Va., BLWt.12458 iss. 5/8/1794
Jesse, Cont., Va., S35557
Nathan, Md., S35550
Richard, Va. See PEEK
Thomas, Cont., Mass., S33458; BLWt.672-100
William, N.Y., BLWt.7604. Iss. 9/25/1790 to D. Hudson & Co., ass. Cert. 2/7/1826. No papers
PEAKE, Christopher, N.Y., Elizabeth, W16675
Jacobus/James H., See PEEK
John, Va., S32439
William, Cont., Dis. No papers; d. in Spottsylvania Co., Va., 8/16/1816
William, Va., Elizabeth, W6863; BLWt.26770-160-55
PEAKES, Eleazer, Mass., Celia,

PEAKES (continued)
BLWt.56953-160-55
PEALE, James, Md., S41056
Jeremiah, Va., Peggy, W5521; BLWt.26742-160-55
PEALLAR, Joseph, N.Y., S43823
PEALLER, Jacob, N.Y., S44241
PEANEY, Simon, Mass. See PERPEANEY
PEARCE, Abraham, Mass., Martha, W26305
Adam, N.J., S34468
Amos, Mass., Hannah, W15190
Aquilla, Md., BLWt.1919-100
Benjamin, N.J., S32438
Caleb, Mass., R.I. See PARCE
Charles, Mass. See PIERCE
David, R.I., R8233
Ezekiel, R.I., Sarah, W18765
Francis, Va. See PIERCE
George, Md., S49294; BLWt.1176-100
Hannah, former wid. of Gideon Church, R.I., which see
Hugh, Md., See PIERCE
Ichabod, R.I., Lucy, W13804; BLWt.26484-160-55
Isaac, R.I., S38994
Israel, Mass., R.I., Hannah, R8030
Israel, N.C., Sea Service, S3660
James, Mass. See PEIRCE
James, N.C., Margaret, W5529
James, N.C., R8031
James, Pa., R8237
Jeremiah, R.I., Nancy/Anna, W26302
Job, Mass., BLWt.4823. Iss. 2/22/1791/1792 to John Peck. No papers
Job, Mass. See PEIRCE
John, Ct., Cont., S43826
John, Md., Sarah, W5527
John, N.J. See PIERCE
John, Not Rev. War, N.W. Indian War. Old War Inv. File No.26342- No bounty land found
Joseph, R.I., S21640
Joshua, Md., BLWt.11594. Iss. 2/7/1790. No papers
Joshua, Md., S39004
Langworthy/Longworthy, R.I., Sally Congdon, former wid., W532; BLWts.102860-40-50 & 2391-120-55 (War of 1812). Her 1st husb., was Eber Sherman who d.in service in War of 1812. She rec'd the BL Wts. noted on this jacket for his service. Her claim for 5 yrs. Half Pay on acct. of his service and death was rejected because she was then in receipt of Rev. War Pension for service of her 2nd husb., Langworthy Pearce
Lawrence S., R.I., Lettice, R8033
Mary, former wid. of Hardy Newson N.C., which see
Michael, N.J., S3674
Michael, Privateer, R.I., Mary, W1069; BLWt.26483-160-55
Miel/Mial, Mass., Dorcas, R8034; BLWt.34623-160-55
Peter, R.I., S23838
Philip, Va., R8035

PEARCE (continued)
Reuben, Navy, R.I., S38999
Robert, Mass., S8241
Robert, Mass., Sea Service, Navy, S.C.; Sea Service, Elizabeth, R8029
Rouse, R.I., Mary, W12613
Samuel, Ct. See PIERCE
Samuel, R.I., after Rev. N.C., R8036
Shubel, Mass., R8037
Stephen, Mass. See PEARY
Stephen, R.I., S14170
Sylvester, R.I., Martha, W12608
William, Mass. See PEIRCE
William, N.C., Nicey, W3590; BLWt.19905-160-55
PEARCY, James, Va. See PIERCY
Thomas, Va., S3679
PEAREA, Allen, Mass., Mary, R8103
PEARL, Frederick, Ct., S36215
James, N.C., BLWt.1757-300-Capt. Iss. 6/1/1792. No papers
Joseph, N.H., BLWt.3385. Iss. 3/25/1790. No papers
Timothy, Ct., Lois, W26292
PEARRE, Joshua, Md., Milly Ann, W5518
Nathaniel, Ga., BLWt.1768-200-Lt. Iss. 8/8/1797 to Abraham Baldwin, ass. No papers. Heitman Hist. Reg. gives this name as Nathaniel Perry.
PEARSALL, Benjamin, Pa., S40251
PEARSE, Daniel, Ct. See PIERCE
Hugh, Md. See PIERCE
Job, Mass., R.I. See PEIRCE
John, N.Y., BLWt.7606. Iss. 3/16/1792 to Nathaniel Platt, ass. No papers
John, R.I., S38995
Richard, Navy, Ct., Candace, W4308
PEARSON, Abel, N.C., S3661
Amos, Cont., Mass., S30025
Benjamin, Mass., S33466
Charles, N.C., R8244
David, Mass., S21418
David, Va., S3662
George, N.C., Arianna, R8042
George, Pa., BLWt.388-100
James, R.I., S45067
Jesse, Ct., Lydia, W16677
John, N.Y., BLWt.2486-120
John, Pa., BLWt.1703-3001-Capt. Iss. 7/2/1795 to Anthony Pearson, Excr. No papers
Jonathan, N.C. Margaret, W10876 BLWt.33769-160-55
Joseph, Mass., Martha, W1468; BLWt.28568-160-55
Joseph, Mass., N.H., Hannah, W21948
Josiah, Mass., Sarah, W18732
Mahlon, S.C. See PIERSON
Mark, Cont., Mass. & Me. res., S36731
Matthew, N.J., BLWt.8631. Iss. 9/12/1789. No papers
Matthias, N.J., S40244
Meshecke/Meshac, Cont., Va., S35555

PEARSON (continued)
Moses, Mass., S41944
Moses, Mass., N.H., Lois, W19980
Nathaniel, Mass., Sarah, W15187
Noah, Cont., N.H., S41945
Parris/Paris, N.C., Mary, W4761
Peter, Ct., S17635
Shadrach, Va., Rachel (?), S35551; BLWt.14129-100. Iss. 8/8/1795. No papers
Silas, Cont., R.I., Susanna, W5512 BLWt.283-60-55
Silas, Mass., Mary, W13799; BLWt. 8176-160-55
Sterling, N.C., R8041
Thomas, Pa., Va., S32440
Thomas, Va., S5910; BLWt.352-200
Timothy M., N.H., S18154
William, Mass., Abiah, W13806
William, Mass., R.I., S45053
William, Va., S16507
William E., Ct., Hannah, W3592; BLWt.31562-160-55
PEARSONS, Job, See PARSONS
John, Pa., BLWt.10214. Iss. 12/13/1791 to Gideon Merkle, ass. of George Pearsons, Admr. No papers
Joseph Jabez, Ct., Hannah, R26148
PEARY, Allen, Mass. See PEAREA
Stephen, Mass., S17014
Winthrop, See PEAVEY
PEASE, Abner, Ct., b. 11/9/1757, S30022
Abner, N.Y., S8948
Asa, Mass., S30643
Charles, Ct., Elizabeth, W10869
David, Ct., Jerusha, W19979
Ebenezer, Ct., N.Y., S41054
Ebenezer, Mass., S41947
Edward, Ct., Abigail, W17431
Edward, Ct., Rhoda, R8049
Ephraim, Ct., R8045
Gideon, Ct., Prudence, R8048
Isaac, Ct., S18545
James, Ct., S14124
Joel, Ct., Cont., Mass., S40252
Joel, Ct., Mass., R8046
John, Cont., Ct., S18544
John, N.J., R8047
Jonathan, N.J., S34470
Joseph, Ct., S41065
Joseph, Ct., Elizabeth, R8044
Moses, Ct., S11225
Noah, Mass., S30020
Peter, Ct., Desire, R8043
Phineas, Ct., S17630
Robert, Ct., Anna, W17432
Samuel, Ct., Lydia, W10873
Samuel, Ct., Sarah, W17430
Samuel, Cont., N.H., S36726
Samuel, N.J., Maria, W15937
Silas, Cont., Ct., Rhoda, W6859
Simeon, Ct., S14151
Stone, Ct., Mary, W26308
Zebulon, Mass., S19423
Zechariah, Mass., R8051
PEASELY, Mary, former wid. of Martin Tubbs, Ct., which see
PEASLEE, Jonathan, Mass., Jane, W13802
Zacheus, Hazen's Regt., BLWt.

PEASLEE (continued)
1763-200-Lt. Iss. 1/22/1790. No papers
PEASLEY, David, See PEESLEY
John, N.C., S3646
Mary, Ct. See Martin TUBBS
PEAVEY, Daniel, Mass., N.H., Mary, W21947; BLWt.26050 1/2-160-55
John, N.H., S22930
Winthrop, N.H., Rachel Frederick, former wid., W11023; BLWts.3386-100-1789 & 358-60-55
PEAVY, Abraham/Abram, N.C., Lydia, W10880
Abram, Va., S31904
PEAY, George, N.C., S3673
PEBBLES, Andrew, Va., S38297
PECARD, Lewis, See PICARD
PECK, Aaron, Ct., Hannah, W21956
Abel, Ct., N.Y., Diadama, W2846; BLWt.24436-160-55
Abel, Va., Lydia, W1989
Abijah, Ct., Sarah, W6856; BLWt.26993-160-55
Abijah, Ct., N.Y., S14153
Abner, Ct., Mass., S30650
Ariel/Arial, Cont., N.Y. res. in 1818, S43836
Asahel, Ct., Anne/Anna, W21957
Augustus, Ct., BLWt.6314. Iss. 12/16/1793 to Eneas Munson, Jr. ass. No papers
Azel, Ct., S11222
Barnabas, See PIKE
Benjamin, Ct., Mary, W3035; BLWt.31557-160-55
Benjamin, Ct., Mary, W16370
Benjamin, Cont., Ct., S15571
Benjamin, Mass., S5148
Benjamin, Pa., S41055
Bezaleel, Ct., S14152
Calvin, Ct., Sarah, W1068; BLWt. 31593-160-55
Cyril, Mass., Clarissa, W26307. Claim not allowed for services of above sold., but on acct. of service of wid's. former husb., Wm. F. Wheeler, a sold. in War of 1812. All papers within
Dan, Ct., S4644
Daniel, Ct., S11228
Daniel, Mass., S7305
David, Ct., S14128
David, Ct., S14156
David, Ct., S43813
David, Ct., Isabel, R8061
David, N.J., BLWt.8632. Iss. 8/29/1789. No papers
David, Va., R8063
Ebenezer, Ct., Cont., S38300
Eleazar, Mass., R8053
Eliphalet, Ct., Abigail, W21946
Elisha, Ct., Lucretia, W15183
Elisha, Ct., Huldah, R8054
Gad, Ct., Mary, W8286; BLWt. 26885-160-55
Gaius, R.I., S19025
Garret, N.Y., S28143
George, Ct., Ann, W19977
George, R.I., Phebe, W21942
Henry, Ga. See PEEK

PECK (continued)
Henry, Mass., R8057
Henry H., N.Y., Elizabeth, W9219; BLWt.26535-160-55
Hiel, Ct., Cont., Hannah, W3294; BLWt.1687-200-Lt. Iss. 9/15/1790 to Harry Williams. No papers
Ichabod, Cont., R.I., S43825
Isaac, Ct., Elizabeth, W9220; BLWt.26312-160-55, d. 12/11/1834 at Berlin
Isaac, Ct., R8059
Isaac, Ct., See PEEK
Isaac, Mass., R.I., Vt., S15557
Jacob, Ct., BLWt.6298. Iss. 9/28/1790 to Bartholomew & Fisher. No papers
Jacob, Ct., Cont., Elizabeth, W26869
Jahleel, N.H., Vt., R8062
James, Cont., Mass., S33457
James, Mass., R.I., Lydia, W18743
Jathleel, Ct., Olive, W26873
Jedediah, Cont., Ct., Tabitha, W16674
Jedidiah/Jedediah, Ct., S14114
Jeremiah, R.I., S33462
Jesse, Ct., Sarah, W1922; BLWt. 31312-160-55
Jesse, Cont., Ct. res., S36213
Joel, R.I., Lucy, W21938; BLWt. 7313-160-55
John, Ct., S14158
John, Ct., Mary, W26301; BLWt. 6299-100. Iss. 10/26/1789. BLWt.300-60-55
John, Ct., Cont., Lois, W21930
John, Navy, Mass., Privateer, b. Boston, pensioner of Ky. Eliza B., W6857; BLWt.53669-160-55
John, N.J., BLWt.1659-200-Lt. Iss. 1/25/1791. No papers
John, N.Y., BLWt.7601. Iss. 7/10/1790 to Quackinboss, ass. No papers
John, N.Y., Hannah, R8055
John, Pa., S5916
Jonathan, Mass., Betty, W21932
Jonathan, R.I., S11220
Joseph, Arty. Artificers, BLWt. 13613. Iss. 12/16/1793 to Eneas Munson, ass. No papers
Joseph, Ct., S29373
Joseph, Ct., Cont., Sarah, W21939
Joseph, Cont., Pd. at N.Y. Agcy., S19023
Joseph, Navy, Va. res. & Agcy. in 1819, Nancy Savage, former wid. W11373; BLWt.44841-160-55
Joseph, N.J., R8065
Joseph, N.Y., R8064
Joshua, Mass., Diodama S., W26874
Josiah, Ct., Hellen, W17428
Judson, Ct., Mary, W17429
Levi, Mass., Hannah, R8056
Loring, R.I., S43811
Lysias, Cont., Ct., Phebe, W26299
Matthew, N.H., Hannah, W24889
Moses, Ct., S14159
Nathaniel, Mass., S33465

PECK (continued)
Nathaniel, Mass., Mary, W18749
Peleg, Mass., Mary, W15192
Peleg, Navy, R.I., Susannah, W2426; BLWt.24153-160-55
Peter, N.C., Mary, W26296
Peter, Va., S18156
Phebe, former wid. of Remember Carpenter, Mass., which see
Reuben, Ct., S22432
Reuben, Ct., S43812
Samuel, Ct., S17012
Samuel, R.I., Olive, W26879
Simon, Cont., Ct., S7304
Stephen, Ct., S36214
Thomas, Ct., S23841
Walter, N.H., Christene, W16676
Ward, Ct., BLWt.6305. Iss. 1/24/1794(?). No papers
Ward, Ct., Dorcas, W26310
William, Ct., Mary, R8066
William, Ct., Cont., Elizabeth, W26875
William, Cont., R.I., S39001; BLWt.1629-400-Maj. Iss. 4/20/1790. No papers
William, Pa., Barbara, W3715
William, Va., S31301
PECKAM, Braddock. See PECKHAM
PECKER, William, Mass., S33450
PECKET, Joseph, Mass., BL Rej.----
PECKHAM, Barber, R.I., Sarah, W13803
Benjamin, Ct., Lucy, W21931
Benjamin, R.I., Mary, W21934
Benjamin L., R.I., S39005; BLWt.1628-300-Capt. Iss. 12/31/1789. No papers. (initial L. omitted)
Braddock, R.I., Silence, R17008
Daniel, R.I., S21924
Enos, R.I., S21420
Jonathan, R.I., Innocent, W26870
Josiah, Mass., S14160
Pardon, Mass., S23839
Peleg, R.I., S11236
Prince, Mass., R8068
Samuel, Navy, R.I., S33464
Samuel, R.I., S15568
Seth, R.I., Mary, W12599
Timothy, R.I., S21919
William, Mass., R8069
Zerviah, former wid. of John Miller, R.I., which see
PECKINPAUGH, Leonard, See BACKENBAUGH
PECOR, Charlotte, former wid. of Thomas B. Sewell, Md. Sea Service, which see
PEDDY, Andrew, N.C., S8945
PEDEN, Alexander, S.C., S21417
Joseph, Pa., Rebecca, R8071
Samuel, S.C., b. Ireland, S30649
PEDRICK, Abijah, N.Y., S9453
Benjamin, N.J., S22436
Joseph, N.H., S43814
Mary, former wid. of Isaac Matlack, N.J., which see
PEEBLES, John, S.C., R8074
Robert, Pa., BLWt.1711-200-Lt. Iss. 7/9/1789. No papers
Thomas, Va., Lucy, W13801; BLWt.

PEEBLES (continued)
86045-160-55
PEECK, Jacobus H., See James H. PEEK
PEED, Richard, Va., R17011
PEEDRICK, Benjamin, See PEDRICK
PEEK, Abel, Va. See PECK
Benjamin, Lamb's Arty., N.Y., BLWt.7649. Iss 10/19/1790. No papers
Christopher/Christophel, N.Y., Deborah, W16371
David, Va. See PECK
Harmanus, N.Y., S14161
Henry, Ga., S16504
Henry H., N.Y. See PECK
Isaac, Ct., R8060
James H/Jacobus H., N.Y., Sarah, W10883
James J./James I., N.Y., S23367
Joseph, N.Y., Catharine, W2568
Lewis D., N.Y., S16222
Richard, Va., S5903
Samuel, Ct., S41064
Samuel, R.I. See PECK
PEEKER, James Hazen's Regt., BLWt. 13584. Iss. 8/11/1790 to Robt. Dunlap, ass. No papers
William, Md., BLWt.11589. Iss. 11/13/1797 to James De Baufre, ass. of the wid. and only child of W.P. No papers
PEEL, Elizabeth, former wid. of David Lemon, which see. Wid's res. was Ala. in 1857. Mar. in Orange Co., N.C. in 1795
Jeremiah, Va. See PEALE
PEELING, Joshua, Pa. Agcy. & res., S5911
Robert, Pa. See PELING
PEER, John, Va., R8076
Mathias, Va., S17009
PEERS, William, Va., Elizabeth, W1921
PEERY, James, Va., Jane, R8132
John, Va. res. of wid. in 1845, Deborah, R8127
PEES, Andrew, Pa., S22433
PEESLEY, David, Mass., S43839
PEESO, William, Mass., Lydia, W26876
PEET, Elijah, Ct., Anna, W18734
John, Ct., Cont., Sally, W17427
John, Mass., BLWt.4802. Iss. 12/2/1791 to Jonathan Tuttle. No papers
John, Mass., Phebe, W13808
John, Lamb's Arty. N.Y., BLWt. 7654. Iss. 9/27/1790 to James F. Sebor, ass. No papers
Lemuel, Ct., S36218
Thaddeus, Ct., S22434
PEEVEY, Daniel, N.H. See PEAVEY
PEGAN, Andrew, Pa., Sea Service, S40249
PEGG, Benjamin, Pa., Ind. War 1792-1795, S40248
Charles, Cont., Va., res. 1832 Madison Co., Ala., S17633
Daniel, N.J., S23840
Elias, Pa., S40250

PEIFER, John George, See PEIFFER
PEIFFER, John George, Pa., Mary Magdalena, R8078
PEIRCE, Abel, Mass., S33463; BLWt.683-100
Abel, Mass., Sally, W15699
Amos, Mass., Vt., S14177
Benjamin, Mass., Lucy, W21975
Benjamin, Mass., Rebecca, W26867
Benjamin, N.H., Nabby, W10900; BLWt.38577-160-55
Benjamin, N.H., See PIERCE
Benjamin, N.H., Lucinda, See PIERCE
Bowen, R.I., S21921
Charles, Mass. See PIERCE
Christopher, Mass., S29378
Daniel, Cont., R.I., Mary, W21973
David, Mass., Keziah, W26900
David, N.H., S36736
Ebenezer, Mass. See PIERCE
Eliab, Mass., S11244
Ezekiel, Mass., S41060
Henry, Mass., Deborah Winslow, former wid., W18350
James, Mass., S36727
James, Mass. See PIERCE
Jesse, Mass., Lydia, W15206
Job, Mass., R.I., Mary, W13814
John, Ct., S3691
John, Mass., S37297
John, Mass. See PIERCE
Jonas, Mass., Susannah, W19990
Jonathan, R.I., Elizabeth, W26319
Joseph, Mass., S34475
Joseph, Mass., Eleanor, W15698
Joseph, Mass. See PIERCE
Joseph, Mass., R8238
Josiah, Mass., S31303
Nathaniel, Mass., S33478
Philip, Mass., Anna, W18763
Richard, Mass., R.I., S33479
Robert, Mass., S5157
Robert, Mass., See PIERCE
Samuel, Ct. See PIERCE
Samuel, Ct., Hannah, W26901
Silas, Mass., BLWt.1644-300-Capt. Iss. 4/2/1791 to John Peck, ass. No papers
Solomon, N.H., S22936
Thomas, Mass. See PIERCE
William, Mass., S15559
William, Mass., Phebe, W19983
William, Mass., Hannah, W26606
Zadock, Mass., S43838
Zebulon, Mass., Mary, W1890
PEIRSON, Abraham, Pa. See PIERSON
Amos, Ct., Sarah, W4765
David, N.J., S40258
John, N.Y. See PEARSON
Stephen, N.J., S16228
Usual, Vt. See Uzal PIERSON
William, N.J., S1081
PELFREY, William, Va., R8079
PELHAM, Abijah, Ct. Sea Service, N.Y., S3667
Charles, Va., Isabella, W3034; BLWt.1735-400-Maj. Iss. 12/3/1792. No papers
Elisha L., N.Y., S14112
William, S.C., Martha, R8080
William, Va., S3678

PELING, Robert, Pa., S41052
PELL, John, Va., Nancy, R8081
Joseph Simon, Va. Sea Service, R84; Va. Half Pay
Josiah, Ct., Pa., N.Y., Elizabeth W2662; BLWt.26661-160-55
Samuel T., N.Y., BLWt.1681-300
Thomas, Mass., Vt., Lydia, W18739
William, Va., S16503
PELLOM, Edward, Ct., S36216
PELLY, John, See PUMPELLY
PELSBURY, Samuel, See PILSBURY
PELTON, Benjamin, Ct., Hannah, W9221
Benjamin, N.Y. & 1812?, Isabella, W1990; BLWts.61054-160-55 & 1651-300-Capt. Iss. 7/14/1791. Also recorded as above under BLWt.2587. No papers
Daniel, Ct., S43827
David, Ct., S33468
Ebenezer, Mass., S43845
Freeman, Ct., Prudence, R8083
Joel, Cont., Mass., Me. Agcy. & res., Ruhamah/Rahamah, W26309; BLWt.41702-160-55
John, Ct., S28842
Joseph, Ct., Abigail, W26303; BLWt.34904-160-55. She also applied for B.L. on acct. of her 1st husb., John Ayres/Ayers, Ct., BL Rej.
Joseph, Ct., N.J., Privateer, S11229
Moses, Ct., Dorothy Phillips/Phillipps, former wid., W17441
Samuel, Mass., S3658
Stephen, Mass., S14119
Thomas, Mass., S33444
PELTS, James, See PATTS
PEMBER, Eli, Ct., Vt., Clarissa, W2335; BLWt.11417-160-55
PEMBERTON, Christian, Pa., S41057
John, Del., Sarah, W10875
John, Sr., Va., S16223
Reuben, Va., R20183
Thomas, Cont., Va., S46403; BLWt.1751-300-Capt. Iss. 8/24/1789. No papers
Thomas, N.Y., BLWt.7589. Iss. 12/8/1792. No papers
PEMBLETON, Jabez, Ct., Lucy, W2557; BLWt.26971-160-55
PEMBROKE, David, Cont., N.Y., 5th U.S. Inf. 1819, S11219
PEMBROOK, David, N.Y., BLWt.7640. Iss. 7/28/1791 to Robert Boyd, ass. No papers
David, Cont., N.Y., S43821
David, Cont. See PEMBROKE
David, Jr., N.Y., BLWt.7643. Iss. 10/27/1791. No papers
James, Lamb's Arty., N.Y., BLWt. 7641. Iss. 8/11/1790 to John Close, ass. No papers
PEN, Benoni, N.J., S46466
PENAX, John, See PINNIX
PENBROOK, David, Cont., N.Y. See PEMBROOK
PENBY, John, N.C., See PENLY
PENCE, John, Va., Nancy, W5511
William, N.J., Elizabeth

PENCE (continued)
Britton, former wid., W398. Her other husb. was pensioned. See claim of Daniel Brittan, N.J.
PENDEGRASS, Job, N.C., S41504
PENDELL, Elizabeth, former wid. of Samuel Osborn, Ct., which see
Jonathan, N.Y., S17013
PENDER, Amos, See PONDER
John, N.H., S36211
Thomas, Md., Anna, W8085; BLWt. 1753-100
PENDERGAST, Edward, Pa., S16505
William, Md., Juliet Onion, former wid., W26596; BLWt.1128-200
PENDERGRASS, David, N.C., Susan, R8086
John, N.C., Mary, W18730
Robert, Sgt. in Proctor's Arty., Pa., BLWt.10232. Iss. 10/28/1789 to M. McConnell, ass. No papers
Thomas, N.J., BLWt.8657. Iss. 6/11/1789 to Matthias Denman, ass. No papers
PENDEXTER, Paul, See PINDEXTER
PENDLETON, Benjamin, Va., S14127
Curtis, Va., Nancy, W8514
Daniel, Cont., Ct., BLWt.2152-300
David, Ct., BLWt.6308. Iss. 4/13/1791 to Victory Wetmore, ass. No papers
David, Ct., S20910
Hiram, N.C., Elizabeth, W5517; BLWt.28549-160-55
James, Va. Arty., BLWt.1749-300-Capt. Iss. 2/18/1793 to Robt. Means, ass. No papers
Joshua, R.I., Nancy, W17438
Micajah, Va., S8951
Nathan, R.I., R8087
Nathaniel, Va., BLWt.1736-300-Capt. Iss. 7/27/1795 to John Bard, ass. No papers
Philip, Va., S18157
Richard, Va., Mary, W5514
Stephen, R.I., S43829
Zebulon, R.I., R8088
PENDOCK, Rufus, Navy, R.I. Agcy. & res., S38997
Samuel, R.I., Anna, W26297; BLWts.3411-100-1792 & 239-60-55
PENEFIELD, Thomas, Md. See PENEFILL
PENEFILL, Thomas, Md., Esther, W9224; BLWt.29741-160-55
PENELL, Clement, Mass., S37295
PENFIELD, Abel, Ct., R8089
Daniel, Ct., R8090
Isaac, Mass., N.Y., S14115
James, Ct., Mary, W26298
Jesse, Ct., Dorinda Shepard, former wid., R9477
Jesse, Cont., Ct., S43834
Nathaniel, Ct., S23369
Peter, Ct., Hannah, W16679
Phineas, Ct., S15558
Samuel, Ct., S5895
Simeon, Ct., S18155
PENHOLLOW, Richard/Richard P. HOLLOW, Ct., Cont., Huldah, W18737
PENICK, John, Va., R8092
PENIMAN, Huldah, former wid. of Barnabas Hollis, Cont., Mass., Which see
PENINGER, Henry, Va., S8946
PENINGTON, James, Va. See PENNINGTON
John, N.J. See PENNINGTON
PENION, Reuben, See PENNEL
PENIX, John, N.C. See PINNIX
John, Va. See PENICK
PENLAND, John, N.C., Alice, R8093
PENLY, John, N.C., S7302
Joseph, Mass., Thankful, W1644; BLWt.19538-160-55
PENN, Benjamin, Md., Rebecca, W8510
Benoni, See PEN
Shadrach, Md. Margaret, W8094
Stephen, Md., Mary, W6858
PENNEFILL, Thomas, Md. See PENEFILL
PENNEL, Hugh, Pa., R17021
Reuben, N.C., Lydia, W5519
PENNELL, Clement, Mass. See PENELL
Jeremiah, Crane's Cont. Arty., Mass., BLWt.4882. Iss. 1/13/1800 to Abijah Holbrook. No papers
Joseph, Mass., Bathsheba, W9222; BLWt.39210-160-55
Robert, N.Y., S14148
PENNETENT, John, Va., S35554
PENNEY, Abraham, Mass., S37296
Benjamin, Mass. See PENNY
David, Mass., Sarah, W15184
Henry, S.C., Mary, W26501
William, N.J., R8097
PENNIFIELD, Thomas, Md., BLWt. 11600. Iss. 3/11/1791. No papers
Thomas, Md. See PENEFILL
PENNIMAN, Adna, Mass., N.H., S45065; BLWt.1624-200-Capt., Lt. Iss. 2/17/1797 to Wm. S Thom, ass. Name also spelled Pennyman. No papers
Ebenezer, Mass., S33460
Huldah, former wid. of Barnabas Hollis, Cont., Mass., which see
James, Mass., S33443
PENNINGER, Martin, N.C., S41951
PENNINGTON, Charles, Pa., R8098
James, Va., S31296
John, N.J., S3670
Kinchen/Kincher, N.C., S.C., S7306
William, Col. Lamb's Regt. of Arty., BLWt.1686-200-Lt. Iss. 7/9/1790 to Theodosius Fowler, ass. No papers
PENNO, Peter, R.I., Sea Service, S39000
PENNOCK, Aaron, See PINNOCK
Haman/Herman, Vt., S18158
Herman, See Haman
PENNOYER, William, Ct., War of 1812, S17631
PENNSINGER, Henry, Pa., S41058
PENNY, Benjamin, Mass., Olive, W10867; BLWt.91015-160-55
John, Md., BLWt.11593. Iss. 9/26/1791 to John McCleland, ass. No papers
John, Mass., S36725
John, N.Y., Desire, W15936
John, N.C., Va., Fanny, W8512
Jonathan, N.Y., BLWt.7602. Iss. 9/9/1790 to Ezekiel Crane, ass. No papers
Pelatiah, Mass., S45066
Salathiel, Cont., Mass., S36728
Simon (Indian), See PERPEANEY
PENNYMAN, Adna, See PENNIMAN
Huldah. See Barnabas HOLLIS
James, Mass. See PENNIMAN
PENOYER, Reuben I./Reuben J., N.Y., R8099
Samuel, Ct., S15573
PENTICOST, Polly, former wid. of Jesse Browder; Va. res. of wid. in 1844. See Jesse Browder
William, Va., S7310
PENTLAND, Thomas, Ct., BLWt.6338. Iss. 5/5/1791 to Benj. Tallmadge, ass. No papers
Thomas, Cont., Ct., S43840
PENTON, Aaron, Pvt., Pa., BLWt. 10221 iss. 4/19/179- to Jacob Clingman, ass. No papers
PEONIX, Overton, Va., Malinda, W5550; BLWt.26752-160-55
PEPIN, Andrew Livingston's Regt. BLWt.1661-200-Lt. Iss. 9/3/1792. Also recorded as above under BLWt.2611. No papers
PEPOON, Daniel, N.Y., Elizabeth, W16363
PEPPER, Elijah, Md., BLWt.11588. Iss. 9/13/1799 to Asahel Phelps, ass. No papers
John, Mass., S19027
William, Del., S5901
PERADY, Emanuel, Navy, R.I., Love, W26312
PERAN, Henry, Hazen's Regt., BLWt. 13587. Iss. 5/7/1790. No papers
Henry, N.Y., S34580
PERCE, James, Mass. See PIERCE
PERCEL, John, N.J., S3666
PERCHMENT, Peter, Va., Mary, W3713
PERCIVAL, John, Mass., S11227
PERCY, David, Mass., R21788
Joseph, Ct., R17029
PERDO, Joseph, Pa. See PARDOE
PEREY, David, Mass. See PERCY
John, N.Y. See PERRY
Joseph, Mass., See PERRY
PEREZ, Peter, German Regt., BLWt. 1717-400-Surgn. Iss. 8/14/1789. No papers
PERHAM, Ezekiel, Mass., Phebe, W2337; BLWt.12716-160-55
Joel W., Mass., S41949
Joseph, Mass., S41946
Oliver, Mass., Anna, W16054; BLWt.11403-160-55
Peter, Mass., S20536
PERIGEN, Molliston, Va., S38992
PERIGO, David, See PERRIGO

PERIGO (continued
Ebenezer, Ct., BLWt.6270. Iss. 9/24/1790 to James F. Sebor, ass. No papers
Ebenezer, Ct., Mary, W17435
PERILL, John, Va., Elizabeth, W5513
PERIN, Daniel, Cont., Mass., Betsey, R8120
Edward, Mass., S43841
John, Cont., R.I. See PERRIN
PERINE, William, Cont., Green Mt. Boys, N.J. & N.Y., S46404
William, N.J., Ann/Anne, W3156
William, N.J. See PERRINE
PERKENS, Thomas, Va. See PERKINS
PERKER, Samuel, Ct., Dis. No papers. See Am. State Papers, Vol. 9, p.112, which shows this sold. was wounded by a cannon ball while on an expedition in R.I. See also p. 61, name spelled Parker
PERKHOLF, Frederick, N.Y., BLWt. 7609. Iss. 8/3/1790 to Cornelius Van Dyck, ass. No papers
PERKHOOF, Frederick, See BARKHUFF
PERKINGS, James, N.Y., S35558
Joseph, N.Y., R20424
PERKINPINE, Elizabeth, former wid. of Bernard Hubley, Pa., which see
PERKINS, Aaron, Ct., S41053; BLWt. 277-100
Abiezer, Cont., Mass., S43835
Abigail, former wid. of David Cook Mass., which see
Abner, Mass., S15195
Abner, Mass., Abigail, W21952
Abraham, Ct., Cert. 3536
Abraham, Mass., Elizabeth Margaret, R8107
Amos, R.I., Cote, W16369
Anthony, Va., S11234
Archelaus, Va., S15570; BLWt.1744-200-Lt. Iss. 2/22/1799 to Wm. R. Bernard, ass. No papers
Azubah, former wid. of Thomas Elgar, Mass., which see
Benjamin, N.H., S15572
Benjamin, Va., S11223
Charles, Cont., Ct., BLWt.340-100
Christian, Va., S25729
Daniel, Ct., S19026
Daniel, Ct., S41063
Daniel, Mass., Sarah, W1991
David, Mass., Nabby, W15185
David, Mass., Sea Service, S3656
Ebenezer, Ct., S36219
Ebenezer, Cont., Mass., S45063
Ebenezer, Cont., Mass., Navy, Sarah, W21954
Ebenezer, Mass., Mary, W21951
Edmund, Mass., S11221
Eliab, Cont., Mass., S43817
Elias, Ct., S14149
Elias, Va., S5908
Elijah, Mass., R8106
Elisha, Ct., S29379
Elisha, Mass., Marcy, W26866
Elizabeth, former wid. of Joseph Darby, Cont., Mass., which see
Enoch, Mass., Susanna, W26878

PERKINS (continued)
Ezekiel, Va., S5905
Francis, Ct., Saloma, W6865; BLWt.6438-160-55
George, N.C., S.C., Keziah, R8113
Henry, Mass., Navy, S29372
Isaac, Ct., S33448
Isaac, Mass., S30647
Isaac, N.C., S41953
Israel, Ct., Lydia, W18748
Israel, Mass., Anna, W21945
Jacob, S.C., Ann, R8105
James, Mass., Cont., S33447
James, Cont., Mass., S37294
James, N.Y., BLWt.7635. Iss. 2/14/1791. No papers
James, N.Y. See PERKINGS
James, N.Y., R8110
Jason, Ct., S43816
Jencks, R.I., Elizabeth, R8108
Jesse, Cont., Mass., Elizabeth, W15938
Joel, Mass., S22437
John, Ga., R8111
John, Mass., S5149
John, Mass., Sarah, W15198
John, Mass., Navy, S15556
John, N.H., BLReg.214778-1855
John/Thomas CARSON, N.C., Va., Francis, W2640; BLWt.86132-160-55
Jonathan, Mass., S5150
Jonathan, N.H., Elizabeth, W16055; BLWt.1625-200-Lt. Iss. 4/24/1798 to Daniel Gookins, ass. No papers
Joseph, Mass., Sarah, W26854
Joseph, Mass., Sea Service, N.H., Hannah, W21944; BLWt.13431-160-55
Joseph, N.H., S14123
Joseph, N.Y., BLWt.7630. Iss. 2/14/1791. No papers
Joseph, N.Y., R8112
Joseph, N.Y., Patience, R8115
Joseph, N.Y., R17033. Sold's. son James, also applied on acct. of his service in War of 1812. See papers within
Joseph, N.Y. See PERKINGS
Joseph, Va., BLWt.12473. Iss. 10/26/1795 to John Stockdell, ass. No papers
Joshua, Mass., S30645
Leonard, Ct., S23366
Lewis, S.C., R8114
Maria, former wid. of Drury Ham, Va., which see
Mark, Mass., S31298; BLWt.15404-160-55
Moses, Ga., S3677
Moses, Mass., S16508
Moses, N.C., Gillean/Gille Ann, R8109
Nathan, Mass., Hannah, W26872
Nathaniel, Cont., N.H., res. at enl. Rochester, N.H., res. in 1821 Waterbury, Vt.; d. 11/1821 Polly, W21935
Nathaniel, Mass., S33451
Nathaniel, Mass., Privateer, Abigail, W26860

PERKINS (continued)
Nathaniel, N.H., Mercy, W26861; res. at enl. Northfield, N.H., res. at application in 1830 Walden, Vt., had lived there 43 yrs. D. 9/5/1842
Nathaniel, R.I., Martha, W2163; BLWt.38570-160-55
Nimrod, Va., S5904
Obadiah, Ct., Dis. No papers. See Am. State Papers, Class 9, p.141 which shows this sold. wounded in the breast by a bayonet, 9/6/1781 at Ft. Griswold. Evidence incomplete
Peletiah, Mass., S20509
Reuben, Ct., S14157
Richard, Cont., Mass., Abigail, R8104
Robert, Mass., Privateer, Mary C. BLWt.56944-160-55
Rufus, Mass., Caroline, W8287
Samuel, Ct., S9454
Samuel, Mass., Mehitable, W21941; BLWt.3622-160-55
Samuel, Va., Susannah, W1992; BLWt.34938-160-55
Sands, R.I., R8117
Theodore, Mass., BLWt.4803. Iss. 3/15/1798. No papers
Theodore, Mass., S36730
Thomas, Cont., Mass., S45061
Thomas, N.C., S9455
Thomas, Va., b. Md., Mary, W5516
Thomas Harden, Va., S3680
Timothy, Cont., Mass.(?), Elizabeth, W13805
Titus, N.Y., BLWts.13593 & 14042 Iss. 12/19/1792 to John Perkins Admr. No papers
Ute/Uta, N.C., R8118
William, Ct., S14126
William, Cont., Mass. Agcy., S36732
William, Mass., BLWt.1639-400-Maj. Iss. 2/7/1794. No papers
William, Mass., Judith, W15177
William, N.C., S8791
Zophar, N.Y., R8119
PERKINSON, Ezekiel, Va., Anna, W5506
James, Cont., Va., S38296
PERLEY, Daniel, Cont., Mass., S17632
Eliphalet, Mass., S33456
Henry, Mass., S33445
Huldah, former wid. of Nathaniel Chamberlain, Mass., which see
Stephen, Mass., S30024
PERMELE, Luther, See PARMLEE
PERON, Henry, N.Y. See PERAN
PEROT, John Baptist, Cont., N.J. res. in 1808; BLWt.973-100
PERPEANEY, Simon, (Indian), Mass. BLWt.1941-100
PERPENER, Simon, See PERPEANEY
PERRE, Joshua, See PEARRE
PERREY, Jeremiah, See PERRY
PERRIGO, David, Cont., N.Y., Eunice, W19981

PERRIGO, Frederick, Vt. & 29th U.S. Inf. War of 1812, Mary, W26858; BLWt.4916-160-50; Inv. File 27303 (1812)
Joseph Hewes, R.I., Miriam, W17436
Rufus, Vt., S19028
William, Ct., BLWt.6264. Iss. 9/24/1790 to Peleg Sanford, ass. No papers
William, Ct., S43818
PERRILL, John, Va. See PERILL
PERRIN, Daniel, Cont., Mass. See PERIN
Jesse, Ct., Cont., Mass., S43819
John, Cont., R.I., S21415
Nathan, Mass. See Nathaniel
Nathaniel/Nathan, Mass., S32437
Nathaniel, Mass., Joanna, W6864; BLWt.3806-160-55
PERRINE, Andrew, N.J., R8122
Henry, N.J., Catharine, R8121
James, N.J., S1077
James, N.J., N.J. service in 1794, d. 1811, Maria, W5510; BLWt.57778-160-55
James D., N.J., S829
Peter, N.J., Sarah, W5520
William, N.J. See PERINE
William, N.J., Margaret, W3859
PERRIT, Needham, N.C., S38998
Peter, Ct., BLWt.1677-300-Capt. Iss. 1/8/1790. No papers
PERROW, Daniel B., Va., R8123
PERRY, Abel, Mass., S18543
Abijah, Ct., S40259
Abner, Cont., Mass., Anna, W18751; BLWt.19770-160-55
Abner, N.C., Sarah Horton, former wid., W4231
Abraham, N.H., BLWt.3397. Iss. 8/10/1789 to Richard Platt, ass. No papers
Abraham, N.H., Mary, W16678
Adam, Mass., Elizabeth, W15191
Adonijah, N.C., Elizabeth, W10882; BLWt.56858-160-55
Almon, Ct., Elizabeth, W18740
Arthur, Ct., S14154
Benjamin, N.H., R8125
Benjamin, Va., S30644
Constant, Mass., Lydia, W15194; BLWt.1890-100
Daniel, Mass., S41059
David, Mass., S29377
David, Mass., S45059
David, N.Y., S28843
David, N.Y., Content, W2643
Diman/Dimond, Mass., Hannah, BLWt.17735-160-55
Dwelly, R.I., Patience, W21936
Ebenezer, Ct./Mass., Dorcas Taylor, former wid.,see case of her 1st husb., Levi Farnam.
Eli, Ct., S14113
Eli, Mass., S19029
Elnathan, Mass., Christania, W1642
Elnathen, Mass., BLWt.4863. Iss. 2/27/1793 to Alexander Power. No papers
Freeman, Ct., N.Y., S14121

PERRY (continued)
Hannah, former wid. of Nathaniel Pettingale, Ct., Mass., N.H., which see. Also served in French War
Henry, Mass., S23368
Henry, N.J., BLWt.8647. Iss. 6/16/1789 to Thomas Coyle, ass. No papers
Ichabod/Jeremiah, Ct., Navy, Rebecca, W17433; BLWt.31558-160-55
Ichabod, N.H., BLWt.3384. Iss. 3/16/1794 to M. Cutler, ass. No papers
Ichabod, N.H., S43815
Isaac, Green Mt. Boys, Cont., Mass., Vt., R8131
Isaac, Mass., S31299
Isaac, Mass., Mary, BLWt.10232-160-55
James, Mass., Abilena, R8124
James, Mass., R.I., S30017
Jeremiah, Ct. See Ichabod
Jeremiah, Privateer, R.I., Amia/Almey/Anna, R18735
Jesse, Cont., Mass., Mary, W26865
Jesse, N.C., S8947
Jesse, S.C., S3655
Job, Mass., S17015
John, Va. See PEERY
John, Ct., S17628
John, Cont., Va. res of heirs in 1830; BLWt.1692-150
John, Mass., S30023
John, Mass., BLWt.131-100; S---
John, Mass., N.J., S33469
John, N.H., S43830
John, N.J., BLWt.8641. Iss. 3/1/1790. No papers
John, N.J., Charity, W5523
John, N.Y., S14155
John/Johannes, N.Y., Elizabeth, R8129
John, N.C. See PARRY
John, Pa., Margaret, R8135
John, Va., S35556
Jonathan, Ct., Hannah, W26295
Jonathan, Mass., S44296
Jonathan, Mass., Betty, W18738
Jonathan, R.I., R8133
Joseph, Ct., Mary, W17434
Joseph, Mass., S33446
Joseph, Mass., See PARRY
Joseph, Mass., Lucy, W5507; BLWt.8461-160-55
Joseph, Sappers & Miners, BLWt. 13579. Iss. 6/29/1789 to Matt. McConnell, ass. No papers
Micah, Mass., Susannah, W2239; BLWt.38571-160-55
Moses, Va., S38295
Nathan, Mass., S30018
Nathaniel, Ct., Eunice, W26864
Nathaniel, Ga. See PEARRE
Nicholas, N.C., S3672
Noah, Mass., BLWt.4839. Iss. 8/24/1790 to Benj. Ives Gilman. No papers
Noah, Mass. See BUMPUS
Obadiah, Mass., Mary, W13807

PERRY (continued)
Ozias, Ct., Cont., S43832
Prince, Mass., Deliverance, W15193
Reuben, Ct., Sally, W2663; BLWt. 54873-160-55
Robert, Va., BLWt.12476. Iss. 5/29/1792 to Francis Graves, ass. No papers
Samuel, Ct., Alice, W15189
Samuel, Ct., Tabitha, W26859; BLWt.15438-160-55
Samuel, Cont., Mass., Anna, W10879; BLWt.80020-160-55
Samuel, Md., S39003
Samuel, N.J., S1078
Seth, Mass., Hannah, W15181
Silas, Mass., S41061
Silas, Mass., Dorcas, W2336; BLWt.10301-160-55
Simon, Md., Elizabeth, W3860
Sylvanus, Ct., S36212; BLWt.1670-200-Lt. Iss. 6/30/1789. No papers
Thomas, Ct., Privateer, S14162
Thomas, Md., BLWt.11612. Iss. 3/11/1791. No papers
Thomas, Md., Mary, W8505; BLWt. 52780-160-55
Thomas, N.J., BLWt.8644. Iss. 1/27/1797. No papers
Thomas, N.J., S34469
Thomas, N.J., Pa., S4647
Thomas, Pa., BLWt.10226. Iss. 8/14/1793 to Jasper Iserloan, ass. No papers
William, Del., BLWt.10865. Iss. 8/?/1789. No papers
William, Mass., BLWt.4814. Iss. 8/23/1796 to Benj. Dana. No papers
William, Mass., Mary, BLWt.1588-150
William, R.I., R8138
William, S.C., S8944
William, Va., W5515
William, Va., Keziah, R8134
William W., Mass., Eleanor Poor, W15188
Willis, N.C., R8139
Winslow, Vt., Rachel, W4309
PERRYMAN, John, N.C., Va., S3682
William, Va., S31300
PERSELL, Jacob, N.Y., R8140
PERSEN, John, N.Y., S14117
PERSINGER, Jacob, Va., S30019
PERSON, Henry, N.C., S30641
Stephen, N.H., S14116
PERSONIUS, Jacobus, N.Y., S43831
PERSONS, Job, Mass. See PARSONS
PESNELL, John, S.C., R8141
PETER, Galloway, Ct., BLWt.6284. Iss. 6/14/1790. No papers
Jonathan, Mass., BLWt.4815. Iss. 2/29/1792 to Moses Beard. No papers
Michael, Cont., Pa., S40255
William, Mass., BLWt.5291. Iss. 1/22/1790 to Benj. Mooers, ass. No papers
PETERMAN, Jacob, Pa., Ann, R8144
PETERS, Absalom, Ct., S14129
Amos, N.J., S1076
Andrew, Mass., BLWt.1634-450-Lt. Col. Iss. 4/1/1796/90. No papers

PETERS (continued)
Anthony, Pa., BLWt.10216. Iss. 7/9/1789. No papers
Anthony, Pa., S40253
Arnold, Pa., BLWt.10222. Iss. 10/21/179? to Daniel Brautigan, ass. No papers
Benjamin, Mass., Martha, W15180
Christian, Va., S5898
Comfort, Mass., Navy, Mercy, W5530
Elias, Pa., BLWt.10212. Iss. 3/23/1791 to Eliz. Peters, Admr. No papers
Elijah, S.C., S38298
Galloway, Ct. (colored), Nancy, W18736; BLWt.6284-100. Iss. 6/14/1790. No papers
Henry, Ark. res. of wid., Catherine, R8145
Hermon, N.Y., S11224
Israel, Mass., Eunice, W26304; BLWt.14509-160-55
Jacob, Cont., Pa., S40246
Jacob, Pvt. in the Arty., Artificers, Pa., BLWt.10205 & 13633 Iss. 5/21/1799 to Abm. Bell, ass. No papers
Jacob, Pa., S5909
James, Mass., BLWt.4850. Iss. 4/19/1792 to Isaac Bronson. No papers
James, Mass., Susannah, W26877
James, Va., Elizabeth, W5503; BLWt.15168-160-55
Jesse, Ga., S16506
Jesse, Va., R8146
John, Mass., S40254
John, Navy, Mass. res. & Agcy., S33454
John, N.H., Betsey, BLWt.1922-100
John, N.J., R8147
John, N.J., Va., S5902
John, N.Y., BLWt.7613. Iss. 9/15/1790 to John S. Hobart et al, assnes. No papers
John, N.Y., BLWt.7618. Iss. 8/24/1790. No papers
John, Va., S5897
John, Va., Nancy, W8511
Jonathan, Ct., BLWt.6275. Iss. 8/21/1789. No papers
Joseph, Ct., S11231
Joseph, see joint petition to Congress in David Gray, Mass., S---
Joseph P., Ct., Lydia, W2338; BLWt.38541-160-55
Levi, N.J., BLWt.8654. Iss. 6/28/1799 to Abraham Bell, ass. No papers
Nathan, Ct., Cont., Mass., Lois, W21937
Peter, Ct., BLWt.6273. Iss. 12/3/1789 to Daniel Watrous, ass. No papers
Peter, Ct., S36210
Philip, N.J., BLWt.8626. Iss. 12/19/1791. Cert. 10/20/1815. No papers
Pomp (colored), Mass., S45062;

PETERS (continued)
BLWt.110-100
Prince, Mass., S41943
Robinson, N.H., Privateer, Mass. S11232
Samuel, Ct., Hannah, W17437
William, Md., BLWt.11596. Iss. 8/8/1794 to Chr. Cusack, ass. No papers
William, N.Y., S19022; BLWt. 1683-150-Ensign. Iss. 2/15/1796. No papers
William, N.Y. See PETTERS
William, N.C., S1580
PETERSON, Abraham, N.J., S34471
Andrew, Mass., S37293
Conrad/Conrod, Va., Mary, W10226
Daniel, Pa., S39006
Eli, Va., S30646
Francis, N.Y., S43824
Gabriel, Pa., Margaret C., W3295; BLWt.27678-160-55 & 1712-200-Lt. Iss. 9/2/1790. No papers
Henry, N.J., S39002
Isaac, N.Y., S14163
Israel, Va., BLWt.12472. Iss. 1/31/1794 to John Stockdale, ass. No papers
Jacob, Mass., S43822
James, N.C., Elizabeth, W4050; BLWt.26665-160-55
John, N.Y. See PATTERSON
John, N.Y., S43842
John, N.C., S7303
John, N.C., b. Pa., S9456
Jonathan, Mass., S30642
Joseph, Mass., Rebecca, W21940
Lemuel, N.J., Privateer, R21900
Lucy, former wid. of Elnathan Darby, Mass., which see
Luther, Mass., Priscilla, W15182
Matson, N.J., S3665
Philip, N.Y., Hannah, W3717; BLWt.26138-160-55
Ruben/Reuben, N.J., S1079
Samuel, N.J., Abigail, W26880
Simon, Pvt. In the Invalid Regt. BLWt.13621. Iss. 7/6/1791 to Carlile Pollock, ass. No papers
Sylvanus, Mass., R8151; BLWt. 34583-160-55
Thaddeus, Mass., S33467
Thomas, N.J., S5899
Turner, Mass., S14118
PETIGRU, William, See PETTIGREW
PETIT, Gideon/Gurdeon, N.C.,S41950
Samuel, N.Y. See PETTIT
Thomas, Md., BLWt.11619. Iss. 1/25/1796 to Samuel Johnston, ass. No papers
PETITT, George, N.C., R8154
Samuel, N.Y.? BLWt.7595. Iss. 7/30/1790 to John Wendall, ass.
PETREE, Peter, N.C., Mary, W4310; BLWt.11061-160-55
PETREY, Martin, Va. See PETRY
PETRI, Johannes, N.Y. Agcy., Dis. No papers
Edward/Edmund PETTIE, Mass., BLWt.4864. Iss. 6/21/1791. No papers

PETRIE (continued)
George, S.C., S38993
Hondedrick M., N.Y. See Richard M.
Richard Marcus/Hondedrick M., N.Y., Catharine Bellinger, former wid., R729
PETRY, Jacob, Pa., S22435
Martin, Va., S17010
PETTAWAY, Micajah, N.C., S3668
PETTEBONE, Stephen, See PETTIBONE
PETTEE, Andrew, N.J., S8950
Nathaniel, See PITTEE
Oliver, Cont., Mass., Abigail, W21953
Oliver, Mass., Elizabeth, W15197; BLWt.3867-160-55
William, Cont., Mass., S14130
PETTENGER, Jacob, N.J., Charity, W810
PETTENGILL, Benjamin, Cont., Mass. N.H., R.I., S11235
Jethro, N.H., S46719
Joseph, N.Y., R8152
Samuel, Mass., R8153
William, N.H. See PETTINGILL
PETTER, Oliver, Mass. See PETTEE
William, Cont., Mass. See PETTEE
PETTERS, John, N.J.,Va. See PETERS
William, N.Y., Lydia, R8148
PETTES, Abial, Cont., Mass., Hannah, W21943
Benjamin, Cont., Privateer, Vt., S17011
PETTEY, Daniel, R.I., S21920
PETTIBONE, Abel, Cont., Mass., S15555
Amos, Mass., S17629
Daniel, Ct., Eunice, W26306; BLWt.39492-160-55
Eli, Mass., Vt., Hannah, W26881
Elijah, Ct., S43837
Jacob, Green Mt. Boys, Mass., S43820
John, Ct., Susannah Pinney, former wid., R8262. Her other husb., Jonathan Pinney, Ct. also served in the Rev. War. Papers in same file.
Samuel, Mass., Rhoda, W18741
Seth, Mass., Vt., Deborah, W26311
Stephen, Ct., BL--
PETTICREW, John, Pa., S29374
Matthew, Va., Ann, W5508
PETTIFORD, Drury, Va., S41954
George, N.C., Tabitha, W9223; BLWt.31309-160-55
Philip, N.C., S41952
William, N.C., S41948
PETTIGREW, James, Pa., Judith, W4760; BLWt.1709-200-Lt. Iss. 7/27/1791. No papers
James, S.C., Jane, W5522
Richard, Va. Sea Service, S46639
William, S.C., S21421
PETTIJOHN, John, N.C., S3669
PETTINGAL, Obadiah, Mass. See PETTINGILL
PETTINGALE, Nathaniel, Ct., Mass., N.H., also French War, Hannah Perry, former wid., W21933

PETTINGELL, Benjamin, Mass.,S30648
Jethro, N.H., BLWt.3375. Iss. 7/21/1789 to Ladd & Cass, assnes. No papers
Jonathan, N.H., BLWt.3387. Iss. 4/5/1796 to O. Ashley, ass. No papers
Joseph, Mass., BLWt.1636-400-Major. Iss. 8/7/1789 to Richard Platt, ass. No papers
PETTINGELL, Joshua, Mass., S29375
William, N.Y., S18163
PETTINGILL, Akerman, Mass., S33455
Benjamin, Mass., S43844
John, Ct., Hannah, W10877; BLWt. 26017-160-55
John, Mass., Elizabeth Dillingham former wid., W24060
Jonathan, N.H., Susanna Bartlett, former wid., R588
Mathew/Matthew, Mass., Navy, S29376
Obadiah, Mass., Eleanor, W26853; BLWt.11188-100-55
William, --, Lydia, W26857. Wid.'s res. Leeds, Maine, 1832
William, N.H., Sarah, W1643; BLWt.11157-160-55
PETTIS, Abial, Cont., Mass. See PETTES
David, Cont., Mass., S43843
Ezekiel, Mass., S14120
John, Va., Martha, W3449
Joseph, Ct., S14164
PETTIT, Ebenezer, Mass., S14122
Gurdeon, N.C. See Gideon PETIT
Henry, S.C., Anna/Ann, W5528
James, Va., S5896
John, Mass., N.Y., S11226
Jonathan, N.Y., S46654
Mathew, Pa., S35553
Samuel, N.Y., S44242
William, N.J., Hannah, R8155
PETTITT, George, N.C. See PETITT
Jabez, Lamb's Arty., N.Y., BLWt. 7652. Iss. 9/24/1791. No papers
Thomas, Md., Sarah, W10874
PETTOT, Enos, Ct., BLWt.6313. Iss. 3/18/1790. No papers
PETTS, David, Mass. See PATTS
James, Cont., Mass. See PATTS
Jonathan, Cont., Mass., S45060
PETTY, Abiel, Lamb's Arty., BLWt. 7637. Iss. 1/7/1796 to Calvin Sangar, ass. No papers
Daniel, N.J., S830
Ebenezer, N.J., R8156
Francis, Ky. Agcy. S---
Jacob, N.J., S29346
John, N.C., R8158
John, N.C., S.C., S39007
Joshua, R.I., S21419
Peter, N.J., S3659
Rodham, Va., Sarah, W2567; BLWt.26911-160-55
Samuel, Mass., S43828
Theophilus, S.C., R8161
Thomas, S.C., S1710
William, N.C., S17016
William, Va., Mildred, W18747
William, Va., R8162

PETTYJOHN, John, Va., R8163
PEUGH, Young, Va., S3633
PEVARE, Noyes, N.H., S11233
PEVEY, Peter, Mass., Lucy, W21929
PEW, Benoni, N.J., BLWt.8624. Iss. 1/6/1790 to Samuel Potter, ass. No papers
Joseph, N.J., S14125
Josiah, See PUGH
Reuben, N.J., Va., Fanny, W9218
William, Cont., N.J., Alice, W2847
PEWIS, James, Lamb's Arty., N.Y. BLWts.7603 & 7434. Iss. 8/12/1790 to John D. Coe, ass. No papers
PEWTERBAUGH, Joseph,See PUTERBAUGH
PEYATT, Lewis, See PIATT
PEYTON, Charles, Va., R8165
George, Va., Susannah, R8166
John, Va., BLWt.1641-300-Capt. Iss. 5/24/1796. Also recorded as above under BLWt.2479. No papers. See N.A. Acc. No.874-050131 Half Pay for John Peyton as possibly the same officer as above.
Valentine, Va., BLWt.2241-300
PFEIFER, John George, See PEIFFER
PFIFER, Martin, N.C., S7312
PHARAOH, Joshua, N.C., S16509
PHARES, Andrew, N.J., Ruth, W4564
PHARIS, Amaziah, N.J., Elizabeth, W5541
Moses, Del., BLWt.10860. Iss. 9/2/1789. No papers
Samuel, N.C., S7309
PHARR, Samuel, N.C., Elizabeth, W4565
PHEARSON, Joseph, See FEARSON
PHEBUS, George, Md., S3683
PHELAN, Edward, See PHELON
Jesse, Cont., Pa., S11237
John, Mass., S35027; BLWt.1121-200 & 2263-200
Patrick, Cont., Mass. See PHELON
Thomas, See PHELEN
PHELEN, Thomas, Pa., R8168
PHELON, Edward, Cont., Mass., BLWt.1076-200. Papers also refer to Patrick Phelon, Cont., Mass., BLWt.1077-200
Patrick, Cont., Mass., BLWt.1077-200. See claim of Edward PHELON
Peter, Pa., BLWt.10195. Iss. 8/5/1796. No papers
PHELPS, Aaron, Ct., Ruth Lewis, former wid., W20438
Abel, Ct., Elizabeth Williams, former wid., W2630
Abijah, Ct., S4648
Alexander, Ct., S11240
Alexander, Ct., N.H., S22933
Amos, Ct., S18160
Anthony, Va., Nancy, W10886; BLWt.30923-160-55
Asahel, Ct., BLWt.6349. Iss. 2/23/1799. No papers
Asahel, Ct., Cont., Margaret, W6866; BLWt.13718-160-55
Austin, Ct., Deborah, W17439

PHELPS (continued)
Azor, Mass., S30028
Beriah, Ct., S23843
Bissell, Ct., Sarah, W175; BLWt.3822-160-55
Cornelius, Ct., Philena, W5536; BLWt.11284-160-55
Daniel, Ct., S14143
Darius, Ct., Mary, R8174
David, Ct., BLWt.6325. Iss. to Samuel Sheldon, ass. Cert. 4/18/1806. No papers
David, Ct., d. 11/3/1834, S11239
David, Ct., d. 4/25/1833, S14141
David, Ct., S41069
Ebenezer, Mass., Polly, W3591; BLWt.67678-160-55
Ebenezer, Mass., N.Y., S14134
Edward, Mass., S33470
Edward, Mass., Eunice, W1924; BLWt.12728-160-55
Eli, Ct., N.Y., Rachel, W26314; BLWt.27592-160-55
Elijah, Ct., BLWt.6290. Iss. 8/23/1790. No papers
Elijah, Ct., Zeruiah, W26313
Elijah, Ct., Cont., Mary, W15846
Elijah, Mass., S29380
Elijah, Mass., R8169
Eliphalet, Mass., Elizabeth, W26889
Elisha, Ct., N.Y., S14135
Erastus, Ct., S14142
Francis, Mass., S22439
George, Mass., R8170
George, Va., BLWt.12449. Iss. 6/20/178?. No papers
Giles, Ct., S9987
Homer, Ct., Adah, W18754; BLWt. 31564-160-55
Ira, Ct., S8952
Israel, N.Y., BLWt.7622. Iss. 11/4/1791. No papers
Israel, Mass., N.Y., S14146
Jacob, Mass., Prudence, R8176
James, Ct., res. prior to 1816, R8171
Jared, Ct., Rowena, W3113
Joel, Ct., Susannah, W18756
Joel, Ct., Cont., Mass., S35028
Joel, N.J., Dis.-- No papers. See Am. State Papers, Class 9, pp.96 & 172. Wounded in the body doing duty at Wyoming in Fort Jenkins that being ordered out on a scout under the command of a Sgt., when they returned the aforesaid Joel Phelps rec'd the aforesaid wound of which he lay confined 18 days at Wyoming
John, Ct., S14137
John, Ct., Sarah, W17447
John, Ct., Catherine, W19986
John, Mass., S14147
John, Mass., Elizabeth, W5545; BLWt.24336-160-55
John, N.H., S45069
John,, N.Y., S16224
John, Va., S38301
Jonathan, Ct., Privateer, Charity W9594; BLWt.26604-160-55

PHELPS (continued)
Joseph, Ct., S15575
Joseph, Mass., S18546
Joshua, Ct., Elizabeth, W21970
Joshua, Mass., Elizabeth, W16680
Josiah, Va., S31451
Judah, Ct., Abigail, W17448
Lancelot, see PHILIPS
Luke, Mass., R8173
Martha, former wid. of John Massey, Cont., Mass., which see
Mary, former wid. of Richard Austin, Ct., which see
Nathaniel, Mass., S5152
Nicholas, Va., R8175
Norman, Ct., S29384
Obadiah, Cont., Arminda Hebard/ Hibbard, former wid. Ohio Agcy. & res., W4985. Her last husb. was a pensioner, William Hibbard Ct., which see
Oliver, Ct., S15574
Oliver, Ct., S22932
Oliver, Ct., Phebe, W5540
Putnam, Mass., Eunice, W18753; BLWt.19619-160-55
Reuben, Ct., Mary, W15214
Roger, Ct., S14144
Rufus, N.Y., BLWt.57525-160-55
Samuel, Ct., S36224
Samuel, Ct., Privateer, S5919
Samuel, Mass., Levina, W4762
Samuel, N.H., Margaret. The two papers in file were found in claim of Samuel Phelps, wid. Hannah, W1470
Samuel, N.H., Hannah, W1470
Seth, Ct., BLWt.1674-300-Capt. Iss. 7/5/1796. No papers
Silas, Ct., Cont., Mary, W26883; BLWt.284-60-55; BLWts.6321 & 284-60-55. Iss. 4/7/1796. No papers
Spencer, Mass., Theodama, W15216
Thomas/Tekel, Ga., W5531
Timothy, Ct., Elizabeth, W26317
William, Ct., R8178
PHENIX, Matthew, N.J., S36225
PHERSON, Joseph, See FEARSON
William, Md., BLWt.11609. Iss. 3/22/1797. No papers
PHETTEPLACE, Eddy, See PHITTYPLACE
John, R.I., Eliza/Elsia, W17446
PHILBRICK, Benjamin, N.H., R8179
Daniel, N.H., Ruth, W21959
Daniel, N.H., Sarah, W26884
David, N.H., Sarah, W18755
Nathaniel, N.H., Tabitha, W26316
Richard, N.H., Olive, R8180
Samuel, N.H., S---
Simon, N.H., Dolly, W21966
PHILBROOK, David, Mass., Catharine W21968
David, N.H. See PHILBRICK
Joel, Navy, Mass., Mary, W5537
Jonathan, N.H., S45070
Samuel, Mass., N.H., Mary,W21962
Thomas, Ct., Mass., Navy, Abigail W21964
William, Mass., S28844
William, Navy, Me. Agcy & res. Lucy, W10889;BLWt. 26746-160-55

PHILE, Charles, Pa., BLWt.1723-300-Capt. Iss. 2/14/1791. No papers
George, N.Y., S40260
Philip, Phila. Agcy., Dis.---. No papers
PHILHOWER, Christopher, N.J., R8181
PHILIPI, Abraham, Pa. See PHILLIPPI
PHILIPPIE, Christopher, Va., R8187; BLWt.34587-160-55
PHILIPS, Abraham, N.Y., S9986
Abraham, N.C., R8184
Adam, N.Y., S14139
Adam, N.C., S8955; BLWt.14987-160-55
Andrew, N.C., S32442
Bennet, N.C., See PHILLIPS
David, N.Y., BLWt.7597. Iss. 7/ 15/1790 to John Hathorn, ass. No papers
Elisha, Ct. See PHILLIPS
Gabriel, Va., Milly, R8208
George/George Nichas, Cont., French, War of 1812, b. in France S31908
Henry, Not Rev. War, Indian War 1786-1787, Va., Old War Inv. Rej. 8193
Isaac, Not Rev. War, Indian Wars 1786-1787, Va., Old War Inv. Rej. 8194
James, Mass., S41072
James, N.Y., Dis. --. No papers. See Am. State Papers, Class 9, p. 94. Wounded in the leg in a battle with the Indians, under Gen. Herkimer, 8/6/1777 at Oriskie. Wound trifling
James, R.I., S39012
James, Va., R8197
John, Mass., S36226
John, N.C., S31905
John, Va., S36223
John, Va., BLWt.1434-100
Joshua, N.Y., BLWt.7598. Iss. 7/ 15/1790 to John Hathorn, ass. No papers
Lambert, Pvt., Md., Wt.11611-100. Iss. 11/29/1790 to Frederick Hall, Admr.
Lancelot, Ct., Jerusha, S21425; W16372
Mitchel, N.C., S41956
Mourning, Va., Elizabeth, R8190; BLWt.44510-160-55
Nehemiah, N.H. See PHILLIPS
Newton, Va., S39008
Norton, Mass., Mary, W24896
Oliver, Mass. See PHILLIPS
Philip, Va., Betsey, W26892
Philo, R.I., BLWt.3417. Iss. 12/ 31/1789. No papers
Philo, R.I., S39013
Spencer, Mass., Dorcas, R8189
Stephen, R.I., Alice Usher, former wid., W26609
Sylvester, Mass., S5922
William, Md., R8213
PHILLEO, Enoch, N.Y., Sarah, R8182
PHILLEY, Remembrance, See FILLEY
PHILLIP, Asa, Ct., Lois, W9229;

PHILLIP (continued)
BLWt.38568-160-55
Elisha, Ct., S21423
Henry W., N.Y., S14133
PHILLIPI, Christopher, Va. See PHILIPPIE
PHILLIPPI, Abraham, Pa., Susanna, W3112
PHILLIPS, Aaron, Cont., N.Y. res. in 1818, S43853
Abiezer, Mass., S29381
Adam, N.C. See PHILIPS
Amos, Mass., Priscilla, W26886
Anderson, Mass., Mary, W21969
Andrew, Mass., Lattice/Letice, R8203
Asa, Ct. See PHILLIP
Asa, Mass., S33472
Ayer, Ct., R8185
Barzilla, Va., S41071
Benjamin, Mass., Sea Service, Naomi, W19984
Bennet, N.C., Isabella, W976
Charles, Mass., S43848
Clemmons, N.C., S3687
Daniel, Mass., S43852
Daniel, Mass., R8188
David, N.Y., Nancy, W4051
David, N.C., Va., b. N.C., Agnes, W10890; BLWt.54235-160-55
David, R.I., Olive, W21961
Dorothy, former wid. of Moses Pelton, Ct., W17441
Ebenezer, Cont., Mass., Charlotte W26315; BLWt.38578-160-55
Ebenezer, Mass., Rachel, W21960
Ebenezer, N.Y., Mary, W10891
Ebenezer H., Mass., S19427
Eleazer, Navy, S.C., Martha, R8205
Eli, N.Y., S22935
Elisha, Ct. See PHILLIP
Elisha, R.I., Wait, W21963
Elizabeth, former wid. of Paris Rathbun, R.I., which see
Elkanah, Mass., S22934
Esquire, Ct., S14145
Ezekiel, Mass., R.I., Mary, R8206; BLWt.34824-160-55
Francis, N.J., BLWt.8656. Iss. 7/ 20/1790. No papers
Gideon, Ct., S14138
Gideon, Mass., S11242
Gideon, Mass., S30027
Hugh, Cont., N.J., b. England, S21923
Ichabod, Mass., S36733
Irby, Va., Elizabeth, R8191
Isaac, Mass., Privateer, S8953
Isaac, N.Y., S7311; BLWt.5373-160-55
Isaac, Pa., S3688
Israel, R.I., Nancy, W18752; BLWt.3998-160-55
Jacob, Md., Va., S35560
Jacob, Mass., Deborah, W26888
Jacob, N.J., R8195
Jacob, N.Y., S11238
Jairus/Jarius, Mass., Silence, W26968
James, Ct., Martha Sarah, W17443
James, Cont., Pa., BLWt.2025-100

PHILLIPS (continued)
James, R.I., Elsie, W18757
Jedediah, Mass., S30651
Jeremiah, R.I., Phebe, W13812
Jeruel, Ct. Prudence, W17440
Job, Ct., S16225
Job, Ct., Mary, W17442
John, Ct., S43846
John, Green Mt. Boys, N.Y., Pa., Vt., S7308
John, Md., S38302
John, Mass., S15957
John, Mass., S18159
John, Mass., S33471
John, Mass., S34472; BLWt.4889-100. Iss. 6/28/1797. No papers. B.L.Reg.232129, Act 3/3/1855
John, Mass., Sarah, W26887
John, Mass., BLWt.75036-160-55
John, N.H., S9457
John, N.H., Anna, W21967; B.L. Reg.251167, Act 3/3/1855. Lucinda Phillips also claimed pension as wid. of above sold.- R file 8204 papers within
John, N.J., Mary, W575
John, N.Y., S23844
John, N.Y., Catharine, R8186
John, N.Y., Hannah, R8192
John, N.Y., R8200
John, N.C., S39010
John, N.C., Sarah, W13811
John, N.C., R8202
John, N.C., S.C., Polly, W3862; BLWt.56570-160-55
John, R.I., S39009
John, S.C., S3684
John, Va., S8954
John, Va., S38303
John, Va., S40261
John, Va., R8201
Jonathan, Mass., R.I., Elizabeth, W15215
Jonathan, N.J., BLWt.1692-300-Capt Iss. 7/16/1789. No papers
Jonathan, Va., Comfort, W5535; BLWt.26910-160-55
Joseph, R.I., Susannah, R8211
Joseph, Va., S3686
Joshua, Mass., S41067
Joshua, Mass., Elizabeth, R17444
Joshua, N.Y., S43849
Lambert, Md., BLWt.11611. Iss. 11/29/1790 to Frederick Hall, Admr. No papers
Levi, N.C., S31906
Levi, Va., S39011
Luke, R.I., S11241
Mark, N.C., S41955
Matthew, Pa., BLWt.10238. Iss. 8/31/1791. No papers
Matthias, Va., S38304
Michael, Ct., S36222
Nancy, former wid. of Benjamin Shenault/Shenall, Va. which see
Nathan, N.Y., S43850
Nathaniel, Cont., Mass., S---
Nathaniel, Mass., Mary, W26890
Nathaniel, R.I., Sarah, W26885
Nehemiah, N.H., BLWt.3376. Iss. 12/17/1795 to Wm. S. Thorn,

PHILLIPS (continued)
ass. No papers
Nehemiah, N.H., S41070
Oliver, Mass., S19031
Pain, Mass., S19428
Pelatiah/Pellaliah, Cont., Mass. S41068
Philip, Ct., Elizabeth, W5532
Richard, Mass., Navy, Olive A., W26891
Richard, Mass., Abigail, W26882
Samuel, Ct., Cont., Millea, W5534; BLWt.11068-160-55
Samuel (colored), Ct., Lydia, W21965
Samuel, N.J., S5923
Samuel, N.Y., S43854
Samuel, Pa., Va., R8210
Samuel, R.I., R8209
Samuel H., Commissary Dept., Ct., S17018
Sarah, former wid. of Samuel Auxer, Va., which see
Seth, Mass., S30652
Silas, Cont., Mass., Susannah, W27459
Solomon, Mass., Susanna/Susannah W1923; BLWt.26816-160-55
Thomas, Ct., Ann Beers, former wid., W25233; BLWt.26391-160-55. Her 2nd & 3rd husbs. were also pensioners. See cases of Joseph Mills, Ct.; Samuel Beers, Ct., Mass.
Thomas, N.C., Hannah, W5533
Thomas, R.I., S23842
Thomas, S.C., Va., R8212
Thomas, Vt., Sally, W6868
Thomas, Va., Sarah, W2848
Timothy, Mass., S29382
Turner, Mass., S14140
William, Cont., R.I., S21922
William, Mass., S36221
William, N.C., S3685
William, Pa., BLWt.10215. Iss. 6/10/1794 to Silas Hart, ass. No papers
William, Va., Mary, W1471
William, Va., Elizabeth, W5538
William Meservy, Mass., Elizabeth Walsh, former wid., W15463
Zachariah, N.C., S35559
Zachariah, Va., Mary, R8207
Zebedee, R.I., R8214
PHILLIS, Jacob, Pa., R8215
PHILLPOTT, Charles, Md., S5924
PHILO, Adams, Ct., R8216
Azor, Ct., S22931
PHILPOT, Bryan, Md., Elizabeth, W5543
John, N.H., S8957
Thomas, S.C., R8217
Warran/Warren, N.C., S31907
PHINNAH, Hannah, former wid. of Lewis Woodruff, N.J. which see
PHINNEY, Asa, Ct., S14136
Ebenezer, Mass., Dis. --- No papers. See Am. State Papers, Class 9, p.135. Wounded in his foot, by the accidental discharge of a gun, which caused

PHINNEY (continued)
an amputation of two of his toes, 7/1777 near Saratoga. Enl. 1/1/1777; dis. 1/1/1780
Ichabod, Mass., Deborah, W21958
Ithaman, See ITHAMAR
Ithamar/Ithaman, Mass., S32441
John, Ct., N.Y., S41066; BLWt. 808-100
John, Mass., S37299
Joseph, Ct., Mary, W16988
Joseph, Mass., S37298
Zenas, Mass., S30026
PHIPPENE, Nehemiah, See PHIPPNE
PHIPPIN, Samuel, Vt., Ruth, W19985
PHIPPNE, Nehemiah, Ct., S14179
PHIPPS, Aaron, N.C., Jane, R8219
Benjamin, S.C., Va., Jean, W5539
Daniel Goffe, Ct., Sea Service, Privateer, S.C., S15860
Jason, Ct., S14131
Jedidiah/Jedediah, Mass., S29383
John, Ga., Va., S14132
John, Mass., Hannah, W27460
Joshua, Va., S35561
Samuel, Mass., BLWt.4797.(See 4120 under F.)Iss. 7/22/1789. No papers
Samuel, Mass., S43851
PHIPS, Benjamin, Va. See PHIPPS
PHIPSE, Harmanus, See FLIPSE
PHITTYPLACE, Eddy, R.I., Mary Smith, former wid., W27487
PHLIPSE, Harmanus, See FLIPSE
PHRENDER, William, Pa., BLWt. 10198. Iss. 7/20/1789. No papers
PIATT, Jacob, N.J., S31310
John D., N.J., Jane, W1473
Lewis, Ct., N.Y., R8220
William, N.J., Indian War of 1791, Sarah Murry, former wid., W7486; BLWt.1691-300-Capt. Iss. 5/26/1791. No papers
William, N.J., U.S.A. 1799 to 1834, R8221
PICARD, Alexander, Hazen's Regt., BLWt.13589. Iss. 8/14/1792 to Benjamin Moore, ass. No papers
Lewis, Cont., Canada, S14175
PICKARD, Adolph, N.Y., S18162; S43861
David, Mass., S37300
Jacob, Mass., Tabitha, W13815
James, Mass., S32448
John, N.Y., Margaret, W26320
John, N.Y., Kinyet/Kynyet, R8224
Thomas, N.C., R8225
PICKENS, Andrew, S.C., S3697
Benjamin, Mass., R.I., Abiah, W21979
Israel, S.C., Sarah, R8226
John, Cont., Mass., S33477
John, Pa., S8959
Thomas, Mass., Elizabeth Olive, W1926
William, S.C., S3699
William Gabriel, S.C., S1244
PICKERD, Isaac, N.Y., Magdalena, W24903
PICKERILL, Samuel, Va., S3703
PICKERING, Anthony, N.H., Privateer, Lovey, W15200

PICKERING (continued)
Benjamin, Mass., R.I., S5156
David, Mass., S33473
James, Pa., Dis. ---. No papers See Am. State Papers, Class 9, p.100. This sold. wounded in the head and in left shoulder; his head was fractured in two places which caused three pieces to be taken out; the shoulder was in that situation that the joint was severely wounded and laid open; he being debilited by much bleeding, was taken prisoner, put on horse, supported, and so conducted to the city of Phila. by the British when they took possession of said city. This happened in Bristol, County of Bucks, Apr. 17, 1778.
Winthrop, N.H., S45073
PICKERTON, Joseph, See PINKERTON
PICKET, Daniel, See SPICKET
Francis, See PRICKETT
John, Cont., Mass., Judith, W21972
PICKETT, Henry, N.C., S31304
John, Mass. See PICKITT
Phineas, Ct., S23373
Robert, N.J., BLWt.8648. Iss. 6/11/1789 to Matthias Denman, ass. No papers
Samuel, Ct., S30031
Stephen, N.J., Elizabeth, W5548
Thomas, Pa., Alice/Allace Whitlock former wid., W4860
William, Mass., Hannah, W5549; BLWt.16135-160-55
PICKHAM, Daniel, See PECKHAM
PICKINS, Alexander, Cont., Mass., S11243
Benjamin, Mass., R.I. See PICKENS
Thomas, Mass. See PICKENS
William, S.C. See PICKENS
PICKITT, John, Mass., S18547
PICKLE, Matthias, N.J., S3700
PICKSLEY, Elijah, See PIXLEY
PIDCOCK, Charles, N.J., R8227
PIDGE, Benjamin, Mass., R8228
Otis, Ct., Jemima, R8229
PIER, Abner, Mass., Lucy, R8230
Isaac, N.J., S1082
John Ernest, N.Y., BLWt.7623. Iss. 12/2/1791 to Edmund Ogden, ass. No papers
John Ernest, N.Y., Mary, W26906
Solomon, Ct., S43856
PIERCE, Abel, Mass. See PEIRCE
Abel, Mass. See PEIRCE
Abner, Mass., S28845
Adam, N.J. See PEARCE
Amos, Del., R26145
Amos, Mass., S5154
Amos, Mass., Vt. See PIERCE
Amos, N.H., Dis.--- No papers. See Am. State Papers, Class 9, p.138. Wounded by a ball in his left hand, which has in a considerable degree, perished. He is 9/10 of his time in a state of delirium. Disability occurred at Bennington, August 1777

PIERCE (continued)
Aquilla, Md. See PEARCE
Augustus, Cont., Mass., S43860
Benjamin, Ct., R8232
Benjamin, Mass., S14172
Benjamin, Mass., S48751; BLWt. 1648-200-Lt. Iss. 12/13/1792. No papers
Benjamin, Mass., Lucy Glass, former wid., W14792
Benjamin, Mass., Lucy,See PEIRCE
Benjamin, Mass. Rebecca, See PEIRCE
Benjamin, N.H., Nabby, See PEIRCE
Benjamin, N.H., Peace, W26863
Benjamin, N.H., Lucinda, R8240; BLWt.19814-160-55
Benjamin, Vt., S11248
Benoni, R.I., S23371
Bezabel, See Bezaleel
Bezaleel/Bezabel, Mass., S40257
Charles, Mass., S36735
Daniel, Ct., S36229
Daniel, Cont., R.I. See PEIRCE
David, Mass. See PEIRCE
David, N.H. See PEIRCE
Deborah, former wid. of Elijah Jones, Mass., which see
Ebenezer, Mass., Pamelia, W8518; BLWt.14966-160-55
Eli, Mass., R.I., Polly, W4499; BLWt.31330-160-55
Eliab, See PEIRCE
Eliphalet, Mass., Tabitha, W15101
Ephraim, N.H., Esther, W21976
Ephraim, N.Y. or Vt., S23372
Ezekiel, R.I. See PEARCE
Francis, Va., S14168
Francis, Va., R8235
George, Md. See PEARCE
Hannah S., former wid. of Gideon Church, R.I., which see
Hardy, Mass., BLWt.1643-200-Lt. Iss. 2/20/1792 to Isaac Pierce, Admr. Also recorded as above under BLWt.2513. No papers
Henry, Mass. See PEIRCE
Hugh, Md., S3690
Hugh, S.C., b. Va., S32445
Israel, Mass., R.I. See PEARCE
Jacob, N.H., Rebecca, W16681
James, Cont., Mass., Abigail, W8288; BLWt.38569-160-55
James, Mass., BLWt.4873. Iss. 4/25/1798 to Joshua Pickering. No papers
James, Mass., S41074
James, Va. See PIERCY
James, Va., Ann, W9596
Jesse, Mass. See PEIRCE
Jesse, R.I.(?) Entered in N.H. list; BLWt.3406. Iss. 8/3/1795 to Wm. Walsworthy, ass. No papers
Job, Ct., Cont., R.I., S14173
Job, Mass., R.I. See PEIRCE
John, Col. Crane's Arty. Regt., BLWt.1653-200-Lt. Iss. 2/20/1790. No papers
John, Ct. See PEIRCE
John, Cont., Mass., Mary, W18766
John, Hazen's Regt., BLWt.13601.

PIERCE (continued)
Iss. 8/10/1789 to Richard Platt, ass. No papers
John, Me., BLReg.272053-1855
John, Md., Va., S38306
John, Mass. See PEIRCE
John, Mass., Elizabeth, W13817
John, N.J., S20521; BLWt.1750-100
John, N.C., S7320
John, S.C., b. N.C., S17021
John, Va., S3692
John, Va., S5933
Jonas, Mass., S30030
Jonas, Mass. See PEIRCE
Jonathan, Mass., Lydia, W15207
Jonathan, Mass., Rebecca, W17454
Joseph, Ct., R8239
Joseph, Mass. See PEIRCE
Joseph, Mass., Eleanor, See PEIRCE
Joseph, Mass., Hannah, W19987
Joseph, Mass. See PEIRCE
Joshua, Mass., BLWt.1660-150-Ens. Iss. 2/23/1796 to Marlborough Turner, ass. No papers
Josiah, Mass. See PEIRCE
Lemuel, Mass., S37301
Lemuel, Mass., Sarah, W1925; BLWt. 3132-160-55
Levi, Ct., Dis. ---. No papers. See Am. State Papers, Class 9, pp.66, 89, 116. Wounded in the right hand by a musket ball which took off two middle fingers, 8/1777 at Croton River, near Valley Forge. Enl. 4/2/1777. Discharged 4/8/1778
Lewis, N.C., R8231
Matthew/Mathew, Mass., Ruth Gibson former wid., W544; BLWt.1969-160-55
Mial, See Miel PEARCE
Nathan, Mass., S14178
Nathan, Mass., Sarah, W15209
Nathaniel, Mass., S20522
Nathaniel, Mass. See PEIRCE
Nehemiah, Mass., Mary, W15201
Richard, Mass., BLWt.4859. Iss. 8/10/1789 to Richard Platt. No papers
Robert, Mass. See PEIRCE
Robert, Mass., Molly, W15202
Robert, Mass. See PEARCE
Ruth, former wid. of Jacob Ormsbee Mass., which see
Samuel, Ct., BLWt.6283. Iss. 3/21/1791 to Josiah Starr, ass. No papers
Samuel, Ct., Dorcas, W5157
Samuel, Ct. See PEIRCE
Samuel, Cont., Mass., S45072
Simon, N.H., Hepsibah, W26903
Solomon, N.H. See PEIRCE
Stephen, R.I. See PEARCE
Susannah, former wid. of William King, Mass., which see
Thaddeas, Mass., Susannah, W13816; BLWt.3136-160-55
Thomas, Cont., Mass., Mary, W17450
Thomas, Cont., Mass., Susannah, W26905
Thomas, Mass., S34473
Thomas, Mass., Sea Service, Navy,

PIERCE (continued)
R8242
Thomas, N.J., S40267; BLWt.8652-100-Pvt. Iss. 7/16/1789 to John Bray, ass. No papers
Thomas, Pa., BLWt.10220. Iss. 7/27/1789 to Richard Platt, ass. No papers.
Willard, Pvt., Invalid Regt., BLWt.13617. Iss. 4/19/1792 to John Peck, ass. No papers
Willard, Mass., S45076
William, Ct., Catharine, W15847
William, Md., S39015
William, Mass. See PEIRCE
William, R.I., Fanny, W977; BLWt.27650-160-55
William L., Va., BLWt.518-300
Zebulon, Mass. See PEIRCE
PIERCEALL, Richard, Md., S1245
PIERCY, Blake, N.C., Mary, R8243
Henry, Pa., BLWt.1707-200-Lt. Iss. 1/7/1794. No papers
James, Va., Betsey, W2849; BLWt.26547-160-55
PIERPOINT, John, Lamb's Arty., N.Y., BLWt.7648 iss. 10/23/1790
Thomas, Ct., S32444
PIERPONT, Eveline, Ct., Rhoda, W19989
John, Ct., S36227
PIERSOL, Samson, Pa., S22937
Stephen, N.J. See PEIRSON
PIERSON, Abraham, Pa., S40256
Amos, Ct. See PEIRSON
Amos, Mass. See PEARSON
Charles, N.C. See PEARSON
Charles, Va., S3695
Daniel, N.J., S40262
Erastus, N.J., S3694
George, Pa. See PARSON
Isaac, N.Y., R8246
James, N.C., S32446
Jesse, Ct. See PEARSON
John, Cont., Md., Elizabeth, W1993
John, Hazen's Regt., BLWt.13594 Iss. 12/4/1790 to Anthony Maxwell, ass. No papers
John, N.J., BLWt.8646. Iss. 6/11/1789 to Matthias Denman, ass. No papers
John, N.Y. See PEARSON
Jonathan, N.C. See PEARSON
Joseph, N.J., S3693
Mahlon, S.C., S3663
Meshac, See Meshecke PEARSON
Moses, N.J., Indian War, R8247
Nathan, Ct., R8248
Robert, Cont., N.J., Margaret, W5561; BLWt.39211-160-55
Samuel, Cont., N.J., S40266
Samuel, N.J., BLWt.8630. Iss. 7/7/1789. No papers
Shadrach, Pvt., Va., BLWt.13609 & 14129
Shadrach, Va. See PEARSON
Stephen, N.J. See PEIRSON
Sylvanus, N.J., Mary, W90
Uzal/Usual, Vt., Dorcas, W15203
William E., Ct. See PEARSON
PIETY, Thomas, Pa., Indian War

PIETY (continued)
1791, Mary, R21475
PIFER, Henry, See PIPER
PIFFANY, Nehemiah, See PHIPPNE
PIGEON, Moses, Mass., Hannah Currier, former wid., W22877
PIGG, Charles, Cont. Va. See PEGG
PIGMAN, Jesse, Pa., R8250
Leonard, N.C., R8251
William, Va., BLWt.12455. Iss. 5/2/1794. No papers
PIGOT, Samuel, R.I., S34474
PIGSLEY, Benjamin, See PITTSLEY
Job, Cont., Mass., R.I., S35562
Paul, Mass., S40263
Welcome, R.I., S43864
PIKE, Aaron, Mass., R8252
Abraham, See PYKE
Barnabas, Ct., Hannah, W26904
Benjamin, Mass., BLWt.1640-300-Capt. Iss. 6/11/1790. No papers
Benjamin, Mass., Dorothy, W15205
Daniel, Mass., S22441
David, Mass., S5153
David, Mass., S14176
Dudley, N.H., Celia, W26896
Ebenezer, Mass., S33475
Elias, Mass., S5935
Elijah, Vt., Martha, W4763; BLWt.30922-160-55
Ephraim, Cont., Mass., Polly, W27595; BLWt.34843-160-55
Ezra, N.Y., Mary, W18764
Henry, Cont., N.H., Dorothy, W18761
Jacob, Mass., Beulah, W17449
James, Ct., Sarah, W4764
James, Mass., S14174
John, Ct., Betsey, W26318; BLWt.18024-160-55
John, Mass., S22440
John, Mass., Ruth, W26907
John, Mass., Ruth, R8255
Jonathan, Ct., S40264
Jonathan, Mass., S29387
Joseph, Mass., Sally, W498; BLWt.9466-160-55
Moses, Mass., S29385
Perkins, N.H., Abigail, W19991
Robert, N.H., Mehitable, W17453
Robert, Va., Anny, R8253
Samuel, Mass., S33476
Samuel, Mass., Sarah, W19998; BLWts.4829-100-1794 & 79-60-55
Timothy, Mass., Anne Stone, former wid., W13927
Willard, Ct., Cont., Molly, W18759
William, Cont., N.H., Phebe, W21977; BLWt.24428-160-55
William, Mass., S11246
William, N.Y., S14167
William, Sheldon's Cavalry, BLWt.1672-200-Lt. Iss. 7/18/1790. No papers
Zebulon, Cont., N.J., Indian War 1790-5 & War of 1812, S36737; BLWt.1716-300-Capt. Iss. 8/27/1789 to John Brown, ass. No papers
PIKINS, William G. See PICKENS
PILE, George, Hazen's Regt.,

PILE (continued)
BLWt.13598. Iss. 7/16/1790. No papers
PILES, Elijah, Va., S32447
Jeremiah, Va., S5155
William, Va., S35563
Zachariah, Va., Susannah, W10896; BLWt.50894-160-55
PILGNITT, Henry, N.Y., BLWt.7605. Iss. 9/15/1790 to John S. Hobart et al, assnes. No papers
PILGRIM, Amos, Va., Rebecca, W1927; BLWt.50897-160-55
Michael, Va., S31909
Thomas, Ct., S36231
Thomas, S.C., Va., S7319
PILKENTON, Richard, N.C., S3701
PILKERTON, Michael, Md., BLWt. 11608. Iss. 1/8/1796 to George Ponsonby, ass. No papers
PILKINGTON, Drura, Va., S9458
PILKINTON, Larkin, Va., S32443
PILLSBURY, Daniel, See PILSBURY
David, See PILSBURY
Eliphalet, See PILSBURY
George, Mass. Sea Service, Polly, W15211
John, See PILSBURY
Joseph, See PILSBERY
Nathan, See PILSBERY
William, See PILSBURY
PILSBERY, Joseph, Mass., S18548
Nathan, Mass., Lucy, W26902
PILSBURY, Amos, Mass., S33480
Daniel, Mass., BLWt.1807-300
David, N.H., S43866
Eliphalet, Mass., S45074
John, Mass. Sea Service, Lydia, R8257
Moses, Mass., S17634
Samuel, Mass., S30021
William, Mass., Sarah G., W26322: BLWt.21837-160-55
PIMPLE, Paul, Pvt., in Proctor's Arty., Pa., BLWt.10231. Iss. 6/29/1789 to M. McConnell, ass. No papers
PINCIN, Benjamin, Mass., Molly, W15204
Simeon, Mass., Sarah, W13818
William, Cont., Mass., Elizabeth, W21971
PINCKNEY, Charles Cotesworth, S.C. BLWt.1759-500-Col. Iss. 2/25/1800. No papers
John E., N.Y., R8259
Jonathan, N.Y., S43865; BLWt. 7619-100-1790. No papers
Thomas, S.C., S46405; BLWt.1760-400-Maj. Iss. 12/28/1798. No papers
William, N.J., Sea Service?; BLWt.473-100
PINDAR, James, Mass., BLWt.4855. Iss. 3/25/1790. No papers
PINDELL, Richard, Md., S30653; BLWt.1730-400-Surgeon. Iss. 9/25/1789.
PINDER (or PINNER, as signed by brother John), Jeremiah, N.H., Hannah, W16056
John, N.H. See PENDER

PINDEXTER, Paul, Mass., S36734
PINE, John, Pvt. in the Art., Pa., BLWt.10228. Iss. 2/7/1792. No papers
Joseph M., Mass., S43862
PINGERY, Stephen, Mass., S5158
PINGREE, Ebenezer, Mass., S11247
Stephen, Mass., S30029
PINGRY, Stephen, Mass. See PINGERY
PINIAM, Reuben, See PENNEL
PINKERTON, Andrew, Pa., BLWt. 10239. Iss. 3/3/1794 to Andrew Pinkerton. No papers
Andrew, Pa., BLWt.223-100
Henry, Pa., Elizabeth, W3114
John, Pa. res. & agcy., Mary, W3450
Joseph, Pa., S39014
PINKHAM, Calvin, R.I., Elizabeth, W26895
Daniel, N.H., BLWt.2300-100
Nathaniel, Mass., Lucy, W9230; BLWt.71210-160-55
Thomas, N.H., Bridget, R8260
PINKNEY, Jonathan. See PINCKNEY
William, See PINCKNEY
PINKSTAFF, Andrew, Va., R8261
PINN, John, Indian, Va., R8264
PINNELL, Peter, S.C., S17019
PINNEO, Joseph, Ct., Azuba, W21978; BLWt.26763-160-55
PINNER, Jeremiah, See PINDER
John, Mass., Ruth, W2339; BLWt. 1952-100; BLWt.319-60-55
PINNEY, Butler, Ct., R8095
Isaac, Ct., S14169
Isaac, Ct., Cont., Vt., Mary, W26971
Jonathan, Ct., Martha, W4766
Jonathan, Ct., Susannah, R---. See case of her other husb., Jone Pettibone, Ct.
Lemuel, Ct., S17020
Nathaniel, Ct., S36228
Philaster, Ct., S43857
PINNIX, John, N.C., Barbara, W18733
Overton, See PEONIX
PINNOCK, Aaron, Vt., R8263
PINSON, Joseph, N.C., Margery, R5560
PINTARD, John, Cont., N.J., N.Y., R8265
PINTO, Solomon, Ct., Clarissa Hall former wid., W11263; BLWts.1673-150 & 1-10-55 iss. 6/3/1795
PINYAN, Reuben, See PENNEL
PIPEN, John, N.C., S8962
PIPER, Amasa, Mass., Mary, W19992
Andrew, N.Y., Elizabeth, W26893
Anna B., former wid. of Jacob Thurston, Ct., Mass., which see
Asa, Mass., S31302
David, N.H., S45071
Frederick, Pa., S8958
Henry, Cont., Pa., S40344
James, Pa., Elizabeth, W5547
John, Mass., S15958
John, N.H., S45075
John, Pa., R8267

PIPER (continued)
John, Va., S5932
John, Va., R17110; Va. Half Pay. N.A. Acc. No. 874. See 050132 Half Pay, John Piper
Judah, Mass., S43855
Lewis, N.Y., BLWt.7620. Iss. 9/15/1790 to John S. Hobart et al, assnes. No papers
Moses, Mass., S33474
Samuel, N.H., Sally, W16057
Simon, Mass., S43863; BLWt.1330-100
Thomas, Cont., N.H., Hannah Danovan/Dunovan/Dunoven, former wid., W24869
Thomas, Mass., R8268
PIPES, John, N.J., Mary, W8517
Joseph, Pa., S11245
PIPKIN, Stephen, N.C., R8269
PIPPEN, Joseph, N.C., Temperance, W5546
Richard, N.C., S8960
PIPPIN, Robert, Md., Mica/Micah, W8519; BLWt.26926-160-55
PIPSICO, John, Va., S36230
PISTOLE, Charles, Va., Elizabeth, W26894
PITCHER, Abner, Ct., S43858
Gottlieb/Gotlieb, N.Y., b. Ger., Mary, W26899; BLWt.9075-160-55
Mehitable, former wid. of John Douglass, Mass., which see
Molly - This is not a pension claim and not to be considered as such, but as it has been often inquired about & there is corresp. in regard to her, it is filed for convenience in reference & searching. Her name was placed upon the list of half pay officers for life. (See Vol. 2, p.155 of Lossing's Pictorial Field Book of the Revolution No record of payments)
Theophilus, Mass., Sarah, W18758
PITCHFORD, Daniel, Va., S30654
PITKIN, John, Ct., S14165
Stephen, Ct., S3675
PITMAN, Ambrose, Va., S30655
Andrew, Va., Margaret Minix/ Minnix, former wid., W9998
Arthur, N.C., R8271
Cary, R.I., S23370
John, N.H., S8961
Jonathan, N.J., Jane Hunt, former wid., W11353
Joseph, N.C., S7314
Mark, Navy, N.H., Mary, R8276
Mathew, N.C., Keziah, R---. See her claim as former wid. of her other husb., Benj. Rodden, Va.
Micajah, N.C., Lydia, R8273
Thomas, N.C., Dicy, R8275
PITMON, Thomas, See PITMAN
PITNEY, Mahlon, N.J., S1080
Rebecca, former wid. of Phinehas Chedister, N.J., which see
PITSLEY, Benjamin, See PITTSLEY
Robert, See PITTSLEY
PITT, Abraham E., N.Y., R8270

PITT (continued)
Henry, N.C., b. Va., S3689
Joseph, N.C., S31305
Richard, Cont., Va., Susannah, W21974
PITTEE, Abner, Mass., S18161
Nathaniel, Mass., S33449
PITTENGELL, William, See PETTINGELL
PITTENGER, Jacob. See PETTENGER
PITTINGER, Abraham, Va., S38305
PITTMAN, James, Ga., Va., S7317
Mathew, N.C. See PITMAN
Micajah, N.C. See PITMAN
William, R.I. Sea Service, R8274
PITTS, George, Cont., Mass., Lydia, W26897
Gideon, Mass., S43859
Henry, S.C., S7316
James, N.C., S7313; BLWt.1962-160-55
Jonathan, See PYTTS
Major, Va., S5931
Philip, Mass., Lovisa, W18762
Richard, Ct., Md., Sarah, W17452
Seth, Mass., Privateer, S19032
Shubael, Mass., S29386
Thomas, R.I., BLWt.3383. Iss. 12/17/1795 to Wm. S. Thorn, ass. No papers
PITTSLEY, Benjamin, Mass., Hannah, W26898
Robert, Mass., Mercy, W15210
PIXLEY, Alexander, Mass., S41073
Asa, Mass., Olive, W10902
Cooper, N.Y., R8277
Elijah, Ct., BLWt.6329. Iss. 3/20/1795 to Elijah Bachus, ass. No papers. Wt. 6329-100 acres -- was also issued to Wyman Parker, Ct. line, 7/19/1798
Elijah, Ct., S40265
Job, See PIGSLEY
John, N.Y., BLWt.7582. Iss. 7/6/1791 to David Pixley, ass. No papers
William, N.Y., Rhoda, W18760
PLACE, Amos, N.H., S37305
Daniel, R.I., Nabby Sibley, former wid., W6062; BLWt.6016-160-55
David, Cont., N.H., S45079
Enoch, R.I., Elizabeth, W21982
Griffin, Vt., S11249
Jeremiah, R.I., S21925
John, R.I., Cynthia, W10905
Joseph, N.H., Anna, W24905; BLWt.34906-160-55
Joseph, R.I., S21926
Peleg, Pa., Ann, W4566
Philip, R.I., Mary, R8278
Reuben, Pa., R8279
Reuben, R.I., Catharine, W2340; BLWt.8374-160-55
Samuel, R.I., S39019
Sarah, former wid. of Thomas Conklin, N.Y., which see
Simeon, R.I., Sarah, W12628
PLAIN, Jacob, Cont., Md., Catharine, W3868
PLAISTED, John, Cont., Mass., Lydia, W21981
Roger, Mass., Margaret, W2240; BLWt.3854-160-55

PLAKARD, Christian, Pa., S4713
PLANK, Asa, R.I., S38307
 George, Pa., Elizabeth, W1994
 Isaiah, R.I., Experience, W5562; BLWt.6017-160-55
 John, Ct., R.I., S39017
PLANT, Eli, Ct., S14180; BLWt. 26111-160-55
 Ethel, Ct., S43870
 Ethil, Sheldon's Dragoons, Ct., BLWt.6340. Iss. 1/28/1790. No papers
 John, Md., Mary, Ann, W26908
 Williamson, Va., S39016
PLANTT, William, Va., S39020
PLASKETT, Joseph, Mass., BLWt. 4861. Iss. 8/24/1790 to Benj. Ives Gilman, ass. No papers
PLASS, Michael, See PLOSS
 Peter, N.Y., S43868
PLATNER, John, Ct., BLWt.6279. Iss. 12/13/1791. No papers
PLATO, Thomas, N.Y., BLWt.7611. Iss. 8/4/1790 to Henry Hart, ass. No papers
 Thomas, N.Y., S43867
PLATT, Daniel, Ct., S23374
 Daniel, Privateer, N.Y., Charlotte D., W19993
 Ebenezer, Ct., Anna, W26323; BLWt.34528-160-55
 Gideon, Ct., S17026
 Isaac, Pvt., Arty. Artificers, BLWt.13616. Iss. 7/12/1792. No papers
 Isaac, Cont., Ct. res. in 1818, S36232
 Jabez, Ct., Jillin, W17462
 James, Ct., Olive, W10903
 John, Ct., S36233
 John, Ct., Sarah, W5563
 John, Del., BLWt.1727-200-Lt. Iss. 5/30/1789. No papers
 John, Pa., S7322
 Joseph, Ct., Mary, W9231
 Joseph, Ct., Lydia, W17459
 Nathan, Ct., Charlotte, R8232; BLWt.90012-160-55
 Olive, former wid. of Eliphalet Smith, Ct., which see
 Richard, N.Y., S46406; BLWt. 348-100
 Samuel, Cont., Ct., Abigail, W21980
 Samuel, Pa., BLWt.1721-200-Surgn's mate. Iss. 5/30/1789. No papers
 Truman, Ct., S18549
 William, N.Y., Lydia Moulton, former wid., W10526; BLWt.75052-160-55
PLATTS, Abel, N.H. res., Meletiah, R8281
 Dan, Ct., S39018
 James, Cont., Mass., Mary, W18767
PLATZ, George, Pa., S23845
PLEASANT, William, Va., S8963
PLEASANTS, Archibald, Va., S5939
 Robert, Va., S8964
PLEDGER, John, Va., S8676
PLEMLINE, Charles, Cont., Pa., Indian Warfare 1785; BLWt.279-100
PLIMLEINE, Charles, See PLEMLINE
PLIMLEY, Henry, N.Y., BLWt.7633. Iss. 6/13/1792 to Abraham Bashman, ass. No papers
 William, See BLIMLY
PLIMLY, Hendrick/Henryk PLUMLY, N.Y., S34476
PLIMPTON, Elias, Mass., Anne/Ann R18768
 Elijah, Mass., Mary, W15212
 Hannah, former wid. of Elisha Fisk, Mass., which see
 John, Mass., Molly, W15199
 Joseph, Mass., Jane Partridge, former wid., W15161
 Oliver, Mass., Lydia, W15213
PLOMONDON, Joseph, Hazen's Regt. BLWt.13590. Iss. 2/4/1790. No papers
PLONK, Jacob, See PLUNK
PLOSS, Michael, N.Y., Elizabeth W17455
PLOTTS, George, See PLATZ
PLOUGH, Aldert, N.J., R8284
 Daniel, N.J., R8285
 Jacob, N.J., S36738
 Jacob, N.J., Lydia, W123
 Samuel, N.Y., S9988
PLUGH, Henry, N.Y., S13462
PLUM, John, N.Y., Tryphena, W3718; BLWt.13015-160-55
PLUMB, Daniel, Sheldon's Dragoons Ct., BLWt.6341. Iss. 12/12/1789 to Theodosius Fowler, ass. No papers
 Hannah, former wid. of Ichabod Talmage, Ct., which see
 Isaac, Ct., Catharine, W6871; BLWt.28583-160-55
 Jared, Cont., Mass., S43869
 Joseph, Ct., S31910
 Joseph, Ct., R8286
 Nathaniel, Ct., Anna, W19994; BLWt.2255-100
 Samuel, Ct., R8287
PLUMBE, Daniel, Ct., S38308
 George, Ct., Eunice, W26909
 William, Cont., Mass., S11250
PLUMER, Isaac, Cont., Mass., Esther, W26911
 Richard, Mass., Patience, W26910
 Simeon, Mass., S5937
 Stephen, Mass., S11251
 Timothy, Mass., Hannah, W17458; BLWt.3831-160-55
 William, Pa., S4649
PLUMLEY, Benjamin, Mass., Anna, R8288
 Ebenezer, Ct., Dorothy, R8289
 Jacob, N.J., BLWt.8660. Iss. 6/15/1795 to John N. Cummings, ass. No papers
 Jonathan, Mass., S41075
 Samuel, Mass., S15196
PLUMLINE, Charles, Pa., S5946
PLUMLY, Henryk/Hendrick, See PLIMLY
PLUMMER, Benjamin, Mass., S19034
 Daniel, Cont., Mass., S37304
 Dicey, former wid. of James Anderson, N.C., which see
 Edward, Cont., Mass., Deborah, W17461
PLUMMER (continued)
 Elisha, Pa., S22938
 Isaac, See PLUMER
 John, Cont., Mass., S37303
 Nathan, N.H., S45078
 Richard, Mass. See PLUMER
 Richard, N.C., R.I., Susanna, W4052
 Robert, Mass., Nancy, W2569; BLWt.24158-160-55
 Samuel, Md., S30656
 Thomas, Mass., S29388
 Timothy, See PLUMER
 William, Del., BLWt.10864. Iss. 9/2/1789 to John Bell, ass. No papers
 William, Mass., S37302
PLUMSTEAD, Nathaniel, N.Y., Sarah Wood, former wid., W22683. She was pensioned erroneously under name of Sarah Atherton for the service of her above named 1st husb., Nathionil Plumstead/ Plumsted/Plumstil, W16814
PLUNK, Jacob, N.C., S7321
PLUNKET, John, Va., BLWt.12463. Iss. 5/8/1794. No papers
 Penelope, former wid. of Joseph Davis, N.J.(?), which see
 Thomas, Va., S38309
PLUNKETT, Reuben, Cont., Va., S25752
PLUNKIT, Penelope, See Joseph Davis, N.J.
PLYLEY, Casper, Pa., S19033
PLYMPTON, Ebenezer, Mass., S5159
 Joseph, See PLIMPTON
 Zeba/Ziba, Mass., Tabitha, W13819
POAGE, William, Va., Elizabeth, W8502
POAK, James S., Pa., S3717
POARCH, Henry, See PORCH
POCKTOR, Thomas, Md., BLWt.11615 Iss. 1/11/1796 or 4 to Joshua Ward, ass. No papers
POCOCK, John, Crane's Cont. Art. Mass., BLWt.4885. Iss. 3/25/ 1790. No papers
POE, Adam, Pa., Elizabeth, R8292
 Benjamin, N.C., S31307
 David, Cont., Md., (Grandfather of Edgar Allen Poe), Elizabeth, R8293
 David, N.C., S41962
 Henry W., N.C. R8294
 John, Cont., Va., S40287
 Stephen, N.C., Mary, R8295
 Virgil, Va., S35565
POENIX, Overton, See PEONIX
POFFENBERGER, Christian, Pa., S9459
POGE, William, See POAGE
POGUE, Joseph, N.C., Nancy, R8297
POH, John, Pa., S5940
POHON, William, Va., R8298
POINDEXTER, Chapman, Va., Elizabeth, W26327; BLWt.38575-160-55
 David, Va., S3723
 Thomas, Va., Sally, W5556; BLWt. 26961-160-55
POKE, George, See POLLOCK

POLAND, Abner, Mass., S33483. His wid., Deborah, was allowed pension as former wid. of Nathaniel Emerson, Mass., which see
Abner, Mass., Sarah, W15262; BLWt. 4871-100. Iss. 1795
Asa, Mass., S44252
Deborah, former wid. of Nathaniel Emerson, Mass., which see
John, N.J., Sarah, W115; BLWt. 2084-100
Joseph, Mass., Hannah, W26913
Moses, Mass., BLWt.4804. Iss. 2/23/1797 to John K. Smith. No papers
Moses, Mass., S37313
Peter, Va., R8300
Samuel, See POLLARD
Seward, Mass., S37308
William, Mass., Betsey, W18770
POLDEN, William, Mass., BLWt.4862. Iss. 6/29/1789. No papers
POLE, Henry, Hazen's Regt. BLWt. 13592-100-Pvt. Iss. 4/12/1790. No papers
POLEN, Joshua, Mass., Ann, W22003
William, Va., S32453
POLERECZKY, John L., Cont., France, Me. res. & agcy., Nancy, W10915
POLHAMUS, John, See POLHEMUS
Rachel, former wid. of John Van Orden, N.Y., which see
POLHEMUS, Cornelius, N.J., S14205
John, N.J., S40271; BLWt.671-300 & 1696-300-Capt. Iss. 7/22/1789. No papers
POLK, Charles, N.C., War of 1812, R8301
Charles, N.C., Philipen, W5571
Ephraim, Pa., Rhoda, R8302
George, Pa. See POLLOCK
Joab, N.J.,S36236. See N.A. Acc. 874-050133, not Half Pay, J. Polk
Job, N.J., BLWt.8627. Iss. 2/25/1792. No papers
William, N.C., S.C., S3706
POLKE, Isaac, Pa., R8303
POLLAND, John, N.J. See POLAND
Joseph, Cont., Can., See MARTIN
Joshua, Mass., BLWt.4836. Iss. 3/25/1790. No papers
Moses, See POLAND
Samuel, Ct. See POLLARD
POLLARD, Absolem/Absolom, Va., Leaner, W8527
Ambrose, Va., Mary Ann, W3865; BLWt.12824-160-55
Barton, Cont., N.H., N.J., Mary, W22001; BLWt.703-100
Braxton C./Braxton, Va., S14194
Chattin, Va., Mary, W4; BLWt. 26428-160-55
Edmund, Va., S16510
Edward, Mass., Mary, W22002
Elijah, N.H., BLWt.3392. Iss. 3/25/1790. No papers
Elijah, Va., R8305
Ezekiel, N.H., BLWt.3391. Iss. 3/25/1790. No papers
Hezekiah, N.H., BLWt.3393. Iss. 3/25/1790. No papers
Isaac, Ct., BLWt.6312. Iss. 10/

POLLARD (continued)
7/1789. No papers
Jacob, N.C., S7325
James, Cont., R.I., Mercy, W18773; BLWt.148-100
James, Va., S32449
John, Mass., S33482
John, Mass., S33495
Jonathan, Mass., S36739
Jonathan, Mass., Keziah, W15794
Jonathan, N.H., Sarah, W15267
Joseph, Va., Catharine, W5555
Richard, S.C., Sarah Whitlow, former wid., R11468; BLWt. 1282-300
Robert, Va., S5944
Robert, Va., Susanna, W811; BLWt.26091-160-55
Samuel, Ct., S40272
Seth, Mass., Hepsibah, W19995
Thaddeus, Mass., Mary, W13824
Thomas, N.H., Olive, W21998; BLWt.56569-160-55
Thomas, N.H. See POLLOCK
Thomas, N.J., BLWt.8625. Iss. 9/8/1789 to Samuel Ruton. No papers
Thomas, N.Y., BLWt.7588. Iss. 7/14/1790, to Richard Platt, ass. No papers
Thomas, Va., R17132; Va. Half Pay
Timothy, Cont., Mass., S37312
Walter, Mass., Sophia, W1931; BLWt.515-160-55
William, S.C., Elizabeth Goodman, former wid., W8862
William, Va., S17638
William, Va., Keziah, W9237
POLLERESKY, John L. See POLERECZKY
POLLET, John, Va., Frances D., R8306
POLLEY, Daniel, Ct., S40285
Hugh, N.Y., BLWt.7639. Iss. 9/15/1790 to Wm. Bell, ass. No papers
John, Cont., Ct., Phebe, W10912; BLWt.3133-160-55
John, Mass., Sally, W6873; BLWt. 19603-160-55
John, Va. See POLLY
Jonathan, Ct., Mehitable/Mehetabel W6872; BLWt.34903-160-55
Joseph, N.H., Rebecca, W4759; BLWt.3758-160-55
Nathaniel, Mass., Eleanor, BLWt. 83501-160-55
Samuel, N.Y., S14202
Uriah, Ct., BLWt.6335. Iss. 1/18/1798 to Uriah Polley. No papers
William, See PAULEY
POLLICK, Thomas, N.H. See POLLOCK
POLLOCK, David, Md., Pa., Ann, W5576
Elias, Md., N.J., S40279. Served under the name of Joseph Smith
Elijah, Ct., Cont., Mass., S40286
George, Pa., Louisa, W1930
Jacob, N.C., Mary Young, former wid., W18247
John, Pa., BLWt.10040 & 10204. Iss. 7/16/1795 to Margaret Pollock, Admr. No papers

POLLOCK (continued)
Mingo, Ct., Molly, W17469
Thomas, N.H., Elizabeth, W26607
POLLY, Edward, Va., Mary, W9236
John, Mass. See POLLEY
John, Va., Susan, W3036
POLOCK, Asher, R.I., BLWt.3410. Iss. 5/4/1791. No papers
POLSTON, Robert, Pa., BLWt.10194. Iss. 12/21/179? No papers
POMEROY, Dan, Cont., Ct., S44251
Daniel, Ct., S3721
Ebenezer, Mass., Sarah, W1996
Elisha, Ct., Mass., Lucy, W26335 BLWt.36552-160-55. She was also pensioned as former wid. of Wm. Rice, her 1st husb., 13th U.S. Inf., War of 1812, which see
Gad, Mass., S30661
Grove, Mass., BLWt.4858. Iss. 8/22/1789. No papers
Grove, Mass. See POMROY
Heman, Mass., R8307
Ichabod, Cont., Mass., S3722
Ira, Mass., Experience, R8308
Jacob, Mass., S30033
Luther, Cont., Mass., S30034
Medad, Ct., S22940
Phinehas, Mass., Rebecca, W2965
Phoebus, Ct., R8310
Pliny, Vt., Dis---. No papers. See Am. State Papers, Class 9, p.155. This sold. ruptured his groin while employed in carrying provisions from Roxbury to Dorchester, Jan. or Feb. 1777, near Boston
Ralph, Ct. See POMROY
POMERY, Daniel, Ct. See POMEROY
Ichabod, See POMEROY
POMPELLY, John, See PUMPELLY
POMPILLY, Bennett, See PUMPILLY
John, See PUMPELLY
POMROY, Amos, Ct., S14215
Gaius, Mass., S33484
Grove, Mass., Eunice Howes, former wid., W14943
Medad, Ct. See POMEROY
Nathaniel, Ct., Martha, W17482
Phinehas, Mass. See POMEROY
Ralph, Ct., S36237; BLWt.100-200
Simeon, Mass., S14190
Simeon, Mass., S14214
POND, Adam, Mass., Sarah, W27606; BLWt.40930-160-55
Adam, Mass., R8311
Barnabas, Ct., Phebe P., W5573; BLWt.31559-160-55
Bartholomew, Ct., S23847
Benjamin, Mass., Polly, W2243
Beriah, Cont., Ct., Silvia/Silva, W18777
Charles, Ct., Sea Service, Catharine, W22005
Dan, Ct., S14218
Elias, Ct., S36239
Elihu, Mass., Marena Allen, W2570; BLWt.18215-160-55
Ezekiel, Mass., S18550
Ezra, Mass., S14181

POND (continued)
Jabez, Mass., Bosmeth/Bosmelt/ Basmeth, W1645
James, N.C. See PAWNS
John H., Va., S18165
Josiah, Mass., S23849
Mijah, Mass., S30036
Oliver, Mass., S33481
Pallu, Mass., S30038
Paul, Cont., Mass., S40277
Phinehas/Phineas, Mass., S44253; BLWt.881-100
Robert, Mass., S30663
Timothy, Ct., Merina, W16374
William, Mass., R8312
Zebulon, Mass., S41959
PONDER, Amos, S.C., Violet, W10920
Thomas, See PANDER
PONE, David, S.C., S7330
PONNIER, Peter, N.Y., BLWt.7592. Iss. 9/21/1790 to Benjamin Elwood, ass. No papers
PONTIGBEAU, See DE PONTGIBAUT
POOBLES, Thomas, See PEEBLES
POOL, Abijah, Mass. See POOLE
David, Navy, Pd. at Ct. Agcy., S20923
Dudly, Va., R8316
Ephraim, S.C., Lucretia, W1475
Henry, S.C., Elinder/Eleanor, R8318
Jacob, Mass., S18552
Jacob, N.J. See VANDERPOOL
James, Md., BLWt.11610. Iss. 11/29/1790 to Frederick Hall, Admr. No papers
James, Va., Ursula, W9233
Jepthah, Mass., S8966
Job, Mass., Mary, W22004
John, Ct., Abigail, W26332
John, Ct., Elizabeth, R8317
John, Mass., S45077. His wid. was pensioned on account of service of her former husb., David Smith, N.H., which see
John, N.J., BLWt.8643. Iss. 11/16/1791 to Adam Nutt, ass. No papers
John, N.J., S3705
John, N.J., S35574
John, N.Y., S19431
John, N.C., S7329
John, S.C., S32450
John Engle, Pa., R8319
Jonathan, N.H., Elizabeth Woodward former wid., W16481
Joshua, Mass., Lucinda, W21990
Oliver, Mass., Sarah, W17465
Peter, Va., S40281
Samuel, Ct., S36234
Samuel, Mass., Abiah, W10911
Samuel, N.C., Agnes, W5552
Thomas, Cont., Ct., Elizabeth, W26922
Thomas, Mass., S37311
William, N.J., Susanna, W5567
William, Va., Catharine, R8315
William Petty, N.C., R8164
Zebinah, Mass., Lurany, W13828
POOLE, Abijah, Mass., S37310; BLWt.1663-200-Lt. Iss. 4/12/1790. No papers
Chester, Ct., Vt., Bridget, W5569; BLWt.14532-160-55
John, See POOL
Mary, former wid. of Davis Smith, N.H., W21987
Samuel, Ct., Ruth, W17466
William W., N.H., R8321
POOLER, Isaac, Mass., Lydia, W26921
POOLLER, George, Ct., Mass., S14198
POOR, Benjamin, Mass., Ann S., W26330; BLWt.17705-160-55
Daniel, Mass., S17025
David, Mass., Abigail, W15268
David, Mass., Jane, R8322; BLWt. 1669-200-Lt. Iss. 2/9/1798 to Addison Richardson, ass. Also recorded as above under BLWt.2696. No papers
George, Mass., Mary, W21995
John, Mass., Navy, See POWERS
John, Va., S38314
John, Va., Jane, W8520
Jonathan, Ct., Cont., S38313
Paul, Mass., Ruth, BLWt.40701-160-55
Robert, Navy, N.H. Agcy. & res., Betsey, W26925
Samuel, Mass., Anna, W21984
Samuel, Mass., Lucy, R8323
Thomas, Va., S11254
Timothy, Mass., S30039
William, Mass., BLWt.4846. Iss. 3/25/1790. No papers
William, Art. Artificers, Pa.,BLWt 13632. Iss. 4/11/1792 to Alexander Power, ass. No papers
William, Pa., S40278
POORE, Thomas, N.C., S39024
POORHAM, John, Hazen's Regt., BLWt. 13606. Iss. 7/18/1795. No papers
POOTMAN, Arent/Aaron, See PUTMAN
POPE, Adam, Pa., Salome, W2851
Arthur, N.C., R8324
Charles, N.C., R8325
Christopher, N.J., Mary, W8779; BLWt.26226-160-55
Elisha, N.C., S8888
Elnathan, Mass., S30658
Ezra, Ct., Mary, R8329
Harwood, N.C., Elizabeth, W4053
Isaac, Mass., S36742; BLWt.1637-400-Maj. Iss. 4/16/1796 to Wm. Sparks, ass. No papers
Isaac Ricks, S.C., Mary, R8330
Jeremiah, N.J., Mary, W138
Jeremiah, N.C., S7333
John, Cont., N.Y., Elizabeth, W26914
John, Md., S35032
John, Mass., S33488
John, Mass., Sarah, W2165; BLWt. 3824-160-55
John, Mass., R8327
John, N.C., Penelope, R8331
John, Va., Lee's Legion, BLWts. 8382 & 12451. Iss. 5/24/1797. No papers. Recorded also under 8623 with no date of issuance with a reference to Wt.8383
POPE (continued)
Matthew/Mathew, Va., R17152; Va. Half Pay. N.A. Acc. No. 874. See 050134 Half Pay Matthew Pope
Philip, N.C., Elizabeth, W55
Poole Hall, N.C., R8333
Ralph, Mass., Abigail Bird, former wid., W14300
Richard, N.C., S8969
Samuel, N.H., War of 1812, Ruth, R8334
Samuel, N.J., Elizabeth Stites, former wid., W978
Samuel, N.Y., Phebe, R8332
Seth, Mass., S30659
Simeon, N.H., Judith, R8328
Thomas, Mass., S33487
Thomas, N.C., Va., Charlotte, R8326
Thomas, Va., BLWt.12456. Iss. 5/2/1794
Thomas, Va., S38310
William, N.C., S35031
POPHAM, Benjamin, Md., S8968
William, Cont., Del., S9989; BLWt.1765-300-Capt. Iss. 9/27/1790
POPKIN, Benjamin, Mass., S33485
POPKINS, John, Crane's Regt. Art. BLWt.1635-450-Lt. Col. Iss. 2/22/1790 to Richard Platt, ass. No papers
POPLIN, George, N.C., S7328
William, N.C., Lucy, W10231
POPPELTON, Samuel, See POPPLETON
POPPENNY, Simon, See PERPEANEY
POPPINO, Daniel, N.Y., Eunice, R8335
John, N.Y., Anna Foster, former wid., R3680
William, N.J., S23848
POPPLE, George, R.I., Hannah Witter, former wid., W18428
Gideon, R.I., Lois, W26328; BLWt.26994-60-55
POPPLESTON, Samuel, See POPPLETON
POPPLESTONE, Gideon, See POPPLE
POPPLETON, Samuel, Green Mt. Boys Vt., Caroline, W9239
POPST, Christian, Pa., S41076
PORCH, Henry, N.C., Rebecca, W9234; BLWt.57777-160-55
PORTER, Aaron, Cont., Mass., Eunice, W13827
Abel, Cont., Ct., S14207
Abijah, Ct., Sarah, W1070; BLWt.26327-160-55
Alexander, Ct., Zerviah, W15261
Amos, Ct., S44254
Andrew, Pa., Arty. BLWt.1699-500. Lt. Col. Cmndt. Iss. 8/20/1789. No papers
Asa, Pvt. in the Invalids; BLWt.13625. Iss. 3/25/179? to David Quinton, ass. No papers
Asa, Mass., S15560
Asa, Mass., S44250
Asa, Mass., BLWt.2098-100
Benjamin, Ct., S23376
Benjamin, Mass., Thankful,W15263

PORTER (continued)
Benjamin Jones, Mass., Elizabeth L., W4714
Billy, Mass., BLWt.1638-400-Maj. Iss. 8/26/1790 to Manassah Cutler, ass. No papers
Charles, Md., b. Pa., Kiturah, R8347
Charles, N.C., S7327
Clara, former wid. of Isaac Reymond/Raymond, which see
Daniel, Ct., BLWt.6300. Iss. 5/26/1790. No papers
Daniel, Ct., S36240
Daniel, Mass., Rachel, W19996
Daniel, Va., R8339
David, Ct., S14216
David, Ct., Sarah, W13821; BLWt. 26136-160-55
David, Va., S36744
Deliverance, former wid. of Michael Doak, Mass., which see
Dudley, Mass., S30037
Edward, Mass., S19036
Eldad, Ct., S44246
Eleazer, Ct., S44258
Eli, Va., Mary, R8349
Elias, Va., R20199
Elijah, Ct., S14219
Elijah, Ct., S40276
Elijah, Ct., Anna Herrington/Harrington, former wid., R8337
Eliphalet, R.I., Mehitable, W5574
Ephraim, Ct., S28846
Ephraim, Md., S15562
Ephraim, Mass., BLWt.1866-100
Ezekiel, Ct., S14199
Ezekiel, Mass., Sarah S., W2664 BLWt.502-160-55
Ezra, Ct., Cont., S35568
Frances, S.C., former wid. of Edward Rowe, which see
Frederick/Fredrik, R.I., S37314
George, Mass., Susannah, W2164; BLWt.13023-160-55
Hancock, S.C., b. Va., S21428
Hugh, Pa., S40289
Isaac, Ct., S14188
Isaac, Ct., R8342
James, Mass., S8971
James, N.C., S25370
James, Pa., BLWt.10199. Iss. 1/14/1791 to Alexander Power, ass. No papers
James, Pa., Polly/Mary, W1478
James, Pa., R8343
Joel, Cont., Mass., S20144
John, Art. Artificer, BLWt.13614. Iss. 11/20/1789. No papers
John, Ct., Lucy, W26336
John, Ct., R8344
John, Ct., Esther, R8346; BLWt. 38839-160-55
John, Ct., Cont., S14195
John, Cont. Ct., Lydia, W8526
John, Cont. Ct., Mary, W21988
John, Cont. Ct., R17154
John, Cont., Mass., S33489
John, Mass., b. 1742, d.1834, S31306
John, Mass., Mary, W15265
John, Mass., Mabel, W17477

PORTER (continued)
John, Va., S39021
John, Va., Roseman, W26329. She also applied for pension as former wid. of John Brady, Va., which see
John W., Va., b. N.C., Martha, W3037; BLWt.26163-160-55
Jonathan, Mass., S29391
Joseph, Ct., Cont., S35572
Joseph, Mass., S8967
Joseph, Mass., S44244
Josiah, S.C., Rachel, R8351
Margaret, former wid. of Wm. Bailey, Va., which see
Martin, Ct., S14213
Mary, former wid. of Nathaniel Cleaves, Mass., which see
Mitchel, Va., Penelope, W1477
Moses, Ct., BLWt.6322 (Land office reported in 1936, this warrant never patented). Iss. 2/5/1790. No papers
Moses, Ct., S35029
Moses, Mass., S37309; BLWt.934-160
Moses, Ct., Sarah, R8354
Nathan, Md., Pa., Md. Sea Service (?), S8970
Nathaniel, Ct., BLWt.6271. Iss. 6/27/1796. No papers
Nathaniel, Sheldon's Dragoons, Ct., BLWt.6342. Iss. 8/7/1789. No papers
Nathaniel, Ct., S44243
Nathaniel, Mass., Sarah, W2852
Nehemiah, N.H., Joanna, W21999
Nicholas Brent/Nicholas B., Va., Gen. Wayne, S32454
Ockelo, Ct., BLWt.6272. Iss. 10/31/1791 to Isaac Bronson, ass. No papers
Oliver, Va., S32452
Philip, S.C., b. N.C., Mary, R8350
Robert, Mass., Elizabeth, W1928
Robert, N.C., See PARTER
Robert, Pa., S3712
Robert, Pa., S4651
Robert, Pa., S35567; BLWt.10287-100. Iss. 5/9/1797. No papers
Robert, Pa. Regt. of Art., BLWt. 1715-200-Lt. Iss. 8/20/1789. No papers
Samuel, Ct., S14191
Samuel, Ct., S14208
Samuel, Mass., Privateer, S8972
Samuel, N.C., S21928
Silas, Mass., S14185
Silas, N.H., BLWt.3377. Iss. 1/11/1791(?). No papers
Simeon, Ct., Sarah, W17468
Solomon, Va., Wincy/Winna, R8357
Stephen, N.Y., Mary, W21986
Thomas, Ct., S17640
Thomas, Md., BLWt.11613. Iss. 11/29/1790 to George Fields, Admr. No papers
Thomas, Va., S8974
Thomas, Va., BLReg.? Papers were found in file of Thomas Porter, S8974
Truman, Ct., S14220
Truman, Ct., R8355

PORTER (continued)
Tyler, Mass., S31914
William, Ct., BLWt.6263. Iss. 12/26/1789 to Isaac Trowbridge, ass. No papers
William, Ct., b. 11/1760, Hannah, W5557; BLWt.3978-160-55
William, Ct., N.Y., b. 1758; BLWt.1519-100
William, Cont., N.Y., S44249
William, Cont., Pa., Eveline, W18778; BLWt.7079-160-55
William, Mass., Mary, W15269
William, Mass., Rebecca, W26333; BLWt.31561-160-55
William, N.H., Deborah, W18700; BLWt.3770-160-55
William, N.C., R8356
William, Va., BLWt.1745-200-Lt. Iss. 4/26/1798. No papers. There are pension claims for two Lts. above name, Va., Cont. Line & Heitman's Hist. Reg. reports three Lts., Va., Cont. Line of above name. But as all the data in regard to the pension claims is vague it could not be decided which drew the above noted Wt.
William, Va., d. 6/20/1807, Elizabeth, W5159
William, Va., d. 1/8/1828, Sally, W24909
William May, Va., S38311
PORTERFIELD, Charles, Va., BLWt. 1145-450
Dennie/Dennis, N.C., BLWt.2254-300
John, Mass., Katharine/Catharine, W21992
John, N.C., Margaret, W1995
Richard, Cont., Va., Louisa, W2341; BLWt.26764-160-55
Robert, Cont., Ohio res. in 1818 Agnes, W5568
Robert, Va., S8965; BLWt.1738-300 Capt. Iss. 9/18/1789. No papers
PORTLOCK, John, Va., S17636
PORTLOW, Orman, See PARTLOW
PORTMAN, John, Pa., Catharine Foster, former wid., W7305
PORTTER, William, Md., BLWt.11590. Iss. 3/21/1794 to Henry Coon, ass. No papers
PORTWOOD, Lloyd, Va., Mary, W1929; BLWt.6398-160-55
Page, Va., S1867
POSEY, Belain, Md., Margaret,W9238
Benjamin, Cont., Md., S36238
Hezekiah, S.C., b. Md., S14192
Michajah, Pa., Rachel, R8358
Thomas, Va., BLWt.1733-450-Lt. Col. Iss. 12/7/1791. No papers
Zephaniah,/Zepheniah, Va., S40268
POSS, Christopher, Va., also 1794, R8359
Nicholas, N.Y., S44248
POST, Abraham, N.J., S831
Abraham, N.J., R8360
Anthony, Cont., N.Y.City res., S46337; BLWt.1650-300-Capt. Iss. 9/7/1790. Also recorded under BLWt.2566, as above. No papers.

POST (continued)
Caleb, Cont., N.J., S32451
Cornelius, N.J., S29389
David, N.J., S18551
Ebenezer, Ct., S36741
Elias, Vt., S15561
Ezra, Ct., S14187
George, Ct., Esther, W17464
Gideon, Mass., S40270
Hendricus, N.Y., S14183
Henry, N.J., S34477
Henry, N.Y., BLWt.7599. Iss. 9/25/1790 to Daniel Hudson & Co., ass. No papers
Henry, N.Y., S34479
Isaac, N.Y., R8361
Jacob, N.J., Vt. res., S19039
Jediah/Jedediah, Ct., Isabella/Isobel, R8362
Jimmy, Ct., S14206
John, N.Y., Margaretta, W15795
John C., N.J., Cornelia, W1071
John H., N.J., Elizabeth, W866
John P., N.J., Catharine, W121
Martin, N.Y., S11253
Patience, former wid. of Peter Lewis, Ct., which see
Reuben, Vt., Esther, W16682
Samuel, N.Y., Gertrude, W21989
Simeon, Ct., Cont., Ct. Sea Service, S22447
Stephen, Ct., S31916
William, N.J., S34478
William, Vt., S22442
POSTENS, Charles, N.J., Hannah, W3157
Jacob, Pa., Ann, W3296
POSTLE, Francis, N.Y., R8363
Henry, Pa., BLWt.10201. Iss. 3/14/1793 to Gideon Markle, ass. No papers
POSTON, John, N.C., Rebecca, W26923
POTEET, Benjamin, Va., Clarinza/Clorinza, W979; BLWt.26104-160-55
POTER, Milton, See POTTER
POSGROVE, Henry, Pa., S23851
POTTAGE, Jabez, Ct., S36241
POTTER, Aaron, Mass., S17637
Aaron, Mass., S41961
Abel, R.I., S14193
Abijah, Mass., S45081
Abraham/Abram, N.C., S30657
Alice/Allice, former wid. of Alvan Goodell/Alvin Goodall, Ct., which see
Amos, N.J., S1075
Anna, former wid. of Thos. Cook, N.H., which see
Barnabas, Mass., Mary, W17481
Benjamin, Ct., BLWt.6310. Iss. 4/15/1790 to Peter DeWitt, ass. No papers
Benjamin, Ct., Rachel, W26326
Borden, Ct., S3710
Caleb, Ct., Mass., Vt., S19037
Caleb, R.I., S14217
Cyrus, R.I., Rebecca, W5564; BLWt.26648-160-55
Daniel, Ct., Martha, W2332; BLWts.64-60-55 & 47-100. Iss. 5/23/1803. No papers

POTTER (continued)
David, Ct., Hannah, W2242; BLWt. 19780-160-55
David, Ct., Rebecca, R8379
David, Ct., R.I., S14189
David, R.I., S22445
Dick, See Richard
Earl, N.Y., R8365
Ebenezer, Ct., Mass., N.H., S11255
Edmund, Mass., BLWt.4828. Iss. 6/30/1789. No papers
Edward, Ct., S14209
Elias C., R.I., R8367
Elisha, Cont., R.I., S14201
Ephraim, Cont., Mass., S33493
Ephraim, Mass., S44245
Ephraim, Mass., N.H., War of 1812, Sarah, W26924
Ephraim, S.C., BLWts.12483 & 13586. Iss. 10/7/1795. No papers
Ezra, Cont., Ct., S35575
Fones, R.I., Martha, W21997
George, Mass., Elizabeth, W26916
George, R.I., S11258
George, R.I., Nancy, W16058
George, R.I., Mary Maxson/Maxon, former wid., W21754. Her last husb., Asa Maxson/Maxon, R.I., was also pensioned.
Gideon, R.I., S14182
Gilbert, Navy, N.Y., Rachel Van Tassel, former wid., R10893
Holliman, Cont., R.I., S39025
Hugh, Mass., S37307
Ichabod, Mass., Sarah, W26920
Income/Incom, R.I., S31911
Israel, Ct., BLWt.1703-200
Israel, Mass., R8368
Israel R., R.I., Sea Service, R8369
Isreal/Israel, S30035
Jacob, Cont., N.J., S3711
Jacob, Mass., R8370
James, Mass., BLWt.4849. Iss. 4/3/1797 to John Jack. No papers
James, Cont., Mass., S36743
James, Mass., S33491
James, R.I., S11261
James, Va., S17023
Jeremiah, R.I., S14212
Joel, Ct., BLWt.6292. Iss. 10/7/1789 to Benjamin Tallmadge, ass. No papers
Joel, Ct., Thankful, W26325
John, Ct., S14203
John, Green Mt. Boys, R.I., Vt., S14184
John, Mass., Rhoda, W15260
John, N.H., S17639
John, R.I., BLWt.3409. Iss. 12/31/1789. No papers
John, R.I., Vt., S19038
John, Va., S14211
Joseph, Cont., Mass., S23850
Joseph, Capt. Cont., N.H., Catharine, W17480; BLWt.1623-300 iss. 10/16/1789 to Theodosius Fowler, ass.
Joseph, Mass., S5941
Joseph, Mass., S40273
Joseph, N.J., S40283

POTTER (continued)
Joseph, N.J., R8373
Joseph, Vt., S22446
Lemuel, Ct., Lydia, W17478
Lemuel, N.Y., R8374
Levi, Ct., Cont., S11262
Lyman, Vt., Abigail, R8364
Mariam, former wid. of Abel Slocum, Privateer, R.I., which see
Medad, Ct., BLWt.6296. Iss. 1/2/1796 to Eneas Munson, ass. No papers
Medad, Ct., S35564
Milton, Ct., S21426
Moses, Ct., BLWt.6332. Iss. 11/2/1791 to Jonathan Tuttle, ass. No papers
Moses, Ct., S35569
Nathan, R.I., Sarah, W12645
Nathaniel, N.Y., R8377
Nicholas, R.I., Phebe, W21994
Noel, Green Mt. Boys, Vt., Mercy, W21991
Noell/Noel, R.I., S14196
Olney, Privateer, R.I., R8378
Pardon, R.I., Mary, W13823
Peter, R.I., S14186
Reuben, R.I., S21927
Richard/Dick (colored), R.I., R8380
Robert, Mass. res. in 1836, Patience Death, former wid., W2821
Robert, Cont., Enl. R.I., S40269
Rouse, R.I., Anna, W21993
Rowland, N.Y., R8381
Samuel, Mass., R.I., S14210
Samuel, N.H., Dis. No papers. BLWt.1990-100. See Am. State Papers, Class 9, p.139. Disabled by ball in his leg, Sept. 1777. Enl. 11/15/1776. Joined Invalids 10/1/1778
Samuel, N.Y., BLWt.7607. Iss. 1/25/1791 to John Chandler, ass. No papers. Wt. cert. 3/5/1814.
Samuel R., R.I., S11257
Sarah, former wid. of John Bidwell N.Y., which see
Sheldin, Ct., Mary, W18775; BLWt. 45-100
Silas, R.I., Elizabeth, W24880
Stephen, Ct., BLWt.1668-300-Capt. Iss. 4/11/1792. No papers
Stephen, R.I., S5942
Stephen, R.I., Susan, BLWt.91504-160-55
Thaddeus, Ct., S23846
Thaddeus, Mass., S21929
Thomas, N.J., BLWt.8658. Iss. 11/16/1791 to Adam Nutt, ass. No papers
Timothy, Ct., Martha, W17479
William, Cont., R.I., S39022; BLWt.1631-300-Capt. Iss. 12/31/1789. No papers
William, Mass., S36745
William, Mass., Sarah, W16373
William, N.C., b. Va., S8910
William, R.I., S23377
William, R.I., Amey/Amy, W26338

POTTER (continued)
Zebedee, R.I., W1313; BLWt. 26229-160-55
POTTERF, Casper, Md., Va., Nancy Arrowsmith, former wid., S17024; BLWt.49468-160-55
POTTISH, Jabez, Ct., BLWt.6343. Iss. 1/28/1790. No papers
POTTLE, Patience, former wid. of Elijah Stanton, Cont., N.H., which see
POTTORF, Casper, See POTTERF
POTTS, Benjamin, Ct., S44247
David, N.Y., S14200
David, Va., S40275
George, Pa., R8382
Isaac, N.J., Rachel, R8385
James, N.C., S3707
James, N.C., Sarah, R8366
Jasper, N.J., BLWt.8650. Iss. 8/7/1789 to Richard Platt, ass. No papers
Jesse, Cont., N.C., S47664
John, S.C., Hannah Parmelia, R8383
John, Va., Susannah, W4767
Jonathan, Va., S40288
Joseph, Pa., BLWt.612-300
Thomas, Md., S7326
Thomas, N.Y., Sarah, W8521; BLWt.8015-160-55
William, N.J., S3709
William, N.C., S.C., S31913
William, S.C., S3708
POTWINE, George, Ct., S14204
POUCHER, Elizabeth, former wid., of Abraham Camer, N.Y., which see. (The name Camer looks like CARNER on register of B.L.)
James, N.Y., R8387
POUGE, Andrew, Pa., BLWt.10209. Iss. 11/9/1792 to Mary Johnson, Admx. No papers
POUL, Frederick, Pa. See POWELL
POULIER, Joseph, Hazen's Regt., BLWt.13605. Iss. 2/4/1790. No papers
POULSON, John, Del., S35033
John, Va., BLWt.1734-400-Maj. Iss. 6/26/1797 to Samuel Marsh, ass. No papers
Michael, N.Y., BLWt.7612. Iss. 3/7/1792 to Jesse Atwater, ass. No papers
POUND, Hezekia/Hezekiah, N.J., Va., S31308
William, Va., Elizabeth, W17467
William, Va., R8388
POUNDS, Samuel, N.C., Sarah, R8389
POURTAR, Solomon, See PORTER
POUSLAND, John, Mass., S29390
POUTY, Bela, See PROUTY
POWARS, Abner, N.H., R8409; see also R8405, same name
Joseph, Mass., S33490
Joseph, N.H., Rebecca, W18772; BLWt.6300-160-55
Noah, Mass., Rhoda, BLWt.38837-160-55
Simeon, See POWERS

POWARS (continued)
Thomas, N.H. See POWERS
POWDER, Tobias, Hazen's Regt., BLWt.13596. Iss. 12/5/1791. No papers
POWDERS, Reuel, Del., R8391
POWE, Rebecca, former wid. of Calvin Spencer, S.C., which see
William, Va., S11252
POWEL, Britain/Briton, N.C., Mary, W4768
Felix, Ct., Cont., S44260
Frederick, See POWELL
Joseph, Pa., R8400
POWELL, Aaron, Va., Susannah,W5566
Abner, N.C., Va., b. Va., S7331
Abraham A., Va., Francis, W1476
Absalom, N.C., Mary, R8401
Ambrose, Va., S14197
Asal/Asahel, Mass., S30660
Benjamin, N.H., BLWt.3380. Iss. 10/12/1795 to James A. Neal, ass. No papers
Benjamin, N.H., S41958
Benjamin, Va., Elizabeth, W5553
Charles, N.C., S7323
David, Pa., S8975
Eleazer, Pa., R8393
Eleven. See Levin H.
Elijah, N.C., Mary, W5570
Elisha, Cont., N.Y., Vt., Eunice, W17470
Felix, Ct., BLWt.6269. Iss. 8/7/1789 to Anspach & Rogers, assnes. No papers
Francis, Va., S31912
Francis, Va., R8404
Frederick, Pa., S40280
George, N.C., S4650
James, N.C., Sarah, W17472
Jeremiah, Mass., R.I., S11259
John, Md., R8397
John, N.H., N.Y., Vt., S22444
John, N.C., Mary, W17471
John, N.C., Mary, W26331; BLWt. 14673-160-55
John, N.C., R8398
John, Va., S25368
John, Va., S38312
John, Va., S39023
John P., Va., See Peyton
Jonathan, N.Y., Eveline, R8396
Levi, Va., S36235
Levin H./Elever, Cont., enl. in S.C., Va. & Ill. res., Elizabeth, R8394; BLWt.1935-100
Lewis, N.C., S31915
Lewis, N.C., Susannah, W4055; BLWt.3972-160-55
Lloyd, Pvt. in Invalids, BLWt. 13628. Iss. 9/4/1789. No papers
Luther, Vt., Theda, R8402
Nathaniel, N.C., S15576
Peter, Ct., Eunice, R8395
Peyton/John Peyton, Va., S46407 BLWt.1743-200-Lt. Iss. 11/22/1791. No papers
Richard, Va., Sarah, W8524
Robert, N.C., Ann, W18771
Robert, Va., Ann, W8525, Va.

POWELL (continued
Half Pay
Stephen, Ct., N.H.(?), Vt.(?), Lurany, W21985
Stephen, N.Y., BLWt.7587. Iss. 12/15/1790. No papers
Stephen, N.Y., Dis. No papers. See Am. State Papers, Class 9, p.126. Sold. rec'd an injury in his left shoulder occasioned by a fall on a stump which dislocated his shoulder 4/1782, Princeton, N.J. Enl. 1/1/1777; on the rolls in 1782
Thomas, Cont., Mass., S44257
Thomas, Del., BLWt.10863. Iss. 12/10/1799 to Alexander McBeath, guardian to Joseph Kirkwood & Mary Kirkwood, orphan children of Robert Kirkwood, ass. No papers
Thomas, Pa., BLWt.10196. Iss. 7/27/1789 to Richard Platt, ass. No papers
Thomas, S.C., BLWts.12482 & 13583. Iss. 5/2/1794. No papers
Truman, Vt., S19040
William, Ct., Cont., Mass., S41957
William, Md., BLWt.11607. Iss. 5/12/1797 to James DeBaufre, ass. No papers
William, Mass., S33494
William, N.Y., Nancy, W2433
William, N.C., b. Md., S17022
William, N.C., S21427
William, N.C., b. Va., Rachel, W4054; BLWt.28506-160-55
William, N.C., Casana, R8392
William, Pa., Elizabeth, R8403
POWELS, Powel, See POWLES
POWELSON, Henry, N.J., Abigail, W3864
POWER, Benjamin, Md., Pa., Wayne's Indian War, S5945
David, Mass., S33496
James, Md., R8406
James, Not Rev. War, Northwest Indian War 1791-1792 & War of 1812. Reg. 18936-50; Reg. 1875-55
Jeremiah, Va. & Indian Spy in 1793, S11260
Jesse, Md., S35030
John, Mass., Anna, W15730
Joseph, Va., Sarah, W9235
Robert, Lee's Legion, BLWt.1755-150. Iss. 2/27/1796 to Edward Kelly, ass. No papers
Robert, Navy, See POOR
Thomas, N.H., BLWt.3378. Iss. 6/24/1793. No papers
William, 4th Regt. Art., BLWt. 1713-300-Capt. Iss. 9/7/1789. No papers
POWERS, Aaron, Ct., BLWt.6350. Iss. 3/19/1792. No papers
Aaron, Ct., S40282
Abner, See POWARS
Alexander, Art. Artificers, BLWt. 1655-200-Lt. & Q.M. Iss. 9/15/1791. Also recorded as above under BLWt.2592. No papers

POWERS (continued)
Amasa, Vt., Lydia Field, former wid., W19268
Asahel, Ct., Mass., N.H., Vt., S22443
Asel, Vt., S22941
Bradly/Bradley, N.C., Sarah, R8410
Charles, Mass., S11256
Charles, N.C., R8412
Cyrus, Ct., Cont., Rachel, W16059
David, Mass., Sarah, W26324
Elizabeth, former wid. of James McClure, N.H., which see
Elizabeth, former wid. of George Gosling, S.C., which see
Ephraim, Mass., Abigail, W16375
Ephraim, N.C., S7332
Francis, S.C., Catharine, R8411
George, N.J., BLWt.8638. Iss. 8/31/1791. No papers
Henry, Cont., N.C., S7324
Isaac, Mass., Lydia, W18774
Jacob, N.Y., R8413
James, Ct., BLWt.6282. Iss. 7/8/1790. No papers
James, Ct., S35570
James, Cont., Mass., S44255
James, N.C., S38315
Jesse, Va., S30662
John, Ct., Cont., Anna, W26337; BLWt.14763-160-55
John, Cont., Mass., S33492
John, Mass. Sea Service, Navy & Privateer, Elizabeth, W13826
John, Rev. War, Navy, Mass., B.L. Reg. 133567-55
John, N.J., S35571
John, Va., Gitty, W8522; BLWt. 17578-160-55
Jonathan, Mass., N.H., Olive, W26918
Jonathan, N.H., Rebecca, W26919
Joseph, Mass., Sybel/Sibil, W5572; BLWt.19506-160-55
Joseph, Mass., R8407
Joseph, N.H. See POWARS
Josiah, N.H., Mary Soper, former wid., W17854
Lewis, Va., S36740
Manassah, Mass., S3716
Moses, N.C., S41963
Moses, Vt., Elizabeth Moore, former wid., W17154
Nahum, N.H., Vt., R8415
Nathan, Ct., Sarah, W17476
Nicholas, N.Y., Hannah, W26917
Nicholas, S.C., S18166
Noah, See POWARS
Oliver, Mass., S44256
Peter, Navy, Mass., Louisa, W5559
Peter, Vt., Sarah, W5575
Pierce, Navy, N.H., Mary Furber, former wid., W24264
Simeon, N.H., S40284; BLWt.489-100
Stephen, Mass., S33486
Stephen, Mass., Phebe Dutton, former wid., W25550. Her last husb., Oliver Dutton, Ct., Cont. & Mass. was also pensioned for service in Rev. War, which see
Stephen, Vt., Mary, W26915
Thomas, Ct., BLWt.6274. Iss. 9/1/1790 to Theodosius Fowler, ass. No papers
Thomas, Cont., Ct. res. in 1818, S35573
Thomas, N.H., S44259
Thomas, Rev. War, d. Pa., Elizabeth, B.L. Reg. 271470-55
Thomas, Vt., Olive, W5554; BLWt. 6458-160-55
Timothy, Ct., Elizabeth, W17473
Whitcomb, Mass., Meriam, W16683
William, Mass., Mary, W26912; BLWt.26225-160-55
William, Va., served till 1792/1793, S18164; BLWt.26471-160-55

POWILL, Elisha, See POWELL
Joseph, See POWL

POWLAS, James, see WAK-AR-AN-THAR-AUS

POWLEES, James, See WAK-AR-AN-THAR-AUS

POWLES, Jacob, N.J., S1083
Paul/Powel, N.J., Maria Blauvelt, former wid., W15877

POWLIS, James, See WAK-AR-AN-THAR-AUS

POWNALL, John, Mass., BLWt.1658-200-Lt. Iss. 4/1/1790 to John May, ass. No papers
Susannah, former wid. of John King, N.H., which see

POYAS, John E., Southern Hospital BLWt.1698-300-Mate. Iss. 6/4/1792 to David Cay, ass. No papers

POYNEER, Reuben I.or J., See PENOYER

POYNER, Thomas, N.C., S7335

POYNTER, Nathaniel, See PAYNTER

PRADDOX/PREDEX, William, Crane's Cont. Art., Mass., BLWt.4888. Iss. 1/26/1790 to John May. Sgt. 100 acres. No papers

PRADY, Christopher, Hazen's Regt. BLWt.13585. Iss. 10/24/1792 to Margaret Stephenson, admx. No papers. Pvt.-100 acres.

PRALL, Edward, Md., BLWt.1729-300-Capt. Iss. 8/14/1789. Only one paper. No original papers. Name also appears as PRAUL in Heitman's Hist. Reg. & the Maryland Archives
John, N.J., Amelia, W3297

PRAMER, Lodowick, N.Y., Dolly Van Schoonhoven, former wid., W18203

PRATER, Jonathan, Va., S7340
Philip, S.C., Susannah Hammond, former wid., W9052

PRATHER, Thomas, N.C., b. Md., S17030
Thomas, Va., also 1793, Delilah, R8419

PRATT, Aaron, Mass., Silence, W13834
Abel, Cont., Green Mt. Boys, N.Y. res. & agcy., S44266
Abiah, Mass., Patience, W15218
Abijah, Ct., Mary, W17483
Abijah, Mass., Mary, W15222
Alderton, Mass., Lucy, R8425
Allen, Ct., BLWt.6277. Iss. 11/19/1789. No papers
Alvin, Mass., Jane, R8421
Asa, Ct., Susannah Starkey, former wid., W11563. BLWt.14955-160-55
Asa, Mass., N.H., S16226
Augustus, Ct., S14233
Benjamin, Ct., Mass., Sarah, R8433
Benjamin, Cont., Mass., Jemima, R8422
Benjamin, Mass., S36746
Benjamin, Mass., Betty, W20004
Bennanuel, Mass., Lucy, W18781
Caleb, Mass., Mary, W1646
Caleb, Vt., S29393
Cary, Ct., S11265
Chalker, N.Y., S44261
Cushing, Cont., Mass., S19044
Cyrus, Mass., Deborah, W15219
Dan, Mass., S31309
Daniel, Mass., S30042
David, Drum Major, Ct., BLWt.6316 Iss. 4/14/1790 to William Wells, ass. No papers
David, Ct., Dis. No papers. See Am. State Papers, Class 9, p.116 Disability. Ruptured by excessive fatigue & hardship in 1780. Enl. 10/12/1777 cont. to end of war.
David, Navy, N.H., Betsey, W10929
Dier, Mass., S18553
Ebenezer, Ct. See PLATT
Ebenezer, Cont., N.H., Susannah, W26926
Edmund, Ct. Navy, Sybil, R8436
Edward, Ct., S5950
Edward, Mass., Elizabeth, W20006
Elam, Mass., Lydia, W26928
Elias, Ct., S29392
Elijah, Mass., S41964
Elnathan, Mass., S18554
Ephraim, Cont., Mass., S40300
Ephraim, Mass., BLWt.4805. Iss. 8/24/1790 to Benjamin Ives Gilman. No papers
Ephraim, Mass., S33504
Ephraim, Mass., d. 6/11/1842, S44265
Ephraim, Mass., Olive, W15225
George, Mass., S37315
Gideon, Cont., Pa., S14226
Hannah, former wid. of Nathan Lewis, Cont., Mass., which see
Isaac, Mass., S30041
Isaac, Mass., Betsey, W10921
Isaiah, Ct., S33506
James, Ct., Cont., S44262
James, Cont., Pa., Susannah, W26340; BLWt.40709-160-55
James, Mass., (Children), W22015
James, Vt., S14222
James, Va., Rebecca, W9599
Jasper, Ct., BLWt.6276. Iss. 1/27/1796. No papers
Jasper/Jesper, Ct., Abigail, S35581 & W17499
Jeremiah, Mass., S41965
Jesse, Mass., Mary, W13832
Joel, Mass., Phebe, W2343; BLWt.

PRATT (continued)
1652-200-Lt. Iss. 4/19/1796 to Joseph Fosdick, ass. No papers
John, Cont., Mass., S33507
John, Mass., S33513
John, Mass., Rebecca, W26931; BLWt.6392-160-55
John, Lamb's Art. N.Y., BLWt. 7653. Iss. 11/27/1790. No papers
John, N.Y., S22942
John, N.Y., S35582
John, Pa., S40296; BLWt.13901-160-55
John, Pa., Elizabeth, W1314; BLWt.1710-200-Lt. Iss. 10/20/1789. No papers
Jonathan, Hazen's Regt., Enl. N.H., Polly Potter, former wid., R---, B.L.Reg. 304209-55 & B.L. Reg.305989-55. Her 2nd husb. was Benjamin Potter.
Jonathan, Ct., Cont., S14221
Jonathan, Mass., S40290
Jonathan, Mass., Martha Sprague, former wid., W17858
Jonathan, Vt., Hannah, W13831; BLWt.38534-160-55
Jonathan, Va., S11263
Joseph, Cont., Mass., S23853
Joseph, Cont., Mass., S33511
Joseph, Cont., Mass., Susanna, W17491
Joseph, Mass., S19045
Joseph, Mass., S33499
Joseph, R.I., Margaret, W9240
Josiah, Cont., N.H., Mary, W27466 BLWt.13582. Iss. 3/25/1790. No papers
Laban, Cont., Mass., S15959
Lemuel, Ct., Cont., Mary, W5577 BLWt.61095-160-55
Levi, Mass., BLWt.4847. Iss. 5/17/1792 to Moses Bissell
Levi, Mass., S11268
Levi, Mass., Mary, W24911
Mary, former wid. of Samuel Dougherty, Mass., which see
Mary, former wid. of Elenezer Field, Navy, Mass., which see
Mathew, Cont., Mass., S41084
Matthew, Mass., Chloe, W22008
Moses, Vt., Green Mt. Boys, Martha, W17488
Nathan, Mass., S15578
Nathan, Mass., S19748
Nathaniel, Mass., Elizabeth,W26930
Noah, Mass., S44264
Noah, Vt., S11266
Olive, former wid. of Caleb Fowler Ct., which see
Paul, Ct., Mass., S9990
Paul, Mass., S33509
Peabody, Ct., Sarah, W26936
Phineas/Phinehas, Ct., Cont., Mass., S40303
Robert, Mass., Rebecca, W22014
Robert, N.Y., S14229
Russell, Ct., R8429
Samuel, Ct., Privateer, R8432
Samuel, Mass., Mary, see her

PRATT (continued)
pension as former wid. of Ebenezer Field, Navy, Mass., S15224
Seth, Cont. Mass., Hannah, W17492
Seth, Mass., BLWt.4806. Iss. 7/20/1797 to Ezra King. No papers
Seth, Mass., Elizabeth, W26934
Silas, Cont., Vt., S41083
Silas, Vt., Catharine, R8434; BLWt.9190-160-55
Simeon, Mass., S5167
Solomon, Cont., Mass., Remember, W17486
Solomon, Mass., Betsey, W5580
Stephen, N.Y.?, R8435
Stephen, Mass., Hannah, W19997
Stephen, Mass., Lucy, R8426
Stephen, Mass., Vt., S19435
Stephen, Vt., Rhoda, R8428
Stephen, Va., Sarah, W8528
Sylvanus, Cont., Mass., Hannah, W20003
Sylvanus, Mass., R.I., S11269
Sylvester, Mass., BLWt.4874. Iss. 1/26/1790 to John May. No papers
Thaddeus, Cont., res. Me., Sarah, W1891; BLWt.1001-160-55
Thomas, Mass., Lydia, W17485
Thomas, Mass., Sarah, W26938
Thomas, Mass., N.H., S45085
Thomas, N.H., BLWt.3389 (or 2389?). Iss. 12/20 or 12/30/1796 to Joel Abbott, ass. No papers
Thomas, N.C., Sally, W1075
Thomas, R.I., Mary, W22011
Tyrus, Mass., Patience, W15220; BLWt.24438-160-55
Whitcom, Ct., Mass., Ruth, R8430
William, Ct., S17029
William, Ct., Zuba/Zaby Byington former wid., R1570
William, Cont., Vt., Rosanna, W15700
William, Mass., S22449
William, Mass., Ruth, W19998; BLWt.13216-160-55
William, N.Y., S.C. res., Amelia, R17199
William, R.I., S33503; BLWt.1630-200-Lt. Iss. 3/5/1800. No papers
William, see papers in claim of Harlehigh SAGE, Va.
Zadock/Zadoc, Ct., Cont., S44263
Zebulon, N.C., S41969
Zimri, Ct., Vt., S19043
PRAUL, Edward, See PRALL
Nathan, Pa., R8438
PRAY, Abraham, Cont., Mass., S17641
Ebenezer, Mass., S33505
John, Cont., Mass., S19041
John, Mass., Jane, W16378; BLWt. 1642-300-Capt. Iss. 8/6/1789. No papers
Joseph, Mass., BLWt.4818. Iss. 1/28/1790 to Joseph May. No papers
Peter, Mass., S17031
Samuel, Cont., Mass., Sarah, W26927
PREAST, Eleazer, See PRIEST

PREBBLE, John, See PRIBBLE
Thomas, See PRIBBLE
PREBLE, David, Mass., BLWt.4809. Iss. 3/25/1790. No papers
Ebenezer, Mass., Martha Hood, former wid., R5194. Her 2nd husb., Robert Hood, also was a sold. in Rev.
James, Mass., Rebecca, W22010
Jedediah, Cont., Mass., Isabella, R8440
Job, Va., R8442
PREISE, George/Georg, Pa., S40294
PRENHOP, Joseph, See PRINTROP
PRENTICE, Asher, Mass., Sarah, W17487
Daniel, Mass., S15199
Elisha, Ct., S15563
Elkanah, Mass., S41082
Jesse, Ct., Elizabeth, W26608
Nathaniel, Ct., Privateer, Margaret, W6750; BLWt.31566-100-55
Samuel, Mass., BLWt.4840. Iss. 4/1/1790. No papers
Valentine, See PRENTISS
William, Ct., Zephrah Kenyon, former wid., W26709
PRENTIS, Jonathan, Ct., R8443
Samuel, Ct., S5949
Thomas, Ct., S21931
PRENTISS, John, Mass., Hannah, W16145
Joshua, Mass., S5164
Samuel, Ct., Lucretia, R8444
Thomas, Cont., Mass., S44273
Valentine, Cont., Mass., S37316; BLWt.749-100
PRESBREY, John, Ct. Sea Service, R.I., Mass., S18555
Seth, Mass., R.I., S19747
Simeon, Mass., Meredith, W1932; BLWt.26382-160-55
PRESBURY, Simeon, See PRESBREY
PRESBY, Richard, N.H., S45083
PRESCOT, Benjamin, N.C., R8445
PRESCOTT, Abel, Mass., Hannah, W1997
Austin, N.C., S41967
Ebenezer, N.H., Phoebe, W16388
Fortunatus, Mass., Phebe, W22013
Jesse, N.H., Judith, W16060
John, S.C., R8446
Jonathan, N.H., S45082
Jonathan, N.H., Catharine, W22009
Joseph, Cont., S3740; BLWt.1697-300-Surgn's Mate. Gen. Hosp. Iss. 7/24/1795. No papers
Mercy, former wid. of John Morrison, N.H., which see
Nathan, See PRESCUTT
Samuel, Cont., Me. pension, Martha W2434
Willoughby, N.C., S41966
PRESCUTT, Nathan,N.H., Dolly, W10923; BLWt.38525-160-55
PRESHO, Asa, Cont., Mass., S33498
Samson, Mass., S33500
PRESLER, Jonathan, N.Y., S14231
PRESLEY, Andrew, N.C., S21434; BLWt.28522-160-55

PRESLEY (continued)
John, N.C., S3738
John, S.C., b. Va., S7338
PRESLOR, Abraham, See PRESSLER
PRESNELL, John, N.C., S8978
PRESSEY, Benjamin, Mass., Rhoda, W16377
James, N.H., Betsey, W2853; BLWt.13208-160-55
John, Mass., S30040
PRESSLER, Abraham, N.Y., R8447
PRESSLEY, David, S.C., b. in Scotland, Ann, W24917
Richard, N.H., BLWt.3398. Iss. 10/12/1795 to James A. Neal, ass. No papers
PRESSON, Lemuel, Mass., Anna, W18780
PRESTON, Abner, N.H., S45084
Amariah, Mass., S33519
Amos, Mass., S41087
Benjamin, N.H., S41078
Benjamin, N.Y., BLWt.7626. Iss. 1/5/1791. No papers
Benjamin, N.Y., Jane, R8449
Calvin, Ct., Rachel, W2690; BLWt.26884-160-55
Daniel, Ct., Esther, W5581; BLWt.6106-160-55
Daniel, Ct., Cont., S35586
David, Ct., S40291
Ebenezer, N.J., S1085
Gardner, Mass., S30044
Hovey, Ct., S35578
Isaac, Mass., Abigail, W17484
Jacob, Va. res. (Fauquier Co.) in 1778, Cecelia, R8448
Jeremiah, Va., R8451
Joel, Va., Lucy, W10229; BLWt. 24165-160-55
John, Del., BLWt.10861. Iss. 9/2/1789. No papers
John, N.Y., R.I., S14223
Joseph, Ct., S36244
Joseph, Del., BLWt.10862. Iss. 9/2/1789. No papers
Joshua, Va., S8981
Levi, Vt., Martha, W2689
Moses, N.H., Tempy, R8453. BLWt. 88011-160-55
Moses, Va., Fanny, W8533
Nathan, Va., Elizabeth, W8532
Noah, Aner/Anor, Ct., W20001
Otheniel, N.Y., BLWt.7625. Iss. 7/22/1790 to Thomas Tillotson, ass. No papers
Othniel/Otheniel, N.Y., S44274
Patrick, Pa., Jemima, R8450; B.L. Reg. 30087-55
Robert, N.H., S41077
Robert, Va., Nancy, W4056
Shubael, Ct., S14230
Stephen, Md., BLWt.11586. Iss. 2/1/1790. No papers
Walter, Va.(?), Letitia, R8452
William, Cont., N.Y., Mary, W2667; BLWt.5079-160-55
William, Cont., N.Y., War of 1812, Rebecca, S40299
William, N.Y., S9991
Zephaniah, Ct., Mary, BLWt. 73547-160-55

PRESTON (continued)
Zera, Mass., S35577
PRESTWOOD, Jonathan, S.C., S8977
Thomas, S.C., S7337
PRETTYMAN, Benjamin, Del., Elizabeth, W9241
PREVEAUX, Adrian, S.C., BLWt.1761-300-Capt. Iss. 6/4/1792 to David Cay, ass. No papers (Heitman's Hist. Reg. gives name as Adrian Proveaux)
PREVOST, John, See PROVOOST
PREWETT, John, Va., S30665
Joshua, Va., Maria Berkshire, former wid., W27643; BLWt. 110265-160-55
Obadiah, Va., R8458
Ransom, See PRUET
Reuben, Va., S39026
Solomon, See PREWITT
William, S.C., R8460
PREWIT, John, Va., Eady/Eddy, R8455
John, Va., Micajah, N.C., Peany, R8459
William, Va., Ellender, R8456
Zachariah, N.C., Va., S5952
PREWITT, Byrd, Va., S35576
John, Va. See PRUETT
Solomon, Va., Mary, W1315
William, S.C. See PREWETT
PREYOR, Jesse, See PURYEAR
PREYS, George, See PREISE
PRIBBLE, James, Va., Pa., b. Md.; Margaret, W3595; BLWt. 34905-160-55
John, Va., S5951
Samuel, Lamb's Art., N.Y., BLWt.7647. Iss. 7/9/1790 to Nicholas Fish, ass. No papers
Thomas, Va., Pa., R8439
PRICE, Abner, N.J., S28848
Adam, N.Y., BLWt.7627. Iss. 8/23/1790 to Chas. Newkirk, ass. Cert. by N. Cutting, 5/9/1820. No papers
Adam, N.Y., S44269
Anjer, Va., Jane, W1073
Benjamin, Md., killed 1791 in St. Clair's Defeat; BLWt.341-300
Benjamin, Mass., Ruth, W4770; BLWt.11060-160-55
Benjamin, N.J., R8461
Burdot, Va., BLWt.12454. Iss. 10/6/1792 to Thomas Newton, ass. No papers
Charles Cully/Charles CULLY, N.Y. R8463
Daniel, S.C., S14227
David, Ct., Susannah, W17493
David, N.J., S16227
David, Va., BLWt.12469. Iss. 3/26/1792 to Francis Graves, ass. No papers
Ebenezer, N.Y., S23854
Edward, N.C., Lucy, W4769
Edward, R.I., Mary, W17498
Elijah, Ct., N.Y., Beulah, R8462
Elijah, Lamb's Art., N.Y.,; BLWt. 7650. Iss. 9/24/1790 to Thomas Lawrence, ass. No papers

PRICE (continued)
Elijah, N.Y., S44268
Elizabeth, former wid. of Benjamin Johnson, Md., which see
Elizabeth, former wid. of Charles Craycraft/Cracraft, Va., which see
Ephraim, N.C., Va., S31919
George, N.J., Sally, W1074
Henry, Pa., S5135
Isaac, N.J., S20534; BLWt.2172-100
Jacob, Va., S3730
James, Va., Esther, R8465
Jesse, S.C., R8468
John, N.J., Hannah, W18782; BLWt. 8636. Iss. 2/10/1790. No papers
John, N.J., Mary, R8472
John, N.Y., S44270
John, N.Y., R8469
John, N.C., Ellen/Elener, R8464
John, Pa., BLWt.10218. Iss. 9/2/1796 to John Price. No papers
John, Va., S5953
John, Va., Mary, R8474
Jonathan, Ct., Jemima, W17497
Joseph, N.J., S1087
Joseph, N.J., Pa., S.C., R8470
Joseph, Pa., S40293
Levi, N.J., Privateer, S3733
Lot, Mass., S33512
Mary, former wid. of Ephraim Smith, Mass., which see
Mathew, R.I., S21930
Nathaniel, Md., S40298
Nathaniel, Lamb's Art., N.Y., BLWt.7644. Iss. 6/24/1793 to Thomas Russell. ass. No papers
Nathaniel, N.Y., S40295
Nathaniel, Pa., R8475
Paul, Ct., BLWt.6289. Iss. 10/30/1789. No papers
Paul, Ct., S35579
Reece, N.C., S3731
Rice, N.J., Phebe Allen, former wid., W5605
Richard, Ct., S36243
Richard, Va., Elizabeth, W2435; BLWt.10244-160-55
Royal, N.C., S3732
Rufus, Ct., Ruth, W16685
Sampson, Va., S18167
Samuel, Ct., BLWt.6304. Iss. 1/11/1794 to John Stephenson, ass. No papers
Samuel, Pa., R8477
Samuel, S.C., S21433
Stephen, N.J., Elizabeth, W16376; BLWt.1557-100
Stephen R., Md., S46467; BLWt. 451-100
Tenrub, N.J., S3734
Thomas, Md., BLWt.1732-200-Lt.
Thomas, N.J., BLWt.2496-100
Thomas, N.C., S7339
Thomas, N.C., Margaret, W1076
Thomas, N.C., Pemina/Pernina, W10227; BLWt.61159-160-55
Thomas, Va., S5954
Thomas, Va., S31917
Thompson, N.J., S7336. BLWt. 13890-160-55
Timothy, N.Y., Polly, W10926;

PRICE (continued)
BLWt.100161-160-55
Tobias, Va., Sarah, W5579
Vincent, N.C., R20176
Walter Lane, Navy, Va. Sea Service, S35036
William, Art., BLWt.1654-200-Lt. Iss. 11/21/1789. No papers
William, N.J., BLWt.8655. Iss. 4/26/1791. No papers
William, N.C., Elizabeth, W1072; BLWt.14969-160-55
William, N.C., R8478
William, N.C., R8479
William, N.C., BLWt.2504-100
William, Va., S35589
William, Va., Hannah, R8467
William, Va., BLWt.1440-200-Capt. Ctf. No. 199; Act of 5/15/1828
William H., N.C. S(?), Ctf.22018
Williamson, Va., Susannah, W5583
PRICHARD, Asahel, Pa., R8480
Benjamin, Ct., S40202; BLWt.6280-100-Pvt. Iss. 5/17/1790. No papers
David, Crane's Cont. Art., Mass., BLWt.4880. Iss. 1/28/1790 to Joseph May. No papers
Edward, N.C., Ruth/Rutha, W8536; BLWt.19810-160-55
George, N.C. See PRITCHARD
James, N.C., Mary, R8490
James, Dragoon, Va., BLWt.12462. Iss. 2/24/1794. No papers
Jared, Ct., S8976
Jeremiah, N.H., Dis. No papers. See Am. State Papers, Class 9, p.58. Wounded 7/1777, at the expedition of Gen. Sullivan against the Indians, by a ball passed through his left shoulder and ruptured in his groin.
John, Va., S32456
Nathaniel, Cont., Comfort, W5582
Thomas, N.C., Mary, R8481
William, N.H., Deidamia, N.H., W22007
William, N.C. See PRITCHARD
PRICHART, John, N.H., Ann, W4501
PRICHETT, George, See PRITCHARD
PRICKETT, Azariah, N.J., BLWt.8651 Iss. 7/29/1794. No papers
Francis, N.J., S3736
John, N.J., S33518
Josiah, Pa., Sarah, W5584
PRIDDY, John, Va., S3741
Richard, Va., Judith, W5593; BLWt.34939-160-55
PRIDE, Absalom, Ct., Cont., S14232
Burton, Ga., N.C., Elizabeth, W10930; BLWt.43521-160-55
James, N.Y., Mehetable/Mehitable W26939
John, Mass., Elizabeth, W2244; BLWt.5069-160-55
Jonathan, Ct., Anna, W15940
Joseph, Mass., S28847
Reuben, Ct., S44276; BLWt.1671-200-Lt. Iss. 11/6/1789 to Reuben Pride/Price. No papers

PRIDE (continued)
Thomas, Mass., S30048
PRIDEMORE, Jonathan, See PRIDMORE
PRIDGEON, Francis, N.C., Mary, W6880
William, N.C., S8982
PRIDMORE, Jonathan, Pa., Rachel, W191; BLWt.26909-160-55
Theodore, Pa., S32457
PRIER, William, See PRIOR
PRIEST, Abel, Mass., Jermiah, W26342; BLWt.11073-160-55
Asa, Mass., S14228
Eleazer, Mass., S33508
Elijah, Mass., Eunice, R8483
Jacob, Mass., Rhoda, W18784
Jeremiah, Va., S8980
Job, Cont., Mass., S33517
Job, Mass., S33510
Joel, N.H., S41080
John, Cont., Ct., Lucy Cook, former wid., W16539; BLWt. 2227-100
John, Cont. Mass. See John J. ATKINS
John, Mass., S19433
John, Mass., S41081
John, S.C., BLWts.12481 & 13580 Iss. 5/2/1794. No papers
John, Va., S3739
Joseph, Mass., S33502
Joseph, Mass., Sally, W812
Levi, Mass., Mary, W15939
Noah, Vt., S30045
Peter, Va., Sarah, W8530
Philemon, Mass., S30043
Samuel, Mass., Susan, W26937
William, N.H., S11267
William, Va., S40292
PRIESTLEY, John, Pa., BLWt.1139-300
PRIESTLY, Charles, S.C., Polly, W981
PRIGG, William, Md., Susan, R8485
PRIM, James, N.C., S3727
John, Va., S32458
PRIME, John, N.Y., Angelica, W22017
John, Va. See PRIM
PRIMES, Record (colored), N.C., R8486. Pensioned as named above erroneously. He gave no surname.
PRIMM, James, Va., S35034
PRIMUS, or LATHROP, Job, Ct., Keturah Smith, former wid., W10256; BLWt.61201-160-55
PRINCE, see Prince SAYWARD(colored)
Ammy, Mass., S17027
Benjamin, Mass., Sarah, W1316
Cato (colored), Mass., S33514
Edward H., Ct., S14224
Henry, S.C., S18168
John, N.C., R8487
Joseph, Ct., N.Y., S23378
Joseph, Va., Rebecca, W8531
Kimball/Kimbell, N.Y., S36245
Nicholas, S.C., Nancy, W8289; BLWt.11053-160-55
Philip, Ct., S35580
Richard, Mass., S33501
Samuel, Cont., N.Y. res., BLWt. 83-100

PRINCE (continued)
Samuel, Mass., Irene, W13830
Timothy, Ct., S41079
William, N.J., Rebecca, W192; BLWts.2476-100 & 196-60-55
PRINDLE, Abijah, Ct., BLWt.6302. Iss. 12/3/1796 to Nathaniel Ruggles, ass. No papers
Abijah, Ct., S35588
Enos J., N.Y., S35584
Joel, Ct., BLWt.6339. Iss. 9/24/1790 to James F. Sebor, ass. No papers
Joel, Cont., Ct., S35585
Jonas Enos, Lamb's Art., N.Y., BLWt.7655. Iss. 8/1/1795. No papers
Jonathan, N.Y., BLWt.7634. Iss. 7/19/1792 to Jesse Atwater, ass. No papers
Jotham, N.Y., S35583
Patience W., former wid. of William Strickland, Mass., which see
Peter, Ct., S31918
Samuel, Ct., S15577
Samuel, Ct., R8488
Samuel, Mass., S44271
Zalmon, Ct., Polly, W24920; BLWts.2397-100 & 26771-160-55
PRINGLE, Joseph, N.Y., S9992
PRINTROP, Joseph, N.Y., S27345
PRINTUP, Joseph, See PRINTROP
PRINTY, William, N.J., S40301
PRIOR, Abner, Ct., Abigail, W4311; BLWt.1666-400-Maj. Iss. 5/20/1791. No papers
Abner, N.Y., BLWt.1685-300 Surgn's Mate. Iss. 9/28/1791. No papers
Azariah, Ct., Alice, W17490
Ebenezer, Ct., Mary, W17496
Gideon, R---
Jesse, Ct., S44275
John, Mass., Privateer, Margaret, W26941
John, Va., S36242
Roswell, Ct., Phebe, W17495
Simeon, Ct., S4652
William, Cont., Ct., Elizabeth, W18783
PRITCHARD, Benjamin, Ct. See PRICHARD
Elizabeth, former wid. of Brampton Hitchcock, which see
George, Ct., Abigail, W2342
George, Va., Elizabeth, W5594
James, Ct., S23852
James, Cont., Va., Phebe, W8534
Nathaniel, See PRICHARD
Rees, Va., S38316
Samuel, Navy, Mass., Martha, W22006
Thomas, Mass., BLWt.987-100
William, Mass., Lydia Dennis, former wid., W14612
William, N.C., R8492
PRITCHART, John, See PRICHART
PRITCHET, Nancy, former wid. of John Montgomery, Va., which see
PRITCHETT, Edward, See PRICHARD

PRITCHETT (continued)
James, Va. See PRITCHARD
John, N.C., R20182
Keziah, former wid. of David Moore, N.C., which see
Stephen, S.C., S36246
PRIVIT, John, N.C., S41968
PROALE, Hannah, former wid. of John Fifield, Navy, N.H., which see
Henry, Mass., S37317
PROBASCO, Gerrit, N.J., S1084
PROCTER, Josiah, Mass., Sea Service, Navy, S30047
Micajah, Va., S21431
Silas, Mass., Olive, W10928
PROCTOR, Abel, Mass., S33515
Benjamin, Va.(?), Susannah, W3594; BLWt.53668-160-55
Daniel, Mass., Hannah, R8494
Ebenezer, N.H., Sarah, W16379
Francis, Cont.-- Commissioned Capt. of the 4th Battn., Cont. Art.
George, Va., S15579
George, Va., S30666
Isaac, Cont., Mass., BLWt.4878. Iss. 10/12/1790
Isaac, N.H., R8495
Joel, N.H., BLWt.3403. Iss. 3/25/1790. No papers
John, Va., R8496
Joseph, Md., R8497
Joseph, N.H., Sybil, W1998; BLWt.34504-160-55
Joseph, Va., S11270
Leonard, Mass., Sea Service, Pedee Bond, former wid., W18631
Levi, Mass., S33516
Little Page, Va., Sarah, W576; BLWt.26622-160-55
Nathaniel, Mass., Mercy, BLWt. 38838-160-55
Nathaniel, Navy, Mass., S21429
Nicholas, Va., Catharine, W8537; BLWt.26634-160-55
Samuel, Mass., S41086
Samuel, Mass., Joanna Thompson, former wid., W26524
Simeon, Mass., S30046
Thomas, Mass., Jane, W15223
Timothy, Mass., Sally, W26933
William, Md., S1711
William, Mass., Mary/Molly, W26929
William, Pa., Elizabeth, W3038
William, R.I., Dis.- No papers. See Am. State Papers, Class 9, p.162. Disability. Ruptured in his belly, occasioned by a stick thrown at him by one Kelly, because he refused to play at cudgels with him. Time 4/1779.
PROFFIT, William, N.C., Elizabeth, R8499
PROFIT, James, Cont., R.I., S39028
PROPER, Frederick, N.Y., Margaret, W17494
PROPPER, Frederick, N.Y., BLWt. 7632. Iss. 2/3/1791 to Hoffman Herman, ass. No papers
PROSSER, Daniel, Va., S40297
John, Va., Elizabeth, R8500
William, Mass. Sea Service, S30664
PROTHERO, Thomas, N.C., Hannah, R8501
PROTZMAN, Peter, Pa., S3742
PROUD, Samuel, R.I., R8502
PROUDFOOT, James, Pa., S22450; BLWt.21827-160-55
PROUGH, Peter, Pa., S40304
PROUSE, Thomas, N.H., BLWt. 3400. Iss. 3/25/1790. No papers
PROUT, James, Ct., N.J., Cloe, W17489
John, Md., BLWt.11618. Iss. 12/12/1792. No papers
Oliver, Ct., S14234
William, Ct., BLWt.6311. Iss. 3/9/1797. No papers
William, Ct., Naomi, W22012
PROUTH, Degorey, N.Y., BLWt. 7624. Iss. 9/4/1790 to John Susfren, ass. No papers
PROUTY, Amos, Cont., Mass., S22448
Bela, Mass., Mary, W4312; BLWt. 13420-160-55
Burpee/Burphy, Mass., Martha, W2665; BLWt.11280-160-55
Burpree/Purpee, Mass., BLWt. 4856. Iss. 3/1/1790 to Elihu Mather. No papers
Caleb, Mass., Navy, S5166
Daniel, Mass., S18169
Eli, Mass., Rebekah, W26935
Elijah, Mass., Anna, W26932; BLWt.14537-160-55
Elisha, Mass., Prudence, W15221
Elisha, Mass., Elizabeth Clark, former wid., W24828
John Warner, Ct., S8983
Johnson, Mass., S15564
Joshua, Mass., S19042
Stephen, Mass., Judith, W5585
PROVANCE, Joseph, See PROVINCE
PROVANDIE, Louis, Cont., enl. in Boston; N.Y. res. & Agcy. S46468; BLWt.4886-100. Iss. 7/12/1797. No papers
PROVEAUX, Adrian, See PREVEAUX
PROVEOST, Samuel, See PROVOST
PROVINCE, Joseph Y., Pa., Va., Rachel, W26341; BLWt.92026-160-55
PROVOOST, John, N.J., Eve, R8454
PROVORSE, Thomas, See PROVOST
PROVOST, Daniel, Ct., S20926
David, N.J., S1086
David, N.J., Barbara, W1479; BLWt.27680-160-55
Robert, N.Y., BLWt.1684-150. Ensign. Iss. 12/15/1789. No papers
Samuel, Ct., Anna, W26339; BLWt.
PROVOST (continued)
40696-160-55
Thomas, Ct., N.Y., Privateer, S17028
PROWS, Thomas, N.H., War of 1812, Margaret, W6878
PROWIT, Degorey, N.Y., S44267. See also Degorey PROUTH
PROWTY, Burpee. See Burpee PROUTY
PRUDDEN, Adoniram, N.J., S44272
PRUDEN, Adoniram, Pvt., N.J., BLWt.8637-100. Iss. 10/4/1790.
Samuel, Sheldon's Dragoons, Ct., BLWt.6345. Iss. 2/25/1790 to John Ludlow, ass. No papers
PRUET, Ransom, N.C., S39029
PRUETT, Archibald, N.C., R8503
John, Va., S35587
John, Va. See PREWIT
Micajah, Va., R8505
PRUIT, Joseph, N.C., b. Va., R8506
PRUITT, Joshua, N.C., S39027
Martin, Va., S32455
Ransom, See PRUET
Samuel, N.C., b. Va., S21432
PRUME, Peter, See PRUYNE
PRUTT, Levi, Mass., S33497
PRUYME, Henry, N.Y., S14225
PRUYNE, Henry, See PRUYME
Lewis, N.Y., R8507
Peter, N.Y., Maria, R8508
PRY, Jesse, Md., R8509
Thomas, Hazen's Regt., BLWt. 1766-300-Capt. Iss. 5/24/1791 to Elizabeth Pry, Admx. No papers
PRYER, Simon, N.J., Susannah, W2854; BLWt.31573-160-55
PRYNE, Henry, N.Y., R202428
PRYOR, John, Cont., Va., Elizabeth Q. Lake, former wid., W12064; BLWt.1750-200-Capt. Lt. Iss. 8/10/1789 to Richard Platt, ass. No papers
Matthew, N.C., S3747
Simon, See PRYER
Thomas, N.J., S35035
William, Va., S8979
PUCKET, William, Va., R8513
PUCKETT, Jacob, Va., Nancy,W8540
John, Va., Rhoda, R8511
Josiah, Pvt. in the Dragoons, Va. BLWt.12457. Iss. 5/5/1790 to Wm. I. Vreedenburgh, ass.
Josiah, Cont., Va., Martha, R8510
Nathaniel, Va., S5958
Thomas, Va., R8512
PUDDING, Conrad, Cont., Va., Elizabeth, W5590
PUDING, Conrad. See PUDDING
PUFFER, Amos, N.H., Esther, W26942
Daniel, Cont., Ct., S43875
Isaac, Mass., Vt., Sarah, W20243
John, Mass., Silence, W15226
Simeon, Cont., Ct., Fanny, W20007
Simeon, N.H., S33524
PUGH, James, Va., Ann, W5588
John, N.C., Va., S7334
Jonathan, Corps of Invalid's, BLWt.1718-200-Lt. Iss. 8/19/

PUGH (continued
1789 to Catharine Pugh, the wid. & legal repr. No papers
Jonathan, Va., R17239; Va. Half Pay
Josiah, Va., Avy, W5586
Lewis, Va., BLWt.12470. Iss. 3/26/1792 to Francis Graves, ass. No papers
Reuben, See PEW
Richard, Va., S38319
Shadrach, N.C., R8514
PULASKI, Count Casimer, d. 10/11/1779. No pension & no B.L. claim on file allowed, but see corresp. with attorneys for his present heirs 1926-1927.
PULCIFER, Joseph, Mass., S37319
Nathaniel, Mass., S29395
PULFORD, Elisha, Ct., BLWt.6295. Iss. 1/15/1796. No papers
Elisha, Ct., S41088
Joseph, Ct., Phebe, W22018
PULIS, John, N.J., S1093
John, N.Y., S43878; BLWt.7600-100. Iss. 3/8/1791. No papers
PULLAM, William, See PULLIAM
PULLEN, Everard, Va., Catharine, W3451
George, Va. See PULLIN
Oliver, Cont., Me. res., S37318
Robert, Va., S16512
Samuel, Hazen's Regt. BLWt.13600 Iss. 7/16/1789. No papers
Thomas, Va., S15847
William, Cont., Mass., R.I., S36747
William, See PULLIN
William, Va., Polly/Mary, W8538
PULLEY, William, Va., Lucy, W1077
PULLIAM, Benjamin, S.C., Jamima, R8516
Drury, Va., R8515
Joseph, Va., R8517
Joseph, Va., R8518
Mosby, Va., S5957
Richard, N.C., S8984
Thomas, Va., S5955
William, Ga., R20425
Zachariah, Va., R8519
PULLIN, George, Cont., Va., Nancy, W8539; BLWt.13724-160-55
John, Va., S3750
William, Va., Mary, W5589
PULLING, John, Mass., Sarah Breed, former wid., W15234
Joseph, Mass., Sarah, W1933
PULLINS, Loftus, Va., S14240
PULLIS, John, N.Y., BLWt.7600. Iss. 3/8/1791. No papers
PULLMAN, John, Ct. Sea Service, R.I., Esther, R8520
Salter, See PULMAN
PULLY, William, Va., S38318
PULMAN, Jonathan, R.I., R8521
Salter, N.Y., Lovisa, W577; BLWts.7586-100-1790 & 163-60-55
PULS, John, Pa., R468
PULVER, Jacob, Cont., N.Y.; Catharine, W17505
John I., N.Y., Ann, W16381

PUMPELLY, John, Mass., Sea Service, Mary, W5558
PUMPHREY, Henry, N.C., or Ga., res. at enl. Natchez, Lucy, W8535
PUMPILLY, Bennet/Bennett, Mass., N.Y., Elizabeth, W27825
PUNCHARD, John, N.H., BLWt. 511-160-55
Samuel, N.H., S33522
PUNDERSON, Ahimaaz, Ct., BLWt. 6318. Iss. 5/14/1790 to Benj. Tallmadge, ass. No papers
John, N.Y., S43872
PUNTENNEY, George H., Md., Pa., Va., R8522
PURBECK, Aaron, Cont., Mass., S19749
PURCELL, Edward, Va., S16230
George, Va., Margaret Chandler, former wid., W6661
Henry D., Pa., BLWt.1708-200
John, Cont., Va., S19046; BLWt. 12453-100-1795; name also appears as PURSELL, PURSLEY & PUSLEY. His 2nd wife was Elizabeth Carter. BLWt.13978-100. Iss. 4/18/1794. No papers. BLWt.354-60-55
William, Md., BLWt.11598. Iss. 8/15/1795. No papers
William, Va., S16229
PURCHASE, Robert, N.J., Eliza, W10936
William, Md., BLWt.11595. Iss. 2/7/1790. No papers
PURCILL, Lawrence, Va., R8524
PURDOM, Thomas, Va., S38321
PURDY, Daniel, Ct., N.Y., S9460
Daniel, Vt., Martha, W17504
Gilbert, N.Y., R20146
Henry, S.C., Nancy, W9602
Jacob, N.Y., Abigail, W17502
James, N.Y., BLWt.7642. Iss. 3/16/1792 to Elias Newman, ass. No papers
James, Cont., N.Y., S43874
Jeremiah, Cont., N.Y., Susannah, W10937; BLWt.7204-160-55
Jonathan, N.Y., S5956
Joseph, Md., BLWt.11592. Iss. 11/9/1792 to John Wright, ass. No papers
Joshua, N.Y., R8256
Josiah, N.Y., S11271
Justus, N.Y., S43873
Obadiah, N.Y., S23855
Patrick B., Pa., Jane, R8525
Solomon, N.Y., S27346
PURGETT, Henry, Va., S18170
PURHAM, Peter, See PERHAM
PURINGTON, Nathaniel. See PURRINGTON
Sylvanus, Mass., S43926
PURINTON, Humphrey, Mass., R8527
James, Mass., R24910
Joseph, Mass., S30667
PURKETT, Henry, See PURKITT
PURKINSON, Jackman, Va., S2012
PURKITT, Henry, Cont., Mass. res. & agcy., Phebe, W2245; BLWts. 6344-100-1797 & 197-60-55
PURNELL, John, Pa., Old War Ind. File 3749 (W.O.31887, W.C.23814 War of 1812). Sarah Ann, R---,

PURNELL (continued)
BLWt.20630-160-12; Reg.62809-55; 16th U.S. Inf.
Samuel, Md., Ann, W13836
PURPLE, John, N.H., S45087; BLWt. 3382-100. Iss. 3/25/1790.
PURRINGTON, Humphrey. See PURINTON
James, See PURINGTON
Nathaniel, Mass., Sea Service, Hepzebeth/Hepsibeth, W21916
Sylvanus, See PURINGTON
PURRINTON, Joseph, See PURINTON
PURSE, William, N.C., S.C., S18171
PURSELL, John, See PURCELL
PURSELLY, William, N.C., Sally, R8523
PURSLEY, James, S.C., Sarah, R8528
John, See PURCELL
John, S.C., Mary, W9242
Peter, See PUSLEY
PURTLE, John, Invalids Regt., BLWt. 13622. Iss. 2/14/1791 to Alexander Power, ass. No papers
Robert, Md., Catherine Wistel/Whistler, former wid., W4397; BLWt.38340-160-55
PURVIANCE, John, See PURVIANS
Joseph, N.C., Patience, W2666
PURVIANS, John, N.C., S.C., S32459
PURVINS, John, See PURVIANS
PURVIS, George, Del., BLWt.1726-300-Capt. Iss. 5/30/1789. No papers
George, Va., Elizabeth, W2691
James, N.C., R8529
James, Va., R17246, Va. Half Pay
William, Va., Jane, W3039
PURYEAR, Jesse, Va., S35590
Reuben, Va., Nancy, W5587
Thomas, Va., Jane, W3452
PUSHEE, David, Mass., S8985
John, Mass., S18557
Nathan, Cont., Mass., Jane, W13835
PUSLEY, John, See PURCELL
Peter, Del., S36247; BLWt.2218-100
PUTERBAUGH, Joseph, Md., R8143
PUTMAN, Aaron/Arent/Arnt, N.Y., Claartje/Clara/Catharine, R8531
Daniel, N.H., BLWt.3388. Iss. 2/16/1795 to Jonathan Grout, ass. No papers
Daniel, S.C., Prudence Key, former wid., W26751
Francis, Cont., N.H., See PUTNAM
Francis, N.Y., S16231
Garret, N.Y., Rebecca, W16687
Peter, N.J., Sarah, W17501
Richard, N.Y., Nelly, W16686
Victor, N.Y., S22944
PUTNAM, Aaron, Ct., Sally, W16146
Aaron, N.Y., See PUTMAN
Asa, Mass., S30049
Daniel, Cont., Ct., Catharine, W17503
Edward, Mass., R8534
Elijah, Mass., S40305
Ezra, Mass., S14236
Francis, Cont., N.H., S43871
Francis, Mass., S17642
Howard, Cont., Mass., S17032
Israel, Cont., Ct., BLWt.1664-1100 Maj.Gen.Iss.12/13/1796. No papers

PUTNAM (continued)
papers
Israel, Mass., S21932
Jacob, Mass., S33520
Jeptha, See John
Jeremiah, Mass., BLWt.1675-150. Ensign. Iss. 2/9/1798 to Addison Richardson, ass. Also recorded as above under BLWt.2698. No papers
Jesse, Cont., N.H., S22451
John, Cont., N.H., Olive, W26943; BLWt.1570-100
John, Cont., Mass., Ann/Anna, W13837
John, Mass., S40306
John/Jeptha, Mass., Mary, W3453
John, N.H., Mary, W5591
John, N.H., Vt., S19047
Joseph, Mass., S29396
Joseph, Mass., Tamar, W26344; BLWt.3538-160-55
Levi, Mass., Hannah, W18785
Nathan, Cont., Mass., S33521
Peter, N.H., Sally, BLWt.54672-160-55
Reuben, Ct., S43876
Rufus, Cont., Mass., BLWt.1633-850. Brig. Gen. Iss. 1/29/1790. No papers
Seth, Green Mt. Boys, N.H., S18556
Stephen, Mass., Sally, W1317
Thomas, Mass., Susanna, R8535
Thomas, N.H., Vt., S16511
Timothy, Mass., S29394
William, N.Y., BLWt.7591. Iss. 9/24/1790 to David Howell, ass. No papers
PUTNEY, Asa, N.H., S22943
David, N.H., R8536
James, N.H., S11272
John, N.H., S45086
Jonathan, N.H., Esther, W16061
Joseph, N.H., Cont., S9993
Joseph, N.Y., R.I., S33523; BLWt.873-100
Samuel, Cont., Mass., Lydia, W26343; BLWt.26769-160-55
Stephen, N.H., Sally, W1999; BLWt.1308-160-55
Thomas, N.H., S45088
William, Cont., N.H., S15960
PUTRIN, William, Cont., Mass., S14237
PYATT, Joseph, Ga., Va., S8986
PYEATT, Robert, Cont., Pa., S8987
PYKE, Abraham, Ct., S5168
PYLES, Joseph, Pa., S5169
PYNCHON, Walter, Mass., Mary, W13838; BLWt.3145-160-55
PYON, Jacob/Jacques, Cont., Canadian, Abigail, W18786
Pierre/Peter, N.Y., S46338; BLWt.1583-100
PYOTT, Ebenezer, Pa., S32460
PYRON, William, N.C., b. Va., S8675
PYTTS, Jonathan, N.C. Winney/Winna, W26321; BLWt.38574-160-55

Q

QUACKENBOSS, Abraham D., N.Y., Caty, W16688
Abraham I., N.Y., Caty, R8537
Isaac, N.Y., S11275
John, N.Y., S23858
John, N.Y., d. 1814, Alida Truax, former wid., W18160
Nicholas, N.Y., Magdalen, W11096
Peter I., N.Y., R8538
QUACKENBOY, Isaac, N.Y., See QUACKENBOSS
QUACKENBUS, Cornelius, N.J.,S4748
QUACKENBUSH, Cornelius, See QUACKENBUS
Daniel, N.Y., S9463
David, N.Y., S23379
John, N.Y. See QUACKENBOSS
Nicholas, See QUACKENBOSS
Sybrant, N.Y., Elizabetth, W20008
QUACKINBUSH, Abraham, Ct., R20426
James, N.J., N.Y., S15200
QUAINTANCE, John, Va., S22945
QUALES, James, Va. , Elizabeth, W8967
QUANCE, Joshua, Mass., BLWts.4890 & 4820. Iss. 5/6/1793
QUARLES, Abner, Va., BLWt.548-100
David, Pickens Dist., S.C. in 1845, Mary, R19426
Francis, Va., S4655
Henry, Va., R17253; Va. Half Pay See N.A. Acc.874. No. 050-135 Half Pay Henry Quarles
James, Va., R17254; Va. Half Pay, See N.A. Acc.874-050136; Half Pay James Quarles
John, Va., R17250; Va. Half Pay
Moses, Va., BLWt.2164-100
Robert, Va., Patsey, W9868; BLWt.1771-150 Ens. Iss. 5/17/1792 to Robert Means, ass.
Thomas, Va., R17251; Va. Half Pay
Wharton, Va., R17252; Va. Half Pay, See N.A. Acc. No.874-050137 Half Pay Wharton Quarles. Iss. 5/6/1793. No papers
William, Mass., Polly, W14219
William, Va., BLWt.1770-200-Lt. Iss. 5/29/1792 to Robert Means ass. No papers
QUARRELL, James, Pa., BLWt.10245. Iss. 7/16/1789 to M. McConnell, ass. No papers
QUARRIER, Alexander, Pa., Sally, W2692
QUARTERFAGE, Peter, Hazen's Regt. BLWt.13637 Iss. 2/20/1792 to Benj. Moore, ass.
QUARTERMAN, John, Pa., S4749
QUAS, Gideon, R.I., Hannah, R8539
QUASH, Gideon, See QUAS
Quomony/Quamony, Mass., Elen Talbot, former wid., R18097
QUAY, John, Va., S33525
QUEEN, Christopher, N.Y., BLWt. 7659. Iss. 11/17/1791 to Elisha Camp, ass. No papers
Christopher, N.Y., S43882
John, Va., S5962

QUEEN (continued)
Marsham, Md., R8542
Samuel, Ga., Dise, R8541
Thomas, N.C., S32280
William L., Ga., S9462
QUEENER, John, Md., S1584
QUEERY, William, N.C., R8544 (Not same as Wm. Quiery, R8540)
QUELLIN, Robert, See QUILLIN
QUENONAULT, Paul, Del., BLWt.287-300. (The papers in file show this name spelled QUENAULT, QUIANAUL, QUENANOLT, QUANAUL, QUEANAULGHT)
QUERRY, Elisha, Pa., Sarah, W7340 BLWt.6262-160-55
QUI, Libbeus. See QUY
QUICK, Abram, N.Y., Jane, W15941
Cornelius, N.Y., Anna, W8965; BLWts.237-60-55 & 7658-100-1792
George, N.Y., Catharine, W24716
George, Pa., S23857
Henry, N.J., Sarah, W22019; BLWts.303-60-55 & 8664-100-1799
Jacob, N.Y., S43881; BLWt.1065-100
James, N.Y., R20189
John, Md., BLWt.11624. Iss. 12/18/1794 to Henry Purdy, ass. No papers
John, N.J., BLWt.8663. Iss. 9/8/1789 to Samuel Rutan, ass. No papers
John, N.J., Margaret/Margeret, W139
John, N.J., Phebe, W3597; BLWt. 18027-160-55
John, N.Y., Mary, W22020
John, Va., Elizabeth, W4313
Levi, S.C., BLWts.12487 & 13640 Iss. 11/24/1795. No papers
Lewis, N.Y., R21681
Moses, N.J., BLWt.8665-100. Iss. 12/29/1790. No papers
Peter, N.J., S1090
Samuel, N.J., R8545
Samuel, N.J., R8546
QUICKEL, Adam, Pa., S11274
QUICKLE, Adam, Md., R8547
QUICKSALL, Jonathan, N.J., R8548
QUIERY, William, N.C., R8540
QUIGLEY, Edward, Hazen's Regt., BLWt.13638. Iss. 9/2/1789. No papers
Edward, Pa., S40307
Isaac, N.J., R8550
James, Cont., Mass., S43880
Samuel, Pa., S4746
Thomas, N.J., Sea Service, S43879
William, Cont., Mass., Thankful, W19890
QUIGLY, Cary, Pa., S22452
QUILLIAN, James, See QUILLIN
QUILLIN, James, N.C., R8551
John, N.C., S9461
Robert, Va., BLWt.392-100
QUILLMAN, Peter, Hazen's Regt., BLWt.13639. Iss. 9/15/1791 to Jacob Barr, ass. No papers
QUIMBY, Benjamin, Cont., N.H., Mary, R8552

QUIMBY (continued)
Benjamin, N.H., S18558
Daniel, Cont., Mass., N.H.,S41089
Eliphalet, See QUINBY
Jacob, Mass., Anna/Nancy, W24714; BLWt.31574-160-55
James, Cont., N.H., Irena Rowe, former wid., W9630; BLWt.96075-160-55
John, Ct., S11273
Jonathan, N.H., S45090
Moses, N.H., S19048
Samuel, Mass., S30050
Samuel, See QUINBY
Zachariah/Zacheriah, N.H., S45089
Zachariah, Pa., BLWt.10244. Iss. 8/24/1790 to Benj. I. Gilman, ass. No papers
QUIN, Francis, Pa., BLWt.10242. Iss. 2/12/1794 to Gideon Merkle, ass. No papers
John, Pa., served until 1794, Elizabeth, R8553
Patrick, Va., BLWt.12484. Iss. 7/14/1792 to Robt. Means, ass. No papers
QUINBEY, John, N.J., S33526
QUINBY, Eliphalet, N.H., BLWt. 3421-100. Iss. 1796
Josiah, N.J., S4033
Moses, N.H. See QUIMBY
Samuel, Mass. See QUIMBY
Samuel, N.J., Acaha/Echsah, W3454; BLWt.26836-160-55
QUINLEY, Thomas, Ct., S35592
QUINLIN, Cornelius, S.C., R8554
QUINN, Benjamin, Va., Franky, W8966
Daniel, S.C., S21435
David, N.C., Esther, W4771
John, Va., S38322
Samuel, Pa., BLWt.1769-200-Lt. Iss. 1/29/1795. No papers
QUINT, Benjamin, Navy, N.H., S45091
John, Navy, N.H. Sea Service, S17643; BLWt.34808-160-55
Mary, former wid. of Thomas Rines, Mass. Sea Service, which see
Thomas, N.H., S45092
William, Mass., Judith, W2693
QUINTARD, Evert, Ct., Hannah,W20009
Isaac, Ct., S17033; BLWt.18011-160-55
James, Ct., S36248
QUINTON, Samuel, S.C., S32461
QUINTORE, William, Md., BLWt.11623 Iss. 1/8/1796 to Geo. Ponsonby, ass. No papers
QUIRK, Thomas, Va., Jane Buford, former wid., W5958, Va. Half Pay. See N.A. Acc. No. 874-050138 Half Pay, Thomas Quirk
QUONT, Frederick, N.Y., S23856
QUY, Lebb, Ct., BLWt.6355. Iss. 12/3/1789. No papers
Libbeus, Ct., S36249

R

RABENSTINE, Dewalt, Pa., S4040
RABER, John, See REBER
RABOLDT, Jacob, See RAYBOLD
RACE, Andrew, Va., S43888
Andrew A., N.Y., R8555
Benjamin, N.Y., S15202
Jonathan W., N.Y., S29399
Phillip, N.Y., S5970
RACINE, Charles, Cont., Canada, Josette/Josephte Migneault, former wid., R7162
Charles, Hazen's Regt., BLWt. 13654. Iss. 10/12/1790. No papers
Pierre, Hazen's Regt., BLWt.13667 iss. 2/20/1792 to Benj. Moore, ass.
RACKET, Noah, N.Y., S14254
RACKLEY, Jeremiah, N.C., S14249
Micajah, N.C., Mary, W26396; BLWt.19620-160-55
Person, N.C., Margaret, R9062
RACKLIFF, Joseph Chandler, Mass., S37321
RADABACH, John Nicholas, Pa., R8556
Peter, Pa. See RADUBACH
RADCLIFF, Philip, Va., S46656
William, Va., S9049
RADCLIFFE, Minus, Del., S31319
RADEMACKER, John, Crane's Cont. Art., Mass., BLWt.4964. Iss. 11/15/1791. No papers
RADER, Conrad, Va., S5973
Henry, Va., S5972
Michael/Michal, Va., S7349
RADFORD, Benjamin, Cont., Mass., S37324
James, Va., Hannah Franklin, former wid., W25605; BLWt.61317-160-55
John, Mass., Sarah, W16383; BLWt. 4949-100. Iss. 12/28/1791 to Abel Wyman, ass. Certified 11/5/1818. No papers
RADIN, Timothy, See RIDIN
RADLEY, Jacob, N.Y., Lucretia Riggs former wid., W26381; BLWt.5081-60-55
William, N.J., BLWt.8683. Iss. 9/12/1789 to Daniel Thompson, ass. No papers
William, N.J. See WRADLEY
RADLOFF, John F., Navy, Mass. res. & agcy., Sarah, W3599
RADUBACH, Peter, Pa., Catharine, R9063; BLWt.2035-100. Name also appears as RADABACH, RODEBAUGH, & EDERBAUGH
RAFFSNYDER, Joseph, N.J., S43904
RAGAINS, Thomas, N.C., Elizabeth, W4502
RAGAN, Bartholomew, Cont., Va., S39032
Daniel, See REAGAN
Jesse, N.C., R8558
Michael, See REAGAN
Owen, N.C., S1585
Richard, Va., Cecelia, R8557
RAGER, Leonard, Va., S40315

RAGIN, Bartholomew, See RAGAN
Thomas, See RAGIN
RAGLAND, Dudley, Va., Margaret S., W5662
Evan, Va. res. 1808, Dis.-- No papers
Finch, Va., S7344
John, Va., S5974
John, Va., S35603
RAGSDALE, Baxter, N.C., Va., S4753
Benjamin, N.C., Martha/Patsey, W1079
Drury, Harrison's Regt. of Art., BLWt.1854-300-Capt. Iss. 8/24/1789. No papers
Godfrey, Cont., Va., Sea Service, Elizabeth, W2966; BLWt.19704-160-55
RAGUE, John, Pa., Hannah, W3600; BLWt.1829-300. Surgeon's Mate. Iss. 9/29/1790 to John Hale, ass. No papers
RAHN, Jonathan, Ga., S32465
Philip, Pa., S4750
RAIDINGAR, Samuel, See REIDINGER
RAIFORD, Robert, N.C., BLWt. 2283-300
RAIMORE, John, Mass. See RAMER
RAINBOULT, Adam, N.C., S32466
RAINE, Nathaniel, Va., S35609
RAINES, Anthony, N.C. See RAINS
John, N.C. See RAINS
Lawrence, See RAYNES
Presley, Va., R8560
Richard, Va. See RAINS
RAINEY, Isaac, N.C., S4545
James, N.C., S35599
John, S.C., S4035
Nathaniel, Va. See RANEY
Stephen, Ct., Esther, W3040; BLWts.1374-450 & 9057-160-55
Williamson, Va., R8563
RAINS, Anthony, N.C., b. Va., Nancy, W1481
Henry, Va., S31317
James, Va., S35600
John, N.C., Letitia, W982
John, Va., S5969
John, Va., Margaret, W4058
John, Va. Nancy, W5659; BLWt. 9548-160-55
Richard, Va., R8562
William, Va., Jane, W4314; BLWt. 34854-160-55
William, Va., Nancy/Anna, R8561
RAINSBURG, John, Md., S7351
RAISSOR, John, See REIZER
RAKE, Henry, Hazen's Regt., BLWt. 13675. Iss. 2/21/1793. No papers
RAKESTRAW, John, Va., Rhoda, R8565
RALEIGH, William, Va., S39030; BLWt.413-100
RALEY, Charles, S.C., Sarah, W5660 BLWt.31337-160-55
RALIEGH, William, See RALEIGH
RALJA, John, N.Y., BLWt.7700. Iss. 8/21/1790 to Abel Belknap, ass. No papers
RALL, Mathew, See Matthias
Matthias/Mathew, S40309; BLWt. 1164-100 (lost) & 1717-100

RALL (continued)
Thomas, S.C., Barbara, R8566; BLWt.82003-160-55
RALLS, John, See ROLLS
Kenaz, Va., S18561
RALPH, Charles, Mass., BLWt.4934. Iss. 8/24/1790 to Benj. Ives Gilman, ass., to Lucy Ralph, legal repr. of Charles Ralph
Jonathan, Cont., Ct., S36251
Thomas, N.C., S38323
Thomas, See RELPH
RALSTON, Andrew, Pa., BLWt.10255. Iss. 7/9/1789. No papers
Andrew, Pa., S40310
John, Cont., N.Y., R8568
John, Pa., Margaret, W3720
John, Va., S31321
RALYA, David, N.Y., S7353
RALYE, John, N.Y., S43899
RAMAGE, John, Pa., S23860
RAMAIR, Philip/Philip B. or Barnet. See REMAIR
RAMBLE, Samuel, Md., BLWt.11637 & 12516. Iss. 1/30/1795 to John Stockdell, ass. No papers
Samuel, Va., S40311
RAMER, Frederick, See RAYMER
Henry, Pa., Mary, W9615
John, Mass., S43894
Philip, Pa. See REMAIR
RAMEY, Archibald, Va., R8569
James, Va. See RAMY
John, Va. See REMAY
Lawrence, Pa., Anna, W4777
RAMIER, Mathias, Armand's Corps, BLWt.13641. Iss. 6/11/1793 to Casper Iserloan, ass. No papers
RAMLEY, Samuel, See RAMBLE
RAMPSON, Garret, See REMSEN
RAMSAY, Daniel, N.C., S4752
David, See RAMSEY
Francis, Va., Lee's Legion, BLWt. 12496 & 13979. Iss. 6/20/1798 to Samuel B. Shapard, ass. No papers
Henry, Md., BLWt.11629. Iss. 5/11/ 1790. No papers
James, Md., Pa., S35038
James, N.H. See RAMSEY
John, Ga., Dis.-- No papers. See Am. State Papers, Class 9, p.169 Wounded in his left thigh & left arm by a broadsword, 7/6/1781 near Long Pane Mills
John, N.Y., Margaret, W26346
John, N.C. See RAMSEY
Joseph, Va. See RAMSEY
Joseph H., Hospital Dept., BLWt. 1873-300-Surgn's. Mate. Iss. 12/31/1796. No papers
Josiah, Va., S17036
Nathaniel, Md., BLWt.1836-500-Col. Iss. 2/11/1791. No papers
Samuel, Ga. See RAMSEY
Thomas, S.C. See RAMSEY
RAMSBOTTOM, Priscilla J., former wid. of Robert Jordan, Mass., which see
RAMSDALE, John, See RAMSDILL
Moses, Mass., Nancy, W26945
RAMSDEL, John, Mass., S4758
RAMSDELL, Amos, Mass., Sarah, W22032
Aquilla, Mass. See RAMSDILL
Ebenezer, Mass., Sea Service, S31322
Ezra, Ct., S35595
Harthan, Cont., Mass., Catharine, W17507
Isaac, Mass., N.H. pension, Abigail Withington, former wid., W17515
James, Cont., Mass., S43898; BLWt.626-100
James, Mass., Juda Robinson, former wid., W24795
Joseph, Mass., Lydia, W13844
Lot, Mass., S33530
Silas, Mass., S33529
RAMSDILL, Aquila, Mass., Lydia, W2247; BLWt.21822-160-55
John, Mass., S45450
Nehemiah, Mass., S18560
Samuel, Mass., S33537
RAMSEN, Luke, See REMSEN
RAMSER, Christopher, N.Y., Deborah R8575
RAMSEY, Alexander, Pa., BLWt.1333-200
Allen, Pa., S32467
Andrew, N.C., b. Pa., S4037
Catharine, former wid. of John Leeper, Pa., which see
Daniel, N.C. See RAMSAY
David, N.C., Margaret, W17511
David, Pa., S40318
Francis, Va., Martha, W8542
Harriet, former wid. of Cornelius Henion, N.J., which see
James, Cont., Va., S46506; BLWt. 1503-100
James, Cont., Va., Frances Ann, W8541; BLWt.1503-100. Iss. 4/28/ 1829. No papers
James, N.H., S45095
James, S.C., R8570
Joel, N.C., S39031
John, N.C., Elizabeth, W42
John, S.C., S31318
Joseph, N.J., S4755
Joseph, Va., S7348, Va. Half Pay
Josiah, Va. See RAMSAY
Nathan, N.Y., BLWt.7716. Iss. 1/ 25/1791 to John Chandler, ass. No papers
Robert, N.C., S4036
Samuel, Ga., S21437
Samuel, N.H., R8571
Samuel, Pa., S31920
Shubridge, Cont., R.I., Marcey, W12829
Thomas, N.H., S15609
Thomas, S.C., b. Pa., S31922
Thomas, Va., S35604
Thomas, Va., R8572
William, N.C., S17035
William, Pa., S7354
RAMSON, Jacob, N.Y., BLWt.7683. Iss. 1/5/1791 to Elisha Millard, ass. No papers
RAMY, James, Va., S31316
RAND, Artemas, Mass., Louisa,W18790
RAND (continued)
Benjamin, Mass., Mary, BLWt. 56855-160-55
Israel, N.H., S14246
James, Mass., S37323
Jasper, Mass., S19752
John/Jack, Mass., S41092
John, N.H., S37322
Lazarus, Mass., Elizabeth, R8576
Michael, Mass., S36870
Reuben, N.H., S36868
Thomas, N.H., S18172
Thomas, N.H., Nabby, W22021
Thomas J., N.H., S22454
Walter, Va., Mary, W4773
William, N.H., Mary, R8577
Zachariah, Mass., Jerusha, W26361
RANDAL, Amos, Ct., Jemima, W24725
David, N.J., Sarah, W5668
John, N.H., R8580
Jonas, Ct., R.I., S11279
Nathaniel, N.H., S43886
Reuben, Cont., Ct., S35608
Samuel, N.H., See RANDEL
Stephen, R.I., Lucina, W24722
RANDALL, Abraham, Mass., S14248
Avery, Mass., Hope, W18791
Benager, N.C., S32469
Benjamin, Mass., BLWt.613-100
Charles, Ct., S4754
Daniel, N.H., Rachel, W22033
Edward, N.H., Sarah, W22034; BLWt.773-100
Elijah, Ct., Judith, W24727
Elijah, Mass., S30668
Elisha, Mass., Navy, S11276
George, S.C., Phoeby, W22031; BLWt.26260-160-55
Gershom/Gersham, Mass., S29401
Henry, R.I., Mary, W22030
Jack, R.I., S35593
Jacob, Mass., S43895
Jacob, Va., Amelia, W5666
James, Cont., Mass., Mary, W24720
James, Md., Elizabeth, W26354
Jedediah, Ct., Martha, W20010
Jeremiah, Lamb's Art., N.Y., BLWt.7719. Iss. 8/25/1790 to Samuel Stringer, ass. No papers
Jethro, Mass., S33538
Job, Mass. See RANDELL
Job, R.I., Sarah, W22037
John, Ct., N.Y., S14245
John, Md., Deborah, W26359
John, Mass., BLWt.4904. Iss. 8/ 10/1789 to Richard Platt. No papers
John, Mass., S33539
John, Mass., S43887
John, N.H., Abigail, W16063
John, N.H., R8581
John, N.C., Pa., or Va., R21892
John, R.I., S21933
John, R.I., Mary, W24717
John, S.C., S18137
Jonathan, N.H., Eleanor, W18788
Joseph, Ct., Cont., Vt., S22453
Joseph, Cont.,Can., Judith, W24719
Joseph, Green Mt. Boys, Vt., S45093
Joseph, N.Y., S16234
Joshua, Mass., S41090

RANDALL (continued)
Joshua, N.Y., R.I., Selah, W27999
Mark, Mass., N.H., Lydia, W16386
Nathaniel, Mass., Navy, Abigail York, former wid., W22711
Nathaniel, N.H., BLWt.3439. Iss. 8/26/1790 to M. Cutler, ass. No papers
Oliver, Mass., War of 1812, See RANDELL
Robert, R.I., Va., Sea Service, S45165
Ruth, former wid. of John Clark, Cont., N.Y., which see
Ruth, former wid. of Lemuel Fox N.Y., which see
Samuel, N.H. See RANDEL
Shubel, Ct. See RANDEL
Stephen, Mass. See RENDEL
Thomas, Md., BLWt.11667. Iss. 7/26/1797 to James DeBaufre, ass. No papers
Timothy, Ct., Eunice, W26350; BLWt.40697-160-55
Waterman, R.I., Marcy, W22041
Ziba, Mass., Amey, R8578
RANDE, Isham, N.C., Va., S31313
RANDEL, Gideon, N.H., R8586
Henry, See RANDOLPH
James, N.H., R8587
Samuel, Cont., N.H., Margaret, W22026; BLWt.10026-160-55
Samuel, N.H., Lucy, W9245; BLWt.31579-160-55
Shubel/Shubal, Ct., Sarah, W22035
RANDELL, Daniel, N.H. See RANDALL
George, N.H., Elizabeth, R8579
Edward, N.H. See RANDALL
Job, Mass., S31320
John, R.I. See RANDALL
Joseph, N.Y. See RANDALL
Oliver, Mass., War of 1812, S19439; Old War Inv. File 5967; BLWt.21760-160-War of 1812
Ziba, Mass. See RANDALL
RANDLE, Isham, See RANDE
Richard, N.C., Va., S32464
RANDLEMAN, Martin, See RUNDLEMAN
RANDLET, William, N.H., S21935
RANDOL, Joshua, Mass. See RANDALL
RANDOLPH, Abraham, N.C., Lydia, W11108
Barzillai F., N.J., Mary F., W2571; BLWt.26861-160-55
Beverly, Va., Martha, W4774
Daniel F., N.J., S904
David Meade, Cont., Va., S36252
Denis/Dennis, N.J., S23381
Henry, Cont., Va., S4038
Henry, Pa., Nancy, W9617
Hugh, S.C., S14252
Ichabod, Pa., R8588
Malichi/Malachi, N.J., Elizabeth, W8544
Matthias, N.Y., S43885
Stelle F., N.J., Hannah F.,W5665
Thomas, Va., S40316
Thomas F., N.J., R8589
Zedekiah F., N.J., Sarah, W16385
RANEY, James, See RAMY
John, N.C., S32462

RANEY (continued)
Nathaniel, Va., S11277
Stephen, Ct. See RANNEY
RANGE, James, Va., Barbara, W310
RANGER, Joseph, Va. Sea Service, S7352
Samuel, Mass., S41091
RANKHORN, Joseph, Navy, N.C., S1712
RANKIN, Andrew, Cont., Navy, Me. res. in 1818, S36869
Daniel, Mass., Sally, W4775; BLWt. 3960-160-55
Daniel, N.Y., S43897
Henry, Pa., S40308
Hugh, Pa., S35605
James, Cont., Mass., Sarah, W22029
James, Del., R8591
James, N.J., Rebecca, W3867
James, N.Y., BLWt.7696. Iss. 8/24/1790 to Cath. Bleeker, et al, Admr. No papers
James, Va., Martha, W4568
John, Pa., S5965
Richard, wid.'s res. Tenn., Jane, R8592
Robert, N.C., S4042
Robert, N.C., Mary, W5664
Robert, Va. See RANKINS
Thomas, N.H., BLWt.3442. Iss. 4/5/1796 to Samuel Stone, ass.
Thomas, N.Y., BLWt.7695. Iss. 7/30/1790 to Edward Compton, ass. No papers
Thomas, N.Y., Catharine, W20012
William, Cont., Va., S31315
William, N.C., S7342
William, Pa., Va., Sarah, W1081
William, Va., S40313
William, Va., Mary, W8543
RANKINS, Daniel, Md., Eleanor Washburn, former wid., W9877
James, N.J., BLWt.8686. Iss. 7/14/1796. No papers
James, N.Y., S14255
John, Cont., Mass., Patience Grant, former wid., W25660; BLWts. 804-100 & 180-60-55
Joseph, Mass., Mehitable, W22022
Robert, Mass., Abigail, W26358
Robert, Va., Peggy, W26365; BLWt.1380-200
RANLET, Jonathan, N.H., S45135
RANN, Solomon, Ct., BLWts.6365 & 5457. Iss. 4/16/1792. No papers
RANNEY, Amos, Ct., Sea Service
George, Ct., Lucy, W16384; BLWt.6377-100. Iss. 7/14/1789
Seth, Ct., N.Y., S11278
Solomon, Ct., S43903
Stephen, Ct., BLWt.6360. Iss. 10/7/1789 to Benj. Tallmadge, ass. No papers
Stephen, Ct., Elizabeth, W22036; BLWt.1518-100
William, Ct., R8593
William, Ct., Cont., S15607
RANNY, David, Ct., Dis.--. No papers. See Am. State Papers, Class 9, p.116. Disability-

RANNY (continued)
Crippled in the left knee by a score occasioned by a fever.
George, Ct. See RANNEY
RANO, John, N.H., BLWt.3433. Iss. 12/?/1796 to H. Olds, ass. No papers
RANSALL, Valentine, Pa., Mary, R8706
RANSDELL, Saul, Mass., BLWt.4946. Iss. 2/7/1799 to John Duncan. No papers.
Thomas, Va., BLWt.1852-300-Capt. Iss. 1/17/1800 to Chilton Ransdell, Grdn. to John & Marcia Ransdell, heirs of T.R. No papers
RANSDILL, John, Mass. See RAMSDILL
RANSFORD, Joseph, Cont., Mass., Navy, Rachel, W10232
RANSIER, George, N.Y., S28849
John, N.Y., BLWt.7689. Iss. 7/22/1789 to Thomas Tillotson, ass. No papers
John, N.Y., S43884
RANSOM, Abner, Ct. Sea Service, Cont. Ct., R8596
Amos, Ct., S15608
Asahel, Ct., S14244
David, Ct., S35597
David, Ct., Mass., Anna/Anne, W20013
Elijah, Ct., S35594; BLWt.1798-200-Lt. Iss. 2/23/1799. No papers
Elisha, Mass., S14247
Ezekiel, Ct., Mass., Lucinda, W5663
George P., Ct., BLWt.6366. Iss. 7/8/1790. No papers
George Palmer, Ct., Elizabeth, W2694
Hazel/Hazael, Mass., R8597
Israel, Ct., Lois, W9616; BLWt.80031-160-55
James, Ct., S15610
Job, Mass., Polly, W26349; BLWt.58686-160-55
Joseph, Ct., Azubah Blish, former wid., W25255; BLWt.47614-160-55
Joseph, Ct., Cont., S18559
Newton, Cont., Mass., Sarah, W16382
Richard, N.C., Kiziah, R8598
Samuel, Ct., alive 1808--?
Samuel, Ct., killed in service 7/3/1778, BLWt.408-300
RANSON, Henry, N.C., S23382
RANSONE, Thomas, Va., Margaret, R17293, Va. Half Pay
RANSTEAD, James, Mass., Jane, W26352; BLWt.57784-160-55
RAPE, Gustavus, S.C., Barbara, W1318; BLWt.28560-160-55
RAPER, Robert, N.C., Nancy, W4569
RAPOLE, George, N.Y., Margaret, W1651; BLWt.14752-160-55
RAPP, George, N.Y., S43883
George, N.Y., Christina. W22039
RARICK, Godfrey, Pa., Catharine,

RARICK (continued)
W3455
RARITY, John, N.J., BLWt.8685. Iss. 2/1/1790. No papers
RARZOR, Paul, Va. See RAZOR
RASAR, Elisha, Ct. See RAZAR
RASBACH, Frederick, See RASBERG
RASBERG, Frederick, N.Y., S27349
RASEY, Joseph, See RAZEY
RASH, Jacob, Sheldon's Dragoons, Ct., BLWt.6409. Iss. 7/22/1789. No papers
Jacob, Ct., Cont., Chloe, W5667
RASIN, William, Md. BLWt.1844-200-Lt. Iss. 10/4/1800. No papers
RASNER, John, Va., S35607; BLWt. 12489-100. Iss. 12/2/1793. No papers
RASOR, Christian, Va., b. N.J., R8599
Jacob, See REESER
Peter, Va., Frances, R8600
RASSLER, Godfrey John, Von Heer's Corps., BLWt.13646. Iss. 9/23/1791. No papers
RATCHFORD, Joseph, S.C., Hannah, W3866
RATCLIFF, James, Cont., Pa.,S35041
John, S.C., R8602
RATCLIFFE, Harper, Va., S31312
RATHBON, Asa, Ct., BLWt.6402. Iss. 1/13/1792. No papers
RATHBONE, Benjamin, Ct., S19438
Edmund, Mass., R.I. See RATHBURN
Jonathan C., Mass. Sea Service, Privateer, R8603
Moses, Ct., Olive, W22040
Tibbits, R.I., Rebecca, W17516
RATHBUN, Ebenezer, R.I., Mary, R8606
Ezra, Ct., S40314
James, R.I. See RATHBURN
Jonathan, Ct., Hannah, W11103; BLWt.8003-160-55
Joseph, Mass. See RATHBURN
Josiah, Mass., Catharine, R8604
Nathan, R.I., Sarah, W2246; BLWt.28578-160-55
Paris, R.I., Elizabeth Phillips, former wid., W24897
Roger, R.I., S39830
Solomon, N.H., Vt., S43900; BLWt.1445-100
Thomas, Ct., Elizabeth, W3115
RATHBURN, Asa, Ct., Ruth, W17508
Edmund, Mass., R.I., Margaret, W26345; BLWt.9494-160-55
James, R.I., S15201
Joseph, Mass., S4047
Solomon, N.H., BLWt.3434. Iss. 6/1/1793 to Stephen Thorne, ass. No papers
Solomon, N.H. See RATHBUN
RATHFON, Jacob, Pa., Elizabeth, W3456
RATLIFF, Nathan, Va., S17034
Reuben, Va., S31311
RATNOUR, George, N.Y., Elizabeth, W11100
RATTENAUER, Jacob, N.Y., S25377
RATTENHOUR, Jacob, See RATTENAUER
RATTI, Charles, Hazen's Regt., BLWt.13665. Iss. 1/22/1790 to Benj. Mooers, ass. No papers
RATTON, Thomas, Pa., S16232
RAVENS, James, Mass., S33535
RAVENSCRAFT, Francis, Va., S38325
Thomas, Va., War of 1812, S1248 & Va. Half Pay. See N.A. Acc. 874-050139 Half Pay Thomas Ravenscroft
RAVIN, James, Mass., BLWt.4917. Iss. 1/26/1790 to John May. No papers
RAWDON, Daniel, Md. Art., BLWt. 11665. Iss. 6/11/1790. No papers
Ezra, Ct., Sarah, W4772
RAWLAND, Henry, See ROWLAND
Samuel, See ROWLAND
RAWLEIGH, Hannah, former wid. of John Wormwood/Wormouth, which see
William, Va. See RALEIGH
RAWLES, John, See ROLLS
RAWLETT, William, See ROWLETT
RAWLEY, Hannah, N.Y. See John WORMWOOD
RAWLINGS, Aaron, Md., BLWt.11626 Iss. 3/11/1791. No papers
Anthony N. See ROLLINS
Eliphalet, N.H., Elizabeth, W26944
Isaac, Md., BLWt.1130-200
John, N.H., S45117
Joseph, Mass., S36867
Moses, See ROLLINS
Nathan, Capt., Pa. Agcy., S4041
Nathaniel, See ROLINGS
Robert, See ROLLINS
Simeon, N.H., S14242
William, Md., BLWt.2429-100
RAWLINGSON, David, S.C., BLWts. 12525 & 13644. Iss. 7/13/1795. No papers
RAWLINS, Francis, N.H., Dorothy, W22025
Nathaniel, See ROLLINS
Richard, S.C., S21934
Solomon, Md., S35039
William, Md. See RAWLINGS
William, Va., S1713
RAWLS, Aaron, Ct., Hannah, R8608
John, See ROLLS
William, S.C., S47905
RAWSEY, James, Cont., res. of son, Va. in 1829; BLWt.1473-100
RAWSON, Abner, Mass., S35037
Bailey, Cont., Mass., Susannah, W22038; BLWt.11089-160-55
Elijah, Mass., S43901
Enoch, Va., Jane, W578
Jonathan, Mass., Esther, W16689
Joseph, Mass., S4757
Joseph, R.I., Elizabeth, W22024
Moses, Mass., S33532
Samuel, Mass., Molly, W15227
Seth, Mass., S33534
Silas, Mass., S14241
Simeon, Cont., Mass., Anna, W20011
RAWSON (continued)
Timothy, Mass., S23859
Wilson, Mass., S4751
RAXFORD, Denison, See REXFORD
Joseph, See RIXFORD
RAY, Andrea, See REY
Andrew, Va., Henrietta, R8611
Benjamin, Cont., Mass., S29397
Benjamin, Md., R8609
Benjamin, Mass., S33536
Benjamin, N.C., Nancy, W26355; BLWt.79035-160-55
Benjamin, Va., Frances, W5657; BLWt.26263-160-55
Caleb, Ct., Cont., S15604
Caleb, Lamb's Art., N.Y., BLWt. 7717. Iss. 9/24/179? No papers
Daniel, Ct., S43891
David, Mass., Eunice, W26357
Ebenezer, Mass., S29402
Francis, N.C., S7350
Frederick, Va., Nancy, W5655; BLWt.38580-160-55
George, Del., R8610
Gershom, R.I., Sally, W26347; BLWt.10240-160-55
Gideon, Ct., Zipporah, W17514
Gilbert, Mass., Rachel, W26353
Isaac, See WRAY
James, N.H., Mehitable, W16062; BLWt.9181-160-55
James, N.J., BLWts.8628, 8667 & 8682. Iss. 3/20/1790 to Jonas Stansbury. No papers
James, N.J., S33531
James, N.Y., BLWt.7697. Iss. 9/28/1790 to Bartholomew & Fisher, assnes. No papers
James, Va. See WRAY
James, Va., S31314
Jesse, N.C., S7345
John, Ga., Mary, R8613
John, Md., Margaret, R8612
John, N.Y., Ester/Esther, W4778; BLWt.6440-160-55
John, N.C., Agness/Nancy Freeland, former wid., W3977
John McCush Robert, Pa., S40990
John P., Ct., S31921
Jonathan, Md., S16513
Joseph, Md., S35040
Joseph, Mass., BLWt.4894. Iss. 12/16/1791. No papers
Joseph, Moses Hazen's Regt., BLWt. 13666-100. Iss. 10/12/1790. No papers
Joseph, N.C., Lydia, W5656
Reuben, Mass., Sarah, W1078
Robert, Mass., S30052
Roswell, N.Y., Leah, W18792
Samuel, N.C., Sarah, R8615
Silas, N.H., S43889; BLWt.1559-100
Thomas, N.C., Elizabeth, W9614
Thomas, R.I., Sarah, W13843
Timothy, Ct., S14250
Warwick, Ct., S35602
William, Mass., R8617; BLWt. 9050-160-55
William, N.C., R8616
William, N.C., b. Pa., S7347
William, Pa., S32470

RAY (continued)
William, Privateer, Mass., Rachel R8614
William, Va., Patty, W5658; BLWt.6446-160-55
Zacheus, N.Y., S21438
RAYBOLD, Jacob, German Regt., commanded by Col. Weltner, BLWt.1845-200-Lt. Iss. 7/9/1789. No papers. (Heitman's Hist. Reg. spells this name RABOLDT)
RAYBURN, George, Va., S38324
Robert, Va., S32463
RAYL, Samuel, N.C., S4034
RAYMER, Frederick, N.Y., Nancy, W17509
Phillip/Philip, Pa., S40312
RAYMON, Isaac, Cont., Pa., S43893
RAYMOND, Aaron, Ct., BLWt.6387. Iss. 6/3/1789. No papers
Abner, Mass., S33533
Amos, Mass., S14243
Benjamin, Mass., BLWt.4952. Iss. 1/26/1790 to John May. No papers
Benjamin, Mass., Betsey/Betty, W15230
Caleb, Mass., Deborah, W22028
Daniel, Ct., Cont., S35601
Daniel, Mass., S30051
Daniel, N.Y., Lucy, R8619
David, Ct., S17037
David, Ct., S35606
Ebur, Ct., S36250
Edward, Mass., S29403
Elisha, R.I., Abigail, W26362
Enoch, N.Y., Susannah, W17510; BLWt.26336-160-55
George, Ct., Navy, Ann, W11111
Isaac, See REYMOND
James, Ct., S35598
James, N.J., BLWt.8692. Iss. 6/3/1799 to Mahlon Dickerson. No papers
James, N.J., S33528
James, N.Y., S23380
John, Cont., Mass., S43896
John, Mass., BLWt.4895. Iss. 8/22/1793 to Samuel Emery. No papers
John, Mass., Priscilla, W15228; BLWt.11425-160-55
John, Mass., Esther/Ester, R8618
Joseph, Mass., Dolly, W24723
Joshua, Ct., Elizabeth, W17512
Lemuel, Ct., BLWt.6408. Iss. 1/25/1796. No papers
Lemuel, Ct., S43890
Lemuel, Mass., Jeddah, W22027; BLWt.31576-160-55
Lemuel, Mass., Abigail Fogg, former wid., W23057
Miriam, former wid. of Benjamin Dimmick/Dimock, which see
Moses, Ct., S20928
Naphtali, Ct., S21436
Nathan, Mass., S29398
Nathaniel, Ct., Dinah, W26356; BLWt.36628-160-55
Nathaniel Lynde, Ct., Navy, Privateer, Louisa, W26351

RAYMOND (continued)
Newcomb, Ct., Lorinda, W26360; BLWt.19804-160-55
Paul, Mass., R8621
Phinehas, Mass., R21673
Rufus, Cont., Mass., Sarah/Serviah, R15231
Samuel, Cont., Mass., S33527
Samuel, Cont., Mass., Elizabeth, W24718
Sands, N.Y., Esther, W11101
Stephen, Ct., Mary, W17513
Stephen, Mass., Ruth, W13840
Sylvanus, Mass., Silence Hatch, former wid., W19724
William, Ct., S35596
William, Cont., Mass., S37320
William, Mass., Sophia, W15229
Zacheus, Ct., Sarah, W3719
Zadok/Zadock, Ct., S16233
Zuriel, Mass., BLWt.4908. Iss. 1/25/1796 to Zuriel Raymond. No papers
Zuriel, Mass., S43902
RAYNER, Amos, N.C., S7355
William, N.Y., 1790 & 1793, R8622
RAYNES, John, Navy, N.H. res. & agcy. in 1818, S45094
Lawrence, Va., Mary, R8623
RAYNOLDS, Benjamin, ---, R8624
John, Md. See REYNOLDS
RAYNOR, William, N.Y. See RAYNER
RAYNSFORD, Joseph, Ct., S40317
RAZAR, Elisha, Ct., Privateer, R8625
RAZEE, Joseph, R.I., Mary Reynolds, former wid., W26368
RAZEY, Joseph, N.H., Letitia, W9243; BLWt.26235-160-55
Pelatiah, N.H., S43892
RAZOR, Paul, Va., Mary E.,R8626
REA, Andrew, See RAY
Benjamin, Mass., S20540
David, N.C., b. Del., S7382
Henry, S.C., Mary, W9246
James, N.H. See RAY
Joshua, Mass., Mary, W15239
Pierce Rogers, Mass., S4763
Robert, N.C., b. Pa., S32474
REAB, George, Mass., S29405; BLWt. 1785-200-Lt. Iss. 4/13/1790. No papers
READ, Abijah, Mass., Susannah, W18794; BLWt.13877-160-55
Abram, Va., S7364 (colored)
Allen, Va. See READE
Ameriah/Amariah, Va., R8627
Amos, Ct., S14261
Amos, Va., R8628
Andrew, Va. See REED
Archibald, Pa., BLWt.1090-200
Bailey, Ct., S23865
Benjamin, Mass., S4055
Benjamin, N.C. See REED
Charles, Pa., BLWt.10300. Iss. 4/13/179? No papers
Clement, Va., R17319. Same no. used for Edmund Read. Va. Half Pay
Daniel, Mass., S17646
Daniel, Mass., 4th U.S. Inf.

READ (continued)
1815, S22461; BLWt.7143-160-12. Old War Inv. File No. 19446
David, Cont., Mass., S45099
David, Mass., R8629
David, N.J., S23867
Ebenezer, Mass. Lydia, See REED
Edmund, Va., S18564
Edmund/Edmond, Va., Paulina Le Grand, former wid., W8084
Edmund, Va., R17319, Va. Half Pay. He also claimed on acct. of services of Col. Clement Read
Eleazer, Mass., Elizabeth, W15237
Elijah, Vt., Elizabeth, W5675; BLWt.26137-160-55
Elisha, Ct., S11286
Elizabeth, former wid. of Seth Martin, N.H., which see
Elnathan, Mass. See REED
Ephraim, Mass., S30672
Ezra, Cont., Mass. See REED
Ezra, Mass. See REED
Frederick, N.H., N.Y., Lavinia, R8665
George, Mass., S19049
George, Mass., S29408
George, Mass., Elizabeth, See REED
Henry, Cont., Va., Betsey, W5679; BLWt.169-100
Isaac, Cont., Navy, R.I., Diodama/Diodamia, W11112
Isaac, Mass., S33547
Jacob, Cont., Mass., Nancy/Anna, W2000; BLWt.26882-160-55
James, See case of Rebecca Read former wid. of Valentine Standley
James, N.J., S23861
James, N.C., Elizabeth, See REED
James, N.C., BLWt.1865-300-Capt. Iss. 11/11/1791. No papers
Jesse, Mass., S43917
Jesse, N.C., BLWt.1864-300-Capt. Iss. 11/10/1796 to Henry Wiggin ass. No papers
Joel, Cont., Elizabeth, Pa. Agcy. & res., W5680
Joel, Mass., S21936
John (alias), Mass. See LOWELL
John, Mass., Mary, W18793; BLWt. 61197-160-55
John, N.C., S14267
John, S.C., See REED
John, Va., S15961
John, Va., S35617
John, Va., R17318, Va. Half Pay, Act of 7/5/1832
Jonathan, Cont., Mass., S41979
Joseph, Mass., S43906
Joshua, Mass. See REED
Levi, Mass., Nancy, R8630; BLWt. 46533-160-55
Noah, Mass. See REED
Robert, N.J. Line in Hazen's Regt. (so recorded) BLWts.8670 & 13660. Iss. 2/22/1799 to Jane Merrill (formerly Read) & Elizabeth Read survivors & heirs and sisters of Robert Read. No papers

READ (continued)
Samuel, Mass., S29407
Samuel, R.I., Anna/Anne, W20015
Thomas, Mass., Navy, R.I. See REED
Thomas, N.Y. See REID
Timothy, Mass., S23387
William, Cont., S.C., S4766; BLWt.1872-450-Surgeon & Physician. Iss. 2/25/1800. No papers
William, Mass., S30670
William, Mass., Ruth, BLWt.50892-160-55
William, Mass., N.H., Abigail, W22049
William, Pa., Susannah Warner, former wid., R11150
William, R.I., S14266
William, R.I., Rebecca, W24750
Zalmon, Ct., Hannah, W178; BLWt. 8458-160-55
READE, Allen, Va., Anne, W5681
Amos, Va. See READ
READEN, William, Va. See READING
William, Va., R8632. (See Wm. READING, S21439, same sold.) Act 1818
READER, Samuel, Pa., Sarah Reed, former wid., R8675
READING, George, Pa., Va., S17038
John, See John M.
John M., Pa., Mary, W579
Samuel,a Maj., Ctf. 270, Act of May 15, 1828. No papers
Samuel, N.J., BLWt.1813-400-Maj. Iss. 11/6/1789. No papers
William, Va., S21439. See Wm. READEN, R8632, same sold. (Act 1832)
William, Va. See READEN
READINGTON, Daniel, See REDINGTON
READY, Dennis, Va., S39040
James, N.Y., BLWt.7669. Iss. 7/27/1797 to Herman Vosbugh, ass. No papers
John Abraham, Pa., S22464
Shadrach, Va., S39035
REAGAN, Daniel, Va., Lydia, W5689
Darby, Ga., S7359
Larkin, N.C., S4058
Michael, Pa., S35614
Philip, Va., S22462
Thomas, S.C., Hannah, W9244
William, Pa., Mary, S1082
REAGAR, Larkin, N.C. See REAGAN
REAGER, Conrad, Pa., S14278
Michael, Cont. Pa. See REGER
REAGIN, Thomas, Pa.,S.C. See REAGAN
REAL, David, Va., S15611
REALE, Nathan, See RIALE
REAM, Adam, Pa., Catharine, W3158
Andrew, Pa., S4067
George, Pa. See REEM
Henry, Pa., S23863
Jacob, Pa., S4765
John Frederick, Pa., S22947
REAMER, David, Cont., Pa., Nancy, W9621
Philip, Pa. See REMAIR
REAMS, Jesse, Va., S4764
Joshua, N.C., S39037

REANY, Joseph, N.C., Mary, W11127; BLWt.40673-160-55
REAR, Martin, Mass. or Pa., R20427
REARDON, George, Va., R8634
James, Md., S7369
John, Va., S38330
John, Va. or Pa., S4064
REASONER, John, Va., BLWt.12489. Iss. 12/2/1793. No papers
REASONS, William, N.C., R8635
REASOR, Michael, Va., S16514
REAVES, Ashur, N.C., Va., S17649
Daniel, S.C. See REEVES
Frederick, N.C. See REEVES
Lazarus, S.C., R8636
Zachariah, N.C., S41973
REAVIS, Harris, N.C., S32472
John, N.C., S7380
REBER, Johannes/John, Pa., S2059
RECE, Allen, Pa., Mary, W5697; BLWt.26762-160-55
RECKART, Earnest A., Cont., (German). See RECKERT
RECKERT, Earnest August, Cont. (German), Mary Elizabeth, R8789
RECKEY, Andrew, N.Y. See RECKIE
RECKIE, Andrew, N.Y., Submit,W17522
RECKLESS, Anthony, Sappers & Miners BLWt.1818-200-Lt. Iss. 5/21/1796. No papers
RECKNER, Daniel, See RICKNER
RECORD, David, Mass., Abigail, W22044
Dominicus, Mass., Jane, W24747
Jonathan, Mass., Nabby, W11114; BLWt.9541-160-55
Nathan, Mass., Anne/Anna, W15702; BLWt.31581-160-55
Samuel, Mass., S23384
Simon, Mass., S29409
RECORDS, Owen, Navy, R.I., S41977
RECTOR, Benjamin, N.C., Nancy, W983 BLWt.26270-160-55
Charles, Va., Catharine, R8637
James, Va., R8638
Jesse, Va., R8639
Lewis, N.C., Frances, W45
Maximillian, Va., Mary Elizabeth, W2002
Nicholas, N.Y. See RICHTER
Uriah, Va., Winefred, W7135; BLWt.26761-160-55
REDD, John, Va., S18174
William, N.C., S7373
REDDEN, Christopher, N.J., S4059
REDDER, Nicholas, Va., Elizabeth, W3458
REDDICK, William, Pa., Margaret, W9620; BLWt.40674-160-55
REDDIN, Christopher. See REDDEN
REDDING, Henry, Md., BLWt.11652. Iss. 2/7/1790. No papers
John, N.H., Dis. --- No papers. See Am. State Papers, Class 9, p.136 Disability - Large putrified ulcers on both legs, occasioned by a cold caught while in a state of perspiration, 8/16/1777 at Bennington.
John, N.C., S41971
Wright, N.J., R8640
REDENOUR, Jacob, See RIDENOUR

REDFARN, James, N.C. res. & agcy. S14934
REDFERN, James, See REDFARN
REDFIELD, Ambrose, Ct., Cont., S45100
Constant, Ct., S17042
Levi, Ct., S14276
Martin, Ct., S17650
Nathan, Ct., S31923
Peleg, Ct., S9464
Roswell, Ct., S17647
Samuel, Ct., R8640 1/2
REDGWAY, Noah, Va. res., R8641
REDHAIR, Frederick, Proctor's Art., Pa., BLWt.10310. Iss. 6/20/1789. No papers
REDICK, John, Pa., Susan, R8642
REDIN, Timothy, See RIDIN
REDINGTON, Asa, N.H., S15962
Daniel, Mass., Anna, W9623
Hannah, former wid. of William Nickels, Mass., which see
Jacob, Mass., Eunice, W20014
John, Ct., Laura Miller, former wid., W10498; BLWt.100371-160-55
REDINHOUR, John, Va., S38329
REDLON, Ebenezer, Cont., Mass., Sarah, W22042; BLWt.27577-160-55
REDLOW, Ebenezer, Cont., Mass. See REDLON
REDMAN, Aaron, Va., Nancy, W9622
Elisha, Md., BLWt.11663. Iss. 3/22/1797 to Abijah Holbrook, ass. No papers
Henry, Va., Irena, W5690; BLWt. 34530-160-55
John, Art. Artificers of Pa., BLWt.13694. Iss. 1/12/1796. No papers
John, Pa., BLWt.10324. Iss. 3/4/1791 to Andrew Neilson, Admr. No papers
John, Va.,Pensioned N.Y., S43913
John, Va., Sarah, W5691
Michael, Pa., BLWt.2070-100
Richard, Va., S38327
Samuel, Va., R8643
Stephen, N.C., R8644
Vincent, Va., BLWt.254-400-Maj. Iss. 12/11/1797. No papers
William, S.C., R8645
REDMON, George, N.C., S.C., S32473
Stephen, N.C. See REDMAN
REDMOND, George, N.C. See REDMON
Michael, Md., BLWt.11669. Iss. 2/7/1790. No papers
REDOUT, William, See RIDEOUT
REDWAY, Comfort, Ct. Roxana, R8646
Joel, Ct., S30057
Preserved, Ct., Azubah, W18796
REECE, John, Pa., R8647
REED, Aaron, N.J., S743
Abijah, Mass. See READ
Abraham, Mass., S37328
Abraham, N.C., S4052
Amesiah, Mass., S17648
Amos, Ct. See READ
Amos, Mass., S14274
Amos, N.J., Gemima, R8657
Andrew, Mass., R8649
Andrew, Va., R8650
Artemas, Mass., S38326

REED (continued)
Benjamin, Ct., S35612
Benjamin, Ct., R8651
Benjamin, Mass. See READ
Benjamin, Mass., Huldah, W24731
Benjamin, Mass., BLWt.29-200
Benjamin, N.C., S41976
Charles, N.J., R8652
Daniel, Ct. res. in 1840,R8653
Daniel, Cont., N.Y., S43905
Daniel, Mass., Anna, BLWt.61170-160-55
David, Mass., S18563
David, Mass., Abigail, W22051
David, R.I., S30674
Diodama, former wid. of Benjamin Rowland, Ct., which see
Ebenezer, Ct., S14275
Ebenezer, Ct., Polly, W18795; BLWt.8185-160-55
Ebenezer, Mass., Sea Service, R.I., Lydia, W24730
Eli, Ct., Meliscent/Melison, W27235
Elihu, Mass., S33545
Elijah/Elijah J., Mass., Susanna, W18802; BLWt.19806-160-55
Elijah, Vt. See READ
Elizabeth, former wid. of Jacob Wilber, N.Y., which see
Elnathan, Mass., Thankful, W5669
Enoch, Ct., BLWt.1794-300-Capt. Iss. 5/29/1789. No papers
Ezra, Cont., Mass., S14265
Ezra, Mass., Hannah, W5677; BLWt. 40705-160-55
Frederic/Frederick, Del., S43911
Frederick, N.H. See READ
Frederick, N.C., R8689
Frederick, Pa., S22460
Garret/Garrett, N.J., N.Y., S14257
George, Md., S30669
George, Mass. See READ
George, Mass., Elizabeth, W15236
George, N.J., BLWt.8691. Iss. 2/10/1795. No papers
George, N.J., S40325
George, N.C., R8658
Giles/Jiles, N.J., S39033
Henry, N.J., S33543
Hezekiah, Mass., BLWt.4911. Iss. 5/14/1790. No papers
Hezekiah, Mass., S43918
Hinds, Cont., N.H., S41975
Howard, Mass., Charlotte, W18800
Isaac, Mass., S29406
Isaac, N.J., d. 7/31/1844, Rebecca W3868
Isaiah, N.J., BLWt.8679. Iss. 7/2/1789. No papers
Isaiah, N.J., Susan, W5678
Isaiah, N.C., S4053
Issachar, Mass., S22455
Ithel, Ct., S16235
Jacob, Cont., BLWt.1810-300. No papers
Jacob, Cont., Mass. See READ
Jacob, Mass., Sarah Holden, former wid., W23338
James, see case of Rebecca Reed, former wid. of Valentine Standley
James, Mass., Ruth, W15238

REED (continued)
James, N.H., S45098
James, N.H., S48869; BLWt.1789-850. Brig. Gen. Iss. 4/1/1790. Also recorded as above under BLWt.2540 & marked Patented in 1800 to Wm. Steel. No papers
James, N.J., S905
James, N.Y., Effa, W15849
James, N.C., Elizabeth, R8655
James, Pa., S16236
James, Pa., S22463
James, Pa., S40324
James, Pa., R8659
James, Va., Sybill/Sabrina, R8676
James R., Hazen's Regt., BLWt. 1874-400-Maj. Iss. 7/3/1789. No papers
Jesse, Mass., BLWt.4954. Iss. 12/23/1791. No papers
Job, Mass., Sally, W18797
Joel, Hazen's Regt., BLWt.13664 Iss. 10/12/1790 to Abel Baynton, ass. No papers
Joel, Mass., Keziah, W22048
John, 2nd. Regt. Art., BLWt.1811-200-Lt. Iss. 9/3/1790. No papers
John, Ct., R8663
John 2nd., Md., S35044
John, Md., Mariam, R8667; BLWt. 44842-160-55
John, Mass., S33544
John, Mass. See LOWELL
John, Mass., Mary, See READ
John, Mass., Rachel, W24744
John, Mass., R8661
John, Mass., N.H., Hannah, W17518
John, N.H., S20163
John, N.H., S43907
John, N.J., BLWt.8689. Iss. 4/20/1790 to Joseph Lyon, Sr., ass. No papers
John, N.J., Leah, W5670; BLWt. 1814-200-Lt. Iss. 4/21/1790. No papers
John, N.J., Ann, W5674
John, N.Y., S14271
John, N.Y. See RIED
John, N.Y., Rebecca, W24740
John, N.C., Sarah, R8674
John, Pa., S25391
John, Pa., R8660
John, Pa., Hayne's Indian War, Martha, R8668
John, S.C., Nancy, W193; BLWt. 34515-160-55
John, S.C., Mar. in Ireland, Elizabeth, R8656
John, Va., S11280
John J. or I., Sr., N.J., S741
John M., R.I., S21441
Jonathan, Cont., Mass., See READ
Jonathan, Mass., S37327
Joseph, Ct., S36253
Joseph, Mass. See READ
Joseph, N.J., S742
Joseph, N.C., Elizabeth, W1484
Joseph, Pa., S40328
Joseph, Pa., Margaret, W9618
Joseph, S.C. See REID
Joshua, Cont.,Mass., Anna, W24735

REED (continued)
Joshua, Mass., S45097
Joshua, Va., S32476
Josiah, Cont., Mass., Privateer, S17039
Josiah, Mass., S30671
Josiah, Mass., S43915
Justus, Ct., Lydia, W814; BLWt. 34847-160-55
Kitchel, Ct., S28851
Lemuel, Mass., S29410; BLWt.9407-160-55
Leonard, N.H., N.Y., S14269
Lovett, N.C., Sibbey, W5671
Lydia, former wid. of John Lothrop Mass., which see
Mary, former wid. of Barnabas McCoy, which see
Moses, N.H., S41978
Moses, N.Y., Permelia/Amelia, W22053
Nathan, Mass., S30056
Nathan, N.C., S31925
Nathan, Va. See RIED
Nathaniel, Mass., Eleanor, W18805
Noah, Mass., Mehitable, W24732
Obadiah, Mass., Elizabeth, W24743; BLWt.9413-160-55
Peter, Mass., Hannah, W20018
Philip, Md., BLWt.1840-300-Capt. Iss. 3/3/1791. No papers
Philip, Pa., S5975
Richard, Ct., S43908
Richard, N.C., Jane, W22054
Robert, N.C., S32471
Robert, N.C., Margaret, R8671
Ruth, former wid. of Daniel Hudson Mass., R.I., which see
Samuel, Ct., Privateer, S11285
Samuel, Cont., Mass., S33549
Samuel, Mass., S33546
Samuel, Mass., S33551
Samuel, Mass., S33553
Samuel, N.Y., S43910
Samuel, N.Y., Lucy, W3601; BLWt. 43512-160-55
Samuel, N.C., S7372
Samuel, Pa., BLWt.1824-200-Lt. Iss. 2/2/1791 to Thos. Reed, Admr. No papers
Samuel, R.I., Ann, See READ
Samuel, S.C., b. Pa., s. of George, S14259
Sarah, former wid. of John Pulling, Mass., which see
Sarah, former wid. of Samuel Reader Pa., which see
Silas, N.Y., Bethiah, W24737
Simeon, Mass., Elizabeth, BLWt. 88010-160-55
Simeon, N.Y., S22456
Solomon, Vt., Rhoda, W24749
Stephan/Stephen, Ct., S43916
Stephen, Mass., S15613
Supply, Mass., S17043
Tallcot, Ct., R8677
Thomas, Cont., Mass., Polly, R8670
Thomas, Mass., S41974; BLWt.71-100
Thomas, Mass., R8690
Thomas, Mass., Navy, R.I., Sarah, R8673
Thomas, N.J., BLWt.8699. Iss. 1/7/

REED (continued)
or 17/1792 to Wm. Lane, ass. No papers
Thomas, N.C., S14263
Thomas, Pa., S31926
Thomas, Vt., U.S.A. 1812, S23383; Old War Inv. file no. 5977; BLWt.7730-160-1812
Timothy, Mass. See READ
Uriah, Cont., Mass., S30673
Ward, Mass., S28850
William, Md., Mass. pension, S33548
William, Mass., Sea Service, S30055
William, N.J., BLWt.8666. Iss. 2/11/1791. No papers
William, N.C., Violett, W5673; BLWt.6271-160-55
William, Pa., BLWt.10272. Iss. 2/3/179? No papers
William, Pa., BLWt.10276. Iss. 6/20/1789. No papers
William, Pa., S4051
William, Pa., See REID
William, Pa., See READ
William, R.I., Rebecca, See READ
Zachariah, Ga., S35615; BLWt. 182-100
Zadock, Cont., N.H., S45096
Zadock, Mass., Lucy, S15235
Zadock, N.H., BLWt.3440. Iss. 3/25/1790. Ctf. of the issue transmitted to Clifton Claggett, M.C. 3/21/1818
REEDER, Andrew, N.J., Sarah, W4059
Benjamin, Md., R17331
Micajah, S.C., b. Va., R8678
Nicholas, See REDDER
William, N.J., S1091
REEDY, Michael, French, Pa., R8679
REEGER, Frederick, Cont., Pa., Margaret Mattox, former wid., W2223; BLWt.13446-160-55
Jacob, Pa., Ann Deborah/Anna Deborah, W5686
REEKIE, Andrew, N.Y. See RECKIE
REEL, John, N.C., Catharine, W9619
REEM, George, Pa., R8633
REEMER, David, See REAMER
REEP, Adam, N.C., Susanna, W4779
Michael, N.C. Agcy., S14280
REES, George, Pa., Rebecca, W5692 BLWt.19622-160-55
Griffith, Pa., S4070
John, Pa., Sea Service, Mary, R19428
Martin, N.Y., BLWt.7706. Iss. 8/20/1790 to James Lowry, ass. No papers
Roger, N.C., Rebecca, R8672
Thomas, N.C., res. of wid. in 1853, Mary, R22016
Thomas, Pa., S7377
REESE, David, Pa., BLWt.10254. Iss. 5/16/1791. No papers
George, N.C., Anna, W8548
Henry, Md., BLWt.11632. Iss. 1/8/1796 to Geo. Ponsonby, ass. No papers
Henry, Pa., Md. Mil. after Rev., Mary, W9247

REESE (continued)
Jacob, Md., R8648
John, Pa., Barbara Margaretta, R17339
John, Va., Lee's Legion, BLWt. 12494 & 13697. Iss. 6/20/1789. No papers
Martin, N.Y., Magdalina Kelly, former wid., W20318
Peter, Pa., S40326
REESER, Jacob, not Rev. War, St. Clair's Indian War, 1791, Pa. & Ky. Agcies. Old War Inv. File 25764
REESOR, Philip, Pa., S23864
REEVE, Elisha, N.Y., S17044
Israel, N.Y., S5978
James, N.Y., S49273
Phebe, former wid. of William Clark, N.Y., which see
William, N.Y., S43914
William, Va., S31924
REEVER, Nathaniel, See REEVES
REEVES, Daniel, Ct., N.Y., R8842
Daniel, S.C., Eleanor, W5687
David, N.J., S33541
Enos, Pa., BLWt.1823-200-Lt. Iss. 11/12/1796. No papers
Frederick, N.C., Elizabeth/Betty, W18801
John, N.C., S7381
John, N.C., Rachael, R8684; BLWt. 31698-160-55
John D., N.C., S7379
Joseph, N.J., S18565
Joshua, Cont., N.J., S4759
Joshua, N.J., S29404
Luther, Ct., BLWt.6388. No papers
Luther, Ct., Anna, W4570
Lydia, former wid. of Benoni Hunt, Mass., which see
Nathaniel, N.Y., Va., b. in N.J. S4760
Pomp (colored), R.I., Thankful Corlis/Colis, former wid. W12762
Puryer, Ct., N.Y., S28852
Richard, N.C., b. Va., Mary,W7133
Robert, Va., S33550
Samuel, N.C., Susannah, W56
Thomas, N.J., Ruth, R8685
William, Mass., Abigail, W1319
William, Va., S17645
REEWARK, James, Md., Susanna & Julia, contesting wids., R9032
REGAN, Charles, N.C., Milly, W5688
Daniel, Va. See REAGAN
Philip, Va. See REAGAN
William, Pa. See REAGAN
REGE, Michel, Pa. See Michael REIGEL
REGER, Michael, Cont., Pa., S23869
Philip, Va., S7383
REGIN, Thomas, Pa. See REAGAN
REGISTER, John, N.C., S7368
John, N.C., Edith, W4318
REHR, Joseph, See ROEHR
REICHART, Charles, Pa. See KIECHART
REICHENBACH, Adam, Pa., S5991
REICHSWICK, Conrad/Conred, Pa., S40323

REID, Alexander, Md., S7371
Alexander, Not Rev. War, Wayne's War, Lydia, BLWt.25358-160-55
Alexander, Va., S1246
Alexander, Va., S36872
Daniel, Mass., R8654
David, Pa., S1870
Ebenezer, Ct. See REED
Frederick, N.C. See REED
George, N.H., BLWt.1772-500-Col. Iss. 1/15/1800 to George Reid. No papers
George, Not Rev. War, Wayne's War, Jane, BLWt.100624-40-50; BLWt.6281-120-55
George, Pa., Ann, R8688
Henry, not Rev. War, Wayne's War, BLWt.22320-160-55
James, Pa., S22457
Joab, Va., S4057; BLWt.26008-160-55
John, N.J., Charity, W26391
John, N.Y., R8662
John, Pa. See ROADS
John, S.C. See REED
John, Va., S10254
John, Va., Keziah, W26946
Joseph, S.C., Isabella, W9249
Richard, N.J., Catharine, W118
Richard, N.C. See REED
Samuel, Mass. See REED
Thaddeus, Ct., Dis.--- No papers See Am. State Papers, Class 9, p.61. Disabled by violent pains & inflamation while in service starting 5/3/1792
Thomas, Cont., N.Y., Catharine, W4317; BLWt.1807-400-Surgeon. Iss. 12/15/1791. No papers
Thomas, N.C., S7366
Thomas, Vt. See REED
William, Pa., Mary, W5676
REIDINGER, Samuel, Pa., S32468
REIFENBERG, Henry, See RYFENBURGH
REIGAL, Michael, See REIGEL
REIGEL, Michael/Michel, Cont., enl. in Pa., S40322
REILAY, John, N.Y., S23386
REILEY, Bennet, Md., Frances, W4315; BLWt.2236-100
Christopher, Pa., S35618; BLWt. 1075-100
George, Va., R8691
James, Mass., BLWt.4905. Iss. 6/24/1793 to Samuel Emery. No papers
John, Pa., BLWt.10249. Iss. 2/14/179? to Alexander Power, ass. No papers
John, Pa. See RILEY
John, Pa., Va., S36871; BLWt. 993-100
John, Va., d. 1818/1819, Christiana, W18798
REILLY, Patrick, Md., BLWt.11649 Iss. 9/20/1799. No papers
Peter, Pa., Abigail Moore, former wid., W4747
REILY, Francis, Navy, Mass., S33552
James, Margaret Yeager, former wid. See her last husb., George Yeager

REILY (continued)
James, Cont., Pa., Va., See RIELY
John, Pa., S35610
John, Pa., BLWt.1820-300-Capt. Iss. 10/10/1789. No papers
John, Va., d. 6/8/1850, Nancy, W7137; BLWt.31575-160-55
William, Md., Barbara, W26377; BLWt.1839-300-Capt. Iss. 7/18/1789. No papers
REINECKER, George, See REINEICKER
REINHARDT, Matthias, N.Y., Sarah, W2467; BLWt.26234-160-55
REINEICKER, George, Cont., Pa., Elizabeth, W26367
REINER, Jacob, Pa., S22458
Martin, Pa., S8694
REINERD, Daniel, See REINERT
REINERT, Daniel, Pa., R8693
REINEY, Joseph, N.C. See REANY
REINFELDER, John, Mass., BLWt. 4909. Iss. 8/7/1789 to Richard Platt. No papers
REINHARDT, Jacob, See RINEHART
REINHARDT, Matthias, See REINEHARDT
REINHART, Johannes/John, N.Y., S42235
John E., Cont., French, R8696
REINICK, Christian, Pa., Christina Watson, former wid., W3199; BLWt.282-300
REINICKER, George, See REINEICKER
REINS, John, Lamb's Art., N.Y., BLWt.7714. Iss. 9/28/1790 to Bartholomew & Fisher, ass., no papers
John, N.Y., S43909
REIS, George, Pa. See REES
REISHER, Christian/Christiann/Christiana, former wid. of John Croft, Md., which see
REITER, Jacob, Pa., S23862
REIZER, John, N.C., S39038
RELAY, Robert, N.Y., Mary, R8697
RELJA, Denier/Dernier, N.Y., Annatje Kniestcarn, former wid., W20365
RELJAT, Simon, See RELYEA
RELPH, Thomas, R.I., Sarah, W22023
RELYEA, Dernier, See Denier RELJA
Henry, N.Y., Elizabeth, W20017
Jacob, N.Y., Charity, W16693
Peter, N.Y., S14279
Simon, N.Y., Deborah, R8698; BLWt.40682-160-55
REMA, Jacob, N.Y., Dorothy, W16387
REMAIR, Philip B./Barnet, Pa., Elizabeth, R---
REMAY, John, Va., Edith, W11104
REMER, David, See REAMER
Lewis, N.Y. res., R8699
REMICK, Elkanah, Mass., Phebe, W22043
James, Mass., Mary, W16690
Samuel, Cont., Mass., N.H., Sarah, W22045
Samuel, N.H., S37325
Timothy, Mass., BLWt.1779-300-Capt. Iss. 11/2/1795 to Joseph Fosdick,

REMICK (continued)
ass. No papers
REMINGTON, Abijah, Ct., Silence, BLWt.24601-160-55
Anthony, Navy, R.I., Hannah, W4791
Benidict/Benedict, R.I., S39831
Benjamin, R.I., S21937
Caleb, R.I., S21940
David, R.I., S11288
Elisha, R.I., S43912
Jabez, R.I., BLWt.7-100. Special Act 6/4/1842. See case of Robert Allen. R.I.
John, Ct., S21944
John, Cont., R.I., Sea Service, S30053
John, Mass., Mary, R8701
Jonathan, Mass., Vt., S21942
Jonathan, R.I., Sarah Greene/Green, former wid., W7559
Joseph, Mass., S21943
Joseph N., R.I., S40320
Joshua, Mass., Vt., S18562; BLWt.28521-160-55
Josiah, Ct., N.Y., R8700
Sally, former wid. of Isaiah Streeter, R.I., which see
Simeon, Ct., S22948
Stephen, R.I., Sarah, W22055
Thomas, R.I., S21938
Thomas, R.I., Mary, W13847
Tiddeman, R.I., S15965
REMMINGTON, Anthony, See REMINGTON
REMSEN, Anne, former wid. of Jacob Onderdonk, which see
Dorcas, former wid. of Pardon Burlingham, N.Y., which see
Garret, N.Y., Catharine, R8702
Luke, N.Y., R8703
REMSON, Christina, former wid. of James Van Wart, N.Y., which see
Dorcas, See Pardon Burlingham, N.Y.
RENDALL, Edward, N.H. See RANDALL
James, Cont.,Mass. See RANDALL
RENDEL, Stephen, Mass., Betsey, W1482
RENEAU, Thomas, Pa., S32477
RENELS, Benjamin, See RENNELLS
RENESON, John, See RENISON
William, Pa., S4060
RENFRO, John, Va., Esther, W9250
RENICK, James, S.C., S14262
RENIFF, Charles, Mass., Almira, W173; BLWt.4950-100. Iss. 8/24/1790; BLWt.113-60-55
RENISON, John, Cont., Pa., Mary, W3298
RENN, Philip, Pa., R8704
RENNELLS, Benjamin, Ct., Cont., Mass., S40327
RENNIFF, Charles, Mass. See RENIF
RENNO, Simeon, N.Y. See RENO
RENNOW, Simeon, See RENO
RENO, Simeon, N.Y., Dorcus Hall, former wid., R22000; BLWt.50896-160-55. (Name also appears as RUNNO, RENNO, RUNNOW & REYNOW)
Zela/Zely, Va., Mary, W8545
RENOLDS, James, N.C., S7370
RENSEL, Valentine, See RANSALL

RENTON, Elizabeth, former wid. of John Richmond, Mass. Sea Service, Navy, which see
RENWAY, Peter, Cont., N.Y., S46339; BLWt.1582-100
REPP, Michael, See REEP
REPPERT, Jacob, Pvt., Von Heer's Corps, BLWt.13643 iss. 1/12/1796 to Jacob Reppert
REPPETOE, William, See RIPPETO
REQUA, Abraham, N.Y., Bethia,W17521
Isaac, N.Y., Henrietta, W24733
John, N.Y., S27367
Joseph, N.Y., S14277
RESSEGUIE, Alexander, Ct., Ruamy, W1483; BLWt.26507-160-55
John, Ct., N.Y., S14268
RESSEQUIE, Abraham, Ct., Ellen Delanoy, former wid., W24054. This woman was rejected as the former wid. of Richard Hill, Mass., which see
Alexander, Ct. See RESSEGUIE
RESTEN, William, N.Y., BLWt.7660 Iss. 7/10/1790 to C.E. Elmandorph, ass. No papers
RESTER, Frederick, Ga., Louisa, R8707
RETER, Thomas, Va. See RUTER
RETHERFORD, Julius, See RUTHERFORD
William, Va. S1869
RETTENHOUSE, Abner, See RITTENHOUSE
REUPKE, Sally, former wid. of Ebenezer Hayden, Mass., which see
REVEL, Holliday/Holladay, Va., S39034; S5980; two claims consolidated 1/26/1934
REVELEY, Francis, Md., BLWt.261-300
REVELL, Michael, N.C., S4077
REVENBARK, Frederick, See RIVENBARK
REVENBURGH, Henry, See RYFENBURGH
REVES, Zachariah, See REAVES
REVIS, Henry, N.C., S32475
REW, Ephraim, Ct., S22946
Memucan, Ct., Hannah, W26363
REWALT, John, Pa., Ann, W17529
REWCY, Thomas, See REWEY
REWEY, Thomas, N.Y., S14281
REWICK, Owen, Ct., "of Invalids"; BLWt.6368 & 13693. Iss. 11/21/1797. No papers
REX, Daniel, Pa., S4066
William, Pa., S4048
REXFORD, Benjamin, Ct., Mary Jane, W5684; BLWt.34529-160-55
Denison, Ct., R8843
Ensign, Cont., Mass., Annis, W18799; BLWt.6123-160-55
Isaac, Ct., S41093
Joseph, See RIXFORD
REXRODE, Zachariah, Va., S5983
REY, Andrea, Va., R17309; Va. Half Pay. See N.A. Acc. No.874. See 050140 Half pay Andrea Rey/Ray
REYMOND, Isaac, Ct., Clara Porter former wid., W26334; BLWt.6397-100-1797 & 238-60-55
REYNOLD, James, Md., BLWt.11647. Iss. 2/1/1790 to Ann Tootle, admx., Janus Williams & Jos. Dawson, admrs. of James Tootle, ass. No papers.

REYNOLDS, Aaron, Va., Indian Wars, S4061
Abijah, N.Y., S40329
Albrow, Ct., S15963
Alexander, Va., S5979
Allen, N.H., BLWt.3422; Iss. 3/9/1791 to Phinehas Knapp, ass. No papers
Allen, Cont., N.H., Deborah, W24745
Benedict, Md., S4065
Benjamin, Mass., Mary, W13846
Benjamin, N.Y., Boat Service, Susannah, W18806
Benjamin, R.I., S30054
Benjamin, R.I., Elizabeth, W12833
Benjamin, Va., R8709
Benoni/Benony, N.Y., Abigail, W12830; BLWt.6113-160-55
Bernard, Va., Lucy, W18804
Betsy, former wid. of John Patch, Mass., which see
Charles, Art. Artificers, BLWt. 13678. Iss. 2/5/1790. No papers
Charles, Cont., Ct., Hannah, W17528
Daniel, Mass., Thankful, W11118
David, Ct., Margaret, W17523
David, Ct., Rebecca, W24738
David, Ct., N.Y., S15964
David, Ct., R.I., S21939
David, Mass., S15612
David, N.Y., S29411
Eliphalet, Ct., S37326
Elisha, N.Y., R.I., Vt., Elizabeth W813; BLWt.11093-160-55
Elisha, N.C., Judith, W4060
Ephraim, N.C., S38328
Ezekiel, N.C., S2013
Ezra, Mass., S33540
Ezra, N.Y., Lurana/Lavina, W26366; BLWt.47746-160-55
Fielding, S.C., b. Va., S17041
Gamaliel, Ct., Mary, W24729
Gardner, R.I., Elizabeth, W24748; BLWt.28515-160-55
George, N.J., S36255
George, R.I., S21443
George, R.I., S22949
Grindall, R.I., Cynthia, W11120; BLWt.40704-160-55
Hamilton, Ga., b. N.C., R8711
Henry, N.C., Va., b. near Phila., Pa., S4079
Hezekiah, N.H., S23868
Isaac, N.C., Anna, W22052
Isaac, Vt., Green Mt. Boys, S14270
Jacob, Ct., S7378
James, Ct., Mary, W22057
James, N.Y., Phebe, R8716
James, N.C. See RENOLDS
James, Pa., Sea Service, S4078
James, R.I., Eunice, W2001
James, Va., BLWt.12491. Iss. 1/7/1793 to Robt. Means, ass. No papers
Jeremiah, Ct., S14256
Jeremiah, Ct., S23385
Jesse, Va., Mary, W5683
Joel, N.Y., S28853
John, Art. Artificers. BLWt.13681 Iss. 2/5/1790. No papers

REYNOLDS (continued)
John, Ct., BLWt.6357 iss. 11/30/1796 to Gideon Buckaway & Bros. ass. No papers
John, Ct., S4762
John, Ct., S22459; BLWt.26540-160-55
John, Md., Sarah, W8290
John, Mass., S33542; BLWt.1838-100
John, Pa., b. Ireland, S4080
John, R.I., S19443
John, Va. Sea Service, R85. Va. Half Pay. See N.A. Acc. No. 837. Va. State Navy. John Reynolds Y.S. File Va. Half Pay
Jonathan, Ct., Mary, W16692
Jonathan, Cont., Ct., S41972
Jonathan, N.Y., S14258
Jonathan, N.Y., Vt., S14264
Jonathan, R.I., S21941
Joseph, Mass., S9997
Joseph, Mass., S29412
Joseph, Mass., Jemima, W22047
Joseph, N.Y. Boat Service, S31928
Joseph, Pa., Barbara, R8708
Joseph, R.I., S35611
Joseph, R.I., Sarah, W24736
Justus, Ct., S40319
Lewis Blew, Va., R8713
Martin, Pa., BLWt.10279 iss. 1/16/1790. No papers
Mary, former wid. of Joseph Razee, R.I., which see
Matthew, Ct., R8714
Nathaniel, N.Y., Hannah, W17527
Nathaniel, Va., S15615
Peter, Mass., R.I., S19051
Reuben, Ct., BLWt.6392 iss. 12/14/1789 to Richard Platt, ass. No papers
Richard D., Va., Nancy, R8715
Robert, See RUNNELS
Robert, Md., S40321
Robert, Rev. War, enl. in Va., Mary, BLReg.223654-55
Robert, R.I., Sarah, W11121; BLWt.28604-160-55
Samuel, N.Y., R8717
Samuel, R.I., S21442
Samuel, S.C., Mary, W1080; BLWt.29027-160-55
Sarah, former wid. of Philip Follett, Ct., Mass., which see
Sarah, former wid. of Spencer Campbell, N.J., which see
Sarah, former wid. of William Dye, Va., which see
Shubel, N.Y., S7374
Silas, Cont.,Vt., War 1812, S14272
Silas, N.Y., R8720
Simeon, Ct., S41094
Simeon, Ct., S41095
Solomon, Ct., Elizabeth, W17517
Stephen, N.H., BLWt.3449 iss. 5/14/1790 to Tallmadge, ass. No papers
Thomas, Md., BLWt.14134 iss. 8/14/1795 to Francis Sherrard, ass. of Charles Reynolds, Admr. No papers
Thomas, Md. See RUNNELS
Thomas, Mass., BLWt.813-100

REYNOLDS (continued)
Thomas, R.I., Sally, W17524
Thomas, Va., R9077
Timothy, N.Y., BLWt.7685. Iss. 10/20/1790. No papers
Timothy, N.Y., S43920
Tobias, Md., S35042
William, Md., S36254
William, N.Y. res. No papers
William, N.C., Catharine, W984
William, Pa., S14273
William, R.I., S21440
William, Va., S5982
William, Va., R17380. Va. Half Pay. See N.A. Acc. No.874-050141 Half Pay William Reynolds
Zachariah, Cont., Vt., War 1812, S11283
REYNOW, Simeon, See RENO
RHAANN, Jacob, Ct., BLWt.6367. Iss. 12/12/1789 to Theodosius Fowler, ass. No papers
RHAME, Ebenezer, S.C., Carah, W8291 BLWt.29015-160-55
RHEA, Aaron, Sheldon's Light Dragoons,BLWt.1803-200-Lt. Iss.6/15/1795 to Jon[a] Rhea, ass. of David Rhea, Admr. of A.R. No papers
David, N.J., S33554; BLWt.1800-450 Lt. Col. Iss. 12/21/1795 to Jon[a] Rhea, ass. Also BLWt.2567. No papers
Jonathan, N.J., BLWt.1816-200-Lt. Iss. 6/11/1789. No papers
Matthew, Va., R17386; Va. Half Pay; BLWt.2451-200
Robert, Va., War of 1812 (Tenn.), b. N.C., Mary, W10235; Inv. file 233; BLWt.22548-160-55
RHEINICK, Christian, See REINICK
RHINEHARD, Jacob, Pa., S31929
RHINEHART, William, See RINEHART
RHINER, George, Va., R8724
RHINEVAULT, William, See RINEVAULT
RHOADES, Ezekiel, N.Y., Anna, W1934 BLWt.29014-160-55
Hezekiah, Va., S7385
Jacob, Mass., Sarah, W11201; BLWt. 10025-160-55
Joseph, Ct., Mass., N.Y. res. in 1832, S23870
Nicholas, Cont., Md. & Ohio res. S46340; BLWt.1169-100
Samuel, Cont., Mass., Mary, W4319
Solomon, Mass., Eleanor, W24753; BLWt.59095-160-55
Timothy, Mass.,N.H., Rowena,W20019
William C., N.Y., Mercy Marsh, former wid., W19855
RHOADS, Cornelius, N.Y., BLWt. 2243-100
Daniel, Mass., Lydia, W13850
Daniel, Pa., Elizabeth, W1485
David, Cont., Mass., S14282
Eliphalet, Mass., S30675
James, Mass., Lydia, W26425
John, N.Y., S46470
Joseph, N.Y., S45583
Moses, Cont., Mass., S37329; BLWt.9052-160-55
Philip, Pa., Susan, W4504
Zebulon, Mass., Relief, R8731
RHODEN, Thomas, N.J., S14284

RHODES, Alexander, N.C., b. Md., S21444
Anthony, Ct., R.I., S14285
Benjamin, N.C., Sobrina, W9251; BLWt.71129-160-55
Benjamin, R.I., Phebe, W22058; BLWt.6122-160-55
Charles, N.C.,Miss. res. in 1833, S7386
Cornelius, N.C., S7387
Daniel, Pa., BLWt.148
Dick, R.I., BLWt.3458. Iss. 12/31/1789. No papers
George, Va., S39041
Jacob, Cont., Va. See RODES
Jacob, Mass. See RHOADES
James, R.I., Betsey, R22059
Jeremiah, N.C., Elizabeth, R8727
John, Mass., Susan, W1647; BLWt. 3144-160-55
John N.Y.; father's name William Rhodes, S14283
John, N.C., d. 10/23/1834, S4084
John, Pa., BLWt.10282. Iss. 10/4/1792 to John Nothstone, admr. No papers
John, R.I., Nancy, W18807; BLWt. 1669-100
Joseph, N.Y., BLWt.7684. Iss. 12/11/1789 to Benj. Brown, ass. No papers
Joseph, N.Y. See RHOADS
Joseph T., N.C., BLWt.1867-300-Capt. Iss. 12/14/1795 to Robert Camp, ass. No papers
Josiah, Mass., S30676
Nathan, N.C., S41981
Nicholas, Cont. Va. See RHOADES
Prime/Prince, R.I., BLWt.3457 Iss. 12/31/1789. No papers
Richard (colored), R.I., Catharine, W22060
Samuel, Mass. See RHOADES
Samuel, R.I., R8732
Samuel, Va., S35045
Sylvester, Navy, Privateer, R.I. Mary, W24752
Thomas, Del., BLWt.2348-100
Thomas, Va., S17045
William, Navy, R.I., Privtr., R8734
William, R.I, S21949
William, Va., S1324; BLWt.1026-100
Zachariah, Cont., Navy, R.I. & Sea Service, S17651
Zachariah, Md., R8735
Zebulon, Mass. See RHOADS
RHORER, John, See ROHRER
RHUFF, Peter, See ROAFF
RIAL, Isaac, N.J., S4770
RIALE, Nathan, Pa., R8737
RIANT, Joseph, See RYANT
RIBBET, Abraham, Pa. See RIBLET
RIBBITS, William, N.J., BLWt.8673. Iss. 1/2/1790 to William Rabbits No papers
RIBLET, Abraham, Pa., S41098; BLWt.10305-100; Pvt. of Mylan's. Iss. 7/16/1789. No papers
Christian, Pa., b. 8/18/1761; Christina Magdalena, S9073. D. in Ohio, 4/6/1844
John, Pa., b. 1756; d. 8/6/1835, S23873

RIBLETT, Peter, Pa., Dragoon. BLWt.10307. Iss. 8/26/1789. No papers
RICE, Abel, Mass., Anna, R8740; B.L. Reg.222341
Abel, Mass., N.H., Anna Gray, former wid., W23160
Abiah, Mass., Sarah, W26390; BLWt. 317-60-55
Abigail, former wid. of Lemuel Carrington, which see
Abijah, Mass., BLWt.4891 & Wt.317-60-55. Iss. 2/21/1792. Wt.4891 to Elijah Austin. No papers
Abiram, Ct., Lucy, W11578
Abner, Cont. Vt.; N.Y. res. in 1832; S14291
Abraham, Mass., N.H., Cynthia, W26371; BLWt.36560-160-55
Allen, See RECE
Amos, Mass., Mary, W2345; BLWt. 19504-160-55
Anthony, R.I., Martha, W22080; BLWt.26171-160-55
Asa, Mass., S14308
Ashbel/Ashbil, Mass., S32482
Bailey, Va., S39044
Bazdale/Basdel, Va., BLWt.1472-100
Benjamin, Mass., S29419
Benjamin, Mass., Betsey, BLWt. 40677-160-55
Calvin, Mass., Betsey, W26387
Charles, Ct., S14292
Charles, Mass., S4091
Charles, N.H., Dis. No papers. See Am. State Papers, Class 9, p.136 Wounded, 6/17/1775 at Bunker Hill by a ball passing through his right shoulder & breast, which prevented him from using his right arm
Chauncey, Ct., S5990
Chauncey, Ct., Mass., S15616
Christian, Pa., R8748
Clark, Vt., S22950
Daniel, Ct., Cont., Jemima, W22086
Daniel, Mass., S19054
Daniel, Mass., R8744
Daniel, R.I., S11307
David, Mass., S15619
David, Mass., Lucy, W13853
David, Navy, Me. res & agcy., S37340
Eber, Vt., Mary, W22085
Edmund, Mass., Betsey, W5698; BLWt.3146-160-55
Eliakim, Mass., S14310
Elijah, Ct., BLWt.6362. Iss. 8/10/1789 to Richard Platt, ass. No papers
Elijah, Ct. See ROYCE
Elijah, Mass., Margaret S., W11144 BLWt.40675-160-55
Elizabeth, former wid. of Josiah Newton, Mass., which see
Enos, Mass., Sarah, W2639
Ephraim, Mass., S18568
Ezekiel, Mass., S19056
Ezra, Mass., S33557
Frederick, Pa., S9085
Frederick, Pa., S40335
George, Va., BLWt.1471-100

RICE (continued)
George, Va., BLWt.1786-300-Capt. Iss. 8/25/1789. Also recorded as above under BLWt.2498. No papers
Gideon, Mass., Elizabeth, W8549; BLWt.7214-160-55. She also claimed B.L. on account of the service of her 1st husb., Benj. Berry, War of 1812, and of her 2nd husb., John Cummings, War of 1812
Holman, Cont., Va., S31327
Isaac, Ct., S4087
Isaac, Mass., S41096
Isaac John, N.H.,R.I. See John
Israel, Mass., S5998
Jacob, Ct., S11298
Jacob, N.H., S43923
James, N.J., BLWt.8677. Iss. 9/6/1791 to James Rice. Certified & sent to A. Gibbs at Ovid, N.Y. 7/1/1818. No papers
James, N.J., Elizabeth, W24770
James, Pa., BLWt.10322. Iss. 2/14/1791 to Alexander Power, ass. No papers
James, Va., S40332
James Brown, Va., R8746
Jason, Cont., Mass., N.H.,S4092
Jason, Mass., S19053
Jedediah, Mass., S22472
Jeduthan, Mass., S18566
Jeptha, N.C., Nancy, W5700
Jesse, Mass., S14289
Jesse, Va., S11300
John, Ct., S11301
John, "in the Invalids", BLWt. 13687. Iss. 8/30/1790 to Simon Veeder, ass. No papers
John, Mass., S23394
John, Mass., Mary, W24760; BLWt. 67-60-55; BLWt.4928-100. Iss. 4/1/1790
John, Mass., Mehitable, W26378
John/John Isaac, N.H., R.I., Anna, R8741
John, N.Y., S43933
John, N.Y., Catharine, W22068
John, N.C., d. 7/22/1837, S9062
John, N.C., age 79 in 1832; S9064
John, N.C., Phebe, W2003; BLWt. 2186-160-55
John, Pa. ----
John, Pa., S41100
John, S.C., R8747
John, Va., S16515
Jonas, Mass., Zilpah, W15253
Jonas, Mass., N.Y., Vt., Elizabeth, W22082
Jonathan, Mass., S29416
Joseph, Cont., R.I., S21446
Joseph, Mass., Mary, W18817
Josiah, Mass., BLWt.4945. Iss. 4/3/1797 to John Jack. No papers
Josiah, Mass., S4769
Josiah, Mass., Betsy Belcher, W15243
Josiah, Mass., Hannah, W15248
Josiah, Mass., R8750
Lemuel, Mass., Anna, W26392
Leonard, N.C., Sally, W3869

RICE (continued)
Luther, Mass., S36874
Martha, former wid. of Stephen Archer, Navy, Pa., Va., which see
Martin, Mass., S30063
Martin, Mass., Ruth, W15247
Merrick, Mass., S41987
Michael, N.J., R8751
Michael, Pa., BLWt.10288. Iss. 3/10/1790. No papers
Moses, Ct., Nancy, W11153; BLWt. 40687-160-55
Nathan, Cont., Mass., S14302; BLWt.1778-400-Major. Iss. 10/26/1789. No papers
Nathan, Mass., S4093
Nathan, Mass., S30060
Nathan, S.C., S18179
Nathaniel, Mass., Sarah, W1488
Naum, See RISE
Nehemiah, Ct., BLWt.1791-300-Capt. Iss. 6/18/1790 to Nehemiah Rice. No papers
Noah, Mass., R8753
Oliver, Mass., S19057; BLWt.1783-200-Lt. Iss. 4/1/1790. No papers
Pelatiah, Vt., S14286
Philip R., Va., Martha M., W3041
Phinehas, Mass., S29415
Phinehas, Mass., Lucy, W15244
Randolph, Va., S14294
Rebecca, former wid. of Phinehas Kimball, R.I., which see
Reuben, Mass., S4802
Richard, Va., Martha, W5694
Right, S.C., S11292
Samuel, Ct., S35631. See paper on Samuel Rice- by Mary Rice, dau. of Samuel Rice. This S.R. may have been her father
Samuel, Mass., Vt., Green Mt. Boys, S30678
Samuel, ----, R----. Dau. resided in Mass. in 1836. She may be the dau. of Samuel Rice, S35631, which see
Samuel, S.C. Sea Service, S39833
Samuel, Va., S14300
Sarah, former wid. of Daniel Benjamin, N.Y., which see
Sarah, former wid. of Peter Hammer, Pa., which see
Shadrack, not Rev. O.W. Inv. File 25398. Wayne's War 1792, Wt. 9698-160-55
Simon, Mass., Sally Harrington, former wid., W24419
Stephen, Mass., BLWt.4932. Iss. 12/12/1792 to Daniel King. No papers
Thaddeus, N.J., S35630
Thomas, Mass., BLWt.4940. Iss. 3/21/1792 to Matthew Park. No papers
Thomas, Pa. res. of heir in 1854; R8755
Uriah, Mass., Molly, W5696
Wait, Ct., S35620
William, Ct., R.I., S14313
William, Cont., Pa., S4090; BLWt.1821-300-Capt. Iss. 3/25/1790. No papers
William, Mass., S14288
William, Mass., S30059
William, N.Y., S6000
William, 13th U.S. Inf. War of 1812, Lucy, W10918. See case of wid's. other husb., Elisha Pomeroy, Ct., Mass.
William, Va., Jemima, W5695
William B., Va., Rebecca, W9625
William H., N.C., b. Va., Elizabeth M., W2437; BLWt.12382-160-55
William S. or N., R.I., S39832

RICH, Amos, Ct., BLWt.6412. Iss. 5/5/1791 to Benj. Tallmadge, ass. No papers
Amos, Ct., S43936
Barnabas, Mass., S33558
Elijah, Mass., S17048
Henry, Cont., Pa., See RICK
Jacob, N.C., Rosanna, W26380; BLWt.26819-160-55
Joel, Cont., Mass., Elizabeth, W24758
John, Mass., Sarah, R8756
John, N.H., Zeruiah, W3602; BLWt. 89515-160-55
Jonas, Mass., S22466
Jonathan, Vt., S14301
Joseph, Mass., S30064
Lemuel, Ct., S5994
Lot, N.C., S9076
Nathaniel, Ct.; BLWt.103-100
Samuel, Ct., S35626; BLWt.6404-100. Iss. 4/15/1800
Stephen, Mass., Rebecca, W18812
Thaddeus, Ct., S14307
William, Mass., N.Y., Thankful, W11150; BLWt.57785-160-55
Zacheus, Mass., S31330

RICHARD, Benjamin, See RICKARD
James, N.J., Sarah, W2857
Jeremiah, N.H., Dis. No papers. See Am. State Papers, Class 9, p.135. Disabled 10/7/1777 at Hubardstown by a musket ball in his left shoulder. Likewise received a rupture in his loin on the Indian expedition under the command of Gen. John Sullivan in the summer of 1779
Lemuel, Mass. See RICKARD
Nathan, Mass., S17655
Silas, Ct., S43921

RICHARDS, Abel, Mass., Mary, W22062
Abijah, Mass., Abigail Bullard, former wid., W15619. Her 2nd husb., Ephraim Bullard, also served, which see
Ambrose, Va., S5999
Amos, Ct., S43925
Amos, N.H., Catharine, W15954
Asa, Mass., Drusilla, W17535
Bartholomew, Cont., N.H., S45108
Benjamin, N.C., Anne, R8757
Bradley, N.H., S37331
Daniel, Mass., Navy, Mercy, W26376
David, Del., Comfort, W3116
David, Mass., Chloe, W15256

RICHARDS (continued)
Edmund/Edmond, Ct., Ruth, W17539
Edward, Va., S39042
Ezrah, N.Y., Ann, W22067
George, Va., S18572
George, Va., S35621
Gershom, Ct., Elizabeth, W22069
Gilbert, N.Y., BLWt.7671. Iss. 10/1/1791 to John Thompson, ass. No papers
Hezekiah, Ct., Jerusha, R8760
Isaac, Ct., S27383
Isaac, Va., S9056
Israel, Ct., R8759
Jacob, Ct., Mary, W2346
Jacob, Va., S40334
James, Mass., S31326
James, Pa., S35627
James, Va. See RICHARDSON
Jesse, Ct., Clarissa, R8758
Jesse, Pa., S4108
Joel, Cont., Mass., S14297
John, Mass., BLWt.4959. Iss. 5/4/1793. No papers
John, Mass., Sally, W15241
John, N.H., S37330
John, Va., S15967
Jonathan, Mass., S29413
Jonathan, Mass., Hannah, W26388
Joseph, Mass., S21448
Joseph, Mass., S28854
Joseph, N.H., S36875
Joseph Anthony, R.I., BLWt.3462 Iss. 3/22/1794. No papers
Joshua, N.C., Margaret, S---; BLWt.11274-160-55. Margaret Richards, wid. of the above sold. rec'd pension as former wid. of William West, S.C., which see
Josiah, Mass., S21445
Lemuel, Mass., Rebecca, W22061
Lewis, Va., S31325
Luther, Ct., R8761
Mark, Ct., S23389
Maurice, See Morris
Mitchell, Mass., S30066
Morris/Maurice, N.C., Sarah, W26383; BLWt.24913-160-55
Nathaniel, Navy, Ct. res. & agcy., S35624
Nehemiah, Mass., Hannah, W20020
Paul, Md., BLWt.11633. Iss. 1/4/1796. No papers
Paul, Md., S35048
Pearson, Va., BLWt.12502. Iss. 10/26/1795 to John Stockdell, ass. No papers
Peter, Ct., S35625
Peter, R.I., S21946
Philemon, Va., S5996
Samuel, Ct., S41985
Samuel, Ct., Cont., S17652
Samuel, Cont., N.H., Margaret, W24773
Samuel, Mass., BLWt.4947. Iss. 8/17/1796. No papers
Samuel, N.J., BLWts.8678 & 14151 iss. 2/28/1799 to David Richard's heir. No papers
Samuel, N.Y., BLWt.1797-200-Lt. Iss. 10/5/1790. No papers

RICHARDS (continued)
Solomon, Mass., S17654
Stephen, N.C., S4772
Theodore, N.H., Lucy, W22066; BLWt.7081-160-55
Thomas, N.H., Cynthia, W5709
Thomas, Va., BLWt.12498. Iss. 10/21/1791 to Elias Parker, ass. No papers
William, Ct., Cont., S35623; BLWt.1796-300-Capt. Iss. 1/28/1790. No papers
William, Pa., BLWt.10264. Iss. 5/27/179? to Francis Kirkpatrick ass. No papers
William, Pa., Anne, W3357
William, Va., R8762
RICHARDSON, Abel, Mass., S5992
Abel, Mass., S33556
Abigail, former wid. of Seth Hunt, Mass., which see
Abijah, Cont., Mass., Hannah, W22063
Abijah, Mass., S33571
Abijah, Mass., Mercy, W3604; BLWt.1781-400-Surgn. Iss. 3/4/1794. No papers
Abijah, Mass., Elizabeth, W24775
Abner, Mass., Anna, W5710; BLWt. 18218-60-55
Abram, S.C., Winney, W13852
Abram, S.C., Mary, R8763
Addison, Mass., BLWt.1805-300-Capt. Iss. 1/30/1787. Also recorded as above under BLWt.2674. No papers
Amasa, Cont., Mass., Lydia, W26375
Amos, N.C., S31932
Amos, N.C., Fanny, W8552
Asa, Ct., Fidelio, S41097
Asa, Mass., Jane, W18809
Benjamin, Mass., Bethiah, W27857
Benjamin, N.C., Mary, W4061. Her former husb., Elijah Bass, was killed at the battle of Eutah Springs.
Caleb, Mass., Huldah, W8553
Caleb, N.H., Martha, W24763
Charles, Md., Nancy, W4320
Daniel, Md., S35047
Daniel, See Daniel Richardson CAMPBELL
Daniel, N.H., S4110
Daniel, N.H., Sarah, W17541; BLWt.2417-400
Daniel, Va., BLWt.414-100. Iss. 4/22/1808
Daniel, Va., Sea Service, R86, Va. Half Pay
David, Ct., Sarah, W5711
David, Md., Wayne's Indian War, War of 1812, S31324
David, Mass., Ebiel, W26374
David, N.H., S19448
David, N.C., S9074
Ebenezer, Cont., Mass., S33567
Ebenezer, Mass., BLWt.4899. Iss. 12/15/1796 to Ebenezer Richardson. No papers
Ebenezer, Mass., Jerusha, W26389
Ebenezer, N.H., S22471

RICHARDSON (continued)
Edward, Mass., S31328
Eliphalet/Elipholet, Mass., Abi Currier, former wid., W2532
Eliphalet, Mass., Elizabeth, W15245
Elizabeth, former wid. of John Manson, Mass., Sea Service, Privateer, which see
Enoch, N.H., S45101
Ezekiel, Mass., S29420
Ezekiel, Mass., Lydia, W24756
Ezekiel, Pa., BLWt.10290. Iss. 5/11/1792 to Isabella Richardson Admx. No papers
Fidelio, Ct. See Asa
George, Cont., Mass., S43927
George, Va., S14293
Gershom, Ct., S16237
Godfrey, Mass., N.H., Martha or Patty, W26370; BLWt.9200-160-55
Humphrey/Humphry, Mass., S41982
Isaac, N.Y., S14311
Jacob, Mass., Ruth, W18789
Jacob, Pa., S40339
James, Mass., Molly, W13851
James, Mass., Sea Service, S17050
James, Mass., War of 1812, Sarah, W22070
James, Navy, Mass., Lucy, W15246
James, N.Y., S23875
James, N.C.,S.C. See RICHESIN
James, N.C., Va., S31323
James, Va., S40345 (Wrongly pensioned twice under names Richardson and Richards)
James, Va., Nancy, R8773
Jason, Mass., S30061
Jeremiah, Mass., S33569
Jeremiah, Mass., N.H., Hannah, W24771; BLWt.13896-160-55
Jesse, Ct., S4775
Jesse, Va., S30680
Job, Mass., S33562
Joel, Mass., Lydia, W22075
John, Ct., S23871
John, Ct., Judith, BLWt.88525-160-55
John, Cont., Md., S46507; BLWt. 1574-100
John, Mass., S18567
John, Mass., S30058
John, Mass., Sarah, W18814
John, N.C., S4113
John, N.C., R8769
John, Pa., BLWt.1832-300-Capt. Iss. 2/14/1791. No papers
John, Pa., S18177
John, Va., BLWt.12495. Iss. 6/6/1797. No papers
John, Va., S4109
Jonas, Mass., BLWt.4951. Iss. 3/25/1790. No papers
Jonas, Mass., S45102
Jonathan, Md., Mary, R8772
Jonathan, Mass., Marcy, W15242
Joseph, Cont., N.H., S20168
Joseph, Mass., S11296
Joseph, Mass., S43922
Joseph, Mass., Molly, W24774
Joseph, N.H., Abigail, W17540

RICHARDSON (continued)
Joseph, N.H., R8770
Joseph, Pa., S22951
Joseph, R.I., S31930
Joseph, Va., Sally, W18810
Joshua, Mass., S40333
Joshua, N.H., Betsey, W24764
Joshua, Va., Mary, W3603
Josiah, Cont., Mass., S33566
Lemuel, N.H., Jerusha, W1486; BLWt.3424-100. Iss. 10/10/1796. No papers. BLWt.302-60-55
Lysander, Mass., Lois, R8771
Moses, Mass., Navy, S29418
Nathaniel, N.H., Mary, W22064; BLWt.1916-100
Nehemiah, Mass., S23872
Nightengale, Pa., BLWt.10302. Iss. 6/11/1793 to Casper Iserloan, ass. No papers
Oliver, Mass., S18571
Randolph, Va., S6003
Reuben, Mass., R8774
Richard, Mass., S18570
Richard, Mass. Sea Service, R1387
Richard, N.H., S45103
Richard, S.C., BLWts.12524 & 13642 Iss. 6/24/1795. No papers
Richard, S.C., Dis.-- No papers. See Am. State Papers, Class 9, pp.106 & 165. Wounded in 1779 at Drawfates, Charleston, by a musket ball, which went through his breast which wound has disabled him from getting a livelihood by labor. Enl. 11/20/1775
Richard, Va., S11304
Richard, Va., S45882
Robert, "in the Invalids", BLWt. 13691. Iss. 12/11/1789 to Richard Rapalje, ass. No papers
Robert, Mass., S33564; BLWt.1725-100
Robert, Va., S39043
Rufus, Cont., Mass., Ruth, W18816
Russel/Rossel, Ct., S43932
Samuel, Ct., Susannah, W17533
Samuel, Md., S40346
Samuel, Md., BLWt.1764-100
Samuel, N.H., S45105
Samuel, N.J., & Hazen's Regt., BLWt.13661. Iss. 2/21/1798 to Samuel Black, ass. No papers
Sanford, Ct., Roxy, W17531
Seth, Mass., Hannah, W20021
Silas, Mass., Abigail, W13856; BLWt.56950-160-55
Stanton, Ct., Vt., Anna, R8764
Stephen, Ct., Hanna, W26386
Stephen, N.H., S45104
Thomas, Md., BLWt.11635. Iss. 12/18/1794 to Henry Purdy, ass. No papers
Thomas, Md., BLWt.11658. Iss. 3/14/1793 to Gideon Merkle, ass. No papers
Thomas, Md. Sea Service, Margaret W2698; BLWt.1972-160-55
Thomas, Mass., BLWt.4910. Iss. 4/1/1790 to John May. No papers
Thomas, N.C., Va.; b. Va., Elizabeth, R8767

RICHARDSON (continued)
Thomas, Va., S9075
Thomas P., Mass., S15618
Timothy, Cont., Mass., Sarah, W20022
William, Ct., Cont., S11291
William, Cont., N.H., Vt., Bethiah, W22083
William, Cont., Pa., and in Whiskey Insurrection in 1794, Mary, W9258; BLWt.82554-160-55
William, Mass., S29417
William, Mass., Levina, W16695
William, Mass., Mary, W26379; BLWt.19719-160-55
William, Mass., R8777
William, Navy, R.I., Nancy, W16696; BLWt.3518-160-55
William, N.H., Esther, W15249
William, N.C., R8778
William, N.C., Va. Indian Wars, 1772;1792; 1793; R8779
William, Va., Elizabeth Caruthers former wid., W6629
RICHARSON, James, Va. See RICHARDSON
RICHART, Charles, Pa. See RIECHART
RICHBOURG, John, S.C., S18175
RICHCREEK, Philip, Pa., Sarah, W4571; BLWt.592-100
RICHEE, James, Va., Martha, R8785
RICHENBACK, Adam, See REICHENBACH
RICHESIN, James, N.C.,S.C., S4112
RICHESON, Jonathan, Md. See RICHARDSON
RICHEY, Abraham, Va., S40347
James, N.H., Abigail, R8782
John, N.C. See RITCHEY
John, Pa., S4101
John, Pa., R8783
John, S.C. See RITCHIE
John, Va., S35628
John, Va., R8780
John, Va., BLWt.2061-100
Robert, Pa. See RICHIE
Robert, Va., S40342
William, Pa., Sarah, W2856
RICHIE, Abraham, Va., See RICHEY
James, Va. See RICHEE
John, Va. See RICHEY
John, Va. See RICHEY
Robert, Pa., S41099
William, Pa. See RICHEY
RICHMAN, Abiathar, Mass., Jemima, W15252
RICHMOND, Abiathar, Mass. See RICHMAN
Abiather, Mass., R8786
Abiezer, Mass., N.Y., Vt., Lydia, W20024
Abner, Ct., Mass., Eunice, W17534
Amaziah, Mass., Sarah, W15240
Amaziah, Mass., R.I., Hannah, W17532
Asa, Mass. Sea Service, Eunice, W18808
Benjamin, Cont., Mass., Betsey, W27478; BLWt.596-150
Christopher, Md., BLWt.1841-300-Capt. Iss. 9/1/1789 to Chs. Richmond. No papers
David, R.I., Nancy, W16388

RICHMOND (continued)
Edward, Mass., S43934
Eliab, Mass., Hannah, W26947
Ezra, Mass., S29414
Gamaliel, Mass., BLWt.4926. Iss. 9/19/1792 to John Blanchard. No papers
Gamaliel, Mass., S33560
George, Mass., S17653
James, Mass., R.I., S30679
James, N.C., b. Scotland, S1714
John, Mass. Sea Service, Navy, Privateer; Elizabeth Renton former wid., R8705
Jonathan, Mass., Meriam, W22079
Jonathan, R.I., Priscilla, W15250
Nathan, Mass., Mary, W22073; BLWt.16134-160-55
Nathaniel, Mass., BLWt.4906. Iss. 5/6/1793. No papers
Nathaniel, Mass., S22465
Nathaniel, Mass., Susannah, W9627
Samuel, Mass., S30677
Seth, Mass., Phebe, W15257
Thomas, R.I., S11303
Vail/Viael, Ct., Navy, Clarissa, W1935; BLWt.38544-160-55
William, R.I., R8787
William, Va., S9088
Zebulon, Cont., Mass., Susanna, W24772
RICHTER, Nathaniel, Pa., R8788
Nicholas, N.Y., S27372 (Not same as Nicholas Rightor, S14309)
RICHTMYER, Johannis, See RIGHTMYER
RICHY, Peter, N.C. See RITCHEY
RICK, Henry, Cont., Pa., BLWt. 275-100
RICKABAUGH, Adam, Va., S4120
RICKARD, Abner, Mass., R.I.,S23393
Benjamin, Mass. Sea Service, Navy S33563
Elijah, Mass., S14298
John, N.C., S9067
Lemuel, Mass., S41986
Samuel, See RECORD
William, Cont., Mass., later in Tenn., BLWt.85-200
RICKART, Leonard, N.C., Mary, W26385
RICKELS, William, Va., Mary, R8790
RICKER, Frederick, Pa., R8792
George, Cont., Mass., Rebecca, W24755
George, N.H., S45106
Henry, Hazen's Regt., BLWt.13656 Iss. 11/12/1796
John, Navy, N.H., S11290
John Berrien, N.J. See RIKER
Joseph, N.H., Sarah, W16694
Maturen/Maturin/Maturian, Cont., Mass., Navy, S19052
Noah, Navy, N.H., Betsy, R8791
Reuben, Navy, N.H., S37334
Reuben, N.H., Mary, S11152
Simeon, Mass., S17040
Simeon, Mass., Dorcas, W26384
Stephen, Mass., S37332
Timothy, Mass., S17049
Timothy, N.H., S45107
Tobias, N.H., Susanna Gammon, former wid., S23090

RICKER (continued)
Tobias, N.H., Privateer, Abigail W24765
Wentworth, N.H., S28855
William, Mass., Amy, W24766
RICKERT, John, N.Y., R8795
Marcus, N.Y., Gertrout/Gertrude W22071
RICKETS, Edward, Pa., R8796
Nicholas, Md., BLWt.1124-200
RICKETSON, Jesse, N.C., Mary, W26382
RICKETTS, Nathan, Pa., S32480
Robert, Pa., S17047
William, N.C., S.C., S9078
William, not Rev., Va., N.W. Indian War 1791. Old War Inv. File 26367
RICKEY, Benjamin, N.J., S4098
Cornelius, N.J., Pa., S4096
Israel, N.J., N.Y., R8797
Jeremiah, N.Y., BLWt.7681. Iss. 7/9/1790 to Elias Benjamin, ass.
Jeremiah, N.Y., See RICKKO
John, N.Y., S23392
John, Proctor's Art., Pa.,BLWt. 10315. Iss. 7/27/1789 to Richard Platt, ass. No papers
Joseph, Md., Pa., S4100
RICKKO, Jeremiah, N.Y., S43928
RICKLES, William, Va. See RICKELS
RICKNER, Daniel, Pa., S35046
RICKS, Edmund, N.C., Va., S9071
RIDDALL, John, N.H., Mary, W9256; BLWt.13185-160-55
RIDDEL, William, Va. See RIDDLE
RIDDLE, David, Cont., Mass., N.H., Mary, W1321
Henry, Gen. Armand's Legionary Corps., BLWt.1876-200-Lt. Iss. 1790. No papers
John, Cont., N.Y., S15617
John, N.J., Privateer, Indian War, R8799
John, Va. See RIDDLEY
John, Va., S9087
John, Va., S31931
Joseph, Mass., S43929
William, Va., Jemima, W11132; BLWt.34936-160-55
RIDDLEY, John, Va., S9069
RIDEN, John, Pa., S5987
RIDENOUR, Jacob, Md. agcy. & res., S4075
RIDEOUT, Abraham, Mass., S37338
Benjamin, Mass., Meriam, W24754
Stephen, Mass. See RIDOUT
William, Mass., Ruth, W1648
RIDER, Adam, Cont., Va., S40341
Asa, Cont., Mass., Esther, W18811 BLWt.1878-100 & 65-60-55
Benjamin, Mass., Sarah, W4781; BLWt.516-160-55
Benjamin, N.Y., S9082
Christain, See RYNDER
Daniel, Ct., Elizabeth, W5705
Daniel, Mass., S11302
David, Cont., Mass., Esther, W24769
David, Mass., Hannah, R8802
Elkanah, Mass., Susannah, W22078

RIDER (continued)
George, N.Y., BLWt.7703. Iss. 8/24/1790 to Glenn & Bleecker, Admr. No papers
Giles, Mass., S33555
James, N.H., R8803
Jeremiah, Ct., S14296
John, Mass., S37333
Joseph, Mass., S1247
Moses, Mass., S11306
Peter, Mass., Dis. ---No papers. See Am. State Papers, Class 9, p.156. Lost sight of his right eye, by a wound with a musket ball in 1776 at Lake Champlain.
Phinehas, Mass., S15968
Reuben, Va., Martha, W2572; BLWt.28530-160-55
Robert, Mass., S19055
Timothy, Mass., S9466
RIDGEWAY, Isaac, Mass., BLWt.4915 Iss. 12/10/1789. No papers
Isaac, Mass. See RIDGWAY
James, Mass., Esther, W17536
John, S.C., Va., b. Va., S21947
Samuel, S.C., S4119
Thomas, Mass., BLWt.4933. Iss. 1/17/1793 to Samuel Emery. No papers
RIDGWAY, Isaac, Mass., S23874. See N.A. Acc. No.874-050142. Not Half Pay. Isaac Ridgeway
James, Hazen's Regt., BLWt.13668. Iss. 8/30/1792 to William Scudder. No papers
James, Mass. See RIDGEWAY
Joseph, Va., R8806
Noah, See REDGWAY
Thomas R., N.J., Mass., R8807
William, S.C., Margaret/Peggy, W22081
RIDIN, Timothy, N.Y., S43935
RIDINGOUR, Andrew, S.C., S32486
RIDLEY, Daniel, Mass., S37339
David, Mass., Mary, W22072; BLWt.14759-160-55
George, Mass., S37336
John, Mass. See RIDLIN
John, Va. See RIDDLEY
Samuel, Md., pensioned in Vt., S41984
Thomas, Va., BLWt.1850-400-Maj. Iss. 2/16/1798 to John Richards, Jr., ass. No papers
William, N.C., S41980
RIDLIN, John, Mass., S40331; BLWt.34855-160-55
RIDLON, Ebenezer, See REDLON
Ephraim, Cont., Mass., S37335
RIDOUT, Giles, Va., S6002
Stephen, Mass., Jane, W580; BLWt.11253-160-55
RIECHART, Charles, Pa., S22467
RIED, John, N.Y., S31927
Nathan, Va., BLWt.522-300. Iss. 7/28/1810
RIEDT, Jacob, Pa., R8809
RIEGELMAN, Conrad, Pa., S22470
RIEL, John, See REEL
RIELEY, Bennet, Md. See REILEY
John, Pa., Va. See REILEY
John, Va. See REILEY

RIELY, James, Cont., Pa., Va., S ?
James, Va., S5981
John, Va., d. 1/18/1847, S31331. See N.A. Acc. 874 No. 050143 not half pay. John Riley
RIENHART, Martin, Pa., S4114
RIFE, Peter, N.C., S9063; BLWt.26406-160-55
RIFFE, Peter, N.C. See RIFE
RIFFEE, Jacob, Va., S9066
RIFFERT, Christian, Pa., S40348
RIFFEY, George, Va., Catharine, W18813
RIFFLE, Melchoir, Pa., R8811
RIFFORD, Frederick, See RUFFORD
RIGBY, James, Pa., BLWt.10285. Iss. 11/27/1794 to Joseph Pall ass. No papers
John, N.C., S9057
William, Md., Ara, W2248; BLWt. 5438-160-55
RIGDEN, James, See RIGDON
RIGDON, James, Md., Elizabeth, W8551; BLWt.26913-160-55
RIGG, Eleazer, Pa., R8812
Hosea, Pa., S32483
RIGGAN, Francis, N.C., S9054
Joel, N.C. See RIGGINS
William P., N.C., S9077
RIGGENS, Joel, See RIGGINS
RIGGESBEE, Jesse, See RIGSBY
RIGGIN, Charles, See REGAN
William, N.C., Jane, R8813
RIGGINS, James, N.J., S906
James, N.C., Jane, W5702; BLWt. 13191-160-55
Joel, N.C., S.C., Nancy, W4322
RIGGS, Abraham, Va., R8814
Bethuel, N.J., N.C., S17046
Charles, Cont., Md., S32484
Daniel, N.Y., BLWt.7675. Iss. 6/24/1790 to Asa Spaulding, ass. No papers
Daniel, N.Y., Susanna, W17537
George, Md., BLWt.11668. Iss. 1/21/1795 to John Faires, ass. No papers
Gideon, Cont., N.J., S40330
Jacob, Md., BLWt.11630 & 12503 Iss. 1/30/1795 to John Stockdale/Stockdell, ass. No papers
James, Ct., R17439
James, N.C., S9068
James, N.C., R8815
James, Pa., Jane, W3042; BLWt. 657-100. No papers
John, Md., BLWt.11627. Iss. 2/1/1790. No papers
John, N.C., Va., Martha, S9079; BLWt.47902-160-55
John, Va., S9081
Jonathan, N.J., S22952
Laban, Ct., Cont., Dorcas, W4780
Lucretia, former wid. of Jacob Radley, N.Y., which see
Moses, Ct., S35629
Reuben, N.C., b. N.J., S45880
Richard, N.C., S1926
Samuel, N.C., S4095
Thomas, N.C., Rhoda, W9252; BLWt.75065-160-55

RIGGS (continued)
Zenas, Cont., N.J., Sarah, W1320
RIGHT, Bazzell/Bazzle, Md., Pa., Nancy, S15966; BLReg. 289222-1885
John, Va., Elizabeth, R8816
RIGHTMYER, Anna, former wid. of Peter Wells, N.Y., which see
Henry/Hendricks, N.Y., S14312
Johannis, N.Y., Maria, W17542
RIGHTON, Joseph, S.C., Elizabeth W22074
RIGHTOR, Nicholas, N.Y., S14309. (Not same as Nicholas Richter, S27372)
RIGLAND, David L., N.Y., Pa., S14287
RIGSBEE, Frederick, See RIGSBY
RIGSBY, Drury, N.C., S30681
Frederick, N.C., Cynthia, W1490 BLWt.8182-160-55
James, N.C., S9060
Jesse, N.C., Elizabeth, R8808
RIKARD, John, S.C., R8820
RIKER, Abraham, N.Y., R8822
Gerardus, N.J., N.Y., S11293. Abigail Riker, wid. of above sold. was pensioned as former wid. of her 1st husb., Jacob Willsey/Wilsie/Woolsey, N.Y. which see
James, N.J., Mary, W2573; BLWt. 27652-160-55
John, N.Y., S6001
John Berrien, N.J., Susannah, W4321; BLWt.1788-400-Surgn. Iss. 11/18/1791 to John B. Ricker. Also recorded as above under BLWt.2528. No papers
John N., N.J., S1092
Matthias, N.J., N.Y., S11294
RILEA, Richard, Cont., Va., Rhoda, W2167
RILEY, Ashbel, Ct., BLWt.6356. Iss. 8/15/1792 to George Wells, ass. No papers
Bennet, Md., Frances, W4315
Charles, N.Y., Catharine Whitford, former wid., W16788
Charles, Va., R8824
Daniel, N.J. See RYLY
Daniel, Va. See RYLIE
James, N.J., BLWt.8675. Iss. 12/15/1792. No papers
James, N.J., Elizabeth, W194
James, N.Y., BLWt.7694. Iss. 7/22/1790 to Thomas Tillotson, ass. No papers
James, N.C. See RYLEE
James, Pa., b. Ireland, S4103
James, S.C., Va., S9061
John, Ct., S14304
John, Ct., BLWt.1792-300-Capt. Iss. 4/22/17--(?). No papers
John, Cont., ----
John, Ct., Pa., b. 3/28/1761 in Eng.; d. 6/29/1837; Nancy, W5703; BLWt.11062-160-55
John, Pa., b. 12/9/1751, S36873
John, Pa., d. 1/30/1811, Sarah, R8692

RILEY (continued)
John, Pa., Va. See REILEY
John, S.C., R8827
John, Va., See RIELY
John, Va., S35622
John, Va. See REILY
John, Va., See RYLEY
Joseph, Ct., S4105
Major, Mass., S11297
Patrick, Md., BLWt.11636. Iss. 3/11/1791. No papers
Roger, Ct., Sarah, W22084
Stephen, Md., Mary, W9255
William, N.C., Nancy, W1083; BLWt.31582-160-55
William, N.C., R8828
William, Va., S4106
RILY, Christopher, See REILEY
RIMEE, Conrad, Pa., Margaret, W3299
RIMMEY, Conrad, Pa. See RIMEE
RINDER, Christiaan, N.Y., BLWt. 7688. Iss. 7/30/1790 to Edward Cumpston, ass. No papers
Christian, N.Y. See RYNDER
RINDGE, Richard, Mass., S41983
Thomas, Ct. See RINGE
RINDRESS, James, N.Y., Sarah, R8829
RINEHART, George Simon, Cont., Pa., S40338
Jacob, N.C., Elender, R8695; BLWt.38835-160-55
Thomas, Md., S5986
William, N.Y., S43937
RINES, Samuel, Mass., S37337
Thomas, Mass., Sea Service, Mary Quint, former wid., W24715
RINESS, James, See RINDRESS
RINEVAULT, William, Ct., Mary, R8830
RINEVOLT, William, Ct., BLWt. 6376. Iss. 4/6/1790. No papers
RING, Jonathan, Mass., Hannah, W26725; BLWt.850-100
Thomas, Ct. See RINGE
Thomas, N.C., Sarah, W5701; BLWt.18204-160-55
RINGE, Richard, Mass. See RINDGE
Thomas, Ct., Anna, W26187; BLWt. 3522-160-55
RINGER, Anna, former wid. of Michael Saylor/George Michael, Md., Pa., R---
Matthias, Md., R8831
RINGO, Burtis, Va., S31329
Cornelius, S.C., Va., Sarah, W10174
John, Va., S14290
RINGSTORPH, Philip, N.Y., Anna, W24767
RINHOLT, Henry, Pa., S5988
RINKER, Abraham, Pa., S40349
George, Va., S32485
Samuel, Pa., U.S.N., Catharine; Old Act. Navy, W1014. See War 1812 pension files for papers. He also served in Rev. War
RION, Thomas, Mass. See RYAN
RIPLEY, Abraham, Ct., S33565

RIPLEY (continued)
Asa, N.Y., Mary/Polly, W22077; BLWt.27654-160-55
Calvin, Mass., S21945
Charles, Ct., N.H., S43931
David, Mass., Jane, W24761
David, N.Y., Priscilla, R8838
Eliphalet, Mass., Rebecca, W13854
Epaphras, Ct., Vt., R8833
Hezekiah/Hezekiel, Ct., Cont. S11305
Hezekiah, Mass., Hannah, W15258; BLWt.1782-200-Lt. Iss. 6/18/1791. No papers
Isaiah, Mass., Jerusha, W20025
Jabez, Ct., Mary, R8836
Jacob, Pa., S4768
Jeremiah, Ct., Mary, R8835
Job (colored), Mass., Sarah, W1487; BLWt.920-100
John, S.C. See MILLS
John A., Ct., Privateer, R8834
Joseph, Mass., Salome, W11134; BLWt.14533-160-55
Joseph, Mass., Elizabeth Lewis W24759
Laban, Mass., S18176
Nehemiah, Ct., Lucy, W1489; BLWt.15196-160-55
Noah, Mass., S30065
Pelham, Mass., Huldah, W2696; BLWt.532-160-55
Peter, Pa., BLWt.10312. Iss. 4/7/1795 to John Nicholson, ass. No papers
Pirum, Ct., Sea Service, Navy, & N.Y., S23388
Richard, Va., S11299
Thadeus, Mass., Mary, W15244
William, Cont., Mass., Lucy, W24762
William, Mass., S33559
RIPPETO, William, Va., Betsey/Elizabeth, W2697; BLWt.19534-160-55
RIPPLE, Job, See RIPLEY
Michael, Pa., S32479
RIPPY, Edward, N.C., S9059
RISDALE, William, N.Y., BLWt. 7690. Iss. 9/15/1790 to John Hinton, ass. No papers
RISDEL, John, Navy, Del., S4117
RISDON, Daniel, Vt., S32481; BLWt.31555-160-55
John, Ct., S18569
Onesimus, Vt., S21447
RISE, Henry B., Cont., D.C. res. in 1820, late of Pa., BLWt. 928-100
Naum, Mass., Ruth, W15259; BLWt.891-100
RISHEL, George, Cont., Pa., S40336
RISING, Abraham, Mass., Vt., S30062; BLWt.26357-160-55
Ben, Ct., S9086
Josiah, Cont., Ct., Huldah, W18818
RISLEY, Allen, Ct., S21449
Asa, Ct., S12226

RISLEY (continued)
Asahel/Asahael, Cont., Ct., BLWt.6410-100 iss. 1790
David, Ct., Cynthia, W24768
David, N.Y., BLWt.7713 iss. 5/27/1791 to Row & Cradet, Admrs. No papers
Eli, Ct., Mindwell, W10236
Elijah, Ct., Cont., S23391
George, Cont., Mass., S17051
Levi, Ct., S35619; BLWt.6407-100. Iss. 2/5/1790. No papers
Moses, Ct., Mass., R8839
Richard, Sheldon's Dragoons, Ct. BLWt.6415. Iss. 2/5/1790. No papers
Richard, Ct., S23390
Samuel, Ct., Stacy O., W26369; BLWt.27587-160-55
Stephen, Sheldon's Dragoons, Ct. BLWt.6389. Iss. 2/5/1790. No papers
Stephen, Ct., Cont., S43930
William, Ct., S14305
RIST, Samuel, Cont., Mass., Rebeckah, W26373
RISTER, Zadock, Md. See RISTON
RISTON, Zadock, Md., S35348
RITCHER, Nicholas, See RICHTER
RITCHEY, Jacob, Pa., S4097
James, N.H., See RICHEY
John, N.C., S9058
Peter, N.C., S32478
RITCHIE, Alexander, Va., Indian War 1786, R8784
John, S.C., Jannet/Jannett, W5707; BLWt.40689-160-55
RITMEYER, Conrad, Md., R8817
RITNER, Henry, See WHRITENHOUR
RITTENHOUSE, Abner, N.J., R8840
Garret, Pa. res. in 1837, R8841
Jacob, Pa., S22469
RITTER, Adam, Va., BLWt.12519. Iss. 6/29/1793 to John Spencer ass. No papers
Ezra, Mass., Jane, W2644; BLWt. 31580-160-55
Frederick, N.Y., Elizabeth, W20026
Henry, N.Y., S19449
Jacob, Pa., S9080. (Not identical with Jacob Reiter)
Killian, N.Y., Hannah, W18815; BLWt.26019-160-55
Thomas, Md., S9065
Thomas, Va. See RUTER
William, Mass., Ruth, W15255
RITZ, Mathias, Pa., S22468
RIVELY, Frederick, Va., S40337
RIVENBARK, Frederick, N.C., Winnefred, W9257; BLWt.75040-160-55
RIVERS, Benjamin, N.C., BLWts. 12522 & 13651. Iss. 12/13/1796 to Gabriel Holmes, ass. No papers
Richard, Md., BLWt.11651. Iss. 1/11/1796 to Joshua Ward, ass. No papers
Samuel, S.C., S21948
RIVES, Daniel, See REEVES
RIX, Adam, Pa., BLWt.10248. Iss. 3/10/1790. No papers

RIX (continued)
Christopher, Mass., BLWt.4925. Iss. 2/6/1797 to Benj. Fessender. No papers
Nathan, Ct., R.I., S14306
Nathaniel, Mass., Lucretia,W22065
RIXFORD, Benjamin, Art. Artrs., BLWt.13680. Iss. 8/23/1790. No papers
Henry, Mass., Catharine, W2344; BLWt.14539-160-55
Joseph, N.Y., Anna, W5708
Samuel, Mass., Elizabeth, W18819
Simon, Mass., S2073
William, Mass., S11289
ROACH, Absalom, Va., S7404
Burdett Price/Burdatt Price, Cont., Va., Elizabeth, W1936
Francis, N.C., S32494
Frederick, Cont., Mass., Margaret W5728
Israel, Mass., Polly, W18828
James, N.C., Ruth, W18830
James, Pa., Frances, R8844
James, Va., Mary, W5727; BLWt.26962-160-55
John, Cont., Va., Patty, W3871
John, Md., BLWt.11644; Iss. 12/23/1795 to George Ponsonby, ass. No papers
John, Mass., Abigail, W22096
John, Va., Elizabeth, W24801
Jonathan, Va., Ruth, W3870
Rachel, former wid. of Thomas Lakeman, Mass., which see
Richard, Va., BLWt.12490. Iss. 5/12/1792 to James Morrison, Admr. No papers
Thomas, Ct., S14373; BLWt. 26121-160-55
William, Pa., S40350
William, Va., BLWt.12510-100. Iss. 1792
ROADS, Anna, former wid. of Frederic Eisenhauer, Pa., which see
John, Pa., War of 1812, R8846
Richard, N.Y., Anna, W16389
Samuel, Mass. See RHOADS
ROAFF, Peter, Cont., Md., S40352
ROAN, John, Pa., S23882
Thomas, N.C. See ROUN
ROANE, Christopher, Va., R--- Va. Half Pay
ROARER, Henry, Va., S19452
ROARK, William, N.J., Pa., S32495
ROASE, Jacob, N.Y., BLWt.7666. Iss. 5/8/1792. No papers
Peter, N.Y., BLWt.7663. Iss. 5/4/1791 to Anthony Maxwell, ass. No papers
ROAT, Christian, N.Y., Elizabeth, W20032; BLWt.18382-160-55
ROATH, Daniel, Ct. See ROTH
Silas, Ct., S36260
ROBARDS, Archibald, Md., Mary, W5737; BLWt.11395-160-55
George, Mass. See ROBERTS
George, Va., S31339

ROBARDS (continued)
Jesse, Va., Francis Ann, W8563; BLWt.31592-160-55
John, Mass. See ROBERTS
Lewis, Va., Hannah, W581
William, Va., Elizabeth, W8562
ROBARSH, Peter, Canadian Regt., N.Y., S43954
ROBARTS, Edward, Pa. See ROBERTS
Gideon, Ct. See ROBERTS
Luke, Ct., BLWt.6380 & 41-60-50 Iss. 2/17/1797. BLWt.6380 to William, Woodward, ass.
Luke, Ct. See ROBERTS
ROBASH, Peter. See ROBARSH
ROBASON, Daniel, See ROBESON
ROBB, John, Jerusha, W (?) The papers herein were found in BL claim of John Robb, War of 1812--BLWt.13654-160-55 to which they do not pertain.
John, Pa., Jane, R8849
John, Pa., BLWt.1830-300-Capt. Iss. 10/24/1789. No papers
Samuel, N.H. See ROBBE
Samuel, N.H., Abigail, R8848
ROBBARTS, Amos, Pa. See ROBERTS
Freelove, Cont., Ct., S41995
ROBBE, John, N.H. Dis. No papers
Samuel, N.H., Mary, W22124
ROBBENS, Miller, N.J., R8858
ROBBINS, Abner, Mass., S33583
Asa, Mass., S30067
Benjamin, Mass., Huldah, W13857
Benjamin, Mass., Keziah, W20030
Brintnal, See ROBINS
Daniel, Ct., Sea Service, See ROBINS
Daniel, Mass. See ROBINS
Daniel, Mass., S37352
Daniel, Mass., Candace, W5743
Daniel, Mass., Mehitable, R8857
David, N.C., Dis. ---. No papers See Am. State Papers, Class 9, p.159. Disability--Eruptions over his body, and great debility occasioned by violent heat of the weather, during the battle of Bunker Hill, 6/17/1775
Ebenezer, Ct., Zeruah, W9636; BLWt.27588-160-55
Ebenezer, Mass., S14357
Ebenezer, Mass., Meribah, W24800
Elijah, N.Y., S32490
Eliphalet, Mass., S37358
Ephraim, Ct., S17052
Ephraim, Mass., S34481
Ephraim, Mass., Hannah, R8851
Evens, N.Y. See ROBINS
Frederick, Ct., Abigail, W26426 BLWt.47767-160-55
Hannah, former wid. of George Roney/Runey, Mass., which see
Henry, Mass., Elizabeth, W20035; BLWt.10224-160-55 & 34937-160-55
Ichabod, Mass., S33579
Jacob, Mass., S33588
John, Cont., Ct. Sea Service, Alice, W17558
John, Md., S35051
John, Mass., S41994

ROBBINS (continued)
John. Lt., Md., Moylan's Dragoons BLWt.1828-200-Lt. Iss. 7/17/1794 to Peter Manifold, Admr.
John, N.J., Pa. Indian War 1791. See ROBINS
John, N.C., S8855
Jonathan, Mass., S37353
Joseph, Sheldon's Dragoons, Ct., BLWt.6413. Iss. 3/25/1790.
Joseph, Cont., Mass., Elizabeth, W15272
Joseph, Cont., Mass., Winnefred, W17548
Joseph, Mass., S19759
Joseph, Mass., Mercy, W16702
Joshua, Ct., R8856
Josiah, Ct., S35633
Josiah, Mass., S15621
Josiah, "Sappers & Miners", BLWt.13647. Iss. 10/16/1789 to Theodosius Fowler, ass. No papers
Lorrin, Ct., Cont., R.I., See ROBINS
Luke, Mass., S33581
Luther, Mass., Anna, W22087
Miller, N.J. See ROBBENS
Moses, Mass., Thirza, W15283; BLWt.34846-160-55
Otis, Cont., Mass., S18185
Paul, Mass., Susanna, W16703
Peter, Navy, R.I., S11313
Samuel, Ct., R.I., S14374
Samuel, Cont., N.H., S43970
Samuel, Mass. See ROBINS
Samuel, Mass., Hanah, W4577; BLWt.19517-160-55
Silas, Ct., Hannah, W17565
Solomon, N.H., R8863
Stephen, Cont., Mass. See ROBINS
Thomas, Mass., S33585
Thomas, N.J., Mary, W11171
William, Cont., Mass., Margaret, W22094
William, Mass., S33576
William, N.H., Nancy, BLWt.96514-160-55
Zachariah, Mass., Abigail, W17549
ROBECHEAU, James, N.Y., BLWt. 1808-300-Capt. Iss. 10/22/1791 to Asa Ballard, ass. No papers
ROBERDS, William, Mass. See ROBERTS
ROBERSON, Charles, Md., S14338
James, N.C., b. Va., S1718
James, Va., S14333
John, Va., S32500
John, Va. See ROBINSON
Judah, former wid. of Henry Miller, Mass., which see
ROBERTS, Aaron, N.J., N.Y., Elizabeth, W2349
Aaron, N.C., S7430
Abigail, former wid. of Samuel Arbuckle, Mass., which see
Abner, Va., S45859
Abraham, N.Y., S14331
Ambrose, Va., S7398
Amos, Ct., S6024
Amos, Pa., S41107

ROBERTS (continued)
Archibald, Md. See ROBARDS
Ashbel, Ct., S18580
Benjamin, Ct. See Benj. SIMMONS
Benjamin, N.H., S45114
Benjamin, Va., S31343; Va. Half Pay
Britain/Brittian, N.C., S7400
Caleb, N.Y., BLWt.7667. Iss. 10/7/1790 to Elijah Hunter, ass. No papers
Clark, Ct., BLWt.6378. Iss. 2/21/1792 to Elijah Austin, ass. No papers
Clark, Ct., Sarah, W17550
Cornelius, Mass., S14348
Cuff, R.I., BLWt.3459. Iss. 1/28/1790. No papers
Cuff/Cuffe (colored), R.I., S33586
Cyrus L., Va., BLWt.2053-300
Daniel, Ct., S31942
Daniel, Ct., Asenath, W16391
David, Cont., Ct., S36256; BLWt.6394-100. Iss. 5/7/1792 to Thomas Stanley, ass. No papers
David, N.C., S32487
David, Vt., Lucy, W2353
Ebenezer, Ct., Cont., S18575
Edmond/Edmund, N.J., S4778
Edmund. See Edmond
Edmund, N.C., S1715
Edward, Md., BLWt.1911-100
Edward, Pa., S22956
Edward, Va., Md. res. at enl., Christena Brag, W8560; BLWt. 34856-160-55
Elijah, Ct., S14314
Elijah, Ct., S14377
Elisha, Cont., Ct., S43939
Elisha, N.H., BLWt.3446. Iss. 3/25/1790. No papers
Ephraim, N.H., Sally, W22111
Esek (colored), R.I., Delana, W2351; BLWt.6027-160-55
Ezekiel, N.Y., S43977
Ezra/Isrey, Va., Patsey, R8874
Francis, Mass., Sarah, W15285
Freelove, Ct., BLWt.6411. Iss. 11/2/1791 to Titus Street, ass. No papers
George, Mass., S37354
George, Navy, N.H., Elizabeth, W22105; BLWt.8462-160-55
George, N.C., S7397; BLWt.31313-160-55
George, Va. See ROBARDS
Gideon, Ct., Jerusha (Pitcher), W2006
Giles, N.H., S33578
Griffith, Hazen's Regt., BLWt. 13671. Iss. 6/12/1797. No papers
Henry/Patrick Henry, Cont., Md., & Pa., Catharine, W164; BLWt. 18018-160-55
Henry, Del., BLWt.10874. Iss. 9/2/1789. No papers
Hezekiah, Va., Agnes, W9631
Isaac, Ct., BLWt.6396. Iss. 8/23/1790. No papers

ROBERTS (continued)
Isaac, Ct., Sally, W26399; BLWt. 29026-160-55
Isaac, Ct., Mass., Sarah, W10243
Isaac, Va., S19453
Isrey, See Ezra
James, Ct., S28862
James, Md., S35052
James, Mass., d. 1780, Martha Whitehouse, former wid., W25992
James, Mass., Navy, d. 5/5/1806, W16701
James, N.C., S4147; BLWt.82519-160-55
James, N.C., Frances, W4063; BLWt.59091-160-55
James, Va., R8867
Jeremiah, Cont., N.H., Mass., S15625
Joel, N.H., Sarah, W5739
John, Ct., French & Indian War 1758-
John, Ct., S11329
John, Ct., Cont., S36259
John, Ct., Privateer, S31939
John, Cont., Vt., Edna, W24796
John, Va., Cont., Lucy Ann, W2347; BLWt.1718-400
John, Del., BLWt.10869. Iss. 9/2/1789 to Andrew Hutton, ass. No papers
John, Mass., S45112
John, Mass., Tabitha, W13863
John, Navy, Pa. res. during Rev. & up to 1815, Old Act Navy, S1308
John, Navy, N.H., S45111
John, N.H., S41998
John, N.J., BLWt.8681. Iss. 8/22/1789. No papers
John, N.J., S16239
John, N.J., S33605
John, N.J., R8870
John, N.C., S7402
John, N.C., R8871
John, N.C., Va., S4148
John, S.C., S18188
John, Va., S4792
John, Va., enl. in N.C., his res. S17061
John, Va., Sarah, R8877
John, Va., R17483; Va. Half Pay. See N.A. Acc. No.874-050144 Half Pay, John Roberts
John, Va., Jane, BLWt.15176-160-55
John T., Mass., S33597
Jonathan, Mass., S45110
Joseph, Cont., Mass., S19058
Joseph, Md., BLWt.11653. Iss. 5/4/1797 to James DeBaufre, ass. No papers
Joseph, Navy, N.H., S16519
Joseph, Navy, N.H., Tamson, R8880
Joseph, Pa., BLWt.10257. Iss. 6/20/1789. No papers
Joseph, Pa., S40358
Joseph, Va., Frances, W8561
Joshua, N.C., b. Va., S7389
Joshua, Va., S17056

ROBERTS (continued)
Josiah, Mass., S41991
Judah, Ct., S15622
Love, Cont., Mass., Betsey, W2169; BLWt.24620-160-55
Lucretia, former wid. of Jeduthan Abbe, Ct., which see
Lucy, former wid. of John Bailey, Mass., which see
Luke, Ct., Catharine/Catherine Jackson, W4326; BLWt.41-60-55
Martin, Va., Elizabeth, W4785
Mary, former wid. of Thomas Sawyer, Mass., which see
Moses, Mass., BLWt.1790-300-Capt.
Mourning, Va., S31342
Nathan, Ct., S43969
Nathan, N.H., Hannah W. Hobbs, former wid., W23297
Nathan, Pa., S6007
Nathaniel, Cont., Ct., S14346
Noah, Ct., S43974
Noman/Namon, Va., S38338
Obadiah, Va., Lee's Legion, BLWt.12512. Iss. 11/2/1792 to Robert Means, ass. No papers
Owen/Owen M., S.C., BLWt.2359-500
Patrick, Pa., BLWt.10261. Iss. 7/9/1789 to Pat. Roberts. No papers
Patrick Henry, Va., See Henry
Paul, N.H., S17060
Pearly, Ct., Submit, W22127
Peter, Cont., Vt., Green Mt. Boys, Jane, R8868
Peter, N.C., S.C., b. Va., S21451
Philip, S.C., b. N.C., Sarah, W2170; BLWt.38566-160-55
Reuben, N.H., BLWt.3429. Iss. 6/17/1790 to B.J. Gilman, ass. No papers
Reuben, N.C., Milly, W1492
Reuben, R.I., BLWt.3461. Iss. 12/31/1789. No papers
Reuben, S.C., b. Va., S31934
Richard, N.C., S38339
Richard, Va., S39052
Richard, Va., Alice, W4573
Richard Brook, S.C., V.S.A., Everada Catherine Sophia, R8866; BLWt.1869-300-Capt. Iss. 4/20/1790. No papers
Robert, S.C., S9468
Rueben/Reuben (colored), R.I., S39834
Rufus, Ct., S44232
Samuel, Ct., BLWt.6395. Iss. 2/5/1790. No papers
Samuel, Ct., S43961
Samuel, N.H., S37342
Samuel, N.J., BLWts.8671 & 14089 Iss. 9/13/1798 to Jonathan & Joseph Roberts, heirs. No papers
Samuel, Va., S21454
Sarah, former wid. of John S. Taylor, Va., which see
Sears, N.J., S4146
Simon, N.H., S31341
Stephen, Ct., BLWt.6390. Iss. 5/7/1792 to Thos. Stanley, ass. No papers

ROBERTS (continued)
Stephen, Ct., Rebecca, W2860
Thomas, Cont., Pa., Catharine, W27872
Thomas, Mass., S30682
Thomas, Mass., Hannah, W24787
Thomas, Va., S4144
Thomas, Va., S31334
Thomas, Va., S38336
Thomas, Va., Nancy, W5738
Timothy, Ct., S14337
Timothy, Navy, N.H., Privateer, Elizabeth, W22113
Warren, N.Y., Debora, R8865
William, Ct., S33611
William, Ct., Abigail, W20033
William, Ct., Mass., Vt., Margaret, W4784
William, Hazen's Regt., BLWt. 13657. Iss. 3/25/1790. No papers
William, Md., BLWt.11628. Iss. 2/1/1790. No papers
William, Md., S35053
William, Mass., S43966
William, Mass., Mercy, W24805
William, N.Y., R.I., Vt., Rachel, R8875
William, N.C., S7418
William, N.C., S17054
William, Pa., BLWt.10246. Iss. 5/20/1791. No papers
William, R.I., Sarah, W12871
William, S.C., S21953
William, Va., S7427
William, Va., Sarah, R8878
William, Va., R17484; Va. Half Pay. See N.A. Acc. No.874-050145 Half Pay William Roberts
William, Va., Indian Wars 1788-1789, S7407
Wilson, Va., S6027
Zaccheus, S.C., Nancy, R8873
Zachariah, Md., S35054
Ziba, Ct., Mary Chase, former wid., W22759
ROBERTSON, Abraham, N.Y. See ROBERTS
Alexander, Pa., S7421
Andrew, Pa., S22479
Benjamin, N.C. See ROBISON
Daniel, Ct., Esther, W16704
David, N.C., S31333
David, Va., BLWt.12518. Iss. 1/6/1795 to John Stockdell, ass. No papers
Ebenezer, N.Y. See ROBINSON
Edward, Cont., Md., S35050
Ephraim, Ct., Priscilla, W17547; BLWt.6399-100. Iss. 2/27/1790 to Theodosius Fowler, ass. No papers
George, Cont., Va., Ann, W18834
George, Va., Judith, W5740
Henry, Va., "3rd Regt. of Va. Dragoons". BLWt.12499 & 14126. Iss. 8/5/1795. No papers
Hugh, Cont., Va., Susan/Susanna, W18836
Isaac, Mass., BLWt.4927. Iss. 4/1/1790. No papers
Isaac, Va., S6009

ROBERTSON (continued)
James, N.Y., BLWt.1573-100. Iss. 12/4/1829
James, N.C., S7405
James, Pa., S38332
James, S.C., b. N.C., S14341
James, Va., S14320
James, Va., S15620
James, Va., S17055
Jemima, former wid. of Joseph Brown, N.C., which see
Jesse, N.C., S39049
Jesse, Va., Sally, W2249
John, Del. See ROBESON
John, Navy, Mass., S17063
John, N.Y., BLWt.1565-100
John, N.C., b. Md., S4793
John, N.C., Va. res.?, R8885
John, Va., S7406
John, Va., Ctf. 30471
John, Va., S38331
John, Va., Elizabeth, W4324
John, Va., Mary, W5742
John, Va., Sarah Angleton, former wid., W8330
John, Va., Frances, R8883; BL Reg.247399-1855
John, Va., BLWt.1861-200-Lt. iss. 10/12/1795. No papers
Joseph, N.C. See ROBESON
Joseph, Va., S38334
Mathew, Va., S31338
Mitchell, Md., S6015
Mordica, Va., BLWt.12514. Iss. 7/14/179? to Robert Means, ass. No papers
Peter, Ct. See ROBINSON
Peter, Mass., N.H. res. in 1807 Mary, R8888
Peter, N.C., Elizabeth, W17569
Richard, Va., S6022
Robert, N.C. See ROBINSON
Seth, Ct., Hannah, W17553
Simeon, Ct. See ROBINSON
Stephen, Va., S35637
Terrence, Hazen's Regt.BLWt.13658 Iss. 6/14/1791 to Ann O'Brien
Thomas, N.C., R8890
Thomas, N.C. See ROBISON
Thomas, Va., S4157
Thomas, S.C. res., R8889
Watson, Mass., BLWt.4900. Iss. 4/1/1790. No papers
William, Cont., Va., W2668; BLWt.16132-160-55
William, N.H., Mary, W17554
William, N.C., son of Chas., b. on Peedee River, S4790
William, N.C.,Va., b. Va.,S14340
William, S.C., S7417
William, S.C. S21951
William, Va. (9th Regt.) res. of Augusta Co., Va., d. 11/12/1831 Lt. BLWt.1860-200 in Rev. War Files
William, Va., BLWt.1860-200
Zachariah, Md., S35632; BLWt. 1055-100. See N.A. Acc. No. 874-050146 Not Half Pay, Zachariah Robertson
ROBESON, Daniel, N.C., Elizabeth W39

ROBESON (continued)
James, N.C. See ROBERTSON
John, Del., S32499
John, N.C., S32488
John, Va. See ROBINSON
Joseph, N.C., S4158
Maximillian, Va. See ROBISON
ROBEY, Richard, Md., S6020
ROBIE, Samuel, N.H., Dorothy, W16699
ROBIN, Va. See Robin LOYD (Indian)
Joseph, Ct., Cont., Elizabeth, W17567
ROBINS, Brintnal, Ct., Mary, W7150; BLWt.26760-160-55
Daniel, Ct., Cont. Sea Service, N.Y., Ruth, W18826; BLWt.8184-160-55
Daniel, Mass., S30070
Daniel, Mass., S33575
Elijah, N.Y. See ROBBINS
Evens, N.Y., Rebecca, R8860
Isaac, N.J., S22954
John, Md., BLWt.11638. Iss. 6/11/1790. No papers
John, N.J., Pa., Indian Wars, R8854
John, N.C., S4150
Joseph, Ct., Mary Mulkin, former wid., W17181
Joseph, Cont., Mass. See ROBBINS
Lorin/Lorron, Ct., R.I., Cont., S14372
Paul, Mass. See ROBBINS
Samuel, Ct., Cont., R.I., Zeruviah W17566
Samuel, Mass., Betsey, W583; BLWt.34842-160-55
Silas, Ct. See ROBBINS
Stephen, Cont., Mass., Sarah, W26393
Thomas, R.I., S15626, Elizabeth Smith
Thomas, Va., S7403
William, N.J., Elizabeth, W4782
William, N.C., Bethiah, W9266
ROBINSON, Abel, Ct., S44235
Alexander, Pa., BLWt.10263. Iss. 2/9/1792 to Sarah Shepperd, ass. No papers
Alexander, Pa. See ROBERTSON
Amasa, Ct., Marcia, W9268; BLWt.1966-160-55
Amos, R.I., S36265
Amos, Vt., S15971
Andrew, Ct., Bethiah/Bethia, W2348; BLWt.26912-160-55
Andrew, Mass., Mehitable, W5746
Andrew, Mass., N.H., S22478
Andrew, Pa., BLWt.1827-200-Lt. Iss. 6/4/1789 to Andrew Robinson. No papers
Asher, Ct., Sarah, W22121
Bartlet/Bartlett, Mass., S43951
Benjamin, Ct., Ruth, R8915
Benjamin, Cont., Ct., S43980
Benjamin, Cont., Va., S9090
Benjamin, N.J. See ROBISON
Benjamin, N.C., S41996
Benjamin, Va., S16516
Caleb, N.H., BLWt.1773-400-Maj.

ROBINSON (continued)
Iss. 1/21/1789 to Eliphalet Ladd & Jonathan Cass, ass. No papers
Caleb, N.J., S23878
Cato, Ct., BLWt.6406. Iss 9/24/1790 to James F. Sebor, ass. No papers
Chandler, Ct., S22957
Charles, Ct., Chloe D., W26409
Charles, Md., Mephyteca, W9267; BLWt.6042-160-55. See Acc. No. 874-050147
Charles, Md. See ROBOSSON
Charles, Mass., S14321
Charles, Va. Agcy. Dis. No papers
Christopher, R.I., Hannah, W26403
Cornelius, N.J., BLWt.8669. Iss. 3/20/1790 to Jonas Stanbury ass. No papers
Daniel, Ct., BLWt.6416. Iss. 2/1790 to Thadius Fowler, ass. No papers
Daniel, Ct., Cont., S11316
Daniel, Cont., Mass., Anna, S33599
Daniel, Mass., S33573
Daniel, Mass., Jane, W584; BLWt. 36562-160-55
Daniel, Mass., Anna, W24819
David, Cont., N.Y., Elizabeth, W24794
David, Mass., S14339
David, N.H., S22961
David, N.Y., BLWt.7720. Iss. 11/27/1790. No papers
David, N.Y., R8896
Ebenezer, Cont., Mass., Privateer S18577; BLWt.3138-160-55
Ebenezer, Mass., S17656
Ebenezer, N.Y., S23401
Eber, Ct., Lucinda, W5745; BLWt.10257-160-55
Edmond, N.Y., BLWt.7661. Iss. 9/24/1792. No papers
Edmund, N.J., S4794
Eleazer, Ct., Mary, W24793; BLWt.851-100
Elias, Ct., Betsey, W11163; BLWt. 31578-160-55
Elias, Ct., Amy/Amie/Annie, R8893; BLWt.1799-200-Lt. Iss. 4/6/1796. No papers
Elizabeth, former wid. of Ebenezer Williams, Mass., which see
Ephraim, Ct., S22474
Francis, Va., S16517
George, Cont., Pa. res., Dis---. No papers. See Am. State Papers Class 9, p.99. Wounded by an accidental fall March 1778 at Lancaster in endeavoring to assist a sick soldier; which fall dislocated his left shoulder & which from that time has not been reduced; that some time in the latter part of 1777, he was discharged as unfit for duty.
George, Mass., Mary, W16707
George, Mass., Isabella, W22088
George, N.Y., BLWt.7678. Iss. 7/14/1790 to Richard Platt, ass.

ROBINSON (continued)
No papers
Hannah, former wid. of James Ferguson, Mass., which see
Hannah, former wid. of Timothy Snow, Mass., which see
Hardy, N.C., S41992
Henry, N.C. See ROBISON
Hugh, N.C. See ROBISON
Increase, Mass., Anne, W22101
Isaac, Mass., BLWt.4907. Iss. 11/4/1794 to Thomas Sheridan. No papers
Isaac, Mass., S43948
Isaac, Va., R8900
Isacher/Isachar, N.Y., S14345
Issachar, Cont., N.Y., S28861
James, Ct., Md., N.J., Pa., S7432
James, Cont., Md., Pa., S39050
James, Mass., S33609
James, Mass., S37347
James, Mass., Judith, W24784; BLWt.7083-160-55
James, N.H., No. 1818 Appl. on file (?)
James, N.Y., BLWt.7673. Iss. 9/15/1790 to John S. Hobart et al, assnes. No papers
James, N.C. See ROBERSON
James, Pa., BLWt.10252. Iss. 3/29/1791. No papers
James, Pa., BLWt.10260. Iss 8/9/1796 to John Broom, ass. No papers
James, Pa., BLWt.10298. Iss. 12/22/1794 to Henry Purdy, ass. No papers.
James, Pa., BLWt.10299. Iss. 6/22/179? No papers
James, Pa., S22960
James, Pa., Hannah, R8901
James, Va. See ROBERSON
James, Va. Agcy. Dis.- No papers
Jared, Ct., S43982; BLWt.1785-200
Jason, Ct., R8904; BLWt.6003-160-55
Jedediah, Mass., Polly, W2699; BLWt.13711-160-55
Jemima, former wid. of Joseph Brown, N.C., which see
Jeremiah, Va., S18180
Jesse, Va., S17466
Joel, Mass., Margaret, W15286
John, Ct., BLWt.6361. Iss. 12/20/1791. No papers
John, Ct., S43979
John, Ct., Sarah, W17573
John, Ct., Esther, W24791
John, Ct., Lucy, W26407
John, Cont., Del., BLWt.1309-100
John, Cont., Mass., Phebe, W22112
John, Cont., Mass., Deborah, W24785
John, Md., S40355
John, Md. or Pa., Jane West, former wid., R8903
John, Mass., Molly, W15282
John, Mass., Susannah, W15291
John, Mass., Martha, W22104
John, Mass., Naomi, W24811
John, N.H., BLWt.3443. Iss. 8/26/1789. No papers

ROBINSON (continued)
John, N.Y., Lydia, W7153
John, N.Y., BLWt.7664. Iss. 9/15/1790 to John S. Hobart et al, ass. No papers
John, N.Y., R8905
John, N.C., b. Va., S31935
John, N.C. See ROBESON
John, N.C., S.C., See ROBISON
John, Pa., S32492
John, Pa., S39055
John, R.I., Peninah, W20028
John, S.C., S32497
John, Va., BLWt.12492. Iss. 4/8/1796 to Wm. Taylor, Henry Bowyer & Thomas Scott, assnes. No papers
John, Va., S6017
John, Va., S6018
John, Va., S40351
John, Va. See ROBERTSON
John, Va., Jeriah, W5747
John, Va., S8884
John, Va., R8907
Jonathan, Ct., S18182
Jonathan, Mass., S14367
Jonathan, Mass., S30072
Jonathan, Mass., S33587
Jonathan, Mass., Hannah, W15288
Jonathan, Pa., S14359
Joseph, Ct., Abbey, W17555
Joseph, Mass., S33598
Joseph, N.H., S45122
Joseph, R.I., Freelove Butterworth former wid., W15613
Joseph, S.C., Rebecca, W10246
Joseph, Va. See ROBISON
Joshua, Ct., Chloe, W2440; BLWt. 13020-160-55
Joshua, Mass., S29425
Josiah, Mass., Sarah, W13859
Juda, former wid. of James Ramsdell, Mass., which see
Keen, Mass., Achsah, W22119
Lambert, Md., S41990
Lemuel, Mass., S33606
Levi, Ct., S33595; BLWt.1291-100
Levi, N.H., S17057
Levi, N.H., S17658
Lewis, N.C., S4153
Martha, former wid. of Thomas Bracket, N.H., which see
Mary, former wid. of George Foss Mass., which see
Matthew, Pa., BLWt.10286. Iss. 3/7/1794 to Gideon Merkle, ass. No papers
Matthew/Mathew, S.C., b. Va., S11309
Meshack, N.H., Sarah, W2352; BLWt. 26899-160-55
Moses, Ct., R.I., Hannah, R8897
Moses, Mass., S31933
Nathan, Mass., Sea Service, Abigail, W13862
Nathaniel, Ct., Susanna, W16706
Nathaniel, Green Mt. Boys, Mass., N.Y., S11323
Nathaniel, Mass., Hannah, W17556
Noah, Ct., N.Y., S23884
Noah, Cont., N.H., Rosamond, W2250 BLWt.1775-200-Capt., Lt. Iss. 3/

ROBINSON (continued)
9/1797 to Wm. S. Thorn, ass. No papers. Her former husb., Wm. Taylor, Cont. & N.H., was a pensioner, which see
Noah, Mass., S21456
Obed, Mass., Abigail, W15281
Oliver, Mass., Betsey, W5748
Otis, Mass., Hannah, W16705
Peter, Ct., BLWt.1795-300-Capt. Iss. 9/14/1789. No papers. Heitman's Hist. Reg. & The Printed Records of Ct. do not show any Capt. Peter Robinson of Ct. They show Capt. Peter Robertson
Peter, Mass., S23881
Peter, Mass., R8913
Peter, N.Y., S23879
Peter, N.Y., S43962
Philip, Mass., S23398
Polly, former wid. of Leme Paige, N.H., which see
Prince, R.I., Ann, R8894
Reuben, Ct., S29421
Reuben, Ct., S36269
Reuben, Ct., Rosannah, W7152; BLWt.7217-160-55
Reuben, Ct., Mass., Vt., S16238
Richard, Ct., S22473
Richard, N.H., BLWt.3432. Iss. 7/21/1789 to Ladd & Cass, assnes. No papers
Richard, N.Y., BLWt.7705. Iss. 7/30/1790 to Edward Cumpston, ass. No papers
Robert, Ct., R8914
Robert, Mass., S43946; BLWt. 133-100
Robert, N.Y., BLWt.7702. Iss. 7/30/1790 to Edward Cumpston, ass. No papers
Robert, N.C., S.C., See ROBISON
Robert, N.C., Susannah, W5741; BLWt.11065-160-55
Samuel, Mass., S14350
Samuel, Mass., Elizabeth, W26415
Samuel, N.C., S4155
Samuel, Vt., Esther, W24817
Simeon, Ct., S43949
Simeon, Cont., N.H., S14378
Simon, Pa., BLWt.10321. Iss. 10/6/1794. No papers
Solomon, N.J., BLWt.2299-100
Stephen, N.Y., S43963; BLWt.7670-100. Iss. 7/7/1791 to Ebenezer Russell. No papers
Susan, former wid. of Alva West, Ct., which see
Thomas, N.H., Molly, W24802
Thomas, N.C. See ROBISON
Thomas, Pa., BLWt.1819-450-Lt. Col. Iss. 7/3/1789. No papers
Thomas, Va., R8916
Tully, Va., R17465. Va. Half Pay
William, Ct., S14315
William, Md., BLWt.1424-100
William, Mass., Sarah, W24781
William, N.H. See ROBERTSON
William, N.J., Sarah, W4572
William, N.Y., BLWt.7708. Iss.

ROBINSON (continued)
3/29/1791 to James Roosevelt, ass. No papers
William (Colored), N.Y., S11320
William, N.C. See ROBISON
William, Pa., Proctor's Art., BLWt.10318. Iss. 6/29/1789 to M. McConnell, ass. No papers
William, Pa., S40359
William, Pa. No papers
William, Pa., Va. See ROBISON
William, S.C. See ROBERTSON
William, Va., BLWt.12509. Iss. 5/2/1794. No papers
William, Va., Mason, R8909
Winthrop, N.H., Privateer, "The Buccanier" was a Mass. Ship. Bulah, W9637
Zachariah, Md. See ROBERTSON
Zacheus, Mass., Bridget, W26411; BLWt.9056-160-55
Zephaniah, Mass., S33593
Ziba, Ct., S14332
Zophar, Ct., Charity, W17564
ROBISON, Benjamin, N.J., Sarah, W15850
Benjamin, N.C., S14361
Henry, N.C., Margery, R8891
Hugh, N.C., Jane, R8902
Isaac, N.Y., R8899
John, Md. or Pa. See ROBINSON
John, N.C., S.C., b. N.C., Abigail, W24798. See N.A. Acc. No.874-050148 Not Half Pay John Robinson
Joseph, Va., Methena, W9635
Macksimilion/Maximillian, Va., S40353
Robert, N.C., S.C., b. Pa., S7426
Thomas, N.C., Mary, R8892
Thomas, N.C., R---
William, N.J. See ROBINSON
William, N.C., b. Pa., Sarah, W18821
William, Pa., Va., S7391
William, S.C., b. Pa., S21452
ROBORSON, Charles, See ROBOSSON
ROBOSSON, Charles, Md., Rebecca, W9273
ROBUCK, George, N.C., S.C., b. Va., S9467
John, S.C., b. Va., R8917
ROBY, Aquilla, Md., R8918
Henry, Mass., R.I., S15624
Joseph, Mass., S18184
Silas, Cont., Mass., N.H., S14319
William, N.H., Hannah, W15273
ROCESTER, Samuel, Ct., BLWt. 6383. Iss. 10/7/1789 to Benj. Tallmadge, ass. No papers
ROCHE, Edward, Del., S36257; BLWt.1835-200-Lt. Iss. 5/30/1789. No papers
Thomas, Crane's Art., BLWts. 13659 & 14090. Iss. 12/31/1794. No papers
ROCHEFONTAINE, Etienne Nicholas, Marie Becket, Engineers, BLWt.1875-300-Capt. Iss. 4/19/1793. No papers

ROCHELLE, John, N.C., Patience, W8567; BLWt.2700-300-Capt. Iss. 6/20/1798. No papers
ROCHESTER, Nicholas, N.C., Ann, W8565
ROCK, Andrew, Md., R8920
John, Cont., Va., Nancy, W985; BLWt.1112-100
William, Md., R8921
ROCKAFELLAR, Peter, Cont., N.J. S34847 (Also written as Peter Rocky Feller)
ROCKAFELLER, John, N.J. Catharine R8919; BLWt.61129-160-55
ROCKAFELLOW, John, See ROCKAFELLER
ROCKEFELLER
Christian, N.Y., Eva, W15798
Diel/Teale, N.Y., Elizabeth, W16392
Peter, Von Heer's Corps, BLWt. 13645. Iss. 1/28/1793. No papers
Teale, N.Y. See Diel
ROCKELD, Thomas, See ROCKHOLD
ROCKETT, John, S.C., S7412
ROCKHILL, William. In the Invalids BLWt.13682. Iss. 6/29/1789 to Matt McConnell, ass. No papers
ROCKHOLD, Thomas T., Md., R8922
ROCKINSTIER, Joseph, N.Y., S22953
ROCKLEY, George, N.J., BLWt.8688. Iss. 7/17/1797 to Abraham Bell, ass. No papers
ROCKLEY, Micajah, See RACKLEY
ROCKWELL, Amasa, Ct., Mass., Prudence, W1086; BLWt.12702-160-55
Clapp, Ct., S17660
Grove, Ct., BLWt.6372. Iss. 11/15/1792. No papers
Grove, Ct., S36268
Jabez, Ct., Betsey B., W3722; BLWt.26759-160-55
Jabez, Ct., Deborah, W22122
Jeremiah, Mass., Abby, W26410; BLWt.19826-160-55
John, Ct., BLWt.6386. Iss. 7/28/1790. No papers
John, Ct., S44237
John, Ct., Abigail, W18838
Joseph, Ct., Esther, W11155; BLWt.31583-160-55
Noadiah, Ct., Cont., S18181
Oswald, Ct., Sarah, W17562
Samuel, Ct., S14356
Samuel, Ct., S23375
Silas, Ct., N.Y., S28856
Simeon, N.Y., S43971
William, Ct., N.Y., Sarah, R8923
ROCKWOOD, Abigail, former wid. of Daniel Knowlton, Mass.,which see
Amos, Mass., S4791
Benjamin, Cont., Mass., Anna, W15294
Ebenezer, Mass., BLWt.4943. Iss. 4/12/1792 to Stephen Thomasson, ass. No papers
Ebenezer, Mass., S37344; BLWt. 927-100
Frost, Mass., Sarah, W15271
Hezekiah, Mass., Betsey, W532; BLWt.6295-160-55

ROCKWELL (continued)
Samuel, Mass., S16518
Samuel, Mass., Vt., Sarah, R8924
Simeon, Mass., S41111
ROCKY FELLER, Peter, See ROCKA-FELLAR
RODAMBER, Christopher, Cont., Pa. S46341
RODAMER, Christopher, See RODAMBER
RODDEN, Benjamin, Va., Keziah Pittman/Pitman, former wid., R8272. See her claim as wid.of other husb., Mathew Pitman/ Pittman, N.C.(?)
RODDEY, Ezekiel, Pa., R8925
RODEBAUGH, Peter. See RADUBACH
RODEN, Jeremiah, S.C., Susanna, R8926
RODERFIELD, William, Crane's Cont. Art., Mass., BLWt.4960 Iss. 9/22/1789. No papers
RODES, Anna, former wid. of Frederic Eisenhauer, Pa., which see
Jacob, Cont., Va., BLWt.510-100
Mark, Cont., Pa., Catharine, W3460
Peter, N.C., R8730
RODGERS, Abraham, Va., S6026
Ahaz, S.C., S21450
Andrew, Pa., BLWt.2165-100
Andrew, Va., S35635
Asa, Mass., S33590
Benjamin, Va. See ROGERS
Daniel, N.C., b. S.C., S1871
Daniel, N.C., See ROGERS
Hugh, S.C., Nancy A., W4327
James, Del., S7410
James, N.J., Massey, W5733
James, Va., S11311
John, Pa., R21679
John, Va., BLWt.2075-100
John R.B., Pa., S4138; BLWt. 1822-400-Surgn. Iss. 9/7/1789 No papers
Joseph, Del., S6019
Joseph, N.Y. See ROGERS
Joseph, S.C., R8930
Margaret, former wid. of Wm. Scott, Pa., which see
Michael, Cont. Pa. See ROGERS
Ralph, S.C., b. N.J., S4788
Shadrach, S.C., Celia, R8928
Stephen, Va., Willa, W5729; BLWt.18372-160-55
Thomas, Ct., S36270
William, Cont., N.C., Sarah, W10239; BLReg.105769-1855
William, S.C., pens. in Ct., S36276
William, Va. See ROGERS
William T., S.C., Ann, W11186
RODMAN, Mingo (colored), R.I., BLWt.1687-100
Philip (colored), R.I., S39835
RODRICQUE, Emanuel, Hazen's Regt., BLWt.13652. Iss. 2/3/ 1792 to John P. Schott, ass. No papers
ROE, Abner, Hazen's Regt., BLWt. 13650. Iss. 7/12/1793 to Reuben Murray, ass. No papers

ROE (continued)
Benjamin, Cont., N.Y., Mary, W15797
Charles, N.C., S7416
Daniel, N.Y., S43973
Henry, N.J., R8931
John, N.J. See ROW
John, Va. (Free man of color), S39045
John, Va., R8932
Joseph, Green Mt. Boys, Vt. See ROWE
Joseph, Pa., BLWt.10297. Iss. 3/10/1795 to Michael Stever, ass. No papers
Matthew, N.C., S20897
Stephen, N.Y., Rebecca, W18829
William, Va. See WROE
William, Va. See ROWE
William, Va Sea Service, R87; Va. Half Pay. See N.A. Acc. No. 837-Va. State Navy. William Roe Y.S. File Va. Half Pay
ROEBUCK, Raleigh, Va., S7425
ROEDER, Conrad, Pa., S23866
ROEHR, Joseph, Pa., R8933
ROEIEAU, Jean Baptist, Cont., N.Y., R20451
ROEMER, Philip, Cont., Pa., Elizabeth, W3301
ROEN, John, See ROWEN
ROESKRANS, Jacobus, See ROSEKRANS
ROFF, Christopher, N.Y., S19454
Henry, See ROLF
Samuel, Mass., S33572
ROGERS, Aaron, Mass., S30073
Aaron, Mass., Hannah, W15280
Abel, Ct., S14322
Abiathar, Ct., Mass., Naomi, W17572
Abijah, Ct., Lydia, W11160
Abisha, Mass., Elizabeth, W20031
Abraham Foster, Mass., Patty, W20027
Alexander, Mass., Rebecca, W1085; BLWt.13209-160-55
Alexander, Pa., BLWt.10265. Iss. 4/29/1793 to Alexander Power, ass. of Wm. Fields, Admr. No papers
Bela, Ct., Rebecca, W18823
Benjamin, Va., Martha, W867
Bias, N.C., Sarah, R8960
Bixbee, Ct., S40357
Boling, Va., Naomi, W1491
Caleb, Mass., S4779
Charles, R.I., S23883
Chester, Ct., Eunice Boynton, former wid., W20744
Daniel, Ct., S11326
Daniel, Cont., Mass., S45119
Daniel, Mass., R.I., S19059
Daniel, N.C., b. Va., Eliza; W5732; BLWt.38565-160-55
Daniel, R.I., Ann, W22117
Daniel, S.C., S18186
Daniel G., N.Y., Elizabeth Galley, former wid., R3970
David, Ct., BLWt.6371. Iss. 12/ 5/1796. No papers
David, Ct., S36274
David, Mass., S37355

ROGERS (continued)
David, N.J., BLWt.8680. Iss. 9/29/1790 to John Hole, ass. No papers
David, N.J., Pa., Insurrection of 1794, Rhoda, W1495
Dorothy, former wid. of Thomas Colby, Mass., which see
Drury, N.C., Frances, R8942
Ebenezer, Ct., S31941
Ebenezer, Ct., Ruth, W17571
Ebenezer, Mass., S43942
Edward, Ct., Hannah, W22118
Edward, Ct. Sea Service, S4795
Edward, S.C., b. Ireland, S31944
Edward, Va., S39054
Edward, Va., Elizabeth, W9261
Eliphalet, Mass., Navy, Privateer, S21954
Elisha, Ct., Anna, W22116; BLWt.6426-160-55
Elkanah, Mass., Tamesin, W15293
Elnathan, Ct., S14376
Ephraim, Ct., Martha, W17561
Ethan, Ct., S4139
Ezekiel, S.C., R8941
George, Va., Elizabeth, W10240; BLWt.31316-160-55
Gideon, Ct., Lucy, W27479
Gurdon, Ct., S31940
Heman, Ct., Hannah, W815; BLWt. 316-60-55. Iss. 1/6/1797
Henry, Mass., S43956
Henry, N.J., S40356
Hezekiah, Ct., BLWt.1793-300-Capt. Iss. 7/21/1789 to Hez. Rogers. No papers
Hezekiah, Mass., S19061
Hosea, Va., S38333
Isaac, Ct., Mary, W11168
Isaac, Cont., Mass., Sarah, W24804
Israel, Ct., S14383
Jabez, Ct., Sarah, W8959
Jacob, N.Y., Sarah, W4574; BLWt.6041-160-55
James, Mass., S15969
James, N.J., BLWt.1817-150-Ens. Iss. 8/8/1791 to Jos. Stanbury Admr.
James, N.Y., Mary, W1895
James, N.C., Judy, W2168
Jedediah, Cont., Ct., Sarah, W17570; BLWt.1802-300-Capt. of Col. Sheldon's Regt. of Cav. Iss. 10/2/1789. No papers
Jeduthun, Ct., Elizabeth, R8940
Jeremiah, R.I., S18576
Jeremiah, Va., S1927
John, Ct., Dis. -- No papers. See Am. State Papers, Class 9, p.126. Sold. wounded at Hackensack, N.J., 11/1779 by musket ball which passed through his left leg and cut off one of the sinews
John, Ct., Privateer, S14380
John, Cont., N.H., Polly, W26948
John, Mass., S33574
John, Mass., S37341
John, Mass., S45120

ROGERS (continued)
John, Mass., Sarah, W18822
John, N.H., BLWt.35-100
John, N.C., Rebecca, W18825
John, Pa. See RODGERS
John, R.I., S11325; BLWt.26-100
John, R.I., S33602; BLWt.1776-200-Lt. Iss. 2/11/1800. No papers
John, R.I., Betsey, W22097
John, S.C., S11330
John, Va., R--- Va. Half Pay. See N.A. Acc. No.874-050149, Half Pay John Rogers
John, Va., R8947
John, Va. Sea Service, R88, Va. Half Pay. See N.A. Acc.837 Va. State Navy, John Rogers Y.S. file, X, Va. Half Pay
Jonah, Ct., R8948
Jonathan, Mass., Phebe, W15287
Jonathan, Mass., R8949
Jonathan, Mass., Sea Service, Hannah, W22102
Jonathan, N.H., S22475
Joseph, Ct., S43978; BLWt.1801-150-Ensign. Iss. 7/21/1789. No papers
Joseph, Ct., S45858
Joseph, N.Y., S11322
Joseph, N.Y., S19063
Joseph, S.C., b. Va., S1928
Joseph, Va., Hester, R8944
Josiah/Josias, Ct., Ruth, W3605
Josiah, Ct., Alice Rogers Hewett former wid., W10099; BLWt. 92107-160-55
Josiah, Ct., Cont., S36272
Josiah, Ct., N.H., Hannah, R8943
Kinsey, S.C., Lydia, R8952
Leonard, Ct., S31937
Levi, Ct., Abigail, W8292; BLWt.26618-160-55
Lewis, N.Y., Effie/Effy, W9632; BLWt.96533-160-55
Lott, Va., Ann, R8938
Lucy, former wid. of Cato Howe/How, Mass., which see
Michael, Cont., Pa., R8956; BLWt.40712-160-55
Mikel, N.Y., R8955
Moses, Mass., Rebecca, W15275
Moses, N.Y., S14323
Nancy, former wid. of Philip Lumpkin, Va., which see
Nathaniel, Ct., S23877
Nathaniel, Mass., S29422
Nathaniel, Mass., Bethiah, W15284
Nathaniel, Mass., Abigail, W17568
Nathaniel, N.H., Eunice, W15279
Nathaniel, N.J., Rachel, W26394
Nathaniel, S.C., Cely/Celly, W9263
Noadiah, Ct., Rebecca, W26413; BLWt.26942-160-55
Noah, Mass., Hannah C., W22095; BLWt.18387-160-55
Oliver, Navy, Ct., S36275
Paul, Mass., S43959
Perley, N.H., S43975
Perley, N.H., Esther, W5730
Peter, Ct., S33582

ROGERS (continued)
Peter, Ct., Nancy, W5731
Randel, N.C., Va., S7428
Reuben, N.Y., S28859
Rhodam, Va., S6021
Richard, Ct., S4784
Richard, Mass., Sea Service, S19062
Robert, Mass., Huldah, W26397; BLWt.9449-160-55
Robert, R.I., S21455
Robert, Va., S6006
Samuel, N.Y. agcy., widow Lydia Ctf. No. 30696
Samuel, Ct., S22482
Samuel, Ct., Privateer, Vt., Mehitable, R8954
Samuel, Mass., Abigail, W22107
Samuel, Mass., R8958
Samuel, N.H., Rhoda, W2669; BLWt.34853-160-55
Samuel, N.H., Sarah, W7147
Samuel, R.I., S14363
Sharp, Ct., BLWt.6384. Iss. 6/10/1790
Simon, Ct., Mary, W27807
Simon, Mass., S14336
Smith, Mass., S33608
Stephen, Mass., S43944
Stevens/Stephen, Ct., Abigail Byrne, former wid., W25319; BLWt.2185-160-55
Thankful, former wid. of Elihu Avery, Ct., which see
Thomas, Ct., S22480
Thomas, Ct., Navy, Privateer, R.I., S14343
Thomas, Mass., Eggatha/Agatha, W15598; BLWt.13872-160-55
Thomas, N.H., S45121
Thomas, Va., b. Md., S7422
Thomas, Va., b. Pa., S31337
Timothy, Ct., Hannah Markham, former wid., W25677. Her last husb., Nathaniel Markham, Cont. Ct., also pensioned, which see
Timothy, Mass., BLWt.4919. Iss. 6/14/1790
William, Cont., N.J., S40365
William, Mass., S31332
William, Mass., S33601; BLWt. 746-100
William, N.H., R8962
William, N.Y., S14330
William, N.Y., Esther, W24813
William, N.C., S21453
William, Pa., b. R.I., Susan/Susannah, W1652
William, Va., S1249
William, Va., S2017
William, Va., R17514; BLWt.2369-300. Va. Half Pay
Williamson, See Wilson
Willoughby, N.C., S3904
Wilson/Williamson, N.C., R8964
Zachariah, N.C., S.C., b. S.C. R8965
Zebadiah/Zebediah, Mass., S18578
Zephaniah, Ct., Elizabeth, W3192

ROGERSON, John, N.C., S41988
John, Pa., S33580
ROHN, Christopher, See ROWEN
ROHR, John, Md., R8934
Joseph, See ROEHR
Philip, Md. res. in 1838, R8936
ROHRER, John, Pa., Elizabeth, W2855
Martin, not Rev. War, U.S.A., Northwest Indian Wars. Pensioned in Ohio, O.W. Inv. File 1341
ROIEAU, Jean Baptist, See ROEIEAU
ROIST, Samuel, Cont., Mass., See RIST
ROLAND, Fendral, N.C., Elizabeth W11166; BLWt.26934-160-55
Jacob, Pa., S7420
James, N.C., S1716
ROLESON, Isaiah, N.J., R8966
ROLF, Henry, Cont., N.J., Patty, W104
James, N.H., BLWt.3424 & 6430 Iss. 3/25/1790
Jeremiah, Mass., Fanny, W22108
Joseph, Mass., Sea Service, Mary, W22106
ROLFE, Jonathan, N.J., Elsy, R8971
William, Mass., S19060
ROLFF, James, N.H. See ROLLF
ROLINGS, Nathaniel, Mass., Privateer, Elizabeth, W24721
ROLINS, Eliphalet, Mass. See ROLLINS
John, Cont., Mass. See ROLLINS
ROLISON, William, S.C., S11310
ROLL, Mathew, See Matthias RALL
Matthias, See RALL
Michael, Pa., S38340
ROLLE, Robert, Md. Sea Service, R20515
ROLLENS, Hananiah, Md., N.J., Martha, R8970
ROLLER, Conrad, Va., Elizabeth, W4325
ROLLF, Ephraim, Cont., N.H., Lucy, W4787
James, N.H., S36876
ROLLINGS, John, Cont., N.H. See ROLLINS
Joseph, N.H. See ROLLINS
Nathaniel, Mass. See ROLINGS
ROLLINGS, Robert, N.H., BLWt. 3451. Iss. 3/10/1797 to Chris. S. Thorn, ass. No papers
Thomas, N.H., Sarah, W15278
ROLLINS, Aaron, N.H., BLWt.3447 Iss. 4/17/1800. No papers
Aaron, N.H., BLWt.3431 & 3477. Iss. 9/17/1800 to Aaron Rollins
Aaron, N.H. See ROWLINS
Aaron, N.H., Catharine Mosley, former wid., W16700
Anthony N., N.H., S14344
Daniel, N.H., S45115
Edward, N.H., Anna Stanton, former wid., W22330
Eliphalet, Mass., S37356
Eliphalet, N.H. See RAWLINGS

ROLLINS (continued)
Hananiah, Md., N.J., See ROLLENS
Jabez, Cont., Mass., N.H.(?), S37351
James, Mass., S29424
Jeremiah, N.H., S45116
John, Cont., Mass., S37349
John, Cont., N.H., Sarah, W24821
John, N.H. See RAWLINGS
Joseph, N.H., Susannah, W24808; BLWt.805-100
Moses, Va., Nancy, W10241; BLWt. 339-60-55 & 499-100
Nathaniel, Mass. See ROLINGS
Nathaniel, N.H., Polly, BLWt. 54234-160-55
Reuben, N.H., Betty, R8969
Robert, N.H., S45118; BLWt.3451-100. Iss. 3/10/1797 to Chris Thorn, ass. No papers (Name spelled ROLLINGS)
Samuel, N.H., Elizabeth, W26402
Sarah, former wid. of James Eveleth, Mass., which see
ROLLO, Zachariah, Ct., S36267; BLWt.1448-100
ROLLS, James, Md., Va., Margaret, R8968
John, Va., S39056
ROLO, Joseph, Ct., Polly, W26405; BLWt.31577-160-55
ROLOO, Daniel, Ct., S11315
ROLPH, Jonathan, See ROLFE
ROLSTON, Isaac, Cont., N.C., Nancy, W26406
ROLSTONE, David, Va., S7431
ROMAINE, Benjamin, N.J., Mary, W18839
ROMAN, Isaac, Va., R8973
ROMANS, Bernard, N.Y., Elizabeth, R8974
ROMER, Hendrick, N.Y., Christina/ Christiana, W16698; BLWt. 10002-160-55
Henry, N.Y., S43965
Luke, N.J., N.Y., S14352
ROMIER, Benjamin, N.Y., BLWt. 7672. Iss. 9/15/1790 to John Hobart et al, assnes. No papers
ROMINE, Benjamin, N.J., S4135
John, Va., S6008
Samuel, N.J., S907
ROMINGER, Michael, N.C., Anna Maria, W17551
ROMMILL, John, Md., BLWt.11656. Iss. 1/11/1796 to Joshua Ward, ass. No papers
RONDE, John/John DeRONDE, N.Y., S28707
RONE, Paul, Md., BLWt.11645. Iss. 2/7/1790
RONEMOUS, Philip, Va., Jane, BLWt.36658-160-55
RONEY, George, Mass., Sea Service, Hannah Robbins, former wid., R8852
Hugh, Md., BLWt.11659. Iss. 4/ 26/1792 to George Stout, ass. No papers
John, Va., BLWt.1856-200-Lt. Iss. 9/4/1792 to Andrew Dunscomb, ass. No papers

RONOMIS, Philip, See RONEMOUS
ROOD, David, Ct., Lucretia, R8981
Eli, N.Y., Mary, W17560
Ezra, Mass., Parthena Brown, former wid., W23694; BLWt.7208-160-55. Her other husb., Nathan Brown, Mass., also served in Rev. War., which see
Ira, Mass., S43952
Jeremiah, Ct., S44231
John, Ct., S20940
Joseph, Ct., R8980
Moses, Cont., Mass., S41997
Roger, Ct., R8982
Rozzel, Ct., Cont., Mass., S23403
Simeon, Ct., S43964
ROODE, Briggs, Ct., R8979
ROODS, John, Pa., War of 1812, See ROADS
ROOF, John, N.Y., S14371
ROOK, Ternon, Pa., BLWt.10281. Iss. 7/16/1789 to Wm. McConnell, ass. No papers
ROOKE, Amos, Pa., R8983
John, Va., BLWt.12493. Iss. 5/12/ 1792 to James Morrison, admr.
ROOKER, John, S.C., Anna, W4786
Joseph, N.Y., S43958
ROOKS, Daniel, Vt., S22483
ROOKSBERRY, Jacob, Ga., N.C., S.C., Eleanor, W3043
ROOLO, Daniel, Ct. See ROLOO
ROOME, Benjamin, N.Y., S43983
Henry, N.J., S1094
Samuel, N.J., S4789
ROOMER, William, N.Y., BLWt.7691 Iss. 8/31/1790 to Richard Plass, ass. No papers
ROORBACK, Marlin, See surname MARLIN
ROOSA, Cornelius, N.Y., Elizabeth, W24786
Jacob, N.Y., Maria, W3160
Jacob J., N.Y., S7414
John A., N.Y., Catharine, W20036
John E., N.Y., S14384
John I/Johannes/Johannis, N.Y., S14375
Peter, N.Y., Leah, W26398
ROOT, Aaron, Mass., Marlow, W4783; BLWt.6412-160-55
Abel, Vt., S4783
Abraham, Mass., BLWt.2485-100
Amos, Ct., S14317
Amos, Mass., Anna, W24812
Asahel, Mass., N.Y., Sally, W16390
Azariah, Mass., S17659
Billa, Ct., Polly, R8991
Daniel, Ct., S11321
David, Mass., BLWt.1810-100
Ebenezer, Mass., Cynthia, W2574; BLWt.7433-160-55
Eleazer, Ct., Lucinda, R8987
Eleazer, Mass., BLWt.4898. Iss. 11/21/1791. No papers
Elias, Mass., S19064
Elihu, Mass., BLWts. 1723-100 & 2225-50
Elijah, Ct., S14386
Elijah, Ct., Mass., S23399
Erastus, Ct., Lucy, W1650; BLWt. 9207-160-55

ROOT (continued)
Ezekiel N., Ct., Cynthia Cowles, former wid., W4927
Israel, Ct., Mass., S15627
Israel, Mass., S43950
Joel, Cont., Ct., S33589
John, Ct., Polly, W26404
Joseph, Ct., S14324
Joseph, Ct., Mary, W4323
Joshua, Ct., S11314
Josiah, Cont., Ct., Sea Service S14328
Josiah, Cont., Mass., Experience Adkins, former wid., W26414; BLWt.6455-160-55
Lemuel, Mass., S22484
Lydia, former wid. of Joseph Waters, Ct., Cont., which see
Moses, Ct., Esther, W24809
Moses, Mass., S22477
Moses, Mass., Lovina, W18827
Moses, Mass., Mary, R8988
Nathan, Ct., S47751
Nathaniel, Ct., S14368
Nathaniel, Ct., S18574
Nathaniel, Ct., S36277
Nathaniel H., Ct., S18573
Oliver, Vt., S14349
Phebe, former wid. of Andrew Colburn, Cont., N.H., which see
Rufus, Vt., S41102
Salmon/Solomon, Ct., Bulah, W1084
Samuel, Art. Artificer, BLWt. 13679. Iss. 11/24/1791 to Isaac Bronson, ass. No papers
Samuel/Salmon, Ct., BLWt.6359. Iss. 2/27/1793 to Alexander Power, ass. No papers
Samuel, Ct., Dinah, W24779
Samuel, Cont., Mass., Lucy, W22092
Seth, Ct., S36273
Solomon, Ct. See Salmon
Thaddeus, Mass., Sarah, W24807
Theodosia, former wid. of Simon Brooks, Mass., which see
Thomas, Ct., S43984
William, Mass., S43972
Zenas, Mass., Mary, W5721; BLWt.507-160-55
ROOTS, Daniel, Ct., Lucy, W22098
Michael, Pa., Va., S10256
ROPER, David, N.C., S30683
Drury, Va., S4133
George, N.C., S36261
James, N.C., S7413
James, N.C., Mary, R8996
John, Mass., Dorcas, W15274
John, N.C., S31945
John, Va., R8995
Nathaniel, Mass., Naomi, R8997
Silas, N.H., Elizabeth, W15292
Sylvester, Mass., S11318
William, Navy, Mass. agcy. & res., S33596
ROREMAN, David, Pa., BLWt.10323. Iss. 3/10/1790 to Alexander Power, ass. No papers
RORER, George, Pa., S22481
RORICK, Gasper, N.J., S833
RORK, Michael, Va., Letty, W5720

ROSA, Abraham, N.Y., S14381
Alias/Elias, N.Y., Nancy/Annatie W17546
Elias, N.Y. See Alias
Storm, N.Y., S23876
ROSAKRANS, Henry, N.Y., Susannah, R9014
ROSAMOND, Samuel, S.C., Sarah, W4579
ROSBROUGH, Isaac, Pa., S41105
ROSCROW, Henry, Pa., BLWt.2064-100
ROSE, Abner, Mass., Abigail, W15276
Abraham, Mass., R.I., Deziar/Deriah, W24780
Abraham, R.I., BLWt.3453. Iss. 4/16/1790
Albert, Pvt., N.Y., BLWt.7692 iss. 12/5/1791 to Albert Rosa, ass.
Alexander, Va., BLWt.1863-300-Capt. Iss. 3/3/1791. No papers
Amos, Mass., S33607
Andrew, N.Y., BLWt.7668. Iss. 7/24/1790 to John Lawrence, ass.
Archibald, Va., BLWt.12500. Iss. 4/12/1792 to Francis Graves, ass.
Archibald, Va., S39046
Benjamin, Mass., S28858
Benjamin, N.Y., R8998
Benjamin B., Va., Sea Service, Susannah, W11162; BLWt.43522-160-55
Charles, N.J., Rebecca, R9010
Charles, Va., Lucinda, W816; BLWt.26292-160-55
Cornelius, Green Mt. Boys, N.Y. Sarah Whaley/Waley, former wid., W19623
David, Pa., S22959
Elijah, Mass., BLWt.4929. Iss. 4/13/1789. No papers
Elijah, Mass., S43945
Elisha, Cont., Mass., S43960
Enoch, Mass., BLWt.1198-100
Evert, N.Y., Margaret, W22126
Gad, Mass., S17657
George, Va., Dicey, W5716
George, Va., R8999
Isaac, Cont., Md., Margaret, W3721
Isaac, Va., S39053
Isaac, Va., Margaret, W5713
Jacob, N.Y., Lisa/Lizzie, W4578
Jacob, N.Y., Jane Woodcock, former wid., R11811
James, N.Y., BLWt.7665. Iss. 7/9/1790 to Nicholas Fish, ass.
James, N.Y., Esther Kylefuss, former wid., W16321
James, N.Y., Elizabeth, W24792; BLWt.36521-160-55
James, Va., Rebecca, W27533; BLWt.6439-160-55. Rebecca received also War of 1812 pension for service of her former husb., Isaac Durham, and BLWt. See War of 1812-Old War Wid. File No.

ROSE (continued)
27539, Isaac Durham; BLWts. are with the pension claims.
Jesse, Va., S35634
Jesse, Va., R9002
Joanna, former wid. of Abraham Wilson, N.Y., which see
John, Ct., BLWt.1804-400-Surgn. Iss. 2/24/1797. No papers
John, Cont., Ct., S43967; BLWt. 1584-150
John, Mass., Sea Service, R9004
John, N.J., BLWt.8659 & 8668. Iss. 8/10/1792. No papers
John, N.J., BLWt.8674. Iss. 4/21/1790. No papers
John, N.J., S4787
John, N.J., Nancy, S43940
John, N.C., b. Va., Rachel, W18824
John, see Gustavus H. HENDERSON, Pa.
John, Pa., BLWt.1825-200-Lt. Iss. 5/18/1789 to Wm. Irvine, his atty.
John, Pa. or Va., also served 1786-1787-1788, R9006
John, Va., d. 1817, Mary, R9008
Jonathan, Ct., Hannah, W26395; BLWt.12565-160-55
Joseph, Mass., S23400
Justus, Mass., R9007
Lemuel, Mass., Achsah, W5715
Lemuel, N.Y., Amy, W22115
Levi, Ct., Mary, W22114
Levi, Mass., S33594
Matthias, Va., S17053
Nathaniel, Mass., Privateer, Polly, W24783
Peleg, Ct., Mary, W22120
Peter, Ct., Cont., Ester Edmonds/Edmunds, former wid., R3244
Peter, N.Y., War of 1812, S19065
Philip, Va., Sarah, W58
Prosper, Ct., S35
Richard, Cont., Va., Mary, W11187 BLWt.75111-160-55
Richard, N.J., S33603
Robert, Cont., BLWt.1855-400-Surgn.
Russel, Cont., Mass., Lydia, W5718; BLWt.7064-160-55
Samuel, Ct., R9011
Samuel, N.C., Mary, W7141; BLWt. 33572-160-55
Sterling, N.C., S4132
Thomas, Mass., N.H., Eunice, W24778
Thomas, Mass., Privateer, S30069
Timothy, Mass., Lydia Dickinson, former wid., W7025
Timothy, N.J., Phebe, W87
William, Ct., S11324
William, N.J., Elizabeth, W18832
William, N.C., Elizabeth, W8554
William, Va., Mary, W9628
Winthrop, Ct., S43968
ROSEBERRY, John M., N.J., S14316; BLWt.12731-160-55
ROSEBOOM, Garret/Garrett, N.J., Gertrude/Tricha, W1494
Hendrick, N.J., S46065

ROSEBOOM (continued)
John, N.J., S32498
ROSEBROOK, Eleazer, N.H., Hannah, R9013
ROSEBROUGH, Isaac, See ROSBROUGH
John, Pa., Aseneth, W11172; BLWt.93085-160-55
ROSECRANSE, James, N.Y., BLWt. 1806-400-Maj. Iss. 7/23/1790.
ROSECRANTZ, Cornelius, N.Y., Jane W20034
ROSEKRANS, Jacobus, N.Y., Blandina Jansen, former wid., W16615
Jacobus, N.Y., Pa., S44234
Peter, N.Y., S14347
Thomas, see Joseph JOHNSON, N.Y.
ROSWELL, Elias, N.J., Deborah, W5735; BLWt.29013
Zachariah, N.J. See ROSSELL
ROSENGRANT, Alexander, N.J., Mary, W15701
ROSENTHAL, Gustavus H. de, see Gustavus H. HENDERSON
ROSER, Abraham, N.J., S41109
ROSETTER, Benjamin, Ct. See ROSSETER
ROSEWATER, Thomas, Pvt., Va., Lee's Legion, BLWts.12497 & 13995 iss. 11/2/1792 to Robert Means, ass.
ROSEWELL, Zachariah, See ROSSELL
ROSIER, Abraham, N.J., BLWt.8687 Iss. 5/27/1793. No papers
Abraham, N.J. See ROSER
John, Mass., See ROZIER
Silas, Mass. See ROSO
ROSMAN, Henry, N.Y., Catharine, W17544
ROSO, Silas, Mass., Phebe Gould, former wid., W14809
ROSS, Adam, Mass., Elizabeth, W18835
Alexander, Md., BLWt.11654. Iss. 11/29/1790 to John Cochran, Admr.
Alexander, Mass. Res., Dis. No papers
Alexander, Va., S14364
Andrew, N.J., S569
Benjamin, R.I., Sarah, W15290; BLWt.1606-100
Charles, Va., S39036
Daniel, Cont., Mass., S30684
Daniel, Mass., Avy, W10237; BLWt.87019-160-55
David, Del., S43981
David, N.C., b. Ct., S7419
Edward, R.I., Tacy, W18820
Edward, Va., R9016
Ezekiel, N.J., S7409
Ezra, N.J., S22955
Finle, N.Y., S4128
George, Mass., S33591
George, S.C., b. Va., S1717
Horatio, Cont., Md., S43938
Isaac, Mass., Elizabeth, W22090
Isaac, N.J., Elizabeth, W4575; BLWt.27583-160-55
Jackson, N.J., S747
James, Cont., Pa., Polly S., W3159
James, Mass., Thankful, W26408

ROSS (continued)
James, N.J., Hannah, R9018
James, N.J., R9019
James, N.C., S35639
James, N.C., Lydia/Liddy, W5722; BLWt.34940-160-55
James, N.C., R9020
James, Pa., Margaret, W2861
Jeremiah, Cont., Mass., S33600
Jesse, Miss. res. in 1850, R9021
John, Cont., N.Y., S43953
John, Cont., Pa., S40363
John, N.H., S18183
John, N.J., Elizabeth, W868
John, N.J., BLWt.1812-400-Maj. Iss. 6/11/1789. No papers
John, N.Y., BLWt.7674 & 13649. Iss. 7/30/1790 to Edward Cumpston, ass. No papers
John, Lamb's Art., N.Y., BLWt. 7710. Iss. 7/24/1790 to John Lawrence.
John, N.Y., S43957
John, N.Y., S43976
John, N.Y., Aramintas, R9015. Also called John Knapp Ross/ John Ross Knapp, Alexander Tagert
John, N.C., S1929
John, N.C., S4131
John, N.C., Lydia Brackett/ Bracket, former wid., R1120
John, N.C., b. Scotland, res. in 1844 Me. & Nova Scotia, R9023 1/2
John, Pa., BLWt.10258. Iss. 6/29/ 1789. No papers
John, Pa., BLWt.10270. Iss. 1/23/ 1793 to John Hoge, ass. No papers
John, Pa., Charlotte, W4062
John, S.C., b. Va., S31336
John, Va., S31335
John, Va., S35636
John Knapp, N.Y. See John ROSS wife Aramintas
Jonathan, Mass., Joanna, W24820
Joseph, Cont., Mass., Sarah, W24789
Joseph, N.J., S4127
Joseph, Va., S7390
Lemuel, Mass., BLWt.4944. Iss. 4/1/1790. No papers
Lemuel, Mass., S33577. See N.A. Acc. No. 874-050150. Not Half Pay
Levi/Levy, N.J., S43947; BLWt. 8694. Iss. 6/11/1789 to Jona. Dayton, ass.
Micah, Mass., Molly How, former wid., W13496
Nathaniel, Cont., N.J., S35638
Oliver, Pa., BLWt.10284. Iss. 7/ 27/1789 to Richard Platt, ass.
Perin, Ct., BL--
Reuben, Cont., Md., S40361
Reuben, Md., R9025
Robert, Cont., N.J. res. in 1818 S33604
Robert, Pa., Lucy, W1496
Robert, Pa., Indian Wars & U.S.A. R9026
Robinson, Md., BLWt.11648. Iss. 9/13/1799 to Asahel Phelps, ass.
Robinson, Md., Sarah, W8556

ROSS (continued)
Rufus, Mass., Vt., S11308
Samuel, Mass., Catharine, W8564
Samuel, R.I., S14370
Seth, Mass., S4776
Seth, R.I., Rebecca, W2004
Thomas, Cont., Mass., S45124
Thomas, Cont., Mass., Hannah, Mass. res. in 1818, W20037
Thomas, N.C., S4126
Thomas, Pa., BLWt.10311. Iss. 11/2/1792 to Mary Johnson, Admx.
Thomas, Pa., Esther, R9017
Thomas, Va., S36877
Timothy, Cont., Mass., S33612
Valentine, Va., S38335; BLWt. 1623-100
Walter, N.C., Margaret, W5723; BLWt.38567-160-55
William, Md., S11331
William, Mass., BLWt.4920. Iss. 3/25/1791 to David Quinton, No papers
William, Mass., Mary, W18831
William, N.J., BLWt.8678. Iss. 3/21/1795. No papers
William, N.Y., S43941
William, N.C., Rachel, R9024
William, R.I., S14325
William, Va., S41989
William, Va., Sally, W8557
William, Va., R9028
William, Va., R9029
Williamson, N.C., S7429
Zachariah, N.J., R9030
Zephaniah, Cont., Mass., S11328
ROSSELL, Elias, N.J. See ROSELL
Jeremiah, Ct., BLWt.6391. Iss. 3/1/1797. No papers
Zachariah, N.J., Mary, W9260; BLWt.256-100
ROSSEN, John, N.C., S9093
ROSSER, Richard, Va., S31344
William, Va., Elizabeth (dau. of Catharine G. Lee), W29945; BLWt.26963-160-55
ROSSETER, Benjamin, Ct., S23395
Noah, Ct., Mass., Amanda, W7156; BLWt.26230-160-55
Samuel, Ct., Dis.-See Am. State Papers, Class 9, p.90. Ruptured by overstraining himself in carrying timber for the erection of a redoubt in the state of N.Y., 8/1781, Neilson's Point
Timothy, Ct., Cont., S44233; BLWt.1604-100
Timothy W., Cont., Mass., Privateer, S4160
ROSSETTER, Bryan, Ct., Sarah, W24782; BLWt.435-100
ROSSGROVE, Henry, Pa. See ROSCROW
ROSSIN, Joseph, Va., Pamela, W8559
Reubin, Va. See ROSSON
ROSSITER, Noah, Ct., Mass. See ROSSETER
Timothy, Ct., S17062
ROSSMAN, Conrad, N.Y., Maria Kilmer, former wid., W20350
Henry, N.Y. See ROSMAN

ROSSON, Archelaus/Archilaus, Va., S1586
Enoch, Va. See RAWSON
James, Va., S7423
John, S.C., R9031
Reubin, Va., S6016
ROSURY, Silas, Mass. See ROSO
ROSWELL, Zachariah, N.J. See ROSSELL
ROTE, Henry, N.Y., S23404
ROTH, Christian, Pa., Catharine, W3191
Daniel, Ct., Hannah, W17559
John, N.Y., Elizabeth Cradle, former wid., W16936
Matthias, Pa., S4125
ROTHMAHLER, Erasmus, S.C., BLWt.2034-150
ROTTENOUR, Jacob, See RATTENAUER
ROUARK, James, Md. See REEWARK
ROUCH, Jonas, Va., S4785
ROUEN, John, Pa., Catharine, W3300
ROUGH, Ludwick, Pa., Jean, BLWt.404-100
ROUGHFCORN, Simon, See RUFFCORN
ROUN, Thomas, N.C., S7415
ROUND, Bartram, R.I., S45860
John, Mass., S30074
Nathaniel, Mass., Martha, W13865
Samuel, Mass., S28857
Simeon, R.I., Anne, W22110
ROUNDEY, Francis, Mass., Sea Service, Privateer, Jane, W18837
Joseph, Mass., S33584. See claim of his wid. as former wid. of John Dupar, Mass.
ROUNDS, Amos, Mass., Polly, W15289 BLWt.18395-160-55
Charles, Mass. See ROUNES
Hezekiah, Mass., BLWt.38836-160-55
James, Mass., Elizabeth, W7149; BLWt.61160-160-55
Joseph, Mass., Susanna, R9033
Jotham, R.I., S32491
Lemuel, Cont., Mass., Mary, W24806
Nathaniel, Mass., R.I., S30068
Oliver, Mass., R.I., S14329
Theodore, Mass., S37350
ROUNDTREE, Nathaniel, Va., S31340
ROUNDY, Luke, Mass., BLWt.2189-150
Uriah, Ct., Lucretia, R9034
ROUNES, Charles, Mass., S40360
ROUNSAVALL, John, N.C., S9091
ROUNSAVELL, John, N.J., BLWt.8684. Iss. 10/3/1799. No papers
ROUNTREE, Job, S.C., S18187
ROURK, James, Md., BLWt.11634. Iss. 5/11/1790. No papers
Martin, Mass., BLWt.4942. Iss. 8/1/1789 to Thomas Cushing. No papers
Timothy, Pa., BLWt.10320. Iss. 4/6/1790. No papers. Notation "on file, not delivered".
ROURKE, Martin, Mass., Elizabeth/ Betty, W24818
ROUS, Jacob, Pa., BLWt.10251. Iss. 11/16/1791. No papers
ROUSE, Henry, Mass., BLWt.4931.

ROUSE (continued)
Iss. 4/1/1790. No papers
Henry, Mass., S42213
Jacob, Va., Anna/Anny, W8558
Jacque, Hazen's Regt., BLWt. 13653. Iss. 4/19/1790 to Gabriel Forman, ass. No papers
John, N.Y., S23396
Jonathan, N.Y., R9035
Joseph, Ct., BLWt.6358. Iss. 5/21/1798 to Solomon Wolcott. No papers
Joseph, Va. See ROUSH
Lewis, Va., Elizabeth, W9259; S25787
Nicholas, N.Y., Olive, W17552; BLWt.31314-160-55
Oliver, Mass., BLWt.1780-300-Capt. Iss. 10/1/1799 to Oliver Rouse, the only surviving heir of O.R.
Peter, Va., S23880
Samuel, Va., S14360
Simeon, Cont., Mass., S42212
Thomas, Mass., S14382
Thomas, Pa., Nancy, W9629; BLWt.61067-160-55
ROUSEY, Edmond, Va. See ROWSEY
ROUSH, George, Pa., Va., S7401; BLWt.31315-160-55
George, Va., S18579
Jonas, Va. See ROUCH
Joseph, Va., R9036
ROUSSE, Oliver, Ct., BLWt.6403. Iss. 9/15/1792 to Samuel Allan, ass.
ROUTON, James, Va., Eliza, W10242; BLWt.40692-160-55
John, Va., Jane, S31943
ROUX, Albert, S.C., BLWt.1818-300
Lewis, S.C., S21952
ROVE, Thomas, Pa. See ROWE
ROW, Hezekiah, N.C., S.C., b. N.C. S32496
John, Cont., Mass., Jane, W1937; BLWt.9533-160-55
John, N.H. See ROWE
John, N.H., S41106
John, N.J., Susannah, W5726
John, N.Y., S14365
John, Pa., Susanna, W3459
John, Pa., Va., Mary, W8555
Joshua, Mass. See ROWE
Philip, N.J., Mary, S2350
Samuel, Mass. See ROWE
Thomas, Va., Sarah, R9044
Webber, Cont., N.H., Rachel, W22091
William, Mass., Betsey, W20029
William, N.H. See ROWE
ROWAN, Benjamin, N.C., S.C., S35049
Henry, Del., BLWt.10867. No papers
James, N.Y. res., R9040
James, Pa., R9041
John, Del., BLWt.10868. Iss. 9/2/1789. No papers
John, N.Y., S14362
John, N.C., Elizabeth, R9038
John, Pa., BLWt.10292. Iss. 5/8/1800. No papers

ROWAN (continued)
John, Pa., S41103
Patrick, Md., BLWt.11642. Iss. 12/23/1795 to George Ponsonby, ass. No papers
Samuel, S.C., Elizabeth, R9039
ROWARK, Elisha, N.C., S7399
ROWDON, George, S.C., b. Md., S15623
ROWE, Andrew, N.C., S.C., Rejected 133970. Widow's claim made under name of Martha ROE
Benjamin, Mass., S37357
Benjamin, S.C., b. Va., Ruth, W57
Caleb, Mass., S37345
Caleb, Mass., S42211
Charles, N.Y., Catherine, W5725; BLWt.27653-160-55
David, Ct., S42214
Ebenezer, Mass., Deborah Cunningham, former wid., W15663
Ebenezer, Mass. Sea Service, S20939
Edward, S.C., Frances Porter, former wid., R8341
Enoch, N.H., S45128
Ezra, Ct., Cont., S15970
Irena, former wid. of James Quimby, Cont., N.H., which see
Isaac, Mass., S29423
Isaiah, Ct., Mary, R9043
Jacob, Mass., Mehitable Chase, former wid., R1888; BLWt.930-100
James, N.C., S41993
James, Va., S31345
Jesse, Va., S4122
John, Ct., Cont., S14358
John, Cont., Mass., Shay's Rebellion, U.S.A., Lydia, W22100; BLWt.1781-150-Ens. Iss. 4/18/1796 to Jeremiah Mason, ass. No papers
John, Mass., Nancy, S24810
John, Mass., Sea Service, Privateer, R9045
John, N.H., BLWt.3444. Iss. 2/3/1792 to N. White, ass. No papers
John, N.H., S37343
John, Sea Service, N.C., Chloe, R9042
John, Va. See ROE
Joseph, Green Mt. Boys, Vt., S14342
Joshua, Mass., Mary, W24803; BLWt.18001-160-55
Joshua, N.C., S14385
Lazarus, N.H., S37346
Moses, Mass., Joice, W24788
Samuel, Mass., Submit, W15270
Shadrach, N.C., R9046
Solomon, Navy, Mass. Agcy. & res., S33592
Thomas, Pa., Milly, W2862
William, Mass. See ROW
William, N.H., S37348
William, Va., Sally, W3044; BLWt.18211-160-55
Zebulon, Mass., S17059
ROWEL, Philander, Ct., S14327
ROWELL, Daniel, N.H., S40364
Enoch, Mass., Rachel, W16393

ROWELL (continued)
Isaac, N.C., Susanna, W9634
Israel, N.H., S45125
James, N.H., S41101
Jesse, N.C., S38337
Jonathan, N.H., res. at enl. Hampstead, N.H., S22476
Jonathan, N.H., d. 12/11/1831, Stafford, Orange Co., Vt., Hannah, W24799. BLWt.13183-160-55
Lemuel, N.H., Sarah, W17563
Moses, N.H., Betsey, W1474
Samuel, N.H., Sarah, W24814
Thomas, N.H., S11319
William, Cont., N.H., S7388
William, N.H., BLWt.1774-300-Capt. Iss. 7/21/1789 to Eliphalet Ladd & Jonathan Cass, ass. No papers
ROWEN, Christopher, Pa., R9049
John, N.H., Sarah, W17474; BLWt. 19511-160-55
John, Pa. See ROUEN
William, Pa., S22958
ROWLAND, Benjamin, Ct., Cont., Diodama Reed, former wid., W24741
Daniel, Ct., S36271
Daniel, N.Y., S28860
David, Ct., S14379
David, S.C., Judith, W9270
George, Pa., BLWt.10287. Iss. 1/5/1792 to Alexander Crawford, ass. No papers
Henry, Va., S40366
Hezekiah, Cont., Ct., Grace, W4328
Jack (colored), Ct., S17058
Jacob, Pa., Christina, R9050
James, N.C. See ROLAND
Jesse, Ct., S36264
John "in the Invalids", BLWt. 13684. Iss. 6/29/1789 to Matt. McConnell, ass. No papers
John, N.Y., S14369
Luke, Ct., Elizabeth, W9271
Nathan, Va., S25408
Peter, S.C., S39047
Samuel, N.J., S32489
Sherman, Ct., BLWt.6381. Iss. 5/26/1790. No papers
Sherman, Ct., S36262
ROWLANDSON, Joseph, Ct., BLWt.6398 Iss. 8/8/1791. No papers
Joseph, Ct. See ROWLINSON
Reuben, Ct., Eunice, W9272
ROWLEE, Samuel, Mass., BLWt.4893 Iss. 3/6/1798 to Sam Rowlee. No papers
ROWLES, William, Md., S6687
ROWLET, William, Va., Rebecca, W26412
ROWLETT, William, Va., R8607
ROWLEY, Abijah, Ct., Cont., S32493
Benjamin, Mass., S33610
Daniel, N.Y., S14318
Eli Smith, Ct., S11312
Israel, Sheldon's Dragoons, Ct., BLWt.6414. Iss. 2/5/1790. No papers
Joseph, Mass., Hannah, R9051
Joseph L., Ct., Sea Service, N.Y., S7408
Nathan, Cont., Vt., Enl. in N.Y.

ROWLEY (continued)
S40354
Philander, Ct. See ROWEL
Reuben, Cont., Vt., Susannah, W2859
Seth, Ct., Cont., N.Y., Innocent W24777; BLWt.5110-160-55
Seth, Mass., N.Y., S42216
Silas, Ct., S14326
Thomas, Ct., Mary, W15277
Timothy, N.Y., BLWt.7701. Iss. 7/10/1790 to C.E. Elmendorph, ass. No papers
Timothy, N.Y., S42215
ROWLING, Eliphalet, N.H., BLWt. 3428. Iss. 7/21/1789 to Ladd & Cass. No papers
ROWLINGS, Joseph, See RAWLINGS
Samuel, N.H. See ROLLINS
ROWLINS, Aaron, N.H., S----
ROWLINSON, Joseph, Ct., S42218
ROWLISON, William, N.J., S6025
ROWNTREE, William, Va., S6028
ROWS, Jacque, Cont., Canada?, S42217
ROWSE, Thomas, Md., S39051; BLWt.74-200
ROWSEY, Edmond, Va., Elizabeth, W1649
ROXBURGH, Alexander, Md., BLWt. 1837-400-Maj. Iss. 6/10/1789
ROXBURY, Reuben, Va., S39057
ROXFORD, Denison, See REXFORD
ROY, Beverly, Va., BLWt.1851-300-Capt. Iss. 5/29/1792 to Robert Means, ass. No papers
ROYAL, Jesse, Del., S36258
John, N.J., Eunice, W17545
John, Va., R9054
William, N.C. See RYALL
ROYALL, Francis, Va., S6023
Grief, Va., Jincey, W18833
Jesse, Del., BLWt.10873. Iss. 12/28/1791 to Wm. Lane, ass. No papers
William, Va., Anne, W8566
ROYALTREE, John, Va., Sally, R9055
ROYALTY, John, Va. See ROYALTREE
ROYCE, Aaron, Ct., S45126
Abiram, See RICE
Asa, Ct., S31936
Elijah, Ct., S23397
Elijah, Ct., Cont., S36263; BLWt. 6362-100. Iss. 8/10/1789. No papers
Isaac, Ct., Abigail, R9056
Lemuel, N.H., Susan, W5724; BLWt. 88-60-55; BLWt.3423-100. Iss. 6/9/1797 to M. Fisk, ass. No papers
Samuel, Ct., Cont., S12256
Stephen, Vt., R9058
ROYER, John, N.C., R9059
ROYS, Silas, N.H., Lois, R9060
ROYSE, Lemuel, N.H. See ROYCE
Solomon, Md., Sarah, W3598; BLWt.26476-160-55
ROYSTAN, James, Md., BLWt.11661. Iss. 9/5/1789. No papers
ROYSTER, David, Va., S11327
ROZAR, Robert, N.C., S.C., S31938

ROZAR (continued)
William, S.C. See ROZIER
ROZELL, Jeremiah, Ct., Cont., S42219; BLWt.6391-100. Iss. 3/1/1797. No papers
ROZER, Charles, Mass., S14351
ROZIER, Charles, Mass. See ROZER
John, Mass., S41110
William, S.C., Chloe, W9264
RUARK, James, See REEWARK
RUBBERT, Adam, Pa. See RUPERT
RUBISON, Calza, N.C., S16240
RUBLE, Christian, Hazen's Regt., BLWt.13676. Iss. 4/21/1791 to Hezekiah Broadwell, ass. No papers
John, Va., S4656
RUCASTLE, John, N.J., BLWt.1815-300-Capt. Iss. 6/11/1789. No papers
RUCKER, Angus, Va., S19068; BLWt.1695-300, N.A. Acc. No. 874-050151 Half Pay Angus Rucker
Colby, N.C., R9061
Daniel, Ct., BLWt.6363. Iss. 2/8/1790. No papers
Elliot, Va., S46408; BLWt.1702-200 Va. Half Pay
John, N.J., BLWt.8690. Iss. 5/27/1790 to Joseph Arrison, ass.
Lemuel, Va., S40372
William, Va., S16520
RUCKMAN, John, N.J., Elizabeth, W6105
RUDD, Andrew, Ct., Cont., S30077
Archer, Va., S6040
Benjamin, Va. Sea Service, Susan, W5756
Bezaleel, N.Y., S10001
Burlingham, N.C., Mary V., W20038; BLWt.28555-160-55
Daniel, Ct., Navy, Abigail W22137; BLWt.7209-160-55
John, Va., S17065
Joseph, Vt., Sarah, W17582
Nathaniel, Ct., S21461
William, Ct., Eunice, W22138
RUDDEEL, James, Va., S4172
RUDDER, Charles, Va., R9064
Edward, Va., Jane, W18844
Epaphroditus, Cont., Va., R17580; BLWt.2472-200 Va. Half Pay
John, Va., S6034
Peyton, Va., R17581; Va. Half Pay
RUDE, Asa, Mass., R9065
Ezekiel, Ct., Phebe, W26417
Isaac, Ct., S17066
Noah, N.J., R9066
William, N.Y., BLWt.7699. Iss. 8/4/1790 to Henry Hart, ass. No papers
William, N.Y., Mary, W16394
William, R.I., S39837
RUDECELLY, Henry, Pa. See RUDECILLY
RUDECILLY, Henry, Pa., S4174
RUDISELLY, Henry, See RUDECILLY
RUDOLF, Jacob, Pa., S4164
RUDOLPH, Christian, Pa., S4797

RUDOLPH (continued)
Christolph, See Johan RUDTOLFH
Christopher, N.Y., BLWt.7704. Iss. 7/28/1790 to Peter Griffin, ass. No papers
David, Lamb's Art., N.Y., BLWt. 7715. Iss. 1/29/1790. No papers
Jacob, Pa. See RUDOLF
John, Pa., BLWt.1183-200
Michael, Cont., Md., BLWt.945-300
RUDTOLFH, Johan Christolfh/Christolph/Christopher, N.Y., S40374
RUDY, Jacob, Pa., S22485
Patrick, Pa., BLWt.10275. Iss. 7/2/1793 to Samuel Quigley, ass.
RUE, Benjamin, Pa., S40370
John, N.J., S908
Richard, Va., S17064
RUFF, Jonathan, N.Y., BLWt.7709. Iss. 5/19/1791 to James Caldwell, ass. No papers
Jonathan, Cont., N.Y., Sarah, W18843
RUFFCORN, Simon, Pa., S40367
RUFFENER, Simon, Pa., Mariah Barbara, W2172
RUFFNER, Simon, See RUFFENER
RUFFORD, Frederick, Cont., Pa., S42227; BLWt. 1321-100
RUFORD, Frederick, See RUFFORD
RUGAN, John, Cont., Pa., S4798
RUGAR, Gideon, N.Y., Mary Wilson former wid., W18459
RUGER, John, N.Y., Elizabeth, W2356; BLWt.7662-100. Iss. 5/19/1791 & 98-60-55
RUGG, Abraham, Mass., Mehitable Darby, former wid., W25512
David, N.H., S41114
Elisha, Mass., Amy Thurston, former wid., W26530
Isaac, Vt., S11334
Joshua, Mass., S21459
Moses, Mass., S40371
Phinehas/Phineas, Mass., Mary, W17581; BLWt.27651-160-55
Stephen, Mass., Elizabeth, W818; BLWt.8163-160-55
Thomas, Cont., Mass., Elizabeth W24825
RUGGLES, Benjamin, Mass., Mary, W24827
Benjamin A., Ct., Betty, W26418
Bostwick, Ct., Lucy, W17576
Daniel, Mass., Lucy, W15298
Ephraim, Mass., Olive, W22128; BLWt.24602-160-55
George, Mass., BLWt.4948. Iss. 11/6/1795 to Jeremiah Hill. No papers
James, Md., R9067
John, Mass., S33613
Joseph, Ct., S14392
Joseph, Mass., S33615; BLWt. 1819-100
Lazarus, Ct. res. Dis. No papers See Am. State Papers, Class 9, p.89-Disabled 10/28/1776 at White Plains by a cannon ball shot in the left wrist & right hand, in the service of the

RUGGLES (continued)
U.S., and that he is disabled so as to prevent him from doing one half the labor he otherwise would have been able to do.
Nathaniel, Mass., N.H., S14390
Seth, Mass., S21955
Timothy, Mass., S30075
Timothy, Mass., Judith, W22133
William, Pa., BLWt.10250. Iss. 7/9/17? No papers
York, Mass., BLWt.4897. Iss. 1/19/1776 to Joseph Fosdick. No papers
RUICK, Owen, Ct., S36034
RUCKER, Jacob, N.J., BLWt.8697. Iss. 1/1/1800 to Joseph Arrison, ass. No papers
RULAND, Benjamin, Cont., N.Y. res., Olive, W11191
Thomas W., Ct., Mary DeForest former wid., W8663; BLWt. 12834-160-55
RULE, Thomas, Pa., S31346
RULIFSON, Harmon, N.J., R9069
RUMALL, Phillip, Pa., BLWt. 10283. Iss. 6/29/1789 to M. McConnell, ass. No papers
RUMBELLO, Thomas, N.Y., BLWt. 7718. Iss. 12/22/1791. No papers
RUMBLEY, John, Md., R9070
RUMERY, Dominicus, See RUMNEY
Jonathan, Mass., Priscilla, W26421
RUMFELT, Henry, Md., Mary, W4789
RUMINGER, George, N.C., R9071
RUMMAGE, George, N.C., Margaret W4065
RUMNEY, Dominicus, Cont., Mass. Pamelia, W22130
RUMPH, Christian, S.C., Elizabeth W22134
RUMRILL, Joseph, Mass., Rebecca, W20041; BLWt.13874-160-55
Peter B., Mass., Joanna, W22131; BLWt.13713-160-55
Thomas, Cont., Mass., Sarah/Sally, W6103; BLWt.3964-160-55
RUMSAY, John, Ct. See RUMSEY
RUMSEY, David, Ct., S42225
Jeremiah, Ct., Aseneth, W3461
John, Ct., BLWt.6379. Iss. 1/24/1792 to Stephen Thorn, ass. No papers
John, Ct., S41970
William, Ct., S18581
RUNDAL, David, N.Y., S14303
RUNDEL, Henry, Ct., R9073
Joseph, Ct., R8582
Phinehas, Ct., S18191
RUNDIO, Peter, Pa. Mil., Susannah
There is no Fed. pension for this Capt., but the Library of Congress (Div. of State Laws) furnished by phone the following info. Pa. State Act No. 166, An Act for the relief of sundry solds. & wids. of the late Rev. War, Section 11 which reads as

RUNDIO (continued)
follows:
"Be it further enacted by the authority aforesaid that the state treas. be & he is hereby authorized & required to pay Susannah Rundio a wid. of Capt. Peter Rundio of Northampton Co., a Rev. War sold. or to her order $40 immedaitely & an annuity of $40 payable one half yearly during life to commence on Jan. 1, 1829"
RUNDLE, Elizabeth former wid. of Moses Hunter, N.Y., which see
John, Ct., Rachel, W11194; BLWt.2170-100
Reuben, Ct., N.Y., S9298
RUNDLEMAN, Martin, N.C., S31946
RUNDLER, Nathaniel, Cont., Mass. See RUNDLET
RUNDLET, Charles, Mass., Anna, R9074
Jonathan, N.H., S18190
Jonathan, N.H. See RANLET
Nathaniel, Cont., Mass., Lydia, W15622
Noah, N.H., Susan, W26416
Theophilus, N.H., S14393; BLWt.11402-160-55
RUNDLETT, Reuben, N.H., Hannah, W22136
RUNELS, Enoch, N.H., Privateer, Francis, R9075
RUNEY, George, Mass. See RONEY
John, Mass., S47735
RUNION, Elijah, Va., R9079
RUNIONS, Benjamin, N.Y., S46342
RUNK, Samuel, N.J., S6030
RUNKLE, Henry, N.Y., S14388
RUNNALD, John, Mass., Rhoda, W26424
RUNNALS, James, N.H., Tamson, W15956
Jesse, Va., Sarah, W4580; see N.A. Acc. No.874-050152. Not Half Pay James Runnals
Miles, N.H., Margaret, W22135
Samuel, Cont., N.H., S18189
RUNNELLS, John, Mass., Rhoda, W26424; BLWt.19903-160-55
Thomas, Va. See REYNOLDS
RUNNELS, Enos, Mass., N.H., Sarah, W20040
James, N.H. See RUNNALS
James, N.C., S7370
Miles, N.H. See RUNNALS
Moses, N.H., BLWt.36-100
Peleg, R.I., Martha, W15295
Robert, Cont., Mass., Sarah, W18842; BLWt.16254-160-55
Samuel, Cont., N.H. See RUNNALS
Samuel, Mass., S20545
Thomas, Md., Pa., in N.H., Elizabeth, W6104
RUNNION, Benjamin, N.Y., BLWt. 7687. Iss. 8/4/1790 to Henry Hart, ass. No papers
Conrad, N.J., S40070
RUNNO, Simeon, See RENO
RUNNOLDS, Silas, N.Y., Indian War 1791 & War 1812, R9078

RUNNOW, Simeon, See RENO
RUNYAN, Anna, former wid. of William Watson, N.J., which see
Coonrad, N.J., BLWt.8672. Iss. 6/11/1789 to Matthias Denman, ass.
Henry, Md., N.J., R9080
Hugh, N.J., S47244
Job, N.J., S6035. No papers on this claim; the same were missing when searched 12/1878. N.J. Rev. War Agcy. Book shows Job Runyon pensioned at Trenton agcy. under Act of 6/7/1832. Ctf. No.424 iss. 9/3/1832, annual rate of $40. Sold, a Pvt., d. 2/12/1835. List of pensioners of Essex Co., N.J. printed 1835, shows Job Runyard, a Pvt. N.J. Mil. Ctf. iss. 9/3/1832 annual rate $40. Act 6/7/1832
Richard, N.J., Jemima, W11197
Samuel, N.J. See RUNYEN
RUNYARD, Job, N.J. See RUNYAN
RUNYEN, Samuel, N.J., R9081
RUNYON, Adam, Va., R9082
George, Pa., Margaret, R17590
Henry, Md. See RUNYAN
John, N.J., Mary, W4790
John, N.C., S4799
Samuel, N.J. See RUNYEN
RUPERT, Adam, Pa., S4800
George, Va., Elizabeth, W4788
Leonard, Pa., R9084
RUPKEE, Sally, former wid. of Ebenezer Hayden, Mass., Which see
RUPLE, John, S.C., R9085
RUPP, Andrew, Pa., S22486
Herman, Pa., R9086
RUPPER, Adam, Pa., BLWt.10268. Iss. 10/31/1791 to Jasper Heiner, ass. No papers
RUPPERT, George, Va. See RUPERT
RUSCO, David, Ct., S41115
Samuel, N.Y., Esther, W17574
RUSE, Aaron, Va., S4162
RUSEL, Samuel, Va. See RUSSELL
RUSH, Benjamin, Cont., Pa., Julia, W4507
Benjamin, Va., Jemima, R9089
Jacob, N.J., R9087
Jacob, Pa., Ann, W11195; BLWt. 105302-160-55
John, N.J., BLWt.8696. Iss. 6/6/1789 to Thos. Coyle, ass. No papers
John, N.J., S42220
John, Va., R9090
Samuel, Mass., S23885
Samuel, Pa. See RUSK
Thomas, Pa., BLWt.10293. Iss. 4/26/1791. No papers
William, N.J., S----
William N.J., Jane, W2863
RUSHING, Philip/Phillip, N.C. S21458
Richard, N.C., b. Va., S21457
RUSHWORM, William,"Proctor's Art." Pa., BLWt.10309 iss. 7/27/1789 to Richard Platt, ass. No papers

RUSK, Jacob, Pa., S40375
James, Pa., S40369. See N.A. Acc. No.874-050153 not Half Pay James Rusk
Samuel, Pa., R9091
RUSS, Asa, Ct., R9093
Epaphras, Ct., BLWt.6374. Iss. 1/23/1796 to Henry Gardner
Epaphras, Ct., S42224
John, N.H., Abigail, R9092
Jonathan, Ct., S42210
Jonathan, Sappers & Miners, BLWt.13648. Iss. 4/9/1791. No papers
Joseph, N.C., S7435
Nathan, Cont., Mass., S45132
RUSSEL, Absalom, Va., S46066
Buckner, N.C., S4166
Elijah, Va., S4169
George, Va., S39059
James, Pa., S4801
James G., Va., S31948
Newton, N.J., S15629
Paul, Pa., Catherine H., R9098
Richard, Va., S7433
Riverus/Riverius, Ct., Cont., Charity, R9105
Samuel, Va., d. 7/26/1831, Hannah, W26423; BLWt.82534-160-55
Simeon, Navy, N.Y., R.I., Jane, R9104
RUSSELL, Abigail, former wid. of James McDonald, Ct., which see
Abner, Mass., S33620
Abraham, N.Y., R9096
Albert, Va., BLWt.1857-200-Lt. Iss. 6/18/1793. No papers
Alexander, Pa., Mary, W3358
Amos, Mass., S33614
Andrew, Mass., S37359
Andrew, Va., BLWt.1047-300; BLWt. 2388-100
Asa, Mass., S21460
Asher/Ashur, Ct., Cont., S40368; BLWt.1195-100
Benjamin, Mass., S30685
Benjamin, Mass., Mehitable, W22139; BLWt.14521-160-55
Benjamin, N.Y., S23405
Betty, former wid. of Daniel Brown, Mass., which see
Bill, Mass., S18582
Calvin, Mass., S37360
Chandler, Mass., S33616
Charles, Va., S46067
Charles, Va., S17603; BLWt.2151-200; Va. Half Pay N.A. Acc. No. 874-050154
Cornelius, Ct., S41112; BLWt. 248-200
Daniel, Mass., S45129
Daniel/David, Mass., Sea Service R9099
Daniel, Navy, S.C., Sarah Susannah W9274
Daniel, N.H. agcy. in 1818, S45131
Daniel, N.H., Betsey, W817; BLWt. 8146-160-55
David, Ct., S15972
David, Ct., Eunice, W26419
David, Mass. Sea Service, See Daniel

RUSSELL (continued)
Ebenezer, Ct., S14387
Eleazer, Ct., S42223
Eleazor, Ct., BLWt.6369 iss. 7/26/? No papers
Elmore, Cont., Ct., S14391
Enoch, Va., Martha, W585; BLWt. 26297-160-55
Evan, Pa., S23886
George, Pa., S31947
Gideon, Ct., S7434
Henry, Mass., S30076
Ichabod, Ct., Hannah, R9101
Isaac, Mass., Hannah, W17580
Isaac, Mass., Mary, W24824
Israel, Mass., S15973
Jacob, Mass., N.H., Dolly Gage former wid., W23077
Jacob, N.J., R9102
James, Mass., Rebecca, W24822
James, N.Y., BLWt.7682 iss. 2/24/1794 to Isaac Davis, ass. No papers
James, N.C., Nancy, W5167; BLWt.61236-160-55
James, Pa., S40376
James, S.C., S39058
James, S.C., Va., R---
James, Va., Ann, R9097
Jedidiah/Jedediah, Cont., Mass., S45127
Jeffrey, Va., Sarah, W5751
John, Ct., S39836
John, Ct., Lovice, W17578
John, Ct., Mass., S42222
John, Cont., Loudoun Co., Va. res., Sarah E., W5755
John, Ct., Mass., Hannah Lyons, dau., W29906
John, Cont., N.Y., S36279
John, Mass., S4796
John, Mass., Nabby, W2251; BLWt. 15183-160-55
John, N.N., Vt., Sarah, W17575
John, N.J., S33618
John, N.J., Lydia, W5752
John, N.Y., BLWt.7711. Iss. 4/21/1791 to Benj. Green, ass. No papers
John, N.Y., S11333
John, Va., S36878
John, Va., BLWt.1856-200. Iss. 5/29/1832
Jonathan, Ct., S10000
Jonathan, Mass., S45130
Jonathan, N.Y., BLWt.7677 iss. 3/31/1793 to Thomas Russell, ass. No papers
Jonathan, N.Y., S6039
Joseph, Mass., BLWt.4935 iss. 3/25/1790. No papers
Joseph, Mass., BLWt.4941. Iss. 7/20/1789 to Reuben Lilley. No papers
Joseph, Mass., S19066; BLWt. 26460-160-55
Joseph, Mass., Margaret, W15799
Josiah, Ct., Cont., S42226
Levi, Cont., Mass., Hannah, W26420
Lodowick, N.Y., Catherine Bear former wid., W16185
Moor, N.H., S11332

RUSSELL (continued)
Moses, Cont., Va., S1872
Moses, Va., Esther, W5754
Oliver, Mass., Betty Goddard, former wid., W14808
Pelatiah, Mass., S33619
Philip, Va., Mary, W2575; BLWt. 26883-160-55
Phillip, Mass., S33617
Phillip M., Surgeon's Mate, Pa. or Va., Esther, W4792
Reuben, Cont., N.H.?, pensioned in Vt., S41113
Robert, N.C., Va., S6041
Robert, Pa., S35056
Robert, Va., Comfort, W5753
Robert S., Va., S14389
Samuel, Mass., Mary, W1938; BLWt.26517-160-55
Samuel, N.Y., S42228
Samuel, Pa., S22962
Samuel, Va., d. 2/4/1831, Tabitia, S38344
Sarah, former wid. of Oliver Frost Mass., which see
Silas, N.H., S45128
Simeon, Mass., Nabby/Abigail, W18841
Solomon, Cont., Mass., S15606; BLWt.705-100
Solomon, Va., S38342
Stephen, Mass., S18583
Thaddeus, N.J., Betsey, W2355; BLWt.24984-160-55
Thomas, Mass., Betsey, W15296
Thomas, N.Y., Elizabeth, R1497; BLWts.168-60-55 & 7676-100-1792
Thomas, N.C., b. Pa., Tabitha, W2700; BLWt.2730-160-55
Thomas, Pa., R9108
Thomas, R.I., BLWt.1777-150--Ens. Iss. 8/31/1791. No papers
Thomas, Va., S38345
Thomas C., S.C., S38343; BLWt. 2361-200
Timothy, Ct., Privateer, Elizabeth, R9100
William, Ct., BLWt.6401. Iss. 7/10/1789. No papers
William, Ct., S42221
William, Ct., Chloe Folker, former wid., W7313
William, Cont., Pa., Magdalena, W3193; BLWt.2421-100
William, Mass. See Bill
William, N.H., BLWt.3445. Iss. 4/28/1794. No papers
William, Mass., N.H., Keziah W24826
William, N.H., BLWt.3445. Iss. 4/28/1794. No papers
William, N.H., Sarah, W15957
William, N.J., S40373
William, N.Y., BLWt.7679. Iss. 10/20/1790. No papers
William, Pa., S6031
William, Pa., Jane, R9103
William, Va., BLWt.1849-500-Col. Iss. 5/9/1794 to Elizabeth Russell, Admx. No papers
RUSSEY, James, Va., W1697; BLWt. 3135-160-55. See N.A. Acc. No.

RUSSEY (continued)
874-050155. Not Half Pay James Russey. Nancy Ayres, former wid.
RUSSWURM, William, N.C., Eleanor Creamer/Kramer, former wid., W3390; BLWt.2234-200. See claim of George Gosnell, Pa., her other husb., for whom she also drew pension.
RUST, Abel, Ct., S42231
Israel, Mass., Jerusha, W15297
Jeremiah, Vt., S19067
John, Va., S15631
John, Va., 1847, Frances, R9110
Justin, Mass., S42230
Oliver, Vt., Lucy, W20039
Peter, N.C., Va., Elizabeth, W4064; BLWt.11261-160-55
Peter, Va., S25415
Quartus, Mass., Anna, W10258
Zebulon, Mass., R9112
RUSTIN, William, Ct., S36278
RUTAN, Abraham, N.J., Lydia, W3606; BLWt.34849-160-55
John, N.J., Jane, W18846
Paul, N.J., S18192
Samuel, N.J., Eleanor, W4506
RUTER, Thomas, Va., S9055
RUTGERS, Harmonus/Harmanus, N.Y. Dorcas Remson/Remsen, former wid. See her claim as former wid. of 2nd husb., Pardon Burlingham, N.Y.
RUTHERFORD, Absalom, Va., Mary, W59; BLWt.35539-160-55
Archibald, Va., Elizabeth, W8571
James, Va., Elizabeth, W9275; BLWt.5208-160-55
John, Mass., Privateer, Mary, W26422; BLWt.13862-160-55
John, Va., S6038
Julius, Va., Rhoda, R9113
Robert, Va., S38341
Thomas, N.C., Sarah, R9114
William, Mass., Sarah, W24823
William, Va., See RETHERFORD
RUTLAND, Abednego, N.C., S4170
RUTLEDGE, Edward, Va., S6032
Joshua, Md., Elizabeth Brooks, former wid., W708; BLWt.505-160-55 & 1843-200-Lt. Iss. 3/7/1791. No papers
Peter, Md., Ruth, R9115
William, N.C., S4171
RUTON, William, N.Y., Rachel, W18845
RUTTER, Jesse, Mass., S42229
RUTTY, Jonah, Ct., Mary, R9116
RYAL, John, N.Y., Elsie, R9117
RYALL, William, N.C., Tabitha/Talitha, W6108; BLWt.2082-100 Iss. 12/20/1836
William, N.C., R9118
Wright, Ga. res. in 1835, Ann, R9119
RYAN, Francis, Mass., Mary Reed former wid. See case of her 1st husb., Barnabas McCoy, Mass.
George, Va., S36879
George, Va. See RHINER
Harris, Va., S38347

RYAN (continued)
James, Cont., N.Y. res. in 1802, BLWt.170-100
James, Md., Eleanor Harper, former wid., W11205. Her last husb. Joseph Harper, Md., was pensioned which see
James, Md., BLWt.1120-100
James, N.C., S32501
James, Pa., BLWt.10294 iss. 11/5/1789. No papers
Jeremiah, Ct., Cont., Mary, R9122
John, Va. agcy., Dis. No papers See 1835 list of Inv. pensioners Vol. H, p.28, Va. agcy.
John, Cont., N.J., S40378
John, Cont., Pa., Va., S42233
John, Del., BLWt.10870. Iss. 9/2/1789. No papers
John, Hazen's Regt., BLWt.13663. Iss. 2/4/1791. No papers
John, Hazen's Regt., BLWt.13670 Iss. 8/3/1789 to Wm. Q. Vredenburgh, ass. No papers
John, Hazen's Regt., BLWt.13672 Iss. 9/19/1799 to Abraham Bell, ass. No papers
John, Md., BLWt.11631. Iss. 12/23/1795 to George Ponsonby, ass.
John, Lamb's Art., N.Y., BLWt. 7707. Iss. 4/21/1791 to David Quinton, ass. No papers
John, Va., S18584
Michael, Navy, N.H., S45133
Michael, Pa., BLWt.10308. Iss. 6/26/1792. No papers
Patrick, N.J., BLWt.8698. Iss. 12/7/1789. No papers
Patrick, Pa., BLWt.10278. Iss. 3/2/179? to Christian Nagle, Admr. No papers
Peter, Md., S7437
Phillip, Va., S7438
Richard, S.C., S4175
Robert, N.Y., Elizabeth, S42236 & W20042; BLWt.7693-100. Iss. 2/14/1791
Rulif, N.Y., R9121
Susannah, former wid. of Neil McGee, Cont., Mass., which see
Thomas, Mass., Charity Springer former wid., W4617; BLWt.33756-160-55
William, in the Inv., BLWt.13683 Iss. 1/17/1793 to Samuel Emery, ass. No papers
William, N.C., S7436
William, Va., R9123
RYANT, Joseph, N.H., S29426
RYBECKER, John, Cont., Pa. agcy. & res., S4179; BLWt.400-100
RYBURN, James, Pa., Elizabeth, W2858
RYCKMAN, Abraham, N.Y., Tamar, R9124
John, N.J., S21462
Wilhelmus, N.Y., S42232; BLWt. 1809-200-Lt. Iss. 10/12/1790. (Name spelled Rykman). No papers
RYDER, Benjamin, Mass. Agcy. Dis.
Christian, N.Y. See RYNDER

RYDER (continued)
Edward, Mass., Mercy, R8804
Elizabeth, former wid. of Philip Grapes, N.H., which see
James, Mass., Tabitha, R9125
Mary, former wid. of John Brown Cont., N.Y., which see
RYEL, Peter, N.Y., Mehitable, W18848
RYERSON, George G., N.J., S1098
John, N.J., R9126
John G., N.J., S1099
Richard G., N.J., S1097
Stephen, N.Y., War of 1812, N.C. Mary, W6107; BLWt.27864-40-50; BLWt.68913-120-55 for War of 1812
Thomas, N.J., S6043
RYFENBURG, Adam, N.Y., Christina, R26149
RYFENBURGH, Henry, N.Y., Hannah, R9128
RYKEMAN, John, N.J. See RYCKMAN
RYKER, Cornelius, See SUYDAM
John, N.J., Va., R9129
RYKMAN, Wilhelmus, See RYCKMAN
RYLAND, John, Cont., Va., Elizabeth, W18847; BLWt.2286-100
John, Va., BLWt.13655 & 13987. Iss. 12/17/1791. No papers
Nicholas N., Cont., Pa., Wayne's Indian Wars, S38346
RYLEE, James, N.C., S31949
RYLEY, John, Va., Julia, R8826
RYLIE, Daniel, Cont., Va., Susannah, W8572
RYLY, Daniel, N.J., Privateer, R8825
RYMER, George, Va., S9469
Phillip, Pa., BLWt.10289. Iss. 11/8/1791 to Peter Rodermal, ass. No papers
RYNDER, Christian, N.Y., R8801
RYNDERS, James, N.Y., BLWt. 7680 & 14133. Iss. 8/11/1798 to Sam Smith. No papers
John, N.Y., S42234
RYNEARSON, Isaac, N.J., Catharine, W3359
RYNEHART, John, See Johannes REINHART
RYNESS, See James RINDRESS
RYNO, Esek, N.J., S1096
RYON, John, Ct., S40377; BLWt. 6364-100. Iss. 9/8/1790. No papers.
John, N.J., S33621
Susannah, former wid. of Neil McGee, Cont., Mass., which see

S

SABEN, Israel, Ct., S11340
SABENS, Isaac, Mass., Lois Colby, former wid., W721
SABIN, Abner, Cont., Mass., S23406
Billings, Ct., S42247
Eldad, Ct., S14395
Elihu, Ct., Cont., Hannah, W17769
Elijah, N.Y., S3853
Hezekiah, Ct., Sarah, W13870
Israel, Ct. See SABEN
Jesse, Mass., S33369
Jonathan, Ct., S31950
Josiah, Green Mt. Boys, Mass., Lydia, W19003
Nathaniel, Ct., Deborah, W26428
Samuel, R.I., S33629; BLWt.994-100
Timothy, Ct., R9133
SABINS, John, Vt., S42244
Nathaniel, Mass., Mary, W1653; BLWt.7437-160-55
SACIA, David, N.Y., Susannah, W17768
SACK, John, Ga., S39062
SACKET, David, Cont., Mass., S40379
Skene Douglass/Skeen DOUGLASS, Ct. Lorrilla, W4619; BLWt.18019-160-55
Zava/Zavin, Mass., S4659
SACKETT, Benjamin, Ct., Mercy, W1940; BLWt.31317-160-55
Buell/Buel, Ct., S14396
Daniel, Ct., N.Y., Martha, W17770
James, N.Y., S7449
Richard, N.Y., Tabitha, W18994
Samuel, Ct., Pa., S4811
William, Ct., Parthena, W26956; BLWt.11282-160-55
Zavin, Mass. See Zava SACKET
SACREY, Isaac, Va., Elizabeth, W10247
James, Va., S35643. See N.A. Acc. No.874-050156. Not Half Pay James Sacrey
SADDLER, Christopher, Cont. (German), Sophia, R9135. His heirs were Wm., Christian & Christopher living in Dover Co., Ohio in 1852
SADDOR, Stephen, Cont., N.Y., Catherine Newell, former wid., W24331
Stephen, Hazen's Regt., BLWt. 13750. Iss. 10/12/1790. No papers
SADLER, Benjamin, Va., S39060
David, S.C., b. Pa., S9471
Eliza, former wid. of John Martin, S.C., which see
Isaac, Pa., S22487
John, Mass., S37363; BLWt.747-100
John, Navy, Mass. res. & Agcy. of wid., Mary, W15302
John, Va., Mary, W9277
John, Va., Leanah, R9136
Robert, Va., S41119
William, Mass., BLWt.4996. Iss. 7/28/1795 to George Brewer, Jr. No papers
SADLERS, James, Va., S41118
SAEGER, Philip, N.J., R9335
SAFFELL, Charles, Md., S7442
SAFFORD, David, Ct., R9137
Gideon, Ct., R6081
Jacob, Cont., Vt., Green Mt. Boys, Elizabeth Tompkins, former wid., W11646; BLWt.102304-160-55
Jesse, Mass., Vt., Abigail, W24904
John, Mass., Martha, W13868
Joseph, Vt., BLWt.1683-200
Rufus, Ct., Mary, R9138
Samuel, Vt., Phebe, BLWt.94503-160-55. She applied for pension based on service of her former husb., Benjamin Morgan, Mass., which see
Samuel, Warner's Regt., BLWt. 1881-450-Lt Col. Iss. /14/1793 No papers
Solomon, Vt., S14400
SAFLEY, Henry, Md., Va., S4809
SAGE, Abraham, Ct., Candace, W24887
Daniel, Ct., Mass., N.Y., S17069
David, Mass., Thirza, W24891
Elias, Mass., Privateer, Elizabeth, W587; BLWts.26222-160-55 & 34989-160-55
Enos, Cont., Mass., S14413
Epaphras, Ct., Elizabeth W., W26430
Harlehigh, Ct., Lucinda, W5972; BLWt.35724-160-55. Her 1st husb., William Pratt, also served in Rev. War.
James, Va., Lovice/Lovise, R9140
John, Va., Mary, W5973
Nathaniel, Cont., Ct., S33624
Samuel, Cont., Pa., S40380
Simeon, Mass., S19460
Stephen, Ct., S30080
William, Va., Mary Ann, R9141
Zadoc/Zadock, Ct., R9142
SAGER, John, N.Y., Catherine, W19001; BLWt.7788-100. Iss. 7/22/1790. No papers
SAILOR, Peter, Pa., BLWt.10341. Iss. 4/19/1792 to John W. Godfrey, ass. No papers
Peter, Pa., S42249
Philip, Pa., S3852
SAILORS, Michael, N.C., S21463
Philip, N.C., Mary Ann, R9143
ST. CLAIR, Arthur, Pa., BLWt.2007-1100-Major Gen. Iss. 1/29/1790. No papers
Daniel, Cont.,Pa., Isabella, W2188
Daniel, Pa.,BLWt.2025-300-Lt. Iss. 2/24/1790. No papers
George, N.J., BLWt.8772. Iss. 3/10/1793 to Jacob Shoemaker, ass. No papers
George, N.Y., BLWt.7834. Iss. 10/27/1791 to Isaac Bogart, ass. No papers
James, N.H., S42397
James, S.C., R9144
William, Md., BLWt.11680. Iss. 3/22/1793. No papers.
ST. GEORGE, George, Ct.,Ga.,S39090
ST. JOHN, Adonijah, Cont., Ct., S36802
David, Ct., Mary, W25104; BLWt.38542-160-55
Enoch, Ct., Maria, W11566; BLWt.9076-160-55
Ezra, N.Y., Abigail, R9145
Jacob, Va., Agnes, W6178
James, Va., S31995
Jesse/Josse, Ct., BLWts.6439 & 6026. Iss. 7/15/1789. No papers
Jesse, Ct., S36804
Jesse, Ct., S42418
John, Ct., Hannah, W19125
John, Pa., BLWt.10390. Iss. 7/27/1789 to Richard Platt, ass. No papers
Justin, Ct., BLWt.6513 & 6037. Iss. 6/3/1789. No papers
Lewis, Cont., Va., S38408
Matthew, N.Y., Jemima, W16737
Matthias, Ct., S18200
Samuel, Ct., R9147
Samuel, Mass., N.Y., Lois, R9146
Samuel, N.Y. res., Thankful, R--
ST. LAURENT, Estienne, Pvt., Hazen's Regt., BLWt.13362 & 13719. Iss. 10/12/1790
ST. LAWRENCE, George, N.Y., BLWt. 7756. Iss. 9/15/1790 to John S. Hobart, ass. No papers
ST. MARIA, LeVacher. See De ST. MARIA
ST. PIERRE, John, Hazen's Regt. BLWts.13608 & 13720. Iss. 10/12/1790. No papers
SALA, Peter, Pa., R9148
SALE, John, Cont., Mass., S30688; BLWt.1933-200. Lt. Iss. 2/22/1799 to John Poor, ass. No papers. Name recorded as John Sale, Jr.
SALEHAMMER, Nicholas, Pa., Elizabeth, W8082
SALEHEIMER, Nicholas, See SALEHAMMER
SALES, Charles, See N.A. Acc. No. 874-050157 Not Half Pay. No pension was found for this veteran
John, R.I. See SAYLES
SALGE, John J., Mass., S46409
SALIER, Zaccheus, N.Y., BLWt.7804. Iss. 10/5/1790. No papers
SALISBURY, Anthony, R.I., Hannah, W22142
Caleb, R.I. See SALSBURY
Charles, R.I., Mehitable, W9152
Edward, Vt., Betsey, W19315
Esther, former wid. of Robert Linsey, Cont., Mass., which see
George, R.I., Abigail, W13874
Gideon, N.Y., b. England, S28863
Hezekiah, Mass., R.I., S19070
John, N.Y., BLWt.7819. Iss. 9/15/1790 to James Caldwell, ass. No papers
John, R.I., S18194
John, R.I., S29433
Jonathan, R.I., Amy, W22157
Joseph, R.I., Lydia, W26954

SALISBURY (continued)
Lawrence, N.Y., S42241
Lucas, N.Y., S28866
Maria A. & Almira Morgan, daus. of Abner Morgan, Mass., which see
Rachel, former wid. of Cornelius Van Deusen, N.Y., which see
Richard, R.I., S28864
Samuel, R.I. See SALSBURY
Thomas, R.I., S42237
Wessell/Wessel, N.Y., S15209
William, Mass., S22490
William, R.I. See SALSBURY
William, R.I., Sarah B., W2173; BLWt.26172-160-55
SALLADY, Daniel, Pa., BLWt.10423; iss. 7/9/1789. No papers
Daniel, Pa., See SALLIDAY
Philip, Md. See SOLLADAY
SALLANHAM, Henry, See SULLENHEIM
SALLE, Peter Benjamin, Va., R9155
SALLEE, James, Cont.,R.I. See SALLY
SALLEY, Daniel, Mass., Cont., Polly, W24885; BLWt.3716-160-55
SALLIDAY, Daniel, Pa., Mary, W3310; BLWt.10423-100. Iss. 7/9/1789
SALLODAY, Daniel, See SALLIDAY
SALLY, Daniel, R.I., S37362
James, Cont., R.I., S33625
John, Pa., BLWt.10397. Iss. 5/21/1792 to John P. Schott ass. No papers
SALMON, Asahel, Ct., S36292
George, S.C., b. Va., Elizabeth, W9640
Gershom, Ct., S14411
Jacob, Va., Lucy, R9157
John, Md., BLWt.11715. Iss. 12/23/1795 to George Ponsonby, ass. No papers
John, N.J., S30686
John, Pa., Va., Sally, W26952
John, Va., Sarah, W5980
Nathaniel, N.J., S3856
Vincent, N.C., BLWts.12581 & 13711. Iss. 5/18/1797 to Gabriel Holmes, ass. No papers
Vincent/Vinson, N.C., Susan, R9156
William, Lamb's Art., N.Y., BLWt. 7858. Iss. 12/2/1791 to John Blanchard, ass. No papers
SALNAVE, Peter, N.J., S42243
SALPAUGH, John, N.Y., Gertrude, W16395
SALSBURRY, Casper, N.Y., BLWt.7831. Iss. 7/22/1790 to Thomas Tillotson, ass. No papers
SALSBURY, Andrew, S.C., S18195
Anthony, R.I. See SALISBURY
Barent S., N.Y., BLWt.1979-200-Lt. Iss. 6/21/1790. No papers
Caleb, R.I., S21469
Gideon, N.Y. See SALISBURY
John, N.Y., S42248
Jonathan, R.I. See SALISBURY
Newman, Va., BLWt.12554. Iss. 1/4/1796 to John Stockdall, ass. No papers
Samuel, R.I., S23409
William, R.I., S42238; BLWt.456-100

SALTER, Francis, Navy, Me. Agcy. & res., Susannah, W24899
James, Va., S41125
John, Mass., S18199
John, N.J., BLWt.8770. Iss. 6/11/1789 to Matthias Denman, ass. No papers
John, N.J., S909
John, Jr., N.J., BLWt.8771. Iss. 7/20/1795. No papers
Michael, Cont., Ky. res. & agcy. in 1828. Osee, W1654; BLWt. 36-60-55 & 13739-100, iss. 3/25/1790
Peter, Mass., BLWt.5040. Iss. 7/31/1797 to Jeremiah Mason. No papers
Peter, Mass., Susannah, W24890
Peter/John Peter, See SARTOR
Samuel, Mass., Catharine/Katherine, R9158
Samuel, Va., S41126
Titus, N.H., S22488
Titus, Sr., Navy, N.H., See Titus Salter
SALTERS, Betsey, former wid. of Gurish Keyes, Mass., which see
SALTONSTALL, Britton, R.I., BLWt. 3520. Iss. 1/28/1790. No papers
Gurdon Flanders, Ct., Navy, R9159
SALTS, Benjamin, N.Y., Jane, W7159; BLWt.9421-160-55
SALTSMAN, George, N.Y., Lavina, Sawina, W22152
Peter, N.Y., BLWt.7786. Iss. 9/7/1790 to William Faulkner, ass. No papers
SALTZMAN, Peter, N.Y., S42239
SALYARS, Dunn, N.C., S.C., Frances, W4795; BLWt.29018-160-55
SALYER, Zaccheus, N.Y., Elizabeth D., W4604; BLWt.43520-160-55
SALYERS, John S.C.? R9160
SAMBORN, Jeremiah, N.H., S15205
SAMBOURN, James, N.H., BLWt.3485 Iss. 3/25/1790. No papers
SAMMONS, Benjamin, N.Y., S11345
Cornelius, See SIMMONS
Frederick, N.Y., S11350
Johannes, N.Y., Margaret, W18998
John, N.J., N.Y., S6045
Newit, Va., S1720
Reuben, N.J See SAMONS
Thomas, N.Y., Mary, W19000
SAMMS, James, Crane's Cont. Art. Mass., BLWt.5103. Iss. 8/1/1789 to Thomas Cushing. No papers
SAMONS, Reuben, N.J., S41121
SAMPLE, David, Wayne's War 1792-1793, Capt. Ballard, Ky. Mil. also War 1812, Mary Turner former wid. BLWts.103423-40-50 & 68752-120-55. See War of 1812 files
James, Va., BLWt.12569. Iss 9/14/1790. No papers
Jesse, S.C. See SAMPLEY
John, Cont., Pa., Barbara, W24898
John, Cont., Pa., R20429
John, Pa., S22964

SAMPLE (continued)
John, S.C., S32505
Nathaniel, S.C., R21850
Robert, Pa., BLWt.2016-300. No papers
Samuel, N.C., Va., S1719
Thomas, See SEMPLE
SAMPLEY, Jesse, S.C., S32503
SAMPSON, Aaron, Pa., BLWt.10408 Iss. 10/12/1792 to John Peters, ass. No papers
Amos, Mass. See SAMSON
Bristol, Ct. See Bristol BUDD
Crocker, Mass., S33623; BLWt.1915-200-Lt. No papers, but with following note: Iss. to himself in Gen. Knox's time, 1/8/1820. Cert. the above for the Hon. Z. Sampson and returned to him.
Ephraim, Mass., Mary Gibbs, former wid., W11053
Etienne, Hazen's Regt., BLWt. 13746. Iss. 10/12/1790. No papers
Francis, Va., R9597
Gideon, Mass., Lydia, W13879
Henry, Cont., N.Y., Sally, W4509; BLWt.9067-160-55
Howland, Mass. See SAMSON
Ichabod, Mass. Deborah, W13872
Isaac, N.Y., BLWt.7783. Iss. 9/15/1790 to Wm. Bell, ass. No papers
Isaac, N.Y., S36280
Isaac, N.C., S35640
Isaac, N.C., S41999
Isaiah, Mass., Betsey, W9161
James, Mass., S18198
James, Va., Mary, R9163
John, N.H., BLWt.3473. Iss. 3/25/1790. No papers
Joseph, Va., S7453
Joshua, Mass., S33632
Luther, Mass., Lydia, W1939; BLWt.11190-160-55
Mary, former wid. of Hugh Mathews, N.H., which see
Moses, Mass., Lucy Dunbar, former wid., W17735
Peleg, Mass., Sarah, W1322; BLWt. 11393-160-55
Philemon, Mass., Vt. See SAMSON
Samuel, Mass., S6047
Samuel, Pa., S32506
Studley, Mass., S30082
William, Va., S17067
William, Va., Elizabeth, W8697
Zephaniah, Ct., Cont., Tamar, R9164
SAMS, Edmund, N.C., R9167
Jonathan, Va., Indian Wars, R9168
Samuel, Va., S6049
SAMSON, Abner, Mass., Ruth, W15306
Ahira, Mass., S33627
Amos, Mass., Joanna, W13866
Andrew, Mass., S30088
Benjamin, Mass., S22492
Colsen/Colson, Mass., Chloe,W15304
Daniel, N.H., R9162
Elijah, Mass., S30078
George, Mass., S22491
Henry, Art. Artificers, BLWt.13773

SANDS (continued)
9/1789. No papers
Andrew, Pa., S40383
Comfort, N.Y. res., Julia, R19408
Edward (colored), Mass., Dinah, W16148
Thomas, Pa., BLWt.10381. Iss. 6/11/1795. No papers
William, Va., Susannah, W986
William, Va., S40386
SANER, Michael, See ZANE
SANFORD, Archibald, Ct., S14412
David, Ct., Abiah, W22151
David, Ct., Hannah, R9195; BLWt. 45718-160-55
David, Mass., S29430
Ebenezer, Ct., Mary, W11382
Edward, Va., S41120
Elihu, Ct., BLWt.6483. Iss. 10/12/1789. No papers
Elihu, Ct., Nancy, W5974
Elisha, Ct., Rhoda, W17772
Elizabeth, former wid. of John Streator, Mass., which see
Ezekiel, Ct., S43103
Ezra, N.Y., Ann, R9192
George, Mass., R9194
George, R.I., S21471
Holsey, Ct., Miriam, W586; BLWt. 31714-160-55
Jairus, Ct., S15207
James, Ct., S43104
James, Ct., Cont., S14410
James, S.C., Va., Esther, R9193
Jesse, Ct., Eleanor, W17774
John, Cont., Mass. See STANFORD
John, Mass., S11336
John, N.Y., Catharine, W5975; S34482; BLWt.2463-100
Jonathan, Ct., S46068
Joseph, Ct., S29434
Joseph, Mass., Eleanor, W19312
Kingsbury, Cont., Ct., Privateer S14398
Lewis, N.Y., S18196
Liffe, Ct., Huldah, W17773
Moses, Ct., Elizabeth, R9196
Robert, Va., Abigail, R9198
Royal, R.I., S21467
Samuel, Ct., BLWt.1947-300-Capt. Iss. 10/30/1789. No papers
Samuel, Ct., S4810; BLWt.26242-160-55
Samuel, Ct., Ruhamah, W19313
Strong, Ct., BLWt.6452. Iss. 4/27/1790. No papers
Strong, Ct., S36289
Susanna, former wid. of Phinehas Brigham, Mass., which see
William, N.J., Jerusha, W5977
William, N.J. See SANDFORD
William, R.I., S11351
Zachariah, Ct., Dis. No papers See Am. State Papers, Class 9, p.116. Disabled at North River by the diseases contracted from hardship in the service.
Zacheus/Zacheous. Cont., Ct., Eunice, W22154
SANGER, Daniel, Ct., S30081
David, Mass., S4808
Pearley, Ct., R9199

SANGER (continued)
Samuel, Mass., BLWt.5080. Iss. 7/6/1796 to Daniel Jackson. No papers
SANKEE, Caesar/Ceasar (colored) N.H., S41124
SANKEY, Ezekiel, Pa., BLWt.10418. Iss. 3/29/179? No papers
Ezekiel, Pa., Catharine, W2864
SANOR, Michael, See ZANE
SANSOM, William, Va., Elizabeth D., W311
SANSOUCI, Guilliame, Hazen's Regt. BLWt.13744. Iss. 9/7/1789 to Wm. I. Vredenburgh, admr. No papers
SANSUM, Philip, Va., BLWt.2060-300-Capt. Iss. 2/23/1796 to Robert Camp, ass. No papers
SANTEE, Caesar, N.C., BLWts.12580 &13710. Iss. 2/13/1797 to Seth Peebles. No papers
John, Pa., Maria Magdalene, W3462
John, See SENTEE
SANTFORD, John, N.Y., BLWt.1083-300
SAP, John, See LAP
SAPP, Jesse, N.C., S1587
Joseph, Del., S41122
William, Ga., R9201
SAPPENFIELD, Michael, N.C., S17068
SAPPINGTON, Hartly, Pa., Va., b. Md., S17072
Richard, Md., Cassandra, W26198
SARDAM, Henry, Ct., Sylvia, W17775
SARGANT, Richard, Pa., S23889
SARGEANT, Daniel, Navy, N.H., Sarah, W16068; BLWt.10052-160-55
Ebenezer, Mass., S4667
Elizabeth, former wid. of John Bryant, N.H., which see
Isaac, Ct. See SERGEANT
Jacob, Ct., Cont., S15208
Richard, Pa. See SARGANT
Samuel, Mass., S33622
Samuel, Mass., Mary, W20044
Sarah, former wid. of Elijah Carpenter, Ct., which see
Solomon, Mass., Lydia, W19011
William, Md., S38350
SARGENT, Amos, Mass., Alice, W26955
Barnard, N.H. See SERGEANT
Benjamin, Mass., S20547
Benjamin, Mass., Eunice, W16710
Charles, Mass., S37365
Chase, Mass., S30079
Daniel, Mass., S37366
Daniel, Mass., Mary, W15305
Daniel, Navy, N.H., Charity, W26950
Ebenezer, Cont., N.H., Phebe, W19340
Ebenezer, Mass., S11342
Ebenezer, Privateer, Mass., R9202
Edward, N.H., R9384
James, Mass., S29431
John, Mass., Grace D., W5982; BLWt.33753-160-55. She also applied for pension as wid. of her former husb., Isaac Denny, Mass.

SARGENT (continued)
John, N.H., S11339
John, Vt., S19069
Jonathan, N.H., S10002
Joshua, Mass., S7439
Mary, former wid. of Samuel Emerson, Cont., N.H., Mass., which see
Mary, former wid. of Timothy Saunders, Mass., which see
Moses, Mass., N.H., S18589
Nelson, See LARGENT
Paul Dudley, Cont., Mass., Lucy, W24894
Phinehas, N.H., Hannah, W24908
Robert, N.H. See SEARGEANT
Samuel, Mass., Martha, W13871; BLWt.24174-160-55
Samuel G., Mass., Privateer, S19072
Timothy, N.H., N.Y., S11362
William, Cont., Mass., S45140
Winthrop, Cont., Mass., BLWt. 2394-300
Winthrop, Mass., S30084
SARJEANT, Elijah, See SERJEANT
SARLE, Thomas, See SEARL
SARLES, Richard, N.Y., Sally, W24900
Thaddeus, See Thaddus SARLLS
SARLLS, Thaddus/Thaddeus, N.Y., S22967
SARRATT, Samuel, N.C. See SARRETT
SARRETT, Allen, S.C., S4661
John, N.C., Mary, W312
Samuel, N.C., Nancy, W5981
SARTAIN, Joel, Va., R9207
SARTELL, John, Mass., S15633
Nathaniel, Cont., Mass., S33631
Nathaniel, Mass., S21473
SARTEN, Claibourn, See Claibourne SARTIN
SARTER, William, S.C. See SARTOR
SARTIN, Clabourne/Claibourn, N.C., Margaret, W9208
SARTOR, John Peter/Peter SALTER, S.C., Sarah, R9209
William, S.C., Rebecca, W8700
SARTWELL, Silvanus/Sylvanus, Mass., Lucy, W26953
SARVEN, Garret, N.Y., S22966
SARVEY, William, Mass., Elizabeth W15303
SARZEDAS, David, Ga., S39061
SASH, Moses, Mass., S36291
SASS, Jacob, N.C., S21956
SASSEN, Abel, N.C., See SASSER
SASSER, Abel, N.C., S7450
Benjamin, N.C., S7446
SATERLEE, James, Ct., BLWt.6490 Iss. 5/15/1790, no papers
William, Gen. Moses Hazen's Regt. BLWt.2112-300-Capt. Iss. 8/22/1789. No papers. Heitman's Reg. spells name as Satterlee
SATTARLEE, Elisha, Ct., BLWt. 6427. Iss. 1/5/1792. No papers
SATTERFIELD, John, Va., R9211
William, Md., BLWt.13730 & 14121 Iss. 5/1/1795 to Francis Sherrard, ass. of Thomas Fulton,

SATTERFIELD (continued)
admr. No papers
William, Md., Unicy, W1088
SATTERLEE, Elisha, Ct., Cynthia, W2967
James, Ct., Desire, W4508; BLWt. 405-100
Samuel, Ct., Sea Service, R9212
William, Hazen's Regt., See SATERLEE
SATTERLEY, John, Ct., R.I. See SATTERLY
Samuel, N.J., S40381
SATTERLY, John, Ct., R.I., Hannah, W18996
SATTERWHITE, John, N.J., BLWts. 8708 & 14039. Iss. 8/28/1792 to James Reynolds, ass. No papers
John S., See John S. WHITE
Robert, Va., S11346
SATWELL, Solomon, Pa., BLWt.10374 Iss. 5/26/1794 to Michael Stiver, ass. No papers
SAUBAT, John Baptiste, Va., R17662; Va. Half Pay
SAULISBURY, Maria A. & Almira Morgan, daus. of Abner Morgan, Mass., which see
SAULS, Henry, N.C., R9213
SAUNDERS, Abel, Ct., S36287
Abraham, Pa., S40382
Augustus, R.I., Elizabeth, W22144
Benjamin, Mass. See SANDERS
Cuff (colored), See Cuff WELLS
Daniel, R.I., S23408
Daniel, Va., S18197
David, N.H., Hannah, See SANDERS
David, Va., S31348
David, Va., War of 1812, Lockey/ Lookey, W3872
George, Md., S35059
George, Va., Elizabeth, W5986
Isaac, Mass. See SANDERS
James, Va., S32502
John, R.I. or N.H., BLWt.3500. Iss. 12/29/1794 to Ephraim Cutter, ass. No papers
John, Va., S6048
John, Va., S7454
John, Va. See SANDERS
Jonathan, N.H. See SANDERS
Joseph, Mass., S6050
Joseph, R.I. See SANDERS
Joseph, Va., S11347
Joseph, Va., Sea Service, S17073. See N.A. Acc. No.837(?), Va. State Navy, Y.S. Files, Va. Half Pay
Martha, former wid. of Solomon Seymour, N.C., which see
Nathaniel, N.C., S.C., b. England S7444
Noah, Mass., S33626
Obed, N.H. See SANDERS
Peter, Ct., S36288
Philemon, Va., S31347
Philip, N.C. See SANDERS
Richard, Va., Ann P., W8699; BLWt.6023-160-55
Robert, Navy, Ct., S36286
Robert, Lamb's Art., N.Y., BLWt.

SAUNDERS (continued)
7848. Iss. 8/20/1790 to Wm. I. Vreedenbaugh, ass. No papers
Robert Hyde, Va., S6046
Solomon, N.C. See SANDERS
Stephen, R.I., S21959
Thomas, N.J., R9220
Thomas, Va., Anna, W5985; BLWt.39500-160-55
Thomas, Va., Mary, R9216
Timothy, Mass., Mary Sargent, former wid., W24892
Uriah, R.I., S21468
Wait, R.I., Lucy, W9278; BLWt. 29028-160-55
William, Md., S36282
William, N.C., R20211; BLWt. 2098-200-Lt. Iss. 11/22/1791. No papers. This BL has no connection with the forged pension claim, but was allowed on the service of the Lt. of the N.C. line on which the forgery was based later.
William, Va., S15974
William, Va. Sea Service, R89. See N.A. Acc. No.837-Va. State Navy. Y.S. File, Va. Half Pay
SAUNDERSON, David, Mass., Hannah Wright, former wid., W20045
Isaac, Crane's Cont. Art., Mass., BLWt.5107. Iss. 10/12/ 1790 to Abel Bayton. No papers
Trial, Armand's Corps. BLWt.4971 & 13704. Iss. 4/1/1790. No papers
William, Va., Jamima, W5987
SAUQUAYUNK, Cornelius, N.Y. res. R9222
SAURMAN, Peter, Pa., Letter of Marque, S36748
SAVACOOL, William, N.J., S15203
SAVAGE, Abijah, Ct., Cont., S36281; BLWt.1954-300-Capt. Iss. 1/28/ 1790. No papers
Abraham, Mass., Sarah Occoman, former wid., W5439
Ebenezer, Mass., R21791
Edward, Mass., R9223
Edward, N.Y., S15204
Francis, Mass., BLWt.4968 & 5302 Iss. 7/31/1797 to Jeremiah Mason No papers
Francis, Mass., S33628
Gideon, Cont., Ct., Sarah, W16064
Henry, Mass., BLWt.1908-200-Lt. Iss. 9/12/1789 to Samuel Phillips Savage, exec. No papers
Hiel, Mass., S14401
Jacob, Navy, Mass., Hannah, W24902
Joel, Mass., Abigail, W22155
John, Ct., S11337
John, Cont., Mass., Privateers, d.1818, Margaret, W19002
John, Cont., Mass., Sea Service? d. 2/27/1815, Sarah, W22147
John, Pa., BLWt.2032-300-Capt. Iss. 4/18/1795. No papers
Joseph, Capt., Cont., Mass. Agcy. & res. in 1838, Catharine H., W18993; BLWt.1928-300 iss. 3/ 21/1791

SAVAGE (continued)
Joseph, Va., BLWt.2088-300-Surgeon's mate. No papers
Leven, N.C., S3849
Luther, Ct., R9225
Nancy, former wid. of Joseph Peck, Navy, Va. res. & Agcy., which see
Nathaniel, Ct., BLWt.6481. Iss. 4/5/1796 to Oliver Ashley, ass. No papers
Nathaniel L., Va., R17665. Va. Half Pay
Richard, Pa., BLWt.10387. Iss. 1/8/1796 to Robert Prise, ass. No papers
Roger, Mass., S28865
Sarah, former wid. of John Jolly, S.C., which see
Selah, Ct., S17071
Seth, Ct., Cont., S15211
Solomon, Ct., Lydia, R9227
Stephen, Art. Artificers, Ct., BLWts.6423 & 13771. Iss. 6/26/ 1789 to James Percival, ass. No papers
Thomas, Ct., Vt., S14402
Thomas, N.C., R9228
William, Ga.?, S.C., R9224
SAVEDGE, Hartwell, Va., S7452
SAVELL, George, Cont., Pa. See SAVILLE
SAVELS, Thomas, Mass., Miriam, W22161
SAVERY, Jonathan, Mass., Sarah, W20047
Thomas, Mass., S18588
SAVIDGE, John, Pa., S40388
SAVILLE, George, Cont., Pa., Mary, W4581
SAVORY, Benjamin, Mass., S29438
SAVOY, Philip, Md., BLWt.11675. Iss. 3/11/1791. No papers
Philip, Md., S35057
SAVY, Stephen, Ct., Cont., N.H., Vt., R17664
SAWEL, John, N.C., S4657
SAWIN, Abner, Mass., S4803. All papers missing from this Old War Inv. Record Book shows Abner Sawin, S4803 Ctf. 15752. Surgeon's Mate, Woodbury's Co., Mass. Line, Rev.
James, Mass., S19459; BLWt.16141-160-55
Jeroham, Vt., S21465; BLWt.2190-160-55
Levi, Mass., S11335; BLWt.26135-160-55
Samuel, Mass., Sarah, W499; BLWt. 10024-160-55
Samuel, Mass., R9230
Thomas, Mass., Abigail, W15308
SAWTELL, Abel, Mass., Sarah, W19309
Benjamin, Mass., Sybel, W4329
Elnathan, Mass., S30083
Hezekiah, N.H., Sarah, R., W24907
Jonas, Mass., Eunice, W24895
Jonathan, Cont., Mass., N.Y., Hannah, W22156
Joseph, Mass., S29432
Richard, Mass., Sarah, W13867

SAWTELL (continued)
Sarah, former wid. of Daniel Townsend, Mass., which see
Solomon, Mass., S11353
SAWYER, Abel, Green Mt. Boys, N.H., S16522
Abel, Mass., Abigail, W19305
Asa, Ct., S36283
Asahel, Ct., S15210
Azariah, Ct., Esther, W26429
Barnabas, Mass., Hannah, W2252; BLWt.3638-160-55
Barzilla, N.H., Jerusha, W24893
Benjamin, Cont., N.H., S15634
Benjamin, Mass., S18586
Benjamin, Mass., S22963
Benjamin, N.H., Abigail Dart, former wid., W22897; BLWt. 24769-160-55
Calvin, Mass., Polly, W15310
Conant, Ct., S41129
Cornelius, Ct., Sarah, W8704; BLWt.18023-160-55
David, Cont., Mass., Judith, W20046
Ebenezer, Mass., S14404
Ebenezer, Mass., S29428
Ebenezer, Mass., S41116
Eber, Cont., Mass., S14399
Edmund, N.H., S11343
Edward, N.H., S22489
Ephraim, Cont., Ct., S36284
Ephraim, Cont., Mass., S41123; BLWt.1930-300-Capt. Iss. 7/5/1797
George, Mass., S30087
Ichabod, N.H., Ann, R9231
Isaac, Mass., S30085
Israel, Mass., S29427
Jacob, Mass., S29437
Jacob, Mass., d. 12/10/1831, Esther, W5978; BLWt.6456-160-55
Jacob, Mass., d. 7/21/1827, Esther, W19316
James, Cont., Mass., N.H., Mary, W22150
James, Mass., Lydia, W19308; BLWt.1921-150-Ens. Iss. 10/28/1791. No papers
James, Va. See SAWYERS
Joatham/Jotham/Jonathan, Mass., N.H., Mary, W21559. (Mass. service appears to have been erased from file jacket)
John, Ct., S9472
John, Cont., Ct. res. of heir in 1830; BLWt.1771-100
John, Mass., S38352
John, Mass., Lettice, W22146
John, Mass., Abigail, W24884
John, Mass., Isabella, W24901
John, Mass., N.H., S17070
John, N.H., S19071; BLWt.77537-160-55
Jonathan, Mass. See Joatham
Jonathan, N.H., S22493
Jonathan, N.H., Jemima, W22143
Joseph, Ct., Cont., S11349
Josiah, Cont., Mass., R.I., Vt., S21464
Josiah, Mass., S37364
Josiah, N.H., Martha, W17771

SAWYER (continued)
Jude, Mass., S4804
Lewis, N.C., S3851
Luke, Mass., Rachel, W24877
Manasseh, N.H., S14406; BLWt. 538-100
Manasseth, N.H., BLWt.3497. Iss. 7/13/1793? No papers
Martha, former wid. of Thomas Stafford, Vt., which see
Mary, former wid. of Daniel Miller, R.I., which see
Nathaniel, Mass., Prudence, R9238
Oliver, Mass., S45137; BLWt.1024-100
Paul, Mass., S42251; BLWt.5049-100. Iss. 1798
Paul, Mass., Keziah, W2175; BLWt. 26303-160-55
Reuben, Mass., R9239
Samuel, Ct., French War 1762, Mary, R9236
Samuel, N.H., Molly, R9237
Sarah, former wid. of Thomas Frothingham, Mass., which see
Solomon, Mass., S19073
Stephen, N.H., S45136
Stephen, N.C., S32504
Thomas, Mass., Mary Roberts, former wid., W2171; BLWt.13437-160-55
William, Ct., S13709
William, Cont., N.H., Privateer, S3850
William, Mass., S18590
William, Va., R9240
SAWYERS, James, Va., Elizabeth, W5979
Joseph, N.C., S9470
William, Cont., S.C. res., Dis. No papers. See Am. State Papers, Class 9, p.106 & 165. Disabled 9/8/1781 at Eutaw Springs. Badly wounded in the head and three places in the right shoulder, and besides he lost both thumbs, which all together prevent him from procuring a livelihood by labor.
SAX, Andrew, Pa., S40384
Jacob, N.Y., S42250
William, Md., BLWts.11174 & 11676. Iss. 1/11/1796 to Joshua Ward, ass. No papers
SAXON, Hugh, S.C., (son of Charles) Mary, R9241
James, S.C., S38348
John, N.Y., S32507; BLWt.9054-160-55
Lewis, S.C., Sally McNess, former wid., W21791
Samuel, See SEXTON
Solomon, N.C., S31951
SAXSON, William, Va., Leah, W8711
SAXTON, Aaron, Vt. See SEXTON
Asher, Ct., Cont., Mass., S29439
James, N.Y., Huldah, R9242
Jared, N.J., See SEXTON
Jesse, N.J., BLWt.8738. Iss. 10/22/1789 to Samuel Potter, William Valentine, Jonathan Valentine, admrs. of Obediah Valentine,

SAXTON (continued)
decd. late assnes. No papers
John, Ct., S42252
John, Mass., Lucy, W13869
Noble, See SEXTON
William, Mass., Mary, W18995
Zephaniah, Ct., Green Mt. Boys, Vt., S14405
SAY, John, N.J., BLWt.8774; iss. 1/28/1793. No papers
SAYER, Nathaniel, Cont., Mass., S19458
Robert, Va., S35641
Robert, Va., BLWt.351-300
SAYERS, Uzal, N.J. See SAYRES
SAYLER, George Michael, Pa., Elizabeth, R9245; BLWt.61332-160-55
SAYLES, Ahab, R.I., Lillis, W5983
Daniel, R.I., S15632
David, R.I., BLWt.1969-300-Capt. Iss. 4/20/1790. No papers
Elisha, R.I., S21470
John, R.I., S21466
Richard, R.I., Rhoda, W16712
Smith, R.I., S21472
Stephen, R.I., Rose, W22159
Stukely, Navy, R.I., S11348
Sylvanus, Navy, R.I., Abigail, W22158
Thomas, R.I., R9244
SAYLOR, George M., See Michael, Md. Pa.
George M., Pa. See George M. SAYLER
Jacob, Cont., Pa., S40389
John, Pa., S40385
Michael/George Michael, Md., Pa., Anna Ringer, former wid., R---
SAYRE, David, N.J., R9247
Ephraim, N.J., Hannah, R9248
Ephraim, Va., R9249
James, N.Y., S22965
Job, N.Y., S23888
Joseph, N.J., S18587
Joshua, Cont., N.Y., S14403
Nathan, N.J., N.Y., S17075
Nathaniel, N.J., S4805
Pierson, N.J., S4806
Reuel/Rauel, N.J., S3855
William, N.J., S33630
SAYRES, Anthony, N.J., S1100
Isaac, See SEARS
Richard, N.J., Privateer, S4660
Uzal, N.J., Phebe, W24886; BLWt. 35692-160-55
SAYRS, Samuel, See SEARS
SAYWARD, George, Mass., Susannah, W22148
Prince (colored), Mass., Dinah, W27467
Richard, See SOWARD
SCAGGS, Mary, former wid. of Fletcher Edwards, S.C., which see
SCAITTS, James, N.Y., BLWt.7722. Iss. 4/16/179? to John Addoms, ass. No papers
SCALES, James, N.C., S7459
Nathan, R.I., Anna, W19328
Nathaniel, N.C., S18201
Samuel, Mass., Privateer, Anna,

SCALES (continued)
W2576; BLWt.5068-160-55
SCALF, John, N.C., Edy, W9280; BLWt.67702-160-55
SCALLY, William, Va., S39065
SCAMMAN, James, Mass., Elizabeth Storer, former wid., W17873
SCAMMEL, Alexander, N.H., BLWt. 1880-500-Col. No papers
SCAMMELL, Samuel L., Mass., BLWt. 2171-150
SCANTLING, Patrick, N.J., BLWt. 8773. Iss. 3/5/1793 to Christien Hubbard, ass. No papers
William, Va., Elizabeth, W19005
SCARBOROUGH, Elisha, Ct., Prudence, W26962
James, N.C., b. Va., S7467
James, Va., Sarah, W17783
John, Ct., S17079
John, Cont., Va., S36293
John, Va., Mary, W6003; BLWt. 1059-200. Iss. 2/10/1823
Samuel, Va., S7457
SCARFF, Joseph, S.C., BLWt.12593. Iss. 11/24/1795; BLWt.13700-100-1795
SCARLET, Thomas, N.C., Anna, W17784
SCARLETT, William, Pa., BLWt.10403-100. Iss. 8/17/1789. No papers
SCARRITT, James, Ct., Eliza, W1942; BLWt.19913-160-55
Nathan, Ct., S45144
SCATES, James, N.Y., S36752
John, Cont., Mass., Navy, S37381
SCAUR, Peter, See SEAUS
SCAUS, Peter, Cont. See SEAUS
SCHAAIEK, Goose Van, BLWt.2146-500 Col. Iss. 9/15/1790 to Mary Van Schaaiek, exec. Also Goose Van Schaaiek, exec. No papers. Heitman's Historical Register and the New York State Archives spell this name as Van Schaick, not Schaaiek
SCHAART, Peter, See SHORT
SCHAECKLER, Fredrick, Pa., R40415
SCHAEFER, Lambert, N.Y., S6059
SCHAFER, Henrich, N.Y., Susannah, W6002; BLWt.7069-160-55
Henricus, N.Y., Sophia, W16397
Henry, N.Y. See SHAFER
Pieter/Peter, N.Y., Engel, W20048
SHAFFNER, Casper, Armand's Corps (Rev. War), BLWt.2127-150-Cornet. Iss. 5/27/1790. No papers
SCHALL, John, See SHAUL
SCHAMP, David, N.J., Lenah, W1089
George, Pa., S6060
SCHANCK, John, N.J., S910
John, N.J., R9251
Koert, N.J., S748
Ralph, N.J. See SCHENK
SCHANK, John, N.J. See SCHANCK
SCHANTZ, Henry, Pa., Magdalena/ Magdalina, W2701; BLWts.271-60-55 & 2-100-55
SCHATZ, Henry, Pa., S3866
John, Md. See SHOTS
SCHAUM, Melchior, Pa., Margaret/ Elizabeth, R9252; BLWt.40716-160-55

SCHAUT, Adam, Pa., See SHOUT
SCHED, Samuel, See SHADE
SCHEDT, Samuel, See SHADE
SCHEEHAN, William, Pa., S3868
SCHEFER, Jacob, See SHAFFER
SCHEIB, William/Wilhelm, Pa., Catharine, W3304
John, Va. See SHEID
SCHELL, Christian, N.Y., R9253
Johannes, N.Y., Dis. No papers. See Am. State Paper, Class 9, p.94. Wounded at Oriskie, in his left side in an action with the Indians
SCHELLENEX, Abraham, See SCHELLENX
SCHELLENGER, Abraham, See SCHELLENX
SCHELLENX, Abraham, Ct., Jane, W16724.
SCHELLINGER, Abraham, See SCHELLENX
SCHENCK, Chrineyonce/Chrincyonce, N.J., Margaret, W3875
Garrit G./Garret G., N.J., S18591
Jacob, N.J., Pa.?, Mary, W2253
John, N.J., See SCHANCK
John, N.J. S9251, See SCHANCK
Koert, N.J. See SCHANCK
Peter T., N.J., Sarah, W22164
Ralph, N.Y., Aleta, W15841; BLWts. 1615-100 & 26970-160-55
William, Cont., N.J., S33633
SCHENK, Henry H., N.J.,Ellen, W989
John H., N.J., N.Y., Eliza, W500
Ralph/Rulef, N.J., Ann, W17788
Rulef, N.J. See Ralph
SCHENNEMAN, John, See SCHUNEMAN
SCHERMERHORN, Bartholomew, N.Y., S17078
Garret, N.Y., S14422
Jacob, N.Y., R9254
John J., N.Y., S23411
John L., N.Y., Anna, W17785
Lawrence, N.Y., Gazona, W19322
Leonard, N.Y., R9556
Richard/Rickart, Cont., N.Y., Annatie, W4331
SCHIFF, Hans George/George, N.Y. See SHEAF
SCHIKER, Frederick, See SCHLIKER
SCHIMFESSEL, Andrew, Pa., Margaret R9510
SCHIMMEL, Valentine, Md., Privateer, R9257
SCHINMELL, Valentine, See SCHIMMELL
SCHISLER, Michael, See SISLER
SCHIVER, Philip Peter, Cont., Pa., S41131
SCHLATTER, Jacob, Pa., Anna Maria, W3302
SCHLEPPY, Jacob, Pa., S7466
SCHLIFE, John, Cont., Md. See SHLIFE
SCHLIKER, Frederick, Cont., Pa. res. in 1828, S46227; BLWt. 1372-100
SCHLOKERMAN, Christopher, Pvt., Pa. BLWt.10433. Iss. 8/4/1797. No papers
SCHLOTT, John Adam, Pa., Catharine W2870
SCHLOTTERER, Gottlieb/Godfrey SLAUGHTER, Pa., Elizabeth, R9258

SCHMALTZ, Elizabeth, former wid. of John Frederick Spotz, Pa., which see
SCHMICK, Christian Carl, See SMICK
SCHMUCK, John, Pa., S22496
SCHNABLE, Joseph, Pa., S6064
SCHNECK, Jacob, Pa., Magdalena, R925
SCHNEIDER, Adam, Pa., S23002
Andrew, Pa. See SNYDER
Hendrichus/Henry, N.Y., Maria, R9925
Jacob, Pa., S22494
John, Md., S41137
SCHNELL, George, Pa., R9261
Lewis, French Sea Service, Indian War1790 (Va.) res. Pa. in 1833; R9262
Philip, Pa., S14419
SCHNIDER, Andrew, See SNYDER
SCHOCKEY, Christian, Pa., See SHOCKEY
SCHOFF, Jacob, N.H., Anna, W26960
SCHOFIELD, David, N.Y., S11101
Gershom, Ct. See SCOFIELD
Jesse, Ct., S31349
William, Pa., S41138
SCHOLEFIELD, James, Cont., N.Y. res. of heirs in 1812, BLWt. 609-100
SCHOLFIELD, Jesse, See SCHOFIELD
Joseph L., Md., Mary, BLWt.31785-160-55
William, Pa. See SCHOFIELD
SCHOLL, Abraham, Va., R9265
David, Pa., R9266
Johan Jost, N.Y., Anna Eva, W16396
SCHOOLCRAFT, Jacob, N.Y., Maria Catrina, W19323
Jacob, Va., R9268
John, N.Y., S15221
John, N.Y., S30689
John, Va., S7468
Lawrence, N.Y., S42260. See N.A. Acc. No. 874-050158. Not Half Pay
Lawrence, N.Y., R9267
Samuel, Ct., Mary, W5999; BLWt. 1108-100
SCHOOLER, William, Va., S46344; BLWt.1827-100
SCHOOLEY, John, N.J., S6058
SCHOOLIN, James, Pa., Mary, W9281
SCHOOLS, George, Va., S6057
SCHOONHOVEN, See SCHOONHOVER
SCHOONHOVER, Christopher, Mass., Hannah, W4330; BLWt.26755-160-55
SCHOONMAKER, Abraham, N.Y., Sarah, W19325
Daniel, N.Y., BLWt.1783-100
Henry, N.Y., Jane, W15800
Johannes, N.Y., S15223
John, N.Y., Magdalena/Helana, R9269
John Ed., N.Y., S14443
Robert, N.Y., BLWt.7739. Iss. 7/ 20/1791 No papers
SCHOONOVER, Christopher, See CRUMB

SCHOONOVER (continued)
Joseph, N.Y., S11359
Thomas, N.J., Margaret, R9270
SCHOTT, John Paul, Armand's Corps., BLWt.2122-300-Capt. Iss. 8/28/1789 to Matthew McConnell, ass. No papers
SCHOUTON, John D., N.Y., War of 1812, Getty Devoe former wid., W10727. She was also pensioned as wid. of Isaac Devoe, Rev. Sold., N.Y. All papers in this claim
SCHOVIL, Jacob, Ct., Green Mt. Boys, S36294
SCHRACK, Andrew, Md., S35061
David, Pa., BLWt.2033-300. Capt. Iss. 11/23/1799. No papers
SCHRADER, Jacob, Md. or Pa., R9271
John, Cont., N.Y., S41134
Philip, Cont., Pa. See SHREDER
Philip, German Regt. See SHRAWDER
SCHRAM, Frederick, N.Y., S15212
Henry, N.Y., R9272
John, N.Y., Lany, W24914
SCHREADER, Jacob, Pa., S42002
John J./John I., BLWt.7824. Iss. 8/31/1790 to Francis Carbines, ass. No papers
SCHREEDER, John I., N.Y., Elizabeth, W19320
SCHRIMSHEAR, John, N.C., R9274
SCHRIMSHER, Robert, S.C., S4666
SCHRIVER, Frederick, Hazen's Regt., BLWt.13751. Iss. 2/23/1792. No papers
Philip Peter, See SCHIVER
SCHROEDER, Anthony, Pa., War of 1812, See Anthoney SHROADER
SCHRYVER, Christain, N.Y., BLWt. 7800. Iss. 6/2/1791 to Jauncey & Given, assnes. No papers
Martinus/Martines, N.Y., Margaret, W19004
SCHULDUS, William, See SCHULTIS
SCHULTIS, William, N.Y., d.4/11/1808 at age of 45 yrs. 3 mo. 24 d. Married Catherine Sternberger at Beaver Dam, Albany Co., N.Y. 6/29/1800. R17684
SCHULTZ, Christian, Hazen's Regt. BLWt.13765. Iss. 6/27/179? No papers
John, Va., S6066
John H., Pa. See SCHUTE
Michael, Pa., S41142
Peter, N.Y., S22982
SCHUMACHER, George, Va., Mary M., W6004
SCHUNEMAN, John, N.Y., S7465
SCHUREMAN, Hercules, N.Y., R9275
SCHUTE, John/John H., Pa., Cont. Mary, W6040
SCHUTT, James, N.Y., Beleche/Belicha, W19326
Solomon, N.Y., Annatie/Anatje, R9276
SCHUYLER, David A., N.Y., S14423
Dirck, N.Y., BLWt.1984-150-Ens. Iss. 2/25/1792. No papers
John S., N.Y., Catharine, R9277

SCHUYLER (continued)
Nicholas, Cont., N.Y., S4665; BLWt.2115-400-Surgn. Iss. 4/29/1791 to Robert Gilchrist, ass. No papers
Nicholas, N.Y., R9278
Peter S., N.Y., Catharine, W17778
Philip S., N.Y., R9279
Reuben, N.Y., S28869
SCHWARTZ, Peter, Mass., Mary, R9280
Philip, Pa., Margaret, R9281
SCHWENCK, Jacob, Pa., S6056
SCIDMORE, Zophar, N.Y., R9283
SCIPIO, Ceaser, Ct., BLWt.6433 Iss. 1/4/179? to Micah Goodwin, ass. No papers
SCIPPERLY, Barent, See SHIPPERLY
SCISCO, Abraham, N.J. See CISCO
Tan, N.J., S4834
William, Cont., N.H. See SISCO
SCISIM, Peter, N.Y., Margaret, R9284
SCISM, Peter, See SCISIM
SCISSON, Robert, Va., S42001
SCOBEY, James, N.J., S42262
SCOFFIELD, Seely, Ct., BLWt. 6489. No papers
SCOFIELD, Asahel, Ct., S28391
Elisha, Ct., N.Y., Abigail, W11399; BLWt.15425-160-55
Else, former wid. of Samuel Comstock, Ct., which see
Enos, Ct., Amy, W17786
Enos, Ct., N.Y., S15219
Ezra, Ct., Milly, W1896
Gershom, Ct., Lydia, W22166
Gideon, Ct., Abigail Garret, former wid., R3922
Hait, Ct., Cont., S17665
Israel, Ct., N.Y., S6052
Jacob, Ct., Abigail, W17779
Jared, Ct., S16242
Josiah Weed, Ct., S17662
Nathaniel, Cont., N.Y. Agcy. & res., S46471
Nathaniel, N.Y., BLWt.7847. Iss. 4/21/1791.No papers
Neazer, Ct., S23892
Peter, N.Y., Hannah, W17782
Reuben, Ct., Cont., S11355
Seely/Selah, Ct., S10004
Silas, N.Y., S14416
Smith, N.Y., Susannah, W19318
Stephen, Ct., S42266
Sylvanus, Ct., Sarah, W17781
William, Ct., S28871
SCOGGIN, Robert, Va., S7458
SCOGGINS, Jonah, N.C., Ann, W24913
Willis, N.C., Unity, W2178
SCOLLAY, John, Mass., Esther, W8705; BLWt.3147-160-55
SCOOLER, William, Va. See SCHOOLER
SCOONE, George, Md., BLWt.463-100
SCOONMAKER, Daniel, N.Y. See SCHOONMAKER
SCOTT, Abel, Mass., S17663
Abraham, Md., Pa., S22497
Alexander, Cont., Va., BLWt. 168-100
Alexander, Md., S42269
Alexander, N.Y., R9287
Alexander, Va., S16244

SCOTT (continued)
Amasa, Ct., S42258
Amasa, Mass., S19763
Andrew, Mass., S6061
Archibald, S.C., Ann McCants, former wid., W8582. Wid's. 2nd husb., John Woodberry, was a Lt. S.C. Militia. See papers in above claim
Arther, Va., S1873
Benjamin, Md., Lotty Furgeson, former wid., W25601; BLWt.88539-160-55
Benjamin, N.Y., Vt., S15213
Benjamin, Pa., Prudence, W1498; BLWt.26325-160-55
Benjamin, Va., S17076
Caleb, Ct., S42267
Charles, Cont., Va., Priscilla, W5996; BLWt.2083-150-Cornet of Va. Iss. 3/6/1797. No papers
Charles, Md., BLWt.11692. Iss. 11/16/1796. No papers
Charles, N.H., Mary, W22167
Charles, R.I., Amey, W22165
Charles, Va., BLWt.2055-850. Brig. Gen. Iss. 4/25/1794. No papers
Christopher, Navy, Pa., S23890
Daniel, Ct., Esther, W9511; BLWt. 3762-160-55
Daniel, Va., S42003
David, Cont., Mass., Sea Service, R.I., Bethiah, W19324
David, Mass., S3860
David, Mass., S15224
David, N.H., BLWt.3481. Iss. 9/29/1791. No papers
David, N.Y., Mary, R9308
David, N.C., S.C., S9473
David, Va., S25425
Dennis, N.C., S39063; BLWt.34831-160-55
Drury, Va., S35644
Ebenezer, Mass., S41135
Eleazer, Ct., S27450
Elijah, Mass., S28870
Elisha, Ct., R9293
Ethiel, Ct., S41132
Ethiel, Ct., BLWt.46-100
Exum, N.C., Alley, W5994
Ezekiel, Ct., S15220
Francis, Va., S37370
George, Pa., S41145
Gideon, Mass., S42257
Henry, N.Y., Christiana, W20049
Hezekiah, N.H., Mary, W15314
Isaac, Md., S17666
Isham, N.C., S42004
James, Cont., Va., S32511
James, Md., BLWt.11742. Iss. 7/17/1797 to Abraham Jarret, ass. No papers
James/James M., Mass., U.S.A., Va. res. after Rev., S38353; BLWt.59-150
James, N.Y., BLWt.7724. Iss. 3/29/1790 to James Rosevelt, ass. No papers
James, N.Y., S14415
James, N.Y., S23894
James, N.C., b. Va., S3864
James, N.C., S6062
James, N.C., S.C., S39064

SCOTT (continued)
James, Pa., S23410
James, Va., S6067
James, Va., S14421
Jeremiah, R.I., Sarah, W22162
Jesse, N.C., Rachel, W4797
Joel, Mass., S3859
John, Ct., S42254
John, Mass., Cont., S16241
John, Cont., Mass., S46520; BLWt.1489-100
John, Cont., Mass., Bethiah, W24918
John, Cont., Va., Betsey/ Elizabeth, W16398
John, Md., BLWt.11687 & 12574. Iss. 1/30/1795 to John Stockdell, ass. No papers
John, Mass., BLWt.5006. Iss. 1/19/1796 to Joseph Fosdick. No papers
John, Mass., S41130
John, Mass., Mehitable, W15312
John, Mass., Mary, W24915
John, N.H., S42253
John, N.J., S6051
John, N.C., S---
John, N.C., b. Pa., S7469
John, Pa., S17077
John, Pa., S37369
John, Pa., Sarah, W5995; BLWt. 26757-160-55
John, Pa., Hannah, R9294
John, Pa., R9302
John, S.C., S1930
John, S.C., S21474
John, S.C., S32508
John, Va., res. of Greene Co., Ky. in 1832, S31351
John, Va., b. 1763, res. of McLean Co., Ill. in 1832, S32509
John, Va., Amelia Co., Va. res. in 1838, S38354; BLWt.819-150-Lt. & Ensign
John, (colored), Va., res. Ohio in 1802, S46522; BLWt.495-100
John, Va., d. 3/24/1843, Sophia, W3046; Va. Half Pay
John, Va., d. 6/1790, Susannah Elizabeth Clark, former wid., R2020; Va. Half Pay
John/John L., Va., d. 1802, Mary, R9309
John, Va., d. Halifax Co., 1/1824, R17708; Va. Half Pay, BLWt.2080. Lt. of Va. Light Dragoons. Iss. 4/18/1796. No papers
Jonathan, Mass., Abigail, W24912
Jonathan, Pa., S41140
Joseph, res. Ind. in 1853, R9304
Joseph, Ct., S15644
Joseph, Ct., S36295
Joseph, Mass., N.H., Betsy, R9288
Joseph, Va., wid. Mary, S9474
Joseph, Va., Elizabeth, W5993; BLWt.2062-300-Capt. Iss. 2/20/ 1799. Name recorded as Joseph Scott, Jr.
Joseph, Va., Drucilla, R9290
Justus, Ct., R9305
Levi, Md., BLWts.11686 & 11782. Iss. 3/11/1791. No papers

SCOTT (continued)
Levi, Md., BLWt.11722. Iss. 3/11/ 179? No papers
Levi, N.C., S30690
Lucy, former wid. of John Fenton, Ct., which see
Matthew, Pa., BLWt.2034-300-Capt. Iss. 7/9/1789. No papers
Micah, N.J., S41141
Moses, Ct., Matilda, W2176; BLWt. 6475-100. Iss. 8/3/1790. No papers
Moses, Ct., Eunice, W15313
Nathaniel, Mass., S42256
Noah, N.J., BLWt.8730. Iss. 8/7/ 1789 to Joseph Jones, No papers
Obadiah, Va., R9310
Oliver, Ct., S41143
Oliver, Ct., Ruth, W19327
Perry, Va. (Lee's Legion), BLWt. 12533 & 13805. Iss. 9/2/1789 to Perry Scott
Philip, Mass., S11356
Phinehas, Mass., Rhoda, W11398
Reuben R., Cont., Va., Margaret, R9306
Richard, S.C., R9311
Robert, N.J., Pa., Sarah, W3305
Robert, Pa., S23896
Robert, S.C., Isabell, W11402; BLWt.86133-160-55
Robert, Va., S31350
Robert, Va., Elizabeth Hord, former wid., W4455
Samuel, Ga., Va., Ann, W5998
Samuel, Md., S35062
Samuel, N.J., N.Y., Sarah, W26431; BLWt.26480-160-55
Samuel, Pa., S41139
Samuel, Va., Martha, R9307
Samuel, Va., Alice, R9312
Severn, Va., S38355
Stephen, Ct., S23895
Sylvanus, Cont., Mass. agcy. & res. in 1838, Deborah, W26958
Thomas, Ct., Ruth, W17780
Thomas, Mass., S42268
Thomas, N.C., b. Md., Lettice, W5997
Thomas, N.C., Va., b. Pa., Sarah, R9313
Thomas, Pa., BLWt.10396. Iss. 6/ 10/1794 to Silas Hart, ass. No papers
Thomas, Pa., Gen. Wayne's Indian War, Elizabeth, W3723; BLWt. 31704-160-55
Thomas, S.C., S3862
Timothy, Hazen's Regt., BLWt. 13755. Iss. 4/19/1792 to Conrad Feger, ass. of Robert Copeland, Admr. No papers
Timothy, Mass., BLWt.5003. Iss. 4/15/1790 to John Warren. No papers
Uri, Ct., S15217
Walter, Va., Va. Half Pay, R17707
William, Ct., Susannah, R17700
William, Ga., Ann, W19329
William, Mass., BLWt.1896-300. Capt. iss. 5/8/1792. No papers
William, Mass., BLWt.5083. Iss.

SCOTT (continued)
2/27/1790 to Theodosius Fowler. No papers
William, N.H., BLWt.3469. Iss. 11/19/1792 to Wm. Hyde, ass. of Abiah Bond. No papers
William, N.H., Disability, BLWt. 1882-400-Maj. Iss. 1/26/1790 to Wm. Scott. No papers. See Am. State Papers, Class 9, p.144. It is stated that he has lost in a great measure the use of his left hand, by a wound received from a musket ball. Likewise wounded in the back by a bayonet at or near the North Castle, in the year 1778
William, N.Y., S10003
William, N.Y., S14418
William, N.Y., Mary, W4582
William, Pa., S41144
William, Pa., Margaret Rodgers/ Rogers, former wid., W7146
William, Pa. (see ltr. relative to 3 bounty claims) BLWts.10344-100-1791; 10366-100-1795; 10450-100-1793
William, R.I., Henrietta, W26959
William, S.C., Mary, W8706; BLWt. 36529-160-55
William, S.C., BLWt.2305-300
William, Va., S6065
William, Va., b. Ireland, S7461
William, Va., S31952
William, Va., S38356
William, Va., Hannah, R9295
William, Va., Seley/Silvy R., R9314
Zerah, Vt., Sybel, W2255; BLWt. 2750-160-55
SCOUTEN, Jacob, N.J., S22495
SCOUTON, Simon S., N.Y., R9317
SCOVEL, Abijah Ct., Rebecca, W2628
Ebenezer, Ct., S42259
Jonah, Ct., Sarah, R9318
Matthew, Ct., Ct. Sea Service, S14414
Michael, Ct., R9321
Samuel, Ct. See SCOVIL
Stephen, Ct., Cont., S42265
SCOVELL, Moses, Ct., Rachel, W4796
Solomon, Ct., 15214
SCOVIL, Abijah, Ct., Mass., R9319
Benjamin, Ct., Eunice, R9320; BLWt.6470-100-Pvt. Iss. 8/25/ 1796 to James A. Neal, ass. No papers
John, Ct., S14420
Joseph, Ct., S23412
Samuel, Ct., S11360
Samuel, Cont., Ct., Lydia, W16714
SCOVILL, Amasa, Ct., S18592
Michael, Ct. See SCOVEL
Timothy, Ct., Chloe, W19006
Westol/Westole Scoville, Ct. S23897
SCOVILLE, Amasa, Cont., Ct., R9322
Michael, Ct., S30691
SCOWDEN, Theodorus, Pa., S23893
SCRAFFORD, George, N.Y., S15216

SCRAMBLING, George, N.Y., R9323
SCRANTOM, Abraham, Ct., S49288
SCRANTON, Abraham, Ct. See SCRANTOM
Abraham, Ct., Lucy, W17787
John, Ct. Sea Service, S17664
Stafford, R.I., Deborah, W22168
Stephen, N.H., Phebe, W2254; BLWt. 40-60-55 & 3472-100. Iss. 2/22/1792 to John Peck, ass. No papers
Thomas, Ct., S15222
Timothy, Ct., Sally, W8707; BLWts. 56-60-55 & 6438-100-1790
Torey/Torry, Ct., BLWt.6485. Iss. 2/24/1790. No papers
Torey/Torry, Ct., S15230
SCRIBER, Peter, N.Y., BLWt.7817. Iss. 7/30/1790 to Wm. Thompson, ass. No papers
SCRIBNER, Abel, N.Y., S42261
Ebenezer, Cont., N.H. res., S45143
Ezra, Ct., Nancy, W26433; BLWt. 40686-160-55
Jared, Ct., R9324
John, N.Y., Eve, W19321
Jonathan, Ct., N.Y., S15215
Levi, Ct., Esther, W26961
Nathaniel, Ct., N.Y., Dis. See Am. State Papers, Class 9, p.116. Capt. in Col. Luddington's Militia. Wounded by a musket ball in his left arm, 6/1/1778
Sarah, former wid. of William Whitteco, Md., which see
Stephen, Mass., S19075
Thaddeus, N.Y., Lydia, W1499
Zadock, N.Y., S41133
SCRIPTER, John, Ct., S42264
SCRIPTURE, Samuel, Mass., N.H., Rebecca, W313; BLWt.19613-160-55
SCRIVEN, James, Ct., R.I., S14417
William, R.I., Mary, W19007
Zebulon, R.I., Mary, W24922
SCRIVER, John, N.Y., BLWt.7784. Iss. 3/7/1792. No papers
SCRIVNER, Benjamin, Pa., Mary, W6000
SCROGGIN, Thomas C., Md., S16524
SCROGGINS, Humphrey, Va., R9325
Thomas, Ga., res. of wid. in 1814 R9326
SCROGGS, Jeremiah, N.C., S7455
John, N.C., S7462
SCROGGY, Thomas, N.J., Ann, W988
SCRUGGS, John, Va., R9328
Samuel/Scott MARTIN, Va., S38357
Timothy, Cont., Va., S35060
William, Va., Elizabeth, W3045
SCRUM, Peter, N.C., S7456
SCRYVER, Martines, See SCHRYVER
SCUDDER, Abijah, N.J., BLWt.8749. Iss. 10/1/1789. No papers
Abner, N.C., S32510
David, N.J., BLWt.298-100
John A., N.J., Pa., Privateer, Elizabeth, W8294
Kenneth A., N.J., Elizabeth, R9331
Philip, N.J., Hannah, R9329
Thomas, N.J., S11358
William, N.Y., BLWt.1978-200-Lt. Iss. 7/7/1790. No papers
William Smith, N.Y. res. Dis. No papers. See Am. State Papers,

SCUDDER (continued)
Class 9, p.126. Lost two fingers and the use of both hands by being frozen in a snow storm when he went with his men to Long Island in a boat to take certain pieces of ordnance that had belonged to the enemy's shipping; which duty he was ordered by Gen. Putnam. Disabled 3/3/1778
SCULL, Mourning, former wid. of Arthur Graham, N.C., which see
SCUREMAN, John, N.J., N.Y., Catharine, W24921; BLWt.34911-160-55
SCURLOCK, James, N.C., BLWt.2048-200
Samuel, N.C., S.C., Martha, R9332
William, N.C., S16523
William, S.C., BLWts.12592 & 13699. Iss. 3/31/1794. No papers
SCUTT, William, N.Y., Hannah, W9279
William, N.Y., Ruth Hollanbeck/Hollenbeck, former wid., W21385
SCYPEART, Robert, See SEYPEART
SEABOURN, Jacob, Va., S37373
SEABRING, Thomas, Pa., S750
SEABROOK, Stephen, N.J., Sarah, W6016; BLWt.28624-160-55
SEABURN, Richard, See SEBRING
SEABURY, Betsey, former wid. of Moses Harris, Mass., which see
Gideon, R.I., Betsey, W27484
John, N.Y., Hannah, R9334
John W., R.I., S15635
Peleg, R.I., S21963
Tilman, N.Y., Catherine, R9333
William, R.I., S21964
SEAGEL, Jacob, N.H., S41147
SEAGER, Darius, Ct., S13713
John, Mass., Mary, R9369. Name also appears as Segor, Seger, Seigar and Segar
Nathaniel, Md., S11365
SEAGO, Robert, See SEGO
SEAGRAVE, Joseph, Cont., Mass., Ct. res., Nancy Morse, former wid., W12509; BLWt.39208-160-55
SEAGRAVES, Jacob, N.C., S39067
John, N.C., S42005
SEAGROVE, John, N.C., S49300
SEAL, Joseph, Cont., Ind. res. in 1828, R20188
SEALE, Jarvis, Va., S11368
SEALS, James, Pa., Sarah, W3117
SEALY, George, Ct., Lois, W19339
Samuel, S.C., Sarah, R9362
SEAMAN, Andrew, Ct., S28872
Catharine, former wid. of Peter Van Kleek, N.Y., which see
Henry, N.Y., S23414
Henry, Pa., Va., Ann, W4583
Isaac, N.Y., Margaret, W16399
Isaac, N.Y., Pa., Charlotte, W19336
James, N.Y., Catharine, W24927
Joseph, N.Y., S10005
Joseph, N.Y., Clarry, W16717
Micah, N.Y., R9337
Paul, N.Y., S22974
Reuben, Mass., Jemima, W24930

SEAMAN (continued)
Stephen, R.I., S29442
SEAMANDS, Jonathan, Va., S1588
SEAMANS, Hezekiah, R.I., Annis, W20153
James, Ct., R.I., S15229
John, R.I., R9338
SEAMEN, Henry, See SEAMAN
James, N.Y. See SEAMAN
SEAMENS, Isaac, N.Y., Mary Teepening, former wid., W15851
SEAMOND, Ephraim, Va., R9336
SEAMONS, Joseph, Va., S3909
SEAMORE, Thomas, See SEYMORE
SEAMSTER, John, Va., S25429
SEARCH, James, N.J., S40390
Lot, N.J., S21961
SEARCY, Asa, N.C., Ind. Wars, Frances Weathered/Weatherhead, former wid., W8992
Jeremiah, S.C., S25811
John, N.C., S31355
John, Va., Barbara, W24934; BLWt.26914-160-55
Luke, N.C., Elizabeth, R9340
Richard, Va., Rebecca, R9341
William, N.C. See SEAREY
SEAREY, William, N.C., Sarah, R9342
SEARFOSS, Benjamin, Pa., left no wid.; one dau., Mary Buck, S23902
SEARGEANT, Robert, N.H., W16150
Ebenezer, See SARGEANT
SEARING, Daniel, R9343, res. in Westchester Co., N.Y.
SEARJEANT, Jeremiah, Va. See SERGEANT
SEARL, Aaron, Mass., S3870
Benjamin B., N.H., S22501
Joseph, Mass., Margaret, W22180
Lemuel, Mass., S30092
Thomas, N.Y., Lois, W24928
SEARLE, Jeremiah, Cont., N.Y., R9344
John, Crane's Cont. Art., Mass., BLWt.4967 & 5177. Iss. 7/21/1798 to Joseph Fosdick. No papers
John, Cont., Mass., S43106
Samuel, Mass., Hannah, W24929; BLWt.242-60-55 & 5028. Iss. 3/25/1790. No papers
William, Mass., Nella, W16069
SEARLES, George S., N.J., S40395
Samuel, N.Y. See SEARLIS
SEARLIS, Samuel, N.Y., R9345
SEARLS, Samuel, Mass. See SEARLE
SEARS, Allen, Mass., S21475
Barnabas, Mass., S33635
Barnabas, Mass., S37377
David, Ct., S17539
David, Cont. Sea Service, Mass., Martha, W17795
Earl, Mass., R.I., Judith, W15315
Ebenezer, Cont., Mass., S22499
Ebenezer, Mass., Privateer, S30090
Elisha, Mass., Hannah, W15316
Elnathan, N.Y., S46523; BLWt.1614-100
Francis, N.Y., Rachel, W16715
Hannah, former wid. of Elias

SEARS (continued)
Wilcox, Cont., Ct., which see
Holmes, Mass., Mercy, W24924
Isaac, Cont., Ct., Grace, W16401
Isaac, N.J., BLWt.8751. Iss. 6/11/1789 to Jonathan Dayton, ass. No papers
Isaac, N.J., S43112
John, Cont., Mass., Mary, W13888
John, Md., BLWt.2049-200-Lt. Iss. 6/19/179? No papers
John, N.Y., Mary, W2471; BLWt. 19730-160-55
Jonathan, Mass., Abagail, W15318
Joseph, Cont., Va., S25810
Lydia, former wid. of Uriah Knight, Cont., Mass., which see
Moses, N.Y., BLWt.7767. Iss. 9/2/1790 to Andrew Thompson, ass. No papers
Nathan, Cont., Mass., S33637
Obadiah, Ct., Hannah Sears, wid. was pensioned as former wid. of Elias Wilcox, which see
Peter, Cont., Mass., S33634; BLWt.1930-200
Roland, Mass., S30692
Samuel, N.J., BLWt.8725. Iss. 7/17/1789 to Betsey Sears, wid. No papers
Samuel, N.J., Betsey Hedden, former wid., W488
Samuel, N.Y., R9350
Silas, Cont., Mass., Betsey, W6009; BLWt.5445-160-55
Willard, Ct., S17667
Willard, Cont., Mass., Lucy M., W6010
SEASE, Michael, Pa. & War of 1812 Rebecca, S9475; BLWt.95227-160-55
SEAT, James, N.C., S7473
SEATON, George, Va., S30693
Thomas, Va., Sarah, W8710
SEAUS, Peter, Cont., Barbara, Pa. res. of wid. in 1820, BLWt. 909-100
SEAVER, Calvin, Cont., Mass., Mary, W19332; BLWt.2089-160-55
Daniel, Mass., Martha, W26439
Ichabod, Mass., S40397
James, Mass. See SEVER
Joseph, Cont., Mass., Abihael, BLWt.38555-160-55; W1655
Joseph, Mass. See SEVER
Joseph, Mass., Abagail, R9351
Luther, Mass., S43117
Nathaniel W., Cont. Vt., Mary Chamberlain, former wid., W22764
Obed, R.I., S.C. Sea Service, S21965
Robert, Cont., Mass., Ann, W19013
Thomas, Mass., BLWt.818-100
William, Mass., Susannah, R9353
SEAVEY, Abigail/Nabby, former wid. of Aden Briggs, Mass.,which see
Daniel, N.H., S45148
Isaac, Cont., N.H., S45151
James, N.H., S31353
Jonathan, Cont.,N.H. res. in 1818, Sarah, W6015; BLWt.8001-160-55

SEAWARD, George, N.H., Mary,W22181
John, Cont., Mass., S4812
John H., Sea Service, N.H., R9355
Joseph, Va. See SEWARD
SEAWELL, Thomas, Mass. See SEWALL
SEAWRIGHT, William, S.C., Mary, W22179
SEAY, Austin, Va., Elizabeth, W19341
Jacob, Va., S25430
Jacob, Va., S31352
James, Va., S9477
James, Va., Sally/Sarah, W8038; BLWt.26165-160-55
Joseph, Va., S7472
Matthew, Va., S7477: BLWt.26247-160-55
Reuben, Va., Mary Ann, R9359
Samuel, Va., Polly, R9358
SEAYRES, John, Va., BLWt.1903-450-Lt. Col. Iss. 8/24/1789. Also recorded under 2520. No papers
Thomas, Va., BLWt.2086-150-Ens. Iss. 9/18/1789. No papers
SEBER, Henry, N.Y. See SEEBER
SEBOTT, Abraham, Pa., S22498
SEBREE, Richard, Va., S14424
William, Va., S38360
SEBRING, Abraham, N.J., S22972
Folkerd, N.J., Mary, W24926
Richard, N.J., S43115
SEBURN, Jacob, Va., BLWt.12547. Iss. 5/1/1792 to Francis Graves, ass. No papers
SECHLER, Michael, Cont., Pa., Rebecca, W1941
SECKLER, Michael, See SECHLER
SECOR, Andrew, N.Y., S15232
Benjamin, N.Y., S22975
Isaac, N.Y., Abigail, W17793; BLWt.527-160-55
James, N.Y., S15227
John, N.Y., S15231
John, N.Y., S43122
Jonas, N.Y., R9348
SECREST, John, N.C., S3875
SEDAM, Cornelius R., N.J. & U.S. Army up to 1792, Nancy Shotwell former wid., R9537; BLWt.2000-150-Ens. Iss. 6/20/1789. She was allowed BL on the service of her husb. Lewis Shotwell, War of 1812 Wt.52592-160-55
Ryke, N.J., S911
SEDGEWICK, Ashur/Asher, Ct., Cont., Temperance, W15026
John, Ct. See SEDGWICK
SEDGLY, John, Mass., Mary, W1656
Joseph, Mass., S30091
SEDGWICK, Asher, See Ashur SEDGEWICK
Ebenezer, Ct., Martha, W17799
John, Ct., Tally, W2007
Samuel, Ct., S43120
Timothy, Ct., Lucy, W26440; BLWt.38547-160-55
William, Ct., S36298
SEDORE, Isaac, N.Y., S29441
SEE, George, Va., R9361
James, N.Y., Dis. No papers. See Am. State Papers, Class 9, p.126 Disability; inflamation caused by

SEE (continued)
hurting his left leg by a fall out of bed, in a fit of delirium, when he had small pox in captivity, in the sugar house, New York in 1779
John, Cont., Va., S17538, alias John Lee
John, Va. see John LEE
SEEBER, Henry, N.Y., S27469
SEEGER, Ezekiel, Cont., Mass., S43114
SEEKELL, Abiathar/Abiather, Mass. R.I., S23901
SEELE, John, Mass., BLWt.5016 iss. 12/7/1791 to Martin Kingsley
SEELEY, Benjamin, Ct. See SEELYE
David, Ct., R9363
Denton, Ct., S17081
Ebenezer, Ct., Betsey, W6013; BLWt.7077-160-55
Isaac, Pa., BLWt.2017-300-Capt. No papers
John, Mass. See SELEY
John, N.J., S33638
SEELY, Benjamin, Cont., Ct., Sarah W2358; BLWt.26562-160-55
Ebenezer, Ct., S13734
Ebenezer, Ct., Cont., Mabel, W3308
Eli, N.Y., S22969
Ephraim, Cont., Mass. See SEELYE
Gideon, N.Y., Patience, R9364
Isaac, Ct., S11369
James, N.Y., S11366
John, N.J., BLWt.8723. Iss. 11/26/1794 to Joseph Wilson, ass. No papers
John, Pa., S15643
Jonathan, Green Mt. Boys, Vt. See SEELYE
Joseph, Ct., N.Y., S36296
Lewis, Lamb's Art., N.Y., BLWt. 7840. Iss. 7/14/1790 to Richard Platt, ass. No papers
Samuel, Pa., Abigail, W3307
Samuel, N.Y., Mercy, W19335
Samuel, Pa., S41146
Samuel C., N.J., Patience, W16402; BLWt.1996-200-Lt. Iss. 9/2/1789 to Daniel Thompson, ass. No papers
Seth, Sappers & Miners, BLWt.13718 Iss. 8/7/1789 to Benjamin Tallmadge, ass. No papers
Silvanus, N.Y. List of Invalid pensioners for Dutchess Co., N.Y. shows that one Silvanus Seely served as a Pvt. in Col. Graham's New York Regt.
Thaddeus, N.Y., Sarah, W19010
SEELYE, Benjamin, Ct., Sarah, W3463; BLWt.15162-160-55
Ephraim, Cont., Mass., Green Mt. Boys, Hannah, S30089; BLWt.19702-160-55
John, Ct., Betsy Campbell, former wid., W4419
John, Ct., Abigail, W22173
Jonathan, Vt., Green Mt. Boys, Freelove Barnes, former wid., W29614; BLWt.30704-160-55

SEELYE (continued)
Seth, Cont., Ct., S43109
SEEMORE, Burges, Va., Dicey, R9365
SEERS, Moses, N.Y., S43113
SEES, Michael, Pa. See SEASE
SEEVER, Jonathan, N.Y. See SEVER
SEGAR, Caleb, Mass. See SEGOR
Ebenezer, Cont., Mass., Mehitable, W27483; BLWt.215-100
Ezekiel, Cont., Mass. See SEEGER
John, Mass. See SEAGER
Peter, N.Y., Mary, W19333
SEGER, Ebenezer, See SEGAR
Elijah, Ct., S21962
Gerret I./Gerrit I., N.Y., Catharine, W19337
John, Mass. See SEAGER
John, N.Y., S23413
Joseph, Ct., Cont., S15228
Nathaniel, Mass., S31356
Peter, See SEGAR
SEGERS, Caleb, Cont., Mass., S33640
SEGERSON, James, Pa., BLWt.10394. Iss. 6/29/1789 to M. McConnell, ass. No papers
SEGO, Robert, S.C., Elender, R9368
SEGOND, James, Chevalier de, Cont. BLWt.65-300
SEGOR, Caleb, Mass., Sally, R9366
John, Mass. See SEAGER
SEGRIST, Melchior, Pa., S6074
SEIBERLING, Frederick, Pa., S4813
SEIBERT, Henry, See SYBERT
SEIDEL, Peter, Pa., S23899
Peter, Pa., Mary Steele, former wid., W6195; BLWt.26299-160-55
SEIDENSBERGER, John, See SIDENBERGER
SEIDLE, Peter, Pa. See SEIDEL
SEIFRET, George, Va., S38132
SEIGAR, John, Mass. See SEAGER
SEIPS, Philip, Md. See SMITH
SEISLAR, Phillip/Philip, Md., S34958
SEITZINGER, Michael, Pa., R17838
Nicholas, Pa., S22968
SEIVERT, Jacob, Pa., S40396
SELAWAY, Reubin, Mass., BLWt. 5086. Iss. 3/25/1790. No papers
SELBY, David Melville, Ct., Hannah, W10249; BLWt.61196-160-55
SELCER, Frederick, Pa., S9476
SELDEN, Asa, Mass., S4814
Benjamin, Ct., R9371
Charles, Mass., BLWt.1911-200. Lt. Iss. 3/1/1800. No papers
Elijah, Ct., S36297
Ezra, Ct., Cont., BLWt.687-300
Samuel, Va., BLWt.2071-200-Lt. Iss. 8/10/1789 to Richard Platt, ass. No papers
Wilson Cary, Va., S4815. Va. Half Pay. N.A. Acc. No. 874-050159. Half Pay Wilson Cary Selden
SELDON, Asa, Mass. See SELDEN
SELEY, Abraham, Ct., S29444
John, Mass., Cont., Mercy, S40392 and W6014
SELF, John, Va., S31358

SELF (continued)
Larkin, Va., S38363; BLWt. 2435-100
Moses, Va., Nancy, W19009
Thomas, Va., S19461
Thomas, Va., Oney, W6008
SELFRIDGE, John, N.Y., Sarah, W4332; BLWt.31718-160-55
Oliver, N.Y., S22973
Robert, Mass., S11367
SELIN, Anthony, Cont., Pa., BLWt.122-300. Iss. 2/8/1804
SELKIRK, James, N.Y., Elizabeth W24932
SELKRIG, Jeremiah, Ct., S29443
SELL, George, Va., BLWt.12568. Iss. 2/18/1793 to Robert Means, ass. No papers.
John, Pa., R9374
Philip, N.C., Dorothy, W4333
SELLACK, Stephen, Ct. See SELLECK
SELLARS, James, Mass., Navy, Privateer, Pamelia, W17794
Jordan, N.C., Mary, W26437; BLWt.36551-160-55
SELLECK, James, Ct. See SELLICK
Joseph, Ct., Phebe, W17796
Peter, Ct., Cont., S15226
Stephen, Ct., Ann, W7170
SELLERS, Conrad, See KELLAR
Daniel, N.C. See Donald
David, N.C. See Donald
Donald, N.C., R9376
Hardy, S.C., R9377
Howel/Howell, S.C., S31357
Isham/Isam, N.C., S14428
James, Mass., Sea Service, See SELLARS
James, N.C., S3872
Jordan, N.C. See SELLARS
Michael, Va., Catharine, W9282
Samuel, Pa., S37371
SELLICK, Gould John, N.Y., Elizabeth, W16400
Henry, Ct., S41149
James, Ct., Chloe, W2256; BLWts. 26231-160-55 & 57783-160-55
James, Ct., Phebe, W19331
Jesse, Ct., R9379
Peter Ct., Cont., See SELLECK
SELLMAN, Jonathan, Jr. See SILLMAN
SELLS, Henry, Pa., R9373
SELMAN, John, Cont., Mass., Privateer, Deborah, W22182
Joseph, Mass., Abigail, W15731
SELMON, Joseph, Va., S38361
SELOOVER, Andrew, N.Y., S16246
SELOVER, John, See SLOVER
SELSBURY, Jonathan, Mass., BLWt. 5019 & 115-60-55. Iss. 2/27/1793. No papers
SEMONS, John, See LEMONS
William, See SIMONS
SEMORE, Thomas, See SEYMORE
SEMOUR, Larkin, Va., R9405
SEMPLE, Thomas, Pa., S.C., S36750
SENATE, Patrick, See SINNETT
SENEVEL, James, Va. See SENEWEL
SENEWEL, James, Va., S17080
SENNETT, Patrick, Va. See SINNETT
SENNIX, James, Crane's Cont. Art. Mass., BLWt.5106. Iss. 8/11/

SENNIX (continued)
1790 to Robert Dunlap. No papers
SENSEBAH, John, See Johann SENSENBACH
SENSENBACH, Johann, Va., Catharine Capshaw, former wid., R1675
SENTEE, John, Va., R17636
SENTELL, Samuel, N.C., Nancy, W6017; BLWt.33754-160-55
William, N.C., Elizabeth, R9382
SENTER, Abel, Mass., N.H., Sarah, W22178
Asa, N.H., S43108; BLWt.1884-300 Capt. Iss. 1/15/1800 to Asa Senter. No papers
Henry, N.C., Rebeccah, R9381
Moses, N.H., Sally, W26436; BLWt. 28642-160-55
Samuel, N.H., Hannah, W15320
Thomas, Mass., S7470
William, See SENTELL
SENTILL, Samuel, N.C. See SENTELL
SEPHTON, Sally, former wid. of Abraham Colby, R.I., which see
SEPT, William, Armand's Corps, BLWt.13702. Iss. 3/8/1791. No papers
SEPTER, Frederick, Pa., R9383
SERGEANT, Abel, R.I., S43119
Barnard, N.H., BLWt.694-100
David, N.J., BLWt.8755. Iss. 6/11/1789 to Matthias Denman, ass. No papers
Ebenezer, Cont., N.H. See SARGENT
Elizabeth, former wid. of John Bryant, N.H., which see
Isaac, Ct., Elizabeth Taylor, former wid., R10414 1/2. She was pensioned as wid. of her other husb., Josiah Taylor, Ct., which see
Jeremiah, Va., S38364
John, Vt. See SARGENT
Timothy, N.H.,N.Y. See SARGENT
Valentine, N.H., S45147
William, Cont., Mass., S19076
SERGENT, Joseph, N.H., S10007
SERING, Samuel, Pa., Sarah, R9386
SERJEANT, Elijah, Md., Va., S16245
James, N.J., S43110
Jeremiah, Va. See SERGEANT
Robert, N.H., BLWt.3471. Iss. 7/6/1792 to John Bridges, ass. No papers
SERJESON, William, N.Y., BLWt. 7723. Iss. 7/9/1790 to Nicholas Fish, ass. No papers
SERLS, Amos, N.Y., Vt., R9346
SERRINE, William, See SIRRINE
SERVAL, Daniel, See SEWAL, also Moses STEVENS for slip relative to this soldier.
SERVANTE, William, Va., S37372
SERVICE, John, Del., BLWt.10878. Iss. 9/2/1789. No papers
Nathaniel, Navy, Mass. res. & agcy., S33639
SERVIS, John, N.J., R9387
SERVOSS, John, N.Y., S22971
SESSIONS, Abijah, Ct.,Hannah,W26434

SESSIONS (continued)
David, Cont., Mass., S37380
John, N.C., S38362
Josias, S.C., S18202
Robert, Ct., Anna, W24925
SESSOMS, Solomon, N.C., Obedience W19330
SESSUMS, Solomon, See SESSOMS
SETCHEL, Isaac, Mass., Sarah Lakeman, former wid., W24469
Jeremiah B., Mary. See case of wid's. former husb., Ebenezer Trusdell, Cont.,Mass.
SETSER, Adam, N.C., R9389
SETTER, Conrad, Hazen's Regt., BLWt.13759. Iss. 5/6/1793. No papers
George, Pa. See SETTLER
SETTLEMYER, Godfrey, Pa., S4643; BLWt.213-100
SETTLER, George, Pa., R9388
SETZER, Adam, See SETSER
SEVA, John, Ga. Agcy. Dis. No papers
SEVARANCE, Joshua, Cont., N.H., Elizabeth, W22174
SEVARTS, Baltus, See SWARTS
Tewalt, See SWARTS
SEVER, Christopher, Mass., S33372
James, Mass., BLWt.717-150
Jonathan, N.Y., Nancy, W24931
Joseph, Mass., S33636
Robert, Mass. See SEAVER
SEVERANCE, Abbe, N.H., Eunice, W26435
Abel, Cont., N.H., S45146
Asa, N.H., S15636
Benjamin, Mass., N.H., Rebecca, W9646
Caleb, Cont., Mass., S37379
Ebenezer, N.H., S22500
Ephraim, See SUFFRANCE
Hannah, former wid. of Daniel Boynton, Mass., which see
Jonathan, N.H., Mehitable, W16151
Joshua, Cont., N.H. See SEVARANCE
Peter, Cont., N.H., S19077
Peter, N.H., Sarah, W19334
Samuel, Mass., Azubah, W3118. See N.A. Acc. No.874-050160. Not Half Pay Samuel Severance wid.- Azubah
SEVERENCE, Joseph, Cont., Mass., S45145; Mass. & N.H. res.
SEVERN, David, Pa., S37374
SEVERNS, Edward, N.J., Hannah, R9394
SEVERS, Daniel, Mass. See SEAVER
SEVERSON, Richard, N.Y., S23900
SEVERY, John, Mass., S11370
Jonathan, Mass. See SAVERY
SEVEY, Eliakim, Mass., S37375
Isaac, See SEAVY
Joseph, N.Y., BLWt.7801. Iss. 2/14/1791 to Elisha Crane, ass. No papers
SEVIER, Abraham, N.C., b. Va., S1589
James, N.C., S45889
John, N.C., Catharine, W6011
Valentine, N.C.,Va., Naomi, W6012
SEVY, Isaac, See SEAVY

SEWAL, Daniel. See Moses Stevens, W22578 for slip relative to this sold. Warranted as Q.M. Sgt.
SEWALL, Charles, Md. See SEWELL
Clement, Md., S20192; BLWt.1444-150. Iss. 12/16/1828
Dummer, Mass., Jenny, W17790
James, Md. See SEWELL
James, Va. See SEWELL
Thomas, Mass., Pricilla, W22175
Thomas, Va. See SEWELL
SEWARD, Daniel, Pa., Elizabeth, W2179
Emanuel/Manuel, Mass., Elizabeth, W13886
Jedediah, Ct., Susan, W1943
Jedediah/Jedadiah, Mass., N.Y., S22970
Jedidiah, Sheldon's Dragoons, Ct. BLWt.6525. Iss. 6/16/1798. No papers
Job, Ct., Lois, W16716
John, Mass., See SEAWARD
Joseph, Va., Martha, W9644; BLWt.71019-160-55
Josiah, Cont., Mass., S45149
Manuel, See Emanuel
Nathan, Ct., Martha, W9283
Samuel, Cont.,Mass., Olive, W24933
Samuel, N.J., S36751
Silas, Ct., S43118
Stephen, Ct., Sarah Lewis, former wid., R6329
Thomas, Crane's Regt. of Art., BLWt.1926-300-Capt. Iss. 1/29/1790. No papers
Timothy, Sheldon's Dragoons, Ct. BLWt.6524. Iss. 7/8/1789. No papers
Timothy, Ct., S43111
Timothy, Ct., Rebecca, W11416; BLWt.38558-160-55
William, Md., Nancy, W9309
SEWELL, Charles, Md., S35064
Dorson, N.C., Mary/Polly, W8712
Henry, Cont., Mass., Elizabeth, W1897; BLWt.1898-300-Capt. Iss. 6/26/1789. No papers
James, Md., S7471; BLWt.554-100
James, Va., Sur. Cft. 7777
John, Md., S35063
Joseph, N.C., S31354
Thomas, Mass. See SEWALL
Thomas, Va., S40394
Thomas B., Md. Sea Service, Charlotte Pecor. former wid.- R8070; BLWt.84056-160-55
William, Md., Rebecca, W9285
SEXTON, Aaron, Vt., Jane, R9398
Charles, N.J., S3874
Elijah, Ct., Thankful, W2444; BLWt.26879-160-55
Ezra, Ct., S3879
Frederick, N.C., Mary, R9399
George, Cont., Vt., Lois, W17789
Jared, N.J., Mary, W3161
John, S.C., Susan, W26432; BLWt. 28630-160-55
John, Va., Mary Ann, W172
Jonathan, N.J., Vt., Elizabeth, R9397
Noble, Mass., N.Y., S43123

SEXTON (continued)
Oliver, Mass., S14427
Samuel, S.C., R9400
Timothy, N.J., Esther, W196
William, See SAXSON
SEYBERT, Christian, Va., S7475
David, Pa., War 1812, Susannah, W10253
SEYMORE, Larkin, See SEMOUR
Thomas, Va., Frances, W17791; BLWt.31706-160-55
SEYMOUR, Anne, former wid. of Tilley Kingsbury, Ct., Mass., which see
Asa, Ct., BLWt.6476. Iss. 2/5/1790. No papers
Asa, Ct., S6072
Asa, Ct., Elizabeth, W17798
Eli, Ct., R9403
George, Ct., Cont., Mabel, W17800
Henry, Ct., R9404
Horace, Sheldon's Dragoons, BLWt. 1966-200-Lt. Iss. 4/28/1795. No papers
James, Ct., Hannah, W11415
James, Ct., Rebecca, W22172
John, Ct., Sally, W24923; BLWt. 26124-160-55
Joseph, Ct., S43116
Nathan, Mass., S41148
Nathaniel, Ct., S15225
Noah, Ct., Miriam, W22171
Samuel, Ct., S28873
Samuel, Ct., Rebecca, W17797
Seth, Ct., Sally, W26438; BLWt. 36536-160-55
Solomon, N.C., Martha Saunders/ Sanders, former wid., W19314
Stephen, Ct., R9406
Stephen, Ct., Cont., S43107
Thomas, Mass., BLWt.4989. Iss. 10/22/1789
Thomas, Va. See SEYMORE
Thomas, Va., also served in 1792, Catharine, R9401
Thomas Young, Cont., Ct., Susan, W19008
William, Ct., S20951
William, Ct., N.Y., Sarah, W19012
William, Del., BLWt.10876. Iss. 12/17/1791 to John Hailey & Eleanor Hailey, Admrs. No papers
William, Mass., Susanna, W11410
Zachariah, Ct., Cont., Elizabeth, W26441
Zadock, Ct., S29440
SEYNER, Michael, See Michael ZANE
SEYPEART, Robert, N.C., S39066
SHACKELFORD, Alexander, Va., S7506
Leonard, Va., S6085
Mary, former wid. of Thomas Dunbar S.C., which see
Mordecai, Va., S21971
Richard, Va., S38369
William, Va., S7499
SHACKFORD, John, Mass., Elizabeth, W7179; BLWt.29724-160-55
Samuel, Mass., S29451
SHACKLEE, Peter, Pa., Barbara Ann, W4799
SHACKLEFORD, Dudley, Va., S6084
Henry, Va., Nancy, W10251;

SHACKLEFORD (continued)
BLWt.61096-160-55
John, Va., Dis. No papers
SHACKLER, Philip, N.C., b. Ger., S39068
SHACKLETON, Richard, N.J., S6231
SHACKLETT, Edward, Cont., Va., Elizabeth, W6037
SHACKLEY, Joseph, Mass., Judith/Judeth, W589; BLWt.538-160-55
SHADDAIN, John, See CHAUDOIN
SHADDICK, William, Cont., res. Del., BLWt.502-100
SHADDOCK, Thomas, See SHATTUCK
William, Cont. See SHADDICK
SHADDUCK, Thomas, N.Y., Evelina, W19027
SHADDY, John, N.C., Mary, W9647; BLWt.26115-160-55
SHADE, Jacob, Md., Va., S6082
Julius, Hazen's Regt., BLWt. 13764. Iss. 11/19/1793. No papers
Samuel, Pa., Catharine, R9408; name also spelled Schedt, Sched, Schede
SHADEICK, William, See SHADDICK
SHADICK, William, See SHADDICK
SHADLEY, Daniel, Va., Elenor, W6043; BLWt.26880-160-55
SHADOW, Deadlove/Dedlove, Pa., S40404
SHADUCK, Joseph, See SHATTUCK
SHADWICK, Levi, See CHADWICK
SHAEFFER, Henry, Pa., Va. See SHAFER
John, Pa., S35069
SHAFER, Adam, N.Y., Delia, W24948
Adam, Pa., R9412
Adam, Pa. See SHAFFER
Andrew, Md., S4820
Christian, N.Y., Elizabeth, R9410; BLWt.99505-160-55
Francis, N.Y., S14445
Henrich, N.Y. See SCHAFER
Henry, N.Y., Elizabeth, W19355
Henry, Pa. or Va., R9413
Jacob, N.J., BLWt.8734. Iss. 3/2/1793. No papers
John Conrad, N.Y. See SHAVER
Peter, N.Y., S15645
Peter/Pieter, N.Y. See SCHAFER
Peter, Pa., S6080
Peter, Pa., R9411
Philip, Pa., BLWt.10405. Iss. 3/16/1793 to John McCleland, ass. of Christain Nagle, admr. No papers
Thomas, Pa. See SHAFFER
SHAFF, Frederick, N.Y., S40407; BLWt.9191-160-55
Henry, N.Y., S14437
William, N.Y., S42288
SHAFFER, Adam, Pa., S6075
Adam, Pa., Sarah, R17758
Andrew, Pa., BLWt.10352. Iss. 1/6/1792 to Sarah Sheppard, ass. No papers
Andrew, Pa., S40403
Charles, See SHEPHERD
David, S.C., enl. N.C., S39069

SHAFFER (continued)
Frederick, Cont., Va., Margaret, W2868
Frederick, Va. See SHAVER
George, N.Y., BLWt.7726. Iss. 9/10/1790 to Wm. Henderson, ass. No papers
George, N.Y., Charity/Gitty/Gertrude, W16723
Jacob, N.J., S40405
Jacob, Pa., S22979
John, Pa. See SHAEFFER
John, Pa., Sally, W6038; BLWt. 28503-160-55
John, Va., b. Pa., S3899. See N.A. Acc. No. 874-050161. Not Half Pay John Shaffer
Thomas, Pa., S40427
SHAFFNER, George, Armand's Corps; BLWt.2120-400-Maj. Iss. 3/31/1797 Certified by N. Cutting 1/15/1822 No papers
SHAFT, John, N.Y., S6081
SHAILER, Hezekiah, Ct., Cont., Navy S17675
SHAIN, Casper, Pa., Deborah, W2867
SHALL, George, Md., Pa., S7493
Henry, N.Y., Catharine, W20051
SHALLIESS, Francis, Ct., Anna, W24943
SHAMEL, Hannah, former wid. of John Houser, N.C., which see
SHANDLER, Robert, See CHANDLER
SHANDLEY, Jacob, Pvt. in the Invalids. BLWt.13784. Iss. 9/14/1789 to Joseph Johnston, exec. certified by N. Cutting,3/19/1820
SHANDS, William, Va., S7492
SHANE, Richard, See SHEAN
SHANER, George, Va., S38370
Henry, See SHOENER
Mathias, See SHEANOR
SHANK, Christian, Md., N.J., b. Ger Julia Ann, W19344
John, Cont., Md., Ellen, W24954
John, Sr., Va., S31961
Manus, Pa., S42006
SHANKLAND, Alexander, N.Y., S9479
William, N.Y., Margaret, W19015
SHANKLE, George, N.C., S7498
SHANKS, John, Md., Ann, S37393; BLWt.262-100
John, Va., Mary, W8713; BLWt. 53749-160-55
Manus, Pa., BLWt.10386. Iss. 2/14/1791 to Alexander Power, ass. of Murtoch Sullivan, Admr. No papers
SHANLEY, Patrick, Mass., BLWt.4973 Iss. 5/1/1791 to Peter Farar. No papers
Patrick, Mass., Dis.-no papers. See Am. State Papers, Class 9, p.59.Wounded in the right ankle and left arm near the wrist at Kingsbury, 1781.
SHANNON, Arthur, Pa., S37385
David, Cont., N.J., Maria Gray, former wid., W16590
David, Pa., BLWt.10436. Iss. 9/19/179? to Abraham Bell, ass. No papers

SHANNON (continued)
George, N.Y., Christina, R9421
George, Pa., Va.?, Ann, R9418
George, not Rev. War, Lewis & Clark expedition & Indian Conductor 1807. Old War Inv. File 24807. See papers in War 1812-Flat files
John, N.H., S18203
John, N.Y., Elizabeth, W15942
John, Va., Ann, R9419
Robert, N.Y., BLWt.7731. Iss. 7/13/1790 to Dirck Van Ingen, ass. No papers
Robert, N.Y., Nancy, W26963
Robert, N.C., Catharine, R9420
Robert, Pa., S22502
Robert, Va. See SHERMAN
Samuel, N.H., Lydia, W16722
Thomas, N.H., Dorothy, W588; BLWt.12821-160-55
William, Pa., S4669
SHANON, Thomas, N.H. See SHANNON
SHANTZ, Henry, See SCHANTZ
SHARKS, Pearl, See SPARKS
SHARLEVILLE, Francis, See CHARLEVILLE
SHARLOCK, Ichabod, Mass., R9423
SHARP, Adam, N.C., S7496
Amos, N.J., S18593
Andrew, N.Y., Green Mt. Boys, S22984
Anthony, N.C., Margaret Hulme, former wid., R5366; BLWt.2095-300-Capt. Iss. 6/1/1792. No papers. Her other husb., George Hulme, Va. was a pensioner
Benjamin, Va., BLWt.12588. Iss. 1/5/1792. No papers
Benjamin, Va., S17086
Elizabeth, former wid. of Uriah McLain, Cont., Mass., which see
George, N.Y., R9432
Gibeon/Gibbeon, Mass., S33642
Isaac, Ct., BLWt.6472. Iss. 11/9/1789 to Reynolds James, ass. No papers
Isaac, Ct., Cont., Green Mt. Boys, Amey, W19358
Isham, N.C., Mary/Polly, W11442; BLWt.36550-160-55
John, Armand's Corps, BLWt.2121-300-Capt. Iss. 6/29/1789 to Matthew McConnell. No papers
John, Ga., b. Va., S31962
John, Pa., S38367
John, Va., S30702
John, Va., Frances, W4336
John, Va., Sarah, W26452; BLWt. 31707-160-55
Josiah, Va., S6086
Moses, Va., Elizabeth, W3047; BLWt.19823-160-55
Peter, N.Y., S42274
Reuben, Ct., Cont., S14450
Richard, N.Y., R9426
Samuel, N.C., Susannah, W9290
Samuel, Va., S3888
Solomon, Va., R9433
Spencer, Va., R9427
Thomas, Hazen's Regt., BLWt. 13732. Iss. 11/8/1791; certified

SHARP (continued)
to Samuel Smith, 3/26/1818. No papers
Thomas, N.C., Rhody, W17803
William, Md., N.C., Elizabeth, R9430
William, Va., S37383
William, Va., Elizabeth, W2473; BLWt.12701-160-55
William, Va., also served in 1764. R9429
SHARPE, Caleb, Ct., S11380
Daniel, Ct., Jemima, W26465
Joseph, N.C., b. Md., S7482
Joseph, Pa., BLWt.10447. Iss. 1/25/179? to Sarah Sharpe, Admr. No papers
Linchfield/Lincefield Linn, Va., R17780. Va. Half Pay
Linee, Va. See Linchfield
Lineefield, Va. See Linchfield
Moses, Va., R9425
William, Va., S37384
SHARPLESS, Robert, Md., BLWt. 11729. Iss. 2/1/1790. No papers
SHARTEL, Jacob, Cont., Pa. res., Dis.- no papers. See Am. State Papers, Class 9, p.1101. Wounded by a party of Indians while on actual duty, by a musket ball, which passed through his right ear, which wound caused dizziness and renders him incapable of following his business. Disabled in 1778 at Muncy Creek. Rank, Capt. in Col. Hartley's Regt.
SHARTS, Nicholas, N.Y., S23905
SHARWOOD, Henry, Va., Fernales, R9501
James, N.Y. See SHERWOOD
SHATSWELL, Isaac, See SETCHELL
SHATTUCK, Abial, Mass., Phebe, W19350; BLWt.34913-160-55
Abraham, Mass., S45152; BLWt. 36747-160-55
David, Ct., S36308
Ebenezer Lakin, Mass., S33652
Ezekiel, Mass., Sarah, W19360
Job, Mass., Elizabeth, W15327
Jonas, Mass., S19462
Joseph, Mass., Phebe, W13892
Nathaniel, Mass., Eunice Bennett former wid., W14291
Nathaniel, Mass., Mary, W19347
Samuel, Mass., S42287
Somers, Mass., Privateer, Esther W26467
Stephen, Mass., S45153
Thomas, Mass., N.Y., Ruth, W2257 BLWt.5101-160-55. Reg. No. 33929-55
Thomas, N.Y. See SHADDUCK
Thomas, N.Y. See SHADDOCK
William, Ct., Cont., S17670
SHAUL, John, N.Y., Elizabeth, W11441
SHAVALIER, John, N.Y., BLWt.6923. Iss. 4/9/1791 to Elisha Canys, ass. No papers
SHAVER, Frederick, Va., S32517; BLWt.17855-160-55
Henry, N.Y., b. 1/15/1760, near

SHAVER (continued
Fort Plain, Montgomery Co., N.Y. Father killed by indians early in Rev. Mother fled to Fort Plank, later known as Minden N.Y., to protect her family. Here Henry Shaver served in the Militia. He was in the battle of Johnstown, N.Y. & the morning after the battle he was among 40 white men and several Indians who were selected by Col. Willett to go in pursuit of the Indians & Tories who were under Walter Butler. They killed Butler on West Canada Creek & took 14 prisoners, S11376
Henry, N.Y., b. 2/15/1758, S11393; had son named Peter, name of wife and other children not given
Jacob, N.Y., S28876; BLWt.31709-160-55
Jacob, Pa., Nancy, W9648
John, N.Y., S22978
John, N.Y., Mary, W19353
John, Pa., Temperance, W9291
John, Va., S36753
John Conrad, N.Y., Dorothy Shepperman, former wid., W15902
John Frederick, Pa., Catharine, W22185
Joseph, N.J., BLWt.8737. Iss. 10/17/1789 to John Pope. No papers
Joseph, N.J., Ann, W9649
Michael, Va., R17776; Va. Half Pay
Paul, Va., S7504
Peter, N.Y., Barbara, W19345
Peter, Pa., Catharine, S22503
SHAVERS, Shadrach, Va., S38368
SHAW, Abiather, Mass., Privateer, Joanna, W4800; BLWt.10261-160-55
Abraham, Mass., Mary, W16070
Abraham, Mass., R9435
Abraham, N.H., R9434
Archibald, Pa., b. Ireland, son of John, S7491
Asa, Mass., S17669
Asa, Mass., Hannah, W6022; BLWt. 36761-160-55
Basil, Cont., Md., S16526
Basil, Md., R9436
Bela, Mass., S41159
Benjamin, Ct., S36305
Benjamin, Cont., Mass., S37390
Benjamin, Mass., S7507
Benjamin, Mass., S14451
Benjamin, Mass., Eunice, W15328
Benjamin, N.C., S3885
Benoni, Mass., Hannah, W26455
Beriah, Mass., S19083
Brackley, Mass., S15978
Caty, former wid. of Valentine Thomas Dalton, Va., which see
Charles, Va., S7484
Chipman, Mass., S11388
Comfort, N.Y., Mary, R9442
Cornelius, N.J., BLWt.8703. Iss. 6/24/1797. No papers
Crispus, Mass., S33658
Crispus, Mass., Fanny, W990; BLWt.2093-160-55

SHAW (continued)
Daniel, Mass., Mabel, W2447; BLWt.26630-160-55
Daniel, Mass., Olive, W19028
Daniel, N.C., BLWt.2096-200-Lt. Iss. 5/18/1797 to Gabriel Holmes
Darling, Mass., S14446
David, Cont., Mass., S11382
David, N.H., Abigail, W22195
David, Pa., R9438
Eliab, Mass., S19082
Elias, Ct., BLWt.6505. Iss. 3/25/1790. No papers
Elijah, Cont., Mass., S33649
Elijah, Mass., S22510
Elisha, Mass., S30093
Ephraim, Mass., Rebecca, W6005; BLWt.11255-160-55
Follansbe, N.H., S17090
George, Mass., Sarah, W10250; BLWt.54116-160-55
George, Navy, N.H., Sea Service, Betsey, W11448
Gilbert, S.C., Mary, W3876
Henry, Md., Va., S36756
Ichabod, Ct., N.Y., S40398
Isaiah, Mass., Anna, BLWt.36548-160-55
Jacob, Cont., Mass., Molly, W17802
Jairus, Mass., S15640
James, Cont., res. Mass., S33651
James, Mass., later lived Vt., S23912
James, Mass., S37389
James, Mass., Lucy, W2474
James, Pa., b. Ireland, Anna, W9288
James, Va., S36757
Jesse, Mass., Sarah, W20052
John, Cont., N.H., Betty, W22186
John, Cont., N.Y., Isabella, W16720; BLWt.1989-200-Lt. Iss. 9/15/1790 to James Cadwell, ass. No papers
John, Md., S40401
John, Md., R9440
John, Mass., BLWt.5084. Iss. 12/14/1793 to Samuel Emery. No papers
John, Mass., S37388
John, Mass., Polly, W13890; BLWt. 24911-160-55
John, Mass., Silence Neal, former wid., R7566
John, Mass., Hannah, R9439
John, Mass., Sally, BLWt.36546-160-55
John, N.H., Ruth, W24951
John, N.J., BLWt.8732. Iss. 10/16/1789 to Benj. Harris, ass. No papers
John, N.C., b. Md., Mary, R9443
John, Pa., BLWt.10364. Iss. 9/19/1795. No papers
John R., Pa., BLWt.10419. Iss. 6/29/1789 to M. McConnell, ass. No papers
Jonathan, N.J., BLWt.8744. Iss. 6/11/1789 to Matthias Denman, ass. No papers
Jonathan, N.J., S36754

SHAW (continued)
Joseph, Cont., N.H., Deborah, W22206; BLWt.19815-160-55
Joseph, Mass., S29450
Joseph, Mass., S30096
Joseph, Mass., S42285
Joseph, Pa., S4819
Joshua, Mass., S11379
Josiah, Cont., Mass., Mary, W1323; BLWt.40685-160-55
Josiah, Mass., S30699
Jotham, Mass., Sarah, W26466
Lemuel, Mass., S15638
Levi, N.H., S29449
Lucy, former wid. of John Goddard/Godard, Mass., which see
Luther, Cont., Mass., S22509
Mason, Mass., Mary, W22183
Michael, N.Y., BLWt.7859. Iss. 4/9/1791. No papers
Michael, Pvt. in Art., Pa., BLWt. 10453. Iss. 3/10/1790. No papers
Michael, Pa., S42008
Nathan, Mass., S23904
Nathan, N.J., Julianna, R9441
Nathaniel, Mass., S18204
Nathaniel, Mass., Betsey, S22203
Nathaniel, Mass., Polly, W26469
Nathaniel, R.I., Prudence, W15334
Noah, R.I., S21969
Obed, Mass., Abiah, W15323
Peter, R.I., Lydia, W22191
Phebe, former wid. of John Ketchum/Ketcham, N.Y., which see
Richard, Ct., Cont., S40402
Richard, Ct., Pa., S22986
Robert, N.C., Elizabeth, W6006; BLWt.7435-160-55
Samuel, Cont., Mass., BLWt.2006-160-55
Samuel, Mass., Navy, S33650
Samuel, Mass., N.H., Patience, R9444
Samuel, N.Y., Zerviah/Zuviah, W16719
Samuel, Pa., S31359
Seth, R.I., S21970
Simeon, Mass., R9445
Stephen, Mass., Betsey, W24940
Sylvanus, Mass., S41151
Sylvanus/Silvanus, Mass., Persis, W13893
Sylvanus/Silvanus, R.I., BLWt. 158-300
Thomas, Cont., Mass., Lydia, W2577; BLWt.13869-160-55
Thomas, Cont., N.H., S43136
Thomas, N.C., Pa., S46070
Victor, Md., S6078
William, Cont., Enl. Ct. or Mass. N.Y. agcy. S42284
William, Cont., N.Y., Ede, W16405
William, Mass., S37382
William, Mass., Olive, W6007
William, N.C., Sarah, W127
William, S.C., S19078
William, S.C., R9446
William, Va., S3881
Zachariah, N.C., S3886
SHAWKE, Jacob, Pa., S4827
SHAWN, Frederick, Md., S7509
SHAY, James, N.J., S42270

SHAY (continued)
Peter, N.J., Catharine, W26470
Timothy, Ct., Hannah, R9447
SHAYES, Daniel, See SHAYS
SHAYLOR, Joseph, Ct., BLWt.1960-200-Lt. Iss. 9/16/1791. No papers
SHAYS, Daniel, Cont., Mass., Rhoda W1945
David, Mass., S41160
SHEA, David, Mass., BLWt.4977. Iss. 10/26/1789 to Joshua Green, Jr. No papers
Dennis, Va., BLWt.12566. Iss. 1/31/1794 to John Stockdell, ass. No papers
John, Va., BLWt.12538. Iss. 4/2/1796. No papers
Michael, Mass., Eleanor, R9448
Patrick?; See N.A. Acc. No.874-050162. Not Half Pay
SHEAD, Amos, Mass. See SHED
Lemuel, Mass. See SHED
SHEAF, George/Hans George, N.Y., Christina/Stena, W19029
SHEAFER, Adam, Pa. See SHAFER
SHEAFFER, John, Pa. See SHAEFFER
Peter, Pa. See SHAFER
Philip, Pa., R9415
SHEAIS, Peter, See SHEARS
SHEALOCK, John W., N.J., BLWt. 8704. Iss. 1/18/1790. No papers
SHEAMAN, John W., Privateer, R.I., S11377
SHEAN, Richard, Cont., Mass., Susannah, W22199
SHEANOR, Mathias, Va., S40422
SHEAR, George, Pa., BLWt.10357. Iss. 2/14/1791 to Alexander Power, ass. No papers
Matthias/Mathias, N.Y., Hannah, W19017
SHEARER, David, Mass., R9449
David, N.H. See SHERER
Jacob, Pa., S22508
James, N.H. See SHERER
James, N.Y., S42286
Robert, N.Y., Mary, W19014
William, Mass., Elinor, R9450
William, N.Y., S43132
SHEARIN, Frederick, N.C., S7495
Lewis, N.C., Susan, W6036
SHEARMAN, Abiel, N.Y. See SHERMAN
Abner, Mass. See SHERMAN
Anthony, N.Y. See SHERMAN
Christopher, R.I. See SHERMAN
Daniel, R.I., S21482
Eber, R.I., S21480
Edward, Mass., Sarah, W24945
George, Va., S9478
George, Va., Mary Magdalen, W6050
Gideon, Cont., Mass., N.Y. res. of heirs in 1844; BLWt.2319-100
Henry, Cont., R.I., S43127; BLWt. 1971-200-Lt. Iss. 12/31/1789. No papers
Job, R.I., S39839
John, Cont., R.I. See SHERMAN
John, Mass., S33644
John, N.J., S33648
John, R.I., Vt., S19086

SHEARMAN (continued)
Lodowick, R.I., S21972
Paul, Cont., N.Y. agcy. & res. S42290
Peleg, Mass., Mary, W22208
Peter, Navy, Mass., S39838
Peter, N.Y., BLWt.7807. Iss. 8/3/1790. No papers
Peter, N.Y., Martha, W27858
Remington, R.I., S21477
Reuben, R.I., Vt., Ruth E. Howard, former wid., W11310; BLWt.100785-160-55
Samuel, Cont., Privateer, R.I., S19463
Solomon, R.I., Susannah, W6051
Stephen, R.I., Rebecca, W19356
Thomas, N.J., R9453
William, R.I. See SHERMAN
William, b. R.I., Vt., S15979
SHEARMON, Job, N.Y., S28874
SHEARS, Peter, Cont., Md., Barbary, W9286
SHEAS, Peter, See SHEARS
SHECKLER, Frederick, See SCHAECKHLER
SHED, Amos, Mass., Tryphena, W15322
Amos, Mass., Lucy Crosby, former wid., R2511
Daniel, Mass., Navy, Sally/Salley, W1944; BLWt.9483-160-55
Daniel, N.H., S36755
David, Mass., Sarah, W22197
Ebenezer, Cont., Mass., Lucy, W22202
Joel, Mass., Dolly, W13891
John, Cont., Mass., Sarah, W16718
John, Mass., S22976
John, Mass., Betsey, W22201
Jonathan, Mass., S15976
Joseph, Mass., Susannah, W26459
Lemuel, Mass., Ruth, W26461; BLWt.561-100
SHEEHANE, Thomas, N.Y., BLWt.7844. Iss. 1/13/1792 to Ezra Blodget, ass. No papers
SHEELDS, James, N.Y. See SHIELDS
SHEELE, John, N.H. See SKEELE
SHEELY, Conrad, N.Y., Elizabeth, R9456
SHEESE, Peter, See SHEARS
SHEETS, Caspar, Cont., Pa. res. in 1795, BLWt.10440-100. Iss. 1790
George, Va., b. Pa., 7479
Jacob, Md., Hannah, W9287
John, Pa., S7483
John, Va. See SHEETZ
Mathias/Matthias, Va., S40423
Philip, Pa. See SHEETZ
SHEETZ, John, Va., R9460
Philip, Pa., S7500
SHEFER, Adam, Pa. See SHAFER
SHEFFER, Teunis, N.Y., S15296
SHEFFIELD, Charles, Mass., S43131; BLWt.19-100
Daniel D., Mass., BLWt.5052. Iss. 3/25/1790. No papers
Dennin, Mass., BLWt.952-100
Ephraim, See SHUFFIELD
George, N.C., Mary, W3611
Joseph, Ct., S42272

SHEFFIELD (continued)
Nathan, N.Y., S14452
Paul, R.I., Hannah, R9463
Robert, N.Y., S36303
Samuel, Navy, res. R.I., S39842
Stanton, R.I., S21479
William, N.C., Elizabeth, W26453; BLWt.36648-160-55
SHEFTALL, Sheftall, Ga., S31959
SHEHAN, Daniel, Pa., BLWt.10330; iss. 1/18/1791. No papers
Daniel, Pa., BLWt.10340. Iss. 12/22/1794 to Henry Purdy, ass. No papers
SHEHEE, John, Armand's Corps, BLWt.13703. Iss. 12/2/1793. No papers
John, Cont., Ga. agcy. & res., S36302
SHEHENA, David, Mass., BLWt.5013. Iss. 9/1/1790 to Theodosius Fowler. No papers
SHEIBELER, Friederich, Va., S23910
SHEID, John, Va., R9464; BLWt. 53501-160-55
SHIELDS, David, Mass., BLWt.5022. Iss. 12/18/1789 to David Shields No papers
SHEITLEFF, William, Mass., S36304
SHELBY, Evan, N.C., Susanna, R9471
James, Va., R17781; Va. Half Pay
SHELCUT, Ezekiel, Pa., BLWt.1261-100
SHELDEN, Ephraim, Mass. See SHELDON
George, N.Y., S17084
Isaac, R.I., S14447
Israel, Mass., Mary, W26460
John, Mass., S19765
Joseph, Cont., N.Y., S42291
William, Mass., S37391
SHELDON, Amos, Mass., S33654
Asa, R.I., Anna, W22204
Caleb, Ct., S19087
Cephas, Mass., S41158
Daniel, R.I., S39841
Ebenezer, Ct., Love, R9466
Elihu, Mass., S43129
Elisha, commanding the 2nd Regt. of Light Dragoons, BLWt.1936-500-Col. Iss. 12/12/17?? to Theodosius Fowler, ass. No papers
Elisha, Mass., S42293
Ephraim, Ct., S14442
Ephraim, Mass., S15642
Ezekiel, R.I., S14434
James, Ct., Abigail, W22184
Jeremiah, Mass., Elizabeth, W26462
Job, R.I., BLWt.3507. Iss. 5/28/1792. No papers
Job, R.I., S42278
John, R.I., S30098
Jonathan, Mass., S19079
Jonathan, R.I., S39840
Joseph, N.Y., BLWt.7810. Iss. 9/4/1790 to John Suffren, ass. No papers
Joseph, N.Y. res. Dis. No papers See Am. State Papers, Class 9, p.95. Wounded in the legs at the battle of Connecticut Farms, N.J.

SHELDON (continued)
Enl. 5/30/1777
Josiah, Mass., Chloe, W6045; BLWt.40683-160-55
Moses, Cont.,Ct.,Vt. res., S15639
Nathaniel, Green Mt. Boys, Vt., S14449
Remembrance, Ct., Phoebe, W24955
Reuben, Mass., S29454
Roger, Ct., Elizabeth, W22189
Roger, Mass., S21968
Samuel, Ct., BLWt.36654-160-55
Samuel, Cont., Mass., S33665
Thomas, Va., BLWt.12553 iss. 12/13/1791 to Francis Graves, ass. No papers
Whiting, Cont., enl. Mass., S42279
William, Mass., S33641
SHELEY, Jacob, N.Y., R9457
Martin, N.Y., R9458
SHELHAMMER, Philip Jacob, Pa., S23907
SHELL, Christian, N.Y. See SCHELL
Elisha, Lamb's Art., N.Y., BLWt. 7833 iss. 9/28/1790 to Bartholomew Fisher, ass. No papers
Elizabeth, former wid. of Abraham Van Deusen, N.Y., which see
George, N.Y., BLWt.7825 iss. 8/28/1790 to C. Yates, exrs., ass. No papers
John, N.C., Catharine Miller, former wid., R7179
Lewis, Armand's Corps. BLWt.13307 & 13717. Iss. 7/20/1792 to Abraham Sheridan, ass. of John Gish, Admr. No papers
Marks, N.Y., S14440
SHELLEHAMER, George, Pa., Mary, R9468
SHELLENX, Abraham, See SCHELLENX
SHELLER, Ludwick, Cont., Pa. res., Rosanna, B.L.Rej.
SHELLEY, Abraham, Cont., Ct., Hannah, W26463
Ebenezer, Ct., S11391
Lewis, Cont., Pa., Rosanna, W4513
Samuel, Ct., S42771; BLWt.1339-100
Samuel, N.J., R9470
SHELLMAN, Ernest Armand's Legion, BLWt.13708 iss. 8/25/1789. No papers
John, Md., S31960
SHELLY, Abraham, Hazen's Regt., BLWt.13725 iss 5/15/1800 to Ithamar Canfield. No papers
Cyrus, N.Y., BLWt.7811 iss. 11/9/1791. No papers
Cyrus, N.Y., S36312
Ebenezer, Ct., BLWt.6479 iss. 9/20/1789. No papers
Medad, Ct., R9469
Rhoda, former wid. of Israel Harrington, which see
Samuel, Ct., S36306; BLWt.1287
Samuel, N.Y., Rebecca, W24942
William, N.Y., Molly, W16721
William, S.C., R9472
SHELOR, Daniel, Md., S6079

SHELP, William, Ct., S17672
SHELTON, Caesar/Cezer (colored) Ct., S19764
Clough, Va., BLWt.740-300
George, N.C., b. Va., S4670; BLWt.26407-160-55
James, Va., S10257
John, Del., S36300
Joseph, Va., S7481
Lemuel, Va., R9474
Matthias. No file found for a sold. with name of Mat(t)hias Chilton/Shelton, or any variation thereof.
Medley, Va., Elizabeth, W8717
Samuel, Va., Jane, W8716
Stephen, Ga., Va., Sinah, W6044
William, Va., Ann, W4335
Wilson, Va., b. Md., S31955
SHELTY, Christopher, See SHULTZ
SHENALL, Benjamin, Va. See SHENAULT
SHENAULT, Benjamin, Va., Nancy Phillips/Philips, former wid., W6867; BLWt.36617-160-55
SHENEFELT, Nicholas, Pa., Anna, W4798
SHEPARD, Abigail, former wid. of Experience Trescott, Cont., Vt. which see
Amos, Ct., S33647
Amos, Ct., Laminta, W22193
Asa, Ct., S14435
Daniel, Ct., S17671
Daniel, N.H., Cont., S43137
David, Mass., Lucinda, W6034
Dorinda, former wid. of Jesse Penfield, Ct., which see
Edward Sears, Ct., R9481
Elijah, Mass., S31954
Elizabeth/Betsey, former wid. of Jesse Hubbell, N.Y., which see
George, Mass., Sea Service, Eunice, W19030
George, N.H., S41155
George, Va. See SHEPHERD
Henry, Ct., S14448
Israel, N.Y., Hannah, R9483
James, Cont., Ct., S33646
James, N.Y., Persis, W24937; BLWt.12833-160-55
Joel, Mass., N.Y., S30695; BLWt.9475-160-55
John, Cont., Ct., Sarah, W11452; BLWts.74-60-55; 13743-100. Iss. to Benj. Tallmadge 10/7/1789. No papers
John, Cont., N.Y., S42292
John, Mass., Sally, W15333
John, Mass., See SHEPERD
John, Mass., Lucy Haven, former wid., W23201. Her 2nd husb.,Wm. Haven, also served in Rev. War
Joseph, Cont., Ct., S33659
Levi, Mass., Elizabeth, W6033; BLWt.13707-160-55
Phineas, Ct., Cont., S3895
Robert, Cont., Pa., S40425
Rufus, N.Y., S14430
Samuel, Ct., S17674
Samuel, Ct., Sabra, W19351
Samuel, N.H., S11372
Samuel, Va. See SHEPHERD

SHEPARD (continued)
Silas, Mass., S42295
Simeon, Mass., Betsey, W2671; BLWt.31588-160-55
Stephen, Ct., S30700
Stephen, Cont., Mass., Prudence, W19357; BLWt.1018-100
Stephen, Mass. res. of wid. in 1836, Margaret, W9487
Thomas, Va., S3901
Thomas Challis, N.H., Lydia, W16725
William, Ct., S22505
William, Mass., BLWt.1918-150-Ens. Iss. 12/6/1791 to Stephen Thorn, ass. No papers
William, N.J., Eleanor/Ellen, W6035
SHEPARDSON, Nathan, Mass., Sarah, W15326
Zephaniah, N.H., S23415
SHEPEARD, Thomas, Ct. See SHEPHERD
SHEPERD, John, Cont.,Ct. See SHEPARD
John, Mass., Elizabeth, W17809
Levi, Mass., Elizabeth, See SHEPARD
SHEPERDSON, Nathan, Mass. See SHEPARDSON
SHEPHARD, Amos, Ct., BLWt.6451. Iss. 6/3/1791 to Isaac Bronson, ass. No papers
Elisha, N.H., S41153
George, N.H., BLWt.3490. Iss. 5/15/1796 to S. Atkinson, ass. No papers
James, Md., BLWt.11693. Iss. 2/1/1790. No papers
Moses, N.J., Rebecca, W6029
Stephen, Ct. See SHEPARD
Whitmore, Ct., S17087
SHEPHERD, Abigail, former wid. of Experience Trescott, Cont., Vt. Which see
Abraham, Cont., Va., Eleanor, W19343; BLWt.1914-300-Capt. Iss. 8/25/1789. Also recorded under Wt.2529. No papers
Amos, Ct. See SHEPARD
Benjamin, N.J., S4826
Charles, Cont., Pa., S43128
Charles, Va., S32516
David, See SHIPHERD
Elisha, Cont., N.J., S17668
Furman, N.J., Hannah, W6031
George, N.J., Catharine, R9480; BLWt.91085-160-55
George, Va., Mary Ann, W8723
Israel, N.Y. See SHEPARD
Jacob, N.J., S3893
Jacob, Pa., Va., Mary, W2008; BLWt.31702-160-55
James, Ct., Dis. No papers. See Am. State Papers Class 9, p.90 Gen. Putnam's Regt. Disabled by a musket ball at the action at Bunker's Hill whereby he lost the use of his left hand, 6/17/1775
James, Cont., Ct. See SHEPARD
James, Mass., Mary, W24939
James, N.Y. See SHEPARD

SHEPHERD (continued)
James, Va. See SHEPPARD
James, Va., R9484
John, Hazen's Regt. BLWt.13743. Iss. 10/7/1789 to Benj. Tallmadge, ass. No papers. Also BLWt.74-60-55
John, Mass., S42296
John, Pa., R9485
John, Va., Eleanor, R9482
Jonathan 3rd., N.H., R9486
Joseph, N.J., Sarah, W7178; BLWt.38563-160-55
Lewis (negro), Mass., Elizabeth, W24944
Morrill, N.H., Olive, W11437; BLWt.31701-160-55
Nathaniel, N.J., BLWt.8718. Iss. 1790
Peter, Va., Mary Ann Wade, W6030
Phineas, Ct., Cont. See SHEPARD
Rachel, former wid. of Michael Parker, N.Y., which see
Samuel, N.C., S21476
Samuel, Va., S3894
Simeon, Mass. See SHEPARD
Stephen, Mass. See SHEPARD
Thomas, Ct., S36311
William, Cont., N.J. or N.Y., S32513; BLWt.566-100. Iss. 11/30/1811
William, Mass., Lucy, W25148
William, N.J. See SHEPARD
SHEPHERDSON, David, Va., S6076
Nathan, Mass. See SHEPARDSON
SHEPLER, George, Va., S7497
SHEPLEY, Adam, Md., Va., S6077
SHEPPARD, Andrew, N.C., R9490
Furman, N.J. See SHEPHERD
James, Cont., Ct. See SHEPARD
James, Va., Priscilla Hay, former wid., W7631
Jonathan, Ct., S41154; BLWt.6464-100. Iss. 5/26/1798 to Isaac Harris, ass. No papers
Jonathan, Md., S38365
Jonathan, N.Y., Sarah, R9489
Joseph, N.Y., S11386
Joseph, Va., S47833
Levi, Mass., See SHEPARD
Nathaniel, N.J., BLWt.8718. Iss. 3/10/1790. No papers
Nathaniel, N.J., See SHEPHERD
Robert, Moylan's Dragoons, Pa., BLWt.10434. Iss. 6/29/1789 to M. McConnell, ass. No papers
Thomas, Crane's Art., Mass., BLWt.5105. Iss. 1/28/1790 to Joseph May. No papers
Valentine/Vallintine, N.C., Zilpha, W6032
William, Cont.,N.Y. See SHEPHERD
William, Ga., R9478
William, N.C., R9479
SHEPPERD, James, Sheldon's Dragoons, Ct., BLWt.6521. Iss. 2/27/1790 to Theodosius Fowler, ass. No papers
Jesse, Ct., S36307
William, Mass., BLWt.1888-500-Col. Iss. 4/1/1790. No papers
SHEPPERMAN, Dorothy, former wid.

SHEPPERMAN (continued)
of John Conrad Shaver/Shafer, N.Y., which see
SHERBORN, Job, N.H., S37387
SHERBURNE, Andrew, Navy, N.H., S42275
Benjamin, Cont., R.I., also in War of 1812, S42276; BLWt.1970-200-Lt. Iss. 11/14/1792. No papers
Henry, R.I., BLWt.1968-500-Col. Iss. 12/31/1789. No papers
John Samuel, N.H., S19767
Pomp (colored), N.H., Flora Bell former wid., W17297
Thomas, Navy, N.H., S43134
SHERER, David, N.H., Hannah, W3464
James, N.H., Betsey, W19348
James, S.C., Theodocia, W4512
SHERFIELD, Ephraim, See SHUFFIELD
SHERIDAN, Abner, N.C., S32519
James, Pa., BLWts.10337 & 13780 Iss. 3/15/1800 to James Sheridan Certified 4/25/1806
James, Pa., Mary, W4511
Martin, Pa., BLWt.10471. Iss. 4/30/1793. No papers
SHERLAY, John, N.H., R20130
SHERLEY, Thomas, S.C., S17083
SHERLOCK, Edward, Pa., S41152; BLWt.10473. Iss. 7/21/179? to David Clarke, ass. No papers
SHERMAN, Abiel, Cont., N.Y., b. 3/11/1761, d. 3/31/1837, S49291
Abiel, N.Y., Mary, b. 3/7/1744; d.7/31/1834, Mary, W19354
Abner, Crane's Art., Mass., BLWt. 5094. Iss. 6/4/1789. No papers
Abner, Cont., Mass., Mary, W2672
Amos P., Mass., S42277
Anthony, N.Y., S31957
Asa, Mass., Polly, W19359
Benjamin, Ct., Lydia, W17806
Benjamin, Mass., S30100
Beriah, Mass., S19080
Caleb, Mass., S30696
Christopher, Mass., S22988
Christopher, Va., S33643
Daniel, R.I., See SHEARMAN
Darius, Cont., N.Y., Anna/Ama, W19020
David, R.I., Hanah, W22192
Edmond, Lamb's Art., N.Y., BLWt. 7851. Iss. 11/4/1791. No papers
Edmund/Edmond, N.Y., S23908
Elijah, Ct., Betty, R9494
Enoch, Ct., Catharine, W15321
Ephraim, Mass., S30694
George, Mass., Vt., Chloe, R9493
George, Va. See SHEARMAN
Gideon, Cont. See SHEARMAN
Gideon, Cornell, R.I., Ruth, W19022; BLWt.27593-160-55
Henry, Cont., R.I. See SHEARMAN
Isaac, Ct., Cont., Mass., S33662; BLWt.1938-500-Col. Iss. 8/7/1789 to Richard Platt, ass. No papers
Isaac, Mass., S29446
Jabez, N.Y., S14438
James, Mass., Peggy, W22200
James, R.I. See SHERMON
Jeremiah, Mass., Eunice, W15325

SHERMAN (continued)
Jesse, Mass., N.Y., R9452
Job, N.Y., See SHEARMAN
John, Ct., Nancy, W8721. BLWt. 1962-200-Lt. Iss. 3/7/1792 to Jonas Prentice, ass. No papers
John, Cont., R.I., Dorcas, W26456
John, Mass., S29453
John, Mass. See SHEARMAN
John, Mass., Chloe, W19346; BLWt. 14515-160-55
John, N.Y., S7503
John W., Privateer, R.I. See SHEAMAN
Joseph, Mass., S23914
Joseph, Mass., S31956
Joseph, Mass., S33655
Mercy, former wid. of Enoch Morgan Mass., which see
Nathan, Mass., S29447
Nathaniel, Ct., S14456
Paul, Cont. See SHEARMAN
Paul, Crane's Cont. Art., Mass. BLWt.5095. Iss 6/2/1789. No papers
Peleg, Mass. See SHEARMAN
Peleg, R.I., S14433
Peter, N.Y. See SHEARMAN
Reuben, R.I., Vt. See SHEARMAN
Reuel, Mass., S19081
Robert, Va., S38366
Rufus, Mass., S30095
Rufus, R.I., S21478
Samuel, Cont.,Privateer, R.I., See SHEARMAN
Samuel, Mass., S33657
Samuel, Mass., Abigail Farrar, former wid., W14711
Stephen, R.I. See SHEARMAN
Thomas, Cont., Mass., Zerniah, W24936
Thomas, Mass., R9496
Thomas, Pa., R20432
Timothy, Cont., Mass., S40400
Timothy, Mass., S33656
William, R.I., S22983
William, R.I., S49212, Rebecca Sherman, wid. of sold., was pensioned as former wid. of John Cunningham, N.J., which see
William, R.I., Margaret, W24950
William B., R.I.,Vt., See SHEARMAN
SHERMON, James, R.I., R9451
SHEROD, Jordan, N.C. See SHERROD
SHERRELL, George, N.C., S3902
SHERRIDAN, Thomas, Crane's Cont., Art., Mass., BLWt.5092 iss. 3/12/1792 to Benjamin Haskell, no papers
SHERRIL, Abraham, N.Y., S9480
Jeremiah, N.Y., S11383
SHERRILL, James, Va., S31362; BLWt.5214-160-55
Lewis, N.C., R9499
Ute, N.C., Elizabeth, R17811
SHERRINER, Lodwick, N.Y., BLWt. 7797. Iss. 7/30/1790 to Edward Cumpston, ass. No papers
SHERROD, Jordan, N.C., S7489
Robert, N.C., S31361
SHERRON, John, N.C., S7501
SHERRY, William, N.C., S11390
SHERTLEFF, William, See SHETTLEFF
SHERWILL, Thomas, Mass., Judith, W16404
SHERWIN, Ahimaaz/Ahimas, Ct., Cont. & Mass. R40424
Daniel, Mass., Abigail, W4510
Elnathan, Mass., S40416
John, Mass., Eunice, W26471
SHERWOOD, Abel, Ct., Mary, W26458
Adiel, N.Y., S42281
Andrew, Cont., N.Y., Judah, W19021 BLWt.249-60-55 & 7853-100-1790
Asa, Ct., BLWt.6461. Iss. 7/27/1789 to Samuel Gibbs, ass. No papers
Asa, Ct., Molly, W26468
Daniel, Ct., Polly, W17812
Eliphalet, Ct., Abigail, W22187; S21485
Isaac, N.Y., BLWt.1905-200-Lt. Iss. 11/9/1791 to Jasper Cropsey, Admr. No papers. Also recorded under BLWt.2563
James, N.Y., BLWt.7752. Iss. 9/13/1791. No papers
James, N.Y. See SHEARER
James, N.Y., Sarah, W24935
Jane, former wid. of David Burr, Ct., which see
Jedediah, Ct., S41156
John, Cont., Mass., Green Mt. Boys, N.Y., S42282
Jonathan, Ct., R9503
Lemuel, Ct., BLWt.1739-100
Moses, Cont., N.Y., Applonea, W19352
Nathan, N.Y., BLWt.7753. Iss. 11/27/1791(?) to Hopkins & Crosby, ass. No papers
Nathan, N.Y., Lucy, W17804
Nehemiah, Ct., S11374
Nehemiah, Ct., S36309
Nehemiah, Ct., S40426
Nehemiah, N.Y., BLWt.7732. Iss. 8/31/1791 to John Watkins, ass. No papers
Nehemiah, N.Y., Mary, W26457
Reuben, Ct., S14455
Seth, Ct., S14431
Seth N., N.Y., Ann, W15801
Seymore/Seymour, Ct., Navy, S42289
Stratton/Stratten, N.J., Barbarey Ann/Barbary Ann, W2445; BLWt.26203-160-55
Thomas, Ct., Cont., N.Y., S15637
William, N.Y., R9504
William, Va., R9506
Zachariah, Ct., Cont., S36313; BLWt.467-100
SHESHING, John, N.H., BLWt.3492 Iss. 3/10/1797 to Chris S. Thom, ass. No papers
SETHAR, John, Cont.,Ct., S11385
SHETTEL, Daniel, Pa., S40561
SHEVER, Frederick, See SHAVER
SHEVERDECKER, Michael, Va., Anna, W6039
SHEW, Henry, N.Y., S29448
Jacob, N.Y., S22985
Stephen, N.Y., Susannah, W1090; BLWt.13417-160-55
SHEWMAKER, Leonard, Va., S17082
SHIBE, William, See SCHEIB
SHIBLEY, John, N.J., S1102
SHICK, Frederick, Ga., BLWt.2109-200-Lt. No date of issue. No papers
SHIELDS, Berry, Va. See Littleberry
Daniel, N.Y., Elizabeth, W2359; BLWt.18-160-55 & 7827-100-1791
David, N.J., S33664
David, Pa., S22989
David, Va., S3891
David L., Mass., S33663
James, Ct., BLWt.6421. Iss. 1/6/1797. No papers
James, Cont., Pa., S40421; BLWt. 2211-100
James, Cont., Va., Rachel, W6027
James, N.Y., Mary, W6026
John, Pa., Elizabeth, W2180; BLWt. 28513-160-55
John, Pa., R9507
John, Pa. Sea Service, S1874
Littleberry/Berry, Va., Susannah, W6024; BLWt.13445-160-55
Thomas, Va., Lydia/Lidia, W6028
Tobias, Pa., S40419
William, N.J., R20433
William, N.C., S.C., Mary H., W6025
SHIERMAN, John, N.J., BLWt.8731; Iss. 9/18/1779 to Abraham Bell, ass. No papers
SHIFF, George, See SHEAF
SHIFFLET, Thomas, Va., Elizabeth, W8718
SHIFLET, Blan, Va., S15641
SHIFLEY, Jacob, Pa., Catharine, W2869
SHILLCUTT, Ezekiel, Pa. See SHELCUT
SHILLING, George, wid. Biddy was former wid. of Patrick Blackstone Pa., which see
SHILLINGSFORD, Thomas, Pa., Rosanna R9509
SHILTY, Christopher, See SHULTZ
SHILTZ, Christopher, See SHULTZ
SHIMEALL, Valentine, See SCHIMMEL
SHIMEL, Richard, N.Y., Maria, W11434; BLWt.39221-160-55
SHIMER, Isaac, Pa., Elizabeth, W3119
James, Pa. See CHAMBERS
SHIMMEL, Richard, N.Y. See SHIMEL
SHIMP, John, Pa., R9511
SHINDEL, Peter, Pa., S23911
SHINDLEBLOWER, George. Hazen's Regt., BLWt.13748
George, Hazen's Regt., S41160 1/2 See BLWt.13748-100. Iss. 3/8/1792 to George Shindleblower. No papers
SHINDLER, John, Cont., Mass., BLWt.1000-100
SHINER, Edward, Mass., BLWt.4984 iss. 4/1/1790
John, See SHRINER
SHINGLETON, William, Va., S38871
SHINKLE, Phillip, Pa., Catharine, R9518
SHINN, Isaac, Va., S7505

SHIPE, Philip, Pa., Anna Catharine, W4334
SHIPHERD, David, Cont., Mass., S23417
SHIPLEY, Adam, See SHEPLEY
Henry, Cont., Md., Ruth, W6046; BLWt.38579-160-55
Samuel, Md., S37392
SHIPMAN, Abraham, Vt., S15977
Benoni, Ct., S36310; BLWt.1955-300-Capt. Lt. Iss. 1/28/1790. No papers
David, N.J., S23416
David, Va., S32518
George, Ct., Mary, W24946
James, Ct., S33645
James, N.C., Lucy, W17810
John, Ct., Mercy/Marcy, W17808
John, N.J., S3906
Samuel, Ct., Sarah, W2670; BLWt. 9523-160-55
Samuel, N.J., S912
Silas, Ct., Sarah, W17807
Stephen, Va., Deborah, R9513
Timothy, N.Y. res. of heir in 1856, Rachel, R9514
SHIPP, Richard, N.C., b. Va., R9515
Thomas, N.C. b. Va., S7487
SHIPPEE, Caleb, R.I., S21483
Christopher, R.I., S30698
Jesse, Mass., Catharine F., W6048; BLWt.17559-160-55
Job, R.I., Margaret, W22196
John, R.I., Sarah, W22207
Nathan, Mass., Mary, W19023
SHIPPERLY, Barent, N.Y., R9283
SHIPPEY, Nancy, former wid. of John Forbes, N.Y., which see
Silas, R.I., Philadelphia, W6047
Solomon, R.I., S21484
Thomas, R.I., Hannah, W19025
William, Ct., N.Y., Pa., S1103
SHIRES, Nicholas, Va., BLWt.12536 & 13939. Iss. 8/4/1789. No papers
Richard, N.J., BLWt.8735. Iss. 9/3/1789 to Wm. I. Vredenburgh, ass. No papers
SHIRK, Jacob, Cont., Pa., S40408
SHIRKEE, Anthony, See CARTER
SHIRKEY, Nicholas, Va., Sarah, W6049
Thomas, N.Y., S42294
SHIRLEY, Alexander, N.H., Mary, W24952
Bennet, Md., Susannah, W3878; BLWt.11706-100. Iss. 1791. Re-iss. 5/27/1839 under Special Act
Daniel, N.H., S40412
James, Mass., N.H., Susan Greenough, former wid., W23156
Job, Mass., S23418
John, Cont., Mass., Sea Service, S11373
John, Va., Frances, W8719
Samuel, Cont., N.H., S43135
Thomas, Pa., S22507
SHIRLOCK, John, N.Y., BLWt.7795. Iss. 7/30/1790 to Edward Cumpston, ass. No papers
SHIRRARD, James, N.J., BLWt.8756. Iss. 6/11/1789 to Thomas Coyle,
SHIRRARD (continued) ass. No papers
SHIRTIFF, John, See SHIRTLIFF
SHIRTLEFF, William, Mass., See SHETTLEFF
SHIRTLIFF, Amasa, Mass., BLWt. 4966. Iss. 7/28/1790. No papers
John, Ct., S21966
Noah, Ct., N.Y., S7478
William, Mass., BLWt.4997. Iss. 3/1/1796. No papers
SHIRTS, David, See CHURCH
Hendrick, N.Y., R9520
Mathias, N.J., BLWt.8764. Iss. 3/1/1796. No papers
Mathias, N.J., N.Y., Susannah, W11453
Peter, N.J., S834
Peter, N.Y., BLWt.7798. Iss. 5/4/1791 to Peter Shirts. No papers
Peter, N.Y., Elizabeth, W19018
SHIRTZER, Caspar, Pa., Elizabeth, W9292
SHITE, Peter, N.Y., S11375
SHITZ, John, Pa., S22504
SHIVE, Lewis, Pa., S22981
SHIVELEY, Jacob, See SHIFLEY
John, Va., R9521
SHIVERICK, Joseph, Mass., S33653
SHIVERS, Jesse, N.C., S42010
Peter, See STIVER
SHLIFE, John, Cont., Md., S40417
SHNEIDER, Frederick, See SNYDER
Henrich, Cont. See Henry SNYDER
SHOALS, Richard, Mass., Sarah, W22194
SHOBE, John William, Pa., S38372
SHOBER, John, Md., Navy, Susannah, W6041
SHOCKEY, Christain, Pa., Mary, W2968; BLWt.10334-100. Iss. 2/17/1800. No papers
SHOCKLEY, John, Md., S35066
Thomas, Va., S3905
SHOCKNEY, Patrick, Pa., S35068
SHOECRAFT, Jacob, N.Y., S14439
John, N.Y., Elizabeth, W16403
SHOEFELT, Christopher, N.Y., Christina, W19024
SHOEMAKER, Abraham, Pa., Margaret, W11456
Abraham, Pa., R9523
Christopher, N.Y., Elizabeth, W19031
Daniel, Pa., S28875
Elizabeth/Eliza, former wid. of David Wilson, Va., which see
Jacob, Pa., Magdalena, W6053
John, N.J., S32515
John, N.Y., Anne Elizabeth, S29452 BLWt.43530-160-55
John, Pa., S22977
Joseph, Pa., War 1812, R9527
Peter, N.Y., Maria, W24947
Peter, Von Heer's Dragoons, BLWt. 18715. Iss. 12/31/1790. No papers
Randal, N.C., S42007
Samuel, Pa., S17089
Thomas T., N.Y., Elizabeth/Betsey
SHOEMAKER (continued) R9525
William, N.J., S7508
Zedekiah, Va., S7480
SHOEMAN, Adam. Pa., BLWt.10426. Iss. 9/22/1791. No papers
Adam, Pa., S40409
Charles, Armand's Corps, BLWt. 13706. Iss. 6/20/1789. No papers
SHOENER, Henry, Pa., Mary Magdalene W6052; BLWt.16105-160-55
SHOES, Frederick, Va., BLWt.12577. Iss. 7/14/1792 to Robert Means, ass. No papers
SHOFNER, Henry, N.C., S14568
SHOLES, Carey Wheeler, Ct., S36314
Cyrus, N.Y. res. about 1822, Polly, R9528
Jabez, See Jabish
Jabish/Jabez, Ct., S11378
John, Navy, Mass, See John SHULTZ
Miner, Ct., S14457
Richard, See SHOALS
SHOME, John, Pa. See SHOMO
SHOMO, John, Pa., S23913
SHONTY, Henry, Pa., R20434
SHOOK, Andrew, N.C., S7485
Jacob, N.Y., S22987
Jacob, N.C., S7486
John, Pa. res., R9529
SHOOTS, John, See SHEETZ
SHOPE, John, Pa., Sarah, R9530
Nicholas, Pa., R9531
William, Va., BLWt.12545. Iss. 4/30/180? No papers
William, Va., Elizabeth, W6054
SHOPP, Peter, Ct., BLWt.1210-100
SHOPPE, Anthony, Mass., Phebe, W24956
SHOPPO, Anthony, See SHOPPE
SHOPTAW, John, Not Rev. War, Pa., Indian Wars 1788-1791, O.W. Inv. Rej. 21684
SHOR, Gabriel, See TZOR
SHORES, Christian, S.C., S32514
Thomas, Va., S6083
Thomas, Va., Elizabeth, W6021
William, Navy, N.H., S43133
SHOREY, John, Cont., Mass., S43126
Samuel, Mass., Bethiah Thurber, former wid., W22411
SHORT, Asa, R.I., Olive, W15943
Benjamin, N.H., BLWt.3467. Iss. 8/26/1790 to M. Cutler, ass. No papers
Henry, N.Y., Sophia, W15332
James, R.I., Anna, W13894
John, Va., S16525
John, Va., Mary, R9534
John, Va., War 1812, S37386
Joshua, Va., S36301
Moses, Mass., Abigail T., W8295; BLWt.13415-160-55
Peter, N.Y., Alida Shultis/Shultz, former wid., W22190
Samuel, Ct., Mary, W2645; BLWt. 35721-160-55
Samuel, R.I., Eleanor Alen/Allen, former wid., W1121; BLWt.9488-160-55

SHORT (continued)
Seth, Ct., S17673
Shubael, Mass., Polly, W24938
Siloam, Ct., S11384
Zachariah/Zacchariah, N.Y., S11389
SHORTER, Rodger, Pvt., Md., BLWt. 11711 iss. 2/7/1790
SHORTMAN, William, Ct., BLWt.6436. Iss. 2/5/1790. No papers
SHORTRIDGE, Andrew, Va., Nancy, W26473; BLWt.26290-160-55
John, N.H., Margaret, W15335
Richard, N.H., Lois, R9535
SHORTT, Archibald, Va., S17085
SHOTO, Anthony D., S.C., R9536
SHOTS, John, Md., Elizabeth, W25128
SHOTT, Richard, Pa., BLWt.10336. Iss. 11/6/1795. No papers
Richard, Pa., Mary, W6019
SHOTTLER, John, Cont., N.J. res. in 1820. BLWt.904-100
SHOTTS, John, Md. See SHOTS
SHOTWELL, James, Va., S17088
Nancy, former wid. of Cornelius R. Sedam, N.J., which see
SHOUFLER, Valentine, Pa., S22506
SHOULER, John, See SHULER
SHOUN, John, Va., S31360
SHOUNTY, Henry, Pa. See SHONTY
SHOUP, Henry, Pa., Elizabeth, R9538
Lewis, Pa. See Ludwig
Ludwig/Lewis, Pa., S40410; BLWt. 2149-100
SHOUPE, William, Va. See SHOPE
SHOUSE, Christain, Pa., S40418
SHOUT, Adam, Pa., S4818
SHOVEL, James, Mass., Priscilla Harrington, former wid. BLWt. 636-100
SHOVELL, John, Md., BLWt.11673. Iss. 2/1/1790. No papers
SHOVER, Francis, Pa., Catharine, W2009; BLWt.5108-160-55
John, See SHOBER
SHRAWDER, Philip, German Regt., BLWt.2029-100-Lt. Iss. 9/12/ 1789. No papers. This name is spelled Schrader in Heitman's Hist. Reg.
SHREAVES, William, See SHRIEVES
SHREDER, Philip, Cont., Pa., Catharine, R9273
SHREEVE, Israel, N.J., BLWt.1993-500-Col. Iss. 11/4/1791. No papers
William, Va. See SHREVE
SHREFLER, Henry, Pa., S4830
SHREVE, Benjamin, N.J., S4832
Godfrey, Mass., BLWt.5015. Iss. 6/24/1795. No papers
Godfrey, Cont., Mass., S42273
John, N.J., S3890
William, Cont., Va., S30697
SHREWSBURY, Allen, Va., Nancy, R9539
SHRIBER, Frederick, Pa., S41136
SHRIEVES, William, Cont., Va., S38358; BLWt.2074-100
SHRINER, John, Md., N.J., Pa., Barbary, R9632
SHRINK, Andrew, Md., BLWt.11740 Iss. 4/7/1791. No papers
SHROADER, Anthoney/Anthony, Pa., War 1812, Elizabeth, S23906 & Wid. Orig. War 1812-20149
SHRODER, Anthony, See Anthoney SHROADER
Godfried Israel, Armand's Legion BLWt.13709. Iss. 1/29/1790. No papers
SHROFE, Adam, Pa., BLWt.10444. Iss. 12/22/179? No papers
SHROM, Henry, Pa. See SHRUM
SHROPSHIRE, Abner, Va., Susannah W8724
Polly/Mary, former wid. of James Welch, N.J., which see
William, N.C., War 1812, Miss. Troops, Elizabeth, W7180; BLWt. 57781-160-55
SHROTT, Samuel, Pa., S40414
SHROUM, Peter, N.C. See SCRUM
SHROYER, Matthias, Cont., Pa. agcy. & res., Mary, W3360
SHRUM, Henry, Pa., Margaret, W2866
SHRUPP, Henry, Cont., Pa., S35065
SHRYOCK, Christain, Cont., Va., S40406
John, Md., S35067
SHUBART, James, Pa., R9542
SHUBERT, John, Cont., Pa., S40413
SHUBRICK, Thomas, S.C., BLWt.2103-300-Capt. Iss. 6/4/1792 to David Cay, ass. No papers
SHUCK, Jacob, Pa., S36299
John, Pa., Mary Ann B., R9543
Mathew, Va. See Mathias
Mathias/Mathew, Va., S14436
Philip, Pa., S31958
SHUFELDT, Christopher, N.Y. See SHOEFELT
John, N.Y., Catharine, W22188
Peter, N.Y., S14444
William, N.Y., S22980
SHUFF, John, Mass., Priscilla, W15330
SHUFFEY, William, N.J., BLWt. 8748. Iss. 7/22/1789. No papers
SHUFFIELD, Ephraim, N.C., Barbara, W8715; BLWt.34860-160-55
SHUGART, Eli, See SUGART
SHULER, Henry, Cont., Pa., S40411
John, Pa., R9545
SHULL, John, N.Y. See SHAUL
John, Pa., R9546
Peter, Pa., Anna Dorotha, W9289
SHULP, John, N.Y., S28877
SHULTER, John, N.Y. See SHULTIS
SHULTIS, Alida, N.Y. See Peter SHORT
Henry, N.Y. See SHULTS
Henry, Pa., R9547
Jacob, N.Y., S15233
John, N.Y., Elizabeth Emerick, former wid., R3340
Philip, N.Y., S--- Dorcas Shultis wid. of sold., was pensioned as former wid. of Samuel Walker, N.Y., which see
SHULTIZ, Alida, former wid. of Peter Short, N.Y., which see
SHULTS, George, N.Y., S14432
Henry, N.Y., S14453
Matthias, Va., Didamah, W8714
SHULTZ, Alida, N.Y. See Peter SHORT
Christopher, Cont., N.Y., Elizabeth, W1091; BLWt.184-60-55 & 7856-100, 1792. Name also appears as Shiltz, Shelty, Shilty
Jacob, N.Y., S11387
John, Navy, Mass., S30094
John, N.Y., BLWt.7815. Iss. 8/3/ 1790 to Cornelius V. Dyck, ass. No papers
John, N.Y., Martha, R9548; BLWt. 34589-160-55
SHUMAKER, Harmon, Md., N.C., S32512
Zedekiah, Va. See SHOEMAKER
SHUMATE, Armstead, Va., Elizabeth R9551
Berryman, Va., Jane, R9552
Samuel, Va., S15646
SHUMAWAY, Isaac Whitney, Mass., S42280
SHUMWAY, Abijah, Mass., Lucy, W17811
Amasa, Mass., Betsey, W24953; BLWt.90036-160-55
Benjamin, Mass., S31953
Cyril, Mass., S21481
Elijah, Mass., Chloe, W19019; BLWt.18369-160-55
Elizabeth, former wid. of Jonathan Morgan, Mass., which see
Isaac Whitney, Mass. See SHUMAWAY
John, Ct., Cont., S41157; BLWt. 1946-300-Capt. Iss. 12/19/1799 to Israel Harris, ass. No papers
Levi, Mass., Chloe, W20050
Peter, Mass., BLWt.5021. Iss. 3/ 30/1796 to Peter Sevier. No papers
Peter, Mass., S40420
Samuel, Mass., S29445
Stephen, Mass., S33660
SHUNTZ, Christian, N.Y., BLWt.7743 Iss. 6/1/1792. No papers
SHUPE, John, Pa., S16247
SHURLEY, Bennet, Md., BLWt.11706. Iss. 3/11/1791. Duplicate iss. 5/27/1839 under a special Act of Congress
Bennet, Md. See SHIRLEY
SHURTLEFF, Benoni, Cont., Mass., Navy, Lucy, W22183 1/2; BLWt. 89528-160-55
David, Mass., S30097
Gideon, Mass., S19085
Robert, Cont., Mass., Mary, W22205
Robert, See Robert GANNETT
Timothy, Mass., S21967
William, Mass. See SHURTLIFF
SHURTLIFF, Amasa, Mass., Sarah, W26464
Simeon, Mass., Submit Baker, former wid., W23550
William, Mass., Lydia, W2472; BLWt.3613-160-55
SHURTS, Mathias, N.J., N.Y., See SHIRTS

SHURTS, Michael, N.J., S4668
SHUSTER, Andrew, Pa., S3898
Martin, Pa., BLWt.58-100
SHUTE, Benjamin, Navy, N.H., S23909
Daniel, Mass., BLWt.1894-400-Surgn. Iss. 10/26/1789. No papers
George, Mass., S43125
John, Mass., Navy, S33661
John, N.H., BLWt.1564-100
Samuel M., N.J., BLWt.1998-200-Lt. Iss. 7/7/1789. No papers
Solomon, Mass., Navy, Elizabeth S30099
Thomas, N.C., S42009
William, N.J. & U.S.A., Anna H., W24949; BLWt.2001-150-Ens. Iss. 6/11/1789. No papers
William, N.Y., S10012
SHUTLEFF, Benoni, See SHURTLEFF
SHUTTELL, Daniel, Pa. See SHETTEL
SHUTTLE, John, Va., R9556
SHUTTS, John, N.Y., Hannah Halleck former wid., W17042
Matthias, Va. See SHULTS
SHY, Jesse, See SKY
SIAS, John, N.H., S19089
SIBBLISS, Thomas, See SIBLISS
SIBERT, David, See SEYBERT
SIBERY, William, Va., S33676
SIBLEY, Aaron, Mass., Lucy, W13902
Archelaus/Archilaus, Mass., Polly W6061; BLWt.40699-160-55
Asa, Mass., Irene, W19036
Daniel, Mass., S30102
David, Mass., S33375
Ezra, Ct., Ann/Anna, W15337
Gibbs, Mass., R9557
James, Mass., S17676
John, Mass., Eulilia, W1946; BLWt.26969-160-55
John, Mass., R9558
John, S.C., S30706
Moses, Ct., S29456
Nabby, former wid. of Daniel Place, R.I., which see
Samuel, Mass., Sarah, W31364
Samuel, N.H., Sarah, W16149
William, Mass., Abigail, W15338
SIBLISS, Thomas, Mass., S40088
SICKELS, John, N.Y. See SICKLES
Samuel, N.J., BLWt.452-100
Zacharias, N.Y., S28880
SICKLE, Charles, Md., BLWt.11712 Iss. 1/11/1796 to Joshua Ward, ass. No papers
David, See VAN SICKLE
SICKLER, William, N.Y., S14465
SICKLES, Abraham, N.Y., BLWt. 7794. Iss. 8/25/1790 to Wm. Sickles. No papers
Daniel, N.J., R9560
Jacob, N.J., BLWt.8728. Iss. 2/25/1792. No papers
Jacob, N.Y., Hannah/Annaetye Van Orden, former wid., W18186
James, N.J., S4841
John, N.Y., Hannah, R9559
Thomas, N.J., Mary, W11430
SIDDALL, Stephen, Va., Rebecca, W6065; BLWt.13738-160-55
SIDDELL, Stephen, Va. See SIDDALL
SIDDLE, George, Pa. See SIDLE
Stephen, Va. See SIDDALL
SIDEBOTTOM, John, See SYDENBOTHOM
Joseph, Va., Agnes, W8727
SIDENBERGER, John, Mass., R9562
SIDES, Philip, Pa., Mary, W4514
SIDLE, George, Pa., S4842
Peter, Pa. See SEIDEL
SIDMAN, Isaac, Pa., Eliza, W3194
John, Pa., R9563
SIDNEY, Joseph, Md., BLWt.11726. Iss. 11/29/1790 to Jeremiah Mudd, ass. No papers
SIDORE, Isaac, See SEDORE
SIDWAY, James, Mass., S29455
SIEGEL, Henry, Pa. See SIGLE
SIFERT, Peter, Cont., Pa., S42304
SIFFIN, John, N.J., BLWt.8714. Iss. 5/31/1790
SIFRITT, Andrew, See CYPRUS
SIGHTS, Jacob, Pa., R6341
SIGLE, Henry, Pa., S22512
SIGLER, Henry, N.J., S33677
John, Pa., R9565
SIGMAN, George, See SIGMON
SIGMON, George, N.C., Catharine, W2969
SIGOURNEY, Andrew, Mass., S21486
SIKES, David, Ct., Lucy, W11425; BLWt.24442-160-55
Francis, Mass., R9567
Gideon, Ct., Mercy, W6066; BLWt.26482-160-55
Jacob, Ct., Mass., Vt., Sarah, W6217
James, N.C., Drucilla, W9653
John, Ct., Vt., Lucy, W19133; BLWt.26020-160-55
John Jones, Mass. See SYKES
Nathan, Mass., R42299
Nathaniel, Mass., Mary, W22211
Thomas A., Va., Sarah, W991
William, Md., BLWt.11174 & 11676. Iss. 1/11/1796 to Joshua Ward, ass. No papers
SILAS, Samuel, Pa., BLWt.10369. Iss. 3/3/1794 to Michael Stiver, ass. No papers
SILENCE, William, Va., S35071
SILK, James, Md., S40431
SILKERK, James, N.Y., BLWt.7734. Iss. 9/25/1790 to William McGill, ass. No papers
SILKWORTH, William, N.Y., Nancy, W24964
SILL, Andrew, Ct., Cont., S10014
David F., Ct., BLWt.1940-450-Lt. Col. Iss. 1/28/1790
Elisha N., Ct., Chloe, W6057
Isaac, Ct., Sarah Brockway, former wid., W17358
Jabez, Ct., R9570
Richard, Ct., BLWt.1950-300-Capt. Iss. 12/15/1790 to Elizabeth Sill et al. No papers
Samuel, Cont., Ct., S36344
Thomas S., Warner's Regt. BLWt. 1932-300-Capt. Iss. 12/27/1799; also recorded W2710
SILLAVEN, William, Md., S7515
SILLAWAY, Daniel, Mass., Privateer, Ann, W13897; BLWt.11283-160-55
SILLCOCK, Joseph, N.J., R9568
SILLCOCKS, Gabriel, N.J., Sarah, R9569
Valentine, N.J., S33675
SILLERY, John, N.C., R9571
SILLEY, Benjamin, Mass., S37401
Thomas, See CILLEY
SILLICK, Benjamin, Ct., BLWt.436-100
James, Ct. See SELLICK
SILLIMAN, Isaac, Ct., Mary, W19033; BLWt.35722-160-55
James, Ct., Huldah, W17818
Samuel, Ct., Navy, Roxillana, W1266; BLWt.27687-160-55
SILLIMAN, Jonathan, Jr., Md., BLWt.2040-400-Maj. Iss. 3/31/1790 No papers. Heitman's Hist. Reg. & the Md. Archives spell this name SELLMAN
SILLOWAY, Daniel, Mass. See SILLAWAY
John, Mass. See SILOWAY
SILLYMAN, Thomas, Pa., Mary, W2881
SILOWAY, John, Mass., Navy, Patience, W19037
SILSBE, David, N.Y., S33669
SILSBURY, Jonathan, Mass., Abigail W24966; BLWt.115-60-55
SILSBY, Lazell, N.H., S14461
Samuel, Cont., Mass., S37400
SILVAR, Aaron, Va., Sarah, W2872; BLWt.53747-160-55
SILVER, Daniel, Mass., S30705
George, Cont., Md., Nancy, R9572
Samuel, N.H., Abigail Clough, former wid., W18908
Zebediah, Mass., S43139
SILVERS, Aaron, Va. See SILVAR
SILVERTHORN, Robert, N.C., Ann, W4802
SILVESTER, Adam, Mass., N.H., S33767
Job, Md., BLWt.11721. Iss. 11/29/1790 to James Moore, admr. No papers
Job, Mass., S37480
Joel, Mass., S33673
Joseph, Cont., Mass., S40432
Joseph, Mass., S4915
Levi, Cont., N.H., Vt., S14464
SILVEY, Stephen, Va. See SILVY
SILVY, Stephen, Va., S31964
SILWOOD, William, Md., BLWt.11698 Iss. 12/23/1795 to George Ponsonby, ass. No papers
SIMANTON, Robert, Pa., S6097
SIMKINS, Gideon, N.Y., BLWt.7826. Iss. 10/12/1790 to Isaac Bogaart, ass. No papers
Isaac, N.Y., R9590
John, N.J. See SIMPKINS
John C., Cont., See SIMPKINS
SIMLER, John Henry, Cont., Pa. res. in 1828, S46331; BLWt. 1403-100
SIMMERLY, John, N.C., R9573
SIMMERS, George, Pa., S22511

SIMMERS (continued)
John, Pa., BLWt.10380. Iss. 2/6/ 179? to John Simmers. Ctfd. 2/ 25/1820
SIMMINS, Henry, N.J., S4838
SIMMON, John, Va., S7512
SIMMONDS, Henry, Pa., BL Rej.
John, N.Y., BLWt.7764. Iss. 8/ 6/1790. No papers
Joshua, Mass. See SIMONDS
Robert, Md., S4836
William, Del., BLWt.1972-100
SIMMONS, Aaron, Md., Sarah, W9293
Aaron, N.Y., Mary, R9575
Abner, R.I., Abigail, W4801; BLWt.17883-160-55
Allen, Mass., Silence, W15340
Benjamin (colored), Ct., Patty, W24974
Benjamin, R.I., Susannah, W22210; BLWt.19607-160-55
Bennett, Mass., BLWt.5060. Iss. 1/26/1790 to John May. No papers
Benoni, Ct., Cont., Navy, R.I., Nancy, W13899; BLWt.18376-160-55
Caleb, R.I., S11394
Chapman, Ct. Sea Service, Elizabeth, W19362
Cornelius, N.Y., S23419
Ensley, N.Y., Lydia, W19032
Ephraim, R.I., S30103
Ezekiel, N.Y., S42303
Ezra, R.I., S11396
Gideon, R.I., S23917
Henry, N.J. See SIMMINS
Ichabod, Mass., Urania, W24971
Ichabod, R.I., Anna, W24961
Isaac, See William Isaac
Isaac, Mass., Elizabeth, W24792; BLWt.80026-160-55
Isaac, R.I., S21973
Isham, N.C., Nancy, W8725
Isles, Pa., BLWt.10424. Iss. 4/ 3/1798. No papers
Ivory, R.I., S29458
James, Va., S39071
James, Va., BLWt.2387-100
Jehu, Va., S6093
Jeremiah, N.C., Lucy, W4803
Jeremiah, Pa. Sea Service, Elizabeth, W6059
Jesse, S.C., Charlotte, W869
Joel, Mass., Artemisia Packard, former wid., W21898; BLWt.36554-160-55
Joel, Va., S17677
John, Ct., Rachel, W24965
John, Mass., BLWt.4983. Iss. 2/29/1792 to Moses Beard. No papers
John, Navy, See SIMONS
John, N.Y., Margaret, W26442; BLWt.19919-160-55
John, N.Y., Mary, W26964
John, N.C., S4672
John, N.C., Mary/Polly, W60
John, N.C., Leodosia, W6063
John, Va., Margaret, R9578
Joseph, See SEAMONS
Joshua, Mass., S14466
Joshua, N.Y., BLWt.7730. Iss. 10/

SIMMONS (continued)
7/1790 to Elijah Hunter, ass. No papers
Joshua, N.Y., Hannah Dep, former wid., W16953
Lemuel, Mass., S30703
Libbeus, Mass. See Lebbeus SIMONS
Nathaniel, Mass., S15981
Nathaniel, Va., R9579
Peleg, Ct., Amy, W11428; BLWt. 26549-160-55
Peleg, R.I., Eliphal, W16727
Reuben, N.J., BLWt.8726. Iss. 12/8/1789. No papers
Reuben, See SAMONS
Robert, Mass., BLWt.4974. Iss. 10/ 12/1790 to William Ely. No papers
Robert, Mass., S42302
Samuel, Ct., S37394
Samuel, Ct., Sarah, W24967; BLWt. 2155-100 & 341-60-55
Sanders, N.C., S7516; BLWt.86543-160-55
Sebre, Mass., Hanah, W22216
Seth, Mass., Abigail, W19363
Stephen, Ct., S32521
Sylvanus, Cont., N.Y., S14484
Thomas, Mass., S15980
Thomas, Mass., S33667
William, Md., S6098
William, Md., S40434
William, Md., Sarah, W17861; BL Reg. 304022-55
William, Mass., S28878
William, R.I., S10013
William, Va., S7514
William, Va., S30704
William Isaac/Isaac, Ga., N.C., R9580
Williamson, Va., BLWt.2386-100
Zarah, R.I., Hannah, R9576. BLWt. 47966-160-55
SIMMS, James, Va., S4840
Micajah, Va. See SIMS
Richard, Va., S17093
William, Va., Judith, R9611
SIMON, Cummy (negro), Ct., S36315
SIMONDS, Ashney/Ashna, See SYMONDS
Benjamin, Mass., S33679
Daniel, See SYMONDS
Jacob, Mass., Mehitable, W24958
James, Mass., Judith, W2181; BLWt.9201-160-55
Jeduthan, Ct., Mary, R9582; BLWt.56917-160-55
Jonas, Col. Proctor's Regt. of Art., BLWt.2026-300-Capt. Iss. 8/19/1789. No papers
Jonathan, Mass. See SYMONDS
Jonathan, Mass., N.H., S16527
Joseph, Mass., BLWt.4986. Iss. 9/ 13/1792 to Jonathan Jenks. No papers
Joseph, Mass., Lucy, W2631; BLWt. 40710-160-55
Joseph, N.H., Bethia/Bethier, W2673; BLWt.33765-160-55
Joshua, Mass., Abigail, W20054; BLWt.33768-160-55
Joshua, N.Y., Mass., Lois, W19365 BLWt.26021-160-55

SIMONDS (continued)
Pomp, Mass., BLWt.5033. Iss. 9/ 10/1789 to Henry Newman. No papers
Robert, Lamb's Art., N.Y., BLWt. 7857. Iss. 10/2/1789. No papers
Silas, See SYMONDS
William, N.H., S43140
SIMONS, Aaron, Ct., Mehitable, W17816
Andrew, Ct., BLWt.6498. Iss. 1/19/1792 to Resolve Waldron, ass. No papers
Andrew, Ct., S42300
Arad, Ct., Sea Service, Cont., Bridget, W15339
Asa, Ct., Mass., S7519
Cornmy, Ct., BLWt.6502. Iss. 1/ 27/1796 to Abijah Curtis, ass. No papers
Eli, Ct., S33668
Elijah, Ct., S15647
Elijah, Ct., Lucy, W17813
Frederick, Md., S6096
Isaac, Ct., R9583
Isham, Ct., Cont., Deborah, W1898 BLWt.5102-160-55
James, Mass. See SIMONDS
Jeduthan, Ct. See SIMONDS
John, Ct., Ann, W16406
John, Navy, res. N.Y., S42301
John, N.H., Susanna, W24969
John, R.I. See LEMONS
Joseph, Ct., S42305
Joseph, Ct., Prudence, W17814
Joseph, Ct., Cont., Mass., S14460
Joseph, Mass., S33678
Joseph, N.H. See SIMONDS
Joshua, Ct., Elizabeth, W24960
Lebbeus/Libbeus, Mass., Mary, W24970
Lycus, Ct., Julia, R9584
Nathan, Ct., S17094
Paul G., Ct., R9585
Reuben, See SAMONS
Robert, S.C., R9586
Sarah, former wid. of David Vibbard/Vibbird, Cont., Ct., which see
Simeon, Mass. See Simon
Simeon, R.I., Sarah, R9587
Simon/Simeon, Mass., S43138
Thomas, Ct., Rebecca Barber, former wid., W20679
William, Ct., Beulah, W17817
SIMONSON, Christopher, N.J., S28883
Simon, N.J., S1104
SIMONTON, Alexander, Pa. agcy. & res., S3914
John, Pa., S40429
Robert, Pa., See SIMANTON
Thomas, Mass., Mary, W24962
Thomas, Pa., Mary, W3880
Walter, Mass., Lucy, W24963
SIMPKIN, Ephraim, N.J., S4673
SIMPKINS, Catharine, former wid. of Thomas Laurence/Lawrence, N.Y., which see
Charles, Md., S39070
Charles, N.J., Barbara, R9588

SIMPKINS (continued)
Ephraim, N.J. See SIMPKIN
Gideon, N.Y., R9589
James, Cont., Va., Patience, W19364; BLWt.18020-160-55
John, N.J., R9591
John G., Cont., Ill. res. in 1829, Margaret, R9592
Prudence, N.Y., former wid. of George Thomas, W19035
Robert, N.Y., S14463
SIMPSON, Aaron, Va., Charlotte, W4337
Alexander, N.H., S4671
Alexander, N.J., Elizabeth, W7182; BLWt.35723
Alexander, Va., Ann, W6060
Benjamin, Mass., S19090
Charles, Mass., S30104
Debrah/Deborah, contesting wid. of John Simpson, N.C., R9594. See file W28011
Edmund, N.C., S21974
Elisha, N.C., S31963
Francis, Va., Sally, R9604
Henry, N.J., S754
Hugh, Va., S.C., Mil. 1787, S31363
Isaac, N.Y., S28884
James, Mass., S11397
James, N.J., R9599
James, N.Y., See SIMSON
James, R.I., Mercy, W15811; BLWt.38560-160-55
James, S.C., S11401
James, S.C., R9598
James, Va., S6102
Jane, former wid. of Thomas Wilson N.H., which see
Jeremiah, Va., S37396
John, Ct., BLWt.1942-400-Surgn. Iss. 9/2/1790. No papers
John, Mass., S33670
John, Mass., R9600
John, N.H., Reuhamah, BLWt.18374-160-55
John, N.J., BLWt.8759. Iss. 7/25/1796. No papers
John, N.Y., S28881
John, N.Y., S43141
John, N.C., Mary, W28011; Debrah/Deborah Simpson also applied for pension as wid. of this sold. & was rejected.
John, Pa., Mary, W19038; BLWt. 27595-160-55
John, Va., S40430
John, Va., Elizabeth, R9595
Joseph, N.Y., S28879
Josiah, N.H., S40428
Lawrence, Md., Sarah, W26443
Mathew, N.J., N.Y., R17851
Michael, Pa., BLWt.2011-300-Capt. Iss. 12/24/1799 to James Johnston ass. No papers
Peter, N.Y., S28882
Rezin, Cont., Md., S35070
Robert, Cont., N.H., S3910
Robert, N.Y., Mary Fuller, former wid., W17000
Robert, Va., S31365
Samuel, N.C., Mary, R9603

SIMPSON (continued)
Simeon, N.J., Sarah, W4586
Southy/Southey, Va., Hannah Topping former wid., W6303. Her late husb., Garret Topping, was a Rev. soldier
Stephen, N.J., S23918
Thomas, Md., S40436
Thomas, Mass., Susannah, W15336; BLWt.16261-160-55
Thomas, N.H., S11395
William, Del., BLWt.10884. Iss. 9/2/1789. No papers
William, Del., S46322
William, Mass., S33666
William, N.H., BLWt.3475. Iss. 2/19/1796 to William Thom, ass. No papers
William, N.H., S11398
William, N.C. See SYMPSON
William, Va., Elizabeth, R9596
William, Va. See SIMSON
Zebadiah, Mass., Lucy, W24959
SIMRALL, Alexander, Pa., S40437
SIMS, Augustin, Va., S32520
Benjamin, Va., Jane, R9608
Curthbert, Va., S33674
Edward, Cont., Va., S46524
Edward, Va., S6104
Francis, Va., S9607
James, Va., S19464
Jeremiah, Cont., Va., Catharine, W1500; BLWt.31586-160-55
John, N.J., S40435
John, N.C., Milly, W10252; BLWt.40695-160-55
John, Va., S7518
John, See SYMMS
Micajah, Va., Elizabeth, W6055
Patrick, Md., S35072
Reuben, Va., S6100
Rhodam, Va., S16925
Samuel, R.I., Anne, R9605
Thomas, N.C., R9610
William, R.I., Rebecca, W22213
William, Va. See SIMMS
William, Sr., Va., S17091
William, Va., S37395
SIMSON, Andrew, N.Y., S29459
James, N.Y., Hannah, W19361; BLWt.7095-160-55
John, N.J., R9601
Simeon, Mass., S37398; BLWt. 8140-160-55
William, Va., S25830
SINCK, Abraham, Pa. See SINK
SINCLAIR, Francis, Mass., Lucinda, W11426; BLWt.100124-160-55
George, Cont., N.Y., S43143
George, Navy, N.J., Pa. Sea Service, S40438
James, N.H., BLWt.3496. Iss. 4/5/1796 to O. Ashley, ass. No papers
James, N.H. See ST. CLAIR
Joshua, N.H., S37399
Noah, N.H., S19770
Richard, N.H., Betsey, W16071
Robert, Va., S17678
Samuel, N.H. See SINCLEAR
SINCLEAR, Jacob, Cont., N.H., Rachael, W15342

SINCLEAR (continued)
James, N.H. See ST. CLAIR
Samuel, N.H., S43142
SINE, Peter, N.J., S1051
SINGER, George, Va., S14462
Henry, Hazen's Regt., BLWt.13758. Iss. 9/10/1789 to Charles Bush, ass. No papers
SINGLETARY, Ithamar, N.C. Dis.- no papers. See Am. State Papers, Class 9, p.171. Wounded in several places in his back by a small sword, as he was retreating from the enemy 6/6/1781 at Rockfish.
Joseph, N.C., Dis. No papers. See Am. State Papers, Class 9, p.106. Wounded in left arm by accidental discharge of a musket while in the actual line of duty in the service of the U.S. that for near two years he continued languishing under the wound, and from the effect of it, and from no other cause the arm is withered, the joint of the elbow is crooked & stiff and the fingers contracted. Disabled at Wilmington, 1776.
Joseph, N.C., S47849
Joseph, S.C., Susannah, R9612
Josiah, N.C., Sarah P., W6064; BLWt.38554-160-55
SINGLETON, Anthony, Harrison's Regt., BLWt.2068-300-Capt. Iss. 8/13/1792. No papers
Edmund, Cont., Va., S38373
John, Pa., BLWt.10451-100. Iss. 3/19/1793. No papers
John, S.C., Elizabeth, W9652
John, Va., Anne, R9613
Joseph, N.C. See SINGLETARY
Joshua, Va., Navy, S7510
Robert, N.C., S39072
SINGLEWOOD, Stephen, Pa., Nancy, R9614
SINGLEY, George, Pa., S6099
SINK, Abraham, Cont., Pa., S6103
Abraham, Pa., Ann, W4587; BLWt. 1414-100
SINKLER, James, See ST. CLAIR
Zebulon, Cont., N.H., Anna, R9616
SINN, Christian, Pa., Margareta, R9617
George, Pa., BLWt.10372. Iss. 1/29/1790 to Andrew Johnston, admr. No papers
SINNAT, Patrick, Va. See SINNETT
SINNAX, William, Crane's Cont. Art., Mass.; BLWt.5112. Iss. 5/22/1798. No papers
SINNETT, Patrick, Va., Catharine W8296; BLWt.26881-160-55
SINNOTT, Patrick, Ct., Mary, W4585
Patrick, N.Y., BLWt.7721. Iss. 6/15/1790. No papers
SINSABAUGH, Adam, N.Y., R6365
Henry, N.Y., Margaret, R9618
SIP, Jesse, Navy, Ct., S36316
SIPES, Daniel, Md., b. Pa., S17092
George, Pa., Rachel, R9619;

SIPES (continued)
BLWt.54117-160-55
SIPPELL, Peter, R.I., S10987
SIPVILL, Nicholas, Pa., S40433
SIRRINE, James, N.Y., R17742
William, N.Y., R9385
SISCHO, Samuel, N.H., Mary, W22217
SISCO, Jacob, N.J., R9620
Peter I., N.J., Elizabeth, W2360; BLWt.11187-160-55
William, Cont., N.H., Abigail, W22209
SISCOW, Nicholas, N.Y., R9621
SISIM, Peter, See SCISIM
SISK, John, Pa., BLWt.10455. Iss. 8/31/1790 to Dudley Woodbridge, ass. No papers
Timothy, Va., Ann, W6058
SISKE, Bartlet, N.C., Va., S1722
SISLAND, William, Md., BLWt.11473 & 11677 iss. 12/18/1794 to Henry Purdy, ass.
SISLER, Michael, Pa., Rachel, R9623
Philip, Md. See Phillip SEISLAR
SISSLER, Michael, Pa. See SISLER
SISSON, Esek, R.I., Sebery, W22212
George, Mass., Anna, W22218
George, R.I., S23916
James, R.I., Sophia, W13898
John, R.I., Susan, W2871
Jonathan, R.I., Betsey, W17815
Peleg, N.Y., Clarissa, W2361; BLWt.26878-160-55
Thomas, R.I., S21867
SITHIAN, John, N.J. See SITHINS
SITHINS, John, N.J., S33671
SITS, Daniel, Mass., N.Y., S22990 BLWt.53741-160-55
SITTERLY, Jacob, N.Y., S23915
SITTINGTON, Robert, Va., S7517
SITTON, William, Va., S39073
SITTS, Henry, N.Y., S42297
Peter, N.Y., Margaret, W6056
SITZLER, Philip, See SEISLAR
SIVER, Thomas, Mass. See SEAVER
SIVOY, Isaac, Pa., BLWt.10452. Iss. 12/28/1793 to Christain Hubbard, ass. No papers
SIX, Henry, Md., S9481
John, Va., S36758
SIZEMORE, Ephraim, Va., Winney, R9625
SIZER, Anthony, Ct., Lucretia, W24550
Daniel, Ct., BLWt.6478. Iss. 11/19/1789. No papers
Daniel, Ct., Cont., S36317
John, Va., S6105
Jonathan, Ct., S14459
Lemuel, Ct., Elizabeth, W22215
William, Cont., Ct., S33672
SKADDIN, Robert K., Pa., R9626
SKAGGS, Archibald, Va., S31367
Henry, Va., b. S.C., S30701
James C., S.C., R9628
William, Va., b. N.C., Polly, W2182; BLWt.27564-160-55
SKAIN, Adam, S.C., S11404
Nicholas, S.C., Rachel, W8728
SKEEL, Amos, Mass., Bethiah/

SKEEL (continued)
Bethuah, W19367
Esther, former wid. of Edward Knapp, Mass., which see
Jonathan, Cont., Mass., S14467
Phebe, former wid. of Robert Hubbard, Ct., which see
William, Mass., BLWt.666-100
SKEELE, Amos, Ct., Lucy, W6070
John, N.H., S19465
SKEELS, Simeon, Cont., Ct., Aseneth Amedon, former wid., W20605
SKEEN, John, N.C., S37404
Peter, N.C., Sarah, R9630
SKEHAN, Jeremiah, N.Y., BLWt. 7829. Iss. 12/11/1789 to Benjamin Brown, ass. No papers
Jeremiah, N.Y., S43130
SKEIN, Adam, S.C. See SKAIN
SKELLENGER, Daniel, N.J., S4844
Elisha P., N.J., S1105
SKELLIE, William, N.Y., S11402
SKELTON, William, Va., S3915
William, Va., S10258
SKERRETT, Clement, Md., BLWt. 2047-200-Lt. iss. 7/14/1789
SKERRITT, Clement, See SKERRETT
SKERRY, John, Mass., N.H., S30106
SKIDMORE, Joseph, Va., Ind. War 1791, S15648
Richard, Mass., S33680
SKIEL, Amos, Mass., See SKEEL
SKIFF, John, Mass., S29460
Obadiah, Mass., Privateer, Lucy, W15329
Prince, Mass., S11405
Stephen, Ct., Adah, W19039
SKIFFINGTON, John, N.Y., BLWt. 7821. Iss. 7/14/1790 to Richard Platt, ass. No papers
SKILES, John, Pa., R9641
SKILLING, John, Pa., S46410
SKILLINGTON, Elijah, Del., BLWt. 2038-200-Lt. Iss. 6/6/1794 to William Brown, ass. No papers
SKILLMAN, Abraham, N.J., Lucretia W197
Abraham, N.J., Mary, W992
Jacob, N.J., S14472
John T., N.J., Mary, W137
Thomas, N. ., S33681
SKIMMER, John, Navy, Mass. agcy. & res., Ruth, W15343
SKINER, David, Ct., Ruth, W2448; BLWt.6422-160-55
SKINNER, Abraham, Cont., Pa., S42309
Adonijah, Ct., Abigail, R9631
Alexander, Va., BLWt.1131-400
Amasa, Mass., Saloma, R9634
Ashbel, Ct., Rhoda, W17819
Benjamin, Ct., Vt., Sarah, W17820
Benjamin, Mass., S19778
Beriah, Ct., S42306
Daniel, Ct., Vt., N.H., Hannah, W24976
Daniel, N.J., N.Y., Pa., S10015
David, Ct. See SKINER
David, N.Y., S11403
Eli, Mass., S31366

SKINNER (continued)
Elisha, Ct., Achsa, W17822
Elisha, Mass., S37402
Ephraim, N.H., S41161
Hannah, former wid. of William Stevens, N.Y., which see
Henry, Mass. Sea Service, Navy, S38374
Henry, Va., S7521; (BLWt.2014-100 fraudulent allowance)
Ira, Ct., Hepsibah, R9633
Isaac, Ct., Mabel, W22220
Isaac, Ct., Lucy, W24975
Isaac, Va., S31368
Israel, Ct., Lovisa, W17821
Israel, Mass., Sally, W24977
James, Mass., Sarah, W22225
James, Va. Sea Service, R91. Va. Half Pay
Jared, Mass., S19091
Jesse, N.Y., S17095
John, Armand's Corps. BLWt.13701 Iss. 12/6/1791 to Stephen Thorn, ass. No papers
John, Ct., S42310
John, Ct., Catharine Emerson, former wid., W24120; BLWt.7097-160-55
John, Ct., Cleopatra, W24980
John, Md.,N.J.,Pa., See SHRINER
John, Mass., S30105
Jonathan, Ct., Judith, W22222
Jonathan, N.Y., S42308
Josiah, N.Y., S23919
Josiah, N.Y., Elizabeth, W16728
Levi, N.Y., S14470
Luther, Ct., Sarah, W22219
Luther, Ct., Temperance, W24978
Micah, N.J., S3916
Richard, Ct., S14471
Richard, Mass. Sea Service, Eleanor Gilbert, former wid., W19505
Samuel, Ct., Elizabeth, W22221
Samuel, Pa., Mary, W6069; BLWt. 19918-160-55
Stephen, Ct., S31965
Thomas, Ct., BLWt.1943-400-Surgn. Iss. 12/3/1789 to Daniel Watrous, ass. No papers
Thomas, Ct., S42307
Thomas, Del., R9635
Timothy, Ct., BLWt.946-100
Timothy, Mass., Ruth, W22224
Uriah, Ct., S22991
Walter, Md., R9636
William, Del., BLWt.10877. Iss. 1/17/1791. No papers
William, Va., R9637
William, Va. Sea Service, R92. Va. Half Pay. See N.A. Acc. No. 837-Va. State Navy Wm. Skinner Y.S. File Va. Half Pay
Zenas, Ct., S14468
SKIPPER, James, N.C., R9639
Nathan, N.C., S39074
SKIPTON, Mathew, Pa., Nancy, W3361
SKOLFIELD, William, Mass., Sarah, W22223
William, Pa., BLWt.2035-200-Lt. Iss. 6/2/1796 to Wm. Skolfield
SKRIGGINS, Thomas, Mass., S37403

SKUTT, Stephen, N.Y., S14469
SKY, Jesse, Va., S31369
SLABACK, William, N.J., S4847
SLACK, Henry, Md., BLWt.1048-100
James, Lamb's Art., N.Y., BLWt. 7837. Iss. 7/28/1790 to G.H.V. Wagener, ass. No papers
John, Md., BLWt.11732. Iss. 3/31/1797 to Jas. DeBaufre, ass. No papers
John, Cont., Md., Margaret, W6072
John, Mass., S22993
John, Pa., Va., S4846
Joseph, N.H., Jerusha, W19371; BLWt.9455-160-55
Thomas, N.J., Rachel, W6077; BLWt.26940-160-55
William, Mass., S42011
SLADE, Abner, Ct., Cont., S16248
Cuff (colored), Cont.,R.I., S33684
Jacob, Ct., R9644
John, Ct., N.H., S21975
Jack, Mass. See Jack GARDNER
Nathan/Nathaniel, N.C., Elizabeth P., W6071
Peleg, Mass., Mary, W22232
Samuel, N.H., S23920; BLWt.9049-160-25
Stephen, N.C., BLWt.1632-200
Thomas, Md., BLWt.11716. Iss. 1/13/1792 to Wm. Lane, ass. of Mary Slade, admr. No papers
William, Ct., S23921; BLWt.15416-160-55
William, N.C., Martha, W4069
SLADOW, Dedlock, Pa. See Deadlock SHADOW
SLADYEN, John, Va., S14476
SLAGHT, John A., N.Y. See SLAIGHT
Mathias/Matthias, N.J., S10017
SLAIGHT, John A., N.Y., R9646
Matthias, N.J. See SLAGHT, Mathias
SLANKARD, George, N.C., R9648
SLAPE, Thomas, Va., S39075
SLAPP, Achilles, Va. See STAPP
SLAPPEY, Henry, S.C., Ann, W6073; BLWt.15437-160-55
SLARROW, Samuel, Mass., N.Y., S14473
SLASON, Ebenezer, Lee's Legion, BLWt.13803. Iss. 3/30/179? to Thomas Russell, ass. No papers
Jonathan, Ct., S22513
Nathaniel, Ct., d. 5/1/1835, Hannah, W24982
SLASSON, Deliverance, Ct., S29461
SLATE, James, Va., BLWt.12561. Iss. 2/24/1794 to Anthony New, ass. No papers
James, Va., S45141
Ruth, former wid. of Moses Ballard Mass., which see
Thomas, Ct., R17896
Zebediah, Mass., Rebecca, W15344
SLATER, Amos, Ct., Rachel, R9651
Edward, Va., S18205
Isaac, Va., Betsey/Elizabeth, W3881; BLWt.26481-160-55
James, Ct., BLWt.6422. Iss. 9/4/1789 to Ezekiel Case, ass. No papers

SLATER (continued)
James, Ct., Esther, W17825
James, Mass., S20959
Robert, N.Y., Margaret, R9650
Silas, R.I., S39843
SLATERBACK, Michael, Pa., BLWt. 10429. Iss. 2/26/1791. No papers
SLATON, James, Va., Martha, W9655
Phebe, former wid. of David Palmer, Mass., which see
SLAUCH, Bernhart, Pa. See Bernhard SLAUGH
SLAUGH, Bernhard/Bernhart, Pa., S15291
SLAUGHTER, Augustine, Va., BLWt.2168-400
Francis L., Pa. agcy. Dis. No papers
George, Va., Mary, W8729
George, Va., Susan, W11458; BLWt.38550-160-55
Godfrey, See Gottlieb SCHLOTTERER
Henry, Pa., BLWt.10432. Iss. 6/20/179? to John Delabarass, ass. No papers
Isaac, N.Y., Jane, W17823; BLWt. 27682-160-55
Jacob, Pa., S39076
James, Va., S31370; Va. Half Pay. See N.A. Acc. 874-050163. Half Pay James Slaughter
John, N.C., S42312
John, Pa., R20516
Philip, Va., Ann Mercer, dau. W29886; BLWt.1653-300. Iss. 7/8/1830 to himself
Thomas, Va., R17889. Va. Half Pay
William, Pa., S4845
William, Va., b.1756, d.1844, S1875
William, Va., Lucy, W19045; BLWt. 1836-150
William, Va., Lucy, R9654
William, Va., d. before 4/1832, Berkeley Co., R17891; BLWt.1899-200 Va. Half Pay. See N.A. Acc. No.874-050164. Half Pay
SLAUSON, Ezra, Ct., S17701
John, N.Y. See SLAWSON
SLAUTER, Ephraim, Ct., Ruth, W6079
Evert, N.Y., BLWt.7729. Iss. 7/10/1790 to C.C. Elmendorph, ass. No papers
SLAUTERBACK, Michael, Pa., S46330 See John Camp, W2177, whose wid. Margaret, this sold. m. in 1834
SLAVEN, Dennis, See Duncan SPIER
Isaiah, Va., S16529
John, N.C., S14480
John, Va., S6110
SLAWSON, Amos, N.Y., Susannah, W19369
Eleazer, Ct., N.Y., S23420
John, N.Y., Rhoda, W24981; BLWt. W24981; BLWt.12573-160-55
Nathan, Ct., d. 10/1844, Hannah, W22226; BLWt.8017-160-55
SLAY, Thomas, S.C., S16540
SLAYTON, Ebenezer, Mass., S6109

SLAYTON (continued)
Jesse, Mass., Betsy/Elizabeth, W19368
SLEAD, John, Ct., S36331
John, Cont., Va., S14479
SLEATH, John, Cont., Va., Anna Parsons, former wid., W7980
SLEDD, John, Va. See SLEAD
John, Va., d. 6/24/1827, Charity W6075
SLEDGE, Jesse, Va., R9657
SLEEPER, Benjamin, Cont., N.H., S43144
John, Mass., Navy, R.I., S18207
Lois, former wid. of James Corbin, Mass., which see
Moses, N.H., Betsey, W22230
Robert, N.H., S17895
SLEET, James, Va., Rachel, R9658
SLEETH, David W., Va., S6111
SLEIGH, John, Pa., R9659
SLEIGHT, Abraham, N.Y., S22995
James, N.Y., S14475
SLEVOGHT, Christian, Von Heer's Dragoons, BLWt.13716. Iss. 11/15/1791. No papers
SLEW, Philip, R.I., BLWt.3510. Iss. 7/3/1795. No papers
SLEWMAN, John, See SLUMAN
SLICHTER, Henry, Pa., R9655
SLICK, William, Md., S22992
SLIEGER, Philip, Hazen's Regt., BLWt.13736. Iss. 4/18/1792 to John Kanter, ass. of Mathias Roland, Admr. No papers
SLIKER, Lucas, Pa., S32523
SLINGERLAND, Peter, N.Y., S9485
SLITER, William, N.Y., S28885
SLITOR, James, N.Y., Fanny, R9660
SLOAN, Bryant, Va. See SLONE
David, Mass., BLWt.5010. Iss. 3/25/1790
David, Mass., S33683
David, Mass., S42012
David, Pa., BLWt.320-200
Ezekiel, Mass., S42013
George, Mass., S14474
George T., Navy, S.C. res. & agcy. b. Ireland, Mary, W22231; BLWt.31713-160-55
Hugh, N.J., BLWt.7789 & 8705. Iss. 2/10/1792. No papers
Israel, Mass., S14478
James, Mass., Phebe, W19044
James, N.C., b. Pa., Frances, R9662
James, Pa., S40439
John, Cont., N.Y., Bethia Bump, former wid., W18675
John, N.C., b. Pa., S1590
John, Pa., BLWt.10406. Iss. 7/9/1789. No papers
John, Pa., Ind. Wars 1791-95, Lavinia/Lavina, R9664
John, S.C., S18206
Joseph, N.H. See SLOANE
Joseph, Va., R9663
Robert, Crane's Cont. Art., Mass., BLWt.5111. Iss. 6/15/1797 to Simeon Wyman. No papers
Samuel, N.C., Elizabeth, R9661

SLOAN (continued)
Sturgin/Sturgeon, Mass., Rachel, W3172. BLWt.1916-200-Lt. Iss. 2/27/1795 to Sturgis Sloan
Thomas, N.C., b. Pa., S32522
William, Mass., S21487
William, Vt., res. N.H., Sarah, W19042
SLOANE, Joseph N.H., Vt., Temperance, W19041
Robert, N.C., S7523
SLOAT, Philip, N.J., Sally, W6076 BLWt.31719-160-55
William, N.Y. See SLUTT
SLOCOMB, John C., N.C. See SLOCUMB
Joshua, Mass. See SLOCUMB
William, Mass., S30107
SLOCUM, Abel, Privateer, R.I., Mariam Potter, former wid., R8376
Edward, R.I., S33682
John, Cont., R.I., Sarah, W22227
Peleg, R.I., Elizabeth, W22228
Primus/Prime, R.I., S39844
William, R.I., S21976
SLOCUMB, Ezekiel, N.C., S7526
John Charles, N.C., S31966
Joshua, Mass., Lucy, W17824
SLONE, Briant, Va., S11406
William, Va., S7528
SLONECKER, John, Pa., S4848
SLOOP, Joseph, Md., BLWt.11689. Iss. 10/6/1794 to Henry Purdy ass. No papers
SLOOT, William, N.Y. See SLUTT
SLOPE, Thomas, Va., BLWt.12548 & 14079. Iss. 5/13/1794. No papers
SLOPER, Henry, N.H., S16528
SLOTE, Peter G., N.Y., S33755
Philip, N.J. See SLOAT
SLOTERBACK, Margaret, former wid. of John Camp, Pa., which see
SLOTTERBACK, Henry, Pa. agcy. Dis. No papers
Margaret, Pa. See John CAMP
SLOTTERBARK, George, Pa., S40440
SLOUGH, Jacob, not Rev. War, Pa. N.W. Ind. Wars 1794. Old War Inv. File 3919
SLOUGHTER, Dedluff, Hazen's Reg BLWt.13734. Iss. 6/28/1791. No papers
John, N.Y., S42313
SLOUT, Philip, N.J., Elizabeth, W19040
SLOUTER, Jacob, N.Y., BLWt.1064-100
John, N.Y., BLWt.7725. Iss. 10/11/1790. No papers
John, N.Y., S14481
John, N.Y. See SLOUGHTER
SLOVER, Daniel, N.J., S919
Isaac, N.J., S913
James, N.J., S921
John, Sea Service, N.J., Margaret W6205; BLWt.10297-160-55
SLOWMELK, Henry, Pa., BLWt.10461. Iss. 11/1/1790(?) to Wm. Lane, ass. No papers
SLOWTER, Andrew, N.Y., S42311; BLWt.1522-100
SLUMAN, John, Cont., Mass., BLWt.

SLUMAN (continued)
1799-300
SLUSHER, John, Md., R9666
SLUTHOUR, Anthony, Cont., Pa., S40441
SLUTS, John, Md., Catharine, R9667
SLUTT, Peter, N.Y., BLWt.7754. Iss. 2/2/1791. No papers
William, N.Y., Susannah, W19370; BLWt.13199-160-55
SLUYTER, Cornelius, N.Y., S22994
Daniel, N.Y., S11407
SLY, Samuel, N.Y., S23421
William, N.Y., R9668
SLYE, William, Md., S1479
SLYTER, Nicholas, N.Y., BLWt.7802 Iss. 6/5/1790 to Jeremiah V. Renselar, ass. No papers
SMACK, Christian, Hazen's Regt., BLWt.13742. Iss. 8/10/1789 to Richard Platt, ass. No papers
SMALL, Andrew, Pa., S3945
Daniel, Mass., S28888. Sarah Small, wid. was pensioned as former wid. of Allison Libbee, Mass., which see
Daniel, Mass., S28890
Daniel, Mass., S32529
Daniel, Mass., S37425
Daniel Jr., Mass., Mary, W2012; BLWt.3614-160-55
Elisha, Mass., S37416
Elisha, Mass., Priscilla, W25013 BLWt.6116-160-55
Ephraim, Mass., Dorcas, W22269
George, N.Y., Elizabeth, W2259; BLWt.27656-160-55
Henry, Mass., Elizabeth, W22253
James, Cont., Mass., S17098
James, Pa., Margaret, W6080
Jeremiah, Mass., S37417
John, N.C., S7537
Nehemiah, Mass., R9669
Samuel, Cont., Mass., N.H., S43147
Samuel, Mass., S30114
William, Mass., S29462
William, N.H., Patience, R9670
Zachariah, Mass., S37424
SMALLEDGE, Samuel, Mass., Elizabeth/Eliza, W25014
SMALLEY, David, Va., S4865
Isaac, N.J., S4866
Isaiah, N.Y., S42331; BLWt.536-160-55
Jacob, N.J., Elizabeth, W6081; BLWt.26143-160-55
Reuben, Vt., S14521
Thomas, N.Y., BLWt.7782. Iss. 3/24/1795. No papers
SMALLING, Jacob, Ct., N.Y., Mary, R9671
SMALLWOOD, Bean/Beane, Va., Elizabeth, W8738
John, Md., BLWt.11713. Iss. 2/1/1790. No papers
John, N.J., S34508
William, Md., BLWt.11701. Iss. 8/14/1797 to James de Baufre, ass. No papers
William, Md., BLWt.656-1100

SMALLWOOD (continued)
William, Va., S3946
SMART, Caleb, N.H., S43151
Dudley, N.H., S15667
Elijah, N.H., Ruth, W22274
John, Mass., BLWt.5069. Iss. 2/27/1790 to Theodosius Fowler, ass. No papers
Jonathan, N.H., Patty, W11467
Laban, N.C., S31375
Moses, N.H., S43148
Nathaniel, N.H., S43152; BLWt. 732-100
Richard, N.H., S37406
Samuel, N.H., Eunice, W25030; BLWt.13013-160-55
Thomas, Pa., S6123
William, Cont., N.H., S49268
SMAW, John, Navy, Va., S42342
SMEAD, Darius, N.H., S35075
Joseph, Mass., Sarah Cook, former wid., BLWt.101355-160-55
Samuel, Mass., S18605
SMEDES, Aldert, N.Y., S11415
SMEDLEY, Jedidiah/Jedediah, Mass., Ruth, W11481
SMEE, Isaac, N.J., S14496
SMELL, Philip, Pa., S11414
SMELLING, Assa, Mass., BLWt.5067 Iss. 7/21/1789 to Jonathan Cass. No papers
SMELTZER, John, Pa., BLWt.10355. Iss. 7/9/1789 (on file "not delivered"). No papers
SMETHERS, John, See SMOTHERS
SMICK, Christian Carl, Pa., Elizabeth, W3362
John, N.J., S34511
Reinard, Pa., BLWt.10457. Iss. 9/19/1795. No papers
William, N.J., R9672
SMIDT, Joseph, Pa., S7543
SMILEY, David, Mass., S43164; BLWt.5216-160-55
James, Mass., S34504
John, Pa., S23424
John, Pa., R17910
Robert, N.J., BLWt.8724. Iss. 12/21/1799. No papers
Robert, N.J., S34489
Samuel, Pa., S40472
William, Mass., Hannah, W13914
SMITH, Aaron, Ct., res. of Haddam, Middlesex Co., Ct. in 1824 at age 87,S20966
Aaron, Ct., res. N.Y.City in 1830 Litchfield, Ct. in 1831. R20435
Aaron/Aran, Cont. Ct., Enl. at Washington, Ct., res. Middlefield Otsego Co., N.Y. in 1818 age 63. S42346
Aaron, Cont., Mass., b. Hardwick, Mass. 9/24/1758, there in 1775, res. Rutland Co., Vt. in 1832 at age 73. S19095
Aaron, Cont. Mass., b. 4/1759, d. 6/19/1824, enl. at Worcester, Mass., res. in 1818 at Cornish, Cheshire Co., N.Y., Huldah, W16729
Aaron, Cont., N.C., b. 4/5/1765, d. 3/1/1841, res. in 1818 Anderson Co., Tenn., Agnes, R9681

SMITH (continued)

Aaron, Mass., b. at Needham, Norfolk Co., Mass., 10/5/1756, d. 4/26/1833, S19097

Aaron, Mass., b. 2/1760, res. at enl. Hadley, Hampshire Co., Mass., res. in 1818 Madison, N.Y., later in Ohio & Wis., d. 9/23/1838, Lydia, S38388

Aaron, N.H., Dis. No papers. Report to Secy. of War, printed in 1838, lists this sold. as res. Cheshire Co., N.H., ensign in Col. Bedell's Regt. Pensioned 11/18/1786

Aaron, S.C., d. 8/5/1850, Elizabeth, R9718

Aaron, S.C., Lt. of S.C. Line; BLWt.2264-200

Aaron, Va., BLWt.12556. Iss. 12/13/1791 to Francis Graves, ass. No papers

Abel, Ct., b. at Brookfield, Fairfield Co., Ct. 5/20/1757, d. 4/27/1849, Sarah, W11479

Abel, Ct., Cont., Mass., b. 10/18/1750. Enl. in Mass., res. in 1818 Windham, Greene Co., N.Y., S43156

Abel, Ct., R.I., res. N.Y. City in 1820 at age 56. S43154

Abijah, Ct., res. at enl. Ashford, Ct., d. 12/9/1831, Judith, R9783

Abisha, Cont., Ct., b. at Haddom, Ct., d. 12/9/1831, S18226

Abisha, Mass., b. Norton, Bristol Co., Mass., 5/8/1761, there at enl., and in 1832. S18603

Abner, Ct., b. Lyme, Ct., 1757, there at enl., res. at Marlow, Cheshire Co., N.H. in 1832, S18232

Abner, Mass., b. Needham, Mass. in 1763, there at enl., res. Dublin, Cheshire Co., N.H. in 1832, S17103

Abner, Mass., enl. at Pelham, Mass., res. Irasburgh, Orleans Co., Vt. in 1818 at age 52, d. 9/11/1825, Sarah, S41176

Abner, N.Y., res. at enl. Westchester Co., N.Y., res. New York City in 1832 age 74. S14527

Abraham, Ct., b. at Woodbridge, Ct. 5/30/1760, res. at enl. Goshen, Ct., res. in 1833 Woodbury, Litchfield Co., Ct., S18225

Abraham, Mass., b. 4/1762, at Lynn Essex Co., Mass., there at enl., res. in 1832 Farmington, Kennebec Co., Me., d. 4/3/1853, S15988

Abraham, N.J., BLWt.8720. Iss. 11/16/1791 to Adam Nutt, ass. No papers

Abraham, N.J., res. Cumberland Co. N.J. in 1818 age 56, res. Cincinnati, Ohio in 1821, S40452

Abraham, N.Y., b. at Hardis, Sussex Co., N.J. in 1760, res. at enl. Warwick, Orange Co., N.Y., res. in 1832 Providence, Saratoga Co., N.Y., d. 8/24/1837, Rachel, W16409

SMITH (continued)

Abraham, N.Y., Sea Service, res. in Bolton, Vt. in 1818 age 61; d. 3/7/1825, W25003

Abraham, Pa., b. Md., 4/11/1755, res. at enl. Northumberland Co., Pa., res. in 1833 Salem, Mercer Co., Pa., S6120

Abraham, S.C., b. 3/12/1754 on Neuse River, N.C., res. at enl. on Broad River, S.C., res. in 1833 Montgomery Co., Mo., R9677 bram, Mass., res. at enl. Middleton, Essex Co., Mass., b. ca. 1755, res. in 1844, Branford Merrimack Co., N.H., S17105

Abram, N.J., res. at enl. Sussex Co., N.J., d. 1779 in Northampton Co., Pa., Elizabeth Gibbs, former wid., W17014

Absalom, N.J., b. 1754 or 1756 in N.J., res. in 1832 Williamsburg, Clermont Co., Ohio, d. 12/28/1834, Susan, W4807

Adam, Cont., Md. res. at enl. Hagerstown, Md., res. in 1819 Huntington Co., Pa., age 66, S40455

Adam, N.H., b. Bedford, Hillsborough Co., N.H. 8/3/1758, there at enl. & in 1838, Anne, d. in 1805, R9679

Adam, Pa., R9680

Albertson, N.Y., res. in 1832 Falesburgh, Sullivan Co.,N.Y., R9683

Alexander, Cont., Mass., enl. at Weston, Middlesex Co., Mass., res. in 1837 Grafton, Worcester Co., Mass. age 74, S30111

Alexander, Ga., S.C., b. York Co. Pa. 1759, res. at enl. Columbia Co., Ga., res. in 1833 Merriwether Co., S16530

Alexander, Md., BLWt.2052-300-Surgn's Mate. Iss. 2/8/1790 to Nath. Fanning, ass. Certified at W.O. 1/18/1813. No papers

Alexander, Mass., in Frederick Co., Va. in 1834 age 76, S19468

Alexander, Pa., b. 10/15/1761 in N.J., d. 6/25/1836, res. at enl. Northumberland Co., Pa., res. 1832 Lycoming Co., Pa., Rebecca, W2011; BLWt.43525-160-55

Alexander Lawson, Cont., Md., d. 1/1802, Martha Jay, former wid., W4247

Allen, Ct., en. at New Haven, Ct. Res. of Plattsburgh, Clinton Co. N.Y. in 1820 age 63, S43161

Allen, Ct., Privateer, b. 1750 in East Haven, New Haven Co., Ct., res. at enl. & in 1834 Branford, New Haven Co., Ct., S17686

Ambrose, Ct., BLWt.6491. Iss. 10/?/1789 to Theodosius Fowler, ass. No papers

Ambrose, Ct. Sea Service, Dis. No papers. See Am. State Papers, Class 9, p.80. Wounded in his right hand by a nine pound shot,

SMITH (continued)

which fractured the bone of his middle finger, 8/1776, at Toppon Bay

Ambrose, Va., b. 3/1/1756. Enl. King & Queen Co., Va., res.in 1833 Logan Co., Ky., S31373

Amos, Ct., b. Lyme, Ct., there at enl., in 1832 res. of Greensboro, Orleans Co., Vt. age 75, S22518

Amos, Ct., b. New London, Ct., 5/5/1757, there at enl., d. 3/17/1836 at Shohone, N.Y., Lydia W24989

Amos, Ct., b. 2/26/1757 at Nine Partners, Dutchess Co., N.Y., res. at enl. Sharon,Ct., res. in 1834 Lewiston, Niagara Co., N.Y., R9685

Amos, Mass., b. 7/5/1762, New Marlborough, Berkshire Co., Mass., there at enl., res. in 1834 Whitestown, Oneida Co., N.Y., S7553

Amos, Mass., in 1829 age 64, res. at Bradford, N.H., where he died 5/12/1832. Wife Eunice d. 5/26/1832, S17687

Amos, Mass., b. Holden, Worcester Co., Mass., d. there 12/17/1825, Sarah, R9850

Amos, Mass., d. 1808, BLWt.1598-100

Amos, R.I., b. So. Kingston, Washington Co., R.I., there up to 1832, S19092

Andrew, Ct., b. Milford, New Haven Co., Ct., 8/14/1762, there up to 1833, S17097

Andrew, Hazen's Regt. BLWt.13729. Iss. 4/30/1792 to Charlotte Smith, ass. No papers

Andrew, Mass., N.Y., b. 12/25/1749, raised on Mohawk River near Schenectady, N.Y., enl. at Stockbridge, Mass., res. 1836 Fairfield Co., Ohio, R9686

Andrew, N.J., b. 8/25/1753 in Hopewell Twp., Hunterdon Co., N.J., there at enl.,in 1834 res. of Romulus, Seneca Co., N.Y., S28889

Andrew, S.C., BLWt.12594 & 13705 Iss. 7/13/1795. No papers

Anthony, Ct., b. 3/15/1752 at West Haven, New Haven Co., Ct., res. at enl. & in 1832 Waterbury New Haven Co., Ct. & d. there 3/3/1838, Esther, W17844

Anthony, N.J., b. 1753 in Monmouth Co., N.J., there at enl., res. in 1832 Greene Co., Pa., d. 8/11/1835-1836, S4856

Anthony, Pa., enl. at Amboy, N.J.; in 1832 res. of Colrain Twp., Bedford Co., Pa., age 67, S23929

Aquilla, Md., b. 3/30/1759. Enl. at Fredericktown, Md., in 1835 Lewis Co., Ky., d. 4/28/1839, Catharine, W8740

Archibald, N.Y., BLWt.7738. Iss.

SMITH (continued)
10/7/1789 to Benjamin Tallmadge, ass. No papers
Arthur, N.C., res. of Sumter Dist. S.C. in 1837, R9690
Arthur, R.I., BLWt.3503 & 14155. Iss. 1/11/1800 to Sarah Smith, heir. No papers
Asa, Ct., Cont., b. 2/8/1761 at Glastonbury, Ct., there at enl., res. of Floyd Co., Ind. in 1834, S32528
Asa, Mass., b. 11/23/1753 at Montague, Hampshire Co., Mass., & there at enl., res. in 1843 Athol, Warren Co., N.Y. S14498
Asa, Mass., b. 5/7/1752 at Belchertown, Hampshire Co., Mass., there at enl., in 1839 res. of Halifax, Windham Co., Vt., d. 2/13/1835, S15986
Asa, Mass., b. 11/5/1744 at Boxford, Mass., there at enl.,in 1832 res. of Vershire, Orange Co., Vt., S22519
Asa, Mass., b. 9/?/1758, enl. at Sandesfield, Mass., res. 1820 in Junius, Seneca Co., N.Y., S43160
Asahel, Green Mt. Boys, Vt., b. 10/5/1756 in Farmington, Ct., res. at enl. Windsor, Windsor Co., Vt. there in 1832, S21979
Asaph, Sheldon's Cavalry, Ct., BLWt.6512. Iss. 6/25/1789. No papers
Asaph, Cont., Ct., enl. at Wethersfield, Ct., res. in 1818 at Berlin, Ct., age 68, S36323
Asher, Ct., res. of Norfolk, Litchfield Co., Ct. in 1824 age 67, d. 1/26/1838 at Norfolk, Ct., Sarah, W17834
Asher, Mass., in 1818 res. of Amherst, Hampshire Co., Mass., age 58, d. 1/20/1827, Anna, W26479
Augustine, Va., b. Westmoreland Co., Va., d. Nelson Co., Va., 12/1/1832 ca. 80 yrs. Res. at enl. Amherst Co., Va., S19466
Aury, N.Y., Gertrude, W15946
Austin, Ct., enl. at Stamford, Ct., in 1820 res. Genesee Co., N.Y. age 66, d. 12/19/1846 in Oswego Co., N.Y., S23426
Austin, N.C., b. 3/4/1763 in Chatham Co., N.C., res. at enl. Guilford Co., res. in 1833 Abbeville District, S.C. S21986
Austin, Va., res. of Lincoln Co. Ga., in 1818, S36318
Azariah, Ct., b. 10/30/1761 in Redding, Fairfield Co., Ct., res. at enl. & in 1832 Ridgefield, Fairfield Co., Ct., d. 5/24/1833, Alathea, W17843
Ballard, Va., BLWt.2075-300-Capt. Iss. 3/20/1792. No papers
Benjamin, Ct., b. 12/31/1761 at Canterbury, Windham Co., Ct., there at enl. & in 1832, S14530

SMITH (continued)
Benjamin, Ct., b. 4/20/1747 in Greenfield Parrish, Fairfield Co., Ct., there in 1833, S17099
Benjamin, Ct., d. 4/24/1834, res. Windham, Windham Co., Ct., Amelia, d. 4/23/1846, R9684
Benjamin, Cont., Ct., enl. at Pomfret, Ct., res. in 1818 Bethel, Windsor Co., Vt. age 64, S41175
Benjamin, Cont., Ct., b. in East Haven, New Haven Co., Ct., d. there 3/22/1794, Lydia, R9792
Benjamin, Cont., Mass., b. in Stoughton, Mass., 7/17/1756, there at enl., res. in 1832 Hope, Waldo Co., Me., d. 8/6/1843, Anna, W22263
Benjamin, Cont., N.Y., b. 7/2/1762 at Smithtown, L.I., res. at enl. Poundridge, Westchester Co., N.Y. City in 1834, S14522
Benjamin, Ga. or S.C., R---
Benjamin, Ga., Va., enl. in Chesterfield Co., Va., there in 1820 age 66, S38387
Benjamin, Md., res. 1828 Nelson Co., Ky., S46547
Benjamin, Mass., res. in 1818 Greenville, Greene Co., N.Y., age 60, d. 9/14/1830, Rachel, W22267
Benjamin, Mass., b. 12/8/175?, enl. from Sandesfield, Berkshire Co., Mass., d. there 4/9/1826, Phebe, R9825
Benjamin, Mass., N.H., b. 1757 at North Hampton, N.H., there at enl. res. in 1832 New Hampton, N.H., S17102
Benjamin, Mass., War 1812, res. in 1818 Needham, Norfolk Co., Mass. age 53, res. in 1820 Woodstock, Ct., later Springfield, Natuck, & Grafton, Mass., d. in Hopkinton, Mass., 6/19/1863, Jerusha, W11470; BLWt.13881-160-55
Benjamin, N.H., BLWt.3468. Iss. 8/26/1790 to M. Cutler, ass. No papers
Benjamin, N.H., BLWt.3476. Iss. 3/25/1790. No papers
Benjamin, N.H., BLWt.3499. Iss. 6/17/1793 to Ephraim True, ass. No papers
Benjamin, N.H., enl. in Temple, N.H., res. 1818 of Dublin, Cheshire Co., N.H. age 66, S43146
Benjamin, N.H., res. in 1818 Wentworth, Grafton Co., N.H. age 62, d. 7/14/1838, Rebecca, W16073
Benjamin, N.H., b. Durham, N.H., res. in 1832 of Newport, Penobscot Co., Me. age 74, d. 12/3/1837, Elizabeth, W25020
Benjamin, N.Y., BLWt.7770. Iss. 7/9/1790 to Theodosius Fowler, ass. No papers
Benjamin, N.Y., res. at enl. on L.I., N.Y., d. 5/1833. Abba/Abigail, R9674
Benjamin, N.C., res. at enl.

SMITH (continued)
Dobbs Co., N.C. & there in 1832 age 73 when it was called Wayne Co., d. 2/23/1840, S7541
Benjamin, N.C., d. 3/15/1785, widow's res. Franklin Co., N.C. (Frances Mills former wid.), W17138
Benjamin, N.C., b. Rowan Co., N.C. in 1763, there at enl. res. in 1833 Tipton Co., Tenn., R9694
Benjamin, N.C.(?), Johnston Co., Martha, R---
Benjamin, R.I., BLWt.3516. Iss. 11/8/1792 to Samuel Emery, ass. No papers
Benjamin, R.I., b. Hoboth, Bristol Co., Mass. in 1760, res. in 1832 Wabash Co., Ill., S32527
Benjamin, R.I., enl. at Providence R.I., res. in 1831 Westport, Essex Co., N.Y. age 76, Anne, S42341
Benjamin, R.I., res. of Johnston, Providence Co., R.I., d. there 9/5/1823, Amey, W25008
Benjamin, R.I., b. North Kingston, Washington Co., R.I. 9/27/1763, there at enl. & up to 1834, R9691
Benjamin L., Navy, N.J., b. Freehold, Monmouth Co., N.J. & there at enl., res. 1833 Wayne Co., N.Y., res.in 1840 Hillsdale, Mich., R9693
Benjamin, see Benjamin N. NESMITH
Benoni, Va., b. 1758/9 in King William Co., Va. & there at enl., in Charlotte Co., Va. in 1833, S7567
Bezaleel, Mass., res. at enl. Whately, Franklin Co., Mass., d. 3/3/1848, Jerusha, W6095; BLWt. 16145-160-55
Bill, Ct., N.Y., b. New London, Ct. in 1753, res. at enl. Middletown, Ct., res. 1832 New Lebanon, N.Y. & Rome, Oneida Co., N.Y., S14528
Billy/Biley/Bailey, Cont., N.H., b. Brentwood, N.H., age 66 in 1818, d. Cornville, Somerset Co., Me. 7/17/1831, Lydia, W17840
Bryant, N.C., b. near Winchester, Va., 8/8/1763, res. at enl. Randolph Co., N.C., res. in 1843 Marshall Co., Ala., R9699
Buckner, N.C., res. in 1832 Pickens District, S.C. age 73, d. 10/27 or 28/1851, W1325; BLWt. 31585-160-55
Caesar (colored), Mass., d. 8/21/1822, Judy, W19380
Caleb, Ct., Sea Service, res. East Haven, Ct., lost at sea about 10/1810, Sarah, W17837
Caleb, Cont.,Mass.,enl. at Hadley, Mass., d. 11/1/1818; Olive,W13910
Caleb, Green Mt. Boys, Vt., res. at enl. Wells, Rutland Co., Vt. d. Middletown, Vt., 7/10/1808 Sarah, R9851

SMITH (continued)
Caleb, N.Y., BLWt.7747. Iss. 4/19/1791 to Abel Woodhull, ass. No papers
Caleb, N.C., en. Henry Co., Va., res. in 1830 Sullivan Co., Tenn. age 60 or over. In 1818 stated that he was aged about 70, S39083
Caleb, Pa. Sea Service, Wayne's Ind. War, 1794 & on the Western Frontiers until 1812, b. Chester Co., Pa. 3/1760, there at enl., res. 1832 Jefferson Co., Ohio, R9700
Calvin, Ct., b. East Haddam, Ct., 11/28/1760, there at enl., d. at Middlefield, Hampshire Co., Mass. 11/18/1832, Anna, R9688
Calvin, Mass., BLWt.1889-500-Col. Iss. 4/1/1790. No papers
Catharine, former wid. of Newbegin Harrison, Mass., which see
Charles, Ct., b. Stamford, Fairfield Co., Ct., 3/1/1764, there at enl., res. 1838 Greenwich, Fairfield Co., Ct., S15983
Charles, Cont., res. 1839 Wilson Co., Tenn. age 69, res. 1843 of Muller Co., Mo., S42325; BLWt. 1520-100
Charles, Cont., Mass., res. 1820 Hope, Lincoln Co., Me. age 65, d. 9/22/1841, Thankful, W24994
Charles, Cont., Mass., b. Kittery, Me., res. Lisbon, Me. in 1818 at age 63, where he d. 12/17/1831, Mary, W25000
Charles, Cont., Va., b. 6/2/1763 in Frederick Co., Va., where he enl., res. Jackson Co. in 1836, S15649
Charles, Md., d. 1787 or 88, Mary, W25002
Charles, Md. Sea Service, b. 5/19/1763 on Tilghman's Island, Talbot Co., Md., res. 1838 St. Michaels District, R9703
Charles, Mass., BLWt.4992. Iss. 1/26/1790 to John May, ass. No papers
Charles, N.J., b. Huntington Co. N.J. 12/24 or 25/1760, res. at enl. Hanover Twp., Morris Co., N.J., res. 1832 Montgomery Co., Ohio, S3932
Charles, N.C., b. Chatham Co., N.C. 3/8/1760, res. 1834 Pendleton Election Dist., S.C., S11431 BLWt.17901-160-55
Charles, N.C., b. 1758 Craven Co. N.C., res. at enl. & in 1832 Pitt Co., N.C., S45777
Charles, S.C., enl. in Fairfield or Chester Dist., S.C., d. 1/28/1845 in Cherokee Co., Ga., Elizabeth, W6122; BLWt.11067-160-55
Charles, Va., res. of Princess Anne Co., Va., S7559
Charles, Va., res. of Iredell Co. N.C. in 1821 age 72, d. 4/19/

SMITH (continued)
1840, Phebe, W4071
Charles, Va.(?), d. 1842, m. in Louisa Co., Va. in 1783, res. of wid., Nancy, S.C., R9812
Charles/Charles L.A., Va., d. 1796, R---
Christian, Cont., Md., res. 1818 Allegany Co., Md., age 66,S35076
Christian, Cont., Pa., res. in 1823 Coshocton Co., Ohio, S1486; BLWt.1122-100
Christopher, Cont., Mass., res. Needham, Norfolk Co., Mass. at age 60, S34499
Christopher, Navy, enl. at Boston Mass., res. 1830 Scituate, R.I., S39845
Christopher, N.Y., BLWt.7746 iss. 6/17/1791 to H. Fisher, admx. (Int. Dept. Archives show Hannah) No papers
Comfort, Mass., b.11/1766 Sandesfield, Berkshire Co., Mass., res. 1847 Wheatland, Monroe Co., N.Y. R9705
Comfort, former wid. of Samuel Hill/Hile Clark, N.H., which see
Conrad, Pa., res. at enl. Shafferstown, Lancaster Co., (Lebanon Co.), Pa., age 80 in 1833 & res. of Greencastle, Franklin Co., Pa., S22517
Conrad, Pa., BLWt.10332-100 iss. 1789. No papers
Conrod/Conrad, Md., enl.Baltimore Md., age 76 in 1818 & res. of Dickenson Twp., Cumberland Co., Pa., d. 1/6/1826, Annie, d. 9/5/1843, W3309; BLWt.2408-100
Cornelius, N.Y., res. 1838 Mohawk Montgomery Co., N.Y. age 94, S22996
Cuff, Ct., res. Haddam, Ct. in 1818 age 54, Mercy, S36321
Curtis, Cont., Vt., b. 10/11/1761 enl. at Rutland Vt., res. in 1818 Murray, Genesee Co., N.Y., d. 2/1828; Mary, W4588
Cushing, Navy, Mass., res. of Falmouth, Barnstable Co., Mass. in 1830, S34494
Cyril, Mass. b. 1/10/1757 at Rehoboth, Bristol Co., Mass. & enl. there, res. in 1832 Attleborough, Mass., S18227
Dan, Ct., Cont., res. at enl. Sharon, Litchfield Co., Ct., res. in 1818 Rutland, Vt. age 60, d. 2/15/1833, Betsey, d. 9/23/1845 W5174
Daniel, Ct., b.East Haven, Ct., 9/23/1762 & there at enl., res. New Haven in 1832, S17681
Daniel, Ct., res. Preston, New London Co., Ct. in 1820 age 74, S36319
Daniel, Ct., res. Stamford, Ct., d. North Castle, Westchester Co. N.Y. 12/18/1831, Mary, W19070; BLWt.26754-160-55

SMITH (continued)
Daniel, Ct.,Cont., res. in 1818 Marcelus, Onondago Co., N.Y., age 62, S45154
Daniel, Ct., R.I., b. Stonington New London Co., Ct. 10/7/1753, res. at enl. Preston/Stonington Ct., res. 1830 Chatham, in 1832 Columbia, Herkimer Co., & in 1833 Niagara Co., N.Y., S11416
Daniel, Cont., Mass., res. 1818 Cambridge, Mass., age 60, S34509
Daniel, Cont.N.H.,Navy, b. Berwick Me., res. Monmouth, Kenebec Co., Me. in 1818 age 61, S37423
Daniel, Cont., N.Y., enl. at Montgomery, Ulster Co., N.Y.,res. New York City in 1832 age 72, S28886
Daniel, Md., b. York Co.,Pa. 9/21/1756, res. Frederick Co., Md. in 1832, S7568
Daniel, Md. See SMYTH
Daniel, Md.,d.prior 9/5/1809, former wid. Rebecca Cook, BLWt. 1513-100
Daniel, Mass., BLWt.5078 iss. 8/26/1790 to Manassas Cutter. No papers
Daniel, Mass., b. Shirley, Middlesex Co., Mass. 10/1/1762 & there at enl., res. Pemberton Island, Me. in 1832, S17101
Daniel, Mass., b. 5/1754 at Ipswich, Essex Co., Mass. & there at enl. and in 1832, S30109
Daniel, N.H., res. at enl. Seabrook, Rockingham Co., N.H., d. 6/1820, Molly, W16074
Daniel, N.H., res. at enl. Kingston, N.H., d. Machiasport, Me. 3/11/1847, Phebe, R9826
Daniel, N.J., b. New Foundland, Bergen Co., N.J. & there at enl. res. Parma, Monroe Co., N.Y. in 1834, R9707
Daniel, N.Y., b. 4/1/1744 in Brookhaven, Suffolk Co., N.Y., there at enl. & in 1832, S14513
Daniel, N.C.,b. 1753/1754 Va., at enl. res. Burke Co., N.C. and in 1835, S7550
Daniel, N.C., res. Rowan & Burke Cos., N.C., d. 5/17/1824, Mary, W6127
Daniel, Moylan's Dragoons, Pa., BLWt.10435 iss. 2/14/1791 to Alexander Power, ass. No papers
Daniel, Pa., d. 5/12/1827, Elizabeth, d. 10/9/1837, R9720
Daniel, Pa.,Va.,b.1755 at Redding Pa. & there 1st enl., 2nd enl. Frederick Co., Va.,res. Harrison Co., Va. in 1833, S18596
Daniel, R.I.,b.Gloucester, Providence Co.,R.I. 4/6/1756 & enl. there, res. Burrellville, Providence Co., R.I., d. 5/27/1835, Thankful, W22241
Daniel, Vt., B. 4/2/1755, res. at enl. Rutland, Vt., d. 5/14/1832 Sarah, R9852
Daniel/Daniel J.,Wayne's Legion

SMITH (continued)
res. Lee Co., Va., d. 8/28/1830 Sally, R17995
Daniel G., N.J., b. 4/10/1760 in Lancaster Co.,res. at enl. Bergen Co.,N.J. & in 1844, S3942
David, Ct., BLWt.1941-400-Major iss. 9/16/1784. No papers
David, Ct.,b.2/16/1763 Stamford, Fairfield Co., Ct. & there at at enl. and in 1832, S17683
David, Ct., b. 3/26/1764 at Vernon, East Windsor, Hartford Co., Ct., there in 1832, S31968
David, Ct., res. Washington Co., Ohio in 1818 age 72, S40468
David, Ct., res. at enl. Derby, New Haven Co., Ct., res. 1832 Auburn, Geauga Co., Ohio, age 69 and d. there 11/19/1852, Hannah, W6123
David, Ct., b. Fairfield, Ct. 6/6/1757 & there at enl., d. 5/31/1835 in Pabakill, Ulster Co., N.Y., Lois, W25016
David, Ct., b. 1758 at Canterbury Ct. & there at enl., res. Braintree, Orange Co., Vt. in 1832, d. 3/23/1840, Mary, R9797
David, Ct., b. 11/30/1756 Milford, Ct. & there at enl. & 1832, d.11/7/1841, Mary, d.12/7/1843, R9798
David, Ct., res. Wayne Co., Ohio in 1829, age 75, Mary, R21792
David, Cont., BLReg.84965-1850
David, Cont., Mass., res. at enl. New Marlborough, Berkshire Co., Mass., res. in 1818 Brutus, Cayuga Co., N.Y., d. 8/30/1822, Abigail, R9675
David, Mass., b. 3/4/1756 in Dedham, Mass. & there at enl., res. New London, Merrimack Co., N.H. in 1832, S11408
David, Mass., res. Lyons, Ontario Co., N.Y. in 1830, Lucretia, S42339; BLWt.109-60-55 & 1-100-55
David, Mass., res. in 1820 Houndsfield, Jefferson Co., N.Y. age 57, Sarah, S42344
David, Mass., res. Oneida Co., N.Y. in 1818 ae 57, d. 7/8/1844 S42351
David, Mass., b. 1753 Sturbridge, Worcester Co., Mass. & there at enl., res. in 1832 Otego, Otego Co., N.Y., R9709
David, Mass., BLWt.841-100. This claim was improperly allowed on service of a man who was alive in 1855, see David SMITH, Mass., S42339
David, N.H., b. Candia, N.H., son of Joseph. Age 16 at enl. when res. of Wentworth, Grafton Co., N.H., d. 11/1799. Mary Poole former wid., W21987. Her 2nd husb. was John Poole, which see
David, N.H., res. in 1820 Burncoat Island, Handcock Co., Me. age 60. He d. 5/27/1840, Betsey, W26484; BLWt.31321-161-55

SMITH (continued)
David, N.Y., BLWt.7780. Iss. 4/26/1791 to Henry Ludlam, ass. No papers
David, N.Y., b. Ridgefield, Ct. 11/25/1751, res. at enl. & in 1833 Salem, Westchester Co., N.Y., S23922
David, N.Y., b. 2/1760, son of John, res. in 1818 Crown Point Essex Co., N.Y., S42333
David, N.Y., b. 3/12/1761, enl. at Fredericksburgh, N.Y., res. in 1818 Fairfield Co., Ohio, d. Delaware Co., Ohio, 10/5/1823, Chloe Main former wid., W4272; BLWt.7761-100. Iss. 12/15/1790 to John Tryon, ass.
David, N.C., res. Cumberland Co. N.C. in 1820 age 63, enl. in Duplin Co., N.C., S42016
David, N.C. War 1812, b. 10/9/1753 in Anson Co., N.C., d. 12/3/1835 in Hinds Co., Miss. Obedience, W25006
David, R.I., b. 12/1761 at Providence, R.I., son of Joshua, res. Londonderry, Windham Co., Vt. in 1832, S18600
David, S.C., served from Abbeville District, S.C., d. Walton Co., Ga. 3/27/1833, Rebecca, W6082
David, Va., enl. in Westmoreland Co., Va. (later in Pa.) res. Henry Co., Ky. in 1818 age 69, d. 8/1/1823, S37418
David E., Pa. Sea Service, b. 11/2/1755 in Chester Co., Pa. & there at enl., res. Mt. Pleasant Twp., Jefferson Co., Ohio in 1832, R9710
Deliverance, N.Y., b. 3/6/1757 at Great Nine Partners, Dutchess Co. N.Y. & there at enl., d. 10/18/1838 at Bern, Albany Co., N.Y., Sarah, W26483; BLWt.34835-160-55
Dennis, Pa., b. Pa., 5/13/1756, res. at enl. Washington Co., Pa. d. in Green Co., Pa. 8/29/1829, Elizabeth, R9721
Doctor, N.Y., b. May 1764 in Greenwich Twp., Ct., res. at enl. Salem, Westchester Co., N.Y., res. in 1832 Westerlo, Albany Co., N.Y., S11425
Dominicus, Cont., Mass., res. in 1818 Biddleford, York Co., Me., S37420
Dow, Ct., b. 3/12/1737 in Branford New Haven Co., Ct. & there at enl. res. in 1832 Middlefield, Otsego Co., N.Y., S14519
Drew, Md., d. 2/12/1815, R22851
Drury, N.C., res. Greenville Dist. S.C. in 1832 age 84, R9713
Duncan, N.Y., BLWt.7791. Iss. 9/7/1790. No papers
Eben/Ebenezer, N.H., res. in 1821 Brentwood, Rockingham Co., N.H. age 55, S43165
Ebenezer, Ct., ?, m. Lucy Stephens,

SMITH (continued)
d. in Rutland Co., Vt. 1835
Ebenezer, Ct., b. 7/27/1763 in Stamford, Fairfield Co., Ct., there at enl. & in 1833, S17108
Ebenezer, Ct., b. 10/3/1761 at Ridgefield, Fairfield Co., Ct., there at enl.,res. Elmira, Tioga Co., N.Y. in 1832, d. 4/1844, Elizabeth, R9722
Ebenezer, Ct., Cont., res. in 1820 Cortland Co., N.Y. age 66, lived in Onondaga Co., N.Y. in 1818, S42343
Ebenezer, Ct., Cont., res. at enl. Fairfield, Ct., d. there 8/14/1832, Naomi, W11471
Ebenezer A., Del. Line, Asst. Surg., Mary, File No. 9299
Ebenezer, Mass., BLWt.1901-300-Capt. Iss. 8/22/1789. No papers
Ebenezer, Mass., b. 12/23/1756/57 at South Reading, Mass. & enl. there, res. Londonderry, Windham Co., Vt. in 1832, S21981
Ebenezer, Mass., b. 5/5/1760 at Tyringham, Mass., res. at enl. & in 1833 Great Barrington, Mass., S30110
Ebenezer, Mass., b. Middleborough, Mass., res. Augusta, Me. in 1818 age 61, Mary (in 1820), S37413; BLWt.216-100
Ebenezer, Mass., son of Abner, b. Ct., d. in Arcadia, Wayne Co., N.Y., m. 3/16/1844, res. at enl. Murraysfield (Chester), Mass., Sally, W1324; BLWt.9411-160-55
Ebenezer, Mass., en. at New Marlborough, Berkshire Co., Mass., res. Walton, Delaware Co., N.Y. in 1818 age 57, d. 2/5/1823, Catharine d. 11/5/1840, W11465
Ebenezer, Mass., War 1812, res. Woolwich, Lincoln Co., (Me.) Mass. in 1818, age 66, d. 9/21/1824, Jennet, W1501; BLWt.1057-300
Ebenezer, Navy, R.I., res. South Kingston, Washington Co., R.I. in 1819 age 61/62, S39846
Ebenezer, N.H. See Eben
Edward, Ct., res. of New Haven, Ct., S20964
Edward, Cont., Md., enl. at Elkton, Md., res. York Co., Pa. in 1828 age 70, S40456
Edward, Cont., Pa., Navy, enl. in Lancaster, Pa., res. of Susquehanna Twp., Dauphin Co., Pa. in 1818 at age 62, S41173
Edward, Md., res. in 1818 Gorham, Ontario Co., N.Y. age 61, formerly in Baltimore Co., Md., S42323
Edward, Mass., res. of New Salem, Franklin Co., Mass. in 1818 age 55, d. 8/20/1834, Annis, W13907
Edward, N.H., enl. in Pembroke, N.H., res. in 1818 Gilmanton, Stafford Co., N.H. age 64, d. 6/6/1833, Abigail, W22248

SMITH (continued)
Edward, N.Y., res. of Franklin, Putnam Co., N.Y., d. 5/25/41 at Freetown, Cortland Co., N.Y. Demeous, d. 5/5/1848, W15854
Edward, N.C., b. Anson Co., N.C. res. Surrey Co., N.C. in 1832 age 73, S7562
Edward, Pa., enl. in Hanover Twp. Dauphin Co., Pa. & there in 1819 when ca. 60/61 yrs., S40454
Edward, Va., b. Culpeper Co., Va. 12/31/1755, & there at enl., res. in 1832 Knox Co., Tenn., S3934
Edward, Va., b. 1/27/1759 in Baltimore Co., Md., res. at enl. Frederick Co., Md., res. of Manchester Twp., Morgan Co., Ohio in 1833, S7566
Edward, Va., reared in Washington Co., Va., res. Lee Co., Va. in 1832 age 71, d. Owsley Co., Ky. 12/6/1852, Hannah, W9301; BLWt. 73591-160-55
Edward Miles, Md., b. Charles Co., Md., d. 1802, Theresa, W8736; BLWt.1800-200
Eleazer, Ct., BLWt.6426. Iss. 6/17/1793. No papers
Eleazer, Ct., Hannah Price, former wid., R8466
Eleazer, Mass., b. 4/1/1755 at Medfield, Norfolk Co., Mass. There at enl., res. Walpole, Norfolk Co., Mass. in 1832, S29467
Eli Ct., res. at enl. Litchfield, Ct., d. there 3/29/1824, Deborah, W17833
Eli, Ct., b. 10/8/1760, res. at enl. Brookfield, Ct., d. 7/17/1819 at Bridgeport, Ct., Phebe Gouge, former wid., W19520; BLWt.24753-160-55
Eli, Mass., res. Medfield, Norfolk Co., Mass. in 1818, d. there 3/21/1830 age 73, Mary C., d. 7/1/1853, R9799
Eli, Va., d. 4/19/1836, widow's res. Campbell Co., Tenn., Jane, R9751
Elijah, Ct., d. 11/21/1824, Prudence, W17829
Elijah, Ct., b. 9/1763 at Norwich, Ct., res. Lebanon, New London Co. Ct. in 1832, d. 3/24/1848, Betsey, W17835; BLWt.33755-160-55
Elijah, Ct., enl. at Ridgefield, Fairfield Co., Ct., d. Scipio, Cayuga Co., N.Y., 7/18/1848 age 88, R9717
Elijah, Ct., Mass., res. of Stafford Ct. in 1775, res. in 1778 Brimfield, Mass., d. 10/2/1824 at Sempronius, Cayuga Co., N.Y., Hannah, R9740
Elijah, Ct., N.Y. res. at enl. Spencertown, N.Y., res of Granfield, Saratoga Co., N.Y. in 1832 age 74, S14493
Elijah, Cont., Mass., N.H., b. Windsor, Ct., res. of Hanover, N.H. at enl., res. of Hatly, Lower Canada in 1832 age 78, S14492
Elijah, Md., BLWt.11684. Iss. 2/7/1790. No papers
Elijah, Md., res. Dorchester Co., Md., res. Baltimore Co., Md. in 1818 age 68, and d. there 3/10/1825, Priscilla, W9302
Elijah, Md., d. 9/15/1831 in Rockcastle Co., Ky., Margaret, R9793
Elijah, Mass., b. 1745 Sunderland or Montague, Hampshire Co., Mass. in Montague at enl., res. of Buckland, Franklin Co., Mass. in 1832, S30709
Elijah, Mass., res. at enl. Hatfield, Hampshire Co., Mass., d. 11/30/1829, Lucy, W15358
Elijah, Mass., b. 1/30/1760 at Waltham, Middlesex Co., Mass., there at enl. & in 1841, R9716
Elijah, Navy, Mass., res. at enl. in Boston, Mass., res. Great Barrington, Berkshire Co., Mass. in 1819, res. Canaan, Columbia Co., N.Y. in 1830 age 75 where he d. ca. 26 yrs. prior to 1854, Abigail, R9676. Widow's 1st husb. Moses Doud/Dowd also served in Rev. War
Elijah, N.J., Va., b.8/13/1755 in N.J., res. Hunterdon Co., N.J. in 1776, res. Washington Co., Va. in 1778; res. in 1832 Rutherford Co. Tenn., d. 3/11/1835 in Jacksonville, Ill., Lucretia Jones, former wid., W1[illegible]504; BLWt.101700-160-55
Elijah, N.Y., enl. at New Marlborough, Ulster Co., N.Y., res. Kingsbury, Washington Co., N.Y. in 1818 age 59, S42324
Elijah/Elidah, N.Y., res. at enl. Old Nackayuna, Albany Co., N.Y., d. in Columbia, Herkimer Co., N.Y., 12/14/1825 age 83, Alida, W19063
Elijah, R.I., b. 4/24/1761 at Smithfield, Providence Co., R.I. and there at enl. & in 1833, S21982
Elijah, Va., enl. in Powhatan, Cumberland Co., Va., res. Davidson Co., Tenn. in 1818 age 57, Jane, S39081
Eliphalet, Armand's Legion, BLWt. 13698. Iss. 7/9/1789. No papers
Eliphalet, Ct., b. 2/25/1761 in Fairfield, Ct. & there at enl., res. Norwalk, Fairfield Co., Ct. in 1832, d. 4/26/1836, Olive Platt former wid., W2241; BLWt. 26996-160-55
Eliphalet, Ct., Cont., Green Mt. Boys, res. in 1820 McConnellsburg, Bedford Co., Pa. age 69, d. 12/31/1839, S40457
Eliphalet, Cont., Mass., Vt., b. 11/16/1759 at Sandisfield, Berkshire Co., Mass. & there at enl., res. Allen, Allegany Co., N.Y. in 1833, S11424
Eliphalet, N.H., res. Sandwich, Strafford Co., N.H. and there at age 70 in 1832, S22997
Elisha, Mass., b. 1758 in New Bedford, Mass. & there at enl., res. Butternutt, Otsego Co., N.Y. in 1832, d. 4/23/1846 in Norwich, Chenango Co., N.Y., S23422
Elisha, Mass., enl. at New Marlborough, Berkshire Co., Mass., res. Monroe Co., Mich. in 1833, S35073
Elisha, Mass., b. Boston, Mass. 2/15/1759, res. Ashfield, Hampshire Co., Mass. at enl., d. at Pompey, Onondaga Co., N.Y., 8/8/1837, Margaret, W1093 BLWt.26223-160-55
Elisha, Mass., res. Worcester Co., Mass. at enl., d. 11/6/1805, Persis, R9822
Elisha, Mass., Vt., b. 4/3/1748 at Old Hadley, Hampshire Co., Mass., res. at enl. Stamford, Bennington Co., Vt., res. in 1833 Gerry, Chautauqua Co., N.Y., S11428
Elisha, N.Y., b. 5/1755, Frederick Town, Dutchess Co., N.Y. (later called Carmel, Putnam Co.) and there at enl., res. in 1832 Coxsackie, Green Co., N.Y., S23425
Elisha, Va., res. at enl. Culpeper Co., Va., later in S.C., d. 3/19/1832, Elizabeth, R9723
Elizabeth, former wid. of Ebenezer Clapp, Cont., Mass., which see
Elizabeth, former wid. of Abijah Northrop, N.Y., which see
Elizabeth, former wid. of John Parmly, N.C., which see
Elkanah, Ct., Mary (her name not listed as part of official file designation), S36320
Elkanah, Mass., b. 8/11/1758 in Lannton, Mass. & there at enl., d. 3/26/1840 at Grafton, Rensselaer Co., N.Y., Hepsibah, W19383
Elnathan, Cont., Ct., res. at enl. Hartford, Ct., res. Fairfield, Ct. in 1830 age 62, d. 7/5/1834, Mary, W24984; BLWt.6518-100
Elwiley, Md., S11412
Enoch, Ct., Cont., Sea Service, b. 12/29/1759, d. 12/1/1824 in N.Y. City, Hannah, W17842; BLWt. 28542-160-55
Enoch, Ct., Cont., b. 1753 in Chatham, Middlesex Co., Ct. & there up to death 3/19/1833, Lydia, S17106
Enoch, Mass., res. Virgil, Cortland Co., N.Y. in 1820 age 59, d. 3/10/1852 at Sempronius, Cayuga Co., N.Y., Abigail, W3728 BLWt.91-100 & 241-60-55

SMITH (continued)
Enoch, N.C., S.C., b. 1759 Orange Co., N.C., res. during Rev. Surry Co., N.C., & Nerberry Dist., S.C., res. Hall Co., Ga. in 1833, S31975
Enos, Ct., b. 7/8/1751 in Greenfield Parish, Fairfield, Ct. & there at enl., res. Beekman, Dutchess Co., N.Y. in 1833, res. in Germantown, Columbia Co., N.Y. in 1838, R9729
Enos, Mass., res. at enl. Belcherstown, Humphries Co., Mass., res. Chelsea, Orange Co., Vt. in 1832 age 71, S23000
Enos, Mass., b. 7/24/1749 in South Hadley, Mass., res. at enl. Ashfield, Franklin Co., Mass., res. Buckland, Enid Co., d. 3/8/1836, Hannah, W15356
Ephraim, Ct., b. 8/28/1759 at Cheshire, New Haven Co., Ct. & there at enl., res. Mendon, Monroe Co., N.Y. in 1832, S23423
Ephraim, Ct., b. 9/5/1762, Lyme, Ct. & there at enl., res. LeRay, Jefferson Co., N.Y. in 1833, d. 8/31/1837, Deborah, R9711
Ephraim, Mass., b. 1/8/1752 at Welfleet, Mass., there at enl., res. Gorham, Cumberland Co., Me. in 1832, S31972
Ephraim, Mass., res. Schoharie, Schoharie Co., N.Y. in 1824 age 59, S42322
Ephraim, Mass., b. 6/23/1758 at Medfield, Norfolk Co., Mass., d. 10/25/1839 at Westminster, Windham Co., Vt., Jerusha, W1947
Ephraim, Mass., res. in Beverly, Mass. in 1775; res. of Ipswich, Mass., d. 4/27/1789, Mary Price former wid., W22016
Eseck, R.I., b. 10/16/1758 in Providence, R.I., moved when young to Northwark, Caledonia Co., Vt., d. 6/22/1840, S15984
Esek, R.I., res. Gloucester, Providence Co., R.I., d. there 2/11/1817, Renew, W12976
Ethan, Ct., res. at enl. Stamford, Fairfield Co., Ct., d. 4/20/1819, Hannah, W17845
Ezekiel, Ct., b. 2/7/1756 in Lyme, New London Co., Ct., res. at enl. New London, Ct., res. Lyme, Ct. in 1832, S18599
Ezekiel, N.Y., b. 7/21/1751/54 in R.I., moved when young to North East, Dutchess Co., N.Y., d. 3/1/1821 in Newfield, Tompkins Co., N.Y., Elsa, W22237
Ezekiel, N.C., res. at enl. Wayne Co., N.C., res. in 1833 Lawrence Co., Ga. age 69, d. 6/1839 in Montgomery Co., Ga., Margaret/Peggy, W26480; BLWt.35690-160-55
Ezra, Ct., BLWt.1959-200-Lt. Iss. 12/18/1789 to Joshua Henshaw, ass. No papers
Ezra, Cont., Ct., res. Stamford, Fairfield Co., Ct. in 1820 age 67, S42319
Ezra, Mass., b. 1754 at Sudbury, Middlesex Co., Mass. & enl. there d. 2/22/1834, son of Henry, Phebe, W27569. Sold's. ch. were Henry, Reuben, Jesse, Ezra, Rebecca wife of John Sergeant, Ruth wife of Abram Sheldon & Lucretia wife of John Osgood.
Fleming, S.C., b. 12/1745 in Fairfax Co., Va., res. at enl. Spartanburg Co., S.C., res. Monroe Co., Ky. in 1833, S30708
Francis, Beaver & Phila. Cos., Pa. Pa. agcy., S15292
Francis, d. 12/5/1827 in D.C., age 71 yrs. 4 mos., son of James Elizabeth, R9724
Francis, Ct., N.H., b. 4/15/1762 at Norwich, Ct. & res. at enl., lived Canaan, N.H., res. Attica, Genesee Co., N.Y. in 1833, R9733
Francis, Mass., enl. at Westford, Mass., res. Rundge, Cheshire Co. N.H. in 1818 age 64, S43162
Francis, Pa., BLWt.10388-100. Iss. in 1789. No papers
Francis, Va., R9732; BLWt.2074-200 Lt. Iss. 4/26/1798. No papers
Frederic/Frederick, Ct., b. 1762 at Norwich, New London Co., Ct. res. at enl. Lebanon, New London Co., Ct. S23428
Frederick, Ct., b. 10/10/1765 at Middletown (Berlin), Ct., there at enl.,res. Manchester, Bennington Co., Vt. in 1834, S19470
Frederick, Ct., Privateer, b. 3/1/1760 in Haddam, Ct., there at enl., res. Jefferson, Schoharie Co., N.Y. in 1832, S11410
Frederick, N.Y., res. at enl. near Fort Dayton, N.Y., d. 6/11/1828 at Herkimer, N.Y., Christina W25015; BLWt.525-160-55
Frederick, N.C., b. 12/25/1755, enl. in Rowan Co., N.C., res. Barren Co., Ky. in 1832, S31381
Frederick, Vt., b. 12/20/1743 in Chatham, Ct., res. at enl. Stafford, Orange Co., Vt., there d. 9/11/1832. S----
Gabriel, Ct., b. 3/11/1761 at Stamford, Fairfield Co., Ct., there at enl., res. Lyons Wayne Co., N.Y. in 1832, S16251
Gad, Mass., native of Whately, Franklin Co., Mass., there at enl., d. 1/1826, R9734
Garnett/Garnet, Va., b. 12/1762, enl. in Montgomery (Wythe) Co., Va., res. Knox Co., Tenn. in 1832, S1724
Garnett, Va., see Jared SMITH
Garret, N.Y., b. 10/6/1757 at Clarkstown, Rockland Co., N.Y. there at enl., res. Pompton Twp., Bergen Co., N.J. in 1832, S1106
Garret, N.Y., enl. at Tappan Orange (Rockland) Co., N.Y., res. in N.Y. City in 1832 age 76, d. 6/16/1847 in Florida, Montgomery Co., N.Y., Maria, W7185; BLWt.31318-160-55
Garrett, Va., See Jared SMITH
George, Cont., N.Y.,res. in 1818 Stratford, Fairfield Co., Ct. age 68, S36769; BLWt.1910-200-Lt. iss. 10/23/1790, also recorded under Wt.2572
George, Mass., b. 1761 in Rutland, Worcester Co., Mass., there at enl., res. of Worthington, Hampshire Co., Mass. in 1832, d. at Orwell, Ashtabula Co., Ohio, d. 6/17/1844, Molly, W6119; BLWt.8475-160-55
George, Mass., b. 8/25/1755 in Middleborough, Plymouth Co., Mass., moved in 1755 to New Salem, Franklin Co., Mass., d. 9/11/1832 at Hardwick, Mass., Sarah, W15351
George, Mass., res. at enl. Grafton, Worcester Co., Mass., d. 3/14/1814, Polly, W25022
George, N.J., b. 1751 in Middlesex Co., N.J., res. at enl. in Freehold Twp., Monmouth Co., N.J. & there in 1832, S755
George, N.Y., res. Walkill, Orange Co., N.Y., d. 3/1803, Mary, W15853
George, N.Y., res. at enl. Herkimer (Ft. Dayton), N.Y., d. 3/29/1809 at Herkimer, N.Y., Maria/Anna Maria, W19064
George, N.Y., b. 1764 in Orange Co., N.Y., there at enl., res. in 1836 Lycoming Co., Pa., R9736
George, N.Y., res. at enl. Palatine, N.Y., d. 3/1816, Hannah, R9741
George, N.C., b. 2/8/1761 in Wake Co., N.C., there at enl., res. in 1833 Davidson Co., Tenn.,S3930
George, N.C., b. 12/24/1763 at Roan Co., N.C., there at enl., res. in 1833 Bedford Co., Tenn., S31969
George, N.C., b. 3/11/1747, d. 4/30/1838, res. Ashe Co., N.C. in 1834, Elizabeth, R9726
George, Pa., BLWt.10395. Iss. 8/6/1792 to Henry Trumheller, ass. No papers
George, Pa., d. 7/1826, Elizabeth, R9725
George, Pa., Ind. res., R9737
George, Pa., b. 7/1/1750 in Lancaster Co., Pa., there at enl., res. in 1834 Campbell Co., Ky., R21853
George, Va., b. 5/6/1764 in Hanover Co., Va., there at enl. and in 1832, S6115
George, Va., res. in 1828 Bedford Co., Va. age 80, S38386
George Adam, Pa., enl. in Berks

SMITH (continued)
Co., Pa., R17924
George P., Va., b. 7/4/1757 in Berkeley Co., Va., res. at enl. Augusta Co., Va., res. Lewis Co., Va. in 1833, S18595
Gershom, N.Y., BLWt.7758. Iss. 9/15/1790 to James Caldwell, ass. No papers
Gideon, Ct., N.H., Vt., b.1760 at Ellington, Ct., res. during Rev. Hanover, N.H. & Hartford, Ct., res. Lyme, Grafton Co., N.H. in 1833, S11409
Gideon, Mass., N.Y.,or Vt., b. 12/28/1752, res. at enl. East Hoosick, Mass., d. 12/13/1798 at Shelburn, Chittenden Co., Vt. & about 2 yrs. later his wid., Patience, m. his brother Zadock, R9821
Gideon, N.Y., b. 1759 at Bedford Worcester Co., N.Y., there at enl., res. Oneonta, Otsego Co., N.Y. in 1832, S11419
Gideon, Pa., b. 5/28/1752 in West Fallowfield Twp., Chester Co., Pa., there at enl., res. Baldeagle Twp., Centre Co., Pa. in 1833, S22515
Godfrey, Cont., Va., enl. in Shenandoah Co., Va., res. Greenup Co., in 1819 age 57, S37426; BLWt.1006-100
Granville, Va., R17957, Va. Half Pay. N.A. Acc. No.874-050165 Half Pay Granville Smith
Gregory, See Thomas ARMISTEAD, Va.
Gregory, Cont.,Ct.,enl. New Britain/West Hartford, Ct., 1818 res. Coxsackie, Greene Co., N.Y. age 56, d. 5/13/1823, Hannah, W16408
Griffith, Pa., res. Montgomery Co., Pa. in 1833 age 69 and there at enl. when it was part of Phila. Co. & was born in that neighborhood, d. there 1/3/1843, Mary, W3467; BLWt.31721-160-55
Hannah, former wid. of Zerubbable Eager, Cont., Mass., which see
Hannah, former wid. of Isaac Thayer, Mass., which see
Hardy, N.C., b. Johnson Co., N.C. res. Laurens Co., Ga. in 1833 age 76, where he d. 2/1852. His wife Rebecca d. 8/1835, S7539
Hardy, N.C., b. 1760 in Warren Co., N.C., there at enl., d. 10/5/1837 in Troup Co., Ga., Elizabeth G., W6096
Hazadiah, Mass., Privateer, b. 2/6/1762, res. at enl. in 1832 Sheffield, Ashtabula Co., Ohio, R9739
Heber, Ct., BLWt.6432 & 13792. Iss. 9/20/1790. No papers
Heber, Ct., Cont., Dis.--no papers. See Am. State Papers, Class 9, p.66 & 116. Wounded by a musket ball through his thigh at White Plains, 10/28/1776

SMITH (continued)
Heman, Ct., b. 1753 at Farmington Ct., res. at enl. Goshen, Ct., res. Oneida Co., N.Y. in 1834, S23427
Heman, Cont., Mass., b. Eastham, Mass., res. Litchfield, Lincoln Co., Me. in 1819 age 71, Sarah Anne, S37405
Henry, ?, Married in Fairfield Co., Ct., d. 1/19/1828, res. of children Ct. & N.Y., Huldah, R18007
Henry, Cont., res. Southfield/ Stroud Twp., Northampton Co., (later Monroe Co.), Pa., d. 6/1801, Mary, W2970
Henry, Cont., Ct., b. 10/13/1758 enl. Middletown, Ct., res. Lee, Berkshire Co., Mass. in 1818, res. Callarine's Town, Tioga Co., N.Y., Susannah, son Henry, S43155
Henry, Cont., Md., b. 1750 in Lancaster Co., Pa. & there until age 25, enl. in Baltimore, Md., res.Anne Arundel Co., Md. in 1842, S14504
Henry, Cont., N.H., enl. at Sanbornton Co., N.H., & there in 1818 age 57, d. 9/25/1842, Lydia W16733
Henry, Cont., N.J., 1st enl. at Bergen, N.J., 2nd at Goshen, N.Y. res. of Middlefield, Otsego Co., N.Y. in 1818 at age 58, d. 9/7/1844 at Brunswick, Rensselaer Co., N.Y., Betsey/Elizabeth, W19055
Henry, Ga., S.C., b. Brunswick Co., Va. & there at enl., res. Harlan Co., Ky. in 1834 age 74/75, d. there 8/15/1836, Elizabeth W9300
Henry, Md., b. 2/26/1759 in Prince George Co., Md., res. at enl. Frederick Co., Md., res. Shelby Co., Ky. in 1834, S31374
Henry, Crane's Cont. Arty., Mass. Pvt., BLWt.5096-100. Iss. 7/18/1791. No papers
Henry, Mass., res. Monroe Co., Ohio in 1818 age 64, d. there 1/30/1825, Catharine, W6089
Henry, Mass., res. at enl. Sandesfield, Berkshire Co., Mass. & d. there 6/11/1787, Elizabeth, W9297
Henry, Mass., res. at enl. Natick, Middlesex Co., Mass. & d. there 11/20/1819, Mary, W15349
Henry, Mass., res. Natick, Mass. Rej. B.L.
Henry, N.Y., b. 3/31/1764 in Catskill, Green Co., N.Y., res. at enl. Stone Arabia, N.Y., d. 5/3/1840 in Ephratah, Montgomery Co., N.Y., Nancy, W6126; BLWt.783-160-55
Henry, N.Y., d. Orange Co., N.Y. 12/20/1829, Maria/Anna Maria, W19069
Henry, N.C., b. 12/25/1741 in

SMITH (continued)
Lancaster Co., Pa., res. at enl. Surry Co., N.C., res. Cabarrus Co., N.C. in 1833, d. 8/28/1835, S32525
Henry, Pa., b. 1752 below Reading Pa., res. at enl. & in 1834 Fayette Co., Pa., S22516
Henry, Pa., b. 1750 in Bucks Co., Pa., there at enl., res. Marlborough Twp., Montomgery Co., Pa. in 1833, S23928
Henry, Pa., b. 7/4/1760 in Lowhill Twp., Northampton (Lehigh) Co., Pa. & there at enl. & in 1832, S23930
Henry, Pa., enl. in Westmoreland Co., Pa., res. Hamilton Co., Ohio in 1822 age 56, S40467
Henry, S.C., b. 8/18/1759 in Rockingham Co., Va., res. at enl. York District, S.C., d. 1/8/1840 in Franklin Co., Ga., Margaret, W2183; BLWt.33764-160-55
Henry, S.C., b. 9/1757 in S.C., res. at enl. Fairfield District, S.C., d. 6/17/1818 in Jaspar Co. Ga., Sally, W27305
Henry, S.C., b. 7/18/1757 and d. in Orangeburg District, S.C. in Oct. 1790, Betty, R9696
Henry, Va., enl. in Pittsylvania Co., Va., res. of McMinn Co., Tenn. in 1832 age 79, S1877
Henry, Va., b. Ireland & came to Va. in 1765, res. at enl. Augusta Co., Va., res. Nelson Co., Va. in 1833 age 84, S6122
Henry, Va., b. 8/1753, res. at enl. Hanover Co., Va., res. Woodford Co., Ky. in 1834, S38384
Henry, Va., b. 8/13/1761 in Caroline Co., Va., res. at enl. Henry Co., Va., res. Franklin Co., Va. in 1832, d. 11/29/1835, Elizabeth W6091; BLWt.26307-160-55
Hezekiah, Art. Artificers, BLWt. 13777. Iss. 8/26/1790 to Jasper Roads, ass. No papers
Hezekiah, Cont., N.J., res. at enl. Canoe Brook, Essex Co., N.J. res. Ulysses, Tompkins Co., N.Y. in 1818 age 55, S17096
Hezekiah, Mass., b. 12/2/1752 at Woodstock, Ct., res. at enl. Colerain, Mass., res. Halifax, Windham Co., Vt. in 1832, d. 7/4/1843, Martha, W25026
Hill/Smith HILL, Va., b. 1761 Chesterfield Co., Va. & there at enl., res. Oglethorpe Co., Ga. in 1833, d. 12/1/1838, Elizabeth W26491
Hiram, N.J., b. 12/22/1756, res. at enl. Hanover Twp., Morris Co., N.J. & there in 1832, S4851
Hope, R.I., res. during Rev., Scituate, R.I. & Killingly, Ct., d. 4/16/1823 at Rome, N.Y., Elizabeth, W22236
Hugh, Mass., b. 11/22/1754, res. in 1828 Verona, Oneida Co., N.Y.

SMITH (continued)
R20204
Ira, Ct., b. 1763 at East Haven, Ct. & enl. there, res. Ulysses, Tompkins Co., N.Y. in 1832, d. 1837, S11417
Ira, Ct., b. 9/7/1757 in Wallingford, Ct. & lived there at enl. when it was Cheshire & in 1832 when it was Prospect, Cheshire Co., Ct., d. there 4/22/1835, Chloe, R9704 (wife was pensioned as former wid. of John Stevens, Ct. which see
Isaac, Ct., BLWt.6441. Iss. 2/21/1797. No papers
Isaac, Ct., res. Greenville, Green Co., N.Y. in 1818 age 56, res. New Canaan, Fairfield Co., Ct. in 1820, S14517
Isaac, Ct., res. at West Boyleston, Worcester Co., Mass. in 1820 age 65, S34516
Isaac, Ct., b. ca. 1758, res. Chittenden Co., Vt. in 1818, res. of Pa. in 1831, and N.Y. in 1834, S42340
Isaac, Ct., res. Greenwich, Fairfield Co., Ct. in 1820 age 63, d. there 7/4 or 12/1829, Mary, W11485; BLWt.75106-100-55
Isaac, Ct., res. at enl. Stamford Fairfield Co., Ct., d. 10/6/1828 Sarah, R9853
Isaac, Ct., N.Y., res. Stamford, Fairfield Co., Ct., d. 2/15/1805 Abigail Finch, former wid.,W3537
Isaac, Mass., b. 1761 at Beverly, Essex Co., Mass. & lived there up to 1832, S29470
Isaac, Mass., b. 2/1/1764 at Lexington, Mass. & d. there 12/6/1840, Sally, W1502; BLWt.3148-160-55
Isaac, Mass., b. 12/2/1752 at Hopkinton, Middlesex Co., Mass. d. there 12/7/1838, Prudence, W15346
Isaac, Mass., b. 1766 at Braintree, Mass. & there at enl., res. Lisbon, Lincoln Co., Me. in 1833, d. 3/29/1838, Mary, W24998
Isaac, Mass., Vt., res. at enl. Guilford, Vt., son of Amos, res. in 1823 Hector, Tompkins Co., N.Y., d. 7/12/1828 at Newfield, Tompkins Co., N.Y., Eunice, W6124; BLWt.45598-160-55
Isaac, N.H., res. at enl. Amherst, Hillsboro Co., N.H., res. Johnson Franklin Co., Vt. in 1818 age 74, S41166
Isaac, N.H., res. of Concord, Grafton Co., N.H. in 1818 age 62, d. 4/15/1819 in Lisbon, N.H., Hannah, W25011
Isaac, N.Y., BLWt.1988-200-Lt. Iss. 6/6/1791 to Mills Philips, ass. No papers
Isaac, N.Y., b. 3/10/1763 in Fredericksburg, Dutchess Co., N.Y. & there at enl., res. in Utica,

SMITH (continued)
Genesee Co., N.Y. in 1832 S14512; BLWt.2191-160-55
Isaac, N.Y., enl. at Brookhaven, Suffolk Co., N.Y. & there in 1819 age 69, S42321
Isaac, N.C., enl. from Wake Co., N.C. & there in 1832 age 72, S7531
Isaac, N.C., res. in 1839 Anson Co., N.C. age 80, S42017
Isaac, R.I., enl. from R.I., res. Greenfield, Saratoga Co., N.Y. in 1821, S42320
Isaac, Va., res. Charlotte Co., Va. in 1832 age 72, S6119
Isaac, Va., b. 1760 in Kingston Parish, Gloucester Co., Va., res. Mathews Co., Va. in 1832, S11427
Isaac, Va., b. New Kent Co., Va. & there at enl., res. Camden, S.C. in 1818 age 61, res. Monroe Co., Ga. in 1832, d. there 7/20/1834, Ann R., W4338
Isaac Sheldon, Ct., Mass., b. 4/11/1765 in Suffield, Ct. & there at enl., res. in White Creek, Washington Co., N.Y. in 1832, R9745
Isabella, former wid. of John Carroll, Md., which see
Isaiah, Ct., BLWt.6506. Iss. 11/15/1792. No papers
Isaiah, Ct., Cont., b. 1/22/1757 enl. at Stamford, Ct., res. Ontario Co., N.Y. in 1818, d. 3/27/1825 at Perry, Genesee Co., N.Y., Nancy/Ann, W17826
Israel, Ct., b. 1759 at Lyme, Ct., & there at enl., res. Dempster, Sullivan Co., N.H., S16531
Israel, Ct., res. Cazenovia, Madison Co., N.Y. in 1818 age 54, d. 12/6/1826 in Chatauqua Co., N.Y., Eleanor, W502; BLWt. 69-60-55
Israel, Ct., R.I., b. 9/22/1754 in Gloucester (later Berrillville) Providence, R.I., there & at Thompson,Ct. during Rev., res. Brookfield, Worcester Co., Mass. in 1833, S14534
Israel, Mass., BLWt.5066. Iss. 8/22/1789. No papers
Israel, Cont., Mass., enl. at Roxbury, Mass., res. in 1818 Edinburgh, Saratoga Co., N.Y., S42317
Israel, Cont., Mass., b. Taunton, Norfolk Co., Mass., there at enl. d. 1/30/1827 age 72 in Greenfield Franklin Co., Mass., Mary, R9800
Israel, Mass., b. 1743 in Middleborough, Plymouth Co., Mass. & there up to 1832, S15985
Israel, N.H., res. in Poplin, N.H. in 1770, res. at enl. Brentwood, N.H. and d. in service 11/15/1775, Hannah, R9743
Israel, N.Y., BLWt.1976-300-Capt.

SMITH (continued)
Iss. 1/5/1791. No papers
Israel, N.Y., b. 9/30/1756 at Trenton, N.J., res. at enl. Stamford, Dutchess Co., N.Y., res. Rensselaerville, Albany Co., N.Y. in 1832, S14516
Ithamar, Ct., Cont., res. at enl. Lyme, New London, Ct., res. Covington, Genesee Co., N.Y. in 1818 age 56, d. there 11/11/1834, Deborah, W19068
Ithamar, Mass., b. 6/13/1756, res. at enl. Wilbraham, Hampshire Co., Mass., res. Marcellus, Onondaga Co., N.Y. in 1832, and Pontiac, Mich. in 1836, S29469
Ithamar, Mass., en. at Western, Mass., res. Enosburgh, Franklin Co., Vt. in 1820 age 73, Abiah, S41162
Ivey, N.C., b. ca. 1759 in Nansemond Co., Va., res. at enl. Duplin Co., N.C., res. Tattnall Co., Ga. in 1833, R9746
Jabez, Ct., b. 9/10/1746 at Stamford, Fairfield Co., Ct. & there up to 1832, res. of N.Y. City in 1836, S14506
Jacob, Ct., Cont., native of Stamford, Ct. & there during the Rev., d. N.Y. City 9/1811, Hannah, W22240; BLWt.26335-160-55
Jacob, Ct. Sea Service, Cont., Mass., b. 1752 at Dedham, Mass., res. Orrington, Penobscot Co., Me. in 1818, d. 5/11/1834, S34503
Jacob, Ct., Green Mt. Boys, Vt., res. Chateaugay, Franklin Co., N.Y. in 1827 age 79, Elizabeth, S43157
Jacob, Cont., N.H., enl. at Sanbornton, N.H., res. Strafford Co., N.H. in 1818 age 74, S43149
Jacob, Md., b. 1758, res. at enl. Sharpsburg, Md., res. Morgan Co., in 1833 where he d. 7/26/1834, Catharine, W7186; BLWt.39337-160-55
Jacob, Mass., N.H., b. Epping, Rockingham Co., N.H. & there at enl., res. Raymond, Rockingham Co., N.H. in 1832 age 77, S18233
Jacob, Mass., Sea Service, Navy, R.I., Privateer, b. Providence, R.I., there & at New Port, R.I. up to 1832 age 72, S21488
Jacob, N.J., b. 1/2/1757 in Lebanon Twp., Huntingdon Co., N.J. & there at enl., res. Oxford Twp., Warren Co., N.J. in 1832, S914
Jacob, Pa., BLWt.10329, iss. 11/5/1791 to Jacob Lunckle, ass. No papers
Jacob, Pa., BLWt.10384. Iss. 3/2/1792 to Jacob Miller, admr. No papers
Jacob, Pa., b. Westmoreland Co., Pa., & there in 1825, age 70, S40471

SMITH (continued)
Jacob, Vt., b. 7/7/1765 in Morris Co., N.J., res. during Rev. Rutland Co., Vt. & Bridport, Addison Co., Vt., d. at Bridport 8/21/1852, Molly, R9748
Jacob, Va., b. 1749/50 in Bucks Co., Pa., enl. in Berkeley Co., Va., res. Washington Co., Ind. in 1832, S16253
Jacob, Va., enl. at Rockingham Co., Va., there in 1818 age 59, d. 8/18/1836, Winna, W19052
Jacob J., N.C., b. 1763 in N.J., res. at enl. Roane Co., N.C., res. Grant Co., Ky. in 1834, R9749
Jacobus, N.Y., b. 1/5/1765 in Marbletown, Ulster Co., N.Y. & there at enl., res. Pamela, Jefferson Co., N.Y. in 1832, S23924
Jairus, Ct., d. 7/3/1803, Sarah, W25032
James, Sheldon's Dragoons, Ct., BLWt.6519. Iss. 1/26/1790 to John May, ass. No papers
James, Ct., b. 1762 at Old Haddam, Ct. & there at enl., res. Harpersfield, Delaware Co., N.Y. in 1832, S11426
James, Ct., b. 7/18/1765, d. 8/2/1827 at Otsego, Otsego Co., N.Y., Marcy, W19372; BLWt. 28582-160-55
James, Ct., b. 1762 at New London North Parish, Ct. & there at enl., res. Westmoreland, Oneida Co., N.Y. in 1834, d. 1/16/1836, Phebe, W27567
James, Ct., Cont., enl. at Lyme, Ct., res. Kent, Putnam Co., N.Y. in 1820 age 62, Nancy, S42349
James, Ct., N.Y., b. 1767 at White Plains, N.Y., res. at enl. Wyoming, Pa., res. Hector, Tompkins Co., N.Y. in 1832, Ruth Ann W26488
James, Cont., res. Addison Twp., Somerset Co., Pa. in 1818 age 73, S40459
James, Cont., Ct., enl. at Southington, Ct. & d. there 3/3/1819, Sarah H., W11482; BLWt. 26502-160-55
James, Cont., Mass., res. Wells, York Co., Me. (Mass.) in 1780, res. Lyman,York Co., Me. in 1818 age 62, d. 5/24/1840, Hannah, W22262
James, Cont., Pa., res. Columbiana Co., Ohio in 1830, Jane, S40453
James, Del., Pa., res. Cecil Co., Md. at enl., res. Monroe Co., Va. in 1818 age 71, d. 11/28/1837, Flora, W6120
James, Ga., Elizabeth, BLWt. 205331-1835
James, Md., BLWt.2046-300-Capt. (recorded on list of officers to whom warrants were iss. prior to 1800)

SMITH (continued)
James, Md., BLWt.11671 iss. 2/1/1790
James 2nd, Md., BLWt.11674. Iss. 7/8/1797 to James DeBaufre, ass. No papers
James, Md., b. 9/1755, res. at enl. Frederick Co., Md., res. Adair Co., Ky. in 1832, res. Gibbon Co., Ind. in 1835, d. 1/29/1838, Margaret, W9657
James, Mass., b. 11/1/1753 at Walpole, Mass. & there at enl., res. Northampton, Hampshire Co., Mass. in 1832, S30710
James, Mass., res. Ipswich, Mass. in 1830, S34514
James, Mass., res. Windham, Vt. in 1818, age 64, S41172
James, Mass., enl. from Lewiston Worcester Co., Mass., res. Peterborough, Hillsboro Co., N.H. in 1818 age 55, d. 6/28/1844 at New Ipswich, N.H., Polly, W10958; BLWt.14513-160-55
James, N.H., res. at enl. Haverhill, N.H., d. 10/8/1844 at Bath, N.H., Ruth, W22276; BLWt.6015-160-55
James, N.J., res. Monmouth Co., N.J. in 1818, d. 8/23/1843 at Howell Twp., Monmouth Co., N.J. Elizabeth, W503
James, N.Y., b. 1761 at Charlotte Dutchess Co., N.Y. & there at enl., res. Canajoharie, Montgomery Co., N.Y. in 1832, S11423
James, N.Y.,res. during Rev. in Dutchess & Columbia Co., N.Y., d. 4/13/1844 at Conquest, Cayuga Co., N.Y., Ann, W19049
James, N.C., BLWts.12591 & 13712 Iss. 5/18/1797 to Gabriel Holmes ass. No papers
James, N.C., res. of Richmond Co. N.C., Dis.- No papers. See Am. State Papers, Class 9, p.164 - Wounded by a musket ball shot through his right thigh, which disabled him from getting a livelihood by labor. Disabled 3/15/1781 at battle of Guilford.
James, N.C., enl. at Williamstown N.C., res. Edgemont Co., N.C. in 1818 age 65, S42018
James, N.C., Va., b. 10/2/1760 in Hanover Co., Va., res. at enl. Buckingham Co., Va., res. Jackson Co., Ala. in 1837, S11432
James, N.C., Va., b. 8/6/1765 in Augusta (Hardy) Co., Va. & there at enl., res. Jefferson Co., Tenn. in 1834, S21489
James, Pa., BLWt.10376. Iss. 1/28/1792. No papers
James, Pa., res. Stoney Creek Twp., Somerset Co., Pa. in 1818 age 59, S40443
James, R.I., res. at enl. Bristol R.I., d. 6/30/1829, Phebe, W12985
James, S.C., b. 6/9 or 1/9/1751 in Prince William Co., Va., res. at

SMITH (continued)
enl. Spartanburgh, S.C., res. Union Dist., S.C. in 1832, S21977
James, Va., BLWts.12528 & 13536. Iss. 11/5/1791 to Robert Means, ass. No papers
James, Va., b. 1752 in Caroline Co., Va., res. at enl. Spotsylvania Co., Va. & there in 1832, S11413
James, Va., res. at enl. Washington Co., Va., res. Scott Co., Va. in 1833 age 80, S11429
James, Va., res. Fayette Co., Ky. in 1833 age 85, S31377
James, Va., enl. in Augusta Co., Va., res. Greenbriar Co., Va. in 1818 age 60, S38385
James, Va., BLWt.459-9-200
James A., Ct., b. 3/16/1763 at Groton, Ct. & there at enl., res. West Stockbridge, Berkshire Co., Mass. in 1840, R9750
James Arrow/James ARROWSMITH, Va., enl. in Fauquier Co. or Stafford Co., Va., res. Fauquier Co. in 1820 age 72, Levina, W5643
James E., Cont., Pa., res. in Philadelphia, Pa. in 1818 age 59, d. 1/14/1835, Jemima, W3727; BLWt.2027-200-Capt. Pa. Art. Iss. 9/9/1790. No papers
Jared/Garrett/Garnett, Va., res. Scott Co., Ky. in 1818, d. 12/11/1820, Margaret, W8743; BLWt. 19722-160-55
Jasiel, Mass., R.I., b. 2/7/1763 in Taunton, Mass. & there at enl. res. Bloomfield, Somerset Co., Me. in 1832, d. 5/15/1848 at Buckfield Me., Mary Ann, W2362; BLWt.43524-160-55
Jedediah, Ct., res. at enl. Ashford Ct., res. Roxbury, Orange Co., Vt. in 1818 age 56 & d. there 2/25/1847, Esther, W22233; BLWts. 6429 & 125-60-55. Iss. 11/24/1791(6429) to Isaac Bronson, ass. No papers
Jedediah, Cont., Mass., res. Hatfield, Hampshire Co., Mass. in 1818, age 64, S34501
Jeffery, Ct., b. 1762 in Haddam, Middlesex Co., Ct., there at enl. res. Madison, New Haven Co., Ct. in 1832, S16250
Jehiel, Ct., BLWt.6462. Iss. 4/6/1790. No papers
Jehiel, Ct., enl. at Branford, Ct. res. Coventry, Chenango Co., N.Y. in 1818 age 57, d. 11/15/1825, Rachel, W22246
Jeremiah, Ct., b. 12/24/1746 in West Haven, Ct., there at enl. when it was part of New Haven & there in 1832 when it was Orange New Haven Co., Ct., d. 7/19/1835 at Orange, S---
Jeremiah, Ct., b. 6/29/1758, res. East Haddam, Middlesex Co., Ct. in 1818 & d. there 12/20/1837, Temperance, W22268

SMITH (continued)
Jeremiah, Ct., b. 6/30/1762 in Norwalk, Fairfield Co., Ct. there at enl., res. Nevisink, Sullivan Co., N.Y. in 1832, d. 7/25/1851, Anna, W26481
Jeremiah, Cont., Mass., res. during Rev. Walpole, Mass. & d. there 5/15/1840, Rachel, W15353
Jeremiah, Cont., N.Y., enl. at Kingsberry, Orange Co., N.Y., res. Schuyler, Herkimer Co., N.Y. in 1820 age 60, S43158; BLWt.7835-100. Iss. 8/10/1790
Jeremiah, Mass., N.H., res. Waterboro, York Co., Me. in 1818 age 62, d. there 8/12/1832, Elizabeth, W22273
Jeremiah, N.H., res. at enl. Sandbornton, Strafford Co., N.H. & there in 1818 age 57, d. 6/3/1827, Lonehannah, W17847
Jeremiah, N.Y., b. 1755 in Claverack, Albany Co. (Columbia Co.), N.Y., & there at enl., d. 1/29/1838 at Davenport, Delaware Co., N.Y., Sophia, W19378
Jeremiah, N.C., res. during Rev. Lincoln Co., N.C., d. 9/1823, Margaret, R9794
Jeremy, Mass., N.H., res. in Epping, Rockingham Co., N.H. in 1818 age 62 & d. there 1/14/1833 Judith, W19048
Jesse, Ct., BLWt.6477. Iss. 3/7/1792 to Jonas Prentice, ass. No papers
Jesse, Ct., res. Woodbridge, New Haven Co., Ct. in 1820, d. 8/15/1831, S36768
Jesse, Ct., b. & lived Stamford, Fairfield Co., Ct., there 1801/1802/1803, R----
Jesse, Ct., enl. at Stratford, Ct., res. Great Barrington, Mass. in 1819 age 62, d. 5/24/1841 at Mexico, N.Y., Susanna, R9861
Jesse, Cont., Mass., res. Salem, Essex Co., in 1820 age 64, S19469
Jesse, Cont., Mass., N.H., res. Washington, N.H. in 1781, res. Bangor, Me. in 1818 age 58 & d. there 11/21/1829, Lucy, W25021
Jesse, Mass., b. 2/10/1759 at Rehoboth, Mass., there at enl. res. Savoy, Berkshire Co., Mass. in 1832 & d. there 12/4/1835, S18601
Jesse, Mass., b. Charlton, Worcester Co., Mass. & d. there 6/12/1826, res. during Rev. Leicester & Charlton, Mass., Sarah, W19381
Jesse, N.Y., res. N.Y.City in 1818 age 59, res. Milton Twp., Saratoga Co., N.Y. in 1822 & d. there 9/1822, Mary, W6084; BLWt. 7776-100-Sgt. Iss. 7/16/1790 to Wm. I. Vreedenburgh, ass. Also

SMITH (continued)
BLWt.189-60-55
Jesse, N.C., b. 3/5/1762 in Chatham Co., N.C., there at enl., res. Pickens Dist., S.C. in 1834, S21490
Jesse, R.I., b. 6/12/1760 at North Providence, R.I., there at enl. & in 1833, S21987
Jesse, R.I., res. Gloucester & Burrilville & Smithfield, R.I. d. 1/8/1805, Sabra, W22270
Jesse, S.C., b. 4/16/1765 in Montgomery Co., N.C., res. at enl. Chester Dist., S.C., res. Franklin Co., Ga. in 1832 & d. there 4/11/1842, Anna, W2450; BLWt.34910-160-55
Jesse, Va., enl. from Henrico Co., Va. & d. there 6/12/1821, Lucy, R9789
Joab, Mass., d. at Chester, Hampden Co., Mass. 2/7/1840 at age 80, Elizabeth, W13911
Job, Ct., res. at enl. Ridgefield Fairfield Co., Ct. & d. there 6/6/1832, Esther, W17831
Job, Ga., S.C., b. 12/25/1748 in York Co., Pa., res. during Rev. St. Paul's Parish, Ga. & in S.C., d. 11/10/1837 in Pickens Dist., S.C., S21983
Job T., R.I., res. Groton, New London Co., Ct. in 1814, in 1832 age 77, S36765
Joel, Ct., b. 11/10/1756 in Reading, Fairfield Co., Ct., there at enl., res. Butternuts, Otsego Co., N.Y. in 1832 & d. there 5/19/1837, Sarah, W19066
Joel, Ct., res. Owego, Tioga Co., N.Y. in 1809; BLWt.198-150
Joel, Mass., b. Sunderland (Lowell), Franklin Co., Mass. & there at enl., res. Deerfield, Franklin Co., Mass. in 1832 age 74, S4862
Joel, N.C., S.C., Va., b. 9/4/1760 in Mecklinburg Co., Va. & 1st enl. there, at 2nd enl. Warren Co., N.C., 3rd enl. York Dist., S.C.; res. White Co., Tenn. in 1833, d. 4/4/1840 in Van Buren Co., Tenn., Nancy, W2260; BLWt. 26916-160-55
John, Art. Artificers, BLWt.13772 Iss. 8/10/1789 to Richard Platt, ass. No papers
John, Col. Lamb's Regt. of Art., BLWt.1990-200-Lt. Iss. 5/18/1790 to Isaac Guion, ass. No papers
John, Ct., b. 6/11/1757 in Springfield, Mass., res. at enl. Suffield, Ct., res. Granville, Hampden Co., Mass. in 1832, d. 9/3/1835, S29468
John, Ct., res. East Haddam, Ct., res. Middlefield, Hampshire Co., Mass. in 1818, S34493
John, Ct., b. 8/4/1741, enl. in Stamford, Ct., res. Lock, Cayuga

SMITH (continued)
Co., N.Y. in 1818, Tamer (wife in 1818), S42352
John, Ct., b. 4/27/1760 at Montville, Ct., res. at enl. New London, Ct., res. at Montville, New London Co., Ct. in 1852, Lydia, W3724
John, Ct., b. 1744, d. 8/5/1827 at New Milford, Litchfield Co., Ct., Anne, W17830
John, Ct., age 57 in 1821, enl. from Kingstreet, Ct., d. 1835 at Lewis, Essex Co., N.Y., Betsy, W22244
John, Ct., b. 6/14/1756 in New Haven, Ct., res. at enl. North Haven, Ct. & there in 1832 & Nov. 1847, Mary, W26965; BLWt. 26722-160-55
John, Ct., res. at enl. New Fairfield, Ct., d. 1818 New Lisbon, N.Y., Nancy Ann Wilbur former wid., R11510
John, Ct. Sea Service, b. 1750, res. of Providence, R.I., d. at sea 9/20/1783, Tabitha, W13915
John, Cont., Ct., b. 3/19/1756 in Farrington, Ct., Chloe, S14497
John, Cont., Ct., res. at enl. & in 1820 Haddam, Middlesex Co., Ct age 64, d. there 5/8/1834, S36772; BLWt.13776-100 Art. Artfc. Iss. 12/6/1799
John, Cont. Ct., res. at enl. & in 1818 Stratford, Fairfield Co., Ct., S36774
John, Cont., Mass., b. Ipswich, Mass. ca. 1759, res. Gloucester Essex Co., Mass. in 1820, S34500
John, Cont., Mass., res. in 1780 Murrayfield, Mass., in Geauga Co., Ohio in 1818 age 64, S40474
John, Cont., Mass., b. 1760, res. Hollis, York Co., Me. in 1818 & 1832, d. 7/18/1836, Anna, W820
John, Cont., Mass., b. 1758, res. at enl. Needham, Mass., res. Grafton, Windham Co., Vt. in 1818, d. 8/4/1838, Sarah, W19377
John, Cont., Mass., b. 1750 near Johnstown, N.Y. & there at Rev., enl. at Stockbridge, Mass., res. Ross Co., Ohio in 1832, R9770
John, Cont., Mass., BLWt.1776-100
John, Cont., N.Y., Mary, S42348; BLWt.1427-100
John, Cont., N.Y., res. Minden, Montgomery Co., N.Y. in 1820, d. 1/27/1852 at Sempronius, N.Y., Abigail, W25004
John, Cont., Pa., b. 1759, d. 10/7/1839. Res. Cumberland Co., Pa. S4857
John, Cont., Pa., enl. at Westmoreland, Pa., res. Harrison Co. Ky. in 1818 age ca. 68, S37411
John, Cont., Pa., b. 1759, d. 10/7/1839, res. at enl. & in 1829 Carlisle, Cumberland Co., Pa., S37412
John, Cont., Pa., enl. in Phila-

SMITH (continued)
delphia, Pa., res. Fauquier Co., Va. in 1818 age 69, Leanner, S38380
John, Cont., Pa., res. Milford Twp., Mifflin Co., Pa. in 1820 age 70, enl. in Pa. (he signs in German), S40451
John, Cont., Pa., also in Gen. Harmars Ind. War, b. 8/26/1758, res. Albemarle Co., Va. in 1820, S38381
John, Cont., Va., b. 1741, probably of Bedford Co., Va., res. in Floyd Co., Ky. in 1818, d. 11/1/1829, Susanna, W8731
John, Ga., b. York Co., Pa. 6/23/1761, res. at enl. Ga., res. Henry Co., Ga. in 1833, S31967
John, Ga., S.C., also served in 1785/1786 against Indians, b. 1761 in York Co., Pa., res. at enl. Richmond,Ga., res. Henry Co., Ga. in 1836, R9769
John, Pvt. Hazen's Regt., BLWt. 13728-100. Iss. 3/25/1790
John, Md. See Joseph SMITH, Md. BLWt.2041 & 2043
John, Md., BLWt.2045-300-Capt. Iss. 1/26/1792. No papers
John, Md., BLWt.11678. Iss. 9/24/1789. No papers
John, Md., BLWt.11699. Iss. 2/7/1790
John, Md., BLWt.11707. Iss. 11/29/1790 to John Smith, Admr. No papers
John, Md., enl. in Fredericktown, Md., res. Baltimore, Md. in 1818 age 67, S---
John, Md., b. 7/17/1760 in Prince George Co., Md., enl. from Frederick Co., Md., res. Harrison Co., Va. in 1833, S6117
John, Md., res. Prince George Co., Md. in 1828, S46521
John, Md., enl. in Fredericksgtown, Md., d. 2/18/1821, Catharine, W170
John, Md., b. 9/30/1748, d. 5/17/1826 in Anne Arundel Co., Md., Sarah, W4070 & W4340
John, Md., b. 2/2/1753, res. at enl. Montgomery Co., Md., res. at ap. Clarke Co., Ky., d. 7/22/1835, Elizabeth, W8741 & S1255; BLWt. 43523-160-55
John, Md., Privateer, b. in Prince George Co., Md. in 1758 & there at enl., res. Iredell Co., N.C. from 1792 to 1832, R9768
John, Md.,Sea Service, res. at enl. Baltimore, Md., res. Beaver Co., Pa. in 1835, R9764
John, Md., Va., res. at enl. Frederick Co., Md., res. Pendleton Co. Va. in 1833 age 63, d. 5/24/1839, Susan, W6117
John, Mass., BLWt.5050. Iss. 8/26/1790 to Manassah Cutler. No papers
John, Mass., b. 1764 Cokiatt (?) Rockland Co., N.Y., res. at enl.

SMITH (continued)
Old Stockbridge, Berkshire Co., Mass., res. Argyle, Washington Co., N.Y. in 1833, S14524
John, Mass., b. 1756 in Stoughton, Mass. & there at enl., res. Wayne Kennebec Co., Me. in 1832, S15650
John, Mass., res. Hadley, Hampshire Co., Mass. in 1818 age over 65, S34498; BLWt.1907-200-Lt. Iss. 4/1/1790
John, Mass., b. 1760, res. Buxton, York Co., Me. in 1818, Elizabeth, S37421
John, Mass., b. 1753, enl. at Boston, Mass., d. Hunterdon Co., N.J., 12/8/1821, Abigail, W1948; BLWt.236-60-55
John, Mass., b. 1760 in Taunton, Mass., there at enl., d. 1845 in Putney, Windham Co., Vt., Mary, W6125; BLWt.8188-160-55
John, (alias Zadock Palmer), Mass. b. 4/25/1757 in Westfield, Hampshire Co., Mass. & enl. there, d. 1833/34 in Clermont Co., Ohio Jane, W8298; BLWt.26298-160-55
John, Mass., res. at enl. Sutton, Worcester Co., Mass. & there in 1793, Molly Banton, former wid., W14258
John, Mass., res. at enl. Worcester Co., Mass., d. 1816 at Shoreham, Addison Co., Vt., Sarah, W17838
John, Mass.,res. at enl. Edgartown Dukes Co., Mass., d. 8/5/1830, Caroline, W20061
John, Mass., b. 1753, res. Mt. Desert, Me. in 1818, d. 1828, Anna, W22266; BLWt.2491-100
John, Mass. B. 1752, res. Northport, Hancock Co., Me. in 1818, d.5/11/1824, Lydia Murch/March, former wid., W23915
John, Mass., b. 9/3/1761, enl. from Ware or Brimfield, Mass., res. in Shrewsbury, Rutland Co., Vt. in 1818, d. 10/2/1840, Dolly, W24985
John, Mass., b. 1757, res. Lexington, Mass. in 1781, d. 1822 at Randolph, Orange Co., Vt., Sarah, W24997
John, Mass., N.H., b. 1749 Ipswich, Mass., d. 1832 at Salisbury, Merrimack Co., N.H., Mary, W15948
John, Mass., Sea Service, b. 1765 at Ipswich, Mass. & there at enl. res. Newburyport, Mass. in 1832, R9759
John, Navy, b. Boston & there in 1819, res. & agcy. Mass., S34496
John, N.H,, BLWt.3465. Iss. 3/25/1790. No papers
John, N.H., res. of Francistown, Dis. No papers. See Am. State Papers, class 9, p.139-Disability wounded in his head by a musket ball which remains lodged there,

SMITH (continued)
about 1781 near Kingsbridge
John, N.H., b. 1759/1760 res. in 1818 New Hampton, Stafford Co., N.H. (not identical with S14489) Phebe, S43150
John, N.H., res. at enl. Londonderry, N.H., res. 1781 Heniper, Merrimack Co., N.H., d. 6/5/1826, Lucy, W22254
John, N.H., Vt., b. 1758 in Hampstead, N.H., res. at enl. Londonderry, N.H., res. Newberry, Orange Co., Vt. in 1832, d. 10/28/1851, Sarah, W3726. This sold. served under the name of John VANCE
John, N.J., BLWt.8727; iss. 10/7/1790 to John Lighton, ass. No papers
John, N.J., BLWt.8763. Iss. 11/19/1780. No papers
John, N.J., b. 3/4/1756 Essex Co. N.J. & there at enl. & in 1832, S4854
John, N.J., b. 6/4/1762 in Hunterdon Co., N.J. & there at enl., res. Butler Co., Ohio in 1832, S4860
John, N.J., b. 1753/54, res. West Bloomfield, Essex Co., N.J. in 1818 & enl. there, S34502
John, N.J., b. 1754/55, res. South Amboy, Middlesex Co., N.J. in 1818, enl. at New Brunswick, N.J. S34507
John, N.J., b. 1749/50, res. at enl. Freehold, Monmouth Co., N.J. d. 9/1799, Rachel, W2479
John, N.J., b. 8/24/1749, res. at enl. Sussex Co., N.J., & lived there after Rev., d. 1/18/1828, wid. Mary living Hunterdon Co., N.J. in 1838, W6129
John, N.J., b. 7/8/1752 or 1750 at Baskinridge, Morris Co., N.J., enl. Monmouth Co., N.J., lived in Saratoga Co., N.Y. about 35 yrs. & in Oswego Co., res. Rochester, N.Y. in 1835, R9760
John, N.Y., BLWt.7763. Iss. 8/24/1790 to Glenn & Bleecker, assnes. No papers
John, N.Y., BLWt.7765. Iss. 8/10/1790. No papers
John, Jr., N.Y., BLWt.7796. Iss. 7/30/1790 to Edw. Cumpston, ass. No papers
John, N.Y., BLWt.7812. Iss. 6/24/1790 to Elkenah Watson, ass. No papers
John, Lamb's Art., N.Y., BLWt.7839 Iss. 9/24/1790. No papers
John, Lamb's Art., N.Y., BLWt.7855 Iss. 9/24/1790. No papers
John, N.Y., res. Bristol, Ct. in 1794, Dis. no papers. See Am. State Papers, Class 9, p.61 & 112 Disabled 2/1783, badly frozen in his feet, upon a tedious march from Oswego to Fort Rensselaer on

SMITH (continued)
the Mohawk River
John, N.Y., b. 1760 Goshen, Orange Co., N.Y., res. there at enl., res. Southport, Troy Co., N.Y. in 1834, S17109
John, N.Y., b. 10/4/1742, res. Rockland Co., N.Y. in 1832, d. 1/12/1832, S22998
John, N.Y., res. Hartford Co., Ct. in 1820 age 62, Nancy, S36760
John, N.Y., res. Kingston, Ulster Co., N.Y. in 1830 age 72, S42318
John, N.Y., b. 2/27/1759 in Beekman, Dutchess Co., N.Y. & there at enl., d. 11/14/1839 in Clinton Dutchess Co., N.Y., Jane, W19061
John, N.Y., res. Smithfield, Madison Co., N.Y. in 1818 age 71, d. ca. 1828 in Oneida Co., N.Y., Elizabeth, W25033
John, N.Y., b. 7/2/1757 in Jamaica Queens Co., N.Y., there at enl. & in 1834, R9761
John, N.Y., b. ca. 1750 Dutchess Co., N.Y. & there at enl., res. Onondaga Co., N.Y. in 1839, R9762
John, N.Y., b. ca. 1761 in Salisbury, Ct., res. at enl. Dutchess Co., N.Y., res. Wayne Co., Mich. in 1841, R9773
John, N.Y., b. 1/28/1757 near Quaker Hill, Dutchess Co., N.Y., res. at enl. Harrison, Westchester Co., N.Y., d. 8/26/1841, Sarah, R9854
John, N.Y., b. 1/1/1755, d. 12/23/1812, Sophia, R9856
John, N.Y., BLWt.1563-100. Iss. 10/26/1829
John, N.C., b. 3/1760, enl. in Burke Co., N.C., res. Hawkins Co., Tenn. in 1833, res. Scott Co., Va. in 1840, S1931
John, N.C., b. 7/1763 in Orange Co., Va., res. at enl. Surry Co. N.C., res. Henry Co., Tenn. in 1832, S4852
John, N.C., b. 1760 in Orange Co. Va., res. at enl. Wilkes Co., N.C., res. Franklin Co., Tenn. in 1832, S4858
John, N.C., b. 10/1/1750 in Bertie Co., N.C., res. at enl. Duplin Co.(later called Sampson Co.), N.C., d. 5/30/1834, S7540
John, N.C., b. 3/15/1763 in Anson Co., N.C. & there at enl., res. Madison Co., Ala. in 1833, res. Jackson Co., Ala. in 1840, S14488
John, N.C., enl. in Greenville Co. N.C., res. Warren Co., N.C. in 1818 age 79, S42014
John, N.C., res. at enl. Lincoln Co., N.C., res. Cape Girardeau Co., Mo. in 1832 age 68, R9772
John, N.C., also served 1789, b. 6/1/1759 in Cumberland Co., Va., res. at enl. Surry Co., N.C., d. 7/18/1838 in Clarke Co., Ga., Polly, R9831
John, N.C., Va., b. 1/5/1754

SMITH (continued)
in Cumberland Co., Va., res. at enl. Granville Co., N.C. & Henry Co., Va., lived in Adair Co., Ky., d. 11/3/1848 in Taylor Co., Ky., Francis, W6085; BLWt.9531-160-55
John, Pa., BLWt.10356. Iss. 12/7/1790. No papers
John, Pa., BLWt.10350. Iss. 12/7/1791 to Aleander William Foster, ass. No papers
John, BLWt.10393. Iss. 7/5/1797 to James DeBaufre, ass. No papers
John, Pa., BLWt.10401. Iss. 12/24/179? No papers
John, Pa., BLWt.10421. Iss. 9/12/1789. No papers
John, Pa., BLWt.10441. Iss. 2/17/179? to John Snell, ass. No papers
John, Pa., BLWt.10463. Iss. 9/24/179? to George Walton, ass. No papers
John, Pa., BLWt.10470. Iss. 1/18/1800 to Peter Eyster, ass. No papers
John, Pa., b. 7/1756 in Berks Co. Pa., res. Lancaster Co., Pa. in 1833, S6113
John, Pa., b. 1755 in Springfield Twp., Bucks Co., Pa., res. at enl. Easton, Northampton Co., Pa. res. Bucks Co., Pa. in 1833, S23927
John, Pa., res. Frederick Co., Va. in 1819 age nearly 62, S38379
John, Pa., res. Westmoreland Co., Pa. in 1818, S40446
John, Pa., res. at enl. Philadelphia, Pa., Agness, R9682
John, Pa., enl. at Lebanon, Lancaster Co., Pa., res. Lebanon Co. Pa. in 1819 age 64, d. 4/6/1834 in Dauphin Co., Pa., Catharine, R9701
John, Pa., res. Baltimore, Md. in 1845 age 86, R9765
John, Pa., b. 4/17/1755 in Germany res. at enl. Lancaster Co., Pa., res. Lewis Co., Va. in 1833, res. Indiana in 1834, R9766
John, Pa., moved from Md. to Pa. & enl. from Washington Co., Pa., d. 2/17/1832 in Tyler Co., Va., Lettuce, R9787
John, Pa., res. Fayette Co., Pa. in 1838 age 71, BLWt.1523-100
John, Pa., Va., b. 11/18/1758 in Philadelphia & there at enl., res. Logan Co., Va. in 1836, R9767
John, Pa., Va., b. near Lancaster, Pa. in 1750, res. at enl. Fayette Co., Pa., res. Wayne Co., Mo. in 1832, R9771
John, Pa., Va., b. 1752 in Frederick Co., Va.,res. at enl. Fayette Co., Pa., d. 10/1/1834 at Woodford Co., Ky., Mary, R9802
John, R.I., BLWt.3509. Iss. 2/24/

SMITH (continued)
1800 to Obh. Sprague, ass. No papers
John, R.I., res. Providence, R.I. in 1820 age 55, S39487
John, R.I., res. at enl. South Kingston, R.I. & there he d. 2/29/1815, Mary, W13913
John, R.I., b. South Kingston, R.I., 12/1759, res. Saratoga Co. N.Y. in 1789, d. 7/16/1810 at Sherburne, Chenango Co., N.Y., Lydia, W25024
John, S.C., lived in Edgefield Dist., S.C., res. Bibb Co., Ala. in 1832 age 73, S32526
John, S.C., res. Fairfield Dist. S.C. in 1818 age ca. 57, S39078
John, S.C., native of N.C., enl. in Abbeville Dist., S.C. & res. there after Rev., d. 5/1/1802, former wid. Barbara Glover, lived Habershaw Co., Ga., R4070
John, Vt., res. Clarendon, Rutland Co., Vt. where he d. 9/1786 Sarah, W22257
John, Va., BLWt.12530. Iss. 11/5/1789. No papers
John, Va., b. ca. 1759, res. at enl. Charlotte Co., Va., res. at ap. in 1832 Green Co., Ky., S---
John, Va., b. 6/30/1760 in Gloucester Co., Va., res. Greenville Co., N.C., S3937
John, Va., b. 10/1/1742 in Amelia Co., Va., res. at enl. Halifax Co., Va. res. Fayette Co., Ohio in 1832, S3939
John, Va., b. 5/7/1750 in Middlesex Co., Va., res. at enl. Frederick Co., Va. & d. there 3/4/1836, S6114
John, Va., b. 1756 in Halifax Co. Va., res. at enl. Franklin Co., Va., res. Giles Co., Va. in 1834, S14482
John, Va., b. 1760 & res. at enl. Spotsylvania Co., Va., res. Orange Co., Va. in 1833, S18229
John, Va., res. King & Queen Co., Va. in 1818 age ca. 61, S38377
John, Va., b. 1743, enl. in Gloucester Co., Va. & there in 1819, S38389
John, Va., b. 1/1763, enl. in Culpeper Co., Va. & there in 1832 d. 9/11/1837 in Rappahannock Co., Va., Delpha, W3465
John, Va., b. 1/14/1762 in Chesterfield Co., Va. & there at enl. & in 1832, d. 5/8/1840, Ann W3466
John, Va., b. 1731, enl. in Shenandoah Co., Va., d. 1819, Nancy, W19051
John, Va., enl. at Spotsylvania Co., Va., d. 1817 in Halifax Co., Va., Elizabeth, R9727
John, Va., b. 1760, res. at enl. Buckingham Co., Va., applied for pension in Surry Co., N.C., d.

SMITH (continued)
in Henry Co., Va. in 1812, Sarah/ Sally, R9844
John Anderson/John ANDERSON, Pa., U.S.A., Wayne's Ind. War, b. 3/ 15/1760 in Donegal Twp., Lancaster Co., Pa., there at enl., res. Derry Twp., Westmoreland Co., Pa. in 1854, R9763; BLWt.56371-80-50; BLWt.44717-80-55 for Ind. War
John Andrew, Va., res. at enl. Fauquier Co., Va., res. Blount Co., Tenn. in 1818, res. Lawrence Co., Ind. in 1824, d. 11/22/1836, S36775
John Carraway, S.C., d. 3/15/1800 in Savannah, Ga., Ann Belcher, former wid., W4890; BLWt.2265-300
John Conradt, N.Y., b. Germany 5/ 1751/52, came from Germany as a British sold., enl. at Claverack, N.Y., res. Sharon, Schoharie Co., N.Y. in 1833, S14514
John Edward, N.Y., b. 4/25/1760 in Clarkstown, Rockland Co., N.Y., there at enl. & in 1832, d. 1/13/ 1848, Mary, W1503
John Eli, N.Y., b. 5/3/1755 at Haverstraw (Clarkstown), Rockland Co., N.Y., there up to 1833, d. 5/19/1840, Rachel, W1657; BLWt. 7094-160-55
John Kilby, Cont., Mass., res. in Portland, Me. in 1818 age 64; d. 8/7/1842. S18231; BLWt.1900-300-Capt. Iss. 4/24/1794
John N., N.J., b. 9/28/1764 in Bergen Co., N.J. & there at enl. res. Morgan Co., Ohio in 1832, S18228
John O.C., N.J., b. 12/1760 in Oxford Twp., Sussex Co., res. Pickaway Co., Ohio in 1832, S3921
John P., N.Y., res. at enl. Claverack, Columbia Co., N.Y., res. Davenport, Delaware Co., N.Y. in 1832 age 83, Gertrude, W19050
Johnson, N.H., b. 6/5/1760 at New Boston, N.H., there at enl., res. Chatham, Lower Canada in 1834, R9774
Johnson, Va., enl. in Albemarle Co., Va., res. Gallia Co., Ohio in 1818 age 53 & d. there 4/4/ 1837, Nancy, R9813
Jonas, Mass., b. Shrewsbury, Mass. res. during the Rev. Rutland, Worcester Co., Mass., d. Leicester, Mass. 5/1818. Elizabeth Flagg former wid., W24404 (2nd. husb. Wm. Flagg, Mass. a sold.)
Jonas, Mass., b. 12/30/1755, Marlborough, Mass. & there at enl., res. Littleton, Middlesex Co., Mass. in 1832, R9775
Jonas, Va., enl. in Washington Co. Va., res. there in 1833 age 83, S7565
Jonathan, Ct., res. at enl. Ashford, Windham Co., Ct., d. 5/2/ 1824, Polly/Molly, W19373; BLWt. 7436-160-55
Jonathan, Ct., res. Haddam, Middlesex Co., Ct. & d. there 8/16/1812, W24990; BLWt.6107-160-55
Jonathan, Ct., b. 1/13/1746 in Groton, New London Co., Ct., res. at enl. Preston, Ct., res. Genoa, Cayuga Co., N.Y. in 1833, R9776
Jonathan, Ct., Navy, enl. at New Haven, Ct., res. Sheffield, Berkshire Co., Mass. in 1818, S34497
Jonathan, Ct., Sea Service, enl. at Chatham, Ct., d. 12/14/1824, Rebecca, R9835
Jonathan, Cont., Mass., N.H., b. 1/7/1755, enl. at Kennebunk, Me. Res. Fairfield Co., Ohio in 1819 d. 3/22/1830, Jemima, W4809
Jonathan, Cont., Vt., enl. in Vt. res. Rutland Co., Vt. in 1839 age 69, S41171
Jonathan, Mass., b. 3/10/1761 in Norton, Bristol Co., Mass., there at enl., res. Coventry, Kent Co. R.I. in 1832, d. 1/3/1855 in Hartford,Ct., Patience, W11469; BLWt.19711-160-55
Jonathan, N.H., enl. Surry, Cheshire Co., N.H., d. 8/1822 in Rockingham, Huldah, W15949
Jonathan, N.J., b. 1/30/1758 Maidenhead Twp., Hunterdon Co., N.J., res. at enl. Princeton, N.J., res. Elkton, Todd Co., Ky. in 1832, S31380
Jonathan, N.C., enl. in Johnston Co., N.C., res. in Wake Co., N.C. in 1832 age 79, d. 1835/36/37, S7556
Jonathan, R.I., b. in Scituate, R.I., 3/11/1746, there at enl. & in 1832, d. 5/2/1841, Freelove, W22259
Jonathan, Va., res. Youngstown, Trumbull Co., Ohio in 1820 age 64, S40473; BLWt.2079-200-Lt. Iss. 10/17/1794
Jonathan, Va., res. during Rev. Taggarts Valley, res. Randolph Co., Va. in 1834, R9777
Jonathan Warren, Mass., res. at enl. Westminster, res. Hubbardston, Worcester Co., Mass. in 1832 & there d. 8/14/1833, Catharine, W22275
Joseph, Ct., b. 1756 at New London, Ct., there at enl. & in 1832, S14511
Joseph, Ct., res. at enl. Derby, New Haven Co., Ct., there in 1820 age 65 & d. there 4/28/1834 Eunice, W6121
Joseph, Ct., b. & always lived in Stanford, Fairfield Co., Ct., d. 8/6/1828, Rebecca, W17827
Joseph, Ct., b. Hebron, Ct. 10/ 18/1760, there in 1781, d. 9/ 12/1821 in Penfield, Ontario Co. N.Y., Elizabeth Chapman, former wid., R1865
Joseph, Cont., BLWt.2126 See Joseph S.
Joseph, Cont., came over with the German troops, res. Greene Co., Pa. in 1818, d. 7/9/1837, Elizabeth, W4515
Joseph, Cont., Mass., res. at enl. Newbury, Essex Co., Mass., res. in Sanbornton, Stafford Co., N.H. in 1818 age 68, S43163
Joseph, Hazen's Regt., BLWt.13760 Iss. 8/14/1792 to Benjamin Moore ass. No papers
Joseph, Md., BLWt.2041-300-Capt. Iss. 6/19/1789. No papers. Also BLWt.2043-300-Capt. Iss. 5/26/ 1798. No papers. On the record book opposite this Wt.2043 are the following entries. "See Jos. Smith No. 2041" & "in the tracts Location Books in the General Land Office it is shown that 2043 was patented in 1803 to Capt. John Smith"-the location was made by Joseph Nourse, & the patent delivered to the Hon. C. Benj. Huger, then a member of Congress
Joseph, Md., b. 2/14/1753 in Cecil Co., Md. there at enl. res. in Wheeling Twp., Belmont Co., Ohio in 1832, S4861
Joseph, Md.,N.J. See Elias POLLOCK
Joseph, Mass., res. New Haven, Ct. in 1818 age 64, S36763
Joseph, Mass., res. Arundel (Kennebunkport) Me., d. 3/10/1825 at Hollis, York Co., Me., Charity W24993
Joseph, Mass., b. 3/18/1759, res. West Springfield, Hampden Co., Mass. & d. there 4/9/1814, Huldah W24999
Joseph, Mass., b. 4/19/1751 at Hadley, Hampshire Co., Mass. & enl. there, there in 1832, d. 9/ 13/1842, Nancy, W25031
Joseph, Mass., res. at enl. Palmer Hampshire Co., Mass., res. Deerfield, Franklin Co., Mass. in 1837 age 79, R9778
Joseph, Mass., had son named Rufus BLWt.1001-200
Joseph, Mass., BLReg.272221-1855
Joseph, N.H., BLWt.3488. Iss. 12/ 17/1795 to William Thorne, ass. No papers
Joseph, N.H., res. Hampton, Strafford Co., N.H. in 1832 age 72, S18234
Joseph, N.H., res. Vershire, Orange Co., Vt. in 1820 age 67, d. 10/ 20/1838, Hannah, W19062
Joseph, N.J., res. Millstone, Middlesex Co., N.J. at enl., d. 5/4/1823, Sarah, R9855
Joseph, N.J., res. Derry Twp., Northumberland Co., Pa., in 1804 BLWt.376-100
Joseph, N.Y., BLWt.7836. Iss. 9/

SMITH (continued)
15/1790 to Wm. Bell, ass. No papers
Joseph, N.Y., b. 1763 at Fishkill, Dutchess Co., N.Y., res. during Rev. Saratoga Co. & Dutchess Co. N.Y., res. Waterford, Saratoga Co., N.Y. in 1834, S10020
Joseph, N.Y., b. 8/18/1757 in South East, Dutchess Co., N.Y., there at enl., res. Dryden, Tompkins Co., N.Y. in 1832, S11418
Joseph, N.Y., b. 3/19/1755 in Amenia, Dutchess Co., N.Y., there at enl., res. Ulster Twp., Bradford Co., Pa. in 1832, S23926
Joseph, N.Y., b. 6/22/1759 in Oswego, Dutchess Co., N.Y., res. at enl. Dutchess Co., N.Y., res. Johnstown, Montgomery Co., N.Y. in 1832, R9779
Joseph, Pa. See SMIDT
Joseph, Pa., b. on Shenandoah River, Va., res. at enl. near Red Stone Fort, Brownsville, Pa. res. Hardin Co., Ky. in 1833 age 71, S31382; BLWt.13722-160-55
Joseph, R.I., enl. at Gloucester, R.I., res. Manchester, Bennington Co., Vt. in 1818 age 80, S41165
Joseph, R.I., b. North Kingston, R.I. in 1754, enl. at South Kingston, R.I., res. Oneonta, Otsego Co., N.Y. in 1832, d. 1/29/1838, Mary, W25025
Joseph, Va., b. 1763 in Md., res. at enl. Halifax Co., Va., res. Pittsylvania Co., Va. in 1832, d. 7/9/1842, Basha, W3725; BLWt.13900-160-55
Joseph, Va., enl. Fairfax Co., Va. & res. there in 1818 age 60, d. 1/4/1824, Lindsey, W19375
Joseph, Va., b. 1754/55 in Orange Co., Va., res. at enl. Rockingham Co., Va., res. Jefferson Co. Ky. in 1835
Joseph S., Cont. Armand's Corp. res. in Taneytown, Frederick Co. Md. in 1806, BLWt.2126-150-Cornet Iss. 5/28/1789
Joshua, Ct., res. at enl. Norwich, Ct., res. Riga, Monroe Co., N.Y. in 1827 age 67, res. Elba, Genesee Co., N.Y. in 1833, d. 2/7/1849 at Oakfield, Genesee Co., N.Y., Polly, S42329
Joshua, R.I., enl. in Westerly Co., R.I., res. Berlin, Rensselaer Co., N.Y. in 1818, wife Elizabeth in 1820, S42336; BLWt. 3502. Iss. 1800
Joshua, R.I., b. 9/2/1754 in Rehoboth, Bristol Co., Mass. & there at enl., res. Seekonk, Bristol Co., Mass. in 1832 & d. there 2/24/1842, Huldah, W15345
Joshua, Va., res. Rutherford Co., Tenn. in 1818 age about 70, S39080
Joshua, Sheldon's Dragoons, Ct.

SMITH (continued)
BLWt.6526. Iss. 6/25/1789. No papers
Josiah, Ct., b. 12/20/1747 in Windham Co., Ct. & there at enl. & in 1832, S14533
Josiah, Ct., b. at New London, Ct. there at enl., res. Tamworth, Strafford Co., N.H. in 1833 age 82, d. 3/1838, S42330
Josiah, Ct., res. Cheshire, New Haven Co., Ct. in 1787 age 28 & there in 1824, res. Geauga Co. Ohio in 1830, d. 11/17/1833, S47992
Josiah, Ct., b. 7/12/1750, res. Poundridge, Westchester Co., N.Y. in 1788, d. 11/29/1830 at Stamford, Ct., Sarah, W25023
Josiah, Ct., Privateer, b. 8/3/1759 at New London, Ct., there at enl., res. Philipstown, Putnam Co., N.Y. in 1818, d. 1/8/1842 in Richmond Co., N.Y., Anna, W25012
Josiah, Cont., res. & agcy. Ct., res. Berlin, Hartford Co., Ct. in 1818 age 62, S36759
Josiah, Mass., BLWt.1895-300-Capt. Iss. 4/1/1790. No papers
Josiah, Mass., res. Wareham, Plymouth Co., Mass. in 1820 age 63 & there in 1828, S34517; BLWt.1913-200-Lt. Iss. 2/22/1790 to Richard Platt, ass. No papers
Josiah, Mass., res. during Rev. South Hadley, Mass., res. Brookfield, Orange Co., Vt. in 1818 age 62, d. 2/15/1823, Persis, W20057
Jotham, Mass., res. during Rev. Leicester, Mass., res. Phillips, Somerset Co., Me. in 1832, S15987
Justin, Mass., b. Springfield, Mass. & there at enl., res. Stratford, Ct. in 1818 age 63, d. 3/27/1835 at Bridgeport, Ct., Molly, W26482
Keturah, former wid. of Job Primus /Lathrop, Ct., which see
Laban, Ct., Privateer, b. 8/14/1765 in New Haven (East Haven) Ct. & lived there up to 1832, S14525
Laban, Cont., Mass., Privateer, b. 7/1/1760 Taunton, Bristol Co., Mass.& there at enl., res. Livermore, Oxford Co., Me. in 1832, S20552
Lambert, Mass., BLWt.5014. Iss. 2/22/1790 to Richard Platt, ass. No papers
Larkin, Cont., Va., Capt. of Cav. His heirs in 1837 were John Hill Smith, Charles Henry Smith, Mary E. Brooke (nee Mary E. Smith), & Mary & Mildred Henderson, ch. of Alexander & Eliza Henderson who was formerly Eliza Smith, BLWt. 2221-300
Larkin, Va., b. Cumberland Co., Va. & there at enl., res. Oglethorpe Co., Ga. in 1832, d. there

SMITH (continued)
10/20/1834, S31974
Laton, Va., b. 1765 in Kent/Sussex Co. (probably in Va.) res. at enl. Washington Co., Va. res. Bledsoe Co., Tenn. in 1833, S1778
Lawrence, Pvt. in the Invalids, BLWt.13779. Iss. 7/16/1789 to Matt. McConnell, ass. No papers
Lawrence, N.C., b. 7/18/1763 in Edgecombe Co., N.C. & there at enl., res. Harne Co., Ga. in 1836, res. Muscogee Co., Ala.in 1839, R9784
Lemuel, Ct., b. 3/1759 in Farmington, Ct., there at enl., res. in Berlin, Hartford Co., Ct. in 1833, d. 1/17/1839, S14502
Lemuel, Mass., BLWt.4980. Iss. 3/25/1790. No papers
Lemuel, Mass., b. 7/15/1759 at Stoughton, Norfolk Co., Mass. & there at enl. & in 1832, S30108
Lemuel, N.Y., b. 2/14/1752 Huntington, L.I., N.Y., there at enl., res. Augusta, Oneida Co., N.Y. in 1832, d. 9/18/1841, Sarah, W19060
Leonard/Leonard B., Md., res. at enl. near Bryantown, Md., res. Columbia Co., Ga. in 1820 age 60 d. there 1/15/1838, Mary, W6098; BLWt.57752-160-55
Leonard, N.Y., b. 1752 in Bedford Worcester Co., N.Y., res. at enl. Newburgh, Orange Co., N.Y. & d. there 4/1840, S46640
Leonard, Pa., BLWt.10361. Iss. 1/13/179? to John Hoover, ass. No papers
Leonard, Pa., b. 1755 in Lehigh Twp., Northampton Co., Pa., there at enl., res. Franklin Twp., Westmoreland Co., Pa. in 1833, d. 2/22/1838, Ann, R9687
Levi, Mass., b. 5/25/1755 at Haddam, Ct., enl. at West Hampton, Mass., res. Henderson, Jefferson Co., N.Y. in 1832, S14505
Levi, Mass., res. Westborough, Worcester Co., Mass. in 1818 & d. there 3/29/1843, Susannah, W24987
Levi, N.Y., b. 3/20/1764 at Derby Ct., res. at enl. Spencertown, N.Y., d. 1/27/1842 or 6/8/1841 at New Milford, Litchfield Co., Ct., W2261; BLWt.31322-160-55
Levi, R.I., res. of Cumberland, Providence Co., R.I., d. there 8/16/1827, Hannah, W22260
Lewis, Ct., Navy, res. at enl. Haddam, Ct., res. Leydon, Lewis Co., N.Y. in 1832 age 80, d. 5/21/1841, Ann, W19059
Lewis, Mass., b. Shrewsbury, Worcester Co., Mass. & always lived there to 1832 at age 72, S19783
Lewis, Mass., res. Shrewsbury, Worcester Co., Mass. in 1782, d.

SMITH (continued)
2/21/1812 at Wardsboro, Windham Co., Vt., Lucy, W19374; BLWt. 26814-160-55
Lewis, N.Y., b. 2/17/1763 at West Springfield, Hampden Co., Mass., res. at enl. Half Moon(Waterford) N.Y., res. Northampton, Hampshire Co., Mass. in 1832, d. 3/15/1838, Eunice, W15352
Lewis (colored), Va., b. Prince George Co., res. at enl. Dinwiddie Co., Va., there in 1832 age 80, S6112
Libbeus, Mass., res. at enl. Medfield, Norfolk Co., Mass., d. 10/16/1828 at Walpole, Mass., Lois, W7187; BLWt.34841-160-55
Liffe, Mass., b. 9/7/1759 at Walpole, Norfolk Co., Mass., there at enl. & death 7/24/1838, Hepsibath, W15347
Lois, former wid. of Samuel Watson Mass., which see
Lorentz, French Army, b. 7/1756 at Strasburgh, Germany, res. Salem Twp., Columbia Co., Ohio in 1833, R9788
Louis, Va., b. 3/4/1763 in Hempfield Twp., Lancaster Co., Pa., res. at enl. Augusta Co., Va., res. Haywood Co., N.C. in 1833, d. 1/4/1842, Mary, W4805
Lucy, former wid. of Wm. French, Ct., W3609 which see
Lue/Lewee, Ct., res. at enl. Plymouth, Litchfield Co., Ct., res. Cornwall, Litchfield Co., Ct. in 1818, age 65 in 1820, Chloe, S36762
Luther, Ct., b. 10/1757 at Voluntown, Ct., res. at enl. Plainfield, Windham Co., Ct. & there in 1823 & d. there 10/3/1839, Ruth, W26486
Luther, Cont., N.H., War 1812, b. 12/30/1764, res. at enl. Lyndesboro, Hillsborough Co., N.H., res. Lewiston, Niagara Co., N.Y. in 1818, d. 8/7/1846, Ayubah/Azubah, W25017; BLWt.79036-160-55
Margaret, former wid. of John Neal Md., N.J., W19054, which see
Mark, Va., b. & reared Pendleton Co., Va., res. Lewis Co., Va. in 1834 age 73, S18594
Marshall, Green Mt. Boys, Vt., res. at enl. Bridgeport, Addison Co., Vt., d. there 8/18/1815, Polly, R9832
Martin, Ct., b. 1762 in Hartford Co., Ct., son of Martin, res. at enl. New Hartford, Ct., res. Vernon Trumbull Co., Ohio in 1832 S18598
Martin, N.J., b. 12/20/1756 in Hunterdon Co., N.J., S4859
Mary, former wid. of John Harris, Mass., which see
Mary, former wid. of Josiah Long, Mass., which see

SMITH (continued)
Mary, former wid. of Zachariah Hall/Hale, Mass.,Navy, which see
Mary, former wid. of Eddy Phittyplace, R.I., which see
Mary, former wid. of Samuel Wheeler, Va., which see
Massa, Ara, See Massey ARRASMITH
Matthew/Mathew, Ct., b. 5/12/1753 at East Haddam, Ct. & there at enl., res. Middlefield, Hampshire Co., Mass. in 1832, S31379
Matthew, Ct., res. at enl. Goshen, Litchfield Co., Ct., d. at Vernon Oneida Co., N.Y., 11/18/1815, Susan, R9860
Matthew, Ct., Vt., b. 1/13/1760 in Pomfret, Windham Co., Ct., there at enl., 3rd enl. at Harland, Vt. res. Chaplain, Windham Co., Ct. in 1832 & d. there 12/25/1841. Emma, W2010; BLWt.27585-160-55
Matthew, N.J., BLWt.8712. Iss. 9/25/1789 to Peter Anspach, ass. No papers
Matthew, Pa., BLWt.10383. Iss. 4/21/1796 to James Morrison, ass. No papers
Matthew, Va., Capt. d. 1777 in service (never married), BLWt. 200-300
Matthias, N.J., b. 8/2/1757 at Freehold Twp., Monmouth Co., N.J. there at enl. & in 1833, S1107
Michael, Ct., res. Chatham, Middlesex Co., Ct., d. 5/10/1828, Mary, W17846
Michael, Md., BLWt.11679. Iss. 6/17/1799 to James DeBaufre, ass. No papers
Michael, Md., BLWt.11694. Iss. 3/18/1795. No papers
Michael, Cont., Md., enl. at Fredericktown, Md., d. 1821 age 63 in Baltimore, Md., Rebecca, W4339; BLWt.352-60-55
Michael, Md., Pa., b. 1752 Washington Co., Md., d. 11/24/1842 in Harrison Co., Ky., Nancy, W6088
Michael, N.J., BLWt.8741. Iss. 6/16/1789 to Thomas Coyle, ass. No papers
Michael, N.Y., War 1812, b. 1760 in N.Y.C., there at enl., res. Cornwall, Orange Co., N.Y. in 1832, S14515
Michael, N.Y., b. 5/24/1748 in Rhinebeck, Dutchess Co., N.Y., res. at enl. Scotchtown, Orange Co., N.Y., res. Glenville, Schenectady Co., N.Y. in 1832, R9808
Michael, Va., BLWt.12535. Iss. 12/14/1795 to Robert Camp, ass. No papers
Michael, Va., enl. in Pa., res. Miami Twp., Hamilton Co., Ohio in 1820 age 57, S40448. His ch. were Elizabeth, Hugh & Mary
Miner, Ct., res. at enl. Windham, Ct., there d. 1/13/1823, Submit, W25010; BLWt.3612-160-55
Moody, N.H., res. at enl.

SMITH (continued)
Hopkinton, Merrimack Co., N.H. there in 1832 age 74, S11422
Moses, Ct., Dis. No papers. See Am. State Papers, Class 9, pps rough, by an accidental fall while at work.
Moses, Cont., Mass., b. 6/12/1756, res. Groton, New London Co., Ct. in 1820, d. 4/15/1822 in Groton (Ledyard), Ct., Lydia W22235; BLWt.25791-160-55
Moses, Mass., b. Exeter, N.H., 10/15/1755, res. at enl. Rowley Mass., res. Greenwich, Washington Co., N.Y. in 1833, d. 6/18/1846, S23925
Moses, Mass., res. Prospect, Hancock Co., Me. in 1818 age 58, S37414
Moses, Mass., res. at enl. alleged to be Northfield, Franklin Co., Mass., d. 12/27/1839 at Pike, Wyoming Co., N.Y., Bethiah, R9695
Moses, N.Y., BLWt.7768. Iss. 1/31/1791. No papers
Moses, N.Y., enl. Orange Co.,N.Y. res. Baltimore, Md. in 1818, res. Baltimore in 1820 age 60, Mary, S35077
Moses, N.Y., enl. at Walkill Twp., Orange Co., N.Y., res. Philadelphia, Pa. in 1818 age 59, S40447
Moses, N.C., b. Cumberland Co., Va. 1761, res. at enl. Halifax Co., N.C., res. Adair Co., Ky. in 1832, S31376
Nahum, Mass., res. Sturbridge, Worcester Co., Mass. in 1818 age 69, S34515
Nancy, former wid. of John Keith, S.C., which see
Nathan/Nathaniel, Ct., BLWt.6443. Iss. 9/8/1790 to James Sebor, ass. No papers
Nathan, Ct., b. 2/1755 at Lyme, Ct., res. at enl. Montville, New London Co., Ct., res. Hebron, Ct. in 1832, S17680
Nathan, Ct., b. Holden, Worcester Co., Mass., res. there in 1818 age 55, res. at enl. on Susquehannah River, in N.Y., d. 8/23/1824 at Holden, Mass., Rachel, W26477, Nathan Smith "of Rutland" m. 8/21/1783 in Princeton, Worcester Co., Mass., Rachael Rolph of said Princeton.
Nathan, Mass., BLWt.4979. Iss. 4/5/1792. No papers
Nathan, Cont., Mass., res. at enl. Pownalborough (Wiscasset) Me., res. Shriley, Middlesex Co., Mass. in 1820 age 89, Ruth,S30112
Nathan, Cont., Mass., res. Weston, Middlesex Co., Mass. in 1818 age 77, S34491
Nathan, Cont., N.H., res. Knox, Hancock Co., Me. in 1820 age 55, where he d. 8/3/1832, Sarah, W24966
Nathan, Md., Va., b. 10/8/1754 in

SMITH (continued)
Harford Co., Md., d. 9/27/1821 in Boone Co., Ky., Ann J., W8730 BLWt.1069-300
Nathan, Mass., res. Sturbridge, Worcester Co., Mass., res. Swanton, Franklin Co., Vt. in 1818 age 74, Sarah, S41167
Nathan, Mass., en. at Lexington, Mass., res. Fitzwilliam, Cheshire Co., H.H. in 1818 age 54, Catharine, S43153; BLWt.6380-160-55
Nathan, enl. at Boston as cook's mate on board the Constitution & served under Capt. Samuel Nichols sold. claims to have been aboard when ship was launched from Navy Yard at (or near) Boston. Rejected 300828
Nathan, N.Y., Privateer, b. 3/27/1763 North Salem, Westchester Co., N.Y., S19096
Nathan, R.I., b. 1755 in Scituate, R.I., there at enl. d. 1/29/1838 at Virgil, Cortland Co., N.Y., Alce/Alice, W19057
Nathan, Vt., b. 1761 in Nine Partners, Dutchess Co., N.Y., res. at enl. Manchester, Vt., d. 8/2/1845 at Lyons, Wayne Co., N.Y., Sally, W24988
Nathan, Va., b. Frederick Co., Va. there at enl., res. Franklin Twp. Washington Co., Ind. in 1836 age 82, R9816
Nathaniel, Ct., res. Lyme, New London Co., Ct., in 1820 age 59, Lucinda, S36764
Nathaniel, Ct., b. 8/11/1761 at Canterbury, Windham Co., Ct. & there at enl., d. there 7/21/1835, Lucy, W17832
Nathaniel, Ct., Cont., res. Litchfield, Ct. in 1820 age 66, S36766
Nathaniel, Ct., b. Rochester, Plymouth Co., Mass., res. Albany N.Y. in 1820 age 57, res. Rochester, Plymouth Co., Mass. in 1841, S34486
Nathaniel, Cont., N.H., b. Epping N.H., res. Monmouth, Kennebec Co., Me. in 1820 age 62, Anna, S37407
Nathaniel, Mass., b. 7/9/1754, res. at enl. Colerain, Franklin Co.,Mass., & there in 1832, d. 5/11/1835, Mary, W20055
Nathaniel, N.H., enl. at Mason, N.H., res. Chester, Windsor Co., Vt. in 1818 age 63, d. there 5/4/1839, Mary, W19376
Nathaniel, Pa., BLWt.2024-200-Lt. Iss. 7/16/1789. No papers
Nathaniel, R.I., res. of Bristol, R.I., d. 3/1821, Elizabeth, W22258
Nathaniel, R.I., b. 11/6/1763 in Newport, R.I. & there at enl., d. there 9/18/1843, Lydia, W22261
Nathaniel, Va., enl. in Culpeper Co., Va., d. 11/1824, Susanna, W1094
Nathaniel, Va., b. 6/30/1763 in Hanover Co., Va. & enl. there, res. Goochland Co., Va. in 1833 where he d. 4/18/1841, Lucy, W5175; BLWt.82570-160-55
Nathaniel, Va., b. 5/5/1762 in Brunswick Co., Va., res. at enl. Henry (later Patrick) Co., Va., res. Maury Co., Tenn. in 1836, R9817
Nehemiah, Cont., Mass., res. Abington, Plymouth Co., Mass. in 1818 age 66, S34505
Nehemiah, Mass., War 1812, N.Y., enl. at Ashfield, Hampshire Co. Mass., res. Meredith, Delaware Co., N.Y. in 1819 age 52 & d. there 12/20/1836, Polly, W2451; BLWts. 31590-160-55 & 91877-40-50
Nicholas, Cont., enl. at Newark, N.J., & Haverstraw, N.Y., res. Salem Twp., Washington Co., Ohio in 1818 age 81, S40462
Nicholas, Lamb's Art. N.Y., BLWt. 7841. Iss. 7/18/1791 to Richard Platt, ass. No papers
Nicholas, N.Y., b. 1755 in Schenectady, N.Y., res. there during Rev. War, res. Orlean, Jefferson Co., N.Y. in 1832, d. 12/13/1845 at Lyme, Jefferson Co., N.Y., S16252
Nicholas/Nichols, Va., b. 6/4/1759 in Germany, res. at enl. Frederick Co., Va., res. Henry Co., Ky. in 1832, d. 12/31/1838, Mary, W8732
Nicholas A., Cont., N.J. See Nicholas ARROSMITH
Noah, Ct., b. 11/1751 at New Fairfield, Ct., res. at enl. Kent, Litchfield Co., Ct., res. Palmyra Ohio, in 1832, Hannah, R9819
Noah, Mass., res. Hollis, York Co. Me. in 1824 age ca. 70, d. there 12/3/1829, Comfort Drew former wid., W22968
Obadiah, N.Y., enl. in Dutchess Co., N.Y., res. Clermont Co., Ohio in 1820 age 61, Peninah, S40458
Obadiah, Va., b. 3/1/1763, Powhatan Co., Va., res. at enl. Buckingham Co., Va., res. Jefferson Co., Tenn. in 1832, S3938
Obed. E., (or C.), Mass., b. 8/8/1757 at Harwich, Barnstable Co., Mass. & there at enl. & in 1832, d. 2/1/1838, Abigail, W13906
Oliver, Ct., res. at enl. Mansfield, Ct., res. Addison, Addison Co., Vt. in 1832 age 68, S21980
Oliver, Cont., N.H., d. 8/14/1811 at Gilford, N.H., Mary, W20059
Oliver, Mass., b. Sowhegan Twp., (New Bedford) N.H., (believed to be Mass., not N.H.), res. at enl. Sturbridge, Worcester Co., Mass., res. Spafford (Marcellus), Onondaga Co., N.Y. in 1823, S29465
Oliver, Mass., res. Pelham, Hampshire Co., Mass. in 1825 age 62, where he d. 8/1/1844, Sarah G., W591
Oliver, Mass., b. 6/14/1761 at Natick, Middlesex Co., Mass. & there at enl., res. Oxford, Worcester Co., Mass. in 1836, R9820
Oliver, Mass., Vt., b. 1752 at Hadley, Hampshire Co., Mass., there at 1st enl., res. Stanford, Bennington Co., Vt. in 1777, res. Clarendon, Orleans Co., N.Y. in 1832, S14500
Oliver, N.H., BLWt.3498. Iss. 7/21/1789 to Ladd & Cass, assnes. No papers
Oliver, R.I., b. 10/26/1757 in Smithfield, Providence Co., R.I. there at enl. & in 1832, d. there 8/16/1842, Aletha, W24991
Oren, Mass., res. at enl. Hampshire (Franklin Co.), Mass., d. there 5/14/1823, Keziah, W15354
Othniel D., Cont., N.Y., enl. at Clinton, Dutchess Co., N.Y. & there in 1820 age ca. 71, S42338
Patrick/Peter, N.C., b. 6/17/1750, res. Robeson Co., N.C.. d. there 7/4/1816, Ann, W4072
Paul, Mass., b. 1758 at South Hadley, Hampden Co., Mass. & there during Rev., res. Royalton, Windsor Co., Vt. in 1832, S21978
Peleg, Mass., res. Waldoboro, Lincoln Co., Me. in 1818 age 67, d. there 6/12/1832, Lucy, S38383
Peleg, N.Y., enl. at Huntington, Suffolk Co., N.Y., there in 1839 age 84, S14518
Peregrine, R.I., res. at enl. Foster (Scituate), Providence Co. R.I., res. after Rev. in Vt., d. 3/20/1813, Jeuriah Tower, former wid., W18147
Peris, Mass., b. 4/7/1763, res. at enl. Sandisfield, Berkshire Co., Mass., res. Genesee Co., N.Y. in 1827, Sarah, W16407
Peter, Ct., res. Stamford, Fairfield Co., Ct. in 1820 age 65, S36767
Peter, Cont., Mass., res. Sudbury, Middlesex Co., Mass. in 1818 age 63, res. Chester, Windsor Co., Vt. in 1826, S41170
Peter, Mass., res. Portland, Me. in 1820 age 60, S37408
Peter, Mass., b. 6/3/1765 at Medfield, Norfolk Co., Mass., there at enl., res. Walpole, Norfolk Co., Mass. in 1832 & d. there 1/21/1834, Nelly, R9818
Peter, N.H., res. Know, Hancock Co., Me. in 1818 age 59, d. 4/18/1837, Hannah, W22347
Peter, N.J., BLWt.8752. Iss. 2/

SMITH (continued)
21/1793 to George Stout, ass. No papers
Peter, N.Y., enl. at North East (Pine Plains), Dutchess Co., N.Y. & there in 1829 age 72, S42335
Peter, N.Y., res. Marbletown, Ulster Co., N.Y., d. 3/22/1834, Agitty, W16732
Peter, N.Y., res. at enl. Rockland Co., N.Y., d. 5/18/1812 in N.Y. City, Catharine, W19065
Peter, N.C., b. 1762, res. at enl. Rowan Co., N.C., S7533
Peter, N.C., b. 4/12/1750 in Lancaster Co., Pa., res. at enl. Surry Co., N.C., res. Stokes (Surry) Co., N.C. in 1832, S7538
Peter, N.C., enl. in Orange Co., N.C., res. Caswell Co., N.C. in 1818 age 71, S42015
Peter, N.C. See Patrick
Peter, Pa., b. 1736 in Berks Co., Pa. & there at enl., other res. Northumberland & Mifflin Cos., Pa., res. Lake Twp., Wayne Co., Ohio in 1833, S4850
Peter, Pa., res. Northampton Co., Pa. in 1830 age 67, S40470; BLWt. 2021-200-Lt. Iss. 10/20/1789
Peter, Pa., res. at enl. Northumberland Co., Pa., d. 9/9/1829, R9824
Peter, Va., res. Montgomery Co., Va. in 1820 age 73, S38378
Peter T., Mass., b. 6/24/1761, res. at enl. Blandford, Hampshire Co., Mass., res. Lexington, Greene Co., N.Y. in 1832,S14491
Phebe, former wid. of John Hopkins Mass., which see
Philemon, Ct., N.Y., b. 9/1/1760 at Stamford, Fairfield Co., Ct. there at enl., res. Phillipstown, Putnam Co., N.Y. in 1832, S14503
Philip, Cont., res. Exeter Twp., Berks Co., Pa. in 1818 age 62, d. 11/30/1837 at Weavertown, Berks Co., Pa., Catharine, W6097; BLWt.535-160-55
Philip, See Philip D. SMYTH
Philip, Hazen's Regt., BLWt.13745 iss. 9/7/1789 to Wm. J. Vredenburgh. No papers
Philip, Md., b. 5/1742 in Delaware Co., Pa., res. at enl. on Thomas Creek, Frederick Co., Md., res. New Sewickley Twp., Beaver Co., Pa. in 1835, R9829
Philip, N.J., b. 3/6/1760 Hunterdon Co., N.J., there at enl., res. Trigg Co.,Ky. in 1833,S31371
Philip, N.C., b. 1757 in York, Pa. res. at enl. Lincoln Co., N.C., res. Monroe Co., Tenn. in 1832, Mary A., S1725
Philip, Pa., b. 1/8/1754, res. 1777 Chester Co., Pa., res. Allegany Co., Pa. in 1834, R9828
Philip, Va., b. 1757 in King & Queen Co., Va., there at enl., res. Spotsylvania Co., Va. in

SMITH (continued)
1832, S6118
Philip, Va., b. 1755 in Amherst Co., Va., there at enl. & in 1832, R9830
Philip D., Cont., Md. See SMYTH
Phineas, Ct., Vt.,b.1761 Suffield, Hartford Co., Ct., res. during the Rev. Winchester, Litchfield Co., Ct., and Rupert, Bennington Co., Vt., in 1833 res. Alburgh, Grand Isle Co., Vt., S19471
Phinehas, Ct., b. 6/1/1759, res. at enl. Roxbury, Ct. & enl. at Woodbury, Ct., d. 11/7/1839 at Southbury, Litchfield Co., Ct. Deborah Ann, W11480
Phinehas, Ct., enl. at New Canaan, Fairfield Co., Ct., d. 3/14/1812 at Norwalk, Fairfield Co., Ct., Abiah, W26487
Pliny, Mass., Vt., b. Sandisfield, Berkshire Co., Mass., res. at en. New Marlborough, Berkshire Co., Mass. & Newport, Bennington Co., Vt., in 1833 Orwell, Rutland Co., Vt. age 70, S15982
Preserved, Mass., b. 1759 at Ashfield, Hampshire Co., Mass., res. in 1832 Rowe, Franklin Co., Mass. d. 8/15/1834, Eunice, W13905
Ralph, Ct., b.1/11/1761 Chatham, Middlesex Co., Ct., there at enl. & 1833, d. 1/24/1838, Mary, W819
Ralph, Ct., res. at enl. Chatham, Middlesex Co., Ct., d. 1807, Hannah, W15945
Ralph, Ct., res. at enl. New Milford, Litchfield Co., Ct., there in 1819, d. 11/13/1825, Anne W17841
Ralph, S.C., b. 8/23 or 24, 1763, res. at enl. York Dist., S.C., res. Lincoln Co., Tenn. in 1832, d. 11/2/1853, Elizabeth, W7184; BLWt.12737-160-55
Randall/Randolph, Cont.,R.I., b. 7/18/1754 Cranston, R.I., enl. there, d. 5/7/1831 Murray, Orleans Co., N.Y., Sarah, W22256; BLWt.645-100
Randol, N.C.,b.4/3/1748 Amelia Co. Va., res. at enl. Wilkes Co.,N.C. res. Carter Co.,Ky. 1843, R9834
Randolph, Cont., R.I., See Randall
Ransom, N.C., b. 4/11/1761 in Hanover Co., Va., res. at enl. Granville Co., N.C., res. Marion Co., Tenn. in 1832, d. 8/12/1855, S3925
Redmond, Va., b. 1/30/1761 in Essex Co., Va., there at enl., res. Fleming Co., Ky. in 1832, d. 12/3/1842, Hannah, W8742
Resolved, R.I., res. Smithfield, Providence Co., R.I., d. 5/9/1826, Mary, W22239
Reuben, Mass., b. 2/1759 at South Hadley, Hampshire (Franklin) Co., Mass., & enl. there, res. Bolton, Warren Co., N.Y. in 1832, d. there 3/20/1842, Miriam, R9810

SMITH (continued)
Reuben, Mass., Vt., b. 7/15/1755 in Brookfield, West Parish, Mass. res. at enl. Guilford, Windham Co., Vt., res. Mentz, Cayuga Co. N.Y. in 1832, res. St. Clair Co., Mich. in 1833, S29463
Reuben, Navy, R.I., b. 11/25/1758 in Cranston, Providence Co., R.I. there at enl., res. Providence, R.I. in 1834, S21494
Reuben, N.Y., b. 7/12/1762 at North Salem Westchester Co., N.Y. there at enl. & in 1832, d. 7/7/1836, Susannah, W15704
Reuben, N.C., b. 2/26/1749 in Pa., res. at enl. Orange Co., N.C. & there in 1832, S7547
Reuben, R.I., res. Burrillville, Providence Co., R.I. in 1831 age 63, Sarah, W1505; BLWts.59-60-55 & 3414-100-(1794)
Reuben, Vt., b. 1/13/1763 in Windsor, Ct., res. at enl. Norwich, Windsor Co., Vt., res Vernon Twp., Scioto Co., Ohio in 1845, d. 12/14/1845, Abigail, S16249
Reuben, Va., res. Pittsylvania Co., Va. in 1839 age 68, d. there 12/2/1831, Elizabeth, W6131; BLWt.9198-160-55
Reuben, Va., res. Floyd Co., Ind. in 1833 age 75, d. there 11/22/1843, Mary, W9659
Reynard/Reynaud, N.Y., Margaret, BLWt.50887-160-55
Richard, Ct., b. 6/5/1758 in Glastonbury, Hartford Co., Ct., there at enl. & in 1832 age 66, S14520
Richard, Cont., N.Y., b. Jamaica Queens Co., L.I., 5/1/1762, d. N.Y.C. 2/29/1832, Susannah, W15947
Richard, Cont., Va., enl. in Prince Edward Co., Va., res. in Franklin Co., Ind. in 1818 (res. Ky. in 1812), S16254; BLWt.570-100
Richard, Md., b.1755 Charles Co., Md., there at enl., res. Rowan Co., N.C. in 1833, d. 6/13/1840 Elizabeth, W4073
Richard, Mass., BLWt.5004. Iss. 6/5/1789 to Edmund Fowle. No papers
Richard, Mass., enl. at New Marlborough, Mass., res. Brutus Cayuga Co., N.Y. in 1818, res. Phelps, Ontario Co., N.Y. in 1830 age 59, d. 1/16/1838 at Milton, Saratoga Co., N.Y., Mary, W25009
Richard, N.H., res. at enl. Hopkinton, N.H., d. 9/19/1807 at Grantham, Sullivan Co., N.H., Edner, W16413
Richard, N.J., b. 12/3/1761 at Maidenhead (Lawrenceville) Hunterdon Co., N.J., there at enl. res. Montgomery Co., Ohio in 1834, S7532

SMITH (continued)
Richard, N.J., b. 8/17/1765 in Hanover Twp., Morris Co., N.J. there in 1832, R9837
Richard, N.Y., BLWt.7751 iss. 7/29/1790. No papers
Richard, N.Y., res. at enl. North Castle Twp., Westchester Co., N.Y., d. ca. 1816, Mary, W22238
Richard, N.C., b.8/24/1743 London, England, res. at enl. Caswell Co. N.C. & there in 1833, S7549
Richard, R.I.,b.4/16/1753 Bristol, R.I., there at enl.& d. there 10/17/1832, Lusanna, R24995
Robert, Ct., Cont., d. before 1828; BLWt.1267-100
Robert, Cont., Ct., b. 1761 Haddam Middlesex Co., Ct. & there at enl., res. Meriden, New Haven Co. Ct. in 1832, S11421
Robert, Cont.,Mass.,b.12/1749, res. at enl. Barre, Worcester Co. Mass., d. there 12/25/1830, Mary, W19382; BLWt.1906-100
Robert, Md., BLWt.11736. Iss. 11/29/1790 to Wm. Smith, Admr. No papers.
Robert, N.Y., BLWt.7818. Iss. 8/10/1790. No papers
Robert, N.Y., b.11/25/1752 N.Y.C. there during Rev. & in N.J., res. Phila., Pa. in 1832, S3926
Robert, N.Y., res. Virgil, Cortland Co., N.Y. in 1828, S46525
Robert, N.Y., res. at enl. Schenectady, N.Y., d. 12/26/1831 Gertrude, R9738
Robert, N.C., b. 4/1/1751, enl. from Johnston Co., N.C., res. Hawkins Co., Tenn. in 1818, d. 1/3/1837, Elizabeth, W1504
Robert, N.C., res. Cabarras Co., N.C., BLWt.57-300
Robert, Pa., b. Ireland, res. at enl. Berks Co., Pa., res. Fayette Co., Pa. in 1834 age 76, S23923
Robert, S.C., b. Ireland, son of Hughy Smith an Irishman who lived in Charleston, S.C. during the Rev. Enl. in Fairfield Co., S.C. d. Butts Co., Ga. 6/19/1853 age ca. 100 yrs., Ferguson, R9731; BLWt.8446-160-55
Robert, S.C., enl. from Orangeburg Dist., S.C., d. 1/22/1781, Hannah, R9744
Robert, Va., enl. in Botetourt Co., Va., d.12/9/1786, Blessing, R9697
Robert, Va., b. 1761 Lunenburg Co., Va. & there at enl. & in 1833 & 1849, res. Charlotte Co., Va. in 1852, R9840
Robert, Va., b. 2/1749, res. at enl. Cumberland Co., Va., res. Oglethorpe Co., Ga. in 1832, R9842
Robin, Va., res. during Rev. King William Co., Va., d. 11/13/1833 in Henrico Co., Va., S14509
Robinson, Cont., N.H., res. at

SMITH (continued)
Deerfield, N.H., res. Murray, Genesee Co., N.Y. in 1818 age 55, S42345
Roger, Ct., Privateer, b. 4/9/1759 at Windham, Ct., there at enl., res. N.Y. after the Rev., res. Columbus, Franklin Co., Ohio in 1833, S14529
Rogers, Mass., res. at enl. Medfield, Mass., res. Pittsford, Rutland Co., Vt. in 1818 age 56, S41168
Roland/Rowland, Mass., b. Middleboro, Mass., res. Augusta, Kennebec Co., Me. in 1818 age 57, d. there 3/27/1840, Nancy, W22348; BLWt.6264-160-55
Rominor, Mass., b. 8/13/1759, res. at enl. Colerain, Franklin Co., Mass., d. 8/23/1827, Hannah, W20056
Roswell, Ct., b. 1758 at East Windsor, Hartford Co., Ct., there at enl. which place was later called Vernon, Tolland Co., Ct., there in 1832, d. 8/15/1844, S17684
Roswell, Vt., b. 10/19/1754 in Farmington, Ct., res. at enl. Windsor, Vt., res. Randolph, Orange Co., Vt. in 1832, S14490
Samuel, Ct. agcy., Dis. No papers
Samuel, Ct., b. 12/25/1749 East Haven, New Haven Co., Ct., there at enl. & in 1832, d. 8/18/1833, Anna, W22265
Samuel, Ct., Ct. Sea Service, b. 3/21/1758 in Southington, Hartford Co., Ct., there at enl., res. Savannah, Chatham Co., Ga. in 1832, S31971
Samuel, Ct., Cont., b. 7/8/1762 at Stratford, Ct. & there at enl., res. Woodbury, New Haven Co., Ct. in 1832, S14494
Samuel, Cont., Ct., res. at enl. Haddam, Ct., res. Wilton, Fairfield Co., Ct. in 1820 age 64, d. there 5/16/1836, Mary, S17107
Samuel, Cont., Mass., res. Monroe Hancock Co., Me. in 1820 age 62, d. 10/29/1842, Mary, W22251
Samuel, Cont., N.H., enl. at Goffstown, N.H., res. Hartford, Windsor Co., Vt. in 1818 age 60, res. Cheshire Co., N.H. in 1837, S43145
Samuel, Cont., N.H., res. Rye, Rockingham Co., N.H. in 1820 age 69, d. 1/4/1824, Elizabeth, W16411
Samuel, Me., B.L.Reg. 334032
Samuel, Md., b. 7/27/1752 in Carlisle, Pa., res. at enl. Harford Co., Md., res. D.C. in 1832 d. 4/22/1839, Margaret, W9303
Samuel, Mass., b. 6/7/1759 at Biddeford, York Co., Me. & there at enl. & in 1832, S18230
Samuel, Mass., res. at enl. Shrewsbury, Worcester Co., Mass. & there in 1832, S19472

SMITH (continued)
Samuel, Mass., b. 1749 in Kittery Me., res. at enl. Arundel (Kennebunkport) York Co., Me. & there in 1832, S30115
Samuel, Mass., b.7/22/1757 Newbury, Genesee Co., N.Y. & there at enl., res. Madison Co., Ohio in 1834, d. 6/6/1844, Sarah,W6090
Samuel, Mass., b. 4/16/1752 in Hatfield, Hampshire Co., Mass., there at enl. & in 1832, d. 10/26/1834, Sarah, W15350
Samuel, Mass., b. 1758 Barre, Worcester Co., Mass. & there at enl. res. Mooers, Clinton Co., N.Y. in 1832, d.1/8/1835, Margaret,W22242
Samuel, Navy, res. Newburyport, Essex Co., Mass. in 1820 age 69, S3929
Samuel, N.H., BLWt.3486 iss. 1/28/ to James Patterson, ass. No papers
Samuel, N.H., b. Exeter, N.H., d. 10/9/1811 at Hallowell, Augusta Co., Me., Hannah, W25028
Samuel, N.Y., b. 10/24/1760 at Fishkill, N.Y., res. at enl. Albany, N.Y., res. Jennings Co., Ind. in 1832, S32530
Samuel, N.Y., b. 6/25/1753, res. Southtown, Suffolk Co., N.Y. & d. there 1/27/1791, Susannah, W17836
Samuel, N.Y., b. 7/13/1757 at Fredericksburg, N.Y., there at enl., d. 11/21/1844 at Seneca, N.Y., Nancy, W19056
Samuel, N.C., b. Bute Co.(Warren Co.), N.C. & lived that area all his life, there in 1833 age 73, S7560
Samuel, N.C., enl. at Hillsboro, Orange Co., N.C., res. Hickman Co., Tenn. in 1820 age 68-70, Sarah, S39082; BLWt.117-100
Samuel, N.C., b.11/16/1758 in Guilford Co. (Rockingham), N.C. & there up to 1832, d. 5/6/1839 Martha, W4808
Samuel, N.C., enl. from Cumberland N.C., d. 12/15/1813 near Columbia S.C., Nancy, R9815
Samuel, N.C.,b. 1755 Pittsylvania Co., Va., res. at enl. Burke Co. N.C., res. Cumberland Co., Ky. in 1832, d.there 6/4/1851, Rachael,R9833
Samuel, Pa., BLWt.2014-200-Lt.Iss. 10/4/1792 to Alexander Bingham, Admr. No papers
Samuel, Pa.,b.3/25/1769, res. of Bucks Co., Pa., d.9/17/1835, Nancy, W3120; BLWt.2006-300 iss. 1/28/1800
Samuel, R.I., BLWt.3517 iss. 5/28/1792 to Israel Angell, ass. No papers
Samuel, R.I., res. Middleborough, Plymouth Co., Mass. in 1820 age 61, Hope, S34487
Samuel, R.I., d. 2/8/1830 in

SMITH (continued)
Swanzey, R.I., Sarah, W12995
Samuel, S.C., b. 12/31/1765 in Spartanburgh Dist., S.C., there at enl. & in 1843, S19093
Samuel, S.C., b. 5/21/1754 in Phila. Co., Pa., res. at enl & 1832 Union Dist., S.C., S21988
Samuel, S.C., res. of Charleston S.C., d. 9/24/1829, Catharine Caroline, W22271
Samuel, Vt., b. 3/17/1759 at Nine Partners, Dutchess Co., N.Y., res. at enl. Salisbury, Rutland Co., Vt., res. Malone, Franklin Co., N.Y. in 1832, S14526
Samuel, Va., b. 4/19/1763 in Northumberland Co., Va., res. at enl. Westmoreland Co., Va., res. Allen Co., Ky. in 1833, S31378
Samuel, Va., b. Ire., res. Bullitt Co., Ky. & d. there in 1832,R9847
Samuel, Va., b. 6/15/1760 in Amherst Co., Va., res. at enl. Montgomery Co., Va., res. Cumberland Co., Ky. in 1834, d. 10/9/1844, Darcus, R9848
Samuel Bryan, Ct., b. 7/18/1755 in Milford, New Haven Co., Ct., lived there up to 1832, S17104
Sarah, former wid. of Robert Stogdill, Ct., which see
Selah/Salah, Mass., b. 1/17/1762 at Deerfield, Mass., d. 3/23/1830 at Waitsfield, Washington Co., Vt., Mary, W20058
Seth, Ct., b. 1/14/1753 at Lyme, New London Co., Ct. & lived there up to 1832, S14507
Seth, Cont., Mass., res. prior to service Suffolk, Ct., enl. at Boston, Mass., res. Norway, Herkimer Co., N.Y. in 1818, d. 7/6/1829, S42347
Seth, Cont. Mass., res. at enl. Norton, Bristol Co., Mass., d. 8/1/1803, Rachael, W15705
Shadrack, Mass., b. 1756 in Smithfield, Providence Co., R.I., res. at enl. Dudley, Worcester Co., Mass., res. New Hartford, Oneida Co., N.Y. in 1832, d. 11/8/1835, Joanna, R9752
Shadrack, N.C., b. 12/26/1752 in Johnston Co. (Wake), N.C., res. at enl. Wake Co., N.C., res. Oglethorpe Co., Ga. in 1832, S31970
Sherman, Ct., res. during Rev. Newtown, Fairfield Co., Ct., d. N.C. in 1811, Amarillas, W25005
Sherwood, Va., b. 1761 in Brunswick Co., Va., there at enl. res. Mecklenburg Co., Va. in 1833, S1591
Shorten, N.Y., BLWt.7741, iss. 10/10/17?? to Anthony Maxwell, ass. No papers
Shubael, R.I., b. 1762 in Rehoboth Mass., there at enl., res. Marshfield, Washington Co., Vt. in 1832, S18602

SMITH (continued)
Sihon/Sion/Simon, N.C., res. at enl. Wake Co., N.C. & d. there 3/19/1832, Sarah, W10268; BLWt. 50941-160-55
Silas, Ct., b. 12/9/1761 at Colchester, Ct., res. at enl. Wyoming, Pa., res. Harlem Twp., Delaware Co., Ohio in 1832, d. 7/17/1839, S18597
Silvanus, Cont., Mass., b. Sept. 1745, res. Shirley, Middlesex Co., Mass. in 1818, d. 5/18/1830, S34490; BLWt.1902-300-Capt. Iss. 3/25/1790
Simeon, Col. Seth Warner's Regt. BLWt.1885-300-Capt. Iss. 7/22/1789 to Thaddeus Thompson, admr. No papers
Simeon, Mass., BLWt.5039. Iss. 3/7/1792 to Jonathan Tuttle, ass. No papers
Simeon, Cont., Mass., enl. at Sandisfield, Mass., res. Cicero Onondaga Co., N.Y. in 1818 age 59, d. 5/4/1841 at Erie, Pa. at age 86, S40449
Simeon, Green Mt. Boys, N.Y., b. 1751 at Brookfield, Mass., enl. at Walpole, Cheshire Co., N.H. res. Erie Co., Pa. in 1832, S4849
Simeon, Mass., b. 10/1753 South Hadley, Mass., res. at enl. & in 1832 West Springfield, Hampshire Co., Mass., S29464
Simeon, Mass., res. Worcester, Worcester Co., Mass. in 1818 age 61, S34513
Simeon, Mass., N.Y., b. 2/29/1756 at Branford, Ct., res. at enl. Harlwood (Washington) Berkshire Co., Mass., res. Westfield Twp., Delaware Co., Ohio in 1832, S17685
Simeon, N.H. b. 2/15/1764 in Raymond, Rockingham Co., N.H., res. at enl. Sandwich, Strafford Co., N.H., d. 7/17/1852 at Campton, Grafton Co., N.H., Mary, R9803; BLWt.13432-160-55
Simeon/Simon, N.C., res. Edgefield Dist., S.C. in 1820 age 69, S39079
Simeon, R.I., b. 10/30/1760 in Gloucester, Providence Co., R.I. there at enl., res. Burrellville Providence Co., R.I. in 1832, S21491
Simeon, R.I., b. 3/4/1746 in Warwick, R.I., res. at enl. Warwick Kent Co., R.I., res. Cranston, Providence Co., R.I. in 1832, d. 3/3/1843, S21492
Simeon, Ct., b. 2/17/1759 in Lyme Ct., res. at enl. Norwich, Ct., res. Westfield, Hampden Co., Mass. in 1832, S11411
Simon, N.C., See Simeon
Simon, N.C. see Sihon
Simon, R.I., res. of Barrington, Bristol Co., R.I., d. 8/1780, Rachel, W22247

SMITH (continued)
Sion, N.C. See Sihon
Skelton, Va., b. 1/19/1762, res. at enl. Hanover Co., Va., res Sumner Co., Tenn. in 1833, Jane Cosby, W2184; BLWt.38556-160-55
Solomon, Mass., b. 6/4/1754, enl. at Belchertown, Mass., res. in Lyme, Grafton Co., N.H. in 1829, d. 5/27/1838, Esther, W16731
Solomon, Mass., b. 1754 in Woburn Middlesex Co., Mass., res. at enl. & in 1832 Acton, Middlesex Co., Mass., d. 7/25/ or 27/1837, Lucy, W19071
Solomon, Mass., res. of Athol, Mass., & Guilford, Windham Co., Vt., d. 11/7/1818, Tabitha, W20060
Solomon, Mass., War 1812, res. Brookfield, Orange Co., Vt. in 1818 age 54, d. there 2/27/1846, Eunice, W19053; BLWt.11161-160-55
Solomon, N.Y., res. Cortright, Delaware Co., N.Y. in 1819 age 59, res. Sheffield, Berkshire Co. Mass. in 1826, S34495
Sparrow, Ct., b. 1760 in Chatham, Middlesex Co., Ct. & there at enl. & d. there 7/14/1842, Eunice W26489
Spencer, Va., enl. from Accomack Co., Va., res. Wayne Co., Tenn. in 1838 age 97, R9858
Stafford, Pa., Va., b. 1752 in Antrim Co., Ireland, res. in Cumberland Co., Pa. in 1776, res. Green Co., Ind. in 1833, R9859
States, N.J., BLWt.8733. Iss. 2/23/1790. No papers
States, N.J., res. Bergen Co., N.J. in 1820 age 66, S34512
Stephen, Ct., b. 4/18/1749 at Haddam, Middlesex Co., Ct., there at enl. & in 1832, d. 4/16/1834, S17100
Stephen, Ct., Ct. Sea Service, b. 4/15/1751 at North Branford, New Haven Co., Ct., enl. at Woodbury Litchfield Co., Ct., S14523
Stephen, Ct.,Cont., enl. Lyme, Ct. res. Covington, Greene Co., N.Y. in 1820 age 64, Theoda, S42337
Stephen, Cont., Mass., res. of Newburyport, Mass., res. Thornton Grafton Co., N.H. in 1818 age 63 & there in 1828, S-Ctf. 12446
Stephen, Mass., b. 1761 at Shrewsbury, Worcester Co., Mass. & there at enl., res. Bath, Steuben Co., N.Y. in 1832, S22999
Stephen, Mass., b. Newcastle, Me., res. Freedom, Kennebec Co., Me. in 1820 age 69, Mary, S37410
Stephen, N.H. (Mass.?), res. of Newbury, Mass. & moved to Sanbornton, N.H. during Rev. & d. there 7/27/1824, Abigail, W25029; BLWt. 5071-160-55
Stephen, N.H. See Stevens
Stephen, N.Y., b. 9/15/1756, res. Mayfield, Montgomery Co., N.Y. in

SMITH (continued)
1818, d. 11/11/1845 at Morristown St. Lawrence Co., N.Y., Elizabeth R9728
Stephen, R.I., b. 12/14/1751 in Gloucester, Providence Co., R.I., there at enl., res. Burrellville, Providence Co., R.I. in 1832 & d. there 10/22/1836, Abigail, W13908
Stephen, Va., res. Louisa Co., Va., moved in 1809 to Pulaski Co., Ky. & d. there 11/28/1811, Nancy, W3049
Stevens, N.H., res. Epping, Rockingham Co., N.H., d. 10/15/1800, Martha, W19067
Stuckley, Mass., BLWt.5023. Iss. 4/20/1709. No papers
Stukeley, Cont., Mass., res. that part of Rehoboth, Mass. later called Seekonk, res. after Rev. Patuxet, R.I. & d. there 9/29/1815, Susanna, W22243
Susanna, former wid. of John Webb, which see
Susannah, former wid. of Abner Everett/Everitt, Pa., which see. She separated from Robert Smith & resumed the name of Everett
Sylvanus, Ct., Cont., res. Davis, Cuyahoga Co., Ohio in 1819 age 60, S40469
Sylvester, Ct., Vt., b. Woodstock, Ct., res. there during Rev. & at Pomfret, Vt., res. Williamstown, Orange Co., Vt. in 1832 age 74, d. 6/8/1839, Hannah, W24983
Thaddeus/Thadeus, N.J., b. 5/6/1742 in Amwell, Hunterdon Co., N.J. & there at enl., res. Rutland, Meigs Co., Ohio in 1832, d. 4/12/1839, Anne, W9658
Theophilus M., Ct., b. 11/9/1757 Milford, Ct., d. 9/1860 at Plymouth, Ct., S14532
Thomas, Ct., b. 1754 Stonington, New London Co., Ct., & enl. there res. Groton, New London Co., Ct. in 1832, d. 12/1/1844 at Franklin Ct., Thankful, W26474
Thomas, Cont., N.Y., enl. at Haverstraw, N.Y., res. Schenectady, N.Y. in 1827 age 67, Agnes, S42326
Thomas, Cont., Va., res. Greene Co., Ky. in 1832 age 70, S11430
Thomas, Md., BLWt.11738. Iss. 5/11/1790. No papers
Thomas, Md., enl. in Md., res. Franklin Co., Ohio in 1826 age 66 S40475
Thomas, Md. See SMYTH
Thomas, Md., enl. Baltimore, Md. res. Indiana Co., Pa. in 1818 age 55, & d. there 3/28/1821, Ann, W26490; BLWt.6280-160-55
Thomas, Mass., enl. at Northampton Mass. Hadley, Hampshire Co., Mass in 1832 age 70, S11433; BLWt. 17853-160-55
Thomas, Mass., b. 1753 in Brunswick, Me., res. during Rev. Bath, Me., res. Litchfield, Lincoln Co., Me. in 1832, S30113
Thomas, Mass., b. 3/10/1762 in Douglas, res. at enl. Sutton, Worcester Co., Mass., there in 1832, d. 10/3/1846, Sally, W1658; BLWt.13740-160-55
Thomas, Mass.. b. Sudbury, Middlesex Co., Mass., there at enl. & in 1832 at age 76, d. 1/2/1837 at Hanover, Worcester Co., Mass., Polly, W15359
Thomas, Mass., res. Kittery, Me. in 1785, res. Fryeburg (York Co., Mass.) Oxford Co., Me. in 1820 age 67, d. 6/1/1827 at Conway, Strafford Co., N.H. (m. Lucretia/Lucy Tefeathering/Tefethner 8 or 9/1785 in Kittery, Me.), W26476
Thomas, N.H., b. 5/10/1764 at Kingston, N.H., res. during Rev. Gilmanton, N.H., res. Cornville, Somerset Co., Me. in 1832 & Dover, Piscataquis Co., Me., R9863
Thomas, N.J., BLWt.8753; Iss. 6/14/1791. No papers
Thomas, N.J., b. 10/11/1751 in Monmouth Co., N.J., & there at enl., res. Harrison Co., Va. in 1833, S15989
Thomas, N.J., res. Monmouth Co., N.J. in 1818, res. South Amboy, Middlesex Co., N.J. in 1820, S34506
Thomas, N.Y., BLWt.7843. Iss. 1/31/1792 to Heil Peck, ass. No papers
Thomas, N.Y., enl. at Westchester N.Y., res Beekman, Dutchess Co., N.Y. in 1820 age 60, S42334
Thomas, N.Y. See Thomas G.
Thomas 2nd, pensioned at Guilford Co., N.C., Dis. No papers
Thomas, N.C., b. Pitt Co., N.C. & there at enl., res. Chowan Co. N.C. in 1833 age 80, S7551
Thomas, N.C., b. 5/5/1741 in Pa., reared in Va., res. at enl. Surry Co., N.C., res. Calloway Co., Ky. in 1833, S31372
Thomas, N.C., b. 1763 in Pittsylvania Co., Va., moved to Washington Co. when about 17, enl. in Hillsborough, Orange Co. N.C., res. Johnson Co., Ind. in 1833, S32524
Thomas, N.C., b. 1754 in Mecklenburg, N.C., there at enl., res. Kanawha Co., Va. in 1833, R9865
Thomas 1st, N.C., res. Cumberland Co., N.C. in 1831, res. Greenville Dist., S.C. in 1836, S10019
Thomas, N.C., S.C., b. Pa., res. at enl. Burke Co., N.C., there in 1832 age 70, d. 12/19/1846, Rachel, W592; BLWt.19914-160-55
Thomas, Pa., BLWt.10354. Iss. 6/20/1789. No papers

SMITH (continued)
Thomas, Pa., b. 1756/1757 in Baltimore, Md., res. at enl. & in 1832 Franklin Twp., Washington Co. (later Greene Co., Pa.) S23931
Thomas, Pa., enl. at Upper Paxton Chester Co., Pa.,res. Barre Twp. Huntington Co., Pa. 1818, S40442
Thomas, Pa., res. Beaver Co., Pa. in 1818 age 67, S40445
Thomas, R.I., b. 4/28/1761 in Scituate, Providence Co., R.I. & there at enl. & in 1832, S21985
Thomas, S.C., b.1/9/1762 in Camden Dist., S.C. & there at enl., res. Barren Co., Ky. in 1833, d. 2/14/1834, Rebecca, W8734
Thomas, S.C., d. 1819, Margaret, R9795
Thomas, Va., BLWt.12529 iss. 5/8/1794. No papers
Thomas, Va., b. Chesterfield Co., Va. & there up to 1832 age 71/72 S6124
Thomas, Va., enl. in Culpeper Co., Va., res. Madison Co., Va. in 1832 age 66, S6125
Thomas, Va., b. 7/23/1752 in Albemarle Co., Va., there at enl., res. Clarke Co., Ky. in 1832, S30707
Thomas, Va., enl. in Amherst Co., Va., res. Washington Co., Ind. in 1818 age 69, S36771
Thomas, Va., b. 1756/1757 in Sussex Co., Va., res. at enl. Brunswick Co., Va., res. Rutherford Co., N.C. in 1833 & d. there 6/16/1843, Judy, W4074
Thomas, Va., b. Hanover Co., Va., there at enl. age 22 yrs., d. 4/9 or 10/1827 in Hanover Co., Va. Susan, W6128
Thomas, Va., res. during the Rev. Henry Co., Va., d.3/1784 Pittsylvania C.H., Va., Sally, R9846
Thomas, Va., b. 3/9/1765,res. at enl. Fairfax Co., Va., res. Fauquier Co., Va. in 1834, R9866
Thomas, Va., b.1763 Pittsylvania Co., Va., there at enl.,res. Henry Co., Ky. in 1834, R9867
Thomas G., N.Y., res. at enl. Orange Co., N.Y., res. Greensburgh, Westchester Co., N.Y.in 1837, R9864
Timothy, Ct., res. Erie Co., N.Y. in 1829 age 69, S42314
Timothy, Ct.,Cont., Privateer, res. Tinmouth, Rutland Co., Vt. in 1818 age 58, Lydia,S41164
Timothy, Mass., res. Genesee Co., N.Y. in 1818 age 60, res. in Medina Co., Ohio in 1830, d. 11/20/1837, S40461
Timothy, Mass., enl. at Sandisfield, Berkshire Co., Mass.,res. Vernon, Oneida Co., N.Y. in 1818 age 56, S42328
Timothy, Mass., enl. from Norton, Bristol Co., Mass. & d. there 1/

SMITH (continued)
9/1794, Anne Lincoln former wid., W4267
Timothy, Mass., res. at enl. Martha's Vineyard, d. 7/27/1818, Mary, W22250
Titus, Mass., res. always at Medfield, Norfolk Co., Mass. & d. there 9/1/1805, Atarah, W15360; BLWt.31708-160-55
Turpin, Mass. Sea Service, Navy, b. 4/4/1751 at Providence, R.I., there at enl. & d. there 8/18/1835, S21984
Valentine, N.Y., b.1764 Ulster Co. N.Y., res. at enl. Marbletown, Ulster Co., N.Y., res. Owasco, Cayuga Co., N.Y. in 1832, S15295
Wait, N.Y., BLWt.7854 iss. ? 1790 to William Bell, ass. No papers
Weden/Weedon, Cont., Va. res. BLWt.523-100
Wells, Cont., Ct., res. Haddam, Middlesex Co., Ct., lost at sea in 1799, Elizabeth, W17848
Wilhelmus, N.Y., d. 9/22/1801, Anna, R9689
Willard, Green Mt. Boys, N.H., res. during Rev. Plainfield, N.H. & Bethel, Vt., Mary, R9804
William, Artillery Artificers, BLWt.13769. Iss. 11/16/1791. No papers
William, Ct., BLWt.1956-200-Lt. Iss. 8/5/1789. No papers
William, Ct., BLWt.6424. Iss. 9/1/1790 to Theodosius Fowler, ass. No papers
William, Ct., BLWt.6448. Iss. 9/22/17?? to Martin Smith, Admr. No papers
William, Ct., m. 11/15/1787, lived in Brooklyn, Windham Co., Ct., Esther, W25018
William, Ct., Cont., res. Bozrah, New London Co., Ct. in 1823 age 67, S14508
William, Ct., Cont., R.I., b. 1758 in North Kingston, R.I., res. at enl. Voluntown, Windham Co., Ct. D. there 7/4/1839, Hannah, W17839
William, Ct., N.Y. See Bill
William, Cont. (Foreign), res. Granby, Hartford Co., Ct. in 1821 age 64, two ch. Gaylord & Anna, S36770
William, Cont., Mass., enl. from Chester, Mass., res. Blandford, Hampden Co., Mass. in 1818, res. Canaan, Litchfield Co., Ct. in 1820 age 62, res. Trumbull Co., Ohio in 1827, S40464
William, Cont., Mass., res. at enl. Rowley, Mass., d. 2/25/1835 at Rome, N.Y., Elizabeth, W22264
William, Cont., Mass., res. Buxton, York Co., Me. in 1818, d. 2/12/1838, Mary, W25007
William, Del., BLWt.10886. Iss. 12/6/1791 to John McCleland, ass. No papers

SMITH (continued)
William, Del., res. Licking Co., Ohio in 1818 age 64 & there in 1821, Elizabeth, S40444
William, Del., age 68 in 1818, res. Darke Co., Ohio in 1820, Nancy, S40460
William, Ga., N.C., S.C., b. 1762 in Derry Co., Ireland, res. at enl. Mecklenburg Co., N.C., after Rev. in Ga., Ala., & Giles Co., Tenn., R9878
William, Ga., S.C.?, d. 11/27/1824 or 1822 in Munroe Co., Ala., Celia, R9701 1/2
William, Hazen's Regt., BLWt. 13753, iss. 6/11/1790. No papers
William, Md., enl. in Frederick Co., Md., res. Berkeley Co., Va. in 1818 age 66, S38376
William, Md., res. of Wythe Co., Va. in 1835 age 81, S38382
William, Md., res. at enl. Charles Co., Md., res. Boone Co. Mo. in 1835 age 74, R9876
William, Md. ?, d. in Queen Anne Co., Md. R---
William, Md., a drummer killed at battle of Guilford, N.H., BLWt. 1119-100
William, Md., Mass., b. in Buckinghamshire, England in 1755- Was in British Army, res. Chatham Co., N.C. in 1834, R9874
William, Mass., BLWt.5005. Iss. 2/27/1793 to Alexander Power. No papers
William, Mass., enl. from Windsor, Berkshire Co., Mass. & there in 1818 age 64, S34488
William, Mass., res. Kittery & Eliot, York Co., Me. in 1818 age 64, S37415
William, Mass., b. 1/1751, m. Thankful Butler in Sept. 1777. She lived in Dukes Co., Mass., d. 9/22/1831, W15355
William, Mass., res. Kittery, Me. d. 8/27/1800, Sarah, W16730
William, Mass., res. at enl. Rochester, Plymouth Co., Mass., d. there 1/16/1817, Desire, W19379
William, Mass., enl. from Taunton Mass., res. Raynham, Mass. & d. there 11/8/1832. M. Thankful Allen in 1815. R9862; BLWt.36531-160-55
William, Mass., N.Y., res. Milan, Dutchess Co., N.Y. in 1818 age 68, S42315
William, N.H. See Billy
William, N.J., b. 3/28/1752 in Somerset Co., N.J., & lived there up to 1832, S915
William, N.J., b. 3/10/1754, res. at enl. Gloucester Co., N.J., d. there 9/7/1832, Martha, R9796
William, N.Y., BLWt.7813. Iss. 3/29/1791 to James Roosevelt, ass. No papers
William, N.Y., b. 5/19/1763 at Canajoharie, N.Y., res. at enl.

SMITH (continued)
Palatine, Montgomery Co., N.Y., res. Ephratah, Montgomery Co., N.Y. in 1832, S11420
William, N.Y., res. at enl. Smithtown, Suffolk Co., N.Y. & there in 1832 age 77, S14499
William, N.Y., b. 5/6/1758 at Livingston Manor, Albany Co., N.Y. & there at enl., res. Pittstown, Rensselaer Co., N.Y. in 1833, S19467
William, N.Y., res. of Westhaven, Rutland Co., Vt. in 1820 age 59, S41169
William, N.Y., b. 10/21/1760 at Esopus, Ulster Co., N.Y. & there at enl., d. 5/4/1843, m. Catharine Woolsey 6/15/1828. W9660
William, N.Y., b. 9/9/1760 at Newburgh, N.Y., there enl. & later lived in Balston, Saratoga Co., then to Amsterdam, Montgomery Co., N.Y., d. 3/26/1837. M. Catharine at Fishkill, Dutchess Co., N.Y. 2/15/1784. Their ch. were James, Reubin, William Jr., Denton, Bebony, David & Arthur, W16410
William, N.Y., res. at enl. Orange Co., N.Y., d. 6/28/1810, Mary, R9805
William, N.C., b. 2/17/1762 at Lunenburg Co., Va., res. at enl. Washington Co., N.C. on the Watauga River, res. Lincoln Co., Tenn. in 1832. Dau. Ida m. Isaac Southworth, living Fayetteville, Tenn. in 1835, S1723
William, N.C., b. 1/25/1758 in Bladen Co., N.C., there up to 1833, S7534
William, N.C., b. 1/16/1762 in Chester Co., Pa., res. at enl. Burke Co. (later Iredell), N.C., res. Iredell Co., N.C. in 1832, S7536
William, N.C., b. Pa., 12/1/1753, res. at enl. & up to 1833 in that part of Orange Co. that became Guilford Co., N.C., S7555
William, N.C., b. Ireland in 1758 res. at enl. & in 1833 Mecklenburg Co., N.C., d. 8/27/1837, S7563
William, N.C., b. Nansemond Co., Va. in 1751, res. during Rev. Cumberland & Moore Cos., N.C., d. 5/8/1852, Meredy, W590; BLWt.13865-160-55
William, N.C., enl. at North Hampden Court House, N.C., d. in Franklin Co., Va. 6/8/1835, Ann, W10257; BLWt.1154-160-55
William, N.C., b. 1763 in Nansemond Co., Va., res. at enl. Bertie Co., N.C., res. Rockingham Co., N.C. in 1832, d. 1/11/1835, Nancy, W17828
William, N.C., enl. in Fayetteville, N.C. & d. there in service Nancy Irwin former wid., R5499. Her 2nd husb. William Irwin also

SMITH (continued)
served in the Rev. See papers in this file.
William, N.C., went to N.C. from New England, m. Milly in March 1770, d. 12/15/1837, R9809
William, N.C.,Va., b. Amelia Co., Va. 1764, res. at enl. Brunswick Co., Va., after Rev. in N.C. & Robertson Co., Tenn. 1832, S4853
William, Pa., BLWt.10375 iss. 9/4/1789 to Ann Short, Admr. No papers
William, Pa., b. Germany 1745/6, res. at enl. Lancaster Co., Pa., res. Washington Co., Tenn. in 1833, d. 10/4/1835, S3928
William, Pa., b. York Co., Pa. 12/3/1760, res. York Co.,(later Adams Co.) at enl., res. Ross Co., Ohio in 1833, S7535
William, Pa., res. York Co., Pa. in 1818 age 68, S40450
William, Pa., enl. from Md./Pa. res. Abbeville Dist., S.C. in 1834 & lived there 44 yrs. All orig. papers sent to John C. Calhoun, R9875 1/2
William, R.I., b. Gloucester Co., R.I. 4/22/1764, there at enl. res. Italy, Yates Co., N.Y. in 1833, S14486
William, R.I., res. at enl. Newport, R.I., d. at Charleston, S.C. in 1807, m. Hannah Carr of Jamestown, R.I. 8/1772, W12993
William, R.I., b. 1756 Kent Co., R.I., d. Butler Co., Ohio 2/20/1845, R9877
William, S.C., b. 1/16/1746 on Shenandoah River in Va., res. at enl. Ninety-Six Dist., S.C., res. Jefferson Co., Tenn. in 1832, d. 1/24/1836, S4855
William, S.C., b. 2/26/1763 Moore Co., N.C., res. at enl. Ninety-Six Dist., S.C., res. Franklin Co., Ga. in 1832, S31973
William, S.C.,b.S.C.,res. Williamsburg Dist., S.C. in 1818, S39077
William, S.C., m. Frances in Edgefield, S.C. 9/2/1784, d. 3/17/1848 in Edgefield, W3729; BLWt. 26259-160-55
William, S.C., b. 9/20/1751 in Bucks Co., Pa., res. at enl. Spartanburg Dist., S.C., m. Mourning Bearden in 1779. Their ch. were Aaron, Lettice, Isaac, Eber, Ralph, William, Eliphas, Elihu, and Dr. J. Winsmith who changed his name from Smith.D. 6/1837, W22272
William, S.C., b. near Dorchester, S.C. in 1764, res. at enl. Beaufort Dist., S.C. & there in 1838, R9875
William, Va., BLWt.12531 iss. 7/7/1792 to Robert Means, ass. No papers.
William, Va., res. N.C. in 1818, Lincoln Co., Tenn.in 1823, S452
William, Va., b. 1761 in York Co.,

SMITH (continued)
Pa., res. at enl. Martinsburg, Va., pensioned in Monroe Co., Ohio, d. 4/23/1833, S3920
William, Va., b. 12/20/1752, res. at enl. Augusta Co., Va., res. Pendleton Co., Va. in 1832, S6121
William, Va., res. at enl. Culpeper Co., Va. & there in 1832 at age ca. 76, d. 11/20/1850, S7548
William, Va., b. 12/20/1762/63 in Morgan Co., Va. & there at enl. & in 1843, S7561
William, Va., b. 4/22/1754 in Sussex Co., Va., res. at enl. Henry Co., Va., res. Clarke Co., Ga. in 1833, S31976
William, Va., enl. in Shenandoah Co., Va., res. Adams Co., Ohio in 1820 at age 68, Hannah, S40463; BLWt.1630-100
William, Va., b. 10/2/1759, res. at enl. Westmoreland Co., Va., res. Hamilton Co., Ohio in 1819 res. Rush Co., Ind. in 1828, S40465
William, Va., b. 7/22/1763 in Staunton, Augusta Co., Va., there at enl., d. 1/26/1842 in Rockbridge Co., Va., Hannah/Hanney, W2629; BLWt.27686-160-55
William, Va., b. Albemarle Co., Va. in 1755, there at enl., m. Elizabeth/Betsey Massie 12/22/1775, d. 12/29/1836, W4806
William, Va., b. Richmond Co., Va., 3/1740, res. at enl. Alleghany Co., Va., d. 2/4/1836, Mary, W6094
William, Va., b. 5/5/1756 in Amelia Co., Va., there at enl., m. Elizabeth Vier/Viah 11/8/1790 or 1792-93, d. Russell Co., Ky., W9298; BLWt.50890-160-55
William, Va., b. Hanover Co., Va. 12/14/1755, res. at enl. Louisa Co., Va. & there in 1833, R9872
William C., N.C., Ga., b. Mecklenburg Co., Va., 3/4/1762, res. during Rev. Wake Co., N.C. & Wilkes Co., Ga., res. Lincoln Co., Tenn. in 1833, S3924
William Pitt, Gen. Hosp., S.C., BLWt.2116-300 Surgeon's Mate. Iss. 9/29/1790. No papers
William S., N.Y., BLWt.1991-450-Lt. Col., Iss. 8/9/1790. No papers
William S., Va., BLWt.2073-200-Lt. Iss. 5/9/1796. No papers
Windsor, Mass., S19094
Zachariah, Ct., S41177
Zachariah, N.C., S3927
Zebina, Ct., Martha, W19047
Zebulon, N.C., S1876
Zephaniah, Mass., S14485
SMITHER, William, Va., S14487
SMITHERS, John, Va. See SMETHERS
John, Va. See SMUTHERS

SMITHERS (continued)
Stephen, Va., R9881
William, Va., S17682
SMITHEY, Reuben, Va. See SMITHY
Thomas, Va., 16532
SMITHART, Darby, S.C., Dorcas, W2635; BLWt.26941-160-55
SMITHPETER, John Michael, N.C.,Va. Christina, W3730;Wt.26006-160-55
SMITHWICK, John, N.C., S7554
SMITHY, Reuben, Va., S3943
William, Va., S1254
SMITTS, John, Cont., Ct. See SMITH
SMOCK, Barnes J., N.J., S1108
Cornelius J., N.J., S29466
George, N.J., R9885
Henry, Va., Margaret, W3048
SMOOT, James, Va., Fanny, W4075
John, Va., S1252
William, Md., BLWt.1234-200
SMOTHERS, Edward, Mass., S34492
John, Va., Elizabeth, W26475
John, Va. See SMUTHERS
William, Va. BLWt.12527 iss.12/31/1791 to Benj. Mifflin, ass. No papers
William, Cont., Va., S38375
SMUTHERS, John, Va., Sea Service, R9880
SMYTH, Ann, former wid. of George Bush, Pa., which see
Daniel, Md., S35074
Daniel, Md. See SMITH
Ezekiel, N.C. See SMITH
James, Md., BLWt.11746 iss. 6/11/1790. No papers
Philip D., Cont., Md.,b.4/26/1759 en. Hagerstown, Md., res. 1825 in Switzerland, Ind., S40466
Thomas, Md., Anna Maria, W25027
SMYTHERS, Stephen, See SMITHERS
SNAGG, Henry, Cont.,N.Y. res. Dis. See Am. State Papers, Class 9, p.126. Wounded in left leg by the drag rope of a field piece at the battle of Princeton, N.J.
SNAIL, Christopher, N.C., S31383
SNAILBAKER, Daniel, See SNELBAKER
SNALE, Thomas, Va. Sea Service, R93, Va. Half Pay
SNAPP, George, Va., S32531
SNARE, William, Pa., R9887
SNEAD, Bowdoin, Va., Mary, W4810 BLWt.29338-160-55
Claibourn, Va., Mildred, W7196; BLWt.3772-160-55
George, Va., Elizabeth Hutchinson former wid., W7839; BLWt.14530-160-55
John, Va. See SNEED
John, Va. D. 1819, Rebecca, W6134
Philip, Va., S38392
Robert, Va., R9891
Robert, Va., Sea Service, R94 Va. Half Pay
Samuel, Mass. See SMEAD
Smith, Va., BLWt.2056-400-Major. Iss. 6/26/1789 to Smith Snead
SNEDEKER, Cornelius, N.J., W6136
Isaac, N.J., S916
William, N.Y., R9888
SNEDEKOR, Isaac, N.Y., R9889
SNEDER, Andrew, See SNYDER

SNEDIKER, Garret, N.J., S6130
SNEDON, Stephen, See SNEETHEN
SNEED, Allen, N.C., R9890
John, Va.,S30711;BLWt.9460-160-55
Robert, Va., S9482
Robert, Va. See SNEAD
Robert, Va. See SNEAD
SNEETHEN, Stephen, N.J., BLWt. 2345-100
SNEIDER, Adam, Pa. See SNYDER
Henrich, Cont. See SNYDER
SNELBAKER, Daniel, Cont., N.J., Mary, R9898; BLWt.310-100
George, N.J., BLWt.2458-100
SNELL, Abraham, Pa., S14535
Anthony, Mass., S15990
Asa, Mass., S33690; BLWt.907-100
David, Mass., Mary, W6137
Gilbert, Mass., S33691
Hanyost/Hans Jost, N.Y., S28607
Henry, N.J., Hannah, R9892
Isaiah, Mass., Lydia, R9895
Jacob, N.Y., S23429 & S28608
James, N.C., S42020
Job, Mass., Abigail, W25037
Job, R.I., S42356
John, Mass., S30117
John, N.Y., S10021
Joseph, Ct., S36776
Joseph, Mass., S33685
Lewis, See SCHNELL
Lewis, Va., Mary, W9305
Peter, N.Y., Susannah/Anna, R9897
Philip, See SCHNELL
Robert, Mass., S19099
Samuel, Cont.,Mass., Mary, W25039
Stephen, N.C., R9896
Thaddeus, Mass., S30116
SNELLBAKER, George, See SNELBAKER
SNELLING, Asa, Mass., S33688
Joseph, Cont., Mass., Rachel, W19075
William, Va., R9899
SNELLINGS, James, Va., S38393
SNELSON, Nathaniel, Va., Sarah, W6135
Thomas, Ga., S.C., S17111
SNETHEN, Waitel, N.J., S6129
SNIDEEKER, Moses, N.Y., BLWt.7771 iss. 3/1/1790 to William Holly, ass. No papers
SNIDER, Christian, Ga., R9900
Christian, Pa. See SNYDEN
Christopher, See George SNYDER
Frederick, Md., Elizabeth, R9918
George Christopher, See SNYDER
Jacob, N.Y., S18604
John, Md. agcy., Invalid, See Archives of Md., Vol. XVIII p. 630 - wounded at White Plains
John, Cont., N.Y., Eme, W19385
John, Cont., Pa., Elizabeth, W8073; BLWt.154-60-55
John, Hazen's Regt., BLWt.13738. Iss. 6/7/1793 to Philip Stout, ass. No papers
John, Va., R9901
John, Va., R9902
John, Va., R21854
John Ludwig, Pa., R9922
Jonathan, Ga., Elizabeth, W2185

SNIDER (continued)
Peter, Pa., R9927
Peter, S.C., R9928
William, N.C., S.C., Sea Service, See William TAYLOR
SNIDOW, Christian, Va., S17112
Jacob, Va., R9903
SNIFFEN, John, N.Y., Mary Ann, W19384
Nehemiah, N.Y., BLWt.7773. Iss. 6/9/1791 to David Hawkins, ass. No papers
Peter, N.Y., Mary, W19072
Reuben, N.Y., S14545
SNIFFIN, Thomas, N.Y., Rachael, W19386
SNIFFING, Amos, N.Y., BLWt.7728-100 Iss. 1790
SNIPE, Nathaniel, Va., S38390
SNODDY, John, N.C., S17110
Samuel, S.C., Elizabeth, W8744; BLWt.18371-160-55
SNODGRASS, Robert, Pa., S6132
Samuel, Pa., S6136
William, Ind. War, res. Tenn., d. 8/28/1855, Margaret, R9904; W.O.38763, W.C.29414; BLWt.23401-160-55
William, Va., d. 9/18/1849. S---
SNOOK, Henry, N.Y., S11435
Peter, N.J., S835
Philip, N.J., R9905
SNOW, Aaron, R.I., Nancy, W11506; BLWt.1262-100
Abner, Mass., Hannah, R9910
Abraham, Ct., Lavina, W504; BLWt. 26727-160-55
Amaziah, Ct., Sarah, R9916
Amos, N.H., Dis.-see Am. State Papers, Class 9, p.155 - Deaf & worn out in service
Asa, Mass., Elizabeth, W25042
Azubah, former wid. of James Nickerson, Mass., which see
Benjamin, Cont., Mass., Elizabeth R9909
Caleb, Mass., S42021
Daniel, R.I., S21989
Ebenezer/Ebinezer, Del., N.C., Sally, W38
Ebenezer, Mass., S33686
Ebenezer, Mass., S33687
Eleazer, Mass., S14543
Ephraim, N.Y., BLWt.1981-200-Lt. Iss. 4/16/1791 to Chloe Snow, Admr. No papers
Eunice, former wid. of Walter Branch, Ct., which see
Ezra, Ct., Lavine, W25036
Hannah, former wid. of Stephen Watson, N.H., which see
Harding, Mass., Mass. & R.I. Sea Service, Betty/Betsey, W25040; BLWt.26441-160-55
Isaac, Ct. Sea Service, Mass., S19098
Ivory, Ct., Mass., Ct. Sea Service S11434
Jacob, Mass., S14538
James, Mass., S6133
James, Mass., S37427

SNOW (continued)
James, Mass., Anna Jeffers former wid., W7886; BLWt.40010-160-55
James, Mass., Alice, W16416; BLWt.4995-100. Iss. 3/1/1790. No papers
James, Mass., Mary, W25043; BLWt. 31320-160-55
Jeremiah, Vt., Cynthia, W15362
Jesse, Mass., R9912
John, Ct., R9913
John, Cont., Va., S38391
John, Mass., S42354
John, Mass., Caroline, W994 BLWt.34514-160-55
John, N.C., S17690
John, Cont., Mass., Vt., Mary, W19073
Jonathan, Ct., S16256
Jonathan, Ct., Mercy, W25038
Joseph, Ct., S14536
Joshua, N.H., S37428; BLWt.3489. Iss. 2/17/1797 to William S. Thorn, ass. No papers
Lemuel, Mass., res. Franklin Co., Ind. in 1818, S40476
Levi, Ct., S17688
Mark, Va., R9914
Mary, former wid. of Solomon Morse, Mass., which see
Nathan, Ct., Mass., S21495
Nathan, Cont., Mass., Deborah, W20062
Nathaniel, Ct., Mehitable, R9915
Nehemiah, N.H., Mariam, W17851
Paul Mansfield, Cont., Mass., War 1812, Mary/Polly, W25035; BLWt. 754-100
Richard, Cont., Va., S14540
Robert, Ct., Anna, W25041; BLWt. 2180-160-55
Samuel, R.I., S17689
Shubeal, Ct., Rachel, W26492; BLWt.45717-160-55
Silas, Ct., S14544
Simeon, Mass., Hannah, R9911
Solomon, Mass., S6134
Thomas, Ct., BLWts.6437 & 14157. Iss. 5/7/1800 to Elizabeth Snow heir
Thomas, Ct., Lucy, W17849
Thomas, Va., Rachel, BLWt.10312-160-55
Timothy, Mass., Hannah Robinson, former wid., W22123
Timothy, Mass., Anna, R9907
William, Cont., Mass., Mercy/ Marcy, W25034
William, Mass., Ruth, W6138
Zephaniah, Mass., Lydia Bugbee, former wid., W18680
SNOWDEAL, John, See DAL
SNOWDEN, Aaron, S.C., Easter, W9665; BLWt.53750-160-55
David, Pa., Nancy, W9308
John, N.Y., BLWt.7766. Iss. 8/ 11/1790 to Patrick Shay, ass. No papers
John, N.Y., S42355
Jonathan, Cont., res. N.J., S574 BLWt.2002-200-Lt. Iss. 8/27/1789 to John Brown, ass. No papers

SNYDER
Abraham, N.Y., Maria, W16414
Abraham, N.Y., Maria, W17850
Adam, Pa. See SCHNEIDER
Adam, Pa., S40477
Andrew, N.Y., Lydia, W19074
Andrew, Pa., S42353; BLWt.2449-100
Christian, Pa., Magdalena, W9306
Christopher, N.Y., S14537
Deiter, Pa., S23001
Elias, N.Y., S14539
Frederick, Pa., Mary, W2873;
BLWt.1950-100
George/George Christopher, Cont.,
wid. res. Pa. in 1838, Catharine,
W3121; BLWt.2145-100
George, Md., S6135
George, N.Y., S14542
Gottleb, N.Y., Rachel, W15361
Henry/Heinrich, Cont., Pa. agcy.
& res., S40478
Henry, N.J., S1109
Henry, N.Y. See Hendrichus
SCHNEIDER
Henry, Pa., Catharine, W3468
Henry, Pa., R9920
Jacob, N.Y., BLWt.7814. Iss. 8/
10/1790 to Stephen Lush, ass.
No papers
Jacob, Pa., S23932
John, Cont., N.Y. See SNIDER
John, Cont., Pa. See SNIDER
John, Md., Privateer, Elizabeth,
W9307
John, N.J., Pa., R9921
John, N.Y., Margaret, W16415
John L., N.Y., Maria, W17852
Jonathan, Ga. See SNIDER
Lewis/Lodowick/Ludwig, N.Y.,
Lucy, R9923
Lodowick, N.Y. See Lewis
Ludowick, N.Y., S11436
Ludwig, N.Y. See Lewis
Margaret, former wid. of Joseph
Thompson, Pa., which see
Nicholas, Pa. res., Elizabeth,
R9919
Peter, Md., S3947
Peter, N.Y., R9926
Peter, S.C. See SNIDER
Philip, Pa., BLWt.1142-150
William, N.Y., S7572
William, N.C.,S.C. S.C. Sea
Service, See William TAYLOR
SOCKMAN, Henry, Pa., S22526
John, Pa., Catharine, W11513;
BLWt.26893-160-55
SODER, John, See SOODER
SODON, Jonathan, R.I., S42357
SOESBE, Daniel, Pa., Rachel,
W9666
SOFIELD, Jonathan, N.J., S7579
Joseph, N.J., S917
Lewis, N.J., Phebe, W8297
SOGOHARASIE, John, Indian Wars,
BLWt.2604-200-Lt. Iss. 3/8/
1792. No papers
SOHAN, William, Mass., BLWt.
5072. Iss. 9/7/1789 to Wm. I.
Vredenburgh. No papers
SOHN, David, Pa., S40481
George Jacob, Pa., S40480

SOLEY, Nathaniel, Mass., S33695
SOLINGER, Adam, Hazen's Regt.,
BLWt.13726. Iss. 2/21/1792 to
Adam Solinger
SOLLACE, Eliza Whitney, former wid.
of David Whitney, Ct., which see
SOLLADAY, Philip, Md., Anna
Christena, R9929
SOLLADY, John, Pa., S22524
SOLLARS, Sabert, N.C., Va., S17113
SOLLEY, Thomas, Cont., Ct.,
Eunice, W17853
SOLLIDAY, Daniel, See SALLIDAY
SOLMES, Nathaniel, N.Y., R9930
SOLOMON, Michael, Pa., BLWt.10402
Iss. 6/10/1794 to Silas Hart,
ass. No papers
SOLOMONS, Cecilia, former wid. of
Abraham Cohen, S.C., which see
SOLT, David, See SULT
Paul, Pa., S7576
SOLTER, Jacob, S.C., S38349
SOMERLY, Moses, Mass., S21496
SOMERS, David, N.J., S4868
George, Pa., BLWt.1844-100
SOMERSETT, Thomas, See SUMMERSETT
SOMERVELL, John, Pa., S37432;
BLWt.1714-100
SOMERVILLE, James, Md., BLWt.2044-
300-Capt. Iss. 2/14/1797. No
papers
John, Pa. See SOMERVELL
SOMES, John, N.H., S11438; BLWt.
26269-160-55
Jonathan, Mass., Anna Leach,
former wid., W9127; BLWt.18250-
160-55
SOMMER, Leonard, Pa., Elizabeth,
W2874
SOMMERS, Simon, Va., S9705; BLWt.
1480-200
Solomon, Md., S35079
SOMMERSETT, Thomas, See SUMMERSETT
SOMMERVILLE, John, Pa., BLWt.10382
Iss. 4/6/1790. No papers. Nota-
tion: Wt. No. 1714 iss. in lieu
of this no. in name of John
Somerville on 3/1/1831
William, Cont., Pa., S41178
SON, Anthony, Va., S36777
Moses, N.Y., R9932
Thomas, N.Y., R9933
SONDAY, Adam, Pa., Mary E., W26495
BLWt.46943-160-55
SONES, Peter, Pa., S23934
SONNER, Anthony, Va., S4870
SOODER, John, Pa., Eva, W3469
SOOP, Conradt, N.Y., S11437
SOOTS, Christian, N.C., Mary M.,
R9934
Frederick, N.C., Peggy/Margaret,
W6153; BLWt.31587-160-55
SOOY, Samuel, N.J., Privateer,
Sophia, W3882
SOPER, Amasa, Mass., S41179
David, N.Y., S23430
Edward, Cont., Vt., Mary, W22278
Henry, N.Y., Hannah, W19387;
BLWt.26435-160-55
Jesse, Ct., N.Y., R9935
Jesse, Vt., Martha, W593; BLWt.
2088-160-55

SOPER (continued)
Mary, former wid. of Josiah
Powers, N.H., which see
Oliver, Cont., Mass., S33698
Prince, Ct., Cont., Green Mt.
Boys, Elizabeth, W25044
Richard, Sheldon's Dragoons,
BLWt.6523. Iss. 12/30/1796. No
papers
Timothy, Ct., S17691
Timothy, N.Y., R9936
SOPERS, Richard, N.J., S756
SORELS, Amos, N.Y., R9937
SORILS, Amos, N.Y. See SORELS
SORK, Michael, N.J., BLWt.8765.
Iss. 6/6/1797 to Valentine
Sork, heir. No papers
SORREL, Edward, Va., Dacris/
Dorcas, W26493; BLWt.9434-
160-55
Elisha, Va., S37190
Mary, former wid. of Andrew
Bankston, Ga., which see
SORRELL, John, Va., S6138
Thomas, Va., S6137
SORRELS, John, N.C., S3953
SORTER, Henry, N.J. See SORTORE
Peter, Pa., S23933
SORTORE, Henry, N.J., Charity,
W22281; BLWt.17953-160-55
SOSBEE, Job, See SOSEBEE
SOSEBEE, Job, N.C., Elizabeth,
R9943
SOSO, Louis, Hazen's Regt.,
BLWt.13735. Iss. 2/20/1792 to
Benjamin Moore, ass. No papers
SOUCEE, Francis, Mass., Susannah
W24674
SOUDER, Christopher, Pa., Sea
Service, Privateer, War 1812,
BLReg. 78264-50, Elizabeth,
W8745; BLWt.26668-160-55
SOUL, Amasa, Mass., Susannah,
BLWt.52781-160-55
Samuel, R.I., S42359
SOULE, Amasa, Mass. See SOUL
Asa, Mass., Ruth H., R9938
Charles W., Mass., S42358
Daniel, Mass., S3951
Ivory, Mass., S17115
James, Cont., Mass., Martha,
S12863
James, Cont., Mass., Molly,
W5176; BLWt.11412-160-55
Jesse, Mass., Abagail, W4620
Jonathan, Mass., Honor, W5177
Jonathan, Mass., Sea Service,
S3952
Simeon, Mass., Aseneth, BLWt.
40700-160-55
SOUTH, Benjamin, N.J., Elizabeth,
R9939
William, N.J., Elizabeth, W4077
Zedekiah, N.J., R9940
SOUTHALL, Henry, N.C., S7574;
BLWt.34908-160-55
Stephen, Va., BLWt.2082-200-Lt.
Iss. 12/13/1791 to Francis
Greaves, ass. No papers
SOUTHARD, Abraham, Mass., S37431
Constant, Mass., S37429
Henry, N.J., S4867

SOUTHARD (continued)
Henry, N.Y., Ruth, W22279
John, N.Y., BLWt.7733. Iss. 10/16/1790 to Thomas Spencer, ass. No papers
John, N.Y., Pvt. in the Marine Corp in 1801, Catharine, W19077
John, Va., S7578
Thomas, Va., Mary Ann, W19076
SOUTHER, Asa, Mass., BLWt.4972 & 13949. Iss. 2/27/1790 to Theodosius Fowler, ass. No papers
Joseph, Cont., Mass. res. & agcy., S33697
Laban, Mass., S4869
Vallentine, Md., N.C., R9942
SOUTHERLAND, Daniel, N.Y., S33692
Daniel, N.C. See SUTHERLAND
James, N.C., S21991
Lawrence, N.Y. See SUTHERLAND
Philip, Va. See SUTHERLAND
Robert, N.C., R10316
Silas, N.Y., S23003
SOUTHERN, Gipson, Ga., S39084
William, N.C., S7575
SOUTHGATE, Elijah, Mass., S19788
Thomas, Mass., S15651
SOUTHLAND, David, Mass., S33694
SOUTHMAYD, Daniel, Ct., S14547
SOUTHWARD, Andrew, Ct., S36778
David, Cont., Mass., S43167
Thomas, Va., BLWt.12579. Iss. 5/7/1793 to Francis Graves, ass. No papers
Thomas, Va., See SOUTHARD
SOUTHWELL, Asahel, Ct., Hannah, W3363
SOUTHWICK, Benjamin, Mass., S33696
David, Mass., BLWt.4999. Iss. 5/8/1792 to Amos Muzzey, ass. No papers
David, Cont., Green Mt. Boys, Mass., S43166
George, Mass., Sea Service, S29472
Lemuel, Mass., Mary, W4589
SOUTHWORTH, Abia, Mass., S29471
Edward, Mass., S30118
Elijah, Ct., S10022
George, Va., Elizabeth, W6142
Isaac, Ct., Vt., S22525
Jasher, Vt., S21990
Joseph, Cont., Ct., S33693
Joseph, Mass., Ct., Lydia, W16417
Lemuel, Ct., S41180
Samuel, Ct., BLWt.6515. Iss. 1/6/1792. No papers
Samuel Wells, Ct., Marcey, W15802
Thomas, Va. See SOUTHARD
Uriah, Mass., Patience, W26494
William, Ct., Cont., Mass., S40479 See N.A. Acc. No. 874-050166 Not Half Pay
William, Va., Lucy, W6141
SOUTS, Christian, N.C. See SOOTS
SOWARD, Richard, Mass., N.H., Navy S37430
William, Md. See SEWARD
William, Md., R9941
SOWDER, Christopher, Pa. See SOUDER
SOWELL, Zadock, N.C., S38394
SOWERS, Frederick, Va., Ann Mary, W6144

SOWERS (continued)
John, N.C., S32532
Michael, Md., S46548; BLWt.1461-100
William, Ct., BLWt.6494. Iss. 4 or 8/18/1789 to Wm. Baldwin, ass. No papers
SOWL, David, Ct., S14546
Job, R.I., S30119
SOWTHER, Vallentine, Md. See SOUTHER
SOYARS, James, Va., Jane, W6140; BLWt.240-60-55 & 387-100
SOYERS, James, See SOYARS
SPACE, John, N.J., Abagail, W4516
John, N.J., BLWt.1738-100
John, N.J., BLWt.7757. Iss. 9/15/1790. No papers
SPADER, Benjamin, N.J., R9944
Bergen, N.J., S31979
William, N.J., R9945
SPAFFORD, Amos, N.H., BLWt.3464. Iss. 3/25/1790. No papers
Amos, N.H., Mary, W22292
Jacob, Mass., S46071
John, Green Mt. Boys, N.H., S14565
John, Mass., R9947
John, Vt., Mary, W25064
Jonathan, Cont., Mass., S33700
Moody, Mass. See SPOFFORD
Tyler, Cont., N.H., Eunice, W1949; BLWt.10033-160-55
SPAHR, Frederick, Pa., R9948
SPAIN, Claiborne, Va., S7591
Peter D., See Peter DE SPAIN
Thomas, N.C., Jemima, R9949
William, N.C., Nancy, W6148
SPAINHOUR, Michael, N.C., Elizabeth/Eliza, W6149
SPALDING, Aaron, Md., BLWt.11672. Iss. 12/18/1794 to Henry Purdy, ass. No papers
Aaron, Md., S37441
Abel, Vt., S3964
Ashbel, See SPAULDING
Barzillai/Brazillai, Ct., N.H., S19101
Benjamin, N.H., S14564
Brazillai, See Barzillai
Daniel, Md., Sea Service, S4877
Darius, Ct., Mary, W1899; BLWt. 27684-160-55
Eleazer, Mass., Sarah, W1659
Ezekiel, Mass. See SPAULDING
Ezra, N.H., S14551
George, Md., Susanna, W1952; BLWt.14970-160-55
Henry, Md., S35082
Henry, N.C., R9950
Jeremiah, Mass., R9951
Job, Mass., BLWt.5075. Iss. 3/25/1790. No papers
John, Ct., Wealthy Ann, W3312
John, Pa., BLWt.10350. Iss. 7/29/1790
Jonas, Mass., Molly, W25053; BLWt.19721-160-55
Joseph, Ct., R9952
Joseph, Ct., Vt., S22529
Joseph, Cont., N.H., S43169
Josiah, Ct., d. 1799, father of

SPALDING (continued)
sold. who rec'd BLWt.75115, Dis.- See Am. State Papers, Class 9, p.153 - Wounded by cannon ball, which passing through a store wall near which he was stationed, forced a stone against the calf of his leg & much injured his knee & tendons. Injured in R.I., 8/27/1778
Josiah, Ct., BLWt.75115-160-55
Philip, Ct., S14567
Reuben, Ct., S17695
Reuben, Vt., Polly, See SPAULDING
Samuel, Cont., N.H. See SPAULDING
Samuel, N.Y., S11447
Silas, Ct., S22530
Simon, Ct., BLWt.1948-300-Capt. Iss. 12/15/1791
Solomon, Mass. See SPAULDING
Stephen, N.H. See SPAULDING
William, Cont., Mass. See SPAULDING
Wright, Ct., Mass., S43168
SPANBERGH, Jacob, N.Y., S14557
SPANGENBERG, John Pa. See SPANGERBURG
SPANGENBERGER, John, See SPANGERBURG
SPANGENBURG, Conrad, Pa., Maria Barbara, R9954
SPANGERBURG, John, Pa., Elizabeth, W3196
SPANGLE, Andrew, Pa., R9955
SPANGLER, Charles, Pa., S14560
George, Pa., Sarah, W3364
SPANKNABLE, John, N.Y., Elizabeth W11519
SPANN, Charles, N.C., S.C., S21497
James, Cont., N.C., S.C., S9484
SPARBACK, Martin, See SPERBECK
SPARBECK, Conrad, N.Y., S10023
SPARHAWK, Jacob, See SPARROCK
Noah, Mass., R9957
Timothy, Mass., S21503
SPARK, Frederick, See SPAHR
SPARKS, Abraham/Abram, N.Y., Leah, W20064
Charity, former wid. of Thomas Champlin, R.I., which see
David, Mass., S37437
Ebenezer, Ct., Margaret, W19395
Henry, Va., Lucy, R9959
James, Pa., Va., S32533
John, Navy, N.J., Lovina/Loviana W19391
John, N.J., S33707
John, N.C., S7580
Joseph, Ct., Eleanor, W20063
Matthew, N.C., S31385
Pearl, N.Y., S27510
Solomon, Pa., S4874
William, N.C., R9960
SPARLIN, John, N.J., S42371
SPARLING, George, N.J., S36783
Heyttje, former wid. of Jeremiah Fleming, N.Y., which see
SPARR, Richard, Va., S40483
SPARRE, John, Pa., S22527
SPARROCK, Jacob, Mass., S37434
SPARROW, Henry, Va., S31384
Jabez, Mass., S19103

SPARROW (continued)
Jacob, Va., S7581
James, See SPANN
Richard, Va., BLWt.12534. No papers
Stephen, Ct., Lydia, W2366; BLWt. 10247-160-55
SPATZ, Michael, Pa., S.C. Sea Service, S3957
SPAULDING, Asahel, N.H., Vt., Alice Tyler former wid., W18179
Ashbel, Mass., Abiah/Abiel, BLWt. 34813-160-55
Benjamin, Mass., Hannah, W19086
Daniel, Mass., Rebecca, W19079
Darius, Ct. See SPALDING
Ebenezer, N.H., Amy, W15369; BLWt.8451-160-55
Edward, N.H., S42369
Eleazer, Mass. See SPALDING
Ezekiel, Mass., Dis. See Am. State Papers, Class 9, p.86 - Received a hurt while in the service of the U.S. by loading a wagon which at time renders him incapable of doing any kind of labor.
Isaac, Mass., Lucy, W25069
Jacob, Mass., N.H., Esther, W15950
Job, Mass., Navy, S33706
John, Cont., Mass., S30124
John, Mass., Elizabeth, W9667; BLWt.2094-160-55
Jonas, Mass. See SPALDING
Joseph, Mass., S42370
Joseph, Mass. See SPALDING
Joseph, N.H., S18208
Josiah, Mass., S30120
Levi, Cont., N.H.?, S42365
Lois, former wid. of George Moore, N.H., which see
Mehitable, former wid. of Ephriam Chamberlain, which see
Nathaniel, R.I., Thankful, W1951; BLWt.29017-160-55
Oliver, Ct., N.H., S14558
Philip, Ct. See SPALDING
Philip, Vt., Hannah, W20065
Phineas, Mass., Sarah, W19085; BLWt.3820-160-55
Phineas, Mass., R9953
Reuben, Ct. See SPALDING
Reuben, Vt., Polly, W2364; BLWt. 9422-160-55
Samuel, Cont., N.H., Eleanor, W22294; BLWt.18002-160-55
Samuel, Mass., S23431
Samuel, Vt., S19100
Solomon, Mass., Jemina, W19397
Stephen, N.H., Lucy, W8299; BLWt.18216-160-55
Thaddeus, Mass., S30121
William, Cont., Mass., S17116
William, Mass., Hannah Adams former wid., W23401
SPEAGLE, Samuel, N.C., Susan, R9963
SPEAK, George, Va., S37435
SPEAKE, Joseph H., Va. Sea Service R95; Va. Half Pay. See N.A. Acc. No. 837 Va. State Navy, Joseph Speake Y.S. File. Va. Half Pay
Richard, S.C., S38395

SPEAKE (continued)
William, Va., S40492
SPEAKS, Hezekiah, Md., Eleanor, W8748
SPEAR, Benjamin, Mass., Elizabeth W19084
Edward, Pa., BLWt.2023-200-Lt. Iss. 9/7/1790
Elijah, Ct., R20436
Elkanah, R.I., S11451
Harmanus, N.J.,N.Y. See Hamonus SPEER
Isaac, Mass., Abagail, W15368
Jacob, Cont., Mass., Navy, Rhoda, W25072
John, Mass., S33699
John, Pa., BLWt.10430. Iss. 6/29/1789 to M. McConnell, ass. No papers
John, Va., Susannah, W2363; BLWt.26915-160-55
Jonathan, Vt., Polly, W7197; BLWt.24618-160-55
Joshua, Ct., S4875
Joshua, N.H., S41183
Luther, Mass., Abagail, W6146; BLWt.8190-160-55
Pearce/Piearc, Navy, R.I., S39852
Richard, Mass., Polly, W20066
Samuel, Cont., Mass., S43171
Samuel, Cont., Mass., Sea Service Elizabeth, W25046
Simeon, Mass., S33703
Stephen, Mass., Mehitable, W25052
Thomas, Mass., N.H., Abigail, W19394
William, Pa., S3955
SPEARES, William, Va., S31980
SPEARING, John, Mass., N.H., Mary W25068
SPEARS, John, Cont., Va., S39851
John, N.Y., BLWt.7785. Iss. 9/27/1790 to Jacob Tremper, ass. No papers
John, N.C., Martha, R9966; BLWt. 7075-160-55
Jonathan, N.Y., BLWt.7806. Iss. 4/21/1791 to Griswald & Starking assnes. No papers
Joseph, N.C., S39086
Joshua, N.C., S.C., R9965
Obadiah, S.C., S7586
Samuel, N.H., Lydia, W25047
Samuel, N.C., S39085
Samuel, Va., S1779
Susannah, former wid. of Sylvanus Chadwich, which see
Thomas, R.I., S21992
SPEARY, Lemuel, Ct., BLWt.6508. Iss. 11/2/1791 to John Heaton, ass. No papers
SPECHT, Adam, Cont., Pa., S40493
Christian, Pa., S4873
SPEDDEN, Edward, Md., Ann, W9312
SPEDDING, Edward, Md. See SPEDDEN
SPEED, Henry, N.Y., Elizabeth, W2262
James, Va., Dis- See Am. State Papers, Class 9, p.171- Wounded in his left leg by a ball which

SPEED (continued)
destroyed two or three of his small ribs, 3/15/1781 at Guilford
SPEEDE, Thomas, N.H., Marcy, W16075
SPEEGLE, Lawrence, Pa., BLWt.10443 Iss. 5/7/179? to Samuel King, ass. No papers
SPEER, Abraham, N.J., S918
Abraham, N.J., S1110
Harmonus/Harmanus, N.J., N.Y., Mary, W201
Joseph, N.Y., Martha, W22282
Samuel, N.H. See SPEARS
William, N.C., S11446; BLWt. 39215-160-55
SPEERLING, William, See SPURLING
SPEIGLAR, Henry, N.Y., BLWt.7787. Iss. 4/5/1793 to James Duggan, ass. No papers
SPEIGLE, Jacob, Pa., Susannah, W2875
SPEKAL, Lawrence, See SPIEGEL
SPELCE, John, N.C. See SPELTS
SPELLMAN, George, See SPILMAN
SPELLMORE, Aaron, N.C. See SPELMORE
SPELMAN, Elihu, Cont., Mass., Mary, W22291
James, Va. See SPILMAN
Jemima, former wid. of Joseph Clark, Ct., which see
SPELMORE, Aaron, N.C., S42023
Asa, N.C., S42022
SPELTS, John, N.C., S14548
SPENCE, Burwell, N.C., Va., Nancy, W11528; BLWt.14753-160-55
David, Pa., BLWt.10358. Iss. 10/31/1795. No papers
James, Hazen's Regt., BLWt.13740 Iss. 9/22/1789 to James Duncan, ass. No papers
James, Ct., d. N.Y.C. 2/10/1825, Elizabeth, W1328; BLWt.50889-160-55
James, N.C., S36782
Nathan, Del., R9971
SPENCER, Aaron, Ct., Mindwell/Mindel, R9980
Abner, N.Y. res., R9972
Alice, former wid. of Ephraim Thornton, R.I., which see
Amasa, Va., b. N.Y., Precilla/Priscilla, W2017
Amos, Va., S40484
Ancel/Ansel, Ct., Loly, W11522; BLWt.26048-160-55
Ann, former wid. of Hosea Hamilton, N.Y., which see
Anthony, Navy, Mass., R.I., S39855
Benjamin, N.C., S.C., Mary, W6158; BLWt.5107-160-55
Beverley, Va., S40491
Calvin, S.C., came from Ct., Rebecca S. Powe, former wid., W21983
Daniel, Ct., S3961
Daniel, Ct., R9976
Daniel, Cont., Ct., S29475; BLWt.53-100
Daniel, N.H., Vt., S29474

SPENCER (continued)
David, Ct., S14563; BLWt.334-200
David, Ct., S36780
David Spencer, R.I. See HOWLAND
Dennis, Mass., S42360
Ebenezer, N.H., b. 1741, S43170
Ebenezer, N.H., b. 1765, Mehitable W19392; BLWt.35691-160-55
Ebenezer, R.I., S21993
Ebenezer, Vt., S31977
Elam, Ct., S23938
Elihu, Ct., Ruth, W26496; BLWt. 11396-160-55
Elijah, Ct., S11453
Elijah, Ct., Sea Service, Hannah, W25062
Emmons, Ct., S14561
Ephraim, Ct., S36779
Gardner, R.I., Mary, W17856
Gideon, Va., Ann, R9973; Va. Half Pay Act, 7/5/1832
Hezekiah, Va., S11440
Humphrey, Md., BLWt.11681. Iss. 5/9/1797. No papers
Ichabod, Ct., Hannah, W22283
Isaac, Ct., S15653
Israel Brainard, N.H., S42361; BLWt.3422-100 iss. 1/23/1799 with note, "warrant presented the 9th day of June 1828. Certified to & sent to Gen. Land Office."
Israel Selden, Ct., Temma, W6154
Jabez, Ct., N.Y., Vt., Patience, W22295
Jacob, N.J., S4879
James, Ct.,Cont., See SPENCE
James, Cont., d. 7/23/1802 in New Hartford, Ct., Thankful, W4811
James, Cont., Ct., d. 3/26/1845 at Somers, Ct., Rachel, W27667; BLWt.19621-160-55
James, Va., Ind. Wars 1791-1795, War 1812, d. Clinton Co., Ohio 10/22/1843, Mary, W4590; BLWt. 38557-160-55
Jared Wilson, Ct., Margaret, W16419
Jehiel, Ct., Anne P., R9975
Jehiel, Ct., Naomi, R9981
Jesse, Va., S7587
Joel, Ct., S36781; BLWt.13898-160-55
John, Ct., Mary, R9979
John, Ct., Cont., Eunice, W6157; Rej. BL
John, Invalids, BLWt.13790. Iss. 5/8/1793. No papers
John, Mass., BLWt.1924-200-Lt. Iss. 7/7/1797 to Anna Spencer an infant & only ch. & heir of John Spencer, subject to the dower of Anna Spencer wid. of said Lt. also recorded as above under Wt. 2688
John, N.J., Charity Wallace, former wid., R11063
John, N.Y., Rebecca, W19389
John, N.C., Sally, W3884; BLWt. 26804-160-55
John, R.I., S21501
John, Va., Mary, W3883
John, Va., Molly, W6156
John, Va., R18077, Va. Half Pay
John, Va., Ind. Wars, War 1812, R9977 & Old War Inv. File 1385, Ind. Wars
Joseph, Va., S37436
Lawton, Navy, R.I. agcy. & res., Abigail, W11520; BLWt.30705-160-55
Matthias, N.Y., S9483
Michael, Mass., Lucinda, W8747
Moses, N.H., BLWt.3479. Iss. 4/20/1797 to Daniel Aiken, ass. No papers
Moses, Va., S39849
Moses, Va., Elizabeth, W41
Moses, Va., Judith, W6155
Nathan, N.J., S14550
Noah, Ct., S28892
Oliver, N.J., BLWt.1994-500-Capt. Iss. 6/11/1789
Orange, N.Y., Sarah, R9985
Peleg, Mass., N.Y., Anne, W19393; BLWt.31324-160-5
Peter, Ct., Jerusha, W7198; BLWt. 31584-160-55
Reuben, Ct., Mehitable, W17857
Reuben, N.H., Alice Mann, former wid., W25871
Robert, Cont., N.J., BLWt.1840-200
Rufus, Mass., S29473
Samuel, Ct., Eunice, W22286
Samuel, Cont., Ct., Sarah, W22288
Samuel, Mass., S40486
Samuel, N.Y., Olive, BLWt.73507-160-55
Samuel B., Ct. Sea Service, S23935
Seth, Ct., S23004
Solomon, Mass., S37440
Theodore, Cont., Ct., Nabby, W26497
Thomas, Ct., Huldah, W2186; BLWt. 49-100
Thomas, Mass., Rebecca, W22293
Thomas, R.I., Mary, W22285
Thomas, Va., Lucy, W19388
Timothy, N.C., W4341
Truman, N.Y., Martha, W25070; BLWt.145[illegible] 160-55
Walter, C[illegible]., S16533
William, Ct., S6143
William, Ct., Phebe, W17859
William, Cont., Va., R9987
William, Mass., BLWt.5024; Iss. 3/25/1790. No papers
William, Mass., Eleanor, W25056
William, N.C., S3960
William, Va., S31386
William, Va. & Ind. Wars, S40487
William, Va., Mary, W9311; BLWt. 26756-160-55
William, Va., R9988
William, Va., R18076. Va. Half Pay. See Acc. No. 874-050167. Half Pay
Wilson, R.I., S21498
Zaccheus, Ct., R9989
SPENSER, Moses, Va. See SPENCER
SPERA, William, Pa., S6141
SPERBECK, Martin, N.Y., R9990
SPERING, John, Pa., Sarah, W2016; BLWt.10413-100. Iss. 8/14/1792
SPERLING, Isaac, N.J., Elizabeth, W6159
SPERRY, Aaron, Mass., Polly, W17855
Armey, Ct., BLWt.6487. Iss. 9/24/1790. No papers
Army, Ct., S42367
Benjamin, Ct., R9991
Ebenezer, Ct., S15652
Elijah, Ct., Cont., Polly, W3885
Elijah, Mass., S33701
Enoch, Mass., S4872
Jacob, Ct., S17693
Jacob, Va., Christina, W2187; BLWt.26144-160-55
Jacob, Va., Elizabeth, W3470; BLWt.26042-160-55
Job, Ct., Rebecca, W17862
John, Va., R9992
Jonathan, Ct., Cont., S11443
Joseph, Ct., Abigail, W16734
Peter, Va., S3959
SPETH, Jacob, Pa., S23936
SPIARS, John, N.C., Va.(?), Frances, R9997
SPICELY, James, Cont., Va., Martha H., W6150; BLWt.53748-160-55
SPICER, Abel, Ct., Sarah, R9995; BLWt.15420-160-55
Asher, Ct., Rebecca, W16418
Jabez, Mass., BLWt.5082. Iss. 7/2/1793 to John Hagamon, ass. No papers
Jabez, Cont., Mass., S42364
Jabez/Jabesh, N.H., S41184
Jacob, N.Y., BLWt.7759. Iss. 1/7/1791
Jacob, N.Y., Sarah, W16735
John, Ct., Mary, W22284
John, N.J., BLWt.8768. Iss. 6/11/1789 to Jonathan Dayton, ass. No papers
John, N.J., S40489
Joseph, Va., S14554
Michael, N.Y., Sarah, W25067
Nathan, N.Y., Catharine Johnson former wid., R5603
Samuel, Md., Pa., S40494
William, Md., Va., S3962
SPICKARD, George, Va., S4880
SPICKET, Daniel, Cont., Md., Privateer, in N.H. in 1818 S43173
SPIEGEL, Lawrence, Pa., S40485
SPIER, Dennis, Del. See Duncan
Duncan/Dennis Slaven, Del., R9996
Joseph, N.Y. See SPEER
SPIERS, Absolom, N.C., Mary, W17860
Charles, Ky., (wid's. res.), Lucy, R9998
John, Md. See SPIRES
Richard, Md. See SPYERS
SPIKE, Daniel, N.Y., S42362
SPILLAR, John, N.C., S28891
SPILLER, John, Cont., Mass., S42172
Samuel, Mass., Annis, W13918
Thomas, Mass., Hannah, W25054

SPILLMAN, James, Va., S16535
SPILMAN, George, Va., S37433
James, Va., S14549
SPINGGER, William M., N.Y., R10018
SPINK, Isaac, Mass., R.I., S11444
John, R.I., S11441
Nicholas, R.I., S42363
Oliver, R.I., S21499
SPINNER, Abraham, Pa., R9999
John, Va., Mary, W2365
Richard, Va., S6140
SPINNEY, Caleb, Mass., N.H., S19473
Hannah, former wid. of Jedediah Witham, Mass., which see
Jeremiah, Mass., S17692
John, Mass., Eunice, R10001
SPIRE, Joseph, N.Y. See SPEER
SPIRES, Absolom, N.C. See SPIERS
John, Md., Mary, W3731
John, N.C., Va.?; See SPIARS
Richard, Md. See SPYERS
SPIRLIN, Thomas, N.H., S22528
SPISER, Samuel, Md., Pa. See SPICER
SPITFATHAM/SPITFATHOM, John, Va., Elizabeth, W6151; BLWt.2240-150
SPIVEY, Edmund, N.C., Elizabeth, R10002
Moses, S.C., Rebecca, R10003
SPLANE, Thomas, Va., S35081
SPOFFNER, Henry, N.C. See SHOFNER
SPOFFORD, Amos, N.H. See SPAFFORD
Moody, Mass., Dolly, W19396
Samuel, Mass., S16534
SPOHN, Philip, Pa., Catharine, R10004
SPOLDIN, John, Va., S6142
SPONG, David, Va., S39848
Jacob, Md., Elizabeth, W3313
John Leonard, Pa., Margaret, W3311
SPONK, Jacob, Md. See SPONG
SPOON, Nicholas, N.Y., Catharine, W17861
SPOONER, Benjamin, R.I., Mary, W25059
Charles, Mass., Polly, W8749; BLWt.8376-160-55
David, Mass., S33704
Gardner, Mass., Vt., S15654
John, R.I., Hannah, W22289
Nathaniel, Ct., Ruth, W2015
Nathaniel, Mass., Mary, W15367
Samuel, Mass., S30712
Thomas, Mass., S30123
William, Cont., Ct., Jerusha, W25071; BLWt.28591-160-55
SPOOR, Abraham, Mass., Comfort/Comnytie, W2480
Abraham, Mass., War 1812, Rebecca W3195
John, N.Y., Rachel, W25065
SPORE, John, N.Y., S16258
SPOTSWOOD, Alexander, Va., R18089 Va. Half Pay
SPOTTEN, Thomas Lewis, N.Y., S14562
SPOTZ, John Frederick, Pa., Elizabeth Schmaltz former wid., W11401
Michael, Pa., S.C. Sea Service, See SPATZ
SPRACHER, John, N.Y., S14555
SPRACKET, Thomas, Pa., BLWt. 10446. Iss. 3/21/1795 to Christian Hubbard, ass. No papers
SPRADLING, James, Va., Sarah, W62
John, N.C., S3963
SPRAGE, Elkanah, See SPRAGUE
SPRAGEN, Thomas, Cont., Va., Elizabeth, W1095
SPRAGGEN, Thomas, See SPRAGEN
SPRAGUE, Abel, Crane's Cont. Art. Mass., BLWt.5099. Iss. 6/20/1789. No papers
Abraham, N.Y., R10005
Abram, Mass., R10006
Andrew, N.Y., Susannah, W19083
Anna, former wid. of William Goodson, R.I., which see
Benjamin, Mass., S14556
Caleb, R.I., S11448
Dan, Ct., S14553
David, Mass., Jane, W25066
Dyer, Ct., Faith, W15365
Ebenezer, Ct., N.Y., R10010
Elijah, N.Y., Nancy, W11523; BLWt.115413-160-55
Elkanah, N.H., Lydia, W19078
Elkanah, Vt., S11445
Frederick, Ct., Mass., Rebecca, R10012
Hosea, Mass., Elizabeth, W19390; BLWt.3957-160-55
James, Cont., Ct., S40482
James, Mass., Nancy, W594; BLWt. 13210-160-55
John, Mass., S37438
John, R.I., S21500
John, R.I., Deliverance, W27488
Jonathan, Mass., Catharine, W13917
Knight, Mass., S30713
Lazarus, N.Y., BLWt.7742. Iss. 9/27/1790. No papers
Martha, former wid. of Jonathan Pratt, Mass., which see
Moses, Mass., S33702
Nathan, Cont., Vt., Sarah, W25051
Philip, Vt., Olive E., W7199; BLWt.3069-160-55
Samuel, Cont., Mass., S29476
Samuel, Cont., Mass., Joanna, W22296
Samuel, Mass., S42372
Samuel, Mass., Amey, R10007
Samuel, Navy, Mass. agcy. & res. Deborah, W15366
Samuel H., Ct., Cont., Mass., R10013
Seth, Mass., S17694
Silas, Mass., S35080
Theodore, Mass., S42368
Timothy, Mass., R10014
Uriah, Mass., S30125
William, Cont., Mass., Anna, W25050
William, Mass., S18606
William, Mass., Mariam, W25057
William, R.I., Mary, W1950
SPRAGUES, Caesar, Mass., Dis.- See Am. State Papers, Class 9, p.110. Had his left foot shot
SPRAGUES (continued)
off by a cannon ball at the action of Monmouth in 1778
SPRAIGE, Nathan, Cont., Vt. See SPRAGUE
SPRAKE, Benjamin, See SPRAGUE
Samuel, Mass., S11442
SPRAKER, John, N.Y. See SPRACHER
SPRIGG, Leven, Va., S14552
SPRING, Isaac B., Mass., Susannah W26498; BLWt.24980-160-55
John, S.C., S31387
Josiah, Mass., Anna, W25058
Seth, Cont., N.H., S18607
Simeon, Mass., BLWt.61-200
Thomas, Green Mt. Boys, Mass., N.H., Vt., S3965
SPRINGER, Abraham, Va., BLWt.12543 & 14030. Iss. 1/30/1792. No papers
Benjamin, Ga., N.C., S1592
Benjamin, R.I., Bersheba, W19082
Charity, former wid. of Thomas Ryan, Mass., which see
Durfee, R.I., S42366; BLWt.3505-100 (name spelled Durphy Springer). Iss. 9/24/1795
Henry, Cont., Mass., N.H., S23937
Isaac, N.Y. See SPRINGGER
Jacob, N.J., S40488; BLWt.1392-100
Jacob, Va., S40495; BLWt.2070-200-Lt. Iss. 1/3/1800
John, Mass., S19104
John, Mass., S31978
John, R.I., Rhoda, W22287; BLWt. 26688-160-55
Knight, R.I., BLWt.3511. Iss. 9/24/1795. No papers
Knight, R.I., S39854
Moses, N.H., BLWt.3478. Iss. 3/25/1790. No papers
Philip, Pa., BLWt.10420. Iss. 7/27/1789 to Richard Platt, ass. No papers
Richard/Derrick/Dedrick/Purdy/Purdick, Pa., R10016; BLWt. 50942-160-55
Sylvester, S.C., BLWt.2107-300 Surgeon's Mate. Iss. 3/2/1791 No papers
Uriah, Va., Sarah, R10017; BLWt. 2001-300-Capt. Iss. 8/22/1791 to John McCleland, ass. No papers. Her former husb. also served in the Rev., William Harrison, Pa. or Va. See this file
William M., N.Y. See SPINGGER
SPRINGFIELD, Moses, N.C., S7590
SPRINGGER, Isaac, N.Y., R10015
William M., N.Y. See SPINGGER
SPRINGS, Micajah, N.C., Laurana Lavicey, W1327
Richard, N.C., b. Del., S7585
Samuel, N.C., Silence, W120
Sedgwick, N.C., Lucy, W6147
SPRINGSTEAD, George, N.Y., S42374
SPRINGSTED, John, N.Y., S23005
SPRINGSTEEN, Abraham, N.Y., BLWt. 7748. Iss. 8/10/1790 to Stephen Lush, ass. No papers

STAATS, Abraham I., N.Y., S14613
John, N.Y., S14597
John, N.Y., Jane, W19103
Philip, N.Y., Anna, W19107
STACEY, Ebenezer, Cont., Mass., Rebecca, W22327
Job, Mass., Betsy Howard, former wid., W23337
John, Mass., S33733
John, Mass., Nancy, W15378
John, Mass., N.H., Eunice, W25158
Joseph, Invalids, BLWt.13793 iss. 9/9/179? to James T. Sebor, ass. No papers
Mahlon, Mass. See Molton STACY
Moses, Mass., Sarah, W19408
Nathaniel, Mass., BLWt.5077 iss. 4/19/1796 to Joseph Fosdick. No papers
Rufus, Mass., S33714
Samuel, Mass., Priscilla, W6193; BLWt.34834-160-55
William, Mass., Mary, W15383
STACK, See John SLACK
Richard, Pa.,BLWt.10389 iss. 7/3/1789 to himself. Cert. 2/24/1820
Richard, Pa., Dis- See Am. State Papers, Class 9, p.128. Rec'd 13 bayonet wounds at the time the American troops under Gen. Wayne were surprised by the enemy at Paoli, 9/1777. Enl. 11/20/1776 for war.
STACKHOUSE, Amos, N.J., S40528, BLWt.509-100
Isaac, Va., S11473
John, Pa., Anna, W25103; BLWt. 85074-160-55
John, Va., S38409
STACKPOLE, James, Va., BLWt.12537 iss. 5/19/1794 to William Ripton, Admr. No papers
John, Pa., BLWt.10415 iss. 11/27/179? to Joseph Pall, ass. No papers
Samuel, N.H., S43989
STACPOLE, Absalom, Mass., N.H., S19105
STACY, Aaron, N.C., Nancy, W19118
Amos, Mass., Abigail, W25097
Benjamin, Mass., R10029
Caleb, Mass., Sarah, W15371
Ebenezer, Mass., S41201
John, Mass., BLWt.5037 iss. 8/12/1793. No papers
John, Mass., Mary, W16423
John, Mass., Mary, W19401
Molton/Mahlon, Cont., Mass., S36807
Nathaniel, Mass., S33758
Nymphas, Mass., Sarah, W25100
Nymphas, Mass., Abigail, W25154
Oliver, res. N.Y., R10030
Thomas, Pa., Mary, W6192; BLWt. 26400-160-55
William, Mass.,BLWt.1891-450-Lt. Col. iss. 4/1/1790. No papers
William, Cont., Mass., Navy, S37446
William, Mass., Elizabeth, W2482
STADDEN, William, Pa., S14586
STADDLEMAN, John, See STUDELLMAN

SQUIER (continued)
Joseph, N.J., S33709
Nathaniel, N.J., R10028
Noble, Mass., Privateer, S14569
Philip, Ct., S36785
Sylvester, Mass., S17696
Thomas, Ct., S11454
SQUIERE, Daniel, Mass., N.H. See SQUIRE
SQUIERS, Elisha, Cont., Ct. See SQUIRE
Seley, Ct. See Selah SQUIRES
SQUIRE, Abner, Ct., S17118
Asa, Ct., BLWt.6522. Iss. 2/7/1800. No papers
Asa, Ct. See SQUYER
Ashur, Ct., BLWt.6447. Iss. 8/23/1790. No papers
Calvin, Ct. See SQUIER
Daniel, Ct. See SQUIER
Daniel, Mass., N.H., d. 4/3/1842; S36784; BLWt.2493-100
David, Ct. agcy., Dis- No papers
Ebenezer, Ct., Lucy, W17864
Ebenezer, Vt., S21994
Elisha, Cont., Ct., Huldah, W4342
Ezra, Vt. See SQUIER
Henry, Va. See ESQUIRE, also given as Henry Winckleblack
Isaac, Ct., Sea Service, Susanna, W17863
Mary, former wid. of Benjamin J. Byrum, Va., which see
Philip, Ct. See SQUIER
William, Ct., Esther, W26966; BLWt.26555-160-55
SQUIRES, Abiather, Ct., Mary, W4591
Ambros/Ambrose, Mass., S42375
David, Mass., S36786
James, N.J., See SQUIER
Jesse, N.Y., S23939
Joel, Mass., N.Y. See SQUIER
Joseph, N.J., BLWt.8709. Iss. 9/10/1790 to Jeremiah Baldwin, ass. No papers
Justus, Ct., Polly, W17865
Pheneas, Ct., BLWt.6480. Iss. 4/2/1793 to Samuel Wild, ass. No papers
Phinehas, Ct., S46401
Samuel, Ct., Ellen Turney, former wid., W22458. Her 2nd husb. was pensioned, see James Chapman, Ct. Her 3rd husb. Aaron Turney, Ct. also pensioned, which see
Selah/Seley, Ct., Hannah, W17866
Stephen, Vt., Betteah Brown, former wid., R---. She was pensioned on acct. of service of her last husb. Abijah Brown, Mass., which see
Thomas, Mass. See SQUYRES
SQUIRRELL, Jacob, N.Y., BLWt.7760 Iss. 5/18/1792. No papers
SQUYER, Asa, Cont., enl. at Ct., S42024
SQUYERS, Thomas, See SQUYRES
SQUYRES, Thomas, Mass., S33708
SROPE, Christopher, N.J., Thankful W202
SRUM, Peter, See SCRUM
STAAB, John, Pa., S23011

SPRINGSTEEN (continued)
Benjamin, N.Y., R10019
George, N.Y., BLWt.7779. Iss. 9/10/1790 to William Henderson, ass. No papers
SPRINGSTIEN, John, N.J., Elizabeth, W3612; BLWt.26037-160-55
SPRINGUM, John, Va., S39850
SPROAT, Thomas, Mass., S30122
William, Pa., BLWt.2019-300-Capt. Iss. 8/14/1789. No papers
SPROUL, Alexander, Va., War 1812, Jane, R10020 1/2
James, N.J., BLWt.1927-150-Ens. Iss. 4/15/1799 to Oliver & Elizabeth Sproul the only ch. & heirs. Also recorded as above under Wt. 2707. No papers
Mary, former wid. of John Little, Mass., War 1812, W25061; BLWt. 67616-160-55
Robert, Mass., Jean, W25048
William, Mass., S19102
SPROULE, Moses, N.J., BLWt.1999-150-Ens. Iss. 10/7/1789. No papers
SPROUSE, David, Va., S3958
SPROUT, Ebenezer, Mass., BLWt. 1890-500-Lt. Col. Cmdt. Iss. 1/29/1790. No papers
James, Mass., S33705
Nathan, Mass., Lucinda, W2014; BLWt.10309-160-55
Nathaniel, Mass., Azubah, W19081
Robert, Mass., S30126
Samuel, Cont., Mass., S14566
SPROWL, Alexander, Va., War 1812, See SPROUL
SPRUCE, John, Va., Mary Jane, W9310
SPRUILL, Jesse, N.C., R10021
William, N.C., S.C.(?), R10022
SPRY, William, Md., S4878
SPURLING, William, Va., S41182
SPURLOCK, William, Va., R10023
SPURR, Enoch, Mass., S17117
John, Cont., R.I., Mass., S39853 BLWt.1892-400-Maj. Iss. 4/20/1790
SPURRIER, Edward, Md., BLWt.2042-300-Capt. Iss. 5/13/1795. No papers
SPYERS, Richard, Md., Rebecca, W6145; BLWt.1672-100
SPYRES, Richard, Md. See SPYERS
SQUARES, Calvin, Ct. See SQUIER
SQUIAR, Daniel, Mass. See SQUIRE
SQUIER, Abiathar, N.Y., Vt., R10024
Calvin, Ct., Mabel, W6160; BLWt. 26204-160-55
Daniel, Ct., S22531; BLWt.26463-160-55
Daniel, Ct., S42376
Edward Adam, Ct., Mary, R10025
Ephraim, Ct., Mass., Priscilla, R10026
Ezra, Vt., Betsey, W4812
Isaac, Ct. See SQUIRE
James, N.J., S22532
Joel, Mass., N.Y., S14570
John, Mass., S23006

STADLEMAN, John, Von Heer's Corps BLWt.13713. Iss. 2/25/1791 to Charles Colver, ass. No papers
STAFFORD, Andrew, R.I., Rachel, W19087
Benjamin, R.I., S17130
David, R.I., Privateer, S23960
David, Va., S38398
Ichabod, R.I., Humility, W19406
James, R.I., S21509
James B., Ltr. of Marque (Mass.) Navy, Abagail, W6216; BLWt.26728-160-55
Joab, Mass., Dis- See Am. State Papers, Class 9, p.95 - Wounded in his foot & nose in an action at Bennington, 8/1777.
John, Cont., Pa., Hannah, S33732
John, Md., Mary J., W11554; BLWt. 50888-160-55
John, R.I., S42410
John, R.I., Orpah, W25157
Joseph, R.I., S17124
Josiah, N.C., S39091
Samuel, R.I., Vt., Privateer, S18612
Stephen, R.I., Abigail, W22304
Stutley, R.I., R10033
Thomas, Ct., BLWt.469-100
Thomas, R.I., S42408; BLWt.1979-100
Thomas, Vt., Martha Sawyer, former wid., R9235
William, R.I., S10024
William, R.I., BL--
STAG, Isaac, N.J., S760
STAGE, Benjamin, N.Y., S23008
William, Pa., S42412
STAGEL, James, Va., R10208
STAGER, Peter, Pa., R10034
STAGG, Benjamin, Pa., S40532
James, N.J., Va., R10035
Jasper, N.Y., BLWt.7792. Iss. 9/15/1790 to John Hobart et al, ass. No papers
John, N.Y., BLWt.7830. Iss. 9/15/1790 to John Hobart, ass. No papers
John, N.J., N.Y., Martha, W2267; BLWt.8166-160-55
John, Jr., Col. Oliver Spencer's Regt. BLWt.1982-200-Lt. Iss. 7/9/1790. No papers
STAHL, Andrew, Pa., R10037
John, Navy, Pa., See John STEELE
STAHLE, Jacob, Pa., Barbara, W3472
STAHLER, Adam, Pa. See STOHLER
STAIRE, Michale, former wid. of William Coombs/Combs,which see
STAKE, Jacob, Pa., BLWt.2018-300-Capt. Iss. 3/14/1794. No papers
John, Cont., N.Y., Sarah, W20068; BLWt.2125-150-Cornet of Von Heer's Corps. Iss. 9/4/1790 to Gerrit H. Van Waggenen, ass. No papers
STALEY, George, N.Y., Janette, W19123
Henry, N.Y., S11490
Jacob, Pa., Va., Barbara, W6179
Matthias, N.Y., S23440
Peter, Pa., Margaret, W6194
STALKER, John, N.Y., S19478

STALKER (continued)
Peter, Ct., Achsah, W19098; BLWt.1381-100
William, Md., BLWt.11735. Iss. 12/29/1791. No papers
STALL, Adam, Pa., S41192
John, Germany, Pa. res. in 1846, R10038
Peter, N.Y., R10039
STALLARD, Nancy, former wid. of Richard Basye/Bayse, Va., which see
Randolph, Va., S6165
STALLINGS, Isaac, N.C., R10040
James, Ga., R10041
Moses, N.C., S31997
STALLIONS, Abraham, Md., BLWt. 11719. Iss. 5/29/1795. No papers
STALLMAN, Wilhelm, Pa., BLWt.10458 Iss. 8/7/1789 to Richard Platt, ass. No papers
STALMACKER, Samuel, See STALNACKER
STALMAKER, Valentine, Va., 1774, R10043
STALNACKER, Samuel, Va., S9487
STAMEY, John, N.C., S.C., S7611
STAMM, George, Md., S36329
STAMPER, Jacob, N.C., S16544
Joel, N.C., S3999
STANALAND, James, S.C., S18215
STANARD, David, Ct. See STANNARD
Larkin, Va., S7607
Oliver, Cont., Mass., Sally, W7225; BLWt.210-160-55
William, Ct., Hannah, W19120
STANBERY, Recompence/Recompense, N.J., Ann C., W2258; BLWt.9538-160-55
STANBRO, John, R.I., Hannah, W11536
STANBROUGH, Lemuel, Ct., Jane, W2453; BLWt.9543-160-55
STANBURY, Elijah, N.Y., BLWt.7774. Iss. 4/16/1791 to John Addams, ass. No papers
James, R.I., S21511
STANCIL, John, N.C. See STANSELL
STANCLIFT, Comfort, Ct., S23949
John, Ct., Cont., S14612
Lemuel, Ct., Mehitable/Mehitabel, W3733; BLWt.2086-160-55
Samuel, Mass., S40518
STANDARD, Oliver, Mass., BLWt.5001 Iss. 3/26/1789. No papers. BLWt. 210-60-55
STANDART, Oliver, Mass. See STANARD
STANDEFER, Benjamin, N.C., Nancy, W822; BLWt.21803-160-55
STANDISH, Amasa, Ct., Mass., S14600
Amos, Cont., Mass., N.Y., Esther W17871
Ebenezer, Mass., Lydia, W26451
Nathaniel, Mass., S33724
Samuel, Mass., Vt., S28899
STANDLEY, Isaac, N.J., Elizabeth, W870
Jacob, N.H., S23943
Kenney, Mass. See STANLEY
Moses, Sea Service, Va. res. in 1818, Mary M., W3886
Peter, Mass. Sea Service, Privateer, Mary, W15406

STANDLEY (continued)
Peter, Pa., BLWt.10392 iss. 9/12/1796. No papers
Valentine, Pa., Sea Service, Rebecca Read/Reed, former wid., W9248. Her last husb. James Read also served in the Rev.
William, Mass., S18617
STANDLY, Noadiah, Ct. See STANLEY
Spirus, N.C., S1726
William, Mass., Sea Service, Jane, R10051
STANDRIDGE, James, N.C., Mary, W9686
STANFIELD, James, N.C., Fanny, W158
John, N.C., Sarah, W6215
Thomas, N.C., R10047
STANFORD, Abner, Mass., BLWt.5047 iss. 4/5/1796 to Oliver Ashley. No papers
Abner, Cont., Mass., Sarah, R10048
John, Mass., BLWt.5057. Iss. 4/2/1796. No papers
John, Cont., Mass., d. 1840, Elizabeth, W22316
John, Mass., Elizabeth, W22318 See her claim for service of 1st husb., John McCaffery, Mass. Sea Service & Navy
Moses, Mass., Jemima, W15400
Samuel, N.C., Margit/Margaret, W2021; BLWt.27655-160-55
Thomas, S.C., S11463
Zachariah, Ct. res. Dis.- See Am. State Papers, Class 9, p.66 - Disabled by cold, being exposed to storm and rain, sleeping on wet ground
STANHOPE, Richard, Ohio res. in 1859, R10049
Samuel, Mass., S6149
STANIFORD, Jeremiah, Mass., Mary, W13921
STANLEY, Adin, Cont., R.I., S18610
Dennis, N.H., Sally, W15396
Elisha, Ct., S29481
Frederick, Ct., S7610
George, Crane's Cont. Art., Mass. BLWt.5104 iss. 6/20/1789. No papers
Isaac, N.J. See STANDLEY
James, Cont., Me. agcy., S37447
John, N.H., Sarah, W15376
Joseph, R.I., R10053
Kenney, Mass., Elizabeth, W25156
Moses, Va. Sea Service, See STANDLEY
Nathaniel, Mass., S15991
Noadiah, Ct., Hannah, W19413
Noah, Ct., Naomi, W25143
Rial, Mass., Abagail, W25089
Richard, Va., R10050
Saladdy, Md., Sarah, R10057
Salmon, Ct., R10055
Solomon, Mass., Patience, W25110
Thomas, Ct., BLWt.6493 iss. 5/7/1792. No papers
Timothy, Ct., S11475
STANLY, Christopher, Cont., Md.

STANLY (continued)
S7609
Hugh, N.C. agcy. & res., S14594
Jesse, Ct., R10052
Joseph, N.H., Martha, W16077
Peter, Mass. Sea Service, Privateer, See STANDLEY
STANNAGE, Thomas, Va., S4905
STANNARD, Abel, Ct., Phebe, W19114
Claudius, Mass., Vt., S4324
David, Ct., Ruth, W25142; BLWt. 36530-160-55
Eliakim, Ct., Cont., S7596
Elijah, Ct., S17709
Ezra, Ct., S7606
Jasper, Ct., S31981
Job, Ct., S17700
John, Ct., S17702
John, Mass., S33719
Joseph, Ct., S41199
Libbeus, Ct., Green Mt. Boys, Vt., S14619
Pliny, Vt., S15660
Samuel, Ct., BLWt.6457. Iss. 9/12/1792 to Stephen Thorn, ass. No papers
Samuel, Ct., Elizabeth, W19119
Seth, Ct., BLWt.6499. Iss. 3/18/1790. No papers
STANPHILL, James, N.C. See STANFIELD
STANSBURY, Elijah, N.Y., Mehitable W16738
Luke, N.C., Nancy, W165
Solomon, Md., N.C., Janett/Jane W8759; BLWt.26103-160-55
Tobias E., Md., Navy, Privateer War 1812, S14604
STANSELL, John, N.C., Edith, W6200 BLWt.43526-160-55
STANSIL, George, N.Y., S27536
STANTON, Anna, former wid. of Edward Rollins, N.H., which see
Benjamin, N.Y., Sarah, W1506
Charles, Cont., N.H., S16543
Daniel, Ct., S20978
Ebenezer, Cont., Ct., Privateer, Mary, W25105
Edward, Ct., Martha, W2481; BLWt.9073-160-55
Elijah, Ct., Cont., Mass., R.I., S14623
Elijah, Cont., N.H., Patience Pottle/Pottles, former wid., W10916; BLWt.104746-160-55
Jason, Ct., Sally, W505; BLWt. 8152-160-55
John, Cont., Md. See STAUNTON
John, Md., BLWt.11682. Iss. 5/4/1797 to James DeBaufre, ass. No papers
John, N.Y., R10060
John, R.I., S22000
Joseph, Ct., Priscilla, W22302
Joseph, Privateer, R.I., S17711
Nathan, Ct., R10061
Paul, Mass., S20554
Robert, N.Y., Sibel, R10062
Samuel, Ct., Hannah, W22305
Stephen, R.I., Sarah, W13934
William, Del., BLWt.10885. Iss. 9/2/1789. No papers

STANTON (continued)
William, Sheldon's Cavalry, BLWt. 1965-300-Capt. Iss. 6/25/1789 to Wm. Stanton. No papers
STANUP, Richard, See STANHOPE
STANWOOD, Ebenezer, Mass., S33738
Joseph, Mass., S29485
Stephen, Mass., BLWt.5090. Iss. 3/25/1790. No papers
Thomas, Mass., BLWt.7297-160-55
William, Mass., S37458; BLWt. 1931-200-Lt. Iss. 4/12/1790. No papers
STAPEL, Mark, See STAPLES
STAPLE, Edward, N.H., S38403
STAPLES, Abel, Ct., S14595
Asa, Ct., S21997
Ebenezer, Ct., S17710
Ebenezer, Mass., S43186
Edward, N.H. See STAPLE
Isaac, Mass., Esther, W25144; BLWt.6425-160-55
Isaac, Va., S14590
John, Cont., Ct. or Pa., Lydia, W6212
John, Cont., Md., Margaret, W4518
John, R.I., Abigail, R10062 1/2
John, Va., Betsey, W22; BLWt. 61340-160-55
Joseph, Mass., Louisa, W22328
Joshua, Mass., BLWt.5076. Iss. 2/29/1792 to Moses Beard
Joshua, Mass., S30130
Margaret, former wid. of Joseph Ham, Mass., which see
Mark, Navy, Mass., Sarah, W22297
Nathan, N.Y., Ruth, W13937
Richard, N.H., R10063
Samuel, Mass., S33720
Sarah, former wid. of James Hill BLWt.36547-160-55
Stephen, Mass., Charity, W25085
William, Mass., S18210
William, Mass., S38404
STAPLETON, Thomas, N.C., Sarah/Sally, W9320
William, Va., Mary, R10064
STAPP, Achilles, Va., Ann, W599; BLWt.34909-160-55
STAPPLEBEEN, Jacob, See STUPPLEBEEN
STARBARD, Anthony, See STARBIRD
STARBIRD, Anthony, Mass., S37462
John, Cont., Mass., N.Y., d. 12/14/1839, Hannah, W2880
John, Mass., d. 11/1824, m. Chloe Bradford, S37461
John, N.H., d. 10/17/1841, S43182
Samuel, Mass., S37444
Solomon, Mass., Eunice, W25086
STARBOARD, Ebenezer, Mass., Margaret Stevens, former wid., W25149. Her other husb. was also pensioned. See William Stevens, Mass., Sea Service & Navy.
STARFIELD, John, See STANFIELD
STARIN, Nicholas, N.Y., Catharine/Catrina, W19124
STARING, Adam, N.Y., Nelly, W19106
Ernestine, former wid. of John Bellinger, N.Y., which see
John, N.Y., Jane, W16741

STARK, Abraham, Ct., See STARKS
Archibald, N.H., BLWt.1886-200-Lt. Iss. 5/20/1796 to John Stark Admr., in trust for the uses of the said will. No papers
Caleb, N.H., Sarah, W15391; BLWt. 1351-200
John, Cont., N.H., S7926; BLWt. 1879-850-Brig. Gen. Iss. 5/20/1796. No papers
John, Cont., N.H., Tryphena, W15405; BLWt.26308-160-55
John, Vt., Eunice, W25130
Joseph, N.J., Pa., Phebe, R10070
Phineas, N.H., Tryphena, BLWt. 11094-160-55
Robert, Va., Sally Graham former wid., W7592
Samuel, Vt., S28895
William, Cont., N.Y., S42387
William, Va., S7592
STARKE, Aaron, Ct., R10073
Amos, N.J., S837
Reuben, S.C., S21996
Richard, Va., Sally, R10071
Richard, Va., BLWt.295-200
William, Va., Mary, R10069; BLWt. 45720-160-55
STARKER, Michael, N.H. See STOCKER
STARKEY, Isaac, Va., S40503
John, Va., Obedience, W19111
Jonathan, N.C., S7612
Jonathan, Va., R10072
Joseph, Mass., N.H., Waitstill, W16745
Joseph, Va., S40525
Susannah, former wid. of Asa Pratt, Ct., which see
STARKS, Abraham, Ct., S42407
Ebenezer, Ct., R10074
Nathan, Cont., Ct., S33723
Pardon T., Mass., S40527
Samuel, Ct., S23959
STARKWEATHER, Billings, Vt., S23434
Elijah, Ct., S46072
Ephraim, Ct., R.I., Rachel, W22308
John, Ct., Hannah, R10075
Prince, Ct., Marcy, R10076
Thomas, Ct., S17126
Thomas, Vt., Sally, R10077
STARLING, Jacob, Ct., S36797
Josiah, Mass., S17127
Levi, N.Y., Pa., S40515
Seth, N.C. See STERLING
STARN, Joseph, Pa., R10088
Nicholas, N.Y. See STARIN
STARNES, Joseph, See STEARNES
Nicholas, Va., Barbary/Barbara, W26445; rejected BL 306817-55 She was really Barbara, wid. of John Hibbin/Hibben of the Ill. Vols., War 1812. See Rej. BL 27375-55 & the former wid. of Nicholas Starnes
STARNS, Charles, Ct. See STEARNS
Joseph, Va., S7600
Jotham, N.H. See STEARNS
Nicholas, Va. See STARNES
Samuel, Mass., S43184
William, Cont., N.H.,N.Y., Vt., Lydia, W19093

STARR, David, Ct., BLWt.1949-300-Capt. Iss. 11/19/1789. No papers
Dumill, Navy, Ct. res., R1418
Eli, Ct., R10078
Elijah, Pa., S40521
George, N.Y., R10080
James, Cont., Pa., res. Md. in 1818, S35087; BLWt.586-100
Jehoshaphat, Cont., Ct., Mary, W22298
Jesse, Cont., Ct., Polly, W19415
John, Ct., Dis- lived in Ohio when pensioned, d. 8/10/1824
John, Pa., Elizabeth, R10079
Jonathan, Ct., R10081
Joshua, Ct., S14609
Josiah, Ct., R10082
Josiah, Ct., BLWt.1935-500-Col. Iss. 10/7/1789. No papers
Robin, Ct., BLWt.6465. Iss. 11/20/1789 to Isaac Trowbridge, ass. No papers
Robin, Ct., S36810
Samuel Moor, Ct., Abigail, W6209
Thaddeus, Ct., S14606
Thomas, Ct., d. 3/5/1801, Lois, W17887; BLWt.1957-200-Lt. Iss. 3/29/1792. No papers
Thomas, Ct., d. 4/21/1806, Dis-See Am. State Papers, Class 9, p.90 - Wounded by a party of British horse, very badly, at the time when Danbury was burnt by the enemy, April 1777
Thomas, Ct., Mass., R10083
William, Ct., S33711
William, Ct., Eunice, W8756
William, Ct., Dis- d. 12/31/1817
William, Va., See LOCKE
STARRETT, John, Pa., Mary, W1423; BLWt.26200-160-55
STARRITT, Benjamin, Lee's Legion, res. Fayette Co., Tenn. in 1849 Ctf. 1027 dated 11/11/30
James, N.C., R10084
STARRY, Tobias, Pa., Elizabeth Catharine, R10234
START, Moses, Md., BLWt.13727 & 1411. Iss. 2/24/1795 to Francis Sherrard, ass. of Aquilla Lanthorn, admr.
Nathan, N.Y., Pa., Jamima, W20067
STATE, Zebediah, See SLATE
STATESER, Isaac, N.J., Zilpha Lefferts former wid., W5316; BLWt.14956-160-55
STATESIR, John, N.J., Agnes, W993
STATINGER, John, Pa., BLWt.10412. Iss. 7/7/1796. No papers
STATLER, Rudolph/Rudy, Fanny, W6211; BLWt.14972-160-55
STATSER, David/Johann David, Elizabeth, W3163
STATZER, David, Pa. See STATSER
STAUCH, Bernhard, See SLAUGH
STAUFFER, Henry, Cont., Pa., BLWt.1182-100
Henry, Pa., Ann Catharine, W3198
STAUGHTON, Alexander, Ct. See STOUGHTON
Gustavus, Mass. See STOUGHTON
STAUNTON, Charles, Ct. See STANTON

STAUNTON (continued)
John, Cont., Md., S35086
Robert, N.Y. See STANTON
STAW, Nicholas, Pa. See STRAW
STAWERS, Samuel, See STOWERS
STAY, William, Del., BLWt.10882. Iss. 5/4/1797 to James De Baufre, ass. No papers
STAYNER, Roger, Pa., S41197; BLWt.1245-300
STAYTON, Joseph, Del., BLWt. 10881. Iss. 7/5/1797. No papers
STEADMAN, Enoch, R.I. See STEDMAN
John, Ct., Matilda, R--- Rev. War
William, R.I., Hannah, W15404
STEAGEL, Conrad, Cont., Pa. res. of dau. in 1838, BLWt.1301-100
STEAR, Nehemiah, R.I. See STEERE
STEARM, Dudly, Mass., BLWt.5030. Iss. 4/19/1792 to John Peck. No papers
STEARMAN, William W., See STEERMAN
STEARNES, Joseph, Mass., Rhoda, W4822
Joseph, N.H., S43179
STEARNS, Abraham, Cont., Mass., Esther, W25106
Asa, Mass., N.H. See STERNES
Ashahel, Mass., Captivity, W22314
Benjamin, Mass., Sarah, W19400
Charles, Ct., Sarah, W6176
Daniel, Mass., S41208
Daniel, Mass., Mary, W15380
Daniel, N.H., S43990
Daniel, Vt., S18608
David, Mass., Mary, W19101
Dudley, Mass., S33737; BLWt.5030-100. Iss. 4/19/1792 to John Peck No papers. See memo relative to name in John Dutch, Mass. BLWt. 4032.
Elias, Mass., N.H., S23007
Ephraim, N.H., Molly, W25134
George, Mass., S4893
Habakkuk, Mass., S33710
Increase, Mass., Mercy, W15375
Isaac, Mass., Lucy, W6177; BLWt. 40698-160-55
Isaac, Mass., Mary, W15953
Jasiel, Mass., S42402
John, Mass., S4887
John, Mass., S41214
John, Mass., N.H., Sarah, W4593
John, Mass., N.H., Sarah, W22300
John, N.H., Sarah, W16153
John, Vt., S23955
Jonathan, Mass., S33741
Jonathan, Mass., S41194
Jonathan, Mass., Mary, W25167
Joseph, Mass., S33713
Joshua, Cont., Mass., S33712
Josiah, Cont., Mass., Sarah, W20074
Jotham, N.H., Abigail, W16428
Levi, Ct., S30716
Nathaniel, Mass., S33721
Nathaniel, Mass., Mary, W2367
Reuben, Mass., S14616
Roswell, Ct., S23439
Samuel, Mass., See STARNS
Samuel, Mass., Alice, W19091
Samuel, Mass., Phebe, R10086

STEARNS (continued)
Samuel, N.H., R10087
Silas, Mass., Lydia, W13930
Stephen, Mass., BLWt.5074. Iss. 2/29/1792 to Moses Beard, ass. No papers
William, Mass., S30135
William, N.Y.,Vt. See STARNS
STEBBENS, Lewis, N.Y., S14626
STEBBINS, Ambrose, Cont., Mass., S19110
Benjamin, Mass., S41210
Darius, Mass., Louisa, W19411
David, Mass., Mary, W19405
Ebenezer, Ct., S41203
Ebenezer, Mass., Diadema, R10089
Gaius, Mass., S7597
James, Mass., S30133
John, Mass., Sarah, W25137
John, Mass., Lydia, R10090
Joseph, Ct., R18144
Jotham, Mass., Hannah, W6213
Samuel, Ct., Ruth, W25135
Samuel, Mass., BLWt.5059. Iss. 4/1/1790. No papers
Samuel, Mass., S14581
Timothy, Mass., S30136
STEBINS, Benjamin, Mass. See STEBBINS
STECHTER, Peter, See STICHLER
STEDMAN, Cato, Ct., BLWt.6434. Iss. 11/15/1791. No papers
David, Mass., Hannah, R10091
Ebenezer, Mass. See STETSON
Enoch, R.I., Hannah, W22315
Isaac, Ct., Lucretia, W2264
James, Ct., S28898
Levi, Ct., Cont., Anna, W19108; BLWts.20-60-55 & 6514-100-1792
Lucy, former wid. of Adriel Huntley, Ct., which see
Nathan, Ct., Privateer, R10093
Philemon, Ct., BLWt.6496. Iss. 9/28/1790 to Theodosius Fowler ass. No papers
Philemon, Ct., S33742
Selah, Ct., S11491
Thomas, Ct., S17121
Thomas, Ct., S36809
Timothy, Col. Swift's Regt. of Ct. Line. In the old Bounty Land Book the following notation was made in the Bounty Land Office & signed "W.M. Stewart: "The discharge of Timothy Stedman of Col. Swift's Regt. of the Connecticut Line, Revolutionary War was presented at this office Feb. 28, 1825 & although returned to the Hon. M. Harvey, it is considered that when the discharge is returned it will be viewed in the same light as though it had remained in the files of this office."
William, Mass. See STEADMAN
STEED, James, Pa., S41212
Jesse, N.C., Sally Williams, former wid., R11616
John, Va., BLWt.2654-300-Capt. Iss. 4/20/1795. No papers
Thomas, Va., Phebe, W6198

STEEDELMAN, John, Pa., BLWt. 10410. Iss. 3/1/1796. No papers
STEEDMAN, Edward, S.C., Agnes, W9676
STEEL, Archibald, Cont., Pa., S7601
David, N.H., Margaret, W15388
David, Pa., BLWt.10425. Iss. 2/3/1794. No papers
David, Pa., Mary, W3162
David, Va., S40516
Eldad, Vt., S15293
Elijah, Ct., Hannah, W25124
Francis, Pa., BLWt.10445. Iss. 4/26/179? No papers
Francis, Va., S7602
James, N.J., Elizabeth, W15804
James, N.Y., Dis- See Am. State Papers, Class 9, p.95 - Wounded in the breast at the taking of Fort Montgomery, 10/6/1777
James, Pa., S4882
John, Ct., R10095
John, Del., Ann, W11540
John, Germany, See STALL
John, Va., S17706
John P., Pa., BLWt.10391. Iss. 6/20/1789. No papers
Joseph, Ct., Olive, W19105
Josiah, Ct., S36791
Perez, Ct., Hannah, W28035
Perez, Ct. See STEELE
Richard, Pa., S6146
Thomas, N.C., S7603
Thomas, Pa., R10100
William, N.C., Cerlia, W6196; BLWt.8156-160-55
STEELE, Ashbell, Ct., Eunice, W25162
Bradford, Ct., Ruth, W17869; BLWt.7085-160-55
David, Ct., Hannah, W25102
David, Cont., Va., S7605
Eliphaz, Vt., S16259
Francis, Pa., Margaret, R10097
Isaac, Ct., Lavina, W17888
Isaac, S.C., Grissell, R10094
James, Ct., Jemima, W26448
James, N.Y., BLWt.7744. Iss. 9/15/1790 to Platt Smith, ass. No papers
John, Ct., S36790
John, Ct., Sarah Hillard former wid., W21331
John, Navy, Pa., Mary Ann/Polly, R10098
John, N.J., S1115
John, N.Y., S28901
John, Pa., R10072 1/2
John, Pa., BLWt.396-300
John, Va., BLWt.2077-200-Lt. Iss. 8/27/1789. No papers
Josiah/Joseph, Ct., BLWt.6420. Iss. 8/10/1789 to Richard Platt, ass. No papers
Josiah, Ct., Phebe, W871
Mary, former wid. of Peter Seidel Pa., which see
Moses, Ct., Amanda, W15372
Perez, Ct. Lucy, R10096
Robert, Mass., Lydia, W600; BLWt.

STEELE (continued)
654-100 & 247-160-55
Rudolph, N.Y., R10099
Samuel, Ct., S17129
Samuel, Ct., Sarah, BLWt.57524-160-55
Samuel, Mass., Rachel, W15386
Samuel, N.C., S17123
Samuel, Va., Hannah, W7208
Thomas, enl. at Crown Point, N.Y., R10101
William, Ct., Rebecca/Renea, W22056
William, N.C., b. Md., S7604
William, N.C., R10105
William, Va., Sea Service, R96 Va. Half Pay. See N.A. Acc. No. 837, Va. State Navy, Wm. Steele Y.S. File, Va., Half Pay
Zadock/Zadok, Ct., Vt., S14571
STEELEY, Jeremiah, N.C., S42028
STEELMAN, James, N.J., S3985
John, N.J., Privateer, Elizabeth W9684; BLWt.86033-160-55
William, N.C., Catharine Hawkins former wid., W8888; BLWt.21806-160-55
Zephaniah, N.J., S3976
STEEN, Edward, Pa., S37459; BLWt.1007-100
STEENBARGER, James, N.Y., Rebecca, W25168
STEENBERGH, Elias, N.Y., Mary, W22312; BLWt.15430-160-55
Elias, N.Y., Katharine, W25099
STEENBURGH, Abraham, N.Y., S42388
Elias, N.Y. See STEENBERGH
John, N.Y., Anna Margaret, R10102
Simon, N.Y., R10103
STEENROD, Ebenezer, N.Y., S14583
STEER, Elisha, R.I., Lois, R10104
STEERE, Asa, R.I., Mary, W22299
Nehemiah, R.I., Rachel, W22306
Reuben, N.Y., S21510
STEERMAN, William Walker, Va., Mary, W8768
STEERS, Hugh, Pa., Mary, W6180
John, Va., S6168
Richard, Va., S6163
STEEVENS, William, Ct., Cont., S11470
STEEVER, Daniel, Pa., S40517
Leonard, Pa., S6144
STEFFEY, John, Pa., War 1812, Rosanna, W7205; BLWt.26543-160-55
Peter, Va., Margaret, W7211; BLWt.34600-160-55
STEGALL, Jesse, Va., S7646
John, Va., Susannah, W4816
STEIGER, Abraham, Pa., S40501
STEIGERWALDT, Frederick, N.C., S7647
STEIN, Edward, Pa. See STEEN
Frederick, Cont., Pa., Elizabeth W3314; BLWt.1312-100. Iss. 5/10/1828
STEINHEISER, John, Hazen's Regt., BLWt.13763. Iss. 7/7/1789 to Henry Ebert. No papers
STEINHYZER, Christopher, Pa.,

STEINHYZER (continued)
Sarah, W4520
STEIRS, Hugh, Pa. See STEERS
STELE, Joseph, N.J., S1113
STELL, Ruel, N.J., BLWt.8702. Iss. 12/28/1789 to John Hollingshead, ass. No papers
STELLE, Joseph, N.J. See STELE
Thomson, N.J., Sarah, W7221
STELLER, Elizabeth, former wid. of John Vanloon, N.Y., which see
STENCEL, John, See STANSELL
STENGEL, Conrad, Cont., Pa., Catharine Brenze/Brenize, former wid., W5926
STENNAGS, Thomas, See STANNAGE
STENT, Eleazer, Ct., Rhoda, R10110
Othniel, Ct., S18221
STEPHENS, Balam, S.C., Mary, R20273
Benjamin, N.C., S31990
Charles, R.I., S36788
Charles, S.C., Barbary, R18173; BLWt.90013-160-55
Coe, N.Y., S42380
Daniel, Ct., BLWt.6467. Iss. 10/7/1789 to Benjamin Talmage, ass. No papers
David, Va., R10111
Ebenezer, N.Y., Rachel, W2018
Henry, N.C., Jane, W6189
Ira, Ct., BLWt.6428. Iss. 1/5/1791 to Ira Stephens
Isaac, N.J. See STEVENS
Isaac, Va., Rebecca, W8767
Jacob, Va., S17703
James, Ct., Vt., S23951
Jehu, Va., S31390
John, Mass., Sea Service, Mary, W19112
John, N.Y., S11458
John, N.C., S42025
John, Va., S31392
John, Va., S46073
John, Va. See STEPHENSON
John, Va., Cont., S37468
John W., Cont., S.C., b. Va., S16536
Joseph L., Va., Lucy, W8764
Laurence, Va., S7639
Mashock, Va., 1794-95, Milly, R10114
Moses, Ct. See STEVENS
Moses, N.C., R10116
Nicholas, Cont., N.J., S40523
Peter, N.H., BLWt.3470 & 307-60-55. Iss. 3/25/1790. No papers
Richard, Navy, Mass., S35085
Robert, Va., S45895
Roswell, Not Rev. War, Wayne's War 1792, BLWt.4384-160-55
Samuel, N.C., b. Va., S7640
Samuel, Pa., Mary, W22332
Silas, Mass., See STEVENS
Silvanus, Mass., S18209
Stephen, N.Y., Jane, W25111
Timothy, N.H., BLWt.3463 & 3430 Iss. 12/24/1789. No papers. 3430 iss. as Ct. but recorded N.H.

STEPHENS (continued)
Uriah, Pa., S11455
William, Ct., Cont. See STEEVENS
William, Cont., Mass., N.H. See STEVENS
William, Mass., S33722
William, Mass. Sea Service, S30140
William, N.C., Mary, R10135
William I., Md., Va. See Wm. STEVENS
STEPHENSON, Abiathar/Abiather, Cont Mass., S42394
Abner, Mass., BLWt.5009; Iss. 4/1/1790. No papers
Abner, Mass., S36787
Alexander, Pa. See STEVENSON
Calvin, Mass., S42399
Daniel, Mass., S33743
David, S.C., Jane, R10141
David, Va., BLWt.2057-400-Maj. Iss. 1/21/1790. No papers
James, Md. Sea Service, Navy, S41188
James, Mass., Elizabeth, W8770; BLWt.28633-160-55
James, N.J., S31388
James, N.C., See STEVENSON
James, Pa. See STEVENSON
James, Pa., Elizabeth, W9677
James, S.C., d. 1817 in Tenn., Rosanna, W596
John, Mass., BLWt.4993. Iss. 4/12/1792. No papers
John, Cont., Mass., S33750
John, N.C., S2020
John, Pa., S40496
John, Va., Sally, W6204; BLWt. 38562-160-55
Moses, S.C., Elizabeth, R21793
Obadiah, Mass., S4012
Thomas, Ct., Hannah Olds, former wid., W15143
William, Cont., Mass. res. & agcy. Hannah, W19414
William, Cont., Pa., S23958
STEPLETON, Andrew, Va., S36799
STEPP, Moses, See STIPP
STEPTO, Simon S., N.C., S3992
STERICHER, Justus, Pa., S41189
STERIGERE, Justus, See STERICHER
STERLING, Henry, Md., R10119
Levi, N.Y., BLWt.7790. Iss. 9/9/1790 to Ezekiel Crane, ass. No papers
Levi, See STARLING
Robert, N.C., R7637
Ruth, former wid. of Samuel Wilson, N.H., which see
Seth, Ct., S15994
Seth, N.C., Comfort, R10118
Silas C., S.C., R10120
Thaddeus, Ct., S17714
STERN, David, Va., BLWts.12546 & 14047. Iss. 5/18/1793 to Francis Graves, ass. No papers
Nicholas, See STARIN
STERNBERGER, James, See STEENBARGER
STERNBERGH, Joseph, N.Y., S14579
STERNE, David, Va., Lucy, W25145; BLWts.195-60-55, 12546-100; 14047-100. Both iss. 5/8/1793 to Francis Graves, ass. BLWt.14047

STERNE (continued)
located in Ohio.
Joshua, Crane's Cont., Mass., BLWt.5091. Iss. 8/10/1789 to Richard Platt, ass. No papers
STERNER, Christain, Pa., S23010
STERNES, Asa, Cont., Mass., N.H., S42378
STERNS, Asahael, Mass., BLWt. 5054. Iss. 4/1/1790. No papers
Isaac, Mass., S39856
Joseph, See STARN
Samuel, Mass. See STARNS
STERRIT, Stewart, Md., S31991
STERRY, Cyprian, Cont., R.I., Polly, W25151
David, Mass., S37454
Silas, Ct., Olive, W22342
STETSON, Abel, Mass., Sally, W15382
Batcheler/Batchelder/Bachelor, Mass., Margaret, W26446
Benjamin, Mass., Mary, W16736
Caleb, Mass., S33745
Ebenezer, Mass., S33717
Elijah, Mass., S19113
Elijah, Mass., S37448
Elisha, Mass., Rebecca, W25150
Gideon, Mass., BLWt.4988. Iss. 2/23/1796 to Marlborough Turner, ass. No papers
Gideon, Mass., S4886
Hezekiah, Mass., S29480
Joseph, Cont., Mass., S37451
Laban, Mass., S30722
[illegible]t, Mass., Joanna, W15394
Micah, Mass., Sarah, W15395
Oliver, Cont., Mass., S14620
Oliver, Mass., Nabby, W25123; BLWt.38553-160-55
Silas, Cont., Mass., Sea Service, Patty, W13922
Snow, Mass., Lydia, W15397
STETZER, Johann David, See David STATSER
STEUART, Charles, Va., R10148
Edward, Va., Mary, W6170; BLWt. 26039-160-55
Joel, Cont., Mass., S43991
John, Va., S19474
STEUBEN, Frederick William Von (Baron), res. N.Y., BLWt. 2126-1100-Maj. Gen. Iss. 6/8/1798
Jonathan, Ct., BLWt.6486. Iss. 4/8/1797 to John Steel, ass. No papers
Jonathan, Cont., Ct., Lucy, W22344
STEURT, Edward, Va. See STEUART
STEVENS, Aaron, Ct., Inv., pens. & BLWt.1945-300. Iss. 4/10/1795. No papers.
Abel, Ct., S11476
Abiel, N.H., BLWt.820-100
Abijah, Mass., S7641
Abraham, Mass., S21515
Adams/Adam, Ct., R.I., Rena, W5185; BLWt.9439-160-55
Alice, former wid. of Lewis George Mass., which see
Amos, Ct., S31986
Amos, Ct., Rachel, W11556; BLWt.

STEVENS (continued)
38543-160-55
Andrew, Vt., Sarah, W15370
Asa, Ct., Lois, R10132
Asa, Mass., Nancy, W2452; BLWt. 11100-160-55
Asa, Vt., R10122
Bartholomew, N.H., Mary, W25074
Barzilla/Barzillai, Mass., S17717
Benjamin, Ct., Cont., S15665
Benjamin, Md., Priscilla, R10138
Benjamin, Mass., S30723
Benjamin, Mass., Elly, W16744
Benjamin, N.H., S41216
Benjamin, N.H., Abigail Tilton, former wid., W27780
Benjamin, Vt., Lydia Allen former wid., W23419
Caleb, Ct., Mary, W19102
Calvin, Cont., Mass., S16541
Charles, S.C. See STEPHENS
Cyprian, Mass., S21514
Daniel, Ct., Pollyphema/Polyphema W11562
Daniel, Mass., N.H., S18223
Daniel, N.H., S19111
Daniel, N.H., Mehitable, W19088
Daniel, N.Y., S11478
Daniel, S.C., S18214
David, Mass., Sarah, W4823; BLWt. 36541-160-55
David, N.Y., S14607
Ebenezer, Cont., Ct., BLWt.625-150
Ebenezer, Cont., R.I., Lucretia, W20076; BLWts.1972-450-Lt. Col., iss. 6/15/1790. No papers
Elias, Ct., Lucretia, W9314; BLWt. 6022-160-55
Elias, Ct., Vt., S14621
Elijah, Mass. Sea Service, Privateer, R10123
Elijah, N.Y., R10124
Elkanah, Ct., N.Y., S15664
Elnathan, Ct., S9486
Ephraim, Ct., S41198
Ephraim, Cont. Mass., N.H., Sybbel, W5182
Ephraim, N.H., S43988
Forward, Ct., Mary, W6185
Gilbert, Va., Nancy, W7213; BLWt.44805-160-55
Giles, Pa., S23436
Henry, Ct., S36805
Henry, Ct., Polly, W821; BLWt. 5104-160-55
Henry, Mass., N.H., S14592
Hubbel, Ct., S42404
Isaac, N.H., S11460
Isaac, N.J., S36798
Isabella, former wid. of Joseph Chaney, Mass., which see
Israel, Ct., Love, R10134
Jacob, Mass., Martha, W25119
Jacob, N.H., R10129
Jacob, Va., Rachel, W2019
James, Cont., Ct., Esther, W6187 BLWt.13775-100. Iss. 1/25/1796. No papers. BLWt.9442-160-55
James, Mass., Hannah, W2265; BLWt.40934-160-55
James, Mass., N.H., b. Andover,

STEVENS (continued)
Mass. 1749, S18220
James, N.H., b. in Hampstead, N.H., 1757, S17128
James, Va., Susanna, W8766
Jeduthan, Mass., Roxanna, W25096
Jeremiah, Ct., S17698
Jeremiah, Cont., Mass., S19476
Jesse, Mass., S23944
Joel, Mass., S29482
Joel, Mass., Olive, W1661; BLWt. 16133-160-55
John, Ct., Chloe Smith former wid., W28034; BLWt.3609-160-55 Her last husb. was also a pensioner, see Ira Smith, Ct.
John, Ct., BLWt.1944-300-Capt. Iss. 6/18/1791. No papers
John, Ct., Mass., res. N.Y., S42431
John, Cont., Md., S6152
John, Cont., Mass., BLWt.1443-100
John, Del., S36327
John, Mass., S33748
John, Mass., S33749
John, Mass., Jerusha, R10131
John, Mass. Sea Service, See STEPHENS
John, N.H., b. Plainfield, Ct. 9/25/1744, S11494
John, N.H., age 74 in 1833, S17133
John, N.J., age 73 in 1833, enl. at Essex Co., N.J., S4891
John, N.J., m. 11/9/1786, d. 8/13/1843 at Mercer, N.J., Phebe, W1092
John, R.I., S33746
John, Va., Eve, R10125
Jonas, Mass., S19475
Jonas, Mass., res. at age 77 in 1832 Wayne Co., N.Y., Mary, W25152
Jonathan, Ct., Elizabeth, W2674; BLWt.6277-160-55
Jonathan, Mass., BLWt.5027. Iss. 3/25/1790. No papers
Jonathan, Mass., d. 2/25/1847, widow's res. St. Laurence Co., N.Y. in 1832, dau. Emma S. Cutler Sarah, W2456
Jonathan, Mass., b. 1747 at Andover, Mass., d. there 4/3/1834, Susanna, W13933
Jonathan, Mass., Portland, Me. res. of wid. in 1847 at age 92, Mary, W25076
Jonathan, N.H., age 87 in 1832, enl. from Sutton, Merrimac Co., N.H., S18218
Joseph, Cont., Mass., b. 10/29/1752, res. Schodeck, Rensselaer Co., N.Y. in 1818, moved to Greenbush in 1820 when wife, Abigail was 58 yrs. old & dau. Eliza age 18, d. 3/10/1836, S42433
Joseph, Mass., enl. from Salisbury Mass., b. there 4/19/1757, S29487
Joseph, Mass., Elizabeth, W22324
Joseph, N.H. Sea Service, lived in Portsmouth, N.H. in 1822, S43175
Josiah, Ct., Ct. agcy. Dis - no

STEVENS (continued)
papers
Josiah, Cont., Mass., age 65 5/19/1820, Mehitable, S43177
Judah, Mass., Abigail, W22335
Lemuel, Ct., Cont., S18217
Levi, Md., Mary, W25147
Moab, N.C., R10115
Moses, Ct., S6148
Moses, Ct., N.Y., S11474
Moses, Mass., S29477
Moses, Mass., Persis Weeks former wid., W22578
Moses, N.H., R10136
Nathaniel, Cont., Ct. res. & agcy. of wid., Amy, W17883 & 17868
Nathaniel, Cont., N.H., S43183
Nathaniel, Mass., Mary, W9313
Nathaniel, N.H., S10027
Nehemiah, Mass., Navy, S11469
Oliver, Ct., Nancy, R10137
Otho, Vt., Sarah, W---. She was also pensioned as former wid. of James Bayley, Vt., which see
Paul, Mass., Esther, W4821
Pelatiah, Cont., Mass., S37456
Peter, Ct., S41186
Peter, Ct., Vt., res. in 1832 Rutland, Vt. age 73, b. 5/6/1759 in Glastonbury, Hartford Co., Ct., son of Joel, S19109
Peter, N.H., Lydia, W8765; BLWt. 307-60-55
Peter, N.H., Molly, W15952
Peter, N.J., BLWt.8706. Iss. 5/9/1792. No papers
Peter, N.J., S33734
Peter, N.Y., Elizabeth, W597; BLWt.27612-160-55
Peter, N.Y., Hannah, R10126
Philip, N.Y., BLWt.7750. Iss. 7/14/1790 to Richard Platt, ass. No papers
Phinehas/Phineas, Ct., S42411
Phinehas, Mass., Lois, R10133
Resalvert/Resolvert, N.Y., S23941
Reuben, Ct., BLWt.6460. Iss. 12/26/1789 to David Knapp, ass. No papers
Reuben, Ct., Jerusha, W17870
Reuben, Ct., N.Y., Molly, W19409
Reuben, N.C., S31983; BLWt.18213-160-55
Richard, Va., Mary Beverly, W6186
Robert, Va., R10139
Roger, N.H., Esther, W25091; BLWt. 243-60-55 & 3466-100-1793
Rusel, N.Y., S6145
Safford, Ct., N.H., S41209
Samuel, Mass., d. 1833, Amy, W25112
Samuel, Mass., R.I., Amey, W25094
Seth, Mass., Sarah, W25165
Silas, Mass., b. 5/20/1755, lived in N.Y. in 1843, S23942
Silas, Mass., b. Worcester Co., Mass. in 1738, dau. Patty m. Eli Jenks, S33739
Silvanus, Ct., Sarah, W19096
Simeon, Mass., age 55 in 1818, S43174
Simeon, Mass., d. 9/18/1799,

STEVENS (continued)
Mariah, W22338
Simeon, Vt., b. 5/1763 in Dutchess Co., N.Y., moved to Vt. when a boy, S22545
Simeon, Vt., Susannah Corliss, former wid., W20918
Solomon, Ct., lived in Green Co., N.Y. when pen., Abelinah, R10121
Solomon, Mass., b. 12/15/1757, S30720
Stephen, Mass., S19794
Theodore, N.Y., BLWt.7846. Iss. 5/22/1793. No papers
Thomas, Ct., b. 5/11/1742, S11492
Thomas, Ct., age 63 in 1820, S36792
Thomas, Ct., enl. from Litchfield Co., Ct., m. Lucy 12/2/1784, d. 12/3/1841, pen. in Pa., W3471
Thomas, Mass., BLWt.5000. Iss. 6/9/1791. No papers
Thomas, Mass., BLWt.5043. Iss. 3/25/1790. No papers
Thomas, Mass., S37450
Thomas, Mass., enl. from Groton, Mass., lived in Hancock Co., Me. in 1818 at age 53, Elizabeth, sold. mentions his ch. as Eliza, Mary, Temperence, Thomas Jr., John & Josiah, S37452
Thomas, Mass., S37469
Thomas, Mass., S42409
Thomas, N.Y., R.I., lived in Niagara Co., N.Y. in 1834 age 80 S23441
Thomas, Va., BLWt.12562. Iss. 1/31/1794 to John Stockdale, ass. No papers
Timothy, Ct., BLWt.6446. Iss. 4/14/1790 to William Wells, ass. No papers
Timothy, Ct., Prudence, W17882
Timothy, Ct., Cont., S36796; BLWt.1286-100
Timothy, N.Y., R10140
Vincent, Pa., S22542
William, Col. Lamb's Art., BLWt. 1973-300-Capt. Iss. 7/15/1790. No papers
William, Cont., Mass., N.H., S19477
William, Md., Va., S36325; BLWt. 2076-200-Lt. Iss. 5/19/1797
William, Mass., S40526
William, Mass. Sea Service, Navy, S---, Margaret Stevens wid. was pensioned as former wid. of Ebenezer Starboard, Mass., which see
William, N.H., Martha, W22346
William, N.Y., Hannah Skinner, former wid., W9294
William, Pa., Margaret, W19109
William Smith, Hosp. Dept., S.C. BLWt.2119-300-Surgeon's Mate. Iss. 12/31/1796. No papers
Zachariah, Mass., Betsey, W314; BLWt.3967-160-55
STEVENSON, Alexander, Md., BLWt. 11717. Iss. 5/11/1790. No papers

STEVENSON (continued)
Alexander, Pa., Susanna, R10145
Charles, Pa., Margaret, W6191
Daniel, Mass., BLWt.139-100
Frederick P., N.Y., Hannah, W2189; BLWt.9447-160-55
George, Pa., Maria, W315; BLWt. 2118-300-Hosp. Mate. Iss. 7/16/ 1789
George, Pa., Catharine, W11534
James, Cont., Pa., S37460
James, Md., Pa., S.C., R---
James, N.J., S42430
James, N.C., b. Pa. in 1754, S4009
James, N.C., b. in Va., S7644
James, Pa., b. Ireland, S3973
James, S.C., b. Pa. in 1764, d. in Ky. in 1857, Ellen, W9685; BLWt. 31717-160-55
John, Del., See STEVENS
John, Md. See STINSON
John, N.C., b. Pa., Elizabeth, W4815
John, N.C. or S.C., b. Ireland, R10142
Nathaniel, Pa., Mary, W2266
Obadiah, Mass. See STEPHENSON
Peter, Mass., Elizabeth, W20072
Robert, Pa., S7643
Robert, Va., R10144
Samuel, Va., Jane, W8769
Stephen, Pa., BLWt.2013-300-Capt. Iss. 1/12/1791. No papers
William, Cont., Va. res. of heirs in 1838, BLWt.2212-200
William, N.J., BLWt.8721. Iss. 2/ 28/1791. No papers
William, Pa., BLWt.10442. Iss. 4/ 9/179? No papers
William, Pa., S23957
William, S.C., R10146
STEVER, Henry, N.Y., S11481
Philip, Pa., Elizabeth, R10108
STEVES, Jeremiah, N.Y., Sarah, W15951
STEWARD, Albert, Ct., Reuana, W19100
Amasa, Cont. Mass., S17120
Benjamin, Mass., Salley, W22323
Charles, Va., S16261
Daniel, Mass., S15996
Eliphalet, Ct., N.Y., R.I., S6156
Elisha, Ct., S11488
Joel, N.H. See STEUART
John, Mass., Marcay Olds former wid., W10841; BLWt.3071-160-55. Name also appears as Stewart & Stuart
Lemuel, R.I. See STEWART
Robert, N.Y. See Budd STUART
Thomas, N.C., R10171
Thomas, Va., Sarah, W4594
William, Ct., S4890
William, Md., BLWt.11725. Iss. 4/ 11/1789 to James DeBaufre, ass. No papers
William, N.H., S41150
STEWART, Alexander, N.J., S36330
Alexander, Pa., BLWt.2010-400-Surgeon. Iss. 5/2/1791 to Alexander Stewart
Alexander, Va., Cont., Dorothy,

STEWART (continued)
W8763
Allan, Mass., N.H., S46074
Amos, S.C., Martha, R10161; BLWt. 55705-160-55
Andrew, Ct., N.Y., b. Scotland, Lucretia, W19099; BLWt.27683-160-55
Archibald, N.J., Catharine, W6161; BLWt.47765-160-55
Barney, Va., S1727
Benjamin, Md., BLWt.11724. Iss. 12/18/1794 to Henry Purdy, ass. No papers
Benjamin, Va., Dorothy, W6162
Budd, N.Y. See Budd STUART
Caleb, Md., S7623
Charles, Ct., BLWt.1922-150-Ens. Iss. 3/1/1797. Also recorded as above under Wt.2677. No papers
Charles, Ct., N.Y., S41196
Charles, Cont., Md., S15656; BLWt. 457-100
Charles, Mass., BLWt.4970. Iss. 2/ 23/1796 to Joseph Brown. No papers
Charles, Mass., BLWt.5011. Iss. 8/ 7/1789 to Richard Platt. No papers
Charles, Mass., S42391
Charles, Mass., R10151
Charles, N.C., Ann, W6171
Charles, N.C., BLWt.2228-300
Charles, Va., S33736
Charles, Va., R10149
Christopher, Pa., Elizabeth, W6169 BLWt.2009-450-Lt. Col. Iss. 12/ 7/1791
Daniel, Ct., Lovisa, W9673; BLWt. 26253-160-55
Daniel, Cont., Mass., Dorothy, W17872
David, Pa. agcy. Dis - no papers
David, N.J., Rachel, W6167
Dempsey (colored), N.C., Lucy, W3734
Edward, N.C., d. 1832, R10152
Ezekiel, N.J., S31393
Finley, N.Y., Isabella, W16421
Francis, Cont., Mass., S41211
George, Pa., S40531
George, Pa., Rebecca, W3365
George, Pa., Susanna/Susannah, W4595
George, Pa. or Va., R10153
Henry, Ct., S23950
Henry, N.H., S38401
Henry, N.C., S31982
Hugh, Cont. Pa., S40499
Hugh, Mass., Mary, W25084
Hugh, Mass., Vt., S4005
Hugh, Pa., BLWt.10378. Iss. 10/ 26/1789 to Hugh Stewart. No papers
Isaac, Md., S7624
James, Ct., N.J., Pa., S40520
James, Ga. See STUART
James, Mass., S31985
James, Mass., Cynthia, W823; BLWt.36535-160-55
James, Mass., d. 1779, wid. lived in Saratoga Co., N.Y. in

STEWART (continued)
1839, Lydia Chase, former wid., W16902
James, Navy, Mass., War 1812, b. in Scotland, m. 1762, son of John the immigrant, who was killed at Battle of Bunker Hill. Served with John Paul Jones on the Ranger. This file contains an interesting account by the sold. of his experiences aboard the Ranger. R10155
James, N.Y., BLWt.8750. Iss. 6/ 16/1789 to Aaron Ogden, ass. No papers
James, N.Y., BLWt.1974-300-Capt. Iss. 9/4/1790 to Gerrit H. Van Wagener, ass. No papers
James, N.C., b. Pa., S7620
James, N.C., lived in Ga. in 1831 S32534
James, Pa., S40513
James, Va., b. 1/2/1757 in Augusta Co. (now Bath), Va., S6159
James, Va., pen. in Ill., S42389
James, Va., Rachel, R10166
James, Va., BLWt.12542-100-1792; BLWt.14024-100. Iss. 12/31/1792. No papers
Jehiel, Mass., Rachel, W25138
Jeremiah, Mass., S33756
Jesse, Mass., S23014
John,(Gen.) Widow's res. Ga., Manning/Mourning, d. 4/23/1830, Parmelia S. Perkins, dau., R10164
John, Ct., BLWt.6469. Iss. 10/9/ 1789. No papers
John, Ct., b. 1762 in East Haddam, Ct., moved after the Rev. to the western part of Ct., then to Mass. & thence to Frankfort, Herkimer Co., N.Y. where he was pen. in 1832, S28902
John, Green Mt. Boys, Vt., m. Susan Smith (or Susannah) in May 1777, d. Fort Edward, Washington Co., N.Y., 8/27/1831 age 77. Among the ch. was a dau. named Susan Wheelock, W19090
John, Md., Pa., b. 2/1/1755, enl. from Hagerstown, Md., moved to Ky. & then to Ohio near the Twp. of Williamsburg, S14585
John, N.H., lived in Thetford, Vt. at age 74 in 1820, S41218
John, N.H., m. Mary Barron, ch. were Sarah, John, Hannah, Lucy, Moses, Mary, Rachel, Thomas, R10162
John, N.H., N.Y., enl. at Cambridge, N.Y., d. 7/30/1829 at age 83, m. Huldah Hubbell, ch. were Cynthia, Aaron, Noble & Ira, R10154
John, N.C., b. in Va., age 76 in 1832, S7619
John, N.C., b. 5/24/1762 in Chatham Co., N.C., moved to Montgomery Co., N.C., then to NcNairy Co., Tenn. in 1836. Had sister named Elizabeth Russell, S21504
John, N.C., R10158

STEWART (continued)
John, Proctor's Art., Pa., BLWt.10448. Iss. 7/27/1789 to Richard Platt, ass. No papers
John, Pa., in Beaver Twp., Pike Co., Ohio in 1829, age 75 in 1833, S7622
John, Pa., age 63 in 1818, d. 7/17/1829, S40508
John, Pa., b. 8/1753 in Paxton Twp., Lancaster Co. (later Dauphin Co.), Pa., held captive in prison ship "Dutton" in N.Y. until 1/12/1777, R21841
John, S.C., b. in N.C., S7621
John, S.C., served under Gen. Sumter, son Levin, Mary, d. 10/31/1842, S19106
John, Vt., pen. from Otsego Co., N.Y., m. Mehitable Hungeford in East Haddam, Ct., in Nov. 1783, d. Frankfort, N.Y., 8/12/1834, W22345
John, Vt., Diadama Fullar, former wid., R3828
John, Va., age 71 in 1832, S6164
John, Va. See STEUART
Joseph, Ct., b. 1759 in East Haddam, Ct., moved to Frankfort, Herkimer Co., N.Y. after Rev. & then to Pulteney, Steuben Co., N.Y., S11484
Joseph, Cont., Ct., Anna Harvey former wid., age 64 in 1819, d. 4/8/1823, m. Anna Preston, 1/22/1774, W13348
Joseph, N.Y., age 79 in 1835, R10159
Jotham, Mass., Hannah, W25093
Jurdon/Jordan, N.C., Va., R10160
Lemuel, Ct., R.I., Rebecca, W15856
Maxey, Va., S38407
Moses, Mass., S11461
Nathan, N.Y., S11493
Oliver, Ct., Rebecca, W26444; BLWt.27657-160-55
Oliver, Cont., N.Y., S14602; BLWt.26120-160-55
Paul, Mass., S4884
Ralph, Va., Mary, W6168
Robert, Ga., R10167
Robert, Md., S39089
Robert, Mass., S43185
Robert, Mass., Sea Service, Mass. & Va. res., Seley, R10169
Robert, Navy, Mass., Margaret, W6165
Robert, N.Y., S23438
Robert, Va., S1256
Sally, former wid. of William Ferbush, Va., which see
Samuel, Ct., R10168; BLWt.26641-160-55
Samuel, Va., Lucy, W7220; BLWt. 26641-160-55
Sarah Ann, former wid. of Thomas Lewis, Va., which see
Thomas, N.C., S31998
Thomas, N.C. See STEWARD
Thomas, N.C., R10172
Thomas, Pa., S6153

STEWART (continued)
Walter, Pa., BLWt.2008-500-Col. Iss. 8/19/1789. No papers
William, Ct. See STEWARD
William, Ct., pen. from Greene Co., N.Y., S42398
William, Ct., Amanda/Maude Darrow W8760
William, Cont., N.Y., See STUART
William, Md., pen. from White Co. Tenn. age 76 in 1826, S39095
William, Mass., War of 1812, Mary, BLWt.67565-160-55
William, Mass., Va., res. Fayette Co., Ky. in 1832 age 69, S30715
William, N.C., living in Scott Co. Va. in 1832 age 76, d. 9/3/1851. Had bro. named David & a half bro. named Loving Bledsoe who also served in Rev., S11472
William, N.C., b. 1/10/1763 in Mecklenburg Co., N.C., moved to Livingston Co., Ky.,in 1806 moved to Crittenden Co., Ky., then to Carmi, White Co., Ill. & there in 1855. S14580; BLWt.13892-160-55
William, N.C., R10173
William, Pa., pen. from Washington Co., Md. at age 58 in 1820, son's name Jeremiah, S35089
William, Pa., age 64 in 1819 & living in Washington Co., Ind. S36803
William, Pa., Mary, R10163
William, S.C., R10174
William, Va. (?)----
William, Va., age 71 in 1832, S6167; BLWt.10005-160-55
William, Va., age 70 in 1820 & living in Madison Co., Tenn., S39097
William, Va., b. 11/8/1762, Martha B. Wilson, 2nd wife, lived in Ga. 40 yrs., had son & grandson named Thomas, Capt. John Stewart, his brother, W11555; BLWt.38559-160-55
William P., Pa., BLWt.10360. Iss. 7/5/179? to Conrad Shindle, ass.
STEYMETS, Jasper, N.Y., Rachel Oppell, former wid., W16666
STICHTER, Peter, Pa., S23945
STICKEL, Valentine/Volentine Stickle, Cont., Pa., S45156
STICKLE, Nicholas N., Cont., N.Y. Jemima, W17886
STICKNEY, Abraham, Mass., Abigail, W25129
Ancill, Mass., S21513
Benjamin, Mass., Nabby/Nabbey, W22320; BLWt.3142-160-55
Daniel, N.H., Sarah, W22313
Jeremiah, Cont., Mass., Elizabeth W22326
John, N.H., Mary, W25140
Jonathan, Mass., N.H., Sarah, W25131
Josiah, Mass., S33760
Levi, N.H., Molly, W22333
Moses, Mass., R10178
Nathan, Mass., Hepsibah/Hepzibah,

STICKNEY (continued)
W4824; BLWt.16117-160-55
Paul, Navy, N.H., S42406
Reuben, Cont., N.H., S42405
Samuel, Mass., Polly, W25159
Simon, Mass., N.H., Zeruiah Colburn, former wid., W17666; BLWt.9074-160-55
Thomas, Cont., N.H., Eunice, W2020; BLWt.31591-160-55
Thomas, Mass., Dorothy, W25121
William, Mass., S14605
Zillia, Mass., Olive, W25115
STIDHAM, Samuel, N.C., S14598
STIDINGER, John, Pa., S40064
STIFF, James, Va., Molly, W4344
STIGEFUSE, John, Pa., BLWt. 10385. Iss. 11/26/1795 to John Shaw, ass. No papers
STILES, Aaron, N.J., S28900
Asa, Ct., War 1812, Olive, R10182, Old War Inv. File 27523 BLWt.26448-160-55
Asahel, Ct., S31987
Asahel, Mass., S14599
Beriah, Ct., S14610
Caleb, N.H., S41219
Caleb, N.H., Elizabeth/Betsey, W25098
Elijah, N.J., Pa. See STITES
Ezra, Cont., Mass., S37445
Gould, Ct., S19108
Henry, Mass., BLWt.5061. Iss. 5/18/1790 to Theodosius Fowler, No papers
Hezekiah, N.J. See STITES
Jacob, Cont., Mass., Privateer, S22539
Jacob, Mass., R20517
Jacob, N.J., R10180; BLWt.14582-1855
James, N.J., Phebe, W10260; BLWt. 47766-160-55
Jeff, See Jeffery BRACE
Job, N.J., BLWt.8729. Iss. 10/29/1792. No papers
Jobe/Job, N.J., S40505
John, Ga., Lucy, W4820; BLWt. 28622-160-55
John, Mass., Ruth, W13923
John, N.J., Mary, R10181
John, not Rev., N.J. Mil., Whiskey Insur. BLWt.75097-160-55. No claim for pension
Jonah, Mass., S47953
Joseph, Ct., BLWt.1043-100
Josiah, Mass. See STITES
Lewis, Ct., S28894
Lincoln, Mass., S41217; BLWt. 31556-160-55
Martin, Ct., Candice/Candace, W25079
Mary, former wid. of Adam Deets, Va., which see
Moses, N.Y., BLWt.7803. Iss. 3/24/1792 to John Wempell, ass. No papers
Moses, N.Y., Catrina Orchard, former wid., W24373
Nahum, Mass., Betsey, W13924
Reuben, Cont., Ct., Submit, W22301

STILES (continued)
Robert, Ct., S42392
Samuel, N.H., R10184
Sarah, former wid. of Isaac Coffing, Ct., which see
Silas, Mass., R10185
STILL, Ebenezer, Mass., Susanna, W17867
John, N.H., BLWt.3484. Iss. 11/19/1792 to Wm. Hyde, ass. & Abijah Bond, ass. No papers
John, N.J., R10186
Ruel/Rual, N.J., S33715
William, Vt., S42393
STILLER, John, Cont., res. Pa. in 1794. Dis. No papers. See Am. State Papers, Class 9, p.99. Capt. Nathaniel Irish's Co. of Artificers. While in the line of duty he received a wound by which he lost two of his fingers of his left hand, which wound rendered him incapable of being a sold., or acting any longer as an artificer. Wounded 3/1780. Res. County of Philadelphia.
STILLING, Benjamin, Md., S4013
STILLINGS, Peter, N.H., S43180
Thomas, Md., S11483
STILLMAN, Benjamin, R.I., BLWt. 47987-160-55
Joseph, Ct., S31988
Nathaniel, Ct., S14603
Roger, Ct., Cont., S14588
Samuel, Ct., Invalid pen., d. 9/27/1821. No papers
Wait, R.I., Welthy, W16427
STILLS, John, N.Y., S30134
Robert, Cont., Va. res of son in 1828; BLWt.1368-100
Samuel, N.H. See STILES
STILLSON, William, Navy, N.H., Sally, W15387
STILLWAGGON, Frederick/Frederic, Pa., S40497
STILLWAGON, Jacob, Pa., Elizabeth W3613; BLWt.84015-160-55
Peter, N.J., Pa., Elizabeth, W3197
STILLWELL, Elias, Ct., BLWt.1952-300-Capt. Iss. 9/29/1790 to Elias Stillwell. No papers
Ezekiel, N.J., S33752
Jacob, N.C., S31993
Jarrat, N.J., S14625
Jasper, N.J., BLWt.8746. Iss. 6/11/1789 to Matthias Denham, ass. No papers
John, N.C. See STILWELL
Joseph, Cont., R.I., S39857
Silas, N.J., Margaret, W25153
William, N.J., BLWt.8757. Iss. 6/11/1789 to Matthias Denman, ass. No papers
William, Cont., N.J., N.Y., S33757
STILPHEN, Cornelius, Mass., Navy, R10187
STILSON, Ebenezer, Ct., S1114
STILWAGON, Philip, Pa., S22536
STILWELL, David, N.C., S36816
Ezekiel, N.J., BLWt.8745. Iss. 6/20/1796. No papers

STILWELL (continued)
Jacob, N.C., See STILLWELL
James, N.Y. See STILWILL
John, N.C., Jane Aspey. W7209; BLWt.53756-160-55
Joseph, R.I., See STILLWELL
Joseph, Va., S41195
Silas, Mass., See STILLWELL
Stephen, N.J., R10188
STILWILL, Elias, Ct., S36806
James, N.Y., Catharine, W16420
STIMMEL, Isaac, Pa., S23952
STIMPSON, Andrew, Mass., S29478
Ebenezer, Mass., Esther, R10189
John, Mass., Betsey, W22329
Thomas, Mass., Abigail, W2268; BLWt.15406-160-55
STIMSON, David, Ct., S14627
Elijah, Pa. See STINSON
Jeremiah, Mass., R10190
Joel, Ct., Susanna, W19095
Lemuel, Mass., Catharine, W7222 BLWt.31720-160-55
Luther, Mass., Sally, W15390; BLWt.17565-160-55
Phinehas, Mass., Lucy, W22337
STINARD, Oglesbery D., N.Y., S23433
STINCHCOMB, Aquilla, widow's res. Md., Catharine, R10191
Christopher, Del., Magdaline, W9319
STINCHFIELD, Ephraim, Mass., Sarah W25078
STINCIPHER, Joseph, N.C., S1891
STINE, Frederick, Md.,Pa. See STEIN
George, N.Y., S11471
Martin, N.J., S4010
Matthias, N.J., R10192
Philip, Pa., S17122
STINGLE, George, Va. See STINGLEY
STINGLEY, George, Va., S32543
STINSON, Elijah, N.C., b. in Va., Rachel, W9678
Elijah, Pa., S4906
James, N.H., Jannet, W19117
James, N.J., S3975
John, Md., S30717
John, N.C., b. Ireland, S7656
Luther, Mass. See STIMSON
Samuel, Mass., Sarah, W7223; BLWt.24335-160-55
Thomas, Mass., S37471
William, Mass., S19114
William, Mass., Abiah, W22325; BLWt.6010-160-55
William, Pa., S22543
STIPE, Frederick, Va., b. Pa., R10193
STIPP, George, Pa., Va., S17697
John, Pa., S30719
Moses, N.C., S.C., S15655; BLWt.34511-160-55
STIPTO, Simon S., N.C. See STEPTO
STIRLING, Robert, Va., S1932
William, Md., BLWt.11723. Iss. 11/29/179? to John Fannier, Admr. No papers
STITES, Elijah, N.J., Pa., S3988
Elizabeth, former wid. of Samuel Pope, N.J., which see

STITES (continued)
Hezekiah, N.J., S16260
Josiah, Mass., Elizabeth Holbrook, former wid., BLWt.50886-160-55
Richard, Va., R10183
STITH, John, Va., BLWt.2064-300-Capt. Iss. 9/9/1789 to Henry Lee, exec. of the last will & test. of Alexander Skinner, decd., late ass of John Stith
Joseph, Va., Nancy, W8750
STITT, William, Pa., S22544
STITZER, Henry, Pa., S7654
STIVER, Peter, Va., Temperance, R10194
STIVERS, Daniel, N.J., Margaret W4345
John, Va., S17707
Peter, Va., S41200
Reuben, Va., S37463
Simeon, N.J., S1112
STIVES, William, N.J., BLWt.8775 Iss. 12/21/1798. No papers
William, N.J., S33728
STOAKES, John, N.C., b. Va., Sarah, W8754
STOBER, Valentine, Pa., S14611
STOCH, Victor C.G., N.Y., BLWt. 7809. Iss. 6/24/1790 to Adam Maynard, ass. No papers
STOCK, George, Pa., S23947
STOCKBRIDGE, John, Cont., Mass., Mary, W25075; BLWt.2233-100
Joseph, Mass., Sarah, W25164
Micah, Mass., S28896
STOCKDILL, Robert, Ct., BLWt. 6444. Iss. 3/2/1792 to Shadrach Mead. No papers
STOCKER, Christopher, Mass., BLWt. 141-100. Claim missing in 1912. Register shows "Issued to Israel Angell 2/28/1804. Not delivered"
Ebenezer, Mass. Regt., BLWt.1909-200-Lt. Iss. 12/12/1791. No papers
Enoch, Mass., S33744
Lamuel, N.H., Dis.- No papers. See Am. State Papers, Class 9, p.137 A violent strain in his back in consequence of carrying a plank, which subjects him to constant discharge of blood when fatigued. Disabled at Mt. Independence in 1776. Res. Hopkinton
Michael, N.H., BLWt.734-100
Samuel, Mass., Sally, W3618; BLWt.13205-160-55
Seth, Lamb's Art., N.Y., BLWt. 7852. Iss. 7/30/1790 to John Gurnee, ass. No papers
Seth, N.Y., S42384
Thaddeus, Ct., S15992
William, N.Y., BLWt.7775. Iss. 5/5/1791 to Wm. Haskin, ass. No papers
William, N.Y., S42381
STOCKHAM, John, N.Y., R10198
STOCKING, Amasa, Ct., S30137
Eber, Ct., S36793; BLWt.581-100
Israel, Cont., pen. in Ct., S36794
Israel, Hazen's Regt., BLWt.13721

STOCKING (continued)
Iss. 1/24/1792 to Stephen Thorne, ass. No papers
Lemuel, Cont., Mass., Ruth, W2269; BLWt.8149-160-55
Moses, Navy, Ct., Elizabeth, W15384
STOCKLON, William, N.J. See STOCKMAN
STOCKLY, Charles, Va., BLWt.1251-200 & 2069-200-Lt. Iss. 9/11/1789. Annulled & Wt.1251 iss. in lieu there of
STOCKMAN, Benjamin, N.J., R10199
Christopher, S.C., S11477
John, Mass., BLWt.5051. Iss. 5/25/1790. No papers
John, Mass., BLWt.5058. Iss. 3/25/1790. No papers
Jonathan, Mass., S30132
William, N.J., Nancy/Nancy Stocklon W6206
STOCKNEY, Patrick, See SHOCKNEY
STOCKTON, Benjamin, Cont., N.J., S3979
Ebenezer, N.H., Elizabeth, W11542 BLWts. 107428-160-55 & 1883-400-Surgeon. Iss. 1/8/1789
James, N.J., Mary, W2485
STOCKWELL, Abel, Ct., BLWt.6509. Iss. 9/1/1790 to Theodosius Fowler, ass. No papers
Eli, Mass., S19793
Elizabeth, former wid. of James Owen, Mass., Navy, which see
Jesse, Mass., S15661
John, Mass., BLWt.5012. Iss. 3/25/1790. No papers
John, Mass., S42385
Levi, Mass., S21995
Levi, N.Y., BLWt.1917-200-Lt. Iss. 3/31/1796. Also recorded as above under Wt. 2616. No papers
Levi, Vt., S23437
Solomon, Mass., Mary, S45155; BLWt.15373
Solomon, Mass., Eunice, W19113
Thaddeus, Mass., Lucy, W17877
STOCUM, Reuben, Ct., N.Y., S11456
STODARD, Melzar, Mass., Lucy, W15381
Samuel, Mass., S33759; BLWt. 1724-100
STODDARD, Abel, Mass., S33731
Amos, Crane's Cont. Art., Mass., BLWt.5109. Iss. 8/10/1789 to Richard Platt. No papers
Brownell, R.I., S21508
Clement, Ct., War 1812, Esther Carpenter, former wid., R10202 & O.W. Widow File No. 12686
Cyrenius/Cyrenus, Ct., S42383
Daniel, Ct., Lucretia, R10204
David, Ct., Elizabeth, R10201
Eleazer, N.H., S18222
Frederick, Ct., BLWt.6488. Iss. 11/2/1791 to Jonathan Tuttle, ass. No papers
Frederick, Ct., S36800
Hosea, Mass., Lucy, W22340
Ichabod, N.Y., S42386
Jacob, Mass., Molly, W15389
James, Ct., S14591
Jonathan, Cont., Mass., S41207

STODDARD (continued)
Lemuel, N.H., S22538
Melzar, Mass. See STODARD
Nathan, Ct., BLWt.106-300
Nathaniel, Cont., Mass., S37470
Noah, Mass., Mary, W9321
Orringh/Orange, Mass., S48619
Philo, Ct., Polly, W2676; BLWt.14952-160-55
Philo, Mass., S31992
Robert, Ct., S14577
Samuel, Ct., BLWt.6455. Iss. 9/16/1791 to Isaac Brooks, ass. No papers
Samuel, Ct., S42377
Samuel, Mass. See STODARD
Simeon C./Simon C., Ct., S43176 BLWt.6500-100. Iss. 8/21/1789. No papers
Simon C., Ct. See Simeon C.
Stephen, Mass., Mary, W20070
Wells, Ct., S18212
William, Ct., S17716
William Trueman, Md., BLWt.2051-200-Lt. Iss. 9/25/1789 to Trueman Stoddard. No papers
STODDART, Philo, Ct. See STODDARD
STODDER, Ebed, Mass., S29486
Isaiah, Mass., Navy, Sally, W19097
James, Cont., Mass., S30128
Samuel, Mass., Sea Service, Susannah, W15398
STOEL, Asa, Ct., Judith, W11535
David, N.H., S11462
Ebenezer, See STOWELL
Samuel, Ct. See STOWELL
STOELL, Stephen, See STOYELL
STOGDILL, Robert, Ct., Sarah Smith, former wid., W22245
STOHLER, Adam, Pa., Eve Maria, W4813
STOKBRIDGE, John, N.Y., BLWt.7838 Iss. 1/25/1791 to Hezekiar Howel, ass. No papers
Joseph, Cont., Mass., See STOCKBRIDGE
STOKELY, Nehemiah, Pa., Susannah, W3165; BLWt.1912-300-Capt. Iss. 11/4/1791 to John McClelland, ass. No papers. Also recorded as above under Wt.2596
Thomas, Pa., Elizabeth, W4079
STOKER, Edward, Va., Anna, W11551
Samuel, N.H. See STOCKER
William, Va., S37472
STOKES, John, N.C. See STOAKES
John, Va., Dis- lost his hand in the battle of Col. Buford's defeat in S.C. Was pensioned for this disability from 9/4/1789. D. in N.C. in 1790. Son John Richmand Stokes was living in Chillicothe, Ohio in 1810. BLWt.526-300-Capt.
Jonathan, Ct., Sea Service, Navy & Privateer, Sally, W25133
Lewis, Va., S6158
Richard, Ct., Jerusha, W11541; BLWt.6020-160-55
Richard, N.C., S42026
Samuel, Va., S10259
Sylvanus, Va., S38397

STOKES (continued)
Thomas, Md., BLWt.11747 iss. 7/9/1799 to Peter, Nelly & Elizabeth Stokes, surviving heirs. No papers
STOLKER, Robert, Mass., S33727
STOLL, Andrew, Pa., Catharine, W1660; BLWt.2248-100
Andrew, Pa. See STAHL
Friedrich, Pa. See Frederick STULL
STOLTS, Jacob, See STULTS
STONE, Abel, N.H., S22540
Abijah, Mass., Abigail, W15393
Abner C., Mass., S33761
Abraham, Mass., S30718
Albemarle, Ct., Navy, Sally/Sarah, W2483; BLWt.6117-160-55
Alexander, R.I., S11459
Alpheus/Alphus, Mass., S33754
Ambrose, Cont., Mass., S19107
Amos, Cont., Mass., S11489
Andrew, R.I., Betsy, W6184; BLWt.10299-160-55
Andrew L., Ct., Mary Hoit former wid., W18056
Anne, former wid. of Timothy Pike, Mass., which see
Baltus, Pa., S41190
Benjamin, Mass., Hannah, W6183
Benjamin, N.H., S22534
Benjamin, N.H., S43987
Betsey, former wid. of Andrew Dewy, Ct., which see
Bille, Ct., Rachael, W2879
Caleb, Sea Service, Mass., R10212
Clark, Mass., Chloe, W3616; BLWt. 75007-160-55
Conway, N.C., War 1812, Elizabeth R10213
Cudbeth/Cutbeth, Md., Sally, W3050
Daniel, Ct., N.Y., S36813
Daniel, Mass., S30714
Daniel, Mass.,N.H., Abigail,W25118
David, Mass., S30129
David, N.J., S1116
Ebenezer, Mass., Esther, W19410
Enos, Mass., BLWt.1929-300-Capt. iss. 8/22/1789. No papers
Ephraim, Mass., Rebeccah, S19112
Ephraim, Mass., S22533
Ephraim, N.H., S42403
Esther, former wid. of Benjamin Fry, R.I., which see
Ezekiel, N.H., S43181; BLWt. 1677-100
Ezekiel, N.C., b. Va., S1933; BLWt.26347-160-55
George, Mass., S23954
George, Mass., S29479
Gregory, Mass., Lucy, W25087
Henry, Va., S6151
Isaac, Mass., S33747
Isaac, Mass., Chloe, W6182; BLWt.512-160-55
Jacob, S.C., S7625
James, Mass., S11479
James, N.H., Lydia Greenfield, former wid., W15908
Jeremiah, N.J., S35088
John, Crane's Cont. Art., Mass., BLWt.5115 iss. 1/28/1790 to

STONE (continued)
Joseph May. No papers
John, Mass., lived in Worthington Co., Mass. in 1832, S30138
John, Mass., lived in Sudbury, Middlesex Co., Mass. at age 75, his ch. were Peter, Walter, Daniel, William, Mary Leanned, Hannah Martings, Nancy Hatch & Abigail, S30139
John, Mass., d. 1/22/1832 in Essex Co., Mass., Hannah, W15377
John, Mass., m. Elizabeth Thayer in Easton, Mass. 9/1772, d. 3/5/1840. Their ch. were Millen, John, Theodore, Betsy, Jerrold, Dolly Niles, Sally Knapp, Laura McCullock, W19122
John, Mass., m. in Templeton, Mass., 11/25/1778, d. 12/6/1813; Lydia, W25092
John, Mass., Abagail, W25155
John, Navy, res. & agcy. in 1818 was Maine, S37453
John, N.H., Rebecca, BLWt.36653-160-55
John, N.Y., BLWt.7808; iss. 8/4/1790 to John N. Bleeker, ass. No papers
John, N.C., Sarah, W19403
John, Pa., S6160
John, Pa., S39096
John, R.I., Phebe, W22309
John Evarts, Ct., S18614
Jonas, Mass., S11485
Jonas, Mass., S19798
Jonathan, Mass., S17125
Jonathan, Mass., Anna, W2454
Jonathan, Mass., Jemima, W15402
Jonathan, Mass., Sally, W25116
Jonathan, Mass., Mary, R10216
Jonathan, Mass., BLWt.1897-300-Capt. Iss. 4/1/1790. No papers
Jonathan, N.C., S9488
Joseph, Mass., S18609
Joseph, Mass., S18616
Joseph, Mass., Elizabeth, R10214
Joseph, R.I., Mary, W25101
Josiah, Mass., Bridget, R10211; BLWt.11272-160-55
Josiah, Mass., Susanna, BLWt. 11191-160-55
Josiah, Mass., N.H., S11486
Lemuel, Mass., S30131
Lemuel, N.Y., S28893
Levi, Ct., S31989
Levi, Ct., Mary, W17875
Nathan, Mass., Alice, R10209; BLWt.19618-160-55
Nathaniel, Mass., S31395
Nathaniel, R.I., Marcy, W22331
Nathaniel, Vt., Lucretia, W25163 BLWt.11063-160-55
Nehemiah, Mass., S19797
Nimrod H., Va., S32535
Olney, R.I., Sea Service, Mary, R10217
Philip, R.I., S42382
Reuben/Rubin, S.C., S32539
Richard, Pa., S40506; BLWt. 1114-100
Rowland, S.C., S1257; see N.A.

STONE (continued)
Acct. No. 847-050168. Not Half Pay.
Samuel, Ct., BLWt.6492. Iss. 12/6/1791 to Stephen Thorn, ass. No papers
Samuel, Ct., S17708
Samuel, Ct., S42401
Samuel, Mass., BLWt.5041. Iss. 12/20/1796 to Oliver Gallup. No papers
Samuel, Cont., Mass., S36808
Samuel, Mass., S6157
Samuel, Mass., S11457
Samuel, Mass., S33725
Samuel, Mass., Hannah, W19399. BLWt.24904-160-55
Samuel, N.H., Hannah, W2190
Samuel, N.H., R10219
Seth, Cont., N.J., Lucy, W595. BLWt.68-60-55 & 6511-100. Iss. 1/14/1799 to Israel Stowell, ass. No papers
Shubael, Cont., Mass., Polly, W20075
Silas, Mass., Polly, W16422
Solomon, N.C., S3990
Stephen, Va., S3966
Thomas, Ct., Cont., S36795; BLWt.6482-100 iss. 10/7/1789 to Benj. Talmadge
Timothy, Mass., Alice, W25113
Uriah, Inv. pen., Vt. agcy. transferred from N.H. No papers
Westcot, R.I., Abigail, W7202; BLWt.31323-160-55
William, Ct., S42429
William, Mass., S4885
William, Mass., S18211
William, Mass., Lucy, W25109
William, Navy, Pa. agcy. & res., Dorothea, W3122
William, N.C., R10222
William, R.I., Lucy, W22307
William, Va., Mary, W8752
William, Va., Sarah, R10220
William, Va., R10221
Windsor, Mass., S46075
STONEBARGER, Lewis, Va. See STONEBERGER
STONEBERGER, Lewis, Va., Mary Ann W9683; BLWt.19807-160-55
STONEBRAKER, Adam, Cont., Pa., S40509
John, Pa., R10223
Sebastian, Pa., S32540
STONECYPHER, John, N.C., b. Va., S16539
STONEHAM, Henry, See STONEUM
STONEKING, Jacob, Pa., R10224
STONER, Abraham, Md., S7634
Casper/Gasper, Pa., S40524
Gasper, Pa. See Casper
Jacob, Pa., S40534
John, Md., Pa., Mary, R10226
John, N.Y., BLWt.7735. Iss. 10/10/1791 to Anthony Maxwell, ass. No papers
John, Pa., S40504
John, Pa., Anna, R10225
Nicholas, N.Y., Hannah, W6181; BLWts.35-60-55 & 7736-100. Iss.

STONER (continued)
5/31/1792. No papers
Peter, N.C., Eve/Eave, W9672
Philip, Pa., Sarah, W4804
STONEUM, Henry, Va., Jane, R22003. BLWt.19522-160-55
STONKARD, John, Pa., S41205
STONNELL, Richard, Va., BLWt. 12575. Iss. 4/13/1791 to James Reynolds. No papers
STOODLEY, William, Mass., S41202; BLWt.38548-160-55
STOOKEY, Jacob, N.J., Keziah, W996
STOOPE, Andrew, Md., Sarah, W2484; BLWt.11186-160-55
STOOPS, Eliakim, N.J., Margaret, R10228
Philip, Del., S4894
STOOTHOFF, Elbert, N.J., Pa., Va., R10227
STOPPLEBEEN, Jacob, See STUPPLEBEEN
STORER, Dorothy H., former wid. of John Courts Jones, Md., which see
Ebenezer, Mass., S18213; BLWt. 1906-500. Iss. 6/17/1794.
Edward, Va. See STOREY
Elias, Mass., S37457
Elizabeth, former wid. of James Scamman, Mass., which see
Henry, Mass., S36817
Isaac, Cont., Mass., Abigail, W22319
Joseph, Mass., Priscilla C., W2368 BLWt.31589-160-55 (wid. pensioned in Va.)
Nehemiah, Navy, Ct., S36801
William, Ct. See STOVER
William, Mass., Sarah, W4818
STORES, Chipman. See STORRS
STOREY, Edward, Va., Joicy, W4348
Enoch, Cont., Mass., Privateer, S14608
James, Ct., S15658
Thomas, Mass. See STORY
William, Cont., Mass. See STORY
STORM, Abraham/Abram, N.J., S40519
David, N.Y., S4900
Isaac, N.Y., S23012
Jacob, Va., R10229
John, Cont., Va., Ann, W1953
John, N.Y., BLWt.7772. Iss. 9/4/1790 to John Suffren, ass. No papers
STORMS, Abraham, Hazen's Regt., BLWt.13724. Iss. 7/14/1790 to Richard Platt, ass. No papers
Abraham, N.Y., Alletta, W19402
John, N.Y., Rebecca, W2876; BLWt.26034-160-55
John, N.Y., Elizabeth, W26449
Nicholas, N.Y., Lana, W16743
STORRS, Augustus, Ct., Anna, W16152
Chipman, Ct., R.I., War 1812, R10231
Ebenezer, Ct., S15995
Justus, Ct., BLWt.1925-300-Surgeon's Mate. Iss. 7/14/1797 . Also recorded as above under Wt.2692. No papers
Lemuel, Ct., Cont., Elizabeth, W25136

STORRS (continued)
Prentiss, Ct., Cont., S11468
STORRY, Nathan, See STORY
STORTS, Jacob, Md., Mary Ann, R10232
STORUM, Charles, N.Y. See STOURMAN
STORY, Andrew, Mass., Molly, W9316
Benajah, Vt., Anne, W19115
Daniel, N.J., S836
Daniel, Va., R10233. See N.A. Acc. No. 874-050169. Not Half Pay
David, See STERRY
Elisha, Cont., Mass., Mehitabel Mehitable, W13928
Henry, Mass., S33735
Henry, S.C., S32537
James, Mass., Sarah, W3732
John, Ct., Cont., S15657
John, N.J., Sarah, W995
John, N.C., Jane, W1507
John, Va., S6155
John, Va., S30721; BLWt.780-100. Iss. 3/16/1819. Act of 4/15/1806
Joseph, Mass., Mary, W4347
Joseph, N.J., Mary, R10235
Lewis, Va., Mildred, R10236
Nathan, Cont., Mass., Elizabeth, W6199. BLWt.5379-160-55
Oliver, Ct., Cont., Lois, W25082
Parker, Mass., Mary, W13929. BLWt.761-100
Primus, Mass., S41215
Roger, Mass., S10028
Solomon, Ct., S36812
Thomas, Mass., R10237
William, Cont., Mass., Lydia Moody former wid., W15088; BLWt.1904-300-Capt. Iss. 3/25/1790. No papers
William, Mass., S31394
William, N.J., S3971
STOTES, John, N.C., R20174
STOTESBURY, John, Pa., Sarah, W105; BLWt.2015-300-Capt. Iss. 8/4/1790 (name spelled Stotsberry)
STOTHARD, Thomas, Va., S40533
STOTLER, Henry, Cont., Md. Ch. were John, Nancy, Elizabeth, W15803
STOTSBERRY, John, See STOTESBURY
STOTT, John, N.C. See STOTES
STOTTLEMEYER, George, Cont., Md. R10238
STOUDEMIER, John, S.C., R10239
STOUFFER, Henry, See STAUFFER
STOUGH, Andrew, N.C., S7630
Andrew, Pa., S6147
Martin, N.C., S7629
Nicholas, Pa. See STROUGH
STOUGHTON, Alexander, Ct., S14596
Augustus, Ct., Cylinda/Celinda, W3315
Gustavus, Mass., S11482
Jonathan, Ct., Hitta, W17874
Livy, Mass., Cynthia, W7207; BLWt.53746-160-55
Russell, Ct., S14622
Shem, Ct., Flora, W17878
William, Ct., Eleanor, W17885

STOURMAN, Charles, N.Y., R10240
STOURNAN, Charles, N.Y. See STOURMAN
STOUSEBERGER, John, Cont., Va. agcy., Maria Margaret, W6207
STOUT, Abraham, N.J., S3969; BLWt.1995-200-Lt. Iss. 5/8/1792
Caleb, N.J., S7593
Catherine/Catharine, former wid. of Ruliff Hagerman, N.J., which see
Daniel, N.J., Anna, W203; BLWt. 28602-160-55
Elijah, N.J., Anna, W8751
Elijah, Va., S15662
Elisha, N.J., Huldah, W4080; BLWt.8707-100
James, Cont., N.Y., Jane, R10241
James, Crane's Cont. Art., Mass. BLWt.5100. Iss. 8/30/1790 to Simon Veeder. No papers
James, N.J., S33730
James, N.J., Esther/Easter, W6197 BLWt.34-60-55 & 8769-100. Iss. to William Garrison, ass. No papers
Jesse, N.J., Mary, W25108
Job, N.J., Pa., Rhoda, W9668
John, N.J., b. 12/25/1747, S1111
John, N.J., b. 6/1760, S4002
John, N.J., Sea Service, N.Y. & Privateer, b. 1755, S3984
John, Pa., age about 80 in 1832, R10243
Joseph, Navy, N.J., Wayne's Army three yrs., Ann Johnson former wid., W4466
Joseph, N.J., BLWt.1920-300-Capt. Iss. 3/23/1796 to John Watson, Admr. Also recorded as above under Wt.2665. No papers
Moses, N.J., Susannah, R10245
Peter, N.C., S32541
Reuben, Va., b. N.J., S14574
Samuel, N.J., S577
Thomas, Va., S7626
Wessel T., N.J., S33729; BLWt. 1997-200-Lt. Iss. 8/30/1790
William, N.J., Rachael, W4078
STOUTENBURGH, Andrew, N.Y., S42396
Benjamin, N.Y., S10026
STOUTENGER, George, N.Y., BLWt. 7805. Iss. 7/22/1790 to Thomas Tillotson, ass. No papers
George, N.Y., S42422
STOVAL, Bartholomew, Va., S1878
George, Va., S31391
Thomas, N.C., Va., S7632
STOVER, Christopher, Cont., Mass. 21" Inf. War 1812, S37455. Old War Inv. File 6171 War 1812
William, Ct., S17705
STOVERS, John, Mass. See STOWERS
STOW, Abijah, Cont., N.Y., Lucinda, W19404
Abijah, Hazen's Regt., BLWt.13768 Iss. 6/21/1791 to Stephen Thorne ass. No papers
Amos, Cont., Vt., Sarah, W2191
Elihu, Cont., Ct., Mary, W20071
Ichabod, Mass., Ruth, W20069

STOW (continued)
Jedediah, Ct., S14593
John, Ct., S11480
John, Mass., R10248
Joshua, Ct., Ruth, W26447
Lazarus, Pa., BLWt.2036-200-Lt. Iss. 6/11/1792
Samuel, Ct., Cont., S36819
Samuel, Cont., Ct., S48632
Samuel, Mass., S14589
Stephen, Ct., Mary, W22311
Timothy, Cont., Mass., Prudence, W22341
William, Va., S7627
Zaccheus, Ct., BLWt.6440. Iss. 6/25/1789. No papers
Zacheus, Ct., S36811
STOWEL, Israel, Cont., Mass., S33751
STOWELL, David, Mass., S33718
Ebenezer, Vt., Pamela, W22280
Isaac, Cont., Mass., S18615
John, N.H., Vt., Joanna, R10247
Nathaniel, Ct., Aurelia Fisk/Fish, former wid., W7266; BLWt.45666-160-55
Samuel, Ct., S42432
Samuel, Mass., Patience, R10249
STOWERS, John, Mass., S41185
John, Pa., BLWt.10404. Iss. 12/24/1790. No papers
John, Pa., Ann C., R10251
Lewis, Va., S31996
Samuel, Cont., Mass., Mary, W22321
STOY, Daniel, Cont., Pa., S40512
John, Pa., BLWt.2020-200-Capt.-Lt. Iss. 3/10/1790. No papers
STOYELL, Stephen, Ct., S11465
STOYER, John Tobias, Pa., S7633
STRACHAN, James, N.J., N.Y., S42420
William, Col. Lamb's Regt. of Art., BLWt.1987-200-Lt. Iss. 6/30/1790. No papers
STRADER, George, N.C., R10253
John, N.C., Elizabeth, W6203
Nicholas, N.Y., Margaret, W16742
STRAHAN, David, N.C., S32538
Gregory, Cont., Pa. res. in 1810 Margaret, W9318; BL rej.
Samuel, Cont., Pa., S37474
STRAHN, John, Cont., Va., Lee's Legion; BLWt.12532 & 13801. Iss. 10/12/1791. No papers
STRAIGHT, Henry, N.Y., S42425
Henry, R.I., Phebe, W26450
Joshua, R.I., S42424
Nathan, R.I., S21516
William, N.Y., S42423; BLWt. 40684-160-55
STRAIN, John, N.C., Isabella, R10255
Robert, Pa., S3989
Samuel, N.C., S.C., Nancy, S4904 BLWt.18206-160-55
Thomas, Pa., S3972
STRAIR, Nicholas, See STRADER
STRAIT, David, R.I., S21512
John, R.I., Sally, W9670; BLWt. 9215-160-55
STRALEY, Andrew, Va., S38406. See

STRALEY (continued)
N.A. Acct. No. 874-050170. Not Half Pay
STRANG, Gilbert, N.Y., Esther, W16426
John, N.J., S3970
Thomas, N.Y., Abigail, R10256
STRANGE, Abner A., Va., Mary S., W25125
Amos, N.C., b. Va., Frances, W6214
David, Va., Elizabeth, W6163
James, S.C., Privateer, S39087
John, R.I., S39858
John, Va., S3995
John, Va., S16537
William, R.I., Hannah, W25083
STRATTEN, William, Cont., Del., S42027
STRATTIN, Hussey, N.Y., BLWt.7793 Iss. 7/10/1790 to John Quackenboss, ass. No papers
STRATTON, Aaron, Mass., BLWt.1899-300-Capt. Iss. 1/6/1792. No papers
Annanias, N.J., BLWt.8715. Iss. 2/1/1790. No papers
Benjamin, Va., S7614
David, Mass., Polly, W19121
Ebenezer, Mass., S19795
Elijah, Mass., S17132
Husey/Hussey, N.Y., S42415
Isaac, Va., S38396
Jabez, Mass., R10257
John, Mass., Hannah, W16740
Jonathan, Mass., S35083
Lot, N.J., S22535
Nehemiah, Cont., N.H., Lois, W25127
Samuel, Ct., S23013
Samuel, Cont., Mass., Martha, W15385; BLWt.5450-160-55
Samuel, Mass., Tabitha, W2455; BLWt.3392-160-55
Seth, Va., BLWt.12551. Iss. 3/4/1796. No papers
Seth, Va., S37473
Stephen, Ct., S23435
Thomas, Ct., S17131
Thomas, Cont., N.Y., N.J., S40507
William, Cont. Del. See STRATTEN
Zebulon, Mass., S11464
STRAUGHAN, James, See STRAEHAN
STRAUSE, Detrick, Pa., BLWts. 10331 & 13714. Iss. 10/21/1791 to John Klein, ass. No papers
STRAW, Daniel, N.H., S32544
Jacob, Cont., N.H., Betty/Betsey R10259
John, N.H., Mary, W22339
Moses, N.H., S43178
Nicholas, Pa., S23956
Richard, N.H., S16542
Samuel, N.H., S17715
William, Mass., S41206
STRAYER, Jacob, Pa., R21856
STRAYHORN, John, N.C., S7655
William, N.C., S7650
STRAYTON, Thomas, Del., S36328
STREATER, Nathan, See STREETER
Ned, Va., S7645
STREATOR, John, Mass., Elizabeth Sanford, former wid., W4794;

STREATOR (continued)
BLWt.6120-180-55
STREBY, Paul, Pa. See STREVE
STREEPS, Robert, Del., BLWt. 2117-100
STREET, Anthony, Va., Trephenia, R10261
David, Va., Letitia, W6164
Isaac, Va., Rhoda/Rhody, W11537
John, Ct., S17712
STREETER, Adams, N.H., R.I., Huldah W25095
Barzillai/Barzilla, R.I., "The Black Regt.", Nancy, W16076
Benjamin, Mass., S42416
Ebenezer, Mass., R.I., S22541
Eleazer, Cont., Mass., R.I., Cynthia, W19412
George, R.I., Rhoda, W22317
Isaiah, R.I., Sally Remington, former wid., W18803
Joel, R.I., S21506
Naphtali, N.H., R.I., Elizabeth, W3617; BLWt.88009-160-55
Nathan, Mass., Naomi, W22343
Nathan, R.I., S21507
Nathaniel, Mass., S42426
Rufus, R.I., Nancy, W4343
Samuel, Mass., S33716
Susannah, former wid. of Abel Johnson, Mass., Vt., which see
STREETOR, Benjamin, Mass., BLWt. 5017. Iss. 12/3/1789 to Moses W. Barker, ass. No papers
STREETS, Robert, Md., BLWt.11708 Iss. 2/1/1790 to Anne Tootle, Admrx. No papers
STREEVY, Paul, See STREVE
STREGEL, Nicholas, Ga., Sarah, W1329; BLWt.28645-160-55
STREMBECK, Jacob, Cont., Pa., S4896
STREPHANE, William, Pa., BLWt. 10469. Iss. 4/21/179? to James Morrison, ass. No papers
STREPS, Robert, See STREEPS
STREVE, Paul, Pa., S41191
STRIBLING, Clayton, S.C., Mary, W6208; BLWt.13987-160-55
Samuel, Va., S37464
Sigismond, Va., BLWt.2066-300-Capt. Iss. 2/24/1796
William, Va., S41204; BLWt.12541. Iss. 4/13/1791 to James Reynolds ass. (Located in Morrow Co., Ohio)
STRICKER, Abraham, Pa. See STRYKER
Adam, N.J., S758
Dennis, N.J., S23432
Henry, Pa., Sarah, W6202
Jacob, Pa., BLWt.10333. Iss. 6/29/1789 to M. McConnell, ass. No papers
Jacob, Pa., S40522
John, Pa., BLWt.2028-200-Lt. Iss. 6/29/1789 to Matthew McConnell, ass. No papers
STRICKLAND, Alexander, Va. See STRICKLING
David, Ct., Cont., S35084
Edward, Va., S42417
James, Mass., Naomi, W19094

STRICKLAND (continued)
Jonah, Ct., R10263
Joseph, N.J., S7636
Roger, Mass., War of 1812, Lydia W6172; BLWt.89519-160-55 & 44651-80-50 & 29820-80-55
Sampson/Samson, N.C., R10264
Seth, Ct., Anna, W17889; BLWt. 9469-160-55
Simeon, Ct., Mary, W17880
Stephen, Ct., R10265
William, Mass., Patience W. Prindle former wid., W19999
STRICKLIN, Frederick, N.C., S39092
Lot, N.C., S7657
Samuel, N.C., R10266
STRICKLING, Alexander, Va., Jane, W6174
STRIKER, Abraham, Pa. See STRYKER
John, Capt-Lt., Col. Proctor's 4th Regt., BLWt.2022-200-Capt.-Lt., iss. 5/19/1789
STRINGER, Fortunatus, Md., BLWt. 11690-14100. Iss. 2/24/1795 to Francis Sherrod, ass. of Leonard Holt, Admr. No papers
John, Crane's Cont. Art., Mass., BLWt.5098. Iss. 1/28/1790 to Joseph May. No papers
John, Va., S16538
Leonard, Sea Service, Va., R10267
STRINGFELLOW, Hannah, former wid. of Jeremiah Moxley, Va., which see
STRINGHAM, Daniel, N.Y., S32536
Henry, N.Y., BLWt.7769. Iss. 12/12/1791 to Samuel Birdsall, ass. No papers
Peter, Hazen's Regt., BLWt.13722 Iss. 3/21/1791 to Josiah Starr, ass. No papers
STROBECK, Adam, N.Y., S26759 & S14584
STROBEL, Albert, S.C., Elizabeth W22354
STROBRIDGE, George, ---, ---, Bethsheba. See widow's claim as former wid. of Jason Crawford Ct.
George, Mass., S11487
Job, See Trowbridge
William, Cont., Mass., res. N.H. for 18 yrs., Hannah, W19398; BLWt.18391-160-55
STROHECKER, John, Pa., S23946
STROHL, Jacob, Pa., Mary, W3164; BLWt.1178-100
STROMAN, John, Pa., S4899
STRON, Richard, N.C., S4675
STRONG, Alexander, N.H., Emelia, W22336
Anthony, Ct., S36814
Asa, Vt., S21505
Barnabas/Barnabus, Ct., S40498
Charles P., N.J., Anne Vanderveere former wid., R10844. Hendrick Vanderveere also served in Rev.
Charles, Va., S31994
Chloe, former wid. of Eli King, Ct., which see

STRONG (continued)
Christopher, S.C., Rosannah, W9315; BLWt.28556-160-55
David, Ct., S14573; BLWt.26346-160-50
David, Ct., BLWt.1951-300-Capt. Iss. 10/17/1789. No papers
David, Mass., S29484
Eleazer, Mass., Mindwell, W25117
Elnathan, Ct., Margaret, W8753; BLWt.29060-160-55
Ephraim, Ct., S18613
Ezekiel, Vt., R10271
Israel, Ct., S11467
Jacob, Ct., Elizabeth, W25146; BLWt.3139-160-55
Joel, Ct., Cont., N.Y., S11466; BLWt.26526-160-55
John, Ct., lived in Torrington then Norfolk, Ct., S15659
John, Ct., lived at Woodbury, Litchfield Co., Ct. age 65 in 1818. Ch. were Fanny & John, S31984
John, Ct., S36818
John, Ct., Mass.(?), Martha, R10274
John, Cont., Ct., S14587; lived in Oneida Co., N.Y. at age 59
John, N.Y., Lydia, W4592
John, Va., S7594
Johnson, Va., S32542
Joseph, Ct., Hannah, R10272
Joseph, Ct., Cont.; son of David Strong, BLWt.1951; lived in Warren Co., Miss. at age 69, S7598
Josiah, Ct., S42428
Levi, War with France 1798-1800 res. Mass., Catharine. O.W. Inv. 48636; O.W. Wid. Rej. 23156
Lydia, former wid. of Oliver Means, which see
Nathan, Mass., S42427
Nathan, N.Y., BLWt.1992-300-Capt. Iss. 3/6/1792. No papers
Nathaniel, Ct., Privateer, S15993
Phineas, Sheldon's Dragoons, Ct., BLWt.6445. Iss. 3/11/1791 to Isaac Bronson, ass. No papers
Phineas, Ct., BLWt.6516. Iss. 11/10/1792. No papers
Phinehas, Ct., S41187
Reuben, Ct., BLWt.6459. Iss. 8/15/1792 to Samuel Allen, ass. No papers
Roger, Ct., Cont., S14575
Roswell, Mass., S14618
Selah, Ct., S29483
Seth, Ct., Rachael, W17879
Solomon, Ct., S41213
Stephen, Ct., S18216
William, Cont., Mass., N.H. & Vt. S14624
William, N.J., S33753
William, Vt., Abigail, W25132; BLWt.8014-160-55
STRONGMAN, William, Cont., Mass. N.H., Vt. See STRONG
STROOP, Henry, Cont., Pa., S7631
John, Pa. See STROUP
STROTHER, Benjamin, Cont., Va., S7635
Benjamin, Va. Sea Service, R97; Va. Half Pay
Daniel, Va., R10275
George, S.C., Jane/Janet, W9317
George, Va., S18611
James, Va., Elizabeth B., W6210
Robert, Va., R10276
William, Va., Lee's Legion, BLWt. 12540 & 13962. Iss. 11/2/1792 to Robt. Means, ass. No papers
STROUD, Abigail, former wid. of Nathaniel Bates, N.H., which see
Hampton, S.C., S36789
Isaac, N.C., S14578
John, N.H., S14614
John, N.C., Delilah, W9675
Mathew/Matthew, N.C., S3980
Sherrod, N.C., Hannah, R10277
William, N.C., R10278
William, Va., S6166
STROUGH, Nicholas, Pa., S23009
STROUP, Adam, N.C., b. Md., S7628
John, Pa., Hannah, S---; BLWt. 40923-160-55
STROUS, George, Pa., S40511
Jacob, Va., S40529
STROUT, Enoch, Mass., Mercy, W25077
Prince, Cont., Mass., Christiana, W25122
STROVER, John, N.Y., Mary, W16425
STROWBRIDGE, George, See file of Jason Crawford, Ct.
STROZIER, Peter, Ga., Margaret, R10279
STRUBIN, Philip, Von Heer's Corp. BLWt.2124-200-Lt. Iss. 1/12/1796. No papers
STRUNK, Henry, Pa., R9554
John, Pa., Barbara, W2878
William, Pa., Mary, W3615
STRUPE, Samuel, N.C., Susannah E. W9671
STRUTHERS, John, Pa., 1794, R18262
STRYKER, Abraham, Pa., Catharine, W25161
John D., N.J., S4889
Peter J., Pa., R10302
Simon, N.J., S920
STUART, Alexander, Md. See John THOMAS, Md.
Benjamin, Mass., Damaris, W15374
Budd/Robert, N.Y., Rebecca, W1662
Charles, Pa., S23948
Daniel, Cont., Mass. See STEWART
Edward, Va., S7617
Edward, Va. See STEUART
George, Pa. See STEWART
James, Ga., S39088
James, S.C., Susan, W8762
John, Del., BLWt.2081-100
John, N.C., S7615
John, Va., R10157
Jordan, N.C. See Jurdon STEWART
Joseph, Ct., S3974
Peter, Mass., S17119
Philip, Cont., Va., S20989; BLWt. 2081-200-Lt. Iss. 2/16/1796
Robert, Mass. Sea Service, See STEWART
Samuel, Ct., Mass., S17713
Samuel, N.H., Hannah, W25088
William, Cont., N.Y., S46472; BLWt.2114-200; Lt. Hazen's Regt., iss. 9/22/1789
William, N.Y., Catharine, W19104
STUBBLEFIELD, Beverly, Va., Mary, W2263; BLWt.2067-300-Capt. Iss. 5/30/1797 to Thomas Overton, ass.
Richard, N.C., R10281
William Seth, Va., Sarah, R10282; BLWt.57782-160-55
STUBBS, Allen, Va., BLWt.12557. Iss. 5/11/1792 to Francis Graves, ass.
Lewis, S.C., S21999
Richard, Mass., S37466
Robert, Pa., BLWt.10474. Iss. 6/20/1789. No papers
Ruth, former wid. of Thomas Hill, Cont., Mass., which see
Samuel, Mass., S38405
William, S.C., Ann F./Annie F., W6188; BLWt.26142-160-55
STUBRACH, Barend, N.Y., Pa., S10029
STUCK, John, Pa., Elizabeth, R10283
STUDELLMAN, John, Cont., Pa., S40510; BLWt.10410-100. Iss. 1796
STUDER, Philip, Md., S40500
STUDLEY, John, Mass., Sarah, W15379
Thomas, Crane's Cont. Art., Mass., BLWt.5116. Iss. 5/8/1792 to Benj. Haskell, ass. No papers
William, Mass., S17699
STUDLY, Consider, Mass., Olive, W15399
STUDTHEM, John, N.C., Martha, W3887 BLWt.28508-160-55
STUDWELL, Henry, Ct., S14617
STUFFLEBEAN, John, N.Y., Elsee, R10283 1/2
STUKEBERY, Jacob, Va., S39094
STUKESBERRY, Jacob, See STUKEBERY
STULL, Andrew, Pa. See STOLL
Andrew, Pa. See STAHL
Frederick, Pa., S40530
George, Pa., BLWt.10379. Iss. 8/5/1796. No papers
Joseph, N.J., S23953
STULTS, Henry, N.J., R10292
Jacob, N.J., Margaret, W1508
STULTZ, Casper, N.C., Anna M., W4819
STUMP, George, Pa., S16262
Jacob, Va., S41193
John, N.Y., BLWt.7762. Iss. 7/16/1790 to William J. Vreedenbugh, ass. No papers
John, N.Y., S42413
Lewis, Va., Margaret, W7201
Michael, Va., R10285
STUPPLEBEEN, Jacob, N.Y., Ann, W16739
STUPPLETON, Jacob, N.Y. See STUPPLEBEEN
STURDEVANT, Caleb, Ct., S35645
James, Ct., S46076
James, Pa. res. in 1789. Dis.
STURDIVANT, Charles, N.C., S36326
Joel, Va., S6150

STURDIVANT (continued)
William, Va., Elizabeth, W4817
STURGEON, James, N.C., b. Va., R10286
Margaret, former wid. of William Jumpt, Pa., which see
Peter, Pa., S4903
Robert, Pa., S40514
STURGES, Aquila, Ct., R10288
Augustus, Ct., Mercy, W17884
Benjamin, Ct., Thankful, W25073
David, Ct., R10289
Hezekiah, Ct., S14601
Joseph, Pa. See STURGIS
Lewis, Ct., S17704
Moris Simmons, Ct., Lois, R10290
Moses, Ct., S36815
STURGIS, Aaron, Ct., S31389
Abram, Ct., Anna, W19407; BLWt. 38561-160-55
Benjamin, N.J., Pa., S3998
Jedidiah, N.J., S3994
Jonathan, Mass., S28897
Joseph, Pa., S6154
STURMAN, William, Va., S39093
William W., Va. See STEERMAN
STURTEVANT, Andrew, Mass., S38400
Asa, Mass., S38402
Barze, Mass., S33726
Dependence, Mass., Abigail, W15407
Ephraim, Mass., Abigail, W15403
Francis, Mass., S30127
Heman, Mass., Betsey, W25107
Hosea, Mass., S18219
Isaac, Mass., Hannah, W25120
Isaac, Mass. res. in 1801, BLWt.4-200
Jesse, Mass., S38399
Jonathan, N.Y., Pegga Ann, W2675; BLWt.6030-160-55
Joseph, Mass., Sarah, W22322; BLWt.8379-160-55
Lemuel, Mass. See STURTVANT
Lemuel, Mass., Priscilla, R10291
Lot, Mass., S37442
Noah, Mass., Ruth, W20073
Seth, Cont., Mass., S37443
Zebedee, Ct., S14615
STURTVANT, Lemuel, Mass., S21998
STUTSON, Levi, Mass., Mary, W15392
STUVER, George, N.Y., Mary, R10107
STYLES, Henry, Pa., S7599
STYMETS, Isaac, Lamb's Art., N.Y. BLWt.7849. Iss. 9/28/1790 to Bartholomew & Fischer, assnes. No papers
Jasper, N.Y. See STEYMETS
STYVERS, Daniel, Pa., S22537
William, Va., S37465
SUBA, Piere, Cont., N.Y. res. in 1831, R20173
SUBBUTH, William, Va., S40538
SUBLETT, Abraham, Va., S31397
SUDDARTH, John, Va., R10293
SUDDOTH, Benjamin, Va., Sea Service, S4015
John, Va., BLWt.2112-100
SUDDUTH, Jared, Va., S32001
William, Va. See SUBBUTH
SUDLOW, Samuel, N.Y., BLWt.7828. Iss. 5/24/1793 to George Stout,

SUDLOW (continued)
ass. No papers
SUDRICK, Joseph, N.H., BLWt. 2312-100
Michael, N.H., Bridget, W25175
SUDTHARD, John, 1st Regt. Light Dragoons, BLWts.13731 & 14124. Iss. 6/19/1795. No papers
SUFFERANCE, Ephraim, Crane's Cont. Art., Mass., BLWt.5110. Iss. to Elephalet Downer, 1/28/1790. No papers
Ephraim, Cont., Mass. See SUFFRANCE
SUFFRANCE, Ephraim, Mass., Cont., Ruth, W25172
SUFFREN, Elizabeth, former wid. of James/Jacobus Bogert, N.J., which see
SUGANNUG, Joel, Mass. See SUGARMUG
SUGARMUG, Joel, Mass., BLWt.985-100
SUGART, Eli, Pa., S40539
SUGGAN, James, Cont., Va., S36821
SUGGITT, John, Va., S14629
SUGGS, George, Va., S38320
SUIDAM, Cornelius, N.J., Margaret W1326; BLWt.6297-160-55
SUIT, Edward, Md., Mary, W13940
Jesse, Md., BLWt.11695. Iss. 9/5/1789 to Jesse Suit. No papers
SUITS, Christian, See SOOTS
Peter, N.Y., Elizabeth, W13941. Her 1st hub. was also in the Rev. Jacob Eply, killed by Indians in April 1779
Peter J., N.Y., d. 1828, Magdalena W19128
SUIYDAM, Cornelius, N.J. See SUIDAM
SULCER, William, Va.,Jane, W9687
SULLARD, Benjamin, N.J., Sarah, W2024
SULLENGER, James, N.C. See SULLINGER
SULLENHEIM, Henry, N.H., S43187
Jacob, N.H. See SULLINGHAM
SULLINGER, Daniel, Md., BLWt.11728 Iss. 12/18/1794 to Henry Purdy, ass. No papers
James, N.C., Sarah, W27638; BLReg. 316805-1855
SULLINGHAM, Jacob, N.H., S16545
SULLINGS, John, Mass., S41220
SULLIVAN, Barnabas, N.C., Pens. in Me. & Mass., Catharine, W20077
Benjamin, Mass., Navy, S43188
Charles, N.Y., Rhoda, R10299
Cornelius, N.J., 1793, S1258
Daniel, Cont., Md., Pa., Sarah, W25169
Daniel, N.J., BLWt.8761. Iss. 6/16/1789 to Thomas Coyle, ass.
Daniel, Pa., BLWt.10427. Iss. 5/16/1791. No papers
Daniel, Va., S7661
David, N.Y., Hannah, W11574
Elijah, Md., BLWt.11685. Iss. 1/11/1796 to Joshua Ward, ass. No papers
George, N.C., Pa., S4025
James, Md., N.Y., S35091

SULLIVAN (continued)
James, N.J., Mary, R10297
John, Invalids, BLWt.13778. Iss. 9/4/1789. No papers
John, S.C., b. 1756 in Va., S18235
John, S.C., b. Ireland 3/31/1760, enl. from Charleston, lived in Fairfield Dist. in 1832, S22002
John, Va., S38410
Larkin, Va., R10296
Murthy, Pa., BLWt.10353. Iss. 8/7/1789 to Richard Platt, ass. No papers
Patrick, N.J., BLWt.8700. Iss. 2/28/1790 to John Ludlow, ass. No papers
Patrick, N.J., Margaret Dearwell, former wid., W24047
Patrick, Pvt., Pa., BLWt.10365. Iss. 7/9/1789
Patrick, Pa., Jane/Christiana Jane R10295
Peleg, R.I., R10298
Perry, Md., BLWt.2058-100
Peter, Va., Katy, W3736
Philip, Md., BLWt.11745. Iss. 6/11/1790. No papers
Pleasant, Va., Milly, W10265
Roger, Hazen's Regt., BLWt.13741 Iss. 10/17/1789 to John Pope, ass. No papers
Solomon, Md., Sarah, W19419
Thomas, Pa., BLWt.10400. Iss. 12/19/1789. No papers
William, Del., BLWt.10887. Iss. 12/28/1790. No papers
William, Md., BLWt.11683-100. Iss. 1792
SULLIVANT, Owen, N.C., Martha/Patty, W11580
SULSER, William, Va. See SULCER
SULT, David, Pa., S40537
SUMERLIN, Winburn, N.C., Milly, W4346
SUMMER, George/George A., S.C., S22001
SUMMERFORD, William, S.C., Piety W11576
SUMMERLIN, Winburn, N.C. See SUMERLIN
SUMMERS, David, Ct., Mary, W2877
Elizabeth, former wid. of George Lewis, Va., which see
Farrel, Lamb's Art., N.Y., BLWt. 7832. Iss. 9/1/1790 to Samuel Cooper, ass. No papers
George, N.C., Mary, W6606
Hezekiah, Md., Ruth, R10304; BLWt.34588-160-55
Horsey, Md., S7664
James, N.C., Lavinia/Levina, W2192 BLWt.61059-160-55
James, Va., R10306
John, Md., BLWt.11718. Iss. 11/29/1790 to Frederick Hall, Admr. No papers
John, Md., Ann, R10303
John, N.C., BLWt.2094-300-Capt. Iss. 11/15/1791
John, N.C., Va., S31999
John, Va., Agnes, W3051
John, Va., R10308

SUMMERS (continued)
Joseph, N.C., S31399
Neram, Ct. See Nirum
Nirum/Neram, Ct., R20186
Peter, Md., Pa. res., S22546
Richard, Md., S7663
Solomon, Md., BLWt.11696. Iss. 2/7/1790
Sylvester, Ct., S16263
Thomas, R.I., S17134
SUMMERSETT, Thomas, Cont., Va. Mary, W4826; BLWt.1171-100
SUMNER, Clement, Mass., S30141
Darius, Mass., Anna, W13938
Ebenezer, Cont., Ct., Sea Service, Jemima, W19418
Ebenezer, Mass., S29488
Eli, Mass., Elizabeth H., W22351
George, Ct., R10311
George, Mass., BLWt.1713-100
Jethro, N.C., BLWt.2092-850-Brgr. Gen. Iss. 2/9/1798 to the heirs, Thomas E. Sumner & Jacky S. Bloun (late Sumner)
Jezeniah, Mass., S31396
Job, Mass., BLWt.1893-400-Maj. Iss. 4/20/1790. No papers
John, Ct., BLWt.1939-450-Lt. Col. Iss. 4/9/1790 to Elizabeth Sumner, admx. No papers
John, Mass., Hannah, W13939
Joseph, Mass., S19804
Robert, Ct., Jemima, W22350
Samuel, Cont., Mass., S33763; BLWt.13795-100. Iss. 7/9/1789
Shubill/Shubell, Ct., S42436
William, Ct., S36820
William, Mass., S4908
William, Mass., Susanna, W15408
William A., N.H., War of 1812, S16264
SUMPTER, Thomas, N.C. See SUMTER
SUMRALL, Moses, N.C., R10310
SUMTER, Thomas, N.C., Lydia, R10312
Thomas, S.C., S19115, son of Brig. Gen. Thomas Sumter
SUNBOURN, Richard, N.H., BLWt. 3487. Iss. 4/7/1795
SUNCKLE, Jacob, Pa., BLWt.10363. Iss. 10/28/1789 to M. McConnell ass. No paper
SUNDERLAND, John, Lamb's Art., N.Y., BLWt.7842. Iss. 9/13/1791. No papers
Joseph, Pa., Elizabeth, W6611; BLWt. 31710-160-55
Nathaniel, 39th U.S. Inf., See file of Edward Nunnelee, Va.
Samuel, Ct., S41221
Samuel, Pa., S6175
Samuel, Pa. See SUNDERLIN
SUNDERLIN, Daniel, Ct., R.I., S17718
Samuel, Ct. See SUNDERLAND
Samuel, Pa., S6176
SUPLER, John, Pa., Rachael, W4521
SURBER, Jacob, Va., S4017
Mary, former wid. of William McClure, Va., which see
SURGENOR, John, N.C., S7662
SURLS, Robert, N.C., S7659
SURRAGE, Isaac, Crane's Cont., Art., Mass., BLWt.5114. Iss. 3/10/1794. No papers
SUSUSEE, Francis, Mass., BLWt. 4969. Iss. 3/1/1792 to D. Quinton, ass. No papers
SUTCH, George, Va., S40535
SUTER, Jacob, N.Y., Margaret, W16429
SUTES, Peter, N.Y. See SUITS
SUTFIN, David, N.J., S4519
John, N.J. See SUTPHIN
Joseph, N.J., Rhoda, W6607
Rachel, former wid. of Minnah Hyatt, N.Y., which see
William, N.J., S14628
SUTHARD, Isaac, Ct. See SOUTHWORTH
SUTHERLAND, Alexander, Md., Va., Elizabeth, W6610
Daniel, N.Y., BLWt.7822. Iss. 4/5/1793 to James Duggan, ass.
Daniel, N.Y. See SOUTHERLAND
Daniel, N.C., S32545
Daniel, N.C., b. Va., Isabella, W6608; BLWt.27685-160-55
George, N.C., Va., S7667
John, Md., b. Scotland, S6173
John, N.C., S39098
John, Pa., BLWt.10342. Iss. 6/11/1795. No papers
Kenneth, Va., S30724
Lawrence, N.Y., R10315
Philemon, Va., Frances, W6609
Philip, Va., Mary, W19417
Samuel, Cont., Va., R21855
Silas, N.Y. See SOUTHERLAND
Traverse, Va., S31398
Walter E., Md., Sarah, W10266; BLWt.24998-160-55
William, Md., Catherine, W8771
William, N.J., Pa., R10318
SUTHIN, John, N.J. See SITHINS
SUTLEY, James, S.C., Mary, W3735; BLWt.61161-160-55
SUTLIEF, Gad, Ct., S23961
Janner/Jonner/Jonah, Ct., War of 1812, Hepsibah Joiner, former wid., R5682
Jonah, Ct. See Janner SUTLIEF
Jonner, Ct. See Janner SUTLIEF
SUTLIFF, David, Ct., R10319
SUTLIFFE, Benjamin, Ct., BLWt. 1681-200
SUTPHEN, Aaron, N.J., S1117
James, N.J., Catharine, W25170
Peter, N.J., S1119
Richard, N.J., S922
Richard, N.J., S15234
Samuel, N.J., R10321
SUTPHIN, Aaron, N.J. See SUTPHEN
Derrick, N.J., Altche, R10320
John, N.J., Privateer, S29489
Rachel, N.Y. See Minnah HYATT
Richard, N.J. See SUTPHEN
SUTS, John I./John J., N.Y., Catherine, W16747
John P., N.Y., Nancy, W25171
Peter, N.Y. See SUITS
Peter P., N.Y., S14630
SUTTEN, David, res. Indiana, Not Rev. War, U.S.A. 1799 O.W. Inv.
SUTTEN (continued)
File 26423
SUTTER, Mary, former wid. of Aaron Whitehead, N.J., which see
SUTTERFIELD, Robert, N.C., Catharine, R10322
SUTTLE, Edward, Va., S4907
SUTTON, Abraham, Lee's Legion; BLWt.13802. Iss. 4/24/1797 to James DeBaufre
Alpheus, Va. See William, Va.
Arad, Pa., Hannah Bailey, former wid., BLReg. 72731-1855
Benjamin, Cont., Ct., Green Mt. S42434
Benjamin, N.J., S38411
Benjamin, Pa., S16266
Benjamin, Va., Mary, W8772
Charles, Md., S42029
Daniel, Pa., BLWt.10472. Iss. 4/18/1796. No papers
Edward, Ct., Abigail Lawrence, former wid., W2897
Elijah, N.J., S6174
Elisha, N.J., N.Y. res. in 1833, R10324
Ephraim, Pa., S40536
Henry, N.J., S923
Jacob, Md. Sea Service, S35090
Jacob, S.C., Nancy, W11577
James, N.C., R10325
John, Cont., N.J., N.Y. res. in 1818, Sarah, W16430
John, Cont., N.C., S.C., Elizabeth, W997
John, Mass., Alice, R10323; BLWt.78019-160-55
John, Mass., Sea Service, Lois, W25173
John, N.H., S15666
John, Pa., BLWt.10439; Iss. 4/16/179? to William Barton, ass.
John, Pa., S6177
John, Va., S6178
Jonathan, N.J., S.C., Mary, R18300
Joseph, N.J., Martha, W872
Joseph, Va., S41223
Michael, N.H., Judith Chenny/Cheney, former wid., W22772; BLWt.16115-160-55
Peter, N.J., S33762
Philip, N.J., S7658
Richard F., Va., Margaret, W9322
Stephen, N.H., Betsey, BLWt. 49467-160-55
Uriah, N.J., S1118
William, N.J., Mary, R10326
William, N.Y., Elizabeth, W19127
William, S.C., Mary, BLWt.79022-160-55
William, Va., S11495
William, Va., Alpheus, S31400
Zachariah, Cont., N.Y., S42435
Zebulon, N.J., S16265
SUYDAM, Cornelius, See SUIDAM
Cornelius, N.J., Ann, R10327
SWADDLE, John, See SWADLE
SWADLE, John, Ct., BLWt.6501 iss. 10/22/1789 to Theodosius Fowler, ass.
John, Ct., S36822

SWADLEY, Mark, Va., S4027
SWAGER, Adam, Pa., S40387
SWAGERS, George, Pa., Elizabeth, W2457
SWAILS, John, N.Y., BLWt.7820. Iss. 8/25/1790 to William Cline
SWAIM, John, N.J., Sarah, W2486
SWAIN, Anthony, N.J., Cont., S7668
Benjamin, Mass., N.H., Privateer, S18236
Charles, Va., S4910
Cornelius, Va., R10328
David, Letter of Marque, Navy, Mass., S30143
Dudley, N.H., S16547
Ebenezer, N.H., Sarah Tucker, former wid., W22462; BLWt.19514-160-55
Ezra, N.Y., S23016
George, Va., Nancy, R10329
Hezekiah, N.H., Mariam, W22354
Ichabod, N.H., Betsey Eaton former wid., R3207 1/2
James, Mass., Rebecca, W13945
Jeremiah, N.H., S16546
Joseph, Cont., Mass., Navy, Meliscent, W20079
Phinehas, N.H., S18237
Richard, N.J., S924
Theophilus, N.H., Elizabeth, BLWt.31786-160-55
SWALLOW, Andrew, Pa., Va., Catharine, W61
SWAN, Adin, Ct., S28903
Caleb, Mass., BLWt.1923-150-Ens. Iss. 11/13/1789. No papers
Charles, Cont., Va., Catharine, W19425
Elias, Ct., Navy, R.I., Anne, R10331
Henry, Mass., S11498
James, Mass., S30142
John, Ct., Sarah, W19422
John, Cont., Md., BLWt.2058-400-Maj. Iss. 5/11/1790
John, Mass., S40545
John, Mass., N.H., S43992
Jonathan, Va., R10332
Joseph F., Cont., Mass., S19480
Joshua, Cont., Pa. res. of heirs in 1835, BLWt.2109-100
Joshua, Mass., S29491
Nathan, Mass., S37476
Robert, Mass., Grace Parker, former wid., W14227
Timothy, Pa., BLWt.10465. Iss. 12/28/1792. No papers
Timothy, Pa., S40548
William, Cont., N.Y., Sarah, W25185
William, N.C., Rachael, R10333
SWANEY, Jacob, Va., R10336
John, Ct., Abigail, W22352
SWANGER, Abraham, Pa., R10338
SWANLEY, Isaac, N.J., BLWt.8762 Iss. 6/6/1797
SWANN, John, N.C., Sarah, R10335
Joseph, N.C., Agnes, R10334
SWANSON, John, N.C., Sarah, W1900 BLWt.26838-160-55
Levi, Va., S38412
William, N.C., R10339
SWANTON, Peter, Md., BLWt. 11691 & 14104. Iss. 2/24/1795 to Francis Sherrard, ass. of John Carbeth/Carbelt, Adm. No papers
SWANY, Timothy, Del., R10337
SWART, Adam, N.Y., R10340
Bartholomew, N.Y., S14637
James, Cont., Va., Margaret, W6112; BLWt. 315-60-55 & 12544 Iss. 6/9/179? to Wm. B. Harrison ass. No papers
Lawrence, N.Y., S11503
Teunis, N.Y., R10341
Teunis, N.Y., R10342
SWARTHOUT, Aaron, N.Y., S11497
Anthony, N.Y., Elizabeth, R10344
Cornelius, N.Y., S26774
Ralph, N.Y., R10343
SWARTOUT, Jacobus, See SWARTWOUT
Thomas, N.Y., S29490
SWARTS, Baltus, N.J., R9390
Tewalt, N.J., R9391
SWARTWOOD, Barnardus, Pa., S22522
Daniel, N.J., Catharine, W25180
Jacob, N.J., S23445
James, N.J., Pa., S14636
John, N.J., Pa., S4913
Moses, Pa., BLWt.10373. Iss. 7/16/1791 to Christian Gross, ass.
Moses, Pa., Mary Magdalena, W6114
Peter, N.J., R10345
SWARTWOUT, Abraham, N.Y., BLWt. 2564-300-Capt. Iss. 7/13/1790. No papers
Bernardus, Jr., N.Y., BLWt.1983-150-Ens. Iss. 7/7/1790. No papers
Cornelius, N.Y., BLWt.1986-200-Capt. Iss. 10/12/1790 to Daniel Ludlow & Edward Gold, assnes. of the est. of C. Swartwout. No papers
Cornelius, N.Y., BLWt.7816. Iss. 10/12/1790 to Henry Platt, ass.
Cornelius, N.Y., Sarah, W29605
Henry, N.Y., BLWt.1980-200-Lt. Iss. 7/7/1791 to John Brinkerhoff, Adm. No papers
Jacobus, N.Y., S28904
Thomas, N.Y. See SWARTOUT
William, N.Y., S23444
SWARTZ, Godfried, See Goofield
Goofield, Armands Corps; BLWt. 2123-200-Lt.
Ludwick, Pa., S23446
Philip, Pa., BLWt.10459. Iss. 1/11/1791. No papers
Philip, Pa., S23964
Phineas/Phinehas, Pa., S15668
SWARTZWALDER, Christian, Pa., R10347. He also claimed pension on acct. of service of his uncle, Peter Swartzwalder. See papers in this file
Peter, See Christian
SWASEY, Richard, Mass., Rachel, W15410
SWATGA, Henry, Pa., S40547
SWATZEL, Philip, Pa., S1593
SWAY, George, Va., S42439
SWAYER, Lambert, N.Y., Eve Allen
SWAYER (continued)
former wid., W15751
SWAYZE, Daniel, N.J., S4911
David, N.J., Alice, W6111
SWAZE, David, N.J. See SWAYZE
SWAZY, Edward, Mass., R10348
SWEARINGEN, Joseph, BLWt.2056-300-Capt. Iss. 8/25/1789. No papers
Richard C., N.C., S31402
Thomas, S.C., b. N.C., Peggy, W6113
Van, Md., Pa., S31401
Van, Pa., Va., Eleanor Newhouse former wid., W5415
SWEAT, Cicero, Mass. See SWETT
David, N.C., S42031
Israel, Mass., S37477
John, N.H. See SWETT
Moses, Mass. See SWEET
Stockman, Cont.,N.H. See SWETT
SWEATLAND, Aaron, See SWETLAND
Luke, Ct. See SWETLAND
SWEATMAN, William, N.C., Lavinia/Lavina, W6116
SWEATT, Abraham Titcomb, N.H., S43190
Daniel, N.H. See SWETT
John, N.H. See SWEET
SWEENEY, Peter, Va., BLWt.12576 Iss. 1/31/1794 to John Stockdale, ass.
SWEENY, Daniel, N.J., BLWt.8711. Iss. 4/20/1790 to Joseph Lyon, Jr. ass. No papers
Edward, BLWt.7845. Iss. 2/28/1794 to Thomas Russell, ass. No papers
Edward, Pa., S40544
Hugh, Pa., BLWt.10338. Iss. 7/9/1789. No papers
Hugh, Pa., S40541
James, Pa., BLWt.10335. Iss. 8/22/1791 to John McCleland, ass. No papers
Joseph, Pa., S23442
Joseph, Va., Nancy, R10349
Moses, Va., enl. from Buckingham Co., Va., d. 3/15/1833, S6180
Moses, Va., S31403, son of John, moved to Jefferson Co., Tenn., then to Cincinnati, & thence to Warren Co., Ky.
Owen, Md., BLWt.13723 & 14103. Iss. 2/24/1795 to Francis Sherrard, ass. of Admr. John Cobeth. No papers
SWEET, Benaiah, R.I., Mary, W13054
Benjamin, R.I., S39859
Caleb, N.Y., BLWt.1985-400-Surgn. Iss. 8/23/1790. No papers
Charles, R.I., S14638
Daniel, R.I., Cynthia, W25183
Ebenezer, Mass., Desire, W25182
Freeborn, R.I., Martha, W19132
Isaac, R.I., Sarah, W20078
Israel, Mass. See SWEAT
Jabez/Jabes, Mass., Hannah, W22362
James, Ct., res. Smithfield, R.I. at age 77, S21518
James, N.Y., R.I., b. North

SWEET (continued)
Kempton, R.I., 4/11/1750, res. in 1779 Shaftsbury, Vt., S21517
James, R.I., res. East Greenwich, Kent Co., S21519
Jeremiah, R.I., Dorcas, W22360
John, Ct., Anna, W19131
John, N.H., Hannah, W19421
John, N.Y., Mary, R10351
John, N.Y., R.I., S14631
John, R.I., S33765
Jonathan, Ct., S14635
Jonathan, Mass., S42440
Joseph, Cont., R.I., Mary, W19130
Joshua, Mass., S40543
Moses, Mass., Priscilla, W15413
Reuben, N.Y., S22521
Rufus, R.I., Elizabeth, W22355
Samuel, R.I., S11502
Samuel, R.I., Hannah, W22357
Samuel, R.I., Elizabeth Griswald, former wid., W24312; BLWt. 35840-160-55
Stephen, R.I., S15997
Thomas, R.I., S23443
Valentine, R.I., S21250
William, R.I., R10352
SWEETEN, Benjamin, N.J., S40540
SWEETING, Lewis, Mass., N.Y., Naomi, W20080
Nathaniel, Mass., N.Y., S14634
SWEETLAND, Arates/Aretas, R.I., Huldah, W25181
Benjamin, Mass., Chloe, W22356
Benjamin, Mass. See SWETLAND
Ebenezer Leach, Ct., S15235
John, Cont., Mass., Sarah, W25184
Nathan, Mass., Rebecca, W25179
Stephen, Mass., S17135; BLWt. 33767-160-55
William, Mass., S17719
SWEETMAN, Richard, Pa., BLWt. 10454. Iss. 11/25/1793 to Christian Hubert. No papers
SWEETON, Richard, N.J., BLWt. 8767. Iss. 6/11/1789 to Jonathon Dayton, ass. No papers
SWEETSER, Benjamin, Mass., Dorothy, R10356
Cornelius, Mass., S30725
John, Mass., Rebecca, W6115; BLWt.18007-160-55
Phillips, Mass., S11500. Betsey Switser/Sweetser, wid. of this sold. was pensioned as former wid. of James Bates, Mass., which see
Richard, Mass., S37478
Samuel, Mass., Lydia, W19129
Stephen, N.H., S42032
SWEEZY, David, N.Y., S14632
SWEGER, John, Pa., S15998
SWEISSHELM, John, Pa., Mary, W8300; BLWt.29016-160-55
SWELLING, George, Martha, R10357
SWEM, Jesse, N.J., Catharine, R10358
SWENTZEL, Frederick, Pa., S22523
SWEPSTON, John, Cont., Va., S15999
SWESEY, Daniel,Pa., S22520
SWETLAND, Aaron, Ct., Cont., Lois, W19423
Ambrose, N.Y., S46199
Aretas, See Arates SWEETLAND
Benjamin, Mass., Rosanna, W10355
Daniel, Cont., Mass., S33764
Ebenezer L., See SWEETLAND
Luke, Ct., S40546; BLWt.477-100
SWETT, Allen, N.C., Nancy, W16
Cicero, Mass., BLWt.5055. Iss. 12/13/1792 to Augustus Blanchard
Cicero, Mass., S43189. Sold. stated he was put in a "black" Co.
Daniel, N.H., Sarah, W6109; BLWt.7449-160-55. See W22361 following
Daniel, N.H., Jane, W22361. This claim should be read in connection with Rev. War claim of Sarah Swett, also a pensioner on acct. of the service of this sold. W6109
John, Mass., Mary, W2023; BLWt. 31711-160-55
John, N.H., Abigail, W25176
Jonathan, Crane's Cont. Art., Mass., BLWt.5118. Iss. 10/10/1796. No papers
Jonathan, Mass., S40549
Joshua, Mass., S28905
Nancy, former wid. of Ezekiel Cobb, Mass., which see
Samuel, Mass., S30144
Stockman, Cont., N.H., Mass., S43191; BLWt.801-100
Thomas R., Mass., N.H., S11496
SWICK, Anthony, Pa., R10360
John, N.J., S10361
SWIFT, Abraham, Mass., S11501
Ambrose, N.Y., R10362
Charles, Ct., Vt., Johannah, W16431
Enoch, Mass., S19116
Heman, Ct., BLWt.1937-500-Col. & later Brevet Brig. Gen. acc. to Heitman
Heman, Mass., Orpha, W15411
Isaac, (Indian), Mass., Patience Crook, former wid., BLWt.1926-100
James, Mass., S29492
John, Ct., d. 3/10/1838, Anna W22353
John, Ct., War of 1812, N.Y., Hepsibar T. Buck, former wid., W8172; BLWt.2505-100
John, Mass., Anne/Ann, W3316
Joseph, Mass., Lucy, W22358
Joshua, Mass., BLWt.4998. Iss. 3/7/1792 to John Heston. No papers
Joshua, Mass., S42438
Lott, N.Y., Elizabeth, W19424; BLWt.27594-160-55
Nathaniel, Ct., S36823
Philetus, Ct., War 1812, Fawnia, W501; BLWt.19156-160-55
Roland/Rowland, Ct., S42437
Samuel, R.I., Vt., Susanna, W4596
Samuel, Va., S38413
SWIFT (continued)
Stephen, Mass., Rebecca, W15412
Thomas, Va., S37475
William, Ct., Eunice, W19420
William, Ct., R10363
SWINDEL, John, N.C., S4031
SWINDLE, John, N.C. See SWINDEL
John, Pa., BLWt.10339 & 13799. Iss. to Christian Hubbert, ass. 7/29/1795. No papers
John, Va., Hannah, W8774
SWINEY, Martha/Patsy, former wid. of William Dunnington, which see
SWING, Mathias, N.C., S7669
SWINGLE, George, Md., S4914
SWININGTON, Joseph, Mass., S23962
SWINK, John, N.C., Mary, W2022; BLWt.3608-160-55
SWINNERTON, James, Mass., S40542
SWINNEY, Jesse, N.C., R10364
Patsey, See file of William Dunnington, Md.
William, N.C., Sarah, W26485; BLWt.26119-160-55
SWINSON, Jesse, N.C., S7670
Richard, N.C., S42033
Theophilus, N.C., S9489
SWISHER, Jacob, Pa., S6179
SWISSHELM, John, Pa. See SWEISSHELM
SWITS, Walter, Cont., N.Y., Sarah, W11585
SWITSER, Betsey, Mass. See James Bates
SWITZEN, George, Pa. See SWITZER
Philip, Va. See SWITZER
SWITZER, Emanuel, Navy, Mass., S42441
George, Pa., S23963
Philip, Va., S4912
SWOOPE, John, Va. Sea Service, See SWOPE
SWOPE, John, Va., Sea Service, R98, Va. Half Pay. See N.A. Acc. No. 837, Va. State Navy, John Swope, Y.S. File
Michael, Va., R10366
SWORD, Michael, Va., S6181
SWORDS, James, Ga., S32002
John, S.C., Eleanor, W8773
William, S.C., Mary, R10367
SWORTS, Twealt, N.J. See SWARTS
SWORTWOUT, Moses, N.Y., S11499
SYBERT, Adam, Cont., Pa., Dis. See Am. State Papers, Class 9, p.99. Wounded in both legs by two musket balls at the storming of one of Cornwallis' redoubts in Va. Mustered in Hazen's Regt. Pa.
Adam, Hazen's Regt.,BLWt.13761 Iss. 11/5/1791. No papers
Henry, Cont., Pa., Mary, W3306
SYBROOK, Henry, See LYBROOK
SYDARS, Solomon, Md., Va., S17136
SYDEBOTHOM, John, Va., Jane, W8775
SYDNOR, Anthony, Va., S6186
Fortunus, Cont., Va., S38160; BLWt.12558-100. Iss. 5/7/1793 to Frank Graves. No papers
SYFAT, Adam, See SYBERT
SYFRITT, Andrew, Va. See CYPRUS

SYKES, Ashbel, Ct., Mass., Vt., S18618
Henry, Va., S6184
Jacob, Ct. See SIKES
James, N.C., b. Va., S1892
John, Ct., Vt., See SIKES
John, Va., S6185
John Jones, Mass., Sarah, W6110; BLWt.3811-160-55
Josiah, N.C., S7673
Thomas A., Va. See SIKES
SYLLIMAN, Thomas, See SILLYMAN
SYLVESTER, Adam, See SILVESTER
Caleb, Mass., S29493
Elisha, Mass., S19482
Gershom, Mass., S42442
Henchman, Mass., Esther, W25177
Isaac, N.J., BLWt.8740. Iss. 2/9/1793. No papers
Job, Mass. See SILVESTER
Joseph, Mass. See SILVESTER
Joseph, Mass., BLWt.885-100
Peter, Mass., S19481
Peter, N.J., BLWt.8758. Iss. 6/16/1789 to Thomas Coyle, ass. No papers
Thomas, Mass., S30145
SYMMES, Ebenezer, Cont., Mass., S37479
John, Mass., Elizabeth, W13946
Presley, Va., S32546
William, Cont., Mass., N.H. & N.J., Mehitabel, W25178
SYMMOND, Henry, Pa., S40550
SYMMONDS, John, Indian War 1790-1795. Old War Inv. File 2643. Res. Ohio
SYMMS, John, Va., S37397
SYMOND, Martin, N.Y., BLWt.7755 Iss. 6/13/1792 to John Hagamon ass. No papers
SYMONDS, Ashna, Ct., S17679
Daniel, Mass., S33766
Henry, Pa. See SYMMOND
John, Mass., S33768
John, Mass., Susanna, W19134
Jonathan, Mass., Jane B., W7176; BLWt.34912-160-55
Joseph, Mass., Susannah, W15414
Levi, N.H., S42443
Nathaniel, Mass., Mary, W16748
Samuel, Ct., BLWts.6442 & 341-60-55. Iss. 11/2/1791 to Titus Street, ass. No papers
Silas, N.H., S41224
Thomas, Mass., S18619
Zebedee, Cont., Mass., Lucy, W15415
SYMONS, Joseph, Ct. See SIMONS
SYMPSON, William, N.C., b. Pa., S15669
SYMS, Cuthbert, Va. See SIMS
SYNG, Abraham, Pa. See SINK
SYNOTT, Thomas, See LYNOTT
SYPE, Christopher, Pa., S40551
Tobias, Pa., Aumney/Anna Maria, W3366
SYPERT, Henry, Pa. See SYBERT
SYPHER, Peter, N.Y., Tamar, W26499
SYPHERD, Mathias/Matthias, Md., S35092

SYTEZ, George, N.Y., BLWt.1975-300-Capt. Iss. 8/23/1790. No papers

T

TABB, Augustin, Va., R18331. Va. Half Pay N.A. Acc. No. 874-050171
TABER, Benjamin, R.I. See TABOR
Earl, R.I. See TABOR
Gideon, R.I. See TABOR
Henry, R.I. See TABOR
Humphrey, Mass., S18623
Ichabod, R.I., S21525
Isaac, R.I., Peace, W26505
John, N.C., Agnes, R10372
John, R.I., Nancy, W22373
Martha, former wid. of Stephen Congdon, which see
Noel, R.I., S33777
Philip, N.H., S43194
Philip, R.I. See TABOR
Samuel, Mass., Deborah, BLWt. 77029-160-55
Samuel, R.I., S22003
William, Ct., Lucinda, W16749
TABOR, Benjamin, Navy, R.I., S39860
Benjamin, R.I., Mercy, W18106
Church, Mass., Betsey, W26507
Earl, R.I., R10373
Gideon, R.I., Hannah, W25469
Henry (colored), R.I., Esther, W1331; BLWts.27-60-55 & 3538-100-1794
Lemuel, R.I., S11514
Pardon, N.H., Ruth, W22380
Philip, R.I., Mary, W16750
Thomas, N.Y., BLWt.7876. Iss. 8/8/179? to Sampson Crossby, ass. No papers
Thomas, N.Y., S46411
William, N.C., Susannah, W6245
TABORN, Joel, N.C. See TABURN
TABOUR, William, N.C. See TABURN
TABOURN, Burrell/Burwell, N.C., S7694
Burwell, See Burrell
TABURN, Joel (colored), N.C., S42037; BLWt.75-100
William (colored), N.C., Nelly, W18115
TACH, Jacob, Va. See TACK
TACK, Jacob, Va., S7677
TACKELS, Alexander, Mass., Philena W18113
TACKLES, Alexander, See TACKELS
TAFF, George, Va., S3753
James, Va., S36825
Peter, Va., S38423
TAFT, Abel, Ct., Vt., S19117
Artemas, Cont., Mass., S41227
Caleb, Mass., S32006
Darius, Mass., Louis/Lois, BLWt. 18029-160-55
Ebenezer, Cont., Mass., Molly, W19426
Ebenezer, Mass., Mary, W8776; BLWt.49265-160-55
Eleazer, Cont., Mass., Relief, W16432
Eleazer, Mass., N.H., S29495
Enos, Mass., S30728
Frederic, Mass., Abigail, W20082
George, Mass., S19806
Hepzibah, former wid. of Peter Blakinton, R.I., which see

TAFT (continued)
Israel, Mass., S30150
Joseph, Mass., S33181
Josiah, Mass., S33769
Matthew, Mass., S3754
Moses, Mass., S30148
Peter, Mass., Mary Daniels, former wid., W14578
Thaddeus, Mass., Silence, W15421
William, Cont., Mass., S14656
TAGER, Jacob, Pa., Susannah, W6244
TAGERT, Alexander, N.Y. See John Ross
James, N.C., Nancy, W4081
TAGGARD, John, N.H. See TAGGART
TAGGART, James, Cont., N.H., S43192
John, N.H., S11520
John, N.H., S38414
Joseph, N.H., Lydia, W20081
Patrick, Pa., Hannah, W2369
Robert, N.H., S38418
William, N.H., S19809
William, N.H. See TAGGERT
William, R.I., Elizabeth, W22370
TAGGERT, William, N.H., BLWt.3521 Iss. 11/8/1792 to S. Emery. No papers
TAILOR, Harman, N.Y., R10416
John, N.H., S43193
John Allen, N.J.,N.C., See John ALLEN
Oliver, N.Y., S11507
Richard, Md. See TAYLOR
TAINTER, Nahum, Mass., Huldah, W13959
Stephen, Mass., S22006
TAIT, Robert L., Va., Mary, W1330; BLWt.26729-160-55
TALADY, Solomon, N.Y., S40557
TALBEE, Stephen, R.I., S21522
TALBERT, Abraham, Mass. See TALBET
Benjamin, Va., S16548
David, Mass. See TALBOT
Samuel, Pa., BLWt.2199-300-Capt.
William, N.Y., BLWt.7884. Iss. 10/11/179? to Henry Tremper, ass. No papers
William, N.Y., S42461
William, Pa., BLWt.10517. Iss. 4/27/1793 to Alexander Power, no papers
TALBET, Abraham, Mass., Mary, W22369
TALBOT, Daniel, Mass., S33772
David, Mass., BLWt.2122-100
David G., Va., S7690
Ellen, former wid. of Quomony Quash, Mass., which see
Enoch, Mass., S30727
Isaac, Mass., Susannah, W13961
Isham, Va., S37482
Jacob, Pa., BLWt.1240-200
James S., Va., R10377
Joseph, Mass. See TOLBUTT
Josiah, Mass., S29494
Levi, Va., S36337
Richard, Md., S40552
Samuel, Mass., Phebe Cobb, former wid., W23867
TALBOTT, Charles, Md., S11519

TALBOTT (continued)
Henry, Md., S11511
James, Md., Nancy, R18337
Rodham, Va., R10378
Silas, R.I., BLWt.2133-450-Lt. Col.
Thomas, Va., S31409
TALBUT, Ebenezer, Ct., S17723
TALCOTT, Aaron, Ct., S36332
Elizur, Ct., Dorothy, W18108
Elizur, Ct., Sally Frisby, former wid., W27522. Her other husb. was a pensioner. See Luther Frisbie, Cont., Ct.
Joseph, Ct., Rebecca, W22377
Justus, Ct., Lydia, W6247; BLWt.28574-160-55
Phineas, Ct., S16001
TALDAY, John, N.Y., R10629
TALERDAY, Solomon, See TALADY
TALIAFERO, Benjamin, BLWt.2217-300-Capt. Iss. 11/14/1794. No papers
Nicholas, BLWt.2220-200-Lt. Iss. 1/31/1794 to Robert Meems, ass. No papers
TALIAFERRO, John, Va., S19483
Richard, Va., S6197
Richard, Va., Mildred, W11597
William, Va., S7695
TALL, William, See Tall WILLIAM
TALLARDAY, Solomon, See TALADY
TALLCOTT, Abraham, Ct., S23452
Daniel, Ct., R10379
TALLEY, Billy, Va., Elizabeth W. W19434
Elisha, Va., R10383
Henry, Va., Edith, W4350; BLWt. 34533-160-55
John, Cont., res. in 1819 in Ga., res. Tenn. in 1830, S38426
John, Sr., Va., BLWt.12601. Iss. 2/14/1797 to Murdock McKenzie, ass. No papers
John, Jr., Va., BLWt.12602. Iss. 2/14/1797 to Murdock McKenzie, ass. No papers
TALLIDAY, John, N.Y., BLWt.7878 Iss. 8/31/179? to Sam Smith. No papers
TALLMADGE, Benjamin, Ct., Cont., S46412; BLWt.2171-400-Major. Iss. 10/7/1789
Daniel, Ct. See TALMAGE
Joel, N.Y., Rhobe, W16754
Samuel, N.Y., S42454; BLWt.2188-200-Lt. Iss. 8/10/1790 to Stephen Lush
Seymour, Ct., S16268
TALLMAN, Abraham, N.Y., Rachael, W15852
Benjamin, R.I., S21524
Dowah H., N.Y., Rachel, W16434
Jacob, N.Y., Hannah, W26511; BLWt.48837-160-55
James, R.I. See TALMAN
Jeremiah, N.J., R10381
John I., N.Y., Fanny, W18111
Peleg, Navy, Ct., Eleanor, W26509; BLWt.35689-160-55
Peter, Ct., Mass.?, Margaret, R10382
Rescom, Mass., S14640

TALLMAN (continued)
Thomas, N.Y., S11522
Tunis, N.Y., S23017
William, N.J., Sarah, W1510; BLWt.31328-160-55
TALLOW, Thomas, Va., Susan, W6334; BLWt.31726-160-55
TALLY, James, N.C., Mildred, W4599
TALMADGE, Ichabod, Ct., Hannah Plumb, former wid., W17460
Joel, N.Y. See TALLMADGE
John, Ct., S11523
Nathaniel, Ct., S18624
Noah, N.J., Elizabeth, W207
TALMAGE, Daniel, Ct., Rebecca, W3737; BLWt.26647-160-55
Elisha, N.Y., S17139
Samuel, Ct., S14653
Samuel, N.Y., See TALLMADGE
Solomon, Ct., S11524
Stephen, N.Y., S28906
Thomas, N.J., S4677
TALMAN, Giles, Art. Artificers, BLWt.13832 iss. 1/26/1790 to John May, ass. No papers
James, R.I., S29499
Thomas, Cont., Mass., Vt., See TOLMAN
William, N.J. See TALLMAN
TAMBLIN, Timothy, Ct., Cont., Mass., Susanna, W19428
TAMBLING, Stephen, Mass., Mary Cogswell, former wid., W15886
TAME, John, Pa., BLWt.10523 iss. 6/29/1789 to M. McConnell. No papers
TAMERLANE, Thomas, S.C., BLWt. 12631 & 13809 iss. 8/5/1796
TANEHILL, James, Pa., S3771
TANKARD, John, Va., S48512
TANKERSLEY, George, Va., R10387
John, Va. Sea Service, Va., Frances, W63
Joseph, Cont., Ga. res. in 1828, R20201
TANKERSLY, Charles, S.C., Catherine, W4602
TANN, Drewry, N.C., S19484
TANNAHILL, Grissal/Gracie, former wid. of Andrew Donnan/ Donnel, N.Y., which see
TANNEHILL, Adamson, Md., BLWt. 2209-300 iss. 6/9/1789
James, Md., S14643
James, Pa. See TANEHILL
Josiah, Md.,Va., Margaret, W8777; BLWt.2219-200-Lt. iss. 6/9/1789
TANNER, Abraham, Va., S6190
Amos, R.I., S23450
Ebenezer, Ct., Lydia, W22372; BLWt.2174-200-Lt. Iss. 12/14/ 1795
Francis, R.I., S23018
Helyer, Navy, b. R.I., res. Vt. S23965
Jacob, N.J., BLWt.8777 & 10493. Iss. 7/29/1796 to William Crawfordly
Jacob, N.Y., S11513
Jacob, Pa. See DANNER
John, R.I., Mass., Vt., Esther, W22376

TANNER (continued)
Josiah, S.C., Martha Lemaster, former wid., W9503
Michael, Va., b. Pa., S32004
Nathan, N.Y., Sarah, W6225; BLWt.38828-160-55
Paul, Va., Mary Ann, W26510
Quom, R.I., S42445; BLWt.1636-100
Samuel, Va., res. Spring Creek, Jackson Co. in 1833; R10389
Samuel, Va., res. Saline Co., Ill., R10390
Thomas, Va., Elizabeth, R10391; BLWt.34819-160-55
Tryal, Ct., S6189
William, R.I. & N.Y., Dis.- Lived in Ohio, d. 6/4/1835
William, R.I., BLWt.3539. Iss. 13/1800 to A. Hobrook. No papers
William, R.I., S4678
William, R.I., Sabrina, W25472
William, Va., S40553
Zopher, N.Y., Mary, R10392
TANNERY, Zopher, See TANNER
TANNEY, Zopher, See TANNER
TAPERVINE, John, See DEOPERVINE
TAPLEY, Asa, Mass., S29498
Thomas, Va., BLWt.12608. Iss. 4/13/1791 to James Reynolds. No papers
TAPLIN, John, Pa., BLWt.10519; Iss. 2/14/1796 to Christian Ives. No papers
John, Vt., R10393
Mansfield, Cont., N.H., Vt., S19118
TAPP, Vincent, Va., S6188
Vincent, Va., S41231
TAPPAN, Daniel, N.Y., BLWt. 7870. Iss. 8/23/1790. No papers
Ebenezer, Mass., S30146
Edward, See TOPPAN
Michael, Mass., Hannah, W6246; BLWt.13706-160-55
William, Mass., S17720
TAPPEN, John, Cont., N.Y., S14641
Peter, Cont., N.Y., S42455; BLWt.2192-200-Lt. Iss. 10/11/1790
TAPPERWINE, Christian, N.Y., BLWt. 7864 & 14099. Iss. 1/30/1795
TAPSCOTT, George, Va., R18351, Va. Half Pay
William, Va., S38416
TAR, David, Mass., BLWt.5173. Iss. 3/25/1790
Melcher, N.C., S7674
TARBELL, Benjamin, Mass., Lydia, W16751
David, Mass., Hannah, W26512
Isaac, Vt., S11504
Joseph, Mass., S38415
Nathan, N.J., BLWt.8783. Iss. 7/7/1783. No papers
Rhoda, former wid. of Jonathan Atherton, Mass., which see
Sarah, former wid. of Samuel Nutting, Mass., which see

TARBELL (continued)
Thomas, Mass., S18620
Thomas, N.H., Sarah, W15422
William, Mass., Sarah, W33182; she was pensioned as former wid. of Samuel Nutting, Mass., which see
TARBELLS, David, Mass., BLWt.5149 Iss. 3/25/1790. No papers
TARBILL, Jonathan, Mass., Mary Cogswell, former wid., R2107. Her 2nd husb. Edward A. Watrous, and 3rd husb. Nathan Cogswell also served in the Rev.
TARBLE, Benjamin, See TARBELL
Nathan, N.J., S33776
TARBOX, Abijah, Mass., Sarah Hooper, former wid., W23329
Caleb, R.I., Sarah, W26504
Nathaniel, Mass., Abigail, W13960
Samuel, Mass., S20557
Temperance, former wid. of John Abbott, Ct., which see
William, Mass., S33180
TARBUSH, Joseph, N.Y., Christiana W19432
TARCOT, Francis, See TEARCOT
TARE, Daniel B. See TARR
Jabez, Mass. See TARR
TARECOTT, Francis, See TEARCOT
TARLTON, James, Del., S3770
Jeremiah, Md., Eleanor, W603
William, N.C., S7693
TARNEUR, Woodhul/Woodhull, N.Y., S14654
TARNEY, Mathew/Matthew, S42460
Matthew, Pa., BLWt.10491. Iss. 1/19/1792 to Sarah Sheppard, ass. No papers
TARP, John, Mass., S39861
TARPENING, Lawrence, N.Y., Lucy, W4828
TARR, Abraham, Mass., S31404
Daniel B., Mass., S30147
David, Mass., S33779
David, Mass., Abigail, W19430
Jabez, Cont., Mass., S30149
John, Mass., Privateer, Annis, W19429
Joseph, Mass., S31406
Joseph, Mass., S38425
TARRANT, Henry, Cont., Va., Osiller R., W998; BLWt.675-100
James, Va., R10395
TARRYBURY, John, N.J., S42462
TART, Thomas, N.C., Privateer, S7676
TARTER, Peter, N.C., Va., S38419
TARVER, Samuel, N.C., Charlotte, W11594
TARVIN, George, Ga., S32003
TASH, Oxford, Cont., Mass., Esther H., W16155
TASKER, James, Va., Mary, R10396
Joseph, N.H., S18242
Richard R., Md., S35093; BLWt. 1113-100
TATE, David, Va., Comfort, R10397
Edmund, Va., Lucy, R10398; BLWt. 52465-160-55; in Va. in 1797

TATE (continued)
James, Va., S42035
John, N.J., Pa., S39101
John, Pa., S32007
John, Va., S6191
Mathew, Va., S11508
Robert, Va., S6192
Robert L., Va. See TAIT
Thomas, N.C., S7675
William, N.C., S3751
William, S.C., BLWt.2229-200-Lt. Iss. to David Cay, ass. 6/4/1792. No papers
William, Va., Margaret, S6193
TATOM, Joshua, N.C. See TATUM
William, N.C., Mary, W2270; BLWt.73589-160-55
TATTON, Phillis, former wid. of Cuff Wells (colored), Ct., which see
TATUM, Henry, Va., Dorothy, W6242; BLWt.316-200. Va. Half Pay.
Howel/Howell, N.C., War of 1812, Rosannah Claxton, former wid., R2027
James, N.C., S39102; BLWt.2226-200-Lt. & Ens. Iss. 1/10/1791
Jesse, Va., Mary, R10401
John, N.C., Mary, W999; BLWt. 35434-160-55
Joshua, N.C., Sarah, W6248
Nathaniel, Va., S3769
Richard, N.C., R20437
Thomas, Va., Margaret, W4601
Zachariah, Va., BLWt.1955-150
TAUCO, Francis, See TEARCOT
TAUCOT, Francis, See TEARCOT
TAULMAN, Jacob, N.Y. See TALLMAN
Peter, Corps of Sappers & Miners, BLWt.2185-300-Capt. Iss. 8/26/1790. No papers
TAUNT, Thomas, N.C., S42036
TAWS, David, N.Y., S11518
TAY, John, Mass., Sarah, W15416
Nathaniel, Cont., Mass., S18240
TAYLAR, Elias, N.H. See TAYLOR
TAYLER, Martin, Ct., R10420
Nathaniel, R.I. See TAYLOR
Richard, Va., S10260
Thomas, Va., R21894
TAYLOR, Aaron, Mass., BLWt.5148. Iss. 3/26/1796 to Peter Sevier. No papers
Aaron, N.C., R10403
Abigail, former wid. of Westwood Waters, S.C., which see
Abner, N.Y., S23451
Abraham, Ct., S7689
Abraham, Cont., Mass., Phebe, W26508
Abraham, Mass., S18621
Abraham, Mass., Rachael, R10423
Absalom, Ct., Sabra, W18118
Adam, Pa., Margaret, W6236; BLWt. 45665-160-55
Andrew, N.C., S3761
Andrew, R.I., Betsey, W22368
Archibald, Va., Rachel, W10319
Augustine, Ct., War of 1812, Huldah, W26502
Azariah, Ct., S14650

TAYLOR (continued)
Bartholomew, Md., S31411
Bartholomew, Va., Frances, W3473 BLWt.24908-160-55
Benjamin, Ct., BLWt.6565 iss. 10/7/1789 to Benjamin Talmadge, ass. No papers
Benjamin, Mass., Eunice, W19427
Benjamin, N.H., Anna, W6226
Benjamin, N.C., b. S.C., Mo. agcy. res. Stoddard Co., S16000
Benjamin, N.C., m. Lydia Evers 8/18/1823, R10406
Benjamin, res. Ga. in 1830, sons John, Willis, & William, lived in Scrivner Co., R10407
Benjamin, Pa., Catherine, W28006
Betty, former wid. of Alexander Debell, Cont., N.H., which see
Billington/Bellington, S.C., b. Va., S31410
Champe, S.C., b. in Va., S22008
Charles, Ga.,S.C., b. Va., S3760
Charles, Va., BLWt.2356-400
Chiles, Ct., Rhoda, W4597
Christopher, Cont., Pa., S42450; BLWt.1335-300
Christopher, N.J., BLWt.8782 iss. 1/6/1792 to John Holmes, ass. No papers
Christopher, N.C., Mary, R10420 1/2
Daniel, Mass., Ruhama, W19435
Daniel, N.J., b. 9/15/1760 Newark Twp., Essex Co., N.J., d. 8/19/1834, S838
Daniel, N.J., b. 1758, res. Hampshire Co., Va. in 1832, S6201
Daniel, Va., b. N.J., S17137
Daniel, Va., b. 8/13/1761 in Va., m. Joan/Jane Howland. His ch. were George, Morgain, Keziah, Grinsfield, Desdamona, Elizabeth Mourning, Daniel, Hughes D., James, Nancy, Jean & William, d. 11/25/1835 in Grainger Co., Tenn. W6232
David, Ct., Cont., S15670
David, Cont., Ct. res. in 1818, Ester/Esther, W4827; BLWt.522-160-55
David, Cont., N.Y., Elizabeth, W22383
David, Mass., b. 6/10/1763 in Eastham (now Orleans), S19120
David, Mass., res. Great Bend, Susquehanna Co., Pa. in 1820, S40554
David, N.J., b. 12/25/1763, res. Bloomfield, Essex Co., N.J., S762
David, N.Y., S23447
David, R.I., S21523
David, Va., S36824
Dempsey, N.C., Sally, R10427
Ebenezer, Mass., S30729
Edmund, N.H., R10412
Edmund, N.C., S1259
Edward, Mass., S41232
Edward, N.H., S43195
Edward, N.J., S7679
Edward, N.Y., S42459; BLWt.972-100

TAYLOR (continued)
Edward, N.C., Va., Ann, W18104
Edward C., Va., Joanna, W8778
Eleazar/Eleazer, Ct., S14639
Eli, Ct., S14646
Elias, Ct., S14642
Elias, Ct., Cont., S17725
Elias, Mass., S31405
Elias, N.H., S41229
Elijah, Ct., Cont., S36335; BLWt.1485-100
Elijah, N.C., Martha, W25471; BLWt.35688-160-55
Eliphalet/Eliphelet, Cont., Mass. S33771. See case of soldier's wid. Betty, who was pensioned as former wid. of Alexander Dobell, Cont., N.H.
Elisha, Ct., S17722, b. in Litchfield, 6/21/1761
Elisha, Ct., S17726, b. 8/7/1760 in Yarmouth, Mass., living in Portage Co., Ohio in 1833
Elisha, R.I., Dilla, W22378
Eliud, Ct., S14644
Elizabeth, former wid. of John Green, Cont., Pa., which see
Elnathan, Ct., Lydia, R10419 1/2
Ephraim, Mass., S38424
Er, Mass., Elizabeth, W6240; BLWt.54197-160-55
Ezekiel, Mass., Mary, W13952; BLWt.12580-160-55
Ferguson/Fergerson, Va., Polly/Sally, W6229
Francis, Va., R19418, Va. Half Pay; BLWt.2478-300-Capt. Iss. 7/5/1799 to James Taylor, ass. BLWt.2443-200-Col. Iss. 2/4/1850
Freegift, N.J., S16267
Gad, Ct., Abigail, W6227
Gamaliel, N.Y., Anna, W18101
George, Ct., R10415 1/2
George, Mass., BLWt.5125. Iss. 8/10/1793. No papers
George, Mass., BLWt.5166. Iss. 9/19/1789. No papers
George, Crane's Cont. Art., Mass. BLWt.5178. Iss. 1/28/1790 to Joseph May. No papers
George, N.J., S925
George, Pa., BLWt.10530. Iss. 9/17/1792. No papers
George, R.I., S42453
George, Va., b. 10/12/1761 Albemarle Co., Va., res. Union Co., S.C., then to Washington & Adair Co., Ky., then to Polk Co., Ill., then to Schuyler Co., Ill. d. 1/12/1834, S32548
George, Va., Catharine/Katherine, R10408
Harman, N.Y. See TAILOR
Henry, N.J., S18622; BLWt.26550-160-55
Henry, Pa., Elizabeth/Betsey, W6231; BLWt.44840-160-55
Hudtson, N.C., S7681
Isaac, Ct., res. East Haddam, Middlesex Co., Ct., d. 1/14/1834, S11516
Isaac, Mass., S41228

TAYLOR (continued)
Isaac, N.H., res. Vt. in 1818, d. 2/27/1828, Betsey, S41233
Isaac, N.J., Sea Service, S7678
Isaac, N.C., Elizabeth, W6235
Isaac, N.C., b. S.C., res. Jasper Co., Ill., Christiana, W22381. This file contains pages from the family Bible with records dating back to 1750
Isaac, Va., BLWt.12614. Iss. 7/14/179? to Robert Means, ass. No papers
Isaac, Va., Margaret, W601; BLWt. 40918-160-55
Jacob, Cont., Mass., N.H., d. 8/5/1838 in Groton, N.H., dau. Betsey m. Benjamin Tenney, W16436
Jacob, N.H., res. Derby, Vt. at age 57, S41230
Jacob, Va., b. 11/12/1758-9, res. Sullivan Co., Tenn. for 31 yrs., d. 8/23/1849 in Kelso Twp., Dearborn Co., Ind., R10416 1/2
James, Cont., Va., m. Sarah Hunt, 12/26/1789 in Orange Co., Va., d. 3/15/1823, W19431
James, Mass., son of Benjamin of Peekskill, N.Y., res. Westford, Chittenden Co., Vt. in 1818, S23967
James, Mass., b. Coventry, Windham Co., Ct., 3/13/1750, res. Pittsfield, Mass. in 1832, S29497
James, Mass., res. Barnstable, Mass. in 1838, m. 11/6/1783, d. 9/15/1843, Susan, W13953
James, N.H., S33781
James, N.Y., m. Elizabeth Thompson 6/17/1782 in Montgomery Co., N.Y., d. 1/8/1832 in Benton, Yates Co., N.Y., W16435
James, N.C., Va., res. Blount Co., Tenn. in 1832, S3764
James, not Rev., Gen. Wayne's N.W. Indian War, res. Phila. then Ohio, Old War Inv. File 26436
James, Pa., b. Lancaster Co., Pa. in 1754, res. "near Wheeling", Licking Co., Ohio in 1804, d. 5/24/1844; ch. James, Cynthia Gill, Nancy Black, and Mary Maholm. S6196
James, Va., S---
James, Va., res. Franklin Co., Tenn. in 1825; d. 8/17/1839, S281
James, Va., res. Mercer Co., Ky. in 1784, then to Franklin Co., Ky. where he d. 12/27 or 28/1844. m. Mary McBride 3/4/1795 in Mercer Co. Son Archibald. W1954; BLWt.27658-160-55
James, Va., Dorothy, R10411
James, Va., R18364; Va. Half Pay Act. 7/5/1832
James, Va., BLWt.1420-100
Jasper, Mass., Sea Service, Privateer, Mary, W13956

TAYLOR (continued)
Jasper, N.Y., S14645
Jedediah, Mass., S30151
Jeremiah, S.C., b. on Va. & N.C. line, S21527
Jesse, Ct., BLWt.6539. Iss. 2/5/1790. No papers
Jesse, Ct., S36336
Jesse, Va., Mary/Polly, W11598; BLWt.12705-160-55
Jesse, Ct., Sarah, W1509; BLWt. 26675-160-55
Job, Ct., Mercy, W26969
Job, R.I., S22004
Joel, Mass., S11506
John, N.Y. agcy., Dis -
John, Ct., BLWt.6559. Iss. 1/25/1796
John, Ct., d. 8/23/1840, S14652
John, Ct., res. Otsego Co., N.Y. in 1832, d. 1/25/1839, Deborah, S29496
John, Ct., Hannah, W18102
John, Ct., Elizabeth, res. Onondaga Co., N.Y. in 1845, W22384
John, Ct., R10419 (had sons John Jr., living in Ohio, Abram, Francis & William living in Greene Co., Pa. in 1852). d. 7/6/1848 in Greene Co., Pa.
John, Ct., BLWt.533-100
John, Cont., res. N.Y. in 1820, BLWt.1740-100
John, Cont., Mass., N.H., Jerusha W602; BLWt.43527-160-55
John, Cont., Va., res. Lincoln Co., Ky. in 1836 then to Ray Co., Mo., S17138
John, Ga., res. Richmond Co., N.C. in 1819, S42034
John, Md., BLWt.11767. Iss. 10/6/1794 to Henry Purdue, ass. No papers
John, Md., 11776. Iss. 8/8/1794 to Chr. Cusack, ass. No papers
John, Md., res. Harrison Co., Va. in 1818, S37483
John, Md., m. Ruth Baily 3/16/1780 in Montgomery Co., Md. Res. Harrison Co. Had nine ch., d. 5/12/1827 in Nicholas Co., Ky. W8780
John, Md., Leggy, W9514; BLWt. 6447-160-55
John, Mass., BLWt.5131 & 13840; iss. 7/11/1791 to Isaac Bronson, ass. No papers
John, Mass., S6200
John, Mass., S14657. Lived in Tioga Co., N.Y. in 1832
John, Mass., S19119, b. 7/13/1760 in Eastham (now Orleans), Mass.
John, Mass., S33770, Lydia, son named Whitfield
John, Mass., S33773. See Am. State Papers, Class 9, p.111. Ruptured by a wound received and injured in his knee 5/20/1780 at West Point.
John, Mass., living in New York in May 1819, S42446
John, Mass., m. Rebecca Hardy

TAYLOR (continued)
12/30/1790, d. 7/27/1823, W13958 Dau. m. Jacob Whitcomb
John, Mass., b. in Pembroke in 1760. After Rev. moved to Duxbury m. Mercy, 9/11/1792 in Duxbury, d. 12/9/1832. W15419
John, Mass., m. Elizabeth Gage, 10/31/1785 in Barnstable Co., Mass., d. 2/17/1836. W15420
John, N.H., living in Sanbornton, N.H. in 1833 age about 70, d. 7/21/1840; S11512
John, N.H., b. 8/25/1760 in Candia N.H., m. Hannah Brown; d. 10/24/1821; W22367
John, N.H., lived in Oxford, Me. in 1840; m. Comfort Burley 2/15/1787; d. 3/25/1840. Ch. were William, George W., Stephen B., Abel W., Comfort Bradbury, Abigail P. Kimball, Rebecca Budgen & Sophronia D., R10410
John, N.J., b. 8/24/1751. Lived in Huron Co., Ohio in 1832; d. 8/2/1841; S16270
John, N.J., lived in York Co., Pa. in 1820 age 73. S40555
John, N.J., son of Jacob & Rachel Taylor of Essex Co., m. Jennet, dau. of Jeremiah & Rachael Fitz Randolph of Woodbridge, N.J., at age 28. Moved to Schenectady, N.Y., d. there in 1801. Ch. were John, Mary E. Seelye wife of Hiram Seelye of Geneva, N.Y., and Augustus Fitz Randolph Taylor a physician in New Brunswick, N.J. in 1837; W18109
John, N.Y. ---
John, N.Y., S42452
John, N.C., b. 1760 in Hertford Co., N.C., S7683
John, N.C., b. 12/4/1756 in Va., d. 4/23/1837; son of John C., lived in Granville Co., N.C. in 1852. Soldier's bros. Richard, Edward, and Lewis referred to as serving in Rev. S7684
John, N.C., res. New Hanover Co., N.C., d. 4/23/1837, S7688
John, N.C., Children Catharine, Nancy, Sally, & Tatum, S42038
John, N.C., War 1812, m. Winifred Horton 11/24/1775; d. 5/28/1826. Their ch. Bethiah, John, Susan, Elizabeth, & Thomas, W18114
John, Pa., lived in Humphreys Co. Tenn. in 1820, moved to White Co., Ill. in 1829. Surviving ch. in 1853 were William, Elizabeth, and Sophia Baker, S24392
John, Pa., m. Peggy/Margaret in 1788 in Co. of Franklin, d. 4/1848 in Tuscarawas Co., Ohio. Two ch., Mary, wife of Jacob Tanner, Peggy, wife of Henry Fancley. W4600
John, R.I., m. Marcy Knight 9/23/1780, d. 1/28/1812. W22374
John, Vt., b. 3/20/1760. M.

TAYLOR (continued)
Triphena Smith, lived in Williston, Chittenden Co.; ch. were Mehitable Cullen, Melindy Joy, Meorra Joy, Otis & Brindage; d. Williston 9/30/1847, S14648
John, Va., b. in Albemarle Co., in 1759. S6194
John, Va. (Rockingham Co.), S7682
John, Va., b. Amherst Co., Va. 4/15/1750? Moved to Albemarle Co. where he enl. Pens. from Washington Co., Ky. in 1832. S30730
John, Va., S38421
John, Va.,War of 1812. Two ch. referred to as Judge John M. Taylor of Ala. and Dr. Gilbert D. Taylor of Tenn. BLWt.1828-200
John B., ---, S11510
John M., Pa., was a Deputy Commissary General in Rev., S22547
John S., Va., Sarah Roberts of Calloway Co., Ky., former wid. m. in Mercer Co., Ky. in March to John S. Taylor, W9265
John V.K., N.J., Lydia, W9512; BLWt.26233-160-55
Joice, Mass., b. 8/31/1753 in Yarmouth; brother Ebenezer also in Rev., S30726
Jonas, N.Y., lived in Niles, Cayuga Co., d. 8/22/1849. Ch. were Jonas, James, Benjamin, Polly, Sally Jones, Catharine Green, and Abraham, S23449
Jonathan, Ct., BLWt.6546 iss. 9/15/1791. No papers
Jonathan, Ct., b. in Greenwich, 2/21/1749, S23448
Jonathan, Ct., m. Nancy 4/19/1789 d. 4/15/1834 Norwalk, Ct.,S18105
Jonathan, Cont., Ct., b. in Middletown, Middlesex Co., Ct., m. Hannah Tuels/Tuells 2/15/1781 d. there 6/21 or 22/1821. W18107
Jonathan, Cont., Va., lived in Edgefield Dist., S.C., there in April 1820; m. Joannah Morris. Many children among them were Pleasant of Dallas Co., Ala., Wyatt A. of Chambers, Ala., Cread of Tenn., Onan of Walton Co., Ga., Elizabeth, wid. of Philip Johnson of Carroll Co., Ga., and Jacky, res. unknown. W4351
Jonathan, Mass., File contains a ltr. of 6/19/1888 from Henry B. Taylor of Mooers, Clinton Co., N.Y. with family data, S21521
Jonathan, Mass., Pens. from Vt., S41225
Jonathan, N.H., enl. from Gilmantown, N.H., where he lived in 1832 at age 88; S18241
Jonathan, N.Y., m. Editha Ingham, 1/27/1777 in Ct., d. 4/25/1835 in Jefferson Co., N.Y. Two sons John and Julius. W15747
Jonathan, R.I., son of William & Deborah Taylor, m. Martha, dau. of William Abishaz Briggs

TAYLOR (continued)
in Little Compton, 6/8/1783, W22371
Joseph Spencer, R.I., Dis- See Am. State Papers, Class 9, p.118 Disorders contacted from exposure and great exertion to save public property lying on the beach at the storming of R.I. in 1778 by Gen. Sullivan
Joseph, Cont., N.J., S33782; BLWt. 2097-100
Joseph, Mass., lived in Windsor Co., Vt. in 1832 age 85, S21526
Joseph, Mass., later lived in Hartford, Washington Co., N.Y., pens. from Berne, Albany Co., at age 56 in 1818, Mary, S42448
Joseph, N.Y., living in Overton Co., Tenn. in 1838 at age 76; sons Moses and Reuben, S6290
Joseph, Va., S16269
Joshua, Ct., BLWt.6552. Iss. 6/24/1789. No papers
Joshua, Ct., son of Mathew, b. in Danbury, Fairfield Co., Ct., brother Levi m. Eunice Seeley, dau. of James, 9/2/1781 in Danbury; d. 8/26/1804. W22375
Josiah, Ct., BLWt.6577. Iss. 7/31/1789. No papers
Josiah, Ct., Elizabeth, W824. Her 1st husb. was Isaac Sergeant/Sargeant, R10414 1/2
Josiah, Va., S6203
Jude, Mass., lived in Westerly, Washington Co., R.I. in 1832, b. 10/10/1753 in Little Compton, R.I., S22005
Laroy/Leroy/Leeroy, N.C., later Tenn. & settled in Washington Co., d. 3/24/1834, survived by granddau., Margaret Irvin, S1934
Lemuel, Ct., b. Danbury, 3/24/1765, d. 10/26/1848; m. Ada Cornwall of Middletown, Ct., 3/16/1787. Had brother named Ira. W11604
Leonard, Mass., pens. from Windsor Co., Vt. in 1833 at age 73. S22007
Leonard, Va., b. 12/22/1757 in Kent Co., lived in Mercer Co., Ky. in 1833 & there d. 9/4/1841 M. Sarah Blasgrave 1/3/1785 in Lunenburg Co., Va., ch. were Elizabeth, Henley, Polley, Leonard, Merston, Bannister, Talitha & Silas (Elizabeth m. Babriel Hutching) W3052
Leroy, N.C. See Laroy
Levi, Ct., enl. from Norwalk, moved to Wilton, Fairfield Co. and living there in 1832, S17724
Levin, Va., living in Worcester Co., Md. in 1818. S35058
Lewis, Mass., BLWt.5167 iss. 5/6/1793
Lewis, Mass., m. Jemima Ford, 6/1784. They lived in Middleford, W19433
Lewis, N.C., S.C., S1728

TAYLOR (continued)
Luke, Mass., living in Cayuga, N.Y. in 1832. S11517
Martin, Ct. See TAYLER
Mathew/Matthew, Pa., Sea Service, enl. at Phila. served as midshipman on the "General Greene". Went to France as Capt. of Marines. Pens. at Baltimore, Md. in 1818 age 61, d. 8/27/1818. S35095
Medad, N.H., BLWt.3525. Iss. 12/6/1791 to Stephen Thorn, ass. No papers
Medad, N.H., living at Hartland, Niagara Co., N.Y. in 1818 age 60. S42449
Meredith, S.C., res. Fairfield Dist., b. near Va. & N.C. line, moved to Pickens Co., Ala. in 1833 in company with his sons. S32547
Nathan, Ct., b. 7/7/1760, d. 9/25/1838 in Essex Co., N.Y., Mehitable, W11596; BLWt.98565-160-55
Nathan, Mass., living in Hartford, Washington Co., N.Y. in 1818; d. there 6/27/1832; m. Lydia Harris 2/17/1784 at Richmond, N.H. W18112
Nathan, N.H., S23966
Nathan, N.H., Rhoda Holt Longley, former wid. (leaf from family bible is in file). Wid. pens. from Me. W24571
Nathan, R.I., m. Prudence Wilcox d. 12/4/1837 in Charleston. W22366
Nathaniel, Mass., b. 12/17/1756 in Lancaster, later called Sterling, four ch. Ebenezer, Jonathan Edward and Sally Blood. S30153
Nathaniel, R.I., age 76 in 1820, ch. Thurston, Eliza, Joseph, Abby, Lucy, and Henry. S39862
Nevil/Nevit/Knevit, Va., Pens. from Worcester Co., Md. at age 65 in 1818. S35094
Niles, Ct., pens. from Saratoga Co., N.Y. in 1818, S42447
Nimrod, Va., pens. from Scott Co. in 1832 at age 76, d. 7/16/1834, Mary. Ch. Henry Davison, Lydia wife of James Johnson, and Nimrod. R10422
Noah, Ct., BLWt.6550. Iss. 7/31/1789. No papers
Noah, Ct., S46513
Noah, Mass., pens. from York Co. Me. S18239
Noah, Mass., R10422 1/2
Obadiah, Cont., Ct., Rhoda, ch. Revad, Rachael, Obadiah, Humphrey, John, Rhoda, Syntha (m. Stevens), Anna Matilda, Sephrona, Quena Clemana (a half brother), Thomas, d. 10/1830 at age 67; W3373; BLWt.1476-100
Obed, Mass., Meriam, W13968; BLWt.9500-160-55
Oliver, N.H. & War 1812, m. Tamar Eaton 10/27/1789, ch. John, Phebe Ebenezer, Nancy, Rebecca,

TAYLOR (continued)
Eliza, Oliver, and Gilman, W22379 BLWt.39219-160-55
Othniel, Mass., res. Canandaigua, Ontario Co., N.Y. in 1818 age 65. d. 8/15/1819. S26776; BLWt.2144-300. Iss. 12/4/1795
Paul, Cont., Pa., res. Berkeley Co., Va. in 1832 age 84. S18238
Peter, N.J., BLWt.8793. Iss. 5/26/1790 to Joshua Mersereau, ass. No papers
Peter, N.J., res. New Utrecht, L.I., King's Co., N.Y. at age 65 in 1820. S42458
Peter, Va., res. Norfolk, Va. in 1818 at age 63(?); m. Elizabeth Kelly in July 1783; d. 5/31/1824 in Norfolk Co. Fam. records show ch. were William, James, Peggy, and Peter. W6239; BLWt.3141-160-55
Philip, N.C., m. Sarah 8/21/1780 W18100
Philip W., Va., res. Spencer Co., Ky. in 1832; res. Shelly Co., Ky. in 1855; S16549; BLWt.38349-160-55
Phineas, Ct., grandson of Hon. Phineas T. Barnum, S14655
Prince, Mass., S42463
Reuben, Ct., Cont., m. Anna Skinner, 12/6/1784 in Hebron, Lebanon Co., Ct., d. 3/9/1833 in Portland, N.Y. W16433
Reuben, Ct., N.Y., Privateer (son of Reuben), b. Norwalk, Fairfield Co., Ct. 11/28/1759, m. Selenda/Celinda Abbott, 6/27/1790 at Wilkesbarre, Luzerne Co., Pa., d. 3/24/1849 at Scott, Pa. Ch. John Abbott, Henry, Polly Abbott, Cynthia, Reuben, Benira, (Henry Brown was the son of Polly Abbott). W2702
Reuben, Mass., res. in 1820 South Hadley, Mass., m. Lucretia Bowers 11/29/1787. She was living in Chatham, Columbia Co. N.Y. in 1851, d. 7/14/1845 at Northampton, Mass. W15417
Richard, Del., BLWt.10896. Iss. 9/2/1789. No papers
Richard, Md., res. in 1831 Preble Co., Ohio, d. there 8/29/1838, Ann, a son James. W4598
Richard, Md., m. Mary in Nov. (about the 14th) 1788, d. 5/15/1815. W9513
Richard, N.H. (also lived in York Co., Me.), S177721
Richard, N.C., S7680
Richard, not Rev., U.S. Indian War 1792, Pa. & Ky. agcy. Old War Inv. File 25876
Richard, Va., m. Dinah, dau. Mary m. Mills Riddick
Richard, Va. See TAYLER
Richard, Va., b. 1755 in Cumberland Co., Va., moved to Bedford

TAYLOR (continued)
Co., Va., then to Smith Co., Tenn. and thence to Pike Co., Ill. in 1832. S32549
Richard, Va., res. Jefferson Co., Ky. in 1809, S46514; BLWt.494-100. Iss. 3/20/1810
Richard, Va., res. Ohio Co., Ky. in 1842 at age 82 and d. there 12/9/1843. R10425
Richard, Va., Sea Service, Va. Half Pay. Res. Louisville, Ky. & there in 1825 at age 81; dau. Matilda Robinson; her ch. were Richard T., Catharine Ann, Eliza wife of Thos. K. Byrne, and Mary wife of James B. Anderson. S25873
Richard C., Va., res. in 1819 Wilkes Co., Ga. at age 74. Lived with son-in-law John Todd in Morgan Co., Ga. in 1820. S42039
Richardson, Va., b. New Kent Co., Va. in 1760; in Ky. in 1834 at age 73. S15671
Robert, Md., BLWt.11171 & 11755. Iss. 5/18/1794 to Christopher Cusack, ass. No papers
Robert, Md., BLWt.11771. Iss. 8/8/1794 to Chr. Cusack, ass. No papers
Robert, Pa., b. Baltimore Co., Md. in 1744. Moved to Rockbridge Co., Va. during the Rev., res. Jackson Co., Ga. in 1833. S32005
Robert, Va., res. Pendleton Co., Ky. in 1833. S38420
Russel, Ct., res. Marcellus, N.Y. in 1832. S11509
Samuel, N.J.res. Dis- See Am. State Papers, Class 9, p.169. Has an ulcerous leg in consequence of wound by cannon ball. Disabled 10/6/1777 at Fort Montgomery, res. Elizabethtown.
Samuel, Ct., son of John and Elizabeth, b. 12/1 or 2/1761 at Dudley, Worcester Co., Mass., res. Palmer, Hampden Co., Mass. in 1833, son Jonathan resided in Palmer in 1851. S11521
Samuel, Ct., b. 1/18/1762 in Danbury, Ct., S14649
Samuel, Mass., res. Hartford, Washington Co., N.Y. in 1818 at age 56; there in 1832. S11515
Samuel, Mass., res. Jefferson, Lincoln Co., Me. in 1832, Hannah, W2370; BLWt.6009-160-55
Samuel, Mass., Lucretia, d. 4/13/1841. W13957
Samuel, Mass., res. Rodman, N.Y., in 1820, Ruth. R10426
Samuel, Mass., brother of Lewis, lived in Aurora Twp., Portage Co., Ohio in 1807, m. Sarah at Washington, Mass., ch. Ella, Samuel, Rebecca, Worthy, Royal, Alvin, Marcus & Melinda, d. 4/10/1813. R10430
Samuel, Mass., Huldah Van Gilder,

TAYLOR (continued)
former wid., m. at Ashfield, Mass. 11/29/1785. Moved to Georgia, Vt., R10867; BLWt. 89509-160-55
Samuel, Navy, res. in 1818 Mass. S33775
Samuel, Pa., BLWt.10501. Iss. 10/12/1792. No papers
Samuel, R.I., S41226
Samuel, S.C., m. Ann Bonneau, W22363
Samuel, Va., b. 8/3/1755, res. Sullivan Co., Tenn. in 1827. R39103
Samuel, Va., wife Elizabeth claimed to be age 104 when pens. W6230
Samuel, Va., R10428
Sarah H.,former wid. of William Osborn, Ct., which see
Silas, Pa., Rebecca Wheatley, former wid., R10432
Simeon, BLWt.6557. Iss. 10/7/1789. No papers
Simeon, Ct., res. Genessee Co., N.Y.in 1818 at age 69, d. Bethany, N.Y. 4/26/1820, m. Sybel/Sibella/Sibilla Hotchkiss 10/7/1772 at Woodbury, Ct. Only child named was Alleythear Huggins who lived in Bethany, N.Y. in 1837. W16753
Simeon, Ct., m. Olive Culver in Litchfield in Sept. 1787, d. 10/4/1840 in Dutchess Co., N.Y. W22385
Simeon, Mass., also lived in Maine, S38417
Simon, Pa., S40556
Solomon, Ct., wid. Abigail lived in Addison Co., Vt., d. 12/31/1825 in Chittenden, Vt. W26513
Solomon, Mass., Anna Weatherbee, former wid., lived in Harvard, Worcester Co., d. 1812. R11360
Spencer, N.Y., Sally, d.10/25/1821 in Warren, Ct. W3620; BLWt. 6411-160-55
Stephen, Ct., m. Prudence Pelton 6/12/1774; d. 9/18/1822 at Torrington, Ct. W22365
Stephen, Mass., age 83 in 1832 and living Worcester, Mass., S14651
Stephen, Mass., res. Alfred, Allegany Co., N.Y. in 1821, Abegail, ch. William, Caroline, Edward, Emeline, and Stephen. Lived in Winona Co., Ter. of Minn. in 1855; S42457; BLWt. 18010-160-55
Stephen, Mass., Mindwell Tolman former wid., m. to Stephen 11/13/1781; d. 6/11/1823. W15436
Tertius, Mass., Elizabeth, sons Tertius and Elias, d. 12/21/1822 in Charlemont. W27491; BLWt.2150-200-Lt. Iss. 10/1/1792 to Isaac Brown, ass. (Name spelled Turtius Taylor)
Theodore, Ct., lived in Glaston-

TAYLOR (continued)
bury, Ct., Betty, S36333
Theophilus, N.C., b. Va. 1759, moved to Chesterfield Co., S.C. then to Franklin Co., Ga. in 1837 (now Haversham Co.), d. 10/4/1845. Ch. William, Salley Holcomb, Jeremiah, Hetty Holcomb and Delpha Johnson. R10433
Thomas, Ct., m. Dorcas Moulton, pens. as former wid. of Levi Farnham, Ct. which see. Pens. from Richland, Oswego Co., N.Y. in 1818 at age 72. S46202
Thomas, Mass., res. Ontario Co., N.Y. in 1818. S42456
Thomas, Mass., m. 3/4/1789, Abigail Brown, former wid. lived in Me. when pensioned. W24667
Thomas, Mass., N.Y., res. Huntington Twp., Luzerne Co., Pa. in 1826, m. Elizabeth 7/15/1835. Son John, brother Cornelius. W6228
Thomas, N.J., Pa., 1812, res. Hampshire Co., Va. in 1833; d. 9/14/1851. S7686
Thomas, R.I., S39863
Thomas, Va., m. Mildred/Milly Markham 12/29/1785 in Cumberland Co., Va., d. 12/17/1839. Pen. from Sumner Co., Tenn. in 1829. Ch. John, Polley, James, Thomas, Betsey, Anney, Gerard, Jonathan, William. W873
Thomas, Va. See TAYLER
Thornton, Va., Elizabeth, sons Woodford and Thornton, BLWt. 1901-150
Timothy, Ct., BLWt.2172-300-Capt. Iss. 5/21/1789. No papers
Walter, N.Y., Anna, W19436
Willet, N.J., S1120
William, Ct., S36334; BLWt.6469-100-Sgt. Iss. 9/4/1789 to Ezekiel Case, ass. No papers
William, Cont., Mass., d. at Rome Mass. 8/5/1837, son William, S33179; BLWt.2152-200-Lt. Iss. 1/23/1799
William, Cont., N.H., S43993; BLWt.40676-160-55. Wid. Rosamond pens. as the wid. of Noah Robinson, N.H., which see
William, Cont., Pa., res. Trumbull, Tenn. in 1823, d. 7/8/1834 S40558
William, Md., BLWt.11760. Iss. 7/22/1797 to James DeBaufre, ass. No papers
William, Md., BLWt.11761. Iss. 9/5/1789 to Keziah Clark, Admx. No papers
William, Md., b. England, res. Ashe Co., N.C. in 1834. S7687
William, Mass., b. 3/20/1753, m. Priscilla 6/16/1784. W13955
William, N.C., S7685
William, N.C., S.C., Sea Service, b. S.C. 1759, res. Lincoln Co., N.C. at enl. Fayette Co., Tenn.

TAYLOR (continued)
in 1832. R10439
William, Pa., R10435
William, Pa., Sea Service, War 1812, b. in Co. Down, Ireland in 1753, drafted in Phila. Pa., res. Jefferson Co., Ohio in 1832. S3755
William, S.C., b. Ireland, res. in Richland Dist., S.C. in 1821, d. 6/10/1828. S39099
William, Va., BLWt.12606. Iss. 1/31/1794 to Robert Means, ass. No papers
William, Va., b. 1758 in Augusta Co., res. Rockcastle Co., Ky. in 1832. S14647
William, Va., S31407
William, Va., daus. Iovey Sarah and Julia Ann, S38422
William, Va., b. May 1754, res. Moreland Twp., Lycoming Co., Pa. in 1818, d. there 3/31/1839. M. Sarah in Amwell Twp., N.J. in Nov. 1783/84. W4603
William, Va., res. Jefferson Co., Ky. in 1818, Louisville in 1820, m. Elizabeth/Eliza Courts, 3/29/1849. Ch. Robert H.C., Eleanor Madison, Caroline Jefferson, Louise Washington, Eliza Ormsby and Richard W. Ferguson. Pension due mother was allowed the following surviving ch.- Richard F. Taylor, Eleanor M. Berry and Eliza O. Horning. D. 3/29/1830 in Oldham Co., Ky. W6233; BLWt. 2501-400-Maj. Iss. 12/8/1797
William, Va., m. Ann/Anna Hensley 1/1/1780 in Culpeper Co. Had bro. Thomas. W6238. BLWt. 26964-160-55
William, Va., m. Agnes Royalty 7/20/1809 in Amherst Co., d. there 6/10/1843 at age 84. R10404
William, Va., R10436
William, Va., R10438
William Tarlton, Va.(?), res. Wayne Co., Ky. in 1836, Elizabeth, R10414. (File contains a leaf from family Bible with many records)
Zachariah, Va., res. Woodford Co., Ky. in 1818 at age 62, Elizabeth, son John, dau. Philadelphia, and other ch. not named. S31408
Zachariah, Va., also 1794, m. Susannah Jarrell/Gerrill, 12/19/1792. W6237; BLWt.11195-160-55
Zalmon, Ct., wid. Hannah pens. from N.Y., m. Hannah 10/26/1780, d. 5/10/1816 in Putnam Co., N.Y. W25470
TAYNTOR, Jedediah, Mass., Mary, W15418
TAYS, Samuel, N.C., S1594
TEACHEY, Daniel, N.C., Mary, W4082 BLWt.19907-160-55
TEAFFE, Henry, Pa., Mary, W2025
TEAGUE, Beni, Mass., S38428
Daniel, Mass., S33785
Jacob, Va., S41235

TEAGUE (continued)
Jesse, Mass., S42468
John, S.C., BLWt.12632-100. Iss. 10/7/1795; BLWt.13811-100-1795
William, S.C., Elizabeth, W208
TEAL, Adam, See TEEL
Emanuel, N.C., Martha, R10440
Jeremiah, Pa., BLWt.10488. Iss. 7/27/1789 to Richard Platt, ass. No papers
John, Pa., Catharine, W2703; BLWt.26003-160-55
John Jeremiah, Pa. See THIEL
Joseph, Ct., Hannah, W18119
Leonard, Pa., BLWt.10478. Iss. 3/29/1792 to Barnard Slauch, ass.
Nathan, Ct., Polly, W19438; BLWt.18221-160-55
Samuel, See DEAL
TEALL, Joseph, Ct., S46473
Oliver, Ct., S11529
TEALS, Joseph, Ct., BLWt.6536 Iss. 4/22/1793 to William Judd. No papers
TEAM, Adam, N.C., S.C., S21528
TEANEY, Daniel, Pa., Catharine, W6252
TEAROOT, Francis, Cont., Canada Mary, W22390; BLWt.14511-160-55. (Name spelled Taucot, Tarcot, Tauco, and Terco)
TEARNEY, Gilbert, Ga., Elizabeth W9850
TEAS, William, Cont., Pa., Sarah W1663; BLWt.2262-100
TEASLY, Silas, N.C., S32009
TEATOR, Henry, N.Y., S11530
TEAZ, William, Cont. See TEAS
TEAZOR, Aaron, Del., BLWt.10889. Iss. 9/2/1789
TEBBETS, Ephraim, N.H. See TEBBITS
Nathaniel, Mass., S19125
Samuel, Cont., Mass., S11560
William, N.H. See TIBBETTS
TEBBETTS, Ephraim, Mass., Rachel, W6286
Isaac, Mass. See TIBBETTS
TEBBITS, Ephraim, N.H., S43201
TEBBS, John, Va. See TIBBS
Willoughby, Va., Betsey, W6284
TEDDERTON, John, N.C., R10441
TEDFORD, John, Va., S3776
Joseph, Va., Mary, R10447
Robert, Va., S3775
TEDRICK, Michael, N.C., S32242
TEED, John, N.J., S6205
William, N.Y., R10442
TEEDER, Michael, Pa. Agcy., Dis-
TEEL, Adam, Pa., S23453
Ezekiel H., Navy, Sea Service, N.J., S23968
John, Pa. See TEAL
Joseph, Mass., S29501
Lodrick, N.C., R10443
Nathan, Ct. See TEAL
TEEPENING, Mary, former wid. of Isaac Seamens, N.Y., which see
TEEPLE, George, N.J., Hannah, R10444
Jacob, Pa., S16552
John, N.J., R10445

TEERPENNING, Jacobus, N.Y., S14142
William, N.Y., S28907
TEETE, James, Va., S7696
TEETER, Conrad, N.J., S23215
Samuel, Va., R10446
TEETS, Peter, N.J., BLWt.8787. Iss. 10/20/1789 to William H. Kerr, ass. No papers
TEFFT, Caleb, R.I., S11531
Daniel, R.I., Sally, W13974
David, R.I., Rheuhamer, W26517
Gardiner, R.I., S11532
TELFORD, Alexander, Va., S4681
Hugh, N.C., S2021
Joseph, Va. See TEDFORD
TELLER, Abraham, N.Y. See claim of Thomas CRUMMELL
Ahasuerus, N.Y., S29500
Tobias, N.Y., S14665
TELLIER, Charles, Hazen's Regt., BLWt.13830. Iss. 7/21/1793. No papers
TELLIS, John, Va., S40559
TELLOTSON, Nathan, N.Y., Phoebe, R10606
TEMPLE, Anna, former wid. of Alexander Hodge, which see
Archelaus, N.H., Eunice, W2882
Benjamin, Va., BLWt.2214-450-Lt. Col., iss. 2/1/1800 to John Marshall. No papers
Ebenezer, Cont., Mass., S14658
Ebenezer, Lamb's Art., N.Y., BLWt.7899. Iss. 4/9/1791 to Jacob Ferris, ass. No papers
Enos, N.H., S14659. His wid. received pension on acct. of the service of her former husb., Alexander Hodge, which see
Ephraim, Mass., S31412
Eppes, Va., Elizabeth, W6255
Frederick, Mass., S41236
James, S.C., Rachel, R10451
Jeremiah, Mass., BLWt.5150. Iss. 3/25/1790. No papers
John, Cont., Mass., Mary, W26515
John, Mass., Polly, W8782. BLWt. 6289-160-55
John, Va., S38431
Jonas, N.H., R10450
Joseph S., Mass., S19813
Salmon, Mass., Mary, W22391
Samuel, Mass., S33183
Samuel, Va., S7704
Silas, Mass., S33787
Stephen, Mass., S33784
Uriah, N.H., BLWt.3529. Iss. 2/21/1795 to Daniel King. No papers
TEMPLEMAN, Samuel, Va., S6204
TEMPLER, Thomas, N.Y., Elizabeth Bunker, former wid., W16880
Thomas, Pa., BLWt.10510. Iss. 6/6/1791. No papers
TEMPLETON, Robert, S.C., S32550
TENAIR, Michael, N.J., BLWt.8807. Iss. 4/26/1792 to William Barton. No papers
TENANT, William, Pa., S35096
TEN BROECK, Adam, N.Y., Hannah, W11614; BLWt.2190-150. Iss.

TEN BROECK (continued)
12/9/1791 to Peter Rockfeller (name also spelled Ten Brook). Also BLWt.4-10-55
John C., N.Y., S42469; BLWt.2184-300-Capt. Iss. 6/2/1792
Leonard, N.Y., Gertrude, R10452
Maria, former wid. of Andrew Hermance, N.Y., which see
Samuel, N.Y., S11526
Samuel J., N.Y., Christina, W18118
TEN BROOK, Adam, See TEN BROECK
TEN BROUK, Samuel J. See TEN BROECK
TENCH, John/John R., Va., S3772
John R., Va. See John
William, Va., S39521
TEN EICK, Andrew J./Andrew G., Sarah, W1096
Coanrod/Conrad, N.J., S14667
Jeremiah, N.J., S4680
TENERY, William, Va., Sarah, W2195; BLWt.19623-160-55
TEN EYCK, Abraham, N.Y., BLWt. 2187-200-Lt. Iss. 8/6/1790
Andrew, N.J. See TEN EICK
Henry, Ct., BLWt.2173-300-Capt. Iss. 3/7/1792. No papers
Jacob T., N.Y., S11527
Jeremiah, N.J. See TENEICK
John D., N.Y., BLWt.2182-300-Capt. Iss. 10/9/1790. No papers
Joseph, N.Y., BLWt.7881. Iss. 8/12/179? to John D. Coe. No papers
Joseph, N.Y., R10456
TENNANT, James, Md., R.I., S22010
John, Ct., R10453
Thomas, Mass., Elizabeth, W18120
William, N.J., BLWt.8789. Iss. 5/26/1796. No papers
TENNELL, George, Va., S37485. BLWt. 206-100
TENNETT, John Peter, Hazen's Regt. BLWt.13817. Iss. 3/25/1790. No papers
TENNEY, Edmund, Mass., N.H., Sarah, W26516
Edward, S.C., S38427
Gideon, Mass., War 1812, Betsey, W20084; BLWt.6401-160-55
James, Mass., Thankful, W3888
Joseph, N.H., R10454
Josiah, Mass. See TENNY
TENNILL, George, Va., S7703
TENNY, Benjamin, Mass., Lydia, W26514
David, N.H., Priscilla, W25474; BLWt.28595-160-55
Joshua, Mass., S19812
Josiah, Mass., Susannah, W6251
Molly, former wid. of Nathan Blake, N.H., which see
Prudence, former wid. of Nathaniel Chamberlain, Mass., which see
Samuel, R.I., BLWt.2135-400-Surgn. Iss. 3/25/1790. No papers
Silas, N.H., Vt., Temperance, W25473
TENYCK, Hendrick, N.Y., Dorcas, W22387
TENYCKE, Joseph, N.Y. See TEN EYCK
TENYKE, Hendrick, See TENYCK
Joseph, N.Y. See TEN EYCK
TERBOSS, Henry, N.Y., R10457
TERBUSH, Peter, N.Y., Sarah, W16985
TERCO, Francis. See TEARCOT
TERHUNE, Abraham, N.J., N.Y., S1122
Cornelius, N.J., S1121
Daniel, N.J., N.Y., S31413
John, N.J., Sarah, W9849
John, N.Y., S14668
TERMS, Peter, Armand's Legion, BLWt.13808. Iss. 5/23/1800. No papers
TERNAN, Dennis, Md., BLWt.11781. Iss. 3/1/1790. No papers
TERNANT, Jean B. See John
John, Foreign, Armand's Legion, BLWt.2241-450-Lt. Col. Iss. 11/26/1796. No papers
TERNEY, Henry, See TURNEY
James, Pa., S40560
TERNURE, James, N.Y., S15672
TERRANT, Henry, Cont., Va., Osiller R., See TARRANT
TERREL, Elihu, Ct., S3773
Jared, Ct., S18625
TERRELL, Asahel, Ct., N.Y., Hannah Blackman, former wid., W17311. Widow's 2nd husb., Nehemiah Blackman, served in Rev.
Enoch, N.J., Nancy, W874
Joel, N.C., agcy. & res., S14664
Richmond, Va., R10459
Simon, N.C., S32008
William, N.Y., S42467
William, S.C., b. N.C., S16550
TERRENCE, Adam, N.C., S14663
TERRIL, Ephraim, Ct., S11528
Presley, Cont., Va., S38430
TERRILL, Amos, Mass., R10458
Hezekiah, Ct., Betsey, W22393; BLWt.36668-160-55
Joel, Ct., Eunice, W4353
John, Cont., Ct., S37484
Nathan, Ct., Dorothy, W4083
Stephen, Ct., S41234
TERRY, Asaph, Ct., Nancy, W6249; BLWt.26938-160-55
Benjamin, N.Y., S49260
David, Mass., S38429
Ebenezer, Ct., S11525
Ebenezer, Ct., N.H., S10661
Elisha, Mass., Phebe, W18121
Gamaliel, Ct., BLWt.6549. Iss. 12/26/1798 to Gam. Tury. No papers
Gamaliel, Ct., Susannah, W16755
Gideon, Va., S41237
Isaac, Mass., R10462
James, Md., BLWt.11753. Iss. 12/12/179? No papers
James, N.C., R10464
James, Va., S17141
John, Navy, Mass., Susannah, W13977; BLWt.53743-160-55
John, N.Y., R10465
John, Va., S7699
Jonathan, N.J., Huldah, W2371
Joseph, Sea Service, Va., S7701
Josiah, Ct., Deborah, W19437
TERRY (continued)
Josiah, Va., See ZERRY
Julius, Ct., R10466
Margaret, former wid. of Wilhelmus Westfall, N.Y., which see
Martin, Ct., S14661
Nancy, former wid. of John Davis N.C., which see
Nathaniel, N.Y., Martha, W22389
Nathaniel, Va., Ann, W3054. BLWt.24435-160-55 & 2216-300-Capt. Iss. 12/14/1796
Obadiah, Va., Sarah, W8781
Richard, N.J., Sarah, W2487
Solomon, Ct., S14662
Stephen, Ct., S17140
Stephen, Va., Dis-
Thomas, Cont., Mass., S14660
Thomas, N.C., b. Va., d. 2/12/1840, Nancy, lived in Smith Co., Tenn., W875
Thomas, Va., son of Wm., S7700
Thomas, Va., Elizabeth (Dunn), b. 1/15/1757, d. 6/10/1837, W2271. Pens. in Ky. Lived in Chesterfield Dist., S.C.
Thomas, Va., Mary, W3053
Thomas, Va., m. Lucy (Lax) in Buckingham Co., 6/30/1786, d. 3/6/1833. W6250
William, Va., m. Susannah Thompson 12/8/1771; d. in Richmond Co., Va. in Dec. 1810, when a member of Va. Legislature. W4196
William Nathan, Ct., Eleanor, R10461
Zeno, Ct., Tabitha, W22392
TERRYBURY, John, See TARRYBURY
TERWILLEGAR, Aaron, N.Y., Keturah, R10470
TERWILLEGER, Benjamin T., N.Y., S13005
Evert, N.Y., Sarah, W18117
James, N.Y., BLWt.7862. Iss. 12/5/1791. No papers
Lucus, N.Y., R10471
TERWILLIGER, Abraham J., N.Y., S14669
Benjamin T., N.Y. See TERWILLEGER
Evert, N.Y., S11533
Harmonius, N.Y., Elizabeth, W22388
James, N.Y., son of Mathew who also served in Rev., S14666. D. 3/10/1834 in Skaneateles, N.Y.
James, N.Y., S42466; d. 9/2/1821; a dau. m. Andrew Kain; res. Shawangunk, N.Y.
James, N.Y., R26157
Josiah, N.Y., m. Rachel Mills, 1/15/1783 in Dutchess Co., W16437
Peter V., N.Y., Rachel, W20083
Simon H., b. 1753 in Schenectady, d. 2/28 or 3/1/1834 at home of his son, Henry S., in Greene Co., N.Y.; m. Sorchy Van Kuren of Shawangunk. R10472
William, N.Y., res. Shawangunk, Ulster Co. in 1818, d. 12/6/1837. S42464
TESHEW, John, Mass., Sea Service, Navy, S33786

TESSIER, Charles, Cont., N.Y., S42465
Peter, Crane's Cont. Art., Mass. BLWt.5185. Iss. 6/5/1789 to Edmund Fowle
TESSIEUR, John, Hazen's Regt., BLWt.13825. Iss. 8/14/179? to Benj. Moore
TETARD, Benjamin, Ga., BLWt.2230-400-Srgn. Iss. 8/20/1799
TETERTON, Thomas, N.C., Anna, R10473
TEULON, Charles, S.C., Christiana R10474; her 1st husb., George Henderson, served in S.C. Militia in Rev.
TEUMEY, John, N.J., S16551
TEW, Benedict, R.I., Rachel (nee Humphrey) Ladieu, former wid., W21552
Henry, R.I., b. 1757, son of James who also served in Rev., S22009
William, R.I., BLWt.2137-300-Capt. (bro. of Benedict, which see)
TEWAHANGARAHKEN, Honyere (Indian) Capt., N.Y., S23019; BLWt.2160-300. Iss. 3/8/1792
Honyost (Indian), N.Y., Jenny, R3065 (bro. of the Capt.)
TEWGOOD, Jonathan, R.I., Mary, S22011
THACHER, Benjamin, Ct., Phebe (Buel/Buell), former wid. who was pensioned in N.H., W2521; BLWt.26736-160-55
Benjamin, Va. See THACKER
Ebenezer, Mass., S33793
Eliakim, Cont., Ct., S23970
James, Cont., Mass., Va., S3788; BLWt.2142-400-Surgn. Iss. 4/9/1790
John, Mass., S14686
John Oxenbridge, Cont., Mass., Lucy, W22415
Nathaniel, Cont., Mass., BLWt. 2475-200
Obadiah, Mass. See THATCHER
Stephen, Pvt., Lamb's Art., N.Y. BLWt.7890-100. Iss. 9/24/1791 to Platt Rogers, ass.
Thomas, Mass. See THATCHER
THACKER, Ambrose, Va., Molly, W6264
Benjamin, Va., S3789
Daniel, Va., S7707
John, Va., Susannah, W6263
Nathaniel, Va., S6225
Reuben, not Rev., Wayne's Indian War, Nancy, res. Va. & Ky. Old War Wid. Rej. 18412
Sackville, Va., S6239
Thomas, Mass., Mary, W14003
William, Va., lived in Washington Co., Tenn. in 1818, S39107
William, Va., Ann, R10476
THACKSTON, Benjamin, Va., Betty Ann, W9855
James, N.C., BLWt.2225-500-Lt. Col. Iss. 11/15/1791
THAOSAGWAT, Hanjoost, BLWt.2161-200-Lt. Iss. 3/8/1792,and 2606
THARP, Abel, Ct., Hannah Austin W20641
Amos, Ct. See THORP
Benjamin, N.J., BLWt.8785. Iss. 7/7/1789. No papers
Charles, N.C., Frances, R10479
Charles, Va., Elizabeth, W1664; BLWt.51759-160-55
David, N.J.. S33800
Earle/Earles, Cont., Ct., Lydia, W19444
James, Va., R10480
John, Cont., N.J. See THORP
John, Va., S38439
John, Va. See Jonathan
Jonathan, Va., Eliza Ann, W3877; BLWt.38348-160-55
Joseph, Ct. See THORP
Paul/Perry, Pa., S22551
Perry, Pa. See Paul
Perry, Pa., Margaret, W2973; BLWt.1477-100
Peter N.J., BLWt.8780 iss. 9/12/1789 to Ebenezer Justin Foote
Peter, N.J., Jemima, W15706
Reuben, N.J. See THORP
Robert, Ga., N.C., R104789
Solomon, N.J., BLWt.8781 iss. 6/11/1789 to Jonathan Dayton
Thomas, Va., S7706
Thomas, Va., Sinah, W6258
THATCHER, Amos, N.J., Pa., Jemima W9854
Asa, Cont., Ct., S41242
Benjamin, Ct. See THACHER
Benjamin, N.H., S22552
Eliakim, Ct. See THACHER
John, Ct., R1439
John O., Cont., Mass. See THACHER
Josiah, Ct., S14670
Levi, Vt., Adocia, R10481
Lot, Mass., S30733
Obediah/Obadiah, Mass., S40568
Peter, N.H., Vt., S11550
Samuel, Ct., N.Y., S11542
Samuel, Vt., S14685
Thomas, Mass., S33797
THAXTER, Gridley, Mass., Privateer S3791
THAXTON, Thomas, N.C., Hannah, R10482
William, N.C., R10483
THAYAR, William, Va. See THAYER
THAYER, Abijah, Mass., S19485
Abner, Mass., Persis, W22412; BLWt.8019-160-55
Abraham, Mass., Lydia, W19446
Alexander, Mass., S33188
Amos, Mass., S33198, res. 1818 Norfolk Co., Mass.
Amos, Mass., S33794, res. 1820 Worcester Co., Mass.
Artemas, Mass., S29504
Asa, Ct., S43199, Res. 1818
Asa, Mass., S33184
Asa, Mass., Mary, W14004
Barnabas, Mass., S30160
Barrick, Mass., Mary, W26521; BLWt.35686-160-55
Bartholomew, Mass., S40577; BLWt.601-200
Benjamin, Mass.,Elizabeth, R10486
THAYER (continued)
Caleb, Sgt.,Crane's Cont. Art. Mass., BLWt.5184 iss. 7/30/1796 to William Blanchard. Card record. No papers
Caleb, Mass., Judy/Judah, W13990
Christopher, Cont., Mass., S43994
Daniel, Mass., Beulah, W19443
David, Cont., Ct., S36338
David, Mass., Anna Packard, former wid., W21891
Eli, Mass., S33200
Elijah, Mass., Phebe, W14012
Elijah, Mass., Hannah, W26531
Elijah, Mass., Mehitable/Mehetabel, W27492; BLWt.38827-160-55
Eliphas, Mass., S6235
Ephraim, Mass., S30157
Ephraim, Mass., Sarah, W14013
Esick, Mass., R.I., Jane, W507; BLWt.19908-160-55
Ezekiel, Mass., S11549
Ezekial, N.Y., S14690
Gideon, Mass., S33196
Gideon, Mass., R.I., S6238
Henry, Mass., Phila., W22407
Isaac, Mass., S23969 (Hannah's husb. d. in 1805 (Isaac Thayer) see papers in her claim under R9742, Isaac Thayer, which were removed from this case 8/23/1939)
Isaac, Mass., Hannah Smith, former wid., R9742
Jacob, Cont., Mass., S42482
Jacob, Cont., Mass., Welthy, W25477
James, Mass., S6234
Jeremiah, Mass., S35651
Jeremiah, Mass., Elizabeth, W22401
Jerijah, Cont., Ct., S41252; BLWt.3768-160-55
Joel, Mass., Susanna, W19448
John, Cont., N.Y. res., S42493
John, Mass., S22013
John, Mass., S30155
John, Mass., Eunice, W14009
John, Mass., Achsah Burgis, former wid., W15617
John, Pvt., Lamb's Art., N.Y., BLWt.7898 iss. 9/27/1790 to James F. Sebor, ass.
Jonathan, Mass., S30739
Jonathan, Mass., Betsey, W16757
Joseph, Cont., Ct., Abigail, W18133
Joseph, Mass., Phebe, W15428
Joseph, Mass., Mary, R10488
Leavitt, Mass., S6236
Levi, Mass., S33186
Levi, Mass., Hannah, R10487
Lydia, Mass., former wid. of Elisha Wales, which see
Nathan, Mass., S33199
Nathaniel, Cont., Mass., Sea Service, Phebe, W14011
Nathaniel, Mass., Rhoda/Rhody, W14007
Obadiah, Cont., Mass., S33195
Oliver, R.I., Deborah, W22402
Paul, Pvt., Mass., BLWt.5134 iss. 5/24/1790. Card record. No papers

THAYER (continued)
Paul, Mass., Elizabeth Estes/ Estus, former wid., W17765
Philip/Phillip, Cont., Mass., Hannah, W2490; BLWt.26646-160-55
Philip, Mass., Lydia, W14002
Randle, Mass., S33187
Richard, Mass., S6208
Rufus, Mass., S30156
Samuel, Pvt., Mass., BLWt.5160 iss. 6/28/1792 to Martin Kingsley Card record. No papers
Samuel, Mass., Abigail, S11547 and R10484
Samuel, Mass., S41246 (in 1820 wife Dinah)
Samuel, Mass., Sarah, W26528
Samuel White, Cont., Mass., Esther, W20086
Shadrach, Mass., Ruth, W14000
Simeon, Mass., S41244
Simeon, R.I., BLWt.2134-400-Maj. Iss. 4/20/1790. Card record. No papers
Solomon, Mass., Elizabeth, W15429
Stephen, Mass., S33193
Stephen, Mass., Anna Otis former wid., W21883; BLWt.5171-100 iss. 1/27/1797
Timothy, Mass., Phebe, W14001
Timothy, Mass., Rachel, W14008
Uriah, Mass., Phebe, W20087; BLWt.13875-160-55
William, Va., Mary, W6265; BLWts. 324-60-55 & 12613-100-179-
Zaccheus, Mass., S33190
Zachariah, Mass., Cont., S33192
Zebah, Mass., Hannah Allen, former wid., W23427
Zebah, Mass., Sarah, R18409
THEAMES, Jonathan, N.C., S42042
THEOBALD, James, Va., S14694
THEPAUTT, William, Pvt., Crane's Cont. Art., Mass., BLWt.5186 iss. 5/17/1792 to Nathaniel W. Appleton
THERRELL, Moses, S.C., Lucretia, R10489
THERWILLAGER, Cleophus, N.Y., R10490
THEUS, Simeon, S.C., BLWt.2227-300-Capt. Iss. 12/31/1796
THEW, Garret, N.Y., R10491
Gilbert, N.Y., Sarah, W15806
THIBOE, Peter, Pvt., Pa., BLWt. 10520 iss. 12/28/1793 to Christian Hubbard, ass. Card record. No papers
THIEL, John Jeremiah, Pa., Maria Rosina/Mary Rosanna, W3474
THIGPEN, Gilead, N.C., Elizabeth R10492
Joseph, N.C., S14684
THIGPHEN, Gilead, See THIGPEN
THING, Jonathan, N.H., S18244
Levi, N.H., Susanna, W18130
Nathaniel, Cont., Mass., N.H., S18626
THISSELL, Jeffry/Jeffrey, Mass., Jemima, W14005
Thomas, Mass., S43196
THISTLE, Samuel, Pvt., Ct.,

THISTLE (continued)
BLWt.6545 iss. 6/25/1789. Card record. No papers
THIVEATT, Edward, N.C., S9490
THOLLY, William, Pvt. in the Art., Pa., Wt. 10527 iss. 2/14/1791 to Alexander Power, ass.
THOM, Mary, N.Y., former wid. of Robert Graham, which see
THOMAS, Aaron, Cont., Ct., S35098
Aaron,, N.C., Sarah, W2704, sold. born N.C.
Abraham, Pa., Va., Polly, W11622 BLWt.84012-160-55
Absalom, N.C., S.C., R10493, b. S.C.
Alexander, N.J., Hannah, W6275
Amos, N.C., S42041
Andrew, Cont., Mass., Vt., S19121
Asa, Pvt., N.J., BLWt.8303 iss. 9/9/179- to John Pope, ass. Card record. No papers
Asa, N.J., S33796
Asa, N.C., R10494
Asa, Pa., Martha, W3475
Beriah, Mass., S14672
Briggs, Mass., S15676
Buckner, Va., S41248 (colored)
Caleb, Ct., S35353
Caleb, Ct., Polly, W6273; BLWt. 28573-160-55
Caleb, Sgt., Mass., BLWt.5168 iss. 12/13/1796. Card record. No papers
Caleb, N.C., S46474, sold. alive in 1828
Caleb, N.C., BLWt.1274-100. Sold. dead March 1828
Catlett, Va., Mary, W1668
Charles, Cont., Mass., R.I., Deborah, W26523
Charles, Mass. See THOMES
Charles, N.C., Va., S31421
Charles, S.C. or Va., S39105
Cornelius, Va. or Va. Sea Service R----. Va. Half Pay
Daniel, Ct., S11536
Daniel, Ct., Eunice, R10496. Sold. d. 1825. Wid. res. Saratoga Co., N.Y. in 1845
Daniel, N.H., Eunice, BLWt.61185-160-55, wid. res. Cheshire Co., N.H. in 1855
Daniel, N.Y., R10495, res. Meigs Co., Ohio in 1858 age 100 years
David, Cont., Mass., S41243
David, N.C., Va., S32552
David, Pa., S40564
Edmund D., N.J., BLWt.2194-200-Lt. Iss. 6/11/1789. Card record No papers
Edward, Mass., S30159
Edward, N.J., Prudence, R10513
Edward, Va., S17147
Eleazer, Mass., Arispey/Arispah W19447
Elijah, Pvt., Ct., BLWt.6542 iss. 7/13/1792. Card record. No papers
Elijah, Ct., S42485, res. Delaware Co., N.Y. in 1818

THOMAS (continued)
Elijah, Mass., S29503, born Barnstable, Mass., 1761
Elisha, N.H., Joanna Hayes former wid., W14860
Elisha, N.H., Sarah Moulton, former wid., W26277
Elisha, Va., S31419; res. Mercer Co., Ky. in 1833
Elisha, Va., Alice/Alcy, W2974, sold. d. Wayne Co., Ky., 12/24/ 1834
Ellis, Md., Mary, W9519
Enoch, Pvt., Ct., BLWt.6750 iss. 8/15/1796 to William Mosely, ass. Card record. No papers
Enoch, Ct., Anne, W16756
Enoch, N.H., Mary, W15431
Ephraim, Pvt., Ct., BLWt.6547 iss.10/22/1789 to Theodosius Fowler, ass. Card record. No papers
Ephraim, N.Y., S6227
Etheldred, N.C., S17143
Evan, N.C., R20518
Evan, Pa., BLWt.2201-100
Evan, Va., S16002, b. 2/28/1753 Chester Co., Pa.
Evan, Va., S17728, b. 2/22/1757 Frederick Co., Va.
Ezekiel, Pvt., N.Y., BLWt.7888 iss. 8/26/1790 to Benj. Townsend ass. Card record. No papers
Ezekiel, N.Y., S40565
Foxwell, Mass., S33788
Francis, Cont., Pa., S35099
Garner, R.I., S39866
George, N.Y., Prudence Simpkins former wid., W19035. Her last husb., Robert Simpkins, N.Y. was pensioned, which see
George, Va., S38440
Giles, Md., S6226
Gregory, Pvt., Ct., BLWt.6556 iss. 1/16/1797. Card record. No papers
Henry, N.Y., S42473; BLWt.7869-100 iss. 7/19/1790. Card record. No papers
Henry, N.C., S1596
Henry, Pa., Mary, W9851
Henry, Va., S38433
Holmes, Mass., Susanna, W22403
Ichabod, Mass., S32018
Isaac, Mass., Averick, W13999
Israel, Mass., S34518
Israel, N.Y., R10498
Jacob, Cont., Va., S39106
Jacob, Pvt., N.H., BLWt.3523 iss. 4/15/1796 to Joseph Conner. Card record. No papers
Jacob, N.H., Ruth, W19445
Jacob, N.Y., Esther, W19440
James, Ct., S18245
James, Cont., Md., Rebecca, W22413
James, Md., BLWt.1433-100
James, Mass., S33194
James, N.C., S6233
James, Pvt., Pa., BLWt.10514 iss. 7/20/1795 to Christian Hubbard, ass. Card record. No papers
James, Pa., S22549

THOMAS (continued)
James, Va., S11548, b. 10/20/1763, Gloucester Co., Va.
James, Va., S17146, b. 1764 Loudoun Co., Va.
James, Va., S32015, res. 1834 in Oglethorpe Co., Ga.
James, Va., S38436, res. 1820 in Amherst Co., Va.
James, Va., S41249, res. 1826 in Pittsylvania Co., Va.
Jason, Mass., S11539
Jeremiah, Mass., R10499
Jesse, Ct., S23454
John, Ct., BLWt.6571 iss. 1790
John, Cont., Ct., Mary, W18136
John, Cont., Mass., S42483; BLWt.2143-100-Surgn. iss. 12/28/1791
John, Pvt., Md., BLWt.11766 iss. 1/21/1795 to John Faires, ass. Card record. No papers
John, Pvt., Md., BLWt.11768 iss. 11/29/179- (torn) to John Gordon, Admr. Card record. No papers
John, Md., Elizabeth, W125. He d. 11/20/1828
John, Md., Elizabeth Stuart/Stewart, former wid., W27527. Her 2nd husb., Alexander Stuart, also served in the Rev. John Thomas d. in 1799
John, Pvt., N.J., BLWt.8800 iss. 1/16/1800 to George Taylor, Jr., ass. Card record. No papers
John, N.J., R10501
John, Pvt., Lamb's Art., N.Y., BLWt.7895 iss. 4/9/1791 to James Wadsworth, ass. Card record. No papers
John/John F., N.Y., R10500
John, N.C., S42040
John, Pvt., Art. Artificer, Pa., BLWts.10479 & 13842 iss. 7/27/1789 to Richard Platt, ass. Card record. No papers
John, Pa., S22548
John, Pa., Va., Indian War 1791, R10503 1/2
John, Va., S3781, b. 1756 Halifax Co., Va.
John, Va., S16271; Sold. b. N.J., res. in 1832 Clermont Co., Ohio; 1837 in Shelby Co., Ind.
John, Va., S22014, res. 1832 in Spartanburgh Dist., S.C.
John, Va., S31416; wid. Sarah, res. in 1833 Owen Co., Ky.
John, Va., S46515; BLWt.1769-300 res. 1828 in Buckingham Co., Va.
John, Va., Catharine, W876; sold. res. in 1833 in Bledsoe Co., Tenn.
John, Va., Sarah/Sally, W6274; res. 1832 in Iredell Co., N.C.
John, Va., R10502; res. 1833 in Albemarle Co., Va.
John, Va., R10503; res. 1832 in Autauga Co., Ala.
John, Va., Rebecca/Mary, R10508 wid. res. 1855 in Macon Co., Mo.
John, Va. sea service, R100; Va.

THOMAS (continued)
Half Pay. He d. 1796; surviving ch. William Thomas, D.C., and Thomas Thomas, Alexandria, Va.
John G., Pvt., Va., Lee's Legion, BLWts.12603 & 13844 iss. 3/4/1796. Card record. No papers
John J., Md., S37488
Jonathan, Pvt., N.H., BLWt.3526 iss. 1/14/1799 to Eln'n Fitch, ass. Card record. No papers
Jonathan, N.H., S35655; res. 1818 in Freedom, Kennebec Co., Me.
Jonathan, N.H., S40574; res. 1820 in Newport Twp., Washington Co., Ohio
Jonathan, N.C., Patience, R10510
Joseph, Ct., Esther, W19452; BLWt.71188-160-55
Joseph, Cont., Mass., S33799; BLWt.2162-300-Capt. iss. 3/26/1792
Joseph, Cont., N.Y., Phebe, W2972
Joseph, Mass. See THOMES
Joseph, Mass., S28911
Joseph, Mass., S42472
Joseph, N.H., Temperance, W15958; BLWt.6294-160-55. He d. in 1825
Joseph, N.H., Huldah, W22406. He d. in 1796
Joseph, N.H., BLWt.1318-200. Iss. 5/22/1828. He d. in 1777
Joseph, N.C., S.C., Va., R10506
Joseph, Va., S38437
Joseph, Va., Rebecca, W6277
Joseph, Va., Mary, W9518
Joseph P., R.I., R10505
Joshua, Cont., Mass., Mary, W26532
Joshua, Mass., Isabella, W20091
Lewis, Va., S37489; BLWt.113-300
Luke, N.J., BLWt.1011-100
Lydia, Mass., former wid. of David Sanders, which see
Mark, Va., R18446; Va. Half Pay. See N.A. Acc. No. 874-050172 Half Pay, Mark Thomas
Massey, Va., Dicey, W8785
Matthew, N.J., Pvt., BLWt.8801 iss. 5/21/1791. No papers
Moses, Mass., S43997
Nathan/Nathaniel, Md., Margaret, R10507
Nathan, Mass., Sarah, W1955; BLWt.9404-160-55
Nathaniel, Mass., Jane, W1667
Nelson, Mass., S33197
Nicholas, R.I., S22017
Noah, Ct., Mary, W18129
Noah, Mass., Vt., S19124
Nothey/Notley, S.C., Temperance, W9517
Oliver, Mass., S42488
Owen, Pa., Va., S3785
Peleg, Mass., Betsey, W18135
Peleg, Mass., R10511
Peter, Pvt., Mass., discharge ctf. attesting to 6 yrs. service in 2nd Mass. Regt. signed by Geo. Washington, 6/10/1783. No other papers on file
Peter, Mass., Happy, W26526

THOMAS (continued)
Peter, Va., 1st Regt. Dragoons, Pvt., BLWt.12615 iss. 8/6/179-
Philemon, N.C., S31417
Philip, Mass., BLWt.2166-300-Capt. iss. 2/3/1792 to Nathan White, ass. No papers
Philip, N.C., Nancy, R10509
Polly, N.Y., former wid. of Walter Vrooman Wemple/Wimple, which see
Priscilla, Va., former wid. of James Lindsey, which see
Richard, Md. See Richard Thomas ATKINSON
Richard, Mass., Joanna, W15425
Richard, N.J., Mary, W11625
Richard, N.C., S14688
Robert, Cont., N.Y., S42479
Robert, Mass., Polly, W26527
Robert, Va., S1880
Rowan, S.C., S22015
Salmon, Mass., Naomi, W15424; BLWt.31727-160-55
Samuel, Ct., BLWt.6573. Iss. 4/15/1790. No papers
Samuel, Cont., Mass., S28909
Samuel, Mass., Phebe, W19451
Samuel, Mass., R10514
Samuel, N.C., S3783
Samuel, R.I., S11544
Seth, Mass., S6209
Seth, R.I., S42470
Simeon, Ct., Lucretia, W18131
Stephen, Ct., Ann, W25479
Stephen, N.C., S289
Thomas, Md., Wt.11758 iss. 1/11/1796 to Josh. Ward, ass.No papers
Thomas, N.J., S22550
Valentine, N.J., BLWt.8786 iss. 8/10/1795 to James Christie, ass. No papers
Valentine, N.J., Elizabeth, W4084
Willard, Mass., S33189
William, res. Brown Co., Ohio in 1855, R10543
William, Mass., fifer, BLWt.5175 iss. 3/25/1790. No papers
William, Mass., Mary, W19441
William, N.C., Elizabeth, S3780
William, N.C., S7711
William, N.C., Agnes, W6279; BLWt.26102-160-55
William, Pa., BLWt.10485 iss. 6/1/1791. No papers
William, R.I., BLWt.3531 iss. 12/31/1789. No papers
William, S.C., Aukey, R10517
William, Va., S3782
William, Va., S36827
William (colored), Va., S38435
Winslow, Mass., Polly, R10512
THOMASON, Byers, Va., Sarah, W6281
Ezekiel, Md., S35100
George, N.C., S7712
George, Va., Catharine, W1097
William, Va., R10518
THOMASSON, John, Va., S6216
John, Va., S7713
William P., N.C., Mary, W6280
THOMBS, Joseph, Mass. See THOMES
THOMES, Charles, Mass., S32013

THOMES (continued)
Joseph, Mass., S28910
Joseph, Mass. See THOMAS
THOMLEY, Thomas, S.C., R20438
THOMLINSON, Jabez, Ct., BLWt. 6593. Iss. 3/21/1791 to Ithamar Canfield, ass. No papers
THOMPSON, Aaron, N.J., S1123
Aaron, N.J., Alletta, W19450; BLWt.9444-160-55
Abel, Mass., Sarah, W15430
Abner, R.I., R10520
Abraham, Ct., S36341
Abraham, Ct., Dorcas B., R10521; BLWt.34599-160-55
Abraham, N.J., S40576
Absalom, N.C., S21533
Alexander, N.Y. res., Cont. & U.S. Army, Amelia, W18128; BLWt.2191-200-Lt. Iss. 5/19/1790. No papers
Alexander, Mass., S----
Alexander, Mass., Lydia, W22417; BLWt.12842-160-55
Alexander, N.Y., R22005
Alexander, Pa., Sarah, S32555; BLWt.31325-160-55
Alexander, Pa., Elizabeth, W3623; BLWt.31723-160-55
Alexander, Va., S14691
Alpheus, Mass., Bula, W16440
Amherst, Mass., S19122; BLWt. 7101-160-55
Amos, Ct., S22016
Anderson, Va., S17145
Andrew, Col. Spencer's Regt., BLWt.2189-200-Lt. Iss. 9/2/1790. No papers
Anthony, Pa., S30736
Asa, Ct. Troops, BLReg.106957
Asa, Cont., Ct., S11541
Asa, Mass., Nancy, W18127
Barabay/Bernard, Cont., Va., S46508; BLWt.1698-100. No papers
Bartholomew, N.C., Martha, W4085
Benjamin, Ga., S32016
Benjamin, Mass., S43996
Benjamin, Mass., Mary, W3738; BLWt.14974-160-55
Benjamin, Mass., Rhoda Johnson former wid., W26686; BLWt.2168-200-Lt. Iss. 5/10/1799 to Marlbry Turner, ass. No papers
Benjamin, Mass., N.H., S19123
Benjamin, N.H., Abigail, W26518
Benjamin, N.J., Melicent, W6269
Benjamin, N.Y., BLWt.7871 iss. 6/2/-- to Thomas Russell, ass.
Benjamin, S.C., See THOMSON
Benjamin, Va., Martha Wade, W1000; BLWt.34994-160-55
Bernard, See Baraby
Brothers, Va., BLWt.12611 iss. 10/22/1791 to Jacob Clingman, ass.
Burwell, N.C., S.C., S3801
Caleb, N.Y., R10526
Charles, N.C., Jemima, W11624; BLWt.26009-160-55
Charles, Va., Mary, W1514
Cornelius, Md., BLWt.11754. Iss.

THOMPSON (continued)
5/11/1790. No papers
Cornelius, Mass., S28908
Daniel, Ct., Dis. No papers
Daniel, Cont., N.Y., S42481
David, Ct., BLWt.6553 iss. 2/24/1795 to Eneas Munson, ass.
David, Ct., S35351
David, Ct., R10527
David, Mass., S35656
David, N.H., Rachel, W22405
David, Va., Elizabeth, R10529
Drewry, N.C., R10528
Drewry/Drury, N.C., Susan, R10640
Ebenezer, Mass., Mercy, W15960
Ebenezer, Pvt., Moylan's Dragoons Pa. line, BLWt.10513 iss. 5/26/1792
Ebenezer, Pa., Hannah, W15807
Edward, Hazen's Regt., BLWt.13823 iss. 3/26/179-
Electious, Md., S32017; his wid. Martha app. as former wid of Francis Holley, N.C., which see
Elias, N.Y., BLWt.7877 iss. 7/14/179- to John W. Watkins, ass.
Elijah, Mass., Keziah, W13984
Epaphras, Sheldon's Dragoons, Ct., BLWt.6587 iss. 1/25/1796 to Reuben Culver, ass.
Epaphras, Cont., Ct., S40566
Ephraim, Mass., S35657
Evan, S.C., Chloe, W2975
Flanders, Va., Elizabeth, W6272; BLWt.2418-100
Francis, Mass., S41245
Frederick, N.C., Frances, W11618; BLWt.28514-160-55
George, Ga., N.C., Jane, R10535
George, Mass., Sally, W22404
George, Pa., BLWt.10499 iss. 6/11/1795. No papers
George, Pa., BLWt.10524 iss. 3/8/1792 to Andrew Fox, ass. No papers
George, Va., S31418
Gideon, N.C., Nancy, R19424
Henry, Ct., S17727
Henry, N.H., BLWt.3522 iss. 4/5/1796 to Samuel Stone, ass.
Hudson, N.C. See THOMSON
Hugh, Ct., S23021
Hugh, Pa., BLWt.10489 iss. 5/18/179- to Isabella M. Clean, late Isabella Thompson, Excx.
Isaac, Cont., Pa., Jane, W4523
Isaac, N.C., S7724
Isaac, Va., R10531
Isaiah, Col. Lamb's Regt. Art., BLWt.2177-200-Capt. Lt. Iss. 7/14/1790. No papers
Jabez, N.J., Mary, W19439; BLWt. 28590-160-55
Jack, Mass., BLWt.5133 iss. 7/15/1797 to Symeon Wyman
Jacob, N.J., S4686
Jacob, Va., S41240
James, res. N.J. Dis.
James, Ct., S14681
James, Ct., N.H., S42487
James, Md., S32553

THOMPSON (continued)
James, Mass., S18243
James, N.H., S11543
James, N.H., S42486
James, N.H., Hannah, W18122
James, N.J., BLWt.8776 iss. 6/2/1797 to Abraham Bell, ass. No papers
James, N.Y., BLWt.7886 iss. 2/14/179-
James, N.Y., Elizabeth, W18125
James, N.C., S32014
James, Pa., BLWt.10508 iss. 3/4/1794 to Michael Stiver, ass. No papers
James, Pa., S6220
James, Pa., R10532 & 10533. Sold. b. Ireland
James, Pa., R10534
James, Pa., S40563, Indian War of 1794 & War of 1812
James, Va., BLWts.12605 & 13982 iss. 7/6/1793 to Francis Graves ass. No papers
James, Va., S3805
James, Va., S41247
Jarrel, N.C., S7722
Jedediah, N.Y., R10536
Jennings, Va., S7717
Jesse, Md., BLWt.11779 iss. 2/1/1790. No papers
Jesse, Md., S35097
Jesse, N.Y., S14678
Joanna, Mass., former wid. of Samuel Proctor, which see
Joel, Mass., S31423
Joel, N.Y., Amy, W2489; BLWt. 29029-160-55
John, Ct., S11534
John/Jonathan, Ct., W508; BLWt. 100290-160-55
John, Ct., Mabel, W3317
John, Ct., Ellis, W25480; BLWt. 26720-160-55
John, Cont., Mass., Jude, W19449
John, Cont., Pa., S7715
John, Pvt., "Invalids", BLWt. 13836-100. Iss. 4/7/1795 to John Nicholson, ass. No papers
John, Md., Elizabeth Jones, former wid., W26687; BLWt.1975-100. Her other husb. was pensioned, see claim of Jason Jones, Md.
John, Mass., BLWt.5129. Iss. 2/22/1792 to John Peck/Peek
John, Mass., S19814
John, Mass., S35654
John, alias Reuben Walton, Mass., which see
John, Mass., Betsey, W1901; BLWt. 9534-160-55
John, Mass., Jannet/Jennet Washburn former wid., W22540. She was wid. of Ephraim Walton, which see
John, Navy, S3796
John, Pvt., N.Y., BLWt.7873 iss. 2/14/179- to James Hamilton, ass. Card record. No papers
John, Pvt., N.Y., BLWt.7885 iss. 5/9/1792. Card record. No papers
John, N.Y., S29505

THOMPSON (continued)
John, N.Y., S40562
John, N.Y., S42476
John, N.Y., S42489
John, N.Y., Rhoda, W18138· BLWt. 7301-160-55
John, N.C., S21534, b. N.C.
John, N.C., Annis, R10524, b. Va.
John, N.C., R10541, heirs res. Wake Co., N.C. in 1855
John, N.C., Va., S41239
John, Pvt., Pa., BLWt.10495 iss. 7/9/1789. Card record. No papers
John, Sgt. Major, Pa., BLWt.10496 iss. 8/7/1789 to Richard Platt, ass. Card record. No papers
John, Pa., S3792
John, Pa., S6219
John, Pa., S23020
John, Pa., S40570
John, Pa., Christiana, W6268
John, S.C., b. Europe, S39104
John, Va., S6223
John, Va., S7716, res. Muskingum Co., Ohio in 1836
John, Va., S17144
John, Va., S31415
John, Va., S36826, res. Mercer Co., Ky. in 1819
John, Va., S36828
John, Va., S41238
John, Va., S41254
John, Va., Elizabeth, W1665; BLWt.13019-160-55
John, Va., Winney, W22418
John, Va., R10540
John, Va., R10544
John, Va., Sarah, R10553
Jonathan, Ct., Mary, see John THOMPSON
Jonathan, Cont., Mass., Lucy, S35653
Jonathan, Mass., Mary, W26529
Joseph, Ct., S42491; BLWt. 1705-100
Joseph, Ct., Ruby, W2488; BLWt. 26862-160-55
Joseph, Mass., BLWt.2139-450-Lt. Col. iss. 10/11/1791. Card record. No papers
Joseph, Mass. See Joseph M.
Joseph, Mass., S35649
Joseph, Mass., S40572
Joseph, Mass., Mary, W14010
Joseph, Mass., Olive, W26522; BLWts.5-60-55 & 5156-100-1789
Joseph, Mass., BLWt.49030-160-55
Joseph, N.H., Lydia, R10548
Joseph, Pa., BLWt.2204-300-Surgeon's Mate, iss. 2/14/1791 to Samuel Nicholson, ass. Card record. No papers
Joseph, Pa., Margaret Snyder, former wid., R9924
Joseph, Va., Harmar's Indian War Susannah, W9853; BLWt.93585-160-55
Joseph M/Joseph, Mass., S20560
Joshua, Ct., Hannah, W22400
Joshua, Cont., N.H., S43995; BLWt.2130-200-Lt. iss. 9/11/1795 to William Thompson, ass.

THOMPSON (continued)
Card record. No papers
Joshua, N.Y., S42477
Lambert, Md., S40569
Lawrence, N.C., S32554
Lawrence, N.C., Keziah, R10546
Loring, Cont., N.H., enl. 1776 in Mass., S41250
Matthew, Cont., Ct., Sea Service Betsey, W25478; BLWt.3140-160-55
Moses, Pvt., Mass., BLWt.5154 iss. 9/13/1792
Moses, Cont., Mass., N.H., S42471
Nathan, Ct., Betty Warner, former wid., W22519
Nathan, Cont., Mass., S14682
Nathan, Mass., S20559
Nathaniel, Cont., Ct., S41241
Nehemiah, Ct., Esther, W827; BLWt.33531-160-55
Nicholas, N.C., Elizabeth, R10530
Peter, N.H., S6214
Price, N.J., Martha, W2273; BLWt. 49-60-55 & 8788-100-Corp., iss. 7/31/1789
Rachel, Pa., former wid. of Ephraim Foster, which see
Ralph, Cont., Mass., S14674
Reuben, Mass., S11540
Richard, Mass., S35658
Richard, Mass., S35659
Robert, Cont., Mass., Hannah, W22398
Robert, Del., S37486
Robert, Pvt., Mass., BLWt.5159 iss. 2/13/1795 to Abner Stow. Card record. No papers
Robert, Mass., S42484
Robert, N.J., S42480; BLWt.2500-100
Robert, N.C., Ursilla, R10551
Robert, Pa., S3800 (includes final payment voucher)
Robert, Va., S6221
Robert, Va., S38441
Roger, Va., R10552
Samuel, Ct., S11537
Samuel, Ct., S43998
Samuel, Ct., Hannah Waldo former wid., W18298
Samuel, Mass., S14680; BLWt.26183-160-55
Samuel, Mass., S42475
Samuel, Mass., Sea Service, Mary, W22408
Samuel, Mass., Privateer, Jane, W14006
Samuel, N.H., BLWt.3530 iss. 10/30/1789 to Ephraim -----, ass. No papers
Samuel, N.H., Dorcas, W19442
Samuel, N.C., Elizabeth, W4605
Samuel, N.C., Va., S3798
Samuel, S.C., S31420
Samuel, Va., Lee's Legion, BLWts. 12604 & 13980 iss. 7/6/1793 to Francis Graves, ass. No papers
Seth, N.C., Judith, R10554
Shadrach, Mass., Martha, W26520
Shearod/Sherrod, Va., S32012. See N.A. Acc. No.874-050173, not Half Pay, Sherod Thompson

THOMPSON (continued)
Sherod, Va. See Shearod
Sherrod, Va. See Shearod
Smith, Va., S38438
Standley/Stanley, N.Y., Susannah, W16441
Stanley, N.Y., BLWt.7866 iss. 11/9/1791 to Burnett Miller, ass. No papers
Stephen, Ct., BLWt.6582 iss. 2/21/1792. No papers
Stephen, Ct., S42478
Stephen, Ct., Abigail, R10519
Stephen, Mass., BLWt.16143-160-55
Stephen, S.C., S1595
Thaddeus, Mass., S3807; BLWt. 2141-400-Surgn. Iss. 7/22/1789
Thadeus, N.Y., Lamb's Art., BLWt. 7896 iss. 12/24/1790. No papers
Theodore, Mass., Elizabeth, BLWt. 49028-160-55
Thomas, Ct., Lydia, W19453
Thomas, Ct., Lucy, R10547
Thomas, Cont., N.Y., BLWt.203-200
Thomas, Cont., Va., S36340
Thomas, Del., BLWt.10891 iss. 5/24/179-. No papers
Thomas, Mass., S7725
Thomas, Mass., S33191
Thomas, Mass., Ruhama, W4830
Thomas, Mass., R10555
Thomas, Mass., N.Y., S14692
Thomas, Mass., N.Y., S14693
Thomas, N.J., R10557
Thomas, N.C., S6215
Thomas, N.C., Va., S3803
Thomas, Pa., R10556
Thomas, Pa., BLWt.1482-200
Thomas, Va., S6222
Thomas, Va., S38432
Timothy, Mass., Mary, W15426
William, Ct., Thankful B., W2275; BLWt.1530-100
William, Cont., Elizabeth, W8787; BLWt.1610-100, res. Ky. in 1829
William, Cont., Mass., S30162
William, Ga., N.C., S.C., R10560
William, Md., S30735
William, Pvt., Mass., BLWt.5158 iss. 5/1/1792 to David Quinton. Card record. No papers
William, Mass., S35660
William, Mass., Rebecca, See TOMPSON
William, Mass., Deborah, W22396
William, Mass., N.H., Dorcas, W18132
William, N.J., S1260
William, N.J., S7720
William, N.J., Margaret, W16758
William, Pvt., N.Y., BLWt.7892 iss. 4/2/179- to John Peck, ass.
William, N.Y., S14677
William, N.Y., R10559
William, N.Y., R21794
William, N.C., S6217
William/Wiliam, N.C., S30731
William, Pa., BLWt.2202-200-Lt. Iss. 4/7/1795 to John Nicholson, ass. Card record. No papers
William, R.I., R20269

THOMPSON (continued)
William, S.C., Mary, W1001; BLWt.5209-160-55
William, S.C., R10561
William, S.C., BLWt.2506-500
William, S.C., Mary, BLWt.51760-160-55
William, Va., S17729
William, Va., R10562
William, Va., R10563; res. in 1833 Campbell Co., Ky.
William, Va., R10564
William, Va., R18477, Va. Half Pay His. wid. Polly, m. Wm. Terry
William Russell, S.C., Elizabeth, W22394
Zebulon, Ct., Lucy, W18134
THOMS, Samuel, Mass., also French & Indian Wars, S35652; BLWt.2165-300 Capt. Iss. 4/12/1790. No papers
William, Mass., Lydia, W4355; BLWt.17732-160-55
THOMSON, Amos, Mass., S14687
Benjamin, S.C., S32551
Edward, Ct., S14683
Gideon, N.C., Nancy, R19424
Hudson, N.C., b. N.C., S1729
James, Ct., S17731
James, Mass., S30158
James, N.Y., S42490
James, N.C., b. N.C., S7718
Job, N.H., S3797
John, Cont., Ct., Pamelia, W26472
John, Va., S40575
John, Va., R10542
Joseph, Ct., S23022
Josiah, Mass., S33791
Moses, Ct., S11177
Moses, Mass., S30161; BLWt.9427-160-55
Nathaniel, Ct., S14695
Rodes/Rhodes, Va., S30737
Rufus, Ct., Salley, W3621
Samuel, Cont., Ct., S35352
Samuel, Mass., Navy, S6218
Thaddeus, Cont., N.Y., Rhoda Augusta, dau., W29931
Thomas, N.Y., Ruhama, W3622; BLWt.13747-160-55. D. 3/14/1848
William, S.C. See THOMPSON
Zebadiah, Mass., S33792
THOMY, Morton, Pa., BLWt.10509. Iss. 3/11/179 . No papers
THORBER, Squire/Squier. See THURBER
THORINTON, Michael, Mass., Sally Munn, former wid., W4748; BLWt.1967-160-55
THORLA, Thomas, Mass., S3790
THORN, George, Pa., Christina, R10565
Henry, R.I., S33798
James, N.H., Nabby/Abigail, W16438
Michael, Va., S16272
Prestley/Presley/Priestley, N.C. R20519
Priestley, N.C. See Prestley
Richard, Va., BLWt.12607 iss. 7/20/1792 to Robert Means, ass. No papers
Samuel/William Samuel, N.Y.,

THORN (continued)
Esther Lefferts former wid., W16326
Samuel, N.Y., Helen/Helena, W18123
Thomas, N.Y., R10568
THORNBURY, Francis, Pa., BLWt.2201-200-Lt. Iss. 3/30/1796 to John Ross, ass.
THORNDIKE, Hezekiah, Mass., Abigail W15432
Joshua, Cont., res. in 1818, Mass. Hannah, W22419
Robert, Mass., Sea Service, S32011
THORNDYKE, Peter, Mass., S14671
THORNE, Daniel, Cont., N.Y., Sarah, BLWt.638-100
Richard, N.J., Margaret, W826
Richard, N.Y., Sarah, W15808
THORNHILL, Henry, Va., S32557
Jesse, Va., S14679
Reuben, Va., S3794
Thomas, Va., BLWt.12609 iss. 7/7/1792 to Robert Means, ass. No papers
Thomas, Va., S46518
William, Va., S14673
William, Va., S15674
THORNING, William, Mass., Eunice, W20090
THORNTON, Borden/Burden, R.I., S22012
Daniel, Ct., BLWt.6567 iss. 2/3/1794. No papers
Elisha, Ct., S14676
Ephraim, R.I., Alice Spencer, former wid., W19080
Frances, former wid. of William Chesterman, Va., which see
George, Va., S7709
James, N.Y., BLWt.7883 iss. 4/9/179-
James, N.Y., Antie/Antia, W18137
James, Va., S41253
John, Cont., Md., S35101
John, N.Y., Ann, W20085
John, Pa., BLWt.10518 iss. 7/24/1792. No papers
John, Va., BLWt.1870-450
Joshua, Mass., N.H., Sarah C., W825; BLWt.31327-160-55
Josiah, S.C., R10570
Michael/Michel, Mass., S35650
Michael, Mass., Sally Munn, former wid. See THORINTON
Patrick, Va., BLWt.12599. Iss. 8/20/1791. No papers
Presley, Va., S3809
Presley, Va., BLWt.553-300
Samuel, N.C., R10571
Stephen, R.I., S21531
Stephen, R.I., Zilpha, W6262; BLWt.16263-160-55
Thomas, Mass., S33790
Thomas, N.Y., Olive, R18456
William, N.Y., BLWt.7891 iss. 5/3/1791 to James Palmer, ass. No papers
William, Cont., N.Y., Mary, W20089
William, Cont., Va., Frances, W6260; BLWt.602-100. See her claim as former wid. of

THORNTON (continued)
William Chesterman, Va.
THOROWGOOD, Lemuel, Va., Sarah Ingram, former wid., R5486
THORP, Amos, Ct., Naomi, R10573
Amos, Ct., BLWt.382-100
Augustus/Eliphalet/Jacob, Cont. Mass., Mary, R10572; BLWt. 2148-300-Capt. Iss. 1/29/1790 under name Eliphalet Thorp
Charles, Va., See THARP
Daniel, Ct., S23023
David, Ct., Elizabeth, W15427
Eliphalet, see Augustus
Ezekiel, Ct., S36339
Ezra, Cont., Ct., S11545
Jacob, See Augustus
James, Ct., Lydia, W26525
John, Cont., N.J., Hannah, W4354; BLWt.1887-200
Joseph, Ct., S6237
Joseph, Ct., Lucy, W15423; BLWt.26419-160-55
Nathan, Ct., Huldah, W6259
Paul, Pa. See THARP
Perry, Pa., S22551
Peter, Ct., S11535
Reuben, N.J., S6229
Reuben, R.I., S39865
Thaddeus, Ct., S15673
Thomas, Cont., Mass., Lucy, W8783; BLWts.1008-100, 92-60-55, and 5169-100-1799
Thomas, Mass., S35647
Thomas, N.Y., BLWt.7897 iss. 10/27/1791. No papers
THRALL, Jesse, Mass., R10574
Lemmy, Ct., R10575
William, Ct., S43198
THRALLS, Richard, Va., S6240
THRASH, Volintine/Valentine, N.C. Barbara, W1332; BLWt.54232-160-55
THRASHER, Aaron, R.I., S31422
Bezaleel/Bazaleel, Ct., Elizabeth, W2372; BLWt.26224-160-55
Charles, Mass., S33789
Daniel, Mass., S30734
George, Mass., Cont., S15675
George, Ga., Saluda, W2373; BLWt. 9424-160-55
George, Mass., S11546
John/Jonathan, Mass., S43197
John, Mass., Bethana/Bethany, W22399
Jonathan, Mass. See John
Joseph, R.I., Pvt., BLWt.3535-100 iss. 5/28/1792 to Israel Angell, ass. No papers
Josiah, Pa., R10578
Seth, Mass., Abiah, R10577
THRAUL, William, Pvt., Ct., BLWt. 6572. Iss. 11/10/1792. No papers
THREADGILL, John, Va., Mary, W18126
Thomas, Ga., Va., S46345; BLWt. 2054-300
THREESHERE, Joseph, R.I., S33185
THRESHER, Ebenezer, Ct., Hannah, W18124
Joseph, R.I., see THREESHERE
THRIFT, John, N.C., b. Va., Elizabeth, W9516
THROCKMORTON, Albion, Va., BLWt.

THROCKMORTON (continued)
2223-200-Lt. Iss. 7/5/1794 to Robert Means, ass. No papers
Holmes, N.J., Cont., S33795
James, N.J., S763
James, N.J., Ctf. 1845
Job, N.J., S764
Job, N.J., Mary, W6256
Joseph, N.J., S14689
Richard, Va., S6212
THROOP, Benjamin, Ct., S42492; BLWt.2170-400-Maj. Iss. 1/28/1790. No papers
Dan, Ct., Mary, W20088
John R., Col. Lamb's Regt., Art. BLWt.2178-200-Lt. Iss. 10/23/1790. No papers
William, N.J., Nancy, See TROOP
THROPP, Benjamin, Ct. See THROOP
THROPTO, Andrew, Pvt., Pa., BLWt.10526. Iss. 10/8/1792 to Paul Lebo, Admr.
THROWER, Benjamin, N.C., Sarah, W6266
THRUSH, Jacob, Pa., S40571
THRUSTON, Benjamin, Pvt., N.J., BLWt.8809 iss. 1/26/1790 to James Bonney, Admr.
Charles Mynn, Dis. No papers. Va. See Heitman, Mayo, and Moulton Pension Laws, under Act of March 3, 1807.
John, Va., R18489, Va. Half Pay
Robert, Va., R18488, Va. Half Pay
THUM, Peter, Cont., Catharine, W6257, m. 1785 in Berks County, Pa.
THUMB, John, Pa., BLWt.2179-150-Ens. Iss. 10/13/1794 to Mary Thumb, admx., also recorded as above under BLWt.2645. No papers
Peter, Pvt., Von Heer's Corps, BLWt.13810 iss. 12/20/179- (torn) to Henry Shoemaker, ass. Card record. No papers
THURBER, Amos, R.I., Mariah, R10581
Benjamin, Mass., Mary Ann, W2274; BLWt.11052-160-55
Bethiah, Mass., former wid. of Samuel Shorey, which see
Darius, R.I., S39864
Francis, N.H., R10580
John, Mass., S21529
Joseph, N.H., Vt., Sarah K., W16439
Nathaniel, Mass., S17730
Samuel, Ct., R.I., S22018
Samuel, R.I., d. 9/11/1832, Elizabeth, W10579
Squier/Squire, R.I., Catharine, W1666; BLWt.26072-160-55
THURLEY, Jonathan, Mass. See THURRELL
THURLO, Asa, Mass., Abigail, W22416
James, Cont., Mass., Elizabeth, W22395
John, Mass., S35661
Joseph, Mass., S29502
THURMAN, Baze, Va., R10583, res. Ky. in 1835
Charles, Va., S31414

THURMAN (continued)
Charles, Va., Barbara, R10582
John, Ga., Deborah, W6267; BLWt. 27565-160-55
John, Va., Nancy, W28009
Philip, S.C., Kesiah, R10584
William, Va., S37487
William, Va., Mary, W169; BLWt. 26953-160-55
THURMOND, David H., Ga., S32010
John, Va., R10585
William, Va., BLWt.1996-100-Ctf. 894, Act of May 15, 1828
THURRELL, Jonathan, Mass., Betty, W26519
THURSTON, Amy, Mass., Elisha Rugg, former wid., W26530. Card record. No papers. Silas written in pencil on card.
Daniel, N.Y., Charlotte, W22410
Daniel, R.I., Privateer, R10586
David, N.J., S23971
Jacob, Cont., Mass., Anna B. Piper, former wid., W10899; BLWt.103980-160-55
Jason, N.Y., S32556
John, Mass., S31424
John, N.H., Else, R10587
John, R.I., S21532
Michael, Pvt. in Proctor's Art., Pa. line, BLWt.10516 iss. 6/20/1789. No papers
Stephen, Mass., R10588
Stephen, Mass., Dolly, BLWt.53755-160-55
Thomas, R.I., S21530
Thomas, S.C., Pvt., BLWts.12633 & 13812 iss. 6/24/1795. Card record No papers
THWEATT, Thomas, Va., S7708; BLWt.2326-300
THWING, James, Ct., S22553
John, Mass., Chloe, W20053
Nicholas, Mass., S30732
TIBBALS, Samuel, Ct., Miriam, W6285
Stephen, Ct., Cont., S11559
Thomas, Ct., Elue (nee Parker), W25482
TIBBEN, Henry, Pa., Mary, R10589
TIBBENS, Henry, Pvt., Hazen's Regt., BLWt.13822 iss. 6/1/1792 to Andrew Bamer, ass. Card record. No papers
TIBBETS, Abner, Mass., R10590
Edmund, N.H., Margery, W22422
Ephraim, N.H., See TEBBITS
George, Mass., R10592
Giles, Mass., S35662
Ichabod, Mass., S18627
James, N.H. Sea Service, S18249
Jedediah, N.H., Dorothy, BLWt. 67607-160-55
John, R.I., S35666
Nathaniel, Mass. See TEBBETS
Simeon, Mass., N.H., Navy, Abigail, W2272; BLWt.10027-160-55
TIBBETTS, Anna, Mass., former wid. of John Johnson, which see
Ephraim, Mass., See TEBBETTS
Isaac, Pvt., Mass., BLWt.5164, iss. 4/25/1798 to Daniel Gookin

TIBBETTS (continued)
Card record. No papers
Isaac, Mass., S40579
Robert, N.H., See TIBBITTS
Samuel, Cont., Mass. See TEBBETS
Stephen, Mass., S35665
William, N.H., Alice, W22421
TIBBITS, Abner, Cont., Ct., S14698
Daniel, Mass., R10591
John, N.H., Margaret, W16442
TIBBITTS, Henry, N.H., Sarah, R10593
Isaac, Mass. See TIBBETTS
Robert, N.H., Tryphena, W16156
Waterman, R.I., S21535
TIBBLES, Thomas, Ct. See TIBBALS
TIBBS, John, Va., BLWt.2477-200-Lt.iss. 7/5/1799 to James Taylor, ass. of Willoughby Tibbs the surviving brother and heir. General Land Office reported that Wt.2417 was patented. In Heitman's Hist. Reg. this man is given as Tebbs. No papers
Joseph, Va., R10594, b. 1/10/1765 Cecil Co., Md., served 1786, 1787 and 1794
Willoughby, Va., Betsey, See TEBBS
TIBETS, Stephen, Mass. See TIBBETTS
TIBO, Michael, Pvt., Hazen's Regt. BLWt.13818 iss. 1/22/1790 to Benj. Mooers, ass. Card record. No papers
TICE, Elias, N.J., Sarah, W6283; BLWt.82539-160-55
Elijah, N.J., Pvt., BLWt.8778 iss. 5/26/1790. Card record. No papers
Henry, N.Y., Huldah, W2705
Jacob, N.J., Ann, W18141
John, N.J., S10035
John, Pvt., N.Y., BLWt.7865 iss. 7/30/1791 to Resolve Waldron, ass. Card record. No papers
John, N.Y., S42500
Joseph, N.Y., Jemima, R10595
Richard, N.J., Privateer, S28912
William, N.H., Ruth, W26534
TICHANAL, David, Va., S7727
TICHENOR, Caleb, N.J., S1127
David, N.J., S3816
Isaac, Cont. service, Vt. res., S22554
Isaac, N.J., S1126
John, N.J. agcy., Invalid pension No papers. Sold. d. 7/27/1810 on List of pensioners reported by Secretary of War in 1835
Joseph, N.J., S1124
Joseph, N.J. See TITCHENOR
Zenas, N.J., Electa, W15961
TICKER, Jared, Pvt., Ct., BLWt. 6543 iss. 12/24/1796. Card record. No papers
TICKNER, Joseph, N.Y., S11557
TIDD, Daniel, Cont., Mass., Anna Chapin, former wid., W23795; BLWt.18003-160-55
Jesse, N.Y., R10599
John, Mass., Abigail, W19455
Jonathan, Mass., S29506
Oliver, Pvt., Crane's Cont. Art.,

TIDD (continued)
Mass., Wt.5179 iss. 8/10/1789 to R. Platt. Card record. No papers
Oliver, Mass., S41257
William, N.J., Pa., Ann, R10598, also served in French & Indian Wars.
TIEBOUT, George, N.Y., Margaret, W20092; BLWt.11084-160-55
Henry, N.Y., BLWt.2183-300-Capt. Iss. 7/22/1790. Card record. No papers
TIERS, Margaret, former wid. of Alexander Leitch Miller, which see
TIFF, Major, Pvt., Ct., BLWt.6588 iss. 3/22/1792. Card record. No papers
Major, Ct., S35354
TIFFANY, Amasa, Ct., Sarah, W15433; BLWt.26603-160-55
Asa, Ct., S17733
Ebenezer, R.I., Mary Ann, R10601
Eleazer, Mass., S30742
Hezekiah, Mass., Betsey, W4833; BLWt.35684-160-55
Hosea, Mass., Anna, W4834
Isaiah, Ct., BLWt.2175-200-Lt. Iss. 8/22/1789. Card record. No papers
Joel, Cont., Mass., S14699
John, Cont., Mass., Ruthey, W16445
Joseph, Mass., S17732
Nathaniel, Ct., S16005
Philemon, Ct., S42498
Simon, Cont., Ct., S11554
Thomas, Cont., Mass., Privateer, S14696
Timothy, Ct., S17149
Walter, Cont., Ct., Osee (nee Dunn), W2976; BLWt.78-60-55 (enl. Hebron, Ct. & later in Boston, lived 1819 in Williamson Co., Tenn.; 1825 in Ky.)
Walter, Cont., Ct., Sally/Sarah Durkel, former wid., W19205; BLWt.2169-100
William, Ct., S7728
Zachariah, Mass., Susannah, W16443
TIFFIN, Thomas, N.C., S38444
TIFFNEY, Benjamin, Mass. See TIFNEY
TIFFT, Caleb, R.I. See TIFT
Robert, R.I., Bridget Coon, former wid., W3514
Rufus, N.Y., S11552
TIFNEY, Benjamin, Mass., Elizabeth, W19456
TIFT, Caleb, R.I., Eleanor, W2458, BLWt.7211-160-55
John, Ct., S23455
Solomon, R.I., S14703
TIGNOR, Isaac, Va., R10602
Thomas, Va., R10603
TILBRY, Peter, N.J., S15237
TILDEN, Charles, Green Mt. Boys, N.H. res., Dis. No papers. On list for appl. for invalid pension from N.H. on 2/28/1795, res. Lebanon, N.H.
Daniel, Ct., Cont., S4683
Ebenezer, Ct., Elizabeth, W25486

TILDEN (continued)
Elisha, Ct., Cont., S33202
Ezra, Mass., Sarah, W14020
Isaiah, Mass., S14704
Job, Mass., Lydia, W15434
John Bell, Pa., S42497, res. 1828 in Frederick Co., Va., BLWt.2200-300-Lt. Iss. 10/10/1796 to John B. Tilden. No papers
Joshua, Ct., S36342
Josiah, N.H., Vt., S11555
Nathaniel, Cont., Mass., S33201
Nathaniel, Mass., Sarah, W26538
Stephen, Ct., Dorothy, W26537
Stephen, Vt., Elizabeth, W1956; BLWt.8013-160-55
Wales, Mass., S30164
William, Mass., Lucy, R10604
TILESTON, Cornelius, Cont., Mass., S6250
TILFORD, William, Va., S16553
TILGHMAN, Tench, Cont., Md., Anna Maria, W9522; BLWt.1158-450
TILL, Peter, N.J., S33803
TILLARD, Edward, Md., BLWt.2207-450-Lt. Col. Iss. 3/4/1800. Card record. No papers
TILLER, William, Cont., Va., S38443
TILLETSON, Simeon, Cont., Ct., S36343
TILLETT, Mary, Md., former wid. of William Jones, which see
TILLEY, Bennet, N.C., S17151
Edmund, N.C., S7732
Henry, N.C., b. Va., S7731
James, Md., S33805
James, Mass., Privateer, S19819
John, N.C., Sally, W4832
Lazarus, N.C., Elizabeth, W6290; BLWt.9524-160-55
Peter, N.J. See TILBRY
Samuel, Sgt., Mass., BLWt.5163 iss. 8/22/1789. Card record. No papers
Samuel, Mass., Hannah, W22426
TILLIEN, Henry, Pvt., Pa. res. Dis. No papers. On list of applicants for invalid pension returned by the Dist Court for Dist. of Pa., submitted to the House of Repr. by the Sec. of War on 4/25/1794 & printed in Am. State Papers, Class 9, p. 100. Capt. O'Hara's independent company.
TILLING, Henry, N.C. See TILLEY
TILLINGHAST, Charles, Cont., N.Y., Catharine, W16444
Daniel, R.I., S11551
Philip, R.I., Frances, W26539
Samuel, R.I., Martha, W22427
TILLISON, Simeon, Ct. See TILLETSON
TILLMAN, Richard, N.Y., Navy, S11178
Tobias, N.C., S6247
TILLOTSON, Abraham, Ct., Cont., Abigail, W22424
Asahel, Ct., S43999
Ashbel, Ct., S1158
Daniel, Ct., S14705

TILLOTSON (continued)
Elias, Ct., Cont., Experience, W18142
George, Ct., Sila, W25489; BLWt. 31729-160-55
Isaac, Ct., Sarah, W1002; BLWt. 40929-160-55
Jacob, Ct., Lovena/Lovina, W25490
Nathan, N.Y., See TELLOTSON
Simeon, Ct. See TILLETSON
Thomas, Cont., res. N.Y., S42495; BLWt.2239-450-Surgn. & Physician of Gen. Hosp. & Md. Line, iss. 10/20/1791 and certified 8/24/1830. No papers
TILLSON, Elisha, Mass., Polly, R10608
Ichabod, Cont., Mass., S33204
Joseph, Mass., See TILSON
William, N.H., S16003
TILLY, Franka, Va., former wid. of Daniel Isbell, which see
TILOTSON, Abraham, Ct., Cont., See TILLOTSON
TILSON, Ephraim, Mass., S6248
Ichabod, Mass. See TILLSON
James, Mass., S6246
Job, N.Y., Hester, W11634; BLWt.13420-160-55
John, Cont., Mass., S33802
Joseph, Mass., Lucinda, W1670
Timothy, N.Y., Sarah, W22430
TILTON, Abigail S., former wid. of Benjamin Stevens, N.H., which see
Daniel, N.H., S18248
Green, N.H., Judith, W26970
Jacob, N.H., S43200
James, BLWt.2238-450, Surgn. & Physician, iss. 5/30/1789. No papers
Jeremiah, N.H., Mehitable, R10611
John, N.J., S581
John, N.J., S765
John, N.J., S16273
John, N.J., Marium/Marian, R10610
John B., N.H., S7733
Joseph, Mass., S19820
Joseph, Sgt., N.J., BLWt.8792 iss. 7/16/1789 to Jonathan Dayton, ass. No papers
Joseph, N.J., S42494
Philip, Cont., N.H., S18250
Salathiel, Mass., Sea Service, R10612
Samuel, N.H., Sally, W14021
Sylvester, N.J., Dis. Am. State Papers, Class 9, res. Stafford Twp., Monmouth Co., p. 121
Timothy, N.H., Sarah, W16080
William, Cont., Mass., Navy, S33801
William, N.H., R10613
TILYON, John, N.J., N.Y. See TILYOU
TILYOU, John, N.J., N.Y., S6251
Peter V., N.J., N.Y., Sarah, W25481; BLWt.34929-160-55
TIMBERLAKE, Francis, N.C., Mary, W19454
John, Va., S37490
Joseph, Cont., Va., S37491;

TIMBERLAKE (continued)
BLWt.2119-100
TIMERMAN, Jacob, N.Y., Magdalena
See ZIMERMAN
John, N.Y., R21795
TIMETT, John Peter, N.Y., Elizabeth, W6289
TIMMERMAN, Henry, N.Y. Agcy., Dis. Report of Sec. of War, 1835, Ensign d. 5/18/1807
Henry, N.Y., Pvt., S14701, res. Jefferson Co., N.Y. in 1821
Henry, S.C., S18247
TIMMONS, George, Ga., Va., S6242, b. S.C., res. 1832 in Dinwiddie Co., Va.
George, Va., S11553, b. Frederick Co., Va., res. 1832 Hopkins Co., Ky.
Joshua, Del., Celia Hancock, former wid., W4483; BLWt.1966-100
Robert, Del., Pvt., BLWt.10897 iss. 9/2/17-- (torn). Card record No papers
Robert, Del., S40580
TIMMS, Absalom, N.J., S40581
Joseph, Md., S36345
TIMPSON, Samuel, Va., R18502, Va. Half Pay
TIMS, Absalom, Pvt., N.J., BLWt. 8804 iss. 6/11/1789 to Mathias Denmon, ass. Card record. No papers
TIMSON, Robert, Mass., S41256
TINAN, Joseph, Mass., S35664
TINCH, James, Va., S6244
TINCKEY, Jacob, N.Y., See TINKEY
TINCUM, Hezekiah, Mass. See TINKHAM
TINDAL, James, N.C., R3546, b. N.C.
TINDALL, John, N.J., Mary L., W11635; BLWt.40905-160-55
William, N.J., Elizabeth, W6288
William, N.J., Hannah, R10614
TINDER, James, Va., S14707
TINDLE, William, N.J. See TINDALL
TINDY, Cuff, Mass. (colored), S33804; res. 1818 in Lancaster, Worcester Co., Mass.
TINER, Joshua, Ga., S32561
TINEY, Moses, Mass., SEE TINNEY
TINGLEY, Ebenezer, N.J., S3815
Lemuel, N.J., Martha, W4831
Samuel, Mass., Amey, W1669; BLWt. 17561-160-55
TINKEE, Conrad, N.J., S6249
TINKER, Absalom, Ct., Mary, W18139
Amos, Pvt., Ct., BLWt.6561 iss. 4/11/1792 to Jonas Prentice, ass. Card record.
Amos, Ct., Hannah, W3624; res. 1818 in Waterbury, New Haven Co., Ct.
Amos, Ct., Mary, W26535; res. of wid. in 1843, Stonington, New London Co., Ct.
Benjamin, Ct., Lucy, W25483
Ezekiel, Ct., Elizabeth Gardiner former wid., R3902
John, Ct., S6245
Nathan, Ct., Privateer, S17413
Polly, Ct., Cont., Navy, former wid. of Samuel Beckwith, which

TINKER (continued)
see
Samuel, Ct., Sally, W4606; BLWt. 33762-160-55
Silas, Ct., R10615
William, Ct., Elizabeth, W25488
TINKEY, Conrad, N.J. See TINKEE
Jacob, N.Y. See TINCKEY
TINKHAM, Ebenezer, Navy, Dis., N.H. res. in 1794, Am. State Papers, Class 9, p.160
Ephraim, Mass., Elizabeth, W14024
Hezekiah, Mass., S41258; BLWt. 954-100
Isaiah, Mass., Susanna, W26536
John, Mass., S35663
Joseph, Mass., Molly, W18140
Levi, Pvt., Mass., BLWt.5132 iss. 3/25/1790. Card record. No papers
Molly, Mass., former wid. of Samuel Wood, which see
Nathan, Mass., Abigail, W16759
Seth, Mass., S22556
TINKUM, Joseph, Mass. See TINKHAM
TINNEN, James, N.C., b. N.C., S3814; res. 1833 in Giles Co., Tenn.
Robert, N.C., b. N.C., S7734; res. 1832 in Orange Co., N.C.
TINNEY, John, Pvt., Va., BLWt. 12598 iss. 2/28/1800. Card record. No papers
John, Va., Jane, W9521
Moses, Mass., Lucy, W22425
TINOR, Joshua, Ga. See TINER
TINSLEY, Cornelius, Va., S3361
Golding, S.C., Va., b. Va., S18246
James, S.C., b. Va., S31426
John, Va., S1951; res. 1832 in Sumner Co., Tenn., d. 11/30/1839
John, Va., S17150; res. 1834 in Henrico Co., Va.
Nathaniel, Va., Lucy, W6291
Samuel, Va., S6243, Va. Half Pay N.A. Acc. No. 874-050174. Half Pay Samuel Tinsley
William, Va., S41255, wid. Delilah res. 1837 in Richmond, Va.
William, Va., Sarah, W8789; BLWt. 53745-160-55
TINTLE, John Peter, N.Y. See TIMETT
TINUM, Hezekiah, Mass. See TINKHAM
TIPPER, Charles, Pa., Mary, W2883
William, N.C., S39109; res. 1823 in Bedford Co., West Tenn.
TIPPET, Notley, Pvt., Md., BLWt. 1770 iss. 2/1/1790 to Ann Tootle, Admx., James Williams & Joseph Dawson, Admrs. of James Tootle, dec'd., late ass. Card record. No papers
TIPPETT, Erastus, N.C., S39108; res. Lawrence Co., West Tenn. in 1820
TIPPIE, Uriah, Pa., Susannah, W25487; BLWt.6034-160-55
TIPPONG, Conrad, N.C., b. Pa., S7729

TIPPS, Jacob, N.C., b. Pa., Margaret, R10616
TIPSONARD, Griffin, N.C. See TIPSOWARD
TIPSOWARD, Griffin, N.C., R10617; res. Coles Co., Ill. in 1835
TIPTON, Abraham, Va., R18512, Va. Half Pay
Jonathan, Md., S3811
Jonathan, N.C., b. Va., Lavina, W1098; BLWt.36523-160-55
Jonathan, N.C., R10618, d. Marshall Co., Ala., 9/4/1848
Luke, Pa., b. Md., S3812, BLWt. 26150-160-55
Thomas, Va., b. Md., S16274
William, Md., R10620, also in 1773; res. 1834 in Fayette Co., Pa.
William, Va., S295; res. Knox Co., Tenn. in 1823
William, Va., b. Md., S14700; res. 1832 in Montgomery Co., Ky., applied as William Tipton, Sr.
TIRELL, Thomas, Mass., Susannah, See TIRRELL
TIRRELL, Benjamin, Mass., S30740
Samuel, Ct., S17148
Thomas, Mass., Susannah, W27493
TIRRILL, Amos, Mass. See TERRILL
Thomas, Mass., S30163
TISDALE, Barnabas, Ct., N.H., S22555
Cudbud, Va., S16554
George, Cont., Mass., S42499
James, Cont., Mass., S33806; BLWt.2145-300-Capt. Iss. 4/1/1790
Joseph, R.I., S21536
TISE, Peter, N.J., S926
TISO, John, N.J., N.Y., S1125
TISON, James, N.C., S38442
TICHENOR, Joseph, N.J., S30741
TITCOMB, Benjamin, N.H., BLWt. 2129-450-Lt. Col., iss. 12/31/1799 to Daniel Titcomb, son of Benjamin Titcomb. Card record. No papers
John, Mass., S31425
John, N.H., Sarah, W22423; BLWt. 540-160-55
Michael, Cont., S33203, res. Newburyport, Mass. in 1818
Nicholas, Mass., Phoebe, W14023
TITLAR, George, N.Y., S14697
TITMAN, Philip, N.J., S7730
TITUS, Abel, Mass., S23972
Benjamin, N.J., Rachel, W6287; BLWt.26740-160-55; wid. res. 1854 in Greene Co., Pa.
Ishmael, N.C., R10623
John, Ct., Vt., War 1812, Mehetable, W25484; sold. d. 3/4/1858 in Moriah, N.Y.
Jonathan, Pvt., N.Y., BLWt.7872 iss. 9/28/179-? Card record. No papers
Jonathan, N.Y., Bathsheba, W22428
Jonathan, N.Y., BLWt.2181-300-Capt. Iss. 1789
Joseph, Ct., S14706
Joseph, Mass., S31427

TITUS (continued)
Samuel, Mass., S16004
Simeon, R.I., S11556
Solomon, N.J., Susanna, W2491
TOBEY, Barnabas, Mass., Thankful, W22441
Isaac, Mass., S11567
Job (Indian), See TOBIAS
John, Mass., Margaret, W2196; BLWt.12558-160-55
Lemuel, Mass., Sea Service, R10624
Matthias, Mass., Hannah, W26545
Stephen, Pvt., Mass., BLWt.5151 iss. 12/14/1793 to Samuel Emery. Card record. No papers
William, Mass., Mary, W26551
TOBIAS, Daniel, Pvt., Ct., BLWt. 6560 iss. 4/27/1792. Card record No papers
Job (Indian), Cont., Mass., BLWt. 1927-100
TOBIN, Edward, Pvt. in the Line Invalids, BLWt.13835 iss. 11/1/1791 to John Addoms, ass. Card record. No papers
Isaac, N.J., S6258
Samuel, Mass., Margaret, W22443
Thomas, Pa., Lydia, W11639
TOBY, Joseph, Mass., Elizabeth, W19461
TOD, Thadeus, Pvt., Ct., BLWt.6544 iss. 2/5/1790. Card record. No papers
TODD, Abraham, N.Y., Deborah, R10626; BLWt.21833-160-55
Archibald, Cont., Mass., Elona/Loney, W19458
Asa, Ct., Abigail, W14034
Benjamin, Ct., Phebe, W26540
Benjamin, N.C., S1597
Benjamin Ichabod, Corp., Ct., BLWt.6533 iss. 5/18/1790 to Theodosius Fowler, ass.
Eli, Cont., Ct., R10627
Jehiel, Ct., S14708
John, Navy, S43202, Me. & N.H. res. & agcy.
John, N.H., S11571
John, N.J., S42510; BLWt.1532-100
Jonathan, Ct., Sally, W2197; BLWt.8160-160-55
Joseph, Mass., S30743
Joseph, N.Y., Patty, W11643
Joseph, N.C., Mary, W3055
Joseph, not Rev. War, St. Clair's Defeat 1791, Ky. Mil., Old War Inv. File 25886; res. 1819 in Switzerland Co., Ind.
Levi, Va., Indian War 1786 R18516, Va. Half Pay
Lewis, N.C., S7736
Paul, Mass., Sally, W1671
Peter, N.C., S31430
Robert, Va., Wayne's 1794 Campaign R18517 Va. Half Pay
Samuel, Ct., Jane, W2276; BLWt. 19507-160-55; B.L.Reg.148241-55
Samuel, Mass., S11566
Samuel, Va., S30744; res. 1833 in Campbell Co., Ky.
Solomon, N.H., Elizabeth Kenaid, former wid., W21524

TODD (continued)
Thaddeus, Ct., S36346
Thomas, Mass., Eunice, W6294; BLWt.8444-160-55
Thomas, N.C., S17736, b. Easton, Pa.
Timothy, Ct., Phebe, W25495
William, N.J., Mary, W6295; BLWt.10234-160-55
William, Pa., S40583; res. 1820 in Chester Co., Pa.
Yale, Cont., Ct., Phebe Davenport former wid., W17710
TODHUNTER, Joseph, Va., S7746; res. 1834 in Hamilton Co., Ohio
TOHN, John F., Ct. See TONE
TOLAND, Adam, Drummer, Del., BLWt.10893 iss. 8/4/1789 to Benjamin Toland, Exr.
John, Cont., Del., S18628
TOLAR, Daniel, S.C., S42043
Nehemiah, N.C., S3822
TALBOT, Jeremiah, Pa., BLWt.2198-400-Maj. Iss. 5/13/1789.No papers
TOLBUTT, Joseph, Sarah, W2194; BLWt.15440-160-55
TOLER, Richard, Va., Mary, W6299 BLWt.40501-160-55
TOLES, James, d. Ga. about 1813, Only surviving son, Sudduth Toles applied 1853 in Rankin Co., Miss., Parcilla, R10630
TOLIN, Elias, Va., S37492
TOLIVER, Jesse, N.C., Frankey/Franky, W4086
John, N.C., BLWt.67685-160-55; res. 1856 in Ashe Co., N.C.
TOLLEN, Cornelius, Pa., S40584; res. Jefferson Co., Ohio in 1818; res. 1833 in Clark Co., Ohio
TOLLES, Amos, N.Y., S32021
Jared, Ct., S11565
TOLLEY, William, N.C., Elizabeth W11648
TOLLIN, Cornelius, Pa. See TOLLEN
TOLLON, Cornelius, Pa. See TOLLEN
TOLLS, Elnathan, Pvt., Ct., BLWt. 6562 iss. 10/22/1789. Card record. No papers
TOLLY, William, Pvt., Crane's Cont. Art., Mass., BLWt.5182 iss. 2/25/1791 to Samuel Whiting. Card record. No papers
TOLMAN, Benjamin, N.H., S15678
Curtis, Mass., R10384
Ebenezer, N.H., S15679
John, Mass., S16006
Lyman, Ct., S22020; BLWt.26348-160-55
Samuel, Mass., S29511; res. Norfolk Co., Mass., 8/16/1832, age 77 yrs.
Samuel, Mass., S31432, b. Boston Mass., 1750; in 1832 res. Augusta Kennebec Co., Me. at age 82
Samuel, Mass., Hannah, W16761. Sold. d. 10/23/1804; wid. res. Hammond, St. Lawrence Co., N.Y. in 1838
Thomas, Cont., Mass., Vt., Lois, W18146; BLWt.2131-200-Lt.,

TOLMAN (continued)
Warner's Regt., iss. 2/14/1793. No papers; name spelled Talman
William, Mass., Jemima, W22431; wid. res. 1836 in Norfolk Co., Mass., age 85 yrs.
William, N.H., Chloe, W19464; wid. res of Dana, Worcester Co., Mass. in 1838
TOLON, Peggy/Becky, former wid. of Aaron Yerks/York, N.Y., which see
TOLSON, Thomas, N.C., R10633
William, Va., R10634
TOM, Henry, Md. See TOMM
Nathaniel, N.Y., Elizabeth, W15962
TOMAR, Christopher, Md., R10637
TOMASON, George, N.C., S7742, b. Johnson Co., N.C., 1749; res. Mecklenburg Co., N.C. in 1833, age 84 yrs.
TOMB, David, S.C., S17155
TOMBS, James, N.Y. See TOMS
Joseph, Mass., S33813
William, Mass., S33205; BLWt. 5136-100-Pvt. iss. 1/26/1796 to William Sparks
TOME, Henry, Pa., S22557
TOMER, Christopher, Md. See TOMAR
TOMKIES, Charles, Va., Anne, W6304
TOMKINS, Abraham, N.Y., BLWt.7889 iss. 10/12/1790 to Henry S. Platt, ass. Card record. No papers
Amos, N.J., S33812
Ichabod, N.J., S766
Joseph, N.J., S6253
Nathaniel, Pvt., N.Y., BLWt.7875 iss. 9/29/179-(?) to John Archer, ass. Card record. No papers
Nathaniel, N.Y., S42505
Phinehas/Phineas, N.Y., S7743
Stephen, N.J., See TOMPKINS
TOMLIN, James, N.J., S6252
John, Va., War of 1812, Jane, W6302
Samuel, Va., S7741; res. Howard Co., Mo. in 1834 age 79 yrs.; b. Fauquier Co., Va., 9/22/1754
William, Cont., Va., S6261; res. in 1832 Fauquier Co., Va., age 74 yrs.
TOMLINSON, Agur, Ct., S14713; not identical with Wm. Agur Tomlinson, W18151; b. 12/1/1757; res. in 1832 Huntingdon, Fairfield Co., Ct., age 74 yrs.
Ambrose, Va. See George
Benjamin, Cont., Ct., S36347
Curtiss/Curtis, Ct., Lucy, W25494; BLWt.26215-160-55
David, Ct., BLWt.1314-150
Eliphalet, Ct., Polly, W18152; BLWts.89-60-55 & 6564-100-1791
George/Ambrose, Va., S31429
Harris, Va., Winifred/Winifield, W9862
Henry, Ct., R10638
Jabez, Cont., Dis., Ct. res. in 1794

TOMLINSON (continued)
Jabez H., Ct., Phebe, W6305
John, Va., S16555
Joseph, Pvt., Ct., BLWt.6540 iss. 12/24/1796. Card record. No papers
Joseph, Ct., Bathsheba, W11638; BLWt.13419-160-55
Joseph, Pa., S7744
Nathaniel, Va., S31431, b. Frederick Co., Md., 10/15/1747
Richard, N.C., S7745; b. Sussex Co., Va.
Samuel, N.J., S6255
William, Corp. in Invalids, BLWt. 13838 iss. 3/10/1790. Card record. No papers
William, Pa., S3779
William Agur, Ct., Phebe, W18151. Not same as Agur Tomlinson S14713. Sold. d. 8/20/1789; res. of wid. Stratford, Ct. in 1838, age 73 yrs.
TOMM, Henry, Md., S35103
TOMPKINS, Amos, N.J., See TOMKINS
Benjamin, R.I., S22019
Christopher, Va. Sea Service, Martha Dameron, former wid., R2636; Va. Half Pay
Elizabeth, former wid., Jacob Safford, Cont., Vt., Green Mt. Boys, which see
Gamaliel, R.I., Mary, W26541
Gideon, R.I., S22023
Gilbert, Navy, R.I., Mary, W22436
Isaac, N.J., Jane, W25492; BLWt. 31725-160-55
James, N.Y., S23456
James, Pvt., R.I., BLWt.3537 iss. 4/25/1794. Card record. No papers
James, R.I., Mary, W26543
John, R.I., Comfort, W22438
Jonathan, N.Y., S11562
Joseph, N.J. See TOMKINS
Laurence, Cont., N.Y., Margaret/ Peggy, W26552
Nathaniel, N.Y. See TOMKINS
Nathaniel, R.I., Sarah, W27494
Robert, Va. Sea Service, R102, Va. Half Pay
Silvanus, N.Y., S28914
Solomon, Ct., Deborah, W19462
Stephen, N.J., S767; res. 1832 in Essex Co., N.J. age 83 yrs.; b. 1/10/1749
Stephen N., N.Y., S23973; b. 1/ 19/1758 in Phillipstown, N.Y.
William, N.Y., R20439
TOMPSON, William, Mass., Rebecca W604; BLWt.19526-160-55
TOMS, Ebenezer, Mass., S30738
James, N.Y., Lucina/Lucinda, R10635
John, N.Y., Sarah, W26554
Seth, Cont., Mass., N.H., Mary, W6271
Thomas, Dis. Va. res. in 1794. Printed Am. State Papers, Class 9, p.105
TONE, John F., Ct., S43986
TONER, James, Va., S33815
TONES, John, R.I. See FONES
TONEY, Abraham, S.C., Elizabeth R10642, b. N.C. Sold. res. Spartanburg Dist., S.C. in 1833, d. 3/8/1837; wid. d. Cherokee Co., Ga., 12/22/1844
Arthur, N.C., Elizabeth, W4835; BLWt.34991-160-55; b. Va., res. 1832 in Caswell Co., N.C. age 67 yrs.; wid. res. of Caswell Co., N.C. in 1854 age 74 yrs.; m. 12/1799 same county
Cary/Carey, Va., Elizabeth, W14029; BLWt.53744-160-55
Jesse, Va., Nancy White, former wid., W11794; BLWt.101695-160-55
Jethro, Pvt., Ct., BLWt.6581 iss. 10/7/1789 to Benj. Tallmadge, ass. Card record. No papers
John, N.C., Martha, W9859
John, R.I. See FONES
John, Va., S17153, res. Powhatan Co., Va. in 1832
TONG, William, Md., Elizabeth, W1333; BLWt.26749-160-55
TONGUE, Naomi, former wid. of John Dailey/Daily, N.J.,see Dailey
TONNER, John, N.C., S3818
TOOCKER, James, Ct., S36349
Phillip, Ct., S36348
TOOKER, Joseph, N.Y., Keturah Blydenburgh, former wid., W25254
TOOL, Edward, Pvt., Art., Pa., BLWt.10522 iss. 3/10/1790. Card record. No papers
Patrick, N.J., BLWt.1038-100
TOOLE, James, Md., S32019
TOOLY, James, Cont., Mass., Navy, Mary Brown former wid., W14398
TOOMBS, Emanuel, Va., Elizabeth, W3477
George, Va., Ann/Nancy, W3476
William, Va., S7740; res. 1832 in Caroline Co., Va., where b. in 1756
TOOMES, William, Va., R10636; res. 1833 in Calloway Co., Mo. age 65 yrs., b. Albemarle Co., Va. 5/8/1768
TOOMEY, John, Md., S35102
TOON, Henry, Md., S14711
TOONE, Argelon, Cont., Va., S41263
TOOPS, Leonard, Pa., Margaret, W5193; BLWt.10-486-100; res. 1818 in Huntingdon Co., Pa. age 58 yrs.; wid. res. in 1840 Harrisburg, Dauphin Co., Pa., age 72 yrs.
TOOTHAKER, Roger, Mass., S42503
Seth, Mass., S35670
TOPHAM, Reuben, N.J., S23026
TOPHAND, Ezekiel, Pvt., Ct., BLWt. 6538 iss. 4/14/1800. Card record. No papers
TOPLIFF, Calvin, Ct., S23028
James, Ct., S16275
TOPP, George, N.C., S42044
TOPPAN, Edward, Mass., S33778
Stephen, Mass., Ednah, R10644
TOPPING, Daniel, N.Y., S42504
Hannah, Va., former wid. of Southy/Southey Simpson; wid's. late husb., Garret Topping was a Rev. sold. See Southy Simpson
Peter, Md., BLWt.2456-100
William, Ct., S13766
TORIAN, Andrew, Va., S17154
TORKEY, Marillis, N.Y., former wid. of Jost Dygert, which see
TORR, Vincent, N.H., S43203
TORRANCE, Joseph, Ct., Sarah, W26547
Thomas, Ct., S23457
Thomas, Ct. See TORRENCE
TORRENCE, Adam, N.C. See TERRENCE
Alexander, Mass., Phebe Hall, former wid., W1758; BLWt.27611-160-55
John, Pa., S6257
Thomas, Mass., S40582
TORRENS, Samuel, Va. See TORRONS
TORREY, Asa, Ct., S42501
Bill, Ct., S14710; b. 1761 Durham Hartford Co., Ct.; res. 1832 in Tioga Co., N.Y.
Elijah, Mass., S11439
Elisha, Mass., S35667
Jesse, Ct., S42509
John, Ct., Abigail, W26542; sold. d. 3/9/1821 at Bethany, Genesee Co., N.Y.
John, Cont., Mass., S42508, res. Cazenovia, Madison Co., N.Y., age 64 yrs; d. 8/23/1833
Jonathan, Pvt., Crane's Cont. Art., Mass., BLWt.5181 iss. 3/ 22/1796. Card record. No papers
Jonathan, Mass., S29507; res. 1832 in Monson, Hampden Co., Mass., age 67 yrs.
Jonathan, Mass., Abigail, W22435; wid. res. 1843 in Hamilton, Madison Co., N.Y. Sold. d. 6/ 14/1837. She d. 9/14/1843
Joseph, Cont., Pa., BLWt.2153-400
Joseph, Mass., S29508; res. 1832 Chesterfield, Hampshire Co., Mass., age 79 yrs.
Josiah, Mass., S19127
Nathaniel, Mass.; res. 1818 in Hampshire Co., Mass.
Nathaniel B., Mass., Sarah, W18153; in 1828 he res. Georgia, Franklin Co., Vt.; 1844 wid. res. Naples, Ontario Co., N.Y., age 73 yrs.
Oliver, R.I., Tamar Torry, W25496; BLWt.26721-160-55
Phillip/Philip, Mass., Rosanda, W4356; BLWt.13003-160-55
Reuben, Mass., S30165
Samuel, Sgt., Hazen's Regt.,BLWt. 13814 iss. 10/12/179- (torn). Card record. No papers
Samuel, Mass., Hannah, W19460
Thomas, Pvt., Crane's Cont. Art., Mass., BLWts.5127 & 5117 iss. 8/24/1796 to Joseph Fosdick
Thomas, Mass., Elizabeth, W14030
Timothy, Mass., Chloe, W20095

TORREY (continued)
William, Cont., W16446; BLWt. 2234-200-Lt. iss. 1/22/1790. Sold. d. 10/8/1831; wid. res. of N.Y.C. in 1838 age 69 yrs., was there 7/30/1793
William, Mass., S33817; BLWt. 2151-200-Lt. Iss. 1/29/1790
TORRONS, Samuel, Va., Anna, W9860
TORRY, Amos, Ct., Sarah, W22437; BLWt.38344-160-55
Asa, Ct. See TORREY
Josiah, Mass. See TORREY
Oliver, R.I. See TORREY
Samuel, Ct., Cont., Green Mt. Boys, S41261
Timothy, Mass. See TORREY
TOSER, Jared, Pvt., Sheldon's Dragoons, Ct., BLWt.6591 iss. 10/16/1789 to Theo. Fowler, ass. Card record. No papers
TOSH, Andrew, Pvt., Va., Lee's Legion; BLWts.12612 & 13981 iss. 11/2/1792 to Robert Means, ass. Card record. No papers
TOTMAN, George, Mass., S6260
John, Cont., Mass., Hannah, W22445; BLWt.8009-160-55
John, Mass., Ruth, R10646
Joshua, Mass., Elizabeth Churchill former wid., W22750
Mindwell, Mass., former wid. of Stephen Taylor, which see
Reuben, Drummer, Mass., BLWt. 5122 iss. 1/28/1790 to Ebenezer Sproat. Card record. No papers
Stephen, Mass., S33783
Stoddard, Mass., S31433
TOTTEN, Levi, N.Y., S21538
Samuel, N.Y., S42502
Thomas, Pvt., N.J., BLWt.8784 iss. 3/13/1790. Card record. No papers
TOTTENDEN, John, Ct., S35355
TOTTINGHAM, David, Mass., Deborah, W21143
TOTTY, Daniel, Va., S13060
Thomas H., Va., Sarah, R10647
TOTUM, Jesse, Va. See TATUM
TOUISSANT, Louis, Mass., S33811; res. 1818 in Williamstown, Berkshire Co., Mass. age 52 yrs.
TOULONG, Leander, R.I., S33809
TOUP, Caleb, N.C., Pa., S7738, b. 6/25/1757 Germany; res. 1832 in Cabarrus Co., N.C., d. 2/23/1835
TOURCOUT, Francis, Pvt., Hazen's Regt., BLWt.13826 iss. 11/4/1789. Card record. No papers
TOURGEE, William, R.I., S21537
TOURJE, Philip, Cont., Mass., R.I. Desire, W16762; sold. res. in 1818 Greenfield, Saratoga Co., N.Y. where he d. 5/8/1826, age 72 yrs.
TOURNOUR, James, N.Y. See TERNURE
TOURTELLOT, Jesse, Mass., R10771, b. 3/6/1749, old style, Gloucester, R.I.
Joseph, Ct., Abigail, W25491
TOURTELLOTT, Reubin/Reuben, R.I.

TOURTELLOTT, (continued)
S35669. Pensioned as Tourtelott
TOURTILLOTT, Abraham, R.I., Leah W23044; entered service at Gloucester, R.I., res. in 1818 Orono, Penobscot Co., Me.
TOUSLEY, Matthew, Vt., S14712
Thomas, Vt., S21539
William, Cont., Vt., Sally, W22433
TOWBERMAN, Henry, Pa., See DOWBERMAN
TOWER, Abraham, Mass., S29510
Augustus, Mass., Polly, W14038
Bela, Mass., Emma, W20093; sold. res. in 1832 Hingham, Plymouth Co., Mass., age 72 yrs. & b. there 5/28/1760
Benjamin, Cont., Mass., Lucy; sold. d. 5/10/1829 Bangor, N.Y. W18145
Benjamin, Mass., R10648; res. 1835 in Cheshire Co., N.H., age 73 yrs.
Gideon, Ct., R.I., Vt., S17735
Hannah, R.I., former wid. of William Emerson, which see
Isaac, Mass., Elizabeth, R10649
Isaiah, Mass., Sylvia, W19457
Jonathan, Mass., S33808
Malichi, Mass., Bathsheba, W14033
Matthew, Mass., Jerusha, W15435; sold. res. 1820 in Scituate, Plymouth Co., Mass. age 65 yrs.
Nathaniel, Mass., Leah, W14037
Nathaniel, Mass., N.Y., Vt., Lucy, W6300; sold. 1832 in Lenox Twp., Susquehanna Co., Pa., age 84 yrs.; d. 4/17/1836, wid. res. there in 1836
Zeruiah, R.I., former wid. of Peregrine Smith, which see
TOWERS, John, Va., Dorcas Henderson former wid., W14896; BLWt.2422-100; her other husb. was a pensioner, see William Henderson, Fairfax Co., Va. service, who d. 11/1834 or 1835, cert. 5446. John Towers d. 12/25/1803, Fairfax Co. Va.; wid. d. 2/3/1841
Lines, Pvt., Mass., BLWt.5143 iss. 11/19/1792 to William Hyde. Card record. No papers
TOWLE, Bracket, N.H., Nelly, W26548
Daniel, N.H., S23029
Jeremiah, N.H., S35672
Jonathan, N.H., Betsey, W2493; BLWt.26732-160-55
Joshua, N.H., Jane Sanborn, former wid., W16067
Josiah, N.H., Jane, W2459; BLWt. 3771-160-55
Levi, N.H., Parna, R10650
Nathan, N.H., S46646
Reuben, N.H., S11564
Solomon, N.H., Polly, W6296; BLWt.33763-160-55
Thomas, N.H., Mary, W22442
William, N.H., S44000; BLWt.836-100
William, N.H., Abigail, W22440

TOWLER, Benjamin, Va., S3821
John, Va., see claim of Thomas ARMISTEAD, Va.
TOWLES, Henry, Va., S8495; res. 6/7/1832 in Madison Co., Va., age 74 yrs. on March 15 last
Henry, Va., Elizabeth, W6298; wid. res. 1837 in Culpeper Co., Va., age 78 yrs.
Oliver, Va., BLWt.2213-450-Lt. Col., iss. 12/7/1791
TOWN, Daniel, Mass., Hetty, W11642; BLWt.19831-160-55
David, Mass., S41262, lived Waterbury in 1827, age 65 yrs.
David D., Mass., S41259, res. of Halifax, Windham Co., Vt. in 1825, age 65 yrs.
Edmund, Mass., S19128
Edmund, Mass., Polly Bliss, former wid., W5831; BLWt.17711-160-55; former husb., Solomon Bliss
Elisha, Mass., S19129
Ephraim, Mass., S41260
Francis, Mass., S33807
Jacob, Mass., BLWt.2499-200
James, Mass., Lucy, W22439
Jonathan, Cont., Mass., S33810
Joseph, Mass. See TOWNS
Joseph, Mass., Hannah, R10651
Moses, Mass., S15677
Noah, Cont., enl. Mass., S35673
Phinehas, Mass., S30745
William, Ct., S32020; res. 1832 in Thompson, Ct.
William, Cont., Ct., Mary, W31
William, Cont., Mass., S42507; res. 1818 in Hebron, Washington Co., N.Y.
William, Mass., S42512; res. 1818 Hartford, Washington Co., N.Y., age 59 yrs.
TOWNE, Archelaus, N.H., Esther, W22432
Elisha, Mass., S14709
Ezra, Cont., N.H., Keziah Hartshorne former wid., W21265
Jacob, Mass., Martha, W11607; BLWt.61053-160-55
Joshua, Mass., S18629
Stephen, Mass., Mary, W18144
TOWNER, Comfort, N.H., Vt., R10653 res. 1832 at Crown Point, Essex Co., N.Y., age 80 yrs.
Elijah, Ct., S11570; res. 1833 in Windham, Greene Co., N.Y.
Elijah, Ct. & boat service Lake Champlain, S22558; res. 1832 in Home Twp., Bradford Co., Pa. age 73 yrs.
Samuel, Ct., Mass., S28913; BLWt. 3389-160-55
TOWNES, Thomas, Va., S6256
TOWNLEY, Dan, Mass. See TOWNSLEY
Evits/Evertts, N.J., Sarah, W2492
George, Somerset, N.J. res., R10655
Henry, Pvt., Md., BLWt.11757-100 iss. 8/19/1791. Card record. No papers
James S., N.J., Catharine, W18150; BLWt.26035-160-55; res. 1833 in

TOWNLEY (continued)
Tompkins Co., N.Y.
Joshua, N.J., S1128
TOWNS, James, N.C., R10652
Joseph, Mass., S35671
TOWNSEN, John, Cont., S42511; BLWt.1490-100; res. 1828 in Carroll Co., Tenn.; 1835 in Calloway Co., Ky.
TOWNSEND, Abraham, Mass., Molly, W26549
Andrew, S.C., S11561, b. S.C., res. 1833 in St. Clair Co., Ala., age 69 yrs.
Bela, Mass., Hannah, W26553
Charles, N.Y., Hannah, W19463
Daniel, Mass., Sarah Sawtell former wid., W24479
David, Gen. Hosp., BLWt.2236-450, Surg. Physician iss. 10/26/1789. Card record. No papers. See ltrs. in James Thatcher file, S3788
David, N.H., Esther, W2277; BLWt. 5206-160-55
George, Mass., Persis, W26550
George, N.C., Elizabeth Mary, W6306; BLWt.34993-160-55
Henry, Va., R10658
Isaac, Cont., Mass., Nancy, W26544 res. 1818 in Hollis, York Co., Mass.
Isaac, N.Y., Hannah, W18148
James, Va., b. Md., S3823; res. 1832 in Lee Twp., Athens Co., Ohio
Jeremiah, Mass., S29512
John, Ct., S11563; res. 1832 in Oneida Co., N.Y., age 74 yrs.
John, Ct., R10659, d. 2/6/1833 In New Haven, Ct.
John, Cont. See TOWNSEN
John, Cont., Mass., S19126; res. 1832 in Middleborough, Plymouth Co., Mass., age 89 yrs.
John, N.J., R10660; res. 1833 in Lewis Co., Va., age 81 yrs.
John, S.C., R10661, b. S.C., res. 1844 in Coosa Co., Ala.
John, Va., Elizabeth, W9861, d. 8/4/1834 Adair Co., Ky.
Jonathan, Ct., Miriam, W18149
Joseph, Cont., Mass., S35674
Joshua, Va., S1730
Mary, N.Y., former wid. of Christopher Midlar, which see
Moses, Mass., S30167
Noe, Pa., Elizabeth, W3166
Oswald, Va., Mary, W605
Reuben, Mass., Margaret, W19459
Richard, N.Y., S11568
Richard, Va., R10662
Robert, R.I., Cont., Rachel, W2375; BLWt.17877-160-55
Robert, Mass., Susan, W22444; BLWt.3980-160-55; also Indian Expedition on Mohawks 1780; res. 1832 Cumberland Co., Maine
Samuel, Pvt., N.Y., BLWt.7879 iss. 11/27/179-. Card record. No papers

TOWNSEND (continued)
Samuel, N.Y., S37493; res. 1818 in Nelson Co., Ky., age 65 yrs.
Samuel, N.Y., Sarah Bennet, former wid., W16839
Samuel, S.C., R10663, b. Va., res. 1841 in Coosa Co., Ala.
Silas, Mass., S30166
Silvanus, N.Y., S14714
Thomas, Md., S11569; res. 1833 in Talbot Co., Md.
Thomas, S.C., Susannah, W3889, b. Augusta Co., Va., d. 1836 in Lumpkin Co., Ga.
Thomas, Va., S31428; res. 1834 in Estill Co., Ky., age 72 yrs.
William, Cont., Va., Lusian/Lucy Ann, W8790; BLWt.2116-100
William, N.C., S17152
TOWNSHEND, George, N.C., Elizabeth Mary. See TOWNSEND
Robert, R.I., Rachel, See TOWNSEND
TOWNSLEY, Dan, Mass., S29509
Gad, Mass., S35668; res. 1818 in Steuben, Washington Co., Me.
Jacob, Cont., Mass., S17734
Moses, Ct. See TOWSLEY
Nicanor, Mass., Orrel, W16760, d. Walpole, Cheshire Co., N.H. 1829 or 1830
Thomas, Pa., S3824
TOWNSON, Elizabeth, former wid. of John Disharoon, N.C., which see
TOWSER, Jeremiah, N.J., S6254
TOWSLEE, Nathaniel, Ct., N.Y., S22022
TOWSLEY, Moses, Ct., Abigail, W6301
TOWSLY, Matthew, Vt. See TOUSLEY
Michael, Pvt., Ct., BLWt.6537 iss. 9/1/1790 to Theodosius Fowler, ass. Card record. No papers
TOWSON, Joshua, Va. See TOWNSEND
William, BLWt.2210-200-Lt. iss. 5/22/1789 to Tom Towson. Card record. No papers
TOY, John, Corp., Armond's Corps, BLWt.13847 iss. 7/27/1789 to Richard Platt, ass. Card record No papers; S18240
Nathaniel, Cont., Mass., See TAY
TOZER, Jared, Ct., Cont., S42506
John, Ct., S42513
John, Mass., N.H., Mary, W21135
Julius, Ct., Elizabeth J., W25493 BLWt.26986-160-55
Peter, N.H., S40585; res. 1823 in Saratoga, N.Y., 1826 res. in Susquehanna Co., Pa.
Richard, Ct., Privateer, R10664
TOZIER, Lemuel, Mass., R10665
TRABIS, William, N.Y., S3830
TRABUE, Daniel, Va., S14727; sold. res. Adair Co., Ky. in 1832, age 72 yrs.; Daniel Trabue, son, Adm. estate, St. Louis Co., Missouri in 1850
James, Va., R18543, Va. Half Pay d. 12/24/1802 Charlotte Co., Va.
John, Va., BLWt.2221-150-Ens. iss. 12/30/1796

TRACEY, John, Pvt., Pa., BLWt. 10503 iss. 2/14/179- (torn) to Alexander Power, ass. of John Stewart, Adm. Card record. No papers
Moses, Ct. res. in 1813. Dis.
Philip, Md., S11581
William, N.C., S18251
William, Va., S7751, res. 1833 in Bedford Co., Va.
William, Va. See TRASEE
TRACY, Calvin, Ct., Elizabeth, W19465
Charles, Cont., Md., S31437
Cyrus, Ct., S19130
Daniel, Ct., Cont., S19823
Dudley, Ct., Cont., Sarah, R10667
Ebenezer, Mass., S42536
Eleazer, Ct., Hannah, W11652; BLWt.31724-160-55; res. 1832 in Franklin, New London Co., Ct.
Elias, Ct., S6269
Elijah, Ct., Vt., Deidomean, W829 BLWt.26805-160-55
Elisha, Ct., Hannah, W18163
Ezekiel, Ct., Patience, W18161
Gamaliel R., Ct., Sarah, W11660
Gilbert, Ct., Privateer, Deborah, W4088
Giles, Ct., Sea Service, S30748
Hezekiah, Ct., BLWt.547-200; res. 1811 in Franklin, New London Co., Ct.
James, S.C., Agnes, W9864; wid. d. 8/9/1844 at home of son Greenberry Tracy, Union Dist., S.C.
James, Vt., Mercy, W2494; BLWt. 11088-160-55
Jedediah, Ct., BLWt.1535-100-Levi Tracy age 75 yrs. res. of Green Co., N.Y., brother and one of heirs in law in 1829
Jeremiah, Ct., R10668
John, Ct., Esther, W16448
Levi, Ct., Vt., S28915
Moses, Ct., Mary, W26555
Philemon, Cont., Ct., Abigail, W3625
Sicha, Mass., former wid. of Lemuel Chapman, which see
Solomon, Ct., Sea Service, Phoebe W20097; res 1818 in Rutland Co., Vt.
Solomon, Ct., Mass., S32025; res. 1832 in Jefferson Co., N.Y., d. 1/21/1849
Solomon, Mass., Dolly, W25499; res. 1832 in Ashford, Cattaraugus Co., N.Y.
Solomon, N.Y., Mary, R10666; res. of wid. in 1845 Allegany Co., N.Y.
Solomon, Va., S36830; res. 1819 in Madison Co., Ky., 1820 in Fayette Co., Ky., moved to Indiana in 1838
Thomas, Mass., Mary, W15438
William, Ct., S35362
TRADER, Arthur, Va., S30169
TRAFFARN, Cromwell, R.I., S42523
TRAFFORD, Joseph, Mass., S33820

TRAFTON, Abial, Mass., S41266
Benjamin, Mass., S35678
Elias D., R.I., Lydia T. Crandall former wid., W27640; BLWt.39483-160-55
Eliphalet, Cont., Mass., S35677
Joshua, Cont., Mass., S18630
Josiah, Mass., S35679
Jotham, Mass., R10669
TRAHAN, Etienne, N.Y., Anastasia, W23062, wid. in 1832 res. of La Cadie, Dist. of Montreal, Canada
Gregory, Cont. See STRAHAN
TRAIL, James, Va., S3828; res. 1832 in Green Co., Tenn. age 75 yrs.
Thomas, Va., S7748; res. 1832 in Floyd Co., Va.
TRAILOR, Cary, Va., R10670
TRAIN, Isaac, Cont., Green Mt. Boys, Mass., S23030
John, Cont., Green Mt. Boys, Mass., S41267
Oliver, Mass., S33823
TRAINUM, William, N.C., S3825; res. 1832 in Sumner Co., Tenn.
TRAMEL, Peter, Ga., N.C., R10674
Sampson, N.C., S.C., Susan, W6313; in 1832 res. Clay Co., Ky. age 82 yrs., 1834 in Morgan Co., Ind.
TRAMELL Dennis, Ga., S.C., Martha R10672; sold. b. Amelia Co., Va. wid. res. 1853 in Taylor Co., Ky.
TRAMMEL, William, S.C., Sarah, W6312; BLWt.17874-160-55
TRAMMELL, Dennis, See TRAMELL
Peter, Ga., N.C. See TRAMEL
Thomas, S.C., Mary, W11655; wid. res. 1846 in Chambers Co., Ala.
William, N.C., S32022
TRANSUE, Philip, Pa., R10676; res. 1834 in Pike Co., Pa.
TRANT, Lawrence, Va., BLWt.1423-300 iss. 12/6/1828 to Obediah Trant, son. BLWt.1858-300 iss. 5/29/1832 to Marg't Bozeman, dau. and others
TRAP, Martin, Va., R10677
TRAPP, James, N.Y., R10678
Jane, N.J., former wid. of John Gardner, which see
TRASEE, William, Va., Lucy, W6307 BLWt.61362-160-55
TRASK, Benjamin, Mass., Hannah, R10682
David, Sgt., Mass., BLWt.5170 iss. 5/31/1790 to Theodosius Fowler. Card record. No papers
Ebenezer, Mass., Hannah, R10681
Ezra, Mass., S29514
Israel, Mass., S30171
Jesse, Mass., S29516
John, Mass., S39869; res. R.I. in 1818
John, Mass., S42515; res. 1819 in St. Lawrence Co., N.Y., age 63 yrs.
John, Mass., S42522; res. 1823 in Clinton Co., N.Y., d. 2/21/1829
Jonathan, Sgt., Mass., BLWt.

TRASK (continued)
5141 iss. 5/31/1790 to Theodosius Fowler. Card record. No papers
Moses, Mass., Anna/Anne, R10679
Nahum, Mass., S11580
Nathaniel, Mass., S31434
Obediah, Mass., Huldah Baker, former wid., S18631; BLWt.10086-160-55
Peter, Mass., Rachel, W14053
Primus, Mass. See Primus HALL
Retire, Mass., S21542; res. 1832 in Rochester, Windsor Co., Vt., b. Mass. 3/6/1751
Retire, Mass., Privateer, S7750; res. 1832 Geauga Co., Ohio, 1841 in Ashtabula, Ohio
Rufus, Mass., S40587
Samuel, Cont., Mass., S19824
Thomas, Cont., R.I., S35357
TRAVER, Adam, N.Y., Anna Maria, R10683
TRAVERS, Elijah, Mass. See TRAVIS
Matthias/Mathias, Md., S7753; res. 1834 Dorchester Co., Md.
Oliver, Mass. See TRAVIS
TRAVERSE, Abraham, N.J., N.Y., Anna, W16449
Andrew, Pvt., Pa., BLWt.10492 iss. 9/2/1796. Card record. No papers
Mathias, Md. See Matthias TRAVERS
Sylvanus, Pvt., Hazen's Regt., BLWt.13816 iss. 1/2/1792 to Jacob Clingman, ass. Card record No papers
TRAVICE, Abraham, Pvt., N.Y., BLWt.7880 iss. 9/9/179- to G. Patterson et al, ass. Card record. No papers
Scott, Pvt., N.Y., BLWt.7861 iss. 6/18/1791 to Peter Learman, ass.
TRAVILLIAN, Joab, See TREVILLIAN
TRAVIS, Amos, N.Y., R10684
Arthur, S.C., S1262
Asa, Mass., Mary, W15964
Edward, Va., Sea Service, R103, Va. Half Pay. See Edward Travis in Va. State Navy. Half Pay. File YS- Edward Travis d. 3/28/1784 James City Co., Va.; sons Joseph E. Travis res. 1846 Brunswick Co. Va., son Edward Travis.
Elijah, Mass., Lydia, W19467
George, N.Y., R10685
James, N.Y., R10686
James, Va., S38445
Jonathan, N.Y., S21540
Joseph, Ct., Cont., S42520
Joseph, Pvt., Lamb's Art., N.Y., BLWt.7893 iss. 7/9/179- to Nicholas Fish, ass.
Nathaniel, Pa., S42534
Oliver, Mass., Milly, R10687
Philip, Ct., N.Y., S42525
Robert, N.Y., S23032
Silvanus, Cont., N.Y. res. & agcy., S46509; en. at Fredericks-town, N.Y.; res. 1828 Lodi, Seneca Co., N.Y.
Thomas, Md., S3826

TRAVIS (continued)
Uriah, N.Y., S42518
TRAY, Elijah, Cont., Vt., res. Bennington. Dis.
TRAYLOR, Cary, Va. See TRAILOR
TRAYNOR, Michael, Pvt., Hazen's Regt., BLWt.13821 iss. 6/29/1789 to Matt McConnell, ass. Card record. No papers
Simon, Pvt., N.J., BLWt.8795 iss. 6/11/1789 to Jonathan Dayton, ass. Card record. No papers
TREACLE, William, Va., Elizabeth, W6309
TREADWAY, Alpheus, Ct., S15680
Daniel, N.C., Mary, W18159
David, Ct., S11578
Elijah, Ct., S16007
Jonathan, Ct., S41265
Josiah, Ct., Rana, W18158
Robert, N.C., Nancy, See TREDWAY
TREADWELL, Abel, Ct., S23458
Benjamin, Ct., Rachel, W2376; BLWt.21832-160-55
Cato, Ct. See TREDWELL
Daniel, Ct., Sarah, W----. She was also pens. as former wid. of Daniel Hoyt, Ct., which see
Marsters/Marstress, Mass., S35675
Moses, Mass., Susanna, W15437; wid. res. Ipswich, Mass. in 1837
Nathaniel, Mass., S11582
Nathaniel, Mass., S33827
Reuben, N.C., Amelia, W6311
Samuel, Mass., Susanna, W22450
Thomas, Mass., Jane, W22446
William, Cont., Mass., Mary, BLWt.93-300
TREAT, Ashbel, N.Y., S29513
Ashbel W., N.Y., S11579
Charles, Mass., S11574
Cornelius, Cont., Mass., Alsy, R10689
James, Ct., Anna, W606; BLWt. 26621-160-55
John, Pvt., Sheldon's Horse, Ct. BLWt.6584 iss. 6/25/1789. No papers
John, Cont., Ct., Elizabeth, W18156
Jonathan, Cont., Ct., Caturah/Katurah, W14051
Joseph, Pvt. Ct. Line, BLWt.6575 iss. 1/28/1790 to William Walter, ass. No papers
Joseph, Cont., Ct., S35360
Maluchi, Gen. Hosp., BLWt.2237-450-Surg. Phys. Iss. 9/29/1790. No papers
Philo, Ct., S35361
Robert, Ct., Content, R10691
Russell, Ct., S35359
Samuel, Mass., BLWt.2155-300-Capt. Iss. 7/27/1798 to the heirs. Also recorded under BLWt.2702-300-Capt Iss. 7/27/1798 to Anna Harrod & Elizabeth Davis, the only surviving heirs and sisters. No papers
Samuel, Mass., S32825; BLWt.794-100

TREAT (continued)
Samuel P., Cont., Ct., S42526
Theaus/Theus/Theodore, N.Y., R10692
Theodore, Cont., Ct., Zippora, W2460; BLWts.486-2275-100; 48-60-55, and 6585-100-1790
Theodore/Theus, See Theaus
Thomas, Ct., Rachel, W25502; BLWt.29007-160-55
Thomas, Mass., Betsey, W4360. She also applied for pension on account of her 1st husband's service. See Joel Boies, Mass.
TREDWAY, Robert, N.C., Nancy, W316
TREDWELL, Cato (colored), Ct., S35358
TREE, John, Cont., Mass., S18253
TREECE, Michael, Pa., Malinda, W7359; BLWt.28600-160-55
TREES, John, Pa., Barbara, R10693
TREET, James, Ct. See TREAT
Russell, Ct. See TREAT
Theodore, Cont., Ct. See TREAT
TREFRY, Edward, Mass., S6267
William, Mass., Mary, W19469
TRELEGAN, John, Pvt., N.J., BLWt.8808 iss. 6/26/1789
TREMAIN, Abner, N.Y. See TREMAN
Daniel, Mass., N.Y., S13078
Gaius, Mass., N.Y., S15126
Nathaniel, Ct., Mass., S30168
TREMAN, Abner, N.Y., Mary, W18157 BLWt.7863-100-Pvt. Iss. 12/15/1790. Name spelled Abner Trimmins
TREMBLE, Jacob, N.J., Phebe, R10704
TREMPER, Jacob, N.Y., R10694
Lawrence, N.Y., S7754
Nicholas, N.Y., Elizabeth, W22453
Valentine F./Volentine, N.Y., Anna, BLWt.85082-160-55
TRENARY, William, Va. See TENERY
TRENCH, James, S.C., S35954
TRENOR, James, Va., S30170
TRENT, Alexander, Va., Jane, R10695
TRESCOTT, Experience, Cont., Vt., Abigail Shepard/Shepherd, former wid., W25114
Jonathan, Mass., S11264
Lemuel, Mass., BLWt.2140-400-Major. Iss. 9/28/1791. No papers
Solon, Mass., S40590
William, Mass., Clarissa, W20096
TRESLER, Frederick, Md., Pa., R10696
TREUTTLE, Jonathan, See TRICKLE
TREVETT, Benjamin C., Cont., Mass. S42532
John, Mass., S35680
John, Navy, R.I., S39868
TREVILLIAN, Hendley, Va., S7756
James, Va., R10698
Joab, N.C., Sarah, R10699
TREVITT, Henry, N.H., S3832
Samuel, Mass., S19132
TREWHIT, Stephen, See TRUHITT
TREWIT, Stephen, See TRUHITT
TREZVANT, John, Va., S41264; BLWt. 2224-400-Surg. Iss. 12/17/1799

TREZVANT (continued)
to Charles Copland, ass.
TRIBBLE, Elijah, N.C., Rachel, R10700
George, Va., Nancy, W27863
James, Va., S17156
TRIBLE, Joseph Fulcher, Va., S40588
TRIBON, William, Mass., Amy/Anna, W15448
TRIBOU, Amasa, Mass., S18252
William, Mass., See TRIBON
TRICE, James, Va., Mary, W9527
TRICKEY, Ephraim, N.H., Lucy, W19466
John, N.H., S18254
Samuel, Pvt., N.H., BLWt.3524. Iss. 2/27/1790 to Theo. Fowler, ass.
Samuel, N.H. See TRICKY
William, N.Y., R10701
TRICKLE, Jonathan, Cont., Pa., BLWt.250-100
TRICKY, Samuel, N.H., S43204
TRIM, Ezra, Ct., Cont., N.Y., S14729
TRIMBEL, John, S.C., S32024
TRIMBLE, George, Cont., N.Y., Mary, R10703
Isaac, Va., S6268
John, N.Y., S22559
John, Pa., S14715
William, Va., Mary, W8791
TRIMINGS, Abner, See TREMAN
TRIMMINS, Abner, See TREMAN
TRINE, George, Pa., S3827
TRINKLE, Christopher, Va., S36829
TRION, Charity, Cont., former wid. of Samuel Grannis, which see
TRIP, Everitt, N.Y., S42531
Joshua, Pvt., R.I., BLWt.3534. Iss. 12/31/1789. No papers
TRIPE, Robert, Mass. See TRIPP
TRIPLET, Nathaniel, Pvt., Va. Lee's Legion. BLWt.12600. Iss. 4/13/1791 to James Reynolds, ass. No papers
TRIPLETT, Daniel, Va., Susannah, W6308; BLWt.26221-160-55
George, Va., Sarah, W607 & Va. Half Pay. BLWt.1766-200. Iss. 9/5/1831 to himself. BLWt. 18373-160-55. See N.A. Acc. No.874-050175. Half Pay. George Triplett
Hedgeman, Va., S11572
Peter, Va., Catherine, W2706
Thomas, Va., S46571; BLWt.1777-300
William, N.C., R10706, b. Va.
TRIPNER, George, Pa., S40591
George, Pa., BLWt.2115-100
George, Jr., Drummer, Pa., BLWt. 10507. Iss. 7/17/1793
TRIPP, Abiel, Mass., Betsey, W14049
Anthony, N.Y., R.I., Mary, W25497; BLWt.2096-160-55
Calvin, Mass., S42516
Charles, N.Y., Jane, W25498
Consider, R.I., S39870
Edward, Navy, R.I., Avis, W22447
Ephraim, Mass., S33824

TRIPP (continued)
Everitt, N.Y., S42531. No papers
Francis, R.I., S18632
Henry Dow, N.J., S42514
John, R.I., Catherine, W14047
Jonathan, Mass., Tamzin, W22451
Othniel, R.I. and "Old French War 1758", S22024
Peleg, N.Y., S23031
Richard, N.Y., S14717
Robert, Mass., S35356
Samuel, Pvt., Mass., BLWt.5130. Iss. 5/18/1792 to John Blanchard No papers
William, N.Y., S42528
TRITT, Peter, Pa., S23974
TROBRIDGE, Benjamin H., Ct., S40592
Ebenezer, Ct. See TROWBRIDGE
Seth, Mass. See TROWBRIDGE
TROGDON, Ezekiel, N.C., R10707
TROLINGER, Henry, Va., Mary, b. N.C., W4087
TROLLINGER, Henry, Va., Mary See TROLINGER
TROOP, William, N.J., Nancy, R10708
TROTTER, Christopher, Cont., Va., S40593
John, Mass., BLWt.2149-300-Capt. Iss. 7/11/1797. No papers
John, Va., S42046
Matthew, N.Y., Margaret, W19471
William, Va., S1598
TROUP, Robert, N.J., Jennet, W16450
TROUSDALE, James, N.C., Elizabeth, W4525
TROUT, Adam, N.Y., S42527
Anthony Daniel, Ga., S.C., Mary Catherine, W9863; BLWt.26294-160-55
Boltzer, Va., S7749
Christian, Md., Elizabeth, W7326
David, Va., R10711; BLWt.35685-160-55
Jacob, N.J., S33822
Jacob, N.C., S1780
Michael, N.Y., S42517. No papers
William, Fifer, Mass., BLWt.5128 iss. 1/26/1790 to John May. No papers
William, N.J., Privateer, S2567
TROUTMAN, Peter, Pa., Catharine, W11651; BLWt.40921-160-55
TROUTT, Michael, Pvt., N.Y., BLWt. 7867. Iss. 9/3/1790 to Resolve Waldron, ass. No papers
Michael, N.Y., S42517
TROVER, John, Va., R10712
TROW, Solomon, Quartermaster Sgt. Col. Lee's Cont. Regt., Mass., BLWt.5137 & 13943 iss. 9/9/1789
TROWAL, William, N.C., R10714
TROWANT, Nathan, Mass., S14720
TROWBRIDGE, Aaron, Mass., S42529
Absalom/Absolem, N.Y., S33818
Benjamin, Ct., S42530
Benjamin H., Ct., S40592. No papers
Billy, Ct., Rhoda James, former wid., W20173
Ebenezer, Ct., Parnel, W4607
Elihu, Ct., S36350

TROWBRIDGE (continued)
Isaac, Mass., S42519; BLWt.1743-100
James, Pvt., Mass., BLWt.5123. Iss. 10/10/1791 to Anthony Maxwell
James, Mass., S43205
James, N.Y., Elizabeth, W16763
Job, N.J., Martha, W5194; BLWt. 34995-160-55
John, Ct., BLWt.2176-200-Lt. Iss. 9/13/1790 to John Trobridge. No papers
John, Cont., Ct., S36352
John, Mass., Mary, W15439
John, Mass., Sarah, W26556
Luther, Mass., Elizabeth, W9865; BLWt.2157-200-Lt. Iss. 1/4/1792 to Jacob Clingman, ass.
Philemon, Cont., Ct., Eunice, W18162
Samuel, Ct., Lydia, W18154
Samuel, Mass., S30747
Seth, Mass., Lucretia, W19470; BLWt.10226-160-55
Stephen, Pvt., Ct., BLWt.6551. Iss. 11/19/1792 to Samuel Miller ass. No papers
Stephen, Ct., S14721
Stephen, Cont., Ct., widow Isabel S46494
Thomas, Ct., S17738
William, Ct., Dorcus, BLWt.36549-160-55
William, Mass., Achsah, W14050
TROWELL, James, N.C., Alcey, W6310; BLWt.27688-160-55
TROWER, Solomon, Va., S31436
TROXEL, Jacob, Va., Elizabeth, R10717
TROY, James, Va., S7747
TRUAIR, Manuel, Cont., Ct., R.I., S42533
TRUAX, Abraham, N.Y., Elizabeth, R10718
Abraham C., N.Y., S13081
Alida, former wid. of John Quackenboss, N.Y., which see
David, Va., b. N.J., S4687
Isaac I., N.Y., S13091
Jacob, N.J., Contente/Constant Truex, W129
Jacob, N.Y., S11577
John, Cont., N.Y., S42537
John, N.J., Mary, W11653; BLWt. 31728-160-55
Joseph, Pa., S6264
Phillip, Pa., Fanny, R10719
TRUBY, Michael, Pa., R10720
TRUCKS, John, Md., Catharine E., W11658; BLWt.53666-160-55
TRUE, Aaron, Mass., N.H., S31435
Abraham, N.H., Anna, W16451
Benjamin, N.H., S18255
Daniel, N.H., Mercy Fryer, former wid., W11026; BLWt.8139-160-55
Edward, N.H., Molly, W22454
Ezekiel, Mass., S19131
Jabez, Mass., S14725
James, Va., S31438
John, Mass., Jemima, W25501;

TRUE (continued)
BLWt.13857-160-55
John, Va., S30746
Jonathan, Mass., Mehitable, W11659
Joseph, N.H., S17737
Martin, Va., S39867
Obadiah, Mass., Mary/Polly, W830; BLWt.13712-160-55
Robert, Va., Nancy, W9526
Sally, Mass., former wid. of Seth Hunt, which see
William, Mass., S29515
Zebulon, Mass., Martha, W22449; BLWt.14981-160-55
TRUEMAN, Alexander, Md., Indian War of 1792; BLWt.2156-300
John, Md., BLWt.2211-200-Lt. Iss. 9/1/1789. No papers
Shem, Ct., S42524. No papers
TRUESDAIL, Hiel, N.Y., S11573
TRUESDALE, Jesse, N.Y., Hannah Van Scoy, former wid., W20106
TRUESDELL, Aaron, N.H., Vt., S14722
Jabish, N.Y., Bethiah, W19468
Jonathan, N.Y., Phebe, W22452
Richard, N.Y., S14728
Samuel, N.Y., S42535
TRUEX, Jacob, N.J. See TRUAX
John, N.J., S33821
TRUFANT, David, Mass., S30749
TRUHITT, Stephen, N.C., S45451
TRUIT, William, Va., S6266
TRUITT, Purnal, Del., N.C., Va., R10723
TRULL, Elijah, Mass., S11575
Willard, Mass., S14719
TRUMAIN, Solomon, Mass. See TRUMAN
TRUMAN, Alexander, See TRUEMAN
Shem, Ct., S42524
Solomon, Mass., Lodema/Lodena, W4829; BLWt.29043-160-55
TRUMBEL, John, Pvt., Mass. BLWt.5138. Iss. 12/6/1791 to Stephen Thorn, ass.
TRUMBULL, David, Cont., Ct., Sarah, W14052
Ezekiel, Ct., S36353
John, Ct., S14718
John, Mass., S31160
John, Mass., S42521; BLWt.1125-100
Jonathon, Ct., BLWt.2169-450-Lt. Col. Iss. 8/7/1789. No papers
Robert, Ct., S21543
Samuel, N.H., Mary, W16081
William, Ct., Rachel, W22456
William, Pa., S35676
TRUMP, George, Pa., Elizabeth, W3374
TRUSDELL, Ebenezer, Cont., Mass., Mary Setchel former wid., W19338. Her 3rd husb. Jeremiah B. Setchel also served in Rev. War
William, Mass., N.Y., S14724
TRUSLER, James, Va., Susannah, W9528
John, Va., Elizabeth, W828
TRUSLOE, Benjamin, Cont., Va., S7757
TRUSSELL, Moses, N.H., S11576 & Q.W. Inv. File No. 20211

TRUX, John, Md. See TRUCKS
TRY, Jacob, Pa., Justina, W7320
TRYALL, Elijah Mass. See TRYON
TRYER, Andrew, Md., Pa., S40589
TRYON, Charity, Cont., former wid. of Samuel Grannis, which see
David, Vt., S19486
Elijah, Mass., S14726
Eliud, N.Y., Bethia Bailey, former wid., W16183
Elizabeth, Ct., former wid. of William Brown, which see
Ezra, Pvt., Ct., BLWt.6574. Iss. 1/18/1800 to Peter Millington, ass.
Ezra, Cont., Ct., S40586
Isaac, Pvt., Art. Artificers, BLWt.13833 iss. 8/23/1790.
Isaac, Cont., Ct., Elizabeth, W25500
Salmon, Ct., R10724
Thomas, Ct., S14716
Thomas, Ct., S32023
William, Sgt., Ct., BLWt.6531. Iss. 2/1790 to Theodosius Fowler ass.
William, Ct., S36351
William, Pvt., Mass., BLWt.5162 iss. 7/7/1797
William, Mass., S33826
TSCHUDI, Martin, Pa., S7758
TUBB, John, N.C., S.C., S32560
TUBBS, Annanius/Ananias, N.H., S41269
Bethuel, Vt., Cynthia, R10726
Clement, N.Y., R10725
Cyrus, Ct., S38448
Enos, Ct., Sarah, W25506; BLWt. 24981-160-55
Ezra, N.H., S42556
Ichabod, N.Y., Sybil/Sibyl, W22460
Isaac, Ct., Eunice Cross former wid., W16937
Jacob, Mass., S35363
John, Ct., S14730
John, N.Y. res. of heir in 1808 B.L.---
Lemuel, Ct., S15687
Martin, Pvt. & Corp., Ct., BLWt. 6534. Iss. 4/21/1796
Martin, Ct., Mary Peasley/Peasely former wid., W19978
Samuel, Ct., S40603; BLWt.378-100
Samuel, Mass. See TUBS
Seth, Mass., S33836
Simon, Cont., Ct., S41272
Thomas, Ct., R10729
TUBS, Enos, Ct. See TUBBS
Samuel, Mass., BLWt.2163-400-Maj. Iss. 2/23/1796 to Marlborough Turner, ass. No papers. Heitman's Hist. Reg. & Mass. Archives spell this name Tubbs
TUCK, Edward, Va., S7760
James, N.H., Deborah, W16452
John, Va., Eady/Edy, W6314
Joseph, Cont., N.H., Navy, Mary, W15443
Thomas, Va., S7761

TUCKER, Abel, Va., S10261
Abraham/Abram, N.J., S42551
Anna, Mass., former wid. of William Goff, which see
Ashbel, Vt., S15683
Benjamin, Ct., Polly, W6317; BLWt.31329-160-55
Benjamin, Ct., Cont., Mass., S42549
Benjamin, N.H., R10731
Benjamin, R.I., Lydia, W15444
Benjamin, S.C., Sea Service, Sarah, R10141
Charles M., N.Y., Hannah C., W18168
Daniel, Pvt., Ct., BLWt.6554 iss. 10/7/1789 to Benj. Tallmadge, ass.
Daniel, Ct., Eunice, W19473
Daniel, Mass., R.I., Susanna, W14062
David, Mass., S33831
David, N.C., Sylvania, W6318
Elisha, Ct., Elizabeth, S17159
Ephraim, Mass., Abigail, R10730
Ezra, Mass., S30172
George, Cont., Md., S36357; BLWt.1571-100
George, Cont., Mass., Sarah, W19476
George, Ga., Martha, W6319
George, Md., S7763
Gray, N.C., Frances, W9867
Harbert, Va., S32027
Henry, Va., S6278
Henry C., Va., R20440
Isaac, Mass., S40596
James, Pvt., Mass., BLWt.5153 iss. 9/1/1790 to Theodosius Fowler
James, Mass., S35364
James, N.C., R10735
James, N.C., R10736
James, Va., S40597
Jarvis, Pvt., Sheldon's Dragoons Ct., BLWt.6589. Iss. 1/9/1794
Jedediah, Mass., Tamer, R10742
Jesse, Va., Nancy King former wid., W7987; BLWt.21818-160-55
John, Ct., S42550
John, Cont., Mass., S33829; BLWt.893-100
John, Cont., Mass., Privateer, S33837
John, Md., Nancy, W2279; BLWt. 15446-160-55
John, Md. or Va., Nancy, R10739
John, N.H., Mass., S19134
John, N.C., S---, enl. in N.C. served as a Pvt. in Capts. Brickle's or Brinkley's Cos. & John Coleman's Co., Col. Archibald Lytle's N.C. Regt., and in battle of James Island
John, N.C., Matilda, R10738; B.L. Rej. 229264-1855
John, R.I., S17739
John, Va., S3837
John, Va., S6274, b. in Md.
John, Va., S40598
Jonathon, N.H., S42545; BLWt. 3527-100. Iss. 10/4/1790

TUCKER (continued)
Joseph, Ct., R.I., S42542; BLWt. 1101-100
Joseph, Pvt., Mass., BLWt.5176 iss. 3/25/1790
Joseph, Mass., S33835
Joseph, Mass., BLWt.2158-200-Lt. Iss. 3/25/1790. No papers
Joseph, Mass., N.Y., S23977
Joseph, N.H., S43206
Joseph, R.I., Drusilla, W14060
Joshua, Mass., S19489
Joshua, Pvt., N.Y., BLWt.7882. Iss. 11/1/179? to Augustus Sacket, ass.
Joshua, N.Y., S42558
Josiah, N.H., Lucy, W2026
Lemuel, Mass., S42557
Lemuel, Mass., BLWt.2129-100
Morris, R.I., S11584
Nathan, Navy, R.I., Privateer, Jemima, W26563
Nathaniel, Mass., S33834
Nathaniel, N.Y., Mary Watson former wid., W19594
Reuben, Ct., R10740
Reuben, Va., Lucy, W6315
Rhodes, R.I., S42546
Robert, R.I., Charity, W18170
Robert, Va., S42047
Samuel, Mass., Anna, W18171
Samuel, Navy, Me. Agcy. & address, S30173
Sarah, N.H., former wid. of Ebenezer Swain, which see
Seth, Mass., S19487; BLWt. 2087-160-55
Shadrach/Shadrack/Shadrich, Va. Elizabeth, W6316; BLWt.36651-160-55
Thomas, Md., S3835
Thomas, N.C., S16556
Thomas, Va., S7762
Thomas Tudor, Military Hosp. for the Southern Dept., BLWt.2240-450-Surg. & Phys. iss. 6/15/1789. No papers
Wait, Ct., Vt., S15681
William, Mass., R10743
William, N.C., Wayne's Indian War, R18574
William, Pa., S40600
William, Va., S7764
William, Va., S38447
Zadoc/Zedick, Del., BLWt.468-100
Zedick, See Zadoc
Zepheniah, Ct., Huldah, W18166
Zoeth, Ct., Mary, W11677
TUCKERMAN, Abraham, BLWt.2164-300-Capt. Iss. 4/20/1790. No papers
TUDER, John, N.C., S14733
Valentine, N.C., S30755
TUDOR, George, Pa., BLWt.2197-400-Maj. Iss. 5/19/1790. No papers
John, N.J., S40604
William, Cont., Mass., Delia, W14059
TUELLS, Benjamin, Ct., S22026
TUELON, Charles, See TEULON
TUELS, Charles, Mass., Molly/

TUELS (continued)
Mary, former wid., W24473
TUERS, Jacob, N.J., Marytze, W6332
TUFFES, William, See TUFFS
TUFFS, William, Mass., S32026
William, Mass., N.Y., Privateer, R10744
TUFFTS, William, Mass., N.Y. See TUFFS
TUFTON, Samuel, Pvt. Crane's Cont. Art., Mass., BLWt.5124. Iss. 8/10/1789 to Richard Platt
TUFTS, David, Mass., Eunice, W831
Ebenezer, Cont., Mass., S43209
Eliakim/Eleakim, Mass., S33828
Francis, Mass., S3834
Francis, Mass., Hannah, W26559; BLWt.2159-200-Lt. Iss. 3/14/1796. No papers
John, Ct., S18635
Nathaniel, Cont., Mass., S41274
Samuel, Mass., BLWt.988-100
William, Mass., BLWt.799-100
Zachariah, Cont., Mass., Va., S44001; enl. at Medford, Mass.
TUGGLE, Charles, Va., S32559
John, N.C.?, Va., Sarah, R10745
Thomas, Va., Nancy, W6335
William, Va., Nancy, W8795
TUKESBURY, Thomas, Mass., N.H., S29518
TUKEY, Benjamin, Mass., Lydia Webb, former wid., W25941. Her last husb. was a pensioner & she was also pensioned on account of his service. See Nathaniel Webb, Cont. & Mass.
William, Mass., S28916; BLWt. 3953-160-55
TULBOTT, Rodham, Va. See TALBOTT
TULL, Charles, N.C., S7759, b. in Md.
Jesse, Del., Rebecca, W9866
Thomas, Pvt., Pa., BLWt.10504. Iss. 10/27/1792 to Frederick Molineaux, ass.
TULLER, Augusta (dau.), Ct., Cont., see Isaac Way
Elijah, Ct., Polly, W18167
Israel, Ct., S35959
Jacob, Ct., Cont., S35960
Joseph, Ct., S17428
TULLERTON, Benjamin, See TUTTERTON
TULLIS, Aaron, Va., S3838, b. N.J.
Michael, Va., b. N.J., Elizabeth W26558
TULLOCK, Magnus, S.C., S6273
TULLOH, Thomas, Va., Susan, See TALLOW
TULLY, Elias, Ct., S32028
James, Pvt. Art. Artificers, Pa., BLWt.13843. Iss. 7/9/1789 notation: "On file not delivered"
Samuel, N.Y., Sylvia, W19474; BLWt.44-60-55 & 7887-100. Iss. 2/14/17??
TUMAN, Peter, N.Y., Olive Charlotte Morton, former wid., W10516; BLWts.357-6055 & 7860-100-1792

TUMBLESTON, Evan, Pvt., Md., BLWt.11775. Iss. 12/22/1794 to Henry Purdy, ass.
TUMEY, Samuel, N.J., Rebecca, W1334; BLWts.149-60-55 & 8794-100. Iss. 9/6/1798. No papers
TUMMEY, Henry, Pvt., N.J., BLWt. 8797 iss. 7/17/179? to Abraham Bell, ass.
TUMY, John, Pvt., N.J., BLWt.8798 iss. 9/6/179? (torn) to Samuel Tumy, heir
Samuel, Pvt., N.J., BLWt.8794 iss. 9/6/1798, and 149-60-55
TUNISON, Anthony, Sgt., Pa., BLWt.10497. Iss. 8/7/1789 to Richard Platt, ass.
Anthony, Pa., Susanna, W4524
Derick, N.J. See Richard
Garret/Garrit, Cont., Va., Sarah W1099; BLWt.2193-400-Surg. Iss. 4/1/1791. No papers. Name spelled Tunnison
Richard/Derick, N.J., Maria, R10746
TUNNISON, Garret, Cont., Va., W1099; BLWt.2193
TUPMAN, John, Va. Sea Service, R104. Va. Half Pay. See N.A. Acc. No.837 Va. State Navy, John Tupman. U.S. File Va. Half Pay
TUPPER, Anselm, Mass., BLWt.2156-200-Lt. Iss. 4/1/1790. No papers
Benjamin, Mass., BLWt.2138-500-Col. Iss. 1/29/1790. No papers
Ezra, Mass., S30754
Ichabod, Cont., Mass., Rebecca, W15440
John, Mass., BLWt.2446-100
Joseph, Mass., Lydia Hill, former wid., W19772
Peleg, Mass., Privateer, R10747
Reuben, Mass., S42559
Samuel, Mass., Patience, W18174
Simeon, Mass., S40578
Thomas, Mass., S33839
William, Qrtmaster Sgt., Ct., BLWt.6568. Iss. 2/20/1790 to Solomon Goss, ass.
William, Ct., S36356
TURBERVILLE, George Lee, Va., BLWt.2153-300-Capt. Iss. 7/15/1789. Also recorded as above under BLWt.2508-300-Capt. No papers
TURBEYFILL, William, Va., S4577
TURBYFILL, John, Va., S7770. See N.A. Acc. No. 874-050176 Half Pay John Turbyfill
TURCK, Henry/Hendrick, N.Y., R20203
John A., N.Y., S14732
William, Phila. Agcy. Dis. No papers. Turck in 1835 list & Turk on old A.B.
TURK, William, S.C., Margaret, W4357
TURKENTINE, Manley, Pvt. Hazen's Regt., BLWt.13827 iss. 6/20/1789
TURLEY, James, Va., S11585
James, Va., S31044
TURNBULL, Charles H., Regt. Art., BLWt.2203-300-Capt. Iss. 5/9/1780 to Charles Turnbull. No papers. Note: 1780 must be in error in recording as this officer served until 1783.
Stephen, Va., R18602. Va. Half Pay. N.A. Acc. No.874-050177 Half Pay. Stephen Turnbull
William, N.Y., S42540
TURNEE, Henry, N.J. See TURNEY
TURNER, Aaron, Mass., Privateer, S11587
Abiel/Abial, Mass., S35681; BLWt.978-100
Alexander, N.J., S9491
Alexander, N.Y., W16765
Alexander, Pa., Jane, W4838
Allen, Cont., Mass., S15684
Andrew, Md., Ct., R10750
Andrew, N.C., Mary, W25505; BLWt.31730-160-55
Asa, Ct., S23975
Asenath, Ct., former wid. of Samuel Dunham, which see
Bates, Cont., Ct., S41275
Benjamin, Md., S7769
Benjamin, Mass., S16557
Bezaleel/Bezalleel, Mass., S31161
Charles, Mass., S42543
Charles, Mass., Hannah, W14063
Charles, Va., S21546
Consider, Pvt. Mass., BLWt.5155 iss. 5/23/1797 to Benj. Dana
Consider, Mass., S43208
Consider, Mass., Sarah Lemont, former wid., W24531
Daniel, Cont., Pa., S40605
David, Mass., Priscilla, W22470
David, Mass., Rhoda, R10761
Edward, Mass., Hannah, W22457
Elias, Va., Nancy, R10758
Elijah, Mass., Hannah, W15442
Elisha, Mass., Lydia, W15445; BLWt.445-100
Elisha, N.Y., S21544
Enoch, Ct., Sylvia, S48697 & R10752
Ephraim, Mass., S33841
Ephraim, Va., Elizabeth, R10753
George, Ga., S39110
George, S.C., S6283; BLWt.2228-300-Capt. Iss. 10/15/1789. No papers
Henry, Ct., Cont., Esther, W25504; BLWt.34992-160-55
Henry, Cont., Vt., S26814
Henry, N.C., b. N.C., R10755
Henry, Drummer, R.I., BLWt.3532. Iss. 3/25/1790
Henry, R.I., S33842
Henry, Va., Rachel, R10759
Hezekiah, Cont., Mass., S19825
Isaac, Mass., Molly, W22463
Jabez, Ct., S31440
Jacob, N.C., BLWt.226-300
James, Pvt., Del., BLWt.10888. Iss. 9/2/1789
James, Md., S3841
James, Pvt. Mass., BLWt.5165 iss. 8/1/1789 to Thomas Cushing
James, Mass., S42538
James, Mass., Isabella Wilkins, former wid., W26016
James, N.C., S1881
James, N.C., b. Pa., Rebecca, W11573; BLWt.38347-160-55
James, Va., S30757
James, Va., Judith, W18172
Jeremiah, Va., Mary, W19472
Joel, Mass., Eunice, W15446
John, Ct., Hannah, W3626
John, Ct., Cont., N.Y., Sarah Lynn, former wid., R6550
John, Cont., Pa., Dis. No papers
John, Pvt. Del., BLWt.10894 iss. 3/6/1790
John, Del., S40594
John, Pvt., Md., BLWt.11765 iss. 6/11/1790
John, Md., S41273
John, Md. Ann Elizabeth, W9529
John, Mass., S30174
John, Mass., S30756
John, N.C., Mary, W8792
John, S.C., b. N.C., R10756
John B., N.J., S3843
John L., Pvt. "in Moylan's Dragoons" Pa., BLWt.10515 iss. 8/10/1789 to Richard Platt, ass.
John T., Pvt., Regt. line of Md. wid. Mary, from 1835 list. Cert. No. 950 iss. 10/13/1829, pensioned from 11/29/1828. Sold. d. 4/27/1831, from Agcy. Book. 185 List shows under Act of 1828 for Stewart Co., Tenn., for John H. Marble, Agent for wid., Mary. Note: "This case was missing in Rev. War pension file 4/30/1940
Jonathan, Mass., S33840; BLWt. 478-300
Joshua, Cont., Mass., W19475
Joshua, Md. See claims of Aquila Corly, R10757
Joshua, Mass., Sea Service, S30758
Josiah, Mass., Lydia, W26560
Laban, Pvt., Del., BLWt.10890 Iss. 5/1/1797 to James DeBaufre ass.
Lemuel, Mass., N.Y., Adah Daniels former wid., R2649
Lewis, S.C., b. in Va., Nancy, W11667
Lewis, Va., S6280
Luther, Mass., S 19133
Marlbry/Marlbury, Mass., S33843 BLWt.2154-200-Lt. Iss. 9/10/1789 to Henry Newman, ass. No papers
Moses, Ct., S41270
Moses, Mass., N.H., S44002
Nathan, Cont., Mass., W19477
Nathan, Mass., S33845
Nathaniel, Ct., Cont., S42544
Noel, S.C., b. in N.C., Sarah W6323; BLWt.54233-160-55

TURNER (continued)
Oliver, Mass., S31439
Patrick, Pa., S40602
Peter, Pvt. N.Y., BLWt.7874 iss. 8/4/179? to Henry Hart, ass.
Peter, N.Y., S42548
Peter, R.I., S4688; BLWt.2136-400-Surg. Iss. 12/31/1789. No papers
Philip, BLWt.199-450-Phys. & Surg. Iss. 3/19/1805
Plato, Mass., S33832
Reuben, N.Y., Jane, W26564
Reuben, N.C., b. N.C., R10760
Richard, Pvt. Md., BLWts.13819 &14120. Iss. 5/1/1795 to Francis Sherrard, ass. of Thomas Felton, Admr.
Robert, Md., R10762
Robert, Mass., Elizabeth, W26561
Robert, N.C., Agnes, R10749
Robin, Va., S7766
Roger, N.C., S14737
Roland, Mass., S6272
Samuel, Cont., Mass., S41271
Samuel, Cont., Mass., Pa., & Privateer, Elizabeth, R10754
Samuel, Mass., Joanna, W8793
Samuel, N.Y., Sarah, R10764
Samuel, S.C., Fanny, W4359; BLWt.17589-160-55
Samuel, Va., S17157
Selah, Ct., Rebecca, W18173
Seth, Ct., Cont., S35365
Seth, Mass., S30753
Simeon, N.Y., Anna, R10751
Simon, Mass., S46201
Smith, Va., S36832
Solomon, Md., Cassandra, W9847
Starbird/Starbard, Mass., S35682
Stephen, Ct., R10765
Stephen, N.Y., Amy, W2198; BLWt.24611-160-55
Stukly/Stukley, R.I., S22025
Thomas, Ct., R10766
Thomas, Ct., Privateer, S11586
Thomas, Cont., Pa., S40599
Thomas, Mass., BLWt.2147-300-Capt. Iss. 9/27/1796. No papers
Thomas, Va., S39111
Titus Jennings, N.C., R20187
William, Ct., S35104
William, Ct., S42547
William, Pvt., Mass., BLWt.5126 iss. 7/13/1792
William, Mass., Joanna, W22469
William, N.J., Hannah, W6322; BLWt.6263-160-55
William, N.Y., S11583
William, N.C., Milly/Milley, W4089
William, Va., S38446
William, Va., Sarah, W6321
William G., Pa., S40601
Zachariah, Va., R20306
Zadock, Mass., Hannah, W15447
Zebedee/Zebadee, Ct., S11590
TURNEY, Aaron, Ct. Sea Service, S18633. Ellen Turney, wid.of above sold. was pensioned as former wid. of 1st husb., Samuel Squires, Ct., which see

TURNEY (continued;
Abel, Ct., Navy, S15682
Asa, Ct., S---. No papers
Clarissa, Ct., former wid. of Gilbert Burr, which see
Hannah, N.J., W11669
Henry, N.C., Nancy, W8794
Toney, Pvt. Ct., BLWt.6578 iss. 9/20/1790
Toney, Ct., Dis. No papers
TURNHAM, Thomas, Cont., Va., S36831
TURNLEY, Francis, Va., S6281
George, N.C., Va., Creek War of 1813, Old Indian War File 1263, S21545
John, Va., Elizabeth, W6327
TURNUER, James, N.Y. See TERNURE
TURNURE, Laurence, Pa., R20441
TURPIN, Alexander, Va., S16008
Horatio, Va., Mary A., W6333; BLWt.51402-160-55
Martin, Va., S30752
Obedieth/Obadiah, Va., S32029
TURREL, Amos, Ct., S14735
TURRIL, Isaac, Ct., S14736
TURRILL, John, Ct., Polly, R10770
TURRYBURY, John, See TARRYBURY
TURS, Eleanor, N.J., former wid. of Robert Woodside, which see
TUTHILL, Azariah, N.Y., BLWt. 2186-200-Lt. Iss. 7/14/1790 to Richard Stall, ass. No papers
Daniel, Ct., N.Y., S14738
David, Ct., S42554
Jonathan, N.Y., Abigail, W4837
Olive, Ct., former wid. of Joseph Crumb, which see (or Oliviet)
William, Pvt. N.Y., BLWt.7900 iss. 7/7/1791 to Jonathon Joyne, ass.
William, N.Y., S42552
TUTLE, Samuel, Cont., Mass., S20566; BLWt.2167-200
TUTT, Charles, Va., BLWt.384-200
Gabriel, S.C., Va., S6279
John, Va., S19135
TUTTERTON, Benjamin, N.C., S6868
TUTTLE, Aaron, Ct., S6284
Aaron, Cont., Ct. Agcy. & res., S46519; BLWt.1496-100
Abel, Ct., S33838
Abijah, N.Y., R10774
Abner, Ct., Elizabeth, W18169
Abraham, Ct., S41268
Andrew, Ct., Betsey, W22464
Asahel, Ct., S17160
Benjamin, Ct., Mass., R10775
Caleb, Ct., S33844
Caleb, N.J., S6277
Charles, Mass., N.H. res. in 1839, Lucy, R10779
Charles, War of 1812, Lucy Hitchcock, former wid., W11293. She was allowed pension as wid. of Ichabod Hitchcock, Ct. Troops. All papers in said claim.
Clement, Ct., S16276
Daniel, Pvt., N.J., BLWt.8790. Iss. 10/30/1789
Edmund, Ct., S17741

TUTTLE (continued)
Enos, Pvt. Ct., BLWt.6579. Iss. 1/16/1797
Enos, Ct., S17440
Hezekiah, Ct., S35366
Hezekiah, Green Mt. Boys, Mass., Lucy, W22467
Isaac, N.H., Elizabeth, W22459
Isaiah, N.J., S40595
James, Mass., R10776
Jared, Ct., Roxanna, W22461
Jedediah, Mass., Lucy, W26562
Jesse, Vt., S42553
Joel, Ct., S42555
John, Mass., S40606
John, N.C., Barbary, W4836
Jonathan, Mass., Catharine, W20098
Joseph, Ct., b. 1761 at Farmington Ct., res. there at enl., Sally, W3627
Joseph, Mass., b. 1760 and enl. at Marlborough, Ct., S18634
Josiah, Ct., Eve Ely, S11589
Lemuel, Cont., Ct., S14734
Levi, Ct., S36355
Lucius, Ct., S14731
Moses, Ct., S11588
Moses, N.Y., S23976
Nathan, N.H., S43207
Nicholas/Nickolas, Va., b. N.Y. State, S17158
Peletiah, Ct., Elizabeth, W15805
Peter, R35697. There are no papers on file in an application for pension made by this sold. under the Act of June 7, 1832. His name is not on old Rejected Register of Rev. War claims, nor on printed list of 1852 Rejected & Suspended Claims. See Rev. War Claim - William Key, R5895 from which this file number was obtained and in which the reference is made to the rejection of Peter Tuttle's claim.
Richard, Mass., S33833
Samuel, Cont., Mass., S20566. BLWt.167-200-Lt. Iss. 8/26/1789 name spelled Tutle
Solomon, Ct., S42539
Thaddeus, Ct., Cont., S19488
Timothy, N.J., Mary, W6326
William, Mass., S33830; BLWt. 697-100
William, N.J., S46476. BLWt.2195-150-Ensign. Iss. 9/30/1789 to William Tuttle
TUTWILER, John, Va., S36354
TUTWILLER, Jonathan, Md., S35105
TWAY, John, N.J., S42048
Timothy, Pvt., N.J., BLWt.8796 iss. 9/7/179? to William Barton, ass.
TWEEDY, Thomas, Cont., Jane, W3478
TWICHEL, Benoni, Ct., S33848
TWICHELL, Abel, Mass., N.H. See TWITCHELL
TWIFORD, George, Va., Director R10782
TWIG, Daniel, N.C., S38449

TWINER, John, Pvt., Md., BLWt. 11764. Iss. 1/8/1796 to George Ponsonby, ass.
John, Md., Judith, R10783
TWINING, Nathan, Mass., R.I., S11591
TWISS, Ebenezer, Mass., S31162
Joseph, Cont., Ct., Lois, W26566
Robert, Mass., S33206
Samuel, Mass., Lydia, W15449
TWIST, Edward, Mass., S33846
Elias, Mass., R10784
Solomon, Cont., Mass., N.C., S19136
Stephen, Mass., also from 1798 to 1828 at various times. Martha, R10785
TWITCHEL, Thomas, Mass., S33847
TWITCHELL, Abel, Mass., N.H., S15685
Benjamin, Mass., R.I., S42560
Daniel, Mass., Eunice, W26565
Eli, Mass., S17742
Ezra, Cont., Mass., S35367
Jacob, Mass., Sarah, R10786
Joshua, Mass., Sarah, W19478
Moses, Mass., Dorcas, W22471
Peter, Mass., S31442
TWITCHETT, Ezra, See TWITCHELL
TWITTY, Russel, N.C., S17161
TWOMBLY, Ebenezer, N.H., S15686
John, N.H., S23033
William, Cont., N.H., Lydia, W6325
TWYMAN, James, Va., S14739
Reuben, Va., S31443
William, Va., S7771
TYCER, Ellis, N.C., S6291
TYCOUNT, Francis, Pvt., Hazen's Regt., BLWt.13828. Iss. 7/16/1789 to Matt McConnell, ass.
TYE, William, Pvt., N.J., BLWt. 8806 iss. 6/11/1789 to Mathias Denman, ass.
William, Pa., S40607
TYLAR, John, Ct. See TYLER
TYLEE, David, Ct., R10787
Edward, N.Y., Rebecca, W1958; BLWt.9068-160-55
TYLER, Abel, Ct., S16009
Abraham, Mass., S35368
Alice, N.H., former wid. of Asahel Spaulding, which see
Amos, Cont., Ct., BLWt.1371-100
Andrew, Mass., S28918
Benjamin, Pvt. Va., Lee's Legion BLWt.12610 iss. 11/2/1792 to Robert Means, ass.
Bezeleel, Mass., Phebe, W16766
Bishop, Ct., S17162
Charles, Va., S37494
Daniel, Ct., Sarah, W18177
Daniel, Ct., N.H., R10789
Daniel, Mass., S11592
Daniel, Mass., S35369
Daniel, Va., Sarah, W4361
David, Ct. See TYLEE
Ebenezer, R.I., Eunice, W15965
Esther, Ct., former wid. of Reuben Moss, which see
George, Va., S41276

TYLER (continued)
George, Va., R10791
Humphrey, Mass., Sarah Wadline, former wid., W18238
Jacob, Ct., Abi, W4839; BLWt. 26939-160-55
Jacob, Ct., Julia, W18176
James, Ct., Sarah, W19479
James, Ct., R10792
James, Cont., N.H., S19138; BLWt.10003-160-55
James, R.I., S23459
Jeremiah, Cont., N.H., S16558
Jeremiah, Mass., S33207
John, Ct., Waity, W3890
John, Ct., Ruth, See FYLER
John, Ct. Anna, W18178
John, Cont., Ct., Mabel, W18175
John, Cont., Mass., Ann, W6330; BLWt.19715-160-55
John, Va., Elizabeth, W6328
Jonathan, Cont., Green Mt. Boys or John McConnell, S42561
Jonathan, Cont., N.H., S23034
Jonathan, Mass., S30178
Joseph, Mass., S35370
Joseph, Vt. Agcy., S--- dis.
Major, Ct. & N.Y., Hannah, W20102
Moses, Mass., S31444
Moses, Mass., Sarah, W25509; BLWt. 524-160-55
Moses, N.C., Mary, W4090
Nathan, Cont., Mass., Olive, W18180
Nathan, Mass., Mary, W26567
Nathaniel, Pvt., Ct., BLWt.6555 Iss. 4/11/1792 to Robert Underwood
Nathaniel, Ct., S42563
Nathaniel, Ct., Cont., Mabel Hotchkiss, former wid., W24450; BLWt.12571-160-55. She was pensioned as wid. of her last husb., Jeremiah Hotchkiss, Ct., same file number
Nehemiah, Ct., Prudence, W25508
Oliver, Ct., S19137
Owen, Pvt., N.C., BLWts.12628 & 13813 iss. 12/13/1790 to Gabriel Holmes, ass.
Parker, Mass., S30759
Peter, Ct., Privateer, S23460
Reuben, Ct., S14740
Rufus, Ct., Mass., S14741
Samuel P., Mass., S30175
Silas, Cont., N.Y., S7774
Simeon, Mass., S30177
Simeon, N.Y., Freelove, R10790
Stephen, Ct., Polly, W18181
William, Cont., N.Y., S42562
William, Mass., Hopeful, W25507 BLWt.10231-160-55
William, Va., S14742
Zelotes, Mass., S30176
TYNER, Benjamin, N.C., S7772
Demsey, S.C., S1599
Joshua, Ga. See TINER
Nicholas, N.C., S7773
TYNEY, Richard, Navy, N.H., S41277
TYNG, Primus (colored),Mass.,R10795

TYREE, William, Va., Sarah, W6331
TYREL, Samuel, N.Y., Eunice, W19480
TYRELL, Hezekiah, See TERRILL
TYRER, Hannah, Ct., former wid. of Silas Nash, which see
TYRRELL, Amos, N.Y., Rachel, BLWt.21821-160-55
Jacob, Mass., S31445
TYRY, William, Va., Sarah, See TYREE
TYSER, Lewis, N.C. See TYSOR
TYSON, Henry, N.C., Sarah, W21860
TYSOR, Lewis, N.C., Susannah/Susanna, W2707; BLWt.26837-160-55
TZOR, Gabriel, Canadian, Marie Margarite, R10796. Name also appears as Girard/Ior/Shor

U

UDELL, William, N.Y., Vt., R10198
UECHRITZ, Louis Augustus de (Baron) Gen. Armand's Legionary Corps. See Lewis D'UTRICK
UFFOOT, Job, Pvt., Ct., BLWts. 6594 & 6600. Iss. 12/12/1792
UFFORD, Samuel M., Ct., S17163
UHLER, Andrew, Navy, Pa., Rachel Bones, former wid., R1004
ULLUM, Shem, Va. See Samuel WULLUM
ULMAN, Frederick, N.Y., Pa., S14743
ULMAR, Jacob, Va., R10799
ULMER, George, Mass., S35683
Philip, Cont., Mass., S19963
ULRICH, John, Pa., S7775
ULTERS, John, Cont., N.Y. See UTTERS
ULTZMAN, Jacob, N.C. See UTZMAN
UMSTED, David, N.C., Elizabeth, R10801
UNCALLS, William, Drummer, Crane's Cont. Art., Mass., BLWts.5191 & 5204. Iss. 8/10/1789 to Richard Platt
UNCAS, John, Ct., Martha, W26610; BLWt.1288-100 & 509-160-55
UNCLES, Benjamin, See UNKLES
UNCOS, John, Ct. See UNCAS
UNDERDOWN, Stephen, N.C., S30760
UNDERHAND, Edward, Mass., Mercy, W25841
UNDERHILL, Gilbert, N.Y., R10803
UNDERWOOD, Amas/Amos, Mass., S15688
Archibald, N.C., S32030
Asa, Mass., Mercy, W26611
Betsey, Ct., former wid. of John White, which see
Howell, N.C., Elizabeth, W19561
Isaac, Mass., S40609
John, Del., S9492
John, Mass., S41279
Jonas, Mass., S42564
Joseph, Mass., S41278
Josiah, Ct., Lucy, W20101
Nathan, Mass., Susanna, W15450
Phinehas/Phinias, Vt., S32562
Shadrach, Ct., S33849; BLWt. 1223-100
Silas, Mass., S14744
Timothy, Ct., S35371
William, N.C., W1003
William, Va. See WEDGBARE
UNGER, Lawrence, See Lorentz
Lorentz, N.C., Anna, W3891
UNGLESBE, William, not Rev. War Service in 1797-Ohio Old War Inv. Rej. File 18617
UNION, John, Mass., S33850
UNKEY, John, Pvt., Pa., BLWts. 10532 & 10537 iss. 12/14/1791
UNKLES, Benjamin, Md., Margaret W3892
UNSELL, Frederick, Pa., Jane, W22472
UPCHURCH, Charles, N.C., S16562
Moses, N.C., S7776
Nathan, N.C., S7777
UPDEGRAPH, Isaac, N.J. See

UPDEGRAPH (continued)
UPTHEGROVE
UPDIKE, Caesar, Pvt., R.I., BLWt.3542 iss. 12/31/1789
Caezer, R.I., S39871
Clement, N.J., S928
Daniel, R.I., Ardelissa/Arteliza W1672
Daniel E., R.I., S22027
James, R.I., S22028
William, N.J., S927
William, N.J. See OBDIKE
UPHAM, Benjamin Allen, Mass., Mary, W4362
Chester, Ct., S35372
Ebenezer, Mass., Tannar, R10806
James, Mass., S41280
Jonathan, Mass., Sarah, W14068
Nathaniel, Mass., S19830
Samuel, Mass., S18636
Thomas, N.H., S23978
Wait, Mass., S42565; BLWt. 5193-100
UPJOHN, James, Pa., S40608
UPP, Jacob, of York, York Co., Pa. Rej. 10807
UPRIGHT, George, N.Y., S42567
Michael, Pvt., N.Y., BLWts.7894 & 7908 iss. 9/28/17-- to Alexander Robertson, ass.
Michael, N.Y., Rosanah, W22473
Nathan, N.Y., Mary, W20099
UPSHAW, James, Va., R18622. Va. Half Pay
John, Va., S16560
Thomas, Va., R18623. Va. Half Pay See N.A. Acc. No. 874-050178 Half Pay Thomas Upshaw
UPSON, Asa, Ct., Ruth, R10809
Ashbel, Ct., Cont., Mary Hungerford, former wid., W18084; BLWt.3994-160-55
Ezekiel, Ct., S42566
James, Ct., Mary, R10808
Jesse, Ct., S768
Joseph, Ct., Mass., S9493
Noah, Ct., Cont., Rachel, W18222
Simeon, Ct., Privateer, S19139
UPTAIN, George, Ga. See UPTON
UPTEGRAFF, Isaac, See UPTHEGROVE
UPTHEGROVE, Isaac, N.J., Mary, W3167
UPTON, Abiel, Mass., Molly, W19562
Amos, Mass., S31446
Cesar, Pvt., Mass., BLWt.5195 iss. 7/9/1794 to John Peck
David, Mass., R10810
Enos, N.H., Sarah, R10812
George, Ga., Charity, W9869; BLWt.61224-160-55
Jeduthun/Jeduthum, Mass., S35684
John, Mass., S29519
John, N.C., R10811
Mehitable, N.H., former wid. of Elijah Averill, which see
Nathaniel, Mass., Sea Service, Jerusha, W22474; BLWt.35831-160-55
Paul, Mass., Jerusha, W14069
Sybil, Ct., former wid. of Abner Lilly/Lilley, which see
URAN, James, Pvt., Mass., BLWt.

URAN (continued)
5190 iss. 7/6/1792 to John Bridges
James, Mass., S35685
James, N.H., S17164
James, N.H., Vt., S14745
Jonathan, Pvt., N.H., BLWt.3541 iss. 1/26/1796 to James A. Neal, ass.
URANE, Jonathan, N.H., Mahitable, See URINE
URE, Uriah, N.C., Nancy, W19563
URICH, John, Pvt. Von Heer's Corps, BLWts.13848 & 13851 iss. 2/22/1791 to Alexander Power, ass.
URINE, Jonathan, N.H., Mahitable W22475
URTON, James, Va., S15690
Peter, Va., S16561
USELTON, George, Md., Margaret, W1100; BLWt.26220-160-55
USHER, Alice, R.I., former wid. of Stephen Philips, which see
John, Mass., S42568
John, R.I., S39872
Robert, Ct., Anna, W3628
Robert, N.H., Lydia, R10813; BLWt.45599-160-55
USSELTON, George, See USELTON
USSERY, Thomas, Va., S7778
UTHEST, John, Pvt., N.Y., Wt. 7923 iss. 2/11/1791
UTLEY, Asa, N.Y., S14746
Burrell, See Burwell
Burwell/Burrell, N.C., Jane, W6336; BLWt.35819-160-55
Jeremiah, N.Y., Elizabeth, W25820; BLWt.31731-160-55
Samuel, Ct., Cont., Sally, W20100
Thomas, Ct., Abigail, W19565
UTLY, Ally, Va., former wid. of Julius Chansley, which see
UTT, Elias, Pa., Lucretia, W7363
UTTER, Abraham, Pa., S32563
Ebenezer, N.Y., S14748
Gilbert, N.Y., BLWt.1579-100
James, Ct., S14747
Jesse, Ct., N.Y., Sarah, R10815
John, Pvt. Lamb's Art., N.Y., BLWt.7939 iss. 9/2/1790 to Philip Van Courtland, ass.
Josiah, N.Y., Mary, R10814
Solomon, Cont., N.Y., Sarah, W19564; BLWt.1651-100 iss. 6/26/1830
UTTERBACK, Benjamin, Va., S16559
Harmon, Va., S31447
UTTERS, John, Cont., N.Y.?, S28205 See Am. State Papers, Vol. 9, p.126 which shows on a list of invalid pension applicants from N.Y. John Utter: Matross, Col. Lamb's Art., enl. for the war on the rolls in May 1783; disabled Dec. 1782 at West Point for lameness from a bruise or wound received when exercising a piece of ordnance; res. Westchester Co. Also,the list of invalid pensioners of Westchester Co., N.Y., printed in

UTTERS (continued)
1835 shows John Utters, Pvt., army of Rev. pensioned from Sept. 4, 1793 under Act Apr. 20, 1796, increased under Acts. 4/27/1810 and 4/24/1816. Died June 11, 1828
UTTLEY, Jeremiah, N.Y. See UTLEY
UTTRICHT, Louis Augustus de (Baron) See Lewis D'UTTRICK (Baron)
UTZMAN, Jacob, N.C., Mary, W22476

V

VACHER, John de Vanbrun C., Md. Ann. See John de Vanbrun LE VACHER
John Francis, N.Y., BLWt.2248-450
Le, De St. Maria, S.C. See DE ST. MARIA, Le Vacher
VACHERAN, Louis, Pvt. Hazen's Regt. BLWt.13857 iss. 2/20/1792 to Benjamin Moore, ass.
VACHEREAU, Louis, Cont., Canada, Rosalie, W18216
VADER, Samuel, N.Y., S11655
VADOREN, Abraham, N.J. See VAN DOREN
VAGHN, William, Ct., S14751
VAIL, Henry, N.J., S6296
Isaac, N.Y., S11625
Jonathan, N.Y., S11129
Joseph, N.Y., Juliana, W212
Solomon, Va., S40611
William, N.Y., Ruth, R10816
VAILE, Christopher, Navy, N.Y., Molly Ann, W26613
VAILL, Peter, Ct., Privateer, Nancy, R10817
VAILS, Nathaniel, Ct., N.Y., R10819
Samuel, N.C., S6300
VANLANDINGHAM, William, N.C., b. in Va., S9505
VALE, Joseph, N.Y. See VAIL
VALENTINE, Bernard, N.Y., S40616
Christopher, N.C. See EATON
Daniel, N.C., R10820. He also applied for pension on account of service of Peter Valentine, see within
David, Va., S9502
Edward, Va., R18626. Va. Half Pay. N.A. Acc. No. 874-050179 Half Pay Edward Valentine
George, Md. See VALLENTINE
Jacob, Pvt., N.J., BLWt.8812 iss. 6/11/1789 to Matthias Denman, ass.
Jacob, N.J., Naomi, R10822
Jacob, Va., Dis. See Jacob Valentine, R18627. May be same
Jacob, R18627. Va. res. of grandson in 1853. See Jacob Valentine, Dis. May be same
John, Cont., N.Y., S11633; BLWt. 5253-160-55
John, Va., Mary, R10821
Josiah, Va., R18628. Va. Half Pay. N.A. Acc. No. 874-050180 Half Pay Josiah Valentine
Luke, Va., S6299
Peter, N.Y., R10823
Peter, N.C., See claim of Daniel Valentine
VALK, Adam, N.Y. See FOLLOCK
VALKENBURGH, Christian, N.Y. See VAN VALKENBURG
VALLANDIGHAM, George, Va., S31448
VALLANDINGHAM, Lewis, Va., Elizabeth, W2977
VALLAW, John, Pvt., Md., BLWts. 11579 & 11787 iss. 6/11/1795 to

VALLAW (continued)
Samuel Johnson/Johnston, ass.
VALLEAU, David, N.J., S839
VALLENTINE, George, Md., Pa., S17171
VALLET, John, R.I., S17744
VAMILIA, Benjamin, See VERMILYEA
VANACKA, George H., Pa., R10825
VANADER, Peter, See VERNADER
VAN AERMAN, John, N.Y., Jane, W18207
VAN AERNAM, Evert, N.Y., S23048
John, N.Y. See VAN AERMAN
VAN AERNUM, John, N.Y. See VAN AERMAN
VANAKEN, Abraham G., N.Y., Maria, W16454
Benjamin, Pa. See VAN AUKEN
Gideon, N.Y., S16277
Joseph, N.J., S6307
VAN ALLEN, Peter, N.J., S6301
VAN ALSTINE, John, N.Y., S9501
Martin A., N.Y., S23036
Nicholas, N.Y., S23982
Peter, N.Y., S14762
VAN ALSTYNE, Jacob, N.Y., S28923
VANAMBURGH, Abraham, Pvt., N.Y., BLWt.7930 iss. 4/21/1791
VAN AMY, Abner, See VAN NAMEE
VAN ANGLEN, John, N.J., BLWt. 2246-300-Capt. Iss. 7/23/1789 Also recorded as above under BLWt.2511. No papers
VAN ANKER, Elias, See VAN AUKER
VANANSDALLEN, Garret, N.J. See VAN ARSDLEN
VAN ANTWERP, John, N.Y., S14761
John, N.Y., Rachel, W19897
Peter, N.Y., Susanna, R10828
Simon, N.J., S28924. It would seem the papers in this jacket pertain to two soldiers with name Simon Van Antwerp
VAN ARNAM, Richard, N.Y., Privateer, S11622
VAN ARSDAELEN, John, N.J., S42584
VAN ARSDALEN, Christopher, N.J., Sarah, W119
Cornelius, N.J., S.F.--- (S. Ctf. 7292) b. Somerset Co., N.J., 7/15/1748. Orderly Sgt. & Lt., res. of Mercer Co., Ky. in 1832. D. 1/5/1840
Minard/Mindart, N.J., S930
Mindart, See Minard
VANARSDALL, Christopher, N.J., S32567
Cornelius, N.J. See VAN ARSDALEN
Cornelius, N.J., Elizabeth, W2978 BLWt.38829-160-55. Pvt. Spy & Wagoner, b. ca. 1760, d. in Mercer Co., Ky. 2/22 or 24/1843
Laurence/Lawrence, Cont., N.J., Tabitha, W6359
VANARSDAIN, John, N.J., Hannah, W4840
VANARSDEALEN, John, See VAN ARSDAELEN
VAN ARSDLEN, Garret, N.J., Pa., S7783
VANARTSDALEN, Garret, Pa., S9510

VAN ARTSDALEN, Jacob C., Pa., Sarah, W3894
VANASDAL, John, N.J., S11611
VAN ASDAL, Tunis, N.Y., Jane, W16767
VANASDALL, Cornelius, Va., S4705 b. Somerset Co., N.J. in 1759, res. of Knox Co., Ohio in 1832
VAN ATTA, John, Pvt., N.Y., BLWt. 7919 iss. 4/21/179? to Hezekiah Broadwell, ass.
Peter P., N.Y., Margaret, See VAN ETTEN
Samuel, N.Y. See VAN NETTER
VAN ATTEN, Abraham, N.Y., R10863
VAN ATTER, James, N.Y., S42599
Joseph, Pvt., N.Y., BLWt.7934 iss. 4/9/1791 to Moses DeWitt, ass.
Joseph, N.Y., S42585
VANATTOR, Isaac, See VAN NATTER
VAN AUKEN, Benjamin, Pa., Margaret W3630
John, Pa. & War of 1812, N.Y., W25827; BLWts.43397-80-50 & 29059-160-55
Levi, N.Y., Elizabeth, W18213
Nathaniel, N.Y. See VANNAKEN
Peter, Pa., R10830
VAN AUKER, Elias, N.Y., S11599
VAN AUKIN, John, Pa. See VAN AUKEN
VAN AULEN, Derick, N.J., S33854
VANAUSDELL, Cornelius, N.J., Va., S15691, b. Somerset Co., N.J. 12/3/1758, res. Greenbrier Co., Va. in 1832; res. Lawrence Co., Ohio in 1841
VAN BENSCHOTEN, Aaron, See VAN BENSCHOTER
Elias, N.Y., S11593
Jaques, N.Y. See BENTSCHOTEN
VAN BENSCHOTER, Aaron, N.Y., Margaret, R10831
VAN BENSCOTEN, Herman, N.Y., S12180
VAN BENTHUSEN, William, N.Y., See VAN BENTHUYSEN
VAN BENTHUYSEN, William, N.Y., Mary, W6356; BLWt.27617-160-55
VAN BERGEN, Peter, N.Y., S19490
VANBIBBER, James, Va., R18641
Peter, Va., S32566
VAN BLARCUM, James, Pvt. N.Y., BLWt.7925 iss. 7/18/1791 to Richard Platt, ass.
James, N.Y., S42580
VAN BOSKERCK, George, N.J., S42601
VANBRUN, John Le Vacher de, Md. See John de Vanbrun LE VACHER
VAN BUNHAGLE, John B.C., Pvt. N.Y., BLWt.7924 iss. 12/9/1791 to Philip Rockefeller, ass.
VAN BUNSCHOTEN, Elias, N.Y., BLWt.2260-300-Capt. Iss. 9/3/ 1792 to John Lawrence, ass. Also recorded as above under BLWt.2612. No papers
VAN BUNSHOOTEN, Peter, N.Y. BLWt.2257-200-Lt. Iss. 9/22/

VAN BUNSHOOTEN (continued) 1790. No papers
VAN BUREN, Abraham, N.Y., S29521
Martin, N.Y., S23461
Martin B., N.Y., R10833
Martin, C., N.Y., S14756
VAN BUSKIRK, Isaac, Va., S17165
Martin, N.Y., Maria, R10832
Peter, Cont., Del., Md., N.J. N.Y. & Pa., and War of 1812, S11613; BLWt.33751-160-55. This claim in two envelopes. See No. 1 corresp. in this envelope. See No. 2 for declarations, affidavits and reports
Richard, N.Y., Rachael, W18218
VAN CAMP, Cornelius, N.Y., Barbara W19569
Isaac, N.Y., S11603
VAN CAMPEN, Abraham, See VAN CAMPER
Daniel, Pa., S11626
John, N.J., S15236
Moses, Pa., S46510; BLWt.2219-200
VAN CAMPER, Abraham, N.J., R10835
VANCE, David, N.C., S32031, b. Va.
James, N.J., S4697
James, Va., S7782
John, Mass., N.H., N.Y., S41282
John, N.C., Vt., W3726. See claim of Sarah, wid. of John Smith
John, N.C., BLWt.2272-200
John, Va., Nancy, W6338
Joseph, Va., S37496
Samuel, Md., R10836
Samuel, N.C., Va., S1882
Thomas, N.J., Sarah, W11689; BLWt.77546-160-55
William, Mass., Charity, W323; BLWt.38830-160-55
William, N.Y., R21895
VAN CLAKE, Henry, N.Y., S42582
VAN CLEAF, Joseph, N.J., S1139
Peter, Cont., N.J., Mary Ann, W6352
William, N.J., Carche, W1102
VAN CLEAVE, Benjamin, N.J., Mary, W6354
VAN CLEEF, Garret, N.J., Dinah, W6353
VAN CLEEVE, Benjamin, N.J., See VAN CLEAVE
Joseph, N.Y., Elizabeth, W211
VAN CLEVE, Benjamin, See VAN CLEAVE
VAN CLIEF, Lawrence, N.Y., S42583
VAN COURT, John, Pa., BLWt.669-200
VAN CURLER, Henry, N.Y., S23467
VANDAL, Abraham, N.Y., S9496
VAN DALSEM, Henry, N.J., N.Y., Eunice, W9870
VANDAMAN, Frederick, Va., Susannah, W6357
VAN DE BOGART, Joseph, N.Y., Rachel, W15968
Minard, N.Y., Elizabeth, W22477; BLWt.13197-160-55
Myndert, N.Y., R10856
VAN DE BOGERT, John, N.Y., S42591
VANDE BURGH, Bartholomeus, N.Y., See Bartholomew VANDERBURGH
VANDEGRIFF, Jacob, Va., Jane, R10839
VANDEGRIFT, Garrett/Garret, Va.

VANDEGRIFT (continued) S7780
VANDEMAN, Frederick, Va. See VANDAMAN
John, Va., Mary, W6355
VAN DEMARK, John, N.Y., Jane, W16557
Joseph, N.Y., S14757
Lodywick, N.Y., Charity Humphrey, former wid., R5372
Solomon, N.Y., Lena, W15827
VAN DE MARKEN, Cornelius, Pvt., N.Y., BLWt.7917 iss. 7/7/ 1791 to Asaph Morse, ass.
VAN DEN BERGH, Evert, N.Y., Jane Lansing, former wid., R6156
Matthias H., N.Y., R10837
Wynant E., N.Y., S6303
VANDEN BOGERT, Nicholas, Corp., N.Y., BLWt.7927 iss. 7/29/ 1790 to John McMillen, ass.
VANDENBURGH, Wynant C., N.Y., S32032
VANDERBECK, Abraham, N.J., S1130
VANDERBELT, Hendrick, N.J., Jane, W3895
Peter, N.J., S11620
VANDERBILT, Cornelius, N.Y., Catharine, R10838
David, Pa., S23985
James, N.Y., S16278
John, N.J., Anna, W18211
John, N.Y., Mary Acker, former wid., W16803. She was pensioned on account of service of last husb. See Jacob Acker, N.Y.
VANDERBOGERT, James, N.Y., Magdelain, W18205
VANDERBURGH, Bartholomew, N.Y., Eve, W22482; BLWt.2259-150-Ens. Iss. 8/30/1790. Name spelled Bartholmeus Van de Burgh
Henry, N.Y., Frances Prouillet, former wid., W9751; BLWt.26928-160-55 & 2250-300-Capt. Iss. 8/4/1791
Henry I./Henry, N.Y., S14760, b. 2/28/1756 and d. 5/15/1841
James, N.Y., S28919
John, N.Y., S16279
John, N.Y., S42600
VAN DER COOK, Henry/Henry Vander, N.Y., Anna Van Ness, former wid., W26615
Isaac, N.Y., S29520
VANDERFORD, Charles, Cont., Mass. State Navy, N.H., S35106
VANDERGRIFF, Jacob, Va., Jane See VANDEGRIFF
VANDERHADEN, Adam, N.Y., Ann, W20105
VANDERHEYDEN, Adam, N.Y. See VANDERHADEN
Daniel, N.Y., S23466
David, N.Y., Elizabeth, W6373; BLWt.90025-160-55
Gershom, N.Y., S42588
Nanning, N.Y., Catharine, W19570
VANDERHOOF, Cornelius, N.J., Mary W4363

VANDERHULE, Abraham/Abram, N.J., Catharine, W18208
VANDERHYDEN, David, N.Y., Elizabeth, See VAN DERHEYDEN
VAN DER LYN, Peter, N.Y., Mary, W4364
VANDERLYNE, Peter, N.Y., Bridget, W18185
VANDERMARK, George, N.Y., S23463
VANDERPOEL, John, N.Y., Gertrude, W18194
VANDERPOOL, Anthony, N.Y., S22560
Jacob, N.J., Julianna, W1104
John, N.Y. See POOL
Malcart, N.Y., S42586
Matthew/Mathew, N.Y., S42594
VANDERSCRIMER, John, Pvt., Pa., BLWt.10541 iss. 10/27/1792 to John Cahill, Admr.
VANDERSLICE, Henry, Pa., S40618
Jacob, Pa., Mary, R10842
VANDERVALL, Marks, Va., See Markes VAN DE WALL
VANDERVEER, Albert, N.J., R22006
Cornelius, N.J., Aulche, R10843
Hendrick, N.J., Rachel, W16453
John, N.J., S1138
Joseph, N.J., S3114
Tunis, N.J., S14752
VANDERVEERE, Hendrick, N.J., Anne See papers in claim of Charles P. Strong, N.J. R file
VANDERVENTER, Christopher, N.J., R10847
VANDERVIER, Joseph N.J. See VANDERVEER
VANDERVOORT, Garret, N.Y., Leah, W18214
James Paul/Jacobus Paul, N.Y., Nancy/Ann/Annatje, W25830
John, N.Y., Privateer, R10849
VANDERWALL, Marks, Va., Markes VAN DE WALL
VANDERWARKER, Gersham, N.Y., S10037
James, N.Y., Eve, W1335; BLWts. 7933-100 & 45-60-55. Iss. 2/14/ 1791
John R., N.Y., R10853
Martin, N.Y., Mary, R10855
VAN DER WERKER, Albert, N.Y. See VAN DER WERKIN
Hendricks, N.Y., Catharine, W18191
James, N.Y., Eve, W1335; BLWt. 45-60-55
VAN DER WERKIN, Albert, N.Y., S42590
Martiness, N.Y., Anna Maria, R10854
VAN DEUSEN, Abraham, Pvt., BLWt. 7926 iss. 10/11/1790 to Henry Tremper, ass.
Abraham, N.Y., Elizabeth Shell, former wid., R9467
Cornelius, N.Y., Rachel Salisbury former wid., W17776
Gloudey, N.Y., S16280
Methew, N.Y., R10851
Peter, N.Y., Catherine, R10850
William, N.Y., Rachel, R10852
VAN DEUZER, Christopher, N.Y., Julianna, W18192
VANDEVENDER, Barnabas, See
VANDEVENDER (continued VANDEVENTER
VANDEVENTER, Barnabas, Va., Elizabeth, W6371; BLWt.29047 160-55
Christopher, N.J., Elizabeth, W1959; BLWt.12723-160-55
James, N.J., R10848
John, N.J., S929
Peter, N.J., Mary, W2979
Peter, Va., S36833
VANDEVER, George, Va., S9504
William, Va. See VANDIVER
VANDEVOUR, John, Pvt., N.Y., BLWt.7941. Iss. 9/6/1791 to George Courtlauld/Courtlanld, admr.
VAN DE WALL, Markes, Va., BLWt. 2270-200-Lt. Iss. 8/10/1789 to Richard Platt, ass. No papers. Heitman's Hist. Reg. gives name as Mark Vandaval. Report of Va. House of Delegates, BL List is Marks Vandervall. Saffells Records of Rev. Va. half pay list is Marks Vanderwall.
VANDIFORD, James, N.C., S4707
VANDIKE, Cornelius, N.J., S4693
David, N.Y., Sabra, W25825; BLWt.82520-160-55
Matthew, N.J., See VAN DYKE
VANDINE, Francis, N.J., S23984
VANDIVER, Cornelius, N.J., Sarah See VANDURER
Edward, S.C., Catharine, R10845
Mathew, N.C., S9500; BLWt.26368-160-55
William, Va., S6308
VANDIVIER, Cornelius, N.J., Sarah R10846
VAN DOREN, Abraham, N.J., Mary Low, former wid., W20519
Bergun, N.J., S4694
Cornelius, N.J., S1135
Hezekiah, Pvt., N.J., BLWt.8810 iss. 1/2/1790
Isaac, N.J., Anna, W1101
Jacob, N.J., Jane, W18209
VAN DORN, Christian, N.J., Nuel, R10858
Peter, N.J., Jane, W6347
VANDORUM, Plato, Pvt., R.I., BLWt. 3543. Iss. 12/31/1789
VAN DRESOR, James, N.Y., S19491
VAN DRIESSEN, Peter, N.Y., Anna, R10859
VAN DUERSEN, William, Ct., Martha W22480
VAN DUSEN, Abraham, N.Y., Annyte, W16456
VAN DUSER, Thomas, Pvt. Sheldon's Dragoons, Ct. BLWt.6602. Iss. 10/26/1789
VANDUVAL, Mark, Va., BLWt.2270-200. See Markes VAN DE WALL
VANDUZER, Henry, N.Y., S19492
VAN DUZOR, Adolf, N.Y., R10860
VANDVENTER, James, See VANDEVENTER
VAN DYCK, Cornelius H., N.Y., Maria, W26612; BLWt.31744-160-55
Peter, Pvt., N.Y., BLWt.7935 iss. 3/1791 to Robert Affleck, ass.
VAN DYK, John, Cont., N.J., Navy, S42592; BLWt.2258-200-Capt. Lt. Iss. 7/18/1789
VAN DYKE, Cornelius, N.Y., BLWt. 2247-450-Lt. Col. Iss. 7/24/ 1790. No papers
Cornelius H., N.Y. See VAN DYCK
Freeman, Va., R20202
Jacob, N.Y., Charlotte, W18217
John, Pa., Martha, W3168
Matthew, N.J., Lydia, W6345
Peter, N.Y., Alida, W16769
VANDYNE, Matthew, N.J., Jane, W6344
VANE, John, Md., S35108
VAN EATON, Samuel, See VAN ETTEN
VANEMAN, Andrew, Pa., S6292
VAN EPS, Abraham I., N.Y., Debora I., W25831
Alexander, N.Y., S6302
Evert, N.Y., Polly, W15969
Garret, N.Y., Sarah, W2200
James, N.Y., Engettye/Engeltje, R10862
John, N.Y., Jane, W27862; BLWt.31760-160-55
John J., N.Y., S17169
VAN ETTE, Benjamin, N.Y., S42597
VAN ETTEN, Abraham, N.Y. See VAN ATTEN
Benjamin, N.Y. See VAN ETTE
Henry, N.Y., S11630
Jacob, N.J., Sarah, W20104
Jacobus, N.Y. See VAN ETTER
James, N.Y. See VAN NATER
John, Pa., Cornelia Labar, former wid., W4474; BLWt.26699-160-55
Levi, N.J., S28921
Peter P., N.Y., Margaret, W25822
Samuel, N.C., R10861
VAN ETTER, Jacobus, N.Y., S42577
Samuel, N.Y. See VAN NETTER
VAN EVERIN, Marten, Pvt., N.Y., BLWt.7922. Iss. 8/4/1790 to E. and Justin Foote, assnes.
VAN EVERY, Martin, N.Y., Sarah, W15967
VAN FLEET, Abraham, Cont., N.Y., S40617
Cornelius, N.J., Sarah, W4527
Daniel, N.Y., S14763
Garret, N.J., S14759
James, N.Y., R10864
John, N.Y., R10898
Joshua, N.Y., S7784
Samuel, N.J., R10900
VANFLIET, Carick. This file contains undated ltr. from John Price asking about a pension for Carick Vanfliet. The reply dated 8/28/1850, states there is no record of such a man. These 2 ltrs. were originally placed in Cornelius Van Fleet's file.
VANFOSSEN, Jacob, Pa., R10865
Leonard, Pa., S22561
VAN GAASBEEK, Thomas, Cont., N.Y. S23045
VANGARDNER, John, Pa., S40612
VAN GELDER, Evout, N.J., S6305

VAN GELDER (continued)
Isaac, N.Y. See VAN GUILDER
VAN GERDER, William, N.J., S17743
VAN GILDER, Daniel, Mass., Ruth, W18195
Huldah, Mass., former wid.of Samuel Taylor, which see
Jacob, Pa., Margaret, R10868
Matthew, N.Y., Ruth, W20103
VAN GORDEN, Alexander, Pa., Hannah, W6349; BLWt.19532-160-55
Jeremiah, N.J. See VAN GORDER
John, N.J. See VAN GORDER
Samuel, N.J., Pa. See VAN GORDER
William, N.J. See VAN GERDER
VAN GORDER, Abraham, N.J., S10751
James, Cont., Elizabeth, W1103. N.J. res. & agcy. in 1818
Jeremiah, N.J., Pa., Hannah, W22481
John, N.J., Agnes, R10870
Samuel, N.J., Pa., S9503
VAN GORDON, Moses, Pa., Elsie, W6348; BLWt.26847-160-55
VAN GUILDER, Daniel, Mass. See VAN GILDER
Isaac, N.Y., BLWt.1658-100. Iss. 7/16/1832 to Jas. Van Guilder
Matthew, Pvt., N.Y., BLWt.7914 Iss. 8/4/1791
Matthew, N.Y. See VAN GILDER
Reuben, Mass., S11618
VANHINING, Henry, N.Y., Prudence, R10871
VAN HOAVANBARGH, Eggo T.H. See VAN HOEVANBARGH
VAN HOESEN, Garret, N.Y., S42598
VAN HOEVANBARGH, Eggo T.H., N.Y. S11615
VAN HOEVENBERGH, Henry, N.Y. See HOEVENBERGH
Rudolphus, N.Y., Lydia, W23324; BLWt.2254-200-Lt. Iss. 5/5/1791
VANHOOK, Jacob, N.C., S9509
VANHOOSEAR, Rinear/Ranear, N.Y. S36358
VAN HOOSEN, Garret, Pvt., N.Y., BLWt.7916. Iss. 2/21/1792 to William Campbell, ass.
VAN HORN, Abraham, Pa., S42589; BLWt.10547-100. Iss. 6/11/1793
Benjamin, Pa., S22562
Cornelius, N.J., S11636
Daniel, N.Y., Hannah, W6346
James, N.J., Leah Earl, former wid., R3190
James, N.J., War of 1812, Mary. R10874
John, Pvt., N.Y., BLWt.7190. Iss. 8/2/1790 to Glenn & Bleecker, assnes.
John, N.Y., Sarah, W16771
Samuel, Pa., S31449
Simon, N.J., S33856
William, N.J., S33852
William, Pa., S23043
VAN HORNE, Abraham, N.J., Anne, R10872
Daniel, N.J., S1132
David, Cont., Sarah C. Ludlow, former wid., W24602; BLWt.2260-

VAN HORNE (continued)
300-Capt. Iss. 2/26/1794. Res. New York City in 1801
Isaac, Pa., Dorothy, W4091; BLWt.2265-300-Capt. Iss. 8/19/1789
Thomas, N.Y., Maria, W18210
VAN HOUSEN, Albert, N.Y., S28925
VAN HOUTEN, Abraham, N.Y., S23046
Claus, N.Y., S23041
John, Cont., N.Y., S---, Eleonard/Ellen/Helen Van Houten, wid. of above sold. was pensioned as former wid. of Isaac Blouvelt, N.Y., which see
John H., N.J., Margaret, W2027
John P., N.J., Hannah, R10876
Peter, N.J., R10877
Ralph, N.J., S840
Resolvert, N.Y., S23037
Tunis, N.Y., Jane, W19568
VAN HOVENBERGH, Henry/Henry V., N.Y. See HOEVENBERGH
VAN HOVENBURGH, Rudolphus, N.Y. See VAN HOEVENBERGH
VAN HUFF, John, Mass., N.Y., S42575; BLWt.1656-100
VAN HUSEN, Albert, See VAN HOUSEN
VAN HUSON, John, N.Y., S23983
VAN HUYSEN, Harmanus, N.J., Rachel, W16772
VAN INGEN, Dirk, Cont., N.Y., BLWt.2181-400
Joseph, N.Y., Eleanor, W25832
VANKAUREN, Hazael, N.Y., S11602
VAN KEINER, John, Pvt., Pa., Wt. 10544. Iss. 7/27/1789 to Richard Platt, ass.
VANKEMAN, Hazael, See VANKAUREN
VAN KIRK, David, N.J., S4698
Jemson, N.J., S22563
John, N.J., S841
John, Pvt., Pa., BLWt.10540. Iss. 1/18/1797 to Henry Apker, Devisee
VAN KLEECK, Henry, Corp., N.Y., BLWt.7904. Iss. 7/9/1790 to Theodosius Fowler, ass.
VAN KLEEFF, Lawrence, Pvt., N.Y. BLWt.7932. Iss. 9/25/1790 to Manuel Waggoner, ass.
VAN KLEEK, Peter, Pvt., N.Y., BLWt.7940. Iss. 7/7/1791 to Robert Wilson, Admr.
Peter, N.Y., Catharine Seaman. former wid., W9284
VAN LANDENGHAM, George, Va., S41281
VAN LEAR, William, Pa., BLWt. 2264-300-Capt. Iss. 7/9/1789
VAN LEUVAN, Christopher, N.Y., S23038
VAN LEW, Frederick/Frederick F., N.J., N.Y., S23035
John, N.J., Margaret, W8797. Pensioned in S.C.
VAN LIEW, Frederick, N.J., S11594
Frederick F., N.Y. See VAN LEW
VANLOON, John, N.Y., Elizabeth Steller, former wid., W19089
VANLUVAN, Christopher, N.Y. See VAN LEUVAN

VAN MATER, Benjamin, N.J., Sarah, W6358
John, Pvt., N.J., BLWt.8811. Iss. 12/5/1791
John, N.J., S42574
John, N.J., Sarah, W20235
William, Cont., N.J., R20190, N.J. res. in 1828
VAN MATRE, Isaac, Va., Jane, W25824 BLWt.28629-160-55
Jacob, Va., Rebecca, See VANMETER
VANMETER, Jacob, Va., Rebecca, W8798
Joseph, Va., S16010
VAN METRE, Isaac, Va. See VAN MATRE
VAN MIDDLESWORTH, Andrew, N.J., S14753
VANN, Edward, S.C., Elizabeth, R10879
Henry, Pvt., Va., BLWt.12636. Iss. 7/14/1792 to Robert Means, ass.
VANNAKEN, Nathaniel, N.Y., Mary, W6360; BLWt.39480-160-55
VAN NAMEE, Abner, N.Y., S11632
VAN NATER, James, N.Y., S23044
VAN NATTER, Isaac, N.Y., R10878
James, N.Y. See VAN NATER
John, Cont., N.J., S33853
VAN NESS, Abraham, N.Y. See David
Adam, N.Y., S11627
Anna, N.Y., former wid. of Henry Van Der Cook, which see
David/Abraham, N.Y., Hannah, W18188
Garret, N.Y., Effe, W18189
Jeronimus, N.Y., S11614
VAN NEST, Jeronimus, See VAN NESS
VAN NESTE, Abraham, N.J., S6295
VANNETTER, Joseph, See VANATTER
Samuel, N.Y., Elizabeth, W18193
VAN NEY, Vincent, Pvt., N.Y., BLWt.7911. Iss. 9/24/1790 to Stephen Cromstock, ass.
VAN NOOY, Peter, N.Y., Mary/Maria R10880
VAN NORDEN, David, N.J., Mary, W6341
VAN NORMAN, Isaac, N.Y., Hannah Page, former wid., W19955; BLWt.7913-100. Iss. 3/14/1793. Her 1st husb., Isaac Van Norman also served in the War of 1812.
James, N.J. See VAN ORMAN
VAN NORSDALL, John, See VAN ARSDAELEN
VAN NORTH, John, Pvt., N.Y., BLWt.7909. Iss. 9/27/1790 to Andrew Stokholm, ass.
VAN NORTHSTRAND, William, N.Y., S17167
VAN NORTWICK, Henry C., N.J., S770
VANNOSS, Cornelius, Pvt., N.Y., BLWt.7907. Iss. 10/27/1791
VANNOSTRAN, George, N.J., S40615
VAN NOSTRANT, Isaac, See NOSTRANT
VAN NOTE, Joseph, N.J., S2895
VAN ORDEN, Albert, Pvt., N.Y., BLWt.7928. Iss. 7/20/1790 to Samuel Curray, ass.
Albert, N.Y., S42576

VAN ORDEN (continued)
Andreas, N.J., N.Y., S11621
Benjamin, N.Y., S11616
Charles, N.Y., Margaret, W19572
Hannah/Annatye, N.Y., former wid. of Jacob Sickles, which see
Jacob, N.Y., S28920
John, N.Y., R10882
John, N.Y., Rachel Polhamus, former wid., R21682
Peter, N.J., N.Y. See VANORDER
Peter, N.Y., S23979
Peter, N.Y., R10885
Peter S., N.J., N.Y., S11160
VANORDER, Peter, N.Y., N.J., S14749
Peter, N.Y. See VAN ORDEN
VANORMAN, Isaac, Ct., (?), Pa., R10886
James, N.J., BLWt.1689-100
VANOSDALN, Garret, Va., R10829
VANOSDOL, Oakey/Okey, N.J., S9507
VANOSDOLL, John, N.Y., S23462
VAN PATTEN, Adam, N.Y., S17168
Frederick, N.Y. See VAN PETTEN
Frederick D., N.Y., S11600
John D., N.Y., Wyntie, W18187; BLWt.9430-160-55
VAN PELT, Hendrick, N.J., Sarah, W1004
Jacob, N.Y., R10887
John, N.J., N.Y., Sarah, R10888
John, Pa., BLWt.1237-200
Peter, Va., Agness, W18198
Rulef, N.J., S4699
Walter, N.J., Nancy, W3893
William, N.J., S6294
VAN PETTEN, Frederick, N.Y., S28926
VANPOOL, Jacob, --, Pa. res. in 1836, R10889
VAN RENSSELAER, Elsie, R.I., former wid. of Nicholas M. Bogart, which see
Henry K., N.Y., Nancy G., W2199; BLWt.31743-160-55
James, N.Y., Elsie R. ----. She was pensioned as former wid. of Nicholas N. Bogart, R.I., which see
Jeremiah, N.Y., BLWt.2253-200-Lt. Iss. 7/15/1790. No papers
Nicholas, N.Y., S42587; BLWt. 2249-300-Capt. Iss. 8/30/1790
VANRIPER, Harman/Harmon, N.J., S1134
VANSANDT, Elisha, Va., Margaret, R10910
VAN SANT, Peter, N.J., S28928
VAN SANTE, John, N.Y., S17172
VAN SANTVOORD, Anthony, N.Y., S28927
Cornelius Z., N.Y., S32035
VAN SAUN, Hester, N.J., former wid. of Carpenter Kelly, which see
VAN SCAAIEK, Goose, N.Y., BLWt. 2245-500-Col. Iss. 9/15/1790 to Mary Van Schaaiek, Exctx. Also recorded as BLWt.2146-500-Col. Iss. 9/15/1790 to Mary Van Schaaiek, exctx. Note: Heitman's Hist. Reg. & the N.Y. Archives spell this name Goose Van SCHAICK
VAN SCHAACK, John, N.Y., S11605
VAN SCHAICK, Goose, N.Y. See Goose VAN SCAAIEK
Hendrick, N.Y., Cathalina, W18215
VAN SCHOICK, Benjamin, N.J., S769
VAN SCHOONHOVEN, Dolly, N.Y., former wid. of Lodowick Pramer, which see
James, N.Y., S46069
VAN SCHOUK, Benjamin, See VAN SCHOICK
VAN SCIVER, Daniel, Mass., N.J. See VAN SCRIVEN
VAN SCOY, Abel, N.Y., S11595
Abraham, N.Y., Hannah, W1902
Hannah, N.Y., former wid. of Jesse Truesdale, which see
Jonathan, N.Y., Abigail, W19899
Samuel, Cont., N.Y., S4695
Timothy, N.Y., S11598
VAN SCRIVEN, Daniel, Mass., N.J. S1131
VANSEES, Abraham, See VANSICES
VANSESE, Abraham, See VANSICES
VAN SICE, John, Pvt., N.Y., BLWt. 7931. Iss. 2/14/1791 to Matthew Visscher, ass.
John C., N.Y., S42572
VANSICES, Abraham, N.Y., S14750
VAN SICKLE, Abraham, Va., Hannah, W93
Corneius/Cornelius, N.J., Mary, W6374; BLWt.38834-160-55
David, N.J., S34485
Peter, N.Y., S9497
Stephen, N.J., S1136
VAN SICKLER, David, N.Y., Mary, W19566
VAN SICKLES, Elias, N.J., R10891
VANSKIVER, William, Pa., S16281
VAN SLIKE, William, See VAN SLYKE
VAN SLYCK, Martin, Pvt., N.Y., BLWt.7929. Iss. 9/21/1790 to Benj. Elwood, ass.
William, N.Y. See VAN SLYKE
VAN SLYK, Nicholas, N.Y., Abigail W18199
VAN SLYKE, George, N.Y., S10016
Martin, N.Y., Maria/Maracha, W15812
Martin, N.Y., Anna, W18196
William, N.Y., Elizabeth, W2461; BLWt.26561-160-55
VAN STEENBERGH, Abraham, N.Y., Catharine, W9530
Benjamin, N.Y., S23039
Elias, N.Y., Mary, See STEENBERGH
Elias, N.Y., Katharine, See STEENBERGH
Thomas G., N.Y., S11631
VAN SURDAM, Anthony, N.Y., R10892
VAN SUYDAM, Andrew, N.Y., Esther, W16773
Anthony, N.Y., See VAN SURDAM
VANSYCKLE, Cornelius, See Corneius VANSICKLE
VAN TASSEL, Abraham, N.Y., Elizabeth, W16770
Cornelius, N.Y., Alsey, W18201
Jacob, N.Y., S23465
Jacob, N.Y., Weentie/Wientie,
VAN TASSEL (continued)
W18183
Rachel, Navy, N.Y., former wid. of Gilbert Potter, which see
Stephen, N.Y., Elizabeth, W4365; BLWt.26219-160-55
VAN TASSELL, Nicholas, N.Y., Mary, W18182
VANTILBURG, Henry, N.J., R10894
VAN TILBURGH, Peter, N.J., S15237
William, N.J., S931
VAN TILE, Egbert, Pvt. Hazen's Regt., BLWt.13855. Iss. 9/25/1789 to Peter Anspach, ass.
VAN TINE, Abraham, N.J., S1133
Jacob, N.J., S9495
Rynear, N.J., Nelly, W107
VANTRESSE, Joseph, Md., S4700
VAN TUYL, John, N.J., Jane, W22483
VANTUYLE, John, N.Y., S11601
VANTYLE, Abraham, N.J., S46077
VAN TYNE, Isaac, N.Y., S42581
VAN VALEN, Samuel, See VERVALEN
VAN VALIET, Joseph, See VAN VLEIT
VAN VALKENBURG, Bernard, N.Y., S11637
Christian, N.Y., Catharine, W15810
VAN VALKENBURGH, Adam, N.Y., See FOLLOCK
Bartholomew, N.Y., R10899. Alive in 1832
Bartholomew J., N.Y., Catharine, W19567; BLWt.2255-200-Lt. Iss. 8/19/1790. Name spelled Barth. Van Volkenburg. D. 8/11/1831
Francis, N.Y., Sylvia, W19571
John A., N.Y. See VAN VALKINBURGH
William, N.Y., S11597
VAN VALKINBURGH, John A., N.Y., Sally, BLWt.71144-160-55
VAN VARCK, James, Pvt., N.J., BLWt.8815. Iss. 7/16/1789 to Rachel Van Varck, legal rep.
VAN VECHTEN, Derick, N.Y., S23047
VAN VEGHTEN, Tobias, N.Y., BLWt. 2261. See Tobias Van VECHTEN
VAN VLACK, Abraham, N.Y., Margaret R10895
VAN VLAIR, Adam, N.J., R10896
VAN VLECK, Benjamin, N.Y., R10897
Samuel, N.Y., Catharine, W16455
VAN VLEEK, Benjamin, N.Y. See VAN VLECK
VAN VLEET, George, N.Y., S11634
John, N.Y., See VANFLEET
Samuel, N.J. See VANFLEET
VAN VLEIT, Joseph, Pa., Susanna, W3629
VAN VLIET, Aaron/Aury/Aurie, Aurant/Arory, N.Y., Maria Norton former wid., W17406; BLWt.8142-160-55
VAN VOAST, Gershom/Joachim, N.Y., R10901
VAN VOLKENBURG, Barth., N.Y. See Bartholomew VAN VALKENBURGH
VAN VOLKENBURGH, Adam, See FOLLOCK
Bartholomew, N.Y. See VAN VALKENBURGH
VAN VOORHASE, William, N.J., S6304
VAN VOORHIS, Albert, N.J., Rachel,

VAN VOORHIS (continued)
W150
VAN VORHASE, William, N.J. See VAN VOORHASE
VAN VORST, Christian, N.Y., BLWt.1921-100
James, N.Y., Wilmot/Williampe, R10902
James J., N.Y., Huldah, W2380; BLWts.1526-100 & 244-60-55
Jelles, N.Y., S42602
Jellis John Baptist, Cont., N.Y., Catharine, W26614
Joachim, N.Y. See Gershom VAN VOAST
John Jacobus, Cont., N.Y., S11624
VAN VOST, Jellis, See Jelles VAN VORST
VAN VRACKEN, Gerret, N.Y., R10903
Claus I./Claus J., N.Y., S32033; b. 7/18/1759
Claus J., N.Y., S28931; b. 1/27/1761
John J., N.Y., R10904
VAN VRANKAN, Richard, N.Y., S11623
VAN VRANKEN, Claus J., N.Y. See VAN VRANCKEN
Derick, N.Y., S28922
Evert, N.Y., S11606
Garret, See Gerret VAN VRACKEN
John G., N.Y., Getty, W18190
Maus, N.Y., Sarah, W15970
Nicholas P., N.Y., S17170
Rebecca, N.Y., former wid. of Nicholas Yates, which see
VAN WAGENEN, Gerrit H., N.Y., S9499
Hendericus, N.Y., R10905
Johannes, N.Y., R10906
Teunis, N.Y., BLWt.2256-200-Lt. Iss. 8/23/1790. No papers
VAN WAGGENER, Conradt/Coonradt, N.J. See Conradt VAN WAGNEN
VAN WAGNEN, Conradt, N.J., Sarah, W19898
VAN WART, Henry, N.Y., S11619
Isaac, N.Y., Amy, W18239
Isaac, N.Y. No pension. No BL. One of Andre's captors and there have been so many inquiries about him that I placed this in file as a memorandum.
Jacob, N.Y., Hester, W18206
James, N.Y., Christina Remson, former wid., W16691
William, N.Y., S46650
VAN WICKLE, Evert, N.J., R10907
VAN WIE, Cornelius, N.Y., Nancy/Ann, R10908
Isaac, N.Y., S23981
John, N.Y., Alida, W16768
VAN WINKLE, Elias, N.J., Hannah, W6351; BLWt.27567-160-55
John, N.J., S32564
William, N.J., Mary, W609; BLWt. 26877-160-55
VAN WOERT, Henry, N.Y., BLWt.2252-200-Lt. Iss. 8/25/1790
Jacob, N.Y., S23040
John, Cont., N.Y., S14758
Rutger, N.Y., S11635
Thomas, N.Y., Diana, R10909
VAN WOMER, Peter, See VAN WURMER
VAN WORMER, Cornelius, N.Y., Catharine, W18197
VAN WURMER, Peter, N.Y., S23464
VAN ZANDT, John, N.J., S1137
John, N.J., See VAN ZANT
John, N.J., Charity, W111
Peter, N.J., See VAN SANT
VANZANT, Garrett, N.C., S.C., Margaret, R10911
George, Pa., S23042
James, Cont., Pa., S32034
John, N.J. See VAN ZANDT
John, N.J., S6306
VAN ZANIT, Barnabus, N.J., S7726 b. on L.I., N.Y.
John, N.Y. See VAN SANTE
VAN ZILE, Abraham, N.J., R10913
VANZILE, Harmonus, N.J., R10912
VARGISON, Elijah, Ct., Margery M.M., W19576
VARICK, Richard, Cont., N.Y., Maria, W15697
VARIEL, Joseph, See VARRIEL
VARIELL, Samuel, Mass., Sarah, W22479
VARLEY, Bernard, Cont., Rachel, W26616; BLWt.7310-160-55. N.Y. res. & agcy. of sold. in 1818
VARMILIYA, Benjamin, N.Y. See VERMILYEA
VARNADORE, Henry, S.C., R10827, b. S.C.
Mathew, S.C., R10914, b. S.C.
VARNEDOORE, Mathew, See VARNADORE
VARNER, Henry, N.C., S4701
John, Mass., Catherine, W25826
Joseph, Cont., Va., Molly, W1762; BLWt.12641-100 & 138-60-55
Matthew/Mathew, N.C., S7787
Phillip, Pa., S40613
VARNEY, Francis, Mass., S35687
VARNON, Joseph, Pvt., Va., BLWt. 12641 iss. 7/14/179- to Robert Means, ass. Also BLWt.139-60-55
VARNUM, Benjamin, Mass., Molly, W25821
Enoch, Va.? Dis. Pa. Agency
James, Cont., Mass., R.I., S48720
James Mitchell, R.I., Martha, W25829
Joel, Mass., Marebah, W22478
John, N.H., Dis--
Jonas, Mass., S18637
Samuel, Cont., R.I., S35686
VARRELL, Joseph, Cont., Mass., See VARRIEL
Samuel, Mass. See VARIELL
VARRIEL, Joseph, Cont., Mass., Elizabeth Herriden/Hariden, former wid., W23272. Her alleged 1st husb. was John Davis, Mass., which see
VARS, Joseph, R.I., S11604
VASCHE, LE, De St. Maria. S.C. See Le Vacher DE ST. MARIA
VASS, Philip V., Va., S19493
Vincent, Va., Caty, W6337; BLWt. 15157-160-55
VASSAL, Benjamin, Mass., S17745
VASSER, Daniel, Va. See VERSER
Micajah, N.C., R10916
Nathaniel, Va., Sarah, W6339
VASTFALL, Abraham, N.Y., See WESTFALL
VAUGHAN, Abram/Abraham, Va., Margaret S., W610; BLWt.16131-160-55
Absalom, Va., Martha, W6343
Almond, Va., Joanna, W6342
Anna, R.I., former wid. of William Lowing, which see
Benjamin, Ct., Vt., S14755
Claiborne, Cont., Va., BLWt. 637-300-Surg. Mate
Claiborne Va., BLWt.2271-300-Capt. Iss. 5/29/1792 to Robert Means, ass. No papers. Note: There was a surgeon's mate of this name whose heirs rec'd Wt.637-300 (See papers). No means of ascertaining whether there were two officers of this name from Va.
Ebenezer, Mass., Joanna, W14077; BLWt.8191-160-55
Ephraim, Va., R10919
Frederick, Ct., S32565
George, Pa., S25466
Ingraham/Ingram, Va., S32568
Jabez, Mass., Violettee, W16157
James, Va., S7779
James, Va., S39497
Jesse, Va., S38450
Joel, N.C., S7781
John, Ct., S42570
John, Del., BLWt.2269-200-Lt. Iss. 6/6/1794 to Wm. D. Brown, ass. No papers
John, Sgt. Md., BLWt.11788. Iss. 9/5/1789
John, Mass., S42579
John/John D., Mass. & Indian War 1785-6, S46292, BLWts.1946-100 & 323-60-55
John, R.I., S22029
John, Va., S7788
John, Va., R18674. Va. Half Pay
Joseph, Del., BLWt.2268-450-Lt. Col. Iss. 5/1/1794 to Hannah Vaughan, Admx. No papers
Obadiah, N.Y., S42571
Prince (colored), R.I., S42603
Samuel, Mass., Mary, W25823
Thomas, Mass., S33851
Thomas, Pa., S40614
Thomas, Va., S6298
Vincent, N.C., Martha, W4366
William, Md., S35107
William, N.C., S9498
William, S.C., Alis/Alice, W11691; BLWt.26110-160-55
William, Va., S14754
Zebulon, Mass., S33208
VAUGHEN, John, Pvt., N.J., BLWt. 8819. Iss. 7/2/1790 to Israel Smith, ass.
Prince, Pvt., R.I., BLWt.3545. Iss. 12/31/1789
VAUGHN, Abner, Va., R10917
John, Cont., Md. or Va., Nancy, R10920
John, Pvt. Crane's Cont. Art., Mass. BLWt.5206 iss. 1/26/1790 to

VAUGHN (continued)
John May
John, N.Y., Lydia, W2884
John, Va. See VAUGHAN
Samuel, N.J., S1129
Thomas, Va., S22030
William, Ct., See VAGHN
William, Va., Elizabeth, W2708; BLWt.29019-160-55
VAWLER, William Va. See VAWTER
VAWTER, William, Va., R10921 Va. Half Pay. BLWt.1699-200. N.A. Acc. No. 874-050181 Half Pay William Vawter
VEACH, Elijah, Va., S37498
VEALE, James Carr, S.C., Levina, W9586
VEASEY, Joshua, N.H., S18257
Thomas, N.H., Lydia, W22484
VEATCH, Daniel, Va.(?), Charity, R10925
Elias, S.C., Jane/Jean, b. Md., R10926
Jeremiah, Md., Priscilla, W8800
VEAZEY, Moses, Mass., S35688
Samuel, N.H., S11607
Thomas, N.H., See VEASEY
VEAZIE, Joseph, Mass., R10922
VECHTEN, VAN, Tobias, N.Y., BLWt. 2261-200-Lt. Iss. 12/21/1790 to Jacob Cuyler & Lydia Cuyler, Admrs. No papers. Heitman's Hist. Reg. gives this man's name as Tobias Van Veghten
VEDDER, Albert L., N.Y., S11840
Cornelius, N.Y., Harriet, R10946; BLWt.43513-160-55
Frederick, N.Y., S21547
Harmanus, N.Y., S6310; BLWt.9545-160-55
John, N.Y., Sarah, W18219
VEDER, Samuel, N.Y., S11655
VEEDER, Garret S., N.Y., S7792
John B., N.Y., R10927
Nicholas G., N.Y., S16283; BLWt. 8448-160-55
Peter V., N.Y., Jane, W19574
Simon, N.Y., S19494
VEGHTE, Henry, N.J., Dorothy, W6361
Rynier, N.J., S1140. Left widow Catharine
VENABLE, William, S.C., Sarah, W7366. b. in Va.
VENABLES, John, N.C., S.C., Mary, W18220
VENALL, John P. See John Peter AHL
VENARD, Thomas, Va., Pa., S16282
William, Va., S14766
VENDRICK, Peter, N.C., S7791
VENNER, John, R.I., S21548
VENUS, John, Pvt., N.Y., BLWt. 7906. Iss. 7/9/1790 to Theodosius Fowler, ass.
John, N.Y., S26845
John, N.Y., S42595
Michael, N.Y., R10928
VERANO, Peter, Cont. (Canada), S18638
VERBACK, Philip, N.H., S14767; BLWt.26109-160-55
VERBELL, Henry, Cont. See WIRBLE
VERBRYCK, Ralph, N.J., S23468
Samuel G., N.J., S23049
William, N.J., Rebecca, W8799
VERDEN, James, S.C., Sarah, W22485
VERDIER, Benedict, Foreign, BLWt. 2276-200-Lt. Iss. 8/29/1794. No papers
VERDIN, James, S.C. SeeVERDEN
VERGASON, Elijah, Ct. See VARGISON
VERGESON, Daniel, Ct., Phebe, R10929
VERGISON, Elijah, Pvt., Ct., BLWt. 6597 iss. 9/9/1790 to James F. Sebor, ass.
VERIEUL, Joseph, Pvt., N.Y., BLWt. 7938 iss. 3/9/1791 to Sam Smith, ass.
VERITY, Samuel, N.Y., R10930
VERLIE, Bernard, Fifer, Hazen's Regt., BLWt.13853 iss.2/4/1790
Francis, Drummer, Hazen's Regt. BLWt.13860 iss. 2/4/1790
VERLIE, Michael, Corp. Hazen's Regt., BLWt.13852. Iss. 9/9/1789 to James Reynolds, ass.
Michael, Mass., S42593
VERMEULE, Cornelius, See VERMULE
VERMILIA, Jacob M., N.Y., Phebe Dominick, former wid., W16960
VERMILLION, Jesse, N.C. See VIRMILLION
Samuel, Md., N.C., S7790
Wilson, N.C. See VIRMILLION
VERMILYA, John, Cont., N.Y., Esther Wells, former wid., W11777; BLWts. 170-60-55 & 228-100 iss. 2/24/1806 "Matross, N.Y."
VERMILYEA, Benjamin, N.Y., R10934
John, Cont., N.Y., Rachel, W2462; BLWt.272-60-55
Philip, N.Y., S42578
William, N.Y., S14764; BLWt.53681-160-55
William Dyckman, N.Y., Frances, R10933
VERMONNET, Jane, Va., former wid. of Samuel K. Bradford, which see
VERMULF, Cornelius, N.J., Elizabeth W19573
VERNADER, Peter, N.J., R10826
VERNER, David, S.C., S21550
John, Pa., S23050
John, Pa., S40619
John, S.C., S7793
John, Pvt. Va., BLWts.10536 & 12637 iss. 1/8/1793 to James McNeal, ass.
Philip, Pvt. Pa., BLWt.10535. Iss. 7/9/1789
Philip, Pa. See VARNER
VERNEY, Francis, Mass. See VARNEY
VERNON, Frederick, Pa., BLWt.2263-400-Major. Iss. 12/29/1792. No papers
Isaac, N.C., S21549
Job, Pa., BLWt.1066-300
Richard, N.C., S1883
Richard, Va., S38451
Thomas, Va., S39112
VERNOOY, Peter, See VAN NOOY
VERONE, Joseph, Va., S41283; BLWt.1327-100
VERONY, Joseph, Va. See VERONE
VERRIAN, John, Pvt., N.Y., BLWt. 7905. Iss. 7/28/1790 to G.H.V. Wagennen, ass.
VERRIL, Edward, N.H., Mary, W22486
VERRITY, Gilbert, Pvt. N.Y., BLWt.7918 iss. 5/3/179? to Abel Henry Smith, ass.
VERRUS, John, N.Y., See VENUS
VERRY, Jonathan, Pvt. Art. Artificers, BLWt.13862 iss. 10/5/1790
Jonathan, Ct., S35373
VERSER, Daniel, Va., Elizabeth, W19575
VERTREES, Isaac, Pa., Elizabeth, R10935
VERVALEN, Abraham, N.J., Elizabeth W2495
Cornelius, N.J., Ann, W18212
Samuel, N.J., Mary, W16774
VERVALIN, Daniel, N.Y., S14765
VERY, George, Mass., N.Y., S33857
Jonathan, Ct. See VERRY
William, Mass., Sally, W15732
VESBROUGH, Isaac, See VOSBROUGH
VESEY, Joshua, N.H. See VEASEY
VEST, George, Va., Nancy, W26617; BLWt.34983-160-55
John, Va., S15692
John, Va., S17173
Philip H., Va., S7789
Samuel, Va., S16563
VETTER, William, N.Y. See FEETER
VIA, Littleberry, Va., R20442
William, Va., S9513
William, Va., Mary, W6363
VIAH, Gideon, Va., S6311
John, Va. See VIER
VIAL, John, R.I. See VIOL
Samuel, Navy (?), R953
VIALL, Allen, R.I., Hannah, W15733
John, R.I., S42596
Nathaniel, Mass., Patience, W3740; BLWt.26280-160-55
Nathaniel, Mass., Betsey, W18221
Nathaniel, R.I., Patience, W25836
Samuel, Sgt., Mass., BLWts.5197 & 5194. Iss. 5/10/1799 to Allen Crocker
Samuel, Mass., S19140
VIARS, William, N.C., S9512
VIBBARD, David, Cont., Ct., Sarah Simons, former wid., W22214
Jesse, Ct. See VIBBART
John, Ct., Cont., Hannah, W18223
Timothy, N.Y., S11628
VIBBART, Jesse, Cont., S35374. Ct. res.
VIBBERT, Jesse, Ct. See VIBBART
John, Ct. See VIBBARD
VIBBIRD, David, Cont., Ct. See VIBBARD
VICALL, Adam, Md., Martin, Ann, former wid., See VIGAL
VICE, John, ____, R10937
VICK, Jesse, N.C., Mary, W19577
John, Va., S6312

VICK (continued)
Joseph, N.C., Dinah, W6364; BLWt.3833-160-55
Joshua, Va., S31452
VICKARY, Robert, Mass., Ruth, See VICKERY
VICKER, Robert, Pvt. in Proctor's Art., Pa., BLWt.10546. Iss. 6/20/1789
VICKERE, Samuel, Mass., S33861
VICKERS, Elijah, N.C. See VICKES
James, N.C., Elizabeth, R10939
John, N.C., Anne, R10938
John, Va., Nancy, R10942; BLWt. 1918-100
Riley, N.C., Mary, R10941
Samuel, S.C., BLWt.2273-450-Surg. Iss. 12/16/1799 to "Mary Lupp & Lucia Vickers, and John Bray, guardian for Sally and Mary the children of Tho. L. Vickers, the Heirs." No papers
William, N.C., S16564
VICKERY, David, Cont., Mass., S35689
Elijah, Cont., Mass., Polly, W20987
Hezekiah, N.C., b. N.C., R10959
John, Mass., enl. from Bedford, R.I., S42605; BLWt.1879-100
Robert, Mass., Ruth, W6366; BLWt. 19909-160-55
Sampson, N.C., b. N.C., R10943
Samuel, Corp. Crane's Cont. Art. Mass., BLWt.5202 iss. 1/26/1790 to John May
Timothy, Ct., R10944
VICKES, Elijah, N.C., Sarah, W4368
VICKOR, William, Pvt. Art. Artificers of Pa., BLWt.13865. Iss. 4/19/1791 to Alexander Power, ass.
VICKORY, Luke, N.C., S1782
Merrifield/Merifield, Cont., N.H. Anny, See VICORY
William, S.C., Susannah, W27307; BLWt.61302-160-55
VICKROY, Thomas, Pa., Sarah Ann, W3632; BLWt.76506-160-55
VICKRY, Elijah, See VICKERY
VICKS, Elijah, N.C. See VICKES
VICORY, Elijah, Pvt. Crane's Cont. Art., Mass., BLWt.5203. Iss. 3/14/1791 to Mace Tisdale
John, R.I., & French & Indian War, Elizabeth, W22488
Merifield/Merrifield, Cont., N.H. Anny, W6365
Merifield, Pvt., Hazen's Regt., BLWt.13856 iss. 4/19/1792 to Isaac Bronson, ass.
VICTOR, Felix, Cont., Canada, Genevieve Boucher, former wid., R1052
John, Cont., Va., Sarah, W5171
VIDETO, Joseph, Mass., S35690
VIELE, John, N.Y., S11609
Philip, N.Y., Rachel, R10947
VIER, John, Va., Sarah, W3896
VIERS, Benjamin, Va., S6313
VIGAL, Adam, Md., Ann Martin, former wid., W24139; BLWt.533-160-55

VILLAS, Noah, Mass. See VILOS
VILLETON, Samuel, Pa., S16565
VILLITON, Samuel, See VILLETON
VILOS, Noah, Mass., S41285
VINCENT, Aaron, Md. See VINSENT
Bethuel, Pa., S22564
David, Mass., S19142
George, N.C., Va., Eleanor, R10948
Jeremiah, N.Y., Mary, W22489
John, Va., S16566
Joseph, Pvt. N.Y., BLWt.7903 iss. 10/15/17-- to James Reynolds, ass.
Joshua, Cont., Mass. See VINSENT
Joshua, R.I., Susannah, W20107
Levi, N.J., S33858
Thomas, N.H., S11608
Thomas, not Rev. War, Indian War 1788. Ky. Agcy., Old War Inv. File 26479
William, N.H., Alice, W16082
VINCINER, George, Va., S32569
VINE, Solomon, Vt., S43213
VINEGARDNER, John, Pvt., Pa., BLWt.10545. Iss. 9/27/1799
VINER, John, Cont., Mass., Sarah, W5424; BLWt.19821-160-55
VINES, John, N.C., R20444
Samuel, N.C., R20443
Thomas, Va., Mary, W2028; BLWt.35683-160-55
VINET, John, N.Y., S43211
VINETTE, John Baptiste, Drummer, Hazen's Regt., BLWt.13861. Iss. 1/22/1790 to Benj. Mooers, ass.
VINEYARD, George, Va., S7794
William, Va., Martha, R10951
VINIAL John alias Jacob, Pvt. Armand's Corps. BLWt.13849 iss. 2/28/1791 to Penelope Butler, ass.
VINING, Ebenezer, Mass., S43212
Elisha, Mass., S33209
George, Mass., S33859
Israel, Mass., S30179
John, Cont., Mass., Mary, W25835
Richard, Mass., S11638
VINNET, John, Pvt., N.J., BLWt. 8817 iss. 6/16/1789 to Thomas Coyle, ass.
VINSEN, John, Mass. See VINSON
VINSENT, Aaron, Md., Rebecca, W4367
Joshua, Cont., Mass., S19143
VINSON, Aaron, Md. See VINSENT
John, Mass., Rebecca, W14078
Thomas, Mass., S30180
William, N.C., R10949
William, N.C., Rebecca, R10952
VINTON, Abiathar, Cont., Mass., Sarah, W1674
John, Ct., Susannah, W16775
John, Cont., Mass., S41284
Joseph, Mass., S33860
Levi, Mass., S43214
Seth, Ct., Mass., Polly, W611
VINYARD, Jacob, Pa., Barbara, R10950
VINZANT, Barnabus, See VAN ZANTT
John, Pa., S14769
VIOL, John, R.I., Sea Service, S39873

VIOLET, John, Va., Constance, W3205; BLWts.1387-100 & 94-60-55
VIRGIL, Abijah, Mass., N.Y., Zipporah, W22487
Asa, Corp., Mass., BLWt.5196 iss. 5/1/1799 to Abijah Holbrook
Asa, Mass., S43210
VIRGINIA, Jeremiah, Vt., S19141
VIRMILLION, Jesse, N.C., Mary, W6362
Wilson, N.C., R10932
VISCHER, John T. See VISSCHER
VISPEE, Jacob, Pvt. Crane's Cont. Art., Mass., BLWt.5205 iss. 3/1790
VISSCHER, John I., N.Y., Annatie/Annatje/Ann, R10956
John T., N.Y., S28929
Matthew, N.Y. See VISSHER
VISSHER, Matthew, N.Y., Lydia, R10954
VITTUM, William, N.H., S23052
VLEIT, David, N.J., Jane, W4369; BLWt.26334-160-55
VLIET, Daniel, N.J., S6314
David, N.J., Jane, See VLEIT
Jaspar/Jasper, N.J., Mary, W3633
William, N.J., R10958
VOGHT, George, Pa., S5420
Peter Christian, N.Y., S42604
VOLENTINE, Barnard, See Bernard VALENTINE
Christopher, N.C. See EATON
VOLK, William, Pa. See FOLK
VOLKENBURGH, Francis, Pvt., N.Y. BLWt.7902 iss. 5/5/1791 to Stephen Hogeboom, ass.
VOLS, Conrad, N.Y., Catharine, See FOLTS
VOLTZ, Joshua, Va. See FOLTZ
VON HEER, Bartholomew, Pa., BLWt.2275-300
VON STEUBEN, Frederick (Baron) Cont., BLWt.2128-1100. Iss. 6/8/1789. See Steuben folder
VOORHEES, Abraham, N.J., S1142
Abraham, N.J., S11610
Albert, Cont., N.J., S33862
Coert, N.J., Ann, W2496
Cornelius, N.J. -- Claim missing 11/24/1928. See report of Sec. War 1835. Pension in Morris Co. N.J., Act of 6/7/1832, etc. Also see Agency Book
David, N.J., S932
Isaac, N.J., Jane, W6368
Isaac, N.J., R10960
John, N.J., Ann Conover, former wid., W146
John, N.J., Maria/Mary, R10963
John J., N.J., Lucy, R10962
Paul, N.J., S6315
Peter, N.J., S1143
Peter, N.J., Mary, W213
Peter L., N.J., BLWt.2262-300-Capt. Iss. 8/18/1795 to John Pool, Jr. Admr. Also recorded as above under BLWt.2656 and name spelled Woorhees
VOORHEIS, Abraham, N.J., S33864
VOORHES, Aaron, N.J., Hannah, W122
Albert, N.J., Margaret, W4370

VOORHES (continued)
James, N.J., Sarah, W25839
John, Pvt., N.J., BLWts.8716 & 8818 iss. 10/13/1792
VOORHIES, Albert, See VAN VOORHIS
John, N.J., Ann Conover, former wid., W146
Minne L., N.J., Dis.
VOORHIS, Garret, N.J., Matildah, W6367
Garrett/Garret, N.J., S47189; BLWt.1411-100. Iss. 11/15/1828
Hendrick/Henry, Cont., N.J., Elizabeth, W16457
Ruliff, N.Y., R10964
VOORHUS, Abraham, See VOORHEES
VORCE, Zeniah/Zeruiah, the wid., R.I., former wid. of Barak Jordan, which see
VORELL, Samuel, Mass. See VARIELL
VORHIS, Henry, See Hendrick VOORHIS
VORIS, James, N.J., S33865
John, N.J. See VOORHEES
John, Va., S14772 b. N.J.--to Pa.-to Va.
VORS, Jesse, Ct., S35375
VORSE, Jesse, Ct. See VORS
VORY, Isaiah, N.J. See VORYS
VORYS, Isaiah, N.J., S6309
VOSBERG, Peter I., Cont., N.Y., See Peter J. VOSBURGH
VOSBROUGH, Isaac, Mass., Polly, W1673; BLWt.35682-160-55
VOSBURGH, Abraham, N.Y., S23471, b. 1755 in Albany, N.Y. and always resided there up to 7/21/1832
Abraham, N.Y., R10967. b. 5/16/1753 at Pownal, Vt. (then Hoosick N.Y.) and resided there up to 4/9/1833
Abraham I., N.Y., S23469. b. 11/4/1757 at Kinderhook, N.Y. & there at enl. Res. Johnstown, Montgomery Co., N.Y. in 1833
Eliakim, Mass., Catharine, W16458
Isaac, Mass., Polly, See VOSBROUGH
Jacob, N.Y., R10968
Jacob, N.Y., R10969
Jehoiakim, N.Y., S23470
Peter, N.Y., S28930
Peter I., Cont., N.Y., Elizabeth, W19578; BLWt.2251-300-Capt. Iss. 8/12/1790. Name spelled Vosberg. His middle name Isaac. See Heitman
William, N.Y., S14771
VOSE, Amariah, Cont., Mass., Jane, W25840
Charles, Ct., Elizabeth, W6375; BLWt.6598-100 iss. 1791, & 132-60-55
Edward, R.I., Rebecca, R10953
Elijah, Cont., Mass., S33863; BLWt.2244-450-Lt. Col. Iss. 4/22/1793 to Calvin Sanger, ass.
Henry, N.Y., R10970
Jesse, Sgt., Ct., BLWt.6596 iss. 5/17/1790
Jesse, Mass., S35691; BLWt.706-100
John, Mass., S33210
John Blake, Mass. See Edward BLAKE

VOSE (continued)
Joseph, Mass., BLWt.2243-500-Col. Iss. 4/18/1796 to Jeremiah Mason, ass. No papers
Samuel, Cont., Mass., Mariam, W20108
Thomas, Cont., Mass., BLWt.723-300
William, Ct., S35376
VOSSELLER, Jacob, N.J., S1141
Luke, N.J., S901
VOUGHT, Godfrey, N.Y., S23051
Henry C., N.Y., S46078
VOWLES, Charles, Va., R18701. Va. Half Pay. N.A. Acc. No.874-050182 Half Pay Charles Vowles
Henry, Va., R18700 Va. Half Pay. N.A. Acc. No.874-050183 Half Pay Henry Vowles
James, Va., Ann, W18224
VRADENBERGH, William, N.Y., S43217
VRADENBURGH, Jacob, N.Y., S11629
Thomas, N.Y., S23987
VREDENBURGH, Isaac, N.J., S771
John, Cont., N.J., S6316
Orra, N.Y., S6317
William, Pvt., N.Y., BLWt.7920. Iss. 7/20/1791 to James Reed, ass.
VREEDENBURGH, Peter, Pvt., N.Y., BLWt.7921 iss. 8/3/1790 to Cornelius V. Dyck, ass.
VREELAND, Abraham, N.J., Rachel, W6369; BLWt.19910-160-55
Abraham, N.J., Elizabeth, W22490
Daniel, Cont., N.J., Betsey, See VRELAND
Garret G., N.J., Rachel, W18225
Jacob, N.J., Jane, R10971
Jemima, N.J., former wid. of Timothy Gould, W6376; BLWt. 38514-160-55
John, N.J., S43216
John, N.J., Elizabeth, W1005
Michael, Pa., See VREELANDT
Peter, N.J., Margaret, W18226
VREELANDT, Daniel, Pvt. Sheldon's Dragoons, Ct., BLWt.6601 iss. 9/2/1789
Michael, Pa., Dytha, W25844
VRELAND, Daniel, Cont., N.J., Betsey, W1515
Peter, N.J. See VREELAND
VREDENBURGH, James, Cont. See VAN GORDER
VROMAN, Bartholomew E., N.Y., Maria, W25842; BLWt.19768-160-55
Isaac Jacob, N.Y., S11612
Peter, N.Y., See VROOMAN
Tunis/Teunis, See VROOMAN
VROOM, Hendrick P., N.J., S1144
VROOMAN, Adam, N.Y., Engelica, W20109
Bartholomew E., N.Y. See VROMAN
Bartholomew I., N.Y., Hannah, R10972
Isaac Jacob, N.Y. See VROMAN
John J., N.Y., Amy, W25843
Lawrence, N.Y., R10973
Peter, N.Y., Angelica, W18673
Simon J., N.Y., Sally, W6370
Teunis/Tunis, N.Y., R10974

VUNCK, Henry/Hendrick, N.J., S11617
VYER, John, Va. See VIER

W

WAALRADT, Isaac, N.Y. See WALLERATH
WABEL, John Henry/Henry, N.Y., See John Henry WAFLE
WACK, Frederick William, Ct., S40647
WACKMAN, Marcus, N.Y., R10975
WADAMS, Caleb, Cont., N.Y., S11643
WADDAMS, Caleb, Mass. See WADHAM
WADDEL, William, N.Y., Olive, W25847; BLWts.7997 & 14-60-55 iss. 12/15/1791, 1855. Wt. 7997 to John Slaughter, ass.
WADDELL, James, S.C., S39114
Nathaniel, Va., S42607
Thomas, Va., S11697
WADDEN, Thomas, Pvt., Mass., BLWt.5305. Iss. 1/20/1796 to Jane Phillips
Thomas, Cont., Mass. See WORDEN
WADDILL, John, Ga., N.C., served also 1788-1791, R10977
WADDLE, George, Md., S9515
John, Va., Phebe, R10978
Joseph, Va. See WOODDELL
Martin, Va., Susan, W1008; BLWt. 26885-160-55
Thomas, Va. See WADDELL
William, N.Y., See WADDEL
William, Pa., S40645
WADDY, Thomas, Pvt., Va., BLWt. 12661. Iss. 1/31/1794 to Francis Graves, ass.
WADE, Abner, Mass., S35707; BLWt. 797-300
Claiborne, Va., S11666
Daniel, N.C., Sarah, W18267
David, ___, Sarah, R10986. S.C. res. in 1853
David E., N.J., R10981
Edward, Pvt. Md., BLWt.11792 iss. 2/1/1790
Edward, N.H., Elizabeth, W1106; BLWts.1812-100 & 181-60-55
Edward, N.H., Mary, R10982
George, Pa., Va., S7829
Henry, Pvt., N.J., BLWt.8836. Iss. 4/20/1793
Hezekiah, Pa., Va., b. Md., Rebecca, W6387
Isaac, Mass., Asenath, R10980
Isaac, Va., Polly, W6389
Jacob, Va., S41290
James, Pvt., Md., BLWts.13891 & 14096. Iss. 1/28/1795 to Francis Sherrard, ass. of Leonard Holt, Admr.
John, Pvt., Ct., BLWt.6666. Iss. 2/5/1790
John, Mass., S33876
John, Mass., Rosanna, W2464; BLWt.14519-160-55
John, Va., S14801
Joseph, N.C., b. N.C., S7826
Joshua, R.I., Mary, W2206
Joshua, Va., Anna, W6388
Jotham, Mass., Margaret, W1516
Moses, Va., S38456
Nathaniel, Cont., Mass., S33234

WADE (continued)
Nathaniel, not Rev. War. N.J. Mil. Whiskey Insurrection, Polly, BLWt.76453-160-55. No claim for pension
Nathaniel, R.I., Molly, W11728
Noadiah, N.J., S33873
Obadiah, N.C., b. N.C., S32576
Obadiah, Va., S16570
Richard, Ga., Entered service in Va., b. in Md.; R10985
Richard, Va., S3443
Robert, Va., S6325
Robert, Va., Ann, R10979
Silvanus/Sylvanus, Mass., Polly/Molly, W2886
Solomon, N.Y., S11677
Thomas, Va., Mary, R10984
Timothy, Ct., Sabra, W19585
Willard, R.I., S21559
William, Pvt., Pa., BLWt.10603 iss. 1/17/1792 to George Moore, ass.
William, Pvt., Pa., BLWt.10640. Iss. 1/5/1796 to Robert Prise, ass.
WADHAM, Abigail, Cont. Ct., Green Mt. Boys, former wid. of Herman Allen, which see
Caleb, Mass., Sarah, BLWt.104423-160-55
WADKINS, Benedict, N.C., Barbara, W11709; BLWt.80036-160-55
John, N.C., S11662
John, N.C., Cynthia, W6415; BLWt.15154-160-55
Thomas, N.C. See WATKINS
William, N.C., S.C., R11197
WADLEIGH, Sgt., N.H., BLWts.3546 & 42-60-55. Iss. 11/28/1789
John, N.H., S18264
John, N.H., Martha Batchelder, former wid., W27661; BLWt.3546 iss. 11/28/1789; BLWt.42-60-55. She applied for BL for her last husb., William Bachelder, N.H. BL Ry. Claim 273093-55
John, N.H., R10988
Jonathan, N.H., Susanna, W18284
Nathaniel, Mass., Nancy, W2032; BLWt.5073-160-55
Simeon, N.H., Abigail, W22538
WADLIA, Daniel, Mass., S35692
WADLINE, Sarah, Mass., former wid. of Humphrey Tyler, which see
WADLINGTON, John, Va. See WATLINGTON
WADSWORTH, Elijah, Sheldon's Horse, BLWt.2357-300
Epaphras, Ct., S22567
Hezekiah, Ct., Cont., S6335
Israel, Ct., S19146
John, Ct., Nela, W18273
John, Mass., S19497
Joseph, Ct., Mass., Chloe, W9155; BLWt.39489-160-55
Joseph, Cont., Mass., S35711
Peleg, Mass., R10991
Reuben, Ct., S32042
Robert, Cont., Va., S41296
Roger, Ct., Ann, W22529

WADSWORTH (continued)
Seneca, Mass., Duesberry, W22500
Thomas, Ct., S11645; BLWt.11080-160-55
Wait, Mass., Sea Service, Priscilla, R10992; BLWt.40012-160-55
William, N.C., S7807
WAFFLE, John Henry/Henry, See John Henry WAFLE
WAFLE, Henry, N.Y. See John Henry
John Henry/Henry, N.Y., Margaret, W22526
WAGER, Charles, N.J., Hannah, W6423
WAGES, Benjamin, Cont., Va., Mary, R10993
WAGG, James, Cont., Mass., S35703. She was pensioned as former wid. of Tobias Gould. (Rhoda Wagg), Mass., which see
John, Cont., Pa., S11640
Rhoda, Mass. former wid. of Tobias Gould, which see
WAGGENER, Andrew, Va., BLWt.2424-400-Maj. Iss. 8/25/1789
Thomas, Va., S31456
WAGGERMAN, Emanuel, Pvt., N.Y., BLWt.7988. Iss. 8/18/1790
Emanuel, N.Y., Rachel Cummings, former wid., R2579
George, Pvt. N.Y., BLWt.7999. Iss. 7/10/1790 to John Quackenbos ass.
WAGGISTER, William, See WAGSTER
WAGGONER, Adam, N.J. See WAGONER
Christopher, N.C., R10995
Daniel, Pa. See WAGNER
George, N.J., Mary, W2314; BLWt.73545-160-55
George, N.J., Mary, W4845; BLWt. 8826-100 iss. 12/7/1789
George, N.Y., S23989
George, N.C., S3484
Henry, ---- Dis. Pa. Agency
Isaac, S.C., b. S.C., S32578
Jacob, Cont., Md., Pa., S40628
Jacob, Cont., N.Y., Salome, W22528
John, Cont., Pa., Sarah, W27855; BLWt.13895-100. Iss. 1/21/1793
John, Va., S7824
Joseph, N.Y., Catharine, W2499
Michael, Pvt. Ct., BLWt.6707. Iss. 8/4/1796
Michael/Michal, Cont., Pa. res. in 1818, S40636
Thomas, Va. See WAGGENER
WAGGONMAN, George, N.Y., S46320
WAGGS, Elisha, Pvt. R.I., BLWt. 3595 iss. 12/31/1789
WAGLE, Isaac, Pa., R11285
John, N.C., Jemima, R10996
WAGNER, Adam, Pa., Margaretta/Margaritta, W4610
Daniel, Pa., S23992
Jacob, Cont.,Md. See WAGGONER
Jacob, Pa., S6320
John, Pvt. Hazen's Regt., BLWt. 13895 iss. 1/21/1793
Martin, Pa., R10997
Philip, Va., S40637
WAGNON, John Peter, Ga., Rebecca W1109; BLWt.2456-200-Lt. Iss.

WAGNON (continued)
4/7/1796
WAGON, James, N.J., S43225.
See James WYGANT S42616;
seems to have been same
veteran
WAGONER, Adam, N.J., S23995
Jacob, Pvt. Pa., BLWt.10604
iss. 5/23/1797
Jacob, Pa. See WAGGONER
John, Pa., S23055
WAGSTAFF, John, Va., R10998
William, Pa., Va., Charity,
W6420
WAGSTER, William, S.C., S38459
WAHR, Frederick, Pa. See WARE
WAID, Abraham, Ct., S35381
Calvin, N.J., Pa., S32575
Henry, Ct., S35705
Increase, Ct., Freelove, W18293
John, Ct., S35378
Pleasant, Va., R11000
Timothy, Ct., Sabra, See WADE
WAIDE, Moses, Va. See WADE
WAIGHT, Assa, Pvt., Mass., BLWt.
5313 iss. 5/1/1792 to David
Quinton
Joseph, Mass., See WAIT
Thaddeus, Mass., Sally, R11001
WAILES, Edward Lloyd, Md.,
Sarah Briggs, W4375
WAINRIGHT, Samuel, Pvt. Sheldon's
Dragoons, Ct. BLWt.6700 iss.
11/16/1789
WAINWRIGHT, Frances, Gen. Hosp.
N.Y., BLWt.2292-300-Mate. Iss.
10/1/1789. Also recorded as
above under BLWt.2534. No
papers
James, Pvt. Del., BLWt.10907 iss.
9/2/1789
John, Mass., S41208
Joseph, N.J., S11002
Thomas, Ct., S36361
WAIR, Elias, Ct., S33226
WAISTCOAT, Benjamin, Mass. See
WESTCOAT
WAIT, Aaron, Mass., R20472
David, Mass., Abigail, W14084
Ezra, Mass., Sarah, W15457
Gardner, Mass., N.Y., S16015
George, N.Y., S11693
Jeduthan, Mass., Naomi, W4842;
BLWt.762-100
John, Va., S7812
Joseph, Mass., Judith, W15465
Joseph, Mass., Hepzibah, W18252
Josiah, Mass., S30189
Nathan, Mass., Lucy, W14109
Nathaniel, Mass., Vt., S11675
Payn, R.I., S11670
Peleg, R.I., R11004
Thomas, Cont., R.I., Naomi,
W15858
William, Cont., Mass., S14788
William, Mass., S29530
Yelverton, R.I., Siporah, W22506
WAITE, Aaron, Mass., S33215
Asa, Mass., Rebeckah, W18256
Daniel/David, Mass., Lydia, W14114
David, Mass. See Daniel
John, R.I., S43224

WAITE (continued)
Jonathan, Mass., Naomi, R11005;
Rejected BL 293559-55
Joseph, Mass., Sarah, W19589
Thaddeus, Mass. See WAIGHT
WAITES, James, Pa. See WAITS
WAITS, James, Pa., Margaret,
W25898; BLWt.27573-160-55
Jenks/Jancks, R.I., S40627
Samuel, S.C., R11006
WAITT, Jacob, Mass., S33227
Jonathan, Mass., Elizabeth, W19580
WAK-AR-AN-THAR-AUS, James, N.Y.,
R11007; BLWt.2348-300-Capt.
Iss. 3/8/1792. Also recorded as
above under BLWt.2602, name
spelled Wakarantharow
WAKEFIELD, Abel, Va., S3475
Daniel, Pvt. Mass., BLWt.5226
iss. 5/6/1789
Ebenezer, Mass., N.H., Abigail,
W18261; BLWt.29009-160-55
Ezekiel, Mass., Molly/Hannah,
W22545
Gibeon, Cont., Nancy, Me. Agcy.
& res., W22499
Henry, N.C. See WEAKFIELD
Isaiah, Mass., Eunice, W18296
Jonathan, Mass., N.H., Elizabeth,
W11711; BLWt.9053-160-55
Joseph, Mass., Mary, W15458
Joseph, N.H., Relief, R11008
Josiah, Mass., Polly, W25859;
BLWt.26735-160-55
Nathaniel, Mass., S29531
Peter, Navy, N.H., S3476
Samuel, Mass., Elizabeth, W18230
Thomas, Mass., S36360
Thomas, N.C., Jemima, W1107
Timothy, Mass., S30561
WAKELAND, James, Ct., Cont.,
Mercy, W25845; BLWt.13877-100-
Pvt. of Hazen's Regt. Iss. 4/
15/1796 to Nath. Ruggles, ass.
WAKELEE, David, Ct., Mary, W6422
James, Ct. See WAKELAND
John, Ct. See WAKLEE
WAKELEY, Henry, Cont., Ct.,
Deborah, W20113
Jonathan, Ct., Esther Parrot,
former wid., W26286
WAKELIE, Henry, Pvt. Ct., BLWt.
6637 iss. 3/21/1795
WAKELIN, Henry, Cont.,Ct. See
WAKELEY
WAKELY, Abel, Ct., BLWt.1337-100
Benjamin, Pvt. Ct., BLWt.6695
iss. 4/9/1791
WAKEMAN, Gershom, Ct., Lucy Ann,
W2282; BLWt.27590-160-55
Gideon, Ct., S14774
Jabez, Ct., S11681
Joseph, Ct., Rachel, R11009
Lyman, Ct., S147777
Seth, Ct., Mary, W18232
Stephen, Ct., S11683
WAKLE, Thomas, Ct., S40638
WAKLEE, Benjamin, Ct., S44004
John, Ct., Elizabeth, W3479;
BLWt.29030-160-55
Joseph, Cont., Ct., S35377

WAKLY, John, Ct. See WAKLEE
WALACE, Christian, See WALLASIE
WALBRIDGE, Ames, Ct., BLWt.2338-
400-Maj. Iss. 10/16/1789 to
Theodosius Fowler, ass. No
papers
Joshua, Ct., Mass., Priscilla,
W3318, BLWt.19515-160-55
Porter, Ct., S36367
Silas, Vt., S11676
WALBURN, Francis, Pvt., N.J.,
BLWt.8821. Iss. 5/2/1797
WALCH, John, Pvt., Md., BLWt.
11829 iss. 10/10/1797
John, Md., S36373
WALCK, Charles, Mass., S35712
WALCKMAN, Michael, Md. See
WALTMAN
WALCOT, Benjamin, Mass. See
WALLCUT
WALCOTT, Benjamin Stewart, R.I.
Marcy, W25865
Clement, Pvt. Pa., BLWt.10585
iss. 12/24/1790
George, R.I., Sabra, W25904
John, Pa., S40634
WALCUTT, Benjamin, See WALLCUT
WALDEN, Alexander, S.C., Va.,
R11011
Ambrose, Cont., Va., S38453
Charles, Va., Mary, W6425
David, N.C., S32570
David, ---, Ct. res., R11013
Drury, N.C., Elizabeth, R11014
Elijah, Va., S3477
George, Va., S9521
Jacob, Navy, N.H., res. N.H.,
S23061
James, R.I., S21558
James, Va., S31454
John, Cont., Va., S40623
John, Cont., Va., Mary, W9878;
BLWt.778-100
John, Va., See WALLING
John, Va., Elizabeth; sold. d.
4/25/1848. W25862
Mary, Ct., former wid. of Andrew
Baker, which see
Nathan, Mass., S43234
Robert, Ct., Lucretia, W8981;
BLWt.16123-160-55
WALDERON, Nathaniel, N.H. See
WALDRON
WALDIN, Ichabod, Ct., See John
WILLIAMS
John, Cont. Va. See WALDEN
WALDING, James, Va., S31454
WALDMAN, Ludwick, Pvt. Pa., BLWt.
10609. Iss. 4/1/1796
WALDNAN, Thomas, N.C., S42057
WALDO, Daniel, Ct., S14782; BLWt.
28501-160-55
David, N.Y., S9522
Edward, N.H., S19389
Hannah, Ct., former wid. of
Samuel Thompson, which see
Jesse, Ct., Martha, W25891
John J., N.Y., S6321
Joseph, Ct., Cont., S11649
Nathan, Ct., Deborah, W22522
Zaccheus/Zacheus, Ct., S16013
Zachariah, Ct., Abigail, W25890;

WALDO (continued)
 BLWt.3805-160-55
WALDON, John, N.C., Catharine, W4374
WALDREN, John, Cont. Va., Mary, W9878; BLWt.778-100
WALDREPE, James, Va., Mary, W2202
WALDROM, Charles, N.C., S32574
WALDRON, Abiather, R.I., Vt., S19502
 Benjamin, N.Y., R11018
 Charles, Md. See WALDROM
 Cornelius, N.Y., Catharine, W16459
 David, N.H., Sea Service, Maria, R11020
 Ebenezer, N.H., S35708
 John, R.I., Elizabeth, W18266
 Nathan, Mass., Mary, W14099
 Nathaniel, N.H., See his signature in Aaron Rollins, W16700 as Walden. S43233; BLWt.209-100
 Oliver, N.Y., R11022
 Philip, Va., Elizabeth, W9154
 Samuel, N.J., Rosanna, W2205
 Samuel, N.J., Va., S11639
 Samuel B., N.Y., S14778
 Thomas, N.C. See WALDNAN
 Thomas, R.I., Ruth, W22517
 William, N.Y., Mary, R11021
WALDROP, John, N.C., S9520
WALDROUP, James, See WALDREPE
WALE, Timothy, Va., S11663
WALER, Asbel, See Ashbel WALLER
WALES, Ebenezer, Ct., BLWt.1895-200
 Eleazer, Ct., S11653
 Eliel, Ct., S40650
 Elisha, Mass., Lydia Thayer, former wid., W15324
 George, Va. See WALLS
 Jacob, Mass., Phebe, W22493
 Jonathan, Mass., Beulah, W15466
 Joseph, Mass., S46289; BLWt. 2317-200-Lt. Iss. 1/11/1793
 Nathaniel, Mass., Mary, W25874
 Samuel, Mass., Abigail, W317; BLWt.58694-160-55
 Samuel, Mass., Mary, W22536
 Shubal, Mass., S18641
 Thomas, Mass., S30184
 Thomas, Va. See WALLS
 Timothy, N.Y., S33235; BLWt. 923-100
WALEY, Sarah, See Sarah ROSE
WALICE, Samuel, Mass., S11674
WALISER, Christian, See WALLASIE
WALKER, Aaron F., N.J., S774
 Abel, Mass., Hannah, W16778
 Abraham, Cont., Dist. Me. in 1818, S35704
 Abraham, R.I., S22036
 Alexander, S.C., Eleanor, W8979
 Alexander, Va., Jane. Also served in 1774, R11040
 Andrew, N.C., b. Ireland, to S.C. & to N.C., S7830
 Andrew, N.C., R11029
 Andrew, Pa., BLWt.2390-300
 Ann, N.C. former wid. of William Lemmond, which see
 Asher, N.J., S3451
 Benjamin, Cont., Mass., S41295.

WALKER (continued)
 His wid., Eunice, was pensioned as former wid. of John Caryl, Mass., which see
 Benjamin, Mass., S21555
 Benjamin, N.J., S7801
 Benjamin, N.Y., BLWt.2364-450-Lt. Col.
 Benjamin, Pa., Sophia, W6402
 Benjamin, Pa., Mary, W14088
 Bruce, N.H., Mehitable, W18272
 Buckley, N.C., Milly/Mildred, b. N.C., W6407
 Calvin, R.I., S11654
 Charles, Mass., S20568
 Charles, Va., S7802
 Daniel, Ga., Hannah, W4613, b. in Ga.
 Daniel, Mass., R11032
 Daniel, N.C., Elizabeth, R11035
 David, N.C., Lydia, R11047, b. in Pa.
 David, Va., R11033
 David, Va., BLWt.345-200
 Edward, Cont., S35706, enl. Cambridge, Mass. Pensioned in Me.
 Edward, Mass., BLWt.2307-200-Lt. Iss. 1/22/1799 to Charles Parsons, ass. No papers
 Edward, Mass., S19147
 Edward, N.Y., Margaret Balcom, former wid., W10388; BLWt.359-60-55 & 7975-100-1790
 Edward, N.C., Jane, R11041, b. N.C.
 Edward, Pvt. Va., BLWt.12651. Iss. 11/5/1789. Note: "On file, not delivered"
 Edward, Va., S40640
 Edward, Va., S41302
 Eliakim, Mass., S16571
 Elijah, Mass., R11034
 Elijah, N.C., Rebecca, W6404; BLWt.35680-160-55. Also served in 1794-1795
 Elizabeth, Mass., former wid. of Samuel Page, which see
 Elizabeth, Mass., former wid. of Peter Dudley, which see
 Eunice, Mass., former wid. of John Caryl, which see
 Ezekiel, Pvt. Mass., BLWt.5316 iss. 2/29/1792 to Moses Beard
 Francis, Pvt. N.J., BLWt.8837 iss. 6/11/1789 to Matthias Denman, ass.
 Francis, Va., Hannah, R11037; BLWt.47812-160-55
 George, Cont., Va., S39115
 George, Mass., S31464
 George, N.J., BLWt.2376-200-Lt. Iss. 9/12/1789. No papers
 George, N.C., S3449, b. Va.
 George R., Va., Lucy, R11046
 Gideon, Mass., Polly, W16463
 Gideon, Mass., Abigail, R11028
 Gideon, Vt., Dis.
 Gordon, Pvt. Mass., BLWt.5289. Iss. 2/27/1793 to Alexander Power
 Gordon, Mass., S43247
 Green, N.C., S7803, b. N.C.
 Henry, Cont., Pa., S40624

WALKER (continued)
 Henry, Va., S31459
 Isaac, Pvt. Mass., BLWts.5216 & 5032; Iss. 12/2/1791 to Martin Kingsley
 Isaac, Mass., S42608
 Isaac, N.C., S3446, b. in Md.
 Jacob, R.I., Hannah, W14090
 James, Pvt. Ct., BLWt.6711 iss. 9/23/1791 to Isaac Bronson, ass.
 James, Ct., S43231
 James, Green Mt. Boys, N.H., N.Y. S11652
 James, Mass., S16572
 James, Mass., S19148
 James, Mass., S19150
 James, Mass., S29522
 James, Mass., S30195
 James, Mass., Susanna, W2207; BLWt.19778-160-55
 James, Mass., Mary, W11718
 James, N.C., S1265, b. Pa.
 James, N.C., S3450, b. Pa.
 James, Va., Elizabeth, R11036
 Jason, N.H., S33216
 Jeremiah, N.C., S31457
 Jeremiah, Va., Mary, W6399
 Jesse, Cont., N.H., W25850
 Jesse, N.C., b. Va., S18261
 Joanna, Ct., former wid. of Cordilla Fitch, which see
 John, Cont., Md., Mary, W6398
 John, Cont., Va., Margaret, S48765
 John, Cont., Va., BLWt.2230-100
 John, Ga., S.C., b. Ireland, W9875
 John, Pvt. Md., BLWt.11791 iss. 2/1/1790
 John, Pvt. Md., BLWt.11801 iss. 11/1/1797 to Elisha Jarrett, ass.
 John, Pvt., Md., BLWts.13892 & 14101 iss. 2/24/1795 to Francis Sherrard, ass. of Acquilla Lanthorn, admr.
 John, Pvt. Mass., BLWt.5211 iss. 1/28/1790 to Joseph May
 John, Pvt. Mass., BLWt.5268 iss. 6/2/1795 to Samuel Emery
 John, Pvt. Mass., BLWt.5278 iss. 12/3/1789
 John, Pvt. Mass., BLWt.5322. Iss. 12/22/1789
 John, Mass., Mary, W25888
 John, Mass., Nancy, W25909
 John, N.H., Hannah, W25851
 John, N.Y., Pa., S43244
 John, N.C., b. N.C., S7796
 John, N.C., Elizabeth, W64
 John, Pa., S16017
 John, Pa., Mary, W6400
 John, S.C., Jane, S39118; R11042
 John, Va., Elizabeth, W4614
 John, Va., Rachel, b. Pa., R11054
 John H., Va., Mariah, b. Md., W27531; BLWt.73590-160-55
 Jonathan, Mass., R11044
 Joseph, Pvt. Ct., BLWt.6609. Iss. 9/9/1790 to James F. Sebor, ass.
 Joseph, Ct., S11672
 Joseph, Ct., Sela, W3368

WALKER (continued)
Joseph, Ct., BLWt.1218-300
Joseph, Cont., Ct., Eunice Eaton, former wid., W17740
Joseph, Mass., S30190
Joseph, Mass., Asenath, W22523
Joseph, Pa., b. Ireland, S11657
Joseph, Va., Amy, W8301; BLWt. 52469-160-55
Josiah, Mass., Mary, W2465
Learned, Mass., Sally, W25854
Lemuel, Mass., N.H., Mass. Sea Service, S17185
Littleberry, Ga., R11045
Mathias, Pvt., N.Y., BLWt.7966 iss. 6/1/1792
Mathias, S.C., b. N.C., R11048
Matthias, N.Y., Hannah, W16779
Memucan, Va., Rachel, R11050
Meshec/Masheck, N.J., S40621; BLWt.362-100
Michael, N.C., Sarah, R11055
Moses, Mass., S31461
Moses, Va., R11051
Nathan, Mass., Sally, W25880; BLWt.8465-160-55
Nathaniel, Ct., S6328
Nathaniel, Ct., S35380
Nathaniel, N.H., Abigail, W25867
Obadiah, Ct., S36834; BLWt. 6631-100-Pvt. Iss. 10/6/1797
Obed, Mass., Sarah, BLWt.73513-160-55
Oliver, Va., S18260
Peter, Ct., S23473
Peter, Cont., Va., BLWt.1483-100
Peter, Pvt. Mass., BLWt.5321. Iss. 3/21/1800. Wt. signed by James McHenry 3/21/1800, Certified 4/21/1818 to Peter Walker & other names, as heirs
Peter, Mass., Diana, W4371; BLWt. 5319-100-Fifer. Iss. 7/30/1790
Peter, Pa., Elizabeth, b. Scotland W5161
Philip, Pa., S38452
Phineas, Ct., Susan, W22534
Reuben, N.C., S3447
Richard, Cont., Va., Anson, W1108; BLWts.2411-100 & 19707-160-55, & Va. Half Pay
Richard, Mass., BLWt.2334-200-Lt. Iss. 9/26/1791 to Peter Edeas, Admr. No papers
Richard, Mass., S31463
Robert, Cont., Mass., S33230; BLWt.2297-300-Capt. Iss. 7/22/1789
Robert, Md., S3444
Robert, N.J., Betsey, W4092
Samson, Mass., Thankful, W19581
Samuel, Ct., S21556
Samuel, Cont., Mass., Mercy/Marcy, W25892
Samuel, Cont., Va., S39117
Samuel, Pvt., Md., BLWts.13893 & 14107 iss. 2/24/1795 to Francis Sherrard, ass. of Acquilla Lanthorn, Admr.
Samuel, Mass., S30194
Samuel, Mass., Judith, W22497
Samuel, N.H., Polly Hoag, former

WALKER (continued)
wid., W11317; BLWt.101245-160-55
Samuel, N.J., Hepzibah, R11039
Samuel, N.Y., S40635
Samuel, N.Y., Dorcas Shultis, former wid., W15331; BLWts.107-60-55 & 7977-100-1790. Her other husb. Philip Shultis, N.Y. was pensioned, which see
Samuel, N.C., S1731
Samuel, Pvt Pa., BLWt.10565 iss. 6/29/1789 to M. McConnell, ass.
Samuel, S.C., S3448, b. Ireland
Samuel, Va., S16567
Sarah, Navy, R.I., former wid. of John Eddy, which see
Seth, Mass., N.H., Privateer, Temperance, W15859
Silas, Mass., BLWt.2332-200-Lt. Iss. 5/19/1797
Simeon, Ct., S23993
Simons, Ct., S17763
Solomon, Cont., Mass.? as Lt. S43245
Solomon, Va., Frances, W4376
Supply, Mass., Rachel, W25916
Tandy, Va., S42058
Thomas, Cont., S43251, N.H. pensioner in 1818
Thomas, N.C., Mary, W6397
Thomas, Pa., Aurilla, R11056
Thomas, Va., S6339
Thomas, Va., Messainiah/Missemiah, W6405
Thomas, Va., R18767, Va. Half Pay
Timothy, Cont., Mass., W14081
Timothy, Cont., Mass., Hannah, W25911
William, Ct., Hannah, W22518
William, Cont., N.H., S---, d. 2/1/1831
William, Del., BLWt.2080-100
William, Pvt. Mass., BLWt.5330 Iss. 5/18/1789 to Martha Walker wid.
William, Mass., S6334
William, Mass., Mary, W15461
William, Mass., Sybil, W22501. Sold. d. 12/1/1833
William, N.H., Elizabeth, W16083
William, Pvt., N.J., BLWt.8856 iss. 9/12/178?
William, N.Y., S32044
William, N.C., S32573, b. N.C.
William, N.C., S.C., Sarah, W6401
William, Pvt. Pa., BLWt.10573 iss. 3/20/1794 to Francis Kirkpatrick, ass.
William, R.I., S32036
William, Va., S6340
William, Va., S7800
William, Va., S14780
William J., Va., S16011
William Leadam/Needham, N.C., S7814
William Needham, See William Leadam
William T., Va., Mary, W6403; BLWt.51765-160-55
Zaccheus, Cont., Mass., S44022
Zebulon, Ct., Hannah, R11057

WALKUP, George, Mass., Lucy, W20116
Samuel, N.C., S30766
WALL, Arthur, N.C., R11058
Edward, Cont., S46346; BLWt. 1644-100. Vt. res. in 1829
Francis, N.H., S36359
Isaac, Pa., S40638
Jacob, N.C., S7836
James, N.J., S3435
James, N.J., Mary, W6391
Jesse, N.C., Molly, R11060
Joel, N.C., Elizabeth, W4095
John, Ct., N.Y., S29529
John, Ga., S38455
John, Md., Pa., Elizabeth, R11059
John, Va., R11089
Jonathan, N.C., S9569
Joseph, N.C., S7823
Millington, N.C., R11061
Peter, Va., Elizabeth, W25857; BLWt.35678-160-55
Richard, Navy, enl. in France, S.C., Sea Service, S22032; b. in Ireland
Richard, N.C., S42054
William, Md., Kitturah, W8971; BLWt.26217-160-55
William, R.I., S21551
William, Va., S17179
WALLACE, Aaron, N.C., R11062
Adam, Va., BLWt.542-300. The papers of the claims of Andrew Wallace, BLWt.543-300 & James Wallace BL are also within
Alexander, Va. See SUTHERLAND
Andrew, Pa., Indian Wars, U.S.A. S3466
Andrew, Va., BLWt.543-300. For papers see claim of Adam Wallace, BLWt.542-300
Benjamin, N.H. See WALLIS
Caesar, Pvt., N.H., BLWt.3568 iss. 1/26/1796 to James A. Neal, ass.
Caesar (colored), N.H., S43250
Charity, N.J., former wid. of John Spencer, which see
Charles, Pa., Abigail, W2286; BLWt.17716-160-55
Cornelius, N.Y., S14790; BLWt. 26520-160-55
Ebenezer, ---, Dis. Vt. res.
Ebenezer, Mass., Fanny, W6409; BLWt.1815-100
Edward, Va., S3469
George, N.C., Jane, W11741; BLWt.40911-160-55
George, Pa., S6326, b. Ireland
Gustavus B., Va., BLWt.2422-450-Lt. Col. Iss. 12/13/1791 to Francis Greaves. No papers
Hannah, Pa., former wid. of Thomas Neal, which see
Hugh, Va., S41306
Isaac H., Vt., R11065
Jacob, N.Y., S23474
James, R.I., S39879
James, S.C., S19145
James, Va., BL---. For papers see claim of Adam Wallace, BLWt.542-300

WALLACE (continued)
James, Va., BLWt.2425-400-Surg. Iss. 3/27/1794 to Wm. B. Wallace, Excr. No papers
James, Va., S7834
James, Va., S9519
James, Va., S38458
James, Va., Ann, W22508. Com. Lt. of S.C. Navy in 1794 or 1795
James, Va., Pa., Sarah, R11072
John, Ct., S22031
John, Mass., S11690
John, Mass., S33214
John, Mass., See WALLES
John, N.H., Mary, W25901, alive in 1832
John, N.H., Phebe, W27852; BLWt. 80012-160-55; d. in 1837
John, N.H., BLWt.1784-100, d. in 1813
John, N.C., S32572
John, N.C., Mary, W6410
John, N.C., Frances, W25897; BLWt.18209-160-55
John, S.C., S9517
John, S.C., S17178
John, S.C., Sarah Locke, former wid., W955
John, S.C. See WALLIS
John, S.C., BLReg.227462-1855
Joseph, Ct., Cont., S40630
Joseph, N.H., S44008
Joseph, Va., R11068
Joshua, S.C., Elizabeth, W11721; BLReg.204730-1855
Josiah, Mass., S35696
Josiah, Mass., Nancy, W22500; BLWt.18384-160-55
Levi, S.C., Jannett, W4528
London, Ct., Phoebe Freeman, former wid., W18290
Nathaniel, N.Y., Lucy Hale, dau., W29797
Oliver, Va., Mary, W22543
Richard, Ct., Vt., S46659
Samuel, Mass., Dorcas, W25872
Samuel, N.C., S7843
Samuel, S.C., Kisiah, W6408; BLWt.27579-160-55
Samuel, Va., Lilly Ann, R11071
Thomas, N.C., S39116
Thomas, N.C., Rebecca, W11739
Thomas, Pvt. Pa., BLWt.10590 iss. 2/14/1791 to Alexander Power, ass.
Uriah, N.Y., Fanny, W25907; BLWt.9456-160-55
Weymouth, N.H., S43240
William, Cont., Ct., Sarah, W18277
William, Mass., Rhoda, R11070
William, Pvt., N.Y., BLWt.8005 iss. 7/24/1790 to John Lawrence, ass.
William, N.Y., S11646
William, N.Y., S26849
William, N.C., S7820
William, Pa., S3470, b. Pa.
William, Pa., S7827, b. Ireland
William, Pa., Mary, R11069
William, S.C., Ruth, W8980
William B., Va. (Art.), S42612; BLWt.2441-200-Lt. Iss. 3/27/

WALLACE (continued)
1794 Kentucky Agcy.
WALLAR, William, Cont., Va., Sarah, W6396
WALLASIE, Christian, N.Y., S43246
WALLCUT, Benjamin, Mass., S33232; BLWt.2328-300-Capt. Iss. 4/22/1793 & presented for certificate on 11/28/1818. Name spelled Walcot
Christopher, Mass., BLWt.2335-150-Ens. Iss. 11/26/1798 to Benj. Wallcut, Thos. Walcutt & Lucy Strafford, Surog-Heirs
Thomas, Cont., Mass., S3482
WALLEN, Elisha, Va., R11075
Jonathan, R.I., S39876; BLWt. 2288-300-Capt. Iss. 2/24/1800
WALLENBACK, John W., N.Y. See WALLINBACK
WALLENGER, Jacob, Drummer, N.J., BLWt.8875 iss. 10/16/1789 to Benj. Harris, ass.
WALLER, Ashbel/Asbel Waler, Ct., Jane, W25861; BLWt.49744-160-55
Daniel, Va., S7838
Daniel, Va., S41303
David, Vt., S14793
Edward, Va., R18768 Va. Half Pay
George, Mass., Margaret, W18289
Hampton, Va., S17182
Jesse, Va., S4719
John, Va., S37503
John C., Vt., Priscilla, W1676; BLReg.231941-1855
Joseph, Vt., R11078
Nathaniel, N.C., S42051
Nelson, Del., BLWt.1958-100
Thomas, Va., Lydia, W1338
Trueman, Vt., Patty, R11079
William, Cont., Va. See WALLAR
WALLERATH, Adolph, N.Y., Anna, W18275
Isaac, N.Y., Margaretta/Margaret W18287
WALLES, John, Mass., Hannah, W2709; BLWt.6402-160-55
John, Mass., R21796
WALLICE, John, N.C. See WALLACE
WALLIN, Daniel, Pa., S6337
WALLINBACK, John W., N.Y., Joanna R11076. Name also appears as Wallenback/Wallingback/Wollenback
WALLING, Carhart/Cohart, N.J., S42050
Cohart, See Carhart
Daniel, N.J., S3480
James, N.J., S33867
John, N.J., Mary, R11080
John, Va., Elizabeth, W171; BLWt. 27690-160-55. Sold. d. 4/18/1836
Joseph, N.J., Margaret, W110
Philip, N.J., S26860
Simeon, R.I., Sarah, W22531
William, N.J., Elizabeth, W19588
William, N.C., S1935
William, S.C., S11642
WALLINGFORD, Cato, N.H., BL109-100
David, N.H., Sarah, R11082; BLWt. 17890-160-55
Jonathan, N.H., Betsey, Wid. Cert.6977; BLWt.47553-160-55

WALLIS, Benjamin, N.H., S44003
Benjamin, N.C., S32571
Curwin, Mass., Thankful, W25915
David, Mass., S30767
Ebenezer, Mass., S30773
Hammond, Ct., N.Y., Rebecca, R11086
Henry, Mass., Sabra, W19586
James, N.C., S7795, b. Jones Co., N.C. in 1743. Consult S7822 also
James, N.C., S7822, b. Craven Co., N.C. in Oct. 1747
John, Cont., Sarah, W11730. Enl. in Va.
John, Mass. See WALLACE
John, Mass., See WALLES
John, Mass., See WALLES
John, S.C., Esther, R11064
John, S.C., R11085
Joseph, Pvt. Ct., BLWt.6650 iss. 1/20/1797
Joshua, S.C., Elizabeth, See WALLACE
London, Ct. See WALLACE
Mathew, Va., Sarah, R11087
Matthew/Mathew, N.C., Mildred, W1519, b. in Pa.
Millicent, Mass., former wid. of Daniel Conant, which see
Moses, Mass., S43227
Robert, Cont., Mass., S41286
Samuel, S.C. See WALLACE
William, Cont., Ct. See WALLACE
Zebulon (colored), Ct., Eleanor R11083
WALLISER, Christian, Pvt. N.Y., BLWt.8020 iss. 7/20/1791
Michael, Pa., BLWt.2480-100
WALLRADT, Henry I. or J., N.Y. S28937
WALLS, Charles, Va., Rebecca, R11091
Francis, N.H., S43252
George, Md., Martha, W8972
George, Va., R18785 Va. Half Pay. N.A. Acc. No.874-050184 Half Pay George Walls
Jacob, Va., Margaret, R18779
John, N.C., Margaret, W18291
John, Pa., S17762
Randolph, Va., R11090
Reuben, Va., S37500
Thomas, Va., R18784 Va. Half Pay
WALLSWORTH, Elijah, See WALSWORTH
WALMSLEY, Philip, R.I. See RODMAN
William, Ct., Cont., S36368; BLWt.2355-150-Ens. Iss. 6/27/1789 to Wm. Walmsley
WALRAD, Henry I. or J. See WALLRADT
WALRADT, Adolphus Jacob, N.Y., S44211
Peter, N.Y., S11684
WALRATH, Adolph, N.Y. See WALLERATH
Henry I. or J. See WALLRADT
Isaac, N.Y. See WALLERATH
Jacob H., N.Y., R11093 & R11904
Nicholas, ---- Dis. N.Y. Agency
WALROND, Noah, Mass., Anna/Ann W14093
WALS, Jacob, N.Y., S43243
WALSER, Frederick, N.C., R11096

WALSH, Elizabeth, Mass., former wid. of William Meservy Phillips which see
James, Va., S40622
John, Md., See WALCH
John, N.Y., S44206
John, N.C., BLWt.2393-300-Capt. Iss. 5/24/1796. Also recorded as above under BLWt.2668. No papers
Thomas, N.Y. See WELCH
William, N.C., S1264
WALSTON, Joseph, Va., R11097
Thomas, N.C., S11661
WALSWORTH, Elijah, Mass., S43223
WALTAMYER, David, Pa., S23056
WALTAR, John, Pa. See WALTERS
WALTER, Adam, N.Y., Elizabeth/ Mariah, R11099
Charles, Ct., S36840
Christian, N.Y., Catharine, W19590; BLWt.24762-160-55
Christopher, Pa., S40632
David, Mass., S10041
David, Pa., Susannah, W6393; BLWt.87029-160-55
Elijah, Ct., R11098
Ephraim, Pa., R11105
Frederick, Pa., S11664
George, N.Y., S10040
Henry, N.J., S3471
Jacob, Pvt. N.Y., BLWt.8010 iss. 2/4/1791
Jacob, N.Y., Pa., S23988
John, Ct., S11673
John, Ct., Rhoda, W2381; BLWt. 11259-160-55
Martin, N.Y., Phebe, W612; BLWts.58-60-55 & 8006-100-1790
Nicholas, Pa., Barbara, W3169
Paul, N.C., S7821
Seth, N.Y., Ruhamah, W16461
William, Pvt. Va., BLWt.12686 iss. 1/31/1793 to John Stockdale, ass.
William, ? , Nancy, R11102. Ill. res.
WALTERS, Foster, N.J., R11100
Jacob, Cont., Pa., Eleanor, W4844
Jacob, Md., Sea Service, R1462
Jacob, N.J., S33874
Jacob, Pa., Va., S23991, b. Md.
John, Pvt. N.J., BLWt.8876. Iss. 7/24/1790
John, N.J., S29524
John, N.C., S30771
John, Pvt. Pa., BLWt.10614 iss. 7/9/1789, also BLWt.21-60-55
John, Pa., S17753
John, Pa., S23053
John, Pa., Catharine, W4372; BLWts.21-60-55 & 10614-100-1789
Michael, Pa., R11106
Nancy, Va., former wid. of John Gray, which see
Peter, Va., Isabella, W2029
Richard C., Va., BLWt.2432-200-Lt.
Solomon, Pvt. N.C., BLWts.12700 & 13885 iss. 8/2/1796 to Griffith John McRae, ass.
WALTHALL, Henry, Va., Elizabeth, W3058; BLWt.27692-160-55

WALTHALL (continued)
William, Senior, Va., S6324
WALTMAN, Lewis, Pa., S40648
Michael, Pvt. Md., BLWt.11811 iss. 2/1/1790
Michael, Md., W25853
WALTON, Benjamin, Mass., S35695
George, Ct., Mary, W15971
George, Pvt. Pa., BLWt.10617 iss. 1/13/1792 to William Lane, ass.
Joel, Va., S6327
John, Ct., Privateer, Mary, R11107
John, N.J., Margaret, W6424
John, Pvt., N.Y., BLWt.8014 iss. 2/23/1792 to Nicholas Everitt, ass.
Josiah, N.H., Dis.
Martin, Va., S3473
Nathan, Mass., Mary, W20115
Newell, Va., S22037
Oliver, Ct., R11108
Oliver, Mass., S30182
Reuben, alias John Thompson, Mass., S35710
Silas, Pvt. Ct., BLWt.6713 iss. 8/23/1790
Silas, Cont., S44017, N.Y. Agcy.
Tilman, Va., Judith, W4373
William, N.J., S23058
William, N.C., Sarah, W1518; BLWt.2445-300-Capt. Iss. 4/27/ 1800
William, N.C., Va., S17184
WALTS, Conrad, N.Y., Elizabeth, W19591
WALTZ, Conrad, N.Y. See WALTS
Conrad, N.Y. See FOLTS
Jacob, N.Y. See WALS
Michael, Md., Pa., S40620; BLWt. 876-100
Peter D., N.Y., Hannah, W3744
WAMACK, Johnson, Ga., N.C., S32577, b. in Va.
WAMBACH, Philip, Pa., S23059
WAMIRE, Frederick, N.Y., S44019
WAMMOCK, Abraham, See WOMACK
WAMPLER, John, Pa., R11109
WAMSLEY, David, Va., S18669
James, R.I. See WORMSLEY
James, Va., S6323
Matthew, R1110, Va. res. in 1834
Philip, R.I. See RODMAN
Thomas, Va. See WARMSLEY
William, Va., S7806
WANDEL, John, N.Y., S40639
WANDELL, Henry, N.Y., Abigail, W11707; BLWt.100790-160-55
Jacob, Pvt., N.Y., BLWt.8043 iss. 6/17/1791 to Hannah Fisher, admx.
Jacob, Cont., N.J., N.Y., S44011
John, N.Y., Hannah, W15816
WANDLE, David, Cont., N.Y., S26886
Jacob, Sgt., N.Y., BLWt.8016 iss. 6/9/1790
WANN, John, Pvt., Pa., BLWt.10563 iss. 5/5/1794 to Alexander Power, ass.
John, Pa., Susannah, W3899

WANN (continued)
Michael, Pvt. Pa., BLWts.10533 & 10549 iss. 11/27/1794 to Joseph Pall, ass.
Michael, Pa., Ann Catharine, W3480
WANNER, Michael, Pa., S41298; BLWt.1279-100
WANSLOW, John, Va., S32045
WANTON, William (colored), R.I., S22035
WAPLES, Samuel, Va., Sabra P., W6427; BLWts.1733-200 & 14529-160-55
WAPSHOTT, Graves, Va., R11111. Also served in 1786 and 1790
WARBELL, Henry, See WIRBLE
WARBLE, Henry, See WIRBLE
WARD, Aaron, Ct., BLWt.1311-100
Aaron, N.Y., S14800
Abijah, Pvt. N.Y., BLWt.7944 iss. 8/1/1791 to Henry I. or J. Van Ranselar, ass.
Abijah, N.Y., Rachel, W18254
Abner, Corp. Mass., BLWt.5259 iss. 4/1/1790
Abner, Mass., Polly, W22513
Abner, Mass., Hannah, W22539
Amos, N.J., S4718
Artemas, Mass., Hannah, R11117
Benjamin, Ct., S7810
Benjamin, Cont., N.H., Elizabeth W18235
Benjamin, Mass., R11113
Bernard, Pa., BLWt.2284-300-Capt. Iss. 5/28/1789; also recorded as above under 2481. No papers
Bernard, Vt., S18639
Caleb, Cont., N.J., S17176
Caleb, Mass., S30775
Caleb, N.J., S3440
Caron H., Va., former wid. of Thomas Fambrough, which see
Charles, N.Y., Mary, R11126
Christopher, Cont., Mass., Sybil/ Sybel, W2201; BLWt.34536-160-55
Christopher, Cont., N.Y., S11650
Christopher, Mass., S33211
Daniel, Pvt., Ct., BLWt.6674 iss. 1/6/1797
Daniel, N.H., S44014
Daniel, N.J., N.Y., S36836
Daniel, N.Y., Martha, R11125
Daniel, N.Y., Susannah, R11127
Daniel A., N.Y., S23476
David, Va., S7818
Dixsey, S.C., S22038
Ebenezer, N.Y., S11641
Edward, Md., Lucy, R11115
Edward, Va., S33871
Elijah, Pvt., Mass., BLWt.5303 iss. 4/13/1795 to Reuben Munn
Elijah, Mass., S44016
Elisha, Mass., S33233
Elisha, Mass., S41291
Elnathan, ? See N.A. Acc. No.874-050185 Not Half Pay. Mass. & Vt. res. No pension file for this veteran
George, Va., Margaret Wintermote, former wid., W6550
Henry, N.C., Charity, R11114
Hopper, Va., S38457

WARD (continued)
Hugh, Pvt. Md., BLWts.11793 & 12675 iss. 1/30/1795 to John Stockdell, ass.
Ichabod, Ct., S40646
Ichabod, Ct., R.I., S14775
Isaac, Pvt. N.J., BLWt.8833. Iss. 6/23/17-- to Elias Dayton and sons, assnes.
Isaac, N.J., Sally, W878
Israel, N.J., S3438
Israel, N.Y., S14797
Jabez, Pvt. Mass., BLWt.5207 iss. 12/6/1791 to Stephen Thorn, ass.
Jabez, Mass., S41305
Jabez, Mass., BLWt.1303-100
Jacob, Ct., S35111
James, Ct., S22568
James, Navy, N.Y., R11118
James, N.Y., R11119
James, N.C., S7819
James, Va., Elizabeth, W1105; BLWt.58685-160-55, m. 1810 d. July 1848
James, Va., Elizabeth, R11116, m. 1779; d. Nov. 1831
Jedediah, Ct., S22566
Jeptha, Pvt. Mass., BLWt.5271 iss. 1/24/1797 to Cesar Diman, father
Jesse, Mass., S23475
John, Ct., Abigail, W22516
John, Cont., Va., Theodosia/ Dosha, W8974; BLWt.1737-100
John, Mass., Navy, S44015
John, Mass., Privateer, R11120 b. in Ireland
John, Pvt. N.J., BLWt.8834 iss. 10/1/1789
John, N.J., S16569
John, N.J., Phoebe, W1110
John, Pvt., N.Y., BLWt.8024 iss. 8/25/1790 to Samuel Stronger, ass.
John, N.Y., Deborah, W4609
John, N.Y., Jane, W19592
John, N.Y., Rebecca, W25858
John, N.C., S16284
John, N.C., S.C., S32579
John, N.C., Va., Rachel, W9872
John, Pa., BLWt.2387-200-Lt. Iss. 8/19/1791 to Alex Power, ass. No papers
John, Pvt. Pa., BLWt.10550. Iss. 2/3/1796
John Sr., Pvt. Pa., BLWt.10551 Iss. 9/26/1791 to John McCleland ass.
John, Pvt. Pa., BLWt.10574 iss. 11/1/1791 to George Walton, ass.
John, Pvt. "in the Artillery", Pa. BLWt.10656 iss. 10/1/1789
John, Pa., Agnes D., R11121
John, Corp., Va. Lee's Legion, BLWt.13924 iss. 4/4/1800
John, Va., Nancy, W1960
John B., Pvt. Lee's Legion, BLWt. 13930 iss. 2/12/1794
John L., N.C., S7804
John P., S.C., BLWt.2453-200-Lt. Iss. 3/19/1800

WARD (continued)
Jonas, Cont., N.J., Chloe, W18248
Jonathan, N.J., Rachel, W18259
Joseph, Cont., Mass., Prudence, W19593
Joseph, Pvt., Md., BLWt.11805 iss. 4/6/1797 to Joseph De Baufre, ass.
Joseph, Mass., S33231
Joseph, Mass., Sarah, W20118; BLWt.11057-160-55
Joseph, Navy, Pa., S40625
Joshua, Ct., Mary, W18276; BLWt.34535-160-55
Joshua, Mass., Huldah, W2498; BLWt.38338-160-55
Josiah, Mass., Hannah, W16777
Josiah, Mass., Privateer, S7813
Kerley/Kerly, Mass., S20224
Laurence, Va., Elizabeth, W8973
Luther, Mass., Anna, W18257
Melcher, Pvt. N.H., BLWt.3569 iss. 7/21/1789 to Ladd & Cass, assnes.
Melcher, N.H., S44018
Moses, Cont., Ct., S36838
Moses, Pvt. Va., BLWt.12655 iss. 5/12/1792 to James Morison, Admr.
Nathan, Ct., Mass., S40629
Nehemiah, Pvt. Mass., BLWt.5300 iss. 10/16/1789 to Theodosius Fowler
Nehemiah, Mass., S33869
Nehemiah, N.J., N.Y., S3439
Nicholas, Mass., S30761
Nicholson, R.I., S21554
Obadiah, Mass., S4716
Reuben, N.Y., Jemima, W22520
Robert, Pvt. N.Y., BLWt.7964 iss. 11/11/1791 to Samuel Broome, ass.
Rufus, Mass., Elizabeth, W6383
Samuel, Ct., Anna, W4843
Samuel, Ct., Mass., S17754
Samuel, Mass., Lois, BLWt.67577-160-55
Samuel, N.H., S43253
Samuel, R.I., BLWt.317-450
Samuel, Va., S32047
Samuel C., N.J., S614
Simon, N.H., Elizabeth N., W11743; BLWt.34516-160-55
Solomon, N.Y., Sarah, W27497
Stephen, Mass., S15694; BLWt. 1399-100
Stephen, Mass., Martha, BLWt. 90014-160-55
Thomas, Ct., S35379
Thomas, Ct., Cont., N.Y., S22569
Thomas, Cont., Dis., N.Y. res.
Thomas, Mass., S35700
Thomas, Pa., Elizabeth, W3741
Thomas, S.C., S14802
Timothy, N.J., S17751
Urial, Ct. See BASCOM
William, Ct., Martha, W25848
William, Ga., S42053. Enl. from Brunswick Co., Va., never resided in Ga. Lived N.C. & Va.
William, Mass., S30769
William, N.J., S33875

WARD (continued)
William, N.C., S7809
William, N.C., S7815
William, N.C., Ledia, R11124
William, Pa., S17181
William, Va., S32048
Willis, N.C., Margaret, W18255
Zadock, Pvt. N.Y., BLWt.7943 iss. 8/4/1791 to Henry I. or J. Van Ranselar, ass.
Zadock, N.Y., S33224
Zebediah, N.J., Harriet Franconi former wid., W16285; BLWt. 108974-160-55
WARDELL, Robert, N.J., S36839; BLWt.155-100. Iss. 3/21/1804
Samuel, Ct., S44010
WARDEN, Barnard, N.Y., R21899
Benjamin, Ct. See WORDEN
Elisha, Va., Fanny, W6428; BLWt.34518-160-55
Ichabod, Ct., Margaret, R11132
James, Ct., N.Y., R11131
James, Md., S40631
John, Ct., N.Y., See WORDIN
Nathan, N.Y., S44024
Samuel, N.C., S32050
Thomas, Mass., Eleanor, W8975
William, Mass., Rev. & War of 1812, Sarah, R11133, Ky. res. of dau. in 1844
WARDLAW, William, S.C., S32040
WARDLEY, Moses, Mass., Patience W25860
WARDROPE, Edward, N.C., S7844
WARDS, Edward, Md. See WARD
WARDWELL, Benjamin, Cont., Mass. Margaret, W25900
Ezekiel, Cont., Mass., S33217
Jacob, Pvt., Ct., BLWt.6681 iss. 1/18/1797 to David Maltbee, ass.
Jacob, Ct., S36837
Joseph, Cont., Mass., S35693; BLWt.2319-150-Ens. Iss. 7/21/ 1789 to Jona Cass, ass.
Joseph, Navy, Me., Elizabeth, W22496
Joshua, R.I., S33222
Nathan, Ct., S29523
Samuel, Pvt. Ct., BLWt.6679 iss. 4/9/1791
Simon, Mass., R.I., Washington's Life Guard, Sarah, W6421; BLWt. 13861-160-55
Stephen, R.I., S22034
William, Ct., Catharine, W2030
WARE, Amos, Mass., S19496
Daniel, Mass., Abigail, W25879
Edward, Va., S32049
Elias, Cont., Mass., Deborah, W15455
Francis M., Md., BLWt.2410-200-Lt. Iss. 9/21/1789 to Francis M. Ware. No papers
Frederick, Mass., Jemima, W25887
Frederick, Pa., R11135
George, Mass. Sea Service, Navy, Priscilla, W19579
Hugh, Pvt., Md., BLWt.11838 iss. 5/1/1797 to James DeBaufre, ass.

WARE (continued)
James, Mass., S29523
James, N.C., S.C., S7816
Jason, Mass., S28935
John, Mass., S18640
John, N.C., S7841, b. N.C.
Joseph, Pvt., Mass., BLWt.5231 iss. 1/7/1796 to Calvin Sanger
Moses, Mass. (?), Ruth Ball, former wid., R11136
Nathan, Cont., Mass., Hannah, W25886
Robert, Pa., R11137, b. Md.
Rowland/Roland, N.C., S3434; BLWt.77006-160-55
Thomas, N.J., S773
Thomas, Va., Mildred, W6385; BLWt.26209-160-55
Thomas, Va., R11138
William, Mass., Sarah Crossman former wid., W18976
William, N.C., Frances, W6386
William, Va., Priscilla, W8969
WAREFIELD, Ephraim, Mass., Julia W2204; BLWt.26681-160-55
WARES, Comfort, Vt., R11139
Elias, Pvt. Ct., BLWt.6615. Iss. 1/28/1792 to Isaac Bronson, ass.
WARFIELD, Aaron, Pvt. Mass., BLWt. 5247 iss. 11/2/1791 to Jon[a] Tuttle
Joseph, Md., Elizabeth, W8978
Joshua, Mass., Prudence, W20117
Reuben, Mass., See WHARFIELD
Samuel, Cont., Mass., R.I., Margery, W14082
Walter, Md., BLWt.2405-400
WARFORD, Benjamin, S.C., Elizabeth W8977, b. S.C.
WARIER, Daniel, Pvt. Md., BLWt. 11803 iss. 12/18/1794 to Henry Purdy, ass.
WARIN, John, Ct., See WARREN
WARING, Abraham, N.Y., Love, W18251
Anthony, Ct., Cont., Mehittable, W11735
Basil, Md., Ann, W25908; BLWt. 1020-200
Gideon, Md., Dis., N.Y. Agcy.
Henry, Ct., Cont., S36372
James, Ct., S17757
Jonathan, Ct., S3460
Joseph, Ct., S11689
Schuder, Ct., S11692; BLWt.36526-160-55
Solomon, Ct., S14787
Thaddeus, Ct., Deborah, W18280
WARLEY, Felix, S.C. See WHARLEY
George, S.C. See WHARLEY
Joseph, S.C. See WHARLEY
WARLICK, Jeremiah, Sgt. Pa., BLWt. 10648 iss. 8/7/1789 to Richard Platt, ass.
WARMACK, William, Va., S37505; BLWt.2140-100. Iss. 3/31/1836 Name shown as Womack/Wommack/ Wormack
WARMAN, Thomas, Cont., Va., BLWt. 1789-300
WARMOUTH, Thadeus Hardwidge, Va.,

WARMOUTH (continued)
Mary, W6419; BLWt.27660-160-55
WARMSLEY, Thomas, Va., Comfort, R11141
WARMSLY, Philip, R.I. See RODMAN
WARMUTH, Christian, N.Y., Mary, W18279
WARN, Benoni, Mass., S44205
William, N.Y., S44208
WARNE, Elijah, N.J., S842
WARNECK, Frederick, Va., Elizabeth Lugg, former wid., W20540
WARNER, Amasa, Pvt. Ct., BLWt. 6655 iss. 9/15/1790 to Nicholas Root, ass.
Amasa, Ct., S44209
Amos, Pvt. Ct., BLWt.6635 iss. 7/6/1795 to Eneas Munson, ass.
Amos, Ct., S36371
Benjamin, Ct., Cont., S14798
Benjamin, Ct., Cont., N.Y., S11644
Benjamin, Mass., Mass. State Navy Mass. Sea Service, S23057
Betty, Ct., former wid. of Nathan Thompson, Which see
Charles, Ct., Sarah, W20111
Charles, Pa., S33877
Christoffel, N.Y. See Christopher WERNER
Cornelius, N.Y., S44013
Daniel, Ct., S11680
Daniel, Ct., S14791
Daniel, Ct., Cont., Mass., Sarah, W25869
Daniel, Pvt. Mass., BLWt.5214 iss. 4/21/1794 to James Battle
Daniel, Mass., Rachel Burleson, former wid., R1470
Daniel, Mass., Sea Service, N.H., Grace, W15453
Daniel, Navy, R.I., Jemima, W25906
Deliverance, Ct., Esther, W18278
Demas, Ct., Rhoda, W18283
Ebenezer, Mass., S30186
Eleazar/Eleazer, Ct., N.Y., S28934
Eleazer, Mass., S22571
Elias, Mass., S30185
Elihu, R.I., Susannah, W2497; BLWt.40942-160-55
George, Ct., Nabby G., W25855
George, N.Y., S28932
Hardin, N.C., Elizabeth, W18253
Holliman, Navy, R.I., Nancy, W25849
Israel, Cont., Vt. & N.Y., S42610 BLWt.26369-160-55
Jabez I., Ct., Mary, W10272
Jacob, Cont., Pa., S46516; BLWt.1642-100
Jacob, Va., R11143
James, Drummer, Mass., BLWt.5237 iss. 4/1/1790
Jason, N.Y., R11144
Jehiel, Mass., N.Y., S14792
Jesse, Mass., R11145
Jesse, R.I., S11651; BLWt.14512-160-55
John, Pvt. Art. Artificers, BLWt. 13899 iss. 11/15/1792 to Jonathan Tuttle, ass.

WARNER (continued)
John, Ct., S6329
John, Ct., S7842
John, Ct., S14786
John, Ct., Abigail, W11736
John, Cont., Hepsibah, W18243; Ct. agcy. and res.
John, Mass., S3639
John, Navy, R.I., S39875
John, Pvt. Pa.,BLWt.10601 iss.4/ 15/1796 to Robert Thomson, ass.
John, Vt., Joanna, W18294
John, Va., S40641; BLWt.1181-100
Jonathan, Mass., Annis, W1337; BLWt.26011-160-55
Jonathan, Mass., Margaret Elizabeth, W11708
Jonathan, Mass., Hannah, W22492
Joseph, R11146. Ohio res. in 1837
Josiah, N.Y., R11147
Loomis/Loome, Ct., Eunice, W18297
Ludwick, Pvt. Pa.,BLWt.10569 iss. 8/8/1796. See card file under Warner-Ludwick, with notation
Michael, Pa., BLWt.10658-100 iss. 7/16/1792 to Gideon Merkle, ass. No papers
Michael, Pa.,S41298;BLWt.1279-100
Molly, Mass., former wid. of Samuel Willard, which see
Moses, Ct., Rachel, W3742
Moses, Mass., S11656
Nathaniel, Ct., S23990
Nathaniel, Ct., Ruth, W10271; BLWt.26232-160-55
Nathaniel, Pvt., Mass., BLWt.5246 iss. 1/26/1790 to John May
Nathaniel, Mass., Sea Service, Privateer, S30191
Nicholas, N.Y., S14789
Noadiah, Mass., S33237
Noah, Mass., Mary, W4093
Omri, Mass., Catharine, W2466; BLWt.31761-160-55
Paul, Mass., S33225
Peter, Pa., R11148
Phineas, Mass., Mary, W20114
Richard, Ct., Merab, W2829; BLWt. 18025-160-55
Robert, Ct., Mary, W18237
Robert, Ct., Cont., S36362; BLWt. 2340-400-Maj. Iss. 4/8/1796
Samuel, Ct., Deborah, W18288
Samuel, Ct., Cont., S11679
Samuel, Ct., Mass., S32041
Samuel, Mass., Elizabeth, W15460
Samuel, Mass., Dis. Res. Mass.
Saul, Ct., S17747
Selden, Ct., Privateer, S16014
Seth, Cont., Green Mt. Boys, N.H. BLWt.2277-500-Col. Iss. 6/29/ 1790 to David Lavensworth, admr. & Esther Warner, admx.
Seth, Mass., Polly, W1517
Solomon, Ct., S11687
Susanna, Pa., former wid. of William Read/Reed, which see
Thomas, Ct., Huldah, W20110
Thomas, Cont., Ct., Belinda, W19584; BLWt.299-60-55
Thomas, Pvt., N.Y., BLWts.8048 & 299-60-1855 iss. 2/24/1791. Wt.

WARNER (continued)
8048 to Shadwick Mead, ass.
Thomas, R.I., Mary, W25870
Timothy, Ct., R11151
William, Pvt., Mass., BLWt.5250 Iss. 8/10/1789
William, Mass., S33220
William, Pvt. Pa., BLWt.10557 iss. 7/6/1791 to Stephen Loudon, ass.
Zaccheus/Zachariah, Pvt., Mass., BLWt.5249 iss. 4/1/1790
Zachariah, Mass., BLWt.2060-100
WARNOCK, John, S.C., Eleanor, W22515
WARRAL, Benjamin, Pa. See WORRAL
WARREN, Aaron, Mass., Keziah, W25913
Aaron, Mass., Sea Service, Navy S30193
Aaron, N.H., Abigail, W2645; BLWt.18220-160-55
Abijah, Mass., S35709
Abraham, Ct., S44007
Adrial, Mass., BLWt.2309-200-Lt. Iss. 4/1/1790. No papers
Ahijah/Elijah, Ct., R11153
Archibald, Va., S16012
Ashbel, Ct., Penelope, W25894
Benjamin, Mass., S33229. Phebe Warren wid. of above sold. rec'd pension as former wid. of Lemuel Doten, which see
Caleb, Vt., S14779
Charles, Mass., S23478
Daniel, Mass., Sarah, W2383; BLWt.3637-160-55
Daniel, Mass., Hannah, W25846; BLWt.19604-160-55
David, Ct., S43230
Drury, Va., S3455
Edward, Pvt., Ct., BLWt.6634 iss. 4/11/1792 to Jonas Prentice, ass.
Edward, Ct., Mary, W25878
Edward, Cont., Pa., S10264
Elijah, Ct. See Ahijah
Elijah, Mass., S6331
Elijah, N.C., S3459
Enoch, Ct., R11155
Ephraim, Mass., S33213
Ephraim, Mass., S44006
Ezra, Ct., S30774
Ezra, Mass., S18263
Henchman, Mass., Esther, W14086
Hugh, S.C., S31453, b. in Va.
Jabez/Jabish, Vt., Hannah, W18260
James, Ct., Cont. See WORREN
James, Mass., Sarah, W22533
James, S.C., S30764
James, Va., R11156
Jason, Mass., S44026
Jeduthan, Mass., S30192
John, Sgt., Ct., BLWt.6604 iss. 4/14/1790 to William Wells, ass.
John, Ct., S36370
John, Ct., Rachel, W18241
John, Ct., Sally, W25884
John, Ct., N.Y., S44012; BLWt. 1341-100
John, Cont., Mass., Elizabeth, W25875; BLWt.2316-200-Lt. Iss. 11/12/1789

WARREN (continued
John, Cont., Va., S3458
John, Md., R11158
John, Mass., S39880
John, Mass., Rebecca, W25914
John, Gen. Hosp. Mass., BLWt.2457-450-Phys. & Surg. Iss. 10/26/1789
John, N.C., S3457
John, Pvt. Va., BLWt.12656. Iss. 3/26/1792 to Francis Graves, ass.
John, Pvt. Va., BLWt.12674 iss. 10/21/1791 to Elias Parker, ass.
Jonas, Mass., Mary, R11165
Jonathan, Ct., Sea Service, R11159
Joseph, Ct., Cont., Hannah, W4378; BLWt.24622-160-55
Joseph, Mass., Rebecca, W25885
Joseph, N.J., R11160
Joshua, Mass., S29525
Josiah, N.H., S43222, wife Jane
Jotham, R11162, Ct. res. in 1851
Moses, Ct., Mary, W25876
Moses, Mass., S3456
Moses, Mass., S31462
Nathan, Ct., S17175
Nathan, Mass., S30768
Nathan, Mass., Lucy, W18244
Nathaniel, Ct., S14773
Nathaniel, Cont., Mass., Margaret W25883
Nathaniel, N.Y., S23477
Neverson, Mass., S33236
Oliver, Mass., Lucy, R11163
Pelatiah, Cont., Mass., Sea Service, Sarah, R11166
Pelatiah/Peletiah, N.H., Peggy Giddings, former wid., W8211
Peter, Mass., S35702
Phebe, Mass., former wid. of Lemuel Doten, which see
Reuben, R11164, Margaret, Miss. res. of wid. in 1855
Richard, Mass., Lydia, W22498
Samuel, Mass., Bettie, W18281
Samuel, Mass., Elizabeth Foster, former wid., W23053
Samuel, S.C., BLWt.1859-300
Seth, Mass., Deliverance, W16776
Silas, Mass., S19495
Simpson, Va., S18262
Stephen, Mass., Hannah, W6429
Stephen, Mass., Mary, W15459
Timothy, Mass., S33228
William, Pvt. Mass., BLWt.5428 iss. 9/13/1791. Official Note: "5428 under Ct. Head, iss. to Wm. Warren of the Mass. Line"
William, Cont., Mass., S43239
William, Cont., Mass., S44025: BLWt.1554-100
William, Mass., S33870
William, Pvt., N.Y., BLWt.7949 iss. 9/13/1792
William, N.C., S42052
William, S.C., Rhoda, W3056, b. Va.
William, Va., S7840
William, Va., S11838
William, Va., R20445
Zenas, Mass., S11691
WARRENER, Aaron, Mass., S44027
Robert, Va., S37506

WARRENER (continued)
Willard, Mass., Lois, W16462
WARRIC, Charles, Cont., Md., See DUNNOM
WARRICK, Charles Donnom, Cont., Md., Jane, W3481
Wyatt/Wiatt/Wiat, N.C. See WARWICK
WARRIN, Jesse, Ct., S17749
WARRINER, Aaron, Pvt. Mass., BLWt. 5217 (see H-4348). Iss. 5/24/1790 Note: I called Int. Dept. Archives and Mr. Flatequal said he found Wt.4348 under Aaron Warriner, but did not find 5217 under Harriner or Warriner
Abner, Mass., Elizabeth, W25896
Benjamin, Mass., S44207
Gad, Mass., S29526, b. 1758
Gad, Mass., Lucy, W18295, b. 1762
Noah, Mass., R18733
Samuel, Mass., Keziah, W20112
Stephen, Mass., S11647
Willard, Mass. See WARRENER
WARRING, Benjamin, Pvt. N.Y., BLWt. 7983 iss. 7/28/1791 to Robert Boyd, ass.
Schudder/Schuder, Ct. See Schuder WARING
Solomon, Ct. See WARING
WARRINGTON, William, Cont., Va., Nancy, W2382; BLWt.78032-160-55
WARSHAM, John, Va. See WORSHAM
WARSON, Thomas, Pvt. Ct., BLWt. 6643 iss. 1/20/1795 to Timothy Benedict, ass.
WARTERFIELD, Peter, Va., S37504
WARTERS, David, N.Y. See WATERS
WARWICK, Wyatt/Wiatt/Wiat, N.C., Sarah, W3898
WASGATE, Davis, Mass. See WASGATT
WASGATT, Davis, Mass., S35701
WASH, John, Ga., N.C., Va., S17183
Thomas, Va., Susannah S., W6381
William, Ga. & Va., S32046
WASHAM, Charles, Va., Polly, W3057
WASHBOURNE, Alden, Cont., Mass., Sarah, W22491
WASHBURN, Abiel, Mass., Navy, Abigail, W8982; BLWt.26984-160-55
Abner, Mass., S15696
Abraham, Mass., S11671
Asa, Mass., S33866
Azel, N.H., BLWt.2279-400-Surg. Iss. 3/5/1798
Bezaliel, Ct. ? Mass. ? R.I. ? Meribah, R11171
Benjamin, Va., S11696
Fildad, Mass., Lucy, W14113
Ebenezer, Mass., Mary, W2284; BLWt.24757-160-55
Eleanor (his name was George), Md., former wid. of Daniel Rankins, which see
Eli, Cont., Ct., Mary, W2031
Eliab, Mass., Mary, W15452
Elijah, Cont., Mass., Elizabeth, W16084
Ephraim, Mass., S30183. His wid. was pensioned as former wid. of John Thompson, which see

WASHBURN (continued)
Hugh, Mass., Catherine, W25902
Isaac, Mass., Betsey, W1677
Isaiah, Mass., Patience, W14080
Isaiah, Mass., R11170
Israel, Mass., S17756
Jannet/Jennet, (his name was Ephraim. His pension No. S30183), Mass., former wid. of John Thompson, which see
Jonah, Mass., S15693
Joseph, Mass., Sarah, W16158
Lemuel, Ct., S44210
Lettice, Navy, Mass., Sarah, W11725
Luther, Mass., S43242
Moses, Va., R11172
Nathan, Ct., Anna/Annah, W25877
Prudence (his name Ebenezer), Mass., former wid. of Stephen Baker, which see
Reuben, Pvt. Mass., BLWt.5223. Iss. 2/27/1793 to John Stevenson
Robert, Cont., Mass., Elizabeth, W19582
Salathiel, Mass., Bathsheba, W18265
Salmon/Solomon, Cont., Mass., Hannah, W14108; BLWt.8455-160-55
Samuel, Ct., S43235
Samuel, Mass., S29527
Samuel, Mass., S33219
Solomon, Mass., See Salmon
Thomas, Mass., S17758
William, Mass., S14794
William, Mass., S44212
WASHER, Elias, Va., Judith, R11174
WASHINGTON, George A., Cont., BLWt.2146-200. Va. res. of heirs in 1836
William, Va., BLWt.2421-450-Lt. Col. Iss. 3/7/1798
William, Dis. Ct. res.
WASHUNKS, Abel, Pvt. Ct., BLWt. 6620 iss. 1/13/1792
WASON, John, N.H., S18265
John, Va., Ellen, W1007; BLWt.27661-160-55
WASSON, James, N.Y., S43241
John, Cont., Ct., Amea, W18268; BLWts.152-60-55; 6708-100-1791
John, Mass., Eunice, W22495
John, N.Y., S11665
John, N.Y., Betshamah, W18236
John, Va. See WASON
Joseph, N.C., S26491
Robert, Ct. Sea Service, Privateer, S17748
Samuel, Mass., S18259
Thomas, Mass., Mary, W22494; BLWt.36534-160-55
William, N.C.? See WAUSON
WASTCOAT, Richard, N.H., S30772
WATCHER, Nicholas, Cont., BLWt. 1671-100. Vt. res. in 1830
WATERBERRY, Nathaniel, Ct., S14796
WATERBURY, Daniel, Ct., N.Y., S28933

WATERBURY (continued)
Deodate, Ct., Mary, W18227
Enos, Ct., Amy, W2280
John, Ct., Hannah, W6432; BLWt. 51762-160-55
Jonathan, Ct., Sally, W18282
Joseph, Ct., S17174
Samuel, Ct., R11177
Samuel, N.Y., Lydia, R----
Thomas, Ct., R11178
William, Ct., S17177
William, Ct., S35697
William, Ct., Sally, R11179
WATERFIELD, John, Va., BLWt.1978-100
Meshack, Va., S38454
Peter, Va. See WARTERFIELD
WATERHOUSE, Ambrose, Ct. See WATROUS
George, Mass., S19498
George, N.H., S17759
John, Cont., Mass., Elizabeth, W27496
Jonathan, Ct. Sea Service, S18258
Joseph, Cont., Mass., S28936
Lucy, Mass., former wid. of Moses McKenney, which see
Lucy, Mass., former wid. of Thomas McKenney, which see
Samuel, Mass., Patience, W25864
William, Pvt. R.I., BLWt.3599. Iss. 8/7/1789 to Richard Platt, ass.
William, R.I., Lavina, W6433
WATERMAN, Abram/Abraham, Ct., Hepsibah/Hepzibah, W2287; BLWt.9405-160-55
Asa, Ct. or R.I., Commissary Dept., Anna S. Lilley, former wid., W21577
Benjamin, R.I., S21560
Calvin, Ct., Priscilla, W8985; BLWt.26934-160-55
Charles, Ct., Sarah, W4611
Chester, Ct., S43221
Darius, Ct., Cont., Ct. Sea Service & Privateer, Rhoda, W1336; BLWt.7207-160-55
David, R.I., S9514
Edward, R.I., Prudence, W2285; BLWt.34503-160-55
Elijah, Ct., S7825
Elijah, Vt., Ruth, W22525
Elisha, Mass., S30763
Elisha, R.I., Elizabeth, R11181
Elisha, Vt., Sarah, W18274
Ephraim, Pvt., Mass., BLWt. 5222 iss. 9/13/1792
Ephraim, Mass., Jerusha, W22509
Glading, Ct., Sea Service, Cont. Charlotte, W15814
Ignatius, Ct., Cont., S40644
Jedediah, Cont., Mass., S43236; BLWt.2321-150-Ens. Iss. 2/6/1792
John, Ct., S43218
John, R.I., Welthian, W22512
John O., Ct., Faith Foster, former wid., R3684
Joseph, Ct., S23054
Joseph, Pvt. Hazen's Regt."of Invalids", BLWt.13914 iss. 9/24/1790 to Peleg Sanford, ass.

WATERMAN (continued)
Joseph, Mass., Navy, S35694
Laban/Laben, R.I., Esther, W25881
Levi, Vt., Hepsibah, W22321
Luther, Ct., Cont., Phebe, W4379
Malachi, Mass., Mary, W25868
Noah, Mass., S19149
Olney, Pvt. R.I., BLWt.3590 iss. 10/7/1798
Olney, R.I., S21552
Robert, Mass., Privateer, S11686
Seth, Mass., S43238
Stephen, R.I., Marcy/Mercy Winsor, former wid., W26087
William, Ct., Privateer, S19838
William, R.I., S21553
William, R.I., S22033
William, Navy, R.I., Esther, W25893
Zebedee, Ct., S17755
Zenas, Mass., S30181
WATEROUS, Benjamin, Ct., Elizabeth W22527
Josiah, Ct., Cont., S3483
Samuel, Ct., Cont., Sarah Eddy, former wid., W21045
WATERS, Abner, Cont., Ct., S3474
Asa, Mass., Susan E., W832; BLWt. 31763-160-55
Benjamin, Ct., Mass., S18642
Benjamin, Mass., Beulah, W3634
Bigelow, Ct., S11667
Daniel, Ct., Sarah, W22542; BLWt. 27568-160-55
David, N.Y., S43249
David, S.C., S7845
Elisha, Cont., S43248; N.Y. res. & agcy.
Henry, N.J., Keziah, W4094
Jacob, Pa., Ann, R11182
James, Pvt., Md., BLWts.11794 & 12678 iss. 1/30/1795 to John Stockdell, ass.
James, Cont., Md., S40642
James, Va., S39113
John, Ct., Mindwell, W15464
John, N.H., Hannah, W25905
John, Va., S11668
Joseph, Pvt. Sheldon's Dragoons Ct., BLWt.6699 iss. 4/11/1792
Joseph, Ct., Cont., Lydia Root, former wid., W17543
Joseph, Mass., Elizabeth, W14110
Joseph, Mass., Sea Service,S30187
Joseph, Dis. Phila., Pa. Agcy.
Judah, Mass., Olive, W18229
Michael V.D., N.Y., Catharine, R11183
Moses, N.C., S9518
Moses, Va., S7828
Oliver, Phebe. See her claim as former wid. of her 1st husb., Samuel Judd, Ct.
Richard, Ct. See WATROUS
Richard, Md., Elizabeth Jane, W11722; BLWt.2409-300-Capt. Iss. 6/7/1789
Theodore, Ct., R11185
Thomas, Cont., N.H., Deborah, W18264
Thomas, Pvt. N.H., BLWt.3562 iss. 7/21/1789 to Ladd & Cass,

WATERS (continued)
assnes.
Thomas, N.Y., S11694
Thomas, Va., S40649
Westwood, S.C., Abigail Taylor, former wid., W26506
William, Pvt., Mass., BLWt.5290 iss. 7/10/1797 to James Adlington, Devisee
William, Va., S41293
Willson, Cont., Md., S7805
WATES, Samuel, S.C. See WAITS
WATESBURY, William, Pvt. Ct., BLWt.6698 iss. 6698 iss. 6/27/1789 to Smith Weed, ass.
WATFORD, Joseph, N.C., R11186
William, N.C., S3463
WATKINS, Abner, Va., S6341
Anna, Navy, R.I., former wid. of Levi P. Cole, which see
Badwell, Ct. See Boadewell
Benjamin, Pvt. N.Y., BLWt.8009 iss. 12/15/1790
Boadewell/Badwell, Ct., S41294
David, Mass., Elizabeth Morris former wid., W25715; BLWt.86043-160-55
Edward, Vt., S11669
Edward, Va., Molly, W6417
Ephraim, Ct., S43220
Gassaway, Md., Eleanor B., W15857 BLWt.2406-300-Capt. Iss. 5/11/1790
Gilbert, Mass., S43219
Jedediah, Ct., French & Indian War, Abigail, R11188
John, Pvt. Ct., BLWt.6625 iss. 11/14/1791
John, Md., R11191
John, N.C., Cynthia, See WADKINS
John, N.C., R11190
John, S.C., Rachel Deavours, former wid., W7003. Her last husb., George Deavours, also served during Rev.
John, Va., S31460
John, Va., S39878
John Watkin, Cont., N.J., Judith, W19583
Jonathan, Pa., Privateer, S17761
Joseph, Va., Susan, W6416
Joseph D., Va., S18266
Leonard, Md., Mary, W8976
Mark, Cont., Mass., Esther, W4847
Michael, Mass., S33218
Moses, Mass., Abial, W14087
Nathan, Ct., S41304
Nathan, Mass., BLWt.2223-300-Capt. Iss. 4/1/1790. No papers
Oliver, Mass., Lucy, W6418; BLWt. 26457-160-55
Richard, Va., R11195
Robert, Ct., S43226
Robert, Va., Hannah, R11189
Samuel, N.C., S3465
Seth, Mass., S21557
Spencer, Va., Sarah, W2283
Stephen, Md., Sarah, W25852; BLWt. 31735-160-55
Stephens, Mass., S22570
Thomas, N.C., Elizabeth, W6779;

WATKINS (continued)
BLWt.45592-160-55
Willard, Cont., Mass., S11678
William, Ct., Lois, R11193
William, Pa., S3464
William, Pa. Sea Service, Privateer, Ann, W11710
Zaccheus, Mass., S33221
Zachariah, Mass., S33212
WATLINGTON, John, Va., Elizabeth, W4097 & Va. Half Pay. N.A. Acc. No.874-050186. Half Pay John Watlington
WATROND, Noah, Mass. See WALROND
WATROUS, Abner, Pvt., Ct., BLWt. 6608 iss. 2/26/1798
Allen, Ct., S4715
Ambrose, Ct., S32043
Benjamin, Pvt. Ct., BLWt.6697 iss. 5/10/1790
Benjamin, Ct., See WATEROUS
John R., Ct., Cont., Lucretia W. Hubbard, former wid., W3018; BLWt.2343-400-Surg. iss. 1/28/1790
Richard, Ct., S36364
William, Ct., S41292
William, Pvt. "in the Invalids" BLWt.13915 iss. 9/25/1790
WATRUS, Richard, See WATROUS
WATSON, Aaron, Mass., S6332
Abner, Va., R11199
Alexander, Mass., S23472
Amariah, Ct., S4717
Benjamin, N.H., Patience, W22511
Benjamin, Pvt., Pa., BLWt.10657 iss. 4/12/1791 to Alexander Power, ass.
Benjamin, Pa., S41299
Caleb, Ct., S44009
Caleb, N.H., Lydia, W25903
Christina, Pa., former wid. of Christian Reinick, which see
Daniel, Cont., Mass., Susannah, W22544
Daniel, N.H., Comfort, W2281; BLWt.13189-160-55
David, Pvt., N.H., BLWt.3553. Iss. 8/24/1790 to B.J. Gilman, ass.
David, N.H., S43229
David, N.H., Alice, W15456
David, Va., S30762
Dudley, N.H., Anna, R11200
Evan T., Va., S30770
Guy, Pvt. R.I., BLWt.3600 iss. 12/31/1789
Guy, R.I., S39874
Jack, Pvt., R.I., BLWt.3594 iss. 12/31/1789
Jack (colored), R.I., S36366
James, Cont., Ct. See John WASSON
James, Mass., Lucy, W15451
James, Mass., BLWt.109010-160-55
James, Pa., S23994, b. Ireland
James, Pa., R11203
James, Va., S40643, Pa. res.
Jesse, Mass., S41297
Jesse, Va., Mary, W6411

WATSON (continued)
John, Pvt. Ct., BLWts.6708 & 152-60-55 iss. 5/5/1791. Wt. 6708 iss to Benjamin Tallmadge, ass.
John, Ct., S32037
John, Dis., Ct. res.
John, Mass., S17186
John, Mass., Eunice, W25889
John, N.H., S43228
John, N.H., Mary, W18262
John, N.C., S16287; b. in Pa.
John, N.C., Lydia, W18292; BLWt. 17957-160-55
John, N.C., Pa., Jane, W3900
John, Pvt. Pa., BLWt.10552. Iss. 1/23/1796
John, Pa., Jane, W22530
John, S.C., Mary Frances, W4846; BLWt.31737-160-55
John, S.C., Bethiah, R11202
John, Va., S15695
John, Va., S31458
John, Va., Hannah, W18258
Joseph, Mass., BLWt.40679-160-55
Joseph, Pvt. N.Y., BLWt.8028 iss. 8/14/1790 to Henry Hart, ass.
Joseph, Va., S11659
Joseph, Va., S31455
Jude, Mass., R11204
Larner, Va., Peggy/Margaret, W6412; BLWt.35677-160-55
Levi, Ct., S32039
Levi, N.Y., S44023
Levin, Ga., S7797
Major, N.Y., S38460
Marston, Cont., Mass., Lucy, W15454
Mary, N.Y., former wid. of Nathaniel Tucker, which see
Micajah, N.C., Barsha, W4096; BLWt.36539-160-55
Nathaniel, N.C., S3454
Neal, N.C., S42056
Oliver, R.I., S11648
Philip, N.C., Hannah, W6413
Rhoda, Mass. former wid. of Luther Jotham (colored), which see
Samuel, Mass., Lois Smith, former wid., W19046
Samuel, R.I., Abiah, W18249
Samuel, S.C., S17187, b. in Pa.
Scip, Pvt. Ct., BLWt.6657 iss. 11/15/1791
Sipeo (colored), Ct., Juda/Judah, W18240
Stephen, N.H., S30188
Stephen, N.H., Hannah Snow, former wid., W22277
Thomas, Ct., S11685
Thomas, Ct., Sarah, W22505; BLWt.10221-160-55
Thomas, Pvt. Md., BLWt.11810 iss. 1/21/1792
Thomas, N.H., Anna, W22507; BLWt.192-60-55 & 3552-100-Pvt. iss. 4/5/1796 to C. Ashley, ass.
Thomas, N.C., R11209

WATSON (continued)
Thomas, Pa., R11208, b. Ireland
Thomas, Va., S17188
Thomas W., Cont., BLWt.476-100 N.J. res. in 1808
Timothy, Ct., Anne, R11201
Titus, Ct., Mercy, W18271
Walter, Md., S41301; BLWt.6407-160-55
William, Cont., Mass., S41300; BLWt.2300-300-Capt. Iss. 8/7/1789 to Richard Platt
William, N.H., Sarah, W22537; BLWt.18375-160-55
William, N.J., N.Y., Anna Runyan, former wid., W8569
William, N.C., S7831, b. Pa.
William, Va., S17180, alive in 1835
William, Va., S17752
William, Va., Tabitha, R11207; d. 2/25/1828
William, Va., R11210
William, Va., R11211
Winthrop, N.H., Mary, W16780
WATT, James, Pa., Sophia, W3367
WATTER, Henry, N.J. See WALTER
WATTERS, Christopher, Pvt. Pa., BLWt.10594 iss. 7/9/1789
Daniel, Ct. See WATERS
James, Cont., Md. See WATERS
Martin, Pa., S23060
Thomas, Va. See WATERS
William, N.J., R11212, Pa. res.
William, N.C., Mary, W3897
WATTERSON, Robert, Va., S39877
WATTLES, Charles, Ct., S14799
Dan, Ct., Cynthia, W3743
David, Ct., S44028
Joshua, Ct., Sarah Ann, W26618; BLWt.3797-160-55
Mason, Cont., Mass.,S43232; BLWt. 2301-300-Capt. Iss. 5/21/1798
William, Ct., N.Y., S14795
WATTS, Benjamin, Va., Elizabeth, R11217
Bennett, Va., Susan, R11221
Charles, Va., R11215
Daniel, Mass., S16016
David, S.C., S18267
David, Va., Elizabeth A.S., W25895; BLWt.40932-160-55
Francis, Pa., BLWt.2114-100
Frederick, Va., R11218
Garret/Garrett, N.C., Anna, R11213
George, S.C., Mary B., W1009
George, S.C., Barbara, R11214
Jacob, N.Y. See WALS
James, N.C., S7817
Jesse, Cont., N.H., Eleanor, W22541
John, Cont., S--- & BLWt.2431-300-Capt. of 1st Regt. of Dragoons. Iss. 8/27/1795 to Smith & Ridgway, assnes.
John, N.H., S11695
John, N.Y., Martha, W18270
John, Va., Lucy, W6382
Mason, Va., S17760
Peter, N.C., S30765, b. Va.
Robert, Pvt., N.J., BLWt.8844

WATTS (continued)
Iss. 6/6/1791
Samuel, Mass., Mary, W2885
William, Md., BLWt.2368-300
William, Va., S16286
William, Va., W19587
WAUFLE, John Henry/Henry, N.Y., Margaret, See John Henry WAFLE
WAUGH, George, Va., Elizabeth, W9873
James, Mass., Bathsheba, W25882
James, Pa., BLWt.2396-300-Capt. Iss. 7/9/1789
Joseph, Ct., Mary, W3745; BLWt. 26478-160-55
Robert, N.H., BLWt.3388-160-55
Samuel, Sgt. Ct., BLWt.6641 iss. 10/7/1789 to Benj. Tallmadge, ass.
Samuel, Ct., N.Y., Elizabeth, W25866
Thaddeus, Ct., Ruth, W22514
Thadeus, Pvt. Ct., BLWt.6640 iss. 12/12/1789 to Theodosius Fowler, ass.
WAUSON, William, N.C., Isabella, R11175
WAUSSON, William, See WASSON
WAX, Peter, Pa., R11222
WAY, Abner, Ct., Eunice, W25899
Asa, Cont., Ct., Susannah, W22504
Durien/Duren, Ct., Sarah, W4612
Elisha, Ct., Hannah, W1006; BLWt.27578-160-55
George, Ct., Mary, W18286
Isaac, Cont., Ct., Augusta Tuller, dau., W29943
Isaac, Va., S16568
John, Ct., Mary, R11223
John, N.Y., S42609; BLWt.7992-100 A. -- Pvt. iss. 3/19/1792
Peter, Ct., Cont., Lucy, W18228
Reynold, Ct., Irene, W15462
Samuel, N.H., Hannah, W25856
Samuel, Pa., BLWt.401-100
Selah, Ct., Lucy, W1675; BLWt. 28570-160-55
WAYLAND, Edward, Ct., Molly, W18242
James, Ct., S6330
James, Pvt. "in the Invalids" BLWt.13917 iss. 2/2/1790
Joshua, Va., S37502
WAYLEY, Aaron, Ct., Hannah, W19895
WAYMAN, Harmon, Va., S32618
WAYNE, Anthony, BLWt.2379-850-Brig. Gen. Iss. 3/5/1796
George, Pa., R11226
John, Pvt., N.J., BLWt.8830 iss. 2/25/1796. Note: See Gilbert Groteclass who is listed with this same Wt. number. In the old book from which this card was copied, Gilbert G's name was placed between Wts. No. 8329 & 8330 - N.J. Line.
WAYT, William, Va., S6333
WEADEN, Peleg, R.I. See WEEDEN
WEAGAR, John, N.Y., R11227
WEAGEAR, John, See WEAGAR
WEAKFIELD, Henry, N.C., Mary, W35

WEAKLEY, Thomas, Va., Prudence, R11229
WEAKS, Job, N.J. See WEEKS
WEAR, Cornelius, Pa., S40658; BLWt.1641-100
James, Pa., Lydia, See WEIR
John, N.C., S1781, b. Pa.
WEARE, James, Cont., BLWt.1437-100, Va. res.
Jeremiah, Cont., Mass., Lucy, W25949
Nathan, N.H., BLWt.2281-200-Lt. Iss. 4/25/1798. No papers
Richard, N.H., BLWt.88-300. Iss. 11/26/1803 to Nathan Weare. Delivered to Samuel Finney
William, Sgt. "in the Invalids" BLWt.13903 iss. 2/5/1790
William, Ct., Cont., S36376
WEASEY, John, Pvt. Pa., BLWt.10606 Iss. 3/16/1793 to Michael Stever, ass.
John, Pa., S40666
WEATHBEE, Jacob, See WETHERBEE
WEATHERALL, John, Cont., Va., Elizabeth, R11187
WEATHERBEE, Abel, See WETHERBEE
Amos, Mass. See WETHERBEE
Anna, Mass., former wid. of Solomon Taylor, which see
Daniel, Cont., Mass. See WETHERBEE
Jacob, N.H. See WETHERBEE
Joab, Mass. See WETHERBEE
Thomas, Mass. See WETHERBEE
Thomas, Mass., Sally, W19602
WEATHERBY, Benjamin, N.J., BLWt. 2374-300-Capt. Iss. 7/24/1790. No papers
Nathaniel, Mass., Elizabeth, W16785
WEATHERED, Frances, N.C., former wid. of Asa Searcy, W8992
WEATHERFORD, Benjamin, Ga., Va., Nancy, W1520
John, Va., R11231
WEATHERHEAD, Amaziah, R.I., S11698
Edmond, Cont., N.Y., Comfort, W19595
Edmund, Pvt. Sheldon's Dragoons Ct., BLWt.6714 iss. 5/15/1790 to Edmund Weatherhead
Levi, R.I., S21565
WEATHERHOLT, Jacob, Va., Jane, W617; BLWt.13723-160-55
WEATHERMAN, Nancy, Va., former wid. of Robert Glasscock, which see
WEATHERN, Micah, See WETHERN
WEATHERS, Elisha, N.C., Sarah, W3901
James, N.H., R11232
Valentine, S.C., Sarah, W25935; BLWt.36818-160-55
Willis, N.C., S7862
WEATHERSBE, Lewis, N.C., R11233
WEATHERSTINE, John, N.Y., Margaret, W18341
WEAVER, Abiel, ? Disability pension, R.I. res.
Abiel, Pvt. R.I., BLWt.3589 iss. 12/31/1789
Abigail, Mass., former wid. of

WEAVER (continued)
David Nason, which see
Adam, Pvt. N.Y., BLWt.8012 iss. 12/28/1791 to Cornelius V. Dyck, ass.
Adam, Pa., S40653
Andrus, Green Mt. Boys, Vt. See WEVER
Anthony, Pvt. Md., BLWt.11821 iss. 1/8/1796 to George Ponsonby, ass.
Anthony, N.J., S23481
Benjamin, R.I., Susannah Davison, former wid., W17707
Caleb, R.I., S33240
Conrad, Pa., See WEVER
Constant, R.I., Molly, W25936
David, Pvt., N.Y., BLWt.7955 iss. 7/22/1790 to Thomas Tillotson, ass.
David, N.Y. & War of 1812, Catharine, R11238
Dutee, R.I., S21563
Edward, N.Y., S43280
Frederick, N.C., Catharine, BLWt.40920-160-55
Frederick, R.I., Polly Blackmer former wid., W18620; BLWt. 6427-160-55
George, Pvt., N.Y., BLWt.8015 iss. 9/7/17-- to Robert Dill, ass. of Michael Overacker, deceased ass.
George, N.Y., S43278
George Michel, N.Y., Catharine, R11237. He d. 12/4/1832. Of Deerfield, Oneida Co., N.Y. in 1832
George N., N.Y., R11241 alive in Oct. 1833, res. in 1833 Jefferson Co., N.Y.
Henry, N.Y., S43284
Henry, Pvt. Pa., BLWt.10621 iss. 9/5/1791
Henry, Pa., See WEBER
Henry, S.C., S39120
Jabez, Cont., Vt., R11242
Jacob, N.Y., Margaret, W25951
Jacob, Pa., BLWt.2371-200-Lt. Iss. 3/14/1794 to Amos Taylor, Admr. Also recorded as above under BLWt.2638. No papers
Jacob, Pvt. Pa., BLWt.10630 iss. 3/19/1792 to Christian Gross, ass.
Jacob, Pa., S40652
Jacob, Pa., See WEAVOR
James, R.I., Mehitable, W22570
James, Va., Nancy, W4581
John, Cont., Va., Patsey, W3635; BLWt.246-60-55
John, N.J. See WEBBER
John, Pvt., N.Y., BLWt.7973 iss. 6/29/1790
John, N.Y., Sarah, W11751; BLWt. 7431-160-55
John, N.C., S42061
John, N.C., Frances, R11239
John, Pvt. Pa., BLWt.10612 iss. 11/4/1791 to John McCleland, ass.
John, Pa., Eve, W3369

WEAVER (continued)
John, R.I., Olive, W22584
John, Va., Sarah, W9158; BLWt. 71029-160-55
John, Va., BLWt.1391-100
John Adam, Pa., Anna Maria, W4383
Joseph, Mass., R.I., Sarah, W18316
Josiah, N.Y., Vt., R11243
Lodowick, Ct., R.I., Polly, W18323
Louden, N.Y., Vt. See ANDREW
Michael, Cont., Md., S40660
Michael, Pa., S16290
Nathan, Mass., S---. See data in claim of Olive, wid. of Nathan Weaver,
Nathan, Mass., Olive, W25926; BLWt.84042-160-55
Nicholas, N.Y., Elizabeth, W15860
Nicholas G., N.Y., Gertrude, W18234
Philip, Va., S14785
Reuben, R.I., S22044
Richard, N.Y., Vt., S11726
Samuel, Ct., BLWt.266-100
Samuel, Ct., Cont., Hannah, W1111; BLWt.13746-160-55
Samuel, N.C., S3516
Samuel, N.C., Va., Mary, W8993
Shadrach, N.C., S3517
Sheffel, Mass., S29539
Thomas, Ct., S35717
Thomas, R.I., Amy, W14419
Timothy, R.I., S11730
William, Cont., R.I., S39885
William, N.C., S7863
William, Pvt., R.I., BLWt.3585 iss. 12/31/1789
William, Va., S17770
WEAVOR, Jacob, Pa., BLWt.2381-300-Capt. Iss. 6/6/1791. No papers
WEBB, Abner, Ct., S14821
Amos, Pvt., N.Y., BLWt.8042 iss. 3/29/1791 to Jonathan Tuttle, ass.
Andrew, Mass., Vt., S11701
Andrew, Pvt. Pa., BLWt.10625 iss. 4/9/1791
Augustin, Va., Frances, W25939; BLWt.26935-160-55
Austin, Ga., Ailsey, W3902
Azariah, N.H., S19151
Bancks/Banks, Barruck, Md. See Barruck
Barnabas, Mass., Anna, W15468
Barruck/Bancks/Banks, Md., S40654
Benjamin, Ct., S11704
Benjamin, Pvt., Mass., BLWt.5279 iss. 2/6/1797
Benjamin, N.C., Pa., S3487, b. Pa.
Benjamin, Va., R11245
Charles, Ct., Dis.
Christopher, Ct., S11705
Constant, Ct., S6349
Daniel, Ct., Luranda, W2291; BLWt.27689-160-55
David, Sgt. Ct., BLWt.6671. Iss. 6/27/1789 to David Webb
David, Ct., Sarah, W6443
David, N.Y., S14803
Ebenezer, Ct., S14824

WEBB (continued)
Ebenezer, Ct., Hannah, W18233; BLWt.12836-160-55
Ebenezer, Ct., Phebe, W25921
Edward, Mass., Sarah, W22549
Francis, Va. Sea Service, R105. Va. Half Pay
George, Cont., Mass., S33887; BLWt.2294-300-Capt. Iss. 12/22/1796
George, N.C., Elizabeth, W6445; BLWt.31780-160-55, b. Pa.
Gideon, Pvt. Lamb's Art., N.Y., BLWt.8047 iss. 4/9/1791 to James Wadsworth, ass.
Isaac, Ct., Cont., Mary, W4851
Isaac, Vt., S11703, b. 10/15/1766 at Williamstown, Mass.
Isaac, Va., S1266
James, Mass., S37522
James, N.C., S42062
Jared, Ct., Prudence, W18300
Jeremiah, R.I., S39887
Jesse, N.C., S3501
Jesse, N.C., Lucretia, W18333
John, Ct., R11253
John, Cont., Ct., S36374; BLWt. 2356-300-Capt. Iss. 11/13/1792
John, Ga., S32055
John, Ga., Elizabeth, R11249
John, Md., S37514
John, Md., Susannah, W4384; BLWt.530-160-55
John, Mass., S17189
John, Mass., S33882
John, Pvt., N.Y., BLWt.7962 iss. 6/20/1791
John, N.Y., S11725
John, N.Y., S46477
John, N.C., S3486
John, N.C., S7849
John, N.C., Charity, R11247
John, S.C., Susanna Smith, former wid., W8735; BLWt. 3143-160-55
John, Va., S41320
John, Va., BLWt.2052-450
Johnson/Johnston, N.C., Grace, W3904; BLWt.6385-160-55
Jonathan, N.Y., Amy, R11244
Joseph, Cont., N.H., Elizabeth, W22586
Joseph, N.Y., S14829
Joshua, N.C., S42059
Joshua, R.I., S32051
Josiah, N.Y., Rhoda, W6444; BLWt.47823-160-55
Lewis, Va., Sea Service, Lucy R., W8990
Libbeus/Libbius, Ct., R11250
Luther, Vt., BLWt.8382-160-55
Mathias, N.J., S23064
Michael, Mass., Navy, Rebecca, W25964
Moses, Ct., Abigail, W25920
Moses, S.C., Va., S35113
Nathaniel, Ct., BLWt.2344-300-Capt. Iss. 5/18/1790 to Theodosius Fowler, ass. No papers
Nathaniel, Cont., Mass., Lydia, W2594 1/2. She was also pen-

WEBB (continued)
sioned as the former wid. of her other husb., Benjamin Tukey, Mass., which see
Reynolds, Ct., Cont., Catharine, W25919
Robert, Sophia, R11256. Widow's res. Miss. in 1849
Samuel, Ct., Abigail, W16781, d. 8/23/1825
Samuel, Ct., Cont., N.Y., R11255 b. North Castle, N.Y. 3/12/1756
Samuel, Mass., Sea Service, Betsey/Betty, R11246, b. Scituate, Mass. 1754, d. 4/14/1839
Samuel B., Ct., BLWt.2337-500-Col. Iss. 1/29/1790
Seth, Ct., Ann, W25922; BLWt. 77513-160-55
Tapley, Va. Sea Service, S14818
Thomas, Mass., S33888
William, Pvt. Lamb's Art., N.Y., BLWt.8037 iss. 10/14/1790
William, N.Y., Mary, W2502
William, N.Y., R11257
William, Pvt. Pa., BLWt.10561 iss. 6/28/1792 to Samuel Alexander, ass.
WEBBER, Benjamin, Cont., S37523, Mass. res. in 1818
Benjamin, Mass., Betsy, W14101
Bradley, Mass., Sibbel, W1339
Charles, Mass., Sarah, R18858
Daniel, Cont., Mass., S37531; BLWt.2313-200-Lt. Iss. 5/14/ 1800 to Joshua Woodman
Edward, N.H., S43285; BLWt.2314-100
Ezekiel, Cont., Mass., Judith, W1961
George, Mass., Abigail, W25943; BLWt.806-100
John, Mass., S30197
John, N.H., S49275; BLWts.51-60-55; 3573-100-1789. Sarah Webber wid. of above sold., rec'd pension as former wid. of Thomas Wiggins, Pa., which see
John, N.J., R11258
Jonathan, Mass., S37515
Joseph, Mass., Elizabeth Woodbury, former wid., W26113
Joseph, R.I., Lussanah/Susannah, W1114; BLWt.26936-160-55
Lewis, Cont., Mass., R.I., S18270
Nathaniel, Pa., S35112
Noah, Mass., Nancy, W25944; BLWt. 14758-160-55
Paul, Mass., S37525
Philip, Va., Mary, W616
Renaldo, Mass., S21564
Reuben, Mass., S36375
Stephen, Cont., Mass., Sally, W4849
William, Cont., Mass., Hannah, W25931; Rej. BL-1855. She was also pensioned as former wid. of her other husb., Thomas Wheeler, Mass., which see
William, Mass., S37524
William, Mass., S43271
William, Mass., Anna, W25925

WEBER, Adam, N.Y. See WEVER
Bradley, Mass., See WEBBER
Henry, Pa., Anna Maria, W2887
Peter, Cont., S33880, Mass. res. & agcy.
WEBSTER, Aaron, Ct., S14815
Abijah, Ct., Olive, R11266; BLWt.36559-160-55
Abraham, Ct., S43272
Allen, Ct., Rebecca, W25963
Amos, Ct., N.Y., R11259
Amos, N.H., BLWt.1005-200
Andrew, Mass., S3520
Asa, Cont., N.H., Vt., Sally, W18329
Ashbell/Ashbil, Ct., Mercy, W18313
Benjamin, Ct., Eve, W2288; BLWts.143-60-55 & 6617-100-1789
Benjamin, Ct., Navy, Lydia, W22562
Charles, Ct., Hannah Loomis, former wid., W20503
Daniel, Ct., S43273
David, Mass., N.H., S15699
Eleazer, Ct., Cont., S33890
Elizabeth, Ct., former wid. of Isaac Goodsell, which see
Isaac, Cont., Ct., Green Mt. Boys, Anna, W20122
Isaac, Mass., N.Y., S11718
Israel, Cont., Ct., Mary Sophia, W18307
Israel, N.H., Betsey, W22550
Jacob, N.H., S18268
James, Ct., R11262
John, Ct., S11728
John, Cont., Va., Maggie, R11263
John, Va., S11700
John B., Cont., Pa., S40663; BLWt.2391-200-Capt. Lt. Iss. 9/12/1789
Joseph, N.H., S14810
Joseph, N.H., Elizabeth, W22563; BLWt.3575-100-Pvt. Iss. 3/25/1790
Joseph, N.Y., Keziah, W19603; BLWt.27691-160-55
Joshua, Ct., S43277
Joshua, Mass., BLWt.5320-100-Pvt. Iss. 3/25/1790
Michael, Ct., S3521
Moses, N.H., S23479
Moses, N.H., Elizabeth, W4850; BLWt.3799-160-55
Nathan, Ct., S14817
Nathan, Ct., S26888
Nathaniel, N.H., Mehitable, W18303 BLWt.24326-160-55
Obed, Ct., Lucy, W613; BLWt.26921-160-55
Richard, N.H., S18269
Samuel, Ct., Margaret, W18318
Samuel, Mass., S33881
Samuel, Mass., Lydia, W14128
Samuel, N.H., S3519
Samuel, N.H., Vt., Elizabeth, W22588
Simeon, Ct., S35715
Stephen, Mass., S14820
Stephen, N.H., Anna, W15467
Stephen, N.H., Catherine, R11260
Thomas, Md., BLWt.2180-100
Thomas, Pvt., N.H., BLWt.3580

WEBSTER (continued
Iss. 8/24/1790 to B.J. Gilman, ass.
Timothy, Ct., Sarah, R11267
William, Ct., Anna, W4848; BLWt. 31773-160-55
William, Va., S3518
Zephaniah, Pvt. Sheldon's Dragoons, Ct., BLWt.6712. Iss. 6/4/1793
WECHTER, Anthony, Sgt. Von Heer's Corps, BLWt.13871 iss. 2/25/ 179- to Chas. Colver, ass.
WEDEMAN, Daniel, N.Y., R11268
WEDGBARE, William, Va., Margaret, W2292; BLWts.72-60-55; 11797 and 12684-100-1795
WEDGE, Samuel, Pvt. Md., BLWt. 11833. Iss. 11/29/1790 to Collin Campbell, admr.
Stephen, N.Y., S35718
WEDGEWOOD, Jesse, Navy, See WEDGWOOD
Noah, N.H. See WEDGWOOD
WEDGWOOD, James, N.H., Anna, W25938
Jesse, Navy, S28939, Me. res.
John, N.H., Mary, R11269; BLWt. 17889-160-55
Noah, N.H., Polly, W1678
WEED, Abishai, Ct., S17191
Abraham, N.Y., S14831
Alexander, Ct., S11717
Andrew, S.C., Mary, BLWt.80034-160-55
Benjamin, Ct., Dis.
Benjamin, Cont., Ct., Hannah, W8986; BLWt.11398-160-55
Benjamin, Mass., S11715
Charles, Ct., Mary, W2501; BLWt.26356-160-55
Charles, Mass., Dorothy, W25945
Charles, N.Y., Mary, W19598
Daniel, Ct., S17768
Daniel, Ct., Elizabeth, R11271
David, Ct., S14825
David, N.Y., S43269
Eleazer, Ct., Cont., Anna, W18302
Elnathan, Ct., S23998
Ephraim, Pvt. Sheldon's Dragoons, Ct., BLWt.6709 iss. 12/10/1789 to Isaac Trowbridge, ass.
Ephraim, Cont., S46347, N.Y. res. in 1828
Ezra, Sgt. N.Y., BLWt.8019 iss. 7/9/1790 to Nicholas Fish, ass.
Ezra, N.Y., S36381
Frederick, Ct., R11272
Gilbert, Ct., Margaret, W18326; BLWt.27659-160-55
Hannah, Ct., former wid. of Joseph Hoyt, which see
Henry, Ct., Rebecca, W2289; BLWt. 51763-160-55
Hezekiah, Ct., Rebecca, W18299
Isaac, Ct., Hannah, W22575
Ithamer/Ithamar, Ct., Delight, W22558
Jabez, Ct., Hannah, W22551
James, Ct., Sarah, W19606
Jared, Ct., Sea Service, R11275
Jehiel, N.Y., Sally, W19608

WEED (continued)
Jesse, Ct., Martha, W18327
John, Ct., S23999
John, Ct., Cont., S11724
John, N.Y., S11727
Jonas, Ct., Abigail Daskam, former wid., W22896; BLWt.32239-160-55. Her other husb. was also a pensioner, William Daskam, Ct. which see
Jonathan, Ct., N.Y., S11682
Jonathan, Ct., Susannah, N.Y., W20119
Jonathan, N.Y., Hannah, W22581
Joseph, Cont., Mass. See William NICKOLS
Nathan, Ct., Mary, W18314
Phineas/Phinehas, N.Y., Abigail, W22583
Reuben, Ct., S11720
Reuben, S.C., R11274, b. N.Y. State
Samuel, N.Y., S43268
Seth, Ct., S6346
Smith, Ct., Sarah, W2290; BLWt.13734-160-55
Stephen, Ct., Elizabeth, W25947
Thadeus, Ct., BLWt.2345-300-Capt. Iss. 6/27/1789. No papers
WEEDEMAN, Peter, S.C., S9523
WEEDEN, Armintus/Mintus, R.I., R11726
Job, Mass., Elizabeth, W22554
John, R.I., S22039, wid. Anna
Mintus, R.I. See Armintus
Peleg, R.I., Sarah, W22552
Thomas, Cont., Mass., S41312
WEEDON, Augustine, Va., S6355
George, Va., BLWt.2418-850-Brig. Gen. Iss. 5/3/1791
Peleg, R.I. See WEEDEN
WEEKES, James, Va., S31467
WEEKLEY, Thomas, Md., S6343
WEEKLY, Samuel, Pvt. Ct., BLWts. 6613 & 8054. Iss. 9/20/1790
WEEKS, Abisha, Mass., S33886
Braddock, Mass., Bethia, W22564
Daniel, R.I., Freelove, W25942
David, Mass., S22577
David, N.C., S31468
Elijah, Mass., Sally wid., and Sarah C. Hurlbutt, dau., W29774
Francis, Ga., Nancy, W25934; BLWt.44287-160-55
Gilbert, N.Y., R20520
Jacob, Pvt. N.Y., BLWt.7994 iss. 7/22/1790 to Thomas Tillotson, ass.
James, Mass., S19154
James, Pvt. N.Y., BLWt.7968 iss. 8/2/1793
James, N.Y., S10043
James (colored), N.Y., S33269
James, Va., See WEEKES
Jedediah, N.H., Lydia, W25946; BLWt.6410-160-55
Job, N.J., S30777
John, Pvt., N.H., BLWt.3572 iss. 9/11/1795 to Wm. S. Thorn, ass.
John, N.H., Susanna, W18324
John, N.C., S3500

WEEKS (continued)
Joseph, Mass., S21562
Joseph, N.C., S3491
Josiah, N.H., Polly, R11281
Leonard, N.H., S43270
Levi, Cont., N.C., Esther, W22580
Micajah, Ct., Bersheba, R11278; BLWt.1592-100
Nathan, R.I., BLWt.2704-Lt. Iss. 1/4/1800 to Joseph Proctor & Melzer Torrey,assnes. of John Weeks, son and only heir. No papers
Nathaniel, Mass., Rachel, W25953
Pelatiah, Mass., N.H., S37527
Persis, Mass., former wid. of Moses Stevens, which see
Samuel, Mass., S6350
Samuel, Mass., Amy, W8302
Sarah, Mass., former wid. of John Mendall, which see
Theophilus, N.C., Ann, W22579
Thomas, Mass., Ruth, BLWt.31787-160-55
Thomas, N.Y., Phebe, W18317
Uriah, Mass., Susannah, W20121
William, Mass., Martha, W20124
William, N.H., Sarah C., W22557; BLWt.11099-160-55
WEEMER, Charles, Pvt. Hazen's Regt. BLWt.13894 iss. 11/29/1792
WEEMS, John, S.C., S7864, b. Va.
WEES, Peter, Va., S1734
WEESE, George, Va., S7850
Michael, Va., S39121
WEGAN, John, Pa., Elizabeth, W4853
WEGER, David, Va., S15698
WEGHAN, Conrad, Pvt. N.Y., BLWt. 7987 iss. 11/11/1791 to Samuel Broome, ass.
WEIBERT, Anthony Felix, See WUIBERT
WEIDA, Michael, Pa., S6356
WEIDELL, Christian, Pvt. Pa., BLWt.10637 iss. 3/19/1792 to George Moore, ass. No papers
WEIDMAN, John, Cont., S46334; BLWt.2392-200-1st Lt. Iss. 7/13/1796; Pa. res. in 1828
WEIDNER, Michael, Mary, R11283 Soldier's res. Pa. in 1845
WEIGAR, David, Va., See WEGER
WEIGELL, Christopher, Pa. See WEIGLE
WEIGHLEY, Isaac, Pa. See WAGLE
WEIGHT, Jacob, Pvt. Ct., BLWt. 6683 iss. 3/25/1790
WEIGHTMAN, Samuel, Pa., Sarah, R11284
WEIGLE, Christopher, Cont., Pa. Catharine, W3320
WEIGLEY, Isaac, Pa. See WAGLE
WEINNAND, Philip, Md., S1267
WEIR, Andrew, Pvt. Pa., BLWt. 10635 iss. 1/18/1794 to Francis Kirkpatrick, ass.
David, S.C., Jane, R11286
George, S.C., S9528, b. in Ireland
James, Pa., Lydia, W22569

WEIR (continued)
James, Va., Margret, R11287
James, N.Y. Agency, Dis.
John, Pa., S22573, b. Pa.
John, Pa., S23065
Samuel, Pvt. Sheldon's Dragoons, Ct., BLWt.6716 iss. 10/26/1789
Thomas, Va., See WARE
WEIRICH, Valentine/Volentine, Pa., S40662
WEIRICK, Michael, Md., Elizabeth, W3321
WEIS, Daniel, N.Y. See WIES
WEISE, Adam, Md., Catharine, W26072; BLWt.26454-160-55
George, Pa., S11711
WEISEL, Jacob, Pa., Ann Maria, W25932; BLWt.79016-160-55
WEISENFELS, Charles Frederick, N.Y., BLWt.2368-200-Lt. Iss. 7/12/1790. No papers
WEISER, John, Cont., Pa., S40659
WEISS, Henry, Pa., Dis.
Jacob, Cont., Pa., Elizabeth, W11769
WEISSENFELS, Charles Frederick, See WEISENFELS
Frederick, N.Y., BLWt.2361-500-a Lt. Col. Commandant. Iss. 1/29/1790
WEITSEL, Abraham, Va., R11288
WEITZEL, Abraham, Va., See WEITSEL
Jacob, Pa., BLWt.2385-200-Lt. Iss. 5/27/1790
John, Pa., Elizabeth, W3319
WEIZER, Henry, Va. See WYSOR
WELBORN, Isaac, N.C. See WELLBORN
Joshua, N.C., S1741, b. N.C.
WELBUR, Record, Mass., See WILBUR
WELBURN, William, Va., S7856
WELCH, Amos, Cont., Ct., S44032
Andrew, Pvt. Pa., BLWt.13890 & 14084. Iss. 8/4/1794
Archelaus, N.H., R11297
Barney, Cont., Ct. or Pa., See WELTS
Benjamin, Cont., Mass., N.H., Thankful, W18306
Benjamin, Ga., R20446
Benjamin, Pvt. N.H., BLWt.3578 iss. 7/21/1789 to Ladd & Cass, assnes
Daniel, Ct., Cont., S36841; BLWt.919-100
Daniel, Cont., Vt., Green Mt. Boys, Mary, W6458
David, Ct., Lurene, W22571
David, Cont., N.Y., Hester Andrews, former wid., R211
David, Dis. Va. res.
David S., Vt., S3504
Dennis, Pvt. Crane's Cont. Art., Mass., BLWt.5336. Iss. 7/15/1797 to Simeon Wyman
Ebenezer, Ct., S40665
Ebenezer, Ct., BLWt.1196-100
Ebenezer, N.Y., Lois, W1903; BLWt.11172-160-55
Edmund, Mass., Hannah, W25965
Edward, Mass., S41315
Hopestill, Ct., S36382

WELCH (continued)
Isaac, Va., S38461
James, Mass., Susannah, W11767
James, Mass., Sarah, R11295
James, N.J., Polly/Mary Shropshire former wid., R9541
James, N.C., S31466
James, Pvt. Pa., BLWt.10566 iss. 7/7/1792 to Joseph Tinker, ass.
James, Va., S6345
John, Ct., Jemima, W8987; BLWt. 34519-160-55
John, Cont., Ct., S14804
John, Cont., R.I., S14822; BLWt. 2287-200-Lt. Iss. 12/14/1796 to John Welch
John, Cont., Vt., Sarah, W22587
John, Pvt. Md., BLWt.11823 iss. 5/4/1797 to James DeBaufre, ass.
John, Mass., S41309
John, N.H., Betsey, W6460; BLWt. 31741-160-55
John, N.H., Mary, R11292
John, Pvt., N.Y., BLWt.8023 iss. 7/2/1790
John, N.Y., Dorcas, W2293; BLWt. 8186160-55
John, N.Y., Polly, W19600
John, Pa., S23066
John, Pa. See WELSH
John, R.I., S36379
John, Va., S3488
John, Va., S7847
Jonas, Mass., Betsey, W25962
Jonathan, Mass., S19503
Joseph, Cont., Mass., S44029; BLWt.2331-200-Lt. Iss. 10/1/1799 to Marlbry Turner, ass. Name spelled Welsh
Joseph, N.H., S11707
Joseph, N.C., S49262
Joseph, Va., Susannah, W8989
Josiah, Vt., R11291
Lemuel, Mass., S37510; BLWt. 889-100
Margaret, Mass., former wid. of John McLucas, which see
Matthias, Pvt., N.H., BLWt.3554 iss. 11/28/1789
Matthias, Mass., N.H., S43255
Michael, Mass. See WELSH
Michael/Michel, N.J., S33878
Moses, N.H., S24000
Nathaniel, Va., R18894. Va. Half Pay. N.A. Acc. No. 874-050187 Half Pay Nathaniel Welch
Patrick, Pvt. "in Moylon's Dragoons", Pa., BLWt.10634 iss. 5/10/1791
Paul, Mass., S37508
Peter, Mass. See WELSH
Richard, Pvt., N.Y., BLWt.8017 iss. 9/20/1790 to Benjamin Elwood, ass.
Robert, Ct., S43282
Robert, Va., S1884
Rossel, Mass., S43265; BLWt. 13887-160-55
Samuel, Ct., Cont., S43263

WELCH (continued)
Samuel, Pa., Wayne's Indian War, War 1812, Old War Inv. File 26494; Rejected file 11294 Rev.
Solomon, Ct., Orpha Dygart, former wid., W14664
Stephen, S.C., S21561
Sylvester, Cont., Va., S6342
Theodosius, Va., Sarah, R11296
Thomas, Cont., Mass. See WELSH
Thomas, Pvt. Hazen's Regt., BLWt. 13880 iss. 11/12/1791 to Timothy Kelly, ass.
Thomas, Pvt., N.H., BLWt.3560 iss. 8/24/1790 to B.J. Gilman, ass.
Thomas, N.H., Lovey, W22566
Thomas, N.H., R26250
Thomas, N.Y., Rebecca, W18309
Thomas, N.C., S1733
William, Ct., R11299
William, Pvt. "in the Invalids", BLWt.13920 iss. 4/19/1792
William, Mass., S37526
William, Mass., N.H., Anna, W25928
William, N.C., Mary Ann, R11293
William, N.C., BLWt.2190-100
WELCHEL, Francis, See WHELCHEL
WELCHONS, William, Pa., Rosanna, W319
WELD, Benjamin, Mass., Nabby, R11301
Calvin, Mass., Eunice, W20120
Edmund G., Mass., Sarah White former wid., W15478
Jacob, Cont., Mass., Sarah, W19601
John, Ct., N.H., S22578
Jonathan, Mass., S19854
Moses, Mass., Mariam, W25966
Samuel, Cont., Mass., R.I., Susannah, W25927
WELDEN, Abraham, Ct., Cont., S35713
Isaac, Ct., S43258
Jesse, Del., Md., See WELDIN
Joshua, Mass., S11722
WELDIN, Isaac, Ct. See WELDEN
Jesse, Del., Md., S3508
WELDING, Isaac, Pvt. Sheldon's Dragoons, Ct., BLWt.6659 iss. 9/15/1796 to Nicholas Root, ass.
WELDON, James, N.Y., BLRej. See papers in BL claim No. 1521-100 Jere/Jeremiah Weldon, N.Y.
Jeremiah, Pvt. N.Y., BLWt.8030 iss ---. Pencil notation "On file not delivered".
Jeremiah/Jere, N.Y., BLWt.1521-100. The Bounty Land papers of James Weldon, Rejected, N.Y. are within
John, S.C., S32053
Jonathan, Vt., R11302
WELDY, George, Va., S39883
WELHITE, Tobias, Va. See WILHITE
WELKER, Daniel, Cont., Pa., S40669; BLWt.450-100
Jacob, Pa., S1602
WELLBORN, Elias, N.C., Mary, W6465, b. in N.C.

WELLBORN (continued)
Isaac, N.C., Mary, W6464, b. in N.C.
WELLER, Amos, Ct., Green Mt. Boys N.Y., Dimis, W25952
Dan, Cont., Mass., Lucinda, W16466
Frederic, N.Y., S14816
John, Pa., S22572
Martin, Cont., Mass., S33238
Philip, N.J., S3498
Thomas, Cont., Green Mt. Boys, N.J., Mary, R11304
WELLES, Bazze/Bayze, See Bayze WELLS
Benjamin, Ct., Mass. See WELLS
Joshua, Pvt. Ct., BLWt.6687 iss. 12/13/1796
Noah, Ct., S23063
WELLING, John, N.J., Mary, BLWt. 45719-160-55
WELLINGTON, Ebenezer, Mass., Rebecca, W22560
Elizabeth, Mass. Sea Service, former wid. of Jacob Homer, which see
Jeduthan, Mass., S18646
John, Mass., S11804
Jonathan, Va., Rachel, R11305
Oliver, Cont., Mass., S18643
Samuel, Mass. See WILLINGTON
WELLIVER, Christian, N.J., S6344
WELLKEY, John, R.I. See WILLKEY
WELLMAN, Abraham, Cont., Mass., Rebecca, W4385
Barnabas, Ct., Cont., S29534
Jacob, Mass., Betsey, W1112; BLWt.70-60-55
Jacob, N.H., S22575
John, Ct., Phebe, See WELLMON
John, Ct., Vt. See Jonathan
John, Cont., Mass., S41317
John, N.H., Anna, W1963
Jonathan/John, Ct., Vt., S15700 BLWt.26108-160-55
Joseph, Cont., Mass., Molly, W25959
Mercy, N.H., former wid. of Aquilla Cleaveland, which see
Oliver, Mass., Thankful, W614; BLWt.61306-160-55
Paul, Ct., S43264
Samuel, Cont., S43276, enl. in Mass., pensioned in N.H.
Samuel, Cont., Martha, W18312. Living Bristol, Mass. in 1847
Silas, Mass., S43261
Timothy, Mass., Lucy, W18315
William, Ct., S17774
William, N.C., BLWt.56857-160-55
Zadock, Ct., Vt., R11306
WELLMON, John, Ct., Phebe, W18325
WELLONS, Charles, Va., Bethany, W3903; BLWt.35676-160-55
WELLS, Abner, Ct., S14805
Abraham, N.Y., Angelica, R11307
Abraham, R.I., S14806
Andrew, S.C., S1600
Asa, Mass., Betsey, W1011
Ashbel, Ct., R11309
Austin, Ct., S32054

WELLS (continued)
Bayze/Bazze, Boat Service on Lake Champlain, Ct., Ruth, W18311
Benjamin, Ct., Mass., Sarah, W6435 BLWt.2352-300-Surgn's Mate iss. 1/17/1793, also recorded as above under BLWt.2622
Benjamin, Privateer of Pa., Mary, W6436; BLWt.31766-160-55. Enl. Md.
Benjamin, Mass., Anna/Anne, W22565 BLWt.2310-200-Lt. iss. 4/1/1790
Benjamin, Vt., Rachel, W18319
Bolling, Va., Elizabeth, W2208
Charles D., Md., Va., S3493
Cornelius, Md., Navy, Sarah Young former wid., W2503; BLWt.79521-160-55
Cuff (colored), Ct., Phillis Tatton, former wid., W18103
Daniel, Ct., N.Y., S6354
David, Mass., S30196
David, Mass., N.H., S41310
Duckett, Md., Sarah, W4380
Ebenezer, N.H., Sarah, W25929
Edward, Pvt. Pa., BLWt.10581 iss. 7/16/1789 to M. McConnell, ass.
Elias, R.I., S14807
Elisha, Ct., S14813
Elisha, Ct., S36377
Esther, Cont., N.Y., former wid. of John Vermilya, which see
Ezekiel, N.H., Alice, W3170
Ezekiel, N.H., Phebe, W15862; BLWt.6253-160-55
George, N.C., R11312; BLWt.18016-160-55
George, R.I., S22041
Gideon, Ct., S18273
Hannah, Ct., former wid. of Henry Main, which see
Henry, Del., S11712
Hezekiah, Ct., Sarah, W25967
Israel, Ct., S40664
Jacob, N.C., Elizabeth, W318; BLWt.28550-160-55
Jacobus, N.Y., Elizabeth, W22572
James, Ct., S17764
James, Cont., Mass., Lucy, W14119 BLWt.2314-200-Lt. iss. 1/12/1792 of Hartford, Ct.
James, N.H., Mary, W22547
James, R.I., Nancy, W8988
James, Va., Sarah Butcher, former wid., W4139; BLWt.10010-160-55
Jedediah F., Ct., Hannah, W22576
Jesse, N.C., S3499
John, Cont., Mass., Amarilons, W18301
John, Cont., Va., S39881; BLWt. 796-100
John, (dec'd), Pvt. Md., BLWt. 11843 iss. 1/12/1792 to John Blair, admr.
John, Md., S6351
John, Pvt. N.Y., BLWt.8031 iss. 7/30/1790 to Edward Cumpston, ass.
John, N.C., S32581, b. in Va.

WELLS (continued)
John, Privateer, R.I., S11729
Jonathan, Ct., S16018
Joseph, Mass., Mary, W14133
Joshua, Mass., Hannah, W16085
Joshua, Mass., Elizabeth, R11311
Joshua, Mass., N.H., S15697
Josiah, Ct., S28938
Littleberry/Littlebury, Va., S31469
Moses, Mass., S33884
Nathaniel, Cont., Va., Agness, W4098; BLWts.1032-100 & 327-60-55
Nathaniel, Mass., N.H., S18276
Nathaniel, N.H., Anna, W18308. She was former wid. of Thomas Wells, which see
Noah, Ct., See WELLES
Obadiah, N.Y., R11315
Oliver, Vt., Rebecca, W25960
Paul, N.H., S41308
Peter, Md., R11317
Peter, Pvt., N.H., BLWt.3547 iss. 4/13/1796 to John Smith, ass.
Peter, N.H., Lois, W11774; BLWt.105452-160-55
Peter, N.Y., S44033
Peter, N.Y., Anna Rightmyer, former wid., W16697
Peter, R.I., S10042
Phineas, Mass., S37507
Richard, Ga., Va., Susanna, W6437; BLWts.26162-160-55 & 52748-160-55
Richard, Pa. See WILLS
Robert, Ct., S16288
Roger, Ct., BLWt.2349-300-Capt. iss. 4/22/1796 to Jemima Wells, admx. No papers
Samuel, Pvt. Ct., BLWt.6706 iss. 5/7/1792 to Thomas Stanley, ass.
Samuel, Ct., Isabel Catharine, W6439
Samuel, N.H., Margaret, W22586
Samuel, Va., S37513
Shalar, N.Y., S23480
Silas, N.Y., S11702
Simeon, Mass., Sarah, W19599
Simon, Ct., Cont., S14809
Solomon R., Va., S14812
Stephen, Mass., N.H., S15703
Thomas, Sgt. Ct., BLWt.6672 iss. 2/5/1790
Thomas, Ct., S11721
Thomas, N.H., Anna Wells, former wid., W22577; BLWts.348-60-55 & 3574-100 iss. 1/28/1790 to James Patterson, ass. of Thos. Wells. His wid. married Nathaniel Wells, W18308
Thomas, Pa., R11318
Timothy, Ct., S40651
Timothy, N.H., S18277
William, Del., Md., S31465
William, Mass., Eleanor, W15815
William, N.Y., S6360
William, N.C., S32582
William, R.I., Martha/Polly/ Patty, R11316

WELLS (continued)
William, Va., S3494
William, Va. See WILLS
William, Pens. at Cincinnati, Ohio agcy. No papers
Youngs, N.Y., S43254
Zachariah, Va., S39119, RG-217 pens. payt. filed inside WDH-6-7-55

WELMAN, Jacob, Pvt., Mass., BLWt.5251 & 70-60-55 iss. 5/1/ 1792 to David Quinton
John, Mass. See WELLMAN
Silas, Pvt. Mass., BLWt.5252 iss. 5/1/1792 to David Quinton

WELP, Anthony, N.Y., BLWt.2366-300-Capt. iss. 12/13/1790 to James Reynolds, ass. of Mary Welp, admx. No papers

WELSCH, John, Pvt. N.Y., BLWt. 8055 iss. 9/15/1790 to John S. Hobart & others, assnes.
Michael, Dis. Pa. res. & troops of Pa.

WELSH, David S., Vt. See WELCH
Deborah, Mass., former wid. of Solomon McFarland, which see
Dominick, Va., Mary, W6461, an Irishman
Edward, Pvt. "in the Invalids" BLWt.13904 iss. 11/9/1789 to James Reynolds, ass.
Henry, Pa., S7867
Isaiah, Va., S7859
James, Mass., Sarah, See WELCH
James, Pa., S14819
John, Mass. See case of Deborah Welsh, former wid. of Solomon McFarland
John, N.H. See WELCH
John, N.H., Mary, See WELCH
John, Pvt. N.Y., BLWt.7950 iss. 9/10/1790 to Justus Banks, ass.
John, Pvt., Pa., BLWt.10580 iss. 5/12/1792
John, Pa., S40657
John, Pa., R11298. He also applied for pension on account of William Welsh, Pa. See papers within
Jonas, Cont., Mass., S18644
Jonas, Mass., Betsey, See WELCH
Jonathan, Pvt. Va., BLWt.12650 iss. 5/12/1792 to James Morrison, admr.
Joseph, Cont., Mass. See WELCH
Joseph, Pvt. N.Y., Invalid, BLWts.7954 & 13905 iss. 2/14/1791 to James Talmage/Tallmadge, ass.
Joseph, Pa., S40655
Michael, Mass., S41318
Michael, Pvt. N.J., BLWt.8860 iss. 3/30/1798 to Michael Welsh
Michael, Pvt. Pa., BLWt.10554 iss. 6/29/1789 to M. McConnell, ass.
Michael, See WELSCH
Michel, See Michael WELCH
Patrick, Va., S40668

WELSH (continued)
Peter, Mass., S33889
Thomas, Cont., Mass., S3502
William, Pvt. Mass., BLWt.5292 iss. 4/3/1797 to Ezra King
William, Pa., R11298. See claim of John Welsh, Pa., R11298
WELTCH, Lemuel, Mass. See WELCH
WELTNER, Ludwick, German Regt., BLWt.2403-500-Col. iss. 9/14/1789 to Mary Weltner, extx. No papers
WELTON, Benjamin, Pvt. Ct., BLWt.6682 iss. 2/--/1790 to Theodosius Fowler, ass.
David, Ct., Sarah, W18250
Eben, Ct., S16577
George, Ct., S18282
Joel, Ct., S35714
Jonathan, Va., Margaret, R11320
Josiah, Ct., R11319
Shubael, Ct., S43283
Solomon, Ct., S36380
WELTS, Barney, Cont., Ct. or Pa., S40670
WELTY, John, Md., S39882
WEMIRE, Frederick, See WAMIRE
WEMPLE, John, N.Y., S23490
Myndert B., N.Y., Catharine, W19604
Walter Vrooman, Cont., N.Y., Polly Thomas, former wid., W6276
WENDELL, Adam, Pvt. Lamb's Art., N.Y., BLWt.8041 iss. 9/8/1790 to Litcher & Smith, Exrs.
Ahasuerus, N.Y., Eve, W25918
David, Cont., N.Y. See WANDLE
Jacob Henry, N.Y., Sarah, W18305; BLWt.2367-200-Lt. iss. 8/2/1791 to Matt Trotter, ass.
John, Pvt. N.Y., BLWt.7979 iss. 8/3/1790 to Cornelius V. Dyck, ass.
John, Pvt. N.Y., BLWt.8000 iss. 6/18/1792
John H., N.Y., S44030
John Y., N.Y. See WANDELL
Robert H., N.Y., R11321
WENDOLPH, Jacob, Pvt. Pa. BLWt. 10588 iss. 6/29/1789 to M. McConnell, ass.
WENSEL, John, Pa., S3511
WENTLING, George, Pa., S6358
WENTWORTH, Alpheus, Ct., Cont., Polly, W22582
Amos, Ct., Sea Service, Lydia, R11325
Andrew, Mass., S37517
Benjamin, Mass., Rachel, W15472
Benning, Mass., S18272
Daniel, Ct., S30776
Daniel, Mass., S41314
Elijah, Cont., Ct., S41311
Enoch, Mass., S37509
Ezekiel, Ct., R11323
Foster, Mass., S19153; BLWt. 21456-160-55
Gibbens, Ct., R11324
Henry, ? , Hannah Gridley, former wid., R4304. Soldier's res.

WENTWORTH (continued)
was N.Y. in 1832
Jedediah, Pvt. Mass., BLWt.5311 iss. 1/26/1790 to John May
John, Cont., Lydia, W22546 Maine res. & agcy. in 1818
John, Mass., S37529
John, Mass., Sarah Eveleth/Everith, former wid., R3400
Josiah H., Ct., S23062
Lemuel, Mass., N.H., S37528
Levi, Ct., S37511; BLWt.55-100
Nathaniel, Mass., Olive, W14123; BLWt.24613-160-55
Paul, Cont., Mass., Mary, W22568
Phinehas/Phineas, N.H., S43267; BLWt.774-100
Richard, Mass., N.H., Joanna, W22553
Samuel, Mass. S33885
Samuel, N.H., S43279
Shubael, Mass., S19152
Sophia, N.Y., Vt., former wid. of Jacob Wheeler, which see
Timothy, Mass., S17190
William, N.H., BLWt.788-100
WENTZ, John, N.C., Catharine, R11326
WENTZEL, John Pa. See WENSEL
WERDEN, Jesse, Ct., R.I., Ruth, W19655
Wait, Ct., Diannah, See WORDEN
WERDIN, Richmond, Green Mt. Boys, Mass., Vt. See WORDEN
WERMSLEY, Philip, R.I. See RODMAN
WERNER, Christopher/Christoffel, N.Y., Maria, R11327
WERNSDARFF, Matthias. Pvt. Pa., BLWt.10558 iss. 7/16/1789 to M. McConnell, ass.
WERNSZ, Philip, See Phillip WERNTZ
WERNTZ, Phillip, Pa., S7860
WERTH, Johannes, N.Y., S11716
WERTS, Jacob, Pa., Catharine, W2980
WERTZ, Daniel, Pa., Catharine, R11328
George, Md., Pa., S11329
Jacob, Pa., Catharine, W2980
WESCOAT, Jeremiah, N.C., R11330
Joseph, Ct., S43281
Joseph, Mass., S29532; BLWt.8011-160-55
WESCOTT, Arnold, R.I. See WESTCOTT
Daniel, Ct., S17767
George, R.I. See WESTCOAT
Isaac, Mass., Abigail, W25930
Joseph, Mass. See WESCOAT
Joshua, Mass., S37516
Thomas, Pvt. Mass., BLWt.5328 iss. 4/5/1793 to "same assignee" could mean to Samuel Emery, the ass. on next line above
Thomas, Mass. See WESTCOAT
Zeba, R.I. See WESTCOT
WESHAM, John, See WYSHAM
WESLER, Jacob, Pvt. "in the Artillery" Pa., BLWt.10650 iss. 2/14/1791
WESLEY, John, Va., S18271
Joseph, Cont., Mass., Margaret,

WESLEY (continued)
See Joseph WESSLEY
WESSELLS, Hercules, Pvt. N.Y., BLWt.8040 iss. 7/26/1791
John, Pvt. Lamb's Art., N.Y., BLWt.8044 iss. 7/16/1790 to Wm. I./J. Vreedenburgh, ass.
Samuel, Pvt. N.J., BLWt.8873 iss. 7/16/1789 to Thomas Coyle, ass.
WESSELS, Hercules, Cont., N.Y., S43274
Samuel, N.J., Hannah Houghton, former wid., R5255. Her last husb., also served in the Rev.
WESSINGER, Ludwick, Md., S23997
WESSLEY, Joseph, Cont., Mass., Margaret, W25924
WESSON, Ephraim, N.H., S22040. He m. Mabel Abbot, wid. of William Abbott, which see
Isaac, Cont., Va., Sally, W6457
James, Mass., BLWt.2289-500-Col. Iss. 7/24/1792. No papers
Joseph, Mass., S37521
Mabel, N.H., former wid. of William Abbott, which see
WEST, Aaron, Ct., Susanna, W19607
Alexander, N.C., Hannah, W18328
Alexander, Va., Mary, W6450
Alva, Cont., Ct., Susan Robinson, former wid., W17557
Amos, Cont., Ct., Helen, W11772 BLWt.31762-160-55
Anah, Mass., Anna, W2294; BLWt. 13888-160-55
Anthony, Ct., S44034
Benjamin, Ct., S29537
Benjamin, Md., S7857
Benjamin, Mass., R21897
Benjamin, Sr., N.C., Nancy, R11345
Bransford, Va., Nancy, W6447
Caleb, Ct., S11723
Caleb, Mass., Bathsheba, W22561
Charles, R.I., N.Y., S17772
Cleamont, N.Y., R11337
David, Ct., S43275
David, N.Y., Hannah, W16464
Edward, Navy, Mass., S23996
Edward, N.H., Merriam, W16783
Elnathan, Mass. Sea Service, S16019
George, N.C., Mary Ann, W6449
George, N.C., R11338
Henry, Navy or Sea Service, N.C. R11339
Hezekiah, S.C., S34519
Ichabod, Ct., Lovina, W1113
Ira, Ct., S32052
Isaac, Mass., S18645
Jackson, Mass., Anna, W14118
Jacob, N.Y., S43260
Jane, Md. or Pa., former wid. of John Robinson, which see; married Enos West
John, Cont., N.J., Margaret, W4530
John, Cont., Pa., Hannah, W6453
John, Pvt. Md., BLWt.11826 iss. 7/31/1789

WEST (continued)
John, Mass., S33239
John, Pvt. N.Y., BLWt.7976 iss. 12/15/1790 to James Aspel, ass.
John, N.Y., Vt., S14811
John, N.C., S32580
John, N.C., R11341
John, R.I., Betsey, W14121
John, Va., S4720
John, Va., S16573
John T., Md. ?, Kitty, R11343
Jonathan, R.I., S29538
Joseph, Ct., Sally, W9157; BLWt.47836-160-55
Joseph, Navy, R.I., Violetta, W4382
Joseph, S.C., S18275, b. N.C.
Joseph, Va., Eleanor, W6446
Joseph, Va., R11342, b. Del.
Josiah, Mass., Abi Gott, former wid., W11068; BLWt.38346-160-55
Judah, Mass., Mary, W6451
Leonard, N.C., S.C., S16574, b. N.C.
Levi, N.C., S39122
Littleton, Va., R11344, b. Del.
Moses, Ct., Mary Wright, former wid., W18387
Nathan, Mass., Marcy, W14131
Nathan, N.H., S11713
Nathan, Fifer R.I., BLWt.3583 iss. 12/14/1789 to Stephen Olney, ass.
Nathan, R.I., Martha, W19596
Nathaniel, R.I., S39886
Nathaniel, R.I. See Nathaniel Hix
Nathaniel, Va., S32583, b. Md.
Nathaniel Hix, R.I., Nelly, W2033
Peter, Mass., S37530
Richard, Ct., S11709
Robert, N.C., S.C., R11347
Samuel, Ct., S17773
Simeon, R.I., Nancy, W22589
Thomas, Mass., S14808
Thomas, Mass., Ann, W6448; BLWt.31777-160-55
Thomas, N.J., S1147
Thomas, N.Y., R11348
Thomas, Pvt., Pa., BLWt.10599 iss. 4/6/1790
Thomas, Pa., R11349
Thomas, R.I., S17769
Thomas, Va., S37512
Thomas, Va., S40667
Thomas L., Not Rev. Indiana Mil. N.W. Ind. War 1811, O.W. Inv. File 24422; BLWts.94551-40-50 & 86980-120-55
Timothy, Mass., S16575
Timothy, Privateer, R.I., S17765
William, Cont.,Vt., Phebe, R11346
William, Md., S42060
William, N.J., S3510
William, N.C., S14827
William, N.C., Susannah, W18304
William, N.C., S.C., Margaret Richards, former wid., W26372; BLWt.274938-1855. Her other husb., Joshua Richards, was also pensioned, which see
William, Pvt., R.I., BLWt.3596 iss. 3/12/1793 to J. Farnham,

WEST (continued)
ass.
William, R.I., S14814
William Blay, Mass., Patience, W22548
Willis, N.C., Silvey, R18901
Willoughby, Va., S7865
WESTBROOK, Aaron, N.J., S1146
Abraham, N.J., S6357
Cornelius B., Pa., S40656
Gideon, N.Y., S22574
Honsiver, N.J., See John I.
Housiver, N.J., See John I.
James, Ct., N.J., R11350
James, N.J., Charity, W15861
John, N.J., N.Y., R11351
John I./Honsiver, N.J., S6359
Josephus, N.Y., R11352
Peter N.J., Lydia, W18321
Richard, Pa., Lydia, W9884
Samuel, N.J., S11714
WESTCOAT, Benjamin, Mass.,S33872
Ephraim, Pvt. Ct., BLWt.6667 iss. 1/11/1797 to Wallace Sunderland, ass.
George, R.I., Phebe, W6455; BLWt.18208-160-55
Samuel, R.I., S35716
Thomas, Mass., S32879
WESTCOOT, Thomas, R.I., S22042
WESTCOT, Amos, Ct., R.I., Abigail, W18330
George, R.I., Phebe, See WESTCOAT
Urian, R.I., Mary, W25940
Ziba/Zeba, R.I., S44031
WESTCOTT, Arnold, N.Y.,R.I.,R11331
Benjamin, Pvt. Mass., BLWt.5324 iss. 1/26/1790 to John May
Caleb, R.I., Lydia, W14132
Daniel, R.I., Marcy, R11332
Foard, R.I., Sarah, W25957
James, Mass., Mary, W25923
Samuel, Mass., Nancy, W25955
Samuel, N.J., S1145
Samuel, R.I., S35716
Stephen, R.I., S17766
Wright, Va., Sea Service, R106 Va. Half Pay. See N.A. Acc. No. 837-Va. State Navy, Wright Wescott, Y.S. File Va. Half Pay
WESTERDALL, Francis, Pvt., N.C., BLWts.12690 & 13873 iss. 1/22/1799
WESTERFELT, Albert, See WESTERVELT
WESTERN, James, Vt. See WESTURN
WESTERVELT, Albert, N.J., Mary, W25933
Benjamin, N.Y., Jane, W1679
Benjamin P., N.J., S1148
Casparas, N.Y., Jane, W25954; BLWt.12838-160-55
Cornelius/Cornelius P., N.J., Maria, W1010
John B., N.Y., S18274
Leah, N.J., former wid. of David Doremus, R11353
WESTFALL, Abraham, N.Y., Dinah/Diana, W4386
Abraham, Va., Massey, W9883
Cornelius, Va., S36842
Cornelius, R11333,Va. res. in 1834

WESTFALL (continued)
Jacob, Va., Mary, W9159
John, Va., S41319
Wilhelmus, N.Y., Margaret Terry former wid., W1511
WESTGATE, James, Mass., R11354
Joseph E., R.I., S15701
Wanton, R.I., S22043
WESTLAKE, Benjamin, N.Y., S29533
Josiah, N.J., R11355
WESTLAND, Joseph, Ct., BLWt.2311-100
Robert, Pvt. Ct., BLWt.6653 iss. 12/14/1789 to Richard Platt, ass.
Robert, Ct., S36378
WESTMORELAND, Jesse, Va., S3526
WESTON, Abner, Mass., Huldah, W25961
Abraham, Ct., Naomi, W19597
Asa, Mass., Abigail, W15470
Benjamin, Ct., Mary, W18320
Betty, Mass., former wid. of Josiah Wright, which see
Daniel, Mass., Lydia, W20123
Daniel, N.H., S37519
David, Mass., S17771
Edmund/Edmond, Mass., S36843
Eliphas, Mass., S18647
Jabez, Mass., S30778
Jacob, Mass., S33883
James, Cont., Mass., S28940
James, Mass., S30198; BLWt.3397-160-55
James, N.C., S7858
John, Ct., Margaret, W4852; BLWt.31769-160-55
Jonathan, Mass., S29535
Joseph, Mass. See WESSON
Joseph, Mass., Sarah, R11358; BLWt.36557-160-55
Josiah, Mass., Hannah, W25948
Levi, Mass., Matilda, W15474
Martha, N.H., former wid. of James Hartshorn, which see
Rachel, Ct., former wid. of Francis Nicholson, which see
Rogers, Mass., N.H., S15702
Rufus, Mass., Abigail, W25956
Samuel, Mass., S37520
Sutherick, N.H., Mary, W16784
Thomas, Pvt. Md., BLWt.11847 iss. 1/8/1796 to George Ponsonby, ass.
William, Cont., Mass., Navy, Elizabeth, W22555
William, N.J., Isabel, W1962; BLWts.33-60-55 & 8858 iss. 7/30/1789
Zachariah, Ct., S43257
Zachariah, Mass., Nancy, R11357 BLWt.45669-160-55
WESTRAY, Daniel, N.C., S7851
WESTURN, James, Vt., S11719
WETHEBEE, Abijah, Mass. See WETHERBEE
WETHEE, Uzziel, Mass., S35137
WETHERALL, John, See WITHERALL
WETHERBEE, Abel, Mass., Sylvia, W2209
Abijah, Mass., Mehetable/Mehitable, W25937

WETHERBEE (continued)
Amos, Mass., Elizabeth, W2468; BLWt.7218-160-55
Caleb, Mass., Mercy, W24337
Daniel, Cont., Mass., Hepsibah, W25958
David, Mass., S31470
Hezekiah, N.H., Lucy Lake, former wid., W20424; BLWt.6389-160-55 Her other husb., Jonathan Lake, was pensioned, which see
WETHERBEE, Isaac, Mass., S11708
Jacob, N.H., S43259
Joab, Mass., Abigail, W16160
Joseph, Mass., Hannah, W2500
Simon, Mass., S43256
Thomas, Mass., S41307
WETHEREL, Simeon, See WITHERELL
WETHERELL, Betsey, N.Y., her former husb., George Hallet/ Hollet, which see
Charles, Mass., Susanna, W9026; BLWt.3620-160-55
David, Mass., R11362
John, Mass., See WITHERALL
Nathaniel, Mass. See WITHERELL
Obadiah/Obediah, Mass., S28949
Samuel, Mass. See WITHERELL
WETHERHEAD, Levi, See WEATHERHEAD
WETHERHOLT, John, N.J., S3523
WETHERICK, George, Pvt., N.Y., BLWt.8022 iss. 1/5/1791
Michael, Pvt., N.Y., BLWt.7986 iss. 1/5/1791
WETHERLY, David, See WITHERILL
WETHERMAN, Nancy, Va. former wid. of Robert Glasscock, which see
WETHERN, Micah, Mass., BLWt. 36525-160-55
WETHERS, Valentine, See WEATHERS
WETHERSTINE, John, Pvt. N.Y., BLWt.8026 iss. 1/5/1791
WETHKNECHT, Martin, Pa., S40661
WETHRELL, William, Mass., former wid. Ruth Atwood, W15714
WETHY, Henry, Ct., Esther, W22574
Jeduthan, Ct., N.Y., R11752
WETMORE, Bela, Mass., W615; BLWt.24328-160-55
David B., Mass., See WHITMORE
Joel, Mass., S43266
WETTER, Henry, N.J., See WALTER
WETTON, Josiah, Ct. See WELTON
WEVER, Adam, N.Y., S43262
Andrus, Green Mt. Boys, Vt., R11236
Conrad, Pa., Feronica, W4854; BLWt.26210-160-55
George, R.I., R11240 1/2
Henry, S.C. See WEAVER
WEYCOPE, Isaac, Pvt., Mass., BLWt.5277 iss. 4/1/1790 to John May
WEYGANT, Tobias, N.Y., Eunice, See WEYGINT
WEYGINT, Tobias, N.Y., Eunice, W2203; BLWt.9527-160-55
WEYMAN, Abel, N.J., BLWt.2375-300-Capt. iss. 4/18/1796 to Marmaduke Curtis, Exr. No papers
WEYMOUTH, Elizabeth, Va., former wid. of Thomas Douglass, Which see
James, Navy, N.H., S29540
Moses, Mass., S37518
WEYSOR, Henry, Va. See WYSOR
WHALAN, Richard, Pvt. N.Y., BLWt.8032 iss. 8/2/1791 to Samuel B. Webb, ass.
WHALAY, Edward, Del., See WHALEY
WHALEN, Jeremiah, R.I., S43292
Joseph, Mass., Meribah, W2034; BLWts.1553-100 & 216-60-55
Walter, N.Y., Catharine, W19611; BLWt.519-160-55
WHALEY, Aaron, Ct. See WAYLEY
Benjamin, Va., S31472
Edward, Del., Elizabeth, R11365; BLWt.1162-100
Ezekiel, Pvt., N.C., BLWts.12699 & 13883 iss. 5/18/1797 to Gabriel Holmes, ass.
Ezekiel, N.C., S42064
George, Va., S40679
Hezekiah, Ct., S36387
James, Va., Elizabeth, W2386
Job, R.I., S22045
Jonathan, Ct., Mercy Lord, former wid., W2739; BLWt.13744-160-55
John, Pvt., Va., BLWt.12664 iss. 5/8/1794
Joseph, R.I., S39891
Reynolds, R.I., S11771
Samuel, N.Y., Olive, R11366
Samuel, R.I., S24005
Sarah, former husb. Cornelius Rose, Green Mt. Boys, N.Y., which see
Theophilus, Ct., Lois, W2038
Theophilus, Vt., S43290
Thomas, R.I., Jerusha, W22098
William, Va., S37532
WHALIN, Walter, Pvt., N.Y., BLWt. 7985 iss. 7/22/1790 to Thomas Tillotson, ass.
WHALING, Richard, N.Y., S43304
Walter, N.Y. See WHALEN
WHAPLES, Samuel, Ct., Huldah, W19613
WHARF, John, Mass., S33241
WHARFIELD, Reuben, Mass., S30779
WHARLEY, Felix, Capt., S.C., BLWt.2448-300 iss. 12/11/1797 Name also spelled "Warley". See BLWt.2451 of his brother, George Warley
George, S.C., See WARLEY
Joseph, Capt., S.C., BLWt.2449-300 iss. 3/1/1799 to Felix Wharley, surviving brother & heir
WHARRY, Daniel, N.Y., S15254
Evans, N.Y., Phebe, W20127
John, N.Y., Esther, W25973
Robert, Pa., BLWt.2239-300
WHARTON, Charles, Pvt., Del., BLWt.10916 iss. 9/2/1789
John, S.C., R11494
Samuel, Pa., S40673
Samuel, Va., Letitia, W6488; BLWt.38832-160-55
WHARTON (continued)
William, Pvt. Pa., BLWt.10661 iss. 5/9/1797 to Daniel Vertner, ass.
William, Pa., S37534
Zachariah, Va., Sarah, W6487
WHATLEY, Daniel, N.C., R11370
Michael, N.C., S7876, b. Va.
Samuel, Ga., Catharine, W6492; BLWt.40901-160-55
William B., Navy, Mass., S33891
WHEADON, Abraham, Ct. See WHEEDON
Ichabod, Mass. See WHEATON
WHEAT, Amos, N.Y., S11756
Daniel, Mass., Betty, W15480
Jacob, Va., Adelaide, W6481
Joseph, Mass., S19156
Joseph, N.H., Bridget, W26008; BLWt.1417-100
Samuel, Mass., S11747
WHEATEN, Jonathan, Ct., S40687
WHEATHERBEE, Joseph, See WETHERBEE
WHEATLEY, Alexander, N.C., Peggy, W102
Andrew, Ct., Rubie, W19614 BLWt.7059-160-55
George, N.C., Mary, W9886
Joseph Hicks, N.J., W1683
Leonard, Va., S30783; BLWt. 26874-160-55
Rebecca, Pa., former wid. of Silas Taylor, which see
William, Md., Rhoda, W9003
WHEATON, Andrew, Ct., Avis, R11372
Benjamin, N.Y., S23067
Benjamin, R.I., S22048
Ephraim, Mass. See WHEDON
Ichabod, Mass., Desiah, W26013; BLWt.17898-160-55
Jeremiah, Ct., S23486
Jesse, Cont., Mass., S21568
John, Mass., R11371
Joseph, Mass., R.I., Bethiah, W26003
Joseph, R.I., War 1812, S48052; BLWt.2286-200-Lt. iss. 7/25/1789
Levi, R.I., S4723
Perez, R.I., Betsey, W14150
Reuben, N.Y., S24010. See N.A. Acc. No.874-050188 - Not Half Pay. Reuben Wheaton
Roswell, Ct., N.H., S36383
Rufus, Ct., S35721
William, Mass., R.I., S11751
WHEDDEN, James, See WHIDDEN
WHEDON, Abraham, Ct. See WHEEDON
Denison, Cont., Mass., S43316
Edmund, N.Y., Dorcas, W4855; BLWt.26614-160-55. She also applied for BL on acct. of the services of her former husb., Zenas Bliss, War 1812, see rejected claim within. Also see pension and BL claim of Zenas Bliss, wid. Hannah, Rev. & 1812,
Ephraim, Mass., Eunice, W6499
Ichabod, Mass., See WHEATON
Rufus, Ct. See WHEATON
WHEEDEN, John, N.C., S7875

WHEEDON, Abraham, Ct., Lydia, W11802; BLWt.12719-160-55
Denison, Mass., See WHEDON
Roswell, Pvt., Ct., BLWt.6624 iss. 12/30/1796
Rufus, Pvt.Ct., BLWt.6605 iss. 7/14/1789 to Rufus Wheedon
Rufus, Ct. See WHEATON
WHEELAN, Martin, Md., R20323
Richard, Md., Margaret/Peggy, See WHELAN
WHEELAND, Michael, Pa., S40674
WHEELER, Aaron, Ct., S11748
Aaron, Ct., S28941
Aaron, Mass., Rachel, W14154
Abner, Mass., S33242
Adam, Mass., BLWt.2322-300-Capt. iss. 1/4/1800. No papers
Amos, Cont., Mass., Elizabeth, W4531
Amos, Mass., Eunice, W18394
Asa, Mass., S41322
Asa, Mass., Polly, W26621
Asahel, Mass., Jerusha, W26011
Benjamin, Ct., Loly/Loby, W6483 BLWt.39-100
Benjamin, Cont., S42063
Benjamin, Md., Pa., S32585
Benjamin, Mass., Celia, W15484
Benjamin, Mass., Robey, W25980; BLWt.16139-160-55
Benjamin, Mass., R11377
Benjamin, Mass., Vt., S11768
Benjamin, N.H., S24003
Beriah, Ct., Sea Service, W25968
Charles, Md., S38465
Charles, N.H., Annis, W16465
Chauncey, Ct. Sea Service, Navy, Caroline Matilda, W25998
Comfort, Ct., N.Y., War of 1812, Permelia/Amelia, R11385; BLWt.105622-160-55
Daniel, Sgt. Ct., BLWt.6606 iss. 9/1/1790
Daniel, Ct., Amy, W18390
David, Ct., S44046
David, Mass., Hannah, R11380
Dimond, Ct., S24006
Ebenezer, N.J., S17775
Edward, Pvt. Mass., BLWt.5212 iss. 11/21/1791
Edward, Ct., Mass., N.Y., S16292
Ezra, N.Y., S11753
Henry, Pvt. N.Y., BLWt.8004 iss. 7/30/1790 to Edward Cumpston, ass.
Henry, N.C., S.C., S7895, b. N.C.
Hezekiah, Ct., Cont., Meribah, W6486; BLWts.95-60-55 & 6685-100 iss. 5/6/1793
Isaac, Mass., Vt., S6374
Isaac, Drummer, N.Y., BLWt.8007 iss. date not shown, to James Lowry, ass.
Isaac, N.Y., S40681
Isaiah, N.H., S30784
Jacob, N.Y., Vt., Sophia Wentworth, former wid., W18310
James, Ct., Elizabeth, W2295; BLWt.31776-160-55
James, Cont., Mass., Mary, W19610
James, Cont., Va., Elizabeth,W9887

WHEELER (continued)
James, Mass., S44053
James, Mass., Sarah Barber, former wid., W15569
James, R.I., Huldah, W22599
James, Va., S32064
Jeremiah, Mass., S11750
Jesse, Mass., S15248
Job, Ct., R11381
John, Dis., Vt. res.
John, Ct., Almira, W25997; BLWt. 36820-160-55
John, Ct., Cont., S40672
John, Mass., S3546
John, Mass., Hannah, W14141
John, Mass., (colored), Ruth, W14148
John, Mass., Sally, W27876
John, Navy, N.H., S37540
John, Pvt. N.Y., BLWt.7945 iss. 2/21/1791 to John Hageman, ass.
John, N.C., Va., Susanna, W8999
John T., Ct., R11382
Jonathan, Ct., S15245
Joseph, Mass., N.H., S6373
Joseph, N.C., S21567
Joseph, R.I., BLWt.5-100 Spec. Act 6/4/1842. For special act and other papers see case of Robert Allen, R.I. BLWt.1-100 Spec. Act 6/4/1842
Joshua, Ct., R11383
Joshua/Joseph, Pvt. "in the Invalids," BLWt.13918 iss. 11/15/1792 to Jonathan Tuttle, ass.
Josiah, Ct., S36388
Josiah, Ct., Hannah, W19628
Lemuel, Mass., S44052
Micajah, Va., S6362
Micajah, Va., S7891
Moses, Mass., S41323
Nathan, Cont., Mass., S40686
Nathan, Mass., S33245
Nathan, Mass., Sarah, W14137
Nathan, Mass., BLWt.2324-200-Lt. iss. 4/15/1796 to Jas. McGregor, ass. No papers. Note: See a statement made by heirs in pension claim of Ens. Nathan Wheeler, Cont. & Mass. and correspondence therein
Nathaniel, Ct., Ellen, W18408
Nathaniel, Mass., Anna, W14153
Peter, Mass., S30792
Phineas, Pvt. Mass., BLWt.5283 iss. 3/16/1792
Phinehas, Mass., S11773
Plomer, N.H., S11733
Prosper, Ct., Sarah, W22604
Randil/Randal, Mass., S22579
Reuben, N.H., S33246
Rhoda F., Ct., former wid. of James Morris, which see
Richard, Cont., N.H., S43309
Richard, Pvt. N.Y., BLWt.7960 iss. 9/1/1790 to Samuel Cooper, ass.
Richard, N.Y., S33243
Rufus, Ct., Mass., N.Y., Sarah

WHEELER (continued)
Wood, former wid., W11881; BLWt. 99516-160-55
Russell/Russel, Mass., Elizabeth W25989
Sabrina/Sabria, Mass., Elihu Hecox, former husb., which see
Sally, Ct., former wid. of Jabez Breed, which see
Sampson, N.H., S46079
Samuel, Ct., Julia, W26002; BLWt.26551-160-55
Samuel, Md., Va., S6364
Samuel, Mass., S17193
Samuel, Mass., S30199
Samuel, Mass., S44043
Samuel, N.H., S43310
Samuel, Pvt., N.Y., BLWt.7967 iss. 7/2?/1790 to Thomas Tillotson, ass.
Samuel, N.Y., Amy, R11375
Samuel, Pa., Elizabeth, R11378
Samuel, Va., Mary Smith, former wid., W25019
Shubael, Mass., Chloe Bosworth, former wid., W15593
Simeon, Ct., S17776
Simeon, Mass., S22052
Simeon, Mass. See Simon
Simon, Mass., Lydia, W15476
Solsbery/Solsberry/Salisberry, Mass., R.I., S15704; BLWt. 26117-160-55
Stephen, N.Y., Lydia Hunt, child, R25546
Thomas, Corp., Ct., BLWt.6644 iss. 3/15/1790
Thomas, Ct., S33903
Thomas, Pvt., Mass., BLWt.5293 iss. 8/13/1795 to Edward Stowe
Thomas, Mass., S19865
Thomas, Mass., S33910
Thomas, Mass., Hannah Webber, former wid., W25931; BLWt.3617-160-55. She was also pensioned as the wid. of her other husb., William Webber, Cont. & Mass., which see
Thomas, Pvt. "in Proctor's Artillery", Pa., BLWt.10652 iss. 6/29/1789 to M. McConnell, ass.
Timothy, Pvt. N.Y., BLWt.7978 iss. 4/2/1792 to Edmund Ogden, ass.
Valentine/Volentine, Mass., Desire, W1682; BLWt.3961-160-55
William, Ct., Anna, R11376
William, Mass., S24001
William, N.H., Lavinna, W15477
William, Pvt. N.Y., BLWt.8035 iss. 4/16/1791 to John Addoms, ass.
William, N.Y., S11749
William, S.C., Nancy, W6485; BLWts.13715-160-55 & 26947-160-55
William F., War 1812, Clarissa Peck, former wid., W26307. See papers and statement on jacket of her last husb., Cyril Peck, Mass.

WHEELER (continued)
Zaccheus, Mass., S19870
Zadock, Ct., Martha, W19620
Zadock Louis, N.H., R11384
Zenas, Mass., S21569
WHEELEY, John, Va., S42072
WHEELOCK, Adam/Adams, Mass., S11761
Alexander, Mass., S33244
Amariah, Mass., Hannah, BLWt.86126-160-55
Archippus, Mass., Julia, W2678; BLWt.26178-160-55
Asa, Mass., S15708
Deneson/Dennison, Mass., S19155
Eleazar, Mass., Vt., S24009
Ithamer/Ithamar, N.H., S43317
John, Cont., Mass., S43295
Jonathan, Mass., S24008
Jonathan, N.H., S41321
Jotham, Mass., S41331
Levi, Pvt. Mass., BLWt.5213 iss. 12/5/1789
Limon/Lyman, Mass., S16021
Obadiah, Mass., S43320
Paul, Mass., S11762
Ralph, Mass., S15253
WHEELWRIGHT, Abraham, Cont., Mass., Privateer, S19158
Joseph, Mass., S29544
Joseph, Mass., S32912
Samuel, Mass., S37556
WHELAN, Richard, Md., Margaret/ Peggy, R11374
WHELCHEL, Davis, S.C., R11388
Francis, S.C., Judah/Judith, R11300. Son res. of Ga. in 1854
John, S.C., Abigail, W6498
WHELEY, John, Va. See WHEELEY
WHELPLEY, Ebenezer, Ct., S29541
James, Ct., S41332
WHERREN, William, Mass., Peggy, W26004
WHETCOMB, Abraham, Mass., S30790
Ephraim, Mass., S41329
WHETMORE, Charles, N.C., S11739
WHETSEL, George, See WHITZELL
WHETSELL, Henry, Va., S7873
WHETSTONE, Daniel, Md., N.C., S32591
WHICKER, James, N.C., Mary, R19003
William, N.C., S3551
William, N.C., S17194
WHIDDEN, James, Mass., Sally, W26622
James, N.H., S22587
Samuel, N.H., S43289
Solomon, Mass., S37557
WHIDDON, Noah, N.C., R11373
WHIGHAM, Robert, N.Y. See WIGHAM
WHIGHT, Jonathan, Va., Hannah, W11803
WHILEBER, John, Dis., N.Y. res.
WHIPLEY, Amos, Mass., W43314; BLWt.1193-100
WHIPPEL, Robert, Cont., Mass., R.I., S11731
WHIPPEN, George, Mass., Navy, S6365
WHIPPING, George, See WHIPPEN

WHIPPLE, Aaron, N.H., S11774
Asa, R.I., Sylvia, W22603
Benjamin, Ct., S11766
Benjamin, Mass., Sarah, W26010
Caleb, Ct., War of 1812, Polly W1965; BLWt.19512-160-50 for War of 1812
Dan, N.H., S11767
Daniel Peck, R.I., Sea Service, Hannah, W8307
David, Mass., S34531
David, Mass., S34532
Elijah, Ct., Cont., S3552
Esek, Navy, R.I., S44048
Ethan, R.I., Lydia, W25994; BLWt.27693-160-55
Frederick, Pvt., Ct., BLWt.6678 iss. 9/24/1790 to Peleg Sanford, ass.
George, R.I., S22053
Ibrook, R.I., S22049
Jabez, R.I., S21572
Job, Cont., R.I., Ruth, W14147
Joseph, Sgt. Ct., BLWt.6639 iss. 2/22/1799
Joseph, Ct., Mary, R11389
Joseph, Va., S40675
Marmaduke, Mass., R.I., Wealthy W22600; BLWt.13194-160-55
Mary, Mass., former wid. of Jeremiah Bingham, which see
Nathan, Pvt. N.Y., BLWt.7952 iss. 9/29/1790 to Melanchton Smith, ass.
Nathan, N.Y., Mary, W18391
Preserved, R.I., Olive, W15479
Robert, Cont., Mass., R.I. See WHIPPEL
Samuel, Mass., Elizabeth, W26012 BLWt.239-100
Simon, R.I., Levina, W22602
Solomon, Mass., S6380
Thomas, Cont., Green Mt. Boys, Mass., S35116
Thomas, Mass., S44047
Thomas, N.H., S11736
Waity, R.I., Dutee Ballou, former wid., which see
William, Mass., S35117
William, Va., S41325
Zebulon, Ct., Lydia, W6491; BLWt.31778-160-55
WHIPPY, John, Mass., S34530
WHIPS, Benjamin, Md., R11391
WHISTLER, Catharine, Md., former wid. of Robert Purtle which see
Sawney, Pvt. Va., BLWt.12683 iss 7/30/179- to Richard Smith, ass.
WHISTON, Joseph, Ct., Elizabeth W16469
WHIT, Charles, S.C., S7889
WHITACAR, John, Va., S36844
WHITACRE, William, Md. See WHITTECO
WHITAKER, Abel, Mass., S30793
Abraham, Ct., S6375
Abraham, N.Y., Ann, W10277; BLWt.24606-160-55
Alexander, N.C., R11392

WHITAKER (continued)
Amos, Mass., Esther, W6496; BLWt.13022-160-55
Benjamin, N.Y., S15242
Catharine, Ct., former wid. of Silas Beardsley, which see
Elizabeth, Va., former wid. of Isaac Chapman, which see
Ephraim, Ct., S9526; BLWt. 1902-300
James, Mass., Susannah, W16787
James, Va., Susanna/Susan, W3482
Jeremiah, Mass., S34528; BLWt. 1732-100
John, Md., Ann, W9001
John, Pvt., N.J., BLWts.8822 & 13948 iss. 2/1/1790 to Abel Whitaker, Admr.
Jonathan, N.J., Mary, W9002
Mark, N.C., S31477
Moses, Mass., S16579
Nathaniel, N.J., S1150
Nell, Ct., S32588
Noah, Mass., S17780
Peter, Mass., Mary, W15483
Philip, Ct., S15255
Richard, N.C., S3596
Robert L., N.C., Nancy, W10276; BLWt.58133-160-55
Silas, Mass., S34529
Stephen, Ct., S34527
William, Cont., Va., Elizabeth, W3905; BLWt.2442-200-Lt. iss. 12/14/1795 to Peter B. Cram, ass.
WHITAM, Jereh/Terey/Jere, Cont., Mass., S37543
Robert, Cont., Mass., Sarah, W22607
WHITBECK, John, N.Y. See WITBECK
WHITCHER, Andrew, N.H., Anna, W16472
Chace, N.H., S7890
WHITCOM, John, Cont., Mass., Navy, S15705
WHITCOMB, Abijah, N.H., S11763
Abraham, Mass. See WHETCOMB
Benjamin, N.H., S42614; BLWt. 2280-400-Major iss. 8/25/1792
Elihu, Mass., Elizabeth, BLWt. 59097-160-55
Ephraim, Mass. See WHETCOMB
Enoch, Mass., Sarah, W22615
Francis, Mass., S19157
Hiram, Ct., Sarah W., W19896
John/John Skinner, Ct., Cont., N.Y., Sarah, W3371
John, Mass., S30786
John, N.H., S23482
John Skinner, See John
Jonathan, Mass., S22584
Josiah, Mass., Rebecca, W18398
Moses, Mass., Rachel, W14144
Nathaniel, N.H., S43315; BLWt. 822-100
Paul, Mass., Eleanor, W11819; BLWt.38339-160-55
Peter, Pvt. Mass., BLWt.5243 iss. 1/26/1790 to John May
Philemon, See case of Urana

WHITCOMB (continued)
Whitcomb, pensioned as former wid. of Amasa Aldrich, Cont. & Mass., which see
Reuben, Mass., N.H., Vt., Esther, W4389
Samuel, Mass., Elenor, W25979
Simon, N.Y., Abigail, R11393
Thomas, N.H., S37546
Thomas, Vt., R11394
Urana, former wid. of Amasa Aldrich, which see
Zelotas, Mass., Sarah, W14140
WHITCRAFT, William, Del., Pa., S24002
WHITE, Abel, Vt., R11398
Abijah, Ct., S28943
Abraham, Md., Va., R11400
Abram/Abraham, Pa., Milly, W6473; BLWt.36540-160-55
Adonijah, Ct., Hannah, W22601
Alexander, Pvt. Hazen's Regt., BLWt.13881 iss. 7/3/1795 to James Lamberton, ass.
Alexander, Pa., Jane, R11418
Alexander Muscle, N.C., R11401
Amariah, Mass., S32059
Ambrous, Va., S31471
Ammi, Cont., Mass., Mary, W18402
Andrew, Pvt. N.H., BLWt.3551 iss. 9/8/1790 to J.F. Sebor, ass.
Andrew, N.C., S17196
Anna, Ct., former wid. of William Johnson, which see
Anthony Walton, Cont., N.J. & U.S.A., Margaret, W6477; BLWt. 2420-500-Col. Iss. 9/18/1789
Antipass, Cont., Mass., Lucinda, W19893
Aquilla, Pa., S37533
Archelaus (colored), Cont., Mass. N.H., S43299
Archibald, Cont., N.H., S41333
Asa, Mass., S34526
Asa, Mass., Lydia, W2298; BLWt. 18005-160-55
Asa, Mass., Sarah Ives, former wid., W26792
Benjamin, Mass., S30201
Benjamin, Mass., S37547
Benjamin, Mass., Philana, W19612
Benjamin, N.Y., R.I., S15249
Benjamin, N.C., S11740
Benjamin, N.C., S39123
Buckminster, Mass., Marcy Bemis former wid., W24651
Caleb, Ct., Privateer, S11758
Caleb, Mass., S6370
Caleb, Va., R20447
Charles, Ct., S11745
Charles, Mass., Sally, W2469; BLWt.3636-160-55
Charles, N.H., S37539
Charles, Pvt. Pa., BLWt.10618 iss. 10/31/1795 to Barnard Merkle, ass.
Charles, Pvt. Va., Lee's Legion BLWts.12660 & 14015 iss. 3/21/ 1794
Charles, Va., S3543
Christopher, R.I., Mary, W19894 d. 12/16/1833

WHITE (continued)
Christopher, Va., S30785
Consider, Ct., Sarah T., W320; BLWt.13196-160-55
Cornelius, Mass., S34533
Daniel, Ct., S15238
Daniel, Ct., Sally, R11443
Daniel, Mass., S18651
Daniel, Mass., S34524
Daniel, Mass., Hannah, W14135
Daniel, Mass., Mary, W19615
Daniel, Mass., Sarah, W26009
Daniel, N.C., S22046
Daniel, N.C., Martha, W6479
Daniel, N.C., R11405
Daniel, N.C., Nelly, R11433
Daniel, Va., S1268
David, Ct., Hannah, W18403 BLWt.26572-160-55
David, Ct., Hannah Wilcox, former wid., R11521
David, Pvt. Mass., BLWt.5220 iss. 5/6/1793
David, Mass., S41334
David, Mass., R.I., S19864
David, Navy, N.H., Anna, W18399
David, N.H., Sarah, BLWt.57523-160-55
David, Pvt., N.J., BLWt.8853 iss. 2/25/1796 to Margaret Nichols, admx.
David, N.C., R11406
David, Pa., S22586
David, Vt., S18653
David, Va., Elizabeth, W4100; BLWt.24983-160-55, b. Ireland
David, Va., Susanna, W8997
Ebenezer, Ct., R11407
Ebenezer, Cont., Mass., Abigail, W1964
Edward, Mass., BLWt.2318-200-Lt. iss. 5/18/1799. No papers
Eli, Mass., S21566
Elias, N.J., Caroline, W22614
Elijah, Cont., Mass., Betsey, W18397; BLWt.31454-160-55
Elijah, Mass., BLWt.142-100
Elijah, Va., S32592; BLWt. 36819-160-55
Elisha, Ct., Abigail, R11408; BLWt.18370-160-55
Elisha, Ct., Cont., S18279
Enoch, Mass., Zerriah, W8309
Ephraim, Ct.,S40676;BLWt.1765-100
Ephraim, Ct., Cont., Mass., Hope, W1680
Ephraim, Pvt.,N.Y., BLWt.7969 iss. 10/12/1790 to Silas Salsey, ass.
Ephraim, N.Y., S43288
Ezekiel/Ezekial, N.C., S42070
Ezra, Ct., Lucy, W22605
Francis, Cont., Mass., Annis, W22617
Francis, Pa., BLWt.2386-200-Lt. iss. 1/28/1791. No papers
Galen, Va., S31476
George, Mass., S37550
George, N.C., S1736, b. Va.
George, N.C., Rachael, R11436; b. N.C.
George, S.C., S32057, b. S.C.

WHITE (continued)
George, Pvt. Va., Lee's Legion, BLWts.12658 & 13933 iss. 6/27/ 1792
George, Va., R11413
Godfrey, R.I., S11752
Gordon, Va., Ann, R11432
Goven, Va., Ann, W1014
Haffield, Mass., BLWt.2295-300-Capt. iss. 1/29/1790
Hampton, N.C., S38467
Henry, Cont., Mass., S34525; BLWt.2306-200-Lt. iss. 10/12/ 1790
Henry, Mass., N.Y., Juliany, W18411
Henry, N.J., N.Y., Sarah, R11440
Henry, N.Y., S3536
Henry, N.C., Esther/Hetty, R11410
Ichabod, Mass., Rhoda, W22612
Isaac, S.C., S11757
Israel, Ct., S6382
Jacob, Ct., Esther, W18407
Jacob, Mass., S18280
Jacob, Pvt. N.J., BLWt.8846 iss. 6/27/179?
Jacob, Pa., Nancy, W833; BLWt. 98058-160-55
Jacob, Pa., R20147
Jacob, Va., Mary Lafoy/Lafo/Lafong former wid., W8076. See John Lefoe (French)
James, Va., S42069
James, Md., S25481; BLWt.1126-100
James, Mass., Dis.
James, Mass., S11760
James, Mass., N.H., S30791
James, Pvt. N.Y., BLWt.7984 iss. 3/6/1792 to Michael Connolly, ass.
James, N.Y., S11754
James, N.Y., S43294
James, N.Y., R11416
James, Va., S3530
James, Va., S32584
James, Va., S37536
James, Va., S38468
James, Va., R11417
James, Lee's Legion or Va. Line, BLWt.12659-100-Pvt. iss. 3/4/ 1794. Also recorded under BLWt.13965
Jedidiah/Jedediah, Ct., S36386
Jenkins/Jinkins, Mass., Sea Service, S23484
Jeremiah, Va., S6376
Jesse, S.C., S32062
Joel, Ct., S11775
Joel, Vt., S22588
John, Pvt. Ct., BLWt.6710 iss. 6/20/1789
John, Ct., S3532
John, Ct., S32589
John, Ct., Betsey Underwood, former wid., W3739
John, Ct., Sarah Millard, former wid., R7172
John, Ct., BLWt.2353-200-Lt. Iss. 7/16/1795 to Eneas Munson, Jr., ass. of Sam Gould, admr. No papers
John, Cont., Ct., Martha, W16786

WHITE (continued)
John, Cont., Md. or Va., Eleanor/ Elenear, W6480
John, Cont., Mass., S34523
John, Cont., Mass., S43286
John, Green Mt. Boys, Mass., S11770
John, Md., BLWt.1933-100
John, Mass., S--- (S. Ctf.11779)
John, Mass., S15252
John, Mass., S34522
John, Mass., S37555
John, Mass., Sarah, W618; BLWt. 7216-160-55
John, Mass., Betsey, W4387; BLWt.8445-160-55
John, Mass., Abigail, W19624
John, Mass., Jane, W25988
John, Mass., Lucy, R11428
John, N.H., Nancy, W6475
John, N.J., S33893; BLWt.2427-100
John, N.Y., S24007
John, N.Y., S32587
John, N.Y., Sarah, R11441
John, N.Y., BLWt.429-100
John, N.C., S7894
John, N.C., S42067
John, N.C., R11426
John, N.C., Va., R11425
John, Pvt. Pa., BLWt.10619 iss. 6/10/1794 to DanDiel Stever, ass.
John, Pa., S32590
John, Pa., S40678
John, Pa., Privateer, R11421
John, R11422. Pa. res.
John, S.C., S3539; BLWt.75041-160-55
John, Va., S3535
John, Va., S32593
John, Va., Elizabeth, W6476
John, Va., R11423
John, Va., BLWt.2439-200-Lt. iss. 12/14/1795 to Peter B. Cram, ass. No papers
John S., Va., S33642; BLWt.1010-100
Jonathan, Mass., Rebecca, W20131
Jonathan, Pvt. Lamb's Art. N.Y., BLWt.8051 iss. 1/29/1793
Jonathan, N.Y., S44051
Jonathan, R.I., S39890
Jonathan, Pvt. Va., BLWts.12662 & 14033 iss. 3/2/1792
Jonathan, Va., S35115
Jonathan, Va., Hannah, W11803
Joseph, Pvt. Ct., BLWts.6610 & 6733 iss. 12/15/1795 to Eneas Munson, Jr., ass.
Joseph, Ct., Mary, W18392
Joseph, Cont., Mass., Mary, W11805 BLWt.19530-160-55
Joseph, Cont., Pa., S40680
Joseph, Md., S38469
Joseph, Mass., S32586
Joseph, Mass., S43307
Joseph, Mass., Jane, W26014; BLWt.19818-160-55
Joseph, Mass., Sea Service, S32060 Ga. res.
Joseph, N.H., Lydia Morrill,

WHITE (continued)
former wid., W21817
Joseph, N.Y., S11769
Joseph, N.Y., S28942
Joseph, Pvt. Pa., BLWt.10610 iss. 6/10/1794 to Silas Hart, ass.
Joseph, Pa., Mary, R11430
Joseph, Va., Mary, W4859; BLWt. 31765-160-55
Joseph, Va., Penelope, W11809; BLWt.26168-160-55
Joshua, Mass., N.H., S37548
Lawrance, Cont., Ct., Eunice, R11411
Lemuel, Ct., S10045
Lemuel, Mass., Matilda, W14138
Levi, Mass., S34521
Lewis, Mass., S30202
Luke, Mass., S15251
Luther, Pvt. Mass., BLWt.5262 iss. date & to whom, not shown
Luther, Cont., Mass., Mary, R11431
Matthew, Ct., Esther, W18409
Micah, Cont., Mass., Sarah, W25987
Moses, Cont., Mass., S11743; BLWt.2378-300-Capt. iss. 11/22/1791
Moses, Mass., S11744
Nancy, Va., former wid. of Jesse Toney, which see
Nathan, Mass., S41328
Nathan, Va., S37535
Nathaniel, Ct., S44040
Nathaniel, Cont., Ct., Abigail, W4532
Nathaniel, Mass., Esther, W16468
Nathaniel, N.H., Vt., Rebekah, W16086
Nathaniel, N.Y., Priscilla, W2299
Nehemiah, Mass., Elizabeth, W8996
Nicholas, Va., S33898
Obadiah, Ct., S15243
Oliver, Ct., S24004
Oliver, Mass., S44050
Oliver, R.I., Cynthia, W20128
Peregrine, Ct., R11434
Peregrine, R.I., S21571
Peter, N.J., BLWt.2136-100
Peter, Pvt., N.Y., BLWt.7953 iss. 1/25/1791 to Silvanus White, ass.
Peter, N.C., S42066
Philip, Ct., Olive, W25969; BLWt.119-60-55 & 6691-100 iss. 4/15/1800
Philip, Mass., S19160
Philip, N.C., Jemima, W6478
Potter, Navy, R.I., Mary, W2036; BLWt.285-60-55
Randolph, Va., Margaret, W9889
Rawley, Va., R11424
Rebecah, N.J., former wid. of Elias Longstreet, which see
Reuben, Mass., S33909
Reuben, Mass., N.Y., S11765
Richard, Va., S6371

WHITE (continued)
Richard, Va., S6384
Robert, Mass., Nancy, W18410
Robert, Pa., S32061
Robert, Va., S7893; BLWt.1678-300
Robert, Va., Betsey, W2300; BLWt.53742-160-55
Royal, Mass., Hannah, W14152
Samuel, Ct., Betsey, W25976
Samuel, Mass., S6383
Samuel, Mass., S11759
Samuel, Mass., S33897
Samuel, Mass., S33905
Samuel, Mass., Petty, W14151
Samuel, Mass., Navy, Lucretia, W15195
Samuel, N.H., S3540
Samuel, N.H., S43305
Samuel, N.J., S933
Samuel, N.J., R11439
Samuel, N.C., S3531; BLReg. 331467-1855
Samuel, N.C., Easter, W4101
Samuel, Pa., R18952
Samuel, Vt., R11438
Samuel, Va., S7871
Samuel B., Md., S25482
Sarah, Mass., former wid. of Edmund G. Weld, which see
Seth, Mass., S29543
Seth, R.I., S6381
Silas, Mass., S43301
Silas, Mass., Bethiah, W22608
Simeon, Mass., S33902
Simpson, Mass., R.I., S18652
Smith, Mass., Mary, W2385
Solomon, Ct., N.Y., S15250
Solomon, Mass., S43313; BLWt. 2304-200-Lt. iss. 4/3/1797 to John Jack, ass.
Solomon, Vt., S11755
Stephen, N.H., Mary, W22610
Stephen, N.C., S3542
Stephen, Not Rev. War, Indian War 1795-1798, BLWts.85871-40-50 & 73589-120-55. Enl. in Va.; later lived in Ala. & Ga.
Tarpley, Va., R18959. Va. Half Pay
Thaddeus, Mass., S22051
Theophilus, Mass., S11732
Thomas, Ct., S15244
Thomas, Cont., Mass., Patience W15481
Thomas, Md., S15240
Thomas, Md., S31474
Thomas, Mass., S33907
Thomas, Mass., Polly Davenport, R11435
Thomas, N.J., S16291
Thomas, N.J., Margaret, W6474; BLWt.8845-100 iss. 1789
Thomas, N.C., Cassandra, W1521, b. in N.C.
Thomas, Pa., S7882
Thomas, Pa., no declaration by soldier
Thomas, R.I., S22050
Thomas, S.C., Elizabeth Jeffors former wid., W21452

WHITE (continued)
Thomas, Va., N.A. Acc. No.874-050189. Half Pay. No pension file identified for this man.
Thomas, Va., S30787
Thomas, Va., S40685
Thomas, Va., Elizabeth, R11409
Thomas, Va., Sarah, R11442
Timothy, Mass., Ruth, W619; BLWt.14663-160-55
Uriah, N.Y., S44041
Vassel/Vassal, Mass., Polly, W22597
Vincent, N.C., R11445
William, Pvt. Ct., BLWt.6670 iss. 3/30/1793
William, Ct., S40684
William, Ct., Zilpha, W22596
William, Ct., R11450
William, Ct., Cont., S36384
William, Cont., Mass., S32058
William, Cont., N.H., S23483
William, Pvt. Hazen's Regt., BLWt.13882 iss. 3/1/1792 to Nathaniel Grimes, ass.
William, Pvt. Mass., BLWt.5318 iss. 8/27/1792 to Samuel Fenny
William, Mass., S23485
William, Mass., S37551
William, Mass., S44035
William, Mass., Jemima, W19609
William, Mass., BLWt.2556-300-Capt. iss. 4/17/1790 to Lydia White, the legal repr.
William, N.Y., S26904
William, N.Y., Huldah, W16471
William, N.Y., Elizabeth, W22606
William, N.C., S42071
William, N.C., Rachel, W65
William, N.C., Jane, R11419
William, Pa., S6363
William, Pa., S40677
William, Pa., R11448
William, Pa., R21898
William, S.C., Mary, W4388
William, S.C., Jane, W8995
William, S.C., R11452, d. 1844
William, Va., S1601
William, Va., S1735
William, Va., Martha, S46512 & R11429; BLWt.2428-300-Capt. iss. 7/5/1789 to James Taylor ass.
William, Va., Caty, W4099; BLWts. 2213-200 & 3190-160-55, sold. d. 12/2/1812
William, Va., Polly Doran, former wid., W7033; BLWt.71128-160-55, d. 1795
William, Va., Hannah, W10275; sold. d. 1/6/1840
William, Va., Dorothy, W18396; sold. d. 1806
William, Va., Elizabeth, W19616, sold. d. 1827
William, Va., R11449
William, Va. Sea Service, R107 1/2 Va. Half Pay. No Va. State Navy Y.S. file, sailing master
William C., Navy, N.H., S43318

WHITE (continued)
William S., Va. Sea Service, R107, Va. half pay. See Acct. 837 Va. State Navy Y.S. file - William S. White
Zachariah, Mass., S30789
WHITECAR, Joseph, N.J., Pa. Sea Service, S6366
WHITECOTTEN, James, Va., S30780
WHITECOTTON, Axton, Va., S6361
WHITED, John, N.C. See WHITEHEAD
WHITEFIELD, William, Va., S38466
WHITEHEAD, Aaron, N.J., Mary Sutter, former wid., W19416
Burrill/Burrell, N.C., Nancy, W4857
Daniel, N.J., Surviah, W19891
David, Ct., Judith, W10278; BLWt.26405-160-55
David, N.J., R11453
Isaac, N.J., R11454
James, Pvt., N.J., BLWt.8861 iss. 9/4/1789 to David Whitehead, ass.
James, N.J., S33894
John, N.Y., Margaret, W19617; BLWt.7982 iss. 3/6/1792
John, N.C., S42065
John, N.C., Sarah, W6495; BLWt.43514-160-55
John, Pvt. Va., BLWt.12669 iss. 7/14/1792 to Robert Means, ass.
Lazarus, N.C. See Lazarus LEWIS
Robert, Va., Barbara, W25999; BLWt.31733-160-55, enl. in N.C.
Samuel, Pvt. N.J., BLWt.8852 iss. 4/14/1792
Samuel, N.J., S40671
Thomas, N.Y., S15246
William, Drummer, N.Y., BLWt. 7890 iss. 6/1/1790 to John Warren, ass.
William, N.Y., Ann, W20126
WHITEHORNE, Samuel, Privateer, R.I., Ruth, W25981; BLWt. 86134-160-55
WHITEHOUSE, Daniel, Mass., S37553
Ebenezer, Pvt. N.H., BLWt.3559 iss. 3/25/1790
Ebenezer, Cont., Navy, N.H., Dorcas, W27502
James, Mass., Mary, W26000
John, N.H., Susanna, W25970; BLWt.6453-160-55
Jonathan, N.H., S43312
Martha, Mass., former wid. of James Roberts, which see
Samuel, Mass., S37538
Samuel, Mass., S37554
Samuel, Privateer, R.I., Ruth, See WHITEHORNE
Thomas, Mass., S36385
WHITEHURST, Anthony, N.C.,R11455
Arthur, N.C., S7878
Richard, N.C., R11456
Simon, N.C., Christiana, W11795; BLWt.31732-160-55
WHITEHURT, Wily, N.C., S.C., R11457
WHITEKER, John, Md., Ann, W9001
William, Ga., S31473

WHITELEY, John, Cont., Ct., Rebecca, W25978
John, Cont., Vt., S40682
Robert, Va., Jane, R11459
William, Ct., S43308
WHITELOCK, John, Mass., N.H., Mary, R11458
WHITEMAN, Frederick, Pa., Sarah W11798; BLWt.52782-160-55
Henry, Pa., Va., S7881
John, Pa., Elizabeth, R11470
John, Pa., Sarah, R20286; BLWt.2011-100
Mathias, N.C., Margaret, R11460
Wollery/Woolery, Pa., S40683
WHITEMORE, Timothy, Mass., S43287
WHITEN, Solomon, See WHIDDEN
WHITENACK, Abraham, N.J., S1149
WHITER, Jacob, Cont., Mass., S43297, N.Y. res.
WHITESIDE, John, N.Y., Margaret, W18405
William, S.C., S1885
WHITFIELD, John, N.C., Mildred, R11396
Solomon, Va., S18281
William, N.C., Mary, R11395
Willis, N.C., Rhoda/Rhody, W1013
Willis, N.C., Nancy, R11397
WHITFORD, Catharine, N.Y., former wid. of Charles Riley, which see
Christopher, R.I., Sarah, W19892
Constant, R.I., S9525
David, Pvt., R.I., BLWt.3586 iss. 11/30/1799 to Abraham Holbrook, ass.
David, R.I., S39892
Job, R.I., S22047
Stukley/Stukeley, R.I., Rose Anna/Rosanna, W4856
Thomas, R.I., Eleanor H., W2470; BLWt.3395-160-55
WHITHAM, Joshua, Mass. See WITHAM
Terey, See Jereh WHITAM
WHITHOUSE, Thomas, See WHITEHOUSE
WHITIKER, Ebenezer, Mass., S11735
WHITIN, Samuel, Mass., Mary, W2384; BLWt.15172-160-55
WHITING, Aaron, Mass., S17779
Asa, Mass., Mary, W25991
Caleb, Mass., S33908
Daniel, Mass., BLWt.2290-450-Lt. Col. iss. 9/7/1789. No papers
Ebenezer, Mass., Elizabeth, W2296
Elihu, Ct., S11776
Elijah, Cont., Ct., Anna, W18412 BLWt.245-60-55
Elizabeth, Ct., Boat Service on Lake Champlain, former wid. of Noble Lyman, which see
Elkanah, Mass., S30200
Francis, 1st Regt. of Light Dragoons, BLWt.2440-200-Lt. iss. 8/25/1789. No papers
Frederick J., Sheldon's Horse, BLWt.2358-200-Lt. iss. 8/23/

WHITING (continued)
1790. No papers
Harvey, Ct., Olive, W11801
Henry, Va., BLWt.2412-200
Isaac, Md., R11461
Isaac, Mass., Mary, W18359
Jacob, Mass., S30788
John, Ct., S15241
John, Ct., Alida, W19618
John, Mass., S22585
John, Mass., Margaret, W1342; BLWt.13705-160-55
John, Mass., BLWt.2312-200-Lt. iss. 1/19/1796 to Joseph Fosdick, ass. No papers
Jonas, Mass., S43298
Joseph, Ct., R11462
Joseph, Ct., Cont., S35724
Joseph, Mass., S21570
Joseph, Mass., Polly, W1115; BLWt.31736-160-55
Joshua, Pvt. Mass., BLWt.5267 iss. 7/6/1792 to James Witham
Joshua, Mass., S30782
Joshua, Mass., Hannah, W22593
Marlborough, Mass., Nabby/Nably, W2210
Nabby, Mass., former wid. of Joseph French, which see
Nathan, Ct., Cont., Navy, R.I., Sarah, W22595
Nathan, Mass., S23069
Nathan, N.H., Phebe, W18404
Nathan H., Ct., BLWt.2351-200-Lt. iss. 2/22/1790 to Theodosius Fowler, ass. No papers
Oliver, Mass., Hannah, W22591
Ozias, Mass., R11463
Samson/Sampson, Mass., S28945
Samuel, Ct., Dis.
Samuel, Ct., Mass., S17777
Samuel, Mass., See WHITIN
Samuel, Mass., Mary, W25972; BLWt.5314-160 iss. 3/25/1790
Samuel, N.H., R11464
Stephen, Mass., BLWt.679-100
Timothy, Mass., Lydia, W1340
William, Ct., S43296 & S11746; BLReg. 181980-1855. He married Elizabeth Noble, wid. of Lyman Noble, which see
William, Mass., S11772
William, Mass., Molly, W22616
WHITINGTON, Faddy, N.C. See WHITTINGTON
John, Del., S35722
WHITLACH, William, Md., Pa., S22583
WHITLEDGE, Ambrose, N.C., S7868
WHITLEY, Joseph, Ct., S44039
Micajah, N.C., S42068
Robert, Va., Jane, See WHITELEY
WHITLOCK, Abel, Ct., Phebe, W18413
Alice/Allace, Pa., former wid. of Thomas Pickett, which see
Ephraim/Ephraim L., N.J., S33900; BLWt.2377-200-Lt. iss. 6/11/1789
Hezekiah, Ct., S15706
James, Cont., N.J., S44042

WHITLOCK (continued)
James, Matross, Pa., BLWt.10645 iss. 6/2/1797
James, Va., S11742
James, Va., R11466
John, Va., S17195
Justus, Ct., Privateer, S18648
Nathan, Ct., S6368
Thomas, Va., S16020
WHITLOW, Benjamin, Qtrm. Sgt. "in Proctor's Artillery", Pa., BLWt.10641 iss. 7/16/1789 to M. McConnell, ass.
Nicholas, Va., R11467
Sarah, S.C., former wid. of Richard Pollard, which see
Solomon, N.C., Mary Hicks, former wid., W8218; BLWt.30783-160-55
Thomas, Va., Hannah Irvin, former wid., W7861
WHITMAN, Abiel, Cont., N.H., Alice, W15485; BLWt.19706-160-55
Benjamin, Cont., R.I., R11469
Benjamin, Green Mt. Boys, R.I., Vt., S18650
Benoni, N.Y., R.I., Esther, W19627
Caleb, R.I., S39889
David, Cont., Mass., Priscilla, W8306; BLWt.36532-160-55
David, Mass., S16578
George, N.Y., R.I., Ruth, W19619
Henry, R.I., Roby/Rhobey, W1681; BLWt.26073-160-55
Jacob, Mass., S19504
Jacob, Pa., Margaret, R11473
John, Ct., S35719
John, Mass., R11474
John, Pa., Elizabeth, See WHITEMAN
John, R.I., Hannah, R11472
John, Va., S2023
John R., N.Y., Mary, R11475; BLWt.51766-160-55
Lemuel, Pvt., Ct., BLWt.6630 iss. 3/12/1792 to John P. Schott, ass.
Lemuel, Ct., S43319
Levi, Pvt., N.H., BLWt.3555 iss. 7/21/1789 to Ladd & Cass, assnes.
Levi, Mass., N.H., S43306
Lucinda, Cont., Va., former wid. of William Kelley, which see
Matthew/Mathew, Va., S18654
Nehemiah, Mass., S17778
Noah, N.H., R11476
Richard, Va., S38464
Samuel, Ct., Abigail, W18402
Stephen, R.I., Lucretia, W25986
Stephen, R.I., See WIGHTMAN
William, Mass., Thorza/Thirza, W2677; BLWt.8145-160-55
Woolery/Wollery, See Wollery WHITEMAN
WHITMARSH, Ebenezer, Mass., Mary, W22590
Ezra, N.Y., Zipporah, W18393; BLWt.11076-160-55
Gideon, Mass., R.I., S15239
Lot, Mass., Susanna, W14139

WHITMARSH (continued)
Micah, Cont., Privateer, R.I., Anne, W25984
Samuel, Mass., S30781
Samuel, Mass., S43293
WHITMILL, Thomas Blount, N.C., Ann, W1522
WHITMOND, Lucinda, Cont., Va., former wid. of William Kelley, which see
WHITMORE, Amos, Pvt. N.Y., BLWt. 8049 iss. 3/15/1791 to John Clarke, ass.
Amos, Cont., N.Y., Mary, W16789
Amos, Pvt. N.J., BLWt.8865 iss. 6/11/1789 to Matthias Denman, ass.
Andrew, Mass., Lucy, R11479
Asa, Pvt. Mass., BLWt.5294 iss. 5/11/1792 to Ezra Blodget
Benjamin, Mass., S41327
Daniel, Mass., Teresa, W8310; BLWt.12562-160-55
David B., Mass., R11478
Edward, Mass., S11734
Enoch, Pvt. Mass., BLWt.5332 iss. 5/31/1790 to Theodosius Fowler
Enoch, Mass., S33904
Everhart, Pvt. Pa., BLWt.10595 iss. 7/7/1797 to Buckner Nance, ass.
Hezekiah, Ct., S32056
Howell/Howel, N.C., Nancy, W509; BLWt.36622-160-55
Isaac, Mass., S33906
Jabez, Ct., BLWt.1537-100
James, Cont.,N.Y., Johannah,W2037 BLWts.188-60-55; 8050-100 iss. 2/28/1791 to John Carpenter, ass.
James, Pvt. Hazen's Regt., BLWt. 13887 iss. 3/25/1790
John, Mass., Rebecca, W11806; BLWt.11077-160-55
John, Va., Ann/Nancy, R11477
John Y., Va., R11480
Joseph, Cont., Mass., Abigail, W22592
Stephen, Md., S35114
Timothy, Mass., S43287
William, Mass., Amey, W22594
WHITMYER, Philip, Pa., S3550
WHITNEY, Abner, Mass., S41324
Abraham, Mass., S37558
Benjamin, Cont., Mass., Delano/Delana, W4858
Benjamin, Mass., S44044
Benjamin, Mass., S44045
Caleb, Cont., Mass., S43323
Caleb, Cont., Mass., S43323
Cornelius, Ct., Hannah, W14136
Daniel, Ct., Hannah, W25995
Daniel, Cont., Mass., Abigail W25983
Daniel, Mass., S18649
Daniel, Mass., Louisa, W25975
David, Ct., Eliza Whitney Sollace former wid., W2013; BLWt.105237-160-55
David, Ct., Nancy, W3636; BLWt. 38341-160-55
David, N.Y., Mary, W6489; BLWt.12572-160-55

WHITNEY (continued)
Ebenezer, Ct., Ruth, W22609
Ebenezer, Cont., Mass., Lovina, W6490; BLWt.15403-160-55
Ebenezer, Mass., Martha, W19625
Ebenezer, Mass., Mehitable, W25977
Eleazer, Mass., Martha, W22611; BLWt.14954-160-55
Elijah, Mass., Vt., S15707
Elisha, Mass., Esther, W3746
Enos, Ct., S22580
Ezekiel, Pvt. Ct., BLWt.6658 iss. 6/27/1789
Ezekiel, Ct., S44036
Ezekiel, Ct., Phebe, W19626
Ezra, N.H., Sally, R11485
Hackaliah, Mass., S6379
Hezekiah, Ct., Olive, W18406
Isaac, Mass., S28944
Isaac, Mass., S37537
Isaac, Mass., Lydia, W15482
Jacob, Mass., Hannah, R11481
Jacob, N.Y., Mabel, W20125
James, Mass., Susanna, R11488
James R., Ct., Navy, S44037
Jesse, Mass., Charity, W1341
Joel, Mass., Lydia, W26620; BLWt.35679-160-55
John, Ct., S17192
John, Mass., S30203
John, Mass., Molly, W4615
John, Mass., Sarah, W16161
Jonas, Mass., Elizabeth, BLWt. 19624-160-55
Jonathan, Mass., S37542
Joseph, Cont., Mass., Mary, W25985
Joseph, R.I.,Sea Service, Mary Hoppin, former wid., W21355
Joshua, Ct., Green Mt. Boys, S41326; BLWt.2354-200-Lt. iss. 5/31/1790 to Theodosius Fowler, ass.
Joshua, Cont., Mass., Electy, W8308
Joshua, Mass., S37549
Joshua, Mass., N.H., Betty/Betsey W15863
Josiah, Pvt. Ct., BLWt.6646 iss. 11/17/1791 to Elisha Camp, ass.
Josiah, Ct., Sally, W2297; BLWt.51764-160-55
Lemuel, Mass., Grace, W9000
Leonard, Mass., S43300
Micah, Cont., Mass., S37545
Moses, Mass., Abigail, W26005
Nathan, Cont., Mass., S11741
Oliver, Mass., Hannah, W20129
Peter, Ct., S41330
Phebe, Mass., former wid. of Elijah Davis, which see
Phineas, Mass., Sally, R11486
Phinehas, Mass., S22581; wife Elizabeth
Phinehas, Mass., S30204. Mary Whitney, wid. of sold., was pensioned as the former wid. of her 1st husb., Isaac Fish, Mass., which see
Phinehas/Phineas, Mass., S38463

WHITNEY (continued)
Phinehas, N.H., Susannah, W16470
Richard, Mass., Ruth, W25996
Roswell, N.Y., Phebe, R11484
Salmon, Mass., Hepzibah, W26619
Samuel, Pvt. Ct., BLWts.6614 & 13913 iss. 12/3/1796 to Nathaniel Ruggles, ass.
Samuel, Ct., S35723
Samuel, Mass., BLWt.5282 iss. 4/8/1796 to Jere Mason
Samuel, Mass., S29542
Samuel, Mass., S33899
Seth, N.Y., S23068
Silas, N.H., Sally, W8311; BLWt. 38336-160-55
Simon, Mass., Lucy, W19622
Stephen, Mass., S31478
Stephen, R.I., S37544
Timothy, Cont., Mass., S33892
Union, Mass., former wid. of Jacob Loomis, which see
Uriel, Cont., Mass., S19159
Walter, Ct., S11737
William, Ct., S35720
William, Mass., S15247
Zebulun, Mass., S31475
WHITON, Abijah, Cont., Mass., Deborah, W14134
Israel, Mass., S33895
Joseph, Ct., Amanda, W14145
Thomas, Ct., Cont., S44049
WHITROW, William, See WHITTECO
WHITT, Hezekiah, Va., S7885
Robert, Va., S7880
William, Va., S7870
WHITTAKER, Ephraim, Ct., S9526; BLWt.1902-300
WHITTECO, William, Md., Sarah Scribner, former wid., W24919
WHITTEKER, John, Va., S36845
WHITTEMORE, Cuff, Pvt., Mass., BLWt.5255-100 iss. 11/2/1795 to Joseph Fosdick
Cuff (colored), Cont., Mass., S33896
Ebenezer, Mass., Sea Service, Isabel Hammond, former wid., W13371
Nathaniel, Mass., S43303
Paul, Mass., BLWt.1013-100
Peter, N.H., S23070
Zebedee, N.H., Prudence, W18400
WHITTEN, Elijah, Sgt. Lamb's Art. N.Y., BLWts.8038 & 245 iss. 7/14/1790, 1855, Wt.8038 to Richard Platt, ass.
John, Mass., Jane, W25974
Jonathan, S.C., S18278, b. Va.
Richard, Mass., S38462
Samuel, Olive, BL files, Act of 1855, Rejected 223820; 1777 Pvt.
WHITTIER, Abner, Mass., Judith, W26001
Andrew, N.H., See WHITCHER
Daniel, Mass., S43322
Daniel, Mass., BLWt.5253-100
Jacob, Corp. Crane's Cont. Art. Mass., BLWt.5338 iss. 9/12/1789 to Ebenezer & Justin Foote

WHITTIER (continued)
assnes. Certified 4/25/1806
Jacob, Cont., Mass. See WHITER
Moses, Sarah Lunt, former wid., R6523. Mass. res. in 1774
Thomas, Mass., Abigail, W1904; BLWt.26216-160-55
WHITTING, John, Ct. See WHITING
Joseph, Mass., S33901
Samuel, Sgt. Mass., BLWt.5314 iss. 3/25/1790
WHITTINGTON, Cornelius, Ga., S.C. b. in Va. , S7892
Faddy, N.C., S32063; BLWt.26174-160-55
Grief, S.C., S7883, b. in Va.
Jarratt, S.C., Polly/Mary, R11491; BLWt.44808-160-55
Nathaniel, S.C., S9527, b. S.C.
Richard, S.C., Mary, W535; BLWt.26973-160-55, b. in Va.
WHITTLE, Thomas, Cont., N.H., R.I., (1775), S43321
William, N.H., Rachil, W26006
WHITTLESEY, Charles H., Ct., S17197
Martin, Dis. paid at Ct. agcy.
Samuel, Mass., Huldah, W6497
WHITTUM, Jeremiah, Pvt. Mass., BLWt.5309 iss. 1/26/1796 to James A. Neal
WHITTY, John, Mass., Dorcas, W4718; BLWt.1452-100
WHITWELL, Samuel, Mass., BLWt. 1778-400
WHITWORTH, Allen, Va., S6367
John, N.C., S7874, b. in N.C.
WHITZELL, George, R11492, Va. res.
WHOOD, Stephen, Mass., S34520
WHOOLEY, Peter Va., (1774), R11493
WHORTON, John, S.C. See WHARTON
Robert, Va., Joley; See HORTON
WHRITENHOUR, Henry, N.J., R11490
WHRITNER, Henry, See WHRITENHOUR
WHYLAND, Leonard, N.Y., S7886
WIARD, Darius, Ct., S28946
WIATT, Pittman, Va., Dis.
WIBERT, Frederick, N.Y., S44088
John, N.Y. See WIBIRT
WIBIRT, John, N.Y., R11495
WICK, John, N.J., Hannah Jane, W4103; BLWt.3189-160-55
Sefrenus/Severenus, N.Y., S28951
William, N.J., S16295
WICKAM, John, S.C., Elizabeth Couzens, former wid. See WICKHAM
Stephen, N.Y. See WICKHAM
WICKE, Severenus, See Sefrenus WICK
WICKER, James, N.C. See WHICKER
Lemuel, Mass., R11496
William, N.C., S.C., S11853
WICKES, Abel, R.I., S21575
Alexander, Ct., S44090
Daniel, R.I. See WEEKS
Oliver, R.I., S21578; BLWt.26146-160-55
Silas, N.Y., S11824
Zophar, N.Y., Jane, W22634; BLWt.10233-160-55

WICKET, Obadiah, Mass., S34535
WICKHAM, Daniel, N.Y., S11798
Isaac, Mass. See WICKHAMS
John, N.Y., S7955
John, S.C., Elizabeth Couzens, former wid., BLWt.125-200
Stephen, Pvt. N.Y., BLWt.7947 iss. 1/5/1791
Stephen, N.Y., Margaret, W26023
William, Ct., Sarah, W26026
WICKHAMS, Isaac, Mass., S34534; BLWt.906-100
WICKLE, John, Pvt. "in the artillery", Pa., BLWt.10655 iss. 7/16/1789 to M. McConnell, ass.
WICKLEY, John, S.C. See WICKLY
WICKLIFFE, Charles, Va., S1271
David, Va., S6409
WICKLY, John, S.C., S39132; BLWt.2452-300-Capt. iss. 1/28/1795 to Wm. Crammond, John Leamy & Hugh Holnies, excrs. of David Cay, dec'd, ass. Name spelled Wickley
WICKOFF, Cornelius, Pa., S11850
Joachan, N.J. See WICOFF
John B., N.J., S6458
Peter, N.J., S3603
William, N.J., Pa., S11858
WICKS, Alexander, Ct. See WICKES
Zophar, N.Y. See WICKES
WICKWIRE, Grant, Ct., S11785
James, Ct., Cont., Sarah, W22629
WICOFF, Joacham, N.J., Hannah, W4401
WIDDER, George, Pa. See WITHERS
WIDDERSTIEN, John, N.Y. See WITDERSTEIN
WIDDOWS, Abraham, Pa., BLWt. 1093-100
WIDENER, Michael, Va., Elizabeth, W8303; BLWt.26617-160-55
WIDGBARE, William, See WEDGBARE
WIDGER, Andrew, Ct., S36390
Eli, Ct., Cont., Navy & Privateer Lucy, W18425; BLWt.3618-160-55
Joseph, Cont., Mass., Rebecca, W19636
Samuel, Ct., R11497
WIDMEYER, Michael, Va., S11857, b. in Md.
WIDRIG, Conrad, N.Y., R11498
Jacob, N.Y., S11839
WIDTERSTINE, John, See WITDERSTEIN
WIER, Cornelius, Pa. See WEAR
George, S.C. See WEIR
James R., Ct., S30802
John, N.H., Rebecca, W26073
WIERS, James, Va., S41358
WIES, Daniel, N.Y., Elizabeth, W15864
WIESNER, Godfrey, Pa., S40720
WIETT, Edward, Va., S3557
WIGGIN, Andrew, N.H., R11500
Benjamin, N.H., S14844
James, N.H., Ruth, W26085
Mark, N.H. See WIGGINS
Nathan, N.H., Elizabeth, W2394
Noah, N.H., Sarah, W16475
Phineas, Cont., N.H., Mehitable, W26049

WIGGIN (continued)
Simon, N.H., S18288
Thomas, Cont., N.H., Elizabeth, W16089
William, N.H., Mary, W9894; BLWt.31455-160-55. She also applied for a pension as the former wid. of Daniel Blanchard and the claim was rejected. See papers within, R924 & duplicate No. R11503
Winthrop, Pvt. N.H., Wt.3579 iss. 1/27/1798 to Jonathan Cass, ass.
Winthrop, N.H., S11820
WIGGINS, Abraham, N.C., R11501
Arthur, N.C., S7952
Benjamin, Cont., Mass., S37560
Jacob, N.Y., S11852
Jesse, S.C., R11502
Mark, N.H., S43325
Thomas, Sgt. Pa., BLWt.10646 iss. 7/9/1799 to Abraham Bell, ass.
Thomas, Cont., Pa., Sarah Webber former wid., W1012. Her other husb., John Webber, N.H., was pensioned, which see
William, N.C., S1739
William, Pa., S17781
William, Pa., Eleanor, W18457
Wilson, Va., S41364
WIGGINTON, Benjamin, Va., S18283
Henry, Va., S31483
John, Cont., Va. See WIGINGTON
WIGGLESWORTH, Edward, Mass., S33920
William, Mass., BLWt.1465-200
WIGGON, James, Pvt. N.J., BLWt. 8851 iss. 1/5/1792
WIGGS, John, N.C., Cherry, W4398
William, N.C., S32608
WIGHAM, Robert, N.Y., Prudence, W6546
WIGHT, Aaron, R.I., S6388
Daniel, Cont., Mass., S37561
Eliab, Mass., S21591
Jabez, Mass., S41350
Jacob, Ct., S33934
Joel, Cont., S42073, enl. in Mass. Me. agcy. and res.
John, Cont., Mass., Olive, W2041; BLWts.710-100 & 308-60-55
Jonathan, Mass., S41349
Joseph, Cont., Mass., Olive, W26047; BLWt.18385-160-55
Lemuel, Mass., S34550
Nahum, Cont., Mass., Nabby, W26141
Nathaniel, Mass., S15714
Samuel, R.I., S22063
William, Ct., S15711
WIGHTMAN, George, Cont., N.Y., S40711; BLWt.1561-100
James, R.I., Mercy, W26054
John, R.I., S48898
Peleg, R.I., Hannah, W620; BLWt.26062-160-55
Stephen, R.I., Deborah, W27499
William, Pa., Mary, W2983
WIGINGS, Joseph, Mass., S33932
WIGINGTON, George, Ga., S.C., S32600

WIGINGTON (continued)
John, Cont., Va., Margaret, W6547
John, Pvt. Va., BLWt.12673 iss. 7/14/1792 to Robert Means, ass.
WIGNER, Daniel, Pa., S3605
WIGTON, John, Pa., BLWt.2388-200-Lt. iss. 8/19/1789. No papers
Thomas, Pa., Elizabeth, R11506
WIKOFF, Garret, N.J., S787
Garrett, N.J., Rachel, R11507
WILARD, Henry, Pa. See WILLYARD
WILBANKS, William, S.C., Abarilla R11508. Name also appears as Woolbanks and Woodbanks
WILBAR, Isaac, Mass., Joanna, W19650
Joshua, R.I., See WILBUR
WILBER, Benjamin, Mass., Vt., R11512
Benjamin, R.I., S14851
Gideon, N.Y., Sarah, See WILBUR
Holden, Mass., Polly, W26043; BLWt.40508-160-55
Jacob, N.Y., Elizabeth Reed, former wid., W24739
Jacob, N.Y., Vt. See WILBUR
John, N.J., S936
John, Privateer, R.I. See WILBUR
Joseph, N.Y., Elizabeth, See WILBOR
Joshua, R.I., See WILBUR
Oliver, R.I., S44086
Uriel/Uriah, R.I. See WILBUR
WILBOR, Joseph, N.Y., Elizabeth, W9167; BLWt.71028-160-55
Thomas, Mass., Sea Service, R.I. See WILBUR
WILBOUR, Aaron, R.I., Elizabeth, W26035
Asa, R.I., See WILLBOUR
John, R.I., Mercy, W14165
Joseph, R.I. See WILBUR
Uriel/Uriah, R.I. See WILBUR
WILBOURN, Lewis, N.C., R11515, b. in Va.
WILBUR, Aaron, R.I. See WILBOUR
Asa, Cont., Mass., S18656
Benjamin, Mass., R.I., S30210
Daniel, R.I., S21573
Francis, R.I., S22057
Gideon, N.Y., Sarah, W23983
Hezekiah, R.I., S22062
Holden, Mass., See WILBER
Jacob, N.Y., Vt., R11513
Jesse, R.I., S22059
John, Privateer, R.I., Elizabeth W1968; BLWt.31451-160-55
John, R.I., Mercy, See WILBOUR
Joseph, N.Y. See WILBOR
Joseph, R.I. See WILBOUR
Joshua, R.I., Elizabeth, W18342 BLWt.26937-160-55
Josiah, Ct., S44220
Nancy Ann, Ct., former wid. of John Smith, which see
Oliver, R.I. See WILBER
Record, Mass., BLWt.21820-160-55
Samuel, Navy, R.I., S22058
Samuel, R.I., S21577

WILBUR (continued)
Thomas, Ct., Dorcas, W10004; BLWt.6007-160-55
Thomas, Mass., Sea Service, R.I. Ruth, W1687; BLWt.19718-160-55
Uriah/Uriel, R.I. See Uriel
Uriel, R.I., Hannah, W22654; BLWt.1853-100
WILBURN, Hezekiah, See WILBUR
WILBY, Jonathan, Ct., See WILLEY
WILCKLOW, Jacob, N.Y., S23078
WILCOX, Abner, Pvt., Ct., BLWt. 6704 iss. 6/1/1793 to Stephens Thorne, ass.
Abner, Cont., N.Y., Lucy, W22618
Abraham, Ct., Cont., Lucretia; W27505; BLWt.26255-160-55
Asa, N.H., Dina, W22660
Billy, Ct., Rebecca, W18423
Borden, Navy, Privateer, R.I., Eunice, W2304; BLWt.26218-160-55
Chloe, Ct., former wid. of Isaac Isaacs, which see
Comfort, Ct., S14848
Consider, N.Y., R11518
Daniel, N.J., S3562. Patience Wilcox, wid. of above sold. was pensioned as former wid. of Aaron Deacon, which see
Edward, R.I., Deborah, W26030
Eleazer, Ct., S16023
Elias, Cont., Ct., Hannah Sears, former wid., W17792. Her other husb., Obadiah Sears, Ct., was pensioned,which see
Elijah, Ct., Lois, W18419
Elijah, Mass., S49277
Elisha, Ct., R.I., S24011
Ezekiel, Ct. See WILLCOX
Ezra, Dis., Vt. ? res.
Ezra, Ct., Rebecca, W18420
George, Mass., R11520
Gideon, R.I. See WILLCOX
Giles, Corp., Ct., BLWt.6675 iss. 2/5/1790
Hannah, Ct., former wid. of David White, which see
Hosea, Ct., S40709
Isaac, Cont., R.I., Mary, W26055
Isaac, N.Y. See WILLCOX
Jacob, Ct., Rachel, W18442
James, Ct., Cont., Lucretia, See WILLCOX
James, Ct., Green Mt. Boys, Mass. & Vt., S19162
Jared, Cont., Mass., S41337
Jehiel, Ct., Catharine, W2211
Jehiel, Ct., Thankful, W6542
Joel, Ct., S40695
John, Ct., S32068
John, N.Y., R11524
John, Privateer, R.I. See WILLCOX
Jonah, Mass., S14869
Jonathan, Ct., S11844
Joseph, Ct., S32073
Josiah, Ct., Rosanna, W26051
Josiah, R.I., S45453; BLWt. 27-100
Lemuel, Pvt., Ct., BLWt.6669 iss. 6/1/1792
Lemuel, Ct., Anste, W22663

WILCOX (continued)
Mary, Mass., former wid. of Elijah Day, which see
Mercy, Ct., former wid. of Daniel Merrell, which see
Nathan, Ct., S36391
Nathaniel, N.Y., S11808
Pardon, R.I., S21574
Phineas, N.H., Dis.
Rebecca, Cont., Ct., former wid. of Richard Doud, which see
Reuben, Ct., S11859
Robert, Navy, R.I., Patience, R11525
Roger, Ct., See WILLCOX
Silvanus, Mass., N.Y., S11783
Stephen, Ct., R11528
Timothy, Ct. See WILLCOX
William, Mass., See WILLCOX
William, Mass., Mary, W18440
WILCOXEN, Daniel, N.C., S16582
David, Ct., S36389
WILCOXON, Daniel, N.C. See WILCOXEN
Elnathan, Ct. See WILCOXSON
WILCOXSON, Daniel, See WILCOXEN
Elnathan, Ct., S15715
Ephraim J., Ct., Mary, W2392; BLWt.27694-160-55
WILCUTT, Jesse, Mass., Katharine, W15491
Zebulon, Mass., S19161
WILD, Daniel, Cont., Mass., S6422
Deborah, Mass., former wid. of William Hayden, which see
Ebenezer, Cont., Mass., Abigail Baxter, former wid., W14225; BLWt.2311-200-Lt. iss. 8/23/ 1791 to Eben Wilds
Jesse, Mass., Mehitable Crittenden, former wid., W15661
John, Mass., Jemima, W26076
Jonathan, Cont., Mass., Deborah, W20135
Jonathan, Cont., Mass., Navy, Privateer, S3553
Levi, Mass., S30216
Micah, Mass., S31163
Thomas, Mass., Anna, W22662; BLWt.31779-160-55
WILDAY, Absalom, N.C. See WILEY
WILDE, John, Mass., Phebe, W9004
Lydia, Mass., former wid. of Enos Dean, which see
Richard, Del., S20575
WILDER, Aaron, Ct., S18655
Abel, Sgt. Mass., BLWt.5285 iss. 4/1/1790
Abel, Mass., Dorothy, W14155
Abel, Mass., N.H., Vt., Mary, W18426
Charles, Vt., Sally/Sarah, W22630
Elijah, Ct., S11779
Ephraim, Mass., S19873
Ephraim, Mass. See WILDS
George, Va., S17204
Jacob, Cont., Mass., Lydia, W18434
Jacob, Mass., Mary, W1523
James, Mass., S30214
Jonathan, Ct., S11793

WILDER (continued)
Jonathan, Mass., S30207
Joseph, Mass., S30798
Joshua, Mass., R11529
Levi, Mass., S41335
Luther, Mass., Phebe, W22623; BLWt.31775-160-55
Nathaniel, Mass., S6385
Peter, Mass., S23491
Peter, N.H., Tamar, W26079
Phineas, Mass., S11790
Reuben, Mass., Thankful, W6463
Reuben W., Mass., Eunice, W6545
Shubael, Mass., S6430
Thomas, Ct., Taphnes/Zahpenes, W22642
Thomas, Mass., Bethiah, W26080
Timothy, Mass., Eunice, W26056; BLWt.31449-160-55
Titus, Mass., Mary, W15489
William, Mass., Relief, R11530
William, N.C., S7948, b. N.C.
Willis, Mass., Relief, W18430
Willis, N.C., S32077
WILDES, Benjamin, Mass., Sarah, W22647
Ezra, Mass., S35134
WILDEY, Edward, Pvt. N.Y., BLWt. 7993 iss. 9/24/1791. Note in pencil: "No.58439 Van Cortlandt's Regt. Page 104. Vol. 3".
WILDMAN, Matthew, Ct., Polly, W18452
WILDRICH, Michael, See WILDRICK
WILDRICK, Michael, N.J., S3522
WILDS, Ebenezer, See WILD
Ephraim, Mass., S20576
Ezra, Mass., See WILDES
Jacob, Mass., Lydia, W15707
WILES, Abraham, Del., S42076; BLWt.2176-100
Henry, N.Y., Elizabeth, W18449
WILEY, Absalom, N.C., S38473
Agnes, Va., former wid. of Hugh McLoughlin, which see
Aldridge/Aldrich, Cont., Mass., BLWt.1673-200
Alexander, N.Y., S29548
Alexander, N.C., S3555
Andrew, Va., S6392
David, Pvt., Mass., BLWt.5230 iss. 8/11/1795
Ebenezer, Mass., S30213
Eleanor, Ct., N.Y., former wid. of David Crouch, which see
Ephraim, Mass., Abigail, W26070; BLWt.3816-160-55
Henry, Va., S38471
James, Ct., See WYLIE
James, N.C., Sea Service, S42075
James, Va., R19086, Va. Half Pay
John, Pvt. Md., BLWt.11798 iss. 2/7/1790
John, Mass., BLWt.2291-400-Maj. iss. 7/22/1789. No papers
John, Mass., S11834
John, N.H., S41338
John, N.J. Dorothy, See WILLY
John, N.Y., S44223
Joseph, Va. See WILLY
Matthew, Pa., R11533

WILEY (continued)
Robert, Mass., Keziah, W18421
Robert, Mass., Elizabeth Winslow, former wid., R11727
Rufus, N.C., S7919
Samuel, Mass., S40689; BLWt. 646-100
Samuel, Pa., S3556
Thomas, Cont., Ga. See WYLLY
Thomas, Cont., Pa., Jane, W4534
Thomas, Cont., Pa., Rebecca, R11534
William, Mass., Hannah, W19630
William, N.C., Ann, W322
William, N.C., Ann, W10002
WILFONG, David, Pvt. Pa., BLWt. 10628 iss. 9/25/1789
John, N.C., S.C. See WILLFONG
John, Pa., S22598
WILFORD, Joseph, Ct. See WILLFORD
Lewis, N.C., Silva, W6548; BLWt. 16126-160-55. Also served in War of 1812 as Wilford Lewis
WILHEID, Frederick, Md., S35138
WILHELM, Baltzer, Cont., N.Y. See Bastinus WILLIAMS
Balzer, Pvt. Von Heer's Corps, BLWt.13872 iss. 3/3/179-
Frederick, Pa., R11539
Henry, Pvt., Pa., BLWt.10632 iss. 3/5/1791
Henry, N.J., Pa., S33936
Peter, S.C., S21579
WILHIDE, Frederick, See WILHEID
WILHITE, John, Va., S14833
Tobias, Va., Polly, R11542
WILKELOW, John, N.Y., Jemima/ Jemime, W22671; BLWts.150-60-55; 7959-100-1791
WILKERSON, Benjamin, Va., Eva, W10001; BLWt.36543-160-55
David, Va., S36847
Francis, N.C., S31482
James, Va., S4727
James, Va. See WILKINSON
John, Ga., S11818; b. in Va.
John, Pvt. Md., BLWt.11796 iss. 4/19/1797 to James DeBaufre, ass.
John, Mass., See WILKINSON
John, N.C., Margaret, W26042; BLWt.40912-160-55, b. in Va.
Joseph, Va. See WILKINSON
Thomas, N.C., S2025, b. N.C.
Thomas, Va. See WILKINSON
Turner, Va., S3601, b. in Va.
William, N.C. See WILKINSON
William, N.C., S32602. See N.A. Acc. No.874-050190 Not Half Pay William Wilkerson, b. Va.
Young, Cont., Md., S35136; BLWt.2414-200-Lt. iss. 9/1/ 1789
WILKERT, John Henry, Cont., Rebecca, R11544; widow's res. N.Y. in 1839
WILKESON, Malachi, See WILKINSON
WILKIE, Augustus, N.Y., S44219
WILKIN, James W., N.Y., S23074
Robert, Pa., BLWt.2383-300-Capt. iss. 3/3/1795. No papers

WILKINGS, John, N.C., S7923
WILKINS, Amos, Mass., S44085
Aquila/Aquilla, Mass., S43328
Asa, Cont., N.C., S44222
Benjamin, Mass., Naomi, W22651
Benjamin, Mass., Sarah, R11547
Benjamin, N.C., R11545
Edward, Cont., Mass., Bridget, W26065
Edward, Mass., S30799
Elisha, N.C., S42078
Gabriel, Va., R11546
George, Md., S6420
George, N.C., S32605
Isabella, Mass., former wid. of James Turner, which see
James, Cont., Pa., S40701
James, S.C., Elizabeth, W9024
John, Corp., Mass., BLWt.5215 iss. 10/26/1789 to Joshua Green, Jr.
John, N.Y., S3606
John, N.C., Sarah, W9893, b. Va.
John, Pa., Catharine, W3123; BLWt.2390-300-Surgn. Mate iss. 12/22/1790
John Henry, Cont. See WILKERT
Jonathan, Mass., Navy, S43326
Nehemiah, Mass., Sarah, W26086
Reuben, Mass., Polly, W14175
Robert Bradford, Cont., N.H., Matilda, W14156; BLWt.2282-200-Lt. iss. 3/25/1790
Thomas, Va., S35742
Thomas, Va., R11548
Uriah, Mass., Phebe, W22626
William, N.C., S3602
WILKINSON, Abel, Ct., R.I., S14842
Amos, Cont., Navy, Pa., S6431
Amos, Mass., R11549
Benjamin, Va. See WILKERSON
Benning, Mass., N.H., War 1812, S19872
Daniel, R.I., Anna, W22653
Daniel, Pvt. Va., BLWt.12645 iss. 1/31/1794 to John Stockdell, ass.
Daniel, Va., Ann, W6551
David, Cont., BLWt.1685-100. N.Y. res. of heirs in 1830
David, Mass., Ruth, BLWt.67532-160-55
David, Pvt., Va., BLWt.12663 iss. 5/8/1794
Edward M./Edward Mott, Ct., S24015 BLWt.26349-160-55
Elisha, Va., S32078
Ichabod, See N.A. Acc.No. 874-050191 Not Half Pay. Ohio res. d. 1820. No pension file identified for this veteran
Ichabod, Ct., Anna Taylor, W3202 and S40710
James, Cont., Md. & N.H. & U.S. Army until 1814, Celestine Charles Laveau, BLWt.7051-160-55
James, N.H., Lydia, See WILKISON
James, Va., S16022
James, Va., Nancy, W6552; BLWt. 28510-160-55
Jeptha, R.I., Lucy, W22672
John, Ct., S11830

WILKINSON (continued)
John, Ga. See WILKERSON
John, Mass., Patience, W19648
John, Mass., N.Y., R.I., S4724
John, Pa., Margaret, W9890; BLWt.33554-160-55
Jonathan, Cont., S23073 enl. in Ct.
Joseph, Ct., R11550
Joseph, Mass., Dorcas, W22645
Joseph, Navy, U.S. Frigate "Boston", S25974; Ky. pensioner
Joseph, R.I., Elizabeth, W14162
Joseph, Va., S17795
Levi, Ct., Cont., Mass., S7913
Malachi, Ct., W4866
Mott, Ct. See Edward M.
Peter, Ct., R11551
Reuben/Reubin, Ct., S44214. See N.A. Acc. No. 874-050192 Not Half Pay Reuben Wilkinson
Robert, Sgt., N.Y., BLWt.7991 iss. 7/20/1790 to John B. Dumond, ass.
Samuel, N.J., S33929
Samuel, R.I., S18659
Thomas, N.Y., S35733
Thomas, Va., S41347
William, N.C., S1937
William, Pvt. Pa., BLWt.10666 iss. 11/5/1789
William, Pa., Frances, W3484
William, R.I., Marcy, W3748; BLWt.26875-160-55
William, R.I., Lydia, W22659
William, R.I., Susan, W26082
William, Va., S6408
Young, Cont., Md. See WILKERSON
WILKISON, Aaron, N.J., S3574
James, N.H., Lydia, W2215
James, N.J., S3600
Samuel, N.J. See WILKINSON
WILKLOW, John, N.Y., See WILKELOW
WILKS, Samuel, Va., Margaret, R11553
Thomas, Va., S7927
WILL, Conrad, Pvt. Pa., BLWt. 10586 iss. 3/19/1792 to George Moore, ass.
WILLARD, Aaron, Mass., Anna, W6553; BLWt.9045-160-55
Artemas, Mass., Ruth Lynn, former wid., W15049
Daniel, Mass., R11555
Eli, Vt., Salome, W2388; BLWt. 13428-160-55
Elias, Ct., Lois, W4715
Elijah, Mass., Betsey, W2213; BLWt.26868-160-55
Ephraim, Cont., Mass., Mindwell W2891
Ephraim, Mass., Sylvia, W14166
Ezra, Mass., Mary, W2301; BLWt.26212-160-55
Humphrey, Cont., Mass., S44068
James, Mass., Elizabeth, W26045; BLWt.33555-160-55
Jeremiah, Mass., N.H., S11088
John, N.H., S11848
John, Pvt. Pa., BLWt.10591 iss.

WILLARD (continued)
iss. 7/10/1794 to Silas Hart, ass.
John, Vt., S14835
John, Va., S41365
Jonathan, Mass., S11842
Jonathan, Mass., Mary, W19646
Jonathan, N.H., S11815
Joseph, Ct., S6432
Joseph, Pvt. Hazen's Regt., BLWt.13884 iss. 3/5/1792 to Michael Bryan, ass.
Joshua, Mass., S23081
Josiah, Mass., S44082
Lizur, Ct., S14850
Longley, N.H., S22593
Moses, N.Y., Arabella, W6554; BLWt.10030-160-55
Peter, Pvt. "in the Invalids," BLWt.13912 iss. 11/30/1799 to Abijah Holbrook, ass.
Peter, Mass., S34548
Reuben, Mass., Catharine, R11554
Samuel, Mass., S34557
Samuel, Mass., Molly Warner, former wid., W18231
Samuel, N.H., Joanna Hall, former wid., W19689
William, Mass., S30206
William, Pa., S40703; BLWt.1710-100
William, Va., S31489
WILLBANKS, Richard, N.C., S.C., Mary, W26069; BLWt.29031-160-55
WILLBER, Benjamin, Mass., Vt. See WILBER
Uriel/Uriah, R.I. See WILBUR
WILLBERT, Jacob, Pvt., N.Y., BLWt.7942 iss. 8/4/1791
WILLBORN, Joshua, See WELBORN
WILLBOUR, Asa, R.I., BLWt.166-100
WILLBUR, Aaron, R.I., Elizabeth, W26035
Uriel/Uriah, R.I., See WILBUR
WILLCOCK, James, N.J., S3604
WILLCOCKS, William, Cont., N.Y. S44070
WILLCOX, Benjamin, Ct., S14852; BLWt.31770-160-55
Daniel, R.I., S14845
Edward, R.I., R11519
Elias, Sgt. Lamb's Art., N.Y. BLWt.8046 iss. 7/14/1790 to Richard Platt, ass.
Ezekiel, Cont., Ct., S34556
Gideon, R.I., S21585
Isaac, N.Y., S32598
Isaiah, R.I., R11522
James, Ct., Elizabeth, W18417
James, Ct., Cont., Lucretia, W9019; BLWt.3192-160-55
Jeremiah, N.Y., R11523
John, Ct., Lois, W10283
John, Pvt., N.Y., BLWt.7961 iss. 11/27/1790
John, N.Y., S44073
John, Privateer, R.I., S29555
Joseph, Ct., BLWt.2350-200-Lt. iss. 1/28/1790. No papers
Joseph, R.I., Nanny, W20134

WILLCOX (continued)
Joseph, Vt., Prudence, R11526
Josiah, Mass., S15716
Nathan, Ct., S19167
Nathan, Ct. See WILCOX
Noah, R.I., S11821
Pardon, R.I., See WILCOX
Robert, R.I., Sarah, W18416
Roger, Ct., Elizabeth, W18453
Stephen, Ct., R.I., S6412
Stephen, Ct., R.I., Sabra, W18454
Sylvester, R.I., S17797
Thomas, R.I., Keziah, W26046
Timothy, Ct., Cont., S41336
William, Cont., Mass., S44092
WILLCUTT, Jesse, See WILCUTT
Thomas, Mass., Susannah, W27498
WILLE, Benjamin, N.H., S44054
WILLEE, William, N.H.See WILLEY
WILLEFORD, Brittain, S.C., S1740
Richard, N.C., S22060, b. N.C.
WILLES, Benjamin, Cont., N.Y., Bridget, see WILLIS
Hezekiah, Ct. See WELLS
James, Mass. See WILLIS
John, Ct., S36848
Silvanus, Ct., N.H., Eunice, W22619
Thomas, N.Y. See WILLIS
WILLESS, William, Pvt. Del., BLWts.10902 & 10405 iss. 12/17/1793 to John Willis, admr.
WILLET, Benjamin, Mass., Lydia Woodwell, former wid., W14186
Christopher, Pvt. Del., BLWt. 10903 iss. 9/2/1789
Cornelius, N.J., S23492
John, N.J., Euphamia, W6538
Samuel, N.J., Elizabeth, W22620
Thomas, Pvt. Pa., BLWt.10578 iss. 3/22/1791
WILLETT, Hartshorne, N.J., S24017
Marinus, N.Y., Margaret, W1525; BLWt.2362-500-Lt. Col. Com[d] iss. 7/30/1790
WILLEY, Abraham, Ct., S24016
Ahimaaz/Ahimaas/Ahimaz, Ct., S34560
Andrew, N.H., S44065
Barzillai, Ct., S16299
Benjamin, Pvt. N.H., BLWt.3563 iss. 3/29/1792 to Gotleib --- and others
Charles, N.H., Comfort, W2214
Ephraim, Ct., Bethia, R11559
Ezekiel, N.H., Patty, W16088
John, N.H., R11560
Jonathan, Ct., S35734
Jonathan, Ct., N.Y., Irene/Irena, W6827; BLWt.517-160-55
Josiah, N.H., Sally, W22649
Paul, N.H., R11562
Robert, N.H., Privateer, Molly, W16473
Samuel, N.H., S9530
William, Corp., N.H., BLWt.3550 iss. 6/17/1790 to Benj. I./J. Gilman, ass.
William, N.H., Deliverance, W16162
WILLFONG, John, N.C., S.C.,

WILLFONG (continued)
S7951, b. in N.C.
WILLFORD, Joseph, Ct., R11537
WILLHELM, Frederick, Pa., S40699
George, Cont., Md., S40700
Michael, Pa., R11540
WILLIAM, Tall/TALL, William, Oneida Indian, Betsey, R21851, N.Y. res.
WILLIAMS, Abel, N.Y., S14863
Abel, Pa., R11593
Abijah, Mass., S32067
Abraham, Md., Survivor-See claim of Elander Williams, W27673, erroneously allowed on this man's service. Her husb., d. in Pulaski Co., Ky. in 1838
Abraham, Mass., BLWt.2303-300-Capt. iss. 4/16/1790. No papers
Abraham, Mass., S34545
Abraham, Va., Elander, W27673; BLWt.114095-160-55
Agnes, Md., former wid. of John Hartshorn, which see
Alexander, Pvt. Ct., BLWt.6688 iss. 2/--/1790 to Theodosius Fowler, ass.
Alexander, Ct., S35740
Alexander, Md., S36392
Alexander, N.C., S39130
Alexander, Va., S6410
Amos, N.H., S37562
Amos, R.I., S17782
Andrew, Ct., S44213
Ann, Mass., former wid. of Timothy Meach, which see
Anna, Ct., Cont., former wid. of Isaac Gallup, which see
Asa, Ct., S14846
Asa, Cont., Ct., Prudence, W2040; BLWt.26182-160-55
Asahel, Ct., S6411
Asahel, Ct., Hannah, W26053
Asher, Ct., Elizabeth, W18445, d. Dec. 1812
Asher, Ct., N.Y., Elizabeth, W2216 BLWt.18009-160-55, d. 11/7/1845
Bartholomew, Cont., Ct., Mary, W2627; BLWt.3754-160-55
Bastinus/Bastian, Cont., N.Y., Elizabeth, R11538
Benjamin, Ct., S11855
Benjamin, Pvt. Md., BLWt.11816 iss. 10/6/1794 to Henry Purdy, ass.
Benjamin, Md., S40691
Benjamin, Md., S40693; BLWt.2083-100
Benjamin, N.H., S11788
Benjamin, N.J., S31479
Benjamin, N.C., S7897
Benjamin, N.C., S7928
Benjamin, N.C., Ann, W26078
Benjamin, N.C., Va., Nancy, W1119; BLWt.26213-160-55
Benjamin Esty, Mass., Mary, W22658
Bennett, N.C., S7956, b. in Md.
Bennett, Va., S35726
Bill, N.Y., S44067

WILLIAMS (continued)
Bostion, Cont., N.Y., See Bastinus
Buckner, N.C., Mary, W4864
Burnet, N.J., S3579
Caleb, Ct., Cont., Eunice, W9165 BLWt.38337-160-55
Caleb, N.C., S3588
Charles, Md., S35122; BLWt.11848-100
Charles, N.H., Deborah, W22650
Charles, Pvt. N.Y., BLWt.7971 iss. 7/9/1790 to Theodosius Fowler, ass.
Christopher, Va., R11564
Constant, Mass., Vt., S32594
Cornelius, N.J., Margaret, R11598
Cornelius, N.Y., Thanaky, W18456
Daniel, Pvt. Artillery Artificers BLWt.13900 iss. 9/29/179- to Cornelius Williams, ass.
Daniel, Ct., S23077
Daniel, Ct., S32074
Daniel, Ct., Hannah, W6512
Daniel, Pvt. Mass., BLWt.5297 iss. 2/22/1790 to Richard Platt
Daniel, Mass., S33933
Daniel, Mass., S44075; BLWt.1299-100
Daniel, Mass., Marcy, W15734
Daniel, Mass., R11567
Daniel, N.C., BLWt.1624-300
Daniel, R.I., R11568
Daniel (colored), Va., R11569
Davenport, Ct., S11813
David, Ct., S11781
David, Ct., Cont., Privateer, Lucy, W22632
David, Md., R11571
David, Mass., Ann, W11836; BLWt.16266-160-55
David, Mass., Navy, S11777
David, N.J., S3585
David, N.J., Elizabeth, W109
David, N.Y., Nancy, W18439
David, N.C., S3578
David, N.C., Elizabeth, W4392
David, N.C., Drucilla/Drusilla, W18347
David, Va., S4729
David, Va., S46517; BLWt.235-200
David, Va., R11572
David, Va., BLWt.2435-200-Lt. iss. 4/19/1792. No papers
David, BLReg.335511-1855 (state not given). Heirs filed from Monroe Co., Wisconsin
Durell, Ct., S14838
Dyer, Navy, R.I., S44094
Eben, Cont., Mass. See Ebenezer
Ebenezer, Ct., S28950
Ebenezer, Ct., S32072
Ebenezer, Ct., S35729
Ebenezer/Eben, Cont., Mass., Sarah, W22661; BLWt.2308-200-Lt. iss. 8/22/1789
Ebenezer, Mass., Elizabeth Robinson, former wid., W22103; BLWt.40004-160-55
Ebenezer, Va., Catharine, W4391

WILLIAMS (continued)
Edward, Ct., Sea Service, Mary, W22633
Edward, N.C., S17199
Edward, N.C., Elizabeth Lambert, former wid., W9116
Eli, Pa., S6396
Elijah, Pvt. Mass., BLWt.5261 iss. 4/1/1790
Elijah, Mass., S41344
Elijah, Va., S11832
Elisha, Ct., S14839
Elisha, Ct., See Elisha Scott
Elisha, Md., Harriet, W26019
Elisha, Mass., R.I., Lydia, W15865
Elisha, R.I., Prudence, W22636; BLWt.26075-160-55
Elisha, Va., S3589
Elisha Scott, Ct., S30796
Elizabeth, Ct., former wid. of Abel Phelps, which see
Elizabeth, Cont., Md., former wid. of Jacob Moser, which see
Elizabeth, N.H., former wid. of Daniel Kidder, which see
Ephraim, R.I., Patience, W26021
Ezekiel, Ct., Lydia Newell, former wid., W5409; BLWt.40681-160-55
Francis, Md., S3575
Francis, Pvt. N.C., BLWts.12698 & 13878 iss. 6/1/1790 to Abishai Thomas, ass.
Francis, R.I., See MUNN
Frederick, N.C., Nancy, R11603
Frederick, Pa. See WILLHELM
Frederick, Pa., S40706
Frederick W., Mass., Mary, R11601
Gabriel, Md., Margaret, W9896
George, Md. See WILLHELM
George, Mass., Mary, BLWt.78040-160-55
George, N.C., S7950
George, N.C., Delpha, R11573
Gerard/Jarratt, Md., Pa., Ruth Ann, W2981
Gilbert, N.Y., Tabitha, W22668
Hannah, Mass., former wid. of Benjamin Hayward, which see
Hardin, N.C., Jane, R11581
Hector, Pvt., Ct., BLWt.6621 iss. 5/17/1790
Henry/Harry, Pvt. Ct., BLWt.6661 iss. 1/19/1792 to Resolve Waldron, ass.
Henry, Ct., Electa, W2889
Henry, Ct., Cont., R.I., Eunice Mott, former wid., W24163
Henry, Cont., N.J., Sarah, W18353
Henry (colored), Md., Esther/Easter, W3638; BLWt.67674-160-55
Henry, Mass., S21580
Henry, N.J., S1153
Henry, N.Y., S35735
Henry, R.I., S11828
Henry, Dis., res. Rowan Co., N.C.
Henry A., N.Y. Art., BLWt.2370-200-Lt. iss. 2/11/1791. No papers
Hickman, N.C., Winna, R11629

WILLIAMS (continued)
Hiel, Ct., Abigail, W6513; BLWt.26176-160-55
Hiram, Mass., N.Y., R11582
Ichabod, N.Y., S28952
Isaac, Ct., S44224
Isaac, Ct., Nancy, W6500; BLWt. 26371-160-55
Isaac, Ct., Cont., S15719
Isaac, Cont., BLWt.971-100 N.J. res. in 1799
Isaac, Mass., Susannah, S34558; S1971
Isaac, Mass., Hannah, W19633
Isaac, Mass., Hannah, W22638
Isaac, Mass., Elizabeth, R11577
Isaac, N.J., S33927
Isaac, Va., S16297
Isaac, Va., S31485
Isaiah, Vt., R11584
Jabez, Pvt., Ct., BLWt.6664 iss. 12/22/1791 to Peter Fairchild, ass.
Jabez, R.I., S17796
Jacob, Ct., Mary, W18422
Jacob, Ct., Frances, R11580
Jacob, Mass., Joanna, R11586
James, Ct., Grace, W19640
James, Del., Eleanor, W6510; BLWt.34820-160-55
James, Md., S40712
James, Md., Pa., Va., S3590; BLWt.26873-160-55
James, Mass., S43327
James, Mass., S44076
James, Mass., Bethiah, W1343; BLWts.96-60-55 & 5281-100-1792
James, Mass., Submit Gould, former wid., W17956. She also applied for pension on account of services of her last husb., Seth Gould, which see
James, N.Y., S23488
James, N.Y., S32070
James, N.Y., Barbara, W26066
James, N.C., S31487
James, N.C., R11585, b. on St. Lawrence River - Parents en route to Ireland
James, Pvt. Pa., BLWt.10560 iss. 10/31/1791 to Jasper Keiner, ass.
James, Pa., S40690
James, Va., Elizabeth, W6502
James, Va., Pattey, W6506
James, Va., Mary, W6515
James, Va., Mary, W9895
James, Va., BLWt.2427-300-Capt. iss. 4/2/1790
James, Va., & War of 1812, S32607
James M., Va., Wilmoth, W6505
Jared, Va., See N.A. Acc. No. 874-050201 Not Half Pay. No pension file identified for this sold.
Jarius, N.J., Lydia, W26058
Jarratt/Gerard, Md., Pa., Ruth Ann, W2981
Jeremiah, Md., Mary, R11602; BLWt.875-100
Jeremiah, Mass., N.H., S11823

WILLIAMS (continued)

Jeremiah, N.C., S42077
Jeremiah, Pa., Mary, W2710; BLWt.29020-160-55
Jeremiah, R.I., Amey N., W14159
Jesse, Md., Va., S30803
Jesse, Vt., S14861
Job, N.C., Celia, W18344
Job, Vt., Alice, W16477
Joel, N.J., Eunice, W215
John, Ct., S11809
John, Ct., S11851
John, Ct., Polly, W26067; BLWt.29008-160-55
John, Ct., Cont., S14873
John, Ct., Navy, S23072
John, Cont., N.Y., S41343
John, Cont., N.C., Martha/Patsey W177; BLWt.2181-160-55, b. N.C.
John, Pvt. Md., BLWt.11827 iss. 5/11/1790
John, Md., S35120
John, Md., S35142
John, Md., Molly, W9016
John, Md., BLWt.1363-100
John, Md., Va., Mildred, W19635, d. 1837 or 1841
John, Mass., S11803
John, Mass., S11860
John, Mass., S34542
John, Mass., S34552
John, Mass., S34555; BLWt.2296-300-Capt. iss. 2/27/1790
John, Mass., S37559
John, Mass., Sea Service, Navy, & Privateers, War of 1812, Sally, W14176
John, Corp., N.J., BLWt.8827 iss. 10/16/178? to Benj. Harris, ass.
John, Pvt., N.J., BLWt.8829 iss. 9/23/1789
John, Pvt. N.J., BLWt.8841 iss. 9/11/1792
John, N.J., S33914
John, N.J., S33926
John, Pvt. N.Y., BLWt.7972 iss. 4/19/1791 to Moses Hetfield, admr.
John, Pvt., N.Y., BLWt.8008 iss. 12/9/1791 to Philip Rockafeller, ass.
John, N.Y., S3593
John, N.Y., S32069
John, N.Y., Nancy, R11605
John, N.Y., Va., S44084
John, N.C., S3592, b. N.C.
John, N.C., Mary Lumpkin, former wid., W9147; BLWt.1586-160-55 Her last husb., John P. Lumkin was a Revolutionary War soldier.
John, N.C., R11587, b. in N.C.
John, N.C., R11588, b. in Va.
John, N.C., R11592
John, N.C., Va., Abiah, W18436, b. in Va.
John, N.C. and 1812, Judith, W9017
John, Not Rev. War, Ky. Mil. Gen. Harman's War -- 1790, Old War Inv. File 26515
John, Pvt. Pa., BLWt.10613 iss. 12/13/1791 to John Paul Schott,

WILLIAMS (continued)

ass.
John, Pvt. Pa., BLWt.10624 iss. 1/17/1792 to George Moore, ass.
John, Fifer, Pa., BLWt.10627 iss. 7/16/1789
John, Pa., S3582
John, Pa., S40692
John, Pa., Susannah, W3124
John, Pa., Susannah, W18348
John, Pa., Va., S40697
John, R.I., S11817
John, R.I., Betsey, W26028
John, Sgt. Va., BLWt.12647 iss. 4/6/1790 to John Williams
John, Va., S3577; BLWt.26145-160-55, res. Morgan Co., Tenn.
John, Va., S6413, res. Hanover Co., Va.
John, Va., S6419, res. Buckingham Co., Va.
John, Va., S14874, res. Mobile Co., Ala.
John, Va., S41348, res. Albemarle Co., Va.
John, Va., Mary, W4390, res. Chesterfield Co., Va. prior to 1842
John, Va., Margaret, W6511; See N.A. Acc. No.874-050193 Half Pay John Williams
John, Va., Winnefred, W9015
John, Va., Nancy, W26060; BLWt. 26743-160-55
John, Va., R11594, res. Forsyth Co., Ga.
John, Va., R19105 Va. Half Pay, Act 7/5/1832. See N.A. Acc. No. 874-050193A Half Pay John Williams
John, Va., R20123, res. Chesterfield Co., Va.
John J., N.C., Nancy, R19099
Jonathan, Mass., S41342
Jonathan, N.J., S1154
Joseph, Ct., S40704
Joseph, Ct., Navy, S14868
Joseph, Cont., Md., S; BLWt.1841-100, res. Md. in 1832
Joseph, Cont., Mass., S11841. Also in French & Indian War and probably in War of 1812
Joseph, Cont., Pa., S40702, res. Pa. in 1818
Joseph, Del., Md., S41341
Joseph, Mass., S29551
Joseph, Mass., BLWt.2298-300-Capt. iss. 4/1/1790 to Joseph Williams. No papers
Joseph, N.H., Abigail Fox, former wid., R3720. See Rev. pen-claim of Ebenezer Fox. The inquirer for this sold's. record should be furnished that one also. Data not quite definite enough to say Abigail was the wid. of Ebenezer Fox
Joseph, N.Y., R11596
Joseph, N.C., S32065, b. N.C.
Joseph, N.C., Sarah, W9891
Joseph, N.C., Christina, R11595

WILLIAMS (continued)

BLWt.45589-160-55
Joseph, Pvt. "in the Artillery" Pa., BLWt.10643 iss. 11/1/1791
Joseph Terry, Va., S32604
Joshua, Pvt. Ct., BLWt.6607 iss. 1/11/1799 to Sylvester Fuller, ass.
Joshua, Cont., Mass., S38470
Joshua, Mass., Sarah, W2390; BLWt.26479-160-55
Joshua, N.J., R11597
Joshua, Pvt. Pa., BLWt.10598 iss. 6/30/1794 to Silas Hart, ass.
Joshua, Pa., Sarah, W2212; BLWt.34907-160-55
Joshua, Pa., BLWt.2395-300-Capt. iss. 12/12/1794 to Joshua Williams
Lawrence, Md., Polly, W9018
Lemuel, Cont., Mass., Anna, W22673
Levi/Levy, Va., S36393
Lew/Lewelling/Lewellen, Va., Winnefred, W1344; BLWt.36621-160-55. See N.A. Acc. No.874-050194 Not Half Pay Lew Williams
Lewellen, See Lew
Lewis, Pvt. Pa., BLWt.10664 iss. 6/27/1796
Lewis, Pa., S40696
Lucy, N.Y., former wid. of Samuel Boughton, which see
Lylburne, Md., BLWt.2408-300-Capt. iss. 2/24/1798
Mathias, Va., S3580
Matthew/Mathew (colored), Va., S6414
Matthias, N.J., S3583
Maurice/Moses, S.C., Martha, See Moses
Michael, Pa. See WILLHELM
Miles, N.J., S17785
Moses, S.C., Martha, W9013
Nathan, Ct., S49269
Nathan, Md., BLWt.1666-200
Nathan, Mass., N.Y., Hannah, W26029; BLWt.9185-160-55
Nathan, Mass., Vt., S7912
Nathan, N.C., Ann, W6514
Nathaniel, Ct., Naomi Menter, former wid., R19136
Nathaniel, Pvt. Mass., BLWt. 5239 iss. 2/28/1794 to Samuel Emery
Nathaniel, Mass., S44055
Nathaniel, Mass., Dinah, W2305
Nathaniel, Mass., Lucilda, W15495
Nathaniel, Mass., Hannah, W26015
Obed, Ct., S35741
Osborn, Md., S35129
Othaniel, Mass., S11795
Otho H., Cont., Md., BLWt.2401-850 Brig. Gen. iss. 5/25/1789
Pearson, Pa., S41354
Peleg, N.H., Sarah, W15493
Perez, Pvt. Mass., BLWt.5295 iss. 4/1/1790

WILLIAMS (continued)
Peter, Ct., S11829
Peter, Ct., Mary, W18435
Peter, Ga., Nancy, W6507
Peter, Pvt. N.J., BLWt.8871 iss. 6/11/1789 to Jonathan Dayton, ass.
Peter, N.Y., S14859
Philip, Va., S1269
Phinehas/Phineas, Vt., S7918
Prince, Ct. See STARKWEATHER
Remembrance, Va., R11612
Richard, Mass., Jane, W18429; BLWt.724-100
Richard, Corp. Lamb's Art. N.Y. BLWt.8053 iss. 6/19/1790
Richard, Va., R11613 Indian Warfare 1774
Richard, Va., R11614
Robert, Margaret, R11599, d. Fayette Co., Ala., 10/4/1845
Robert, Ct., Hannah Fitch, former wid., W10990
Robert, Ct., Cont., S17200
Robert, Cont., Mass., S19508; BLWt.2315-200-Lt. iss. 1/29/1790, d. 11/16/1834
Robert, Cont., Mass., S46081, d. 9/10/1818
Robert, Md. & Indian War, S26512
Robert, Mass., Navy, N.H., S43324
Robert, N.C., S7922, b. N.C.
Robert, N.C., S39129
Robert, Va., S41355
Robinson, Ct., S23493
Roger, Va., R11615
Roger M., Va., R11626
Ruth, N.Y., former wid. of Daniel Parrish, which see
Sally, N.C., former wid. of Jesse Steed, which see
Samuel, Mass., S30208
Samuel, Mass., Mercy, W16163
Samuel, N.H. & 21st Inf. War of 1812, S4725; O.W. Inv. File 26509, War of 1812; BLWt.1164-160-12
Samuel, N.J., Eunice, W2387
Samuel, N.C., S1738
Samuel, N.C., S7957
Samuel, N.C., R11617
Samuel, S.C., S11833
Samuel, S.C., R11619, b. N.C
Samuel F., N.C., R11618
Samuel William, Ct., Cont., Emily, W26071; BLWt.2347-300-Capt. iss. 5/14/1796
Shadrack/Shadrick, Va. Hannah, W154
Silas, Ct., Vt., R11620
Silas, Mass., S11778
Simeon, Ct., Prudence, R11609
Solomon, Ct., S14862
Solomon, Ct., Lucy, W20133
Solomon, Ct., Cont., S14867
Solomon, N.C., S3591
Sophia, Ct., former wid. of Enos Crane, which see
Squire, R.I., S21576
Stacey, Pvt. Pa., BLWt.10587 iss. 4/28/1791

WILLIAMS (continued)
Stacey/Stacy, Pa., S40688
Stephen, Mass., S18658
Stephen, N.C., S36846
Stephen, N.C., Mary/Polly, W9897; BLWt.98059-160-55
Stephen, N.C., Bidianee/Bediana, W26063
Stimson, Mass., Sally, W2308; BLWt.26043-160-55
Tall, See WILLIAM
Thaddeus, Ct., Dis.
Thomas, Ct., S6421
Thomas, Ct., S6428
Thomas, Ct., Content, W19645
Thomas, Ct., BLWt.1275-100 iss. 3/17/1828
Thomas, Cont. Mass., Elizabeth, R11578
Thomas, Cont., Pa., S34559 pens. in Ct.
Thomas, Del., S35728
Thomas, Ga., S.C., S7933
Thomas, Pvt., Md., BLWt.11845 iss. 12/24/1794 to John Hailey, admr.
Thomas, Mass., S6397
Thomas, Mass., S41340
Thomas, Mass., S44221
Thomas, Mass., Polly, W26038
Thomas, N.H., Olive, W18338
Thomas, N.C., Rebecca, R11611, Pvt. & Lt.
Thomas, N.C.(?), S.C., Rachel, R11610; BLReg. 276381-55, b. in Pa.
Thomas, Pvt. Pa., BLWt.10605 iss. 5/21/1792 to Moses Dill, ass.
Thomas, Pa., S40698, Pvt.
Thomas, R.I., Penelope, W26077
Thomas, Va., S3584, Pvt.
Thomas, Va., S11836, Pvt.
Thomas, Va., S14843, Pvt.
Thomas, Va., S31488, Pvt.
Thomas, Va., R11621, Pvt.
Thomas C., N.C., Nancy, W6509, b. in N.C.
Thomas P., N.Y., Elizabeth, R11579
Thomas P., N.C., S7940
Timothy, Privateer, R.I., Dinas W18444
Tobias, N.C., Jemima, W6516
Uriah, Cont., Ct., Johannah/Jehannah, W22665
Uriah, Pvt. N.Y., BLWt.8018 iss. 9/25/1790 to John Thompson, ass.
Uriah, N.Y., Polly, W15486
Veach, Ct., S17789
Warham/Wareham, Ct., Anna, W11856
Waring, N.C., S7946
Weeks/Wilks, See Wilks
Wilks, Ct., Tamer, W26059
William, Pvt., Ct., BLWt.6662 iss. 4/19/1792 to Isaac Bronson, ass.
William, Ct., S14832; BLWt.26358-160-55
William/William R., Ct., R11624

WILLIAMS (continued)
William, Cont., BLWt.2284-100 Mich. res. of heir in 1842
William, Cont., Mass., S19513
William, Cont., Mass., Susanna, W22652
William, Cont., N.C., BLWt.2202-300
William, Cont., Va., S36394
William, Pvt., Md., BLWts.11795 & 12681 iss. 1/30/1795 to John Stockdell, ass.
William, Md., S3587
William, Md.(?) - N.Y., S33928 pens. in Pa. and N.J.
William, Md., Va., R11627
William, N.J., Mary Ann, W4861; BLWt.12724-160-55
William, Dis. N.J. Agency
William, N.Y., S14853
William, N.Y., Va., Honour, W2307; BLWt.26185-160-55
William, N.C., S46082
William, N.C., Mary, W3907
William, N.C., Nancy, R11606
William, N.C., R11628
William, Pvt., Pa., BLWt.10553 iss. 12/20/1791 to George Walton, ass.
William, Pvt. Pa., BLWt.10567 iss. 7/16/1792
William, Pvt., Pa., BLWt.10579 iss. 12/13/179? to John Paul Schott, ass.
William, S.C., S32595, b. S.C.
William, S.C., Lucy, W9166
William, Va., S3576, b. Pa.
William, Va., S11831, b. Md.
William, Va., S32597, wid. Suzanne
William, Va., S38474
William, Va., S40694
William, Va., Margaret, W1967, b. in Pa.
William, Va., Mary, W3747; BLWt.11166-160-55
William, Va., Mary, W4102
William, Va., Elizabeth, W9014; BLWts.47-60-55 & 12666-100 iss. 5/8/1794
William, Va. (?), R11625, res. at time of application N.Y., wife Sarah
William R., Ct. See William
Willoughby, N.C., Nancy McMinn former wid., W36; BLWt.15177-160-55
Zebedee, N.C., S39131
WILLIAMSON, Alexander, Md., S7954
Calvin, S.C., S7949
Charles, N.C., S7939
Cuthbert, Va., Susannah, W4394
Deborix, N.C., Martha, W6521
Eleazer, Pa., S3597
Elijah, S.C., Sarah, W6518
Elizabeth, Cont.,Va., former wid. of Joseph Johnson, which see
Garrett, N.J., Johanna, W1019
George, Cont. Mass., S41346
Henry, N.J., Anna, W22670
Henry, Va., R11632

WILLIAMSON (continued)
Isaac, N.J., Anna, W6250
Isaac, N.C., Mary, W6522
Isaac, S.C., S7911
Jacob, N.J., S33917
Jacob, N.J., Martha, W2393; BLWt.26211-160-55
James, N.Y., S23487; BLWt.7970-100-Pvt. iss. 8/30/1790 to Volkert Veeder, ass.
James, Pa., S22597
James, Va., Nancy, R11604
Jedidiah, N.Y., Sophia, W19643
John, N.J., Sarah, W1016
John, Pvt., N.Y., BLWt.8101 iss. 9/15/1790 to John Post and Cornelius Haring, assnes.
John, N.Y., S11784
John, N.Y., S11854
John, N.Y., Hannah, W18447
John, Pvt., Pa., BLWt.10555 iss. 10/27/1792 to Frederick Mollineaux, ass.
John, Pa., S40705
John, S.C., BLWt.2363-300
John, Va., Martha, W6523
John, Va., Cynthia, W26061; BLWt.33529-160-55
John, Va., R11635
Joseph, Pa., S7908
Littleton, Ga., S3594
Marcus, N.Y., Mary, W26084
Matthias, N.J., S1152
Nathan, Ct., S11789
Nicholas, N.Y., Elizabeth, W22622
Peter, N.J., S3598
Peter, Not Rev., N.W. Indian War-St. Clair; BLWts.33418-80-50 & 48439-80-55,enl. in Md.
Robert, N.C., R11636
Samuel, N.Y., R11637
Thomas, Va., S16580
William, N.J., Helena, W4862
William, N.J., Lenah, W6519
William, N.C., Elizabeth, W1686; BLWt.18013-160-55
William, N.C., Polly, W18356
William, Pa., Elizabeth, R11638
William, Va., Rosa, W3637; BLWt.26667-160-55
WILLIFORD, Jacob, N.C., S1737, b. in Va.
Jesse, Va., Cherry, W4865; BLWt.15169-160-55
Jordan, Va., S6404; BLWt.26148-160-55
Nathan, S.C., S32066, b. in Va.
Richard, N.C. See WILLEFORD
Willis, N.C., S42074
WILLIGER, Peter V. See TERWILLIGER
WILLIN, Levin, Md., Sea Service, S7921
WILLING, John C., Mass., S33912
John Christopher, Pvt. Crane's Cont. Art., Mass., BLWt.5343 iss. 3/10/1796 or 1790
WILLINGTON, Elisha, Mass., BLWt. 2397-200-Lt. iss. 2/27/1797 to John Kessler, ass., also recorded as BLWt.2679. No papers

WILLINGTON (continued)
Jonathan, Pvt. or Drum Major, Mass., BLWt.5232 iss. 7/-/----
John, Mass., See WELLINGTON
Josiah, Cont., Mass., S34547; BLWt.2330-200-Lt. iss. 4/18/1796 to Jeremiah Mason, ass.
Oliver, Cont., Mass. See WELLINGTON
Samuel, Mass., S11801
Thomas, Mass., BLWt.2327-300-Capt. iss. 3/12/1792 to Benj. Haskell, ass. No papers
WILLIS, Abisha, Mass., S30205
Andrew, Md., S35141
Azariah, Mass., S34536
Bailey, Va., S39894
Benjamin, Cont., N.Y., Bridget W19634; BLWt.18217-160-55
Benjamin, Pvt. Lee's Legion, BLWt.13928 iss. 7/16/1790 to Wm. I. or J. Vreedenburgh, ass.
Britton, S.C., S1270
Caleb, Mass., S44217
Caleb, Mass., former wid. Patty Wood/Woods, former wid., W22696
Charles, Navy, Mass., S34543. Also in service on land
Daniel, Cont., Ct., S44064
Daniel, Md., BLWt.2440-100
Ebenezer, Mass., Thankful, W14178
Edmund, Mass., S16024
Edward, Va., Hannah, W9005; BLWt.31739-160-55
Ezra, Mass., Susannah, W19632
George, N.C., R11639
George, N.C., R11661
Henry, N.J., S3560
Henry, N.Y., S11782
Hezekiah, Cont., Mass., Abigail W18343
James, Mass., Allice, W18427
James, Mass., Sarah, W22644; BLWt.12708-160-55
James, Mass., BLWt.951-100
James, Va., S6417
Jarvis, Md., S39128
John, Mass., S6402
John, Mass., S11805
John, N.Y., R11640
John, Va., S1603
John, Va., S41351
John, Va., BLWt.2423-400-Major
Jonathan, Mass., S41360
Joseph, Pvt. Mass., BLWt.5296 iss. 3/10/1790
Joseph, Mass., S34537
Joseph, Mass., S44057
Joseph, N.J., Grace, W3639
Joseph, N.C., Jemima, W1017; BLWt.14990-160-55
Lewis
Meshach, Ga., S39124
Russell, N.J., Mary, W19629; BLWt.26038-160-55
Silas, Mass., S22061
Silvanus, Ct., N.H., Eunice, See WILLES
Smith, Pa., Eleanor, W321; BLWt.67580-160-55
Thomas, N.Y., Huldah/Huldeh, W1015

WILLIS (continued)
Thomas, N.Y., Anna, W6526; BLWt.26824-160-55
William, Mass., Sea Service, Pa., S7900
William, N.J., S845
William, N.J., Phebe Kitchel, former wid., W949
William, Pvt. Va., BLWt.12687 iss. 1/31/1794 to Francis Graves, ass.
William, Va., S39125
Zacharias, Pvt. Mass., BLWt.5241 iss. 12/22/1791
Zenas, Mass., See WYLLYS
WILLISON, William, Pa., N.Y., S11812
WILLISTON, Caleb, Mass., Mary, W22640; BLWt.26521-160-55
Godfrey, Mass., Lydia, W22631
Ichabod, R.I., S21586
Payson, Ct., S17787; BLWt.26118-160-55
WILLIT, John, N.J. See WILLET
Samuel, N.J. See WILLET
WILLITS, Isaac, Sgt. N.J., BLWt. 8843 iss. 4/8/1791 to James Hyndshaw, ass.
WILLKEY, John, R.I., S39888
WILLMAN, Benoni, Cont., Mass., S14858
John, Ct., Phebe, See WELLMON
WILLMARTH, Amos, Mass. See WILMARTH
Nathaniel, Mass., S22602
Thomas, Mass., S33918
WILLMOT, John, Pvt. N.Y., BLWt. 7951 iss. 10/11/1790 to Henry Tremper, ass.
Timothy, Ct., Cont., Polly, W26036
WILLMOTH, William, See WILMOT
WILLMOTT, William, See WILMOT
WILLOUGHBY, Alexander, Va., S31481
Bliss, Ct., S7914
Ebenezer, N.H., R11643
Edlyne, Va., S7941
Henry, Va., S6415; BLWt.15434-160-55
Josiah, Vt., Susannah, W26050
Salmon, Ct., Ruby, W2634; BLWt.28598-160-55
Samuel, Ct., Privateer, S11807
William, Ga., S36396
William, Va., Sarah, W18345
WILLOUGHLY, Edlyne, See WILLOUGHBY
WILLS, Conrad, Pa., S40707
Enoch, Pvt. Pa., BLWt.10589 iss. 11/27/1794 to Joseph Pall, ass.
James, Mass., R.I., Patty, W2306; BLWt.13710-160-55
James, Va., S17198
Joel, Ct., S19166
John, Dis. Md. Agency
John, Mass., Navy, Mary, W14172
Jonathan, Ct., Cont., Lydia, W19644
Leonard, N.C., Sarah, W26027; BLWt.31715-160-55
Lewis, Va., Elinder, W1018
Nathaniel, Pvt. Va., BLWt.12665

WILLS (continued)
iss. 2/18/1793 to Robert Means, ass. Note: "Iss. a cert. of this record 8/26/1818 to a man who called himself Nathaniel Walls who I take to be the same."
Nathaniel, Cont., Va., Mildred, R11645
Richard, Pa., S42615
Thomas C., Md., S3561
William, Cont., Va., S3494
William, Va., S31484
WILLSE, Abraham, N.Y., S28947
Henry T., N.Y., Margaret, W26034
Jacob, Cont., N.Y., Bethia, W22628
James, N.Y., Dorothy, W6539; BLWt.28623-160-55
WILLSEY, Henry T., See WILLSE
Jacob, Cont., N.Y., Abigail Riker, W28001. Her last husb., Gerardus Riker, N.J. & N.Y., was also a pensioner, which see
William, Pvt. N.Y., BLWt.8029 iss. 8/4/1791
WILLSIE, William, N.Y., S44063
WILLSON, Alexander, Mass., Catharine, W11834, b. 6/15/1761. Enl. in Mass. In 1818 res. of Chautauqua Co., N.Y., d. 9/7/1843 at Harbour Creek Twp., Erie Co., Pa.
Andrew, N.Y., S11849, b. 1/16/1761 Montgomery, Orange Co., N.Y. & res. there at enl. and in 1832.
Andrew, N.Y., S16293, res. during Rev. Cherry Valley & Florida, N.Y.; res. in 1832 Middlefield, Otsego Co., N.Y. aged 75 yrs.
Hue/Hugh, N.H., S41339, enl. at Salem, N.Y. In 1820 aged about 56 yrs., res. Springfield, Windsor Co., Vt., wife Betsey. In 1825 res. Lisbon, St. Lawrence Co., N.Y.
Isaac, Mass., Vt., See WOOLSON
James, Mass., S6398, son of William, b. 4/4/1754 at Graystreet, 7 mi. from Londonderry, Ireland; res. from 1772 to 1832 Oakham & Barre, Worcester Co., Mass.
James, N.J., S33916. In 1820 aged 68 yrs. & res. Franklin Twp., Somerset Co., N.J.
James, N.C., Amelia/Milly, W9008; BLWt.31742-160-55, res. during Rev. about 30 mi. from Guilford Co., N.C., d. 10/17/1811 at his res. in Livingston Co., Ky.
John, Ct., S15713, b. 1/23/1764 at Fairfield, Fairfield Co., Ct. & res. there at enl. and in 1832
John, Ct., R11668, b. 12/1760; wives Keziah & Mariam; res. at enl. Middletown, Middlesex Co. Ct., d. 7/6/1843 at Whitestown,

WILLSON (continued)
Oneida Co., N.Y.
John, Mass., S11796, b. 4/16/1764 at Petersham, Worcester Co., Mass.; res. at enl. Bolton Worcester Co., Mass.; res. after Rev. N.H. and Vt. Res. in 1832 Louisville Twp., St. Lawrence Co., N.Y., d. 10/16/1847
John, Mass., S15710, b. 1755 in York, Me. (Mass.) & res. there at enl.; res. 1832 in Castine, Hancock Co., Me.
John, N.J., S844, b. 1/13/1755 at Potterstown, Hunterdon Co., N.J.; res. at enl. Bloomsbury, Hunterdon Co., N.J.; res. in 1832 Mansfield Twp., Warren Co., N.J.
John, N.J., War of 1812, S33915; b. N.J. & res. in 1818 at Warren Twp., Somerset Co., N.J., aged 53 yrs.
John, N.C., Va., Elizabeth, W2391 b. 11/30/1756 in Md., res. at enl. Albemarle Co., Va., and Surry Co., N.C.; res. in 1833 Pulaski Co., Ky. & there d. 10/26/1844
Joseph, Ct., Eleanor, W18443; res. at enl. Fairfield Co., Ct. d. at Weston, Fairfield Co., Ct. 9/7/1830 aged 76 yrs.
Joseph, Mass., S6429, b. 1/16/1762 at New Braintree, Worcester Co., Mass. & res. there at enl.; res. in 1833 Leicester, Worcester Co., Mass.
Josiah, N.J., N.Y., S44093; in 1819 res. Morris Co., N.J., in 1821 aged 62 yrs. res. New York City, and wife Jemima
Luke, Mass., S41361; in 1820 aged 66 yrs. res. Putney, Windham Co., Vt., wife Anna
Moore, Cont., Va., S44078; enl. in Westmoreland & Richmond Cos. Va. In 1821 aged 71 yrs. res. Wayne, Steuben Co., N.Y., wife Christina
Nathaniel, N.J., S3567, b. 12/23/1750. In 1832 res. Morris Co., N.J.
Nathaniel, R.I., S39896; in 1823 aged 69 yrs. res of Bristol Co., R.I., d. 5/31/1826
Paul, Cont., Mass., S35732, b. 7/21/1755 at Bolton, Worcester Co., Mass. & res. there at enl.; in 1818 and 1834 res. Saratoga Co., N.Y.; in 1842 res. Caldwell Co., Ky.
Richard, Cont., Md., S35121; res. of Queen Anne Co., Md.; in 1818 aged 63 yrs. & res. of Baltimore, Md.
Robert, Pa., S33937; enl. at Chambersburgh, Cumberland Co., Pa.; in 1818 aged 74 yrs. res. Morris Co., N.J.

WILLSON (continued)
Samuel, Cont., Mass., S44074 enl. at Concord, Mass. In 1820 aged 61 yrs. & res. Stoddard, Cheshire Co., N.H.
Samuel, Mass., Ann, W16474; in 1820 aged 59 yrs. & res. Saratoga Co., N.Y., d. 1/7/1834
Samuel, Pvt. N.H., BLWts.3173 & 3549 iss. 12/28/1796 to Christopher S. Thorn, ass.
Samuel, N.Y., Helen, W22656; BLWt.6419-160-55; b. 11/18/1754 in Glasgow (Blanford), Berkshire Co., Mass.; res. at enl. Cherry Valley, Otsego Co., N.Y. & Florida, N.Y; res. in 1832 Middlefield, Otsego Co., N.Y. & d. there 8/25/1836
Samuel, Pa., S22591; b. 3/17/1748, res. at enl. Cumberland Co., Pa. and in 1833
Sarah, Ct., former wid. of Samuel Dix, which see
Solomon, Mass., S21587, b. 9/26/1760 in Petersham, Worcester Co., Mass. & res. there at enl.; in 1832 res. of Chester, Windsor Co., Vt.
Thomas, Ct., S44091, enl. at Stamford, Ct. In 1820 aged 60 yrs. res. Brutus, Cayuga Co., N.Y., wife Phebe
William, Pvt. Mass., BLWt.5234 iss. 8/18/1797 to Simeon Wyman
William, N.C., Elizabeth, W18352; res. of Johnston Co., N.C. & d. there in Oct. 1830
William, R.I., S11822, b. South Kingston, Washington Co., R.I. and always lived there to 1832, then 71 yrs. old.
William, S.C., R11689, b. 6/30/1747 on Potomac near location of Washington, D.C., res. at enl. York Co., S.C., wife Anne, d. 4/18/1842 in Jackson Co., Ga.
William, Va., S6393; also served in 1774, Ind. War; b. 11/7/1745 in Augusta Co., Va. & res. there always up to 1832
WILLY, John, N.J., Dorothy, R11532
Joseph, Va., Mary, R11561
WILLYARD, Henry, Pa., Agnes, W9892; BLWt.26151-160-55
WILLYS, Thomas, Ct., Cont., S17784
WILMARTH, Amos, Mass., Eunice, W15494
Benjamin, Mass., Huldah, W18415
Ebenezer, Mass., S33922
Ebenezer, Mass., R11646
Eliphalet, Mass., S17788
Ephraim, Vt., Dis.
Jonathan, Mass., S31492
Joseph, Mass., S30209
Nathaniel, Mass., S22602
Samuel, Mass., S35737
Stephen, Mass., R11647
Thomas, Mass. See WILLMARTH
WILMORE, Christopher, Va., Peggy,

WILMORE (continued)
W6557
John, Pvt. Md., BLWt.11809 iss. 4/24/1797 to James De Baufre, ass.
WILMOT, Timothy, Ct. See WILLMOTT
Walter, Cont., Ct., S35736
William, Md., BLWt.281-300
WILMOTH, Francis, Pvt. N.Y., BLWt. 8002 iss. 7/17/1792 to Jasper Cropsey, ass.
William, N.C., S32596
WILMOTKNOT, George, Pvt. Pa., BLWt.10639 iss. 7/22/1799 to Abraham Dell, ass.
WILMOTT, Elijah, Ct., R11648
Robert, Md., BLWt.2415-200-Lt. iss. 1/28/1800. No papers
WILRICK, Jacob, Pvt. Pa., BLWt. 10568 iss. 3/8/1793
WILSEY, Isaac, Pvt. N.Y., BLWt. 7956 iss. 8/4/1790 to Ebenezer and Justin Foote, assnes.
James/Jacobus, Cont., N.Y., R11650
James, N.Y. See WILLSE
William, N.Y., R11651
WILSHIRE, John, Ga., Va., S6425
WILSIE, Jacob, Pvt. N.Y., BLWt. 8036 iss. 10/12/1790 to Henry S. Platt, ass.
Jacob, Cont. N.Y., See WILLSE
WILSON, Aaron, Mass., N.H., Betsey W26044, res. at enl. Kittery, York Co., Me., d. 7/17/1825
Aaron, N.H., S11827, b. 1758 at Petersham, Mass.; res. at enl. Keene, Cheshire Co., N.H., res. in 1833 Swansey, Cheshire Co., N.H.
Abiel/Abial, Ct., S35739; enl. at Windsor, Hartford Co., Ct. & res. there in 1818 aged 64 yrs.
Abiel, Mass., S44080; enl. at Andover, Essex Co., Mass. In 1819 aged 59 yrs. & res. of Wilton, Hillsborough Co., N.H.
Abraham, N.Y., Joanna Rose, former wid., W5714; BLWts.7948-100; 318-60-55. Son of Thomas; res. during Rev. Washington Co. N.Y., also lived in Rensselaer Co., N.Y., d. in summer of 1805 in Otsego Co., N.Y.
Abraham, Va., Elizabeth, W6532, b. 1759 in Spotsylvania Co., Va. & lived there in 1832, res. at enl. Culpeper Co., Va. d. 8/10/1841
Albert, N.J., N.Y., S3566, b. 2/14/1755 at Woodbridge, N.J., res. during Rev. New York City, Haverstraw, N.Y., Bergen Co., N.J. In 1832 res. Bergen Co., N.J.
Alexander, Cont. Pa., S44061; enl. at Allentown, Pa. In 1820 aged 66 yrs. & res. Phila., Pa. In 1822 res. N.Y.
Alexander, Pvt. Mass., BLWt.

WILSON (continued)
5307 iss. 10/4/1790 to Th. Shenkland
Andrew, Cont., Pa., S39900. In 1820 aged 61 yrs. & res. Lycoming Co., Pa., wife Elizabeth
Andrew, N.Y., Nelly, R11679; res. during Rev. Hampstead, Orange Co. (later called Rampo, Rockland Co., N.Y.) N.Y., d. 11/9/1822, b. 3/10/1762
Andrew, N.C., Mary, R11674 (went to service from East Tenn., d. 12/11/1811)
Andrew, Pa., S35725; in 1818 aged 63 yrs. & res. of Fleming Co., Ky.
Andrew, Va., S3570, b. 7/15/1761 in Ireland, enl. in Rockbridge Co., Va.; in 1832 res. Fairfield Twp., Butler Co., Ohio
Andrew, R11653, b. 1741 in Tyrone Co., Ireland, came to U.S. from Ireland after Rev., in 1833 res. of Lewis Co., Va.
Archibald, Pa., Mary, R11694, res. at enl. Milestown, Phila. Co., Pa., d. 7/2/1817
Archibald, Va., Martha, W4863; res. of Mecklenburg Co., Va. In 1820 aged 64 yrs. & res. Guilford Co., N.C., d. 12/21/1828
Artemas, Mass., Cata, W26025; b. 2/14/1757 in Westminster, Mass. & res. there at enl., res. in 1833 Fitzwilliam, Cheshire Co., N.H., d. 4/30/1847
Asa, Ct., Joanna, W26037; res. at enl. Enfield, Ct., res. in 1832 Fairfield, Franklin Co., Vt., aged 69 yrs., d. 9/1/1837
Asa, N.J., S17203, b. near New Brunswick, N.J. & res. there at enl., in 1834 res. Greene Co., Pa., aged 73 yrs. In 1840 res. Preston Co., Va.
Augustin, N.C., S7920, b. 8/4/1755 in Lunenberg Co., Va., res. at enl. Dobbs Co., N.C., res. in 1833 Washington Co., Ga.
Augustin/Augustus, See Augustus
Augustus, N.C., R11654. Also served in 1790 & 1794, b. 5/4/1759 in Md., res. at enl. N.C. (in what was later Sullivan Co. Tenn.); res. in 1848 Anderson Co., Tenn.
Barnaby, Pvt. Md., BLWt.11819 iss. 3/11/1791. Offical Note: "On 3/24/1835 this Wt. was sent from Gen. Land Office to this office and returned with a cert. that it had never been registered on the books of this office and that Wt. No.2067 for 100 acres had been iss. 9/22/1834 to the heirs of Barney Wilson, that being the name as found in the final settlement of cert. in the 4th Md. Regt."

WILSON (continued)
Barney, Md., BLWt.2067-100; d. at Baltimore in 1799/1800
Benjamin, Cont.,Pa., Hannah, W9162; res. at enl. York Co., Pa., d. 7/12/1825 in Nicholas Co., Ky.
Benjamin, Mass., Nabby/Abigail, W26022, b. 11/25/1748 at Northborough, Worcester Co. & res. there at enl., d. 12/20/1832 at Paxton, Worcester Co., Mass.
Benjamin, N.J., S3568, b. 3/29/1762 at Middletown, Monmouth Co., N.J. & res. there at enl. and in 1832
Benjamin, N.J., S6424, b. 6/25/1751 in Somerset Co., N.J. & res. there at enl., in 1832 res. of Washington Co., Pa.
Calvin, Pvt. Ct., BLWt.6656 iss. 10/16/1789 to Theodosius Fowler, ass.
Calvin, Ct., Submit, W18424, res. at enl. & until death 5/20/1808 was Windsor, Hartford Co., Ct., Pognonock Parish
Charles, Mass., Experience Jordan former wid., W26798; d. 7/30/1778
Daniel, N.J., S843, b. 8/4/1755 in West Windsor, Middlesex Co., N.J., there at enl. In 1832 res. of East Windsor, N.J.
Daniel S., Ct., S14837, b. 1/2/1757 at Harwinton Co., Ct. & res. there at enl., d. 5/25/1834
David, Ct., Cont., S39898
David, Cont. Mass., S33930. In 1820 aged 75 yrs. & res. Middlesex Co., Mass.
David, Pvt. Md., BLWt.11799 iss. 10/6/1794 to Henry Purdy, ass.
David, Md., S35119; enl. at Chester Town, Eastern Shore of Md. In 1820 aged 64 yrs. res. Washington Co., Md. (a colored man)
David, Pa., S3563, res. at enl. York Co., Pa. In 1832 aged 80 yrs. & a res. of Adams Co., Pa., d. 7/22/1846
David, Va., Elizabeth/Eliza Shoemaker, former wid., W11445; BLWt.113205-160-55. In 1819 aged 66 yrs. res. Wilson Co., Ky. & d. there 12/18/1835
David, Va., Elizabeth, BLReg. No. 94814-55
Ebenezer, Mass., S44058; res. at enl. in vicinity of Salem & Beverly, Mass. In 1820 aged 56 yrs., res. Troy, Rensselaer Co., N.Y.
Edward, Mass., S35124; in 1820 aged 58 yrs. res. North Yarmouth Me., wife Elizabeth
Edward, Va., S41362; in 1829 aged about 70 yrs. & res. of Mecklenburg Co., Va.

WILSON (continued)
Eli B., Va., S6401, b. Augusta Co. (later Pendleton Co.) Va., res. at enl. & in 1832 Pendleton Co., Va., aged 77 yrs., d. 11/11/1845; widow Hannah.
Elizabeth, Cont. Pa., former wid. of Andrew Besterfield, which see
Elnathan, Ct., S24014, b. 2/23/1762 at Horseneck, Greenwich Twp., Fairfield Co., Ct., res. at enl. Horseneck, Ct., res. in 1832 Wilkesbarre, Luzerne Co., Pa.
Enoch, Mass., S30211, b. 11/4/1758 in Needham, Norfolk Co., Mass. & res. there at enl. In 1837 res. of Wrentham, Norfolk Co., Mass.
Ephraim, Cont., Mass., S33931. In 1820 aged 59 yrs., res. Carlisle, Middlesex Co., Mass. wife Alice
Ephraim, Mass., Privateer, S29554 b. 2/14/1762 at Northboro, Worcester Co., Mass. & res. at enl., res. in 1832 Barre, Worcester Co., Mass.
Ephraim, Pa., S32609, b. 7/18/1756 in Sussex Co., Del., res. at enl. Washington Co., Pa.
Francis, Mass., S34546. In 1818 he was 76 yrs. old & res. of Holden, Worcester Co., Mass.; b. about 1740
Galbreath, Pvt. Va., BLWt.12654 iss. 11/5/1789
George, Pvt. Ct., BLWt.6690 iss. 1/28/1792 to Moses Sill, ass.
George, Ct., S23079, b. 1757 at Simsbury, Hartford Co., Ct. & res. there at enl. In 1832 res. Phelps, Ontario Co., N.Y.
George, Md., S32076, b. 7/1/1750 res. at enl. Talbot Co., Md., res. in 1832 Walton Co., Ga.
George, N.C., Va., S6391; res. at enl. Anson Co., N.C., in 1833 aged 73 yrs. & res. Lewis Co., Va.
Gilbreath, Cont., Md., S39903; enl. in Md. In 1820 aged 78 yrs., res. Allegheny Co., Pa., wife Christina
Goodwin, Gen. Hosp., Pa., BLWt. 2458-450-Surg. Iss. 10/27/1789 to Jos. Crocker, admr. of Job Sumner, late ass. No papers
Gowen, Mass., Abigail, R11652, res. of Chemsfield & Columbia, Washington Co., Me., d. 6/22/1825
Henry, Cont., Mass., Eunice, W22643; in 1818 aged 57 yrs. & res. Rowe, Franklin Co., Mass., d. 4/14/1826 at Sherburne, Rutland Co., Vt.
Henry, N.C., Mary, W11852; BLWt. 31768-160-55, b. 9/4/1763 on Tarr River, N.C., res. at enl. Dobbs. Co., N.C., res. in 1832 Darlington Dist., S.C., d. 11/22/1838
Henry, Va., S30795, b. in Augusta Co., Va. & res. there at enl., in 1832 res. of Montgomery Co., Ky., aged 71 yrs.
Henry, Va., S41356; enl. in Rockbridge Co., Va. In 1820 aged 92 yrs. & res. of Augusta Co., Va.
Hosea, Del., BLWt.1793-100, d. 11/12/1798
Isaac, Mass., S34538; in 1820 aged 54 yrs. & res. Bedford, Middlesex Co., Mass.
Isaac, Mass., Vt., See WOOLSON
Isaac, N.H., BLReg.311642-1855
Isaac, Pa., S18661, b. 10/22/1758 in Morris Co., N.J., res. at enl. Northumberland Co., Pa., res. in 1832 Clark Co., Ohio; d. 5/11/1841
Isaac, Va., 1785 Ind. War, R11656, res. in 1833 Washington Co., Ohio
Israel, N.Y., S40718; in 1824 aged 68 yrs. & res. Canajoharie, Montgomery Co., N.Y. In 1836 res. Geauga Co., Ohio
Jacob, Ct., Cont., Ruth, W22621; res. at enl. Plainfield, Ct., d. 8/15/1833 at Sardinia, Erie Co., N.Y.
James, Cont., Ct., R11658, b. Middletown, Ct., 11/18/1764, res. there at enl. In 1832 res. Whitestown, Oneida Co., N.Y.
James, Cont., N.Y., Pa., R11657 b. 1759 in Pa., res. at enl. Skenesborough (Whitehall), Washington Co., N.Y., d. 4/21/1836 at Whitehall
James, Ga., R11664, b. 4/11/1761 in Raferts Fort, near Broad River, S.C., res. at enl. Richmond Co., Ga., res. in 1835 Sumter Co., Ala.
James, Pvt. Md., BLWt.11831 iss. 11/29/1790 to Barney Wilson, admr.
James, Md., S35727, b. 3/12/1763, enl. at Frederick Town, Md.,in 1804 res. of Clarke Co., Ky.
James, Mass. See WILLSON
James, N.H., Hitty H./Hetty H., W1966, b. 11/17/1750, enl. at Chester, Rockingham Co., N.H., d. 9/6/1824 at Chester, N.H.
James, N.H., R---, b. 7/13/1757 in Plainfield, Ct., res. at enl. Planfield, N.H.; after Rev. in Vt., res. in 1832 Marcy, Oneida Co., N.Y.
James, Pvt., N.J., BLWt.8867 iss. 10/24/1792 to John Phillips, ass.
James, N.J., S3571, b. 1748 in Monmouth Co., N.J. & res. there at enl. In 1832 res. Trumbull Co., Ohio
James, N.J., S36850; in 1820 aged 67 yrs. & res. of Litchfield Co., Ct.
James, Pvt. N.Y., BLWt.8013 iss. 5/14/1793 or 1790 to Thomas Russell, ass.
James, N.Y., S23076, b. 1748 on Long Island, res. at enl. & in 1832 Clarkstown, Rockland Co., N.Y.
James, N.Y., Elizabeth, W16479; d. 9/28/1807
James, N.Y., Martha, W18431, b. 5/15/ or 26/1747 at West Greenwich, R.I., res. at enl. Claverack, Columbia Co., N.Y., d. 4/7/1823
James, N.C., S3565, b. 9/25/1757 in Mecklenburgh Co., N.C. & res. there at enl., d. 4/11/1843
James, N.C., S7938, b. 1760 in Rowan Co., N.C. & res. there at enl. In 1832 res. Iredell Co. (Rowan), N.C.
James, N.C., Amelia, See WILLSON
James, N.C., Phebe, R11684, res. at enl. Burke Co., N.C., d. 1834
James, N.C., S.C., R11663, b. 7/12/1758 in Pa., res. at enl. Orange Co., N.C., res. in 1832 Franklin Co., Ga.
James, Pvt. Pa., BLWt.10642 iss. 9/7/1790 to Joseph Ashton, ass.
James, Pa., S7898, b. Tyrone Co., Ireland, res. at enl. Oxford, Chester Co., Pa., res. in 1832 Youngstown, Trumbull Co., Ohio, aged 86 or 87 yrs., d. 11/29/1835
James, S.C., Martha Anderson, former wid., R195, res. during Rev. Abbeville District, d. 1/1781
James, S.C., R11660, b. 3/24/1760 in Antrim Co., Ireland, son of Robert, res. at enl. Craven Co. (Fairfield District) S.C., res. in 1838 Fairfield District. S.C.
James, Va., S30801, b. 7/1756, res. at enl. Albemarle Co., Va., res. in 1833 Nicholas Co., Ky.
James, Va., S41352, res. at enl. Berkeley Co., Va. In 1820 aged 70 yrs. and res. Berkeley Co., wife Elizabeth
James, Va., Catharine, W4716; BLWt.10248-160-55; res. at enl. & in 1830 Spotsylvania Co., Va., aged 77 yrs., d. 8/8/1839 in Muskingum Co., Ohio
James, Va., Agnes, W9012, son of Abraham; b. 12/10/1763 in Caroline Co., Va. & res. there at enl., d. 8/12/1829 at Falmouth, Pendleton Co., Ky.
James, Va., Sarah, W10000, b.

WILSON (continued)
8/28/1761 in Frederick Co., Va. enl. in Frederick Co., Va., after Rev. res. in Pa., Ky. & Ind., d. 9/7/1834 in Lawrence Co., Ind.
James Armstrong, Pa., Margaret Henderson, former wid., W3140; BLWt.2304-300, res. of Carlisle, Cumberland Co., Pa. & there d. in 1788
James S., Va., R11659, b. 2/6/1765 in Cumberland Co., Va., son of Ben, and there at enl., res. of Kanawha Co., Va. in 1837
Jane, Pa., former wid. of William McClure, which see
Jared, Mass., S21582
Javin, Pvt. Ct., BLWt.6623 iss. 10/22/1789 to Theodosius Fowler, ass.
Javin, Ct., S35738
Jeremiah, N.H., R11666
Jeremiah, Pvt. N.J., BLWt.8869 iss. 4/25/1791 to William Piatt, ass.
Jeremiah, Va., S31491
Jeremiah, Dis. Phila., Pa. agcy.
Joab, Ct., S17783
John, Pvt. Ct., BLWt.6619 iss. 6/3/1791 to Isaac Bronson, ass. of Ann Wilson, admr.
John, Ct., S16296, b. 1760
John, Ct., Sally, W2679; BLWt. 13736-160-55, b. 1762
John, Ct., Cont., Pa., S44069
John, Ct., N.Y., S32075, b. 1762
John, Ct., Privateer, S14847, b. 1749
John, Cont., N.Y., Betsey, W11855 BLWts.1525-100 & 207-60-55
John, R---, d. in 1809 probably in Tenn.
John, Del., BLWt.2400-300-Capt. iss. 9/2/1789 to Simon Wilmer Wilson, admr. No papers
John, Pvt., Md., BLWt.11830 iss. 2/1/1790
John, Mass., S34551; BLWt.2346-100
John, Mass., S35135
John, Mass., Rachel, W26052
John, alias John FURGUSON, Mass. N.H., Mary, W25575; BLWt.14528-160-55
John, N.H., S18287
John, Pvt., N.J., BLWt.8840 iss. 4/24/1791. Also BLReg.103526-55
John, N.J., Sarah, W1526
John, N.J., Mary, W9163
John, N.Y., S14864
John, N.Y., S44077
John, N.C., S---
John, N.C., S17205, b. in N.C.
John, N.C., S21581, b. Pa.
John, N.C., Elizabeth, W4395
John, N.C., Elizabeth, W6540; BLWt.79529-160-55. She was the former wid. of John Lindsey who d. in service in the War of 1812

WILSON (continued)
and for whose service she also received a pension Old War Wid. File 27765. Also, BLWt.56897-80-50 & 2473-80-55 (all papers in these War of 1812 claims are within this jacket).
John, N.C., Patty, R11680
John, N.C., Va., S3573
John, Pa., S14865
John, Pa., S39902
John, Pa., Nancy, W3372
John, Pa., Mary, R11675
John, Pa., Lucy, R11691
John, Pa., Elizabeth Biggs, former wid., R19029
John, Vt., S11810
John, Va., S1936
John, Va., S40714
John, Va., Anna B., W6533
John, Va., Polly/Mary, W26081
John, Va., R11670
John, Va., Mary, R11676
John, Va., Elizabeth, R21437
John, Va., BLWt.1626-200
John G., Mass., R11667
John Overing, Mass., Nancy, R11678
Jonathan, Ct., S17791
Jonathan, N.H., Eleanor, W26039
Jonathan, N.Y., R1834
Jos. (Josh), Pvt. Mass., BLWt. 5219 iss. 4/19/1792 to Nathan White
Joseph, Mass. See WILLSON
Joseph, Mass., Elizabeth, W14157
Joseph, Mass., Hannah, W26018, res. at enl. Falmouth, Cumberland Co., Me., d. 10/2/1823 at Portland, Me.
Joseph, Mass., Letter of Marque Margaret, W19639
Joseph, N.H., S35127
Joseph, N.C., Indian War 1791, S3569, b. in Va.
Joseph, Pa., S22596
Joseph, Va., S38475
Joshua, N.C., S32599, b. Va.
Josiah, N.C., S14855
Josiah, Pa., Hannah, W9009
Lewis, Ct., R11673
Mahlon, Va., BLWt.482-100
Mark, Mass., Olive, W22637
Mary, N.Y., former wid. of Gideon Rugar, which see
Mathew, Md., S7902
Matthew, Cont., Pa., S16294
Michael, Va., S36849
Mindart, N.J., S3564
Moses, Ct., S17792
Nathan, Mass., Sarah, W18349
Nathaniel, Ct., Navy, Ruth, W26062
Nathaniel, Mass., Ann/Anna, W1684; BLWt.8020-160-55
Nathaniel, Mass., Abigail, W19631, d. 1/3/1817
Nathaniel, Mass., Mary, R11677
Nathaniel, Mass., Abigail, BLWt.18396-160-55, d. in 1825
Nehemiah, Ct., Rachel, W18437

WILSON (continued)
Nehemiah, Mass., Polly, W2890
Newhall, Mass., S30800
Newman, N.C., S22055
Noah, Cont., Mass., Sea Service, Vt., S22595
Obadiah, Pa., S40708
Peter, Ct., R11681
Peter, Ga., Va., Dice, R11662
Richard, Va., S6416
Richard James, Cont., N.Y., Mary, W1969; BLWt.7096-160-55
Robert, Cont., Pa., Martha, W18448
Robert, Pvt., Hazen's Regt., BLWt.13886 iss. 6/29/1789 to Matt. McConnell, ass.
Robert, N.H., S24012
Robert, N.J., S17786
Robert, N.Y., Amelia Hickox, former wid., W7746; BLWt.2369-150-Ens. iss. 8/25/1790 to William Cline, ass.; also BLWt.3-10-55
Robert, N.C., S38476
Robert, N.C., S.C., & Indian Wars, Jane, W216
Robert, N.C., Va., S7924, b. in Va.
Robert, N.C., Va., S32603, b. in Va.
Robert, Pa., Dis.
Robert, Pa., S39905
Robert, Pa., Jane, W9010, Capt.
Robert, S.C., Sarah, W2302; BLWt.6043-160-55
Robert, Va., S6433
Robert M., Navy, Janet, W4533, Pa. Agcy. and res.
Ruby, N.H., former wid. of Benoni/Benjamin Hill, which see
Samuel, Ct., S15709
Samuel, Ct., Eleanor, W18438
Samuel, Mass., Lydia, W18357
Samuel, Pvt., N.H., BLWts.3549 & 3173 iss. 12/28/1796 to Christr. S. Thorn, ass.
Samuel, N.H., Ruth Sterling, former wid., W25139
Samuel, N.J., R22011
Samuel, N.Y., Margaret, W9161; BLWt.39220-160-55
Samuel, N.C., S7944, b. in Pa.
Samuel, N.C., S.C., S7915, b. in Va.
Samuel, Pa., S2844
Samuel, Va., S11811
Samuel, Va., Sea Service, R108; Va. half pay
Stafford, N.J., Agnes, W879
Supply, N.H., S11825
Thaddeus, N.H., S22601
Thomas, Pvt. Ct., BLWt.6692 iss. 6/3/1791 to Isaac Bronson, ass.
Thomas, Ct., N.Y., Sarah, W10280; BLWt.61162-160-55
Thomas, Cont., N.Y., S23071
Thomas, Mass., S11846; BLWt. 12567-160-55
Thomas, N.H., S44083

WILSON (continued)
Thomas, N.H., Margaret, W11860; BLWt.85083-160-55
Thomas, N.H., Jane Simpson, former wid., W16072
Thomas, N.J., Sarah, W16790
Thomas, Pvt. N.Y., BLWt.7963 iss. 9/6/1791
Thomas, Sgt. "in Moylan's Dragoons," Pa., BLWt.10633 iss. 6/29/1789 to M. McConnell, ass.
Thomas, Pa., R20148
Thomas, Pa., R---
Thomas, R.I., S21584
Thomas, S.C., S18285
Thomas, Va., Mary, W9007 & Va. half pay. See N.A. Acc. No. 874-050195 Half Pay, Thomas Wilson
Thomas, Va., Mary, W27589. In British service in 1762, 1763, and 1764
Valentine, N.Y., Amy, W18418
Wallis, Va., S6418
Walter, N.Y., S14860
Warren, N.H., Shuah, W1524
William, Pvt. Md., BLWt.11850 iss. 11/29/1790 to Barney Wilson, admr.
William, Md., Sarah, W2303
William, Mass., S34540
William, Mass., Susannah, W15866
William, Mass., Lovina Bingham former wid., W17300
William, Mass., Cristeen, R11655
William, Mass., R.I., W22627
William, N.J., S937
William, N.J., S1151
William, N.Y., Elizabeth, W15817
William, N.Y., Mary, W19642
William, N.C., Nancy, W1116
William, N.C., Rachel, W2218
William, N.C., R11687
William, Pvt. Pa., BLWt.10660 iss. 4/10/1793 to Philip Stout, ass.
William, Pa., S----
William, Pa., S3572
William, Pa., S22600
William, Pa., Sarah, W3201
William, Pa., Jane, W4396
William, Pa., Sarah, W9898
William, Pa., BLWt.2382-300-Capt. iss. 8/26/1789
William, Sea Service, S32606, res. Newcastle Co., Del., and Henry Co., Ind.
William, S.C., Mahalah, R11688
William, S.C., Va., R---
William, Va., S6393
William, Va., S7907, b. in Md.
William, Va., S46083
William, Va., R11686
William, Va., R11690
Willis, N.C., Elizabeth, W6531, b. in N.C.
Willis, Va., BLWt.2434-200-Lt. iss. 1/28/1800
Willis, Va., Sea Service, R109 Va. Half Pay. See N.A. Acc.

WILSON (continued)
837-Va. State Navy, Willis Wilson, Y.S. File Va. Half Pay
Zachariah, Va., Luranah, R11672; BLWt.39498-160-55
WILT, Jacob, Pa., R11693
Thomas, Pa., Barbara, W3322
WILTON, George, Ct. See WELTON
WILTS, Michael, N.J. See WELCH
WILTSEE, Jacobus, Cont., N.Y. See James WILSEY
WILTSIE, Isaac, N.Y., S44079
WILTY, James, N.C. See WITTY
WILYARD, Henry, Pa. See WILLYARD
WIMAN, William, Vt., Melinda, W1974; BLWt.36624-160-55
WIMBISH, James, Va., Lucy, W19641
WIMBRO, Thomas P., Md., BLWt. 2267-100; Pension Act of 5/15/1828 - Md. Agcy.
WIMBROUGH, Richard, Va., S9529
WIMBROW, Thomas P., See WIMBRO
WIMER, Adam, Pa., R11695
WIMMER, John, Pa., S40717
WIMPLE, Walter Vrooman, former wid., Polly Thomas, See WEMPLE
WIMSET, Raphael, Md. See WINSETT
WIMYRE, Frederick, Pvt., N.Y., BLWt.7946 iss. 2/21/1792 to Moses Wells, ass.
WINANS, Abraham, Cont., N.J., Martha, W18346
John, Cont., N.Y., S44059
John, N.Y., Catharine, W16799
Silas, Cont., N.Y., Elizabeth Calkins, former wid., W16527
William, Pvt. Ct., BLWt.6689 iss. 8/10/1797
William, N.Y., S44056
William, N.Y., R11919
WINARD, John, Pa., Jane, W6560
WINBORNE, John, N.C., S7937
WINCH, Abijah, Mass., S11792
Jason, Mass., S19165
Joseph, N.H., Anna, W26624; BLWt.13704-160-55
Silas, Mass., S29553
WINCHEL, James, N.Y., S14854
Jedediah/Jeddediah, Mass., S44062
John, Ct., S17790
Justus, Mass., Aphia/Apphia, W16791
William, Ct., Elviry, W19651
WINCHELL, Daniel, Pvt. Ct., BLWt.6676 iss. 9/24/1790 to James F. Sebor, ass.
Ezekiel, Drummer, Ct., BLWt. 6680 iss. 12/14/1789 to Richard Platt, ass.
John, N.Y., Mary, R11696
WINCHESTER, Amariah, Cont., Mass., R.I., Betsey Hart, former wid., W1856
Amariah, N.Y., S14834
Asa, Vt., Sarah, W19638
Benjamin, Mass., R11698
Benjamin, Vt., S22594
Benjamin, Vt., Ruth, W18355; BLWt.7441-160-55
Charles, Cont., Mass., Irena,

WINCHESTER (continued)
W26068; BLWt.50-60-55
Daniel, N.C., Rosanna, W1117; BLWt.92108-160-55
David, Mass., N.H., S15712
Henry, Mass., Lois, W16478
Jabez, Ct., S14871
Jacob B., Pvt. Mass., BLWt.5233 iss. 12/23/1796
James, Md. & U.S.A., Susan, W23; BLWt.2407-300-Capt. iss. 12/22/1796
John, Drummer, Mass., BLWt.5236 iss. 12/3/1789 to Daniel Watrous, ass.
Jonathan, Cont. Mass., S34539
Lemuel, Mass., S29547
Richard, Ct., Lydia, W9027
Samuel, Mass., Hannah, BLWt. 75112-160-55
Silas, Cont., Mass., Sarah, W22669
William, Cont., Mass., S18657
William, Mass., BLWt.2329-200-Lt. iss. 3/26/1796 to Peter Surer, ass. No papers
WINCHIP, Joel, Mass., S28953
WINCKLEBLACK, Henry, Va., S6389
WINDER, Levin, Md., BLWt.2404-450-Lt. Col. iss. 6/2/1789. No papers
WINDERS, John, N.C., R11699
WINDFIELD, Daniel, N.J.(?), N.Y., Hannah, See WINFIELD
Henry, N.Y., S785
William, N.Y., See WINFIELD
WINDHAM, George, Md. See WINHAM
Sarah, Md., former wid. of Joshua Lamb, which see. She was also pensioned as wid. of Thomas Windham, Md.
Thomas, Md., Sarah, W9020. She was also pensioned as former wid. of Joshua Lamb, which see
William, S.C., R11701
WINDLE, John P., Va., R11702
WINDOLPH, Jacob, Pa., S39906
WINDOWS, Henry, Pvt. Md., BLWt. 11828 iss. 7/9/1799
WINDSOR, Christopher, Va., Prudence, W9025
John, Pvt., N.Y., BLWt.8033 iss. 8/28/1790 & 91--60-1855. BLWt. 8033 to C. Yate's Exrs., assnes.
Jonathan, Va., R11703
Philip, Drummer, Del., BLWt. 10901 iss. 8/8/1797 to Thomas Gould, ass.
WINE, Kallion, N.Y., Rachel, W2039; BLWt.2497-160-55
WINEGAR, Garret, N.Y., Lois/Louis, W26075
Samuel, N.Y., R11705
WINEGARDNER, Joseph, Cont., French R11706; res. Ohio in 1833
WINFIELD, Abraham, N.Y., S44060
Benjamin, N.Y., Anna, R11707
Curtis, Va., R20524
Daniel, N.J. (?), N.Y., Hannah, R11708; BLWt. 7298-160-55
David, N.Y., S14870

WINFIELD (continued)
Emanuel, N.J., S17201
Harris, Va., S7910
William, N.Y., Margaret, R11709
WINFORD, Henry, Pvt. N.Y., BLWt. 8025 iss. 4/2/1792
Henry, N.Y., S44089
WINFREY, John, Va., Elizabeth, W6543
Philip, Va., S31486
WING, Aaron, Mass., Sylvina P., R11711; BLWt.71115-160-55
Bani, Mass., Thirza, W622; BLWt.12581-160-55
Benjamin, N.Y., Sarah, R11710
Daniel, N.Y., S11780
Eli, Mass., S34549
Gideon, Va., Abigail, W26020
Isaiah, Mass., S11799
Israel, N.H., S34541
James, Mass., S29549
Jonathan, Mass., BLWt.2320-150-Ens. iss. 2/16/1799 to Marlbry Turner, ass.
Moses, Cont., Mass., Navy, Privateer, Martha, W5168
Nathan, Mass., Love, W22639
WINGATE, Daniel, N.H., S44087
David, N.H., Lydia, W26083
Enoch, N.H., Mary, R11713
John, Mass., S35132
John, N.C., R11712
John, Va., S35731
Jonathan, N.H., S31490
WINGEROW, Joseph, Cont., French See WINEGARDNER
WINGFIELD, Enoch, Va., S16581
John, Va., Mary, R11714
William, Va., R11715
WINGHART, Adam, Pvt. Pa., BLWt.10584 iss. 6/20/1789
WINGO, John, Va., R11716
William, Va., S7896
WINGROVE, John, Va., S11856
WINHAM, George, Md., Mary, W4535
WININGHAM, James, N.C., Sarah, R11724
WINK, Jacob, Cont., Md., S35118
WINKLER, Frederick, Pvt. "in the Artillery" Pa., BLWt.10644 iss. 7/27/1789 to Richard Platt, ass.
Henry, N.C., Susannah/Susan, W3061
Johannes Ardulph, Pa. See John
John/Johannes Ardulph, Pa., R11718
Joseph, Pa., BLWt.2454-100
WINKLES, James, N.C., R11717
WINLOCK, Joseph, Va., Effey, W3060; BLWt.2433-200-Lt. iss. 2/10/1800 to Lucas Sullivant, ass.
WINMER, Jacob, N.J., S17794
WINN, Elisha, Va., S38477
Galanus, Va., S14849
Henry, N.J., Catharine, R11720
John, Pvt., Ct., BLWt.6702 iss. 5/21/1794
John, Cont., S26922, N.Y. res. & Agcy.
John, Cont., Thankful Denton,

WINN (continued)
former wid., R2889; N.Y. res. in 1806
John, Cont. Va., S39127
John, Mass., Abigail, W20132
John, Pa., S35140; BLWt.10562-100-Sgt. iss. 7/16/1789
John, Va., S7899
Jonathan, Mass., S29550
Joseph, Mass., S29552
Joseph, N.Y., R11722
Josiah, N.J., Susanna, W3225
Peter, N.Y., BLWt.1106-100
Richard, Va., Jane, W6558
Samuel, R.I., BLWt.2660-200-Lt. iss. 1/5/1796. No papers
William, Va., S11699
Zachariah, N.C., S18286
WINNA, John, N.Y., Anna, W19637
WINNE, Aaron, N.Y., S11847
Casper, N.Y., S24018
Cornelius, N.Y., S14841
Jacob, N.Y., Susannah, W18455
Jacobus, N.Y., S14856
John, N.Y., Mariah, R11723
John D., N.Y., S11806
Kallione, N.Y. See Kallion WINE
Peter J., N.Y., S11835
WINNEE, Kallian, See WINE
WINNIFORD, David, Va., Judith, W9021
WINNING, James, Pa., S39901
WINNINGHAM, Joseph, S.C., S9531
WINSETT, Raphael, Md., Susannah, W621
WINSHIP, Abel, Cont., Mass., Elizabeth, W11837
Ebenezer, Cont., Mass., Mary, W22667
Jabez, Ct., Hannah, R11725
John, Mass., S33923
John, Mass., Betty, W22625
Richard, Mass., S11786
WINSLOW, Abraham, Cont., Mass., Elizabeth, W26623
Asa, Pa., S11861
Benjamin, Mass., S35126
David, Mass., N.H., S35125
Deborah, Mass., former wid. of Henry Peirce/Pierce, which see
Elizabeth, Mass., former wid. of Robert Wiley, which see
Ezekiel, Mass., Sedona, W4402
George, R.I., S30215
Hannah, Ct., former wid. of Oliver Brown, which see
Jennett, Mass., former wid. of Timothy Partridge, which see
Job, Cont., Mass., S44218
John, Cont., Mass., Polly, W26017
John, Cont., Mass., Ann, R11726
Kenelm, Mass., S40716
Lemuel, Mass., R.I., Sylvina, W14181; BLWt.18397-160-55
Nathan, Mass., Bethiah, W15488
Nathaniel, Mass., Hannah, R11728
Nathaniel, Mass., BLWt.446-400
Oliver, Mass., S33913
Samuel, N.H., Betsey, W26031; BLWt.33530-160-55
Stephen, Mass., Privateer, S4726

WINSLOW (continued)
Timothy, Mass., R11731
Tisdale, Mass., Jane, W18340
William, Pvt. Mass., BLWt.5257 iss. 11/18/1794 to Asa Spaulding
WINSOR, Christopher, See WINDSOR
John, Mass., Sea Service, S11787
John, N.Y., Lydia, W22646; BLWt. 91-60-55
Marcy, R.I., former wid. of Stephen Waterman, which see
Olney, R.I., S22054
Peter, Mass., Charlotte, W14161; BLWts.721-100 & 336-60-55
Samuel, R.I., Hannah, W2633; BLWt.26944-160-55
William, Mass., S30217
WINSTEAD, Francis, Va., S3607
Mandley, N.C., S14836
WINSTON, Anthony, Va., S6390
Isaac, Mass., Hannah, W26041; BLWt.26917-160-55
Isaac, N.C., R11732
Nathaniel, N.C., S6406
Robert, Va. See William Bobby
William, Lee's Legion, BLWt. 2443-200-Lt. iss. 9/9/1789 to Henry Lee, Exr. of Alex Skinner late ass. of Wm. Winston
William Bobby/Robert, Va., S41357
WINTER, Abigail, Mass., former wid. of Jacob Lewis, which see
Abner, Ct., Anna, R11733
Asa, Ct., Lydia, W14158
Benjamin, Mass., Hannah, W22657
Frederick, Pa. (1774), Va., R11734; b. in N.Y.
John, Mass., Phebe Hawks, former wid., W14891
John, Pa., S24013
Jonathan W., Ct., S17202
Joseph, Mass., Betsey Morse, former wid., W24012; BLWts.783-100 & 62-60-55
Joshua, Pvt. Mass., BLWt.5276 iss. 4/1/1790
Joshua, Mass., S33921
Nicholas, Ct., S11797
Peter, N.J., See WINTERS
Peter, N.Y., Elizabeth, W6559; BLWt.13006-160-55
Stephen, Pa., S18660
WINTERMOTE, Margaret, Va., former wid. of George Ward, which see
WINTERS, Jacob, N.J., S39897
James, N.J., Pa., S40719
Juvenil/Juvenal, Ct., Amelia, W2217; BLWt.3818-160-55
Peter, N.J., S29545
Thomas, Sgt., N.Y., BLWt.8039 iss. 7/14/1790 to Richard Platt ass.
Timothy, Corp., Pa., BLWt.10571 iss. 7/9/1789
WINTERSTEEN, James, N.J., Ariantee W6561
WINTON, James, Pvt., N.H., BLWt. 3548 iss. 9/9/1789
Joseph, Ct., Cont., Privateer, S11814
Nathan, Ct., S39899
WINTREE, Francis, Pvt., Armand's

WINTREE (continued)
Corps, BLWt.13870 iss. 8/3/1793 to Casper Iserloan, ass.
WINTWORTH, Alpheus, Cont., Ct., See WENTWORTH
Levi, Ct., See WENTWORTH
WIRBLE, Henry, Cont., Margaret, W9023; BLWt.13897-100; Ky. agcy. and res.
WIRE, Rhinehart, Pa., S39908
Samuel, Cont., Ct., Eunice, W18441
WIREY, Michael, Pvt. Md., BLWt. 11812 iss. 12/22/1794
WIRS, John, Mass., Miriam, W19647
WIRT, Philip, Pa., Dorothy, R11735
WIRTZ, John, Pa., S22590
William, Pa., R11736
WISCARVER, George , See WISECARVER
WISE, Abner, N.H., R11737
Adam, Md., Catharine, See WEISE
Daniel, Mass., Lydia, W22664
Daniel, Mass., Navy, N.H., Privateer, Hannah, W22635
Daniel, N.Y., See WIES
Ebenezer, Cont., N.H., Mary, W26074
Henry, Pa., S35139
Jacob, Pa., S6387
Jacob, S.C., S18284
John, N.C., S36395
John, R.I., S39895
Peter, Pa., S3554
Peter, Pa., S4728
Samuel, Va., S35730
William, Cont., Ct., S11791
William, Pvt., N.Y., BLWt.8045 iss. 10/10/1791 to Anthony Maxwell, ass.
WISECARVER, George, Va., S22589
WISEMAN, Caleb, Pa., S41353
Frederick, Pa. See WHITEMAN
George, Pa., S39904
James, N.C., S16298
Joseph, N.C., Pa., Elizabeth, R11741
Thomas, Md., S39126
WISEMORE, Abram/Abraham, See WISMORE
WISER, John, N.Y., R11739
Michael, Md. See WISOR
Solomon, Pvt., Pa., BLWt.10597 iss. 12/6/1791
Solomon, Pa., R11740
WISHAM, John, Cont., Md., See WYSHAM
WISHART, Thomas, Va., BLWt.1795-200 iss. 12/27/1832
WISLER, Micheal, Pa., S39907
WISMORE, Abraham/Abram, Pa., BLWt.2468-100
WISNAR, Adam, N.Y. See WISNER
WISNER, Adam, N.Y., Pa., R11742
David, N.Y., Deliverance, W6549; BLWt.26863-160-55
Henry, Pvt. Von Heer's Corps, BLWt.13874 iss. 12/9/1793 to Alexander Power, ass.
Jacob, Md., R11743
Jacob, Pa., Sarah, W26040; BLWt.

WISNER (continued)
BLWt.36627-160-55
Jehiel, N.J., N.Y., S29546
John, N.Y., Sarah, R11744
Samuel, N.J., N.Y., Julaner, W2711 BLWt.28559-160-55
WISONG, Fayett/Fiatt, Va., Susannah W8305; BLWt.26215-160-55
Fiatt, Va. See Fayett
WISOR, George, Va., S11843
Michael, Md., Nelly, W3906
WISSEMORE, Abram/Abraham, See WISMORE
WISSENBAGH, Henry, Pvt., N.Y., BLWt.7990 iss. 4/17/1792 to Noah Johnson, ass.
WISSWELL, Israel, Mass., S40713
WISTEL, Catharine, Md., former wid. of Robert Purtle, which see
WISWALL, Daniel, Pvt. Mass., BLWt. 5331 iss 8/17/1796
Daniel, Mass., S33925
Jonathan, Mass., Sarah, W14160
Samuel, Vt., S19164
WISWELL, Daniel, Mass., Abigail, W26064
David, Mass., S33919
David, Mass., R11745
Enoch, Mass., Jane, R11746
Israel, Md. See WISSWELL
WITBECK, Abraham, N.Y., R11509
Andries, N.Y., S15256
John, N.Y., Lena VanDenburgh, W18458
WITBEEK, Abraham L., N.Y., S14866
WITCHEL, Jacob, N.J., S33911
Jacob, Pvt. N.J., BLWt.8850 iss. 6/23/1789 to Elias Dayton & Son, assnes.
WITCHER, James, Va., S2024
WITDERSTEIN, John, N.Y., Margaret W18341
WITDERSTONE, John, N.Y. See WITDERSTEIN
WITHAM, Aaron, Mass., Abigail Harris, former wid., W23189
Andrew, Navy, Lydia, R11748; Mass. res. & Me. Agcy., d. in N.H.
Bartholomew, Cont., Mass., Elizabeth, W26048
Caleb, Mass., Lucretia, W26024
Elijah, Cont., Mass., Mehitable, R11749
James, Pvt. Mass., BLWt.5227 iss. 12/13/1792
James, Mass., S35131
James, Mass., S44225
Jedediah, Mass., Hannah Spinney, former wid., W25049
Jere, Cont., Mass. See Jere[h] WHITAM
John Spence, Mass., S35128
Joshua, Mass., S37541
Moses, Mass., Jane, W26057
Nathan, Mass., Rhoda, W16476
Pelatiah, Mass., Sarah, W18433
Peter/Petter, Va., S32071
Thomas, Privateer, Mass., S19876
Thomas B., Privateer, Mass., R11747

WITHEE, Uzziel, Mass. See WETHEE
Zoe, Cont., N.H., Sally, W22655; BLWt.3193-160-55
WITHERALL, John, Mass., S29536
WITHERELL, Abel, Mass., S34561
Charles, Mass., See WETHERELL
James, Mass., Amy, W6556; BLWt. 1835-150
John, Mass. See WITHERALL
John, Mass. See WITHRELL
Nathaniel, Mass., S21583
Obadiah, Mass., See WETHERELL
Samuel, Mass., S41316
Simeon, Mass., Hannah, R11751
WITHERFORD, William, Cont., Va., Mary, W4400
WITHERHAM, John, Pvt. Pa., BLWt. 10607 iss. 5/20/1791 to Precilla Davis, ass.
WITHERILL, David, Ct., Cont., R11750
WITHERINGTON, Daniel, N.C., S7932
Joseph, N.C., S1938
Solomon, N.C., S7936
William, N.C., S7953
WITHERLY, William, Pvt. "in the artillery" Pa., BLWt.10667 iss. 6/25/1794
WITHERS, George, Pa., Anna, W6555 BLWt.57779-160-55
James, Va., Susannah, W4399; BLWt.1938-200 & Va. Half Pay. See N.A. Acc. No. 874-050199 Half Pay James Withers (Papers once on file under S7942 & R19187 are within)
Jesse, Va., S11819
Spencer, Va., S6400
William Ramblin, Cont., S.C., Va., Martha A., W18351; BLWt. 760-150
WITHERSPOON, Ann, N.H., former wid. of James Moore, which see
David, S.C., Mary, W1685
James, N.J., BLWt.1754-400-Brigade Major iss. 5/7/1789 to Rev. Dr. John Witherspoon, legal rep. also recorded as above under BLWt.2283
John, N.C., S3610
John, N.C., S32601
William, N.C., S7901
WITHERSTINE, John, N.Y. See WITDERSTEIN
WITHEY, Jeduthan, See WETHY
WITHINGTON, Abigail, Mass., former wid. of Isaac Ramsdell, which see
Ebenezer, Cont., Mass., S30794
Elijah, Mass., BLWt.678-100
James, Sgt. Mass., BLWt.5315 iss. 1/25/1790 to John May
John, Mass., S33924
Lemuel, Mass., S33935
Richard, S.C., Mary, R11753
Robert, Mass., S35133
Thomas, Mass., Elizabeth, W2389; BLWt.18006-160-55
WITHRELL, John, Mass., S30212
William, Mass., See WETHRELL
WITHRINGTON, John, Pvt. Mass. BLWt.5245 iss. 4/17/1792 to Thomas Seward

WITHROW, James, N.C., S6403
James, N.C., S7945
Samuel, Pa., S22599
WITMAN, Abraham, Pa., Elizabeth W2888
John, Pa., Anna Maria, R11754
WITT, Abner, Mass., Molly, W15487
Aires, N.C. See Earis
Artemas, N.H., Eunice, W15492
Benjamin, Mass., S34554
Benjamin, Mass., Olivia Bacon former wid., W14260
Burgess, N.C., Elizabeth, W54; BLWt.31738-160-55
Caleb, Va., Miriam, R11755
Earis, N.C., Rebecca, W623; BLWt.36623-160-55
Egbert D./Egbert, N.Y., S12757
Elisha, Va., Phebe, W3059
Eris, N.C. See Earis
Jacob, Pa., S22592
Jesse, Va., S39893, d. 1846 in Va.
Jesse, Va., Alice/Alcy, W6524, d. in 1842 in Va.
Joseph, Mass., S19163
Moses, N.H., R11756
Stephen, Mass., S34553
WITTEN, Thomas, Va., S6407
WITTER, Ebenezer, Ct., Mass. Sea Service, S11802
Hannah, R.I., former wid. of George Popple, which see
Jonah, Ct., S17793
Joseph, Mass., S40715
Josiah, Ct., Mass., S41359
William, Ct., R11757
WITTERS, Conrad, Pa., Susanna, R11758
WITTUM, Malachi, Green Mt. Boys, Vt., Sarah, R11759
WITTY, Andrew, N.C., R19064
James, N.C., S18662
WITZ, John, Pa., S23075
WIXOM, Shubael, Mass., S35130
WIXON, Daniel, N.Y. See WIXSOM
WIXSOM, Daniel, N.Y., S11800
Shubael, Mass. See WIXOM
WIZER, Michael, Md. See WISOR
WOELPER, David, Pa., BLWt.2394-300-Capt. iss. 8/19/1789 to John Phillips, ass. No papers
WOGLAM, John, N.J. See WOGLOM
WOGLOM, Abraham, N.J., Annabell, W19654
John, N.J., Elizabeth, W26098
WOHLEBEN, Abraham, N.Y. See WOLLEBER
Peter, N.Y., Catharine, See WOLEVER
WOLCATT, Solomon, Ct. See WOLCOTT
WOLCOT, Oliver, Mass., S19172
Solomon, Mass., S35147
WOLCOTT, Abiel, Ct., R11761
Benajah, Ct., S40729
David, Mass., S16300; BLWt. 5067-160-55
Elijah, Ct., Mary, W22678
Erastus, Ct., BLWt.2346-300-Capt. iss. 2/23/1799 to Chloe Wolcott,

WOLCOTT (continued)
guardian to Erastus, Chloe, Jr. Edward, Julia, otherwise called Julah, and Helen Wolcott (minors) the only surviving heirs of ___ No papers
Giles, Cont., N.H., S44106; BLWt. 2278-300-Capt. of N.H., iss. 12/12/1797
John, Ct., Boat service on Lake Champlain, Martha, W20137
John, Mass., Lydia, R11764
John, Pa. See WALCOTT
Joseph, Ct., Sarah Hixon, former wid., W21336. Her last husb., Elkanah Hixson, also pensioned which see
Josiah, Ct., Elizabeth, W9034; BLWt.17733-160-55
Oliver, Ct., R11763
Samuel, Ct., Jerusha, W22535
Samuel, Ct., R.I., Sarah, R11765
Silas, Pa., Margaret, See WOLCUT
Solomon, Ct., Cornelia, W26096; BLWt.26527-160-55
William, Ct., Huldah, W26090; BLWt.11070-160-55
William, Md., S40728
William, N.Y., See WOOLCOTT
WOLCUT, Silas, Pa., Margaret, W2982
WOLCUTT, Joseph, Ct. See WOLCOTT
WOLEBER, Abraham, N.Y. See WOLLEBER
John, N.Y. See WOOLAVER
Peter, N.Y. See WOLEVER
WOLEVER, John, See WOOLAVER
Peter, N.Y., Catharine, W19659. Also spelled WOLLEBER, WOOLEVER, WOOLEBEN, WOLEBER, WOHLEBEN, WOOLIVER
Phillip/Philip, Pa., S3615
WOLF, Adam, Pa., S3615
Andrew, Va., S46413
David, Md., Va., R11767
Frederick, Cont. See WOOLF
George, Not Rev. N.W. Ind. War 1792 Old War Inv. File No. 26521. Res. Pa. & Ohio
George, Pa., Charity, R11766
Jacob, Pa., S24023
Levy/Levi, Ct., See DE WOLF
Lewis, N.C., Mary, W4403
Michael, Cont., Md., Va., S40726
Michael, Pa., S24024
Peter, Pa., S7963
Seth, Ct. See D'WOLF
WOLFE, Adam, Pa., S4731
Christian, Pvt., Hazen's Regt. BLWt.13898 iss. 9/23/1789
David, Cont., N.Y., S14888
Henry, Pvt. N.J., BLWt.8828 iss. 7/2/1789
John, Pa., Mary, W3324; BLWt.2432-100
William, Pa., S24020
WOLFENBARGER, Philip, Cont., Va. Catharine, W6575
WOLFINBARGER, Peter, Va., R11770
WOLFINBERGER, Philip, Va., See WOLFENBARGER

WOLFORD, John, Md., R11027
John, N.J., S11898
Michael, Md. See WOOLFORD
WOLLARD, John, N.C., S1732
WOLLEBER, Abraham, N.Y., Dorothy R17772. Also spelled as WOLEBER WOLLEBUR, WOHLEBEN, WOLLEBEN
John, N.Y., R11771
Peter, N.Y. See WOLEVER
WOLLENBACK, John W. See WALLINBACK
WOLLEY, Austin, N.Y., Margaret, R11851
David, Mass., See WOOLEY
WOLOVER, John, N.Y. See WOOLAVER
WOLVEN, John H., N.Y., S6440
WOMACK, Abner, N.C., S30804, b. Va.
Abraham, N.C., Lucy, W6602; BLWt.38342-160-55
Massanello, Va., S16584
WOMBLE, John, N.C., S42083
WONACOTT, Richard, See WONICUTT
WONDER, Andrew, Pa., S11880
WONEYCUTT, Edward, Va. Sea Service R110 Va. Half Pay. See N.A. Acc. No.837- Va. State Navy, Edward "Honeycott" U.S. File Va., Half Pay
WONICUTT, Richard, Pa., R11773
WOOD, Aaron, Md., N.C., Matilda, W6566; BLWt.10008-160-55
Aaron, Mass., Olive, W22691
Aaron, Corp., N.H., BLWt.3576 iss. 10/12/1795 to James A. Neal ass.
Abel, Mass., S30219
Abijah, Mass., S30224
Abner, Ct., Betsey, W18377
Abner, Mass., S29556
Abner, R.I., S11895
Abraham, Pvt., N.J., BLWt.8870 iss. 6/11/1789 to Jonathan Dayton, ass.
Abraham, Cont., N.J., Nancy, W6563
Abraham, N.Y., S14880
Abraham, N.C., S32611
Abraham, R.I., Susannah, W26111
Alexander, N.Y., S44099
Amos, Mass., S18666
Amos, Mass., Lovice, W14184
Amos, Mass., R11777
Amos, Mass., R.I., Vt., R11778
Asa, Ct., S17798
Asa, Mass., Abigail, W16164
Asahel, Mass., S33947
Bartholomew, N.C., S.C., Martha Ann, R11797
Barzillai, Mass., S33946
Belfield, N.C., Nancy Milsaps, former wid., W4492; BLWt.94052-160-55
Benjamin, Ct., S40732
Benjamin, Ct., R11779
Benjamin, Mass., S14876
Benjamin, Mass., Ruth, R11802
Benjamin, N.J., Lydia, W6567
Benjamin, N.Y., R11780
Benjamin C., Md., S11890
Caldwell, Va. See WOODS
Caleb, Cont., Mass., S11887
Charles, Ct., S39916

WOOD (continued)
Charles, N.Y., R11781
Charles, Pvt. N.C., BLWts.12697 & 13875 iss. 8/14/1792 to Isaac Cole, ass.
Charles, N.C., S42084
Charles, R.I., Mary, W6569
Charles, Rosa, R11801, N.C. or S.C.
Clement, N.J., S44098
Consider, Mass., S39917
Coolidge P., Mass., Navy, Patience, W15499. She was pensioned as former wid. of Nathaniel Parker, which see
Daniel, Ct., Vt., S14898
Daniel, Cont., N.Y., Catharine, W18382; BLWt.2373-300-Capt. iss. 4/28/1791
Daniel, Mass., S30808
Daniel, Mass., S44108
David, Ct., Electa, W6564; BLWt. 12848-160-55
David, Mass., S22609
David, Mass., S29558
David, Mass., Princess, W18381; BLWt.3619-160-55
David, N.Y., Elizabeth, R11782
Dempsey, S.C., S47990
Ebenezer, Cont., N.J., S40722
Ebenezer, Mass., S41379
Ebenezer, Mass., Celinda M.S.D. W10285; BLWt.79023-160-55
Ebenezer, Mass., Phebe, W16165
Ebenezer, Pvt. Va., Lee's Legion BLWts.12657 & 13926 iss. 9/15/1790
Edward, Mass., S34563
Eleazer, Mass., S41366
Eli, Ct., N.Y., Rhoda, W16480
Eli, Mass., S33953
Elias, Pvt. N.J., BLWt.8832 iss. 7/7/1789
Eliphalet, Cont., Mass., S15723
Elisha, Ct., R.I., S14902
Elisha, Mass., Lovene, R11795
Ellit, Va., S1605
Enoch, Mass., Olive, W1688
Enoch, N.Y., Lydia, W9030; BLWt. 9192-160-55
Enos, Vt. & War of 1812, S11863
Ephraim/Ephriam, N.H., Vt., S14895
Ezra, Pvt. Mass., BLWt.5275 iss. 10/1/1791
Francis, Mass., S15724
Francis, Va., S18290
George, N.Y., S11872
Gerard, Md., BLWt.2160-300
Gideon, N.H., S41378
Henry, N.Y., S10050
Henry, N.C., Nancy, R11785; BLWt. 45590-160-55, b. N.C.
Holland, Cont. Mass., Abigail, W14188
Ichabod, Mass., S30805
Ichabod, Mass., Sarah, R11803
Isaac, Mass., S33943
Isaac, N.J., BLWt.221-100
Isaac, N.C., Lucy Fields, former wid., R3530

WOOD (continued)
Isaac, R.I., S23494
Isaiah, Mass., S35149
Israel, N.Y., S14897
Jacob, Pvt. Ct., BLWt.6611 iss. 3/19/1792
Jacob, Ct., S44095
Jacob, Ct., S44102
Jacob, Mass., Lydia, W22693
Jacob, N.J., R11786
Jacob, Vt., Martha, R11796
James, Cont., Mass., R.I., S11876
James, Cont., Va., Jemima, W4717
James, Ga., Elizabeth, W4405, b. Va., res. at enl. in Va.
James 1st, Pvt. Md., BLWt.11789 iss. 7/8/1797 to James DeBaufre, ass.
James, Mass., S16586
James, Mass., S44097
James, Pvt. N.Y., BLWt.7981 iss. 8/4/1790 to Henry Hart, ass.
James, N.Y., Mary, W19653
James, N.C., Sarah, W6571
James, Pvt. Va., Lee's Legion, BLWt.12672 iss. 4/8/179- to William Taylor, Henry Bowyer, Thomas T. Scott, assnes.
James, Va., S6445
James, Va., BLWt.2419-500-Col. iss. 2/14/1792
Jared, Ct., N.Y., S11882
Jason, Mass., Sarah, W16794
Jeremiah, N.J., R11788
Jesse/Jessey, Pvt. Lamb's Art. BLWts.13889 & 13958 iss. 6/8/1791 to Richard Allison & Daniel Conklin admrs.
Jesse, Mass., Lois, W22689
Jesse, Va., S7962
Jesse, Va., Nancy, W6572
Job, N.Y., R.I., Jane, W22687; BLWt.6384-160-55
Joel, Ct., Cont., S17206
John, Ct., S18663
John, Ct., Nabby/Nebby, W26110
John, Ct., Abigail, R11774
John, Ct., Cont., Privateer, S11868
John, Ct., N.H., R11790
John, Md., Rachel, W2311; BLWt. 11171-160-55
John, Md., Elizabeth, W6573; BLWt.9525-160-55
John, Mass., Susanna, W14182
John, Mass., R21797
John, N.J., S11875
John, N.Y., S24021
John, N.Y., Margaret, W4104; BLWt.38833-160-55
John, N.C., S1887
John, N.C., See WOODS
John, N.C., R11792
John, N.C., S.C., S3613
John, N.C., Va., Elizabeth, W9028
John, R.I., S22069
John, R.I., Phebe, W22698
John, Va., R11791
Jonathan, Cont., N.H., S41369
Jonathan, Md., S11899

WOOD (continued)
Jonathan, Mass., R.I., Mehitable, R11798
Jonathan, Grace, N.H., W18380
Jonathan, R.I., S11869
Jonathan, Vt., S3614
Jonathan, Va., R11793
Joseph, Ct., R.I., S23084
Joseph, Cont., N.J., Joanna, R11789
Joseph, Cont., Va., S16583
Joseph, Pvt. Md., BLWt.11854 iss. 10/26/1792 to James Williams, ass. of Benj. Burch, Admr.
Joseph, Mass., S11901
Joseph, Mass., Bethiah, W26128
Joseph, N.H., S17209; BLWt.9051-160-55
Joseph, N.J., Pa., S24019
Joseph, N.Y., R11794
Joseph, Pvt., Va., BLWt.12649 iss. 6/18/1795 to Joseph Wood
Joseph, Dis. Phila. Agency
Joshua, Mass., S41377
Joshua, Mass., Martha, W1345; BLWt.38831-160-55
Joshua, Mass., Esther, W26125; BLWt.9047-160-55
Josiah, Cont., Mass., S41374
Josiah, Mass., S35152
Judah, Mass., S19169
Lemuel, Pvt. Ct., BLWt.6626 iss. 1/26/1790 to John May, ass.
Lemuel, Ct., Elizabeth/Elizebeth W4106
Levi, Ct., Vt., S6446
Levi, Mass., Bethany, W20139
Lillis, R.I., former wid. of Spencer Beers, which see
Mary, Ct., former wid. of Jonathan Kneeland, which see
Matthew/Mathew, N.C., S39135
Mathias, Va., Ann, W1527
Misael, N.C., S32079, b. in Md.
Moses, Mass., S11902
Nathan, Ct., S11870
Nathan, Cont., Mass., Susannah, W26114
Nathan, Mass., S19514
Nathan, Mass., S30220
Nathaniel, Ct., Green Mt. Boys Vt., Lois Collins, former wid., W16928
Nicholas, Cont., Del., S40723
Nicholas, Pvt. "in the artillery" Va., BLWt.12677 iss. 5/5/1790 to Wm. J./F. Vredenburgh, ass.
Nichols, Mass., Hope, W14187
Obadiah, N.C., S32613
Pardon, R.I., S22066
Patty, Mass., former wid. of Caleb Willis, which see
Peter, Mass., Sarah, R11804
Reuben, R.I., Mercy/Marcy, W22675; BLWt.9454-160-55
Richard, Mass., S44100
Richard, N.Y., Lydia, W22697
Robert, N.Y., Abigail, W26109
Robert, R.I., S23083
Robert, Va., S39909
Robertson, Pvt., Md., BLWt.11790

WOOD (continued)
iss. 1/11/1796 to Joshua Ward, ass.
Sampson, N.C., S42079
Samuel, Pvt. Ct., BLWt.6612 iss. 6/24/1797 to John Duncan, ass.
Samuel, Ct., S35748
Samuel, Ct., S44101
Samuel, Cont., Mass., S33951
Samuel, Pvt., Lee's Legion, BLWt. 13927 iss. 8/21/1790
Samuel, Mass., S31498
Samuel, Mass., S33945
Samuel, Mass., Molly Tinkham, former wid., W14022
Samuel, N.Y., S28955
Samuel, Pa., S39910
Samuel, S.C., S35744
Samuel, Va., S7959
Sarah, Ct., Mass., N.Y., former wid. of Rufus Wheeler, which see
Sarah, N.Y., former wid. of Nathaniel Plumstead, which see
Seth, Mass., Persis, W26099
Silas, Pvt. Ct., BLWt.6684 iss. 11/30/1799 to Abijah Holbrook, ass.
Silas, Ct., S35747
Silas, Mass., Sibyl, W18363
Silvanus/Sylvanus, Mass., Joanna, W22681
Simeon, Mass., Rhoba, W26126
Solomon, Cont., Ct., Christiana, W2427; BLWt.31764-160-55
Solomon, Vt., Perthena/Parthena, W18376; BLWt.12714-160-60
Solomon, Va., S18668
Squier/Squire, Mass., N.Y., Vt., S14893
Stephen, Mass., Jemima, W20138
Stephen, Va., S7966
Susan, N.Y., former wid. of Thomas Bunting, which see
Sylvanus/Silvanus, Cont., Mass., Deborah, W19657
Thomas, Ct., Abigail, W27506
Thomas, Ct., Mass., S14879
Thomas, Cont., N.H., S44104
Thomas, Cont., Pa., Sea Service, S44096
Thomas, Sgt. Md., BLWt.11800 iss. 2/1/1790
Thomas, Md., S35154
Thomas, Mass., Lois, W22694
Thomas, Mass., Vt., Amity, W18374
Thomas, Va., S1604
Thomas, Va., Mary, W6568
Thomas V., N.Y., S14894
Thurston, N.Y., Catherine, W1973; BLWt.28541-160-55
Timothy, Mass., Annar, W18383
Timothy, N.Y., S23495
Titus, Cont., Mass., S11836
William, Cont., Mass., N.H., Lusanna, W16793
William, Cont., Va., Jincy, W11883 BLWts.12646-100 & 57-60-55. BLWt. 298-60-55 cancelled
William, Mass., S14900
William, Mass., S19170
William, Mass., S45462

WOOD (continued)
William, Mass., Phebe, W26120
William, N.J., Sarah, See WOODS
William, N.C., S7971
William, N.C., Sarah, W4868, b. in N.C.
William, N.C., Va., R11809, b. in Va.
William, Pa., R11808, b. in Pa.
William, S.C., S21589
William, Va., S32615
Zadok/Zadoh, S.C., S3612, b. in Va.
Zephaniah, Mass., Susanna, W6574; BLWt.9547-160-55
WOODALL, Charles, Va., S11878
Joseph, N.C., S32081
Samuel, Va., Joanna, W3909
WOODARD, Artemas, Mass., S22607
Asa, N.J., See WOODWARD
Daniel, Cont., N.H., R.I., R21852
Daniel, Mass., Olive, W22682
Ebenezer, Vt., Elizabeth, W18378
George, Va., Charlotte, W2506; BLWt.26506-160-55
Jacob, Mass., See WOODWARD
Jacob, Va., S17208
James, Ct., See Josiah WOODARD
Jesse, Ct., Vt., S14967 1/2
Jesse, N.C., R11840, b. in N.C.
John, Pvt. Mass., BLWt.5306 iss. 4/1/1790
John, Mass., Sarah, W22688; BLWt.14543-160-55
John, N.Y., S29557
John, Vt., R11842
Josiah/James, Ct., Jane, W26100
Nathaniel, Mass. See WOODWARD
Richard, Va., S31493; b. Md.
Samuel, Mass., Ann, W26122
Samuel, Vt., R11845
Samuel, Va., Sarah, W5169; BLWt. 2178-160-55
Seth, Mass., Elizabeth, W14196
Thomas, N.C., R11844, b. N.C.
Thomas, R.I. See WOODWARD
Timothy, Cont., Mass., Elizabeth W6578; BLWt.7309-160-55
WOODBANKS, William, S.C. See WILBANKS
WOODBERRY, Benjamin, Mass., S33942
Daniel, Mass., S33940
Jacob B., Mass., Hannah, W15736
John, S.C., See papers in claim of Archibald Scott, W8582
Mager, Mass., S30218
Nathan, Mass., S3618
Robert, Mass., Rebecca, W15498
WOODBERY, Luke, Mass., S45159
WOODBRIDGE, Christopher, Mass., Sarah, W26130; BLWt.2299-300-Capt. iss. 8/1/1789 to Thomas Cushing, ass.
Dudley, Mass., S33955
George, Ct., Privateer, S11877
Theodore, Ct., BLWt.2339-400-Major iss. 4/4/1790 to Wm. Wells ass.
WOODBURN, Jonathan, Md., S35144
Moses, Ct., Privateer, S22605
WOODBURY, Anna, Mass., former wid.

WOODBURY (continued)
of Joshua Bangs, which see
Benjamin, Mass., S35145
Benjamin, Mass., Rhoda, W22685
Ebenezer, Cont., N.H., S35151
Elisha, Cont., N.H., S18289
Elisha, Cont., N.H., Rhoda Clough, former wid., W260; BLWt.18017-160-55
Elizabeth, Mass., former wid. of Joseph Webber, which see
Israel, Mass., S31499
Israel, N.H., S18291; BLWt. 11152-160-55
James, Mass., S44105
James H., Cont., N.H., S45158
Jesse, N.H., Abigail, R11810; BLWt.19783-160-55
John, Cont., Eliza/Elizabeth, W15739; enl. in N.H.
John, Mass., Sarah, W16796
Jonathan, Mass., Hannah, W26127
Joseph, Mass., Nancy, B.L.Reg. 96920-55
Josiah, N.H., S30806
Lot, Mass., Elizabeth, W22676
Lott/Lot, Mass., Martha, W18361
Luke, N.H., Elizabeth, W16795
Mary, Mass., former wid. of Zebulon Ingersoll, which see
Nathaniel, Mass., Mary, W15496
Peter, Mass., S19171
William, Mass., S33948
WOODCOCK, Bartholomew, Mass., S30222
Benjamin, Mass., Ruth, W624; BLWt.51929-160-55
Jane, N.Y., former wid. of Jacob Rose, which see
John, Ct., R11812
John, Va., S41381
Jonathan, Mass., Caroline, W19652
Peter, Pvt. N.Y., BLWt.8003 iss. 7/30/1790 to Edward Compston, ass.
Peter, N.Y., S45157
Samuel, Ct., Rhoda, W9169
William, Del., S32082
WOODDAY, John, N.C., S1886
WOODDELL, Joseph, Va., S11883
WOODILL, John, N.C., Catharine, W3911
WOODDIN, Jeremiah, Ct., BLWt. 1891-100
WOODELL, John, N.C. See WOODDILL
Joseph, Va., S11883
WOODEN, Abner, Mass., Hannah Holmes, former wid.,See WOODIN
Amos, Mass., S24022
Charles, Ct., S15722
Daniel, N.Y., See WOODIN
James, Pvt., Crane's Cont. Art. Mass., BLWt.5337 iss. 4/9/1791 to James Ross
Jeremiah, Ct., See WOODIN
John, Pvt. Pa., BLWt.10654 iss. 5/11/1792
Reuben, N.Y., Patience, W26124; BLWt.57780-160-55
WOODETH, Benjamin, Cont., Ct., S16025

WOODFORD, Bissel, Ct., S11873
Joseph, Ct., S29561
Timothy, Ct., S41370
WOODHAM, Robert, Pvt. Md., BLWt. 11852 iss. 9/12/1792 to John Wright, ass. of Sarah Mantts/ Mantle?
WOODHOUSE, Henry, Mass., Sea Service, Catharine, W26626; BLWt.34517-160-55 (also served in War of 1812)
Samuel, Ct., Abigail, W26108
WOODILL, John, N.C. See WOODDILL
WOODIN, Abner, Mass., Hannah Holmes, R5167. Her 2nd husb., Asa Holmes, was also a sold. in the Revolution
Aner, Cont., Ct., Ruth, W18365
Daniel, N.Y., S28956
Jeremiah, Ct., BLWt.1891-100
John, N.Y., Rebecca, W19658
Philo, Ct., S45161
Reuben, N.Y., Patience, See WOODEN
Samuel, Pvt. Del., BLWt.10911 iss. 9/1/179?. Notation: "Certified by N. Cutting, January 14, 1822".
WOODLAND, Rhode, Pvt. Md., BLWt. 11836 iss. 11/29/1790 to John Fannier, Admr.
WOODMAN, Abner, Mass., N.H., R11816
Benjamin, Cont., Mass., S35146
Dan (colored), N.H., S44103
David, N.H., S11888
Edward, N.C., Sarah, W2893
Edward, R.I., S22067
Ephraim, Mass., Elizabeth, W1689; BLWt.6031-160-55
James, Cont., Mass., S19168
Jeremiah, N.H., Mary/Polly, W22684; BLWt.19912-160-55
John, Mass., S35153
John, Pvt., Va., BLWt.12652 iss. 8/12/1791
Jonathan, Mass., S33949
Joseph, Mass., Elizabeth, W14199
Joseph, Mass., N.H., S17210
Joshua, Mass., Navy, Sarah, W22692; BLWt.26202-160-55
Robert, R.I., S22070
Silvester, Pvt. R.I., BLWt.3584 iss. 6/27/1798 to Andrew Taylor ass.
Sylvester, R.I., S45160
Thomas, N.H., S7969
William, R.I., S22064
WOODMANCY, David, See WOODMANSEE
Joseph, Ct., Dis.
Reuben, R.I., Sarah Hicks, former wid., W21319
WOODMANSEE, David, N.J., Elizabeth, W6576; BLWt.31767-160-55
David, R.I., S10048
Gideon, Mass., S39911
Joseph, Ct., Dis. See WOODMANCY
Squire, Mass., R.I., S22065
WOODMORE, Cornelius, Pvt., N.Y., BLWt.7957 iss. 7/16/1790 to Wm. I. Vreedenburgh, ass.

WOODOTH, John, Pvt., Lee's Legion, BLWt.13931 iss. 2/ 12/1800
WOODRING, Peter, Pa., S3617
WOODROE, Simeon, Pa., Elizabeth W3910
WOODROOF, Harden/Harding, Va., Sally, W3485; BLWt.1892-100
Jesse, Va., Esther, W2397
WOODROW, Simeon, Pa. See WOODROE
WOODRUF, Baldwin, Pvt. Sheldon's Dragoons. Ct., BLWt.6705 iss. 8/23/1790
WOODRUFF, Aaron, Pa., BLWt.2316-300
Amos, Ct., S14901
Amos, Mass., Lura Belding/Belden former wid., W12268; BLWt.9481-160-55
Asaph, Mass., Ruth, R11823
Baldwin/Nathaniel Baldwin, Cont. Ct., Bede Hough, former wid., W14926
Benjamin, N.J., S29563
Benjamin, N.J., Catharine, W26097 BLWt.77547-160-55
Benjamin, N.C., Va., Sarah, W6583 BLWt.35681-160-55
Caleb, N.J., S46084
Cornelius, Pa., R11818
Ephraim, Cont., N.J., Frances, W2309; BLWt.6445-160-55
Ephraim, N.Y., S33938; BLWt.2372-200-Lt. iss. 9/24/1790
Gad, Mass., Azubah Comes, former wid., W18967
Gedor, Ct., Sarah, W26102
Harding/Harden, See WOODROOF
Henlock, N.Y., BLWt.2363-400-Surg. iss. 8/16/1790. No papers
Ichabod, N.J., Abigail, W16792
Isaac, N.J., S39912
Jason, Ct., R11819
Jesse, Va., See WOODROOF
John, Ct., Sarah, W16483
John, Ct., Privateer, S15721
John, N.J., N.Y., S45457; BLWt. 600-100
Jonathan, Pa. Sea Service, R11820
Joseph, Cont., Ct., S14889
Joseph, N.J., Mary, W625; BLWt. 14661-160-55
Josiah, N.J., Susan, W26094; BLWt.86041-160-55
Lambert, Ct., R11821
Lewis, N.J., Hannah Phinnah, former wid., R8218
Nathaniel Baldwin, See Baldwin
Noadiah, Ct., Dorcas, W18366
Noadiah, N.Y., R11822
Oliver, Ct., Privateer, S14885
Philo, Ct., S15720
Robert, N.J., S3616
Samuel, Ct., S7964
Samuel, Ct., S14875
Samuel, Ct., Chloe, W4406; BLWt.36545-160-55
Samuel, Ct., Cont., S39915
Samuel, N.J., S22608
Samuel, N.Y., BLWt.2460-300-Hosp. Mate iss. 6/26/1789. No papers

WOODRUFF (continued)
Selah, Ct., Caroline, W11882
Solomon, Ct., Chestinah/ Christina, W18367
Thomas, N.J., S935
William, Ct., Ruth, W20136
WOODRUM, Stephen, Cont., Va., S35745; BLWt.12670-100-Pvt. iss. 2/10/1800 to Robert Means, ass.
WOODS, Abel, Mass., S23082
Amos, Mass., Betsy, W22674
Archibald, Va., S14892
Archibald, Va., R11825
Azariah, N.J., Jean, W11866
Caldwell, Va., Nancy, W9033
Christopher, Pa., Margaret, W26103
Cornelius, Pvt. Hazen's Regt., BLWt.13879 iss. 7/27/1789 to Richard Platt, ass.
Daniel, N.H., S41368
Elisha, Cont., Mass., S44109
Henry, N.C., S7968
Henry, Pa., Indian War 1790-1791 S22604
Isaac, N.C. See WOOD
John, Cont., Mass., Vt., Abigail, W18368
John, Pvt. Mass., BLWt.5286 iss. 5/19/1797
John, Mass., BLWt.5286 iss. 5/ 19/1797
John, Mass., S33952
John, N.C., S2026, b. in N.C.
John, N.C., See WOOD
John, Pa. & Indian Wars 1794-1795 Sarah, W3323
Joseph, Mass., Keziah, W4105
Joseph, Mass., N.H., Vt., S22068
Josiah, Va., R11831
Justus, Cont., Ct. Sea Service, S35746
Samuel, Mass., Mary Nye, former wid., S41367; BLWt.92087-160-55 She was pensioned on acct. of the service of her last husb., Solomon Nye, Ct., which see
Samuel, Pvt. Pa., BLWt.10575 iss. 2/3/1792 to Stephen Loudon, ass.
Samuel, Pa., S41382
Samuel, Va., S35743
Seth, Mass., Persis, See WOOD
Thomas, Pa., Ann, R11826
Thomas, S.C., S32614, b. S.C.
Timothy, Mass., S30223
William, Pvt., N.J., BLWt.8849 iss. 3/10/1796
William, N.J., Sarah, R11805
William, N.C., Ruth, W6565
William, Pa., S31496
William, Pvt. Va., BLWt.12646 iss. 8/20/1791, also BLWt.57-60-55
William, Pvt. Va., BLWt.12653 iss. 7/14/1792 to Robert Means, ass.
WOODSIDE, Archibald, N.C., S7967
John, N.C., Jane, W6585; BLWt. 18205-160-55
John, Pa., S11889; BLWt.2398-200-Lt. iss. 5/13/1789. See papers within

WOODSIDE (continued)
Robert, N.J., Eleanor Turs, former wid., W4358
Samuel, S.C., Jane, R11833
William, N.C., S7960
WOODSIDES, Robert, Pvt. N.J., BLWt.8877 iss. 2/25/1793
WOODSON, Charles, Va., Judith, W6580
Frederick, Va., R19214, Va. Half Pay. N.A. Acc. No.874-050196. See Half Pay Frederick Woodson
Hughes, Va., R19215 Va. Half Pay
Jacob, Va., S11894
John, Va., S6434
John, Va., S39137
John Stephen, Va., R11835
Joseph, Va., S6437
Robert, Va., BLWt.2426-300-Capt. iss. 3/9/1795 to Tucker W. Woodson, heir-at-law. No papers
Samuel, Va., S31495
Wade N., Va., S30807
WOODSTOCK, William, Corp., Crane's Cont. Art., Mass., BLWt.5339 iss. 6/2/1790
William, Mass., S45461
WOODSUM, David, Navy, Mass., Abigail/Nabby, W26088
Samuel, Mass., S29562
WOODWARD, Aaron, Ct., R11836
Abner, Ct., S11866
Asa, Ct., S41371
Asa, Ct., Sea Service, Cont., Sally, W26129
Asa, Ct., Mass., Vt., Ruth, W6579
Asa, N.J., S33954
Benedict, N.Y., Elizabeth, W18373
Benjamin, Mass., S35150; BLWt. 843-100
Benjamin, N.Y., S46478
Benjamin, Va., S6435
Daniel, Cont., N.H., R.I., R21852
Daniel, Mass., S30227
David, N.H., Tabitha, W15497
Dolly, Cont., Mass., former wid. of Calvin Cowing, which see
Ebenezer, Ct., S41372
Ebenezer, Vt., See WOODORD
Eliphalet, Cont., Mass., N.H., Martha, W18371
Elizabeth, N.H., former wid. of Jonathan Pool, which see
Frederick, Ct., R11838
Gideon, Ct., S11897
Hezekiah, Ct., Aseneth, W3640
Hezekiah, N.Y., S11865
Jacob, Mass., Mercy, W22675
Jacob, Va., See WOODARD
James, Ct. See WOODARD
James, Mass., See WOODWORTH
Jehiel, N.H., Vt., R11839
Jesse, N.C. See WOODARD
John, Ct., Vt., S14877
John, Mass., S11862
John, Mass., Sarah, See WOODARD
John, Vt. See WOODARD
Jonathan, Mass., S28954
Jonathan, Mass., S30221
Jonathan, N.H., Vt., S16585

WOODWARD (continued)
Joshua, Ct., S11879
Joshua, R.I., BLWt.150-100. Claim missing in 1912. Register shows "issued 2/28/1804. Delivered to Mich[l] Nourse."
Josiah, Mass., Patty, W26101
Jourdan, N.C., S7972, b. in N.C.
Levi, Mass., S6439
Nathan, Mass., S21590
Nathaniel, Mass., S33939
Nathaniel, Mass., Sea Service, R11843
Nehemiah, R.I., S41375
Noah, Ct., S11874
Oliver, Ct., S40727
Peter, Cont., Mary, W19656; BLWt. 2359-200-Lt. iss. 10/23/1790
Pompey (colored), Mass., Mary, W4867; BLWt.26731-160-55
Reuben, Ct., S11864
Samuel, Crane's Art., Mass., BLWt.2293-300-Surgeon's Mate, iss. 4/10/1790 to Martha Woodward wid. & legal repr. Also recorded as above under BLWt.2541. No papers
Samuel, Mass., Eunice, W18370
Samuel, Mass., Ann. See WOODARD
Samuel, Va., Sarah, W5169; BLWt. 2178-160-55
Seth, Mass., See WOODARD
Theodorus, N.H., Vt., S14881
Thomas, N.C. See WOODARD
Thomas, R.I., S41376
Timothy, Mass., See WOODARD
Topsail, Mass., S33941
William, Cont., Mass., Lydia, W26089
William, Sgt. Hazen's Regt., BLWt. 13876 iss. 8/22/1789
WOODWELL, Gideon, Navy, Mass., S33944
Lydia, Mass., former wid. of Benjamin Willet, which see
WOODWORTH, Abel, Navy, Ct., S23496
Asa, Mass., BLWt.830-100
Azel, Ct., Dis.
Benjamin, Ct., S11881
Daniel, N.Y., S32612
Darius, Ct., S36851
Dyer, Ct., N.Y., S17799
Elisha, R.I., Edith, W22677
Ezekiel, Mass., S40733
Ezra, Ct., S4733
Ichabod, Ct., S32080
James, Mass., Ruth, W26104
Jedediah, Ct., Adah, W18362
Joel, N.H., S45455
Joseph, Cont., Ct., Wayty, W6854
Josiah, Cont., Ct., S14890
Reuben, N.Y., Olive, W26118
Richard, Pa., S40731
Roger, Ct., S41373
Roswell, Ct., N.H., Phebe, W18369
Roswell, Mass., Celia, R11846
Samuel, Ct., Sally, W26095; BLWt. 26922-160-55
Swift, Ct., S29560
Timothy, Ct., Lydia, W2475; BLWt.6290-160-55
William, Ct., S29559

WOODWORTH (continued)
William G., N.Y., S17207
Ziba, Ct., Lucy, R11848
WOODY, Benjamin, Va., Martha, W6577 BLWt.28650-160-55
James, N.C., S31497; BLWt.26147-160-55
Jonathan, N.C., S17211
Martin, Va., Susanna, W3912
WOODYARD, Calvert, Md. See MASON
Richard, Va. See WOODARD
WOOLARD, James, N.C., S42082
John, Va. See WOOLLARD
WOOLAVER, Jacob, N.Y., Susanna, W18372
John, N.Y., Catharine, W18375
Peter, N.Y. See WOLEVER
WOOLBANKS, William, S.C. See WILBANKS
WOOLBRIDGE, William, See WOOLDRIDGE
WOOLCOT, Benajah, Pvt. Ct., BLWt. 6627 iss. 8/23/1790
Elijah, Pvt. Ct., BLWt.6693 iss. 9/24/1790
Joseph, Pvt. Ct., BLWt.6677 iss. 6/23/1791 to John Birch, ass.
Solomon, Mass. See WOLCOT
WOOLCOTT, John, Ct. See WOLCOTT
John, Mass. See WOLCOTT
Joseph, N.Y., S32610
Silas, Pa. See WOLCUT
Solomon, Ct., Cornelia, See WOLCOTT
William, N.Y., S45458
WOOLDREDGE, John, R.I., S34564
WOOLDRIDGE, James, Va., S11884
John, Va., Fleming/Flemming, W6582
Joseph, Va., S7965
Josiah, Va., Martha T., W22686
Thomas, Va., S31494
William, Ct., War of 1812, Catharine Austin, former wid., W10359 BLWt.80028-160-55
WOOLEBEN, Peter, See WOLEVER
WOOLEBER, Jacob, N.Y. See WOOLAVER
WOOLEVER, Peter, See WOLEVER
WOOLEY, Asa, N.J., Catharine, R11849
David, Cont., Mass., See WOOLLEY
Isaac, Pvt. N.J., BLWt.8838 iss. 9/15/1789
Jacob, Pvt. N.J., BLWt.8839 iss. 9/25/1789
Samuel, N.J., Privateer, R11850
Stephen, N.J., Jane, W11880; BLWt.26450-160-55
William, N.J., Sophia, W2505; BLWt.26516-160-55
WOOLF, Frederick, Cont. (French) See WOLF
Lewis, Cont., Pa., S39913
Vallentine, N.Y., R11852
WOOLFOLK, Robert, Va., S11896
WOOLFORD, Michael, Md., BLWt. 648-100
Thomas, Md., BLWt.2402-500-Col. iss. 2/20/1794 to Thomas Woolford. No papers
Thomas, Md., S14882
WOOLHAVE, William, Pvt. Hazen's Regt., BLWt.13888 iss. 3/1/

WOOLHAVE (continued)
1792 to Nathaniel Grimes, ass.
WOOLHEATER, Adam, Md., R11854
WOOLIVER, Peter, See WOLEVER
WOOLLARD, John, Va., S4732
John, Va., Susannah, W2398; BLWt.18021-160-55
WOOLLEY, Asa, N.J., Catharine, See WOOLEY
Austin, N.Y., Margaret, R11851
David, Cont., Mass., Hannah, W26107; BLWt.31453-160-55. Name also appears as WOOLEY & WOLLEY
Jacob, N.J., Hannah, W3908
Jonathan, Mass., N.H., Anna, W29941; BLWt.36620-160-55. Dau. Phoebe Maria Palmeter
Nathan, Cont., Mass., Lucy, W18384
William, N.J., Sophia, W2505; BLWt.26516-160-55
WOOLLY, David, Mass., Sarah, W15735
WOOLMAN, Ralph, Pvt. Crane's Cont. Art., Mass., BLWt.5335 iss. 12/15/1795 to Levi Stoughton
Ralph, Mass., S39914
WOOLOVER, John, N.Y. See WOOLAVER
WOOLRIDGE, John, R.I., S34564
WOOLSEY, Daniel, N.Y., R11856
Gilbert, Ct., S14884
John, Ct., S10047
Melancthon Lloyd, Cont., N.Y., Alida, W18379; BLWt.2326-200-Lt. iss. 3/6/1792. Recorded as of Mass. Troops
WOOLSON, Isaac, Mass., Vt., S45454, b. 11/1757, in 1820 res. of Lewiston, Niagara Co., N.Y., wife Mercy. D. 10/11/1820
WOLVERTON, John, N.J., Rachel, W2507
WOOLWINE, Philip S., Va., Indian War 1790, Elizabeth, R11858
WOOLWORTH, Ebenezer, Ct., BLWt. 1023-100
Levi, Ct., S45456
WOORHEES, Peter L., See VOORHEES
WOOSELY, Aaron, Pvt., Va., BLWt. 12668 iss. 7/14/1792 to Robert Means, ass.
WOOSLEY, Aaron, Va., S39134
Moses, Va., S6442
Thomas, Pvt. Va., 5 entries. BLWts.12267 & 12648 iss. 5/8/1794 14091 (with note: 12267) iss. 1/8/1795; 14091 & 12671 iss 1/8/1795 to Robert Means, ass.
Thomas, Cont., Va., Jane S., W10005
William, Va., S42080
WOOSTER, Benjamin, Ct., Sally, W2396
David, Brig. Gen., BLWt.2285-850 acres; BLWt.2514-850 acres
Ephraim, Ct., S14883
James, N.H., Hannah, See WORCESTER
John, Mass., Olive, W26091
Lemuel, Ct., S14887
Moses, Ct., Cont., S46333; BLWt. 1806-100
Thomas, Ct., BLWt.2360

WOOSTER (continued)
300-Capt. Iss. 7/27/1789
Walter, Ct., Ursula, W26106
WOOTEN, Dolby, Pvt. Del., BLWt. 10913 iss. 4/15/1799 to Mitchell Kershaw, ass. Notation:"Certified 3/3/1813"
Thomas, Ga., Susanna, S11892 & R11861
Turner, Va., Nancy, R11860
William, Frances Bachelor, former wid., R350. N.C. res. of wid. in 1843
WOOTERS, Marclin, N.C., S7958
WOOTON, Silas P., Va., S40730
WORCESTER, Eldad, Mass., S18665
Eleanor, Mass., former wid. of Mark Hanscom, which see
James, N.H., Hannah, W26092; BLWt.755-100
Jesse, N.H., Sarah, W26117
Noah, Mass., N.H., S11867
Samuel, Mass., S18664
Samuel, Mass. See WORSTER
Samuel, Mass., Isabel, R11863
Thomas, Mass., See WORSTER
William, Mass. See WORSTER
WORD, Thomas, Va., S39133
WORDEN, Arnold, R.I., W6581
Barnard, N.Y. See WARDEN
Benjamin, Ct., S40724
Benjamin, N.Y., S23497
Billings, Ct., S14886
Elizabeth, Ct., former wid. of Obed Holcomb, which see
Gilbert, N.Y., S14899
Ichabod, Ct. See WARDEN
Isaac, N.Y., S11871
James, Ct., N.Y. See WARDEN
Jesse, Ct., R.I. See WERDEN
John, Mass., S11885
Joseph, Ct., Cont., S35749
Paul, Cont., Sarah, BLWt.992-100. N.Y. res. of wid. in 1819
Richmond, Green Mt. Boys, Mass., Vt., S14878
Roger, Ct., N.Y., S14891
Sylvester/Silyester, Cont., Ct., S45463
Thomas, Ct., Cont.,Jemima, W4407
Thomas, Cont., Mass., S44005
Wait, Ct., Diannah, R11864
William, Ct. See WORDIN
WORDIN, Elizabeth, Ct. See WORDEN
John, Ct., N.Y., S14776
William, Ct., Dorcas, W22679
WORK, Asa, Mass., R11869
David, Pa., S7961
James, Mass., S30226
WORKMAN, Abraham, Va., R11868
Daniel, Va., S40725
Hugh, Pa., S22603
James, Pa., S22606
Peter, N.C., S39136
Samuel, Pvt., N.J., BLWt.8863 iss. 5/9/1792
WORKS, James, Mass., S30226
WORLDLEY, Polley, Ga., former wid. of David Hill, which see
WORLEN, John, Pvt. Pa., BLWt. 10577 iss. 1/11/1791

WORLEY
David, Md., R11870
Joshua, Va., S18667
Lovett, N.C., Mary, R7391
Zachariah, Va., Milley, W1972; BLWt.18388-160-55
WORMELL, John, Mass., S35143
Nathaniel, Navy, R.I., Susannah W26121
WORMOOD, John/Joshn, See WORMWOOD
WORMOUTH, John, N.Y. See WORMWOOD
WORMSLEY, James, R.I., S23498
WORMUD, John/Joshn, See WORMWOOD
WORMWELL, Nathaniel, Navy, R.I. See WORMELL
WORMWOOD, Amos, Mass., Lydia, W26105
James, Mass., S20578
John, N.Y., Hannah Rawley/Rawleigh former wid., W24797
John/Joshn, N.Y., Catharine, W26093; BLWt.31734-160-55
Joseph, Mass., R11872
Matthias, N.Y., S45459
Peter, Cont., N.Y., Sarah, W22680
WORNELL, James, Va., Charlotte/Sharlotte, W2892; BLWt.26919-160-55
WORNER, Abner, Ct., S34569
Peter, Md., R11149
WORRAL, Benjamin, Pa., S3478
WORRALL, William, N.J., S34562
WORRELL, Nicholas, N.J., S934
William, N.J. See WORRALL
WORREN, James, Ct., Cont., S45452
WORRICK, Wyatt/Wiatt/Wiat, N.C. See WARWICK
WORSELEY, Joseph, Mass., Sea Service, Elizabeth, W9035; BLWt.13423-160-55
WORSHAM, Essex, Va., S6447
John, Va., S11658
Joshua, Pa., Va.?, S41380
Richard, Va., S38478; BLWt.2438-200-Lt. Iss. 3/19/1794
William, 1st Regt. Light Dragoons BLWt.2380-200-Lt. iss. 6/19/1795 to Richard Worsham, admr., also recorded as above under BLWt. 2655. No papers
William, Va., S6436
WORSLEY, Joseph, Mass., Sea Service, Elizabeth, See WORSELEY
Robert, N.H., Abigail, W16482
Thomas, N.C., S42081
WORSTER, Benjamin, Mass., Navy, S43188
James, N.H., See WORCESTER
Samuel, Mass., Relief, W15737
Thomas, Mass., Susannah, W14183
William, Mass., S35148
WORT, John, Pa., Mary, W6562
Peter, Pvt. Art. Artificers "of Pennsylvania", BLWt.13923 iss. 6/26/1792
WORTH, William, Pvt. N.J., BLWt. 8854 iss. 6/15/1795 to John N. Cumming, ass.
William, N.J., S33950
WORTHEN, Benjamin, Mass. See WORTHER

WORTHEN (continued)
Isaac, Navy, N.H., Judith, W18364
Michael, N.H., Dorothy, W26112
Stephen, Cont. Mass., S44107
WORTHER, Benjamin, Mass., S31500
WORTHINGTON, Benjamin, Pvt. Md., BLWt.11817 iss. 8/10/1790
Charles, Md., S4734
Edward, Va., R19205. Va. Half Pay. N.A. Acc. No.874-050197 Half Pay Edward Worthington
Eliphalet, Mass., Meletiah, W2310
Heman, Mass., S34567
Stephen, Mass., S34566
William, Pa., S1272
William, Pa., Ann, W1346; BLWt. 9193-160-55
WORTHLEY, Jonathan, N.H., Tamar, W2395; BLWt.11095-160-55
WORTHLY, Daniel, Mass., Dorcas, W22690
WORTMAN, Abraham, N.J., Abigail, W4404; BLWt.31571-160-55
John, N.J., Charity, W100
John, N.J., Sarah, W1020
WOSSON, William, Pa., Va., S18670
WOTTON, Henry, Mass., S34568
John, Mass., S34565
WRADLEY, William, N.J., Elizabeth W626
WRAY, Benjamin, Va. See RAY
David, Va., S7973
George, Va., Sea Service, R111, Va. Half Pay
Henry, Va., Clarissa, W6380; See N.A. Acc. No.874-050198 Not Half Pay Henry Wray
Isaac, N.Y., S14251
James, Pa., S3619
James, Va., S5971
WREN, Bates, Va. See WRENN
Joseph, N.C., Nancy, W18386
Joseph, Pvt. Pa., BLWt.10631 iss. 7/11/1791
Joseph, Pa., S39921
WRENN, Bates, Va., R11875
John, Cont., S7979. Sussex Co., Va. in 1832
WRIGGINS, Thomas, N.J., S34570
WRIGHT, Aaron, Mass., S30809
Aaron, Mass., Mary, W15972
Aaron, Pa., Jane, W2894, d. 1816
Abel, Vt., Sybel Ford, former wid., W1406; BLWt.17868-160-55
Abijah, Ct., Sally, W2477; BLWt. 26876-160-55
Abner, Cont.,Mass.?, Jane, W15818
Abraham, Ct., Rebecca, W22699
Abraham/Abraham B., Mass., S44114
Abraham, N.Y., S24025
Abraham, N.Y., R11876
Absalom, Md., Mary, W6589; BLWts. 11808-100 iss. 12/18/1794 & 148-60-55
Alexander, Pvt. "in the Artillery Artificers" Pa., BLWts.10556 & 13922 iss. 6/22/1796
Andrew, Mass., S24027
Andrew, Va., Lucy, W6587
Archibald, Va., Mary, W18460
Asa, N.Y., S23499

WRIGHT (continued)
Asa, N.C., S18292, b. in Va.
Asa, Pa., S11907
Asahel, Mass., S6454
Asahel, Mass., S41386; BLWt. 1509-100
Asher, Ct., Bulah, W22700
Asher, Cont. Ct., S36854
Azariah, Vt., S24026
Barruck, Pvt. N.Y., BLWt.7958 iss. 7/16/1790 to Wm. I. Vreedenburgh, ass.
Bazeliel/Bezelel, Mass., S45465
Bazzell, Md., Pa., See RIGHT
Benjamin, Ct., S36852
Benjamin, Cont., Ct., Susanna, W19662
Benjamin, N.H., S22610
Benjamin, Pvt. N.Y., BLWt.8021 iss. 9/9/1790 to Ezekiel Crane, ass.
Bilya/Billya, Mass., Patience, W26140
Bledso, Va., Sarah, R19267
Bolling, Va., Milley, W5183; BLWt.26982-160-55
Caleb, Vt., Charlotte, W19661
Carmi, Mass., S32084
Charles, Ct., Betsey, W3486; BLWt.6391-160-55
Cornelius, Ct., S45467
Cyprion, Sgt. Mass., BLWt.5256 iss. 4/1/1790
Daniel, Pvt. Ct., BLWt.6636 iss. 4/14/1790 to William Wells, ass.
Daniel, Ct., S32086
Daniel, Ct., Mabel, W26133
Daniel, Cont., N.H., S45163
Daniel, Mass., Chloe/Cloe, W20140
Daniel, Mass., N.Y., Lovina, W22703
Daniel, N.J., R11880
Daniel, N.C., S32616
Darius, Mass., Louisa/Lovisa, W14203
David, N.H., Vt., S44110
David, N.C., S6448
David, Pa., S49261
Deborah, Ct., former wid. of Samuel Bates, which see
Dennis, N.Y., S16302
Ebenezer, Ct., res. of Wethersfield Ct., d. 1808. No number
Ebenezer, Mass., S34574
Edmund, Mass., S30228
Edward, Md., S39919
Edward, Pvt. N.Y., BLWt.7998 iss. 2/14/1791 to James Sheldon, ass.
Edward, N.Y., Freelove, W18388
Edward, N.C., S7977
Eldad, Mass., S34573
Eleazer, Vt., S11904
Eliab, Mass., See WIGHT
Elijah, Ct., Jane, W26135
Elijah, Cont., Md., Pa., S1273
Elijah, N.H., Meriam, W26137
Elisha, Mass., S23500
Ely, N.H., S46348
Ephraim, Ct., S19515
Francis, Ct., BLWt.1118-100
George, Ct., Elizabeth, W22702; BLWt.7062-160-55

WRIGHT (continued)
George, Cont. Va., S38480
George, Pa., S7978
George, Va., S31501
George, Va., Sarah, W3062; BLWt.31452-160-55
Hannah, Mass., former wid. of David Saunderson, which see
Henderson, Pvt. Pa., BLWt.10602 iss. 7/27/1789 to Richard Platt, ass.
Henry, Mass., S34572
Isaac, Cont., N.Y., S14906
Isaac, Mass., Selah, W26139
Isaac, Mass., N.H., S30229
Isaac, S.C., R11886
Israel, R11887, Ky. res. in 1837
Jacob, Mass., S44113
Jacob, N.J., S6452
Jacob, N.J., Ann, W1021
Jacob, N.Y., BLWt.2365-300-Capt. iss. 8/10/1790 to Samuel Stringer and Stephen Luske, assnes. No papers
Jacob, N.Y., S14903
James, Pvt., Ct., BLWt.6647 iss. 10/7/1789 to Benj. Tallmadge, ass.
James, Ct., Elizabeth, W9038
James, Ct., Navy, S36857
James, Pvt. Mass., BLWt.5327 iss. 5/2/1795 to Samuel Emery
James, Mass., S18671
James, N.C., S9532
James, Va., S30232
James, Va., S31504
James, Va., S35750
James, Va., R11889
James, Va., Peggy, R11901
James, Va., BLWt.2429-300
Jarrett, Va., Elizabeth, W627
Jehiel, Mass., Catharine, W15708
Jeremiah, Ct., S36856
Jeremiah, Va., S32617
Jesse, Pvt. Md., BLWt.11806 iss. 6/10/1789
Jesse, Mass., S14905
Joab, Ct. & N.Y. in War of 1812, Peninah, W6598; BLWts.41741-40-50 & 3827-120-55
Joel, Cont., Mass. See WIGHT
John, Ct., S36858
John, Ct., Cont., S45464
John, Ct., Cont., S45466
John, Cont. Md., S45469
John, Cont., Pa., S10299
John, Cont., Va., S41384; BLWt. 1499-100
John, Pvt. Lee's Legion, BLWt. 13929 iss. 2/4/1793
John, Pvt., Mass., BLWt.5263 iss. 12/31/1795 to Joseph & Allen Crocker
John, Pvt. Mass., BLWt.5274 iss. 11/14/1789 to Sarah Green, wid.
John, Mass., S18672
John, Mass., S30234
John, Pvt., N.Y., BLWt.7974 iss. 10/12/1790 to Conrad Seeber, ass.
John, N.Y., S45470

WRIGHT (continued)
John, N.C., Nancy Dew, former wid. See her case as wid. of John Dew, N.C.
John, N.C., S7974, b. in N.C.
John, N.C., S31502, b. in Va.
John, N.C., R11894, b. in Va.
John, Pa. See LAMBRIGHT
John, Pa., Elizabeth, R11882
John, Pa., R11892
John, S.C., Alsey, R11877
John, Va., S6449
John, Va., Margaret, S41387
John, Va., Elizabeth, W6588
John, Va., Mary, W6599
John, Va., Elizabeth, See RIGHT
John, Va., R11893
John A., Va., S17214
John G., Cont.,N.Y., Charity, W6594; BLWt.2005-300
Jonathan, Ct., S11908
Jonathan, Ct., Margaret/Pegga, W11895
Jonathan, Mass., Rachel, W26142
Jonathan, N.H., S45471
Jonathan, N.H., Vt., R11896
Jonathan, Va. See WHIGHT
Joseph, Pvt., Ct., BLWt.6618 iss. 4/14/1790 to William Wells, ass.
Joseph, Cont., Mass., S34575
Joseph, Cont., Mass., S45468
Joseph, Mass., S18673
Joseph, Pvt., N.J., BLWt.8859 iss. 6/16/1789 to Thomas Coyle, ass.
Joseph, N.C., R11898
Joseph, Va., S31503
Joseph Allyn, Ct., Cont., S36855 BLWt.2342-400-Major iss. 10/30/1789
Joseph H., N.Y., R11897
Joshua, Cont., Mass., Susannah, W19660
Josiah, Cont., Mass., Mary, W26627
Josiah, Cont., N.H., S44112
Josiah, Mass., Betty Weston, former wid., W18331
Josiah, Vt., Susannah, R11908
Jotham, Art. Artificers, N.Y., BLWt.2325-200-Lt. iss. 6/2/1790 Also recorded as above under BLWt.2558
Jude, Mass., Roxanna, R11903
Lemuel, Mass., N.H., Mary, W26131
Lemuel, N.H., R11904
Levi, Mass., Mercy, W835; BLWt. 12582-160-55
Lewis, Va., wid. Elizabeth, wid. Ctf. 31569
Luther, Mass., Lorain, W22701
Mary, Ct., former wid. of Moses West, which see
Moses, Ct., Abigail, W18385
Moses, Mass., S9711; BLWt.15184-160-55
Moses, Va., S39923
Moses, Va., Elizabeth, W6591
Nahum, Cont., Mass. See WIGHT
Nathan, Md., BLWt.1220-200

WRIGHT (continued)
Nathan, S.C., Va., S32083
Nathaniel, Mass. See WIGHT
Nehemiah, N.H., Mary/Polly, W16166
Noah, Mass., S30230
Obadiah, Mass., S30233
Oliver, Mass., S30231
Oliver, Mass., N.H., S15725
Paul, Va., S41383
Perez, Mass., Lucy Frye, former wid., W11022; BLWt.18201-160-55
Peter, Mass., S34571
Peter, Mass., Abigail, W26132
Phinehas/Phineas, Cont., Mass. Vt., S45472
Reuben, Ct., Cont., S17212
Richard, Va., S39922
Richard, Va., Anna/Ann, W6590
Robert, Cont., Mass., N.J., S7975
Robert, Pvt., Md., BLWt.11807 iss. 1/11/1796 to Joshua Ward, ass.
Robert, N.Y., BLWt.2333-300-Capt. iss. 7/20/1791 to Lucretia Allen Admx. Also recorded as above under BLWt.2586. No papers
Robert, Pvt., N.Y., BLWt.7989 iss. 7/30/1790 to Edward Cumpston, ass.
Robert, N.Y., S36853
Robert, Pa., S3620
Robert, Va., S6450
Robert, Va., Mary Goodwin, former wid., W25638; BLWt.96061-160-55
Roswell, Ct., Abigail, W26134
Roxavene, Ct., former wid. of Martin Denslow, W6593; BLWt. 3191-160-55
Samuel, Ct., S14904
Samuel, Ct., or Mass., Jemima, R11890
Samuel, Mass., Navy, Hannah, W26138
Samuel, Pvt. N.J., BLWt.8864 iss. 9/28/1790 to Nathaniel Leonard, ass.
Samuel, Pvt. N.Y., BLWt.7995 iss. 7/12/1790 to C.F. Weisenfels, ass.
Samuel, N.Y., Phebe, W18461
Samuel Turbutt, Md., Ann, W4408
Seth, Mass., Sarah, W19663 & W14200
Silas, Mass., Mercy, W6592
Simeon, Ct., Sarah, W16797
Simeon, Green Mt. Boys Vt., R11905
Simeon, Mass., S3621
Solomon, Cont., Mass., S45162
Solomon, S.C., R11906
Solomon, Vt., Eunice, W15740
Starke, Va., S6451
Stephen, Mass., Sarah, W14202
Stephen, Mass., BLWt.19501-160-55
Stephen, Va., Sea Service, R11907

WRIGHT (continued)
Thadeus, Mass., S11909
Thomas, Cont., Mass., N.H., S44111
Thomas, Pvt. Mass., BLWt.5210 iss. 1/28/1790 to James Patterson
Thomas, Mass., Privateer, S41385
Thomas, N.C., S7976
Thomas, N.C., Mary, R11899, b. in Va.
Thomas, Va., S6453
Thomas, Va., S38479
Thomas, Va., Mary, W2984
Thomas, Va., Indian War 1788 & 1792, Elenor, R11881
Thomas M., Mass., S18674
Uriah, Mass., S11903
William, Cont., Va., S17213, b. in England
William, Pvt. Del., BLWt.10905 iss. 9/2/1789
William, N.Y., S11906
William, N.C., S16301
William, N.C., Elizabeth, R11884
William, N.C., R11910
William, Pa., S4735
William, Va., S11905
William, Va., S32087
William, Va., Elizabeth, W6596
William, Va., Mary, R11900
WRIGHTINGTON, George, Mass., S45473
Robert, Mass., Sally Omans, former wid., W27495
Thomas, Mass., S35155
WRIGHTMIRE, George, Pa., S39920
WRISLE, George, Ct., S17800
WRISLEY, Samuel, Cont., Ct., S32085
WRITHINGTON, Robert, Pvt. Mass., BLWt.5317 iss. 7/16/1792
WROE, William, Va., S39918
WUERTZ, William, Pa. See WIRTZ
WUIBERT, Anthony Felix, Engineers BLWt.2461-450-Lt. Col. iss. 11/5/1789. No papers. This name is spelled Weibert; see Heitman's Hist. Reg.
WUINS, William, Pvt. N.Y., BLWt. 8011 iss. 4/5/1793 to George Stout, ass.
WULLUM, Samuel/Shem, Va., Hannah, W4841
WUNDER, George, Pa., Ann, R11911
WURTZ, Philip, Pa. See WIRT
WYATT, Benjamin, Mass., Mary, W26144; BLWt.28537-160-55
Francis, Cont., Va., Frances, W2042
Henry, Va., Elizabeth, W836
Jeremiah, N.C., R11916
John, Pvt. N.Y., BLWt.8034 iss. 1/25/1791 to Samuel Stringer, ass.
John, N.C., S17215; B.L. Rej. 40073-55
John, Va., S16303, b. in England
John, Va., Mary, W6595
Simon, Cont., Mass., S34577
Spievy/Spivey, Va., S6456

WYATT (continued)
Stephen, Mass., Hannah, W14209
Theophilus, Va., Sally, W2478; BLWt.31450-160-55
Thomas, Pa. & Dunmore's War 1774, S35159
WYBERT, Frederick, Pvt. N.Y., BLWt.8027 iss. 9/24/1791 to Platt Rogers, ass.
WYCHOFF, Cornelius, See WYCKOFF
WYCKOFF, Cornelius, Cont., N.J. Alice, W19664
John, N.J., S1155
John, N.J., Johannah, W6604
John B., N.J., See WICKOFF
John C., N.J., S938
Samuel, Md., S4736
WYER, George, Va., R11917
John, Mass. See WIRS
Josiah, Mass., S35157
WYETH, Ebenezer, Mass., S34576
Jonas, Mass., Navy, Elizabeth W14205
Joshua, Mass., S40734
WYGANT, James, N.J., S42616
See James WAGON, S43225, seems to have been same veteran
Martin, N.Y., S19517
WYKOFF, Jacob, N.J., S32619
WYLEY, James, Va., See WYLY
John, N.J., S3622
Robert, Mass., Dis.
WYLIE, Francis, S.C., S21592
James, Ct., S11816
James, Mass., See WYLLIE
Peter, Ct., S41392
Simeon, N.Y., S39924
Thomas, Pa., BLWt.2302-300-Capt. iss. 3/20/1798 to Alex Power, ass. Also recorded as above under BLWt.2549. No papers
WYLLIE, James, Mass., R11918
WYLLIS, John Palsgrave, Ct., BLWt.2336-400-Major iss. 7/27/1789. No papers
Joseph, Cont., N.J. See WYLLYS
WYLLY, Thomas, Cont., Ga., Sarah, R11535
WYLLYS, Joseph, Pvt. Ct., BLWt. 6628 iss. 1/28/1790 to William Walter Parsons, ass.
Joseph, Pvt. Ct., BLWt.6701 iss. 7/6/1791 to Silas Pepoon, ass.
Joseph, Cont., N.J., Elizabeth, W26147
Samuel, Ct., BLWt.2341-500-Col. iss. 10/12/1789. No papers
Zenas, Mass., S44216
WYLY, James, Va., Mary, W26145; BLWt.26214-160-55, b. in N.C.
WYMAN, Asa Miller, Mass., S41391; BLWts.394-100 & 15-60-55
Benjamin, Mass., S45475
Daniel, 1st., Cont.,Mass., S35158 Res. 1818 Chesterville, Kennebec Co., Me. age 63 yrs., wife Ruth. Daniel Wyman 2nd testified both served in same Co. & Regt.
Daniel, 2nd., Cont., Mass., S35160 Res. of Fairfield, Somerset Co., Mass. in 1818 aged 70, wife Esther. He d. 1/16/1827. He

WYMAN (continued)
served in the same Co. & Regt. with Daniel Wyman 1st and testified for him. See S35158
David, Mass., S30235
David, Mass., Sarah, W18462
Deen/Dean, Mass., War 1812-34th U.S. Inf. S35156; BLWt.728-100
Ezra, N.H., Hannah, BLWt.61131-160-55
Francis, Cont., Mass., Lucy, W15743
Henry, Mass., Sarah, W18332; BLWt.19518-160-55
Isaac, Cont., N.H., S11910
James, Mass., Mary, R11913
Jeduthan, Cont., Mass., Dorcas, W26148
John, Cont., Mass., R.I., S41389
John, Mass., S7980
John, Mass., S41390; BLWt.395-100
Jonas, Mass., Elizabeth Colburn, former wid., W14513. Her last husb. was pensioned. See Joseph Colburn, Mass.
Jonas, N.H., Lydia, W16484
Joseph, Mass., S29564
Josiah, N.H., Aphia, W26143
Nehemiah, Mass., Susanna, W14204
Reuben, Mass., Olive, W4869; BLWt.3194-160-55
Samuel, Mass., S45474
Samuel, Mass., Abigail Adams, former wid., R23
Seth, Mass., S19888
Seth, Mass., S22611
Silas, Mass., Susanna, W15742
Stephen, Cont., Mass., Olive, W16090
Thomas, Mass., Sarah, W21859
Uzziah, Mass., Lydia, W26146
William, Mass., S19173; BLWt. 29750-160-55
William, Vt., Melinda, See WIMAN
WYMER, Henry, Pa., S41388
John, Pa. See WIMMER
WYNANS, John, N.Y. See WINANS
William, N.Y., See WINANS
WYNKOOP, Hezekiah, N.Y., S11911
WYNN, Henry, N.J., Catharine, See WINN
Josiah, N.J., See WINN
Webster, Pvt., Pa., BLWt.10665 iss. 1/21/1792
Webster, Pa., S46332
William, Va., R11920
WYRICK, Peter, Pa., Sarah, W11899
WYSEMORE, Abram/Abraham, See WISMORE, Abraham
WYSHAM, John, Cont., Md., BLWt. 2196-100
WYSHOVER, Jacob, Pvt., N.Y., BLWt.7996 iss. 10/31/1791
WYSONG, Jacob, Va., Mary, W18463
WYSOR, Henry, Va., S7854

Y

YACOBI, Philib/Philip, Pa., S39768
YADER, Joseph, Va., S1742
YAGER, Samuel, Va. See YEAGOR
YAIL, Wait, Cont., Mass. See YALE
YALE, Daniel, Ct., S11912
James, Ct., S11914
Wait, Cont., Mass., Sarah, W22704
Waitstill/Wate, Ct. See Wate YALE
Wait /Waitstill, Ct., S36860
YAMANS, Nathan, Mass., S45479
YANCEY, Ambrose, Va., S46059, b. in Va.
Austin, N.C., S.C., R11921
Layton/Leighton/Leyton, Cont., Va., Fanny/Frances, W7380; BLWt.2467-200-Lt. iss. 9/5/1796
Lewis, Cont., Va., Phebe/Pheby, W2508; BLWt.36522-160-55
Philemon, Va., S1274
Robert, Cont., Va., S35752; BLWt.2465-300-Capt. iss. 5/5/1790 to Wm. I. Vredenburgh, ass.
YANCY, Elizabeth, wid. of John. This is listed in the 1852"Rejected & Suspended Pensions" - res. Gallatin, Sumner Co., Tenn. Notation in large Rejected & Suspended Book - claim missing - 1877
Philemon, Va., S1274
YANSON, Henry, N.Y., S23501
John/Johannes, N.Y., Margaret, W20144
YAPLE, John Nicholas, N.Y., Catherine, W25565
YARBORAUGH, Nathan, N.C., Mary, W4870
YARBOROUGH, Davis, N.C., S1606
Edward, N.C., Sarah, W4776; BLWt.2470-300-Capt. iss. 5/10/1790
Elisha, Va., S7984
Henry, N.C., S1607
Joel, Va., Agness, See YARBROUGH
John, N.C., Joanna, R11923
Joseph, N.C., S7981
Lewis, S.C. See YARBROUGH
Nathan, N.C., See YARBORAUGH
Randolph, N.C., Mary, R11924
YARBROUGH, Charles, Cont., Va., BLWt.1923-200
Joel, Va., Agness, W7382
John, N.C., See YARBOROUGH
John, Va., S36861
Lewis, S.C., Elizabeth, W1120
Nathan, N.C., Mary, W4870
YARD, Daniel, N.J., Mary, W2399
George, N.J., R11925
Isaiah, N.J., S1156
YARINGTON, Daniel, Ct., S45478
YARRINGTON, Daniel, See YARINGTON
Ephraim, Pvt. Sheldon's Dragoons Ct., BLWt.6720 iss. 9/29/1790
William, Pvt., N.Y., BLWt.8058 iss. 7/9/1790 to Nicholas Fish, ass.
William, N.Y., S45477
YATER, John, N.J., BLWt.98-100

YATES, Barzillai, See YEATS
Benjamin, Md. See YEATS
Christopher P., N.Y., Maria, W16486
George, Va., BLWt.2469-300-Sur. Mate, iss. 1/17/1800 to Reuben Zimerman, guardian to Lawrence Catlett Yates, heir.
George James, Mass., Nancy, W26500
Hannah, Mass., Navy, former wid. of Charles Muncriff, which see
Jacob, N.Y., Elizabeth, W20141
John, Mass., Sea Service, S30236
John, N.C., Jemima, W20142
John, N.C., R11928
John, Va. See YEATES
John, Va., Courtney, R11926
Joseph, Sgt. N.J., BLWt.8883 iss. 7/1/1790
Joseph, N.J., S45476
Nicholas, N.Y., Rebecca Van Vranken/Van Vrenken, former wid. W18200
Robert, Md., S35754
Samuel, N.C., Jane, R11927
Thomas, N.C., See YEATES
William, Dis., Vt. res.
William, Pvt., N.J., BLWt.8885 iss. 6/16/1789 to Thomas Coyle, ass.
William, N.J., S7982
YAW, Amos, Vt. See YEAW
Sarah, Mass., former wid. of Preserved Bullock, which see
YAXTHEIMER, Henry, Pa. See YOXTHEIMER
YEADEN, Joseph, Va. See YADER
YEAGER, Elisha, Va., S16587
George, War of 1812, Margaret, R11930, Pa. res. of wid. in 1850. Her other husb., James(?) Reily, also served in the Rev. See papers within
Henry, Pa., Privateer, R11929
John, Va., S7985
Solomon, Va., Phebe, W2043; BLWt.51767-160-55
YEAGOR, Samuel, Va., S35751
YEAMANS, Jonathan, Mass., BLWt. 2462-200-Lt. iss. 12/31/1789. No papers
YEARGAN, Thomas, Va., S7987
YEARGIN, John, Va., Mildred, R11931
YEARLY, James, N.C., R11932
YEARWOOD, John, N.C., R11933
YEAST, Jacob, Md., Elizabeth, R11934
Philip, Md., S7986
YEASTING, Peter, Pvt., N.J., BLWt.8879 iss. 6/11/1789 to Matthias Denman, ass.
YEATES, Benjamin, Md. See YEATS
John, Va., S7988. See N.A. Acc. No. 874-050200 Half Pay John Yeates
Samuel, N.C. See YATES
Thomas, N.C., Rebecca, W7335
YEATON, Hannah, Mass., former wid. of Samuel Bradbury,

YEATON (continued)
which see
James, Mass., Lucy, W26628
John, Mass., R11935
Jonathan, N.H., Jane, W6377; BLWt.26747-160-55
Moses, N.H., Sea Service, Sally, W22706
Paul, N.H., S35161; BLWt.3793-160-55
Samuel, Cont., N.H., S43329; BLWt.1325-100, a res. of Durham N.H.; enl. 1775
Samuel, N.H., BLWt.2351-100; a res. of Tamworth & Ossipee, and enl. in 1782
YEATS, Barzillai, Mass., R.I., S14908
Benjamin, Md., Sarah, W8202; BLWt.3134-160-55
George James, Mass. See YATES
Samuel, N.C. See YATES
Thomas, N.C. See YEATES
YEATTS, William, Pa. See YETTS
YEATY, John, Pvt., N.J., BLWt. 8884 iss. 11/12/1796
YEAW, Amos, Vt., Eunice, W9039; BLWt.19531-160-55
YEBEL, Henry, Cont., Pa., Anna Maria, W3326
YEBLE, Henry, Pa. See YEBEL
YELTON, James, Va., S30810
William, Va., S35753
YELVERTON, Anthony, N.Y., S11917
YENDALL, Samuel, See YENDELL
YENDELL, Samuel, Mass. Sea Service, S30237; BLWt.26417-160-55
YENGLING, John Frederick, N.Y., Margaret, W11610
YENTZER, John, Pa., Mary, R11937
YEOMAN, Solomon, N.C., S32088
YEOMANS, Edward, Ct., Gratis, W11902; BLWt.8181-160-55
Eleazer, Pvt., N.Y., BLWt.8057 iss. 7/16/1790 to Philip Van Cortland, ass.
Isaac, N.Y., Nancy, See YOUMANS
Jeremiah, Pvt. N.Y., BLWt.8059 iss. 8/12/1790 to Benjamin Coe ass.
John, Mass., Martha, W26629
Jonathan, N.Y., R11938
Joshua, Ct., Elizabeth, W20145
Moses, N.Y., BLWt.2468-200-Lt. iss. 10/23/1790. Also recorded as above under BLWt.2574. No papers
Samuel, Ct., S22612
YERKS, Aaron, N.Y., Peggy/Becky Tolon, former wid., R10631
Hermanus, Pvt. Crane's Cont. Art., Mass., BLWt.5354 iss. 8/7/1789 to Richard Platt
James, N.Y., Auley, W16487
John, N.Y., S23502
YERRY, John, N.Y., Maria, W25475
YETMAN, James, N.J., S2222
YETTEN, James, Mass. See YEATON
Samuel, N.H., See YETTON
YETTON, George, N.H.,N.Y., S11916

YETTON (continued)
James, Va. See YELTON
Samuel, N.H., S46237
YETTS, William, Pa., Elizabeth R11950
YEULEN, William, See YEULIN
YEULIN, William, Mass., S35162
YEULING, William, See YEULIN
YEW, Andrew, Mass., R.I., S11915
YINGLING, John F., Pvt. N.Y., BLWt.8061 iss. 8/23/1790 to Charles Newkerk, ass.
YOAHUM, Jacob, Va. See YOAKUM
YOAKHUM, Jacob, See YOAKUM
YOAKUM, Jacob, Va., Magdalen, R11939. Name also appears as YOAKHUM/YOAHUM/YOCUM/YOKUM
YOCOM, George, Va., R11941
Jacob, Va. See YOAKUM
Jesse, Va., R11940
John, Va., S32622
YOCUM, Peter, Pa., S22616
YOHE, George, Pa., S23086
YOHO, Henry, Va., S7996
YOKUM, Jacob, Va. See YOAKUM
YOMANS, Edward, Ct. See YEOMANS
YONES, Michael, Pa. Katherine, W7376
YONG, Andrew, N.C., S30812
Ebenezer, Ct. See YOUNG
YONGER, Jacob, N.Y. See YOUGER
YONKER, Frederick, See JUNGKURTH
YONTZ, George Frederick, N.C., Maria Barbara, W7378
YORDAN, John, N.Y., S26982, d. 2/18/1840
John P., N.Y., R11943, alive in 1845
YORDEN, John, N.Y. See YORDAN
Nicholas, N.Y., Catharine, S26971 & R11942
YORDON, John, N.Y. See YORDAN
YORESS, John, Pvt. N.Y., BLWt. 8056 iss. 10/11/1790 to Lewis Graham, ass.
YORK, Aaron, N.Y. See YERKS
Abigail, Mass, Navy, former wid. of Nathaniel Randall, which see
Allan, Ct., S17217
Benjamin, Navy, N.H., S16026
Benjamin, N.H., S7999
Daniel, N.H., S46479
Daniel, N.Y., S23504
Elisha, Ct., Sarah, W18246; BLWt.14959-160-55
Gersham, Cont., N.H., S41395
Isaac, Cont., Mass., Polly, W837 BLWt.3621-160-55, born, lived & died 11/24/1846 in Standish, Cumberland Co., Me.
Isaac Ilsly, Cont., Mass., S17801 res. during Rev. at Standish & Bethel, Me.; res. in 1818 Bethel Oxford Co., Me., wife Betsey, d. 8/5/1844
Jacob, Mass., S19175
James, Ct., S17218
Jeremiah, Ct., Thankful, W2045; BLWt.27662-160-55
Jeremiah/Jeramiah, Va., Pa.,

YORK (continued)
Joanna, W10006; BLWt.94059-160-55
John, Mass., S16027
John, N.Y., S11927
John, Pvt., R.I., BLWt.3605 iss. 6/24/1793
John, Va., S35757
Joseph, Pvt. N.H., BLWt.3603 iss. 6/17/1790 to B.J. Gilman, ass.
Joseph, N.H., S43336
Joseph, N.H., R11944
Joshua, Pa., S36864
Robert, N.H., S43332
Samuel, Pvt. N.H., BLWt.3601 iss. 5/17/1792 to S. Finney/Tinney?, ass.
Samuel, N.H., S43334
Sawney/Sawney Crosby, Ct., S36862
Solomon, Mass., Patience, W26630 BLWt.26567-160-55
William, Mass., S22071
William, N.H., Betsey, W2044; BLWt.26306-160-55
William, N.C., S38481, d. 1830
William, N.C., R11946, d. 1839
William, N.C., BLWt.120-100
William, Ring, Mass., Mary, W26631 BLWt.31782-160-55
YORKSHIRE, Thomas, Va., S41394
YORRENCE, Thomas, Dis., Vt. res.
YOST, John, Pvt., Pa., BLWt.10680 iss. 3/21/1792
Martin, Pvt., Pa., BLWt.10677 iss. 7/9/1789. Notation: "Certified 4/18/1806"
Philip, N.C., R11948
YOUGER, George, N.Y. See YOUKER
Jacob, N.Y., S11925
YOUKER, George, N.Y., S29566
Jacob, N.Y., See YOUGER
John, N.Y., Anna Catharina, W22709
YOUMAN, Nathan, N.Y., S45485
YOUMANS, Isaac, N.Y., Nancy, W7381
Jeremiah, N.J., S33957
Jonas, N.Y., S11919
YOUNG, Aaron, Pvt. N.J., BLWt.8881 iss. 1/29/1799 to Aaron Young
Aaron, N.J., S33956
Abiather, R.I., Mary, W11967
Abraham, Mass., S35163
Alexander, Cont., N.Y., S45480
Alexander, S.C., S35755
Andrew, N.C. See YONG
Andrew, Pa., S39138
Archibald, Va., Sarah, W206
Arthur Dobbs, N.C., S7994
Asa, R.I., Nancy, W16488
Barent/Barney, N.Y., See Barney
Barney, N.Y., Elizabeth, W22715
Beniah, Mass., N.H., S17216
Benjamin, Md., S35164
Benjamin, Mass., Mary, W22707
Benjamin, Mass., Sea Service, Mary, W15746
Benjamin, R.I., Waity, W20149
Caleb, Mass., N.H., Vt., Miriam W26632
Charles, Cont., Pa., S19896

YOUNG (continued)
Charles, Not Rev. War, Va., Indian Wars 1790-1794. O.W. Rej. 11954
Charles, Pa., S7995
Christian, N.Y., S4740
Christian, Pa., BLWt.1811-100
Christian, Va., R19323
Christopher, N.Y., S45481
Christopher, Va., S40735
Clark/Edward Clark, Cont., N.H. Ruth, W18245
Daniel, Mass., Patty, W15744; BLWt.71155-160-55
Daniel, N.H., S46026
David, Pvt., Md., BLWt.11858 iss. 3/11/1791
David, Mass., S18675
David, Pvt. N.J., BLWt.8880 iss. 1/5/1791
David, R.I., Zeruria/Zeruia, W14215
David, Keturah, BLWt.36245-160-55; N.J. res. of wid. 1855
Ebenezer, Ct., Elizabeth, W22713
Edward Clark, See Clark
Eleazer, N.H., Hannah, W15974
Eli, Ct., S11920
Elias, R.I., S17802
Elisha, Mass., Hannah, W14213
Esek/Eseck, Cont., R.I.? S43331
George, Cont., Md., S41397
George, N.J., Mary, W7379; BLWt. 26153-160-55
George, N.Y. or Pa., Catharine, R11951
Gideon, Mass., S33958
Gotfried/Godfrey, N.Y., S26974
Guy, N.Y., S41393; BLWt.2464-300-Capt. iss. 11/20/1792
Henry, Cont., Mass., Zeruah, W14214
Henry/John Henry, Cont., Pa., S35165; BLWt.635-100
Henry, Md., Mary Sanders, former wid., R9182
Henry, N.Y., S24031
Henry, N.Y.?, Mary, R11968; N.Y. res. of wid. in 1838
Henry, Pa., S4739
Henry, Pa., Catharine, R11952
Henry, Va., R19332
Henry, Va., BLWt.2466-300-Capt. iss. 6/23/1795 to Robert Means, ass.
Isaac, Ct., S22615
Isaac, Pvt. Md., BLWt.11856 iss. 6/8/1797 to James DeBaufre, ass.
Isham, Ga., N.C., S1889
Israel, Cont., Mass., S45487
Israel, Mass., Privateer, S29565
Israel, N.Y., Lydia, W16485
Jacob, N.C., S31506
Jacob, Pvt., Pa., BLWt.10682 iss. 4/6/1790
Jacob, Pa., S7997
Jacob, Pa., Anna Maria, W27800
Jacob A., N.Y., R11960
Jacob W., Md., Privateer, S3954
James, N.H., S19174
James, N.J., S795

YOUNG (continued)
James, N.J., S2151
James, N.Y., S23503
James, N.Y., S23505
James, N.Y., Elizabeth, R11974
James, Pa., Mary/Maria Clearwater former wid., W20885
James, R.I., S22614
James, S.C., R11977
James, Va., S7998
James, Va., Vina, R11976
Jaret, S.C., S16304
Jedediah, Mass., S19176
Jeremiah, N.Y., S28958
Johannis/Johannes, N.Y., Elizabeth W20147, d. in 1815
John, Ct., N.Y., S14912
John, Cont., Mass., S4738
John, Cont., Mass., Hannah, W22714
John, Cont., Mass., Navy, S45482
John, Cont., N.H., Yonnaca, W15745
John, General Hosp., BLWt.2463-300-Surgeon's Mate iss. 9/8/1790 Also recorded as above under BLWt 2567. No papers
John, Pvt., Md., BLWt.11855 iss. 12/22/1794
John, Corp., Mass., BLWt.5350 iss. 1/26/1790 to John May
John, Mass., Hannah, W11908; BLWt. 101. 305-160-55. This is Brigham Young's father
John, Navy, R.I., Rebecca, W4719
John, Disability Pension, res. N.J.
John, Pvt. N.Y., BLWt.8060 iss. 8/3/1790 to Cornelius Van Dyck, ass.
John, N.Y., Elizabeth Beebe, former wid., R703
John, N.C., Cynthia, W9042
John, Pvt., Pa., BLWt.10684 iss. 6/10/1793 to Christian Hubbart, ass.
John, Pa., S24030
John, Pa., Elizabeth, W3488
John, S.C., Nancy, W1976; BLWt. 18212-160-55
John, Pvt., Va., BLWt.12701 iss. 6/22/179-
John, Va., S16588
John, Va., Margaret, W1975; BLWt. 92042-160-55
John, Va., Keziah, W7377; BLWt. 39499-160-55, also Indian Spy from 1783 to 1793
John, Va., Elizabeth, R11957
John, Va., R11962
John, Va. & Indian Warfare in Ky. S30811; B.L.Reg. 275729. 1855. Son of Reuben Young. Sold. m. Mary Moore
John D., N.Y., R11964
John Henry/Henry, Cont., Pa., See Henry
Jonathan, Cont., Mass., S43333
Joseph, Ct. See YOUNGS
Joseph, Ct., Mass., S11926
Joseph, Cont., BLWt.10683-100-Pvt. iss. 12/28/1793
Joseph, Pvt. Mass., BLWt.5351

YOUNG (continued)
iss. 1/26/1796 to James A. Neal
Joseph, Corp., Mass., BLWt.5352 iss. 12/3/1789 to Moses W. Barker
Joseph, Cont., Mass., S34578
Joseph, General Hosp., BLWt.2471-450-Physician & Surgeon, iss. 7/14/1790. No papers
Joseph, Mass., Patty, W22712; BLWt.1479-100
Joseph, N.H., Eunice, W1690
Joseph, N.H., BLWt.776-100
Joseph, N.Y., Jane, W20146
Joseph, Pvt. "in Moylan's Dragoons", Pa., BLWt.10683 iss. 12/28/1793
Joseph, Pa., Elizabeth, W628
Levi, Ga., N.J., S.C., Nancy, W9040, b. in N.J.
Marcus, Pa., BLWt.428-200
Mark/Marks, Pa., S23085
Mary, N.C., former wid. of Jacob Pollock, which see
Matthias, Md., Anna Barbara, R11949
Matthias, Pa., R11970
Michael, N.C., S35758
Michael, Pa., Martha, W3171; BLWt.36232-160-55
Morgan, N.J., S4741, b. Morris Co., N.J. in Oct. 1752
Morgan, N.J., S17804, b. Mendham Twp., Morris Co., N.J. in 1762
Moses, Cont., Mass., S18293
Nathan, Va., S-35756
Nathaniel, Mass., Chloe/Cloe, W22710; BLWt.31781-160-55
Othaniel, Cont., R.I., S21593
Peter, N.J., R11973
Peter, N.Y., S11922
Peter, N.Y., R11972
Philip, N.J., S22613
Philip, N.J., S24029
Ralph, Va., S31507
Reuben, Va., Ann, W9041
Richard, Cont., R.I., S35166
Richard, N.Y., S11923
Robert, Ct., N.Y., Abigail, W20150
Robert, Cont., Pa., S39139
Robert, Cont., R.I., Polly Downing, former wid., W4944. His wid., Polly Young, later m. Phineas Downing, which see
Robert, N.J., S7993
Robert, N.C., R1932
Robert, Pvt., Pa., BLWt.10681 iss. 8/19/1789 to Richard Murthwaite, ass.
Robert, Va., Judith, W3063; BLWt.1860-200
Ruth, N.Y., former wid. of Robert Dickson, which see
Samuel, Pvt. Md., BLWt.11857 iss. 6/11/1793 to Luke Reiley ass.
Samuel, N.Y., Margaret, R11966
Samuel, N.C., S1888
Samuel, Pa., Va., S32621
Samuel, R.I., S17803

YOUNG (continued)
Samuel, Va., S38482
Samuel, Va., Frances, W5196
Sarah, Md., Navy, former wid. of Cornelius Wells, which see
Simeon, Mass., S19177
Solomon, Ct., S14911
Stephen, Ct., Cont., R.I., S22072
Stephen, Mass., Mercy, R11971
Sylvester, Pvt. N.J., BLWt.8886 iss. 6/11/1789 to Matthias Denman, ass.
Thomas, Cont., Mass., S43330
Thomas, N.J., See YOUNGS
Thomas, Pvt., N.J., BLWt.8882 iss. 6/16/1789 to Thomas Coyle, ass.
Thomas, S.C., S10309, b. S.C.
Thomas, Va., S11921
Vachel, N.C. See Vetchell
Vetchell, N.C., Catherine, R11953
William, ? , Deborah, R11956, res. of son William, Decatur Co. Tenn. in 1854
William, Ct., Navy, Privateer, Mary, W20148
William, Md., Rebeca/Rebecca, W2509; BLWt.26901-160-55
William, Mass., Margaret, W26633
William, Mass., BLWt.10398-100
William, N.C., S4737, b. Pa.
William, N.C., S31505
William, N.C., Mary, R11969, b. N.C.
William, N.C., War of 1812, Margaret, W11; BLWt.71078-160-55; b. in Va.
William, Pa., Jemima, W3487
William, R.I., Mary, W22708
William, S.C., S4742, b. York Co., Pa. 10/15/1744. In 1832 res. of Perry Co., Tenn.
William, S.C., Mary, W10008, d. 11/7/1826 in Greenville Dist., S.C.
William, S.C., Rej. -
William, Va., S14913
Zebulon, Mass., S20579
YOUNGBLOOD, Jacob, S.C., S17219
Joseph, S.C., Mary, R11978; S.C. res.
YOUNGER, Joshua, Va., Catharine, W10009; BLWt.39222-160-55
Kanard, Md., S32620
YOUNGLOVE, David, Dis.,N.Y. Agcy.
John, Cont., Ct., S45486
John, N.Y., S26972
Moses, Ct., N.Y., Polly, W4410
Samuel, Cont., N.Y., S14910
YOUNGMAN, Jabez, Cont., N.H., S43335
Peter, Mass., S41398
Stephen Wright, Cont., N.H., Abigail, W15973
Thomas, N.H., S41396
YOUNGS, Benjamin, Ct., S36863
Benjamin, N.Y., S11918
Jeremiah, N.Y., S9533
John, N.Y., S14909
Joseph, Ct., S24032

YOUNGS (continued)
Joseph, Mass., S45483
Joseph, N.Y., Jane, W20146
Samuel, N.Y., S45484
Thomas, N.J., BLWt.97-100
YOUNKER, Frederick, Pa., See JUNGKURTH
YOUNT, John, Pa., S---
YOUNTZ, George Frederick, See YONTZ
YOURING, Joseph, Mass., S15726
YOUSE, John, Cont., Pa., S39140
YOUST, Philip, N.C. See YOST
YOWELL, William, Va., Nelly, W5551; BLWt.26208-160-55
YOXTHEIMER, Henry, Pa., S3495
YULE, James, Cont., Mass., Md. Q.M. Dept., Margaret, W20152
YUNGST, Peter, Pa., See JUNGST
YUNKER, Frederick, See JUNGKURTH
YUNT, George, Pa., Polly, W9044
YURKSE, John, Pvt., N.Y., BLWt. 8063 iss. 9/24/1791 to Platt Rogers, ass.

Z

ZACHARY, William, S.C., R11982
ZADO, Congo, (pencil notation only Fado) Pvt., Ct., BLWt. 6721 iss. 9/24/1790
ZAHNER, Michael, Pa. See ZANE
ZALLAR, Michael, Pa. See ZALLER
ZALLER, Michael, Pa., S39100
ZANE, Michael, Pa., Mary, R6141 (also spelled ZANER/ZAHNER/ SEYMER/SANER/SANOR/SENIOR
Samuel, Pa., See LANE
ZANER, Michael, Pa. See ZANE
ZANES, John, Pvt., Pa., BLWt. 10686 iss. 6/17/1799 to Abraham Bell, ass.
ZEA, Martin, Va., Ann, R11984
ZEANES, John, Pa. See ZEANS
ZEANS, John, Pa., S39142
ZEASTER, Michael, Pvt. N.Y., BLWt.8066 iss. 2/14/1791
ZECHMAN, George, Pa., S24034
ZECK, Jacob, Pa., Va., S3101
ZECKLER, Michael, ? (book torn) BLWt.13936 iss. 3/29/1792
ZEE, Nicholas, N.Y., R11985
ZEECH, Nicholas, See ZEE
ZEGAR, Casper, Pa., S8002
ZEGLER, Christopher, Cont., N.Y. See ZEIGLER
ZEH, David, N.Y., S24033
Nicholas, N.Y. See ZEE
ZEHNER, Michel, Pa. See ZANE
ZEIGLER, Charles, Pa., BLReg. 296-488-1855
Christopher, Cont., N.Y., R11987
David, Pa., BLWt.2472-300
Manuel, Pa., S8001
ZEILLEY, Thomas, N.Y. See ZIELLEY
ZELIE, Martinus/Martinis, N.Y. See Martinis ZIELIE
ZELLAR, Conrad, Pa. See KELLAR
ZELLARS, Michael, Pvt., N.Y., BLWt.8064 iss. 8/18/1790 to Joseph Stringham, ass.
ZELLNER, John, Pa., S39143
ZELUFF, Daniel, N.J., Catharine, W1528
ZERENIOUS, Christopher, Pvt., N.Y., BLWt.8065 iss. 6/12/1792 to William Kline, ass.
ZERRY, Josiah, Va., S31508
ZETTLEMOYER, Martin, Pa., S8004
ZIBBERE, Bristo, Silvia, R11986, Ct. res.
ZIEGLER, George, Cont., Pa., S39141
ZIELIE, Martinis/Martinus, N.Y., S28960
ZIELLEY, Catharine, N.Y., former wid. of Andrew Dillenbach, which see
Thomas, N.Y., R11988
ZIGLAR, Leonard, Va., Nancy, W4107 BLWt.29058-160-55
ZIMERMAN, Jacob, N.Y., Magdalena/ Lena, W20002
John, N.Y., Elizabeth, W16489
William, N.Y. See ZIMMERMAN
ZIMMER, George, N.Y., S23507; BLWt.61052-160-55
ZIMMERMAN, Abraham, Pa., S23088
Christian, N.Y., S11928
Frederick, Va., Judith Bourne, former wid., W8374
George, Md., R11991
Jacob, N.Y. See ZIMERMAN
John, N.Y., See ZIMERMAN
William, N.Y., Catharine, R11990
ZINN, John, Va., Nancy, W6379; BLWt.34520-160-55
ZOBEL, Christopher, Pa. See ZUBER
ZOLL, Jacob, Md., R11992
ZOLLINGER, Alexander, Pa., R11993
Peter, Pa., S8005
ZORNES, Andrew, Pa., S35759
ZUBER, Christopher, Pa., S23089 (name also appears as Stuphol ZUBER, Christopher ZOBEL, and Stophel ZUBLY)
Stuphol, See Christopher
ZUBLY, Stophel, See Christopher ZUBER
ZUFELD, Christopher, N.Y. See SHOEFELD
ZUMBRO, Jacob, Pa., S23087
ZUMWALT, Adam, Va., French War, Mary, W9651
ZWEIER, John, Pa., Eve Fricker, former wid., R3803

SUPPLEMENT

In addition to the 2669 rolls of microfilm for which the preceding index was made, there is Roll 2670 of miscellaneous records.

These records consist mainly of documents that presumedly were accidentally separated from the Revolutionary War pension and bounty-land warrant files to which they belonged. The pertinent files could not be subsequently identified on the basis of the incomplete information contained in the individual records thus separated. Also present are some documents that were deliberately removed by previous custodians from files where they did not belong, although no other pertinent files were found in which they could be properly refiled.

Many of the documents are letters to the Commissioner of Pensions and other U.S. Government officials from heirs of Revolutionary War veterans and their attorneys seeking to establish eligibility for pensions or bounty land, and copies of replies. Other documents include pension applications (declarations) of claimants, powers of attorney, annotated paper jackets used to hold other documents in pension and bounty-land application files, and an original journal and account book kept during the Revolutionary War. Dates of the documents range from 1776 to 1920, with one undated item possibly of pre-Revolutionary War origin.

The documents are arranged in two groups. The first and larger group in terms of individual documents is arranged alphabetically by the name of the veteran or, lacking that, the name of some other significant persons referred to in the record, such as an heir or attorney. The second group consists of documents containing no names or many names. These documents are described in terms of the type of record involved and are unarranged.

Each folder containing a miscellaneous record has been microfilmed before the document or related documents it contains; the brief captions on these folders, prepared by the National Archives and Records Service staff, identify the record or records. The following lists were prepared from the folder labels:

DOCUMENTS IDENTIFIED BY NAMES OF PERSONS

Black, Robert
Boyd, William
Boynton
Brown, James
Brown, William
Caldwell, James
Campbell, Elizabeth
Campbell, James
Campbell, John
Cawby, Martin
Clark, George Rogers
Clark, John
Clinton, George
Cole, Jacob S.
Compton, John
Cook, Sylvanus
Cooper, Leonard
Davidson, David
Davis, John
Dovall, Richard
Dudley,
Dunlap, William
Dygert, Safrinus
Eames, Samuel

Eisenlord, John
Elliott, Richard
Evans, Edward
Fagg, John
Faulkner, John
Fowler, William
Fralix, Simon
Gay, Samuel
Griffis, Thomas
Hammon, Isaac
Harvey, James
Haughten, John
Hawley, Lewis
Heough, Joseph
Hogan, John
Howell, David
Hughes, John
Hull, Still
Hurtwell, Oliver
Jennings, William
Kimberly, Z.
King, William
Lighton, Reuben
Lockey, Nathan
Luce, Lockard
Lunsford, Reuben
Lynn, William
Marshall, Thomas
Martin, Reuben
McCormick, William
Miller, Peter
Miller, Richard
Myer, J.
Neely, Robert
Nelson, William
Newman, Thomas
Osgood, Walter F.
Pannel, James
Porter, William
Robbins, John
Root, Erastus
Rudolph, William
Seab, Soloman
Smith, Dianna
Smith, John
Smith, L. (Mrs.)
Smith, Solomon
Stewart, William
Thompson, John
Vosburgh, Peter
Vroman, (Col.)
Weaver, William
Weeks, John
Weiss, Thomas
White, John
Williams, John
Willis
Wilson, James
Wilson, John
Wood, Allen
Woodruff, John H.
Yates, Christopher

DOCUMENTS IDENTIFIED BY TYPES OF RECORDS

Wadsworth and Carter Day Book
Continental Currency ($45 bill)
Pay Account for the Sloop "Count Polaska", 1779
List of Officers and Seamen Belonging to the Brig Hazard
Commanded by Capt. Simeon Samson
Printed Orders of Gov. Jonathan Trumbull of Conn., Dec. 14, 1776
Undated Autobiographical Manuscript Sketch of Unidentified Person,
Born in Princess Ann County, April 3, 1760